A Dictionary of British and Irish History

A Dictionary of British and Irish History

Edited by

Robert Peberdy and Philip Waller

WILEY Blackwell

This edition first published 2021
© 2021 John Wiley & Sons Ltd; © editorial matter and organisation Robert Peberdy and Philip Waller.

The right of Robert Peberdy and Philip Waller to be identified as the authors of the editorial material in this work has been asserted in accordance with law.

Registered Offices
John Wiley & Sons, Inc., 111 River Street, Hoboken, NJ 07030, USA
John Wiley & Sons Ltd, The Atrium, Southern Gate, Chichester, West Sussex, PO19 8SQ, UK

Editorial Office
111 River Street, Hoboken, NJ 07030, USA

For details of our global editorial offices, customer services, and more information about Wiley products visit us at www.wiley.com.

Wiley also publishes its books in a variety of electronic formats and by print-on-demand. Some content that appears in standard print versions of this book may not be available in other formats.

Library of Congress Cataloging-in-Publication Data

Names: Peberdy, Robert, editor. | Waller, P. J. (Philip J.), editor.
Title: A dictionary of British and Irish history / edited by Robert Bernard
    Peberdy and Philip John Waller.
Description: First edition. | Hoboken : Wiley, 2021.
Identifiers: LCCN 2020012769 (print) | LCCN 2020012770 (ebook) | ISBN
    9780631201540 (cloth) | ISBN 9780631201557 (paperback) | ISBN
    9781119698425 (adobe pdf) | ISBN 9781119698449 (epub)
Subjects: LCSH: Great Britain–History–Encyclopedias. |
    Ireland–History–Encyclopedias.
Classification: LCC DA640 .D53 2020 (print) | LCC DA640 (ebook) | DDC
    941.003–dc23
LC record available at https://lccn.loc.gov/2020012769
LC ebook record available at https://lccn.loc.gov/2020012770

Cover design: Wiley
Cover images (top to bottom): Stonehenge, near Amesbury, Wiltshire, England, UK: John Evans/Shutterstock
Rock of Cashel, Co. Tipperary, Republic of Ireland: travelbild.com/Alamy Stock Photo
Dugald Stewart Monument and Edinburgh skyline, Scotland, UK: Norbert Achtelik, MITO images GmbH/Alamy Stock Photo
Pontcysyllte Aqueduct, Denbighshire, Wales, UK: Kelly Rann/Alamy Stock Photo

Set in 9/10.5pt Minion by SPi Global, Pondicherry, India
Printed by CPI Group (UK) Ltd, Croydon CR0 4YY

10 9 8 7 6 5 4 3 2 1

Contents

Preface   vii

Advisers   ix

Contributors   x

Abbreviations   xii

Acknowledgements   xiv

DICTIONARY ENTRIES A–Z   1

Maps   695

Preface

Readers who chance upon this work may wonder why its editors have created a reference book when so much information is now freely available through the Internet. The explanation is the editors' conviction that the book remains an effective medium for the presentation and communication of knowledge.

The content of books represents the desire of editors and authors to communicate with particular readers and users, and to address their perceived interests or requirements. Long-established facilities, namely the book trade, book reviews and libraries, enable them to reach intended audiences. The Internet, despite its advantages for many purposes, can be a sprawling, uncertain medium. Although authors of websites can communicate potentially with over 4 billion people, they cannot necessarily reach interested readers; publishing through a website is rather like posting an announcement in the hope that someone might notice it. This absence of channelled interaction tends to encourage authors to give unlimited expression to their own concerns and enthusiasms, rather than providing what an audience wants. Books have other advantages. Many people find that they can browse more easily through printed books than through electronically held material and can absorb content more effectively from print than from a screen.

All facets of *A Dictionary of British and Irish History* have been carefully designed for particular users and purposes. It is aimed, in the first instance, at history students in universities, colleges and schools, in Britain and Ireland and worldwide. Like all reference books, it provides items of information that may be required instantly, such as definitions of concepts and dates of births, deaths, treaties and battles. But it also offers further assistance. Two difficulties often encountered in studying historical topics are ascertaining essential elements and appreciating them within broader contexts. The latter problem occurs particularly when history is studied as 'modules' covering brief periods or narrow topics. This *Dictionary* provides numerous short synoptic entries on broad subjects from which students can quickly absorb basic subject-matter and appreciate it as part of a larger story. The provision of extensive cross-referencing also enables students to expand their learning immediately. Content is deliberately factual and chronological in emphasis, rather than analytical; and brevity necessarily excludes deeper matters such as causation, consequences and alternative theories. The production of short entries has inevitably required simplicity, ruthless selection of facts and sometimes sharp generalization. The editors hope that use of the *Dictionary*'s entries will leave students with a clear grasp of basic information with which they can then tackle more detailed and discursive publications.

The editors further hope that the book will prove useful to other groups who need to obtain basic historical information rapidly and easily, such as teachers, journalists, museum curators, tourism promoters, civil servants, diplomats and politicians — not to mention readers who have a natural curiosity about the past.

In providing a reference work on British and Irish history, the editors have sought to be even-handed in dealing with the component parts of the British Isles. This is done in a flexible way. For some topics (e.g., housing, the Reformation) there are separate entries on the constituent parts of Britain and on Ireland. In other instances (e.g., divorce law), a single entry covers different jurisdictions.

The editors wish to draw attention to and explain certain features of the *Dictionary*.

- **Cross-references**: these occur within and at the end of entries and are shown by capitalization of words. Capitalized words within entries do not always correspond exactly to the headings of other entries; nevertheless they will be similar and easy to follow. Sometimes a key word within a phrase is capitalized to indicate an entry heading (e.g., 'Church of SCOTLAND' refers to 'Scotland, Church of').

- **Personal names**: people are generally referred to by their normally used names rather than full names (the latter are mentioned mostly to elucidate use of initials; e.g., 'William Ewart Gladstone' to explain the entry heading 'Gladstone, W.E.').

- **Historical periods**: common period names (e.g., early medieval, Regency, Victorian) have been used sparingly; periods are frequently described in terms of centuries. This has been done partly to assist users who are unfamiliar with period names and partly because some names are used differently in the various parts of the British Isles. Period names are discussed in the entry 'historical periods'.

- **Dates between 5 Oct. 1582 and 2 Sept. 1752**: these are given as 'Old Style' dates as were used officially in Britain and Ireland (rather than as the 'New Style' dates that were used in Continental Europe following adoption of the Gregorian Calendar).

- **Start of year**: this is taken throughout as 1 January, as became official in Scotland after 31 Dec. 1599 and in England, Wales and Ireland after 31 Dec. 1751.

- **References to shires/counties and kingdoms**: where a place is located by reference to a shire or county (from the 10th century in England, later elsewhere), the unit is normally the contemporaneous one (e.g., before 1965 some places now within London, such as Chiswick, are located by reference to the former county of Middlesex). Places are also sometimes located by reference to a contemporaneous kingdom (e.g., Gwynedd, Mercia).

- **Places of birth and death in biographies**: these are usually located partly by reference to the relevant contemporaneous kingdom, country or other territory, except that after the formation of Great Britain in 1707 places within Britain continue to be specified in relation to England, Scotland or Wales. In Ireland following partition (1921), places are located by reference to southern or Northern Ireland.

- **Numbering of rulers**: because of the varying geographical extents of rulers' authority within the British Isles, some rulers of 'multiple kingdoms' or unified kingdoms have conventionally been known by different numbers in each kingdom or by a particular numbering. The *Dictionary* uses the following conventions. James VI of Scotland is normally called 'James VI/I' after his accession as James I in England and Ireland (1603), and his later namesake is 'James VII/II'. English numbering is used for rulers called Henry (Henry II to Henry VIII) as lords of Ireland; William III as king of Ireland (its first William) and Scotland (the second William); the following as rulers of the United Kingdom: William IV, Edward VII and Edward VIII (the first and second Edwards for Scotland) and Elizabeth II (Scotland's first Elizabeth).

- **Use of term 'lord'**: references to the *creation* of a man as a 'lord' (from 1387 in England, 1462 in Ireland), or inheritance of such status, normally refer to the peerage rank of 'baron'; other ranks, such as viscount, are usually designated. Note, however, that some men who ranked higher than baron are commonly referred to as 'Lord' (e.g., the 3rd Viscount Palmerston is usually called 'Lord Palmerston').

Advisers

BRITISH AND IRISH PREHISTORY
John Collis, *Emeritus Professor of Archaeology, University of Sheffield*

ROMAN BRITAIN
Martin Millett, FBA, *Laurence Professor of Classical Archaeology, University of Cambridge*

WALES, 5TH—15TH CENTURIES
T.M. Charles-Edwards, FBA, *Emeritus Jesus Professor of Celtic, University of Oxford*

WALES, 16TH—21ST CENTURIES
Aled Gruffydd Jones, *formerly Sir John Williams Professor of Welsh History, Aberystwyth University, and National Librarian of Wales*

NORTHERN BRITAIN & SCOTLAND, 5TH—15TH CENTURIES
Alexander Grant, *Reader in Medieval History, University of Lancaster*

SCOTLAND, 16TH—21ST CENTURIES
Keith Brown, *Professor of History, and Vice-President and Dean of the Faculty of Humanities, University of Manchester*

IRELAND, 5TH—15TH CENTURIES
Seán Duffy, *Associate Professor of Medieval History, Trinity College, Dublin*

IRELAND, 16TH—21ST CENTURIES
R.F. Foster, FBA, *Emeritus Professor of Irish History, University of Oxford; Professor of Irish History and Literature, Queen Mary University of London*

SOUTHERN BRITAIN & ENGLAND, 5TH—11TH CENTURIES
Pauline Stafford, *Emeritus Professor of Early Medieval History, University of Liverpool*

ENGLAND, 11TH—12TH CENTURIES
John Hudson, FBA, *Bishop Wardlaw Professor of Legal History, University of St Andrews*

ENGLAND, 13TH—15TH CENTURIES
James G. Clark, *Professor of History, University of Exeter*

ENGLAND, 16TH CENTURY
Andrew Pettegree, *Professor of Modern History, University of St Andrews*

ENGLAND, 17TH CENTURY
Clive Holmes, *Emeritus Fellow, Lady Margaret Hall, Oxford*

ENGLAND & GREAT BRITAIN, 18TH CENTURY
Sir David Eastwood, *Vice-Chancellor, University of Birmingham*

ENGLAND & GREAT BRITAIN, 19TH CENTURY
Janet Howarth, *Emeritus Fellow, St Hilda's College, Oxford*

ENGLAND & GREAT BRITAIN, 20TH—21ST CENTURIES
J.S. Rowett, *Emeritus Fellow, Brasenose College, Oxford*

IMPERIAL HISTORY
T.N. Harper, *Professor of the History of Southeast Asia, University of Cambridge; Fellow of Magdalene College, Cambridge*

ADVISER FOR SCHOOLS
Andrew White, *formerly history teacher, Cherwell School, Oxford, and tutor at the Oxford University Department of Education*

CARTOGRAPHER
Giles Darkes, *Oxford*

Contributors

David Ashton, *Deputy Principal, Royal Holloway, University of London*

Brian Blacker, *independent scholar*

James S. Bothwell, *Lecturer in Later Medieval History, University of Leicester*

Richard Brickstock, *formerly Lecturer and Researcher in Archaeology and Ancient History at the Universities of Durham and Leeds*

James G. Clark, *Professor of History, University of Exeter*

Simon Coates†, *sometime British Academy Postdoctoral Research Fellow, King's College London*

John Collis, *Emeritus Professor of Archaeology, University of Sheffield*

Gabriel Cooney, *Adjunct Professor of Archaeology, UCD School of Archaeology, University College Dublin*

David Crook, *formerly Reader in Education, Brunel University, London*

John Davies†, *sometime Senior Lecturer in Welsh History, University College of Wales, Aberystwyth*

Mark Edmonds, *Emeritus Professor of Archaeology, University of York*

Janet Foggie, *Church of Scotland Chaplain to the University of Stirling*

Austin Gee, *Tutor in History, Otago University, New Zealand*

Colin Haydon, *Fellow of the Society of Antiquaries and of the Royal Historical Society*

Stuart Hunn, *Head of Politics, Bancroft's School, London*

Mike Keoghan, *Chief Economic Adviser of the Department of Business, Energy and Industrial Strategy, UK Government*

Alan R. MacDonald, *Senior Lecturer in History, University of Dundee*

Alastair Macdonald, *Mackie Lecturer in History, University of Aberdeen*

Christine McGladdery, *Associate Lecturer and Director of Teaching, School of History, University of St Andrews*

Ailbhe Mac Shamhráin†, *sometime Lecturer on the Medieval Irish Studies Programme at NUI Maynooth*

Chris Murray, *Editor,* The Hutchinson Dictionary of the Arts

Helen Parish, *Professor of Early Modern History, University of Reading*

Robert Peberdy, *formerly Assistant Editor, Victoria County History of Oxfordshire*

Mark Philpott, *Fellow of Keble College, Oxford; J.M. Neale Fellow in Church History, St Stephen's House, Oxford*

Barry Raftery†, *sometime Professor of Celtic Archaeology, University College Dublin*

Paul Seaward, *British Academy/Wolfson Research Professor, History of Parliament, London*

Susan Skedd, *independent scholar and heritage consultant*

Glenn A. Steppler, *military historian*

Ann Swailes, OP, *Assistant Chaplain, Fisher House, Cambridge*

Richard Tames, *Adjunct Professor of History at Syracuse University's London Centre*

Andrew Thompson, *Professor of Global Imperial History, University of Oxford*

David E. Thornton, *Assistant Professor of History, Bilkent University*

Jason Tomes, *Lecturer in London for Boston University*

Matthew Vickers, *Chief Executive of Ombudsman Services, UK*

Andrew Wareham, *Reader in Medieval Economic History, University of Roehampton*

Ian Whyte†, *sometime Emeritus Professor, Lancaster Environment Centre, University of Lancaster*

Abbreviations

AD	Anno Domini (Latin, 'In the year of our Lord'; year 1 and forwards)
Aug.	August
b.	born
bap.	baptized
BC	Before Christ (before year 1 and backwards)
BP	Before Present
C	central
c.	about (Latin *circa*)
d.	died
d.	pence (Latin *denarius/denarii*)
Dec.	December
E	east
EEC	European Economic Community
est.	estimated
EU	European Union
Feb.	February
fl.	flourished
Fr.	French
ft	foot or feet
ha	hectare or hectares
HMS	His (or Her) Majesty's Ship
Jan.	January
km	kilometre or kilometres
N	north
m	metre or metres
ME	Middle English
mi	mile or miles
MP	Member of Parliament, referring 14th century—1707 to the English Parliament (including Wales from 1544); 1707—1800 to the British Parliament; 1801—1922 to the UK Parliament (for Great Britain and Ireland); from 1922 to the UK Parliament (for Great Britain and Northern Ireland)
Mt	Mount
N	north

NATO	North Atlantic Treaty Organisation
Nov.	November
Oct.	October
OE	Old English
OFr.	Old French
OIr.	Old Irish
popn	population
R.	River
S	south
s.	shilling or shillings (Latin *solidus/solidi*)
Sept.	September
sq	square
St	Saint
TD	Teachta Dála (officially 'Deputy to the Dáil', the lower house of the Irish Parliament)
US	United States
USA	United States of America
USSR	Union of Soviet Socialist Republics
W	west

Acknowledgements

In addition to the Advisers and Contributors listed on previous pages, we are indebted to numerous people for assistance of various kinds. In the first instance we wish to acknowledge former and current members of staff at the publishers, particularly the late John Davey who commissioned the book, Tessa Harvey who long provided wise counsel, and Ajith Kumar who advised on production-related matters. We are especially grateful to Jennifer Manias for encouragement and help during the final stages of preparation.

We wish to express thanks too for comments on draft entries and other kinds of support from the following: Dr Kate Adcock, Dr Virginia Bainbridge, Professor Jeremy Black, Professor Paul Brand, Kevin Brown, Dr Beatrice Clayre, Professor Peter Coss, the late Michael Crosby, the late Professor R.R. Davies, Charles Dickerson, Dr Rosamond Faith, Dr Dorian Gerhold, Alan Godwin, Dr Matthew Grimley, Professor Steven Gunn, Dr Andrew Hegarty, Arkady Hodge, Revd Dr Gordon Jeanes, David Lane, the late Aidan Lawes, Dr Chris Lewis, Revd Raymond and Joan Moody, Professor Richard Moore-Colyer, Dr Pamela Nightingale, Professor Nicholas Orme, Bernard and May Peberdy, Ian and Linda Peberdy, Dr Max Peberdy, Dr David Pelteret, Professor Carl and Dr Gill Petrokofsky, Professor Charles Phythian-Adams, Dr Nigel Ramsay, the late Dr J.M. Roberts, the late Professor Jack Simmons, Dr Graham Speake, John and Elaine Steane, Rosalind Tolson, Peter Truesdale, Jane Waller, Dr Peter Watson, Dr Elizabeth Wells, Dr Hilary Davan Wetton, Professor Chris Wickham, Roger Willson, the late Patrick Wormald. We are also grateful to the staff of the Bodleian Library in Oxford, particularly at the History and Law libraries, and thank Holly Regan-Jones for checking the text and Giles Darkes for composing the maps.

A

ABBOT, GEORGE (b. 29 Oct. 1562 at Guildford, Surrey, England; d. 4 Aug. 1633 at Croydon, Surrey, aged 70). A clothworker's son and Church of ENGLAND clergyman, Abbot was appointed bishop of Coventry and Lichfield (1609), bishop of London (1610), and archbishop of CANTERBURY and privy councillor (1611) by JAMES VI/I. He lost favour with the king in 1613 for opposing annulment of the countess of Essex's marriage (*see* SOMERSET, ROBERT EARL OF). As a CALVINIST who tolerated moderate PURITANISM, Abbot welcomed the condemnation of ARMINIANISM in 1619 by the international Synod of Dort in the Dutch Republic. In July 1621 he accidentally killed a gamekeeper with a crossbow while hunting. Thereafter he was frequently taunted about the incident.

Abbot was disregarded by CHARLES I (king from 1625) who preferred advice from the anti-Puritan William LAUD. He was effectively suspended from office during 1627–8 for rejecting a royal order: he had refused to license publication of a sermon that advocated absolute obedience to the king.

ABDICATION CRISIS Events of 1936 which led EDWARD VIII to renounce his position as king of Great Britain and Ireland. On 16 Nov. Edward expressed determination to marry Wallis Simpson, an American socialite. The prime minister, Stanley BALDWIN, and archbishop of Canterbury, Cosmo Lang, judged it impermissible for the titular head of the Church of ENGLAND to wed a twice-divorced woman. DOMINION premiers agreed. The British press refrained from reporting the matter until 3 Dec. By then the authorities had ruled out a morganatic marriage (i.e., Mrs Simpson remaining a commoner rather than becoming queen). Edward abdicated (11 Dec.) in favour of a brother (*see* GEORGE VI). He went abroad, as duke of Windsor, and married in June 1937.

ABDICATION CRISIS AND IRISH FREE STATE The premier, Éamon DE VALERA, opportunistically used the ABDICATION CRISIS (late 1936) to minimize the role of the British Crown. Meeting in emergency session, the Free State's Parliament passed a constitutional amendment Act (11 Dec.) which removed all references to the Crown from the constitution (and thereby eliminated the Crown's role in internal affairs, such as appointment of the premier and ministers by the governor-general). The External Relations Act (12 Dec.) confirmed the abdication of EDWARD VIII and permitted his successors to represent the IFS in foreign relations. (The post of governor-general was abolished in May 1937.)

This legislation prepared the way for de Valera's 1937 CONSTITUTION, which instituted an elected president, although it remained unclear whether president or monarch was head of State. The situation was clarified in 1948 when the External Relations Act was repealed and a republic, outside the COMMONWEALTH, was declared (effective from 1949).

A Dictionary of British and Irish History, First Edition. Edited by Robert Peberdy and Philip Waller.
© 2021 John Wiley & Sons Ltd; © editorial matter and organisation Robert Peberdy and Phillip Waller.
Published 2021 by John Wiley & Sons Ltd.

ABERCONWY, TREATY OF Agreed on 9 Nov. 1277 (at Aberconwy, GWYNEDD, NW Wales); between LLYWELYN AP GRUFFUDD, prince of Gwynedd, and EDWARD I, king of England; it followed Edward's 1277 invasion. Llywelyn retained the title PRINCE OF WALES, but was fined for disobedience; he conceded territories (including Y BERFEDDWLAD) and the release of DAFYDD AP GRUFFUDD (brother). *See also* ANGLO-WELSH RELATIONS, 6TH–13TH CENTURIES.

ABERDEEN A city in NE Scotland. Centre of Aberdeen sheriffdom 12th century–1975; a unitary authority from 1996.

Founded as a BURGH by King DAVID I (between 1124 and 1132), Aberdeen (originally Brittonic, meaning 'Mouth of the Don') became the principal port of NE Scotland, exporting hides, wool and fish to Continental Europe. After the local bishop's see was moved to Aberdeen (by 1132), a second burgh developed around the new cathedral. Universities were founded in 1495 (King's College) and 1593 (Marischal College) and united in 1860. SHIP-BUILDING flourished in the late 18th century, and FISHING (cod-trawling) from the 1880s to the late 20th century. The city expanded again from the 1970s as the principal centre of the oil industry. An institute of technology was upgraded as Robert Gordon University in 1992. *See also* NORTH SEA GAS AND OIL INDUSTRIES.

Est. popn: 1300, 2000; 1600, 10,000; 1800, 27,000; 1900, 153,000; 2000, 213,000.

ABERDEEN, 4TH EARL OF (b. 28 Jan. 1784 at Edinburgh, Scotland; d. 14 Dec. 1860 at London, England, aged 76). Twice British foreign secretary; prime minister of a WHIG–PEELITE coalition 1852—5.

George Gordon was an orphan. His guardians, William PITT the Younger and Henry Dundas, arranged his education and introduced him to TORY politics. He inherited his earldom in 1801 and sat in the House of Lords as a Scottish representative peer from 1806.

As special ambassador to Austria (1813–14), Aberdeen was not conspicuously successful. He occupied himself with archaeology and estate management until called to be foreign secretary under the duke of WELLINGTON (1828–30), when he negotiated the borders of GREECE. Again foreign secretary (1841–6), in the ministry of Sir Robert PEEL, he conciliated the USA and improved relations with FRANCE.

When the Conservative Party split in 1846, Aberdeen supported Peel. A convinced 'free trader', he emerged as leader of the PEELITES (1850) and formed a coalition government (1852) with Lord RUSSELL, Lord PALMERSTON and W.E. GLADSTONE in key offices. The ministry lacked unity, Aberdeen appeared irresolute, and Great Britain

drifted into the CRIMEAN WAR against his better judgement (1854). Mismanagement of the campaign forced his resignation in Jan. 1855. Succeeded by Palmerston.

ABERFAN DISASTER Accident on 21 Oct. 1966, when a coal tip (waste and sludge) at the village of Aberfan (near Merthyr Tydfil, Glamorgan, Wales) collapsed. The ensuing avalanche buried a school and neighbouring streets, killing 116 children and 28 adults. *See also* COAL INDUSTRY, WALES.

ABERNETHY, TREATY OF The submission (terms unknown), in autumn 1072 (at Abernethy, E Scotland), which was imposed on King MALCOLM III of Scotland by King WILLIAM I of England, who had invaded following Scottish raids. It was ineffective: Malcolm resumed raids. ROBERT CURTHOSE (1080) and King WILLIAM II (1091) tried to reimpose the agreement. Malcolm died while attacking N England in 1093. *See also* SCOTTISH–ENGLISH RELATIONS BEFORE 1290.

ABJURATION ACT Legislation by the English Parliament, Jan. 1702, which required office-holders and Church of ENGLAND clergy in England and Wales to take an abjuration oath (oath of renouncement) recognizing WILLIAM III as the rightful king and denying that the Stuart claimant 'James III' had any right. The Act was occasioned by the recent death of JAMES VII/II (Sept. 1701) and recognition of his son as king by Louis XIV of France. A modified oath was reimposed by later Acts, and replaced by a new oath of allegiance in 1858. *See also* JACOBITISM, IMPACT ON BRITISH POLITICS.

ABLETT, NOAH (b. 4 Oct. 1883 at Ynys-hir, Glamorgan, Wales; d. 3 Oct. 1935 at Merthyr Tydfil, Glamorgan, aged 52). Miners' leader; campaigner for confrontation between Capital and Labour (owners and employees). Ablett and colleagues wrote *The Miners' Next Step* (1912), a syndicalist manifesto which advocated the overthrow of coalowners by industrial action. *See also* TRADE UNIONISM, WALES; SYNDICALISM.

ABORTION, GREAT BRITAIN The aborting (killing) of human foetuses was made illegal by the UK Parliament in 1861. Termination of pregnancies up to 28 weeks was permitted from 1968 under the 1967 Abortion Act (proposed by Liberal MP David Steel with support from the Labour government), and reduced to 24 weeks in 1990. Two doctors were required to certify that a woman would be harmed mentally or physically by giving birth. By end 2015, about 8.5 million foetuses had been aborted. Feminists have strongly opposed further restrictions on abortion, while the Catholic Church has consistently opposed its provision.

ABORTION, IRELAND Abortion was made illegal in Ireland by the UK Parliament in 1861. In the Republic of Ireland in 1983, in response to pressure for decriminalization and following a referendum, unborn children were also protected by a constitutional amendment. However, abortion remained contentious, with the Catholic Church strongly opposed.

In March 1992 the Republic's Supreme Court ruled that abortion was allowed when a mother's life was in danger, including by risk of suicide. This prompted referendums on three further amendments (Nov. 1992). Two were accepted, allowing procurement of abortions abroad and distribution of information about services in other jurisdictions. (The rejected amendment would have prohibited abortion for risk of suicide.) In 2002 another referendum sought prohibition of abortion for risk of suicide, and proposed new penalties for performing or assisting an abortion. It was narrowly rejected (50.42% to 49.58%).

In 2010 the European Court of Human Rights accepted that there was no right to an abortion in the Republic, but advised that clarification was needed about permissible medical circumstances for abortions. That judgment and the death (2012) of a woman denied an abortion on medical grounds resulted in legislation (2013) specifying allowable medical circumstances, including risk of suicide.

After the 2016 election the FINE GAEL-led government of Enda KENNY held a Citizens' Assembly to consider changes to the 1983 amendment. Its report (June 2017) recommended liberalization. A referendum, held under Kenny's successor Leo VARADKAR, approved replacement of the amendment with authorization for abortion (May 2018). Legislation in Dec. 2018 repealed the 2013 Act and allowed abortions up to 12 weeks' gestation.

In NORTHERN IRELAND, abortion was permitted from 1945 if a mother's life was at risk. In 2017–18 there were 44 legal abortions. In July 2019, while Northern Ireland's devolved ASSEMBLY and EXECUTIVE were suspended, the UK Parliament decriminalized abortion in Northern Ireland and required regulations for abortion to be implemented by April 2020. *See also* CHURCH–STATE RELATIONS, SOUTHERN IRELAND FROM 1922; WOMEN'S MOVEMENT FROM 1960s, IRELAND.

ABRAHAM, WILLIAM *see* MABON

ABSOLUTISM A form of government in which a ruler theoretically has unlimited power. European monarchies developed in this direction in the 16th–18th centuries. Certain features were considered characteristics of absolutism: a standing army, a compliant bureaucracy, the capacity to levy taxes without legislative approval, and the ability to pursue policies without consent from representative institutions.

In England such features were most apparent in the reigns of CHARLES I (1625–49) and JAMES VII/II (1685–8), and to a lesser extent in the reign of CHARLES II (1660–85). But these kings were restrained by a relatively strong legal and political culture. The increased strength of Parliament, resulting from the GLORIOUS REVOLUTION, ended absolutist developments. *See also* BALANCED CONSTITUTION; CHARLES I, PERSONAL RULE; STANDING ARMY, ENGLAND; KINGSHIP AND MONARCHY, ENGLAND 1066 TO 1680s.

ACADEMIES OF ART A Royal Academy of Arts was founded in England in 1768 to raise the status of art and artists. Located in London, its first patron was King GEORGE III. The first president was Joshua REYNOLDS. It has run a school and has held an annual summer exhibition since 1769. A Royal Hibernian Academy was founded in Ireland in 1823 (in Dublin), and a Scottish Academy in 1826 (in Edinburgh; granted royal charter 1838). *See also* VISUAL ARTS, BRITAIN/IRELAND.

ACRE, FALL OF The capture, on 18 May 1291, of the most important remaining Latin (or European) stronghold in Syria by Muslim forces under al-Ashraf, sultan of Egypt. It led to the evacuation of the remaining Christian forts in the Middle East, effectively ending two centuries of European crusading involvement in the Holy Land. *See also* CRUSADES.

ACT OF UNION *see* UNION OF WALES WITH ENGLAND

ACT RECISSORY An Act passed by the Scottish Parliament on 28 March 1661 repealing most Acts since 1633. (Recissory means 'revoking'.) It thus abolished all public legislation, religious and secular, introduced by the Covenanting regime (1638–50), thereby restoring royal authority and the institutional structure of the early 17th century. *See also* COVENANTING REVOLUTION; RESTORATION, SCOTLAND.

ADAMS, GERRY (b. 6 Oct. 1948 at Belfast, Northern Ireland). Reputedly a leading member of the PROVISIONAL IRISH REPUBLICAN ARMY (PIRA) in NORTHERN IRELAND in the early 1970s, Adams was interned (imprisoned without trial) in 1972, 1973–6, and imprisoned in 1978. He helped to organize the 1981 HUNGER STRIKES which encouraged PROVISIONAL SINN FÉIN (PSF) to exploit electoral politics alongside violent activity. In 1982 Adams was elected for PSF to the new ASSEMBLY (abstained). From 1983 to 2018 he was president of PSF.

From 1988 Adams engaged with John HUME in secret discussions about achieving Irish nationalist ambitions (principally a united Ireland). Their joint statement (24 April 1993) and report to the Irish taoiseach (premier) encouraged a PEACE PROCESS. From Sept. 1997, following a second PIRA ceasefire, Adams participated in the multi-party talks that culminated in the BELFAST AGREEMENT (1998). He was a member of another Assembly (1998–2010), and PSF participated in multi-party EXECUTIVES (1999–2002, 2007–17). Adams was also an abstentionist member of the UK Parliament 1983–92, 1997–2011. From 2011 to 2020 he sat in the Dáil of the Republic of Ireland. *See also* TROUBLES; McGUINNESS, MARTIN.

ADDINGTON, HENRY (b. 30 May 1757 at London, England; d. 15 Feb. 1844 at Richmond, Surrey, England, aged 86). A doctor's son and childhood friend of William PITT the Younger, Addington became an MP in 1784 and served as speaker of the House of Commons from 1789. An opponent of CATHOLIC EMANCIPATION, he was chosen by King GEORGE III to replace Pitt as PRIME MINISTER (first lord of the Treasury) in March 1801, during the NAPOLEONIC WARS. Addington's ministry negotiated the Peace of AMIENS with France (March 1802) but proved inadequate when war resumed (May 1803). The ministry collapsed in April 1804. Pitt resumed office.

Addington was created Viscount Sidmouth in 1805. He held posts in the ministries of Pitt (1805) and Lord GRENVILLE (1806–7), and was home secretary 1812–21 (under Lord LIVERPOOL), a period of social unrest. Sidmouth took harsh action against LUDDITES and introduced the repressive SIX ACTS (1819).

ADDLED PARLIAMENT In England, the PARLIAMENT convened in 1614 by King JAMES VI/I who sought taxes to pay off debts. It met on 5 April and was dissolved on 7 June. As in the 1610 Parliament, opposition to IMPOSITIONS prevented agreement. It was nicknamed 'Addled' because, like an addled egg that produces no chicken, it failed to pass any Bills.

ADEN AND ADEN PROTECTORATE Former British territories in S Arabia. In 1839 the EAST INDIA COMPANY annexed the town of Aden, near the Red Sea; islands and other lands were later included. A coaling station for ships, Aden became especially important after the opening of the SUEZ CANAL (1869).

After 1839, informal agreements were made with rulers in Aden's eastern hinterland, and from 1886 to 1954 Great Britain made formal treaties, creating the so-called Aden Protectorate. Administration of the territories was transferred from India to London in 1917. Aden itself became a CROWN COLONY in 1937.

In 1959 some rulers in the protectorate formed the 'Federation of Arab Emirates of the South' (renamed Federation of South Arabia in 1962). Aden, under British sovereignty, joined the Federation in 1963; protected territories outside the Federation became the Protectorate of South Arabia. But from 1965 civil war spread into the FSA from North Yemen, and 129 British troops were killed (1965–7). Britain withdrew in Nov. 1967, whereupon the FSA and protectorate became the People's Republic of South Yemen. *See also* BRITISH SOMALILAND.

ADOMNÁN (b. 627 or 628 in N Ireland; d. 23 Sept. 704 on Iona, Scottish Dál Riata, aged 76). In 679 Adomnán became ninth abbot of IONA (off Mull, W of Scotland, in the kingdom of DÁL RIATA), chosen probably for both learning and kinship with its founder Colum Cille (or COLUMBA). After his friend Aldfrith became king of NORTHUMBRIA, Adomnán rescued Irish captives from Northumbria (687). According to BEDE, Adomnán accepted the Roman timing of Easter from Northumbria and persuaded many Irish churches to adopt it, but not his own Ionan monasteries. In 697 Adomnán supported the adoption in Ireland of the 'Law of Innocents', which protected women, children and clergy in warfare. Adomnán wrote a *Life of Columba* and was venerated as a saint. *See also* EASTER CONTROVERSY.

ADRIAN IV (b. *c*.1100 at Abbot's Langley, Hertfordshire, England; d. 1 Sept. 1159 at Anagni, Italy, aged about 59). Nicholas Breakspear, an abbot in France, was created a cardinal in 1149. After serving as papal legate in Scandinavia (1152–4), he was elected Pope (Dec. 1154) – the only Englishman to hold the office. He allegedly issued the bull *LAUDABILITER*, sanctioning involvement in Ireland by HENRY II.

ADULLAMITES Nickname of a WHIG faction in the UK Parliament which resisted any significant widening of the electorate, 1866–7, viewing it as a transfer of power to the ignorant. John BRIGHT likened their leader, Robert LOWE, to King David calling the discontented into the cave of Adullam (a reference to the Bible, 1 Samuel 22: 1–2). The Adullamites' opposition to PARLIAMENTARY REFORM caused the fall of Lord John RUSSELL's Liberal government in 1866.

ADVENTURERS, ACT FOR Act of the English Parliament, passed 19 March 1642, to pay for suppression of Irish rebels (*see* IRISH WARS, 1641–52). It offered financial investors ('Adventurers') land which would be confiscated from rebels (total 2.5 million acres; 1 million ha). One-third of the target £1 million was raised. Land was allocated from 1654 (*see* CROMWELLIAN LAND SETTLEMENT).

ADVERTISING Information was spread in TOWNS, possibly by the 12th century, by criers (or bellmen), and shops advertised their presence with signs (e.g., striped pole for a barber). Shop fascias, with lettering, spread from the late 18th century.

Printing extended possibilities. From the mid 17th century NEWSPAPERS carried advertisements, and handbills were produced (e.g., advertising coffee). By the 18th century the term 'advertisement' (meaning 'notification') was restricted to business announcements. The first 'advertising agent', William Taylor, is recorded in 1786 in Maidstone (SE England), and an agency, Reynell & Son, was founded in LONDON in 1812.

In the 19th century the development of mass-produced branded goods for large markets, resulting partly from the INDUSTRIAL REVOLUTION, required efficient, large-scale advertising. Manufacturers of patent medicines notably invested heavily (e.g., on posters, newspaper advertisements). From the later 19th century advertisements were painted on buildings, and hoardings (billboards) were used. Agencies became more numerous, producing copy and artwork, and (from 1920s) organizing 'campaigns'.

Film advertising began in 1897 (with an advert for custard powder), but TELEVISION and RADIO advertising were resisted in the UK until 1955 and 1973 respectively, although commercial radio stations broadcast advertisements from Continental Europe from the 1920s. In the Republic of Ireland, advertising began on radio in 1989, on television in 1998. The Internet became an important medium from the 1990s.

Industry self-regulation schemes for handling complaints were introduced in the UK in 1962 and in the Republic of Ireland in 1981. Several British agencies were successful internationally from the later 20th century, notably WPP, developed by Sir Martin Sorrell, which in 2000 became the world's largest advertising company.

ADVOWSON The right to present a clergyman to a Church benefice (living). It arose from the foundation of local churches by lords (and creation of the PARISH SYSTEM) – in England in the 10th–12th centuries, later elsewhere. Advowsons were often associated with MANORS. As MONASTICISM expanded from the late 11th century, many advowsons were granted to religious houses. They often returned to lay ownership in the 16th century through the DISSOLUTION OF RELIGIOUS HOUSES.

The preference for presbyterianism in the Church of SCOTLAND made private patronage contentious: it was abolished in 1649, restored in 1661, transferred to heritors and elders in 1690, restored in 1712, and abolished in 1874. It was also abolished in the Church of IRELAND from 1871, and in the Church in WALES from 1920.

As a property right, advowsons have been dealt with by royal rather than Church courts. Sale of advowsons in the Church of England was prohibited from 1924.

ÆLFGIFU (fl. from c.1006; d. after 1037, probably in England). The daughter of an EALDORMAN, Ælfgifu 'of

Northampton' married CNUT (of Denmark) in England probably c.1013–14. She bore two sons, Swein and Harold. After Cnut became king of England (1016), he married again (1017) without repudiating Ælfgifu (see EMMA).

From 1030 Ælfgifu and Swein lived in Norway (conquered by Cnut in 1028), where Ælfgifu was regent for Swein. They were driven out in 1034. Ælfgifu returned to England and probably helped Harold to become king (see HAROLD 'HAREFOOT').

ÆLFRIC (b. c.950 in England; d. c.1010 at Eynsham, Oxfordshire, England, aged about 60). Educated at WINCHESTER under ÆTHELWOLD, the monk Ælfric absorbed the ideals of the TENTH-CENTURY REFORMATION. Based at Cerne Abbas monastery (Dorset, from c.987) and then Eynsham (first abbot, from 1005), he was a prolific author and stylish writer of Old English. His works included homilies, saints' lives, translations of scripture, and grammatical works. See also EDUCATION AND LEARNING, ENGLAND BEFORE 1066.

ÆLFTHRYTH (fl. from c.956; d. c.1000 in England). Ælfthryth married EDGAR, king of England, in 964 as second or third wife. She was crowned alongside him in 973. When Edgar died (975), his and Ælfthryth's surviving son, ÆTHELRED, was denied the kingship in favour of his older half-brother Edward.

In 978 Ælfthryth's retainers murdered Edward, resulting in Æthelred's succession as king. Ælfthryth's culpability is suspected but unproved. She was an important figure at Æthelred's court. See also EDWARD THE MARTYR.

ÆTHELBALD (fl. from c.709; d. 757, at Seckington, Mercia). A member of the royal kindred of MERCIA (C England), Æthelbald lived in exile during the reign of his rival King Ceolred (709–16). Soon after Ceolred's death Æthelbald became king. He expanded Mercian-controlled territory, taking LONDON and the Middle Saxon province from ESSEX, and absorbing the MAGONSÆTE (by 740). After the abdication of INE of WESSEX (726), Æthelbald became overking in southern England (by 731), even exercising some authority in Wessex. But he was defeated by King Cuthred of Wessex (752), and later murdered by his bodyguard. See also KINGSHIP, ANGLO-SAXON.

ÆTHELBERT (fl. from late 6th century; d. 24 Feb. 616, probably in Kent). Son of Eormenric, king of KENT (SE England), Æthelbert married Bertha, a Christian princess from Francia by 581. He succeeded as king c.590. Æthelbert's marriage enabled AUGUSTINE to undertake his Christian mission to the Anglo-Saxon kingdoms (597). Æthelbert allowed Christian worship, supported church-building, and issued the first English law code. He was the first Anglo-Saxon king to espouse Christianity, and facilitated its spread (to ESSEX, EAST ANGLIA). BEDE claimed that Æthelbert was the third overking of the southern Anglo-Saxons. *See also* KINGSHIP, ANGLO-SAXON; LAW, ENGLAND BEFORE 1066.

ÆTHELFLÆD (b. in 870s in Wessex; d. 12 June 918 at Tamworth, Mercia). The first-born child of King ALFRED of WESSEX (S England), Æthelflæd married (by 887) Æthelred, ruler ('EALDORMAN') of western Mercia (W Midlands). After his death (911) she was accepted as his successor and called 'Lady of the Mercians'.

Æthelflæd constructed BURHS (fortified centres) in western Mercia and collaborated with her brother EDWARD THE ELDER of Wessex in conquering Danish-held eastern Mercia. She received the submission of Danes at Derby (917) and Leicester (918). *See also* ENGLAND, FORMATION OF.

ÆTHELING In Anglo-Saxon England, term applied to candidates for kingship; OE *æthel* means 'noble', *-ing* means 'originating from' or 'son of'.

In the 6th–9th centuries an ætheling had to claim descent through a male line from the accepted founder of a royal kindred (in 5th or 6th century). In the 9th–11th centuries 'ætheling' designated a narrower group of sons or grandsons of a king. The position existed because there was no automatic succession to kingship. (Succession was influenced by kindred members, queens, other nobles and churchmen.)

The last ætheling was Edgar ætheling (*c.*1052–1125 or later), grandson of EDMUND IRONSIDE. In 1066, after the deaths of EDWARD THE CONFESSOR and HAROLD II, Edgar was widely considered the legitimate claimant to the English kingship. He submitted to WILLIAM I in Dec. 1066; rebelled 1068–72; resubmitted 1074. His sister MARGARET married MALCOLM III of Scotland. *See also* KINGSHIP, ANGLO-SAXON.

ÆTHELRED II, 'THE UNREADY' (b. *c.*967; d. 23 April 1016 at London, England, aged about 49). Æthelred became king of England after the murder of his older half-brother EDWARD THE MARTYR (18 March 978). From 980 England was raided by VIKINGS (mainly Danes). In 991 a large army was paid to move elsewhere (*see* MALDON, BATTLE OF), and Æthelred made a similar payment in 994. Raids nonetheless continued (997–1000, 1001–2, 1003, 1006–7, 1009–12). Æthelred also countered the Viking threat with a marriage alliance with Normandy (*see* EMMA).

In 1012 Thorkell, a Danish leader, became Æthelred's (paid) supporter. Denmark's king, SWEIN FORKBEARD, probably fearing attack, made a pre-emptive invasion (summer 1013). Æthelred fled to Normandy (Dec. 1013). Swein's death (Feb. 1014) enabled him to return, but Swein's son CNUT invaded (1015) and quickly conquered much of England. Æthelred died in early 1016, leaving his son EDMUND IRONSIDE to continue resistance.

Æthelred (meaning 'noble counsel') was nicknamed *Unræd* (OE, meaning 'no-counsel' or 'ill-advised') from the 12th century. This was later corrupted to 'Unready'. *See also* GELD.

ÆTHELWOLD (b. between 904 and 909 at Winchester, Hampshire, Wessex; d. 1 Aug. 984 at Beddington, Surrey, England, aged around 78). A monk at Glastonbury under DUNSTAN, *c.*954 Æthelwold was given the MINSTER at Abingdon (modern Oxfordshire) where he created a Benedictine monastery. As bishop of WINCHESTER (from 963) he extended monastic reform, replacing clergy at the Old and New Minsters with Abingdon monks and refounding religious houses elsewhere (e.g., Peterborough, Ely). He consolidated reform by compiling the *Regularis concordia* ('Monastic agreement', early 970s), a rule for English religious houses based on St Benedict's rule. Æthelwold also promoted liturgical change, and was an important adviser to the young King ÆTHELRED II. *See also* TENTH-CENTURY REFORMATION.

ÆTHELWULF (fl. from 825; d. 858). Æthelwulf succeeded his father EGBERT as king of WESSEX (S England) in 839 after ruling subordinate territories (SE England) as subking. (His son Athelstan succeeded as subking.) From the 840s Wessex suffered frequent VIKING (Danish) raids. Æthelwulf won a famous victory in 851, reported even in Francia.

In 855–6 Æthelwulf made a pilgrimage to Rome. During his absence, his son Æthelbald rebelled (856). On return, Æthelwulf had to cede much of Wessex to Æthelbald. *See also* KINGSHIP, ANGLO-SAXON; ALFRED.

AFFINITY *see* BASTARD FEUDALISM

AFGHANISTAN, BRITISH RELATIONS WITH The aim of British policy in the 19th century was to exclude Russian influence from Afghanistan as a buffer state to protect India (*see* GREAT GAME). The First Afghan War (1838–42) involved a British attempt to restore a pro-British ruler. The Second (1878–80) forcibly installed a British envoy at Kabul who was promptly murdered. Lord ROBERTS then briefly occupied Kabul and relieved a garrison near Kandahar (1879–80). After another conflict, Britain recognized the independence of Afghanistan by the treaty of Rawalpindi (Aug. 1919). Britain again undertook military operations in Afghanistan in the early 21st century as part of the US-led 'War on Terror' (*see* AFGHANISTAN WAR (2001–14), BRITISH INVOLVEMENT). *See also* RUSSIA AND USSR, ENGLISH AND BRITISH RELATIONS WITH; ANGLO-RUSSIAN CONVENTION.

AFGHANISTAN WAR (2001–14), BRITISH INVOLVEMENT After hijackers associated with the radical Islamic group al-Quaeda crashed three passenger aircraft into prominent buildings in the USA on 11 Sept. 2001 (called '9/11' in USA), the USA intervened in Afghanistan, hunting al-Quaeda's leader Osama bin Laden. Afghanistan was dominated by the Taliban, a fundamentalist Islamic movement. Working with anti-Taliban forces, the USA drove the Taliban from government (Oct.–Dec.), though bin Laden remained at large (killed in Pakistan in 2011). US and international forces stayed in Afghanistan to eliminate terrorist bases and promote democratic society, but were challenged by resurgent Taliban until 2009, when a 'surge' (deployment expansion) again repulsed them. Combat operations formally ceased in Dec. 2014.

British forces participated from the start with missile attacks (7 Oct. 2001). Troops were deployed from Nov., and joined 'ISAF' (International Security Assistance Force), a force authorized by the United Nations (Dec.) to train Afghan forces (police, army) and fight insurgents. From summer 2006 Helmand Province in S Afghanistan (population 880,000) was the main area of British activity, starting with 6000 troops who were tasked to suppress Helmand's opium industry (responsible for 80% of world production). Some economic and social development work occurred, but forces were mostly involved in military operations. By 2009 Britain's Helmand deployment exceeded 9000 troops. Extra US forces were then introduced (2010), and a British withdrawal began (2011). It ended in Oct. 2014, leaving a small training force. British forces suffered 456 deaths. *See also* UNITED STATES OF AMERICA, BRITISH RELATIONS WITH; BLAIR, TONY.

AFRICAN CARIBBEANS IN GREAT BRITAIN A few immigrants from English (later British) colonies in the WEST INDIES settled from the 17th century. During the 19th century small communities became established in ports (e.g., LONDON, CARDIFF, LIVERPOOL).

Large-scale immigration, predominantly from JAMAICA, began in 1948, symbolized by arrival of the ship *Empire Windrush* carrying 492 Jamaicans. By the early 1960s, there were about 300,000 African Caribbean immigrants, who sought a better life. Settled mainly in cities, they remained the largest minority group until the late 1970s. Though westernized, English-speaking and often Christian, they encountered discrimination in public housing and employment (e.g., exclusion from employment on buses in BRISTOL, provoking the 'Bristol bus boycott' in 1963). Disturbances occurred in African Caribbean areas (late 1950s–mid 1980s; e.g., NOTTING HILL RIOTS, 1958, BRIXTON AND TOXTETH RIOTS, 1981).

Numerous African Caribbeans became prominent in sport and music, and 'countercultures' flourished. A majority of African Caribbean families have been single-parent households, usually headed by a mother. By the early 21st century, African Caribbeans were the fifth-largest minority (about 600,000 in 2011, mostly in England and Wales). High levels of intermarriage or cohabitation took place mainly with the white population. *See also* ETHNIC AND NATIONAL MINORITIES, ENGLAND/WALES.

AFRICANS IN GREAT BRITAIN A few black Africans lived in England from the mid 16th century, often originating from the SLAVE TRADE and working as personal servants. By the 18th century, there were possibly 15,000 in LONDON. (Slavery was not recognized in England and Wales, as Somerset's case confirmed in 1772.)

In the 1960s–70s, thousands of black Africans from former British colonies in WEST AFRICA settled, many coming initially as university students. Continuing immigration from sub-Saharan countries expanded rapidly from the later 1990s, from former British territories (e.g., Zimbabwe) and elsewhere (e.g., Congo). In 2011 there were 1,016,000 black Africans in Britain, of whom two-thirds lived in London and most of the remainder in other cities and towns in England and Wales. About 25% of men and 18% of women married or cohabited outside their own group (2010).

From the late 1980s African immigrants included refugees from civil war in Somalia – some from former BRITISH SOMALILAND, most from former Italian Somaliland. As Muslims from rural backgrounds, with a clan-based social structure and often illiterate, Somalis tended to form exclusive communities. With only 30% of adults employed, they depended extensively on State benefits. About 60% of households were headed by a single parent. The few Somalis who prospered included the champion runner Sir 'Mo' Farah (b. 1983 in Somalia). In 2011, there were about 103,000 Somalis (two-thirds resident in London). *See also* ETHNIC AND NATIONAL MINORITIES, ENGLAND/SCOTLAND/WALES.

AGADIR CRISIS A dispute provoked by France's military occupation of Fez, the capital of Morocco (NW Africa), in May 1911 (to suppress riots), effectively establishing a PROTECTORATE. France's action threatened a Franco-German agreement concerning interests in Morocco (1909). Germany responded by stationing a gunboat off the Moroccan port of Agadir (1 July). Great Britain's chancellor of the Exchequer, David LLOYD GEORGE, publicly supported France (21 July), to Germany's consternation. Britain's stance reinforced the ANGLO-FRENCH CONVENTION (1904) and raised tension with GERMANY. The matter was settled by negotiations. *See also* GREY, EDWARD; GUNBOAT DIPLOMACY.

AGINCOURT, BATTLE OF *see* HUNDRED YEARS WAR

AGREEMENT OF THE PEOPLE A proposed radical constitution for England and Wales which was drawn up by LEVELLERS in the NEW MODEL ARMY and presented to the Army's Council on 28 Oct. 1647, following the First CIVIL WAR (*see* PUTNEY DEBATES). Parliament would have full powers and be elected by an extensive franchise. There would also be religious toleration. Two further versions were published and, while uninfluential at the time, they affected later radical thinking. *See also* CIVIL WARS, POLITICAL ASPECTS.

AGRICOLA (b. 13 June 40 at Forum Julii/Fréjus, SE Gaul; d. 93 at Rome, Italy, aged about 53). A distinguished Roman senator, Gnaeus Julius Agricola owes his fame to a biography by his son-in-law TACITUS. After an early career which included two postings in Britain (*c.* 61, 70–3 or 74), Agricola was consul in 77. As governor of Roman Britain (77–83) he completed the conquest of W Britain (Wales) and advanced into N Britain (Scotland), defeating the CALEDONIANS at MONS GRAUPIUS (83). *See also* ROMAN BRITAIN.

AGRICULTURAL CO-OPERATIVES, IRELAND Societies formed from 1889 mainly by farmers to improve efficiency. Following Continental European models, co-operatives operated creameries for butter production, bought seeds and fertilizers in bulk, marketed produce, and provided credit. The movement was promoted by the Irish Agricultural Organisation Society, founded 1894 (*see* PLUNKETT, HORACE). By 1914 there were about 1000 societies. In the later 20th century, many became large businesses through mergers. *See also* AGRICULTURE, IRELAND 17TH CENTURY TO 1921.

AGRICULTURAL DEPRESSION, LATE 19TH CENTURY From the late 1870s, AGRICULTURE in Great Britain and Ireland suffered from a substantial decline in food prices and profitability caused by the influx of cheaper foreign foodstuffs. Wheat producers (e.g., in S England, SE Scotland) were worst hit, undercut by US and Russian wheat. Livestock producers were affected by American chilled beef (from 1875) and by Australian and New Zealand frozen meat (from 1880). Many left farming; landlords lost rental income. The depression encouraged dairying and diversification, and in Ireland contributed to LAND AGITATION. Conditions improved slowly from *c.*1900. *See also* FOREIGN TRADE, GREAT BRITAIN FROM LATER 18TH CENTURY.

AGRICULTURAL REVOLUTION Historians' term for substantial increases in agricultural output and productivity involving innovation and social change. It was adopted in the 1880s by the English historians Arnold Toynbee and R.E. Prothero (later Lord Ernle) for developments in England, approximately 1760–1840.

The Revolution was considered complementary to the INDUSTRIAL REVOLUTION, and derived similarly from the work of 'great men', such as Jethro Tull, inventor of the seed drill (1701); Viscount TOWNSHEND ('Turnip Townshend'), who promoted the 'Norfolk rotation' of crops (1730s); and the animal breeder Robert Bakewell (active by 1760s). Landowners' replacement of open-field farming with large, tenant-held capitalist farms was also deemed important (*see* ENCLOSURE).

The original conception was challenged. Earlier revolutions were proposed: 1560–1650, which saw innovations such as 'convertible husbandry' (alternating land use between cultivation and pasture) and irrigated meadows; or 1650–1760, when new crop rotations were spreading and CAPITALISM was influential. Though output growth is difficult to quantify, the original proposal has remained persuasive because farming became based on large units of production (farms) employing a workforce of labourers, and agriculture supported an expanding industrial sector. Developments are sometimes seen as culminating in a 'Second Agricultural Revolution' of so-called HIGH FARMING (from 1840s). The Revolution also affected parts of Scotland and Wales but had little impact in Ireland. From 1945 far greater increases in productivity were obtained by mechanization, intensive use of chemicals, new strains of plants and improved animal breeds.

AGRICULTURE, ENGLAND BEFORE MID 18TH CENTURY In the 5th–6th centuries, GERMANIC IMMIGRATON made no observable differences to agricultural practices. Livestock rearing, especially of cattle, was important. Sufficient cereals were grown for domestic needs and élites. Changes in the 8th–9th centuries included increasing arable cultivation, larger fields, and more sheep- and pig-keeping. Possibly in the 9th–10th centuries, extensive open fields emerged, associated with villages, mainly in a 'central region' (NE England across Midlands to S coast), though chronology and causation are obscure. Elsewhere, small fields remained normal.

By the 12th century, open-field agricultural systems were well developed, regulated by lords' manorial courts (*see* MANOR). They typically comprised two or three fields divided into 'selions' (strips of land). 'Mixed farming' was practised, whereby crops were grown (variously barley, wheat, oats, rye, peas, beans) and sheep kept for manure (as well as wool). One field was annually left fallow for manuring. Upland areas were dominated by livestock. In the 12th–13th centuries, agriculture was stimulated by COMMERCIALIZATION and POPULATION increase. Population decline from the mid 14th century, and increased labour costs, eventually caused contraction of arable farming and (in 15th century) widespread sheep grazing on permanent pasture (*see* ENCLOSURE). Many tenants acquired larger holdings (origin of 'yeoman farmers').

Re-expanding population from the 16th century increased demand for grain. Arable farming was extended, and yields were increased by more intensive manuring and 'convertible husbandry' (alternating periods of cultivation and pasture). Irrigation of meadows in southern England (from early 17th century) increased hay production for livestock. When population stagnated in the later 17th century, grain prices and profitability fell (despite the CORN LAWS), enabling landlords to buy farmers' lands or introduce shorter leases. Livestock rearing increased, facilitated by new crop rotations involving nitrogen-fixing grasses (e.g., clover) and turnips. Agricultural production probably doubled in the 16th–18th centuries, enabling the population to be fed without significant imports. *See also* FENS; ENCLOSURE AND ENGROSSING, ENGLAND 1480s–1630s; TENURES, ENGLAND FROM 1066; RURAL SETTLEMENT AND SOCIETY, ENGLAND.

AGRICULTURE, ENGLAND FROM MID 18TH CENTURY

The gradual spread of new crop rotations (cereals, clover, turnips), sowing by seed drill (from 1770s) and selective stock-breeding increased output. Open-field systems disappeared from the mid 18th century as land was enclosed under parliamentary legislation (at peak, 1790–1815; *see* ENCLOSURE). Loss of grazing worsened conditions of the poor.

In the 19th century, industrialization meant that agriculture ceased to be the basis of the economy: in 1800 it employed a third of the workforce, by 1900 only a tenth (*see* INDUSTRIAL REVOLUTION). Industrial interests seemingly triumphed over the 'landed interest' with repeal of the CORN LAWS (1846), which ended protection for arable farming, though HIGH FARMING helped to sustain profitability. RAILWAYS stimulated dairying by enabling rapid transport of milk. There was a long-term trend towards larger units of cultivation, although farms of over 500 acres (200 ha) remained rare outside East Anglia.

Large-scale imports of chilled meat from 1875, grain from the late 1870s, and frozen meat from 1880 reduced prices and profits, and encouraged change from arable to livestock, and rural depopulation (*see* AGRICULTURAL DEPRESSION, LATE 19TH CENTURY). From 1908, the National Farmers' Union operated as a pressure group. WORLD WAR I (1914–18) stimulated grain production, and provided an opportunity (1919–21) for large-scale land sales by landlords to tenants (36% of land was owner-occupied by 1927). Renewed price falls left agriculture depressed in the 1920s–30s, eventually provoking government intervention (*see* AGRICULTURE, STATE INVOLVEMENT, GREAT BRITAIN).

By the 1930s, 70% of food was imported, but agricultural output nearly doubled during WORLD WAR II (1939–45), with little extra labour, due to more mechanization

(tractors, milking machines, combine harvesters). From the mid 20th century, intensive methods became prevalent (e.g., spraying crops with chemical pesticides). From 1973, agriculture was subject to the COMMON AGRICUTURAL POLICY of the European Union. *See also* AGRICULTURAL REVOLUTION; TENURES, ENGLAND FROM 1066; RURAL SETTLEMENT AND SOCIETY, ENGLAND.

AGRICULTURE, IRELAND BEFORE 17TH CENTURY

Until the late 12th century, agriculture was mostly pastoral, predominantly cow keeping (sheep were less important). Cattle were measures of value for social status and wealth, and conflicts between kingdoms often consisted of cattle raids. Cow keeping involved transhumance (or booleying, i.e., seasonal movement to upland pastures). Cereals were also cultivated (mostly oats), and bees were widely kept for honey. Flax was widely grown for domestic linen production.

Following the Anglo-Norman invasion (1169–70), agriculture in English-inhabited areas was organized within MANORS, as elsewhere in Europe (*see* NORMANS, IMPACT ON IRELAND). Cultivated land expanded greatly, especially in E and S Ireland, with wheat and oats as the main crops. Sheep were kept to provide manure (so-called 'sheep–corn husbandry'). Individual holdings consisted of small strips of land distributed among a few large, open fields. Agricultural regimes were subject to communal organization. Lords' unfree tenants were predominantly Gaelic Irish (so-called betaghs), who undertook LABOUR SERVICES, though they were less onerous than in lowland England to attract settlers. Much labour was hired.

The reduced POPULATION of the late 14th and 15th centuries resulted in a contraction of arable cultivation and expansion of sheep-farming in English areas. The shrinkage of English-occupied areas led to an expansion of Gaelic pastoralism, though around English areas (in E and SE Ireland) English and Gaelic practices were intermixed. In the 16th century, English PLANTATIONS attempted to expand arable cultivation in Gaelic areas. *See also* TENURES, IRELAND; RURAL SETTLEMENT AND SOCIETY, IRELAND.

AGRICULTURE, IRELAND 17TH CENTURY TO 1921

Pastoral farming (cattle, sheep) continued to predominate in W and N Ireland, while arable farming or 'tillage' remained prominent in E and parts of S Ireland. Demand from England for live cattle and wool stimulated pastoral farming, though warfare in the 1640s–50s depressed activity (*see* IRISH WARS, 1641–52). In the mid 1660s, half of Ireland's exports by value were cattle or cattle-based products (hides, beef, tallow, butter).

From the mid 18th century, landowners raised arable productivity and rents by enclosing open fields and converting pasture. The government from 1758 provided bounties (incentive payments) on exports of corn and flour to expand tillage and employment (reinforced 1784 by FOSTER'S CORN LAW). Grain exports increased until the 1840s, turning Ireland into Great Britain's 'bread basket'. (Grain exports rose c.1815–45 from 125,000 to 513,000 tons per year.) Exports of cattle and pigs also grew. But population also rose substantially (4.4–8.5 million, 1781–1845). Most holdings were very small (69% under 15 acres in 1845), and held on lease. Labourers cultivated potatoes for subsistence in gardens or tiny plots.

The GREAT FAMINE (1845–9) eliminated overcrowding and tiny landholdings, and accelerated a reversion to pastoral farming (e.g., cattle increased 1850–79 from 1.4 to 3.8 million). Incomes and conditions improved, though depressions impeded progress (1859–64, 1879–90). Related unrest, exploited by politicians, resulted in legislation that extended landownership by small farmers (see LAND AGITATION AND REFORM, IRELAND). Other means employed to improve agriculture included AGRICULTURAL CO-OPERATIVES (from 1889) and the CONGESTED DISTRICTS BOARD (1891). When Ireland was partitioned in 1921, it remained a largely agricultural country. See also TENURES, IRELAND; RURAL SETTLEMENT AND SOCIETY, IRELAND.

AGRICULTURE, NORTHERN IRELAND In 1926, following the PARTITION OF IRELAND (1921), 26% of the total workforce was occupied in agriculture (147,000 people). Most landholdings were small (70% under 30 acres or 12 ha). Livestock (especially cattle) and livestock products dominated (80% of output by value). Arable farming occupied 23% of agricultural land. Agriculture was regulated by the province's PARLIAMENT and affected by British government policies.

During the 1920s, under FREE TRADE, prices fell. Protection from 1932 improved conditions (see TARIFF REFORM; OTTAWA AGREEMENTS). Arable production declined during the 1920s–30s. In the 1930s, pig numbers increased threefold, encouraged by cheap foodstuffs and a marketing board (1933). Sheep and poultry numbers also rose. Agriculture benefited from the Anglo-Irish ECONOMIC WAR (1932–8) and UK Wheat Act (1932). A subsidy for 'fat cattle' (1934) encouraged 'finishing' instead of raising cattle, using 'store cattle' from southern Ireland.

During WORLD WAR II (1939–45) cow herds and arable expanded, while sheep numbers fell. Afterwards, previous trends were resumed, with the British government providing new financial support from 1947. Beef production and pig numbers expanded (latter peaking in 1965). In 1960, pig and poultry production were half of output by value, declining to 21% by 1985. The number of labourers declined drastically as tasks (e.g., milking) were mechanized. Dairy production expanded from the 1960s. By 1985, arable, now more productive, occupied only 9% of land. Holdings remained small (average of 48 acres, 19 ha, in 1980), with many worked part-time or leased out.

From 1973, conditions were determined by the COMMON AGRICULTURAL POLICY of the European Economic Community. In 2015, livestock accounted for 80% of output by value. Agriculture engaged 3.2% of the workforce. See also AGRICULTURE, STATE INVOLVEMENT, GREAT BRITAIN/NORTHERN IRELAND; RURAL SETTLEMENT AND SOCIETY, IRELAND.

AGRICULTURE, SCOTLAND BEFORE 18TH CENTURY From the 13th century onwards, arable farming was organized on an infield–outfield system, a variant of open-field agriculture (see AGRICULTURE, ENGLAND BEFORE MID 18TH CENTURY). The distinction between infield and outfield developed from earlier, simpler 'infield-only' systems. Open-field farming may have been introduced with FEUDALISM (from the 12th century), replacing earlier systems based on small enclosed fields.

The infield, on the best soils, was relatively small (at most, a third of total area), but received most manure and was intensively cropped with bere (a form of barley), oats and sometimes wheat, rye and legumes. The more extensive outfields, producing only oats, received little manure and were regularly rested as fallow to restore fertility. Crop yields were low; a return of three times the seed sown was considered acceptable, though infields sometimes produced more. Arable land was frequently held in shares, with holdings fragmented into intermixed parcels under the RUNRIG system. An eight-oxen team, ploughing land as ridge and furrow, was normal. In the W Highlands, population growth from the late 16th century encouraged a shift from plough to intensive spade cultivation in 'lazy beds' (heavily manured hill-side strips).

All communities produced some grain for subsistence, and most farms kept cattle and sheep. There was an emphasis on arable in the eastern Lowlands, while the eastern Borders specialized in sheep farming from the 12th century. Galloway (SW Scotland) concentrated on cattle rearing. In the medieval Lowlands, and in the Highlands into the late 18th century, cattle were driven to summer pastures, or shielings, among hills and mountains. During the 17th century, arable farming expanded with population growth and, around the major towns, became more intensive with liming and improved rotations. Enclosure of land on estate policies (parks) and home farms began in the later 17th century. See also TENURES, SCOTLAND; RURAL SETTLEMENT AND SOCIETY, SCOTLAND.

AGRICULTURE, SCOTLAND FROM 18TH CENTURY Free trade with England, introduced by the UNION OF ENGLAND AND SCOTLAND (1707), stimulated sheep and cattle farming in the Borders. Tenants were removed, particularly in the 1720s, to provide pastures (see LEVELLERS'

REVOLT). In the eastern Lowlands multiple tenancies were gradually replaced by single tenancies.

Between the 1760s and 1820s, growing towns and industrial regions stimulated the transformation (or 'improvement') of Lowland agriculture. Landowners terminated leases and enclosed open fields (both in- and outfields), creating compact large farms (often over 100 acres, 40 ha) with single tenants. Commonties (common lands) were made private and enclosed. Farmers adopted techniques for improving fertility (intensive liming; increased stocking of sheep and cattle, to provide dung, fed on sown grass and turnips). Crop yields doubled or tripled. Little mechanization occurred, though the light two-horse plough became common. In the HIGHLANDS large sheep farms were created (1770s–1840s) by removal of tenants (see CLEARANCES; CROFTING). Better roads and CANALS improved access to markets.

Prosperity continued until the 1870s. From the 1820s, fat cattle were exported to London by steamship (from the 1850s by RAILWAYS). The NE became famous for beef. Arable yields were raised in mid century by HIGH FARMING techniques. Scotland suffered from the AGRICULTURAL DEPRESSION of the 1880s–90s, though less than most of the UK.

In the 20th century, the World Wars (1914–18, 1939–45) created temporary demand as imports were cut, but prices fell afterwards. From the 1950s, arable farming became totally mechanized (tractors, harvesters), and from 1973, agriculture was subject to the COMMON AGRICULTURAL POLICY of the European Economic Community. Having employed 150,000 people in 1881, by 2000 agriculture required only 25,000 workers. See also TENURES, SCOTLAND; RURAL SETTLEMENT AND SOCIETY, SCOTLAND.

AGRICULTURE, SOUTHERN IRELAND Agriculture predominated in the economy of the IRISH FREE STATE (founded 1922), accounting in 1926 for 53% of the total workforce (648,000 people) and 34% of national income. Livestock (especially cattle) and livestock products (e.g., butter) were the main concerns. In the 1920s, prices declined though exports (mainly to Great Britain) rose 12% in value 1925–30.

From 1932, the FIANNA FÁIL government of Éamon DE VALERA sought to increase self-sufficiency by encouraging arable farming with price support (1932). But expansion was modest, and de Valera's ECONOMIC WAR with Britain greatly reduced agricultural exports and incomes (e.g., cattle exports fell by two-thirds in value 1931–4).

Increased overseas demand in WORLD WAR II (1939–45) and afterwards improved conditions, but in the 1950s–60s prices declined and farmers depended considerably on State aid. The difficult situation produced a 'flight from the land'. By 1971, agriculture employed 25% of the workforce, less than now occupied in industry.

The Republic of Ireland's entry into the European Economic Community (1973) brought agriculture under its COMMON AGRICULTURAL POLICY (CAP), which raised incomes. Cattle remained pre-eminent, with beef cattle becoming more important. The CAP's terms favoured capital-intensive large farms, which increased production and productivity. Dairy farms fell from 86,000 in 1984 to 25,000 in 2005. By 2011, only 4.7% of the workforce remained in agriculture, though food processing was an important industry. See also AGRICULTURE, STATE INVOLVEMENT, SOUTHERN IRELAND; RURAL SETTLEMENT AND SOCIETY, IRELAND.

AGRICULTURE, STATE INVOLVEMENT, GREAT BRITAIN From the 1660s to 1840s the English (later British) government encouraged stability of arable agriculture through the CORN LAWS. Following their abolition (1846), LAISSEZ-FAIRE prevailed.

The need for increased home food production during WORLD WAR I (1914–18) provoked intervention. From 1917, some permanent pasture was ploughed up, under local direction, to expand cereal production (mostly in 1918). The 1917 Corn Production Act (for UK) introduced minimum prices for wheat and oats, and minimum wages for labourers. They were continued by the 1920 Agriculture Act (for Great Britain), but it was repealed in 1921 because of farmers' opposition and cost. Wage regulation was reinstituted (1924) in England and Wales (in Scotland, 1937). Minor support measures were introduced (e.g., sugar beet subsidy, 1925). De-rating of land and agricultural buildings (in stages, 1923–9) reduced costs.

In the 1930s, in response to difficult economic conditions, the government sought to sustain agriculture and increase efficiency. The 1931 Agricultural Marketing Act authorized marketing boards in Britain, and the 1932 Wheat Act (for UK) guaranteed minimum prices for wheat. The 1937 Agriculture Act began war preparations, including subsidies to expand wheat acreage and for additional crops. The 1939 Agricultural Development Act subsidized ploughing of grassland for cereal production. Support was extended in 1944 (during WORLD WAR II), and the post-war 1947 Agriculture Act guaranteed prices in the UK for most products (basis of support altered 1953). Arrangements continued until the UK joined the European Economic Community (1973; see COMMON AGRICULTURAL POLICY).

AGRICULTURE, STATE INVOLVEMENT, NORTHERN IRELAND The provincial government formed in 1921 included a Ministry of Agriculture. In the 1920s–30s, it sought to raise standards of produce partly to increase exports. Initiatives included the 1922 Livestock Breeding Act, which required the licensing of bulls, the 1924 Eggs Marketing Act, the 1925 Drainage Act, and the 1934–8 Milk Acts.

Farming was assisted by de-rating of agricultural land from 1923. During WORLD WAR II (1939–45), State incentives and requirements increased production, especially of crops (ploughed acreage almost doubled 1939–43). Land improvement was further encouraged by the Drainage Act of 1947.

Between 1947 and 1954, UK legislation guaranteed prices for main produce. In 1973, agriculture became subordinate to the COMMON AGRICULTURAL POLICY of the European Economic Community.

AGRICULTURE, STATE INVOLVEMENT, SOUTHERN IRELAND In the 1920s, government initiatives attempted to increase output and exports (mostly pastoral products sold to Great Britain). Improvement of quality was emphasized. Creameries were reorganized, a sugar-beet factory was built, and an Agricultural Credit Corporation was founded (1927). Import duties were imposed on a few products (butter, oats, oatmeal) for protection. State-sponsored transfer of land ownership from landlords to tenants continued (Land Acts 1923, 1927).

The government of Éamon DE VALERA (premier 1932–48) sought agricultural self-sufficiency by expanding grain production. It introduced price support for dairy products (1932) and grain crops (1933). But the ECONOMIC WAR provoked by de Valera in 1932 reduced exports and farmers' incomes.

Renewed decline of farmers' incomes from the 1950s was countered by government contracts for some agricultural products, and in the 1960s by subsidies and an Anglo-Irish Free Trade Agreement (1965). From 1973, agriculture was subject to the COMMON AGRICULTURAL POLICY of the European Economic Community.

AGRICULTURE, WALES BEFORE 18TH CENTURY Agriculture was strongly influenced by varying physical geography – with much upland, mountainous regions and forest – and by variable land quality. Until the 17th century, crop yields were generally below those of England except in the fertile SE. In lowland regions (along the S coast and BORDER lands), mixed agriculture (arable and stock keeping) was the norm. In the uplands, pastoral farming predominated, with animals being moved annually to summer pastures (transhumance) until the late 18th century. Cattle were the main animals in the rural economy, and also a principal export to England.

Much arable farming was based on the open-field system (see AGRICULTURE, ENGLAND BEFORE MID 18TH CENTURY), though in uplands the infield–outfield system was probably common (see AGRICULTURE, SCOTLAND BEFORE 18TH CENTURY). Because many uplands were of poor quality, more particularly of high acidity, the main crop was oats. Barley and wheat were more common on lowland parts of the MARCH OF WALES. Sheep farming on uplands

was a relatively late introduction, and was developed particularly by Cistercian monasteries in S Wales in the 12th century. It expanded significantly in the 15th century, partly because of the decline of arable farming in the wake of the BLACK DEATH (1349). From the late 17th century, some wealthier farmers adopted new husbandry techniques. See also TENURES, WALES; RURAL SETTLEMENT AND SOCIETY, WALES.

AGRICULTURE, WALES FROM 18TH CENTURY Stock rearing remained the predominant activity, so innovations relating to animals were most important. From the late 18th century, new breeds were produced by cross-breeding with English sheep and cattle; some were widely adopted. The Welsh Black cattle breed, created in the mid 19th century from two PEMBROKESHIRE varieties, was notably successful. In arable-based lowlands, landowners used extended rotations (including turnips) on home farms and participated in mid 19th-century HIGH FARMING. But tenant farmers were notably less enterprising. Investment in some areas was stimulated by demand from industrial TOWNS and availability of RAILWAYS. During the AGRICULTURAL DEPRESSION (1880s–90s), about 40% of arable land was converted to pasture.

Demand during WORLD WAR I (1914–18) brought prosperity, while post-war land sales increased owner-occupied land from 10 to 39%. But price falls depressed agriculture; recovery began only in the late 1930s, with expansion of dairying, and became widespread during WORLD WAR II (1939–45).

After 1945, selective herbicides, improved fertilizers and machinery (tractors, harvesters) increased arable productivity. From 1973, agriculture was subject to the COMMON AGRICULTURAL POLICY of the European Economic Community. By 1990, the number of farms had halved, though 72% of holdings remained smaller than 123 acres (50 ha). In the late 1990s, price falls again threatened both upland sheep farming and all aspects of cattle production. In the early 21st century, farming remained primarily pastoral, though in dairying only large herds of cows (several hundred head) were viable. Many farmers engaged in diverse activities (e.g., provision of accommodation) to provide sufficient income. See also TENURES, WALES; ENCLOSURES, WALES; RURAL SETTLEMENT AND SOCIETY, WALES; AGRICULTURE, STATE INTERVENTION, GREAT BRITAIN.

AHERN, BERTIE (b. 12 Sept. 1951 at Drumcondra, Co. Dublin, Republic of Ireland). A FIANNA FÁIL TD (1977–2011), Ahern served in the governments of Charles HAUGHEY and Albert REYNOLDS. Elected party leader after Reynolds (1994), he was unable to become taoiseach (premier) because Fianna Fáil's coalition partner (Labour) changed alliance (see BRUTON, JOHN).

After the 1997 general election, Ahern became taoiseach of a coalition government, continuing with coalitions after the 2002 and 2007 elections. With Tony BLAIR, he reinvigorated the Northern Ireland PEACE PROCESS, resulting in the BELFAST AGREEMENT (1998), modification of the Republic's constitutional claim to Northern Ireland (1999), and devolved government in Northern Ireland (1999–2002). During Ahern's premiership, the Republic entered the euro currency (1999) and accepted the European Union's treaty of Nice (2002, by second referendum). In early 2002, the government accepted a payment from Catholic religious orders for indemnification against child abuse claims. A proposed tightening of the ABORTION prohibition was rejected by referendum (2002). Economic expansion continued.

Suspicions about personal finances raised by the Mahon Tribunal into political corruption caused Ahern to resign as taoiseach and party leader (effective May 2008). After the economic crash of Sept. 2008, he was widely blamed for Ireland's plight. *See also* SOCIAL PARTNERSHIP; COWEN, BRIAN; CHURCH–STATE RELATIONS, SOUTHERN IRELAND FROM 1922.

AIDAN (fl. from 635; d. 31 Aug. 651 near Bamburgh, Bernicia). In 635 Aidan, an Irish monk at IONA (off W Scotland), offered to serve as bishop and missionary in BERNICIA and DEIRA (NE England), to meet a request from King OSWALD. After being consecrated, he settled on Lindisfarne, where a monastery was founded, and from where he made preaching tours on foot. After Oswald's death (642), he continued work under OSWIU and Oswine (subking in Deira). *See also* CONVERSION OF ANGLO-SAXONS; CHAD.

AIRCRAFT INDUSTRY, UNITED KINGDOM Short Brothers was the first company in the world to manufacture aircraft, from 1909 in London. A sizable industry developed primarily because of military demand. During WORLD WAR I (1914–18), employment reached 112,000, and 58,000 planes were produced (from 1918 mainly for the ROYAL AIR FORCE). Contraction followed, with employment reduced to 30,000 by 1930. About 15 companies made airframes, and five made engines, mainly for the RAF, although aircraft were also produced for commercial AIR TRANSPORT and private flying. Re-expansion of military production began in 1934.

During WORLD WAR II (1939–45), employment reached 340,000 and 131,000 planes were manufactured. An outstanding innovation was the jet engine (in service from 1944; *see* WHITTLE, FRANK).

Aircraft development was extensively funded by the government from the mid 1940s to sustain a substantial industry. New military planes included the Canberra bomber (in RAF service 1951–2006), Hunter fighter (1951–1990s) and Lightning supersonic fighter (1959–88). Civil planes included the first jet-powered airliner, the Comet (from 1952). Its grounding (1954–8), after crashes, allowed the US industry to overtake. The VC-10 (produced 1962–70) was the last British long-haul airliner.

From the late 1950s the government encouraged company mergers and international collaborations. The latter produced the Anglo-French supersonic airliner Concorde (in service 1976–2003). From 1967, wings were contributed to European 'Airbus' aircraft.

In 1971, following collapse, engine manufacturer ROLLS-ROYCE was nationalized, and in 1977 most other manufacturing was consolidated in the State-owned British Aircraft Corporation (both privatized in 1980s). New military aircraft were collaborations, notably the Tornado (manufactured 1979–98) and Typhoon (from 1994).

The creation of the defence company BAE Systems in 1999 subsumed most aircraft production. Production of civil aircraft (small airliners) ended in 2013. In 2017, aircraft and related aerospace manufacturing employed 120,000 people. Rolls-Royce remained a world leader in jet engines. *See also* INDUSTRY, NORTHERN IRELAND.

AIR FORCE, SOUTHERN IRELAND *see* DEFENCE FORCES, SOUTHERN IRELAND

AIR FORCE, UNITED KINGDOM *see* ROYAL AIR FORCE

AIRGIALLA (ORIEL OR URIEL) A kingdom in central N Ireland (broadly between Loughs Erne and Neagh). It existed by the 5th century when it may have changed allegiance from the Ulaid (retreating eastwards) to the advancing Northern Uí NÉILL (*see* ULSTER). Its name, meaning 'Eastern hostages', was bestowed by the latter. Airgialla supposedly comprised nine dynasties, one holding a high-kingship. During the 7th and 8th centuries lands were lost to the Cenél nEógain branch of the Northern Uí Néill (modern Co. Tyrone).

By the 11th century the Ua Cerbaill dynasty was dominant (English, O'Carroll). Donnchad Ua Cerbaill (d. 1168) added lands to the SE (modern Co. Louth) by 1142. After his son Murchad's death (1189), Prince JOHN of England granted lands to the Anglo-Normans Bertram de Verdon and Gilbert Pipard (1189 or 1190). Settlement by their retainers caused Ua Cerbaill authority to collapse.

From the early 13th century, the Mac Mathgamna (MacMahon) dynasty dominated the reduced kingdom (modern Co. Monaghan). In 1590, Hugh Roe MacMahon was executed for treason by the English and his lordship was divided (1591). *See also* NIALL NOÍGIALLACH; ARMAGH.

AIR TRANSPORT, GREAT BRITAIN AND NORTHERN IRELAND Aeroplanes flew in Britain from 1908, and were soon used for military purposes (*see* ROYAL AIR FORCE). State regulation of civil aviation, and scheduled services (initially to Paris, France), began in 1919, the latter operated by British and overseas companies. The earliest international airports were near LONDON at Hounslow Heath (1919–20) and Croydon (1920–39). From 1924, the main British airline was Imperial Airways (created by a merger), which pioneered routes across the BRITISH EMPIRE. In the 1930s several companies developed domestic routes (e.g., to MANCHESTER, BELFAST, GLASGOW); a merger created British Airways (1935), which served domestic and Continental European destinations. Imperial and BA merged in 1940, under State ownership, as the British Overseas Airways Corporation (BOAC). Pan American Airways operated scheduled trans-Atlantic flights in 1939. Commercial flying was restricted during WORLD WAR II (1939–45).

From 1946, Heathrow London (created for military use) was the primary civil airport (busiest in Europe by 1955). Gatwick was expanded from 1958 as London's second airport. The designation of Stansted in 1969 as the third reflected the growth of flying as a mass activity (e.g., for holidays). London City Airport, near central London, opened in 1987 for smaller aircraft; Luton Airport was renamed 'London Luton' in 1990. Regional airports were also expanded. By the early 21st century there were 15 major airports.

In 1947, several companies were absorbed by State-owned British European Airways (BEA, formed 1946), establishing a State 'duopoly' of British-based passenger air transport. BOAC introduced jet airliners (Comet) in 1952. From 1960, competition was allowed from independent airlines (e.g., British United Airways). BOAC and BEA merged in 1974 as British Airways (privatized 1987). Further liberalization from the 1980s enabled 'low-cost' airlines to flourish from 1995. In 2015, airports handled about 260 million passengers.

AIR TRANSPORT, SOUTHERN IRELAND After the first aeroplane flight in Ireland, in 1910 (by Harry Ferguson of BELFAST), recreational flying developed. Military airfields and seaplane bases were opened in 1917–18 (during WORLD WAR I), notably Baldonnel Aerodrome near DUBLIN which became southern Ireland's main military airfield (renamed Casement Aerodrome in 1965).

The IRISH FREE STATE founded a military Air Service in 1922 (*see* DEFENCE FORCES, SOUTHERN IRELAND), but eschewed civil aviation until 1935 when it agreed to provide facilities for trans-Atlantic flights by the W coast. The Foynes flying boat terminal by the Shannon estuary serviced flights 1939–45, and was superseded by Shannon Airport, at which flights from the USA terminated under a 1945 agreement with the USA. Meanwhile, a State airline, Aer Lingus, was started (1936), operating from Baldonnel to Great Britain; Aer Rianta was created as a civil aviation and ownership authority (1937); and Dublin Airport was opened (1940).

Further expansion included flights to Continental Europe (from late 1940s), Aer Lingus services to the USA (1958), and the opening of CORK Airport (1961). Smaller regional airports were created in the later 20th century, including Knock International (Co. Mayo) for visitors to Knock Shrine (1985). The requirement for flights from the USA to use Shannon Airport was modified in 1994 and ended in 2008. New Irish airlines included Ryanair (1985), a 'low-cost carrier' which became one of Ireland's largest companies, by 2015 operating over 350 aircraft. In 2015, the Republic's airports handled almost 30 million passengers, with Dublin accounting for 81% of flights.

AIX-LA-CHAPELLE, TREATY OF Peace treaty signed on 7 Oct. 1748 at the free imperial city of Aix-la-Chapelle (German, Aachen), ending the War of the AUSTRIAN SUCCESSION. It largely restored wartime conquests to their pre-war rulers. It also renewed the trading contract (Spanish *asiento*) granted to Great Britain by Spain in 1713, and reconfirmed recognition of the HANOVERIAN SUCCESSION (*see* UTRECHT, PEACE OF). Britain subsequently surrendered the *asiento* in return for other concessions (treaty of Madrid, 24 Sept. 1750). *See also* ROBINSON, THOMAS.

***ALABAMA* AFFAIR** A dispute between Great Britain and the USA. In 1862, during the AMERICAN CIVIL WAR, the British government failed to impound a vessel built at Birkenhead (NW England) for use as a cruiser by the breakaway American Confederacy. As the *Alabama*, it inflicted considerable damage on US Federal shipping. The USA demanded compensation and, after protracted negotiations, Britain agreed in 1872 to pay $15.5 million for damages caused by the *Alabama* and ten other British-built ships.

ALBANY, 2ND DUKE OF *see* STEWART, MURDOCH

ALBANY, 3RD DUKE OF *see* STEWART, ALEXANDER

ALBANY, 4TH DUKE of *see* STEWART, JOHN

ALBANY, ROBERT DUKE OF *see* STEWART, ROBERT

ALBERT OF SAXE-COBURG (b. 26 Aug. 1819 at Schloss Rosenau, Saxe-Coburg-Saalfeld, Germany; d. 14 Dec. 1861 at Windsor, Berkshire, England, aged 42). In 1840 Albert, a younger son of Duke Ernst I of Saxe-Coburg-Gotha, married his first cousin VICTORIA, queen of Great Britain and Ireland.

Intensely serious and obviously foreign, he was never widely popular, but his intelligence gradually won the respect of senior politicians. Under his influence, Victoria became an impartial (though still active) constitutional monarch, and respectable domesticity characterized the royal family. Eager to advance art, science and technology, Albert promoted the GREAT EXHIBITION (1851). He was given the title of 'prince consort' in 1857. He died of typhoid. *See also* KINGSHIP AND MONARCHY, ENGLAND AND GREAT BRITAIN FROM 1680s.

ALCHEMY A mixture of pseudo-scientific and philosophical thought which sought the 'philosopher's stone', a substance that would turn base metals (e.g., lead, copper) into gold or silver. Alchemy flourished in England during the 14th–17th centuries and is recorded in Scotland in the early 16th century. It declined after the SCIENTIFIC REVOLUTION of the 17th century. *See also* DEE, JOHN; NEWTON, ISAAC.

ALCUIN (b. *c.*740 in Northumbria; d. 19 May 804 at Tours, Francia, aged about 64). Master of the cathedral school at YORK, Northumbria (NE England), Alcuin was invited by Charlemagne, king of the Franks, to advise on educational and Church matters (781). He lived in Francia from 786 (returned to Northumbria 790–3), and was abbot of St Martin at Tours from 796. He revised the Frankish liturgy, wrote books on many subjects, participated in theological disputes, and corresponded with English kings and clergy (over 300 letters survive). *See also* EDUCATION AND LEARNING, ENGLAND BEFORE 1066.

ALEHOUSES, TAVERNS, INNS Alehouses were ordinary houses in which people bought and consumed ale (barley-based alcohol), which was usually brewed on the premises, sometimes by women. In existence by the 11th century, they were widespread in towns and the countryside in the 14th century, their presence indicated by signs. Poorer people could augment their income by running an alehouse. In England in the late 16th and 17th centuries, as probably elsewhere, alehouses became more numerous in relation to the population. Beer replaced ale, sometimes provided by commercial 'common brewers'. Authorities viewed alehouses as unruly and subversive places, and attempted to control them through LICENSING and other means. They were called 'public houses' (or 'pubs') from the 18th century, and from the 1820s onwards were often purpose-built.

Taverns were rooms or buildings for the sale and consumption of wine. As it was more expensive than ale, taverns attracted a better-off clientele, and occurred mainly in towns. Well established by the 13th century, by the 16th century they also provided meals. Taverns lost their distinctiveness from the 18th century.

Inns provided lodgings for travellers and usually also stabling for horses. Although of earlier origin, they were familiar in towns from the late 14th century, with most small towns having two or three inns and larger towns many more. Some were substantial businesses with numerous rooms, and innkeepers might be important local figures. Inns were used as meeting places, and in the late 17th–early 19th centuries some were social centres for GENTRY. During the same period, inns on main roads facilitated stage-coaching. Inns were superseded from the 19th century by hotels, which concentrated on provision of accommodation.

ALEXANDER, WILLIAM (b. *c.*1567 in Scotland; d. 12 Sept. 1640 at London, England, aged about 73). As tutor to Prince HENRY, eldest son of King JAMES VI of Scotland, Alexander moved to England with James on the UNION OF CROWNS (1603). He was knighted (1609) and, on Henry's death (1612), transferred to the household of Henry's younger brother Charles.

In 1621 Alexander was granted NOVA SCOTIA, where he attempted, unsuccessfully, to establish a Scottish colony. From 1626 until his death, he was CHARLES I's SECRETARY OF STATE for Scotland (based in England); he remained a staunch royalist. He was created Viscount (1630) and earl of Stirling (1633).

ALEXANDER I (b. *c.*1077; d. 23 April 1124 at Stirling, C Scotland, aged about 48). King of Scots (Scotland) 1107–24.

The fifth son of MALCOLM III and MARGARET (both d. 1093), Alexander succeeded his brother EDGAR (8 Jan. 1107). By 1113, he ceded subordinate rule of S Scotland to his younger brother (*see* DAVID I). Alexander championed autonomy for the Scottish Church (against claims from archbishops of YORK, England): in 1109 his new bishop of ST ANDREWS, Turgot (d. 1115), probably withheld obedience when consecrated by the archbishop. Alexander also brought Augustinian canons from England to SCONE (*c.*1115). Succeeded by David I. *See also* MAC MALCOLM RULERS; RELIGIOUS ORDERS.

ALEXANDER II (b. 24 Aug. 1198 at Haddington, Lothian, SE Scotland; d. 8 July 1249 at Kerrera, Argyll, W Scotland, aged 50). King of Scots (Scotland) 1214–49. Alexander succeeded WILLIAM I (father) aged 16 (4 Dec. 1214) and joined the rebellion against King JOHN of England, seeking to regain northern English counties (*see* DAVID I). In Aug. 1216, he led an army to Dover, SE England, where he did homage to Prince Louis of France for the counties, agreeing they would remain within England. But Alexander's assertion of authority over the territories in spring 1217 (following John's death in Oct. 1216) caused the papal legate in England to place Alexander and leading subjects under an interdict. On 1 Dec. he surrendered CARLISLE in return for absolution, and soon afterwards did homage to HENRY III for other English lands. In 1221 Alexander married Henry's sister Joan.

Alexander exerted authority within Scotland by suppressing rebellions in MORAY, NE Scotland (1228–30), and GALLOWAY, SW Scotland (1235). In 1237 he renounced claims to N England (treaty of YORK). Following another treaty with England (1244), Alexander sought to acquire the WESTERN ISLES. He died while expelling Ewen, son of Duncan, agent of King Haakon IV of Norway. Succeeded by ALEXANDER III. *See also* MAC MALCOLM RULERS; ENGLAND, FRENCH INVASION (1216–17).

ALEXANDER III (b. 4 Sept. 1241 at Roxburgh, SE Scotland; d. 8 March 1286 near Kinghorn, Fife, E Scotland, aged 44). King of Scots (Scotland) 1249–86. Alexander succeeded ALEXANDER II (father) aged 7 (8 July 1249). In 1251 he married Margaret, daughter of King HENRY III of England. During his minority, until 1260, rival factions (particularly the COMYN family and Alan Durward) periodically replaced each other in royal offices. Henry III also intervened.

Alexander acquired suzerainty of the WESTERN ISLES and Isle of MAN from Norway in 1266 (*see* LARGS, BATTLE OF; PERTH, TREATY OF). Thereafter his reign was peaceful (including good relations with England), and probably highly successful. Alexander died after falling from his horse. His children were already dead; he was succeeded by his grand-daughter, MARGARET, 'THE MAID OF NORWAY'. *See also* MAC MALCOLM RULERS.

ALFRED (b. 848 or 849 at Wantage, Wessex; d. 26 Oct. 899 in Wessex, aged about 50). The fourth son of King ÆTHELWULF to rule WESSEX (S England), Alfred succeeded his brother Æthelred as king in April 871. VIKINGS were attempting to overrun Wessex (one of only three remaining Anglo-Saxon kingdoms). In 878 much of Wessex capitulated; Alfred fled into hiding at Athelney (Somerset). Soon afterwards, he defeated a Viking army at EDINGTON (Wiltshire) and made terms with their leader, Guthrum (treaty of Wedmore). He constructed BURHS (fortresses) around Wessex to increase its security. By 883, Alfred was overking of (western) MERCIA, and in 886 he captured LONDON and the Thames Valley. He successfully countered further Viking attacks (892–6).

Alfred recruited scholars from Francia, Mercia and Wales to help raise standards of LITERACY and Christian knowledge among the Wessex clergy and nobles (*see* ASSER). He himself translated several books from Latin into Old English, and commissioned the *ANGLO-SAXON CHRONICLE*. He adopted the title 'king of the Anglo-Saxons'. The legend of Alfred, at Athelney, allowing cakes to burn while he pondered his future dates from the 10th century. *See also* KINGSHIP, ANGLO-SAXON; ANGLO-SAXONS.

ALIEN ACT Legislation passed by the English Parliament in Feb. 1705 in response to anti-English Acts of the Scottish Parliament, especially the Act of SECURITY. It required Scotland to begin negotiations for union by 25 Dec. 1705 or accept the HANOVERIAN SUCCESSION. If ignored, punitive measures would follow (including the treatment of Scots coming to England as aliens). It stirred anti-English feeling in Scotland (*see* WORCESTER AFFAIR) but succeeded in its purpose. *See also* UNION OF ENGLAND AND SCOTLAND.

ALIEN PRIORIES, ENGLAND AND WALES Religious houses, generally small (some very small, with two or three monks), which were founded mainly in the late 11th and 12th centuries following the NORMAN CONQUEST. Perhaps totalling about 100, they were controlled and often staffed from overseas monasteries, many in NORMANDY.

During conflict with France, the king seized the priories' estates to obtain their revenues (1295–1303, 1337–60, 1369–99). Several larger houses obtained independence (so-called 'denization'), but many of the smaller ones were confiscated and suppressed by 1414. Their estates were used to endow new institutions such as colleges in OXFORD and CAMBRIDGE. *See also* MONASTICISM, MEDIEVAL ENGLAND/WALES; EDWARD I; HUNDRED YEARS WAR.

ALLECTUS (d. 296 in S Britain). Of unknown origin, Allectus was probably the chief finance minister of the usurper CARAUSIUS, whom he assassinated in 293, thereby replacing him as ruler of ROMAN BRITAIN. Allectus held power for three years (293–6), until he was defeated and killed by Asclepiodotus, praetorian prefect of Emperor Constantius I, at an unknown site in S Britain (perhaps in modern Hampshire).

ALLENBY, EDMUND (b. 23 April 1861 at Brackenhurst Hall, Nottinghamshire, England; d. 14 May 1936 at London, England, aged 75). A soldier from 1881, Allenby held commands in the (Second) BOER WAR (1899–1902) and WORLD WAR I (from 1914). As commander of the Egyptian Expeditionary Force from June 1917, he led campaigns against the Ottoman Turks in PALESTINE. The Third Battle of Gaza (Oct.–Dec.) resulted in the capture of Jerusalem, which Allenby entered dramatically on 11 Dec. He commanded a final offensive northwards in Sept.–Oct. 1918, which left him in charge of an extensive area. Allenby served as special high commissioner to EGYPT (1919–25), when he oversaw its recognition as a sovereign state. He was created Viscount Allenby in 1919.

ALLIANCE PARTY A political party in NORTHERN IRELAND, founded on 21 April 1970. Originating in the CIVIL RIGHTS MOVEMENT, it sought to be non-sectarian, centrist and liberal. It drew support mainly from urban middle-class Unionists (initially former supporters of Terence O'NEILL) and nationalists (many formerly supporters of the Northern Ireland Labour Party).

Alliance joined the power-sharing Executive of 1974. It supported the BELFAST AGREEMENT (1998), and was usually the fifth largest party in the subsequent ASSEMBLY. From 2010, it participated in the EXECUTIVE, but became critical of the power-sharing system, claiming that 'horse trading' between the major sectarian parties deepened sectarian divisions. It left the Executive for opposition in 2016.

AMBROSIUS AURELIANUS (fl. in mid 5th century in Britain). A British military leader, from a Roman background. According to GILDAS, he roused defeated Britons (in W or SW Britain) to challenge rebellious 'Saxons' (possibly in 440s). The Britons were successful, though a long period of indecisive conflict followed, lasting until the battle of MOUNT BADON. *See* POST-ROMAN BRITAIN; VORTIGERN.

AMERICAN CIVIL WAR AND GREAT BRITAIN British opinion was divided over the secession of the proslavery southern states of the USA in 1861. Many British aristocrats favoured the southern plantation owners, and some traders anticipated free markets in the newly formed Confederate States of America. Radicals such as John BRIGHT, however, passionately supported the Union. The *TRENT* INCIDENT (Nov.–Dec. 1861) and the *ALABAMA* AFFAIR (from 1862) created ill feeling between Britain and the USA, but Lord PALMERSTON, the British prime minister, withheld recognition from the Confederacy and preserved neutrality.

Sympathy for the southern states waned after President Abraham Lincoln's 'Emancipation Proclamation' (1 Jan. 1863), which freed slaves in rebellious areas. British ships did not break the Union's blockade, despite the impact of the COTTON FAMINE. The anti-slavery campaign reinvigorated British Radicals, and working-class support for a moral cause impressed the leading Liberal W.E. GLADSTONE. Thus the American Civil War indirectly helped to revive the British movement for PARLIAMENTARY REFORM. The Confederate States surrendered in April 1865. *See also* UNITED STATES OF AMERICA, BRITISH RELATIONS WITH.

AMERICAN INDEPENDENCE In 1776, THIRTEEN COLONIES in the Americas declared independence from Great Britain as the United States of America. Their action resulted from disputes over taxation for defence costs, and the outbreak of war (*see* AMERICAN INDEPENDENCE, ORIGINS OF). It was the first secession from the BRITISH EMPIRE.

Colonies co-operated against Britain from Oct. 1765, when nine held the 'Stamp Act Congress' in New York to denounce Britain's Stamp Act. The INTOLERABLE ACTS of 1774 provoked the First Continental Congress, at Philadelphia (Sept. 1774–Aug. 1776), representing 12 colonies (GEORGIA was unrepresented). It petitioned GEORGE III for redress, organized resistance, and rejected union.

After war broke out in April 1775, colonial royal governors fled and colonial congresses seized power. During the ensuing AMERICAN WAR OF INDEPENDENCE (1775–81), Congress provided co-ordination. It authorized a 'Continental Army' (May 1775) and again petitioned King George (July). Radical opponents of Britain, notably Thomas PAINE, urged independence. In May 1776, Congress advised colonies to form independent governments as 'states'. Congress voted for independence (2 July) and issued a Declaration of Independence (4 July). Eleven states also adopted new constitutions (1776–80; CONNECTICUT and RHODE ISLAND were exceptions). A Second Continental Congress, including Georgia, met from Sept. 1776. In Nov. 1777, it approved Articles of Confederation (approved by States by Feb. 1781).

On 2 March 1781 the States, still individually sovereign, inaugurated the Confederation. As it lacked a central government, the Congress of the Confederation co-ordinated policy. Following the British surrender at YORKTOWN (19 Oct.), Congress obtained recognition of independence from Britain (in treaty of Paris, 1783). But the Confederation was considered ineffective. In 1787 a Federal Convention, convened to revise the Articles, produced a constitution. It prescribed a federal State with an elected president, government, army and navy, and bicameral legislature (implemented 2 July 1788). George WASHINGTON became president in 1789.

AMERICAN INDEPENDENCE, ORIGINS OF When the SEVEN YEARS WAR ended in 1763, Great Britain became the dominant imperial power in N America. But its acquisition of 'New France', including land along the Mississippi parallel to its east-coast colonies, required provision of an army for defence. Attempts to fund this partly through taxation on the colonies were resisted.

In 1764–5 the ministry of George GRENVILLE in Britain promoted legislation affecting the colonies: the Currency Act (1764), which regulated colonial currency; the Sugar Act (1764), which increased import duties; and the Stamp Act (1765), which imposed a duty on publications and documents. Violent resistance led the ministry of the earl of ROCKINGHAM, in March 1767, to pass the Declaratory Act, which affirmed the British Parliament's right to legislate for the colonies, while also repealing the Sugar and Stamp Acts. But in June the new ministry, headed by the earl of Chatham (William PITT the Elder), imposed the 'Townshend duties' on the colonies (on tea, glass, paper, etc.). Protests followed, with colonists asserting there must be 'no taxation without representation'. Most duties were withdrawn (1770).

In 1773 the Tea Act, passed for the ministry of Lord NORTH, allowed tea to be exported directly from India to America. It affected mercantile interests in Massachusetts. The violent response, notably the BOSTON TEA PARTY (Dec.), provoked coercive measures from North's government (1774; see INTOLERABLE ACTS). Skirmishes between colonists and British troops in 1775 led to war. On 4 July 1776, a congress of 13 colonies at Philadelphia declared independence. See also NORTH AMERICAN COLONIES; AMERICAN WAR OF INDEPENDENCE.

AMERICAN WAR OF INDEPENDENCE The attempt by Great Britain to assert authority over THIRTEEN COLONIES in N America, 1775–81, following disputes (see AMERICAN INDEPENDENCE, ORIGINS OF).

Skirmishes broke out on 19 April 1775 in the northern colony of MASSACHUSETTS (at Lexington and Concord). Colonial militias then besieged British forces at Boston, while another colonial force invaded CANADA (May 1775–May 1776). British troops evicted a threatening force at Creed's Hill near Boston (17 June, battle of Bunker Hill). Meanwhile the colonies' Continental Congress had authorized (May) a 'Continental Army' (George WASHINGTON appointed commander-in-chief, June). From Oct., William HOWE commanded British forces, and Britain imposed an embargo on colonial exports (Dec.). British forces left Boston by sea in March 1776. On 4 July the Congress formally declared independence.

Britain attempted to isolate NEW ENGLAND by capturing New York City (achieved July–Sept. 1776). Its forces (including German mercenaries) then marched S into NEW JERSEY, but were defeated by Washington's army at Trenton (26 Dec.) and Princeton (3 Jan. 1777).

In July 1777, British forces sailed to Chesapeake Bay. They defeated Washington's army at Brandywine Creek (11 Sept.) and occupied Philadelphia, PENNSYLVANIA (26 Sept.). From June 1777, a British force also invaded from Canada to divide the colonies (British surrendered at Saratoga, 17 Oct.). In 1778, Henry Clinton replaced Howe (May), and led British forces from Philadelphia back to New York (June). The colonies were strengthened by alliance with France (Feb. 1778).

The British attempted to conquer the southern colonies, starting with GEORGIA (from Oct. 1778; captured Savannah, 29 Dec., Augusta, Jan. 1779). In SOUTH CAROLINA they took Charleston (12 May 1780) and were victorious at Camden (16 Aug.). In NORTH CAROLINA they fought at Guildford Courthouse (15 March 1781). After resting at Wilmington (April), they moved N into VIRGINIA, but were besieged at YORKTOWN, where George

CORNWALLIS surrendered (19 Oct.). See also AMERICAN INDEPENDENCE.

AMERICAN WAR OF INDEPENDENCE, IMPACT ON IRELAND The war (1775–81) dramatically affected Ireland, partly because of inept reactions by the British and Irish governments. After war began, the British government imposed additional restrictions on Irish food exports (3 Feb. 1776), to sustain supplies to Britain. This plus a trade recession caused resentment, eventually provoking the NON-IMPORTATION MOVEMENT (1778–9). The Irish government's refusal to fund a militia in 1778, after troops were redeployed to coastal areas (following France's alliance with the USA, Feb. 1778), resulted in the formation of the VOLUNTEERS (voluntary militia), who became politically active.

After a British army in N America surrendered at YORKTOWN (1781), PATRIOT members of the Irish Parliament (e.g., Henry GRATTAN; earl of CHARLEMONT) recruited Volunteer support and pressed for greater autonomy for Ireland. The result was the CONSTITUTION OF 1782. See also PROTESTANT ASCENDANCY; BUCKINGHAM-SHIRE, 2ND EARL OF.

AMERY, LEOPOLD (b. 22 Nov. 1873 at Gorakhpur, North Western Provinces, India; d. 16 Sept. 1955 at London, England, aged 81). As a writer and editor in Great Britain for *The Times* 1899–1909, concerned with SOUTH AFRICA, Amery admired the imperial policies of Alfred MILNER. He became a prominent champion of the BRITISH EMPIRE. A Conservative MP 1911–45, he held government posts from 1917. As colonial secretary 1924–9, and also dominions secretary 1925–9, he supported 'imperial preference' (see TARIFF REFORM) and advocated the idea of a 'co-operative Commonwealth'. He was secretary of state for INDIA and BURMA 1940–5. See also DOMINION; COMMONWEALTH.

AMICABLE GRANT In England, a TAX instigated in 1525 by Thomas WOLSEY for King HENRY VIII, to fund an invasion of France. It was imposed by ROYAL PREROGATIVE, rather than granted by Parliament, and was to be levied on clergy and laity. Following soon after other heavy taxation, the collection (from April) generated popular resistance and was abandoned (by 13 May).

AMIENS, PEACE OF A truce between Great Britain and France concluded at Amiens, France, on 27 March 1802 (negotiated for the ministry of Henry ADDINGTON). It halted hostilities during the NAPOLEONIC WARS by fudging controversial strategic issues. Terms included the abandonment by the British Crown of its 14th-century claim to the French Crown (see FRANCE, CLAIMS BY RULERS OF ENGLAND). French intervention in Italy and Switzerland, coupled with Britain's refusal to evacuate MALTA, sparked renewed conflict in May 1803.

AMRITSAR MASSACRE A notorious incident in the city of Amritsar (NW India) on 13 April 1919 (also known as the Jallianwala Bagh Massacre), when a British commander, Brigadier-General Sir Reginald Dyer, ordered troops (mostly Indians) to fire on a large crowd of protestors in a walled recreation ground. It happened soon after wartime emergency powers in India had been extended (so-called Rowlatt Act), and in reprisal for recent violent protests in Amritsar. Possibly 500–600 people were killed and 1500 were wounded. The event discredited British rule in INDIA.

ANARCHISM A political creed based on the belief that government is evil and can be abolished. Anarchists reject restraints on spontaneous action and generally favour violent revolution. Developed in 19th-century Europe, the doctrine spread from foreign exiles to a few British extremists.

ANARCHY Term used to describe conditions in NORMANDY and England (especially the latter) during struggles to oust STEPHEN as ruler (in Normandy 1138–44, in England 1139–54). Based on contemporary accounts, the term suggests a total breakdown of authority. Modern study has shown that in England, each side exercised some authority over extensive areas (including issue of CURRENCY), and that disorder was often circumscribed (e.g., by local pacts between opponents). *See also* MATILDA; DAVID I.

ANCIENT CONSTITUTION A concept formulated in England in the early 17th century, particularly by Edward COKE (d. 1634), which claimed that royal power had been regulated by COMMON LAW since at least the time of King ÆTHELBERT of Kent (d. 616). Englishmen therefore possessed inherited liberties. The concept influenced opponents of JAMES VI/I and CHARLES I, who by contrast claimed unfettered prerogative rights of divine origin (*see* DIVINE RIGHT MONARCHY).

ANCIENT ORDER OF HIBERNIANS A Catholic men's charitable society (with women's branch), which was refounded in the USA in 1838. After Church condemnation (for secrecy) was lifted in 1904, the small Irish branch was reorganized by Joseph DEVLIN, who presided over its controlling 'Board of Erin' 1905–34. The Order expanded rapidly, mainly in N Ireland, to 60,000 members in 1909, 120,000 in 1915. They provided a 'power base' for Devlin and the IRISH PARLIAMENTARY PARTY, and countered the Protestant ORANGE ORDER. Membership fell rapidly from c.1970.

ANDERSON, ELIZABETH GARRETT (b. 9 June 1836 at London, England; d. 17 Dec. 1917 at Aldeburgh, Suffolk, England, aged 81). Elizabeth Garrett joined the LANGHAM PLACE CIRCLE in the mid 1850s. Inspired by Elizabeth Blackwell, an English woman with a US medical degree, she qualified as an apothecary (1865), obtained a medical degree from Paris University (1870), and joined the British Medical Association (1873), making her England's first qualified woman doctor. She also founded the New Hospital for Women (1868) and promoted women's medical education. (She married in 1871.) In retirement Anderson became England's first woman mayor (1908). *See also* FAWCETT, MILLICENT; WOMEN'S MOVEMENT 1850s TO 1918, GREAT BRITAIN.

ANDERSON, JOHN (b. 8 July 1882 at Edinburgh, Scotland; d. 4 Jan. 1958 at London, England, aged 75). A distinguished British civil servant, Anderson served as governor of Bengal, INDIA, 1932–7, and was an Independent MP 1938–50 (for Scottish universities). From 1938 he contributed to preparations for wartime conditions in the UK. A prefabricated domestic bomb shelter which he commissioned (Nov. 1938) became known as the 'Anderson shelter'. After the outbreak of WORLD WAR II, he was appointed home secretary (Sept. 1939). He then dominated civil administration as lord president of the Council with responsibility for economic mobilization (1940–3) and as chancellor of the Exchequer (1943–5). Anderson was created Viscount Waverley in 1952.

ANEIRIN (fl. in early 7th century). A Welsh 'early poet'. His poem *Y Gododdin* ('The Gododdin') celebrates an unsuccessful raid c.600 by Britons from EDINBURGH in GODODDIN (SE Scotland) against SAXONS probably at Catterick (N Yorkshire, England). Originally composed in Primitive Welsh, it survives in Old Welsh (9th–11th centuries) copied c.1250. *See also* POST-ROMAN BRITAIN; WELSH LANGUAGE AND LITERATURE.

ANGEVIN EMPIRE Historians' term for territories in France and the British Isles accumulated in the 11th–12th centuries by the 'Angevins', i.e., counts of Anjou (vassals of the king of France).

Count Fulk IV (ruled 1068–1109) conquered Touraine, and Fulk V (1109–29) acquired Maine by marriage to an heiress. His son Geoffrey Plantagenet acquired a claim to NORMANDY and England through marriage (1128) to MATILDA, daughter of HENRY I. Geoffrey succeeded as count in 1129 (father's abdication) and conquered Normandy (1142–4; *see* STEPHEN).

Angevin rule reached its zenith under Geoffrey's son Henry (*see* HENRY II), who was duke of Normandy from 1150 (grant from father) and count of Anjou (by hereditary succession) from 1151. From 1152, he was also duke of Aquitaine (through marriage to ELEANOR OF AQUITAINE), and from 1154 king of England (succession by treaty). Between 1166 and 1178 he established control over Brittany, and in 1171 assumed the lordship of Ireland (*see* HENRY II AND IRELAND). In 1174 he imposed terms on the king of Scotland (*see* FALAISE, TREATY OF).

Henry and his successors RICHARD and JOHN allowed territories to retain their customs and governments. John lost most of his French lands in 1202–4 (seized by Philip II of France), retaining only the CHANNEL ISLANDS, part of Poitou and GASCONY (latter two territories from duchy of Aquitaine). Poitou was lost in 1224, though attempts were made to recover it in 1225–7, 1230 and 1242 (*see* HENRY III). *See also* NORMAN EMPIRE; FRANCE, CLAIMS BY RULERS OF ENGLAND.

ANGLES Name applied in the 7th–10th centuries (OE, Engle) to inhabitants of Germanic culture in eastern parts of Britain, roughly (N–S) from the Firth of Forth to the R. Stour (in East Anglia). According to BEDE (in 731), they were derived from Continental Angles, who lived in and were named after Angeln on the Jutland peninsula (in modern N Germany), and who were one of three Continental peoples who produced migrants to Britain (5th–6th centuries). The connection between Angeln and Britain is affirmed by archaeological evidence (e.g., cruciform brooches worn by women). In Britain, 'Angles' formed one of two large groupings of Germanic inhabitants (alongside SAXONS).

By the late 6th century there was a kingdom of EAST ANGLIA (roughly modern Norfolk and Suffolk in E England), although its rulers may have been of Swedish rather than Anglian origin; its inhabitants are recorded as 'East Angles' (e.g., in the TRIBAL HIDAGE). According to Bede, peoples W of East Anglia were 'Middle Angles' (though there was no Middle Anglian kingdom), and rulers and inhabitants of MERCIA, DEIRA and BERNICIA were also Angles. (The Anglian area must have included Britons and other inhabitants.)

The name Angles was used in Latin ('Angli') by Gregory the Great (Pope 590–604) for all Germanic inhabitants of Britain, a practice followed by Bede (though he also distinguished Angles, Saxons and others) and other 8th-century writers. From the later 9th century, Anglian identity was the basis for the promotion of a broader 'English' identity, which eventually superseded narrower identities (*see* ENGLISH). *See also* GERMANIC IMMIGRATION, SOUTHERN BRITAIN.

ANGLESEY An island off NW WALES; from Old Norse, Ongulsey, meaning 'Ongull's island' (Welsh, Môn, meaning unknown).

Until late 1282 Anglesey contained the chief court (Welsh *llys*) of the kings of GWYNEDD at Aberffro. After the English conquest of native Wales, Anglesey became a shire (1284–1974; then a district within Gwynedd county; a unitary authority from 1996). Once renowned for agricultural wealth, Anglesey was linked to the mainland by the Menai suspension bridge designed by Thomas TELFORD (built 1819–26), and by the Britannia railway bridge (1846–9).

ANGLICAN COMMUNION An international association of autonomous Churches, mostly derived from the Church of ENGLAND and in communion with the see of CANTERBURY (SE England), dating from the 19th century. The Churches of England and Ireland were informally associated in the 16th–18th centuries (united 1801–70), and those churches with the EPISCOPAL CHURCH IN SCOTLAND (from early 18th century).

Churches based on the Church of England's episcopal organization, liturgy and doctrine were created after AMERICAN INDEPENDENCE, starting with the Protestant Episcopal Church in the USA (1789). Thereafter, Churches were founded in the BRITISH EMPIRE through the consecration of bishops in England (e.g., bishop for NEW SOUTH WALES, 1836) and development of provinces (groups of dioceses). In 1867, at the request of the Canadian Church, Archbishop Charles Longley held the first 'Lambeth Conference' of bishops (in England) to consider problems of doctrine and governance. Conferences were held thereafter at roughly 10-year intervals (without legislative authority). In 2015, the Communion comprised 38 provinces and six other jurisdictions. *See also* MISSIONARY SOCIETIES.

ANGLICIZATION, IRELAND English and Welsh immigrants settled widely after the Anglo-Norman invasion (1169–70), and English institutions and culture were introduced (*see* NORMANS, IMPACT ON IRELAND). But Gaelic culture endured and aspects were adopted by Anglo-Irish inhabitants despite prohibition (*see* KILKENNY, STATUTE OF).

From the 1530s the English government aspired to 'civilize' the Gaelic Irish by spreading English culture and reformed Christianity. In the 16th–17th centuries, the reassertion of English government, immigration by English and Scots for PLANTATIONS, and the CROMWELLIAN LAND SETTLEMENT spread English and English customs. During the 18th century, following the demise of the Gaelic LEARNED CLASSES, Gaelic Irish people (including Catholic clergy) increasingly adopted English. By 1851, only 5% of the population were monoglot Irish speakers. In the 20th century, English remained the primary language, and English law and culture persisted in southern Ireland. *See also* IRISH LANGUAGE AND LITERATURE.

ANGLICIZATION, SCOTLAND Most English influences have been imported rather than imposed from outside. Scots, derived from northern English, replaced Gaelic in the Lowlands in the 12th–16th centuries, and English Bibles were influential from the REFORMATION (1560).

After the UNION OF ENGLAND AND SCOTLAND (1707), English influences steadily increased. They were transmitted by nobles (especially peers), who lived and married in England and educated their children there, while writers of the Scottish ENLIGHTENMENT purged their language of Scottish idioms. Connections with England were strengthened from the 1840s by RAILWAYS. In the late 19th century landlords and urban upper middle classes became increasingly anglicized, through adherence to the EPISCOPAL CHURCH, which was strongly influenced by the Church of ENGLAND, and through attendance at new schools modelled on English 'public schools'. Many institutions, however (in LAW and EDUCATION, and the presbyterian churches), and aspects of life (e.g., DIET) were resistant to English influences. See also SCOTTISH LITERATURE IN ENGLISH; SCOTS LANGUAGE AND LITERATURE; GAELIC LANGUAGE AND LITERATURE, NORTH BRITAIN AND SCOTLAND; GAELDOM, SCOTLAND.

ANGLICIZATION, WALES In 1800, probably 80% of the population of Wales spoke Welsh, and the great majority knew no other language. By 1900, the number of Welsh speakers doubled, but the proportion fell to 50%. Most subsequent censuses registered decline. By 1991, 18.7% of the inhabitants of Wales (511,000) claimed a knowledge of Welsh. However, the situation appeared to be stabilizing and centres of growth could be discerned.

Causes of the decline in the proportion of Welsh speakers included the impact of immigration; the influence of English mass media; the assumption that English is more genteel and more useful; and indifference or hostility of schools – though from the 1940s schools generally supported Welsh and many WELSH-MEDIUM SCHOOLS were established. In 2011 Welsh was spoken by 19% of usual residents aged 3 and over. See also WELSH LANGUAGE AND LITERATURE; BROADCASTING, WALES.

ANGLO-DUTCH WARS Three naval wars between England and the Dutch Republic, between 1652 and 1674. Their principal cause was commercial rivalry, in Africa, Asia and N America, but dynastic and religious factors were involved.

The first war, during the COMMONWEALTH period, was triggered by Dutch resentment of the 1651 NAVIGATION ACT. Fleets clashed in April 1652, and England declared war on 30 June. The war was ended by the treaty of Westminster (5 April 1654). The Dutch accepted the Navigation Act and agreed to deny assistance to the exiled King CHARLES II.

After Charles's RESTORATION (1660), suspicions of Dutch ties with English republicans contributed to war from Feb. 1665. James, duke of York, defeated the Dutch at the battle of Lowestoft (3 July). In 1666, fleets clashed in the North Sea on 1–4 June (so-called 'Four Days Battle'). In 1667 the Dutch attacked English ships on the R. Medway (12 June, the 'Black Day'). Peace was agreed on 21 July (treaty of Breda, including confirmation of England's possession of NEW YORK). The earl of CLARENDON was dismissed in Aug.

England again declared war on 17 March 1672, in conjunction with France (under treaty of DOVER, 1670). Fleets clashed on 28 May at Southwold Bay, England. Parliament forced Charles to withdraw a recent Declaration of INDULGENCE and accept a TEST ACT (March 1673) in return for funds. Political opposition forced Charles to make peace in 1674 (treaty of Westminster, 19 Feb.). See also STOP OF THE EXCHEQUER; JAMES VII/II.

ANGLO-FRENCH CONVENTION An agreement signed on 8 April 1904 at Westminster, London, by the British foreign secretary, the marquess of LANSDOWNE, to settle Anglo-French colonial disputes, notably regarding Egypt, Morocco and W Africa. It established the *Entente cordiale* (French, meaning 'friendly understanding') between Great Britain and France which developed into a defensive arrangement by 1914. See also FRANCE, ENGLISH AND BRITISH RELATIONS WITH; AGADIR CRISIS.

ANGLO-GERMAN NAVAL AGREEMENT An arrangement concluded on 18 June 1935 whereby Great Britain accepted a German demand for agreement to expand its naval forces to 35% of British naval strength, enabling Germany to surpass French naval forces. Ostensibly a measure of arms limitation, it constituted APPEASEMENT because German naval construction contravened the treaty of VERSAILLES (1919). See also GERMANY, BRITISH RELATIONS WITH.

ANGLO-IRISH AGREEMENT (1985) see HILLSBOROUGH AGREEMENT

ANGLO-IRISH AGREEMENTS (1938) Agreements on defence, finance and trade signed 25 April 1938 in London by delegations of the British and Irish governments, ending the six-year 'Economic War'. Great Britain would return three 'treaty ports' in southern Ireland (retained since Irish independence). Southern Ireland would pay £10 million to settle unpaid land annuities. Both countries would remove penal customs duties. See also ECONOMIC WAR; SOUTHERN IRELAND FROM 1922.

ANGLO-IRISH LITERATURE Term used to distinguish literature of Irish origin written in English from literature in Irish. It often refers specifically to writing by Irish authors of English descent, starting as early as the 14th century, and to writers associated with the Protestant ASCENDANCY (18th–20th centuries). In the later 19th and early 20th centuries, such literature was condemned as 'un-Irish' by leaders of the GAELIC REVIVAL, though W.B. YEATS and others argued that literature in both English and Irish contributed to the development of a national canon. English literature of Irish origin since the 1920s–30s is usually described as 'Irish'.

Notable Anglo-Irish authors include Jonathan SWIFT (1667–1745), George Berkeley (1685–1753), Edmund BURKE (1729–97), Oliver Goldsmith (1730–74), Maria Edgeworth (1767–1849), Augusta Gregory (1852–1932), Oscar Wilde (1854–1900), George Bernard SHAW (1856–1950), 'Somerville and Ross' (cousins Edith Somerville, 1858–1949, and Violet Martin, known as Martin Ross, 1862–1915), Yeats (1865–1939) and Elizabeth Bowen (1899–1973). *See also* IMMIGRATION TO IRELAND.

ANGLO-IRISH SOCIETY *see* NORMAN IRISH FAMILIES OR OLD ENGLISH

ANGLO-IRISH TREATY Signed 6 Dec. 1921 at 10 Downing St, London (residence of the British prime minister), by members of the British government (including David LLOYD GEORGE) and representatives of the Dáil Éireann or 'Assembly of Ireland' (including Arthur GRIFFITH and Michael COLLINS).

The treaty provided for an effectively independent 'Irish Free State', with informal DOMINION status, from which Northern Ireland (six counties) could (and did) opt out. It was ratified by the Dáil (7 Jan. 1922), but rejected by many republicans (including Éamon DE VALERA) because it confirmed the PARTITION OF IRELAND and retained allegiance to the British Crown. Divisions over the treaty escalated into the IRISH CIVIL WAR. *See also* IRISH FREE STATE, FOUNDING OF; BOUNDARY COMMISSION.

ANGLO-JAPANESE ALLIANCE A treaty concluded on 30 Jan. 1902 at Westminster, London, by the British foreign secretary, the marquess of LANSDOWNE, and the Japanese representative Baron Tadasu Hayashi. The countries undertook to defend each other's interests in E Asia against attack by any two powers. Initially aimed at curbing Russian expansionism, the alliance was strengthened in 1905, modified in 1911, and abandoned in 1921. *See also* JAPAN, BRITISH RELATIONS WITH.

ANGLO-PERSIAN OIL COMPANY A commercial company formed in 1909 with support of the British government following the discovery of oil in Persia (Iran). Great Britain acquired a controlling interest in 1914 to obtain a reliable fuel supply for its NAVY. The government supervised policy but avoided involvement in commercial administration. The company was renamed the Anglo-Iranian Oil Company in 1935, and British Petroleum in 1954. From 1954 Iran's oil was exploited by a consortium including British Petroleum. *See also* OIL INDUSTRY.

ANGLO-POLISH GUARANTEE An undertaking announced by the British prime minister Neville CHAMBERLAIN on 31 March 1939, whereby Great Britain would resist any threat to the independence of Poland. Provoked by the German invasion of CZECHOSLOVAKIA, it was reinforced by an Anglo-Polish alliance (25 Aug. 1939). Germany's attack on Poland on 1 Sept. caused Britain to declare war (3 Sept.), but it was unable to defend Poland. *See also* POLAND, BRITISH RELATIONS WITH; WORLD WAR II, BRITISH INVOLVEMENT.

ANGLO-RUSSIAN CONVENTION A treaty signed on 31 Aug. 1907 at Westminster, London, by government representatives to reduce friction between Great Britain and RUSSIA in Asia. The powers agreed spheres of influence in PERSIA (Iran), AFGHANISTAN and Tibet (under Chinese suzerainty). With the ANGLO-FRENCH CONVENTION (1904), it furthered the development of an anti-German bloc. *See also* RUSSIA AND USSR, ENGLISH AND BRITISH RELATIONS WITH.

ANGLO-SAXON CHRONICLE An account of events mainly in Anglo-Saxon England, arranged by year and written in Old English. It was originally compiled from various sources in the late 9th century, probably for King ALFRED. The earliest content is dubious. From 648 some entries may be contemporary. The *Chronicle* was continued in separate versions to the mid 11th century, and in one text until 1154.

ANGLO-SAXONS Term used from 883 (alongside others) in writings connected with the court of ALFRED, king of WESSEX (e.g., Latin description of Alfred as *Angulsaxonum rex*, 'king of the Anglo-Saxons'). It recognized peoples combined under Alfred's rule: SAXONS of Wessex (S England) and ANGLES of (western) MERCIA (W Midlands).

After Alfred's death (899), the term was retained by his son EDWARD THE ELDER (ruled 899–924), but dropped by Edward's successor ATHELSTAN from 927 when he expanded the territory under his rule (*see* ENGLISH). The term is used more broadly by historians to describe Germanic rulers and culturally Germanic inhabitants in southern Britain in the 5th–10th centuries (sometimes until the Norman invasion of 1066). *See also* GERMANIC IMMIGRATION, SOUTHERN BRITAIN; KINGSHIP, ANGLO-SAXON.

ANGLO-SCOTTISH BORDER *see* BORDER, ANGLO-SCOTTISH

ANGLO-SPANISH WAR A conflict of varying intensity, 1585–1604. It arose largely from Spain's attempt to suppress a revolt (from 1566) in the Netherlands (modern Netherlands, Belgium, Luxembourg and part of NE France), which then belonged to the king of Spain, Philip II. England's ruler, ELIZABETH I, feared that if (Catholic) Spain suppressed local liberties and established absolute rule, (Protestant) England's security and commercial interests would be threatened. Spain sought to re-establish Catholicism in England.

Relations deteriorated from Dec. 1568 when Genoese-owned bullion was seized from Spanish ships taking shelter in English ports. Retaliation, ordered by Spain's ambassador, included banning English imports into the Netherlands. In 1570–1, following the Pope's excommunication of Elizabeth, Philip encouraged the RIDOLFI PLOT. Relations improved, and trade restarted, in 1573 (convention of Nijmegen). Elizabeth ostensibly acted as mediator in the Netherlands, despite pressure to intervene from English Protestants, while allowing English seamen to attack Spanish ships in the Americas.

In Aug. 1585, fearing a Spanish victory, Elizabeth agreed to assist (Dutch) rebels in the northern Netherlands. She dispatched military forces (from Aug. 1585), and a naval expedition attacked Spanish ports in the Americas (1585–6). The land force, as initially led by Robert, earl of LEICESTER (1585–6, 1587), had limited effect (although troops remained). Philip responded by planning an invasion of England. Delayed in 1587 by an English raid on Cádiz (SW Spain), it was thwarted in 1588 (*see* SPANISH ARMADA). The English attempted a revenge attack on Spanish-ruled Lisbon (Portugal) in 1589, commanded by Francis DRAKE.

In the 1590s England mounted five major naval expeditions, including another attack on Cádiz (1596). Spain sent three expeditions, two of them to Ireland (*see* NINE YEARS WAR). English troops also supported Dutch land forces. Peace was concluded in 1604 by JAMES VI/I of England. *See also* SPAIN, ENGLISH AND BRITISH RELATIONS WITH.

ANGLO-WELSH RELATIONS, 6TH–13TH CENTURIES During this period, relations were usually antagonistic, with English rulers normally in the stronger position, but positions often varied according to shifting political conditions, especially in England.

In the 6th and 7th centuries Welsh and English kings sometimes made equal alliances (*see* CADWALLON AP CADFAN). But Mercian expansion in the 7th and 8th centuries confined Welsh rulers (*see* BORDER, ANGLO-WELSH). The rise of WESSEX (9th and 10th centuries) and creation of England increased subjugation: in the 10th century Welsh kings were compelled to acknowledge the English king, at his court, as overlord (*see* ENGLAND, FORMATION OF). In the early 11th century Welsh kings, such as GRUFFUDD AP LLYWELYN, exploited political instability in England by raiding England.

The advent of NORMANS from the 1070s further disadvantaged Welsh rulers. With the creation of the MARCH OF WALES, they additionally confronted Norman (later English) lords, whose outlook generally (but not always) reflected English royal policy. Norman and Angevin rulers of England (respectively 1066–1154, 1154–1216) generally sought to maintain overlordship over Welsh rulers rather than attempt conquest. Relations were sometimes peaceful (*see* SIWAN), and Welsh fortunes flourished under OWAIN GWYNEDD of Gwynedd and RHYS AP GRUFFUDD of DEHEUBARTH in the 12th century, and under the princes of Gwynedd in the 13th century, until the breakdown of relations under LLYWELYN AP GRUFFUDD of Gwynedd led to the conquest of 1282–3 under EDWARD I (*see* WALES, ENGLISH CONQUEST OF). *See also* WALES.

ANGUS, DOUGLAS EARLS OF A Scottish noble family, known as the 'Red Douglases'; flourished 1389–1761. They were descendants of George Douglas (*c*.1378–1402 or 1403), illegitimate son of William, (1st) earl of Douglas, and Margaret Stewart, countess of Mar and heiress to the Angus earldom. In 1389 Margaret Stewart resigned the earldom (in E Scotland) to George Douglas. The 'Red Douglases' became the senior Douglas family in 1455 (*see* DOUGLAS, EARLS OF). *See also* DOUGLAS, ARCHIBALD (*c*.1489–1557).

ANNALES CAMBRIAE (Latin, meaning 'Annals of Wales'). Latin annals recording events in Welsh history to the 13th century; probably started at ST DAVIDS in the 8th century. Three versions survive: two from St Davids (from *c*.955, 1288) and one from Neath (*c*.1286). *See also* BRUT Y TYWYSOGION.

ANNE (b. 6 Feb. 1665 at Westminster, Middlesex, England; d. 1 Aug. 1714 at Westminster, aged 49). The second daughter of James, duke of York (JAMES VII/II from 1685), Anne was raised as a Protestant. She married in 1683. She supported the accession in 1689 of WILLIAM III and MARY II (her elder sister), following James's flight (*see* GLORIOUS REVOLUTION), and accepted succession arrangements made after her heir's death in 1700 (*see* SETTLEMENT, ACT OF).

Anne succeeded William on 8 March 1702, becoming queen of England, Ireland and Scotland. Her reign was dominated by the War of the SPANISH SUCCESSION, struggles between WHIGS and TORIES, and UNION OF ENGLAND

AND SCOTLAND (1707). Until 1710 Anne was guided by Lord GODOLPHIN.

Anne's attachment to the Church of ENGLAND made her sympathetic to Tories. But their objections to the war led to reliance on Whig ministers from 1704. Her resentment of this contributed to estrangement from her confidante Sarah CHURCHILL (duchess of Marlborough), and appointment of Tory ministers including Robert HARLEY (both 1710). The Army commander, the duke of MARLBOROUGH, was dismissed in 1711, and peace was negotiated.

Anne dismissed Harley in July 1714. Her appointment of the duke of SHREWSBURY as treasurer facilitated the succession of GEORGE I. *See also* CABINET; OCCASIONAL CONFORMITY; UTRECHT, PEACE OF; HANOVERIAN SUCCESSION.

ANNE OF CLEVES (b. 22 Sept. 1515 in duchy of Cleves, Germany; d. 16 July 1557 at Chelsea, Middlesex, England, aged 41). The sister of William, duke of Julier-Cleves, Anne became the fourth wife of King HENRY VIII of England (married 6 Jan. 1540). The marriage was negotiated by Thomas CROMWELL to provide an alliance with an important German state. Henry found Anne unattractive and the marriage was unconsummated. Cromwell subsequently fell from office. The marriage was declared annulled on 9 July 1540. Anne remained in England. *See also* HENRY VIII, WIVES OF.

ANNEXING ACT An Act of the British Parliament, passed in 1752, which annexed to the Crown 13 estates forfeited by Jacobites; one of the punitive measures taken after the JACOBITE REBELLION of 1745. Income was assigned to a Board of Annexed Estates, which was established in 1755 and consisted of 28 government appointees (mostly Scotsmen). It funded education and promoted Protestantism in the HIGHLANDS. The estates were restored to their owners, and the Board disbanded, in 1784. *See also* SOCIETY IN SCOTLAND FOR PROPAGATING CHRISTIAN KNOWLEDGE.

ANSELM (b. 1033 at Aosta, Italy; d. 21 April 1109 at Canterbury, Kent, England, aged 76). Anselm became a pupil of LANFRANC at Bec monastery, NORMANDY (1059), then a monk (1060), prior (1063) and abbot (1078). In 1093 he was appointed archbishop of CANTERBURY in England by King WILLIAM II.

Relations with William were difficult. Eventually, when William forbad an appeal to the Pope, Anselm went into exile (1097). He was recalled (1100) by Henry I. But Anselm opposed royal investiture of bishops and returned to exile (1103–6). He and Henry agreed a compromise (1106, confirmed 1107; *see* HENRY I). Anselm wrote influential theological works, including the *Proslogion* which propounds an all-inclusive single proof for the existence of God. He was canonized in 1494.

ANTARCTIC, BRITISH INVOLVEMENT From the 1760s, the British asserted a presence in the Pacific Ocean and searched for a long-suspected southern continent. Following expeditions commanded by John Byron (1764–6), Samuel Wallis (1766–8) and James COOK (1768–71), the second expedition of Cook (1772–5) included three ice-edge cruises (without sighting land) and discovery of South Georgia and the South Sandwich Islands.

In 1819 British commander William Smith made the first sighting of land S of 60° latitude (Feb.) and the first landing (Oct.), thereby discovering the South Shetland Islands. In Jan. 1820, while surveying, Smith and Edward Bransfield (of the Royal Navy) saw the Antarctic mainland (Antarctic Peninsula), just after a Russian expedition. A US crew probably made the first landing (1821). British sealer George Powell and an American discovered the South Orkney Islands (also 1821), and an expedition by whaler John Biscoe (1830–2) circumnavigated Antarctica. Sporadic later expeditions included those of James Ross (1839–43) and George Nares (1872–4).

More expeditions followed from the 1890s. The Southern Cross Expedition of Norwegian-British explorer C.E. Borchgrevink (1898–1900) overwintered on the mainland. The National Antarctic Expedition under Robert Scott (1901–4) included inland journeys. The Scottish expedition of W.S. Bruce (1902–4) studied the Weddell Sea. Ernest Shackleton's expedition (1907–9) included a journey to within 97 mi (155 km) of the South Pole. During another expedition (1910–12), Scott reached the Pole (17 Jan. 1912), but had been narrowly beaten by Norwegian Roald Amundsen. (Scott's polar party died during the return journey.) Shackleton's 1914–17 expedition failed. Scientific expeditions occurred in the 1920s–30s, and permanent stations were established from 1943. Vivian Fuchs made the first Antarctic crossing in 1957–8.

British exploration included claims to sovereignty and establishment of a British presence: *see* ANTARCTIC AND SOUTH ATLANTIC, BRITISH TERRITORIES.

ANTARCTIC AND SOUTH ATLANTIC, BRITISH TERRITORIES Islands in the southern Atlantic Ocean were claimed for Great Britain in the mid 18th century: the FALKLAND ISLANDS in 1765 by Captain John Byron of the Royal Navy; South Georgia and the South Sandwich Islands in 1775 by Captain James COOK. Lands in the Southern Ocean were claimed in the early 19th century: the South Shetland Islands in 1819 by ship commander William Smith; the South Orkney Islands in 1821 by sealer and co-discoverer George Powell. Graham's Land (part of the Antarctic Peninsula) was claimed by ship commander John Biscoe in 1832.

The Falklands were constituted as a CROWN COLONY in 1841. Following inquiry from Norway, sovereignty over the other territories was reasserted in 1908, to facilitate regulation and taxation of whaling, and part of Antarctica also claimed. The lands became a crown colony known as the Falklands Islands Dependencies, administered from the Falklands. (The claim was modified in 1917, including extension of the Antarctica sector to the South Pole.) From the 1920s other countries asserted claims in Antarctica, some of which challenged the British claim. In 1959, the UK was a signatory to the Antarctic Treaty whereby claims were frozen and Antarctica reserved for peaceful uses (effective from 1961).

In 1962, the South Orkney Islands, South Shetland Islands and British Antarctica were separated as a colony called British Antarctic Territory. The Falklands, Falklands Dependencies (South Georgia, South Sandwich Islands) and British Antarctic Territory colonies were retitled 'British dependent territories' in 1983. The Falklands Dependencies became a separate dependent territory, with a constitution, in 1985 (called South Georgia and the South Sandwich Islands). 'British dependent territories' were renamed 'British overseas territories' in 2002.

ANTI-CATHOLICISM, BRITAIN Hostility to CATHOLICS grew from the late 16th century following the REFORMATION, grounded on horror of 'popish cruelty' (as experienced in England and Wales with burnings under Queen MARY I), rejection of doctrines (e.g., TRANSUBSTANTIATION), and fear of papal intervention (exemplified by the excommunication of ELIZABETH I, 1570) and Catholic countries.

Anti-Catholic laws were passed for England and Wales until 1605, treating promotion of Catholicism as treason rather than heresy, and in the late 17th century (*see* RECUSANCY, ENGLAND AND WALES). (Executions were by hanging rather than burning.) In Scotland from 1560, the saying and hearing of Mass were punishable; more anti-Catholic laws and proclamations were issued into the 17th century, and extra disabilities imposed from the later 17th century (e.g., 1700, comprehensive anti-popery Act barred inheritance of property). In the 18th century enforcement of some measures declined, and prohibitions were eventually removed, despite popular opposition, initially to legalize recruitment for the ARMY (Relief Acts for England and Wales 1778, 1791; for Scotland 1793).

Anti-Catholicism was expressed notably in fears of Catholic coups or risings in the 1640s, during the POPISH PLOT and EXCLUSION CRISIS (1678–81), and in JACOBITE times (1689–1745); and also in riots (e.g., GORDON RIOTS, 1780; Stockport Riots, 1852; 'Murphy Riots' in various English towns, 1867–8, provoked by anti-Catholic preacher William Murphy). It was strengthened by the seeming Romanism of RITUALISM in the Church of England (from 1840s). Anti-Catholicism also excited political controversy (e.g., over MAYNOOTH GRANT, 1845). The establishment of

a Catholic hierarchy in England and Wales (1850) was branded 'papal aggression', and provoked the Ecclesiastical Titles Act (1851) banning territorial titles (replaced 1871). Irish immigration made sectarianism significant in LIVERPOOL (from 1830s) and GLASGOW. Protestants associated Catholicism with authoritarianism, Protestantism with liberty. Although anti-Catholicism declined in the 20th century, it remained pronounced in parts of Scotland in the 21st century. *See also* CATHOLIC EMANCIPATION, IMPACT ON BRITISH POLITICS.

ANTI-CATHOLIC LEGISLATION, ENGLAND, SCOTLAND AND WALES *see* RECUSANCY, ENGLAND AND WALES; ANTI-CATHOLICISM, BRITAIN

ANTI-CATHOLIC LEGISLATION, IRELAND, 1691 TO 1740s After Catholic forces were defeated in the WILLIAMITE WAR (1688–91), laws were passed (some violating the treaty of LIMERICK) which denied Catholics political power, minimized their threat to the State, and stifled the Catholic Church. They helped to secure the PROTESTANT ASCENDANCY, i.e., the domination of Ireland by Protestant (Church of Ireland) landed and professional families, which lasted formally until 1800.

Catholics were excluded from the Irish House of Commons by England's Parliament; from Dec. 1691 it required members to repudiate Catholic doctrines and the Pope's claimed power to depose a monarch. (The terms were also applied to public offices.) But qualified Catholics could continue to vote in elections.

From 1695 the Irish Parliament passed anti-Catholic Acts, known as 'Popery Laws' or 'Penal Laws'. The Disarming Act (1695) forbade Catholics to keep weapons or a horse worth more than £5. The Education Act (1695) prohibited Catholics from keeping or teaching in schools. The BANISHMENT ACT (1697) banned bishops and religious orders. The Act to Prevent the Growth of Popery (or 'Popery Act', 1704) prohibited Catholics from buying land or from leasing it for more than 31 years. It also imposed partible inheritance (division of land between sons) unless the eldest conformed to the Church of Ireland. An Act of 1709 required Catholic clergy to take an oath of abjuration (denying the Stuart claim to the throne); it was largely ineffective. Catholic peers were excluded from the House of Lords in 1716, and the few remaining Catholic voters lost their franchise in 1729. Later legislation banned Catholic lawyers from practising at the Irish bar (1733) and disallowed 'mixed marriages' (1745). Land legislation was strictly enforced, other Acts less so.

The last attempt at major legislation took place in 1748 (defeated in Lords). From the 1750s Catholic groups organized campaigns against restrictions. *See also* CATHOLIC RELIEF AND EMANCIPATION, IRELAND.

ANTI-CORN LAW LEAGUE A pioneering pressure group founded by businessmen in MANCHESTER, England, in 1839 to agitate for FREE TRADE, particularly repeal of the protective CORN LAWS. Led by Richard COBDEN and John BRIGHT, the League staged mass meetings throughout Great Britain, distributed pamphlets and lobbied MPs. It disbanded after achieving its main objective (1846).

ANTI-VIVISECTIONISM Vivisection (experiments on living animals) was criticized in Great Britain from the 18th century. As experiments proliferated, Frances Cobbe (1822–1904) campaigned against vivisection from 1863. In 1875 a royal commission was appointed, and Cobbe founded the Victoria Street Society in London to intensify pressure. The Cruelty to Animals Act of 1876 introduced licensing for vivisection. In 1897 Cobbe's society was renamed the National Anti-Vivisection Society; it agreed to accept increased controls on vivisection prior to abolition. Cobbe responded by founding the British Union for the Abolition of Vivisection (1898). Both societies continued in the 21st century, along with other anti-vivisection organizations. *See also* SOCIETY FOR THE PREVENTION OF CRUELTY TO ANIMALS.

ANTONINE WALL A Roman defensive wall across the FORTH–CLYDE ISTHMUS in N Britain (modern Scotland). It was built after *c*.142 at the instigation of the Roman emperor Antoninus Pius (138–61), replacing HADRIAN'S WALL as the formal northern limit of ROMAN BRITAIN. It consisted of turf laid on a stone foundation. Punctuated by forts, it was 37 mi (60 km) long. The wall's history is uncertain: the evidence suggests that it was probably abandoned gradually in favour of Hadrian's Wall in the later 150s or 160s.

APPEALS, ACT IN RESTRAINT OF In England, legislation by the REFORMATION PARLIAMENT, promoted by Thomas CROMWELL, passed in April 1533. It described England as an 'Empire', meaning that all jurisdiction depended on the king. It banned appeals to the papal court in Rome concerning matrimony, testaments and tithes, effectively removing England (and Wales) from papal jurisdiction. The Act enabled the first marriage of King HENRY VIII to be annulled without subsequent appeal to the Pope. *See also* GREAT MATTER; REFORMATION, ENGLAND.

APPEASEMENT The policy of negotiation and concession adopted by the British government towards GERMANY, ITALY and JAPAN in the 1930s. It aimed to prevent war by satisfying grievances within legally binding arrangements. Examples include: the ANGLO-GERMAN NAVAL AGREEMENT (June 1935), HOARE–LAVAL PACT (Dec. 1935), and Munich Agreement (Sept. 1938; *see* MUNICH CRISIS). Great Britain also accepted Japanese conquest of Manchuria (1931) and acquiesced in German occupation of the Rhineland (1936), absorption of Austria (13 March 1938), and invasion of CZECHOSLOVAKIA (15 March 1939). Overt appeasement ended with the ANGLO-POLISH GUARANTEE (31 March 1939).

Appeasers were influenced by popular PACIFISM. Some thought the treaty of VERSAILLES (1919, following WORLD WAR I), too harsh. Others wanted disengagement from Continental Europe. The GREAT DEPRESSION hindered rearmament against the threat from Nazi Germany. Britain also felt uneasy about confronting three potential enemies simultaneously.

Appeasement has been defended for securing necessary 'extra time' for rearmament before the outbreak of WORLD WAR II (Sept. 1939). It has also been damned as a shameful attempt to buy peace at others' expense. Many historians think it was the only realistic strategy for an overstretched power. *See also* CHAMBERLAIN, NEVILLE; HALIFAX, VISCOUNT; DAWSON, GEOFFREY; CHURCHILL, WINSTON; EDEN ANTHONY.

APPELLANTS Name given initially to three English MAGNATES – the duke of Gloucester (Thomas of Woodstock), earl of Arundel (Richard FitzAlan), and earl of Warwick (Thomas Beauchamp) – who 'appealed' against five favourites of King RICHARD II at a royal Council on 17 Nov. 1387. Later joined by the earl of Derby (Henry Bolingbroke) and earl of Nottingham (Thomas Mowbray), they defeated a royalist army at Radcot Bridge (Oxfordshire) on 20 Dec. and had the favourites convicted for TREASON in the MERCILESS PARLIAMENT (1388).

Richard took revenge from 1397: Gloucester was murdered in CALAIS, Arundel was executed, and Warwick was exiled (Sept.); Bolingbroke and Nottingham were banished (1398). But soon afterwards Bolingbroke overthrew Richard (*see* HENRY IV).

APPROPRIATION OF CHURCHES, ENGLAND Appropriation was the legal transfer of a church's revenues from its incumbent priest to a religious corporation, usually a monastery which already possessed the church. It was widespread in the 1180s–1230s to combat inflation, but continued until the early 16th century. About a third of livings were appropriated in England.

A portion of a church's revenues, often 'small tithes' on livestock and minor produce, was usually reserved for the incumbent, who was styled 'vicar'. (Incumbents who retained full revenues were styled 'rector'.) The appropriator received 'great tithes' of grain and hay. After the DISSOLUTION OF RELIGIOUS HOUSES (1530s), most appropriated incomes were acquired by laymen, who were known as 'lay rectors' or impropriators. *See also* TITHE; CHURCH, MEDIEVAL ENGLAND.

APPROPRIATION OF CHURCHES, IRELAND

Mainly from the 13th century, revenues intended for the clergy of local churches, principally TITHES, were often transferred to monasteries, with a small proportion retained for local clergy (*see* MONASTICISM, MEDIEVAL IRELAND). An estimated 60% of livings were 'appropriated' (legally acquired), though proportions varied regionally with the highest in E Ireland. Following the DISSOLUTION OF RELIGIOUS HOUSES (16th century), monastic livings were acquired by secular lords, who were known as 'impropriators'. Some revenues were restored to the Church of IRELAND in the early 17th century (*see* LAUDIANISM, IMPACT ON IRELAND). *See also* CHURCH, MEDIEVAL IRELAND.

APPROPRIATION OF CHURCHES, SCOTLAND

In the 12th and 13th centuries the endowing of monasteries and cathedral clergy usually included the formal appropriation of rectories (clergy livings), whose revenues (mainly TEINDS) were diverted to the new legal owners. To support clergy, rectories were replaced by vicarages (lower stipends). Vicarages were also appropriated (replaced by small allowances). By *c.*1300 the revenues of half of Scotland's parishes had been appropriated; more were later appropriated for COLLEGIATE CHURCHES and university colleges (*see* UNIVERSITIES, SCOTLAND). By 1550, 86% of rectories and 56% of vicarages had been appropriated.

From the late 15th century appropriated incomes increasingly passed temporarily to laymen through the COMMENDATION OF ABBEYS. In 1587 many appropriated revenues were annexed to the Crown by King JAMES VI, who used them to form new secular lordships. *See also* CHURCH, MEDIEVAL SCOTLAND.

APPROPRIATION OF CHURCHES, WALES

Between *c.*1070 and 1400 Welsh monasteries appropriated the revenues of many parish churches, to which they appointed poorly paid vicars. At the DISSOLUTION OF RELIGIOUS HOUSES (1536–9), the revenues passed to the Crown which sold them (mainly 1539–58). Most purchasers were GENTRY who thereby controlled clerical appointments (until 1920), though the percentage of appropriated livings was much smaller than in England. *See also* CHURCH, MEDIEVAL WALES.

ARBROATH, DECLARATION OF

A letter dated at Arbroath (E Scotland) on 6 April 1320 from 39 Scottish nobles to Pope John XXII, who had put Scotland under an interdict because King ROBERT I had refused a truce with King EDWARD II of England. Famous since the 17th century, it powerfully argues Scotland's case for independence from England. *See also* SCOTTISH–ENGLISH RELATIONS 1290 TO 1357.

ARCHITECTURE, BRITAIN

Among earlier structures are prehistoric stone monuments (e.g., STONEHENGE, *c.*2000 BC), BRONZE AGE and IRON AGE settlements, and sites from ROMAN BRITAIN (e.g., HADRIAN'S WALL). In the 7th–11th centuries the Anglo-Saxons, influenced by Continental architecture, built small plain churches and larger abbeys (e.g., at WINCHESTER). Romanesque architecture, imported by the NORMANS in the late 11th century, brought a new scale and confidence to Church architecture (e.g., DURHAM Cathedral) and in CASTLES. Gothic architecture was introduced from France in the later 12th century: its three main phases in Britain (Early English, Decorated, Perpendicular) were employed in numerous churches, cathedrals and abbeys during the next 350 years (e.g., WESTMINSTER Abbey).

In the 16th century, the DISSOLUTION OF RELIGIOUS HOUSES and REFORMATION severely reduced Church patronage, preventing full assimilation of Italian Renaissance styles, although they influenced the design of grand houses. A true Renaissance architecture arrived in the early 17th century with the Palladianism of Inigo JONES. Baroque style developed after the GREAT FIRE OF LONDON (1666), when Christopher WREN was commissioned to rebuild the capital's churches, including St Paul's Cathedral. A restrained Neo-classicism dominated the 18th century, with the Scottish architect Robert Adam (1728–92) creating distinctive town and country houses.

The restless 19th century was characterized by revivals, the most distinctive being Neo-Gothic, seen in churches and public buildings (e.g., Houses of Parliament, Westminster). Notable at the end of the century were the Art Nouveau designs in Scotland of Charles Rennie Mackintosh (1868–1928).

During the 20th century, British architects responded to international influences. Post-modern buildings by such architects as Richard Rogers (e.g., Lloyd's building, London, completed 1986) and Lord Foster (e.g., 'The Gherkin', London, 2004) won international acclaim.

ARCHITECTURE, IRELAND

The earliest remains are remarkable NEOLITHIC tombs (e.g., NEWGRANGE, *c.*3000 BC) and IRON AGE fortifications (e.g., at TARA). From the 6th century Christian monks, at first adapting indigenous styles, built small beehive huts (as on Skellig Michael, Co. Kerry), and later simple oratories, churches, monasteries and (almost unique to Ireland) tall, free-standing towers (e.g., at GLENDALOUGH).

The 12th century marked a turning point, the Cistercians notably building large monasteries (e.g., Jerpoint Abbey, Co. Kilkenny), and the Gothic style arriving in the wake of the Anglo-Norman invasion of 1169–70.

In the 16th century the dissolution of monasteries, REFORMATION, and reassertion of English authority greatly reduced religious building. Houses built then and in the 17th century (often fortified) were based on English and Scottish models. In the more settled conditions of the late 17th and early 18th centuries, classical styles appeared (e.g., Beaulieu House, Drogheda, Co. Louth), and Palladianism was introduced from England (e.g., Castletown House, Co. Kildare, built for William CONOLLY). From the mid 18th century, Neo-Classicism became dominant, resulting in distinctive Georgian areas in many towns and cities, notably DUBLIN where James Gandon (1743–1823) designed prominent buildings (e.g., Custom House).

During the 19th century there was a revival of styles, the most distinctive being Gothic Revival. It was used for both Protestant and Catholic churches, the latter including new cathedrals (e.g., ARMAGH Cathedral, 1854–73). Irish architecture in the 20th century reflected international developments (e.g., the modernist Dublin airport terminal, 1940).

ARCTIC, ENGLISH AND BRITISH EXPLORATION In the 16th–18th centuries English merchants and others invested in seaborne expeditions into the Arctic area to find a trade route to E Asia, to circumvent Spanish and Portuguese routes. 'Passages' were sought mostly to the NW (around N America) and NE (around Eurasia).

Searches to the NW started in the early 16th century (*see* NORTH-WEST PASSAGE). Achievements included discovery of the Hudson Strait (by Martin FROBISHER, 1578); exploration of the Davis Strait (by John Davis, 1586, 1587); exploration of the Hudson Strait and discovery of Hudson Bay and James Bay (by Henry HUDSON, 1610); discovery of Baffin Bay (by William Baffin and Robert Bylot, 1616).

Expeditions for the North-East Passage occurred in 1553 (leading to formation of the MUSCOVY COMPANY), 1556, and 1580. Hudson attempted a transpolar sailing in 1607, and in 1608 sailed to the NE. His discovery of whales in the Greenland Sea (1607) stimulated whaling, which expanded knowledge of conditions.

In the late 18th century the British Admiralty, pursuing scientific ideas, looked for expansive ice-free sea in the Arctic Ocean. Though this proved illusory, C.J. Phipps achieved a new 'northing' (northwards advance) in 1773, and James COOK discovered the Bering Strait between N America and Asia in 1778. In 1806 William Scoresby, with son William, achieved a new northing while whaling; Scoresby junior made important discoveries in geography, currents, etc., in 1813–17 and 1822. New searches for a North-west Passage between 1818 and the 1840s were eventually successful.

Meanwhile in 1827, Edward Parry sought the North Pole using sledge-boats. Attempts by various countries from the 1860s included a British expedition (under George Nares, 1875–6). The first undisputed land crossing to the Pole (an American expedition by snowmobile) occurred in 1968.

British explorer Wally Herbert (1934–2007) was the first man recognized as reaching the Pole on foot (1969). *See also* ANTARCTIC, BRITISH INVOLVEMENT.

ARGYLL, 2ND DUKE OF (b. 10 Oct. 1680 at Petersham, Surrey, England; d. 4 Oct. 1743 at Petersham, aged 62). John Campbell succeeded as duke in 1703. In 1705, aged 24, he was appointed QUEEN'S COMMISSIONER in Scotland and obtained agreement from the Scottish Parliament for union negotiations with England and authorization for Queen ANNE to appoint Scotland's commissioners (leading to the UNION OF ENGLAND AND SCOTLAND). In reward, he was granted an English peerage as earl of Greenwich (Nov. 1705).

In 1706–9 Argyll served in the War of the SPANISH SUCCESSION. On the accession of GEORGE I (1714), he was appointed commander-in-chief in Scotland and the following year suppressed a JACOBITE REBELLION. He was suddenly deprived of his offices in June 1716, but restored to favour in 1719 (created duke of Greenwich, April 1719). In the British Parliament he headed the 'Argathelian' party which he put at the disposal of the administration of Robert WALPOLE (1720s–30s). *See also* HAMILTON, 4TH DUKE OF; ISLAY, EARL OF; PARLIAMENTARY REPRESENTATION, SCOTLAND; PORTEOUS AFFAIR; ARGYLL, EARLS AND DUKES OF.

ARGYLL, 8TH EARL OF (b. March 1607 in Argyll, W Scotland; d. 27 May 1661 at Edinburgh, SE Scotland, aged 54). A member of the Privy COUNCIL from 1626, Archibald Campbell (earl from late 1638) nevertheless subscribed to the NATIONAL COVENANT (1638) and fought for the Covenanters in the Wars of the COVENANT (1639–40). In 1644–5 his forces were attacked by the Royalist earl of MONTROSE. He opposed the ENGAGEMENT with King CHARLES I (Dec. 1647) and was a leader of the radical government of 1648–50.

After the English invasion of 1650, Argyll briefly supported CHARLES II, but during the 1650s complied with Oliver CROMWELL's occupation and helped to suppress the GLENCAIRN RISING (1653–4). He was executed for his complicity after the RESTORATION (1660). *See also* COVENANTING REVOLUTION; ARGYLL, 9TH EARL OF; ARGYLL, EARLS AND DUKES OF.

ARGYLL, 9TH EARL OF (b. 26 Feb. 1629 at Dalkeith, SE Scotland; d. 30 June 1685 at Edinburgh, SE Scotland, aged 56). Unlike his father the 8th earl of ARGYLL, Archibald Campbell was a Royalist and fought for King CHARLES II against Oliver CROMWELL at DUNBAR (1650), WORCESTER (1651), and during the GLENCAIRN RISING (1653–4). He was imprisoned in 1657, and again after the RESTORATION (1661–3, for criticising Charles's government). On his release he received his father's earldom and lands.

In 1681 Argyll, a strong Protestant, was arrested by the Catholic duke of Albany (the future JAMES VII/II), then

KING'S COMMISSIONER in Scotland, and convicted of treason for refusing to acknowledge royal supremacy. He escaped (Dec. 1681) and fled abroad, only to be captured and executed after the ARGYLL RISING. *See also* CIVIL WARS, SCOTTISH PARTICIPATION; MACKENZIE, GEORGE; ARGYLL, EARLS AND DUKES OF.

ARGYLL, EARLS AND DUKES OF The principal titled family of the Campbell CLAN (originally from STRATHCLYDE; in Argyll, W Scotland, from the 13th century). Colin Campbell (fl. 1431–93) was created earl by King JAMES II (1457 or 1458); his successors (dukes from 1701) were constantly prominent in Scottish and British political life. *See also* ARGYLL, 8TH EARL OF; ARGYLL, 9TH EARL OF; ARGYLL, 2ND DUKE OF; ISLAY, EARL OF.

ARGYLL RISING A rebellion in Scotland in 1685 against King JAMES VII/II led by Archibald Campbell, (9th) earl of ARGYLL, intended to coincide with MONMOUTH'S REBELLION in England. Argyll returned from the Dutch Republic, to which he had escaped in 1682 after being condemned to death for treason (following arrest by James, then duke of Albany). Argyll landed in the WESTERN ISLES (mid May), moved to the mainland, but was captured (18 June) and executed (30 June).

ARISTOCRACY *see* NOBILITY

ARISTOCRACY OF LABOUR Term coined in 1871 by Russian anarchist theorist Mikhail Bakunin for élite workers, such as printers and ENGINEERING craftsmen. They were considered to exhibit the hallmarks of an aristocracy: higher living standards, collective pride and hereditary recruitment. Skilled workers dominated British TRADE UNIONISM and other working-class movements (e.g., CHARTISM) from the 1820s until the rise of general unionism in the 1880s.

ARKWRIGHT, RICHARD (b. 23 Dec. 1732 at Preston, Lancashire, England; d. 3 Aug. 1792 at Cromford, Derbyshire, England, aged 59). Originally a wig maker, Arkwright in 1767 designed a machine for spinning threads using rollers, the 'water frame'. It enabled fine, strong thread to be produced, suitable for warps, and could be driven by external power. By 1772 he established a FACTORY at Cromford (on R. Derwent), which spun cotton and silk yarns using water power. Arkwright became England's largest cotton spinner, with numerous factories and several thousand employees. He was knighted in 1786. *See also* COTTON INDUSTRY, ENGLAND.

ARLINGTON, EARL OF (b. autumn 1618 in England; d. 28 July 1685 at Westminster, Middlesex, England, aged

66). A Royalist in the CIVIL WARS, Henry Bennet lived in overseas exile 1647–61, variously serving Prince Charles (CHARLES II from 1649) and James, duke of York. As a SECRETARY OF STATE to Charles from 1662 he was a rival of the earl of CLARENDON. He was created Lord Arlington in 1665.

After Clarendon's fall (1667), Arlington became an influential minister (one of the CABAL group). In foreign affairs, he created a 'triple alliance' with the Dutch and Sweden (1668), but negotiated with France after Charles changed policy. He signed the secret treaty of DOVER (1670). In April 1672 he was created an earl, after the start of war against the Dutch.

In 1674 Arlington was impeached for promoting popery, advising war, and self-aggrandizement. Though successful in defence, he sold his secretaryship (Sept.) and lost influence to the earl of DANBY. He declared himself Catholic on his deathbed. *See also* ANGLO-DUTCH WARS; IMPEACHMENT.

ARMADA *see* SPANISH ARMADA

ARMAGH A city in Northern Ireland, centre of Co. Armagh; from Irish, Árd Macha, meaning 'Macha's height'.

Associated with PATRICK (5th century), Armagh was an ecclesiastical centre (monastic and lay settlement) which developed proto-urban characteristics. From the 7th century its bishops, as successors of Patrick and supported by the Uí NÉILL, claimed pre-eminence over Ireland's churches. Armagh's monastery had strong scholarly traditions; its scriptorium produced the Book of ARMAGH (807). Its community was dominated by hereditary abbots. Canons replaced the community in the early 12th century.

Armagh became the centre of a territorial diocese and province in 1111, and was granted primatial status in 1152 (at the synod of Kells), though this was subsequently challenged by archbishops of Dublin (*see* PRIMACY DISPUTE, DUBLIN AND ARMAGH). From 1545 (except 1553–8) there were Church of IRELAND and Catholic primates, and a Catholic cathedral was built 1840–73. Armagh's city status, removed in 1840, was formally restored in 1994. *See also* MONASTICISM, MEDIEVAL IRELAND; CAPITALS.

Est. popn: 1300, 1000; 1600, 800; 1800, 4000; 1900, 7000; 2000, 14,000.

ARMAGH, BOOK OF A small-format manuscript book (in Trinity College, Dublin, Ireland). It originated as a copy of the New Testament made in 807 for Abbot Torbach of ARMAGH (N Ireland), but further texts were added, notably the *Confession* of PATRICK and other Patrick-related documents. It was later kept as a relic by the coarb ('heir') of St Patrick and then by the hereditary steward of Armagh (until late 17th century).

ARMENIAN MASSACRES (1896) The mass murder of Armenian revolutionaries by Turks in Constantinople (Istanbul), capital of the OTTOMAN EMPIRE, Aug. 1896. The massacres provoked protests in Great Britain led by journalist W.T. STEAD and former prime minister W.E. GLADSTONE. Diplomatic efforts by the serving prime minister, Lord SALISBURY, to reform the Ottoman Empire proved ineffectual. Henceforth British public opinion balked at supporting Turkey over the EASTERN QUESTION.

ARMINIANISM A theological movement in the 17th century deriving from the rejection by the Dutch Protestant theologian Jacobus Arminius (1560–1609) of Calvinist doctrine on predestination, and his acceptance of man's free will (*see* CALVINISM). Calvinists regarded Arminianism as a betrayal of Protestantism.

In England, during the reigns of JAMES VI/I (1603–25) and CHARLES I (1625–49), anti-Puritans (in the Church of ENGLAND), particularly Archbishop William LAUD and his followers, were often (inaccurately) described by opponents as Arminians. *See also* MONTAGU, RICHARD; GRAND REMONSTRANCE.

ARMSTRONG, WILLIAM (b. 26 Nov. 1810 at Newcastle upon Tyne, Northumberland, England; d. 27 Dec. 1900 at Cragside, Northumberland, aged 90). A lawyer who was fascinated by machines, Armstrong in 1847 formed a company which manufactured hydraulic devices (lifts, cranes) at Elswick near Newcastle. In the 1850s, he was involved in designing guns and mines (knighted 1859), and in 1859 started his own ordnance factory, also at Elswick. From 1875 Armstrong lived mainly on his country estate at Cragside. His firm merged with a warship builder in 1882, becoming Sir William Armstrong, Mitchell & Co., Ltd; it became one of the world's largest engineering companies. Armstrong was created Lord Armstrong in 1887. *See also* ENGINEERING, GREAT BRITAIN.

ARMY, ENGLISH AND BRITISH England's first regular army was Parliament's NEW MODEL ARMY (1645). Disbanded by King CHARLES II in 1661–2, it was replaced with a small force of 'guards and garrisons' based on 'regiments' (9000 troops by 1685). Forces were also established elsewhere (e.g., Ireland, TANGIER). Subsequent expansion (to 35,000 troops, including Catholic officers) contributed to the overthrow of JAMES VII/II (1688). People feared a STANDING ARMY, and saw defence as depending primarily on the NAVY. The requirement for substantial parliamentary funding from the 1690s facilitated civilian control.

Between 1689 and 1815, the Army (British from 1707) participated in six major wars (*see* FISCAL–MILITARY STATE), each entailing rapid expansion (from around 20,000) and contraction. For example, strength during the

War of the AUSTRIAN SUCCESSION (1740–8) averaged 62,000. Expansion during the FRENCH REVOLUTIONARY AND NAPOLEONIC WARS (1793–1815) peaked at 250,000 (1813). Domestic roles included defence (e.g., against JACOBITE REBELLIONS) and 'police' work (e.g., suppressing riots). Some regiments were stationed overseas.

After 1815, the Army was again reduced, declining to 88,000 in 1838, then re-expanded, partly for imperial defence; in 1846, two-thirds of infantry were stationed abroad. Between 1815 and 1899 the Army undertook colonial campaigns. The only major war, the CRIMEAN WAR (1854–6), found the Army wanting. Reforms implemented by Edward CARDWELL (1868–71) introduced short service, abolished purchase of officers' commissions, and created specific regimental districts. Further reforms after the (Second) BOER WAR (1899–1902) included creation of a general staff (1906).

Unprecedented expansions, involving CONSCRIPTION, were required by WORLD WAR I (1914–18, to 3.5 million in 1918) and WORLD WAR II (1939–45, 3 million in 1945). Imperial commitments shrank with DECOLONIZATION (1947–8, 1957–1960s), but were counterbalanced by the COLD WAR (1947–91) and TROUBLES in Northern Ireland (1969–90s). Army strength of 152,000 in 1990 was reduced to 91,000 by 2014. *See also* MILITARY SERVICE, ENGLAND FROM 1066 TO MID 17TH CENTURY; ESHER, 2ND VISCOUNT; HALDANE, R.B.; WORLD WAR I, BRITISH ARMY; MILITIAS, ENGLAND AND WALES.

ARMY, ENGLISH AND BRITISH, IN IRELAND, LATE 17TH-18TH CENTURIES In May 1660 the Parliamentary army of occupation, comprising possibly 11,000 Protestant soldiers, switched allegiance to King CHARLES II. Reduced to 7000 by the mid 1660s and dispersed, it was reorganized into regiments between 1677 and 1683. Kilmainham Hospital (Ireland's largest civil building, in Co. Dublin) was completed in 1684 for injured and retired soldiers.

From 1686 (under JAMES VII/II), the earl of TYRCONNELL extensively replaced Protestants with Catholics and expanded the Army to 45,000 (so-called 'Jacobite Army'). After defeat in the WILLIAMITE WAR (1688–91), 12,000 soldiers left Ireland under the treaty of LIMERICK and the remainder were disbanded.

In 1699 (under WILLIAM III), the English Parliament authorized 12,000 (Protestant) soldiers of the English Army to be stationed in Ireland (increased to 15,000 in 1769), and civil administrative departments were developed. The 'Irish establishment' was funded by the Irish Parliament, necessitating biennial meetings to pass supply Acts (*see* PARLIAMENT, IRELAND). Army units were based in specially built barracks around the country, and sometimes assisted EXCISE and CUSTOMS officers and JUSTICES OF THE PEACE, underpinning the PROTESTANT ASCENDANCY. Catholics were recruited from the 1750s (at first covertly), and the need for recruits encouraged concessions (*see* CATHOLIC RELIEF AND EMANCIPATION). Military forces (of various kinds) expanded to 76,000 during the French Wars of the 1790s, and were reduced drastically after 1802.

After the UNION OF IRELAND AND GREAT BRITAIN (1801), the Irish military establishment was brought under British administration. Up to 30,000 soldiers continued to be stationed in Ireland until 1922. *See also* IRISH BRIGADES; MILITIAS, IRELAND; CURRAGH 'MUTINY'.

ARMY, SOUTHERN IRELAND *see* DEFENCE FORCES, SOUTHERN IRELAND

ARMY COMRADES' ASSOCIATION In the IRISH FREE STATE, a political-military organization founded on 9 Feb. 1932, mainly by ex-members of the National Army, to uphold the State and provide physical support for CUMANN NA NGAEDHEAL. From 24 March 1933, when it adopted a new uniform, the organization's members (about 30,000) were popularly called 'Blueshirts'. Eoin O'DUFFY became leader in July and it adopted the name 'National Guard'. It was declared unlawful on 22 Aug., but became part of FINE GAEL (2 Sept.) and was reconstituted as a party section called 'Young Ireland Association'. *See also* POLITICAL PARTIES, SOUTHERN IRELAND FROM 1922; FASCISM, SOUTHERN IRELAND.

ARMY MUTINY, IRELAND An incident in the IRISH FREE STATE (IFS) when two disaffected officers of the National Army, belonging to a faction called 'Old IRA', presented demands directly to the Executive Council of the IFS (6 March 1924). They demanded abolition of the (executive) Army Council and suspension of demobilization. Their arrest provoked 50 officers to resign. Though informal concessions were made, many mutineers were arrested (18–19 March), demonstrating that the government possessed authority over agencies of the new State. *See also* SOUTHERN IRELAND FROM 1922; O'HIGGINS, KEVIN; DEFENCE FORCES, SOUTHERN IRELAND.

ARNOLD, THOMAS (b. 13 June 1795 at West Cowes, Isle of Wight, England; d. 12 June 1842 at Rugby, Warwickshire, England, aged 46). Educated at WINCHESTER College (from 1807) and OXFORD University (from 1811), Arnold ran a private school from 1819. In 1828 he was ordained in the Church of ENGLAND and became headmaster of Rugby School. He strengthened discipline through use of prefects (sixth-formers), and regular examinations and reports to parents, and sought to produce Christian gentlemen of strong moral character. His ideals were spread by colleagues and pupils, thereby helping to revitalize public schools. He also became regius professor of modern history at Oxford in 1841. *See also* GRAMMAR AND PUBLIC SCHOOLS, REFORM OF, ENGLAND AND WALES.

ARRAN, EARL OF *see* STEWART, JAMES

ARRAN, 2RD EARL OF (b. *c*.1519 at Hamilton, C Scotland; d. 22 Jan. 1575 at Hamilton, aged about 56). James Hamilton succeeded as earl in 1529. In 1542, as closest heir, he was appointed regent for MARY, QUEEN OF SCOTS. Inclined to Protestantism, Arran allied with King HENRY VIII of England (Aug. 1543), but was soon forced to renege (*see* BEATON, DAVID), provoking invasions (1544, 1545, 1547). He then co-operated with the pro-French policy of Beaton and MARY OF GUISE, receiving the dukedom of Châtelhérault, France (1549), and resigning the regency to Mary in 1554.

From Sept. 1559 Arran supported the pro-Protestant LORDS OF THE CONGREGATION. In 1565, after refusing a summons to court from Mary, Queen of Scots, Arran was proclaimed a traitor and fled. He returned in 1569, following her abdication (1567), and led the pro-Mary party in the MARIAN CIVIL WAR until 1573, when he acknowledged JAMES VI. *See also* SCOTTISH–ENGLISH RELATIONS 1357 TO 1603.

ARRAS, CONGRESS OF Peace negotiations, during the HUNDRED YEARS WAR, held from 5 Aug. 1435 at St Waast Abbey, Arras, Flanders (a territory of the duke of BURGUNDY), involving English, French and Burgundian delegations. The unwillingness of the English and French to compromise caused stalemate. The English withdrew (6 Sept.). Philip the Good, duke of Burgundy, then rejected the English and the treaty of TROYES (1420), and recognized Charles VII as king of France (confirmed 21 Sept.).

ARRAY, COMMISSIONS OF In England and Wales, groups of men appointed to recruit able-bodied freemen for the king's army. First used in the late 13th century by King EDWARD I, their use declined during the HUNDRED YEARS WAR (1337–1453), but they continued until the mid 16th century when LORD LIEUTENANTS became responsible for recruitment. Commissions were reintroduced by CHARLES I in 1640 (for war against Scotland) and in May 1642 (declared unlawful by Parliament). *See also* MILITARY SERVICE, ENGLAND 1066 TO MID 17TH CENTURY.

ARTHUR (possibly fl. late 5th century in Britain). A Briton first mentioned in the 7th-century Welsh poem *Y Gododdin* (*see* ANEIRIN). He was celebrated in the 9th-century *Historia Brittonum* as a commander who defeated SAXONS 12 times (*see* NENNIUS). From the 12th century King Arthur was a major figure in European literature. He probably never existed. *See also* POST-ROMAN BRITAIN.

ARTHUR, PRINCE OF WALES (b. 19 Sept. 1486 at Winchester, Hampshire, England; d. 2 April 1502 at Ludlow, Shropshire, England, aged 15). Eldest son and heir of King HENRY VII, Arthur was created PRINCE OF WALES on 29 Nov. 1489. He was married to KATHERINE OF ARAGON (14 Nov. 1501), under the treaty of MEDINA DEL CAMPO, but died possibly before consummating the marriage (the matter was disputed). He was succeeded as heir by his brother Henry who married Katherine (*see* HENRY VIII). *See also* COUNCIL IN THE MARCHES OF WALES.

ARTHUR OF BRITTANY (b. 29 March 1187 at Nantes, Brittany; d. allegedly 3 April 1203 at Rouen, Normandy, aged 16). The posthumous son of Geoffrey, duke of Brittany (fourth son of King HENRY II), Arthur was a threat to JOHN (fifth son). In 1199 he and supporters attempted, unsuccessfully, to control parts of the ANGEVIN EMPIRE. Although John recognized Arthur's position in Brittany (1200), he was captured (Aug. 1202) by forces loyal to John and disappeared. He was allegedly murdered by John himself.

ARTICLES OF RELIGION List-like statements of religious doctrine issued by national churches in the 16th and 17th centuries to resolve questions of doctrine and ceremonial.

After the English Church left papal jurisdiction (confirmed 1534), traditional doctrine was largely reaffirmed in the TEN ARTICLES (1536) and SIX ARTICLES (1539). But a reformed theology was asserted by Thomas CRANMER in the Forty-Two Articles of 1553 (e.g., justification by faith), and some Catholic doctrines were condemned (e.g., TRANSUBSTANTIATION). The Articles were mostly reissued in 1563, following the ELIZABETHAN SETTLEMENT, as the Thirty-nine Articles, which remained a document of belief in Anglican churches.

A less precise statement was issued for the Church of IRELAND in 1567 in the Twelve Articles, which were expanded, under the influence of CALVINISM, into 104 Articles (1615). In 1634 the Church was forced to adopt the English Thirty-nine Articles (*see* LAUDIANISM, IMPACT ON IRELAND). The Church of SCOTLAND adopted articles influenced by Calvinism in the SCOTS CONFESSION of 1560. *See also* ENGLAND, CHURCH OF; TEST AND CORPORATION ACTS.

ARTIFICERS, STATUTE OF Legislation by the English Parliament, 1563, which sought economic and social stability through regulation. It specified a minimum term of seven years for apprenticeships, and one year as the minimum employment period in many occupations. It required JUSTICES OF THE PEACE to set maximum wage rates annually according to prevailing conditions. Many requirements were abandoned in the 18th century and repealed in 1813–14. *See also* ECONOMY, STATE INVOLVEMENT, BRITAIN.

ARTS AND CRAFTS MOVEMENT A movement mainly in the decorative arts which flourished in England in the 1880s–90s in reaction to mass-produced objects and formal design. Influenced by William MORRIS and John RUSKIN, it valued natural and local materials, craft techniques and informal designs, and was promoted by various groups and individuals, including C.R. Ashbee, founder of the Guild of Handicraft (1888). The movement produced architecture, furniture, textiles, wallpaper, metalwork, paintings and gardens. It was influential in Continental Europe and the USA. *See also* VISUAL ARTS, BRITAIN.

ARUNDEL, THOMAS (b. mid 1353 in England; d. 19 Feb. 1414 at Canterbury, Kent, England, aged 60). Arundel, an earl's son, served as bishop of Ely from 1373, archbishop of YORK from 1388, and as CHANCELLOR 1386–9, 1391–6. He was appointed archbishop of CANTERBURY in 1396. In 1397 Arundel was condemned as a traitor for sympathizing with the APPELLANTS against King RICHARD II in 1386–8. He was nominally demoted to bishop of St Andrews and exiled.

Arundel eventually joined Henry Bolingbroke in Paris (France), and they landed in England in July 1399. Arundel supported Richard's enforced abdication (Sept.) and Henry's seizure of the throne (*see* HENRY IV). He was reinstated as archbishop of Canterbury. In 1407 he was reappointed chancellor, but was dismissed in 1409 under pressure from Prince Henry. Though reinstated in 1412, he was removed after Henry succeeded as king (*see* HENRY V). From the mid 1390s Arundel combated LOLLARDY and defended the Church against demands for disendowment. *See also* BEAUFORT, HENRY.

ASCENDANCY, IRELAND *see* PROTESTANT ASCENDANCY

ASIENTO **(1713–50)** *see* UTRECHT, PEACE OF; AIX-LA-CHAPELLE, TREATY OF

ASQUITH, H.H. (b. 12 Sept. 1852 at Morley, Yorkshire, England; d. 15 Feb. 1928 at Sutton Courtenay, Berkshire, England, aged 75). Leader of the LIBERAL PARTY 1908–26, British prime minister 1908–16.

A lawyer, Herbert Henry Asquith was a Liberal MP from 1886 who won respect as home secretary (1892–5). A Liberal imperialist, he served Henry CAMPBELL-BANNERMAN as chancellor of the Exchequer 1905–8, introducing differential TAX rates for earned and unearned income (1907) and PENSIONS (implemented 1909).

As prime minister from April 1908, Asquith oversaw reforms. His talented cabinet included David LLOYD GEORGE, Winston CHURCHILL, John MORLEY, and Sir Edward GREY. The crisis over the PEOPLE'S BUDGET (1909–10) ended in a qualified success, but Irish HOME RULE approached disaster.

Asquith led Great Britain and Ireland into WORLD WAR I (1914), but criticism forced him to create a coalition government (May 1915). His leadership appeared lethargic in disputes over strategy and CONSCRIPTION. Faced with demands for a war committee (excluding himself), he resigned and entered Opposition (5 Dec. 1916). When Lloyd George became prime minister, Liberals were divided. Asquith lost his seat in Dec. 1918. He returned as MP 1920–4, but antipathy to Lloyd George prevented Liberal reunion. He was created earl of Oxford and Asquith (1925).

ASSEMBLIES, NORTHERN IRELAND During the TROUBLES, the province's PARLIAMENT was succeeded by Assemblies elected by proportional representation to facilitate better representation of a disparate society and encourage coalition government. The first Assembly (with legislative power), elected in June 1973, was suspended on 29 May 1974 after its EXECUTIVE collapsed. ('Direct rule' from WESTMINSTER was reimposed.) A Constitutional Convention was elected in 1975 to negotiate power-sharing arrangements. Dominated by Unionists who preferred majority (Unionist) rule, it was dissolved in 1976. A consultative Assembly, to advise the secretary of state for Northern Ireland, existed 1982–6.

In June 2008 an Assembly with 108 members and legislative power was elected under the BELFAST AGREEMENT. Although suspended in 2000, 2001 (briefly) and 2002–7, when direct rule was again imposed, it proved a more successful institution. It was suspended again in Jan. 2017 when the power-sharing Executive collapsed, and was reinstated in 2020. *See also* PEACE PROCESS, NORTHERN IRELAND.

ASSER (fl. from 870s; d. 909). A Welsh monk and priest, Asser was educated at ST DAVIDS in DYFED (SW Wales). From probably 885, he spent periods at the court of King ALFRED of WESSEX (S England). Alfred presented him with MINSTERS and made him bishop of Sherborne (in modern Dorset). In 893, Asser composed (in Latin) a *Life of Alfred, King of the Anglo-Saxons* to present a favourable portrait to Welsh kings. *See also* ANGLO-SAXONS.

ASSIZE Term meaning 'sitting' (from OFr. *asise*), used in England for several aspects of law: (a) laws and orders issued by the king and COUNCIL (mid 12th–mid 13th centuries), e.g., the Assize of CLARENDON; (b) procedures established by laws and orders (e.g., the POSSESSORY ASSIZES); (c) courts or bodies involved in implementing laws and orders (e.g., juries of assize); (d) some trials.

From *c.*1370 until 1972, assize courts (so-called 'assizes'), derived from commissions for possessory assizes and goal delivery (clearing), were the senior local courts. Presided over by itinerant justices of assize, they were usually held twice-yearly in major towns (arranged on 'circuits') for serious criminal matters and civil cases. Similar courts were also held in Ireland and later in Wales. *See also* COMMON LAW; COURTS, ENGLAND BEFORE 1660; COURTS, IRELAND; COURTS, WALES.

ASTELL, MARY (b. 12 Nov. 1666 at Newcastle upon Tyne, Northumberland, England; d. 9 May 1731 at Chelsea, Middlesex, England; aged 64). A coal merchant's daughter and TORY, Astell moved to London in the late 1680s and later settled at Chelsea. She established a reputation with *A Serious Proposal to the Ladies* (1694), which advocated an educational academy for women. She also contributed to theological and social debates (e.g., *Letters Concerning the Love of God*, 1695, with John Norris; *Some Reflections Upon Marriage*, 1700).

ASTOR, NANCY (b. 19 May 1879 at Danville, Virginia, USA; d. 2 May 1964 at Grimsthorpe Castle, Lincolnshire, England, aged 84). The first woman to sit in the UK House of Commons. She replaced her husband, William Waldorf Astor, as MP for Plymouth (SW England), through a by-election (28 Nov. 1919) after he succeeded to a viscountcy. A Conservative, she represented her constituency until 1945. She campaigned for TEMPERANCE, moral reform and family issues (e.g., provision of nursery schools). In the late 1930s her circle, the 'Cliveden set' (named after the Astors' country house in Buckinghamshire), strongly supported APPEASEMENT. *See also* MARKIEVICZ, COUNTESS; PARLIAMENT, UNITED KINGDOM 1801 TO 1921.

ATHELSTAN (b. 893 or 894 in Wessex; d. 27 Oct. 939 at Gloucester, Gloucestershire, England, aged 45 or 46). The eldest son of EDWARD THE ELDER, king of the ANGLO-SAXONS, Athelstan was raised in MERCIA (W Midlands) by his aunt ÆTHELFLÆD. On Edward's death (17 July 924) Athelstan succeeded immediately in Mercia, but his accession in Wessex (S England) was delayed by the 16-day rule of his half-brother Ælfweard.

In 927, after the death of King Sihtric, Athelstan seized the kingdom of YORK and effectively annexed NORTHUMBRIA (former BERNICIA), giving England a border with Scotland. Kings from N Britain and Wales acknowledged Athelstan's overlordship. He claimed to be king 'of the whole of Britain'. In 934 Athelstan invaded Scotland. Subsequently, in 937, England was invaded by Scots, Dublin Vikings and allies, but Athelstan defeated them at BRUNANBURH.

Athelstan held large councils, issued law codes, made gifts to monasteries, and collected relics. He developed extensive relations in Continental Europe. Succeeded by EDMUND. *See also* ENGLAND, FORMATION OF; ENGLISH; BORDER, ANGLO-SCOTTISH; TITHE.

ATHELSTAN 'HALF-KING' (born by *c*.915; d. after 957, probably at Glastonbury, Somerset, England). A member of the royal kindred of WESSEX (S England), Athelstan was appointed EALDORMAN (governor) of East Anglia by King ATHELSTAN (932). He was influential during the reigns of EDMUND (939–46) and EADRED (946–55), and was given authority additionally in eastern and C Mercia (949, 951), making him responsible for English rule in former Danish-ruled territory.

Athelstan resigned after King EADWIG exiled DUNSTAN, and retired to Glastonbury Abbey (956 or 957). His father, three brothers and two sons were also ealdormen, the last in East Anglia (958–92). *See also* ENGLAND, FORMATION OF.

ATHOLL, KINGDOM OF A Pictish kingdom in highland (modern) E Scotland (N of R. Tay, within modern Perth and Kinross county). It was mentioned in 739 when its king Talorcan was drowned by ONUIST SON OF VURGUIST, king of FORTRIU. Its name (Gaelic, Athfotla, meaning 'New Ireland') may indicate immigration by SCOTS (Irish). Atholl may have been the centre of a Pictish kingship S of the MOUNTH, and have become subordinate to Fortriu from the later 7th century. By 966, much of Atholl was ruled by a regional governor (*see* MORMAER). *See also* PICTS; KINGSHIP, NORTH BRITAIN.

ATLANTIC, BATTLE OF THE A war of attrition in the Atlantic Ocean between British and Allied ships, and German vessels (mostly submarines) 1939–45; part of WORLD WAR II. It was mainly an Allied struggle to protect eastbound merchant ships from submarine attacks. Shipping losses were most severe between March 1941 and April 1943. The name was coined by Winston CHURCHILL on 6 March 1941.

ATOMIC AND NUCLEAR WEAPONS The atomic bomb, of huge destructive force, was developed during WORLD WAR II as a UK–American joint project (based on the Quebec Agreement, Aug. 1943). Bombs were deployed against Japan, destroying the cities of Hiroshima (6 Aug. 1945) and Nagasaki (9 Aug.). But in Aug. 1946 the USA ended co-operation with the UK. Prime Minister Clement ATTLEE resolved (1947) to create an independent nuclear deterrent.

The UK built an atomic bomb (1952) and hydrogen (thermonuclear) bomb (1957), but fell behind in missile technology, though other delivery methods were employed (e.g., aircraft; *see* ROYAL AIR FORCE). It arranged to buy US 'Skybolt' missiles (1960), but the Americans cancelled the project (1962).

In Dec. 1962 Harold MACMILLAN secured the US submarine-launched 'Polaris' missile system to carry British warheads on British-built Resolution-class submarines

(operational 1968–1996). From 1949 the US Air Force kept atomic bombs at its British bases, their use requiring British approval. In 1980, the government of Margaret THATCHER accepted 160 US 'Cruise' missiles on these terms (operational 1983–91), and ordered US 'Trident' missiles to replace Polaris.

The Trident system, based on four Vanguard-class submarines, was introduced from 1994, and other types of nuclear weapons used by British forces (e.g., free-fall bombs) were withdrawn (completed 1998), leaving Trident as the sole system. In 2006 the Labour government of Tony BLAIR decided to replace the submarines, but in 2010 the coalition government of David CAMERON postponed a final decision about manufacture. Following the Conservative election victory in 2015, the House of Commons voted in 2016 to renew the Trident system, and soon afterwards construction of the first new Dreadnought-class submarine began. *See also* CAMPAIGN FOR NUCLEAR DISARMAMENT.

ATREBATES *see* BELGAE

ATTAINDER Forfeiture of estates and titles imposed for felony or TREASON (from OFr. *ataindre*, meaning 'to condemn'). In England from 1459, individuals were attainted by PARLIAMENT using a Bill of attainder, a non-judicial conviction which declared the victim's blood to be corrupted and disinherited his heirs. Victims were usually executed. Many noblemen were attainted during the YORKIST–LANCASTRIAN CONFLICT and in the 16th century. Later victims included the earl of Strafford (Thomas WENTWORTH, 1641) and William LAUD (1644). The last victim was Lord Edward FITZGERALD (attainted posthumously by Irish Parliament, 1798).

ATTERBURY, FRANCIS (b. 6 March 1663 at Milton Keynes, Buckinghamshire, England; d. 22 Feb. 1732 at Paris, France, aged 68). A Church of ENGLAND clergyman, Atterbury became prominent as a HIGH CHURCH and TORY preacher in London in the 1690s. In 1710 he assisted Dr Henry SACHEVERELL with his defence. He was appointed dean of Christ Church, Oxford, in 1711. In 1713, thanks to patronage from Viscount BOLINGBROKE, he became bishop of Rochester (1713).

Atterbury accepted the accession of King GEORGE I (1714), despite his preference for the 'Old Pretender' (Stuart claimant). George refused to favour him and Atterbury was enticed into Jacobite conspiracies. Arrested in Aug. 1722, he was deprived of his bishopric and exiled (1723). He served the Pretender 1725–8. *See also* JACOBITISM, IMPACT ON BRITISH POLITICS.

ATTLEE, CLEMENT (b. 3 Jan. 1883 at Putney, Surrey, England; d. 8 Oct. 1967 at London, England, aged 84).

Leader of the LABOUR PARTY 1935–55; British prime minister 1945–51.

Attlee became a barrister, taught at the London School of Economics, undertook social work in E London, and during WORLD WAR I rose to major. After serving as mayor of Stepney (1919–20), he became an MP (1922) and held junior office (1930–1). Taciturn by nature, he seemed an uninspiring choice as Party leader in Nov. 1935, but he skilfully consolidated his authority.

After Labour entered coalition government during WORLD WAR II (May 1940), Attlee was lord PRIVY SEAL, dominions secretary (1942–3), and lord president of the Council (1943–5), as well as deputy prime minister (1942–5).

As head of the first majority Labour government from July 1945, Attlee presided over NATIONALIZATION, INDIAN INDEPENDENCE and creation of the WELFARE STATE. His Cabinet included such strong personalities as Ernest BEVIN, Herbert MORRISON, Hugh DALTON, Stafford CRIPPS and Nye BEVAN. The 1950 election almost eliminated his majority and splits emerged over rearmament and NATIONAL HEALTH SERVICE charges. After losing the 1951 election, Attlee gave priority to Party unity. He retired in 1955 and was created Earl Attlee.

ATTWOOD, THOMAS (b. 6 Oct. 1783 at Halesowen, Worcestershire, England; d. 6 March 1856 at Great Malvern, Worcestershire, aged 72). A banker's son, Attwood founded the Birmingham Political Union in Jan. 1830 and orchestrated agitation in Britain for PARLIAMENTARY REFORM. He welcomed the Reform Act of 1832, but later endorsed CHARTISM. As an MP (1832–9), he repeatedly advocated paper money (*see* CURRENCY SCHOOL).

AUDEN, W.H. (b. 21 Feb. 1907 at York, Yorkshire, England; d. 29 Sept. 1973 at Vienna, Austria, aged 66). A doctor's son, educated at OXFORD University (1925–8), and schoolmaster (1930–5), Wystan Hugh Auden became a prolific writer. His early works, expressing an anti-fascist outlook, reflected concerns of the 1930s. They included the poem *Spain* (1937), based on brief participation in the SPANISH CIVIL WAR. After moving to the USA in Jan. 1939, Auden published overtly Christian work and co-wrote the libretto for Igor Stravinksy's opera *The Rake's Progress* (1951). He returned to Oxford as professor of poetry (1956–61). *See also* ENGLISH LITERATURE, ENGLAND.

AUGHRIM, BATTLE OF The final major battle of the WILLIAMITE WAR (1688–91), fought at Aughrim Hill in Co. Galway (W Ireland) on 12 July 1691. Protestant forces supporting King WILLIAM III ('Williamites'), commanded by Baron van Ginkel (a Dutchman), defeated mainly Catholic forces supporting (the former king) JAMES VII/II ('Jacobites'), commanded by the marquis of St-Ruth (a Frenchman). Ginkel's victory led to the surrender of Jacobite forces. *See also* LIMERICK, TREATY OF.

AUGUSTINE (fl. from 596; d. 26 May between 604 and 609). A monk in Rome, Augustine was chosen by Pope Gregory the Great (596) to lead a Christian mission to the Anglo-Saxon kingdoms. In 597, he and companions landed in KENT (SE England), where King ÆTHELBERT permitted them to preach. Soon afterwards Augustine was consecrated bishop (in Francia).

In 601 Gregory appointed Augustine as archbishop (effectively first archbishop of CANTERBURY) and instructed him to consecrate 12 bishops for southern England and one for YORK. (Only two consecrations happened.) Augustine sought co-operation with British bishops, meeting them twice (near R. Severn) and asking them to adopt certain Roman customs. They refused. *See also* CONVERSION OF ANGLO-SAXONS.

AULD ALLIANCE *see* SCOTTISH–FRENCH ALLIANCE

AUSTEN, JANE (b. 16 Dec. 1775 at Steventon, Hampshire, England; d. 18 July 1817 at Winchester, Hampshire, aged 41). A clergyman's daughter who lived mainly in rural England, Austen began writing in 1787. She wrote six major novels, generally considered literary masterpieces. Four were published anonymously in her lifetime (from 1811), the others posthumously. They portray, in a gently comic way, the world of minor GENTRY (including single women and professional men), exploring restrictions and opportunities within their social stratum. *See also* ENGLISH LITERATURE, ENGLAND.

AUSTRALIA A former British DOMINION in the SW Pacific. James COOK annexed Australia's E coast for Great Britain in 1770, naming it NEW SOUTH WALES. It became a colony in 1788, initially for transported convicts (*see* TRANSPORTATION), and included eastern and C Australia.

Some convicts chose to remain, settlement spread, and free settlers arrived in significant numbers from the 1830s. Pastoral farming became prominent. Parts of New South Wales were demarcated as separate colonies: VAN DIEMEN'S LAND (1825), SOUTH AUSTRALIA (1842), VICTORIA (1851), and QUEENSLAND (1859). Other areas were also developed: NORTHERN TERRITORY from 1824, WESTERN AUSTRALIA from 1826 (colony from 1829). After 1850 colonies established RESPONSIBLE GOVERNMENT, although aborigines did not secure full citizenship rights until 1967. The mid 19th century witnessed exploration of the interior, while gold rushes from 1851 stimulated immigration and economic growth. AUSTRALIAN FEDERATION in 1901 united six colonies as the Commonwealth of Australia (capital at Canberra from 1913).

A 'White Australia Policy' determined immigration controls 1902–74. During WORLD WAR I (1914–18), 300,000 Australians fought in Europe as volunteers, notably at GALLIPOLI. Approx. population in 1921: 5,436,000. The Statute of WESTMINSTER (1931) confirmed Australia's equality with Britain within the Empire. During WORLD WAR II (1939–45) Australia sent troops to Europe, N Africa, Malaya, and New Guinea. Japan bombed Northern Territory and Western Australia. An appeal to the USA for military assistance (Dec. 1941) marked a shift away from an exclusive Anglo-Australian relationship.

In the later 20th century, the expansion of Australian industry and British membership of the EUROPEAN ECONOMIC COMMUNITY redirected trade towards E Asia. The 1986 Australia Act of the UK Parliament removed the vestiges of British legal authority, though the British monarch remained sovereign. *See also* MENZIES, ROBERT.

AUSTRALIAN FEDERATION The process in the later 19th century whereby Great Britain's six Australian colonies (NEW SOUTH WALES, VICTORIA, QUEENSLAND, TASMANIA, SOUTH AUSTRALIA, WESTERN AUSTRALIA) united to create the Commonwealth of AUSTRALIA, a DOMINION within the British Empire. The move reflected growing Australian patriotism, concern to control defence and immigration, and desire for continental free trade. Victoria was keen but New South Wales was wary.

Conventions in Australia in 1891 and 1897–8 negotiated a federal constitution which was approved in referendums, except that NEW ZEALAND decided against joining. The Commonwealth was established by the Commonwealth of Australia Constitution Act passed by the UK Parliament in 1900, and instituted on 1 Jan. 1901. The colonies became states, and the Commonwealth was provided with a governor-general, bicameral Parliament, government and High Court. *See also* DEAKIN, ALFRED; NORTHERN TERRITORY.

AUSTRIAN SUCCESSION, WAR OF THE A complex European war, 1740–8, when countries sought to partition the Austrian HABSBURG EMPIRE following the accession of Empress Maria Theresa. Great Britain was concerned to counter the power of France (an imperial and naval rival) and of Spain.

Britain was already at war with Spain (*see* JENKINS' EAR, WAR OF). It now subsidized the empress's forces, organized an allied army against France in the Austrian Netherlands,

and challenged Franco-Spanish naval activity. On 16 June 1743 an allied army (British, Austrian, Dutch and some German troops), led by King GEORGE II, defeated the French at Dettingen in Germany. But in 1745 allied forces were defeated by the French (30 April) at Fontenoy (in Austrian Netherlands), and British forces were withdrawn to confront the JACOBITE REBELLION.

British naval forces were successful against the French in 1747: off Cape Finisterre, Spain (3 May), and off Belle Île, France (Oct.). The war was ended by the treaty of AIX-LA-CHAPELLE. *See also* CARTERET, LORD; NEWCASTLE, DUKE OF; HARRINGTON, EARL OF; DIPLOMATIC REVOLUTION.

AUTARKY Term meaning 'self-sufficiency', often applied to self-contained national economies. It was used to characterize the economic policy of southern Ireland 1932–late 1950s. Pioneered by the FIANNA FÁIL government of Éamon DE VALERA, it included the imposition of tariffs and import quotas, and legislation to preserve Irish ownership of industry (1932, 1934). *See also* SOUTHERN IRELAND FROM 1922.

AVEBURY A monument complex of the Late NEOLITHIC (i.e., *c.* 2800 BC) at the head of the Kennet Valley in Wiltshire, S England. It comprises a massive HENGE enclosure with internal stone arrangements, and avenues that link the monument to others such as the Sanctuary. Nearby are contemporaneous monuments such as SILBURY HILL and older sites such as West Kennet LONG BARROW and Windmill Hill CAUSEWAYED ENCLOSURE. The scale of the complex suggests use for periodic social gatherings, rites of passage and important political events.

AXE INDUSTRY, PREHISTORIC BRITAIN The making of ground and polished axes of flint and stone was an important activity during the NEOLITHIC (*c.*4300–*c.*2300 BC). Made at flint mines and highland stone sources, these practical tools also circulated between communities as tokens of identity and value.

AXE INDUSTRY, PREHISTORIC IRELAND A range of stone and rock sources were used to make axeheads in NEOLITHIC Ireland (i.e., *c.*3800– *c.*2500 BC). Porcellanite was the single most important source. Two known porcellanite axe quarry sites are at Tievebulliagh and Brockley on Rathlin Island, both in Co. Antrim (NE Ireland).

B

BABBAGE, CHARLES *see* COMPUTING

BACON, ANTHONY (b. 1718, probably at London, England; d. 21 Jan. 1786 at Cyfarthfa, Glamorgan, Wales, aged 67). The leading industrialist in the development of MERTHYR TYDFIL (S Wales) as the world's greatest iron-working town; he founded the Cyfarthfa ironworks there in 1765. Bacon made a fortune from supplying munitions to the British government during the AMERICAN WAR OF INDEPENDENCE (1775–81). *See also* CRAWSHAY FAMILY; IRON AND STEEL INDUSTRIES, WALES.

BACON, FRANCIS (b. 22 Jan. 1561 at London, England; d. 9 April 1626 at Highgate, Middlesex, England, aged 65). A royal minister's son, Bacon became a barrister and (1584) MP. Distrusted by Queen ELIZABETH I and her chief minister Lord Burghley (William CECIL), Bacon joined the supporters of the 2nd earl of ESSEX (1591), but abandoned him before Essex rebelled (1601).

Knighted by JAMES VI/I (1603), Bacon held royal offices from 1607. After the fall of Edward COKE, he was appointed (1618) lord CHANCELLOR (also created Lord Verulam, Viscount St Albans from 1621). But he was impeached by Parliament for accepting bribes, and dismissed by James (1621).

Bacon was also an influential philosopher. His *Novum Organum* (1620) argued that the material world should be understood through experimental investigation rather than ancient knowledge and logic, an approach fundamental to the SCIENTIFIC REVOLUTION.

BADEN-POWELL, ROBERT (b. 22 Feb. 1857 at Paddington, Middlesex, England; d. 18 Jan. 1941 at Nyeri, Kenya, aged 83). A soldier from 1876, Baden-Powell wrote training manuals, books and articles. His leadership at MAFEKING (1899–1900, during Second Boer War) made him a hero in Great Britain.

Influenced by concerns about NATIONAL DETERIORA-TION, Baden-Powell realized that military training methods could be adapted for boys. In 1907 he drafted a manual and experimented with a camp on Brownsea Island (Dorset). The manual, published in 1908 as *Scouting for Boys*, stimulated the formation of scouting groups, and launch of the Boy Scouts organization by Baden-Powell (1908). After retiring from the Army (1910), he continued to promote scouting. Baden-Powell was knighted (1909), and created a baronet (1922) and Lord Baden-Powell (1929). *See also* YOUTH ORGANIZATIONS.

BAGEHOT, WALTER (b. 3 Feb. 1826 at Langport, Somerset, England; d. 24 March 1877 at Curry Rivel, Somerset, aged 51). Educated at University College, London, Bagehot worked in his family's bank (1852–61), in Langport and BRISTOL, while also publishing articles on current affairs. In 1852 he co-founded the *National Review*. A contributor to *The Economist* from 1857, he was editor

---

A Dictionary of British and Irish History, First Edition. Edited by Robert Peberdy and Philip Waller.
© 2021 John Wiley & Sons Ltd; © editorial matter and organisation Robert Peberdy and Phillip Waller.
Published 2021 by John Wiley & Sons Ltd.

from 1861 (resident in London). He is best known for *The English Constitution* (1867). It notably distinguished between the 'dignified' part of the constitution (primarily the monarchy), which created legitimacy for government by attracting popular support, and the 'efficient' part (House of Commons, executive), which exercised authority. *See also* CONSTITUTION, UNITED KINGDOM.

BAIRD, JOHN LOGIE (b. 13 Aug. 1888 at Helensburgh, Dunbartonshire, Scotland; d. 14 June 1946 at Bexhill-on-Sea, East Sussex, England, aged 57). After studying electrical engineering at the Royal Technical College, GLASGOW, and attending the university (1914–15), Baird was involved in various ventures. In 1922, while recuperating from illness at Hastings (SE England), he began development of a partly mechanical system for the transmission and reception of visual signals. On 1 Jan. 1926 he gave the first recognized demonstration of television (at the ROYAL INSTITUTION, London). Afterwards he filed patents and formed companies to exploit his inventions.

The BRITISH BROADCASTING CORPORATION used Baird systems for television in 1929 (experimental broadcast) and 1932–5 (the world's first service). From 1936, a Baird system was used alongside an all-electronic system, which was preferred from 1937. Baird continued to develop television systems, and demonstrated colour television (1938). *See also* TELEVISION, GREAT BRITAIN AND NORTHERN IRELAND.

BALANCED CONSTITUTION An idealized characterization of the English constitution which was developed during the early stages of the First CIVIL WAR (from 1642). The constitution was viewed as a balance of the king's rights and prerogatives and the people's liberties and property, with king and Parliament sharing sovereign power. Later commentators saw this as disrupted by CHARLES I and JAMES VII/II, restored by the GLORIOUS REVOLUTION (17th century), and subverted by GEORGE III (late 18th century). In practice, royal powers declined from the late 17th century. *See also* ANCIENT CONSTITUTION.

BALANCE OF POWER An international system in which power is so distributed among states (or alliances) that no one state (or alliance) is predominant and peace is maintained. In the 16th–20th centuries English/British foreign policy in Europe generally sought to preserve such a situation. *See also* FOREIGN RELATIONS, ENGLAND 16TH CENTURY TO 1707; FOREIGN RELATIONS, GREAT BRITAIN.

BALDWIN, STANLEY (b. 3 Aug. 1867 at Bewdley, Worcestershire, England; d. 14 Dec. 1947 at Astley, Lancashire, England, aged 80). Leader of the British CONSERVATIVE PARTY 1923–37; prime minister (1923–4, 1924–9, 1935–7).

Baldwin succeeded his father as MP for Bewdley in 1908 and held junior posts at the Treasury (1917–21) before becoming president of the Board of Trade. Hostile towards the Liberal prime minister David LLOYD GEORGE, he condemned the coalition government at the CARLTON CLUB MEETING (Oct. 1922).

Chancellor of the Exchequer from Oct. 1922 to May 1923, Baldwin then succeeded Bonar LAW as prime minister. His decision to fight an election on TARIFF REFORM (Dec. 1923) dismayed many Conservatives, as did tolerance of a Labour government (from Jan. 1924), but electoral victory in Oct. redeemed him. He ran his CABINET on a loose rein and, despite the GENERAL STRIKE (1926), acquired a reputation for moderation. This was insufficient to secure re-election in May 1929, but he repelled attacks on his leadership before taking the Conservatives into the NATIONAL GOVERNMENT (1931).

Baldwin was lord president of the Council 1931–5. During his final premiership, he handled the ABDICATION CRISIS (1936). Succeeded by Neville CHAMBERLAIN, Baldwin was later accused of complacency about defence. *See also* MACDONALD, RAMSAY.

BALE, JOHN (b. 21 Nov. 1495 at Cove, Suffolk, England; d. Nov. 1563 at Canterbury, Kent, England, aged 67 or 68). A friar, Bale left his order in 1536 and became a secular priest. He married, and promoted religious reform by satirizing the Western Church in polemical plays. Deprived of protection by the fall of Thomas CROMWELL, Bale lived in Continental Europe 1540–8.

In early 1553 Bale was sent to Ireland by Edward VI as bishop of OSSORY. Based at KILKENNY, he sought to introduce the 1552 Protestant PRAYER BOOK but met resistance from clergy. After the accession of the Catholic Queen Mary I, he fled to Continental Europe (late 1553), returning to England after the accession of Elizabeth I. *See also* REFORMATION, IRELAND.

BALFOUR, A.J. (b. 25 July 1848 at Whittingehame, East Lothian, Scotland; d. 19 March 1930 at Woking, Surrey, England, aged 81). British prime minister 1902–5; leader of the CONSERVATIVE PARTY 1902–11.

Balfour's career was advanced by his uncle Lord SALISBURY, who helped him into Parliament (1874) and as prime minister appointed him president of the Local Government Board (1885–6) and Scottish secretary (1886–7). Balfour made his reputation as Irish secretary (1887–91). He led the Conservatives in the House of Commons 1891–2, 1895–1902 (entitled first lord of the Treasury), and sponsored the BALFOUR EDUCATION ACT (1902).

As prime minister, Balfour established the Committee of Imperial Defence (1904) and oversaw the ANGLO-FRENCH CONVENTION (1904). But TARIFF REFORM, advocated by

Joseph CHAMBERLAIN, proved divisive. Eventually, Balfour resigned (Dec. 1905), allowing the Liberals into government (*see* CAMPBELL-BANNERMAN, HENRY). In Jan. 1906 the Conservatives suffered electoral defeat. Balfour quit as leader after two more lost elections.

Balfour returned to government in coalitions: as first lord of the Admiralty (1915–16) and foreign secretary (1916–19). He signed the BALFOUR DECLARATION (1917) and attended the PARIS PEACE CONFERENCE (1919). He ended his career as lord president of the Council (1919–22, 1925–9), becoming earl of Balfour (1922). *See also* BALFOUR, A.J., AND IRELAND; BALFOUR DEFINITION.

BALFOUR, A.J., AND IRELAND Balfour was (Conservative) CHIEF SECRETARY FOR IRELAND March 1887–Nov. 1891, during the anti-landlord PLAN OF CAMPAIGN. He responded uncompromisingly, obtaining extra powers with the Criminal Law and Procedure (Ireland) Act (July 1887). After police fired on demonstrators in the 'Mitchelstown Massacre' (Co. Cork, 9 Sept. 1887), Balfour was dubbed 'Bloody Balfour'.

Balfour attempted to diminish popular support for Home Rule by promoting land reform and economic development. Measures included the Land Law (Ireland) Act of 1887, Light Railways (Ireland) Act of 1889 and Purchase of Land (Ireland) Act of 1891. The last created the CONGESTED DISTRICTS BOARD. The 1903 Land Act was passed during his premiership. *See also* HOME RULE MOVEMENT, IRELAND; LAND AGITATION AND REFORM, IRELAND; TRANSPORT COMMUNICATIONS, IRELAND.

BALFOUR DECLARATION A statement of support for the creation of a 'national home' for Jews in PALESTINE made on 2 Nov. 1917 by the British foreign secretary, A.J. BALFOUR, in a letter to Lord Rothschild as a Zionist representative. It also required the safeguarding of non-Jewish communities. Its purpose was to secure international Jewish support for the Allies in WORLD WAR I. The declaration was implemented when the LEAGUE OF NATIONS made Palestine a British MANDATE (1920), and led eventually to the foundation of ISRAEL.

BALFOUR DEFINITION A statement about the constitutional relationship of Great Britain and its DOMINIONS formulated in 1926 by a committee of dominion prime ministers chaired by Earl BALFOUR. It stated that Britain and the dominions were autonomous and equal in status within the British Empire, though Britain retained some responsibility for foreign affairs and defence. It was later endorsed by the Statute of WESTMINSTER.

BALFOUR EDUCATION ACT Popular name for the Education Act of 1902, passed by the UK Parliament for England and Wales under A.J. BALFOUR (as leader of the House of Commons and then prime minister). It transferred the supervision and funding of board and voluntary schools to county, county borough, and some borough and urban district councils, which became 'Local Education Authorities' (supervised by the central Board of Education, established 1899). Authorities were authorized to support post-elementary (or secondary) education. Nonconformists protested about the funding of Church of England schools by ratepayers. *See also* MORANT, ROBERT; BALFOUR EDUCATION ACT AND WALES; GRAMMAR SCHOOL; EDUCATION, ENGLAND/WALES.

BALFOUR EDUCATION ACT AND WALES The provision in the 1902 Education Act for rate-based support of Church of England schools in Wales generated hostility because most Welsh ratepayers were nonconformists. Encouraged by David LLOYD GEORGE (a Liberal), county councils refused to comply – action known as the 'Welsh Revolt'. The (Conservative) British government responded with the Coercion of Wales Act (1904), enabling the Board of Education to assume councils' responsibilities. The controversy diminished with the government's fall in 1905 and the Act was largely implemented. *See also* EDUCATION, WALES; NONCONFORMITY AND DISSENT, WALES.

BALKANS, BRITISH INVOLVEMENT Prime Minister William PITT the Younger was the first British statesman to express concern at the influence of RUSSIA in SE Europe – in 1788, with the formation of a short-lived triple alliance against Russia. But the nationalism of Christian peoples subject to the Muslim OTTOMAN EMPIRE made outright British support for the Empire difficult in this aspect of the EASTERN QUESTION. Long-term British policy aimed at peaceful contraction of Ottoman-ruled territory in Europe and limitation of Russian gains therefrom. The Royal Navy was ready to defend Istanbul to prevent Russian seizure of the Turkish Straits.

Great Britain helped GREECE to independence (proclaimed 1822) and approved the autonomy of ROMANIA after the CRIMEAN WAR (in treaty of Paris, 1856). Prime Minister Benjamin DISRAELI overturned the treaty of SAN STEFANO at the Congress of BERLIN (1878), but Lord SALISBURY hoped the enlargement of Bulgaria in 1885 would strengthen its resistance to Russian expansion. The subsequent decline of British naval power in the Mediterranean dictated a less active policy. By seeking balance between Russian and Austrian interests, the British foreign secretary Edward GREY worked to contain the Balkan Wars at the Conference of London (1912–13).

In 1918, following WORLD WAR I, a Kingdom of Serbs, Croats and Slovenes was created in the western Balkans with British support (renamed Yugoslavia in 1929). Britain was among the powers drawn into its disintegration in the 1990s (*see* YUGOSLAV WARS, BRITISH INVOLVEMENT).

BALLADS Simple songs, with each verse sung to the same melody, which narrate a story, often about love, legendary figures (e.g., Robin HOOD; ROB ROY), or historical events. Documented in England from the 13th century, they flourished throughout the British Isles. Ballads were originally transmitted orally, but in the 16th–19th centuries they were also printed, usually on single sheets or 'broadsides'. Printing encouraged the writing of new ballads, including socially critical ballads (from the 17th century), and ballads about sensational events. Ballads were spread by emigration to N America and elsewhere. They were collected and edited mainly from the early 19th century.

BALLIOL, DERVORGUILLA (b. *c.*1209; d. 28 Jan. 1290 at Buittle Castle, SW Scotland, aged about 81). A daughter of Alan, lord of GALLOWAY, and his second wife Margaret (eldest daughter of David earl of HUNTINGDON), Dervorguilla married John Balliol (1233). She founded Sweetheart (Cistercian) Abbey (SW Scotland) in his memory (1273) and completed (1282) his foundation for scholars at OXFORD University (*see* BALLIOL FAMILY). Her royal descent from Earl David enabled their son John BALLIOL to become king of Scots.

BALLIOL, EDWARD (b. *c.*1283 at Buittle Castle, SW Scotland; d. Jan. 1364, near Doncaster, Yorkshire, England, aged about 80). Eldest son of John BALLIOL (king of Scots 1292–6); claimant to the Scottish kingship.

Having lived abroad during the reign of King ROBERT I (1306–29), Balliol took advantage of the minority of DAVID II to invade E Scotland (Aug. 1332). Victorious at DUPPLIN, he was crowned (24 Sept.) and did homage to King EDWARD III of England (23 Nov.) but was expelled by Dec.

In March 1333 Balliol invaded again and, with Edward's help, was victorious at HALIDON HILL (12 July). He reestablished himself, held a Parliament near Edinburgh (Feb. 1334), but fled to England in late 1334. Another invasion led by Edward and Balliol (July–Aug. 1335) reinstated Balliol, but his supporters lost ground after the battle of CULBLEAN (Nov. 1335) and he was undermined by Edward's war against France from 1337 (*see* HUNDRED YEARS WAR). Balliol was driven out by late 1338.

After King David was captured at NEVILLE'S CROSS (1346), Balliol invaded again (May 1347), restoring much of S Scotland to English administration and holding his ancestral castle until 1354. On 21 Jan. 1356, as Edward III prepared to invade Scotland, Balliol resigned his claim. *See also* DISINHERITED; SCOTTISH–ENGLISH RELATIONS 1290 TO 1357.

BALLIOL, JOHN (b. *c.*1250; d. April 1313 at Bailleul, France, aged about 63). King of Scots 1292–6. In 1290 Balliol claimed the vacant kingship of Scotland through his mother, Dervorguilla BALLIOL. He was selected as king by King EDWARD I of England in the GREAT CAUSE. John was inaugurated on 30 Nov. 1292 and did homage to Edward (26 Dec.), recognizing him as overlord of Scotland.

Edward soon restricted John's authority (e.g., by hearing appeals from Scotland in England). In June 1294 Edward demanded military service in France from Scottish magnates. Scots resisted. In July 1295, 12 'guardians' took government from John's control and allied with France (23 Oct.; *see* SCOTTISH–FRENCH ALLIANCE). Edward invaded Scotland (30 March 1296) and defeated John's forces at Dunbar, SE Scotland (27 April). John was deposed (10 July) and stripped of his regalia (from which he was called 'Toom Tabard' or 'empty coat').

John was imprisoned in London until 1299, and later retired to France. Meanwhile, the guardians fought the English in Balliol's name until 1304. *See also* SCOTTISH–ENGLISH RELATIONS 1290 TO 1357; ROBERT I; BALLIOL, EDWARD.

BALLIOL FAMILY From Picardy, NE France, the Balliols held land in NE England from the late 11th century and in Scotland from the mid 12th century; they flourished until 1368. John Balliol (d. 1268) married Dervorguilla, heiress of Alan of Galloway, and later founded a student hostel in OXFORD, England (by 1266; from 1282, Balliol College). Through her royal descent their son John BALLIOL became king of Scots. *See also* BALLIOL, DERVORGUILLA; BALLIOL, EDWARD; GALLOWAY.

BALMERINO TRIAL The trial in Scotland (at EDINBURGH), in March 1635, of James Elphinstone, (2nd) Lord Balmerino, for sedition: he had retained possession of a nobles' petition complaining about innovations in government by King CHARLES I (e.g., the prominence of bishops). Charles had rejected the petition in 1633. Balmerino was tried as an example to the king's opponents. Though convicted and sentenced to death, he was pardoned for fear his execution would provoke popular revolt. *See also* COVENANTING REVOLUTION.

BALTIC STATES, BRITISH RELATIONS WITH British naval operations in the Baltic Sea (1918–21) helped to liberate Estonia, Latvia and Lithuania from Bolshevik-ruled Russia (agreed by treaties 1920). Full diplomatic relations were established (1921–2). Aside from Anglo-German commercial rivalry, Great Britain viewed the three nations with benevolent detachment. It refused to compromise their independence during talks regarding an Anglo-Soviet alliance (1939), but the British in practice accepted their annexation by the USSR (1940) while never formally acknowledging Soviet sovereignty. Britain recognized the renewed independence of Estonia, Latvia and Lithuania in 1991. In 2004 the States became members of the NORTH ATLANTIC TREATY ORGANIZATION and European Union. *See also* RUSSIA AND USSR, ENGLISH AND BRITISH RELATIONS WITH.

BANCROFT, RICHARD (b. Sept. 1544 at Farnworth, Lancashire, England; d. 2 Nov. 1610, at Lambeth, Surrey, England, aged 66). Ordained a Church of ENGLAND priest in 1574, Bancroft seized the press that printed the MARPRELATE TRACTS (1589). An opponent of PURITANISM and defender of episcopacy, he was appointed bishop of London in 1597.

In 1604 Bancroft participated in the HAMPTON COURT CONFERENCE (Jan.), called by King JAMES VI/I. Following the death of Archbishop John WHITGIFT (Feb.), he presided over the southern Convocation (Church assembly), which adopted his own compilation of 141 constitutions and canons (April). In Oct. he was appointed archbishop of CANTERBURY. Bancroft enforced the canons: about 80 clergy were deprived of their livings for refusing to assent. He also sought to defend Church courts from challenges from COMMON LAW courts.

BANGORIAN CONTROVERSY Dispute about Church–State relations in England and Wales soon after the accession of King GEORGE I, provoked by Benjamin Hoadly, bishop of BANGOR and a WHIG. In two pamphlets, published 1716–17, Hoadly defended State authority over the Church and denied that clergy had spiritual authority. He implied that the Church of ENGLAND and DISSENTERS' churches were essentially alike. His views offended HIGH CHURCH clergy. In May 1717 the lower house of Convocation (Church assembly) condemned Hoadly. The Whig ministry discontinued Convocation (until 1842), weakening the High Church faction.

BANGOR (IRELAND) A town in Co. Down, Northern Ireland; from Irish, Beannchar Árd Uladh, meaning 'Peaked hill'.

Originally an ecclesiastical centre (monastic and lay settlement) founded by Comgall (d. 603), Bangor was dominated in its early years by the founder's lineage, the Dál nAraide (later replaced by the Dál Fiatach). Though in ULSTER (N Ireland), it maintained links with LEINSTER (E Ireland). It quickly became a considerable intellectual centre, with COLUMBANUS among its scholars. It declined due to VIKING impact (early 9th century), but was replaced by an Augustinian house in 1124, founded by MALACHY. A small town was founded in the 12th or 13th century which became a borough in 1612 and was a centre of the COTTON INDUSTRY in the later 18th and 19th centuries. *See also* MONASTICISM, MEDIEVAL IRELAND.

BANGOR (WALES) A city in Gwynedd unitary authority, NW Wales; Welsh, meaning 'Wattle-fence enclosure'. Bangor was originally the location of a monastery and bishop's seat founded by DEINIOL (d. 584). A new cathedral, dedicated to St Deiniol, was started between 1120 and 1139 and remained the pre-eminent church of GWYNEDD. A town is first mentioned in 1211. *See also* CHURCH ORGANIZATION, WALES; UNIVERSITIES, WALES.

Est. popn: 1300, 300; 1600, 900; 1800, 1800; 1900, 11,000; 2000, 13,000.

BANISHMENT ACT Legislation by the Irish Parliament, passed 25 Sept. 1697, which banned Catholic bishops, other senior clergy and regular clergy (i.e., monks, friars) from Ireland. At first it was enforced: 424 regular clergy were expelled in 1698, and only three bishops remained by 1703. But the episcopate and religious orders revived soon afterwards. (The Act was repealed in 1878.) *See also* ANTI-CATHOLIC LEGISLATION, IRELAND, 1691 TO 1740s; RELIGIOUS ORDERS AND REGULAR CLERGY, IRELAND FROM 16TH CENTURY.

BANK CHARTER ACT Legislation by the UK Parliament, 1844, affecting banking mainly in England and Wales. It sought to reduce economic instability by encouraging country banks to cease note issuing (completed 1921), and by amending the Bank of England's charter so that 'issue' and 'banking' departments were separated and note issue was based on rules ('fiduciary' or unbacked note issue was limited to £14 million; other notes could be issued backed by gold equivalent). The Act remained fundamental until 1914. *See also* BANKING, ENGLAND AND WALES; CURRENCY SCHOOL.

BANK HOLIDAYS Days when banks are closed by law, which are generally observed as public holidays. The UK Parliament, acting on proposals by Sir John Lubbock, specified dates from 1871: four in England, Wales and Ireland (St Stephen's Day, Easter Monday, Whit Monday, and first Monday in Aug.), five in Scotland (New Year's Day, Good Friday, first Monday in May, first Monday in Aug., Christmas Day). Subsequent additions included St Patrick's Day in Ireland (1903). In 1939 southern Ireland replaced bank holidays with 'public holidays'; from 2007 St Andrew's Day was also a holiday in Scotland. *See also* HOLIDAYS.

BANKING, ENGLAND AND WALES Banking businesses developed in the 1640s–70s in LONDON, when some goldsmiths provided financial services for merchants and others, such as holding cash, discounting (buying) bills of exchange (contracts for payments), issuing promissory notes (early banknotes) and transferring funds. Parliament in 1697 confined JOINT-STOCK banking to the recently founded BANK OF ENGLAND, and in 1708 limited private banks to six partners. Early expansion of banking mostly occurred in London: in 1750 about 50 'City banks' served mercantile businesses, while 'West End banks' provided for landowners. There were only 12 elsewhere.

So-called 'country banks' increased thereafter: to 370 by 1800 and possibly 780 by 1810. Many were conducted alongside other businesses. Their notes circulated as local currency, and bill discounting provided working capital to businesses (to late 19th century). London banks facilitated the transfer of surplus funds of agricultural regions to industrial regions. Banks were liable to collapse during financial crises.

From 1826 joint-stock banking, including note issuing, was allowed beyond 65 mi (104 km) from London (limit removed, without note issuing, 1833). By 1841 there were 115 joint-stock banks, which opened branches and took over partnership banks, though note issuing was discouraged from 1844 (see BANK CHARTER ACT). LIMITED LIABILITY was available from 1858. From the later 19th century, joint-stock banks also merged. By 1914 there were about 20 partnership and 40 joint-stock banks, and 7000 branches. 'Merchant banks' undertook overseas business.

By the mid 1920s, domestic banking was dominated by a 'big five': Barclays, Lloyds, Midland, National Provincial, Westminster. The last two merged in 1968 (renamed 'National Westminster' 1970; acquired by Royal Bank of Scotland 2000); Midland was bought by the Hongkong and Shanghai Banking Corporation in 1992. From the 1980s some building societies became banks, increasing competition. In 2009, following a crisis, the British government acquired majority ownership of Royal Bank of Scotland and part-ownership of Lloyds (latter terminated 2017). *See also* BANKING, SCOTLAND; CURRENCY, ENGLAND AND GREAT BRITAIN FROM 1660s.

BANKING, IRELAND Banks were started from the 1720s (six in DUBLIN by 1730s). They were usually operated by merchants, who bought bills of exchange (thereby providing capital), transmitted money and issued notes. Economic crises usually resulted in bank collapses.

In 1782, supported by PATRIOTS, Parliament founded the Bank of Ireland (opened 1783), and encouraged its pre-eminence by limiting other note-issuing banks to six business partners. Following a crisis in 1820, the Bank of Ireland Act (1821) permitted joint-stock banks with unlimited partners over 50 (Irish) mi (100 km) from Dublin. New banks included the Hibernian Bank (1825) and Ulster Bank (1836). The Bank of Ireland acted as a central bank in assisting other banks. The 1845 Bank Act limited note

issuing to six banks. By 1914, about 860 bank branches existed. During the 19th century SAVINGS BANKS and building societies were also formed.

Co-operation between banks from the later 19th century culminated in the Irish Banks' Standing Committee formed by nine banks in 1920. Co-ordination continued despite the PARTITION OF IRELAND (1921). Suspicion of banks caused the IRISH FREE STATE government to undertake investigations (1926, 1934–8) and found State-sponsored credit providers. IFS banks maintained close relations with the Bank of England until WORLD WAR II, when an Irish Central Bank was created (1942).

Mergers in the 1950–60s left four main banks: Bank of Ireland and Allied Irish Banks based in the Republic of Ireland; Northern Bank and Ulster Bank based in Northern Ireland (subsidiaries of British banks). Rapid expansion of lending from the later 20th century left many banks and other financial institutions potentially insolvent when a financial crisis erupted in 2008. The Republic's government was forced to guarantee deposits and nationalize companies, including Anglo-Irish Bank, Allied Irish Banks and Bank of Ireland. *See also* CURRENCY, IRELAND FROM 16TH CENTURY.

BANKING, SCOTLAND The first bank, the Bank of Scotland (in EDINBURGH), was incorporated by Scotland's Parliament in 1695 with a 21-year monopoly. Its purpose was to encourage commerce by expanding credit (gold and silver coins were scarce). It discounted bills, lent money, and from 1704 issued notes. Two similar banks followed (founded by royal charter): Royal Bank of Scotland (1727) and British Linen Company (1746), the latter to promote the linen industry but which specialized in banking and pioneered a branch network. From 1747 banks were also founded in provincial centres, notably GLASGOW. Financed mainly by merchants, they provided services for trade, agriculture and industry, including cash accounts (overdrafts), deposit accounts, and note issuing. (Parliament's prohibition on joint-stock companies in 1720 was not applied in Scotland.) By 1826 there were 36 banks. In 1810 Henry Duncan, minister of Ruthwell (Dumfriesshire), founded a parish savings bank for the poor. His idea spread: by 1818 there were 182 such banks (see SAVINGS BANKS).

In the 1840s restrictive legislation halted expansion and encouraged conservatism: the 1844 Bank Charter Act effectively prevented new banks from issuing notes; from 1845 note issuing beyond an authorized amount had to be backed by specie. Crashes (e.g., large Western Bank in 1857) and amalgamations reduced numbers: to ten by 1878, eight by 1914, five by 1958, three by 1971 (Bank of Scotland, Royal Bank of Scotland, Clydesdale Bank, founded 1838 and owned by Midland Bank since 1920).

Categorized from 1971 as 'clearing banks', in the 1970s–90s they developed business both within and outside Scotland.

From the late 1990s Royal Bank of Scotland expanded rapidly, briefly becoming the world's largest bank, and in 2001 Bank of Scotland merged with Halifax Building Society as HBOS. But in 2008 both faced collapse. The former was taken largely into government ownership, and the latter was acquired by Lloyds (2009) with government support. *See also* CURRENCY, SCOTLAND.

BANKING SCHOOL *see* CURRENCY SCHOOL

BANK OF ENGLAND Originally a JOINT-STOCK COMPANY incorporated in 1694 by royal charter, comprising subscribers to a £1.2 million loan to the English government (for funding the War of the GRAND ALLIANCE). Enlarged from 1696, the Bank became the government's main source of short-term loans and its own bank (e.g., holding balances, providing bullion for CURRENCY), and also London's leading bank. It enjoyed a monopoly of joint-stock banking in England and Wales (1697–1826), was the leading issuer of notes, discounted bills of exchange (contracts for payments), and provided accounts to other banks. From 1763 (financial crisis), it was regarded as 'lender of last resort'. Its support for other banks gave it considerable influence, a situation enhanced from 1797 when convertibility of its notes into gold was suspended, compelling other banks to hold its notes as reserves.

When convertibility was restored in 1821, the Bank operated the GOLD STANDARD to encourage economic stability. After a financial crisis in 1825, it opened provincial branches to improve the distribution of notes and sovereigns. Crises in 1836 and 1839 resulted in the BANK CHARTER ACT (1844) which encouraged a monopoly in England and Wales for Bank of England notes, and regulated note issue. The Bank was now effectively a British 'central bank'. A liaison committee with other banks was formally established in 1911. In the later 19th and early 20th centuries the Bank exerted influence internationally through London's world pre-eminence as a financial centre.

Following suspension of convertibility in 1919 (after WORLD WAR I), the gold standard was restored in 1925, only to be abandoned in 1931. Nationalization of the Bank (1 March 1946) enabled central government from the 1950s to use the BANK RATE for its monetary policy. Control was redelegated to the Bank in 1997, though another authority undertook supervision of banks and insurance companies (restored 2013). *See also* FINANCIAL REVOLUTION; BANKING, ENGLAND AND WALES.

BANK OF IRELAND *see* BANKING, IRELAND

BANK OF SCOTLAND *see* BANKING, SCOTLAND

BANK RATE Originally the 'discount rate' of the BANK OF ENGLAND (for discounting bills of exchange, 18th–19th centuries), normally above other rates. From the 1860s to 1930s it protected gold and other UK reserves (by attracting inflows at a high interest rate), and from the 1950s was part of government monetary policy (influencing commercial interest rates and general economic activity). Replaced Oct. 1972 by 'minimum lending rate', to encourage competition among banks. *See also* GOLD STANDARD.

BANKS, JOSEPH (b. 13 Feb. 1743 at London, England; d. 19 June 1820 at Isleworth, Middlesex, England, aged 77). Interested in botany from school days, Banks attended OXFORD University. The inheritance of an estate soon afterwards (1764) enabled him to pursue natural history. Encouraged by Daniel Solander, a follower of the Swedish botanist Linnaeus, Banks participated in three overseas expeditions as a naturalist: to NEWFOUNDLAND and Labrador (1766), around the world with James COOK (1768–71), and to Iceland (1772). In 1766 he was elected a fellow of the ROYAL SOCIETY.

Banks created an outstanding herbarium (collection of dried plants, now at the Natural History Museum, London). From 1773, as effectively the director, he made the Royal Botanical Gardens at Kew (Surrey) a leading research centre. As the longest serving president of the Royal Society (1778 to death), Banks encouraged the exchange of scientific ideas within Great Britain and overseas. He was created a baronet (1781).

BANNOCKBURN, BATTLE OF Fought S of STIRLING (C Scotland) on 23–24 June 1314. About 8000 Scots under King ROBERT I defeated about 17,000 English under King EDWARD II. The English were seeking to prevent the surrender of Stirling Castle (a last English stronghold in Scotland). Robert afterwards dealt with his enemies in Scotland (*see* CAMBUSKENNETH PARLIAMENT). The defeat worsened Edward's position in England, although England withheld recognition of Scotland's independence (until 1328). *See also* SCOTTISH–ENGLISH RELATIONS 1290 TO 1357.

BAPTISTS, ENGLAND Protestant Christian DISSENTERS who practise baptism of adult believers (not infants). Influenced by John Smyth (d. 1612), who rebaptized himself, English Baptists established a church in LONDON in 1612. From 1633 they divided into General and Particular Baptists, the latter adhering to CALVINISM. Baptists contributed to radical politics in the mid 17th century (*see* ENGLISH REVOLUTION SECTS). They were persecuted after the RESTORATION (1660) but granted freedom of worship by the TOLERATION ACT (1689).

Numbers declined from the early 18th century. Congregations formed county associations from 1764.

In 1770, after many congregations had drifted into UNITARIANISM, evangelical General Baptists created the New Connexion. In 1790 there were 2800 New Connexion and 17,000 Particular Baptists. The latter created a General Union in 1813.

Baptists increased rapidly in the 19th century, sustained by prominent preachers such as C.H. Spurgeon (1834–92). In 1891 the General Union and New Connexion formed the Baptist Union of Great Britain and Ireland. English membership peaked in 1907 at almost 268,000 (attendance at services differed). Membership then declined to 173,000 in 1970, 130,000 in 2010. *See also* NONCONFORMITY AND DISSENT, ENGLAND.

BAPTISTS, IRELAND *see* NONCONFORMITY AND DISSENT, IRELAND

BAPTISTS, SCOTLAND *see* DISSENT, SCOTLAND

BAPTISTS, WALES *see* NONCONFORMITY AND DISSENT, WALES

BARBADOS An island and former English colony in the WEST INDIES (British from 1707). It was uninhabited when English settlers arrived in 1627. After initially cultivating tobacco as an export crop, they switched in the 1640s to sugar, which thereafter dominated the economy and stimulated the SLAVE TRADE. Sugar was grown on PLANTATIONS owned by a 'plantocracy' and worked by slaves from WEST AFRICA. Barbados was a 'proprietary colony' (colony held by owners under the Crown). A House of Assembly was founded in 1639. Slaves outnumbered free men after 1650.

A major slave revolt occurred in 1816, and emancipation was granted in 1834. Barbados became a CROWN COLONY in 1885. The Assembly was elected by universal suffrage from 1951. Barbados belonged to the Federation of the West Indies 1958–62 and became independent in 1966 (with the British monarch as head of State). Approx. population in 1921, 156,000; in 1965, 244,000.

BARBER, ANTHONY (b. 4 July 1920 at Hessle, Yorkshire, England; d. 16 Dec. 2005 at Ipswich, Suffolk, England, aged 85). A tax barrister, Barber was a Conservative MP (1951–64, 1965–74), and held posts in the British government in the 1950s–60s. He was Party chairman 1967–70. In 1970 he succeeded Ian MACLEOD as chancellor of the Exchequer, under Edward HEATH. He initially reduced public spending, but fear of rising unemployment prompted a reflationary Budget (March 1972). The ensuing 'Barber boom' (1973) resulted in accelerating INFLATION, a statutory INCOMES POLICY, a MINERS' STRIKE and the government's downfall. Barber left politics in 1974 and was created Lord Barber.

BAREBONE'S PARLIAMENT In England, 1653, during the Commonwealth, a single-chamber assembly which replaced the RUMP PARLIAMENT. Its 137 members were nominated by the Army Council to represent English counties, Wales, Scotland and Ireland. Convened on 4 July, it surrendered power to Oliver CROMWELL on 12 Dec. after moderates became alarmed by demands for radical reform of law and tithes. The Parliament's nickname, derived from London MP and preacher Praise-God Barebone, was intended to defame the assembly as a body of religious fanatics. *See also* COMMONWEALTH AND PROTECTORATE.

BARING, EVELYN (b. 26 Feb. 1841 at Cromer, Norfolk, England; d. 29 Jan. 1917 at London, England, aged 65). From a banking family, Baring became a financial administrator in Egypt (1876–80; controller-general of finance from 1879), and India (1880–3). In 1883, following Great Britain's intervention, he was appointed consul-general to EGYPT, becoming effectively its ruler. He reformed Egypt's finances and introduced agricultural, social and legal improvements. He supported reconquest of SUDAN (undertaken 1896–8) and creation of a condominium (jointly ruled country). Baring was created Lord Baring (1892), Viscount Cromer (1899) and earl of Cromer (1901). He retired in 1907.

BARLOW, WILLIAM (b. *c*.1480 in Essex, England; d. 13 Aug. 1568 at Chichester, Sussex, England, aged about 88). Originally an Augustinian canon, by 1535 Barlow supported Church reform (*see* REFORMATION, ENGLAND) and was appointed prior of Haverfordwest (SW Wales) by Anne BOLEYN. In 1536 he became bishop of ST ASAPH (NE Wales), then of ST DAVIDS (SW). He attacked popular devotion to relics, saints and pilgrimages.

Under King EDWARD VI, Barlow moved (1548) to Bath and Wells (SW England), but resigned after MARY's accession (1553). Imprisoned, he recanted and then fled abroad. Under ELIZABETH, he was bishop of Chichester (S England) from 1559. His five daughters all married bishops. *See also* REFORMATION, ENGLAND/WALES.

BARNETT, SAMUEL (b. 8 Feb. 1844 at Bristol, Gloucestershire, England; d. 17 June 1913 at Hove, East Sussex, England, aged 69). A Church of England clergyman who ministered in London from 1867, Barnett helped to found the CHARITY ORGANISATION SOCIETY (1869). In 1884 he started Toynbee Hall in the deprived East End where university students could live among the poor (he was warden 1884–1906). It inaugurated the UNIVERSITY SETTLEMENT MOVEMENT. Barnett also catered for spiritual and recreational deprivation by founding the Whitechapel Art Gallery (1901) and supporting country holidays for slum children.

BARON In England, term used in the late 11th–14th centuries for an important tenant-in-chief of the king (derived from Latin *baro*, meaning 'man'). Barons, including EARLS, comprised the upper NOBILITY. In the 13th century they were known collectively as the 'baronage'. During the 14th century the summoning of earls and selected barons to PARLIAMENT, and the creation of new ranks of nobility, transformed the status of baron to that of the lowest rank in the PEERAGE (lords summoned individually to Parliament). *See also* SOCIAL STRUCTURE, ENGLAND 1066 TO 16TH CENTURY.

BARONET A hereditary status and title bestowed in England and Wales from 1611, ranking below the PEERAGE (nobility) and above KNIGHTS (i.e., part of the GENTRY). It was created by King JAMES VI/I as a means of raising money to tackle the Crown's shortage of funds after the failure of the GREAT CONTRACT. Income from sales of baronetcies was used to defend English settlements in ULSTER (N Ireland). Baronetcies were conferred for Ireland from 1619, and for Scotland and NOVA SCOTIA from 1625.

BARONIAL CONFLICT AND WARS In England, struggles 1258–67 between King HENRY III and BARONS alienated by Henry's reckless foreign policy, oppressive government and favouring of foreign relatives.

On 30 April 1258, after Henry had supported a relative in a dispute against a baron, leading nobles demanded reform of government (*see* LUSIGNANS). In June Henry accepted, by oath, the Provisions of OXFORD which subordinated his government to an elected Council and required co-operation with PARLIAMENT. The reforms were extended in Oct. by the Provisions of WESTMINSTER. The Council collapsed in late 1260, enabling Henry to regain authority (e.g., appointing supporters to offices). On 12 June 1261 a papal bull was published which released Henry from his oath, causing the reformer Simon de MONTFORT to go abroad (July).

In 1263 Montfort returned (April), and reformers attacked royalists' estates. The Provisions of Oxford were reimposed (16 July), with Montfort dominating government. During the summer, some reformers (e.g., Roger BIGOD) changed sides. On 1 Nov. a truce was agreed and Louis IX of France was asked to arbitrate. He condemned the reformers (Mise of Amiens, 23 Jan. 1264), yet opposition continued. On 14 May, at the battle of Lewes (Sussex), reformers captured Henry and his heir Edward. Montfort effectively ruled in the king's name, looking to Parliament for support.

In 1265 Edward escaped (May), rallied support and defeated opponents at Evesham, Worcs. (4 Aug). Montfort was killed. Henry conciliated opponents with moderate reforms and land restitution (*see* KENILWORTH, DICTUM OF), though fighting continued until July 1267.

BARONY, IRELAND Name used from the 16th century for subdivisions of SHIRES (or counties), totalling about 250. They are based on the Gaelic Irish unit the *trícha cét* (meaning 'thirty hundred'), which refers to military musters and is recorded as a territorial unit from the 11th century. It has been suggested that most of the territories represent the areas of small kingdoms (*see* TÚATH).

After the Anglo-Norman invasion (1169–70), the *trícha cét* was equated with the Welsh CANTREF. From the late 17th to 19th centuries baronies were important in county-based government – used for assessing public works and levying CESS. In 1715 the Irish Parliament authorized the appointment of constables for baronies. *See also* LOCAL GOVERNMENTAL STRUCTURES, IRELAND.

BARONY, SCOTLAND A basic unit of local (judicial) administration from the 13th century to the 18th; until the later 15th century, most were roughly equivalent to parishes, and probably contained a dozen or so FERMTOUNS. Many were continuations of early THANAGES and 12th-century knights' fees.

Formal development into baronies resulted from royal grants of judicial powers (over, e.g., theft, assault, accidental homicide). There were over 400 baronies *c.*1400, and more than 1000 in the 17th century. Barons' powers were reduced in the 1650s, and although they were not abolished by the Heritable Jurisdictions Act (1747), they fell into disuse. *See also* LOCAL GOVERNMENTAL STRUCTURES, SCOTLAND; LAIRD.

BARTHOLOMEW'S DAY EVICTIONS In England and Wales, 1662, following RESTORATION of the monarchy, the resignation of about 1000 clergy from their Church of ENGLAND livings for rejecting the Church's ceremonies as prescribed in the newly revised PRAYER BOOK. Under the 1662 Act of Uniformity, clergy were required to accept the book by oath, and renounce the SOLEMN LEAGUE AND COVENANT (1643), by St Bartholomew's Day (24 Aug.), when TITHES were payable. The eviction of so-called 'Bartholomew men' strengthened NONCONFORMITY. *See also* CLARENDON CODE.

BASTARD FEUDALISM Term invented in 1885 by the English historian Charles Plummer to describe lordship and political society in late-medieval England (14th–15th centuries). It described a situation in which lords obtained services and military support by recruiting and retaining followers mainly with money payments (instead of with land, as in a 'traditional' feudal system; *see* MILITARY SERVICE, ENGLAND 1066 TO MID 17TH CENTURY). Payments were made as either annual fees (annuities) or daily wages, and were sometimes agreed by contract (or indenture). Lords also provided uniforms or other insignia and food (so-called 'livery and maintenance'). Uniforms and insignia indicated allegiance. The 'retaining' of GENTRY and others provided magnates with 'retinues' (effectively private armies) which they could use for feuding, influencing legal proceedings and warfare. A lord's total body of followers was called an 'affinity'.

Bastard feudalism has a longer and wider history than Plummer envisaged, and political society was arguably more fluid, and less contractual. Retaining existed by the mid 12th century though it grew during the 14th century. The House of Commons complained about its effects (e.g., lawlessness) from the 1370s onwards, and bastard feudalism facilitated the YORKIST–LANCASTRIAN CONFLICT (1450s–80s). Similar developments occurred in Wales and parts of Ireland, and to a lesser extent in Scotland (see MANRENT).

From the late 13th century, English rulers relied on retinues recruited by noblemen to provide military forces, but in the late 15th and 16th centuries they sought to control retaining. It remained a means of raising armed forces for the Crown until the CIVIL WARS (1640s), although its importance declined in the later 16th century with the revival and development of the MILITIA. See also PATRONAGE.

BATH A city in SW England, by the R. Avon; centre of Bath and North East Somerset (unitary authority). Site of natural hot springs.

Bath flourished as a spa under the Romans (1st–4th centuries; called Aquae Sulis, meaning 'Springs of Sulis'), then declined in the 5th century. The site was taken by the Gewisse in the late 6th century (see WESSEX), and named after the ruins of Roman baths. A MINSTER was founded in the late 7th century, and a small town later developed. Bath was a bishop's see 1088–1206 and a joint see thereafter (with Wells, Somerset).

In the 18th century Bath became England's premier spa and pleasure capital, over which Beau Nash (1674–1762) presided. Splendid houses, streets, squares, crescents and facilities (e.g., pump house) were built. After bombing in WORLD WAR II, buildings were subsequently restored. Bath gained two universities: Bath University of Technology (chartered 1966), Bath Spa University (upgraded college, 2005). See also EDGAR; TOWN PLANNING; CONSUMER REVOLUTION; HIGHER EDUCATION, EXPANSION OF.

Est. popn: 1086, 1500; 1300, 1500; 1600, 2000; 1800, 35,000; 1900, 52,000; 2000, 83,000.

BATH, EARL OF see PULTENEY, WILLIAM

BAXTER, RICHARD (b. 12 Nov. 1615 at Rowton, Shropshire, England; d. 8 Dec. 1691 at London, England, aged 76). A Church of ENGLAND clergyman from 1638, with PURITAN sympathies, Baxter served as a preacher in Kidderminster (Worcestershire) 1641–2, and as a chaplain in Parliament's NEW MODEL ARMY 1645–7. He returned to Kidderminster in 1648 as vicar. He became well known in the 1650s for his writings (notably *The Saint's Everlasting Rest*, 1650), and in 1652 founded the Worcestershire Voluntary Association of Ministers to encourage unity.

After the RESTORATION (1660), Baxter declined the offer of a bishopric from King CHARLES II. He participated in discussions towards a Church settlement encompassing a broad range of Protestants (see WORCESTER HOUSE DECLARATION; SAVOY CONFERENCE). When these failed, he left his living (1662). Thereafter he devoted himself to writing and preaching.

BAYEUX TAPESTRY An embroidery, at Bayeux Cathedral (in Normandy, N France), depicting the Norman invasion of England (1066). The surviving work measures 223 ft by about 20 in (68 m by about 50 cm). The end is lost. Its early history is unrecorded. It was probably made in England for ODO OF BAYEUX before 1082. See also NORMAN CONQUEST OF ENGLAND.

BAYLY, LEWIS (b. in 1570s, probably at Carmarthen, Carmarthenshire, Wales; d. 26 Oct. 1631, probably in Wales, aged around 65). A combative personality and adherent of PURITANISM who wrote the popular devotional work *The Practice of Piety* (1611). The Welsh translation, *Yr Ymarfer o Dduwioldeb* (1630), was influential into the 19th century. Bayly held Church posts in England, and was bishop of BANGOR 1616–31 and patron of John DAVIES.

BBC see BRITISH BROADCASTING CORPORATION

BBC WORLD SERVICE Name used from 1965 for the international radio transmissions (or 'external services') of the BRITISH BROADCASTING CORPORATION. An 'Empire Service' in English was started in 1932, followed by an Arabic service in Jan. 1938 and French, German and Italian services during the MUNICH CRISIS (Sept.). By the end of 1940, during WORLD WAR II, the BBC broadcast in 34 languages, rising to 45 in 1945. The Empire Service was renamed the Overseas Service (Nov. 1939), General Overseas Service (1943), and World Service (1965). Though the BBC's overseas broadcasts were supported financially by the British government, they were considered trustworthy around the world, and sustained British influence following the decline of the BRITISH EMPIRE. In 2015 over 300 million people listened to BBC services in 29 languages. A television service was started in 1991.

BEAGHMORE STONE CIRCLES A complex of STONE CIRCLES, rows and cairns in Co. Tyrone, N Ireland. The exposed part consists of seven circles, including three pairs. The circles consist of many small, closely spaced stones, and are associated with pre-existing small cairns. The long rows lead tangentially onto the circles. Use of the site centres on *c.*1600 in the early Middle BRONZE AGE.

BEAKER CULTURE, BRITAIN A prehistoric culture defined by the appearance in the very late NEOLITHIC of ceramic vessels with an 'S'-shaped profile and incised decoration; made and used over the period *c.*2700 BC–1000 BC (including most of the BRONZE AGE). Beaker culture is often associated with the first metals. Although Beaker culture has traditionally been taken as evidence for the immigration of an ethnic group or 'culture', it is now thought to reflect more complex networks of contact and exchange and the use of Beakers in new ceremonial and sacred events.

BEAKER CULTURE, IRELAND Beaker pots, dating from *c.*2500– *c.*1700 BC (CHALCOLITHIC PERIOD and Early BRONZE AGE), occur in settlements, ritual sites and in burials sometimes accompanied by copper daggers and an archer's equipment. They were once regarded as evidence of an intrusive 'Beaker Folk', but their generally indigenous contexts imply no significant population influx.

BEATLES, THE A pop music group from LIVERPOOL (NW England), consisting from 1962 of John Lennon (1940–80), Paul McCartney (b. 1942), George Harrison (1943–2001) and Ringo Starr (b. 1940). They dominated popular music in Great Britain from 1963 until their break-up in 1970, performing many songs by Lennon and McCartney. They achieved immense success in the USA. The Beatles' music energized 1960s YOUTH CULTURE, and remained popular worldwide.

BEATON, DAVID (b. *c.*1494 at Markinch, Fife, E Scotland; d. 29 May 1546 at St Andrews, Fife, aged about 52). Clergyman; appointed bishop of Mirepoix, France (1537), cardinal (1538), and archbishop of ST ANDREWS (1539). As an adviser of King JAMES V from 1528, Beaton negotiated his French marriages and in 1541 persuaded him to avoid a meeting arranged by King HENRY VIII, provoking the English invasion of 1452.

On 10 Jan. 1543, following James's death, the regent, the earl of ARRAN, appointed Beaton as CHANCELLOR (replacing Gavin DUNBAR), only to arrest and remove him (27 Jan.). Arran then arranged peace and marriage treaties with England (agreed Aug. 1543). Beaton meanwhile constructed a large opposition. In Sept. Arran capitulated to Beaton; in Dec. Parliament cancelled the treaties and Beaton was reappointed chancellor. He was also a PAPAL LEGATE from 1544. As a fervent opponent of Church reform, Beaton had George WISHART burnt for heresy (1 March 1546), provoking his murder by Wishart's supporters. *See also* SCOTTISH–ENGLISH RELATIONS 1357 TO 1603.

BEAUFORT, EDMUND (b. *c.*1406; d. 22 May 1455 at St Albans, Hertfordshire, England, aged 49). Beaufort was involved in the French wars in the 1420s–30s (*see* HUNDRED YEARS WAR). He was created earl of Dorset in 1442, marquess in 1443. In 1444 he succeeded his brother as earl of Somerset, becoming the head of the Beaufort faction in English politics. He replaced Richard, duke of YORK, as lieutenant of France and Normandy in 1447 and was created duke of Somerset in 1448.

Somerset's direction of the war was disastrous: by June 1450 the remaining English-held lands in N France were lost. Yet Somerset remained in favour with King HENRY VI until Henry fell ill and York became 'protector'. Somerset was imprisoned 1454–5. On release, he rejoined the king. He was killed when royalist ('Lancastrian') forces clashed with 'Yorkists' at the first battle of St Albans. *See also* BEAUFORT FAMILY; YORKIST–LANCASTRIAN CONFLICT.

BEAUFORT, HENRY (b. *c.*1375; d. 11 April 1447 at Winchester, Hampshire, England, aged about 71). The second illegitimate son of JOHN OF GAUNT and Katherine SWYNFORD, Beaufort was appointed bishop of LINCOLN (1398), then of WINCHESTER (1404). Under King HENRY IV (half-brother) he was CHANCELLOR 1403–5 and a leading member of government 1410–12.

Under HENRY V (nephew, ruled 1413–22), Beaufort served as chancellor (1413–17) and provided loans for war in France (*see* HUNDRED YEARS WAR). During the (Church) Council of Constance he was appointed cardinal (1417), but Henry compelled him to refuse (1419).

Under HENRY VI (great-nephew), Beaufort was chancellor from 1424, vying with the duke of GLOUCESTER for authority in government and over the king (a minor); in Oct. 1425 their forces met on London bridge. Their conflict was settled by the duke of BEDFORD and Beaufort resigned as chancellor (1426) with the concession of taking the cardinalate (1427). In France 1430–1, he presided at the trial of JOAN OF ARC and crowned Henry VI as king of France. He remained excluded from English government until 1435, when he also joined peace negotiations with France. After Henry VI was declared ruler (1437), Beaufort was effectively his chief minister until 1443. *See also* BEAUFORT FAMILY.

BEAUFORT, MARGARET (b. 31 May 1443 at Bletsoe, Bedfordshire, England; d. 29 June 1509 at Westminster, Middlesex, England, aged 66). Margaret was the surviving child of John Beaufort, duke of Somerset (d. 1444). Her royal lineage made her marriage prospects political. After the duke of SUFFOLK attempted a union with his heir, her wardship passed to King HENRY VI's half-brothers Edmund and Jasper TUDOR. She married Edmund in 1455 but he died before their son Henry was born (1457). Later she married Henry Stafford (d. 1471) and Thomas Stanley (d. 1504), a YORKIST.

When HENRY VI died (21 May 1471), Henry Tudor became a LANCASTRIAN claimant to the English throne held by the Yorkist EDWARD IV. Margaret urged him into exile in Brittany. He invaded in 1485 to depose RICHARD III. Margaret lived through Henry's reign, honoured as 'the king's mother' (see HENRY VII). She was patron of William CAXTON (by 1489) and founded colleges at CAMBRIDGE. See also BEAUFORT FAMILY; YORKIST–LANCASTRIAN CONFLICT.

BEAUFORT FAMILY A noble family whose blood-link to the English Crown underpinned the Tudor claim in 1485. The Beauforts originated in the extramarital liaison between JOHN OF GAUNT, third son of King EDWARD III, and Katherine SWYNFORD (1370s). Their four children were legitimized in 1396 (papal bull) and 1397 (letters patent). The family name derived from a French lordship formerly held by Gaunt. The Beauforts became key supporters of their relatives the LANCASTRIAN kings.

The leading members were: Henry BEAUFORT (c.1375–1447), Gaunt's second Beaufort son; Edmund BEAUFORT (c.1406–55), second son of Gaunt's oldest son (John) and counsellor of HENRY VI; Margaret BEAUFORT (1443–1509), niece of Edmund by his older brother (John). Edmund Beaufort's older sister Joan married JAMES I of Scotland (1424). Margaret's son Henry Tudor seized the throne of England in 1485 (see HENRY VII). See also YORKIST–LANCASTRIAN CONFLICT.

BEAVERBROOK, LORD (b. 25 May 1879 at Maple, Ontario, Canada; d. 9 June 1964 at Cherkley Court, Surrey, England, aged 85). A self-made tycoon, Max Aitken emigrated to England in 1910, became a confidant of Bonar LAW, and was elected a Conservative MP (Dec.). He was created a baronet (1911) and Lord Beaverbrook (1917), and served as British minister of information (Feb.–Oct. 1918) under David LLOYD GEORGE.

During the 1920s, Beaverbrook developed his popular *Daily Express* newspaper. It was strongly imperialist and critical of Conservative leader Stanley BALDWIN, and advocated 'imperial preference' (from 1929; see TARIFF REFORM) and APPEASEMENT (late 1930s). During WORLD WAR II, Beaverbrook served Winston CHURCHILL, another friend, as minister of aircraft production (1940–1), minister of supply (1941–2) and lord PRIVY SEAL (1943–5). See also NEWSPAPERS, ENGLAND.

BECHUANALAND A former British territory in southern Africa. European travellers and missionaries (including Robert MOFFAT) were active N of CAPE COLONY in the early 19th century, and from the 1830s Boers from the Transvaal claimed land in the area. German colonization to the W in the 1880s caused the British to establish the CROWN COLONY of British Bechuanaland (1885) and Bechuanaland PROTECTORATE to the N (1885, extended 1892). The colony was annexed to Cape Colony in 1895 (later included in SOUTH AFRICA).

In 1895 African chiefs, visiting London, persuaded the British government to retain the protectorate rather than cede control to the BRITISH SOUTH AFRICA COMPANY, though the company used Bechuanaland as a base for expansion northwards (see SOUTHERN RHODESIA). British administration operated through native rulers. Self-government was granted in 1965, and the protectorate became an independent republic as Botswana in 1966. Approx. population in 1921, 153,000; in 1965, 525,000.

BECKET, THOMAS (b. 21 Dec. 1120 at London, England; d. 29 Dec. 1170 at Canterbury, Kent, England, aged 50). A merchant's son, Becket rose under the patronage of THEOBALD OF BEC, archbishop of CANTERBURY. In Jan. 1155 he was appointed CHANCELLOR by King HENRY II. They became close friends. In 1162 Becket was elected archbishop of Canterbury despite the claims of Gilbert FOLIOT.

To Henry's dismay, Becket resisted his attempts to assert jurisdiction over the English Church. After Becket rejected the Constitutions of CLARENDON (issued Jan. 1164), Henry sought to ruin him. Becket was charged with offences at a royal council (Oct.) but fled into exile in France (2 Nov.).

Becket returned (1 Dec. 1170), having excommunicated bishops who had crowned HENRY THE YOUNG KING. His headstrong behaviour angered Henry. An outburst from Henry provoked four knights to murder Becket in his cathedral. He was canonized in 1173, and his tomb in Canterbury Cathedral became a major pilgrimage destination. See also CHAUCER, GEOFFREY.

BEDCHAMBER CRISIS A constitutional dispute which prevented a change of government in Great Britain, 1839. After the WHIG prime minister Viscount MELBOURNE resigned, Queen VICTORIA invited the CONSERVATIVE Sir Robert PEEL to form a minority government (8 May). He asked the queen to indicate support by replacing some ladies of her bedchamber who were related to Whigs. When the queen refused, Peel declined to become prime minister and Melbourne resumed office (10 May). The queen's apparent partisanship was criticized. See also KINGSHIP AND MONARCHY, ENGLAND AND GREAT BRITAIN FROM 1680s.

BEDE (b. 673 or 674 in Bernicia; d. 26 May 735 at Jarrow, Northumbria, aged about 61). Around 680 Bede, aged 7, entered Monkwearmouth monastery. From 682 he lived at its nearby 'twin' house of Jarrow.

Bede became one of the most learned and prolific authors in Europe, producing biblical commentaries, saints' Lives, studies of chronology and computation, and the *Ecclesiastical History of the English People* (completed 731). An outstanding historical source, the *History* narrates the progress of Christianity among Anglo-Saxon kingdoms, and demonstrates how virtuous kings are rewarded on Earth. *See also* BENEDICT BISCOP; NORTHUMBRIA.

BEDFORD, 4TH DUKE OF (b. 30 Sept. 1710 at Streatham, Surrey, England; d. 15 Jan. 1771 at London, England, aged 60). John Russell, a WHIG, succeeded as duke in 1732. Following the fall of Robert WALPOLE (1742), he was a reforming first lord of the Admiralty (1744–8), (southern) SECRETARY OF STATE (1748–51), lord lieutenant of Ireland (1755–61), and lord PRIVY SEAL (1761–3). In Sept. 1762 he was sent to Paris, France, by the earl of BUTE to negotiate a treaty to end the SEVEN YEARS WAR.

Bedford became president of the Council in the ministry of George GRENVILLE (1763). He feared that Bute remained influential with King GEORGE III and sought to have him banned from office. Bedford was dismissed in 1765. Some of his followers joined the ministry of William PITT the Elder in late 1767.

BEDFORD, JOHN DUKE OF (b. 20 June 1389 in England; d. 14 Sept. 1435 at Rouen, Normandy, aged 46). John of Lancaster, first brother of King HENRY V, was created duke of Bedford in 1414. After Henry renewed war against France (1415; *see* HUNDRED YEARS WAR), Bedford served as 'lieutenant' (regent) in England in 1415, 1417–19, 1421–2. He defeated a Franco-Genoese fleet off Harfleur in 1416, and campaigned in France 1420–1. When HENRY VI succeeded (1 Sept. 1422), Bedford became heir presumptive and 'protector'.

As the young king's regent in France, Bedford married (1423) Anne, sister of Philip, duke of BURGUNDY, a union intended to cement the Anglo-Burgundian alliance. He strengthened England's hold on Normandy, achieving a heavy defeat of Franco-Scots forces at Verneuil (17 Aug. 1424). He was recalled to England to resolve disputes between (his brother) the duke of GLOUCESTER and (his uncle) Henry BEAUFORT (1425–7), and his regency was suspended 1430–2 for Henry's coronation in Paris.

The English position in France weakened after defeat at ORLÉANS (1429). Bedford returned to England to obtain reinforcements (1433–4). Peace negotiations began but failed at the Congress of ARRAS (Aug.–Sept. 1435), with the Burgundian alliance also ending. Bedford died soon afterwards. *See also* WOODVILLE FAMILY.

'BEECHING REPORT' Popular name for a plan for the modernization of Great Britain's nationalized RAILWAYS (full title, *The Reshaping of British Railways*), published 1963, which was prepared by Richard Beeching, chairman of the British Railways Board. Beeching proposed closure of 280 economically unviable lines and 1850 stations to restore profitability. The 18,000 route mi (28,800 km) of railways were reduced by 1969 to 12,000 mi (19,200 km), and stations from 7000 to 3000.

BEHN, APHRA (b. 14 Dec. 1640 in Kent, England; d. 16 April 1689 at London, England, aged 48). Behn possibly served as a Royalist spy in the 1650s, and in 1666 was an agent for Lord ARLINGTON in Antwerp (Spanish Netherlands). A playwright from 1670, she had at least 19 plays staged, including *The Rover* (1677) about a comic rake. Many reflected strong Royalist views. She became a TORY propagandist during the EXCLUSION CRISIS (1679–81). From 1684 Behn published prose fiction, including *Oronooko* (1688), a story which attacked slavery. *See also* ENGLISH LITERATURE, ENGLAND.

BELFAST The capital city of Northern Ireland, by the R. Lagan; from Irish Béal Feirste, meaning 'Mouth of Farset stream'.

Belfast town was developed from 1603 by the English soldier Sir Arthur CHICHESTER (granted charter of self-government by King JAMES VI/I in 1613). In the later 17th century it became the centre of the rural Ulster LINEN INDUSTRY and an important port (Ireland's fourth-largest town in 1680s).

Late 18th-century Belfast became an industrial centre. Cotton-spinning factories flourished in and around Belfast *c*.1780–1870s. (By 1811, 15 of 33 Belfast factories were steam powered.) Flax-spinning mills operated from the 1820s (29 by 1850), and linen weaving was mechanized in factories from the 1850s. SHIP BUILDING became substantial with the expansion of Harland and Wolff (from 1860s). By the 1880s Belfast produced a third of Ireland's net industrial output and two-thirds of industrial exports. It received city status in 1888 and became the capital of NORTHERN IRELAND in 1921.

Aircraft manufacturing was started in 1937, but Belfast's economy declined from the 1960s and life was disrupted 1969– *c*.2000 by sectarian conflict (*see* TROUBLES). *See also* INDUSTRY, NORTHERN IRELAND.

Est. popn: 1800, 20,000; 1900, 349,000; 2000, 280,000.

BELFAST AGREEMENT Signed on 10 April 1998 (Good Friday) at BELFAST, Northern Ireland, by representatives of the British and Irish governments and of eight political parties; part of Northern Ireland's PEACE PROCESS. It provided for an elected ASSEMBLY and devolved power-sharing EXECUTIVE in Northern Ireland; bodies representing both Northern Ireland and the Republic of Ireland; and a British–Irish Council. Prisoners associated with PARAMILITARY ORGANIZATIONS would be released, and the Republic would revoke its constitutional claim on Northern Ireland. The Agreement was endorsed by referendums in Northern Ireland and the Republic of Ireland on 22 May. *See also* NORTHERN IRELAND.

BELGAE A confederation of Gallic tribes in NW Europe (between the Rivers Rhine, Seine and Marne) which was defeated by the Roman general CAESAR (57, 52 BC). Commius, leader of the Atrebates tribe, fled to Britain, establishing a Belgic kingdom of the Atrebates in S Britain. His son Verica's expulsion by the CATUVELLAUNI provided the pretext for the Roman invasion of AD 43 (*see* CLAUDIAN INVASION). In Roman Britain (1st–5th centuries), the Atrebates' territory comprised two *civitates*, named for the Atrebates and Belgae (*see* CIVITAS). *See also* IRON AGE TRIBES, BRITAIN; WINCHESTER.

BELGIUM (SOUTHERN NETHERLANDS), ENGLISH AND BRITISH RELATIONS WITH From 1689 England (Great Britain from 1707) fought repeatedly to prevent French domination of the (largely Catholic) southern Netherlands (Spanish ruled to 1714, then Austrian ruled). But they were conquered by the French in 1794 (annexed 1795). In 1815, following the fall of the French emperor Napoleon Bonaparte, the British foreign secretary Viscount CASTLEREAGH arranged their unification with the (mainly Protestant) northern (Dutch) NETHERLANDS in a 'United Kingdom of the Netherlands'. When the southern Netherlands revolted in 1830, Lord PALMERSTON recognized their independence, as 'Belgium', rather than drive them into the arms of FRANCE. Having forced a Dutch withdrawal, he later sponsored international guarantees of neutrality (by treaty of London, 1839).

Revulsion at King Leopold's misrule in the Belgian Congo was overlaid when Germany invaded Belgium on 4 Aug. 1914, in violation of the 1839 treaty. This became the immediate cause of British entry into WORLD WAR I. Belgian troops operated with the Allies (1914–18). Having guaranteed the Belgian–German frontier under the treaty of LOCARNO (1925), Britain briefly intervened in May 1940 (early in WORLD WAR II), following sudden Belgian capitulation to Germany. British forces participated in Belgium's liberation in 1944, and from 1949 both countries were allies within the NORTH ATLANTIC TREATY ORGANIZATION.

BELIZE *see* BRITISH HONDURAS

BELL, ALEXANDER GRAHAM (b. 3 March 1847 at Edinburgh, Scotland; d. 2 Aug. 1922 at Beinn Bhreagh,

Nova Scotia, Canada, aged 75). After brief periods in Scotland and England as a teacher, university student and elocutionist, Bell emigrated with his parents to CANADA (1870). He moved to the USA, becoming professor of vocal physiology and elocution at Boston University (1873) and a citizen (1874).

Interested in telegraphy and familiar with types of apparatus that turned sound into images, Bell produced an 'ear phonautograph' (1874), a machine that recorded speech on glass employing a human ear and part of a skull. It stimulated the idea of using a membrane to transmit speech electrically. In 1876 and 1877 he filed the fundamental patents that established him as inventor of the telephone. Bell also developed a 'photophone' for transmission of speech by light beam, and was interested in numerous other scientific matters (e.g., aeroplanes). *See also* ELECTRONIC COMMUNICATIONS, GREAT BRITAIN/IRELAND.

BELL, HENRY (b. 7 April 1767 at Torpichen, Linlithgowshire, Scotland; d. 14 Nov. 1830 at Helensburgh, Dunbartonshire, Scotland, aged 63). In 1807, after working as a stonemason, millwright, engineer and builder, Bell opened the Baths Inn at Helensburgh on the Clyde estuary. Interested in applying steam propulsion to ships, he designed and built *Comet*, which was launched on the Clyde in 1812. Propelled by paddles, it was the first successful steam-powered passenger vessel in Europe (wrecked 1820). Bell sought to develop steamship services, and in 1825 inaugurated a service from GLASGOW to Inverness via the Caledonian Canal. *See also* HOLIDAYS; CANALS, SCOTLAND.

BEND OF THE BOYNE An island-like area by the R. Boyne, Co. Meath (E Ireland), where the river changes course. Known in Irish as Brú na Boinne, this was a focus of NEOLITHIC settlement. Around 3000 BC, the large passage tombs at KNOWTH, Dowth and NEWGRANGE were constructed. Ceremonial activity later shifted to open-air enclosures and HENGES.

BENEDICT BISCOP (b. *c*.628 in Bernicia; d. 12 Jan. 689, probably at Monkwearmouth, Northumbria, aged about 61). An Anglian nobleman who entered monastic life in Francia (mid 660s), Biscop founded (673 or 674) St Peter's monastery at Monkwearmouth in BERNICIA (NE England). A 'twin' house, St Paul's, was founded at Jarrow (681 or 682). Using books acquired in Rome (671–2, 685), Biscop created one of the finest libraries in Europe. It made possible the work of BEDE. *See also* EDUCATION AND LEARNING, ENGLAND BEFORE 1066.

BENEFIT OF CLERGY The principle that clergy should be tried in Church courts. It was conceded in England for some felonies by King HENRY II in 1176, following the murder of Thomas BECKET (1170), but remained contentious. By the mid 14th century, clergy were commonly transferred from royal to Church courts if found guilty in the former, enabling them to be acquitted or convicted with a lesser punishment in the latter. By 1400 reading was used as a test of clerical status, enabling laity to claim it.

The benefit was removed for murder and theft from churches in 1532 by the REFORMATION PARLIAMENT. Burglary and rape were excluded in 1566. The benefit was largely abolished in 1827. *See also* CHURCH, MEDIEVAL ENGLAND.

BENN, TONY (b. 3 April 1925 at London, England; d. 14 March 2014 at London, aged 88). A Labour MP from 1950 and heir to a viscountcy (and membership of the UK House of Lords), Benn sought to renounce his succession. On becoming (2nd) Viscount Stansgate (1960), he was barred from the House of Commons (ban maintained after re-election in by-election, 1961). He succeeded in obtaining the Peerage Act (1963), under which he disclaimed his peerage. He was re-elected as an MP (held seats 1963–83, 1984–2005).

Benn held British government offices under Harold WILSON (1964–70, 1974–6) and James CALLAGHAN (1976–9). As the controversial champion of Labour's left wing, he sought to become deputy leader of the Party in 1981, but lost narrowly to Denis HEALEY. *See also* PEERAGE, DISCLAIMING OF.

BENSON, E.W. (b. 14 July 1829 at Birmingham, Warwickshire, England; d. 11 Oct. 1896 at Hawarden, Flintshire, Wales, aged 67). A Church of England clergyman, Edward White Benson was the first master of Wellington College (1858–72), a school which commemorated the duke of WELLINGTON. In 1877 he became bishop of the new diocese of Truro (for Cornwall, SW England). As archbishop of CANTERBURY from 1883, he encouraged overseas missions and the creation of new Anglican churches. In 1889 Benson revived the archbishop's court to consider an accusation of RITUALISM against Bishop Edward King of Lincoln. His judgment (1890) generally supported King. He died while visiting W.E. GLADSTONE. *See also* ANGLICAN COMMUNION.

BENTHAM, JEREMY (b. 4 Feb. 1748 at London, England; d. 6 June 1832 at Westminster, Middlesex, England, aged 84). After attending OXFORD University (1760–3) and studying law, Bentham published critical works about government, law, economics and education (from 1776). He sought to establish fundamental principles. His most influential work, *An Introduction to the Principles of Morals and Legislation* (1789), propounded

UTILITARIANISM: that human actions should be judged by their effect on society's general happiness. He particularly influenced the PHILOSOPHIC RADICALS.

BENTINCK, LORD WILLIAM (b. 14 Sept. 1774 at Piccadilly, Middlesex, England; d. 17 June 1839 at Paris, France, aged 64). A son of the 3rd duke of PORTLAND, and a WHIG, Bentinck joined the British Army in 1791. He served as governor of Madras (now Chennai), SE India (1803–7), when he was blamed for the anti-British 'Vellore Mutiny' (July 1806), and as an envoy in Sicily (1811–15).

As governor-general of INDIA from 1828, Bentinck made economies in expenditure, revenue reforms in NW India, and increased the employment of natives in official positions. He extended Anglicization by instituting English in higher courts and government business, and prohibited *suttee* (burning of widows). He retired in 1835 and became an MP.

BEOWULF The longest heroic poem in Old English. Its time of composition is uncertain; suggestions range from the 8th to early 11th century. It survives in a single 11th-century manuscript. Though written in Anglo-Saxon England, its story is set in pre-Christian Denmark and Sweden. It displays the working of Germanic kingship, expressed through gift giving, feasting and feud. *See also* KINGSHIP, ANGLO-SAXON.

BERESFORD, JOHN (b. 14 March 1738 at Dublin, Ireland; d. 5 Nov. 1805 at Walworth, Co. Londonderry, Ireland, aged 67). A member of the Irish House of Commons from 1760, Beresford was appointed a commissioner of revenue in 1770, during the reorganization of government patronage instigated by Viscount TOWNSHEND. As chief commissioner, from 1780, he commissioned James Gandon to design Dublin's new Custom House.

After William PITT the Younger became prime minister of Great Britain (Dec. 1783), he recruited Beresford as an adviser on Irish affairs (with John FITZGIBBON and John FOSTER). Beresford supported Pitt's decision to unite Ireland with Britain, but opposed Catholic Emancipation. After the union he sat in the UK House of Commons. *See also* PROTESTANT ASCENDANCY; UNION OF IRELAND AND GREAT BRITAIN.

BERFEDDWLAD, Y (Welsh, meaning 'The middle country'). A region in N WALES, between the Rivers Conwy and Dee, which was contested by Normans (later English) and Welsh; called 'The Four Cantrefs' in English.

It comprised the CANTREFS of Rhos, Rhufoniog, Dyffryn Clwyd, and Tegeingl (English, Englefield). It was alternatively known in Welsh as Gwynedd-is-Conwy, i.e., 'GWYNEDD below [east of] the Conwy', as distinct from

Gwynedd proper, or Gwynedd-uwch-Conwy ('Gwynedd above the Conwy').

In the early Middle Ages (6th–9th centuries) the cantrefs were not combined; Rhos and Rhufoniog, at least, had independent rulers. In the 9th century, they fell to Gwynedd, though English settled in Tegeingl by the late 10th century. Y Berfeddwlad came under early Norman pressure, from c.1070 (see ROBERT OF RHUDDLAN). In the 12th and 13th centuries it moved between English and Welsh control, according to the fortunes of the rulers of Gwynedd.

BERLIN, CONGRESS OF A meeting of leaders of European Great Powers in Berlin, Germany, from 13 June to 13 July 1878, held to negotiate revision of the treaty of SAN STEFANO. It was called following protests by Great Britain and Austria. The vigorous diplomacy of the earl of Beaconsfield (Benjamin DISRAELI) helped to restore territory to the OTTOMAN EMPIRE and check the advance of Russian influence in the BALKANS.

BERLIN AIRLIFT An operation by Western powers (USA, Great Britain, France), during the COLD WAR, to sustain part of Berlin. In 1945, following WORLD WAR II, both Germany and Berlin were divided into four zones, occupied by the USA, Great Britain, France and the USSR. Berlin lay within the USSR's German zone; its western zones (population, 2 million) were sustained by a railway and motorway from the W.

On 24 June 1948, three days after the Western powers announced the introduction of a new currency to Berlin, the USSR, ruled by Josef Stalin, stopped road and rail traffic to its western zones. Stalin intended to force the Western powers from Berlin or possibly to disrupt their economic revival of western Germany. They responded with a continuous cargo airlift of food and other supplies, supported by other countries. In the face of Western determination, the USSR lifted its blockade on 12 May 1949, and the airlift ended on 30 Sept. Flights totalled over 277,000, carrying 1.6 million tons.

BERMUDA A British overseas territory in the NW Atlantic, consisting of 130 coral islands, 20 of which are inhabited. Settlement began after an English ship, sailing to VIRGINIA, was shipwrecked in 1609. Men remained behind to preserve a claim. The islands were initially known as the Somers Islands after the shipwrecked admiral Sir George Somers (1554–1610). They were governed 1612–14 by the VIRGINIA COMPANY (London group), and from 1615 by the Somers Islands Company. They were soon known as 'Bermuda' after an earlier Spanish discoverer. An assembly met from 1620. After a rebellion in 1684, Bermuda became a CROWN COLONY. African slaves were brought to work on PLANTATIONS from 1616.

During the 20th century, tourism, banking and insurance became mainstays of the economy. Bermuda was granted internal self-government in 1968 (with the British monarch remaining head of State). Bermuda became a British DEPENDENT TERRITORY in 1983, and an overseas territory in 2002. Approx. population in 1921, 23,000; in 2010, 64,000.

BERNARD OF NEUFMARCHÉ (b. c.1045, probably in Normandy; d. c.1125, aged about 80). A Norman who went to England with WILLIAM I; through marriage he acquired land in Herefordshire (W England, abutting Wales). Bernard invaded C Wales c.1093 and created the Marcher lordship of Brecon, founding also the town of Brecon and St John's Priory, Brecon. See BRYCHEINIOG; NORMANS, IMPACT ON WALES; MARCH OF WALES.

BERNARD OF ST DAVIDS (fl. from 1115; d. between 30 June and Dec. 1148). The first Norman bishop of ST DAVIDS, SW Wales, 1115–48; imposed by King HENRY I of England against local wishes. Bernard resisted URBAN OF LLANDAFF's attempt to expand the Llandaff diocese into SW Wales (1127–33); he then sought, unsuccessfully, metropolitan (archiepiscopal) status for St Davids in Wales. See also NATIONAL PATRON SAINTS; CHURCH, MEDIEVAL WALES.

BERNERS-LEE, TIMOTHY (b. 8 June 1955 at London, England). After studying physics at OXFORD University, Berners-Lee worked in telecommunications and in the COMPUTING industry as a software designer. In 1980, while briefly at CERN (the European particle physics laboratory), he designed a program to store files that included connections between texts (hyperlinks), and on returning in 1984 developed procedures that allowed computers to communicate with each other.

In 1989 Berners-Lee proposed an arrangement for enabling information to be accessed through the Internet (the recently created global network of interlinked computer networks), using a standard 'address' for sources, and he wrote software for the first 'web server' and 'web browser' (1990–1). Placed in the public domain by CERN in 1993, the system expanded rapidly into the resource called the 'World Wide Web'. After leaving CERN (1994), Berners-Lee remained involved in computing, artificial intelligence and Web development. He was elected a fellow of the ROYAL SOCIETY (2001) and knighted (2004).

BERNICIA A kingdom (6th–7th centuries) which initially occupied modern Co. Durham, Tyne and Wear, and Northumberland (NE England). Bernicia's Brittonic name (of unknown meaning) suggests a British origin (5th or 6th century; see POST-ROMAN BRITAIN). By the mid 6th century, following moderate Germanic settlement (by 'Angles'), a Germanic dynasty ruled.

In the 7th century the royal dynasties of Bernicia and DEIRA (to the S) sought to rule both kingdoms. Æthelfrith of Bernicia (ruled 592–616) also ruled Deira from 604. EDWIN of Deira ruled both kingdoms 616–33 (permitted Christianity 619, with short-lived see at YORK from 627). The kingdoms had separate rulers 633–4 (Eanfrith in Bernicia). OSWALD of Bernicia ruled both kingdoms 634–42 and extended Bernicia northwards (see GODODDIN). (635, Oswald reintroduced Christianity with see at Lindisfarne; see AIDAN.) Oswiu, ruled 642–70, overcame resistance in Deira. His successor, EGFRITH, annexed Deira (679), creating NORTHUMBRIA. See also KINGSHIP, ANGLO-SAXON.

BERWICK, (1560) TREATY OF Agreed on 27 Feb. 1560 (at BERWICK-UPON-TWEED, adjacent to NE England), between Scotland's pro-Protestant LORDS OF THE CONGREGATION and English representatives (following the deposition of the Catholic MARY OF GUISE, regent for MARY, QUEEN OF SCOTS). The treaty permitted English intervention against French troops in Scotland while guaranteeing Scotland's independence. Religion was not mentioned. See also EDINBURGH, (1560) TREATY OF; REFORMATION, SCOTLAND.

BERWICK, (1639) TREATY OF Signed on 18 June 1639 (at BERWICK-UPON-TWEED, adjacent to NE England), between King CHARLES I and leaders of Scottish COVENANTERS. It ended the First Bishops' War. Scots would disband; Charles would withdraw his army and attend a General Assembly of the Church of SCOTLAND and a meeting of the Scottish Parliament. His failure to do so provoked the Second Bishops' War. See also COVENANT, WARS OF THE, OR BISHOPS' WARS; COVENANTING REVOLUTION.

BERWICK-UPON-TWEED (English, meaning 'Barley farm on R. Tweed'). A coastal town in Northumberland, NE England, on the N bank of the R. Tweed; the chief town on the eastern Anglo-Scottish BORDER.

Made a BURGH and head of a SHERIFFDOM by King DAVID I (ruled 1124–53), Berwick was until 1296 Scotland's leading international port. It was captured by King EDWARD I of England in 1296; retaken by ROBERT I of Scotland in 1318; captured by EDWARD III of England in 1333 and held until 1461 (ceded by HENRY VI). The English recaptured it in 1482. Berwick was given independent status in 1551, but remained an English garrison town (refortified 1558–69) and was incorporated into England in 1844. Since 1296 it has been mainly a market town.

Est. popn: 1300, 2000; 1600, 1800; 1800, 7000; 1900, 13,400; 2000, 12,800.

BESANT, ANNIE (b. 1 Oct. 1847 at London, England; d. 20 Sept. 1933 at Adyar, Madras Province, India, aged 85). In 1873, after becoming a freethinker, Besant left her clergyman husband and rural home. She moved to London where she collaborated with the atheist Charles BRADLAUGH (1875–86), became a public speaker, and earned notoriety for advocating contraception (see BIRTH CONTROL). A member of the FABIAN SOCIETY, in 1886–8 she helped to unionize unskilled workers (so-called 'New Unionism' movement). From 1889 Besant was involved in the syncretic mysticism of theosophy. In India from 1893, she promoted education, and from 1909 campaigned for Indian independence. She joined the Indian National Congress in 1913 and presided at its national meeting in 1917. See also THEOSOPHICAL SOCIETY.

BEUNO (fl. in 7th century; d. perhaps in 642). The founder and abbot of a monastery at Clynnog, GWYNEDD (NW Wales); dedicatee of other churches in N Wales. Beuno was later regarded as a saint. His life was written in Welsh in the 14th century. See also MONASTICISM, MEDIEVAL WALES.

BEVAN, BRIDGET (b. probably Oct. 1698 at Carmarthen, Carmarthenshire, Wales; d. 11 Dec. 1779 at Laugharne, Carmarthenshire, aged 81). Of GENTRY stock (born Bridget Vaughan, married 1721), 'Madam Bevan' was chief patron and adviser of Griffith JONES who launched 'circulating schools' in the 1730s. She continued them after his death in 1761 and bequeathed £10,000 to perpetuate them. Unfortunately, her will was disputed and, starved of funds, the schools withered. See also EDUCATION, WALES.

BEVAN, NYE (b. 15 Nov. 1897 at Tredegar, Monmouthshire, Wales; d. 6 July 1960 at Chesham, Buckinghamshire, England, aged 62). A coalminer, Aneurin Bevan (known as 'Nye') became a trade union official and a Labour MP (1929). Famed for radical oratory, he established the British NATIONAL HEALTH SERVICE while minister of health (1945–51) in the post-war government of Clement ATTLEE. Transferred to the Ministry of Labour in Jan. 1951, he resigned on 21 April in protest at the introduction of health service charges by Hugh GAITSKELL, chancellor of the Exchequer. In Dec. 1955 he unsuccessfully contested the Party leadership, but became deputy leader in 1959 (to Gaitskell).

BEVANITES An informal left-wing faction within the British LABOUR PARTY, headed by Nye BEVAN. It emerged in March 1952 when 57 MPs voted against the Party's defence policy. Bevanites opposed increased military spending and German rearmament, but were divided when Bevan voiced approval for ATOMIC WEAPONS (1957).

BEVERIDGE, WILLIAM (b. 5 March 1879 at Rangpur, Bengal, India; d. 16 March 1963 at Oxford, Oxfordshire, England, aged 84). Welfare promoter. Concerned about social problems (from 1900s), especially UNEMPLOYMENT, Beveridge worked for the British CIVIL SERVICE from 1908 (knighted 1919). In 1909, he established State-funded labour exchanges (bureaux for job finding). As director of the London School of Economics (1919–37), he encouraged sociological research with practical applications; while master of University College, OXFORD (1937–44), he returned to government service (1940, during WORLD WAR II). In Dec. 1942, as a committee chairman, Beveridge produced *Social Insurance and Allied Services*, the visionary 'Beveridge Report' which proposed comprehensive welfare provision to eradicate poverty. It was substantially enacted (*see* WELFARE STATE). Beveridge was a Liberal MP (1944–5), and created Lord Beveridge (1946).

'BEVERIDGE REPORT' *see* BEVERIDGE, WILLIAM; WELFARE STATE

BEVIN, ERNEST (b. 9 March 1881 at Winsford, Somerset, England; d. 14 April 1951 at London, England, aged 70). A farm labourer, carter and trade unionist, Bevin in 1921 amalgamated almost 50 unions into the TRANSPORT AND GENERAL WORKERS' UNION. He served as its general secretary 1921–40. In 1939 he was instrumental in securing trade union support for the UK war effort (*see* WORLD WAR II).

In May 1940 Bevin was appointed minister of labour and national service in the wartime coalition government under Winston CHURCHILL and elected a Labour MP. As foreign secretary (1945–51), in the post-war Labour government of Clement ATTLEE, he shaped British policy towards the COLD WAR (in defiance of left-wing critics) while helping to implement MARSHALL AID and create NATO (NORTH ATLANTIC TREATY ORGANIZATION). His handling of PALESTINE was controversial. *See also* WORLD WAR II, IMPACT ON BRITISH ECONOMY.

BIBLE, ENGLISH Parts of the Latin Bible were translated into Old English in the 8th–11th centuries (e.g., by ÆLFRIC), and in the 12th–14th centuries into Middle English, though latterly translation was discouraged. The first full translation was produced in OXFORD in the 1380s, influenced by John WYCLIF (d. 1384). Its association with heresy caused Convocation (Church assembly) to condemn it (1409) and prohibit unauthorized translations (*see* LOLLARDY, ENGLAND; CENSORSHIP, ENGLAND AND WALES). William TYNDALE, who translated the New Testament from Greek and part of the Old Testament from Hebrew (1520s–30s), had to work abroad and was executed.

A favourable attitude developed after England's break from papal jurisdiction (confirmed 1534). Miles Coverdale published a complete translation in Germany (1535), and in 1536 Thomas CROMWELL ordered churches to provide English Bibles. Coverdale's version was reissued (1536); it was followed by Matthew's Bible (1537, a compilation from Tyndale and Coverdale) and the Great Bible (1539, edited by Coverdale).

In 1560 English Puritans in Geneva (Switzerland) produced the popular Geneva Bible. Its radical commentary provoked Archbishop Matthew PARKER to commission the Bishops' Bible (1568), a revision of the Great Bible. It was replaced in 1611 by a version ordered King JAMES VI/I (*see* HAMPTON COURT CONFERENCE). Later known as the Authorized Version or King James Bible, it became regarded as a literary masterpiece. Meanwhile Catholics had produced the Douai–Reims Bible (New Testament 1582, Old Testament 1610).

The Authorized Version was revised in the late 19th century (published 1881–5, American Version 1901). Since then numerous new translations and versions have been made, including the Jerusalem Bible (1966) and New English Bible (1970). *See also* ANGLICIZATION, SCOTLAND.

BIBLE, IRISH Elizabeth I, as ruler of Ireland, decided by 1564 that an Irish-language Bible translation should be produced to encourage the conversion of Gaelic Irish people to Protestantism. The New Testament was published in 1603, translated from Greek by William Daniel (a Church of IRELAND archbishop). A translation of the Old Testament, organized by Bishop William Bedell, was completed in 1640 and printed in 1685. A complete Bible was issued in 1690. The translations were used by both Protestants and Catholics. A translation authorized by the Catholic Church, the Maynooth Irish Bible, was published in 1981. *See also* REFORMATION, IRELAND.

BIBLE, WELSH Extensive translations first appeared in the 16th century, during the REFORMATION. William SALESBURY published Bible readings in 1551 and helped to obtain an Act of 1563 which required Welsh bishops to provide every parish with a printed Welsh Bible by 1567. That year saw publication of the New Testament, largely Salesbury's work. The entire Bible, translated or revised by William MORGAN, was published in 1588, and a revision in 1620 (by Richard Parry and John DAVIES). A new translation appeared in 1988.

BICYCLES AND BICYCLE INDUSTRIES Two-wheeled, feet-propelled 'hobby-horses' were made in England from the early 19th century. A mechanically propelled bicycle, with treadles driving a rear wheel, was invented in 1839 in Scotland by Kirkpatrick Macmillan but not manufactured. Following developments in France, pedal-driven bicycles were manufactured in England from the 1860s. Further advances included the chain drive (patented 1876) and tubular, diamond-shaped frame (basis of so-called 'safety bicycle', created 1884–5). Hard wheel rims made early machines uncomfortable.

Bicycles and cycling were transformed by the invention in 1887 of the pneumatic tyre (by Scotsman J.B. Dunlop, in BELFAST, NE Ireland). Bicycles with pneumatic tyres were manufactured in Ireland from 1889 (in DUBLIN), then in England where mass production rapidly developed, especially in the W Midlands. From the mid 1890s, people of all classes in Great Britain could purchase cycles, though in Ireland they remained luxury items until c.1918. Touring and racing became widespread, encouraged by clubs. In Ireland, the organization of sports cycling was fractured by national divisions and disputes after the PARTITION OF IRELAND (1921), lasting until 2006. British competitive cycling attained high-profile success in the early 21st century – in 2012 Bradley Wiggins was the first British competitor to win the prestigious 'Tour de France' race.

In 1960, following a merger, Raleigh (at Nottingham, C England) became the world's largest bicycle manufacturer. Its output declined severely in the 1980s due to overseas competition; volume production ceased in 1999. In the Republic of Ireland, bicycle manufacturing ceased in 1976 (burning of Raleigh factory, Dublin) but was revived in 2014.

BIG BANG Nickname for reforms to the LONDON Stock Exchange, implemented 27 Oct. 1986. Under pressure from the British government, 'restrictive practices' were abolished, principally the division between jobbers (dealers in shares at the Exchange, so-called 'market makers') and brokers (traders of shares with jobbers on behalf of investors). The 'trading floor' was replaced with electronic trading, and the Exchange changed from an association into a company. A main purpose of 'big bang' was to increase foreign investment. *See also* YUPPIE OR YUPPY.

BIGOD, ROGER (b. c.1215 in England; d. 1270 at Thetford, Norfolk, England, aged about 55). Son of Hugh Bigod, 3rd earl of Norfolk (d. 1225), Roger Bigod was invested as earl in 1233 and succeeded as MARSHAL (by right of his mother) in 1246. From 1255 he was hostile to King HENRY III and his French relatives (*see* LUSIGNANS), and from 1258 helped to lead the party that imposed reforms (*see* OXFORD, PROVISIONS OF). He served on the barons' supervisory Council (to early 1260), before Henry regained authority.

In 1263, after the reformer Simon de MONTFORT had imposed his authority on the king, Bigod rejoined Henry's side; then, after Henry was captured (May 1264), he cooperated with Montfort's (second) government (1264–5). *See also* BARONIAL CONFLICT AND WARS.

BIMETALLISM The practice of basing currency value on gold and silver reserves, according to a fixed relative value between the two metals. Used by some countries in the 19th century, it was advocated in Great Britain (e.g., by the Bimetallic League) between the late 1870s and 1890s, and adoption was considered by a Gold and Silver Commission (1887—90). Supporters argued that it would allow expansion of money supply and facilitate trade with silver-using countries. The GOLD STANDARD was retained.

BIRGHAM, TREATY OF Ratified on 18 July 1290 (at Birgham, SE Scotland) by the 'guardians' of Scotland, who had agreed with King EDWARD I of England that his heir, EDWARD (II), would marry the infant Scottish queen, MARGARET, 'THE MAID OF NORWAY'. Their heir would rule England and Scotland, the latter remaining independent. The treaty became irrelevant with Margaret's death (Sept. 1290). *See also* GREAT CAUSE; SCOTTISH–ENGLISH RELATIONS 1290 TO 1357.

BIRMINGHAM A city and metropolitan borough in C England; formerly in Warwickshire.

Birmingham was a settlement from the 6th or 7th century until the 1160s when a small town was developed. (Its name means 'Village of the family or followers of Beorma'.) Metal working was prominent by the 15th century.

During the 17th century, thanks to local iron ore, coal and wood, Birmingham emerged as a major industrial centre, producing and trading metal products (e.g., knives, scythes). During the 18th century, the population expanded ten-fold. Products increased to include screws, buttons, jewellery, and guns. From 1775, Matthew BOULTON and James WATT built steam engines at nearby Handsworth. Birmingham was a CANAL hub by 1790 and a RAILWAY centre from 1837.

Birmingham became associated with religious NONCONFORMITY and political radicalism (*see* RADICALS). It gained parliamentary representation (1832) and a town council (1838). Municipal improvement was later promoted by Joseph CHAMBERLAIN. Birmingham acquired city status (1889), a university (1900), and a bishop (1904). Boundary changes in 1911 made it England's second largest city.

In the 20th century Birmingham's manufacturing diversified to include MACHINE TOOLS, BICYCLES, MOTORCYCLES, MOTOR VEHICLES, CHEMICALS and plastics. The city attracted considerable immigration by AFRICAN CARIBBEANS and SOUTH ASIANS in the 1950s–1960s. The centre was transformed by the Bull Ring shopping centre (1964), and four additional universities were created (by upgrading): Aston (1966), Birmingham City (1992), University College (2012), Newman (2013). *See also* HIGHER EDUCATION, EXPANSION OF.

Est. popn: 1300, 1000; 1600, 2500; 1800, 73,000; 1900, 552,000; 2000, 1,025,000.

BIRMINGHAM CAUCUS Name for the Birmingham Liberal Association, founded 1865 in the English town of BIRMINGHAM; the first permanent local party organization in Great Britain. In a three-member constituency, where each elector had two votes, it directed supporters so as to secure three Liberal MPs. It became the power base of Joseph CHAMBERLAIN. *See also* LIBERAL PARTY.

BIRRELL, AUGUSTINE (b. 19 Jan. 1850 at Wavertree, Lancashire, England; d. 20 Nov. 1933 at London, England, aged 83). A lawyer, prolific author and (Liberal) member of the UK Parliament (1889–1900, 1906–18), Birrell served as CHIEF SECRETARY FOR IRELAND from Jan. 1907. He encouraged the HOME RULE MOVEMENT, established the National University of Ireland, acceptable to Catholics (1908; *see* UNIVERSITIES, IRELAND), and compelled the sale of some estates (1909 Land Act, the 'Birrell Act'). Birrell failed, however, to appreciate the growing strength of republicanism and was surprised by the EASTER RISING of 1916. After it had been crushed, he resigned (3 May). *See also* LAND AGITATION AND REFORM, IRELAND.

BIRTH CONTROL Artificial methods (alternatives to long-used 'natural' methods) spread in Great Britain from the 1870s with the manufacture of rubber sheaths or condoms and development of women's products (e.g., Dutch cap). The distribution of condoms to soldiers in WORLD WAR I (1914–18), to combat venereal disease, extended awareness. Artificial birth control contributed to declining fertility in Britain into the 1930s, leading to a smaller average family size. Its use was controversial, particularly in the 1920s (e.g., when promoted publicly by Marie STOPES), but was accepted by the Church of England in 1930. The Roman Catholic Church remained opposed. Contraceptive pills for women, available from 1961, notably changed sexual behaviour. *See also* BRADLAUGH, CHARLES; BESANT, ANNIE.

BIRTH CONTROL, SOUTHERN IRELAND In 1935 the IRISH FREE STATE prohibited the import or sale of contraceptive devices. The availability of contraceptive pills from 1961 (not prohibited) led to challenges against legislation (e.g., 1971, overt import of devices from NORTHERN IRELAND on the 'contraceptive train'). In 1973 the Republic's Supreme Court deemed the importation ban illegal (McGee case). The 1979 Family Planning Act, passed despite Catholic opposition, allowed contraceptives to married couples on prescription. Sales to all persons over 18 were allowed in 1985. *See also* WOMEN'S MOVEMENT FROM 1960s, IRELAND; CHURCH–STATE RELATIONS, SOUTHERN IRELAND FROM 1922.

BISHOPS' BOOK A comprehensive doctrinal statement compiled by bishops and other clergy for the English Church (full title, *Institution of a Christian Man*), authorized Sept. 1537 by King HENRY VIII for three years. More conservative than the TEN ARTICLES (1536), the book affirmed Catholic sacraments and the doctrine of purgatory. Nevertheless, its theology allowed a Lutheran interpretation, and it was hostile to the Catholic cult of images. *See also* KING'S BOOK; REFORMATION, ENGLAND.

BISHOPS' EXCLUSION BILL Legislation proposed in the English Parliament in 1641–2 to exclude bishops from the House of Lords, to overcome their resistance to political and ecclesiastical reforms. It was passed by the House of Commons on 23 Oct. 1641, by the Lords on 13 Feb. 1642. King CHARLES I accepted the Bill on 14 Feb. to buy time and enable Queen HENRIETTA MARIA to escape abroad. The Act was repealed by the CAVALIER PARLIAMENT in 1661. *See also* LONG PARLIAMENT.

BISHOPS' WARS *see* COVENANT, WARS OF THE, OR BISHOPS' WARS

BLACK, JOSEPH (b. 16 April 1728 at Bordeaux, France; d. 6 Dec. 1799 at Edinburgh, Scotland, aged 71). The son of an Ulsterman in the wine trade, Black studied at GLASGOW University from 1744, eventually specializing in medicine, and at EDINBURGH University from 1752. His doctoral thesis (1754) indicated the existence of a gas distinct from 'common air'. Further experiments, published in 1756, showed that a 'fixed air', derived from a solid, could be distinguished from air in the atmosphere, launching the crucial idea that gases could be differentiated in the same way as liquids and solids.

Black succeeded William CULLEN at Glasgow as lecturer in chemistry (1756), and soon became a professor. He developed the concept of 'latent heat' (the energy absorbed by a substance which causes change, as ice is affected before melting). James WATT was a friend. Succeeding Cullen as professor of chemistry at Edinburgh in 1766, Black undertook research to improve industrial processes and public health. Though he published little, he was influential internationally through his students. *See also* ENLIGHTENMENT, SCOTLAND.

BLACK ACT Name for legislation, passed by the British PARLIAMENT in 1723, which created over 50 new capital offences in England and Wales connected with poaching and property. An addition to the GAME LAWS, it was provoked by the activity of poaching gangs who blackened their faces. The Act was the most severe statute passed in the 18th century. It was regularly renewed until most provisions were repealed in 1827. *See also* LAW, ENGLAND FROM 1066; LEGAL REFORMS, ENGLAND AND WALES, 1820s.

BLACK ACTS Name (of obscure origin) for Acts of the Scottish Parliament in May 1584 reflecting the anti-presbyterian influence of James STEWART, earl of Arran and chancellor (1584–5). They denounced presbyteries, proclaimed royal supremacy over matters spiritual and temporal, confirmed the authority of bishops and made them primarily responsible to the Crown rather than the General Assembly (altering the Concordat of LEITH). *See also* CHURCH ORGANIZATION, SCOTLAND FROM 16TH CENTURY.

BLACK AND TANS Nickname for British ex-soldiers who served during the War of IRISH INDEPENDENCE as reinforcements to the Royal Irish Constabulary, March 1920–July 1921. The name, taken from a pack of hunting hounds in Co. Limerick, was first used in April 1920 when a group rampaged through Limerick. Their initial 'uniform' was a mix of dark green (RIC) and khaki (army). They became notorious for violent reprisals against republican sympathizers. *See also* IRISH FREE STATE, FOUNDING OF.

BLACK BOOK OF CARMARTHEN An important Welsh manuscript (in the National Library of Wales, Aberystwyth) which was copied *c.*1250 in CARMARTHEN Priory (SW Wales). It includes early poetry (religious poetry; prophetic poems linked to Merlin; *Stanzas of the Graves*) and work by 12th- and 13th-century poets including CYNDDELW BRYDYDD MAWR. *See also* WELSH LANGUAGE AND LITERATURE.

BLACK DEATH, IMPACT ON ENGLAND The bubonic and pneumonic plague known (from the 16th century) as the 'Black Death' affected England in 1348–9. Originating in Asia, it swept through Europe from 1347 and entered England in June 1348, probably at Melcombe Regis (Dorset), coming from CALAIS with imported cloth bales. Transmitted by rats and fleas, the plague spread through southern counties and into the Midlands in 1348 and early 1349. After subsiding, it revived in March 1349 and advanced through northern England. All communities and social groups suffered, though to varying extents. Probably over 2 million people died out of 5 million. A second outbreak in 1361–2 killed about 1 million.

The population fall had far-reaching social and economic consequences. Labour shortages caused wage rises and internal migration. Lords could not enforce LABOUR SERVICES, and eventually leased their directly managed lands ('demesnes') to tenants (*see* MANOR). Statutes to protect lords' interests caused unrest (*see* LABOURERS, ORDINANCE AND STATUTE OF), culminating in the PEASANTS' REVOLT. *See also* PLAGUE, ENGLAND.

BLACK DEATH, IMPACT ON IRELAND The plague reportedly arrived via the east-coast port of Howth (Co. Dublin) in July 1348. It spread quickly to DUBLIN and Drogheda and across the country. According to the Franciscan friar John Clyn, Dublin and other Anglo-Irish towns became almost uninhabited. Archbishop Richard FITZRALPH claimed that two-thirds of the Anglo-Irish population were killed, but that Gaelic Irish were less affected. The plague hastened the shrinkage of the English colony as inhabitants moved to towns or England. *See also* PLAGUE, IRELAND; IRELAND, ENGLISH COLONY IN, 13TH–15TH CENTURIES.

BLACK DEATH, IMPACT ON SCOTLAND The plague arrived from England in autumn 1349 and spread through 1350. Although it made the most savage cut of population in Scottish history, chroniclers' claims that a third perished may imply lower mortality than elsewhere in Britain. Few MAGNATES died. As elsewhere, plague returned several times later in the 14th century.

The long-term consequence was to reduce the population by over a half, creating a new relationship between population and resources. Its effects included shortage of labour, more livestock farming, falls in rents, larger landholdings, and leasing of lords' demesnes (*see* MANOR). Population recovery, however, was probably under way by the mid 15th century, significantly earlier than in England. *See also* PLAGUE, SCOTLAND; POPULATION, SCOTLAND.

BLACK DEATH, IMPACT ON WALES The plague entered SE Wales by March 1349, reached CARMARTHEN, SW Wales, by sea by late March and swept through the Anglo-Welsh border country to NE Wales by June. Dispersal continued until the autumn. Perhaps a third of the population was killed.

Afterwards, migration to find good-quality vacant land accelerated the decline of native tenures (*see* TENURES, WALES). The 1349 and later plagues (e.g., 1361–2, 1369) encouraged contraction of arable farming and expansion of sheep farming. *See also* PLAGUE, WALES; AGRICULTURE, WALES BEFORE 18TH CENTURY.

BLACK DINNER *see* JAMES II

BLACK HOLE OF CALCUTTA Name used for a notorious incident in INDIA in 1756. After the nawab (ruler) of Bengal, Siraj-ud-Daulah, seized control of CALCUTTA (a British headquarters in NE India) on 20 June, captives were imprisoned in a small cell (the 'Black Hole'). By the following morning, most had died by suffocation or heat exhaustion. The incident was reported in Great Britain as evidence of Indian brutality. The numbers involved are uncertain: 60–200 were incarcerated, 40–140 died. *See also* CLIVE, ROBERT.

BLACK PRINCE *see* Edward the Black Prince

BLACKSTONE, WILLIAM (b. 10 July 1723 at London, England; d. 14 Feb. 1780 at London, aged 56). An unsuccessful barrister, Blackstone instead lectured on English law at Oxford University from 1753 (also Vinerian professor of law 1758–66). He was elected an MP in 1761 and became a judge in 1770 (also knighted). Blackstone is famous for his *Commentaries on the Laws of England* (4 volumes, 1765–9), an elegant, systematic exposition aimed at laymen which was influential in England and N America for over a century.

BLACK WATCH A distinguished Scottish regiment in the British Army, which was authorized by King George II in 1739; it was constituted from six Highland Companies of Foot (formed from 1725) and four new companies. The original companies represented attempts to secure the support of loyal Highland clans following the Jacobite Rebellion of 1715. During the Jacobite Rebellion of 1745, the regiment was stationed in S England for fear of unreliability. Its name, originally a nickname, referred to the dark tartan worn by soldiers and their role of watching the Highlands. In 2006 the regiment was amalgamated with other units as the Royal Regiment of Scotland.

BLACK WEDNESDAY Nickname for Wednesday 16 Sept. 1992 when the British Conservative government was compelled to withdraw sterling from the European Economic Community's Exchange Rate Mechanism (ERM). During the day, speculators' currency sales forced the government to raise the base interest rate from 10% to 12%, and declare a rise to 15%, to protect sterling's ERM value. These actions failed; at 7.30 pm the chancellor of the Exchequer, Norman Lamont, announced withdrawal. The humiliation damaged the Conservatives' reputation for financial management and the premiership of John Major. *See also* European Economic Community/European Union, impact on British politics.

BLAIR, TONY (b. 6 May 1953 at Edinburgh, Scotland). Leader of the Labour Party 1994–2007; British prime minister 1997–2007.

A barrister and MP (1983–2007), Blair became Party leader with acquiescence from rival Gordon Brown (*see* Granita Accord). With Alastair Campbell and Peter Mandelson, he 'modernized' Labour as New Labour with centrist policies (e.g., abandoning nationalization, 1995) and won an unprecedented three general elections for Labour (1997, 2001, 2005). Brown, as chancellor of the Exchequer, received extensive authority in domestic policy.

Blair implemented devolution in Scotland and Wales (1997–9), achieved a peace settlement for Northern Ireland

(1998; *see* Belfast Agreement), reinstated city-wide government in London (1999–2000), and removed most hereditary peers from the House of Lords (1999). He pursued an interventionist foreign policy (*see* Kosovo War; Sierra Leone). His government sought 'modernization' of public services and encouraged immigration.

In Blair's second term, he controversially committed military support to US-led campaigns in Afghanistan (from 2001) and Iraq (from 2003). Domestic developments included legal civil partnerships for same-sex couples (2004).

Involvement in Iraq damaged Blair's popularity and authority. On 7 Sept. 2006, under pressure from Brown's supporters, he announced a resignation plan. He was succeeded by Brown in June 2007.

BLENKINSOP, JOHN (b. 1783 at Felling, Co. Durham, England; d. 22 Jan. 1831 at Leeds, aged 47). A supervisor of coal mines, Blenkinsop experimented with steam engines. In 1812–13 he built four two-cylinder railway locomotives, which hauled coal waggons along tooth-racked cast-iron rails from Middleton colliery to Leeds (to loading staithes on the R. Aire). It was the world's first practical, commercial steam-powered railway system. The locomotives operated until 1835. Blenkinsop's work influenced George Stephenson. *See also* railways, England.

BLIGH, WILLIAM (b. 9 Sept. 1754 at Plymouth, Devon, England; d. 7 Dec. 1817 at London, England, aged 63). A career sailor in the British Navy, Bligh suffered a mutiny (cause unknown) on 28 April 1789 as captain of HMS *Bounty*. He and 18 others were put adrift in a longboat in the Pacific. They eventually reached Timor (14 June). Bligh was afterwards exonerated of blame for the mutiny.

Bligh's crews also participated in the Spithead and Nore munities in England (1797). As governor of New South Wales (from 1805), he was deposed in 1808 by the 'Rum Rebellion' (reaction to his attempt to suppress illegal rum trading). He returned to England in 1810.

BLITZ Nickname used by people in Great Britain and Northern Ireland in World War II for German large-scale bombing: of London (Sept. 1940–May 1941) and of provincial towns (Oct. 1940–Sept. 1941); also for the 'Little Blitz' on London, southern England and some other places (Jan.–April 1944). The press derived it from the German *Blitzkrieg*, meaning 'lightning war' (referring to fast-moving warfare using motorized land forces and air support). *See also* evacuation, World War II.

BLOODY ASSIZES In England, name for trials of participants in Monmouth's Rebellion, 1685. The presiding judge was Lord Jeffreys (George Jeffreys, 1645–89), lord chief justice. The trials took place from 2 to 23 Sept. at

WINCHESTER (Hampshire) and in Somerset and Dorset. About 1300 people were tried; about 250 were executed and at least 850 were transported abroad. (Monmouth was executed in London.)

BLOODY SUNDAY (1920) Name applied to the most murderous day during the War of IRISH INDEPENDENCE, 21 Nov. 1920. In the morning, in DUBLIN, members of the IRISH REPUBLICAN ARMY, commanded by Michael COLLINS, killed 14 British intelligence agents. In the afternoon, at a Gaelic football match, police reinforcements (so-called 'Auxiliaries'), allegedly searching for a wanted man, opened fire, killing 12.

BLOODY SUNDAY (1972) Popular name for the day (30 Jan.), during the TROUBLES in Northern Ireland, when British Army soldiers shot dead 13 participants at an illegal march in LONDONDERRY (against internment of suspected terrorists). Another victim died later. The incident discredited British security forces, increased recruitment to the PROVISIONAL IRISH REPUBLICAN ARMY, and persuaded the British prime minister Edward HEATH to introduce 'direct rule' of Northern Ireland (24 March).

An official report on the event ('Widgery Report'), published in April 1972, relied mainly on the soldiers' evidence and largely exonerated them, creating long-lasting resentment. In Jan. 1998 Tony BLAIR established a new inquiry as part of the Northern Ireland PEACE PROCESS. Its outcome, the 'Saville Report' published in 2010 (costing £191 million), concluded that victims had been unarmed and their deaths unjustifiable. Prime Minister David CAMERON made a public apology for the deaths. *See also* NORTHERN IRELAND.

BLOOMSBURY GROUP A small group of influential English writers and artists who met informally at homes in the Bloomsbury district of LONDON between *c*.1907 and *c*.1930. Principal members were: novelists Virginia Woolf (1882–1941), E.M. Forster (1879–1970); art critics Clive Bell (1881–1964), Roger Fry (1866–1934); painters Vanessa Bell (1879–1961), Duncan Grant (1885–1978); biographer Lytton Strachey (1880–1932); political theorist Leonard Woolf (1880–1969); economist J.M. KEYNES (1883–1946). They combined serious concern for artistic and philosophical principles with irreverence towards personal morality.

BLOUNT, CHARLES *see* MOUNTJOY, LORD

BLUE BOOKS, TREACHERY OF THE *see* EDUCATION IN WALES, INQUIRY INTO

BLUESHIRTS *see* ARMY COMRADES' ASSOCIATION; FASCISM, SOUTHERN IRELAND

BOADICEA *see* BOUDICCA

BODICHON, BARBARA (b. 8 April 1827 at Whatlington, Sussex, England; d. 11 June 1891 at Scalands Gate, Sussex, aged 64). Barbara Leigh Smith, an independent writer and painter, campaigned from 1854 for reform of property law relating to women and other rights. In 1857, when leader of the LANGHAM PLACE CIRCLE, she published *Women and Work* and married French physician Eugène Bodichon. Thereafter she divided her time between Algiers and England (until 1877). She co-founded the *English Woman's Journal* (1858–64) with Bessie Rayner Parkes, and helped Emily Davies to found the College for Women at Hitchin in 1869 (near CAMBRIDGE from 1873, as Girton College). *See also* WOMEN'S MOVEMENT 1850S TO 1918, GREAT BRITAIN.

BOER WAR, FIRST *see* SOUTH AFRICA

BOER WAR OR SECOND BOER WAR A conflict in southern Africa between British forces and the Boer-ruled Transvaal (or South African Republic) and Orange Free State, 1899–1902, provoked by British expansionism. In the late 1890s, Joseph CHAMBERLAIN, the British colonial secretary, and Alfred MILNER in southern Africa, pressurized Paul Kruger, the Transvaal's president, to enfranchise *uitlanders* (British and other immigrants in Transvaal). In response, Kruger demanded withdrawal of British troops from the region (9 Oct. 1899). His ultimatum was rejected.

The ensuing war had three phases. The first, from 11 Oct. 1899 to Jan. 1900, saw Boer incursions into British territory, with sieges of Ladysmith, Kimberley and MAFEKING, and heavy British losses in the 'Black Week' of Dec. 1899. Great Britain sent reinforcements, with Lord ROBERTS as the new supreme commander.

In the second phase, Feb.–Aug. 1900, Roberts launched counter-offensives, raising the sieges, defeating the Boers at Paardeburg (27 Feb.) and capturing the Transvaal capital Pretoria (5 June). Britain annexed the Orange Free State (24 May) and Transvaal (1 Sept.).

Finally, from Nov. 1900, there was guerrilla warfare, to which Lord KITCHENER (new British commander) responded by destroying Boer farms and interning occupants in concentration camps. Boer resistance ended in May 1902 (*see* VEREENIGING, TREATY OF).

About 22,000 British troops died (two-thirds from disease and illness), at least 25,000 Boers (most in concentration camps), and 12,000 Africans. The war also had profound consequences for British society, provoking debates about Army reform, social welfare and the morality of imperial rule. *See also* SOUTH AFRICA; NATIONAL DETERIORATION; ESHER, 2ND VISCOUNT; HALDANE, R.B.

BOHUN FAMILY A noble family prominent in England from the mid 12th century; they were important in the MARCH OF WALES 1241–1373 through the marriage of Humphrey of Bohun (d. 1265) to Eleanor, daughter of William de BRAOSE (d. 1230). Eleanor inherited (1241) lordships of Brecon and Hay (C Wales) and Haverfordwest (SW Wales).

In the reign of King EDWARD II of England (1307–27), Humphrey de Bohun (c.1276–1322) opposed PIERS GAVESTON and the DESPENSERS. Humphrey de Bohun (1342–73) died without a male heir.

BOLEYN, ANNE (b. c.1500, probably at Blickling, Norfolk, England; d. 19 May 1536 at London, England, aged about 36). A courtier's daughter, Anne was courted by King HENRY VIII from 1526 although he was married to KATHERINE OF ARAGON. (Divorce proceedings began in April 1527; see GREAT MATTER.) Anne was created marchioness of Pembroke in Sept. 1532. She slept with Henry from Nov. and became pregnant. They were married secretly on 25 Jan. 1533 (marriage publicized at Easter, Anne crowned 1 June). On 7 Sept. Anne gave birth to a daughter (see ELIZABETH I). At court Anne sponsored evangelical clergy and writers.

Anne's failure to produce a male heir disenchanted Henry. She was imprisoned for treasonable adultery (2 May 1536). Her marriage was declared invalid (17 May) and she was executed. See also HENRY VIII, WIVES OF; BROWNE, GEORGE.

BOLINGBROKE, VISCOUNT (b. 16 Sept. 1678, probably at Lydiard Tregoze, Wiltshire, England; d. 12 Dec. 1751 at Battersea, Surrey, England, aged 73). An MP from 1701 and a TORY, Henry St John collaborated with Robert HARLEY. He was secretary at war 1704–8 and SECRETARY OF STATE from 1710. From 1711 he supervised negotiations with France which resulted in the Peace of UTRECHT (1713), ending the War of the SPANISH SUCCESSION. He was created Viscount Bolingbroke in 1712. Like other Tories, Bolingbroke became dissatisfied with Harley (see OCTOBER CLUB). In 1714 he persuaded Queen ANNE to dismiss Harley, but the earl of SHREWSBURY succeeded as leading minister.

In Aug. 1714 Bolingbroke was dismissed by the pro-WHIG King GEORGE I. Fearful that Whigs would seek his execution for Jacobite plotting, he fled to France and served the Jacobite claimant as secretary of state (1715–16). Allowed to return in 1723, he became an opponent of Robert WALPOLE, notably attacking his Excise Bill (1733). See also JACOBITISM, IMPACT ON BRITISH POLITICS; EXCISE CRISIS; WYNDHAM, WILLIAM.

BONDFIELD, MARGARET (b. 17 March 1873 at Chard, Somerset, England; d. 16 June 1953 at Sanderstead, Surrey, England, aged 80). A shopworker from 1887, Bondfield became involved in trade unionism. She was the first woman chairman of the TRADES UNION CONGRESS (1923) and a LABOUR PARTY MP 1923–4, 1926–31. In 1924 she became the first woman minister in a British government (as parliamentary secretary to the Ministry of Labour), and from 1929 the first woman CABINET member (as minister of labour) and privy councillor. In both instances, she served under Ramsay MACDONALD. In 1931 she refused to join his NATIONAL GOVERNMENT.

BONIFACE (b. early 670s in Wessex; d. 5 June 754 near Dokkum, Frisia, aged about 80). Responding to a missionary vocation, the monk Wynfrith lived in Frisia (modern Netherlands) in 716. In 719 the Pope commissioned him to evangelize pagans and named him Boniface. He worked with WILLIBRORD in Frisia (719–21). In 722, while revisiting Rome, he was made bishop and authorized to preach E of the R. Rhine (eastern Francia). He founded monasteries and churches, and recruited assistants from England.

In 732 Boniface was appointed archbishop. He reorganized dioceses in Bavaria (739), founded new bishoprics to the N (741–2), and founded Fulda monastery. Around 746 he adopted Mainz (in modern Germany) as his see. After resigning (753), he returned to Frisia, where he was martyred (buried at Fulda). See also LEOBA; MISSIONS TO CONTINENTAL EUROPE, ANGLO-SAXON.

BONNER, EDMUND (b. probably at Hanley, Worcestershire, England; d. 5 Sept. 1569 at London, England). Bonner, a clergyman, served King HENRY VIII as a diplomat (late 1520s–1540s). He accepted Henry's supremacy in the English Church (confirmed 1534). He was appointed bishop of Hereford (1538), then of London (1539). But during the reign of EDWARD VI (1547–53) Bonner resisted Protestant reforms. He was imprisoned and deprived of his bishopric (Oct. 1550).

Restored as bishop by MARY I (Aug. 1553), Bonner promoted Catholicism and combated heresy in his diocese – 113 heretics were burnt (1555–8). After the accession of ELIZABETH I (1558), Bonner refused to acknowledge her supremacy in the Church. He was again deprived (May 1559) and later imprisoned (1560). See also REFORMATION, ENGLAND.

BOOKLAND In Anglo-Saxon England, land held by written CHARTER or 'book' (OE bocland). Unlike other land, bookland was given (e.g., by kings) with freedom to alienate (by grant, sale or bequest). Kin had no entitlement to inherit. Bookland tenure was introduced in the 7th century to endow MINSTER churches. From the late 8th century, senior lay people also held (and alienated) bookland.

Bookland was replaced by new tenures in the late 11th century. *See also* TENURES, ENGLAND BEFORE 1066; THREE PUBLIC SERVICES.

BOOK OF ORDERS In England and Wales, instructions issued Jan. 1631 by the PRIVY COUNCIL to JUSTICES OF THE PEACE requiring quarterly reports about the administration of laws relating to the poor. Although the Book arose from short-term problems (e.g., grain shortage), and did not represent the policy of THOROUGH, it reflected the concern of Charles I for maintaining social harmony and avoiding disorder. *See also* CHARLES I, PERSONAL RULE.

BOOT, JESSE (b. 2 June 1850 at Nottingham, Nottinghamshire, England; d. 13 June 1931 at Vallée, Jersey, Channel Islands, aged 81). Boot became a medical herbalist and, facing competition from new patent medicines, from 1877 sold medical products in quantity at reduced prices. From 1883 he developed a retail business that employed pharmacists and sold other products (e.g., books, stationery). His company manufactured medical products from 1892. By 1914 Boot's company had 560 outlets, including DEPARTMENT STORES. Boot sold a controlling interest in 1920. He was created a knight (1909), a baronet (1916) and Lord Trent (1928).

BOOTH, CHARLES (b. 30 March 1840 at Liverpool, Lancashire, England; d. 23 Nov. 1916 at Gracedieu Manor, Leicestershire, England, aged 76). Sociologist. Booth, a businessman involved in shipping, became disenchanted with politics and religion. Influenced by positivism from the 1860s, he studied the lives of the poor in LONDON from 1887, including employment, poverty and religious influences. His investigations, published in *Life and Labour of the People in London* (17 volumes, 1889–1902), demonstrated that about a third of Londoners lived in poverty. From these, he argued for old age PENSIONS and TARIFF REFORM. *See also* NATIONAL DETERIORATION.

BOOTH FAMILY The English family which developed the SALVATION ARMY. William Booth (1829–1912) was active in Wesleyan METHODISM from the 1840s. In 1865 he founded the independent East London Christian Mission, which established 'stations' elsewhere. The organization was renamed the Salvation Army in 1879, with Booth as 'general'. Booth's wife Catherine (1829–90) conducted mission services from 1860 and campaigned for the PURITY MOVEMENT. Their son Bramwell Booth (1856–1929) was involved in his parents' work from 1870, becoming chief organizer of the Army from 1881, general from 1912. His sister Evangeline Cory Booth (1865–1950) led the Army in the USA from 1904 and was general 1934–9. His daughter Catherine Bramwell-Booth (1883–1987) was in charge of

Army social work among women in Great Britain 1926–46. Other family members were also Salvationists.

BORDER, ANGLO-SCOTTISH The historical border between England and Scotland follows natural features, running (NE–SW) along the R. Tweed and across the Cheviot Hills to the Solway Firth. First established in the later 11th century, and more firmly from the mid 12th century, it represents the line at which England finally halted southward expansion by the kingdom of Scotland. (There is no compelling natural border across N Britain.)

Scotland originated in the UNION OF SCOTS AND PICTS from *c*.842. Their kingdom (called 'Alba' meaning 'Britain' from *c*.900, 'Scotland' from the 11th century) was mostly N of the FORTH–CLYDE ISTHMUS. To the SE, it abutted the Anglian (English) kingdom of NORTHUMBRIA, and to the SW the British kingdom of STRATHCLYDE. In the 10th or 11th century (probably by 1026), Alba/Scotland acquired the LOTHIAN part of Northumbria, extending to the R. Tweed. From 1018 it had authority over Strathclyde (including Cumbria in modern NW England).

In 1092, King WILLIAM II of England seized the southern part of former Strathclyde, pushing the border back northwards, to the Solway Firth (*see* CARLISLE). Scottish expansionist ambitions nonetheless continued. King DAVID I regained former southern Strathclyde in 1136, obtained NE England in 1139, and from 1141 ruled southwards to a line from the R. Tees to the R. Ribble. In 1157, however, HENRY II of England forced MALCOLM IV to surrender N England, restoring the Tweed–Solway line.

The border remained largely unchanged (*see* BERWICK-UPON-TWEED), though Scottish claims were maintained until 1237 (abandoned in treaty of York). Local cross-border relations fell under special laws (codified 1249 as the 'Laws of the Marches').

The border area remained turbulent in the 14th–16th centuries, often with recurrent warfare. Conditions became peaceful with the UNION OF CROWNS (1603). Following the UNION OF ENGLAND AND SCOTLAND (1707), the border ceased to be an international boundary, becoming an internal border of GREAT BRITAIN. *See also* SCOTTISH–ENGLISH RELATIONS; RAIDING, CROSS-BORDER; COUNCIL OF THE NORTH.

BORDER, ANGLO-WELSH W Britain (WALES) was severed from direct land contact with other British areas by Germanic (English) kingdoms probably in the early 7th century. Soon afterwards, the advance of the English kingdom of MERCIA against the Welsh kingdom of POWYS pushed the border back to a N–S line between the Dee and Severn estuaries, which was roughly marked from the late 8th century by OFFA'S DYKE. For over 400 years, political and settlement borders fluctuated around that axis (from the mid 10th century dividing the Welsh kingdoms from a united England).

English settlement moved W even after construction of the dyke; English lived around Radnor (C Wales) by the late 10th century, and in NE Wales before 1066. Though NORMANS invaded Wales from the late 11th century, the lordships they founded, constituting the MARCH OF WALES, were treated as territories *within* Wales.

BORDER COMMISSIONS In the 14th–16th centuries, disorder was endemic in the Anglo-Scottish border country, with cross-border raids for cattle thieving. After the UNION OF CROWNS (1603), both sides came under King JAMES VI/I, who appointed ten border commissioners (five Scots, five English) to administer justice (1605). By often brutal means, they largely pacified the area. The commission was renewed in 1618 but disbanded in 1621. Disorder revived, prompting CHARLES I to establish new commissions (1630, 1635). *See also* BORDER, ANGLO-SCOTTISH; RAIDING, CROSS-BORDER.

BORNEO An island in SE Asia within which Great Britain acquired territories. In 1842 the sultan of Brunei in N Borneo gave the Sarawak River area (later named Kuching) to the Englishman James Brooke, inaugurating rule by members of the BROOKE FAMILY (to 1946). It was extended by further grants between 1846 and 1905. The territory was known as Sarawak.

In 1880 the Englishman Alfred Dent acquired an existing foreign jurisdiction in part of NE Borneo, called North Borneo. It was governed from 1882 by Dent's BRITISH NORTH BORNEO COMPANY.

Both territories, together with Brunei, were made British PROTECTORATES in 1888. Timber and rubber were exported. Approx. total population in 1921: 1,846,000. Sarawak and Brunei were occupied by Japan 1941–5, North Borneo 1942–5. Sarawak and North Borneo became CROWN COLONIES in 1946, and joined the Federation of Malaysia in 1963, when British forces helped to defend them from Indonesia. (North Borneo was renamed Sabah.) Brunei was granted internal self-government in 1971 and independence as a sultanate in 1983.

BOROUGH A settlement, usually a TOWN, where some inhabitants enjoy particular rights, privileges or liberties. Some were personal, such as the right to sell or bequeath property; others were corporate, such as the right to elect officers and administer the town. The term is derived from OE *burh*, which originally referred to a fortified centre.

By the mid 11th century, larger BURHS (in England) probably had courts and customs. During the 12th and 13th centuries, kings granted charters of liberties to many English towns, especially larger ones, often including

confirmation of existing customs and self-government (e.g., to OXFORD, *c.*1155). Lords also founded, and granted varying liberties to, numerous small towns (e.g., Maurice de Gant to LEEDS, 1207), which historians sometimes designate as 'seigneurial boroughs'. From the 13th century, some boroughs were represented in PARLIAMENT, and are often designated 'parliamentary boroughs' by historians. Boroughs sometimes received extensive legal rights from the mid 14th century and are regarded as 'incorporated boroughs', while from the late 14th century a few towns received county status, becoming 'county boroughs' (*see* INCORPORATION OF BOROUGHS). Kings and lords created boroughs in Wales (from late 11th century) and Ireland (from late 12th century), following invasions; similar developments occurred in Scotland (*see* BURGH).

The organization of TOWN GOVERNMENT – including the holding and definition of borough status and borough FRANCHISES – was controlled from the 19th century by the UK Parliament, and also from the 1920s by the parliaments in Ireland. *See also* GUILD; ROTTEN BOROUGH; LOCAL GOVERNMENT, NORTHERN IRELAND/SOUTHERN IRELAND.

BOSTON TEA PARTY A protest at Boston, MASSACHUSETTS (N America), on 16 Dec. 1773 when men disguised as Indians threw 342 chests of tea from three ships into the harbour. They were objecting to the British Tea Act (1773), which permitted the EAST INDIA COMPANY to send tea directly to British colonies. The Act threatened local mercantile interests because the Company's tea would undercut their trade. The British Parliament responded with the INTOLERABLE ACTS. *See also* AMERICAN INDEPENDENCE, ORIGINS OF.

BOSWORTH, BATTLE OF Fought on 22 Aug. 1485 about 3 mi (5 km) SW of Market Bosworth (Leicestershire, C England), between armies supporting King RICHARD III (YORKIST) and Henry Tudor, claimant to the throne (LANCASTRIAN). Richard was defeated and killed when Lord Stanley (Henry's step-father) and his brother Sir William Stanley intervened on Henry's side. Henry succeeded as king (*see* HENRY VII). *See also* YORKIST–LANCASTRIAN CONFLICT; BEAUFORT, MARGARET; STANLEY FAMILY.

BOTANY BAY An inlet in SE Australia, on the coast of NEW SOUTH WALES, which was the original landing site in AUSTRALIA of James COOK (29 April 1770). Cook applied the name because of the diverse flora. It became associated with the TRANSPORTATION of British and Irish convicts, who first arrived there on 18 Jan. 1788, though the penal settlement was established at Sydney.

BOTHA, LOUIS (b. 27 Sept. 1862 near Greytown, Natal; d. 27 Aug. 1919 at Pretoria, Transvaal, South Africa, aged

56). A Boer farmer, Botha was elected to the Parliament of Transvaal (or South African Republic) in 1897. During the (Second) BOER WAR he became commander-in-chief of Transvaal forces (1900), but in May 1902 advised peace making.

When Transvaal (now a British CROWN COLONY) was granted self-government (1907), Botha became prime minister. He supported the proposed federal SOUTH AFRICA and served as its first prime minister (1910–19). During WORLD WAR I he suppressed the pro-German Maritz Rebellion (1914–15) and occupied German South West Africa (1915, modern Namibia). Botha's assertion of South African influence within the BRITISH EMPIRE alienated many Boers. *See also* SMUTS, JAN.

BOTHWELL, 4TH EARL OF (b. 1534 or 1535 in Scotland; d. 14 April 1578 at Drachsholm, Denmark, aged about 43). James Hepburn inherited his earldom in 1556. Although he adopted Protestantism before the REFORMATION (1560), he remained pro-French and supported the Catholic MARY OF GUISE (regent 1554–9) and MARY, QUEEN OF SCOTS. He was suspected of involvement in the murder of her (second) husband, Lord DARNLEY (10 Feb. 1567). He then divorced his wife and married Mary (15 May 1567) but his enemies forced Mary to abandon him (and to abdicate). Bothwell fled to Orkney, then to Denmark where he died in prison. *See also* CONFEDERATE LORDS.

BOTHWELL, 5TH EARL OF (b. Dec. 1562; d. April 1612 at Naples, Kingdom of Naples, aged 49). Francis Stewart, a grandson of King JAMES V, was recognized as earl of Bothwell in Nov. 1577, succeeding his uncle the 4th earl before his death. He rose to prominence following the RUTHVEN RAID (22 Aug. 1582). His pro-English beliefs faltered after the execution of MARY, QUEEN OF SCOTS (Feb. 1587), and he rebelled alongside the northern earls in April 1589. Appointed assistant governor during JAMES VI's absence abroad (1589–90), he retained royal confidence until implicated in witchcraft by the North Berwick witch trials (Nov. 1590; imprisoned April–June 1591). Thereafter he attempted to recover favour through a series of armed confrontations with James (1591–4). In March 1595, having lost Protestant support, he went into exile in Continental Europe.

BOTHWELL BRIG, BATTLE OF Fought near Hamilton (S Scotland) on 22 June 1679. A Scottish government force, commanded by the duke of MONMOUTH, routed an army of COVENANTERS, killing 200–400 men. The battle was the culmination of the RISING OF 1679. Thereafter, support for Covenanting waned, leaving the CAMERONIANS as the main group of radical Covenanters.

BOTSWANA *see* BECHUANALAND

BOUDICCA (d. 61 in C Britain). The last queen of the Iceni, a British tribe whose territory (modern Norfolk, E England) was absorbed into the province of ROMAN BRITAIN on the death of her husband King Prasutagus (60 or 61). Flogged by the Romans, who also raped her daughters, Boudicca (also known as Boadicea) led a rebellion (61) while the Roman governor, C. Suetonius Paulinus, was campaigning in W Britain (Wales). The rebels sacked Camulodunum (COLCHESTER), Londinium (LONDON) and Verulamium (ST ALBANS) before being defeated in battle by Paulinus, after which Boudicca took poison.

BOULTER, HUGH (b. 4 Jan. 1672 at London, England; d. 27 Sept. 1742 at Westminster, Middlesex, England, aged 70). In 1724 Boulter, a bishop in England, was appointed (Church of Ireland) archbishop of ARMAGH and primate to strengthen British influence in Ireland during the WOOD'S HALFPENCE affair. (He sat on the Irish COUNCIL and in the Irish House of Lords.) From 1730 (recall of Governor CARTERET), he was the British government's main adviser on Irish policies. He supported ANTI-CATHOLIC LEGISLATION, opposed Protestant demands for legislative independence (*see* PATRIOTS), and recommended English candidates for government and Church posts. Boulter also promoted education and charities, and contributed to relief during the 1740–1 famine. *See also* PROTESTANT ASCENDANCY.

BOULTON, MATTHEW (b. 14 Sept. 1728 at Birmingham, Warwickshire, England; d. 17 Aug. 1809 at Handsworth, Warwickshire, aged 80). Boulton expanded his father's silver-stamping business (in BIRMINGHAM), building the 'Soho' factory (finished 1766, at Handsworth, near Birmingham) and becoming the leading manufacturer in the W Midlands of 'toys' (small metal items such as buckles).

In 1768 Boulton met the Scottish inventor James WATT, and in 1773 he accepted a share in Watt's patent for an improved steam engine. From 1775 their business manufactured engines, producing over 500 by 1800. They pioneered the application of steam power to a variety of industrial processes. *See also* INDUSTRIAL REVOLUTION; LUNAR SOCIETY OF BIRMINGHAM.

BOUNDARY COMMISSION A committee of three representatives, established in 1924 (under the 1921 ANGLO-IRISH TREATY), to review and adjust the boundary between the Irish Free State (IFS) and Northern Ireland. Many politicians in the IFS expected the Commission to reduce Northern Ireland's size, possibly making it economically unviable. On 7 Nov. 1925 a British newspaper revealed that only minor changes were proposed, causing the Commission to collapse. (The IFS commissioner, Eoin MacNeill, and chairman resigned.) The British, IFS and Northern Ireland governments revoked the Commission (3 Dec.). The boundary remained unchanged. *See also* Irish Free State, founding of.

BOW GROUP A discussion group within the British Conservative Party which first met in Feb. 1951 at the Bow and Bromley Constitutional Club in the East End of London. Membership was originally restricted to university graduates aged under 36. Its influence on party thinking fluctuated, as did its own ideological complexion. Its chairmen included Geoffrey Howe (1955–6).

BOXER RISING An outbreak of violence against foreigners in China in 1900. With official connivance, the 'Society of Harmonious Fists' besieged European legations in Beijing from 19 June. Great Britain contributed to the international force which relieved them (14 Aug.), and sought to avoid this intervention precipitating partition of the Chinese Empire. *See also* China, English and British relations with.

BOYCOTT, CHARLES (b. 12 March 1832 at Burgh St Peter, Norfolk, England; d. 19 June 1897 in Suffolk, England, aged 65). A land agent in Ireland (Co. Mayo) from 1873, Boycott suffered ostracism in 1880, at the behest of the Land League, for evicting tenants; for example, on 24 Sept. tenants refused to harvest crops under his management. He imported Orangemen volunteers from Ulster (N Ireland), who were protected by 1000 troops (12–26 Nov.). The case generated publicity and Boycott's name was immediately used to denote non-violent intimidation. Boycott left Ireland in 1886. *See also* land agitation and reform, Ireland; Orange Order, Ireland.

BOYLE, HENRY (b. between 1681 and 1687 at Castlemartyr, Co. Cork, Ireland; d. 27 Dec. 1764 at Dublin, Ireland). A member of the Irish House of Commons from 1707, Boyle (a Whig) was elected speaker in Oct. 1733. To secure his support, the government appointed him to lucrative posts (e.g., chancellor of the Exchequer from Nov. 1733). He and his allies dominated the Commons until 1753 when they were challenged by allies of Archbishop George Stone. Boyle responded by allowing the defeat of a money Bill. The government retaliated by dismissing Boyle and others from their government posts (spring 1754).

In 1756 a new chief governor made a 'peace' agreement: Boyle would retire as speaker, be created earl of Shannon, and receive a pension. Though now based in the House of Lords, he controlled the largest Commons faction until his death. *See also* undertakers; Money Bill dispute; Protestant Ascendancy.

BOYLE, ROBERT (b. 25 Jan. 1627 at Lismore, Co. Waterford, Ireland; d. 30 Dec. 1691 at London, England, aged 64). Educated in England, Boyle travelled in Continental Europe 1639–44. On returning, he became involved with leading natural philosophers (scientists) and undertook research. Based in Oxford 1654–68, and associated initially with the group of natural philosophers centred on Wadham College, Boyle studied the properties of air through experiments using an air pump, publishing his discoveries in *New Experiments …* (1660). A second edition (1662) included what became known as 'Boyle's Law' – that the volume of a gas varies inversely to the pressure on it – though it was discovered by an assistant, Richard Towneley. Boyle also advocated a 'corpuscularist' theory of matter (that matter is constituted from indivisible corpuscles). He was a founder of the Royal Society (1660). *See also* Scientific Revolution.

BOYNE, BATTLE OF THE Major battle of the Williamite War (1688–91), fought near the R. Boyne in Co. Meath (E Ireland), near Drogheda, on 1 July 1690. Protestant forces commanded by King William III (English, Irish, Huguenots, Danish, Germans, totalling 36,000; 'Williamites') defeated forces commanded by (the former king) James VII/II (Irish, French, mostly Catholics, totalling 25,000; 'Jacobites'). Afterwards James fled abroad (4 July), while William took E Ireland. War continued for another year. *See also* James VII/II and Ireland; Orange Order, Ireland.

BOYNE VALLEY *see* Bend of the Boyne

BRACTON Commonly used name for the 13th-century legal treatise *On the Laws and Customs of England* (written in Latin). It was named after its supposed author, the justice Henry of Bratton or Bracton (d. 1268). But much of the treatise was written by the mid 1230s when Bratton was young. The justice and bishop William of Raleigh (d. 1250), for whom Bratton worked as clerk, is the likely author. Bratton probably revised the work (1240s–50s) before it was circulated. The major concerns of *Bracton* are criminal and property law. *See also* law, England from 1066.

BRADLAUGH, CHARLES (b. 26 Sept. 1833 at London, England; d. 30 Jan. 1891 at London, aged 57). Propagandist for atheism, republicanism and birth control. Elected a Liberal MP in 1880, Bradlaugh objected to swearing an oath on the Bible for admission to the UK House of Commons. Denied his request to affirm instead, he asked to take the oath but was refused. The Fourth Party exploited his expulsion and repeated re-election to embarrass W.E. Gladstone. Bradlaugh was permitted to take the oath and admitted in 1886. An Act to allow affirmation was passed in 1888.

BRAOSE FAMILY An important noble family in the MARCH OF WALES *c*.1165–1230, originally from NORMANDY (N France); they descended from Philip de Braose, who settled at Radnor (C Wales) by *c*.1095 (*see* BUILTH).

William Braose (d. perhaps 1175) acquired Brecon *c*.1165 by marriage; by the early 13th century his descendants had accumulated vast territories in SE Wales. Braose involvement ended with William Braose (d. 1230); succeeded by the BOHUN and MORTIMER families. *See also* JOHN.

BREADALBANE, 1ST EARL OF (b. *c*.1635 in Scotland; d. 19 March 1717 in Scotland, aged about 80). A powerful HIGHLAND chief (of the Campbell CLAN of Glenorchy) and presbyterian, John Campbell was granted titles in 1677 and made earl of Breadalbane in 1681. In 1689 he reluctantly supported the accession of William of Orange (*see* WILLIAM III). Afterwards, with Sir John DALRYMPLE, Breadalbane was required to obtain loyalty oaths from dissident chiefs. A consequence was the GLENCOE MASSACRE (1692), in which Breadalbane was implicated. In 1695 he was briefly imprisoned for suspected JACOBITISM. Breadalbane opposed the UNION OF ENGLAND AND SCOTLAND (1707) but sat in the British House of Lords (1713–15). He contributed troops to the JACOBITE REBELLION of 1715, but escaped punishment on account of his age.

BRÉAUTÉ, FALKES DE (b. in Normandy; d. 1226 at Rome, Italy). Of obscure origin, de Bréauté was in the service of King JOHN in England by 1207. During John's conflict with rebel barons in 1215–16, he was a commander of royalist forces (*see* MAGNA CARTA), and was rewarded with marriage to an earl's widow, thereby gaining extensive estates.

After the accession of HENRY III, de Bréauté helped to defeat French and baronial forces at Lincoln (May 1217; *see* ENGLAND, FRENCH INVASION (1216–17)), and he remained a leading government officer. But in Dec. 1223, having made enemies, he agreed to resign his sheriffdoms and castles though he resisted loss of his estates. Having submitted to Henry (19 Aug. 1224), he went into overseas exile (Oct.).

BREDA, DECLARATION OF The statement issued at Breda in the Dutch Republic on 4 April 1660 by CHARLES II, exiled king of England, Ireland and Scotland. Prepared at the suggestion of General MONCK, it was issued during elections in England and Wales to the CONVENTION PARLIAMENT. Charles, who was seeking to regain his thrones, promised conditional pardons to former enemies, settlement of pay arrears for the Army, that Parliament could resolve disputed land titles, and advocated religious liberty. The Declaration was read in Parliament on 1 May and encouraged the RESTORATION. *See also* CLARENDON, EARL OF.

BREHON *see* BREHON LAW

BREHON LAW Term used for Old Irish laws, which were written down from the 8th century in such tracts as *Senchas Már* (OIr., meaning 'Great Tradition'); derived from OIr. *brithem* ('brehon' in English), meaning 'judge' or 'jurist'. Law making and justice were usually the preserve of the *brithemain*, who comprised one of the LEARNED CLASSES. Although kings were not lawgivers, they could issue emergency provisions.

Ireland in effect lacked a concept of criminal law. All felonies and misdemeanours were civil offences. While certain laws dealt with such crimes as murder, assault and theft, they were concerned with the provision of compensation for a victim and his kin rather than punishment of criminals. Various tracts dealt with land, contracts and pledges, personal injuries, SOCIAL STRUCTURE, and FAMILY AND KINSHIP (including related obligations such as fosterage and marriage).

Although society was generally patriarchal, the laws accorded women considerable status. Women could not normally give legal witness, and could inherit only a life-interest in property, but they had rights in marriage and divorce based on the property they had contributed to a marriage. Women were jointly responsible with their husbands for rearing children.

Despite reinterpretations, brehon law survived in Gaelic Irish areas, particularly ULSTER (N Ireland), until the end of the 'Gaelic era' (early 17th century). In 1920–2 revolutionary courts run by SINN FÉIN admitted citations from 'early Irish law-codes', but the IRISH FREE STATE (founded 1922) in principle followed the English legal system.

BRÉIFNE A kingdom in NW Ireland, between CONNACHT (W Ireland) and AIRGIALLA (N Ireland), created in the late 8th century by the Uí Briúin Bréifne dynasty from Connacht. By the 10th century they had expanded south-eastwards (modern Co. Cavan); in the 12th century they governed part of MEATH (E Ireland). By then, their ruling family had adopted the surname Ua Ruairc (English, O'Rourke).

After the death of Tigernán Ua Ruairc (1172), the dynasty's power collapsed and Meath was taken by Anglo-Normans (*see* LACY, HUGH DE). The remainder of Bréifne remained outside direct Anglo-Norman control, but by the mid 13th century broke into two: W Bréifne (modern Co. Leitrim) under the O'Rourkes, E Bréifne (modern Co. Cavan) under the O'Reillys (Irish, Ó Ragallaig). Both dynasties survived until the late 16th century. Brian O'Rourke was hanged by the English in 1591 and his kingdom was later included in the ULSTER PLANTATION. *See also* MAC MURCHADA, DIARMAIT.

BRÉTIGNY, TREATY OF Concluded on 8 May 1360 at Brétigny (N France), between English and French representatives, ending the first phase of the HUNDRED YEARS WAR. The ransom for releasing King John II of France from English custody was reduced. John would cede lands and sovereignty in SW and N France, including the duchy of Aquitaine and CALAIS, to King EDWARD III of England. Edward would cede Normandy and Touraine, and renounce his claim to the French Crown. It was a poor outcome for Edward given his military dominance. The treaty was replaced (24 Oct.) by the treaty of Calais, which omitted John's cession of sovereignty and Edward's renunciation of his claim. *See also* GASCONY.

BRETTON WOODS AGREEMENTS Arrangements made in July 1944 by 44 Allied powers, including the UK (represented by J.M. KEYNES), at the United Nations International Monetary and Financial Conference, Bretton Woods, New Hampshire, USA. They created a monetary system, for implementation after WORLD WAR II, designed to provide stability: it involved fixed exchange rates based on the dollar and gold, an International Monetary Fund to provide liquidity, and a World Bank for longer-term loans. Currency values could be changed only in exceptional circumstances. The pound sterling was devalued from $4.03 to $2.80 (1949), and to $2.40 (1967). The system collapsed from 1971 and currencies 'floated' (sterling from 23 June 1972).

BREWING INDUSTRY, ENGLAND AND WALES Ale-brewing, with malted barley or oats, was undertaken widely in rural households until the 18th century. In towns, women brewed ale for sale. It was also brewed at alehouses and inns.

Beer-brewing, using hops for flavouring and preservation, was introduced by German immigrants in the late 14th century. During the 16th and 17th centuries 'common breweries' (businesses usually run by men which sold to inns and individuals) were founded in towns, but LONDON remained the major centre until the 19th century. Around 1700 it produced a quarter of England's beer, though there were prominent businesses elsewhere (e.g., Burton-on-Trent, Staffordshire, with high-quality water). London brewers used coal instead of wood for heating from the 16th century, and coke from the mid 17th century.

In 1722 'porter' (strong, dark beer) was invented near London. It was suitable for large-scale production and kept well. For over 50 years several London breweries were the largest industrial businesses (e.g., Whitbread's). From the 1820s 'pale ale' beer was popular and widely exported (e.g., to India).

The spread of RAILWAYS from the 1830s increased marketing areas. Brewing expanded notably at Burton-on-Trent (26 breweries by 1869). Specializing in 'pale ale', its production surpassed that of London. Brewing by retailers

and public houses declined rapidly. In Wales, brewing expanded in industrial areas from the 1830s.

In the 20th century commercial breweries in England and Wales declined from over 3000 in 1900 to under 200 in 1980, with many Welsh brewers being absorbed by English companies. But a 'Campaign for Real Ale' later encouraged a growth of 'microbreweries' serving small areas.

BREWING INDUSTRY, IRELAND Ale was widely brewed in rural households until at least the 17th century, when commercial beer-brewing became established, using imported hops. Most breweries (probably over 1000 in 1700) were small and produced for direct retail sale. Large-scale production was concentrated in DUBLIN.

By the 1770s breweries faced strong English competition. (Beer imports rose from 15,000 barrels in 1750 to 100,000 in 1792.) Some responded by expanding output, and by 1814 exports exceeded imports, though breweries declined (937 in 1790 to 247 in 1837).

Output continued to rise during the 19th century, with Dublin and CORK as primary centres and GUINNESS (Dublin), producing 'stout', predominant by 1840. Beer output trebled between the 1850s and 1914. By 1900 Dublin breweries produced about three-quarters of total beer output, with two-thirds of that brewed by Guinness. Forty per cent of production was exported, mostly by Guinness. Brewery numbers declined to 28 by 1914.

Guinness remained Ireland's pre-eminent brewer, also producing lager from 1952. In the early 21st century there were 16 breweries in the Republic of Ireland and three in Northern Ireland, and some new 'microbreweries'.

BREWING INDUSTRY, SCOTLAND References to brewing date from the 12th century onwards. By the 15th century domestic brewing was widespread, often carried out by women. Ale was the staple drink. By the 17th century commercial brewing was established in Lowland towns.

In the 18th century numerous large breweries were founded such as H. & R. Tennent (Glasgow, 1740) and William Younger (Leith, 1749), which also produced beer and soon superseded domestic production. They usually continued as family businesses. By *c.*1850 there were nearly 300 breweries. From the late 19th century Scotland produced light ales and lager. Exports were considerable between *c.*1850 and 1914.

By the 1990s takeovers had reduced numbers to a mere seven large brewers, though smaller breweries were also reappearing. By 2017 there were about 115 breweries, most operated by 'craft' brewers. Scottish beers have a more malty and less hoppy flavour than their English counterparts.

BREXIT Shorthand term for 'British Exit' from the European Union (EU), coined in May 2012 by the British pro-EU campaigner Peter Wilding by analogy with 'Grexit' (invented Feb. 2012 for a possible 'Greek Exit' from the euro currency). Originally considered hypothetical, Brexit became possible in 2015 when the UK's (Conservative) government legislated for a referendum on membership, to negate electoral pressure from the anti-EU UNITED KINGDOM INDEPENDENCE PARTY and anti-EU sentiment within the Conservative Party by settling the issue. Prime Minister David CAMERON expected to win endorsement of membership.

The referendum (23 June 2016) produced a majority for 'leave' (52% to 48%), causing Cameron to resign. He was succeeded by Theresa MAY, previously a 'remainer'. Notice of departure, authorized by Parliament, was served on the EU on 29 March 2017, to become effective two years later.

In June 2017 May held a general election to assist Brexit: she expected to strengthen her authority by increasing her House of Commons majority. The reverse happened. The majority was lost and May became reliant on support from DEMOCRATIC UNIONIST PARTY (DUP) MPs from NORTHERN IRELAND. Her withdrawal strategy ('Chequers Plan', July 2018) prompted two Cabinet ministers to resign (including Boris JOHNSON), and her withdrawal agreement with the EU was rejected three times by the Commons (Jan.–March 2019). It was opposed by many Conservatives for alleged excessive concessions, by the LABOUR PARTY Opposition mainly for party advantage, and by other parties (e.g., LIBERAL DEMOCRATS, SCOTTISH NATIONAL PARTY) because they opposed Brexit. DUP MPs and many Conservatives particularly resisted an 'Irish backstop', which might leave Northern Ireland indefinitely subject to EU regulations (to prevent a 'hard border' in Ireland). Brexit was eventually postponed to 31 Oct. Conservatives reacted to the impasse by pressurizing May into resignation.

May was replaced by 'Brexiteer' Boris Johnson (July). His willingness to countenance a 'no deal' departure was stymied by opponents in Parliament, who legislated (Sept.) for the prime minister to request a three-month extension if Parliament had not accepted a deal or a no-deal departure by 19 Oct. Although Johnson obtained a revised withdrawal agreement (17 Oct.), continuing opposition resulted in postponement of the UK's departure. Conservative victory in a general election (12 Dec. 2019) enabled the UK to leave the EU on 31 Jan. 2020. *See also* ROYAL PREROGATIVE; EUROPEAN ECONOMIC COMMUNITY/EUROPEAN UNION, IMPACT ON BRITISH POLITICS.

BRIAN BÓRUMA (BRIAN BORU) (b. *c*.941 at Béal Boru, Munster, S Ireland; d. 23 April 1014, Clontarf, Leinster, E Ireland, aged about 73). Brian succeeded as high-king of the Dál Cais in MUNSTER in 976 and by 982 was Munster's high-king. He then intermittently fought MÁEL SECHNAILL MAC DOMNAILL, high-king of the Southern Uí Néill (E Ireland) and of Ireland. By 996 Brian was dominant in S Ireland.

In 997 Brian pressurized Máel Sechnaill into sharing the high-kingship (S Ireland to Brian), and in 1002 obtained Máel Sechnaill's submission, ending Uí Néill monopoly of the high-kingship. Brian then campaigned in N Ireland, securing widespread recognition as high-king by 1011. In 1012 Leinstermen and their Scandinavian allies began to rebel. Brian defeated them at CLONTARF in 1014, but was then killed. In the late 11th century his descendants adopted his name as their surname; *see* O'BRIEN FAMILY.

BRIDEI SON OF BELI (fl. from 671; d. 692, probably in N Britain). From 671 Bridei ruled the northern Pictish kingdom of FORTRIU (in modern NE Scotland), and is the first to be named as its king (in Irish sources). But he was an outsider; his family was southern Pictish (probably from Fife), his father was a king in Brittonic STRATHCLYDE, and his mother was a daughter of King EDWIN of Northumbria. Through her, he was a cousin of the dominant Northumbrian king EGFRITH, who controlled southern Pictland and probably installed Bridei as a puppet in northern Pictland. But Mercians defeated Egfrith in 679, and thereafter Bridei exerted his own power, devastating the ORKNEY ISLANDS (681) and capturing strongholds in southern Pictland. Egfrith reacted by leading an army north in 685, but was defeated and killed probably near (modern) Forfar (see DÚN NECHTAIN, BATTLE OF). That ended Northumbrian power north of the R. Forth, and enabled Bridei to dominate both northern and southern Pictland. *See also* PICTS; KINGSHIP, NORTH BRITAIN.

BRIDEI SON OF DER-ILEI (fl. from 696; d. 707, probably in N Britain). From 696 Bridei ruled FORTRIU and the other Pictish areas, thus creating a unified Pictish realm stretching S to the FORTH–CLYDE ISTHMUS. His right to the kingship came from his Pictish mother Der-Ilei; his father was from Scottish (i.e., Irish) Argyll, which helped him have good relations with DÁL RIATA. Moreover, after 698, when he defeated a Northumbrian effort to reverse the takeover of southern Pictland, he also established good relations with Aldfrith, king of NORTHUMBRIA. The most striking aspect of his reign, however, is his relationship with IONA (where Aldfrith had been a monk). Working with Abbot ADOMNÁN (biographer of Columba), and with Aldfrith's encouragement, he brought previously independent religious settlements scattered across Pictland into a much more episcopal structure under Ionan primacy. *See also* PICTS.

BRIDEI SON OF MAILCON (fl. from *c*.556; d. 586, probably in N Britain). A king of PICTS from *c*.556, Bridei's power base appears to have been the former Verturiones tribe (see FORTRIU), whose heartland was in the coastal region from the inner Moray Firth to the R. Don (in NE of modern Scotland); but his sway probably stretched across the central and northern Highlands, and also the ORKNEY ISLANDS (which suggests he had naval resources). Early in his reign (c.558) he defeated a force of SCOTS (Irish) from (Scottish) DÁL RIATA. Later, he was visited by the Irish monk COLUMBA (from IONA monastery, founded 563), at a stronghold in or near either (modern) Inverness or Dunkeld. After initial hostility, Bridei eventually treated Columba with honour, but seems not to have espoused Christianity. *See also* KINGSHIP, NORTH BRITAIN.

BRIDGEWATER, 3RD DUKE OF (b. 21 May 1736, probably at Westminster, Middlesex, England; d. 8 March 1803 at Westminster, aged 66). Francis Egerton inherited his dukedom in 1748. From 1755, after seeing the Languedoc Canal in France and studying engineering, he planned a canal to exploit his coalmines at Worsley (Lancashire). He obtained Acts of Parliament in 1759, 1760 and 1762. Under the second he built a canal to MANCHESTER (engineered by James Brindley), the first 'arterial canal' to be built in England for many centuries. Successfully operating by the early 1760s, this encouraged his further investment in canal-building. *See also* CANALS, ENGLAND.

BRIGANTES *see* CARTIMANDUA; VENUTIUS

BRIGHT, JOHN (b.16 Nov. 1811 at Rochdale, Lancashire, England; d. 27 March 1889 at Rochdale, aged 77). Bright, a Quaker cotton mill-owner, was chief orator of the ANTI-CORN LAW LEAGUE (1839-46). A Radical MP from 1843, he opposed the CRIMEAN WAR (1854-6); later he campaigned for PARLIAMENTARY REFORM, before holding office under W.E. GLADSTONE (president of the Board of Trade 1868-70, chancellor of the duchy of Lancaster 1873-4, 1880-2).

BRIGIT (fl. in possibly early 6th century in Ireland). By the mid 7th century Brigit was claimed as the founder of a church and monastery at KILDARE (E Ireland). Her historical existence is doubtful; her cult may have started as the Christianization of devotion to a pagan goddess of the same name. Brigit nevertheless became the most popular saint in Ireland after PATRICK. *See also* CONVERSION OF IRELAND.

BRISTOL A city, port and unitary authority in SW England, at the confluence of the Rivers Avon and Frome.

A town was founded by the 10th century. Its name means 'Place by the bridge'. Bristol has been important for trade and communications with Ireland. In the 14th–16th centuries it was also a substantial centre of the CLOTH INDUSTRY. Divided between Gloucestershire and Somerset, Bristol was the first English town to receive county status (1373). England's exploration of N America started from Bristol in 1497 (*see* CABOT, JOHN). It was a bishop's see from 1542 (except for 1836–96; joined with Gloucester).

Bristol expanded enormously from the late 17th century with the development of trade with the WEST INDIES, NORTH AMERICAN COLONIES and WEST AFRICA (notably the SLAVE TRADE). During the 18th century it superseded NORWICH as the largest and wealthiest city after London. The first METHODIST chapel opened there in 1739. Although Bristol was disadvantaged by the rise of LIVERPOOL and abolition of the slave trade (1807), it continued to process sugar and tobacco, and manufacture chocolate. It was assisted from 1841 by a RAILWAY to London.

Foreign trade diminished after WORLD WAR II (1939–45), but Bristol remained an important industrial and financial centre. It gained two universities (both by upgrading): Bristol University (1909), University of the West of England (1992).

Est. popn: 1086, 4000; 1300, 12,000; 1600, 12,000; 1800, 64,000; 1900, 330,000; 2000, 635,000.

BRITAIN The largest island within the BRITISH ISLES, about 570 mi (920 km) in length (N–S). Continuously inhabited from c.11,000 BC, it finally became separate from Continental Europe between 5800 and 5400 BC (*see* GLACIATIONS). Inhabitants adopted Brittonic (or Common Brittonic) language in the 1st millennium BC.

The island's Brittonic name was probably Albion, meaning 'The land' or 'Mainland'. Britain is recorded in the 1st century BC as Prettanike (Greek), and as Brettania or Britannia (Latin), meaning 'Land of the Prettanoi' or 'Pretani' or 'Britanni', i.e., 'painted ones', similar to the later PICTS. ('Pretani' was probably the Brittonic name for its inhabitants.) The island was later known in OE as Bryten. 'Britain' is derived from OFr., Bretaigne.

Britain was also known as Great Britain (in Greek) from the 2nd century AD, to distinguish it from Little Britain (Ireland). From the 12th century, the name differentiated Britain from Brittany in France (Lesser Britain).

Following eleven millennia with varying cultures (*see* PREHISTORIC BRITAIN), over half of southern Britain was ruled by Romans (1st–5th centuries AD; *see* ROMAN BRITAIN). British kingdoms emerged to the N.

GERMANIC SETTLEMENT (5th–6th centuries) changed British culture in much of southern Britain to Germanic (or 'Anglo-Saxon') culture (e.g., language). Germanic rulers displaced British kingdoms. The main exception was W Britain (modern Wales). In N Britain, immigration introduced Irish rule and culture (*see* DÁL RIATA). Britain was disrupted by VIKINGS (8th–9th centuries).

N Britain became a single large kingdom in the 9th–11th centuries (*see* SCOTLAND), and much of S Britain in the 10th century (*see* ENGLAND, FORMATION OF). W Britain was taken under English rule in the 11th–13th centuries and annexed in 1536 (*see* WALES). Union of England and Scotland was attempted in 1604–8, and existed briefly in the 1650s. It took place in 1707, creating GREAT BRITAIN. *See also* POST-ROMAN BRITAIN; DUMNONIA; UNION OF CROWNS, ENGLAND (WITH IRELAND) AND SCOTLAND; UNION OF ENGLAND AND SCOTLAND, 1650s.

BRITAIN, BATTLE OF During WORLD WAR II, the acute contest for air superiority over the English Channel, fought 10 July–31 Oct. 1940 between the British ROYAL AIR FORCE and German Luftwaffe. The British lost 915 aeroplanes, the Germans 1733. The successful British defence of air space caused Adolf Hitler to postpone his intended invasion of Great Britain. *See also* DOWDING, HUGH.

BRITANNIA *see* ROMAN BRITAIN

BRITISH ASSOCIATION FOR THE ADVANCEMENT OF SCIENCE An organization founded in 1831 at YORK to encourage scientific research and seek support from the British government. Suggested by the editor and scientist David Brewster (1781–1868), who feared that British science was declining compared with science in Continental Europe, it was organized by clergyman and geologist William Harcourt (1789–1871). It also reflected concern that the ROYAL SOCIETY had become complacent.

The Association has held annual meetings in major towns in the British Isles and occasionally overseas, and published reports on the state of science. Its 1860 meeting in OXFORD famously featured a confrontation between Bishop Samuel Wilberforce and T.H. HUXLEY over the claim of Charles DARWIN that humans resulted from EVOLUTION. In the 1990s the Association's annual meeting was developed into the British Science Festival, and in 2009 the Association was renamed the British Science Association.

BRITISH BROADCASTING CORPORATION A public corporation (abbreviated as 'BBC') established by royal charter on 1 Jan. 1927 with a monopoly of RADIO broadcasting in Great Britain, NORTHERN IRELAND, the CHANNEL ISLANDS and Isle of MAN. Superseding the commercial British Broadcasting Company (created 1922), and funded by an annual radio licence, the BBC was independent of overt commercial or political influence. Its first director general was John REITH. From the 1930s the BBC developed TELEVISION broadcasting.

The charter was periodically renewed, modified or supplemented. The BBC's work was supervised by its trustees, the Board of Governors. This model of 'public broadcasting' was emulated worldwide. The BBC lost its monopolies of television and radio in 1954 and 1972 respectively. In 2007 a regulatory BBC Trust replaced the Board.

BRITISH BROADCASTING CORPORATION WORLD SERVICE *see* BBC WORLD SERVICE

BRITISH COMMONWEALTH *see* COMMONWEALTH

BRITISH COUNCIL An organization which promotes knowledge of British culture (e.g., arts) and the English language overseas, founded in 1934 by the British government as the 'British Committee for Relations with Other Countries' to counter ideologies such as communism and fascism. It began work in E Europe and the Middle East in 1934, opening its first overseas offices in 1938, and was incorporated by royal charter as the British Council in 1940. Autonomous, but partly financed by the Foreign Office, the Council has projected British influence following the decline of the BRITISH EMPIRE. In the early 21st century it operated in over 100 countries.

BRITISH EMPIRE The term 'British Empire' has covered varying territories and types of activity. England founded an empire of commerce, settlement and commodity production in N America and the WEST INDIES in the 17th century, which was partly lost when most American colonies declared independence in 1776 (*see* NORTH AMERICAN COLONIES). An empire was developed in E Asia from the 17th century when the EAST INDIA COMPANY established trading posts. It was greatly extended in the later 18th century through territorial acquisitions (*see* INDIA), and more trading posts and territories were added later, often as PROTECTORATES (*see* SINGAPORE, MALAYA, BORNEO, HONG KONG). Trading posts were founded in W Africa from the late 17th century (*see* ROYAL AFRICAN COMPANY).

A new empire of white settlement was created during the later 18th century and first half of the 19th century. Control over French CANADA was established during the SEVEN YEARS WAR (1756–63), while peace settlements of 1814–15 secured a foothold in southern Africa (*see* CAPE COLONY). Colonies were founded in AUSTRALIA as penal settlements (*see* TRANSPORTATION). NEW ZEALAND was acquired in 1839–40.

Britain's dependent empire was expanded considerably during the era of so-called NEW IMPERIALISM in the later 19th century. In WEST AFRICA, Britain's coastal presence was extended inland (*see* GAMBIA, SIERRA LEONE, GOLD COAST, NIGERIA); in N Africa, EGYPT and SUDAN were brought under British rule; and three protectorates were established in EAST AFRICA. Britain also acquired influence in S America and China (*see* INFORMAL EMPIRE). After WORLD WAR I (1914–18), territories were acquired as MANDATES (in Africa and Middle East).

The British Empire was most extensive in the 1920s. Thereafter it contracted; the Statute of WESTMINSTER (1931) recognized self-governing DOMINIONS as effectively independent, and many territories became self-governing between 1947 and 1964 (*see* DECOLONIZATION). In 2015 the UK retained 14 overseas territories (*see* DEPENDENT TERRITORY). *See also* CROWN COLONY; SLAVE TRADE, ENGLISH AND BRITISH INVOLVEMENT.

BRITISH EMPIRE, GOVERNMENT OF English colonies in the Americas (from 1607) were minimally supervised by the king and PRIVY COUNCIL until CHARLES II increased control through the lords of trade and plantations (from 1675), who oversaw the NAVIGATION ACTS and heard appeals. They were replaced by the Board of TRADE (1696–1782), though the SECRETARY OF STATE (southern) was also involved from the 1720s. After disputes began with NORTH AMERICAN COLONIES (1760s), a separate colonial secretaryship was created (1768–82). Colonial affairs were then handled by the home secretary (1782–1801), secretary for war and the colonies (1801–54) and colonial secretary (1854–1966). PROTECTORATES created in the late 19th century were briefly administered by the foreign secretary, then transferred to the colonial secretary.

From the 17th century until 1858 administration of British INDIA remained with the EAST INDIA COMPANY, though Parliament imposed State supervision (Regulating Act 1773, providing Crown appointment of governors and presidency councils; India Act 1784, creating a Board of Control). There was a secretary of state for India 1858–1947 (with BURMA from 1937, to 1948).

From 1925 there was also a secretary for DOMINION affairs (renamed COMMONWEALTH relations, 1947), a position often held by the colonial secretary. The post absorbed the colonial secretaryship in 1966, but was taken over by the foreign secretary in 1968 (his department became the Foreign and Commonwealth Office).

Within colonies, administration varied, notably between 'direct' and 'indirect' rule. Colonies under direct rule usually had a governor and council, and often an assembly. Later administration in India operated through the INDIAN CIVIL SERVICE, backed by a police force and Indian Army. Indirect rule, or governance through native authorities with British 'guidance', was the preferred method in Indian princely kingdoms, MALAYA (from 19th century), and most of tropical Africa (e.g., NIGERIA). Other types of government included RESPONSIBLE GOVERNMENT. *See also* NORTH AMERICAN COLONIES, GOVERNMENTS OF; MANDATE OR MANDATED TERRITORY; INFORMAL EMPIRE.

BRITISH GUIANA A former British colony on the N coast of S America. The area known as Guiana (larger than the later colony) was visited by Walter RALEGH (1595,

1617–18), who sought the fabled wealthy city of Eldorado, and by other Englishmen. During the 17th century the Dutch established sugar PLANTATIONS worked by slaves.

Great Britain occupied Guiana in 1796 to exclude French influence and retained the W part (1814) which it unified as the CROWN COLONY of British Guiana in 1831. After SLAVERY was abolished in 1834, sugar production declined. Following instability in the 1950s, British Guiana was granted independence as Guyana under the British Crown in 1966, and became a republic in 1970. Approx. population in 1921, 301,000; in 1965, 645,000.

BRITISH HONDURAS A former British possession in C America. Settled by English buccaneers and log cutters from 1638, the territory was long denied formal recognition for fear of Spanish hostility. Great Britain appointed a superintendent in 1786 and declared a CROWN COLONY in 1862. British Honduras became self-governing in 1964, and was renamed Belize in 1973, but territorial claims by neighbouring Guatemala delayed independence. It was granted in 1981 with the British monarch as head of State. Approx. population in 1921, 45,000; in 1980, 145,000.

BRITISH–IRISH RELATIONS FROM 1922 *see* IRISH–BRITISH RELATIONS FROM 1922

BRITISH ISLES The archipelago NW of Continental Europe, named from its largest island, BRITAIN. It comprises about 4400 islands of at least 0.5 acre (0.2 ha), of which about 200 are inhabited. The second-largest island is IRELAND. Other significant, though much smaller, islands or subsidiary archipelagos are Isles of Scilly, Aran Islands, ANGLESEY, Isle of MAN, WESTERN ISLES (or Hebrides), ORKNEY ISLANDS, SHETLAND ISLANDS, Isle of Wight. The CHANNEL ISLANDS are often associated with the British Isles though they lie close to Continental Europe (France).

The islands contain five sovereign jurisdictions: UNITED KINGDOM of Great Britain and Northern Ireland (UK); Isle of Man (British Crown 'dependency' outside UK); bailiwicks of Guernsey and Jersey (two British Crown 'dependencies' outside UK, the Channel Islands); Republic of Ireland. Est. total popn in 2015: 69,909,000.

The islands have never been a single political entity, but they belonged to a single monarch as kingdoms or lordships from 1603 (succession of JAMES VI of SCOTLAND as king of ENGLAND, with the Channel Islands and Man, and as king of Ireland) to 1949 (change of status by SOUTHERN IRELAND to a republic).

BRITISH LEGION The main voluntary social and welfare organization for veterans of the British armed forces, founded in 1921 (after WORLD WAR I) by merger of four organizations. Earl HAIG was its first president; 'Royal' was prefixed in 1971. The Legion provides care with funds raised by an annual 'poppy appeal'. In the early 21st century it had branches in the UK, Republic of Ireland and other countries, and over 300,000 members.

BRITISH NATIONAL PARTY *see* FASCISM, GREAT BRITAIN

BRITISH NORTH BORNEO COMPANY A commercial company founded in 1881 by Alfred Dent, and granted a British royal charter, which in 1882 took over jurisdiction in North Borneo (part of Borneo). The sultans of Sulu and Brunei had earlier granted jurisdiction to Baron von Overbeck, Austro-Hungarian consul at HONG KONG, and Overbeck had conveyed his rights to Dent (1880). The charter obliged the company to administer justice with regard to native law, and to preserve native religion and customs. A British PROTECTORATE was established in 1888. The company administered North Borneo until it became a CROWN COLONY in 1946 (except during Japanese occupation, 1942–5).

BRITISH SCIENCE ASSOCIATION *see* BRITISH ASSOCIATION FOR THE ADVANCEMENT OF SCIENCE

BRITISH SOMALILAND A former British territory on the Gulf of Aden in E Africa (now part of Somalia). British forces occupied the coast in 1884 to secure the sea route to ADEN and supplies. After treaties had been negotiated with various sultans, a PROTECTORATE was declared in 1888. Tribal raiding, led by Mahommed bin Abdullah Hassan (the so-called 'Mad Mullah'), hindered administration inland until 1920. The territory was united with Italian Somaliland in 1960 to form the independent Somali Republic. Approx. population in 1921, 345,000; in 1959, 500,000. *See also* EAST AFRICA, BRITISH INVOLVEMENT.

BRITISH SOUTH AFRICA COMPANY A commercial company incorporated in 1888 and led by Cecil RHODES (d. 1902). In 1889 it was authorized by royal charter to administer and exploit a large area of SE Africa. It created and ran the territories known as SOUTHERN RHODESIA and NORTHERN RHODESIA, retaining sovereign rights until 1924 (expiry of charter). In 1965 the company merged its business with other companies and continued as a non-trading entity.

BRITONS IN ANGLO-SAXON KINGDOMS From the 5th century men of Germanic origin established kingdoms in southern Britain which contained a majority of British (Brittonic-speaking) inhabitants. British inhabitants are acknowledged in the laws of King ÆTHELBERT of KENT (d. 616). Their social structure included nobles, freemen and unfree peasants, but they were reckoned at lower status than corresponding Germanic inhabitants (*see* WERGELD). A similar situation appears in the laws of INE of WESSEX (d. *c*.726). The majority Britons eventually assimilated to the culture of the Germanic minority (by 9th century). *See also* GERMANIC IMMIGRATION, SOUTHERN BRITAIN; CEMETERIES, EARLY GERMANIC.

BRITTEN, BENJAMIN (b. 22 Nov. 1913 at Lowestoft, Suffolk, England; d. 4 Dec. 1976 at Aldeburgh, Suffolk, aged 73). An accomplished composer as a teenager, Britten studied at the Royal College of Music (1930–3) and developed a modernist idiom without abandoning tonality. He quickly built a reputation with both instrumental and vocal works (e.g., song-cycle *Our Hunting Fathers*, 1936). A conscientious objector to war, Britten lived in the USA 1939–42, during WORLD WAR II. After his return to Great Britain, he composed *Peter Grimes* (performed 1945), the first of several operas to join the international repertoire, and founded the Aldeburgh Festival (1948). Later works include the *War Requiem* (1961). Created Lord Britten (1976), he was the first composer to become a peer.

BRIXTON AND TOXTETH RIOTS In Great Britain, two large outbreaks of urban disorder in 1981, a period of high unemployment, inflation and widespread disturbances. Both occurred in areas with substandard housing and AFRICAN CARIBBEAN populations.

In Brixton, S London, on Saturday 11 April 1981 a predominantly black crowd attacked a heavy police presence, following a week of intensive policing and, on the previous evening, a battle between black youths and police. For the first time in Britain, petrol bombs were thrown at police; police vehicles were burned, 28 buildings were torched and 117 other buildings damaged. A visit the next day by the home secretary, William Whitelaw, provoked more rioting and looting, also involving white gangs.

In Toxteth, LIVERPOOL (NW England), rioting by black and white youths took place from 4 to 12 July, following a confrontation between youths and the police on 3 July. 500 people were arrested, 460 police were injured and 70 buildings were demolished. Police used CS gas for the first time in Britain.

Responses included the government-commissioned 'Scarman Report' on the Brixton Riots (1981), by the senior judge Lord Scarman, which criticized the treatment of black people by the police and urged tackling of racial disadvantages. After the Toxteth Riots Michael HESELTINE, the environment secretary, encouraged regeneration in Liverpool, and Robert RUNCIE, archbishop of Canterbury, commissioned a report on inner-city problems, *Faith in the City* (1985). *See also* ETHNIC AND NATIONAL MINORITIES, ENGLAND.

BROADCASTING, ENGLAND *see* RADIO BROAD-CASTING, GREAT BRITAIN AND NORTHERN IRELAND; TEL-EVISION, GREAT BRITAIN AND NORTHERN IRELAND

BROADCASTING, NORTHERN IRELAND From 15 Sept. 1924 the British Broadcasting Company (BBC) radio station '2BE' transmitted the BBC's national programme and local items over a limited area from BELFAST. When the BBC became a corporation (1927), it was renamed BBC Northern Ireland. A new transmitter covered the entire province from 1936. Music predominated in local programming until *c.*1933 when speech programmes (e.g., talks, plays) became more prominent. Apart from news, current affairs were avoided to placate the Unionist government, thereby alienating Catholics, though the BBC co-operated with southern Ireland's station despite criticism.

During WORLD WAR II (1939–45), local programming ceased. On resumption, broadcasts included programmes from NE England because of a wavelength shortage (to 1963). The station sought to present Northern Ireland positively but was criticized for limited interest in Gaelic Irish culture; requests for Irish language programmes were refused, although Irish music was broadcast.

The threat of commercial radio provoked the BBC into transforming its station into Radio Ulster (1975), giving local programmes priority. From 1979 BBC Radio Foyle provided programmes for Co. Londonderry within Radio Ulster's schedule. Commercial broadcasting began with Downtown Radio (1976). The Belfast CityBeat station (1996–2015) won numerous awards.

The BBC relayed television to Northern Ireland from 1953. During the 1950s local programming gradually expanded, spurred from 1959 by competition from the commercial station Ulster TV (part of the Independent Television Network). BBC Two was inaugurated in 1964. Television broadcasting notably made the world aware of the TROUBLES (1968–90s) and influenced their course. *See also* BRITISH BROADCASTING CORPORATION.

BROADCASTING, SCOTLAND The first radio stations of the commercial British Broadcasting Company (BRITISH BROADCASTING CORPORATION from 1927) included four in Scotland: Glasgow and Aberdeen (1923), Edinburgh and Dundee (1924). They broadcast both London-originated and locally produced programmes. In 1930, except for Aberdeen, they were replaced by a single National Region for Scotland which produced some programming. After restructuring of 'BBC' radio programmes into four services in 1967, most Scottish material appeared as 'opt-outs' on Radio 4.

The development of commercial radio in Scotland began with Radio Clyde (1973) in Glasgow. It prompted the BBC to develop its services. It inaugurated BBC Radio Orkney,

BBC Radio Shetland (both 1977) and BBC Radio Scotland (1978). From 1985 BBC Radio nan Gàidheal broadcast material in Gaelic. By 2017 there were about 36 local commercial stations as well as smaller community stations and other forms of radio broadcasting.

The BBC began television broadcasts in Scotland in 1952, although few programmes were originated locally. Under the 1954 Television Act two commercial stations were started within Scotland: Scottish Television (1957, later STV), covering C Scotland; Grampian (1961), for NE Scotland (also N Scotland from 1982). Border TV (1961) covered the border region and SW from NW England. The BBC started a second channel in 1964, with its channels becoming known as BBC1 Scotland and BBC2 Scotland. In 1997 the owner of STV acquired Grampian, and in 2006 rebranded the stations as STV Central and STV North.

New technologies developed in the 1980s–90s were utilized to provide television in Gaelic. The commercial digital channel TeleG operated from 1999 to 2011, and the satellite and cable service BBC Alba from 2008 (a partnership with the Gaelic Media Service, created by the UK 2003 Communications Act). *See also* GAELDOM, SCOTLAND.

BROADCASTING, SOUTHERN IRELAND Regular radio broadcasts began in the IRISH FREE STATE on 1 Jan. 1926 with a speech by Douglas HYDE, mostly in Irish. The station, '2RN', operated under the Department for Posts and Telegraphs with some State funding. It was renamed Radio Athlone (1933) and Radio Éireann (1937). Programmes included Irish language lessons, sports reports and music, but little news reporting. A committee, Comhairle Radio Éireann, provided independent supervision 1953–60.

In 1960 a State-sponsored, public-service authority was established, Radio Éireann (renamed Radio Telefís Éireann, RTÉ, in 1966), which was charged with promoting Irish language and culture. During the 1970s–80s its monopoly was challenged by unauthorized 'pirate' stations, including an Irish-language station (1970). It responded with new services: Raidió na Gaeltachta (1972), an Irish-language for the GAELTACHT, and Radio 2 (1979) for young people. Legislation in 1988 suppressed the 'pirates' and created the Independent Radio and Television Commission with licensing powers. A commercial station was launched in 1989. In 2015 there were nine RTÉ stations, two commercial national stations, and digital and local stations.

RTÉ inaugurated television broadcasting on New Year's Eve 1961, including an address by President Éamon DE VALERA. Due to restricted funds, extensive programming was bought from the USA. Home productions included *The Late Late Show*, a 'chat show' which tackled social issues (presented 1962–99 by Gay Byrne). Colour broadcasting started in 1971. RTÉ initiated RTÉ 2 in 1978 (UK programmes and Irish material) and Telefís na Gaeilge in

1996 (Irish-language programmes). TV3, a commercial channel, began in 1998. Satellite and cable television expanded from the 1990s, and another commercial channel, Channel 6, operated 2006–9.

BROADCASTING, WALES Radio broadcasting was initiated in 1923, from a studio in CARDIFF serving S Wales and SW England, by the British Broadcasting Company (Corporation from 1927). Wales received its own wavelength in 1937, and the few programmes produced there were divided equally between Welsh and English. Two full home services, BBC Radio Wales (English) and BBC Radio Cymru (Welsh), were established in 1978 and 1979 respectively. The first commercial radio station, Swansea Sound, operated from 1974.

BBC TELEVISION was extended to Wales in 1952, serving S Wales and SW England, as did the commercial company Television Wales and West (TWW) from 1958. Other areas were covered by the commercial Wales (West and North) Television from 1962, and in 1964 Wales received a BBC service (BBC Wales Television). The paucity of Welsh-language programmes on BBC Wales and HTV (Harlech TV, successor to TWW from 1968) caused protests. In 1979 political parties agreed to provide a Welsh-language channel, but the elected Conservative government reneged. The intention was reinstated after Gwynfor EVANS threatened to undertake a hunger strike. S4C, the Welsh Fourth Channel, was inaugurated on 2 Nov. 1982.

In 2017 there were four Welsh television services (BBC1 Wales, BBC2 Wales, ITV Cymru Wales, S4C), three national radio stations (BBC Radio Wales, BBC Radio Cymru, BBC Radio Cymru 2), 14 commercial radio stations, and community radio stations.

BROCH A type of multi-storey, circular stone house found in the northern Hebrides, northern Scotland, Orkney and Shetland. Its origins lie in the early IRON AGE (from c.700 BC), but brochs were common in the 1st centuries BC and AD. Compared with WHEELHOUSES, they may represent élite dwellings. *See also* PREHISTORIC BRITAIN, HOUSING.

BRONZE AGE, BRITAIN The period c.2300– c.700 BC, when copper, bronze and gold artefacts were produced. Developing out of the NEOLITHIC, it is often divided into Early (to c.1600 BC), Middle (to c.1200 BC) and Late phases. Evidence for the Early Bronze Age is dominated by STONE CIRCLES, rock art, ROUND BARROWS and HENGE MONUMENTS. Later phases are commonly traced through field systems and other land divisions. Increasingly varied forms of metalwork – weaponry, tools and bodily ornaments – were used, displayed and circulated during the period. Succeeded by the IRON AGE.

BRONZE AGE, IRELAND The period c.2300–to c.700 BC, often divided into Early (to c.1700 BC), Middle (to c.1200 BC) and Late phases. Apart from the many metal objects that give the period its name, the earlier phases are marked by single burials containing food vessels and cinerary urns, while the later phase has few burials but numerous settlements. It developed from, and overlapped with, the CHALCOLITHIC PERIOD and was succeeded by the IRON AGE.

BROOKE, ALAN (b. 23 July 1883 at Bagnères-de-Bigorre, France; d. 17 June 1963 at Hartley Wintney, Hampshire, England, aged 79). A soldier in the British Army, Brooke became chief of the imperial general staff in Dec. 1941, playing a major part in formulating Allied strategy in WORLD WAR II. His relations with Prime Minister Winston CHURCHILL were stormy but productive. In 1945 he retired and was created Lord Alanbrooke (created Viscount Alanbrooke 1946).

BROOKE, BASIL (b. 9 June 1888 at Colebrooke Park, Co. Fermanagh, Ireland; d. 18 Aug. 1973 at Colebrooke Park, Northern Ireland, aged 85). Brooke succeeded as baronet in 1907, and was an ULSTER UNIONIST PARTY member of Northern Ireland's House of Commons 1929–68. As prime minister, from 1 May 1943, he increased war-related industrial production (1943–5) and co-operated with the social policies of Britain's post-war Labour government (1945–51), introducing free health care and secondary education (1946–8). After southern Ireland became a republic (1949) he obtained the Ireland Act, whereby the UK Parliament guaranteed Northern Ireland's position within the UK. Brooke sought to maintain Unionist cohesion and ignored Catholic grievances, perpetuating sectarianism. Northern Ireland's longest-serving prime minister, he resigned (25 March 1963) because of increasing unemployment and the electoral threat from the Northern Ireland Labour Party. He was created Viscount Brookeborough (1952). *See also* NORTHERN IRELAND; WELFARE STATE.

BROOKEBOROUGH, VISCOUNT *see* BROOKE, BASIL

BROOKE FAMILY The English family who ruled Sarawak in BORNEO, 1842–1946. James Brooke (1803–68), a soldier and adventurer, helped to suppress a rebellion in the Sarawak River area (1840). In return, he was made governor (1841) by a local rajah (prince) and then installed as rajah (1842), under the overlordship of the sultan of Brunei. Ruling with a government of natives and white officers, he introduced laws, encouraged trade, countered piracy, and explored the interior. He received the island of Labuan (1846), and additional land (1862).

James Brooke was succeeded in 1868 by his nephew Charles Brooke (1829–1917). He acquired more lands from the sultan of Brunei, and in 1888 allowed Sarawak to become a British PROTECTORATE. In the early 20th century he encouraged rubber cultivation. In 1917 he was succeeded by his son Vyner Brooke (1874–1963), who developed oil and introduced a written constitution (Sept. 1941) but was forced out by the Japanese (Sarawak occupied 1941–5). He ceded Sarawak to Britain in 1946. The Brookes were nicknamed 'white rajahs'.

BROUGHAM, HENRY (b. 19 Sept. 1778 at Edinburgh, Scotland; d. 7 May 1868 at Cannes, France, aged 89). British WHIG politician, lawyer and popular educator. Brougham was a Whig MP 1810–12 and from 1816. He won popularity defending Queen CAROLINE (1820). Created Lord Brougham and appointed lord CHANCELLOR in 1830, he piloted the Great Reform Act through the House of Lords (1832). After losing office in 1834, he was never reappointed. (Lord MELBOURNE found his vanity insufferable.) Brougham wrote on numerous subjects and designed the four-wheeled horse-drawn carriage named after him. *See also* PARLIAMENTARY REFORM.

BROWN, GEORGE (b. 2 Sept. 1914 at Lambeth, London, England; d. 2 June 1985 at Truro, Cornwall, England, aged 70). A van driver's son, Brown became a trade unionist and LABOUR PARTY activist. Elected as an MP in 1945, he opposed the BEVANITES (1950s) and served as deputy leader of the Party (1960–70). Harold WILSON appointed him (1964) as the first economic affairs secretary, charged with economic planning and modernization of industry. He was British foreign secretary from 1966, but resigned (15 March 1968) over Wilson's failure to consult him. Volatile and fond of drink, Brown lost his seat in 1970 and was created Lord George-Brown. He joined the SOCIAL DEMOCRATIC PARTY in 1985.

BROWN, GORDON (b. 20 Feb. 1951 at Glasgow, Scotland). Leader of the LABOUR PARTY and British prime minister 2007–2010.

A student politician (at EDINBURGH University), lecturer and journalist, Brown became a Labour MP (1983) and Opposition spokesman. Though ambitious, he did not contest the 1992 Party leadership election; in 1994 he stood aside for rival Tony BLAIR (*see* GRANITA ACCORD).

As chancellor of the Exchequer in Blair's government from 1997, Brown delegated control of interest rates to the BANK OF ENGLAND and created the Financial Services Authority to regulate financial companies. Prioritizing economic stability, he regularly claimed to have abolished cycles of 'boom and bust'. Against Blair, he blocked entry to the euro (European currency), and considerably directed domestic policy (e.g., introducing TAX CREDITS). He sought trade union support against Blair's more inclusive approach

(*see* SPENCE AFFAIR). The government divided into 'Brownites' and 'Blairites'.

When Blair resigned under pressure in 2007, the Labour Party enabled Brown to become leader without opposition. Succeeding as prime minister, he failed to exploit public popularity by holding a general election. In 2008–9 an international financial crisis triggered bank failures, increased unemployment and inflated the government's deficit. Labour lost the 2010 election; Brown resigned as prime minister and Party leader. He left Parliament in 2015. *See also* MANDELSON, PETER; CAMERON, DAVID.

BROWNE, GEORGE (fl. from 1520s in England; d. after 25 Nov. 1556 in Ireland). Religious reformer in Ireland. Originally a friar and priest in England, Browne from 1532 advocated annulment of Henry VIII's marriage. At Easter 1533, during a sermon in London, he revealed Henry's remarriage (to Anne Boleyn; *see* GREAT MATTER). He supported royal supremacy over the English Church.

Appointed archbishop of DUBLIN in 1536, Browne went to Ireland where he publicized Henry's headship of the Irish Church (1538, in prescribed prayers called 'The Form of the Beads') and issued injunctions against 'superstitious' practices (e.g., pilgrimages to shrines). But he resisted further reforms under Edward VI (1547–53), and was deprived of his archbishopric (1554) by the Catholic Mary I for an earlier marriage (1536–c.1540). Browne obtained a pardon for misdemeanours from Cardinal POLE (1555) and died a Catholic. *See also* REFORMATION, IRELAND.

BROWNISTS Term used in England from the 1580s to mid 17th century for members of 'separatist' Church congregations (i.e., independent Protestant congregations outside the Church of ENGLAND). They were named after Robert Browne (c.1550–1633), who founded a congregation at NORWICH (E England) in 1581 (transferred to Netherlands 1582). Leaders were usually radical Puritans, and congregations were persecuted. *See also* PURITANISM, ENGLAND; CONGREGATIONALISTS; NONCONFORMITY AND DISSENT, ENGLAND.

BRUCE, EDWARD *see* BRUCE INVASION OF IRELAND

BRUCE FAMILY A Scottish noble and royal family from NW NORMANDY (N France); descendants of Robert de Brius (now Brix) who received lands in NE England from King HENRY I of England and the lordship of Annandale (SW Scotland) from King DAVID I of Scotland in 1124. In 1291 Robert Bruce (1210–95) claimed the Scottish kingship (as grandson of David, earl of HUNTINGDON; *see* GREAT CAUSE). His grandson Robert, and Robert's son David, ruled Scotland (*see* ROBERT I; DAVID II).

BRUCE INVASION OF IRELAND A Scottish attempt to conquer the English colony in Ireland, thereby pressurizing King EDWARD II of England on a 'second front'; led by Edward Bruce (c.1275–1318), brother of King ROBERT I.

Bruce landed at Larne, NE Ireland, on 26 May 1315 and was crowned king of Ireland shortly afterwards. His main supporter was Domnall O'Neill of Ulster (*see* O'NEILL FAMILIES), who rebutted papal condemnation with a 'Remonstrance of the Irish Princes' (1317). Expeditions into English-held lands (1315–16, 1317, 1318) won little support because the Anglo-Irish viewed Bruce as an Irish king. He was killed on 14 Oct. 1318 during the battle of Faughart (E Ireland). The invasion permanently reduced revenues received by the English colony's government. *See also* SCOTTISH–ENGLISH RELATIONS 1290–1357; GAELIC REVIVAL, IRELAND 13TH–15TH CENTURIES.

BRUCE KINGS *see* BRUCE FAMILY

BRUNANBURH, BATTLE OF Fought at an unidentified location in NE England or the E Midlands in 937. West Saxons and Mercians (English), led by King ATHELSTAN, defeated an invading army led by Kings CONSTANTINE II of Scotland, Owain of STRATHCLYDE, and Olaf Guthfrithson of DUBLIN. The invasion was probably revenge for Athelstan's invasion of Scotland (934) and intended to enable Olaf to re-establish the Viking kingdom of YORK.

BRUNEI PROTECTORATE *see* BORNEO

BRUNEL, ISAMBARD KINGDOM (b. 9 April 1806 at Portsmouth, Hampshire, England; d. 15 Sept. 1859 at Westminster, Middlesex, England, aged 53). The son of Marc Isambard Brunel (1769–1849), a French royalist émigré civil engineer, Brunel was educated in England and France. In England from 1822, he worked from 1825 as assistant engineer on his father's Thames tunnel at London, but suffered injury (1828). While recovering at Clifton (near BRISTOL, SW England), he won a design competition for a bridge across the Avon Valley (completed posthumously).

In 1833, aged 27, Brunel was appointed chief engineer of the Great Western Railway, for which he constructed over 1000 mi (1600 km) of 'broad gauge' track and innovatory structures (e.g., Saltash Bridge). He also designed three pioneering large steamships: SS *Great Western* (inaugurated 1838), the first successful trans-Atlantic steamship (paddle-driven); *Great Britain* (1845), the first large iron-hulled and screw-propelled steamship; *Great Eastern* (1859), the first ship with a double iron hull. Brunel was one of Great Britain's greatest civil engineers. *See also* RAILWAYS, ENGLAND; ENGINEERING, GREAT BRITAIN.

BRUTON, JOHN (b. 18 May 1947 at Dunboyne, Co. Meath, southern Ireland). A barrister and farmer, Bruton became a FINE GAEL TD (1969) and served in the governments of Liam COSGRAVE (1973–7) and Garret FITZGERALD (1981–2, 1982–7). In 1990 he was elected party leader, succeeding Alan Dukes with whom Fine Gael TDs had become dissatisfied.

In Dec. 1994, following collapse of the FIANNA FÁIL–LABOUR coalition government of Albert REYNOLDS, Bruton became taoiseach (premier) of a coalition with Labour and the Democratic Left, nicknamed the 'Rainbow Coalition' (Ireland's first instance of a new coalition government formed without a general election). During Bruton's premiership divorce was legalized by referendum (1995), economic growth accelerated (reaching 10% in 1997), and the Northern Ireland PEACE PROCESS was pursued vigorously. Bruton lost office in 1997 because of Labour's losses in a general election. He was replaced as party leader in 2001 for fear that Fine Gael would perform badly at the 2002 election. *See also* SOCIAL PARTNERSHIP; AHERN, BERTIE.

BRUT Y TYWYSOGION (Welsh, meaning 'Chronicle of the Princes'). A late 13th-century chronicle, in Middle Welsh; an outstanding source for Welsh history 682–1282. Three versions survive, probably separate translations of a lost version of the *ANNALES CAMBRIAE*. At least one came from STRATA FLORIDA.

BRYCHEINIOG An early medieval kingdom in WALES (5th or 6th–10th centuries); later a lordship in the MARCH OF WALES (11th–16th centuries) based around the upper R. Usk and encircled by mountainous terrain. It was named after Brychan, a legendary Irish immigrant (5th or 6th century).

An Irish-style CRANNOG at Llangorse (possibly the seat of Brycheiniog's kings) and Irish OGHAM stone inscriptions give plausibility to the legend of Irish foundation. Brycheiniog is mentioned from the mid 8th century. Around 885 King Elise ap Tewdwr, under pressure from the dynasty of RHODRI MAWR of GWYNEDD, submitted to the overlordship of King ALFRED of WESSEX (SW England). But relations with England were sometimes stormy (e.g., in 916 ÆTHELFLÆD attacked Llangorse, capturing the king's wife and 33 others). The dynasty survived until the 930s: the last known king, Tewdwr, submitted to ATHELSTAN in 934. By the 980s Brycheiniog had fallen to DEHEUBARTH (SW Wales).

In 1093 King RHYS AP TEWDWR of Deheubarth was killed in Brycheiniog by NORMANS – probably followers of BERNARD OF NEUFMARCHÉ, who took over Brycheiniog and founded the lordship of Brecon. It passed to the earls of Hereford (c.1125), to the families of BRAOSE (c.1165) and BOHUN (1241), and eventually (1399) to the duchy of

LANCASTER. In 1536 Brecon was combined with BUILTH to form Breconshire. *See also* IRISH COLONIZATION OF BRITAIN, 4TH–6TH CENTURIES.

B SPECIALS *see* ULSTER SPECIAL CONSTABULARY

BUCHANAN, GEORGE (b. Feb. 1506 at Moss, C Scotland; d. 29 Sept. 1582 at Edinburgh, SE Scotland, aged 76). In 1538 Buchanan, a private tutor who had studied at French and Scottish universities, was imprisoned by David BEATON for writing a satire on Franciscan FRIARS (commissioned by King JAMES V). He escaped abroad (1539) and was imprisoned for heresy (Protestantism) in Portugal (1548–51).

In Scotland again from 1561, Buchanan became tutor to MARY, QUEEN OF SCOTS. He accepted Protestantism (*see* REFORMATION, SCOTLAND), and though a layman was moderator of the General Assembly of the Church of SCOTLAND (June 1567). In the MARIAN CIVIL WAR after Mary's forced abdication (1568–73) he supported JAMES VI's party, and was tutor to the king (1570–8). Buchanan developed views about limited monarchy to justify Mary's deposition, which remained politically controversial well into the 17th century. He was also the first to claim, in his 20-volume (Latin) *History of Scotland*, that the Scots, Welsh and Irish were Celts (*see* CELTIC CULTURE). *See also* HUMANISM.

BUCKINGHAM, DUKE OF (b. 28 Aug. 1592 at Brooksby, Leicestershire, England; d. 23 Aug. 1628 at Portsmouth, Hampshire, England, aged 35). George Villiers met King JAMES VI/I in 1614. Knighted in 1615, he replaced the earl of SOMERSET as royal favourite and became influential. He was created Viscount Villiers (1616), earl of Buckingham (Jan. 1617), appointed a privy councillor (Feb.) and raised to marquess (1618) and duke (1623). In 1623 Buckingham accompanied James's heir Charles to Spain (*see* SPANISH MATCH). His subsequent demand (1624) for war against Spain won popularity. But an expedition against Catholic Habsburg forces in Germany, Jan.–March 1625, failed.

Buckingham's continuing influence after the accession of CHARLES I (1625) caused Parliament to limit further funds (summer). After a naval expedition against Cádiz, Spain, failed (Oct.), Parliament attempted to impeach Buckingham (May 1626). Charles dissolved Parliament and ordered a FORCED LOAN. Buckingham led a naval expedition to aid French Protestants in La Rochelle, to weaken France (July–Nov. 1627). After its failure Parliament attacked Buckingham in a remonstrance (June 1628). Buckingham was murdered by John Felton, a discontented soldier.

BUCKINGHAM PALACE The principal LONDON residence of monarchs of Great Britain and Northern Ireland. It is the second royal residence on its site. The first was Buckingham House (built 1702–5), which was acquired in 1762 by King GEORGE III and renamed the Queen's House, for Queen Charlotte.

GEORGE IV, king from 1820 (formerly prince regent, resident at Carlton House), thought the monarchy required a more imposing residence. The government funded a new palace (1825–30, 1832–7), designed by John Nash and completed by Edward Blore. It comprised three ranges of buildings round a courtyard with a triumphal arch on the east side. The palace was occupied by VICTORIA (from 1837) and subsequent monarchs.

The east side was enclosed with a building in 1846–50 (and the 'Marble Arch' relocated). In 1913 a new façade was added to the east range (designed by Aston Webb), providing an imposing public frontage. The palace is used for numerous State occasions. The State Apartments were opened annually to visitors from 1993.

BUCKINGHAM PALACE CONFERENCE In Great Britain, a meeting of British and Irish political leaders at Buckingham Palace, LONDON, 21–24 July 1914. It was called by King GEORGE V, at the British government's request, in response to the situation in Ireland: supporters and opponents of Home Rule had armed themselves in anticipation of its introduction. The Conference failed because Irish nationalists (John REDMOND, John DILLON) and Unionists (E.H. CARSON, James CRAIG) could not agree a scheme for the exclusion of ULSTER (N Ireland). *See also* HOME RULE MOVEMENT, IRELAND.

BUCKINGHAMSHIRE, 2ND EARL OF (b. 17 Aug. 1723 at Greenwich, Kent, England; d. 3 Sept. 1793 at Blickling Hall, Norfolk, England, aged 70). John Hobart succeeded as earl in 1756, and in 1777 was sent to Ireland as chief governor (lord lieutenant). He encountered unrest caused by British restrictions on food exports (imposed 1776, to help the British Army in the AMERICAN WAR OF INDEPENDENCE). The crisis worsened; Buckinghamshire faced the rise of the VOLUNTEERS and of the NON-IMPORTATION MOVEMENT (1779), and Parliament's refusal to grant new taxes (Nov. 1779). He proved unable to master the situation, and the British government was forced to lift trade restrictions (1780). Buckinghamshire was recalled in late 1780. *See also* PROTESTANT ASCENDANCY.

BUCKINGHAMSHIRE ELECTION AFFAIR In England, a crisis in 1604, after the accession of King JAMES VI/I, when the Court of CHANCERY annulled the election of Francis Goodwin as an MP for Buckinghamshire (because he was an outlaw). The House of Commons challenged James's referral of the matter to the Court (March). A new election was held, with James conceding that the House was entitled to settle disputed elections (11 April). *See also* PARLIAMENTARY PRIVILEGE.

BUILTH A minor medieval kingdom in C WALES, first recorded *c*.800. In the 9th century its kings were said to rule over the neighbouring Gwerthrynion and claimed descent from VORTIGERN. Builth was ruled in the late 11th century as a CANTREF by descendants of RHODRI MAWR. Its name (Welsh, Buellt, from *bu* and *gelt*) means 'cow pasture'.

Builth was among the first lordships established by NORMANS in Wales: it was conquered *c*.1095 by Philip de BRAOSE, lord of Radnor. The lordship, though small, was important: its castle guarded the route from England into C Wales along the Wye Valley. In 1228 Builth passed as dowry to DAFYDD AP LLYWELYN of Gwynedd when he married Isabel Braose.

Builth was among the first Welsh lands taken by King HENRY III of England in 1241. It subsequently passed between Henry (later EDWARD I) and LLYWELYN AP GRUFFUDD of Gwynedd according to political fortunes, until 1277 when the English established control and rebuilt the castle. Thereafter the lordship was leased to Marcher families, notably the MORTIMERS, and was included in Breconshire in 1536; *see* UNION OF WALES WITH ENGLAND.

BULGARIAN ATROCITIES Name given to the brutal reprisals which Turkish leaders took against a revolt by Bulgarian guerrillas in May 1876. In Great Britain, reports of massacres brought the EASTERN QUESTION to the forefront of politics (1876–80). While the Conservative prime minister, Benjamin DISRAELI, persisted in supporting the OTTOMAN EMPIRE, the Liberal W.E. GLADSTONE conducted a campaign of moral outrage, demanding expulsion of the Turks from Europe.

BUNYAN, JOHN (b. Nov. 1628 at Elstow, Bedfordshire, England; d. 31 Aug. 1688 at London, England, aged 59). After fighting in a Parliamentary army 1644–6 (during the First CIVIL WAR), Bunyan became a Puritan, author, and preacher at an Independent church in Bedford in the mid 1650s. Following the RESTORATION of the monarchy (1660), he was regularly imprisoned.

Released under the 1672 Declaration of INDULGENCE, Bunyan preached widely in the Midlands and in London. His publications drew on his earlier religious conversion. They included *Grace Abounding* (1666) and *The Pilgrim's Progress* (2 parts, 1678, 1684). The latter became one of the most influential works in the English language. *See also* PURITANISM, ENGLAND; NONCONFORMITY AND DISSENT, ENGLAND.

BURDETT, FRANCIS (b. 25 Jan. 1770 at Foremark, Derbyshire, England; d. 23 Jan. 1844 at London, England, aged 73). An MP from 1796 (and baronet from 1797), Burdett was a FOXITE Whig until 1806. Increasingly radical thereafter, he became a leading national campaigner for PARLIAMENTARY REFORM (until 1820). He presented reform Bills to the UK Parliament in 1809, 1817 and 1818 (the last including manhood suffrage). He became a popular hero in 1810 when he was imprisoned for publishing a parliamentary speech (a breach of parliamentary privilege).

From 1825 Burdett campaigned for CATHOLIC EMANCIPATION. He remained an MP until his death, supporting the Conservatives from 1837.

BURGESS In England from the late 11th century, a male inhabitant of a TOWN (from OFr. *burgeis*, meaning 'town dweller'), implying the acquisition of liberties (e.g., as a tenement-holder) and belonging to a town's community. The term spread to other parts of the British Isles. As TOWN GOVERNMENT changed, the term acquired narrower meanings: either a man who had been admitted to a town's body of freemen (inhabitants entitled to trade, elect town officers and hold office) or a member of a town's self-perpetuating authority (or 'closed corporation'). (Non-burgess inhabitants were sometimes called 'foreigners'.) The term largely disappeared with the reform of town corporations, when authorities became composed of councillors – two-thirds elected, one-third aldermen elected by other councillors (Scotland, 1833; England and Wales, 1835; Ireland, 1840).

BURGESS, THOMAS (b. 18 Nov. 1756 at Odiham, Hampshire, England; d. 19 Feb. 1837 at Salisbury, Wiltshire, England, aged 80). As bishop of ST DAVIDS 1803–25, Burgess strove to improve the Church of England in Wales. In 1822 he founded St David's College, Lampeter (Cardiganshire), which raised the educational standard of clergy. He also encouraged clergy interested in Welsh literature and supported Welsh cultural societies. He was bishop of Salisbury (England) 1825–37. *See also* UNIVERSITIES, WALES.

BURGH Term for an urban settlement in Scotland, with privileges of trade and self-government; the term is derived from OE *burh* (*see* BURH).

The earliest burghs were royal foundations, started by King DAVID I (ruled 1124–53). By 1306 there were 38 royal burghs (many the heads of SHERIFFDOMS and alongside castles), and 18 non-royal burghs (founded by churchmen or secular lords). From the late 14th century older foundations encouraged a distinction between 'royal burghs' (including some Church burghs) and 'burghs of barony', recent or new towns founded by secular lords. Royal burghs managed to establish monopolies of trade in their areas or 'liberties' and of foreign trade, in return for contributions to taxation. (Baronial burghs monopolized trade only within their boundaries.) Royal burghs co-ordinated policy, allocated taxation and encouraged uniformity in town government through the Court of the FOUR BURGHS and CONVENTION

OF ROYAL BURGHS. Their independent and influential position within the political framework was unique in Europe.

New baronial burghs were founded in the 15th century, and some 270 between 1500 and c.1720, challenging the position of royal burghs; they lost their monopoly of foreign trade in 1672. In the 19th century burghs and populous places lacking burgh status could adopt powers under 'Police Acts' (1833–67) and be classified as 'police burghs'.

In 1929 surviving burghs were reorganized into three categories (effective from 1930): cities (ABERDEEN, DUNDEE, EDINBURGH, GLASGOW), large burghs (19), and small burghs (178). Burghs were abolished in 1975. *See also* TOWN GOVERNMENT, SCOTLAND; TOWN SOCIETY, SCOTLAND.

BURGH, HUBERT DE (b. c.1170, probably in Norfolk, England; d. May 1243 at Banstead, Surrey, England, aged about 73). In the 1190s de Burgh entered the service of Prince JOHN (king from 1199) and was seneschal of Poitou 1212–15. Having remained loyal during the crisis of 1215, he was appointed CHIEF JUSTICIAR as someone acceptable to John's opponents (by 25 June).

After John's death (Oct. 1216), de Burgh supported the accession of HENRY III, a minor, and remained justiciar. From Oct. 1221 he was pre-eminent in the government, having sidelined Peter des ROCHES. He also married Margaret, sister of ALEXANDER II of Scotland (his second marriage).

After Henry took power (Jan. 1227), he made de Burgh earl of Kent (Feb.) and confirmed the justiciarship for life (1228). But on 29 July 1232 Henry dismissed de Burgh for allegedly inciting anti-Italian riots. Imprisoned, he later escaped and was pardoned. *See also* BURGH OR BURKE FAMILY, IRELAND.

BURGHAL HIDAGE Name given to a memorandum which lists: (a) 30 BURHS (fortified places), mainly in WESSEX (S England), (b) the HIDES allocated for the maintenance and manning of each burh's defences (due from estates). It probably dates from after 914 (in the reign of EDWARD THE ELDER). The list demonstrates the sophistication of royal government in Anglo-Saxon England. *See also* THREE PUBLIC SERVICES.

BURGH OR BURKE FAMILY, IRELAND An Anglo-Irish noble family, descended from the Englishman William de Burgh (d. 1205) who arrived in Ireland in 1185 (with Prince JOHN) and received land in MUNSTER (S Ireland, 1185) and title to CONNACHT (W Ireland, c.1194). His son Richard (d. 1243) was granted most of Connacht (1227, forfeited 1232–4). Richard's second successor Walter (d. 1271) received the earldom of Ulster in 1263 from the Lord Edward (*see* EDWARD I AND IRELAND). His son Richard, the 'Red Earl' (c.1259–1326, minor until 1280),

was pre-eminent in Ireland and fought the BRUCE INVASION. Richard's grandson and successor William de Burgh (1312–33) left an heiress who married Lionel, son of King EDWARD III. Lionel was recognized as earl of Ulster and was later sent to Ireland (*see* IRELAND, ENGLISH EXPEDITIONS TO, LATE 14TH CENTURY).

After the murder of William de Burgh (1333), most of his estates in Connacht were retained by kinsmen who established their own landed families. By the mid 15th century Gaelicized Burgh families were predominant in Connacht. Later descendants included the earls of Clanricarde (descendants of Ulick de Burgh, created earl 1543, d. 1544) and the political philosopher Edmund BURKE.

BURGH REFORM ACTS Two Acts of the UK Parliament, 1833, which reformed town government in Scotland. They followed the first Scottish REFORM ACT (1832) and preceded the MUNICIPAL CORPORATIONS ACT for England and Wales (1835). The Royal Burghs (Scotland) Act instituted elected councils in royal burghs using the burgh franchise introduced in 1832 for parliamentary elections, thus ending 'closed corporations' (self-perpetuating councils). The Parliamentary Burghs (Scotland) Act implemented similar arrangements in newly created parliamentary burghs. *See also* TOWN GOVERNMENT, SCOTLAND.

BURGUNDY, ENGLISH RELATIONS WITH In the late 14th and 15th centuries the Valois dukes of Burgundy, with lands in France and the Netherlands, were important for England, which had strong economic ties with the Netherlands. There were four dukes: Philip the Bold (duke 1363–1404), John the Fearless (1404–19); Philip the Good (1419–67), Charles the Bold (1467–77). After Charles's death, the Burgundian lands were contested. Charles's heiress, Mary, married Maximilian of Austria (1477), and eventually the main northern lands (Artois, Flanders) were annexed to the HABSBURG EMPIRE (1493).

In France, a quarrel from 1404 between John the Fearless and Louis, duke of Orléans, developed into civil war between so-called 'Burgundians' and 'Armagnacs' (1410). The dissension facilitated King HENRY V's invasion of France (1415; *see* HUNDRED YEARS WAR). After John the Fearless was murdered (1419) by agents of the French dauphin (heir to the king), Philip the Good allied with the English and affirmed the treaty of TROYES (1420). The alliance was strengthened by marriage of Philip's sister Anne to John, duke of BEDFORD (1423), but endangered when Humphrey, duke of GLOUCESTER, sought lands in the Netherlands claimed by Philip (1424–5). Philip abandoned the alliance in 1435 (*see* ARRAS, CONGRESS OF).

In 1468 EDWARD IV of England made a marriage alliance, whereby his sister Margaret of York (1446–1503) married Charles the Bold. Edward and Charles agreed

(1474) that Edward would invade France in pursuit of the English claim to the French Crown and cede territory to Charles. Though invasion followed (1475), Edward was bought off by the French king (*see* PICQUIGNY, TREATY OF).

Margaret became dowager duchess when Charles the Bold died (1477). Following the accession of HENRY VII in England (1485), her court was a place of refuge (until 1496) for Henry's YORKIST opponents, and she supported Perkin WARBECK.

BURH OE term for a fortified centre. It was notably used for the forts and fortified towns founded by King ALFRED (ruled 871–99) to defend WESSEX (S England) against VIKINGS. More burhs were founded by EDWARD THE ELDER (ruled 899–924) and ÆTHELFLÆD (ruler of MERCIA 911–18).

During the 10th century 'burh' became increasingly synonymous with royal urban centres with mints and markets. By the 14th century it had developed into the ME term BOROUGH, which often denoted a self-governing town. *See also* BURGHAL HIDAGE; TOWN GOVERNMENT, ENGLAND.

BURKE, EDMUND (b. 1 Jan. 1729 or 1730 at Dublin, Ireland; d. 9 July 1797 at Beaconsfield, Buckinghamshire, England, aged 67 or 68). After graduating from Trinity College, Dublin, and studying law in England (from 1750), Burke became a prolific writer. He was secretary to the 2nd marquess of ROCKINGHAM from 1764, and an MP 1765–94, mostly in opposition. His rhetoric much influenced the ROCKINGHAM WHIGS. Burke himself attacked the alleged 'secret influence' of the Crown; he advocated conciliation with the rebellious N American colonies in the 1760s–70s; and as paymaster-general in 1782 he achieved some ECONOMICAL REFORM. Also interested in India, in 1787 he instigated the impeachment of Warren HASTINGS.

Burke is best known for his *Reflections on the Revolution in France* (1790), a denunciation which became an influential expression of CONSERVATISM. *See also* BURGH OR BURKE FAMILY, IRELAND; FRENCH REVOLUTION, IMPACT ON ENGLAND.

BURMA A former British territory in SE Asia. British India annexed the kingdom of Burma in three stages: after wars in 1824–6, 1852 and 1885. Burma was governed as a province of INDIA until 1937, when it became a separate CROWN COLONY with limited self-government. The British expanded rice growing and forestry. Burma was occupied by the Japanese 1942–5, during WORLD WAR II, though part was recaptured in 1945. Independence was granted in 1948, when Burma became a republic outside the COMMONWEALTH. It changed its name to Myanmar in 1989. Approx. population in 1921, 13,212,000; in 1947, 18,000,000. *See also* ORWELL, GEORGE; WINGATE, ORDE.

BURNET, ALEXANDER (bap. 6 Aug. 1615 at Edinburgh, SE Scotland; d. 22 Aug. 1684 at St Andrews, Scotland, aged 69). Burnet served as a priest in the Church of England until ejected by Parliamentarians for Royalist sympathies (1650). After the RESTORATION (1660) he was appointed bishop of ABERDEEN (1663), then archbishop of GLASGOW (1664). Although he implemented government policy by persecuting COVENANTERS in W Scotland, he opposed the 1669 Act of Supremacy (making the king head of the Church of SCOTLAND) and was deposed. He was restored in 1674 and became archbishop of ST ANDREWS in 1679.

BURNS, JOHN (b. 20 Oct. 1858 at London, England; d. 24 Jan. 1943 at London, aged 84). Burns, who left school aged ten, was an Independent Labour MP 1892–1918. He co-operated with the Liberals, and became the first working-class member of the British CABINET as president of the Local Government Board (1905–14, serving under Henry CAMPBELL-BANNERMAN and H.H. ASQUITH). Opposition to war prompted his resignation in Aug. 1914 (*see* WORLD WAR I).

BURNS, ROBERT (b. 25 Jan. 1759 at Alloway, Ayrshire, Scotland; d. 21 July 1796 at Dumfries, Dumfriesshire, Scotland, aged 37). Scotland's national poet. A son of a market gardener (later farmer), Burns became famous with the publication of *Poems, Chiefly in the Scottish Dialect* (1786) and was lionized by EDINBURGH literati. He also collected folk songs and wrote songs to old tunes. After failing as a farmer, he was an EXCISE man in Dumfries (from 1791). His works satirize social divisions and CALVINISM, and celebrate love. From 1801 Burns clubs were founded, which began the tradition of holding 'Burns suppers' on the poet's birthday, celebrated with poetry, songs and speeches. *See also* SCOTS LANGUAGE AND LITERATURE.

BURTON, RICHARD (b. 19 March 1821 at Torquay, Devon, England; d. 20 Oct. 1890 at Trieste, Austro-Hungarian Empire, aged 69). After working in India for the EAST INDIA COMPANY (1842–9), Burton became an explorer. He visited the Muslim cities of Mecca and Medina (in modern Saudi Arabia) in 1853, and explored NE Africa in 1855. While seeking sources of the White Nile in E Africa, 1857–8, he discovered Lake Tanganyika (his collaborator John Speke found Lake Victoria, a Nile source). In 1861 Burton explored the GOLD COAST (W Africa). From 1861 Burton worked for the British consular service. He was a prolific author and translator. *See also* NILE, BRITISH INTERESTS.

BUSINESS ORGANIZATION Most businesses in the British Isles have been controlled by a single operator (so-called 'sole trader', e.g., farmer, merchant, manufacturer) with unlimited liability for debts. Partnerships (typically with family or friends) have also existed, particularly in trade and industry (again with unlimited liability). In the 12th–16th centuries town craftsmen and traders often belonged to GUILDS; they regulated rather than conducted economic activity. Likewise, most OVERSEAS TRADING COMPANIES (from 14th century) regulated merchants.

JOINT-STOCK COMPANIES were formed in England from 1553 (1567 in Scotland), capitalized by shareholders with transferable shares, and managed by directors and officers. Most received legal corporate status through a Crown charter. Mainly from the late 17th century, companies were also formed under articles of association. In Scotland, the Council for Trade, established 1661, authorized companies and granted privileges (to over 50 undertakings, 1661–1707). Companies developed ways to limit risks (e.g., in 18th century by vesting assets in trustees). Following the SOUTH SEA BUBBLE, the 1720 'Bubble Act' (for Great Britain) discouraged formation of joint-stock companies by requiring a charter or legislation. It was unenforced in Scotland, where some legal personality also became recognized for partnerships (retaining unlimited liability).

Repeal of the Bubble Act in 1825 reauthorized joint-stock companies without charter or legislation. From 1844, UK companies could be incorporated by registration, and from 1856 most registered companies could declare LIMITED LIABILITY (using abbreviation 'Ltd'). Registration was compulsory for larger companies from 1862. From the 1880s many partnerships became limited-liability companies; public companies (with publicly traded shares) generally adopted limited liability. UK companies increased from 9300 in 1885 to 62,700 in 1914.

Legislation affecting partnerships began in 1890; company legislation was consolidated in 1908. From 1974 'public limited companies' were distinguished (as 'PLCs') from private companies. After 1921, Northern and southern Ireland developed their own company law (former reintegrated with UK 2006).

BUTE, 3RD EARL OF (b. 25 May 1713 at Edinburgh, SE Scotland; d. 10 March 1792 at London, England, aged 78). John Stuart succeeded as earl in 1723 and lived in England from 1745. In 1747 he met FREDERICK, PRINCE OF WALES (son of King GEORGE II), while attending horse races and became a favourite of the prince (d. 1751) and a confidant of his son George.

After George became king (1760; see GEORGE III), he appointed Bute as (northern) SECRETARY OF STATE (March 1761). Bute also entered the House of Lords as a Scottish representative peer. By Nov. he was chief minister, and was appointed first lord of the Treasury in May 1762, succeeding the earl of NEWCASTLE. He sought to build a non-party ministry based on the KING'S FRIENDS.

Bute's ministry declared war on Spain (Jan. 1762), and negotiated the Peace of PARIS, ending the SEVEN YEARS WAR (Feb. 1763). Bute then removed the surviving ministers from Newcastle's administration. But he encountered resistance with a proposed CIDER TAX (1763). He was mercilessly satirized, especially by John WILKES. Worn down, he resigned in April 1763 (succeeded by George GRENVILLE).

The ROCKINGHAM WHIGS claimed that Bute's 'secret influence' undermined later ministries, but by 1765 he was politically inactive. See also BUTE FAMILY; PITT, WILLIAM, THE ELDER.

BUTE, 2ND MARQUESS OF (b. 10 Aug. 1793 at Dumfries House, Ayrshire, Scotland; d. 18 March 1848 at Cardiff, Glamorgan, Wales, aged 54). A great-grandson of the 3rd earl of BUTE, John Crichton Stuart inherited his grandfather's title and widespread estates in 1814, including CARDIFF and much of the S Wales coalfield. He built Cardiff's first substantial dock (opened 1839), inaugurating development that eventually resulted in Cardiff becoming the world's chief coal-exporting port. See also BUTE FAMILY; COAL INDUSTRY, WALES.

BUTE FAMILY A Scottish noble family (a branch of the STEWART FAMILY, descended from an illegitimate son of King ROBERT II); important in Great Britain in 18th–20th centuries. Members include the prime minister in 1762–3 (see BUTE, 3RD EARL OF).

In 1766 John Stuart (1744–1814), the 3rd earl's son and heir, married the heiress of the CARDIFF Castle estate (Glamorgan, Wales) and in 1796 was created marquess of Bute. His grandson and heir, John Crichton Stuart (1793–1848), invested heavily in Cardiff (see BUTE, 2ND MARQUESS OF). John Patrick Crichton Stuart (1847–1900), the 3rd marquess, considerably rebuilt Cardiff Castle, which was presented to Cardiff in 1947 by John Crichton Stuart (1907–56), the 5th marquess.

BUTLER, JOSEPHINE (b. 13 April 1828 at Glendale, Northumberland, England; d. 30 Dec. 1906 at Wooler, Northumberland, aged 78). From a landed background, Butler in the 1850s–60s helped poor women in OXFORD, Cheltenham and LIVERPOOL, and from the late 1860s campaigned for women's rights (e.g., education, property ownership). Convinced that the INDUSTRIAL REVOLUTION had disadvantaged women economically, she pressed reforming ideas in about 90 books and pamphlets. From 1869 she was a leading campaigner against the CONTAGIOUS DISEASES ACTS (repealed 1886) and female prostitution although she was critical of the coercive approach of the PURITY MOVEMENT.

BUTLER, 'RAB' (b. 9 Dec. 1902 at Attock Serai, Punjab, India; d. 8 March 1982 at Great Yeldham, Essex, England, aged 79). Richard Austen Butler (known as 'Rab') was a Conservative MP 1929–65, a minister in the British NATIONAL GOVERNMENT from 1931, and education minister (1941–5) in the wartime coalition. His name became associated with the 1944 Act that expanded secondary education (*see* BUTLER EDUCATION ACT).

After the war Butler led the Conservatives in adopting full employment and social security as central policies. The congruence with Labour was nicknamed 'BUTSKELLISM'. Butler became a central figure in Conservative governments. His offices included chancellor of the Exchequer (1951–5), lord PRIVY SEAL (1955–7), home secretary (1957–62) and foreign secretary (1963–4). Butler failed to obtain the Party leadership in 1957 and 1963. He was created Lord Butler in 1965. *See also* EDEN, ANTHONY; MACMILLAN, HAROLD.

BUTLER EDUCATION ACT Popular name for the Education Act of 1944, promoted by R.A. BUTLER, president of the Board of Education, and passed by the UK Parliament for England and Wales. It divided public education into primary, secondary and further, and required education authorities to plan and provide separate secondary schools for children of all abilities. The leaving age would be raised to 15 and later 16. Other provisions included school meals and free milk. Most authorities instituted 'multilateral' secondary education based on selection (usually at age 11) for GRAMMAR, 'modern' and sometimes technical schools (as recommended by the 'Spens Report' of 1939) although a few pursued COMPREHENSIVE EDUCATION. *See also* EDUCATION, ENGLAND/WALES.

BUTLER FAMILY, IRELAND An Anglo-Irish noble family. Its members were descended from Theobald Walter (d. 1205), who went to Ireland with Prince JOHN (1185), was given lands, and was appointed chief butler (by 1192). The post became hereditary and the family adopted the surname Butler.

In 1328 James, 7th butler (*c.*1305–38), was created earl of Ormond. He and his successors were dominant in E MUNSTER (S Ireland), and were rivalled in Ireland until the 16th century by only the 'Geraldine' earls of KILDARE and DESMOND (*see* BUTLER–GERALDINE FEUD). James Butler (1390–1452, 4th earl from 1405) feuded with the Talbot family (*see* TALBOT–ORMOND FEUD). The 5th, 6th and 7th earls lived mainly in England (1450s–1515). Butler influence in Ireland was revived by the 7th earl's cousin Piers Butler (*c.*1467–1539, 8th earl from 1515), who served as chief governor (lord deputy) 1522–4.

James Butler (1610–88) dominated Ireland in the 1640s and 1670s–80s and was created duke of Ormond in 1661 (*see* ORMOND, 12TH EARL OF). His grandson and successor James Butler (1665–1745) supported King WILLIAM

III and Queen ANNE, but became a Jacobite in 1715, after George I's accession, and fled abroad (Irish estates forfeited 1716). In 1721 his brother Charles Butler (1671–1758) was permitted to buy the estates and succeed as 3rd duke. He died without direct heir. The earldom of Ormond descended in another line into the 21st century. *See also* KILKENNY.

BUTLER–GERALDINE FEUD In Ireland, feuding between the BUTLER FAMILY (led by the earls of Ormond) and the GERALDINES (led by the earls of Kildare and Desmond) which frequently disrupted Anglo-Irish political life between the 1450s and 1560s. During the YORKIST–LANCASTRIAN CONFLICT in England (1450–90s), Butlers sympathized or allied with Lancastrians, Geraldines with Yorkists. In 1522–4 Geraldines undermined the 8th earl of Ormond's governorship. In the 1560s inter-party rivalry contributed to the First DESMOND REBELLION. *See also* KILDARE ASCENDANCY.

BUTSKELLISM Term denoting the consensus between leading members of the British LABOUR and CONSERVATIVE PARTIES in the 1950s in accepting the mixed economy (nationalized and private industry), WELFARE STATE and Keynesian economics (*see* KEYNES, J.M.). Formed from the names of 'Rab' BUTLER (Conservative) and Hugh GAITSKELL (Labour), the word first appeared in *The Economist* on 13 Feb. 1954.

BUTT, ISAAC (b. 6 Sept. 1813 at Glenfin, Co. Donegal, Ireland; d. 5 May 1879 near Dundrum, Co. Dublin, Ireland, aged 65). A (Protestant) economist and lawyer, Butt long supported the UNION OF IRELAND AND GREAT BRITAIN but was shocked by the British government's weak response to the GREAT FAMINE (1845–9). From 1852 to 1865, as a member of the UK Parliament (Conservative, then Liberal), he attempted unavailingly to reform landholding in Ireland. He also defended participants in the RISING OF 1848 and INSURRECTION OF 1867.

These experiences led Butt to promote 'Home Rule' (a separate Irish Parliament); in 1870 he founded the federalist HOME GOVERNMENT ASSOCIATION (superseded by the HOME RULE LEAGUE, 1873). He was re-elected to Parliament in 1871, but from 1875 was overshadowed by C.S. PARNELL. *See also* HOME RULE MOVEMENT, IRELAND.

BYNG, JOHN (b. Oct. 1704 at Southill, Bedfordshire, England; d. 14 March 1757 at Portsmouth, Hampshire, England, aged 52). A sailor from 1718, Byng held numerous British naval commands. In 1756, early in the SEVEN YEARS WAR, he was sent as commander with a fleet to defend MINORCA (W Mediterranean). After discovering that French troops had landed, and encountering a French fleet, he withdrew to GIBRALTAR. The British garrison on Minorca surrendered (June).

On returning to England Byng was arrested (July) and convicted of negligence (Jan. 1757), though recommended for clemency. King GEORGE II insisted on his execution (by firing squad). His role in the loss of Minorca was controversial. Many viewed him as a scapegoat for incompetence by the ministry of the duke of NEWCASTLE. The French writer Voltaire, who knew Byng, claimed his execution was simple brutality: an admiral was executed 'to encourage the others' (*Candide*, 1759).

BYRD, WILLIAM (b. 1542 or 1543, probably in London, England; d. 4 July 1623 at Stondon Massey, Essex, England, aged about 80). Though a Catholic, Byrd was a gentleman (lay singer) of the Chapel Royal (1572 until death) under the Protestant rulers ELIZABETH I and JAMES VI/I. From 1577 he lived outside London, in Middlesex, then in Essex (from 1590s). He composed music for the Church of ENGLAND as well as Catholic Mass settings and motets for RECUSANTS and secular music. He is regarded as the greatest English composer of his time. *See also* TALLIS, THOMAS.

C

CABAL In England, nickname of ministers who gained influence under King CHARLES II following the fall of the earl of CLARENDON in 1667, so-called from the initial letters of their names. They were: Sir Thomas Clifford, Lord ARLINGTON, the 2nd duke of Buckingham, Lord Ashley (later earl of SHAFTESBURY), and the earl of LAUDERDALE. They were not a cohesive group, and disagreed on policies, though they generally favoured religious toleration. Most lost office in 1673–4, when the earl of DANBY became pre-eminent.

CABINET Term for senior ministers of a country in a collective capacity (as a government or administration), or for a meeting of such ministers, usually chaired by a PRIME MINISTER. In England it derives from the practice by King CHARLES II (ruled 1660–85) of occasionally meeting a few ministers in a cabinet (a small, private room) for policy making, in preference to working with the larger PRIVY COUNCIL.

The nature and use of Cabinets developed markedly during the next 50 years. WILLIAM III (1689–1703) held regular meetings of both the Privy Council and some office-holders, the latter called a Cabinet-council (including officers of the royal household). He also sometimes allowed officers of State to meet separately. Queen ANNE considered the Cabinet-council more important than the Privy Council; a small subgroup also met to prepare recommendations (*see* LORDS OF THE COMMITTEE). Parliament was suspicious of Cabinets and prohibited their use by future rulers (Act of SETTLEMENT, 1701; clause repealed 1706).

Although GEORGE I (1714–27) initially continued arrangements, Robert WALPOLE, first lord of the Treasury and effectively prime minister, developed the small 'inner Cabinet' as the principal policy-making forum, under his chairmanship, eclipsing the royal court. Cabinet members included the lord CHANCELLOR, two SECRETARIES OF STATE and lord president of the Council. Their recommendations were conveyed to the king, who continued to appoint ministers. The Cabinet-council (or 'outer Cabinet') met occasionally into the 19th century.

In the 19th century the Cabinet became politically more homogeneous, with invariably party affiliation. It acquired strength from collective responsibility: ministers were expected to show support for policy agreed by the Cabinet when speaking in Parliament or meeting the king or queen. The prime minister appointed and dismissed ministers. Standing committees assisted Cabinet government from the later 19th century. Minute taking for public record began when David LLOYD GEORGE introduced a secretariat (1916). Cabinet size grew from 12 members under Benjamin DISRAELI (1874) to 20 under Stanley BALDWIN (1935). *See also* CLOSET; GOVERNMENT, GREAT BRITAIN 1707 TO LATER 18TH CENTURY; WAR CABINET; KITCHEN CABINET.

A Dictionary of British and Irish History, First Edition. Edited by Robert Peberdy and Philip Waller.
© 2021 John Wiley & Sons Ltd; © editorial matter and organisation Robert Peberdy and Phillip Waller.
Published 2021 by John Wiley & Sons Ltd.

CABOT, JOHN (b. *c.*1451 in Italy; d. 1498 at sea, aged about 47). An Italian seaman (Giovanni Caboto) who had probably met the trans-Atlantic explorer Christopher Columbus, Cabot moved to BRISTOL (SW England) *c.*1495 because inhabitants were interested in Atlantic exploration. In 1497, with support from Bristol merchants and authorization from King HENRY VII, he commanded the first English-sponsored trans-Atlantic voyage, probably seeking a westward route to Asia. Cabot landed on NEWFOUNDLAND (24 June), annexed territory for England, and discovered a rich fishery nearby. He began a second voyage in May 1498 only to disappear. *See also* NORTH AMERICA, ENGLISH EXPLORATION.

CADE'S REBELLION In England, a popular revolt against the government of King HENRY VI, particularly against followers of the duke of Suffolk (William de la POLE). It erupted in May 1450 in Kent and spread through southern England. Kentish rebels, led by the obscure Jack Cade, held LONDON 3–5 July. Following a battle on London bridge (5–6 July), many rebels withdrew. Cade was captured on 12 July and died soon afterwards. Disturbances continued until 1454. *See also* YORK, RICHARD DUKE OF.

CADWALLON AP CADFAN (fl. from *c.*600; d. 634 at Heavenfield, near Hexham, Bernicia). King of GWYNEDD (NW Wales) from *c.*625, involved with Anglo-Saxon kings.

In 633 Cadwallon, a Christian, with the pagan PENDA of MERCIA (C England), killed EDWIN of DEIRA and BERNICIA (NE England) at Hatfield Chase, ELMET (NE England). (Edwin had previously besieged Cadwallon on Priestholm island, off Anglesey, Gwynedd.) In 634 Cadwallon killed and supplanted Edwin's successors (Osric in Deira, Eanfrith in Bernicia), but was killed by OSWALD of Bernicia. *See also* ANGLO-WELSH RELATIONS, 6TH–13TH CENTURIES.

CAERNARFON A town in NW Wales, by the Menai Strait; centre of Gwynedd unitary authority; Welsh, meaning 'Fort in Arfon [CANTREF]'.

In 1283, following the English conquest of native Wales, a Welsh royal court (Welsh *llys*) and town were replaced by a castle and walled town, which served as the administrative centre for N Wales. English inhabitants predominated until the early 16th century. In the 19th century Caernarfon was notable for slate exporting (Victoria Dock built 1870s); *see* SLATE INDUSTRY, WALES. Caernarfon was the centre of Caernarfonshire 1284–1974, of Gwynedd county 1974–96. *See also* CHARLES, PRINCE OF WALES.

Est. popn: 1300, 300; 1600, 1200; 1800, 3500; 1900, 9000; 2000, 9000.

CAESAR, JULIUS (b. 12 July 100 BC, probably at or near Rome, Italy; d. 15 March 44 BC at Rome, aged 55). Gaius Julius Caesar was responsible for the Roman conquest of Gaul (58–51 BC) and the first Roman expeditions against Britain (55, 54 BC). His victory over his rival Pompey (48 BC), and subsequent campaigns, made him undisputed master of the Roman world until his assassination. He described his campaigns in Gaul and Britain in *The Gallic War. See also* CAESAR'S EXPEDITIONS; BELGAE.

CAESAR'S EXPEDITIONS The Roman general Julius CAESAR twice invaded SE Britain. His first campaign (55 BC) met with near disaster; he extricated his forces with difficulty after his fleet was destroyed on a Kentish beach by storms; but the exploit was hailed in Rome as a triumph. The second, larger, expedition (54 BC) experienced similar difficulties, but more genuine success, defeating a large native force led by CASSIVELLAUNUS. Before withdrawing, Caesar imposed a treaty on the south-eastern tribes, who promised hostages, tribute and obedience to Rome. *See also* IRON AGE TRIBES, BRITAIN.

CAIRD, JAMES (b. 10 June 1816 at Stranraer, Wigtownshire, Scotland; d. 9 Feb. 1892 at London, England, aged 75). Caird was a farmer 1841–60 and estate owner from 1860. He attracted attention in 1849 with his pamphlet *High Farming under Liberal Covenants*, which argued that efficient farmers with supportive landlords could flourish despite the recent repeal of the CORN LAWS. He also produced a comprehensive survey, *English Agriculture in 1850–1* (1852), following a commission from *The Times* newspaper. As an MP (Whig) 1857–65, Caird pressed the government to collect agricultural statistics (started 1866). He remained prominent in official bodies and public societies (retired 1891). *See also* HIGH FARMING; AGRICULTURE, ENGLAND FROM MID 18TH CENTURY.

CALAIS A coastal port, formerly in Flanders (now in NE France), which was captured from the French by an English army led by King EDWARD III in 1347 (after a long siege, 4 Sept. 1346–4 Aug. 1347). French inhabitants were replaced with English settlers. English soldiers under a Crown-appointed captain provided security.

Calais was of strategic importance during the remainder of the HUNDRED YEARS WAR, and from 1363 it was the usual location of the English wool STAPLE (taxation point), governed by the Company of the Staple (merchants). A mint was also established. Calais remained under English rule until recaptured by the French on 7 Jan. 1558. England accepted its loss in the Anglo-French treaty of Troyes (1564). *See also* WOOL TRADE, ENGLAND; MARY I; CATEAU-CAMBRÉSIS, TREATY OF; FRANCE, ENGLISH AND BRITISH RELATIONS WITH.

CALCUTTA A city on the Hooghly River in NE India (renamed Kolkata in 2001). It developed from a trading post founded in 1690 by the EAST INDIA COMPANY in the cotton-weaving district of Bengal. After being fought over in 1756–7, Calcutta became a great commercial centre and the capital of British India (1774–1912). *See also* INDIA; DELHI.

CALEDONIANS A confederation of British (or Pictish) tribes in N Britain (within modern Scotland), who were defeated by the Roman governor AGRICOLA at MONS GRAUPIUS (83). They remained outside ROMAN BRITAIN, posing an occasional threat to its northern frontiers, especially during the reign of Emperor Septimius Severus (193–211). They are thought to have lived N of the MAEATAE.

CALLAGHAN, JAMES (b. 27 March 1912 at Portsmouth, Hampshire, England; d. 26 March 2005 at Burgess Hill, West Sussex, England, aged 92). Leader of the LABOUR PARTY 1976–80; British prime minister 1976–9.

A sailor's son, Callaghan became a civil servant and trade unionist. An MP from 1945, he held junior office under Clement ATTLEE. After coming third in the 1963 leadership contest, he served as chancellor of the Exchequer under Harold WILSON (1964–7). His department squabbled with the new Department of Economic Affairs, and sterling's value was threatened. Eventually the pound was devalued ($2.80 to $2.40, on 17 Nov. 1967). Callaghan became home secretary (1967–70). He won trade union support by blocking *IN PLACE OF STRIFE* (1969). As foreign secretary (1974–6) he renegotiated membership terms of the EUROPEAN ECONOMIC COMMUNITY.

In April 1976 Callaghan defeated Michael FOOT to succeed Wilson as prime minister. Inflation was high and unemployment rising. Moderate and avuncular, Callaghan soon had to rely for a parliamentary majority on the LIB-LAB PACT and Nationalist MPs. After deciding against an election in 1978, he suffered the WINTER OF DISCONTENT and lost the election of May 1979. Callaghan retired as Party leader in 1980 and as an MP in 1987 (created Lord Callaghan). *See also* JENKINS, ROY; HEALEY, DENIS; THATCHER, MARGARET.

CALVINISM Protestant Christian theology derived from writings of Swiss reformer John (Jean) Calvin (1509–64). Calvin systematized the Lutheran theologies of justification by faith and scripture as the rule of faith, and added predestination and a distinctive theology of the Eucharist. Calvinist churches were often directed by presbyters (ministers and elders).

Calvinism was most influential in Scotland. Calvinist theology was accepted in the SCOTS CONFESSION (1560) and presbyterianism in the 'First Book of DISCIPLINE' (1560). It was also influential in England 1560s–1660, though presbyterianism was rejected for the Church of ENGLAND. Calvinism influenced the Church of IRELAND in

the 17th century, and also English and Welsh dissenting churches from the late 17th century. *See also* LUTHERANISM; PURITANISM, ENGLAND; REFORMATION, SCOTLAND; METHODIST REVIVAL, WALES.

CALVINISTIC METHODISTS A voluntary Protestant church; the only church of Welsh origin and the main nonconformist church in Wales from the mid 19th century. It emerged from the METHODIST REVIVAL in the Church of England in Wales (from 1730s), separating in 1811 (*see* THOMAS, CHARLES). It perpetuated the Methodist structure of local society, district meeting (held monthly), presbytery (association of districts), and regional association (quarterly meeting). In 1823 the church adopted a Confession, modelled on the Calvinistic Westminster Confession (*see* WESTMINSTER ASSEMBLY), and in 1826 a Constitutional Deed, vesting property in the whole church (or connexion). A General Assembly of associations met annually from 1864. The church was also known from the 1840s as the Presbyterian Church of Wales.

The church was initially conservative in political outlook, but from the mid 19th century supported nonconformist causes (*see* NONCONFORMITY AND DISSENT, WALES). At its peak in 1905–6 there were 189,000 members, which fell to 150,000 in 1960, 63,000 in 1990, and 20,000 in 2017. Calvinistic Methodists have been especially concerned for Welsh language and culture. *See also* ELIAS, JOHN; EDUCATION IN WALES, INQUIRY INTO; SPORT, WALES.

CAMBRAI, BATTLE OF An offensive action during WORLD WAR I, on 20 Nov. 1917, when a British force of 381 massed TANKS broke through German defences near Cambrai (N France) and reached open country. The only major breakthrough on the Western Front, it could not be exploited due to insufficient infantry resources, but it demonstrated the tank's potential.

CAMBRIDGE A city in E England, by the R. Cam or Granta; centre of Cambridgeshire.

Originally the location of a Roman fort (on N bank, 1st–4th centuries), Cambridge became the site of an Anglo-Saxon BURH or fortified centre (8th century) and a bridge (by 875) which controlled a route into EAST ANGLIA. In the 9th century Danes built a burh on the S bank, which was extended under English rule in the early 10th century. Normans built a castle on the N bank by 1086. An annual fair was started at nearby Stourbridge *c.*1200. In 1209, during a closure of OXFORD University, scholars settled in Cambridge; under royal protection from 1231, the community developed into a university, with endowed colleges from the late 13th century.

In the 12th–19th centuries Cambridge was an important centre of corn exporting (by river). Stourbridge fair was of national importance in the 16th–18th centuries. The university grew strongly from the late 19th century. Science-based businesses expanded from the 1970s.

Cambridge was granted city status in 1951, and in 1992 a polytechnic received university status (Anglia Polytechnic University, renamed Anglia Ruskin University 2005). In 2019 Cambridge University included 31 colleges. *See also* UNIVERSITIES, ENGLAND.

Est. popn: 1086, 1500; 1300, 5000; 1600, 5000; 1800, 10,000; 1900, 38,000; 2000, 108,000.

CAMBRIDGE, RICHARD EARL OF (b. July 1385 at Conisbrough, Yorkshire, England; d. 5 Aug. 1415 at Southampton, Hampshire, England, aged 30). The second son of Edmund Langley, duke of York (d. 1402), Richard of Conisbrough fought against OWAIN GLYN DŴR (1403–4). He was created earl of Cambridge by King HENRY V in May 1414. He intended to serve in France in 1415, but in the summer organized a conspiracy to depose Henry in favour of Edmund Mortimer, earl of March (his former brother-in-law). The plot was betrayed and Cambridge was tried and beheaded. Richard, duke of YORK, was his son, and EDWARD IV his grandson. *See also* SOUTHAMPTON PLOT; MORTIMER FAMILY.

CAMBRIDGE, WILLIAM DUKE OF (b. 21 June 1982 at Paddington, London, England). Prince William, eldest son of CHARLES, PRINCE OF WALES, and DIANA, PRINCESS OF WALES, was encouraged to become involved in charitable activity by his mother. In 1997, aged 15, he suffered her death.

After studying at ST ANDREWS University, William travelled in Latin America and Africa (2005–6) before joining the British Army. He also undertook attachments to the Royal Air Force and Navy (2008) before serving as a search-and-rescue helicopter pilot (2010–13) and then devoting himself to royal duties. In 2011 he married Kate Middleton, whom he had met at university (they were created duke and duchess of Cambridge). Their relaxed, youthful style at public engagements regained support for the British monarchy. *See also* ELIZABETH II.

CAMBUSKENNETH PARLIAMENT A meeting of the Scottish Parliament at Cambuskenneth Abbey, near Bannockburn (C Scotland), four months after the battle of BANNOCKBURN. On 6 Nov. 1314 Parliament disinherited (of land and status) those who had not made peace with King ROBERT I, creating the DISINHERITED. *See also* SCOTTISH–ENGLISH RELATIONS 1290 TO 1357.

CAMERON, DAVID (b. 9 Oct. 1966 at London, England). Leader of the CONSERVATIVE PARTY 2005–16; British prime minister 2010–16.

Educated at Eton College school and OXFORD University, Cameron worked for the Conservative Research Department (1988–92), and as a 'special adviser' (at Treasury 1992–3, Home Office 1993–4). Head of corporate affairs for a media company 1994–2001, he became an MP (2001–16), Conservative leader (elected by membership) and Opposition leader (2005).

The 2010 UK election left the Conservatives as the largest party but without a majority in the House of Commons. Cameron formed a coalition government (the first since 1945) with the LIBERAL DEMOCRATS, prioritizing reduction of expenditure to curtail the Budget deficit (*see* BROWN, GORDON). In 2011 British aircraft helped to overthrow Libya's ruler, Muammar al-Qaddafi. Against strong Conservative opposition, Cameron extended civil marriage to same-sex couples in England and Wales (implemented 2014). He also allowed a referendum on Scottish independence (2014; *see* SALMOND, ALEX).

After the 2015 election Cameron formed a Conservative government. He sought to end Conservative and other opposition to membership of the EUROPEAN UNION by obtaining revised terms and holding a referendum (2016). When the public voted to leave, Cameron resigned as Party leader and prime minister (*see* BREXIT). Succeeded by Theresa MAY. *See also* PHONE-HACKING SCANDAL.

CAMERONIANS Strict COVENANTERS (also called Society People or Hillmen), mainly in SW Scotland, who continued to reject royal and Church authority after the RISING OF 1679. Organized in local societies and meeting in CONVENTICLES, Cameronians were led by field preachers including Richard Cameron (1648–80), after whom they were named. Most refused to re-join the Church of Scotland after episcopacy was abolished (1689) because it failed to adhere to the NATIONAL COVENANT (1638). In the late 1730s most joined the SECESSION CHURCH, leaving a remnant who developed the REFORMED PRESBYTERIAN CHURCH.

CAMPAIGN FOR NUCLEAR DISARMAMENT A pressure group (popularly known as 'CND') which was founded on 17 Feb. 1958 by Bertrand RUSSELL and Canon John Collins to rally mass opposition to the British nuclear deterrent and to ATOMIC AND NUCLEAR WEAPONS in general. Especially active 1958–63 and 1980–7, it helped to win LABOUR PARTY support for unilateral nuclear disarmament in 1960 and between 1981 and 1987. *See also* PRIESTLEY, J.B.; HESELTINE, MICHAEL.

CAMPBELL, ALASTAIR (b. 25 May 1957 at Keighley, Yorkshire, England). A 'tabloid' journalist, mainly for Labour-supporting newspapers, Campbell also advised LABOUR PARTY leader Neil KINNOCK (1985–92). After

Tony BLAIR was elected leader (1994), Campbell became his press secretary and close adviser. As a SPIN DOCTOR, he discredited the Conservative government of John MAJOR and broadened Labour's appeal (e.g., implementing the name NEW LABOUR).

After Blair became prime minister (1997), Campbell remained influential as government chief press secretary (1997–2001) and director of communications and strategy (2001–3, including control over media presentation by civil servants). He edited two collections of intelligence information to magnify the threat posed by 'weapons of mass destruction' allegedly possessed by Iraq (published Sept. 2002, Feb. 2003). The latter was revealed to include plagiarized material (and nicknamed the 'Dodgy Dossier'). On 29 May 2003 radio reporter Andrew Gilligan alleged that the former had been 'sexed up', and afterwards accused Campbell of including dubious material. Gilligan's alleged source, former weapons inspector David Kelly, apparently committed suicide (July). Campbell left office in Aug. although the subsequent 'Hutton Report' largely cleared him of unjustified exaggeration. *See also* IRAQ WAR, BRITISH INVOLVEMENT.

CAMPBELL, ARCHIBALD *see* ARGYLL, 8TH EARL OF

CAMPBELL-BANNERMAN, HENRY (b. 7 Sept. 1836 at Glasgow, Scotland; d. 22 April 1908 at Westminster, London, England, aged 71). Leader of the LIBERAL PARTY 1898–1908; British prime minister 1905–8.

The son of a lord provost of GLASGOW, Henry Campbell studied at CAMBRIDGE University and became an MP (1868). He added 'Bannerman' in 1871, on inheriting property. 'C-B' served W.E. GLADSTONE as Irish secretary (1884–5) and war secretary (1886). He headed the War Office again 1892–5.

In 1898 Campbell-Bannerman seemed a suitable compromise figure to lead the divided Liberals in the House of Commons, in succession to William HARCOURT. His opinions became more radical: he criticized the (Second) BOER WAR (1899–1902), condemning concentration camps as 'methods of barbarism'. This troubled Liberal imperialists such as H.H. ASQUITH, Sir Edward GREY and R.B. HALDANE, although they joined his government in Dec. 1905.

Following a landslide general election victory (Jan. 1906), Campbell-Bannerman advanced reforms, despite obstruction in the House of Lords. The Trade Disputes Act (1906) overturned the TAFF VALE judgment and self-government was granted to the defeated Boer states in SOUTH AFRICA. Illness forced Campbell-Bannerman's resignation (6 April 1908). He died at his official residence in Downing Street, Westminster. Succeeded by Asquith.

CAMPBELL FAMILY *see* ARGYLL, EARLS AND DUKES OF

CANADA A former British DOMINION in N America, formed in 1867; its name probably derived from *kanata*, a native word meaning 'community'.

Despite English claims to NEWFOUNDLAND, the French led the settlement of northern regions of N America in the 16th and 17th centuries, though they competed with English colonists over NOVA SCOTIA (17th century), and the HUDSON'S BAY COMPANY (a fur-trading enterprise, established 1670) asserted English control over vast lands around Hudson Bay (*see* RUPERT'S LAND).

British forces conquered French Canada during the SEVEN YEARS WAR (ended 1763). It became a CROWN COLONY in 1774 with rights for French inhabitants (*see* QUEBEC ACT), but was divided in 1791 into Upper Canada (Ontario) and Lower Canada (Quebec). Both colonies repelled US invasions in the 1812 Anglo-American War. NEW BRUNSWICK was separated from Nova Scotia in 1784.

Large-scale British immigration into Canada from the 1820s upset French-speaking Canadians concentrated in Lower Canada. This, and discontent with oligarchic rule, erupted in rebellions in 1837–8, led by Louis-Joseph PAPINEAU (Lower Canada) and W.L. Mackenzie (Upper Canada). In 1840 the Canadas were united as the Province of Canada (*see* DURHAM, EARL OF), which gained RESPONSIBLE GOVERNMENT in 1849. But in 1867 CANADIAN CONFEDERATION redivided Canada and created a dominion with Nova Scotia and New Brunswick.

Canada expanded W in 1870 with the addition of Rupert's Land and North-Western Territory, parts of which became the provinces of Manitoba (1870), Alberta (1905), and Saskatchewan (1905). British Columbia (1871), Prince Edward Island (1873) and Newfoundland (1949) also joined the confederation. Wheat farming and mining flourished. Canada participated in the WORLD WARS, and the STATUTE OF WESTMINSTER (1931) confirmed its autonomy within the Empire. Rapid industrialization after 1945 encouraged closer ties with the USA. The UK Parliament surrendered residual constitutional powers in 1982. Approx. population in 1921, 8,700,000; in 1930, 10,208,000 (28% of French origin). *See also* NORTH AMERICA, ENGLISH EXPLORATION.

CANADIAN CONFEDERATION Term used for the process whereby three British colonies in N America (CANADA, NEW BRUNSWICK, NOVA SCOTIA) were united as the dominion of CANADA, a federal State with four provinces. (Canada East and Canada West, united in 1840, were separated as Quebec and Ontario.) The scheme was devised by the Quebec City Conference (Oct. 1864) and enacted by the UK Parliament in the British North America Act (1867). Implemented on 1 July 1867. Confederation was intended to end conflict between representatives of East and West Canada, and to facilitate protection of fishing rights, acquisition of the far west (preventing loss of land to the USA) and railway construction (*see* FLEMING, SANDFORD).

CANALS, ENGLAND Artificial waterways were cut in the 2nd–4th centuries by the Romans (e.g., Foss Dyke, Lincolnshire), and short channels were dug in the 10th–13th centuries. The 16th–18th centuries saw river improvements. The Exeter Ship Canal, 5 mi (8 km) in length, was made 1564–6 (reconstructed 1698–1701).

The major period of construction began with the Bridgewater Canal (early 1760s) which linked Lancashire coalmines to the R. Mersey (*see* BRIDGEWATER, 3RD DUKE OF). Its engineer, James Brindley (1716–72), subsequently worked on the 'Grand Cross' network (completed 1790). Centred on BIRMINGHAM, it connected the industrial Midlands with LIVERPOOL, Hull, LONDON and BRISTOL (ports), via the Rivers Mersey, Humber, Thames and Severn respectively. 'Canal mania' in the 1790s added subsidiary routes. Total length reached about 3600 mi (5800 km). Canals aided the INDUSTRIAL REVOLUTION by reducing transport costs for minerals. In 1894 the Manchester Ship Canal enabled ocean-going vessels to reach MANCHESTER.

Competition from RAILWAYS diminished activity after 1830. Although steam-powered barges were introduced, barge size was constricted by locks built for horse-hauled barges. In the 20th century, the advent of lorries accelerated decline. Canals were nationalized in 1948. The navigable network halved by the 1960s, when recreational boating supplanted freight traffic. Most canals in England and Wales were transferred to a trust in 2012. *See also* TRANSPORT COMMUNICATIONS, ENGLAND.

CANALS, IRELAND *see* TRANSPORT COMMUNICATIONS, IRELAND

CANALS, SCOTLAND Because of unfavourable topography only seven notable canals were built (1768–1822), amounting to 135 mi (220 km). Two canals were especially important: the Forth and Clyde Canal (started 1768, completed 1790), linking the N Sea and Atlantic, and the Monkland Canal (opened 1793) joining the N Lanarkshire coalfield to GLASGOW. The Union Canal (1822) joined EDINBURGH to the Forth and Clyde Canal. In the W the Crinan Canal through Kintyre (Argyllshire) shortened the journey from Glasgow to the WESTERN ISLES (1801). In the HIGHLANDS the Caledonian Canal (1822) linked the Moray Firth and Inverness to the western coast.

Commercial traffic on inland Lowland canals was reduced by the RAILWAYS and ceased between 1854 and 1962. Most canals became dilapidated and passed into public ownership (under the British Waterways Board from 1962). In 2012 the Board's Scottish division became a public corporation of the Scottish government. Operating as

'Scottish Canals', it continued to manage the Caledonian, Crinan, Forth and Clyde, Monkland and Union canals, and promoted their use for leisure purposes. *See also* TRANSPORT COMMUNICATIONS, SCOTLAND.

CANALS, WALES About 180 mi (290 km) were constructed, between 1766 and 1825, starting with short channels linking coalmines to shipping places (typically 1–2 mi, 1.6–3.2 km). Three canals in S Wales, joining industrial areas to seaports, were most important: the Glamorganshire Canal to CARDIFF (opened 1794), the SWANSEA Canal (1798), and the Monmouthshire Canal to NEWPORT (1799). By providing transport for coal and iron exports, they permitted development of the S Wales coalfield. In rural Wales the major canals (for agricultural produce) were the Montgomeryshire (1795, 1819), Llangollen (1808), and Brecknock and Abergavenny (1800) canals.

Rural canals were unremunerative, but industrial canals prospered until the 1860s–80s, when closure of ironworks and transfer of business to RAILWAYS greatly reduced traffic. Commercial use had generally ended by 1939, but rural canals were revived in the late 20th century for leisure boating. In 2012 surviving canals were transferred to a trust. *See also* TRANSPORT COMMUNICATIONS, WALES.

CANMORE DYNASTY *see* MAC MALCOLM RULERS

CANNING, GEORGE (b. 11 April 1770 at Marylebone, Middlesex, England; d. 8 Aug. 1827 in Chiswick, Middlesex, aged 57). The orphaned son of an actress and a disinherited Irish gentleman, Canning became an MP in 1793 as a protégé of William PITT the Younger and held junior offices under Pitt (1796–1801, 1804–6). When foreign secretary (1807–9), under the duke of PORTLAND, he supported the Peninsular campaign until a quarrel with Lord CASTLEREAGH led to his resignation.

Appointed president of the Board of Control for India in 1816 (under the earl of LIVERPOOL), Canning resigned again in 1820 because he opposed the treatment of Queen CAROLINE. Eloquent and opinionated, he provoked strong reactions. William HUSKISSON and Lord PALMERSTON were devoted followers. ULTRA TORIES detested his Liberal Toryism and advocacy of CATHOLIC EMANCIPATION.

Castlereagh's suicide in 1822 allowed Canning to become foreign secretary and leader of the House of Commons. He distanced Great Britain from RUSSIA, PRUSSIA, and the HABSBURG EMPIRE, and sympathized with independence movements in LATIN AMERICA and GREECE.

In April 1827 King GEORGE IV appointed him as prime minister (succeeding Liverpool). Half the TORY Cabinet refused to serve, so he formed a coalition with the WHIG faction of the marquess of LANSDOWNE. He died four months later. *See also* FRENCH REVOLUTIONARY AND

NAPOLEONIC WARS, BRITISH INVOLVEMENT; GODERICH, VISCOUNT; CANNINGITES.

CANNINGITES In the UK Parliament from the early 19th century, followers of the 'Liberal Tory' George CANNING. They supported CATHOLIC EMANCIPATION. Some joined the ministry of the earl of LIVERPOOL from 1822, and were leading exponents of LIBERAL TORYISM. They served in the TORY–WHIG coalitions of Canning (April–Aug. 1827) and Viscount GODERICH (1827–8) but resigned from the ministry of the duke of WELLINGTON in May 1828 when the House of Lords rejected the redistribution of some parliamentary seats. They joined the government of Earl GREY in 1830 and were assimilated into the WHIGS. They included William HUSKISSON (d. 1830) and Lord PALMERSTON.

CANONS, BOOK OF A codification of Scottish Church law, drafted by Scottish bishops, revised in England by Archbishop William LAUD, and published in Jan. 1636 by authority of King CHARLES I (rather than a General Assembly). It ignored presbyterian Church structure and included the (disliked) FIVE ARTICLES OF PERTH. Its publication contributed to the REVOLT OF 1637 and COVENANTING REVOLUTION. *See also* GLASGOW ASSEMBLY.

CANTERBURY A city in SE England, by the R. Stour; centre of Kent and the prime see in the Church of ENGLAND.
Originally an IRON AGE settlement site, a Roman city flourished in the 1st–5th centuries (called Durovernum, meaning 'Walled town by alder swamp'). By the late 6th century it belonged to the Germanic kingdom of KENT (called Cantwaraburh, OE, meaning 'Town of the men of Kent'). A cathedral was established by missionaries (*c.*600) which remained the seat of the chief bishop in the English church (*see* AUGUSTINE).
After the murder of Archbishop Thomas BECKET in the cathedral (1170) Canterbury was a pilgrimage destination (until 16th century). Cloth making flourished in the 12th–16th centuries, silk weaving and paper making in the 17th–18th centuries. Tourism expanded from the late 19th century. The University of Kent was founded at Canterbury in 1965.
Est. popn: 1086, 6000; 1300, 5000; 1600, 5000; 1800, 9000; 1900, 24,000; 2000, 40,000.

CANTERBURY AND YORK PRIMACY DISPUTE *see* PRIMACY DISPUTE, CANTERBURY AND YORK

CANTILUPE, THOMAS DE (b. *c.*1220 at Hambleden, Buckinghamshire, England; d. 25 Aug. 1282 in France, aged about 62). A scholar and clergyman, Cantilupe presented the baronial case to Louis IX at Amiens in Jan. 1264 and served as CHANCELLOR under Simon de MONTFORT (Feb.–May 1265; *see* BARONIAL CONFLICT AND WARS).

After returning to academic life, Cantilupe was appointed bishop of HEREFORD (1275). He supported King EDWARD I against Archbishop John PECHAM, who excommunicated him in 1282. Cantilupe died while travelling to the papal court to challenge Pecham's claims. Renowned for holiness, he was canonized in 1320.

CANTREF (Welsh, meaning 'hundred townships'; plural, cantrefi). A large administrative district in medieval Wales; some were perhaps originally kingdoms (from 5th century); by *c.*1100 a cantref was usually a subdivision of a kingdom (comprising two or more COMMOTES). Cantrefs disappeared in the MARCH OF WALES from the 12th century, and elsewhere after the English Conquest (1282–3), though a few were combined as new lordships. *See also* LOCAL GOVERNMENTAL STRUCTURES, WALES.

CAPE COLONY A former British colony in southern Africa. Cape Town was established by the Dutch East India Company in 1652 as a provisioning port for its ships. During the late 17th and 18th centuries Dutch and others settled across a large area to the N and E.
In 1795, after France had invaded the Netherlands, Cape Town was occupied by Great Britain (repossessed by Dutch 1802–6). The British paid the Dutch £6 million to retain it in 1814. Resentment at the abolition of slavery (1834) and other matters caused 10,000 Boers (Calvinist farmers) to make the 'Great Trek' from Cape Colony to other areas (1835–7).
Cape Colony was granted internal self-government in 1872, and BECHUANALAND colony was annexed in 1895. It became a province of SOUTH AFRICA in 1910. Approx. population in 1904: 2,410,000 (of whom 580,000, about 24%, were white). *See also* NATAL; RHODES, CECIL.

CAPITAL EXPORTS *see* FOREIGN INVESTMENT

CAPITALISM Term used from the early 19th century for economic activity based on investment of 'capital' (money or other resources) to produce profit (rather than for subsistence or constant consumption). Karl MARX (1818–83) made capitalism a distinctive stage in his historical scheme, succeeding FEUDALISM after a part-capitalist 'transition' (*see* MARXISM). In Marx's view, capitalism, like feudalism, created exploitative, alienating conditions for workers, and antagonistic class relationships.
Historians have further distinguished types of capitalism, including 'merchant capitalism', in which merchants invest in small-scale production or specialized trading (e.g., in luxury goods); 'agrarian capitalism', in which agricultural production is primarily market oriented; 'industrial capitalism', i.e., machine-based manufacturing for markets. Capitalist economies tend to be dynamic rather than static.

It has been argued that capitalism developed in England on a small scale from as early as the 11th century when merchants invested in urban cloth industries (*see* CLOTH INDUSTRY, ENGLAND). Textile industries also developed elsewhere in the British Isles in later centuries, often organized by merchants who employed domestic workers ('putting out system'). Such developments, and later capitalism, were facilitated by COMMERCIALIZATION. Agrarian capitalism is evident from the 15th century, when 'farmers' (rent payers) leased land for large-scale sheep farming (perhaps the start of 'transition', as feudalism waned). Small-scale agrarian capitalism expanded in the 16th–17th centuries, whereby hired labour was used alongside family labour to produce for the market. By the early 18th century it was dominant in southern and eastern England, and becoming significant elsewhere in Britain.

Industrial capitalism developed rapidly in Britain from the late 18th century, and to a lesser extent in Ireland. It involved organization of production by 'capitalists', using FACTORIES, machines and a disciplined workforce or 'proletariat' (*see* INDUSTRIAL REVOLUTION). By the early 19th century much of Britain and parts of Ireland were predominantly capitalist economies. *See also* COTTON INDUSTRY, ENGLAND/SCOTLAND; ENTREPRENEUR; BUSINESS ORGANIZATION; HOLIDAYS.

CAPITALS There have been recognized or designated capitals (chief centres) since late PREHISTORY. The earliest in BRITAIN were probably some OPPIDA (1st centuries BC–AD), e.g., Camulodunon (at modern COLCHESTER), Verlamion (ST ALBANS).

In ROMAN BRITAIN (from AD 43), the original province capital was Camulodunum (Colchester), which was replaced, perhaps by 60, by Londinium (LONDON). Division produced additional capitals (*see* ROMAN BRITAIN, GOVERNMENT). From *c*.300 Londinium was also capital of Britannia diocese. Tribal areas also had capitals (*see* CIVITAS).

Post-Roman kingdoms (from 5th century), ruled by itinerant kings, generally lacked capitals. From *c*.600, CANTERBURY was head see of the English Church, with YORK as head of a northern province from 735. London re-emerged as a commercial capital (late 7th century). From the 10th century, WINCHESTER (Hampshire) was effectively capital of the kingdom of ENGLAND. It was succeeded by the late 12th century by WESTMINSTER, W of London, which became part of London's built-up area in the late 17th century. London has since been the capital of England, Great Britain (from 1707) and the United Kingdom (from 1801), though Westminster remained the political centre, and the City of London the commercial centre.

In Scotland, EDINBURGH emerged as capital in the 15th century (designated 1633). CARDIFF was designated capital of Wales in 1955.

In Ireland, there were provincial ceremonial capitals possibly from the 4th or 5th century, or even by the late 1st millennium BC: EMAIN MACHA (Navan Fort, Co. Armagh) for the Ulaid; Cruachain (Rathcroghan mound, Co. Roscommon) for CONNACHT; Dún Ailinne (Knockaulin, Co. Kildare) for LEINSTER. CASHEL became the centre for MUNSTER. The centre of high-kingship was TARA (Co. Meath). ARMAGH claimed pre-eminence over the Church from the 7th century, and officially became the head see in 1152. DUBLIN became Ireland's pre-eminent town in the 10th century, and capital for the English lordship in 1171. When Ireland was partitioned in 1921, BELFAST was designated capital of Northern Ireland.

CARATACUS (fl. from 40 or 41 in Britain; d. after 52 in Italy). Son and joint heir of CUNOBELIN of the CATUVELLAUNI (an IRON AGE TRIBE), Caratacus opposed the Roman invasion of 43. Overwhelmed in SE Britain, he organized resistance in W Britain (Wales) until his defeat by the Roman governor Ostorius Scapula (51). Although he was surrendered to the Romans (51) by CARTIMANDUA, queen of the Brigantes, his bravery earned him honourable retirement in Rome. *See also* CLAUDIAN INVASION.

CARAUSIUS (d. 293). A low-born Menapian (from the Low Countries), M. Aurelius Mausaeus Carausius was appointed commander of a Roman fleet in the English Channel under Maximian (emperor 1 April 286–305). Carausius seized control of ROMAN BRITAIN in 286 or 287 (provoked by being condemned for corruption). He ruled it and part of Gaul until 293, when his hopes of recognition as a legitimate ruler were dashed: Maximian's deputy Constantius I retook Boulogne (NE Gaul) and Carausius was assassinated by ALLECTUS.

CARDIFF A city in SE WALES; capital of Wales and centre of Cardiff unitary authority; from Welsh, Caerdydd, earlier Caerdyf, meaning 'Fort on R. Taff' (after a Roman fort).

Founded probably in the 1090s by Robert FITZ HAMO, Cardiff was laid out alongside a castle at an important river crossing and was the centre of the lordship of GLAMORGAN. Expansion in the 13th century (shoe making, glove making, trade, etc.) made it Wales's largest town. But in the 14th century it declined (overtaken by CARMARTHEN), and remained a small market town.

The opening of the Glamorganshire Canal in 1794 inaugurated a new era by improving transport from MERTHYR TYDFIL and the S Wales coalfield (*see* COAL INDUSTRY, WALES). New docks constructed between 1798 and 1907 provided deep-water facilities for marine shipping (*see* BUTE, 2ND MARQUESS OF). By the late 19th century, Cardiff was the world's greatest coal-exporting centre: at its peak in

1913, 10.5 million tons were shipped. Copper and iron-works were also established (1866 and 1888 respectively).

Around 1920 industrial decline began – coal exports ceased in 1963 – but from c.1945 light industry expanded (e.g., engineering, food processing) and government departments were located there.

Cardiff was the centre of Glamorgan 1536–1974. It was created a city in 1902, and national capital in 1955. It became a district within South Glamorgan county in 1974, and part of a unitary authority in 1996. *See also* LLANDAFF; TOWNS, WALES; UNIVERSITIES, WALES.

Est. popn: 1300, 2000; 1600, 1300; 1800, 1800; 1900, 160,000; 2000, 290,000.

CARDWELL, EDWARD (b. 24 July 1813 at Liverpool, Lancashire, England; d. 15 Feb. 1886 at Torquay, Devon, England, aged 72). An MP 1842–52, 1853–74, Cardwell was a PEELITE Conservative who became a LIBERAL. He held various government offices in the 1850s–60s. As secretary of state for war 1868–74, in the ministry of W.E. GLADSTONE, he reduced expenditure while implementing far-reaching reforms to the ARMY. In 1870 the War Office was reorganized and short-term service introduced (six years' service, six years in reserve). In 1871 the purchase of officers' commissions was abolished. From 1872 'pairing' of battalions was introduced (one stationed in Britain, the other overseas). Cardwell was created Viscount Cardwell in 1874.

CARHAM, BATTLE OF Fought in the earldom of Northumbria (in modern Northumberland, NE England), at Carham by the R. Tweed (location of a ford), probably in 1018. A military force invading from the N, led by King MALCOLM II of Scotland and King Owain the Bald of STRATHCLYDE, defeated an English force probably under Eadulf Cudel, earl of Bamburgh. The battle's significance is unclear. Some have considered it unimportant while others have claimed that it resulted in the cession of LOTHIAN (or part of Lothian) to the Scots. *See also* NORTHUMBRIA; BORDER, ANGLO-SCOTTISH.

CARLISLE A city in NW England, by the R. Eden; centre of Cumberland (12th century–1974), then of Cumbria.

Originally a Roman town (called Luguvalium, Latin from Brittonic, meaning 'Place belonging to Luguvallos', 1st–4th centuries), Carlisle was selected in 1092 by King WILLIAM II as the location for a castle and town to guard land seized from the Scottish kingdom. (Its name, combining Brittonic and Romano-British words, means 'Fort of Luguvallos'.) Carlisle remained the principal English stronghold at the western end of the Anglo-Scottish BORDER (except 1136–57; *see* DAVID I, MALCOLM IV). A cathedral and bishopric were founded in 1133 by HENRY I. In the 12th and 13th centuries Carlisle traded with Scotland and

Ireland. It declined in the mid 14th century and remained small. It was the focus for the manufacturing of woollen textiles (17th–18th centuries) and of calico (late 18th–19th centuries).

From 1836 Carlisle developed into a railway centre with associated industries (e.g., manufacture of signalling equipment). In 1916, in a unique scheme (the 'Carlisle Experiment'), public houses in and near Carlisle were taken into public ownership and regulated to discourage intemperance among workers at a nearby munitions factory (estate privatized 1971). In 2007 the University of Cumbria was founded with its headquarters at Carlisle and campuses elsewhere.

Est. popn: 1300, 1100; 1600, 2000; 1800, 9000; 1900, 45,000; 2000, 70,000.

CARLTON CLUB A select political-cum-social club in WESTMINSTER, London, England, which served as a meeting place for Tory (Conservative) gentlemen from its foundation in 1832. After a committee began collecting constituency information from members in 1835, the club became the effective headquarters of the CONSERVATIVE PARTY (until 1870).

CARLTON CLUB MEETING The gathering of British Conservative MPs at the CARLTON CLUB in London on 19 Oct. 1922, following the CHANAK CRISIS. Stanley BALDWIN and Bonar Law demanded withdrawal by Conservatives from the coalition government. Despite opposition from Austen CHAMBERLAIN, the meeting agreed (185 to 88 votes). The Liberal prime minister, David LLOYD GEORGE, resigned immediately. Succeeded by Law.

CARLYLE, THOMAS (b. 4 Dec. 1795 at Ecclefechan, Dumfriesshire, Scotland; d. 5 Feb. 1881 at Chelsea, Middlesex, England, aged 85). A farmer's son, Carlyle became a writer and translator in the 1820s, mainly concerned with literary topics. In 1834 he left Scotland and settled in Chelsea where he wrote essays and histories (e.g., *The French Revolution*, 1837), and became a literary celebrity. His vehemently expressed philosophy stressed the significance of heroic individuals (e.g., in *On Heroes, Hero-Worship and the Heroic in History*, 1841) and esteemed hard work and duty. He was dubbed the 'Sage of Chelsea'.

CARMARTHEN A town in SW Wales by the R. Tywi; centre of Carmarthenshire unitary authority; from Welsh Caerfyrddin, meaning 'Fort at Moridunum'.

Carmarthen was founded in 1109, on the site of a former Roman town, on the instruction of HENRY I of England. It passed periodically between Welsh rulers and the king of England until 1241, when HENRY III of England began developing Carmarthenshire. In 1284 EDWARD I made

Carmarthen the governmental centre of newly conquered S Wales (*see* LOCAL GOVERNMENTAL STRUCTURES, WALES). Carmarthen became an important wool-exporting centre, and in 1353 the wool STAPLE for Wales. From then until the late 18th century it was usually the largest town in Wales, serving as a market centre for the fertile Tywi Valley and as a tidal port. It was also notable for cloth manufacturing, tanning and rope making, which were superseded by milk processing in the 20th century. Carmarthen was the centre of Carmarthenshire until 1974, then of Dyfed county (to 1996), then of Carmarthenshire unitary authority.

Est. popn: 1300, 1000; 1600, 2250; 1800, 5500; 1900, 10,000; 2000, 13,700.

CARNEGIE, ANDREW (b. 25 Nov. 1835 at Dunfermline, Fife, Scotland; d. 11 Aug. 1919 at Lenox, Massachusetts, USA, aged 83). A Scottish weaver's son, Carnegie emigrated with his family to the USA in 1848. He held various jobs, made money by speculation, and from 1873 concentrated on steel manufacturing, becoming one of the world's richest men. He retired in 1901 to distribute his wealth to worthy causes, including Scottish UNIVERSITIES. *See also* PUBLIC LIBRARIES.

CAROLINE OF BRUNSWICK (b. 17 May 1768 in Brunswick-Wolfenbüttel, Germany; d. 7 Aug. 1821 at London, England, aged 53). Caroline married her cousin George, prince of Wales, the heir to King GEORGE III, in England on 8 April 1795. He found her repellently coarse. They separated after a daughter was born in Jan. 1796. Princess Caroline went abroad in 1814.

She returned in 1820 after George's accession as king of Great Britain and Ireland to claim her rights as queen consort (*see* GEORGE IV). The king and government attempted controversially to dissolve her marriage in Parliament, provoking attacks from RADICALS. The Bill was withdrawn when adultery could not be proved. Caroline was refused admission to the king's coronation (19 July 1821). *See also* CANNING, GEORGE; COBBETT, WILLIAM.

CARSON, E.H. (b. 9 Feb. 1854 at Dublin, Ireland; d. 22 Oct. 1935 at Minster, Kent, England, aged 81). As a forceful barrister, Edward Henry Carson helped A.J. BALFOUR to combat the PLAN OF CAMPAIGN (from 1887). In 1892 he was appointed Irish solicitor-general and elected to the UK Parliament (as a Liberal Unionist), where he opposed the 1893 Home Rule Bill. He served as solicitor-general for the (Conservative) British government 1900–5.

In 1910 Carson became leader of the Irish Unionist Parliamentary Party. Seeing that Home Rule was likely to be enacted, he led the opposition in ULSTER where resistance was strongest, helping to organize ULSTER'S SOLEMN LEAGUE AND COVENANT (1912), the ULSTER VOLUNTEER FORCE (1913), and a provisional government (1913). During WORLD WAR I Carson held senior government posts (1915–18) while continuing to press for Ulster's exclusion from Home Rule. In 1920 Carson reluctantly accepted the government's plan for separate Home Rule in N and S Ireland. He resigned as Party leader in 1921 and served as an appeal lord until 1929 (as Lord Carson of Duncairn). *See also* HOME RULE MOVEMENT, IRELAND; UNIONISM, IRELAND.

CARSTARES, WILLIAM (b. 11 Feb. 1649 at Cathcart, W Scotland; d. 28 Dec. 1715 at Edinburgh, SE Scotland, aged 66). The son of a minister who was deposed after the PENTLAND RISING, Carstares was educated partly in the Dutch Republic (*c.*1669–72). Having been imprisoned for complicity in the RYE HOUSE PLOT (1683), he returned to the Republic and in 1687 was appointed a chaplain to William of Orange (*see* WILLIAM III). He accompanied William's invasion of Britain (1688), persuaded him to allow presbyterianism in Scotland, and remained an adviser until William's death (1702). In 1703 he became principal of Edinburgh University. Carstares won support from the Church of SCOTLAND for the UNION OF ENGLAND AND SCOTLAND by helping to obtain the Protestant Religion and Presbyterian Church Act (1707).

CARTERET, LORD (b. 22 April 1690, probably in England; d. 2 Jan. 1763 at Bath, Somerset, England, aged 72). John Carteret succeeded as Lord Carteret aged 5 and attended the House of Lords from 1711. A WHIG, he was appointed SECRETARY OF STATE (southern) in March 1721, just before Robert WALPOLE became first lord of the Treasury. Mistrusted by Viscount TOWNSHEND, the northern secretary, he was dismissed in 1724 and sent to Ireland (*see* CARTERET, LORD, AND IRELAND). After returning (1730), he was a leader of opposition to Walpole in the Lords.

After Walpole's fall (1742), Carteret became northern secretary and chief minister. He was forced to resign in Nov. 1744 because the PELHAMS thought he was enabling King GEORGE II to keep HANOVER out of the War of the AUSTRIAN SUCCESSION. (He had succeeded as Earl Granville in Oct. 1744.)

In 1746, after the Pelhams' ministry resigned, George appointed Granville as secretary of state. But he and the earl of BATH were unable to form a ministry and resigned (10–14 Feb.). *See also* WILMINGTON, EARL OF; PITT, WILLIAM, THE ELDER.

CARTERET, LORD, AND IRELAND Carteret's opposition to British Prime Minister Robert WALPOLE included encouragement of resistance in Ireland to WOOD'S HALFPENCE. Walpole responded by sending him to Ireland as chief governor (lord lieutenant), to obtain acceptance of the coinage (Oct. 1724). Although Carteret failed, he created an alliance with William CONOLLY which enabled him to obtain supply grants (funding) from the Irish Parliament (1726, 1728). He returned with his reputation intact (April 1730), and resumed opposition in England. *See also* PROTESTANT ASCENDANCY.

CARTIMANDUA (fl. from 43; d. 68 or 69 or later). Queen of the Brigantes of C Britain (modern N England) at the time of the CLAUDIAN INVASION (43), Cartimandua remained in power as a client ruler, providing a buffer state on ROMAN BRITAIN's northern border. Her expulsion by VENUTIUS (68 or 69) precipitated the incorporation of her kingdom, Brigantia, into Roman Britain (70s). *See also* CARATACUS.

CARTWRIGHT, EDMUND (b. 24 April 1743 at Marnham, Nottinghamshire, England; d. 30 Oct. 1823 at Hastings, Sussex, England, aged 80). A Church of England clergyman and poet (and brother of John CARTWRIGHT), Edmund Cartwright proposed, after a chance meeting with some men from Manchester (1784), that weaving should be mechanized (to match yarn spinning). He was stimulated to design a 'power loom' (patented 1785), which he developed after moving (1785) from Leicestershire to Doncaster (Yorkshire). He also patented a wool-combing machine (1789) which was widely adopted. In London from 1793, Cartwright remained an inventor and experimenter. Effective power looms became established in the Lancashire COTTON INDUSTRY in the 1820s–30s.

CARTWRIGHT, JOHN (b. 17 Sept. 1740 at Marnham, Nottinghamshire, England; 23 Sept. 1824 at London, England, aged 84). 'Major' Cartwright (so called as a MILITIA officer) supported AMERICAN INDEPENDENCE (declared 1776). It persuaded him that Great Britain's Parliament needed reform. In *Take Your Choice* (1776) he advocated manhood suffrage, annual Parliaments and secret ballots, and in 1780 helped to found the Society for Constitutional Information to campaign for these ends. During the 1770s–90s he also worked with Charles James FOX and Christopher WYVILL. Cartwright supported the FRENCH REVOLUTION (from 1789).

In 1812 Cartwright founded the first Hampden Club to seek PARLIAMENTARY REFORM, and began campaigning tours. In 1821 he was convicted of sedition and fined. He rejected the use of violence for political purposes. *See also* CARTWRIGHT, EDMUND.

CARTWRIGHT, THOMAS (b. 1534 or 1535, probably at Royston, Hertfordshire, England; d. 27 Dec. 1603 at Warwick, Warwickshire, England, aged 67 or 68). In early 1570 Cartwright, a Puritan clergyman, scholar and preacher, became a professor of divinity at CAMBRIDGE University. He claimed that scripture supported only a presbyterian-type organization for the Church, and denounced the episcopal structure of the Church of ENGLAND. John WHITGIFT, as vice-chancellor, deprived him of his chair (Dec.).

Cartwright spent most of the 1570s–mid 1580s abroad, though he contributed publications to the 'Admonition Controversy' (1573–7), a dispute about Church government. He was master of the earl of LEICESTER's hospital in Warwick from 1586. In 1589 Cartwright was imprisoned for offences relating to presbyterian activities. Released in 1592, he served as a chaplain and presbyterian minister in Guernsey 1596–1601. *See also* PURITANISM, ENGLAND; FIELD, JOHN.

CASEMENT, ROGER (b. 1 Sept. 1864 at Kingstown, Co. Dublin, Ireland; d. 3 Aug. 1916 at London, England, aged 51). As a British diplomat (1892–1912) Casement exposed cruelty by traders in the Congo (1904) and Peru (1911). (He was knighted in 1911.) After retirement he helped to form the IRISH VOLUNTEERS (1913).

When the UK entered WORLD WAR I (Aug. 1914) Casement was in the USA. He went to Germany (Nov.), seeking help to achieve Irish independence. He returned to Ireland in 1916, in a German submarine, ostensibly to rendezvous with a German arms shipment but in reality to halt the planned anti-British rising (he feared failure). Casement landed in Co. Kerry on 21 April and was quickly arrested. Following the EASTER RISING he was convicted of treason and hanged. Pleas for clemency were countered by private circulation of his diaries, which revealed homosexual activity. *See also* DEVOY, JOHN.

CASHEL A town and former royal centre in Co. Tipperary, Republic of Ireland; from Irish, Caiseal Mumhan, meaning 'Stone fort of Munster'.

A limestone outcrop at Cashel, called the Rock of Cashel, was the seat of the high-kings of MUNSTER (S Ireland) from possibly the 5th century to the 12th century. Donated to the Church in 1101 by Muirchertach UA BRIAIN, high-king of Munster, it was made the centre of a diocese in 1111 and of a province in 1152. 'Cormac's Chapel', Ireland's finest Romanesque building, was built on the Rock 1127–34 for Cormac Mac Carthaig; a new cathedral was constructed in the 13th century (abandoned 1748 and replaced). A town was laid out nearby in the 12th or 13th century. *See also* CAPITALS; TOWNS, IRELAND.

CASKET LETTERS Letters from MARY, QUEEN OF SCOTS, to her future husband the (4th) earl of BOTHWELL (whom she married in May 1567) which were found in a casket. 'Discovered' by Mary's enemies on 20 June 1567, the letters implicated her in the murder of her previous husband, Lord DARNLEY, and contributed to her forced abdication (July). The originals were destroyed in 1584, but copies have survived. The letters' authenticity is uncertain.

CASSIVELLAUNUS (fl. *c.*54 BC in Britain). Leader of a powerful people N of the R. Thames (probably the CATUVELLAUNI), Cassivellaunus led a coalition of British tribes to resist the second of CAESAR'S EXPEDITIONS (54 BC). After the Romans stormed his capital (probably modern Wheathampstead, Hertfordshire, England), Cassivellaunus submitted, technically becoming a Roman client king while probably remaining largely independent. *See also* IRON AGE TRIBES, BRITAIN.

CASTLE A fortified building or buildings designed as both fortress and residence for a king or lord; from Old Northern French *castel*. Castles became widespread in Continental Europe around 1000, as part of the 'feudal revolution' (*see* FEUDALISM). Though a few were possibly built in Herefordshire (W England) in the 1050s, they are associated with the NORMAN CONQUEST OF ENGLAND (1066–70s). King WILLIAM I built castles at major towns to secure control of SHIRES, and he and followers constructed castles elsewhere as residences, symbols of lordship and estate centres (*see* HONOUR). The Norman invasion of Wales (from late 11th century) and Anglo-Norman invasion of Ireland (from 1169) likewise involved castle buildings (*see* MARCH OF WALES; NORMANS, IMPACT ON IRELAND). Castles were introduced to Scotland from the 1120s (*see* NORMANS, IMPACT ON SCOTLAND). Edward I's conquest of native Wales in 1282–3 was secured with castles (*see* WALES, ENGLISH CONQUEST OF).

The earliest 'motte and bailey' castles consisted of a large earthen mound (motte) surmounted by a wooden fortress set within a protected courtyard (bailey). They could be built quickly. Soon afterwards, more substantial castles were built in stone. They proliferated in the 12th century. Some of the largest castles were those built for Edward I in NW Wales.

By the 16th century, lords preferred undefended houses. Many castles were reused as fortresses during the CIVIL WARS (1642–8). Afterwards they were either demolished or allowed to decay. Later castles in the British Isles were romantic evocations of medieval tradition.

CASTLE CHAMBER, COURT OF In Ireland, a central PREROGATIVE COURT, derived from the PRIVY COUNCIL, which operated 1563–6, 1571–1640s (abolished 1662). Based at DUBLIN Castle, and comprising the CHIEF GOVERNOR and senior officers (e.g., chancellor), it focused on major breaches of peace (e.g., disputes between magnates) and other courts' inadequacies (e.g., failure to convict

recusants). Its procedure was based on STAR CHAMBER in England. In the 1630s it was used by Thomas Wentworth, lord deputy, to reacquire Church lands (*see* LAUDIANISM, IMPACT ON IRELAND). *See also* COURTS, IRELAND; EQUITY COURTS.

CASTLEREAGH, VISCOUNT (b. 18 June 1769 at Dublin, Ireland; d. 12 Aug. 1822 at North Cray, Kent, England, aged 53). Robert Stewart became an MP in Ireland in 1790 and in Great Britain in 1794. He was known as Viscount Castlereagh from 1796. As chief secretary for Ireland (1798–1801) in the government of William PITT the Younger, Castlereagh suppressed the RISING OF 1798 and helped to push the UNION OF IRELAND AND GREAT BRITAIN through the Irish Parliament (1800). He resigned with Pitt (1801) following the rejection of CATHOLIC EMANCIPATION by King GEORGE III.

Castlereagh held office again as secretary for war in 1805–6 (under Pitt) and 1807–9 (under the duke of PORTLAND). He devised reforms of the Army and domestic militia (implemented 1808) and appointed Arthur Wellesley as commander of the Peninsular campaign (1809; *see* WELLINGTON, DUKE OF). He was a successful foreign secretary 1812–22, and negotiated the Peace of Paris (1815). His scheme to ensure peace in Europe through congresses of leading powers (the 'Congress System') ultimately failed.

As leader of the Commons (from 1812) Castlereagh was associated with post-war repressive actions and policies (*see* PETERLOO; SIX ACTS). He succeeded as 2nd marquess of Londonderry in 1821. Overworked and mentally disturbed, he committed suicide.

CATEAU-CAMBRÉSIS, TREATY OF Agreed on 2 April 1559 at Cateau-Cambrésis in the Spanish Netherlands between representatives of England, France, and Spain and the Netherlands (in the reign of Queen ELIZABETH I of England). It concluded the war of 1557–8 between an Anglo-Spanish alliance and France, and awarded CALAIS to France for eight years after which England would regain it or receive 500,000 crowns. A second treaty (3 April) settled numerous disputes between France and Spain. *See also* FOREIGN RELATIONS, ENGLAND 16TH CENTURY TO 1707.

CATECHISMS Manuals for teaching basic Christian doctrines to children and prospective communicants at the Eucharist, usually constructed as a dialogue of questions and answers. Examples exist from the 15th century but the term was used from the 16th. Early catechisms include those of John COLET (d. 1519) in England and of the Catholic reformer John HAMILTON (1552) in Scotland.

Catechisms proliferated from the REFORMATION. In England and Wales a catechism was included in editions of the Book of COMMON PRAYER (from 1549), which was also used in Ireland. Irish Catholic catechisms were produced from 1593, based on the 'Roman Catechism' (1566). The Church of SCOTLAND in 1648 adopted two catechisms produced by the WESTMINTER ASSEMBLY.

CATHACH (OIr., meaning 'battler'). In Ireland, a holy relic carried into battle to invoke a saint's support (a practice widespread in medieval Europe). The most famous *cathach* is that of Colum Cille (or COLUMBA): a 6th-century manuscript psalter (at the Royal Irish Academy, Dublin) which was borne in a reliquary by Colum Cille's kinsmen.

CATHOLIC APOSTOLIC CHURCH A Protestant Christian denomination which developed in England from 1832. It arose from conferences held by Henry Drummond (1786–1860) which encouraged premillennialism (the belief that Christ would return before the millennium). Drummond and J.B. Cardale toured England and Scotland in 1834–5 ordaining ministers. A complex hierarchy of ministers eventually included 12 apostles. Services featured speaking in tongues. Members were sometimes called 'Irvingites' after Revd Edward Irving (1792–1834), a former presbyterian minister and early member. When the last apostle died in 1901 there were about 315 congregations in England, 28 in Scotland, six in Ireland, and others overseas. The Church declined in the 20th century.

CATHOLIC ASSOCIATION OF IRELAND A political organization founded on 12 May 1823 by Daniel O'CONNELL to campaign for 'Emancipation' of Catholics (principally admission to the UK Parliament). It became a mass organization in 1824 by recruiting associate members who paid 1*d.* (minimum) per month (so-called 'Catholic rent'). The Association helped to win the COUNTY CLARE BY-ELECTION (1828), which resulted in Emancipation (April 1829). It was suppressed by the Emancipation Act. *See also* CATHOLIC RELIEF AND EMANCIPATION, IRELAND.

CATHOLIC COMMITTEE In Ireland, a national political organization founded in DUBLIN by GENTRY in 1760 to seek removal of ANTI-CATHOLIC LEGISLATION. It was dominated from early 1791 by radicals whose campaign (including a national convention of 3–8 Dec. 1792) helped to obtain HOBART'S ACT (April 1793). The Committee dissolved itself in 1793 (to comply with legislation prohibiting assemblies).

A new Committee ('General Committee of the Catholics of Ireland') was formed in May 1809 to end exclusion of Catholics from the UK Parliament. It was suppressed in July 1811. *See also* CATHOLIC RELIEF AND EMANCIPATION, IRELAND; TONE, WOLFE.

CATHOLIC CONFEDERATION In Ireland, an organization created by Catholic clergy and laity, meeting at KILKENNY (Co. Kilkenny) 10–13 May 1642, to prosecute the existing anti-English rebellion and obtain recognition of Catholicism from King CHARLES I (*see* IRISH WARS, 1641–52). It comprised a Supreme Council, in continuous session at Kilkenny, elected General Assembly (met nine times in 1642–9), and a council in each of Ireland's four PROVINCES. The Confederation supported an army in each province. Individual Catholics adhered by oath. The Confederation was a tense alliance of OLD ENGLISH and Gaelic Irish.

From 1643 the Confederation negotiated with Charles's representatives. Because of anti-Catholic feeling in England and Scotland, Charles could not openly recognize Catholicism. Confederation leaders (mainly Old English) agreed compromises in 1645 and 1646, but were thwarted by the Pope's nuncio Archbishop RINUCCINI (supported by Gaelic Irish). He pressed for the original aims despite the threat that England's (anti-Catholic) Parliament would win the English CIVIL WAR (*see* GLAMORGAN TREATIES; ORMOND TREATIES). In Aug. 1646 Rinuccini imprisoned most of the Council and controlled the Confederation until its Munster army was defeated by the Parliamentarian Lord INCHIQUIN at Knocknanuss, Co. Cork (13 Nov. 1647).

After Inchiquin declared for Charles (April 1648) the Confederation agreed a truce with him (20 May), against Rinuccini's opposition. On 17 Jan. 1649 it joined Governor ORMOND's Royalist coalition. But Charles was executed soon afterwards and Ireland was conquered by Parliamentary forces (1649–52).

CATHOLIC CONVENTION *see* CATHOLIC COMMITTEE

CATHOLIC EMANCIPATION, IMPACT ON BRITISH POLITICS William PITT the Younger, prime minister of Great Britain, wished to grant civil and political rights (e.g., eligibility for higher civil offices and election to the new UK Parliament) to Roman Catholics after the UNION OF IRELAND AND GREAT BRITAIN (1801) because Catholics comprised a majority in Ireland. King GEORGE III rejected Emancipation because it would break his coronation oath. Pitt resigned (1801). George's heir, Prince George (regent 1811–20, king 1820–30), also opposed Emancipation. The issue affected British politics for almost 30 years.

While most WHIGS supported Emancipation, TORIES became divided. Lord LIVERPOOL (prime minister 1809–27) remained neutral, but the duke of WELLINGTON and Robert PEEL refused in 1827 to serve under George CANNING because he favoured Emancipation, splitting the party. Then, 18 months later, fear of civil war in Ireland forced Wellington to concede reform (April 1829; *see* COUNTY CLARE BY-ELECTION). ULTRA TORIES, outraged by this, attacked their party leaders, and the Tories lost the 1830 general election. *See also* RECUSANCY, ENGLAND AND WALES.

CATHOLIC MISSIONARIES, ENGLAND AND WALES, LATE 16TH–MID 17TH CENTURIES From 1574 secular clergy who had trained in Continental Europe returned to support Catholics who had separated from the Church of ENGLAND and to encourage general reconversion. Many had studied at the seminary at Douai (Netherlands) founded in 1568 by William Allen (1532–94). From 1580 missionaries included Jesuits from Rome. In 1640 there were about 400 secular clergy, 200 Jesuits and 100 Benedictine monks.

Missionaries faced legal persecution. From 1581 it was treasonable to convert someone to Catholicism, and from 1585 for priests to be in England and Wales and for laity to shelter them. They had to operate covertly. By 1640, 144 priests had been executed. Missionaries nevertheless ensured that Catholicism survived. *See also* RECUSANCY, ENGLAND AND WALES; CATHOLICS AND CATHOLIC CHURCH, ENGLAND/WALES.

CATHOLIC PLOTS, ENGLAND Attempts by Roman Catholics to overthrow the country's Protestant rulers and restore Catholicism as the national religion, mainly late 16th–early 17th centuries. Between 1568 and 1587 conspirators envisaged replacing Queen ELIZABETH I with her Catholic cousin MARY, QUEEN OF SCOTS. They were encouraged by the papal bull *Regnans in excelsis* (1570) which exhorted Catholics to depose Elizabeth. Plotters usually sought help from foreign Catholic powers, especially Spain.

Catholics became involved in the NORTHERN REBELLION (1569). Later plots included those of Roberto di RIDOLFI (1571), Francis THROCKMORTON (1583), William Parry (1583) and Sir Anthony Babington (1586). The GUNPOWDER PLOT (1605) aimed to assassinate King JAMES VI/I. Later conspiracies were mostly products of anti-popery and xenophobia, notably the spurious POPISH PLOT (1678).

CATHOLIC RELIEF AND EMANCIPATION, IRELAND Catholics sought 'relief' from extensive legal restrictions, imposed by the British and Irish Parliaments, from the 1750s (*see* ANTI-CATHOLIC LEGISLATION, IRELAND, 1691 TO 1740s). A national CATHOLIC COMMITTEE was formed (1760), and from 1768 relief Bills were presented to the Irish Parliament. Only two concessions were granted: 61-year bogland reclamation leases were permitted (1772), and a revised loyalty oath was introduced (1774).

The first major Act was passed during the AMERICAN WAR OF INDEPENDENCE under pressure from the British government which sought to encourage military recruitment of Catholics. Called GARDINER'S ACT, it permitted long leases and land inheritance (1778). Acts passed in 1782 allowed purchase of rural land, and removed many restrictions on Catholic clergy and education.

After the FRENCH REVOLUTION (1789) Catholics pressed for more concessions. British pressure resulted in Langrishe's Act (1792), which removed some disabilities (e.g., Catholics could become barristers). This encouraged radical campaigning for 'Emancipation' (political rights), including a national convention in DUBLIN (3–8 Dec. 1792). It resulted in HOBART'S ACT (1793), which granted the parliamentary franchise and opened many public offices but not membership of Parliament.

At the UNION OF IRELAND AND GREAT BRITAIN (1801), Catholics were excluded from the UK Parliament. From 1808 the (Protestant) Irish MP Henry GRATTAN frequently proposed Emancipation (e.g., Bill in 1813). After Grattan's death (1820), the Catholic lawyer Daniel O'CONNELL led the Emancipation campaign. Forced to work outside Parliament, he founded the CATHOLIC ASSOCIATION (1823) which became a mass organization and influenced the 1826 general election in Ireland by encouraging support for sympathetic candidates. The British government remained opposed until O'Connell was elected to Parliament at the COUNTY CLARE BY-ELECTION (1828), despite his ineligibility. Fearing unrest, the prime minister, the duke of WELLINGTON, yielded; Catholics were admitted to Parliament and most high offices, though the FRANCHISE requirement was also increased (1829). *See also* CATHOLICS AND CATHOLIC CHURCH, IRELAND FROM 16TH CENTURY.

CATHOLICS AND CATHOLIC CHURCH, ENGLAND Following re-establishment of the Protestant Church of England (1559; *see* ELIZABETHAN SETTLEMENT), Roman Catholics emerged as a mistrusted minority, known as 'recusants'. They suffered legal disabilities (*see* RECUSANCY, ENGLAND AND WALES), and sometimes persecution, though some plotted to overthrow the monarch (*see* CATHOLIC PLOTS, ENGLAND). From 1574 secular priests from overseas seminaries and Jesuits sought to sustain the faith in, and import Counter-Reformation ideology to, the English 'mission territory'. Success was limited, and 'seigneurial Catholicism' became characteristic: priests acted as chaplains to landed families and ministered to Catholic tenants. In 1600 Catholics numbered about 40,000, with concentrations in Lancashire, the NE and London. An archpriest was appointed for the territory in 1598, and an apostolic vicariate (territory under vicar apostolic) was instituted in 1623.

ANTI-CATHOLICISM was strong among Parliamentarians in the 1640s, and under King Charles II (1660–85; *see* TEST AND CORPORATION ACTS; POPISH PLOT; EXCLUSION CRISIS). From 1685 the Catholic King JAMES VII/II sought to provide liberty and prominence for Catholicism. (In 1688 England and Wales were divided into four apostolic vicariates.) James's fall (1688) was disastrous: until 1746 Catholics suffered harassment as JACOBITES. Yet numbers grew, notably in towns, reaching 80,000 in 1770 (England and Wales). Many anti-Catholic measures fell into disuse, and Relief Acts (1778, 1791) removed many disabilities, the latter Act allowing exercise of religion, including chapels. CATHOLIC EMANCIPATION was conceded in 1829.

During the 19th century Catholicism burgeoned, boosted by Irish IMMIGRATION and converts from Protestantism. Chapels were built in working-class districts of LONDON and industrial towns. A new hierarchy was instituted in 1850 (archbishop of WESTMINSTER and 12 suffragan bishops), and Catholic parishes established in 1918. Nicholas WISEMAN and others provided leadership.

In the 20th century the diocesan structure was reorganized (reaching four provinces in 1965), and the Catholic population peaked in 1993. Yet in the 21st century Catholics constituted the largest body of regular Christian worshippers. *See also* NEWMAN, JOHN HENRY; MANNING, HENRY; HUME, BASIL; PAPAL VISITS, GREAT BRITAIN.

CATHOLICS AND CATHOLIC CHURCH, IRELAND FROM 16TH CENTURY From the 1570s a majority of the population (Gaelic Irish and OLD ENGLISH) abandoned the State-controlled Church of Ireland. A separate Catholic Church developed, loyal to the papacy (*see* REFORMATION, IRELAND; RECUSANCY, IRELAND). (The papacy had appointed bishops as rivals to royal appointees from the 1530s.) Secular and regular clergy were increasingly trained overseas (in Irish colleges from the 1590s). By the 1630s the Church operated throughout Ireland. Mass was said in houses or outdoors.

In the 1640s Catholics sought official acceptance through rebellion, only for Ireland to be conquered by anti-Catholic, English Parliamentary forces, and for Catholic landowners to be extensively dispossessed (*see* IRISH WARS, 1641–52; COMMONWEALTH AND PROTECTORATE, IRELAND). Another bid for toleration, following the RESTORATION (1660), was thwarted by clergy (*see* LOYAL REMONSTRANCE). The promotion of Catholicism from 1685 for King JAMES VII/II provoked ANTI-CATHOLIC LEGISLATION (1691–1740s). Despite this, in 1732 there were at least 890 Mass-houses (chapels), 1400 secular priests and 250 friars.

Anti-Catholic restrictions were largely removed between the 1770s and 1820s (*see* CATHOLIC RELIEF AND EMANCIPATION, IRELAND), and a national seminary was founded (1795; *see* MAYNOOTH SEMINARY). From the 1790s cathedrals and churches were built. During the 19th century a 'devotional revolution' gained strength: the Church discouraged 'semi-pagan' activities (e.g., wakes) and promoted Church-based alternatives (e.g.,

confraternities). It also gained increased involvement in EDUCATION (*see* NATIONAL EDUCATION, IRELAND).

After the PARTITION OF IRELAND (1921), the Church continued as an all-Ireland organization. It remained powerful in southern Ireland (e.g., recognized in the CONSTITUTION of 1937) until greatly weakened from the 1990s by socially 'permissive' influences, scandals (e.g., revelation of child abuse by clergy) and IMMIGRATION. Attendance at Mass and vocations to the priesthood fell. In NORTHERN IRELAND, where Catholics were a minority, inequitable treatment contributed to the TROUBLES (1968–90s). *See also* CHURCH, MEDIEVAL IRELAND; RELIGIOUS ORDERS AND REGULAR CLERGY, IRELAND FROM 16TH CENTURY; CHURCH–STATE RELATIONS, SOUTHERN IRELAND FROM 1922; CULLEN, PAUL; McQUAID, J.C.

CATHOLICS AND CATHOLIC CHURCH, SCOTLAND During the 1560s, despite the State's repudiation of Catholicism (*see* REFORMATION, SCOTLAND), the Church's structure continued and many people remained Catholics, including MARY, QUEEN OF SCOTS, and Archbishop John HAMILTON. But the loss of bishops (by exile, execution or conformity) removed leadership, and from 1573 (Act of Conformity) Catholic clergy in parish livings were deprived. Catholics became a minority, concentrated in the NE, N and SW, who were ministered to clandestinely by priests protected by nobles (e.g., 6th earl of HUNTLY). Anti-Catholic legislation was passed in the late 16th and 17th centuries.

During the 17th century Catholicism largely disappeared from the Lowlands, but survived in the HIGHLANDS and WESTERN ISLES, strengthened by missions from Irish Franciscans (1619–37), and in the NE. The papacy established a prefecture apostolic for Scotland in 1653, which was replaced by an apostolic vicariate in 1694 (two vicariates from 1729, three from 1827). The first seminaries were founded (Loch Morar, N, 1714; Scalan, NE, 1716). Catholics were suspected of JACOBITISM and many emigrated after the 1745 JACOBITE REBELLION. In 1755 there were 16,500 Catholics. Many penal laws were repealed in 1793.

Numbers increased from the 1790s with Irish immigration. By 1830 the GLASGOW area contained 50,000 Catholics. Schools were founded and churches built, especially from mid century. In 1878, delayed by Protestant hostility, the papacy restored a hierarchy, consisting of the archbishop of ST ANDREWS and EDINBURGH with four suffragans and the archdiocese of GLASGOW (directly subject to the Pope). (Glasgow was raised to a province with two suffragans in 1947.) In 1878 there were 300,000 Catholics, mainly in W Scotland. Around 1980 Catholics (est. 828,000) became the largest denomination of churchgoers in Scotland. In 2011, 840,000 people claimed Catholic affiliation. *See also* ANTI-CATHOLICISM, BRITAIN; OGILVIE, JOHN; IMMIGRATION, SCOTLAND; WHEATLEY, JOHN.

CATHOLICS AND CATHOLIC CHURCH, WALES Catholics were a distinctive religious minority from 1559, when most people in Wales acquiesced in the re-establishment of the Protestant Church of ENGLAND (*see* REFORMATION, WALES). Led by GENTRY and largely concentrated in the NE (Flintshire) and SE (Monmouthshire), Catholics received missionary priests trained in Continental Europe from 1577 and were fined for RECUSANCY (1580s–1620s). From 1623 Wales, along with England and Scotland, became part of an apostolic vicariate (territory headed by a vicar apostolic).

Persecution flared again during the POPISH PLOT of 1678–9. From 1688 Welsh Catholics, numbering under 2000, belonged to a western apostolic vicariate of England and Wales. Numbers fell during the 18th century.

Catholics increased from the 1790s with Irish immigration to S Wales, and benefited from CATHOLIC EMANCIPATION (1829). Churches were built. Under the hierarchy established in 1850, S Wales (and Herefordshire, England) became the diocese of NEWPORT and Menevia, and N Wales became part of the diocese of Shrewsbury (in Shropshire, England). Both dioceses were part of WESTMINSTER province. (Menevia is a Latin name for ST DAVIDS.)

In 1895 part of the southern diocese became the diocese of Newport (including Herefordshire). The remainder of Wales became the vicariate of Wales, and then the diocese of Menevia (1898). The dioceses were assigned to the new BIRMINGHAM province in 1911. Wales (with part of England) became a province in 1916 when Newport diocese was elevated to an archdiocese (CARDIFF), with Menevia as a suffragan see. N Wales was separated from Menevia in 1987 as the diocese of WREXHAM. From the 1920s the Church contributed to national life. Converts included Saunders LEWIS (1932). In 2010 Catholics, numbering around 200,000, formed Wales's second largest Christian denomination.

CATO STREET CONSPIRACY In England, a conspiracy in 1820 to overthrow the government of the earl of LIVERPOOL. Encouraged by a government spy, the conspirators, led by Arthur Thistlewood, met on 23 Feb. in Cato Street, London, and plotted to assassinate the CABINET at dinner. They were arrested, and five were later hanged. The conspiracy appeared to justify the recent SIX ACTS.

CATUVELLAUNI A powerful tribe of S Britain (N of the R. Thames) in the 1st centuries BC and AD. Their rulers included CASSIVELLAUNUS (probably), Tasciovanus and his son CUNOBELIN (father of CARATACUS). The Romans organized the Catuvellauni as a *CIVITAS*, with its capital at Verulamium (ST ALBANS). *See also* IRON AGE TRIBES, BRITAIN.

CAUSEWAYED ENCLOSURE A hill top enclosed by a single interrupted ditch dating to the first half of the NEOLITHIC (i.e., *c.*4300– *c.*3300 BC), found in S Britain. Many enclosures, such as Windmill Hill (Wiltshire, S England), were gathering places for dispersed populations, used on a seasonal or periodic basis for rites of passage, exchange and other ceremonies. Some may have also seen limited use as settlements.

CAVALIER PARLIAMENT The English Parliament which met on 8 May 1661, succeeding the CONVENTION PARLIAMENT. It was so called because it expressed loyalty to the RESTORATION monarchy of CHARLES II (recalling earlier CAVALIERS) through its legislation of 1661–5, which confirmed royal rights (e.g., affirming command of the militia), reinstated bishops to the House of Lords, and attempted to reimpose religious uniformity (*see* CLARENDON CODE).

From 1672, fear that Charles would impose 'popery' and arbitrary government encouraged the growth of a 'country' opposition within the Cavalier Parliament, despite efforts by the earl of DANBY to recruit a 'court party' of supporters (e.g., with payments). The Parliament was dissolved on 24 Jan. 1679 following its attempt to impeach Danby. *See also* TEST AND CORPORATION ACTS; EXCLUSION CRISIS.

CAVALIERS, ROUNDHEADS In England and Wales, names applied to the partisans of respectively king and Parliament during the CIVIL WARS (1642–8). They originated in late 1641 in London as derogatory terms. 'Cavalier' alluded to cruel Spanish troops (Spanish *caballeros*) and also to the arrogance and debauchery of young courtiers, but it became associated with honour and loyalty to CHARLES I. 'Roundhead' implied the short hair supposedly characteristic of Puritans (*see* PURITANISM, ENGLAND).

CAVALIERS, SCOTLAND Name given to Jacobites (supporters of the exiled Stuart claimant) in the Scottish Parliament of 1703–7 (about 70, elected 1702). In 1703 they co-operated with the COUNTRY PARTY to pass the Act of SECURITY, which threatened the HANOVERIAN SUCCESSION already adopted by England. (They also passed the Act anent WAR AND PEACE.) *See also* JACOBITISM, IMPACT ON BRITISH POLITICS; UNION OF ENGLAND AND SCOTLAND.

CAVELL, EDITH (b. 4 Dec. 1865 at Swardeston, Norfolk, England; d. 12 Oct. 1915 at Brussels, Belgium, aged 49). From 1907 Cavell was director of a training school for nurses and clinic in Brussels. After the outbreak of WORLD WAR I and German occupation of Belgium (Aug. 1914), she became involved in organizing the escape of Allied soldiers. Arrested by the Germans on 5 Aug. 1915, she confessed and was executed by firing squad. In Great Britain and elsewhere Cavell was regarded as a heroine and martyr.

CAVENDISH, FREDERICK (b. 30 Nov. 1836 at Eastbourne, Sussex, England; d. 6 May 1882 at Dublin, Ireland, aged 45). Brother of the 8th duke of DEVONSHIRE, Lord Frederick Cavendish was a Liberal MP (1865–82) and protégé of the Liberal prime minister W.E. GLADSTONE, who appointed him chief secretary for Ireland (May 1882). He was assassinated on the day after his arrival in Dublin: *see* PHOENIX PARK MURDERS.

CAXTON, WILLIAM (b. *c.*1420 in Kent, England; d. early 1492 at Westminster, Middlesex, England, aged in 70s). A London mercer (cloth dealer), active in the Low Countries from the 1450s, Caxton moved to Cologne in Germany in 1471 and became involved in printing and publishing. By late 1472 he had established a press in Bruges on which he printed two books in English, *History of Troy* and a chess manual. In 1475 or 1476 he moved the press to WESTMINSTER, becoming England's first book printer. He published over 100 books, mainly in English. *See also* MALORY, THOMAS; PRINTING, ENGLAND.

CECIL, ROBERT (b. 1 June 1563 at Westminster, Middlesex, England; d. 24 May 1612 at Marlborough, Wiltshire, England, aged 48). The younger son of William CECIL (chief minister of Queen ELIZABETH I), Robert Cecil was an MP from 1584. In 1591 he was knighted, made a privy councillor, and unofficially began government administrative work. He was appointed SECRETARY OF STATE in 1596, and succeeded his father (d. 1598) as chief minister. From 1601 Cecil corresponded secretly with King James of Scotland to facilitate his accession to the English throne (1603; *see* JAMES VI/I).

Cecil was created Lord Cecil (1603), Viscount Cranborne (1604) and earl of Salisbury (1605). Retained as secretary, Salisbury was also lord TREASURER from 1608. He led peace making with Spain (1604), and sought to reduce the king's indebtedness, but James resisted Salisbury's appeals for reduction of expenditure. He was more successful at increasing income (e.g., with additional taxes on imports, 1608; *see* IMPOSITIONS). Salisbury's attempt at a permanent solution (1610) failed (*see* GREAT CONTRACT).

CECIL, WILLIAM (b. 18 Sept. 1520 at Bourne, Lincolnshire, England; d. 4 Aug. 1598 at Westminster, Middlesex, England, aged 77). A courtier's son, Cecil served Edward, duke of SOMERSET, protector of the Protestant King EDWARD VI, from 1547. Following Somerset's fall (1549), Cecil served the earl of Warwick (1550; SECRETARY OF STATE to 1553; knighted 1551). Despite supporting Lady Jane GREY (1553), he lived peacefully under the Catholic MARY I (1553–8).

Cecil knew Mary's half-sister Elizabeth from 1548. On her accession (1558) he was appointed secretary of state and remained her chief minister, transferring to lord TREASURER in 1572. He was created Lord Burghley in 1571 (*see* ELIZABETH I).

Cecil organized the Protestant settlement of the English Church in 1559 (*see* ELIZABETHAN SETTLEMENT), and persuaded Elizabeth to expel French forces from Scotland (*see* BERWICK, (1560) TREATY OF). He sought to prevent an alliance between Spain and France, both Catholic powers, and encouraged foreign Protestants, if possible without going to war. He supported proposals for Elizabeth to make a foreign marriage. From the early 1590s he increasingly delegated work to his son Robert CECIL. *See also* ESSEX, 2ND EARL OF.

CELTIC CULTURE, BRITAIN Ancient sources locate Celts in S and C France, N Italy and Spain, but not in Britain or Ireland. The belief that the early British and Irish were Celts starts with George BUCHANAN, who in 1582 argued a Celtic origin for Irish and Scots on linguistic grounds. In 1874 H. Hildebrand divided the IRON AGE into earlier Hallstatt and later La Tène periods; afterwards, these were redefined as 'cultures' with distinctive burial rites, ceramics and metal artefacts and art styles. The 'La Tène culture and art' has been claimed as 'Celtic' and used to document the 'spread' of the Celts, including immigration into Britain.

Such ethnic interpretations are now largely rejected by archaeologists, and the modern definition of 'speakers of Celtic languages' as Celts cannot be imposed on the past. The 'Celtic' languages of Britain in the IRON AGE (*c.*700 BC–AD 43) are developments of an earlier Indo-European language. Continental contacts are explained in terms of trade and social relationships as well as immigration. The concept of an *ethnic* 'Celtic Britain' is thus a modern fabrication.

CELTIC CULTURE, IRELAND By *c.* AD 500 the Irish language (Goidelic) was spoken in all parts of the country. In linguistic terms, therefore, Ireland was 'Celtic'. There is, however, no agreement about how or when the language was introduced, and there are serious difficulties in attempting to link the language with surviving material culture. Philologists insist that only large-scale folk intrusions at some time in late PREHISTORY can explain the introduction of the Irish language to Ireland. But the Continental culture often associated with 'Celts', 'La Tène', is almost entirely absent from much of southern Ireland. Where La Tène does occur, it is, with very few exceptions, of native character. Most especially, the normal burial form of the last centuries BC in Ireland is unrelated to outside developments and has its roots in indigenous BRONZE AGE traditions. It is thus possible that small, powerful groups, perhaps accompanied by craftsmen, entered Ireland in the last centuries BC, but the mechanism by which the country became Irish speaking remains to be explained.

CEMETERIES, EARLY GERMANIC Cemeteries provide evidence about settlers and societies in early Anglo-Saxon England (5th–8th centuries). About 1500 have been excavated. Burials are either cremations (bones, usually in bags or urns) or inhumations (remains of bodies). Cremations predominate N of the R. Thames, inhumations to the S. Cremated remains were sometimes buried with small goods (e.g., combs). Inhumations were sometimes accompanied by swords, spears and other goods.

Interpretation is difficult. Britons cannot be confidently identified, and there is no clear correlation between grave goods and religious context (paganism or Christianity). Burial of goods ceased in the 8th century. *See also* GERMANIC IMMIGRATION, SOUTHERN BRITAIN; BRITONS IN ANGLO-SAXON KINGDOMS.

CENSORSHIP, ENGLAND AND WALES In the 15th–17th centuries censorship was used to defend religious and political cohesion. In 1409 constitutions against LOLLARDY prohibited the reading of works by John WYCLIF, unauthorized English translations of the BIBLE, and possession of an English Bible. Theological writings had to be inspected (to 1530s).

Under King HENRY VIII, the import of LUTHERAN writings and the English New Testament of William TYNDALE were resisted by proclamations and seizures (1520s–30s). In 1536 publications supporting papal supremacy were banned, though the English Bible was allowed. From 1538 a licence was required for printing and importing English books. The first censorship statute (1543) penalized unlicensed printing and importing, and restricted reading of the English Bible.

Incorporation of the Stationers' Company of LONDON by Philip and MARY I (1557), with powers to regulate printing and register publications, restrained subversion. ELIZABETH I renewed licensing (injunctions 1559; arrangements simplified 1586). Play licensing had started in 1549 (allocated to master of the revels 1574).

Censorship was largely ineffective 1640s–1655, and attacked by John MILTON (*Areopagitica*, 1644), though theatres were closed 1642–60 because of PURITAN hostility. Following the RESTORATION, licensing was revived and offensive books banned (Licensing Act, 1662). Intermittently renewed, the Act was allowed to lapse in 1695 because enforcement was considered impracticable.

Censorship then relied on other means (e.g., laws against seditious libel). In 1737 obscene libel (intent to corrupt) became a COMMON LAW offence (Curll's case), and play censorship was transferred to the lord chamberlain (Licensing Act). Sale of obscene material became a

statutory offence in 1857 (Obscene Publications Act, UK except Scotland), and Hicklin's case (1868) defined obscene content. A less restrictive replacement Act (1959) was famously tested in 1960 (*see* LANE, ALLEN). Play censorship was abolished in 1968.

The British film industry organized censorship from 1913 (renamed 'classification' 1984). RADIO and TELEVISION were regulated through charters and legislation. The Internet (1990s) created new problems because of its decentralized organization. *See also* REFORMATION, ENGLAND/WALES; PRINTING, ENGLAND/WALES.

CENSORSHIP, IRELAND The appointment of royal printers in the 16th–17th centuries provided considerable control over publications. Imported Catholic writings were sometimes seized. In the late 17th–19th centuries, libel and blasphemy laws were used for suppressing some publications. In 1857 the UK Parliament included Ireland under the Obscene Publications Act. In the later 19th century Catholic concern about the content of some British popular newspapers caused 'vigilance committees' to intercept and destroy imports.

After foundation of the IRISH FREE STATE, routine censorship of films and publications was introduced (respectively 1923, 1929), reflecting Catholic moral concerns (e.g., publications advocating BIRTH CONTROL were banned). (The 1929 legislation repealed and replaced the 1857 Act.) Censorship of publications peaked in the early 1950s, when over 600 books were banned annually. Its stringency then declined and restrictions were modified. Film censorship was replaced by 'classification' in 2008. The theatre was exempt from direct censorship. *See also* PRINTING, IRELAND.

CENSORSHIP, SCOTLAND The Scottish Parliament banned the import of LUTHERAN publications (1525, 1535), and from 1551 required examination and licensing of publications (reiterated 1646). After the Restoration, the Scottish Privy Council made orders for censorship (1661, 1680). Publication of obscene works was also an offence under COMMON LAW. This was considered sufficiently stringent for Scotland to be excluded from the 1857 Obscene Publications Act (applicable elsewhere in UK), though publication of obscene material was made a statutory offence in 1892 (Burgh Police (Scotland) Act; replaced by Civic Government (Scotland) Act 1982. *See also* REFORMATION, SCOTLAND.

CENSUSES *see* NATIONAL AND IMPERIAL CENSUSES

CENTRAL AFRICAN FEDERATION *see* FEDERATION OF RHODESIA AND NYASALAND

CENTRAL BELT, SCOTLAND *see* FORTH–CLYDE ISTHMUS

CENTRAL HEATING The circulation of hot water or air around a building, heated at a central point. Systems were used in public buildings or very large houses in Great Britain and Ireland by the mid 19th century. Domestic central heating was common in the UK from the 1960s: it was installed in 25% of houses by 1970, 75% by 1990, 90% by 2011. (NORTH SEA gas became the main fuel in Britain from the 1970s.) In the Republic of Ireland, 59% of households had central heating in 1991, 90% in 2001 (half of systems using oil, 25% mains gas).

CENWULF (fl. from 796 in Mercia; d. 821 at Basingwerk, Mercia). Cenwulf seized the kingship of MERCIA (C England) after the death of Egfrith, son of OFFA (796). But he faced rebellions in subordinate areas outside Mercia. He possibly reasserted authority over EAST ANGLIA, and put down a rebellion in KENT (798). Cenwulf apparently lacked authority in WESSEX. In 812–14 he deprived Sigered, king of ESSEX, of royal status. In 803 Cenwulf permitted abolition of the archbishopric of Lichfield (created for OFFA, 787), returning authority to the archbishop of CANTERBURY. *See also* KINGSHIP, ANGLO-SAXON; EGBERT.

CEREDIGION An early medieval kingdom (5th–9th centuries) in W WALES, between the Rivers Teifi and Dyfi. It was named after Ceredig ap Cunedda who may have conquered the area from Irish settlers in the 5th century. His line claimed affiliation to the main line of GWYNEDD (NW Wales). Ceredigion's last independent king, Arthen, was drowned in 872. It passed ultimately (by the early 11th century) to the descendants of RHODRI MAWR who ruled DEHEUBARTH (SW Wales).

After the death of King RHYS AP TEWDWR in 1093, Ceredigion passed to POWYS (C Wales) until 1110, when Gilbert fitz Richard de CLARE was created lord of Ceredigion (or Cardigan) by King HENRY I of England. Welsh resurgence in 1135–6 returned Ceredigion to native control, firstly of Gwynedd, then (from the 1150s) of Deheubarth. Except for a brief return of Clare control in the reign of RHYS AP GRUFFUDD (1155–97), Ceredigion remained effectively part of Deheubarth until 1277, when most was conquered for EDWARD I of England and became Cardiganshire. S Ceredigion was left under RHYS AP MAREDUDD until he revolted in 1287, when it was taken by the English Crown. The name Ceredigion was reused from 1974 for a district council (reconstituted as a unitary authority and county in 1996). *See also* IRISH COLONIZATION OF BRITAIN, 4TH–6TH CENTURIES.

CESS A tax, as in 'county cess' or 'Church cess' (derived from 'assessment'). In 16th-century Ireland cess referred particularly to levies in kind (e.g., foodstuffs, provision of carts) and money for the household and military retinue of the CHIEF GOVERNOR. Raised mainly from Palesmen (inhabitants of the PALE), cess became more burdensome from 1548.

In 1575 a crisis developed when Palesmen rejected a COMPOSITION (fixed payment) in lieu. Sir Henry SIDNEY then sought a heavy cess, provoking a petition to ELIZABETH I (1577) which claimed that cess required approval from PARLIAMENT or a Great Council. As a compromise, the Palesmen accepted a one-year composition (renewed 1584, 1586). *See also* ROYAL REVENUES, IRELAND.

CESSATION In Ireland, the ceasefire for a year agreed on 15 Sept. 1643 between Royalist forces and Catholic rebels. Made on the instructions of King CHARLES I (issued April), it enabled 5000 Protestant troops to be sent to England to aid the Royalist cause in the CIVIL WAR, though they had little military impact. *See also* IRISH WARS, 1641–52; ORMOND, 12TH EARL OF.

CEYLON A former British territory in the Indian Ocean. The Portuguese and then the Dutch held the island before the EAST INDIA COMPANY captured the coastline in 1796. The French (occupiers of the Netherlands) recognized Great Britain's possession of Ceylon in the Peace of AMIENS (1802), and it became a CROWN COLONY. The British took full control after deposing the king of Kandy in 1815. They brought INDENTURED LABOUR from S INDIA to work on coffee PLANTATIONS, but tea and rubber became staple products in the 1880s. Ceylon was granted DOMINION status in 1947, and became independent under the British Crown in 1948. It changed name to Sri Lanka, and became a republic, in 1972. Approx. population in 1921, 4,405,000; in 1947, 7,037,000.

CHAD (fl. from 651; d. 2 March 672 at Lichfield, Mercia). An English disciple of AIDAN, Chad was appointed bishop of Northumbria (NE England) by King OSWIU (664). He resigned (669) at the request of Archbishop THEODORE because he had been consecrated by an illegal bishop (succeeded by WILFRID). In 669 Theodore appointed Chad as bishop of MERCIA (C England). He established a see and monastery at Lichfield (in modern Staffordshire), from where he spread Irish-influenced Christianity. *See also* CONVERSION OF ANGLO-SAXONS; WULFHERE.

CHADWICK, EDWIN (b. 24 Jan. 1800 at Longsight, Lancashire, England; d. 5 July 1890 at East Sheen, Surrey, England, aged 90). Social reformer. An assistant to Jeremy BENTHAM 1830–2, Chadwick worked for the Royal Commission on the Poor Laws and was also seconded (1833) to the Royal Commission on Factories. Their reports resulted in the 1833 Factory Act and the 1834 POOR LAW AMENDMENT ACT. Chadwick implemented the latter

(1834–9) as secretary of the Poor Law Commission. He then obtained authorization for a parliamentary inquiry into public health, to which he was seconded. His report *The Sanitary Condition of the Labouring Population* (1842) led to a Royal Commission on the Health of Towns (1843), the 1848 PUBLIC HEALTH ACT, and establishment of a General Board of Health (1848) including Chadwick. When its authorization expired (1854), Chadwick's enemies forced him into retirement. In tackling social problems, Chadwick advocated strong State supervision rather than local autonomy. *See also* FACTORY LEGISLATION.

CHADWICK, JAMES (b. 20 Oct. 1891 at Bollington, Cheshire, England; d. 24 July 1974 at Cambridge, Cambridgeshire, England, aged 82). After studying physics and holding short-term posts at MANCHESTER and CAMBRIDGE Universities (also in Germany 1913–18, interned from 1914), Chadwick was appointed assistant director of research at the Cavendish Laboratory in Cambridge (1923). He was both a student and colleague of Ernest RUTHERFORD, and in 1927 was elected a fellow of the ROYAL SOCIETY. In 1932, through study of radiation from beryllium, Chadwick discovered the neutron (electrically neutral constituent of the atomic nucleus), for which he received the 1935 Nobel Prize in Physics.

While professor of physics at LIVERPOOL University (from 1935), Chadwick largely wrote the 'MAUD Report' (1941, during WORLD WAR II), which convinced the British and US governments that an atomic bomb was feasible. He spent 1943–6 in the USA as head of the British Mission at the Manhattan Project, which created the bomb. Knighted in 1945, Chadwick was master of Gonville and Caius College, Cambridge, 1948–58. *See also* ATOMIC AND NUCLEAR WEAPONS.

CHALCOLITHIC PERIOD OR COPPER AGE Terms used to demarcate the period of PREHISTORY in Ireland from *c*.2500 to *c*.2000 BC, following the NEOLITHIC PERIOD and overlapping with the Early BRONZE AGE from *c*.2300 BC. (Chalcolithic means 'copper stone'.) They denote the earliest use of metal. The period coincides with the advent of BEAKER CULTURE.

The period's most important site is Ross Ireland (Co. Kerry), where substantial surface deposits of copper were extracted and worked from *c*.2400 BC. The major product was axe heads, which were exported to Britain. Prehistorians have considered the possible existence of a Chalcolithic period in Britain, but it has not found general acceptance.

CHALMERS, THOMAS (b. 17 March 1780 at Anstruther, Fife, Scotland; d. 31 May 1847 at Edinburgh, Scotland, aged 67). Following conversion to EVANGELICALISM in 1811, Chalmers, a Church of SCOTLAND minister, served the poverty-stricken parish of St John's in GLASGOW from 1819 to 1823 where he attempted to raise religious and moral standards by establishing schools and encouraging personal responsibility by both poor and well-off. In the 1830s, as leader of the Church's evangelical party, he organized church building and led opposition to private patronage of Church livings. After the courts rejected the Church's bid for a congregational veto on appointments, Chalmers reluctantly led the DISRUPTION (1843) and was first moderator of the FREE CHURCH OF SCOTLAND. His ideal of moral self-help was widely influential.

CHAMBERLAIN, AUSTEN (b. 16 Oct. 1863 at Birmingham, Warwickshire, England; d. 16 March 1937 at London, England, aged 73). The eldest son of Joseph CHAMBERLAIN, Austen was a LIBERAL UNIONIST MP from 1892. In 1902 he joined the Cabinet of A.J. BALFOUR as postmaster-general, continuing after his father resigned as colonial secretary (over TARIFF REFORM, Sept. 1903). He was promoted to chancellor of the Exchequer (1903–5). From 1906 he continued his father's tariff reform campaign. In Nov. 1911 Chamberlain withdrew from a contest for leadership of the CONSERVATIVE PARTY in favour of Bonar Law (Nov. 1911). He became India secretary in May 1915 (during WORLD WAR I), but resigned (July 1917) over mishandling of the Mesopotamian campaign.

Chamberlain re-entered the Cabinet, under David LLOYD GEORGE, as minister without portfolio (April 1918). He was again chancellor of the Exchequer (1919–21), and led the CONSERVATIVE PARTY between March 1921 and the CARLTON CLUB MEETING (Oct. 1922). As foreign secretary 1924–9 he negotiated the treaty of LOCARNO (1925). Briefly first lord of the Admiralty (1931), Chamberlain was latterly critical of APPEASEMENT. *See also* BALDWIN, STANLEY; CHAMBERLAIN, NEVILLE.

CHAMBERLAIN, JOSEPH (b. 8 July 1836 at London, England; d. 2 July 1914 at London, aged 77). Controversial LIBERAL UNIONIST politician who advocated social reform and IMPERIALISM.

Son of a UNITARIAN shopkeeper, Chamberlain made a fortune manufacturing screws in BIRMINGHAM, where he was mayor (1873–5). He became a Liberal MP in 1876 and served W.E. GLADSTONE as president of the Board of Trade (1880–5). A leading British radical, he devised the UNAUTHORIZED PROGRAMME. His opposition to HOME RULE for Ireland in 1886 split the LIBERAL PARTY.

From 1895 to 1903, Chamberlain was a key figure as colonial secretary in the Conservative-Unionist governments of Lord SALISBURY and A.J. BALFOUR. His handling of the (Second) BOER WAR (1899–1902) revealed characteristic dynamism and abrasiveness. He resigned (18 Sept. 1903) to campaign for TARIFF REFORM, which bitterly divided the CONSERVATIVE PARTY. A crippling stroke suddenly silenced him (1906). His sons became prominent politicians: *see* CHAMBERLAIN, AUSTEN; CHAMBERLAIN, NEVILLE.

CHAMBERLAIN, NEVILLE (b. 18 March 1869 at Birmingham, Warwickshire, England; d. 9 Nov. 1940 at London, England, aged 71). British prime minister and leader of the CONSERVATIVE PARTY 1937–40.

The second son of Joseph, and half-brother of Austen, CHAMBERLAIN, Neville Chamberlain became a businessman. He was lord mayor of BIRMINGHAM 1915–16. Appointed director-general of national service in 1917, he clashed with Prime Minister David LLOYD GEORGE and soon quit. An MP from 1918, he served as paymaster-general (1922–3) and chancellor of the Exchequer (1923–4). Reforms at the Ministry of Health (1924–9) enhanced his standing.

In the NATIONAL GOVERNMENT, Chamberlain was chancellor of the Exchequer (1931–7). He rejected the ideas of J.M. KEYNES, but rejoiced at the OTTAWA AGREEMENTS (1932). He was the obvious successor to Stanley BALDWIN as prime minister (May 1937).

Chamberlain's premiership was dominated by attempted APPEASEMENT of Nazi Germany. After the MUNICH CRISIS (1938) he predicted 'peace for our time'. The fall of CZECHOSLOVAKIA discredited his policy. Party pressure compelled him to declare war (3 Sept. 1939). Chamberlain resigned on 10 May 1940 (succeeded by Winston CHURCHILL). He was lord president of the Council until 30 Sept., Party leader until 4 Oct. His reputation stands or falls by appeasement. *See also* WORLD WAR II.

CHAMBERLAIN, SCOTLAND The chief financial officer and head of the (itinerant) ROYAL HOUSEHOLD (usually a layman); the office was introduced from England *c.*1125 by King DAVID I. The chamberlain received ROYAL REVENUES, disbursed moneys at court, and supervised BURGHS through visitations (ayres). In 1424 JAMES I gave the chamberlain's headship to a new officer, and *c.*1426–8 removed all other powers, except for supervision of burghs; ayres ended after 1517. The office continued until 1705 (held heritably by the dukes of Lennox 1583–1672).

CHAMBERS OF COMMERCE OF THE UNITED KINGDOM, ASSOCIATION OF An organization formed in 1860 to represent general commercial interests. It held annual conferences and lobbied the British government on trade legislation. Local chambers had been founded from the 18th century (e.g., for Jersey 1768, Glasgow 1783), though most dated from after 1850.

CHANAK CRISIS An Anglo-Turkish war scare in 1922. After WORLD WAR I, the Allies occupied parts of Turkey (Nov. 1918) and proposed partition but Turkish nationalist forces defeated GREECE and confronted British troops at Chanak on the Dardanelles (Sept. 1922). The perceived belligerence of the British prime minister David LLOYD GEORGE appeared troubling until the immediate crisis was resolved by negotiation (11 Oct.). Most Conservatives in Lloyd George's coalition Cabinet had opposed war. The division created by the crisis resulted in Lloyd George's downfall (*see* CARLTON CLUB MEETING). *See also* OTTOMAN EMPIRE, ENGLISH AND BRITISH RELATIONS WITH.

CHANCELLOR, ENGLAND A principal royal officer; originally a chaplain in the king's household who organized document writing and kept the great seal. The first known chancellor was Regenbald (1060s).

The chancellor's importance grew in the 12th century as document production increased. He attended the EXCHEQUER (to early 13th century), and by the reign of King HENRY II (1154–89) a settled 'Chancery' department existed at WESTMINSTER. The chancellor was a leading member of the king's COUNCIL. From the 14th century he presided over the lords in PARLIAMENT and increasingly acted as judge in a separate Court of Chancery. Chancellors were usually senior clergy until the mid 16th century, then laymen (lawyers).

In 1873 the Court of Chancery became part of the High Court, and the chancellor a member of the Court of Appeal and head of the judiciary and courts. His responsibility for courts was removed in 2003, and most of his remaining roles in 2006. The title of lord chancellor was given to the minister for justice in the House of Commons. *See also* EQUITY COURTS, ENGLAND.

CHANCELLOR, IRELAND *see* CHANCERY AND COURT OF CHANCERY, IRELAND

CHANCELLOR, SCOTLAND The most senior royal officer, until 1546 usually (but not invariably) a churchman. The office was introduced from England *c.*1123 by David, heir to Alexander I (when ruling S Scotland). The chancellor supervised the royal 'chapel' or Chancery, which produced royal documents; acted as the ruler's senior adviser; and was a leading member of the COUNCIL and PARLIAMENT. From 1546 the post was given to a leading nobleman. The last holder was the earl of SEAFIELD (d. 1730). *See also* SECRETARY OF STATE, SCOTLAND; KING'S (OR QUEEN'S) COMMISSIONER, SCOTLAND.

CHANCERY, COURT OF, ENGLAND A court of law, based in WESTMINSTER HALL, which developed from the late 14th century under the CHANCELLOR and provided justice when COMMON LAW remedies were unavailable (e.g., due to deficiency of written evidence). It expanded in the 15th century when cases concerning USES were prominent. Proceedings began with a petition, and business was in English or French (rather than Latin). From the 16th century the court's flexible mode of law was called EQUITY.

From the late 17th century the court's operation became more expensive and slower. Plaintiffs sometimes waited years for judgments. Despite reforms in the 1830s–40s, the court was satirized by Charles DICKENS in *Bleak House* (1852–3). It was abolished in 1873 (by the Judicature Act) though equity was retained in the legal system. *See also* COURTS, ENGLAND BEFORE 1660/FROM 1660.

CHANCERY, SCOTLAND *see* GOVERNMENT, SCOTLAND BEFORE 1707

CHANCERY AND COURT OF CHANCERY, IRELAND A Chancery (writing office) was established in 1232 by the English GOVERNMENT in Ireland. Headed by a chancellor, it accompanied the CHIEF GOVERNOR, issued WRITS, and kept copies of documents (similar to English CHANCERY ROLLS). In the later 13th century the chancellor overtook the treasurer as second in importance to the governor.

The Chancery lost work in the later 15th century to the Privy Seal Office, but by 1534 was developing as a court of EQUITY (in DUBLIN). Its procedures notably appealed to plaintiffs from Gaelic lordships. From the 18th century its jurisdiction included inheritance and bankruptcy. The court became a division of the new High Court of Justice in 1878. The post of lord chancellor was abolished by the UK Parliament in 1922. *See also* COUNCILS, IRELAND, LATE 12TH–16TH CENTURIES; COURTS, IRELAND.

CHANCERY ROLLS A type of record created by the English Chancery (royal writing office), probably instigated by Hubert WALTER. From 1199 clerks routinely copied outgoing letters on parchment sheets which were sewn together as rolls. Different types of business were entered on separate rolls (e.g., letters to named individuals on 'close rolls'). Chancery rolls are a rich source for English history. Some series continued into the 21st century in book form.

CHANNEL ISLANDS An archipelago in the English Channel, off NW France, most of which belongs to the British Crown. The islands have been organized since the late 15th century as two bailiwicks. Each is now a self-governing Crown 'dependency' associated with, but outside, the UNITED KINGDOM. The bailiwick of Jersey comprises Jersey island and uninhabited islands. The bailiwick of Guernsey consists of three autonomous sub-jurisdictions: Guernsey island, with three other inhabited and some uninhabited islands; Alderney, with uninhabited islands; and Sark, with inhabited Brecqhou and uninhabited

islands. Est. popn in 2015: Jersey, 102,000; bailiwick of Guernsey, 62,000 (most on Guernsey). A lieutenant-governor represents the monarch in each bailiwick.

The islands were probably granted in 933 by the king of France to William Longsword, count of Rouen, whose lands developed into the duchy of NORMANDY. (Normandy became associated with England in 1066; *see* NORMAN CONQUEST OF ENGLAND.) The islands were retaken by the king of France, with the rest of Normandy, between 1202 and 1204, but quickly reseized by JOHN, king of England and duke of Normandy. In 1254 King HENRY III regarded them as English Crown possessions, but they were claimed until the late 15th century by France, which attacked and sometimes occupied them. (Jersey relinquished Chausey in 1499.) The Channel Islands were the only part of the duchy of Normandy to remain with the English Crown, though French influences remained strong (e.g., in law).

The islands became Protestant (Calvinist) under EDWARD VI (reigned 1547–53) and were transferred from a French diocese to the Church of England (WINCHESTER diocese) in 1569. The islands were occupied by Germany 1940–5 (during WORLD WAR II).

The islands' economies were historically agricultural/horticultural, supplemented with textile manufacturing in the 16th–18th centuries and tourism growing from the early 1950s. From the early 1960s Guernsey and Jersey developed into 'offshore' financial centres (so-called 'tax havens'). *See also* NEW JERSEY.

CHANNEL TUNNEL A tunnel under the English Channel connecting France to Great Britain, for horse-hauled coaches, was proposed in 1802 during the short-lived peace of Amiens by the French mining engineer Albert Mathieu to Napoleon Bonaparte. Development was prevented by hostilities (*see* FRENCH REVOLUTIONARY AND NAPOLEONIC WARS, BRITISH INVOLVEMENT). Another French engineer, Aimé Thomé de Gamond, suggested various links from the 1830s. His 1857 proposal for a railway tunnel won British–French official approval in 1867. Tunnelling started in 1878, but was halted in 1883 because British military and parliamentary committees deemed the venture a security risk. The British opposed further proposals for similar reasons until 1955.

Research recommenced in 1957, and a decision to proceed was taken in 1966, only for the British government to cancel the project (1975) because of cost and opposition. Yet discussions continued, and in 1986 the treaty of Canterbury authorized the Anglo-French company Eurotunnel to finance, construct and operate a tunnel. It was dug between Folkestone (SE England) and Calais (NE France), comprising two parallel railway tunnels and a smaller service tunnel, 31 mi (50 km) long. The tunnel was inaugurated on 6

May 1994, for use by vehicle-carrying shuttle trains and long-distance trains. *See also* FRANCE, ENGLISH AND BRITISH RELATIONS WITH.

CHANTRIES, ENGLAND AND WALES A chantry was an endowment, made most often by individuals but latterly also by fraternities and guilds, to fund the perpetual celebration of Mass for the souls of specified deceased people at an existing altar or purpose-built chapel within any church. Originating in the 12th century out of earlier arrangements for intercessory prayer and Masses (the Latin term *cantaria* meant originally a licence to say Mass), chantries proliferated in the 13th–16th centuries.

Chantries were attacked from the 1520s by evangelical reformers as a visible symbol of the doctrine of purgatory. King HENRY VIII sought to suppress them under the 1545 Chantries Act, but little was done before it lapsed at his death (1547). Chantries were dissolved at Easter 1548, under the 1547 Chantries Act, by the reforming government of Edward, duke of SOMERSET. *See also* REFORMATION, ENGLAND/WALES.

CHANTRIES, SCOTLAND *see* COLLEGIATE CHURCHES

CHAPLIN, CHARLIE (b. 16 April 1889 at Kennington, London, England; d. 25 Dec. 1977 at Corsier-sur-Vevey, Switzerland, aged 88). Raised in poverty, Chaplin became a child entertainer (1897). In the USA from 1913, he was recruited as an actor for pantomime-based 'silent' films. His character, the 'little tramp' (1914–36), made him the world's leading star and rich. *The Gold Rush* (1925) is considered his masterpiece. In the 1930s Chaplin transferred successfully to 'talkies' (e.g., *Modern Times*, 1936). His 1940 parody *The Great Dictator* infuriated its target, Adolf Hitler. Threatened from the late 1940s by the US government for alleged communist associations, Chaplin lived in Europe from 1952. He received a special 'Oscar' award in the USA in 1972, and was knighted in Great Britain in 1975. *See also* CINEMA AND FILM INDUSTRY, GREAT BRITAIN.

CHARITY COMMISSIONS A commission was appointed in 1819 to investigate charities in England and Wales after concerns were raised about misapplication of funds, and was extended until 1840. A permanent Charity Commission was established in 1853 to guard against abuses. It has maintained a register and has supervised charitable organizations. In Ireland, Commissioners of Charitable Donations and Bequests were established in 1845 and continued after foundation of the IRISH FREE STATE (1922). Charities in Scotland were supervised by the Office of the Scottish Charity Regulator from 2003, and in Northern Ireland by a Charity Commission from 2009.

CHARITY ORGANISATION SOCIETY An influential voluntary society founded in London in 1869 to improve the efficiency with which private charities dispensed funds to the poor. It sought to replace indiscriminate relief by assessing the needs of individuals and families; it insisted that the poor should accept responsibility, even in times of mass unemployment and distress. It issued guidance for charity workers, and publicized the extent of poverty and disability. By 1892, 88 similar local societies existed in England, Scotland and Wales. The 'COS' was renamed the Family Welfare Association in 1946. *See also* BARNETT, SAMUEL.

CHARLEMONT, EARL OF (b. 18 Aug. 1728 at Castle Caulfeild, Co. Tyrone, Ireland; d. 4 Aug. 1799 at Dublin, Ireland, aged 70). James Caulfeild succeeded as (4th) Viscount Charlemont in 1734. He was created earl of Charlemont in 1763 for suppressing rural disorder in Co. Armagh.

From 1773 Charlemont campaigned (e.g., in the Irish House of Lords) for Irish parliamentary independence. As commander-in-chief of the VOLUNTEERS he drafted the pro-independence resolutions which were adopted at the Volunteers' Dungannon Convention (Feb. 1782) and resulted in the CONSTITUTION OF 1782. But Charlemont opposed allowing political power to Catholics and chaired a Volunteer convention in Dublin in Nov. 1783 (about parliamentary reform) to prevent adoption of pro-Catholic demands. He later opposed the UNION OF IRELAND AND GREAT BRITAIN. *See also* PROTESTANT ASCENDANCY.

CHARLES, PRINCE OF WALES (b. 14 Nov. 1948 at Buckingham Palace, London, England). Eldest son and heir of ELIZABETH II, queen of Great Britain and Northern Ireland, Prince Charles attended CAMBRIDGE University, becoming the first immediate heir to the English or British Crown to earn a degree (1970). During a break from Cambridge, he studied Welsh and was invested at CAERNARFON Castle as PRINCE OF WALES (1 July 1969). He also became a jet pilot (1971) and served in the Royal Navy (1971–6). He has spoken out controversially on inner-city deprivation, ecology and modern architecture (*see* TOWN PLANNING). The Prince's Trust (founded 1976), which helps disadvantaged children, provided an important focus for social work.

In 1981 Prince Charles married Lady Diana Spencer, producing two children, but continued a long-standing involvement with Camilla Parker Bowles. His separation (1992) and divorce (1996) from Diana damaged his and the monarchy's standing. Following her death (1997), he eventually married Mrs Parker Bowles (2005). *See also* DIANA, PRINCESS OF WALES; CAMBRIDGE, WILLIAM DUKE OF.

CHARLES, THOMAS (b. 14 Oct. 1755 at Llanfihangel Abercywyn, Carmarthenshire, Wales; d. 5 Oct. 1814 at Bala, Merionethshire, Wales, aged 58). A clergyman in the Church of England, which included Wales, Charles settled in his wife's home town of Bala, from where he was among the first to spread Methodism in N Wales (from 1784). He organized the Welsh SUNDAY SCHOOL MOVEMENT and in 1811 ordained the first CALVINISTIC METHODIST ministers, taking Welsh Methodism out of the Church of England to become a separate denomination. *See also* METHODIST REVIVAL, WALES; NONCONFORMITY AND DISSENT, WALES.

CHARLES I (b. 19 Nov. 1600 at Dunfermline, Fife, E Scotland; d. 30 Jan. 1649 at Westminster, Middlesex, England, aged 48). Charles succeeded JAMES VI/I (father) as king of England, Ireland and Scotland on 27 March 1625. Parliament had agreed to war against Spain but an expedition failed (Oct.), provoking an attempt (1626) to impeach Charles's favourite the duke of BUCKINGHAM and refusal of funds. Charles levied a FORCED LOAN. His third Parliament (1628–9), held after disastrous intervention in France, presented a PETITION OF RIGHT (1628). Members prevented adjournment to criticize Charles's policies (*see* HOLLES, DENZIL).

Charles made peace overseas (1629) and ruled without Parliament (*see* CHARLES I, PERSONAL RULE). In 1640, after military confrontation in Scotland (*see* COVENANT, WARS OF THE, OR BISHOPS' WARS), he summoned Parliament but members attacked his religious and taxation policies (*see* SHORT PARLIAMENT). After Scots invaded England, Charles called another Parliament (Nov.), but had to make concessions (*see* LONG PARLIAMENT).

From 1642 Charles and Parliament were at war (*see* CIVIL WARS). Charles surrendered to Scottish invaders (May 1646), but was passed to parliamentary commissioners (Jan. 1647), and seized by Parliament's Army (June). Following further war (1648), he was executed (*see* CHARLES I, TRIAL AND EXECUTION). Succeeded in Scotland by CHARLES II. Monarchy was abolished elsewhere. *See also* SPANISH MATCH; HENRIETTA MARIA; LAUD, WILLIAM; WENTWORTH, THOMAS; ENGAGEMENT; JAMES VII/II.

CHARLES I, PERSONAL RULE Term applied to the period from 1629 when Charles ruled without calling PARLIAMENT and without funds authorized by Parliament. He made peace with France (April 1629) and Spain (Nov.) to avoid expenditure on war. He augmented ROYAL REVENUES by reviving long-abandoned practices such as fining landowners for failing to take up knighthood and fining offenders against ancient FOREST LAW. His imposition of SHIP MONEY nationally in 1635 was especially unpopular. With his ecclesiastical adviser William LAUD, Charles encouraged greater emphasis on ceremonial in church services, decency within churches (such as protective rails for COMMUNION TABLES), and a relaxed attitude to Sunday recreation. Their attempt to impose reforms on the Scottish Church provoked rebellion (*see* REVOLT OF 1637). When Charles failed to suppress this with military force (First Bishops' War, 1639), he recalled Parliament to obtain funds for further warfare (1640), whereupon MPs attacked him for levying arbitrary taxation and religious innovations (*see* SHORT PARLIAMENT). The struggle between king and Parliament culminated in CIVIL WAR. *See also* WESTON, RICHARD; COTTINGTON, FRANCIS; TONNAGE AND POUNDAGE; THOROUGH; COVENANT, WARS OF THE, OR BISHOPS' WARS.

CHARLES I, TRIAL AND EXECUTION On 6 Jan. 1649 England's RUMP PARLIAMENT, claiming authority from the people, established a High Court of Justice with 135 nominated commissioners (judges) to try Charles for treason (by levying war against Parliament and the people). The trial was held in WESTMINSTER HALL on 20–27 Jan. Charles refused to plead. He was sentenced to death, with 57 commissioners signing the death warrant. Charles was executed in Whitehall (street), Westminster (Middlesex), on 30 Jan. *See also* CHARLES I.

CHARLES II (b. 29 May 1630 at Westminster, Middlesex, England; d. 6 Feb. 1685 at Westminster, aged 54). Son and heir of CHARLES I, Charles went overseas in 1646, during the CIVIL WARS. After his father's execution (1649), monarchy was abolished in England. Charles went to Scotland, took the Covenant, and unsuccessfully invaded England (1650–1; *see* COVENANTING REVOLUTION; WORCESTER, BATTLE OF). He escaped abroad.

Recalled in 1660 (*see* CONVENTION PARLIAMENT), Charles regained most royal powers, but had to accept Parliament's religious settlement (*see* RESTORATION, ENGLAND AND WALES). In foreign affairs Charles fought the Dutch Republic (1665–7), allied with the Dutch and Sweden against France (1668), then allied with France (1670) and fought the Dutch (1672–4). Charles's main ministers were the earl of CLARENDON (to 1667), the CABAL (to 1673–4) and the earl of DANBY (to 1679). He had numerous mistresses.

In the 1670s people feared that Charles would restore Catholicism and impose arbitrary government. Parliament forced him to withdraw a Declaration of INDULGENCE and passed a TEST ACT (1673). After a POPISH PLOT was revealed, WHIGS tried to exclude Charles's Catholic heir, his brother James (1678–81; *see* EXCLUSION CRISIS). From 1681 customs revenues enabled Charles to govern without Parliament, and Whigs were removed from offices. *See also* RESTORATION, IRELAND/SCOTLAND; ANGLO-DUTCH WARS; DOVER, TREATY OF; PORTSMOUTH, DUCHESS OF; RYE HOUSE PLOT.

CHARTERS, ANGLO-SAXON ENGLAND Documents recording the conveyance of estates in perpetuity. Based on Italian models, they were probably introduced by Roman missionaries *c.*600; the earliest surviving original charter dates from 679. Usually written in Latin, charters are also known as diplomas or *bocs* (OE). About 1000 survive (originals or copies). They were superseded in the mid 11th century by smaller writ-charters (*see* WRIT). *See also* BOOKLAND.

CHARTER SCHOOLS In Ireland, popular name for schools supported by the Society in Dublin for Promoting Christian Knowledge (founded 1717). It received a royal charter in 1733 as the Incorporated Society in Dublin for Promoting English Protestant Schools, and was supported by grants from the Crown (1738–94) and Irish and UK Parliaments (1751–1831). Charter schools sought to turn Catholics and poor Protestants into industrious Protestants, but educated relatively few children and declined in the early 19th century. *See also* EDUCATION, IRELAND.

CHARTISM, ENGLAND A British working-class mass movement which sought enfranchisement and PARLIAMENTARY REFORM. It was named after 'The People's Charter' (1838), a list of six demands largely drafted by William Lovett (1800–77). The Charter called for universal male suffrage, equal electoral districts, payment of MPs, abolition of the property qualification for MPs, voting by ballot and annually elected Parliaments. Feargus O'CONNOR publicized the Charter and Thomas ATTWOOD summoned a National Convention in London (Feb. 1839). This raised a petition of 1.2 million signatures which was vainly presented to the UK Parliament in July 1839.

The Chartists divided over tactics. Lovett sanctioned only 'moral force' but others, such as O'Connor and James Bronterre O'Brien (1805–64), hinted at 'physical force'. Chartism was most radical in northern cities, where it expressed industrial discontent. Parliament rejected a second Chartist petition of 3 million signatures in May 1842.

In 1848 O'Connor staged a mass rally at Kennington, Surrey, near London (10 April). The government feared revolution, but a third and final petition was delivered without violence. Chartism faded away without securing its aims, although all of the Chartists' demands except annual Parliaments were subsequently granted.

CHARTISM, SCOTLAND Support grew quickly; by spring 1839 there were 130 Chartist associations. It declined after Parliament's rejection of the second petition (May 1842), but revived in 1848 when 10,000 demonstrated in Edinburgh for the third petition (April). Scottish Chartists also advocated reform of the CORN LAWS, educational reform and trade union rights. The movement was divided between 'physical force' Chartism (Glasgow based and proletarian) and a stronger 'moral force' Chartism (Edinburgh based and artisan). Religion was influential in the latter: 20 Chartist churches were formed by early 1841. TEMPERANCE was also championed.

CHARTISM, WALES The movement (1838–*c.*1850) attracted widespread support, particularly in the S Wales coalfield, in CARMARTHEN (SW Wales) and in mid-Wales wool towns. Dramatic incidents occurred, such as riots in Llanidloes (a Montgomeryshire wool town) in April 1839 and the NEWPORT RISING (1839).

In the 1840s Chartists published newspapers, fostered TRADE UNIONISM and sought to organize a general strike. Welsh Chartism ceased to be a mass movement by 1850, although individual Chartists remained in the 1860s.

CHATHAM, EARL OF *see* PITT, WILLIAM, THE ELDER

CHAUCER, GEOFFREY (b. *c.*1340 in England; d. possibly 25 Oct. 1400 at Wesminster, Middlesex, England, aged about 60). Son of a London vintner, Chaucer fought in France 1359–60 under Lionel, duke of Clarence, and possibly EDWARD THE BLACK PRINCE. He joined the household of King EDWARD III by 1367 and led several overseas diplomatic missions. He was controller of the London customs 1374–86, clerk of the king's works 1389–91, and royal forester 1391–9. He lived in Kent in the 1380s–90s.

Chaucer began writing by the 1360s. He is celebrated for his (unfinished) *Canterbury Tales* (1390s), a collection of verse stories told by pilgrims journeying to the tomb of Thomas BECKET in CANTERBURY. Its prologue portrays 14th-century society. *See also* ENGLISH LITERATURE, ENGLAND.

CHEDDAR The site in Somerset (SW England) of an (excavated) estate centre which belonged to the kings of WESSEX (later of England), late 9th–early 11th centuries. It was used as a hunting centre and meeting place for the WITAN (council). The site included a large hall. A replacement hall and stone chapel were built *c.*930. *See also* KINGSHIP, ANGLO-SAXON.

CHEMICALS INDUSTRY, ENGLAND AND GREAT BRITAIN Chemical production was limited before the 18th century. In the late 16th–19th centuries, copperas stones, found in SE England, were processed in coastal plants to produce copperas (a blackening agent and dye fixative) and sulfuric acid (for textile bleaching). Large-scale production of sulfuric acid (or 'vitriol') was achieved in 1736 by Joshua Ward, using glass vessels, and improved in 1746 with the 'lead-chamber process' invented by John Roebuck who established a manufacturing plant in Scotland.

From the 1790s a 'chemicals revolution' of innovations made crucial contributions to the INDUSTRIAL REVOLUTION, especially textiles: chlorine-based bleach was devised by 1793, and a bleaching powder was patented in 1799 by Charles Tennant. His chemicals factory at St Rollox (near GLASGOW, Scotland) became one of the largest in Europe by the 1840s. Synthetic soda (for textiles, soap making, etc.) was made from 1816 using the French 'Leblanc process' (by R. Tyne, NE England; also later at St Rollox and by R. Mersey, NW England). Britain had the world's largest chemicals industry until the 1880s.

Subsequent significant developments included formation of Brunner Mond (1873) to exploit the Belgian 'Solvay process' for synthetic soda making (*see* MOND, LUDWIG); merger of 'Leblanc' companies as United Alkali (1890), the world's largest chemicals company; and foundation of British Dyestuffs (1915), with government support, to promote a weak area. In 1926 they merged (with Nobel Explosives) as IMPERIAL CHEMICAL INDUSTRIES, which remained a pre-eminent company until the 1990s.

The industry expanded through the 20th century, boosted by requirements during WORLD WAR II and developing areas (e.g., fertilizers, plastics, pharmaceuticals). Large companies invested in laboratories; university-based research also produced commercial products. In the early 21st century there were over 3000 companies (excepting pharmaceuticals and petroleum), with concentrations in N England and Scotland, which employed over 210,000 people and produced 12% of UK manufactures (by sales).

CHESTER, EARLS OF, AND WALES The earldom of Chester (Cheshire) was created by WILLIAM I in 1070 to guard NW England against the Welsh. Hugh d'Avranches, 2nd earl (d. 1101), invaded N Wales in the mid 1070s; he and successors controlled NE Wales until OWAIN GWYNEDD retook it in the 1150s and 1160s. Thereafter earls were less active in Welsh affairs. The earldom escheated (reverted) to the English Crown in 1237, making the Crown a neighbour of Gwynedd. *See also* NORMANS, IMPACT ON WALES; ROBERT OF RHUDDLAN.

CHICHELE, HENRY (b. *c*.1362 at Higham Ferrers, Northamptonshire, England; d. 12 April 1443 at Canterbury, Kent, England, aged about 81). A clergyman, lawyer and administrator, Chichele was bishop of ST DAVIDS from 1407 and archbishop of CANTERBURY from 1414. He supported King HENRY V in war against France (from 1415), negotiating the surrender of Rouen in 1419 (*see* HUNDRED YEARS WAR).

Under HENRY VI (from 1422) Chichele was a leading member of the COUNCIL until 1435 and sought to reconcile the duke of GLOUCESTER and Henry BEAUFORT. His opposition to Beaufort's cardinalate grew into general resistance to papal influence, resulting in his 1423 condemnation by Pope Martin V. Chichele also instigated trials of lollards (1416–20), and founded St Bernard's and All Souls Colleges in OXFORD (both 1438). *See also* LOLLARDY, ENGLAND.

CHICHESTER, ARTHUR (b. May 1563 at Raleigh, Devon, England; d. 19 Feb. 1625 at London, England, aged 62). A naval officer and soldier (knighted 1596), Chichester was sent to Ireland by Queen ELIZABETH I in 1599 where he helped Lord MOUNTJOY to defeat the rebellion of the 2nd earl of Tyrone (*see* NINE YEARS WAR). He was rewarded with BELFAST Castle (in NE Ireland) and nearby lands (1603).

Chichester served as chief governor of Ireland (lord deputy) 1605–16, under JAMES VI/I. He supported the gradual elimination of Irish customs and Catholicism. After the earls of Tyrone and Tyrconnell fled in 1607, he seized their lands for plantation, intending a generous allocation to native Irishmen. But O'DOHERTY'S REBELLION (1608) caused a change of policy to large-scale immigration (*see* ULSTER PLANTATION). Chichester was created Lord Chichester of Belfast in 1613. He was buried in Carrickfergus (NE Ireland). *See also* FLIGHT OF THE EARLS.

CHIEF GOVERNOR, IRELAND After HENRY II made himself lord of Ireland (1171), rulers of England were represented by governors with various titles, who acted as head of GOVERNMENT and administration, chief judge and military commander. Until the 15th century they were a mixture of locally based men and ones sent from England.

From the early 13th century the governor was usually styled 'justiciar', though high-ranking noblemen, who were often appointed in the 14th and 15th centuries, were styled 'king's lieutenant' in honour of their rank. Until the late 15th century governors from England usually lived in Ireland for some of their term. When absent, they were represented by a 'deputy justiciar' or (from late 14th century) 'deputy'. Between 1471 and 1534 earls of Kildare (Anglo-Irish magnates based in Ireland) were usually governors, with various titles (*see* KILDARE ASCENDANCY).

In the 16th and early 17th centuries, governors were usually Englishmen and styled 'lord deputy'. From the later 17th century they tended to be English noblemen and called 'lord lieutenant'. In the 18th century (until *c*.1780) the governor was usually of CABINET rank, and between 1700 and 1767 governors usually resided in Ireland when PARLIAMENT was in session (six months in two years), delegating authority to three 'lords justices' in their absence. Governors resided continuously from 1767. The office survived the UNION OF IRELAND AND GREAT BRITAIN (1801), but became mainly ceremonial (*see* CHIEF SECRETARY FOR IRELAND). From Dec. 1922 the IRISH FREE STATE and NORTHERN IRELAND had separate governors.

CHIEF JUSTICIAR In England, an officer who acted as head of government and sometimes regent in the king's absence (from Latin *justiciarius*, meaning 'a justice'). The post is recorded from the 1150s (reign of King HENRY II) and probably dates from the reign of HENRY I (1100–35). Kings had delegated similar authority to important followers or servants from the 1060s (e.g., ODO OF BAYEUX, RANULF FLAMBARD). The post lapsed in 1234 and was revived 1258–65 by the Provisions of OXFORD. The term was also employed in other situations (e.g., in Wales after the English invasions of 1277 and 1282–3; *see* COURTS, WALES). *See also* WALTER, HUBERT; GEOFFREY FITZ PETER; BURGH, HUBERT DE.

CHIEF SECRETARY FOR IRELAND The British government minister who was responsible for administration and policy in Ireland after the UNION OF IRELAND AND GREAT BRITAIN (1801). The post originated (by 1566) as secretary to the CHIEF GOVERNOR of Ireland (styled 'chief secretary' by 1701). From 1777, when a second under-secretary was appointed, the chief secretary's office developed into a department that instructed other Irish departments. Viscount CASTLEREAGH (chief secretary 1798–1801) developed a co-ordinating role for the British government when he obtained support for Union in the Irish PARLIAMENT and afterwards established an Irish Office at WESTMINSTER.

Post-Union chief secretaries were usually CABINET members. Notable secretaries included Robert PEEL, A.J. BALFOUR, George WYNDHAM and Augustine BIRRELL. The post ended in Oct. 1922 (resignation of Sir Hamar Greenwood). *See also* GOVERNMENT, IRELAND 19TH–20TH CENTURIES.

CHILD WELFARE Until the 1880s fathers and masters were mostly responsible for children. In England and Wales from the 16th century, overseers of the poor could provide for orphans (e.g., with apprenticeships).

In the 18th century, increasing numbers of abandoned and orphaned children in large towns were tackled by philanthropic responses (e.g., Thomas Coram's Foundling Hospital, London, 1742; Female Orphan House, Dublin, 1790). Workhouses sometimes supplied relief and education.

In the 19th century legislation protected working children (*see* FACTORY LEGISLATION), and specialist institutions and procedures were developed for problem children. Imprisoned juveniles were segregated (1838), and summary trials provided (1847, England and Wales). Official support was given in Great Britain to 'reformatory schools' for delinquent children (1854) and 'industrial schools' for vagrant children (1857). (Authorized for Ireland 1858, 1868.)

From the 1870s activists and the State promoted a caring approach. Thomas Barnardo established homes for destitute children (from 1870); voluntary societies (from 1883) exposed child abuse. From 1886 UK courts could override paternal custody. 'Probation' (release during good behaviour) was introduced (1887, for England and Wales). Legislation against cruelty (1889, for UK) allowed police to intervene in family relations. Free school meals for children were authorized (England and Wales 1906, Scotland 1908, Ireland, in towns, 1914). The landmark 1908 Children's Act (for UK) introduced 'juvenile courts' and 'Borstals' (reformatories for convicts aged 16–21).

From the 1920s psychologists and educationists encouraged greater sympathy, and State involvement increased. Adoption was regulated (England and Wales 1926, Northern Ireland 1929, Scotland 1930); many reformatory and industrial schools closed (1920s–30s), and the remainder became 'approved schools' (1933). Local authorities developed child-related services (e.g., maternity hospitals). Other important changes included family allowances (1945; *see* WELFARE STATE); priority for children's welfare in legal proceedings (1975 Children Act, for Britain); children's rights (1991, UK ratification of United Nations Convention); greater childcare funding (1990s). *See also* NATIONAL SOCIETY FOR THE PREVENTION OF CRUELTY TO CHILDREN; NATIONAL DETERIORATION.

CHILD WELFARE, SOUTHERN IRELAND The IRISH FREE STATE (from 1922) retained protective powers under the 1908 Children Act but increased reliance on 'industrial schools' for housing and training orphaned, neglected and abandoned children (about 50 schools accommodating roughly 6000 children), and on 'Magdalene laundries' (10) as asylums for a variety of 'fallen' girls and women. Although State funded, the institutions were run mostly by Catholic religious orders. Nuns also ran maternity homes for unmarried mothers from which children were taken for adoption, sometimes to the USA.

State support for children was expanded from 1944 with children's allowances (extended 1952, 1963). Adoption was regulated from 1952 (Adoption Act), and health care provided for most mothers and children from 1953 (Health Act, following failure of the MOTHER AND CHILD SCHEME). Fosterage was further regulated from 1957 (Children Act). Between the early 1950s and 1986 child mortality dropped from 40 to 7.5 deaths per thousand live births.

Industrial schools were closed in the 1960s–70s and Magdalene laundries by 1996. From the 1990s there were revelations of extensive physical and sexual abuse in the institutions, for which the government apologized.

In 1992 the Republic of Ireland ratified the United Nations Convention on the Rights of the Child. Following criticism by the United Nations, it established an Ombudsman for Children (1998) and modified the 1937 CONSTITUTION to include recognition of children's rights and permit greater State intervention for welfare purposes (approved by referendum 2012, implemented following legal challenges 2015).

CHINA, ENGLISH AND BRITISH RELATIONS WITH The English East India Company (British from 1707) traded with China from the early 17th century – it imported tea from 1644. In the late 18th century the Company became China's main supplier of opium, which Chinese merchants imported through Guangzhou (Canton).

After Chinese officials seized British-owned opium in 1839 (to enforce an import ban), Great Britain forced China to open markets to Western trade. During the First Opium War (1839–42), British forces bombarded Guangzhou and seized Hong Kong Island. The treaty of Nanjing (1842) ceded Hong Kong and provided access to other ports (*see* Chinese Treaty Ports). Chinese detention of the crew of the vessel *Arrow* led to the Second Opium War (1856–60), when Anglo-French military action won further concessions. Britain obtained additional territory near Hong Kong Island in 1860 and 1898. British Christian missionaries were active in China 1860s–1940s.

Commerce flourished until encroachments by rival European powers on China challenged British dominance in the 1890s (provoking the Boxer Rising of 1900). The Anglo-Japanese alliance (1902) was an effective short-term riposte, but the growth of Japanese influence and rise of Chinese nationalism eroded British interests in E Asia in the early 20th century. Britain tolerated Japanese involvement in China in the 1930s but was an ally of China 1941–5, during World War II. Britain recognized China's new communist regime in 1950, but joined in the Korean War (1950–3).

From 1972 Britain followed the USA in developing relations with China (e.g., 1979, visit to Britain by Chairman Hua Guofeng). A major issue was the future of Hong Kong, much of which was held on lease. Its return to China was agreed in 1984 (implemented 1997). As Chinese power and influence continued to grow, British involvements with China expanded (e.g., in trade, education, cultural exchanges). Queen Elizabeth II made a State visit to China in 1986.

CHINESE IN GREAT BRITAIN Chinese, including seamen, settled from the early 19th century, coming from Hong Kong (British from 1842) and other Chinese treaty ports, especially Tianjin and Shanghai. By 1900 small 'Chinatowns' existed in ports (e.g., London, Cardiff, Liverpool).

Large-scale immigration developed, via Hong Kong, after the Communist takeover of China (1949). First-generation immigrants, mainly Cantonese speaking, were concentrated in catering and maintained a separate identity. Chinese also came from Malaysia and Singapore in the 1960s–70s, and from mainland China from the 1990s. Chinese children achieved above-average results in education and entered commercial and professional careers. In 2011 there were about 387,000 Chinese (over 90% in England and Wales). Over 30% of women married into the indigenous white population. *See also* Ethnic and National Minorities, England/Scotland/Wales.

CHINESE TREATY PORTS Trading places in China which were opened to foreigners by pressure and where foreigners received legal rights. The arrangement was started by the British following the Opium War of 1839–42. The 1842 treaty of Nanjing ceded Hong Kong Island to the British and access to four other ports, including Shanghai (in addition to Guangzhou, or Canton, the previous main trading port). China's ratification of the treaty of Tianjin (1860), following the Second Opium War of 1856–60, granted access to eleven more ports. Diplomatic representation was permitted, and British citizens were exempted from Chinese jurisdiction. The ports were part of Great Britain's so-called Informal Empire. They were captured by the Japanese in 1941, and Britain surrendered its rights to the Chinese government in Jan. 1943. *See also* China, British relations with.

CHIVALRY A code of social, cultural and to some extent spiritual values arising from the theory and practice of knighthood (*see* Knight). The term is derived from OFr. *chevalerie*, which is related to *chevalier*, meaning 'knight', and *cheval*, meaning 'horse'.

Emerging in the 12th century, chivalry was cultivated in royal and noble circles throughout Western Europe until the early 16th century (with later revivals). At its core were beliefs in the honour and Christian virtue to be won from martial deeds; the obligation of a knight to his king, fellow warriors and his lady; an idealized notion of 'true' love which could exist between men and women; and the importance of legendary martial figures as exemplars of manhood and knighthood (e.g., Achilles, Alexander, Arthur). In Britain these values were expressed in art, literature, noble recreations (e.g., tournaments), knighting ceremonies, fellowships (e.g., Order of the Garter), and even in education. *See also* Froissart, Jean; Thistle, Order of the.

CHOLERA Epidemics of cholera overwhelmed Europe in the 19th century; four included the British Isles. Originating in the Indian subcontinent, the disease caused diarrhoea and dehydration. High mortality ensued.

Cholera arrived in Sunderland (NE England) in Oct. 1831, then spread into Scotland and through England and (from March 1832) Ireland. Wales was lightly affected. The epidemic faded in Great Britain in early 1833, but in Ireland persisted into 1834. Est. deaths: England, 21,000; Scotland, 9600; Wales, 500; Ireland, 25,000.

The second epidemic was the worst. Cholera appeared in LONDON in Sept. 1848, and expanded across Britain and Ireland, continuing through 1849. S Wales was badly affected; in Ireland cholera aggravated the GREAT FAMINE. Deaths: England, 48,700; Scotland, 8000; Wales, 4500; Ireland, 30,000.

In autumn 1853 cholera reappeared in NEWCASTLE UPON TYNE (NE England) and across N England. In 1854 serious outbreaks occurred elsewhere in Britain (especially London), though Ireland was largely spared. Deaths: England, 19,000; Scotland, 6000; Wales, 1000; Ireland, 1700.

In autumn 1865 cholera broke out in and around SOUTHAMPTON (S England). An epidemic followed in 1866, though Scotland mostly escaped. Deaths: England, 12,000; Scotland, 400; Wales, 2200; Ireland, 2400.

Cholera provoked early government intervention in public health. A Central Board of Health was established in England before the first epidemic (1831, superseding one created by the Royal College of Physicians), which issued recommendations for local boards. Similar policies were pursued in Scotland and Ireland. Ignorance about cholera's cause and spread impaired responses. Theories included infection by interpersonal contact ('contagion') or foul air ('miasma'). Exposure of insanitary urban conditions encouraged policy development (see PUBLIC HEALTH ACTS). In 1854 the physician John Snow demonstrated, by disabling a waterpump in London, that cholera spread in polluted water (not air). Improvement of water supplies helped to prevent further outbreaks. Cholera's cause was discovered by Continental European scientists. See also SLUMS; MEDICINE AND PUBLIC HEALTH.

CHRISTIAN BROTHERS Popular name for the Congregation of Christian Brothers, a Catholic order of laymen who live under vows and specialize in school teaching. It was founded in Ireland in 1808 by Edmund Rice (1762–1844), who began teaching at WATERFORD in 1802. Awarded papal recognition in 1820, the order ran 300 schools in Ireland by 1900 and more overseas, notably contributing to the provision of Catholic education in urban areas. See also EDUCATION, IRELAND.

CHRISTIAN SOCIALISM A variety of political movements which either emphasize the social teachings of Jesus Christ or consider SOCIALISM complementary to Christian ethics. Christian socialism began with the efforts of Church of ENGLAND philanthropists to alleviate industrial conditions in the mid 19th century. See also MAURICE, F.D.

CHRISTINA OF MARKYATE (b. c.1096 at Huntingdon, Huntingdonshire, England; d. after 1155 at Markyate, Hertfordshire, England). A merchant's daughter with a vocation to a hermit's life, Christina thwarted attempted seduction by RANULF FLAMBARD (c.1114) and escaped from a forced marriage. She settled as a hermit at Markyate (c.1123). A French speaker (like some other hermits), Christina was influential in religious circles. She became a nun in 1131 and her cell was elevated into a nunnery in 1145.

CHURCH, ENGLAND AND WALES, 1640s–50s In June 1643, during the First CIVIL WAR, the LONG PARLIAMENT authorized an assembly to plan reform of the Church of ENGLAND. It met from July (see WESTMINSTER ASSEMBLY). After Parliament allied with the Scots (Aug.), there was pressure to adopt a presbyterian-type organization (see SOLEMN LEAGUE AND COVENANT). In Jan. 1645 Parliament ordered the use of a Directory of Public Worship, prepared by the Assembly, and in Aug. prohibited the PRAYER BOOK. In 1646 it authorized a presbyterian organization (March) and abolished episcopacy (Oct.). In 1650 the RUMP PARLIAMENT repealed legislation requiring Church attendance.

A presbyterian-type Church government was established in some areas, but not throughout the country. It comprised presbyteries (parish meetings of clergy and lay elders), classes (district meetings) and provincial assemblies. Worship continued at parish churches, with many pre-War clergy retaining their livings. TITHES were retained. In 1654 'tryers' were established to examine candidates for parish livings, and county committees of 'ejectors' to remove unworthy clergy. Alongside the State Church were numerous independent congregations (e.g., over 200 Baptist churches by 1660). The reformed Church was terminated in 1662. See also COMMONWEALTH AND PROTECTORATE; CLARENDON CODE.

CHURCH, MEDIEVAL ENGLAND In the 5th–6th centuries Christianity largely disappeared from eastern areas of former ROMAN BRITAIN, with natives adopting PAGANISM from Germanic settlers. During the 7th century monk-missionaries converted Germanic kings (see CONVERSION OF ANGLO-SAXONS). Dioceses were created based on kingdoms or subkingdoms, with CANTERBURY as centre of an English 'province'. (YORK headed a northern province from 735.) Communities of monks or secular clergy based at MINSTER churches provided care for smaller territories. In the later 8th–9th centuries VIKINGS disrupted the Church in E England.

In the 10th century, kings re-established dioceses in former Viking areas, and Scandinavian settlers adopted Christianity. Monasticism was revitalized (see TENTH-CENTURY REFORMATION). During the 10th–11th centuries minor lords founded churches within minster territories, establishing about 9000 parish churches with their own clergy (*see* PARISH SYSTEM, ENGLAND, FORMATION OF).

From the late 11th century the papacy and Continental movements were more influential, and the Church became more autonomous. Hundreds of monasteries were founded in the late 11th–12th centuries, many belonging to Continental orders (*see* MONASTICISM, ENGLAND). Secular clergy were required to be celibate. From the 12th century Church courts regulated the clergy and aspects of ordinary life (e.g., marriage) using canon law. Conflicts with kings regularly occurred (*see* ANSELM; BECKET, THOMAS; PECHAM, JOHN; PRAEMUNIRE, STATUTES OF).

From the 13th century the Church strove harder to educate laity and encourage discipline. The advent of FRIARS increased preaching. The laity were required to attend confession and communion annually (at Easter). Concern for souls in purgatory encouraged the foundation of CHANTRIES and GUILDS, and making pilgrimages to win INDULGENCES. Lay piety also flourished through observance of Corpus Christi (from 14th century, *see* MYSTERY PLAYS), rebuilding of churches and use of devotional literature. The only major challenge came from LOLLARDY (late 14th–15th centuries), though other critics attacked abuses (e.g., John COLET, d. 1519). *See also* CHURCH ORGANIZATION, ENGLAND; APPROPRIATION OF CHURCHES, ENGLAND/WALES; ENGLISH MYSTICS; GREAT SCHISM; HUNNE AFFAIR; REFORMATION, ENGLAND.

CHURCH, MEDIEVAL IRELAND Christianity was adopted from *c*.400 (*see* CONVERSION OF IRELAND). Although bishops governed the Church, MONASTICISM became prominent. Communities of men and women devoted themselves to religious life, and produced high-quality manuscripts (e.g., Book of KELLS) and artefacts (e.g., Ardagh Chalice). Historians have dubbed the 7th–9th centuries the GOLDEN AGE. From the 7th century ARMAGH claimed pre-eminence over Ireland's churches.

Churches ministered to society by providing religious services, sanctuary, hospitality, education and care for the sick and orphaned. Some communities (e.g., at CLONMACNOIS, GLENDALOUGH, KILDARE) attracted agricultural tenants, craftsmen and traders, creating proto-towns (*see* TOWNS, IRELAND). The prestige of such centres caused kings and later VIKINGS (9th–10th centuries) to fight for dominance. They also succumbed to hereditary control by local lay families.

Increasing contact with Continental Europe stimulated change and reform from the 12th century (*see* CHURCH REFORM, MEDIEVAL IRELAND). Plain architectural styles were succeeded by elaborate Romanesque (as at CASHEL), and a new type of CHURCH ORGANIZATION was introduced, based on territorial dioceses. Many communities were replaced by houses belonging to Continental religious

orders, and houses of FRIARS were founded from the 13th century (continuing to 16th century). A PARISH SYSTEM was created, with clergy supported by tithes (levy of tenth of produce), though a requirement for clerical celibacy was widely ignored. In reaction, conservative ecclesiastical schools attempted to preserve traditional learning (e.g., in Book of Leinster, late 12th century).

Following the Anglo-Norman invasion (1169–70), the Church became divided into Gaelic and English spheres. Nine bishoprics were usually held by Englishmen, 13 by Gaelic Irish, while nine varied. Most clergy livings were poor (the Statute of KILKENNY, 1366, sought to exclude Gaelic clergy from the few wealthy livings). From the 15th century a revival in religious life, mainly in English areas, included the foundation of confraternities, chantries and performance of MYSTERY PLAYS. *See also* LEARNED CLASSES, IRELAND; APPROPRIATION OF CHURCHES, IRELAND; REFORMATION, IRELAND.

CHURCH, MEDIEVAL NORTH BRITAIN AND SCOTLAND Early Christianity in N Britain was based on monastic churches and diocesan organization. From possibly the late 4th century it spread northwards from ROMAN BRITAIN across the Brittonic area S of the FORTH–CLYDE ISTHMUS (5th–6th centuries), where emergent kingdoms probably served as dioceses (*see* RHEGED; NINIAN OR NYNIA; STRATHCLYDE (CLYDE ROCK), KINGDOM OF; KENTIGERN OR MUNGO; GODODDIN). It also diffused into Pictish areas to the N. To the NW, SCOTS from Ireland also spread Christianity (from 6th century). Some monasteries were established from the monastery at IONA (founded 563).

The Roman observance of Easter was possibly adopted in Clyde Rock (Strathclyde) in the 680s–90s, and in Pictish churches from probably 715 (*see* NAITON SON OF DER-ILEI). Monasteries associated with Iona changed in 716. Monasteries were devastated by VIKINGS (late 8th–late 9th centuries). After the UNION OF SCOTS AND PICTS (from *c*.842), DUNKELD became the pre-eminent church (succeeded by Kilrimont/ST ANDREWS in the 10th century).

The 12th and 13th centuries saw transformation along European lines. Dioceses developed internal structures (including 1100 parishes and churches), and Continental (especially French) monastic orders were introduced followed by FRIARS. A close relationship with the papacy developed after Celestine III uniquely placed dioceses under papal supervision (between 1189 and 1192) as a 'Special Daughter'. (Because of pressure from archbishops of YORK, Scotland had no archbishop.) The Church also reinforced Scotland's identity: from 1296 clergy supported anti-English resistance (*see* LAMBERTON, WILLIAM; WISHART, ROBERT).

In the 14th–15th centuries parish clergy became poorer as livings were APPROPRIATED. Few parish churches were rebuilt, although heresy and anti-papal feeling were rare (*see* LOLLARDY, SCOTLAND) and conscientious bishops (e.g., James KENNEDY, William ELPHINSTONE) founded colleges for training clergy. *See also* CHURCH ORGANIZATION, NORTH BRITAIN AND SCOTLAND BEFORE THE REFORMATION; MONASTICISM, MEDIEVAL NORTH BRITAIN AND SCOTLAND; GREAT SCHISM; REFORMATION, SCOTLAND.

CHURCH, MEDIEVAL WALES Christianity was practised in W Britain (later Wales) in the late Roman period (3rd and 4th centuries) and continued afterwards (*see* CONVERSION OF WALES). The early medieval Church (5th–11th centuries) developed a distinctive character. It was strongly monastic (*see* MONASTICISM, MEDIEVAL WALES), and was influenced by 6th-century holy men such as ILLTUD, TEILO, DEINIOL and DAVID.

The advent of NORMANS in the late 11th century greatly altered the Welsh Church, even in native-ruled kingdoms. The Church became integrated with that of England (from 1107 bishops professed obedience to the archbishop of CANTERBURY). Important churchmen (e.g., BERNARD OF ST DAVIDS, URBAN OF LLANDAFF) were nominees of Normans or later the English. The 12th and 13th centuries saw the development of (four) dioceses with demarcated territories and internal structures including the PARISH SYSTEM. The Normans also introduced Continental monastic orders (*see* MONASTICISM, MEDIEVAL WALES) and FRIARS, who helped to shape devotional and intellectual life in the 14th and 15th centuries.

The BLACK DEATH (1349) and revolt of OWAIN GLYN DŴR (1400–10) severely reduced financial resources but recovery began *c.*1430. Between *c.*1460 and *c.*1530 many churches in the NE and SE were rebuilt; elsewhere roodlofts and additional altars were installed. Local Church life often flourished, though most bishops in the 14th and 15th centuries were English and absentees. Monasteries also were in poor condition. *See also* CHURCH ORGANIZATION, WALES; APPROPRIATION OF CHURCHES, WALES; REFORMATION, WALES.

CHURCH BUILDING COMMISSION An official body established by the UK Parliament in 1818 to assist the building of new churches for the Church of ENGLAND, particularly where provision was scarce (e.g., in expanding towns). Parliament provided £1 million, augmented in 1824 by £500,000. The Commission funded or contributed to almost 100 churches under the 1818 Act and about 500 under the 1824 Act (including some in Wales). It was merged in 1857 with the ECCLESIASTICAL COMMISSIONERS.

CHURCH COUNCILS, ANGLO-SAXON ENGLAND Quasi-national assemblies of bishops and other clergy were held from 672 or 673, when Archbishop THEODORE organized the council of Hertford. (It was made possible by the synod of WHITBY, 664, when the Church in BERNICIA and DEIRA adopted the 'Roman' customs followed elsewhere in Anglo-Saxon England.) The Hertford council designated 'Clofesho' (possibly Brixworth in modern Northamptonshire) as the future meeting place, but meetings were held at several places.

Councils authorized the creation of new dioceses, legislated on doctrinal matters and the behaviour of clergy and laity, and considered disputes about ecclesiastical property. Major canons (decrees) survive from Hertford, Clofesho (747) and Chelsea (816), and from a legatine council in 786 (council presided over by papal legates). The holding of councils was interrupted by Viking raids (9th century); thereafter they were associated with meetings of the king's WITAN. *See also* CONVERSION OF ANGLO-SAXONS.

CHURCHILL, JOHN (b. 26 May 1650 at Ashe, Devon, England; d. 16 June 1722 at Windsor, Berkshire, England, aged 72). An Army officer from 1667, Churchill became a protégé of James, duke of York (JAMES VII/II from 1685), and helped to defeat MONMOUTH'S REBELLION (1685). But in Nov. 1688 he defected to James's opponent (and successor) William of Orange (WILLIAM III). Churchill was created earl of Marlborough by William (1689) and fought in Ireland (*see* WILLIAMITE WAR). His connection with Princess ANNE, through his wife, Sarah CHURCHILL, created difficulty with William (1692–4), but provided influence after Anne's accession as queen (1702).

Marlborough commanded the allied armies during the War of the SPANISH SUCCESSION, defeating the French in battles and sieges 1702–11 while Lord GODOLPHIN maintained political support at home. He was created a duke in 1702, and in 1705 was given land and funds for building Blenheim Palace (Oxfordshire).

In 1710 Anne dismissed Marlborough's wife (April), and appointed a TORY ministry which wanted peace (Aug.). Marlborough was dismissed in Dec. 1711. His military commands were restored by King GEORGE I (1714).

CHURCHILL, RANDOLPH (b. 13 Feb. 1849 at Blenheim Palace, Oxfordshire, England; d. 24 Jan. 1895 at London, England, aged 45). British politician whose meteoric rise and fall galvanized the CONSERVATIVE PARTY in the 1880s.

Third son of the 7th duke of Marlborough, Lord Randolph Churchill became an MP in 1874. His egotism alienated many, but the audacity of the FOURTH PARTY and TORY DEMOCRACY, accompanied by a threat to empower constituency representatives, compelled Lord SALISBURY to conciliate him. Churchill served as secretary for India (1885–6) and chancellor of the Exchequer (July–Dec. 1886), but a rash resignation over defence estimates terminated his short career. *See also* CHURCHILL, WINSTON.

CHURCHILL, SARAH (b. 5 June 1660 at Holywell, Hertfordshire, England; d. 18 Oct. 1744 at London, England, aged 84). Sarah Jenyns was a friend from childhood of Lady Anne, younger daughter of James, duke of York. In 1678 she married John CHURCHILL (earl of Marlborough from 1689, duke from 1702).

After Anne's accession as queen (1702), the influence of the countess of Marlborough helped to secure her husband's position as commander in the War of the SPANISH SUCCESSION. But their relationship deteriorated from 1707, because the queen received political advice from Abigail MASHAM. In 1710 the duchess of Marlborough was dismissed by Anne – they never met again. After her husband's death (1722), the duchess oversaw the completion of Blenheim Palace (Oxfordshire).

CHURCHILL, WINSTON (b. 30 Nov. 1874 at Blenheim Palace, Oxfordshire, England; d. 24 Jan. 1965 at London, England, aged 90). British prime minister 1940–5, 1951–5; CONSERVATIVE PARTY leader 1940–55.

The elder son of Lord Randolph CHURCHILL, Winston Churchill won fame reporting the (Second) BOER WAR. An MP 1900–22, he changed from Conservative to Liberal (1904) to oppose TARIFF REFORM. As under-secretary for the colonies (1905–8), president of the Board of Trade (1908–10) and home secretary (1910–11), he was rated a reformer.

From 1911 Churchill served as first lord of the Admiralty, but failure of the GALLIPOLI CAMPAIGN (during WORLD WAR I) prompted demotion to chancellor of the duchy of Lancaster (May–Nov. 1915). After Army service, he was minister of munitions (1916–19), secretary for war and air (1919–21) and colonial secretary (1921–2).

Re-elected in 1924, Churchill rejoined the Conservatives. As chancellor of the Exchequer (1924–9), he readopted the GOLD STANDARD. Excluded from the NATIONAL GOVERNMENT, he condemned APPEASEMENT.

When WORLD WAR II began, Churchill rejoined the Admiralty (Sept. 1939), and became coalition prime minister (10 May 1940). He led the UK to victory. In Opposition after 1945, he remained a world figure. Old age overshadowed his second premiership. *See also* TONYPANDY INCIDENT; ATTLEE, CLEMENT.

CHURCH ORGANIZATION, ENGLAND When Pope Gregory I sent missionaries to Anglo-Saxon kingdoms (596), he envisaged two provinces, each of 13 dioceses, with metropolitan sees (centres) at LONDON and YORK. Dioceses were founded during the 7th century, but producing a pattern based on fewer kingdoms. CANTERBURY (in KENT) became a metropolitan see (601; *see* AUGUSTINE); York was similarly recognized in 735. Technically the Canterbury and York provinces were

separate Churches, but were usually regarded as one. (Lichfield was also a metropolitan see 787–803; *see* OFFA.) In the mid 9th century, there were 16 dioceses, each with a cathedral (bishop's seat). Subordinate churches were also founded, so-called MINSTERS. In western areas, a few churches probably survived from the pre-Gregorian era.

Some dioceses and churches in eastern areas were disrupted in the late 9th–10th centuries by VIKING activity. Following reinstatement, there were in the 1060s 15 dioceses of varying sizes. After the NORMAN CONQUEST (1066–70s), four sees were relocated (e.g., Dorchester to LINCOLN, Elmham to NORWICH), and two dioceses created (Ely, 1109; Carlisle, 1133). WHITHORN diocese (in modern SW Scotland) was nominally subject to York 8th–14th centuries.

Between the mid 10th and 13th centuries, churches were built within territories of minster churches to serve small estates; as 'parishes' they became the basic local territory (*see* PARISH SYSTEM, ENGLAND, FORMATION OF). During the 12th century, large areas within dioceses were demarcated as 'archdeaconries' and small groups of parishes as rural 'deaneries'. Following the DISSOLUTION OF RELIGIOUS HOUSES (1536–40), six new dioceses were created by subdivision (one soon suppressed). Former monastic churches served as cathedrals.

The Church adapted belatedly to industrialization and urban expansion (from later 18th century). During the 19th and 20th centuries new parishes and dioceses were created (e.g., MANCHESTER diocese, 1847). In 2015 there were 42 dioceses. From the mid 20th century rural parishes were grouped or amalgamated. *See also* CHURCH, MEDIEVAL ENGLAND; CANTERBURY AND YORK, PRIMACY DISPUTE; REFORMATION, ENGLAND; ENGLAND, CHURCH OF.

CHURCH ORGANIZATION, IRELAND From its beginning (5th century) the Church was episcopal (governed by bishops). Early bishops, including PALLADIUS and PATRICK, apparently established sees (centres) at or near royal sites. Accorded high status within the SOCIAL STRUCTURE, bishops exercised authority within areas which seemingly corresponded to the *TÚATH* (small kingdom). But because *túatha* fluctuated in size and numbers, and lacked urban centres for sees, a fixed diocesan system was impracticable. There was no established hierarchy of bishops, though association with senior kings conferred prestige. As a result, abbots and abbesses of important churches also gained power through acquiring dependent churches across adjacent *túatha* (though the Church was not, as some have claimed, 'abbatial' or 'monastic' in character).

The CHURCH REFORM movement from the late 11th century included organizational reform: in 1111 the synod of Ráith Bressail (possibly in modern Co. Cork) legislated for two provinces each with an archdiocese and 12 dioceses. The province sees were ARMAGH and CASHEL. The synod of Kells in 1152 (in modern Co. Meath) subdivided the provinces, designating DUBLIN and Tuam as other province sees. Eventually 35 dioceses resulted. Further reform after the arrival of Anglo-Normans (1169–70) included the creation of PARISHES and their grouping into deaneries. A few dioceses were united in the 14th–15th centuries.

After the REFORMATION (16th century) the structure was retained by both the Protestant Church of IRELAND and the continuing Catholic Church. In many areas Church of Ireland clergy served groups of parishes, and sometimes dioceses were joined. The provinces of Tuam and Cashel were abolished, and bishoprics amalgamated, after 1833 (*see* CHURCH TEMPORALITIES (IRELAND) ACT). In 2014, following further reorganization, the Church comprised two archdioceses and ten dioceses. The Catholic Church's structure remained largely unaltered except for the partition or amalgamation of parishes according to changing population distribution. *See also* CHURCH, MEDIEVAL IRELAND; MCQUAID, J.C.

CHURCH ORGANIZATION, NORTH BRITAIN AND SCOTLAND BEFORE THE REFORMATION In

the 5th–7th centuries kingdoms S of the FORTH–CLYDE ISTHMUS probably each served as a diocese under a bishop based in a monastery (*see* RHEGED; STRATHCLYDE (CLYDE ROCK), KINGDOM OF; GODODDIN). To the NW (Irish dominated) and NE (PICTS) monasteries ministered to areas with some abbots doubling as bishops.

After NORTHUMBRIA's conquest of Gododdin (by 638) and Rheged (by 685), new dioceses were created (Abercorn, 681–5, for Gododdin; then under LINDISFARNE; Whithorn for Rheged by 731). Likewise, Pictish kings probably created dioceses in the E and NE (sees at Brechin, DUNKELD, Dunblane, Mortlach (ABERDEEN by 1132), and Kilrimont/ST ANDREWS).

The Scots king KENNETH I MAC ALPIN, also ruler of the Picts from *c*.842, made Dunkeld the pre-eminent church (superseded by Kilrimont/St Andrews by early 10th century). 12th-century kings founded dioceses in the NE (Moray by 1124), N (Ross by 1131, Caithness by 1147) and W (Argyll, taken from Dunkeld *c*.1190). PARISHES were also established (late 11th–mid 13th centuries), which bishops governed through 'officials', archdeacons and 'deans of Christianity' (clergy supervising groups of parishes).

In the 12th century archbishops of YORK (in England) claimed jurisdiction over the Church in Scotland. Scottish kings opposed this and sought recognition of a Scottish province from the papacy. Popes resisted the request, for fear of offending the king of England, until between 1189 and 1192 when the papacy uniquely assumed control of effectively ten dioceses as a 'special daughter' (coordinated from 1225 by a CONSERVATOR). Whithorn (or GALLOWAY) remained with York, and Sodor (or the Isles) with Nidaros (or Trondheim,

Norway), until *c*.1350. In 1472 St Andrews was raised to an archbishopric (*see* GRAHAM, PATRICK), and Orkney (including the SHETLAND Islands) was officially transferred from Nidaros. Glasgow became an archbishopric in 1492 (initially with four subordinate dioceses), creating rival camps. *See also* CHURCH, MEDIEVAL NORTH BRITAIN AND SCOTLAND; CULDEES; WESTERN ISLES; CHURCH ORGANIZATION, SCOTLAND FROM 16TH CENTURY.

CHURCH ORGANIZATION, SCOTLAND FROM 16TH CENTURY Reformers rejected episcopacy and clerical hierarchy. A new order was proposed (in the 'First Book of Discipline', 1560): parishes served by 'ministers'; dioceses (10), each containing 100 parishes, under a 'superintendent'; and a council (General Assembly), chaired by a 'moderator'. Its creation began; five superintendents were appointed and the Assembly met. But because three Catholic bishops conformed to Protestantism, their dioceses were retained and the neat system was never realized. From 1567 ministers were appointed to historical parish livings, and in 1572 bishops were accepted, using historical dioceses but responsible to the Assembly (*see* LEITH, CONCORDAT OF; TULCHAN BISHOPS).

In 1578 a 'Second Book of Discipline' advocated 'presbyterian' organization, derived from Geneva, Switzerland (*see* DISCIPLINE, BOOKS OF), in which bishops and dioceses would be replaced by 'presbyteries' (courts of ministers and elders, supervising groups of parishes). Presbyteries, based on BURGHS, were formed from 1581. They were banned in 1584 (*see* BLACK ACTS) but permitted in 1586, with bishops as 'moderators', creating an episcopal-presbyterian system. A fully presbyterian system (without bishops) was authorized in 1592, including regional synods (*see* GOLDEN ACT).

In 1606 King JAMES VI restored bishops as moderators of presbyteries and synods, and no assembly was called after 1618. In 1638 the GLASGOW ASSEMBLY abolished episcopacy. It was restored in 1662 (*see* RESTORATION, SCOTLAND), but condemned in 1689. From 1690 organization was fully presbyterian (KIRK SESSIONS, presbyteries, synods, General Assembly). Synods were abolished in 1992. Most groups of seceders also retained presbyterian government. *See also* SCOTLAND, CHURCH OF; DISSENT, SCOTLAND; CATHOLICS AND CATHOLIC CHURCH, SCOTLAND.

CHURCH ORGANIZATION, WALES From at least the 6th century, the Church in W Britain (later Wales) comprised independent, monastic 'mother churches' (Welsh *clasau*; singular, *clas*). Each was headed by an abbot (sometimes doubling as bishop), who governed a community of male clergy. Each *clas* influenced lesser churches (Welsh *llannau*; singular, *llan*), often dedicated to a local saint.

Between 1107 and 1143, under Norman influence (*see* NORMANS, IMPACT ON WALES; URBAN OF LLANDAFF), four *clasau* became cathedrals with large, defined dioceses: LLANDAFF (SE Wales), ST DAVIDS (SW and C), BANGOR (NW), and ST ASAPH (NE). Other developments followed. BERNARD OF ST DAVIDS (bishop 1115–48) created four archdeaconries within St Davids; other dioceses had archdeacons by the 13th century. Below archdeaconries, rural deaneries were formed by the late 13th century, often corresponding to CANTREFS or COMMOTES. Meanwhile the PARISH SYSTEM developed. Norman bishops also replaced cathedral communities with individually funded canons.

The Norman system continued largely intact until the 20th century. (Two detached parts of Bangor were added physically to Bangor and St Asaph respectively in 1859.) After DISESTABLISHMENT (1920), part of Llandaff became Monmouth diocese (1921), and part of St Davids Swansea and Brecon diocese (1923). *See also* CHURCH, MEDIEVAL WALES; MONASTICISM, MEDIEVAL WALES; REFORMATION, WALES; ENGLAND, CHURCH OF; WALES, CHURCH IN.

CHURCH RATES Payments levied in England, Wales and Ireland from inhabitants of parishes by the 17th century for the upkeep of Church of England or Church of Ireland churches. Rates were fixed by parish meetings and collected by churchwardens. In the early 19th century DISSENTERS and CATHOLICS demonstrated considerable resentment. Rates were abolished in Ireland by the 1833 Church Temporalities (Ireland) Act, and in England and Wales by the 1868 Compulsory Church Rate Abolition Act.

CHURCH REFORM, MEDIEVAL IRELAND A movement in the later 11th and 12th centuries which reorganized the Church and raised standards, reflecting the European Gregorian reform movement (inspired by Gregory VII, Pope 1073–85). It owed much to LANFRANC, the Italian archbishop of CANTERBURY in England (1070–89), who in 1074 urged the holding of a synod to address abuses and corresponded with Toirrdelbach Ua Briain (d. 1086), high-king of MUNSTER (S Ireland) and Ireland. Toirrdelbach presided over a synod in DUBLIN in 1080–1.

In 1111 Muirchertach UA BRIAIN, Toirrdelbach's successor, presided over a synod at Ráith Bressail which created two provinces, each with 12 dioceses, mostly superseding older major monastic churches. Cathedral building followed. Territories were reorganized at the synod of Kells (1152) as four provinces and 34 dioceses, with ARMAGH as the primatial see. Reforming clergy, such as Archbishop MALACHY (d. 1148), promoted more regular religious observation and regularization of marriage for the laity, and renewed discipline for the clergy, the last based on observances of new Continental religious orders. *See also* PRIMACY DISPUTE, DUBLIN AND ARMAGH.

CHURCH–STATE RELATIONS, SOUTHERN IRELAND FROM 1922 The population of the IRISH FREE STATE, which excluded Protestant-dominated NORTHERN IRELAND, was overwhelmingly Catholic (90%). This and the identification of Irish nationalism with Catholicism gave the Church authority to shape southern Ireland's social and moral ethos.

The CUMANN NA NGAEDHEAL government introduced film and book censorship (1923, 1929), restricted liquor sales (1924) and removed facilities for DIVORCE (1925). The FIANNA FÁIL government of Éamon DE VALERA banned contraceptive devices and regulated dance halls (1935). The 1937 CONSTITUTION recognized 'the special position of the Holy Catholic Apostolic and Roman Church', reflected Catholic teaching on family life and women, and banned divorce. In 1951 bishops' opposition to the MOTHER AND CHILD SCHEME undermined the inter-party government.

Cultural changes from the 1960s reduced Church influence. Censorship of films and books was relaxed (1964, 1967), and a referendum (1972) approved removal of the Church's 'special position' (to conciliate northern Protestants). The WOMEN'S MOVEMENT undermined Catholic morality; sale of contraceptive devices was increasingly allowed from 1979, although referendums approved a constitutional ban on ABORTION (1983) and continuing prohibition of divorce (1986). Church control of education was reduced (e.g., by school management boards from 1975).

From the 1990s the Church weakened (e.g., fall in priestly ordinations) and its authority declined. Homosexual activity was decriminalized (1993) and legalization of divorce approved (1995). Abuse of children by clergy, and its concealment by some bishops, were exposed (e.g., in inquiry reports, 2005, 2009, 2011). The Church's diminished status was demonstrated in 2011 when the taoiseach (premier) Enda KENNY attacked the Church and the Vatican for downplaying the scale of child abuse. In 2018 Leo VARADKAR secured support for legalization of abortion and informed Pope Francis that religion would no longer be at the centre of a profoundly changed Irish society (*see* PAPAL VISITS, IRELAND). *See also* CATHOLICS AND CATHOLIC CHURCH, IRELAND FROM 16TH CENTURY; SOUTHERN IRELAND FROM 1922; HOMOSEXUALITY, LAW RELATING TO.

CHURCH TEMPORALITIES (IRELAND) ACT Legislation by the UK Parliament, enacted Aug. 1833, which reformed the Church of IRELAND. It reduced bishoprics from 22 to 12 and abolished the Church CESS. Livings were to be reorganized, and tenants of Church land could convert leaseholds into virtual freeholds. In England, opposition to the State's interference with Church affairs provoked the OXFORD MOVEMENT.

CIDER TAX An EXCISE (sales tax) on cider sold in Great Britain which was proposed in 1763 by Sir Francis DASHWOOD, chancellor of the Exchequer, to help repay debt after the SEVEN YEARS WAR. It provoked riots in the cider-producing areas of SW and W England, and increased the unpopularity of the government of the earl of BUTE. It was introduced in modified form (repealed 1766).

CINEMA AND FILM INDUSTRY, GREAT BRITAIN Films were first shown publicly on 20 Feb. 1896 in LONDON by the French inventors of film cinematography, the Lumière brothers. Cinema developed rapidly from a fairground and MUSIC HALL attraction to mass entertainment, using purpose-built buildings from 1907. By 1914 there were 3800 cinemas. During the 1920s–30s, many luxurious 'picture palaces' were constructed. After reaching 4400 in 1946, the number of cinemas fell to 3000 in 1960, 1500 in 1970 and 730 in 2014. (The first multi-screen cinema, or 'multiplex', opened at Milton Keynes in 1985.) Annual admissions correspondingly peaked at 1600 million in 1946, then declined because of alternative entertainment, reaching a low of 54 million in 1984 and reviving to 165 million in 2013.

After 1896, film studios were quickly established, but US films soon dominated cinemas, from 1914 featuring British star Charlie CHAPLIN. The 1927 Cinematographic Films Act, provoked by a decline in British film making, imposed compulsory quotas of British films on cinemas to encourage production (continuing with modifications until 1983). US films nonetheless remained popular. Sound films were introduced in 1928 (Britain's first was Alfred Hitchcock's *Blackmail*, 1929), and colour films in the mid 1930s. The Hungarian immigrant Alexander Korda was a successful producer in the 1930s. The 1940s are considered a 'golden age' (e.g., *The Third Man*, 1949). 'Ealing Comedies' (1947–57) were popular; James Bond films (from 1962) were worldwide successes. In the early 21st century, films reflecting South Asian culture were made in Britain. By this time films often derived their impact from special-effects technology.

CINEMA AND FILM INDUSTRY, IRELAND The first exhibition of films, produced by the Lumière brothers, was held on 20 April 1896, and the first purpose-built cinema opened in 1909, both in DUBLIN. By 1930 significant towns had cinemas, which showed mainly American or British films. After the IRISH FREE STATE was created, national censorship was quickly introduced (1923) in response to Catholic moral concerns yet attendance increased, peaking in 1954 when there were about 320 cinemas. It declined, with cinemas closing, until 1985. During the 1990s attendances in the Republic of Ireland were the highest per head in Europe. In 2000 there were about 60 commercial cinemas in the Republic and 30 in Northern Ireland, most with multiple screens. The first purpose-built 'multiplex' opened in 1990 at Tallaght, Co. Dublin.

An industry did not develop in the early 20th century, but some film making occurred, often involving expatriates and with nationalist content. The Kalem Co. of the USA shot films on Irish subjects 1910–14, and the Film Company of Ireland made romantic and historical films 1916–20. The first sound film was the travelogue *The Voice of Ireland* (1932). The first feature-length Irish-language film, *Mise Éire* ('I am Ireland'), was made in 1959 by the Irish language and arts organization Gael Linn.

Film making developed strongly in the Republic from the 1970s, often tackling universal subjects and encouraged from 1981 by the official Irish Film Board. Successes included the Oscar-winning *My Left Foot* (1989). In Northern Ireland film making thrived from the 1990s. Notable films included *Good Vibrations* (2013), set in BELFAST during the TROUBLES.

CINQUE PORTS A federation of towns in SE England (originally OFr. *cink porz*, meaning 'five ports'), which provided ships for the king for war-related operations in return for privileges (mainly rights of jurisdiction). The arrangement predated the Norman invasion (1066). In the 12th century there were five ports: Sandwich, Dover, Hythe, Romney, Hastings, which were joined as 'head ports' by Rye and Winchelsea. Eventually another 25 towns became affiliated. The Crown appointed a warden from 1268, and granted a charter of liberties in 1328. In the 13th century the federation provided 57 ships.

The federation provided ships throughout the HUNDRED YEARS WAR (1337–1453) and later contributed to the fleet that countered the SPANISH ARMADA (1588). Most of its privileges were abolished in the 1830s but the federation survived, with its wardenship remaining a position of honour. *See also* NAVAL FORCES, ENGLAND BEFORE LATE 11TH CENTURY; NAVY, ENGLISH, BEFORE 1660.

CIRCULATING SCHOOLS *see* JONES, GRIFFITH

CIRCUMNAVIGATIONS A Spanish expedition made the first journey around the globe in 1519–22, finding a westward route to the 'spice islands' of Asia. Francis DRAKE unintentionally made the first English circumnavigation in 1577–80. After sailing through the Strait of Magellan to the W coast of S America, he returned via the Pacific to avoid repassing the strait. Thomas Cavendish commanded a similar journey in 1586–8. The next circumnavigation did not happen until William Dampier circumnavigated the globe on various vessels in 1679–91. He commanded a circumnavigation 1703–7. Circumnavigations were frequent thereafter. *See also* NORTH-WEST PASSAGE.

CITRINE, WALTER (b. 22 Aug. 1887 at Liverpool, Lancashire, England; d. 22 Jan. 1983 at Brixham, Devon, England, aged 95). As acting general secretary of the TRADES UNION CONGRESS, Citrine was prominent in organizing, and abandoning, the GENERAL STRIKE in Great Britain (1926). He served as general secretary 1926–46. A skilful administrator on the right wing of the LABOUR MOVEMENT, Citrine built the TUC into an organization which governments of all parties and businesses were prepared to consult. He was knighted in 1935 and created Lord Citrine in 1946. He chaired the British Electricity Authority 1947–57.

CIVIL LIST Term originally used for the expenditures involved in supporting the English monarch, royal household and civil government, which were funded separately by PARLIAMENT from 1697 (under the Civil List Act). The list excluded military and naval expenditure. Parliament's control of the civil list increased its influence over the Crown (following the GLORIOUS REVOLUTION), although the Crown's powers of appointment provided continuing authority through PATRONAGE. From 1831 the civil list covered only expenses of the royal household. *See also* GOVERNMENT, ENGLAND WITH WALES 1642 TO 1707.

CIVIL REGISTRATION The registration of births, marriages and deaths with civil authorities became compulsory in England and Wales from 1837, and in Scotland from 1855. Civil registration of births and deaths was introduced in Ireland from 1864. Civil registration was sought partly because PARISH REGISTRATION had ceased to be comprehensive, and because social commentators, professional groups and government officials sought reliable statistical information.

CIVIL RIGHTS MOVEMENT, NORTHERN IRELAND A social and political campaign, in the 1960s, to improve the conditions of the minority Catholic population.

The appointment of the reformist Terence O'NEILL as prime minister (March 1963), and the civil rights movement in the USA, encouraged the formation of campaigning groups. The first main organization, the Campaign for Social Justice (launched Jan. 1964), publicized alleged discrimination (e.g., 'gerrymandered' electoral wards) and pressurized the British government. A Campaign for Democracy in Ulster was launched in Great Britain by Labour Party MPs (June 1965).

Initial lack of success led to the formation in April 1967 of the NORTHERN IRELAND CIVIL RIGHTS ASSOCIATION, which organized marches (provoking Unionist counter-demonstrations). Clashes with police appeared on television, notably violence during a march in LONDONDERRY on 5 Oct. 1968. O'Neill proposed additional reforms (22 Nov.), but they failed to quell the disruption. The situation deteriorated, resulting in the so-called TROUBLES. *See also* NORTHERN IRELAND; PEOPLE'S DEMOCRACY.

CIVIL SERVICE, ENGLAND AND GREAT BRITAIN The British government's civilian officials were called a 'Civil Service' from 1816, copying the INDIAN CIVIL SERVICE. They were previously known as 'king's servants' or 'officeholders'.

Specialist royal officials emerged in England in the 12th century through development of royal household departments and separate administrative departments (e.g., EXCHEQUER). Officers and clerks were normally clergy. By *c*.1200 WESTMINSTER had become the fixed centre of GOVERNMENT (including principal COURTS). Laymen occasionally held senior offices from the mid 14th century.

Clergy were generally superseded by laymen in the 16th century. Appointment was frequently by patronage. From 1546 (institution of naval council) there were departments for military purposes. In 1600 officials numbered about 1200.

Between the 1660s and 1720s the sophistication and size of government increased. As the Treasury developed controls over other departments, and 'political' ministers changed, senior Treasury officials provided continuity. From 1683 the EXCISE became the first large-scale department, with officials throughout England and Wales. By the 1720s, including Scotland, there were 12,000 permanent government officials. From 1782 some reforms were implemented (*see* ECONOMICAL REFORM).

Reforms advocated by the 'NORTHCOTE–TREVELYAN REPORT' (1853) changed the service's character. A Civil Service Commission was created and examinations introduced for junior posts (both 1855). From 1870 appointment to many departments was by open competitive examination. Impartiality became a leading principle. In 1874 there were 54,000 civil servants. By the 1920s many departments were organized into three levels of ranks and work: 'clerical', 'executive' (management and cases), 'administrative' (control of departments, policy).

As the scope of government expanded during the 20th century, staffing increased dramatically (including women), and offices were established throughout Great Britain. Staffing reached 371,000 by 1939 and peaked at 747,000 in 1975, before declining through efficiency reductions. From 1999 sections served devolved governments in Scotland and Wales. In 2017 there were 419,000 civil servants (including part-time staff). *See also* PLACEMAN; INDUSTRIAL DEMOCRACY; QUANGO.

CIVIL SERVICE, IRELAND Government employees increased considerably from the later 17th century. By 1800 the GOVERNMENT and COURTS employed about 5000 people, including 3000 under the revenue commissioners. Appointment was usually by patronage (rather than suitability), and promotion by seniority. Following the UNION OF IRELAND AND GREAT BRITAIN (1801), many departments were amalgamated with British departments (e.g., customs and excise in 1823), and efficiency was improved.

The Irish Civil Service adopted qualifying examinations for entrance in 1855 (recommended by the 'NORTHCOTE-TREVELYAN REPORT' of 1853). As in Britain, open competition for posts began in 1870, and the service was divided into upper and lower divisions from 1876 (there was also a clerical grade). The most senior posts were dominated by Protestants, the remainder by Catholics.

CIVIL SERVICE, NORTHERN IRELAND

A Northern Ireland Civil Service was organized from Sept. 1920 by Sir Ernest Clark, an English civil servant. Because few staff transferred from the Dublin-based Irish Civil Service, it depended mainly on local recruitment. Despite non-sectarian intentions, it became overwhelmingly Protestant. Recruitment and promotion of Catholics were deterred partly by pressure from Unionist politicians and the ORANGE ORDER. The percentage of Catholics 1927–59 was 6%. In 1972 there were 15,000 civil servants.

After British 'direct rule' was imposed (1972), the NICS worked mainly under the Northern Ireland Office of the British government. Increased recruitment of Catholics reduced Protestants to 59% by 1985. From 1999 (with interruptions), the service again served devolved government (see EXECUTIVES, NORTHERN IRELAND). In 2014, over 27,000 civil servants supported 12 ministerial departments and other offices. See also GOVERNMENT, NORTHERN IRELAND.

CIVIL SERVICE, SOUTHERN IRELAND

The provisional government of the IRISH FREE STATE (formed Jan. 1922) retained most UK civil servants in Ireland (about 21,000). Though the new service was influenced by the independence movement (e.g., reservation of some posts for Army veterans; requirement of Irish for employment from Jan. 1923), it largely maintained the British ethos of impartiality. A Civil Service Commission was established (1923) to manage appointments (by competitive examination). From 1935 women were required to resign on marriage (rescinded 1973). The language requirement was abolished in 1974.

Until the late 20th century many entrants attended leading Catholic schools, and the service was criticized for being excessively conservative, though in the late 1950s T.K. WHITAKER redirected economic policy. It failed to anticipate the banking collapse of 2008. In 2010 there were about 34,000 civil servants. See also GOVERNMENT, SOUTHERN IRELAND.

CIVIL WARS

The struggle, principally in England, for predominant authority between King CHARLES I and supporters ('Royalists' or 'Cavaliers') and the LONG PARLIAMENT and supporters ('Parliamentarians' or 'Roundheads'), 1642–6, 1648. Parliament's support was strongest in E and SE England, including London; the king's in SW England and Wales.

Both sides recruited forces from early 1642 (see MILITIA ORDINANCE). Parliament appointed the earl of ESSEX as commander on 12 July; Charles symbolically raised his standard at Nottingham on 22 Aug. Armies fought, inconclusively, at Edgehill (Warwickshire) on 23 Oct. A Royalist advance on London was blocked on 13 Nov. (at Turnham Green, Middlesex). OXFORD became the Royalist capital.

In April 1643 Charles sought forces from Ireland (see CESSATION), and on 26 July Royalists captured BRISTOL. Parliament allied with Scottish presbyterians (Aug.), agreeing to Church reform (see SOLEMN LEAGUE AND COVENANT). In 1644 Parliamentarians and Scots were victorious at Marston Moor, Yorkshire (2 July) and dominated N England, but in Sept. Essex's army surrendered to Royalists in Cornwall. Repercussions included Parliament's creation of the NEW MODEL ARMY (April 1645), commanded by Thomas FAIRFAX and Oliver CROMWELL. It defeated Royalists decisively at Naseby, Northamptonshire (14 June), and at Langport, Somerset (10 July), and recaptured Bristol (10 Sept.).

In 1646 Royalist armies surrendered in Cornwall (13 March) and Gloucestershire (21 March). Charles left Oxford (27 April) and surrendered to Scots in Nottinghamshire (5 May). Oxford capitulated on 24 June.

A second war originated with an alliance made on 26 Dec. 1647 between Charles (imprisoned on Isle of Wight) and Scottish representatives (see ENGAGEMENT). Royalists mounted risings in April and May 1648. Though they were quickly suppressed, Royalists in Colchester held out until Aug. A Scottish army invaded on 8 July and was defeated at PRESTON (Lancashire) by Cromwell (17–19 Aug.). Charles was executed in 1649 and monarchy abolished (see COMMONWEALTH AND PROTECTORATE). See also CAVALIERS, ROUNDHEADS; CIVIL WARS, POLITICAL ASPECTS.

CIVIL WARS, IMPACT OF

The CIVIL WARS (1642–6, 1648) were the longest period of warfare on the British mainland after the YORKIST–LANCASTRIAN CONFLICT (15th century). They caused the deaths of around 190,000 people in England and Wales. Possibly a tenth of the adult male population was usually in arms. Soldiers were billeted on the civilian population, and horses and carts were taken for military use. The passage of armies brought devastation, and sieges caused considerable destruction. Parliamentarian forces destroyed altars and other church furnishings. From 1643 Parliament introduced the assessment, a weekly tax mainly on land, and a sales tax (*see* EXCISE).

To some, the wars appeared to have far-reaching social consequences: Royalist GENTRY suffered sometimes crippling fines and were displaced as local rulers by minor gentlemen (*see* COUNTY COMMITTEES). Adherents of some religious movements (e.g., QUAKERS) rejected social hierarchy. The important role played by women in many sects caused some Royalists to claim that traditional family roles were being inverted. *See also* CHURCH, ENGLAND AND WALES, 1640s–50s; ENGLISH REVOLUTION SECTS.

CIVIL WARS, POLITICAL ASPECTS War began in 1642 after a two-year struggle between King CHARLES I and opponents in Parliament. Having made concessions in 1641 (*see* LONG PARLIAMENT), Charles rejected most further demands (e.g., parliamentary approval of ministers, control of armed forces, abolition of episcopacy and ceremonies; *see* GRAND REMONSTRANCE; BISHOPS EXCLUSION BILL; NINETEEN PROPOSITIONS). Supported by Royalist MPs and peers, he sought to preserve his powers.

Parliamentarians became divided: a 'peace party' wanted a quick settlement; a 'middle group' sought victory and a negotiated agreement; a 'war party' wanted victory and an imposed settlement. On 1 Feb. 1643 Parliament presented propositions, including abolition of bishops and control of military forces ('treaty of Oxford'). Charles countered with demands.

In 1643 Parliament's aims became firmer when it accepted Scottish demands for radical Church reform, probably along presbyterian lines (*see* SOLEMN LEAGUE AND COVENANT). Parliament's main leaders also died: John HAMPDEN (June), John PYM (Dec.). During 1644 a new fault line emerged, between 'political' Presbyterians (the larger group) and Independents, the former favouring a reformed national Church, the latter opposing uniformity. The Scots, fearful of Independents, sent terms to Charles in Nov. 1644. Negotiations at Uxbridge, Middlesex (Jan.–Feb. 1645) were inconclusive.

After Charles surrendered to the Scots in 1646, Parliament made proposals (July; *see* NEWCASTLE PROPOSITIONS). Discussions followed but no solution. In 1647 Parliament's NEW MODEL ARMY, influenced by Independents, became increasingly political. After it seized Charles (June) it made proposals, which Charles rejected (July), and debated a radical settlement (*see* HEADS OF PROPOSALS; PUTNEY DEBATES).

In Dec. 1647, Charles (now imprisoned on Isle of Wight) sought victory through alliance with Scots (*see* ENGAGEMENT). After a Scottish invasion was defeated (1648), Presbyterian MPs wanted peace. The Army demanded trial of the king. It excluded Presbyterian MPs (Dec.; *see* PRIDE'S PURGE), enabling Independents to execute Charles (*see* CHARLES I, TRIAL AND EXECUTION). *See also* HOLLES, DENZIL; IRETON, HENRY; CROMWELL, OLIVER; CHURCH, ENGLAND AND WALES, 1640s–50s.

CIVIL WARS, SCOTTISH PARTICIPATION Intervention was intended mainly to secure Scotland's presbyterian form of CHURCH ORGANIZATION. During the 1630s King CHARLES I alienated much of Scottish society by his religious policies (*see* REVOLT OF 1637). It united behind the NATIONAL COVENANT (1638). COVENANTERS took control of government and in 1640 invaded England (*see* COVENANT, WARS OF THE, OR BISHOPS' WARS). After Civil War broke out in England in 1642, a Scottish Convention and the General Assembly of the Church agreed to ally with the Parliamentarians, making the SOLEMN LEAGUE AND COVENANT (1643) which offered the prospect of extending presbyterianism to England and Wales. In Jan. 1644 a Scottish army entered England and helped Parliamentarians to defeat Royalists at Marston Moor (2 July).

On 5 May 1646 Charles surrendered to the Scots at Southwell (Nottinghamshire, C England), but failed to agree terms (*see* HENDERSON, ALEXANDER). They ransomed him to the Parliamentarians (30 Jan. 1647). Meanwhile the Parliamentarians failed to implement the religious section of the Solemn League. Royalist Scots negotiated with Charles and agreed the ENGAGEMENT (26 Dec. 1647): Scots would help restore Charles in return for a trial period of presbyterianism in England. Scottish 'Engagers', led by the marquis of HAMILTON, invaded England (July 1648) but were defeated at Preston, Lancashire (17–19 Aug.).

Radical presbyterians then took power in Scotland. In Jan. 1648 a Convention repudiated the Engagement and renewed the Solemn League. Radicals dominated Scotland until the arrival of CHARLES II (24 June 1650), which provoked intervention by Oliver CROMWELL leading to the UNION OF ENGLAND AND SCOTLAND in the 1650s. *See also* COVENANTING REVOLUTION.

CIVIL WARS, WALES In 1642 Wales was so Royalist that it was later described as 'the nursery of the king's infantry' (Arthur Trevor, 1645). Only PEMBROKESHIRE and some border areas supported Parliament. Most fighting was related to attempts by both sides to control routes through N and S Wales from Ireland. Parliamentarian invasions were repulsed until autumn 1645 (following the battle of Naseby, England, in June) when most areas were taken by, or declared for, Parliament. The last Royalist stronghold, Harlech, fell in March 1647.

The Second Civil War began in Wales, when the disaffected Parliamentarian John Poyer, governor of Pembroke Castle, declared for CHARLES I (10 April 1648), attracting intervention by Oliver CROMWELL (rising suppressed by

July). *See also* WILLIAMS, JOHN; COMMONWEALTH AND PROTECTORATE, WALES.

CIVITAS Originally the Roman (Latin) term for an autonomous state, it later came to denote any self-governing community. In ROMAN BRITAIN, indigenous tribes were organized (from the mid 1st century) as *civitates*; each had magistrates and a council of local aristocracy, and a central town (the *civitas* capital). *See also* IRON AGE TRIBES, BRITAIN; ROMAN BRITAIN, TOWNS; ROMANIZATION.

CIVITAS CAPITAL *see* CIVITAS; ROMAN BRITAIN, TOWNS

CLAN, SCOTLAND A social group, comprising a kindred and its clients, which gives allegiance to a chief; from *clann*, Gaelic, meaning 'children'. Clans apparently developed in the HIGHLANDS of Scotland in the 14th century among both native Gaelic kindreds and the kindreds of landowners of Anglo-Norman origin. They enabled local leaders to protect themselves and their followers without the support of central authority (due to the declining power of the monarchy in the region.) As well as providing protection, chiefs allocated land. Clan surnames were adopted in the 17th century, when chiefs also established legal ownership of clan land. Some clans remained Catholic after the REFORMATION (1560) and supported JACOBITISM in the 18th century. After CULLODEN (1746) the estates of rebellious chiefs were confiscated. The 1746 Disarming Act banned Highland clothes (except in the British Army) and condemned bagpipes.

The suppression of clan culture stimulated the foundation of the Highland Society of London (1778), which achieved the unbanning of Highland dress in 1782. Individual clans now adopted particular designs or 'tartans'. Forfeited estates were restored in 1784. The distinguished service of Highland regiments in overseas wars, especially the FRENCH REVOLUTIONARY AND NAPOLEONIC WARS (1793–1815), created awareness of Highland culture. Royal approval was bestowed in 1822 when clansmen paraded in Edinburgh before King GEORGE IV, who also wore Highland dress. 'Scottishness' was increasingly identified with clan culture.

While clan culture gained prestige, society was weakened by CLEARANCES (from 1770s), when Highland inhabitants were removed to coastal areas or emigrated. Clan culture survived in British overseas territories, and was strengthened from the late 20th century by international clan gatherings, made possible by affordable air travel.

CLAN NA GAEL *see* FENIAN BROTHERHOOD

CLANN NA POBLACHTA (Irish, meaning 'Family of the Republic'). A political party founded by Seán MacBride and other ex-members of the IRISH REPUBLICAN ARMY, launched 6 July 1946. It sought the transformation of southern Ireland into a republic and greater emphasis on social reform (though conformable to Catholic teaching). It won ten seats in the Dáil in 1948 and participated in two inter-party governments (1948–51, 1954–7), before declining and being wound up (1965). *See also* POLITICAL PARTIES, SOUTHERN IRELAND FROM 1922.

CLAPHAM SECT In England, a small informal group of wealthy EVANGELICAL Christians (members of the Church of ENGLAND), which flourished approximately 1790–1830. It was named after Clapham village in Surrey (now within London), where leading members lived, including Henry Thornton (1760–1815) and William WILBERFORCE. The group promoted moral concerns, notably the anti-slavery movement and reformation of manners. The name was invented in 1844 by former member James Stephen.

CLARE, RICHARD FITZ GILBERT DE *see* STRONGBOW

CLARE FAMILY A prominent family in England, Wales and Ireland, 1066–1314, established by Richard fitz Gilbert (d. *c*.1090), from NORMANDY. Their family name is derived from Clare, Suffolk (E England), the centre of Richard's estates.

Richard's second son, Gilbert fitz Richard (d. *c*.1115), received the lordship of CEREDIGION (W Wales) from King HENRY I of England. Gilbert's second son, Gilbert fitz Gilbert (d. *c*.1148), was created earl of Pembroke in 1138. His son, STRONGBOW, invaded Ireland.

Richard de Clare (d. 1217) and son Gilbert (d. 1230), descendants of Gilbert fitz Richard's eldest son, were leading opponents of King JOHN of England. By marriage, Richard acquired GLAMORGAN (S Wales). Gilbert married a daughter of William MARSHAL; their son Richard (1222–62) inherited Kilkenny, SE Ireland, and Caerleon and Usk in S Wales (making Richard the greatest lord in S Wales; *see* MARCH OF WALES).

Richard's son Gilbert de Clare (1241–95) supported SIMON DE MONTFORT, but deserted him in 1265. His son Gilbert (1291–1314) was prominent in the reign of EDWARD II of England (1307–27). He died at BANNOCKBURN (Scotland), ending the male line. His youngest sister, Elizabeth (d. 1360), founded Clare College, CAMBRIDGE (1326).

CLARENCE, GEORGE DUKE OF (b. 21 Oct. 1449 at Dublin, Ireland; d. 18 Feb. 1478 at London, England, aged 28). Third surviving son of Richard, duke of YORK, and brother and heir (until Nov. 1470) of King EDWARD IV, George Plantagenet was created duke of Clarence in 1461 after Edward seized the throne. In 1469 he married Isabel Neville, daughter of Richard, earl of WARWICK, who was now disaffected with Edward. In 1469–70 Clarence supported Warwick in conflict with Edward's supporters. Exiled in France (1470), he supported Warwick's restoration of HENRY VI but reconciled to Edward, he fought against Warwick at Barnet (2 April 1471; *see* YORKIST–LANCASTRIAN CONFLICT). He was created earl of Warwick and Salisbury in 1472.

In 1477 Clarence's sympathy for condemned traitor Thomas Burdet led to imprisonment. Convicted of TREASON, he was allegedly drowned in a butt (barrel) of malmsey wine.

CLARENDON, ASSIZE OF Orders made by King HENRY II and his COUNCIL in 1166 requiring local juries throughout England (irrespective of lords' rights) to name people suspected of criminal acts. They would be arrested by a SHERIFF and judged in public by ordeal of water, i.e. immersion in a water-filled pit. (Sinking demonstrated innocence; floating demonstrated guilt.) From 1174 the assize was enforced by itinerant justices, the so-called 'general eyre' (*see* EYRE), and procedures were revised by the Assize of NORTHAMPTON (1176). *See also* ASSIZE.

CLARENDON, CONSTITUTIONS OF A schedule of alleged customs which King HENRY II of England presented to a royal Council at Clarendon Palace (Wiltshire) on 29 Jan. 1164. They specified the authority of the Crown in Church affairs (e.g., involvement by royal courts in cases of indicted clergy), though some were possibly contrary to canon law. Thomas BECKET, archbishop of CANTERBURY, accepted the Constitutions, then reneged and eventually went into exile (Nov.).

CLARENDON, EARL OF (b. 18 Feb. 1609 at Dinton, Wiltshire, England; d. 9 Dec. 1674 at Rouen, France, aged 65). Edward Hyde, a lawyer, co-operated (as an MP) with critics of King CHARLES I in 1640–1 (*see* SHORT PARLIAMENT; LONG PARLIAMENT). But from Feb. 1642, fearful of radicalism, he served the king, continuing during the CIVIL WARS (knighted and appointed privy councillor 1643). He served Charles's son Charles 1645–6 and from 1654 (following Charles I's death in 1649). Hyde lived in overseas exile 1646–60 (appointed CHANCELLOR 1658).

In the 1650s, during the COMMONWEALTH AND PROTECTORATE, Hyde advocated restoration of the monarchy by reconciliation rather than force. In 1660 he drafted the Declaration of BREDA (April), which assisted Charles's return to England (May) as king (CHARLES II), and then became his leading minister. In Sept. Hyde's daughter Anne married Charles's heir, James, duke of York. In 1661 Hyde was made earl of Clarendon. His desire to accommodate presbyterians within the Church of ENGLAND was thwarted by the CAVALIER PARLIAMENT.

Clarendon was blamed for failure in the second ANGLO-DUTCH WAR and dismissed as chancellor (30 Aug. 1667). Threatened with IMPEACHMENT, he fled abroad. During his periods in exile he wrote an influential Royalist history of the Civil Wars. *See also* RESTORATION, ENGLAND AND WALES; JAMES VII/II.

CLARENDON CODE Term applied to four Acts of Parliament for England and Wales, passed 1661–5 by the CAVALIER PARLIAMENT (in reign of CHARLES II), which sought to reimpose uniformity within the Church of ENGLAND and suppress Protestant dissent and Catholicism.

The Corporation Act (1661) required members of town corporations to swear an oath of loyalty and take Holy Communion in the Church of England. The Act of Uniformity (1662) required clergy and schoolmasters to assent to a revised PRAYER BOOK, and to take an oath abjuring the SOLEMN LEAGUE AND COVENANT. The Conventicle Act (1664) prohibited large conventicles (private meetings for worship involving more than five people). The Five Mile Act (1665) banned dissenting clergy from being within 5 mi (8 km) of corporate towns or a previous living. The legislation was named after the earl of CLARENDON, though it was not instigated by him. Most provisions were repealed in the 19th century. *See also* CHURCH, ENGLAND AND WALES, 1640s–50s; BARTHOLOMEW'S DAY EVICTIONS; INDULGENCE, DECLARATIONS OF; TOLERATION ACT, ENGLAND AND WALES.

CLARKE, TOM (b. 11 March 1858 at Hurst Park, Isle of Wight, England; d. 3 May 1916 at Kilmainham, Co. Dublin, Ireland, aged 58). Raised in N Ireland (as a Catholic) from 1865, Clarke lived in the USA from 1880 where he joined Clan na Gael, an American-Irish republican organization affiliated to the IRISH REPUBLICAN BROTHERHOOD (IRB). He went to Britain in 1883 to organize bombings, but was arrested and served 15 years of penal servitude.

After release (1898), Clarke returned to the USA where he worked with John DEVOY. He moved to Ireland in 1907, established a shop in DUBLIN, and joined the Supreme Council of the IRB. After the UK entered WORLD WAR I (Aug. 1914), Clarke participated in the IRB's planning for an uprising, maintaining contacts with Devoy. During the Dublin EASTER RISING (1916), Clarke was based in the General Post Office. He was afterwards court-martialled and shot. His widow, Kathleen Clarke (1878–1972), was prominent in IRISH FREE STATE politics.

CLAS CHURCH *see* CHURCH, MEDIEVAL WALES

CLASSES, ACT OF An Act of the Scottish PARLIAMENT, passed on 23 Jan. 1649, debarring from military and civil offices most Scots who had supported King CHARLES I and those deemed ungodly (defined by categories or classes). It enabled the radical presbyterian government (in power Sept. 1648 to Dec. 1650) to purge Royalists and others considered as enemies of the regime. It was revoked in May 1651, after the coronation of CHARLES II. *See also* COVENANTING REVOLUTION.

CLASSICAL AND NEOCLASSICAL ECONOMICS A tradition of Scottish and English economic thought. Classical economics began with Adam SMITH (notably in *The Wealth of Nations*, 1776) and was developed by such writers as David RICARDO and J.S. MILL. It was reinvigorated ('neoclassical economics') by Alfred MARSHALL (d. 1924). A basic concept was competition, which arose from individual self-interest but was beneficial to society. *See also* LAISSEZ-FAIRE; POLITICAL ECONOMY.

CLAUDIAN INVASION In AD 43 the Roman emperor CLAUDIUS I sent a force of some 40,000 men, commanded by Aulus Plautius, to invade Britain. Claudius himself followed, staging a triumphal entry into Camulodunon (COLCHESTER; Roman Camulodunum), capital of the defeated CATUVELLAUNI. He accepted the surrender of 11 native kings and established a new Roman province, Britannia (in SE Britain). *See also* ROMAN BRITAIN.

CLAUDIUS I (b. 1 Aug. 10 BC at Lugdunum/Lyons, S Gaul; d. 13 Oct. AD 54 at Rome, Italy, aged 63). Tiberius Claudius Nero Germanicus was proclaimed Roman emperor by the praetorian guard (imperial bodyguard) after the assassination of his nephew Gaius (Caligula) in Jan. 41. A member of the ruling Julio-Claudian family, but lacking experience and prestige, Claudius began the Roman Conquest of Britain, largely to enhance his political standing. *See* CLAUDIAN INVASION.

CLEARANCES The removal of agricultural tenants and communities from long-settled lands in Scotland in the 18th–19th centuries. Clearances occurred in the Lowlands (particularly in the early 18th century), the HIGHLANDS (1770s–1840s), and the SHETLAND ISLANDS (early 19th century and from 1860s), though the term is associated with Highland clearances.

Landowners saw the process as economic 'improvement'. In the western Highlands and WESTERN ISLES, cleared land was used for large-scale sheep-farming while tenants were resettled on coastal crofts (smallholdings) to undertake agricultural and other work. EMIGRATION is often associated with clearances, though it usually followed later and resulted from overcrowding of croft lands, lack of secondary employment and failed harvests. *See also* AGRICULTURE, SCOTLAND FROM 18TH CENTURY; LEVELLERS' REVOLT; CROFTING; SUTHERLAND CLEARANCES.

CLERICIS LAICOS Title of the bull issued in 1296 by Pope Boniface VIII which declared that taxation of the clergy by laity required papal authority, on pain of excommunication. It sought primarily to restrain the kings of England and France. In England a crisis followed (*see* WINCHELSEY, ROBERT), but King EDWARD I circumvented the prohibition. Thereafter kings levied taxes by claiming the necessity of a national emergency. *See also* CHURCH, MEDIEVAL ENGLAND.

CLIMACTERIC Term for a decisive period of change, resulting from the fulfilment of developments or trends. Historians have argued for two climacterics in modern British economic history. The first is the 1870s, when growth generated by steam power and FACTORIES reached its greatest magnitude. The other is the period 1899–1913, when the average annual increase in gross domestic product (GDP) fell to 1.4% from 2.1% (1873–99). *See also* INDUSTRIAL REVOLUTION.

CLIVE, ROBERT (b. 29 Sept. 1725 at Styche, Shropshire, England; d. 22 Nov. 1774 at London, England, aged 49). Employed by the EAST INDIA COMPANY (EIC) at Madras (now Chennai, SE India) 1743–53, Clive won renown by capturing Arcot, near Madras (31 Aug. 1751), to undermine a pro-French Indian commander, and by organizing anti-French guerrilla activity.

Back in India from 1755, Clive was involved mainly with Bengal (NE India). He recaptured the British fort at CALCUTTA from the nawab (ruler) of Bengal, Siraj-ud-Daulah (2 Jan. 1757), then overthrew him at PLASSEY (June). The 'client' successor, Mir Ja'far, rewarded the EIC and Clive. Clive was appointed EIC governor of Bengal. He returned to England in 1760; created Lord Plassey 1762 (Irish peerage), knighted 1764, elected MP.

As governor again of Bengal, 1765–7, Clive agreed an annual payment to the Mughal emperor in return for authority to collect imperial revenues (the *diwani*). The EIC also exercised authority under the nawab. It was now effectively a territorial ruler. After the EIC fell into financial difficulties (1772), Clive's administration was attacked. He defended himself in Parliament (1773), but the pressure drove him to suicide. *See also* INDIA.

CLONMACNOIS A former ecclesiastical centre (monastic and lay settlement) in Co. Offaly, Republic of Ireland, containing churches and the magnificent 'Cross of the Scriptures' (9th or 10th century); from Irish, Clúain moccu Nóis, meaning 'Meadow of the son of Noss'.

Founded by Ciarán (d. 549), Clonmacnois was in MEATH (E Ireland) but near CONNACHT (W). It was dominated by the Southern Uí NÉILL until the 11th century. Created a diocesan see in the late 12th century, it became an important centre of trade and craftwork. It declined from the 13th century. Little habitation remained by the 16th century. *See also* MONASTICISM, MEDIEVAL IRELAND.

CLONTARF, BATTLE OF Fought on 23 April 1014 (Good Friday) at Clontarf, LEINSTER (E Ireland). Brian BÓRUMA, high-king of Ireland (from MUNSTER), defeated rebellious Leinstermen and their allies (Norsemen from DUBLIN and VIKINGS from the Isle of MAN and WESTERN ISLES). Brian was killed afterwards in his tent. Clontarf was an incident in the history of Ireland's high-kingship rather than a decisive battle between Irish and Vikings. *See also* MÁEL SECHNAILL MAC DOMNAILL; KINGSHIP, IRELAND.

CLONTARF MEETING The intended final 'monster meeting' of Daniel O'CONNELL's 1843 campaign in Ireland for repeal of the union of Ireland and Great Britain. Scheduled for Sunday 8 Oct. at Clontarf (Co. Dublin), it was banned by the government on 7 Oct., then cancelled by O'Connell. He was arrested a week later and agitation collapsed. *See also* UNION REPEAL MOVEMENT, IRELAND.

CLOSET A small room in royal residences where British monarchs received individual ministers in private audience. The closet became an important place for the expression of royal opinion and power in the 18th century, when the king ceased regular attendance at CABINET, and a PRIME MINISTER needed 'the favour of the closet' (i.e., royal support) as well as parliamentary support.

CLOTH INDUSTRY, ENGLAND In the 5th–11th centuries, women spun woollen yarn and wove cloth on upright looms mostly for family use. Cloth-making industries developed from the 11th century in TOWNS (mainly large centres, e.g., OXFORD, YORK), producing 'broadcloths' on two-man horizontal looms, introduced from abroad. Cloth 'finishing' became more elaborate. From the late 12th century fulling (pounding cloth with water and soap to strengthen the web) was mechanized with water-driven fulling mills.

In the later 14th century cloth became England's leading export commodity by value (overtaking WOOL), partly because heavy duties had encouraged diversion of wool from exports to cloth manufacturing; by the 1430s wool exported as cloth also exceeded raw wool exports. Much additional output came from pastoral areas where part-time family cloth making developed. They included Devon and Somerset; W Wiltshire and adjacent areas; N Essex and S Suffolk; W Yorkshire and E Lancashire. Production was often organized by merchants as piecework ('putting out system'), though some weavers worked independently. Despite fluctuations in output and changes in production areas, cloth's pre-eminence among exports lasted until the later 18th century (overtaken by COTTON).

From the 1560s, partly through the influence of immigrant craftsmen, lighter, more attractive cloths were produced, so-called 'new draperies' (e.g., perpetuanas, serges). Production of worsteds (light cloths made from long wool) grew strongly in Norfolk (including NORWICH) and W Yorkshire, which by the late 18th century became the leading production areas (others declined).

Between the 1790s and 1850s worsted manufacturing became factory based and highly mechanized, foremost in Yorkshire (*see* INDUSTRIAL REVOLUTION). (The Norfolk industry ended in the 1840s.) Continuing expansion required imported wool (70% by 1890s). In 1911, over 220,000 people worked in woollen and worsted manufacturing. The industry then declined because of overseas tariffs and competition from artificial fibres and overseas woollens. In the 1950s, Pakistanis were recruited (*see* SOUTH ASIANS IN GREAT BRITAIN). Production dwindled in the 1970s–80s.

CLOTWORTHY, JOHN (b. *c.*1600 in Ireland; d. 23 Sept. 1665 at Dublin, Ireland, aged about 65). A Puritan (Protestant) landowner in NE Ireland, Clotworthy (knighted 1626) openly opposed Ireland's chief governor (from 1632) Viscount WENTWORTH. In 1640–1, as a member of the English House of Commons, he helped to organize the impeachment of Wentworth. During the 1640s he moved between England and Ireland. Expelled from the Commons in PRIDE'S PURGE (Dec. 1648), he was imprisoned (to Nov. 1651). In the 1650s Clotworthy increased his Irish estates under the CROMWELLIAN LAND SETTLEMENT and through speculative purchases.

Clotworthy supported the RESTORATION (1660), and helped to preserve the recent land settlement by representing landowners to King CHARLES II. He was created Viscount Massereene in Nov. 1660. *See also* IRISH WARS, 1641–52.

CLUB A group (about 70) in the Scottish PARLIAMENT who successfully opposed royal ministers in the 1689 and 1690 sessions, achieving the REVOLUTION SETTLEMENT. Using prearranged tactics, they undermined Crown control of Parliament through abolition of the LORDS OF THE ARTICLES, and obtained the restoration of presbyterianism in CHURCH ORGANIZATION and reinstatement of Church ministers deposed in 1662. Thereafter opposition continued as the looser COUNTRY PARTY.

CLUBMEN In England, during the First CIVIL WAR, a rural resistance movement against military forces on both sides, wanting peace and an agreement between king and Parliament. Originating in Shropshire (W England) in Dec. 1644, it spread through SW and S England in 1645. Clubmen were named after their basic weapon. Ostensibly neutral, they sometimes acted with the side that was locally most powerful.

CLYDE ROCK, KINGDOM OF *see* STRATHCLYDE (CLYDE ROCK), KINGDOM OF

CLYDESIDE An area in W-C Scotland bordering the banks of the R. Clyde, W of GLASGOW, where SHIP BUILDING expanded from the 1820s. (An adjacent area on the N bank became industrialized from the 1870s and known as Clydebank.) Clydeside was a focus of labour militancy in 1915–22 (*see* RED CLYDESIDE). Its industries declined from the 1920s.

CLYDESIDERS Nickname given to ten members of the INDEPENDENT LABOUR PARTY who were elected to the UK Parliament in 1922 by constituencies in GLASGOW (Scotland), which included the CLYDESIDE area. During WORLD WAR I (1914–18) the Glasgow area had seen militant opposition to DILUTION from shipyard unions (e.g., a short-lived workers' soviet in 1917), and had been nicknamed RED CLYDESIDE.

CLYNES, J.R. (b. 27 March 1869 at Oldham, Lancashire, England; d. 23 Oct. 1949 at London, England, aged 80). John Robert Clynes was president of the National Union of General and Municipal Workers 1912–37, and a Labour MP 1906–31, 1935–45. He led the British LABOUR PARTY 1921–2. Left-wing support enabled Ramsay MACDONALD to supplant him as leader. He served in government under MacDonald as lord PRIVY SEAL (1924) and home secretary (1929–31).

CND *see* CAMPAIGN FOR NUCLEAR DISARMAMENT

CNUT (b. late 10th century in Denmark; d. 12 Nov. 1035 at Shaftesbury, Dorset, England). A younger son of SWEIN FORKBEARD, king of Denmark, Cnut participated in Swein's invasion of England (1013–14). In 1015–16 he led another invasion, which resulted in division of England with EDMUND IRONSIDE (Oct. or Nov. 1016). After Edmund's death (30 Nov.), Cnut succeeded as king of all England. He strengthened his position by marrying (1017) EMMA, widow of King ÆTHELRED II (without repudiating his first wife, ÆLFGIFU).

Cnut also sought power around the North Sea. He took control of Denmark in 1019–20 (revisited 1023), fought in Sweden (1026), and overthrew Olaf, king of Norway (1028).

In England Cnut gave land to Danish followers (*see* HOUSECARL), yet two English earls became pre-eminent advisers, Leofric and GODWINE. The legend of Cnut trying to turn back the sea (demonstrating his human weakness) appeared in the 12th century. *See also* SCANDINAVIAN EMPIRE, ENGLAND'S POSITION IN; EARLS, ANGLO-SAXON ENGLAND.

COAL–CATTLE PACT A trade agreement between the IRISH FREE STATE (IFS) and UK which moderated the so-called 'Economic War'; announced 3 Jan. 1935. The IFS agreed to import coal only from UK suppliers; the UK increased its quota for imported Irish cattle. The Pact was renewed, with modifications, in 1936 and 1937. *See also* ECONOMIC WAR.

COAL INDUSTRY, ENGLAND By the 13th century, coal was cut from hillsides or river banks. Shaft mines, descended by ladders, are recorded from the 15th century. Workings were often exploited part-time, sometimes by families. Water and gases in mines hampered coal extraction.

In 1200 mining particularly flourished around NEWCASTLE UPON TYNE (NE England), supplying LONDON and overseas markets by ship. It expanded spectacularly from the late 16th century, using deeper and larger mines, and waggonways (*see* RAILWAYS, ENGLAND). Shipments rose from 36,000 tons in 1551 to 522,000 in 1631, 800,000 in 1690. Other coalfields were also developed. Coal was used for domestic heating and metalwork, and substituted for wood and charcoal in other industrial processes.

From the 18th century steam-powered pumping permitted deeper mines (*see* NEWCOMEN, THOMAS), while improved river navigability and CANALS (from 1760s) reduced transport costs and expanded markets. The INDUSTRIAL REVOLUTION (from later 18th century) depended on coal (as steam engine fuel; as coke, for iron smelting). 'Safety lamps' (invented 1815) stimulated the cutting of larger underground workings.

Demand from steam-powered RAILWAYS (from 1830s) and industrial expansion further expanded output, as did overseas sales (from 1860s). In 1851 there were 100,000 miners in England (excepting MONMOUTHSHIRE). Output in Great Britain rose from 10 million tons in 1800 to 287 million in 1913 (peak), with 184.5 million tons (64%) cut in England, mostly by hand.

The government controlled the industry 1915–21 (during and after WORLD WAR I). Employment in England reached 754,000 in 1921, then declined, initially because of falling exports, reaching 553,000 in 1933. At NATIONALIZATION (1947) there were 369 collieries. Employment fell to 440,000 in 1960, 183,500 in 1980. Bitter strikes occurred, notably in 1921, 1926, 1972, 1974, and 1984–5. The small surviving industry was privatized in 1994. England's last deep mine (Kellingley, N Yorkshire) closed in 2015, though opencast mining continued. *See also* MINERS' UNIONS.

COAL INDUSTRY, IRELAND Mining started in the mid 17th century in three main areas: (a) E Tyrone in N

Ireland; (b) in the Leinster coalfield around Castlecomer (Co. Kilkenny), yielding anthracite for industrial use; (c) Slieveardagh (Co. Tipperary), an extension of the Leinster coalfield, also producing anthracite. Output met only a small proportion of demand. Most coal was imported from Britain.

In the 18th century more mines were opened, including one in Co. Tyrone at Brackaville (1723), which was renamed Coalisland. The Newry Canal was built for transporting Tyrone coal to DUBLIN (opened 1742). Leinster coal was carried down the R. Barrow for malting and brewing, and from 1791 sent to Dublin via canals. Coal was also dug at Ballycastle (Co. Antrim) from the mid 18th century, at Arigna (Co. Roscommon) from 1765, and in W MUNSTER. Around 1800, Irish sources supplied less than 10% of consumption.

Mining largely ceased at Ballycastle by the mid 19th century, in Munster by the 1870s, and in Tyrone and Slieveardagh in the early 20th century. Revival was attempted in Tyrone in the 1920s, and production reoccurred in Slieveardagh in the 1940s–80s. Mining continued on the Leinster field until 1969, and at Arigna until 1990, supplying a power station from 1958. See also TRANSPORT COMMUNICATIONS, IRELAND

COAL INDUSTRY, SCOTLAND Coal was used for brine boiling by the 13th century, for domestic heating by the 16th, and by the late 16th century was exported. Found in the C Lowlands, it was cut from outcropping seams or dug from bell-shaped holes. The industry grew in the 17th century, as Edinburgh merchants invested in mines, and expanded possibly ten-fold in the 18th century. Important new uses were for coke smelting of iron from 1760 and fuelling of steam engines from the 1780s (see COTTON INDUSTRY, SCOTLAND). Transport costs were reduced by waggonways (from 1722), CANALS (from 1790s) and steam RAILWAYS (from 1830s). A legal restriction on employment from c.1600, colliery serfdom, was formally abolished in 1799.

By c.1800 mining took place from Ayrshire (W) through Lanarkshire (S) and into Fife (E) and Lothian (SE). In 1870, 47,000 men worked in over 400 mines, producing 15 million tons. From the mid 1870s the more productive eastern collieries (Fife and Lothian) became predominantly export oriented. Coal production peaked in 1913 at 42.5 million tons and employment in 1920 at 147,000.

Decline followed: by 1933, 81,000 were employed. At NATIONALIZATION in 1947 there were 187 collieries. Employment fell to 72,000 in 1960, 20,500 in 1980, collieries to 71 in 1965, 15 in 1980, one by 1992 (Longannet, privatized 1994). The last colliery closed in 2002, following an underground flood. Opencast coal extraction continued. See also FOREIGN TRADE, N BRITAIN AND SCOTLAND

BEFORE 17TH CENTURY; FOREIGN TRADE, SCOTLAND FROM 17TH CENTURY; INDUSTRY, SCOTLAND BEFORE/FROM LATE 18TH CENTURY.

COAL INDUSTRY, WALES Between 1870 and 1960 coal dominated Wales's economy to an extent unparalleled in any country. The industry's modern development, from the early 18th century, was stimulated by metal industries (e.g., in W Glamorgan), and facilitated by CANALS (built 1760s–90s) and especially RAILWAYS (1830s–40s) which enabled large-scale exporting. From the 1860s the RHONDDA VALLEYS (C Glamorgan) were a major coalmining area (see DAVIES, DAVID; LEWIS, WILLIAM THOMAS). In 1911 a third of the world's exported coal originated in Wales. Output in S Wales peaked in 1913 at 57 million tons (N Wales produced 3 million tons). Coalminers increased from 60,000 in 1851 to 275,000 in 1921 (S Wales, including MONMOUTHSHIRE, 257,000; N Wales, 18,000), a third of the male labour force. The growth concentrated population in the S and SE, encouraged TRADE UNIONISM (see MABON) and the LABOUR PARTY, and gave rise to SYNDICALISM (see ABLETT, NOAH).

The collapse of international trade in the 1920s produced grievous depression (1925–39). Employment in S Wales fell to 126,000 by 1936. Contraction continued in spite of NATIONALIZATION in 1947, when there were 203 collieries in S Wales (including Monmouthshire) and eight in N Wales. By 1960 mining employed 106,000; by 1980, 26,000, producing 7.7 million tons. Most remaining mines were closed after the MINERS' STRIKE of 1984–5. The last deep mine, Tower Colliery in S Wales, closed in 1994 but was reopened by a workers' company (1995). It closed again in 2008 when workable reserves ran out. Opencast mining and extraction from small drift mines continued. See also INDUSTRY, WALES, BEFORE/FROM 18TH CENTURY; IRON AND STEEL INDUSTRIES, WALES; CARDIFF; MINERS' UNIONS; INDUSTRIAL DECLINE, WALES; ABERFAN DISASTER.

COALMINERS' UNIONS see MINERS' UNIONS

COBBETT, WILLIAM (b. 9 March 1763 at Farnham, Surrey, England; d. 18 June 1835 at Ash, Surrey, aged 72). A publican's son with little education, Cobbett served as a soldier (1783–91), then became a prolific author and editor, initially of TORY outlook. In the USA 1792–1800, he wrote pamphlets condemning the FRENCH REVOLUTION and Thomas PAINE. Back in England, he published the *Porcupine* newspaper (1800–1) and the periodical *Political Register* (from 1802).

From c.1804 Cobbett became increasingly radical, supporting CATHOLIC EMANCIPATION and PARLIAMENTARY REFORM, and publicizing rural poverty. Imprisoned 1810–12, he spent 1817–19 again in the USA to avoid rearrest for agitation. In 1820–1 he advised Queen CAROLINE, and from 1832 served as an MP. He is famed for *Rural Rides* (1830), observations of country life in southern England in the 1820s. *See also* HUNT, HENRY 'ORATOR'.

COBDEN, RICHARD (b. 3 June 1804 near Midhurst, Sussex, England; d. 2 April 1865 at London, England, aged 60). Cobden, who ran a calico-printing mill in Lancashire, was a leader of the ANTI-CORN LAW LEAGUE (1839–46) and a Radical MP (1841–57, 1859–65). Dominant in the MANCHESTER SCHOOL, he argued that FREE TRADE would ensure prosperity and peace. Admirers founded the Cobden Club (1866) to disseminate his ideas.

COBHAM'S CUBS Nickname of WHIG opposition politicians in the British Parliament led by Viscount Cobham (Richard Temple) in the 1730s–40s. Cobham, in the House of Lords, opposed the policies of the Whig prime minister Robert WALPOLE from 1733 (*see* EXCISE CRISIS). He was supported in the House of Commons from 1734 by George Lyttelton, Thomas Pitt and William PITT, and from 1741 by George GRENVILLE, all kinsmen. They alleged that Walpole (resigned 1742) was an agent of corruption.

COCKAYNE PROJECT A scheme to make England's CLOTH INDUSTRY and trade more profitable. In 1616, on advice from the London merchant Sir William Cockayne, King JAMES VI/I prohibited exports of 'unfinished' (undyed and undressed) cloth, allowing only more valuable 'finished' cloth to be traded. The dyeing industry could not meet the extra demand, and the Dutch imposed a trade embargo. James cancelled the prohibition in 1617. The cloth industry and James's reputation were badly damaged.

COCKCROFT, JOHN (b. 27 May 1897 at Todmorden, Yorkshire, England; d. 18 Sept. 1967 at Cambridge, Cambridgeshire, England, aged 70). After studying in MANCHESTER and CAMBRIDGE, and service in WORLD WAR I, Cockcroft was a research student in physics at the Cavendish Laboratory in Cambridge (1924–8). He became a fellow of St John's College (1928–46) and Jacksonian professor of natural philosophy (1939–46). In 1932 Cockcroft and Ernest Walton (1903–95) achieved the first disintegration of atoms, for which they received the 1951 Nobel Prize in Physics.

During WORLD WAR II (1939–45), Cockcroft was involved in RADAR development (from 1940), and headed nuclear research facilities in Canada (1944–6). In 1945 he was appointed to create a British nuclear research laboratory: it started in 1946 as the Atomic Energy Research Establishment, at Harwell, Berkshire (included in UK Atomic Energy Authority from 1954). Cockcroft was knighted in 1948 and remained director until 1958, serving

as founding master of Churchill College, Cambridge, from 1959. *See also* RUTHERFORD, ERNEST.

CO-EDUCATION The education of boys and girls together rather than in separate schools, classes or colleges. Some girls were probably educated alongside boys in elementary schools in the British Isles from the 15th century, including Scottish parish schools (from 17th century). Elementary charity and voluntary schools (18th–19th centuries) were usually co-educational, as were most State-funded elementary schools (from 19th century).

Girls' post-elementary education and higher education (from 19th century) tended to be single-sex, though some universities and colleges were co-educational. COMPREHENSIVE EDUCATION in Great Britain (from 1949) was usually co-educational. Women's colleges in universities became co-educational from the 1960s, and most boys' INDEPENDENT SCHOOLS admitted girls from the later 20th century. By the 21st century co-education was extensive in Britain but limited in Ireland. *See also* GIRLS' AND WOMEN'S EDUCATION, BRITAIN.

COERCION ACTS, IRELAND Legislation granting special powers to combat unrest, referring either to all coercive Acts from the late 18th century or to coercive legislation of the UK Parliament 1833–87 (replacing INSURRECTION ACTS). Legislation was usually time limited, and permitted arrest on suspicion and short-term detention without trial. The Criminal Law and Procedure (Ireland) Act of 1887 was applied until the 1920s.

COGIDUBNUS (fl. from 43; d. late 70s or later). Tiberius Claudius Cogidubnus (or Togidubnus) was installed by the Romans as a client king after the CLAUDIAN INVASION (43). He ruled the tribal areas (in SE Britain) of the Atrebates, BELGAE and Regni (capital Chichester, with Fishbourne palace nearby) until at least the 70s. *See also* IRON AGE TRIBES, BRITAIN.

COKE, EDWARD (b. 1 Feb. 1552 at Mileham, Norfolk, England; d. 3 Sept. 1634 at Stoke Poges, Buckinghamshire, England, aged 82). A prominent lawyer, Coke was solicitor-general from 1592, attorney-general from 1594 (knighted 1603). As chief justice of common pleas from 1606 he defended COMMON LAW against other jurisdictions (e.g., Church courts), annoying JAMES VI/I. He was nonetheless appointed chief justice of King's Bench (Oct. 1613) and privy councillor (Nov.).

In 1616, after resisting royal intervention in a case, Coke was dismissed. He returned to the Privy Council in 1617 after marrying a daughter to the brother of James's favourite the duke of BUCKINGHAM, only to be imprisoned 1621–2 for opposing the SPANISH MATCH. In 1628, as an

MP, Coke proposed the PETITION OF RIGHT and condemned Buckingham. His legal publications were influential. *See also* ANCIENT CONSTITUTION.

COLCHESTER A town in Essex, SE England, by the R. Colne. It was originally Camulodunon (Brittonic, meaning 'Fort of Camul'), an OPPIDUM and capital first of the Trinovantes (1st century BC), then of the CATUVELLAUNI. It became Camulodunum, first capital of ROMAN BRITAIN, in 43 (first *colonia* in 49), but was probably abandoned in the 5th century.

The site was revived in the 9th or 10th century (called in OE Colneceaster, meaning 'Walled town on R. Colne'). Domestic cloth making flourished *c.*1350–1450 and late 16th–18th centuries. Industrial development in the 19th century included clothing and boot factories, breweries and flour mills, followed by Marconi wireless and electronics in the 20th. It was also famous for oyster beds, until pollution largely killed them. *See also* ROMAN BRITAIN, TOWNS.

Est. popn: 200, 15,000; 1086, 2500; 1300, 3000–4000; 1600, 10,000; 1800, 11,000; 1900, 38,000; 2000, 104,000.

COLD WAR, BRITISH INVOLVEMENT The term 'Cold War' refers to hostility between Western powers led by the USA and the 'eastern bloc' of the USSR and its satellites, 1947–91, which was manifest in diplomatic rivalry, proxy conflicts worldwide, and an arms race. The USA actively promoted 'containment' of communism from 1947 (e.g., with MARSHALL AID).

Great Britain was a firm ally of the USA. Disputes from 1944 over POLAND, GERMANY, IRAN and GREECE had raised British fears of post-war expansionism by the USSR. Ernest BEVIN, British foreign secretary 1945–51, favoured independent British ATOMIC WEAPONS (rather than reliance on US weapons) and welcomed commitment by the USA (1949) to the NORTH ATLANTIC TREATY ORGANIZATION (NATO).

British statesmen viewed the Cold War primarily as power politics in Europe and the Middle East. They paid less attention to ideology and E Asia, despite involvement in the KOREAN WAR (1950–3). British mediation between the USA and USSR (1955, 1959–60) was ineffective. The Cuban Missile Crisis (Oct. 1962, when the USA forced the USSR to remove missiles from Cuba) demonstrated superpower dominance. The retention of US forces in Europe and NATO unity remained priorities of British foreign policy. In the 1980s Britain supported US pressure on the USSR (e.g., stationing of cruise missiles in Britain and elsewhere from 1983), which contributed to the eventual dissolution of the USSR (Dec. 1991). *See also* RUSSIA AND USSR, ENGLISH AND BRITISH RELATIONS; BERLIN AIRLIFT; CONSCRIPTION.

COLET, JOHN (b. Jan. 1467 at London, England; d. 16 Sept. 1519 at Sheen, Surrey, England, aged 52). A clergyman and scholar, Colet became renowned for his public lectures on St Paul's letters at OXFORD University (from *c.*1496). From 1499 he became close to the Dutch humanist Erasmus. In 1504 Colet was appointed dean of St Paul's Cathedral in London. He denounced abuses in the Church and urged moral reform of the clergy. But that and his critical approach to scripture created suspicion of heresy. He refounded St Paul's School (1510). *See also* HUMANISM; REFORMATION, ENGLAND.

COLLEGIATE CHURCHES Churches endowed with lands and TITHES for supporting a college (or self-governing body; Latin *collegium*) of secular clergy, who prayed for their founder's and benefactors' souls. Some colleges in England provided a school or supported poor men (Eton College, founded 1440 by King HENRY VI, did both).

Collegiate churches were popular in Scotland; 42 existed by 1560, most founded by MAGNATES. The earliest dated from the 13th century, 36 from after 1400. Most colleges were dissolved in the 16th century along with RELIGIOUS HOUSES.

COLLINS, MICHAEL (b. 16 Oct. 1890 at Clonakilty, Co. Cork, Ireland; d. 22 Aug. 1922 at Beal na mBlath, Co. Cork, Southern Ireland, aged 31). While working in England (from 1906), Collins joined the IRISH REPUBLICAN BROTHERHOOD and SINN FÉIN. He returned to Ireland in Jan. 1916, participated in the EASTER RISING (April), and was interned (released Dec.). Thereafter he was a leading republican and rival of Éamon DE VALERA.

In 1919 Collins joined Sinn Féin's self-proclaimed Dáil Éireann ('Assembly of Ireland', formed Jan.), and its government (established 1 April). During the War of IRISH INDEPENDENCE (1919–21) he organized attacks by the IRISH REPUBLICAN ARMY (IRA) on the police and British Army. After a truce was arranged (11 July 1921), he helped to negotiate the ANGLO-IRISH TREATY (Dec.) which created the IRISH FREE STATE. Collins became chairman of its provisional government, aged 31 (14 Jan. 1922). During the ensuing IRISH CIVIL WAR (from June) he commanded the National Army (from 12 July) against the IRA. He was killed in an ambush.

COLOMBO PLAN A scheme proposed at a meeting of COMMONWEALTH foreign ministers in Colombo, Ceylon (now Sri Lanka), Jan. 1950, whereby richer countries (Great Britain, Canada, Australia, New Zealand) would finance development in poorer Asian countries (e.g., India, Ceylon, Malaya). Initially intended to resist COMMUNISM, it expanded to include non-Commonwealth countries (e.g., USA). It continued to run programmes in the early 21st century, when there were 27 members.

COLONIA see ROMAN BRITAIN, TOWNS

COLONIAL OFFICE *see* BRITISH EMPIRE, GOVERNMENT OF

COLONY *see* PLANTATION; CROWN COLONY

COLUMBA (COLUM CILLE) (b. 520 or 521 in N Ireland; d. 9 June 597 at Iona, Scottish Dál Riata, aged about 76). Born into the Northern Uí Néill (Cenél Conaill kindred), Columba in 563 founded a monastery on IONA (off Mull, W of Scotland, in kingdom of DÁL RIATA), followed by daughter houses in the WESTERN ISLES and Ireland (including Durrow). He travelled among the Picts (*see* BRIDEI SON OF MAILCON) and attended the meeting at DRUIM CETT. His ordination of Áedán mac Gabráin of Dál Riata as king (*c.*574) is the first known priestly ordination of a king in western Europe (though some historians consider the record as fictitious). After his death Columba was venerated as a saint. *See also* SELF-EXILE FROM IRELAND, 6TH–8TH CENTURIES; ADOMNÁN; CONVERSION OF NORTH BRITONS, PICTS AND SCOTS.

COLUMBANUS (b. possibly in 560s in Leinster, E Ireland; d. 23 Nov. 615 at Bobbio, N Italy). Columbanus studied at BANGOR (N Ireland) before leaving (*c.*591) for Gaul. There he founded monasteries (e.g., Luxeuil, Burgundy) which followed Irish customs (including the 'Irish Easter'). Criticized by local bishops, he appealed to the Pope. Though expelled by the king of Burgundy, he founded a monastery at Bobbio. His writings included an austere monastic rule. He was later venerated as a saint. *See also* SELF-EXILE FROM IRELAND, 6TH–8TH CENTURIES; EASTER CONTROVERSY; GOLDEN AGE.

COLUM CILLE *see* COLUMBA

COMBINATION ACTS Legislation which prohibited 'combinations' of craftsmen or workers for collective purposes. During the 18th century the British Parliament passed about 40 Acts against combinations in particular trades (e.g., 1721 Act relating to London tailors). A Combination Act of 1799, passed alongside other repressive legislation, introduced a universal ban, strengthening a COMMON LAW prohibition of conspiracies against trade. A replacement Act in 1800 allowed individual workmen to negotiate wages with their master and provided for arbitration and appeal to a magistrate. The 1800 Act was repealed in 1824, effectively legalizing trade unions, though an Act of 1825 penalized intimidation. *See also* TRADE UNIONISM, ENGLAND/SCOTLAND/WALES; FRENCH REVOLUTION, IMPACT ON ENGLAND.

COMMENDATION OF ABBEYS, SCOTLAND Commendation (the temporary holding of a Church office

and its revenues 'in trust'; Latin *in commendam*) was exploited by rulers from 1488, when Pope Innocent VIII granted King JAMES III power to nominate to vacant senior Church positions. Rulers granted abbacies and abbeys to senior officers, relatives (including three illegitimate sons of JAMES V) and nobles. Recipients, known as lay abbots or 'commendators', sat in PARLIAMENT in the clerical estate. By 1560 most abbots were laymen who retained clerical estates after the REFORMATION.

In 1587 King JAMES VI annexed ecclesiastical lands and appropriated revenues, and began 'erecting' (converting) lay abbacies into hereditary temporal lordships with peerages (21 of 30 abbeys by 1625). So-called 'lords of erection' belonged to Parliament's noble estate. *See also* PEERAGE, SCOTLAND.

COMMERCIALIZATION Term used by historians for the process whereby an economy and society become significantly changed by development of commercial institutions and practices. It has been argued (e.g., by R.H. Britnell) that England underwent extensive commercialization between the late 11th and early 14th centuries, proportionately greater than simultaneous increases in POPULATION and cultivated land. (Commercialization may have encouraged population increase.) A larger proportion of people became dependent on, or involved in, market transactions. In the longer term, commercialization facilitated CAPITALISM.

England became more densely urbanized, with perhaps 20% of the population becoming town dwellers (*see* TOWNS, ENGLAND). Well over a thousand MARKETS AND FAIRS were licensed. TRANSPORT COMMUNICATIONS were improved (e.g., by bridge building), which enabled market integration. There was probably an increase in the money stock per person. Wealthier peasants became more actively involved in trading. Though England's population fell heavily in the 14th century, and the money supply declined, much of the commercial framework survived and was revitalized from the 16th century. Commercialization was less intense elsewhere in the British Isles, with some areas of Ireland and Scotland becoming affected only from the 17th and 18th centuries.

COMMERCIAL REVOLUTION Term denoting the dramatic expansion of English and British trade in respectively the late 17th and 18th centuries and its economic and social effects. Improved internal communications and agriculture stimulated domestic commerce, while the pattern of FOREIGN TRADE was reshaped through trade with S Europe and Asia, and development of colonies in N America and the West Indies. *See also* FINANCIAL REVOLUTION; INDUSTRIAL REVOLUTION.

COMMISSIONERS OF SUPPLY In Scotland, shire-based committees usually of LAIRDS, nominated by government advisers; first appointed in 1667 to levy the reintroduced cess (*see* TAXATION, SCOTLAND). The commissioners subsequently received more powers and were important shire authorities until they were largely superseded by elected county councils (1890). Commissioners ceased to collect tax in 1839 but remained on county police committees until 1930, when they were abolished. *See also* LOCAL GOVERNMENTAL STRUCTURES, SCOTLAND; POLICE, SCOTLAND.

COMMON AGRICULTURAL POLICY A central policy regime of the EUROPEAN ECONOMIC COMMUNITY (European Union from 1993) which regulated AGRICULTURE in the UK and Republic of Ireland after their admission (Jan. 1973). Intended to support farmers' incomes, the policy used mechanisms such as import tariffs and 'intervention' purchasing of surplus produce to support prices. Its creation of substantial surpluses and expense were countered with reforms, notably 'milk production quotas' (adopted 1984); SET-ASIDE SCHEME (1988); 'MacSharry reforms' (1992), including reduction of 'intervention prices' and introduction of fixed compensation payments; replacement of production subsidies by 'single payments' to farmers for land and environmental maintenance (2003). The Set-aside Scheme was suspended in 2008 and milk quotas abolished in 2015. The UK's decision to leave the European Union (2016) entailed development of new national agricultural policies (*see* BREXIT). *See also* FARM MODERNISATION SCHEME.

COMMON LAW A type of law which developed in medieval England and became one of the world's principal legal systems; originally so named because it became common to the kingdom of England. The term was widely used from the 1270s.

Common law originated in the assertion of royal authority from 1166, when judges were sent regularly and frequently throughout England to try criminal cases and property disputes (*see* CLARENDON, ASSIZE OF; POSSESSORY ASSIZES). By 1300 a system had developed whereby professional royal judges presided over local and central courts (*see* WESTMINSTER HALL), and cases were settled according to established rules and previous decisions (i.e., applying precedent rather than abstract legal principles). From the late 13th century courts took account of parliamentary STATUTES. Common law reduced the role of local custom and lords' private jurisdiction.

From the 14th century 'equity' (justice based on fairness) developed alongside common law, effectively to circumvent rigid aspects (e.g., when required evidence was lacking). Common law absorbed much commercial law in the 17th and 18th centuries, and took over business from

Church jurisdiction in the 19th century (e.g., probate). From 1973 it could be overridden by European law.

Common law was imposed in English-governed Ireland in the 13th century, and applied in Wales from the 1280s and 1543 (*see* GREAT SESSIONS, COURT OF). It was spread worldwide through the expansion of the English (or British) Empire in the 17th–19th centuries. *See also* BRACTON; CHANCERY, COURT OF, ENGLAND; EQUITY COURTS; LAW, ENGLAND.

COMMON ORDER, BOOK OF The first service book of the Church of SCOTLAND, introduced soon after the REFORMATION. It was compiled in Geneva, Switzerland, by John KNOX (1556), who drew on prayers and writings of the Swiss Church reformer John Calvin, and was formally adopted by the Church's General Assembly in 1562. Enlarged in 1564, it was replaced in 1645.

COMMON PRAYER, BOOK OF *see* PRAYER BOOKS, ENGLAND

COMMONWEALTH A voluntary association of independent states comprising the UK and mostly former territories of the BRITISH EMPIRE. The term 'Imperial Commonwealth' was used from 1917 to refer to Great Britain and its DOMINIONS. 'British Commonwealth' appeared in the BALFOUR DEFINITION in 1926, which affirmed the equality of dominions (recognized by the Statute of WESTMINSTER, 1931). 'British' was dropped in 1949.

The Commonwealth's structure was changed by DECOLONIZATION, making it more multi-racial. Following India's independence (1947), it was agreed in 1949 that republics could join the Commonwealth without declaring allegiance to the British Crown (India remained a member on becoming a republic in 1950). In 1957 GHANA began a wave of applications from 'black Africa'. In 2015 there were 53 members, including 31 republics.

Until 1962 all Commonwealth citizens possessed British citizenship or equivalent status and the right to enter the UK. Immigration was then restricted. Although the Commonwealth has been a heterogeneous body, some unity was maintained by meetings of government heads, a secretariat (established 1965), financial and cultural ties (e.g., Commonwealth Games), the English language, and the commitment of Queen ELIZABETH II as its head.

COMMONWEALTH AND PROTECTORATE The constitutional positions of England, Wales and Ireland following the execution of King CHARLES I: Commonwealth 1649–53 (under the RUMP PARLIAMENT), Protectorate 1653–9, restored Commonwealth 1659–60. The period 1649–60 is also called the 'Interregnum' (interval between kings' reigns). Ireland was conquered for Parliament in

1649–52 (*see* CROMWELL, OLIVER, AND IRELAND). Scotland remained a kingdom until conquered in 1650–1.

The Rump House of Commons decided to abolish the monarchy and House of Lords (6 and 7 Feb., implemented 17 and 19 March). On 19 May it declared England a 'Commonwealth or a Free State' and established a Council of State as an executive, under a chairman. Scotland was added in Oct. 1651.

By 1653 the Army was frustrated by the Rump's resistance to social, legal and political reform, religious toleration, and elections. Its commander Oliver CROMWELL terminated the Rump and Council (20 April 1653), replacing them with a smaller Council, chaired by himself, and a nominated assembly (met July–Dec.; *see* BAREBONE'S PARLIAMENT).

On 16 Dec. 1653, under a new constitution, the INSTRUMENT OF GOVERNMENT, Cromwell assumed executive power as 'lord protector'. He held a Parliament Sept. 1654–Jan. 1655, dissolving it after disagreements. Following PENRUDDOCK'S RISING (March 1655), Cromwell placed England and Wales under district governors (Aug. 1655–Jan. 1657; *see* MAJOR-GENERALS, RULE OF). A second Parliament (Sept. 1656–Feb. 1658) amended the constitution (*see* HUMBLE PETITION AND ADVICE).

On Cromwell's death (Sept. 1658) his son Richard CROMWELL became protector. Parliament met in Jan. 1659. The Army, fearing reorganization, forced Richard to dissolve Parliament (22 April) and then deposed him. It recalled the Rump (6 May), only to dismiss it on 13 Oct. (restored 26 Dec.). The intervention of General George MONCK in 1660 ended with RESTORATION of the monarchy. *See also* ENGLISH REVOLUTION; UNION OF ENGLAND AND SCOTLAND, 1650s; COMMONWEALTH AND PROTECTORATE, IRELAND; ANGLO-DUTCH WARS.

COMMONWEALTH AND PROTECTORATE, IRELAND

England's Parliament was actively involved in Ireland from 1647 (*see* IRISH WARS, 1641–52). After the execution of King CHARLES I (30 Jan. 1649), Ireland was subordinate to England's sovereign bodies and then to the Protectorate (inaugurated 16 Dec. 1653). In March 1653 Ireland was given 30 seats in England's Parliament.

Parliament imposed its authority by conquest (1649–52; *see* CROMWELL, OLIVER, AND IRELAND), and from Oct. 1650 it delegated government to four 'commissioners of Parliament' (most were 'Army radicals'). They divided the country into 'precincts' (initially six, eventually 12), each under a military governor or commissioner of revenue. In Nov. 1651 England's Parliament abolished the historical governorship (offices of lieutenant and deputy), and in July 1652 it appointed Charles Fleetwood as 'principal commissioner of government'. Garrisons of Parliament's NEW MODEL ARMY remained in Ireland during the 1650s.

Parliament and Cromwell sought to impose major changes on Irish society. The most drastic was the extensive transfer of land from Catholics to Protestants (*see* CROMWELLIAN LAND SETTLEMENT). They also attempted to convert the episcopal (Protestant) Church of IRELAND into a Congregationalist- (or Independent-) type Church, by appointing State-paid 'ministers of the Gospel', and banned the Book of Common Prayer. Other Protestant denominations were tolerated. Catholicism was undermined by transporting clergy.

In July 1654 Fleetwood was appointed chief governor (lord deputy), and a Council of State was appointed (Aug.). The English regime became less stern and by 1656 most of Ireland's historical governmental structure was restored. *See also* GOVERNMENT, IRELAND 12TH–MID 17TH CENTURIES; RESTORATION, IRELAND.

COMMONWEALTH AND PROTECTORATE, SCOTLAND *see* UNION OF ENGLAND AND SCOTLAND, 1650s

COMMONWEALTH AND PROTECTORATE, WALES

The Parliamentarians' victory in the CIVIL WARS of 1642–8 aroused little enthusiasm. COUNTY COMMITTEES, established in 1647 to sequester funds, continued as supervisory local governments. In the early 1650s they drew contempt from Welsh GENTRY for consisting of men considered to be of low birth. Wales also experienced the Commonwealth leaders' attempt to spread Puritan ideals by the Act for the Better Propagation of the Gospel in Wales (1650), under which Commissioners ejected 278 clergy, and 60 schools were established (*see* PURITANISM, WALES; EDUCATION, WALES). The military government of 1655–7 was particularly resented (*see* MAJOR-GENERALS), such that the RESTORATION of the monarchy in 1660 won enthusiastic approval. *See also* POWELL, VAVASOR.

COMMON WEALTH PARTY

A radical British political party founded in July 1942, during WORLD WAR II, by Sir Richard Acland (a Liberal Party MP) with support from listeners to the radio talks of J.B. PRIESTLEY. During the wartime electoral truce, it contested by-elections where 'reactionary' candidates were otherwise unopposed, winning three. The single Common Wealth MP elected at the 1945 general election joined the Labour Party in 1946.

COMMORTH

(anglicized form of Welsh *cymorth*, meaning 'aid', 'help'). In Wales (possibly from 5th or 6th century), a biennial or triennial render of cattle from freemen and bondmen to their ruler. From the late 11th century renders were also made to Norman (later English) lords in the MARCH OF WALES. They were abolished by the English Parliament in 1534. *See also* ROYAL REVENUES, WALES.

COMMOTE (Welsh *cwmwd*; plural, *cymydau*). By *c.*1100 the basic local administrative unit in native Wales. Each had a lordly centre or royal court (Welsh *llys*) at which bondmen and freemen paid dues, and where justice was administered. After the English Conquest (1282–3), commotes became hundreds, i.e., subdivisions of new SHIRES. *See also* CANTREF; LOCAL GOVERNMENTAL STRUCTURES, WALES.

COMMUNES, ENGLAND Communes were associations of men bound by oath. Many were formed in Continental European cities in the late 11th and 12th centuries, to seek freedom from external rulers, but few in England. Communes were formed briefly in LONDON (1141, 1191), and were attempted in Gloucester (1170) and YORK (1176). During the BARONIAL CONFLICT AND WARS a 'commune of the middling people' (Latin *communa mediocris populi*) held power in London in support of Simon de MONTFORT (July 1263–Oct. 1265).

COMMUNION TABLES From the mid 16th century Protestant Church reformers sought the replacement of stone altars in churches with wooden tables, in accordance with their understanding of the Eucharist (as memorial rather than sacrifice). In England and Wales, congregations were ordered to replace altars in 1550 (in reign of King EDWARD VI) and 1559 (in ELIZABETHAN SETTLEMENT). Altars were reinstated under MARY I (1553–8). In the 1630s Archbishop LAUD controversially encouraged the protection of tables with rails (forbidden 1643–60). Tables replaced altars in Scotland and the Church of IRELAND from 1560. Protestant dissenting churches (from 17th century) also used tables. *See also* REFORMATION, ENGLAND/IRELAND/SCOTLAND/WALES; LAUDIANISM, IMPACT ON IRELAND.

COMMUNISM A political ideology which advocates the creation of social and economic equality through common ownership of the means of production and exchange. Modern communism, derived from MARXISM (theory formulated by Karl MARX, d. 1883), began to influence politics in Britain through the SOCIAL DEMOCRATIC FEDERATION (founded 1881). A British COMMUNIST PARTY was founded in 1920, inspired by the communist seizure of power (Bolshevik Revolution) in Russia (1917), but remained a fringe group. Working-class radicals mostly supported the constitutional SOCIALISM of the LABOUR PARTY.

Anti-fascism won recruits for communism in the 1930s, and many intellectuals became Communist Party members (e.g., Hugh MacDIARMID, Denis HEALEY). But communism appeared treacherous during the COLD WAR against the USSR and its allies (1947–91), and erstwhile sympathizers became disillusioned by the Soviet suppression of the Hungarian uprising (1956). The collapse of the USSR (1989–91) left the communist movement moribund. A few Irish communists operated as the Communist Party of Ireland (1921–4, 1933–), Irish Workers' League (1923–4), and other organizations. *See also* CAPITALISM.

COMMUNIST PARTY The Communist Party of Great Britain (CPGB) was founded in July 1920. During the 1920s–30s it alternated vainly between trying to supplant the LABOUR PARTY and trying to affiliate to it. While Harry Pollitt was general secretary (1929–39, 1941–56), its loyalty to the Communist Party of the USSR was unshakable. Membership peaked at around 18,000 in 1939. Concentrated support in West Fife (Scotland) and the RHONDDA VALLEYS (Wales) secured two Communist MPs (1945–50). In 1950 the CPGB fielded 100 candidates at the general election, its largest contingent.

The CPGB changed its name to Democratic Left in 1991 and dissolved itself in 1999. Various groups vied over the British communist tradition, with the Communist Party of Britain (founded 1988) emerging in the 21st century as the principal successor. *See also* COMMUNISM.

COMMUNITY CHARGE A local tax introduced in Scotland in 1989 and in England and Wales in 1990 to replace domestic rates. Popularly known as the 'poll tax', it was levied at a flat rate on all resident adults (with rebates for the very poor). Margaret THATCHER, the prime minister, intended it to promote accountability and economy in local government, but it proved difficult to administer and unpopular. Widespread protests included mass non-payment and a riot in central London (31 March 1990). It contributed to Thatcher's downfall (Nov.). From 1993 a property-based Council Tax replaced the Charge. *See also* POLL TAXES, ENGLAND.

COMMUNITY OF THE REALM Term used in England from the 1250s to early 14th century, initially to denote the body of BARONS, KNIGHTS and burgesses (leading townsmen) who, although below the king and his most intimate councillors, were involved in national politics, particularly through PARLIAMENT. By the 1320s the concept was becoming identified with the 'Commons' in Parliament (shire and borough representatives), who from the 1330s formed Parliament's lower house (House of Commons). *See also* COMMUNES, ENGLAND.

COMPOSITION Term used for fixed monetary taxation in place of exactions which Sir Henry SIDNEY advocated to make Ireland's government self-funding. His attempt from 1575 to introduce a composition in the PALE (E Ireland), in place of levies, met resistance, though a compromise was reached (*see* CESS). Compositions were achieved in MUNSTER (1575–8) and CONNACHT (1577).

Gaelic chieftains and Anglo-Irish lords were required to abandon 'coign and livery' (exactions of billeting and supplies) and pay taxation derived from tenants' payments.

In 1586, after revising the Connacht composition (1585), John PERROT sought a general composition, but it was rejected by the Irish PARLIAMENT. (He then negotiated a revised composition with Palesmen.) Some composition payments continued into the 18th century. *See also* ROYAL REVENUES, IRELAND.

COMPREHENSIVE EDUCATION A type of secondary-level education whereby children of all abilities are taught in the same 'comprehensive schools', usually co-educational. The idea was developed in the 1920s, adopted in principle by London County Council in 1936, implemented by some educational authorities in England and Wales under the BUTLER EDUCATION ACT (1944), and recommended for Scotland in 1947.

The first reorganized school opened in 1949 (Holyhead County School, Anglesey), the first purpose-built school in 1954 (Kidbrooke School, SE London). In 1965 the British Labour government instructed education authorities to prepare plans for comprehensive education (replacing selective systems). By the 1980s 'comprehensivization' had been implemented in Scotland, Wales and most of England. Some comprehensives were founded in the Republic of Ireland from 1966. *See also* EDUCATION, ENGLAND/SCOTLAND/WALES.

COMPTON, HENRY (b. 1631 or 1632 at Compton Wynyates, Warwickshire, England; d. 7 July 1713 at Fulham, Middlesex, England, aged about 82). A soldier then clergyman, Compton was appointed bishop of Oxford (1674) and bishop of London (1675). He served from 1676 as a privy councillor. In 1676 Compton helped to organize the 'Compton Census', an enumeration of religious dissenters in England and Wales. It was intended to dissuade King CHARLES II from granting religious toleration by demonstrating that the number of dissenters was negligible.

In 1685 Compton was removed from the Privy Council and other posts for criticizing the illegal appointment of Catholic Army officers by the new Catholic king JAMES VII/II. He was then suspended as bishop for supporting an anti-Catholic preacher (Sept. 1686–Sept. 1688). He encouraged the bishops imprisoned in June 1688 for refusing a royal order (*see* SEVEN BISHOPS' CASE), and signed the invitation to the prince of Orange which initiated the GLORIOUS REVOLUTION (June). Compton was subsequently reappointed a privy councillor (1689).

COMPUTING Important contributions to the development of computing were made in Great Britain. A program-instructed 'Analytical Engine' was proposed in 1834 by the CAMBRIDGE University mathematician Charles Babbage (1792–1871), but only a fragment was built. In 1936 Alan TURING, also at Cambridge, published principles for a program-based digital computer.

Turing's ideas were soon developed because of WORLD WAR II (1939–45). The Government Code and Cipher School (code-breaking centre) at Bletchley Park (Buckinghamshire) recruited Turing and his former mathematician colleague Max Newman (1897–1984). In 1942–3, at Newman's suggestion, an electro-mechanical machine, the 'Heath Robinson', was built for fast decryption of messages. Its mechanical shortcomings stimulated Tommy Flowers (1905–98) to design an electronic machine with 1500 valves, which operated from Dec. 1943. Named 'Colossus', it is considered the world's first program-controlled electronic computer. Ten machines were built, including the faster Mark II, but most were destroyed, and Colossus remained secret until the 1970s.

In 1946 Turing designed the ACE (Automatic Computing Engine), but it was not constructed. Newman moved to MANCHESTER University, where he commissioned the first stored-program computer, nicknamed 'Baby' (operational from 21 June 1948). Britain's first commercially produced computer, the Ferranti 1, was delivered in 1951.

A British computer industry grew during the 1950s, but by 1960 IBM and other US companies were dominant worldwide. Britain's industry responded with consolidation (company mergers, from 1959), eventually producing (1968) a 'national champion' in ICL (International Computers Ltd), part-owned by the government. Acquired by a British company in 1984, ICL was sold to a Japanese company in 1990.

COMYN FAMILY A prominent family in Scottish political life mid 12th–early 14th centuries; probably from NORMANDY (N France). Supporters of John BALLIOL, king of Scots 1292–6.

William Comyn (fl. 1178–1233) was the first Scottish lord of Anglo-French origin to acquire an earldom, through marriage in 1212 to the (Gaelic) heiress of Buchan (NE Scotland). Their son Earl Alexander (fl. 1244–89) was prominent under King ALEXANDER III. Alexander's son Earl John submitted to King EDWARD I of England, conqueror of Scotland, in 1304 and opposed Robert Bruce's seizure of the Scottish kingship in 1306 (*see* ROBERT I). Robert routed John's forces at Inverurie (23 May 1308), after which he ravaged and broke up the earldom. (John died later that year.)

The second son of William Comyn's first marriage, Walter Comyn (*c*.1190–1258), became lord of Badenoch (in the C Highlands) and earl of Menteith (1234). His great-nephew John ('John the Black'; d. *c*.1302) was a 'guardian' of Scotland 1286–92 and supported King John

Balliol, to whose sister he was married. After Balliol's deposition (1296) he submitted to Edward I, but supported William WALLACE by Dec. 1297. His son John ('John the Red') continued to support Balliol (his uncle), but submitted to Edward I in 1304. He was killed by Robert Bruce in Dumfries on 10 Feb. 1306, probably for rejecting Bruce's claim to the kingship.

CONCEALED LANDS Term used for lands in England and Wales once held by religious houses (before 1530s) or by CHANTRIES (before 1548) which were allegedly not surrendered to the Crown when the institutions were dissolved. From 1559 Queen ELIZABETH I granted individuals the right to search for concealed lands. Commissions were appointed to examine suspected illegal landholders. Their activities, funded by the grantees, generated complaints. Eventually, in 1624, Parliament prohibited the search for defective titles over 60 years old. *See also* DISSOLUTION OF RELIGIOUS HOUSES, ENGLAND/WALES.

CONCERT OF EUROPE The informal system of occasional conferences held by Great Powers between 1815 and 1914 to try and resolve disputes that endangered international stability (e.g., the Congress of BERLIN, 1878). Great Britain, France, Russia, the Habsburg Empire, and Prussia (Germany from 1871) were essential participants; also Italy (from 1860) and sometimes the Ottoman Empire. *See also* FOREIGN RELATIONS, GREAT BRITAIN.

CONFEDERATE LORDS Title adopted by Scottish nobles (Catholic and Protestant) who rebelled after the marriage (15 May 1567) of MARY, QUEEN OF SCOTS, to the earl of BOTHWELL. They were offended by Mary's hasty marriage to a suspected murderer of her previous husband, and by Bothwell's elevation as consort. On 15 June the Lords confronted Mary and Bothwell at Carberry Hill (SE Scotland). Bothwell fled, while Mary was imprisoned and later abdicated (24 July). The earl of MORAY became regent. *See also* CASKET LETTERS.

CONFEDERATION OF BRITISH INDUSTRY *see* FEDERATION OF BRITISH INDUSTRIES

CONGESTED DISTRICTS BOARD, IRELAND A body established by the British government in 1891, on the initiative of Irish secretary A.J. BALFOUR, to assist impoverished areas. Funded partly from former endowments of the Church of Ireland, and working predominantly in W Ireland, it acquired estates and reorganized them with larger landholdings (for sale); built roads, bridges and harbours; and promoted industry (e.g., fishing, lace making). Though considerable amounts were spent, conditions were not fundamentally improved. It was dissolved in 1923.

See also DISESTABLISHMENT, CHURCH OF IRELAND; LAND REFORM LEGISLATION, IRELAND 19TH AND EARLY 20TH CENTURIES.

CONGESTED DISTRICTS BOARD, SCOTLAND A body established by the British government in 1897, modelled on the Irish Board, to tackle overpopulation and poverty in crofting areas in the Scottish Highlands and Islands, partly by making crofters self-reliant. It promoted agriculture, fishing and extension of smallholdings, but having only modest funds it failed to improve underlying conditions. It was wound up in 1912. *See also* CROFTING.

CONGREGATION, LORDS OF THE *see* LORDS OF THE CONGREGATION

CONGREGATIONALISTS, ENGLAND Dissenting Christian denomination, originally influenced by CALVINISM and consisting of autonomous congregations. Congregationalists were called Independents from the 1640s to the late 18th century.

(Protestant) 'separatist' congregations were formed from the 1560s. Their leaders included Church of ENGLAND clergy who were expelled from livings in London for objecting to vestments (*see* PURITANISM, ENGLAND). From the 1580s separatists were often called 'BROWNISTS'. Congregations were also established overseas, notably in NEW ENGLAND. Independents were important politically in the mid 17th century (*see* CIVIL WARS, POLITICAL ASPECTS). Persecuted after the RESTORATION (1660), their worship was legalized by the TOLERATION ACT (1689).

In the early 18th century there were 60,000 Independents, and 15,000 members in 1750 (attendance was higher). County Associations were formed from the 1790s and a Congregational Union of England and Wales in 1832. English membership grew to 35,000 in 1800, 165,000 in 1850, and peaked at 291,000 in 1908, then declined to 151,000 in 1970. In 1972 most Congregational churches united with the Presbyterian Church of England to form the United Reformed Church. *See also* NONCONFORMITY AND DISSENT, ENGLAND/WALES; DISSENTERS, SCOTLAND.

CONNACHT A provincial kingdom in W Ireland, between the Atlantic and R. Shannon, extending N–S from Sligo Bay to Lough Derg. Connacht had a separate identity in the 5th–6th centuries, when it contained dynasties claiming descent from Conn Cétchathach (Conn 'Hundred-battler'), after whom it was named. (Conn was probably a deity claimed as a historical figure.) High-kings of LEINSTER (E Ireland) possibly exercised overlordship. A high-kingship of Connacht is recorded from the mid 7th century (reign of Ragallach mac Uatach, d. 649).

In the 5th–mid 8th centuries Connacht's pre-eminent dynasties were the Uí Fiachrach (federations in N and S Connacht). They were challenged from the mid 7th century by the Uí Briúin Aí (including Ragallach), situated around Cruachain hillfort (near modern Tulsk, Co. Roscommon), who monopolized Connacht's high-kingship from 773. (A related dynasty created the kingdom of BRÉIFNE.) From 973 the high-kingship was held by one line, which adopted the surname Ua Conchobair (English, O'CONNOR) by the 11th century. Toirrdelbach (d. 1156) and Ruaidrí UA CONCHOBAIR (resigned 1193) were high-kings of Connacht and Ireland.

After a succession dispute (to 1202), Cathal Crobderg Ua Conchobair (d. 1224) became king (recognized by King JOHN of England 1215). In 1226 the English government confiscated Connacht from Cathal's son Áed and granted most of it as a lordship to the Englishman Richard de Burgh (1227). The BURGH FAMILY dominated Connacht until 1333 (death of William de Burgh). During the 14th century the Dublin-based government gradually lost authority within Connacht.

The O'Connors survived as kings until the mid 15th century, but failed to restore province-wide rule. By c.1450 Gaelicized junior branches of the Burgh family were predominant. Connacht was later defined geographically by an English presidency (1569–1651, 1660–72). See also IRELAND, ENGLISH CONQUEST, 12TH–13TH CENTURIES; PROVINCES, IRELAND.

CONNECTICUT A former English colony in N America (in NEW ENGLAND), formally constituted in 1662 (British from 1707). It comprised an area S of MASSACHUSETTS around the Connecticut River valley, where Dutch people and English Puritan separatists had settled from 1633. Several settlements agreed an arrangement for government in Jan. 1639. A Puritan settlement at New Haven (founded 1637) and five other settlements, W of the Connecticut River, also formally united as New Haven Colony in 1643. The latter was included within the 1662 charter (issued by King CHARLES II) without consultation, but assented in 1665.

Connecticut was effectively self-governing, with authority to elect its own governor (subject to Crown approval). Est. population 1770: 175,000. Connecticut supported AMERICAN INDEPENDENCE and became a State of the USA in 1776. See also NONCONFORMITY AND DISSENT, ENGLAND; NORTH AMERICAN COLONIES; NEW ENGLAND, DOMINION OF.

CONNOLLY, JAMES (b. 5 June 1868 at Edinburgh, Scotland; d. 12 May 1916 at Kilmainham, Co. Dublin, Ireland, aged 47). A son of Irish emigrants, Connolly, a Marxist, moved in 1896 to Ireland where he was active in socialist and republican circles. From 1910 he worked with Jim LARKIN, founder of the Irish Transport and General

Workers' Union, and led strikers during the 'Dublin lock-out' (1913–14). From Oct. 1914, in Larkin's absence, he led the Union and its associated IRISH CITIZEN ARMY (ICA).

On 9 Sept. 1914 Connolly and Tom CLARKE (representing the IRISH REPUBLICAN BROTHERHOOD) agreed to use the European war as cover for an anti-British rebellion. It began on Easter Monday 1916, when Connolly, leading the ICA, proclaimed a republic (see EASTER RISING). After the Rising was crushed, Connolly was court-martialled and shot. See also WORLD WAR I, IMPACT ON IRELAND.

CONOLLY, WILLIAM (b. 1662 at Ballyshannon, Co. Donegal, Ireland; d. 30 Oct. 1729 at Dublin, Ireland, aged 66 or 67). A Protestant lawyer who became wealthy from dealings in confiscated Catholic estates (1690s), Conolly sat in the Irish House of Commons 1692–3, 1695–9 and 1703–29 (adopted WHIG affiliation 1703). After the Whig election victory of 1714, he was appointed chief commissioner of Irish revenues, thereby gaining extensive patronage.

In Nov. 1715 Conolly was elected speaker of the Commons. He used the position to advance government business in return for influence and patronage, making him the first 'UNDERTAKER' (parliamentary power-broker) in 18th-century Ireland, though his prominence was challenged by Alan Brodrick (chancellor 1714–25; Viscount Midleton from 1717). Conolly's influence was at its height in 1726–8 (see CARTERET, LORD, AND IRELAND). Conolly collapsed in Sept. 1729 and resigned as speaker (13 Oct.). See also PROTESTANT ASCENDANCY; ARCHITECTURE, IRELAND.

CONSCRIPTION In the late 17th–early 20th centuries, concern in England and Great Britain about State power discouraged military conscription, except that the NAVY was manned partly by impressment (forcible recruiting), and the ARMY expanded likewise during emergencies. In WORLD WAR I (1914–18), Britain's Liberal government retained voluntary enlistment until declining recruitment and manpower management forced a change. The first legislation for extensive conscription was passed in Jan. 1916, though recruitment continued to decline due to the physical inadequacy of candidates. Of the 4.9 million soldiers recruited in wartime, 1.3 million were conscripted (see WORLD WAR I, BRITISH ARMY). Conscription was retained until 1920. Legislation to extend conscription to Ireland (April 1918) exacerbated conflicts that resulted in partition and civil war (see WORLD WAR I, IMPACT ON IRELAND).

In May 1939, as war loomed, conscription was introduced in Britain for the first time in peacetime (military training for men aged 20–22). When WORLD WAR II began (3 Sept.), men aged 18–41 were immediately made liable for 'national service' (with skilled workers exempted). Conscription was extended to women in 1942, for work in industry or service in military auxiliary branches. From Dec. 1943 some men were selected by ballot for work in coalmines (so-called 'Bevin boys', named after Ernest BEVIN). NORTHERN IRELAND was exempted from conscription.

After the war (1945) conscription of men continued under wartime legislation (from May 1946 for two years' service). In 1947 new conscription legislation was passed to ensure forces sufficient for military commitments and the COLD WAR. From 1949, British males aged 17–21 undertook 18 months of 'national service' (extended 1950 to two years, because of the KOREAN WAR). In 1957 it was decided to reduce forces (to decrease expenditure) and return to voluntary enlistment. Conscription was phased out (last national serviceman released 1963). Between 1949 and 1963, 1.5 million men undertook national service.

CONSERVATISM A political outlook which considers the existing social order preferable to any 'engineered' alternative. It cherishes tradition and defends established institutions. British conservatism became explicit in reaction to the FRENCH REVOLUTION (1789). Though never an absolute consideration, it has always influenced the British CONSERVATIVE PARTY.

CONSERVATIVE AND UNIONIST PARTY, SCOTLAND As Party identities revived from c.1800 most members from Scotland in the UK House of Commons were TORIES but between 1832 and 1918 Tories (or Conservatives) held a minority of seats (10–21 of 45–74 seats). They were strongest in the shires, where they were supported by small landowners. From the 1870s they gained support by resisting disestablishment of the Church of Scotland. Local organization improved with the foundation of the National Union of Conservative Associations (1882). From 1886 Conservatives co-operated with LIBERAL UNIONISTS (breakaways from the LIBERAL PARTY), making local pacts to avoid competition. In the 'KHAKI ELECTION' of 1900 they jointly won a majority of seats (Conservatives 21, Unionists 17) and merged, as the Scottish Unionist Party, in 1912. In 1918 Unionists won 32 seats (of 74).

After falling back in 1922 and 1923 (15, 16 seats), Unionists won 38 seats (a majority) in 1924. Until 1959 Unionists won 22–50 seats and achieved majorities in 1931 and 1935. From 1931 to 1959 they were supported by 5–8 National Liberals. The Party was renamed the Conservative and Unionist Party in 1965. From 1964 to 1983 Conservatives won 16–23 seats.

From the mid 1980s national Conservative policies and Scottish nationalism generated unpopularity in Scotland: Conservatives won 10 seats in 1987, 12 in 1992, 0 in 1997, one in 2001, 2005, 2010 and 2015, 13 in 2017 and six in 2019.

When a Scottish Parliament was reinstituted, Conservatives came third in elections from 1999 to 2011, winning 17–18 seats (of 129). In 2016 they came second (to the Scottish National Party) with 31 seats. Their prospect for participating in an administration seemed poor. *See also* DEVOLUTION, SCOTLAND.

CONSERVATIVE PARTY A mainly British political party which developed in the 1830s from the modernization of the TORIES. Led by Sir Robert PEEL, it tempered CONSERVATISM with support for moderate reforms (*see* TAMWORTH MANIFESTO). In government 1841–6, Peel tried to recognize both industrial and landed interests, but repeal of the CORN LAWS split the Party, with PEELITES joining the Liberals. The remaining Conservatives were mostly landowners. Although briefly in office under the earl of DERBY, they failed to win a majority until 1874, when Benjamin DISRAELI had infused the Party with IMPERIALISM and broadened its class appeal (*see* CRYSTAL PALACE SPEECH).

The adhesion of the LIBERAL UNIONISTS made the Conservatives the dominant party after 1886. The parties merged in 1912, and were known as Unionists until 1922 because they opposed HOME RULE for Ireland. Lord SALISBURY and A.J. BALFOUR were sceptical of social reform. Their faith in free enterprise won business support, but divisions over TARIFF REFORM contributed to severe defeat in 1906.

The decline of the LIBERAL PARTY allowed the Conservatives to dominate politics in the 1920s–30s by consolidating the middle-class anti-socialist vote. Though Stanley BALDWIN (leader 1923–36) was popular, unemployment and APPEASEMENT tarnished the Conservatives' reputation. Despite the prestige of Winston CHURCHILL, the Conservatives lost the 1945 election, but they reconciled themselves to many Labour reforms. BUTSKELLISM characterized the Conservative governments of 1951–64.

After the failure of Edward HEATH (prime minister 1970–4), Margaret THATCHER restored the emphases on free enterprise, anti-socialism, and patriotism, and sought to reverse many post-war trends. After governing for 18 years (1979–97), the Conservatives suffered a heavy defeat, losing all their MPs from Scotland and Wales. The Party returned to government in 2010 under David CAMERON (in coalition with LIBERAL DEMOCRATS to 2015). Theresa MAY became leader and prime minister in 2016. She was succeeded in 2019 by Boris JOHNSON. Support for the Conservative Party has always been strongest in England. *See also* CARLTON CLUB; CONSERVATIVE AND UNIONIST PARTY, SCOTLAND; CONSERVATIVE PARTY, WALES; PARLIAMENTARY REPRESENTATION, ENGLAND/IRELAND; BREXIT.

CONSERVATIVE PARTY 1922 COMMITTEE Popular name for the 'Conservative Private Members' Committee' of 'backbench' members of the UK House of Commons. Formed in April 1923, it consisted of MPs elected in 1922. MPs elected in 1923 and 1924 subsequently joined, and all backbenchers were eligible from 1926. 'The 1922' was important from the 1940s as a channel of communication to Party leaders. From 1965 its chairman presided over Party leadership elections as returning officer. 'Frontbenchers' (ministers) were allowed to attend meetings from 2010.

CONSERVATIVE PARTY, WALES Most Welsh members of the UK Parliament were Conservatives (and GENTRY) from the beginnings of Party organization in the early 1830s until the 1865 general election (overtaken by LIBERALS). Thereafter Conservatives remained a minority, supported by (at most) one-third of the electorate in the 20th and 21st centuries, though in the 1906, 1997 and 2001 general elections no Conservative MPs were elected in Wales. The Party won three seats in 2005, eight in 2010, 11 in 2015, eight in 2017 and 14 in 2019 (of 40). Local organization developed in conjunction with arrangements in England; *see* CONSERVATIVE PARTY.

CONSERVATOR OF THE PRIVILEGES OF THE SCOTTISH CHURCH A diocesan bishop, often of GLASGOW or ST ANDREWS, who presided over general councils of the Scottish Church and represented the Church. The position existed from 1225 to 1472, for lack of a primate (archbishop). *See also* CHURCH ORGANIZATION, NORTH BRITAIN AND SCOTLAND BEFORE THE REFORMATION; GRAHAM, PATRICK.

CONSTANTÍN SON OF VURGUIST (fl. from 789; d. 820, probably in N Britain). Constantín was probably a kinsman, two generations later, of ONUIST SON OF VURGUIST (d. 761). He is the first king in the British Isles known to have been named after the Roman emperor Constantine (which probably reflects the growing Pictish cult of St Andrew, patron saint of Constantinople). Unfortunately, chronicle sources for his reign are scanty; all they relate is that in 789 he defeated Conall mac Tadg (who finished up in Kintyre), and that he died peacefully. But since Conall was king of Picts 785–9, Constantín presumably replaced him.

The length of Constantín's reign implies success – as does the magnificent Dupplin Cross bearing his name that was erected above the royal centre of Forteviot (modern C Scotland). He also probably founded the church at DUNKELD. Most significantly, his son Domnall is recorded as king of (Scottish) DÁL RIATA 811–35: Onuist's earlier lordship over Dál Riata had lapsed but Constantín clearly restored it. After his death, his brother (another) Onuist continued to rule uneventfully until 836. Unfortunately, three years later, in 839, there was a great battle against invading Norsemen: the Pictish and Dál Riatan kings were killed and their army was destroyed. *See also* KINGSHIP, NORTH BRITAIN.

CONSTANTINE II (Gaelic, Causantín mac Aeda; fl. from *c*.900; d. 952 at St Andrews, E Scotland). King of Scots (Scotland) 900–40 (or later).

After succeeding DONALD II (cousin), Constantine faced continuing VIKING attacks. He defeated Danes at Strathearn (E Scotland) in 904, possibly ending Danish incursions for a half century. In 918, with King Ealdred of NORTHUMBRIA (former BERNICIA), he fought an indecisive battle with the Irish-Norse leader Ragnall near Corbridge (NE England).

In the early 10th century power within Britain was affected by the expansion of territory ruled by kings of WESSEX. In 920 and 927 Constantine temporarily submitted to King ATHELSTAN of Wessex, who in 934 invaded Alba (Scotland). In 937 Constantine, with allies from STRATHCLYDE and the kingdom of YORK, invaded southwards, but was defeated by Athelstan at BRUNANBURH (NE England). He retired to ST ANDREWS (as monk) between 940 and 945; succeeded by MALCOLM I (second cousin). *See also* MAC ALPIN KINGS.

CONSTANTINE III (fl. from 407; d. 411). The third pretender to take power in ROMAN BRITAIN in the period 406–7 (following Marcus in 406, Gratian in 407). Constantine won control of much of Gaul and Spain. He gained temporary recognition from the legitimate Roman emperor, Honorius, in 409, before being defeated and executed (summer 411).

CONSTITUTION, UNITED KINGDOM The UK is a 'constitutional monarchy' with a system of governance consisting pre-eminently of democratic representation in the House of Commons within a sovereign PARLIAMENT (legislature) comprising monarch, House of Lords and Commons. Government (the executive) and law making rely on controlling a Commons majority. Unlike most States, the UK lacks a written constitution (authoritative legal text). Governance is regulated by conventions (practices), laws and an independent judiciary, resulting from periodic adaptations.

The UK's hereditary monarch is head of State. He or she formally appoints the head of government (the PRIME MINISTER) and judges, and retains 'reserve powers'. In practice the prime minister is the leader of the largest POLITICAL PARTY in the Commons. Most senior ministers are MPs and answerable to the Commons. Parliament's second chamber, the Lords (mostly nominated life peers), can amend legislation.

The constitution derives mainly from English and British history. (ENGLAND with WALES combined with

Scotland in 1707 as Great Britain. Britain and Ireland formed the United Kingdom in 1801. Southern Ireland received independence in 1922.) Formed in the 10th century, the kingdom of England was ruled by king and nobility; central administration and common law emerged from the royal household (12th century). Royal authority was limited by Magna Carta (1225 version) and Parliament's development (from 13th century); the monarchy re-emerged after Civil Wars (1642–8) and the Commonwealth and Protectorate (1649–60). After James VII/II attempted to reassert Catholicism, a Convention Parliament (1689) removed the monarch's ability to govern without Parliament (see Glorious Revolution).

Policy making passed to a prime minister in the 1720s (see Walpole, Robert), and democratic representation expanded between 1832 and 1928 (see parliamentary reform). The Lords surrendered power to veto legislation in 1911, and most hereditary nobles were removed in 1999. Accession to the European Economic Community (1973) and the Human Rights Act (1998) limited Parliament's authority. See also royal prerogative; law, England from 1066; England, Church of; ancient constitution; balanced constitution; Settlement, Act of; Bagehot, Walter; Dicey, A.V.

CONSTITUTION OF 1782 Term denoting constitutional changes in Ireland, during the Protestant Ascendancy. They increased the authority of Ireland's Parliament and reduced Ireland's subordination to Great Britain, although Ireland's government remained under British control.

Following a campaign by Patriot MPs (notably Henry Grattan) and Volunteers, the British government (led by the marquess of Rockingham) repealed the (British) 1720 Declaratory Act (21 June 1782; see Sixth of George I). This removed the British Parliament's claimed right to legislate for Ireland and restored judicial supremacy to the Irish House of Lords (judicial independence). The government allowed Ireland's Parliament to pass Yelverton's Act (27 July), which modified Poynings' Law, enabling it to initiate legislation (legislative independence). (Ireland's Parliament became known as 'Grattan's Parliament'.) The changes were confirmed by the British Renunciation Act (1783). Though many members of the Irish House of Commons welcomed the 'Constitution', they rejected parliamentary reform and Catholic Emancipation (see Flood, Henry). The 'Constitution' lasted until the Union of Ireland and Great Britain (1801). See also American War of Independence, impact on Ireland; Parliament, Ireland; courts, Ireland.

CONSTITUTIONS, SOUTHERN IRELAND On 21 Jan. 1919 the Dáil Éireann ('Assembly of Ireland') formed by Sinn Féin MPs adopted a provisional constitution prescribing a single-chamber legislature (Dáil) and small executive government.

It was superseded in 1922 by a constitution for an Irish Free State (IFS) drafted for the 'Second Dáil' under the 1921 Anglo-Irish Treaty. Approved by a 'Third Dáil' (25 Oct.), it was ratified by the UK Parliament on 5 Dec. The constitution affirmed membership of the Commonwealth (making the IFS effectively a dominion), derived civil authority from the people, and prescribed a legislature (see Parliament, southern Ireland). It could be amended by legislation for eight years (extended 1930), thereafter by referendum. Major amendments were made in 1936 (see Abdication Crisis and Irish Free State).

In 1937 Éamon de Valera organized a replacement constitution which asserted that Ireland (Irish, Éire) was sovereign and independent, and replaced the king's representative with a popularly elected president. The 'national territory' was controversially defined as the entire island (amended 1999), but Ireland's government would operate in 26 counties until Northern Ireland was reincorporated. The constitution recognized the 'special position' of the Catholic Church (removed 1973), and reflected Catholic teaching by prohibiting divorce (removed 1996) and protecting the family and women's domestic importance. After ratification by referendum, it came into force on 29 Dec. 1937. Southern Ireland formally became a republic outside the Commonwealth on 18 April 1949 under the Republic of Ireland Act (1948). Thirty-two amendments to the constitution were made up to 2019, following approval by referendum.

CONSUMER REVOLUTION A concept concerning social change, proposed in 1982 by English historian Neil McKendrick. He observed that in the later 17th and 18th centuries sections of English society markedly increased their consumption of goods and services. Developments involved primarily 'middling ranks' (e.g., professional people, urban gentry, merchants, yeomen farmers), and also landowners, though probably not poor people.

Facilitated by rising disposable incomes linked to more prosperous agriculture, foreign trade and financial investments, the Consumer Revolution was evidenced by new types of furniture (e.g., mirrors) and fabrics (e.g., cottons), carpets, ceramics, clocks and pictures, and by greater use of lawyers, physicians, hairdressers, etc. More time was spent on leisure activities such as attending plays, horse racing and gaming. The Consumer Revolution stimulated growth of county and cathedral towns, inland spas and coastal resorts (see holidays), and permanent shops in towns. Sensibilities changed as people became more preoccupied with fashions and luxuries. The Consumer Revolution affected other parts of the British Isles. From the early 19th century it was accelerated by the INDUSTRIAL REVOLUTION. *See also* MEDICINE AND PUBLIC HEALTH; PROFESSIONS.

CONTAGIOUS DISEASES ACTS Legislation passed by the UK Parliament in 1864, 1866 and 1869 to suppress venereal disease in the Army and Navy. It authorized police to arrest, medically examine and confine suspected prostitutes in 18 garrison or port towns in England and Ireland. Opposition to State-regulated prostitution came from moral reformers, working people and above all Josephine BUTLER's Ladies' National Association (1870–86), which mobilized opinion against this recognition of a sexual double standard. The Acts were repealed in 1886. *See also* PURITY MOVEMENT.

CONVENTICLES, ENGLAND AND WALES *see* CLARENDON CODE

CONVENTICLES, SCOTLAND Conventicles (private religious meetings) were held in the 1620s–30s by people opposed to Church innovations of King JAMES VI and King CHARLES I; they declined after innovations were abolished in 1638 (*see* GLASGOW ASSEMBLY).

Conventicles were revived, especially in the SW, by COVENANTERS opposed to the religious settlement of 1661–2 (*see* RESTORATION, SCOTLAND). Often led by ejected clergy, conventicles were persecuted in 1661–9 and 1673–9. They declined after the 1689–90 REVOLUTION SETTLEMENT, although CAMERONIANS continued to meet in conventicles into the 18th century. *See also* DISSENT, SCOTLAND.

CONVENTION OF ESTATES *see* COUNCIL-GENERAL

CONVENTION OF ROYAL BURGHS In Scotland, the assembly of representatives of royal BURGHS (towns); a continuation of the Court of the FOUR BURGHS, perhaps initially constituted in 1487. Its principal role was the allocation of royal taxation between burghs. In the late 16th and early 17th centuries it considerably influenced government economic policy. After 1707 it mainly represented trade and industry to government. It was abolished by the UK Parliament in 1976.

CONVENTION PARLIAMENT, ENGLAND AND WALES (1660) The Parliament elected in April 1660 after the dissolution of the LONG PARLIAMENT. Comprising House of Commons and House of Lords, it met on 25 April. Members were Parliamentarians and Royalists. On 1 May it voted for RESTORATION of the monarchy. It was declared a legal Parliament in June.

The Convention Parliament pronounced legislation passed since 1641 without royal authority as void. It mostly disbanded the NEW MODEL ARMY. It pardoned the king's enemies with a few exceptions (Act of Indemnity and Oblivion), and allowed unordained clergy to remain in post, but rejected the WORCESTER HOUSE DECLARATION for settlement of religion. Dissolved 29 Dec. and succeeded by the CAVALIER PARLIAMENT. *See also* BREDA, DECLARATION OF.

CONVENTION PARLIAMENT, ENGLAND AND WALES (1689–90) The assembly summoned by William of Orange following the flight of JAMES VII/II (elections ordered 28 and 29 Dec. 1688). It met on 22 Jan. 1689, with WHIGS forming a majority in the House of Commons.

The Convention declared that James had abdicated (6 Feb.) and offered the throne jointly to William and his wife Mary (accession proclaimed 13 Feb.). It also passed the TOLERATION ACT (May) and Bill of RIGHTS (Dec.). Dissolved 6 Feb. 1690. It was not strictly a Parliament but followed the precedent of the 1660 CONVENTION PARLIAMENT. *See also* WILLIAM III; GLORIOUS REVOLUTION.

CONVENTION PARLIAMENT, SCOTLAND A Convention of Estates, part elected, held in 1689 to consider the Crown's future following William of Orange's invasion of England and the flight of King JAMES VII/II (23 Dec. 1688). It met on 14 March; heard letters from William and James on 16 March; and overwhelmingly voted on 4 April that James had forfeited the Crown. On 11 April it accepted a 'Claim of Right' specifying constitutional principles and proclaimed William and Mary as rulers. They formally accepted Parliament's offer of the Crown and took oaths (at WESTMINSTER, England) on 11 May. The Convention continued as a Parliament until prorogued on 2 Aug. *See also* COUNCIL-GENERAL; GLORIOUS REVOLUTION, SCOTLAND; WILLIAM III; REVOLUTION SETTLEMENT, SCOTLAND.

CONVERSION OF ANGLO-SAXONS Germanic-settled areas of Britain were converted to Christianity through the haphazard establishment of bishoprics and MINSTERS in individual kingdoms. (Christianity survived to some extent in western, Brittonic areas; *see* POST-ROMAN BRITAIN.)

Conversion was initiated by missionaries sent by Pope Gregory the Great. Led by AUGUSTINE, they landed (597) in KENT (SE England). King ÆTHELBERT accepted Christianity and influenced Sæbert of ESSEX and RÆDWALD of EAST ANGLIA to do likewise. Sees were founded at CANTERBURY, Rochester (Kent) and LONDON (kingdom of Essex). After Æthelbert's death (616) the bishops of London and Rochester were expelled. Christianity was later rejected in Essex and East Anglia.

Christianity was taken N when Æthelbert's Christian daughter Æthelburg married EDWIN of DEIRA (625). She was accompanied by Bishop Paulinus. Edwin accepted Christianity (627), and Paulinus preached widely. But after

Edwin's death (633) Paulinus fled. Meanwhile (630s) Christianity was re-established in East Anglia and introduced to the Gewisse (*see* WESSEX).

Christianity made renewed progress in N England from 635 when OSWALD, king of BERNICIA and Deira, requested a bishop from IONA, the leading Irish monastery in N Britain. As a result AIDAN spread Christianity in Oswald's kingdoms, and other Irish or Irish-trained men – Diuma, Ceollach, Cedd and Trumhere – reconverted Essex and spread Christianity to MERCIA and the MIDDLE ANGLES.

Iona-linked 'Irish' churches followed different customs from other churches (e.g., in the timing of Easter). In 664 the Northumbrian church opted for 'Roman' customs (*see* WHITBY, SYNOD OF). The increased uniformity enabled Archbishop THEODORE to hold a first quasi-national council (672 or 673). SUSSEX and the Isle of Wight were converted in the 670s–80s. *See also* PAGANISM, ANGLO-SAXON ENGLAND; BEDE; YORK.

CONVERSION OF IRELAND Archaeological evidence from the S coast suggests that Christianity arrived by *c*.400. Channels of transmission can only be conjectured: trade with ROMAN BRITAIN and Continental Europe, kinship with Irish settlers in W Britain, and slave-trading and raiding. Female Christian slaves, acquired from Britain to nurse the children of high-ranking Irish, may have been influential.

By 431 Ireland's Christian community was sufficiently large to justify provision of a bishop, PALLADIUS, who worked probably in E Ireland. Later bishops included PATRICK (5th century), whose missionary work promoted MONASTICISM. He was active in N Ireland, especially the NE. His converts included young royal women, many of whom became nuns. His male disciples founded churches. Though poorly recorded, Christianity spread steadily, giving Irish society a distinctly Christian character by the mid 6th century. *See also* ROMAN BRITAIN AND IRELAND; CHURCH, MEDIEVAL IRELAND.

CONVERSION OF NORTH BRITONS, PICTS AND SCOTS Christianity reached the Britons of southern N Britain (modern southern Scotland and NE England) from ROMAN BRITAIN possibly in the late 4th century. In the 5th century the presence of Christianity is suggested by the possible association of Coroticus (a Christian magnate excommunicated by PATRICK) with the kingdom of Clyde Rock; an episcopal see may have been founded within the kingdom at GLASGOW in the later 6th century (*see* STRATHCLYDE (CLYDE ROCK), KINGDOM OF). Christianity probably began to spread among the PICTS of N Britain from the 5th century.

From *c*.500 SCOTS from Ireland, probably including Christians, settled in the western part of N Britain and on the WESTERN ISLES. Their Christianity was reinforced by COLUMBA from NE Ireland who established a monastery on IONA in 563. During the 6th and 7th centuries Columban monasteries became widely established among the Picts. *See also* CHURCH, MEDIEVAL NORTH BRITAIN AND SCOTLAND.

CONVERSION OF WALES The conversion of W Britain (i.e., the later Wales) to Christianity cannot be distinguished as a series of events or linked to specific individuals. Christianity must originally have penetrated W Britain when Britain belonged to the Roman Empire, perhaps in the 3rd century. But it probably made less headway there than elsewhere in Britain (*see* ROMAN BRITAIN, CHRISTIANITY IN), except in the heavily Romanized SE.

In the post-Roman period (5th and 6th centuries) western Britain absorbed MONASTICISM from Continental Europe (especially Gaul), which accelerated the spread of Christianity among the Britons of W Britain. This probably owed much to such monks as ILLTUD, TEILO, DEINIOL and DAVID (all 6th century). *See also* CHURCH, MEDIEVAL WALES.

COOK, JAMES (b. 27 Oct. 1728 at Marton-in-Cleveland, Yorkshire, England; d. 14 Feb. 1779 at Kealakekua Bay, Hawaii, aged 50). A labourer's son who worked in coastal shipping and then joined the British NAVY (1755), Cook became renowned for surveying skills. He led three explorations across the Pacific, which greatly enlarged geographical knowledge. The first (1768–71), westwards from S America, showed that NEW ZEALAND was separate from a supposed southern continent. Cook also explored, and annexed, the E coast of Australia (*see* BOTANY BAY; NEW SOUTH WALES), and discovered that Australia was separated from New Guinea.

During the second voyage (1772–5), eastwards from Africa, Cook proved (by approaching Antarctica) that there was no southern continent, and discovered various Pacific islands. During the third voyage (from 1776) Cook explored the N Pacific, looking for the NORTH-WEST PASSAGE (1778). He died in a fight with natives on Hawaii, caused by misunderstanding.

COOKE, HENRY (b. 11 Feb. 1788 at Grillagh, Co. Londonderry, Ireland; d. 13 Dec. 1868 at Belfast, Ireland, aged 80). A presbyterian clergyman, Cooke held ministerial positions from 1808, becoming a renowned preacher and upholder of presbyterian orthodoxy (e.g., he attacked the Belfast Academical Institution for Arianism 1822–6). He ministered at May Street church, BELFAST (1829–53), which was built for him. His influence increased following a withdrawal of presbyterian 'liberals' from the Synod of Ulster (1829).

Cooke opposed CATHOLIC EMANCIPATION (conceded 1829) and NATIONAL EDUCATION (introduced 1831), but supported the Church of IRELAND (as a fellow Protestant body). In 1853 he became first president of the Presbyterian College, Belfast (retired 1867). He is acknowledged as strengthening evangelicalism and anti-Catholicism in ULSTER. *See also* PRESBYTERIANISM, IRELAND.

COOPER, ANTHONY ASHLEY *see* SHAFTESBURY, EARL OF

CO-OPERATIVE MOVEMENT Co-operative trading associations flourished in Britain from the 18th century. An influential movement grew from the example of the Rochdale Society of Equitable Pioneers (in Lancashire, NW England): it opened a shop in 1844 and paid a 'dividend' (profit share) to members. By 1860 over 1000 similar societies existed. Membership reached almost 3 million by 1914. Co-operative wholesale societies, for supplying retail societies, were founded in N England in 1863 and in Scotland in 1868. Activities expanded, including banking, industrial production and dairy farming. A Co-operative Central Board was founded in 1869 to co-ordinate activity (renamed Co-operative Union in 1870, Co-operatives UK from 2001).

Government hostility to the movement during WORLD WAR I resulted in the formation of the Co-operative Party (1917) and election of MPs from 1918. Following an agreement with the LABOUR PARTY in 1927, politicians represented both parties in Parliament and local government, an arrangement that continued in the 21st century. *See also* SHOPS AND RETAILING.

COPPER AND ZINC INDUSTRIES, WALES From the 1560s significant copper works were established in the S (Monmouthshire, W Glamorgan), though until 1693 the monopoly of the Mines Royal Company discouraged expansion (*see* INDUSTRY, WALES BEFORE 18TH CENTURY). Sir Humphrey Mackworth (1657–1727) then pioneered copper smelting at Neath (W Glamorgan) with ore from Cornwall (England) and local anthracite coal. Soon afterwards nearby SWANSEA emerged as the main centre. The discovery of ore at Mynydd Parys (Anglesey) in 1768 led to smelting at Holywell (Flintshire), controlled by Thomas Williams (1737–1802), who also developed works at Swansea and dominated the world copper trade. By 1820, 90% of Great Britain's copper and much zinc were smelted around Swansea, causing enormous pollution. Copper smelting effectively ended by the 1920s and zinc working soon afterwards. *See also* BRONZE AGE, BRITAIN.

COPYHOLD In England and Wales, customary land tenures which developed from the later 14th century, replacing villeinage. Tenants continued to hold land from MANORS, according to manorial custom, but paid a low fixed annual rent instead of undertaking LABOUR SERVICES.

The name is derived from the copy of the record of a tenant's admission (from the manor court record) which was given to the tenant and served as his proof of title.

Most copyhold tenancies were heritable. From the mid 15th century they were protected by royal law courts. Copyhold was replaced from the 16th century and abolished by the 1922 Law of Property Act (effective in 1925). *See also* TENURES, ENGLAND FROM 1066; SERFDOM.

CORCORAN, TIMOTHY (b. 17 Jan. 1872 at Honeymount, Co. Tipperary, Ireland; d. 23 March 1943 at Dublin, Ireland, aged 71). A Jesuit priest and schoolteacher, Corcoran became professor in the theory and practice of education at University College, DUBLIN (1909–42). As a member of commissions of education in the IRISH FREE STATE (founded 1922), Corcoran strongly promoted Irish-medium education and influenced the curriculum at primary and secondary levels. He advocated a Catholic ethos in education. *See also* EDUCATION, SOUTHERN IRELAND.

CORK A city and port in the Republic of Ireland, by the R. Lee; centre of Co. Cork; from Irish, Corcaigh, meaning 'Swampy place'.

Cork (in MUNSTER, S Ireland) was originally an ecclesiastical centre (monastic and lay settlement) founded in the 7th century by Finbarr. It was raided in the 9th century by VIKINGS, who established a trading centre (915) which developed into a town. In 1171 it was captured by King HENRY II of England, and Anglo-Normans created a city on islands which traded with England (notably BRISTOL and LONDON), France and the Iberian Peninsula.

Cork expanded in the late 17th century from trade in cloth, live cattle and butter, becoming Ireland's second largest urban centre (overtaken by BELFAST in later 19th century). During the 18th century it prospered from trade with N America and ship provisioning, but declined economically in the 19th century, especially after the GREAT FAMINE (1845–9). After the partition of Ireland (1921) it was southern Ireland's second largest city.

The US manufacturing companies Ford (cars) and Dunlop (tyres) opened factories in 1919 and 1935 respectively (both closed 1984). Renewed industrial development in the later 20th century included chemicals and electronics. Queen's College was founded in 1845 (1908, renamed University College Cork; 1997, awarded university status). *See also* TOWNS, IRELAND; IRISH INDEPENDENCE, WAR OF.

Est. popn: 1300, 2000; 1600, 2400; 1800, 80,000; 1900, 76,000; 2000, 125,000.

CORNISH REBELLION A protest in 1497 by inhabitants of Cornwall (SW England) against taxation which had been granted (Jan.) to King HENRY VII to fund war against JAMES IV of Scotland. (James was harbouring Perkin

WARBECK.) Led by the lawyer Thomas Flamank, the rebels marched (from May) to LONDON to petition Henry. They were defeated by Henry's army at Blackheath (Kent), near London (17 June).

CORN LAWS Legislation enacted from the mid 17th century onwards, initially for England and Wales, which influenced grain prices and supplies. Previously the government had protected consumers in difficult situations (e.g., prohibiting exports after bad harvests). It now sought domestic market stability, greater exports and expansion of shipping (*see* MERCANTILISM).

The 1663 Corn Law set prices below which exports were allowed and deterrent duties were charged on imports (modified 1670 with a sliding scale – high import duties when prices were low, and vice versa). From 1673 bounties encouraged exports of wheat, barley and rye (renewed 1698). Scotland also introduced a corn bounty (1695), and came under the English laws in 1707. Until the mid 18th century, production increased, prices fell and exports grew. But as population increased, exports declined and prices rose. In 1773 exports were banned when prices were high.

From 1815, after the NAPOLEONIC WARS (a period of high prices), a new law sustained prices by prohibiting imports to the UK when prices were low (replaced by sliding scale of prices and duties in 1828). Though protection was intended to support Irish producers and British farmers working marginal soils, it was condemned by opponents (e.g., the ANTI-CORN LAW LEAGUE from 1839) for favouring landlords at the expense of industrial workers. Sir Robert PEEL, a supporter of FREE TRADE, reduced duties in 1846, but at the cost of dividing the CONSERVATIVE PARTY. Nominal duties continued until 1869. *See also* FOSTER'S CORN LAW.

CORNWALL, DUCHY OF A landed estate which traditionally supports the eldest son of the ruler of England before his accession to the throne. The position of duke of Cornwall (the first ducal title in England) and the duchy were created in 1337 for Prince Edward, eldest son of King Edward III (*see* EDWARD THE BLACK PRINCE). Before 1832 the duchy controlled the selection of MPs by many BOROUGHS in SW England, giving the duke considerable political influence.

CORNWALLIS, CHARLES (b. 31 Dec. 1738 at London, England; d. 5 Oct. 1805 at Ghazipur, Bengal, India, aged 66). A soldier from 1757, Cornwallis served in the SEVEN YEARS WAR and (from 1776) in the AMERICAN WAR OF INDEPENDENCE. Though compelled to surrender at YORKTOWN (1781), his reputation survived.

As governor-general of INDIA, 1786–93 (the first appointed by the British government), Cornwallis led a successful military campaign (1791–2) against Tipu Sultan,

ruler of Mysore (S India). He also undertook judicial, administrative and revenue reforms (enacted in the 'Cornwallis Code', 1793). Back in Britain, he was created Marquess Cornwallis.

From June 1798 Cornwallis served as lord lieutenant of Ireland. He completed the suppression of the RISING OF 1798, and implemented the UNION OF IRELAND AND GREAT BRITAIN, but resigned (Feb. 1801) after King GEORGE III rejected CATHOLIC EMANCIPATION. He helped to negotiate the Peace of AMIENS with France (1802). Cornwallis returned to India in 1805 as governor-general but died. *See also* INDIAN CIVIL SERVICE.

CORONATION, ENGLAND Ceremonies for inaugurating kings in early Anglo-Saxon kingdoms (5th–8th centuries) are undocumented. They possibly included the bestowal of a helmet to symbolize a king's role as war leader. By the late 8th century anointing was introduced, following precedents from Continental Europe. It presented kings as Christian rulers endowed with holiness. (For the first recorded anointing *see* OFFA.) A (Latin) anointing service existed by the early 9th century.

The first king to be crowned was probably EDWARD THE ELDER, king of the Anglo-Saxons (Whit Sunday, 900). He was also invested with other regalia (ring, sword, sceptre), and placed on a throne. His (second) wife Ælfflæd was probably the first queen to be anointed. Most 10th-century coronations took place at KINGSTON UPON THAMES.

A more elaborate service was prepared for the 'second coronation', at BATH, of EDGAR (973). It comprised: (a) consecration and oath taking; (b) anointment; (c) investiture and coronation; (d) enthronement; (e) acclamation. This scheme was largely retained thereafter.

From 1066 (HAROLD II) most coronations were held in WESTMINSTER Abbey. A new coronation chair was commissioned in 1297 by EDWARD I to hold the captured Scottish STONE OF DESTINY. From 1603 the coronation service was in English. Most regalia were destroyed during the 1650s (*see* COMMONWEALTH AND PROTECTORATE) and replaced for CHARLES II (1661). The regalia (or 'Crown Jewels') are kept in the Tower of London. *See also* KINGSHIP, ANGLO-SAXON.

CORONATION, SCOTLAND In 1329, at the request of King ROBERT I, Pope John XXII granted privileges of coronation and unction (replacing INAUGURATION and giving Scottish and English rulers equal status). From DAVID II (1331) to CHARLES II (1651) kings were crowned at SCONE. (JAMES VII/II was never crowned; William and Mary (1689) and Anne (1702) took oaths at WESTMINSTER, England.)

CORONER In England, an officer who investigates deaths from unknown, unnatural or violent causes by holding an inquest. The post originated in 1194 when freemen in each county were required to elect 'keepers of pleas of the Crown' (usually 2–4) to investigate criminal matters. From 1246 coroners were elected for life. Elections continued until 1888; thereafter coroners were appointed. From 1926 coroners had to be barristers, solicitors or legally qualified medical practitioners.

CORRUPT PRACTICES ACT The first effective legislation against bribery in UK general elections, enacted 1883. It set maximum election expenses for constituencies on a per-head basis, required candidates to present certified accounts, and introduced severe penalties for malpractice. Election spending by parliamentary candidates halved between 1880 and 1892. *See also* PARLIAMENTARY REFORM.

COSGRAVE, LIAM (b. 13 April 1920 at Templeogue, Co. Dublin, Ireland; d. 4 Oct. 2017 at Dún Laoghaire, Dún Laoghaire-Rathdown County, aged 97). A son of W.T. COSGRAVE, Liam Cosgrave entered the Dáil in 1943 as a FINE GAEL TD. He served as minister for external affairs 1954–7, when he led Ireland into the United Nations (1955).

In 1965 Cosgrave was elected party leader, and from Feb. 1973 was taoiseach (premier) of a coalition government (with LABOUR). Cosgrave supported the SUNNINGDALE AGREEMENT (Dec. 1973) and Northern Ireland's unsuccessful power-sharing Executive (Jan.–May 1974). He lost the June 1977 election to FIANNA FÁIL, and resigned as party leader (succeeded by Garret FITZGERALD). *See also* SOUTHERN IRELAND FROM 1922; EXECUTIVES, NORTHERN IRELAND.

COSGRAVE, W.T. (b. 5 June 1880 at Templeogue, Co. Dublin, Ireland; d. 16 Nov. 1965 at Dublin, Republic of Ireland, aged 85). William Thomas Cosgrave, a nationalist, participated in the republican EASTER RISING (1916), the Dáil Éireann (self-proclaimed 'Assembly of Ireland'; from Jan. 1919) and the Dáil government (from April). He supported the ANGLO-IRISH TREATY (Dec. 1921) and joined the provisional government of the Irish Free State (Jan. 1922), succeeding Michael COLLINS as chairman (Aug.). He also succeeded Arthur GRIFFITH as president of Dáil Éireann (Sept.–Dec.). When the Irish Free State's constitution was inaugurated (6 Dec.), Cosgrave became president of the Executive Council (premier).

In 1923 Cosgrave founded (and led) CUMANN NA NGAEDHEAL. His government won the IRISH CIVIL WAR and established new institutions (police, judiciary, etc.). In 1927, after the murder of Kevin O'HIGGINS, a proposed Electoral Amendment Act forced abstaining members of FIANNA FÁIL to take their Dáil seats. Cosgrave lost power to Fianna Fáil in 1932. He resigned as party leader (1933), but led his party's successor, FINE GAEL, from 1934 to 1944

(retirement). *See also* IRISH FREE STATE, FOUNDING OF; GOVERNMENT, SOUTHERN IRELAND; SOUTHERN IRELAND FROM 1922; O'DUFFY, EOIN.

COSTELLO, JOHN (b. 20 June 1891 at Dublin, Ireland; d. 5 Jan. 1976 at Dublin, Republic of Ireland, aged 84). A lawyer, Costello was a FINE GAEL TD 1933–43, 1944–69. In 1948 he was appointed taoiseach (premier) of Ireland's first inter-party government (because Fine Gael's leader was unacceptable to other coalition parties). He oversaw Ireland's conversion into a republic (1949), but was weakened by controversy over the MOTHER AND CHILD SCHEME, and fell when independent TDs withdrew support (1951). He led a second inter-party government (1954–7), which sponsored economic development but faced renewed terrorism by the IRISH REPUBLICAN ARMY. *See also* SOUTHERN IRELAND FROM 1922.

COTTINGTON, FRANCIS (b. probably 1579 in Somerset, England; d. 19 June 1652 at Valladolid, Spain, aged about 73). A courtier and diplomat, Cottington was appointed a privy councillor (1628) and chancellor of the Exchequer (1629) by King CHARLES I. As also ambassador to SPAIN (1629–31) he negotiated a peace treaty (treaty of Madrid, 1630). Created Lord Cottington in 1631, he resigned as chancellor of the Exchequer in 1641, during the LONG PARLIAMENT. In 1643, during the CIVIL WARS, he joined Charles in OXFORD and was appointed TREASURER. He oversaw the surrender of Oxford to Parliamentarians in June 1646 and then went abroad. *See also* CHARLES I, PERSONAL RULE.

COTTON FAMINE An economic and social crisis in Lancashire and N Cheshire (NW England), caused by a shortage of raw cotton for the COTTON INDUSTRY, 1861–5, when the USA, during the AMERICAN CIVIL WAR, blockaded the ports of the breakaway Confederate States of America (the main source of cotton). The Famine created severe unemployment among the area's workforce (including 420,000 cotton workers). It was partly alleviated from 1863 by government-supported work schemes (e.g., road building), and later by alternative supplies from Egypt and India. Despite the suffering, workers supported the anti-slavery northern states.

COTTON INDUSTRY, ENGLAND In Lancashire (NW England) from the later 16th century, fustian (cotton mixed with linen) was made using cotton from the Levant (eastern Mediterranean). Town-based merchants organized domestic spinning and weaving. The damp climate suited cotton fibres. A major industry, producing yarn and cloth, developed from the later 18th century based on increasingly productive equipment. The scale of expansion made cotton a leading sector in the INDUSTRIAL REVOLUTION.

The 'flying shuttle', used in weaving from the 1750s (invented by John KAY), stimulated development of yarn-spinning machines, notably the 'spinning jenny' (c.1764; see HARGREAVES, JAMES). Richard ARKWRIGHT, inventor of the water-powered 'water frame' (1767), created England's largest yarn-spinning business, centred on FACTORIES in Derbyshire. The hand-operated 'spinning mule' (1779), invented by Samuel CROMPTON, created rapid industrial growth in S Lancashire, around MANCHESTER, from the 1780s. Spinning was powered by steam engines from 1785. The expansion of spinning caused handloom weaving to grow in the 1790s–1820s. Power-driven weaving became established in the 1820s–30s, leading to decline in handweaving (see CARTWRIGHT, EDMUND). From the 1790s the USA was the main source of cotton, imported through LIVERPOOL. By 1830 cotton goods accounted for half of British exports by value.

The industry expanded until 1913, when about 500,000 people were employed in Lancashire and the county supplied two-thirds of world trade in cotton goods. But from the 1920s overseas industries captured British markets. Companies amalgamated and reduced capacity: 25% in spinning by 1938, 33% in weaving. Decline resumed in the 1950s: between 1950 and 1980 cloth output fell from 2207 to 399 million yards. During the 1960s most of the surviving industry was absorbed into larger textile companies. See also COTTON FAMINE.

COTTON INDUSTRY, IRELAND Water-powered yarn-spinning mills were built in various places (e.g., around DUBLIN and CORK) from the 1780s, following the introduction of the 'spinning jenny' to BELFAST (1778–9). By 1811 the largest centre, Belfast (in ULSTER), had 33 mills (15 steam powered). Most mills outside Ulster closed by 1830, due to British competition. The Ulster industry, including weaving, declined from the 1870s, the last mill (in Belfast) closing in 1919. See also INDUSTRY, IRELAND 18TH CENTURY TO 1921.

COTTON INDUSTRY, SCOTLAND From the mid 1750s domestic workers mixed cotton yarn with linen yarn. A separate industry developed in the 1770s with the development of water-powered cotton-spinning mills using English technology. In the 1780s–90s the industry expanded spectacularly in the GLASGOW–PAISLEY area (W-C Scotland), promoted by leading figures in the linen industry. By 1787 there were 19 mills; by 1795, 91. Imports of raw cotton to the R. Clyde (from the West Indies and USA) increased 80-fold between 1775 and 1812. From the 1780s mills were increasingly situated in towns and driven by steam engines. The industry achieved great success in fine printed fabrics, notably the eastern-inspired Paisley pattern shawls. The growth of spinning stimulated expansion in the number of handloom weavers but mechanization of weaving, especially from the 1820s, reduced numbers and caused hardship.

After 1860 the industry became uncompetitive and declined in the face of English competition. Firms closed or amalgamated. By 1910 only nine companies remained, most of which closed by 1929. One survivor was J. & P. Coats, created by amalgamation in 1896, which dominated the world market in cotton thread. See also INDUSTRY, SCOTLAND FROM LATE 18TH CENTURY.

COUNCIL, ANGLO-SAXON ENGLAND see WITAN

COUNCIL, SCOTLAND The small body of royal officers, noblemen and clergy which advised the ruler on day-to-day political, administrative and legal business. It existed probably by the mid 13th century, having developed from informal meetings of king and senior household members. From the 1420s legal business was often cleared by special 'sessions', and from 1503 was regularly delegated to a separate council which developed into the Court of SESSION. Fewer than ten councillors normally attended. The Council issued proclamations and Acts, and influenced PARLIAMENT. From the 16th century it was also known as the 'Privy' or 'Secret' Council. After King JAMES VI moved to England in 1603 the Council was the main agency exercising royal powers, chaired by the CHANCELLOR until 1626 when a president was appointed. In 1638–41 and 1643–51 it was marginalized by a Committee of Estates. (From 1641 councillors required Parliamentary approval; see COVENANTING REVOLUTION.) During the English occupation of 1651–60 it was effectively non-existent, but was restored in 1661 with councillors appointed by ROYAL PREROGATIVE. The Council was abolished by the British Parliament in Feb. 1708 (soon after the UNION OF ENGLAND AND SCOTLAND), at the behest of JUNTO WHIGS and the SQUADRONE who wanted to remove the court's influence on elections.

COUNCIL FOR SCOTTISH AFFAIRS An advisory council in England established in 1662 by King CHARLES II at the instigation of his chief minister the earl of CLARENDON. Based at Whitehall Palace, WESTMINSTER, with mainly English members, it was Clarendon's instrument for influencing Scottish affairs (usually under the king's control). It was abolished after Clarendon's fall (1667), on insistence of the (2nd) earl of LAUDERDALE.

COUNCIL-GENERAL In Scotland, a body similar to PARLIAMENT in composition and authority, but smaller and convenable at shorter notice. It probably developed in the 13th century as an augmented king's COUNCIL of MAGNATES and prelates. It was known as the Council-General from the

1360s when it included BURGH commissioners (representatives). Shire commissioners attended from 1587. Councils-General legislated, ratified treaties and raised taxation, lacking only Parliament's authority as a court.

Decreasing in frequency after c.1450, Councils-General were replaced in the early 16th century by Conventions of Estates with similar composition and powers. After 1660 meetings were rare but the last Convention, from 14 March 1689, enacted the Glorious Revolution in Scotland (see CONVENTION PARLIAMENT, SCOTLAND).

COUNCIL HOUSING, GREAT BRITAIN A modest amount of housing was built by local authorities under the permissive Housing of the Working Classes Acts of 1890 (UK) and 1900 (England and Wales). After WORLD WAR I, central government assumed responsibility for providing decent 'homes for heroes', operating through local authorities. Legislation in 1919 required authorities to survey needs, and provided subsidies. Though government policies frequently changed (sometimes emphasizing SLUM clearance), 1.1 million homes were provided in England by 1939 (and more elsewhere in Great Britain), predominantly on low-density suburban estates. Some authorities also built blocks of flats, usually up to five storeys.

After WORLD WAR II, renewed commitment to provision of housing under the WELFARE STATE saw nearly 3 million council dwellings built in Britain 1945–85. In the 1950s–60s slums were sometimes demolished and replaced by new estates on town peripheries. Many high-rise blocks of flats were built until the Ronan Point disaster (partial collapse of a tower block in London, 1968) shook confidence.

From the 1980s central governments reduced the role of local authorities. From 1980 council tenants could become freeholders under 'right to buy' legislation, and from 1988 estates were transferred to other landlords (e.g., HOUSING ASSOCIATIONS). Local authority building was restricted, and funding directed to alternative housing providers. In 2011–12, local authorities retained 2.1 million dwellings in Britain while other providers of 'social housing' owned 2.7 million. See also HOUSING LEGISLATION, ENGLAND AND WALES/SCOTLAND.

COUNCIL HOUSING, IRELAND see HOUSING, IRELAND, STATE INVOLVEMENT

COUNCIL IN THE MARCHES OF WALES An English royal administrative council and law court which operated from 1476 in Wales and in English border shires (Gloucestershire, Worcestershire, Herefordshire, Shropshire, and until 1569 Cheshire); generally based at LUDLOW (W England).

It originated with EDWARD IV's 1476 grant of judicial powers to the PRINCE OF WALES's council (1471–83), an arrangement revived by HENRY VII for Prince ARTHUR (1489) which survived Arthur's death (1502). The Council was expanded by Cardinal WOLSEY (1526), invigorated by Rowland LEE (president 1534–43), and made permanent by STATUTE in 1543. It functioned under the English PRIVY COUNCIL.

After the UNION OF WALES WITH ENGLAND (1536–43) the Council heard appeals from the COURT OF GREAT SESSIONS. From 1586 its president was LORD LIEUTENANT in most shires. It was abolished as an organ of central government in 1641; judicial work also stopped (1642) but was revived in 1660 (see RESTORATION) and continued until abolished in 1689 (see GLORIOUS REVOLUTION). See also SIDNEY, HENRY; PREROGATIVE COURTS; EQUITY COURTS.

COUNCIL OF THE NORTH A royal council and law court which operated periodically in N England 1480s–1641. It developed from the council of Richard, duke of Gloucester, when he governed N England for King EDWARD IV (1470s–80s). As king, Richard reconstituted the council (1484) as a judicial body for Yorkshire, Westmorland and Cumberland (see RICHARD III). It lapsed in 1485; reinstated (1502–7) for Yorkshire by HENRY VII.

A similar council was re-established for Yorkshire by Thomas WOLSEY in 1525. It was reorganized in 1537, following the PILGRIMAGE OF GRACE (1536), by Thomas CROMWELL, acting for the royal Council in Yorkshire, Co. Durham, Northumberland, Westmorland and Cumberland. It suppressed the NORTHERN REBELLION (1569). Its final president was Thomas WENTWORTH. Abolished 1641. See also PREROGATIVE COURTS.

COUNCILS, ENGLAND 1066 TO 1530s Kings continued as necessary to hold small Councils of nobles, senior clergy (bishops, abbots) and officers (see WITAN). A Council assisted royal officers during the absence of RICHARD I (1190–9) and the minority of HENRY III (1216–27). Kings also convened 'Great Councils' (assemblies of BARONS and clergy) and other large Councils (e.g., including merchants), intermittently until the early 16th century, despite the rise of PARLIAMENT (from 13th century).

From the 1230s Henry III held more regular Council meetings. Men were appointed as councillors and required to swear an oath. The Council helped to operate the government, with the PRIVY SEAL being used to authorize orders. When barons rebelled against Henry's rule in 1258 they imposed a Council as the centre of government (see BARONIAL CONFLICT AND WARS). Kings appointed numerous councillors (e.g., possibly 70 in reign of EDWARD I), but only a few attended meetings regularly.

From the 1350s (reign of EDWARD III) the Council was an established part of government, with a small core of active councillors (sometimes around ten) who met regularly without the king. They advised the king and handled his business. The CHANCELLOR, TREASURER and keeper of the privy seal were leading members. Others included bishops, magnates, KNIGHTS, judges and other royal officers. The Council was served by a clerk from *c*.1392. Its business included negotiations with foreign envoys, receiving petitions and judicial decisions. It was replaced in the 1530s by the PRIVY COUNCIL. *See also* GOVERNMENT, ENGLAND 1066 TO 1509.

COUNCILS, IRELAND, LATE 12TH–16TH CENTURIES Assemblies for advising the CHIEF GOVERNOR. Initially, magnates were convened as necessary. Regular meetings were held by the mid 13th century, also including senior officers (treasurer, chancellor, escheator), and a clerk assisted by the mid 14th century. A royal ordinance of 1479 requiring majority support for Council Acts encouraged some governors to obtain that by threats. A smaller Council was instituted in 1520 (*see* PRIVY COUNCIL, IRELAND).

In the 14th–16th centuries (and possibly earlier) governors also convened 'Great Councils', i.e., meetings with a large attendance of nobles, which assented to legislation and granted taxes. They were often indistinguishable from PARLIAMENT.

COUNCILS, WALES, 12TH–13TH CENTURIES In 13th-century kingdoms, councils were meetings of a ruler with his *DISTAIN* (steward), nobles, senior clergymen, and senior servants to consider judicial matters and such issues as relations with other Welsh rulers and England; they were the main instrument of royal government and administration. Councils probably developed in the late 12th century from occasional meetings of a ruler and noble freemen. *See also* KINGSHIP, WALES 5TH–13TH CENTURIES.

COUNTIES *see* SHIRES

COUNTRY PARTY OR COUNTRYMEN Names given to the main opposition group in the Scottish Parliament 1690–1707. A looser grouping than its predecessor the CLUB, the Country Party opposed continental war and the growth of central government in the 1690s. From 1700 its leader was the 4th duke of HAMILTON. After the 1702 election, it attempted to extend parliamentary control of Scottish affairs by passing (1703) the Act of SECURITY and the Act anent PEACE AND WAR in co-operation with the CAVALIERS. It failed to prevent the UNION OF ENGLAND AND SCOTLAND (1707).

COUNTY CLARE BY-ELECTION An election in Ireland to the UK Parliament which was used by the CATHOLIC ASSOCIATION to challenge the British government's opposition to Catholic Emancipation (principally admission of Catholics to Parliament). It was won, on 5 July 1828, by the ineligible Catholic candidate, Daniel O'CONNELL, the Association's leader. Emancipation was quickly granted for fear of unrest (April 1829). *See also* CATHOLIC RELIEF AND EMANCIPATION, IRELAND.

COUNTY COMMITTEES In England and Wales, committees for local government established by the LONG PARLIAMENT in counties under its control from 1642, during the CIVIL WARS. Although intended mainly to collect taxes, they became involved with most aspects of local government and superseded existing authorities. Their most significant powers were removed by the RUMP PARLIAMENT in 1649, and none survived to the RESTORATION (1660).

COUNTY COMMUNITY Historians' term for the leading men of a county (or SHIRE), especially when involved in local political activity. Particularly in England, county-based institutions (created by the monarch) provided occasions for social gatherings by senior inhabitants (e.g., landowners), notably the SHIRE COURT (or 'county court', from mid 10th century), ASSIZE courts (from late 13th century), and quarter sessions (courts of JUSTICES OF THE PEACE, from mid 14th century). In the early 13th century, the men of some counties even paid collectively for favours (e.g., *c*.1221, men of Cornwall paid for having a local man as SHERIFF).

County communities, consisting of GENTRY, yeomen, other freemen, etc., became politically active in the early 17th century because of concerns about royal policies (e.g., SHIP MONEY, ARMINIANISM in 1630s). Local opinion could vary between bitter factionalism and consensus. When the SHORT PARLIAMENT met in 1640, county petitions of grievances were presented.

From soon after the RESTORATION (1660), many leading landowners gradually withdrew from active engagement in local administration and politics, leaving the work to lesser figures. Although counties remained central in royal administration, they largely ceased to be centres of political resistance. In the 18th–19th centuries new county institutions developed (e.g., agricultural associations), and for some counties a hall was built (e.g., shire hall, HEREFORD, 1817–19). Authority within counties was removed from social élites when elected county councils were instigated in England and Wales in 1889.

COUNTY COURT *see* SHIRE COURT

COUNTY SCHOOLS Secondary schools in Wales founded under the Welsh Intermediate Education Act, 1889, to counter the poor availability of such education; based on a recommendation of Aberdare Report (1881).

Schools were non-denominational, and were controlled and funded by the new county councils. By 1902, 95 existed, providing relatively greater secondary provision (for both sexes) than was available in England. County schools became grammar schools under the BUTLER EDUCATION ACT (1944). *See also* EDUCATION, WALES.

COUPON ELECTION Nickname given to the UK general election of 14 Dec. 1918, held after WORLD WAR I. Candidates endorsed by the governing coalition of Liberals and Conservatives received a letter from party leaders David LLOYD GEORGE and Bonar Law. The leader of the Independent Liberals (in Opposition), H.H. ASQUITH, derided this as a coupon (suggesting war-time rationing). The coalitionists won an overwhelming 478 seats. Sinn Féin MPs elected in Ireland formed their own assembly (*see* IRISH FREE STATE, FOUNDING OF).

COURCY, JOHN DE (b. *c.*1140 possibly in NW England; d. 1219 in England, aged about 79). First recorded in Ireland in 1176 (in DUBLIN), in early 1177 de Courcy deposed and replaced the high-king of ULSTER (NE Ireland) and in 1180 married Affreca, daughter of Godred, king of MAN. He settled NE Ireland with men from NW England. Though he lived as an independent king, he served as justiciar (the English king's representative in Ireland) 1185–92.

In 1204 de Courcy was deposed by Hugh de Lacy (d. 1242), whose conquest was confirmed by King John (1205). De Courcy returned to Ireland with John in 1210, but failed to regain his lands. He then remained in England. *See also* JOHN AND IRELAND; IRELAND, ENGLISH CONQUEST, 12TH–13TH CENTURIES.

COURT AND COUNTRY In England, terms used by 17th-century political commentators for groups in Parliament. 'Court' indicated government officials and courtiers who promoted the king's interests; 'country' referred to men who generally opposed royal plans on principle, tending to view the court as decadent and corrupt.

The labels were particularly appropriate in the 1620s (reigns of JAMES VI/I, CHARLES I), and 1660s–70s (reign of CHARLES II). From the 1680s parliamentary groups were more commonly described as TORIES and WHIGS, though into the 18th century both groups contained 'court' and 'country' sections. The labels can be misleading, because the strongest opposition to royal policy often came from within the court.

COURT WITS In England, a group at the court of King CHARLES II (ruled 1660–85), including the 2nd duke of Buckingham (George Villiers), the 2nd earl of ROCHESTER (John Wilmot), Sir Charles Sedley and Thomas Shadwell,

whose scandalous activities were generally condoned by the king. Some were patrons of the arts; a number were poets and playwrights.

COURTAULD, SAMUEL (b. 7 May 1876 at Bocking, Essex, England; d. 1 Dec. 1947 at Westminster, London, England, aged 71). Of HUGUENOT background, Courtauld joined his family's eponymous textile company in 1898. As chairman 1921–46, he developed it into the world's largest manufacturer of 'rayon' (so-called 'artificial silk', used notably for women's hosiery and underwear), with factories around Great Britain and overseas subsidiary companies. A prominent art collector, he helped to found (1932) the Courtauld Institute of Art (within London University), to which he donated an outstanding collection of French Impressionist paintings.

COURTS, ENGLAND BEFORE 1660 In the 6th–10th centuries justice was obtainable in Anglo-Saxon kingdoms at folk (public) assemblies, presided over by a 'doomsman' (judgment-giver). In WESSEX, by the late 9th century, courts were held under royal authority in SHIRES (subdivisions), attended for the king by an EALDORMAN and bishop. In the 10th century public courts were instituted across England in shires, hundreds or wapentakes (subdivisions of shires) and BURHS. Lords probably held 'private' MANOR courts, and controlled some hundred courts.

After the NORMAN CONQUEST (1066–70s), major lords introduced private 'honour courts' (*see* HONOUR). King HENRY I (ruled 1100–35) briefly strengthened public justice by sending justiciars to attend shire courts and hold separate courts. The EXCHEQUER developed partly as a court, Church courts were established, and TOWNS had courts.

Royal justice was asserted from 1174, when HENRY II sent judges on circuits to hold 'general eyres' (to 1294; *see* EYRE). From the 1190s the Court of Common Bench (later 'Common Pleas', for civil cases) developed at WESTMINSTER (from the Exchequer), and from 1234 'King's Bench' (for royal matters, later criminal cases). Royal law became known as COMMON LAW.

From the 13th century other judicial commissions operated: of OYER AND TERMINER, gaol delivery (clearing), and ASSIZES. Between 1350 and 1370 a new local system emerged: 'quarter sessions' held by JUSTICES OF THE PEACE for lesser crimes, and 'assizes', held twice yearly in larger towns by itinerant justices for major crimes and civil matters.

More flexible justice became obtainable from the Court of CHANCERY (from late 14th century) and other EQUITY COURTS. Kings founded new courts (from late 15th century) to extend authority (*see* PREROGATIVE COURTS). Some of the latter were abolished by the LONG PARLIAMENT (1641). In the 1620s the House of Lords in Parliament became recognized as a superior appellate court (abolished 1649–60). *See also* LAW, ENGLAND BEFORE/FROM 1066; TOWN GOVERNMENT, ENGLAND; WARDS AND LIVERIES, COURT OF.

COURTS, ENGLAND FROM 1660 At the RESTORATION, most abolished PREROGATIVE COURTS were not restored, and Parliament confirmed the abolition (1646) of the Court of WARDS AND LIVERIES. (The COUNCIL IN THE MARCHES OF WALES was revived for civil pleas; abolished 1689.) This left COMMON-LAW courts as the principal courts: the House of Lords, King's Bench and Common Pleas at WESTMINSTER; twice-yearly provincial assize courts held by itinerant justices; quarter sessions held by JUSTICES OF THE PEACE (JPs) and town courts, both for lesser offences. The main EQUITY COURTS, CHANCERY and EXCHEQUER, also persisted.

By now, hundred and MANOR courts had weakened, although some lasted until, respectively, the 19th and 20th centuries. Church courts lost authority over behaviour in the 18th century, and most remaining jurisdiction (e.g., probate) in the 19th century.

Industrialization, urbanization and public criticism generated pressures for reform in the 19th century. A Central Criminal Court, supplanting London's 'Old Bailey' court, was established for London and adjacent areas (1834); new county courts were started for minor disputes (1846); and Divorce and Probate Courts were created (1857). The 1873 Judicature Act (effective from 1875) provided comprehensive reform: it created a Supreme Court of Judicature, comprising a High Court of Justice (incorporating older central courts) and Court of Appeal, with authority over assizes and JPs' (or magistrates') courts. Intended abolition of the House of Lords' judicial role was revoked (*see* LAW LORDS). Most town courts disappeared by 1914.

In 1956, to expand capacity, 'Crown Courts' were established in LIVERPOOL and MANCHESTER, largely superseding assizes and including quarter sessions. The 1971 Courts Act (implemented 1972) created similar arrangements elsewhere. It abolished assizes and quarter sessions, replacing them with a Crown Court (local courts, including magistrates' courts). In 2009 a UK Supreme Court replaced the House of Lords' judicial role (the existing Supreme Court became the 'Senior Courts of England and Wales'). *See also* LEGAL REFORMS, ENGLAND AND WALES, 1870s.

COURTS, IRELAND Following the Anglo-Norman invasion (1169–70), English-type courts were developed in English-controlled areas. The court and COUNCIL of the CHIEF GOVERNOR heard suits; by the early 13th century the EXCHEQUER also operated as a court, and justices made tours (to early 14th century; *see* EYRE). By the late 13th century royal courts were established in DUBLIN: Common Pleas and King's Bench (latter derived from the governor's court). Their justices also later undertook circuits to hold assizes. The royal courts applied English COMMON LAW. Local courts were held by SHERIFFS, lords of liberties and MANORS, and by town and Church authorities. By the early 16th century the CHANCERY (central writing office) also developed as a court (in Dublin), based on EQUITY. The area within which courts were held shrank in the 14th–15th centuries as Gaelic Irish lordships expanded.

The reassertion of English authority from the mid 16th century included use of new courts alongside existing types: quarter sessions held by JUSTICES OF THE PEACE; Court of CASTLE CHAMBER (1563–6, 1571–1640s); PRESIDENCY courts (1569–1640s, 1660–72); and Court of WARDS AND LIVERIES (1622–40s). The Court of High Commission, which operated intermittently 1561–1641, sought to enforce religious change (*see* REFORMATION, IRELAND).

In the 17th century the House of Lords in the Irish PARLIAMENT functioned as an appeal court, but lost jurisdiction to the British House 1720–82 and again from 1801 (*see* SIXTH OF GEORGE I; UNION OF IRELAND AND GREAT BRITAIN). In 1796 the Exchequer, Chancery, Common Pleas and King's Bench moved to a prominent new 'Four Courts' building in Dublin. During the 19th century improvements to local justice were attempted through appointing RESIDENT MAGISTRATES. In 1877 the Irish Judicature Act merged the central courts into the Supreme Court of Judicature consisting of a High Court and Court of Appeal (effective from 1878).

COURTS, SCOTLAND Before the 12th century kings and MORMAERS held assemblies at which hereditary lawmen (similar to Irish BREHONS) declared legal knowledge. King DAVID I (ruled 1124–53) developed specialized local courts: itinerant JUSTICIARS' courts, run by MAGNATES, handling serious matters (murder, rape, arson, violent robbery); sheriffs' courts for lesser offences (*see* SHERIFFDOM). The king's COUNCIL heard cases, as did the COUNCIL-GENERAL and PARLIAMENT (from 13th century). The Church, BURGHS and lords also held courts, especially barony courts with similar powers to sheriffs' courts.

From the 14th century magnates increasingly received 'grants in REGALITY' (quasi-royal jurisdiction over estates). During the 15th–17th centuries regalities and baronies increased, placing possibly half the country mainly under private jurisdiction (though ultimate Crown control remained). At the highest level, Council's legal business was delegated from 1503 to a separate council which became the Court of SESSION; from 1672 the justiciars' courts were reinvigorated as the High Court of JUSTICIARY. JUSTICES OF THE PEACE were introduced in 1609 but proved ineffectual. KIRK SESSIONS judged moral offences (late 16th–18th centuries).

After Scotland's union with England (1707), Parliament was closed and the Council abolished (1708), leaving the Session and Justiciary courts supreme in, respectively, civil and criminal matters, although the British House of Lords assumed civil superiority (*see* GREENSHIELDS' CASE). JPs' powers were also increased.

After the 1745 JACOBITE REBELLION, regalities were abolished (1747) and royal justice reasserted (barony courts declined). The Sheriff Court re-emerged as the main lower court (under a sheriff depute, usually a lawyer; renamed sheriff in 1818). From 1926 a Court of Criminal Appeal heard appeals from the High Court of Justiciary.

In 1975 JPs' and Burgh Courts were replaced by District Courts (for minor offences) under JPs, and sheriffdoms by six regional sheriffdoms (under sheriff principals). District Courts were replaced by Justice of the Peace Courts in 2008–10. *See also* LAW, SCOTLAND; CROFTING; EUROPEAN INSTITUTIONS, GREAT BRITAIN AND.

COURTS, SOUTHERN IRELAND The attempt from 1919 by the republican Dáil Éireann ('Assembly of Ireland') to supplant British authority included creation of courts. By 1921 there were about 900 parish and 70 district courts, and a Supreme Court. (Many previous lower-level courts had ceased.) They were abolished in Oct. 1922 by the provisional government of the IRISH FREE STATE (IFS).

The 1922 IFS CONSTITUTION authorized a new structure. It was created under the 1924 Courts of Justice Act, which prescribed: District Court (for minor criminal and civil matters); Circuit Court (more important cases); High Court (major cases, sitting as the Central Criminal Court for serious criminal offences); Supreme Court. Appeals could also be made to the UK PRIVY COUNCIL (abandoned 1930s). The 1937 constitution ratified the system, but required legislation was not enacted until 1961. Tribunals were also created for non-criminal matters (e.g., employment disputes). A Court of Appeal, intermediate between the High Court and Supreme Court, was added in 2014 to increase capacity for high-level appeals.

Ireland's adherence (1953) to the European Convention on Human Rights entailed access (from 1959) to the European Court of Human Rights. Entry to the EUROPEAN ECONOMIC COMMUNITY (1973) gave superior jurisdiction to the European Court of Justice. *See also* LAW, SOUTHERN IRELAND.

COURTS, WALES From the late 11th century, lordships in the MARCH OF WALES (created by Anglo-Norman lords) were governed through a court and subsidiary courts (usually for COMMOTES); new MANORS and TOWNS also had courts. Church courts were started in the 13th century.

The English conquest of lands in native Wales in 1277 was consolidated by development of judicial authority and

courts: commissions of justices were appointed for (a) the March and Wales, (b) S (i.e., W and SW) Wales (1278), and a justiciar for S Wales (1280). Lands in NE Wales were eventually (1281) placed under the justiciar of Chester (NW England).

After further English invasions (1282–3), and issue of the Statute of RHUDDLAN (1284), new jurisdictions and courts were organized. Flintshire was created in NE Wales (superseding earlier arrangements) and governed by the justiciar of Chester. Lands in NW Wales were placed under a justiciar and divided into counties (Anglesey, Caernarfonshire, Merionethshire); counties and subsidiary commotes had courts. In S Wales, the justiciarship was revitalized, and Cardiganshire and Carmarthenshire developed as county jurisdictions. The justiciars of N and S Wales, effectively the king's provincial governors, held 'Great Sessions' for major crimes and protecting royal rights (fitfully in the 15th century). Courts were also held in new towns and lordships.

From the 14th century itinerant judges held courts in some lordships in S Wales and in Cardiganshire and Carmarthenshire (often 'redeemed' or cancelled for payment, until the practice was prohibited in 1526). A COUNCIL IN THE MARCHES OF WALES exercised superior jurisdiction 1476–1642, 1660–89.

Under the UNION OF WALES WITH ENGLAND (1536–43), shires (with courts) replaced the March. 'Quarter sessions', held by JUSTICES OF THE PEACE, operated throughout Wales and (except in MONMOUTHSHIRE) Courts of GREAT SESSIONS. The last were replaced by assizes in 1830. Subsequent reforms in England usually included Wales. *See also* COURTS, ENGLAND FROM 1660; WELSH LANGUAGE ACTS.

COURTS AND LAW, NORTHERN IRELAND At the province's creation (1921), existing 'inferior' (lower) courts were retained (county and magistrates' courts). A 'superior' (higher) Supreme Court of Judicature was created under the GOVERNMENT OF IRELAND ACT (1920), comprising a High Court (with King's Bench and Chancery divisions) and Court of Appeal. Judgments remained ultimately appealable to the UK House of Lords (UK Supreme Court from 2009). Justices also held local ASSIZES. A Court of Criminal Appeal was added to the Supreme Court in 1930. In 1935 the judicial work of (unpaid) justices of the peace (JPs) in the magistrates' courts was transferred to (paid) RESIDENT MAGISTRATES.

In response to the TROUBLES, so-called 'Diplock Courts' also operated (1973–2007) in which a single judge, without a jury, tried terrorism-related offences (e.g., murder, bombing). They were named after Lord Diplock, chairman of the commission that recommended them.

Reforms in 1978 merged the Court of Criminal Appeal with the Court of Appeal, added a Family Division to the

High Court, and replaced assizes with a Crown Court (part of the Supreme Court). ('Supreme' was dropped in 2009.)

Numerous sources of law have been applicable, including: (a) COMMON LAW from England and Ireland; (b) judgments by pre-1921 Irish courts and by courts in Northern Ireland, southern Ireland and England; (c) legislation by the PARLIAMENTS of England, Ireland, Great Britain, the UK, Northern Ireland; (d) legislation by Northern Ireland ASSEMBLIES; (e) orders in Council (UK Privy Council) during periods of direct rule (intermittently from 1972); (f) law of the European Economic Community (from 1973). In 1998 the UK Parliament included Northern Ireland under the Human Rights Act, which made the European Convention on Human Rights applicable in domestic law.

COVENANT, 1638 *see* NATIONAL COVENANT

COVENANT, WARS OF THE, OR BISHOPS' WARS Military campaigns in 1639 and 1640 involving English and Scottish forces which arose from religious innovations in Scotland promoted by King CHARLES I (e.g., Book of CANONS, 1636; PRAYER BOOK, 1637). Opposition was focused by the REVOLT OF 1637 and a resistance movement which developed in 1638 (*see* NATIONAL COVENANT). Charles suspended some innovations and allowed the GLASGOW ASSEMBLY to meet. But it condemned and reversed the Crown's religious policy (Nov.–Dec. 1638).

Charles responded with military force (First Bishops' War); in late May 1639 an English army marched to the vicinity of BERWICK-UPON-TWEED where it confronted an army of Scottish Covenanters in SE Scotland. Charles agreed to accept the treaty of BERWICK (18 June).

The Covenanting army did not disband and Charles broke the terms of the treaty and sought financial aid in England (*see* SHORT PARLIAMENT). Covenanters invaded England on 20 Aug. 1640 (Second Bishops' War), defeating an English force at Newburn, Northumberland (28 Aug.), and occupying NEWCASTLE UPON TYNE (30 Aug.). To secure their withdrawal Charles agreed to pay them £860 a day (treaty of Ripon), pending a settlement. This led to the recall of the English Parliament (*see* LONG PARLIAMENT) and CIVIL WARS. *See also* COVENANTING REVOLUTION.

COVENANTERS In Scotland, those who supported the principles of the NATIONAL COVENANT (1638). The first Covenanters organized a national movement of opposition to the religious policies of King CHARLES I, including most nobility, clergy, and townsmen as well as rural tenants. (The NE, including ABERDEEN, was the main anti-covenanting area.) In 1638–40 its leaders took control of the Church of SCOTLAND and of national government in the COVENANTING REVOLUTION. The movement was

weakened by the ENGAGEMENT (1647) and the split between REMONSTRANTS and RESOLUTIONERS (1650).

After the RESTORATION (1660), when most nobles and many clergy acquiesced in the re-establishment of episcopacy in 1662, Covenanters formed a large dissenting, anti-episcopal minority outside the Church, led mainly by clergy who had been ejected from their livings. Strongest in the SW, Covenanters met in CONVENTICLES, often with armed protection. The government sought to suppress them with penal laws and military action. Most Covenanters rejoined the Church after the settlement of 1689–90, which again did away with episcopacy. *See also* PENTLAND RISING; RISING OF 1679; REVOLUTION SETTLEMENT, SCOTLAND; DISSENT, SCOTLAND.

COVENANTING REVOLUTION In Scotland, the seizure of control of Church (1638) and government (1640) from King CHARLES I by COVENANTERS (supporters of the 1638 National Covenant), in reaction to Charles's political and religious policies (*see* REVOCATION OF 1625; BALMERINO TRIAL; REVOLT OF 1637; NATIONAL COVENANT).

In late 1638 a General Assembly of the Church defied Charles by abolishing religious innovations and episcopacy (*see* GLASGOW ASSEMBLY). After military action (*see* COVENANT, WARS OF THE, OR BISHOPS' WARS), an Assembly and PARLIAMENT re-enacted the Assembly's legislation (Aug. 1639). In June 1640 Parliament, meeting on its own initiative, abolished its clerical estate, passed a Triennial Act (meetings required every three years), and established a Committee of Estates (standing committee), displacing the COUNCIL. In 1641 Parliament enacted a veto on appointments to royal offices and the Council. In 1643 Covenanters, meeting in a CONVENTION, allied with English Parliamentarians (*see* SOLEMN LEAGUE AND COVENANT) and invaded England (1644; *see* CIVIL WARS, SCOTTISH PARTICIPATION).

The failure of England's Parliament to introduce presbyterianism, as expected under the Solemn League, caused one party to ally with Charles (Dec. 1647; *see* ENGAGEMENT), thereby dividing the Covenanters. 'Engagers', including most nobles, now invaded England on Charles's behalf. Their defeat at Preston (17–19 Aug. 1648) enabled anti-Engagement radicals to take power, exclude Engagers and others, repudiate the Engagement, and renew the Solemn League (*see* ARGYLL, 8TH EARL OF; CLASSES, ACT OF).

The arrival of CHARLES II (24 June 1650), after taking the Covenant, caused new division. In Oct. radicals called for more purges (*see* REMONSTRANTS), while others called for union behind the king (*see* RESOLUTIONERS). The latter prevailed; Charles was crowned (1 Jan. 1651) and the Act of Classes revoked (May). Soon afterwards, however, the regime was swept aside by English Parliamentarian invaders; *see* DUNBAR, BATTLE OF; UNION OF ENGLAND AND SCOTLAND, 1650s.

COVENANTS, SCOTLAND The practice of making covenants or solemn binding agreements was a distinctive feature of Protestant Christianity and society in 16th- and 17th-century Scotland. It originated in bonds of MANRENT, made from the 15th century, in which members of the landed class bound themselves together for mutual protection and support. This took on a religious aspect in the three bonds of the LORDS OF THE CONGREGATION (1557, 1559, 1560), by which nobles swore, to each other and God, to strive for the overthrow of Catholicism and for the Reformation of Christianity.

After the REFORMATION (1560) the reformed Church assumed the idea with the NEGATIVE CONFESSION (1581), a repudiation of Catholicism intended for national circulation and subscription. The word 'covenant', however, only appeared in 1596 when, in a period of insecurity, the Church's General Assembly called for a national 'renewal of the covenant with God'.

The covenant idea reach its apogee with the NATIONAL COVENANT of 1638, a protest against religious policies of King CHARLES I, which led to the COVENANTING REVOLUTION. It assumed a pan-British dimension with the SOLEMN LEAGUE AND COVENANT of 1643. *See also* COVENANTERS.

COWEN, BRIAN (b. 10 Jan. 1960 at Clara, Co. Offaly, Ireland). A FIANNA FÁIL TD (1984–2011), Cowen served in the governments of Albert REYNOLDS (1992–4) and Bertie AHERN (1997–2008), from 2004 as minister for finance. On Ahern's resignation (May 2008), he was elected party leader and taoiseach (premier).

Soon afterwards, Ireland's economy crashed (part of a worldwide recession), leaving banks and other financial institutions liable to collapse. Cowen's government guaranteed extensive bank liabilities (Sept. 2008), and injected capital into the main banks (Dec.) and then nationalized them (2009–10). The cost of rescues and a rapidly expanding government deficit required a 'bailout' loan from the European Union and International Monetary Fund (Nov. 2010). During Cowen's premiership, the Republic accepted the European Union's treaty of Lisbon (2009, by second referendum). Official reports on child abuse by Catholic clergy were published (2009).

In early 2011 a loss of trust caused the Green Party to withdraw from Cowen's government. He resigned as party leader but remained taoiseach to pass financial legislation. At the ensuing general election (Feb.), Cowen retired from the Dáil. His party suffered its worst result. *See also* SOCIAL PARTNERSHIP; KENNY, ENDA.

CRAIG, JAMES (b. 8 Jan. 1871 at Belfast, Ireland; d. 24 Nov. 1940 at Craigavad, Co. Down, Northern Ireland, aged 69). A Unionist MP (1906–21), Craig worked with E.H.

CARSON from 1910 to oppose Irish HOME RULE. He helped to organize ULSTER'S SOLEMN LEAGUE AND COVENANT (1912) and the ULSTER VOLUNTEER FORCE (1913).

In 1920, as Great Britain developed new plans for Ireland's government, Craig accepted the principle of a self-governing 'Northern Ireland' of six counties, which Protestants could control. He succeeded as Unionist leader on 24 Feb. 1921 and became Northern Ireland's first prime minister (from 7 June). His government crushed violence by the IRISH REPUBLICAN ARMY (1921–2). Craig supported policies that entrenched Protestant domination (e.g., gerrymandering of electoral boundaries) and made little effort to conciliate the Catholic minority. He died in office. He was created a baronet (1918) and Viscount Craigavon of Stormont (1927). *See also* GOVERNMENT, NORTHERN IRELAND.

CRAIGAVON, VISCOUNT *see* CRAIG, JAMES

CRANFIELD, LIONEL (b. March 1575 at London, England; d. 5 Aug. 1645 at London, aged 70). A wealthy merchant and financier, Cranfield was involved in government from 1613, initially as surveyor-general of CUSTOMS (knighted 1613). From 1615 he collaborated with Viscount Villiers (later duke of BUCKINGHAM), the favourite of King JAMES VI/I. As master of the royal wardrobe from 1618 he reduced expenditure by a third but failed to solve James's financial problems. He was appointed a privy councillor (1620), created Lord Cranfield (1621), appointed lord TREASURER (1621), and made earl of Middlesex (1622).

By 1624 Buckingham considered the parsimonious Middlesex as an impediment to his pro-war policy and brought about his IMPEACHMENT by Parliament for corruption. Though pardoned by CHARLES I, he retired from politics.

CRANMER, THOMAS (b. 2 July 1489 at Aslockton, Nottinghamshire, England; d. 21 March 1556 at Oxford, Oxfordshire, England, aged 66). A scholar at CAMBRIDGE University and clergyman, Cranmer from 1529 assisted the quest to annul the first marriage of King HENRY VIII (*see* GREAT MATTER). Henry appointed him archbishop of CANTERBURY in late 1532. In 1533, following passage of the Act in Restraint of APPEALS, Cranmer judged Henry's first marriage as invalid (23 May) and his second marriage valid (28 May). Cranmer was by now influenced by Continental evangelical theology. Renewed religious conservatism threatened him from the late 1530s (*see* SIX ARTICLES), but he survived two plots (1543) thanks to Henry's support.

During the reign of EDWARD VI (1547–53), Cranmer instituted reformed doctrine and observances in the Church, including the PRAYER BOOKS (1549, 1552) and Forty-Two ARTICLES (1553).

After the accession of MARY I (1553), Cranmer was imprisoned (14 Sept.) and condemned for treason for supporting Lady Jane GREY (13 Nov.). He was moved to OXFORD (March 1554) and tried for heresy (Sept. 1555). Although he signed submissions, he was burnt, and before dying condemned the Pope and the Mass. *See also* REFORMATION, ENGLAND; CROMWELL, THOMAS.

CRANNOG An artificial platform of wood, stones, animal bones and other refuse, usually constructed on the muddy foreshore of a lake to provide a dry occupation site (from Irish *crann*, meaning tree). Crannogs were in use by 900 BC, during the Late BRONZE AGE, and probably earlier; they flourished in the early historic and medieval periods (i.e., to roughly AD 1500).

CRAWSHAY FAMILY Ironmasters in Glamorgan, S Wales. Richard Crawshay (1739–1810), from Yorkshire (NE England), became by 1790 the sole owner of the Cyfarthfa ironworks near MERTHYR TYDFIL by buying out the family of Anthony BACON. He made a fortune from supplying cannons during the NAPOLEONIC WARS (1799–1815), becoming one of Great Britain's first industrialist millionaires. The ironworks remained in Crawshay's family until they were absorbed into the Guest, Keen company in 1902. Richard's grandson, William Crawshay II (1788–1867), built a grandiose castle at Cyfarthfa. *See also* IRON AND STEEL INDUSTRIES, WALES.

CRÉCY, BATTLE OF *see* HUNDRED YEARS WAR

CRICK, FRANCIS (b. 8 June 1916 at Weston Favell, Northamptonshire, England; d. 28 July 2004 at San Diego, California, USA, aged 88). From 1947 Crick, a physicist curious about biophysics, undertook biological research at CAMBRIDGE, moving in 1949 to the Medical Research Council Unit at the Cavendish Laboratory to study large molecules by X-ray crystallography. He collaborated from 1951 with James D. Watson, a young researcher from the USA, on DNA (deoxyribonucleic acid), a constituent of chromosomes. Watson suspected that DNA carried genetic information.

In 1953, influenced by photographs and a report by Rosalind FRANKLIN in London, Crick and Watson completed a model of the DNA molecule, consisting of two intertwined helical strands, which could separate and instigate replication. It was a major scientific breakthrough. Crick and Watson announced their achievement at the nearby Eagle pub (28 Feb.) and in two papers (April). Crick was elected a fellow of the ROYAL SOCIETY (1959) and received the 1962 Nobel Prize in Physiology or Medicine (with Watson and Maurice Wilkins). From 1977 Crick developed the Salk Institute for Biological Studies at San Diego, where he specialized in neuroscience and consciousness.

CRIMEAN WAR Fought by Great Britain, FRANCE, and the OTTOMAN EMPIRE against RUSSIA, 1854–6. The conflict originated in the EASTERN QUESTION. A Franco-Russian dispute over guardianship of Holy Places in Palestine led to Russia occupying Moldavia and Wallachia (Ottoman provinces) in order to reassert its claim to protect Eastern Christians (June 1853). The Turks retaliated by declaring war (Sept. 1853), and Britain and France intervened (Britain declared war 31 March 1854). Russia promptly withdrew, but the allies decided to secure Turkey against future coercion by destroying the Russian Black Sea naval base at Sevastopol in the Crimea.

Allied forces landed (14 Sept. 1854), won the battle of Alma (20 Sept.), and laid siege to Sevastopol. Lord Raglan (1788–1855) commanded the British Army. Russian counter-attacks failed at Balaclava (20 Oct.) – famous for the 'charge of the Light Brigade' (charge by British light cavalry) – and Inkerman (5 Nov.). Winter then caught the allies unprepared. Reports of squalor, disease and chaos in the British camp forced Lord ABERDEEN to resign as prime minister. Lord PALMERSTON sent more men and supplies, and Florence NIGHTINGALE organized hospitals.

After determined Anglo-French assaults, the Russian garrison abandoned Sevastopol on 8 Sept. 1855. The treaty of Paris (30 March 1856) prohibited warships and fortifications on the Black Sea (until Russia violated it with impunity in 1870). Deaths: 45,000 British, 180,000 French, 450,000 Russian, mainly from disease.

CRIMINAL LAW AMENDMENT ACT, 1885 Legislation applicable to the UK which prohibited the procuring of girls and young women as prostitutes (so-called trafficking of 'white slaves'), banned brothel keeping and raised the age of consent from 13 to 16. It also outlawed public and private acts of gross indecency between males (i.e., homosexual behaviour). *See also* PURITY MOVEMENT; HOMOSEXUALITY, LAW RELATING TO.

CRIPPS, STAFFORD (b. 24 April 1889 at London, England; d. 21 April 1952 at Zurich, Switzerland, aged 62). A prominent barrister (knighted 1930), Cripps became a Labour MP in 1931. He was expelled from the British LABOUR PARTY (Jan. 1939) for advocating co-operation with the COMMUNIST PARTY. Though not formally readmitted until 1945, he served as ambassador to the USSR (1940–2), lord PRIVY SEAL (1942) and minister of aircraft production (1942–5) in the wartime coalition of Winston CHURCHILL.

In the post-war government of Clement ATTLEE, Cripps was president of the Board of Trade (1945–7) and chancellor of the Exchequer (1947–50). He earned respect despite devaluation of sterling in Sept. 1949. Ill health caused his resignation. The necessary 'austerity' policies of the post-war period chimed with Cripps's ascetic persona. *See also* DALTON, HUGH.

CROFTERS' WAR Protests by crofters in the Highlands and Islands of Scotland 1882–8 (especially Skye and Harris). Triggered by economic depression, they began in spring 1882 with a rent strike at Braes on Skye and demands for the return of former grazing lands. The British government established a royal commission (1883–4) and conceded security and heritability of tenure, and fair rents, in the Crofters Holdings (Scotland) Act of 1886. This failed to satisfy all crofters and trouble continued until economic conditions improved. *See also* CROFTING; CONGESTED DISTRICTS BOARD, SCOTLAND.

CROFTING A form of rural life in coastal areas of the western Scottish Highlands (Fort William northwards) and WESTERN ISLES based on townships of smallholdings ('crofts') and protective legislation. It was developed by landlords from the 1770s for tenants forcibly moved from inland townships (*see* CLEARANCES). 'Crofters' received separate holdings, insufficient for subsistence, and had to take secondary occupations (e.g., fishing, kelp gathering). Their main crop was potatoes. Secondary income fell after 1815 (end of NAPOLEONIC WARS), and in 1846–56 potato failures threatened starvation (prevented by outside food supplies, public works and EMIGRATION).

Renewed economic crisis in 1881–2 triggered the widely publicized CROFTERS' WAR. Great Britain's Liberal government accepted crofters as a special case and the 1886 Crofters Holdings (Scotland) Act, providing security of tenure and fair rents, inaugurated crofting legislation. Later provisions included the CONGESTED DISTRICTS BOARD (1897–1912), to provide economic investment; the 1919 Land Settlement (Scotland) Act, to fund augmentation of holdings; the 1955 Crofters' Commission, to reorganize crofts; and the 1976 Crofting Reform Act, to facilitate purchase. In the mid 1990s there were 18,000 crofts (average size, 4 acres, 1.6 ha). Secondary employment now included providing tourist accommodation. The Scottish Executive (established 1999) expressed continuing support for crofting. There have also been crofts on the SHETLAND ISLANDS and to a lesser extent on the ORKNEY ISLANDS.

CROMDALE, BATTLE OF *see* KILLIECRANKIE, BATTLE OF

CROMPTON, SAMUEL (b. 3 Dec. 1753 at Tonge, Lancashire, England; d. 26 June 1827 at Bolton, Lancashire, aged 73). A cotton spinner and weaver, Crompton in 1778–9 invented the 'spinning mule', a machine which spun high-quality yarn. It combined the 'moving carriage' of the

'spinning jenny' (*see* HARGREAVES, JAMES) and rollers (as pioneered by Richard ARKWRIGHT). Crompton did not patent his invention. Mules were cheap to produce, and contributed to the rapid expansion of the Manchester-centred cotton industry. From 1791 to 1815 Crompton ran a factory. He became a Swedenborgian. *See also* COTTON INDUSTRY, ENGLAND.

CROMWELL, OLIVER (b. 25 April 1599 at Huntingdon, Huntingdonshire, England; d. 3 Sept. 1658 at Westminster, Middlesex, England, aged 59). Lord protector of England (with Wales), Ireland and Scotland 1653–8.

A Puritan and MP without military experience, from an obscure GENTRY family, Cromwell became an outstanding (Parliamentarian) commander during the 1642–6 CIVIL WAR (second-in-command in the NEW MODEL ARMY from 1645). In 1646–7 he sought to reconcile the disputatious Army and Parliament. He defeated the Scottish Royalist invasion of 1648 (Second Civil War). As an Independent he supported PRIDE'S PURGE (Dec.), execution of King CHARLES I, and abolition of monarchy (1649).

In 1649–50 Cromwell conquered Ireland (*see* CROMWELL, OLIVER, AND IRELAND), and in July 1650, as commander-in-chief, he invaded Scotland. In Aug. 1651 he pursued CHARLES II from Scotland, defeating him at WORCESTER.

By 1653 the Army was discontented with the RUMP PARLIAMENT. Cromwell ejected it (April), briefly replacing it with BAREBONE'S PARLIAMENT (July–Dec.). On 16 Dec. Cromwell became 'lord protector' (*see* INSTRUMENT OF GOVERNMENT). Parliaments were held in 1654–5 and 1656–8.

In 1657 Cromwell, who felt guided by God, refused to become king and was reinaugurated as protector. Though a son succeeded him (*see* CROMWELL, RICHARD), his death led to RESTORATION of the monarchy. *See also* CIVIL WARS, POLITICAL ASPECTS; COMMONWEALTH AND PROTECTORATE; WESTERN DESIGN; HUMBLE PETITION AND ADVICE.

CROMWELL, OLIVER, AND IRELAND Cromwell was sent to Ireland by England's RUMP PARLIAMENT, as chief governor (lieutenant) and general, to overthrow the coalition of Royalist Protestants and the CATHOLIC CONFEDERATION. When he landed at Dublin (15 Aug. 1649), Parliament held only DUBLIN and LONDONDERRY (N Ireland). His Army comprised 20,000 men from the NEW MODEL ARMY.

Cromwell captured Drogheda, N of Dublin, killing its garrison as an example (11 Sept.). He then marched S and seized WEXFORD (11 Oct.), where 1500 soldiers were killed. New Ross, to the W, surrendered on 19 Oct. Soon afterwards CORK and other towns in MUNSTER (S Ireland) defected to Parliament. WATERFORD withstood Cromwell's siege (abandoned early Dec.).

In Jan. 1650 English forces restarted operations. By 30 March all major towns in Munster were in English hands except for Waterford, Clonmel and Limerick. KILKENNY surrendered to Cromwell on 28 March, followed by Clonmel (18 May). Cromwell left Ireland on 27 May (from Youghal, Co. Cork), leaving other commanders to advance the conquest (completed June 1652). In nine months he had taken most of E and S Ireland.

In 1653 Cromwell issued orders resulting in the CROMWELLIAN LAND SETTLEMENT. His family became involved in Ireland's government, with his son Henry serving as governor 1657–9. *See also* IRISH WARS, 1641–52; JONES, MICHAEL; COMMONWEALTH AND PROTECTORATE, IRELAND.

CROMWELL, RICHARD (b. 4 Oct. 1626 at Huntingdon, Huntingdonshire, England; d. 12 July 1712 at Cheshunt, Hertfordshire, England, aged 85). The eldest surviving son of Oliver CROMWELL (by mid 1640s), Richard Cromwell succeeded as lord protector in the British Isles and commander-in-chief of the NEW MODEL ARMY, by his father's nomination, on 3 Sept. 1658. The Army, fearing reorganization, forced Cromwell to dissolve the 'Protectorate Parliament' (22 April 1659). It recalled the RUMP PARLIAMENT (met 6 May) and then deposed Cromwell (confirmed to Rump 25 May). He lived thereafter in obscurity in Continental Europe and England. *See also* COMMONWEALTH AND PROTECTORATE.

CROMWELL, THOMAS (b. *c*.1485 at Putney, Surrey, England; d. 28 July 1540 at London, England, aged about 55). A self-taught lawyer, Cromwell worked for Cardinal Thomas WOLSEY from 1524. After Wolsey's fall (1529) he served King HENRY VIII (from mid 1530; councillor from late 1530). During 1532–6 Cromwell helped to arrange Henry's divorce from KATHERINE OF ARAGON and masterminded the separation of the English Church from papal jurisdiction with Henry as head (*see* REFORMATION PARLIAMENT). He was Henry's chief minister by late 1533 (king's secretary from April 1534).

In Jan. 1535 Cromwell was appointed Henry's vicegerent (deputy) in spiritual affairs, to enforce Henry's supremacy over the Church. He organized the DISSOLUTION OF RELIGIOUS HOUSES (1536–40) and promoted evangelical reform (e.g., condemning pilgrimages and relics, 1538). He started to lose authority after arranging Henry's disastrous marriage to ANNE OF CLEVES (Jan. 1540), though he was created earl of Essex (April). He was arrested on 10 June, attainted by Parliament for treason and other crimes (29 June) and executed. *See also* TUDOR REVOLUTION IN GOVERNMENT; NORFOLK, 3RD DUKE OF; REFORMATION, ENGLAND.

CROMWELLIAN LAND SETTLEMENT The redistribution of land in Ireland undertaken after conquest by armies of the English Parliament (1649–52). It was made to reward investors under the 1642 Act for ADVENTURERS, to settle soldiers' arrears of pay, and to reduce the political influence of Catholics. Under the Settlement of Ireland Act (passed 12 Aug. 1652) the RUMP PARLIAMENT in England designated classes of people (mostly Catholics) who would forfeit their estates. Detailed decisions about land clearance and resettlement were made by Oliver Cromwell and the English Council of State on 2 July 1653.

Some 11 (of 20) million acres were confiscated. Many Catholic landowners were entirely dispossessed; 3000 others resettled in CONNACHT (W Ireland) on much smaller holdings. By 1660, 500 'Adventurers' became landowners and about 12,000 former soldiers (all Protestants) settled on forfeited lands. The Settlement was not reversed after the RESTORATION (1660), and provided the basis for the PROTESTANT ASCENDANCY. *See also* IRISH WARS, 1641–52; CROMWELL, OLIVER, AND IRELAND; PETTY, WILLIAM.

CROMWELLIAN UNION, ENGLAND AND SCOTLAND *see* UNION OF ENGLAND AND SCOTLAND, 1650s

CROSSMAN, RICHARD (b. 15 Dec. 1907 at London, England; d. 5 April 1974 at Prescote Manor, Oxfordshire, England, aged 66). A philosophy don at OXFORD University (1930–7), involved in LABOUR PARTY politics from the mid 1930s, Crossman became an MP in 1945. He drew close to Nye BEVAN (*see* BEVANITES), then to Harold WILSON. He served Wilson as minister of housing (1964–6), leader of the House of Commons (1966–8), and health and social security secretary (1968–70). His political diaries, providing a vivid insider's account of British government, were published soon after his death, as he wished, despite resistance from the Labour government.

CROWN COLONY Term used for English or British colonies under the direct authority of the monarch (or Crown), with rule usually exercised by a governor on the monarch's behalf. The term is used for colonies in the Americas established in the 17th–18th centuries by emigration (starting with VIRGINIA). In the 19th century it was the basic form of government for British possessions in which the population was overwhelmingly non-European and considered unfit for representative government. *See also* DEPENDENT TERRITORY.

CRUSADES Term denoting primarily military expeditions from W Europe in the 11th–13th centuries to recover the Holy Land from Muslim rule and re-establish Christian rule. It refers to the cross worn by participants. The main such Crusades were: First Crusade, 1096–1102, instigated by Pope Urban II, which captured Jerusalem (1099) and enabled four 'Latin kingdoms' to be established (by 1120); Second Crusade, 1147–9, which challenged a Muslim resurgence; Third Crusade, 1189–92, provoked by Saladin's capture of Jerusalem (1187), which recovered coastal territory but not Jerusalem; Fourth Crusade, 1202–4, which was diverted to Constantinople; Fifth Crusade, 1217–29, which recovered Jerusalem (held 1229–44). Despite further expeditions, European Christians were effectively expelled by 1291 (*see* ACRE, FALL OF).

As military undertakings promoted by Popes, Crusades appealed to kings, nobles and knights from the British Isles. Eminent participants included Bishop ODO OF BAYEUX; King RICHARD I; Bishop Hubert WALTER; RICHARD, EARL OF CORNWALL; Simon de MONTFORT; the Lord Edward (*see* EDWARD I). Other kinds of people also volunteered (e.g., craftsmen, labourers), attracted by potential posthumous reward, though Welsh and Irish participation was less common. Taxation was sometimes levied, such as the 'Saladin tithe' in England (1188). The international religious and military orders of the Knights Hospitaller and Knights Templar, which assisted crusading, received estates in Britain and Ireland. (The Templars were suppressed in the early 14th century and their lands transferred to the Hospitallers.)

Crusades to the Holy Land were part of a broader movement, continuing until the 16th century, which included Crusades in Spain (against Muslims from N Africa) and the Baltic (against pagan Slavs). They also saw involvement from the British Isles (e.g., Scots in Baltic Crusades).

CRYSTAL PALACE *see* GREAT EXHIBITION

CRYSTAL PALACE SPEECH An address given by the leading Conservative Benjamin DISRAELI at the relocated Crystal Palace, Sydenham, Kent (SE England) on 24 June 1872. He expounded his view of the CONSERVATIVE PARTY, emphasizing commitment to the constitution, monarchy, British Empire, and social reform. The speech was a notable event in the Party's recovery from defeat in the 1868 general election.

CULBLEAN, BATTLE OF Fought in Culblean Forest (NE Scotland), on 30 Nov. 1335. Andrew MURRAY and supporters of King DAVID II killed David of Strathbogie, earl of Atholl, Edward BALLIOL's lieutenant in N Scotland. Culblean began the final decline of Balliol's fortunes. *See also* SCOTTISH–ENGLISH RELATIONS 1290 TO 1357.

CULDEES Monks in Ireland (from Irish *Céli Dé*, meaning 'Clients of God') who, in the 8th–12th centuries as anchorites, communities or bishops' households, lived a more devout life (e.g., observing celibacy and regular prayer). They spread to N Britain (modern Scotland) and included communities at DUNKELD and ST ANDREWS (by 9th century). Households generally became cathedral canons in the 12th century, serving their church rather than

their community, though a few (e.g., at ARMAGH, St Andrews) became independent and lasted longer.

CULLEN, PAUL (b. 29 April 1803 at Prospect, Co. Kildare, Ireland; d. 24 Oct. 1878 at Dublin, Ireland, aged 75). Cullen was based in Rome from 1820 (ordained a Catholic priest 1829). He advised the papacy not to condemn NATIONAL EDUCATION in Ireland (1841), but supported condemnation of the non-denominational Queen's Colleges (1848; *see* UNIVERSITIES, IRELAND).

In Ireland from 1850 as archbishop of ARMAGH, Cullen held the synod of Thurles (Aug.), Ireland's first Catholic bishops' synod since 1642, which promoted Roman devotional practices. As archbishop of DUBLIN from 1852, he was resented by Archbishop MACHALE, but Cullen isolated his rival. He rejected FENIANS and other secular nationalists, supporting instead the NATIONAL ASSOCIATION (1864). In 1866 Cullen was created Ireland's first cardinal. As an ULTRAMONTANIST, he supported the declaration of papal infallibility (1870). *See also* CATHOLICS AND CATHOLIC CHURCH, IRELAND FROM 16TH CENTURY.

CULLEN, WILLIAM (b. 15 April 1710 at Hamilton, Lanarkshire, Scotland; d. 5 Feb. 1790 at Edinburgh, Scotland, aged 79). A physician (from late 1720s), Cullen practised in GLASGOW from 1744, and lectured at its university from 1746, also teaching chemistry and other subjects from 1747 and becoming professor of medicine (1751). His pupils included Joseph BLACK. He moved by invitation to EDINBURGH University where he held professorships of chemistry (from 1755), medical theory (1766) and medical practice (1773). He also lectured at Edinburgh's Royal Infirmary.

As a chemist, Cullen classified substances and studied effects of heat and cold. His medical writings (e.g., *First Lines of the Practice of Physic*, four volumes, 1777–84) classified diseases. He introduced the concept of 'neurosis' for disorders lacking a fever or local cause (e.g., convulsions), arguing that the nervous system could contribute to illness. Cullen was an influential figure of the Scottish ENLIGHTENMENT.

CULLODEN, BATTLE OF Fought on Drumossie Moor, near Culloden village, 5 mi (8 km) E of Inverness (Inverness-shire, N Scotland), on 16 April 1746; the final battle of the JACOBITE REBELLION of 1745. A largely Highland army under the 'Young Pretender', Charles Edward Stuart, fighting on a badly chosen site, was crushed by British government forces under the duke of CUMBERLAND.

CUMANN NA NGAEDHAEL (Irish, meaning 'Party of the Irish'). A cultural society founded on 30 Sept. 1900 by Arthur GRIFFITH. It merged with the FENIAN Dungannon Clubs in April 1907 to form the Sinn Féin League (*see* SINN FÉIN).

The name was reused for a political party founded by W.T. COSGRAVE to unite supporters of the ANGLO-IRISH TREATY (1921) and IRISH FREE STATE; launched 8 April 1923. As the Free State's first governing party, Cumann na nGaedhael promoted Irish culture but pursued conservative fiscal and social policies. It was defeated in March 1932 (by FIANNA FÁIL) and was the main party which formed FINE GAEL in 1933. *See also* POLITICAL PARTIES, SOUTHERN IRELAND FROM 1922.

CUMBERLAND, DUKE OF (b. 15 April 1721 at London, England; d. 31 Oct. 1765 at London, aged 44). Prince William, the second surviving son of George, prince of Wales (King GEORGE II from 1727), was created duke of Cumberland in 1726. A soldier from 1740, he fought at Dettingen (1743) in the War of the AUSTRIAN SUCCESSION, but as commander of allied forces was defeated at Fontenoy (April 1745). Cumberland then crushed the JACOBITE REBELLION of 1745-6 in Scotland, gaining the nickname 'Butcher'. During the SEVEN YEARS WAR (from 1756) Cumberland surrendered HANOVER (1757). His father repudiated the agreement and Cumberland resigned his commands.

In the 1760s (reign of GEORGE III), Cumberland encouraged opposition to the prime ministers the earl of BUTE and George GRENVILLE. When Grenville resigned (July 1765), Cumberland advised the king to appoint the marquess of ROCKINGHAM. *See also* FREDERICK, PRINCE OF WALES.

CUNNINGHAME GRAHAM, ROBERT BONTINE (b. 24 May 1852 at London, England; d. 20 March 1936 at Buenos Aires, Argentina, aged 83). Of aristocratic descent, Cunninghame Graham frequently visited South America from 1869, to work with gauchos. In 1883 he inherited his father's Scottish estate.

In 1886 Cunninghame Graham was elected Liberal MP for NW Lanarkshire. He soon became a radical socialist; with Keir HARDIE he founded the Scottish Parliamentary Labour Party (1888). Out of Parliament from 1892, he advocated Scottish Home Rule, helping to refound the Scottish Home Rule Association (1918). He became first president of the National Party of Scotland (1928) and of the SCOTTISH NATIONAL PARTY (1934). He wrote travel books and fiction. *See also* DEVOLUTION, SCOTLAND.

CUNOBELIN (fl. from *c*.1; d. 41 or 42). Son of Tasciovanus of the CATUVELLAUNI, Cunobelin (William SHAKESPEARE's Cymbeline) ruled an increasingly powerful kingdom in SE Britain for perhaps 40 years. He conquered the neighbouring Trinovantes, making Camulodunon (COLCHESTER) his capital, and was succeeded by his sons Togodumnus and CARATACUS just before the CLAUDIAN INVASION of 43. *See also* IRON AGE TRIBES, BRITAIN.

CURRAGH 'MUTINY' An incident on 20 March 1914 when 58 British ARMY officers stationed at the Curragh Military Camp in Co. Kildare, Ireland, offered their resignations when required to move to ULSTER (N Ireland). The officers presumed, mistakenly, that they were being deployed against opponents of Irish Home Rule. The incident (strictly not a mutiny) implied that the British government could not rely on the Army to impose Home Rule on Ulster. *See also* HOME RULE MOVEMENT, IRELAND.

CURRENCY, ENGLAND BEFORE 1066 In the 6th and 7th centuries Anglo-Saxon kingdoms used gold coins from Francia, in two denominations: (Latin) *solidus* and *tremissis* (third of a *solidus*). *Tremisses* (OE *thrymsas*) were minted locally, by hand hammering, from the early 7th century.

Minting of gold coins ceased in the late 7th century, as elsewhere in northern Europe. Kings issued small silver coins (pennies, commonly called *sceattas* by numismatists), similar to coins from Frisia (modern Netherlands). Successive issues were debased by reduction of silver content.

Around 760 Kings Beonna of EAST ANGLIA and OFFA of MERCIA introduced high-quality silver pennies. Similar coins were minted elsewhere, except in NORTHUMBRIA (which retained *sceattas*, called *stycas*). In the late 9th century VIKING rulers in YORK and East Anglia issued coins, while the kings of Wessex and Mercia and the archbishop of Canterbury adopted common designs.

In the 10th century kings of England established moneyers in royal burhs (fortified centres) who issued coins of standard design and quality. From late in the reign of EDGAR (d. 988) they were regularly reminted from new dies. (The number of mints peaked at 71 *c*.1017–23, in the reign of CNUT.) The system survived the NORMAN CONQUEST (1066–70s). *See also* KINGSHIP, ANGLO-SAXON ENGLAND.

CURRENCY, ENGLAND 1066 TO 1650s Kings retained authority over minting through issuing dies (except *c*.1140–54; *see* ANARCHY). The silver penny remained the only coin into the 13th century; from the 1080s it was called a 'sterling' (possibly from OE *ster*, referring to strength), a term later used for England's currency. Pennies were often cut into halves or quarters for small transactions. During the 12th century mints were reduced (30 in 1158, ten by 1216). Frequent recoinages ended in 1158. A gold 'penny', worth 20*d*., was briefly issued from 1257. From 1279 minting of silver halfpennies, farthings (¼*d*.) and groats (4*d*.) diversified the coinage.

Lasting production of gold coins started in 1344 to facilitate international trade, with the noble (6*s*. 8*d*.), half-noble and quarter-noble becoming standard. The angel, replacing the noble, was issued from 1465, and a half-angel from 1472. In 1489 HENRY VII issued a gold pound coin, the largest denomination yet. Between 1344 and 1464 (as in Continental Europe) silver pennies were steadily debased by production of smaller coins.

The money supply, which also determined credit within society, expanded considerably from the 1170s to 1320s; it then contracted, generating concern such that in 1363 a mint was opened at CALAIS (in Continental Europe) to which merchants were required to bring bullion. From the 1380s to 1460s severe shortage of bullion and coin constrained economic activity.

Both silver and gold coinages were debased 1544–51 by reduction in the purity of metal. (From 1544 minting was normally confined to the Tower of London.) They were restored by ELIZABETH I in 1560–1 (commemorated on her tomb). Afterwards silver largely replaced gold coinage, though shortage of small change caused local issuing of tokens. Bills of exchange (contracts for payments) were also increasingly used as alternatives to coins. During the CIVIL WARS (1642–8) both sides issued coinage. *See also* INFLATION AND DEFLATION.

CURRENCY, ENGLAND AND GREAT BRITAIN FROM 1660s
Following the RESTORATION coins were reminted (1662–3), using machines instead of hand hammering. New gold coins of several values, made of W African gold, became known as 'guineas' (*see* ROYAL AFRICAN COMPANY). Royal copper coinage was minted from 1672. An important development was the expansion of other media: bills of exchange (contracts for payment), government tallies (acknowledgements of debts), 'promissory notes' (banknotes, including BANK OF ENGLAND notes from 1694). The issuing of 'paper' in excess of coin deposits expanded the money stock. From 1707 English and Scottish coinages were unified.

Parliament's specification of high silver content for silver coins (1696) encouraged their export, leaving gold and 'paper' predominant by the mid 18th century. Few silver and copper coins were then minted until the later 18th century, causing shortages in industrial areas. 'Country banks' became prominent note issuers.

The suspension of convertibility of Bank of England notes to gold coin 1797–1821, because of war, increased reliance on paper money. In 1816 the Coinage Act introduced a GOLD STANDARD (currency valuation by gold rather than silver). Guineas were replaced by 'sovereigns' in 1817. Note issuing, considered a problem, was controlled from 1844 (*see* BANK CHARTER ACT). By the 1860s the Bank of England managed sterling through the BANK RATE. It became a currency of worldwide importance.

The gold standard was suspended, and notes increased, in 1914 because of WORLD WAR I; circulation of gold coins

largely ceased in 1915. A modified gold standard was restored 1925–31. From 1944 to 1972 sterling's international value was based on fixed exchange rates (*see* BRETTON WOODS AGREEMENTS); it then 'floated', its value determined by markets. The pound was decimalized (divided into 100 pence) in 1971. In 1991 the UK rejected involvement in a European currency (*see* MAASTRICHT, TREATY OF). Polymer banknotes replaced paper from 2016. *See also* BANKING, ENGLAND AND WALES; CURRENCY, IRELAND FROM 16TH CENTURY; BIMETALLISM.

CURRENCY, IRELAND, 9TH–16TH CENTURIES
Coins were introduced in the 9th century after the arrival of VIKINGS. In the 990s Sitric Silkbeard, Norse ruler of DUBLIN 989–1036, established a mint and issued English-style pennies. Dubliners produced pennies into the 12th century. In the mid 12th century the O'CONNOR FAMILY possibly established a mint at CLONMACNOIS.

Following the Anglo-Norman invasion (1169–70), coins based on English coins were produced from the mid 1180s at a royal mint in Dublin and elsewhere. JOHN, lord of Ireland, confined minting to Dublin (1204); there was a major recoinage in 1251–4. No Anglo-Irish coins were struck from 1330 to 1425, and many remaining coins were sheared. New coins were issued in 1425 and from 1460 onwards which were imitated by Gaelic chiefs, notably the O'Reillys of BRÉIFNE. The Irish mint was closed in 1505, and English silver coins were imported.

CURRENCY, IRELAND FROM 16TH CENTURY
From 1534 coins were usually minted in England for Ireland. HENRY VIII issued silver sixpences (worth an English groat, i.e., 4*d*.), and threepences, which were progressively debased. Under EDWARD VI production in Ireland was briefly resumed (several poor-quality denominations), retaining Henry's name (1548–52). MARY I restored minting to England. Under ELIZABETH I, English sterling was used, though with lower worth (1560s–1601); coinage (shillings, sixpences, threepences) then reverted to poor standards. Copper pennies and halfpennies were also issued. JAMES VI/I minted high-standard silver shillings and sixpences. From 1607 English-type coins with lower values circulated.

During the IRISH WARS of the 1640s, both sides issued coins. The CATHOLIC CONFEDERATION also authorized certain foreign coinages, while the earl of ORMOND minted Ireland's only premodern gold coins (1646), and after Charles I's death issued coins for CHARLES II (1649). From *c*.1653 the first unofficial tradesmen's tokens were produced (farthings to twopences). Under Charles II (from 1660), the supply of official small denominations improved. Halfpennies issued from 1680 were worth twelve-thirteenths of the English halfpence, a difference that became standard between the two currencies. During the intervention of JAMES VII/II (1689–90), Jacobites issued high-denomination coins in low-value alloys.

After copper halfpennies were issued in the 1690s, no new coinage was produced until 1722, when an issue was resisted (*see* WOOD'S HALFPENCE AFFAIR). The supply of large denominations expanded from the 1720s with banknotes (also Bank of Ireland notes from 1783). Coinage consisted of foreign silver, official small denominations (halfpences, farthings), and unofficial tokens. Ireland's currency was abolished in 1826, although banks still issued notes.

The IRISH FREE STATE (founded 1922) introduced currency at parity with British currency in 1928 (decimalized 1971). Parity ended in 1979, and the European Union's 'euro' was adopted in 1999. Notes were issued for NORTHERN IRELAND by local banks from 1929. *See also* BANKING, IRELAND.

CURRENCY, SCOTLAND The earliest coins struck in Scotland were silver pennies of *c*.1136 (*see* DAVID I); the earliest known gold noble (6*s*. 8*d*.) dates from 1357 (reign of DAVID II). By 1153 there were five mints (including BERWICK-UPON-TWEED, EDINBURGH and ABERDEEN); by 1250, the high point, mints existed in 16 BURGHS. Under JAMES I (king 1406–37) pennies and half-pennies of billon (silver alloyed with base metal) were introduced, and copper farthings under JAMES III (king 1460–88).

Currency retained parity with English coinage until 1367, when devaluations began to reduce relative value. By the late 15th century the Scots pound was worth one-third of the English pound, and by the UNION OF CROWNS (1603) only one-twelfth. It was revalued to parity at the UNION OF ENGLAND AND SCOTLAND (1707), and the coinages were unified. Minting in Scotland was not proscribed, but ceased in 1709. Paper money was issued by Scottish banks (the first founded 1695). Three banks issued notes in the 21st century. *See also* BANKING, SCOTLAND.

CURRENCY SCHOOL Name for theorists who in the late 1830s argued that stability in money supply and value could be achieved through confining banknote issuing to the BANK OF ENGLAND, regulation of note issue, and the GOLD STANDARD. Their opponents, the 'Banking School', argued that bankers should influence money supply by issuing notes according to 'needs of trade'. The Currency School influenced the 1844 BANK CHARTER ACT. *See also* BANKING, ENGLAND AND WALES.

CURZON, LORD (b. 11 Jan. 1859 at Kedleston Hall, Derbyshire, England; d. 20 March 1925 at London, England, aged 66). A Conservative MP from 1886, George Curzon held government offices from 1891. Created Lord Curzon (Irish peerage) in 1898, he served as viceroy of INDIA from 1899. Efficient and authoritarian, and opposed to native participation in government, he alienated Hindu opinion, notably with the partition of Bengal (implemented 1905). In 1903 Curzon organized a durbar (assembly) of native rulers to honour the coronation of EDWARD VII. He resigned (1905) after friction with Lord KITCHENER (commander-in-chief of Indian Army).

Curzon entered the UK House of Lords in 1908 as an Irish representative peer, and was created Earl Curzon in 1911 (marquess from 1921). He served as lord PRIVY SEAL under H.H. ASQUITH (1915–16), as a member of the WAR CABINET of David LLOYD GEORGE (1916–19), and as foreign secretary (1919–24). Denied the premiership in 1923, he was reappointed as lord privy seal by Stanley BALDWIN (1924).

CUSTOMS, ENGLAND AND WALES BEFORE 1689 English kings occasionally levied duties in the 12th–13th centuries. Permanent customs began in 1275 when merchants granted EDWARD I perpetual duty on exports of wool and hides ('ancient custom') to repay ITALIAN BANKERS. Charges yielded £10,000 annually. Various assemblies authorized further short-term levies (often renewed). Extra duty (or 'subsidy') on wool (nicknamed MALTOLT) was imposed to fund warfare 1294–7 (*see* GASCON WAR). A 'new custom' was levied from alien (foreign) merchants 1303–9, 1310–11, and from 1322, comprising additional wool duty; charges on wine imports ('tonnage') and general merchandise ('poundage', on imports and exports). Duties were collected at some Welsh ports.

From 1336 EDWARD III raised funds for warfare largely from wool subsidies (*see* HUNDRED YEARS WAR). Native merchants also paid poundage, and (low) duty on cloth, from 1347, and tonnage from 1350. Collection was sometimes 'farmed' (leased for advance payments). Average annual yield in the 1350s was £87,500. In 1362 Edward conceded that duties required PARLIAMENT's authorization.

High wool subsidies continued but declining wool exports reduced revenues – to £20,000 by 1432. Income revived to £25,000 (1460s) and £34,000 (1470s). In 1398 RICHARD II forced Parliament to make a life-time grant of wool customs. HENRY IV (1399), HENRY V (1415) and HENRY VI (1454) also received life-time grants of customs; from 1484 (RICHARD III) each ruler usually received a life-time grant from their first Parliament.

A 'Book of Rates' (valuations of merchandise) was introduced from 1502–3. Income rose to £48,000 (1507–8) before declining. A revised Book (1558) boosted income to £83,000. Royal exploitation of customs became controversial in the 17th century (*see* IMPOSITIONS; TONNAGE AND POUNDAGE). After the LONG PARLIAMENT took control of customs (1641), income was allocated to the Navy. At the RESTORATION (1660), it was granted to CHARLES II. When farming ceased (1671), a Customs Board was established. *See also* ROYAL REVENUES, ENGLAND; WOOL TRADE, ENGLAND; CLOTH INDUSTRY, ENGLAND.

CUSTOMS, ENGLAND, WALES AND GREAT BRITAIN FROM 1689

In England and Wales government ministers and PARLIAMENT largely appropriated control of customs. Duties were increased and expanded to help fund the Wars of the GRAND ALLIANCE (1689–97) and SPANISH SUCCESSION (1702–13). This unintentionally provided protection for new manufacturing industries (e.g., paper making; *see* MERCANTILISM), and also encouraged smuggling. The Customs Board became one of government's largest departments (1900 regular employees in 1708). The UNION OF ENGLAND AND SCOTLAND (1707) included internal free trade and a customs union.

Reforms by Robert WALPOLE in 1721–5 included removal of duties from many exports, bonded warehouses, integration of collection in Scotland (1723). Duties were increased further for warfare (1748, 1759, 1779–82), though reduced on tea, wine and spirits (1784) to undermine smuggling. The UNION OF IRELAND AND GREAT BRITAIN (1801) included phased internal free trade.

In the 1820s (bilateral agreements), 1845–6 and 1850s duties were lowered or abolished to make FREE TRADE the basis of UK international commerce (including repeal of the CORN LAWS, 1846). Although TARIFF REFORM was advocated from the 1880s, free trade continued until WORLD WAR I, when duties were imposed on luxuries (so-called 'McKenna duties', 1915); it was abandoned in 1931–2, during the GREAT DEPRESSION, to protect industries. A general tariff was imposed in 1932, which was modified by limited imperial preference (*see* OTTAWA AGREEMENTS) and other treaties.

Tariffs and imperial preference were reduced in the 1950s–60s under the General Agreement on Tariffs and Trade (1947), and from 1960 to 1973 the UK belonged to the European Free Trade Association (EFTA), which eliminated duties on industrial goods between members. It then participated in the internal market and external tariff régime of the EUROPEAN ECONOMIC COMMUNITY. The decision (2016) to leave the now European Union required new customs arrangements (*see* BREXIT). *See also* AMERICAN INDEPENDENCE, ORIGINS OF; HUSKISSON, WILLIAM; GLADSTONE, W.E.

CUSTOMS, IRELAND

The central GOVERNMENT levied customs intermittently on exports (including trade to England) in the 13th century, and regularly on wool, woolfells and hides from 1275. Collected at major ports, customs income totalled about (Irish) £1400 per year in the 1280s but later declined dramatically, yielding only £100 by 1420. Income rose from the 1460s, though ports outside the PALE were allowed to retain receipts to fund defences.

The Irish PARLIAMENT granted poundage (an additional charge on exports and imports) from 1474, and an impost on imported wines from 1569. Reorganization in 1613 included recentralization of customs income and extension to more goods. Collection was sometimes farmed (i.e., leased to private contractors for a fixed payment).

In 1662 Parliament granted customs income (with EXCISE) to the monarch in perpetuity. When farming arrangements (1669–82) collapsed, revenue commissioners resumed management. Their departments became the largest part of the Irish government (3000 employees in late 18th century), an importance symbolized by the new DUBLIN Custom House (completed 1791). The Crown surrendered control to Parliament in 1793.

After the UNION OF IRELAND AND GREAT BRITAIN (1801), charges on trade with Britain were gradually removed and the customs and excise departments were merged with their British counterparts (1823). In the IRISH FREE STATE (founded 1922), customs were supervised by the Department of Finance.

CUSTOMS, SCOTLAND

Duties on foreign trade were introduced in the late 13th century, on wool and leather exports. They were trebled in 1358, and quadrupled in 1368, to meet the ransom of King DAVID II. During the 1360s–70s export boom they generated annually over £10,000 Scots, but only around £3000 in the 15th and 16th centuries. In 1426 JAMES I cut duties on wool exports to boost trade, compensating with duties on cloth, salmon, salt and other exports.

Receipts rose in the late 16th century, but fell in real terms because of inflation (or PRICE RISE). In 1597 export duties were raised substantially, and a general tariff on imports was introduced (*see* OCTAVIANS). In 1600 wool, hides, cloth and fish generated the largest export customs.

The UNION OF ENGLAND AND SCOTLAND (1707) included a customs union, with rates set by the British government and Parliament. From 1723 the (English) Customs Board administered collection in Scotland. *See also* ROYAL REVENUES, SCOTLAND.

CUTHBERT

(b. *c.*635 near Melrose, Bernicia; d. 20 March 687 on Inner Farne island, Northumbria, aged about 51). A monk (from 651), who accepted Roman customs after the synod of WHITBY (664), Cuthbert lived a mainly solitary life on the Farne Islands (from 670s). In 684 he was appointed bishop of Hexham by EGFRITH, king of NORTHUMBRIA (NE England/SE modern Scotland). He preferred to be bishop of Lindisfarne (consecrated 685). In 687 he returned to the Farne Islands.

The discovery of Cuthbert's incorrupt body in 698 started a cult. The body and relics were removed from Lindisfarne in the mid 9th century and eventually arrived in DURHAM (995) where they remain. He became the most popular saint in northern England.

CYMMRODORION, HONOURABLE SOCIETY OF *see* WELSH NATIONAL SOCIETIES

CYMRU FYDD see YOUNG WALES

CYNDDELW BRYDYDD MAWR (fl. from *c*.1155; d. *c*.1200). A 'court poet' of the Middle Welsh period who *c*.1155 won the position of *pencerdd* ('chief poet') and praised King MADOG AP MAREDUDD of Powys (C Wales). He was later associated with OWAIN GWYNEDD of Gwynedd (NW Wales) and with RHYS AP GRUFFUDD of Deheubarth (SW Wales). *See also* WELSH LANGUAGE AND LITERATURE.

CYPRUS A former British island in the E Mediterranean with Greek and Turkish inhabitants. The OTTOMAN EMPIRE ceded Cyprus to British administration as a PROTECTORATE in 1878 in return for conditional guarantees of its territory. Great Britain annexed the island in Nov. 1914, after the outbreak of WORLD WAR I, and declared it a CROWN COLONY in 1925.

Riots in 1931 marked the start of a Greek Cypriot movement for *enosis* (union) with Greece, which was opposed by Turkish Cypriots. Greek Cypriots belonging to EOKA ('National Organization of Cypriot Fighters') attacked British forces 1955–9. Cyprus was granted independence as a republic in 1960 with a constitution that ruled out both *enosis* and partition, and guaranteed rights for the Turkish minority. The compromise soon broke down, and Turkey invaded northern Cyprus in 1974 (separate State proclaimed 1975). Britain retained two military bases on the island. Approx. population in 1921, 310,000 (20% Muslim); in 1959, 553,000.

CZECHOSLOVAKIA, BRITISH RELATIONS WITH

At the end of WORLD WAR I (Nov. 1918), Great Britain favoured the dissolution of the HABSBURG EMPIRE, which included lands occupied by Czechs and Slovaks. In Aug. 1918 it had recognized the Paris-based Czechoslovak National Council of Tomáš Masaryk as a representative body, and it confirmed the independence of Czechoslovakia at the PARIS PEACE CONFERENCE (1919).

Czechoslovakia became an ally of FRANCE (from 1924). Britain refused to guarantee its frontiers in the treaty of LOCARNO (1925). In 1938 the British prime minister, Neville CHAMBERLAIN, assisted in partitioning the country (*see* MUNICH CRISIS; APPEASEMENT), and British guarantees given to the rump State were declared inoperative when (the renamed) Czecho-Slovakia disintegrated and Germany invaded Bohemia (15 March 1939). Chamberlain's successor, Winston CHURCHILL, in 1940 proclaimed the restoration of Czechoslovakia as a British war aim (achieved 1945).

The communist takeover of Czechoslovakia (1948) increased British enthusiasm for the creation (1949) of the NORTH ATLANTIC TREATY ORGANIZATION (NATO). Britain condemned the invasion by USSR forces in 1968. Following the fall of communism (1989), Prime Minister Margaret THATCHER expressed British shame at 1930s appeasement when she visited Czechoslovakia in 1990. On 1 Jan. 1993, Czechoslovakia was divided into the Czech Republic and Slovakia. Both joined NATO (respectively 1999, 2004) and the EUROPEAN UNION (2004).

D

___

DAFYDD AP GRUFFUDD (b. *c*.1235; d. 3 Oct. 1283 at Shrewsbury, Shropshire, England, aged about 48). Rebellious younger brother of LLYWELYN AP GRUFFUDD (prince of GWYNEDD, NW Wales, 1246–82).

Dafydd revolted three times against Llywelyn: in 1255 (reconciled 1257, after invasion by King HENRY III of England); in 1263, when he fled to England (reconciled after treaty of MONTGOMERY, 1267); in 1274 (reconciled 1277; *see* ABERCONWY, TREATY OF). On 22 March 1282 he initiated a Welsh revolt against the MARCH OF WALES, provoking invasion (*see* WALES, ENGLISH CONQUEST OF). After Llywelyn's death (Dec. 1282), Dafydd led the revolt, but was captured (June 1283), tried and executed.

DAFYDD AP GWILYM (b. *c*.1320, possibly at Bro Gynin, Cardiganshire, Wales; d. *c*.1349, aged about 29). A famous early Modern Welsh bard; poet of love and nature; pioneer of the seven-syllable *cywydd* metre. Dafydd ap Gwilym introduced the European cult of 'courtly love' into Welsh poetry. He died possibly in the BLACK DEATH. *See also* WELSH LANGUAGE AND LITERATURE.

DAFYDD AP LLYWELYN (b. *c*.1205; d. Feb. 1246 at Aber, Gwynedd, aged about 41). Welsh prince; son of LLYWELYN AP IORWERTH and SIWAN; ruler of GWYNEDD (NW Wales) 1240–6.

During the 1220s and 1230s Dafydd's father sought recognition from King HENRY III of England of Dafydd as his sole successor (he had an elder half-brother), so Gwynedd would preserve its unity and its dominance in Wales. After Dafydd's accession, however, Henry compelled him to do homage alongside other Welsh rulers (15 May 1240), and in Aug. 1241 Henry invaded N Wales and extracted concessions and territory. Dafydd responded by seeking papal overlordship (1244) and by styling himself PRINCE OF WALES. War was renewed in Aug. 1245 with inconclusive outcome; Dafydd died before further conflict occurred. Succeeded by LLYWELYN AP GRUFFUDD (nephew). *See also* ANGLO-WELSH RELATIONS, 6TH–13TH CENTURIES.

DÁIL ÉIREANN *see* PARLIAMENT, SOUTHERN IRELAND

DALHOUSIE, 10TH EARL OF (b. 22 April 1812 at Dalhousie Castle, Midlothian, Scotland; d. 19 Dec. 1860 at Dalhousie Castle, aged 47). James Ramsay succeeded as earl in 1838. While serving at the British Board of TRADE (1843–6) he was involved with railways.

In Jan. 1848, aged 35, Dalhousie was the youngest person to become governor-general of INDIA. He faced unrest among the sikhs: war followed (Nov. 1848–March 1849), after which the Punjab was annexed. Dalhousie was created a marquess. He exploited opportunities to annex other territories, notably part of BURMA (1852) and Oudh (1856). Dalhousie promoted economic development by constructing roads, introducing telegraphs and planning railways. He also imposed uniformity on British administration.

A Dictionary of British and Irish History, First Edition. Edited by Robert Peberdy and Philip Waller.
© 2021 John Wiley & Sons Ltd; © editorial matter and organisation Robert Peberdy and Phillip Waller.
Published 2021 by John Wiley & Sons Ltd.

He energetically opposed notorious Indian customs (e.g., female infanticide) and the slave trade. He left India in 1856. *See also* SIKH WARS.

DÁL RIATA An Irish overkingdom in both NE Ireland and western N Britain (adjoining the Northern Channel), 6th–7th centuries, which continued in N Britain until the 9th century. Its name means 'The share of Riata' (a personal name).

'Irish Dál Riata' was formed by *c*.500 (in northern modern Co. Antrim). (Its inhabitants were possibly successors of the Robogdii tribe mapped by Greek geographer Ptolemy in the 2nd century AD.) By then migration from Ireland to N Britain (modern Argyll and Bute) was probably long established. Around 500 Dál Riata's high-king, Fergus Mór, is said to have moved to N Britain.

In the 6th century Dál Riata in N Britain comprised three kingdoms, each with a ruling dynasty and king: Cenél Loairn, Cenél nOengusa, and Cenél nGabrain. (A fourth kingdom, Cenél Comgaill, emerged by the late 7th century.) The king of Cenél nGabráin was usually high-king. In the early 7th century Irish Dál Riata became subject to the Ulaid and separate (*see* ULSTER).

'Scottish Dál Riata' profoundly influenced N Britain. From the 6th century it transmitted Irish Christianity to the Picts (*see* CONVERSION OF NORTH BRITONS, PICTS AND SCOTS). From 741 it was associated with the Picts, often as a subordinate kingdom. This pattern culminated in permanent union from the 840s under Irish-speaking kings (*see* MAC ALPIN KINGS). By *c*.1000 Irish culture largely superseded Pictish culture throughout N Britain. Ultimately the unified kingdom's name referred to its Irish origin: from the 12th century it was commonly called Scotland, the 'Land of the Irish', derived from Scotti (Latin, meaning 'Irish'). *See also* DRUIM CETT, MEETING AT; UNION OF SCOTS AND PICTS; GAELIC LANGUAGE AND LITERATURE, NORTH BRITAIN AND SCOTLAND.

DALRYMPLE, JAMES *see* STAIR, VISCOUNT

DALRYMPLE, JOHN (b. 1648 in Scotland; d. 8 Jan. 1707 at Edinburgh, SE Scotland, aged about 59). The son of James Dalrymple (later Viscount STAIR), John Dalrymple was appointed LORD ADVOCATE of Scotland (1687–8) by King JAMES VII/II, but supported his replacement by William of Orange (*see* WILLIAM III). In 1689, on behalf of the CONVENTION PARLIAMENT, he offered the Scottish Crown to William. Dalrymple was reappointed lord advocate (1689–92) and made SECRETARY OF STATE (1691), in which capacity he sought oaths of loyalty from Jacobite chiefs. When some refused, he decided to make an example, resulting in the GLENCOE MASSACRE (1692) and Dalrymple's eventual resignation (1695). He succeeded his father as viscount in 1702 (created earl of Stair 1703) and

advised Queen ANNE's government on Scottish affairs. *See also* GLORIOUS REVOLUTION, SCOTLAND.

DALTON, HUGH (b. 26 Aug. 1887 at Neath, Glamorgan, Wales; d. 12 Feb. 1962 at London, England, aged 74). An academic economist, Dalton was a Labour MP 1924–31, 1935–59. During the British wartime coalition of Winston CHURCHILL he served as minister of economic warfare (1940–2) and president of the Board of Trade (1942–5). As chancellor of the Exchequer (1945–7) in the post-war government of Clement ATTLEE, at a time of grave economic difficulty, Dalton nationalized the BANK OF ENGLAND (1946) and restored sterling to convertibility before resigning over accidental Budget leaks (13 Nov. 1947). He returned to the Cabinet in 1948, and served as minister of town and country planning 1950–1. He was created Lord Dalton in 1960. *See also* CRIPPS, STAFFORD.

DALTON, JOHN (b. 6 Sept. 1766 at Eaglesfield, Cumberland, England; d. 27 July 1844 at Manchester, Lancashire, England, aged 77). The son of a QUAKER weaver, Dalton became a schoolmaster (1778). Self-educated in natural philosophy (science), he taught mathematics and natural philosophy at Manchester Academy from 1793, becoming a private teacher in 1799. From 1787 he kept a daily meteorological diary, which stimulated thought about substances.

Dalton's principal achievement was a developed atomic theory, including the propositions that each chemical element (e.g., oxygen) consists of identical atoms; that the atoms of elements have different weights; and that chemical compounds have compound atoms. He published a rudimentary table of atomic weights in 1803, and an extensive account of his theory in part one of *A New System of Chemical Philosophy* (1808). Involved in the Manchester Literary and Philosophical Society, Dalton was elected a fellow of the ROYAL SOCIETY (1822).

DANBY, EARL OF (b. 20 Feb. 1632 at Kiveton, Yorkshire, England; d. 26 July 1712 at Easton Neston, Northamptonshire, England, aged 80). An MP from 1665 (reign of King CHARLES II), Thomas Osborne profited from the disintegration of the CABAL group of ministers. In 1673 he was appointed TREASURER and made Viscount Latimer. As Charles's leading minister he undertook financial reforms and advocated an anti-French foreign policy. He was created earl of Danby in 1674. From 1675 he used government funds to award pensions and posts to MPs to create a 'court party'. He arranged the marriage of Charles's niece Mary to the Dutch Protestant William of Orange (1677). From late 1678 Danby's enemies attempted to impeach him. He resigned as treasurer (March 1679) and was imprisoned until 1684.

Danby refused to support the Catholic JAMES VII/II, and in 1688, though a TORY, he signed the letter inviting William of Orange to invade England. From 1689, as president of the Council, he helped WILLIAM III to manage ministers and MPs. He was created marquess of Carmarthen (1689) and duke of Leeds (1694). His influence declined from 1695 (subject of attempted impeachment) and he lost his offices in 1699. *See also* PARLIAMENT, ENGLAND AND WALES 1660 TO 1707.

DANEBURY A HILLFORT near Andover, Hampshire, S England, constructed within a Late BRONZE AGE enclosure *c.*450 BC. The defences, enclosing 12 acres (5 ha), were enlarged and elaborated, before abandonment *c.*100 BC. Silos and granaries indicate storage, but the fort's social status and function are disputed.

DANEGELD *see* GELD

DANELAW Term for areas of England under Danish rule and influence (derived from OE *Dena lage*, which was first used in the early 11th century). It can refer to the eastern Midlands, East Anglia and north-eastern England, which were ruled by Danes in the late 9th and early 10th centuries and where Danish influence remained strong (until 12th century). Alternatively it can refer to the smaller area of Yorkshire, Lincolnshire, Nottinghamshire, Derbyshire, Leicestershire and Rutland, where rural society exhibited distinctive features (e.g., large numbers of freemen). *See also* VIKINGS, IMPACT ON ENGLAND; HIDE.

DARBY, ABRAHAM (b. 14 April 1678 at Wrens Nest, Worcestershire, England; d. 5 May 1717 at Madeley, Shropshire, England, aged 39). A QUAKER and businessman involved in metal-related activities, Darby leased a blast furnace for iron making at Coalbrookdale (Shropshire) from *c.*1706. He pioneered the use of coke, instead of the more expensive charcoal, for smelting iron, drawing on earlier experience of malting with coke. Darby also made cast-iron products. His business expanded under his son (1711–63) and grandson (1750–89), both namesakes. The latter constructed the world's first cast-iron bridge at Ironbridge (1777–9). *See also* IRON AND STEEL INDUSTRIES, ENGLAND.

DARIEN SCHEME The principal colonization project of the Company of Scotland, which was incorporated in 1695 to establish colonies and trade worldwide, thereby countering Scotland's exclusion from English colonies under the NAVIGATION ACTS. The Company was damaged when King WILLIAM III, pressurized by English trading interests, banned English investment.

In 1698 the Company founded the colony of 'Caledonia' on the Darien isthmus in (Spanish) C America (modern Panama), as an entrepôt between the Atlantic and Pacific but most settlers (3000) died. A relief expedition surrendered to the Spanish in 1700. The Scheme wasted possibly a quarter of Scottish liquid assets, thereby weakening the economy and strengthening the economic case for the UNION OF ENGLAND AND SCOTLAND. The Company was wound up in 1707. *See also* WORCESTER AFFAIR; EQUIVALENT.

DARNLEY, LORD (b. 7 Dec. 1545 at Temple Newsam, Yorkshire, England; d. 10 Feb. 1567 at Kirk o'Field, Edinburgh, SE Scotland, aged 21). Heir of the exiled 4th earl of LENNOX, Lord Darnley (the courtesy title of Henry Stewart) went to Scotland in 1565 and married the widowed MARY, QUEEN OF SCOTS (29 July). As her cousin (descended from Margaret, sister of King HENRY VIII of England), the marriage strengthened STEWART claims to the English Crown (Darnley claimed right of succession after Mary). But Darnley became estranged from Mary. After involvement in David RIZZIO's murder (1566), he sought the Scottish Crown and negotiated with the papacy, promising the restoration of Catholicism (*see* REFORMATION, SCOTLAND). He was murdered – probably strangled while fleeing from a gunpowder attack. *See also* BOTHWELL, 4TH EARL OF.

DARWIN, CHARLES (b. 12 Feb. 1809 at Shrewsbury, Shropshire, England; d. 19 April 1882 at Downe, Kent, England, aged 73). A grandson of the evolutionist Erasmus Darwin (1731–1802), Charles Darwin decided to study the natural world. In 1831–6 he served as naturalist on a survey voyage by HMS *Beagle*, visiting Atlantic and Pacific islands and the southern seas. It stimulated Darwin to consider connections between similar animal species on different continents, and between living and fossil species. After returning he was influenced by the geologist Charles LYELL. From 1842 Darwin lived and studied privately in Kent (SE England).

In the late 1830s Darwin conceived the theory of 'natural selection', an explanation of how species evolve through natural occurrence of variations, and preservation of some variations by advantageous circumstances. He refrained from publicizing his idea until A.R. Wallace produced a similar theory in 1858: their ideas were then announced to the Linnean Society and published. Darwin issued a substantial exposition in *On the Origin of Species by Means of Natural Selection* (1859).

Darwin's theory was considered scandalous for excluding divine agency and envisaging man as an evolved species. Darwin expanded the latter idea in *The Descent of Man* (1871). *See also* EVOLUTION; GEOLOGY.

DARWIN, ERASMUS *see* EVOLUTION

DASHWOOD, FRANCIS (b. Dec. 1708 at London, England; d. 11 Dec. 1781 at West Wycombe, Buckinghamshire, England, aged 80 or 81). An independent MP from 1741, Dashwood was appointed chancellor of the Exchequer in 1762 in the ministry of the earl of BUTE. Needing to reduce debts caused by the SEVEN YEARS WAR he proposed a CIDER TAX in 1763. It provoked fierce opposition. Though it was approved by Parliament in modified form, Bute and Dashwood resigned (April 1763).

Dashwood succeeded an uncle as Lord Le Despencer (1763). He served as paymaster-general from 1766 until his death. A patron of the arts, he was also notorious as a member of the Hellfire Club.

DAVID (b. *c.*530; d. 589, aged about 59). The founder of a monastery at ST DAVIDS (DYFED, SW Wales); dedicatee of churches in S Wales, Cornwall (SW England), and Brittany (NW France). David (Welsh, Dewi) became famous for ascetic monasticism. He was regarded as a saint by the 9th century and the cult received papal approval in 1120. He has been venerated as the patron saint of Wales since the 12th century. *See also* MONASTICISM, MEDIEVAL WALES; NATIONAL PATRON SAINTS.

DAVID I (b. *c.*1082; d. 24 May 1153 at Carlisle, Cumberland, annexed to Scotland, aged about 71). King of Scots (Scotland) 1124–53.

The youngest son of MALCOLM III and MARGARET, exiled from Scotland to England after their deaths (1093), David was raised at the courts of King WILLIAM II and King HENRY I, experience that made him Scotland's most innovative ruler. By 1113 he was ruling S Scotland, under his brother ALEXANDER I.

King from 23 April 1124, David granted hereditary lordships to Anglo-Normans mainly from England. He also founded SHERIFFDOMS and BURGHS, introduced JUSTICIARS, minted Scotland's first CURRENCY, imported new monastic orders, and reorganized the ROYAL HOUSEHOLD.

From 1135 David supported Empress MATILDA (cousin) against King STEPHEN in England (*see* ANARCHY), and sought extra territory. By the 1st treaty of Durham (Feb. 1136, following a Scottish invasion), David received CARLISLE (probably with Cumberland and Westmorland, NW England) from Stephen. David invaded again in July 1138; although defeated (*see* STANDARD, BATTLE OF THE), his son Henry (d. 1152) received the earldom of Northumberland (NE England) by the 2nd treaty of Durham (9 April 1139). David then supported Stephen until Stephen was captured (Feb. 1141). David resumed support of Matilda and occupied N Lancashire (NW England). Succeeded by MALCOLM IV. *See also* MAC MALCOLM RULERS; NORMANS, IMPACT ON SCOTLAND; BORDER, ANGLO-SCOTTISH.

DAVID II (b. 5 March 1324 at Dunfermline, Fife, E Scotland; d. 22 Feb. 1371 at Edinburgh, SE Scotland, aged 46). King of Scots (Scotland) 1329–71.

David succeeded ROBERT I (father) aged 5 (7 June 1329). His minority was overshadowed by the attempt of Edward BALLIOL to obtain the Scottish kingship. After Balliol's invasions of 1332 and 1333, David was sent to France (1334) while 'guardians' ruled Scotland (*see* DUPPLIN, BATTLE OF; HALIDON HILL, BATTLE OF). Successful resistance permitted David's return, and the start of his personal rule, in June 1341.

In 1346 Scots invaded England to support the French (at war with England), but were defeated at NEVILLE'S CROSS. David was captured and held in England until ransomed in 1357; meanwhile Balliol and King EDWARD III caused trouble in Scotland. David's release cost 100,000 marks (10,000 marks per year; stopped 1360, resumed 1365). The need for cash stimulated 'intensive government', including a new assessment of landed incomes (1366) and quadrupling of CUSTOMS (1368). David used lesser nobles, knights and burgesses as advisers, creating anger among magnates. In 1363 several rebelled, partly because David refused to dismiss his counsellors. The rebellion collapsed when David attacked the earl of DOUGLAS. David died childless; succeeded by ROBERT II. *See also* SCOTTISH–ENGLISH RELATIONS 1290 TO 1357.

DAVIDSON, RANDALL (b. 7 April 1848 at Edinburgh, Scotland; d. 25 May 1930 at Chelsea, London, aged 82). Originally a presbyterian, Davidson was ordained priest in the Church of ENGLAND (1875). Chaplain to Archbishop TAIT 1877–82, he became an informal adviser to Queen VICTORIA (e.g., on Church appointments) and a bishop.

As archbishop of CANTERBURY 1903–28, Davidson resisted disestablishment of the Church in Wales (enacted 1914; *see* DISESTABLISHMENT, CHURCH OF ENGLAND IN WALES). During WORLD WAR I (1914–18) he avoided bellicosity and privately criticized military strategy. Davidson supported creation of the Church Assembly, with delegated authority from Parliament (1919), and ecumenism (e.g., 'Malines Conversations' with Roman Catholic theologians, 1921–5). In 1926 he attempted to end the GENERAL STRIKE.

DAVIES, DAVID (b. 18 Dec. 1818 at Llandinam, Montgomeryshire, Wales; d. 20 July 1890 at Llandinam, aged 71). The most successful entrepreneur in Welsh history. Initially a bridge- and railway-builder, Davies became a coalowner in the RHONDDA VALLEYS (1864). He developed the Ocean Coal Company and was chief promoter of Barry docks, SE Wales (opened 1889, part of the port of CARDIFF). Davies was chief patron of University College, Aberystwyth (*see* UNIVERSITIES, WALES).

Davies's grandson, Lord Davies (1880–1944), championed the LEAGUE OF NATIONS. Lord Davies's sisters, Gwendoline (1882–1951) and Margaret Davies (1884–1963), collected French Impressionist paintings which they bequeathed to the National Museum of Wales, Cardiff. *See also* COAL INDUSTRY, WALES.

DAVIES, JOHN (b. *c*.1567; d. 15 May 1644 at Harlech, Merionethshire, Wales, aged about 77). Clergyman and scholar; known as Dr John Davies of Mallwyd (Merionethshire), after his home from 1604. Davies sought to raise Welsh to European standing as a language of scholarship and literature; his publications included a Welsh Grammar (1621) and Latin–Welsh Dictionary (1632), which provided foundations for later study. He contributed to revision of the Welsh BIBLE (1620) and Prayer Book (*see* SERVICE BOOKS, WALES). *See also* WELSH LANGUAGE AND LITERATURE; HUMANISM.

DAVIES, JOHN (b. April 1569 at Tisbury, Wiltshire, England; d. 8 Dec. 1626 at Westminster, Middlesex, England, aged 57). A lawyer and poet, Davies served the government in Ireland as solicitor-general (1603–6) and attorney-general (1606–19; knighted 1609.) He believed that Gaelic Irish society should be anglicized, by government, law and forced cultural change. His ideas influenced the 1609 plans for the ULSTER PLANTATION, which envisaged immigrants outnumbering natives. They were also expounded in his book *A Discoverie of the True Causes why Ireland was never entirely Subdued … until … his Majesties happie Raigne* (1612).

DAVIS, THOMAS (b. 14 Oct. 1814 at Mallow, Co. Cork, Ireland; d. 16 Sept. 1845 at Dublin, Ireland, aged 30). A (Protestant) writer, Davis joined the REPEAL ASSOCIATION in 1841. In Oct. 1842 he co-founded the weekly *Nation*, around which the YOUNG IRELAND MOVEMENT developed. Davis promoted cultural nationalism embracing Catholic and Protestant, which he expressed in poems and ballads (e.g., 'A Nation Once Again'). In May 1845 he quarrelled with Daniel O'CONNELL over the non-denominational Queen's Colleges founded by Sir Robert PEEL. He died of an infection.

DAVITT, MICHAEL (b. 25 March 1846 at Strade, Co. Mayo, Ireland; d. 31 May 1906 at Dublin, Ireland, aged 60). The son of an evicted (Catholic) Irish farmer, Davitt grew up in Lancashire (England) and joined the IRISH REPUBLICAN BROTHERHOOD (1865). While imprisoned (1870–7), he devised a scheme for combining rural agitation with parliamentary pressure to further Irish nationalist ambitions. It was rejected by the IRB, but Davitt later convinced C.S. PARNELL.

Davitt founded the Land League of Mayo (Aug. 1879), then the national LAND LEAGUE (Oct.), with Parnell as president, which campaigned against landlords. He was reimprisoned (Feb. 1881–May 1882). Afterwards he campaigned for land nationalization, but Parnell repudiated the policy (9 April 1884). Davitt sat in the UK Parliament 1893, 1895–9 (as an anti-Parnellite), and helped to found the UNITED IRISH LEAGUE (1898). *See also* LAND AGITATION AND REFORM, IRELAND.

DAVY, HUMPHRY (b. 17 Dec. 1778 at Penzance, Cornwall, England; d. 29 May 1829 at Geneva, Switzerland, aged 50). Apprenticed to an apothecary-surgeon (1795), Davy educated himself in natural philosophy (science). The *Traité élémentaire de chimie* by French chemist Antoine Lavoisier stimulated him to experiment with heat. In 1798 Davy was appointed chemical superintendent of the Pneumatic Medical Institute near BRISTOL to investigate therapeutic uses of gases. He discovered the euphoric effect of nitrous oxide, which he nicknamed 'laughing gas'. Publication of *Researches, Chemical and Philosophical* (1800) established Davy's reputation.

In 1801, by invitation, Davy joined the ROYAL INSTITUTION in London, where he worked on tanning and agriculture (appointed professor of chemistry 1802; elected to ROYAL SOCIETY 1803). Exploiting the power of electricity for decomposing substances, he isolated the chemical elements potassium and sodium (1807) and while studying acidity, he concluded that 'green gas' derived from sea salt was an element, which he named 'chlorine' (1810).

Knighted in 1812, Davy retired from the Institution. After touring Continental Europe (1813–15), he invented a safety lamp for miners, though George STEPHENSON challenged his claim as an innovator. Davy was created a baronet (1818) and served as president of the Royal Society (1820–7). He died during further travels. *See also* FARADAY, MICHAEL.

DAWSON, GEOFFREY (b. 25 Oct. 1874 at Skipton, Yorkshire, England; d. 7 Nov. 1944 at London, England, aged 70). Geoffrey Robinson (so named until 1917) joined the British Civil Service (1898) and went (1901) to SOUTH AFRICA as private secretary to the high commissioner, Lord MILNER. He edited the *Johannesburg Star* 1905–10, and the London *Times* 1912–19, leaving the latter because of tensions with owner Lord Northcliffe. In Dec. 1916 *The Times* campaigned to oust Prime Minister H.H. ASQUITH. Editor again 1923–41, following Northcliffe's death, Dawson supported APPEASEMENT of Nazi Germany, especially the MUNICH agreement (1938).

DAYLIGHT SAVING Advocated in Great Britain from 1907, 'British Summer Time' (BST) was introduced from

1916, during WORLD WAR I, to extend daylight during the working day. Time was advanced from Greenwich Mean Time (GMT) by an hour for spring and summer months. Ireland also used BST from 1917 (following replacement of Dublin Mean Time with GMT in Oct. 1916).

In the UK during WORLD WAR II (but not in southern Ireland), BST replaced GMT from Feb. 1940 to Oct. 1945, and 'Double Summer Time' (time advanced by a further hour) was applied in 1940 (May–Aug.) and 1941–5 (April–Aug.). Double Summer Time was reapplied during the 1947 fuel crisis, and BST adopted experimentally as standard time 1968–71. Ireland similarly adopted BST as its legal 'Standard Time' in 1968, reverting to GMT for autumn and winter from late 1971.

D-DAY *see* OVERLORD

DEAKIN, ALFRED (b. 3 Aug. 1856 at Melbourne, Victoria; d. 7 Oct. 1919 at Melbourne, Victoria, Australia, aged 63). A lawyer and journalist, Deakin was a Liberal member of Victoria's Parliament 1879, 1880–1900, and a government minister 1883–90. During the 1890s he campaigned for an Australian federation, attending inter-colony constitutional conventions. In 1900 he participated in discussions in Britain on the Australia Constitution Bill, securing a limitation on appeals to the PRIVY COUNCIL.

Deakin sat in the new Australian federal Parliament 1901–13, and in 1901 became attorney-general. As Protectionist prime minister 1903–4, 1905–8, supported by Labour, he introduced social reforms (e.g., sickness benefits). Prime minister again 1909–10, as leader of the new Commonwealth Liberal Party, Deakin advocated 'imperial preference' to consolidate the British Empire (*see* TARIFF REFORM). He described himself as an 'independent Australian Briton'. *See also* AUSTRALIAN FEDERATION.

DECOLONIZATION The process of granting independence to colonies. The end of the BRITISH EMPIRE by decolonization is usually divided into two periods. The first, 1947–8 (during the Labour government of Clement ATTLEE), saw the termination of British rule in the Indian subcontinent (*see* INDIAN INDEPENDENCE; CEYLON; BURMA) and the surrender of Britain's mandate in PALESTINE. In the second period, from 1957 to the mid 1960s (during the Conservative governments of Harold MACMILLAN and Alec DOUGLAS-HOME), independence was granted to territories in Africa, the Mediterranean, the Caribbean, and to MALAYA. By 1964 decolonization was almost complete though British economic influence persisted.

Decolonization stimulated debate about its causes. Explanations included the rise of nationalism, which had made imperial rule unworkable; the poor economic value of the Empire, which made it not worth defending; and Britain's relative financial and military decline (compared with the USA and USSR), which made it too weak to maintain the Empire. *See also* MACLEOD, IAIN.

DEE, JOHN (b. 13 July 1527 at London, England; d. 26 March 1609 at London, aged 81). A clergyman, influential mathematician and astrologer, Dee lived at Mortlake (Surrey) 1565–83 where he practised ALCHEMY. He advocated English expansion overseas and advised explorers such as Martin FROBISHER. He was the first to use the term 'British Impire' (1577). In 1583, at the invitation of a nobleman, Dee moved to Poland and practised alchemy there. After travelling in Central Europe, he returned to England in 1589. From 1595 Dee was warden of the collegiate church at MANCHESTER (returned to Mortlake 1605).

DEFENCE FORCES, SOUTHERN IRELAND During 1922 the IRISH FREE STATE government created a National Army, initially from members of the IRISH REPUBLICAN ARMY who supported the ANGLO-IRISH TREATY, and started an Air Service. From June 1922 to May 1923 the Army fought anti-treaty forces, expanding to about 58,000 men (*see* IRISH CIVIL WAR). On 1 Oct. 1924, following a drastic reduction in the Army's size and an ARMY MUTINY, the Defence Forces (Irish, Óglaigh na hÉireann) were established (Air Service renamed Air Corps). The Army was temporarily re-expanded, from 10,000 to 40,000, during WORLD WAR II (1939–45), in which southern Ireland remained neutral. A Naval Service was started in 1946.

From 1958 Irish troops participated continuously in United Nations peace-keeping operations. Women were admitted to all positions in 1992. Personnel strengths in 2014 were: Army, about 7300; Naval Service, 990; Air Corps, 750. The Naval Service operated eight ships, the Airs Corps 27 aircraft.

DEFENCE OF THE REALM ACTS Legislation by the UK Parliament during WORLD WAR I (1914–18) which gave the British government extensive control over society and the economy throughout the UK (with qualifications). A brief Act of 8 Aug. 1914 authorized regulations for public safety, defence and control of transport. Six amending Acts (including a Consolidation Act, Nov. 1914) included requisitioning of resources, press censorship, imprisonment without trial, restrictions on movement, and regulation of public houses and alcohol (*see* LICENSING OF DRINKING PREMISES, ENGLAND AND WALES/IRELAND/SCOTLAND).

DEFENDERS In Ireland, a rural SECRET SOCIETY formed from 1784 to defend Catholics against Protestant PEEP O'DAY BOYS. It began in Co. Armagh (NE Ireland) and by 1795 spread to 14 counties and many towns. Its members were influenced by the FRENCH REVOLUTION. From 1794 Defenders were recruited by the UNITED IRISHMEN and participated in the RISING OF 1798. *See also* ORANGE ORDER, IRELAND.

DEFOE, DANIEL (b. autumn 1660, probably at London, England; d. 24 April 1731 at London, aged 70). From a dissenting and trading family, Defoe became a prolific journalist and propagandist. He produced WHIG propaganda in the 1690s. A verse satire defending King WILLIAM III, *The True-Born Englishman* (1701), made him well known. He served Robert HARLEY as an agent 1704–8, 1710–14, and continued as a propagandist for successive ministries after the accession of King GEORGE I (1714). His *Tour Thro' the Whole Island of Great Britain* (1724–7) presents a vivid picture of economic activity. From 1719 Defoe published NOVELS, notably *Robinson Crusoe* (1719) and *Moll Flanders* (1722). *See also* ENGLISH LITERATURE, ENGLAND.

DE HERETICO COMBURENDO In England, a statute enacted in 1401, in opposition to LOLLARDY, which introduced capital punishment for heretics. (Its popular Latin title means 'Regarding the burning of a heretic'.) It required alleged heretics to be tried under Church law. Convicted heretics who refused to recant were to be handed over to secular justices for burning at the stake.

The Statute was repealed in 1547 (reign of King EDWARD VI), reinstated in 1555 (reign of MARY I), and repealed in 1559 (reign of ELIZABETH I). It was copied in Scotland in 1425.

DEHEUBARTH An important medieval kingdom in SW WALES (10th–13th centuries), with its principal seat at Dinefwr. Its name Deheubarth Cymru (Latin, Dextralis pars Britanniae), meaning 'the righthand [or southern] part of Wales', referred to all S Wales but was taken to mean the SW, comprising the earlier kingdoms of DYFED, CEREDIGION and Ystrad Tywi.

Deheubarth emerged in the late 10th century, under the southern branch of the dynasty of RHODRI MAWR in Dyfed. But after the death of King RHYS AP TEWDWR in 1093, Deheubarth suffered the NORMANS' appropriation of PEMBROKESHIRE in the SW. By 1133 the dynasty was effectively restricted to Cantref Mawr (NE Deheubarth).

After 1165 RHYS AP GRUFFUDD restored and expanded the kingdom's earlier extent. But after his death in 1197, fighting between his heirs left Deheubarth permanently divided between his sons and their nephews by 1216. Further fragmentation followed after 1240; Deheubarth became a collection of minor principalities variously influenced by GWYNEDD or the English Crown. The old line became nearly extinct after the revolt of RHYS AP MAREDUDD in 1287 (though *see* OWAIN GLYN DŴR).

DE-INDUSTRIALIZATION The decline of manufacturing within an economy, measured variously by share of gross domestic product (GDP), employment or output. In Great Britain, manufacturing employment peaked in 1965–6, whereas GDP share peaked in 1972. De-industrialization has been associated with expansion of financial and consumer services, concentration of economic activity in London and SE England, and higher employment of women. Commentators dispute whether it represents economic 'maturity' or 'decline'. NORTHERN IRELAND also experienced substantial de-industrialization from the 1970s.

DEINIOL (fl. in 6th century; d. 11 Sept. 584). A bishop and founder of the important monastery at BANGOR in GWYNEDD (NW Wales), which had a daughter house at Bangor-is-Coed (NE Wales). He is the dedicatee, as saint, of churches in N Wales and of several in the S. *See also* MONASTICISM, MEDIEVAL WALES.

DEIRA A kingdom (6th–7th centuries) occupying the historical county of Yorkshire (NE England). Its Brittonic name (unknown meaning) suggests a British origin (5th or 6th century; *see* POST-ROMAN BRITAIN). Settled by Germanic people ('Angles') from the 5th century, a Germanic dynasty ruled by the late 6th century. The first documented king (ruling in 597) is Ælle. Around 600 Deirans repulsed an incursion by northern Britons (*see* ANEIRIN).

During the 7th century Deira's royal kindred struggled against BERNICIA (to the N). Deira was ruled from 604 by Æthelfrith of Bernicia. EDWIN of Deira ruled both kingdoms 616–33 (619, permitted Christianity; 627, founded short-lived see at YORK). The kingdoms had separate rulers 633–4 (Osric in Deira), but Oswald of Bernicia regained control of Deira (ruled 634–42). His successor, Oswiu, ruled 642–70 but met resistance in Deira. Oswiu's successor, EGFRITH, incorporated Deira (679) in a single kingdom called NORTHUMBRIA. *See also* KINGSHIP, ANGLO-SAXON.

DEISM A creed developed in England in the late 17th century which accepted the existence of God but denied divine intervention in the world and the doctrine of the Trinity. Influenced by John LOCKE (though he denied being a deist), it stressed the importance of reason in theology. John Toland's *Christianity Not Mysterious* (1696) was particularly notorious. Deism flourished into the 18th century when rebuttals were published (e.g., *Analogy of Religion* by Joseph Butler, 1736).

DELAWARE A former English territory in N America (British from 1707). Delaware Bay was named in 1610 after Lord De La Warr, governor of VIRGINIA. The area was settled continuously from 1638 by Swedes, Finns and

Dutch as part of 'New Sweden' (*see also* PENNSYLVANIA). It was captured by Dutch Americans in 1655, and by English in 1664 (with New Netherland; *see* NEW YORK). The Dutch repossessed Delaware 1673–4.

In 1681, when William PENN obtained land from King CHARLES II for Pennsylvania, he also leased the Delaware area from James, duke of York (*see* JAMES VII/II). Inhabitants increasingly resented association with QUAKER-influenced Pennsylvania. Delaware remained under the governor of PENNSYLVANIA until 1776, but with authority delegated to a deputy governor from 1691. In 1701 Penn allowed Delaware a law-making assembly (met from 1704), effectively separating it. An executive council was instituted in 1710. Est. population 1770: 35,000. Known as the 'Three Lower Counties on the Delaware', Delaware was not recognized as a colony by the British Crown. The name Delaware State was adopted in 1776 after the territory joined the USA. *See also* NORTH AMERICAN COLONIES.

DELHI A city in N India. Capital of the Mughal Empire from 1658, Delhi was captured by British forces from the Marathas in 1803. When CALCUTTA (in NE India) became the administrative centre of a reunified Bengal in 1912, Delhi replaced it as capital of British India. An official quarter and new capital, 'New Delhi', was inaugurated in 1931 and remained the capital and seat of government after independence (1947). *See also* INDIA.

DEMOCRATIC UNIONIST PARTY A political party in NORTHERN IRELAND, founded on 14 Sept. 1971 by Ian PAISLEY and Desmond Boal to provide a focus for Unionists who opposed concessions to nationalists (*see* TROUBLES). After Great Britain imposed 'direct rule' (March 1972), the DUP generally favoured restoration of devolved government to Northern Ireland under exclusive Unionist control.

The DUP opposed the SUNNINGDALE AGREEMENT (1973) and first power-sharing Executive (1974), and the HILLSBOROUGH AGREEMENT (1985). During the 1990s the DUP, unlike the ULSTER UNIONIST PARTY, opposed talks with nationalists unless the PROVISIONAL IRISH REPUBLICAN ARMY (PIRA) first 'decommissioned' its weapons. It participated in talks from 1996 while PROVISIONAL SINN FÉIN (linked to the PIRA) was excluded, but withdrew in 1997 when PSF was admitted. It also opposed the BELFAST AGREEMENT (1998), and though it participated in the subsequent Assembly and Executive, refused to attend Executive meetings (1999–2002). (Devolved government was suspended in 2002.)

At the 2003 Assembly elections the DUP became the largest party, but rejected renewed devolution without PIRA arms decommissioning. After the PIRA was pressurized into formally abandoning its armed campaign (2005), the DUP accepted new governmental arrangements (ST ANDREW'S AGREEMENT, Oct. 2006) and from May 2007 was the principal party in a new Executive; Paisley was first minister with the PSF activist Martin MCGUINNESS as deputy. Paisley was succeeded (as Party leader and first minister) by Peter Robinson (first minister 2008–16) and Arlene Foster (from 2016). (The arrangement collapsed in 2017 when McGuinness resigned. An Executive, with Foster as first minister, was restored in Jan. 2020.) *See also* UNIONISM, IRELAND; EXECUTIVES, NORTHERN IRELAND.

DENNING, LORD (b. 23 Jan. 1899 at Whitchurch, Hampshire, England; d. 5 March 1999 at Winchester, Hampshire, aged 100). Alfred Denning became a justice of the British High Court in 1944 (also knighted), a lord justice of appeal in 1948, and a LAW LORD in 1957 (as Lord Denning). In 1962 he returned to the Court of Appeal as master of the rolls and became famous for his personal style and innovative rulings. He was popularly viewed as a champion of ordinary people against the power of the State. Denning also conducted the official enquiry into the PROFUMO AFFAIR (1963). He retired in 1982.

DEPARTMENT STORES Large retailers which sell a variety of goods arranged in separate departments. The first in Great Britain was probably Bainbridge's at NEWCASTLE UPON TYNE, which developed in the 1840s and had 23 separately accounting departments by 1849. Ireland's first store was Delany's New Mart in DUBLIN, which was purpose-built in 1853. Most large British and Irish towns had such stores by 1900. Several in London became internationally famous, notably 'Selfridges' (opened 1909). *See also* SHOPS AND RETAILING.

DEPENDENT TERRITORY Term used by Great Britain from 1968 as a replacement for CROWN COLONY. It was given legal status by the 1981 British Nationality Act (effective from 1983). 'British dependent territories' were under the jurisdiction of the British Crown and government but not part of the UK. In 2002 the term was changed to 'British overseas territory'. In 2015 there were 14 overseas territories, including BERMUDA, the FALKLAND ISLANDS, and GIBRALTAR.

DERBY, 14TH EARL OF (b. 29 March 1799 at Knowsley Hall, Lancashire, England; d. 23 Oct. 1869 at London, England, aged 70). Leader of the CONSERVATIVE PARTY 1846–68 and three times British prime minister without a majority. Known as Lord Stanley 1834–51.

Edward Stanley entered Parliament as a WHIG MP (1820) and held office under Viscount GODERICH (1827–8) and Earl GREY (1830–4). He introduced proposals to abolish colonial SLAVERY (1833), but then left the government and drifted towards the Conservatives. Sir Robert PEEL appointed him secretary for war and the colonies (1841). He entered the House of Lords early, in 1844.

Stanley resigned in Dec. 1845 in protest at repeal of the CORN LAWS, which he thought essential to the landed interest. After the Conservatives split (1846), he and Benjamin DISRAELI led the protectionist rump.

Derby was prime minister only when Whig coalitions collapsed; he vainly sought reunion with PEELITES or a deal with Lord PALMERSTON. His first ministry survived ten months (Feb.–Dec. 1852). His second, lasting 16 months (Feb. 1858–June 1859), abolished the EAST INDIA COMPANY. The Reform Act of 1867, which dominated his final term (July 1866–Feb. 1868) was largely Disraeli's work. Derby called it 'a leap in the dark'. *See also* STANLEY FAMILY.

DERBY, 15TH EARL OF (b. 21 July 1826 at Knowsley Hall, Lancashire, England; d. 21 April 1893 at Knowsley Hall, aged 66). Son of the 14th earl of DERBY, Edward Stanley became a Conservative MP in 1848. Known as Lord Stanley 1851–69, he served his father, when prime minister, as under-secretary for foreign affairs (1852) and secretary of state for India (1858–9). He pursued conciliatory policies as foreign secretary under Benjamin DISRAELI (1867–8, 1874–8), fearing Disraeli's belligerent approach to the EASTERN QUESTION. He resigned on 27 March 1878 in protest at plans to seize territory from the OTTOMAN EMPIRE.

In 1880 Derby left the Conservative Party over the Afghan War. He joined the Liberals and as colonial secretary under W.E. GLADSTONE (1882–5) resisted expansion in Africa. He led the LIBERAL UNIONISTS in the House of Lords 1886–91. *See also* STANLEY FAMILY; AFGHANISTAN, BRITISH RELATIONS WITH.

DERRY *see* LONDONDERRY

DESMOND, EARLS OF An Anglo-Irish noble family. The earldom of Desmond was created in 1329 for Maurice fitz Thomas (1293–1356), a descendant of Maurice fitz Gerald who invaded Ireland in 1169 (*see* GERALDINES). The earldom's main lands were in W MUNSTER (S Ireland), in Cos. Limerick and Kerry, making it the most isolated Anglo-Irish lordship. It became Gaelicized, and Gerald fitz Maurice, 3rd earl of Desmond (*c.*1338–98, earl from 1363), wrote poems in Irish.

The 7th earl, Thomas Fitzgerald (*c.*1426–68, earl from 1462), served as chief governor of Ireland (deputy lieutenant, 1463–5) but was wantonly executed by the (English) earl of Worcester. Subsequent earls avoided involvement with government. The 9th earl (Maurice Fitzgerald, earl from 1488, d. 1520) supported Perkin WARBECK against HENRY VII.

The 13th earl (James Fitzgerald, earl from 1540, d. 1558) allowed the revival of royal government in the earldom (1541). The 14th earl (Gerald Fitzgerald, *c.*1533–83, earl from 1560) joined the Second DESMOND REBELLION and forfeited the earldom (1582). His lands were seized for the MUNSTER PLANTATION. His son James Fitzgerald (1570 or 1571–1601) was created earl in 1600. The title was bestowed on members of other families in the 17th century. *See also* BUTLER–GERALDINE FEUD; IRELAND, ENGLISH CONQUEST, 16TH CENTURY.

DESMOND, KINGDOM OF *see* MUNSTER

DESMOND REBELLION, FIRST An anti-English rebellion by Anglo-Irish and Gaelic Irish lords in MUNSTER (S Ireland), led by James Fitzmaurice Fitzgerald, cousin of the (imprisoned) 14th earl of Desmond. It was provoked by plans to subordinate local magnates to a PRESIDENCY, and by the favour shown by Queen ELIZABETH I to Desmond's rival, the 11th earl of Ormond.

The Rebellion began in June 1569. It was largely suppressed by end 1569 (by Henry SIDNEY and Humphrey GILBERT), and near extinguished in 1571–2 (by John PERROT). Fitzgerald surrendered on 23 Feb. 1573. *See also* DESMOND, EARLS OF; BUTLER–GERALDINE FEUD; IRELAND, ENGLISH CONQUEST, 16TH CENTURY.

DESMOND REBELLION, SECOND A further rebellion against English government in MUNSTER (S Ireland); launched by James Fitzmaurice Fitzgerald (18 July 1579; killed 18 Aug.). It was joined by Sir John of Desmond (1 Aug.) and the 14th earl of Desmond (Oct.), and reinforced by Viscount Baltinglass (revolt in LEINSTER, July 1580) and Italian and Spanish troops (arrived Sept.). Though the Rebellion was largely suppressed by spring 1581, Sir John and the earl fought on (killed, respectively, early 1582 and 2 Nov. 1583). Lands were seized for the MUNSTER PLANTATION. *See also* DESMOND, EARLS OF; IRELAND, ENGLISH CONQUEST, 16TH CENTURY.

DESPENSER FAMILY AND WALES Despensers entered the MARCH OF WALES through the marriage (1306) of Hugh Despenser the Younger to a CLARE co-heiress (inherited 1317). Patronized by King EDWARD II of England, they amassed estates in S Wales (especially GLAMORGAN), their power contributing to civil war in the March in 1321.

After Hugh the Elder and Hugh the Younger were executed in 1326, their estates were forfeited, but were restored in 1337 to Hugh the Younger's son Hugh (*c.*1308–49). Despensers remained involved until the execution of Thomas Despenser (1400).

DESPENSERS Term used for two members of the Despenser family of middle-ranking BARONS, based in the English Midlands, who became prominent in the later years of King EDWARD II of England (ruled 1307–27). Their influence grew after Hugh Despenser the Younger (fl. from 1306) was appointed chamberlain in Edward's household (Oct. 1318). Hugh Despenser the Elder (b. 1261) had served Edward and his father, EDWARD I, as diplomat and soldier.

Edward's favouritism for the Despensers angered magnates who attacked their Welsh lands in May 1321. On 14 Aug. Parliament banished them. Hugh the Elder went to GASCONY; Hugh the Younger marauded in the English Channel. The Despensers returned in early 1322 and helped Edward to attack his enemies. His main opponent, THOMAS OF LANCASTER, was killed in March. In May, Hugh the Elder was made earl of Winchester.

The Despensers dominated government until 1326 when Queen ISABELLA and Roger MORTIMER invaded England (landed 24 Sept.). On 15 Oct. they denounced the Despensers who fled westwards from London. Hugh the Elder surrendered on 26 Oct. at BRISTOL and was executed the next day. Hugh the Younger and Edward were captured on 16 Nov. at Neath (Glamorgan, S Wales). Hugh was hanged at HEREFORD on 24 Nov. *See also* DESPENSER FAMILY AND WALES.

DE VALERA, ÉAMON (b. 14 Oct. 1882 at New York, USA; d. 29 Aug. 1975 at Dublin, Republic of Ireland, aged 92). Raised in Ireland (from 1885), de Valera joined the GAELIC LEAGUE (1908) and IRISH VOLUNTEERS (1913). He participated in the 1916 EASTER RISING (imprisoned to June 1917).

In 1917 de Valera was elected a SINN FÉIN MP (10 July, at by-election) and party president (25 Oct.), but was rearrested (May 1918; escaped from prison in England Feb. 1919). He became president of Sinn Féin's republican Dáil Éireann ('Assembly of Ireland') on 1 April 1919. He spent June 1919–Dec. 1920, during the War of IRISH INDEPENDENCE, in the USA. De Valera helped to end the war, but rejected the treaty that created the IRISH FREE STATE. He supported 'Anti-treatyites' in the IRISH CIVIL WAR (from June 1922), but eventually urged cessation of hostilities (24 May 1923). He was imprisoned Aug. 1923–July 1924.

De Valera founded FIANNA FÁIL (1926), and entered the Dáil (1927). In 1932 he became president of the Executive Council (premier; from 1937 'taoiseach'), serving until 1948. He instigated an 'ECONOMIC WAR' with Great Britain (1932–8) and new CONSTITUTION (1937). He served again 1951–4, 1957–9, and was president 1959–73. *See also* COLLINS, MICHAEL; SOUTHERN IRELAND FROM 1922.

DEVLIN, JOSEPH (b. 13 Feb. 1871 at Belfast, Ireland; d. 18 Jan. 1934 at Belfast, Northern Ireland, aged 62). A Catholic from ULSTER, Devlin sat for the IRISH PARLIAMENTARY PARTY in the UK Parliament 1902–22. In June 1916, during an attempt to settle the Home Rule problem, he persuaded fellow Ulster Irish nationalists to accept Ulster's temporary exclusion (to win support from Unionists), a stance that damaged his reputation.

After Ireland was partitioned (1921), Devlin was the leading Irish Nationalist in NORTHERN IRELAND. As a member of its Parliament 1921–34 (abstained until 1925) he spoke for the Catholic minority, but was unable to influence the dominant Unionists. He also sat in the UK Parliament 1929–34. *See also* HOME RULE MOVEMENT, IRELAND; ANCIENT ORDER OF HIBERNIANS.

DEVOLUTION, SCOTLAND Reconsideration of Scotland's position within the UK was sought from the 1850s, and in the early 1880s Scots campaigned for a Scottish secretaryship. The latter was created in 1885, together with the SCOTTISH OFFICE, starting administrative devolution. The espousal of HOME RULE for Ireland by W.E. GLADSTONE in Dec. 1885 encouraged further claims; the Scottish Home Rule Association was founded in 1886, and from 1888 the Scottish LIBERAL PARTY campaigned for Home Rule, later gaining LABOUR PARTY support. Although six Home Rule bills failed in Parliament in 1908–14, eventual success was anticipated when the House of Commons approved Irish Home Rule in May 1914.

World War I (1914–18) and the Liberal Party's decline broke the momentum. Conservatives remained opposed, Labour was uninterested. Campaigners formed their own parties, culminating in the separatist-inclined SCOTTISH NATIONAL PARTY (SNP), founded in 1934. In 1939 Conservatives sought to appease Nationalists by moving the Scottish Office to Edinburgh.

SNP activity in the 1960s provoked Conservatives (1968) and Labour (1973) to espouse devolution, leading to a referendum for a Scottish Assembly on 1 March 1979. Although it was narrowly approved, support fell below the required 40% of the Scottish electorate. Labour revived the issue in the 1990s: a referendum on 11 Sept. 1997 approved a Parliament with tax-varying powers. It was inaugurated in 1999 (*see* PARLIAMENT, SCOTLAND). A Scottish Executive headed by a 'first minister' was also established, which was renamed a 'government' from 2007 by the SNP administration (legally recognized 2012). The Parliament and Executive received extensive authority over domestic matters (e.g., economic affairs, education, health, justice, policing), and were supported by a 'Devolved Civil Service'.

In 2011 the SNP's victory in the Scottish election enabled it to obtain a referendum on independence. Held on 18 Sept. 2014, it rejected the proposal (55.3% to 44.7% on turnout of 84.6%). *See also* SALMOND, ALEX.

DEVOLUTION, WALES Alien rule was imposed in the 11th–13th centuries (*see* MARCH OF WALES; WALES, ENGLISH CONQUEST OF), and from the 1530s Wales was subject to legislation by the English Parliament (*see* UNION OF WALES WITH ENGLAND). Devolution of power to a separate parliament was proposed in the 1840s by Irishman Thomas DAVIS and championed by Welsh Radicals from the 1880s (*see* YOUNG WALES). Separate legislation for Wales began in the 1880s (*see* TEMPERANCE MOVEMENT, WALES), and the UK House of Commons considered Home Rule Bills between 1890 and 1914.

Administrative devolution within the British government began with a Welsh Department of the Board of Education in 1907 (*see* EDWARDS, OWEN MORGAN) and culminated with creation of the WELSH OFFICE in 1964.

Campaigning for a Welsh Parliament was renewed in the 1950s and became prominent in the 1960s thanks to PLAID CYMRU. The UK Parliament's Wales Act of 1978 provided for a Welsh Assembly, but the people of Wales rejected it in a referendum on 1 March 1979. Another plan, promoted by the LABOUR PARTY, was narrowly approved on 18 Sept. 1997.

In 1999 the National Assembly for Wales (Welsh *Cynulliad Cenedlaethol Cymru*) was inaugurated, with powers previously vested in the secretary of state for Wales (mainly concerning expenditure). It delegated powers to an Executive Committee headed by a first secretary (called 'first minister' from 2000). In 2007 the Committee was replaced by a Welsh government, with the first minister being appointed by the monarch; the Assembly received power to enact legislation in specified areas (called 'Measures'). From 2012, following a referendum (2011), the Assembly was empowered to pass Acts, and in 2014 taxation legislation was permitted. From 2017 the Assembly and government were given permanent status (abolition would require popular approval) and the Assembly's powers were broadened. The Assembly was renamed the Welsh Parliament (Welsh *Senedd Cymru*) in May 2020.

DEVOLUTION CRISIS An episode in Irish and British politics 1904–5. It began when the Irish Reform Association, an organization of reform-minded southern Unionists, published proposals for moderate devolution (26 Sept. 1904). They envisaged an Irish Financial Council, with nominated and elected members, which would control expenditure.

Other Unionists, especially in ULSTER, saw the plans as a step to HOME RULE. They organized opposition and formed the ULSTER UNIONIST COUNCIL. Although the British (Conservative) government repudiated the scheme, the chief secretary for Ireland, George WYNDHAM, was forced to resign (6 March 1905). *See also* UNIONISM, IRELAND.

DEVONSHIRE, 4TH DUKE OF (b. May 1720, probably at Westminster, Middlesex, England; d. 2 Oct. 1764 at Spa, Austrian Netherlands, aged 44). William Cavendish was styled marquess of Hartington from 1729. A well-connected WHIG, he was an MP from 1741 and admitted to the House of Lords in 1749. He succeeded as duke in Dec. 1755 and was lord lieutenant of Ireland April 1755–Jan. 1757.

In Nov. 1756, following the resignation of the duke of NEWCASTLE, King GEORGE II appointed Devonshire as first lord of the Treasury (prime minister), though William PITT the Elder was effectively leader of the ministry. They prosecuted the SEVEN YEARS WAR. When Pitt resigned in April 1757 the ministry was damaged. Devonshire helped to form a new ministry led by Newcastle and Pitt (July 1757). Devonshire continued as lord chamberlain, resigning after the earl of BUTE replaced Newcastle (1762).

DEVONSHIRE, 8TH DUKE OF (b. 23 July 1833 at Lower Holker, Lancashire, England; d. 24 March 1908 at Cannes, France, aged 74). Spencer Cavendish became a Liberal MP in 1857 and was Lord Hartington from 1858 until he succeeded as duke in 1891. He held posts in the British government from 1863 and led the Liberals in the House of Commons 1875–80.

In Feb. 1886 Hartington rejected the policy of Irish HOME RULE being promoted by W.E. GLADSTONE (*see* HAWARDEN KITE). He became leader of the WHIG faction of the LIBERAL UNIONISTS. He served Lord SALISBURY, the Conservative prime minister, as lord president of the Council from 1895. His resignation as a 'free trader' in Oct. 1903 weakened the government of A.J. BALFOUR. *See also* CAVENDISH, FREDERICK.

DEVOY, JOHN (b. 3 Sept. 1842 at Kill, Co. Kildare, Ireland; d. 30 Sept. 1928 at Atlantic City, New Jersey, USA, aged 86). Active in Ireland in the IRISH REPUBLICAN BROTHERHOOD (IRB) from 1861, Devoy was imprisoned 1866–71. He moved to the USA where from *c*.1873 he led Clan na Gael (American-Irish republican organization affiliated to the IRB). In 1879, in the so-called 'New Departure', he gave republican support to the campaign for land reform waged by Michael DAVITT and C.S. PARNELL (*see* LAND AGITATION AND REFORM, IRELAND).

In 1907 Devoy sent Tom CLARKE to Ireland to revive the IRB. After WORLD WAR I began (1914) he sought German support for an Irish rebellion, agreed to Roger CASEMENT's visit to Germany (1914–16), and encouraged preparations for the EASTER RISING (1916). He supported the ANGLO-IRISH TREATY of 1921 and IRISH FREE STATE.

DEWAR, DONALD (b. 21 Aug. 1937 at Glasgow, Scotland; d. 11 Oct. 2000 at Edinburgh, Scotland, aged 63). A solicitor, Dewar from the 1960s supported Home Rule (or devolution) for Scotland. As a LABOUR PARTY MP (1966–70, from 1978) he held Opposition posts (1980–97).

While shadow secretary of state for Scotland (1983–92) Dewar helped to initiate the cross-party SCOTTISH CONSTITUTIONAL CONVENTION which formulated a Home Rule scheme (announced 1990). As Labour secretary of state for Scotland (1997–9), under Tony BLAIR, he held a referendum on Home Rule (Sept. 1997), led the pro-devolution campaign, and largely instituted the Convention's scheme (in 1998 Scotland Act). In May 1999 Dewar became the inaugural first minister of the Scottish Executive. *See also* DEVOLUTION, SCOTLAND.

DIALOGUE OF THE EXCHEQUER A (Latin) treatise written in England *c*.1179 by Richard Fitz Neal, the royal TREASURER. Intended as a guide to procedure in the EXCHEQUER, it takes the form of a student asking questions and his master providing replies. The *Dialogue* provides detailed evidence of 12th-century English GOVERNMENT.

DIANA, PRINCESS OF WALES (b. 1 July 1961 at Sandringham, Norfolk, England; d. 31 Aug. 1997 at Paris, France, aged 36). An earl's daughter, Lady Diana Spencer on 29 July 1981 married CHARLES, PRINCE OF WALES, heir to Queen ELIZABETH II. Youthful and stylish, she attracted worldwide attention and became known for charitable work (e.g., with sufferers from HIV/AIDS). In 1992 a book alleged that her marriage had deteriorated and that she had been mistreated by the royal household. Although the claims were denied, the couple separated (Dec. 1992) and divorced (1996). Media preoccupation with Princess Diana's situation damaged the monarchy's reputation.

In 1997, in Paris, Diana and boyfriend Dodi Fayed were pursued into a road tunnel by photographers. Their car, driven by an inebriated employee of Fayed's father, Mohamed Al-Fayed, crashed. Diana, Fayed and the driver were killed (a guard survived). Diana's funeral, at WESTMINSTER Abbey (6 Sept.), was watched worldwide on television by an estimated 2 billion people. Immediately after her death, Tony BLAIR had dubbed Diana 'the people's princess'. *See also* CAMBRIDGE, WILLIAM DUKE OF.

DICEY, A.V. (b. 4 Feb. 1835 at Claybrooke Parva, Leicestershire, England; d. 7 April 1922 at Oxford, Oxfordshire, England, aged 87). A barrister from 1863, Albert Venn Dicey became Vinerian professor of law at OXFORD University in 1882. He published several influential books. They included *Introduction to the Study of the Law of the Constitution* (1885), which viewed COMMON LAW as central to English liberty and argued that the British CONSTITUTION was based on the rule of law; and *A Digest of the Law of England* (1896). Though a Liberal, Dicey opposed HOME RULE for Ireland, regarding devolved government as inherently weak.

DICKENS, CHARLES (b. 7 Feb. 1812 at Portsea, Hampshire, England; d. 9 June 1870 at Gad's Hill Place, Kent, England, aged 58). A son of a poor clerk, Dickens became a journalist in London and achieved fame as a novelist with such works as *Oliver Twist* (1837–9), which attacked the POOR LAW, and *Nicholas Nickleby* (1838–9). Later works include *David Copperfield* (1850), *Hard Times* (1854), *Little Dorrit* (1855–7), *Great Expectations* (1860–1) and *Our Mutual Friend* (1864–5). His writings vividly depict English life while criticizing many social and personal values. He is one of the greatest English novelists. *See also* ENGLISH LITERATURE, ENGLAND; NOVEL.

DIET, ENGLAND BEFORE 16TH CENTURY The staple foodstuff in peasant households was cereal, mostly barley but also rye, oats or combinations. It was eaten mainly as small loaves. Peasants also consumed thick soup (OE *briw*) made of beans, peas, leeks, cabbage, turnips, carrots and parsnips. Diets included cheese, butter, milk, eggs, fish (especially herrings) and eels but little meat. Pork was the main meat, especially as bacon and sausage. Naturally occurring fruits, berries and nuts were eaten, such as apples, pears, raspberries and cherries. The main drink was ale, made of barley. In the late 14th and 15th centuries the relatively greater wealth of many peasant households permitted a greater consumption of meat.

Before the 11th century the NOBILITY and other wealthy people ate more red meat, including venison, and wheaten bread, and drank mead and imported wine. In the 11th–13th centuries the diets of the wealthy became richer and more varied. They consumed more varieties of meat and fish (including pike and bream from specially built ponds), and dishes containing imported spices. *See also* AGRICULTURE, ENGLAND BEFORE MID 18TH CENTURY.

DIET, ENGLAND FROM 16TH CENTURY In the 16th–17th centuries diets remained similar to earlier ones. Families of small-scale farmers, craftsmen and labourers ate bread made from barley, or sometimes rye or oats, together with cheese, butter, bacon. They consumed milk, and pottages of beans, peas and other vegetables (also potatoes and turnips by the late 17th century). Ale remained the main drink, but in towns was superseded by beer (from 18th century in the countryside). The diet of larger farmers included wheat bread and beef.

The wealthy (e.g., landowners, merchants) enjoyed more varied and richer diets. Meats included beef, mutton, venison and wildfowl. Dishes were flavoured with spices (e.g., pepper, nutmegs). Desserts included fruit (apples, pears), puddings and cakes. Drinks included wines and spirits.

Coffee and tea were introduced in the 1640s, chocolate in the 1650s. They were frequently drunk by 'middling' people at town coffee-houses. Tea spread widely during the

18th century (sweetened by sugar, derived from slave-worked plantations), as did wheat bread. Wealthier people obtained more varied meats (e.g., Norfolk turkeys) and fruit (e.g., oranges, lemons).

Diets in industrial towns (from late 18th century) resembled those of the rural poor. Factory workers typically lived on bread, potatoes, bacon and tea. Adulteration by retailers was a problem. RAILWAYS (from 1830s) improved supplies of vegetables, fruit and milk.

From the 1870s, diets were affected by numerous changes. Imports reduced prices (meat consumption notably increased). Convenience (pre-prepared) foods became available, starting with 'fish and chips'. Use of canned food expanded rapidly. Domestic cooking was improved by affordability of gas stoves (from 1880s), electric stoves (1930s) and refrigerators (1950s). American-style breakfast cereals became popular (1920s–30s). IMMIGRATION (from 1940s) established new cuisines (e.g., in restaurants). Supermarkets (from 1950s) enormously enlarged choice. But by the 21st century, high consumption of 'processed' and 'fast' foods had contributed to an obesity crisis. See also AGRICULTURE, ENGLAND BEFORE/FROM MID 18TH CENTURY; BREWING INDUSTRY, ENGLAND AND WALES.

DIET, IRELAND Before the late 17th century the diet of Gaelic Irish was dominated by products of pastoral farming, such as milk, curds, butter, butter-milk, cheese. Oats were the main cereal, eaten as porridge, gruel and especially oatcakes. They were also malted to make ale. Barley was also used for making bread and ale. Additional foods included nuts, berries, apples and freshwater fish. Wealthier people ate beef.

Following the Anglo-Norman invasion (1169–70), cereals were more widely grown and consumed, mainly by Anglo-Irish. Wheaten bread and meat were eaten regularly by lords and wealthier townspeople. Fish, especially herring, became important supplementary foods.

From the early 17th century potatoes supplemented the diets of all groups. (They are first mentioned in 1606.) During the 18th century more peas and beans were consumed, though milk consumption declined. Except among the poor, tea became widely drunk. Bread became a staple among Anglo-Irish and presbyterians. Wealthy people enjoyed a wide variety of foods.

By the 1780s potatoes had become the main subsistence for growing numbers of poor people, and by the 1830s were the dietary staple for a third of the population (see POPULATION, IRELAND). Such reliance on a single food had devastating consequences when potato blight struck in 1845 (see GREAT FAMINE).

Following the famine, potatoes declined in importance. More bread, oatmeal and Indian meal were eaten, together with bacon, sausages and eggs. Rising wages and falling prices enabled the poor to purchase a wider variety of foods. In the 1960s diets were broadened and improved by the spread of tinned and frozen foods, and in the later 20th century the Irish were introduced to overseas cuisines as a result of immigration, for example at restaurants opened by immigrants. See also AGRICULTURE, IRELAND BEFORE 17TH CENTURY/17TH CENTURY TO 1921; BREWING INDUSTRY, IRELAND; WHISKY INDUSTRIES.

DIET, SCOTLAND In the 6th–14th centuries oats were the principal foodstuff, eaten as gruel, porridge or oatcakes (the last accompanied with cheese, butter or honey). They were supplemented with vegetables: kail, onions and leeks (as broth) in the Lowlands, nettles in the HIGHLANDS. Herrings were also popular (preserved by smoking or salting). Meat was a luxury, with mutton being most common. The main drink was ale, made of bere (a kind of barley). Lords and merchants enjoyed greater variety (e.g., beef, spices, fruit, wine).

From the late 14th century, when pastoral farming became more extensive, ordinary people consumed considerable amounts of meat, cheese, butter and milk. Animal-derived foods declined in the Lowlands in the 16th century and in the Highlands in the 17th century, in favour of oatmeal. During the 18th century, rising wages allowed the consumption of tea and sugar.

From c.1750 potatoes were widely grown. They dominated CROFTING areas (Highlands) and became a staple alongside oats of poor people in industrializing towns. Their importance declined after crop failures in 1846–56. During the 19th century haggis (sheep's stomach containing oatmeal and offal) became renowned as Scotland's 'national dish'.

From the 1860s a less nutritious 'new diet' of white bread and tea with sugar replaced oats, first in the towns, then in the countryside (by the 1930s). From the 1950s rising living standards enabled more food (e.g., meat) to be afforded. Although tinned and frozen foods became more widely available, biscuits and sweets were popular and intake of vegetables and fruit remained low. After the end of WORLD WAR II (1945), and again in the later 20th century, immigrants introduced overseas cuisines in major urban centres. See also AGRICULTURE, SCOTLAND BEFORE/FROM 18TH CENTURY; FISHING INDUSTRY AND WHALING, SCOTLAND; BREWING INDUSTRY, SCOTLAND; WHISKY INDUSTRIES.

DIET, WALES Until the late 19th century the staple diet in rural areas consisted of oat or rye bread, cheese, and vegetable or bread soup, supplemented by meat (usually pork) and wild fruit, with ale as the main drink. Potatoes were important in the diets of the poorest from the late 18th century. In industrial areas in the late 18th and 19th centuries the basic diet was often narrower, consisting of mainly bread, butter and tea. Richer people (e.g., GENTRY from the 15th century) enjoyed a more varied diet, including wheat bread, beef, mutton, apples, pears and wine.

Average conditions improved in industrial areas in the late 19th century, though malnutrition was widespread during the depression of the 1920s–30s. Nutrition improved from the 1940s, when a wider range of foods, especially meat, became affordable. In cities and large towns in the late 20th century processed and standardized foods became prominent as supermarkets increasingly dominated retail food sales. In the early 21st century people experienced a wider range of foodstuffs from restaurants opened by members of new ETHNIC MINORITIES. *See also* AGRICULTURE, WALES BEFORE/FROM 18TH CENTURY.

DILKE, CHARLES (b. 4 Sept. 1843 at London, England; d. 26 Jan. 1911 at London, aged 67). A Liberal MP 1868–86 and 1892–1911, Dilke inherited a BARONETCY in 1869. He was both an imperialist, noted for his book *Greater Britain* (1868), and a radical, notorious for republican views (*c.*1870–2). Dilke held government offices under W.E. GLADSTONE (1880–5), but his reputation never recovered from involvement in a scandalous divorce suit (1886).

DILLON, J.B. (b. 5 May 1814 at Ballaghaderreen, Co. Roscommon, Ireland; d. 15 Sept. 1866 at Killiney, Co. Dublin, Ireland, aged 52). A (Catholic) lawyer, John Blake Dillon joined the REPEAL ASSOCIATION in 1841 and co-founded *The Nation*, the newspaper of the YOUNG IRELAND MOVEMENT (Oct. 1842). He seceded from the Association with other 'Young Irelanders' in July 1846.

The conviction of John MITCHEL (May 1848) provoked Dillon to violence: he participated in the REBELLION OF 1848. After its suppression he escaped overseas (to France, USA). He returned to Ireland under an amnesty (1856) and helped to found the anti-Fenian NATIONAL ASSOCIATION OF IRELAND (1864). As an MP from 1865, he advocated land reform and DISESTABLISHMENT of the Church of Ireland, and denounced Fenianism. *See also* FENIAN BROTHERHOOD; DILLON, JOHN.

DILLON, JOHN (b. 4 Sept. 1851 at Blackrock, Co. Dublin, Ireland; d. 4 Aug. 1927 at London, England, aged 75). A son of J.B. DILLON, John Dillon (a Catholic) sat for Irish constituencies in the UK Parliament 1880–3, 1885–1918. He gave vigorous leadership in Ireland to the LAND LEAGUE (1880–1) and PLAN OF CAMPAIGN (1886–91), resulting in imprisonment (1881, 1881–2, 1888).

When the IRISH PARLIAMENTARY PARTY split (Dec. 1890), Dillon joined anti-Parnellites (from 1896 led Irish National Federation). After reunification (1900) he served under the leadership of the former Parnellite John

REDMOND, whom he succeeded (March 1918). But at the UK general election in Dec. 1918, the Party was swept aside by SINN FÉIN, with Dillon losing his seat to Éamon DE VALERA. *See also* HOME RULE MOVEMENT, IRELAND.

DILUTION OF LABOUR The practice of substituting unskilled or semi-skilled workers in jobs previously reserved for skilled workers. Large-scale dilution first occurred when women workers entered the munitions industry during WORLD WAR I (1914–18). In March 1915 the chancellor of the Exchequer David LLOYD GEORGE negotiated the 'Treasury Agreement' whereby trade unions accepted temporary dilution but the continuing concerns of skilled workers caused intermittent strikes. *See also* WORLD WAR I, IMPACT ON BRITISH ECONOMY.

DIPLOMATIC REVOLUTION Term for the reversal of European alliances 1756–7. In the War of the AUSTRIAN SUCCESSION (1740–8), Great Britain and the HABSBURG EMPIRE (frequent allies since 1688) had opposed FRANCE and PRUSSIA. In Jan. 1756, partly to protect HANOVER (in Germany), Britain signed a treaty with Prussia. It prompted the Habsburgs to align with France in the SEVEN YEARS WAR (1756–63). *See also* NEWCASTLE, DUKE OF; FOREIGN RELATIONS, GREAT BRITAIN.

DIRECT-GRANT SCHOOL From 1919, an independent fee-paying GRAMMAR SCHOOL in England and Wales which received a State grant solely from the Board of Education in return for allocating a proportion of places free to pupils from State-funded primary schools. Such schools had previously received funds under the BALFOUR EDUCATION ACT (1902) from both the Board and Local Education Authorities. In the 1930s, about 230 direct-grant schools provided a 'bridge' between independent and State schools. The system was phased out from 1975, with many schools becoming financially independent.

DISCIPLINE, BOOKS OF Manifestos prescribing Church organization compiled for the Church of SCOTLAND. The 'First Book of Discipline', compiled by six clergy including John KNOX in May 1560 during the REFORMATION crisis, envisaged a hierarchy of parishes (under ministers), dioceses (under superintendents), and council (General Assembly). It was rejected by a Convention of Estates (Jan. 1561) for demanding restoration of alienated parish revenues (held by laity and bishops through APPROPRIATION and COMMENDATION). The 'Second Book of Discipline' (completed 1578) replaced dioceses with presbyteries (courts of ministers and elders). It influenced the GOLDEN ACT (1592). *See also* CHURCH ORGANIZATION, SCOTLAND FROM 16TH CENTURY; THIRDS OF BENEFICES.

DISESTABLISHMENT, CHURCH OF ENGLAND IN WALES A major popular cause in Wales 1840s–1914 (*see* LIBERATION SOCIETY); it sought removal of the endowments and privileged legal status of the Church of ENGLAND in Wales (e.g., as recipient of compulsory TITHES and rates). The disestablishment movement resulted from the expansion of NONCONFORMITY, which reduced churchgoers to a minority by 1851, and Welsh nationalism, and was supported officially by the LIBERAL PARTY from 1891 (*see* NEWCASTLE PROGRAMME). Disestablishment motions were presented to the UK Parliament from 1879, and Bills from 1894, but the latter were doomed to fail because of opposition of the House of Lords.

Removal of the Lords' veto in 1911 (*see* PEOPLE'S BUDGET) permitted the enactment of disestablishment in Sept. 1914, but implementation was delayed by WORLD WAR I (1914–18). It took place on 31 March 1920. Confiscated endowments were shared between the University of Wales and local authorities. *See also* TITHE WAR; EDWARDS, ALFRED GEORGE; WALES, CHURCH IN.

DISESTABLISHMENT, CHURCH OF IRELAND Disestablishment of Ireland's unrepresentative State Church (i.e., removal of State control and endowments) was proposed by the British Liberal politician W.E. GLADSTONE from 1865 to conciliate Catholic Irish to the union with Great Britain. It was implemented by the UK Parliament in 1869 with the Irish Church Act.

On 1 January 1871 the Church became a voluntary body, governed by bishops, a synod and commissioners. Extensive endowments were confiscated and shared between the voluntary Church, the Catholic MAYNOOTH SEMINARY, presbyterian churches (replacing the *REGIUM DONUM*), and public works. Disestablishment also ended the union with the Church of England (from 1801). *See also* IRELAND, CHURCH OF.

DISINHERITED Term for landholders in Scotland, opposed to King ROBERT I and DAVID II, whose Scottish possessions were forfeited in 1314 after Robert's victory at the battle of BANNOCKBURN (*see* CAMBUSKENNETH PARLIAMENT), and who then lived in England. They supported the bids by Edward BALLIOL for the Scottish kingship (1332–47), and the later involvement in Scotland by King EDWARD III (1356), but failed to recover their lands.

DISRAELI, BENJAMIN (b. 21 Dec. 1804 at London, England; d. 19 April 1881 at Hughenden Manor, Buckinghamshire, England, aged 76). Leader of the CONSERVATIVE PARTY 1868–81; British prime minister 1868, 1874–80.

Born a Jew but baptized in 1817, Disraeli made his name with the novel *Vivian Grey* (1826). After failing as a Radical,

this dandy became a TORY MP in 1837. Sympathy for YOUNG ENGLAND inspired the novels *Coningsby* (1844) and *Sybil* (1845). Advancement appeared unlikely until his Party split over the CORN LAWS (1846). Disraeli excoriated Sir Robert PEEL and won the leadership in the House of Commons (1848). He served the earl of DERBY as chancellor of the Exchequer (1852, 1858–9, 1866–8).

Disraeli discarded Conservative resistance to PARLIAMENTARY REFORM and devised the Second Reform Act (1867). This initial bid for working-class support failed when his first premiership (Feb.–Dec. 1868) ended in electoral defeat, but his relaunch of the Conservatives as an inclusive national party secured a majority in 1874.

Disraeli's government introduced social reforms affecting HOUSING and PUBLIC HEALTH. It secured shares in the SUEZ CANAL and thwarted RUSSIA at the Congress of BERLIN. Disraeli was created earl of Beaconsfield (1876). His enthusiastic IMPERIALISM encountered set-backs in AFGHANISTAN and the ZULU WAR.

DISRUPTION The secession in 1843 of two-fifths of clergy and laity from the Church of SCOTLAND. It began on 18 May when a third of the ministers (mainly evangelicals) attending the Church's General Assembly withdrew to a nearby hall and, with other ministers (total about 450), founded the FREE CHURCH OF SCOTLAND. They withdrew in protest at the courts' and government's rejection of the Assembly's 1834 Veto Act, which allowed congregations to veto patrons' nominees to Church livings. *See also* PATRONAGE ACT, 1712; CHALMERS, THOMAS; MILLER, HUGH.

DISSENT, ENGLAND *see* NONCONFORMITY AND DISSENT, ENGLAND

DISSENT, IRELAND *see* NONCONFORMITY AND DISSENT, IRELAND

DISSENT, SCOTLAND From the mid 17th century disputes over government in the Church of SCOTLAND created dissenting groups. Secession began in 1662 when opponents of newly restored episcopacy formed independent congregations (*see* COVENANTERS). Most rejoined after the RISING OF 1679 or abolition of episcopacy in 1689. The latter act, though, caused secession by episcopalians (*see* EPISCOPAL CHURCH IN SCOTLAND).

The first presbyterian dissenting church was the SECESSION CHURCH, founded in 1733 by opponents of private patronage of livings. The REFORMED PRESBYTERIAN CHURCH was developed from 1743 by strict Covenanters (*see* CAMERONIANS), while the more liberal RELIEF CHURCH, founded 1761, also opposed patronage. Though these churches fragmented, from *c*.1780 presbyterian dissenters increased, to 29% of the population in the 1820s.

In 1843 the Disruption, which created the Free Church of Scotland, made dissenting presbyterians a majority (59%) of Scots churchgoers by 1851. They generally adhered to evangelicalism and supported the Liberal Party. The Free Church, once settled, attracted other dissenting churches. It united in 1876 with the Reformed Presbyterian Church and in 1900 with the United Presbyterian Church, creating the United Free Church of Scotland, Scotland's largest Church. Its union in 1929 with the Church of Scotland (now independent of State control) largely ended presbyterian dissent.

Small groups nonetheless continued, notably the Free Presbyterian Church (formed 1893) and a continuing Free Church (1900) which remained vigorous in the Western Highlands and Islands. Other non-presbyterian dissenters became established from the 18th century (e.g., Quakers, Methodists, Congregationalists, Baptists, Plymouth Brethren) but attracted relatively few supporters. *See also* Catholics and Catholic Church, Scotland.

DISSENTERS *see* nonconformists, dissenters

DISSENTING ACADEMIES, ENGLAND Private academies which flourished in the late 17th and 18th centuries to provide Dissenters with higher education, because they were barred from Oxford and Cambridge Universities by religious tests (e.g., subscription to the Thirty-nine Articles of the Church of England). Some academies were founded by clergymen who left Church livings in 1660–3 (*see* Clarendon Code). Tories sought to suppress academies with the Schism Act of 1714 (repealed 1719 by Whigs).

Many subjects were taught, including science, though some students were prepared for religious ministry. Radical theological and political ideas were sometimes developed. Famous academies included those at Northampton (under Philip Doddridge) and Warrington (where Joseph Priestley taught). Academies declined in the 19th century, hastened by the founding of secular university colleges and removal of university religious tests (1854, 1856, 1871). *See also* nonconformity and dissent, England; education, England; university reform, England.

DISSENTING ACADEMIES, WALES Private academies were first started by clergymen who left the Church of England, which included Wales, in 1660–2 (*see* Clarendon Code). They enabled dissenting ministers to earn a living, and provided university-level education for dissenters' children (prevented until 1854 from attending Oxford University and until 1856 from graduating at Cambridge University). Adherents of the Church of England also attended.

The first academy in Wales was started by Samuel Jones at Brynllywarch (Glamorgan) by 1672; many were short-lived. Academies also educated trainee ministers, sometimes for several denominations. During the 18th and 19th centuries denominations founded their own colleges, which usually also admitted non-trainees. Academies run by individuals were largely superseded by university colleges in the late 19th century (*see* universities, Wales). Denominational colleges continued into the 20th century as clergy-training colleges.

DISSOLUTION OF CHANTRIES *see* chantries, England and Wales

DISSOLUTION OF RELIGIOUS HOUSES, ENGLAND The closure of monasteries, nunneries and friaries, 1536–40. It arose from the assertion of royal authority after England's separation from papal jurisdiction (ratified 1534). The inspection of houses in 1535 for the *Valor Ecclesiasticus* suggested to Thomas Cromwell, vicegerent (deputy) in spiritual affairs to King Henry VIII, a means for increasing royal wealth. He used evidence of abuses, collected by a visitation of houses in late 1535, to defame the religious and justify his policy.

In March 1536 an Act of the Reformation Parliament closed and confiscated smaller, poorer monasteries and nunneries (with incomes under £200 per year). About 280 of 370 small houses were affected. Inhabitants were allowed to move to larger houses. Some larger houses in N England were suppressed following the Pilgrimage of Grace (Oct.–Dec. 1536).

From spring 1538 the remaining houses, including friaries, were compelled to close by 'voluntary' surrender. The last, Waltham Abbey (Essex), surrendered in April 1540. Another Act (1539) confirmed the second wave of closures. In all about 800 houses were closed, and 11,000 monks, nuns and friars were evicted. Many monks and nuns received pensions. Monastic property passed to the Crown. *See also* monasticism, England; friars, England; concealed lands; Reformation, England.

DISSOLUTION OF RELIGIOUS HOUSES, IRELAND In late 1537, after opponents caused delay, Ireland's Parliament agreed to dissolve 13 monasteries to strengthen defence of the Pale. Soon afterwards (Sept. 1538) Henry VIII decided to close all houses, extending the policy implemented in England and Wales.

In 1539–40 commissioners forced houses mainly in the Pale, the earldom of Ormond and the SE to close by 'voluntary' surrender; some houses beyond this area surrendered from 1542 (e.g., in W Ireland). By Henry's death (1547), over half of monasteries and under half of friaries had been suppressed. Many monks and friars became secular clergy;

some monks and nuns received pensions. Monastic lands were acquired by local lords, and some churches became parish churches. Many remaining religious houses closed or were suppressed as English authority was asserted in the later 16th century. *See also* MONASTICISM, MEDIEVAL IRELAND; FRIARS, IRELAND BEFORE 1530s; REFORMATION, IRELAND; IRELAND, ENGLISH CONQUEST, 16TH CENTURY; RELIGIOUS ORDERS AND REGULAR CLERGY, IRELAND FROM 16TH CENTURY.

DISSOLUTION OF RELIGIOUS HOUSES, SCOTLAND There was no dissolution by legislation. Before the REFORMATION (1560) many houses were effectively under lay control because of COMMENDATION, though they operated as religious institutions. Proscription of the Mass in 1560 made religious houses (including COLLEGIATE CHURCHES) redundant. Their members either converted to Protestantism and departed or remained in their houses on pensions while properties belonging to houses were taken by the Crown or remained with their commendators (and often their descendants). Houses of mendicant FRIARS were the only buildings in Scotland to suffer significant material destruction at the Reformation (1559–60).

DISSOLUTION OF RELIGIOUS HOUSES, WALES Houses were dissolved contemporaneously with those in England by Thomas CROMWELL's agents (including John PRICE), to enrich the Crown, after the 1534 break from papal jurisdiction (*see* REFORMATION, ENGLAND/WALES). All but three wealthier monasteries (STRATA FLORIDA, Neath and Whitland) and some dependencies were dissolved in 1536; friaries surrendered in Aug. and Sept. 1538; remaining monasteries went in 1539. In all 47 houses closed, without resistance. Monastic estates (10% of Wales) passed to the Crown which sold them to GENTRY families from 1539 onwards. Monks and some nuns were given pensions; friars received nothing. *See also* APPROPRIATION OF CHURCHES, WALES.

DISTAIN (Welsh, meaning 'steward', derived from OE *discthegn*, meaning 'dish-servant'). A royal officer in kingdoms of medieval Wales; originally responsible for provisioning the royal household. During the late 12th century he became the ruler's chief adviser and head of the council (*see* COUNCILS, WALES, 12TH–13TH CENTURIES). *See also* EDNYFED FYCHAN; KINGSHIP, WALES 5TH–13TH CENTURIES.

DIVINE RIGHT MONARCHY The claim that royal authority was derived from a direct grant of power by God to a king. Divine attributes had been claimed for rulers since at least the 8th century (*see* KINGSHIP, ANGLO-SAXON; CORONATION, ENGLAND), but a divine basis for kingship was stressed in Europe from the 16th century. It was forcefully expressed in late 16th-century Scotland by King JAMES VI (e.g., in *The True Lawe of Free Monarchies*, 1598), and in England by James (from 1603) and his descendants CHARLES I, CHARLES II, and JAMES VII/II. Another leading theorist was Sir Robert Filmer in *Patriarcha* (1642, published 1680). Filmer's version was strongly attacked by John LOCKE in his *Two Treatises of Government*. *See also* KINGSHIP, SCOTTISH; KINGSHIP AND MONARCHY, ENGLAND 1066 TO 1680s.

DIVORCE, LAW RELATING TO By the 12th century marriage in western Europe was deemed a Christian sacrament and marriages were therefore indissoluble. Church courts could annul marriages (declare them invalid, e.g., for non-consummation), enabling remarriage, or approve separations (e.g., for adultery).

After the REFORMATION (16th century), different modifications arose. In England and Wales, the (Protestant) Church of ENGLAND maintained indissolubility, except that from 1670 (case of Lord Roos) separated wealthy people could obtain private Acts of Parliament permitting remarriage. In 1857 legislation abolished matrimonial jurisdiction of Church courts and established the Court for Divorce and Matrimonial Causes. It authorized divorce for adultery, but required an additional offence (e.g., desertion) for divorce by a wife (law equalized 1923). Grounds for divorce were extended in 1937, and in 1969 'irretrievable breakdown' (for specific reasons) became the basis (implemented 1971).

In (Protestant) Scotland, the Commissary Court of Edinburgh was established (1563) to provide divorce for adultery (allowing remarriage); desertion also became a ground (1573). In 1938 the 1573 Act was replaced with amended arrangements, and 'irretrievable breakdown' became the sole basis for divorce in 1976 (implemented 1977).

In Ireland marriage remained indissoluble under the (Protestant) Church of IRELAND, although private divorce Acts were obtained (18th–20th centuries). In 1870, alongside disestablishment of the Church of Ireland, a Court for Matrimonial Causes was established to provide annulments and separations.

In Northern Ireland (from 1921) divorce Acts continued until 1939, when the High Court was empowered to provide dissolutions. 'Irretrievable breakdown' was introduced by a British order in Council (1978). In (largely Catholic) southern Ireland divorce Acts were precluded (1925), and legislation was prohibited by the 1937 CONSTITUTION. A referendum confirmed the prohibition (1986), but was soon reversed (1995). Legislation (1996) provided no-fault divorce based on marital breakdown (implemented 1997).

Legislation for same-sex civil partnerships and marriage from 2005 included provision for dissolutions (*see* HOMO-SEXUALITY, LAW RELATING TO).

DOCK STRIKE, 1889 In England, a four-week strike by London dock workers (19 Aug.–14 Sept.) who sought a minimum wage of 6*d*. an hour. Encouraged by recent successful strikes by match girls and gas workers, it involved well-organized picketing, orderly demonstrations, £30,000 from Australian sympathizers, and mediation by Cardinal Henry MANNING. The dockers' victory led to formation of a dockers' union and growth in unionization of less skilled workers (part of 'New Unionism'). *See also* TRADE UNIONISM, ENGLAND.

DOMESDAY BOOK Nickname for a comprehensive record of landholders, estates, tenants and resources in England in the late 11th century, assembled in two different-sized books (known as 'Great Domesday', 'Little Domesday'). The content, arranged by county, is derived from a survey ordered by King WILLIAM I at Christmas 1085. Its purpose was to produce a working document for use by officials in the royal Treasury to manage royal rights over lords' estates.

Information was collected in 1086 by SHERIFFS from landholders and communities, and then checked by panels of commissioners (e.g., bishops) who compiled reports for groups of counties. Preparation of Domesday Book involved the reordering of material for each county from a geographical arrangement into a structure arranged by landholders. It was possibly completed in 1088 (in reign of WILLIAM II). The record was called 'The book of Judgement' by *c*.1179 (in *DIALOGUE OF THE EXCHEQUER*), and is held at The National Archives, London.

DOMINION Term used for territories, usually involving British settlement, which had virtual autonomy in domestic affairs through a grant of RESPONSIBLE GOVERN-MENT. It was first used in that sense for the dominion of Canada in 1867 (*see* CANADIAN CONFEDERATION). Other self-governing British territories were designated British dominions from 1907. The 'Balfour Definition' (1926) and Statute of WESTMINSTER (1931) propounded the principle that dominions were equal in status to Britain. Dominions have also included AUSTRALIA, CEYLON, GHANA, INDIA, IRISH FREE STATE, NEWFOUNDLAND, NEW ZEALAND, PAKISTAN, SOUTH AFRICA.

DONALD II (Gaelic, Domnall mac Causantín; fl. from *c*.889; d. 900, probably at Dunnottar, E Scotland). King of Scots (Scotland) *c*.889–900.

A grandson of KENNETH I MAC ALPIN, Donald's reign saw continuing attacks by VIKINGS, whom he defeated at least once. Donald was the first ruler to be called 'king of Alba' (Gaelic *rí Alban*), i.e., king of Britain (i.e., Scotland) rather than of the Picts (whose name disappeared). Succeeded by CONSTANTINE II (cousin). *See also* UNION OF SCOTS AND PICTS; MAC ALPIN KINGS.

DONALD III (Gaelic, Domnall mac Donnchada; b. *c*.1033; d. 1100 at Rescobie, Angus, N Scotland, aged about 66). King of Scots (Scotland) 1093–4, 1094–7.

A son of King DUNCAN I, Donald succeeded his brother MALCOLM III (13 Nov. 1093) in a backlash against English at the court provoked by Malcolm's death (*see* MARGARET). Those driven out probably included Malcolm's sons. With English support, two sons dislodged Donald: DUNCAN II (May–Nov. 1094) and EDGAR (from Oct. 1097). Donald, who was nicknamed 'the Fair' (Gaelic, Bán), died in captivity. *See also* MAC MALCOLM RULERS.

DOUGLAS, ARCHIBALD (b. *c*.1369 in Scotland; d. 16 Aug. 1424 at Verneuil, Normandy, France, aged about 55). (4th) earl of Douglas from 1400.

Around 1387 Douglas married a granddaughter of King ROBERT II, and possibly in 1398 was assigned the lands of his father, Archibald, (3rd) earl of Douglas (to ensure succession), becoming the dominant MAGNATE in S Scotland. He began fighting the English, attacking English-held Roxburgh (1398) and invading England (1399). He acquired royal offices, and used patronage to secure a widespread following.

In 1401–2, effectively allied to the duke of Albany (Robert STEWART, brother of ROBERT III), Douglas promoted continuing military action. But in Sept. 1402, while campaigning in NE England, he was defeated and captured (*see* HUMBLETON, BATTLE OF). Held by the PERCY FAMILY, he joined their rebellion (1403) against HENRY IV of England, only to become a royal prisoner. He absconded (during parole) in 1408.

Douglas reinforced his liberty with an agreement of mutual friendship (1409) with Albany (now 'governor' for JAMES I). But rivals began to emerge in S Scotland. In 1424, by invitation, Douglas led an army to France to assist the dauphin against the English (*see* HUNDRED YEARS WAR). He was created duke of Touraine, only to die in battle. *See also* SCOTTISH–ENGLISH RELATIONS 1357 TO 1603.

DOUGLAS, ARCHIBALD (b. *c*.1489 in Scotland; d. Jan. 1557 at Tantallon Castle, SE Scotland, aged about 67). (6th Douglas) earl of ANGUS from 1513 or 1514, Douglas married Margaret Tudor (1514), widow of King JAMES IV of Scotland and (pro-English) regent for JAMES V (until 1515; replaced by the pro-French (4th) duke of Albany).

In Nov. 1520, following a quarrel with the earl of Arran, Angus was forced into exile by the regent. He returned in

1524, gained custody of the young king (1526), and governed Scotland under the king's nominal authority until 1528 when James escaped and proscribed Angus.

Angus lived in England until James's death in 1542, when he was restored by the regent, the (2nd) earl of ARRAN. The experience of England's 1544 invasion made Angus anti-English; he fought against them at the battle of Pinkie (1547). Thereafter he was little involved. *See also* ANGUS, DOUGLAS EARLS OF; STEWART, JOHN; SCOTTISH-ENGLISH RELATIONS 1357 TO 1603.

DOUGLAS, EARLS OF A Scottish noble family, known as the 'Black Douglases'; flourished 1358–1455. They were descendants probably of an immigrant of Flemish background of the early 12th century. William Douglas (*c*.1327–84, a kinsman of James DOUGLAS) was raised to the status of earl in 1358. Subsequently the family's territories were greatly increased by marriage and inheritance. William DOUGLAS (1424–52), 8th earl and dominant in S Scotland, was Scotland's most powerful MAGNATE until killed by JAMES II. James Douglas (1426–91), 9th and last earl, rebelled, fled to England, and was attainted (1455). *See also* ANGUS, DOUGLAS EARLS OF; DOUGLAS, ARCHIBALD; EARLDOMS, SCOTLAND.

DOUGLAS, JAMES (b. *c*.1288; d. 25 Aug. 1330 at Teba, Granada, S Spain, aged about 42). A Scottish lord and companion of King ROBERT I, for whom he organized guerrilla warfare against the English in Scotland (1306–14) and subsequently in northern England. Douglas was rewarded with extensive estates and jurisdictional powers. He was knighted in June 1314, on the eve of the battle of BANNOCKBURN. He died fighting the Moors, while taking Robert's embalmed heart to the Holy Land to redeem his pledge to go on CRUSADE. *See also* DOUGLAS, EARLS OF.

DOUGLAS, WILLIAM (b. late 1424 in Scotland; d. 22 Feb. 1452 at Stirling, C Scotland, aged 27). (8th) earl of Douglas from 25 March 1443 and probably 'lieutenant' (regent) of Scotland July 1444 to July 1449 (*see* JAMES II); a predominant Scottish MAGNATE, based in southern Scotland. Douglas's power, and his disregard for the Crown, threatened King James. In 1452 they quarrelled and James killed him. *See also* DOUGLAS, EARLS OF.

DOUGLAS-HOME, ALEC (b. 2 July 1903 at London, England; d. 9 Oct. 1995 at Coldstream, Berwickshire, Scotland, aged 92). Leader of the CONSERVATIVE PARTY 1963–5; British prime minister 1963–4.

A grandson of the 12th earl of Home, Douglas-Home was known as Lord Dunglass from 1918. Elected as an MP in 1931, he served Neville CHAMBERLAIN as parliamentary private secretary (1937–9). In 1951 he succeeded his father as earl and moved to the House of Lords.

A Scottish Office minister (1951–5), Home was then minister for Commonwealth relations (1955–60) and foreign secretary (1960–3). He was nevertheless comparatively little known, so his appointment as prime minister on 19 Oct. 1963, as a compromise alternative to 'Rab' BUTLER and Lord HAILSHAM, caused general surprise. He renounced his PEERAGE and won a by-election (8 Nov.) to return to the House of Commons. (Created a knight of the THISTLE in 1962, he was known as Sir Alec Douglas-Home.) An imminent general election dominated Douglas-Home's term in office; the Conservatives narrowly lost (15 Oct. 1964) and Harold WILSON became premier.

Douglas-Home retired as Party leader in July 1965, but served Edward HEATH as foreign secretary (1970–4) before accepting a life peerage as Lord Home of the Hirsel. *See also* HOME FAMILY.

DOVER, TREATY OF A secret agreement made on 22 May 1670 at Dover, Kent (SE England), by CHARLES II, king of England, and his sister Henrietta, duchess of Orléans, acting for Louis XIV of France. They agreed to: war against the Dutch Republic; payment of cash subsidies by Louis to Charles; conversion by Charles to Roman Catholicism at a time of his choice. A second, 'public' treaty, the treaty of London, providing only for war against the Dutch, was signed by English ministers on 21 Dec. *See also* ANGLO-DUTCH WARS.

DOWDING, HUGH (b. 24 April 1882 at Moffat, Dumfriesshire, Scotland; d. 15 Feb. 1970 at Tunbridge Wells, Kent, England, aged 87). A British Army airman from 1914 (in the ROYAL AIR FORCE from 1918), Dowding became head of Fighter Command in 1936. He organized new air defences combining coastal radar stations, operations rooms and interception fighter aircraft (constructed 1937–9). In 1940, during WORLD WAR II, he insisted on retention of fighters to defend Britain (rather than extensive deployment in France). His system proved crucial in winning the battle of BRITAIN, though it was unable to counter night-time bombing effectively. Alleged shortcomings led to Dowding's removal from office in Nov. 1940. He was created Lord Dowding in 1943. *See also* WATSON-WATT, ROBERT.

DOWNING STREET DECLARATION A statement made on 15 Dec. 1993 outside 10 Downing St, London, by the British and Irish prime ministers, John MAJOR and Albert REYNOLDS. The British government renounced any strategic role in NORTHERN IRELAND, and both leaders affirmed that a united Ireland required the consent of all people in Ireland (including Unionists). The Declaration led to a ceasefire by the PROVISIONAL IRISH REPUBLICAN

ARMY (31 Aug. 1994) and the BELFAST AGREEMENT (1998). *See also* PEACE PROCESS, NORTHERN IRELAND.

DOWRIS HOARD The largest recorded hoard of bronzes from Late BRONZE AGE Ireland (*c*.1200– *c*.700 BC), found in the 1820s in a bog at Dowris (Co. Offaly, C Ireland). It comprised at least 218 objects, including weapons, tools, buckets, cauldrons, 'crotals' (rattles), and no fewer than 26 bronze horns.

DRAKE, FRANCIS (b. early 1540 at Crowndale, Devon, England; d. 27 Jan. 1596 off Porto Bello, New Spain, aged 55). Seaman. After shipping slaves from Africa to S America (1560s, with his kinsman John HAWKINS), Drake raided the Spanish West Indies and America (1570s). Between 13 Dec. 1577 and 26 Sept. 1580 he commanded the first English CIRCUMNAVIGATION, attacking Spanish settlements and ships in America, and prospecting for unoccupied land. He returned with treasure and spices (knighted 1581).

During England's war with Spain from 1585, Drake delayed the SPANISH ARMADA (with raid on Cádiz, SW Spain, 1587), and contributed to its defeat (1588). A revenge attack on Spanish-ruled Lisbon (1589) failed; Drake was court-martialled. He died during another raiding expedition (with John Hawkins). *See also* PIRACY AND PRIVATEERING; SPAIN, ENGLISH AND BRITISH RELATIONS WITH.

DRESS, MEN'S In the 5th–14th centuries men typically wore a knee-length woollen tunic (sometimes with an under-tunic or shirt, and loincloth), breeches (short baggy trousers) and hose (stockings, over lower legs and feet), leather shoes and possibly a cloak. In Ireland, from the 8th century, long trousers and long cloaks (OIr. *brata*) became common. The Anglo-Irish invasion (1169–70) resulted in two 'dress cultures', though incomers often adopted Gaelic dress, despite condemnation (*see* KILKENNY, STATUTE OF).

From the mid 14th century 'tailored' tight-fitting clothes, fastened with buttons and often colourful, were introduced from abroad, notably the gipon or doublet. Originally designed for wearing with plate armour, it was a padded ('doubled') jacket of waist length which was worn (over a shirt) with long hose. New overgarments (late 14th–15th centuries) included the cotehardie (tight, knee-length coat) and houppelande (gown), followed (from 15th century) by the jerkin, an outer jacket, often of leather. By the 16th century labourers might wear linen shirt and underwear, woollen doublet, jerkin (wool or leather), knee breeches and woollen stockings, and cloak.

From the 1660s the doublet and jerkin were replaced by a 'vest' (long buttoned waistcoat) and outer long coat. Shirts, breeches and hose continued, and cravats (neckcloths) were popular. Wealthy men wore wigs from the 1660s to early 19th century. In the 18th–19th centuries, rural labourers often wore a smock (shirt-like outer garment). In the Scottish HIGHLANDS, the short kilt was developed (by 1730s; *see* CLAN, SCOTLAND).

In the early 19th century long trousers replaced breeches, and clothes became sombre. Fabrics (including COTTON) were woven by machine. 'Suits' of various styles became common (including professional uniforms), and flat caps were popular (19th–20th centuries). In the 20th century, the main items of dress comprised underclothes, shirt, necktie (from 1920s), suit (waistcoat, jacket, trousers). Affluence from the 1950s made more varied and less formal clothes (e.g., leather jackets) affordable.

DRESS, WOMEN'S In the 5th–14th centuries women typically wore an ankle-length under-tunic (later known as a smock, shift or chemise) with long sleeves, a shorter woollen outer tunic, hose (stockings) and leather shoes. A cloak and headcovering (shoulder-length veil) were additionally worn outdoors. From the 12th century wealthier women wore fabrics from the Levant (eastern Mediterranean), such as silk.

Women's dress became more close-fitting from the mid 14th century. The outer tunic was gradually replaced by a dress with a tight-fitting upper 'bodice' and, below the waist, a flared skirt. Exotic headdresses were created. Like men, women wore (late 14th–15th centuries) the cotehardie (tight, ankle-length coat) and houppelande (gown). Poorer women also wore aprons from the 15th century.

In the 16th and early 17th centuries the farthingale (a framework of hoops, used to support a skirt), derived from Spain, was popular among the wealthy. Ruffs (projecting linen neckpieces) were popular with wealthy men and women from the 1550s to 1620s. From *c*.1550 the bodice and skirt were often separate items, and from the 1590s an under-bodice (or corset) stiffened with whalebones became fashionable. Wealthy women wore looser, long skirts from the 1620s.

In the 17th–19th centuries fashions changed regularly, often in response to Continental influences (e.g., from the 1820s women typically wore corsets and long dresses over several petticoats), but garment types remained essentially unchanged. (Drawers were adopted from *c*.1800.) Greater change occurred in the 20th century. From the 1920s mass-produced bras were worn, and skin-toned stockings (of silk or rayon, nylon from *c*.1946) accompanied blouses, jackets and short dresses or skirts. From the 1960s dress became ever more varied, individualistic and youthful, epitomized by the miniskirt (1961). As women's occupations broadened they also wore or adapted male professional dress (e.g., as police, clergy, etc.). From the 1980s women increasingly wore trousers. A sophisticated international fashion industry encouraged rapid change in styles.

DRUIDS *see* PREHISTORIC BRITAIN, RELIGIOUS PRACTICES; ROMAN BRITAIN, INDIGENOUS RELIGIONS; INAUGURATION, IRELAND

DRUIM CETT, MEETING AT A meeting in summer 575 (or more likely *c*.590) in N Ireland (at Druim Cett, modern Mullagh, Co. Londonderry) at which Áed mac Ainmerech, high-king of the Northern Uí Néill, and Áedán mac Gabráin, high-king of Dál Riata, probably confirmed an alliance against Báetán mac Cairill, high-king of the Ulaid, to prevent Báetán's expansion around the Irish Sea (and thereby infringement of their interests). Participants included Áed's kinsman Colum Cille (or COLUMBA). *See also* ULSTER.

DRUMMOND, THOMAS (b. 10 Oct. 1797 at Edinburgh, Scotland; d. 15 April 1840 at Dublin, Ireland, aged 42). An engineer, Drummond served as under-secretary for Ireland 1835–40. He implemented government policies agreed under the LICHFIELD HOUSE COMPACT (1835), e.g., TITHE reform (1838), appointment of Catholics as law and police officers. He also implemented the POOR RELIEF (IRELAND) ACT, 1838, and envisaged a national railway system. He famously said that 'Property has its duties as well as its rights'.

DRYDEN, JOHN (b. 9 Aug. 1631 at Aldwincle, Northamptonshire, England; d. 1 May 1700 at London, England, aged 68). Dryden's family was Puritan and Parliamentarian in the CIVIL WARS (1642–8), but he attracted the patronage of King CHARLES II in the 1660s with his plays, and was appointed the first official poet laureate in 1668 (dismissed 1689 by WILLIAM III). *All for Love* (1677) is considered his best play. In the early 1680s Dryden composed anti-WHIG verse satires and essays. After the accession of JAMES VII/II, he converted to the Catholic Church (1686), which he defended in his poem *The Hind and the Panther* (1687). He was England's major literary figure of the late 17th century. *See also* ENGLISH LITERATURE, ENGLAND.

DUBLIN City in E Ireland, by the R. Liffey; capital of the Republic of Ireland; from Irish, Dubh Linn, meaning 'Black pool' (alternative Irish name: Baile Átha Clia, meaning 'Town of the hurdle ford').

From 841 to *c*.902 VIKINGS operated from a *longphort* (ship-camp) by the Liffey. Around 917 they established a trading centre on the S bank, possibly at a new location, which became the main Viking town in Ireland, with a sizeable population, streets, churches and earthen defences. Situated in LEINSTER, it remained Ireland's pre-eminent urban centre. Its Hiberno-Scandinavian kings extended authority into the hinterland (including FINGAL), though from 944 they submitted to Irish high-kings, and from 1014 were dominated by Irish rulers (*see* TARA).

In 1170 Dublin was captured by the Cambro-Norman invader STRONGBOW, but was handed to HENRY II, king of England, in 1171. It remained the centre of English (later British) GOVERNMENT until 1922. A castle and stone walls were built (*see* JOHN AND IRELAND), and religious houses were founded. Dublin traded with England, France and the Mediterranean. It declined in the 14th and 15th centuries (*see* PALE).

Economic expansion in the 17th century caused building to spread well beyond Dublin's medieval walls (including N bank). During further growth in the 18th century, squares were created, and elegant houses and public buildings were constructed (e.g., Custom House, 1781–91). Now the centre of the PROTESTANT ASCENDANCY, Dublin enjoyed vibrant cultural activity (e.g., première of *Messiah* by G.F. HANDEL, 1742). Economic development included grain exporting, sugar baking and large-scale brewing (*see* GUINNESS COMPANY AND FAMILY).

Dublin stagnated economically in the 19th century, and was the focus of the 1916 EASTER RISING. It became the capital of the IRISH FREE STATE in 1922, and expanded vigorously from the 1950s. By the early 21st century its area accommodated 1.2 million people, almost a third of the Republic's population. *See also* TOWNS, IRELAND; OSTMEN; CAPITALS; UNIVERSITIES, IRELAND; COMMUNICATIONS, IRELAND.

Est. popn: 1300, 8000; 1600, 5000; 1800, 200,000; 1900, 290,000; 2000, 493,000.

DUBLIN AND ARMAGH PRIMACY DISPUTE *see* PRIMACY DISPUTE, DUBLIN AND ARMAGH

DUBLIN CASTLE PLOT In Ireland, a conspiracy in 1641 to seize DUBLIN Castle, in order to incapacitate the government as part of a broader anti-English rebellion (*see* ULSTER RISING). A few hours before implementation, on 23 Oct., an informer revealed the rebels' plans. Government forces arrested the rebel leaders, Connor MAGUIRE and Hugh Óg MacMahon, and mustered men to deter further attack. *See also* IRISH WARS, 1641–52.

DUDLEY, EDMUND (b. *c*.1462 possibly at Atherington, Sussex, England; d. 17 Aug. 1510 at London, England, aged about 48). A lawyer and undersheriff of London (1496–1502), by 1504 Dudley worked with Richard EMPSON for King HENRY VII. As members of the Council Learned in the Law, they exacted feudal payments (e.g., inheritance charges) and fines, making them extremely unpopular with noblemen and other landowners. Dudley was also president of the royal COUNCIL 1506–9.

HENRY VIII, on his accession, won popularity by allowing the arrest of Dudley and Empson (24 April 1509) and their execution for TREASON. Dudley's son John was protector under EDWARD VI (*see* NORTHUMBERLAND, JOHN DUKE OF); his grandson Robert Dudley was a royal favourite (*see* LEICESTER, ROBERT EARL OF).

DUFFY, C.G. (b. 12 April 1816 at Monaghan, Co. Monaghan, Ireland; d. 9 Feb. 1903 at Nice, France, aged 86). A (Catholic) journalist, Charles Gavan Duffy co-founded (and owned) *The Nation* (Oct. 1842), the newspaper of the YOUNG IRELAND MOVEMENT. He was imprisoned before the REBELLION OF 1848 (9 July). After his release (April 1849) Duffy campaigned for land reform, in *The Nation* and as an MP (1852–5). In Oct. 1855, disillusioned by failure, he emigrated to Australia and entered politics there (1856–80; prime minister of Victoria 1871–2; knighted 1873). He later retired to Nice and wrote memoirs of Young Ireland which transmitted their ideals to later nationalists. *See also* LAND AGITATION AND REFORM, IRELAND.

DUMBARTON ROCK, KINGDOM OF *see* STRATHCLYDE (CLYDE ROCK), KINGDOM OF

DUMNONIA The British (Brittonic-speaking) kingdom descended from the IRON AGE TRIBE of the Dumnonii which occupied SW England (the later Cornwall, Devon and W Somerset).

Formed in the 5th or 6th century, Dumnonia intermittently lost territory to the (Germanic-ruled) kingdom of WESSEX: the NE in the 7th century, SE by the late 7th century, the eastern part (Devon) in the 8th century. King EGBERT of Wessex probably established control over Cornwall after defeating Cornishmen and Vikings at Hingston Down (835). The last recorded king of Cornwall, Dungarth, drowned in 876. The name Devon is derived from Dumnonii. *See also* POST-ROMAN BRITAIN.

DUNBAR, BATTLE OF Fought on 3 Sept. 1650 at Dunbar (SE Scotland); a section of the English NEW MODEL ARMY under Oliver CROMWELL, retreating southwards, defeated a larger Scottish army. (Cromwell had invaded Scotland in July 1650 in response to King CHARLES II's arrival there on 24 June.) Dunbar led to English rule in Scotland and UNION OF ENGLAND AND SCOTLAND.

DUNBAR, GAVIN (b. *c*.1495; d. 30 April 1547 in Scotland, aged about 51). Tutor of King JAMES V *c*.1520 and archbishop of Glasgow from 1525, Dunbar was appointed CHANCELLOR by James after he escaped (1528) from the captivity of the earl of Angus (*see* DOUGLAS, ARCHIBALD). In 1532 Dunbar persuaded James to establish a College of Justice to fund judges of the judicial council (*see* SESSION, COURT OF). Opposed to Protestant Church reformers, Dunbar supported the burnings of Patrick HAMILTON

(1528) and George WISHART (1546). In 1543, following King James's death (1542), he was removed from the chancellorship (Jan.), briefly restored (late Jan. to Sept.), and again removed, losing office both times to his rival David BEATON.

DUNBAR, WILLIAM (b. *c*.1460; d. *c*.1520, aged about 60). Scots poet; the greatest poet at the court of King JAMES IV. Dunbar's work ranges from eulogies to sharp social satires. His greatest poems include *Lament for the Makaris* (poets), with the sonorous refrain 'Timor mortis conturbat me' ('Fear of death troubles me'). *See also* MAKARIS; SCOTS LANGUAGE AND LITERATURE.

DUNCAN I (Gaelic, Donnchad ua Maíl Cholium; d. 14 Aug. 1040 at Pitgaveny, Moray). King of Scots (Scotland) 1034–40.

Duncan ruled STRATHCLYDE under his grandfather King MALCOLM II, whom he succeeded in Scotland (through his mother Bethóc, Malcolm's daughter). (Duncan's father was Crinán, abbot of DUNKELD.) In 1039 Duncan invaded NE England, but was defeated at DURHAM. He was killed in Moray, while challenging MACBETH. Macbeth seized the Scottish kingship; Duncan's sons fled to England. *See also* DONALD III; MAC ALPIN KINGS.

DUNCAN II (Gaelic, Donnchad mac Mael Coluim; b. *c*.1060; d. 12 Nov. 1094 at Mondynes, Mearns, E Scotland, aged about 34). King of Scots (Scotland) 1094.

A son of King MALCOLM III and his first wife Ingibiorg, Duncan was exiled from Scotland to England on his father's death (1093). Duncan returned in 1094 (supported by King WILLIAM II of England). He ousted DONALD III (May) but was murdered. Donald returned. *See also* MAC MALCOLM RULERS.

DUNDAS, HENRY (b. 28 April 1742 at Arniston, Midlothian, Scotland; d. 28 May 1811 at Edinburgh, Scotland, aged 69). A son of Robert Dundas, president of the Court of SESSION, Henry Dundas became an advocate (1763). He was MP for Midlothian (1774–90, except 1782) and for Edinburgh (1790–1802), and LORD ADVOCATE (1775–83). For 30 years (1775–1805) Dundas controlled political patronage in Scotland. In the 1780s and 1790s he was also involved in Indian affairs.

Dundas held high office under his friend William PITT the Younger (home secretary, 1791–4; secretary for war, 1794–1801; first lord of the Admiralty, 1804–5). He also fought radicalism in Scotland and was active in the prosecution of Thomas MUIR. Henry ADDINGTON created him Viscount Melville (1802). In 1805 Dundas was accused of corruption and resigned. Though acquitted in an impeachment trial (1806) he never again held office.

DUNDEE A city in E Scotland (formally designated 1889), on the N bank of the Firth of Tay; a unitary authority from 1996.

Dundee (possibly from Gaelic, meaning 'Fort of Daigh') was founded as a BURGH *c.*1190 by King WILLIAM I and quickly became a major port, exporting to England, the Baltic and the Low Countries (especially wool and hides). It flourished in the 18th and 19th centuries from linen manufacturing (steam powered from the 1790s) and from the 1830s from jute weaving. Both industries declined in the 1920s–30s. Light industry developed from *c.*1950. University College (founded 1881) became the University of Dundee in 1967. An institute of technology was upgraded as the University of Abertay Dundee in 1994.

Est. popn: 1300, 2000; 1600, 3000; 1800, 26,000; 1900, 161,000; 2000, 154,000.

DUNDEE, VISCOUNT *see* GRAHAM, JOHN, OF CLAVERHOUSE

DUNFERMLINE A town in Fife, E Scotland. Originally a fort (Gaelic *dun*; meaning of other name-elements unknown).

Dunfermline was a royal residence by 1070, when King MALCOLM III married MARGARET of England there. She probably founded Dunfermline priory (abbey from 1128; suppressed 1560), the first Benedictine house in Scotland and principal medieval royal burial place (succeeding IONA).

DAVID I (ruled 1124–53) founded a BURGH, which was later superseded by the abbot's burgh. From the 18th century Dunfermline prospered from coal mining and linen manufacturing, boosted by the Rosyth naval dockyard from 1903. Textiles and mining declined from the 1920s but new industries (e.g., electronics) developed from the 1960s. *See also* CHARLES I; CARNEGIE, ANDREW.

Est. popn: 1300, 500; 1600, 1000; 1800, 10,000; 1900, 25,200; 2000, 39,000.

DUNKELD A town in Perthshire and Kinross, C Scotland. A church was founded there in the early 9th century probably by CONSTANTÍN SON OF VURGUIST, which became a house of CULDEES. King KENNETH I MAC ALPIN adopted Dunkeld as his ecclesiastical centre *c.*849, importing relics of COLUMBA. Bishops are recorded in 865 and from *c.*1127 (continuing until 1689). The BURGH (founded by 1512 – probably much earlier) was damaged in 1689 (after the battle of KILLIECRANKIE), when JACOBITES unsuccessfully attacked CAMERONIANS holding the town.

DUNKIRK A town and port in N France, by the Strait of Dover (within the English Channel), which belonged to England 1658–62. In March 1657 England, ruled by Oliver CROMWELL, lord protector, agreed to joint attacks with France in the Spanish Netherlands. Mardyck fort, near Dunkirk, was captured on 19 Sept. and ceded to the English; Dunkirk was besieged from 15 May 1658. On 4 June the Anglo-French army defeated Spain's Army of Flanders (reinforced by English Royalists) at the battle of the Dunes as it sought to relieve the siege. Dunkirk surrendered on 14 June and was handed to England the following day by King Louis XIV of France. The acquisition provided control of the strait, thereby deterring any Royalist invasion of England from the Netherlands.

At the RESTORATION (1660) Mardyck and Dunkirk passed under the rule of King CHARLES II. Expensive to garrison, they were sold to Louis in 1662 for 500,000 *livres* (about £375,000). *See also* FRANCE, ENGLISH AND BRITISH RELATIONS WITH.

DUNKIRK, WITHDRAWAL FROM The emergency evacuation in 1940 of the British Expeditionary Force from France after the German invasion. Between 27 May and 3 June, 860 ships (many of them small private vessels) transported 338,000 troops to England, though heavy weapons had to be abandoned. *See also* WORLD WAR II, BRITISH INVOLVEMENT.

DÚN NECHTAIN, BATTLE OF Irish name for a battle fought in territory of the PICTS (N Britain) on Saturday 20 May 685. Picts led by King BRIDEI SON OF BELI defeated an invading force of Northumbrians (English) led by King EGFRITH. Defeat of the Northumbrians ended their dominance over the southern Pictish area: thereafter they remained S of the R. Forth.

The battle's location is uncertain. Two possibilities (in modern Scotland) have been suggested: Dunnichen Hill (near Forfar in Fife, E Scotland) and Dunachton (near Kingussie in Highland, N Scotland). The location is called Nechtansmere in Old English.

DUNNICHEN, BATTLE OF *see* DÚN NECHTAIN, BATTLE OF

DUNNING'S RESOLUTION A motion proposed by the opposition WHIG MP John Dunning and passed by the British House of Commons on 6 April 1780 which asserted that 'the influence of the Crown has increased, is increasing, and ought to be diminished'. It represented the widespread belief that the 'secret influence' of King GEORGE III had reduced the independence of Parliament. Although it was a victory by campaigners for ECONOMICAL REFORM over the ministry of Lord NORTH, it stiffened the king's resolve to support the ministry against its opponents.

DUNSTAN (b. *c.*910 near Glastonbury, Somerset, Wessex; d. 19 May 988 at Canterbury, Kent, England, aged about 78). Abbot of Glastonbury from 940, Dunstan was chief adviser of Kings EDMUND and EADRED, but was exiled by EADWIG (956). Living at Ghent (Flanders), he experienced reformed Benedictine monasticism.

Dunstan was recalled in 957 or 958 by EDGAR, ruler of MERCIA, and made bishop of Worcester and soon afterwards bishop of London. After Edgar became king of England (959) he made Dunstan archbishop of CANTERBURY (960). Dunstan promoted reform (*see* TENTH-CENTURY REFORMATION), organized Edgar's 'second coronation' (*see* CORONATION, ENGLAND), and probably ensured the accession of EDWARD THE MARTYR (975).

DUPPLIN, BATTLE OF Fought SW of Perth (C Scotland) on 11 Aug. 1332. Edward BALLIOL, claimant to the Scottish kingship, and the DISINHERITED defeated Scots loyal to King DAVID II. The victory enabled Balliol to be crowned at nearby SCONE and encouraged later intervention by King EDWARD III of England. *See also* SCOTTISH–ENGLISH RELATIONS 1290 TO 1357.

DURHAM A city in NE England, by the R. Wear; centre of Co. Durham.

Centred on a defensible peninsula, Durham originated in 995 when the clergy of St CUTHBERT, including a bishop, settled there with the saint's relics. (The name means 'Island with a hill'.) A cathedral was built and a town developed. After the NORMAN CONQUEST (1066–70s) a castle was built (1070s), the clergy were replaced by a priory of Benedictine monks (1083), and a new cathedral was started (1093). The priory was replaced by a secular chapter in 1541.

Durham remained a small county centre and cathedral city. The bishop's diocese comprised Co. Durham and Northumberland until 1882 when Northumberland was removed (*see* NEWCASTLE UPON TYNE). Within Co. Durham the bishop exercised palatine rights until 1836 (*see* PALATINATE). Durham University was founded in 1832.

Est. popn: 1300, 1500; 1600, 4000; 1800, 7000; 1900, 14,000; 2000, 43,000.

DURHAM, EARL OF (b. 12 April 1792 at London, England; d. 28 July 1840 at Cowes, Isle of Wight, England, aged 48). John Lambton, a WHIG, became an MP in 1812.

From 1819 he supported parliamentary reform, and was nicknamed 'Radical Jack'. He was created Lord Durham in 1828. As lord PRIVY SEAL 1830–3, under the 2nd Earl GREY, he drafted the Bill that became the 'Great Reform Act' of 1832. He became an earl in 1833, and was ambassador to Russia 1835–7.

In 1838–9 Durham was governor-general of the Canadas (following risings in 1837–8), and spent May–Nov. 1838 in Upper and Lower Canada. His *Report on the Affairs of British North America* (1839, the 'Durham Report') recommended the union of the two Canadas to Anglicize French Canadians (implemented 1840–1). *See also* CANADA.

DYCK, ANTHONY VAN (b. 22 March 1599 at Antwerp, Spanish Netherlands; d. 9 Dec. 1641 at London, England, aged 42). A former assistant of Peter Paul Rubens, van Dyck moved to England in 1632 at the invitation of King CHARLES I. He painted numerous portraits of Charles, his family, nobles and courtiers. He interpreted Charles's vision of monarchy while also introducing a new sophistication into English portrait painting. *See also* VISUAL ARTS, BRITAIN.

DYFED An early medieval kingdom in SW WALES (6th–10th centuries), with its principal seat at Narberth (or Arberth). It was named from the Demetae, an IRON AGE TRIBE which formed a *CIVITAS* in ROMAN BRITAIN (1st–5th centuries), centred on Moridunum (CARMARTHEN).

Dyfed emerged probably in the 6th century, with a ruling line perhaps derived from 5th-century Irish settlers. In the 6th century King Vortipor of Dyfed was chastised by GILDAS. The dynasty apparently died out in the male line during the 9th century. By the early 10th century Dyfed was controlled by the dynasty of RHODRI MAWR in the person of HYWEL DDA. His descendants continued to rule after Dyfed was expanded into DEHEUBARTH, perhaps in the late 10th century.

The Normans' creation of PEMBROKESHIRE in the early 12th century led to the permanent removal of SW Dyfed from Welsh control. The name Dyfed was reused 1974–96 for a region incorporating parts of Pembrokeshire, Cardiganshire and Carmarthenshire. *See also* IRISH COLONIZATION OF BRITAIN, 4TH–6TH CENTURIES.

E

EADGIFU (b. by 904; d. in or after 966 in England). The daughter of an EALDORMAN, Eadgifu married King EDWARD THE ELDER c.919 (his third wife). She bore EDMUND and EADRED, and was influential during their reigns (939–46, 946–55). She supported leading churchmen, and persuaded Eadred to give the royal estate of Abingdon (Berkshire) to ÆTHELWOLD where he established a Benedictine abbey.

Eadgifu was deprived of her lands by her grandson EADWIG (king 955–9). They were restored by EDGAR (king of England from 959). Eadgifu thereafter lived in religious retirement. *See also* TENTH-CENTURY REFORMATION.

EADRED (b. c.923; d. 23 Nov. 955 at Frome, Somerset, England, aged about 32). The younger son of EDWARD THE ELDER and EADGIFU (third wife), Eadred succeeded his brother EDMUND as king of England in May 946. (Edmund's sons were young boys.)

Like Edmund, Eadred suffered the loss of part of N England to Vikings. It was held by the Norwegian Eric Bloodaxe (947–8); by Olaf Sihtricson from Dublin (949–52); and again (952–4) by Eric Bloodaxe (*see* YORK, VIKING KINGDOM OF). Eadred's advisers included Eadgifu, DUNSTAN, and ATHELSTAN 'HALF-KING'. Succeeded by EADWIG. *See also* ENGLAND, FORMATION OF; YORK, VIKING KINGDOM OF.

EADWIG (b. c.940; d. 1 Oct. 959 in England, aged about 19). The eldest son of King EDMUND, Eadwig succeeded his uncle EADRED as king of England on 23 Nov. 955, aged about 15. He immediately began removing his uncle's close supporters, depriving EADGIFU of lands and exiling DUNSTAN (Jan. or Feb. 956). ATHELSTAN 'HALF-KING' withdrew. Eadwig sought to win new supporters by making numerous land grants (956). By summer 957 his brother EDGAR had been accepted as king in Mercia, and by 958 in Northumbria. (Edgar eventually succeeded as king of England.)

EALDORMAN OE term meaning 'elder' or 'great man'. By the 7th century it referred to senior noblemen in Anglo-Saxon kingdoms (e.g., members of royal kindreds, kings' leading supporters). It increasingly denoted responsibility for military leadership and government; for example, from the 8th century each SHIRE in WESSEX was headed by an ealdorman. In the 10th century King EDWARD THE ELDER and King ATHELSTAN reduced the number of ealdormen, making them effectively regional governors (*see* ATHELSTAN 'HALF-KING'). *See also* SOCIAL STRUCTURE, ENGLAND BEFORE 1066; EARLS, ANGLO-SAXON ENGLAND.

EARLDOMS, SCOTLAND Originally discrete large territories (about 12), each headed by a MORMAER who raised military forces and exercised judicial authority. Probably in existence by the 10th century (N of the FORTH–CLYDE ISTHMUS), they were once thought to represent downgraded, Pictish kingdoms, but this seems unlikely.

A Dictionary of British and Irish History, First Edition. Edited by Robert Peberdy and Philip Waller.
© 2021 John Wiley & Sons Ltd; © editorial matter and organisation Robert Peberdy and Phillip Waller.
Published 2021 by John Wiley & Sons Ltd.

From the early 12th century, starting with Constantine MacDuff of FIFE (recorded in 1107), the English term 'earl' replaced mormaer, and mormaers' territories became earldoms. Kings also converted earls into 'feudal' tenants by regranting earldoms as 'fiefs' held for service and descending by male primogeniture rather than TANISTRY (e.g., regranting of Fife c.1136 to Duncan MacDuff, 3rd earl). In 1286 there were 13 earldoms, eight held by indigenous families (originating before the arrival of NORMANS), and five held by families of outside origin (the first acquired in the early 13th century; see COMYN FAMILY). Earldoms existed alongside 15 other large territorial lordships created in the 12th–13th centuries (e.g., Annandale, created 1124; see BRUCE FAMILY).

The existence of earldoms and large lordships meant that Scotland had strong regional power structures, through connections between earls and major lords and lesser lords within their territories. The pattern remained strong until the later 14th century, but began to change slowly from the early 14th century when kings started granting rights of REGALITY to numerous lords. From 1358 the status of earl was granted in recognition of personal importance and accumulated scattered lordships, rather than in association with a historical territory (see DOUGLAS, EARLS OF), and in 1401 an Act of Parliament diluted earls' powers by transferring superior lordship over vacant BARONIES to the Crown. Kings JAMES I and JAMES II retained vacant earldoms and lordships. By the 1460s only five 'old' earldoms and lordships did not belong to the Crown. A different kind of upper nobility emerged, recognized through personal summons to Parliament (see PEERAGE, SCOTLAND). See also EARLS, ANGLO-SAXON ENGLAND; FEUDALISM; NORMANS, IMPACT ON SCOTLAND; NOBILITY.

EARLS, ANGLO-SAXON ENGLAND During the reign of CNUT (1016–35) the OE term eorl, derived from Norse/Danish jarl (meaning 'nobleman'), replaced EALDORMAN. Like late 10th-century ealdormen, some earls were regional governors, administering earldoms (groups of SHIRES) for the king (e.g., holding shire courts, from which they received a third of the profits of justice).

During the reign of the EDWARD THE CONFESSOR (1042–66) the earldoms were dominated by the GODWINE FAMILY (they held seven in 1066). After the Norman invasion (1066), King WILLIAM I dispensed with regional earldoms and worked through shires. The title 'earl' became a personal dignity. See also SHERIFF.

EAST AFRICA, BRITISH INVOLVEMENT Concern for the sea route to INDIA and opposition to the SLAVE TRADE led Great Britain to take an interest in ZANZIBAR from the 1820s. Missionaries went inland in the 1860s. After an Anglo-German deal on spheres of influence (1886), the Imperial British East Africa Company began to penetrate the areas that became UGANDA and KENYA (see MACKINNON, WILLIAM). These were made PROTECTORATES (respectively 1894, 1895) because the British sought to safeguard the source of the NILE at Lake Victoria. Britain also established a protectorate over part of Somaliland for strategic purposes (1888; see BRITISH SOMALILAND), and over Zanzibar (1890), and later acquired part of German East Africa (1919; see TANGANYIKA). In 1940–1 British forces expelled ITALY from E Africa (see WINGATE, ORDE). Growing African nationalism in the 1950s, and diminishing strategic value (following Indian independence, 1947), prompted British withdrawal (1960–3). See also DECOLONIZATION.

EAST ANGLIA, KINGDOM OF A Germanic-ruled kingdom (6th–9th centuries), occupying modern Suffolk and Norfolk (E England). The area was settled by Germanic people ('Angles') from the 5th century. It was under a single dynasty by the late 6th century, probably based in SE Suffolk, an area which included SUTTON HOO and (from 7th century) Ipswich, an international trading centre. The first well-documented king is RÆDWALD (early 7th century), who exercised authority over other kingdoms. Christianity was established by Sigebert (ruled c.631–c.645).

In the 7th–9th centuries there was intermittent conflict with MERCIA (C England); both OFFA and CENWULF of Mercia sometimes exercised authority in East Anglia. The last independent Anglo-Saxon king, Edmund, was killed by VIKINGS (Danes) in 869. They ruled until 917 (submission to EDWARD THE ELDER). See also KINGSHIP, ANGLO-SAXON.

EASTER CONTROVERSY Disputes in Ireland and Britain in the 7th–8th centuries over computing the annual date of Easter. Around 500 the British and Irish Churches adopted the 'Celtic cycle', an 84-year scheme of solar and lunar cycles. When it was extended to Gaul, in monasteries founded by the Irishman COLUMBANUS (from 590s), it seemed anachronistic – Gaul's other monasteries employed the 19-year 'Victorian cycle' (tabulated by Victorius of Aquitaine). Around 627 Columbanus's monasteries in Gaul accepted the Victorian cycle, and the Irish Church preferred it in 629 or 630 (synod of Mag Léne), though not all monasteries complied, especially those associated with IONA (in N Britain). Many Irish churches later moved to the 19-year 'Dionysiac cycle', espoused by the Roman Church by 640.

In Germanic-ruled kingdoms in Britain, the 19-year cycles were widely used, under Roman influence, but BERNICIA and DEIRA, influenced by Iona, retained the 84-year cycle. In 664, under pressure from WILFRID, they agreed to the Dionysiac cycle and also abandoned other 'Irish' practices (see WHITBY, SYNOD OF).

More monasteries in northern Ireland, and probably STRATHCLYDE Britons, followed the Dionysiac cycle from the 680s or 690s, as did Pictish monasteries from probably 715 (*see* NAITON SON OF DER-ILEI). Iona and its associated monasteries changed in 716. *See also* CONVERSION OF ANGLO-SAXONS; ADOMNÁN.

EASTER RISING In Ireland, an attempt to replace British rule forcibly with a republic, organized by leaders of the IRISH REPUBLICAN BROTHERHOOD and IRISH CITIZEN ARMY. Plotting began in mid Aug. 1914, to exploit Britain's distraction by WORLD WAR I. In Dec. 1915 or Jan. 1916 it was decided to rebel at Easter. The leaders planned to seize cities and towns, with German military assistance (*see* CASEMENT, ROGER). Widespread support was expected.

The Germans supplied only a shipload of arms, which was intercepted on the Rising's eve (Sat. 22 April). 'Exercises' by IRISH VOLUNTEERS, which were to have provided a 'front', were also cancelled at the last minute (*see* MACNEILL, EOIN). Rebel commanders nevertheless decided to proceed on Easter Monday (24 April). Rebels (about 1800) seized major buildings in DUBLIN, and Patrick PEARSE, at the General Post Office (the rebels' headquarters), proclaimed a republic. The British declared martial law in Dublin (25 April) and recaptured rebel strongholds. The rebels surrendered on Sat. 29 April. Sixty-four rebels, 116 military personnel and about 270 other people died.

The Rising won little support but the execution of 15 leaders by firing squad (3–12 May), followed by Casement's execution, caused outrage and helped to precipitate the radicalization of the nationalist movement in favour of SINN FÉIN and away from the IRISH PARLIAMENTARY PARTY. The ensuing guerrilla war led to establishment of the IRISH FREE STATE. *See also* WORLD WAR I, IMPACT ON IRELAND; CLARKE, TOM; CONNOLLY, JAMES; DE VALERA, ÉAMON.

EASTERN QUESTION Term used for a major issue in late 18th- and 19th-century European international politics, created by the weakness of the OTTOMAN EMPIRE (the lands governed by Muslim Ottoman emperors from Istanbul) and by the efforts of rival powers to exploit it. Great Britain was chiefly concerned to prevent RUSSIA from gaining unhindered access to the Mediterranean Sea from the Black Sea, thereby threatening its route to INDIA through the Middle East. *See also* CRIMEAN WAR; BULGARIAN ATROCITIES.

EAST INDIA COMPANY An English overseas trading company (British from 1707) which was granted a monopoly of trade with the East Indies by royal charter in 1600. It organized trading voyages from 1601 and founded trading centres (e.g., Surat, NW India, 1612). The company soon concentrated on INDIA (e.g., acquiring pepper). From the later 17th century its main centres were the 'presidency' headquarters of Bombay (now Mumbai), Madras (now Chennai) and CALCUTTA. By the mid 18th century the company's trade was important in the British economy – 13% of imports, 5% of exports. It also wielded political influence.

Commercial rivalries between British and French companies resulted in confused fighting during the 1740s–50s, eventually ending with defeat of the French in 1760 at Wandiwash (or Vandivasi, SE India). In Bengal, conflict with nawabs (rulers) led to the loss of Calcutta, but it was recovered (1757) by the company's army under Robert CLIVE (*see* PLASSEY, BATTLE OF). During the 1760s the company became a territorial ruler (C eastern coast, Bengal).

By now company agents were considered corrupt, so the British government began to exert influence through statutes, notably the 1784 India Act. Promoted by William PITT the Elder, it established a Board of Control responsible to the British Parliament and made the governor-general a Crown appointee. Company territories were greatly expanded under Richard WELLESLEY (governor-general 1797–1805). In 1813 the company's monopoly was broken, although it retained territories and powers until 1858 (*see* INDIAN MUTINY). *See also* OVERSEAS TRADING COMPANIES; SEVEN YEARS WAR; INDIAN CIVIL SERVICE.

ECCLESIASTICAL COMMISSIONERS An official body established by the UK Parliament in 1835 to review and strengthen the state of the Church of ENGLAND. They appropriated endowments (e.g., from cathedrals) and used them to increase stipends of parish clergy or create new livings and parishes, envisaging a standard population of 3000–4000. The Commissioners absorbed the CHURCH BUILDING COMMISSION in 1857 and merged with Queen Anne's Bounty in 1948 to form the Church Commissioners, who continued to manage the Church's central assets in the 21st century. *See also* HOWLEY, WILLIAM.

ECCLESIOLOGISTS Name given to members and supporters of the Cambridge Camden Society, founded at CAMBRIDGE University in 1839, who promoted the revival of Gothic architecture in the Church of ENGLAND. Their name was derived from the Society's journal, *The Ecclesiologist* (published from 1841). Ecclesiologists influenced the building or restoration of hundreds of churches in England and elsewhere. The Camden Society changed name to the Ecclesiological Society in 1845. It survived until 1868, and was seen as supporting the OXFORD MOVEMENT.

ECONOMICAL REFORM Term used for the ambitions of a political movement in the 1770s–80s which sought to reduce the alleged influence of the Crown in the British House of Commons (a belief exemplified by

DUNNING'S RESOLUTION). It sought reforms, notably the reduction of PLACEMEN, to eliminate corruption.

Opposition WHIG MPs proposed several reform Bills in 1780 but were defeated by supporters of the prime minister Lord NORTH. In 1782 the ministry of the marquess of ROCKINGHAM implemented reforms: Crewe's Act disfranchised revenue officers; Clerke's Act excluded government contractors from the House of Commons; and the Civil Establishment Act, proposed by Edmund BURKE, abolished many court and other posts. The legislation started a new phase of reduction in the PATRONAGE available to the Crown and government ministers. *See also* PETITIONING MOVEMENT.

ECONOMIC EXPANSION, PROGRAMMES FOR

Three programmes in the Republic of Ireland, 1959–72, which sought to accelerate economic growth by facilitating inward investment and free trade. T.K. WHITAKER and Seán LEMASS were architects of the first two (for 1959–63, 1964–70). The second was abandoned in 1967 and replaced by a third (1969–72). Such planning then ceased. *See also* SOUTHERN IRELAND FROM 1922.

ECONOMIC WAR

Term used for a trade conflict between southern Ireland and the UK 1932–8. It began when the Irish Free State government of Éamon DE VALERA refused to pay annuities for land purchase to the British Exchequer (30 June 1932), seeking to repudiate liabilities to Great Britain. The British government responded by imposing tariffs on Irish goods. The conflict was moderated by the COAL–CATTLE PACTS (1935–7) and ended by the 1938 ANGLO-IRISH AGREEMENTS. Ireland suffered more than Britain, and NORTHERN IRELAND was hit badly by increased food costs. *See also* SOUTHERN IRELAND FROM 1922.

ECONOMY, STATE INVOLVEMENT, BRITAIN

Provision of CURRENCY has been a basic responsibility of monarchs and governments: Anglo-Saxon kings issued coins from the 7th century, Scottish kings from the 12th century. From the 1340s bullion for coinage was a concern: exports were restricted or merchants were required to bring foreign coins or silver to mints. Kings encouraged social fairness by promoting standard weights and measures (from 10th century in England, 12th century in Scotland) and price regulation (from 12th century; e.g., bread). Labour legislation began in England after the 'Black Death' (1348–9; *see* LABOURERS, ORDINANCE AND STATUTE OF).

In the 16th century numerous STATUTES on economic matters were enacted by England's PARLIAMENT, often for social stability (e.g., Statute of ARTIFICERS). English governments welcomed skilled immigration to promote industrial advancement (e.g., *see* CLOTH INDUSTRY,

ENGLAND). An important development was legalization of interest (England 1545–52, 1571; Scotland 1587).

From the 17th century English governments pursued more strategic policies, later called MERCANTILISM. Legislation from 1650 sought to exclude the Dutch from overseas trade and create a monopoly, stimulating inflow of bullion (*see* NAVIGATION ACTS). Tariffs were used to promote agriculture and manufactures (*see* CORN LAWS).

The rise of industrial society (from 1780s) and CLASSICAL ECONOMICS encouraged FREE TRADE to expand overseas trade (by 1850s, including repeal of the Corn Laws and Navigation Acts), and minimal government involvement (so-called LAISSEZ-FAIRE). Governments regulated currency (*see* GOLD STANDARD; BANK CHARTER ACT), and industrial conditions (*see* FACTORY ACTS).

In the 20th century the world wars (1914–18, 1939–45) necessitated extensive State economic control. The Labour government of 1945–51 created a 'mixed economy' by NATIONALIZATION, and governments sought to 'manage' the economy (*see* KEYNES, J.M.; BUTSKELLISM). The Labour government of 1964–70 attempted to rationalize and modernize manufacturing industries, with little success. From the 1980s governments reduced their role (*see* PRIVATIZATION). *See also* ENCLOSURE AND ENGROSSING, ENGLAND 1480s TO 1630s; FISHERIES AND MANUFACTURES, BOARD OF TRUSTEES FOR; BANK RATE.

ECONOMY, STATE INVOLVEMENT, IRELAND 18TH–20TH CENTURIES

In the 18th century some Protestant landowners promoted economic development or 'improvement' by using PARLIAMENT to establish agencies and provide funds. A Linen Board (1711–1828) encouraged linen manufacture by subsidizing flax seeds and equipment, and supervising quality of output. A Tillage Commission (from 1730) encouraged arable farming, draining of bogs, inland navigation, and construction of CANALS. It was reformed in 1752 as the Inland Navigation Commission (dissolved 1787). Another Inland Navigation Board operated 1800–31. Parliament made grants for individual projects (e.g., roads) in supply Acts.

State support persisted after the union (1801), funded by the UK Parliament, despite LAISSEZ-FAIRE ideals and concern for economic efficiency. New agencies included a Drainage Commission (1809–14), Fishery Board (1819–30), and Board of WORKS (1831–1922). The last provided some relief during the GREAT FAMINE (1845–9) by creating employment on public works. State subventions included support for RAILWAYS (e.g., Dublin–Kingstown railway, opened 1834).

Later initiatives tackled particular problems. The CONGESTED DISTRICTS BOARD (1891–1923) focused on poorer areas, and the government's Department of Agriculture and Technical Instruction (created 1899) addressed perceived agricultural backwardness.

EDEN, ANTHONY (b. 12 June 1897 at Windlestone Hall, Co. Durham, England; d. 14 Jan. 1977 at Alvediston, Wiltshire, England, aged 79). British prime minister and leader of the CONSERVATIVE PARTY 1955–7.

Eden was an MP 1923–57 with foreign policy as his primary interest. He was parliamentary private secretary to Austen CHAMBERLAIN (1926–9), under-secretary for foreign affairs (1931–4), and minister for League of Nations affairs (1934–5). A popular figure, he became foreign secretary in Dec. 1935, but resigned (Feb. 1938) after disagreements with Neville CHAMBERLAIN. He emerged as a critic of APPEASEMENT.

During WORLD WAR II Eden served as dominions secretary (1939–40) and war secretary, before becoming foreign secretary (Dec. 1940–May 1945). Detractors have argued that he made a better diplomat than policy maker. Having worked closely with Winston CHURCHILL throughout the war, he was again Churchill's foreign secretary (1951–5).

The obvious successor to the premiership in April 1955, Eden tried to improve relations between the USA and USSR. He dominated the British response to the SUEZ CRISIS, and its dramatic failure discredited him. His debonair manner concealed a highly strung temperament and his health gave way. He resigned on 9 Jan. 1957. Created earl of Avon in 1961.

EDEN TREATY A commercial treaty, lowering duties on trade, between France and Great Britain, signed 26 Sept. 1786 at Versailles, France; named after the chief British negotiator, William Eden. Required by the 1783 Peace of Versailles, after the AMERICAN WAR OF INDEPENDENCE, it was part of a movement for encouraging trade by means of international agreements. *See also* PITT, WILLIAM, THE YOUNGER.

EDGAR (b. 943 or 944; d. 8 July 975 in England, aged 31 or 32). The younger son of King EDMUND, Edgar was educated by ÆTHELWOLD, abbot of Abingdon. In 957 and 958 respectively he was accepted as ruler of MERCIA and NORTHUMBRIA (C and N England) while his brother EADWIG was still king of England. He immediately (957 or 958) recalled DUNSTAN (exiled by Eadwig) and made him bishop of Worcester. Edgar succeeded Eadwig as king of England on 1 Oct. 959. During his reign England was spared VIKING attacks.

Edgar supported leaders of the TENTH-CENTURY REFORMATION. He promoted Dunstan to bishop of London (959) and archbishop of CANTERBURY (960), OSWALD to bishop of Worcester (962; also archbishop of YORK from 971), and Æthelwold to bishop of WINCHESTER (963). On Whit Sunday 973, in his thirtieth year, Edgar underwent a 'second coronation' at BATH, influenced by Carolingian and Ottonian ceremonies. Soon afterwards, at Chester,

Edgar was acknowledged by eight northern kings (including KENNETH II, king of Scots), who rowed him on the R. Dee. (Edgar possibly made a formal cession of LOTHIAN to Kenneth in 973 or 975.) Late in his reign Edgar inaugurated a system of regular recoinages.

EDGAR (b. *c*.1074; d. 8 Jan. 1107 at Edinburgh, SE Scotland, aged about 33). King of Scots (Scotland) 1097–1107.

A son of MALCOLM III and MARGARET (both d. 1093), Edgar was exiled in England during the reign of Malcolm's successor, Edgar's uncle DONALD III. In 1097, with English support, Edgar invaded Scotland and ousted Donald (Oct.). Thereafter he had good relations with King WILLIAM II and King HENRY I of England, who regarded him as their vassal; his sister Edith/Maud married Henry in 1100. Edgar probably introduced the sealed WRIT from England. He also recognized Norwegian sovereignty of the WESTERN ISLES in 1098 (thereby abandoning IONA). He died childless; succeeded by a younger brother, ALEXANDER I. *See also* MAC MALCOLM RULERS.

EDGAR ÆTHELING *see* ÆTHELING

EDINBURGH City in SE Scotland, with its centre on a prominent rock; capital of Scotland from the 15th century (designated as capital 1633).

Originally a fortified centre in the British kingdom of GODODDIN (and called Din Eidyn; Brittonic, meaning 'The fortress Eidyn'), Edinburgh belonged to the Anglian (English) kingdom of BERNICIA by 638 and was called 'Edwin's burh'. Captured by Indulf, king of Scots (reigned 952–62), it became a royal residence. A castle was built on the rock by the early 12th century.

Two towns developed E of the Castle: Edinburgh royal BURGH, probably founded by King DAVID I (ruled 1124–53); and Canongate, to the E, founded by the nearby Augustinian Holyrood Abbey (itself founded 1128; suppressed 1559). From 1329 Edinburgh controlled Leith, a port on the Firth of Forth, and benefited from trade re-routed after the English occupied BERWICK-UPON-TWEED in 1333. By the 1530s, Edinburgh handled more than two-thirds of Scottish exports. A wealthy merchant élite emerged.

Political importance increased from *c*.1440 when PARLIAMENT met regularly in Edinburgh (until 1707); *c*.1501 a royal residence was built at Holyrood. In 1532 the College of Justice was founded in Edinburgh (*see* SESSION, COURT OF) and a university in 1583. Canongate became a social centre, and from the later 17th century Edinburgh developed as a financial centre (*see* BANKING, SCOTLAND). Consequently the city became cramped, a problem solved from 1767 with the building of the 'New Town' to the N (*see* TOWN PLANNING).

In the 21st century Edinburgh remained an administrative and financial centre, enhanced by its annual arts festival (founded 1947) and by the presence of the Scottish Parliament and Executive/government (inaugurated 1999).

Est. popn: 1300, 2000; 1600, 17,000; 1800, 83,000; 1900, 395,000; 2000, 430,000.

EDINBURGH, (1328) TREATY OF Concluded 17 March 1328 (at Edinburgh, SE Scotland); between King ROBERT I of Scotland and envoys of King EDWARD III of England (a minor); ratified by the English PARLIAMENT at Northampton (C England), 4 May 1328. The treaty conceded Robert's demand for recognition of Scotland's independence. It lasted only four years. *See also* SCOTTISH–ENGLISH RELATIONS 1290 TO 1357.

EDINBURGH, (1560) TREATY OF Signed on 6 July 1560 (at Edinburgh, SE Scotland); between English and French representatives, following the death of MARY OF GUISE. English and French forces would withdraw from Scotland. MARY, QUEEN OF SCOTS, who claimed the English throne, would cease using the English royal arms, thereby implicitly recognizing ELIZABETH as queen of England. It also specified the constitution of the next Scottish Parliament. *See also* BERWICK, (1560) TREATY OF; REFORMATION, SCOTLAND.

EDINBURGH LETTER An open letter sent from Edinburgh, Scotland, by the WHIG leader Lord John RUSSELL to his London constituents on 22 Nov. 1845. It announced that Russell favoured abolition of the CORN LAWS. His move encouraged the CONSERVATIVE prime minister, Sir Robert PEEL, to declare his own support for repeal (2 Dec.).

EDINGTON, BATTLE OF Fought near Edington, NE WESSEX (Wiltshire, SW England), between 6 and 12 May 878. West Saxons led by King ALFRED defeated VIKINGS led by Guthrum (a Dane), enabling Alfred to recover Wessex from near-conquest by Vikings.

EDITH (b. between 1020 and 1033; d. 18 Dec. 1075 at Winchester, Hampshire, England). The eldest daughter of GODWINE, earl of Wessex, Edith was married to Edward the Confessor, king of England (23 Jan. 1045), to strengthen the friendship between earl and king. The marriage was childless. During the exile of the GODWINE FAMILY (1051–2), Edith was banished to a nunnery (*see* EDWARD THE CONFESSOR).

In 1066 Edith's brother HAROLD succeeded as king, only to be ousted by WILLIAM I. Edith remained in England and retained her land, possibly because she had supported William's seizure of the Crown.

EDMUND (b. 920 or 921; d. 26 May 946 at Pucklechurch, Gloucestershire, England, aged 24 or 25). The elder son of EDWARD THE ELDER and EADGIFU (third wife), Edmund succeeded his half-brother ATHELSTAN as king of England on 27 Oct. 939. He faced a resurgence of VIKING force. Olaf Guthfrithson, from DUBLIN (Ireland), seized northern England (probably late 939) and invaded eastern MERCIA (940). Edmund agreed to cede the territories.

In 942 Edmund recovered eastern Mercia, and in 944 expelled Olaf Sihtricson and rival Ragnall Guthfrithson from York. Edmund was murdered while trying to stop a brawl. Succeeded by brother EADRED. *See also* ENGLAND, FORMATION OF; YORK, VIKING KINGDOM OF.

EDMUND IRONSIDE (b. in 980s; d. 30 Nov. 1016 at London, England). A younger son of ÆTHELRED II, king of England, Edmund became his heir in June 1014. In 1015 he rebelled, probably seeking to counter the influence of Eadric Streona, ealdorman of MERCIA (C England). Edmund was accepted as ruler in eastern Mercia and N England.

Soon afterwards CNUT invaded (Sept. 1015). Edmund led the resistance. (He succeeded Æthelred in April 1016.) After fighting Danes in WESSEX, Edmund relieved London from attack, but was defeated (18 Oct.) at Ashingdon (Essex) and again in W England. He and Cnut agreed a division of England (Oct. or Nov.), which left Wessex (S England) under Edmund. He died soon afterwards. His nickname may be contemporary. *See also* ÆTHELING.

EDMUND OF ABINGDON (b. *c*.1174 at Abingdon, Berkshire, England; d. 16 Nov. 1240 at Soisy-Bouy, France, aged about 66). A notable scholar at OXFORD University and in Paris, Edmund was elected archbishop of CANTERBURY in 1233. After Richard Marshal, earl of Pembroke and opponent of King HENRY III, was murdered in Ireland (April 1234), Edmund forced Henry to expel his foreign favourites, preventing civil war. He died while travelling to Rome. Celebrated for devoutness, Edmund was canonized (1247). He is commemorated at Oxford by St Edmund Hall (formerly an academic hall, a college from 1957).

EDNYFED FYCHAN (fl. from 1200; d. 1246). *Distain* (steward) of LLYWELYN AP IORWERTH and DAFYDD AP LLYWELYN of GWYNEDD, NW Wales (served *c*.1212–46); ancestor of the TUDOR FAMILY. In the 1230s and 1240s Ednyfed conducted diplomatic negotiations between Welsh rulers and King HENRY III of England. He was rewarded with land grants in ANGLESEY and E Gwynedd.

EDUCATION, ENGLAND BEFORE 1066 *see* EDUCATION AND LEARNING, ENGLAND BEFORE 1066

EDUCATION, ENGLAND FROM 1066 Monasteries continued to provide teaching, and separate town schools are recorded from the late 11th century. Later called GRAMMAR SCHOOLS, and funded by fees, they taught reading, writing and Latin grammar. Boys often became clergy or proceeded to university. Basic education (e.g., reading) was also obtained from clergy. From the 1380s benefactors endowed teaching posts, providing free places; from the 1440s small schools were founded, often with a CHANTRY. Classical studies became important from the late 15th century.

The DISSOLUTION OF RELIGIOUS HOUSES (1536–40) and dissolution of chantries (1548) reduced provision. New schools were founded (*see* EDUCATIONAL REVOLUTION). From the 1660s, Protestant dissenters ran rival schools.

During the 18th century, subscription-based co-educational elementary 'charity schools' were started (*see* SOCIETY FOR PROMOTING CHRISTIAN KNOWLEDGE), and small private schools, sometimes teaching non-classical subjects (mathematics, accountancy). Women ran 'dames' schools' for young children. A few grammar schools became recognized as 'public schools' for the élite.

Urban expansion (later 18th century) stimulated new methods. The SUNDAY SCHOOL MOVEMENT (from 1780s) provided basic education, and economical 'monitorial systems' (teaching by older children) devised by Andrew Bell (1796) and Joseph Lancaster (1798) attracted support, resulting in: Royal Lancasterian Institution (1808, interdenominational; British and Foreign Schools Society from 1814); National Society (1811, Church of England). Their 'voluntary schools', supported from 1833 by State grants, provided most elementary education.

FORSTER'S EDUCATION ACT (1870) began State provision (additional elementary schools). Education became compulsory in 1880 (ages 5–10; to 11 from 1893, 12 from 1899), and free from 1891. The BALFOUR EDUCATION ACT (1902) placed voluntary and State schools under Local Education Authorities and increased post-elementary education. From 1921 the leaving age was 14. The BUTLER EDUCATION ACT (1944) instigated compulsory secondary education (to 15 from 1947). Usually selective, it was largely replaced by COMPREHENSIVE EDUCATION (from 1965; to age 16 from 1972–3). *See also* UNIVERSITIES, ENGLAND; GRAMMAR AND PUBLIC SCHOOLS, REFORM OF, ENGLAND AND WALES; HIGHER EDUCATION, EXPANSION OF; DIRECT-GRANT SCHOOL; INDEPENDENT SCHOOL; NATIONAL CURRICULUM; LITERACY, ENGLAND.

EDUCATION, IRELAND In Gaelic Irish society from the 1st millennium BC to 17th century AD, intellectual and artistic learning was transmitted within hereditary LEARNED CLASSES (e.g., by bardic schools). Fosterage (child-rearing by foster parents) conveyed practical learning (e.g., horsemanship). Monasteries flourished as centres of learning in the 6th–11th centuries (*see* GOLDEN AGE). In the 12th–16th centuries, reformed monasteries, major churches, and friaries (from 13th century) provided education (in Gaelic and Anglo-Irish areas). No university was founded: would-be students went overseas, mainly to OXFORD.

During the 16th century the DISSOLUTION OF RELIGIOUS HOUSES reduced educational provision. The government attempted to spread reformed Christianity through legislation requiring parish and diocesan schools (respectively 1537, 1570; *see* IRELAND, CHURCH OF). Success was limited, though a Protestant university college was founded (Trinity College, Dublin, 1592). Schools were established in the ULSTER PLANTATION (early 17th century). Education remained available to Catholics in private schools and overseas colleges. Catholic education was hindered 1690s–1780s by ANTI-CATHOLIC LEGISLATION, though secretive HEDGE SCHOOLS extensively provided elementary education. Protestants attempted proselytization of Catholics through charity schools (*see* CHARTER SCHOOLS).

From the later 18th century, political leaders proposed non-denominational education, and from 1816 the UK Parliament supported non-denominational schools of the KILDARE PLACE SOCIETY. State-funded non-denominational elementary education was implemented nationally from 1831, but became denominational (Catholic, Church of Ireland, presbyterian) through modifications (*see* NATIONAL EDUCATION). University education was expanded from the 1840s (*see* UNIVERSITIES, IRELAND). A modest increase of private intermediate (secondary) education (for children about 12–16) was also provided, mostly by Catholic orders and organizations. The State subsidized intermediate education from 1878 through grants based on examination results, and provision was made from 1889 for TECHNICAL EDUCATION. Education became compulsory for town children aged 6–14 in 1892. Schools or classes were mostly single-sex. *See also* EDUCATION, NORTHERN IRELAND/SOUTHERN IRELAND; HIGHER EDUCATION, EXPANSION OF.

EDUCATION, NORTHERN IRELAND Following the creation of Northern Ireland (1921), arrangements in England and Wales were influential. Its government assumed supervision of school education from Feb. 1922. The 'Londonderry Act' (1923) then created supervisory educational committees under county and county borough councils, made schooling compulsory from 6 to 14 (with exemptions), and enabled schools to be vested in educational committees. By 1930, 430 Protestant voluntary schools were transferred. Catholic schools remained separate (with continuing State funding). Local-authority schools were intended to be non-denominational, but legislation (1925, 1930) provided for Bible teaching and denominational management. From 1938 it was planned to raise the leaving age.

The Education Act of 1947, influenced by the BUTLER EDUCATION ACT, developed free secondary education, instituting selection at age 11 by examination for academic (grammar) or intermediate school. Councils also took over TECHNICAL EDUCATION. The leaving age was raised to 15 in 1957, to 16 in 1972. In 1973, area boards replaced educational committees. From 1981 some 'integrated' (non-denominational) schools were opened, and a new curriculum in 1989 included study of Irish 'cultural traditions' to encourage tolerance. The '11-plus' examination was abolished in 2009, though many grammar schools introduced their own admission examinations. *See also* EDUCATION, IRELAND; UNIVERSITIES, IRELAND; HIGHER EDUCATION, EXPANSION OF.

EDUCATION, SCOTLAND Little is known about schools before the REFORMATION (1560). Cathedrals had song schools and (like major towns) GRAMMAR SCHOOLS for teaching Latin. References to rural schools are rare.

The Reformers aimed to establish an elementary school in each parish, grammar schools in BURGHS, and colleges in larger towns; but lack of funds limited implementation. Progress occurred mainly in the 17th century, with State support. In 1616 the Privy COUNCIL authorized a school for every PARISH. More significant was the 1696 statute which provided for proper funding of parish schools by landowners (*see* HERITORS). By the late 17th century many Lowland parishes had a school, although provision in remoter areas (e.g., GALLOWAY, SW Scotland) remained meagre. Burgh schools took children from age 7 or 8. They taught Latin and sometimes Greek and, by the early 18th century, such subjects as book-keeping, geography and navigation. Provision of schools in the HIGHLANDS was poor until well into the 18th century though the SOCIETY IN SCOTLAND FOR PROPAGATING CHRISTIAN KNOWLEDGE (founded 1709) established many schools there.

The education system expanded significantly in the 18th century, while the 19th century saw development of technical institutes (*see* TECHNICAL EDUCATION) and greater provision for working-class children in urban areas. The Education (Scotland) Act of 1872 transferred parish schools to elected parochial school boards and made education compulsory from age 5 to 13 (raised to 15 in 1918, to 16 in 1972). The 1918 Education Act integrated denominational schools (mainly Roman Catholic) into the State system. Secondary schools developed from the late 19th century and were replaced by COMPREHENSIVES in the 1960s and 1970s. *See also* UNIVERSITIES, SCOTLAND; LITERACY, SCOTLAND; LOCAL GOVERNMENTAL STRUCTURES, SCOTLAND; GOVERNMENT, SCOTLAND FROM 1707; HIGHER EDUCATION, EXPANSION OF.

EDUCATION, SOUTHERN IRELAND After independence (1922), school management remained mostly with religious authorities. The IRISH FREE STATE government assumed supervision from boards of elementary and intermediate (secondary) education (1922) and of technical education (1924). From 1926 education was compulsory for children aged 6–14 (with exemptions). A few vocational schools for children aged 14–16 were developed from 1930, though most children continued to attend only elementary school.

The State's priority was to use education for reviving Irish. From 1922 Irish had to be taught or used for an hour a day in elementary schools; from 1926 Irish was theoretically used for the first two years of schooling. It was included from 1929 in the voluntary primary certificate (compulsory from 1943). In intermediate education, a pass in Irish was required for the intermediate examination from 1928, and for the leaving examination from 1934.

From the 1960s intermediate education was expanded to aid economic development. Co-educational comprehensive schools were opened from 1966 alongside existing grant-aided voluntary schools (mostly run by religious orders) and vocational schools. Secondary education was free from 1967. The leaving age was raised to 15 in 1973, to 16 in 2000. Church influence diminished with the spread of school management boards from 1975 (established on statutory basis 1998). Curricula were extensively revised in the late 20th century. *See also* EDUCATION, IRELAND; UNIVERSITIES, IRELAND; TECHNICAL EDUCATION; HIGHER EDUCATION, EXPANSION OF.

EDUCATION, WALES In medieval Wales (6th–15th centuries) learning was mainly restricted to clergy or bards, though both taught pupils. By 1500 GRAMMAR SCHOOLS existed; more were founded from the 1540s – 27 are recorded before 1640. There were also private schools and tutors. Education catered mainly for sons of wealthier townspeople and farmers. (GENTRY sons were generally sent to England.) Development was impeded by the scattered population and lack of books in Welsh.

Between 1650 and 1870 religious groups periodically broadened opportunities. About 60 schools were started (mainly in towns) under the PURITAN-inspired Propagation Act of 1650, but disappeared after the RESTORATION (1660). The WELSH TRUST, promoted by Anglicans and DISSENTERS, briefly supported 300 schools, using English (1674–81). Between 1699 and 1737 the Anglican SOCIETY FOR PROMOTING CHRISTIAN KNOWLEDGE founded 96 schools (some using Welsh); but finance withered and schools closed. More successful were the 'circulating schools' of Griffiths JONES, which provided part-time teaching (mainly in Welsh) in over 1600 places (1731–1800). Then the Anglican National Society (founded 1811) sought to establish a school in every parish. By mid century, over 1000 Anglican schools existed, and by 1870 about 300 nonconformist British schools.

The 1870 Education Act advanced elementary education throughout Wales by requiring local boards to establish schools where none existed. Under the BALFOUR EDUCATION ACT (1902), elementary schools were transferred to county councils (*see* BALFOUR EDUCATION ACT AND WALES). Meanwhile the Welsh Intermediate Education Act of 1889 established COUNTY SCHOOLS, providing academic secondary education. These became grammar schools under the BUTLER EDUCATION ACT (1944), alongside new secondary modern schools. Both were replaced from the 1960s by comprehensive schools (*see* COMPREHENSIVE EDUCATION).

University education was absent until 1872 (though *see* DISSENTING ACADEMIES, WALES). Welshmen went abroad, many to Jesus College, OXFORD, England (founded 1571). *See also* UNIVERSITIES, WALES; HIGHER EDUCATION, EXPANSION OF.

EDUCATION ACT, 1870 *see* FORSTER'S EDUCATION ACT

EDUCATION ACT, 1902 *see* BALFOUR EDUCATION ACT; BALFOUR EDUCATION ACT AND WALES

EDUCATION ACT, 1944 *see* BUTLER EDUCATION ACT

EDUCATIONAL REVOLUTION A concept proposed in 1964 by English historian Lawrence Stone. He argued that in England between 1560 and 1640 the provision of education expanded and was available to males in most social classes. Almost half of the male population was alleged to have obtained basic LITERACY. The number of schools increased, including 278 new GRAMMAR SCHOOLS. Attendance at UNIVERSITIES grew from the 1560s, until in the 1630s about 2.5% of the relevant male cohort attended.

Critics argued that expansion was modest rather than revolutionary. Most men and women remained illiterate, and many boys lived beyond reach of secondary schools. The proportion of the male population attending university remained tiny. *See also* EDUCATION, ENGLAND.

EDUCATION AND LEARNING, ENGLAND BEFORE 1066 Latin-based education entered Anglo-Saxon culture with AUGUSTINE's Christian mission (from 597). Schools for clergy were founded at CANTERBURY and elsewhere. They spread as MINSTERS were founded. Subjects taught included scripture, metre and astronomy. The Canterbury school was reinvigorated by THEODORE (archbishop 669–90). Its pupils included Aldhelm (d. 709 or 710), author of treatises, poems and letters.

Learning also flourished in NORTHUMBRIA (NE England), often under Irish influence. Notable centres included Lindisfarne (from 635), Monkwearmouth-Jarrow (from late 7th century; *see* BENEDICT BISCOP, BEDE), and YORK (*see* ALCUIN). Teaching also took place at some royal courts.

Latin declined in the 9th century, and VIKING attacks caused schools to close. ALFRED of WESSEX (ruled 871–99) started a revival of learning by importing books and scholars (e.g., ASSER). It gathered strength from the mid 10th century, using Latin and the vernacular (Old English), as schools were founded at revived or new monasteries (*see* TENTH-CENTURY REFORMATION). Notable scholars included ÆLFRIC (d. *c.*1010) and Byrhtferth of Ramsey (*c.*970–*c.*1020). *See also* CONVERSION OF ANGLO-SAXONS.

EDUCATION IN WALES, INQUIRY INTO Initiated by Welsh-born MP William Williams, who sought to improve education in Wales, the inquiry was conducted in 1846 by three young English lawyers (members of the Church of England) who were ignorant of Wales. Their report (1847) asserted that Welsh people were dirty, ignorant, and promiscuous (etc.), were confined by Welsh, and that Welsh religion (nonconformity) was primitive. Outraged Welshmen castigated the report as 'the Treachery of the Blue Books'. The offence politicized Welsh nonconformity (especially Methodists), encouraged association of Welshness with nonconformity, and stimulated nationalism. *See also* EDUCATION, WALES; NONCONFORMITY AND DISSENT, WALES.

EDWARD I (b. 17 or 18 June 1239 at Westminster, Middlesex, England; d. 7 July 1307 at Burgh-by-Sands, Cumberland, England, aged 68). Eldest son of King HENRY III, Edward was given various lordships in 1254 (e.g., Ireland, Gascony). In 1260 he briefly supported Henry's opponents (reconciled spring 1260). He was captured by rebel barons at Lewes (Sussex) in 1264, but escaped in 1265 and defeated the rebels (*see* BARONIAL CONFLICT AND WARS). In 1271 he embarked on CRUSADE.

Edward succeeded as king of England on 20 Nov. 1272 but remained abroad until Aug. 1274. During 1275–90 he instituted LEGAL REFORMS and fiscal improvements (*see* SUBSIDIES). In 1276–7 he crushed rebellion in Wales (*see* ABERCONWY, TREATY OF). Another rebellion in 1282 resulted in further land seizures (*see* WALES, ENGLISH CONQUEST OF).

In 1292 Edward settled the contested succession to the Scottish kingship (*see* GREAT CAUSE). Conflict with France erupted in 1294, though Edward was diverted by rebellion in Wales (crushed 1295) and Scotland (seized Scottish kingship 1296). In 1297 Edward's demands in England for military service and taxation almost caused civil war (*see*

REMONSTRANCES), and he had to make a truce with France (1298; *see* GASCON WAR). From 1298 to 1305 Edward led campaigns against Scotland. He died while travelling to Scotland. *See also* WINCHELSEY, ROBERT; SCOTTISH–ENGLISH RELATIONS 1290 TO 1357; EDWARD I AND IRELAND; EMPIRE, ENGLISH IDEAS OF, 11TH–15TH CENTURIES.

EDWARD I AND IRELAND While heir to the English throne, Edward was granted most of Ireland by his father, HENRY III (14 Feb. 1254), though Henry remained titular 'lord of Ireland'. Edward never visited Ireland, but exploited it as a source of troops, revenues and foodstuffs. Troops from Ireland helped him to defeat Simon de Montfort at Evesham in 1265 (*see* BARONIAL CONFLICT AND WARS). As king (1272–1307), Edward moved Irish troops to Wales (1282–3), Scotland, GASCONY and Flanders.

Edward's policy reduced the resources available to the Dublin-based government for sustaining the English colony in Ireland, resulting in increased lawlessness. It thereby also assisted the GAELIC REVIVAL. *See also* IRELAND, ENGLISH COLONY IN, 13TH–15TH CENTURIES.

EDWARD II (b. 25 April 1284 at Caernarfon, Caernarfonshire, Wales; d. possibly 21 Sept. 1327 at Berkeley, Gloucestershire, England, aged 43). After succeeding EDWARD I (father) as king of England and lord of Ireland (7 July 1307), Edward recalled Piers GAVESTON from exile and made him earl of Cornwall. He married ISABELLA, from France (Jan. 1308). Gaveston's prominence at Edward's coronation (Feb.) angered magnates who insisted on banishment (June 1308–June 1309). Unrest continued. Parliament imposed reforming ORDINANCES (1311). Gaveston was exiled again (Nov.–Jan. 1312) and executed (June).

After Edward was defeated at BANNOCKBURN, Scotland (June 1314), he conceded control of government to opponents led by THOMAS OF LANCASTER, though Lancaster withdrew (May 1316). In 1318 Edward became intimate with Hugh DESPENSER and his father Hugh. But they were banished (Aug. 1321–early 1322). From late 1321 Edward confronted opponents. His supporters executed Lancaster (March 1322); Parliament revoked the Ordinances (May).

Edward's favouritism for the Despensers antagonized Isabella. In late 1326, after she and Roger MORTIMER invaded England from France, the Despensers were executed and Edward was imprisoned. Parliament deposed him (13 Jan. 1327) and he abdicated (21 Jan.). Though his death was reported in Sept., he possibly survived as a fugitive until 1341. Succeeded by EDWARD III. *See also* SCOTTISH–ENGLISH RELATIONS 1290 TO 1357.

EDWARD III (b. 13 Nov. 1312 at Windsor, Berkshire, England; d. 21 June 1377 at Sheen, Surrey, England, aged

65). In 1325 Edward did homage to the king of France for GASCONY for King EDWARD II (father). He returned with the invasion force of Queen ISABELLA (Sept. 1326). Declared regent (26 Oct.), he succeeded as king of England and lord of Ireland (25 Jan. 1327) following his father's deposition. Isabella and Roger MORTIMER dominated government until Edward overthrew them (Oct. 1330).

In the 1330s Edward campaigned in Scotland, briefly restoring Edward BALLIOL. In 1337, following disputes over Gascony, Edward declared war against France, initiating the HUNDRED YEARS WAR. He defeated the French fleet at Sluys (June 1340). In 1346 he invaded France and was victorious at Crécy (Aug.), and (1347) captured CALAIS. From 1347 to 1355 he enacted legislation in England (e.g., Statutes of LABOURERS, PROVISORS, PRAEMUNIRE) and founded the GARTER fellowship. Further warfare in France in 1355 and 1359–60 ended with the BRÉTIGNY treaty (1360).

In the 1360s political tensions increased and peace collapsed (1369). In the 1370s Edward was senile. Government was influenced by his mistress Alice PERRERS and JOHN OF GAUNT (from 1374) until challenged by the GOOD PARLIAMENT (1376). Edward was succeeded by RICHARD II. *See also* LANCASTER, HENRY EARL OF; SCOTTISH–ENGLISH RELATIONS 1290 TO 1357; EDWARD THE BLACK PRINCE.

EDWARD IV (b. 28 April 1442 at Rouen, Normandy; d. 9 April 1483 at Westminster, Middlesex, England, aged 40). Edward supported his father Richard, duke of YORK, against King HENRY VI of England (*see* YORKIST–LANCASTRIAN CONFLICT). At York's death (30 Dec. 1460), Edward succeeded as duke and 'YORKIST' leader. After defeating royalists ('LANCASTRIANS') at Mortimer's Cross, Herefordshire (2 Feb. 1461), he sought the throne, proclaiming himself king (4 March). Following heavy defeat of Lancastrians at Towton, Yorkshire (29 March), he returned south for coronation (28 June), also claiming lordship of Ireland. Henry fled to Scotland.

Edward's secret marriage to Elizabeth WOODVILLE (1 May 1464, publicized Sept.) and favouritism for her family aroused opposition. In 1469 the earl of WARWICK attempted deposition; a second attempt (Sept. 1470) forced Edward into exile in Flanders (3 Oct.). Henry VI was restored.

Edward returned on 14 March 1471, defeated Warwick at Barnet, Hertfordshire (14 April), and Lancastrians at Tewkesbury, Gloucestershire (4 May), and regained the throne. (Henry was afterwards killed.)

Edward increased his income through improvements in financial administration. In July 1475 he invaded France but failed to draw Louis XI to battle (concluded treaty of PICQUIGNY). In 1478 he had the duke of CLARENCE (brother) executed for TREASON. Succeeded by EDWARD V. *See also* NEW MONARCHY, ENGLAND.

EDWARD V (b. 2 Nov. 1470 at Westminster, Middlesex, England; d. between June and September 1483 at London, England, aged 12). Edward Plantagenet succeeded his father EDWARD IV as king of England and lord of Ireland on 9 April 1483, aged 12. As he travelled to WESTMINSTER to be crowned, he was wrested from control of the WOODVILLE FAMILY by his uncle Richard, duke of Gloucester (30 April). Edward was lodged at the Tower of London (mid May; joined by brother Richard, duke of Norfolk, on 16 June). He was deposed (25 June), because his parents' marriage was allegedly invalid. Gloucester became king (see RICHARD III). Edward and his brother were almost certainly murdered.

EDWARD VI (b. 12 Oct. 1537 at Hampton Court, Middlesex, England; d. 6 July 1553 at Greenwich, Kent, England, aged 15). The son of HENRY VIII and Jane Seymour, Edward succeeded his father as king of England and Ireland on 28 Jan. 1547 aged 9. He was controlled during 1547–9 by a Protestant faction led by a protector, his maternal uncle Edward, duke of SOMERSET. Somerset continued Henry's war in Scotland (1547) and allowed Archbishop Thomas CRANMER to introduce Protestant reforms in the Church, including a CATECHISM (1548) and liturgy (Jan. 1549). The latter provoked the PRAYER-BOOK REBELLION.

On Somerset's fall (Oct. 1549) the earl of Warwick seized control of Edward and ruled as chief minister (created duke of NORTHUMBERLAND Oct. 1551). He ended the Scottish war (1550) and continued to promote Protestant reforms. Edward's final illness, from May 1553, caused Northumberland to alter the succession (see GREY, LADY JANE). The failure of his scheme (July 1553) allowed the succession of Edward's Catholic half-sister MARY I. See also REFORMATION, ENGLAND/IRELAND.

EDWARD VII (b. 9 Nov. 1841 at Buckingham Palace, London, England; d. 6 May 1910 at Buckingham Palace, aged 68). The eldest son of Queen VICTORIA, Edward was created PRINCE OF WALES soon after his birth. His pleasure-loving nature dismayed his parents, but others appeared tolerant of his devotion to women, high society and horse-racing. So did Alexandra of Denmark, his wife from 1863.

Personal charm and love of pageantry proved assets when Edward succeeded as king of Great Britain and Ireland, and emperor of India, on 22 Jan. 1901, aged 59. Having cosmopolitan tendencies, he acquired a reputation for diplomacy, but his political understanding was shallow (partly because Victoria had long excluded him from official business). In the crisis over the PEOPLE'S BUDGET (1909–10), he refused to create new peers until a general election had tested public attitudes. Succeeded by GEORGE V. See also ESHER, 2ND VISCOUNT.

EDWARD VIII (b. 23 June 1894 at Richmond, Surrey, England; d. 28 May 1972 at Paris, France, aged 77). The eldest son of George, duke of York (later GEORGE V), Prince Edward was informally known as David. Having had a naval education, he was a British Army staff officer during WORLD WAR I (1914–18). Between 1919 and 1925 he made several successful tours of the British Empire. Seemingly impatient of formality, he appeared especially popular with his own generation. Otherwise a playboy, he publicly expressed concern about poverty (see GREAT DEPRESSION, IMPACT ON GREAT BRITAIN).

Edward succeeded as king of Great Britain and Ireland on 20 Jan. 1936 but, determined to marry the American divorcée Wallis Simpson, he was compelled to abdicate (11 Dec.). Afterwards, as duke of Windsor, he lived mainly in France, though acted as governor of The Bahamas (1940–5), during WORLD WAR II. See also ABDICATION CRISIS; MONCKTON, WALTER.

EDWARDS, ALFRED GEORGE (b. 2 Nov. 1848 at Llanymawddwy, Merionethshire, Wales; d. 22 July 1937 at St Asaph, Flintshire, Wales, aged 88). Bishop of ST ASAPH from 1889 (to 1934), Edwards vigorously opposed DISESTABLISHMENT of the Church of England in Wales. When it became probable (1914), he advocated the formation of a separate Welsh Church and province and was elected first archbishop of the Church in WALES (7 April 1920).

EDWARDS, OWEN MORGAN (b. 25 Dec. 1858 at Llanuwchllyn, Merionethshire, Wales; d. 15 May 1920 at Llanuwchllyn, aged 61). A tutor at Lincoln College, OXFORD, from 1889, Edwards published popular Welsh books and magazines on Welsh history and traditions, contributing to national awareness. From 1907, as chief inspector of schools for Wales under the Welsh Department of the Board of Education (see DEVOLUTION, WALES), he attacked rote learning and pressed for education in Welsh. He was knighted in 1916. See also LITERARY REVIVAL, WELSH; WELSH LEAGUE OF YOUTH.

EDWARD THE BLACK PRINCE (b. 15 June 1330 at Woodstock, Oxfordshire, England; d. 8 June 1376 at Westminster, Middlesex, England, aged 45). The eldest son of King EDWARD III, Edward was created duke of Cornwall (1337) – England's first duke – and prince of Wales (1343). He fought in France under his father (1346–7), participating in victory at Crécy (1346). He was later a victorious commander at Poitiers (1356).

After Aquitaine was ceded to England (1360), Edward was created prince of Aquitaine (1362). In 1367 he intervened in Castile (Spain), defeating enemies of Pedro the Cruel at Nájera and restoring Pedro as king. But his forces failed to suppress a revolt in Aquitaine (1368–70). He returned to England in 1371, a sick man, and surrendered Aquitaine to his father (Oct. 1372). He predeceased King Edward, who was succeeded by the Black Prince's son (see RICHARD II). The prince's nickname dates from 1569; it refers to an alleged preference for black armour. *See also* HUNDRED YEARS WAR.

EDWARD THE CONFESSOR (b. c.1004 at Islip, Oxfordshire, England; d. 4 or 5 Jan. 1066 at Westminster, Middlesex, England, aged about 61). A son of King ÆTHEL-RED II and Emma, Edward went to NORMANDY with his mother in 1013 (see EMMA). He returned permanently in 1041 and succeeded HARTHACNUT (died 8 June 1042).

Like his predecessors, Edward favoured GODWINE, earl of Wessex, and married Godwine's daughter EDITH (1045). But in 1051 Godwine defied Edward's order to punish men of Dover (SE England) for fighting with retainers of Eustace of Boulogne (Edward's former brother-in-law). The GOD-WINE FAMILY fled (1051), and Edward made Robert of Jumièges, a Norman and archbishop of Canterbury, his leading adviser. When the Godwine family forced Edward to reinstate them (1052), Robert fled.

After Godwine's death (1053), his son HAROLD became Edward's principal adviser. Harold challenged incursions by the Welsh king GRUFFUDD AP LLYWELYN (d. 1063), while Edward rebuilt WESTMINSTER Abbey. Edward died without direct heir, having allegedly nominated Harold as successor despite the claim of WILLIAM, duke of Normandy. In 1161 Edward was canonized and titled 'Confessor'.

EDWARD THE ELDER (b. in 870s in Wessex; d. 17 July 924 at Farndon, Mercia). Edward succeeded his father ALFRED as king in Oct. 899. He ruled WESSEX (S England) while his brother-in-law Æthelred (d. 911) ruled western MERCIA (W Midlands) probably as a subordinate EALDOR-MAN. (Former English areas elsewhere were ruled by Danes.) Edward's accession was opposed by a cousin, Æthelwold, who took refuge with Danes. Æthelwold attacked Wessex until he was killed in battle (902).

From 909 West Saxons and Mercians attacked the Danes. In 910 they crushed northern Danes at TETTENHALL, which enabled them to conquer eastern Mercia and E England. Edward collaborated with his sister ÆTHELFLÆD, 'Lady of the Mercians' (d. June 918), and built burhs (fortified centres). In Dec. 918 he deposed Æthelflæd's successor in Mercia, Ælfwynn, ending Mercia's autonomy.

By late 918 Edward's territory extended to the Humber estuary. In 920 rulers of YORK, NORTHUMBRIA, STRATH-CLYDE and Alba (modern Scotland, N of the FORTH–CLYDE ISTHMUS), meeting at Bakewell (N Mercia), acknowledged his overlordship. Edward died while campaigning against rebellious men of Chester (NW Mercia). He was called 'the Elder' from c.1000 to distinguish him from EDWARD THE MARTYR. Succeeded by ATHELSTAN. *See also* ENGLAND, FORMATION OF; BURGHAL HIDAGE; SHIRE; WINCHESTER.

EDWARD THE MARTYR (b. between 957 and 960; d. 18 March 978 at Corfe, Dorset, England, aged about 19). A son of EDGAR, king of England, by his first union, Edward succeeded as king (by late 975) thanks to support from DUNSTAN, archbishop of CANTERBURY. His accession was opposed by some nobles and clergy (including Edgar's widow ÆLFTHRYTH and possibly Bishop ÆTHELWOLD), who had favoured Ælfthryth's son (and Edward's younger half-brother) ÆTHELRED.

Edward was murdered by Ælfthryth's retainers while visiting Ælfthryth and Æthelred. In 980 his body was reinterred at Shaftesbury Abbey (Dorset), where it reputedly worked miracles. Edward was succeeded by Æthelred, and called 'the Martyr' from c.1000.

EDWIN (b. 584 or 585; d. 12 Oct. 633 at Hatfield Chase, Deira, aged 48). King of DEIRA and BERNICIA (NE England) 616 or 617–33. In 604 Edwin, a member of Deira's royal kindred, fled into exile when King Æthelfrith of Bernicia took over Deira. Edwin returned in 616 with his protector, RÆDWALD of East Anglia, who killed Æthelfrith (in Deira). Edwin became king of Deira and Bernicia.

After Rædwald's death (between 616 and 627) Edwin became overking of Anglo-Saxon kingdoms. In 625 he married the Christian princess Æthelburg from KENT, who was accompanied by the bishop Paulinus. According to BEDE he reluctantly accepted baptism (12 April 627 at YORK). He made Paulinus bishop of York. He was killed by PENDA of Mercia and CADWALLON AP CADFAN of Gwynedd. (Paulinus returned to Kent.) *See also* CONVER-SION OF ANGLO-SAXONS; KINGSHIP, ANGLO-SAXON; ELMET; OSWALD.

EGBERT (fl. from 786; d. 839). Egbert was possibly from KENT (SE England), then subordinate to MERCIA (C England). In 802 he seized the kingship of WESSEX (S England). In 825 the West Saxons repulsed a Mercian invasion, winning victory at 'Ellendun' (Wroughton, Wiltshire). Egbert then (826) took control of Mercia's subordinate territories in S and SE England. His son Æthelwulf expelled the Mercian subking of KENT; afterwards the men of ESSEX, Surrey and SUSSEX submitted. EAST ANGLIA (E England) also acknowledged Egbert's authority.

In 829 Egbert conquered Mercia, expelling King Wiglaf, and obtained acknowledgement of his authority from NORTHUMBRIA. He was probably expelled from Mercia in 830, but retained S and SE England. In the late 830s he defended Wessex against Danish incursions. Succeeded by ÆTHELWULF. The Wessex-English-British royal family is descended from Egbert. *See also* KINGSHIP, ANGLO-SAXON.

EGFRITH (b. 645 or 646; d. 20 May 685 at Dún Nechtain, Pictland, aged 39). In 670 Egfrith, a Bernician, succeeded his father OSWIU as king of BERNICIA and DEIRA (NE England/SE modern Scotland). He ruled Deira through a subking, Ælfwine, after whose death (679) the kingdoms remained united (*see* NORTHUMBRIA).

Egfrith expanded Bernicia to its greatest extent by taking over LINDSEY to the SE (by 675) and probably absorbing ELMET and RHEGED to the W. But he was defeated by Æthelred of Mercia in 679 (battle of the Trent) and lost Lindsey. He attempted to exert authority to the N and W: he founded a bishopric for the southern PICTS (681) at Abercorn (W of EDINBURGH), and raided Ireland (684). In 685, while invading Pictland, he was attacked at DÚN NECHTAIN and killed. The defeat ended Northumbrian dominance over the southern Pictish area. *See also* KINGSHIP, ANGLO-SAXON; BRIDEI SON OF BELI.

EGYPT A country in NE Africa which was formerly under British control. In the mid 19th century Egypt was technically a province of the OTTOMAN EMPIRE but was effectively independent (under khedives from 1867). Government bankruptcy in 1876 led to Anglo-French financial management. British troops intervened in 1882 to suppress a nationalist revolt, and remained to protect the SUEZ CANAL (constructed 1859–69), while Evelyn BARING governed the country (from 1883).

When Great Britain went to war with the Ottoman Empire in 1914 it declared a PROTECTORATE over Egypt; but to appease nationalist feeling it recognized nominal independence in 1922 (under a king), retaining control over defence and foreign policy. Approx. population in 1921: 13,387,000. The protectorate was replaced in 1936 with a 20-year alliance, which retained British military protection of the canal zone. The British resisted attacks on Egypt during WORLD WAR II (1942). The withdrawal of the British garrison protecting the canal in June 1956 precipitated the SUEZ CRISIS. *See also* SUDAN.

ÉIRE *see* SOUTHERN IRELAND FROM 1922

EISTEDDFOD (Welsh, meaning 'Gathering' or 'Congress'). A gathering of Welsh poets. Gatherings are recorded from 1176 and the term *eisteddfod* was used for assemblies in the 15th and 16th centuries. By the 18th century, after the decline of the bardic tradition (i.e., professional poets), gatherings were private, sometimes drunken meetings of poets.

New poetry festivals were launched in 1789 and provincial eisteddfods were held in the early 19th century. The Carmarthen eisteddfod in 1819 also included a meeting of the druidical *gorsedd* founded by Edward WILLIAMS, and his druidical ceremonies were performed at eisteddfods from 1858 onwards. A National Eisteddfod was held intermittently from 1861 and near annually from 1881, following the foundation of the National Eisteddfod Assocation (1880). In the 21st century it remained the principal cultural gathering of Welsh-speaking Welsh, awarding prizes for poetry and music and hosting druidical ceremonies. *See also* WELSH NATIONAL SOCIETIES; WELSH LEAGUE OF YOUTH.

EL ALAMEIN, (SECOND) BATTLE OF A decisive battle in NE Africa, 23 Oct.–4 Nov. 1942, during WORLD WAR II. British and Commonwealth troops of the Eighth Army (commanded by Bernard MONTGOMERY), initially based at El Alamein (W of Alexandria, Egypt), forced Germans and Italians into a retreat which ended in their expulsion from Africa (May 1943).

ELDON, EARL OF (b. 4 June 1751 at Newcastle upon Tyne, Northumberland, England; d. 13 Jan. 1838 at London, England, aged 86). A coal merchant's son, John Scott became a barrister. An MP from 1783, he served as solicitor-general (1788–93) and attorney-general (1793–9) in the ministry of William PITT the Younger. He promoted repressive domestic legislation (e.g., Treasonable Practices Act, 1795). In 1799 he was appointed lord chief justice and created Lord Eldon.

Eldon served as lord CHANCELLOR 1801–27 (except 1806–7), in the ministries of Henry ADDINGTON, Pitt, the duke of PORTLAND, Spencer PERCEVAL, and the earl of LIVERPOOL. He was created earl of Eldon in 1821. He opposed CATHOLIC EMANCIPATION and legal reforms, and in the early 1830s campaigned against PARLIAMENTARY REFORM.

ELEANOR OF AQUITAINE (b. *c.*1122, probably near Bordeaux, Aquitaine; d. 31 March 1204 at Poitiers, Aquitaine, or Fontevrault, Anjou, aged about 82). Inheritor of the duchy of Aquitaine (W France, April 1137), Eleanor married (July) King Louis VII of France (ruler from Aug.). After the marriage was annulled (March 1152) she married (May) Henry, count of Anjou and duke of NORMANDY. The marriage gave Henry control of her lands. (He also succeeded as king of England in 1154; *see* HENRY II.) Their eight children included HENRY THE YOUNG KING, RICHARD and JOHN.

Eleanor supported the REVOLT OF 1173–4 against her husband. Afterwards she was confined (1174–83). Following Henry's death (1189) Eleanor was involved in political affairs in the ANGEVIN EMPIRE. In 1199 and 1202 she rebuffed attacks in John's Continental territories by ARTHUR OF BRITTANY (her grandson). Eleanor was renowned for her patronage of troubadours.

ELECTRICITY INDUSTRY AND ELECTRIFICATION, GREAT BRITAIN From the 1870s, dynamos driven by steam engines provided electricity at individual premises, mainly for lighting. The 1882 Electricity Lighting Act (for UK), allowing cables below or over public streets, encouraged local generating stations. By 1913 there were 230 power-supply companies, 327 municipal suppliers, and private sources, mainly supplying urban areas. Coal-fired steam turbines were widely used (invented 1884).

The 1919 Electricity (Supply) Act began rationalization by establishing an Electricity Commission (regulator) and regional 'joint electricity authorities' (suppliers). The Central Electricity Board (instigated 1927) constructed a National Grid to provide country-wide supply (completed 1933, fully operational 1938), reduced suppliers and constructed new generating stations, mostly coal-fired. By 1939 electricity reached two-thirds of houses though only 10% of farms. (Rural electrification continued until the 1970s.)

In 1948 the industry was nationalized (under 1947 Electricity Act), with a British Electricity Authority (BEA) responsible for generation and distribution, and 14 regional boards as suppliers. (The North of Scotland Hydro-Electric Board, created 1943, remained separate.) The BEA was replaced in 1954 by a Central Electricity Authority (CEA) for England and Wales and South of Scotland Electricity Board (generation and supply). Another reorganization (1957) replaced the CEA with the Central Electricity Generating Board, which owned the Grid and sold power to boards. An Electricity Council co-ordinated policy making. Following restructuring, most of the industry was privatized in 1990–1.

Britain's first nuclear power station supplied the Grid from 1956. By 1989, 19 stations were operational (nuclear power peaked in 1997 at 27% of supply). From the early 1990s, gas increasingly replaced coal for power-generation, and 'renewables' (e.g., wind turbines) were promoted. Scotland's electricity system was integrated with England and Wales in 2005.

ELECTRICITY INDUSTRY AND ELECTRIFICA-TION, IRELAND Power stations, using imported coal, were developed from 1892 mainly by urban authorities. Following the PARTITION OF IRELAND (1921), the IRISH FREE STATE expanded availability of power with the SHANNON HYDROELECTRIC SCHEME (constructed 1925–9) and foundation of the Electricity Supply Board (1927) which gradually established a monopoly of production and supply. Most urban populations were supplied by 1943. Electricity was extended across rural areas mainly in the 1950s–60s. Peat was also used for power generation from the 1950s, oil from the 1970s, natural gas from the late 1970s, wind from the 1990s. An Electricity Board of Northern Ireland (founded 1931) likewise acquired generating capacity, and extended supplies to rural areas from the late 1940s. From the 1990s the industry was extensively reorganized throughout Ireland, including the creation in 2007 of an all-Ireland wholesale market.

ELECTRONIC COMMUNICATIONS, GREAT BRITAIN
The world's first effective electrical telegraph system was inaugurated in July 1839 (on Great Western Railway), following 70 years of experimental transmission of messages by electrical impulses. Telegraphs became integral to railway operations. Public services developed from the 1840s, and a cable was laid across the English Channel in 1850. An effective connection with N America was inaugurated in 1866 (see ELECTRONIC COMMUNICATIONS, IRELAND). Public systems were nationalized under the Post Office in 1869. Use of telegraph services declined steeply in the 1960s.

A practical telephone (apparatus for speech transmission) was patented in 1876–7 in the USA (see BELL, ALEXANDER GRAHAM), and used in Britain from 1879 (starting in London). Judged a form of telegraphy (1880), telephony was assigned to the Post Office, which licensed companies and then acquired a near monopoly (by 1912). Subscribers reached 1 million by 1922, 3 million by 1939 (mainly business users and wealthier individuals). In 1985 there were over 20 million lines. Electro-mechanical direct dialling, developed from the 1920s, was replaced by electronic equipment from the 1980s. The Post Office's telephone business was separated in 1980 as British Telecommunications (privatized 1984). Mobile telephone services started in 1985 and rapidly became popular. Electronic facsimile ('fax') machines became widely used from the late 1970s, and electronic mail ('email') from the mid 1990s.

Wireless (or radio) telegraphy was patented by Guglielmo MARCONI in 1896, and from 1900 developed for ship-to-shore communications. The development of radio telephony (in Germany from 1906) enabled public RADIO BROADCASTING to start in 1922.

ELECTRONIC COMMUNICATIONS, IRELAND
Telegraph lines were installed from 1844, including the first cross-channel line in 1852 (to Holyhead, NW Wales) and the first durable trans-Atlantic line in 1866 (from Valentia Island, Co. Kerry). The first telephone exchange was established in DUBLIN in 1880. Telephone communications with Britain began in 1893. In 1918 Ireland had 12,000 telephones. Mobile telephones were introduced in both NORTHERN IRELAND and the Republic in 1985, and electronic mail ('email') became widespread from the mid 1990s. See also BROADCASTING, IRELAND.

ELGAR, EDWARD (b. 2 June 1857 at Broadheath, Worcestershire, England; d. 23 Feb. 1934 at Worcester, Worcestershire, aged 76). Elgar became the first internationally renowned English composer since Henry PURCELL (d. 1695), despite a lack of formal musical training. His first successful work was *Enigma Variations* for orchestra (performed 1899). His orchestral *Pomp and Circumstance March* no. 1, with added words ('Land of Hope and Glory', 1902), became an unofficial national anthem. His other works include *The Dream of Gerontius* (1900), a setting for choir and orchestra of extracts from a poem by Cardinal John Henry NEWMAN (Elgar was a Roman Catholic), and concertos for violin (1910) and cello (1919). Elgar was knighted in 1904.

ELIAS, JOHN (b. April or May 1774 at Abererch, Caernarfonshire, Wales; d. 8 June 1841 at Fron, Anglesey, Wales, aged 67). A charismatic preacher widely known in Wales from 1794, Elias was among the first ministers ordained for the CALVINISTIC METHODIST church (1811). A high Calvinist, he influenced the church's Confession (1823) and Constitutional Deed (1826), and as a TORY encouraged conservative attitudes, opposing, for example, CATHOLIC EMANCIPATION, PARLIAMENTARY REFORM, and CHARTISM. He was called the 'Pope of Anglesey'. *See also* NONCONFORMITY AND DISSENT, WALES.

ELIOT, GEORGE (b. 22 Nov. 1819 at Chilvers Coton, Warwickshire, England; d. 22 Dec. 1880 at Chelsea, Middlesex, England, aged 61). From an EVANGELICAL background, Mary Ann Evans became sceptical about Christian teaching. In London from 1851, she was sub-editor of the *Westminster Review* 1851–3. From 1854 she lived with the writer G.H. Lewes (1817–78), who was separated from his wife. From 1857 Evans published fiction under the pseudonym George Eliot. Most of her novels, pre-eminently *Middlemarch* (1871–2), are set in provincial England and explore the psychology of individuals and their relationships. *See also* ENGLISH LITERATURE, ENGLAND; NOVEL.

ELIOT, T.S. (b. 26 Sept. 1888 at St Louis, Missouri, USA; d. 4 Jan. 1965 at London, England, aged 76). A student of philosophy, Thomas Stearns Eliot studied at Harvard, Paris and OXFORD Universities. Resident in London from 1915, he became a poet, playwright, and publisher. In 1927 he was baptized in the Church of ENGLAND and acquired British citizenship. Eliot became famous with *The Waste Land* (1922), a long poem evoking post-war desolation. Also a critic, he argued that English literary culture had become impoverished since the 17th century. His poems about time and eternity, *Four Quartets* (1943), are considered his finest. A central figure in modernism, Eliot was awarded the 1948 Nobel Prize in Literature. *See also* ENGLISH LITERATURE, ENGLAND.

ELIZABETH, QUEEN (b. 4 Aug. 1900 at St Paul's Walden, Hertfordshire, England; d. 30 March 2002 at Windsor, Berkshire, England, aged 101). Of Scottish descent, Lady Elizabeth Bowes-Lyon in 1923 married Albert, duke of York, the younger son of King GEORGE V. She was privately dismayed in 1936 when York unexpectedly became king (as GEORGE VI) of Great Britain and Ireland and emperor of India, following the ABDICATION CRISIS. She provided

important support for a diffident ruler, helping to invest the monarchy with an attractive family image. After the king's death (1952), as the 'Queen Mother', she supported her daughter ELIZABETH II for 50 years. Her social ease and devotion to public duties generated great popularity.

ELIZABETH I (b. 7 Sept. 1533 at Greenwich, Kent, England; d. 24 March 1603 at Richmond, Surrey, England, aged 69). The daughter of King HENRY VIII and Anne BOLEYN, Elizabeth succeeded her Catholic half-sister MARY I (d. 17 Nov. 1558) as queen of England and Ireland. William CECIL served as chief minister until his death (1598). In 1559 they restored Protestantism to the English Church with Elizabeth as 'supreme governor' (*see* ELIZABETHAN SETTLEMENT). England assisted Protestants to remove French troops from Scotland (1560).

During the 1560s–70s possible husbands were considered for Elizabeth. They included: her favourite the earl of LEICESTER; Archduke Charles of Austria (negotiations 1563–7); Henri, duke of Anjou, France (considered 1570–2); François, duke of Alençon and Anjou, France (intermittently considered 1572–81). Elizabeth's throne was claimed by MARY, QUEEN OF SCOTS, whose asylum in England from 1568 provoked CATHOLIC PLOTS. Mary was executed in 1587.

Elizabeth sought to avoid foreign wars, but from 1585 aided Protestants fighting the Spanish in the Netherlands. There was open war with Spain 1588–1604 (*see* ANGLO-SPANISH WAR).

The 1590s saw rivalry between Elizabeth's new favourite, the earl of ESSEX, and Robert CECIL. It ended with Essex's rebellion (1601). Elizabeth was succeeded by JAMES VI/I. *See also* PURITANISM, ENGLAND; IRELAND, ENGLISH CONQUEST, 16TH CENTURY.

ELIZABETH I AND IRELAND *see* IRELAND, ENGLISH CONQUEST, 16TH CENTURY; REFORMATION, IRELAND

ELIZABETH II (b. 21 April 1926 at Buckingham Palace, London, England). Eldest daughter of Albert, duke of York, Elizabeth became heir apparent in 1936 when her father unexpectedly became king of Great Britain and Ireland (*see* GEORGE VI). In 1947 she married Philip Mountbatten (created duke of Edinburgh).

Succeeding as ruler, aged 25, on 6 Feb. 1952 (in KENYA), Elizabeth performed royal duties with dignity, including her role as head of the COMMONWEALTH. Her Silver Jubilee (1977) was a popular celebration. But on 24 Nov. 1992, following the marital troubles of her children Andrew (separation), Anne (divorce) and CHARLES (allegations), and a destructive fire at WINDSOR Castle (20 Nov.), she admitted that she had endured an 'annus horribilis' (Latin, meaning 'horrible year'). Under public pressure, she agreed to pay tax on her private income. The marital difficulties of Prince

Charles and his popular wife DIANA (d. 1997) continued to weaken the monarchy.

Elizabeth's Golden Jubilee (2002), the marriage of her grandson William (2011; *see* CAMBRIDGE, WILLIAM DUKE OF), and her Diamond Jubilee (2012) raised the monarchy's popularity. The queen contributed to the PEACE PROCESS for Northern Ireland by making a State visit to the Republic of Ireland (17–20 May 2011). On 9 Sept. 2015 Elizabeth became Britain's longest-ruling monarch. *See also* ELIZABETH, QUEEN.

ELIZABETHAN SETTLEMENT Term used for the alteration of religion in England and Wales in 1559, following the accession of Queen ELIZABETH I, which re-established the Church of ENGLAND. The Settlement was planned by William CECIL and the queen, and imposed by PARLIAMENT and the queen, after initial rejection by the House of Lords.

An Act of Supremacy restored royal authority over the Church (in place of the Pope), designating the monarch 'supreme governor'. The Act of Uniformity reinstated the English PRAYER BOOK of 1552 with modifications to conciliate conservatives. Later royal injunctions required the use of traditional clerical vestments, including the surplice. The Settlement combined a traditional structure with Protestant theology. *See also* REFORMATION, ENGLAND; PARKER, MATTHEW; PURITANISM, ENGLAND; JEWEL, JOHN; HOOKER, RICHARD.

ELIZABETHAN SETTLEMENT, IRELAND In 1560, following the accession of Queen ELIZABETH I, Ireland's Parliament reinstituted a State Church under royal authority. An Act of Supremacy made Ireland's ruler 'supreme governor' of the Church of IRELAND (in place of the Pope), and required acknowledgement of this from clergy and some civil officers by an oath of supremacy. An Act of Uniformity prescribed the English PRAYER BOOK (1559 version) and required attendance at the reformed Church. *See also* REFORMATION, IRELAND; RECUSANCY, IRELAND.

ELIZABETH OF YORK (b. 11 Feb. 1466 at Westminster, Middlesex, England; d. 11 Feb. 1503 at London, England, aged 37). Elizabeth was the eldest child of the YORKIST king EDWARD IV and Elizabeth WOODVILLE. In May 1483, after her brother EDWARD V (a minor) was seized by their uncle Richard, duke of Gloucester, she entered sanctuary at Westminster Abbey with her mother. But after Richard usurped the throne (26 June; *see* RICHARD III), she eventually became reconciled (1 March 1484) and left sanctuary.

After Richard was deposed by the LANCASTRIAN claimant Henry Tudor (1485), Elizabeth married Henry (18 Jan. 1486; *see* HENRY VII), uniting their lineages. Their children included Prince ARTHUR and HENRY VIII. *See also* YORKIST–LANCASTRIAN CONFLICT.

ELLIOT, WALTER (b. 19 Sept. 1888 at Lanark, Lanarkshire, Scotland; d. 8 Jan. 1958 at Bonchester Bridge, Roxburghshire, Scotland, aged 69). Educated in science and medicine at GLASGOW University, Elliot served as a Conservative MP for Scottish constituencies (1918–58, except 1923–4, 1945–6). After holding junior posts at the SCOTTISH OFFICE (1923, 1924–9), he became minister for agriculture (1932), secretary of state for Scotland (1936) and minister for health (1938). He remained in government under Neville CHAMBERLAIN (from 1937), despite doubts about Chamberlain's APPEASEMENT policy. For his apparent inconsistency he was dropped by Winston CHURCHILL in 1940. Elliot later held many honorary public positions.

ELLIS, TOM (b. 16 Feb. 1859 at Cefnddwysarn, Merionethshire, Wales; d. 5 April 1899 at Cannes, SE France, aged 40). MP for Merionethshire 1886–99, Liberal chief whip 1894–9; the most revered figure in late 19th-century Welsh Liberal politics. Ellis pioneered causes later pursued by David LLOYD GEORGE (Church DISESTABLISHMENT, Welsh DEVOLUTION, land reform).

ELMET A British (Brittonic-speaking) kingdom in the northern part of former Roman Britain (modern West Yorkshire); probably founded in the 5th century. It survived the establishment of adjacent Germanic kingdoms (DEIRA to NE, MERCIA to S). But they competed for control of Elmet during the 7th century. EDWIN of Deira expelled a king in 616; Elmet paid tribute to Mercia in mid century (*see* TRIBAL HIDAGE). Elmet was probably incorporated into Deira by EGFRITH (king 670–85). *See also* POST-ROMAN BRITAIN.

ELPHINSTONE, WILLIAM (b. 1431 at Glasgow, W-C Scotland; d. late Oct. 1514 at Edinburgh, SE Scotland, aged 82 or 83). A student at Glasgow University and Paris, Elphinstone later taught in France. Returning to Scotland *c.*1471, he became rector of Glasgow University (1474), bishop of Ross (1481) and bishop of ABERDEEN (1483). He served King JAMES III as a diplomat and CHANCELLOR (1488), and JAMES IV as a diplomat and lord privy seal (1492–1514).

Elphinstone founded a university college at Aberdeen (papal bull 1495) and commissioned the Aberdeen Breviary (two volumes, printed 1509, 1510), which listed 70 Scottish saints for commemoration.

EMAIN MACHA The nominal 'seat' or capital of the kings of ULSTER (N Ireland), 4th–12th centuries, known from historical and literary sources. It is identified with Navan Fort (Co. Armagh, Northern Ireland), a hillfort in the centre of a complex of prehistoric monuments. Tradition claims that its Irish name means 'Twins of Macha' (a goddess). *See also* KINGSHIP, IRELAND; CAPITALS.

EMERGENCY *see* WORLD WAR II, IMPACT ON IRELAND

EMIGRATION FROM ENGLAND From the later 11th century English people migrated to lordships within Wales created by Normans (*see* MARCH OF WALES). There were similar movements into Scotland in the 12th century (*see* NORMANS, IMPACT ON SCOTLAND), to Ireland after 1169–70 (*see* NORMANS, IMPACT ON IRELAND), and to new parts of Wales after 1283 (*see* WALES, ENGLISH CONQUEST OF). Each movement involved several thousands and transplanted English culture.

From the 1530s, so-called NEW ENGLISH migrated to Ireland, some to reassert English authority, others to populate colonization schemes (or PLANTATIONS, 1550s–1630s). In the 1650s, 12,000 ex-soldiers settled on confiscated land (*see* CROMWELLIAN LAND SETTLEMENT).

Sustained emigration to the Americas began in the early 17th century: to Chesapeake Bay from 1607 (*see* VIRGINIA; MARYLAND); BERMUDA from 1615; NEW ENGLAND from 1620 (*see* PLYMOUTH PLANTATION OR COLONY); WEST INDIES from 1624. Motives included self-advancement and (in New England) religious separatism (*see* PURITANISM, ENGLAND). Some 50,000 people migrated by 1650, another 400,000 by 1700 (200,000 to the Caribbean, 120,000 to Virginia/Maryland, 80,000 to New England and 'middle colonies').

During the 18th century personal emigration to the Americas declined below 100,000. Emigration was also imposed on felons as punishment; they were sent mainly to Virginia/Maryland (to 1775), then to AUSTRALIA (1787–1868).

Between the 1790s and 1850s, 500,000 English people emigrated, often fleeing poverty; four-fifths went to the USA, the remainder to British N America (*see* CANADA), southern Africa and Australian colonies. Emigration increased markedly until WORLD WAR I (1914–18), afterwards continuing at a lower level (4.2 million emigrated from England and Wales 1860–1900). Emigrants included orphaned or destitute children resettled by philanthropic societies. Although numerous, English emigrants did not create culturally distinctive communities, except for expanding the Church of England.

From 1973 to 2020, UK citizens freely migrated within the EUROPEAN ECONOMIC COMMUNITY/EUROPEAN UNION. Significant numbers of older people retired to France and Spain. *See also* EMPIRE, MEDIEVAL ENGLISH IDEAS OF; ROANOKE SETTLEMENTS; TRANSPORTATION; NEW ZEALAND.

EMIGRATION FROM IRELAND Emigration has been a recurrent feature of Irish history. Irish people settled in Britain in the 4th–6th centuries (*see* IRISH COLONIZATION IN BRITAIN, 4TH–6TH CENTURIES). In the late 14th and 15th centuries, the contraction of English-dominated areas, following the BLACK DEATH, caused some Anglo-Irish migration to England. In the late 16th and 17th centuries, various Gaelic Irish left after unsuccessful rebellions (e.g., DESMOND REBELLIONS) or because of religious pressures (e.g., expulsions of clergy). From the early 17th century Irish migrated to English territories in the WEST INDIES (e.g., Montserrat) and N America (southern colonies).

Between 1700 and 1815 possibly 200,000 Irish emigrated to N America, three-quarters of them presbyterians from N Ireland. Emigrants also flocked to English towns, notably LIVERPOOL, MANCHESTER and LONDON.

Emigration then increased substantially: between 1815 and 1845 over 1.5 million people emigrated, predominantly to the USA. Presbyterians dominated to the 1830s, then Catholics. Destinations also now included AUSTRALIA. Irish also migrated seasonally to Great Britain for agricultural work. The GREAT FAMINE (1845–9) swelled the exodus: over 2.1 million left between 1846 and 1855, mainly to the USA (1.5 million), Britain (315,000), CANADA (300,000), Australia and NEW ZEALAND, reinforcing the diaspora. Many travelled in over-crowded vessels nicknamed 'coffin ships'. Another 4 million emigrated by 1914.

Between 1921 (PARTITION OF IRELAND) and 2001, 1.5 million emigrated from SOUTHERN IRELAND and 500,000 from NORTHERN IRELAND. Britain was the main destination, due partly to US immigration restrictions and the 1930s Great Depression. Emigration rates chiefly reflected economic conditions. Emigration from southern Ireland remained high until the 1960s, then declined; it surged again in the 1980s–early 1990s, reviving again from 2008 (economic crash). Emigration from Northern Ireland was strong from the 1960s. In relation to its population size, Ireland in the 19th–20th centuries had the highest level of emigration in Europe. *See also* POPULATION, IRELAND.

EMIGRATION FROM SCOTLAND Scots emigrated from at least the 13th century, mainly to trade (e.g., in Bruges by the 1290s, later in Scandinavia and the Baltic area) or to fight (e.g., in Ireland, *see* GALLOGLASSES; in France, against the English, in the HUNDRED YEARS WAR).

From *c*.1570 population expansion stimulated large-scale emigration: between 1600 and 1650, 85,000–115,000 Scots emigrated, mostly from the Lowlands. Some joined existing communities (notably in Poland), others became mercenaries (e.g., in the Thirty Years War, 1618–48). Around 20,000–30,000 settled in Ulster (*see* ULSTER PLANTATION). In the late 17th century total emigration was 78,000–127,000, mainly to Ulster (60,000–100,000), but also to the Americas (7000), especially the Caribbean. Between *c*.1700 and the 1760s the principal destination was N America (30,000).

From the 1770s renewed population growth and agricultural change increased emigration, including many people from the HIGHLANDS; between 1830 and 1914, despite industrial expansion, 2 million emigrated overseas and 600,000 to England. (Many emigrants were skilled men seeking better opportunities.) The main overseas destinations were the USA, British N America (later CANADA) and, from the 1850s, AUSTRALIA and NEW ZEALAND. Large-scale emigration continued until the 1960s (apart from the war years). *See also* CLEARANCES; POPULATION, SCOTLAND.

EMIGRATION FROM WALES Since the 10th century England has been the main destination (*see* ASSER), particularly English border towns (e.g., Chester). After the UNION OF WALES WITH ENGLAND (1536–43), many Welshmen flourished at the English royal court and in law and the Church (e.g., John WILLIAMS). In the 18th century and later, LONDON and LIVERPOOL were the chief centres of Welsh migration. Industrial expansion in Wales restrained emigration in the late 18th and 19th centuries, but the 1920s–30s depression caused a mass exodus: in 1951, 600,000 Welsh-born people lived in England.

Overseas emigration was important from the late 17th century when religious dissenters settled in N America. By 1830 the USA contained 330,000 people of Welsh stock. Continuing migration included settlement in industrial areas of Pennsylvania. In the late 19th century there was substantial migration to Canada, S Africa, and Australasia, and also a fascinating settlement in Patagonia, Argentina, launched in 1865. *See also* POPULATION, WALES.

EMMA (b. 980s in Normandy; d. 7 March 1052, probably in Winchester, Hampshire, England). A sister of Richard II, duke of NORMANDY, Emma was married to ÆTHELRED II, king of England, as a marriage alliance against the VIKINGS (1002). She lived in Normandy in 1013–14, following a Viking invasion of England (*see* SWEIN FORKBEARD).

In 1017 Emma married England's new king, CNUT (Swein's son), on condition that their children (rather than Cnut's other children) should succeed to the kingship. On Cnut's death (1035) their son HARTHACNUT (nominally) became king, but stayed in Denmark. (Emma was in England.) By late 1037 Harthacnut's older half-brother and regent, HAROLD HAREFOOT, seized the kingship. Emma fled to Flanders. After Harold's death (1040) she returned. Her older son by Æthelred, EDWARD THE CONFESSOR, became king in 1042, but turned against his mother, seizing her treasure (Nov. 1043). *See also* ÆLFGIFU.

EMMET'S RISING In Ireland, a rising principally in DUBLIN on 23 July 1803; the final rebellious act by members of the UNITED IRISHMEN. Rebels led by Robert Emmet (b. 1778) intended to seize the Castle and establish a provisional government and republic. They were easily dispersed. Emmet was captured on 25 Aug. and executed on 20 Sept.

EMPIRE, ANGLO-SAXON IDEAS OF BEDE mentioned (731) that seven 6th- and 7th-century kings had authority (Latin *imperium*) over other kingdoms S of the R. Humber. (The kings included: ÆTHELBERT, RÆDWALD, EDWIN, OSWALD, OSWIU.) Their authority largely reflected military power. There was no heritable 'high kingship'.

Powerful 8th-century kings of MERCIA also made claims: ÆTHELBALD claimed to be king of the Southern English, and once to be king of Britain (736); OFFA claimed once to be king of England (774).

Kings of England in the 10th century (ATHELSTAN to ÆTHELRED II), claimed to be kings of Britain, drawing on imperial ideas expressed by Ottonian kings in Germany. Their claims were sometimes expressed symbolically, e.g., when eight northern kings rowed EDGAR on the R. Dee (973). *See also* KINGSHIP, ANGLO-SAXON; TRIBAL HIDAGE.

EMPIRE, ENGLISH IDEAS OF, 11TH–15TH CENTURIES Between 1066 and 1204 England belonged to collections of territories which historians have called the NORMAN EMPIRE and ANGEVIN EMPIRE. Some have viewed England as a colonial territory ruled from a 'core' area elsewhere. England nonetheless retained its own administration.

Welsh historian R.R. Davies (1938–2005) and others have argued that in the 11th–14th centuries English expansionist aspirations within the British Isles persisted. Between *c*.1070 and *c*.1170, parts of Wales were conquered and became lordships held from the English Crown (*see* MARCH OF WALES). Parts of Ireland were conquered from 1169 (*see* IRELAND, ENGLISH CONQUEST, 12TH–13TH CENTURIES). English immigrants, forms of government and economic organization were introduced. Scotland was not conquered but aspects of Norman and English society were instituted (*see* NORMANS, IMPACT ON SCOTLAND).

Expansion culminated in the conquest of native Welsh kingdoms and seizure of Scotland by King EDWARD I (late 13th–early 14th centuries). Though English influences then declined, England sought territory in France (*see* HUNDRED YEARS WAR) and later exerted authority in Ireland and Wales (*see* RICHARD II AND IRELAND; OWAIN GLYN DŴR).

English-ruled lands were not designated an empire, nor did kings claim an imperial title. The term *dominium* (Latin, meaning 'lordship') was much used by Edward I.

EMPIRE, ENGLISH IDEAS OF, FROM LATER 15TH CENTURY Expansionary activities were undertaken for varying purposes. Envy of Portuguese and Spanish expansion partly motivated early English searches for oceanic routes to Asia for trade (*see* NORTH-WEST PASSAGE;

MUSCOVY COMPANY), and for gold, although John CABOT annexed NEWFOUNDLAND (1497; reclaimed 1583).

Colonization in the Americas was advocated from the 1560s to export surplus population, who would provide agricultural products and buy manufactures (*see* GILBERT, HUMPHREY; HAKLUYT, RICHARD). Success in growing tobacco enabled VIRGINIA (1609) to become England's first permanent colony (in N America), and sugar cultivation (from 1640s) supported colonies in the WEST INDIES; both commodities became dependent on the SLAVE TRADE (abolished 1807). Other colonies reflected religious aspirations (e.g., PLYMOUTH PLANTATION; MASSACHUSETTS), while the HUDSON'S BAY COMPANY (1670) pursued furs. Ventures around Africa to Asia (from 1601) sought exotic goods (e.g., spices; *see* EAST INDIA COMPANY) and were facilitated by coastal trading posts. Government valued the Empire as a commercial entity and protected it through legislation (*see* NAVIGATION ACTS). Colonies were also used for TRANSPORTATION. (From 1707 the Empire was a British entity.)

Significant acquisitions of territories with non-British populations started from the 1760s, for particular reasons. In N America, conquered French territories were retained to provide security (1763; *see* PARIS, PEACE OF); in INDIA, the East India Company acquired Bengal (1765) to entrench its presence and for financial gain, and made further defensive acquisitions. From 1788, following AMERICAN INDEPENDENCE, convicts were sent to NEW SOUTH WALES.

New factors influenced expansion in the 19th century, such as MISSIONARY SOCIETIES and exploration societies, increasing trade driven by the INDUSTRIAL REVOLUTION, population growth (resulting in emigration to AUSTRALIA, NEW ZEALAND, CANADA), and rivalry with other powers (*see* SCRAMBLE FOR AFRICA; NEW IMPERIALISM). Britain's imperial endeavours were often presented as a 'civilizing mission', spreading Protestant Christianity, law and economic development; celebration of 'Empire Day' spread (from Canada) from 1897. *See also* OVERSEAS EXPLORATION, ENGLISH AND BRITISH; BRITISH EMPIRE; IMPERIALISM OF FREE TRADE; INFORMAL EMPIRE; CHINESE TREATY PORTS; GREAT GAME.

EMPSON, RICHARD (b. *c.*1450, probably at Towcester, Northamptonshire, England; d. 17 Aug. 1510 at London, England, aged about 60). Empson, a lawyer, worked by 1504 with Edmund DUDLEY for King HENRY VII. As members of the Council Learned in the Law, they exacted feudal payments and fines. Their efficiency made them widely hated. When Henry died, HENRY VIII allowed Empson and Dudley to be arrested (24 April 1509) and convicted of TREASON (1 Oct. 1509). Empson was executed with Dudley.

ENCLOSURE The replacement of intermixed lands, usually subject to some common use (including arable

fields, meadow, pasture, heath), with compact, individually managed farms. Enclosure was undertaken in areas of open-field farming throughout the British Isles, and also affected upland pasture elsewhere.

Enclosure by local agreement happened by the 12th century, and was fairly common in the 15th–16th centuries (usually for sheep grazing). From the mid 18th century open-field land was enclosed in England and Wales mostly under private Acts of Parliament (so-called 'parliamentary enclosure'). The movement peaked in 1790–1815. Open-field farming largely disappeared by 1870. *See also* AGRICULTURE, SCOTLAND FROM 18TH CENTURY; ENCLOSURES, WALES; AGRICULTURAL REVOLUTION.

ENCLOSURE AND ENGROSSING, ENGLAND 1480s TO 1630s During this period enclosure and engrossing provoked legislation, government action and popular resistance. Enclosure refers to the formation of compact and bounded agricultural units, often involving suppression of common rights, engrossing to the amalgamation of landholdings. Both usually entailed conversion of arable land to pasture. Previously during the 15th century, engrossing and enclosure for sheep grazing had been undertaken without controversy in response to population decline (*see* POPULATION, ENGLAND).

Attitudes changed from the 1480s. Legislation prohibited engrossing on the Isle of Wight (1488) and more generally (1489), because it allegedly caused decay of arable farming, unemployment and loss of manpower for defence. An Act of 1515, possibly caused by corn shortage, required repair of decayed buildings and the restoration to arable of land converted to pasture since February 1515; in 1517–18 a commission established by Thomas WOLSEY, the king's chief minister, enquired into depopulation since 1488, resulting in prosecutions. (Excessive conversion to pasture was attacked in 1516 by Thomas MORE in *Utopia*.) Further Acts and proclamations followed in the 1530s. In 1548 Protector SOMERSET, concerned about social conditions, instigated an enquiry into enclosures, and introduced (1549) a tax on sheep. Attacks on enclosures and popular uprisings (PRAYER-BOOK REBELLION; KETT'S REBELLION) diverted his attention and both were cancelled. Further pro-arable legislation ensued in the 1550s–60s.

Bad harvests in the 1590s revived activity; in 1597 engrossing was prohibited and another Act required restoration to arable of recently converted pastureland. Another enquiry was provoked in 1607 by a revolt against enclosures in the Midlands, and in the 1630s the government again investigated enclosures and fined enclosers. By then, however, enclosure was advocated for agricultural improvement, and landowners were registering enclosures at the Court of CHANCERY to establish legal security. *See also*

AGRICULTURE, ENGLAND BEFORE MID 18TH CENTURY; ECONOMY, STATE INVOLVEMENT, BRITAIN.

ENCLOSURES, WALES In the late 16th century arable open fields existed mainly in S Wales and W of the Anglo-Welsh BORDER (formerly the MARCH OF WALES). Most fields in S Wales were enclosed by 1640, by landowners acting individually or in concert. Enclosure of pasture and moor also began.

Private enclosures continued throughout the 18th and 19th centuries, but from 1753 parliamentary Acts or Orders were often used: 227 were passed covering almost 10% of Wales. They were overwhelmingly (99%) concerned with common and waste, often upland sheep-grazing areas, and most were passed during the French Revolutionary and Napoleonic wars (1792–1815) when prices and rents reached unprecedented levels. *See also* AGRICULTURE, WALES BEFORE/FROM 18TH CENTURY.

ENGAGEMENT An agreement made on 26 Dec. 1647 (at Carisbrooke Castle, Isle of Wight, England) between King CHARLES I and three commissioners representing Scots (including many Royalists) who were dismayed by the English Parliament's failure to introduce presbyterianism (*see* SOLEMN LEAGUE AND COVENANT). The Scots agreed to help restore Charles as king of England on condition that he established presbyterianism for three years. The change of sides divided the Covenanting movement (*see* COVENANTING REVOLUTION). The consequent Scottish invasion of England was defeated (battle of Preston, 17–19 Aug. 1648), enabling radicals to take power. Supporters of the Engagement included the (2nd) earl of LAUDERDALE and (3rd) marquis of HAMILTON. Opponents included the (8th) earl of ARGYLL and Archibald JOHNSTON. *See also* CIVIL WARS, SCOTTISH PARTICIPATION.

ENGINEERING, GREAT BRITAIN Civil engineering (i.e., 'civilian' rather than military, concerned with structures) developed as a distinctive PROFESSION from the 1690s with such works as harbours, bridges, roads and CANALS (last from 1760s). Early civil engineers were often craftsmen from other specialisms; for example, the canal engineer James Brindley (1716–72) was originally a millwright. The versatile John Smeaton (1724–92) is regarded as the 'father of civil engineering'. In 1771, in London, the Society of Civil Engineers was founded, the world's first such society.

Mechanical engineering (concerned with mechanisms, usually of metal) emerged from the later 18th century from the INDUSTRIAL REVOLUTION. Engineering skills developed strongly from the 1770s at the Soho works of Matthew BOULTON and James WATT for building steam engines (near BIRMINGHAM, C England). An industry manufacturing textile machinery developed around the Lancashire COTTON INDUSTRY (NW England). The spread of RAIL-

ways (from 1830s) included the creation of engineering workshops (e.g., for building locomotives). The making of MACHINE TOOLS also progressed. Until *c.* 1850 Britain was the world's leading producer of machinery.

Although Britain's share then declined, new specialisms appeared, sometimes with strong regional concentrations. They included agricultural machinery, light engineering (e.g., nail-making machines), electrical engineering (from 1880s), and shoemaking machinery. Engineering was further stimulated by the BICYCLE, MOTOR and AIRCRAFT industries, but also affected by the decline of 'staples' (e.g., textiles). In the later 20th century aerospace engineering was important, and in the 21st century such areas as autosport, renewable energy (e.g., wind turbines) and healthcare technology. *See also* ARMSTRONG, WILLIAM; TECHNICAL EDUCATION.

ENGINEERING, IRELAND *see* INDUSTRY, NORTHERN IRELAND

ENGLAND A jurisdiction within the UNITED KINGDOM comprising southern BRITAIN (except WALES) and offshore islands; formerly a kingdom. Area: 50,200 sq mi (130,000 sq km). Est. popn in 2015: 54,786,000. English is the main language, though in 2011 almost 300 languages were spoken. The landscape is mountainous or hilly in the N, W and SW.

During the 5th–7th centuries, following Roman rule, much of southern Britain, inhabited by Brittonic-speaking people, experienced Germanic (or 'Anglo-Saxon') immigration and establishment of kingdoms (*see* KINGSHIP, ANGLO-SAXON); Christianity was widely adopted in the 7th century (*see* CONVERSION OF ANGLO-SAXONS). By the 9th century, the majority indigenous population had espoused Germanic culture (e.g., language), making the area different from other parts of Britain (*see* BRITISH IN ANGLO-SAXON KINGDOMS). Following disruption by VIKINGS, kings of WESSEX created a single kingdom in the 10th century, and developed relatively sophisticated government (*see* ENGLAND, FORMATION OF). In the early 11th century, during the reign of the Dane CNUT, it was first called 'Engla lond', the 'Land of the Angles'.

In 1066 England was invaded by Normans (*see* NORMAN CONQUEST OF ENGLAND), causing considerable social and cultural change (*see* FEUDALISM). England became part of the NORMAN EMPIRE and ANGEVIN EMPIRE (to 1204). But in the 12th–14th centuries English rule and lordship were imposed within the British Isles and in France (*see* EMPIRE, ENGLISH IDEAS OF, 11TH–15TH CENTURIES); in 1536, Wales was annexed; and in the late 16th–17th centuries English-ruled territories were established beyond Europe (*see* BRITISH EMPIRE).

England separated from the Catholic Church in 1534 and adopted reformed Christianity (*see* REFORMATION, ENGLAND; ENGLAND, CHURCH OF). From 1603, by the

UNION OF CROWNS, England and Scotland had the same ruler. Government and society were dislocated in the mid 17th century (see CIVIL WARS; COMMONWEALTH AND PROTECTORATE). In 1707 England and Scotland were united as GREAT BRITAIN. See also ENGLISH; DUMNONIA; OFFA'S DYKE; LONDON; BORDER, ANGLO-SCOTTISH.

ENGLAND, CHURCH OF England's legally established State Church from 1534 (except 1554-9), including Wales until 1920; united with the Church of IRELAND 1801-70.

A separate English Church was created in 1534 when Parliament, at the instigation of King HENRY VIII, replaced papal with royal jurisdiction (see GREAT MATTER). Episcopacy continued, and doctrine remained largely unchanged, though religious houses were dissolved (1536-40). Under EDWARD VI, English services, published in a PRAYER BOOK, replaced Latin services (1549); a more Protestant version (1552) replaced Mass with Holy Communion. Following disruption under MARY I, Edwardian arrangements were reinstated (1559; see ELIZABETHAN SETTLEMENT). CALVINISM became widely accepted. The reformed Church was rejected by radical Protestants (see BROWNISTS) and continuing Catholics (see RECUSANCY, ENGLAND AND WALES).

'Puritans' sought further reforms (e.g., abolition of ceremonies). Though stifled in the 1620s-30s (see LAUD, WILLIAM), they achieved many aims in the 1640s-50s (see CHURCH, ENGLAND AND WALES, 1640s-50s), but more radical dissenting groups also emerged (e.g., QUAKERS). An attempt to reimpose uniformity (1660s; see CLARENDON CODE) was thwarted by persistent dissent, suspension of penal laws by JAMES VII/II (1687), and by the TOLERATION ACT (1689) which many assumed made church attendance voluntary.

In the 18th century the Church remained strong in society, but lost vigour and shunned revivalist METHODISM. As POPULATION increased and industrial towns developed (1780s-1820s), urban working-class populations became 'unchurched' or preferred NONCONFORMITY (a census in 1851 showed roughly equal attendance at Church of England and nonconformist places of worship). The weakening situation stimulated responses, notably EVANGELICALISM, investment in church-building and EDUCATION, and the OXFORD MOVEMENT, though developments from the last caused great controversy (see RITUALISM).

Church attendance fell heavily during the 20th century, and proposed union with Methodists failed (1972). By the 21st century the Church's social influence had declined. Women were increasingly preponderant within congregations, and prominent as officers and clergy (see WOMEN, ORDINATION OF). See also CHURCH, MEDIEVAL ENGLAND/WALES; CHURCH ORGANIZATION, ENGLAND/WALES; REFORMATION, ENGLAND/WALES; PURITANISM, ENGLAND/WALES; ANGLICAN COMMUNION; WALES, CHURCH IN.

ENGLAND, DANISH CONQUEST The phase of Viking raids on England that began in the 980s culminated with conquest by CNUT of Denmark (1016). This brought peace, strengthened contacts with Scandinavia, and made Cnut a leading ruler in northern Europe.

Cnut (ruled 1016-35) emphasized continuity with the English kingdom: he married (1017) EMMA, widow of King ÆTHELRED II, and publicly supported the Church. But he levied heavy taxation to pay for the ships needed to sustain his empire. There was little Scandinavian settlement after 1016, though North Sea commerce expanded and London grew as a trading centre.

Cnut was succeeded by his sons HARTHACNUT (1035-7, 1040-2) and HAROLD HAREFOOT (1037-40). The accession of EDWARD THE CONFESSOR (1042) restored the English royal line. See also VIKINGS, IMPACT ON ENGLAND; SCANDINAVIAN EMPIRE, ENGLAND'S POSITION IN; EARLS, ANGLO-SAXON ENGLAND.

ENGLAND, FORMATION OF A single kingdom, uniting lands mainly populated by ANGLO-SAXONS, was created in the 10th century by kings of WESSEX (S England). They conquered Danish-held territory and annexed two Anglo-Saxon kingdoms (see KINGSHIP, ANGLO-SAXON; VIKINGS, IMPACT ON ENGLAND).

When EDWARD THE ELDER became king of Wessex in 899, Danes ruled eastern England and much of the N. Only three Anglo-Saxon kingdoms remained: Wessex, (western) MERCIA (W Midlands), and (northern) NORTHUMBRIA (NE England). From 909 Edward attacked the Danes. With his sister ÆTHELFLÆD, wife of Æthelred of Mercia (d. 911), Edward conquered Danish territories in the E Midlands and East Anglia (910-18). They consolidated their conquests by constructing BURHS (fortified centres). Æthelflæd died in June 918; in Dec. Edward deposed her daughter and successor, Ælfwynn. When Edward died (924) his kingdom extended to the R. Humber. In 927 King ATHELSTAN seized the Danish-ruled kingdom of York and annexed Northumbria.

It proved hard to hold the conquered territories. For periods between 939 and 954 Vikings re-established rule in NE England (see YORK, VIKING KINGDOM OF). From 940 to 942 Olaf Guthfrithson and Olaf Sihtricson also held eastern Mercia (see EDMUND).

England's kings enhanced their authority by creating new SHIRES (governed through EALDORMEN and REEVES). The kingdom was integrated through the WITAN.

ENGLAND, FRENCH INVASION (1216-17) An intervention against King JOHN made at the request of rebel BARONS. French forces, led by Prince Louis, landed in Kent (SE England) on 21 May 1216. They captured much of SE England by Oct., when John died. Supporters of HENRY III (John's successor) defeated Louis' army and English barons at LINCOLN on 20 May 1217, and a French fleet off Sandwich (Kent) on 24 Aug. Louis concluded a treaty near KINGSTON UPON THAMES (12 Sept.) and withdrew. *See also* BRÉAUTÉ, FALKES DE; ALEXANDER II.

ENGLISH Term for (a) the culturally predominant inhabitants of the kingdom of England (10th century to 1707, excepting WALES), or (b) similar inhabitants of the former kingdom within GREAT BRITAIN (from 1707), or (c) some peoples of English culture outside England or Great Britain (e.g., in LOTHIAN after its inclusion in Scotland). The term descends ultimately from 'ANGLES' (OE, Engle).

English identity is derived from the culture (especially language) of Germanic immigrants to southern Britain in the 5th–6th centuries, although they and assimilated Britons were mostly called either Angles or SAXONS until at least the 10th century. The preference for 'Angles' to denote all Germanic people in Britain appears to have originated with Gregory the Great, Pope 590–604, who used the Latin 'Angli'. His practice was imitated by BEDE (in 731), who considered Angles and Saxons as a single Christian people, and by other clerical writers (e.g., BONIFACE).

This probably influenced ALFRED, king of WESSEX, in using the 'Anglian' term 'Angelcynn' (OE, meaning 'English people') from the 880s (alongside ANGLO-SAXONS) to promote a common, Christian identity for Angles and Saxons under his rule. It was replaced by 'Engle' after King ATHELSTAN seized the Viking kingdom of YORK (927); in the 10th century OE 'Englisc' came into use. Although a strong kingdom of England and English identity developed, the former included inhabitants with Scandinavian identities (*see* VIKINGS, IMPACT ON ENGLAND). English identity withstood the NORMAN CONQUEST (1066–70s), after which inhabitants were often described in records as 'French and English' (to early 13th century). *See also* ENGLISH LANGUAGE; ETHNIC AND NATIONAL MINORITIES, ENGLAND.

ENGLISH EMPIRE *see* EMPIRE, ANGLO-SAXON IDEAS OF; EMPIRE, ENGLISH IDEAS OF, 11TH–15TH CENTURIES; EMPIRE, ENGLISH IDEAS OF. FROM LATER 15TH CENTURY; BRITISH EMPIRE

ENGLISH LANGUAGE English is derived from Old English, a variant of West Germanic languages which emerged in southern BRITAIN during the 5th–7th centuries through contact between Germanic peoples from coastal areas in NW Europe (*see* GERMANIC IMMIGRATION, SOUTHERN BRITAIN). Old English had three grammatical genders, and was heavily inflected. Few words were absorbed from indigenous Brittonic, which it extensively replaced, though borrowings were made from LATIN. Old English was written in runes, and from the 7th century in

the Latin alphabet (with modifications). It was used for literature and records, with West Saxon dialect becoming the standard written form (late 9th–11th centuries).

Old English evolved into Middle English between *c*.1050 and *c*.1150, partly through influence from VIKINGS and the NORMAN CONQUEST (1066–70s), though until the 14th century it was considerably displaced as a written and élite language by FRENCH and Latin. English inflexions became simpler, and vocabulary larger, with borrowings from Scandinavian languages and French. Middle English blended French sounds with Germanic sounds. Spelling was highly variable. In the 15th century London English, influenced by East Midland dialect, became influential. Northern English developed in Scotland into the SCOTS LANGUAGE.

By the late 15th century Early Modern English developed, with fewer inflexions. A 'Great Vowel Shift' (*c*.1400–*c*.1600) made English sound less like Continental languages. Influenced by HUMANISM, vocabulary was enlarged, drawing on classical Latin and other languages. Printing (from 1476) and use of English BIBLES and the PRAYER BOOK encouraged a written standard form.

By *c*.1700 written English reached a form, Late Modern English, which has remained largely standard, encouraged by prescribed grammar and spelling (e.g., in dictionaries). It was spread abroad through imperial expansion (*see* BRITISH EMPIRE), and from the 19th century became a major international language with numerous varieties. In the 21st century 1 billion people worldwide had some familiarity with English.

ENGLISH LITERATURE, ENGLAND Early 'Old English' literature (7th century onwards) is mainly alliterative poetry (e.g., *BEOWULF*), originating in oral tradition. King ALFRED (d. 899) encouraged prose writing (e.g., *ANGLO-SAXON CHRONICLE*); later writers include ÆLFRIC and WULFSTAN.

'Middle English' literature (12th–15th centuries) was influenced by French literature, especially chivalric romances. Outstanding writers included William LANGLAND, Geoffrey CHAUCER and Thomas MALORY. Drama flourished as MYSTERY PLAYS.

During the 'Early Modern English' period (16th–17th centuries) drama and poetry flowered, the latter influenced by Italian forms. Playwrights included Christopher MARLOWE, William SHAKESPEARE, Ben JONSON; poets included Philip Sidney, Edmund SPENSER, Shakespeare, Jonson. In the 17th century prose developed greater force (e.g., 'Authorised Version' of BIBLE, 1611; works by John BUNYAN); poetry expressed new religious sensibility (e.g., works by John Donne, George Herbert, John MILTON). Drama, banned during the COMMONWEALTH, flourished after the RESTORATION of 1660 (e.g., plays by Aphra BEHN, John DRYDEN).

The 18th century saw the emergence of the NOVEL (as composed, e.g., by Daniel DEFOE) and vigorous prose writing (e.g., by Samuel Johnson, Edward Gibbon). Poetry was often characterised by wit and classical restraint (e.g., by Alexander Pope).

The 19th century included the Romantic movement (e.g., poets John Keats, William Wordsworth); development of the novel (by Jane Austen, the Bronte family, George Eliot, Charles Dickens); poetry reflecting religious doubt (e.g., by Matthew Arnold, Alfred Tennyson); novels presenting psychological complexity (e.g., by Henry James, Joseph Conrad, Thomas Hardy).

After World War I (1914–18), a 'modernist' sensibility was expressed in novels (e.g., by D.H. Lawrence, Virginia Woolf) and poetry (by T.S. Eliot). Some writers of the 1930s–40s reflected social concerns (e.g., George Orwell, W.H. Auden). Themes explored after World War II (1939–45) included everyday life (e.g., by Philip Larkin, Kingsley Amis). Immigration from the mid 20th century produced writers who presented experiences of new ethnic groups (e.g., Meera Syal).

ENGLISH LITERATURE, IRELAND *see* Anglo-Irish literature

ENGLISH LITERATURE, SCOTLAND *see* Scots language and literature; Scottish literature in English

ENGLISH MYSTICS Name applied to several authors in England, mainly of the 14th century, who wrote about religious experience and developed the English language accordingly. The earliest, Richard Rolle (*c*.1300–49), lived as a hermit in Yorkshire. His writings, in Latin and English, include *The Form of Perfect Living* and *Commandment of Love to God*. The Augustinian canon Walter Hilton (*c*.1343–96), in Nottinghamshire, is best known for *The Scale of Perfection*, about man's search for God. Julian (or Juliana) of Norwich (1342–*c*.1416) related visions of the crucified Christ in *Revelations of Divine Love* (two versions). In later life she was an anchoress. In the late 14th century an unknown author wrote *The Cloud of Unknowing* about seeking God through contemplation. Although the Mystics focused on knowing God through individual striving rather than the corporate Church, they refrained from criticism of the clergy, and evaded suspicion of heresy. Rolle and Hilton influenced 15th-century English religious culture. *See also* Church, medieval England.

ENGLISH REVOLUTION Term applied generally to events of 1640–60 (*see* Long Parliament; Civil Wars; Commonwealth and Protectorate). Contemporaries used it to indicate their 'circular' nature: from monarchy to republic, and eventually back to monarchy.

Modern historians have used the term to indicate the radicalism that was unleashed by the Civil Wars, by the defeat and execution (1649) of King Charles I, and by the collapse of religious uniformity. It included demands for a wide expansion in political participation (*see* Levellers), and the placing of individual conscience above religious authority. Many influential political leaders, however, were conservative men (e.g., Oliver Cromwell), who resisted demands for a wider franchise and suppressed religious groups that appeared to threaten social hierarchies. *See also* English Revolution Sects.

ENGLISH REVOLUTION SECTS During the 1640s legislation against religious dissent became unenforceable (repealed 1650). The situation permitted the expansion or formation of religious and political sects.

Many religious sects rejected Calvinist orthodoxy (*see* Calvinism). Most drew on a sense of personal contact with God and distaste for an established Church. 'Baptists' (already in existence) condemned infant baptism and professed their faith through rebaptism. 'Seekers' rejected Church discipline. 'Ranters' were supposedly contemptuous of religious orthodoxy, although they probably did not form a single sect. 'Muggletonians', in the 1650s, denied doctrines such as the Trinity and believed that Ludowicke Muggleton (1609–98) was a prophet. Some sects, such as 'Fifth Monarchists' in the 1650s, were influenced by the millenarian belief that the kingdom of heaven would soon be established on Earth. In the 1650s many sectaries were drawn into the Quaker movement (*see* Fox, George). Political sects included Levellers and 'Diggers' (*see* Winstanley, Gerrard). Women played prominent roles.

Sects were thought to threaten social and political hierarchies. They were persecuted in the 1650s and after the Restoration (1660). *See also* Church, England and Wales, 1640s–50s.

ENGLISHRY The part (usually lowland) of a lordship in the March of Wales where English immigrants were settled and an English-type manor instituted (in the late 11th or 12th century). English identity declined with Welsh immigration after 1349 (*see* Black Death, impact on Wales). *See also* Welshry.

ENLIGHTENMENT A movement in European and American thought in the later 17th and 18th centuries which sought a rational understanding of the world (in place of religious or customary understanding), criticized social and political organization, and advocated the application of reason to society, including provision of rights. The English term 'Enlightenment' was used from the early 19th century.

Eighteenth-century French thinkers credited the Englishmen John Locke (d. 1704) and Isaac Newton

(d. 1727) as leading originators of Enlightenment rationalism. Though Enlightenment thinking was influential in England, and applied to Christianity (producing DEISM and UNITARIANISM), it generally avoided or rejected the strong anti-religious views formulated in France (e.g., by Voltaire). Some historians even doubt that there was an 'English Enlightenment'. Enlightenment thought flourished in Scotland (*see* ENLIGHTENMENT, SCOTLAND). The US historian Gertrude Himmelfarb has proposed a 'British Enlightenment' to recognize that contributions came from all parts of the British Isles. Enlightenment thought also influenced British colonies in N America to seek independence, and affected both the Constitution of the USA and the FRENCH REVOLUTION. Enlightenment thought, while countered by Romanticism, strongly persisted.

Notable British Enlightenment figures (excepting Scotsmen) include: theologian and philosopher Joseph Butler (1692–1752), philosopher and political theorist Richard PRICE, historian Edward GIBBON, scientist Joseph PRIESTLEY, theologian William PALEY, radical Thomas PAINE, social theorist and novelist William GODWIN. *See also* SCIENTIFIC REVOLUTION; AMERICAN INDEPENDENCE.

ENLIGHTENMENT, SCOTLAND The 18th-century ENLIGHTENMENT movement flourished in Scotland, especially at its universities. Centred on EDINBURGH, but with notable contributions from GLASGOW and ABERDEEN, it drew on a long-standing HUMANIST educational tradition and encapsulated philosophy, economics, science and the arts. A Scottish characteristic was the marrying of theory and practice. Activities influenced by the Enlightenment included agricultural 'improvement' and FREE TRADE.

Notable figures of the Scottish Enlightenment include: legal theorist and philosopher Henry Home, Lord Kames (1696–1782), chemist and medical professor William CULLEN, philosopher David Hume (1711–76), historian William Robertson (1721–93), economist Adam SMITH, sociologist Adam Ferguson (1723–1816), chemist Joseph BLACK, geologist James HUTTON. *See also* AGRICULTURE, SCOTLAND FROM 18TH CENTURY; SCOTLAND, CHURCH OF; STATISTICAL ACCOUNTS.

ENTENTE CORDIALE see ANGLO-FRENCH CONVENTION

ENTREPRENEUR (French, meaning 'one who undertakes'). Term used in Great Britain from the late 19th century for economic agents. In economic theory an entrepreneur has three functions: providing capital, managing an enterprise, taking commercial risk. The term is applied until the 18th century to 'merchant capitalists' in Britain and Ireland who organized domestic INDUSTRY (e.g., textiles) and marketed products. It then refers more typically to the owner-manager of a commercial or industrial business. In Ireland the related term 'undertaker' was used for middlemen in PLANTATIONS.

ENVIRONMENTAL MOVEMENT A broad reform movement concerned with protecting the natural world from human damage. Prominent from the 1960s, its manifestations have ranged from anti-litter campaigns to repudiation of industrial society, with strong links to FEMINISM, vegetarianism and mysticism.

Leading environmentalist pressure groups included Friends of the Earth (launched in UK 1971), which campaigned for recycling and renewable energy; and Greenpeace (founded in USA 1971, in UK 1977), which challenged whaling, nuclear testing and dumping of toxic materials. The Green Party, founded in 1975 as the Ecology Party, won an unprecedented (and unrepeated) 15% of the vote in European Parliament elections in 1989 after 'global warming' made environmental pollution a matter of general public concern. Slow regrowth of its support from the late 1990s culminated in election of an MP in 2010 (Party leader Caroline Lucas, for Brighton Pavilion; re-elected 2015, 2017, 2019).

From the 1980s environmentalism influenced the main political parties and government policies. The Conservative prime minister Margaret THATCHER warned in speeches about the effects of pollution on the climate (1988–90). Labour passed the 2000 Utilities Act, under Tony BLAIR, subsidizing power generation from renewable sources (e.g., wind), and the 2008 Climate Change Act, under Gordon BROWN, setting a drastic target for reduction of six 'greenhouse gases' by 2050. It also created a Department of Energy and Climate Change (1998). From 2007 inshore 'hydraulic fracking' (use of underground explosions to release gas and petroleum) became controversial. The EUROPEAN ECONOMIC COMMUNITY (European Union) also issued extensive legislation on environmental matters, and the UK participated in United Nations environmental conferences from 1972.

EÓGANACHTA *see* MUNSTER

EPISCOPAL CHURCH IN SCOTLAND A dissenting Church, governed by bishops, formed by clergy and laity who rejected the (final) establishment of presbyterian government in the Church of SCOTLAND in 1690 (*see* REVOLUTION SETTLEMENT, SCOTLAND). Episcopalians established meeting-houses (notably in NE Scotland) but were persecuted as alleged Jacobites (supporters of the deposed King JAMES VII/II) and 'papists'. Congregations which prayed for the reigning sovereign ('Juring' or 'Qualified' congregations) were authorized by the 1712 TOLERATION ACT; but most remained illegal ('Non-juring' congregations). Episcopalians provided the majority of

Jacobite troops in the 1715 and 1745 JACOBITE REBELLIONS and were subjected to penal laws (e.g., closure of meeting-houses, 1719). Yet the Church developed, consecrating new bishops from 1704, establishing a college of bishops in 1720, and electing a 'primus' (head bishop) from 1731. In 1784 bishops consecrated the first bishop for the Episcopal Church in the independent USA.

After the death of the Jacobite 'pretender' Charles Edward Stuart in 1788 Non-jurors recognized the reigning king (George III), and were effectively granted legal tolera-tion (1792). In the 19th century the Church attracted landowners (an estimated two-thirds by 1851) and the Anglicized upper classes. Adherents rose from 12,000 (est.) in 1790 to 45,000 in 1851, 146,000 in 1914. Churches and cathedrals were built, and the OXFORD MOVEMENT and RITUALISM were influential.

Numbers fell rapidly from 1945, to 56,000 by 1995. The name Scottish Episcopal Church was adopted in 1979. Women were ordained as priests from 1994, and as bishops from 2018. In 2017 the Church controversially became the first major Church in the UK to decide to provide same-sex weddings. In 2018 it had about 300 congregations and 31,000 members (with a larger number of attendees). *See also* DISSENT, SCOTLAND; ANGLICAN COMMUNION.

EQUITY COURTS Term for certain royal courts of law and councils in England, Wales and Ireland which operated alongside COMMON LAW courts. Concerned mainly with civil business, they could provide remedies for alleged unjust acts according to flexible principles of justice or fairness rather than narrow rules and precedents. This form of justice – called 'equity' by the 16th century (from OFr. *equité*, derived from Latin *aequitas*, meaning 'fairness') – was seen as supplementing or correcting common law. Proceedings were recorded in English or French (rather than Latin). Procedures included a suitor's initial petition or bill; issue of the writ *subpoena* (Latin, meaning 'under penalty') against the defendant; defendant's response; written answers to questions by witnesses ('depositions'); arguments in court by the parties' lawyers; ruling by a judge (rather than jury).

In England, the main equity court, CHANCERY, devel-oped from the late 14th century. Other courts included the Court of REQUESTS (by 1483–1642), STAR CHAMBER (*c.*1515–1641) and Exchequer (equity side 1540s–1841). Administrative courts which utilized equity included: COUNCIL IN THE MARCHES OF WALES (1476–1689, with interruptions); COUNCIL OF THE NORTH (1484–1641, with interruptions); Court of Duchy Chamber (by 1480s, for duchy of Lancaster); Augmentations (1536–54); First Fruits and Tenths (1540–54); WARDS AND LIVERIES (1540–1646); General Surveyors (1542–7). In Ireland the main bodies were: Court of CHANCERY (from early 16th century); Court

of CASTLE CHAMBER (1563–6, 1571–1640s); PRESIDENCY courts (1569–1640s, 1660–72); WARDS AND LIVERIES (1622–40s). In the later 19th century, English and Irish equity courts were amalgamated with other courts, and equity became available in all superior courts (*see* LEGAL REFORMS, ENGLAND AND WALES, 1870s; COURTS, IRELAND).

EQUIVALENT Term used for the £398,000 (sterling) granted in 1707 by the English government to Scotland under the treaty of Union in return for Scotland's future contribution to England's pre-union NATIONAL DEBT. The money was disbursed to creditors of the Scottish government and stockholders of the Company of Scotland (*see* DARIEN SCHEME). Some regarded the Equivalent as a bribe. *See also* UNION OF ENGLAND AND SCOTLAND.

ERSKINE, EBENEZER, CASE OF A dispute in the Church of SCOTLAND. In 1733 Erskine (1680–1754), min-ister of STIRLING, was suspended by the Church's General Assembly for attacking its support of private patronage (*see* PATRONAGE ACT, 1712). He and other ministers formed a presbytery which became the nucleus for the separate SECESSION CHURCH. Erskine was formally expelled by the Church in 1740.

ESHER, 2ND VISCOUNT (b. 30 June 1852 at Kensington, Middlesex, England; d. 22 Jan. 1930 at London, England, aged 77). As secretary of the Office of Works 1895–1902, responsible for State buildings, Reginald Brett (Viscount Esher from 1899) was concerned to strengthen the British monarchy. He strongly influenced the staging of grand public celebrations for the diamond jubilee of VICTORIA (1897) and coronation of EDWARD VII (1902), and the creation of a processional way along the Mall in LONDON (1903–4). A confidant of A.J. BALFOUR (prime minister) and Edward VII, Esher chaired the 'Esher Committee' (1903–4) to reform the War Office and ARMY command following the (Second) BOER WAR. During WORLD WAR I he provided informal liaison between Allied commanders and politicians. Esher was a discreet but influential Establishment 'insider'. *See also* KINGSHIP AND MONARCHY, ENGLAND AND GREAT BRITAIN FROM 1680s.

ESSEX, 1ST EARL OF (b. 16 Sept. 1539 at Chartley, Staffordshire, England; d. 22 Sept. 1576 at Dublin, Ireland, aged 37). A courtier and soldier, Walter Devereux suc-ceeded as Viscount Hereford in 1558. In 1569 he helped to crush the NORTHERN REBELLION against Queen ELIZABETH I. He was created earl of Essex in 1572.

As a private adventurer, Essex attempted to colonize the Irish province of ULSTER (from July 1573) but failed because of plague and shortage of supplies. After obtaining reinforcements he led raids, killing members of the

O'NEILL clan. Elizabeth appointed him earl marshal of Ireland (March 1575). Essex ordered a siege of Rathlin Island, during which possibly 400 were killed (22–6 July). He was recalled to England soon afterwards. He was reappointed as earl marshal in July 1576 and returned to Ireland. *See also* PLANTATIONS, IRELAND.

ESSEX, 2ND EARL OF (b. 10 Nov. 1565 in England; d. 25 Feb. 1601 at London, England, aged 35). Robert Devereux succeeded as earl in 1576. He had martial aspirations: he fought in the Netherlands (1585–6) and later in Portugal (1589). Introduced to Queen ELIZABETH I in 1586, he was her favourite by May 1587 (June, confirmed as master of the horse, succeeding stepfather Robert, earl of LEICESTER). Despite a secret marriage (1590), which angered Elizabeth, he was appointed a privy councillor (1593).

Essex sought to succeed Lord Burghley (William CECIL) as Elizabeth's chief minister. He also favoured aggression against Spain. In 1596 he attacked Cádiz, but Elizabeth was uninfluenced. In 1597 he failed to capture the Spanish treasure fleet (from the Americas). In 1599 Essex went to Ireland (as lord lieutenant), where he concluded a truce with Irish rebels (9 Sept.) without royal authority (*see* NINE YEARS WAR).

After his return (Sept. 1599), Essex was excluded from the royal court. On 8 Feb. 1601, he and 300 followers sought help from the mayor of London to overthrow his enemies (so-called 'Essex Rebellion'). The mayor refused. Essex surrendered and was executed for TREASON. *See also* CECIL, ROBERT.

ESSEX, 3RD EARL OF (b. 11 Jan. 1591 at London, England; d. 14 Sept. 1646 at London, aged 55). Son of the disgraced 2nd earl of ESSEX (executed 1601) and a Puritan, Robert Devereux was granted his heritable titles by King JAMES VI/I (1603). His marriage was annulled in 1613 to enable his wife to marry a royal favourite (*see* SOMERSET, ROBERT EARL OF). In the 1620s Essex served abroad as a soldier. During the LONG PARLIAMENT (from 1640) he supported the House of Commons' demands of CHARLES I.

On 12 July 1642 Essex was appointed captain-general (commander) of Parliament's armies. During the CIVIL WARS he fought Royalists at Edgehill, Warwickshire (23 Oct. 1642), and blocked their approach to London (20 Nov., at Turnham Green, Middlesex). On 21 Aug. 1644 his army surrendered after being defeated near Lostwithiel (Cornwall), though Essex escaped. He resigned on 2 April 1645, anticipating exclusion by the SELF-DENYING ORDINANCE.

ESSEX, KINGDOM OF A Germanic-ruled kingdom (6th–9th centuries), occupying modern Essex (E England) and, initially, adjacent lands (historical Middlesex, part of Hertfordshire, and intermittently Surrey). 'Saxons' settled in the area from the 5th century. The kingdom was formed by the late 6th century. Christianity was finally adopted, after reverses, in the mid 660s. From the early 7th century LONDON was the principal trading centre.

Essex declined from the early 8th century. Its western lands, including London, were annexed by King ÆTHELBALD of MERCIA (ruled 716–57). In 812–14 King CENWULF of Mercia demoted Sigered from king to subking. In 825 Essex surrendered to King EGBERT of WESSEX. It retained its identity as a SHIRE within Wessex. *See also* KINGSHIP, ANGLO-SAXON.

ESSEX REBELLION *see* ESSEX, 2ND EARL OF

ÉTAPLES, TREATY OF Signed on 3 Nov. 1492 at Étaples (N France), between King HENRY VII of England and Charles VIII of France. It ended Henry's brief siege of Boulogne, by which he had shown displeasure at France's absorption of Brittany (Dec. 1491). Henry would withdraw his army; Charles agreed to pay Henry £149,000 and undertook not to support claimants to Henry's throne. *See also* FRANCE, ENGLISH AND BRITISH RELATIONS WITH.

ETHNIC AND NATIONAL MINORITIES, ENGLAND Germanic immigrants to southern Britain (5th–6th centuries), who settled amongst Britons, became culturally dominant (e.g., Britons' adoption of Germanic language). Scandinavian successors (late 9th–10th centuries) in the E and NE both occupied unsettled lands and concentrated in towns (e.g., YORK). They were eventually absorbed.

The NORMAN CONQUEST (1066–70s) established a mainly Norman French élite; some towns acquired 'alien' communities. Incomers eventually assimilated except for JEWS (expelled 1290). Scots, Welsh and Irish also steadily immigrated. In the 15th century Dutch and Flemings lived in larger towns. In 1500, 6% of London's population were foreigners.

Protestant refugees (Dutch, Walloons, French) in the 1560s–70s established large communities in London and NORWICH, and smaller ones elsewhere (in SE England, East Anglia), introducing manufacturing innovations (e.g., in textiles). French Protestant refugees after 1685 created communities and invigorated industries (e.g., silk textiles; *see* HUGUENOTS). A Jewish community also developed in London, and Indian sailors ('lascars') settled there.

Irish immigrants in the 18th century formed communities principally in London, LIVERPOOL and MANCHESTER, while Scots usually dispersed. Black AFRICANS were mostly servants, and clustered in London and Liverpool.

Large-scale Irish immigration occurred particularly following the GREAT FAMINE (1845–9); by the 1890s, 5–10% of city populations were Irish-born. East European Jewish immigrants in the 1880s–90s settled mainly in

London's East End, LEEDS and Manchester. CHINESE immigration created 'Chinatowns' in ports (e.g., Liverpool). In the 1940s, the main minorities were Jewish and port communities.

Immigration in the 1950s–70s added communities of AFRICAN CARIBBEANS (London, other large cities), Kashmiri Pakistanis (northern textile-manufacturing towns) and other SOUTH ASIANS (London, Midlands). From 1998 immigration rapidly expanded minorities (e.g., Poles in small towns and agricultural areas). By 2011, 20% of England's population were minorities; London and other towns had 'majority-minority populations'. *See also* IMMIGRATION TO ENGLAND; MUSLIMS IN GREAT BRITAIN; MULTICULTURALISM.

ETHNIC AND NATIONAL MINORITIES, IRELAND
Various peoples have historically settled among the Gaelic Irish population, notably Britons, Scandinavians, 'Old English', Welsh, 'New English' and Scots (*see* IMMIGRATION TO IRELAND). In the 13th century there was also a small Jewish community. New Jewish settlement began *c*.1500, and a synagogue was founded in DUBLIN in 1660. The Jewish population throughout Ireland peaked at 5500 in the 1940s. In the early 21st century it totalled about 2000, with synagogues in CORK, Dublin and BELFAST.

After the PARTITION OF IRELAND (1921), southern Ireland's population was predominantly of Gaelic origin and Catholic until the mid 1990s, when rapid economic expansion attracted new immigration, predominantly from the European Union. By 2011 (census), immigrants accounted for 12% of the population. They included: 112,000 from the UK, 63,000 Poles, 24,000 Lithuanians, 16,000 Nigerians, 19,000 other Africans, 11,000 Chinese, 36,000 other Asians.

Until the late 1990s the population of NORTHERN IRELAND remained mainly of Scottish or English background (majority, mostly Protestant), or Gaelic Irish (minority, usually Catholic). More peaceful conditions, following the TROUBLES, and expansion of the European Union (2004) encouraged immigration. By 2011 the immigrant population reached 11%, including 19,000 Poles and 7000 Lithuanians. The increased immigration (including many Catholics) and emigration from the established population had reduced the Protestant majority over Catholics to only 3% (48% to 45%).

ETHNIC AND NATIONAL MINORITIES, SCOTLAND
Immigration in the 19th and 20th centuries implanted distinctive minority communities, especially in GLASGOW and its region (W-C Scotland). Protestant Irish (immigrated 1790s–1880s) worked in the cotton and linen industries, later (from mid 19th century) in the coal, metal and engineering industries. As presbyterians they were

soon assimilated, but retained distinctiveness through the ORANGE ORDER. Catholic Irish (1790s–1920s) usually did unskilled casual work (labouring, building, etc.) and were visible as poor Catholic communities. Many presbyterians considered them an 'alien presence', particularly in the 1920s–30s. They rose socially from the 1950s as children increasingly attended university and became professionals (*see* CATHOLICS AND CATHOLIC CHURCH, SCOTLAND).

Lithuanians (immigrated 1880s–1914) established communities in the C Lowlands which retained their culture until the 1920s–30s. Lithuanian men worked mainly in coalmining. Jews (immigrated 1880s–1914) also established communities, the largest in Glasgow. During the 20th century many Jews were successful in business and the professions (*see also* SHINWELL, EMANUEL). Italians (1880s–1914) were more widely dispersed, often running cafes, though in 1914 3000 lived in Glasgow and 1000 in Edinburgh. Italians were assimilated from the 1950s. Asians (immigrated in 1950s–60s) also formed communities in cities. Many worked in transport or ran grocery shops.

The size and number of distinctive minority groups rose from 1998 with a new wave of immigration from overseas. In 2011 there were significant new groups from Poland, India, Republic of Ireland, USA and Pakistan, and smaller groups from many other countries. Asians were the largest ethnic minority group (3% of population), though 9% of the population had been born in England. The places with the largest proportionate ethnic minority populations were: Glasgow (12%), Aberdeen (8%), Edinburgh (8%) and Dundee (6%). *See also* IMMIGRATION TO SCOTLAND.

ETHNIC AND NATIONAL MINORITIES, WALES
Immigration from the 18th century created distinctive minority communities. In the late 20th century the largest were the English, though few of the English in Wales considered themselves a 'minority'. Former coalfields (NE and S Wales) and major ports contained communities of Irish ancestry, while CARDIFF (SE Wales) had Caribbean, African and Asian communities dating back to the late 19th century. Wales also contains a small Jewish community and scattered groups of Italian, Spanish and Polish ancestry.

From the 1950s immigration from 'New Commonwealth' countries in the West Indies, Asia and Africa created new communities, particularly in NEWPORT and Cardiff, although numbers were relatively small; in 1991, 1.9% of the population had been born in the 'New Commonwealth' compared with 4.9% for the entire UK. Relations with Welsh people were generally harmonious, though riots against Irish, Chinese, Jews and black communities occasionally occurred, as well as arson attacks on English-owned holiday homes in the 1980s. Large-scale immigration from 1998 increased the number and size of minority communities. In 2015 there were significant populations from

Poland, India, Germany, Republic of Ireland, China and Pakistan, and small groups from over 50 other countries. *See also* IMMIGRATION TO WALES, 18TH–21ST CENTURIES.

EUGENICS The science of improving human offspring (from Greek *eugenes*, meaning 'well born'). It was developed in Great Britain from the late 19th century, initially by Francis GALTON. His argument that mental characteristics were largely inherited, and the observation that families of the intellectual and enterprising middle classes were shrinking (but not those of other classes), produced concern that the quality of the population would deteriorate. Such views influenced fears about NATIONAL DETERIORATION from *c*.1902.

In 1909 a Eugenics Education Society was founded to campaign for segregation of the 'feeble minded', attracting support from many eminent people. Renamed the Eugenics Society in 1926, it also advocated voluntary sterilization of the mentally abnormal. Eugenic practices were discredited by authoritarian and genocidal policies in Germany in the 1930s–40s. In 1989 the Eugenics Society became the Galton Institute, concerned primarily with the scientific study of human heredity.

EUROPEAN ECONOMIC COMMUNITY/EURO-PEAN UNION, IMPACT ON BRITISH POLITICS From the 1960s attitudes towards European integration changed between and within the major political parties, affecting British politics. When in 1961 the CONSERVATIVE government of Harold MACMILLAN attempted entry to the European Economic Community (EEC, or 'Common Market', founded 1958), LABOUR was hostile. Yet the second attempt was made by Labour prime minister Harold WILSON (1967), despite Party resistance.

After the Conservative Edward HEATH secured agreement for entry (1971), Labour opposed the terms (as did some Conservatives), but pro-European Labour MPs supported the government (vote on membership, 28 Oct.). (The UK entered in 1973.) After succeeding Heath (1974), Wilson conducted superficial renegotiations and obtained approval in a referendum (5 June 1975, 67% in favour). But by 1983 Labour advocated withdrawal at the general election.

The Conservative Margaret THATCHER exhibited a mixed attitude: she accepted the Single European Act, which strengthened European powers (1986), but from 1988 opposed planned Economic and Monetary Union (EMU) while permitting entry into the EXCHANGE RATE MECHANISM (Oct. 1990). As EMU developed, tenacious 'Europhile' and 'Eurosceptic' factions divided the Conservatives. Although John MAJOR negotiated 'opt-outs' from the currency ('euro') and employment regulations ('social chapter'), Eurosceptics almost thwarted ratification of the treaty of MAASTRICHT (1992, creating the European Union or EU). Conservative divisions continued but Labour grew more pro-European.

After election in 1997, Labour accepted the social chapter and allowed large-scale IMMIGRATION from new members, but Gordon BROWN (chancellor of the Exchequer) prevented entry to the euro. His subsequent government accepted the treaty of Lisbon (with opt-outs), which increased the EU's legal powers (ratified by UK 2008). Brown's successor (from 2010), Conservative David CAMERON, was pressurized by both Conservative Eurosceptics and the UNITED KINGDOM INDEPENDENCE PARTY. In 2016 he completed superficial renegotiation of membership terms and called a referendum, expecting it to endorse membership. Instead the public voted to leave (*see* BREXIT). *See also* COMMON AGRICULTURAL POLICY; LIBERAL DEMOCRATS.

EUROPEAN ECONOMIC COMMUNITY/EUROPEAN UNION AND REPUBLIC OF IRELAND The European Economic Community (European Union, or EU, from 1993) admitted Ireland on 1 January 1973. Membership subordinated aspects of Irish law to European law, and representatives joined the Community's institutions. Ireland entered the European Monetary System (1979), which uncoupled the Irish pound's value from sterling, and subsequently the euro (1999). Concerns about domestic autonomy caused voters to reject the treaties of Nice (2001) and Lisbon (2008) in referendums (amended versions were accepted).

Ireland received considerable funding in relation to population size (IR£14 billion 1973–91): the COMMON AGRICULTURAL POLICY supported prices and raised farm incomes while regional funds financed infrastructure (e.g., roads). The economy diversified, though various uncompetitive firms closed. Membership changed Ireland's relationship to the UK; they became equal partners within the Community, and exports to the UK declined (61% to 35% by 1988). European law influenced social legislation (e.g., as affecting women), and immigrants from the EU altered society's composition. In 2010, following the near collapse of Ireland's banking system, the EU contributed rescue funding. The UK's decision in 2016 to leave the European Union had considerable implications for Ireland (*see* BREXIT). *See also* FARM MODERNISATION SCHEME; MAASTRICHT, TREATY OF.

EUROPEAN INSTITUTIONS, GREAT BRITAIN AND In its relations with Western Europe after WORLD WAR II (ended 1945), Britain was initially anxious not to loosen ties with the COMMONWEALTH and USA. It joined purely inter-national institutions such as the Council of Europe (1949) and Western European Union (1955–2011). It shunned supra-national authorities such as the European Coal and Steel Community (1950) and the European Economic Community or EEC (1958). Britain tried to incorporate the EEC into a looser FREE TRADE agreement, but succeeded only in forming non-EEC members into the European Free Trade Association (EFTA, founded 1960).

Prime Minister Harold MACMILLAN initiated a change of policy. From 1961 Britain sought EEC membership, but applications were vetoed by France in 1963 and 1967. Edward HEATH secured entry on 1 Jan. 1973, but EEC institutions and financial arrangements often seemed uncongenial. Britain accepted the Single European Act (1987), which created an EEC-wide internal market, but opted out of new employment regulations and the single currency envisaged by the treaty of MAASTRICHT (1992), which also renamed the EEC the European Union (effective from 1993). Continuing opposition to European integration, promoted by the UNITED KINGDOM INDEPENDENCE PARTY and Conservative 'Eurosceptics', eventually caused David CAMERON to hold a referendum on membership. Against his preference, the UK public voted to leave (2016; see BREXIT).

EUROPEAN UNION *see* EUROPEAN ECONOMIC COMMUNITY/EUROPEAN UNION, IMPACT ON BRITISH POLITICS; EUROPEAN INSTITUTIONS, GREAT BRITAIN AND; EUROPEAN ECONOMIC COMMUNITY/EUROPEAN UNION AND IRELAND

EVACUATION, WORLD WAR II Evacuation from British cities was planned by the government in 1938 in response to fear of German bombing. Implemented on 1 Sept. 1939 (two days before war was declared), about 1.5 million persons, mostly children, were moved to safer areas. When bombing failed to occur, many returned home (almost two-thirds by Jan. 1940). Further evacuations from LONDON occurred during the BLITZ (German heavy bombing, from Sept. 1940) and in June–Aug. 1944 during attacks by 'V1' flying bombs. Evacuation of poor children revealed urban poverty to better-off families, encouraging support for post-war social reform (see WELFARE STATE).

In NORTHERN IRELAND, small-scale evacuations took place mainly from BELFAST in 1940 (5600 persons in July, 1,00 in Aug.). German raids in April 1941 forced the private evacuation of over 30,000 children from Belfast to rural areas

EVANGELICALISM A form of Protestant Christianity which emphasizes the need for heartfelt conversion to produce a conviction of personal salvation. Evangelicals also stress the doctrines of Christ's atonement (reconciling man with God through his death), regeneration by the Holy Spirit and justification by faith alone. Evangelicals base faith firmly on the Bible, and express 'vital religion' in endeavours to spread the Gospel, promote good causes, and lead holy lives.

Evangelicalism became a powerful force in the Churches of England, Ireland and Scotland from the 1730s, and in other movements (e.g., METHODISM). It was influential in the 19th century (e.g., through the CLAPHAM SECT) and continued in the 21st century. 'Evangelical' is also used for opponents of Catholicism in the 1520s–50s, before 'Protestant' came into common use. *See also* EVANGELICAL MOVEMENTS; PLYMOUTH BRETHREN.

EVANGELICAL MOVEMENTS The promotion of doctrines and principles of EVANGELICALISM in the British Isles from the 18th century was influenced by a 'Protestant Awakening' in Europe and N America. In Wales, itinerant preachers spread the Gospel (*see* METHODIST REVIVAL, WALES). In Scotland the Kirk (Church of SCOTLAND) sought to evangelize in the Gaelic HIGHLANDS. From 1739 George WHITEFIELD and John WESLEY began open-air preaching, touring Great Britain and Ireland. Their movement, METHODISM, eventually broke with the Church of ENGLAND, but an evangelical party developed within the Church in which Charles Simeon (1759–1836) was influential.

Evangelicals promoted causes such as the abolition of the SLAVE TRADE and missionary work in the British Empire (*see* MISSIONARY SOCIETIES). Their ideals had a profound impact on 19th-century culture. Evangelical bishops included J.B. SUMNER (1780–1862) and his brother C.R. Sumner (1790–1874, bishop of WINCHESTER 1827–69).

From the mid 20th century divisions developed among evangelicals over fundamentalist and liberal attitudes to Scripture, but conversion campaigns (e.g., led by US evangelist Billy Graham), the Charismatic movement and acceptance of extrovert worship influenced by popular culture succeeded in winning converts. *See also* FREE CHURCH OF SCOTLAND.

EVANS, GWYNFOR (b. 1 Sept. 1912 at Barry, Glamorgan, Wales; d. 21 April 2005 at Pencarreg, Ceredigion, Wales, aged 92). President of PLAID CYMRU 1945–81; MP for CARMARTHEN, 1966–70, 1974–9. Evans' initial election victory (at a by-election) made him his Party's first MP and moved DEVOLUTION to the forefront of Welsh politics. In 1980 he threatened a hunger strike to force the British government to maintain its commitment to a Welsh-language television service. *See also* BROADCASTING, WALES.

EVESHAM, BATTLE OF *see* BARONIAL CONFLICT AND WARS

EVOLUTION The hypothesis that species of living organisms on Earth have arisen through biological development from simpler forms, rather than by divine creation. Before the mid 19th century it was commonly argued that the complexity of the animal world represented God's design of species with the attributes required for particular habitats (*see* PALEY, WILLIAM). But during the 18th century, as awareness of the living world expanded through exploration, plants were classified, and knowledge of fossils and GEOLOGY increased, a few people suspected that the living world represented evolution rather than design.

A British pioneer was the doctor Erasmus Darwin (1731–1802), who translated works by the Swedish botanist Carl Linnaeus (1707–77). In *Zoonomia* (two volumes, 1794, 1796) Darwin argued that parents could transmit acquired characteristics to offspring, and that animals had developed over a long period of time from a few living beings. His posthumous poetic work *The Temple of Nature* (1803) envisaged life originating in chemical actions and developing through increasingly sophisticated forms. But it was unclear how different species were formed.

A natural means of species development and survival, 'natural selection', was announced and published in 1858 by the naturalists Alfred Russell Wallace (1823–1913) and Charles DARWIN (grandson of Erasmus Darwin). The latter elaborated his theory in larger works, and it was promoted by T.H. HUXLEY (nicknamed 'Darwin's Bulldog'). Darwin's denial of divine creation, and the associated proposal that humans were an evolved species, distressed churches, though some theologians soon showed sympathy (e.g., John Henry NEWMAN in 1868). The concepts of evolution and natural selection were also applied to social analysis (e.g., by Herbert SPENCER).

The biological mechanisms of variation and inheritance still remained unknown until a model of the DNA (deoxyribonucleic acid) molecule was created in 1953 in CAMBRIDGE (*see* CRICK, FRANCIS).

EWORTH, HANS (fl. from 1540 at Antwerp, Netherlands; d. after 1574, possibly at London, England). A painter of portraits and allegorical scenes, Eworth became a freeman of the Antwerp guild of painters in 1540. Recorded in England from 1549, he made several portraits of Queen MARY I (d. 1558). He remained in England under the Protestant ELIZABETH I, though many of his works depict Catholics. *See also* VISUAL ARTS, BRITAIN.

EXCHANGE RATE MECHANISM The system established in 1979 by the EUROPEAN ECONOMIC COMMUNITY to constrain fluctuations of participants' currencies against each other and encourage convergence of national economies in preparation for a single currency. The UK (alone) declined to join. During the 1980s Margaret THATCHER (prime minister) remained hostile despite support for entry from ministers Geoffrey HOWE and Nigel LAWSON. Lawson's attempt from 1988, as chancellor of the Exchequer, to 'shadow' the Deutschmark, mimicking the mechanism, led to his resignation (1989).

In 1990 Lawson's successor John MAJOR persuaded Thatcher to accept sterling's participation (announced 5 Oct.). The entry rate of DM 2.95 to the pound proved unsustainable. Sterling was forced out in 1992, damaging the Conservatives' reputation for economic management (*see* BLACK WEDNESDAY). *See also* EUROPEAN ECONOMIC COMMUNITY/EUROPEAN UNION, IMPACT ON BRITISH POLITICS.

EXCHEQUER, ENGLAND A department of royal GOVERNMENT responsible for receiving and issuing money, and for keeping accounts, 12th–19th centuries. It was named after the chequered tablecloth on which accounting was done.

The Exchequer was probably created *c*.1110 by ROGER OF SALISBURY, linked to the royal treasury at WINCHESTER Castle. Located at WESTMINSTER from the late 12th century, it then comprised a lower exchequer, where payments and receipts were made, and an upper exchequer where the king and officials (CHANCELLOR, TREASURER, etc.) met as a court twice a year to receive sheriffs' accounts. The Exchequer's main accounts were called PIPE ROLLS. From the late 12th century some officers sent deputies, and from the early 13th century the chancellor was represented by his clerk, the chancellor of the Exchequer.

The Exchequer expanded as new departments and accounts were created, but became subordinated to the separated Treasury from the later 17th century. Its main accounting practices continued until the 19th century. Much of the Exchequer was abolished in 1834 and the remainder in 1866. *See also* DIALOGUE OF THE EXCHEQUER.

EXCHEQUER, IRELAND A department of GOVERNMENT in the English lordship (later kingdom) of Ireland, based at DUBLIN, which received revenues (e.g., profits from MANORS), and kept and audited accounts, 12th–19th centuries. Created by 1185, following the Anglo-Norman invasion (1169–70), it was probably the first department to become separate from the itinerant household of the CHIEF GOVERNOR. Its head, the treasurer, was second in importance to the governor until the later 13th century.

From *c*.1285 treasurers were required to present accounts in England, strengthening English control, and from the later 15th century the Exchequer's effective head was an under-treasurer. During the 16th century an Exchequer Court also evolved, based on equity. The Exchequer's importance declined from the late 17th century; it was amalgamated with the English Exchequer in 1817 (*see* EXCHEQUER, IRELAND, ABOLITION OF).

EXCHEQUER, IRELAND, ABOLITION OF The Exchequer was abolished on 5 Jan. 1817, following the merger of Irish and British national debts and revenues as envisaged under the UNION OF IRELAND AND GREAT BRITAIN. The Irish Treasury (part of the Exchequer) was retained and amalgamated with the British Treasury. Fiscal affairs were thereafter overseen by a vice-treasurer at the

British Treasury (at WESTMINSTER) and deputy at DUBLIN. *See also* GOVERNMENT, IRELAND 19TH–20TH CENTURIES.

EXCHEQUER, SCOTLAND A commission (not permanent office) comprising the CHANCELLOR, royal councillors and clerks, which was usually convened annually to audit the accounts of royal household officers (CHAMBERLAIN, comptroller, treasurer) and local officers (sheriffs, custumars, bailies of royal BURGHS). The Exchequer was started *c*.1180–1200, continued after the UNION OF ENGLAND AND SCOTLAND (1707), and was merged into the Court of SESSION in 1856.

EXCISE Inland taxation levied on the sale of commodities such as ale, beer, salt, meat, soap and hats. Excise was introduced in parts of England in 1643, during the CIVIL WARS, by the LONG PARLIAMENT to raise war finance. Devised by John PYM in imitation of Dutch practice, it was copied by Royalists in their territories (including Wales).

Excise continued after the wars (1648) and RESTORATION (1660). It was a principal source of government income until the early 19th century, and remained important thereafter (under various names). It was long disliked partly because of the many 'excisemen' (petty officials) involved in its collection. Excise was introduced in Ireland in 1643 and in Scotland in 1644. *See also* FISCAL–MILITARY STATE.

EXCISE CRISIS A major political crisis in Great Britain, in 1733, during the premiership of Robert WALPOLE. He proposed to extend EXCISE duties to include imported wine and tobacco, in order to hold down the LAND TAX. It generated popular opposition, which feared tyrannical behaviour by additional excise officials. When MPs appeared likely to defeat the scheme, Walpole withdrew it (11 April). *See also* COBHAM'S CUBS; PULTENEY, WILLIAM.

EXCLUSION CRISIS A political crisis in England, 1678–81, in the reign of King CHARLES II, when politicians tried to exclude the heir to the throne, James, duke of York, from the succession because of his Catholicism. Charles frustrated the movement.

James's conversion to Catholicism (1669, publicized 1673) raised fears about his future behaviour as king (*see* ABSOLUTISM). These were exacerbated when the POPISH PLOT (revealed Sept. 1678) envisaged the assassination of Charles and replacement by York. The earl of SHAFTESBURY and others proposed exclusion of James in Parliament (Oct.–Nov.). Charles dissolved Parliament in Jan. 1679 (*see* CAVALIER PARLIAMENT).

In May 1679 the House of Commons accepted an Exclusion Bill; Charles prorogued and later dissolved Parliament ('First Exclusion Parliament', March–July 1679).

In 1679 'Exclusionists' and 'Anti-Exclusionists' became known as WHIGS and TORIES, and people outside Parliament (e.g., pamphleteers) campaigned for exclusion. In Nov. 1680 the Commons accepted, but House of Lords rejected, an Exclusion Bill (during 'Second Exclusion Parliament', Oct. 1680–Jan. 1681). In 1681 Parliament, meeting in OXFORD, threatened to approve Exclusion. Charles dissolved it ('Third Exclusion Parliament', March 1681). Thereafter Charles ruled without Parliament, despite the 1664 TRIENNIAL ACT, and excluded Whigs from corporations and government posts. *See also* JAMES VII/II.

EXECUTIVES, NORTHERN IRELAND During the TROUBLES, the British government sought to replace Unionist government with coalition government to encourage social reconciliation. Following the election of an ASSEMBLY, a multi-party Executive Council, led by Brian FAULKNER, held authority Jan.–May 1974. It was undermined by the ULSTER WORKERS' STRIKE.

Following the BELFAST AGREEMENT, a power-sharing Executive was formed in Dec. 1999, led by David TRIMBLE of the ULSTER UNIONIST PARTY (UUP) with the SOCIAL DEMOCRATIC AND LABOUR PARTY (SDLP) as principal partner. It was suspended Feb.–May 2000, and from Oct. 2002 after the discovery of spying by PROVISIONAL SINN FÉIN (a coalition party). A resumption was prevented by the rise of the anti-Agreement DEMOCRATIC UNIONIST PARTY, until its leader, Ian PAISLEY, agreed to head an Executive (implemented May 2007). Martin McGUINNESS of Provisional Sinn Féin became deputy first minister. Paisley retired in 2008. He was succeeded by Peter Robinson (2008–16) and Arlene Foster. The Executive collapsed in Jan. 2017 when McGuinness resigned, mainly over the Renewable Heat Incentive (an allegedly abused energy scheme in which Arlene Foster had previously been involved). A new Executive was instituted in Jan. 2020 with Foster as first minister and Michelle O'Neill (Provisional Sinn Féin) as deputy first minister. *See also* PEACE PROCESS, NORTHERN IRELAND.

EXPLANATION, ACT OF *see* SETTLEMENT AND EXPLANATION, ACTS OF

EXTERNAL RELATIONS ACT, IRELAND *see* ABDICATION CRISIS AND IRISH FREE STATE

EYRE OFr. term, meaning 'journey', used especially for a journey or circuit made by kings or judges. In England itinerant judges, sent out from the royal court, are first recorded under King HENRY I (ruled 1100–35). The term 'general eyre' is used for the teams of justices who were sent to groups of counties from 1174 when they implemented the Assize of CLARENDON (1166). General eyres occurred regularly until 1294. *See also* ASSIZE; COMMON LAW; JUSTICIARS, SCOTLAND.

F

FABIAN SOCIETY An organization founded in Great Britain in Jan. 1884 to promote SOCIALISM through peaceful evolution. It was named after the Roman general Quintus Fabius Maximus Rullianus (fl. 325–295 BC), who triumphed by dint of patience. Members included George Bernard SHAW and Sidney and Beatrice WEBB. The Fabians helped to form the LABOUR PARTY (1900) and continued to operate as an affiliated research agency in the early 21st century.

FACTORY Term originally used for an overseas trading station (16th–19th centuries), sometimes combining a residence and warehouse (derived from 'factor', meaning 'agent'). From the 18th century it also referred to a building or range of buildings with manufacturing machinery. The earliest large mechanized factory in the British Isles was the silk-throwing factory built in 1715–19 at Derby (Derbyshire, C England) for John and Thomas Lombe. Five storeys high, it accommodated 300 employees.

Capital-intensive modes of production and machinery (e.g., for textiles) moved much manufacture from homes and workshops into specialized large units. Early factories were located by watercourses to employ water power. (Factories were often called 'mills'.) From the later 18th century steam power facilitated other locations, requiring access to coal; and 'factory towns' developed (e.g., MANCHESTER). *See also* INDUSTRIAL REVOLUTION.

FACTORY LEGISLATION Factory conditions caused concern from the later 18th century. The UK Parliament enacted legislation for cotton factories in both Great Britain and Ireland in 1802, 1819, 1825 and 1831, regulating cleanliness, ventilation and education for apprentices. The first effective Factory Act, applicable in all UK textile factories, was that of 1833, which prohibited children under nine, restricted working time for under-18s, and instigated inspectors. An Act in 1844 limited daily work to 6½ hours for children aged 10–12 and 12 hours for women (the latter reduced by the Ten Hours Act of 1847). Legislation in 1864 and 1867 included other factories and workshops. Legislation for factories continued until the mid 20th century. Thereafter it was included in 'health and safety' legislation in both Britain and Ireland.

Alongside factory legislation, women and boys under ten in Britain and Ireland were prohibited from working underground by the Mines Act of 1842. The 1908 Coal Mines Act began regulation of men's work. *See also* INDUSTRIAL REVOLUTION; COTTON INDUSTRY, ENGLAND/SCOTLAND; SHAFTESBURY, 7TH EARL OF.

FAIRFAX, THOMAS (b. 17 Jan. 1612 at Denton, Yorkshire, England; d. 12 Nov. 1671 at Nun Appleton, Yorkshire, aged 59). Fairfax gained military experience in Continental Europe (1629–31). He fought for King CHARLES I in the Wars of the COVENANT (1639–40;

A Dictionary of British and Irish History, First Edition. Edited by Robert Peberdy and Philip Waller.
© 2021 John Wiley & Sons Ltd; © editorial matter and organisation Robert Peberdy and Phillip Waller.
Published 2021 by John Wiley & Sons Ltd.

knighted 1641). But from 1642 he supported Parliament in the CIVIL WARS, winning a national reputation with the capture of Selby (Yorkshire) on 11 April 1644. He also fought at Marston Moor, Yorkshire (2 July).

On 21 Jan. 1645 Fairfax was appointed commander of Parliament's NEW MODEL ARMY, shortly before other senior officers were removed by the SELF-DENYING ORDINANCE. He decisively defeated Royalists at Naseby, Northamptonshire (14 June), captured BRISTOL (10 Sept.), and accepted surrender of the Royalist capital, OXFORD (24 June 1646). In 1648 he became Lord Fairfax by inheritance (Scottish title). In 1650 Fairfax resigned rather than lead an invasion of Scotland. In 1660 he captured YORK for General MONCK (Jan.) and supported the RESTORATION.

FAIRS *see* MARKETS AND FAIRS

FAIR TRADE MOVEMENT In the late 19th century, a campaign in Great Britain for PROTECTIONISM to apply in commercial dealings with countries that would not agree to FREE TRADE. It protested at the 'unfair' competition which British industries were facing from countries that used subsidies and tariffs. The Fair Trade League was founded in 1881.

FALAISE, TREATY OF Sealed 8 Dec. 1174 (at Valognes, NORMANDY); imposed by King HENRY II of England on King WILLIAM I of Scotland. It acknowledged that William had done homage to Henry for Scotland (probably in Falaise, Normandy). (William had been captured in NE England in July; *see* REVOLT OF 1173–4.) Cancelled 1189. *See also* SCOTTISH–ENGLISH RELATIONS BEFORE 1290.

FALKIRK, BATTLE OF Fought near Falkirk, SE of Stirling (C Scotland), on 22 July 1298. An English army under King EDWARD I defeated a Scottish army under William WALLACE (reversing defeat of the English at STIRLING BRIDGE). The battle of Falkirk ended Wallace's leadership of resistance to English rule in Scotland, although Edward was unable to pacify Scotland. *See also* SCOTTISH–ENGLISH RELATIONS 1290 TO 1357.

FALKLAND ISLANDS A British overseas territory in the S Atlantic Ocean, comprising East and West Falkland and a hundred smaller islands; named in 1690 after Viscount Falkland, recently treasurer of the English Navy. From 1764 Great Britain, France, Spain and Argentina all established short-lived settlements; Britain claimed the islands in 1765. In 1833 a British naval ship reasserted sovereignty, and a CROWN COLONY was established in 1841. Sheep farmers from Scotland settled permanently on the islands, whose economy henceforth depended on sheep. Argentina also claimed sovereignty and in 1982 invaded the islands (*see*

FALKLANDS WAR). The Falklands became a British DEPENDENT TERRITORY in 1983, and an overseas territory in 2002. Approx. population in 1921, 2000; in 2010, 2900.

FALKLANDS WAR The armed campaign by Great Britain in 1982 to recapture the FALKLAND ISLANDS. On 2 April, following a reduction of British naval strength in the S Atlantic, Argentine troops invaded the Islands, in furtherance of a territorial claim. The British government, led by Margaret THATCHER, pledged to restore British sovereignty (favoured overwhelmingly by Falklands inhabitants).

A 'task force' of ships sailed on 4 April, and naval conflict began on 2 May. Mediation by the USA failed, and British troops liberated the Islands by force (21 May–14 June). The war cost 255 British lives. *See also* WAR CABINET.

FAMILY AND KINSHIP, ENGLAND Among Anglo-Saxons, the 'nuclear' family (husband, wife, two or three children) was central. Wider kinship also mattered, based on 'agnatic' (male) relationships within a kindred group (7th–9th centuries). Kinsmen were involved in WERGILD payments, landholding and marriage arrangements. Stronger lordship and royal authority reduced their importance. The Church exercised jurisdiction over marriage in the 12th–19th centuries. Hereditary surnames were adopted in the 12–14th centuries.

By the late 14th century and probably earlier, family formation matched the 'Western European marriage pattern', whereby adults married relatively late (mid 20s), when able to establish a household, and many (perhaps 10%) remained single. Families remained small due to late marriage, high child mortality, and suckling of children to reduce fertility. About 3% of births were illegitimate. Recognition of wider kindred varied; they were particularly valued for PATRONAGE. Households often included servants and apprentices (one-sixth of rural households, one-third of urban households in late 14th century). Average household size was 4.75; noblemen's households were much larger.

From the mid 18th century, average marriage age fell (from 26 to 23 for women by 1800) and more people married: fertility rose, families became larger, POPULATION increased (aided by lower mortality). Around 1840 there were eight births per family (average). The illegitimacy rate was (temporarily) 7%.

The marriage age rose from the 1870s; births per family also declined due to BIRTH CONTROL. By 1920 the average number of children per family was 2.8.

From the 1960s divorce increased significantly, and many adults preferred cohabitation or raised children in single-parent households, eroding family and kinship. Between 1961 and 1992 illegitimate (or non-marital) births rose from 6% to 31%, reaching 47% by 2010. Civil partnerships for same-sex couples were introduced in the UK in 2005 and civil marriage in England in 2014. Children were created for such couples by artificial methods. Opposite-sex civil partnerships were made available from Dec. 2019. *See also* DIVORCE, LAW RELATING TO; HARDWICKE MARRIAGE ACT; CIVIL REGISTRATION; ABORTION, GREAT BRITAIN.

FAMILY AND KINSHIP, IRELAND BEFORE 18TH CENTURY In the 7th century the most significant grouping was the *derbfine* ('certain-kindred'), consisting of a man and three generations of patrilineal (agnatic) male descendants (up to second cousin). (From *c.*700 it contracted to the *gelfine*, 'white kindred', of three generations.) This property-owning unit was responsible for its members' liabilities. A senior kinsman (OIr. *aire coisring*, meaning 'lord of a kindred') represented the group in external dealings. The importance of the kin-group for inheritance (including KINGSHIP) explains the preoccupation of kings and nobles with genealogy.

The conjugal family, parents and children, had its place within this kin-group. The bond of *lánamnas* ('marriage') united father, mother, son and daughter. Both parents shared responsibility for rearing children. Through marriage, women left their paternal kin-group and joined that of their husband. An important function of marriage was to produce children, especially sons. Ties of another kind were created by fosterage. Royal and noble children were customarily fostered – boys from 7 to 17, girls to 14. Foster parents supported and educated children in accordance with their status.

English settlers after the Anglo-Norman invasion (1169–70) had a narrower view of kinship: estates and landholdings were usually held by individuals and transmitted to a single heir. Wider kin were of little significance. Some Anglo-Irish adopted fosterage, or married Gaelic Irish, practices that were prohibited in the 14th century to resist absorption of the Anglo-Irish into Gaelic society (*see* KILKENNY, STATUTE OF). English practices, especially primogeniture (succession by eldest son) were spread by the reassertion of English authority and law, new settlement, and dispossession of Gaelic landowners in the 16th–17th centuries. Gaelic customs collapsed. *See also* BREHON LAW; TENURES, IRELAND.

FAMILY AND KINSHIP, IRELAND FROM 18TH CENTURY Rising POPULATION in the late 18th century was probably caused by changing family characteristics, though data shortage hampers explanation. Women's age of marriage possibly fell to the low twenties, or marital fertility in rural areas was high, facilitated by potatoes and subdivision of landholdings. After 1800, population increase generated considerable EMIGRATION, and women's average

(mean) marriage age may have risen slightly (to 24.5 in 1845). The separation of Catholics and Protestants within society was maintained partly by discouragement of intermarriage.

After the GREAT FAMINE (1845–9), the marriage rate fell, and average age of marriage rose, because of reduced economic opportunity: many young women emigrated, and increased proportions of women and especially men remained single. (Ireland's population declined until the 1920s, southern Ireland's until the 1960s.) Ireland's marital fertility was lower than elsewhere in Europe, though it became relatively high from the 1870s as fertility elsewhere declined. In the late 1950s, in the Republic of Ireland, average marriage ages were 31 for men, 27 for women. The total fertility rate peaked at 4.1 children in 1964 (compared with 2.1 for replacement). Protestants in NORTHERN IRELAND had smaller families from the 1920s. The IRISH FREE STATE reinforced Catholic teaching: divorce was prevented (1925), contraceptive devices banned (1935), and the family protected under the 1937 CONSTITUTION, including prohibition of divorce. (ABORTION was already illegal.)

From the late 20th century the Republic underwent a 'demographic transition', changes in values, and erosion of kinship. BIRTH CONTROL was widespread by the 1970s (contraception was officially allowed from 1979). From the 1980s the birth rate declined, falling below replacement after 1991. Cohabitation and illegitimacy increased, the latter reaching 36% by 2015. Divorce was introduced in 1997, legal provisions for cohabitants and same-sex civil partnerships in 2010, same-sex marriage under the constitution in 2015, and liberal abortion provision was legalized in 2018. In 2019 the UK Parliament legislated for the introduction of same-sex marriage, opposite-sex civil partnerships and liberal abortion provision in Northern Ireland from 2020.

FAMILY AND KINSHIP, SCOTLAND Before the 12th century the kindred group was a central social institution. Kindreds made retribution for kinfolk and influenced descent of land (*see* LAW, SCOTLAND; KIN-BASED SOCIETY). From the early 12th century kings modified relations among nobles by requiring descent by primogeniture (to eldest son) for lordships and EARLDOMS. Lineages became important; but in the absence of male heirs, lands and titles passed through female connections (an aspect of 'cognatic kinship').

In the 14th–15th centuries kin-based society revived, but acknowledged only male lines ('agnatic kinship'). Landed families established 'cadet' branches whose male members shared a surname. (Married women retained their original kin surname.) As lands descended to successive generations, localities in both Lowlands and HIGHLANDS became identified with particular surnames. Kin-based justice and bloodfeud persisted, in the

Lowlands until the late 16th century, in the Highlands until the 18th century.

Families generally lived as small 'nuclear' households. From 1560, when the REFORMATION changed marriage from sacrament to contract, society tolerated various marital practices. 'Irregular marriages' were legally valid (by private vows, promise to marry and intercourse, or tacit marriage 'by cohabitation and repute'); divorce was permitted (from 1560 for adultery, 1573 for desertion). During the 17th century population mobility in the Lowlands probably reduced the density of kinship, thereby re-emphasizing the nuclear family. High mortality kept family size low; rural families typically included only two children.

During the 19th century family size increased, reaching 5–7 children (average) among working-class families. From the 1870s it fell, through use of family limitation methods, returning by the 1990s to two children. Irregular marriage, except for 'cohabitation and repute', was prohibited in 1939 (Marriage (Scotland) Act) but from the 1960s intentional cohabitation increased. By 2017 a majority of births (50.9%) were non-marital. UK legislation introduced same-sex civil partnerships (2005), and Scottish legislation provided same-sex marriage (2014). *See also* CLAN, SCOTLAND.

FAMILY AND KINSHIP, WALES BEFORE 15TH CENTURY The kindred group (Welsh *cenedl*) was the key element in social and economic life, making kinship an important feature of society. The inner kindred comprised male descendants of a great-grandfather (a form of 'agnatic kinship'). Land, for example, was controlled by kindreds (*see* TENURES, WALES); although land was farmed individually, alienation of land was subject to the consent of kinsmen. The principle caused tension when applied to the succession of kingdoms (*see* KINGSHIP, WALES 5TH–13TH CENTURIES). The kindred group also had social roles; e.g., exacting revenge if a member was murdered (*see* LAW, WELSH).

People lived in 'nuclear' family households of husband, wife, and children (sometimes with servants or aged parents). New families were formed by marriage, with individuals exercising choice of marriage-partner. Marriage was considered a terminable contract, so divorce was a regular custom. Men sometimes had children by several wives or concubines. Children of irregular liaisons could be adopted into the kindred group (Welsh *cynnwys*), giving legitimate and illegitimate children similar status. Within marriage the husband was in theory pre-eminent. Women's main social role was to bear children. In practice, women provided links between families and between kindred groups. Literary sources testify to affection within marriage.

In English-inhabited parts of the MARCH OF WALES (late 11th–16th centuries) English customs prevailed (*see* FAMILY AND KINSHIP, ENGLAND).

FAMILY AND KINSHIP, WALES FROM 15TH CENTURY From the 15th century the kindred group (Welsh *cenedl*) became less important. The GENTRY pioneered the replacement of partible inheritance (division between heirs) with primogeniture (inheritance by eldest son), which created unequal lineages within kin-networks. They also replaced patronymics (using *ap*, meaning 'son of', or *ferch*, 'daughter of') with heritable surnames. The UNION OF WALES WITH ENGLAND (1536–43) abolished partible inheritance and imposed English COMMON LAW, thereby displacing kin-based Welsh customary law (*see* LAW, WELSH). By the 19th century heritable patrilineal surnames were almost universal. The common family remained the 'nuclear' unit of husband, wife and two or three children, with servants in wealthier households. High mortality kept families small.

Infant mortality fell from the early 20th century, and BIRTH CONTROL was widely used to limit family size. From the 1960s a substantial minority preferred cohabitation to marriage or raised children in single-parent households, further diminishing family and kinship roles. Between 1961 and 1992 illegitimate (or non-marital) births rose from 4% to 34% of live births, and reached 58% by 2010. Civil partnerships for same-sex couples were introduced in the UK in 2005 and civil marriage in Wales in 2014. Artificial methods were used to create children for such couples. Opposite-sex civil partnerships were made available by the UK Parliament from Dec. 2019.

FAMINES, BRITAIN Occasional famines are recorded from the late 10th century. In 1315–17 Britain suffered in the 'Great European Famine', when bad weather and harvest failure may have killed 15% of England's population. (The crisis was prolonged by an epidemic that killed sheep and cattle, 1319–21.) Famine is recorded in England in 1437–40, and in England and Wales in 1582–3 and in the late 1590s. A severe famine in northern England in 1622–3 was the last in England. England and Wales avoided further famines because of increased and more resilient agricultural productivity and better integration of regions by transport and marketing systems.

Scotland was more vulnerable than England and Wales because of its colder climate, limited agriculture (e.g., extensive dependence on oats) and low commercialization. From the mid 16th century, as population grew, dearths of foodstuffs frequently occurred, either nationally or regionally. Most of the country was affected in 1623, the 1640s and 1696–9. The last occasion reduced population by about 13%, and was the final time when large numbers died in the Lowlands. There were further crop failures in the northern Highlands and islands from the 1740s to 1840s, though relief was more effective. *See also* POPULATION, ENGLAND/SCOTLAND/WALES.

FAMINES, IRELAND Bad weather intermittently caused localized or widespread famine in the 5th–15th centuries. For example, Ireland shared in the 'Great European Famine' of 1315–17. After a pause in the 16th and 17th centuries, a famine in 1740–1 killed 200,000–400,000 people (10–20% of the population). Famine affected Ireland again in 1816 and 1822, and finally with the GREAT FAMINE of 1845–9, which possibly killed proportionately fewer people than in 1740–1 but had far-reaching political consequences. *See also* POPULATION, IRELAND.

FARADAY, MICHAEL (b. 22 Sept. 1791 at Newington Butts, Surrey, England; d. 25 Aug. 1867 at Hampton Court, Middlesex, England, aged 75). Apprenticed as a bookbinder (1805), Faraday educated himself in chemistry. Enthused by the lectures of Humphry DAVY at the ROYAL INSTITUTION, he obtained employment there as a laboratory assistant (1813), and accompanied Davy on a Continental tour (1813–15).

In 1821 Faraday made a major discovery: when he electrified a wire suspended near a magnet protruding from a bowl of mercury, it rotated. The phenomenon, called 'electro-magnetic rotation', was later exploited for electric motors. Faraday was elected to the ROYAL SOCIETY (1824), despite friction with Davy (resulting from a recent experiment), and promoted to laboratory director (1825).

In 1831 Faraday discovered 'electro-magnetic induction' through two experiments. After wrapping separate coils of insulated wire on opposite sides of an iron ring, he found that an electric current in one coil stimulated electricity in the other (the basis for the transformer). He also created an electrical charge in a coil of wire by moving a magnet within the coil (the basis for the dynamo). Faraday's discoveries made him famous. In the 1840s–50s he made further progress in understanding light and magnetic effects. *See also* MAXWELL, JAMES CLERK.

FARM MODERNISATION SCHEME A European Economic Community scheme (under the COMMON AGRICULTURAL POLICY) to increase farmers' incomes by reducing farm numbers, which was adopted by the Republic of Ireland in 1974. Farmers were classified as 'commercial' (4.3%), 'development' (23.6%) or 'other' (72.1%). Investment grants were available mainly for 'development' farmers. A related scheme encouraged 'other' (smaller) farmers to retire. Results were disappointing (e.g., only about 600 farmers retired). The

modernization scheme was replaced in 1986. *See also* AGRICULTURE, STATE INVOLVEMENT, SOUTHERN IRELAND.

FARM OF THE SHIRE In England, a sum paid annually by the SHERIFF of each SHIRE to the ROYAL HOUSEHOLD or Exchequer in place of variable royal revenues. Farms (from Latin *firma*, meaning 'fixed payment') were generally introduced possibly after the Norman Conquest (1066–70s) or slightly later (after 1086). In 1129–30 they provided 40% of Exchequer income. Their importance declined in the 13th century when some revenues were excluded and collected separately. *See also* EXCHEQUER; ROYAL REVENUES, ENGLAND.

FASCISM, GREAT BRITAIN The main organization was the British Union of Fascists (BUF), formed Oct. 1932 through a renaming of the New Party. It eclipsed various petty precursors. Led by Oswald MOSLEY, the BUF advocated the corporate State, anticommunism, and (later) antisemitism, and included a uniformed 'National Defence Force' (nicknamed 'Blackshirts'). Despite secret funding from Italy and Germany, the BUF failed to attract a mass membership. Violence at prominent events in London alienated Conservative sympathizers (e.g., at Olympia, 1934, at Cable Street, 1936). It attempted to stir up resentments in poor districts of East London. The BUF was proscribed in 1940 but there were continuities between Mosley's post-war Union Movement and later groups (e.g., National Front, founded 1967; British National Party, founded 1982).

FASCISM, SOUTHERN IRELAND A quasi-fascist party appeared in the Irish Free State from March 1933 when the ARMY COMRADES' ASSOCIATION adopted its 'Blueshirt' uniform. Its leader (from July), Eoin O'DUFFY, had met Italy's fascist leader, Benito Mussolini (Sept. 1928), and admired his 'corporate State'. O'Duffy planned a Blueshirts' march for 13 Aug. 1933, which many presumed would resemble Mussolini's ceremonial 'March on Rome' (1922) and culminate in an attempt to seize power. It was prohibited by the government of Éamon DE VALERA, which also later banned the party (22 Aug.). O'Duffy subsequently formed the short-lived Fascist National Corporate Party or 'Greenshirts'.

FASHODA CRISIS A dispute between Great Britain and France in 1898 after British military forces in SUDAN discovered (Sept.) a French force, commanded by Colonel Jean-Baptiste Marchand, at the village of Fashoda. It had been sent from W Africa to claim sovereignty over the Upper Nile (an area of British interest). The British prime minister, Lord SALISBURY, rejected talks until French troops were withdrawn. France agreed on 4 Nov. 1898, and renounced claims on the Nile Valley in 1899. *See also* NILE, BRITISH INTERESTS; SCRAMBLE FOR AFRICA.

FAULKNER, BRIAN (b. 18 Feb. 1921 at Helen's Bay, Co. Down, Ireland; d. 3 March 1977 at Saintfield, Co. Down, Northern Ireland, aged 56). An ULSTER UNIONIST PARTY member of Northern Ireland's Parliament from 1949, Faulkner became prime minister on 23 March 1971 (in succession to James Chichester-Clark), during a period of increasing violence. He combated terrorism with 'internment' (detention without trial, from 9 Aug. 1971), which increased alienation of Catholics. His position was undermined by 'BLOODY SUNDAY' (30 Jan. 1972). He lost office when the British government imposed 'direct rule' (24 March).

From 1 Jan. 1974 Faulkner led a new power-sharing Executive, but Unionist opposition to the SUNNINGDALE AGREEMENT, which involved the Republic of Ireland, forced him to resign as Party leader (7 Jan.). The Executive was undermined by the ULSTER WORKERS' STRIKE and Faulkner resigned (30 May). He formed the Unionist Party of Northern Ireland, but retired soon afterwards (1975). Created Lord Faulkner in Jan. 1977, he died shortly afterwards in a hunting accident. *See also* NORTHERN IRELAND; EXECUTIVES, NORTHERN IRELAND.

FAWCETT, MILLICENT GARRETT (b. 11 June 1847 at Aldeburgh, Suffolk, England; d. 5 Aug. 1929 at London, England, aged 82). Sister of Elizabeth Garrett ANDERSON and wife of Liberal politician and political economist Henry Fawcett, Millicent Garrett Fawcett became a writer and public speaker, and was co-founder with Henry Sidgwick and others of Newnham College for women, CAMBRIDGE (1872). She campaigned for women's suffrage from 1869 and the PURITY MOVEMENT from 1885. As leader from 1897 of the NATIONAL UNION OF WOMEN'S SUFFRAGE SOCIETIES (president 1907–19), she followed constitutional methods, rejecting suffragette violence, and after 1914 she rejected feminist criticism of British participation in WORLD WAR I. In 1917 she accepted the limited enfranchisement of women over 30 but lived to see universal adult suffrage achieved in 1928. *See also* WOMEN'S SUFFRAGE MOVEMENT, GREAT BRITAIN.

FEDERATED MALAY STATES Former British-controlled territories on the Malay Peninsula. After British influence had spread inland from the settlements of Penang and Malacca (part of a CROWN COLONY from 1867), Great Britain declared PROTECTORATES (1873–88) over the sultanates of Perak, Selangor, Negri Sembilan and Pahang. They formed the Malay Federation from 1895, with Kuala Lumpur as capital. Approx. population in 1921: 1,325,000. In 1946 Britain united the Federation with the UNFEDERATED MALAY STATES, Penang and Malacca to form the Malayan Union, a crown colony. It was replaced in 1948 by the Federation of Malaya (*see* MALAYA).

FEDERATION OF BRITISH INDUSTRIES A leading organization of industrialists, founded in 1916 to represent its members' interests to government. It merged with the National Association of British Manufacturers and the British Employers' Confederation in 1965 to form the Confederation of British Industry (CBI), which held annual conferences from 1977.

FEDERATION OF RHODESIA AND NYASALAND A former British territory in SE Africa, also called the Central African Federation, created by the union of SOUTHERN RHODESIA, NORTHERN RHODESIA and NYASALAND in 1953. Intended by the British to assist economic development (especially of copper deposits in Northern Rhodesia), and to exclude South African influence, it was seen by black Africans as a device to extend and entrench the power of whites in Southern Rhodesia (the location of its capital, Salisbury). Approx. population in 1961: 8,630,000.

After black opposition led to unrest and a state of emergency (1959), Great Britain dismantled the federation in 1963. Northern Rhodesia and Nyasaland were granted independence under black majority rule, while the white government of Southern Rhodesia declared independence (*see* RHODESIA PROBLEM).

FEIS TEMRO (OIr., meaning 'Festival of Tara'). In Ireland, a ritual festival held at TARA (E Ireland) at which a high-king asserted his overlordship. It is recorded between the mid 5th century (in reign of Ailill Molt, king of CONNACHT, d. 482) and the mid 6th century (in reign of Diarmait mac Cerbaill, king of the Southern Uí NÉILL, d. 565). *See also* KINGSHIP, IRELAND.

FEMINISM The advocacy of the claims of women to equality in the political, economic and social realms. The term came into use in Great Britain in the 1890s, long after the writings of Mary WOLLSTONECRAFT (d. 1797) and Harriet MARTINEAU (d. 1876) had propagated the idea and inspired the WOMEN'S MOVEMENT.

FENIAN BROTHERHOOD A secret society based in the USA which advocated the establishment of an Irish republic, if necessary by force. It was founded by John O'MAHONY in New York in 1858, concurrently with the IRISH REPUBLICAN BROTHERHOOD (IRB) in Ireland. Its name referred to medieval Gaelic soldiers. The Brotherhood recognized the Supreme Council of the IRB as the provisional government of an Irish republic. Members of both organizations were popularly known as 'Fenians', and their cause as 'Fenianism'. The movement was denounced by the Roman Catholic hierarchy and considered tainted with anti-clericalism.

In June 1866 several thousand American Fenians raided Canada, attempting to seize land for bargaining with the British over Ireland. Americans also participated in the unsuccessful INSURRECTION OF 1867 in Ireland. Splits in the Brotherhood led to the establishment of the rival Clan na Gael group (June 1867). The Brotherhood declined after O'Mahony's death (1877), though the terms 'Fenians' and 'Fenianism' remained in widespread use. The Clan continued as the principal American Irish nationalist organization. Under John DEVOY it became formally linked with the IRB in the late 1870s, and later helped to mount the EASTER RISING (1916).

FENS An area in E England (encompassing parts of Lincolnshire, Norfolk and Cambridgeshire) which formerly consisted of wetlands with islands and margins of drier ground (from OE *fen*, meaning 'marsh').

During the MESOLITHIC period (*c*.8500–*c*.4300 BC) gatherers and hunters used drier areas, which often supported dense vegetation. During the NEOLITHIC (*c*.4300–*c*.2300 BC) and BRONZE AGE (*c*.2300–*c*.700 BC), communities developed settlements and ceremonial sites on drier margins; they undertook stock husbandry (sheep and cattle) and cultivation. In late PREHISTORY, periodic marine flooding became widespread, contributing to a build-up of peat across the southern fenland. From at least the 5th to the 17th centuries AD this area was an abundant source of reeds, birds and fish (especially eels), and contained rich grazing lands.

Large-scale drainage was first undertaken systematically in the Roman period (1st–4th centuries), by means of channels such as Car Dyke. In 1631 the Bedford Level Corporation was founded. Advised by Dutch engineer Cornelius Vermuyden (*c*.1594–1683), it dug drains and rivers and reclaimed large areas of the southern fens, including the 'Bedford Level' (completed 1637) and the 'Great Level' (1649–52). Extensive arable cultivation was introduced. The peak period of drainage, however, was the late 18th and early 19th centuries.

Drainage caused the peat to sink below the level of the drainage rivers, threatening the reclamation. So from the late 17th century, windmills were introduced to pump water from drainage channels into the higher rivers. Steam engines were used from 1819, diesel engines from *c*.1917, and electric engines from the mid 20th century. *See also* GUTHLAC.

FERMTOUN OR TOUN (Gaelic *clachan*). A grouping of one-storey longhouses (typically four to six); the main form of RURAL SETTLEMENT in Scotland (except the SE) from the 13th century (and probably earlier) to the 18th. Fermtouns usually belonged to lords and were held from them by tenants, often with householders acting as joint tenants. Associated AGRICULTURE normally operated on the infield–outfield system. In the Lowlands, most fermtouns were replaced by villages or isolated farmhouses. *See also* THANAGE; BARONY.

FETHARD-ON-SEA BOYCOTT Sectarian controversy in Ireland, 1957. From May, Catholics in the town of Fethard-on-Sea (Co. Wexford, Republic of Ireland), with clerical support, boycotted businesses belonging to Protestants. They were alleged (wrongly) to have assisted a Protestant (Church of IRELAND) woman, Sheila Cloney, who had left her Catholic husband and taken her children away rather than educate them at a Catholic school (defying the Church's requirement for children of mixed marriages to be raised as Catholics).

Publicized internationally, the boycott was deplored by (Protestant) Unionists in NORTHERN IRELAND as exemplifying Catholic power in the Republic. It was condemned publicly by the Republic's premier, Éamon DE VALERA (4 July), who worked secretly to solve the problem. The boycott was called off in Nov. An apology was made by the Catholic diocese's bishop in 1998. *See also* CHURCH–STATE RELATIONS, SOUTHERN IRELAND FROM 1922.

FEUDAL INCIDENTS Historians' and lawyers' term for occasional payments due to a lord, and some other rights, arising from feudal land TENURE, especially 'incidents' due to a king as lord-in-chief from his tenants-in-chief (direct holders of estates). The major incidents were: (a) 'aid', payments in emergency circumstances (e.g., to ransom a king or lord) or occasional customary exactions (e.g., on knighting of an eldest son, or marriage of an eldest daughter); (b) 'relief', payment from an heir for succession to his inheritance and restoration of his estate; (c) 'wardship', control over the person and estate of an underage heir, including arrangement of the heir's marriage.

In England, feudal incidents were an important part of ROYAL REVENUES from the Norman Conquest (1066–70s) to 1640s. Limits were placed on their exploitation in MAGNA CARTA (1215) because of abuse by JOHN. From the 14th century tenants-in-chief sought to avoid liability through the USE (vesting of lands in trust). Rulers responded with measures to protect their rights (e.g., Statute of Uses, 1536; Court of WARDS, 1540). Liability by lords for incidents was extended to Wales in the late 11th–13th centuries through establishment of the MARCH OF WALES and conquest elsewhere. Many incidents in England and Wales were abolished with feudal tenures by Parliament in 1660. Incidents were also introduced to Ireland following the Anglo-Norman invasion (1169–70); they were abolished with feudal tenures in 1662. Rulers of Scotland received feudal incidents from some lords in the 12th–18th centuries. Incidents were also levied by lords from tenants (*see* MANOR). *See also* FEUDALISM; WARDS AND LIVERIES, COURT OF, ENGLAND AND WALES/IRELAND.

FEUDALISM Term used to characterize economic and social conditions based primarily on personal dependence (often contrasted with a society administered by 'public' authorities). It was devised by the English lawyer Sir Henry Spelman (1563 or 1564–1641) for land tenure based on 'fees' (Latin singular *feodum*), i.e., lands held for service, and has been applied in various ways to mainly medieval conditions.

The broadest feudalism is the 'feudal mode of production', whereby lords (or nobles, or an aristocracy) possess land and exploit their dominance to extract rent (as produce, money or services) from dependent peasants. Karl Marx (1818–83) designated this as a stage in his historical scheme (*see* MARXISM). England's economy approximated to such feudalism in the 9th–14th centuries, and it was extended lightly to parts of Wales from the late 11th century (*see* MARCH OF WALES), and to Ireland from the late 12th century (*see* NORMANS, IMPACT ON IRELAND).

Historians also envisage 'feudal society', in which lords exercise 'private' justice over subordinates. It is argued that a 'feudal revolution' occurred in Continental Europe around 1000, when central authority collapsed and lords dominated local society, their power based on CASTLES and armed and mounted KNIGHTS. After the NORMAN CONQUEST (1066–1070s), private lordship was exercised in England through HONOURS and MANORS and their courts, and was extended to parts of Wales, Ireland and Scotland (*see* BARONY; REGALITY), but declined from the late 14th century. *See also* SERFDOM; TENURES, ENGLAND FROM 1066; MILITARY SERVICE, ENGLAND FROM 1066 TO MID 17TH CENTURY; BASTARD FEUDALISM.

FEUING MOVEMENT In Scotland, the process in the 16th century whereby rulers and the Church alienated extensive lands as heritable feus (fees or fiefs) in feu-ferme tenure (perpetual leases) to 'tenants' (effectively owners). Recipients made a large initial payment (the 'grassum') and paid a fixed annual rent ('feu-duty'). Grants were made on unprecedented scale mainly to raise money. (Feuing enabled the Church to raise money from land without breaking canon law's prohibition on selling land given for pious purposes.)

King JAMES IV made numerous grants in 1508–13 (for military purposes and building), as did JAMES V in 1538–42. Thereafter the feuing of royal lands was modest. An Act of 1584 required remaining lands to be feued. Church lands were feued from the 1530s to the 1560s, especially in the

1540s, to raise money for taxes and, in the Borders, for building repairs after English invasions.

Recipients ('feuars') included magnates, sitting tenants, lawyers and merchants. The movement was important socially for increasing the importance of LAIRDS. The Crown's financial gains were lost when INFLATION reduced the value of feu-duties. *See also* TENURES, SCOTLAND; ROYAL REVENUES, SCOTLAND; FRANCHISE, SCOTLAND.

FIANNA FÁIL (Irish, meaning 'Soldiers of Destiny'). A political party launched at Dublin in the IRISH FREE STATE on 16 May 1926 by Éamon DE VALERA and supporters. Drawing membership from republican SINN FÉIN, whose elected deputies abstained from the Dáil (lower house of Parliament), it intended to remove deputies' oath to the Crown and join parliamentary politics. After the party came second at the June 1927 election, elected representatives abstained from the Dáil until threatened emergency legislation pressurized them into swearing the oath (12 Aug.).

Fianna Fáil was southern Ireland's largest party in the Dáil 1932–2011, and held office 1932–73 (except for 1948–51, 1954–7), and frequently thereafter. Until 1989 it refused to join coalitions, and sometimes formed minority governments. Thereafter, except for brief 'caretaker' periods, Fianna Fáil formed coalitions, often with the PROGRESSIVE DEMOCRATS (formed in 1985 by dissatisfied Fianna Fáil TDs).

The party's leaders after de Valera were: Seán LEMASS (1959–66), Jack LYNCH (1966–79), Charles HAUGHEY (1979–92), Albert REYNOLDS (1992–4), Bertie AHERN (1994–2008), Brian COWEN (2008–11), and Micháel Martin (from 2011).

Claiming to be Ireland's national party, Fianna Fáil initially sought reunification of Ireland as a republic; restoration of the Irish language to primacy; land reform; economic self-sufficiency (*see* AUTARKY). The party appealed notably to small farmers. From the late 1950s the party promoted economic expansion and development (*see* ECONOMIC EXPANSION, PROGRAMMES FOR), and from the late 1980s contributed to the Northern Ireland PEACE PROCESS; in 1998 Bertie Ahern's government sponsored modification of the Republic's constitutional claim to Northern Ireland. From the late 20th century the party won considerable support in urban areas. *See also* POLITICAL PARTIES, SOUTHERN IRELAND FROM 1922.

FIELD, JOHN (b. *c.*1545 at London, England; d. March 1588 at London, aged about 43). A clergyman in the Church of ENGLAND (from 1566), Field became a leading promoter of presbyterian Church organization. From *c.*1570 he organized meetings of clergy in London that resembled Calvinist presbyteries (governing councils). In

1572, with Thomas Wilcox, he published *An Admonition to the Parliament*, which attacked episcopacy (Church government by bishops) and advocated presbyterian structure. It ignited the 'Admonition Controversy', a dispute about Church government. Field and Wilcox were briefly imprisoned.

Field was licensed to preach again from 1579. After Archbishop John WHITGIFT required clergy to accept articles of religion (1583–4), Field responded with renewed presbyterian activity, including organization of 'classes' (clergy conferences). *See also* REFORMATION, ENGLAND; PURITANISM, ENGLAND; CARTWRIGHT, THOMAS.

FIELD OF CLOTH OF GOLD Name given to the ceremonial meeting between Francis I of France and King HENRY VIII of England in Picardy (France), near CALAIS, 7–24 June 1520. Proposed by the French, it was used by Cardinal Thomas WOLSEY to enhance Henry's international status. Tournaments and banquets were held ostensibly to symbolize friendship. The reality was different: in July Henry made a treaty with Emperor Charles V. *See also* FOREIGN RELATIONS, ENGLAND 16TH CENTURY TO 1707; FRANCE, ENGLISH AND BRITISH RELATIONS WITH.

FIFE, EARLDOM OF A territory in E Scotland, between the Firth of Tay (N) and Firth of Forth (S); formerly an important area within southern Pictland, in which ONUIST SON OF VURGUIST (king of PICTS 732–61) probably founded the church at Cennrígmonaid (*see* ST ANDREWS). Possibly by the 10th century, Fife was governed by a MORMAER. It was considered an earldom from the early 12th century.

In the 11th century Fife belonged to descendants of Kenneth III, king of Scots (son of King Dubh), probably as compensation for the exclusion of their kindred (the MacDuffs) from succession to the Scottish kingship (*see* KENNETH II). The mormaer, and later the earl, was regarded as Scotland's senior nobleman and assisted at the king's INAUGURATION. Around 1136 Fife was the first existing extensive territory to be regranted by the king (DAVID I) as subject to Anglo-Norman feudal practices. MacDuffs held the earldom until the mid 14th century. *See also* EARLDOMS, SCOTLAND; TENURES, SCOTLAND.

FIFTEENTH AND TENTH In England, a tax levied intermittently with the authority of PARLIAMENT on the movable property of laity, 1332–1624. Householders in many towns and on 'ancient demesne' (royal estates) paid a tenth of the assessed value of their goods; householders elsewhere paid a fifteenth. Kings had levied 'fractional taxes' since 1166, with Parliament granting such taxes from 1237. Differential rates began in 1294. From 1334 a fixed rate was levied on each community.

From the mid 13th century, a tenth was the usual rate of taxation levied by the Church on its property through Convocation (Church assembly); the valuation made for the 1291 tenth was used until 1535, when, under the Act of First Fruits and Tenths (1534), there was a new assessment, the *VALOR ECCLESIASTICUS*, and a new requirement for Convocation's grant to be subject to Parliament's authority. Convocation surrendered its right to self-taxation in 1664, though levying of tenths continued. *See also* TAXATION, ENGLAND AND WALES BEFORE 1660.

FIJI A former British colony in the S Pacific consisting of 844 islands and islets. Visited by James COOK in 1774, Fiji attracted missionaries and sandalwood traders from the 1830s. Settlers from AUSTRALIA and NEW ZEALAND started cotton PLANTATIONS in the 1860s. Subsequent internal disorder led the king of Fiji to offer his realm to Great Britain. It accepted without enthusiasm in 1874, creating a CROWN COLONY. After a measles epidemic in 1875–6 killed thousands, planters imported INDENTURED LABOUR from India (1879–1916). By the 1960s Indians were as numerous as indigenous Fijians. Fiji became independent under the British Crown in 1970, and a republic in 1987. Approx. population in 1921, 157,000; in 1969, 506,000.

FINANCIAL REVOLUTION The creation of financial institutions in England in the 1690s to provide the government with a sophisticated system of public borrowing, which made secure long-term debt available as a form of investment. The principal cause was the heavy expenditure required for wars with France 1689–1713 (*see* GRAND ALLIANCE, WAR OF THE; SPANISH SUCCESSION, WAR OF THE).

The main developments were the establishment of the NATIONAL DEBT (1693) and BANK OF ENGLAND (1694), secured by Acts of Parliament. The government's flotations of debt encouraged a rapid increase in the market for securities. Financial investments became an alternative to landownership. By the 1720s London became the world's leading centre for the flotation of public loans, foreign trade, insurance, and dealings in gold and jewels.

FINCH, DANIEL *see* NOTTINGHAM, 2ND EARL OF

FINE GAEL (Irish, meaning 'Tribe of the Gaels'). A political party established on 2 Sept. 1933 by CUMANN NA NGAEDHAEL, the ARMY COMRADES' ASSOCIATION and the National Centre Party (all opposition parties). Though one of southern Ireland's main parties (alongside FIANNA FÁIL), Fine Gael has entered government only by making coalitions. It led 'inter-party governments' in 1948–51, 1954–7, and coalition governments 1973–7, 1981–2, 1982–7, 1994–7, 2011–2016, from 2016. Except for the 2016 government, all of Fine Gael's governments included the LABOUR PARTY.

Fine Gael's leaders have been: Eoin O'DUFFY (1933–4), W.T. COSGRAVE (1934–44), Richard Mulcahy (1944–59), James Dillon (1959–65), Liam COSGRAVE (1965–77), Garret FITZGERALD (1977–87), Alan Dukes (1987–90), John BRUTON (1990–2001), Michael Noonan (2001–2), Enda KENNY (2002–17) and Leo VARADKAR (from 2017).

Fine Gael was initially conservative, valuing maintenance of law and order, and stable government. Supporters included shopkeepers, professional men and more prosperous farmers. From the 1970s Fine Gael advocated policies for promoting peace in Northern Ireland (*see* SUNNINGDALE AGREEMENT; NEW IRELAND FORUM; PEACE PROCESS, NORTHERN IRELAND). In the 1980s FitzGerald encouraged Fine Gael to be socially more liberal. Under Alan Dukes, Fine Gael (in Opposition) co-operated with the Fianna Fáil government in tackling economic problems. Leo Varadkar, as taoiseach (premier), promoted radical social liberalization. *See also* COSTELLO, JOHN; POLITICAL PARTIES, SOUTHERN IRELAND FROM 1922.

FINGAL In Ireland, the area N of DUBLIN, which was settled by VIKINGS from the mid 9th century. Its Irish name, Fine Gall, means 'Territory of the foreigner'. Controlled in the 10th–12th centuries by Hiberno-Scandinavian kings of Dublin, it supplied grain, wood, fuel and livestock. Inhabitants described themselves as OSTMEN. Following the Anglo-Norman invasion (1169–70), part of the area became royal land. A lordship of Fingal was recognized in 1208, and Fingal county was created in 1994 when Co. Dublin (in Republic of Ireland) was divided.

FIRST WORLD WAR *see* WORLD WAR I

FISCAL–MILITARY STATE Term proposed in 1989 by the English historian John Brewer to characterize the English and British State in the later 17th and 18th centuries. It acknowledges a capacity to fund a large NAVY and sustained warfare primarily from substantial tax-raising (LAND TAX, EXCISE, CUSTOMS). A large contribution also came from long-term borrowing, the outcome of the FINANCIAL REVOLUTION (e.g., NATIONAL DEBT, BANK OF ENGLAND). A prominent feature of the fiscal–military State was a large and pervasive bureaucracy.

Conflicts included: War of the GRAND ALLIANCE (1689–97), War of the SPANISH SUCCESSION (1702–13), War of the AUSTRIAN SUCCESSION (1740–8), SEVEN YEARS WAR (1756–63), War of AMERICAN INDEPENDENCE (1775–81), FRENCH REVOLUTIONARY AND NAPOLEONIC WARS (1793–1815).

It can be countered that fiscal capacity and large military forces were developed earlier, during the CIVIL WARS (1642–8). Naval and military funding also remained important aspects of State expenditure long after the 18th century. *See also* GOVERNMENT, ENGLAND WITH WALES 1642 TO 1707; GOVERNMENT, GREAT BRITAIN 1707 TO LATER 18TH CENTURY.

FISH, SIMON (b. possibly in Kent, England; d. early 1531 at London, England). An anti-clerical lawyer, Fish wrote *A Supplication for the Beggars* probably in 1528 while exiled in the Low Counties. It attacked the wealth and vices of the English clergy and advocated reform, stirring anti-clericalism at the start of the REFORMATION PARLIAMENT (1529). The *Supplication* also provoked a rebuttal in *Supplication of Souls* by Thomas MORE (1529). Fish died of plague. *See also* REFORMATION, ENGLAND.

FISHER, JOHN (b. *c.*1469 at Beverley, Yorkshire, England; d. 22 June 1535 at London, England, aged about 65). A scholar and clergyman, Fisher was appointed confessor to Margaret BEAUFORT, mother of King HENRY VII (1497). In 1504 he became bishop of Rochester and chancellor of Cambridge University. During the 1520s he wrote and preached against LUTHERANISM.

From 1527 Fisher supported KATHERINE OF ARAGON in resisting HENRY VIII's attempts to obtain a divorce. He spoke in Convocation (Church assembly) against Henry's assertion of authority over the English Church, opposing Henry's assumption of supremacy (1531) and the 'Submission of the Clergy' (1532). In 1534 Fisher refused the oath to the Act of Succession, which deemed Katherine's marriage as invalid, and was imprisoned (April). In 1535 he denied Henry's status as supreme head of the Church. He was convicted of treason (17 June) and beheaded. Fisher was created a cardinal on 21 May 1535 and canonized in 1935. *See also* REFORMATION, ENGLAND; MORE, THOMAS.

FISHER, LORD (b. 25 Jan. 1841 at Rambodde, Ceylon; d. 10 July 1920 at London, England, aged 79). Admiral John Fisher (known as 'Jacky') was a belligerent first sea lord (1904–10). He modernized the Royal NAVY, including administration, strategy and ship construction, to win the so-called NAVAL RACE (with Germany). Created Lord Fisher in 1909, Fisher was recalled to service in Oct. 1914, after the outbreak of WORLD WAR I, but resigned (May 1915) over disagreements concerning the GALLIPOLI CAMPAIGN.

FISHERIES AND MANUFACTURES, BOARD OF TRUSTEES FOR A British government agency in Scotland, established in 1727 (following the SHAWFIELD RIOTS), belatedly implementing Article 15 of the treaty of Union (1707). It allocated subsidies for economic development, notably supporting technical development of the linen industry (from 1740s) and the Forth and Clyde Canal (built 1768–90). Wound up 1844. *See also* TEXTILE INDUSTRIES, SCOTLAND.

FISHING INDUSTRY, IRELAND Sea fish (especially herring) were an important export in the 14th–early 17th centuries, with WATERFORD (S Ireland) serving as the main fishing port. In the 19th century the industry was stimulated by a Fishery Board (1819–30) and the CONGESTED DISTRICTS BOARD (1891–1923), although only 8000 men were employed full-time in 1907. In decline from 1918, sea fishing re-expanded from the 1950s from the Republic of Ireland, overseen from 1952 by the Bord Iascaigh Mhara and subject from 1983 to the European Economic Community's Common Fisheries Policy. In 2013 there were about 5000 fishermen and 1700 fish farmers. Some 870 sea fishermen worked from Northern Ireland in 2016 (about a fifth part-time).

FISHING INDUSTRY AND WHALING, ENGLAND AND WALES Fishing took place in rivers, estuaries and at sea by the 6th century; DOMESDAY BOOK (1086) records herring fishermen. Before the 15th century sea fishing concentrated on inshore waters. The main areas were off NE England, East Anglia, Kent, SW England, and parts of Wales, with herring and cod as primary concerns. Great Yarmouth (East Anglia) was pre-eminent for herring by the 13th century. Dutch competition undermined the herring trade in the 15th–17th centuries. Trawling (dragging of nets along the seabed) was recorded from the later 14th century.

Offshore fishing flourished from the 15th century, when fishermen visited Icelandic waters (to later 17th century). Between the 1570s and later 18th century, grounds off NEWFOUNDLAND were also exploited, with much of the catch exported to the Iberian Peninsula. Pilchards and herring were likewise exported from SW England.

Sea fishing expanded from the later 18th century through offshore trawling with 'smacks' (sailing vessels). Steam-powered trawlers (from 1880s) revived deep-sea fishing around Iceland and elsewhere. In 1909, 1300 steam trawlers operated, with Grimsby and Hull (NE England), and Fleetwood (NW England), as pre-eminent bases. Railways enabled rapid inland distribution of fish. In 1920 sea fishing employed 34,400 men and boys.

Sea fishing was damaged by 'Cod Wars' with Iceland (1958–61, 1972–3, resulting from extensions of territorial waters), then contracted severely because of the opening of UK waters to European fleets (1973, on entry to the EUROPEAN ECONOMIC COMMUNITY), the Third Cod War (1975–6), and introduction of large vessels. In 2016 there were 5300 sea fishermen in England, 750 in Wales (a fifth part-time). Newlyn and Brixham (SW England) remained significant fishing ports.

Whaling also took place: in northern waters (early 17th–early 20th centuries), southern oceans (1775–1859), and the Antarctic region (1904–60s). Hull and Whitby (NE England) were important whaling centres.

FISHING INDUSTRY AND WHALING, SCOTLAND Until the mid 19th century sea fishermen, many based in specialist villages on the E or SW coast, usually worked from small boats in inshore waters (within 15 mi, 24 km), using lines to catch herring, cod and haddock. From the 1840s larger boats and drift-nets were used to catch herring farther offshore. In 1865 Wick (Caithness), with 800 boats, was deemed the herring capital of Europe.

After steam-powered trawlers were introduced c.1882, ABERDEEN (NE Scotland) developed by 1911 into one of Great Britain's largest fishing ports, with 230 trawlers (catching cod and haddock). Other ports used steam-trawlers from c.1900 to catch herring, mainly for export. Fraserburgh (Aberdeenshire) and Mallaig (Inverness-shire) became major processing centres. In 1920, 26,800 men and boys were employed in sea fishing.

The industry survived difficult conditions in the 1920s–30s, and converted to diesel power from 1945. It was damaged by 'Cod Wars' with Iceland (1958–61, 1972–3, resulting from extensions of territorial waters), and then shrank dramatically (1970s–90s) due to the opening of UK waters to European fleets (1973, on entry to the EUROPEAN ECONOMIC COMMUNITY), the Third Cod War (1975–6), introduction of large boats operating enormous nets, and depletion of fish stocks. In 2016 there were about 4800 sea fishermen (about one-fifth part-time).

Arctic whaling also flourished from the mid 18th century until the 1830s (notable centres were Aberdeen, DUNDEE and Dunbar) and again from c.1860 to c.1914. *See also* FOREIGN TRADE, SCOTLAND BEFORE/FROM 17TH CENTURY.

FITZALAN FAMILY AND WALES The FitzAlans became an important noble family in the northern MARCH OF WALES. William FitzAlan, the second son of Alan (from Brittany, France; in England from c.1102), became lord of Oswestry by 1127. The family added the lordships of Clun (c.1200 by marriage), Chirkland (1322), and Bromfield and Yale (1347). Despite periodic forfeitures, the FitzAlan earls of Arundel remained important in NE Wales until 1536 (UNION OF WALES WITH ENGLAND). *See also* STEWART FAMILY.

FITZGERALD, GARRET (b. 9 Feb. 1926 at Ballsbridge, Dublin, Irish Free State; d. 19 May 2011 at Dublin, Republic of Ireland, aged 85). The son of a Catholic father and mother from a Protestant background, FitzGerald, a university lecturer, was elected to the Irish Senate (1965) and then became a FINE GAEL TD (1969). He served as minister for foreign affairs 1973–7 under Liam COSGRAVE whom he succeeded as party leader (1977).

FitzGerald was taoiseach (premier) June 1981–March 1982 and Dec. 1982–March 1987, in coalition with the LABOUR PARTY. His governments struggled with economic recession and high unemployment. FitzGerald aspired to conciliate Unionists in NORTHERN IRELAND by reducing Catholic influence on social legislation in the Republic and removing disliked aspects of its constitution. He sponsored the NEW IRELAND FORUM to develop fresh approaches to Ireland's future (1983–4). Though its proposals were rejected in Great Britain by Margaret THATCHER, she accepted the HILLSBOROUGH AGREEMENT (1985) to encourage northern 'constitutional nationalists'. FitzGerald liberalized BIRTH CONTROL availability (1985) but a referendum to permit divorce was defeated (1986). In Jan. 1987 Labour left the government over proposed budget cuts. FitzGerald then lost an election and resigned as party leader, retiring from the Dáil in 1992. *See also* HAUGHEY, CHARLES; TROUBLES; SOUTHERN IRELAND FROM 1922.

FITZGERALD, LORD EDWARD (b. 15 Oct. 1763 at London, England; d. 4 June 1798 at London, aged 34). A son of the duke of Leinster and a soldier, Fitzgerald was attracted by ideals of the French Revolution. He spent autumn 1792 in Paris where he met Tom PAINE (Oct.). He also toasted the abolition of hereditary titles (18 Nov., at a banquet), and was dismissed from the British Army.

From 1796 Fitzgerald was involved with the UNITED IRISHMEN, and from Feb. 1798 led the planning for an uprising. He secretly continued preparations after many conspirators were arrested (12 March), only to be captured (19 May) just before the rising. He died soon afterwards from wounds. *See also* KILDARE, EARLS OF; RISING OF 1798; FRENCH REVOLUTION, IMPACT ON IRELAND; ATTAINDER.

FITZGERALDS *see* GERALDINES

FITZGIBBON, JOHN (b. 1749 at Donnybrook, Co. Dublin, Ireland; d. 28 Jan. 1802 at Dublin, Ireland, aged 53 or 54). Fitzgibbon, a lawyer, entered the Irish House of Commons in 1778 and reluctantly accepted legislative independence (*see* CONSTITUTION OF 1782). In Dec. 1783 he was appointed attorney-general by the new British prime minister, William PITT the Younger, and thereafter was a leading member of the Irish government (appointed lord chancellor and created Lord Fitzgibbon in 1789, created earl of Clare in 1795). He repressed rural unrest, and helped to quell the RISING OF 1798. He reluctantly accepted a Catholic relief Act in 1793, and assisted Pitt in implementing the UNION OF IRELAND AND GREAT BRITAIN (1801). His funeral attracted a hostile crowd. *See also* PROTESTANT ASCENDANCY.

FITZ HAMO, ROBERT (b. *c.*1050, probably in Normandy; d. March 1107, aged about 57). A Norman who supported King WILLIAM II against the revolt of ODO OF BAYEUX (1088); was rewarded *c.*1090 with lands in Gloucestershire (SW England). From there he invaded S Wales, founded CARDIFF castle and town, and became first lord of GLAMORGAN and Gwynllŵg. His daughter Mabel married ROBERT OF GLOUCESTER. *See also* NORMANS, IMPACT ON WALES.

FITZRALPH, RICHARD (b. late 1290s at Dundalk, Louth, Ireland; d. 16 or 20 Nov. 1360 at Avignon, France). A theologian, Richard became archbishop of ARMAGH (N Ireland) in 1346. A promoter of Church reform, he held synods in the early 1350s at which he criticized the moral deficiencies of clergy, warfare between Gaelic Irish and English, and the exclusion of Gaelic Irish from guilds and professions. He sought recognition of his rights as primate of Ireland, especially within the archbishopric of Dublin, and criticized mendicant friars for disrupting the authority of parochial clergy. *See also* PRIMACY DISPUTE, DUBLIN AND ARMAGH.

FIVE ARTICLES OF PERTH Articles requiring certain religious observances, disliked by presbyterians, which were passed by a General Assembly of the Church of SCOTLAND at Perth (C Scotland) in 1618, under coercion from King JAMES VI, and by Parliament in 1621, after a struggle. (Assemblies had rejected them in 1616 and 1617.) The observances were: private baptism; private communion (both only on the verge of death); kneeling at communion; celebration of major festivals (Christmas, Good Friday, Easter Sunday, Ascension and Whit Sunday); confirmation by bishops. *See also* HAMILTON, THOMAS; SPOTTISWOODE, JOHN; GLASGOW ASSEMBLY.

FIVE KNIGHTS' CASE In England, an episode when five knights imprisoned for refusing payment of the FORCED LOAN of 1626, levied for King CHARLES I, challenged their imprisonment by legal petition (Nov. 1627). Judges accepted that the king could imprison without showing cause or expediting a trial, but refused to validate the loan. The attorney-general altered the case record to imply that they had supported the loan. Many MPs feared that this smacked of arbitrary royal government (March 1628). *See also* PETITION OF RIGHT.

FIVE MEMBERS INCIDENT In England, the attempt on 4 Jan. 1642 by King CHARLES I and 80 armed men to arrest five MPs in the House of Commons who had been charged (with one peer) with TREASON. The members, who included John PYM, John HAMPDEN and Denzil HOLLES, had already escaped. Charles's action embittered relations with Parliament and hastened war. *See also* LONG PARLIAMENT; CIVIL WARS.

FLEMING, ALEXANDER *see* PENICILLIN

FLEMING, SANDFORD (b. 7 Jan. 1827 at Kirkcaldy, Fife, Scotland; d. 22 July 1915 at Halifax, Nova Scotia, Canada, aged 88). Fleming emigrated to CANADA in 1845 and became a prominent railway engineer (chief engineer of Northern Railway 1855–63, for Nova Scotia 1864–6). Following CANADIAN CONFEDERATION, he was appointed chief engineer (1867) for the strategic line of the Inter-Colonial Railway to Halifax, Nova Scotia (completed 1876). When British Columbia joined the dominion of Canada (1871), Fleming surveyed the route of the associated Canadian Pacific Railway (active 1872–80). From 1879 he successfully lobbied for the 'Pacific Cable' (completed 1902). Fleming was knighted in 1897.

FLETCHER, ANDREW (b. 1653 at Saltoun, SE Scotland; d. Sept. 1716 at London, England, aged 62 or 63). A member of the Scottish Parliament in 1678 and 1681, Fletcher (often called 'Fletcher of Saltoun') opposed the administrations of, respectively, the dukes of LAUDERDALE and Albany (future King JAMES VII/II). After refusing the 1681 Test Oath (recognizing the king as head of the Church), Fletcher fled overseas and then went secretly to England where he briefly supported MONMOUTH'S REBELLION (1685). He fled again, to the Dutch Republic, and returned to England in 1688 with William of Orange (see WILLIAM III).

In 1703 Fletcher re-entered Parliament where he sought to limit royal and English power, influencing the Act of SECURITY (1704). He was the foremost campaigner against the incorporating UNION OF ENGLAND AND SCOTLAND. After it happened (1707), Fletcher retired from politics. He wrote many publications on Scottish affairs.

FLETCHER, ANDREW (1692–1766) see MILTON, LORD

FLIGHT OF THE EARLS The sudden departure from Ireland (from Lough Swilly in NW ULSTER), on 4 Sept. 1607, of the earls of Tyrone (Hugh O'NEILL) and Tyrconnell (Rory O'Donnell) with supporters. The earls feared accusation by the English of seeking foreign support for another rebellion (see NINE YEARS WAR). (During summer 1607 Tyrconnell had communicated with the Spanish, but about fighting in the Netherlands.) The English confiscated the earls' lands (Dec.) and later established the ULSTER PLANTATION on them. See also O'DOHERTY'S REBELLION.

FLINTS, PREHISTORIC IRELAND The only major occurrence of chalk with flint seams occurs in NE Ireland. It was exploited from the MESOLITHIC (c.8000– c.3800 BC) onwards. Elsewhere flint in glacial and beach deposits was exploited, as well as other stone sources such as chert. Distinct alterations in the working of flint occur over time with accompanying changes in diagnostic artefact types, such as projectile points (small flints for insertion in wooden spears).

FLINTS AND FLINT MINING, PREHISTORIC BRITAIN The main raw material used in PREHISTORY, flint was procured and worked in many different ways. During the NEOLITHIC PERIOD (c.4300– c.2300 BC) in the S and E, shafts and galleries were cut into chalk to recover nodules of workable flint. Flint mines were used periodically for several centuries and often associated with the production of tools such as AXES. Mines of the earlier Neolithic (c.4000– c.3500 BC) include Blackpatch and Cissbury (Sussex, S England). Those of the later Neolithic and Early BRONZE AGE (c.2800– c.1600 BC) include GRIMES GRAVES (Norfolk, E England). Neolithic mines have also been identified at the Den of Boddam (Grampian, NE Scotland).

FLODDEN, BATTLE OF Fought in NW Northumberland (NE England) on 9 Sept. 1513. A Scottish army under King JAMES IV (invading England seven weeks after King HENRY VIII had invaded France) was heavily defeated by English forces under the earl of Surrey (Thomas Howard). King James, nine earls and other senior Scots were killed. See also SCOTTISH–ENGLISH RELATIONS 1357 TO 1603; JAMES V.

FLOOD, HENRY (b. 1732 at Donnybrook, Co. Dublin; d. 2 Dec. 1791 at Farmley, Co. Kilkenny, aged about 59). Flood, a (Protestant) lawyer, entered the Irish House of Commons in 1759 and became leader of the PATRIOTS, pressing for reforms such as shorter Parliaments (granted 1768; see OCTENNIAL ACT). During the governorship of Viscount TOWNSHEND (1767–72), he moved votes against augmentation of the Army (April 1768) and funding (Dec. 1769). But in 1774–5 he accepted government posts and salaries, thereby losing popular support and allowing Henry GRATTAN to overshadow him.

Flood rejoined the Patriot movement in 1778 (when the VOLUNTEER movement developed) and worked with the Commons opposition (1779–80). In consequence he was dismissed from government posts (late 1781). He participated in the campaign that achieved parliamentary independence in 1782, and in 1783 supported demands for parliamentary reform: he proposed a motion and Bill in the Commons (defeated 29 Nov. 1783, 20 March 1784). He also sat in the British Parliament from 1783. Flood lost both seats in 1790 and retired. See also PROTESTANT ASCENDANCY; CONSTITUTION OF 1782.

FLOREY, HOWARD see PENICILLIN

FOLIOT, GILBERT (b. c.1110 in England; d. 18 Feb. 1187 in England, aged about 77). Bishop of HEREFORD from 1148, Foliot opposed the election of Thomas BECKET as archbishop of Canterbury (1162). Becket sought Foliot's support by securing his appointment as bishop of LONDON

(1163). Foliot nevertheless became a leading opponent of Becket in the latter's struggle with King HENRY II (to 1170).

FOOD RIOTS A form of social protest and action. Recorded in England from the 14th century, riots occurred frequently in Britain and Ireland in the 18th and 19th centuries, and in bad years were widespread (e.g., in 1766 at least 40 places in England were affected). They were usually triggered by sharp increases in grain prices, rumours of increases or grain shortages, but also reflected the wider trading of foodstuffs that had resulted from urbanization and COMMERCIALIZATION. In Britain, the main participants were industrial workers, such as coalminers, tin miners and cloth workers, who depended on markets for food supplies. Women were also prominent.

Rioters seized grain at ports or from carts, warehouses or barns. They also attacked mills or forced dealers at markets to lower prices. Attacks often sought to prevent exports from inland areas. Sometimes rioters sold seized grain at a claimed 'fair price', a practice which the English historian E.P. Thompson (1924–93) claimed as exemplifying a 'moral economy' (economy based on fairness). Riots were rare in LONDON, its food-supply system being sophisticated. Riots decreased in Britain after 1818 as workers acted through TRADE UNIONISM, real wages gradually rose, and the food market became efficient, although instances occurred until 1867.

In Ireland, riots occurred from 1709, in ports and large towns in the S and E. During the famine of 1740–1 they erupted in all provinces. Riots also took place in small towns and the countryside from the 1770s. In the early 19th century they were mainly confined to the W, and became hard to distinguish from other agitation. The most intense rioting happened in 1846–7, during the GREAT FAMINE. It then largely ceased due to population decrease and improved conditions.

FOOT, MICHAEL (b. 23 July 1913 at Plymouth, Devon, England; d. 3 March 2010 at London, England, aged 96). Foot, a socialist journalist, was a Labour MP 1945–55, 1960–92. Though a BEVANITE (1950s) and rebellious backbencher, he eventually held office in the British government: as employment secretary 1974–6, leader of the House of Commons 1976–9. In 1980 he succeeded James CALLAGHAN as LABOUR PARTY leader (with Denis HEALEY as deputy), but suffered a heavy defeat in the 1983 general election and resigned. Succeeded by Neil KINNOCK. *See also* THATCHER, MARGARET.

FORCED LOAN In England and Wales, an involuntary loan of money to the Crown, usually required from wealthier subjects for one or two years. Though loans were meant to be repaid, this did not always happen. The first general loan was levied in England by King RICHARD II in 1397. Loans were extracted by most rulers until the 1640s. They were condemned in the PETITION OF RIGHT (1628). *See also* FORCED LOAN, 1626; TAXATION, ENGLAND AND WALES BEFORE 1660.

FORCED LOAN, 1626 In England and Wales, effectively a tax ordered in Sept. 1626 by the Privy Council for King CHARLES I (without Parliament's consent), to fund warfare in France. Although it raised over £243,000, payments were sometimes extracted by coercion. Many people refused to pay (over 100 were imprisoned), and the loan's legality was challenged (*see* FIVE KNIGHTS' CASE). It soured relations between Charles and Parliament. *See also* BUCKINGHAM, DUKE OF; PETITION OF RIGHT.

FOREIGN INVESTMENT British people made investments overseas (also called 'capital exports') from the 1820s through merchant bankers, attracted by higher rates of return than were obtainable domestically. Destinations of funds included Latin America and the USA. In the 1830s–40s Continental European railways were lucrative. Total investments are difficult to estimate but until 1850 were relatively modest, amounting perhaps to £200 million.

Investments then grew significantly, reaching £1 billion by 1870 and £4.2 billion by 1913 (44% of world's total). Railways remained important, notably in India, the USA and Argentina. Investment in mining was also popular in the 1890s. In 1913, 41% of investments were in railways, and 47% in the BRITISH EMPIRE. Foreign investment often benefited British industry because recipients bought British capital goods. Income from investments (£200 million in 1913) and 'INVISIBLES' enabled imports to exceed the value of exported goods.

Little was invested abroad during WORLD WAR I (1914–18). By 1929 investments stood at £3.7 billion, by 1939 at £4 billion. Sales worth £1.1 billion were made during WORLD WAR II (1939–45). Afterwards renewed activity increased investments to £11.8 billion by 1961. Money was invested in oil, and in Canada and Australia, both COMMONWEALTH countries.

During the 1960s foreign investment expanded strongly, partly to enlarge markets and partly because domestic opportunities were less attractive. In 1980 it stood at £48.3 billion. Dramatic expansion followed, as capital became more mobile and industrial production was increasingly organized on an international basis: to £324 billion in 1989, £11 trillion in 2017 (over five times GDP) with 31% in the USA, 9% in France, 7% in Germany.

FOREIGN RELATIONS, ENGLAND BEFORE 1066 Anglo-Saxon kingdoms had extensive trading connections (from 6th century), and the CONVERSION OF

ANGLO-SAXONS (7th century) created ties with Continental European churches and the papacy (*see*, e.g., WILFRID). Missionaries were influential abroad in the 8th century (*see* MISSIONS TO CONTINENTAL EUROPE, ANGLO-SAXON). Otherwise kingdoms in the 6th–9th centuries were involved with each other or British kingdoms (*see* KINGSHIP, ANGLO-SAXON). OFFA of MERCIA exceptionally sought an equal marriage alliance with Charlemagne, emperor of the Franks (*c*.790). Insulted, Charlemagne banned English merchants.

Later kings of WESSEX valued overseas alliances for prestige. ÆTHELWULF married a Frankish princess (856). ALFRED married a daughter to the count of Flanders (890s). EDWARD THE ELDER married a daughter to the king of the West Franks (*c*.918).

Overseas rulers sought alliances with ATHELSTAN (king of England 924–39) because of his importance. Hugh, duke of the Franks, married Athelstan's sister Eadhild (926). The German king Henry the Fowler married his son Otto to Athelstan's sister Eadgyth (929). When Otto invaded Lotharingia (939) Athelstan sent a fleet in support.

VIKING attacks from the 980s caused King ÆTHELRED II to ally with nearby NORMANDY (*see* EMMA). Under CNUT (ruled 1016–35) England became more involved in Scandinavia (*see* SCANDINAVIAN EMPIRE, ENGLAND'S POSITION IN). The accession of the half-Norman EDWARD THE CONFESSOR (1042) resulted in Norman involvement and the Norman invasion (1066). *See also* EMPIRE, ANGLO-SAXON IDEAS OF; FOREIGN TRADE, ENGLAND BEFORE 1066.

FOREIGN RELATIONS, ENGLAND 1066 TO 16TH CENTURY England's principal relations were with six neighbours or powers: Wales (Brittonic kingdoms), Ireland (Gaelic kingdoms), Scotland, France, Holy Roman Empire and HOLY SEE (or papacy). For the first four, relations involved aggression.

Parts of Wales were conquered between *c*.1070 and *c*.1170 (*see* NORMANS, IMPACT ON WALES; MARCH OF WALES). In the 12th and 13th centuries, kings had fluctuating relations with the main kingdom, GWYNEDD, which ended in conquest (*see* GRUFFUDD AP CYNAN; OWAIN GWYNEDD; LLYWELYN AP IORWERTH; DAFYDD AP LLYWELYN; LLYWELYN AP GRUFFUDD). HENRY II assumed lordship over Ireland in 1171, following an invasion; by *c*.1250 many Gaelic kingdoms were displaced by English lordships (*see* IRELAND, ENGLISH CONQUEST, 12TH–13TH CENTURIES). Relations with Scotland were frequently antagonistic (*see* SCOTTISH–ENGLISH RELATIONS), with Scotland from 1295 often seeking French assistance against England (*see* SCOTTISH–FRENCH ALLIANCE).

England's main involvement was with France. From 1066 kings of England were of French origin (also dukes of NORMANDY), and from the mid 12th century had lordship

over large areas of France (*see* ANGEVIN EMPIRE). After most lands were lost in 1202–4, kings aspired to regain French territory but faced powerful kings. Territorial disputes were addressed by the treaty of PARIS (1259), but friction continued over GASCONY (an English-held lordship in SW France). From 1337 to 1453 England was at war with France, with kings claiming the French Crown (*see* HUNDRED YEARS WAR). England sought to use the Holy Roman Empire as a counterbalance in the first phase (1337–60), and later allied with BURGUNDY (1419–35).

England had varying relations with the papacy, which tended to act as a mediator between England and France. This was hampered by the 'Avignon Papacy' (1309–77), when the papacy was based within France, and during the GREAT SCHISM (1378–1417). *See also* FRANCE, CLAIMS BY RULERS OF ENGLAND; SPAIN, ENGLISH AND BRITISH RELATIONS WITH; HENRY VII.

FOREIGN RELATIONS, ENGLAND 16TH CENTURY TO 1707 King HENRY VIII (ruled 1509–47) pursued a vigorous foreign policy, mounting military expeditions against FRANCE (1512–14, 1522, 1544) and Scotland (1542, 1545). With the REFORMATION, religion became a factor, but hostility between France and the HABSBURG EMPIRE, both Catholic powers, permitted diplomatic manoeuvring. While France suffered civil war (with limited intervention by England in 1562–3 to support Protestants), ELIZABETH I from 1585 provided military assistance to Protestant rebels in the Spanish-ruled NETHERLANDS, producing intermittent conflict with Spain (*see* ANGLO-SPANISH WAR).

The UNION OF CROWNS (1603), whereby JAMES VI of Scotland also became king of England, improved security, and James secured peace with Spain (1604). He largely avoided involvement in the Thirty Years War (1618–48), despite the eviction of his son-in-law Frederick V from Bohemia (1620) and his palatinate (1622), funding only an unsuccessful overseas expedition in 1625–6. Strategic confusion led to disastrous and humiliating clashes with Spain and France early in the reign of CHARLES I (raid on Cádiz, Spain, 1625; expeditions to the Isle of Rhé, 1627, and La Rochelle, 1628, to assist French Protestants).

Oliver CROMWELL (lord protector 1653–8) restored English prestige as growing trading interests inspired colonial expansion and conflict with the NETHERLANDS (*see* ANGLO-DUTCH WARS). CHARLES II made a secret alliance with France (1670; *see* DOVER, TREATY OF), but the GLORIOUS REVOLUTION (1688–9) transformed foreign policy. England opposed French dominance of Europe in the Wars of the GRAND ALLIANCE (1689–97) and SPANISH SUCCESSION (1702–13). *See also* SCOTTISH–ENGLISH RELATIONS 1357–1603.

FOREIGN RELATIONS, GREAT BRITAIN In the 18th century Britain was concerned to prevent French domination of Europe. It made alliances with the HABSBURG EMPIRE, PRUSSIA and RUSSIA, and fought the Wars of the SPANISH SUCCESSION (1702–13) and AUSTRIAN SUCCESSION (1740–8), the SEVEN YEARS WAR (1756–63), and the FRENCH REVOLUTIONARY AND NAPOLEONIC WARS (1793–1815). Naval superiority enabled Britain to triumph over FRANCE in colonial contests in INDIA and CANADA. Only when lacking Continental allies in the War of AMERICAN INDEPENDENCE (1775–81) was it defeated.

With the peace settlement of 1814–15, Viscount CASTLEREAGH was able to establish a BALANCE OF POWER which largely left Britain free to enjoy paramountcy outside Europe. It sought peace and FREE TRADE to pursue commercial interests as the first industrialized nation (*see* INDUSTRIAL REVOLUTION). In the mid 19th century Lord PALMERSTON expressed cautious sympathy for European liberal and nationalist movements. Anxiety about Russia menacing India prompted participation in the EASTERN QUESTION.

As industrialization strengthened rival powers after 1870, imperial defence seemed to require strategic expansion in Asia and Africa. Disputes with Russia and France inclined Lord SALISBURY to limited co-operation with GERMANY. However, when Germany began in 1900 to build a substantial navy, SPLENDID ISOLATION gave way to rapprochement with France (*see* ANGLO-FRENCH CONVENTION) and then involvement in WORLD WAR I (1914–18) to prevent German domination of Europe. German expansionism in the 1930s, coupled with the rise of JAPAN, gravely challenged the British Empire.

Though WORLD WAR II (1939–45) eliminated these threats, the UNITED STATES and USSR emerged as pre-eminent superpowers. Reluctantly accepting this, Britain allied with the USA in the COLD WAR, implemented DECOLONIZATION and joined (1973) the EUROPEAN ECONOMIC COMMUNITY. Called the European Union from 1993, it proved unpopular and in 2016 the UK public voted to leave, requiring Britain to fashion a new independent role (*see* BREXIT). *See also* FISCAL–MILITARY STATE.

FOREIGN RELATIONS, IRELAND BEFORE EARLY 17TH CENTURY The competitive nature of Irish kings impeded common relations with foreign powers (*see* KINGSHIP, IRELAND). From the 9th century individual kings sometimes made alliances (e.g., with VIKINGS) to improve their situations. In 1166–7 Diarmait MAC MURCHADA likewise recruited Anglo-Normans to recover LEINSTER from his Irish enemies. Even after their invasion (1169–70), Irish kings were reluctant to co-operate to expel them (*see* NORMANS, IMPACT ON IRELAND).

The first united approach to a foreign power was the invitation by Gaelic Irish rulers to Edward Bruce of Scotland in 1315 to become king of Ireland, made to obtain support from his brother King ROBERT I (*see* BRUCE INVASION OF IRELAND). They also entreated papal support for Bruce's kingship. In the early 15th century the Welshman OWAIN GLYN DŴR requested Irish support for his rebellion against English rule.

Foreign intervention was again sought in the 16th century when England was re-exerting authority (*see* IRELAND, ENGLISH CONQUEST, 16TH CENTURY). Spanish arms and money equipped the Irish during the NINE YEARS WAR (1593–1603), and troops landed at Kinsale (1601). In the 1640s the papacy became involved in Irish affairs (*see* RINUCCINI, GIOVANNI BATTISTA).

FOREIGN RELATIONS, MANAGEMENT OF, GREAT BRITAIN Foreign policy is the constitutional responsibility of the CABINET, but the need for specialized knowledge has normally limited effective participation to a small group of ministers. Diplomatic secrecy can render parliamentary scrutiny superficial or purely retrospective. Treaties do not require ratification by Parliament, but from 1924 members were permitted to examine and, if desired, to debate them before ratification (so-called Ponsonby Rule), a convention formalized by the 2010 Constitutional Reform and Governance Act.

The Foreign Office was established as a distinct government department in 1782. Its head, the foreign secretary, has often operated with considerable autonomy. This was especially true of Viscount CASTLEREAGH, George CANNING, Lord PALMERSTON and Edward GREY, and, to a lesser extent, Austen CHAMBERLAIN and Ernest BEVIN. It is nevertheless common for the prime minister to take a close interest in international affairs. Benjamin DISRAELI, W.E. GLADSTONE, David LLOYD GEORGE, Neville CHAMBERLAIN, Anthony EDEN, Margaret THATCHER and Tony BLAIR were notably active. The marquess of SALISBURY was his own foreign secretary (1886–92, 1895–1900). Foreign Office reforms in 1905 freed senior officials from routine clerical work and created a new class of advisers.

Britain has maintained permanent embassies to the Great Powers. Legations in less important capitals were upgraded in the 20th century, while consular and commercial services developed gradually to meet local needs. Improvements in communications, starting with telegraphs in the 1850s, progressively reduced ambassadorial discretion, but the diplomatic service long retained an aristocratic ethos: private means were required until 1920. In 2015 Britain maintained overseas relations with about 180 countries through 270 diplomatic offices. *See also* SECRETARY OF STATE.

FOREIGN RELATIONS, MANAGEMENT OF, SOUTHERN IRELAND *see* FOREIGN RELATIONS, SOUTHERN IRELAND

FOREIGN RELATIONS, NORTH BRITAIN AND SCOTLAND Relations were shaped mainly by the proximity of England (see SCOTTISH–ENGLISH RELATIONS), although other important relations existed. The arrival of SCOTS from *c*.500 reflected persistent connections with Ireland (see also BRUCE, EDWARD), while a legacy of the VIKING onslaught (late 8th–mid 10th centuries) was lasting contact with Norway (see NORWAY, 'MATTER OF'; JAMES III). From the 12th century the wool trade with Flanders assumed major economic importance.

Immigration by NORMANS and Flemish lords in the 12th and 13th centuries gave Scotland a NOBILITY with strong cultural links to Continental Europe. Alliances were made with France, and from 1295 to the 1420s, and from 1512 to 1560, its support was a crucial counterweight to English aggression.

As the English threat diminished in the 15th century, STEWART RULERS established more ties with Continental rulers and projected themselves as international players. But their lofty self-image masked a weak reality. In 1513, for example, the invasion of England by King JAMES IV, to support France, ended in disaster at FLODDEN. Scotland was then either wooed or dominated by England or France, until the REFORMATION (1560) brought Scotland closer to Protestant England than Catholic France. The realignment was entrenched by the accession of JAMES VI to the English throne (1603). *See also* SCOTTISH–FRENCH ALLIANCE.

FOREIGN RELATIONS, SOUTHERN IRELAND The 'Dáil government' of 1919–22 included a minister for foreign affairs and appointed some foreign envoys (see GOVERNMENT, SOUTHERN IRELAND). It sought recognition for an Irish republic at the 1919 PARIS PEACE CONFERENCE and from overseas Irish communities.

The IRISH FREE STATE (from 1922), a British Empire DOMINION, used foreign relations to assert autonomy. It joined the League of Nations (1923) and against British opposition registered the ANGLO-IRISH TREATY as an international treaty (1924). It also appointed representatives to the USA (first dominion representative, 1924) and to France, Germany and the Holy See (1929). It sought formal autonomy for dominions partly as a basis for reducing the British role in its internal affairs (established 1931). From 1931 the IFS obtained accreditation for its diplomats directly from the king.

From 1932 to 1948 Éamon DE VALERA was minister for external affairs as well as premier. He kept Ireland out of the Spanish Civil War and supported APPEASEMENT of Germany. When WORLD WAR II broke out he declared neutrality (Sept. 1939), which caused tension with the USA after it entered the war (1941), although afterwards Ireland accepted US MARSHALL AID to assist economic development (1948–9).

After southern Ireland became a republic (1949), President Seán O'Kelly undertook overseas State visits to express the new status, and the first ambassadors were appointed. The Republic continued neutrality (e.g., declining membership of NATO, 1949) and sought foreign support against the PARTITION OF IRELAND. Though eager to join the United Nations, Ireland was denied membership by the USSR until 1956. Thereafter it supported DECOLONIZATION, and from 1958 joined UN peacekeeping operations.

Following entry to the EUROPEAN ECONOMIC COMMUNITY (1973), Ireland became increasingly concerned with maximizing influence within Europe. In 2000, Ireland maintained diplomatic relations with 95 countries through 53 overseas diplomatic missions. Visiting heads of State have included US presidents John F. Kennedy (1963), Barack Obama (2011) and Donald Trump (2019). *See also* IRISH–BRITISH RELATIONS FROM 1922.

FOREIGN RELATIONS, WALES In the 5th–11th centuries foreign relations meant mainly contact with Ireland and Anglo-Saxon kingdoms (see ANGLO-WELSH RELATIONS), though there were trading and cultural links with France and kings went to Rome on pilgrimage.

With the advent of NORMANS (late 11th century), Wales came closer to Continental Europe (see CHURCH, MEDIEVAL WALES). Rulers of GWYNEDD (NW Wales) periodically established diplomatic relations with Continental rulers, usually to counter kings of England. For example, OWAIN GWYNEDD (ruled 1137–70) sought support from King Louis VII of France against HENRY II. In 1212 LLYWELYN AP IORWERTH made a treaty with Philip Augustus of France against King JOHN; Llywelyn seems also to have gained Pope Innocent III's support. In 1244 DAFYDD AP LLYWELYN attempted to place Gwynedd under the pope's overlordship, to avoid subordination to HENRY III.

OWAIN GLYN DŴR revived the policy of seeking foreign support: his embassy to Charles VI of France resulted in a treaty (July 1404) and a French military expedition to Wales (1405). Welshmen also maintained informal links with the Continent during the HUNDRED YEARS WAR (1337–1453); *see* OWAIN LAWGOCH.

FOREIGN SECRETARY *see* SECRETARY OF STATE

FOREIGN TRADE, ENGLAND BEFORE 1066 Early Anglo-Saxon kingdoms (6th–7th centuries) traded with northern Europe (Francia, Scandinavia) and the Mediterranean area (Italy, Byzantine Empire). Byzantine silver has been found, for example, in EAST ANGLIA (though it was possibly acquired by gift exchange). Slaves constituted a major export throughout the Anglo-Saxon period.

In the 7th–9th centuries trade around the North Sea flourished, organized largely by traders from Frisia (modern Netherlands; *see* WIC). English exports included cloth. Imports included glass, pottery, wine, silk, precious stones. Trade with Francia is implied by Charlemagne's embargo against English ships (*c.*789, following a dispute) and his commercial treaty with OFFA (*c.*796).

VIKING activity and settlement (9th–11th centuries) expanded the geographical range and content of trade because parts of England became linked to Viking trading networks that extended from Ireland to modern Russia. Imports included amber, walrus ivory, and furs. By the mid 11th century bulkier commodities had become more significant as exports, for example timber, fish, cheese and possibly wool. *See also* FOREIGN RELATIONS, ENGLAND BEFORE 1066; CURRENCY, ENGLAND BEFORE 1066.

FOREIGN TRADE, ENGLAND 1066 TO EARLY 17TH CENTURY In the 11th–14th centuries trade expanded, mostly with Flanders (part of modern Belgium and adjacent areas), northern France and the Rhineland; also with the Baltic and W Mediterranean (and elsewhere in the British Isles). Around 1300, LONDON handled 40% of exports, E coast ports (e.g., Boston) and SOUTHAMPTON 50%. Exports were mainly primary products: pre-eminently WOOL, but also hides, tin, COAL and (intermittently) grain. Imports comprised wine (particularly from GASCONY), salt, preserved fish (mostly herrings), materials for craftwork and manufacturing (e.g., iron; pitch and canvas for SHIP BUILDING; woad and ashes for cloth making), and luxury items (e.g., silks, furs).

Wool exports peaked in 1304–11 and declined significantly from the 1360s (directed from 1363 through the Calais STAPLE). In the later 14th century, exports of woollen cloth overtook wool (in value); it remained England's pre-eminent export commodity until the later 18th century (*see* CLOTH INDUSTRY, ENGLAND). European bullion shortages depressed trade 1390–1415, 1445–65.

From the mid 15th century London's share of trade increased, with Antwerp (in Flanders) being the outstanding trading centre for Continental markets *c.*1480–1586 (with disruptions). Replacement centres included Amsterdam (in Dutch Republic). Annual cloth exports (handled by 'merchant adventurers') rose from 38,000 (late 1460s) to 126,000 (1540s); trade then stagnated. Wine, cloth-making and ship-building materials, and luxuries remained significant imports.

From *c.*1550 merchants, organized in OVERSEAS TRADING COMPANIES, sought mainly luxury items (e.g., spices, silks) from a geographically wider range of places. Trade was revitalized in the Baltic (1550s), and around SW Europe and in the Mediterranean (1570s). From 1551 merchants traded with Morocco (NW Africa), and explored the W

African coast. Trade with Russia began in 1555, and with the OTTOMAN EMPIRE *c.*1580. Trading voyages to E Asia started in 1601–3, and colonies were established in N America from 1607. *See also* ARCTIC, ENGLISH AND BRITISH EXPLORATION; NORTH AMERICA, ENGLISH EXPLORATION.

FOREIGN TRADE, ENGLAND EARLY 17TH TO LATER 18TH CENTURIES Until the mid 17th century the main areas for trade remained N and C Europe (70% in 1640). Trade with the Iberian peninsula and Italy continued to expand, and OVERSEAS TRADING COMPANIES developed more distant markets (e.g., eastern Mediterranean). Woollen cloth was still the major export commodity, increasingly the lighter 'new draperies' (40% of woollens by value by 1640); imports were varied.

Trans-oceanic trade also began, with E and S Asia, and with colonies in the Americas. From 1601 the EAST INDIA COMPANY traded in the Indonesian archipelago and India, importing pepper and other spices, and (from 1613) calicoes (Indian cottons). From 1614 tobacco was imported from VIRGINIA (N America), and from the 1620s from WEST INDIES colonies. From the 1630s commodities (e.g., fur) were imported from NEW ENGLAND. Re-exporting started, mainly of colonial products to Continental Europe (6% of London's exports by value by 1640).

Competition from Dutch shipping, and concern to strengthen trading relationships, prompted legislation from 1651 requiring use of English ships and initial importation to England rather than elsewhere (*see* NAVIGATION ACTS). In mid-century England also entered the SLAVE TRADE; a 'triangular trade' emerged whereby Englishmen exchanged woollens and metals (e.g., copper) in W Africa for slaves, shipped slaves to the Americas and imported colonial goods.

Trade expanded greatly from the 1660s: tobacco and sugar became major colonial imports; tea, coffee and cottons came from Asia. Restrictive policies (later called MERCANTILISM) helped to make England an entrepôt (trading centre) for Continental Europe; by 1700, 30% of imports were re-exported.

By 1780 trade doubled in volume, mainly from extra-European activities (in N America, West Indies, Africa, India, E Asia). Woollen textiles remained the largest export commodity, and re-exports continued at around a third of exports. Expansion particularly benefited England's western ports (e.g., BRISTOL, LIVERPOOL). *See also* COMMERCIAL REVOLUTION.

FOREIGN TRADE, GREAT BRITAIN FROM LATER 18TH CENTURY By 1780 the main export markets were Europe and the Americas (two-fifths each) and Asia. Woollen textiles were the principal commodity. Exports of cotton yarn and cloth rose rapidly (*see* INDUSTRIAL

REVOLUTION), overtaking woollens. Textiles remained pre-eminent (75% in 1830s, over 50% in 1870s). Imports c.1780 were dominated by foodstuffs (33%, including sugar, tobacco, tea) and textile raw materials (about 20%). Subsequent developments included abolition of the SLAVE TRADE (1807); increasing exports to the USA and Asia, especially INDIA (main market by 1850s); moves towards FREE TRADE. Imports exceeded exports in value, creating a 'trade gap' (covered by 'invisible exports', e.g., insurance, shipping).

From the 1870s food imports grew dramatically, meeting half of requirements by 1913. Imports of raw materials and even manufactured goods (e.g., electrical equipment) also increased. Exports were hampered by competition and tariffs (e.g., from USA), although coal exports expanded markedly. Trade with many countries was imbalanced (i.e., mostly exports or imports).

During WORLD WAR I (1914–18) markets were lost and exports slumped, especially textiles and coal. Thereafter imports mostly exceeded pre-war levels; exports remained lower. In 1932 the government implemented protectionism and 'imperial preference' (see TARIFF REFORM).

Trade fell heavily during WORLD WAR II (1939–45). Afterwards conditions necessitated an 'export drive' (1947–51), primarily of manufactured goods. During the 1950s food imports declined (to 36%) while others increased: manufactures (28%), raw materials (25%), fuel (11%). In the 1960s trade with the EUROPEAN ECONOMIC COMMUNITY (EEC) expanded. Exports of goods peaked at 20% of UK gross domestic product (GDP) in 1977.

From 1973 the UK operated under EEC trading arrangements. Exports to EEC countries peaked in 1999 at 55% of total. In the 21st century, leading export markets were the USA and Germany, the main suppliers Germany, China and USA. Major exports and imports included manufactured goods, machinery, chemicals, fuels, foodstuffs. In 2017 goods exports were 17% of UK GDP. See also CHINESE TREATY PORTS; FAIR TRADE MOVEMENT; COAL INDUSTRY, WALES; BREXIT.

FOREIGN TRADE, IRELAND BEFORE 17TH CENTURY

From at least the 5th century pottery and glass were imported from Continental Europe, and probably also wine, olive oil and other commodities. Amber from Scandinavia reached Ireland from the 9th century. The main exports were probably hides (from cattle and sheep) and wool. Foreign trade benefited mainly élite members of society.

In the early 10th century VIKINGS established trading centres by rivers near eastern and southern coasts which developed into TOWNS (e.g., DUBLIN). They involved Ireland in more vigorous trade between Scandinavia, N Europe, Britain (notably Chester and BRISTOL) and west-ern Continental Europe. Among Viking imports were furs, ivory, wine and silver.

Following the Anglo-Norman invasion (1169–70), the Viking (or Hiberno-Norse) towns remained important trading centres in the new lordship (see NORMANS, IMPACT ON IRELAND), with Dublin rapidly becoming the leading centre of foreign trade. Other towns were reduced to regional centres. New ports were established (e.g., Drogheda, Dundalk, Galway), though they remained less important than existing ports. Ireland's main trading partner, and greatest export market, was England. Major exports included hides, wool, timber and linen, while the main imports (from various sources) included wine, salt, iron, dyes and spices. In the 13th century Ireland produced and exported surplus cereals, but this declined during the 14th century, and in the 15th century grain was imported. Herring and other sea fish were important exports from at least the 14th century. Trading patterns changed little in the 16th century, except that Parliament sought to prevent wool exports (prohibited 1521). They re-expanded in the later 16th century, under licences, to supply some English cloth industries.

FOREIGN TRADE, IRELAND FROM 17TH CENTURY

In the early 17th century hides remained the main export commodity, alongside wool, fish, timber, and some linen, linen yarn and friezes (low-quality cloth). Wool exports to Britain grew, and large-scale exporting of store cattle developed (for fattening for LONDON), together with cattle-based products (barrelled beef, tallow, butter) and sheep. Wine was probably the main import (from various sources), alongside pottery and expensive commodities such as glassware, sugar and spices. Important imports from England included broadcloth and coal. Tobacco was imported from the Americas.

After disruption in the 1640s (see IRISH WARS, 1641–52), trade revival was damaged by restrictions against live cattle exports (1663) and prohibition of cattle and sheep imports to England (1667). Butter and wool became the main exports to England, while more salted beef and other provisions were exported to American colonies. More trade also went to Continental Europe, notably France. Linen exports grew strongly from the 1680s. After stagnation in the early 18th century, foreign trade resumed strong growth from the 1740s. Cattle exporting to England resumed in 1759.

From the 1770s demand from an urbanizing and industrializing Britain expanded the value of exports within Ireland's national income (to a fifth by 1845). In 1825, 87% of recorded foreign trade was with Britain. By 1835, linen accounted for 32% of exports (by value), grain for 29%, other foodstuffs for 26%. Important imports included sugar, tea, coffee, wine, coal, cotton and woollens. Trade was disrupted 1845–9 by the GREAT FAMINE.

In the later 19th century some agricultural exports to Britain (e.g., grain) declined due to competition (e.g., from American grain from 1870s). Linen exports remained strong, and several industries were successful in world markets, notably SHIP BUILDING, engineering (NE Ireland), BREWING and distilling. In 1914, food, drink and farm produce accounted for 54% of exports, manufactured goods for 40%.

FOREIGN TRADE, IRELAND, ENGLISH AND BRITISH REGULATION

From the 13th century trade was affected by English law and legislation (e.g., English measures and duties). In the 14th–15th centuries wool and hides were exported through the STAPLE system (with modifications).

In 1569 and 1571 Ireland's Parliament, on English instruction, imposed heavy duties on wool exports to inhibit supplies to the Spanish Netherlands. Ireland's CHIEF GOVERNOR subsequently influenced exports through licensing, reinforced from 1617 by use of staple towns (designated ports in Ireland and England), to direct supplies to the English cloth industry.

From the 1660s English economic policy took regular account of Ireland. In 1660 England's Parliament favoured Ireland under an anti-Dutch NAVIGATION ACT (Ireland could trade with English colonies, using Irish ships). Conversely the 1663 Staple Act confined colonial trade to English ships (except for exports of Irish provisions and horses); direct imports from colonies were banned. Also in 1663, sectional interests persuaded England's Parliament to restrict imports of (Irish) live cattle (forbidden July–Dec.); in 1667 cattle imports were banned together with imports of sheep, swine, beef and pork (Cattle Acts). Following a lapse, bans were reimposed in 1681 and extended to mutton, butter and cheese. In 1699 the English Woollen Act prohibited the export of Irish wool and woollen cloth except to England and Wales, and imposed heavy duties on woollen cloth. (It sought to suppress Irish clothmaking and secure wool for England.) More considerately England abolished import duties on Irish linen in 1696.

Great Britain readmitted some Irish exports to trans-Atlantic markets from 1731, and allowed cattle imports from 1759. Campaigning by PATRIOTS in the 1770s achieved removal of many British restrictions (1780). After the UNION OF IRELAND AND GREAT BRITAIN (1801) duties between Ireland and Britain were removed, creating a free market, though this undermined certain industrial concerns (see INDUSTRY, IRELAND 18TH CENTURY TO 1921).

FOREIGN TRADE, NORTH BRITAIN AND SCOTLAND BEFORE 17TH CENTURY

Kingdoms in N Britain from the 5th century (later Scotland) imported pottery, glass and wine, probably in exchange for furs, hides and wool. With minting of coins from the 12th century (see CURRENCY, SCOTLAND) trade expanded but the content remained similar. The export of wool to Flanders (part of modern Belgium and adjacent areas) was dominant. England (until 1296) and France were also major trading partners.

Patterns of trade changed slowly. In the Low Countries, Bruges (in Flanders) came to dominate Scottish trade. A STAPLE was established there by the mid 14th century, which moved to Middelburg in 1407 and to Veere (both SW modern Netherlands) from 1507 or 1508 (lasting until 1799). In the 14th and 15th centuries E-coast ports, and increasingly EDINBURGH, dominated foreign trade.

Expansion occurred in the later 16th century, with increasing imports of timber from Norway. Baltic ports supplied iron, hemp, pitch and tar, and grain in time of dearth. The 'auld alliance' (see SCOTTISH–FRENCH ALLIANCE) gave Scots preferential treatment in many French towns, and much wine was imported from Bordeaux (SW France). Exports of coal, salt, lead and coarse cloth developed, along with hides and fish. Trade with England increased following the REFORMATION (1560). By the UNION OF CROWNS (1603) England was again a major trading partner.

FOREIGN TRADE, SCOTLAND FROM 17TH CENTURY

From c.1600 until disruption in the 1640s–50s (see COVENANTING REVOLUTION) Scotland's principal trading partners were England, the Low Countries, the Baltic area, and increasingly NE Ireland (see ULSTER PLANTATION). Major export commodities remained hides, wool, coarse woollen cloth, linen and fish (herrings and salmon), together with coal, lead and salt. Imports included manufactured goods (e.g., furniture, fine cloths), timber, iron and wine. From the 1660s exports to England revived (especially cattle, sheep, linen, coal), though European markets declined. Scotland also became prominent in the expanding 'Atlantic economy', exporting linen and other manufactures to the WEST INDIES and N America in return for sugar and tobacco (despite English NAVIGATION ACTS). The trade stimulated the rise of GLASGOW (W-C Scotland) to second-largest city by 1670.

Free trade with England from 1707 (see UNION OF ENGLAND AND SCOTLAND) further stimulated exports (cattle, sheep, grain, coal, iron). The tobacco trade experienced a 'golden age' from the 1740s until reduced from 1775 by the AMERICAN WAR OF INDEPENDENCE. Based on re-exporting to France, the Low Countries, and Germany, it amounted to half of exports (by value) in the 1750s. From the late 18th century trade was developed with INDIA, AUSTRALIA and S America, including export of linen, cotton (from early 19th century) and jute (from 1830s).

From the 1830s iron and coal were exported worldwide, especially to the BRITISH EMPIRE and S America, followed from mid century by ships, railway locomotives and steel, making Scotland a leading exporter in the world economy. Markets slumped during the 1920s–30s, but revived after 1945 (end of WORLD WAR II). In the 1950s–80s exports declined severely as other countries undercut Scottish industry, although financial services and electronics provided some replacement from the 1980s. *See also* INDUSTRY, SCOTLAND FROM LATE 18TH CENTURY; INDUSTRIAL DECLINE, SCOTLAND.

FOREIGN TRADE, WALES *see* FOREIGN TRADE, GREAT BRITAIN FROM LATER 18TH CENTURY

FOREST LAW In England, law developed by NORMAN KINGS (from late 11th century) to protect hunting land (not necessarily wooded). King HENRY II extended forest law over a third of the country and consolidated law and customs (Assize of Woodstock, 1184). Some grievances were remedied in MAGNA CARTA (1215) and the Charter of the Forest (1217). Extensive areas were 'disafforested' in the 14th century.

FORSTER, W.E. (b. 11 July 1818 at Bradpole, Dorset, England; d. 5 April 1886 at London, England, aged 67). A Yorkshire mill-owner from a QUAKER family, William Edward Forster became a Liberal MP in 1861. As vice-president of the Council (1868–74) under W.E. GLADSTONE, he oversaw the Education Act of 1870 and the Ballot Act of 1872 which introduced secret ballots. He was chief secretary for Ireland from 1880, resigning in 1882 in protest at the KILMAINHAM TREATY. *See also* FORSTER'S EDUCATION ACT.

FORSTER'S EDUCATION ACT Popular name for the UK Parliament's Elementary Education Act of 1870, which was overseen by W.E. FORSTER. It instituted elected school boards in England and Wales where elementary education was unavailable. They provided schools for children aged up to 12 which could charge fees. The Act inaugurated direct provision of schooling by the State. The resulting 'dual system' of board and voluntary schools lasted until 1902 (*see* BALFOUR EDUCATION ACT). *See also* EDUCATION, ENGLAND/WALES.

FORTH–CLYDE ISTHMUS The relatively narrow and low-lying area of N Britain (modern SCOTLAND) between the estuaries of the Rivers Forth (E) and Clyde (W), about 25 mi (40 km) wide at its shortest extent. There are wider upland areas to N and S.

The isthmus has been prominent in the history of N Britain. The Romans built a defensive wall across the isthmus (2nd century; *see* ANTONINE WALL), and it became the southern border area of the PICTS (3rd–10th centuries). In the 15th century, EDINBURGH, by the Forth estuary, became Scotland's capital; from the later 18th century GLASGOW, by

the Clyde, was a major industrial centre. Continuing economic expansion within and around the isthmus created a 'Central Belt', which dominated Scotland in its population: in 2015 it contained about 65% of inhabitants (3.5 million of almost 5.4 million people). *See also* STIRLING.

FORTRIU A Pictish (Brittonic-speaking) kingdom in N Britain recorded from the 7th century. Its name is derived from the IRON AGE TRIBE the Verturiones. From the 19th century Fortriu was equated with Strathearn in C Scotland (N of Stirling, W of Perth), but a more northerly location now seems more likely, SE of the Moray Firth (modern NE Scotland). The prominent fort at Burghead (in modern Moray), where 7th-century carvings have been found, may have been an important centre within Fortriu.

From the late 7th century kings of Fortriu probably ruled PICTS both N and S of the MOUNTH, though possibly through a subordinate king to the S (*see* ATHOLL, KINGDOM OF). References to Fortriu continue until the disappearance of Pictish identity *c*.900. *See also* KINGSHIP, NORTH BRITAIN.

FOSTER, JOHN (b. Sept. 1740 possibly at Dunleer, Co. Louth, Ireland; d. 23 Aug. 1828 at Collon House, Co. Louth, aged 87). A member of the Irish House of Commons from 1761, Foster was an ally of the government in Ireland from 1777. In 1783 Great Britain's new prime minister, William PITT the Younger, recruited him (with John BERESFORD and John FITZGIBBON) as an adviser. He served as chancellor of the Irish Exchequer (1784–5) and was elected (last) speaker of the Commons (1785). He promoted economic activity (e.g., 'Foster's Corn Law', 1784, which encouraged grain exports), but opposed Catholic relief, though in 1793 he reluctantly accepted a relief Act. He opposed the UNION OF IRELAND AND GREAT BRITAIN (1801), instigated by Pitt, and refused to surrender the mace. He and Pitt were later reconciled. He was created Lord Oriel in 1821. *See also* PROTESTANT ASCENDANCY.

FOSTER'S CORN LAW Legislation by the Irish Parliament, 1784, promoted by John FOSTER, chancellor of the Irish Exchequer. It regulated export subsidies for grain when prices were low (except from DUBLIN) and prohibited exports when prices were high. It is credited with further encouraging grain cultivation and also flour milling as higher bounties were paid on ground corn. It operated into the 19th century. *See also* AGRICULTURE, IRELAND 17TH CENTURY TO 1921.

FOUR BURGHS, COURT OF THE In Scotland, an assembly of representatives from BERWICK-UPON-TWEED, EDINBURGH, Roxburgh and STIRLING (four royal BURGHS); formed by the early 13th century. In 1369 Lanark and Linlithgow replaced English-held Berwick and Roxburgh;

additional towns were represented in the 15th century. The Court allocated royal taxation between burghs, influenced PARLIAMENT and COUNCILS-GENERAL, and encouraged consistency in burgh government. It was continued (after 1487) by the CONVENTION OF ROYAL BURGHS.

FOUR CANTREFS *see* BERFEDDWLAD, Y

FOURTH PARTY A splinter group of Conservatives in the UK Parliament of 1880–5, consisting of Lord Randolph CHURCHILL, John Gorst, Sir Henry Drummond-Wolff and A.J. BALFOUR. Flouting Sir Stafford NORTHCOTE, they excoriated the Liberal government (and especially the prime minister, W.E. GLADSTONE) in an opportunistic fashion.

FOX, CHARLES JAMES (b. 24 Jan. 1749 at Westminster, Middlesex, England; d. 13 Sept. 1806 at Chiswick, Middlesex, aged 57). A son of Henry FOX and a WHIG, Charles James Fox became an MP in 1768 and served in the ministry of Lord NORTH (1770–2, 1772–4), despite being disliked by King GEORGE III. Through friendship with Edmund BURKE he joined the ROCKINGHAM WHIGS in opposition. In 1782, after North's resignation, he served under the marquess of ROCKINGHAM as foreign secretary (the first), but resigned over the king's appointment of the earl of SHELBURNE as prime minister. His short-lived coalition with North in 1783, nominally led by the duke of PORTLAND, involved further service as foreign secretary, but exacerbated the king's loathing for him. George dismissed the ministry (Dec. 1783) and appointed William PITT the Younger as prime minister.

Fox spent 1784–1806 leading the opposition Whigs. His early enthusiasm for the FRENCH REVOLUTION (from 1789) helped to split the Whigs in 1794, with Portland and others joining Pitt's ministry. Fox allied with Lord GRENVILLE in 1804, and in 1806 re-entered government as foreign secretary.

A liberal, Fox was a dominant force in London society. His supporters, known as FOXITES, were fiercely loyal to him.

FOX, GEORGE (b. July 1624 at Fenny Drayton, Leicestershire, England; d. 13 Jan. 1691 at London, England, aged 66). A weaver's son, Fox began to wander through the English countryside from 1643 (during the CIVIL WARS). From 1647 he undertook charismatic preaching tours, emphasizing the 'inner light of the living Christ' within each individual. He rejected formal ceremonies, religious doctrine, and any need for clergy. He went to N England in 1651 where he made contact with other 'separatist' groups, and in 1652, in Westmorland (NW England), formed the Society of Friends (nicknamed 'Quakers'). Thereafter he travelled in Britain, Ireland, Continental Europe, the West Indies and N America, promoting the Society and forming structured organizations. Although frequently imprisoned, Fox created a new religious movement, which was well established by his death. *See also* ENGLISH REVOLUTION SECTS; QUAKERS; NONCONFORMITY AND DISSENT, ENGLAND.

FOX, HENRY (b. 28 Sept. 1705 at Chiswick, Middlesex, England; d. 1 July 1774 at Kensington, Middlesex, aged 69). An MP from 1735 and WHIG, Fox supported the ministry of Robert WALPOLE (resigned 1742). He held office from 1743 under Henry PELHAM, serving as secretary at war from 1746. He became SECRETARY OF STATE (southern) in the ministry of the duke of NEWCASTLE in 1755 (resigned Oct. 1756, unwilling to defend the loss of MINORCA). Fox was paymaster-general in the PITT–Newcastle ministry from 1757. He used the office to enrich himself massively, earning a reputation for gross corruption.

Remaining in office under the earl of BUTE (from 1761), Fox carried the Peace of PARIS, which ended the SEVEN YEARS WAR, through the House of Commons (approved 9 Dec. 1762). He was created Lord Holland (April 1763) after Bute's resignation, but was ousted by George GRENVILLE (1765). He was the father of Charles James Fox.

FOXE, RICHARD (b. 1447 or 1448 at Ropsley, Lincolnshire, England; d. 5 Oct. 1528 at Winchester, Hampshire, England, aged about 80). Foxe was a leading minister and bishop under King HENRY VII. From 1485 he was king's secretary (to 1487) and a councillor, and from 1487 keeper of the PRIVY SEAL. He was appointed successively bishop of Exeter (1487), Bath and Wells (1492), DURHAM (1494), and WINCHESTER (1501). He negotiated important treaties, including those of MEDINA DEL CAMPO (1489), ÉTAPLES (1492) and Ayton (1502, for marriage of Margaret Tudor to JAMES IV of Scotland).

Under HENRY VIII (king from 1509), Foxe became overshadowed by Thomas WOLSEY (by 1513). He resigned as keeper of the privy seal in 1516. A patron of humanist scholarship, Foxe founded Corpus Christi College, Oxford (1517). *See also* HUMANISM.

FOXE'S 'BOOK OF MARTYRS' The popular title for *The Acts and Monuments of the Church* by John Foxe (1517–87), published in England in 1563 (in reign of Queen ELIZABETH I). Based on an earlier Latin work by Foxe (1559), it provided a Church history for Protestants, identifying the papacy as the Antichrist and vividly portraying the sufferings of English Protestants under MARY I. Highly influential, especially among PURITANS and later dissenters, it was continually reprinted until the mid 19th century. *See also* REFORMATION, ENGLAND.

FOXITES Name used for the supporters of the English WHIG leader Charles James Fox (1749–1806), particularly after the Whigs divided over attitudes to the FRENCH REVOLUTION in 1794. Derived from the ROCKINGHAM WHIGS, the Foxites advocated PARLIAMENTARY REFORM and peace with France, and opposed repressive legislation and Crown influence. They seceded from Parliament 1797–1801. After Fox's death the Foxites continued under the leadership of Charles Grey (Earl GREY), who eventually led a reforming Whig ministry from 1830. *See also* PORTLAND, 3RD DUKE OF.

FRANCE, CLAIMS BY RULERS OF ENGLAND In 1202–4 lands held by King JOHN of England as a French nobleman (Normandy, Anjou with Touraine and Maine, much of Aquitaine) were seized by King Philip II. (From 1066 kings of England had been dukes of NORMANDY, and other French lands were acquired later: *see* ANGEVIN EMPIRE.) John managed to retain the CHANNEL ISLANDS (from duchy of Normandy) and two areas of Aquitaine – part of Poitou (lost in 1224) and GASCONY (in SW France). Retention of Gascony was not accepted by French kings.

John (d. 1216) and his successor HENRY III claimed and sought to regain lost territories. (In 1254 Henry regarded the Channel Islands as English possessions.) The situation was regularized in 1259 by the treaty of PARIS, under which Henry renounced claims and Gascony was recognized as a lordship held from the king of France, though difficulties ensued (*see* GASCON WAR). Henry also did homage for the Channel Islands.

When Charles IV of France died in 1328 without a direct heir, EDWARD III had a matrilineal (female-line) claim to the French Crown through his mother ISABELLA, Charles's sister. It was rejected by French authorities who preferred the male descent of Philip of Valois (Philip VI). Philip's confiscation of Gascony in 1337 caused Edward to commence war and (from 1340) style himself 'king of France' (*see* HUNDRED YEARS WAR). The title was dropped briefly (1360–9), following the treaty of BRÉTIGNY.

Under the treaty of Troyes (1420), HENRY V was recognized as heir to Charles VI of France, implicitly recognizing Charles's legitimacy as ruler; on Charles's death (1422) HENRY VI was proclaimed king. Though most English-held and -conquered lands were lost by 1454, rulers of England retained the title 'king/queen of France' until 1801 (dropped at the UNION OF IRELAND AND GREAT BRITAIN). It was formally abandoned in 1802 (*see* AMIENS, PEACE OF). *See also* FRANCE, ENGLISH AND BRITISH RELATIONS WITH; CALAIS.

FRANCE, ENGLISH AND BRITISH RELATIONS WITH In the late 11th and 12th centuries, England was ruled by kings who held territories in France and had uneasy relationships with kings of France, their feudal superiors (*see* NORMAN EMPIRE; ANGEVIN EMPIRE). From the 14th century English kings claimed the kingship of France and attempted to conquer the country (*see* HUNDRED YEARS WAR). The loss of CALAIS (1558) effectively ended this phase.

England intermittently supported French Protestants or HUGUENOTS (1559–98) and tried to exploit conflicts between France and the HABSBURG EMPIRE. Oliver CROMWELL sided with France rather than Spain (*see* DUNKIRK). King CHARLES II accepted French subsidies (1670; *see* DOVER, TREATY OF), but England (Great Britain from 1707) was at war with France for nearly half the time between 1689 and 1815, a period when Britain helped to limit French power in Europe, won a global contest for colonies, opposed the French Revolution and defeated the French emperor Napoleon Bonaparte (*see* GRAND ALLIANCE, WAR OF THE; SPANISH SUCCESSION, WAR OF THE; SEVEN YEARS WAR; FRENCH REVOLUTIONARY AND NAPOLEONIC WARS, BRITISH INVOLVEMENT).

Mistrust persisted, despite co-operation in the CRIMEAN WAR (1854–6), until 1904 when the ANGLO-FRENCH CONVENTION marked a rapprochement. That culminated in alliance against GERMANY in WORLD WAR I (1914–18). Differences soon re-emerged, and Britain restricted its commitment to France to the treaty of LOCARNO (1925). They were again allies in WORLD WAR II (1939–40, 1944–5) and in the NORTH ATLANTIC TREATY ORGANIZATION (founded 1949).

France twice vetoed UK entry into the EUROPEAN ECONOMIC COMMUNITY (1963, 1967), but eventually relented (the UK joined in 1973). Thereafter relations were generally cordial, although in 2003 France, unlike Britain, opposed the US-led invasion of IRAQ. In 2010 the countries made two defence treaties for sharing military resources, but France was angered in 2016 by the UK population's decision in a referendum to leave the European Union. *See also* FRANCE, CLAIMS BY RULERS OF ENGLAND; CHANNEL TUNNEL.

FRANCE, SCOTTISH RELATIONS WITH *see* SCOTTISH–FRENCH ALLIANCE

FRANCHISE Old French and Anglo-Norman term for a privilege or freedom. Used in England from the 12th century, it was absorbed into Middle English, referring to a jurisdiction or rights which normally belonged to the Crown but were exercised by an individual or corporate body by presumption or royal authorization (e.g., jurisdiction of a PALATINATE).

Some franchises predated the NORMAN CONQUEST (1066–70s); by the late 13th century they were so numerous that Edward I investigated their legality (*see* QUO

WARRANTO INQUIRIES). Thereafter franchises were normally granted by ROYAL PREROGATIVE. They also existed elsewhere in the British Isles.

From the 18th century the term has commonly meant an 'elective franchise', i.e., the privilege or right of voting in public elections, especially for members of a local authority or national legislature. It also denotes the qualifications required for voting.

FRANCHISE, ENGLAND AND WALES *see* PARLIAMENTARY CONSTITUENCIES AND ELECTIONS; PARLIAMENTARY REFORM

FRANCHISE, IRELAND BEFORE 1801 In the late 14th–16th centuries, Anglo-Irish landholders chose SHIRE (or county) representatives for the House of Commons in the Irish PARLIAMENT, and town freemen (privileged Anglo-Irish inhabitants) chose town representatives.

In 1542 Parliament enacted the English county franchise qualification: ownership, or life leasehold, of land worth 40*s*. per year (rental value). The electorate expanded in the late 16th–early 17th centuries with the foundation of additional counties and boroughs. A majority of boroughs had 'closed corporations' (self-perpetuating governments) which elected MPs and from which Catholics were excluded. From 1603 the provost, fellows and scholars of Trinity College, Dublin, also elected two MPs.

Catholics were effectively barred from voting in 1709 (imposition of oath of abjuration), and formally disfranchised in 1728, creating a Protestant electorate (*see* PROTESTANT ASCENDANCY). They were readmitted to franchises in 1793 (*see* HOBART'S ACT). Most of the 117 boroughs in the 18th century were controlled by landowners who nominated candidates.

FRANCHISE, IRELAND 1801 TO 1921 At the UNION OF IRELAND AND GREAT BRITAIN (1801), 84 of 117 boroughs were disfranchised. Franchises otherwise continued, but when Catholic Emancipation was conceded in 1829 the UK Parliament reduced the electorate from about 216,000 to 37,000 by increasing the county land qualification from 40*s*. to £10.

The 1832 Irish Reform Act re-expanded the electorate to 90,000 by adding some long leaseholders to county electorates, and in boroughs by enfranchising occupiers of property worth £10 and resident freemen (qualified by inheritance or apprenticeship). The 1850 Irish Franchise Act expanded mainly the county electorate by enfranchising tenants of land worth £12 a year (total electorate increased to 163,000). The 1868 Irish Reform Act enlarged the borough electorate (31,000 to 45,000) by reducing the franchise for occupiers to over £4.

Subsequent franchise extensions were uniform with England and Wales: 1884, to male householders in boroughs and counties (738,000); 1918, to men aged 21 or over, women aged 30 or over. The 1918 extensions contributed to the success of SINN FÉIN at the 1918 UK general election. *See also* PARLIAMENTARY REPRESENTATION, IRELAND.

FRANCHISE, SCOTLAND From the early 14th century to 1587 the only elected members of the Scottish PARLIAMENT were representatives of royal BURGHS. In the 14th–15th centuries they were probably elected by all BURGESSES; from 1469 only by councillors (*see* TOWN GOVERNMENT, SCOTLAND). In 1587 shire representatives (or commissioners) were included in Parliament, elected by freeholders of land worth at least 40*s*. (Scots) per year. Other categories of landholders were added in the 17th century.

After the UNION OF ENGLAND AND SCOTLAND (1707) the same groups elected burgh and shire representatives to the British Parliament. There were 1500 electors for 15 burgh seats (14 representing groups of burghs), 2600 for 30 shire seats.

The First Scottish Reform Act (1832) enfranchised male householders in burghs with property worth at least £10 per year, and £10 proprietors and £50 (short-lease) and £10 (long-lease) tenants in shires. The electorate increased to 60,000. The Second Scottish Reform Act (1868) enfranchised all rate-paying male householders (owners or tenants) in burghs and lodgers occupying premises worth at least £10 per year in rent, and £5 proprietors and £14 tenants in shires. The electorate rose to 230,000. Further extensions were uniform with England and Wales: 1884, to male householders in both burghs and shires (560,000); 1918, to men aged 21 or over, women 30 or over; 1928, to women 21–29; 1969, men and women 18–21. The voting age was lowered to 16 in 2013 for the independence referendum, and in 2015 for elections to the Scottish Parliament and local government.

FRANCHISE, SOUTHERN IRELAND The 1922 constitution of the IRISH FREE STATE enfranchised all citizens aged 21 or over for Dáil elections and referendums, and citizens aged 30 or over for Seanad elections (*see* PARLIAMENT, SOUTHERN IRELAND). (Only one Seanad election was held, in 1925.) Under the 1937 constitution Dáil electors could also elect the new president, and 49 members (of 60) of the replacement Seanad were elected by: (a) Dáil members, senators and local councillors (from 'vocational panels' of nominated members), (b) university graduates.

Under referendums, the minimum voting age was reduced to 18 in 1972; the university franchise was extended in principle to graduates of all Irish university-level institutions in 1979 (unimplemented by 2019); participation in Dáil elections was permitted for residents who were not Irish citizens in 1984 (granted in 1985 to UK citizens). From 1979 all European Economic Community citizens could vote in elections to the European Parliament.

FRANKLIN, ROSALIND (b. 25 July 1920 at Notting Hill, London, England; d. 16 April 1958 at Chelsea, London, aged 37). After studying chemistry at CAMBRIDGE University (1938–41), and starting research, Franklin undertook war-related scientific research in London (1942–6), meanwhile obtaining a Cambridge doctorate (1945). Her experience of X-ray diffraction methods in France (1947–50, in Paris) led to appointment at King's College, London, to examine DNA (deoxyribonucleic acid), an important constituent of chromosomes in cell nuclei.

By May 1952 Franklin had obtained excellent diffraction photographs. In early 1953 her colleague Maurice Wilkins (1916–2004) showed these to James Watson from Cambridge, and directed him to a recent unpublished report by Franklin. The information enabled Watson and Francis CRICK to complete their DNA model (in March), one of the greatest scientific achievements (providing a chemical understanding of heredity). Franklin moved to Birkbeck College (1953), and died young from cancer. Her importance in scientific history only became widely appreciated in the 1990s.

FREDERICK, PRINCE OF WALES (b. 20 Jan. 1707 at Hanover, Germany; d. 20 March 1751 at Kew, Surrey, England, aged 44). Frederick lived in Hanover until Dec. 1728, moving to England after his father became king of Great Britain and Ireland (see GEORGE II). As heir, he was created prince of Wales in Jan. 1729.

Relations between Frederick and his parents soon deteriorated, and he encouraged politicians opposed to the king's chief minister, Robert WALPOLE. In 1737 Frederick was expelled from court and established a rival court at Norfolk House. Relations improved after Walpole's resignation (1742) but remained strained. Frederick moved to LEICESTER HOUSE in 1743. He died in 1751 after being hit by a real tennis ball. His son George succeeded as king in 1760 (see GEORGE III). See also CUMBERLAND, DUKE OF.

FREE CHURCH OF SCOTLAND A dissenting presbyterian Church formed in 1843 by two-fifths of Church of SCOTLAND ministers and laity, led by Thomas CHALMERS, who desired a Church more independent from the State and who objected particularly to private patronage (see DISRUPTION). By 1845, 500 churches had been built. The Church was strong in towns and cities, and in CROFTING areas of the Highlands and Islands. In 1892 relaxation of its adherence to the Westminster Confession (1647) caused a secession (see FREE PRESBYTERIAN CHURCH). Most of the

Free Church merged with the UNITED PRESBYTERIAN CHURCH in 1900 to form the UNITED FREE CHURCH OF SCOTLAND.

A minority, concentrated in N and W Scotland (including the WESTERN ISLES), maintained a continuing Free Church. It split in 2000 over the handling of allegations of misconduct against a college principal. In 2015 the Free Church had about 100 congregations in Scotland and 12,000 attendees, and the Free Church (Continuing) 29 congregations and about 1000 members. See also DISSENT, SCOTLAND.

FREE PRESBYTERIAN CHURCH A Scottish dissenting Church formed in 1893 by the secession of members of the FREE CHURCH OF SCOTLAND after it removed (1892) the necessity of absolute adherence to the Westminster Confession (1647). The Free Presbyterian Church retained the exclusive use of unaccompanied metrical psalms (no hymns) and practised strict sabbatarianism. In its heartland, NW Scotland (including parts of the WESTERN ISLES), it campaigned against Sunday ferries.

The Church split again in 1989 after a prominent elder, Lord Mackay of Clashfern (the lord CHANCELLOR), attended a former colleague's Catholic requiem mass. The more liberal wing formed the Associated Presbyterian Churches. In 2018 the Free Presbyterian Church had about 30 congregations in Scotland, and the Associated Presbyterian Churches eight congregations. See also DISSENT, SCOTLAND.

FREE TRADE The practice and doctrine of unrestricted commerce. Free trade between Scotland and England was introduced by the UNION OF ENGLAND AND SCOTLAND (1707). In the 18th century Adam SMITH (d. 1790) expounded the economic rationale for free trade, and William PITT the Younger started lowering British import duties (1783–93). The UNION OF IRELAND AND GREAT BRITAIN (1801) included free trade between Britain and Ireland. Trade treaties were made with several European States under the 1823 Reciprocity of Duties Act (see HUSKISSON, WILLIAM). The decisive advance was the repeal of the CORN LAWS (1846). W.E. GLADSTONE removed most remaining tariffs in the 1850s, and free trade became an established tenet of British economic policy.

A campaign for TARIFF REFORM 1903–6 was resisted, but PROTECTIONISM was adopted in the face of high unemployment in 1932. In 1947 the UK recommended a policy of dismantling barriers to trade. See also ECONOMY, STATE INVOLVEMENT, BRITAIN; MERCANTILISM.

FRENCH, JOHN (b. 28 Sept. 1852 at Ripple, Kent, England; d. 22 May 1925 at Deal, Kent, aged 72). Following the outbreak of WORLD WAR I, French served as commander-in-chief of the British Expeditionary Force in France and Belgium (Aug. 1914–Dec. 1915). He proved unable to counter the development of trench warfare, and his relations with the other Allied armies were strained. Undermined by Douglas HAIG, he was compelled to resign after the failed offensive at Loos (created Viscount French). French was lord lieutenant of Ireland 1918–21 (see IRISH FREE STATE, FOUNDING OF).

FRENCH, USE IN BRITISH ISLES Connections between King EDWARD THE CONFESSOR and NORMANDY resulted in some use of French in English royal circles during his reign (1042–66). The NORMAN CONQUEST (1066–70s) placed England under a French-speaking élite (king, NOBILITY, senior clergy, etc.). Norman French became used at court, in law courts, in education and elsewhere. Literary works were written in French from the early 12th to early 15th centuries (e.g., *Voyage of St Brendan* by the monk Benedeit, 1120s).

Although the invaders' descendants soon became bilingual (with English), an 'Anglo-Norman' dialect developed by the mid 12th century which remained socially and culturally dominant until the early 15th century. (Some clergy and lawyers also spoke LATIN. Ordinary people continued to speak English.) From the mid 13th century manuals were produced for people who sought French for social advancement, and French became a written language of law and government, reflecting the prestige of French culture in Continental Europe.

French was replaced by English from the mid 14th century: in schools in the 1350s–80s, in legal pleadings from 1363, and in PARLIAMENT from the 1390s. HENRY IV (ruled 1399–1413) conducted government business in English, and HENRY V replaced French with English in his correspondence from Aug. 1417. Some record keeping in French continued until the 18th century.

The immigration of noble families into Scotland in the 12th and early 13th centuries extended Anglo-Norman French. Its cultural impact was small (e.g., little literary writing in French). Knowledge of French declined among landed families in the 14th century.

Anglo-Norman French was used in Ireland after the Anglo-Norman invasion (1169–70), spoken by nobles, Anglo-Irish senior clergy and urban merchants until the early 14th century. Literary writing was produced in the 13th century, notably the verse chronicle *The Song of Dermot and the Earl*, which recounts the Anglo-Norman invasion. *See also* NORMANS, IMPACT ON SCOTLAND/IRELAND.

FRENCH REVOLUTION, IMPACT ON ENGLAND The Revolution (from 1789) was widely welcomed, especially by RADICALS. In 1791–2 they formed Corresponding Societies in cities and leading towns (e.g., LONDON, MANCHESTER, SHEFFIELD) and called for extensive parliamentary reform and other changes (e.g., land nationalization). *Rights of Man* (1791–2) by Thomas PAINE was influential. Conservatives became especially alarmed from 1792, although Edmund BURKE had expressed fears in Nov. 1790 in his *Reflections*. After the French monarchy was overthrown (Sept. 1792), they organized Associations for the Preservation of Liberty and Property to suppress radical activity.

War with France from Feb. 1793 increased tensions. Fear of unrest and rebellion caused the government of William PITT the Younger to intervene. Several Radicals were tried in 1794 (see TREASON TRIALS, 1794), and protest meetings in 1795 were countered with Acts of Parliament against 'seditious meetings' and 'treasonable practices'. Radical activity was largely suppressed by 1797, though COMBINATION ACTS against trade unions were passed in 1799–1800.

The Revolution also divided WHIG politicians in 1794, when conservative Whigs led by the 3rd duke of PORTLAND joined Pitt's government, leaving a remnant supporting Charles James Fox. Radicalism flourished again during the difficult economic conditions of 1807–12 (see CARTWRIGHT, JOHN; BURDETT, FRANCIS; LUDDITES). *See also* GODWIN, WILLIAM; WOLLSTONECRAFT, MARY; FRENCH REVOLUTIONARY AND NAPOLEONIC WARS, BRITISH INVOLVEMENT.

FRENCH REVOLUTION, IMPACT ON IRELAND The Revolution initially reinvigorated existing political causes. In autumn 1791 Radicals in BELFAST and DUBLIN founded clubs of 'UNITED IRISHMEN' to intensify the campaign for parliamentary reform (e.g., a broader franchise), while Catholics called for further relief from legal disabilities. The British government, concerned to retain Catholic loyalty, forced Ireland's Parliament to make concessions (1792, 1793; see CATHOLIC RELIEF AND EMANCIPATION, IRELAND).

From Feb. 1793, when France declared war on Britain, Irish radicalism was increasingly feared. Ireland's Parliament passed the Convention Act (Aug.), which prohibited meetings for the purpose of petitioning, and the government abolished the VOLUNTEERS (voluntary militia). The United Irishmen were suppressed in May 1794. Parliament rejected calls for parliamentary reform and Catholic Emancipation (principally admission to Parliament). From 1795 it passed increasingly repressive legislation (notably the Insurrection Act of March 1796 which extended the powers of local justices).

Ireland's government primarily feared the United Irishmen, who had re-emerged as a secret society committed to establishing a republic. In 1798 United Irishmen attempted a rebellion (see RISING OF 1798), which was followed by a French invasion (see HUMBERT'S EXPEDITION). These events persuaded the British prime minister, William PITT the Younger, to undertake the UNION OF IRELAND AND GREAT BRITAIN (1801). *See also* FITZGERALD, LORD; TONE, WOLFE.

FRENCH REVOLUTION, IMPACT ON SCOTLAND

Middle-class and artisan reformers welcomed the Revolution, and the Scottish journalist James MacKintosh, in his *Vindiciae Gallicae* ('Gaul's Justification', 1791), countered the anti-Revolution *Reflections* (1790) by Edmund BURKE. After attempts were made from May 1792 to suppress Thomas Paine's *Rights of Man*, demands for reform increased. In June 1792 the Edinburgh mob burned Henry DUNDAS, Viscount Melville, in effigy and from July 'Friends of the People' and other societies were founded; they held three conventions in 1792–3.

These developments, and the execution of Louis XVI in France (21 Jan. 1793), provoked reaction. Five convention leaders (the 'Scottish martyrs', including Thomas MUIR) were transported in 1793 and other movements collapsed or were suppressed. Revolutionary ideals survived to inspire 19th-century radicalism.

FRENCH REVOLUTION, IMPACT ON WALES

The Revolution (1789) was welcomed by Welsh RADICALS, such as Richard PRICE, and encouraged the formation of Unitarian congregations (*see* UNITARIANISM) and druidism (by Edward WILLIAMS). Most people were apathetic or hostile while supporters were repelled by revolutionary violence in France (1792–5), war with France (from 1793), and by the French landing at Fishguard (Pembrokeshire) in 1797. Government oppression and their fundamentalist beliefs prompted the infant Methodist Church to adopt Conservative attitudes (*see* NONCONFORMITY AND DISSENT, WALES). But as the 19th century advanced, revolutionary ideas influenced Welsh CHARTISM and radical LIBERALISM. *See also* NEWSPAPERS, WALES.

FRENCH REVOLUTIONARY AND NAPOLEONIC WARS, BRITISH INVOLVEMENT

The French Republic was at war in Europe from 1792, and declared war on Great Britain and the Dutch Republic in 1793. In the War of the First Coalition (1793–6), against France, Britain seized French 'sugar islands' in the Caribbean (1793–4), and an army fought alongside Hanoverians and Austrians in Continental Europe (1793–5). After the Dutch (now the Batavian Republic) allied with France in 1795, Britain seized their colonies in Africa and Asia. But peace treaties between Continental powers and France (1795–7) left Britain isolated. A British fleet, commanded by Horatio NELSON, destroyed a French fleet near Egypt (battle of the Nile, 1 Aug. 1798), preventing French intervention in India.

In 1798–9 Britain assembled another coalition against France (effectively ruled from Nov. 1799 by Napoleon Bonaparte). French successes (War of the Second Coalition, 1799–1801) forced countries to make peace, and Britain agreed the Peace of AMIENS (March 1802).

In 1803 war was resumed. The French seized HANOVER. In 1805–6 Britain constructed a third coalition (active 1805–7) and in Oct. 1805 Nelson's victory over a Franco-Spanish fleet at TRAFALGAR prevented a French invasion. The French sought to undermine Britain with a trade blockade (1806–13), and defeated Austria and Prussia (1806).

In 1808 British land forces began operations in the Iberian Peninsula. Between 1809 and 1814 Viscount WELLINGTON expelled the French and entered France. After Napoleon's failed invasion of Russia (1812), Britain subsidized a fourth coalition (1813–14). Napoleon abdicated in April 1814 and entered exile. He returned in 1815 only to be defeated at WATERLOO. *See also* JAY'S TREATY; HUMBERT'S EXPEDITION; MALTA; VOLUNTEERS.

FRIARS, ENGLAND

Orders of mendicant friars, founded in Continental Europe from the early 13th century, spread quickly to England where they established houses in towns and cities. The Dominican Order of Friars Preachers (black friars, founded 1216) settled in LONDON and OXFORD in 1221 and eventually had about 54 houses. The Franciscan Order of Friars Minor (grey friars, authorized 1210) arrived in 1224 and founded about 62 houses. Other orders had a smaller presence. The Carmelites (white friars, organized 1226) founded about 36 houses from 1240. The Augustinian Order of Hermit Friars (organized 1256) established their first community in 1257. Friars of the Sack and Friars of the Cross also founded houses from 1244 and 1257, though communities were short-lived. Much later, King HENRY VII founded six houses of stricter Observant Franciscans (1482–1507). As preachers, confessors, scholars, politicians and especially everyday pastors, friars were influential in national and regional (urban) life until the DISSOLUTION (1530s). *See also* GROSSETESTE, ROBERT; PECHAM, JOHN; OCKHAM, WILLIAM; RELIGIOUS ORDERS; CHURCH, MEDIEVAL ENGLAND.

FRIARS, IRELAND BEFORE 1530s

Dominicans established houses in DUBLIN and Drogheda (E Ireland) in 1224, and then in other major English centres (23 houses by 1300). Franciscans spread likewise, with a house in Dublin (1231) followed by foundations elsewhere (32 houses by 1325). Houses of Carmelite friars were also founded from c.1272, and Augustinians established 11 houses between 1282 and 1341. Friars attracted support in Gaelic Irish areas (e.g., Dominican house at LIMERICK founded 1227 by Donnchad O'Brien, king of Thomond).

Between 1349 and 1539 about 60 new houses were founded, encompassing all orders. Many were in CONNACHT (W Ireland) and ULSTER (N Ireland) under the patronage of Gaelic Irish chiefs. From the 1420s, some houses joined the 'Observant' (i.e., stricter) section of their order. By the 1530s there were 38 Dominican houses, 61 Franciscan (38 Observant), about 20 Augustinian, and a few Carmelite houses. *See also* RELIGIOUS ORDERS; CHURCH, MEDIEVAL IRELAND; DISSOLUTION OF RELIGIOUS HOUSES, IRELAND.

FRIARS, IRELAND FROM 1530s *see* RELIGIOUS ORDERS AND REGULAR CLERGY, IRELAND FROM 16TH CENTURY

FRIARS, SCOTLAND Dominicans settled (from England) from 1230, Franciscans from 1231, and Carmelites from 1267. By 1300 each had, respectively, 11, five and four houses, most in BURGHS, while Augustinians had one house (at BERWICK-UPON-TWEED). Franciscans formed a separate Scottish vicariate by 1329, but Dominicans remained in the English province until 1482. Between 1458 and 1513 nine houses of Observant Franciscans were founded (a province from 1467). There were also two houses of Franciscan nuns (at Aberdour and DUNDEE), and one of Dominican nuns (at EDINBURGH, founded 1517). Friaries were apparently flourishing before their destruction in the REFORMATION (1559–60). *See also* RELIGIOUS ORDERS; CHURCH, MEDIEVAL NORTH BRITAIN AND SCOTLAND.

FRIARS, WALES Mendicant friars founded only 12 houses in medieval Wales, most in the mid 13th century. But friars had considerable impact, possibly eclipsing the previously influential Cistercian monks.

The Franciscans founded three houses (at Llanfaes, CARMARTHEN and CARDIFF); the Dominicans, five (at BANGOR, Rhuddlan, Haverfordwest, Cardiff, and Brecon); the Carmelites, three (Denbigh, Ruthin and Cardiff). The Austin friars founded a house at NEWPORT in the 14th century.

Like the Cistercians, friars were active in both English-controlled and native Wales. Their patrons included Welsh rulers, such as LLYWELYN AP IORWERTH. But friars encouraged popular devotion, helped by their willingness to use Welsh, and by their translations into Welsh. The most important devotional work written in medieval Wales, *Y Cysegrlan Fuchedd* ('The Consecrated Life'), was probably composed by a Dominican.

Welsh friaries were impoverished in the late Middle Ages, and were dissolved in 1538 (*see* DISSOLUTION OF RELIGIOUS HOUSES, WALES). *See also* RELIGIOUS ORDERS; CHURCH, MEDIEVAL WALES.

FRIENDLY SOCIETIES Independent non-profitmaking voluntary associations of working people, who pay regular contributions to receive financial benefits in the event of sickness or unemployment. Starting in the 17th century, they multiplied in the 18th and 19th centuries in

Great Britain and Ireland, often adopting whimsical rituals and names (e.g., Oddfellows, Rechabites, Antediluvian Buffaloes). Officially regulated from 1793, the societies formed a major part of the NATIONAL INSURANCE system in Britain (1911–48), when membership peaked at around 14 million. (Friendly societies were less important for national insurance in Ireland.) The UK WELFARE STATE made friendly societies largely redundant, though some continued in the 21st century.

FROBISHER, MARTIN (b. *c*.1535 at Altofts, Yorkshire, England; d. 22 Nov. 1594 at Plymouth, Devon, England, aged about 59). Seaman. After involvement in trading voyages to W Africa (1550s) and PRIVATEERING (1560s), Frobisher in 1576 revived English interest in the NORTHWEST PASSAGE (to Asia) by leading an expedition to the NW Atlantic. He seemingly found the passage's end (Baffin Island). In 1577 and 1578 he revisited the area to mine a promising black ore, but it proved worthless, though he discovered the Hudson Strait (1578). Frobisher later commanded ships against the SPANISH ARMADA and was knighted (1588). *See also* NORTH AMERICA, ENGLISH EXPLORATION.

FROISSART, JEAN (b. 1337 at Valenciennes, Hainault; d. *c*.1404, aged about 67). Author of French poetry and romances, Froissart was in England 1361–8 under the patronage of Philippa of Hainault (d. 1369), wife of King EDWARD III; among royalty he travelled in Scotland, Spain and Italy. He returned to the Low Countries, becoming a priest and patronized by Wenceslas, duke of Brabant (d. 1383), and Guy de Châtillon, count of Blois (d. 1397). He visited England again in 1395, when he met King RICHARD II.

Knowing key witnesses, and gathering their testimony from *c*.1370, Froissart composed the *Chroniques* ('Chronicles'), an account of the HUNDRED YEARS WAR which glorified CHIVALRY.

FRY, ELIZABETH (b. 21 May 1780 at Norwich, Norfolk, England; d. 13 Oct. 1845 at Ramsgate, Kent, England, aged 65). A QUAKER, Fry in 1813 visited the women's part of Newgate Prison, London. In 1817 she founded a society to improve conditions, and from 1818 visited prisons in Great Britain and Ireland. She published her discoveries in *Observations on the Visiting … of Female Prisoners* (1827) which proved influential. Between 1838 and 1843 she visited Continental prisons. Fry sought to transform prisons into 'schools of industry and virtue' by treating prisoners humanely. *See also* HOWARD, JOHN; GAOLS AND PRISONS, ENGLAND AND WALES.

FYRD *see* MILITARY SERVICE, ENGLAND BEFORE 1066.

G

GAELDOM, SCOTLAND The area in which Gaelic language and culture have persisted (Gaelic, Gaidhealtachd). Between *c*.1600 and 1891 it covered most of the HIGHLANDS and WESTERN ISLES. In 1801 there were 300,000 Gaelic-speakers (19% of Scotland's total population). During the 19th century bilingualism spread: in 1891, 44,000 people were monolingual, 211,000 bilingual. By 1931 the Gaeldom effectively contracted to the Western Highlands and Isles (136,000 speakers, most bilingual), by 1971 to the Isles (88,000 speakers), when only a few mainland areas had a majority of Gaelic-speakers. An association to promote Gaelic language and culture, An Comunn Gàidhealach, was founded in 1891, and regular Gaelic radio broadcasts were provided from 1935 and television from the early 1960s.

Attempts were made to arrest decline. Gaelic-medium education began in 1958 (expanded from *c*.1980) and schools broadcasting was started in 1970. Comunn Na Gàidhlig, a Gaelic language promotion agency, was formed in 1984, and from 1985 BBC Radio nan Gàidheal broadcast material in Gaelic. During the 1980s–90s the British government made funding available to increase Gaelic television programmes. A limited Gaelic channel TeleG operated from 1999 to 2011, and BBC Alba from 2008.

The establishment of a Scottish Parliament and Executive in 1999 also provided impetus. The Gaelic Language (Scotland) Act of 2005 gave formal recognition to Gaelic as a national language and established the Bòrd na Gàidhlig as a public body to promote use of the language, particularly by public authorities and in education. In 2011 there were about 57,000 Gaelic speakers (1.1% of the population). *See also* GAELIC LANGUAGE AND LITERATURE, NORTH BRITAIN AND SCOTLAND; HIGHLAND SOCIETY OF EDINBURGH.

GAELIC LANGUAGE AND LITERATURE, IRELAND *see* IRISH LANGUAGE AND LITERATURE

GAELIC LANGUAGE AND LITERATURE, NORTH BRITAIN AND SCOTLAND Old Irish or Gaelic, a 'Q-Celtic' language, was carried from NE Ireland to N Britain by Irish migrants from *c*.500 (*see* DÁL RIATA). Through missionaries and expansion of Dalriadic power, Gaelic had spread through N Britain by *c*.1000 (S to the R. Tweed and Solway Firth), superseding Brittonic ('P-Celtic').

Between the 11th and 14th centuries Gaelic retreated to the HIGHLANDS, partly because of the spread of English-style rural settlement; however, it also survived in Aberdeenshire (NE Scotland) and GALLOWAY (SW) into the 17th century. Gaelic culture was transmitted orally, so relatively little of a rich tradition has survived. Much comes from two manuscript collections, the Book of the Deans of Lismore (15th century) and the Red Book of Clanranald (17th century). Formal bardic poetry declined in the later 17th century with a reduction of aristocratic patronage, giving way to freer vernacular styles of verse, exemplified by Iain Lom (*c*.1620–*c*.1707). Roderick Morison (*c*.1656–*c*.1714), Alasdair MacMhaighstir Alasdair (*c*.1695–*c*.1770),

A Dictionary of British and Irish History, First Edition. Edited by Robert Peberdy and Philip Waller.
© 2021 John Wiley & Sons Ltd; © editorial matter and organisation Robert Peberdy and Phillip Waller.
Published 2021 by John Wiley & Sons Ltd.

Robb Donn Mackay (1714–78) and Duncan Ban MacIntyre (1724–1812).

In the 18th century Church and government mounted a concerted attack on Gaelic, which retreated to the far N and W. In 1991 there were 65,000 Gaelic speakers in Scotland, which fell to 57,000 by 2011. *See also* SCOTS LANGUAGE AND LITERATURE; GAELDOM, SCOTLAND.

GAELIC LEAGUE *see* GAELIC REVIVAL, IRELAND 19TH–20TH CENTURIES

GAELIC NAMES OF SCOTTISH KINGS Kings from KENNETH I MAC ALPIN (d. 858) are conventionally known by English names; recurrent names are numbered (with Kenneth starting the first sequence). This is misleading. Until the late 11th century kings bore a Gaelic (Irish) name and patronymic (father's name). Moreover, reference to Kenneth I as first ruler of a united kingdom arguably overstates his and the kingdom's importance (*see* UNION OF SCOTS AND PICTS). Gaelic names are often used for the MAC ALPIN KINGS (840–1042) and for the next six kings (to DONALD III, ruled 1093–4, 1094–7). Many subsequent rulers bore non-Gaelic names.

GAELIC REVIVAL, IRELAND 13TH–15TH CENTURIES A movement which revitalized the power of Irish ruling dynasties and Irish culture more generally. It contributed to the reversal of English expansion.

Between 1169 and *c.*1250 Anglo-Normans (or English) had suppressed Ireland's high-kingship and provincial high-kingships, and imposed their rule on two-thirds of the country (*see* IRELAND, ENGLISH CONQUEST, 12TH–13TH CENTURIES). In the mid 13th century Irish local kings managed briefly to halt English expansion (CONNACHT, 1240s–70s; ULSTER, 1250s; MUNSTER, 1250s–60s), but it resumed until *c.*1300 (1320s in Ulster). Major Irish royal dynasties survived independently in the N (notably the O'NEILLS and O'DONNELLS), mid-W (O'BRIENS in Thomond), and SW (MacCarthys), and within English areas (notably the MacMurroughs in SE Ireland).

Irish rulers gained strength from the 1270s when the MacMurrough, O'Toole and O'Byrne dynasties within LEINSTER (E Ireland) began to harass the English in Cos. Dublin and Carlow. The BRUCE INVASION (1315–18) stimulated Irish kings to oppose the English and caused the Dublin-based government to lose regular contact with parts of the English colony. From 1333 (death of William de Burgh) it gradually lost authority within Connacht (W Ireland) and much of Ulster (NE), enabling Irish kings to assert authority. By the mid 15th century, English lordship had been reduced to a small government-controlled area in the E (*see* PALE, IRELAND) and Anglo-Irish lordships in the E and S. Irish military revival was accompanied by a revival in Irish literary forms, especially poetry. *See also* IRELAND, ENGLISH COLONY IN, 13TH–15TH CENTURIES.

GAELIC REVIVAL, IRELAND 19TH–20TH CENTURIES A social and political movement which, following the GREAT FAMINE (1845–9), sought to arrest the decline of the Irish language and Gaelic culture. A Society for the Preservation of the Irish Language was started in 1876, and in 1884 the Gaelic Athletic Association (GAA), which organized hurling, football and other games throughout Ireland. The Gaelic League, founded 1893, held language classes and promoted music, dancing, poetry and story telling. By 1908 there were 800 GAA and 500 League branches. The organizations attracted nationalists and republicans (e.g., members of the IRISH REPUBLICAN BROTHERHOOD), and from 1915 the League supported Irish independence. The government banned it in 1919.

Support for cultural organizations declined after the establishment of the IRISH FREE STATE (1922), and the revival was seen by the avant-garde Irish writers James Joyce and Samuel Beckett as culturally regressive. Despite the designation of Irish as Ireland's 'first official language' in 1937, English remained the main language. The GAA and League continued to be influential. *See also* HYDE, DOUGLAS; EDUCATION, SOUTHERN IRELAND.

GAELIC SOCIETY, IRELAND *see* SOCIAL STRUCTURE, GAELIC IRELAND 5TH–12TH CENTURIES/12TH–17TH CENTURIES

GAELIC SOCIETY, SCOTLAND *see* SOCIAL STRUCTURE, NORTH BRITAIN AND SCOTLAND

GAELS English version of the Irish term Goídil, which was used by the Irish, by the 8th century, to refer to themselves. It was derived from Brittonic (Welsh) *gwyddyl*, meaning 'wild men'. From the 9th century it distinguished native Irish from invaders and their descendants (such as VIKINGS, NORMANS). The related adjective 'Gaelic' refers to Irish culture in Ireland and elsewhere. *See also* SCOTS; IRISH; IRISH LANGUAGE AND LITERATURE; GAELIC LANGUAGE AND LITERATURE, NORTH BRITAIN AND SCOTLAND.

GAELTACHT, IRELAND The Irish term Gaedhealtacht (later Gaeltacht, meaning 'Gaelic entity') was used from the later 19th century for Irish-speaking areas, mostly small rural districts in NW, W, SW and S Ireland. By 1891 Ireland had only 38,000 monolingual inhabitants, mostly in the Gaeltacht. (About 680,000 people, 14.5% of the population, spoke Irish.) Leaders of the Gaelic League (founded 1893) valued the Gaeltacht as a repository of culture (e.g., folklore, music).

In 1925 the IRISH FREE STATE government established a commission to devise ways of preserving the Gaeltacht, partly as a basis for reviving Irish as the national language. The subsequent Housing (Gaeltacht) Act of 1929, which provided grants for housing and farm buildings, defined the Gaeltacht (main areas in seven counties, smaller areas in another six counties). In 1956 a government department was created for the Gaeltacht, which was redefined (areas in seven counties). A State-sponsored body to promote economic development, Gaeltarra Éireann, was founded in 1958. But by the 1960s few monolingual inhabitants remained.

Further initiatives to sustain the Gaeltacht included an Irish-language radio station (launched 1972), the language agency Bord na Gaeilge (1978), the development authority Údarás na Gaeltachta (1980, superseding Gaeltarra Éireann), and an Irish-language television service (1996). In 2011 the Gaeltacht's population was 96,628, of whom 23,175 (24%) spoke Irish daily outside the education system. Fear that community use of Irish would cease resulted in the 2012 Gaeltacht Act which promoted language plans (between communities and government) and related Language Planning Areas within the Gaeltacht. *See also* IRISH LANGUAGE AND LITERATURE; BROADCASTING, IRELAND.

GAITSKELL, HUGH (b. 9 April 1906 at London, England; d. 18 Jan. 1963 at London, aged 56). Leader of the British LABOUR PARTY 1955–63.

Gaitskell taught economics at University College, London (1928–39), and worked with Hugh DALTON as a civil servant during WORLD WAR II. Elected as an MP in 1945, he was minister of fuel and power (1947–50), minister for economic affairs (1950) and chancellor of the Exchequer (1950–1), under Clement ATTLEE. His introduction of health charges (April 1951) and support for rearmament angered BEVANITES, but he easily defeated Nye BEVAN in a leadership contest (Dec. 1955). He toiled to improve Party unity while resisting unilateral nuclear disarmament. Despite Labour's defeat in the 1959 general election, Gaitskell appeared a credible contender for the premiership until his sudden death. *See also* BUTSKELLISM.

GALLIC EMPIRE A breakaway Roman state established by Postumus (ruler 259–68), Roman commander on the R. Rhine. Rebelling against the emperor Gallienus, he took control of Gaul, Britain and Spain, and established his capital at Augusta Treverorum (Trier). Postumus' successors, notably Victorinus (268–70) and Tetricus (270–3), held the Empire until 273 when the central emperor, Aurelian, defeated Tetricus. *See also* ROMAN BRITAIN.

GALLIPOLI CAMPAIGN An Allied offensive during WORLD WAR I against the OTTOMAN EMPIRE, intended to open a supply route to Russia and defeat the Ottoman

Turks. After a failed naval assault on the Dardanelles in March 1915, British troops and ANZACs (men of the Australian and New Zealand Army Corps) invaded the Gallipoli peninsula on 25 April. They met fierce resistance, suffered heavy casualties, and were evacuated (9 Dec.–9 Jan. 1916). ANZAC heroism and bitterness against incompetent British planning and execution became important national legends.

GALLOGLASSES Scottish mercenaries (from Argyll and the WESTERN ISLES) who were hired by Irish kings and chiefs (from Irish *gallóglaigh*, meaning 'Hebridean warriors'). They helped to resist English expansion in ULSTER and N CONNACHT in the late 13th and 14th centuries, and were employed by Anglo-Irish lords in the 15th and 16th centuries. Heavily armoured, they fought with long-handled axes, spears and swords.

GALLOWAY The far SW area of Scotland (within modern Dumfries and Galloway county). It was inhabited by the Novantae IRON AGE TRIBE (1st–5th centuries), and was in the British kingdom of RHEGED (6th–late 7th centuries) and in the English kingdom of BERNICIA (late 7th–9th centuries). In the 8th–10th centuries it was settled by Irish and became GAELIC-speaking. ('Galloway' is derived from Gaelic *Gall-ghaidhil*, meaning 'Foreign Gaels'. Gaelic continued until the 17th century.) Galloway had its own ruler or lord until 1234 (death of Alan of Galloway); thereafter kings of Scotland had greater control. In the 17th century there was a strong presence of COVENANTERS. *See also* WILLIAM I; ALEXANDER II; BALLIOL FAMILY.

GALTON, FRANCIS (b. 16 Feb. 1822 at Birmingham, Warwickshire, England; d. 17 Jan. 1911 at Haslemere, Surrey, England, aged 88). After studying medicine and mathematics, Galton became financially independent on his father's death (1844). He toured the Middle East (1845–6) and Africa (1850–2) before settling in LONDON (1853). The theory of 'natural selection' proposed by his cousin Charles DARWIN (in *On the Origin of Species* ..., 1859) made Galton wonder if human mental traits resulted from experiences or inheritance. He concluded by 1865 that inheritance was primary, and that the marriage of intelligent partners could improve the human race.

Galton developed the understanding of inheritance by expanding statistical techniques. Through studies of sweet peas (1870s) he established an inheritance pattern between two generations; he then collected data about humans. Galton coined the term 'eugenics' (1883) for the science and practice of improving the human race, and summarized his work in *Natural Inheritance* (1889). Knighted in 1909, he endowed a professorship of eugenics at University College, London. *See also* EUGENICS.

GAMBIA A former British territory in W Africa. Englishmen traded at the mouth of the Gambia River from 1587, and in 1663 seized a fort. In the late 17th century traders of the ROYAL AFRICAN COMPANY obtained gold and slaves from the area.

The settlement of Bathurst was developed from 1816. The coastal territory became a CROWN COLONY in 1843 (to 1866, re-established 1888), while the hinterland was briefly a PROTECTORATE (1894–1902), then part of the colony. Great Britain granted self-government in 1963, and independence under the British Crown in 1965. Gambia became a republic in 1970. Approx. population in 1921, 201,000; in 1964, 372,000. *See also* WEST AFRICA, ENGLISH AND BRITISH INVOLVEMENT.

GAME LAWS Legislation that restricted the hunting of game (deer, hares, rabbits, pheasants, etc.) to wealthier landed people. In England in the 11th–14th centuries, FOREST LAW protected game for hunting by kings, and in 1390 Parliament prohibited ordinary people from hunting.

A new era of legislation began with the 1671 Game Act for England and Wales, which restricted hunting mainly to wealthy landowners and some lessees. The BLACK ACT (1723) notoriously created numerous capital offences, and trade in game was banned in 1755. But poaching became highly organized and pervasive. Although some Acts were repealed from the 1820s, laws against poaching remained controversial into the 20th century. *See also* LEGAL REFORMS, ENGLAND AND WALES, 1820s.

GANDHI, MOHANDAS (b. 2 Oct. 1869 at Porbandar, Porbandar State, India; d. 30 Jan. 1948 at Delhi, East Punjab, India, aged 78). Gandhi trained as a barrister in England, and became a political activist while living in southern Africa (1893–1914). After returning to India (1915), he campaigned against British rule with non-violent activity (e.g., his 'salt march', 1930, when thousands broke the government monopoly on salt collection). He was called 'Mahatma' ('great soul'). During the 1920s–30s he was intermittently imprisoned. In 1931, after consultation by the viceroy, Lord Irwin, Gandhi discontinued resistance and participated in talks in London, but achieved little.

Gandhi exploited WORLD WAR II by developing an anti-British 'Quit India' campaign, only to be imprisoned (1942–4). After the war he co-operated with the pro-Independence British government of Clement ATTLEE, but opposed independence based on religious partition (implemented 1947). He was shot dead by a militant Hindu. *See also* INDIAN INDEPENDENCE.

GAOLS AND PRISONS, ENGLAND AND WALES Some English royal gaols existed by the later 9th century; more gaols were provided from the late 11th century in CASTLES and TOWNS. The Assize of CLARENDON (1166) ordered provision in counties without gaols. Until 1865 the main gaols (also in Wales) were locally controlled 'county gaols' (often in castles) and town gaols. They usually held persons until trial or punishment, rather than as punishment. County gaols and some LONDON gaols also confined debtors for long periods.

From c.1560 large towns also created 'bridewells' (lock-ups) to discipline troublesome poor people (e.g., vagrants), imitating London's Bridewell Hospital (1556). They were authorized for counties, as 'houses of correction', in 1576. From the 17th century brief confinement in bridewells was formally used as punishment.

From the 1770s reformers (e.g., John HOWARD) advocated imprisonment as punishment (alternative to TRANSPORTATION) and sought better conditions. When war interrupted transportation, the government became involved through providing ships as gaols (so-called 'hulks', used 1776–1859). Parliament authorized two 'penitentiaries' (1779) for imprisonment and moral reform, but until c.1815 new gaols resulted from local initiatives.

Millbank Penitentiary in London, accommodating 860, opened in 1816. It was replaced by Pentonville Prison (1842), which was designed for solitary confinement (so-called 'separate system') and influenced further government prisons. From 1850 they were supervised by 'directors of convict prisons'. Gaols were regulated from 1823. In 1865 local gaols and houses of correction were designated 'local prisons' and required to meet prescribed conditions; they were centralized in 1877 under a Prison Commission which imposed severe conditions (e.g., punitive labour). The 1898 Prison Act re-emphasized rehabilitation and transferred convict prisons to Prison Commission members.

In the 20th century new types of facilities were introduced (e.g., 'open prison', 1933) and harsh treatments outlawed (1948). The Home Office took direct control in 1963. In 2015, 120 establishments held 85,000 prisoners. *See also* LOCAL GOVERNMENTAL STRUCTURES, ENGLAND/WALES; FRY, ELIZABETH; INFANT AND CHILD WELFARE, BRITAIN; HABEAS CORPUS.

GAOLS AND PRISONS, IRELAND By the 13th century gaols probably existed in castles and towns in Anglo-Irish areas, to hold prisoners before trial or punishment. In 1635 Parliament legislated for 'houses of correction' (for detention of idle poor, e.g., vagrants). They were widespread in the 18th century; some were converted into gaols. From 1708 gaols were supervised by county grand juries.

In the 1760s, when over half of prisoners were debtors, squalid gaol conditions were criticized, partly for engendering disease. Legislation in 1763 required exercise grounds and segregation of prisoners. Further concerns were expressed from the 1770s, from 1783 involving physician Sir Jeremiah Fitzpatrick; he influenced the 1786 Prisons Act which provided for chaplains, physicians and inspectors, and became chief inspector. He advocated 'penitentiaries' for punishment and moral reform, though only one was opened briefly (1790, in DUBLIN, for juveniles and women). Some other prisons were built (e.g., Kilmainham, for Co. Dublin, 1796).

Following the UNION OF IRELAND AND GREAT BRITAIN (1801), government-funded prisons were constructed (from 1820s), sometimes as holding depots before TRANSPORTATION (to 1867). They included the UK's first penitentiary for women (1836, at Grangegorman, Co. Dublin). Government prisons were supervised from 1854 by 'directors of convict prisons', who pioneered the 'progressive stage system' (using rewards to encourage reform). From 1826 basic standards (e.g., for hygiene) were prescribed for all prisons. In 1877 prisons were transferred to a Prisons Board.

In NORTHERN IRELAND (from 1921), prisons were controlled by the Home Affairs ministry. Crumlin Road gaol, BELFAST, became the main prison (closed 1996). During the TROUBLES, the Maze Prison (Co. Down) was a principal detention centre (1971–2000). In the IRISH FREE STATE, the Prisons Board was abolished (1928) and prisons transferred to the Department of Justice. In 2015, 14 establishments in the Republic of Ireland held 3700 prisoners; three establishments in Northern Ireland held 1600. *See also* LOCAL GOVERNMENTAL STRUCTURES, IRELAND; HABEAS CORPUS.

GAOLS AND PRISONS, SCOTLAND From the 12th century persons awaiting trial or punishment were detained in various places: gaols or pits in royal or private CASTLES, houses in villages and BURGHS, and burgh tolbooths (market and court houses). From the 1560s, KIRK SESSIONS sometimes imposed imprisonment to punish moral offences. Political opponents or religious dissenters tended to be imprisoned in royal gaols.

In 1597 Parliament required burghs to provide gaols and ward houses, and to receive prisoners from county authorities (continued to 1839). Legislation in 1672 stipulated that burghs should build correction houses for vagabonds (similar to English 'houses of correction'), but this was apparently ineffective. As in England, new local prisons were constructed from the later 18th century, notably at EDINBURGH (1795), GLASGOW (1798), ABERDEEN (1809) and Greenock (1810).

In the 19th century imprisonment became the main means of punishment, subject to government regulation and control. From 1835 regulatory powers over Scottish prisons were exercised by the British home secretary, and in 1839 local prisons were placed under county management boards and a supervisory General Board. A government-funded 'convict prison', designed for solitary confinement and supervised by the General Board, was opened at PERTH (1843). The General Board was abolished in 1860 (powers granted to home secretary), and in 1877 a Prison Commission for Scotland took over prison management. The home secretary's responsibilities were transferred to the SECRETARY FOR SCOTLAND in 1885–9. By 1898 there were only 14 prisons.

In 1929 management was transferred from the Prison Commission to the SCOTTISH OFFICE. Harsh conditions (e.g., punitive labour) were ended in 1949. In 1999 prisons became a responsibility of the Scottish Executive. In 2015, 15 establishments held 8000 prisoners. *See also* LOCAL GOVERNMENTAL STRUCTURES, SCOTLAND; INFANT AND CHILD WELFARE, BRITAIN.

GARDEN CITY, GARDEN SUBURB A garden city was an ideal type of self-sufficient settlement for about 32,000 inhabitants, combining residential and industrial areas within a rural belt, which was proposed in 1898 by Ebenezer Howard in *Tomorrow: A Peaceful Path to Real Reform* (reprinted 1902 as *Garden Cities of To-morrow*). Garden cities were promoted from 1899 by the Garden City Association, and implemented at Letchworth (from 1903) and Welwyn (from 1919), both in Hertfordshire (SE England). The concept influenced the 1946 New Towns Act (for Great Britain) and other planning legislation, and some subsequent new towns.

A garden suburb was a residential development based on the garden-city idea, including low-density, cottage-type housing. It was promoted by the architectural planner Raymond Unwin in *Cottage Plans and Common Sense* (1902). The most famous example is Hampstead Garden Suburb in N London (planned from 1905). *See also* TOWN PLANNING.

GARDINER, STEPHEN (b. *c.*1497 at Bury St Edmunds, Suffolk, England; d. 12 Nov. 1555 at London, aged about 58). A clergyman and lawyer, Gardiner became involved (1527) in seeking annulment of the marriage of King HENRY VIII and KATHERINE OF ARAGON. He was appointed king's secretary (1529) and bishop of WINCHESTER (1531). In the 1530s he was distrusted by Thomas CROMWELL and Thomas CRANMER. Replaced as secretary (1534), he sought favour with Henry by writing *De vera obedientia* ('Of True Obedience', 1535), a defence of Henry's supremacy in the English Church. After a period in France (1535–8), he helped to bring about Cromwell's downfall (1540). During the 1540s he wrote defences of Catholic theology.

Gardiner spent most of EDWARD VI's reign in prison for opposing Protestant reform in the Church and was deprived of his bishopric (1551). He was released by MARY I (1553), restored to Winchester, and appointed CHANCELLOR. *See also* REFORMATION, ENGLAND.

GARDINER'S ACT Popular name for the Catholic Relief Act passed in 1778 by the Irish Parliament; the first major legislation for Catholic relief, named after MP Luke Gardiner. It allowed Catholics to inherit land on the same terms as Protestants and to take 999-year leases. *See also* CATHOLIC RELIEF AND EMANCIPATION, IRELAND.

GARTER, ORDER OF THE A fellowship of knights, modelled on the legendary knights of the 'Round Table' of King ARTHUR, instituted in 1349 at WINDSOR by EDWARD III, king of England. Membership comprised the king, prince of Wales and 24 knight companions. Appointment to the Order later became an honour granted by the ruler. Members wear a garter, and the Order's motto is *Honi soit qui mal y pense* ('Shame on him who thinks evil of it'). Both were probably adopted from an earlier fraternity. 'Lady companions' were admitted from 1990, and the Order continued in the 21st century. *See also* KNIGHT; HONOURS SYSTEM.

GAS AND OIL INDUSTRIES, REPUBLIC OF IRELAND Gas production companies, using coal, operated in Ireland from the 1820s. From 1969, encouraged by NORTH SEA discoveries, a US company explored offshore under licence, and in 1971 found the Kinsale Head gas field (off S coast). The Republic asserted involvement in resource exploitation (1975) by requiring a 50 per cent holding and royalties (abolished after industry lobbying 1987). Production of natural gas started in 1978, initially for the CORK area; it was then supplied to DUBLIN via a pipeline (1982). New fields in the Kinsale Head region were discovered from 1989; their output was routed via the Kinsale platforms. Output from Kinsale Head peaked in 1995. In 2010 the region's fields met about 9% of gas consumption.

From 1994 the Republic also imported gas from Britain (via a pipeline). In 1996 the Corrib field (off W coast), was discovered, but exploitation plans were resisted by environmentalists and other protesters, delaying production until 2015. The field promised to meet about 60% of gas requirements.

Oil was discovered at the Barryroe field, near the Kinsale Head field, in 1973. Although later deemed commercially viable, exploitation had not begun by 2019. Prospectors hoped to find more viable sources of gas and oil.

GASCON WAR Conflict between King EDWARD I of England and Philip IV of France 1294–7. Following disputes between Gascon and French (Norman) sailors, Philip in March 1294 confiscated GASCONY (SW France), which Edward held from Philip as a vassal. French forces seized areas. English and Gascon troops recaptured parts of Gascony (1294–7). After dealing with problems in Wales and Scotland, Edward landed in Flanders (in modern Belgium) in Aug. 1297, but had insufficient forces for effectively waging war in France. A truce was agreed (Sept. 1297) followed by a settlement (1303) which restored the pre-war situation. *See also* REMONSTRANCES; *MALTOLT*.

GASCONY Name used for territory in SW France (between R. Charente and Pyrenees) which was held by kings of England in the 13th–15th centuries. It was part of the former duchy of Aquitaine which had become associated with England in 1154 (*see* HENRY II; ANGEVIN EMPIRE). In 1206, after most of King JOHN's French lands had been lost to the French king, John reconquered Gascony from a brief Castilian (Spanish) occupation. When Poitou was lost to the French (1224), Gascony was the only surviving English possession in Continental Europe. It was an important source of wine for England.

In 1259, under the treaty of PARIS, Gascony (called Guienne by the French) was recognized as a fief (lordship under feudal law) held by the king of England from the king of France. It proved a source of conflict. Edward I had to recover it in the 1290s (*see* GASCON WAR). Its confiscation in 1337 started the HUNDRED YEARS WAR. In 1360 EDWARD III regained the former duchy of Aquitaine (*see* BRÉTIGNY, TREATY OF), but in the 15th century English lands in SW France were gradually taken by the French. Their conquest was completed in 1453 following the battle of Castillon. *See also* FRANCE, CLAIMS BY RULERS OF ENGLAND.

GAS INDUSTRY, GREAT BRITAIN Gas derived from heated coal was used for lighting in 1794 by William Murdock (1754–1839) in Cornwall. From 1805 gas plants and lights were installed at factories. The first gas business, the Gas Light and Coke Company, was started in 1812 for LONDON. By the mid 19th century most towns had a municipal or private gasworks which fed lights in streets and large buildings. Domestic lighting, cooking and heating developed from the 1880s. Although in the 1920s–30s electricity replaced gas for lighting, production doubled to meet industrial and other domestic demand. The 1948 Gas Act nationalized over 1000 concerns as 12 area gas boards under a Gas Council.

Between 1967 and 1977 'natural gas' from the North Sea replaced coal gas. Gas boards were merged in 1972 as the British Gas Corporation (privatized as British Gas 1986, reorganized from 1997). Production of North Sea gas peaked in 2000. Importing had started in 1998, initially via a pipeline, and Britain became a net importer from 2004. *See also* NORTH SEA GAS AND OIL INDUSTRIES.

GATHERING AND HUNTING A strategy for acquiring food, and a mode of life, followed worldwide by most human species for most of PREHISTORY (and sometimes later). In Britain, people lived in small bands (perhaps 20–30 members in the PALAEOLITHIC, 15–20 in the MESOLITHIC), which moved between a few temporary camps, according to season, in an annual cycle. They gathered food (nuts, berries, fruit, fungi, etc.) from the surrounding area (usually within two hours' walk), which was supplemented by the hunting of animals (mammoths, elks, horses, deer, cattle, pigs, etc., according to climate), and fishing. Gathering was probably done mainly by women, hunting by men. An annual cycle may have covered 50 mi (80 km). Camps comprised huts made of branches covered by bark, turf or skin. Clothes were made from skins. It was an efficient, subsistence way of life.

Gathering and hunting was practised in Britain throughout the Palaeolithic (*c*.450,000 BP– *c*.8500 BC, with interruptions – *see* GLACIATIONS) and Mesolithic (*c*.8500– *c*.4300 BC), and in Ireland during the Mesolithic (*c*.8000– *c*.3800 BC). It was supplanted by agriculture (*see* PREHISTORIC BRITAIN/IRELAND, AGRICULTURE).

GAUNT, JOHN OF *see* JOHN OF GAUNT

GAVESTON, PIERS (b. early 1280s in Gascony; d. 19 June 1312 at Blacklow Hill, Warwickshire, England, aged about 30). Gaveston joined the household of Prince Edward, heir to King EDWARD I, in 1300, but was exiled to GASCONY by King Edward because of his intimacy with the prince (Feb. 1307). He was recalled after Prince Edward became king (July) and created earl of Cornwall (6 Aug.). He married Edward's niece Margaret of Clare (Nov.). His prominence at Edward's coronation (Feb. 1308) and influence infuriated nobles who forced his banishment (June; sent to Ireland as lieutenant).

Gaveston returned (June 1309) and served in the 1310– 11 Scottish campaign, but was banished in Nov. 1311 (went to Brabant; *see* ORDINANCES). After returning (Jan. 1312), he was besieged in Scarborough Castle (April–May 1312). He surrendered (19 May) and was executed. It is unclear whether Gaveston and Edward had a homosexual relationship or formed a compact as 'adoptive brothers'. *See also* EDWARD II.

GEDDES, JANE *see* REVOLT OF 1637

GEDDES, PATRICK (b. 2 Oct. 1854 at Ballater, Aberdeenshire, Scotland; d. 17 April 1932 at Montpellier, France, aged 77). Trained as a biologist by the Darwinian T.H. HUXLEY, Geddes sought to understand human social evolution through sociology (1870s). In the 1880s he helped to organize urban renewal (preservation and new building) in EDINBURGH, though achieved fame with *The Evolution of Sex* (1889, co-author with J. Arthur Thomson) and became a professor of botany (1889–1919). From 1904

(commission for Pittencrief Park, DUNFERMLINE), Geddes was involved in town planning, continuing his work in Ireland (1911–13) and India (1914–24). His ideas, summarized in *Cities in Evolution* (1915), proved influential. He was knighted in 1932.

GEDDES AXE Nickname given to cuts of £64 million in expenditure made in 1922 by the British government (coalition of 'Lloyd George Liberals' and Conservatives), so called because they arose from reports of the Committee on Government Expenditure (Feb.) chaired by Sir Eric Geddes. Affecting education, health and defence, the economies undermined pledges to undertake social reform made by the prime minister, David LLOYD GEORGE.

GEE, THOMAS (b. 24 Jan. 1815 at Denbigh, Denbighshire, Wales; d. 28 Sept. 1898 at Denbigh, aged 83). The chief figure in Welsh-language publishing in the mid and late 19th century. Working from 1838 in his father's printing business in Denbigh, Gee published the quarterly *Y Traethodydd* ('The Essayist', from 1845) and the weekly *Baner Cymru* ('Banner of Wales', from 1857; retitled *Baner ac Amserau Cymru* from 1861). The *Baner* was the pre-eminent voice of nonconformist LIBERALISM, campaigning for TEMPERANCE, DISESTABLISHMENT and other causes. *See also* NEWSPAPERS, WALES.

GELD OE term meaning 'render' or 'payment'; used for tax collected in coin and other metal by kings of England in the 10th–12th centuries. Levies were assessed mainly on land.

From 991 to 1018 income from geld funded payments to VIKINGS for peace, known as *gafol* (OE, meaning 'tribute'). A tax called *heregeld* ('army geld') was collected from 1012 to 1051. Geld, modelled on the *heregeld*, was levied after the Norman invasion (1066) and often called 'Danegeld'. Income declined in the 12th century. The last collection was made in 1162. Levies were initially made through SHIRES and their subdivisions (hundreds or wapentakes), but later (by late 11th century) through estate structures. *See also* ROYAL REVENUES, ENGLAND BEFORE 1066.

GENERAL STRIKE In Great Britain, 3–12 May 1926, industrial action called by the TRADES UNION CONGRESS (TUC) in support of coalminers who had been locked out for resisting pay cuts and longer hours. Work halted in heavy industry, transport, engineering, construction and printing. The success of the government in maintaining essential services and good order led the TUC to call off the strike after nine days and accept a compromise. The miners rejected this, and stayed out in vain for six months. The failure of the General Strike strengthened moderates within the LABOUR MOVEMENT. *See also* MINERS' UNIONS; CITRINE, WALTER; BALDWIN, STANLEY.

GENTRY A superior stratum within SOCIAL STRUC-TURES comprising lesser landowners and some PROFES-SIONALS (e.g., lawyers) and urban property-owners, who dominated SHIRE (or county) government. In England the gentry emerged as self-conscious communities among the lesser NOBILITY (below BARONS) between the mid 13th and mid 14th centuries, although the term (from OFr. *gentrice*, meaning 'gentle born') was little used until the 16th century.

Various developments contributed to the English gentry's formation, based around KNIGHTS. From the 1250s onwards knights were more regularly involved as leaders (e.g., SHERIFFS) in county government and as representatives in PARLIAMENT (becoming part of the House of Commons in the 14th century). From the late 13th century knights assisted in combating disorder as 'keepers of the peace'; after acquiring judicial powers, keepers were known from 1361 as JUSTICES OF THE PEACE (JPs) and exercised considerable authority. Men of slightly lower standing also participated, and were accorded the social ranks of 'esquire' (by 1363, from OFr. *esquier*, meaning 'shield-bearer') and 'gentleman' (by 1413). Moreover, emergence of the PEERAGE differentiated the gentry, but its identification with nobility relegated gentry to non-noble status (16th century).

In Wales, gentry evolved in the 15th century among Welsh freemen and other landowners (*see* GENTRY, WALES). In Scotland, some small landowners acquired gentry-like status and roles in the 17th–19th centuries (*see* LAIRD). In Ireland, gentry appeared in the PALE in the 15th century. Small landowners described as 'squires' and 'gentlemen' were active in county government throughout Ireland from the 17th century, but became identified with the larger PROTESTANT ASCENDANCY. In the N, in the 18th century, some prosperous dissenters acquired estates, joined the Church of IRELAND, and established themselves as gentry.

Gentry lost power, and their social identity faded, from the later 19th century with the decline of LANDED SOCIETY, although in NORTHERN IRELAND some remained influential (1921–80s). *See also* COUNTY COMMUNITY; BASTARD FEUDALISM; TACKSMAN; SOCIAL CLASS TERMINOLOGY.

GENTRY, WALES A stable élite of small landowners emerged in the 15th and early 16th centuries consisting of families descended from Welsh freemen (Welsh *uchelwyr*) or royal kindreds, or from English knightly families, some of whom had adopted Welsh culture. Stability resulted largely from the replacement of partible inheritance (division between heirs) by primogeniture (inheritance by eldest son), which preserved estates. By English standards, most gentry outside SE Wales were poor.

Gentry were formally made the governing élite by the UNION OF WALES WITH ENGLAND (1536–43), which provided for JUSTICES OF THE PEACE and other officers to be selected from the gentry. The gentry predominated over the nobility, considerably influencing the Church (of England) and town politics, though their patronage of Welsh culture began to dwindle in the late 17th century.

In the 18th century (1720s–60s) many families failed to produce male heirs. Heiresses inherited and their marriages combined estates. Some married Englishmen. The gentry evolved into a smaller, wealthier landed class (some richer than aristocrats), remote from rural people, a situation exacerbated as gentry increasingly spoke English and as most Welsh country people became nonconformists in the early 19th century. In 1873 the landlord class (gentry and absent aristocracy) owned 60% of Welsh land, with most possessing 1000–3000 acres (400–1200 ha). They were considered aliens by many, and attacked by radical liberals; from 1889, with the election of county councils, their power was rapidly eroded. Many estates were sold or diminished between 1914 and 1922. *See also* DISSOLUTION OF RELIGIOUS HOUSES, WALES; LANDED SOCIETY, DECLINE OF, WALES.

GEOFFREY FITZ PETER (fl. from 1166 in England; d. 2 Oct. 1213 in England). Geoffrey, a layman, worked as a royal administrator during the absence of King RICHARD I (ruled 1189–99). In 1198 he succeeded Hubert WALTER as CHIEF JUSTICIAR (served until death). He was made earl of Essex by JOHN (1199), for whom he raised money. Geoffrey campaigned in Wales (1198, 1206, 1210) and twice served as regent (1204, 1210).

GEOFFREY OF MONMOUTH (b. *c.*1100, probably at Monmouth, SE Wales; d. 1155, aged about 55). Author (in Latin). His *Historia regum Britanniae* (*History of the Kings of Britain*, completed *c.*1135–6) and *Vita Merlini* (*Life of Merlin*, *c.*1150) elaborated and spread the legend of King ARTHUR. He lived in OXFORD (England) by 1129, in LLANDAFF (SE Wales) from the late 1140s, and was bishop of ST ASAPH (NE Wales) from 1152, but never visited his diocese for fear of OWAIN GWYNEDD.

GEOLOGY In the 18th–19th centuries British natural philosophers (scientists) contributed to geological understanding with profound consequences. Robert HOOKE (1635–1703) was a pioneer in arguing that the Earth's form had resulted from natural processes rather than divine action. However, his posthumous *Discourse of Earthquakes* (1705) had little influence.

Curiosity developed in Europe from the mid 18th century, influenced by the Lisbon earthquake in Portugal (1750) and eruptions of Mt Vesuvius in Italy (e.g., 1760, 1767), and in Great Britain also by canal building. James HUTTON began investigations (1750s) and the CAMBRIDGE don John Michell published a theory of earthquakes (1760). Geology interested the LUNAR SOCIETY, particularly John Whitehurst. His *Inquiry into the Original State and Formation of the Earth* (1778) included the first illustrations of rock strata, but he struggled to reconcile evidence with religious beliefs, envisaging divine action operating with natural forces. Hutton's theory of 'actualism', published in 1788 (in a paper) and 1795 (*Theory of the Earth*), described processes forming the Earth's surface through immense periods of time, implicitly denying Bible-based chronology.

Around 1800 activity expanded: e.g., from 1803 Robert Jameson promoted geology at EDINBURGH University; from 1805 there were lectures at OXFORD; in 1807 the Geological Society of London was founded; in 1815 William 'Strata' Smith issued the first geological map of Britain. Study of fossils increased; e.g., James Parkinson published a treatise (three volumes, 1804–8) arguing that fossils resulted from the biblical 'great flood', an idea that became popular. *Outlines … of Extraneous Fossils* by William Martin (1809) correlated fossils with rock strata. This phase culminated in *Principles of Geology* by Charles LYELL (three volumes, 1830–3), which explained geological formations by natural processes ('uniformitarianism'), and demonstrated from fossils the appearance and disappearance of species. Lyell's ideas influenced the evolutionary theory of his cousin Charles DARWIN (publicized 1858). *See also* SCIENTIFIC REVOLUTION.

GEORGE, HENRY (b. 2 Sept. 1839 at Philadelphia, Pennsylvania, USA; d. 29 Oct. 1897 at New York, USA, aged 58). A journalist (1858–80) and politician, George developed the economics of David RICARDO. He believed that the concentration of unearned wealth, primarily in land, was the main cause of poverty. In his influential book *Progress and Poverty* (1879), he proposed that the State should tax the unimproved value of land to transfer wealth from landlords to the general population. In the 1880s he made lecture tours in the British Isles which encouraged political movements directed against landlords.

GEORGE I (b. 28 May 1660 at Hanover, Germany; d. 11 June 1727 at Osnabrück, Germany, aged 67). Georg Ludwig, elector of HANOVER, became king of Great Britain and Ireland on 1 Aug. 1714 in succession to ANNE (*see* HANOVERIAN SUCCESSION). The domination of the PRIVY COUNCIL by WHIGS prevented an immediate Stuart challenge, enabling George to succeed peacefully (*see* JACOBITISM, IMPACT ON BRITISH POLITICS).

George appointed a largely Whig ministry, having been angered by TORIES' neglect of Hanover in the Peace of UTRECHT. Whigs won a general election in 1715. George then excluded Tories from central and local offices. In Sept.

Jacobites attempted to depose George (*see* JACOBITE REBELLION, 1715).

James STANHOPE, Viscount TOWNSHEND and Robert WALPOLE emerged as leading ministers. In 1717 the ministry split, with Townshend and Walpole going into opposition (they criticized the ministry's favourable attitude to Hanover's interests). Soon afterwards George quarrelled with his heir, Prince George, who promoted opposition (*see* LEICESTER HOUSE). They were reconciled in 1720, when Townshend and Walpole returned to office.

After the SOUTH SEA BUBBLE crisis (1720), Walpole defended involvement by the king and ministers. George rewarded him with promotion again to first lord of the Treasury (1721). King George died while travelling to Hanover. Succeeded by GEORGE II. *See also* SHREWSBURY, 12TH EARL OF; SUNDERLAND, 3RD EARL OF; CABINET.

GEORGE II (b. 30 Oct. 1683 at Hanover, Germany; d. 25 Oct. 1760 at Kensington Palace, Middlesex, England, aged 76). Georg August, son of the elector of Hanover, moved to England in 1714 when his father also became king of Great Britain and Ireland (*see* GEORGE I). In 1717, following disagreement over a choice of godparents, he was banished. He established a rival court which attracted opposition politicians (*see* LEICESTER HOUSE). Prince and king were reconciled in 1720.

George succeeded his father on 11 June 1727 and retained the WHIG Robert WALPOLE as prime minister. After Walpole, George's chief ministers (all Whigs) were: Lord CARTERET, Henry PELHAM, duke of NEWCASTLE, duke of DEVONSHIRE. In 1737 George expelled his son FREDERICK from court; he then established a centre of opposition (until 1751). George was forced by the PELHAMS to remove Carteret (1742) and to accept ministerial appointments he disliked (1746).

During George's reign Britain was involved in the War of JENKINS' EAR (from 1739), War of the AUSTRIAN SUCCESSION (1740–8), and the SEVEN YEARS WAR (from 1756). George was the last British monarch to command an army in battle: at Dettingen (June 1743). In 1745 the largest JACOBITE REBELLION was suppressed (*see* CUMBERLAND, DUKE OF). George died in his CLOSET. Succeeded by GEORGE III.

GEORGE III (b. 4 June 1738 at London, England; d. 29 Jan. 1820 at Windsor, Berkshire, England, aged 81). The son of FREDERICK, PRINCE OF WALES, George succeeded his grandfather GEORGE II as king of Great Britain and Ireland, and elector of HANOVER, on 25 Oct. 1760. His tutor the earl of BUTE inspired his idea of becoming a 'patriot king' heading a non-party government. His attempt to implement this contributed to political instability in the 1760s. George also obstinately refused to countenance AMERICAN INDEPENDENCE and kept Lord NORTH in office (prime minister 1770–82). He became adept at manipulating the political process (e.g., destroying the 1783 coalition between Lord NORTH and Charles James FOX, and appointing William PITT the Younger).

George became increasingly popular as Britain faced (from 1789) the anti-royalist French Revolution and the FRENCH REVOLUTIONARY AND NAPOLEONIC WARS. This was reinforced by his piety, happy domestic life and interest in agriculture (he was nicknamed 'Farmer George'). Wartime danger brought about the UNION OF IRELAND AND GREAT BRITAIN in 1801, but George's opposition to CATHOLIC EMANCIPATION caused political problems.

George suffered bouts of insanity in 1765, 1788–9, and from 1810, which caused constitutional crises. His son Prince George served as regent 1811–20. *See also* KING'S FRIENDS; GRENVILLE, GEORGE; PORTLAND, 3RD DUKE OF; DUNNING'S RESOLUTION; GRENVILLE, LORD; GEORGE IV.

GEORGE IV (b. 12 Aug. 1762 at Westminster, Middlesex, England; d. 26 June 1830 at Windsor, Berkshire, England, aged 67). Eldest son of GEORGE III, Prince George (nicknamed 'Prinny') pursued a dissolute life. His secret marriage in 1785 to Maria Fitzherbert (1756–1837) was invalid because she was a Roman Catholic (*see* ROYAL MARRIAGES ACT). When George's debts became a political issue, he encouraged opposition WHIGS led by Charles James FOX, and vainly hoped to be made regent during his father's illness in 1789. He married CAROLINE OF BRUNSWICK in 1795 but they soon separated.

George became regent of Great Britain and Ireland in Feb. 1811. By now he had turned against the Whigs. He retained the TORY Spencer PERCEVAL, whom he disliked, as prime minister (followed 1812 by earl of LIVERPOOL). George succeeded as king (including HANOVER) on 29 Jan. 1820. An unsuccessful attempt to divorce his wife overshadowed the start of his reign, when he visited Ireland (1821) and Scotland (1822). By selecting George CANNING, a LIBERAL TORY, as prime minister in 1827, he alienated other Tories. But George's resistance to CATHOLIC EMANCIPATION exasperated the duke of WELLINGTON.

George was a patron of the arts and promoted the monarchy. He built Brighton Pavilion and BUCKINGHAM PALACE, and renovated WINDSOR Castle. Succeeded by WILLIAM IV. *See also* GODERICH, VISCOUNT.

GEORGE V (b. 3 June 1865 at London, England; d. 20 Jan. 1936 at Sandringham, Norfolk, England, aged 70). A younger son of Edward, prince of Wales (later EDWARD VII), George appeared unlikely to reign until Prince Albert Victor died in 1892. By then, naval service had moulded a dutiful and gruff character. Created duke of York in 1892, George married Mary of Teck in 1893. He was PRINCE OF WALES from 1901.

George succeeded as king of Great Britain and Ireland, and emperor of India, on 6 May 1910. When faced with awkward political situations, he acted with scrupulous respect for the constitution. He co-operated with H.H. ASQUITH over the PARLIAMENT ACT crisis (1910–11), chose Stanley BALDWIN (in the House of Commons) over Lord CURZON as prime minister in 1923, and encouraged the formation of the NATIONAL GOVERNMENT (1931). His changing of his family name from Saxe-Coburg-Gotha to Windsor in June 1917 (during WORLD WAR I) appeased anti-German feeling. George instituted the annual royal Christmas radio broadcast (1932), and celebrated his Silver Jubilee (1935). Succeeded by EDWARD VIII.

GEORGE VI (b. 14 Dec. 1895 at Sandringham, Norfolk, England; d. 6 Feb. 1952 at Sandringham, aged 56). The second son of George, duke of York (later GEORGE V), George was originally called Prince Albert. After serving in the British Royal Navy and Royal Air Force (1909–20), he was created duke of York (1920) and became known for factory visits. Afflicted by a stammer, he married Elizabeth Bowes-Lyon in 1923 (*see* ELIZABETH, QUEEN).

York appeared an unlikely monarch until the ABDICATION CRISIS placed him on the throne (replacing EDWARD VIII): he succeeded on 11 Dec. 1936 as king of Great Britain and Ireland, and emperor of India. (Southern Ireland and India became republics in 1949 and 1950 respectively.) George's modesty and conscientiousness progressively won respect. He paid official visits to France (1938), Canada and the USA (1939), and South Africa (1947). His decision to stay in London during wartime bombing boosted national morale (*see* WORLD WAR II).

GEORGIA A former British colony in N America. In 1732 the Englishman James Oglethorpe obtained a charter from King GEORGE II for a colony S of SOUTH CAROLINA (named after George). The grant was supported financially by the British PARLIAMENT, with power granted to trustee proprietors for 21 years. Georgia was intended for the relatively poor who would establish themselves as soldier-farmers on smallholdings.

Oglethorpe and the first settlers arrived in 1733. In 1735, slavery was outlawed (rescinded 1750 at behest of immigrants from South Carolina). After war against Spain began in 1739 (*see* JENKINS' EAR, WAR OF), Oglethorpe attacked St Augustine in Spanish Florida (1740) and repelled Spanish invaders at the battle of Bloody Swamp (July 1742).

When the royal grant expired in 1753, Georgia became a CROWN COLONY with a Crown-appointed governor and council, and elected assembly. PLANTATION agriculture expanded. Est. population 1770: 26,000. Georgia reluctantly supported AMERICAN INDEPENDENCE and became a State of the USA in 1776. *See also* NORTH AMERICAN COLONIES.

GERALDINES Name used by the writer GERALD OF WALES (in Latin *Giraldide*) for his relatives (including illegitimate ones) who invaded Ireland in 1169–70. It referred to Gerald's grandfather Gerald of Windsor (d. by 1136), the Norman constable of PEMBROKE (SW Wales) who married the Welsh princess NEST. The Geraldines comprised: descendants (sons and grandsons) of Gerald of Windsor and Nest; descendants of Nest and other men; and other relatives (about 30 in all).

The term is also used for descendants of Gerald of Windsor's third son, Maurice fitz Gerald (d. 1176), many of whom bore the surname Fitzgerald. The most important were the families who held the earldoms of KILDARE (created 1316) and DESMOND (created 1329). With the BUTLER family, they were the leading Anglo-Irish families in the 15th and early 16th centuries. *See also* NORMANS, IMPACT ON IRELAND; IRELAND, ENGLISH COLONY IN, 13TH–15TH CENTURIES; BUTLER–GERALDINE FEUD.

GERALD OF WALES (b. 1145 or 1146 at Manorbier, Pembrokeshire, Wales; d. 1223, aged 77). A cleric and author, of Norman and Welsh parentage (*see* NEST); known in Latin as Giraldus Cambrensis. Gerald visited Ireland (*see* GERALD OF WALES AND IRELAND) and toured Wales with Archbishop Baldwin of Canterbury in 1188, which resulted in his *Journey through Wales* (1191) and *Description of Wales* (1194). Gerald was archdeacon of Brecon (1175–1204) and twice sought election as bishop of ST DAVIDS (1176, 1199–1203). *See also* CHURCH, MEDIEVAL WALES.

GERALD OF WALES AND IRELAND Gerald was related to many Anglo-Norman invaders of Ireland (*see* GERALDINES). He visited Ireland with his brother Philip de Barry (1183–4) and with Prince JOHN (April 1185, remaining until spring 1186). He wrote the *Topography of Ireland* (completed 1188) and *Conquest of Ireland* (1189), which are based on observation and information obtained from Anglo-Normans. They present the Gaelic Irish as barbarous and semi-pagan, the Anglo-Normans as bringers of civilization. *See also* IRELAND, ENGLISH CONQUEST, 12TH–13TH CENTURIES.

GERMAIN, GEORGE (b. 26 Jan. 1716 at Westminster, Middlesex, England; d. 26 Aug. 1785 at Stoneland Lodge, Sussex, England, aged 69). George Sackville served as a soldier from 1737 and became an MP in 1741. During the SEVEN YEARS WAR he was blamed for ineptitude as a commander at the battle of Minden (Aug. 1759). He was dismissed (1759) and convicted of disobedience (1760).

Sackville was restored to favour by King GEORGE III. He held government office in 1765 under the marquess of ROCKINGHAM (1765), and in 1770 changed his surname

after inheriting estates. In the 1760s–70s he supported the assertion of Parliamentary authority over Great Britain's American colonies, and from 1775 to 1782 was secretary of state for the colonies. In 1780 he initiated a strategy of reoccupation of colonies from the south but it led to defeat (*see* AMERICAN INDEPENDENCE, WAR OF). After leaving office he was created Viscount Sackville.

GERMANIC IMMIGRATION, SOUTHERN BRITAIN In the early 5th century, after the end of Roman imperial rule, Germanic men were used as mercenaries by British rulers (*see* VORTIGERN). Substantial immigration followed from the mid 5th century; by the mid 6th century, despite British resistance (*see* AMBROSIUS AURELIANUS), numerous people from (modern) NW and N Germany and Denmark had settled in eastern and south-eastern areas, and in the Midlands (via river valleys).

Groups in SE Britain called themselves SAXONS, after (Old) Saxony, except for people in KENT (and also the Isle of Wight) who were JUTES, from Jutland. Groups N of the Saxons were ANGLES, after Angeln in Schleswig (N Germany). Other immigrants included Frisians (from modern Netherlands).

Immigrants settled among Brittonic-speaking natives. Despite disparate Continental origins, they quickly developed a common language, the precursor of Old English (related to Frisian), and resisted assimilation. Their fighting units conquered British kingdoms or created their own (*see* KINGSHIP, ANGLO-SAXON). By *c*.700 Anglo-Saxon kingdoms occupied much of former Roman Britain. The majority British population eventually adopted Germanic culture (by 9th century). *See also* POST-ROMAN BRITAIN; BRITONS IN ANGLO-SAXON KINGDOMS; CEMETERIES, EARLY GERMANIC.

GERMANUS (b. *c*.375, probably in Gaul; d. 31 July 448 at Ravenna, Italy, aged about 73). Bishop of Auxerre, NE Gaul (modern France), from 407 or 418; visited Britain (429; 446–7) to combat Pelagianism (*see* PELAGIUS). In 429 Germanus confronted Pelagians in public, visited Alban's shrine (*see* ST ALBANS), and led Britons in a victory over PICTS and SAXONS. He was remembered in Wales as 'Garmon' or 'Harmon', who allegedly helped Cadell Deyrnllug found the dynasty of POWYS. *See also* POST-ROMAN BRITAIN.

GERMANY, BRITISH RELATIONS WITH After the proclamation of German unification (18 Jan. 1871), Great Britain's relations with Germany were broadly harmonious (1870s–90s), because both nations regarded FRANCE and RUSSIA as their principal potential enemies. The ruler (Kaiser) from 1888, William II, was a grandson of Queen VICTORIA. But attitudes were already changing when informal alliance talks took place in 1898 and 1901. German jealousy of the British Empire, combined with commercial rivalry and intimidating German diplomacy in Europe, were stirring antagonism which fuelled the NAVAL RACE (from 1900) and culminated in WORLD WAR I (1914–18).

At the PARIS PEACE CONFERENCE (1919), Britain's concern for the BALANCE OF POWER led it to oppose French plans to dismember Germany. The spirit of reconciliation which infused LOCARNO merged into APPEASEMENT (1930s). This was abandoned in 1939 when Britain entered WORLD WAR II to oppose aggressive German expansionism (1939–45).

After Germany's defeat, Britain occupied NW Germany (1945–55), and co-operated with the Federal Republic of Germany (or West Germany, created in 1949 and sovereign from 1955). The Republic was an ally in the NORTH ATLANTIC TREATY ORGANIZATION from 1955. Relations cooled in 1989–90 because the prime minister Margaret THATCHER was antagonistic to rapid German reunification. (Unification of West and East Germany took place on 3 Oct. 1990.) Subsequent policies on the EUROPEAN ECONOMIC COMMUNITY/EUROPEAN UNION were divergent, with Germany favouring greater European integration and the UK eventually deciding to leave (2016). *See also* PRUSSIA, BRITISH RELATIONS WITH.

GHANA *see* GOLD COAST

GIBBON, EDWARD (b. 27 April 1737 at Putney, Surrey, England; d. 16 Jan. 1794 at London, England, aged 56). From a landed family and resident for periods in Switzerland, Gibbon was the greatest 18th-century English historian. While visiting Rome (Italy) in 1764, during a GRAND TOUR, he conceived the idea of a history of the Roman Empire. His *Decline and Fall of the Roman Empire* (six volumes, published 1776–88), a masterpiece of style and wit, displays massive learning and a profound debt to ENLIGHTENMENT thought, notably in its critical treatment of Christianity and admiration of classical values.

GIBBON, LEWIS GRASSIC (b. 13 Feb. 1901 near Auchterless, Aberdeenshire, Scotland; d. 7 Feb. 1935 at Welwyn Garden City, Hertfordshire, England, aged 33). Writer; pseudonym of James Leslie Mitchell. After working in journalism in Aberdeen and Glasgow, Mitchell served in the British Army (1917–23) and Royal Air Force. From 1929 he concentrated on writing. His major success was the trilogy of novels *A Scots Quair* (1932–4), which vividly portray Scottish life in the early 20th century. *See also* SCOTTISH LITERATURE IN ENGLISH.

GIBRALTAR A British territory on the Iberian Peninsula. Known as 'The Rock', Gibraltar is a strategic promontory (2.25 sq mi, 5.8 sq km) commanding the entrance to the Mediterranean Sea (N side). Captured by

England during the War of the SPANISH SUCCESSION (1704), it was ceded by SPAIN to Great Britain under the Peace of UTRECHT (1713). Gibraltar withstood a Franco-Spanish siege 1779–82.

From the early 19th century Gibraltar was an important British naval base, and was made a CROWN COLONY in 1830. Later developments included an enclosed harbour (established 1903–6) and airport (1939). After receiving internal self-government in 1964, Gibraltarians voted overwhelmingly to retain British sovereignty in a referendum in 1967 (confirmed 2002). Spain, which has demanded reversion of the territory, closed the frontier from 1969 to 1985. Gibraltar became a British DEPENDENT TERRITORY in 1983, and British overseas territory in 2002. Approx. population in 1921, 18,500; in 2012, 29,000.

GIBSON, EDMUND (b. autumn 1669 at Bampton, Westmorland, England; d. 6 Sept. 1748 at Bath, Somerset, England, aged 78). Of modest origins, Gibson was a prolific author and Church of ENGLAND clergyman. He became bishop of Lincoln in 1716. As bishop of London from 1723 and a WHIG, Gibson advised the prime minister, Robert WALPOLE, on the appointment of bishops, recommending fellow Whigs who would support Walpole's ministry in the House of Lords. He was nicknamed 'Walpole's Pope'. But Gibson was concerned to protect the Church of England's privileges: in 1736 he organized opposition to a Quaker Tithe Bill and resigned as Walpole's adviser.

GILBERT, HUMPHREY (b. early 1537 at Greenway, Devon, England; d. 9 Sept. 1583 in N Atlantic, aged 46). Soldier and explorer. While in Ireland, 1566–70, Gilbert became involved in PLANTATION schemes (knighted 1570), and in 1572 led an expedition to the Netherlands to support Dutch rebels against the Spanish. From the 1560s he also advocated overseas colonization and exploration for the NORTH-WEST PASSAGE.

Gilbert began English attempts to colonize N America. In 1578 he attempted a trans-Atlantic voyage, possibly for colonization, and in 1583 he crossed the Atlantic. He appropriated St John's harbour, NEWFOUNDLAND, and reclaimed extensive adjacent lands for Queen ELIZABETH I (3 Aug.) but failed to settle a colony. He drowned while sailing home. Gilbert's ambitions were continued by his half-brother Walter RALEGH. *See also* NORTH AMERICA, ENGLISH EXPLORATION.

GILBERT, WILLIAM (b. 1544 at Colchester, Essex, England; d. 30 Nov. 1603 at London, England, aged about 59). After studying at CAMBRIDGE University, Gilbert may have undertaken experiments on magnetism in the early 1570s, using naturally occurring (magnetic) lodestones. From 1573 he practised as a physician in London, becoming a physician to Queen ELIZABETH I (1601) and King JAMES VI/I (1603).

In 1600, in his treatise *De Magnete …*, Gilbert was the first person to expound scientific method in print (hypotheses tested by experimentation). He advanced the understanding of electricity and magnetism, and perceived the Earth as a spherical magnet surrounded by a magnetic field. Gilbert argued that the Earth rotates in a vacuum, and indicated support for the Sun-centred understanding of planetary motion published by Copernicus in 1543. *See also* SCIENTIFIC REVOLUTION.

GILBERT AND ELLICE ISLANDS A former British possession in the SW Pacific, comprising two archipelagos. They became a PROTECTORATE in 1892 and a CROWN COLONY in 1915. Japan occupied the Gilbert Islands 1942–3. The archipelagos became separate political entities in 1975.

The Ellice Islands became independent under the British Crown as Tuvalu in 1978. Approx. population in 1921, 3500; in 1977, 7000. The Gilbert Islands became the republic of Kiribati in 1979. Approx. population in 1921, 21,300; in 1978, 56,500.

GILDAS (fl. late 5th–mid 6th centuries in Britain). British Christian priest; author of *De excidio Britanniae* (*On the Ruin of Britain*), a warning about the consequences of sinful behaviour. Gildas argued that the behaviour of earlier British kings and clergy had provoked divine retribution in the Germanic conquest of eastern Britain. Written in sophisticated Latin (presumably for learned readers), possibly *c*.540, the *De excidio* contains the only substantial 6th-century account of POST-ROMAN BRITAIN. Gildas probably lived in S Britain (modern Dorset or Wiltshire). *See also* AMBROSIUS AURELIANUS; VORTIGERN.

GIN CRAZE Episode in England, 1720s–40s, when gin was cheap because of increased production and low malt prices. A perceived boom in consumption and drunkenness generated moral panic. Parliament reacted with legislation from 1729, which imposed duties and required vendors to be licensed. It culminated in the 1751 Gin Act which additionally banned various retailers. Consumption was reduced by increased malt prices from the mid 18th century. *See also* LICENSING OF DRINKING PREMISES, ENGLAND AND WALES.

GIRLS' AND WOMEN'S EDUCATION, BRITAIN In the 15th–19th centuries girls from better-off families often received an elementary education from private teachers, occasionally reaching high levels (e.g., in languages). Parish schools in Scotland, developed in the 17th century, included girls, and there were girls' academies in towns. Private girls' boarding schools existed in England from the early 17th century. Charity schools and Sunday schools founded in Great Britain in the 18th century included girls. Girls' education stressed domestic skills (e.g., needlework) and accomplishments (e.g., singing).

Provision expanded in England and Wales from the mid 19th century, sometimes in the form of 'sister schools' such as Queen's College, London (1848), and Cheltenham Ladies' College (1854). For working-class girls there was elementary education in voluntary or board schools: this became compulsory in 1880. Girls' grammar schools were founded under the Endowed Schools Act (1869), by the Girls' Public Day School Company (1872), and under the BALFOUR EDUCATION ACT (1902). A few girls' boarding schools modelled themselves on boys' public schools, and women's colleges opened at OXFORD and CAMBRIDGE in the 1870s. In 1878 London University opened its degrees to women, as by 1895 did all British Universities except Oxford and Cambridge. Women could graduate from Oxford from 1920 but the Cambridge MA remained closed until 1948. *See also* CO-EDUCATION.

GIRLS' AND WOMEN'S EDUCATION, IRELAND *see* EDUCATION, IRELAND; UNIVERSITIES, IRELAND

GLACIATIONS The spreading of ice sheets, and associated long periods of cold climate (also called 'Ice Ages'), which in parts of the world have influenced the areas in which humans can settle and the resources available to them (food, building materials). The long-run PREHISTORY of Britain was shaped by alternating glaciations and generally short, warmer periods called 'interglacials'. Glaciations were punctuated in turn by short warm periods called 'interstadials', and interglacials by short cold periods called 'stadials'. During glaciations, the N ice cap spread southwards, covering much of Britain and Ireland. The absorption of water as ice lowered the sea level, joining Britain to Continental Europe, and possibly Ireland to Britain.

There have probably been five periods of human occupation of Britain, mostly during interglacials and interstadials: (a) by the early human species *Homo heidelbergensis* *c*.450,000 BP, during an interstadial in the 'Anglian glaciation' (470,000–400,000 BP); (b) during the subsequent 'Hoxnian interglacial', *c*.400,000– *c*.350,000 BP, especially the so-called 'mid-Hoxnian expansion' when bands of *Homo heidelbergensis* occupied much of Britain and the climate was mild; (c) *c*.225,000 BP, during the second, 'Ilfordian interstadial' of the 'Wolstonian glaciation' (*c*.350,000–130,000 BP), when both *Homo heidelbergensis* and Neanderthals may have been present; (d) during the 'Devensian interglacial' (*c*.80,000–*c*.27,000 BP), when Neanderthals and from *c*.40,000 BP bands of modern man, *Homo sapiens sapiens*, spread into Britain (this period was curtailed by increasingly cold conditions which peaked *c*.18,000 BP); (e) from *c*.11,000 BC to the present, the 'Flandrian interglacial' (with Ireland inhabited from *c*.8000 BC). Ireland became separated *c*.9000 BC, and Britain was finally separated from the Continent between 5800 and 5400 BC. Prehistory to *c*.8500 BC is called the PALAEOLITHIC, the next period the MESOLITHIC. *See also* PREHISTORIC BRITAIN/IRELAND; GATHERING AND HUNTING.

GLADSTONE, W.E. (b. 29 Dec. 1809 at Liverpool, Lancashire, England; d. 19 May 1898 at Hawarden, Flintshire, Wales, aged 88). Leader of the LIBERAL PARTY 1866–75, 1880–94; four times British prime minister.

William Ewart Gladstone, a merchant's son, went to Eton College school and OXFORD University. Entering Parliament as a TORY MP in 1832, he was president of the Board of Trade (1843–5) and colonial secretary (1845–6).

A PEELITE (nominally until 1865), Gladstone advanced FREE TRADE and retrenchment as chancellor of the Exchequer (1852–5, 1859–66). He moved towards LIBERALISM and PARLIAMENTARY REFORM. Lord John RUSSELL's resignation left him leading the Liberals.

Gladstone's first ministry (1868–74) saw reforms of the ARMY, EDUCATION and COURTS, and efforts to pacify Ireland. He retired from leadership in Opposition, but denunciation of BULGARIAN ATROCITIES and Benjamin DISRAELI's foreign policy helped sweep him back to power after the MIDLOTHIAN campaign.

Gladstone's second ministry (1880–5) was troubled. Though averse to colonial expansion, Gladstone faced imperial problems, in SOUTH AFRICA, EGYPT and the SUDAN. The Third Reform Act (1884) was the main domestic achievement. During his final two terms (Feb.–July 1886, 1892–4), Irish HOME RULE preoccupied him. When the 'Grand Old Man' finally resigned he was 84.

GLADSTONE, W.E., AND IRELAND Responding to the 1867 'Fenian outrages' (*see* INSURRECTION OF 1867) and Irish discontent, Gladstone declared in 1868 'my mission is to pacify Ireland'. During his first ministry (1868–74) Gladstone disestablished the Church of Ireland (1869) and passed a Land Act (1870). During his second ministry (1880–5) he faced rural unrest and demands for Home Rule, both promoted by Irish leader C.S. PARNELL. Gladstone's government passed COERCION and Land Acts (1881), and arrested Irish leaders, including Parnell (Oct. 1881). But turmoil continued and Gladstone conceded Parnell's release (1882; *see* KILMAINHAM TREATY). Unrest declined after the PHOENIX PARK MURDERS (1882).

On 17 Dec. 1885, following a general election, Gladstone's 'conversion' to Home Rule was disclosed. It was caused partly by external pressures, but was consistent with Liberal principles of self-government. Irish support enabled Gladstone to resume office (1886), but his Home Rule Bill was defeated in the Commons (8 June) and he resigned. (The Bill also divided the Liberal Party.) During Gladstone's fourth ministry (1892–4) a second Home Rule Bill passed the Commons but was defeated in the Lords (1893). *See also* MAYNOOTH GRANT CONTROVERSY; DISESTABLISHMENT, CHURCH OF IRELAND; HOME RULE MOVEMENT, IRELAND; LAND AGITATION AND REFORM, IRELAND.

GLAMORGAN, LORDSHIP OF An important Norman, later English, lordship in SE WALES (1090s–1536); part of the MARCH OF WALES; centred on the lowland region of the kingdom of GLYWYSING/Morgannwg. The name derives from Welsh, Gwlad Morgan, meaning 'Land of Morgan'.

The lordship was founded in the 1090s by Robert FITZ HAMO, who built on initial Norman penetration into SE Wales *c*.1070 (*see* NORMANS, IMPACT ON WALES). Fitz Hamo built a castle at CARDIFF (administrative centre of the lordship) and parcelled out land in the Vale of Glamorgan to his followers as knights' fees and MANORS. Name evidence shows considerable English immigration. Upland areas were held from fitz Hamo by Welsh rulers.

On fitz Hamo's death (1107) the lordship passed to his son-in-law ROBERT OF GLOUCESTER and then (1147) to Robert's son William (d. 1183). After a period in royal custody, it passed (1217) by marriage to Gilbert fitz Richard de CLARE. Clares held the lordship until 1314, and brought the entire lordship under their court at Cardiff (at the expense of upland rulers). The lordship was held from 1317 to 1400 (with interruptions) by the DESPENSERS, and in 1502 it passed to the English Crown.

On the abolition of the March in 1536 the lordship provided the basis for the county of Glamorgan (*see* UNION OF WALES WITH ENGLAND), which became heavily industrialized and densely populated from the late 18th century with the exploitation of the S Wales coalfield (mostly in Glamorgan). In 1971 the county's 1,258,000 inhabitants constituted 45% of Wales's population. Glamorgan was abolished in 1974.

GLAMORGAN TREATIES Two secret treaties made in 1645 by the (Catholic) earl of Glamorgan, envoy for King CHARLES I in Ireland. The first, agreed 25 Aug. with leaders of the CATHOLIC CONFEDERATION, allowed Catholic worship in Catholic-held churches. The Confederation would also send 10,000 troops to England. The papal nuncio, Archbishop RINUCCINI, considered it insufficient and negotiated a second treaty which allowed the Catholic Church a prominent place in Ireland (agreed 20 Dec.).

The first treaty was discovered in late Oct. and publicized. Charles, fearing anti-Catholic attitudes in England and Scotland, disowned Glamorgan's activities (letter to English Parliament, 29 Jan. 1646). The treaties were superseded by the ORMOND TREATIES. *See also* IRISH WARS, 1641–52.

GLANVILL Commonly used short name for the *Treatise on the Laws and Customs of the Kingdom of England*, a manual compiled (in Latin) *c.*1187–9. Although associated with Ranulph de Glanville, chief justiciar 1180–9, the work's authorship is unknown. It illuminates legal developments under King HENRY II (1160s–80s), stressing the importance of royal power. *See also* COMMON LAW.

GLASGOW (Brittonic, meaning 'Green hollow'). A city in W-C Scotland, by the R. Clyde. It originated as an ecclesiastical centre in the British kingdom of Clyde Rock (STRATHCLYDE), possibly as early as the later 6th century (*see* KENTIGERN). The cathedral is first recorded in 1136; the adjacent BURGH (possibly founded by King DAVID I, ruled 1124–53) was given to the bishop between 1175 and 1178. Glasgow University, founded 1451, increased the clerical element, and the bishop was elevated to archbishop in 1492. Until the 17th century, Glasgow's economic importance was only local, mainly because of the concentration of Scottish exporting on E coast ports. Glasgow became a royal burgh in 1611; the bishopric was abolished in 1689.

Glasgow expanded in the late 17th and 18th centuries from trade with the Americas, especially in sugar and tobacco. (Tobacco-trading was greatly reduced from 1775 by the AMERICAN WAR OF INDEPENDENCE.) Industry expanded vigorously from the late 18th century, especially TEXTILES (linen, then COTTON), which remained the main source of employment until the later 19th century, and COAL and IRON. The latter industries provided the basis for heavy industries in the late 19th century, above all SHIP BUILDING, which peaked *c.*1912. The city acquired splendid Victorian architecture, but also slums. Social conditions generated tensions, exacerbated by strikes during WORLD WAR I (1914–18) and afterwards. Radical politics emerged (*see* RED CLYDESIDE) and Irish immigration generated sectarian tensions.

Industry declined from the 1920s and worsened during the 1930s. From the 1960s ship building contracted. But Glasgow rebounded in the 1980s and celebrated 1990 as 'European City of Culture'. *See also* TOWNS, SCOTLAND; TRANSPORT COMMUNICATIONS, SCOTLAND; ETHNIC AND NATIONAL MINORITIES, SCOTLAND.

Est. popn: 1300, 1500; 1600, 7000; 1800, 77,000; 1900, 953,000; 2000, 1,200,000.

GLASGOW ASSEMBLY A meeting of the General Assembly of the Church of SCOTLAND held at GLASGOW Cathedral, 21 Nov.–20 Dec. 1638; the first allowed by rulers since 1618. In defiance of royal authority, it abolished the FIVE ARTICLES OF PERTH (1618), Book of CANONS (1636), PRAYER BOOK (1637), and episcopacy (Church government by bishops). Intended by King CHARLES I to conciliate opponents, following the signing of the NATIONAL COVENANT (Feb. 1638), the meeting led to the Wars of the COVENANT and the COVENANTING REVOLUTION. *See also* HAMILTON, 3RD MARQUIS OF; HENDERSON, ALEXANDER.

GLASS INDUSTRY, IRELAND Manufacture of lead glass was started at DUBLIN in 1690 and spread to other towns. It flourished especially in the mid 18th–early 19th centuries, with larger firms being formed in the 1770s–80s to counter English competition. Businesses produced mainly domestic glassware (bottles, glasses). Manufacturing ceased by 1900, apart from bottle-making, though it was revived at WATERFORD in 1947. *See also* INDUSTRY, IRELAND 18TH CENTURY TO 1921.

GLENCAIRN RISING A Royalist rising in Scotland against English occupation, from Aug. 1653; led by the (9th) earl of Glencairn (William Cunningham) and John MIDDLETON, under commission from King CHARLES II. The rising had considerable support, especially in the HIGHLANDS, but was uncoordinated. It was largely suppressed by July 1654. *See also* UNION OF ENGLAND AND SCOTLAND, 1650s; MONCK, GEORGE.

GLENCOE MASSACRE The killing, as an exemplary punishment, of MacIan, chief of the Glencoe MacDonald clan, and 37 others by government troops, near Glencoe village (W Scotland) during the night of 13 Feb. 1692. The massacre arose from the government's attempt to secure the loyalty of HIGHLAND clans to the new rulers, William and Mary (*see* GLORIOUS REVOLUTION, SCOTLAND).

Chiefs were required to sign a loyalty oath by 1 Jan. 1692. Several failed, though MacIan signed five days later. The government singled out his clan because it was small and unpopular (due to cattle thieving). The killings damaged King William's reputation and strengthened JACOBITISM. *See also* DALRYMPLE, JOHN; BREADALBANE, 1ST EARL OF; WILLIAM III.

GLENDALOUGH The site of a former ecclesiastical centre in Co. Wicklow, Republic of Ireland; from Irish, Gleann Dá Locha, meaning 'Valley of two lakes'.

Glendalough, in LEINSTER (E Ireland), was originally the location of a hermitage allegedly founded in the 6th century by Cóemgen (St Kevin, d. 618). An ecclesiastical centre (monastic and lay settlement) developed, which was dominated in the 8th–12th centuries by the Uí Máil and Uí Dúnlainge dynasties. Abbot Lorcán Ua Tuathail (Laurence O'TOOLE) reformed the religious community as an Augustinian house *c.*1160 (suppressed 1539). A diocesan see from 1111, Glendalough diocese was united with Dublin in 1213. A tower, churches and former cathedral survive. *See also* MONASTICISM, MEDIEVAL IRELAND.

GLOBE THEATRE A theatre, circular in layout, which was built in 1599 on the S bank of the R. Thames near LONDON, England. It was named after its sign, which showed Hercules carrying the world. Many plays by William SHAKESPEARE were performed there. The Globe burnt down in 1613 and was rebuilt in 1614. It was closed by PURITANS in 1642; demolished 1644. A reconstruction was opened near the original location in 1997.

GLORIOUS REVOLUTION Term used from the 18th century for the replacement in 1688–9 of the Catholic king JAMES VII/II by the Protestants William of Orange (WILLIAM III), stadholder (lieutenant) of the Dutch Republic, and MARY II as rulers of England (with Wales), Ireland and Scotland, and for associated constitutional developments.

From 1687 unrest arose in England when James prepared to secure a Parliament favourable to repeal of anti-Catholic laws. William became alarmed in 1688 as it became known that James's wife, Mary of Modena, was expecting a child: it might supplant his wife (James's elder daughter) as heir in England with a Catholic male and possibly encourage England to ally with Catholic France. A son was born in June, though people alleged that it was not the queen's child.

Seven politicians who feared the continuance of a Catholic monarchy invited William to intervene (30 June 1688). His army landed at Brixham, Devon (SW England), on 5 Nov. and entered London on 18 Dec. James was captured, but escaped on 23 Dec. William called an election. A CONVENTION PARLIAMENT (met 22 Jan. 1689) decided that James had abdicated, and invited William and Mary to become joint rulers (13 Feb.).

Existing limitations on Crown powers were affirmed by a Declaration and Bill of RIGHTS (1689), which also prohibited a STANDING ARMY without Parliament's consent. The Bill additionally prohibited a Catholic from becoming ruler. The TOLERATION ACT (1689), passed to secure Protestant support for William, gave limited liberty to DISSENTERS.

The Crown subsequently became more dependent on Parliament. William and ANNE required grants of funds for Continental warfare, and the TRIENNIAL ACT (1694) instituted frequent Parliaments and elections. The Civil List Act (1697) inaugurated the separate provision of funds by Parliament for the royal household and civil government. The Act of SETTLEMENT (1701) imposed further restrictions. POLITICAL PARTIES increasingly influenced the Crown's choice of ministers. *See also* ANCIENT CONSTITUTION; FINANCIAL REVOLUTION; JACOBITISM, IMPACT ON BRITISH POLITICS.

GLORIOUS REVOLUTION, IRELAND *see* JAMES VII/II AND IRELAND

GLORIOUS REVOLUTION, SCOTLAND Although King JAMES VII/II fled abroad in 1688 (23 Dec.), following invasion of England by William of Orange, he was replaced in Scotland by William and his wife Mary under separate arrangements and for different reasons.

As KING'S COMMISSIONER in Scotland (for King Charles II) in 1681 James (then known as the duke of Albany) had obtained the Test Act requiring clergy and royal office-holders to acknowledge royal supremacy in Church and State by oath. Many clergy lost their livings for refusing. As king (from 1685), James had sought toleration for CATHOLICS against popular opinion. After Parliament refused (1686), he imposed toleration by ROYAL PREROGATIVE (Feb., June 1687).

After James's flight, William assumed responsibility for government. James was formally deprived for arbitrary rule in Scotland, and William and Mary were offered the Crown, in 1689 by a Scottish CONVENTION PARLIAMENT, which also enacted a substantial REVOLUTION SETTLEMENT. *See also* WILLIAM III; CORONATION, SCOTLAND.

GLOUCESTER, HUMPHREY DUKE OF (b. autumn 1390 at Eaton Tregoes, Herefordshire, England; d. 23 Feb. 1447 at Bury St Edmunds, Suffolk, England, aged 56). Humphrey of Lancaster, the youngest brother of King HENRY V (ruled 1413–22), was created duke of Gloucester in 1414. He served in Henry's French campaigns (*see* HUNDRED YEARS WAR), and was 'keeper' of England for Henry 1419–21, 1422.

After the accession of HENRY VI, a minor (1422), in England and France, the duke of BEDFORD (older brother) was regent in France with Gloucester as 'protector' in England. Gloucester contended with Henry BEAUFORT, and also attempted to seize his wife's claimed inheritance in Hainault (1424–5), endangering the Anglo-Burgundian alliance. Bedford intervened in 1426: Beaufort was removed but Gloucester remained protector until 1429 and was 'lieutenant' 1430–3. Bedford finally ousted Gloucester in 1433 but at Bedford's death (1435) he became heir and 'chief councillor', again governing with Beaufort. After Henry was declared ruler (1437), Beaufort was the dominant influence. In 1441 Gloucester was discredited when his (second) wife was convicted of treasonable witchcraft. Later arrested on suspicion of treason (1447), he died while awaiting trial. He was a patron of scholarship and donor to the library of OXFORD University. *See also* HUMANISM.

GLYWYSING An early medieval kingdom in SE WALES (6th–11th centuries); said to be named after King Glywys (6th century) but which was ruled by the dynasty of Meurig ap Tewdrig (fl. *c*.600) until the late 10th century. The Book of LLANDAFF illuminates some of its history in unusual detail.

At times Glywysing probably comprised all of SE Wales, including Gwent and Ergyng (English, Archenfield); but areas were sometimes ruled independently and Ergyng was lost to England probably in the 9th century. Glywysing is notable for not falling under the dynasty of RHODRI MAWR of Gwynedd during the late 9th and early 10th centuries.

From *c.*930 to 974 Glywysing was ruled by Morgan Hen ('the Old') who imposed such unity that it was renamed Morgannwg, 'Morgan's Land'. After Morgan, DEHEUBARTH (SW Wales) detached Gower, and new dynasties took the kingship, including that of GRUFFUDD AP RHYDDERCH (ruled Morgannwg 1045–55). Gruffudd's heirs dominated Morgannwg in the late 11th century, though Morgan's descendants held some power. This fragmentation may partly explain the ease with which NORMANS conquered Morgannwg in the 1090s, enabling Robert FITZ HAMO to establish the lordship of GLAMORGAN.

GODERICH, VISCOUNT (b. 1 Nov. 1782 at Newby Hall, Yorkshire, England; d. 28 Jan. 1859 at Putney, Surrey, England, aged 76). Frederick Robinson, a Tory MP from 1806, was president of the Board of Trade (1818–23) and chancellor of the Exchequer (1823–7) in the government of the earl of LIVERPOOL. He worked with William HUSKISSON for freer trade. In April 1827 he was created Viscount Goderich and became colonial secretary and leader of the House of Lords under George CANNING.

In Aug. 1827 Goderich succeeded Canning as PRIME MINISTER. Unable to consolidate his coalition of LIBERAL TORIES and moderate WHIGS at a time of confused party politics, he resigned in Jan. 1828 with a reputation for tearful indecisiveness. His moderate opinions later secured him office under both Earl GREY (1830–4) and Sir Robert PEEL (1841–6). In 1833 he was created earl of Ripon.

GODODDIN A British (Brittonic-speaking) kingdom, based in LOTHIAN (modern SE Scotland). Descended from the IRON AGE TRIBE the Votadini, from which its name is derived, the kingdom is first recorded in the 6th century, when it was threatened by the Anglian (Germanic) kingdom of BERNICIA to the S (*see* POST-ROMAN BRITAIN). Gododdin was probably conquered by OSWALD, king of Bernicia and Deira (Northumbria), by 638. A raid by men from Gododdin against Saxons in Deira is celebrated in a poem originally written in the early 7th century (*see* ANEIRIN). *See also* KINGSHIP, NORTH BRITAIN.

GODOLPHIN, EARL OF (b. 15 June 1645 at Breage, Cornwall, England; d. 15 Sept. 1712 at St Albans, Hertfordshire, England, aged 67). Sidney Godolphin entered service at court in 1662 (reign of King CHARLES II) and became a friend of John CHURCHILL. An MP from

1668, he was a commissioner of the Treasury 1679–84, 1684–9, 1690–7, and 1700–1, under Charles (d. 1685), JAMES VII/II (to 1688), and WILLIAM III (1689–1702). He was created Lord Godolphin in 1684. In 1696–1700 he worked closely with Robert HARLEY.

As lord TREASURER from May 1702, Godolphin was a leading minister under Queen ANNE. A non-party manager, he drew support from WHIGS and TORIES. He provided finance for the War of the SPANISH SUCCESSION, while Churchill conducted the war, and also brought about the UNION OF ENGLAND AND SCOTLAND (1707), to safeguard the HANOVERIAN SUCCESSION. From 1706 he was forced to rely increasingly on Whigs and remove Tories. He was created an earl in Dec. 1706.

Growing discontent with the war and about the Whigs, shared by the queen, enabled Robert Harley to persuade Anne to dismiss Godolphin (8 Aug. 1710).

GODWIN, WILLIAM (b. 3 March 1756 at Wisbech, Cambridgeshire, England; d. 7 April 1836 at Westminster, England, aged 80). A dissenting clergyman, Godwin lost his Christian faith and took up writing. In London from 1782, he became prominent with *An Enquiry Concerning Political Justice* (1793). In March 1797 he married Mary WOLLSTONECRAFT (d. Sept.). Godwin also published *Memoirs of the Author of a Vindication of the Rights of Woman* (1798) and several novels, including *Caleb Williams* (1794). He argued for the reorganization of society and politics according to rational principles. *See also* ENLIGHTENMENT.

GODWINE (fl. from 1014; d. 15 April 1053 at Winchester, Hampshire, England). An English supporter of CNUT, king of England and Denmark, Godwine was made an earl in 1018 (earl of all WESSEX from 1023). By Cnut's death (1035) he was England's most powerful secular lord. He supported HARTHACNUT as Cnut's successor, though Harthacnut remained in Denmark while HAROLD 'HAREFOOT' (half-brother) was regent. In 1036 Godwine was allegedly involved in the blinding of Alfred ætheling (another half-brother), who then died.

In 1037 Harold Harefoot appropriated the kingship of England, probably with Godwine's support. After Harthacnut succeeded Harold (1040), Godwine placated him with a gift (a manned ship) and by publicly condemning Alfred's blinding.

Godwine's power increased after the accession of Edward the Confessor (1042): his daughter EDITH married Edward (1045), and five sons became earls. But in 1051 Godwine refused a royal order (*see* EDWARD THE CONFESSOR). The Godwine family fled into exile. They were reinstated in Sept. 1052. Godwine died soon afterwards. *See also* GODWINE FAMILY.

GODWINE FAMILY In England, the family of GODWINE, earl of Wessex (d. 1053), which was influential under King Edward the Confessor (ruled 1042–66). Five of Godwine's sons were made EARLS: Swein (1043), HAROLD (1044), Tostig (1055), Gyrth (1057 or 1058) and Leofwine (1057). Their sister EDITH married Edward (1045). The family spent 1051–2 in exile (*see* EDWARD THE CONFESSOR).

Swein died in 1052. Tostig was ousted as earl of Northumbria by a rebellion (1065; died at STAMFORD BRIDGE). Harold succeeded King Edward but, like Gyrth and Leofwine, was killed at HASTINGS (1066).

GOLD COAST A former British territory in W Africa. The coast was a source of gold and slaves for British traders from the mid 17th century, and trading ports were established (*see* ROYAL AFRICAN COMPANY). In 1874 a CROWN COLONY was created. It expanded inland 1874–1902, when military expeditions against the Ashanti ended in annexations and PROTECTORATES. The latter were treated as effectively part of the colony. A section of former German Togoland was added in 1919.

Reliant on cocoa farming, the Gold Coast became independent in 1957 as the DOMINION of Ghana (under the British Crown). It was the first British colony in Africa to receive independence. Ghana became a republic in 1960. Approx. population in 1921, 2,108,000; in 1956, 5,484,000. *See also* WEST AFRICA, ENGLISH AND BRITISH INVOLVEMENT; NKRUMAH, KWAME.

GOLDEN ACT An Act of the Scottish Parliament, passed 1592, which authorized a presbyterian structure of Church government (KIRK SESSIONS, presbyteries, synods, General Assembly). The king could set the date and meeting place of Assemblies. It was named with reference to the BLACK ACTS. *See also* CHURCH ORGANIZATION, SCOTLAND FROM 16TH CENTURY.

GOLDEN AGE Historians' term for the 7th–9th centuries in Ireland when monastic-based Christian culture flourished. Ecclesiastical craftsmen produced illuminated manuscripts (e.g., Book of KELLS) and magnificent metalwork (e.g., Ardagh Chalice, Tara Brooch). Learning in Irish and Latin flowered, notably in grammar, biblical studies and computus (study of the ecclesiastical calendar). Scholars such as COLUMBANUS (d. 615) and JOHN SCOTTUS ERIUGENA (d. c.870) transmitted Irish Christian learning to Continental Europe. The end of the Golden Age is attributed to the impact of VIKINGS. *See also* CHURCH, MEDIEVAL IRELAND; LATIN, USE BY IRISH.

GOLDIE, GEORGE (b. 20 May 1846 at The Nunnery, Isle of Man; d. 20 Aug. 1925 at London, England, aged 79). Businessman and imperialist. Involved in trading with the Niger area (in modern NIGERIA) from 1875, George Goldie-Taubman sought a monopoly. In 1879 his company formed the United African Company with rivals. A successor National African Company was authorized (1882) to acquire territorial sovereignty. It established control around the lower Niger through treaties with African rulers (1883), and acquired French companies (1884). It was chartered (1886) as the Royal Niger Company (Goldie-Taubman knighted 1887, also changed name).

Goldie organized government for his company's territories (judiciary, local agents, Army). But the British colonial secretary, Joseph CHAMBERLAIN, deemed it inadequate. Although Goldie asserted authority over Muslim areas (1897), partly against French threats, the charter was revoked (1900) and Britain assumed authority. Goldie withdrew from Africa. *See also* LUGARD, FREDERICK; WEST AFRICA, ENGLISH AND BRITISH INVOLVEMENT; SCRAMBLE FOR AFRICA.

GOLD STANDARD The use of gold to value currency units. The link between gold, a country's balance of payments, and money supply can provide a self-regulating process: if too many goods are imported, gold flows out, money supply shrinks, domestic prices fall, and imports become more expensive. Equilibrium then returns.

Great Britain officially adopted a gold standard by the 1816 Coinage Act which abandoned bimetallism (reckoning in silver and gold) and issued small-denomination coins valued in relation to gold. Its use was extended in 1821 when convertibility of notes for coin at the BANK OF ENGLAND was reintroduced. (It had been suspended in 1797, during the FRENCH REVOLUTIONARY WARS.) Irish currency was assimilated in 1826. The UK left the gold standard in 1919 (after WORLD WAR I), readopted it in 1925, and left again in 1931 because of the international financial crisis. *See also* CURRENCY, ENGLAND AND GREAT BRITAIN FROM 1660s; KEYNES, J.M.

GOOD FRIDAY AGREEMENT *see* BELFAST AGREEMENT

GOOD PARLIAMENT Name applied to the English PARLIAMENT of 28 April–10 July 1376 (the longest hitherto, held at WESTMINSTER), which saw a serious attack on the conduct and costs of the government of King EDWARD III. The Commons condemned the corruption of the king's chamberlain, his mistress Alice PERRERS, and of several London merchants. For the first time their charges were presented to the Lords by a spokesman, Peter de la MARE, effectively the first Commons 'speaker'. The Lords examined and punished the government officers, the first instance of IMPEACHMENT. Their sentences were quashed by the Parliament of Jan. 1377, influenced by JOHN OF GAUNT.

GORDON, CHARLES GEORGE (b. 28 Jan. 1833 at Woolwich, Kent, England; d. 26 Jan. 1885 at Khartoum, Sudan, aged 51). A distinguished soldier in the CRIMEAN WAR (served 1855–6) and in China (1858–64), Gordon was nicknamed 'Chinese Gordon'. After a chance meeting he served as governor of Equatoria in Egyptian-ruled SUDAN (1874–7), where he suppressed the slave trade. As governor-general of Sudan 1877–9, he crushed rebellion in Darfur province.

In 1884 the British government sent Gordon to Sudan to quash the MADHI REBELLION. In Khartoum from Feb. (as governor-general), he evacuated Egyptian civilians and soldiers, only to be besieged from March by rebels. Though a relief force was sent (Sept.), Gordon was killed. His resistance of 317 days was portrayed as heroic.

GORDON RIOTS In England, anti-Catholic riots in LONDON, 2–9 June 1780. They were precipitated by Parliament's rejection of a petition, presented by Lord George Gordon (while demonstrators waited in Parliament Square), which demanded cancellation of the first Catholic Relief Act (1778). Rioting was eventually suppressed by the Army. It was the worst breakdown of order in Great Britain in the 18th century. Possibly a thousand people were killed. Around 450 people were taken prisoner, of whom 25 were hanged. Gordon was acquitted of TREASON (Feb. 1781). *See also* ANTI-CATHOLICISM, BRITAIN.

GORE, CHARLES (b. 22 Jan. 1853 at Wimbledon, Surrey, England; d. 17 Jan. 1932 at Kensington, London, England, aged 78). Gore was attracted to 'Anglo-Catholic' worship at school (*see* RITUALISM), and also became concerned about social issues. Ordained in the Church of England (1876), he was the first principal of Pusey House, OXFORD (1884–93). In 1889 he helped to launch the Christian Social Union to study social problems, and edited *Lux Mundi* ('Light of the World'), an essay collection. His contribution shocked conservative theologians. In 1892 Gore founded the Community of the Resurrection, a men's religious community. As bishop of WORCESTER from 1902, he decided that BIRMINGHAM should be separated. He became its first bishop (1905), and then bishop of Oxford (1911–19). His numerous writings were influential.

GORHAM JUDGMENT A controversial decision by the Judicial Committee of the British PRIVY COUNCIL, issued 8 March 1850. It upheld an appeal from Revd George Gorham after he was refused admission to a Church of ENGLAND living (Brampford Speke, Devon, SW England) by Bishop Henry Phillpotts who objected to Gorham's evangelical understanding of baptism. Gorham was instituted under the authority of Archbishop J.B. SUMNER. The readiness of State authority to rule on a doctrinal issue

precipitated several Roman Catholic conversions, including that of Henry MANNING. *See also* SURPLICE RIOTS.

GOVERNMENT, BRITISH EMPIRE *see* BRITISH EMPIRE, GOVERNMENT OF

GOVERNMENT, ENGLAND BEFORE 1066 Early Germanic kingdoms (by 6th century), which included British inhabitants, were governed by itinerant kings and royal officers (e.g., REEVES). Peasants were required to provide *feorm* (renders of food, drink) for consumption by ROYAL HOUSEHOLDS. Kings also imposed services such as repairing royal halls. Kings subordinate to overkings had to raise and pay tribute (*see* TRIBAL HIDAGE). Renders, services and tribute were often organized within small units known as SHIRES which were assessed in HIDES. Kings also gave authority to LAWS and customs, and issued coins (from early 7th century). The advent of literate clergy (7th century) enabled kings to issue documents written in Latin or Old English (e.g., land CHARTERS, laws).

Government developed as kingdoms became larger (*see* KINGSHIP, ANGLO-SAXON). In WESSEX, large shires were formed from the 8th century, each supervised by an EALDORMAN as king's deputy. Similar arrangements, using provinces, possibly operated in NORTHUMBRIA and MERCIA. Kings also levied tolls at WICS (7th–9th centuries). Kings of Mercia imposed or formalized onerous services in the 740s (*see* THREE PUBLIC SERVICES).

From the mid 10th century shires were created across the recently created kingdom of England, which were overseen for the king by ealdormen, bishops and reeves (including SHERIFFS). Some ealdormen or earls supervised several shires. Within shires were smaller hundreds (or wapentakes) and townships, and also BURHS (royal urban centres). Courts were held at all levels (*see* SHIRE COURT), and used for peace-keeping and to raise MILITARY SERVICE and taxes (*see* GELD).

The king's itinerant household remained the centre with royal chaplains preparing written instructions to localities (WRITS). EDWARD THE CONFESSOR (d. 1066) is the first king known to have authenticated documents with a seal. In the 1060s a chaplain who organized document-writing and kept the seal was designated CHANCELLOR, the first title to be applied to an important individual officer.

GOVERNMENT, ENGLAND 1066 TO 1509 The king's itinerant household remained central, with the CHANCELLOR supervising the writing office (Chancery) and keeping the 'great seal'. Latin was the main language of documents from the 1070s. WILLIAM I (ruled 1066–87) retained local units (SHIRE, hundred or wapentake, and township), but ended earls' supervision of shires (or 'counties'). SHERIFFS administered local units and additionally enforced royal rights in lords' estates (*see* HONOUR). When kings went overseas they delegated authority (to CHIEF JUSTICIARS from 1150s).

Government tended to become more elaborate, with some functions going 'out of court' as activity expanded. From *c.*1110 an auditing office, the EXCHEQUER, supervised sheriffs (based at WESTMINSTER by 1200). By the 1130s the ROYAL HOUSEHOLD was organized as departments, and included a TREASURER. The reassertion of royal authority from the 1160s (after the ANARCHY), involving justices and new legal procedures, resulted in COMMON LAW (*see* EYRE; POSSESSORY ASSIZES). From 1194 the Crown required shire communities to elect keepers of pleas to assist justices. By the 1250s, much of the Chancery and central courts also operated at Westminster.

JOHN (ruled 1199–1216) governed from his 'chamber' and authenticated documents with a PRIVY SEAL. HENRY III (from 1227) preferred the 'wardrobe' and relied more on his Council. From the early 14th century the privy seal had a keeper and office. EDWARD III revived the chamber as an accounting department (1330s).

By the 1350s the Council had become a central institution, its members including the 'great officers' (chancellor, treasurer, keeper of privy seal). Local justice was strengthened through JUSTICES OF THE PEACE. After weak rule in the 1440s–50s, EDWARD IV reasserted royal power by establishing relatives as informal local lieutenants (1470s), and giving judicial powers to regional councils (*see* COUNCIL IN THE MARCHES OF WALES; COUNCIL OF THE NORTH). He and successors managed finances through the chamber. *See also* DOMESDAY BOOK; WESTMINSTER HALL; PARLIAMENT, ENGLAND 1230s TO 1520s; SECRETARY OF STATE; NEW MONARCHY, ENGLAND; COURTS, ENGLAND BEFORE 1660.

GOVERNMENT, ENGLAND WITH WALES 1509 TO 1642

Under King HENRY VIII (ruled 1509–47) central government became extensively dominated by chief ministers, more assertive, and more Council based. Thomas WOLSEY supervised government 1514–29 and pursued 'prerogative justice' by developing the Courts of STAR CHAMBER and REQUESTS, and the COUNCIL IN THE MARCHES OF WALES and COUNCIL OF THE NORTH (so-called PREROGATIVE COURTS). Thomas CROMWELL directed government 1533–40, bestowing importance on the post of 'king's secretary' and utilizing a few advisers. After his fall they became the PRIVY COUNCIL, which remained powerful until the 1640s. Cromwell also created (1536) the Court of Augmentations for revenues from the DISSOLUTION OF RELIGIOUS HOUSES. (Courts of First Fruits and Tenths, and WARDS, were also instituted in 1540, and of General Surveyors in 1542.) The royal chamber's financial administration dwindled. (Cromwell's initiatives have

been claimed as a TUDOR REVOLUTION IN GOVERNMENT.) Wales was annexed to England in 1535.

From 1540 there were usually two SECRETARIES OF STATE (ranking below the CHANCELLOR, TREASURER and keeper of the PRIVY SEAL). MARY I united the Courts of Augmentations (including from 1547 General Surveyors) and First Fruits and Tenths with the EXCHEQUER (1554).

The government of ELIZABETH I (ruled 1558–1603) was managed by William CECIL (to 1598) and Robert CECIL (continuing to 1612). Authority in localities was strengthened. By 1585 a nobleman was appointed for each SHIRE as LORD LIEUTENANT – effectively head of its government (with deputies). Ranking above the SHERIFF, he supervised JUSTICES OF THE PEACE and the MILITIA. The PARISH was used for civil purposes.

The use of government agencies (including courts) by JAMES VI/I (1603–25) and CHARLES I to raise money and exert authority contributed to conflict with Parliament (*see* IMPOSITIONS; SHIP MONEY; PETITION OF RIGHT; CHARLES I, PERSONAL RULE). In 1641 Parliament compelled Charles to accept abolition of the Courts of Star Chamber, the Marches and the North (and High Commission).

GOVERNMENT, ENGLAND WITH WALES 1642 TO 1707

During the First CIVIL WAR (1642–6), King CHARLES I retained traditional offices and departments when possible, while Parliament operated mainly through committees (e.g., county committees, superseding JUSTICES OF THE PEACE or JPs) and treasuries. Warfare required greater tax raising: from 1642 Parliament levied 'assessments' (regular payments from individuals), and from 1643 EXCISE (tax on commodities). Royalists did likewise.

Following the abolition of monarchy (1649), various forms of governance were tried (*see* COMMONWEALTH AND PROTECTORATE), with the NEW MODEL ARMY remaining influential. Some traditional elements were reinstated (e.g., JPs, replacing county committees; national Exchequer, 1654). But an effective structure proved elusive.

In 1660 monarchical government was restored, although without most PREROGATIVE COURTS and the Court of WARDS AND LIVERIES. The CHANCELLOR, TREASURER, and SECRETARIES OF STATE remained important officers. CHARLES II also maintained an ARMY. Government was funded mainly by revenues awarded by Parliament. Lord lieutenants were reappointed for counties.

Rulers determined policies, working with individuals or groups who could obtain parliamentary funding (e.g., earl of DANBY). The PRIVY COUNCIL became less important, although significant committees were formed. Financial difficulties and warfare had influential consequences. Crucially, from 1667 (during the Second ANGLO-DUTCH WAR) the Treasury was developed as a department separate from the EXCHEQUER, controlling revenues and expenditures (so-called 'Treasury supremacy').

After the fall of JAMES VII/II (1688), William III was reliant on Parliament for funding the War of the GRAND ALLIANCE (1689–97). The war also resulted in scrutiny of government expenditure by the House of Commons (*see* PUBLIC ACCOUNTS, COMMISSIONS OF), and long-term borrowing authorized by Parliament (*see* FINANCIAL REVOLUTION). From 1697 civil and military expenditure were distinguished (*see* CIVIL LIST). Government's greater dependence on Parliament was reinforced by the War of the SPANISH SUCCESSION (1702–13). Anne (1702–14) governed partly through a Cabinet-council influenced by LORDS OF THE COMMITTEE. *See also* STOP OF THE EXCHEQUER; GLORIOUS REVOLUTION; CUSTOMS, ENGLAND, WALES AND GREAT BRITAIN FROM 1689; FISCAL–MILITARY STATE; CABINET.

GOVERNMENT, GREAT BRITAIN 1707 TO LATER 18TH CENTURY
After 1707 Scotland was soon brought under government from England (*see* GOVERNMENT, SCOTLAND FROM 1707). Britain's first Hanoverian ruler, King GEORGE I (1714–27), initially determined policy and selected ministers (with statutory limitations; *see* SETTLEMENT, ACT OF). He replaced the TREASURER with a Treasury Board or commission ('lords of the Treasury'), an arrangement that proved permanent. Like ANNE, George held Cabinet-council meetings, with leading ministers also meeting separately as an inner Cabinet (first lord of the Treasury, two SECRETARIES OF STATE, lord CHANCELLOR, president of the Council). His choice of ministers was constrained by requiring support from Parliament, especially funding. It remained essential to have a leading minister in the House of Commons, usually the first lord of the Treasury, though most ministers were peers.

Robert WALPOLE, as first lord 1721–42, extensively shifted policy making to the inner CABINET, under his chairmanship; he is considered Britain's first PRIME MINISTER. He and successors collaborated with the king in agreeing policy (sometimes ratified by the outer Cabinet), recommending ministers and obtaining Commons support. However, GEORGE III (from 1760) extensively reasserted royal powers.

The government's main concerns were diplomacy, colonial affairs and sometimes warfare; NATIONAL DEBT management and taxation; the NAVY and ARMY; and (especially to 1745) security of the régime against JACOBITISM. As revenues expanded, government collectors increased (to 14,300 revenue staff in 1782); the Excise and Customs Boards were the largest departments. In 1782 the secretaryships were reorganized, creating the Foreign and Home Offices, the latter handling domestic, colonial and war-related business.

After 1707 county government was developed in Scotland (*see* LOCAL GOVERNMENTAL STRUCTURES, SCOTLAND). Elsewhere local government became more active, with local élites obtaining authorization for administrative bodies from Parliament. For example, TURNPIKE TRUSTS were formed for road maintenance and improvement, and improvement commissions were established in towns (*see* IMPROVEMENT ACTS). *See also* TRADE, BOARD OF; BRITISH EMPIRE, GOVERNMENT OF; FISCAL–MILITARY STATE.

GOVERNMENT, GREAT BRITAIN LATER 18TH–LATER 19TH CENTURIES
The PRIME MINISTER remained central, based on support in PARLIAMENT, authority in the CABINET and control of the Treasury. By the 1840s the monarch lost political power. The Cabinet included 11–14 other ministers, principally the lord CHANCELLOR, foreign secretary, and home secretary. Ministers' departments were small (e.g., 24 administrative staff at Foreign Office, 1807). Revenue offices (e.g., Customs, Excise) had large staffs (20,000 in 1815). After union with Ireland (1801), parts of its government were integrated (*see* GOVERNMENT, IRELAND, 19TH–20TH CENTURIES).

Most central government expenditure (65% in 1880) serviced the NATIONAL DEBT and military requirements, despite the infrequency of major wars after 1815. Home security, diplomacy, and colonial affairs and defence remained important; conditions in Ireland were a recurrent concern.

Although governments were based on POLITICAL PARTIES in Parliament, attitudes to policy were similar (e.g., acceptance of FREE TRADE to promote prosperity). Government activity was broadened by changing economic and social conditions, though policymakers sought to minimize intervention and preferred collaboration with local élites (the influence of LAISSEZ-FAIRE). Local administration tended to expand more than central bureaucracy. Campaigning about conditions in textile factories, resulting from the INDUSTRIAL REVOLUTION, produced legislation from 1802 and oversight by government inspectors from 1833 (*see* FACTORY LEGISLATION). Reform of poor relief by the 1834 POOR LAW AMENDMENT ACT introduced locally elected boards operating under central supervision. From 1848 similar arrangements tackled insanitary conditions in towns (*see* PUBLIC HEALTH ACTS). Central government also instigated paid local POLICE forces.

Governments also reformed institutions, sometimes reflecting critical ideological precepts (e.g., by PHILOSOPHIC RADICALS). Instances included: LEGAL REFORMS (1820s); PARLIAMENTARY REFORM; TOWN GOVERNMENT; Church reforms (*see* ECCLESIASTICAL COMMISSIONERS); UNIVERSITY REFORM; GRAMMAR AND PUBLIC SCHOOLS.

Outside corporate towns, JUSTICES OF THE PEACE dominated local government until 1889. The functions of PARISHES were eroded by new local authorities. *See also* ECONOMICAL REFORM; KINGSHIP AND MONARCHY, ENGLAND AND GREAT BRITAIN FROM 1680s; CIVIL SERVICE; POST OFFICE; BRITISH EMPIRE, GOVERNMENT OF.

GOVERNMENT, GREAT BRITAIN FROM LATER 19TH CENTURY

Organization and purposes began to change significantly. Many towns already had elected authorities which provided utilities such as water supply, SEWERAGE and GAS (so-called 'municipal socialism'); elected school boards existed throughout Scotland and in parts of England and Wales. In response to public demands, other elected local councils were introduced (1880s–90s), with county councils receiving powers from JUSTICES OF THE PEACE. Theorists advocated greater activity concerning social problems (*see* NEW LIBERALISM). In 1902 most elementary education in England and Wales was assigned to local government (*see* BALFOUR EDUCATION ACT); after 1906 Liberal governments implemented radical social changes throughout the UK (e.g., old-age PENSIONS, NATIONAL INSURANCE).

The scale of WORLD WAR I (1914–18) required unprecedented controls over the economy (e.g., COAL INDUSTRY, RAILWAYS) and society (e.g., CONSCRIPTION, RATIONING). Prime Minister David LLOYD GEORGE (from 1916) improved executive efficiency with new ministries, a small WAR CABINET and Cabinet secretariat (this last permanent). Controls were reduced post-war, and devolved government was established (1921) in NORTHERN IRELAND (southern Ireland became independent). Assertive government continued (e.g., COUNCIL HOUSING, ELECTRICITY), but responses to the GREAT DEPRESSION (1930s) were limited.

During WORLD WAR II (1939–45) central government again obtained extensive powers; sustainment of morale included plans and legislation for social reform (e.g., 'Beveridge Report', BUTLER EDUCATION ACT, family allowances). The post-war Labour government (1945–51) nationalized major industries (e.g., coal, electricity, railways) and created a WELFARE STATE (e.g., free healthcare), expanding bureaucratic control. DECOLONIZATION (1940s–60s) reduced imperial responsibilities.

Government's expanded roles were widely accepted (*see* BUTSKELLISM) until they seemed responsible for fostering inefficiency (1970s; *see* THATCHERISM): nationalized industries were privatized in the 1980s–90s. Governments were established in Wales and Scotland by DEVOLUTION (1999). As DE-INDUSTRIALIZATION changed the economy, the WOMEN'S MOVEMENT became influential, and large-scale immigration created a MULTICULTURAL SOCIETY, governments focused more on regulating social relations (e.g., 2010 Equality Act).

GOVERNMENT, IRELAND 12TH–MID 17TH CENTURIES

The head of English government and military forces (from 1170s) was the king's representative, the CHIEF GOVERNOR (variously designated), who was advised by a COUNCIL. Development of government involved replication of English offices and posts. An EXCHEQUER handled ROYAL REVENUES by 1185 (housed after 1204 in the new DUBLIN Castle; *see* JOHN AND IRELAND); by 1212 it was headed by a treasurer. A CHANCERY (writing office) was created in 1232 under a chancellor (also represented at the Exchequer). By 1250 an escheator managed estates temporarily in royal possession (belonging to underage wards or vacant bishoprics). At local level, government operated through SHIRES (territories administered by SHERIFFS) and liberties (areas held by Anglo-Irish magnates). Courts administering COMMON LAW developed from the early 13th century (*see* COURTS, IRELAND).

The recapture of land by Gaelic kings from the 13th century reduced the area administered by the Dublin government, confining it by the mid 15th century mainly to parts of E Ireland (the PALE and WEXFORD areas). Between the 1450s and 1534 control of government was frequently delegated to Anglo-Irish magnates (*see* KILDARE ASCENDANCY).

The reassertion of English authority in the 16th–early 17th centuries expanded administration throughout Ireland (*see* IRELAND, ENGLISH CONQUEST, 16TH CENTURY). Shires (or 'counties') were instituted W of the PALE from 1557 (*see* LEIX-OFFALY PLANTATION). The appointment of regional presidents for CONNACHT (W Ireland, 1569) and MUNSTER (S, 1570) was followed by the institution of shire administration and judicial activity (*see* PRESIDENCIES, IRELAND). Administration was extended to ULSTER (N Ireland) in the early 17th century. Central authority was strengthened by a PRIVY COUNCIL (1520), Court of CASTLE CHAMBER (1571), and Court of WARDS AND LIVERIES (1622). Following the IRISH WARS of the 1640s, English Parliamentary officers introduced new structures (*see* COMMONWEALTH AND PROTECTORATE, IRELAND). *See also* JUSTICES OF THE PEACE, IRELAND.

GOVERNMENT, IRELAND MID 17TH–18TH CENTURIES

From 1654 the Protectorate regime extensively restored earlier organization (e.g., sheriffs, JUSTICES OF THE PEACE, assize courts). After the RESTORATION of the monarchy (1660), King CHARLES II conceded formal abolition of the disliked Courts of CASTLE CHAMBER and WARDS AND LIVERIES (1662), though the Munster and Connacht PRESIDENCIES were briefly reinstated (abolished 1672). A board of revenue commissioners was established (1662) to supervise CUSTOMS and EXCISE revenues.

The CHIEF GOVERNOR (usually styled 'lord lieutenant') remained head of government and armed forces (assisted by the PRIVY COUNCIL), though in the 18th century he became more accountable to the British PRIME MINISTER than the king. From the 1690s he had to obtain regular revenue grants from PARLIAMENT, mainly to fund the ARMY, through exercising patronage (*see* UNDERTAKERS). Unlike in Great Britain, central government remained largely separate from the legislature. (Many senior officers were Englishmen.) From 1777 the office of the governor's secretary expanded and came to instruct other departments (*see* CHIEF SECRETARY FOR IRELAND).

From 1682, after the 'farming' (delegated private collection) of customs and excise revenues collapsed, collection was managed by the revenue commissioners who were accountable to the English (later British) Treasury. Their departments became a major section of central government, with employees throughout Ireland. They raised three-fifths of total income, and from 1791 operated from Dublin's new Custom House. Other extensions of government included a Stamp Office (1773), Lottery Office (1782) and Post Office (1784).

Agencies were also created to promote economic development, notably the Linen Board (1711–1828) and commissioners for improving inland navigation (1758–87). Concern about efficiency resulted in the appointment of supervisory commissioners of accounts (1761) and Treasury commissioners (1795). Civil management departments were also developed for the Army (*see* ARMY, ENGLISH AND BRITISH, IN IRELAND). *See also* ROYAL REVENUES, IRELAND.

GOVERNMENT, IRELAND 19TH–20TH CENTURIES

After the UNION OF IRELAND AND GREAT BRITAIN (1801), Britain increased control. The CHIEF SECRETARY FOR IRELAND, a British government minister and spokesman in the UK Parliament, supervised policy. Financial and other aspects of administration were integrated with British government, including Army financial administration (by 1820s), the Treasury section of the Exchequer (1817; *see* EXCHEQUER, IRELAND, ABOLITION OF), customs and excise (1823), Stamp Office (1827) and Post Office (1831).

The lord lieutenant was retained despite abolition of the Irish Parliament (*see* CHIEF GOVERNOR, IRELAND). State activity within Ireland was expanded to encompass peace keeping, improvement of social conditions, and reduction of religious-based privilege (*see* PROTESTANT ASCENDANCY). Administration was often supervised by boards of commissioners and local inspectors.

Central policing was developed from 1814 (*see* POLICE, IRELAND), together with a system of RESIDENT MAGISTRATES. Economic development was facilitated through a Drainage Commission (1809–13), Fishery Board (1819–30) and Board of WORKS (1831–1922). A Board of Education implemented NATIONAL EDUCATION from 1831, and an Ecclesiastical Commission undertook reform in the

Church of IRELAND. Poor relief was introduced under the Poor Law Commission for England and Wales but transferred to an Irish Commission in 1847 (*see* POOR RELIEF, IRELAND). Further Church reform began in 1868 (*see* DISESTABLISHMENT, CHURCH OF IRELAND), and from 1872 a Local Government Board supervised local government, poor relief and public health.

More agencies were created for particular concerns, including the Intermediate Education Board (1878) for secondary education, the Land Commission (1881) for LAND REFORM LEGISLATION, the CONGESTED DISTRICTS BOARD (1891–1923) for impoverished areas, the Department of Agriculture and Technical Instruction (1899) for the rural economy, and the Irish National Health Commission (1912) for health and unemployment insurance. The British government surrendered authority in southern Ireland on 16 Jan. 1922 (*see* IRISH FREE STATE, FOUNDING OF). *See also* CIVIL SERVICE, IRELAND.

GOVERNMENT, NORTHERN IRELAND

In 1920 the UK Parliament authorized a government for six counties, empowering the local PARLIAMENT to create ministries, and the governor of Ireland to appoint ministers (*see* GOVERNMENT OF IRELAND ACT, 1920). Ministers formed an Executive Committee of the Irish Privy Council but in practice were called a Cabinet and were answerable to the Northern Ireland Parliament. (Northern Ireland had its own governor and Privy Council from Dec. 1922.)

On 7 June 1921 a Department of the Prime Minister and six ministries (Finance, Home Affairs, Labour, Education, Agriculture, Commerce) were announced. Powers were transferred between Nov. 1921 and Feb. 1922. Taxation remained mainly under the British government. Most ministers were Unionists.

Additional ministries were created for new concerns: Public Security (1940–4, during WORLD WAR II), Health and Local Government (1944–65), Development (1965–74), Community Relations (1969–74).

In 1972, following the imposition of 'direct rule' (*see* TROUBLES), the British government created a Northern Ireland Office and vested government in a SECRETARY OF STATE who with under-secretaries supervised the Northern Ireland ministries. The governorship and Ministry of Home Affairs were abolished in 1973.

Devolved government, with coalitions controlling ministries (renamed 'departments' 1974), was reinstated in 1974 (Jan.–May) and in 1999 (suspended 2000, 2002–7, Jan. 2017–Jan. 2020). In 2015 there were 11 main departments. *See also* CIVIL SERVICE, NORTHERN IRELAND; EXECUTIVES, NORTHERN IRELAND.

GOVERNMENT, SCOTLAND BEFORE 1707

Before the 12th century authority was exercised mainly by

itinerant kings and MORMAERS, who received tribute in kind, generally through appointed officials (*see* THANAGE). Elaboration, along Anglo-Norman lines, began *c.*1120 when David (heir to King Alexander I) founded SHERIFF-DOMS in SE Scotland. As king, DAVID I (ruled 1124–53) introduced itinerant JUSTICIARS (usually MAGNATES) to deal with serious crimes, increased the number of sheriff-doms (basing many on thanages), and presumably started sheriffs' courts for lesser offences. His reorganized ROYAL HOUSEHOLD included a CHAMBERLAIN to receive revenues and supervise BURGHS, and a CHANCELLOR, whose 'chapel' or Chancery produced documents. By *c.*1250 the king conducted day-to-day administrative and judicial business with a COUNCIL and held COUNCILS-GENERAL and PARLIAMENTS. During royal MINORITIES, government was usually directed by 'guardians'. JAMES I transferred most financial responsibilities to a treasurer and comptroller (*c.*1426–8). From the 15th century EDINBURGH was increasingly the centre of government.

Most of the structure survived into the 18th century, but particularly from the 14th century kings granted royal rights to lords, placing perhaps a half of the kingdom outside the jurisdiction of royal law officers (*see* REGALITY). Personal royal involvement in justice declined following the foundation of the College of Justice (1532; *see* SESSION, COURT OF).

From 1603, when JAMES VI moved to England, the Privy Council (continuation of the Council) took on even more importance as the focus of daily government. James attempted, unsuccessfully, to institute JUSTICES OF THE PEACE (1609). The Privy Council was effectively replaced by a Committee of Estates in 1638–41 and 1643–51, and by English occupiers 1651–60, but was restored in 1661. From 1667 the treasurer's importance increased as taxation grew. *See also* COURTS, SCOTLAND; LOCAL GOVERNMENTAL STRUCTURES, SCOTLAND.

GOVERNMENT, SCOTLAND FROM 1707 The UNION OF ENGLAND AND SCOTLAND (1707) left Scotland's CHURCH ORGANIZATION and legal systems intact. Institutions of central government were quickly removed: the Privy COUNCIL was abolished in 1708, the post of SECRETARY OF STATE in 1709. (Some other offices survived as sinecures.) Scottish affairs were thereafter supervised mainly by the British SECRETARY OF STATE for the Northern Department, though a WESTMINSTER-based third secretaryship with responsibility for Scotland occasionally existed. In 1782, when the secretaryships were reorganized, responsibility passed to the new HOME OFFICE. Government attempted to secure loyalty within Scotland through 'management'; i.e., use of patronage (*see* ISLAY, EARL OF; MILTON, LORD; DUNDAS, HENRY).

As State intervention in social and economic matters increased in the 19th century, Scotland's different legal arrangements encouraged the formation of separate supervisory boards responsible to the Home Office; e.g., for poor relief (1845), lunacy (1857), and prisons (1877). In 1872 a Scotch Education Department was established, under the PRIVY COUNCIL. The disparate elements of Scottish government were brought together in 1885 under the SCOTTISH OFFICE, headed by a SECRETARY FOR SCOTLAND. The Office's responsibilities were gradually increased, and it was moved to EDINBURGH in 1939 and reorganized.

In 1999 responsibility for most aspects of domestic government in Scotland was devolved to a separate Scottish Executive (responsible to a Scottish PARLIAMENT), which took over most Scottish Office departments. *See also* LOCAL GOVERNMENTAL STRUCTURES, SCOTLAND; DEVOLUTION, SCOTLAND.

GOVERNMENT, SOUTHERN IRELAND On 1 April 1919 the Dáil Éireann ('Assembly of Ireland'), recently formed in DUBLIN by SINN FÉIN members of the UK Parliament, appointed a (republican) government (*see* PARLIAMENT, SOUTHERN IRELAND). Operating clandestinely, it tried to replace the existing government (e.g., organizing COURTS, obtaining adherence from local authorities). It continued under the Second and Third Dáils until Sept. 1922.

A government was also authorized for Southern Ireland by the UK Parliament's GOVERNMENT OF IRELAND ACT, 1920, but not implemented (*see* PARTITION OF IRELAND).

On 14 Jan. 1922, the House of Commons of Southern Ireland (Second Dáil and non-republican members) approved the recent ANGLO-IRISH TREATY and constituted a 'provisional government' for the IRISH FREE STATE (IFS) chaired by Michael COLLINS. It received authority on 16 Jan. For nine months the IFS had two governments, with some common members.

The 1922 CONSTITUTION prescribed an Executive Council of president and ministers (all Dáil members). The Dáil nominated the president, and he nominated ministers for Dáil approval. There could be additional 'extern' ministers, who were not necessarily Dáil members (discontinued 1927). The president and ministers were confirmed by the governor-general. The Ministers and Secretaries Act of 1924 defined a structure of 11 departments.

When the governor-general's powers were removed in 1936, his executive authority was vested in the Executive Council, and the Dáil elected the chairman, and he appointed ministers (*see* ABDICATION CRISIS AND IRISH FREE STATE). The 1937 constitution renamed the chairman as 'taoiseach' (nominated by the Dáil, appointed by the State president), and stipulated an executive government of 7–15 members (including the taoiseach, who nominated other ministers). Though ministers' responsibilities and titles were subsequently changed, the basic structure continued in the 21st century.

GOVERNMENT OF IRELAND ACT, 1920 Legislation by the UK Parliament (passed 23 Dec. 1920) which replaced the 1914 Home Rule Act. It enacted HOME RULE in Ireland by providing for: (a) two jurisdictions, Northern Ireland (six counties) and Southern Ireland (26 counties), each with a two-chamber Parliament and government; (b) a Council of Ireland through which Ireland could eventually be reunited.

The northern province was quickly established (*see* NORTHERN IRELAND), but SINN FÉIN rejected the Act and attempted to achieve an all-Ireland republic. The Act was superseded partly by the ANGLO-IRISH TREATY of 1921 and other legislation. It was repealed under the BELFAST AGREEMENT (1998). *See also* IRISH FREE STATE, FOUNDING OF.

GOVERNOR, IRELAND *see* CHIEF GOVERNOR, IRELAND

GOWRIE CONSPIRACY An incident when King JAMES VI of Scotland was lured on 5 Aug. 1600 to Alexander Ruthven's house in Perth (C Scotland). During a fight Alexander and his brother John Ruthven, (3rd) earl of Gowrie, were killed. The 'conspiracy' was possibly an attempt to seize James, or James's revenge for the RUTHVEN RAID (organized by the Gowries' father).

GRACES, IRELAND Concessions ('graces') offered by King CHARLES I in the 1620s in return for taxes (so he could redirect English funds from Ireland for expenditure on foreign policy). They attracted support from (Catholic) OLD ENGLISH, who sought to improve their status, but (Protestant) NEW ENGLISH resisted concessions to Catholics. Twenty-six Graces offered in Sept. 1626 were declined; 51 offered in May 1628 (after negotiations) were unadopted (Parliament failed to meet).

In July 1634 Viscount Wentworth, the chief governor, obtained subsidies from Parliament by implying that the 51 Graces would be enacted. But in Nov. he withheld two important Graces (extending the English Statute of Limitations to Ireland, guaranteeing land titles in CONNACHT), provoking Catholics to reject the rest. Graces were solicited until the 1640s. *See also* WENTWORTH, THOMAS, AND IRELAND.

GRAFTON, 3RD DUKE OF (b. 28 Sept. 1735 in England; d. 14 March 1811 at Euston, Suffolk, England, aged 75). Augustus Fitzroy, a WHIG, was elected an MP in 1756 and succeeded as duke in 1757. He served as SECRETARY OF STATE (northern) in the ministry of the marquess of ROCKINGHAM (1765–6), and became first lord of the Treasury in the ministry of William PITT (1766).

From 1767, when Pitt fell ill, Grafton effectively led the ministry. (Pitt resigned in 1768.) He handled the WILKES AFFAIR and early stages of the American crisis, but was violently attacked in the Letters of JUNIUS. Following growing divisions, Grafton resigned in Jan. 1770.

Grafton served as lord PRIVY SEAL in Lord NORTH's administration from 1771, resigning in 1775 because he preferred conciliation of the American colonies (*see* AMERICAN INDEPENDENCE, ORIGINS OF). He was again lord privy seal in the ministries of Rockingham (1782) and the earl of SHELBURNE (1782–3). After retiring he wrote religious tracts.

GRAHAM, JOHN, OF CLAVERHOUSE (b. *c.*1648 in Scotland; d. 27 July 1689 at Killiecrankie Pass, near Pitlochry, C Scotland, aged about 41). Previously a mercenary in Continental Europe, Graham commanded government troops against COVENANTERS during the RISING OF 1679. He was defeated at Drumclog (1 June) but contributed to victory at BOTHWELL BRIG (22 June). In 1682–5 he again suppressed Covenanters, who called him 'Bluidy Clavers'. He was created Viscount Dundee in 1688.

In 1689, following the flight of King JAMES VII/II, the conservative Dundee attended Scotland's CONVENTION PARLIAMENT. Dismayed at its hostility to James, he withdrew (18 March) and was declared a rebel (30 March), making him one of Scotland's first Jacobites. Government supporters pursued Dundee into the HIGHLANDS. In July, supported by new troops, he defeated a government army at KILLIECRANKIE but died from gunshot. *See also* GLORIOUS REVOLUTION, SCOTLAND; JACOBITISM, IMPACT ON BRITISH POLITICS.

GRAHAM, PATRICK (fl. from 1457; d. 1478 at Loch Leven, Fife, E Scotland). Bishop of Brechin from 1464, Graham was moved to ST ANDREWS in 1465, succeeding his uncle James KENNEDY. In 1472, in Rome, he obtained papal bulls making St Andrews an archbishopric with authority over other Scottish bishops (to their and King JAMES III's anger). Back in Scotland by 1474, he suffered a mental breakdown (*c.*1475), and was tried, deprived (9 Jan. 1478) and imprisoned. *See also* CHURCH ORGANIZATION, NORTH BRITAIN AND SCOTLAND BEFORE THE REFORMATION.

GRAMMAR AND PUBLIC SCHOOLS, REFORM OF, ENGLAND AND WALES In the early 19th century RADICALS criticized schools for outdated curricula (based on classical languages) and decay (misuse of endowments, lack of pupils). Developments at Rugby School (Warwickshire) from 1828, emphasizing discipline and character, began a revitalization (*see* ARNOLD, THOMAS), including emphasis on sport. It was strengthened by the foundation of new public schools (e.g., Marlborough College, 1843).

Nine public schools deemed 'the chief nurseries of our statesmen' (including Eton and Winchester) were reformed by the Public Schools Act of 1868, implementing recommendations of the Clarendon Commission. Governing bodies were reorganized, and scholarships awarded by examination. Other schools were reformed by the Endowed Schools Act of 1869, following the Taunton Commission. It reorganized endowments and increased provision for girls. Schools were encouraged to broaden curricula (e.g., to include science). The new schools and reforms strengthened educational provision for the upper and middle classes. *See also* GIRLS' AND WOMEN'S EDUCATION, BRITAIN; SOCIAL STRUCTURE, ENGLAND FROM LATER 18TH CENTURY.

GRAMMAR SCHOOL A type of post-elementary school concerned primarily with teaching the Latin language. In English towns there were such schools, for boys, from the 11th century, under Church control. By 1300 they took varied forms, including monastic schools for poor and fee-paying boys, and schools attached to major parish churches. From 1380 patrons endowed teaching posts or schools. Over 100 endowed schools were founded before 1530, among them WINCHESTER (1381) and Eton (1440). From the 18th century the larger, prestigious schools were called 'public schools'. Grammar schools were founded in many Scottish towns by the 15th century, and in Wales and Ireland from the 16th century. Girls' grammar schools were started from the mid 19th century.

From 1902 Local Education Authorities throughout Great Britain founded grammar schools or funded places at older ones (*see* BALFOUR EDUCATION ACT, BUTLER EDUCATION ACT). The majority were closed from the late 1960s (*see* COMPREHENSIVE EDUCATION). Many pre-1902 schools survived as fee-paying INDEPENDENT SCHOOLS.

GRAND ALLIANCE, WAR OF THE War by allied European powers against French expansion, 1689–97. The allies were led by William of Orange, stadholder (lieutenant) of the Dutch Republic, France by King Louis XIV.

In Sept. 1688 France invaded the Rhineland Palatinate (in Germany). William was already planning intervention in England; in 1689 he became joint ruler with his wife (*see* GLORIOUS REVOLUTION). Though this prevented England from supporting France, large English and Dutch forces were tied up in Ireland 1689–91, where former English king JAMES VII/II tried to re-establish himself with French support (*see* WILLIAMITE WAR). Meanwhile in May 1689 the Dutch allied with the Habsburg Empire, and were joined in 1689–90 by England, several German states, and Spain.

In 1692 an English fleet prevented a French invasion of England by defeating a French fleet at La Hogue, off N France (19–24 May). In 1694–5 another English fleet saved Barcelona (Spain) from capture by France. A brutal war of raid and reprisal was begun between English and French colonists (and their respective native American allies) in NE America.

William campaigned in Continental Europe from 1690, his army including English troops. After difficult years he recaptured the important centre of Namur in the Spanish Netherlands in 1695. By now the French were concerned about having scope to secure a French successor in Spain, and agreed to make peace. The treaty of Rijswijk, 1697, restored most captured territories.

In England the war effort was supported by Whig leaders (*see* WHIG JUNTO). The financial requirements helped to stimulate the FINANCIAL REVOLUTION, including creation of the NATIONAL DEBT (1693) and foundation of the BANK OF ENGLAND (1694). *See also* ORFORD, EARL OF; FRANCE, ENGLISH AND BRITISH RELATIONS WITH; SPANISH SUCCESSION, WAR OF THE.

GRAND REMONSTRANCE In England, the address presented by the House of Commons to King Charles I on 1 Dec. 1641. It attacked abuses of 1625–40, claiming there was a plot to subvert 'the fundamental laws and principles of government' and promote ARMINIANISM (*see* CHARLES I, PERSONAL RULE). It asked Charles to appoint only councillors approved by Parliament, to exclude bishops from Parliament, and to abolish some Church ceremonies. Charles's reply, published 23 Dec., rejected or evaded the Commons' demands. *See also* LONG PARLIAMENT.

GRAND TOUR A tour across Continental Europe (chiefly to France and Italy but also Switzerland, Germany and Spain) undertaken by young wealthy men, mainly from England, to complete their cultural education. Tours were made from the late 16th century to the 1830s, but their heyday was the late 17th and 18th centuries. Travellers acquired paintings and sculpture, experienced foreign regimes, worship and culture, and enjoyed sexual adventures.

GRANITA ACCORD In Great Britain, a private oral agreement made at the Granita restaurant in Islington, LONDON, on 31 May 1994, by the prominent LABOUR PARTY MPs Tony BLAIR and Gordon BROWN, following the sudden death of Party leader John SMITH. Blair obtained Brown's support for his leadership candidacy, and agreed, if elected, to pursue 'fairness' as the Party's policy priority. He had already accepted that Brown would be chancellor of the Exchequer in a future Labour government, with extensive power over domestic policy. It was later alleged (though disputed) that Blair envisaged retiring after two terms as prime minister in favour of Brown.

GRANT-MAINTAINED SCHOOL A type of State-funded school introduced in England and Wales by the (Conservatives') 1988 Education Reform Act, intended to weaken control by Local Education Authorities (LEAs). Existing schools became entitled to 'opt out' of LEA control and receive funding directly from central government. New schools could also be founded. Grant-maintained schools received considerable control over admissions, staffing and finance. Almost 1,200 were created, mostly secondary schools. Grant-maintained status was abolished by the Labour government in 1998, although its introduction of city academies in 2000 (later 'academies') created similar schools.

GRANVILLE, EARL see CARTERET, LORD

GRANVILLE, 2ND EARL (b. 11 May 1815 at London, England; d. 31 March 1891 at London, aged 75). British Liberal politician, known as Lord Leveson 1833–46.

Granville Leveson-Gower was elected as an MP in 1836 and held office under Viscount MELBOURNE, Lord John RUSSELL and the earl of ABERDEEN before leading the Liberals in the House of Lords (1855–91). Loyal to W.E. GLADSTONE, he served as colonial secretary (1868–70, 1886) and foreign secretary (1870–4, 1880–5). Though not an outstanding minister, he was a tactful intermediary between the prime minister and fractious colleagues.

GRATTAN, HENRY (b. June or July 1746 at Dublin, Ireland; d. 4 June 1820 at Marylebone, Middlesex, England, aged 73). A (Protestant) barrister, protégé of the earl of CHARLEMONT, and powerful orator, Grattan entered the Irish House of Commons in 1775 where he became leader of the PATRIOTS. After the Dungannon Convention (Feb. 1782), at which extra-parliamentary VOLUNTEERS called for legislative independence for Ireland, Grattan moved a declaration in the Commons (16 April). It persuaded the British government to grant independence (see CONSTITUTION OF 1782). Ireland's Parliament was thereafter popularly called 'Grattan's Parliament'.

During the 1780s–90s Grattan supported campaigns for parliamentary reform and Catholic relief. He retired in 1797, but returned briefly to the Commons in 1800 to oppose the intended UNION OF IRELAND AND GREAT BRITAIN. In 1805 he was elected to the UK Parliament where he campaigned for Catholic Emancipation until his death. See also PROTESTANT ASCENDANCY; CATHOLIC RELIEF AND EMANCIPATION, IRELAND.

GRAVAMINA (Latin, meaning 'grievances'). In England, a written statement of complaints presented by clergy to

the monarch. First presented in 1237 to King HENRY III, they were used in 1297 during negotiations with Edward I over taxation (see WINCHELSEY, ROBERT). It became customary to produce them at the opening of the southern Convocation (Church assembly). In the 1560s Puritan clergy used *gravamina* to seek changes to Church practices (see PURITANISM, ENGLAND). See also CHURCH, MEDIEVAL ENGLAND.

GREAT BRITAIN The longer name for the island of Britain, and name of the kingdom created by the union of ENGLAND (including Wales) and SCOTLAND, later incorporated in the UNITED KINGDOM.

'Great Britain' was used originally by authors writing in Greek or Latin to distinguish Britain from IRELAND or from Brittany in Continental Europe (see BRITAIN). After King JAMES VI of Scotland also became king of England he proclaimed himself 'king of Great Britain' (1604) as part of an attempted unification of the kingdoms (see UNION OF CROWNS, ENGLAND (WITH IRELAND) AND SCOTLAND). When England and Scotland were united in 1707, the new kingdom was officially called 'Great Britain' (see UNION OF ENGLAND AND SCOTLAND). The English PARLIAMENT at WESTMINSTER was expanded as the new kingdom's legislature, and Scotland was soon brought under a single British government (see GOVERNMENT, SCOTLAND FROM 1707). People from both countries participated in subsequent imperial expansion (see BRITISH EMPIRE). From the late 18th century, Britain experienced the world's first INDUSTRIAL REVOLUTION and rapid decline in the relative importance of AGRICULTURE.

After Great Britain was united with Ireland in 1801 (as the 'United Kingdom of Great Britain and Ireland'), a UK Parliament and government dealt with Britain within the context of the larger kingdom (e.g., legislating as considered necessary for the UK, Britain, or lesser jurisdictions). Government became more focused on Britain after NORTHERN IRELAND became self-governing (1921) and southern Ireland became independent (1922). The UK government's authority within Britain was reduced from 1999 by DEVOLUTION of government to Scotland and Wales.

GREAT CAUSE Term for the legal process (May 1291–17 Nov. 1292) that followed the death of MARGARET, 'THE MAID OF NORWAY', by which King EDWARD I of England and 104 auditors considered 13 claims to the vacant Scottish kingship. Edward required claimants to recognize his overlordship of Scotland. John BALLIOL was, correctly, selected. See also SCOTTISH–ENGLISH RELATIONS 1290 TO 1357.

GREAT CONTRACT In England, a scheme proposed in Feb. 1610 by the TREASURER, the earl of Salisbury (Robert CECIL), to solve the financial problems of King

JAMES VI/I. Parliament would pay off James's debts and grant taxes to meet regular expenditure. In return, some royal rights would be modified or abolished, e.g., purveyance (compulsory cheap provisioning). Opposition in the House of Commons and James's reluctance to abandon IMPOSITIONS caused the project to collapse (Nov.).

GREAT COUNCIL *see* COUNCILS, ENGLAND 1066 TO 1530s

GREAT DEPRESSION, IMPACT ON GREAT BRITAIN The worldwide economic depression, caused by collapse of trade following the 'Wall Street Crash' (fall of US stock market, Oct. 1929), produced the greatest economic crisis in Britain since the early 19th century. Conditions deteriorated until 1933, then slowly improved, but remained difficult until WORLD WAR II (1939–45).

The Depression increased already high unemployment. It peaked at 3.7 million in Sept. 1932. Struggling 'staple industries' fared worst: in 1932 unemployment reached 59% in SHIP BUILDING, 48% in iron and steel, 41% in COAL MINING, 31% in COTTON textiles. The worst affected areas were S Wales, C Scotland and N England.

Financial problems also brought about a NATIONAL GOVERNMENT (Aug. 1931), which abandoned the GOLD STANDARD and cut expenditure. The latter included a 'means test' (scrutiny of household income) of the long-term unemployed (Jan. 1932), which was especially resented (to 1940s). From 1932 protectionist tariffs were reintroduced, formally abandoning 'free trade'. *See also* KEYNES, J.M.; TARIFF REFORM; WELFARE STATE.

GREAT DEPRESSION, IMPACT ON IRELAND NORTHERN IRELAND probably fared worse, because its industry relied on the international economy. Unemployment rose from 19% of insured workers in 1923–30 (average) to 28% in 1932, reaching 29.5% in Feb. 1938. SHIP BUILDING was hit hard: employment at Harland and Wolff fell from 10,400 in 1930 to 1500 in 1932, though re-expanded from 1934 with new orders and through diversification (e.g., locomotive building). The smaller Workman Clark company closed in Jan. 1935 after orders ceased. Contraction of LINEN manufacturing continued an existing decline. (AGRICULTURE fared relatively well though incomes remained low.) The industrial situation generated protest: in 1932 an Unemployed Workers' Committee organized marches, and unemployed workers undertaking task work went on strike for increased relief payments (3–14 Oct.). A demonstration in BELFAST on 11 Oct. resulted in deaths and injuries.

In SOUTHERN IRELAND, the government supported dairy products and grain (1932–3) to counter declining world prices, and government-sponsored import substitution (to encourage self-sufficiency) modestly increased industrial employment. Because of the Depression, the main destination of EMIGRATION changed from the USA to Great Britain. The country was affected primarily by the ECONOMIC WAR (1932–8) provoked by Éamon de Valera. For example, cattle exports fell 1931–4 by almost two-thirds in value.

GREAT EXHIBITION In England, an international exhibition of craftwork and industrial products at Hyde Park, London, 1 May–15 Oct. 1851, organized partly by Prince ALBERT. Over 14,000 exhibits were displayed in the 'Crystal Palace', a prefabricated building of iron and glass designed by Joseph Paxton. Visited by 6 million people, many of whom travelled by RAILWAY, the exhibition testified to Great Britain's position as a leading industrial power (*see* INDUSTRIAL REVOLUTION).

GREAT FAMINE Name for the disastrous famine in Ireland of 1845–9. Staple potato crops were repeatedly devastated by 'potato blight', causing widespread starvation. The British government of Sir Robert PEEL initially funded provision of meal and employment schemes. Its successor, led by Lord John RUSSELL (from June 1846), added soup kitchens (1847). But in 1847 Russell transferred responsibility for relief to the Irish poor law system which proved inadequate.

Around 1.1 million people died (out of 8.5. million), and over 1.3 million people emigrated between 1846 and 1852 (double the previous level of outflow). The authorities' alleged callousness radicalized many Irish nationalists. *See also* TREVELYAN, CHARLES; FAMINES, IRELAND; POPULATION, IRELAND; POOR RELIEF, IRELAND; EMIGRATION FROM IRELAND.

GREAT FIRE OF LONDON In 1666, a fire which destroyed England's commercial capital. It burnt from 2 to 7 Sept., destroying 13,200 houses and 87 churches, including St Paul's Cathedral, though only nine people were killed. Most houses were replaced by 1672; church rebuilding continued into the 18th century. Although the fire began accidentally in a bakery, Roman Catholics were blamed. *See also* GREAT PLAGUE; WREN, CHRISTOPHER.

GREAT GAME Term coined by Arthur Conolly (1807–42) and popularized by Rudyard KIPLING to describe the rivalry in C Asia between the British and Russian Empires during the 19th and early 20th centuries. Russian expansion threatened the security and stability of INDIA. In response, Great Britain tried to extend India's frontier up to the NW mountain ranges, and to construct a zone of buffer states (e.g., Afghanistan, Tibet). British military officers were sent to the region to monitor Russian activities and recommend responses.

GREAT MATTER Term used for the attempt from 1527 by HENRY VIII of England and Ireland to obtain the annulment (declaration of invalidity) of his marriage to KATHERINE OF ARAGON, who had failed to produce a male heir, so he could remarry. Henry believed that God had punished him for breaking biblical law by marrying his brother's widow (see ARTHUR, PRINCE OF WALES). An annulment required overturning an earlier papal dispensation (exemption from ecclesiastical law) which had been needed for Henry's marriage. Pope Clement VII, under pressure from Emperor Charles V (Katherine's nephew), was reluctant to invalidate the earlier dispensation.

In 1529 Pope Clement appointed cardinals Thomas WOLSEY and Lorenzo Campeggio as a legatine commission to consider the case in England (court held in London, May–July). Campeggio adjourned the hearing without a decision. (As a result Wolsey fell from power.) To sway the Pope, Henry applied threatening pressure on the English Church; in 1531 he was recognized as its head by Convocation (see REFORMATION PARLIAMENT).

In 1533 Henry secretly married Anne BOLEYN (Jan.). Papal jurisdiction was terminated by the Act in Restraint of APPEALS (April), and the new archbishop of Canterbury, Thomas CRANMER, considered the case under Henry's authority. He declared Henry's first marriage invalid (23 May) and his second marriage valid (28 May). Anne Boleyn failed to produce a male heir. A third marriage was required. See also REFORMATION, ENGLAND/IRELAND; HENRY VIII, WIVES OF.

GREAT PLAGUE The last major outbreak of bubonic plague in England. LONDON was worst affected. The epidemic there began in April 1665, peaked in Sept., and petered out by autumn 1666, killing between 70,000 and 100,000 people. The Great Plague extensively disrupted economic activity and caused social unrest. Soon afterwards London was devastated by the GREAT FIRE. See also PLAGUE, ENGLAND.

GREAT REFORM ACT see PARLIAMENTARY REFORM

GREAT SCHISM Term for the division of the Catholic Church and European countries, 1378–1417, in allegiance to rival Popes. After the election of Urban VI (April 1378), some cardinals, dissatisfied with Urban for his authoritarian behaviour, elected another Pope, Clement VII (Sept.). Urban remained in Rome; Clement settled in Avignon, a papal territory in modern S France. Successors were elected for each.

The Council of Pisa (NW Italy) attempted to end the schism in 1409 by deposing the Popes and electing another. It failed because the 'deposed' Popes refused to withdraw, leaving three Popes. Another Council, at Constance (in modern SW Germany), was successful. The 'conciliar' Pope, John XXIII, fled (1415); the Roman Pope, Gregory XII, resigned (1415); and the Avignonese Pope, Benedict XIII, was deposed (1417). A new Pope, Martin V, was elected in 1417.

Because Clement VII was elected with French support, the English government – nominally at war with France – adhered to the Roman Popes until 1409, when it supported the Council of Pisa and transferred to the conciliar Pope (as did France). It also pushed for a solution at Constance. (England's authority covered Wales and Ireland.) Scotland, linked with France, supported the Avignonese Popes, and withheld obedience from Martin V until Oct. 1418.

Popes interfered in areas not professing adherence: Clement VII (Avignon) appointed Cardinal Walter Wardlaw as legate for Ireland alongside Scotland (1384), and appointed an archbishop of Tuam in Ireland; Roman popes attempted to appoint Englishmen to Scottish bishoprics. Popes also attracted support from dissidents; for example, in 1406 Welsh rebels expressed adherence to the Avignonese Pope. See also HUNDRED YEARS WAR; SCOTTISH–ENGLISH RELATIONS 1357–1603.

GREAT SESSIONS, COURT OF A superior royal law court in Wales. Following the English conquests of lands in native Wales in 1277 and 1282–3, the justiciar (or justice) of N Wales and justiciar of W (and SW) Wales each a held a Court of Great Sessions in his area. They dealt with criminal and civil cases under English COMMON LAW.

In 1543, under the UNION OF WALES WITH ENGLAND, a Court of Great Sessions was instigated throughout Wales (except MONMOUTHSHIRE), operating in four circuits of three SHIRES each and held in each county town twice a year for six days. Judges were usually English barristers. Business included debt, TENURE disputes, and murder. Cases were received from JUSTICES OF THE PEACE; civil suitors could appeal to the COUNCIL IN THE MARCHES OF WALES (until 1689).

The Court was abolished in 1830 when Wales was placed under the central courts at WESTMINSTER (England) and added to the English assize circuits. See also COURTS, WALES; COURTS, ENGLAND FROM 1660.

GREAT WAR see WORLD WAR I

GREECE, BRITISH RELATIONS WITH British sympathy for Greek liberation from the OTTOMAN EMPIRE (proclaimed 13 Jan. 1822) was tempered by official concern for the EASTERN QUESTION. The foreign secretary George CANNING determined to match intervention by RUSSIA and FRANCE: the three powers secured Greece's independence by destroying the Ottoman fleet at the battle of Navarino (20 Oct. 1827).

The Royal Navy then ensured effective British dominance over Greece, as exemplified by the PACIFICO INCIDENT (1850). Greek irredentism (expansionist ambition to include other Greek populations) was restrained by Anglo-French occupation of Piraeus (1854–7) and British blockades (1885, 1897).

Anglo-French intervention decided Greece's tortuous eventual entry into WORLD WAR I (1917) on the Allied side, before David LLOYD GEORGE encouraged the disastrous Greek occupation of Smyrna (in Ottoman-ruled Anatolia) in 1919.

A British guarantee (13 April 1939) led to joint military action in WORLD WAR II, but Greece was occupied by Germany (1941–4). Britain made strenuous efforts (1944–7) to prevent a communist takeover, and Greece joined the NORTH ATLANTIC TREATY ORGANIZATION in 1952. In the 1950s relations were soured by British refusal to permit the union of CYPRUS with Greece. (Cyprus became independent in 1960.) Britain maintained relations during military rule in Greece (1967–74). Following the 1974 Turkish invasion of northern Cyprus, Greece accused Britain of failing to uphold the 1960 Cyprus settlement. Relations have since been generally good, although Greece demands that the 'Elgin Marbles' (sculptures removed from Athens to Britain in 1801–12) be returned.

GREEN, T.H. (b. 7 April 1836 at Birkin, Yorkshire, England; d. 26 March 1882 at Oxford, Oxfordshire, England, aged 45). Thomas Hill Green was a tutor at Balliol College in OXFORD University from 1866 and a professor of moral philosophy from 1878. He argued that the moral goodness of individuals should ideally seek expression through aiding the well-being of society. A Liberal, he supported the TEMPERANCE MOVEMENT, admission of women to university, franchise extension and other causes. Through sermons, publications and pupils (e.g., H.H. ASQUITH, Charles GORE) he was influential in national life, providing a rationale for the State to promote social welfare. *See also* JOWETT, BENJAMIN; NEW LIBERALISM.

GREEN PARTY *see* ENVIRONMENTAL MOVEMENT

GREENSHIELDS' CASE A legal case affecting Scotland's position within Great Britain. In 1710 James Greenshields, a Scottish Episcopalian clergyman banned from preaching in Edinburgh, appealed to the British House of Lords after the Court of SESSION had refused to suspend the ban. The Lords overturned the Session's judgment, thereby establishing the Lords' status as an appeal court in civil matters following the 1707 UNION OF ENGLAND AND SCOTLAND. The case also led to the TOLERATION ACT and PATRONAGE ACT (both 1712). *See also* EPISCOPAL CHURCH IN SCOTLAND.

GREGORY, JAMES (b. Nov. 1638 at Drumoak, NE Scotland; d. Oct. 1675 at Edinburgh, SE Scotland, aged 36). Educated at ABERDEEN (Marischal College), Gregory moved to London in 1662. In 1663 he published *Optica Promota*, which described his idea of a 'reflecting telescope' (using mirrors rather than lenses to avoid distortion, as later constructed by Isaac NEWTON). Gregory visited Italy 1664–8 to improve his mathematics, and published outstanding advances in pure mathematics (1667, 1668). He was professor at mathematics at ST ANDREWS University (1668–74) and EDINBURGH (1674–5).

GRENADA An island and former British colony in the WEST INDIES. First colonized by France in 1650, Grenada was British 1762–79 and from 1783. The island developed a PLANTATION economy with slavery (until emancipation in 1834). Part of the Federation of the West Indies 1958–62, Grenada was granted internal self-government in 1967 and independence in 1974 (with the British monarch remaining head of State). Approx. population in 1921, 66,000; in 1973, 95,000. *See also* SLAVE TRADE, ENGLISH AND BRITISH INVOLVEMENT; PARIS, PEACE OF.

GRENVILLE, GEORGE (b. 14 Oct. 1712 at Wotton Underwood, Buckinghamshire, England; d. 13 Nov. 1770 at Piccadilly, Middlesex, England, aged 58). An MP from 1741, Grenville joined the opposition WHIGS known as COBHAM'S CUBS. After the fall of Robert WALPOLE (1742), he became lord of the Admiralty (1744) in the ministry of Henry PELHAM, then treasurer of the NAVY (1754) under the earl of NEWCASTLE. He was dismissed in 1755 for criticizing foreign policy.

Grenville served again as treasurer of the Navy from 1756 in the PITT–DEVONSHIRE ministry (resigned April 1757) and in the Pitt–Newcastle ministry of 1757–61. He remained in office after Pitt's resignation in 1761 and succeeded the earl of BUTE as (northern) SECRETARY OF STATE (May 1762), resigning to become first lord of the Admiralty (Oct.).

In 1763 Grenville succeeded Bute as first lord of the Treasury (PRIME MINISTER), though he was distrusted by King GEORGE III who continued to consult Bute. In 1764–5 Grenville's ministry introduced measures to raise money in the N American colonies to meet defence costs, notably the Stamp Act. Colonists protested fiercely (*see* AMERICAN INDEPENDENCE, ORIGINS OF). Grenville was dismissed in July 1765 (replaced by marquess of ROCKINGHAM). In opposition he defended the Stamp Act. *See also* GRENVILLE-TEMPLE, RICHARD; SEVEN YEARS WAR; GRENVILLE, LORD.

GRENVILLE, LORD (b. 25 Oct. 1759 at Wotton Underwood, Buckinghamshire, England; d. 12 Jan. 1834 at Dropmore, Buckinghamshire, aged 74). A son of the British prime minister George GRENVILLE (d. 1770), and cousin of

William PITT the Younger, William Grenville was an MP from 1782. In 1790 he was created Lord Grenville and became chief spokesman for Pitt's ministry in the House of Lords. He served as home secretary (1789–91) and foreign secretary (1791–1801). Fearful of influence from the FRENCH REVOLUTION, Grenville supported repressive legislation. He resigned with Pitt because of King GEORGE III's opposition to CATHOLIC EMANCIPATION.

In 1802 Grenville joined Charles James FOX in opposing the Peace of AMIENS with France, made by the ministry of Henry ADDINGTON. He refused to join Pitt in government again in 1804 because King George blocked the appointment of Fox. Grenville and Fox came to power in 1806, after Pitt's death, in the 'Ministry of All the Talents', with Grenville as PRIME MINISTER. The ministry abolished the slave trade in British possessions (25 March 1807). It resigned on 24 March because of the king's renewed opposition to Catholic Emancipation. Grenville continued as a Whig opposition leader until c.1812. See also SLAVE TRADE, ABOLITION OF.

GRENVILLE-TEMPLE, RICHARD (b. 26 Sept. 1711 at Westminster, Middlesex, England; d. 11 Sept. 1779 at Stowe, Buckinghamshire, England, aged 67). Brother of George GRENVILLE and an MP from 1734, Richard Grenville joined the opposition WHIGS known as COBHAM'S CUBS. He was an ally and brother-in-law of William PITT the Elder. Having changed his surname, he succeeded as 2nd Earl Temple in 1752.

Temple was appointed first lord of the Admiralty in the Pitt-Devonshire coalition (1756). Disliked by King GEORGE II, he was dismissed (April 1757) but returned to office as lord PRIVY SEAL (1759) in the Pitt-Newcastle ministry. He resigned with Pitt in 1761 and became an active opponent of the earl of BUTE, providing financial support to Bute's radical critic John WILKES. In 1766 he quarrelled with Pitt (now earl of Chatham). They were reconciled in 1768. Temple opposed the ministry of the duke of GRAFTON (1769–70).

GRESHAM COLLEGE In England, an academic institution founded by Sir Thomas Gresham (c.1518–79); inaugurated in 1597 in his house in LONDON, following his widow's death. Vested in the Corporation of London and Mercers' Company, Gresham College supported seven residential professors, who gave weekly lectures. Subjects included astronomy, geometry and physic (medicine). In the 17th century the college was important for research in natural philosophy (science) and dissemination of new ideas (see SCIENTIFIC REVOLUTION), and as home of the ROYAL SOCIETY (1660–1710).

Having survived the GREAT FIRE (1666), the college's building was demolished in 1768. The college then operated from various locations, and became independent in 1984. In the early 21st century ten part-time professors, and visiting professors, delivered over 130 public lectures annually.

GREY, 2ND EARL (b. 13 March 1764 at Falloden, Northumberland, England; d. 17 July 1845 at Howick, Northumberland, aged 81). Charles Grey became an MP in 1786. A FOXITE Whig, he helped to found the Society of the Friends of the People (1792) to campaign for fairer representation in Parliament. He criticized the war against revolutionary France (from 1793).

Grey served under Lord GRENVILLE as first lord of the Admiralty (1806) and foreign secretary (1806–7). After inheriting an earldom in 1807, he led Whig opposition in the House of Lords. His support for CATHOLIC EMANCIPATION caused King GEORGE III and GEORGE IV to resist his inclusion in government.

After the Tory government was defeated in the Commons in 1830, the new king, WILLIAM IV, appointed Grey as prime minister. He advocated PARLIAMENTARY REFORM to broaden support for the constitution and to separate the responsible middle class from Radicals. The 'Great Reform Act' became law in June 1832 after 18 months of controversy, a general election (May 1831), confrontation with the House of Lords, disputes with the king, and popular protest.

Grey's ministry also abolished SLAVERY within the British Empire (1833) and introduced the POOR LAW AMENDMENT ACT (1834) before Cabinet disagreements over Irish policy prompted his retirement (July 1834). See also FRENCH REVOLUTIONARY AND NAPOLEONIC WARS, BRITISH INVOLVEMENT.

GREY, EDWARD (b. 25 April 1862 at London, England; d. 7 Sept. 1933 at Fallodon, Northumberland, England, aged 71). Grey, a baronet, became a Liberal MP in 1885. He supported Lord ROSEBERY as under-secretary for foreign affairs 1892–5, and was foreign secretary from Dec. 1905 (under Henry CAMPBELL-BANNERMAN to 1908, then H.H. ASQUITH). Grey wanted Great Britain to draw closer to France and Russia, to counterbalance German power. In Jan. 1906 he authorized secret military talks with the French which transformed the ENTENTE CORDIALE. He negotiated the ANGLO-RUSSIAN CONVENTION (1907), and upheld France when threatened by Germany in the AGADIR CRISIS (1911). Subsequent efforts to improve Anglo-German relations were largely unavailing.

In 1914 Grey insisted on prompt intervention in WORLD WAR I, and continued in office until Dec. 1916 despite failing eyesight. (He was created Viscount Grey of Fallodon in July 1916.) An elusive personality, Grey professedly preferred fishing and bird watching to politics.

GREY, JANE (b. Oct. 1537 at Bradgate, Leicestershire, England; d. 12 Feb. 1554 at London, England, aged 16). Lady Jane Grey, a Protestant, was among the relatives designated by King EDWARD VI in 1553 as his successors (to exclude his half-sisters MARY, a Catholic, and ELIZABETH). On 21 May she was forcibly married to Guildford Dudley, fourth son of the duke of NORTHUMBERLAND, president of the Council. Probably under pressure from Northumberland, Edward nominated Jane as his successor (21 June).

Edward died on 6 July 1553; Jane was proclaimed queen on 10 July. But Mary rallied support and Jane was deposed (19 July). She pleaded guilty to TREASON (19 Nov.) and was executed following WYATT'S REBELLION.

GRIFFITH, ARTHUR (b. 31 March 1871 at Dublin, Ireland; d. 12 Aug. 1922 at Dublin, Irish Free State, aged 51). A journalist and nationalist, Griffith founded Cumann na nGaedheal ('Society of the Irish') in Sept. 1900, and the National Council (a nationalist forum) in 1903. In 1905 he propounded his policy, known as 'Sinn Féin' ('We Ourselves'), to the Council: independence under the British Crown (rather than 'Home Rule' under the UK Parliament), to be won by 'moral force' (rather than violence). (The Society became the Sinn Féin League in April 1907, which in 1908 merged with the Council as SINN FÉIN.) Griffith joined the Irish Volunteers (1913), and participated in gun running (1914), but played no part in the 1916 EASTER RISING. He was nevertheless imprisoned for complicity (May–Dec.).

On 20 Jan. 1919 Griffith was elected vice-president of the Dáil and republic proclaimed by Sinn Féin MPs in Dublin. After a period of British–Irish conflict, he led the delegation which negotiated the ANGLO-IRISH TREATY (Dec. 1921). On 9 Jan. 1922, following the Irish Dáil's acceptance of the Treaty, Griffith briefly succeeded Éamon DE VALERA as Dáil president. *See also* IRISH FREE STATE, FOUNDING OF.

GRIFFITHS, JAMES (b. 19 Sept. 1890 at Ammanford, Carmarthenshire, Wales; d. 7 Aug. 1975 at London, England, aged 84). A Welsh miners' leader 1925–36; Labour MP for Llanelli, Carmarthenshire, 1936–70. Griffiths served as a minister in the Department of National Insurance (1945–50), contributing to the formation of the WELFARE STATE, and in the Colonial Office (1950–1). He was deputy leader of the Labour Party (1955–9) and first secretary of state for Wales (1964–6; *see* WELSH OFFICE).

GRIMES GRAVES Large-scale flint mines near Thetford, Norfolk, E England. Shafts, galleries and flaking floors reflect periodic flint procurement and tool production in the later NEOLITHIC and Early BRONZE AGE (*c.*2500–1600 BC). Formal deposits in several shafts suggest the source was of ceremonial as well as practical importance for various groups. The area became a focus for settlement in the Later Bronze Age after mines had fallen out of use.

GRIMOND, JO (b. 29 July 1913 at St Andrews, Fife, Scotland; d. 24 Oct. 1993 at Kirkwall, Orkney, Scotland, aged 80). A Liberal MP 1950–83, Grimond was Party leader 1956–67. In 1957 there were only five Liberals in the UK of House of Commons, but Grimond revitalized the Party as a radical alternative to Labour, increasing its popular vote and seats (12 were won in the 1966 general election). In 1977 he opposed the LIB–LAB PACT. He was created Lord Grimond in 1983. *See also* LIBERAL PARTY.

GRINDAL, EDMUND (b. between 1516 and 1520 at St Bees, Cumberland, England; d. 6 July 1583 at Croydon, Surrey, England, aged in 60s). A scholar and clergyman who adopted reformed theology (late 1540s), Grindal became chaplain to King EDWARD VI (1551) but went into overseas exile (1554) under the Catholic MARY I. In 1559 he returned, following the accession of the Protestant ELIZABETH I, and reluctantly became bishop of London. Despite holding reservations about the ELIZABETHAN SETTLEMENT, Grindal sought in 1565–7 to enforce correct vestments among his clergy. As archbishop of YORK from 1570 he combated Catholic practices (e.g., by removing altars).

In 1575 Elizabeth, with recommendation from Lord Burghley (William CECIL), nominated Grindal as archbishop of CANTERBURY. In June 1576 she ordered him to act against 'prophesyings' (meetings of clergy to hear sermons on scripture). Grindal refused and was effectively suspended (May 1577). *See also* REFORMATION, ENGLAND; PURITANISM, ENGLAND.

GROSSETESTE, ROBERT (b. *c.*1170 in Suffolk, England; d. 9 Oct. 1253 at Buckden, Huntingdonshire, England, aged about 83). A clergyman, outstanding writer on scientific subjects (to *c.*1220) and theologian, Grosseteste taught at OXFORD University from 1225 and became its chancellor by 1230. From 1231 he was *lector* (teacher) to Oxford's recently founded house of Franciscan friars. As bishop of LINCOLN from 1235, Grosseteste sought high standards from secular clergy and religious houses. In 1250 he attacked Church corruption while visiting the Pope at Lyons (France). *See also* FRIARS, ENGLAND.

GROUNDNUT SCHEME A plan adopted by the British Labour government in 1946 to grow peanuts in TANGANYIKA (now Tanzania) to produce vegetable oil for cooking (in Britain). The soils proved unsuitable, and the scheme was abandoned in Jan. 1951 after expenditure of £49 million. It was attacked as an example of the potential wastefulness caused by economic planning.

GRUFFUDD AP CYNAN (b. *c*.1055 at Dublin, Ireland; d. 1137, probably in N Wales, aged about 82). King of GWYNEDD (NW Wales) 1090–1137.

Though Gruffudd was descended from RHODRI MAWR of Gwynedd, his mother was Irish-Scandinavian and he grew up in DUBLIN. He arrived in Wales in 1075 and, helped by the Norman ROBERT OF RHUDDLAN, challenged King Trahaearn ap Caradog of Gwynedd. He slew Trahaearn at MYNYDD CARN in 1081 but almost immediately afterwards was imprisoned by Hugh, 2nd earl of CHESTER. He was free – and king of Gwynedd – possibly by 1090, definitely by 1094 when he and Cadwgan ap Bleddyn of Powys (C Wales) rebelled against the Normans. This led to an attack on Anglesey (NW Wales) by Earl Hugh (1098), forcing Gruffudd to flee to Ireland; but he returned (1099) after the timely arrival of Magnus Barelegs of Norway.

In 1114 Gruffudd's growing power was a cause of King HENRY I of England's invasion of N Wales: Gruffudd was compelled to submit. In the 1120s and 1130s Gruffudd's sons (including his successor OWAIN GWYNEDD) gained territory on his behalf. Gruffudd was the only Welsh king commemorated in a medieval biography. *See also* ANGLO-WELSH RELATIONS, 6TH–13TH CENTURIES.

GRUFFUDD AP LLYWELYN (fl. from 1023; d. 5 Aug. 1063 in N Wales). King of GWYNEDD (NW Wales) 1039–63, and of DEHEUBARTH (SW Wales) 1055–63, whose raids into Herefordshire (W England), permitted Welsh recolonization beyond the earlier BORDER. Though probably not descended directly from RHODRI MAWR of Gwynedd, Gruffudd assumed the kingship of Gwynedd (and possibly of Powys, C Wales) in 1039. He finally gained control of Deheubarth in 1055, having slain GRUFFUDD AP RHYDDERCH. English attempts to curb him apparently failed, though he was compelled to swear loyalty to EDWARD THE CONFESSOR in 1056. On the death of his long-time ally Ælfgar, earl of Mercia (probably in 1062), Earl Harold renewed English pressure (*see* HAROLD II). In 1063 he invaded N Wales, prompting Gruffudd's men to kill him. Harold had Gruffudd's head sent to King Edward. *See also* ANGLO-WELSH RELATIONS, 6TH–13TH CENTURIES.

GRUFFUDD AP RHYDDERCH (b. *c*.1020; d. 1055, aged about 35). King of DEHEUBARTH (SW Wales) and MORGANNWG (S Wales) 1045–56. The son of King Rhydderch ab Iestyn (d. 1033), whose family probably originated in GWENT (SE Wales), Gruffudd first appears active *c*.1043, leading VIKINGS against Morgannwg (then ruled by Meurig ap Hywel).

In 1045 Gruffudd apparently asserted a claim to rule S Wales, which generated rivalry with GRUFFUDD AP LLYWELYN of GWYNEDD (NW Wales). The latter sought unsuccessfully to oust Gruffudd ap Rhydderch in 1046

(assisted by the English earl Swein, son of GODWINE). Thereafter Gruffudd was secure in S Wales and even attacked England. In 1053, however, his brother Rhys was killed by EDWARD THE CONFESSOR; and Gruffudd ap Rhydderch was killed by Gruffudd ap Llywelyn's forces in 1055.

GUERNSEY *see* CHANNEL ISLANDS

GUEST FAMILY Ironmasters in Glamorgan, S Wales. John Guest (1722–85), from Shropshire (W England), was appointed manager of the Dowlais ironworks near MERTHYR TYDFIL in 1763 and became their main owner by 1782. His descendants retained the works until they were absorbed into the Guest, Keen company in 1900. In the 1840s Sir Josiah John Guest (1785–1852) had more employees than any man on earth. His wife, Lady Charlotte Guest (1812–95), translated *Y MABINOGI* into English. *See also* IRON AND STEEL INDUSTRIES, WALES.

GUILD A voluntary organization that provides mutual aid for its members or furthers a common purpose; the term (OE *gyld*) refers to payment or sacrifice. Guilds are recorded in England from the 9th century, associated with MINSTERS. They fetched members' bodies for burial, financed Masses for the souls of dead members, and promoted conviviality. From the late 11th century, merchant guilds (associations of traders) were sometimes granted exclusive rights of trading within TOWNS by kings or lords, and often developed into urban governing bodies. There were also guilds of craftsmen, which protected their members' interests and regulated standards. Religious guilds, which held feasts and funded commemorative Masses, were widespread in the 13th–16th centuries.

Religious guilds were dissolved in the 16th century (*see* CHANTRIES, ENGLAND AND WALES). Some town guilds became corporations, and craft guilds declined in the 17th–18th centuries. Guilds had similar histories elsewhere in the British Isles.

GUINNESS COMPANY AND FAMILY The Irish brewer Arthur Guinness (1725–1803) acquired a brewery in DUBLIN in 1759. Under his son Arthur (1768–1855) it became by 1840 Ireland's largest commercial enterprise, producing stout (strong, dark) beers. A public company from 1886, Guinness was the world's largest brewer by the 20th century, selling in Ireland, Great Britain, and elsewhere. Large-scale production also took place in England (Park Royal, London) 1936–2005. Guinness merged into 'Diageo' in 1997, the name becoming a brand.

Members of the Guinness family, adherents mostly of the Church of IRELAND, continued in the business until the later 20th century. They funded many philanthropic projects (e.g., restoration of St Patrick's Cathedral, Dublin, 1860–5), and contributed to Irish and British public life. *See also* BREWING INDUSTRY, IRELAND.

GUNBOAT DIPLOMACY The pursuit of foreign policy objectives involving a display of military power, especially naval power. It is associated with British naval supremacy in the 19th century, particularly with Viscount PALMERSTON. Great Britain sometimes sent warships to prominent locations to increase its leverage in international disputes (e.g., in the PACIFICO INCIDENT). *See also* NAVY, ENGLISH AND BRITISH, FROM 1660; AGADIR CRISIS.

GUNPOWDER PLOT In England, a Catholic conspiracy against King JAMES VI/I. From early 1604 Robert Catesby, provoked by renewed enforcement of anti-Catholic laws, planned to assassinate James and royal officers. The government was warned (26 Oct. 1605). Around midnight on 4–5 Nov., prior to the state opening of Parliament, barrels of gunpowder were found below the House of Lords' chamber, together with Guy Fawkes who was due to ignite them. Fawkes and other conspirators were arrested and executed for TREASON. *See also* CATHOLIC PLOTS, ENGLAND.

GUTHLAC (b. 674 in Mercia; d. 3 April 715, probably at Crowland, Mercia, aged about 40). A member of the Mercian royal kindred and warrior, Guthlac became a monk (698). From 700 he lived a hermit's life on Crowland island in the FENS, where he was visited by both poor and eminent people. The latter included the exiled Mercian royal kinsman ÆTHELBALD. He is the subject of a (Latin) *Life of St Guthlac*.

GUTUN OWAIN (b. probably at Maelor Saesneg, Flintshire, Wales; fl. from *c*.1460; d. *c*.1498). A Welsh scholar who compiled important collections of Welsh genealogies and versions of the BRUT Y TYWYSOGION. Also known as Gruffudd ap Huw ab Owain, he composed early Modern praise poetry in the *cywydd* metre. *See also* WELSH LANGUAGE AND LITERATURE.

GUYANA *see* BRITISH GUIANA

GWENT An early medieval kingdom in SE WALES (6th or 7th–11th centuries), originally including S Wales (the later GLAMORGAN), but soon restricted to the area between the Rivers Usk and Wye; named from the Roman CIVITAS capital Venta Silurum (Welsh, Caerwent).

Men of Gwent allegedly defeated SAXONS *c*.630, thereby impeding Germanic settlement in SE Wales. Gwent was usually overshadowed by GLYWYSING/Morgannwg to the W, but periodically asserted independence. It was conquered by NORMANS between *c*.1070 and 1085, who formed the lordships of Monmouth, Chepstow, Caerleon and Usk (*see* MARCH OF WALES).

In 1536 MONMOUTHSHIRE replaced the lordships (*see* UNION OF WALES WITH ENGLAND). The name Gwent was revived for the regional authority that succeeded Monmouthshire (1974–96), and for a successor unitary authority and county borough, Blaenau Gwent (from 1996).

GWYNEDD The pre-eminent kingdom of medieval WALES (6th–13th centuries), in NW Wales. Its core was the NW corner, Gwynedd-uwch-Conwy ('Gwynedd above the Conwy'), but it often incorporated areas to the E and S. Its rulers' principal court was at Aberffro (on ANGLESEY). The meaning of 'Gwynedd' is uncertain. (The Latin name, Venedotia, is derived from an early form of the Welsh name.)

Tradition claimed the foundation of Gwynedd in the 5th century by Cunedda Wledig; the historical record begins with King MAELGWN GWYNEDD (d. 547). In the 7th century Cadfan (d. *c*.625) was described as 'most wise and renowned of all kings'; his son CADWALLON AP CADFAN (ruled *c*.625–34) challenged Anglo-Saxon rulers. In the early 9th century Gwynedd passed to MERFYN FRYCH (ruled 825–44), founder of a new dynasty. His son RHODRI MAWR (844–78) and Rhodri's sons ruled much of Wales. Subsequently the dynasty divided into a northern branch in Gwynedd and a southern one in DEHEUBARTH (SW Wales).

In the 11th century Gwynedd was ruled by usurpers, including GRUFFUDD AP LLYWELYN (ruled 1039–63); and NORMANS may have been briefly in control (*see* ROBERT OF RHUDDLAN). The main line returned with GRUFFUDD AP CYNAN (ruled *c*.1090–1137) who re-established Gwynedd's predominance within Wales. It was reaffirmed by his son OWAIN GWYNEDD (ruled 1137–70) and later by LLYWELYN AP IORWERTH (ruled 1199–1240) and LLYWELYN AP GRUFFUDD (1246–82).

After the English conquest of native Wales in 1282–3 Gwynedd was divided into Anglesey, Caernarfonshire and Merionethshire (*see* RHUDDLAN OR WALES, STATUTE OF). The name Gwynedd was later reused for a regional authority based on the three counties (1974–96).

H

HABEAS CORPUS A Latin phrase which usually refers to the WRIT (written order) known as *habeas corpus ad subjiciendum* ('that you have the body for submitting'), though other habeas corpus writs existed. From the later 15th century it was used to test the legality of someone's detention. During the FIVE KNIGHTS' CASE (1627), one of the detained found that the writ was nullified because he had been imprisoned by the king's command. Parliament complained about such prerogative power in the PETITION OF RIGHT (1628), and in 1641 legislated for a right to the writ even when detention had been ordered by the king or PRIVY COUNCIL (Habeas Corpus Act).

The Habeas Corpus Act of 1679 made access to the writ easier for persons imprisoned on criminal charges and extended it to Wales, BERWICK-UPON-TWEED, Jersey and Guernsey (*see* CHANNEL ISLANDS). It was made available for non-criminal matters in 1816 and also applied to the Isle of MAN. The writ was sometimes issued into Ireland, and the 1679 Act was effectively replicated by the Irish Parliament in 1781–2. Habeas corpus did not exist in Scotland, but from 1701 means were developed for prevention of unlawful detention. In 1998 the HUMAN RIGHTS ACT, applicable throughout the UK, also provided an entitlement to take legal action concerning the lawfulness of detention.

HABSBURG EMPIRE, ENGLISH AND BRITISH RELATIONS WITH From the 16th to the 19th century, common hostility to FRANCE often resulted in co-operation. Emperor Charles V, who ruled both Spain (and its empire) and lands in C Europe, allied with King HENRY VIII (1543), despite Henry's break from the Roman Church (*see* REFORMATION, ENGLAND). After the Empire was divided (1555–6), England was concerned more with SPAIN than C Europe (the part generally denoted by the name 'Habsburg Empire'). English intervention (1625) against the Habsburgs in the Thirty Years War was ineffectual.

Between 1689 and 1815, military coalition against FRANCE was the norm (albeit with notable exceptions such as the SEVEN YEARS WAR). The British feared French conquest of the Spanish/Austrian Netherlands (roughly equivalent to modern BELGIUM).

Habsburg hostility to liberalism and nationalism caused tension in the 19th century, especially over ITALY, but shared mistrust of RUSSIA in respect of the EASTERN QUESTION gave rise to loose alliance in the Mediterranean Agreements (1887–92). As the Empire (or 'Austria-Hungary') was allied to GERMANY (from 1882), Great Britain declared war on 12 Aug. 1914 and supported partition of Habsburg lands by the peace treaties of 1919–20 (*see* PARIS PEACE CONFERENCE). *See also* GRAND ALLIANCE, WAR OF THE; SPANISH SUCCESSION, WAR OF THE; AUSTRIAN SUCCESSION, WAR OF THE; DIPLOMATIC REVOLUTION.

HADRIAN'S WALL The main Roman defensive wall across N Britain. It was built after Emperor Hadrian's visit

A Dictionary of British and Irish History, First Edition. Edited by Robert Peberdy and Philip Waller.
© 2021 John Wiley & Sons Ltd; © editorial matter and organisation Robert Peberdy and Phillip Waller.
Published 2021 by John Wiley & Sons Ltd.

to Britain in 122. Originally 70 mi or 76 Roman mi (113 km) long, and approximately 15 ft (4.6 m) high, it spanned the Tyne–Solway isthmus and provided a northern frontier for ROMAN BRITAIN. Punctuated by forts and milecastles, its eastern half was built in stone and the western in turf (though later replaced by stone). A ditch to the N provided protection; a *vallum* (ditch and bank) to the S delineated a military zone. Although it was briefly superseded by the ANTONINE WALL, it remained in use until at least the late 4th century.

HAIG, DOUGLAS (b. 19 June 1861 at Edinburgh, Scotland; d. 29 Jan. 1928 at Bemersyde, Berwickshire, Scotland, aged 66). Educated at OXFORD University, Haig served in the (Second) BOER WAR (1899–1902) before holding various staff appointments. During WORLD WAR I (1914–18) he led the First Army (Jan.–Dec. 1915) and succeeded John FRENCH as commander-in-chief of the British Expeditionary Force (Dec. 1915–April 1919).

Dogged and unimaginative, Haig insisted that the war could be won only by massive offensives on the Western Front, which entailed huge loss of life. After the SOMME (1916) and Third Battle of YPRES (1917) campaigns, he lost the confidence of the prime minister, David LLOYD GEORGE, who tried to subordinate him. After the war Haig headed the BRITISH LEGION, a welfare organization for ex-servicemen. His war strategy remains controversial.

HAILSHAM, LORD (b. 9 Oct. 1907 at London, England; d. 12 Oct. 2001 at Putney, London, England, aged 94). Quintin Hogg, a barrister, became a Conservative MP at a by-election for OXFORD in 1938 expressly as a supporter of the Munich Agreement (*see* MUNICH CRISIS). His treatise *The Case for Conservatism* (1947) proved influential. He succeeded as Viscount Hailsham and moved to the House of Lords in 1950.

Hailsham held various offices in the British governments of Anthony EDEN and Harold MACMILLAN, including first lord of the Admiralty (1956–7), education minister (1957), minister for science and technology (the first, 1959–64), and leader of the Lords (1960–3). In Oct. 1963, hoping to succeed Macmillan as Conservative leader, he announced the intention to disclaim his peerage (implemented Nov.). He accepted a life peerage in 1970 to serve as lord CHANCELLOR under Edward HEATH. He held the office again under Margaret THATCHER (1979–87). *See also* PEERAGE, DISCLAIMING OF.

HAKLUYT, RICHARD (b. *c*.1552 at London, England; d. 23 Nov. 1616, probably at Westminster, Middlesex, England, aged about 64). Hakluyt became a clergyman (by 1580) but was primarily interested in geography and overseas colonization. His book *Divers Voyages Touching the Discoverie of America* (1582) supported colonization proposals by Humphrey GILBERT (implemented 1583), and he wrote 'Discourse on Western Planting' (1584) for Walter RALEGH to seek support from Queen ELIZABETH I (*see* ROANOKE SETTLEMENTS).

Hakluyt's major work, *The Principal Navigations ... of the English Nation* (1589; expanded edition 1598–1600), argued that PLANTATIONS could provide more than treasure: benefits would include cheap raw materials, markets, prevention of bullion loss to foreign economies, and relief of population pressure. Hakluyt also assisted the EAST INDIA COMPANY and VIRGINIA COMPANY. *See also* NORTH AMERICA, ENGLISH EXPLORATION; MERCANTILISM.

HALDANE, R.B. (b. 30 July 1856 at Edinburgh, Scotland; d. 19 Aug. 1928 at Cloan, Perthshire, Scotland, aged 72). Educated at Edinburgh and Göttingen Universities, Richard Burdon Haldane became a barrister (1876) and Liberal MP (1885). As war secretary (1905–12), under Henry CAMPBELL-BANNERMAN and H.H. ASQUITH, he introduced comprehensive Army reforms (e.g., creation of an Expeditionary Force and a part-time Territorial Force, and of a general staff). He was created Viscount Haldane in 1911, and was lord CHANCELLOR from 1912 until excluded in May 1915, during WORLD WAR I, because of supposed German sympathies. Haldane returned as lord chancellor in the first Labour government (1924). *See also* ARMY, ENGLISH AND BRITISH.

HALIDON HILL, BATTLE OF Fought NW of BERWICK-UPON-TWEED (SE Scotland) on 19 July 1333. King EDWARD III of England heavily defeated a Scottish army which was seeking to break his siege of Berwick. Edward BALLIOL, claimant to the Scottish kingship (supported by Edward), then invaded Scotland for a second time. *See also* SCOTTISH–ENGLISH RELATIONS 1290 TO 1357.

HALIFAX, EARL OF (b. 16 April 1661 at Horton, Northamptonshire, England; d. 19 May 1715 at London, England, aged 54). Charles Montagu became an MP in 1689, a Treasury commissioner in 1692, and chancellor of the Exchequer and privy councillor in 1694. As a member of the WHIG JUNTO, he was a leading member of the ministry (under King WILLIAM III). He was involved in financing the War of the GRAND ALLIANCE and financial reforms, including the foundation of the BANK OF ENGLAND (1694). The Junto's influence declined from 1697, and Montagu resigned as chancellor in 1699. He was created Lord Halifax in 1700.

After the accession of Queen ANNE (1702), Halifax was dismissed from the Privy Council. He was reappointed to the Council and Treasury Board, and created earl of Halifax, in 1714, after the accession of King GEORGE I.

HALIFAX, 2ND EARL OF (b. 5 or 6 Oct. 1716 in England; d. 8 June 1771 at Horton, Northamptonshire, England, aged 55). George Montagu, a WHIG, succeeded as earl in 1739. Following marriage into a wealthy mercantile family (1741) he used the surname Montagu-Dunk. In politics Halifax adhered to the opposition party of Prince FREDERICK (1742–4), then supported the PELHAMS. He was president of the Board of Trade in their ministries, 1748–61 (except 1756–7; *see* DEVONSHIRE, 4TH DUKE OF). He promoted Great Britain's overseas trading interests, especially in N America, and was popular with merchants. Halifax in NOVA SCOTIA was named after him (1749). He was then lord lieutenant of Ireland (1761–3).

Halifax served as first lord of the Admiralty under Lord BUTE (1762–3) and SECRETARY OF STATE (southern) 1763–5 under George GRENVILLE. He regained office under his nephew Lord NORTH: as lord PRIVY SEAL 1770–1, secretary of state (northern) 1771. Under Bute he signed the general warrant by which John WILKES was arrested. *See also* TRADE, BOARD OF.

HALIFAX, MARQUESS OF (b. 11 Nov. 1633 at Thornhill, Yorkshire, England; d. 5 April 1695 at Westminster, Middlesex, England, aged 61). George Savile was created Lord Savile of Halifax in 1668. In 1679 King CHARLES II appointed him to the Privy Council and made him earl of Halifax to help prevent the exclusion of the Catholic James, duke of York, from succession to the throne (*see* EXCLUSION CRISIS). Halifax helped to defeat an Exclusion Bill (Nov. 1680) and became regarded as Charles's chief minister. He supported repressive measures against WHIGS. In 1682 Halifax was created a marquess and appointed lord privy seal.

After the accession of JAMES VII/II (1685), Halifax became president of the Council, but was dismissed (Oct.) for opposing James's catholicizing policies. He supported the accession of WILLIAM III and MARY II in 1689, and served as lord privy seal 1689–90 (*see* GLORIOUS REVOLUTION). As someone detached from party allegiances, who sought political compromises, he was happy to be nicknamed 'the Trimmer'.

HALIFAX, VISCOUNT (b. 16 April 1881 at Powderham Castle, Devon, England; d. 23 Dec. 1959 at Garrowby, Yorkshire, England, aged 78). A Conservative MP 1910–25, Edward Wood held office in the British governments of David LLOYD GEORGE, Bonar LAW and Stanley BALDWIN. Created Lord Irwin in 1925, he served as viceroy of INDIA 1926–31. His 'Irwin Declaration' (1929) promised India eventual DOMINION status.

After returning to Great Britain, Irwin served in the NATIONAL GOVERNMENT: as education minister (1932–5), war secretary (1935), lord PRIVY SEAL (1935–7), and president of the Council (1937–8). (He succeeded as Viscount Halifax in 1934.) As foreign secretary from Feb. 1938, Halifax espoused APPEASEMENT, although his attitude to Germany hardened from March 1939. He rejected offers of the premiership in May 1940 and went to the USA as ambassador (Jan. 1941–May 1946). He was created earl of Halifax in 1944.

HALLEY, EDMOND (b. 29 Oct. 1656 at London, England; d. 14 Jan. 1742 at Greenwich, Kent, England, aged 85). Interested in astronomy as a child, Halley was encouraged from 1675 by John Flamsteed, the astronomer royal. He won a reputation in 1679 by publishing a catalogue of stars of the southern hemisphere, derived from observations made on St Helena during an expedition (1676–8). Halley also commanded England's first naval expedition for scientific purposes (1698–1700) and an expedition to study tides (1701). He was professor of geometry at OXFORD University from 1703, and succeeded Flamsteed in 1720. Halley excelled in extracting patterns from data collections. He famously calculated the orbits of comets, and correctly predicted the return of one comet (seen 1682) which was named after him. *See also* SCIENTIFIC REVOLUTION.

HAMILTON, 4TH DUKE OF (b. 11 April 1658 at Hamilton Palace, S Scotland; d. 15 Nov. 1712 at London, England, aged 54). James Hamilton opposed the forfeiture of JAMES VII/II as king of Scotland and was imprisoned (1688–9, 1689–90). He was created a duke in 1698 (after his mother resigned the title). From 1700 to 1707 Hamilton led the COUNTRY PARTY in the Scottish Parliament, which opposed union with England, but susceptibility to court pressure made him ineffectual (e.g., in Sept. 1705 he proposed that Scotland's commissioners for negotiating the treaty of Union should be the queen's nominees, thereby ensuring pro-union appointments).

After union took place (1707) Hamilton joined the English TORIES and was elected a Scottish 'representative peer' in the British House of Lords (1708). He also received a British dukedom (1711), only to be barred, by English opponents, from sitting by right of his British title. He died in a duel. *See also* UNION OF ENGLAND AND SCOTLAND; PEERAGE, SCOTTISH.

HAMILTON, 3RD MARQUIS OF (b. 19 June 1606 in England; d. 6 March 1649 at London, England, aged 42). Of Scottish parents, James Hamilton was raised in England. He succeeded as marquis in 1625 and joined the English PRIVY COUNCIL (1628). In 1638 he was King CHARLES I's commissioner to the GLASGOW ASSEMBLY, which he left in protest at its intention to abolish episcopacy (28 Nov.).

Hamilton returned to Scotland with Charles in 1641 and attempted, unsuccessfully, to conciliate leading

COVENANTERS. Further missions in 1642 and 1643 failed to prevent Scots from joining the CIVIL WARS. Charles imprisoned him for his failure (1644–6), but Hamilton remained loyal and in 1648 raised support in Scotland for the ENGAGEMENT. He led a Royalist army into England only to be defeated at Preston by Oliver CROMWELL (17–19 Aug.). He was captured and executed by Parliamentarians. Hamilton was created a duke in April 1643. *See also* COVENANTING REVOLUTION.

HAMILTON, JOHN (b. *c*.1511 in Scotland; d. 6 April 1571 at Stirling, C Scotland, aged about 60). Clergyman; archbishop of ST ANDREWS 1547–71. Hamilton attempted to reform the Scottish Church through Church councils (1549–59). They condemned immoral behaviour by clergy, required more frequent preaching (1549), and authorized a SCOTS catechism (1552). But this failed to prevent the REFORMATION (1560).

Under MARY, QUEEN OF SCOTS, Hamilton remained Catholic and was quiescent until 1563 when he said Mass in public (imprisoned 1563–5). He supported Mary after her deposition (1567), and was executed by the regent the (4th) earl of LENNOX for complicity in the murder of Lord DARNLEY (Lennox's son). *See also* MYLN, WALTER, EXECUTION OF; CATHOLICS AND CATHOLIC CHURCH, SCOTLAND.

HAMILTON, PATRICK (b. *c*.1498 in Scotland; d. 18 Feb. 1528 at St Andrews, Fife, E Scotland, aged about 30). An early proponent of LUTHERANISM in Scotland. Hamilton probably encountered Martin Luther's ideas at Paris University, France, *c*.1518–20. At ST ANDREWS University by 1523, his Lutheran sympathies became evident. In 1526 he fled to Germany, meeting Luther and writing *Patrick's Places* (Lutheran theology). Hamilton returned to St Andrews in 1527 and was burnt for heresy, the first death caused by religious conflict in 16th-century Scotland.

HAMILTON, THOMAS (b. 1563 in Scotland; d. 29 May 1637, probably in Scotland, aged about 74). An advocate, Hamilton was appointed a lord of SESSION (1592, as Lord Drumcairn). As LORD ADVOCATE (1596–1612) and SECRETARY OF STATE (1612–27), he was one of King JAMES VI's principal officers. Hamilton probably suggested appointment of the OCTAVIANS (1596–7). As a keen promoter of James's ecclesiastical policy, he obtained a majority (by intimidation) in a General Assembly for the FIVE ARTICLES OF PERTH (1618). He was also president of the Court of Session (1616–27). He was created Lord Binning (1613), earl of Melrose (1619) and earl of Haddington (1627). *See also* SCOTLAND, CHURCH OF.

HAMPDEN, JOHN (b. mid 1595, probably at Great Hampden, Buckinghamshire, England; d. 24 June 1643 at Thame, Oxfordshire, England, aged 47 or 48). First elected an MP in 1621, Hampden was put under restraint 1627–8 for refusing to pay the FORCED LOAN levied by King CHARLES I. In 1637–8 his unsuccessful challenge to the legality of SHIP MONEY made him a national hero. He was among the king's critics in the SHORT PARLIAMENT (1640). In the LONG PARLIAMENT he supported the MILITIA ORDINANCE from Dec. 1641, and was one of the FIVE MEMBERS whom Charles tried to arrest in Jan. 1642.

After CIVIL WAR broke out in Aug. 1642 Hampden became a military commander. He was fatally wounded while advancing on OXFORD. *See also* ST JOHN, OLIVER.

HAMPDEN, RENN (b. 29 March 1793 in Barbados; d. 23 April 1868 at London, England, aged 75). A Church of England clergyman and professor of philosophy at OXFORD University, Hampden was nominated as regius professor of divinity in 1836 by Viscount MELBOURNE (prime minister). The choice provoked protests from OXFORD MOVEMENT clergy (e.g., John Henry NEWMAN) because they disapproved of Hampden's undogmatic approach to Christian theology. The dispute strengthened theological parties within the Church. More protests followed in 1847 when Hampden was nominated as bishop of HEREFORD.

HAMPTON COURT A royal palace in SW London, England (originally in rural Middlesex). Situated on the N bank of the R. Thames, it was built for Thomas WOLSEY *c*.1515–25 but presented by him to King HENRY VIII in 1529 to curry favour. It remained a royal residence until the mid 19th century. In the 1690s Christopher WREN added ranges in classical style for WILLIAM III and MARY II. *See also* HAMPTON COURT CONFERENCE; ROYAL HOUSEHOLD, ENGLAND.

HAMPTON COURT CONFERENCE In England, a conference of Church of ENGLAND theologians convened by King JAMES VI/I in 1604 in response to the 'Millenary Petition', a petition supposedly from a thousand Puritan clergy requesting reform of the Church's doctrine and ceremonies, and correction of abuses. Comprising panels of senior clergy and moderate Puritans, the conference met at HAMPTON COURT (Middlesex) on 14–16 Jan. James rejected most proposals, but agreed to a revised English Bible (published 1611, the so-called 'King James Bible' or 'Authorized Version'). *See also* PURITANISM, ENGLAND; BIBLE, ENGLISH.

HAMWIC *see* SOUTHAMPTON; WIC

HANDEL, GEORGE FREDERICK (b. 23 Feb. 1685 at Halle, Brandenburg, Germany; d. 14 April 1759 at Westminster, Middlesex, England, aged 74). Handel (German, Händel) wrote operas from 1705 and visited Italy

1706–10. In 1710 he was appointed Kapellmeister (music director) to the elector of Hanover.

Handel visited England 1710–11 and returned in 1712. Enthusiasm for his work encouraged him to remain, a decision made easier by the elector's accession as king in 1714 (*see* GEORGE I). Handel received commissions from nobles and royalty, and provided operas for the commercial theatre. From the 1730s he composed English oratorios (e.g., *Messiah*, premiered 1742), which became established in English culture.

HANKEY, MAURICE (b. 1 April 1877 at Biarritz, France; d. 25 Jan. 1963 at Redhill, Surrey, England, aged 85). Civil servant. As secretary of the Committee of Imperial Defence (1912–38), secretary of the WAR CABINET (1916–19), and Cabinet secretary (1919–38), Maurice Hankey devised much of the administrative machinery of 20th-century British CABINET government. Created Lord Hankey in 1939, he was a government minister without portfolio 1939–42. *See also* WORLD WAR I, IMPACT ON BRITISH POLITICS AND GOVERNMENT.

HANOVER, IMPACT ON BRITISH POLITICS The kings of Great Britain and Ireland also ruled this state in NW Germany 1714–1837 (an electorate to 1806, kingdom from 1814). Under the 1701 Act of SETTLEMENT, Parliament's approval was required for any war involving the ruler's possessions in Continental Europe. British opposition politicians complained that GEORGE I (ruled 1714–27) and GEORGE II (1727–60) sacrificed British interests in Europe in defence of Hanover, especially during the War of the AUSTRIAN SUCCESSION (1740–8). Foreign powers saw attacking Hanover as a means of attacking Britain. This happened during the SEVEN YEARS WAR (1756–63) and FRENCH REVOLUTIONARY AND NAPOLEONIC WARS (1793–1815). Hanover was under foreign rule 1803–13.

Under Hanoverian succession rules (Salic law), female heirs were excluded unless there were no male heirs. When VICTORIA succeeded in Britain and Ireland in 1837, Ernest August, son of GEORGE III, became king of Hanover. *See also* HANOVERIAN SUCCESSION; CUMBERLAND, DUKE OF; DIPLOMATIC REVOLUTION.

HANOVERIAN SUCCESSION The transfer of the kingships of Great Britain and Ireland to the Protestant ruler of Hanover, Germany, in 1714, following the extinction of the line of Protestant Stuart rulers.

Provision for the succession became necessary in 1700, if Catholics were to be avoided, when the second and final prospective heir to King WILLIAM III died (namely William's nephew William, duke of Gloucester, the only child of King William's sister-in-law ANNE). In 1701 the English Parliament vested the succession in Sophia, electress of Hanover (granddaughter of JAMES VI/I by his daughter Elizabeth; *see* SETTLEMENT, ACT OF).

Scottish leaders were angered by lack of consultation and threatened an alternative arrangement (*see* SECURITY, ACT OF). This provoked the UNION OF ENGLAND AND SCOTLAND (1707). On Anne's death, Sophia's son Georg succeeded in Britain and Ireland as GEORGE I. The succession was challenged until the mid 18th century (*see* JACOBITISM, IMPACT ON BRITISH POLITICS). *See also* STEWART RULERS.

HANSON, LORD (b. 20 Jan. 1922 at Golcar, Yorkshire, England; d. 1 Nov. 2004 at Winterbourne, Berkshire, England, aged 82). Starting in haulage, James Hanson developed, bought and sold businesses in the 1940s–60s, working from 1954 with Gordon White (1923–95). From 1964 they operated through Wiles Group (renamed Hanson Trust, 1969), acquiring conglomerate businesses for break-up: parts were sold, the remainder made more profitable.

From 1973 White operated as a deal-maker from the USA, leaving management to Hanson (knighted 1976). Their large acquisitions included Imperial Tobacco (1986) and Consolidated Goldfields (1988). Prime Minister Margaret THATCHER admired their 'buccaneering' approach: Hanson was created Lord Hanson (1983), and White was knighted (1979) and created Lord White (1990). But in 1991 Hanson Trust's threatened bid for IMPERIAL CHEMICAL INDUSTRIES was rebuffed. After White's death, Hanson Trust was reorganized (1996) and Hanson retired (1997).

HARCOURT, WILLIAM (b. 14 Oct. 1827 at York, Yorkshire, England; d. 1 Oct. 1904 at Nuneham Courtenay, Oxfordshire, England, aged 76). A lawyer, Harcourt became a LIBERAL PARTY MP in 1868. He served as solicitor-general 1873–4 (also knighted 1873), and was British home secretary 1880–5 and chancellor of the Exchequer 1886, 1892–5. Disappointed of succeeding W.E. GLADSTONE as prime minister in March 1894, he made a difficult colleague for the earl of ROSEBERY, whose imperialism he opposed. His 1894 Budget introduced graduated death duties, to the dismay of hereditary landowners (Rosebery included). Harcourt led the Liberals in the House of Commons 1894–8. *See also* LANDED SOCIETY, DECLINE OF, ENGLAND.

HARDIE, KEIR (b. 15 Aug. 1856 at Legbrannock, Lanarkshire, Scotland; d. 26 Sept. 1915 at Glasgow, Scotland, aged 59). Raised in poverty, Hardie was a coalminer 1866–78, a shopkeeper, journalist and (1879–81) union official, and from 1886 secretary of the Ayrshire Miners' Union. In 1892 he was sensationally elected as an 'independent Labour' MP, representing an English constituency (West Ham South, London). Hardie helped to form the INDEPENDENT LABOUR PARTY (1893) and continued as an ILP MP until 1895. He was re-elected in 1900 for MERTHYR TYDFIL, representing the recently founded Labour Representation Committee (renamed LABOUR PARTY in 1906). He remained an MP until his death. Hardie advocated a wide variety of personal, radical and socialist causes: temperance, land reform, graduated taxation, provision of employment, free schooling, pensions, universal suffrage, abolition of the House of Lords, and pacifism.

HARDWICKE, LORD (b. 1 Dec. 1690 at Dover, Kent, England; d. 6 March 1764 at London, England, aged 73). Philip Yorke, a WHIG, became a barrister in 1715. He was elected an MP in 1719, under the PATRONAGE of the duke of NEWCASTLE, and appointed solicitor-general (1720). During the ministry of Robert WALPOLE he was appointed attorney-general (1724), lord chief justice (1733, also created Lord Hardwicke) and lord CHANCELLOR (1737).

After Walpole's resignation, Hardwicke remained in office, and from 1744 was a leading colleague of the PELHAMS. He promoted punitive legislation after the 1745 Jacobite Rebellion (see JACOBITE REBELLIONS, CONSEQUENCES IN SCOTLAND) and the so-called HARDWICKE MARRIAGE ACT (1753).

Having been created earl of Hardwicke in 1754, he retired as lord chancellor when Newcastle resigned as first lord of the Treasury in 1756, then negotiated the arrangement whereby Newcastle returned to office in 1757 in association with William PITT the Elder. See also GEORGE I; GEORGE II.

HARDWICKE MARRIAGE ACT Legislation by the British Parliament, 1753, which sought to deter clandestine marriages in England and Wales, thereby preventing the abduction of heiresses for their property. Marriages had to be celebrated by a clergyman of the Church of England, after the calling of banns. Parents or guardians had to give consent for the marriage of minors. JEWS and QUAKERS were excepted, but not other DISSENTERS or CATHOLICS. The Act was named after the lord chancellor, Lord HARDWICKE. It was extended to Scotland in 1784 and repealed in 1823.

HARDY, THOMAS (b. 2 June 1840 at Upper Brockhampton, Dorset, England; d. 11 Jan. 1928 at Dorchester, Dorset, aged 87). A stonemason's son, Hardy trained as an architect (in London from 1862). In the 1870s he achieved success as a novelist. Most of his novels are set in 'Wessex', a fictionalized version of S and SW England. Works such as *Far from the Madding Crowd* (1874), *Tess of the D'Urbervilles* (1891) and *Jude the Obscure* (1896) reflect the clash of rural custom with modern forces. *Tess* and *Jude* both offended conventional morality. The furore created by *Jude* (e.g., it was burnt by a bishop), together with the attainment of a sufficient income, caused Hardy to concentrate on poetry. See also ENGLISH LITERATURE, ENGLAND; NOVEL.

HARGREAVES, JAMES (b. late 1720 or Jan. 1721 at Oswaldtwistle, Lancashire, England; d. 18 April 1778 at Nottingham, Nottinghamshire, England, aged 57). A handloom weaver, Hargreaves c.1764 invented the 'spinning jenny', a machine for spinning several threads simultaneously. ('Jenny' means 'engine'.) Patented in 1770, it provided an increase in spinning productivity (for weft yarn) alongside the improved productivity in weaving produced by the 'flying shuttle' (patented 1733; see KAY, JOHN). The invention was widely adopted in the textile industries. See also ARKWRIGHT, RICHARD; COTTON INDUSTRY, ENGLAND.

HARLAW, BATTLE OF Fought NW of Aberdeen (NE Scotland) on 24 July 1411. Donald, lord of the Isles, was repulsed by forces under the earl of Mar, representative of the duke of Albany, governor of Scotland (see STEWART, ROBERT). Donald probably sought to defeat Mar and seize Ross (N Scotland). See also ISLES, LORDSHIP OF THE.

HARLEY, ROBERT (b. 5 Dec. 1661 at London, England; d. 21 May 1724 at London, aged 62). An MP from 1689, Harley was a 'country' WHIG (in the reign of King WILLIAM III). In the mid 1690s he and some country TORIES formed the 'New Country Party'. From 1698 the ministry sought his support and he became a court politician: he was elected speaker of the House of Commons (1701) with the ministry's support.

Under Queen ANNE (from 1702), Harley worked with Lord GODOLPHIN and the duke of MARLBOROUGH to prosecute the War of the SPANISH SUCCESSION. He was appointed a SECRETARY OF STATE in 1704. But factional and personal rivalries ended with Harley's resignation in 1708. In 1710 Harley used his continuing influence with Anne to obtain the dismissal of Godolphin (Aug.) and appointment of Tory ministers. Harley was chancellor of the Exchequer from 1710, TREASURER from 1711, and was created earl of Oxford in 1711. He brought about peace (1712, withdrawal from war).

Oxford was dismissed by Anne shortly before her death (1714), through intrigues by Viscount BOLINGBROKE. After the accession of GEORGE I, Harley's Whig enemies accused him of TREASON. He was imprisoned 1715–17, but attempted IMPEACHMENT of Oxford failed. See also MASHAM, ABIGAIL; COURT AND COUNTRY.

HAROLD 'HAREFOOT' (b. c.1016; d. 17 March 1040 at Oxford, Oxfordshire, England). Harold was a son of King CNUT of Denmark (king of England from 1016) and ÆLFGIFU (first wife). After Cnut's death (Nov. 1035), Harold was accepted in England as regent for his younger half-brother HARTHACNUT (son of Cnut by EMMA), who remained in Denmark. In 1036 Harold ordered the blinding of Alfred ætheling, another half-brother (son of ÆTHELRED II and Emma). (Alfred died soon afterwards.)

By late 1037, after winning support from GODWINE and others, Harold had become widely recognized as king. Emma fled abroad. Harthacnut was preparing to invade England when Harold died. He was succeeded by Harthacnut, who had Harold's body exhumed and dumped in a marsh. Harold's nickname probably dates from 12th century. *See also* ÆTHELING.

HAROLD II (b. *c*.1020; d. 14 Oct. 1066 near Hastings, Sussex, England, aged about 46). The second son of GODWINE, earl of Wessex, Harold was made earl in eastern England (1044) by King Edward the Confessor. During the crisis of 1051-2 he fled to Ireland (*see* EDWARD THE CONFESSOR). He succeeded to his father's earldom in 1053, becoming England's most important secular lord. He notably countered Welsh incursions (*see* GRUFFUDD AP LLYWELYN). Around 1064, while in NORMANDY, Harold swore an oath of loyalty to Duke William (possibly under duress).

On 5 Jan. 1066 Harold succeeded as king, allegedly nominated by the dying Edward. On 28 Sept., while Harold was in Yorkshire (N England), William and an army landed in England. Harold marched S, only to be killed in battle at HASTINGS. The depiction of Harold on the 11th-century BAYEUX TAPESTRY with an arrow in an eye may be the creation of 19th-century restoration work. *See also* STAMFORD BRIDGE, BATTLE OF.

HARRINGTON, EARL OF (b. *c*.1683, probably in Derbyshire, England; d. 8 Dec. 1756 in England, aged about 73). William Stanhope, a WHIG and cousin of Earl STANHOPE, was an MP 1715-22, 1727-30. After service as a diplomat, he was created Lord Harrington (Jan. 1730) and appointed SECRETARY OF STATE (northern) in the ministry of Robert WALPOLE, succeeding Viscount TOWNSHEND (Feb.).

After Walpole resigned (1742), Harrington became president of the Council in the ministry of Lord CARTERET and was created an earl. Following Carteret's fall (1744) he continued under Henry PELHAM as secretary of state (northern), resigning with the ministry in Feb. 1746. After reappointment he resigned (Oct.) because he favoured making peace in the War of the AUSTRIAN SUCCESSION, rather than prosecuting the war more vigorously as the PELHAMS preferred. He was lord lieutenant of Ireland 1746-50.

HARRIS, ARTHUR (b. 13 April 1892 at Cheltenham, Gloucestershire, England; d. 5 April 1984 at Goring, Oxfordshire, England, aged 91). In 1915 Harris joined the Royal Flying Corps of the British Army (Royal Air Force from 1917). By the mid 1930s he firmly believed that bombing could expedite victory in wartime and prevent wasteful losses of ground troops. From Feb. 1942 to 1945, during WORLD WAR II, as commander-in-chief of RAF Bomber Command, he effected the bombing of German cities. His single-minded approach made him the most controversial British military leader. Nicknamed 'Bomber Harris', he was created a baronet (1953). *See also* WORLD WAR II, BOMBING OFFENSIVE AGAINST GERMANY.

HARRIS, HOWEL (b. 23 Jan. 1714 at Trefecca, Breconshire, Wales; d. 21 July 1773 at Trefecca, aged 59). Passionate leader of early Welsh Methodism. Following a spiritual awakening in 1735 Harris, a schoolmaster, became an itinerant preacher but was refused ordination in the Church of England. From 1737 he collaborated with Daniel ROWLAND in developing Methodist societies and associated with George WHITEFIELD and the WESLEYS in England.

In 1750 Harris was expelled by the Welsh (Methodist) Association for unorthodox beliefs and his irregular relationship with 'Madam (Sidney) Griffith'. He retired in 1752, following Griffith's death, and established a community at Trefecca. An attempted return to public preaching in 1763 largely failed. *See also* METHODIST REVIVAL, WALES.

HARRYING OF THE NORTH Devastation of the countryside mainly in northern England (parts of Yorkshire, Cheshire, Staffordshire, Derbyshire, Shropshire) by Normans Oct. 1069–Feb. 1070, during the NORMAN CONQUEST OF ENGLAND. The action avenged a revolt by English magnates and Danish allies, which included the killing of Normans in YORK (21 Sept. 1069). Afterwards King WILLIAM I replaced most remaining English magnates with Normans. *See also* SWEIN ESTRITHSON.

HARTHACNUT (b. *c*.1018; d. 8 June 1042 at Lambeth, Surrey, England, aged about 23). A son of CNUT and EMMA (second wife), Harthacnut succeeded his father (d. 12 Nov. 1035) as king of Denmark and England. He remained in Denmark (threatened by Norway) while his older half-brother HAROLD 'HAREFOOT' became regent in England. By late 1037 Harold was widely accepted as king. Harthacnut prepared to invade (1038-9), but Harold's death (17 March 1040) made this unnecessary.

Harthacnut landed in England on 17 June 1040. His rule was often harsh (e.g., in 1041 he devastated Worcestershire after two tax collectors were killed). He died at a wedding feast, having probably nominated EDWARD THE CONFESSOR (half-brother) as successor. Harthacnut's death ended Danish rule of England.

HARVEY, WILLIAM (b. 1 April 1578 at Folkestone, Kent, England; d. 3 June 1657 at Roehampton, Surrey, or London, England, aged 79). After studying at CAMBRIDGE University, Harvey went to Italy and obtained a doctorate in medicine from Padua University (1602). Admitted to the Royal College of Physicians in London (1604), he was physician to St Bartholomew's Hospital 1609–43. He also served King JAMES VI/I, and was physician to CHARLES I, on whom he attended during the First CIVIL WAR (1642–6), also becoming warden of Merton College, OXFORD (1645–6).

Through painstaking anatomical research Harvey discovered that the heart acts as a pump that circulates blood round the body (published 1628 in *De Motu Cordis*, 'On the Motion of the Heart'). He also explored embryology (findings published 1651 in *De Generatione Animalium*, 'On the Generation of Animals'). *See also* SCIENTIFIC REVOLUTION; MEDICINE AND PUBLIC HEALTH.

HASTINGS, BATTLE OF Fought near Hastings (Sussex, England), at the place subsequently called Battle, on 14 Oct. 1066. An invading army of Normans and allies, commanded by Duke William II, defeated an English army led by King HAROLD II. Those killed included Harold, two brothers, and numerous English nobles. William's victory began the NORMAN CONQUEST OF ENGLAND. *See also* WILLIAM I OR WILLIAM THE CONQUEROR.

HASTINGS, FRANCIS (b. 7 Dec. 1754 at Dublin, Ireland; d. 28 Nov. 1826 at sea near Naples, Italy, aged 71). Hastings, styled Lord Rawdon (Irish title) from 1762, joined the British Army in 1771 and served in the AMERICAN WAR OF INDEPENDENCE (1775–81). Between 1783 and 1812 he held various appointments in England. He was created Lord Rawdon (English peerage) in 1783 and succeeded as earl of Moira in 1793 (Irish peerage).

As governor-general of India from 1813, Moira pacified Nepal (1814–16) and established supremacy in C India (1817–18). He was created marquess of Hastings in 1817. A reformer, he encouraged education, and improved the legal system and Civil Service. He supported the acquisition of SINGAPORE (1819). Hastings resigned in 1821 after being accused of corruption. He served from 1824 as governor of MALTA.

HASTINGS, WARREN (b. 6 Dec. 1732 at Churchill, Oxfordshire, England; d. 22 Aug. 1818 at Daylesford, Worcestershire, England, aged 85). Controversial governor in INDIA. Hastings worked in India for the EAST INDIA COMPANY from 1750, serving on its councils for Bengal

(1761–4) and Madras (now Chennai, 1769–72). In 1772 he became governor-general of Bengal (est. population 20 million), and from 1774 was the first governor-general of British India under the 1773 Regulating Act. Between 1774 and 1780 he struggled against opposition from his executive council.

Hastings attempted to increase company revenues through reorganization. He also created civil courts, waged wars (e.g., defending Madras, 1780–2), and acquired territories (e.g., Benares, 1781). After resigning in 1785, because of ill health, he was accused of ruthlessness and arrogance. Complaints were pursued in Britain by Edmund BURKE. Hastings was impeached for corruption (1787) but acquitted (23 April 1795) after a seven-year trial.

HATTON, CHRISTOPHER (b. *c.*1540 at Holdenby, Northamptonshire, England; d. 20 Nov. 1591 at London, England, aged about 51). Hatton attracted the attention of Queen ELIZABETH I in 1561 and became a favourite courtier. As an MP from 1571 he increasingly acted as her intermediary and manager in the House of Commons. He was created a privy councillor and knighted in 1577. Through his closeness he was able to influence the queen. From 1583 he supported Archbishop John Whitgift's drive for uniformity in the Church (*see* PURITANISM, ENGLAND), and from 1587 served as CHANCELLOR.

HAUGHEY, CHARLES (b. 16 Sept. 1925 at Castlebar, Co. Mayo, Irish Free State; d. 13 June 2006 at Kinsealy, Dublin, Republic of Ireland, aged 80). A FIANNA FÁIL TD from 1957, Haughey served in the governments of Seán LEMASS and Jack LYNCH (1960s). Dismissed as finance minister by Lynch (1970), he was tried for conspiracy to import arms illegally (for the PROVISIONAL IRISH REPUBLICAN ARMY in NORTHERN IRELAND). Acquitted, he returned to government (1977). Haughey replaced Lynch as party leader and taoiseach (premier) in 1979, serving as taoiseach until June 1981, in 1982, and Feb. 1987–Jan. 1992.

Ostensibly 'hardline' regarding Northern Ireland, Haughey called for British withdrawal during the NEW IRELAND FORUM (1983–4) and opposed the HILLSBOROUGH AGREEMENT (1985). Disaffection with his leadership caused some Fianna Fáil TDs to form the PROGRESSIVE DEMOCRATS (Dec. 1985).

From 1987 Haughey's minority government tackled economic problems through SOCIAL PARTNERSHIP and with support from FINE GAEL, and continued the Hillsborough Agreement. After the 1989 election, Haughey formed a coalition with the Progressive Democrats, but allegations about his involvement in illegal phone-tapping (in 1982) caused them to withdraw, forcing Haughey's resignation. Official reports in 1997 and 2006 revealed that Haughey's opulent life-style had been funded by embezzlement and payments for favours. *See also* SOUTHERN IRELAND FROM 1922; FITZGERALD, GARRET; AHERN, BERTIE; REYNOLDS, ALBERT.

HAWARDEN KITE Nickname given to the revelation by Herbert Gladstone, published on 17 Dec. 1885, that his father, Liberal leader W.E. GLADSTONE, favoured Home Rule for Ireland. (Hawarden was Gladstone's home in N Wales.) He had privately decided this months earlier, and the revelation looked like an opportunistic bid for support from Irish MPs (needed if the Liberals were to form a government following the Nov. 1885 general election). *See also* HOME RULE MOVEMENT, IRELAND.

HAWKINS, JOHN (b. 1532 at Plymouth, Devon, England; d. 12 Nov. 1595, off Puerto Rico, Spanish Indies, aged about 63). Based at London from *c.*1559, Hawkins was the first English trader to ship slaves from WEST AFRICA to Spanish America (1562–3, 1564–5, 1567–9), in an attempt to become established in the SLAVE TRADE. He abandoned the trade following a clash with Spanish ships near Veracruz (in modern Mexico). Hawkins later strengthened the English NAVY (as treasurer from 1577, comptroller from 1589). Knighted while fighting the SPANISH ARMADA (1588), he died while raiding the West Indies with his kinsman Francis DRAKE. *See also* SPAIN, ENGLISH AND BRITISH RELATIONS WITH.

HEADS OF PROPOSALS In England, after the First CIVIL WAR, a draft constitution prepared by Henry IRETON for the General Council of the NEW MODEL ARMY and shown to King CHARLES I on 23 July 1647. It proposed biennial Parliaments elected on a broad franchise, which would control appointments to principal public offices for ten years, and toleration for Protestants, though an episcopal Church was permitted. Charles rejected the proposals on 28 July. (A reform and rationalization of parliamentary constituencies, proposed in the 'Heads', was adopted in 1653.) *See also* CIVIL WARS, POLITICAL ASPECTS; COMMONWEALTH AND PROTECTORATE.

HEALEY, DENIS (b. 30 Aug. 1917 at Mottingham, Kent, England; 3 Oct. 2015 at Alfriston, Sussex, England, aged 98). A Labour MP 1952–92, Healey was an effective British defence secretary 1964–70, under Harold WILSON. As chancellor of the Exchequer 1974–9, under Wilson and James CALLAGHAN, he adopted essentially MONETARIST policies to secure a loan from the International Monetary Fund (Jan. 1977), enraging left-wingers.

In Nov. 1980 Healey narrowly failed to become Party leader (losing to Michael FOOT). He served as deputy leader 1980–3. As foreign affairs spokesman 1980–7, for Foot and Neil KINNOCK, he had to present policies (e.g.,

unilateral nuclear disarmament) apparently inconsistent with his own views. He was created Lord Healey in 1992. *See also* BENN, TONY.

HEALY, T.M. (b. 17 May 1855 at Bantry, Co. Cork, Ireland; d. 26 March 1931 at Chapelizod, Co. Dublin, Ireland, aged 75). Timothy Michael Healy (a Catholic) entered Irish politics in NE England (1870s) and sat in the UK Parliament from 1880, supporting Irish leader C.S. PARNELL. He contributed the 'Healy Clause' to the 1881 Irish Land Act, which protected tenants' improvements from rent increases.

When the IRISH PARLIAMENTARY PARTY split (Dec. 1890), Healy, a sharp-tongued lawyer, led the clericalist opposition to the Parnellite group of MPs (1891–1900). After the Party reunited (1900), Healy, having promoted John REDMOND for the leadership against John DILLON, became estranged and grew closer to William O'BRIEN. From 1917 he showed sympathy for the political ideals, though not the violent methods, of SINN FÉIN (he resigned his parliamentary seat to a Sinn Féin prisoner in 1918). Healy served as first governor-general of the IRISH FREE STATE (1922–8). *See also* HOME RULE MOVEMENT, IRELAND.

HEARTH TAX A property tax granted in England and Wales in 1662 (following the RESTORATION) by the CAVALIER PARLIAMENT as a perpetual addition to the Crown's 'ordinary' income. Charged on the number of fireplaces in each dwelling, it proved unpopular. It was surrendered in 1689 by King WILLIAM III in order to obtain support from the CONVENTION PARLIAMENT. The Irish Parliament also granted a hearth tax for Ireland's government in 1662 which continued until the 19th century (*see* TAXATION, IRELAND). *See also* TAXATION, ENGLAND, WALES AND GREAT BRITAIN FROM 1660.

HEARTS OF STEEL *see* STEELBOYS

HEATH, EDWARD (b. 9 July 1916 at Broadstairs, Kent, England; d. 17 July 2005 at Salisbury, Wiltshire, England, aged 89). Leader of the CONSERVATIVE PARTY 1965–75; British prime minister 1970–4.

A builder's son, educated at OXFORD University, Heath became an MP in 1950. He served as a whip (1952–9) and minister of labour (1959–60). As lord PRIVY SEAL (1960–3), he tried to negotiate UK membership of the EUROPEAN ECONOMIC COMMUNITY (EEC). He was president of the Board of Trade under Alec DOUGLAS-HOME (1963–4).

In 1965 Heath won the Conservative leadership under a new contested system. Despite losing the 1966 election, he led the Party to victory in 1970, promising expenditure cuts and criticizing INCOMES POLICIES and industrial intervention. His government assumed direct rule over NORTHERN IRELAND (1972) and took the UK into the EEC (1973).

After a policy 'U-turn' (1971–2), Heath and Anthony BARBER pursued reflation and an incomes policy, and funded ailing businesses (e.g., ROLLS-ROYCE). A MINERS' STRIKE led to electoral defeat (Feb. 1974). Appeals for national unity failed in another election (Oct.).

Heath lost the Party leadership to Margaret THATCHER (Feb. 1975). He vehemently criticized THATCHERISM, which repudiated his record. Knighted in 1992, he remained an MP until 2001. *See also* WILSON, HAROLD.

HEBRIDES *see* WESTERN ISLES

HEDGE SCHOOLS Popular name for clandestine, rural elementary schools for Catholics in Ireland, 18th–early 19th centuries. Held outdoors, or in cottages or barns, they circumvented ANTI-CATHOLIC LEGISLATION of 1695–1740 that inhibited Catholic schools. Teachers charged fees, and English was widely taught, though some schools helped to perpetuate Gaelic Irish culture. They were superseded by NATIONAL EDUCATION. *See also* EDUCATION, IRELAND.

HELIGOLAND A tiny island in the North Sea, seized by Great Britain from Denmark in 1807 and annexed in 1814. Lord SALISBURY ceded it to Germany (1 July 1890) in return for a reduction of German claims in E Africa (*see* EAST AFRICA, BRITISH INVOLVEMENT). This was regretted when Germany used Heligoland as a naval base in WORLD WAR I (1914–18) and WORLD WAR II (1939–45). *See also* GERMANY, BRITISH RELATIONS WITH.

HELY-HUTCHINSON, JOHN (b. 1724 at Gortroe, Co. Cork, Ireland; d. 4 Sept. 1794 at Buxton, Derbyshire, England, aged about 70). Originally John Hely, Hely-Hutchinson, a lawyer, entered the Irish House of Commons in 1759 and soon became a leading member and holder of government posts and salaries. In 1768 he endangered his position by helping to defeat a government Bill (for Army augmentation); but he quickly resumed support (and received another pension). In 1774, with government backing, he was controversially appointed provost of Trinity College, Dublin. During the economic crisis of 1779 he published, anonymously, *Commercial Restraints of Ireland*, which influenced the campaign for removal of British restrictions on Irish trade. He also supported CATHOLIC RELIEF. *See also* NON-IMPORTATION MOVEMENT; PROTESTANT ASCENDANCY.

HENDERSON, ALEXANDER (b. *c*.1583 in Creich parish, Fife, E Scotland; d. 19 Aug. 1646 at Leith, SE Scotland, aged about 63). An academic theologian and then parish minister (from 1612), Henderson opposed the FIVE ARTICLES OF PERTH (1618) and the 1637 Prayer Book (*see* REVOLT OF 1637). In 1638, with Archibald JOHNSTON,

he drafted the NATIONAL COVENANT (Feb.) and was elected moderator of the GLASGOW ASSEMBLY (23 Nov.), though he was less zealous than many COVENANTERS.

In 1643, as a commissioner to the WESTMINSTER ASSEMBLY, Henderson contributed to the SOLEMN LEAGUE AND COVENANT. In Aug. 1646 he tried to persuade King CHARLES I (in Newcastle upon Tyne, NE England) to accept the National Covenant. He failed, and died soon afterwards. *See also* COVENANTING REVOLUTION; SCOTLAND, CHURCH OF.

HENDERSON, ARTHUR (b. 20 Sept. 1863 at Glasgow, Scotland; d. 20 Oct. 1935 at London, England, aged 72). Henderson, a trade unionist and Methodist lay preacher, became a Labour MP in 1903. He led the British LABOUR PARTY 1908–10, 1914–18, and in May 1915 became Labour's first CABINET minister (as president of the Board of Education in the coalition government; paymaster-general from Aug. 1916). He served in the WAR CABINET, under David LLOYD GEORGE, 1916–17. As Labour Party secretary (1912–34) he built up the Party's organization.

Henderson was home secretary (1924) and foreign secretary (1929–31) in the Labour governments led by Ramsay MACDONALD, but refused to join MacDonald's NATIONAL GOVERNMENT. He succeeded MacDonald as Party leader (Aug. 1931–Oct. 1932), but lost his seat at the Oct. 1931 election. He chaired the World Disarmament Conference (1932–4). *See also* LANSBURY, GEORGE.

HENDREGADREDD MANUSCRIPT A 14th-century Welsh manuscript (in National Library of Wales, Aberystwyth), which was copied at STRATA FLORIDA (W Wales). It is the main source for writings by Welsh court poets of the 12th and 13th centuries, including the family of MEILYR BRYDYDD, CYNDDELW BRYDYDD MAWR, and HYWEL AB OWAIN GWYNEDD. *See also* WELSH LANGUAGE AND LITERATURE.

HENGE MONUMENTS, BRITAIN Ceremonial enclosures with up to four entrances and a ditch within an external bank, dated to the Later NEOLITHIC and Early BRONZE AGE (*c*.2500–1600 BC). Reworked over many generations, henges were foci for ritual, feasting and other politically charged events. They are often associated with stone or timber settings, and are varied in scale and duration of use. Examples have been identified in many regions, from Orkney to SW England.

HENGE MONUMENTS, IRELAND Monuments (also known as 'embanked enclosures') that comprise a flat-topped earthen bank enclosing a circular to oval space with a domed or hollowed interior and a single entrance. In most cases there is no evidence of a construction ditch.

Henges occur singly, in pairs or in threes. They are normally located in areas that were already ceremonial foci, particularly where there were PASSAGE TOMBS, such as the BEND OF THE BOYNE, Fourknocks (Co. Meath, E Ireland) and Ballynahatty (Co. Down, NE Ireland). They date from the Late NEOLITHIC (c.2700– c.2500 BC) and may incorporate earlier monuments or activity.

HENRIETTA MARIA (b. 16 Nov. 1609 at Paris, France; d. 31 Aug. 1669 at Colombes, France, aged 59). Henrietta Maria, a French Catholic princess, married the Protestant King CHARLES I by proxy in 1625 and went to England. After the death of the duke of BUCKINGHAM (1628) her relationship with Charles became close and affectionate. She was attacked (e.g., in House of Commons, 1629) for attempting to advance Catholicism.

In Feb. 1642, as CIVIL WAR loomed, Henrietta Maria went abroad to raise money, returning with munitions in Jan. 1643. She spent 1643–4 at the Royalist capital of OXFORD (at Merton College), then went to France (July 1644). She never saw Charles again (he was executed in 1649). After the RESTORATION (1660) she made three visits to England. Her children included CHARLES II and JAMES VII/II. *See also* SPANISH MATCH.

HENRY, PRINCE OF WALES (b. 19 Feb. 1594 at Stirling, C Scotland; d. 6 Nov. 1612 at Westminster, Middlesex, England, aged 18). The eldest child of King JAMES VI/I, Henry became a strong Protestant and an enthusiast for military and artistic activities (e.g., collecting paintings). Created prince of Wales in 1610, his early death was widely seen as robbing England and Scotland of an exceptional future monarch. His younger brother Charles became heir (*see* CHARLES I). *See also* ALEXANDER, WILLIAM; SPANISH MATCH.

HENRY I (b. 1068 or 1069 possibly at Selby, Yorkshire, England; d. 1 Dec. 1135 at Lyons-la-Forêt, Normandy, aged 66 or 67). The third surviving son of King WILLIAM I, Henry succeeded WILLIAM II (older brother) as king of England (2 Aug. 1100). He sought popular support by denouncing William's policies (in 'coronation charter', 5 Aug.), arresting RANULF FLAMBARD, and marrying (Nov.) the half-English Edith (or Matilda, d. 1118), daughter of Queen MARGARET of Scotland. Henry also recalled Archbishop ANSELM from exile.

Henry's position was challenged by his older brother ROBERT CURTHOSE, duke of Normandy, who landed in England (July 1101). Henry forced Robert to abandon his claim (treaty of Alton). In 1106 Henry defeated Robert at TINCHEBRAI and appropriated Normandy.

Henry found his authority within the Church challenged by Anselm's desire to implement a Church council decree

(1099) against lay investiture of churchmen. They eventually agreed (1106) that bishops could be elected but their appointment would require Henry's approval.

Henry fathered at least 24 bastards (e.g., ROBERT OF GLOUCESTER) but only one legitimate male heir, who died in 1120 (*see* WHITE SHIP DISASTER). A second marriage proved childless. So Henry sought to ensure the succession of his daughter MATILDA. On his death STEPHEN (nephew) seized the kingship. Conflict ensued. *See also* GOVERNMENT, ENGLAND 1066 TO 1509.

HENRY II (b. 5 March 1133 at Le Mans, Maine; d. 6 July 1189 at Chinon, Touraine, aged 56). Henry's childhood was overshadowed by his parents' attempt to capture NORMANDY (duchy) and England (kingdom) from STEPHEN. (His father was Geoffrey of Anjou, his mother was Empress MATILDA.) Henry received Normandy from his father in 1150, and succeeded him as count of Anjou in Sept. 1151. Through marriage to ELEANOR OF AQUITAINE (1152) he controlled extensive lands in W France. He succeeded Stephen as king of England on 25 Oct. 1154.

Henry's priority in England was to reassert royal authority. He demolished 'adulterine' (unlicensed) castles, and in 1157 recovered lands from Scottish rule (*see* DAVID I; MALCOLM IV). He strengthened the justice system (*see* COMMON LAW; CLARENDON, ASSIZE OF; POSSESSORY ASSIZES). But his assertion of royal rights in the Church was resisted by Archbishop Thomas BECKET (1160s). The murder of Becket (1170) damaged Henry's reputation.

Henry's authority was often challenged. In 1171–2 he intervened in Ireland to prevent STRONGBOW (a subordinate lord) from establishing royal authority (*see* HENRY II AND IRELAND). His family proved troublesome (e.g., *see* REVOLT OF 1173–4). Henry allegedly died on hearing that his favourite son, JOHN, had joined a rebellion. Succeeded by RICHARD I. *See also* ANARCHY; ANGEVIN EMPIRE; PLANTAGENETS.

HENRY II AND IRELAND England's rule in Ireland started during Henry's reign. Henry possibly considered invasion in 1155 but refrained (*see* LAUDABILITER). In 1166 he permitted Diarmait MAC MURCHADA, an ousted Irish high-king, to recruit mercenaries from his lands. Their success, especially the succession (1171) of STRONGBOW as high-king of LEINSTER (E Ireland), provoked Henry to visit Ireland (17 Oct. 1171–17 April 1172), where he made himself lord of Ireland. Henry forced Strongbow to surrender Leinster, retained DUBLIN, WEXFORD and WATERFORD as royal lands, and established subordinate territories by granting Leinster to Strongbow and MEATH to Hugh de Lacy as lordships. Many Irish kings also submitted, but not the high-king, Ruaidrí Ua CONCHOBAIR (submitted in 1175; *see* WINDSOR, TREATY OF).

In 1177 Henry granted away more lands in Ireland. He also decided to make Ireland a kingdom under his son John. He transferred the lordship in March 1185 and sent John to Ireland (*see* JOHN AND IRELAND). Though the Pope provided a crown (1187), it was never used. Ireland remained a royal lordship. *See also* NORMANS, IMPACT ON IRELAND.

HENRY III (b. 1 Oct. 1207 at Winchester, Hampshire, England; d. 16 Nov. 1272 at Westminster, Middlesex, England, aged 65). Henry succeeded JOHN (father) as king of England and lord of Ireland while a minor (crowned 28 Oct. 1216). A Council was formed with William MARSHAL as regent; French invaders were expelled (*see* ENGLAND, FRENCH INVASION). Marshal resigned in 1219. From Oct. 1221 Hubert de BURGH was pre-eminent, retaining influence after Henry took power (Jan. 1227).

Henry desired to regain lost French lands and in 1230 attempted to recover Poitou (*see* ANGEVIN EMPIRE). In 1232 he replaced de Burgh with Peter des ROCHES and Peter de RIVALLIS. But following a rebellion by Richard Marshal (1233), Henry was forced to oust them (1234; *see* EDMUND OF ABINGDON). He then relied mainly on administrators and foreign relatives (*see* LUSIGNANS). In 1242 Henry campaigned again in Poitou. He began rebuilding WESTMINSTER Abbey in 1245.

Henry's campaign to pacify GASCONY in 1253 generated indebtedness. His acceptance of the Sicilian Crown for his son Edmund (1254), involving payments to the Pope, and favouritism for the Lusignans aggravated the situation. In 1258 magnates revolted, demanding reforms. For seven years Henry struggled against BARONS, including Simon de MONTFORT (*see* BARONIAL CONFLICT AND WARS). Henry eventually prevailed. Succeeded by EDWARD I.

HENRY IV (b. 3 April 1367 at Bolingbroke, Lincolnshire, England; d. 20 March 1413 at Westminster, Middlesex, England, aged 45). Henry Bolingbroke, son of JOHN OF GAUNT, was created earl of Derby (1377) and of Hereford (1384). In 1387–8 he campaigned against counsellors of King RICHARD II (*see* APPELLANTS; MERCILESS PARLIAMENT), but later (1397) supported Richard's attack on the duke of Gloucester and earls of Arundel and Warwick, and was made duke of Hereford.

In 1398 Richard exiled Bolingbroke for accusing the duke of Norfolk of conspiracy. After Gaunt died and Bolingbroke became duke of Lancaster (Feb. 1399), Richard confiscated Bolingbroke's inheritance. While Richard was in Ireland (from June), Henry recruited supporters in France. Landing in Yorkshire (July), he captured the returning Richard at Conwy, Wales (Aug.). Richard was deposed and Henry became king and also lord of Ireland (30 Sept.), ignoring another claim (*see* MORTIMER FAMILY).

Henry soon faced rebellions. A revolt spread through Wales from 1400 (*see* OWAIN GLYN DŴR). Henry also defeated Henry PERCY (1403), and a revolt involving Archbishop Richard SCROPE (1405). From *c*.1405 Henry suffered illness. He pursued negotiations with France, and civil war there led him to plan a campaign (1411–12), but illness prevented it and his health collapsed (late 1412). Succeeded by HENRY V. *See also* LANCASTRIANS; BEAUFORT, HENRY; HUNDRED YEARS WAR.

HENRY V (b. 16 Sept. 1387 at Monmouth, March of Wales; d. 31 Aug. or 1 Sept. 1422 at Vincennes, France, aged 34). The eldest son of HENRY IV (king of England and lord of Ireland from 1399), Henry was created prince of Wales in Oct. 1399 and duke of Lancaster in Nov. During 1402–8 he fought against the Welsh revolt (*see* OWAIN GLYN DŴR), and in 1403 against Henry PERCY. He joined the king's Council (1406) and with Henry BEAUFORT assumed control after the dismissal of Thomas ARUNDEL (1409). But in Nov. 1412 Prince Henry and other councillors were dismissed by the king, possibly because the Beauforts sought the king's abdication.

After succeeding as king (21 March 1413), Henry negotiated with France while preparing for war. After defeating OLDCASTLE'S RISING (1414) and discovering the SOUTHAMPTON PLOT (1415), he invaded France (Aug. 1415). He besieged Harfleur (Aug.–Sept.), defeated the French at Agincourt (25 Oct.), and returned. He invaded again in Aug. 1417, and conquered Normandy by summer 1419. After allying with the duke of BURGUNDY (25 Dec.), Henry concluded the treaty of TROYES (May 1420), becoming regent of France and the king's heir. In 1421 Henry campaigned N of Paris, but died from dysentery during the siege of Meaux. Succeeded by HENRY VI. *See also* LANCASTRIANS; HUNDRED YEARS WAR.

HENRY VI (b. 6 Dec. 1421 at Windsor, Berkshire, England; d. 21 May 1471 at London, England, aged 49). Henry succeeded HENRY V (father) as king of England and lord of Ireland on 1 Sept. 1422, aged 8 months, and was recognized as king of France (21 Oct., under treaty of TROYES). The duke of BEDFORD became regent in France. In England the duke of GLOUCESTER and Henry BEAUFORT vied for control. As ruler from 1437, Henry favoured Beaufort (d. 1447) and the earl of Suffolk (William de la POLE). Suffolk arranged (1444) a French truce and Henry's marriage to MARGARET OF ANJOU. When Normandy was lost (1449), Suffolk was impeached. Edmund BEAUFORT, duke of Somerset, was now favoured.

From 1450 Henry's rule was attacked by Richard, duke of YORK. On Henry's mental collapse, York became 'protector' (March 1454–Feb. 1455); after Somerset was killed (22 May) he acted again (Oct. 1455–Feb. 1456). Queen Margaret then took control.

War erupted in 1459. In 1461 Henry was deposed by York's son Edward. Exiled in Scotland, he was captured in 1465. When Richard, earl of Warwick, rejected Edward, Henry was reinstated (3 Oct. 1470–11 April 1471) but was deposed again and executed. He was briefly revered as a saint. *See also* YORKIST–LANCASTRIAN CONFLICT; EDWARD IV; WARWICK, RICHARD EARL OF.

HENRY VII (b. 28 Jan. 1457 at Pembroke, Pembrokeshire, Wales; d. 21 April 1509 at Richmond, Surrey, England, aged 52). A LANCASTRIAN claimant to the English throne and lordship of Ireland from 1471, Henry Tudor lived in exile in Brittany and France 1471–85. In 1485 he landed in Wales (7 Aug.) and deposed King RICHARD III at BOSWORTH (22 Aug.).

Henry's initial priority was securing the throne against YORKIST challengers. His marriage to ELIZABETH OF YORK (18 Jan. 1486) failed to reconcile Yorkists. Insurrections followed: LOVELL'S CONSPIRACY (1486), the invasions of Lambert SIMNEL (1487) and Perkin WARBECK (1497), SUFFOLK'S REBELLION (1501). Henry's foreign policy sought to win recognition and exclude Yorkist pretenders. He allied with Spain (1489; *see* MEDINA DEL CAMPO, TREATY OF), exacted a treaty with France (1492; *see* ÉTAPLES, TREATY OF), and made peace with Scotland (treaty of Ayton, 1502). His heir ARTHUR married KATHERINE OF ARAGON (1501), his daughter Mary married JAMES IV of Scotland (1503).

From 1501 Henry increasingly enforced his rule by imposing recognizances (contracts for good behaviour) on noblemen and others. He also greatly increased royal revenues. From 1504 his principal agents were Edmund DUDLEY and Richard EMPSON. He was succeeded by HENRY VIII. *See also* TUDOR FAMILY; BEAUFORT, MARGARET; YORKIST–LANCASTRIAN CONFLICT; NEW MONARCHY, ENGLAND; MORTON, RICHARD; HENRY VII AND IRELAND; ROYAL HOUSEHOLD, ENGLAND.

HENRY VII AND IRELAND Henry's interventions were mainly responses to rebellions. When Henry Tudor, a Lancastrian, became king of England and lord of Ireland (1485), most Anglo-Irish MAGNATES were Yorkists, including the governor, the (8th) earl of Kildare (*see* YORKIST–LANCASTRIAN CONFLICT, ROLE OF IRELAND). Yorkist rebels therefore used Ireland as a base.

In 1487 the rebellion of Lambert SIMNEL was launched in Ireland. Henry sent Sir Richard Edgecombe to take oaths of loyalty from Simnel's supporters (May–July 1488). In 1491–2 the rebel Perkin WARBECK recruited in Ireland. Henry removed Kildare from office (20 May 1492) and sent Sir Edward POYNINGS (Oct. 1494–Dec. 1495), who asserted English control over the Irish government and Parliament (*see* POYNINGS' LAW). On 6 Aug. 1496 Henry reappointed

Kildare as deputy, after he had sworn to uphold royal interests. Kildare remained in office beyond Henry's death (*see* KILDARE ASCENDANCY).

HENRY VIII (b. 28 June 1491 at Greenwich, Kent, England; d. 28 Jan. 1547 at Westminster, Middlesex, England, aged 56). Henry succeeded HENRY VII (father) as king of England and lord of Ireland on 22 April 1509, aged 17. He waged war against France 1512–14, then pursued a pacific foreign policy directed by chief minister Thomas WOLSEY. Treaties were concluded with the Holy Roman Emperor (Charles V, 1522), and France (1525).

By 1527 Henry worried about lack of a male heir. Wolsey failed to obtain papal annulment of Henry's marriage, so he could remarry, and lost office (1529; *see* GREAT MATTER). Thomas CROMWELL restricted APPEALS to Rome, enabling Thomas CRANMER (archbishop of Canterbury) to declare Henry's marriage invalid (23 May 1533). In 1534 Henry was confirmed as head of the English Church. Cromwell also organized the DISSOLUTION OF RELIGIOUS HOUSES (1536–40) and promoted evangelical reforms. Henry's third wife, Jane Seymour, produced a male heir, Edward, in 1537.

From 1536 Henry's religious views became conservative (*see* TEN ARTICLES). Cromwell was dismissed in 1540, following the failure of Henry's fourth marriage. Thereafter Henry ceased to rely on pre-eminent ministers. During 1542–5 he resumed warfare with Scotland and France. His health declined in late 1546. Succeeded by EDWARD VI. *See also* HENRY VIII, WIVES OF; SUCCESSION ACTS; REFORMATION, ENGLAND; HENRY VIII AND IRELAND; SCOTTISH–ENGLISH RELATIONS 1357 TO 1603.

HENRY VIII, WIVES OF Henry VIII, king of England and ruler of Ireland 1509–47, married KATHERINE OF ARAGON on 11 June 1509. Her sole child to survive infancy, MARY, was born on 18 Feb. 1516. The marriage was annulled on 23 May 1533. Henry had already married Anne BOLEYN (25 Jan. 1533). She gave birth to ELIZABETH on 7 Sept. Anne was executed for treasonable adultery on 19 May 1536.

Anne's enemies had introduced Jane Seymour (b. 1508 or 1509) to Henry. They married on 30 May 1536. She gave birth to EDWARD (VI) on 12 Oct. 1537 but died (24 Oct.). Henry's subsequent marriage, to ANNE OF CLEVES on 6 Jan. 1540, was soon annulled (9 July). Henry's next wife, Katherine HOWARD, was put forward by the religious conservatives Stephen GARDINER and the (3rd) duke of NORFOLK. She and Henry married on 28 July 1540 but Katherine was executed for treason (13 Feb. 1542). Henry married his final wife, Katherine PARR, on 12 July 1543. She survived him, dying in 1548. All of Henry's wives were descendants of King EDWARD I. *See also* SUCCESSION ACTS.

HENRY VIII AND IRELAND Henry continued Henry VII's delegation of government to the (Anglo-Irish) earls of Kildare (*see* KILDARE ASCENDANCY). But he resented his weak position (most of Ireland lay outside royal authority), and distrusted the 9th earl of Kildare (*see* SURREY EXPEDITION).

The KILDARE REBELLION (1534) caused a policy change: governors were now sent from England and Henry's authority was enhanced. In 1536 Lord Grey removed the Irish Church from papal jurisdiction and made Henry its head (as in England). In 1541 Henry's style was raised from 'lord' to 'king', and royal government was reintroduced to some Anglo-Irish lordships (*see* ST LEGER, ANTHONY; DESMOND, EARLS OF). 'Conquest by conciliation' was attempted (1540–3): many Gaelic Irish lords accepted Henry's rule together with English law and customs (*see* SURRENDER AND REGRANT). The policies had limited success: new initiatives were required after Henry's death (1547). *See also* IRELAND, ENGLISH CONQUEST, 16TH CENTURY.

HENRY OF BLOIS (b. *c*.1096 or *c*.1100 in Blois, France; d. 8 or 9 Aug. 1171 at Winchester, Hampshire, England, aged in 70s). A monk, abbot of Glastonbury (from 1126) and also bishop of WINCHESTER (from 1129), Henry helped STEPHEN (brother) to become king of England (1135). Offended at not being elected archbishop of Canterbury (1138), he briefly defected to MATILDA, challenger to Stephen's rule (March–July 1141).

Henry helped to negotiate a settlement between Stephen and Henry Plantagenet (treaty of Winchester, 1153), and later tried to mediate between Henry and Thomas BECKET. His considerable income enabled Henry to be a castle-builder and opulent patron of the arts, including illuminated manuscripts and enamels. *See also* THEOBALD OF BEC; HENRY II.

HENRY THE YOUNG KING (b. 28 Feb. 1155 at London, England; d. 11 June 1183 at Martel, Aquitaine, aged 28). The eldest surviving son of King HENRY II, Henry was (unusually for England) crowned during his father's lifetime (14 June 1170). He nonetheless joined the REVOLT OF 1173–4 against his father, and supported a rebellion against RICHARD (brother) in Aquitaine (1182–3). He predeceased his father, dying of dysentery.

HEPTARCHY Term meaning 'seven governments', used from the 12th century to describe Anglo-Saxon England in the 7th century; it refers to the kingdoms of NORTHUMBRIA, MERCIA, EAST ANGLIA, ESSEX, KENT, SUSSEX and WESSEX. It implies misleadingly that the kingdoms were coherent and stable, and ignores smaller kingdoms and peoples. *See also* KINGSHIP, ANGLO-SAXON.

HERBERT FAMILY A Welsh gentry family which originated in GWENT (SE Wales) and was active in Welsh and English affairs 15th–17th centuries. Sir William Herbert ('Black William', *c*.1423–69) was a leading Welsh YORKIST (created earl of Pembroke 1468). His grandson (by an illegitimate son) William Herbert (*c*.1506–70) was an influential courtier during the reigns of HENRY VIII to ELIZABETH (earl of Pembroke by second creation 1551). Later descendants included the poet George Herbert (1593–1633). *See also* GENTRY, WALES.

HEREFORD A city in W England, by the R. Wye; centre of Herefordshire.

Hereford originated in the 7th century as a Germanic settlement by a strategic river-crossing (leading to Wales). Its name means 'Army ford'. An episcopal see was founded for the MAGONSÆTE (by 680), and later a BURH (possibly late 8th century). Hereford was a shire centre from the mid 10th century.

In the 12th–16th centuries Hereford was important for wool exporting and cloth making. Thereafter it served as a local market and county town, growing in the late 20th century as small-scale industry expanded (e.g., electronics).

Est. popn: 1086, 2000; 1300, 4000; 1600, 4000; 1800, 6800; 1900, 24,000; 2000, 40,000.

HERITABLE JURISDICTIONS, SCOTLAND, ABOLITION OF Private heritable jurisdictions and offices, such as REGALITIES and sheriff posts, were abolished by the British government, by the Heritable Jurisdictions (Scotland) Act of 1747 (effective from 25 March 1748). Responding to the JACOBITE REBELLION of 1745, the government's aim was to reduce the power of Highland CLANS, though rights were abolished throughout Scotland. Crown jurisdiction was restored to perhaps half the country. (BARONIES retained minor rights.) *See also* COURTS, SCOTLAND; LOCAL GOVERNMENTAL STRUCTURES, SCOTLAND.

HERITAGE INDUSTRY Term coined by the British cultural critic Robert Hewison (b. 1943) for his book *The Heritage Industry: Britain in a Climate of Decline* (1987). It refers to the manufacture and promotion of a particular view of the past by so-called 'heritage organizations' (e.g., museums, NATIONAL TRUST, government agencies). Hewison argued that they created a sanitized idea of history – based on a sense of contemporary decline and disintegration, and on nostalgia for a safe, non-existent golden age – and distracted interest from modern art and culture.

HERITOR Term (meaning 'one who inherits') used in Scotland, particularly from the 17th century, for an owner of heritable landed property (either freeholder or feuar).

Heritors were required to support the parish church and manse (1663–1925), and parish schools and schoolmasters (1646–61, 1696–1872). *See also* POOR RELIEF, SCOTLAND.

HESELTINE, MICHAEL (b. 21 March 1933 at Swansea, Glamorgan, Wales). A successful publisher, Heseltine was a Conservative MP 1966–2001. He held posts in the British government under Edward HEATH (1970–4), and served Margaret THATCHER as environment secretary 1979–83. As defence secretary from 1983 he vigorously contested the CAMPAIGN FOR NUCLEAR DISARMAMENT (over stationing of US missiles in Britain) before resigning in the WESTLAND CRISIS (1986). Ambitious and pro-European, he disliked the COMMUNITY CHARGE and challenged Thatcher for the Party leadership (Nov. 1990), winning sufficient support to oust her but not to succeed her.

Under John MAJOR, Heseltine was environment secretary (1990–2) and president of the Board of Trade (from 1992). In 1995 he supported Major's re-election as leader, and was rewarded with appointment as deputy prime minister (1995–7). He was created Lord Heseltine in 2001. *See also* HOWE, GEOFFREY; BRIXTON AND TOXTETH RIOTS.

HICKS, JOHN (b. 8 April 1904 at Warwick, Warwickshire, England; d. 20 May 1989 at Blockley, Gloucestershire, England, aged 85). An economist, Hicks held academic posts from 1926, including a professorship at OXFORD University (1946–65). His publications, notably *Value and Capital* (1939), included reassessments of basic economic concepts. His model summarizing the macroeconomics of J.M. KEYNES, and propositions regarding such matters as wages, consumers and price changes, and welfare economics widely influenced other economists and policy-making. Knighted (1964), Hicks was the first British person to be awarded the Nobel Prize in Economics (1972).

HIDE In Anglo-Saxon England, a term which originally (from 5th century) referred to land sufficient to sustain a 'family' (freeman and dependant tenants), usually reckoned at 120 acres. (OE *hid* and the related terms *hiwisc* and *hiwscipe* mean 'family' or 'household'.) The hide became an assessment unit: for tribute liability (by mid 7th century, *see* TRIBAL HIDAGE), other services (by 8th century, *see* THREE PUBLIC SERVICES), and taxation (*see* GELD). In the DANELAW the carucate replaced the hide; 'sulungs' were used in KENT. Use of hides largely ceased in the 12th century. *See also* BURGHAL HIDAGE.

HIGH CHURCH Term used from the 1690s to describe mainly clergy of the Church of ENGLAND who promoted an exalted view of the Church's authority, the office of bishop, and ceremonies and sacraments. They looked back to positions taken by anti-Puritans of the early 17th century,

notably Archbishop William LAUD, and had become numerous since the RESTORATION (1660). Usually TORIES, they opposed DISSENTERS, LATITUDINARIANS and Low Churchmen. In the 1690s, following the TOLERATION ACT, they resented WHIG support for dissent.

High Churchmen were politically weak after the accession of King GEORGE I (1714) because of Whig dominance. Their principles were reasserted against EVANGELICALISM in the late 18th century, and were largely subsumed by the OXFORD MOVEMENT in the 19th century. *See also* NON-JURORS; SACHEVERELL AFFAIR; ATTERBURY, FRANCIS.

HIGHER EDUCATION, EXPANSION OF Before the 1820s, post-school education was available from two UNIVERSITIES in England, five in Scotland, one in Ireland, and from DISSENTING ACADEMIES. Various concerns expanded higher education, still catering for a small minority until the late 20th century.

A need for more school teachers motivated religious societies to start training colleges from the 1820s. New universities were founded: in England as a result of religious rivalry and civic aspirations (another nine by 1914); in Ireland by State and Catholic initiatives (two universities); in Wales by nationalist ambitions (federal university). From 1873 the 'university extension' movement provided academic lectures in English towns, reinforced from 1903 by Workers' Educational Association classes, initially in England. Anxieties about inadequate technical and scientific education produced specialist institutions from 1880, and in 1889 authorization for local funding of technical colleges (*see* TECHNICAL EDUCATION).

From 1919 government financial support for universities was provided through a University Grants Committee (for Great Britain from 1922). In Britain from the 1950s the government periodically expanded higher education: from 1956 some colleges became Colleges of Advanced Technology to expand technical education; university places were increased following the 'Robbins Report' (1963); more colleges were upgraded from 1969 as 'polytechnics' ('central institutions' in Scotland) mainly to provide degree-level vocational education; an Open University (started 1969) offered 'distance learning' for older adults. By 1972 the age-related participation rate was 14%. From 1992 the 'élite system' was changed to a 'mass system' to provide a larger, more educated workforce: polytechnics and various colleges became universities, and institutions increased places. In 2009–10 the participation rate reached 46%.

In the Republic of Ireland, nine regional technical colleges were opened in the 1970s, and expanded from 1992 into 14 Institutes of Technology. More universities were created from 1989; by 2019 there were eight. The participation rate in 2009–10 was 53%. *See also* MECHANICS' INSTITUTES.

HIGH FARMING Term widely used from the 1840s for farming that invested in new advances, such as under-drainage of land, phosphate fertilisers and mechanized threshing. It also referred to more efficient feeding arrangements for cattle which increased manure and improved meat. Though considered as 'superior' farming, it was expensive, and risky when grain prices were falling. 'High farming' techniques were applied in mixed-farming areas of the British Isles until the AGRICULTURAL DEPRESSION (from 1870s). *See also* CAIRD, JAMES; AGRICULTURE, ENGLAND FROM MID 18TH CENTURY.

HIGHLAND GATHERINGS Annual meetings held in the Scottish HIGHLANDS for sports and cultural activities. Originating in celebrations at cattle fairs and in tests of military strength, many gatherings were started between 1781 and 1820, during the development of CLAN culture. Events included caber tossing, running, piping, dancing and even dismembering stunned cows. Without the last, gatherings remained popular in the early 21st century. *See also* SPORT, SCOTLAND.

HIGHLANDS The mainly rugged and mountainous northern and western parts of Scotland, sharply divided from the Lowlands; until the mid 18th century they contained 40% of the POPULATION. With few extensive areas of good soils, the Highlands were an essentially pastoral region. They were distinguished from the 14th century onwards by the continuing predominance of Gaelic speech (ebbing elsewhere in Scotland) and development of CLAN-based society. Remote from central authority, the Highlands were difficult to control until the JACOBITE REBELLION of 1745. *See also* AGRICULTURE, SCOTLAND BEFORE/FROM 18TH CENTURY; HIGHLAND GATHERINGS; HIGHLAND SOCIETY OF EDINBURGH.

HIGHLAND SOCIETY OF EDINBURGH An organization founded by Highland landowners in 1784 to improve the agriculture and economy of the HIGHLANDS, and to preserve and promote their culture. It supported a Gaelic piper and bard, collected Gaelic manuscripts, and sponsored a Gaelic dictionary (published 1828). From 1844 it operated mainly as an agricultural society (as the Royal Highland and Agricultural Society). *See also* GAELIC LANGUAGE AND LITERATURE, NORTH BRITAIN AND SCOTLAND.

HIGH POLITICS Historians' term, popular from the late 19th century, for interactions within élites in distinct arenas, such as a royal court, government, legislature, party-political leadership. The term 'low politics' has sometimes been used for underhand political behaviour (e.g., bribery). From the 1970s political scientists defined 'high politics' as matters relating to the survival of a State (e.g., security policy, defence provision) and 'low politics' as domestic matters (e.g., economic policy, social welfare), while acknowledging their interdependence.

HILD (b. 614 in Deira; d. 17 Nov. 680 at Whitby, Northumbria, aged 65 or 66). A member of the royal kindred of DEIRA (NE England), Hild was baptized in 627 and became a nun and abbess by 651. In 657 she founded a monastic 'double house' (communities of men and women) at Whitby of which she was abbess. In 664 it hosted the synod at which Northumbria abandoned Irish customs (*see* WHITBY, SYNOD OF).

HILL, OCTAVIA (b. 3 Dec. 1838 at Wisbech, Cambridgeshire, England; 13 Aug. 1912 at London, England, aged 73). In the 1850s Hill was shocked by poverty and insanitary housing in London. From 1865, with financial support from John RUSKIN, she refurbished and rented out cottages, and helped tenants to find employment. Her example proved influential. Hill was also involved in the CHARITY ORGANISATION SOCIETY (founded 1869), and from 1884 managed properties in London for the ECCLESIASTICAL COMMISSIONERS. She was a co-founder of the NATIONAL TRUST (1895), to conserve 'places of historic interest or natural beauty'.

HILL, ROWLAND (b. 3 Dec. 1795 at Kidderminster, Worcestershire, England; d. 27 Aug. 1879 at Hampstead, Middlesex, England, aged 83). A schoolmaster who became concerned about inefficient and expensive postal services, Hill wrote the pamphlet *Post Office Reform* (1837). He proposed cheap uniform postage rates and prepayment, which would provide social and commercial benefits and be self-funding through increased volumes of mail (an example of UTILITARIANISM). The scheme was adopted, and Hill worked at the Treasury (1839–42) to assist implementation (1840, throughout the UK). He served as secretary to the postmaster-general 1846–54, and as secretary of the POST OFFICE 1854–64 (knighted 1860).

HILLFORTS, BRITAIN Hillforts are earthworks with defences, usually following the contours of a hill. Ranging from defended farmsteads to villages, pastoral enclosures and storage centres (e.g., DANEBURY), they flourished from *c*.600 to *c*.300 BC (in the IRON AGE), though NEOLITHIC and BRONZE AGE examples occur; some were reoccupied in post-Roman times. Sites in SW England (e.g., MAIDEN CASTLE) were used during the CLAUDIAN INVASION of Britain. About 3,600 hillforts are known.

HILLFORTS, IRELAND About 500 hillforts have been identified. Usually less than 25 acres (10 ha) in area, they do not appear to represent significant centres of population. Defences are uncomplex (e.g., a single rampart) and entrances are simple. Their principal period of use was *c*.1000– *c*.700 BC, i.e., during the Late BRONZE AGE. It is unlikely that they were built by invaders and their purposes remain uncertain.

HILLSBOROUGH AGREEMENT Signed 15 Nov. 1985 at Hillsborough, Co. Down, Northern Ireland, by the British and Irish prime ministers (Margaret THATCHER, Garret FITZGERALD). It sought to support the SOCIAL DEMOCRATIC AND LABOUR PARTY in Northern Ireland against pressure from PROVISIONAL SINN FÉIN by conceding a role in Northern Ireland to the government of the Republic of Ireland (through an Inter-Governmental Conference). It also affirmed that a change in Northern Ireland's status required majority consent. 'Hillsborough' was denounced by Unionists. *See also* NORTHERN IRELAND; TROUBLES.

HILLSBOROUGH DISASTER An incident in SHEFFIELD (N England) at the Hillsborough Stadium of Sheffield Wednesday Football Club on 15 April 1989, during a match between LIVERPOOL Football Club and Nottingham Forest. Police allowed Liverpool fans without tickets to enter the stadium, resulting in overcrowding and 96 deaths, all except one of Liverpool supporters. Some media commentators influenced by the police claimed that the drunkenness of fans caused the disaster, and inquests recorded verdicts of accidental death (1991).

Families of the deceased campaigned to disclose how the police and other authorities had concealed the extent of official incompetence at the stadium. In 2000 the match commander, David Duckenfield, was tried on two specimen charges of manslaughter under a private prosecution but the jury was unable to reach a verdict. In 2012 new inquests were ordered. Held from 2014 to 2016 (the longest jury proceedings in British legal history), they concluded that the deceased had been unlawfully killed. Duckenfield was retried on manslaughter charges in 2019 but again the jury was unable to deliver a verdict (April). A retrial was held (Oct.—Nov.) which resulted in Duckenfield's acquittal.

HISTORICAL PERIODS History, as differentiated from PREHISTORY, refers to the past that is knowable from written sources. For southern Britain (most of modern England, and Wales) the earliest historical period is the Roman period (AD 43–early 5th century; *see* ROMAN BRITAIN). For northern Britain (including modern Scotland) and Ireland, which were outside Roman rule, history generally begins in the 5th century, though sources for the former are poor until the 12th century.

The 5th–15th centuries are conventionally called the 'Middle Ages', a concept invented in 15th-century Italy to denote the interval between 'classical' Greek and Roman culture and its revival (*see* HUMANISM). The Middle Ages are sometimes divided into 'Early' (5th–10th centuries), 'High' (11th–13th centuries) and 'Late' (14th–15th centuries). The 5th and 6th centuries are also termed the 'Dark Ages', because developments are unclear due to paucity of sources and difficulty of interpretation (*see* POST-ROMAN BRITAIN). In English history the period from the 5th century to 1066 is often called the 'Anglo-Saxon period', referring to the presence of Germanic culture and kingdoms (differing from the Brittonic and Gaelic societies elsewhere). A key aspect of the Middle Ages was the assimilation of the British Isles to the Western Christian Church. There is no generally accepted definitive end-point.

The 16th–late 18th centuries are frequently called the 'Early Modern period', acknowledging such developments as assertive central government (*see* NEW MONARCHY, ENGLAND/SCOTLAND); establishment of State churches by the REFORMATION; agrarian and mercantile CAPITALISM; OVERSEAS EXPLORATION and imperial expansion (*see* BRITISH EMPIRE). The INDUSTRIAL REVOLUTION from the late 18th century is conventionally held to mark the start of the 'Late Modern' or 'Modern' period (to present).

History within the British Isles is also divided into periods named after ruling dynasties (e.g., 'Tudor period' for England, Wales and Ireland 1485–1603) or individual monarchs (e.g., 'Victorian period' for 1837–1901). *See also* IRELAND; DE-INDUSTRIALIZATION.

HOARE–LAVAL PACT An Anglo-French exercise in APPEASEMENT of Italy after its invasion of Abyssinia (Ethiopia) in 1935. On 8 Dec., the British foreign secretary, Sir Samuel Hoare, and the French premier, Pierre Laval, secretly proposed a partition of Abyssinia, awarding some territory to Italy. When the proposal was leaked, public indignation at betrayal of the LEAGUE OF NATIONS, which had begun imposing sanctions, forced the British government to disown the plan. Hoare resigned (18 Dec.). Italian forces occupied the entire country. *See also* ITALY, BRITISH RELATIONS WITH.

HOBART'S ACT Popular name for the Catholic Relief Act passed by the Irish Parliament in Feb. 1793; named after Robert Hobart (chief secretary for Ireland). It was passed under pressure from the British government following a campaign by the CATHOLIC COMMITTEE. Britain was anxious to retain Catholic loyalty following the FRENCH REVOLUTION. The Act extended the parliamentary franchise, and opened many Crown offices, to Catholics. Catholics became eligible to study at, and obtain degrees from, the University of Dublin (Trinity College). They could also hold arms on the same terms as Protestants. *See also* CATHOLIC RELIEF AND EMANCIPATION, IRELAND.

HOBBES, THOMAS (b. 5 April 1588 at Malmesbury, Wiltshire, England; d. 3 Dec. 1679 at Hardwick, Derbyshire, England, aged 91). In 1608, after studying at OXFORD University, Hobbes became private tutor to a nobleman. Dismissive of traditional scholasticism, he formulated a moral philosophy based on mathematical reasoning, and developed his interests partly by visiting Continental Europe (1629–30, 1634).

In the late 1630s Hobbes appeared to be a supporter of royal prerogative rights (*see* CHARLES I, PERSONAL RULE). Fearful of radicals, he fled to France in 1640. In 1651 he published *Leviathan*, a political treatise which seemingly justified the transfer of allegiance by a people to a new sovereign power. Many viewed it as supportive of England's ruling RUMP PARLIAMENT, which had executed King CHARLES I, and disloyal to the exiled CHARLES II. After returning to England (1652), Hobbes was accused of atheism. His lifetime's writings made him one of England greatest philosophers.

HOBSON, J.A. (b. 6 July 1858 at Derby, Derbyshire, England; d. 1 April 1940 at Hampstead, London, England, aged 81). Originally a schoolmaster and lecturer, John Atkinson Hobson from 1889 became a prolific author, eventually writing over 50 books. Interested in economics and ethics, he influenced NEW LIBERALISM and later the WELFARE STATE. His visit to southern Africa in 1899, to report on the (Second) BOER WAR for the *Manchester Guardian*, resulted in his most important work: *Imperialism: A Study* (1902). It argued that IMPERIALISM was driven partly by the need for countries to acquire new markets in which rich people could invest surplus wealth, thereby encouraging greed and militarism. Hobson rejected socialism while advocating redistribution of resources.

HODGKIN, DOROTHY (b. 12 May 1910 at Giza, Egypt; d. 29 July 1994 at Ilmington, Warwickshire, England, aged 84). Interested in crystals from childhood, Dorothy Crowfoot (Hodgkin from 1937) studied chemistry at OXFORD University (1928–32) where she used the relatively new technique of X-ray diffraction for investigating the atomic and molecular structure of crystals. Briefly in CAMBRIDGE (1932–4), she returned to her Oxford college, Somerville, and soon began studying insulin. Her pupils included a future prime minister (*see* THATCHER, MARGARET). She retired in 1977.

In 1939 Hodgkin agreed to work out the structure of PENICILLIN, and succeeded (1945). By 1957 she discovered the structure of vitamin B12 (important for human health), and in 1969 finally determined the structure of insulin, her greatest achievement. She was elected a fellow of the ROYAL SOCIETY (1947) and received the 1964 Nobel Prize in Chemistry. Hodgkin was involved in international scientific and political activities (e.g., visiting scientists in China).

HOLBEIN, HANS, THE YOUNGER (b. 1497 or 1498 at Augsburg, Germany; d. Nov. 1543 at London, England, aged about 45). A painter of religious works and portraits, Holbein worked mainly in Basel, Switzerland, 1515–26, and then in England, 1526–8, where he undertook commissions for German merchants and painted the family of Thomas MORE. Holbein returned to Basel, but the Reformation there (1528) caused him to seek patrons abroad. By 1532 he had returned to England. Probably in 1535 he was appointed court painter. He projected the image of King HENRY VIII and created a powerful representation of the early 16th-century élite. *See also* VISUAL ARTS, BRITAIN.

HOLIDAY CAMPS Enclosed sites providing holiday accommodation and entertainment. The first camps, with accommodation in huts, were opened in Great Britain soon after 1900, provided by firms, trade unions and other organizations. By 1939 there were 200 small camps. Large, commercial seaside camps were developed from the 1930s, notably by Harry Warner (from 1931), Billy Butlin (from 1936), and Fred Pontin (from 1946). Offering chalet accommodation, leisure activities and entertainment, they attracted mainly lower middle-class families. Most were in Britain (a few in Ireland). After flourishing in the 1950s–60s, camps declined as overseas holidays became popular. *See also* HOLIDAYS.

HOLIDAYS Possibly by the 8th century, people in Britain and Ireland took breaks mainly on Sundays and at other religious occasions such as Christmas, shrovetide, Easter, Whitsun and saints' days (hence 'holiday' derived from 'holy day'). Local festivals (or wakes) were held on patron saints' commemoration days or at annual fairs. Other breaks were associated with older calendrical events (e.g., start of summer on May Day, midsummer), or agricultural occasions (e.g., end of sheep shearing, harvest). Breaks were often celebrated with games and feasts.

Such customs survived into the 19th century, though in Britain religious festivals were reduced during the REFORMATION (e.g., in England, 1536). During FACTORY-based industrialization from the later 18th century (e.g., in N England), employers grudgingly accepted traditional holidays (e.g., closing for wakes), though they curtailed routine absenteeism (e.g., on Mondays, so-called 'Saint Monday'). From 1850 many UK factory workers had Saturday afternoons free. From 1871, BANK HOLIDAYS increased regular breaks.

Only wealthy people enjoyed extensive, travel-based leisure. In England from the 18th century they frequented inland medicinal spas (e.g., BATH, Tunbridge Wells) and seaside bathing centres (e.g., Margate, Brighton). Activities included assemblies and balls.

From 1812 steamships stimulated resorts on major rivers (e.g., Clyde, Forth, Thames) for excursions and holidays, mainly by middle-class people. RAILWAYS, from the 1840s, facilitated more widespread developments: larger numbers of people made excursions, usually to the seaside, sometimes arranged by agents or railway companies. In England, Lancashire COTTON INDUSTRY workers pioneered unpaid week-long holidays (usually at Blackpool). They became increasingly popular in Britain from the 1870s as wages rose, stimulating development of resorts and HOLIDAY CAMPS.

Entitlements to paid holidays were introduced in 1938 (Great Britain, Northern Ireland) and 1939 (southern Ireland). Resorts flourished until the 1950s but declined from the 1960s as overseas holidays, using cheap air travel, grew in popularity. *See also* SABBATARIANISM; SPORT.

HOLLES, DENZIL (b. 31 Oct. 1598 in England; d. 17 Feb. 1680 at London, England, aged 81). On 2 March 1629 Holles, a Puritan MP, and others restrained the speaker of the House of Commons to prevent adjournment (ordered by King CHARLES I). Holles denounced unauthorized TONNAGE AND POUNDAGE and alleged that ARMINIANISM was being encouraged in the Church of England (imprisoned to Oct.). In Jan. 1642 Charles sought his arrest (*see* FIVE MEMBERS INCIDENT). From summer 1642 Holles fought for Parliament in the CIVIL WAR, but desired a negotiated settlement.

In 1647, following Charles's capture, Holles, now a leading 'Presbyterian' MP, sought disbandment of the NEW MODEL ARMY. This provoked political organization by officers within the Army and its march on London (Aug.). Holles fled abroad. He returned in 1648 and in Dec. advocated a settlement with the king, provoking PRIDE'S PURGE. He returned to exile (1648–54). After RESTORATION of the monarchy he was made a baron (1661) and remained involved in politics until the mid 1670s. *See also* CIVIL WARS, POLITICAL ASPECTS.

HOLOCAUST AND BRITISH GOVERNMENT In Dec. 1942, during WORLD WAR II, the British accused Nazi Germany of a 'bestial policy of cold-blooded extermination', but assumed that it was deporting Jews in Continental Europe mainly as slave labour. Only in June 1944 did they become convinced of the true function of the Auschwitz-Birkenau camp in Poland as a centre for the mass extermination of European Jews. The prime minister, Winston CHURCHILL, rejected German attempts to barter Jewish lives for concessions, and considered bombing the gas chambers and railway lines. The chances of success were judged too low to warrant the diversion of resources. In retrospect, the large-scale killing of Jews (6 million), subsequently known as the Holocaust, made Britain's pre-war limited admission of Jewish refugees seem shameful.

HOLY SEE, ENGLISH AND BRITISH RELATIONS WITH The excommunication of ELIZABETH I, ruler of England and Ireland, by Pope Pius V (1570) ended long-established direct contacts with the Holy See. England was not prominent in papal diplomacy in the 17th and 18th centuries, although three papal envoys were sent to King CHARLES I (ruled 1625–49), and relations were briefly resumed under the Catholic JAMES VII/II (1687). Jacobite claimants received half-hearted support (*see* JACOBITISM, IMPACT ON BRITISH POLITICS).

Papal recognition of GEORGE III as legitimate ruler of Great Britain and Ireland (1792), and the visit of Cardinal Ercole Consalvi to Allied sovereigns in 1814, improved relations. Britain then kept a diplomat in Rome until 1874 (notably Odo Russell, 1860–70) to discuss Irish affairs and Italian unification through intermediaries. King EDWARD VII met Pope Leo XIII privately (1903).

The British opened formal diplomatic relations to counter German propaganda in 1914. In the 1920s–30s Maltese affairs dominated low-level diplomacy (*see* MALTA). The British legation at the Vatican was a conduit of information during WORLD WAR II. Post-war relations were increasingly normalized, and included a State visit to the Vatican by Queen ELIZABETH II (1980) and PAPAL VISITS to Britain. *See also* FOREIGN RELATIONS, SOUTHERN IRELAND.

HOME, 14TH EARL OF *see* DOUGLAS-HOME, ALEC

HOME FAMILY A Scottish noble family; a leading family in SE Scotland where they effectively replaced the earls of Dunbar (flourished from late 11th century to 1435). Sir Alexander Home (d. *c.*1492) was created a LORD OF PARLIAMENT in 1473. In 1488 the Homes were instrumental in the defeat and death of King JAMES III. The 6th lord, Alexander Home (*c.*1566–1619), was created an earl in 1605. The 14th earl was prime minister of Great Britain (1963–4; *see* DOUGLAS-HOME, ALEC).

HOME GOVERNMENT ASSOCIATION In Ireland, a political organization founded by Isaac BUTT in DUBLIN on 19 May 1870, supported by Catholics and some Protestants disillusioned by W.E. Gladstone's disestablishment of the Church of Ireland. It promoted parliamentary candidates who favoured an Irish Parliament within a federal UK. Few candidates were elected. It dissolved itself in Nov. 1873 and was replaced by the HOME RULE LEAGUE. *See also* HOME RULE MOVEMENT, IRELAND; GLADSTONE, W.E., AND IRELAND.

HOME RULE, SCOTLAND *see* DEVOLUTION, SCOTLAND

HOME RULE, WALES *see* DEVOLUTION, WALES

HOME RULE LEAGUE In Ireland, a political organization formed in DUBLIN in Nov. 1873 to replace the HOME GOVERNMENT ASSOCIATION with a stronger organization. Led initially by Isaac BUTT, the League advocated self-government within a federal UK. Its candidates won 59 seats in the 1874 general election. It survived into the early 1880s and was absorbed by the NATIONAL LEAGUE (founded Oct. 1882). *See also* HOME RULE MOVEMENT, IRELAND.

HOME RULE MOVEMENT, IRELAND A campaign for an Irish Parliament subordinate to the UK Parliament; started in 1870 by Isaac BUTT as a moderate alternative to 'Fenian' republican ambitions (*see* INSURRECTION OF 1867; MANCHESTER 'MARTYRS'). Pro-Home Rule MPs were elected from Jan. 1871 (at by-elections), and 59 in 1874 who founded the IRISH PARLIAMENTARY PARTY (IPP). But the Conservative-dominated House of Commons rejected Home Rule motions (1874, 1876), inducing C.S. PARNELL and others to disrupt Commons business and support LAND AGITATION (1879–82).

From Dec. 1885 the support of Liberal leader W.E. Gladstone made Home Rule possible. His (third) government, with IPP support, presented a Bill; but it was defeated in the Commons (June 1886). A second Bill passed during Gladstone's fourth ministry, but was defeated in the House of Lords (Sept. 1893). In Ireland 'Unionists' campaigned against both Bills.

The cause languished until Jan. 1910 when the Liberal government became dependent on IPP support. Following removal of the Lords' veto, the government introduced a third Bill (April 1912) which passed the Commons (Jan. 1913). But fear of armed resistance in Ulster (N Ireland) provoked consideration, from autumn 1913, of the exclusion of northern counties (*see* BUCKINGHAM PALACE CONFERENCE). Home Rule was enacted on 18 Sept. 1914 but suspended because of WORLD WAR I.

After the unforeseen EASTER RISING (April 1916), David LLOYD GEORGE attempted to negotiate a settlement (May–July), but failed because of southern Unionists' opposition and John REDMOND's rejection of Ulster's exclusion. Delegation of the problem to an IRISH CONVENTION (May 1917–April 1918) also failed.

After the war the British government decided to create two devolved Parliaments (Government of Ireland Act, Dec. 1920). Northern Ireland's Parliament was opened on 22 June 1921, but SINN FÉIN, now dominant in the S, rejected 'Southern Ireland' and sought Irish unity and independence. *See also* GLADSTONE, W.E., AND IRELAND; UNIONISM, IRELAND; 'CURRAGH MUTINY'; IRISH FREE STATE, FOUNDING OF.

HOME SECRETARY *see* SECRETARY OF STATE

HOMILDON HILL, BATTLE OF *see* HUMBLETON, BATTLE OF

HOMOSEXUALITY, LAW RELATING TO Before the 16th–17th centuries the sin of 'sodomy' (sexual intercourse between males) was countered mainly by the Church through confession and penance or courts. In 1534 the English Parliament's Buggery Act made anal intercourse (with man, woman or animal) a felony punishable by death. It was possibly aimed at clergy, particularly monks, because BENEFIT OF CLERGY was denied (*see* REFORMATION PARLIAMENT). Also applicable in Wales from 1536, the Act was repealed in 1547, replaced by the 1548 Sodomy Act (repealed 1553), and reinstated in 1563 (Sodomy Act). The last was replaced in 1828 by provisions in the Offences Against the Person Act (England and Wales). The Irish Parliament passed a Buggery Act in 1634 (replaced 1829). In Scotland, sodomy was a criminal and capital offence under common law, though few cases occurred. It ceased to be a capital offence in England, Wales and Ireland in 1861, in Scotland in 1889. In 1885 the Criminal Law Amendment Act (for UK) made gross indecency between males a criminal offence.

Decriminalization of private homosexual behaviour between consenting adult males was recommended for the UK in 1957 by the WOLFENDEN COMMITTEE. It was implemented for England and Wales in 1967, for Scotland in 1980, and for Northern Ireland in 1982, the last following a case in the European Court of Human Rights. Decriminalization in the Republic of Ireland (1993) followed a similar case.

From the 1970s campaigners sought legal standing for homosexual relationships. Civil partnerships for same-sex couples were introduced in the UK in 2005 and in the Republic of Ireland in 2011, and civil marriage in England and Wales in March 2014, in Scotland in Dec. 2014, in the Republic of Ireland in 2015, and in Northern Ireland in 2020. In the UK the 2010 Equality Act was used to suppress opposition to homosexual activity based on religious teaching.

HONG KONG A former British colony on the coast of SE China, by the Pearl River estuary. British forces seized Hong Kong Island (1841) during the First Opium War, and China ceded it by the treaty of Nanjing (1842). A CROWN COLONY from 1843, Hong Kong was enlarged by acquisition of the adjacent Kowloon Peninsula (1860) and 'New

Territories' (1898, on a 99-year lease). The colony was developed as a trading post and naval base, but occupied by Japan 1941–5 (during WORLD WAR II).

After 1949, refugees from communist China increased the population. From the 1950s Hong Kong grew into a major industrial and financial centre. Its status changed to British DEPENDENT TERRITORY in 1983. Under a Sino-British Agreement (1984), the whole territory reverted to the People's Republic of China on 1 July 1997 with a 50-year guarantee of basic constitutional and economic freedoms. Approx. population in 1921, 662,000; in 1996, 6,218,000. *See also* CHINA, BRITISH RELATIONS WITH.

HONOUR In England, after the NORMAN CONQUEST (1066–70s), a collection of estates held from the king by a major lord (so-called 'tenant-in-chief'), usually with knights holding estates from the lord (as 'knights' fees'). Its centre was a CASTLE or chief MANOR, where a court was held. Honours were created in Wales, Scotland and Ireland in the 11th–13th centuries. Honours lost importance from the 13th century. *See also* BARON; FEUDALISM.

HONOURS SYSTEM From the 14th to 19th centuries, rulers bestowed civil ranks in Britain and Ireland (e.g., knighthoods, PEERAGES, BARONETCIES from 17th century) mainly to elevate recipients in social status. From the 1770s men were appointed to the chivalric Order of the Bath (created 1725) also for military, naval or diplomatic achievement. Queen VICTORIA founded the Victoria Cross in 1856 to recognize valour by all ranks in the Army and Navy, starting with participants in the CRIMEAN WAR. Areas of recognition were increased in 1902 with creation of the Order of Merit for exceptional service by men or women in art, literature and science (also awarded for military service).

The most substantial expansion of honours took place in 1917, during WORLD WAR I, with establishment of the Order of the British Empire, for service to charitable and welfare organizations, and in arts, sciences and public service (except Civil Service). It was divided into five ranks: two ranks of knight or dame, commander, officer and member; there was also a British Empire medal. Awards were made in the UK, DOMINIONS and India, though dominions later established their own Orders. The George Cross, to recognize heroism in great danger, was instituted in 1940, during WORLD WAR II.

Honours have been conferred since the 18th century mainly on recommendation from the PRIME MINISTER. From 1993 the UK public were encouraged to recommend recipients. In the early 21st century about 3000 honours were awarded annually.

During the 20th century appointments to peerages were often made for political purposes (creation of hereditary peerages and titles mostly ceased from 1964). Appointments to orders of chivalry tended to recognize service or distinction, as did some appointments to non-judicial life peerages (introduced 1958). The CONSTITUTIONS of southern Ireland (1922, 1937) prohibited titles of nobility; other national honours were not created. *See also* NOBILITY; KNIGHT; GARTER, ORDER OF THE; THISTLE, ORDER OF THE.

HOOKE, ROBERT (b. 18 July 1635 at Freshwater, Isle of Wight, England; d. 3 March 1703 at London, England, aged 67). At OXFORD University from 1653, Hooke became involved with the group of natural philosophers (scientists) centred on Wadham College, and from 1655 assisted Robert BOYLE. In 1662 he was appointed curator of experiments for the recently founded ROYAL SOCIETY in London (also fellow from 1663, a secretary 1677–83). His provision of experiments at meetings encouraged the Society to focus on research. Hooke lectured at GRESHAM COLLEGE from 1664 (also professor of geometry from 1665).

With wide interests, Hooke invented a spring-regulated watch (*c.*1659), and published *Micrographia* (1665), a collection mainly of microscopical illustrations (e.g., astounding pictures of insects) but also including a theory of light and first use of the term 'cell'. From 1679 Hooke expressed resentment towards Isaac NEWTON, claiming Newton had failed to acknowledge indebtedness for ideas about gravity and the orbital motion of planets. *See also* SCIENTIFIC REVOLUTION; GEOLOGY.

HOOKER, RICHARD (b. April 1554 at Exeter, Devon, England; d. 2 Nov. 1600 at Bishopsbourne, Kent, England, aged 46). Hooker obtained a place at Corpus Christi College, OXFORD (1569), with support from Bishop John JEWEL (d. 1571), and was a clergyman from 1579. He was master of the Temple Church, London, 1585–91, and lived in Kent from 1595.

Hooker published *Of the Laws of Ecclesiastical Polity* (four books 1593, fifth book 1597), a defence of the ELIZABETHAN SETTLEMENT against Catholics and Puritans. Influenced by Erastian ideas (principally that the Church should be subordinate to civil power), it argued that the English Church and State formed an organic unity ruled by the monarch and supreme governor and by laws made by Parliament, and that the Church was guided by the Bible, tradition and reason. (Three more books of the *Laws* were published in the 17th century.) *See also* REFORMATION, ENGLAND; ENGLAND, CHURCH OF.

HORE-BELISHA, LESLIE (b. 7 Sept. 1893 at London, England; d. 17 Feb. 1957 at Reims, France, aged 63). A Liberal MP 1923–45, Hore-Belisha supported John SIMON in the 1930s and served in the British NATIONAL GOVERNMENT as transport minister (1934–7). He introduced the driving test and illuminated pedestrian crossings (nicknamed 'Belisha beacons'). As a reforming war secretary (1937–40), he improved terms of service in the ARMY and helped to persuade the prime minister, Neville CHAMBERLAIN, to introduce CONSCRIPTION. He was created Lord Hore-Belisha in 1954. *See also* MOTOR VEHICLES AND MOTORING, GREAT BRITAIN.

HORSE RACING, BRITAIN Horses were raced in ROMAN BRITAIN (1st–4th centuries), and at LONDON (Smithfield) in the 1170s. Racing (with wagers) often accompanied fairs. The oldest racecourse (1539) still in use is the Roodee at Chester (NW England).

Horse racing became more formal in the early 17th century, when King JAMES VI/I and CHARLES I encouraged flat racing. After the RESTORATION (1660), rulers resumed patronage, and regular meetings were held in England at Newmarket (Suffolk), Epsom (Surrey), Doncaster (Yorkshire) and YORK. The 'thoroughbred' racehorse breed was created in the late 17th and early 18th centuries from domestic mares and imported Oriental stallions. Favoured by aristocrats, horse racing was a widely popular diversion by 1750, when the Jockey Club began regulation. Distinctive 'classic' flat races have included the St Leger (founded 1776), Oaks (1779), and Derby (1780). Standardized procedures developed in the early 19th century, when organized racing also expanded in Scotland with new courses at Musselburgh (1816) and Kelso (1822). Steeplechasing (racing over fences, initially cross-country between churches) originated in Ireland in 1752 and quickly spread to Great Britain. Its pre-eminent race, the Grand National, began in 1839.

The legalization of off-course betting in the UK (from 1961) intensified public interest; horse racing became the second most televised sport after football. In 1993 the British Horseracing Board (BHB) was created as a governing body, and in 2006 the Jockey Club transferred regulation to the Horserace Regulatory Authority (HRA). The BHB and HRA merged in 2007 as the British Horseracing Authority. In 2015 there were 51 racecourses in England, five in Scotland, three in Wales. *See also* SPORT, ENGLAND/SCOTLAND/WALES.

HORSE RACING, IRELAND *see* SPORT, IRELAND

HOSPITALS Starting in England (1070s), hospitals proliferated throughout Britain and Ireland in the 11th–13th centuries, exceeding 150 in Scotland and (by 1340s), 650 in England and Wales. A quarter were leper-houses, located outside towns. Others were usually on town edges, catering for travellers, the poor (by alms giving) and the sick. Hospitals accommodated a few people to over 200. Terms for hospitals included the English 'spital' (from OFr.

hospitale, meaning 'place of hospitality'). Intended as charitable works, hospitals often had a religious character (e.g., clergy, a chapel). Continuing foundations included numerous 'almshouses' for the infirm.

Because of their religious aspects, many hospitals were closed during the DISSOLUTIONS OF RELIGIOUS HOUSES (1530s–60s). Almshouses tended to survive, and town authorities retained some hospitals.

A new hospital movement flourished in the 18th–19th centuries, reflecting medical progress and philanthropy. Starting in Ireland (Charitable Infirmary, DUBLIN, 1718), voluntary hospitals for the sick poor were founded in major towns, supported by subscriptions (e.g., Westminster Infirmary, 1720). From 1770 outpatient dispensaries were also provided. In Ireland, Catholic involvement became prominent in the 19th century.

State participation started with legislation for Ireland authorizing county infirmaries (1765), dispensaries (1805), and fever hospitals (1818), with local public funding. Except in Scotland, workhouse infirmaries were developed from the 1830s; in Ireland they admitted non-destitute sick from 1862. In Scotland, parochial boards could support hospitals from 1845, as could local authorities from 1867. The medical importance of hospitals expanded from the 1880s with the development of sterile operating theatres.

In the 1920s–30s workhouse infirmaries were often converted into local-authority hospitals (Great Britain) or county homes and hospitals (IRISH FREE STATE). In southern Ireland a horse-racing sweepstake supported hospitals 1930–86. When centralized health systems were created in the UK (late 1940s), hospitals were nationalized (*see* NATIONAL HEALTH SERVICE). Southern Ireland retained voluntary, State and private hospitals.

HOTEL CECIL Nickname of the last British government headed by the 3rd marquess of SALISBURY (1900–2), whose family name was Cecil; so called because it involved many family members and relatives. They included his nephew A.J. BALFOUR, as leader of the House of Commons; his son-in-law the 2nd earl of Selborne, as first lord of the Admiralty; his son Viscount Cranborne, as under-secretary for foreign affairs. A real 'Hotel Cecil' had been opened in LONDON in 1896.

HOUGHERS Irish term for cattle maimers. It was applied from *c*.1700 to rural protesters (smallholders, labourers) in Connacht (W Ireland) who used intimidation and cattle maiming to oppose the spread of grassland and stock rearing (at the expense of small-scale tillage farming), which reduced demand for labour. The authorities countered with repressive legislation in 1710. 'Houghing' faded after an amnesty in 1713. *See also* AGRICULTURE, IRELAND 17TH CENTURY TO 1921.

HOUSECARL In England, term used from the reign of CNUT (1016–35) to the 1080s (OE *huscarl*, derived from Old Norse words meaning 'house-man'). It referred to Cnut's Danish household followers, and generally to land-holders of Danish or other foreign origin. Housecarls were probably not a distinctive fighting force. *See also* MILITARY SERVICE, ENGLAND BEFORE 1066.

HOUSING, ENGLAND BEFORE 1066 From the 5th century there were two main types of wooden building, both rectangular. The 'sunken-floor building' (German *Grubenhaus*) was derived from Continental Europe. It had a post at each end, ridge post, and turf walls. Its floor was below ground level. Average ground area was 10 × 6.5 ft (3 × 2 m). Sunken-floor buildings largely disappeared in the 8th century.

The 'hall' type consisted of pairs of posts joined by ridge posts, usually with wattle walls. A partition sometimes provided a 'private' internal area. Both house types were used as living accommodation and for other purposes (animal shelters, grain storage, weaving). *See also* WEST STOW; CHEDDAR; YEAVERING.

HOUSING, ENGLAND 1066 TO 16TH CENTURY From the NORMAN CONQUEST (1066–70s) kings and higher nobles lived mainly in CASTLES (fortified residences), which asserted their dominance. By 1100 there were well over 100, and in the 13th and 14th centuries around 350. They were built initially of wood, then of stone (from 12th century). Castles comprised a fence or wall, often with ditch or moat, and buildings (hall, chambers, kitchen, chapel, etc.) or a tower (keep) containing rooms for different functions. From the 14th century, buildings and rooms became grander and defences less important. Kings and magnates remained itinerant, moving between estates.

Lesser nobles continued to use single-storey wooden halls with associated buildings (e.g., storage rooms, kitchen), often surrounded by a fence and possibly a moat. During the 12th century a chamber (domestic room) and storage rooms were sometimes combined as a two-storey block, possibly joined to the hall. By 1250 a tripartite arrangement had been evolved: central hall with service rooms (buttery, pantry) at one end and chamber at the other. It quickly became widespread. In the 15th century more elaborate plans were created with buildings round courtyards.

Townsmen created multi-storey, complex buildings from the 1180s when timber framing was developed in LONDON, partly to utilize narrow plots. Techniques spread widely in the 13th century. A common arrangement consisted of a workshop or retail shop by the street, chamber over the shop, hall behind the front block, and service rooms. Most townspeople, however, lived in cottages.

Peasants lived in wooden cottages or halls. Longhouses accommodating people and animals became widespread in the 12th century (replaced in lowland areas by separate buildings from 14th century). Buildings were improved from the 13th century by widespread use of crucks (paired inward-curved timbers) or box frames on stone foundations. Wealthier peasants copied the arrangement of hall with adjacent rooms.

HOUSING, ENGLAND FROM 16TH CENTURY From *c*.1500 noblemen built 'country houses' – large houses usually without defences. Many were 'courtyard houses' (courts with surrounding buildings). Brick was sometimes used (introduced in 1430s); glazed windows were prominent. The architectural high-point, 1700–60, included classical designs influenced by the Italian Andrea Palladio (1508–80). Numerous houses were destroyed in the 20th century or put to other uses (*see* LANDED SOCIETY, DECLINE OF, ENGLAND).

From the late 16th century the houses of lesser landowners (or GENTRY) were often compact two- or three-storey buildings with a symmetrical façade (classical designs in late 17th–18th centuries). Many were rebuilt in the late 18th–late 19th centuries. In the 20th century, businessmen and celebrities acquired gentry houses.

Between *c*.1570 and *c*.1640 prosperous yeomen (larger farmers) improved houses (with ceilings in halls, fireplaces, chimneys) or built new ones, part of a phenomenon named the 'Great Rebuilding' by English historian W.G. Hoskins (1908–92). During the period of parliamentary ENCLOSURE (mid 18th–mid 19th centuries) large, brick farmhouses emerged. Cottages were also built for labourers. The Great Rebuilding included modernization of town houses. Classical influences and brick became prominent in towns in the late 17th and 18th centuries, when sometimes just frontages were replaced. Terraces of classical-style houses were popular.

The INDUSTRIAL REVOLUTION (from 1780s) saw thousands of houses for workers added to mainly Midland and northern towns (e.g., MANCHESTER), as terraces or around courts. Overcrowded and insanitary neighbourhoods degenerated into SLUMS. Standards were raised by philanthropic societies (from 1840s), PUBLIC HEALTH ACTS, HOUSING LEGISLATION and councils (from 1890s). Detached and semi-detached houses were built in separate areas for middle-class people from the 1790s.

From the 1920s large public-authority and private estates were created, largely of semi-detached houses (typically with three bedrooms); high-rise blocks of flats were also favoured in the 1950s–60s. In the 21st century private house building predominated. *See also* RURAL SETTLEMENT AND SOCIETY, ENGLAND; TOWNS, ENGLAND; TOWN PLANNING; SUBURBS AND SUBURBIA; COUNCIL HOUSING, GREAT BRITAIN.

HOUSING, IRELAND From the 5th century houses remained circular, with wattle-and-daub walls and thatched roofs, some situated within RINGFORTS or on CRANNOGS. Rectangular houses with timber structures were increasingly built from the 9th century. Viking-founded towns (10th–13th centuries) included rectangular buildings with wattle walls, steep-pitched, thatched roofs and interior aisles.

After the Anglo-Norman invasion (1169–70), lords constructed CASTLES that included timber buildings (stone from 13th century). English tenants probably had rectangular single-storey houses with timber structures, wattle-and-daub walls and thatched roofs, or sometimes in E Ireland 'longhouses' for families and cattle. Multi-storey timber-framed houses were erected in towns from the 13th century. The poor occupied windowless wattle or mud cottages (or 'cabins'). In the late 14th–17th centuries Anglo-Irish and Gaelic Irish lords preferred stone tower-houses of two or three storeys, within fortified enclosures. Chimneys became common from the 16th century. Brick was familiar in DUBLIN from the late 16th century.

In the late 17th and 18th centuries, landowners built undefended country houses often in classical style. In towns, wealthier townsman began to prefer stone, and in Dublin grand brick terraces and fashionable squares appeared. Larger farmers built improved houses, with two storeys, internal plaster walls and slate roofs. Brick was widely used in Ulster (N Ireland). As the Gaelic Irish population increased – rapidly from the mid 18th century – the majority lived in one- or two-room cabins; many decayed after the GREAT FAMINE (1845–9). Between the 1880s and 1914, 43,000 labourers' cottages were provided by public authorities. In Dublin SLUMS expanded as buildings were subdivided, whereas in Belfast good-quality brick terraces were built. Middle-class people moved to substantial suburban houses.

In the 20th century housing was improved with plumbing and electrification. Settlement expansion from the 1960s included suburban estates with detached and semi-detached brick houses, and widespread building of bungalows in the countryside. *See also* PREHISTORIC IRELAND, HOUSING; RURAL SETTLEMENT AND SOCIETY, IRELAND; TOWNS, IRELAND; HOUSING, STATE INVOLVEMENT, IRELAND.

HOUSING, SCOTLAND From *c*.500 farmers in N Britain (later Scotland) probably built longhouses, accommodating people and animals (separated by a partition). They were supported by cruck-pairs (upright, inward-curved timbers, often obscured by walls). Walls were normally of turf or clay, roofs were thatched. Poorer people lived in one-room cottages. Such arrangements continued until the 18th century (until the 20th century in parts of the HIGHLANDS and Islands). Until the 12th century kings and nobles lived in timber halls (also cruck-built); thereafter

they built CASTLES following English styles, though in the 14th–mid 17th centuries defensible stone tower-houses were popular with lords (housing animals on the ground floor). In towns, merchants' houses were probably of two or more storeys, built of timber frames with walls of planks or wattle and daub (interwoven rods covered with mud) and roofs of tiles or slates. From the 16th century town houses were rebuilt in stone.

From the mid 18th century farmhouses were usually two-roomed (living room, parlour/bedroom), with animals housed separately. LAIRDS typically occupied two-storey rectangular houses with a central staircase, while magnates built large country houses. In industrializing towns from the late 18th century, tenement blocks were built, usually of stone with slate roofs and containing four or five storeys with one or two rooms per tenement (or flat). Facilities (e.g., water supply) were poor. Tenement building continued into the 20th century. In 1871, 70% of dwellings consisted of one or two rooms.

Improvement began in the 1920s–30s when councils built two- and three-storey tenement blocks and semi-detached houses on town fringes, often using bricks and brick tiles. Private developers built 'bungalow belts'. During a second phase of clearance and replacement in the 1960s–70s people were rehoused in concrete tower blocks, especially in GLASGOW. Considered unsuccessful, many were later demolished. *See also* PREHISTORIC BRITAIN, HOUSING; RURAL SETTLEMENT AND SOCIETY, SCOTLAND; FERMTOUN OR TOUN; TOWNS, SCOTLAND; COUNCIL HOUSING, GREAT BRITAIN; HOUSING LEGISLATION, SCOTLAND.

HOUSING, STATE INVOLVEMENT, GREAT BRITAIN *see* COUNCIL HOUSING, GREAT BRITAIN; HOUSING LEGISLATION, ENGLAND AND WALES/SCOTLAND

HOUSING, STATE INVOLVEMENT, IRELAND In the late 19th century concern about housing conditions in the UK included Ireland. The 1878 Public Health (Ireland) Act authorized local housing regulations. Legislation from 1883 enabled local authorities to borrow money to provide cottages for agricultural labourers (43,000 built by 1914). Similar arrangements from 1890 funded working-class housing in towns and cities.

In the 1920s the IRISH FREE STATE funded at most only 2400 houses per year due to economic stringency. But in 1932 the new FIANNA FÁIL government launched an ambitious programme under which 9000 houses on average were built annually 1932–42. The number of families living in one or two rooms fell by 50% in DUBLIN. After decline during WORLD WAR II, building revived in the 1950s. From 1948 Dublin Corporation developed suburban estates (including the Ballymun Flats, 1966) so that city-centre SLUMS could be cleared. By the late 20th century these had become extensive though social conditions often deteriorated (e.g., high unemployment).

In NORTHERN IRELAND only 8000 publicly funded houses were built 1921–45. Bombing and investigations during WORLD WAR II (1939–45) revealed an extensive need for new housing. In 1945 the provincial government established the Northern Ireland Housing Trust (NIHT) to provide additional public housing for allocation on a non-sectarian basis (48,500 dwellings built by 1971). Because local authorities remained involved, some housing continued to be built or allocated on sectarian considerations. From the early 1960s Catholics complained about unfair treatment by some (Protestant) Unionist authorities. Grievances contributed to the outbreak of the TROUBLES (1969). In 1971 a Northern Ireland Housing Executive was created to transcend sectarianism. It took over the NIHT and local-authority housing, and in 2015 owned about 89,000 dwellings and supported other provision of 'social housing'.

HOUSING, WALES From at least the 6th to the 16th centuries structures were usually of wood. The basic type was the hall, made of cruck-pairs (upright, inward-curved timbers) joined by planks to make bay-units, with walls of wattle and daub (interwoven rods covered with mud); roofs were thatched with reeds or straw. A fire provided heating (smoke escaping through a roof-hole). Size reflected importance: kings and senior freemen (*uchelwyr*) had the largest halls (perhaps five bays), with a bay at each end partitioned off for sleeping and cooking respectively. Lesser freemen and bondmen had one- or two-bay hall-houses. The poorest lived in single-bay (one-room) huts. In the MARCH OF WALES (late 11th–16th centuries), lords built stone castles while knights had timber halls.

In the late 16th century the hall was superseded by the box-frame house, two-storeyed with parlour, hall, and kitchen on the ground floor and sleeping chambers above reached by a staircase (often by the parlour end-wall). Heating came from an enclosed fireplace. Windows contained glass. Many such houses were built between 1550 and 1640 by GENTRY, farmers, and merchants, particularly in E Wales. Stone was also used. Between 1660 and 1740 the central passage house replaced the box-frame, with an entrance hall containing the staircase. Poor homes in rural areas remained largely unchanged until the mid 19th century, when two storeys became common. Town housing was similar to rural housing.

During town expansion in S Wales in the 19th century, industrialists and speculative builders built brick or stone terraces. Sanitation usually remained poor. Standards rose from the later 19th century (*see* COUNCIL HOUSING, GREAT BRITAIN). After 1945 slums were cleared and municipal estates laid out (some on exposed upland sites), with numerous semi-detached houses. Bungalows became familiar in rural areas. *See also* PREHISTORIC BRITAIN, HOUSING; ROMAN BRITAIN, SETTLEMENT AND AGRICULTURE; RURAL SETTLEMENT AND SOCIETY, WALES; TOWNS, WALES.

HOUSING ASSOCIATIONS Independent not-for-profit organizations which provide housing mainly for rent. They developed in Great Britain and Ireland from the 1840s. In Scotland, associations were empowered by legislation in 1855 to acquire dilapidated property. Many associations were started after WORLD WAR I (ended 1918) to supply housing for working-class people; in England and Wales they could receive public funds under the 1919 Housing and Town Planning Act. Associations became a leading source of new 'social housing' in Britain from the 1980s, partially offsetting the diminution of COUNCIL HOUSING, though in 2000 they owned only about 6% of dwellings in England and Scotland, 3% in Wales.

HOUSING LEGISLATION, ENGLAND AND WALES In the 1840s–60s, major towns tackled insanitary conditions with by-laws to disseminate minimum standards. The 1851 Lodging Houses Act (UK except Scotland) began permissive national legislation, allowing authorities to purchase or build lodging houses. The 1868 Artizans and Labourers Dwellings Act ('Torrens Act', UK) empowered authorities to compel the repair or demolition of insanitary houses, and the 1875 Artizans' and Labourers' Dwellings Improvement Act ('Cross Act', UK except Scotland) permitted compulsory purchase for SLUM clearance and housing programmes. The 1890 Housing of the Working Classes Act (UK) strengthened clearance powers and permitted housing schemes funded by local rates; London authorities were required to rehouse displaced persons. The 1900 Housing of the Working Classes Act (England and Wales) allowed schemes outside a council's area of jurisdiction. In 1915, during WORLD WAR I, legislation introduced rent controls (continued to 1970s).

The 1919 Housing and Town Planning Act ('Addison Act', England and Wales) promoted large-scale house-building by local authorities through subsidies (reduced 1921). The 1923 Housing Act ('Chamberlain Act', Great Britain) subsidized mainly private house-building (to 1930). The 1924 Housing Act ('Wheatley Act', Britain) reintroduced subsidies for council house-building (to 1933). The 1930 Housing Act (mostly England and Wales) emphasized slum clearance (implemented mainly by 1933 Housing Act).

Housing Acts in 1946 and 1952 (England and Wales) re-encouraged large-scale building with subsidies. They were reduced under the 1954 Housing Repairs and Rents Act, which promoted slum clearance. General subsidies were reintroduced by the 1961 Housing Act. The 1964 Housing Act (Britain) established the Housing Corporation to regulate HOUSING ASSOCIATIONS and fund social housing (replaced 2008).

Among later Acts, the 1980 Housing Act awarded tenants of local authorities and other bodies in England and Wales a 'right to buy'. In 2014 the Welsh Assembly passed a Housing Act, strengthening regulation of the rental market and combating homelessness. *See also* PUBLIC HEALTH ACTS; COUNCIL HOUSING, GREAT BRITAIN.

HOUSING LEGISLATION, IRELAND *see* HOUSING, STATE INVOLVEMENT, IRELAND

HOUSING LEGISLATION, SCOTLAND From the 19th century the UK Parliament affected housing through local Acts, Scottish Acts and Acts for Great Britain or the UK. The flexibility partly reflected distinctive urban housing (e.g., preponderance of tenement blocks) and gross overcrowding.

Early 'permissive' legislation included the 1855 Dwelling Houses (Scotland) Act, which authorized associations to acquire dilapidated housing (*see* HOUSING ASSOCIATIONS). In 1866 the Artizans and Labourers Dwellings Act ('Torrens Act', UK) permitted action over insanitary houses by local authorities and brought Scotland under the 1851 Lodging Houses Act. Improvement Trusts, with power to clear SLUMS, were authorized for GLASGOW (1866), EDINBURGH (1867) and DUNDEE (1871). The 1875 Artizans' and Labourers' Dwellings Improvement (Scotland) Act (Scotland's 'Cross Act') envisaged building programmes. Scotland was included in the 1890 Housing of the Working Classes Act which allowed rate-funded schemes.

During WORLD WAR I the Glasgow Rent Strike (1915), against rent increases, forced the imposition of controls (Rent Restrictions Act, 1915, UK), and a Royal Commission on Housing in Scotland (established 1912, in response to trade union complaints about colliery-owned housing) recommended State action (1917). The 1919 Housing and Town Planning (Scotland) Act ('Addison Act' for Scotland), providing subsidies, initiated large-scale building by local authorities (1920s–30s). Arrangements were altered by Scottish Housing Acts (1925, 1930, 1935) and British legislation.

Later Acts included the 1946 New Towns Act (Britain), under which five towns were created, and the 1957 Housing and Town Development (Scotland) Act, which enabled Glasgow to disperse 'excess' population. The Housing Corporation (established 1964) covered Scotland. In 1980 public tenants received a 'right to buy' (Tenants' Rights, Etc. (Scotland) Act).

In 1999 legislative authority was devolved to the new Scottish Parliament. By 2017 it passed six major Acts, creating elaborate regulations. It terminated the 'right to buy' for new social housing and tenants in 2010, and for other tenants in 2014.

HOWARD, JOHN (b. 2 Sept. 1726 at Hackney or Enfield, Middlesex, England; d. 20 Jan. 1790 at Kherson, Russia, aged 63). A businessman's son and DISSENTER, Howard was appalled by the conditions and compulsory discharge fees which he discovered at Bedfordshire gaol after he became SHERIFF in 1773. When other officers rejected changes he began to campaign for general improvements. He visited prisons in England, Wales and overseas, reporting his findings in *The State of the Prisons in England and Wales* (1777). From 1784 he studied management of plague. Howard died while visiting a Russian army unit. *See also* FRY, ELIZABETH; GAOLS AND PRISONS, ENGLAND AND WALES.

HOWARD, KATHERINE (b. by 1524 in England; d. 13 Feb. 1542 at London, England). A niece of Thomas Howard, 3rd duke of NORFOLK, Katherine was familiar with King HENRY VIII by April 1540. The relationship was possibly encouraged by the conservative bishop Stephen GARDINER because Katherine was a Catholic. Katherine and Henry were married on 28 July. She was Henry's fifth wife. But premarital sexual relationships were reported to Henry on 2 Nov. Angry, he deserted Katherine on 6 Nov. She was attainted by Parliament for treason (11 Feb. 1542) and executed. *See also* HENRY VIII, WIVES OF; HOWARD FAMILY.

HOWARD FAMILY An English noble family which was prominent in the 16th century. In 1483 John Howard was created duke of Norfolk and earl marshal by King RICHARD III. He died at BOSWORTH (1485) and was attainted. His son Thomas Howard (1443–1524) was also created duke of Norfolk, by HENRY VIII (1514). Thomas's son Thomas, 3rd Howard duke, was influential in Henry's reign (*see* NORFOLK, 3RD DUKE OF), and was uncle of Anne BOLEYN and Katherine HOWARD. In 1547 he and his son Henry, earl of Surrey, were attainted and the son was executed. The 3rd duke was restored in 1553. His grandson, Thomas Howard (1538–72), 4th duke, was executed for involvement in the RIDOLFI PLOT. Thomas's son Philip Howard (1557–95), a convert to Catholicism, was convicted of TREASON in 1589 for allegedly favouring the SPANISH ARMADA (canonized 1970).

Philip Howard's son Thomas (1585–1646) was restored in 1604 to the earldoms of Arundel and Surrey (titles once held by his father) and in 1644 created earl of Norfolk. Thomas's grandson Thomas (1627–77) was restored to the dukedom of Norfolk (1660). His relative Henry Howard (1815–60), 14th duke, took the surname Fitzalan-Howard (1842). He and his successors were influential lay Catholics. Other branches of the Howard family have also held peerages. *See also* ATTAINDER; MARSHAL, ENGLAND.

HOWE, GEOFFREY (b. 20 Dec. 1926 at Port Talbot, Glamorgan, Wales; d. 9 Oct. 2015 at Idlicote, Warwickshire, England, aged 88). Howe, a barrister, was a Conservative MP 1964–66, 1970–92. He served in the British government under Edward HEATH as solicitor-general (1970–2; knighted 1970) and as trade and consumer affairs minister (1972–4).

Howe served Margaret THATCHER as chancellor of the Exchequer (1979–83) and foreign secretary (from 1983), until differences over Great Britain's approach to the EUROPEAN ECONOMIC COMMUNITY became irreconcilable. Appointed leader of the House of Commons and deputy prime minister in 1989, he resigned on 1 Nov. 1990. His 'resignation speech' in the Commons (13 Nov.) encouraged Michael HESELTINE to challenge Thatcher for the Party leadership, precipitating her downfall. He was created Lord Howe (1992). *See also* BOW GROUP.

HOWE, WILLIAM (b. 10 Aug. 1729 at London, England; d. 12 July 1814 at Plymouth, Devon, England, aged 84). A soldier from 1746, Howe distinguished himself in N America during the SEVEN YEARS WAR (1756–63). He was also an MP 1758–80. In 1775 he was appointed second-in-command of British forces in N America. He hoped to promote conciliation with rebellious colonists, but arrived in Boston, Massachusetts (25 May), after war had broken out. He succeeded as commander-in-chief in Oct.

Howe captured NEW YORK City in 1776 but his forces were defeated at Trenton, New Jersey (Dec.). In 1777 he had mixed success and asked to resign. He passed the command to Henry Clinton in May 1778 and returned to England where he was blamed to failing to end the rebellion. Howe remained in the Army, holding commands in England during the French wars from 1793. *See also* AMERICAN WAR OF INDEPENDENCE.

HOWELL, GEORGE (b. 5 Oct. 1833 at Wrington, Somerset, England; d. 16 Sept. 1910 at London, England, aged 76). A bricklayer in London from 1855, Howell became a trade unionist and labour leader. He was secretary from 1865 of the REFORM LEAGUE, which campaigned for franchise reform (achieved 1867), and of the Parliamentary Committee of the TRADES UNION CONGRESS 1873–6. He was a Lib-Lab MP 1885–95. *See also* TRADE UNIONISM, ENGLAND.

HOWLEY, WILLIAM (b. 12 Feb. 1766 at Ropley, Hampshire, England; d. 11 Feb. 1848 at Lambeth, Surrey, England, aged 81). A Church of England clergyman and TORY, Howley became bishop of LONDON (1813). In 1828, despite his opposition to CATHOLIC EMANCIPATION, he was appointed archbishop of CANTERBURY by the duke of WELLINGTON (after enactment of Emancipation). In

1831–2 Howley opposed PARLIAMENTARY REFORM, provoking popular protest. But he was concerned to reform the Church, and supported training colleges for clergy and the ECCLESIASTICAL COMMISSIONERS. His attitude to the OXFORD MOVEMENT was mixed: he welcomed its assertion of apostolic succession while disapproving of seemingly Catholic tendencies.

HUDSON, GEORGE (b. March 1800 at Howsham, Yorkshire, England; d. 14 Dec. 1871 at London, England, aged 71). Using inherited wealth and political connections in YORK (NE England), Hudson became involved in railway development (from 1833) and a company chairman (1837). By 1844 he controlled over 1000 mi (1600 km) and was nicknamed the 'railway king'. He was elected as an MP in 1845 (Conservative). But economic depression exposed (1849) fraudulent behaviour (e.g., payment of dividends from capital). Forced to resign directorships, Hudson spent parliamentary recesses abroad to avoid arrest. After losing his seat he retired to France (1859–65). *See also* RAILWAYS, ENGLAND.

HUDSON, HENRY (b. at London, England; d. 1611 in Hudson Bay, N America). Hudson commanded seaborne expeditions in search of northern sea routes from Europe to E Asia. Three major geographical features were named after him: the Hudson River (now in USA), and the Hudson Strait and Hudson Bay (in Canada).

Hudson's first expedition, in 1607 for the English MUSCOVY COMPANY, sailed northwards between E Greenland and Spitsbergen seeking a transpolar route. A second, in 1608 for the same company, went northeastwards into the Barents Sea seeking a North-east Passage. A third, in 1609 for the Dutch East India Company, also entered the Barents Sea. Hudson then diverted in search of the NORTH-WEST PASSAGE: he sailed to N America, went southwards, and ascended the Hudson River.

In 1610, while leading another expedition to N America (for an English syndicate), Hudson explored the Hudson Strait and discovered Hudson Bay. But after wintering, his crew mutinied over diminishing provisions. Hudson was set adrift in a small boat with his son John and six others (22 June 1611). *See also* ARCTIC, ENGLISH AND BRITISH EXPLORATION; HUDSON'S BAY COMPANY.

HUDSON'S BAY COMPANY An English mercantile company which formerly governed a large area of N America. Following exploration, the company received a charter in 1670 from King CHARLES II granting rights in land around Hudson Bay, which it named RUPERT'S LAND. Its principal business was fur-buying, which it undertook from coastal forts. Many forts were held by the French from 1686 until restored in the Peace of UTRECHT (1713).

From the 1770s the company was forced to build forts inland to defend its interests against a rival North West Company. It also developed trading in the adjacent North-Western Territory. A replacement charter in 1821 united the company with its rival, and granted monopoly trading rights also over North-Western Territory and the Pacific area. In 1846 the company built Fort Victoria on Vancouver Island, and from 1849 ran Vancouver colony. (Great Britain reacquired the Pacific area and Vancouver Island in 1858.) The company surrendered its charter to the British Crown in 1869, and its territories were transferred to CANADA in 1870. The company remained a commercial enterprise.

HUGUENOTS Term used in France from the mid 16th century for Protestant Christians (referring to confederates bound by oath). Facing Catholic hostility, thousands fled to England between the 1540s and 1590s. They were granted religious and political freedoms in France in 1598, at the end of the 'Wars of Religion', by the Edict of Nantes.

In Oct. 1685, King Louis XIV revoked the Edict, causing 400,000 Huguenots to flee abroad. Some 40,000–50,000 took refuge in the British Isles, of whom over 20,000 settled in and around LONDON. Numerous woollen weavers became established in provincial English towns, and in Scotland and Ireland. Huguenot immigrants also included skilled workers in other trades (e.g., glass making, silk weaving, printing), and experts in finance. Some distinguished business families have been descendants of Huguenots. *See also* STRANGER CHURCHES, ENGLAND; COURTAULD, SAMUEL; ETHNIC AND NATIONAL MINORITIES, ENGLAND/SCOTLAND/WALES.

HUMANISM A movement in European thought, education and arts, 14th–17th centuries, which advocated understanding from a human rather than divine perspective (e.g., using human motivation rather than a providential scheme to interpret history). Originating in Italy and associated with the Renaissance, it emulated the approaches and standards of Roman and Greek 'classical' writings.

Italian humanism spread into England in the 1430s through patronage of Italian scholars by Humphrey, duke of GLOUCESTER (d. 1447). Greek was studied (in addition to Latin) from the 1460s; soon afterwards English UNIVERSITIES and schools introduced classical studies. St Paul's School, London (refounded 1510 by John COLET), and Corpus Christi College, OXFORD (founded 1517 by Richard FOXE), were humanist institutions. Humanism influenced early legislation for POOR RELIEF. Scotland was influenced from the early 16th century, with the Italian Giovanni Ferrerio (1502–79) notably spreading humanist ideas (1528–37, 1541–5), and George BUCHANAN (d. 1582) becoming an outstanding figure. Humanist influences improved Welsh prose (e.g., by William SALESBURY, d.

c.1584, and John DAVIES of Mallwyd, d. 1644). Humanism reached Ireland in the late 16th century from both England and Continental European colleges.

Humanism weakened in the 16th century when the REFORMATION activated religious disputes. But classical education remained influential into the 20th century.

HUMAN RIGHTS ACT Legislation of the UK Parliament, passed in 1998 (effective from 2000), which incorporated rights from the European Convention on Human Rights (1950) into LAW throughout the UK. Although the UK was a signatory to the Convention, cases appealing to Convention Rights previously had to be taken to the European Court of Human Rights at Strasbourg (France).

The Act prohibits public authorities from acting in ways that conflict with Convention Rights, and requires judges to interpret UK legislation in accordance with such rights. Where legislation is deemed incompatible, judges can make a declaration and require the government and Parliament to ensure compatibility. The Act represented the 'modernizing' approach of NEW LABOUR. Similar legislation was adopted in the CHANNEL ISLANDS (2000) and Isle of MAN (2001), with effect from 2006, and in the Republic of Ireland (2003).

HUMBERT'S EXPEDITION A French invasion of W Ireland in 1798, intended to revive rebellion against the Irish government following the RISING OF 1798. About 1000 men, led by General Joseph Humbert, landed at Kilcummin (Co. Mayo) on 22 Aug. They marched inland, accompanied by several thousand Irishmen, until forced to surrender by government troops at Ballinamuck (Co. Longford) on 8 Sept. The French were allowed to depart. *See also* FRENCH REVOLUTION, IMPACT ON IRELAND.

HUMBLE PETITION AND ADVICE In England, 1657, during the Protectorate, a revised constitution intended to remedy defects of the INSTRUMENT OF GOVERNMENT. It was presented by Parliament to Oliver CROMWELL, lord protector, on 31 March. It added a nominated 'Other House' to the legislature alongside the House of Commons and readopted the name 'Privy Council' for the Council of State. It asked Cromwell to become king and nominate a successor. Cromwell refused the kingship. He accepted a revised version of the Petition on 25 May and was reinstalled as protector on 26 June. *See also* COMMONWEALTH AND PROTECTORATE.

HUMBLETON, BATTLE OF Fought near Wooler in Northumberland (NE England) on 14 Sept. 1402. A Scottish raiding army led by the (4th) earl of Douglas (*see* DOUGLAS, ARCHIBALD), taking revenge for an English invasion in 1401, was heavily defeated by English forces while returning from NEWCASTLE UPON TYNE. Douglas and two other earls, and Murdoch STEWART, were captured. Humbleton concluded a period of Scottish exertion against England. *See also* SCOTTISH–ENGLISH RELATIONS 1357 TO 1603.

HUME, BASIL (b. 2 March 1923 at Newcastle upon Tyne, Northumberland, England; d. 17 June 1999 at London, England, aged 76). Originally named George, the Benedictine abbot Basil Hume in 1976 became archbishop of WESTMINSTER and a cardinal. From 1979 he led Catholics in England and Wales as president of the countries' Bishops' Conference.

In 1982 Hume oversaw the first PAPAL VISIT to Great Britain. Friendly with Church of England leaders, from the late 1980s he supported Catholic involvement in ecumenical activity, although he arranged for Church of England clergy opposed to women's ordination to become Catholic priests (1990s). His self-effacing character had strong appeal beyond the Catholic Church (e.g., Queen ELIZABETH II attended Vespers in Westminster Cathedral, 1995).

HUME, JOHN (b. 18 Jan. 1937 at Londonderry, Co. Londonderry, Northern Ireland). Active in the CIVIL RIGHTS MOVEMENT (1960s), Hume was elected to the NORTHERN IRELAND Parliament (1969–73). In 1970 he cofounded the moderate nationalist, mainly Catholic, SOCIAL DEMOCRATIC AND LABOUR PARTY, which he led 1979–2001. Hume was a member of the Northern Ireland ASSEMBLY of 1973–5, power-sharing EXECUTIVE of 1974, Constitutional Convention of 1975–6, Assembly of 1982–6, and of the European Parliament (1979–2004) and UK Parliament (1983–2005).

Concerned to establish peace in Northern Ireland, Hume contributed to the NEW IRELAND FORUM (1983–4). From 1988 he held secret periodic discussions with Gerry ADAMS, president of PROVISIONAL SINN FÉIN, about means for achieving nationalist aspirations. Their joint declaration (24 April 1993) accelerated the Northern Ireland PEACE PROCESS, and Hume participated in negotiations from 1996 that resulted in the BELFAST AGREEMENT (1998). He was (jointly) awarded the 1998 Nobel Peace Prize. Hume served in the new Northern Ireland Assembly (1998–2000) before becoming a professor of peace studies (2002–10). *See also* TRIMBLE, DAVID.

HUNDRED YEARS WAR Conflict between England and France 1337–1453, involving France's allies (Scotland, Castile), which originated in disputes over GASCONY, SW France (English possession; *see* PARIS, TREATY OF).

In 1337 Philip VI of France (d. 1350) confiscated Gascony from King EDWARD III. In 1338 Edward landed in Flanders and (1340) reclaimed the French Crown (as grandson of Philip IV, d. 1314). English ships defeated French ships off Sluys (24 June 1340). A truce was concluded; Edward departed.

In July 1346 Edward invaded Normandy, defeating the French at Crécy (26 Aug.); but not exploiting the victory, he captured CALAIS (taken Aug. 1347) and made peace. Hostilities resumed in 1355 with EDWARD THE BLACK PRINCE campaigning from Bordeaux (Gascony). On 19 Sept. 1356 the French were defeated at Poitiers (W France) and King John II (d. 1364) was captured. Peace was agreed in 1360 (*see* BRÉTIGNY, TREATY OF). But after Charles V accepted a Gascon appeal, hostilities resumed (1369). Warfare and truces in the 1370s–90s culminated in a 28-year truce (1396).

In 1415 HENRY V invaded France, defeated the French at Agincourt (25 Oct.) and conquered Normandy (1417–19). The murder of John, duke of BURGUNDY (Sept. 1419), by men of the dauphin (French heir) resulted in an Anglo-Burgundian alliance. In 1420 Henry was recognized as regent and heir to Charles VI (*see* TROYES, TREATY OF). Henry's and Charles's deaths (1422) left the duke of BEDFORD as regent.

In 1429 the English siege of ORLÉANS was defeated, enabling the dauphin Charles to be consecrated at Reims. The French recaptured territory, and in 1435 the Burgundians changed sides (*see* ARRAS, CONGRESS OF). Fighting was intermittent until a truce was agreed in 1444 (*see* MARGARET OF ANJOU). In 1448 Henry VI of England secretly surrendered Maine. The French reconquered Normandy in 1449–50 and Gascony by 1453. England retained Calais until 1558. *See also* SCOTTISH–ENGLISH RELATIONS 1290 TO 1357/1357 TO 1603; SCOTTISH–FRENCH ALLIANCE; FRANCE, CLAIMS BY RULERS OF ENGLAND; GREAT SCHISM.

HUNGER MARCHES In Great Britain in the early 20th century, a form of working-class protest about economic problems. The first march was undertaken in May 1905 by bootmakers from Raunds (Northamptonshire), who went to LONDON to urge the War Office not to undercut union-recommended prices. Next month, unemployed men from Leicester (C England) attempted to petition King EDWARD VII about their plight. The term 'hunger march' was coined in 1908 for a march from MANCHESTER (abortive).

In 1922, during the post-WORLD WAR I depression, the National Unemployed Workers' Committee Movement organized a national march to London from several starting places. Others were held in 1927, 1930, 1932, 1934, 1936; there were also local marches. The 1932 march was the largest, involving 100,000 marchers; it ended in riot. The most famous was the 'Jarrow Crusade', part of the 1936 march, in which 200 unemployed men from Jarrow (NE England) petitioned Parliament for new industry. The marches had negligible effect. *See also* NATIONAL

UNEMPLOYED WORKERS MOVEMENT; GREAT DEPRESSION, IMPACT ON GREAT BRITAIN.

HUNGER STRIKES, NORTHERN IRELAND A series of hunger strikes, during the TROUBLES, staged by republican prisoners at the Maze Prison who demanded the restoration of 'special status'. They started on 1 March 1981, led by Bobby Sands (elected MP in by-election 9 April; died 5 May). Ten prisoners died in May–Aug. Great Britain's refusal to compromise provoked unrest, and increased popular support for republican nationalism persuaded PROVISIONAL SINN FÉIN to exploit electoral politics alongside continuing violence. *See also* NORTHERN IRELAND.

HUNNE AFFAIR In England, an episode resulting from the imprisonment by Church authorities of Richard Hunne, a London merchant tailor (2 Dec. 1514), for alleged heresy while he was prosecuting clergy in the secular courts. On 4 Dec. Hunne was found hanged. The authorities claimed he had committed suicide. A coroner's jury suspected murder. Dr Horsey, a Church officer, and two servants were accused, but an inquiry failed to settle the case. The affair exacerbated tensions between laity and clergy, and provoked debates about the Church's privileges. *See also* CHURCH, MEDIEVAL ENGLAND.

HUNT, HENRY 'ORATOR' (b. 6 Nov. 1773 at Upavon, Wiltshire, England; d. 13 Feb. 1835 at Alresford, Hampshire, England, aged 61). A farmer, influenced by William COBBETT, Hunt agitated from 1812 for far-reaching PARLIAMENTARY REFORM, including manhood suffrage. A demagogic speaker, he was nicknamed 'Orator Hunt' in 1816 by writer Robert Southey. He spoke at mass meetings from 1816. His arrest near Manchester in 1819 resulted in the 'PETERLOO Massacre'. He was imprisoned 1820–2. Hunt continued to campaign, and served as an MP 1830–2. He opposed the Great Reform Act (1832) as an inadequate measure.

HUNTING AND GATHERING *see* GATHERING AND HUNTING

HUNTINGDON, DAVID EARL OF (b. 1152; d. 17 June 1219 at Yardley Hastings, Northamptonshire, England, aged 66 or 67). Brother of WILLIAM I, king of Scots; recipient of extensive royal grants of land, and William's agent in N Scotland. In 1185 David became a vassal of King HENRY II of England, when William resigned the earldom of Huntingdon (C England) to him (from which David recruited settlers for Scotland). In 1290 the chief claimants to the vacant Scottish kingship (John BALLIOL, Robert Bruce, John Hastings) were each descended from one of David's daughters. *See also* NORMANS, IMPACT ON SCOTLAND; GREAT CAUSE.

HUNTLY, 4TH EARL OF (b. 1513 in Scotland; d. 5 Nov. 1562 at Corrichie, NE Scotland, aged 48 or 49). George Gordon succeeded as earl in 1524 and was CHANCELLOR from 1546 (until death). During the regency of MARY OF GUISE (1554–9) he was overshadowed by his French deputy, de Roubay, and in spring 1560 reluctantly joined the pro-Protestant LORDS OF THE CONGREGATION. He supported the Catholic MARY, QUEEN OF SCOTS, until she gave the earldom of Moray (under Huntly's administration) to her half-brother James Stewart in 1562 (*see* MORAY, JAMES EARL OF). Huntly rebelled, but was defeated by Stewart, dying soon afterwards. *See also* HUNTLY, EARLS AND MARQUISES OF.

HUNTLY, 6TH EARL OF (b. 1562 in Scotland; d. 13 June 1636 at Dundee, E Scotland, aged about 74). Educated in France, George Gordon succeeded as earl in 1576. As Scotland's foremost Catholic he was censured in the 1580s by the Church of SCOTLAND, but protected by the king, the Protestant King JAMES VI, who resented Church pressure. Huntly conspired with Spain (1588–9) and was implicated in the murder of the earl of MORAY (1592), but was punished lightly.

In 1594 James, seeking Church support, marched against Huntly: he went into exile (March 1595), but returned in 1596 and formally joined the Church (June 1597). Thereafter he kept relatively quiet but continued to be harried for his reputed Catholicism. He was created a marquis in 1599, and died a Catholic. *See also* HUNTLY, EARLS AND MARQUISES OF; CATHOLICS AND CATHOLIC CHURCH, SCOTLAND.

HUNTLY, EARLS AND MARQUISES OF A noble family, based in NE Scotland, which was prominent in Scottish political life mid 15th–mid 17th centuries. They were descendants of Sir Alexander Seton (d. 1470), who was created earl of Huntly in 1455. He adopted the surname Gordon (for distinction from the main Seton family) from his mother Elizabeth Gordon, an heiress from whom his father had acquired most of his extensive estates.

Alexander Gordon (d. 1524), 3rd earl, made the family the most powerful in N and NE Scotland. The 4th and 6th earls of HUNTLY (the latter a marquis from 1599) were involved in internal conflict. Other family members have included the earl of ABERDEEN, prime minister of Great Britain (1852–5).

HUNTSMAN, BENJAMIN (b. 4 June 1704 at Epworth, Lincolnshire, England; d. 20 June 1776 at Attercliffe, Yorkshire, England, aged 72). A clockmaker living near SHEFFIELD (Yorkshire) from 1742, Huntsman (a Quaker) experimented with purifying steel by melting it at extreme heat. He invented cast, or crucible, steel, and worked as a steelmaker by 1751. His invention was the major improvement in steel making before the invention of the Bessemer process (1856). The eventual adoption of Huntsman's process led to Sheffield's pre-eminence in steel manufacturing. *See also* IRON AND STEEL INDUSTRIES, ENGLAND.

HUSKISSON, WILLIAM (b. 11 March 1770 at Birtsmorton, Worcestershire, England; d. 15 Sept. 1830 at Liverpool, Lancashire, England, aged 60). Huskisson became an MP in 1796 and served as joint secretary to the Treasury 1804–6, 1807–9, under William PITT the Younger and the duke of PORTLAND. He led debates on the CORN LAWS and GOLD STANDARD.

Huskisson perceived the growing importance of manufacturing exports for Great Britain's economy. As president of the Board of Trade (1823–7), he lowered import duties, reformed the NAVIGATION ACTS and made trade treaties with several European States. Viscount GODERICH made him colonial secretary and leader of the Commons (1827), but he resigned from the duke of WELLINGTON's government in 1828. A LIBERAL TORY, Huskisson was killed accidentally by a steam locomotive (*Rocket*, designed by George STEPHENSON) at the opening of the Liverpool and Manchester railway.

HUTTON, JAMES (b. 3 June 1726 at Edinburgh, SE Scotland; d. 26 March 1797 at Edinburgh, aged 70). After studying (in 1740s) at the universities of EDINBURGH and Paris, Hutton became wealthy from co-founding a chemical manufactory. As a farmer in SE Scotland 1754–c.1767, he introduced advanced techniques. He then lived in Edinburgh, primarily pursuing scientific interests.

Interested in geology from the 1750s, Hutton toured Great Britain to study rock formations and collect specimens (to 1770s). He perceived that rocks in the Earth's surface are subject to a constant process of erosion, reconsolidation and uplift, which necessarily operated through an immense period of time. This implicitly undermined Bible-based history of the Earth (*see* USSHER, JAMES). Hutton published his theory, named 'actualism', in a paper (1788) and in *Theory of the Earth* (two volumes, 1795). His friend John Playfair provided a more accessible presentation in *Illustrations of the Huttonian Theory of the Earth* (1802), though Hutton's theory was not widely accepted until the mid 19th century (as 'uniformitarianism'). *See also* GEOLOGY; ENLIGHTENMENT, SCOTLAND.

HUXLEY, T.H. (b. 4 May 1825 at Ealing, Middlesex, England; d. 29 June 1895 at Eastbourne, Sussex, England, aged 70). Thomas Henry Huxley obtained a basic medical qualification (1845), served in the Royal Navy (1846–54) and became a lecturer. From the 1840s he made important biological and zoological discoveries. He was a fellow of the ROYAL SOCIETY from 1851 (secretary 1871–80, president 1883–5).

After the publication of *Origin of Species* (1859) by Charles DARWIN, a hypothesis about the evolution of new animal species, Huxley provided scientific support from research on fossils. He also concluded that religious belief must be subordinated to evidence and reason. He rejected atheism, coining the term 'agnosticism' (1869), meaning that knowledge of God's existence or non-existence is impossible. Nevertheless, he encouraged Bible study in schools because he considered religious sentiment the basis of moral conduct.

HWICCE A Germanic group which in the 7th–8th centuries inhabited a kingdom around the Severn Valley (modern Gloucestershire and Worcestershire, W England). They were a 'buffer' between MERCIA and WESSEX. The kingdom's origin is obscure. It was possibly created by King PENDA of Mercia (d. 655) as a subordinate kingdom. A bishopric was founded at WORCESTER (679 or 680). The Hwiccian kingdom became an ealdomanry of Mercia c.780. *See also* KINGSHIP, ANGLO-SAXON.

HYDE, DOUGLAS (b. 17 Jan. 1860 at Frenchpark, Co. Roscommon, Ireland; d. 12 July 1949 at Dublin, Republic of Ireland, aged 89). A (Protestant) Gaelic scholar, Hyde was first president of the Gaelic League (1893–1915). He sought to preserve the Irish language while resisting the increasing politicization of Gaelic culture. Professor of modern Irish at University College, Dublin (1909–32), following the foundation of the IRISH FREE STATE (1922) Hyde served as a senator (1925) and was elected first president of southern Ireland under the 1937 CONSTITUTION (1938–45). *See also* GAELIC REVIVAL, IRELAND 19TH–20TH CENTURIES.

HYDE, EDWARD *see* CLARENDON, EARL OF

HYDE, LAURENCE *see* ROCHESTER, EARL OF

HYNDMAN, H.M. (b. 7 March 1842 at London, England; d. 22 Nov. 1921 at London, aged 79). An admirer of Karl MARX, Henry Mayers Hyndman in 1881 published *England for All* and founded the Democratic Federation. Avowedly socialist from 1883 (e.g., in advocating NATIONALIZATION), it was renamed the SOCIAL DEMOCRATIC FEDERATION in 1884 and merged into the British Socialist Party in 1911. Hyndman and others left the BSP in 1916 because of its opposition to WORLD WAR I and founded the National Socialist Party (affiliated to LABOUR PARTY 1918). In 1920 it readopted the name Social Democratic Federation.

HYWEL AB OWAIN GWYNEDD (b. c.1120; d. 1170 at Pentraeth, Anglesey, Gwynedd, aged about 50). A poet of the Middle Welsh period; son of King OWAIN GWYNEDD of Gwynedd (NW Wales). His life was often violent, but his poetry is romantic, concerned with women and nature. *See also* WELSH LANGUAGE AND LITERATURE.

HYWEL DDA, LAWS OF Welsh laws, contained within legal collections of the 13th century onwards, which were said to have been compiled for HYWEL DDA, king of GWYNEDD 942 or 943–50. Though collections incorporate early material, Hywel's reputed contribution was probably invented in the 12th century to confer status and counter English criticism of Welsh customs. *See also* LAW, WELSH.

HYWEL DDA, 'THE GOOD' (b. *c.*880; d. 950, aged about 70). King of DYFED (SW Wales) 904 or 905–50; king of GWYNEDD (NW Wales) 942 or 943–50. Though descended from RHODRI MAWR of Gwynedd, Hywel acquired Dyfed on the death of his father-in-law. He submitted in 926 (with other Welsh kings) to ATHELSTAN and subsequently to later English kings. In 942 or 943 Hywel's rival, King Idwal Foel of Gwynedd, died, enabling Hywel to control Gwynedd. He thus ruled much of Wales until his death. His sons lost Gwynedd, but most subsequent rulers of Dyfed were his descendants. Hywel is famous for allegedly promulgating laws: *see* HYWEL DDA, LAWS OF; ANGLO-WELSH RELATIONS, 6TH–13TH CENTURIES.

I

ICE AGES *see* GLACIATIONS

ICI *see* IMPERIAL CHEMICAL INDUSTRIES

ILLTUD (b. *c.*470; d. *c.*530, aged about 60). A renowned scholar, possibly from Brittany; founder and abbot of the monastery of Llantwit Major (S Wales), where DAVID, Samson of Dol, and GILDAS are said to have studied. Illtud is the dedicatee (as saint) of churches in SE Wales and Brittany. *See also* CONVERSION OF WALES; MONASTICISM, MEDIEVAL WALES.

IMMIGRATION AND ASYLUM LEGISLATION, SOUTHERN IRELAND The IRISH FREE STATE (founded 1922) initially maintained UK legislation, and effectively remained a single area with the UK (except during WORLD WAR II, 1939–45, with restrictions until 1952 for Great Britain). It enacted legislation concerning 'aliens' (non-native immigrants) in 1935 after passing citizenship legislation: its Aliens Act replaced the 1914 and 1919 UK Aliens Restriction Acts with similar provisions, authorizing the minister for justice to consider immigration applications, prohibit admissions, undertake deportations, and operate residence requirements. Entry of the Republic of Ireland to the EUROPEAN ECONOMIC COMMUNITY (EEC) in 1973 included right of residence for EEC citizens. From 1986 some non-EEC citizens associated with business investment were allowed residence. The State's power to deport was upheld by a legal judgment (1986), but another judgment affirmed that foreign-born parents of an Irish-born child were entitled to reside (1989). IMMIGRATION was relatively low until the mid 1990s.

Although the Republic ratified the United Nations Refugee Convention in 1956, refugee status was not legally recognized until 1996; following a rapid rise in asylum applications, legislation stipulated arrangements (Refugee Act, implemented 2000). In 1999 deportation powers were given statutory authority (in Immigration Act, specifying a deportation process), after their delegation to a minister was deemed unconstitutional. The Immigration Acts of 2003 and 2004 tightened procedures (e.g., carriers required to validate landing documents).

A judgment of Jan. 2003 allowed deportation of some non-Irish parents of Irish children but was considered ambiguous. Motivated by concern about visitors giving birth in Ireland to obtain residency, a referendum in 2004 endorsed diminution of the constitutional right to citizenship (implemented by the Irish Nationality and Citizenship Act of 2004, requiring parental qualification).

IMMIGRATION AND ASYLUM LEGISLATION, UNITED KINGDOM BEFORE 1973 The British and Irish Parliaments passed Aliens Acts in Jan. 1793 in response to the FRENCH REVOLUTION to counter trouble-makers (e.g., insurrectionaries). British legislation specified arrival ports for aliens (subjects of other States), controlled movement and residence, and enabled expulsion of undesirable aliens. Similar legislation (for UK from 1801) was enacted until 1836 (Registration of Aliens Act), with expulsion excluded from 1824, allowing asylum.

Agitation against mass immigration mainly by JEWS (1880s–90s) resulted in the 1905 Aliens Act (replacing the 1836 Act), restricting immigration from outside the BRITISH EMPIRE. It authorized rejection of undesirables, specifically pauper and diseased aliens, but retained right of asylum from persecution.

Restrictions during WORLD WAR I affected immigration. The 1914 emergency Aliens Restriction Act authorized orders to exclude or expel aliens. The 1914 Status of Aliens Act defined British subjects (citizens) as essentially persons born in the British Empire. Provisions in the former Act were extended (Aliens Restriction Act, 1919).

Freedom of immigration from within the Empire was confirmed by the 1948 British Nationality Act, enacted after COMMONWEALTH countries agreed to introduce citizenships. It created 'Citizenship of the United Kingdom and Colonies' and gave British-subject status to citizens of nine other Commonwealth countries, permitting residence in the UK by 700 million persons. From 1954 the UK accepted obligations under the 1951 United Nations Refugee Convention (amended 1967).

'New Commonwealth' immigration provoked limitation: under the 1962 Commonwealth Immigrants Act, entry required 'employment vouchers', although dependents and UK passport-holders could enter. The 1968 Commonwealth Immigrants Act, intended to prevent immigration of E African Asians, removed rights of passport-holders; free entry now required 'patriality' (UK-born parent or grandparent, favouring the 'Old Commonwealth'). An appeals system was introduced in 1969 (Immigration Appeals Act), and the 1971 Immigration Act consolidated immigration law ahead of entry to the EUROPEAN ECONOMIC COMMUNITY. *See also* DECOLONIZATION.

IMMIGRATION AND ASYLUM LEGISLATION, UNITED KINGDOM FROM 1973

The UK's entry in 1973 to the EUROPEAN ECONOMIC COMMUNITY or EEC (European Union or EU from 1993) divided immigration into two types: entry by citizens of other EEC countries, under the EEC's requirement for 'free movement'; non-EEC/EU immigration, regulated by UK legislation and international law.

Continuing concern about non-EEC immigration resulted in the 1981 British Nationality Act. It replaced the 1948 'United Kingdom and Colonies' citizenship with full citizenship for the UK and two other categories for remaining British territories; right of residence in the UK applied only to full citizenship. Further legislation in the 1980s–90s tackled smuggling and employment of illegal immigrants and asylum seekers.

In 1997 a rule change by the new Labour government (relaxation of the 'primary purpose' rule, allowing entry to more dependents), helped to fuel a rapid, large increase in non-EU immigration. It included many thousands who entered as tourists and sought to settle by claiming refugee status. Frequent legislation ensued, partly to placate the UK public by suggesting that immigration was under control, partly to deter immigrants by trying to demonstrate that the UK was not a 'soft touch'. It had little effect. Numerous Acts included regulations for handling of asylum seekers (1999), introduction of a citizenship test (2002), restrictions on appeals (2006), the concept of probationary citizenship (2009), and limitation of facilities for illegal immigrants (2014). Major revisions were made in 2016. The scale of immigration (including substantial immigration from new EU countries from 2004) contributed to the UK's decision to leave the EU (2016), thereby to enable the UK Parliament to legislate again for all types of immigration (*see* BREXIT).

IMMIGRATION TO ENGLAND GERMANIC IMMIGRATION to southern Britain in the 5th–6th centuries created a culturally Germanic ('Anglo-Saxon' or 'English') society by *c.*900. Danes and Norwegians settled in some areas in the late 9th–10th centuries but were eventually absorbed (*see* VIKINGS, IMPACT ON ENGLAND).

The NORMAN CONQUEST (1066–70s) replaced the English élite (e.g., landholders, senior clergy) with immigrant French and others. JEWS also settled in TOWNS. Immigrants (possibly 10,000 altogether) were generally soon absorbed, but their culture remained influential to the 15th century (*see* FRENCH, USE IN BRITISH ISLES; ENGLISH LANGUAGE). Jews were expelled in 1290. In the 13th–15th centuries immigration was small (e.g., merchants, Flemish and Dutch craftsmen). As in later centuries, Irish, Welsh and Scots immigrated, especially to towns. In 1500 London contained possibly 3000 immigrants (of 50,000 inhabitants).

Religion then became influential. Marranos (crypto-Jews) from the Iberian Peninsula settled in London and BRISTOL, and in the 1540s–90s thousands of Protestants arrived from France and the Low Countries, incidentally helping development of INDUSTRY. More French Protestants followed from 1685 (*see* HUGUENOTS), and Jewish immigration increased. Involvement in the SLAVE TRADE resulted in immigration of AFRICANS.

In the 19th century Irish immigration was considerable, driven by poverty and the GREAT FAMINE (*see* EMIGRATION FROM IRELAND). In 1861 Irish-born inhabitants totalled 499,000 (in a population of 18.3 million). In the 1880s–90s over 100,000 Jews arrived from Prussia and Russia, fleeing pogroms. Smaller groups included Germans, Poles, Italians, Indians, CHINESE.

Substantial immigration occurred again from 1948 (to 1970s), mostly from the 'New Commonwealth' (e.g., AFRICAN CARIBBEANS; SOUTH ASIANS). By 1971, 6% of the population was foreign-born. From 1997 large-scale immigration was encouraged: net immigration to 2009 was 2.2 million; by 2017, 15% of the population was foreign born. Immigrants came predominantly from Africa and Asia, and from 2004 from eastern Europe (notably POLAND). *See also* ETHNIC AND NATIONAL MINORITIES, ENGLAND; IMMIGRATION AND ASYLUM LEGISLATION, UNITED KINGDOM BEFORE/FROM 1973; MULTICULTURAL SOCIETY.

IMMIGRATION TO IRELAND The island was settled from Britain and the Isle of MAN from *c*.8000 BC; immigrants in the last centuries BC were possibly responsible for development of the Irish language (*see* PREHISTORIC IRELAND; CELTIC CULTURE, IRELAND). Small-scale immigration probably continued through the 1st millennium AD (*see* IRISH COLONIZATION IN BRITAIN, 4TH–6TH CENTURIES).

Later immigrants created minority populations and cultures which shaped Irish history through interaction with the majority Gaelic Irish population. VIKINGS settled in some coastal areas from the mid 9th century, and founded TOWNS which retained Scandinavian identities into the 13th century (*see* OSTMEN; FINGAL).

An invasion of Anglo-Normans in 1169–70 led to English rule of Ireland and settlement by several thousand English and Welsh people (*see* NORMANS, IMPACT ON IRELAND), though the population of immigrant origin declined in the 14th–15th centuries. During the REFORMATION (16th century) most inhabitants of English descent remained Catholic, and became known as OLD ENGLISH, retaining their identity into the 18th century.

Between the 1530s and mid 17th century another stream of English immigrants held government posts, settled on PLANTATIONS, or came as soldiers (1649–52). Many received land in the CROMWELLIAN LAND SETTLEMENT. As Protestants they dominated Ireland until the late 19th century (*see* PROTESTANT ASCENDANCY). Meanwhile there was considerable settlement in NE Ireland in the 17th century by presbyterians from Scotland, who created a distinctive society (*see* PRESBYTERIANISM, IRELAND). There was an inflow of French Protestants in the 1690s (*see* HUGUENOTS).

Though British rule ended in southern Ireland in 1922, English culture remained influential. Between the mid 1990s and 2008, economic expansion attracted a diverse wave of immigrants, amounting by 2010 to 10% of the population (from 188 countries). In NORTHERN IRELAND, there was considerable net immigration from 2001, including settlement from Eastern Europe after the expansion of the EUROPEAN UNION in 2004. *See also* ETHNIC AND NATIONAL MINORITIES, IRELAND.

IMMIGRATION TO SCOTLAND The most important early phase occurred in the 12th–13th centuries when men immigrated from England (many from Anglo-Norman families) to acquire estates (*see* NORMANS, IMPACT ON SCOTLAND; SOCIAL STRUCTURE, SCOTLAND). They imported English tenants, though they were quickly absorbed into the host population.

Significant immigration resumed in the 1790s with Irish migration, which continued until the late 19th century. Over 100,000 Irish arrived by the 1830s, three-quarters of whom were Catholics. They settled mainly in the GLASGOW region (W-C Scotland). The GREAT FAMINE (1845–9) increased numbers: in 1851 there were 207,000 Irish-born inhabitants (7.2% of total population). English people also immigrated steadily during the century: in 1921 there were 190,000 English-born inhabitants (4% of total).

Between the 1880s and 1914 new groups arrived: Lithuanians escaping Russification (8000); Jews from Russia fleeing pogroms (10,000 in Glasgow in 1914); and Italians, who arrived from particular villages by arranged migration (5500 by 1914).

During the 20th and 21st centuries English immigration persisted; in 1971, 280,000 residents (5.3% of total) were English-born, and in 2011, 475,000 (9%). During the 1940s Poles also settled. They were followed in the 1950s–60s by Asians moving from England (16,000 by 1970). Another strong wave of immigration occurred from 1998, growing strongly from 2003. By 2011, 7% of the population had been born outside the UK. The largest number lived in the Edinburgh area (75,000), though between 2001 and 2011 the largest proportional increase occurred in ABERDEEN (167%, from 6% to 16% of total population). *See also* POPULATION, SCOTLAND; ETHNIC AND NATIONAL MINORITIES, SCOTLAND; CATHOLICS AND CATHOLIC CHURCH, SCOTLAND; ORANGE ORDER, SCOTLAND.

IMMIGRATION TO WALES, LATE 11TH–14TH CENTURIES The development of the MARCH OF WALES (late 11th–12th centuries) included settlement by English immigrants, normally on lowlands. In such places as PEMBROKESHIRE (SW Wales) and the Gower Peninsula (S Wales) immigrants replaced natives; elsewhere they occupied vacant land. Early immigration also included French, and *c*.1107–10 Flemings settled DYFED (SW Wales). Marcher lords also populated new TOWNS with English immigrants.

A second phase of English immigration occurred after the conquest of 1282–3 (*see* WALES, ENGLISH CONQUEST OF). In NE Wales, English settled on appropriated land; in the NW they inhabited new towns.

Immigrants' descendants maintained English identity and language into the 14th century, though Welsh people moved into English-populated towns in the 12th and 13th centuries. After the BLACK DEATH (1349), Welsh migrated into English areas, while English learnt Welsh. Most English areas became bilingual. By c.1550, only S Pembrokeshire, the Gower, and the Chepstow area (SE Wales) remained wholly English-speaking.

IMMIGRATION TO WALES, 18TH–21ST CENTURIES

Industrialization during the 18th century increased immigration from England (historically the main origin of immigrants), including skilled men attracted by the COPPER and IRON industries. Industrializing towns (e.g., SWANSEA, MERTHYR TYDFIL) developed English enclaves. As expansion accelerated from the 1790s, immigration from Ireland also increased (until 1880s). English immigration was further boosted from the 1860s by the expanding COAL INDUSTRY. By 1911, 19% of the population was English born. Depression in the 1920s–30s halted the flow, but it revived from the 1960s as English people bought second homes in Wales or retired there. Other groups were small. By 1900 CARDIFF had communities from the Caribbean, India and China, and a Jewish community. After 1945 Poles settled in rural areas. From the 1970s there was a considerable influx from India, Bangladesh, and Somalia.

As elsewhere in the UK, there was significant immigration from 1998. By 2011, 5.5% of residents had been born outside the UK. Most had settled in S Wales, with Cardiff having both the largest number of immigrants (46,000) and highest proportion (13%). Between 2001 and 2011 the biggest increase occurred at Merthyr Tydfil (227%). *See also* POPULATION, WALES; ETHNIC AND NATIONAL MINORITIES, WALES; ANGLICIZATION, WALES; CATHOLICS AND CATHOLIC CHURCH, WALES.

IMPEACHMENT

In England, a method of trying public officers on serious charges in PARLIAMENT. Impeachment reached developed form in the GOOD PARLIAMENT of 1376, when the House of Commons presented charges and the House of Lords acted as judges. Little used after 1459, when rulers tended to control ministers' careers, impeachment was revived in 1621 and continued until 1806 (against Henry DUNDAS), though convictions were rare. Warren HASTINGS of the East India Company was famously impeached in 1788–95 (acquitted). Impeachment was included in the constitution of the USA (1787).

IMPERIAL CHEMICAL INDUSTRIES

A major British industrial company, created in 1926 by merger of four chemical companies including Brunner Mond (*see* MOND, LUDWIG). Products included bulk chemicals, explosives, dyestuffs and paints. Marketing concentrated initially on the British Empire. Heavily engaged in research, 'ICI' proved innovative and successful. It established a separate pharmaceuticals division in 1957.

In 1993, after repulsing a takeover and breakup threatened by Hanson Trust (1991), ICI demerged its profitable pharmaceuticals division (renamed 'Zeneca'). The remaining business was acquired in 2008 by the Dutch firm Akzo Nobel, ending ICI's business identity. *See also* CHEMICALS INDUSTRY, ENGLAND AND GREAT BRITAIN; HANSON, LORD.

IMPERIAL CONFERENCES

Meetings of representatives of Great Britain and countries in the BRITISH EMPIRE, known as 'colonial conferences' until 1907. The first met in London in 1887 (the year of Queen VICTORIA's diamond jubilee), partly as a result of campaigning by the IMPERIAL FEDERATION LEAGUE, the second in 1894 (in Canada). Further conferences took place in 1897 and 1902, in which Joseph CHAMBERLAIN played an important role, and in 1907, 1911, 1917, 1923, 1930, and 1937. The main subjects debated at conferences were: communications, defence, emigration, foreign relations, trade. Conferences were purely consultative. INDIA was not admitted until 1917. Conferences continued as COMMONWEALTH conferences.

IMPERIAL FEDERATION LEAGUE

A popular organization founded in Great Britain (in London) in 1884 to mobilize public support for strengthening relations between Britain and the self-governing territories of its Empire. It advocated an imperial Parliament and was involved in convening the first colonial conference (1887). The British branch was dissolved in 1893 but overseas branches survived into the 20th century. *See also* IMPERIAL CONFERENCES.

IMPERIALISM

Term used for the establishment and maintenance of rule by one people or country over other peoples, countries and lands (derived from Latin *imperium*, meaning 'supreme authority'). It usually involves government of dependent areas (rather than acknowledgement of superiority by payment of tribute). Imperial expansion has included English overseas expansion from the 16th century (British from 1707). The ways in which power was exercised took many different forms, institutionalized as CROWN COLONIES, PROTECTORATES and DOMINIONS. *See also* BRITISH EMPIRE.

IMPERIALISM OF FREE TRADE

Phrase coined in 1953 by the English historians John Gallagher and Ronald Robinson to summarize their criticism of the claim that in the mid 19th century Great Britain was indifferent to its Empire. They argued that Britain's adoption of FREE TRADE in the 1840s–50s contributed to continuing economic and imperial expansion, using whatever means seemed locally appropriate (e.g., territorial power, economic influence). *See also* INFORMAL EMPIRE; CHINESE TREATY PORTS; NEW IMPERIALISM; FOREIGN INVESTMENT.

IMPERIAL PREFERENCE *see* TARIFF REFORM

IMPOSITIONS Additional taxes on English imports, imposed from 1558. In 1606 (in the reign of King JAMES VI/I), John Bates, a London merchant, challenged a new levy on currants in the Exchequer Court ('Bates' case'), arguing that as a tax it required approval by Parliament. The Court adjudged the levy a legal exercise of the ROYAL PREROGATIVE over foreign relations. The judgment enabled the TREAS-URER, the earl of Salisbury (Robert CECIL), to extend imposi-tions to other commodities. The House of Commons, fearful of arbitrary taxation, challenged impositions (1610, 1614). They were condemned by the GRAND REMONSTRANCE (1641). *See also* GREAT CONTRACT; ADDLED PARLIAMENT; CUSTOMS, ENGLAND AND WALES BEFORE 1689.

IMPROVEMENT ACTS Legislation of the British, Irish and UK Parliaments which authorized boards of com-missioners in individual TOWNS to provide improvements, such as STREET LIGHTING, pavements, street cleaning, SEW-ERAGE and water supplies. Starting in 1725, about 600 Acts were passed in Great Britain, mainly between 1750 and the 1830s. Boards functioned alongside existing authorities, and funded improvements through special rates. Their responsibilities were taken over by other bodies in the 19th and 20th centuries.

INAUGURATION, ENGLAND *see* CORONATION, ENGLAND

INAUGURATION, IRELAND Possibly from the IRON AGE (700 BC–AD 400), a king was symbolically 'married' to his kingdom at a ceremony on a mound or hill (Irish *banais ríghe*, meaning 'marriage of the king'). The senior druid walked round the king and handed him a hazel rod. After the introduction of Christianity (5th century), coarbs ('heirs' of monastery founders) or bishops often replaced druids.

As kingship changed to lordship or chieftainship from the 11th century, chiefs were inaugurated by their chief vassal or nominal overlord who proclaimed the chief's name. The rod now symbolized possession of territory and lordship. Inaugurations ended *c.*1600. *See also* KINGSHIP, IRELAND.

INAUGURATION, SCOTLAND Probably from the mid 9th century until 1292 (John BALLIOL) kings were inaugurated on a mound at SCONE (C Scotland, in modern Perth and Kinross) where the so-called STONE OF DESTINY is also recorded from 1249. The ceremony symbolized the marriage of king to kingdom. (ROBERT I was inaugurated at Scone in 1306, but after the stone had been removed.) Replaced from 1331 by CORONATION. (Earlier forms of inauguration in N Britain are unrecorded.) *See also* KENNETH I MAC ALPIN; FIFE, EARLDOM OF.

INCHIQUIN, 6TH LORD (b. *c.*1614 in Ireland; d. 9 Sept. 1674 in Ireland, aged about 60). The Protestant Murrough O'Brien succeeded as Lord Inchiquin in 1624. When the Catholic rebellion began in 1641, Inchiquin, strongly anti-Catholic, commanded government forces in MUNSTER, S Ireland (*see* IRISH WARS, 1641–52). On 17 July 1644 he declared for England's Parliament (against King CHARLES I). He defeated the Munster army of the CATHOLIC CONFEDERATION at Knocknanuss (Co. Cork) on 13 Nov. 1647.

In April 1648, alarmed at Parliament's treatment of Charles, Inchiquin rejoined the Royalists and made a truce with the Confederation (20 May). It divided Catholics, but encouraged the marquess of ORMOND's return to Ireland. In 1649–50 Inchiquin sought unsuccessfully to obstruct Oliver CROMWELL's conquest. He left Ireland in Dec. 1650.

In 1654 Inchiquin was created Earl Inchiquin and con-verted to Catholicism. He returned to Munster in 1663 and lived quietly. *See also* O'BRIEN FAMILY.

INCOMES POLICIES Modern economic strategies to combat INFLATION by limiting wage increases, usually involving legal powers. The Conservative chancellor Selwyn LLOYD announced the first 'pay pause' in the UK in July 1961 (control of public-sector wages for 1961–2). The Labour prime minister Harold WILSON agreed voluntary restraint with trade unions (Dec. 1964), but later resorted to a pay and price freeze for six months (July 1966) and legal powers to regulate wages and prices (Oct.). Similar policies adopted by the Conservative Edward HEATH (Nov. 1972) were wrecked by a MINERS' STRIKE (1973–4). From July 1975 Wilson again sought to limit increases, relying on Labour's SOCIAL CONTRACT with the unions (1973). The policy broke down by 1978 (under James CALLAGHAN). Margaret THATCHER, prime minister from 1979, who accepted a MONETARIST analysis of inflation, rejected incomes policies as useless. *See also* ECONOMY, STATE INVOLVEMENT, BRITAIN.

INCOME TAX Term for tax on the incomes of individ-uals or businesses derived from varied sources (a form of 'direct taxation'). The world's first successful income tax was introduced in Great Britain in 1798 by William PITT the Younger to help fund war against France (*see* FRENCH REVOLUTIONARY AND NAPOLEONIC WARS, BRITISH INVOLVEMENT). Initially charged at graduated rates from 2*d.* in the pound on incomes of £60 to 2*s.* (10%) on incomes over £200, it lapsed in 1802 (after the Peace of AMIENS), but was reintroduced (1806). Deeply unpopular, it ceased in 1816 after MPs rejected continuation.

Income tax was reintroduced in Britain in 1842 by Sir Robert PEEL as a short-term measure to eliminate the gov-ernment's deficit and facilitate CUSTOMS reductions.

Extensions were made, and from 1853 Ireland was included. Although abolition was intended, income tax became indispensable (by mid 1870s).

In 1907 a LIBERAL government introduced separate rates for 'earned' and 'unearned' income, and in 1909 added 'super-tax' on very high incomes for social and military purposes (*see* PEOPLE'S BUDGET). WORLD WAR I (1914–18) required unprecedented increases: standard rate rose from 1*s*. 2*d*. to 6*s*. (30%); tax-payers increased from 1.3 to 7.8 million, including some working-class people for the first time.

From 1923 to 1939 the UK standard rate averaged 4*s*. 6*d*., before rising to 10*s*. (50%) during WORLD WAR II (1939–45). Relatively high rates persisted afterwards, partly to support the WELFARE STATE. In 1974 LABOUR increased the top rate for earned income to 83%, and for unearned income to 98%.

From 1979 the CONSERVATIVES espoused lower rates, notably reducing the top rate for earned income to 60%, then 40% (1988). Their stance was largely retained by Labour after 1997. In 2014–15 income tax provided 29% of UK government revenue, and was paid by 30.7 million people (25.1 million paying at basic rate). *See also* TAXATION, ENGLAND, WALES AND GREAT BRITAIN FROM 1660.

INCORPORATION OF BOROUGHS Term used for royal grants of liberties which constituted the governing bodies of TOWNS as legal personalities. Liberties included the right to sue and be sued, make by-laws and hold lands. The grant to Coventry (C England) of 1345 is regarded as the first instance, though many towns already had extensive liberties. Incorporation continued in England, Wales and Ireland until the early 18th century, and occurred in Scotland from the later 15th to mid 17th century. From 1373 some larger towns were also granted county status (*see* BRISTOL). *See also* TOWN GOVERNMENT, ENGLAND/IRELAND/WALES.

INDENTURED LABOUR Indentured (contracted) labour was used in English colonies from the 17th century. English emigrant labourers sometimes agreed to work in a colony for a fixed period in return for passage. Indenturing was used after the abolition of slavery (1834), e.g., by owners of sugar PLANTATIONS in the British WEST INDIES. Intended initially as a transitional arrangement, its use continued (*see* SLAVERY IN BRITISH EMPIRE, ABOLITION OF). Over a million indentured labourers were transported from INDIA, and the British government approved the system until 1920.

INDEPENDENCE, SCOTTISH WARS OF *see* SCOTTISH–ENGLISH RELATIONS 1290 TO 1357

INDEPENDENT IRISH PARTY *see* PARLIAMENTARY REPRESENTATION, IRELAND

INDEPENDENT LABOUR PARTY A socialist political party founded in Bradford (NE England) in Jan. 1893 to win seats in the UK Parliament for representatives of working men (separate from the LIBERAL PARTY). One of its founders, the MP Keir HARDIE, sat henceforth as an ILP MP until defeated in 1895. The ILP helped to found the Labour Representation Committee in 1900 (LABOUR PARTY from 1906), from which it remained separate although ILP candidates were endorsed by the Committee/Party.

The ILP's influence declined after Labour admitted individual members from 1918. In 1932 the ILP disaffiliated from Labour, disenchanted by its moderate policies. Its MPs fell from 46 in 1921 to three in 1945. Its strength was in Scotland: its MPs there included Tom JOHNSTON, James MAXTON and John WHEATLEY. In 1947 its MPs defected to Labour; no more were elected. The Party continued until 1975 when it was renamed as Independent Labour Publications and became a pressure group within the Labour Party.

INDEPENDENT SCHOOL Term used in the UK for self-governing, fee-paying schools (i.e., private schools not funded by Local Education Authorities or central government). Such schools are long established, and generally divided into 'preparatory schools' (for ages 8–13) and 'public schools' (ages 13–18). The term became more widely used from 1975 when the Labour government abolished 'hybrid' DIRECT-GRANT SCHOOLS in England and Wales. *See also* GRAMMAR SCHOOL.

INDIA A former British territory in S Asia. India was ruled by Mughal emperors when the EAST INDIA COMPANY founded trading centres at Surat (1612), Madras (1642, now Chennai), Bombay (1668, now Mumbai), CALCUTTA (1690, now Kolkata), and elsewhere.

As Mughal power declined in the early 18th century, Great Britain and France competed for influence among native kingdoms. After victories by Robert CLIVE at PLASSEY (1757) and Buxar (1764), the East India Company gained control of Bengal (NE India). Warren HASTINGS, first governor-general of British India (1774), raised a native army, but from 1785 the British government supervised the company's activities (under India Act, 1784). British traders made fortunes. Richard WELLESLEY (governor-general 1797–1805) used force to eradicate French influence and induce native kingdoms (e.g., Hyderabad, Mysore), to recognize British overlordship. Regional wars in the early 19th century helped the company extend its supremacy across India with direct and indirect rule.

In the 1830s, the INDIAN CIVIL SERVICE started westernization policies, resistance to which contributed to the INDIAN MUTINY (1857–8). Afterwards the British government assumed responsibility for India (1858, represented by a viceroy). In 1876, Queen VICTORIA took the title 'empress of India'. The British promoted economic development with road and railway building and irrigation schemes. India's defence became a strategic preoccupation (*see* Great Game).

Educated Indians resented their subordination, and the Indian National Congress (founded 1885) called for greater self-government. The Morley-Minto Reforms (1909) extended representative government, and the Montagu-Chelmsford Reforms (1919) conceded some responsible government at provincial level. Indian troops supported Britain in World War I, but the Amritsar Massacre (1919) led nationalists to support civil disobedience campaigns led by Mohandas Gandhi. Constitutional reforms promised by the India Act 1935 were delayed by World War II and divisions between Hindus and Muslims. Indian independence came in 1947, when partition also created Pakistan. Approx. population in 1921, 318,900,000; in 1946, 415,000,000. *See also* Burma.

INDIA, BRITISH RELATIONS WITH The guiding principles of Indian foreign policy from its independence (as a Dominion) in 1947 – anti-colonialism and non-alignment – prevented the Commonwealth from developing into a political–military bloc. Great Britain was conciliatory. From 1950 it accepted India as a republic within the Commonwealth, and refused to condemn Indian neutrality in the Cold War, though in 1961 India's prime minister, Jawaharlal Nehru, denounced British policy in Africa and Britain condemned India's seizure of Portugal's Indian territories. Britain nonetheless provided military aid when China attacked Assam (1962).

Britain has professed impartiality regarding conflicts between India and Pakistan. Relations have generally remained cordial, though sensitive, with disagreements over the Rhodesia problem, South Africa and migration to Britain (*see* South Asians in Great Britain). In the early 21st century Indian companies became substantial investors in the British economy (e.g., in 2008 Tata bought the luxury car manufacturer Jaguar Land Rover).

INDIAN CIVIL SERVICE The small, élite professional bureaucracy that governed British India. It developed from *c.*1790 when Charles Cornwallis, the governor-general, introduced salaried civil administration (separated from trading activity). Appointees were British and employed by the East India Company. Recruits attended a training college 1805–58, and thereafter took university courses. Competitive entrance examinations were introduced in 1853. Total strength was about a thousand men.

After the British government superseded the company in 1858, Indians were admitted though few were recruited until the later 19th century. The proportion increased from 1917, but power remained with white officials until

independence in 1947, when control was transferred to the new governments of India and Pakistan.

INDIAN INDEPENDENCE India's independence was obtained mainly by the Indian National Congress, which was formed in 1885 by westernized Indians to seek greater involvement in government. The British permitted election of Indians to provincial councils from 1892, though Lord Curzon (viceroy 1899–1905) rejected further concessions. By 1908 the Congress, dominated by Hindus, sought a self-governing Dominion. Britain's sympathetic Liberal government allowed election of a majority of provincial council members (Morley-Minto Reforms, 1909). Meanwhile, Muslims had founded the Muslim League (1906).

From 1915, during World War I, Mohandas Gandhi encouraged mass protests. Reforms were promised to retain Indian support. From 1919, elected representatives could become ministers in provincial councils (Montagu-Chelmsford Reforms). But the Amritsar Massacre (April 1919) discredited British rule and provoked protests. Gandhi demanded self-government and independence, while the British offered compromises. Dominion status was promised ('Irwin Declaration', 1929), yet Gandhi broke the salt laws in protest (1930). Following concessions in 1935, Congress formed provincial governments, but resigned when the viceroy declared war against Germany (1939). In 1942 Gandhi launched a 'Quit India' campaign. By now the Muslim League was demanding a separate 'Pakistan'.

The post-war British Labour government accepted withdrawal. In Sept. 1946 it created a government of Indians, with Jawaharlal Nehru as effectively prime minister. Independence was implemented on 15 Aug. 1947, with the subcontinent partitioned as the dominions of India and Pakistan. India became a republic in 1950, Pakistan in 1956. *See also* Mountbatten, Lord; Burma.

INDIAN MUTINY The most substantial rebellion against British rule in India, 1857–8. It began at Meerut, near Delhi (N India), on 10 May 1857 when Indian soldiers killed their British officers and the officers' families. They marched to Delhi and restored the Mughal emperor. The rebellion spread across northern India. Its causes were complex, but included grievances about conditions, including the use of 'unclean' animal fat on gun cartridges. The uprising was crushed within months, and peace proclaimed on 8 July 1858. Afterwards the British government assumed control of India from the East India Company.

INDULGENCE A pardon granted by the Pope or his bishops to remit further punishment due for committed sins. Indulgences became common in western Europe in the 12th century. They were believed to shorten the torment of souls in purgatory (the place where souls awaited entry to heaven). Criticized by reformers in the early 16th century, they were banned in England and Wales by royal proclamation (1536) and apparently disappeared in Scotland (mid 16th century). *See also* REFORMATION, ENGLAND.

INDULGENCE, DECLARATIONS OF Attempts in the 1660s–80s by King CHARLES II and King JAMES VII/II to remove legal restrictions on separate worship by Protestant dissenters and Roman Catholics in England and Wales (so-called 'penal laws'; *see* RECUSANCY, ENGLAND AND WALES; CLARENDON CODE).

In the first Declaration (26 Dec. 1662), Charles stated an intention to obtain statutory power to suspend the penal laws. They were suspended by Charles's Declaration of 15 March 1672, but Parliament forced him to revoke it (8 March 1673; *see* ANGLO-DUTCH WARS). James's Declaration of 4 April 1687 (reissued 27 April 1688) provided a general liberty of worship.

The kings' attempts to introduce toleration by Declarations (primarily for Catholics) implied a belief in having power to override STATUTE law. It was condemned in the Declaration of RIGHTS. *See also* SEVEN BISHOPS' CASE; GLORIOUS REVOLUTION.

INDUSTRIAL DECLINE, ENGLAND Decline was experienced in two broad phases, involving different sets of industries. From the 1920s, the 'staple industries' of the INDUSTRIAL REVOLUTION markedly contracted, principally COTTON and woollen textiles, COAL, IRON AND STEEL, and SHIP BUILDING. Overseas competition and failure to innovate caused loss of markets. Although there was respite during and after WORLD WAR II (1939–45), the cotton industry largely closed by the late 1960s, woollen textiles by the late 1980s, and coal mining by the mid 1990s. The decline of iron and steel was slowed from the 1930s by demand from new industries, but in the 1970s production became concentrated in three areas, and by 2000 only a few thousand people were employed. Ship building became insignificant by the 1990s.

From the 1890s the manufacturing sector was sustained by new industries, notably BICYCLES, MOTORCYCLES, the MOTOR INDUSTRY, electrical engineering and the AIRCRAFT INDUSTRY. During the 20th century CHEMICALS and pharmaceuticals also expanded, and after World War II, COMPUTING and nuclear power were developing areas. Many of these also declined mainly from the 1970s. Motorcycle production shrank rapidly in the 1970s, mainly because of Japanese competition. The motor industry also faltered, due to competition and internal problems (e.g., strikes). In the 1980s bicycle production fell severely, and manufacturing of goods vehicles collapsed. Manufacture of computer hardware and building of nuclear power stations ended in the 1990s. Decline greatly reduced industrial employment, and

left the economy based to a far greater extent on services (e.g., banking, insurance). *See also* INDUSTRY, ENGLAND FROM LATE 18TH CENTURY; DE-INDUSTRIALIZATION.

INDUSTRIAL DECLINE, IRELAND *see* INDUSTRY, IRELAND FROM 18TH CENTURY TO 1921; INDUSTRY, NORTHERN IRELAND/SOUTHERN IRELAND

INDUSTRIAL DECLINE, SCOTLAND Around 1900 Scotland's economy was dominated by heavy industry (coal mining, iron and steel making, ship building, locomotive building, engineering machinery) and textiles. Much production was exported. Innovation was already faltering (e.g., failure to adopt the diesel engine in ship building). Until the late 1950s production fluctuated according to worldwide economic conditions, though the 1930s slump caused many companies to amalgamate. In the 1950s government encouraged expansion, for example by lending funds for the Ravenscraig steelworks (inaugurated 1960).

By the mid 1960s sectors were nevertheless failing, partly because of foreign competition. Coal was losing to electricity and oil: from 1965 to 1980 mines were reduced from 71 to 15. Struggling ship-building companies on the R. Clyde were amalgamated into two combines in 1967–8. Jute production effectively ended in the mid 1960s while employment in other textiles fell. In 1979–81 national recession induced further contraction and during the 1980s most shipyards and coalmines were closed, followed by the Ravenscraig steelworks in 1993, symbolically ending Scotland's reliance on heavy industry. *See also* INDUSTRY, SCOTLAND FROM LATE 18TH CENTURY; DE-INDUSTRIALIZATION.

INDUSTRIAL DECLINE, WALES In the early 19th century Wales was the world centre of the IRON, COPPER and TINPLATE industries, and in the late 19th century it dominated the world export trade in COAL and had the world's chief SLATE INDUSTRY. The primary role in iron making was lost by the 1860s, though steel making developed. From the late 19th century copper working suffered from overseas competition and effectively ended by the 1920s, while slate quarrying declined from the 1890s and had virtually ended by the 1960s because of industrial disputes and the popularity of clay tiles. Coal maintained its supremacy until the early 1920s, but use of oil, changing trade patterns and industrial disputes caused contraction and virtual closure by the 1990s. Steel and tinplate were depressed in the 1930s and revived after 1945. But the domination of heavy industry was over by the 1960s. *See also* INDUSTRY, WALES FROM 18TH CENTURY; DE-INDUSTRIALIZATION.

INDUSTRIAL DEMOCRACY Term used for formal involvement by employees in top-level management of organizations. Industrial democracy in the UK has been slight. The 1917 'Whitley Report' (named after the deputy speaker of the House of Commons J.H. Whitley), an outcome of 'reconstruction' ideas during WORLD WAR I, proposed 'joint industrial councils' of employers and employees at national, district and works levels. Though the 1918 Trade Boards Act authorized their creation, they became established mostly in government service (so-called 'Whitley Councils').

In the 1970s the TRADES UNION CONGRESS and LABOUR PARTY advocated industrial democracy. The 1977 'Bullock Report' (named after Sir Alan Bullock), commissioned by a Labour government, recommended inclusion of worker and shareholder representatives on boards of large companies, the former elected by trade unions. A minority report by the commission's employer members disagreed, fearing union control of industry. Broad hostility to the recommendations deterred legislation. In the 1980s the Conservative government encouraged 'worker participation', mainly through share acquisition at PRIVATIZATIONS. *See also* WORLD WAR I, IMPACT ON BRITISH SOCIETY.

INDUSTRIAL DISPUTES Strikes became common in Great Britain in the 18th and 19th centuries as economic organizations became larger, but they were hampered by divisions within workforces, low levels of unionization, import of strike-breaking labour, restrictive legislation, and costs of disputes. A well-publicized action was the 1889 London DOCK STRIKE. The first major national strike resulted from the lockout of engineering workers by the Employers' Federation of Engineering Associations, July 1897–Jan. 1898.

Major strikes in the early 20th century included ones by cotton workers (1910), railwaymen and dockers (1911) and miners (1912), and by dock workers in Ireland (*see* LARKIN, JIM). The formation of a TRIPLE ALLIANCE (1914) threatened crippling strikes, but during WORLD WAR I (1914–18) trade unions accepted arbitration. Many 'unofficial' strikes nonetheless occurred. Increased material expectations created by the war were quashed by falling wages and rising unemployment. Bitter strikes to resist pay cuts (by miners 1921, engineers 1922, boilermakers 1923, builders 1924) culminated in the 1926 miners' lockout and GENERAL STRIKE.

Major disputes recurred from the 1950s, many in the 1960s–70s involving public-sector workers. In 1958–67, an average of 144 working days per thousand were lost annually in Britain. In 1972–3, strikes cost 23 million working days. Such disruption, especially during the WINTER OF DISCONTENT (1979), provoked legal restrictions on union activity (1980s). Militancy declined after the failure of the anti-government MINERS' STRIKE of 1984–5. By 1995, only 415,000 days were lost to industrial action. *See also* SYNDICALISM; TRADE UNION LEGISLATION.

INDUSTRIAL REVOLUTION Term applied to a turning point in world history whereby economies accomplished prodigious increases in industrial productivity; sustained economic growth began; and economies and societies became dominated by industry rather than agriculture. The Revolution occurred first in Great Britain (from 1780s), then spread abroad. The term was originally promoted by the English historian Arnold Toynbee (1852–83).

The Revolution emerged in Britain from developing conditions in the 16th–18th centuries. British society became more urbanized, INDUSTRY became economically more important, and the SCIENTIFIC REVOLUTION encouraged technological developments (e.g., steam engine exhibited by Thomas NEWCOMEN in 1712). It resulted more particularly from technological innovations intended to obtain large increases in industrial productivity, initially in the COTTON INDUSTRY (machines for high-volume spinning of yarn, driven by hand or water). It was greatly furthered by improvement of steam engines and the invention of mechanically driven rotary motion, which enabled engines to drive productive machinery. The Revolution was facilitated by availability of COAL and iron ore, and by new processes for smelting and refining IRON. Once started, the development of processes and equipment continued, and applied in new areas (e.g., mechanized transport, such as steamships and steam-powered railways).

Various reasons have been proposed for the Revolution's British origin, including a Protestant work ethic, absence of absolutism, strong property rights, and exceptionally high wages which stimulated development of productive machinery to cut costs. Industrialization spread to Ireland, but declined outside the NE in the 19th century (*see* INDUSTRY, IRELAND 18TH CENTURY TO 1921). In the 20th century steam power was replaced by oil (or petrol) and electricity (so-called 'Second Industrial Revolution'). Both Britain and Northern Ireland experienced DE-INDUSTRIALIZATION from the 1960s–70s.

INDUSTRY, ENGLAND BEFORE LATE 18TH CENTURY In the 5th–11th centuries, non-agricultural production comprised mainly small-scale craftwork. Some was widespread. For example, most women made woollen yarn and cloth. IRON working occurred widely. Less common pursuits included stonework, high-quality metalwork (e.g., sword making), glasswork, leatherwork, salt preparation, fishing, mill construction.

Increased urbanization (from 12th century) concentrated much craftwork in TOWNS. By 1300, craftsmen in over 600 towns produced mainly for local consumption. They included foodstuff processors (e.g., brewers, butchers), textile workers (e.g., tailors), leatherworkers (e.g., shoemakers), and metalworkers (e.g., smiths). Larger-scale and specialist industries also emerged, some in particular areas. Cloth-making industries developed in larger towns from the 11th century (*see* CLOTH INDUSTRY, ENGLAND). From the late 14th century, cloth was England's primary export commodity (to 18th century), with much production in rural areas. The Forest of Dean (Gloucestershire) and Weald of Kent and Sussex became iron-making areas (12th–13th centuries); metal working was established in the W Midlands by 1400. By 1300 COAL was supplied from NE England to LONDON and overseas. Building expanded for cathedrals, churches and CASTLES. Tin was mined in Devon and Cornwall (SW England). Salt manufacturing and fishing continued. Industrial activities engaged 10–15% of the workforce.

In the 16th–18th centuries, industry expanded and changed, sometimes influenced by IMMIGRATION. Output of cloth, iron and coal increased; urban crafts grew more diverse. New products were manufactured (e.g., light cloths or 'new draperies', paper, gunpowder, copperas). New techniques were developed (e.g., coke in malting, mid 17th century). Specialisms grew in new areas (e.g., hosiery knitting in E Midlands from late 17th century). Large-scale enterprises were created (e.g., naval dockyards in late 17th century, London breweries in 18th century), and FACTORIES were built (from 1715–19). By the 1770s almost half of the population depended on manufacturing and mining, sometimes combined with agriculture. *See also* AGRICULTURE, ENGLAND BEFORE MID 18TH CENTURY; FOREIGN TRADE, ENGLAND BEFORE 1066/FROM 1066 TO EARLY 17TH CENTURY.

INDUSTRY, ENGLAND FROM LATE 18TH CENTURY From the 1780s, thanks to technological innovations and rising demand, the output of some industries increased dramatically and their organization changed, developments known as the INDUSTRIAL REVOLUTION. The 'spinning mule', invented by Samuel CROMPTON, enabled cotton yarn production to expand rapidly in Lancashire (NW England). Initially powered by water, mules were driven by steam from 1785, and power-driven weaving became established in the 1820s–30s (*see* COTTON INDUSTRY, ENGLAND). Cotton textile production became concentrated in FACTORIES, and 'factory towns' emerged (e.g., MANCHESTER). Iron making also grew significantly, facilitated by innovations (*see* IRON AND STEEL INDUSTRIES, ENGLAND). In the 1790s–1850s the worsted branch of the CLOTH INDUSTRY became mechanized, mainly in W Yorkshire (NE England). Mechanization was based on improved steam engines (*see* WATT, JAMES) and advances in ENGINEERING, including MACHINE TOOLS. Technological improvements also enabled the COAL INDUSTRY to expand. Domestic industry slowly declined.

Industrialization diversified during the 19th century, although textiles, iron making and coal remained leading 'staple industries'. Steam-powered RAILWAYS were built (from 1830s); mechanization of shoe making and tailoring began (from 1850s); SHIP BUILDING expanded in NE England (from 1860s), based on iron construction and steam propulsion. From the 1860s new processes reduced steel production costs, and output enlarged.

From the 1880s inventions generated new industries: ELECTRICITY INDUSTRY (1880s), BICYCLE INDUSTRY (1890s), MOTOR INDUSTRY (1900s), AIRCRAFT INDUSTRY (1910s), domestic appliances; additionally (from 1950s) nuclear power and COMPUTING. CHEMICALS and pharmaceuticals also expanded during the 20th century. The W Midlands notably became a major centre of vehicle manufacturing.

Older staple industries declined in output from the early 20th century, as did many newer industries from the 1960s (*see* INDUSTRIAL DECLINE, ENGLAND). During the 1970s–80s, DE-INDUSTRIALIZATION accelerated, reducing industry to about 10% of the economy in the early 21st century. The main surviving areas were car manufacturing, aircraft and aerospace, chemicals and pharmaceuticals. *See also* LUDDITES; FOREIGN TRADE, GREAT BRITAIN FROM LATER 18TH CENTURY.

INDUSTRY, IRELAND BEFORE 18TH CENTURY
Activity was minimal in the 5th–9th centuries. Woollen cloth and clothes were made by individual households. Professional ironworkers probably made agricultural equipment and items such as knives. Little pottery was produced. From the 6th century ecclesiastical centres (in E and SE Ireland) stimulated quarrying, bronzework (e.g., production of bowls) and gold working. Industrial output increased with the foundation of several TOWNS by VIKINGS (early 10th century). Their inhabitants engaged in metal and leather working, comb making (from bone and antlers), and in wood-based activities (e.g., ship building, carpentry).

Numerous small towns established in English areas after the Anglo-Norman invasion (1169–70) included craftsmen (weavers, shoemakers, smiths, etc.), and pottery making expanded greatly. In the late 14th and 15th centuries the production of linen and coarse woollen cloths increased in both English and Gaelic Irish areas. Some PLANTATIONS of the late 16th and early 17th centuries also encouraged cloth production. In the later 17th century linen became an important product and Ireland's leading manufactured export. Yet the country remained predominantly agricultural, and important industries involved the processing of agricultural products. *See also* AGRICULTURE, IRELAND BEFORE 17TH CENTURY; FOREIGN TRADE, IRELAND BEFORE/FROM 17TH CENTURY.

INDUSTRY, IRELAND 18TH CENTURY TO 1921
During the 18th century, the range and scale of activity increased, alongside ubiquitous craftwork (e.g., smithing, shoe making, cloth production). There was organized

domestic spinning of LINEN and woollen (worsted) yarn. Linen cloth was produced mainly in NE Ireland, woollen cloth in E and S Ireland. Food processing developed on a considerable scale in and around towns, principally malting, BREWING, sugar refining, and (from 1760s) whiskey distilling. Large water-powered flour mills were built from the 1760s (e.g., five-storey mill at Slane, Co. Meath). Other notable industries included paper making, iron working and GLASS manufacturing. From the 1770s–80s some firms (e.g., leading brewers) expanded to meet competition from Britain while others failed.

From the 1780s aspects of the British INDUSTRIAL REVOLUTION spread into Ireland. Factory-based cotton spinning, sometimes using steam engines, flourished in various areas (e.g., around CORK) from the 1780s. Linen spinning was mechanized from 1825 and became a major industry in Belfast and the Lagan Valley. But from the 1820s to the 1870s, partly because of free trade with Britain, urban and rural industrial activity and employment declined outside NE Ireland, increasing impoverishment.

Several industries, mainly based in ULSTER (N Ireland), flourished in the late 19th and early 20th centuries through success in exporting, notably linen manufacturing and SHIP BUILDING. The GUINNESS brewing company, based in Dublin, was also a major exporter. *See also* AGRICULTURE, IRELAND 17TH CENTURY TO 1921; FOREIGN TRADE, IRELAND FROM 17TH CENTURY.

INDUSTRY, NORTHERN IRELAND After the PARTITION OF IRELAND (1921) the province contained almost two-thirds of Ireland's manufacturing industry and workforce. Although manufacturing accounted for 35% of the workforce (1926), there were only two staples and both were vulnerable to overseas competition: SHIP BUILDING and LINEN textiles.

Linen declined through the 1920s–30 because of changes in fashion and competition from synthetic fibres (employment, mainly of women, fell from 75,000 in 1924 to 57,000 in 1935). Ship building fared reasonably well until hit in 1930 by the GREAT DEPRESSION. Some industrial recovery occurred in the late 1930s through diversification (e.g., establishment of Short and Harland aircraft factory at BELFAST, 1936). Increased industrial output and employment (including linen) were temporarily stimulated by WORLD WAR II (1939–45).

Linen declined through the 1950s–60s to insignificance, while ship building flourished until the 1960s when demand for its main vessel-types (e.g., liners) collapsed and it faced overseas competition. Around 1960 the Republic of Ireland overtook Northern Ireland in manufacturing output. Government incentives attracted some new industries (e.g., electronics, engineering, synthetic fibres). By 1970 half of employees worked for externally owned firms.

Between 1973 and 1983 manufacturing output fell by one-third, and employment by 40%, because of the TROUBLES and DE-INDUSTRIALIZATION. Following the BELFAST AGREEMENT (1998) some growth occurred in such areas as chemicals and engineering. In 2015, services dominated the economy, with manufacturing accounting for 10% of employment and 14% of gross domestic product. The largest employer was Bombardier Aerospace (continuation of Short and Harland) with 5400 staff.

INDUSTRY, SCOTLAND BEFORE LATE 18TH CENTURY Until the later 16th century industry was small scale and unspecialized. BURGHS, founded from the 12th century, contained such craftsmen as smiths, weavers, tailors, tanners and potters. Manufactures were also imported in return for exports of raw materials (*see* FOREIGN TRADE, NORTH BRITAIN AND SCOTLAND BEFORE 17TH CENTURY).

In the later 16th and 17th centuries coal mining and salt making expanded, especially around the Forth estuary, with lead mining at Leadhills (C Scotland). Early manufactories included glass, gunpowder, and soap works. Production of coarse woollen plaiding developed on a large scale, especially in the NE. The later 17th century saw encouragement of fine woollens, the rise of the linen industry, and sugar refining in GLASGOW.

Access to English and colonial markets after the UNION OF ENGLAND AND SCOTLAND (1707) encouraged linen production, which doubled every 20–25 years. Coal mining expanded steadily, iron smelting more slowly. Blast furnaces in the HIGHLANDS used local charcoal but imported English ore. The foundation of the Carron Ironworks (1759) near Falkirk (C Scotland) marked the shift to large-scale integrated production. Glasgow's tobacco trade (supplying N Europe from N America) encouraged linen and other manufactures in W-C Scotland as return cargoes. From the 1770s cotton-spinning mills led the move into the INDUSTRIAL REVOLUTION. *See also* AGRICULTURE, SCOTLAND BEFORE LATE 17TH CENTURY; FOREIGN TRADE, NORTH BRITAIN AND SCOTLAND BEFORE 17TH CENTURY; FOREIGN TRADE, SCOTLAND FROM 17TH CENTURY.

INDUSTRY, SCOTLAND FROM LATE 18TH CENTURY From the 1780s increased use of mechanical equipment and new processes enabled a rapid expansion of production which transformed Scotland's economy and society (*see* INDUSTRIAL REVOLUTION).

Water-powered mills, often in the countryside, were used in linen manufacturing from the 1750s and in cotton from the 1770s (*see* TEXTILE INDUSTRIES, SCOTLAND). Steam power was then applied to cotton spinning, creating spectacular growth in the GLASGOW–PAISLEY area (W-C Scotland) in the 1780s–90s (*see* COTTON INDUSTRY, SCOTLAND). Expansion of textiles encouraged development of CHEMICALS (bleaching agents, dyestuffs) and steady expansion of the COAL INDUSTRY and iron output. (Steam engines were built in Scotland from 1800.) People were drawn into the C Lowlands, where half the population lived by 1820 (*see* FORTH–CLYDE ISTHMUS).

In the 1830s–40s the leading sectors changed. Technical developments stimulated expansion of the IRON INDUSTRY from the 1830s, which facilitated expanding production of ships, railway locomotives, and engineering machinery from the 1840s, also concentrated in the Glasgow area. Momentum continued until 1914, with innovations, increased exports and from the 1870s the use of steel. (Before 1914 Glasgow was Europe's largest locomotive-building centre.) The jute industry developed in DUNDEE from the 1830s, though cotton declined from the 1860s. Scotland was prominent in beer BREWING and WHISKY distilling from the 1850s, and ABERDEEN became Great Britain's largest fishing port by 1911.

Heavy industry dominated until the 1950s, although production and employment fluctuated. Sectors failed from the mid 1960s and most closed in the 1980s (*see* INDUSTRIAL DECLINE, SCOTLAND). Fishing declined in the 1970s–90s. Successful new developments were electronics (from the 1950s) and oil (from the 1970s), while TOURISM and financial services helped to replace lost industrial income. *See also* AGRICULTURE, SCOTLAND FROM 18TH CENTURY; FOREIGN TRADE, SCOTLAND FROM 17TH CENTURY.

INDUSTRY, SOUTHERN IRELAND In the IRISH FREE STATE (founded 1922) 14% of the workforce was in manufacturing (1926). The largest sector was food processing (e.g., baking, brewing) followed by clothing (e.g., dressmaking). Raw materials and manufactured goods were extensively imported. Though modest duties were introduced (1924–5), the government held costs down to benefit agriculture and agricultural exports.

From 1932 the FIANNA FÁIL government of Éamon DE VALERA sought 'import substitution' by imposing high tariffs to promote industry. Irish part-ownership of industries was required. There was success in such areas as footwear, textiles, clothing and MOTOR VEHICLE assembly. Industrial employment rose from 110,000 to 166,000 (1931–8). During WORLD WAR II (1939–45), shortages of materials and difficult economic conditions depressed output (by a quarter, 1938–43). Restored by 1947, it expanded slowly through the 1950s, assisted by the Industrial Development Authority (created 1949). Output exceeded that of Northern Ireland from *c.*1960.

From 1959 policy changed: economic expansion was stimulated through outside investment and free trade (*see* ECONOMIC EXPANSION, PROGRAMMES FOR). Foreign owners established production (e.g., chemicals, electrical equipment). By 1971 almost 30% of the labour force was in manufacturing, with a third employed in externally owned

firms in 1973. During the 1960s, industrial exports overtook agricultural exports.

After entry to the EUROPEAN ECONOMIC COMMUNITY (1973) many domestically owned businesses declined while externally owned firms increased; in the 1980s, production of motor vehicles, textiles and leather goods collapsed. Industrial employment peaked in the early 1980s at 32%. It fell to 28% by 2001 and 18% by 2011 when the leading sectors were pharmaceuticals, chemicals, food processing and electrical equipment. Services were now the predominant economic sector. *See also* AGRICULTURE, SOUTHERN IRELAND; DE-INDUSTRIALIZATION.

INDUSTRY, WALES BEFORE 18TH CENTURY Little evidence survives before the 14th century. In the 14th–17th centuries woollen cloth and leather working were important, with cloth production (mainly coarse cloths) concentrated in rural areas (Glamorgan, Carmarthenshire, Merionethshire, Denbighshire). Cloth was exported to Ireland and Continental Europe via English border towns (e.g., Shrewsbury, BRISTOL).

Small-scale mineral exploitation also occurred: coal mining (Flintshire, Denbighshire), lead mining (Flintshire, Cardiganshire) and slate quarrying (Caernarfonshire). Iron making was revived by Cistercians (*see,* MONASTICISM, MEDIEVAL WALES) and expanded after the import of the blast furnace in the late 16th century, when some English ironmasters established businesses in Denbighshire and S Wales. Coal and iron were exported via Chepstow and Welsh ports. In 1568 the new Mines Royal Company received monopoly mining rights in Wales (except Monmouthshire) and sponsored mainly lead and copper mining.

From *c.*1660 estate-owners started small enterprises (usually mineral related), which expanded after the Mines Royal's monopoly was broken in 1693. During the French wars of 1689–1714, naval demand stimulated copper and tin smelting in the SWANSEA–Neath area (S Wales). Influential here was the Englishman Sir Humphrey Mackworth (1657–1727) who developed coal mining and lead and copper smelting at Neath, and laid Wales's first tramway. *See also* AGRICULTURE, WALES BEFORE 18TH CENTURY.

INDUSTRY, WALES FROM 18TH CENTURY Around 1700 the principal industry was woollen cloth manufacturing. It was eclipsed by 1730 in S Wales by the COAL INDUSTRY and by metal industries, especially COPPER and TINPLATE (around SWANSEA, W Glamorgan) and IRON. From the 1790s there was industrial 'take-off': rapid expansion of output and employment such that by the 1840s dependence on industry exceeded dependence on agriculture (*see* INDUSTRIAL REVOLUTION). An industrial area dominated by coal and iron also developed in the NE, particularly around WREXHAM (Denbighshire).

From *c*.1870 to the 1920s coal mining dominated the economy, and steel making largely replaced iron. Cloth retained its importance in mid Wales, until undermined in the late 19th century by competition from the industry in northern England. Industrialization stimulated POPULATION increase, migration to the S and SE, IMMIGRATION from Ireland and England, and expansion of TOWNS.

INDUSTRIAL DECLINE was a major feature from the 1920s to the 1940s. In the early 21st century steel and tinplate remained important, together with industries that had developed since 1945, such as oil refining, plastics, manufacturing of car components, and electronics. *See also* LEAD INDUSTRY, WALES; SLATE INDUSTRY, WALES; CANALS, WALES; RAILWAYS, WALES; AGRICULTURE, WALES FROM 18TH CENTURY.

INE (fl. from 688 in Wessex; d. in or after 726 at Rome, Italy). King of WESSEX (S England) from 688, Ine maintained rule over an extensive territory, including the recently annexed kingdoms of Surrey and SUSSEX. He also fought in DUMNONIA (710) and against the Mercians (716).

Ine probably divided Wessex into large SHIRES. He was the first king of Wessex known to have issued a law code (by 694). He possibly founded (or promoted) the port of Hamwic (*see* SOUTHAMPTON). Ine supported the creation of new dioceses, endowed churches, and freed churches from paying tribute. In 726 he abdicated. He died in Rome on pilgrimage. *See also* KINGSHIP, ANGLO-SAXON; EALDORMAN.

INFLATION AND DEFLATION Sustained changes of money prices (differentiated from short-term fluctuations) occurred from the late 12th century, particularly in England where COMMERCIALIZATION was affecting economic activity. Between the 1170s and 1320s, prices rose by three to four times. Consequences included resumption by lords of 'direct management' of MANORS (instead of long-term leasing), to increase profits.

In the 14th–15th centuries several cycles occurred: 1320s–1345, deflation; 1345–70s, inflation. Prices then fell to the 1450s–60s, before rising. From the 1350s landlords leased out demesne lands within manors.

From *c*.1515 to the mid 17th century the British Isles experienced severe inflation, the so-called 'Price Revolution'. Agricultural prices rose by 585%, prices of manufactures by 224% (*see* PRICE RISE, 16TH–MID 17TH CENTURIES).

From the 1660s to *c*.1700 prices were stable; they then declined to *c*.1730 and were static to *c*.1760, before rising steadily. During the FRENCH REVOLUTIONARY AND NAPOLEONIC WARS (1792–1815), there was rapid inflation, followed by sharp deflation. Until the 1780s price-change patterns were related to changing money supply and population.

Prices remained fairly stable until 1914, restrained by the GOLD STANDARD, although food prices fell during the AGRICULTURAL DEPRESSION (1880s–90s). From 1914 to 1920, during and after WORLD WAR I, prices doubled, mainly due to shortages. Monetary policy then produced deflation (consumer prices fell by 30%, 1920–39). High inflation returned during WORLD WAR II (1939–45) and the KOREAN WAR (1950–3).

Inflation persisted during the 1950s–60s (annual average 1964–72, 5.4%), then surged, because of domestic problems and increased oil prices (1973–4). In Aug. 1975 it reached 26.9% and remained high. Inflation was reduced in the 1980s with MONETARIST policies, and controlled from the late 1980s primarily by the base interest rate. In 1997 the BANK OF ENGLAND was given responsibility for maintaining low inflation (*see* BROWN, GORDON). *See also* INCOMES POLICIES; MINERS' STRIKE AND ENERGY CRISIS, 1973–4.

INFORMAL EMPIRE A concept referring to areas of the world in which Great Britain exercised political power, derived from naval, industrial or financial power, without making legal claims to territory. Britain's informal empire included parts of South America (1820s–90s), China (1860s–90s) and the Middle East (1920s–50s). *See also* BRITISH EMPIRE; CHINESE TREATY PORTS; FOREIGN INVESTMENT.

IN PLACE OF STRIFE The title of proposals issued on 17 Jan. 1969 (as a government 'white paper') by the British employment minister Barbara Castle to modernize industrial relations (e.g., by requiring strike ballots) and outlaw unofficial strikes. Trade unions opposed the scheme. It was abandoned by the prime minister, Harold WILSON, under pressure from James CALLAGHAN (18 June). *See also* TRADE UNION LEGISLATION.

INSTRUMENT OF GOVERNMENT The constitution under which the Protectorate was established in 1653 for England and Wales with Scotland and Ireland, replacing the Commonwealth. Drafted by John LAMBERT and accepted by Army officers on 13 Dec., it made Oliver CROMWELL head of state as 'lord protector'. It provided for a Council of State, and for Parliaments elected on a reformed franchise at least every three years. Cromwell was admitted to office on 16 Dec. *See also* HUMBLE PETITION AND ADVICE; COMMONWEALTH AND PROTECTORATE.

INSURRECTION ACTS, IRELAND Legislation empowering JUSTICES OF THE PEACE (JPs) to combat unrest. The first Act, passed by the Irish Parliament in 1795 to counter revolutionary agitation, empowered the CHIEF GOVERNOR (lord lieutenant) to designate areas as disturbed, and permitted JPs to search for arms, introduce curfews, and sentence disorderly men to naval service. Similar Acts were passed for Ireland by the UK Parliament (1807, 1814, 1822, and 1835, last expired 1840). *See also* COERCION ACTS, IRELAND; FRENCH REVOLUTION, IMPACT ON IRELAND.

INSURRECTION OF 1867 An attempt to overthrow British rule in Ireland organized by 'Fenians' (supporters of the IRISH REPUBLICAN BROTHERHOOD and FENIAN BROTHERHOOD). On 5–6 March participants gathered S of Dublin, near Cork, and in Cos. Clare, Limerick, Louth and Tipperary. They also attacked police barracks, trains and telegraph wires. The rebels were easily dispersed by government forces. *See also* HOME RULE MOVEMENT, IRELAND.

INTOLERABLE ACTS Term applied to Acts of the British Parliament, passed March–April 1774 for the government of Lord NORTH, which sought to suppress opposition to British policy in the N American colony of MASSACHUSETTS following the BOSTON TEA PARTY.

Two Acts strengthened the Massachusetts governor's powers, a third 'punished' Boston by removing its customs house, and another enabled citizens to be tried outside the colony. Colonists associated the Acts with the QUEBEC ACT of April 1774, which inflamed American Protestant opinion by accepting Catholicism in CANADA. The Acts were denounced in N America and led to AMERICAN INDEPENDENCE.

'INVISIBLES' Term which usually refers to intangible income-producing services provided to overseas parties, sometimes called 'invisible exports'. They can contribute to a country's 'balance of trade' alongside tangible exports or imports (i.e., goods such as foodstuffs, raw materials and manufactures).

Invisibles contributed markedly to British trade from the 18th century. They included provision of shipping for foreign parties; insurance of foreign vessels; repatriated incomes from overseas residents and officials; fish caught abroad (e.g., near NEWFOUNDLAND) and sold to foreigners. In the 19th century, according to financial estimates, invisibles facilitated imports of greater value than that of tangible exports, even though Great Britain's economy had become industrialized. Income from invisibles increased markedly from the 1850s, rising from £23.7 million in 1851–5 (annual average) to £152.6 million in 1911–13. This represented largely the expansion of shipping and associated financing and insurance, centred on LONDON. (However, income from FOREIGN INVESTMENT overtook invisibles in the 1890s.)

Income was reduced in 1915–18, due to WORLD WAR I. It then revived and helped to cover the trade gap in the 1920s, but fell from 1929, because of the contraction of world trade in the Great Depression, contributing to the UK's financial difficulties. After some recovery it was reduced by WORLD WAR II (1939–45). From the late 1940s to late 1980s, exports of 'services' accounted for 5–7% of UK GDP; they then rose to 14% in 2017 (compared with 17% for goods exports). *See also* FOREIGN TRADE, GREAT BRITAIN FROM LATER 18TH CENTURY.

IOLO GOCH (b. *c.*1325; d. 1398, aged about 73). An early Modern Welsh poet; an author of praise poetry (eulogy and elegy) addressed to freemen (Welsh *uchelwyr*), reflecting their ideals (*see* SOCIAL STRUCTURE, WALES). His patrons included OWAIN GLYN DŴR and the TUDOR FAMILY. He was an exponent of the *cywydd* metre. *See also* WELSH LANGUAGE AND LITERATURE.

IOLO MORGANWG *see* WILLIAMS, EDWARD

IONA A small island off Mull, W of Scotland; site of the monastery founded in 563 by COLUMBA (from NE Ireland), in (Scottish) DÁL RIATA. Ionan monks founded other monasteries, and Iona headed a confederation of monasteries in Ireland and N Britain until the mid 9th century. Learning and art flourished until VIKINGS attacked Iona in the 790s. It was the royal burial place until the 11th century.

A Benedictine monastery and an Augustinian nunnery replaced the original monastery in 1203. The monastery's church was also the cathedral of the WESTERN ISLES 1500–1689. It was reopened, after rebuilding, in 1912; other buildings were restored by the Iona Community founded in 1938 by George MacLeod (1895–1991). *See also* CHURCH, MEDIEVAL NORTH BRITAIN AND SCOTLAND; KENNETH I MAC ALPIN; AIDAN; CHAD; SMITH, JOHN.

IONA, STATUTES OF Terms for release exacted on IONA in 1609 by Andrew Knox (1559–1633), bishop of the Isles, from nine CLAN chiefs of the WESTERN ISLES who had been imprisoned in 1608. They agreed to promote settlement by ministers of the Church of SCOTLAND and to suppress violence. The statutes were part of King JAMES VI's policy of quelling disorder in Scotland's outer regions.

IRAN, BRITISH RELATIONS WITH *see* PERSIA (IRAN), BRITISH RELATIONS WITH

IRANIAN EMBASSY SIEGE A dramatic incident in Great Britain in 1980. Iranian Arab gunmen seized 20 hostages at the Iranian embassy in Knightsbridge, London (30 April), and demanded the release of prisoners in Iran. The embassy was successfully stormed (5 May) by the Special Air Service (SAS), an action that epitomized the government's determination to resist international terrorism.

IRAQ, BRITISH MANDATE A former British territory in the Middle East, created in 1920 from territories previously belonging to the OTTOMAN EMPIRE (including Mesopotamia). Great Britain governed it as a MANDATE of the LEAGUE OF NATIONS. It had been conquered by the British in 1917–18 (during WORLD WAR I). Approx. population in 1920: 2,849,000. In 1921 Britain established a monarchy, and Iraq became nominally independent in 1932, though British influence remained strong (e.g., in oil exploitation) until the monarchy was overthrown in 1958.

IRAQ WAR, BRITISH INVOLVEMENT On 20 March 2003 the USA, supported by Great Britain, invaded Iraq, because it allegedly possessed 'weapons of mass destruction' ('WMD'), which threatened international peace, and had defied a United Nations resolution (Nov. 2002). The invasion aimed to replace the dictator Saddam Hussein with democracy. US forces took control of Baghdad on 9 April, and Saddam Hussein was captured on 13 Dec. (later executed). But violence by Sunni and Shi'ite Muslim sects prolonged the occupation. A 'surge' (increased deployment) in 2007 enabled US troops to be largely withdrawn by Aug. 2010.

British forces (with other national units) were involved mainly across S Iraq. The deployment reached 46,000 in April 2003. Iraq's second city, Basra, was entered on 6 April. Troop numbers were reduced drastically from May. As elsewhere, sectarian and tribal fighting became endemic. British forces withdrew to Basra airport in Sept. 2007, and combat operations ended in April 2009, leaving 179 military personnel dead.

Britain's involvement was controversial. A pre-war dossier of evidence for the Iraqi threat (published 3 Feb. 2003) appeared dubious (nicknamed 'dodgy dossier'). On 15 Feb., 1 million people protested in LONDON. Failure to obtain a second United Nations resolution, authorizing invasion (Feb.–March), suggested the war was illegal. (In all, four government ministers resigned.) Allegations in May–June concerning an earlier dossier caused a former weapons investigator to commit suicide and prompted an inquiry (*see* CAMPBELL, ALASTAIR). WMD were not found, prompting another inquiry ('Butler Review', report published July 2004). It was also alleged in early 2004 that official legal advice before the invasion had been made more favourable. The controversies weakened the prime minister, Tony BLAIR (left office 2007). The 'Chilcot Report' into Britain's involvement (2016) concluded that Iraq had presented no immediate threat, and that the invasion was based on flawed intelligence, presented with unjustifiable certainty, and unsatisfactory authorization. *See also* UNITED STATES OF AMERICA, BRITISH RELATIONS WITH.

IRELAND The second-largest island within the BRITISH ISLES, about 220 mi (360 km) in length (N–S), comprising the Republic of Ireland and Northern Ireland (part of the UNITED KINGDOM). Area: 32,600 sq mi (84,400 sq km). Est. popn in 2015: Republic, 4,635,000; Northern Ireland, 1,852,000. The landscape includes a Central Plain. Until the 18th century, Irish was the majority language (superseded by English). In 2015, about 180 languages were spoken.

Immigration started *c*.8000 BC, after Ireland became separated from Britain (*see* GLACIATIONS). Many subsequent cultural changes were similar to those elsewhere (*see* PREHISTORY, IRELAND). The IRISH LANGUAGE became established probably by the mid 1st millennium BC. Ireland's Irish name, Éire (recorded in the 1st century BC in Greek, Ierne), is derived from a goddess's name (OIr., Ériu). Its Latin name was Hibernia. The English name is recorded from the 9th century AD.

Christianity reached Ireland by *c*.400 (*see* CONVERSION OF IRELAND). A land of numerous kingdoms (*see* KINGSHIP, IRELAND), Ireland in 1171 became a lordship ruled by kings of England. Invaders extensively introduced English-type economic and social arrangements, though Irish kings reduced the Anglo-Irish area (*see* NORMANS, IMPACT ON IRELAND; GAELIC REVIVAL, IRELAND, 13TH–15TH CENTURIES). English rule was reasserted in the 16th century, with Ireland becoming a kingdom (1541) and experiencing 'NEW ENGLISH' immigration. But reformed Christianity was rejected by the majority Gaelic Irish and many Anglo-Irish, who remained Catholics (*see* REFORMATION, IRELAND).

Rebellion by Catholics in the 17th century resulted in dispossession of land, and domination by an élite of Church of IRELAND adherents (*see* PROTESTANT ASCENDANCY). Meanwhile Scottish presbyterians settled in NE Ireland. A UNION OF IRELAND AND GREAT BRITAIN was instigated by Great Britain (1801) for security reasons. Later agitation for, and opposition to, HOME RULE, and nationalism produced division (1921–2) into a Protestant-dominated NORTHERN IRELAND and a largely Catholic IRISH FREE STATE (republic from 1949). *See also* IRISH; GOLDEN AGE; CHURCH, MEDIEVAL IRELAND; CATHOLICS AND CATHOLIC CHURCH, IRELAND FROM 16TH CENTURY; PRESBYTERIANISM, IRELAND; SOUTHERN IRELAND FROM 1922.

IRELAND, CHURCH OF Ireland's State Church 1536–1870 (except 1557–60), Protestant in theology from 1560; a voluntary (disestablished) Church from 1871.

Papal jurisdiction over the Irish Church was replaced by royal authority in 1536, with Ireland's ruler becoming 'supreme governor' in 1560 (*see* REFORMATION, IRELAND). The Church retained episcopacy (government by bishops) and parochial organization, together with existing buildings and endowments, but from the 1570s it was rejected by most Gaelic Irish and OLD ENGLISH. Its main supporters were NEW ENGLISH in major towns and southern PLANTATIONS; elsewhere congregations and clergy were scattered. CALVINISM was influential from the 1580s, but challenged in the 1630s (*see* USSHER, JAMES; LAUDIANISM, IMPACT ON IRELAND). Between 1647 and 1659 English Parliamentarians prohibited episcopacy and the Church's Prayer Book, creating effectively a congregational Church (*see* COMMONWEALTH AND PROTECTORATE, IRELAND).

Episcopacy was restored from 1660, and the 1666 Act of Uniformity imposed a revised Prayer Book (*see* RESTORATION, IRELAND). Adherents are estimated at 100,000 in 1672. The Church accepted the replacement of King JAMES VII/II by WILLIAM III (*see* WILLIAMITE WAR; KING, WILLIAM), and it became identified with Ireland's Protestant landowners (*see* PROTESTANT ASCENDANCY). It was united with the Church of England 1801–70 (*see* UNION OF IRELAND AND GREAT BRITAIN).

Opposition to the Church's privileged position (e.g., from Catholics) provoked reforms from the British government in 1833 and disestablishment from 1871 (*see* CHURCH TEMPORALITIES (IRELAND) ACT; DISESTABLISHMENT, CHURCH OF IRELAND). The Church remained an all-Ireland body after the PARTITION OF IRELAND (1921). Women were admitted to the priesthood from 1990, and were ordained as bishops from 2013. Estimated membership in 2010 was 390,000, two-thirds in NORTHERN IRELAND. *See also* PRAYER BOOKS, IRELAND; BIBLE, IRISH; ARTICLES OF RELIGION; TITHE ISSUE, IRELAND.

IRELAND, ENGLISH COLONY IN, 13TH–15TH CENTURIES In 1250, two-thirds of Ireland was under English lordship and government. (The largest Gaelic area was in the N.) But control was already deteriorating. Some major English lordships in LEINSTER and MEATH (E Ireland) had been divided between absentee heiresses (1240s), and Irish kings were harassing English areas (*see* GAELIC REVIVAL, IRELAND 13TH–15TH CENTURIES). From the 1280s the government was weakened by withdrawal of men and funds for overseas wars (*see* EDWARD I AND IRELAND).

In the 14th century various developments further diminished the government's influence: devastation caused by the BRUCE INVASION (1315–18); the death of William de BURGH without male heir (1333), which reduced authority in W and NE Ireland; and mortality and dislocation resulting from the BLACK DEATH (1348). English areas contracted, and many inhabitants adopted Irish customs, despite prohibitions (*see* KILKENNY, STATUTE OF). Expeditions from England to arrest decline were ineffectual (*see* IRELAND, ENGLISH EXPEDITIONS TO, LATE 14TH CENTURY).

In the 15th century the areas of Anglo-Irish lordships, mostly in E, S and SW Ireland, remained stable, preserved by 'tail male' inheritance. The most important were the earldoms of ORMOND, DESMOND and KILDARE, though the Dublin-based government had minimal authority within them. By the 1420s it controlled only part of E Ireland (*see* PALE). Governors lacked funds for expansion, and the TALBOT–ORMOND FEUD (*c*.1414–1440s) was divisive.

From the 1450s, several Anglo-Irish magnates became YORKISTS, thanks to Ireland's connections with Richard,

duke of YORK, who fled to Ireland in 1459 (*see* YORKIST–LANCASTRIAN CONFLICT, ROLE OF IRELAND). Though his son became king of England in 1460 (as EDWARD IV), England was little involved in Ireland. During the 1460s–70s it was governed by Anglo-Irish lords, and from 1471 to 1534 dominated by the earls of Kildare (*see* KILDARE ASCENDANCY). English authority was then reasserted (*see* IRELAND, ENGLISH CONQUEST, 16TH CENTURY). *See also* IRELAND, ENGLISH CONQUEST, 12TH–13TH CENTURIES.

IRELAND, ENGLISH CONQUEST, 12TH–13TH CENTURIES Bands of adventurers from S Wales (conventionally called 'Anglo-Normans'), operating with Henry II's authorization, arrived in 1169–70 to help their employer, Diarmait MAC MURCHADA, regain his high-kingship of LEINSTER (E Ireland). In 1169 they captured WEXFORD (5 May) and helped to restore Diarmait in Leinster; in 1170 they captured WATERFORD (25 Aug.) and DUBLIN (21 Sept.). In 1171 their principal leader, STRONGBOW, succeeded Diarmait. But Henry, during a visit to Ireland (1171–2), confiscated Leinster, assumed the lordship of Ireland, and granted Leinster and adjacent MEATH as subordinate lordships to Strongbow and Hugh de LACY (*see* HENRY II AND IRELAND). England's territory was defined, and accepted, by Ireland's high-king, in the treaty of WINDSOR (1175).

Despite the treaty, in 1177 John de COURCY conquered NE Ireland (modern Cos. Down and Antrim) and Henry granted the kingdoms of Desmond and Thomond in S Ireland to Anglo-Normans (*see* MUNSTER). In 1185 his son JOHN granted other lands in Munster (modern Cos. Waterford and Tipperary) and lands N of Meath (modern Co. Louth). By *c*.1200 English immigrants had settled in NE, E and S Ireland.

Land acquisition in W Ireland began after HENRY III granted most of CONNACHT to Richard de BURGH in 1227. Settlement also expanded along the N coast in the 1230s–40s. In mid century Irish resistance halted expansion (Connacht, 1240s–70s; Ulster, 1250s; Munster, 1250s–60s); yet it resumed, continuing until *c*.1300 (1320s in Ulster).

England appropriated three-quarters of Ireland, in which a colony was established with a social structure and institutions derived from England. But Irish kings survived in the N, in 'rump' kingdoms elsewhere, and within English areas. In the 14th century they reasserted themselves. *See also* NORMANS, IMPACT ON IRELAND; IRELAND, ENGLISH COLONY IN, 13TH–15TH CENTURIES.

IRELAND, ENGLISH CONQUEST, 16TH CENTURY Around 1500 Henry VII's government controlled only part of E Ireland (PALE; WEXFORD area). Most of Ireland belonged to autonomous lordships, held mainly by Anglo-Irish lords (about 20) in LEINSTER (E Ireland) and MUNSTER (S), and mainly by Gaelic chieftains (about 50) in

CONNACHT (W) and ULSTER (N). The chief governor, acting for the lord of Ireland (king of England), was an Anglo-Irish earl (see KILDARE ASCENDANCY).

After the KILDARE REBELLION (1534), Henry VIII sent governors from England to extend English authority (partly to prevent interference by foreign powers), and to reshape Gaelic society. Under Anthony ST LEGER, Henry was declared 'king of Ireland' (1541). Government authority was reintroduced to some Anglo-Irish lordships (see DESMOND, EARLS OF). Although many chieftains recognized royal authority and accepted English law and customs (1540–3; see SURRENDER AND REGRANT), little changed. Edward Bellingham (governor 1548–9, under Edward VI) strengthened the Pale against Gaelic attacks by establishing English seneschals (military captains) to the S, and forts to the W (see LEIX-OFFALY PLANTATION).

In 1562, under Queen ELIZABETH I, the earl of SUSSEX advocated presidents for Munster, Connacht and Ulster, to displace lords' power and maintain peace (see PRESIDENCIES, IRELAND). Henry SIDNEY nominated a president for Munster (1566), but the earl of Ormond obtained cancellation (appointment made 1570, following the First DESMOND REBELLION). A presidency was instituted in Connacht in 1569 (see COMPOSITION).

By the 1580s government officers operated everywhere except Ulster, where the chieftains Shane O'NEILL (d. 1567) and Turlough Luineach O'Neill (d. 1595) remained strong. The English applied pressure by nominally founding lieutenancies (1584; replaced by shires 1585), by supporting Turlough's rival, Hugh O'NEILL, and by abolishing (1591) peripheral lordships (see BRÉIFNE; AIRGIALLA). Gaelic lords responded with warfare (1593), supported by Hugh O'Neill from 1595 (see NINE YEARS WAR).

The English completed the conquest by defeating O'Neill (1603). But failure to impose Protestantism impaired their authority. See also HENRY VII AND IRELAND; REFORMATION, IRELAND; PLANTATIONS, IRELAND; IRISH WARS, 1641–52.

IRELAND, ENGLISH EXPEDITIONS TO, LATE 14TH CENTURY Between 1361 and 1399 English kings attempted to halt the contraction of English authority and territory in Ireland with five major expeditions. They largely failed.

In 1361, following a halt in the HUNDRED YEARS WAR, EDWARD III sent his son Lionel (absentee earl of Ulster and Connacht) as lieutenant with 1500 men. During this expedition (15 Sept. 1361–7 Nov. 1366, except 22 April–Dec. 1364), Lionel campaigned against the Gaelic Irish, moved government offices from Dublin south-west to Carlow, and sponsored the Statute of KILKENNY (1366). (Lionel, earl of Clarence from 1362, died in 1368.)

William of Windsor, a soldier, led two expeditions. During the first (1369–72) he campaigned in LEINSTER (E Ireland) and suppressed a revolt in Thomond (mid-W Ireland). During the second (1374–6) he campaigned in Leinster and Thomond, and attempted to raise money from Anglo-Irish. In the 1390s Richard II made two expeditions (see RICHARD II AND IRELAND). See also IRELAND, ENGLISH COLONY IN, 13TH–15TH CENTURIES.

IRELAND, IMPACT ON ENGLISH AND BRITISH POLITICS Ireland has frequently affected and complicated English and British affairs. Leaders have particularly feared foreign involvement in Ireland. English rule was provoked (1171) by the need to prevent the establishment of a separate Anglo-Norman kingdom (see HENRY II AND IRELAND; NORMANS, IMPACT ON IRELAND). The intervention of Edward Bruce from Scotland (1315) widened the scope of Anglo-Scottish warfare and threatened English rule in Ireland (see BRUCE INVASION OF IRELAND; SCOTTISH–ENGLISH RELATIONS, 1290–1357). The presence of RICHARD II in Ireland (1399) provided opportunity for Henry Bolingbroke to seize the English throne (see HENRY IV). In the late 15th–16th centuries Anglo-Irish provided strong support for Yorkists in England (see YORKIST–LANCASTRIAN CONFLICT, ROLE OF IRELAND).

During the 16th century Gaelic Irish leaders and Anglo-Irish rebels sometimes sought support from Spain – it finally became involved during the NINE YEARS WAR (1593–1603). The ULSTER RISING of 1641 and subsequent Catholic demands increased the difficulties of CHARLES I in England and inflamed PURITAN fears, eventually resulting in Parliamentary conquest to destroy Royalist sympathies (see IRISH WARS, 1641–52; COMMONWEALTH AND PROTECTORATE, IRELAND). In 1689–90 JAMES VII/II sought to regain his lost English and Scottish thrones by rallying support in Ireland (see WILLIAMITE WAR). In the late 1790s Ireland's vulnerability to French invasion persuaded William Pitt to instigate UNION OF IRELAND AND GREAT BRITAIN.

After union (1801), Irish MPs and concerns became important in the UK Parliament at WESTMINSTER, and from the 1870s the campaign for Home Rule deeply influenced British politics (see HOME RULE MOVEMENT). Protestant resistance in Ulster and militant Irish republicanism eventually resulted in the PARTITION OF IRELAND (1921) and foundation of the IRISH FREE STATE (1922). The continuance of NORTHERN IRELAND within the UK perpetuated Irish influence within British politics, especially during the TROUBLES (1968–90s) and PEACE PROCESS. See also BREXIT.

IRELAND, PARTITION OF see PARTITION OF IRELAND

IRELAND, REPUBLIC OF see SOUTHERN IRELAND FROM 1922; COSTELLO, JOHN

IRELAND ACT Legislation by the UK Parliament, passed 2 June 1949 in response to the inauguration of a Republic of Ireland (18 April 1949). It recognized that southern Ireland had ceased to be part of the king's dominions, but affirmed that NORTHERN IRELAND could only leave the UK if its Parliament agreed. After the abolition of the Northern Ireland Parliament, the Northern Ireland Constitution Act specified that withdrawal from the UK required a majority vote in a referendum (1973). *See also* SOUTHERN IRELAND FROM 1922.

IRELAND AND ROMAN BRITAIN *see* ROMAN BRITAIN AND IRELAND

IRELAND (SOUTHERN) FROM 1922 *see* SOUTHERN IRELAND FROM 1922

IRETON, HENRY (b. late 1611 at Attenborough, Nottinghamshire, England; d. 26 Nov. 1651 at Limerick, Co. Limerick, Ireland, aged 40). A lawyer and Puritan, Ireton commanded troops for Parliament during the CIVIL WARS (from 1642) and became an officer in the NEW MODEL ARMY (from 1645). In June 1646 he negotiated the surrender of OXFORD (Royalist capital) and married Bridget, daughter of Oliver CROMWELL.

In 1647–9 Ireton, a political 'Independent', contributed to the Army's political documents (e.g., HEADS OF PROPOSALS, 1647), but opposed the broad parliamentary franchise proposed at the PUTNEY DEBATES. He sought agreement with King CHARLES I until late 1647. Thereafter he supported deposition of the king. He helped to instigate PRIDE'S PURGE (Dec. 1648) and was a commissioner (judge) at Charles's trial (*see* CHARLES I, TRIAL AND EXECUTION).

From Aug. 1649 Ireton was second-in-command to Cromwell in Parliament's military campaign in Ireland, succeeding as commander and lord deputy in May 1650. He died after besieging Limerick. *See also* CIVIL WARS, POLITICAL ASPECTS; CROMWELL, OLIVER, AND IRELAND.

IRISH Although Ireland's earliest extensive historical sources (6th–8th centuries) reveal linguistic and cultural uniformity among the island's inhabitants, they were not known by a single name; several were used. This may indicate that local identities were primary (*see* TÚATH).

The earliest general name for inhabitants of IRELAND was the Latin Scotti, possibly meaning 'swordsmen'. Of non-Irish origin, it was used by Roman writers from the 4th century when it may have referred to a federation of peoples in N Ireland. In the 5th century PATRICK used the term for all inhabitants. By the 7th century it was employed by writers in Ireland and elsewhere for both inhabitants of Ireland and people of Irish culture in N Britain; by the 10th century it was usually restricted to the latter. Names derived from Scotti, initially meaning 'Irish', were formed in Old English (Scottas, by later 9th century) and other languages, but not in Irish.

The name Érainn (OIr.) was also applied to inhabitants of Ireland (sometimes excluding the Ulaid in NE Ireland) by the 7th century. It is derived from the island's early name Ériu (OIr.), which refers to a goddess. Érainn is associated with Latin Iverni recorded in the 2nd century for a people in SW Ireland. Other peoples in southern Ireland were later associated with the Érainn. The island was called Irland in Old English by the later 9th century, and inhabitants were termed Irisce (ME) by the 13th century.

By the 8th century inhabitants of Ireland also adopted the Brittonic (Welsh) name for Irish attackers, *gwyddyl* ('wild men'), as Goídil (OIr.). Their language became known as *Goídelc* (OIr.). Later corresponding English words were GAELS and Gaelic (by 17th century).

Érainn and Goídil survived into modern Irish as Éireannaigh and Gaeil, denoting respectively affinity with the island and with Gaelic culture. The Irish language is called *Gaeilge*. *See also* CELTIC CULTURE, IRELAND; SCOTS; SCOTLAND.

IRISH BRIGADES Military units in Continental European armies, mainly in Catholic countries (e.g., France, Spain), which were created from 1587 for Catholic Irishmen. Some soldiers returned from brigades for the IRISH WARS of 1641–52 and the WILLIAMITE WAR (1688–91). Brigades became more prominent following the 'Flight of the Wild Geese' (1691), the emigration of 12,000 Jacobite soldiers under the treaty of LIMERICK. The last unit, the Irish Legion in France, disbanded in 1814.

IRISH–BRITISH RELATIONS FROM 1922 The government of the IRISH FREE STATE (a British Empire DOMINION) co-operated with Great Britain while asserting autonomy in other FOREIGN RELATIONS. For example, it agreed secretly (1923) to continue payment of land annuities (for earlier land purchases by tenants), and accepted the collapse of the BOUNDARY COMMISSION (1925), though the PARTITION OF IRELAND remained a grievance. The UK remained the IFS's major trading partner.

Relations were antagonistic under Éamon DE VALERA (premier and minister for external relations 1932–48). He claimed greater independence by withholding annuities (1932, provoking an ECONOMIC WAR), and reducing the monarch's role (1936; *see* ABDICATION CRISIS AND IRISH FREE STATE). Disputes were settled in 1938 (*see* ANGLO-IRISH AGREEMENTS), but relations were tense during WORLD WAR II (1939–45) because of Ireland's neutrality. Southern Ireland became a republic outside the COMMONWEALTH in 1949.

From the 1960s Ireland sought closer relations, making a free-trade agreement in 1965. Entry into the European Economic Community (1973) reduced the proportion of trade with the UK. From 1968, conflict in Northern Ireland was a central concern (see TROUBLES). Despite recurring disagreements, the governments collaborated at creating peace through power-sharing, with Ireland conceding constitutional amendments (see SUNNINGDALE AGREEMENT; HILLSBOROUGH AGREEMENT; PEACE PROCESS, NORTHERN IRELAND). Improved relations culminated in State visits by Queen ELIZABETH II to Ireland (2011) and by President Michael D. Higgins to Britain (2014). See also BREXIT.

IRISH CITIZEN ARMY A small military force founded on 19 Nov. 1913 in DUBLIN by James CONNOLLY to defend strikers and pickets against police attacks during the 'Dublin lockout'. It was revived in early 1914 and collaborated with the IRISH REPUBLICAN BROTHERHOOD and IRISH VOLUNTEERS. The Army aspired to establish a workers' republic; some 200 members participated in the EASTER RISING of 1916. See also TRADE UNIONISM, IRELAND.

IRISH CIVIL WAR Conflict in the Irish Free State (IFS) which followed acceptance of the 1921 ANGLO-IRISH TREATY. The Treaty, which created the IFS, was ratified by the Dáil Éireann ('Assembly of Ireland') of SINN FÉIN MPs on 7 Jan. 1922 (see IRISH FREE STATE, FOUNDING OF). Supporters (so-called 'Treatyites') formed a provisional government and began creating State institutions, including a National Army. Opponents ('Anti-treatyites'), many of whom remained in the IRISH REPUBLICAN ARMY (IRA), repudiated the treaty and expressed loyalty to the republic declared during the 1916 EASTER RISING. In March 1922 they elected Liam Lynch as chief-of-staff. On 14 April an IRA unit, acting independently and emulating 1916 rebels, occupied the 'Four Courts' building in DUBLIN.

Warfare began on 28 June 1922 when the new National Army sought to retake the Four Courts. Though the operation was successful (30 June), fighting between the Army and IRA broke out throughout the IFS. Ambushes and assassinations were frequent: victims included the Army's commander, Michael COLLINS (22 Aug. 1922), and Lynch (10 April 1923). From Nov. 1922 the government of the IFS executed anti-treatyite prisoners.

The Army gradually established control and on 24 May 1923 the IRA suspended resistance, though arrests of IRA men continued. About 2000 people were killed (including 77 executed prisoners) and bitterness persisted long afterwards. See also IRISH FREE STATE, FOUNDING OF.

IRISH COLONIZATION IN BRITAIN, 4TH–6TH CENTURIES Well-evidenced migration of this period was probably part of longer-term, two-way movements. People from LEINSTER (E Ireland) colonized parts of W Britain (Wales), the Laigin leaving their name on the Lleyn Peninsula (NW Wales). Others also settled in the Isle of MAN and in N Britain (Argyll, W Scotland). Extensive contact of this kind between Ireland and Britain continued until the 8th century. Irish involvement with Britain included slave raiding (see PATRICK), and some emigration might have been caused by internal disputes.

From c.500 SCOTS from NE Ireland settled in western N Britain, a movement that resulted eventually in the formation of the kingdom of the Scots and the Gaelicization of N Britain (see DÁL RIATA). The Eóganachta kindred of MUNSTER (S Ireland) were apparently returners from Britain (5th century). Irish OGHAM writing was a by-product of interaction between Ireland and Britain. See also BRYCHEINIOG; CEREDIGION; DYFED; EMIGRATION FROM SCOTLAND.

IRISH CONVENTION An assembly of 95 Irish political representatives which met intermittently at Trinity College, DUBLIN, Ireland (and occasionally elsewhere), from 25 July 1917 to 5 April 1918. It was convened by the British prime minister, David LLOYD GEORGE, in the hope that supporters and opponents of Home Rule might negotiate a compromise agreement on Ireland's future governance. Representatives were unable to reach a unanimous settlement. See also HOME RULE MOVEMENT, IRELAND; REDMOND, JOHN; PLUNKETT, HORACE.

IRISH FREE STATE, FOUNDING OF From 1910 the British government seemed likely to grant Home Rule to Ireland (self-government within the UK), despite opposition (see HOME RULE MOVEMENT, IRELAND; UNIONISM, IRELAND). The policy was supported by most Irish nationalists, represented by the IRISH PARLIAMENTARY PARTY. But from May 1916, when leaders of the republican EASTER RISING, were executed, nationalists changed party. From Feb. 1917, SINN FÉIN republicans won parliamentary by-elections. They gained more support in April 1918 when the British government took power to impose military conscription. At the UK general election of Dec. 1918, Sinn Féin won a large majority of Irish constituencies.

On 21 Jan. 1919 many Sinn Féin MPs met in DUBLIN as a self-proclaimed Dáil Éireann ('Assembly of Ireland') and re-proclaimed a republic. The Dáil later appointed a government (1 April) and started 'arbitration courts' (June). Meanwhile the IRISH REPUBLICAN ARMY (IRA) attacked Crown forces (see IRISH INDEPENDENCE, WAR OF). The British government responded by combating violence and by proscribing Sinn Féin, the IRA (starting 4 July 1919 in Co. Tipperary) and the Dáil (12 Sept.). It legislated for separate Parliaments in Northern and Southern Ireland (see GOVERNMENT OF IRELAND ACT, 1920). The northern

Parliament was established (22 June 1921), but Sinn Féin rejected the Act.

On 9 July 1921 the British and the Dáil agreed a truce. The ensuing ANGLO-IRISH TREATY (6 Dec.) provided for an Irish Free State (Irish, Saorstát Éireann) with DOMINION status, including Northern Ireland (with opt-out provision). The (Second) Dáil accepted the treaty (7 Jan. 1922), and a provisional government was formed (14 Jan.) which received power from Great Britain (16 Jan.). But many IRA members rejected partition and a non-republican State: the IRISH CIVIL WAR followed. The (Third) Dáil ratified a CONSTITUTION on 25 Oct. 1922; the (all-Ireland) State was inaugurated on 6 Dec.; Northern Ireland opted out on 7 Dec. *See also* BOUNDARY COMMISSION; SOUTHERN IRELAND FROM 1922.

IRISH INDEPENDENCE, WAR OF A period of guerrilla conflict, 1919–21, when the IRISH REPUBLICAN ARMY (IRA), supporting SINN FÉIN, sought to establish a republic comprising all of Ireland. The 'War' took place alongside the British government's attempt to implement 'Home Rule'.

The killing of two policemen on 21 Jan. 1919 at Soloheadbeg (Co. Tipperary), during an IRA robbery, is considered as the start. (It coincided with the first meeting of Sinn Féin's Dáil Éireann or 'Assembly of Ireland'.) Thereafter IRA units, often acting independently, attacked mainly members of the Royal Irish Constabulary (RIC). In autumn 1919 the RIC evacuated remote barracks in W and S Ireland, and the British government decided to reinforce the RIC.

From early 1920 IRA attacks increased. During Easter (April) they burnt about 300 abandoned barracks. Reinforcements for the RIC had recently started to arrive, the BLACK AND TANS (British ex-soldiers). They were followed from July by the 'Auxiliary Division' (British ex-Army officers). British forces struggled to identify IRA men, who wore civilian dress; from July 1920 they frequently retaliated with attacks on property (e.g., burning of CORK, 11 Dec. 1920, as reprisal for IRA ambush). The violence alienated public opinion in Great Britain and the USA, as did the deaths of hunger strikers (Oct. 1920) and execution of Kevin Barry, aged 18 (1 Nov., All Saints' Day). The most violent day was 'BLOODY SUNDAY' (21 Nov. 1920).

Sinn Féin rejected the British government's Home Rule scheme (GOVERNMENT OF IRELAND ACT, Dec. 1920), and violence continued. Attempts to arrange a truce had started in late 1920. On 22 June 1921 King GEORGE V, while opening the new Northern Ireland Parliament, called for peace. Soon afterwards the British prime minister, David LLOYD GEORGE, arranged a truce with Sinn Féin leader Éamon DE VALERA, starting on 11 July. About 1200 died. *See also* IRISH FREE STATE, FOUNDING OF; COLLINS, MICHAEL.

IRISH LANGUAGE AND LITERATURE Irish belongs to the Goidelic division of Celtic languages, and was used by the mid 1st millennium BC. Archaic Old Irish features in OGHAM inscriptions of the 4th–6th centuries. The CONVERSION OF IRELAND (5th–6th centuries) introduced LITERACY in Latin and the Latin alphabet; by the 8th century a diverse literature in Old Irish had developed, including genealogies, BREHON LAW, verse, and historical works.

The period of Middle Irish (10th–12th centuries) saw new genres, including hagiography (previously in Latin). The VIKINGS influenced vocabulary relating to seafaring and commerce, and introduced new story motifs. Works of pseudo-history and epic tales, exemplified by the Ulster Cycle, reached great heights by the 12th century.

After the Anglo-Norman invasion (1169–70), Gaelic literature and culture became markedly conservative. (The 13th–17th centuries were the period of Early Modern Irish.) Nonetheless, bardic poetry represented a new development, while popular lyrics about Fianna warriors largely displaced the grandiose Ulster epic. The collapse of Gaelic society following the English conquest of the 16th century and wars of the 17th century drove the LEARNED CLASSES underground. Clandestine 'courts of poetry' produced ballads and patriotic 'vision' poems.

Modern Irish developed from the 17th century. By the 19th century Irish survived principally in remote areas as a peasant patois with associated folklore. Revival movements, notably the Gaelic League from 1893, began teaching the language to nonspeakers and generated a modern printed literature. Governments of the IRISH FREE STATE (from 1922) required schools to revive Irish, but with little success as a spoken medium. Nonetheless, a rich literature developed with particular advances in the novel, short story, poetry and drama. In the late 20th century a popular revival of Irish in the Irish Republic included an Irish-medium school movement. Gaelic-language newspapers and radio also appeared, with a television station from 1996. *See also* ANGLICIZATION, IRELAND; GAELIC REVIVAL, IRELAND 19TH–20TH CENTURIES.

IRISH LOYAL AND PATRIOTIC UNION *see* IRISH UNIONIST ALLIANCE

IRISH PARLIAMENTARY PARTY An organization founded in DUBLIN on 3 March 1874 by 45 (of 59) newly elected pro-Home Rule Irish MPs, to co-ordinate activity in the UK House of Commons; also known as the Irish or Home Rule Party. The first chairmen were Isaac BUTT (1874–9) and William Shaw (1879–80). From 1877 C.S. PARNELL was most prominent (elected chairman 1880). The Party won 86 seats in Dec. 1885, giving it the balance of power. (It supported W.E. GLADSTONE, who introduced a Home Rule Bill.) The Party was supported locally by the HOME RULE LEAGUE, from 1882 by the NATIONAL LEAGUE.

On 6 Dec. 1890, after Parnell had admitted involvement in adultery, the Party and League split into Parnellite and anti-Parnellite factions. Though Parnell died in 1891, the Party's division persisted until 30 Jan. 1900, when it reunited under John REDMOND (a Parnellite). From June 1900 the UNITED IRISH LEAGUE served as principal local organization.

From Jan. 1910 the Party again held the balance of power in the Commons. It supported the Liberals in return for enactment of Home Rule. But implementation was delayed by WORLD WAR I and, following the EASTER RISING (1916) public sympathy swung to SINN FÉIN: at the UK general election in Dec. 1918 the Party won only seven seats. After the PARTITION OF IRELAND (1921) the Party continued as the NATIONALIST PARTY in Northern Ireland but ceased to function in the IRISH FREE STATE. *See also* HOME RULE MOVEMENT, IRELAND; PARLIAMENTARY REPRESENTATION, IRELAND.

IRISH REPUBLICAN ARMY The name used from 1919 for the IRISH VOLUNTEERS (military organization), following the re-proclamation of a republic by the Dáil Éireann ('Assembly of Ireland') of SINN FÉIN MPs (21 Jan.). During the War of IRISH INDEPENDENCE (1919–21) the 'IRA' attacked government forces, seeking to make the republic a reality. When the Dáil accepted the ANGLO-IRISH TREATY (7 Jan. 1922), which retained the Crown and accepted partition of Ireland, most of the IRA rejected the decision. It subsequently repudiated the Dáil's authority (26–7 March). Civil War ensued (June 1922–May 1923).

Despite losing the Civil War, the IRA reaffirmed its commitment to a republic, and created a General Army Convention as its supreme authority (Nov. 1925). But the foundation of FIANNA FÁIL (1926), anti-IRA legislation passed after the murder of Kevin O'HIGGINS (July 1927), and Éamon DE VALERA's quasi-republican policies (1930s) caused membership to decline. On 18 June 1936, following the killing of policemen, de Valera banned the IRA.

From Dec. 1938 the IRA claimed to be the government of the Irish republic (as originally proclaimed in 1916; *see* EASTER RISING). It mounted a bombing campaign in Great Britain in 1939. From 1941 it concentrated within Ireland on NORTHERN IRELAND, and in 1948 formally ended operations in the S. In 1956–62 it attacked police and other authorities in the border area of Northern Ireland, but achieved little. Its preoccupation with Marxist ideology in the 1960s caused disaffected members to found the PROVISIONAL IRISH REPUBLICAN ARMY (1970). The remnant organization became known as the 'Official IRA'. It declared a ceasefire and effectively disbanded in 1972. *See also* IRISH FREE STATE, FOUNDING OF; IRISH CIVIL WAR; MacBRIDE, SEÁN.

IRISH REPUBLICAN BROTHERHOOD A secret society committed to the overthrow of British rule in Ireland and establishment of a republic. It was founded by James STEPHENS in DUBLIN on 17 March 1858 (St Patrick's Day), concurrently with the FENIAN BROTHERHOOD in the USA, with which it had close links. The society was initially known by various names, including 'The Society' and 'The Brotherhood'. It was soon called the Irish Revolutionary or Republican Brotherhood (IRB). Activists were popularly called 'Fenians'. The society's attempted rising in 1867 was quickly suppressed (*see* INSURRECTION OF 1867), but its reputation was boosted by the execution of the MANCHESTER 'MARTYRS'.

During the late 19th century the IRB was relatively inactive, though it organized explosions in England in the 1880s and members participated in the HOME RULE MOVEMENT. It was revived by Tom CLARKE in the early 20th century, when it infiltrated Gaelic cultural organizations and the IRISH VOLUNTEERS (1913). It took advantage of WORLD WAR I to stage the EASTER RISING (1916). Afterwards it was reorganized, but it split during the IRISH CIVIL WAR and dissolved itself in 1924. *See also* DEVOY, JOHN.

IRISH TENANT LEAGUE An organization founded in Ireland in 1850 by C.G. DUFFY and Frederick Lucas to campaign for statutory improvement of tenancy conditions, partly by co-ordinating TENANT PROTECTION SOCIETIES. Its advocacy of the so-called 'THREE Fs' made them central to LAND AGITATION AND REFORM. It was also called the 'League of North and South' because the aims included the extension of 'Ulster Custom' (a tenant's right to sell a lease) throughout Ireland. At the 1852 general election it supported sympathetic candidates (about 48 were elected). It continued until 1858. *See also* PARLIAMENTARY REPRESENTATION, IRELAND.

IRISH UNIONIST ALLIANCE A political organization founded on 1 May 1885 in Dublin, as the Irish Loyal and Patriotic Union, to oppose the HOME RULE MOVEMENT; it was renamed on 6 April 1891. The Alliance effectively represented southern Unionists (i.e., Unionists outside ULSTER). From late 1917, during the IRISH CONVENTION, its leader, Viscount Midleton (St John Brodrick), sought a Home Rule settlement acceptable to both 'Home Rulers' and Unionists. But his opponents resisted, eventually causing Midleton to establish a rival 'Anti-Partition League' (Jan. 1919). Thereafter the Alliance was impotent. *See also* ULSTER UNIONIST PARTY; UNIONISM, IRELAND.

IRISH VOLUNTEERS A voluntary militia founded in DUBLIN on 25 Nov. 1913, in reaction to the creation of the ULSTER VOLUNTEER FORCE, to pressurize the British government into implementing Irish Home Rule (due for enactment in 1914). Commanded by Eoin MacNEILL, the Volunteers quickly recruited over 100,000 members. In June 1914 John REDMOND, leader of the IRISH

PARLIAMENTARY PARTY, was granted considerable influence (through nomination rights). In late Sept. 1914, after Redmond encouraged Volunteers to enlist in the British Army (in WORLD WAR I), the Volunteers split. The majority re-formed as the 'National Volunteers' and joined the British Army.

Two or three thousand men, including MacNeill, retained the old name. Some participated in the EASTER RISING of 1916, while many later joined the IRISH REPUBLICAN ARMY. *See also* HOME RULE MOVEMENT, IRELAND.

IRISH WARS, 1641–52 In Oct. 1641 (Catholic) Gaelic Irish in Ulster (N Ireland) rebelled against the DUBLIN-based royal government (*see* DUBLIN CASTLE PLOT; ULSTER RISING). Demanding tolerance of Catholicism, they seized parts of Ulster. From Dec. they were supported by (Catholic) OLD ENGLISH in LEINSTER and MUNSTER (E and S Ireland). In response Ulster Protestants organized armies, and the English government sent Scottish troops (spring 1642). By late spring 1642 Protestants had recovered ground in Ulster. Meanwhile Catholics created the CATHOLIC CONFEDERATION (May 1642).

From Aug. 1642 the conflict was complicated by war in England between King CHARLES I and Parliament (*see* CIVIL WARS). Charles wanted peace in Ireland, but open conciliation of Catholics would alienate Protestant Royalists in England and Scotland. Old English were prepared to compromise, Gaelic Irish were reluctant.

On 15 Sept. 1643 most combatants agreed a one-year 'CESSATION'. But Scots in Ulster – supporters of the English Parliament – resolved to fight on. In July 1644 the (Protestant) commander in Munster, Lord INCHIQUIN, joined the Parliamentary side. The Catholic Confederation attempted, unsuccessfully, to defeat them (Ulster 1644, Munster 1645). In Dec. 1645 Charles's envoy Lord Glamorgan agreed a secret treaty with Archbishop RINUCCINI, papal nuncio to the Confederation. But Charles had to disavow Glamorgan's work (*see* GLAMORGAN TREATIES). Ireland's chief governor, the marquess of ORMOND, agreed a treaty in 1646, but Rinuccini blocked it and took control of the Confederation (*see* ORMOND TREATIES). With Charles now captive (in England), Ormond surrendered Dublin to Parliament and left (July 1647).

On 13 Nov. 1647 Inchiquin defeated the Confederation's Munster army at Knocknanuss, weakening Rinuccini's influence. When, in 1648, Inchiquin rejoined the Royalists, the Confederation accepted a truce (May) and Ormond returned (Oct.). He agreed a treaty with the Confederation (17 Jan. 1649), creating a Royalist coalition. But Charles was executed (30 Jan.) and Parliament then conquered Ireland (1649–52). *See also* O'NEILL, PHELIM; ADVENTURERS, ACT FOR; JONES, MICHAEL; CROMWELL, OLIVER, AND IRELAND.

IRON AGE, BRITAIN The period of PREHISTORY defined by the introduction of iron working *c.*700 BC; it succeeded the BRONZE AGE. Throughout the Iron Age, Continental styles of metal working, ceramics and art were adopted. Iron Age societies are known mainly from settlements such as HILLFORTS. Burials are rare, except for the Arras group (Yorkshire, NE England) and the Aylesford group (Kent, SE England), which are wrongly ascribed to the BELGAE.

In most of Britain the period ended with the Roman Conquest, starting in AD 43 (*see* ROMAN BRITAIN). In 'Scotland' the period lasted until *c.*1000, with the period 400–1000 being known as the Late Iron Age or early historic period.

IRON AGE, IRELAND The period *c.*700 BC– *c.* AD 400. There are indistinct hints of an incipient Iron Age (succeeding the BRONZE AGE) *c.*700 BC, displaying links with the European Hallstatt world. With the appearance of La Tène influences *c.*300 BC, however, a more established Iron Age presence in the country is recognizable with the widespread use of iron for weapons and tools, and occasionally also for horse-trappings and personal ornaments. Burials were simple cremations in pits, generally with few grave goods, which were placed in low barrows or in earlier burial mounds. Little is known of settlements of the period but several royal sites of presumed ritual character have been identified. Most important are the embanked hilltop enclosures at TARA, Co. Meath (E Ireland), and Navan Fort, Co. Armagh (NE Ireland; *see* EMAIN MACHA).

IRON AGE TRIBES, BRITAIN The names of tribes and sub-tribal groupings of pre-Roman Britain (i.e., before AD 43) are known almost exclusively from later Roman sources – historians' accounts of the conquest, geographers' lists of towns, and inscriptions; there is no clear information on tribal boundaries. Some names, such as BELGAE and Regnenses, may relate to post-conquest administrative reorganizations rather than reflect tribal entities. Only one of the four tribes mentioned by Julius CAESAR in 54 BC reappears in later sources, the Trinovantes of Essex; by the time of the conquest their capital at Camulodunon (COLCHESTER) was under Catuvellaunian control, and is named as the capital of CUNOBELIN.

Most tribes in S and E Britain were ruled by kings, known from both coinage and Roman sources. Reconstructions of conflicts between the Trinovantes, Catuvellauni and Atrebates based on these sources must be treated with scepticism as little is known about the basis of royal power. *See also* CLAUDIAN INVASION.

IRON AGE TRIBES, IRELAND Little is known of Ireland's IRON AGE tribes. Ptolemy's map of the 2nd century AD displays several tribal names, some of indigenous character and others also found in Britain (e.g., Brigantes) and NW Europe (e.g., Manapii). Opinions are divided as to the historical accuracy of these names.

IRON AND STEEL INDUSTRIES, ENGLAND Iron ore was widely smelted in bloomeries (furnaces) using charcoal from the 6th century, for making weapons (swords, shields), agricultural equipment (e.g., horseshoes), tools and domestic equipment (e.g., wool combs). Low-carbon steel was produced for strengthening swords and knives. In respectively the 12th and 13th centuries, the Forest of Dean (Gloucestershire) and Weald of Kent and Sussex became leading iron-making areas, using local ore and wood (latter for charcoal making). Metal working was prominent in the W Midlands by 1400.

Smelting was improved by introduction of blast furnaces (late 15th century) which used water-powered bellows to raise temperatures. By the 1550s the Weald contained 26 furnaces, notably producing iron for cannons and shot. Furnaces were also built in the W Midlands (including Shropshire), Staffordshire and S Yorkshire (in all, over 80 by 1650s). Iron smelting and working expanded into the 18th century, with iron also imported. Production was constrained by the cost of charcoal. (Coal was unsuitable because its sulfur contaminated iron.) From *c.*1706 Abraham DARBY pioneered coke smelting.

Iron production expanded rapidly from the late 1780s (part of the INDUSTRIAL REVOLUTION) with the production of malleable wrought iron using coke smelting, rolling and puddling (latter two inventions patented by Henry Cort, 1783–4). Great Britain's iron industry was internationally paramount until *c.*1870. Meanwhile, 'crucible steel' made SHEFFIELD pre-eminent in steel making (*see* HUNTSMAN, BENJAMIN). From the 1860s, new processes (e.g., Henry Bessemer's, 1856) reduced steel prices and increased output (so-called 'steel revolution'). New production areas developed (e.g., Teesside, NE England).

Following decline in the 1920s, output (iron and steel) recovered from the 1930s with new demand (e.g., MOTOR INDUSTRY). The British industry was nationalized (1949), privatized (1953), renationalized (1967), reprivatized (1988). Concentration of production (1970s) left S Yorkshire, Scunthorpe (Lincolnshire) and Teesside as England's main steel-producing areas. The British industries employed 145,000 in 1924, 38,000 in 1994, 18,000 in 2014. *See also* IRON AGE, BRITAIN.

IRON AND STEEL INDUSTRIES, SCOTLAND Iron smelting with charcoal began by the late 1st millennium BC; the first blast furnace, by Loch Maree (N Scotland), was operating by 1610, though Lowland merchants preferred to import iron from abroad. In the 18th century furnaces were established in Argyllshire (W) where wood was plentiful. In 1760 coke smelting was introduced by the new Carron Works near Falkirk (Stirlingshire), which specialized in guns, but subsequent expansion was modest. Rapid expansion began in the 1830s, following J.B. Neilson's invention of the 'hot blast' (1828) which reduced fuel costs and worked on blackband ironstones from the C Lowlands (discovered 1801). Blast furnaces increased from 27 in 1830 to 133 in 1860. The main product was pig iron, of which half was exported.

Steel making developed after the Siemens open-hearth process was introduced in 1872. (Local ores were unsuitable for the Bessemer process invented in 1856.) By *c.*1900 Scotland produced 20% of British output, though efficient integrated iron-and-steel plants were not built. Demand from SHIP BUILDING was vitally important, lasting until the mid 1920s.

Between 1929 and 1934 most firms were absorbed into Colville's (nationalized 1951, denationalized 1953). In 1960 it inaugurated Scotland's first integrated plant at Ravenscraig (Lanarkshire), adding a strip-mill under government pressure in 1962. The industry was renationalized in 1966 but demand fell. Ravenscraig closed in 1993, soon after privatization (1988). In 2018, two steel mills survived. *See also* INDUSTRY, SCOTLAND BEFORE/FROM LATE 18TH CENTURY.

IRON AND STEEL INDUSTRIES, WALES Iron was smelted with charcoal in small furnaces from the 7th century BC (*see* IRON AGE, BRITAIN), and in taller, more productive blast furnaces from the late 16th century. From the mid 18th century munitions demand encouraged the foundation of larger enterprises in the NE and SE, which usually smelted with coke derived from local coal. Companies included those of the MERTHYR TYDFIL 'iron kings' (*see* BACON, ANTHONY; CRAWSHAY FAMILY). Production expanded rapidly from *c.*1790, thanks to military demand; in 1830 Wales produced 40% of Great Britain's pig iron. Demand for RAILWAY construction then sustained production.

From the 1860s new steel-making processes reduced demand for iron. Steel plants were opened in Wales, many near the S Wales coast (to facilitate exporting). Inland ironworks closed. Steel output remained steady until the 1930s and then declined.

In 1947 several companies combined as the Steel Company of Wales and built Britain's largest steelworks at Port Talbot (Glamorgan; opened 1951). Steel making was nationalized in 1951, denationalized in 1953 and renationalized in 1966. Costs became uneconomic: two of four large plants in S Wales were closed (1970s), and the Shotton works in the NE (1983). The industry was privatized in 1988. In 1985 the iron and steel industries employed about 20,000 people, but in 2015 only 6400 people. *See also* INDUSTRY, WALES FROM 18TH CENTURY; COAL INDUSTRY, WALES; CANALS, WALES.

IRON INDUSTRY, IRELAND After the IRON AGE, iron working continued among proto-urban and urban populations and probably elsewhere (*see* TOWNS, IRELAND). In the 13th–17th centuries iron was largely imported from Spain and England.

From the later 16th century, (Protestant) organizers of PLANTATIONS included ironworks among economic development schemes, motivated by availability of wood for charcoal making. Using immigrant specialists, ironworks were started in MUNSTER, ULSTER and at Mountrath (Queen's Co., modern Co. Laois). The first blast furnace is recorded in 1593 (in Co. Cork). Most ironworks were destroyed by rebels in 1641–2 (*see* IRISH WARS 1641–52). Landowners resumed development from the 1650s, using local or imported ore (e.g., ironworks started by William PETTY at Kenmare, Co. Kerry).

As charcoal became expensive in the 18th century, due to deforestation, the industry contracted and the last charcoal-fuelled furnace closed in 1798. The total number of furnaces is estimated at 160. A 'modern' works at Arigna in Co. Roscommon (NW Ireland), based on local ore and coal, operated briefly (1788–1808). Ireland became reliant on imported iron, which was used by foundries at ports and elsewhere for making agricultural, industrial and other products.

IRVINGITES *see* CATHOLIC APOSTOLIC CHURCH

ISABELLA (b. late 1295 in France; d. 23 Aug. 1358 at Hertford, Hertfordshire, England, aged 63). Isabella, daughter of King Philip IV of France, married King EDWARD II of England (25 Jan. 1308). In the 1320s she was alienated by Edward's favouritism for the DESPENSERS. In March 1325 she went to France, to negotiate about GASCONY (confiscated 1324 by her brother King Charles IV). Joined by her son Edward (Sept.), she refused to return unless the Despensers were removed.

In Paris, Isabella became the lover of the exile Roger MORTIMER (by March 1326). They invaded England (landed 24 Sept.), won extensive support, and denounced the Despensers (15 Oct.). Prince Edward was made guardian of England (26 Oct.). King Edward was deposed (20 Jan. 1327). Isabella's collaboration with Mortimer's accumulation of estates, offices and incomes alienated the BARONS. She was arrested with Mortimer in Oct. 1330. He was executed but she survived. *See also* EDWARD III.

ISANDLWANA, BATTLE OF Fought at Isandlwana, in Zululand (in southern Africa), on 22 Jan. 1879, during the ZULU WAR. About 20,000 Zulus made a surprise and overwhelming attack on a smaller invading force of British and native troops (about 1700). About 850 British and 470 native defenders were killed, and about 2000 Zulus. The

scale of the defeat shocked British opinion, though it was negated by successes elsewhere.

ISLAY, EARL OF (b. June 1682 at Petersham, Surrey, England; d. 15 April 1761 at London, England, aged 78). A younger brother of John Campbell, 2nd duke of ARGYLL from 1703, Archibald Campbell was educated at Eton (England) and GLASGOW University. He was created earl of Islay in 1706, and from 1707 until his death (except for 1713) was a Scottish 'representative peer' in the British House of Lords. He was appointed lord justice-general of Scotland (1710), lord clerk register (1714), and keeper of the privy seal (1721) and of the great seal (1733).

From 1725, following the SHAWFIELD RIOTS, Islay organized government affairs in Scotland, influencing the award of government-controlled posts and obtaining the return of loyal MPs and representative peers to the British Parliament. He was based in London and operated through local agents, especially Lord MILTON, though he made annual visits to Scotland. He was nicknamed 'king of Scotland'. Islay succeeded his brother as duke in 1743. *See also* ARGYLL, EARLS AND DUKES OF.

ISLES, LORDSHIP OF THE An important lordship, or quasi-kingdom, in late medieval Scotland, comprising most of the WESTERN ISLES and western HIGHLANDS; held by the MACDONALD family. By 1346 John of Islay (d. 1387) reacquired, by royal grant and marriage, most lands held by his ancestor SOMERLED (d. 1164). From the 1350s he styled himself 'lord' ('king' in Gaelic). He and successors encouraged GAELIC culture. From 1389 lords clashed with rulers (*see*, e.g., HARLAW, BATTLE OF). King JAMES IV annexed the lordship in 1493. *See also* EARLDOMS, SCOTLAND.

ISLES, LORDS OF THE *see* MACDONALD, LORDS OF THE ISLES

ISRAEL, BRITISH RELATIONS WITH When Great Britain relinquished its PALESTINE mandate on 14 May 1948, the Jewish People's Council declared a Jewish State of Israel and the first Arab–Israeli War ensued. Britain recognized Israel (27 April 1950) without accepting the armistice lines as definitive borders. In 1956 the two countries colluded (with France) in military action against Egypt (*see* SUEZ CRISIS), but Britain otherwise promoted compromise in Israel's dealings with neighbouring countries and Palestinians. While upholding Israel's right to exist, it has sought Israeli withdrawal from territories occupied in 1967.

Prime Minister James CALLAGHAN advocated a homeland for Palestinian Arabs (1977), and his successor Margaret THATCHER backed calls for Palestinian self-determination (1980). After Israel invaded Lebanon, Britain imposed an arms embargo (1982–94). But relations improved, and Thatcher became the first serving prime minister to visit Israel (1986). Tony BLAIR aspired to be a peacemaker; in 1998 he held a summit in London between the Israeli prime minister Benjamin Netanyahu and the Palestinian leader Yasser Arafat; and in 2001–2 he encouraged the US president, George W. Bush, to balance threats against Iraq with concern for the Israeli–Palestinian dispute. But British influence was minimal, and continuing conflict between Israelis and Palestinians prevented significant progress. In 2014 the UK House of Commons voted in favour of recognizing the Palestinian State (declared 1988).

ITALIAN BANKERS, MEDIEVAL ENGLAND Companies operating as deposit-takers, lenders, papal agents and merchants provided crucial finance for the Crown 1250s–1340s. King HENRY III borrowed from Sienese merchants 1254–8. EDWARD I borrowed from the Frescobaldi in the 1270s–80s (e.g., to fund the conquest of WALES). EDWARD III began the HUNDRED YEARS WAR (1338–9) with loans from the Peruzzi and Bardi, causing them to go bankrupt (respectively 1343, 1346). Italian

bankers also made large loans to some religious houses. *See also* ROYAL REVENUES, ENGLAND 1066 TO 1603.

ITALY, BRITISH RELATIONS WITH In the mid 19th century British liberal opinion applauded Italian nationalism. Lord PALMERSTON, who favoured a unified Italy but was concerned about French influence, prevented European intervention when Giuseppe Garibaldi conquered the kingdom of the Two Sicilies (1860) in the name of a United Italy (proclaimed 17 March 1861).

Conscious of Britain's naval power in the Mediterranean, Italy sought good relations and accepted a Mediterranean Agreement (1887). It entered WORLD WAR I on the Allied side (1915), but afterwards felt cheated of promised territories. In the 1930s, despite British appeasement regarding Italy's invasion of Abyssinia (Ethiopia) in Oct. 1935 (*see* HOARE–LAVAL PACT), Benito Mussolini favoured alliance with Germany. During WORLD WAR II, Italy declared war on Britain (10 June 1940) in a bid for Mediterranean supremacy. The Anglo-American invasion of Sicily forced Italy's capitulation (3 Sept. 1943). After the war, Italy and Britain were allies in the NORTH ATLANTIC TREATY ORGANIZATION from 1949.

J

JACOBITE REBELLION, 1689 *see* GRAHAM, JOHN, OF CLAVERHOUSE; KILLIECRANKIE, BATTLE OF

JACOBITE REBELLION, 1708 The first rebellion since 1689, in Scotland, exploited the failure of the DARIEN SCHEME and the unpopularity of the UNION OF ENGLAND AND SCOTLAND (1707). It was supported by France, which recognized James Edward Stuart (1688–1766), son of JAMES VII/II, as king. France used the rebellion as a diversionary attack on Great Britain, which it was fighting in the War of the SPANISH SUCCESSION. A fleet carrying 'James VIII' and troops left France in mid March, sailed to the Forth estuary (to meet Jacobites), but was forced by the British Navy to flee without landing (24 March). *See also* TREASON; FRANCE, ENGLISH AND BRITISH RELATIONS WITH.

JACOBITE REBELLION, 1715 Resentment at the succession of King GEORGE I (1714), in England and Scotland, and in Scotland continuing unpopularity of the UNION OF ENGLAND AND SCOTLAND (from 1707), provided the opportunity for another rising. In Scotland it was started by the (6th) earl of MAR, who had been dismissed by George (Sept. 1714). He launched his campaign at Braemar (Aberdeenshire, NE Scotland) on 6 Sept. 1715. Inverness (N) and Perth (C) were taken on 14 Sept. On 13 Nov. Mar's forces clashed indecisively with troops under the (2nd) duke of ARGYLL at Sheriffmuir (near Dunblane, Perthshire), though Jacobite support afterwards declined.

In England, a rising was planned in the SW, but was prevented by the arrest of leading Jacobites (Sept.–Oct. 1715) and the securing of BRISTOL and BATH by troops (end Sept.). A complementary rising began in Northumberland (NE England) on 6 Oct. A Jacobite force failed to take NEWCASTLE UPON TYNE; after joining Jacobites from Lowland Scotland it marched into Lancashire (NW England), where it surrendered (at Preston, on 14 Nov.). The Pretender, 'James VIII', landed in Scotland (at Peterhead, Aberdeenshire) on 22 Dec., only to leave Montrose (Angus) on 4 Feb. 1716 and retreat to France.

JACOBITE REBELLION, 1719 Hostilities between Great Britain and Spain led the Spanish government, under King Philip V, to plan invasions of Britain via SW England and NW Scotland. 'James VIII' was to accompany the former, which was thwarted by storms. The diversionary northern invasion proceeded. About 300 Spaniards and exiled Jacobite nobles landed at Kintail, opposite the Isle of Skye, and took Eilean Donan Castle. They were defeated nearby at Glenshiel (10 June) by government troops while a frigate destroyed the castle. The Spanish surrendered (11 June) and sailed home.

JACOBITE REBELLION, 1745 The last and largest attempt to restore the exiled Stuarts, and the only true Highland rising. It was the initiative of the 'Young Pretender', Charles Edward Stuart (1720–88), son of 'James

A Dictionary of British and Irish History, First Edition. Edited by Robert Peberdy and Philip Waller.
© 2021 John Wiley & Sons Ltd; © editorial matter and organisation Robert Peberdy and Phillip Waller.
Published 2021 by John Wiley & Sons Ltd.

VIII', undertaken after France had abandoned planned invasions in early 1744.

Prince Charles landed near Arisaig (NW Scotland) with seven companions and formally began his campaign on 19 Aug. Within six weeks they rallied massive support from the HIGHLANDS, took Inverness (N Scotland) and Perth (C), and Edinburgh (SE, 17 Sept.) and defeated a government army (21 Sept.) at Prestopans, E of Edinburgh. But little support was forthcoming from the Lowlands. It was decided, against the wishes of Lord George MURRAY, to invade England (from the NW). The Jacobites reached Derby (4 Dec.), and London was in panic, but little English support materialized. The Jacobites withdrew (from 6 Dec.) back into Scotland, defeating government forces at Falkirk (C Scotland) on 17 Jan. 1746.

The Jacobites then withdrew to the Highlands. Some commanders favoured a switch to guerrilla tactics. Prince Charles wanted a pitched battle. An unfavourable site was chosen, at CULLODEN, resulting in massive defeat (16 April). The British commander, the duke of CUMBERLAND, ordered savage reprisals, earning the nickname 'Butcher'. Prince Charles avoided capture and eventually left for France in Sept. 1746.

JACOBITE REBELLIONS, CONSEQUENCES IN SCOTLAND The government's response to the 1715 Rebellion was relatively lenient: 19 peers were attainted and their estates forfeited but only two were executed; estates were returned after six years. A Disarming Act was passed (1716) but proved ineffective; loyal clans handed over weapons while Jacobites delivered broken and rusty equipment. Individual town councillors, clergy, teachers and academics who had supported the Jacobites were removed from office, especially in the north-eastern shires and Perthshire. Government concern persisted, particularly about the HIGHLANDS: the seizure of weapons was authorized in 1725, and 240 mi (385 km) of military roads were built (see WADE, GEORGE).

The 1745 Rebellion provoked a more ruthless response, aimed mainly at the Highlands. In 1746-7 forces under 'Butcher' CUMBERLAND ravaged the Fort Augustus area (Inverness-shire), confiscating thousands of cattle. Rebels' estates were forfeited and 13 annexed to the Crown (see ANNEXING ACT). In 1746 a Disarming Act banned Highland dress and the carrying of weapons, while in 1747 HERITABLE JURISDICTIONS and military tenures were abolished. The meeting houses of Non-juror Episcopalians were suppressed. To deter further rebellion, Fort George was built near Ardersier in Inverness-shire (1748-69) and another 750 mi (1200 km) of military roads were constructed. See also CLAN, SCOTLAND.

JACOBITISM, IMPACT ON BRITISH POLITICS Jacobitism was the cause of restoring Catholic members of the Stuart family as rulers of England, Ireland and Scotland after King JAMES VII/II was replaced by the Protestants WILLIAM III and MARY II in 1689. James died in 1701. Thereafter 'Jacobites' (from Latin for James, 'Jacobus') supported his son James Edward Stuart (1688-1766), the 'Old Pretender', and his sons Charles Edward Stuart (1720-88), the 'Young Pretender', and Henry Stuart (1725-1807), cardinal duke of York.

In England the cause was supported by many ROMAN CATHOLICS and NON-JURORS and by some HIGH CHURCHMEN; in Scotland by EPISCOPALIANS, Catholics and Highlanders disgruntled with the UNION OF ENGLAND AND SCOTLAND (1707). It also received aid or encouragement from France and other powers. Robert WALPOLE (prime minister 1721-42) promoted a peace policy to discourage foreign support for Jacobitism.

JACOBITE REBELLIONS, which attempted to restore the Stuarts, failed in: 1689-91 (Ireland and Scotland, see WILLIAMITE WAR), 1708 (Scotland), 1715-16 (Scotland and England), 1719 (Scotland), 1745-6 (Scotland and England). After the 'Forty-five' Jacobitism withered.

Jacobitism bound GEORGE I (ruled 1714-27) and GEORGE II (1727-60) to WHIG politicians; they feared that TORIES were Jacobites and favoured a Stuart restoration. See also STEWART RULERS; JACOBITE REBELLIONS, CONSEQUENCES IN SCOTLAND; JACOBITISM, WALES.

JACOBITISM, WALES In the early 18th century many GENTRY families were sympathetic to restoration of the STUARTS and formed Jacobite societies. The main stronghold was NE Wales, where Sir Watkin Williams Wynn (1692-1749) led the Cycle of the White Rose (founded 1710), which met by rotation in members' homes. But few joined the JACOBITE REBELLIONS of 1715 and 1745, preferring to preserve their lives and estates. Some Welsh Jacobites later became involved in freemasonry.

JAMAICA An island and former English colony in the WEST INDIES (British from 1707). Captured from Spain in 1655 (during the PROTECTORATE; see WESTERN DESIGN), it was under military government until 1661. It then became a CROWN COLONY. Jamaica quickly developed into the world's largest sugar producer, with slaves working on PLANTATIONS and outnumbering the white population. Slaves were emancipated in 1834, after which sugar production declined. Following an uprising in 1865, the governor took control of government. Popular involvement was reintroduced in 1884 through a partially elected legislative council.

Jamaica belonged to the Federation of the West Indies from 1958, and became independent on leaving in 1962 (retaining the British monarch as head of State). Approx. population in 1921, 858,000; in 1961, 1,646,000. See also SLAVE TRADE, ENGLISH AND BRITISH INVOLVEMENT.

JAMES I (b. July 1394 at Dunfermline, Fife, E Scotland; d. 21 Feb. 1437 at Perth, C Scotland, aged 42). King of Scots (Scotland) 1406–37.

In 1406 James, aged 11 and heir to his father King ROBERT III, was dispatched by ship to France for safety. (His elder brother had died in imprisonment in 1402; *see* STEWART, DAVID.) James was captured by English pirates (14 March). The news killed King Robert. James succeeded (4 April 1406) but remained captive. Scotland remained under his uncle Robert STEWART, duke of Albany and 'guardian', who became 'governor' and resisted James's return.

Following Albany's death (1420), terms for James's release were agreed (finalized 4 Dec. 1423). He returned to Scotland, newly married to Joan Beaufort, on 5 April 1424 (*see* BEAUFORT FAMILY). Determined to predominate, he destroyed Albany's successor, Murdoch Stewart (1425), and other nobles. In Aug. 1428 he arrested about 50 northern magnates at Inverness; some were executed. He also reorganized GOVERNMENT, sponsored law-making and economic regulation, and increased ROYAL REVENUES by retaining forfeited and vacant estates. In foreign policy James inclined towards France, but abstained from practical commitment until 1436 (daughter sent to marry the dauphin). James was assassinated in 1437 by several disaffected nobles; succeeded by JAMES II. *See also* HUNDRED YEARS WAR.

JAMES I OF ENGLAND *see* JAMES VI/I

JAMES II (b. 16 Oct. 1430 at Edinburgh, SE Scotland; d. 3 Aug. 1460 at Roxburgh, S Scotland, aged 29). King of Scots (Scotland) 1437–60. Succeeding his father King JAMES I when aged 6 (21 Feb. 1437), James remained effectively a minor until 1449. Meanwhile factions contested control of government.

Archibald Douglas, (5th) earl of Douglas, was 'lieutenant' (regent) until he died in 1439. The Livingston and Crichton families then dominated, executing William, (6th) earl of Douglas, and his brother after seizing them at the 'Black Dinner' (Edinburgh Castle, 24 Nov. 1440). In 1443 or 1444 William, (8th) earl of DOUGLAS, divided the families, allying with the Livingstons and becoming lieutenant (July 1444–July 1449). In autumn 1444 the COUNCIL declared the Crichtons outlaws. Under William Douglas the Scots renewed the French alliance (1448) and married James to Mary of Guelders (1449).

After his marriage (3 July), James exerted authority, but initially in Douglas's shadow. The Livingstons were arrested (Sept.); two were executed (Jan. 1450). In 1452 James killed Douglas, and in 1455 attacked Douglas lands which were forfeited, destroying Scotland's most powerful family (*see* DOUGLAS, EARLS OF). Thereafter James ruled most effectively but in 1460 he was killed by an exploding canon when

besieging English-held Roxburgh. Succeeded by JAMES III. *See also* EARLDOMS, SCOTLAND; MINORITIES, ROYAL.

JAMES II OF ENGLAND *see* JAMES VII/II

JAMES III (b. May 1451 at St Andrews, Fife, E Scotland; d. 11 June 1488 at Sauchieburn, C Scotland, aged 37). King of Scots (Scotland) 1460–88.

James succeeded his father King JAMES II on 3 Aug. 1460, aged 9. During his minority, Scotland was governed by a regency council, dominated by Mary of Guelders (1461–3) and Bishop James KENNEDY (1463–5). On 9 July 1466 James was abducted by the Boyd family, under whose control he remained until he overthrew them in Nov. 1469 and began his personal rule. The Boyds arranged his marriage (on 13 July 1469) to Margaret, daughter of King Christian I of Denmark-Norway who pledged the ORKNEY ISLANDS and SHETLAND ISLANDS to the dowry. (James annexed the islands in 1472.)

In 1482 James was captured by several leading nobles and held in EDINBURGH. He was released by an English army, accompanied by his brother Alexander STEWART, (3rd) duke of Albany (who had fled to England in 1479). In 1488 another magnate rebellion broke out. James fought the rebels (nominally led by his son and heir) at SAUCHIEBURN, near Stirling. He was defeated and killed, probably after the battle. Succeeded by JAMES IV. *See also* HOME FAMILY.

JAMES IV (b. 17 March 1473 at Stirling, C Scotland; d. 9 Sept. 1513 at Flodden, Northumberland, England, aged 40). King of Scots (Scotland) 1488–1513.

James succeeded King JAMES III (father) after the battle of SAUCHIEBURN (11 June 1488), when he was nominal leader of a magnate revolt. Although a minor (until spring 1495), he participated in government, pursuing peace with England (truce agreed 1491) and extending authority over the WESTERN ISLES (four campaigns 1493–8).

James began his personal rule by invading NE England (Sept. 1496), ostensibly to support the claim of Perkin WARBECK to the English Crown, but reverted to a pro-English policy (truce 1497; treaty 1502; marriage to Margaret Tudor, daughter of King HENRY VII, 1503). Peace enabled James to rebuild palaces and construct a NAVY (from 1505), using money came from diverted Church revenues (*see* COMMENDATION OF ABBEYS, SCOTLAND), taxes on clergy, and FEUING of royal lands. Between 1497 and 1512, income grew at least six-fold.

In June 1509, following the accession of King HENRY VIII in England, James renewed the treaty with England; but he was soon persuaded to renew the SCOTTISH–FRENCH ALLIANCE (1512). In 1513, after Henry invaded France, James invaded England (22 Aug.) only to be killed at FLODDEN. Succeeded by JAMES V. *See also* NEW MONAR-CHY, SCOTLAND; ROYAL REVENUES, SCOTLAND; SCOTTISH–ENGLISH RELATIONS 1357 TO 1603.

JAMES V (b. 10 April 1512 at Linlithgow, Lothian, SE Scotland; d. 14 Dec. 1542 at Falkland, Fife, E Scotland, aged 30). King of Scots (Scotland) 1513–42.

James succeeded King JAMES IV (father) on 9 Sept. 1513, aged 1. His minority lasted 15 years, during which leading figures competed for influence: the pro-English Margaret Tudor (king's mother) was dominant 1513–15; the pro-French (4th) duke of Albany to 1524 (with interruptions; *see* STEWART, JOHN); Margaret again until 1525, when she divorced her second husband, Archibald DOUGLAS, earl of Angus. Angus then took James under control.

In 1528 James escaped and outlawed the Angus Douglases. He increased income by obtaining papal grants (1531) of a perpetual tax on clergy (used to found the College of Justice, 1532) and nomination to bishoprics (many were given to his illegitimate infants, for their revenues).

James made peace with England (treaty 1534) while cultivating France – he married Madeleine Valoise (Jan. 1537, d. by July) and MARY OF GUISE (1538). In 1541 relations with England deteriorated when James snubbed planned discussions with King HENRY VIII at York. A Scottish army invaded NW England in 1542, but was defeated at Solway Moss, Cumberland (24 Nov.). James died soon afterwards, leaving a young heiress, MARY, QUEEN OF SCOTS. *See also* MINORITIES, ROYAL; COMMENDATION OF ABBEYS, SCOTLAND; SCOTTISH–ENGLISH RELATIONS 1357 TO 1603.

JAMES VI/I (b. 19 June 1566 at Edinburgh, SE Scotland; d. 27 March 1625 at Theobalds, Hertfordshire, England, aged 58). James became king of Scotland (James VI) as a minor (24 July 1567), succeeding his mother MARY, QUEEN OF SCOTS. His minority saw the DOUGLAS WARS (1568–73) and regencies of the earls of MORAY (1567–70), LENNOX (1570–1), MAR (1571–2), and MORTON (1572–8). James was then dominated by Esmé STEWART (1580–2), the 'Ruthven regime' (1582–3; *see* RUTHVEN RAID), and James STEWART (1583–5), and was threatened by Catholic 'northern earls' (including HUNTLY) and the Protestant BOTHWELL. He accumulated large debts (*see* OCTAVIANS).

James succeeded Queen ELIZABETH I in England and Ireland (24 March 1603). From England he reimposed bishops on the Church of Scotland (1606) and reformed worship (*see* FIVE ARTICLES OF PERTH). He returned only once to Scotland (1617).

James made peace with Spain (1604). Influenced by favourites, the earl of SOMERSET (to 1615) and duke of BUCKINGHAM, he spent excessively. Attempts at financial reform by Robert CECIL (d. 1612) and Lionel CRANFIELD (from 1618) had limited success (*see* IMPOSITIONS; GREAT

CONTRACT). Relations with Parliament were strained (*see* ADDLED PARLIAMENT). In religion James avoided extremes (*see* PURITANISM, ENGLAND; ARMINIANISM). Succeeded by CHARLES I. *See also* UNION OF ENGLAND AND SCOTLAND, 1606 SCHEME; FOREIGN RELATIONS, ENGLAND 16TH CENTURY TO 1707; SPANISH MATCH; ULSTER PLANTATION.

JAMES VII/II (b. 14 Oct. 1633 at Westminster, Middlesex, England; d. 5 Sept. 1701 at St Germain, France, aged 67). Second son of King CHARLES I, James was created duke of York (1634). He lived in exile 1648–60 (*see* COMMONWEALTH AND PROTECTORATE). From 1649 York was immediate heir to his brother CHARLES II. He participated in the ANGLO-DUTCH WARS (1665–7, 1672–3) as lord high admiral. But having become a Catholic (1669), he resigned (1673) to avoid anti-Catholic oaths required by the 1673 TEST ACT. He lived in exile in 1679 (Netherlands) and 1679–80, 1680–2 (Scotland) while Charles resisted his exclusion from the succession (*see* EXCLUSION CRISIS).

York succeeded as king of England and Ireland (James II) and Scotland (James VII) on 6 Feb. 1685. After crushing rebellions (ARGYLL RISING, MONMOUTH'S REBELLION), he advanced Catholicism (e.g., appointing Catholic Army officers, suspending laws against Catholics and Protestant dissenters). The birth of a son on 10 June 1688 threatened perpetuation of a Catholic monarchy. On 30 June, seven noblemen invited William of Orange to intervene (landed 5 Nov.). James fled abroad (23 Dec.). A CONVENTION PARLIAMENT decreed his abdication.

James attempted to regain his thrones by capturing Ireland (*see* JAMES VII/II AND IRELAND), and descendants thereafter claimed them. *See also* INDULGENCE, DECLARATIONS OF; SEVEN BISHOPS' CASE; GLORIOUS REVOLUTION; GLORIOUS REVOLUTION, SCOTLAND; JACOBITISM, IMPACT ON BRITISH POLITICS.

JAMES VII/II AND IRELAND King James's intention to promote Catholicism enjoyed the best prospects in Protestant-dominated Ireland, where most inhabitants were Catholics who desired (at the least) tolerance of Catholicism. 'Catholicization' was implemented by James's Catholic friend and agent Tyrconnell, who appointed Catholics to the Army, judiciary and government (*see* TYRCONNELL, EARL OF). James also encouraged activity by the Catholic Church (e.g., public presence of bishops). Such developments alarmed Protestants in Ireland and Britain.

After James fled from England (Dec. 1688), Tyrconnell held Ireland for him. James went there from France (landed at Kinsale, Co. Cork, 12 March 1689), planning to use Ireland as a base for recovering England and Scotland. But his first military move, against (Protestant) Londonderry, failed (April–July; *see* LONDONDERRY, SIEGE OF). When

James held a Parliament to raise funds, he was forced to concede the restoration of dispossessed lands to Catholics, thereby increasing Protestant fears (May–July; *see* PATRIOT PARLIAMENT).

In 1689–90 forces supporting Ireland's new rulers, WILLIAM III and MARY II, arrived, and armies commanded by James and William clashed at the BOYNE (1 July 1690). James was defeated. He returned to Dublin and left Ireland on 4 July (from Kinsale). His policies made Irish Protestants determined to prevent any reassertion of Catholicism. *See also* RESTORATION, IRELAND; WILLIAMITE WAR; PROTESTANT ASCENDANCY.

JAMES VII/II AND NORTH AMERICA *see* NEW ENGLAND, DOMINION OF.

JAMES OF ST GEORGES (b. *c.*1235, possibly at St George d'Esperanche, Savoy; d. between Sept. 1307 and May 1309, aged probably over 70). Architect and mason.

James was recruited by King EDWARD I of England from Savoy between Oct. 1275 and 1278. During the 1280s–90s James (as master of the king's works) and other Savoyards designed and built Edward's most famous castles in Wales, e.g., Beaumaris, CAERNARFON, Conwy, Harlech. James later worked in Scotland, but financial restraints produced lower standards. *See* WALES, ENGLISH CONQUEST OF.

JAMESON RAID In southern Africa, starting on 29 Dec. 1895, an invasion from (British) Bechuanaland into the (Boer) Transvaal Republic by 600 men led by L. Starr Jameson, a British administrator. It was intended to provoke an uprising and overthrow the government of President Paul Kruger, but failed. Cecil RHODES, prime minister of CAPE COLONY, had to resign for complicity, though Joseph CHAMBERLAIN, British colonial secretary, was exonerated of involvement. Strained relations between Great Britain and the Boers led eventually to the (Second) BOER WAR. *See also* SOUTH AFRICA.

JAPAN, BRITISH RELATIONS WITH After the USA forcibly opened Western relations with Japan (1853–4), Great Britain made treaties in 1854 and 1858. The latter, an 'unequal treaty', included representation at Edo (Tokyo) and access to three ports and their hinterlands with 'extra-territorial' legal jurisdiction. The Iwakura Embassy, an investigative diplomatic mission, visited numerous places in Britain in 1872, particularly industrial centres, and was received by Queen VICTORIA. The surrender of British extra-territorial rights in 1894 (effective 1899) equalized relations and facilitated the ANGLO-JAPANESE ALLIANCE (1902) which protected Japan from French intervention in the Russo-Japanese War (1904–5).

During WORLD WAR I Japan joined the Allies (1914–18), to the extent of occupying German possessions in E Asia.

Friction between Japan and the USA led to abandonment of the Anglo-Japanese Alliance in 1921 (superseded by new international treaties in 1922). British toleration of Japanese expansion in China from 1931 failed to prevent Japanese occupation of British possessions in E Asia in 1941–2, during WORLD WAR II (e.g., HONG KONG, MALAYSIA, SINGAPORE, BURMA). The Japanese took almost 140,000 Allied prisoners (over 30,000 died).

After Japan's surrender (1945) and disarmament, Britain largely withdrew from E Asia (by 1970s). From the 1960s Japanese industrial production undermined some British industries (e.g., MOTORCYCLE manufacturing) and imbalance of trade became a major issue, although official relations were amicable. Japanese emperors made State visits to Britain from 1971, and Prince Naruhito (emperor from 2019) studied at OXFORD University (1983–5, at Merton College).

JARROW CRUSADE *see* HUNGER MARCHES

JAVA, BRITISH INTERREGNUM IN Term referring to the British occupation of Java in the Dutch East Indies 1811–16, during the NAPOLEONIC WARS in Europe. The British captured Java from the French, who had seized it from the Dutch (1808). It was governed by Stamford RAFFLES, who envisaged it as a centre for British rule in E Asia. He reorganized the government (e.g., extensively abolished forced labour), before Java was restored to the Dutch.

JAY'S TREATY Signed 19 Nov. 1794 in London, England, by US envoy John Jay and Lord GRENVILLE, the British foreign secretary. It obtained US neutrality in the war between Great Britain and revolutionary France. Britain ceded military outposts on the American frontier and limited access to West Indies trade. Denounced in the USA because not all issues were settled, it was eventually ratified (June 1795) to avoid war. *See also* FRENCH REVOLUTIONARY AND NAPOLEONIC WARS, BRITISH INVOLVEMENT.

JEFFREYS, ALEC (b. 9 Jan. 1950 at Oxford, Oxfordshire, England). Interested in science as a young child, Jeffreys studied biochemistry and took at doctorate (1975) at OXFORD University. After undertaking research on genes in the Netherlands, he joined Leicester University (1977), becoming a professor in 1987.

In 1984, while studying the DNA (deoxyribonucleic acid, the carrier of genetic information) of several members of a family, Jeffreys noticed that repetitive patterns of DNA are unique to each individual except for identical twins, and could be used for identification, a technique he named 'genetic fingerprinting'. Its potential was demonstrated in 1987 when DNA evidence exonerated the prime suspect for two murders near Leicester and identified the killer. Jeffreys' discovery enabled DNA evidence to be used worldwide for criminal investigations and other purposes (e.g., confirmation of the presumed remains of RICHARD III). Jeffreys was elected a fellow of the ROYAL SOCIETY (1986) and knighted (1994).

JEFFREYS, GEORGE *see* BLOODY ASSIZES

JELLICOE, JOHN (b. 5 Dec. 1859 at Southampton, Hampshire, England; d. 19 Nov. 1935 at Chelsea, London, England, aged 75). Jellicoe joined the British Royal NAVY in 1872 and became interested in gunnery. During WORLD WAR I he commanded the Grand Fleet (from July 1914), and fought the battle of Jutland (in N Sea), the war's major surface naval battle (31 May–1 June 1916). Although indecisive in outcome, it persuaded the Germans to avoid further surface engagements.

As first sea lord (from Dec. 1916), Jellicoe faced unrestricted German submarine warfare and huge shipping losses (from Feb. 1917). He introduced convoys for merchant vessels. But the prime minister, David LLOYD GEORGE, considered him pessimistic and he was eventually dismissed by the head of the Admiralty, Eric Geddes (Dec. 1917). Jellicoe was created Viscount Jellicoe (1918) and Earl Jellicoe (1925). He served as governor of NEW ZEALAND 1920–5.

JENKINS, ROY (b. 11 Nov. 1920 at Abersychan, Monmouthshire, Wales; d. 5 Jan. 2003 at East Hendred, Oxfordshire, England, aged 82). An MP's son, Jenkins was a Labour MP 1948–76. As British home secretary (1965–7) under Harold WILSON he supported liberalization of laws on HOMOSEXUALITY and ABORTION. He replaced James CALLAGHAN as chancellor of the Exchequer (1967–70). Elected deputy Party leader in 1970, he resigned (1972) over Labour's opposition to the terms for membership of the EUROPEAN ECONOMIC COMMUNITY. Jenkins nevertheless served again as home secretary (1974–6). He led the 'Yes' campaign in the referendum on EEC membership in 1975, and served as president of the European Commission 1977–81.

Disenchanted with Labour, Jenkins encouraged the foundation of the SOCIAL DEMOCRATIC PARTY in Britain (1981), serving as an SDP MP 1982–7 and as leader 1982–3. He was created Lord Jenkins in 1987.

JENKINS' EAR, WAR OF A mainly maritime war between Great Britain and Spain, 1739–48. It arose from Spanish attempts to suppress illicit British trade with its American colonies (alongside trade permitted under the Peace of UTRECHT).

In March 1738 British opinion was inflamed when Captain Robert Jenkins claimed that in 1731 the Spanish had raided his ship and cut off his ear. An attempted settlement (Convention of Prado, 4 Jan. 1739) failed. On 8 Oct.

1739 the British prime minister, Robert WALPOLE, declared war. The war became part of the War of the AUSTRIAN SUCCESSION (from 1740).

JENKINSON, CHARLES (b. 26 April 1729 at Winchester, Hampshire, England; d. 17 Dec. 1808 at London, England, aged 79). Elected an MP in 1761, Jenkinson became one of the KING'S FRIENDS. He held office in the ministries of the earl of BUTE (1761–3), George GRENVILLE (1763–5), William PITT the Elder (1766–7), the duke of GRAFTON (1767–70), and Lord NORTH (from 1770). In Dec. 1778 he was appointed secretary at war, an important post as Great Britain was at war with rebellious American colonies. He left office with North after Britain's defeat in 1782.

In 1786 Jenkinson was created Lord Hawkesbury and appointed president of the Board of TRADE in the ministry of William PITT the Younger, serving until 1803. He was created earl of Liverpool in 1796. *See also* AMERICAN WAR OF INDEPENDENCE; LIVERPOOL, 2ND EARL OF.

JENNER, EDWARD (b. 17 May 1749 at Berkeley, Gloucestershire, England; d. 26 Jan. 1823 at Berkeley, aged 73). After studying medicine locally and in London (1770–2), Jenner worked as a general practitioner in Gloucestershire (W England). He was intrigued by the popular belief that survival of cowpox, a mild disease caught from cows, conferred protection against smallpox, a fatal or disfiguring disease. (Since 1721 smallpox had been combated by the unreliable technique of 'variolation', the creation of a mild smallpox infection to provide immunity.) In 1796, after studying cowpox cases, Jenner inoculated cowpox matter into a young boy. Several weeks later he variolated the boy for smallpox, but he failed to develop the disease. Jenner published his findings privately in *Inquiry into the Causes and Effects of the Variolae Vaccinae ...* (1798). Jenner encouraged 'vaccination' (from Latin *vacca*, meaning 'cow'), initially through the Royal Jennerian Society (1803–8) which achieved a dramatic reduction in smallpox deaths. Vaccination subsequently became an important method for tackling diseases. *See also* MEDICINE AND PUBLIC HEALTH.

JERSEY *see* CHANNEL ISLANDS

JEVONS, W.S. (b. 1 Sept. 1835 at Liverpool, Lancashire, England; d. 13 Aug. 1882 at Bulverhythe, Sussex, England, aged 46). After studying at University College, London, William Stanley Jevons worked in AUSTRALIA (1854–9, at the Royal Mint), becoming interested in POLITICAL ECONOMY, philosophy and social problems. He taught at Owens College, MANCHESTER (1863–76), and at UCL (professor of political economy, 1876–80). Jevons attracted attention with *The Coal Question* (1865), which argued that Great Britain's economic strength depended on cheap coal which would diminish in 50 years. He also made important contributions to economic theory and logic. Jevons drowned while swimming.

JEWEL, JOHN (b. 24 May 1522 at Bowden, Devon, England; d. 23 Sept. 1571 at Monkton Farleigh, Wiltshire, England, aged 49). A clergyman and scholar at OXFORD University, Jewel adopted evangelical theology in the 1540s. During the reign of the Catholic Queen MARY I he went into exile (by 1555). He returned in 1559, after the accession of the Protestant ELIZABETH I, and was appointed bishop of Salisbury (consecrated 1560). In 1562 Jewel published the *Apologia pro ecclesia Anglicana*, an official defence of the ELIZABETHAN SETTLEMENT of the English Church against charges of heresy from Catholic critics. *See also* REFORMATION, ENGLAND.

JEWS, ENGLAND AND GREAT BRITAIN FROM 16TH CENTURY After 1290 (expulsion from England), few Jews remained (*see* JEWS, ENGLAND TO 1290). During the 16th century, Marranos (outwardly Christian crypto-Jews) of Spanish and Portuguese origin (Sephardim) settled in LONDON and BRISTOL, alongside the few professing Jews.

Legitimation of Jewish life began in 1656 when the Council of State, possibly influenced by Protector Oliver CROMWELL, granted a petition from London Jews for worship in a house. They started a synagogue, and the (Sephardim) community was protected after the RESTORATION (1660) by CHARLES II and JAMES VII/II, though disabilities applied. In 1697, 12 Jewish merchants were formally admitted to the Royal Exchange. From the late 17th century immigrants of German or Polish origin (Ashkenazim) formed a community. In 1753 legislation for naturalization of foreign-born Jews was quickly repealed because of popular protest.

By 1760, 6000 Jews lived in Great Britain, most in London. New communities were being established (the first at Portsmouth, Hampshire, from 1747). Collaboration by community representatives in the 1760s developed into the Board of Deputies, and by the early 19th century the rabbi of the Ashkenazi 'Great Synagogue' was regarded as 'chief rabbi'. In 1815 Jews numbered 20,000. 'Reformed' synagogues opened from 1842.

From the 1830s major restrictions were removed (e.g., eligibility for parliamentary franchise granted 1835, for municipal offices 1845). The first MP was elected in 1847 though excluded until 1858 (following changes to oaths). The first Jewish government minister was appointed in 1871.

Large-scale immigration fleeing pogroms in the Russian Empire and Prussia in the 1880s–90s increased the population from 65,000 in 1880 to 200,000 in 1905. Immigrants initially dominated the clothing trades. In 1933–9, 60,000 refugees from Nazi Germany were admitted. Jews extensively assimilated to British society and prospered while retaining cultural identity. The population, divided between different 'denominational' outlooks, peaked c.1955 at 410,000, declining to 291,000 by 2012. *See also* DISRAELI, BENJAMIN; HOLOCAUST AND BRITISH GOVERNMENT; ETHNIC AND NATIONAL MINORITIES, ENGLAND/SCOTLAND/WALES.

JEWS, ENGLAND TO 1290 Jews immigrated from northern France after the NORMAN CONQUEST (1066–70s). Many operated as money-lenders, a role difficult for Christians because the Church prohibited usury (lending at interest). Based in towns, Jews lent to kings, nobles, merchants and religious houses. They were taxed heavily, providing by the 1180s one seventh of royal income. From 1194 lending was increasingly supervised through a department of the EXCHEQUER and local centres (eventually 27) which stored agreements. Under King JOHN (1199–1216) and HENRY III (1216–72) taxation reached new heights, impoverishing the community. Jews also experienced physical attacks.

During the 13th century the Church pressed for suppression of usury. English kings resisted until 1275 when usury was forbidden (by Statute of Judaism). The community failed to adapt, and many continued lending. EDWARD I decided on expulsion: on 18 July 1290 Jews were ordered to leave England by 1 Nov. About 3000 migrated to Continental Europe.

JEWS, IRELAND *see* ETHNIC AND NATIONAL MINORITIES, IRELAND

JINGOISM Term denoting vulgar and aggressive nationalism or imperialism. It derives from the exclamation 'by jingo' as used in an English MUSIC HALL song written by G.W. Hunt in 1877 to support the stand of Great Britain's prime minister, Benjamin DISRAELI, against Russian expansion in the BALKANS.

JOAN *see* SIWAN

JOAN OF ARC (b. 1412 at Domrémy, France; d. 30 May 1431 at Rouen, Normandy, aged 18). Peasant girl who, inspired by visions, persuaded French leaders, including the dauphin Charles (unconsecrated king), to allow her to challenge the English siege of ORLÉANS. Her force raised the siege (6–8 May 1429). Further victories followed, and Charles was consecrated (17 July) in Reims Cathedral, the traditional coronation place of French kings.

Joan was captured by Burgundians (allies of the English) on 23 May 1430. Sold to the English for 10,000 francs (by Jan. 1431), she was tried for heresy and burnt in English-held Normandy. She was canonized in 1920. *See also* HUNDRED YEARS WAR.

JOHN (b. 24 Dec. 1167 at Oxford, Oxfordshire, England; d. 18 or 19 Oct. 1216 at Newark, Nottinghamshire, England, aged 48). John was the youngest and favourite son of HENRY II, ruler of the ANGEVIN EMPIRE (*see* REVOLT OF 1173–4). After RICHARD I succeeded (1189), he gave John titles and lands. Yet in Richard's absence, John conspired with Philip II of France against Richard.

John succeeded Richard as king of England (6 April 1199) and duke of NORMANDY but was resisted elsewhere. His succession was recognized by Philip (as feudal overlord) in 1200 in return for concessions (treaty of Le Goulet). John's second marriage (1200) provoked rebellion (1201) in Poitou (W France). It escalated into war with Philip (1202–4), who seized most of John's French lands. John quarrelled with Pope Innocent III (Dec. 1206), refusing to admit Stephen LANGTON as archbishop of Canterbury. He submitted on 13 May 1213, surrendering England and Ireland to papal overlordship (i.e., becoming the Pope's vassal).

John failed to reconquer lost territories (Feb.–Oct. 1214). In England, civil war developed. John agreed peace terms (June 1215; *see* MAGNA CARTA), but reneged with papal support. Fighting resumed. At John's death a French army, supporting rebels, held nearly half of England. HENRY III succeeded. *See also* JOHN AND IRELAND; ARTHUR OF BRITTANY; ENGLAND, FRENCH INVASION (1216–17).

JOHN AND IRELAND John (aged 9) was nominated as king of Ireland by his father, Henry II of England, in 1177. In 1185 Henry formally granted him the lordship of Ireland and requested a crown from the Pope (arrived 1187 but never used). John then visited Ireland (25 April–Dec. 1185), to restrain the leading Anglo-Norman, Hugh de LACY (d. 1186), and establish royal government. Little was achieved, though John retained the lordship.

On his accession in England (1199), John was the first ruler also to be styled 'lord of Ireland'. He developed English government in Ireland (e.g., in 1204 he ordered the building of Dublin Castle). In 1210 he planned an expedition in pursuit of the rebel William de Braose. Though Braose then fled Ireland, the expedition proceeded (20 June–late Aug.): John expelled Braose's protectors, Walter and Hugh de Lacy (sons of the earlier Hugh), and received submissions from English lords and Irish kings. *See also* HENRY II AND IRELAND; IRELAND, ENGLISH CONQUEST, 12TH–13TH CENTURIES.

JOHN, KING OF SCOTS *see* BALLIOL, JOHN

JOHN OF GAUNT (b. March 1340 at Ghent, Flanders; d. 3 Feb. 1399 at Leicester, Leicestershire, England, aged 58). The third surviving son of King EDWARD III of England, Gaunt married (1359) Blanche (d. 1368), daughter of Henry of Grosmont, earl of Lancaster (d. 1361). After the death of Blanche's sister (1362), Gaunt inherited Lancaster's estates and was created duke of Lancaster (1362). Through marriage (1371) to Constanza of Castile (d. 1394) he claimed the Crown of Castile and Léon (Spain). He campaigned in France in the 1370s (*see* HUNDRED YEARS WAR) and defended royal authority during the GOOD PARLIAMENT (1376).

After Edward III's death (1377), Gaunt helped RICHARD II to defeat the PEASANTS' REVOLT (1381). In 1386–7 he unsuccessfully asserted his claim in Castile and afterwards renounced it (1388). Back in England, he attempted to defend Richard against the APPELLANTS. (His son Henry later overthrew Richard: *see* HENRY IV.) Gaunt's liaison with Katherine SWYNFORD (1370s) produced four children (*see* BEAUFORT FAMILY). They married in 1396. John's childhood name 'of Gaunt' (i.e., Ghent) was popularized by Shakespeare's play *Richard II*. *See also* LANCASTRIANS.

JOHN SCOTTUS ERIUGENA (fl. 843– *c*.870). An outstanding philosopher-theologian from Ireland ('Eriugena' means 'born in Ireland'), John attended the court of Charles the Bald, king of the western Franks, in 843. He was fluent in Latin and Greek. His *On Divine Predestination* (850 or 851) was commissioned by Archbishop Hincmar of Reims to rebut arguments for predestination, but was itself condemned (855, 859). His *Periphyseon* ('On the Nature of Things', 860s) was the first major philosophical treatise of medieval Western Europe. John attracted many pupils and followers. *See also* GOLDEN AGE.

JOHNSON, BORIS (b. 19 June 1964 at New York, USA). Leader of the CONSERVATIVE PARTY and British prime minister from 2019.

Of British parents, with Turko-German-Russian ancestry, Johnson studied at Eton College school and OXFORD University (1983–7) and became a journalist. Sacked by *The Times* for fabricating a quote (1988), he joined the *Telegraph*. As its Brussels correspondent (1989–94), he created a reputation for criticism of the EUROPEAN ECONOMIC COMMUNITY (renamed European Union (EU) 1993). Johnson edited the *Spectator* magazine 1999–2005, continuing while an MP (2001–8). In 2008 and 2012 he was elected mayor of LONDON, defeating Labour's Ken LIVINGSTONE. He was re-elected an MP in 2015.

During the 2016 referendum on UK membership of the EU, Johnson was prominent in the successful 'Leave' campaign. In an election for a new Conservative leader (and prime minister), he withdrew after an ally, Michael Gove, revoked support. Appointed foreign secretary by Theresa MAY, Johnson resigned over her proposed EU withdrawal agreement (2018). When Parliament's rejection of the agreement compelled May's resignation, Johnson was elected as successor. His readiness to accept a 'no deal' departure, if necessary, provoked resistance in Parliament, where he lacked a Commons majority. Despite negotiating a revised withdrawal agreement (17 Oct.), he was forced to obtain postponement of the UK's departure from the EU. On 30 Oct. he received parliamentary authority for a general election. Held on 12 Dec., it resulted in a large Conservative majority and approval for withdrawal from the EU (implemented on 31 Jan. 2020). *See also* BREXIT; CAMERON, DAVID.

JOHNSON, SAMUEL (b. 18 Sept. 1709 at Lichfield, Staffordshire, England; d. 13 Dec. 1784 at London, England, aged 75). Unsuccessful as a schoolmaster, Johnson went to London in 1737 where he lived by writing (producing poems, reviews, essays, etc.). Famous for defining 40,000 words in his *Dictionary of the English Language* (from 1746, published 1755), he became a central figure in literary and intellectual life. Politically a TORY, he was known as 'Dr Johnson' after receiving a doctorate from DUBLIN University (1765). His friend James Boswell immortalized him in the *Life of Johnson* (1791).

JOHNSTON, ARCHIBALD, OF WARRISTON (b. Feb. or March 1611 at Edinburgh, SE Scotland; d. 23 July 1663 at Edinburgh, aged 52). An advocate, Johnston helped to draft the NATIONAL COVENANT, was clerk to the GLASGOW ASSEMBLY (both 1638), and supported the Covenanting government. In 1641 the embattled King CHARLES I, seeking supporters, made him a lord of SESSION (as Lord Warriston). Johnston supported the SOLEMN LEAGUE AND COVENANT (1643) and attended the WESTMINSTER ASSEMBLY (1644).

In 1648 Johnston led opposition to the ENGAGEMENT with Charles (Dec. 1647), but after Charles's execution (1649) briefly supported CHARLES II (created lord clerk register 1649). In late 1650 he broke with Charles and led the REMONSTRANTS. From 1657 he served Oliver CROMWELL (as lord clerk register).

At the RESTORATION (1660) Johnston fled abroad and in his absence was condemned to death for treason (1661). He was captured in France in 1663, taken to Scotland, and hanged. *See also* COVENANTING REVOLUTION; SCOTLAND, CHURCH OF; HENDERSON, ALEXANDER.

JOHNSTON, TOM (b. 2 Nov. 1881 at Kirkintilloch, Dunbartonshire, Scotland; d. 5 Sept. 1965 at Milngavie, Dunbartonshire, aged 83). Johnston founded and edited the socialist weekly *Forward* (1906–33) and was Labour MP for West Stirlingshire (1922–4, 1929–31, 1935–45) and Dundee (1924–9). He served in the Labour government of 1929–31.

At the outbreak of WORLD WAR II (1939), Johnston was appointed regional commissioner for Scotland, in charge of EVACUATION. As secretary of state for Scotland (1941–5) he developed hydro-electric power generation in the HIGHLANDS

and introduced free health-care, anticipating the post-war NATIONAL HEALTH SERVICE. He left politics in 1945, and served as chairman of the North of Scotland Hydro-Electric Board (1945–59). *See also* RED CLYDESIDE; ELECTRICITY INDUSTRY AND ELECTRIFICATION, GREAT BRITAIN.

JOINT-STOCK COMPANY A form of BUSINESS ORGANIZATION in which capital is divided into shares to spread risk. Such companies were created in England and Scotland from the mid 16th century under the Crown (e.g., Muscovy Company, England, 1555), and also from the later 17th century by articles of association, and in Scotland by the Council for Trade (established 1661). The 'Bubble Act' passed by the British Parliament in 1720 restricted their formation by requiring a royal charter or Act of Parliament, though it was unenforced in Scotland (repealed 1825). From 1844 companies could be incorporated by registration. Joint-stock companies were used for building CANALS and RAILWAYS, and by some BANKS. They became popular for industrial concerns from the late 19th century because they facilitated large enterprises.

JONES, GRIFFITH (b. 1683 at Penboyr, Carmarthenshire, Wales; d. 8 April 1761 at Laugharne, Carmarthenshire, aged 77). Educator. Ordained a priest (1708) in the Church of England, which included Wales, Jones became a powerful preacher. He was rector of Llanddowror (Carmarthenshire) from 1716. In the 1730s he started 'circulating schools', initially in Carmarthenshire, to enable children and adults to read the Bible. Taught by itinerant teachers, they met in churches, barns and houses. By 1761, 3325 schools had been held in 1600 places, educating perhaps 250,000 people. Jones's work was supported and continued by Bridget BEVAN. *See also* EDUCATION, WALES; LITERACY, WALES; ROWLAND, DANIEL.

JONES, INIGO (b. 15 July 1573 at London, England; d. 21 June 1652 at London, aged 78). Jones visited Italy *c.*1600. Soon afterwards he was employed at the English royal court as a designer of MASQUES, sometimes with Ben JONSON (1605–31). He visited France in 1609 and Italy again in 1613. Appointed surveyor-general to King JAMES VI/I in 1615, he designed classical-style buildings influenced by the Italian architect Andrea Palladio (1508–80). They included the Banqueting House in Whitehall, WESTMINSTER (1619–22). He was England's first Renaissance architect. *See also* TOWN PLANNING.

JONES, JOHN VIRIAMU (b. 2 Jan. 1856 at Swansea, Glamorgan, Wales; d. 1 June 1901 at Geneva, Switzerland, aged 45). Physicist and first principal of University College, CARDIFF; appointed in 1883, aged 27. A supporter of the Welsh language, Jones was the leading figure in the establishment of the federal University of Wales (1893), of which he was the first vice-chancellor. *See also* UNIVERSITIES, WALES.

JONES, MICHAEL (b. between 1606 and 1610 in Ireland; d. 10 Dec. 1649 at Dungarvan, Co. Waterford, Ireland, aged about 41). An Irish Puritan, Jones became a Parliamentarian in England in spring 1644, fearing that King CHARLES I would make extensive concessions to Irish Catholics. He fought for Parliament in England 1644–6.

In June 1647 Jones returned to Ireland as commander of Parliamentary forces in Leinster (E Ireland) and secured DUBLIN (surrendered to him by the Royalist chief governor the marquess of ORMOND). On 2 Aug. 1649 Jones destroyed Royalist forces at Baggotsrath and Rathmines (near Dublin), which enabled Oliver Cromwell to conquer E and S Ireland rapidly in 1649–50. Jones served as Cromwell's second-in-command. He died of disease. *See also* IRISH WARS, 1641–52; CROMWELL, OLIVER, AND IRELAND.

JONES, THOMAS (b. 27 Sept. 1870 at Rhymney, Monmouthshire, Wales; d. 15 Oct. 1955 at Birchington, Kent, England, aged 85). Civil servant; deputy secretary of the British CABINET 1916–30, chosen by David LLOYD GEORGE. Jones was involved in negotiations for the ANGLO-IRISH TREATY of 1921. From 1933 he led organizations relieving social distress in Wales (*see* GREAT DEPRESSION, IMPACT ON GREAT BRITAIN). President of University College, Aberystwyth, 1944–54.

JONSON, BEN (b. 11 June 1572 in SE England; d. Aug. 1637 at Westminster, Middlesex, England, aged 65). An actor and playwright by 1597, Jonson composed mainly comedies and satires, but also political tragedies (e.g., *Sejanus*, 1603). He was regularly employed by the court of King JAMES VI/I to compose MASQUES, often in collaboration with Inigo JONES (from 1605 until they fell out in 1631). Jonson's works display classical learning and elegance, but also mordant social observations. *See also* ENGLISH LITERATURE, ENGLAND.

JORDAN, BRITISH RELATIONS WITH After independence (1946), the kingdom of TRANSJORDAN (Jordan from 1949) initially remained firmly allied to Great Britain. But the principal British adviser, Sir John Glubb (nicknamed 'Glubb Pasha'), was dismissed in March 1956 because Arab nationalists believed him too influential. Some British influence survived the SUEZ CRISIS (July–Dec. 1956), and in July 1958 British troops intervened to defend King Hussein after the monarchy had been overthrown in neighbouring Iraq.

After 1967, when Israel seized the 'West Bank' from Jordan, Jordan sought closer alliance with other Arab states. But it remained pro-Western, despite sympathy for Iraq during the IRAQ WAR (1990–1), a tendency assisted by its peace treaty with Israel (1994). There have been strong links between the British and Jordanian military forces and royal families. From 2012 Britain provided financial support for Syrian refugees in Jordan.

JOWETT, BENJAMIN (b. 15 April 1817 at Camberwell, Surrey, England; d. 10 Oct. 1893 at Headley Park, Hampshire, England, aged 76). A fellow of Balliol College at OXFORD University from 1838 and Church of England clergyman, Jowett studied Biblical texts using the critical approach applied to classical texts. His publications (e.g., commentary on four Pauline Epistles, 1855) caused controversy. As master of Balliol from 1870, he made it the leading Oxford college and influential in public affairs. Middle-class and overseas boys were persuaded to enter the college, and Jowett encouraged them into political life or the CIVIL SERVICE. As vice-chancellor of Oxford 1882–6, Jowett implemented reforms (e.g., creation of faculty boards). *See also* GREEN, T.H.

JULIAN OF NORWICH *see* ENGLISH MYSTICS

JUNIUS, LETTERS OF In England, a series of 70 letters signed by 'Junius' which appeared in the *Public Advertiser*, a popular newspaper, between Jan. 1769 and Jan. 1772 and were widely reprinted. They were bitterly critical of the ministries of the duke of GRAFTON and Lord NORTH, and attacked the influence of King GEORGE III. The author was probably Philip Francis (1740–1818), a clerk at the War Office.

JUNTO *see* WHIG JUNTO

JUSTICES OF THE PEACE, ENGLAND Crown-appointed judicial and administrative officers who were important in the government of counties (or SHIRES) 14th–19th centuries. Their office developed from that of 'keeper of the peace', which was established to assist SHERIFFS following the BARONIAL CONFLICT AND WARS (1258–67). Under King EDWARD II (ruled 1307–27) keepers also led commissions to restore order, and from 1330 dealt with felonies and made arrests. From 1361 keepers were titled 'justices of the peace' (JPs) and required to hold trials four times a year ('quarter sessions'). The Crown appointed a 'commission of the peace' annually for each county. Justices were often called 'magistrates', were usually GENTRY, and were unpaid.

From the 16th century justices were given considerable additional responsibilities: maintaining unfunded bridges (1531), licensing inns and alehouses (1552), supervising local road repairs (1555), licensing itinerant traders (1563–1772), implementing other economic legislation (e.g., Statute of ARTIFICERS, 1563), and (from 1572) supervising operation of the poor laws (*see* POOR RELIEF, ENGLAND AND WALES).

From 1605 the PRIVY COUNCIL encouraged 'petty sessions' (sessions for minor business held by single magistrates), and from 1631 JPs were required to report regularly to the Council (*see* BOOK OF ORDERS). New responsibilities from the late 17th century were often political and religious: checking Anglican allegiance under the 1673 TEST ACT, registering dissenters' meeting houses (1688), registering FRIENDLY SOCIETIES (1793). From the late 18th century lay gentry became reluctant to serve and many justices were Church of England clergymen (25% by 1800).

JPs lost many administrative functions in 1889 (transferred to county councils). They continued to undertake judicial work and license public houses. From 1972 quarter sessions ceased. Magistrates' courts became part of the Crown Court, undertaking preliminary hearings (before transfer to a higher court) and dealing with lesser offences. *See also* COURTS, ENGLAND BEFORE/FROM 1660; LAW, ENGLAND FROM 1066.

JUSTICES OF THE PEACE, IRELAND 'Keepers of the peace', mentioned from 1277, were appointed in Crown-controlled SHIRES from among Anglo-Irish lords to help sheriffs deal with felons and rebels (particularly Gaelic Irish), and supervise Anglo-Irish military forces.

By the mid 16th century keepers (or 'magistrates', or 'justices of the peace', JPs) in the English PALE held judicial 'quarter sessions' for lesser criminal and civil matters. By the early 17th century sessions were held throughout Ireland, following the reassertion of English authority. (JPs were appointed to shire or county commissions by the chancellor and were unpaid.) Catholics were denied office from 1607, though some were appointed in the mid and later 17th century. In the 18th century JPs were central to the PROTESTANT ASCENDANCY; quarter sessions were the most important local courts (with mayors and aldermen serving as magistrates in towns), and JPs supervised other local officials (*see* LOCAL GOVERNMENTAL STRUCTURES, IRELAND).

From the later 18th century JPs struggled to suppress unrest and radicalism, despite receiving special powers (*see* INSURRECTION ACTS). Though Catholics were permitted from 1793 (*see* HOBART'S ACT), most JPs were Protestants and considered partial. Barristers were appointed as assistants from 1796; in the 19th century the parallel paid office of RESIDENT MAGISTRATE was developed. More Catholics and liberal Protestants were appointed from the late 1830s. 'Petty sessions' (hearings for minor offences by an individual JP) were introduced in the 1820s.

In the IRISH FREE STATE, JPs were replaced by 'peace commissioners' (1924). In NORTHERN IRELAND, JPs' judicial powers were transferred to resident magistrates in 1935.

JUSTICES OF THE PEACE, SCOTLAND An Act of the Scottish Parliament attempted to introduce shire justices (or commissioners), similar to those in England, in 1587. It failed, as largely did an Act of 1609 which instituted JPs to indict malefactors, combat vagrancy and oversee roads, alehouses, weights and measures, and wages.

A national system was established more effectively after the UNION OF ENGLAND AND SCOTLAND (1707), when JPs supervised weights and measures, wages, working hours and prisons, and from 1718 roads, poor law and vagabonds (working with COMMISSIONERS OF SUPPLY). Justices held district and shire courts (or sessions), which increased in importance after the abolition of HERITABLE JURISDICTIONS (1747).

During the 19th century JPs lost administrative powers to other bodies, particularly from 1890 to county councils. From 1975 sessions were replaced by new District Courts in which JPs dealt with minor criminal matters (e.g., breaches of the peace, petty vandalism). When District Courts were abolished (2008–10), new Justice of the Peace Courts were established, organized by sheriffdoms. *See also* COURTS, SCOTLAND; POLICE, SCOTLAND.

JUSTICES OF THE PEACE, WALES The institution of justices (or JPs) in Wales, to combat disorder, was a central purpose of the UNION OF WALES WITH ENGLAND. The policy involved the creation of SHIRES where none existed, so that arrangements in England were replicated throughout Wales. Justices were selected from local GENTRY, thereby giving Wales native governors. They began work in 1541–3, holding 'quarter sessions' in main towns and providing local justice and government. Courts dealt with such matters as theft, assault, selection of parish officers, and repair of bridges.

JPs lost administrative duties to county councils after the Local Government Act of 1888 but judicial work continued. Sessions ceased in 1972 when JPs became part of the Crown Court (*see* COURTS, ENGLAND FROM 1660). *See also* LOCAL GOVERNMENTAL STRUCTURES, WALES; GREAT SESSIONS, COURT OF.

JUSTICIARS, SCOTLAND The highest royal officers responsible for justice (especially major crimes and appeals); the post was copied from England by King DAVID I (ruled 1124–53); justiciars operated through ayres and courts. Separate appointments were made (usually of MAGNATES) for LOTHIAN (SE Scotland) and Scotia (N of R. Forth); also for GALLOWAY (SW Scotland) in later 12th and later 13th centuries. From the early 16th century only one officer was appointed, the justice-general.

In 1672 the former justiciars' courts were reinvigorated as the High Court of JUSTICIARY. From 1837 the post of justice-general was held by the lord president of the Court of SESSION. *See also* COURTS, SCOTLAND; EYRE; REGALITY.

JUSTICIARY, HIGH COURT OF A criminal court for major cases in Scotland. It was established in 1672, to reinvigorate royal criminal jurisdiction. It originally comprised the justice-general, justice-clerk, and five judges of the Court of Session (as commissioners of justiciary), who sat in Edinburgh and elsewhere on circuit. Its importance increased after the abolition of HERITABLE JURISDICTIONS in 1747. A superior Court of Criminal Appeal was founded in 1926. *See also* COURTS, SCOTLAND; JUSTICIARS, SCOTLAND.

JUTES One of three Continental Germanic peoples which, according to BEDE (in 731), produced migrants to southern Britain (5th–6th centuries). Originating in the Jutland peninsula in N Europe (modern Denmark and adjacent N Germany), after which they are named, Jutes (OE, Iotas) migrated to two areas: (modern) E Kent and (farther westwards) the Isle of Wight and the mainland to the N (in modern Hampshire). Bede's statement is supported by archaeological evidence (e.g., pottery).

Kings of KENT (6th–8th centuries) were probably of Jutish origin, although the kingdom's inhabitants were known in the 7th century as Cantwara ('Men of Kent'). Kings of Jutish origin apparently ruled the Isle of Wight until the late 7th century, though the adjacent mainland was probably controlled by rulers of the Gewisse (i.e., WESSEX) from the 660s. The Isle of Wight was conquered by King Cadwalla of Wessex in 686. *See also* GERMANIC IMMIGRATION, SOUTHERN BRITAIN.

K

KAILYARD Scots term, meaning 'cabbage patch', which was applied pejoratively in 1895 to a school of Scottish fiction (popular 1880–1914). Kailyard writers typically set stories in idyllic, pre-industrial Lowland rural communities in which old-fashioned values prevailed. Events usually had happy endings. Notable Kailyard writers included J.M. Barrie (1860–1937) and S.R. Crockett (1859–1914). Kailyard novels were particularly popular in overseas Scottish communities. *See also* SCOTS LANGUAGE AND LITERATURE.

KATHERINE OF ARAGON (b. 16 Dec. 1485 at Alcalá de Henares, Castile, Spain; d. 7 Jan. 1536 at Kimbolton, Huntingdonshire, England, aged 50). Originally married in England (14 Nov. 1501) to Prince ARTHUR (d. 1502), Katherine subsequently married his brother King HENRY VIII (11 June 1509). She bore six children (1510–18) but only one, MARY, survived infancy. Failure to produce a male heir caused Henry to seek a divorce (from 1527). Katherine resisted and the couple lived apart (final meeting 11 July 1531). The marriage was pronounced invalid in 1533. *See also* HENRY VII; MEDINA DEL CAMPO, TREATY OF; GREAT MATTER; HENRY VIII, WIVES OF.

KAY, JOHN (b. 16 July 1704 at Walmersley, Lancashire, England; d. 1780 or 1781 in France, aged about 76). A maker of reeds (weaving devices), Kay invented the 'wheel-shuttle' (later known as the 'flying shuttle'). Patented in 1733, it could double a hand weaver's work rate. It was quickly adopted in the woollen industry, and used in the cotton industry from the 1750s. Kay emigrated to France in 1747 where he improved card-making machinery and produced other innovations. *See also* COTTON INDUSTRY, ENGLAND.

KAY-SHUTTLEWORTH, J.P. (b. 20 July 1804 at Rochdale, Lancashire, England; d. 26 May 1877 at London, England, aged 72). James Phillips Kay (Kay-Shuttleworth from 1842) became concerned about the poor from the 1820s, while studying medicine in EDINBURGH and practising in MANCHESTER. An assistant poor law commissioner from 1835 (in E England), he concluded that improvement in social conditions required better schooling. He served 1839–48 as assistant secretary to the PRIVY COUNCIL Committee on Education (for England and Wales). He sought to raise standards through schools inspectors, by using promising children as pupil-teachers, and by founding Battersea College (Surrey) for teacher-training (1840). He advocated state provision of education. *See also* EDUCATION, ENGLAND.

KEBLE, JOHN (b. 25 April 1792 at Fairford, Gloucestershire, England; d. 29 March 1866 at Bournemouth, Dorset, England, aged 73). A fellow of Oriel College, OXFORD, from 1812, and Church of England clergyman, Keble became friendly in the 1820s with John Henry NEWMAN and E.B. PUSEY. He ministered in rural parishes from 1825, and in 1827 published the popular poetry collection *The Christian Year*. He was professor of poetry at Oxford 1831–41.

A Dictionary of British and Irish History, First Edition. Edited by Robert Peberdy and Philip Waller.
© 2021 John Wiley & Sons Ltd; © editorial matter and organisation Robert Peberdy and Phillip Waller.
Published 2021 by John Wiley & Sons Ltd.

On 14 July 1833, in his 'assize sermon' at St Mary's Church, Oxford, Keble attacked the British government for assuming authority to reorganize the Church in Ireland. The event is regarded as the start of the OXFORD MOVEMENT. *See also* IRELAND, CHURCH OF.

KELLS, BOOK OF A large-format manuscript book (in Trinity College, Dublin, Ireland) containing the Gospels and 40 full-page illustrations (showing Christ, the Evangelists, etc.); an outstanding example of Irish culture of the GOLDEN AGE. Started in the late 8th century on IONA (off Mull, W of Scotland), it was taken to Kells (in modern Co. Meath, E Ireland), and probably finished there, because of VIKING raids on Iona. (Iona and Kells were both founded by COLUMBA.)

KELVIN, LORD *see* THOMSON, WILLIAM

KEMPE, MARGERY (b. *c.*1373 at Bishop's Lynn, Norfolk, England; d. in or after 1438 in England). After experiencing visions during childbirth, Margery embarked on an independent religious life. Though married she took a vow of chastity (1413), made pilgrimages in England and overseas, and sought spiritual counsel from senior clergy, some of whom considered her a heretic. She recorded her life in a vivid autobiography, *The Book of Margery Kempe*, which she dictated in old age to a priest at Syon Abbey (Middlesex).

KENILWORTH A town in Warwickshire (C England). Its name, derived from an earlier settlement, means 'Cynehild's enclosure'. The town and a castle were founded in the 1120s by a BARON.

In 1253 Kenilworth Castle was granted by King HENRY III to Simon de MONTFORT, who used it as a power base. After Montfort's death (Aug. 1265), some of his supporters were besieged in the castle by royalists (June–Dec. 1266). In the late 14th century a great hall and apartments were built for JOHN OF GAUNT. In 1562 the castle was granted by ELIZABETH I to Robert, earl of LEICESTER (d. 1588). Sections were demolished in 1649 by Parliamentarians to make it untenable (*see* CIVIL WARS). The town was essentially a market centre for its area. *See also* KENILWORTH, DICTUM OF.

Est. popn: 1300, 800; 1600, 700; 1800, 900; 1900, 4500; 2000, 22,000.

KENILWORTH, DICTUM OF In England, a declaration issued on 31 Oct. 1266 by an elected committee of 12 BARONS and bishops to govern the restoration of disinherited estates (confiscated from supporters of Simon de MONTFORT) following the BARONIAL CONFLICT AND WARS. It ruled that lands could be recovered on payment of a sum equal to half of their total value.

KENNEDY, JAMES (b. *c.*1408; d. 24 May 1465 at St Andrews, Fife, E Scotland, aged about 57). A grandson of King ROBERT III (d. 1406), Kennedy was appointed bishop of DUNKELD (1437) by JAMES I against the wishes of Pope Eugenius IV; but he won favour by supporting the papacy against Scottish conciliarists (supporters of Church councils) and was appointed bishop of ST ANDREWS (1441).

In 1444 (during the minority of JAMES II), after William, (8th) earl of Douglas, secured a dominant position in government with the Livingston family, Kennedy was threatened with deprivation and his lands were harried. He withdrew from politics and spent periods abroad. In 1450 he founded St Salvator's College at St Andrews for promoting theology and training parish clergy.

Kennedy returned to prominence in 1461, during the minority of JAMES III when James's mother, Mary of Guelders, was dominant. She sought agreement with the Yorkist EDWARD IV in England whereas Kennedy advocated restoration of the Lancastrians (*see* YORKIST–LANCASTRIAN CONFLICT). Kennedy directed the government after Mary's death (1463).

KENNETH I MAC ALPIN (Gaelic, Cináed mac Alpin; fl. from 836; d. 13 Feb. 858 at Forteviot, C Scotland). King of SCOTS 840–58 and of PICTS *c.*842–58.

Probably a Scot of obscure origin, Kenneth exploited disruption caused by VIKING attacks to establish authority over (Scottish) DÁL RIATA (W Scotland) and, in a longer process, over the Picts (840s). To consolidate union, he moved relics of COLUMBA from IONA (off W Scotland) to DUNKELD (C Scotland) in 848 or 849. Likewise he made SCONE (C Scotland) a primary political centre (*see* INAUGURATION, SCOTLAND). Scots and Picts had sometimes had common rulers; the MAC ALPIN KINGS made union permanent. Kenneth also raided LOTHIAN (in English NORTHUMBRIA) six times, but was attacked by Britons from STRATHCLYDE.

Kenneth died of cancer and was succeeded by his brother Donald I (Gaelic, Domnall mac Alpin; ruled 858–62) and by his sons Constantine I (Causantín mac Cináedon, 862–76) and Aed (Áed mac Cináedon, 876–8); by Donald's son Giric (Giric mac Dúngaile, *c.*878– *c.*889) perhaps ruling concurrently with Eochaid, son of Kenneth's daughter, and by Constantine I's son DONALD II. *See also* MAC ALPIN KINGS; KINGSHIP, SCOTTISH; UNION OF SCOTS AND PICTS.

KENNETH II (Gaelic, Cináed mac Maíl Choluim; fl. from 971; d. 995 at Fettercairn, Mearns, E Scotland). King of Scots (Scotland) 971–95.

A younger son of MALCOLM I, Kenneth succeeded Culen (cousin). He raided STRATHCLYDE unsuccessfully in 971, and more successfully in 972. He also raided England. In 973 EDGAR, king of England, may have recognized Scottish control of LOTHIAN (modern SE Scotland). Within Scotland, feud persisted within the royal dynasty: Kenneth killed his predecessor's brother Olaf (977), but was later killed by internal enemies.

Kenneth was succeeded by a cousin (son of Culen), Constantine III (Gaelic, Causantín mac Cuilén; ruled 995–7), who was killed and succeeded by Kenneth II's nephew Kenneth III (Cináed mac Duib; 997–1005). The latter was killed and succeeded by Kenneth II's son MALCOLM II. *See also* MAC ALPIN KINGS.

KENNY, ENDA (b. 24 April 1951 at Islandeady, Co. Mayo, Republic of Ireland). Kenny succeeded his father as a FINE GAEL TD in 1975 (at a by-election), and served in the government of John BRUTON (1994–7). After Fine Gael's disastrous performance in the 2002 general election, he was elected party leader (succeeded Michael Noonan). At the 2011 election, following the financial crisis of 2008, Fine Gael became the largest party and Kenny became taoiseach (premier) of a coalition with LABOUR.

Kenny's premiership saw the State visit of Queen ELIZABETH II (2011). More capital was provided for Ireland's main banks, but in Dec. 2013 the financial 'bailout' by the EUROPEAN UNION and International Monetary Fund was terminated. Thereafter Kenny's government sought to maintain disciplined management of the public finances while prioritizing job creation. At the 2016 election Fine Gael remained the largest party but Labour collapsed. After ten weeks of negotiations, Kenny continued as taoiseach in coalition with TDs from 'small' parties and with some support from Fianna Fáil. He was the first Fine Gael leader to achieve re-election. He retired as party leader and taoiseach in 2017 (succeeded by Leo VARADKAR). *See also* CHURCH–STATE RELATIONS, SOUTHERN IRELAND FROM 1922.

KENSINGTON PALACE A royal residence in England, formerly in Middlesex (now within London). It was the main home of the royal family in the later 17th–mid 18th centuries.

Dating from *c.*1605 and named Nottingham House in 1681, the building with its grounds was purchased by King WILLIAM III and Queen MARY II in 1689 because they found WHITEHALL PALACE unhealthy. They commissioned enlargements from Christopher WREN. The palace was also the home of ANNE, GEORGE I and GEORGE II. After further enlargement for George I, it comprised buildings around three courtyards.

After GEORGE III moved (1762; *see* BUCKINGHAM PALACE), Kensington Palace was frequently inhabited by secondary members of the royal family, including Princess VICTORIA (until 1837), Prince CHARLES and Princess DIANA (from 1981), and the duke and duchess of CAMBRIDGE (from 2011). Victoria's grandson Prince Arthur

of Connaught nicknamed the palace 'the aunt heap'. Its State Apartments were open to the public from 1899.

KENT, KINGDOM OF A Germanic-ruled kingdom (6th–8th centuries), occupying the historical county of Kent (SE England) and adjacent lands. It was based on the Roman *CIVITAS* of the Cantiaci, from which its name was derived (OE, Cænt). The Roman territory possibly became independent (early 5th century). Settlement by JUTES took place in the 5th century, and a kingdom was formed in the 6th century which possibly reunited small territories. W Kent remained under a subking.

The first documented king is Eormenric (late 6th century). His son ÆTHELBERT (d. 616) was the first Anglo-Saxon king to accept Christianity. He established bishoprics at CANTERBURY and Rochester. By 764 King OFFA of MERCIA exercised authority, though he was temporarily dislodged (776–85). Kent was ruled by a Mercian subking from 798, ruled directly by Mercia from 807, and absorbed by WESSEX in 825. *See also* KINGSHIP, ANGLO-SAXON.

KENTIGERN OR MUNGO (d. between 612 and 614, probably in N Britain). A monk and bishop; the presumed founder in the later 6th century of a monastery in the British kingdom of Clyde Rock, possibly at GLASGOW (*see* STRATHCLYDE (CLYDE ROCK), KINGDOM OF). He is the dedicatee (as saint) of Glasgow Cathedral, where his relics were venerated until the REFORMATION (1560). He was also known by pet-forms of his name, in Gaelic and Brittonic, which became Mungo in English. *See also* CHURCH, MEDIEVAL NORTH BRITAIN AND SCOTLAND; ST ASAPH.

KENYA A former British colony in E Africa. It originated in 1888 when the Imperial British East Africa Company leased a coastal area from ZANZIBAR. In 1895 the British government assumed control, claimed the hinterland, and declared the East Africa Protectorate. This was converted into a CROWN COLONY in 1920 and renamed Kenya. White farmers had been encouraged to settle but in 1923 were refused self-government. Indian labourers were imported to help build railways.

The MAU MAU REVOLT (1952–4) disrupted constitutional reforms, but Kenya was granted independence under the British Crown in 1963. It became a republic in 1964 with Jomo KENYATTA as president. Approx. population in 1921, 2,529,000; in 1962, 8,636,000. *See also* EAST AFRICA, BRITISH INVOLVEMENT.

KENYATTA, JOMO (b. *c.*1895 at Ngenda, British East Africa; d. 22 Aug. 1978 at Mombasa, Kenya, aged about 83). Kenyatta visited Great Britain, Europe and the USSR 1929–30 as a representative of Kikuyu people, and worked and studied in Britain from 1931 (in USSR 1932–3). Returning to KENYA in 1946, he became leader of the Kenyan African Union, but in 1952 was convicted by the colonial authorities of involvement in the MAU MAU REVOLT and imprisoned. Released in 1961, he became leader of the Kenya African National Union, a member of Kenya's Parliament (1962), and prime minister (May 1963). Following independence (Dec. 1963), Kenyatta served as president (Dec. 1964 until death).

KERNS In Ireland, term used by Anglo-Irish for lightly armed Gaelic Irish infantry. They served Anglo-Normans as mercenaries after the Anglo-Norman invasion (1169–70), and remained important in Irish warfare until the 17th century. Lacking armour, they fought with swords, bows and javelins, and mainly engaged in harrying and plundering.

KETTLE, THOMAS (b. 9 Feb. 1880 at Artane, Co. Dublin, Ireland; d. 9 Sept. 1916 at Givenchy, France, aged 36). A lawyer and, as MP (1906–10), a strong advocate of the constitutionalist Home Rule cause, Kettle was professor of National Economics of Ireland at the National University of Ireland from 1910. When the UK entered WORLD WAR I (Aug. 1914), Kettle supported Irish participation (unlike many nationalists) and served in the British Army. He died at the battle of the SOMME. *See also* HOME RULE MOVEMENT, IRELAND.

KETT'S REBELLION A revolt in Norfolk (E England) in 1549, during the reign of King EDWARD VI. Provoked by economic grievances, especially enclosure of common lands, the rebellion began in early July and was led by landowner Robert Kett. By 16 July the rebels numbered 16,000. After occupying NORWICH (23 July), they repulsed a royal army (30 July). They were eventually defeated at nearby Dussindale by an army commanded by the earl of Warwick (27 Aug.). Kett was executed by being suspended in chains against the wall of Norwich Castle (7 Dec.). *See also* NORTHUMBERLAND, JOHN DUKE OF.

KEYNES, J. M. (b. 5 June 1883 at Cambridge, Cambridgeshire, England; d. 21 April 1946 at West Firle, East Sussex, England, aged 62). Economist, member of the BLOOMSBURY GROUP, and (from 1909) fellow of King's College, CAMBRIDGE.

A temporary British Treasury civil servant 1915–19, and adviser at the PARIS PEACE CONFERENCE, (John) Maynard Keynes was made famous by his attack on the treaty of VERSAILLES, *The Economic Consequences of the Peace* (Dec. 1919); it claimed that reparations imposed on Germany would create harsh conditions throughout Europe. In 1924 he criticized Great Britain's proposed return to the pre-war GOLD STANDARD for endangering industrial competitiveness. His book *The General Theory of Employment, Interest and Money* (1936) argued that economic depression could

become sustained for lack of savings and private investment. He advocated increased government expenditure to generate economic growth, an idea that remained influential. Keynes also contributed to the BRETTON WOODS AGREEMENTS (1944). *See also* GREAT DEPRESSION, IMPACT ON GREAT BRITAIN; ECONOMY, STATE INVOLVEMENT, BRITAIN.

KHAKI ELECTION In Great Britain, nickname for the general election of Oct. 1900, held during the (Second) BOER WAR. The CONSERVATIVE PARTY exploited successes in the war, over which the LIBERAL PARTY was divided, and won with a slightly increased majority. Lord SALISBURY remained prime minister. Khaki was the colour of the new army uniform.

KILBLEAN, BATTLE OF *see* CULBLEAN, BATTLE OF

KILDARE A town in Co. Kildare, Republic of Ireland; from Irish, Cill Dara, meaning 'Church of the oak'.

Situated in LEINSTER (E Ireland), Kildare was originally an ecclesiastical centre (monastic and lay settlement), allegedly founded by BRIGIT (early 6th century) and dominated by Uí Dúnlainge kings in the 7th–9th centuries. It survived VIKING attacks and became a diocesan see in 1111. A town was founded in the 12th or 13th century which remained a local market centre. *See also* MONASTICISM, MEDIEVAL IRELAND.

KILDARE, 8TH EARL OF (b. 1456 in Ireland; d. 3 Sept. 1513 at Athy, Co. Kildare, Ireland, aged about 57). Gerald Fitzgerald (known in Irish as Gearóid Mór, Gerald 'the Elder') succeeded as earl in 1478 and from 1479 was the English king's governor in Ireland. As a Yorkist his position was threatened when Henry Tudor, a Lancastrian, seized the English throne (1485). Kildare survived involvement in the Yorkist SIMNEL rebellion (1487), but his suspected support for Perkin WARBECK (1491–2) provoked replacement (20 May 1492). He was arrested by Edward POYNINGS and sent to England (1495–6). After Henry strengthened English control over the Irish government, Kildare was reappointed (4 Aug. 1496) and served until his death. *See also* YORKIST–LANCASTRIAN CONFLICT, ROLE OF IRELAND; HENRY VII AND IRELAND; KILDARE ASCENDANCY.

KILDARE, 9TH EARL OF (b. 1487 in Ireland; d. 2 Sept. 1534 at London, England, aged 46 or 47). Gerald Fitzgerald was raised in England (1493–1503). In 1513 he succeeded his father as earl, and as the leading Anglo-Irish magnate and chief governor of Ireland (lord deputy) but he faced interventions by Henry VIII.

Kildare served as governor 1513–20, 1524–8 and 1532–4. In each period he was summoned to court in England to answer complaints (absent 1515, 1519–23, 1526–30, 1534) and lost office; but Henry reappointed him because replacement governors failed to keep peace and raise funds. His final deprivation (June 1534) occurred after his son attacked Henry's rule (*see* OFFALY, LORD). Kildare was imprisoned in the Tower of London (29 June), where he died. *See also* KILDARE ASCENDANCY; HENRY VIII AND IRELAND; SURREY EXPEDITION.

KILDARE, 10TH EARL OF *see* OFFALY, LORD

KILDARE, 11TH EARL OF (b. 28 Feb. 1525, probably in Ireland; d. 16 Nov. 1585 at London, England, aged 60). Gerald Fitzgerald was a son of the 9th earl of KILDARE and half-brother of Lord OFFALY (10th earl), whose rebellion (1534) resulted in forfeiture of his family's estates and titles (*see* KILDARE REBELLION). Following his father's death (1534), Fitzgerald was protected by relatives and then taken abroad (1540).

In 1552, to conciliate the Anglo-Irish, Protector SOMERSET allowed Fitzgerald to return to Ireland. Queen MARY I created a new Kildare earldom for him and returned most estates (1554). Under ELIZABETH I he conformed to Protestantism and regained all estates and titles (1569). Though he enjoyed great prestige, Kildare was unable to restore his family's previous dominant position in Ireland. *See also* KILDARE ASCENDANCY.

KILDARE, EARLS OF An Anglo-Irish noble family. The earldom of Kildare was created in 1316 for John fitz Thomas (fl. from 1287; d. 1316), a descendant of Maurice fitz Gerald who invaded Ireland in 1169 (*see* GERALDINES). Its chief estates were in Co. Kildare (in Leinster, E Ireland). The 7th, 8th and 9th earls dominated Ireland between 1471 and 1534 (*see* KILDARE ASCENDANCY). The 7th and 8th earls also sympathized with YORKISTS in England (*see* YORKIST–LANCASTRIAN CONFLICT, ROLE OF IRELAND; BUTLER–GERALDINE FEUD). The 9th earl's son, Lord OFFALY (Thomas Fitzgerald), rebelled against HENRY VIII of England (1534), resulting in his forfeiture of the earldom (1536) and execution (*see* KILDARE REBELLION).

Thomas's half-brother, Gerald Fitzgerald (1525–85), was created earl of Kildare (new grant, 1554), and restored to the historical earldom (1569). He conformed to Protestantism under ELIZABETH I. The 20th earl, James Fitzgerald (1722–73, earl from 1744), held government posts and was created duke of Leinster (1766). Maurice FitzGerald (b. 1948) succeeded as 9th duke in 2004.

KILDARE ASCENDANCY Historians' term for the period 1471 to 1534 in Ireland when the English government was headed (with interruptions) by the Anglo-Irish magnates the 7th, 8th and 9th earls of Kildare, with various official titles. (Before and afterwards, governors were fre-

quently sent from England.) With estates near the PALE, the Kildares were able to organize its defence. They used PATRONAGE to control the Council and Parliament, and established authority over many Anglo-Irish and Gaelic lords.

The 7th earl (Thomas Fitzgerald) was appointed governor in 1471 by EDWARD IV, a YORKIST, after he had been restored as king of England and lord of Ireland. (Kildare had intermittently been governor from 1454.) He continued until 1475 and was reappointed in 1478, when he died.

The 8th earl (Gerald Fitzgerald) was governor for most of the period from 1479 to 1513 (death). Though a Yorkist, he survived the seizure of the English kingship by the LANCASTRIAN Henry Tudor (1485). His suspected involvement with Perkin WARBECK resulted in removal (1492–6), while Henry strengthened control over the Irish government (*see* HENRY VII AND IRELAND). He was retained by Henry VIII (from 1509).

The 9th earl (Gerald Fitzgerald) proved weaker than his father. He was deprived of the governorship in 1534 after his son, Lord OFFALY, rebelled against Henry. *See also* KILDARE, 8TH EARL OF; KILDARE, 9TH EARL OF; HENRY VIII AND IRELAND.

KILDARE PLACE SOCIETY Popular name for the Society for Promoting the Education of the Poor in Ireland, founded in 1811 to provide non-denominational elementary schools and based at Kildare Place, DUBLIN. Supported from 1816 by UK parliamentary grants, in 1820 it ran 381 schools with about 26,400 children. In the 1820s it was accused of proselytizing for Protestantism (e.g., by John MACHALE) and shunned by Catholics. It closed in 1831. *See also* EDUCATION, IRELAND.

KILDARE REBELLION In Ireland, an Anglo-Irish rebellion against Henry VIII; raised in July 1534 by Lord OFFALY, following Henry's imprisonment (in London) of his father, the 9th earl of KILDARE. (Offaly had provoked the imprisonment by resigning as vice-deputy and denouncing Henry; 11 June.)

Offaly's supporters besieged DUBLIN Castle and secured other areas. Henry sent an army to Ireland under Sir William Skeffington (arrived Oct.). Offaly surrendered on 24 Aug. 1535 and was executed, with five uncles, in London (Feb. 1537). The Rebellion ended the KILDARE ASCENDANCY. *See also* HENRY VIII AND IRELAND.

KILKENNY A city in the Republic of Ireland, by the R. Nore; centre of Co. Kilkenny; from Irish, Cill Chainnigh, meaning 'Canice's church'.

A monastic centre by the 10th century, Kilkenny became the see for OSSORY diocese in 1111. In 1172 STRONGBOW built a castle there, and William MARSHAL developed a town (1190s), which became one of Ireland's few important inland towns and sometimes a meeting-place for PARLIAMENT (late 13th–early 15th centuries). Until 1843 Kilkenny comprised two jurisdictions: 'Irishtown' and 'Hightown' (English). The castle was bought by the 3rd earl of Ormond in 1391 (*see* BUTLER FAMILY, IRELAND). Formally a city from 1609, Kilkenny was the centre for the CATHOLIC CONFEDERATION 1642–8 (surrendered to Oliver CROMWELL 1650). It prospered in the 18th century and remained a market town. In the 1960s it became the centre of an innovative design industry, and from 1974 was the home of a celebrated arts festival. *See also* KILKENNY, STATUTE OF.

Est. popn: 1300, 1000; 1600, 1200; 1800, 15,000; 1900, 10,000; 2000, 20,000.

KILKENNY, CONFEDERATION OF *see* CATHOLIC CONFEDERATION

KILKENNY, STATUTE OF In Ireland, laws proclaimed by PARLIAMENT, meeting at KILKENNY, on 19 Feb. 1366 which attempted to halt the decline of the English colony. They identified 'degeneracy', i.e., adoption of Gaelic Irish culture by Anglo-Irish, as the main problem. To prevent this they required Anglo-Irish to use English law, dress and customs. Alliances between Anglo-Irish and Gaelic Irish (marriage, trade) were also forbidden. The Statute enshrined separation in law but was ineffectual. Attempts were made in 1614–15 to declare it obsolete. It was repealed by the Republic of Ireland in 1983. *See also* IRELAND, ENGLISH COLONY IN, 13TH–15TH CENTURIES; GAELIC REVIVAL, IRELAND 13TH–15TH CENTURIES.

KILLIECRANKIE, BATTLE OF Fought in Killiecrankie Pass, near Pitlochry (C Scotland) on 27 July 1689. A Jacobite army (supporters of the deposed King JAMES VII/II), led by John GRAHAM, Viscount Dundee, put to flight a government force which was trying to reach Jacobite-held Blair Castle. Though victorious, Dundee was mortally wounded. The Jacobite remnant was defeated at the battle of Cromdale (NE Scotland) on 1 May 1690. *See also* JACOBITISM, IMPACT ON BRITISH POLITICS.

KILMAINHAM TREATY A tacit agreement between C.S. PARNELL, imprisoned leader of the IRISH PARLIAMENTARY PARTY, and W.E. GLADSTONE, British prime minister, which was announced by Gladstone to the UK House of Commons on 2 May 1882. Parnell would be released from Kilmainham Gaol (Ireland) and discourage rural agitation; the British government would assist indebted Irish tenant farmers. The 'treaty' was intended to stop rural unrest. It was overshadowed by the PHOENIX PARK MURDERS (6 May). *See also* LAND AGITATION AND REFORM, IRELAND.

KIN-BASED SOCIETY A society in which access to land, social status and the operation of authority were related to membership of a kindred. Aspects of kin-based societies remained important in the SOCIAL STRUCTURES of Wales and Ireland to the 17th century. In Scotland kindreds were particularly strong in areas in which central control was weak, notably the Borders until the late 16th century and the HIGHLANDS (with its CLAN system) until the mid 18th century.

KINDLY TENURE In Scotland, types of tenure which were theoretically for limited terms (e.g., tenancies at will, rental tenancy, leasehold) but which by custom included a right (recognized by law courts) for succession by an heir. ('Kindly' is derived from 'kinship'.) Kindly tenure was widespread from the 15th century and declined in the 18th century, though the 'king's kindly tenants' of Lochmaben barony (SW Scotland) survived into the 21st century. *See also* TENURES, SCOTLAND.

KING, GREGORY (b. 15 Dec. 1648 at Lichfield, Staffordshire, England; d. 29 Aug. 1712 at London, England, aged 63). After acquiring experience in heraldry, King went to London in 1672 where he worked for a printer and mapmaker, and as a surveyor in the planning of Soho (1675–80). From 1677 to 1694 he was active in heraldic work; he then undertook statistical work for the English government. In 1696 he compiled, probably for Robert HARLEY, his 'Natural and Political Observations and Conclusions upon the State and Condition of England' (published 1801), an ambitious attempt to estimate England's population, age distribution, wealth and other characteristics in 1688.

KING, MACKENZIE (b. 17 Dec. 1874 at Berlin, Ontario, Canada; d. 22 July 1950 at Kingsmere, Quebec, Canada, aged 75). A lawyer, King was a Liberal member of the Canadian Parliament 1908–11, 1919–48, and minister of labour under Wilfrid LAURIER (1909–11). Elected Party leader in 1919, he served as prime minister 1921–6, 1926–30, and 1935–48. He insisted on Canadian autonomy within the BRITISH EMPIRE, rejecting the idea of Jan SMUTS that DOMINIONS should act together. In 1939 Canada supported Great Britain in declaring war on Germany, but King opposed conscription. After it was approved by plebiscite (1941), conscription was introduced for home defence and in Nov. 1944 for overseas military service. King resigned office because of illness. *See also* CANADA.

KING, WILLIAM (b. 1 May 1650 at Antrim, Co. Antrim, Ireland; d. 8 May 1729 at Dublin, Ireland, aged 79). A Church of IRELAND clergyman, King became dean of St Patrick's Cathedral, DUBLIN, in Feb. 1689. During the WILLIAMITE WAR, he was imprisoned by Jacobites for supporting the

Williamites (1689, 1690). Following Williamite successes he was appointed bishop of DERRY (Dec. 1690). He justified opposition to (the former king) JAMES VII/II in *The State of the Protestants of Ireland* (1691), but discountenanced harsh anti-Catholic legislation.

As archbishop of Dublin from 1703, King opposed concessions to presbyterians (e.g., in Irish Toleration Act, 1719), and WOOD'S HALFPENCE (1722–5). A distinguished theologian, he was a leading Protestant churchman of his time.

KING AND COUNTRY DEBATE The occasion on 9 Feb. 1933 when the Oxford Union, a student debating society associated with OXFORD University (C England), passed the motion: 'this House will in no circumstances fight for its King and its Country'. Much publicized, this manifestation of PACIFISM impressed foreign opinion, notably in Germany.

KING'S BOOK A statement of doctrine for the English Church, published May 1543 as a revision and replacement of the BISHOPS' BOOK of 1537 (full title, *Necessary Doctrine and Erudition for any Christian Man*). Produced by bishops and other clergy with involvement from King HENRY VIII, it mostly affirmed Catholic doctrine (e.g., prayers for the dead) and also rejected reformed theology (e.g., justification by faith). *See also* REFORMATION, ENGLAND.

KING'S FRIENDS Name adopted by British MPs who supported the earl of BUTE in the early 1760s (e.g., Charles JENKINSON). They saw themselves as servants of King GEORGE III, above party politics, which paradoxically contributed to political instability. They were seen as a threat to the constitution by the ROCKINGHAM WHIGS (1760s–90s). King's Friends (e.g., Edward THURLOW) were included in most ministries until the early 19th century. *See also* POLITICAL PARTIES.

KINGSHIP, ANGLO-SAXON From the mid 5th century leaders of Germanic warbands ruled eastern and southern parts of southern Britain (*see* POST-ROMAN BRITAIN). By *c.*600 there were at least 30 Germanic-ruled (or Anglo-Saxon) kingdoms. The most important were: BERNICIA, DEIRA, MERCIA, EAST ANGLIA, ESSEX, KENT, SUSSEX, and the Gewisse kingdom (later WESSEX).

Kings sought to dominate and sometimes absorb other kingdoms. During the 7th century the Northumbrian kingdoms (Bernicia, Deira) and Mercia (C England) were most aggressive. In the 8th century Mercia was pre-eminent and incorporated lesser kingdoms. By *c.*800 it included SE England (Essex, Kent, Sussex), but the area was seized by EGBERT of Wessex (826). At his death (839) four kingdoms remained: Northumbria, East Anglia, Mercia, Wessex.

In the mid 9th century VIKINGS (mainly Danes) conquered East Anglia and parts of other kingdoms. In Wessex, ALFRED (ruled 871–99) prevented collapse. In the 10th century his descendants annexed Mercia and Northumbria, and conquered Viking-held lands, creating a single kingdom (*see* ENGLAND, FORMATION OF).

A kingdom usually belonged to a kindred, whose members claimed descent from a common ancestor. Various members were considered as possible kings (*see* ÆTHELING), but kings usually sought the succession of their sons and had rival candidates killed. Pre-Christian inauguration ceremonies for kings are unrecorded. Christian ceremonies developed from the 8th century, giving kings a sacred character (*see* CORONATION, ENGLAND).

Kings and their households lived itinerant lives, supported by food renders, tribute and tolls (*see* ROYAL REVENUES, ENGLAND BEFORE 1066). They exerted power by maintaining and rewarding a warband, which was reinforced as necessary with other nobles and free peasants (*see* MILITARY SERVICE, ENGLAND BEFORE 1066). Kings also expressed authority through licensing or issuing coinage (*see* CURRENCY, ENGLAND BEFORE 1066). From the 8th century increasingly sophisticated methods of GOVERNMENT were developed, adding a further dimension to royal authority (*see* THREE PUBLIC SERVICES; EALDORMAN; SHIRE; WITAN. *See also* HEPTARCHY; EMPIRE, ANGLO-SAXON IDEAS OF; ROYAL HOUSEHOLD, ENGLAND.

KINGSHIP, IRELAND From at least the IRON AGE (700 BC–AD 400) there were over 100 petty kings with queen-consorts. Evidence from the 5th–10th centuries reveals a hierarchy of: local (petty) king (OIr. *rí*), regional overking (*ruiri*), and provincial high-king (*rí ruirech*). From at least the 8th century, the Uí NÉILL provincial high-kings claimed a high-kingship of Ireland based on possession of TARA (*rí Temrach*). While all rulers had royal status and powers, sub-kings were tributary to overkings. The ancient sacredness of kingship is echoed in INAUGURATION rituals.

Regnal succession was through the male line (though not by 'primogeniture,' succession by eldest son). All male members of a royal *derbfine* (four-generation kin-group) were theoretically eligible; in practice the strongest candidates prevailed. As new kings sometimes married the widows of predecessors, royal women enjoyed considerable influence. Wealth and family connections bestowed importance in regnal succession.

From the 11th century kingship evolved. Stronger dynasties suppressed lesser ones, created stronger provinces, and strove for effective high-kingship. Sovereignty became more concentrated, with lesser rulers reduced to the status of 'lord' (Irish *tigerna*). These developments were arrested by the arrival of NORMANS (or Anglo-Normans, from 1169).

In the 15th–16th centuries surviving kings, who used mercenaries to maintain authority, were called 'lord' or 'chief' (*tigerna*). Such rulers survived, notably in ULSTER, until the early 17th century. *See also* TÚATH; FEIS TEMRO; ÓENACH TAILTEN.

KINGSHIP, IRON AGE BRITAIN/IRELAND *see* PREHISTORIC BRITAIN/IRELAND, SOCIAL STRUCTURE

KINGSHIP, NORTH BRITAIN Kingship as evidenced from the 6th century may have originated from earlier tribes (16 within modern Scotland were mapped in the 2nd century). Tribes elsewhere in Britain had been ruled by kings (*see* IRON AGE TRIBES, BRITAIN).

British (Brittonic-speaking) kingdoms S of the FORTH–CLYDE ISTHMUS indicate continuity. GODODDIN derived its name from a tribal name, and RHEGED was apparently based on a tribe (both in 6th–7th centuries). The kingdom of Clyde Rock or STRATHCLYDE (to 11th century) was related to two earlier tribes.

N of the isthmus, the kingship pattern among the PICTS (also Brittonic-speaking) is unclear. It was once thought to resemble Irish kingship, with local kingdoms N and S of the MOUNTH and one or two high-kings. But kings are only extensively documented from one area, FORTRIU (from the 7th century), the name of which was derived from a tribe. Its location was probably E of the Moray Firth (in modern NE Scotland), near the base of an earlier king (*see* BRIDEI SON OF MAILCON). Fortriu probably dominated Pictland from the later 7th century (southwards to the Forth estuary). A king of ATHOLL (in modern E Scotland) is mentioned in 739, which may imply a kingdom in the southern Pictish area. BEDE claimed (731) that succession was matrilineal (through female line), but this is unsupported by other evidence.

Around 500, SCOTS from Ireland (Gaelic-speaking) expanded DÁL RIATA into western N Britain, establishing four kingdoms under a high-king. Succession within local kingdoms was probably by TANISTRY, and the high-kingship was associated with the dominant local kingdom. From *c*.842 the high-kings of the Scots also ruled the Picts (*see* UNION OF SCOTS AND PICTS).

Kings expressed authority by obtaining tribute from local inhabitants and by leading warbands to acquire prestigious goods (e.g., cattle, slaves) from other kingdoms. *See also* ROYAL REVENUES, SCOTLAND; INAUGURATION, SCOTLAND; KINGSHIP, SCOTTISH.

KINGSHIP, SCOTTISH From *c*.842 to 1034 MAC ALPIN KINGS originating from DÁL RIATA (modern W Scotland) ruled SCOTS and PICTS N of the FORTH–CLYDE ISTHMUS, though the WESTERN ISLES, ORKNEY ISLANDS and SHETLAND ISLANDS were lost (9th–10th centuries). Initiated by INAUGURATION, kings were essentially war leaders. From *c*.889 to 1005 succession alternated between two lineages. Under the Mac Alpins, Gaelic culture largely replaced Pictish culture. Expansion southwards began probably under MALCOLM II (ruled 1005–34).

Following transmission by female line and disruptions (1034–97), kingship was held by MAC MALCOLM RULERS, succeeding by male primogeniture (by eldest son), which sometimes produced MINORITIES. David, as ruler of S Scotland (by 1113) and king (1124–53), replicated 'feudal' and administrative arrangements from England and NORMANDY (*see* DAVID I). They included lordships held for military service; SHERIFFDOMS; BURGHS (towns). Royal GOVERNMENT remained household-based into the 15th century. ALEXANDER III regained suzerainty over the Western Isles (1266).

In 1286 PARLIAMENT accepted a female ruler, albeit a minor (*see* MARGARET, 'THE MAID OF NORWAY'). Events after her death led to seizure of Scotland by EDWARD I of England (1296). Robert Bruce restored native kingship (ruled 1306–29; *see* ROBERT I), and obtained CORONATION rights.

From 1333 to 1356 Bruce rule was challenged (*see* BALLIOL, EDWARD), and kingship remained weak to the 1420s, due to minorities, rule by proxies and magnate power. (From 1371 Scotland was under STEWART RULERS.) Scotland's coherence was preserved partly by the Church and growing national identity. In the 15th century JAMES I and JAMES II exerted authority against MAGNATES, and JAMES III annexed the Orkney Islands and Shetland Islands. JAMES IV (1488–1513) has been characterized as representing NEW MONARCHY.

In the 16th century divisions over foreign policy and religion made minorities fractious (e.g., *see* MARY OF GUISE). JAMES VI claimed 'divine right' for kingship (1580s–90s), before moving to England. *See also* ROYAL REVENUES, SCOTLAND; UNION OF CROWNS, ENGLAND (WITH IRELAND) AND SCOTLAND; ROYAL PREROGATIVE; COVENANTING REVOLUTION.

KINGSHIP, WALES 5TH–13TH CENTURIES Kingship emerged after the end of Roman rule in the 5th century, to provide political and military leadership (*see* POST-ROMAN BRITAIN): rulers styled 'king' (Welsh *brenin*; Latin *rex*) are first attested in the mid 6th century. Early kingdoms included GWYNEDD, POWYS, DYFED, GLYWYSING and GWENT. CEREDIGION and BRYCHEINIOG appeared by the 8th century. By the early 10th century the dynasty of RHODRI MAWR (d. 878) ruled in most kingdoms.

During the 12th century kings were increasingly styled 'prince' (Welsh *tywysog*; Latin *princeps*), perhaps reflecting a more precise concept of kingship (a Europe-wide development). From *c*.1210 the style was applied to only Gwynedd's ruler; others were called 'lord' (Welsh *arglwydd*), 'magnate' or 'baron'. Princes of Gwynedd also aspired to be PRINCE OF WALES.

Royal dynasties often divided into rival branches, forming 'segmentary lineages'. Succession did not necessarily pass from father to (eldest) son; close kinsmen frequently made claims and contested them, often violently. The 11th century in particular saw the intrusion of numerous minor lines.

Early kings were leaders of warbands (Welsh *teulu*); there were few restraints on their actions. They did not normally promulgate laws (*see* LAW, WELSH). By the 12th century kings worked within structured arrangements, such as the organized household (*see* ROYAL HOUSEHOLDS, WALES) and council (*see* COUNCILS, WALES), and were served by a *DISTAIN* and other officers. The form of inauguration is unknown. *See also* WALES; TANISTRY.

KINGSHIP AND MONARCHY, ENGLAND 1066 TO 1680s After the NORMAN CONQUEST kings remained military leaders, animators of government, and sacred figures. They additionally became 'feudal' lords-in-chief (of nobles holding land for MILITARY SERVICE; *see* FEUDALISM). Succession remained disputable (*see* ROBERT CURTHOSE; ARTHUR OF BRITTANY), and accession by a woman was rejected (*see* MATILDA). Male primogeniture (succession by eldest son) was established in 1216 (accession of HENRY III as minor).

Effective rule required co-operation with the NOBILITY. Authoritarian (or 'tyrannical') behaviour provoked resistance and restrictions (*see* MAGNA CARTA; BARONIAL CONFLICT AND WARS; ORDINANCES) – even deposition (EDWARD II, RICHARD II). By 1300 feudal relations weakened (e.g., use of contracted military forces). From the 13th century kings were criticized in PARLIAMENT.

Henry Bolingbroke's seizure of the throne in 1399 (as HENRY IV), invoking a weak claim, eventually became the basis for factional conflict and depositions (1450s–85; *see* YORKIST–LANCASTRIAN CONFLICT). HENRY VII, who overthrew Richard III (1485), strove to end factionalism.

TUDOR rulers (1485–1603) asserted authority through PREROGATIVE COURTS, limiting numbers of noblemen, and through supremacy over the Church (confirmed 1534; *see* REFORMATION, ENGLAND). They relied extensively on ministers of non-noble origin (e.g., Thomas WOLSEY, William CECIL), and sometimes Parliament's endorsement (*see* REFORMATION PARLIAMENT). MARY I (ruled 1553–8) was effectively England's first female monarch. ELIZABETH I (1558–1603) settled the English Church's Protestant character (*see* ELIZABETHAN SETTLEMENT).

After 1603 (succession of JAMES VI/I from Scotland), relations with Parliament were difficult. The attempt by CHARLES I to rule without Parliament (1629–40), including controversial religious policies, resulted in CIVIL WARS (1642–6, 1648) and abolition of monarchy (1649). It was restored (1660) following failure to establish alternative governance. Parliament sought to secure its own existence, and restrain CHARLES II, mainly through restricting finance. But his heir's Catholicism

threatened Protestant uniformity and generated fear of ABSOLUTISM (*see* JAMES VII/II). *See also* NORMAN KINGS; PLANTAGENETS; ROYAL REVENUES, ENGLAND FROM 1066; ROYAL PREROGATIVE; NEW MONARCHY, ENGLAND; DIVINE RIGHT MONARCHY; COMMONWEALTH AND PROTECTORATE; RESTORATION, ENGLAND AND WALES.

KINGSHIP AND MONARCHY, ENGLAND AND GREAT BRITAIN FROM 1680s In 1678–81 the prospect of a Catholic ruler (James, duke of York) caused dispute about the nature of monarchy, dividing England's (Protestant) political élite into parties (*see* EXCLUSION CRISIS). WHIGS argued that monarchy could be altered for the people; TORIES generally supported hereditary succession as divine right. Such ideas influenced developments that resulted in decline of royal powers.

James's promotion of Catholicism from 1685 (*see* JAMES VII/II), the birth of a male heir (June 1688) threatening a Catholic succession, and fear of alliance with Catholic France against the Protestant Dutch Republic provoked opposition and a Dutch invasion. James fled abroad (Dec.). A CONVENTION PARLIAMENT then created a limited monarchy largely on its terms (1689; *see* GLORIOUS REVOLUTION). It declared that James had abdicated, and decided the succession (partly on hereditary right); new monarchs WILLIAM III and MARY II agreed to respect parliamentary STATUTES; and legislation enshrined conditions, including prohibition of Catholic rulers (*see* RIGHTS, DECLARATION AND BILL OF). (Even stronger rights were asserted in Scotland; *see* REVOLUTION SETTLEMENT, SCOTLAND.) In 1701 the English Parliament ensured a continuing Protestant succession (effective from 1714; *see* SETTLEMENT, ACT OF; HANOVERIAN SUCCESSION).

Financial requirements strengthened Parliament's role (*see* FISCAL–MILITARY STATE). Rulers' choice of leading ministers became limited to influential supporters within Parliament who directed royal patronage (effectively led by a head of government from 1721; *see* PRIME MINISTER). A ruler last vetoed legislation in 1707. However, GEORGE III (ruled 1760–1811) frequently asserted independence (e.g., rejection of CATHOLIC EMANCIPATION).

From the 1780s royal influence within Parliament declined (*see* ECONOMICAL REFORM). From 1830 governments were usually determined by general elections (*see* WILLIAM IV). VICTORIA (reigned 1837–1901) accepted a non-partisan political role (*see* BAGEHOT, WALTER). Expansion of the BRITISH EMPIRE and greater ceremonial raised the monarchy's prestige; it evolved into a focus for unity (*see* ELIZABETH II). In 2013 Parliament ended male priority in the succession. *See also* ROYAL PREROGATIVE; BALANCED CONSTITUTION; JACOBITISM, IMPACT ON BRITISH POLITICS; GEORGE II; BEDCHAMBER CRISIS; ALBERT OF SAXE-COBURG; ESHER, LORD; ABDICATION CRISIS; COMMONWEALTH; SUCCESSION TO THE CROWN ACT.

KINGSLEY, CHARLES (b. 12 June 1819 at Holne, Devon, England; d. 23 Jan. 1875 at Eversley, Hampshire, England, aged 55). A Church of England clergyman who became concerned about rural poverty while serving in Dorset (S England), Kingsley participated in the CHRISTIAN SOCIALIST movement from the late 1840s. From 1848 he also wrote novels (e.g., *Westward Ho!*, 1855), becoming best known for his children's fable *The Water Babies* (1863). He was regius professor of history at CAMBRIDGE University 1860–9. In 1864, in a review, Kingsley questioned the honesty of J.H. NEWMAN, provoking Newman to write his autobiographical *Apologia pro vita sua*.

KING'S LIEUTENANT *see* LORD LIEUTENANT

KING'S LIST Following the UNION OF ENGLAND AND SCOTLAND (1707), the list of 16 nobles nominated by the British government as preferred candidates for election as Scotland's 'representative peers' in the British House of Lords. The list was sent covertly to Scotland in the king's name each year until 1781. The nominees were normally elected, thereby providing reliable support for the government in the Lords. *See also* ISLAY, EARL OF; PEERAGE, SCOTLAND.

KING'S (OR QUEEN'S) COMMISSIONER, SCOTLAND A person commissioned by the ruler of Scotland (of Great Britain from 1707, of the UK from 1801) to act in Scotland as his or her representative. The term is notably used for the king's (or queen's) commissioner to Parliament in the period 1660–1707, when the commissioner acted as head of government (effectively replacing the CHANCELLOR). From 1689, when Parliament met regularly and was difficult to control, the commissioner's work included the building of support among members for royal policies (see PARLIAMENT, SCOTLAND). Commissioners included: the earl of Middleton (John MIDDLETON), the (7th) earl of ROTHES, the (2nd) earl of LAUDERDALE, the duke of Albany (see JAMES VII/II), and the (2nd) duke of QUEENSBERRY.

KINGSTON UPON THAMES A former small town in Surrey (S England); part of SW London from 1965. It was the site of a MINSTER church by the 8th century and is recorded as a royal estate (in WESSEX) in 838. (Kingston means 'King's settlement'.) Kingston was the coronation place of seven kings. The first was EDWARD THE ELDER, king of Wessex (in 900); the last was ÆTHELRED II, king of England (in 979). *See* CORONATION, ENGLAND.

KINNOCK, NEIL (b. 28 March 1942 at Tredegar, Monmouthshire, Wales). Kinnock became a Labour MP in 1970 as a supporter of Michael FOOT. As Party and Opposition leader from 1983 he worked to reunify the LABOUR PARTY and make it electable by suppressing troublesome left-wingers and disposing of unpopular policies (e.g., unilateral nuclear disarmament). The Party's unexpected defeat in the 1992 UK general election prompted his resignation (succeeded by John SMITH). He was the longest-serving Opposition leader not to become prime minister. Kinnock left Parliament in 1995 to become a UK commissioner of the EUROPEAN UNION (served 1995–2004). He was created Lord Kinnock in 2005. *See also* THATCHER, MARGARET; SOCIAL DEMOCRATIC PARTY; TROTSKYITES.

KINSALE, BATTLE OF Fought near Kinsale, Co. Cork (S Ireland), on 24 Dec. 1601. A mainly English army commanded by Lord MOUNTJOY intercepted and defeated a Gaelic Irish army, mainly from ULSTER (N Ireland), commanded by the 2nd earl of Tyrone (Hugh O'NEILL). Tyrone intended to relieve a Spanish army besieged in Kinsale (had landed 21 Sept.). Mountjoy's victory broke Tyrone's anti-English campaign (*see* NINE YEARS WAR). (The Spanish surrendered on 2 Jan. 1602.)

KIPLING, RUDYARD (b. 30 Dec. 1865 at Bombay, India; d. 18 Jan. 1936 at London, England, aged 70). Kipling won a reputation as an author of stories, poems and sketches in the 1880s while working as a journalist in India. He lived in the USA 1892–6. Writings such as the 'Jungle Books' (1894–5), *Stalky and Co.* (1899) and *Kim* (1901) made him immensely popular. From 1902 to 1908 he generally wintered in SOUTH AFRICA, using a house initially provided by Cecil RHODES. Many honoured him as the 'Bard of Empire' who celebrated the civilizing mission of the British Empire, though critics accused him of JINGOISM. Kipling received the 1907 Nobel Prize in Literature. *See also* ENGLISH LITERATURE, ENGLAND.

KIRIBATI *see* GILBERT AND ELLICE ISLANDS

KIRK SESSION The administrative court of parish churches of the Church of SCOTLAND. Sessions were established in the Lowlands between 1559 and the 1630s, but took until the late 18th century to cover the HIGHLANDS. They consist of the parish minister (chairman) and 'ruling elders' (lay Church officers, appointed for life from *c*.1578). Sessions were responsible for POOR RELIEF and EDUCATION until the mid 19th century, and were forceful regulators of moral behaviour until the late 18th century (or later), although the TOLERATION ACT of 1712 withdrew authority over people outside the Church. Kirk sessions also operated in N Ireland by the 18th century (*see* PRESBYTERIAN SOCIETY, IRELAND). *See also* CHURCH ORGANIZATION, SCOTLAND FROM 16TH CENTURY; COURTS, SCOTLAND.

KITCHEN CABINET Term, originating in the USA, which refers to an informal clique of friends and advisers whom a leader may consult in preference to his official colleagues. In Great Britain the term is especially associated with the coterie around the Labour leader and prime minister Harold WILSON, 1964–76, headed by his political secretary Marcia Williams (later Baroness Falkender).

KITCHENER, LORD (b. 24 June 1850 at Gunsborough Villa, Co. Kerry, Ireland; d. 5 June 1916 in North Sea, aged 65). Educated in England at the Royal Military Academy, Woolwich (Kent), Horatio Kitchener served in CYPRUS and EGYPT, taking command of the Egyptian Army in 1889. His reconquest of the SUDAN (1896–8) made him a British national hero. Created Lord Kitchener (1898), he then led British forces in the (Second) BOER WAR (1900–2). Kitchener quarrelled violently with Lord CURZON while commander-in-chief of the Indian Army (1902–9).

When war broke out in 1914, Kitchener was appointed war secretary by the prime minister H.H. ASQUITH (5 Aug.), despite his status as a serving officer. He inspired public confidence but failed to work effectively with politicians. His chief initiative was to raise a mass volunteer army (*see* WORLD WAR I, BRITISH ARMY). He drowned when the ship on which he was travelling to Russia struck a mine off Orkney.

KNIGHT A man esteemed or formally honoured for military or other service. Knights are recorded in late Anglo-Saxon England (10th–11th centuries) as horse-mounted, armed associates of noblemen (ranking alongside thegns). The OE term *cniht* means 'boy' or 'retainer'.

Following the NORMAN CONQUEST (1066–70s) several thousand men of similar status from NORMANDY and elsewhere settled in England. Some lived off wages from lords; others received modest amounts of land (so-called 'knights' fees') and were expected to undertake 40 days' military service per year. Around 1150 there were 4000–5000 knights. During the 12th century concepts of CHIVALRY developed around knighthood.

From the late 12th century men refused knighthood. Causes included: (a) requirement to serve on juries and hold local offices, instigated by King HENRY II; (b) inflation, which reduced income; (c) expense of more elaborate armour and larger horses; (d) cost of new 'knighting' ceremonies. From 1224 the Crown tried, ineffectually, to force ('distrain') men to become knights. By *c*.1300 there were about 1250 knights (usually called 'knights bachelor'). Many continued to perform military service, though they were numerically unimportant (*see* MILITARY SERVICE, ENGLAND 1066 TO MID 17TH CENTURY). Knighthood remained a personal (not hereditary) honour. From the mid 13th century knights became the basis for the development of the social stratum of GENTRY.

From the reign of EDWARD IV (1461–70, 1471–83) rulers also knighted leading merchants. Knighthood increasingly rewarded service and denoted status. A female equivalent, 'damehood', was introduced in 1917. In the 20th and 21st centuries knights included sportsmen and pop stars. *See also* FEUDALISM; HONOURS SYSTEM; SOCIAL STRUCTURE, ENGLAND 1066 TO 16TH CENTURY.

KNIGHTS OF COLUMBANUS An Irish Catholic social, charitable and religious organization, founded in BELFAST (N Ireland) in 1915 to encourage fraternity among professional men (and to oppose socialism and the ORANGE ORDER). A DUBLIN branch was established in 1917. It was recognized by the Catholic Church in 1934. Many leading politicians in southern Ireland have been members. The secrecy surrounding its membership and organization has prompted comparisons with freemasonry.

KNOWTH A passage tomb complex at the W end of the BEND OF THE BOYNE (Co. Meath, E Ireland). The central mound is 310 ft (95 m) in diameter, 33 ft (10 m) high, covering two back-to-back tombs and surrounded by 127 kerbstones. It dates from *c*.3000 BC, in the NEOLITHIC. Around it are 19 smaller tombs. Ceremony and settlement continued at the site after the Neolithic (i.e., beyond *c*.2500 BC). During the IRON AGE (*c*.700 BC–*c*. AD 400) the central mound was a defended site; a cemetery lay nearby. *See also* PASSAGE TOMBS.

KNOX, JOHN (b. *c*.1514 at Haddington, SE Scotland; d. 24 Nov. 1572 at Edinburgh, SE Scotland, aged about 58). Leader of the Scottish Reformation.

A Catholic priest, Knox adopted Protestantism *c*.1544 under the influence of George WISHART. In 1547 he joined Protestants besieged by French troops in St Andrews Castle, but was captured and taken to France (1547–9). In 1549 he went to England and served as a chaplain to the Protestant King EDWARD VI, but fled overseas after the accession of the Catholic MARY I (1553) and met the Swiss Protestant John Calvin in Geneva (Switzerland).

In 1559 Knox returned to Scotland at the invitation of the LORDS OF THE CONGREGATION. On 11 May his preaching in PERTH provoked attacks on churches which led to the official repudiation of Catholicism in 1560 (*see* REFORMATION, SCOTLAND). Knox became minister of Edinburgh (1560–72) and with others drafted the 'First Book of Discipline' and SCOTS CONFESSION. His writings were largely political, e.g., *The First Blast of the Trumpet against the Monstrous Regiment of Women* (published 1558), which attacked government ('regiment') by women, specifically MARY OF GUISE and Mary of England (and also offended ELIZABETH). He also wrote a *History of the*

Reformation (completed 1566). *See also* CALVINISM; DISCIPLINE, BOOKS OF; COMMON ORDER, BOOK OF.

KOREAN WAR, BRITISH INVOLVEMENT Occupation zones established in Korea by the USSR and USA in 1945, at the end of WORLD WAR II (replacing Japanese occupation), developed into client states (1948). On 25 June 1950 communist North Korea invaded South Korea. The USA led a United Nations operation to repel the attack. Great Britain gave immediate support and committed troops to a Commonwealth Division. Defence spending doubled.

United Nations forces liberated South Korea and advanced into North Korea. Millions of Chinese 'volunteers' then intervened to help the North (Nov. 1950). The British prime minister, Clement ATTLEE, discouraged the USA from bombing China or using atomic weapons. The Battle of Imjin River (22–25 April 1951) halted the Chinese offensive. Prolonged truce talks began in July 1951. An armistice (27 July 1953) left the front line as the border between North and South Korea.

The war involved 100,000 British servicemen and 1078 died. The total death toll was around 3 million.

KOSOVO WAR, BRITISH INVOLVEMENT In 1999, during the YUGOSLAV WARS, British forces participated in action against Serbian 'ethnic cleansing' (killing or expulsion based on ethnic background) in Kosovo, a province of Serbia with a majority population of Albanians.

In Jan. 1999, after a ceasefire between Serbs and the Kosovo Liberation Army (KLA) collapsed, Serbs responded to KLA murders with extensive killing of Albanians. Following failure of a peace conference (Feb.–March), a small international monitoring force was withdrawn, and from 24 March US and British aircraft attacked military sites in Serbia. Serbian ethnic cleansing increased, with over a million Albanians leaving their homes by late April. The British prime minister Tony BLAIR publicized their plight with visits to refugee camps (3 and 18 May).

Persuaded by Blair, the US president Bill Clinton threatened deployment of ground forces (18 May); the Russians meanwhile pressurized Serb leaders. The Serbs announced withdrawal (2 June) and bombing was halted (10 June). A multinational peacekeeping force, including 12,000 British troops, was deployed. When Blair visited Kosovo (31 July), he was fêted by Albanians. Numerous Albanian baby boys were named 'Toni' or 'Tonibler'. *See also* UNITED STATES OF AMERICA, BRITISH RELATIONS WITH.

KUWAIT An Arab emirate in the PERSIAN GULF, formerly under British protection (but not part of the BRITISH EMPIRE). In 1899 the sheik of Kuwait granted Great Britain control of foreign relations to prevent the OTTOMAN EMPIRE intruding a German-built railway. After the outbreak of WORLD WAR I (1914), Britain recognized Kuwait as an independent sheikdom under its protection. From 1936 British and US firms developed an OIL INDUSTRY. Britain relinquished its rights in Kuwait in June 1961 (when the ruler became styled emir), but then had to deter an invasion threat from Iraq by sending troops. British forces helped to liberate Kuwait from Iraqi occupation in the GULF WAR (1991).

L

LABOURERS, ORDINANCE AND STATUTE OF In England, legislation passed by the royal COUNCIL and PARLIAMENT (respectively June 1349, Feb. 1351) to counter the labour shortage and higher wages that resulted from the BLACK DEATH (1348–9). The Ordinance required able-bodied landless men and women to accept any available work at pre-plague rates (among other restrictions). The Statute fixed rates for agricultural work. The legislation was enforced vigorously until the 1370s. *See also* PEASANTS' REVOLT; ECONOMY, STATE INVOLVEMENT, BRITAIN.

LABOURIST Term applied to British working-class politicians in the late 19th and early 20th centuries who were keener to advance trade union rights and working-class representation than to pursue SOCIALISM. Labourists collaborated with the LIBERAL PARTY and were later involved in the LABOUR PARTY.

LABOUR MOVEMENT Term used to refer generally to campaigns and organizations which sought to improve the conditions of, and opportunities for, working people in industrial society. In Great Britain the term encompasses CHARTISM (early 19th century), TRADE UNIONISM (from early 19th century), the CO-OPERATIVE MOVEMENT (from late 19th century), public EDUCATION, and the LABOUR PARTY (founded 1900). In Ireland a significant movement began to develop from the later 19th century (*see* TRADE UNIONISM, IRELAND; LABOUR PARTY, IRISH).

LABOUR PARTY A British political party founded in London on 27 Feb. 1900 as the Labour Representation Committee (LRC). It linked SOCIALISTS of the INDEPENDENT LABOUR PARTY (formed by Keir HARDIE in 1893) and FABIAN SOCIETY with trade unions which desired more working-class representation in the UK Parliament. It subsidized only 15 candidates in 1900, but many unions affiliated after the TAFF VALE CASE (1906).

An anti-Conservative pact with the Liberals (1903) helped secure the election of 29 Labour MPs in 1906, and the LRC renamed itself the Labour Party. Support was concentrated among urban industrial workers. Though divided over WORLD WAR I, Labour officially supported the coalition government (1915–18), its influence enhanced by growing union power. Arthur HENDERSON reorganized the Party, which adopted a SOCIALIST constitution (1918).

Benefiting from the coincidence of PARLIAMENTARY REFORM (1918) and LIBERAL PARTY disunity (1916–23), Labour became the main Opposition in 1922. Ramsay MACDONALD formed minority Labour governments (Jan.–Nov. 1924, 1929–31), but schism over the NATIONAL GOVERNMENT reduced Labour to 52 MPs (1931). It recovered to serve in the coalition government of WORLD WAR II and win a landslide majority in 1945. The government of Clement ATTLEE (1945–51) implemented NATIONALIZATION and the WELFARE STATE.

Thereafter Hugh GAITSKELL, Harold WILSON and James CALLAGHAN managed division between consolidators and

A Dictionary of British and Irish History, First Edition. Edited by Robert Peberdy and Philip Waller.
© 2021 John Wiley & Sons Ltd; © editorial matter and organisation Robert Peberdy and Phillip Waller.
Published 2021 by John Wiley & Sons Ltd.

advocates of more SOCIALISM. The left wing criticized the pragmatism of Labour governments (1964–70, 1974–9). Internal strife peaked under Michael FOOT, when the SOCIAL DEMOCRATIC PARTY seceded (1981). Labour suffered four election defeats (1979, 1983, 1987, 1992).

After Neil KINNOCK and John SMITH moderated policy, Tony BLAIR reconciled his followers to policies adopted by the Conservative Margaret THATCHER (e.g., abandoning nationalization) and won three elections as NEW LABOUR (1997, 2001, 2005). His successor Gordon BROWN lost the 2010 election and resigned (succeeded by Ed Miliband to 2015, Jeremy Corbyn to 2020, then Sir Keir Starmer).

LABOUR PARTY, IRISH A political party, founded by the Irish Trade Union Congress on 28 June 1912, which initially advocated an Irish republic. It abstained from both the 1918 UK general election and 1921 Irish election to help SINN FÉIN. In 1922, following creation of the IRISH FREE STATE, it won 17 seats in the Dáil and acted as the Opposition (in the absence of Sinn Féin members).

From 1927, when FIANNA FÁIL deputies joined the Dáil, the Labour Party was usually the third-largest party. From 1932 its support enabled Fianna Fáil to hold office, and it later participated in coalition governments mostly alongside FINE GAEL (1948–51, 1954–7, 1973–7, 1981–2, 1982–7, 1994–7, 2011–16). In 1993–4, after winning a record 33 seats, it exceptionally allied with Fianna Fáil (under Albert REYNOLDS), but withdrew over a controversial judicial appointment. Labour then joined a government with Fine Gael and Democratic Left (so-called 'Rainbow Coalition') without an election. Labour's leader from 1982 to 1997 was Dick Spring. At the 2011 election, during an economic crisis, Labour won 37 seats and joined a government under Enda KENNY. But in 2016 its representation collapsed to seven seats. (Its sole minister left the government in 2017.) In 2020, Labour won six seats.

Labour has won support among farm labourers, in larger towns, and among middle-class liberals but has lacked strong appeal to industrial workers. It has advocated a controlled economy and expansive welfare. *See also* POLITICAL PARTIES, SOUTHERN IRELAND FROM 1922; ROBINSON, MARY.

LABOUR PARTY, SCOTLAND Two attempts were made to establish a Scottish working-class party. In 1888 Keir HARDIE and R.B. CUNNINGHAME GRAHAM founded the Scottish Parliamentary Labour Party; it merged in 1894 with the (British) INDEPENDENT LABOUR PARTY (ILP). In Jan. 1900 working-class organizations founded the Scottish Workers' Parliamentary Elections Committee ('Representation' Committee from 1902), to seek representation in Parliament. In June 1906, following the renaming of the (London-based) Labour Representation Committee (LRC) as the LABOUR PARTY, it renamed itself Labour Party

(Scottish Section). It amalgamated with main party in 1909. A Scottish Advisory Council was instituted in 1915 (later replaced by an elected Scottish National Executive Committee) and constituency organizations were widely established in the 1930s.

Two MPs (LRC-sponsored) were elected in 1906 (re-elected Jan. 1910), three in Dec. 1910, six in 1918. By 1915 there were also 69 town and 13 county councillors. In 1922 Labour, allied with the ILP, became the largest Scottish parliamentary party (winning 29 of 74 seats), thanks largely to newly registered voters (enfranchised 1918).

Until the 1960s Labour vied with Unionists (Conservatives). Except in 1931 (7), it won 20–38 seats (including ILP seats, 1922–45), achieving majorities in 1923, 1929, 1945, 1950, and 1959. It also dominated many local authorities from the 1930s. From 1964 Labour consistently won majorities in parliamentary elections (40–56 seats), until 2015 when it was dramatically displaced by the SCOTTISH NATIONAL PARTY (SNP): it collapsed to one seat, recovering slightly in 2017 (seven seats). In 2019, representation fell back to one seat.

At DEVOLUTION, Labour became the largest party in the Scottish Parliament, winning 56 seats (of 129) in 1999 and 50 in 2003, and forming coalition administrations with the LIBERAL DEMOCRATS (1999–2003, 2003–7). In 2007 it slipped to second (46 seats), enabling the SNP to become the governing party. Labour won 37 seats in 2011, and came third in 2016 with 24.

LABOUR PARTY, WALES The 1890s LABOUR MOVEMENT found considerable support in industrial areas, with branches of the INDEPENDENT LABOUR PARTY (founded 1893) being started from 1897. In 1900 Keir HARDIE was elected to the UK Parliament as ILP MP for MERTHYR TYDFIL, supported by the Labour Representation Committee (founded 1900, renamed LABOUR PARTY 1906).

From the 1922 general election onwards the Labour Party won the majority of Welsh parliamentary constituencies (except in 1924 and 1931). MPs from Wales included five leaders of the parliamentary Party: Hardie, Ramsay MACDONALD, James CALLAGHAN, Michael FOOT, and Neil KINNOCK. From the 1920s Labour dominated local government (supplanting the LIBERAL PARTY) and in 1999 won the largest number of seats (28 of 60) in the new Welsh Assembly (*see* PARLIAMENT, WALES). Thereafter it formed either minority governments in Wales or coalitions with a junior partner.

Local organization initially developed as part of the British Party, with Arthur HENDERSON rejecting Welsh demands for autonomy *c*.1918. Welsh agents and organizers (of both sexes) were appointed in the 1920s–30s, and they and their successors became increasingly powerful. A S Wales Regional Federation was established in the late

1930s. After 1945 it was replaced by an all-Wales organization with its own staff and annual conference. It clashed at times with Labour's national headquarters, notably over devolution in the 1960s–70s. *See also* DEVOLUTION, WALES.

LABOUR SERVICES Agricultural tasks, such as ploughing, sowing, reaping and managing livestock, which unfree peasant tenants were obliged to perform on their lord's directly managed (or 'demesne') lands in return for holding their own land (*see* MANOR). Some were undertaken weekly, others at busy times such as harvest. Services are recorded throughout the British Isles in the 12th–14th centuries though they doubtless existed much earlier. The obligation to undertake services was recognized as evidence for unfree social status.

Lords abandoned services under pressure from tenants mainly in the 14th–15th centuries, especially after the BLACK DEATH (1348–50). 'Servile' tenure was replaced by contract-like TENURES. *See also* SERFDOM; SOCIAL STRUCTURE, ENGLAND 1066 TO 16TH CENTURY.

LACY, HUGH DE (fl. from 1162 in England; d. 26 July 1186 at Durrow, Meath lordship, E Ireland, aged about 46). De Lacy went to Ireland in Oct. 1171 with HENRY II. In April 1172, to counter the power of STRONGBOW, he was granted MEATH as a lordship. There he settled followers from England.

After Strongbow's death (1176), de Lacy was the pre-eminent Anglo-Norman in Ireland. In 1180 he married a daughter of the high-king of Ireland, Ruaidrí UA CONCHOBAIR. De Lacy was suspected of wanting to succeed Ruaidrí, prompting Henry II to send John to Ireland in 1185 (*see* JOHN AND IRELAND). De Lacy was assassinated on the order of a minor Irish king, possibly in revenge for the earlier killing of the king's son. *See also* NORMANS, IMPACT ON IRELAND.

LAIRD (Scots, meaning 'lord'). In Scotland, a landowner or landholder below the PEERAGE, possibly owning a BARONY; similar to GENTRY or yeoman farmers in England. Originally noblemen, they were considered non-noble by the late 16th century. Lairds benefited from the 16th-century FEUING MOVEMENT, were represented in PARLIAMENT (by shire commissioners) from 1587, and were prominent in local government in the 18th century. Their numbers fell from the 1760s as landownership became concentrated. *See also* SOCIAL STRUCTURE, SCOTLAND; LOCAL GOVERNMENTAL STRUCTURES, SCOTLAND.

LAISSEZ-FAIRE (French, meaning 'let [people] do'). Term used by French economists from the early 18th century to denounce State interference, especially in trade. The principle of State restraint was supported by English classical economists of the 18th and 19th centuries, who held that the free working of markets ensured maximum economic welfare. The State should therefore remove obstacles to trade. Laissez-faire influenced the UK's adherence to FREE TRADE from the 1840s to 1930s. *See also* CLASSICAL AND NEOCLASSICAL ECONOMICS; MANCHESTER SCHOOL; CORN LAWS.

LAMBERT, JOHN (b. summer 1619 at Calton, Yorkshire, England; d. March 1684 at St Nicholas Island, Devon, England, aged 64). Lambert fought for Parliament in the CIVIL WARS (from 1642), and became a commander in the NEW MODEL ARMY (from 1646). In 1647 he was among officers who negotiated with Parliament. He was prominent in the English invasion of Scotland (1650–1).

Lambert drafted the INSTRUMENT OF GOVERNMENT, the basis for the Protectorate established in Dec. 1653. He was thought likely to succeed Oliver CROMWELL as lord protector. But in 1657 he opposed enhancement of the protector's position and was forced to resign his commands (*see* HUMBLE PETITION AND ADVICE). Restored in late 1659, after dismissal of the RUMP PARLIAMENT, he attempted in 1659–60 to prevent the RESTORATION. He was convicted of high TREASON in 1662 and exiled. *See also* COMMONWEALTH AND PROTECTORATE.

LAMBERTON, WILLIAM (fl. from 1292; d. 1328, probably at St Andrews, Fife, E Scotland). Clergyman. After King EDWARD I of England seized Scotland in 1296, Lamberton did homage (as chancellor of Glasgow Cathedral). But in Nov. 1297, after the Scottish victory at STIRLING BRIDGE, he was elected to the pre-eminent bishopric of ST ANDREWS on the instruction of William WALLACE. Lamberton also served as a 'guardian' of Scotland (chosen by MAGNATES) 1299–1301.

After Scottish nobles resubmitted to Edward in Feb. 1304, Lamberton secretly agreed (11 June) to support Robert Bruce (*see* ROBERT I). He co-operated with Edward in 1305, but backed Robert's seizure of kingship in Feb. 1306. Captured in June, Lamberton was imprisoned in England until 1309. He remained a senior bishop for most of King Robert's reign.

LAMBETH A borough in S LONDON which became notorious in 1985 when its LABOUR PARTY council, led by Ted Knight (nicknamed 'Red Ted'), refused to set a budget in protest against the British Conservative government's 1984 Rates Act. Thirty-two councillors were surcharged and banned for five years. The council was widely seen as a leading example of irresponsible and inefficient management, based on political PATRONAGE, and was even disowned by the national Labour Party. *See also* LONDON, GOVERNMENT OF.

LANCASTER, DUCHY OF In England, a landed estate formed from 1267 when Edmund Crouchback, a younger son of King HENRY III, was created earl of Lancaster. His earldom included royal estates in Lancashire. In 1351 Henry of Grosmont, the 4th earl (d. 1361), was created a duke and given palatine powers in Lancashire (e.g., appointment of county officers). In 1362 the duchy's estates passed to Henry's son-in-law JOHN OF GAUNT, who was created duke of Lancaster.

In 1399, when Gaunt's son Henry Bolingbroke seized the throne, the duchy became an asset of the Crown but retained its own administration (*see* HENRY IV). Since the 18th century the duchy's chancellor has usually been a member of the British government and CABINET. *See also* PALATINATE.

LANCASTER, HENRY EARL OF (b. *c.*1280 in England; d. 22 Sept. 1345 in England, aged about 65). A younger brother of THOMAS OF LANCASTER (d. 1322), Henry of Lancaster opposed King EDWARD II (his cousin) and the DESPENSERS from 1322, and supported Edward's deposition by Queen ISABELLA and Roger MORTIMER (1326–7). He was styled earl of Lancaster from Oct. 1326 and had custody of Edward (Nov. 1326–April 1327).

After Edward II abdicated (Jan. 1327), Lancaster was president of the regency COUNCIL. But in 1328 he became estranged from the court, which was dominated by Mortimer. Around 1329 Lancaster became blind. Though disenchanted with Mortimer and Isabella, he was not involved in their overthrow (Oct. 1330). Thereafter he assisted various royal commissions. *See also* EDWARD III.

LANCASTRIANS Historians' term for: (a) three kings of England descended from JOHN OF GAUNT (d. 1399), duke of Lancaster and third son of EDWARD III, namely HENRY IV, HENRY V, HENRY VI, and their supporters and servants; (b) supporters of HENRY VI and MARGARET OF ANJOU during their struggles with 'Yorkists' in the 1450s, and of their efforts to reclaim the throne 1461–71 (*see* YORKIST–LANCASTRIAN CONFLICT). The term is also sometimes applied to supporters of Henry Tudor (i.e., HENRY VII) against EDWARD IV and RICHARD III.

The Lancastrian kings' claim to the throne was based on their descent in the male line from Edward III. They argued that the Yorkist claim was invalid because it involved descent through the female line (*see* YORKISTS).

LAND AGITATION AND REFORM, IRELAND After the failure of the UNION REPEAL MOVEMENT, some nationalist politicians exploited agricultural unrest. In 1850, following the GREAT FAMINE, C.G. DUFFY and Frederick Lucas founded the IRISH TENANT LEAGUE to campaign for statutory rights for tenants (*see* 'THREE FS').

About 48 Irish pro-reform MPs were elected in 1852, but failed to obtain legislation. (The League ceased in 1858.) Reforms were enacted by (the British Liberal) W.E. Gladstone (1869, provision for sale of land to tenants in disestablishment of Church of Ireland; 1870, Land Act giving statutory recognition to ULSTER CUSTOM).

The LAND LEAGUE, founded Oct. 1879 by Irish republican Michael DAVITT (following bad harvests), waged a 'Land War', encouraging tenants to ostracize 'unco-operative' landlords. Gladstone's government passed coercive legislation (March 1881) and a Land Act (Aug.), the latter conceding the 'Three Fs' and a Land Court for rent adjudication. But agitation continued, despite proscription of the League and imprisonment of its leaders, including C.S. PARNELL (Oct. 1881). It declined after the KILMAINHAM TREATY (May 1882), under which Parnell discouraged unrest and the government helped indebted tenants (Arrears of Rent Act, Aug. 1882).

Agitation was revived by the NATIONAL LEAGUE following Gladstone's failure to enact Home Rule (June 1886); its PLAN OF CAMPAIGN (Oct.) encouraged tenants to set rents. The ensuing unrest was combated by (the British Conservative) A.J. BALFOUR, who pursued land reform to diminish support for Home Rule (1887, Land Act permitting rent adjustments and regulating evictions; 1888, 1891, Land Purchase Acts providing purchase loans).

New agitation was inflamed in 1898 by the UNITED IRISH LEAGUE (so-called 'Ranch War'). Pressure from William O'BRIEN led to a LAND CONFERENCE (1902) and the 1903 Land Act which encouraged sales and provided loans. By 1920, 9 million acres were purchased, making Ireland substantially a land of small owner-occupiers. *See also* GLADSTONE, W.E., AND IRELAND; WYNDHAM, GEORGE; HOME RULE MOVEMENT, IRELAND.

LAND CONFERENCE In DUBLIN, Ireland, a meeting of representatives of landowners and tenants, Dec. 1902, convened by landowner John Shawe-Taylor to settle the Irish 'land question'. Its recommendation that tenants should receive government loans to buy their land formed the basis of the 1903 Land Act ('Wyndham Act'). *See also* O'BRIEN, WILLIAM; WYNDHAM, GEORGE; LAND REFORM LEGISLATION, IRELAND 19TH AND EARLY 20TH CENTURIES.

LANDED SOCIETY, DECLINE OF, ENGLAND Despite the INDUSTRIAL REVOLUTION, political power (outside industrial towns) was largely based on concentrated landownership until the late 19th century. In the late 1870s, nearly 80% of land was owned by 7000 families. In the UK PARLIAMENT, most peers in the House of Lords were landowners or members of landed families, as were a majority of Commons members. Within counties, administrative and judicial authority was exercised by LORD LIEUTENANTS (usually aristocrats) and JUSTICES OF THE PEACE (JPs, usually GENTRY).

Landed political power slowly diminished from the 1880s as a result of political developments and economic pressures. From 1885, MPs from landed backgrounds were a minority in the Commons, and the proportion of landed peers declined (half of new peers 1886–1914 were from non-landed backgrounds). Legislation in 1889 transferred JPs' administrative powers to elected county councils. Many landed families suffered financial pressure from the AGRICULTURAL DEPRESSION (1880s–90s), graduated death duties (from 1894), high income tax during and after WORLD WAR I (1914–18), and adoption of market values for death duties (1919). The Parliament Act of 1911 ended the Lords' veto of legislation (see PARLIAMENT, UNITED KINGDOM 1801 TO 1921).

After the war, in which many landowners and heirs were killed, land seemed to have lost its political prestige. In 1919–22 a quarter of English land was sold as landowners reduced or disposed of estates. Sales persisted, and hundreds of country houses were demolished or abandoned, or sold for non-domestic purposes. After WORLD WAR II (1939–45) estates (including houses) were also donated to the NATIONAL TRUST. By 1982 large landowners retained only a third of agricultural land, although landownership remained socially prestigious and land was bought, for example, by successful businessmen. See also PEERAGE, BRITISH AND UNITED KINGDOM.

LANDED SOCIETY, DECLINE OF, IRELAND In the late 18th century most land belonged to about 2000 estates, the majority consisting of 2000–4000 acres (800–1600 ha) and several dozen of over 50,000 acres (20,000 ha). Most owners were of NEW ENGLISH descent (from 16th or 17th century) and comprised the PROTESTANT ASCENDANCY; few were Gaelic Irish, OLD ENGLISH or presbyterian. Landowners' involvement in Irish society and affairs diminished when the UNION OF IRELAND AND GREAT BRITAIN (1801) terminated Ireland's PARLIAMENT. Some landowners moved to England or became part-time absentees. Unlike in Great Britain, many left investment in landholdings to tenants.

From 1879 deterioration in tenants' conditions caused by the AGRICULTURAL DEPRESSION generated agitation against landowners. The British government initially reformed tenancy conditions, but from 1885 legislation by the UK Parliament included provision of loans for tenants to acquire holdings, and from 1891 the CONGESTED DISTRICTS BOARD acquired estates for reorganization. The most far-reaching measure was the 1903 Land Act, which induced landlords to sell holdings by providing cash (rather than stock) for sales and a bonus. Immediately afterwards, for example, the duke of Leinster's trustees sold 45,000 acres (18,000 ha) to tenants.

By 1920 'landlordism' had been largely extinguished by State action. It was attacked symbolically during the War of Irish Independence (1919–21) and Irish Civil War (1922–3) with the burning of over 300 'big houses'. Many survivors were acquired by institutions (e.g., schools, religious orders). See also TENURES, IRELAND; LAND AGITATION AND REFORM, IRELAND; SOCIAL STRUCTURE, IRELAND FROM 17TH CENTURY.

LANDED SOCIETY, DECLINE OF, WALES From the 16th century landed wealth and power were highly concentrated. GENTRY and English peers owned over 60% of land, and the gentry provided JUSTICES OF THE PEACE, MPs, and influenced towns and the Church (of England). The gentry became distanced from ordinary rural society, in the 18th century by their adoption of the English language, and in the 19th century by the espousal of nonconformity by many country people.

Landed power declined from 1865, when landlords became a minority of MPs (see LIBERAL PARTY, WALES). JPs lost administrative powers to new county councils in 1889 (usually dominated by Liberals), while the AGRICULTURAL DEPRESSION of the 1880s–90s reduced rental incomes and the new death-duty system of 1894 threatened the viability of estates. Many were sold or reduced between 1919 and 1922, leaving landowners with about a third of agricultural land. Country houses decayed or were adapted as schools or hotels. See also SOCIAL STRUCTURE, WALES; CONSERVATIVE PARTY, WALES.

LAND LEAGUE In Ireland, an organization inaugurated in DUBLIN on 21 Oct. 1879 (as the Irish National Land League) to seek rent reductions and facilitate landownership by tenants. It was founded by Michael DAVITT, partly to create unrest for nationalist purposes. C.S. PARNELL was president.

From Sept. 1880 the League campaigned against landlords by encouraging the withholding of 'excessive' rents and co-operation. ('Victims' included Charles BOYCOTT.) The government responded by arresting Parnell (13 Oct. 1881) and proscribing the League (20 Oct.). It was supplanted by the NATIONAL LEAGUE. See also PARNELL, ANNA; LAND AGITATION AND REFORM, IRELAND.

LAND REFORM LEGISLATION, IRELAND 19TH AND EARLY 20TH CENTURIES Between 1870 and 1909 the UK Parliament passed legislation that increased tenants' rights and extensively replaced landlords with owner-occupiers (almost 500,000 by 1920).

The Landlord and Tenant (Ireland) Act of 1870, promoted by W.E. GLADSTONE ('First Gladstone Land Act'), gave legal recognition to ULSTER CUSTOM where established (recompense of tenant's 'interest' in his land) and prescribed compensation for tenants' improvements to holdings.

Agricultural depression, rural unrest (the 'Land War'), and agitation by the LAND LEAGUE resulted in the Land Law (Ireland) Act of 1881 ('Second Gladstone Land Act'). It conceded the 'THREE Fs' throughout Ireland (fair rent, fixity of tenure, free sale of tenancies), and established a Land Court to adjudicate rents and a Land Commission to provide tenants with loans for purchase of holdings (to 75% of value). The 1885 Purchase of Land (Ireland) Act ('Ashbourne Act') raised the loan limit to 100%, and the 1887 Land Law (Ireland) Act empowered the Land Court to fix leaseholders' rents and revise other rents.

The 1891 Purchase of Land (Ireland) Act ('Balfour Act') enabled landlords to receive bonds for land sales, and established the CONGESTED DISTRICTS BOARD. The 1903 Land Act ('Wyndham Act') provided standard terms for land sales (based on agreement at the 1902 LAND CONFERENCE). Its terms were modified by the 1909 Irish Land Act ('Birrell Act'). See also LAND AGITATION AND REFORM, IRELAND.

LAND TAX A tax authorized for England and Wales by legislation in 1692, to help fund the War of the GRAND ALLIANCE; extended to Scotland in 1707. It was influenced by the 'assessment' introduced by Parliament in 1643. Renewed annually, land tax was the only direct tax in Great Britain during the 18th century. It was levied initially on personal estate, offices and land, at 4s. in the pound (i.e., a 20% tax rate), but developed into a tax on land, buildings and rents. Until 1714 it provided a third of government revenue. Thereafter the rate was usually lower (with EXCISE duties mainly used to provide additional revenue).

From 1798 land tax was perpetual, but could be redeemed by payment of a capital sum (to benefit the SINKING FUND). Redemption was made compulsory on the sale of property in 1949, and unredeemed tax was abolished in 1963. See also FISCAL–MILITARY STATE.

LAND WAR, IRELAND see LAND AGITATION AND REFORM, IRELAND

LANE, ALLEN (b. 21 Sept. 1902 at Bristol, Gloucestershire, England; d. 7 July 1970 at Northwood, London, England, aged 67). Allen Williams joined the London-based Bodley Head publishing company, and changed surname, in 1919. In the 1930s he discerned a mass market for well-designed, cheap paperback books. His first ten 'Penguin paperbacks', all novels, were issued by Bodley Head in June 1935; following their success Lane founded Penguin Books (1936). Series were started for non-fiction and children's books. Lane was knighted in 1952. A risk-taker, Lane in 1960 published the long-banned (1928) novel *Lady Chatterley's Lover* by D.H. LAWRENCE, testing the 1959 Obscene Publications Act. Penguin Books was indicted, and acquitted in a celebrated trial (20 Oct.–2 Nov. 1960).

LANFRANC (b. c.1010 at Pavia, Lombardy, Italy; d. 24 May 1089 at Canterbury, Kent, England, aged about 79). In NORMANDY from c.1039, Lanfranc became a monk at Bec (c.1042) where he attracted outstanding pupils (including ANSELM). He became prior of Bec c.1045, then abbot of St Stephen's, Caen (1063).

In 1070 Lanfranc was appointed archbishop of CANTERBURY in England. Working closely with King WILLIAM I, he replaced English abbots and bishops with Normans and promoted Church reform (e.g., adoption of celibacy by secular clergy). He helped WILLIAM II to become king (1087), and suppressed the rebellion of ODO OF BAYEUX (1088). See also PRIMACY DISPUTE, CANTERBURY AND YORK.

LANGHAM PLACE CIRCLE An informal group of English middle-class women who campaigned for the Married Women's Property Bill (1857) and other women's causes (until 1866). They included Barbara BODICHON, Bessie Parkes (1829–1925) and Emily Davies (1830–1921). Several wrote for the *English Woman's Journal* (1858–64), based in Langham Place, London. See also ANDERSON, ELIZABETH GARRETT; WOMEN'S MOVEMENT 1850S TO 1918, GREAT BRITAIN.

LANGLAND, WILLIAM (b. c.1325 at Cleobury Mortimer, Shropshire, England; d. c.1390 at London, England). Langland was probably the author of *The Vision of Piers Plowman*, an alliterative English poem written in the 1360s–70s and later revised which satirized contemporary society through the medium of a 'dream-vision'. The son of an Oxfordshire landowner, Langland took minor clerical orders and was employed as a chaplain and CHANTRY priest by wealthy patrons. See also ENGLISH LITERATURE, ENGLAND.

LANGSIDE, BATTLE OF Fought in W Scotland, SW of Glasgow, on 13 May 1568. MARY, QUEEN OF SCOTS, who had abdicated in 1567, and her supporters were defeated by the regent James, earl of MORAY. Mary was attempting to rally support after escaping from prison (2 May 1568). After the battle Mary fled into England while war continued in Scotland (see MARIAN CIVIL WAR).

LANGTON, STEPHEN (b. c.1150 at Langton, Lincolnshire, England; d. 9 July 1228 at Slindon, Sussex, England, aged about 78). A teacher at Paris University, Langton was elected archbishop of CANTERBURY (Dec. 1206) in Rome by Canterbury monks influenced by Pope Innocent III. But King JOHN, denied his own nominee, refused to admit Langton. Innocent placed England under an interdict (prohibition of sacraments, from March 1208) and excommunicated John (Nov. 1209). Eventually John conceded. Langton entered England on 9 July 1213.

During the crisis that culminated in MAGNA CARTA, Langton advised John's opponents while seeking conciliation with the king (1213–15). He was abroad 1215–18, 1220–1, but involved in English politics in the 1220s (*see* HENRY III). In 1222 Langton held a Church council which issued influential canons (e.g., setting a minimum income for vicars).

LANSBURY, GEORGE (b. 22 Feb. 1859 at Halesworth, Suffolk, England; d. 7 May 1940 at Golders Green, Middlesex, England, aged 81). A navvy's son, involved in London politics from 1886, Lansbury was a CHRISTIAN SOCIALIST and pacifist. A Labour MP 1910–12, he was involved in the 'Poplar rates rebellion' of 1921 (*see* POPLARISM). Re-elected as an MP in 1922, Lansbury served as commissioner for works under Ramsay MACDONALD 1929–31 but refused to join MacDonald's NATIONAL GOVERNMENT (Aug. 1931).

The only former Labour Cabinet minister (other than National Labour ministers) re-elected to Parliament in Oct. 1931, he became Labour's parliamentary leader, and succeeded Arthur HENDERSON as Party leader in Oct. 1932 (resigned leadership 1935). He maintained his strong pacifist outlook despite the rise of European fascism in the 1920s–30s.

LANSDOWNE, 3RD MARQUESS OF (b. 2 July 1780 at London, England; d. 31 Jan. 1863 at Bowood, Wiltshire, England, aged 82). A son of the WHIG earl of SHELBURNE, Henry Petty (Petty-Fitzmaurice from 1818) was elected an MP in 1802. He succeeded as marquess in 1809.

Previously chancellor of the Exchequer 1806–7 (under Lord GRENVILLE), Petty offended partisan Whigs by serving George CANNING and Viscount GODERICH (LIBERAL TORIES) as home secretary (1827–8); but his moderation as lord president of the Council (1830–4, 1835–41, 1846–52) and minister without portfolio (1853–63) helped CABINET cohesion.

LANSDOWNE, 5TH MARQUESS OF (b. 14 Jan. 1845 at London, England; d. 3 June 1927 at Clonmel, Co. Tipperary, Irish Free State, aged 82). LIBERAL UNIONIST politician. Henry Petty-Fitzmaurice succeeded as marquess in 1866. He was governor-general of Canada (1883–8) and viceroy of India (1888–94) before serving as war secretary (1895–1900), when defeats in the (Second) BOER WAR damaged his reputation. As foreign secretary (1900–5) he negotiated the ANGLO-JAPANESE ALLIANCE (1902) and ANGLO-FRENCH CONVENTION (1904); as leader of Conservative peers (1903–16) he opposed the PEOPLE'S BUDGET (1909). His 'Lansdowne Letter' in a national newspaper (29 Nov. 1917), which called for a compromise peace in WORLD WAR I, excited vilification.

LARGS, BATTLE OF Fought near Largs on the W coast of Scotland on 2 Oct. 1263. An indecisive clash between Scottish forces and Norwegians from King Haakon's naval expedition (which aimed to prevent King ALEXANDER III from seizing Norwegian territories off Scotland). The expedition failed. *See also* PERTH, TREATY OF.

LARKIN, JIM (b. 21 Jan. 1876 at Liverpool, Lancashire, England; d. 30 Jan. 1947 at Dublin, southern Ireland, aged 71). Of Irish parentage, Larkin went from England to Ireland in 1907 to organize BELFAST dockers for the National Union of Dock Labourers. A lockout ensued (May–Nov.), which English trade unionists settled without Larkin's involvement. He therefore founded the separate Irish Transport and General Workers' Union (Dec. 1908), provoking the bitter 'Dublin lockout' (Aug. 1913–Feb. 1914; defeat for Union).

In Oct. 1914 Larkin went to the USA (imprisoned 1920). He returned to Ireland (Irish Free State) in 1923, but was prevented from resuming his union leadership. He founded the Workers' Union of Ireland in 1924 and served as an Independent Labour TD (1926–32) and Labour Party TD (1943–4). *See also* TRADE UNIONISM, IRELAND; LABOUR PARTY, IRISH; CONNOLLY, JAMES.

LATIMER, HUGH (b. *c*.1485 at Thurcaston, Leicestershire, England; d. 16 Oct. 1555 at Oxford, Oxfordshire, England, aged about 70). A scholar at CAMBRIDGE University 1510s–20s, Latimer was attracted by the theology of Continental reformers from the mid 1520s. In the 1530s he attacked aspects of traditional Christianity (e.g., doctrine of purgatory). In 1535, supported by Anne BOLEYN, he was appointed bishop of Worcester but resigned in July 1539 in response to the reaffirmation of conservative doctrine by King HENRY VIII (*see* SIX ARTICLES).

During the reign of EDWARD VI (1547–53) Latimer preached widely in favour of reformed theology. When MARY I became queen, he was arrested (Sept. 1553), taken to OXFORD (March 1554), tried, and burnt for heresy. *See also* REFORMATION, ENGLAND.

LATIN, USE BY IRISH Contacts with Roman Britain brought awareness of Latin to Ireland from the 2nd century (*see* ROMAN BRITAIN AND IRELAND). It became familiar from the 5th century as the language of the Christian Church (*see* CONVERSION OF IRELAND). Latin (or 'Hiberno-Latin') writing and learning flourished in monasteries in the 6th–8th centuries, making Ireland an intellectual centre of European stature; they remained vibrant among Irishmen in Continental Europe through the 9th century (*see* GOLDEN AGE). Writings included grammars, biblical commentaries, penitentials, saints' lives, and annals. Irish Latinists developed the extravagant 'Hisperic style' (named after the 7th-century *Hisperica famina*, 'Western Sayings', implying elegance). Influential abroad, it featured long phrases and new words. Latin writing was minimal in Ireland in the 10th–12th centuries.

Following the Anglo-Norman invasion (1169–70), Anglo-Norman Latin was the main language of government documents and Church records (to 16th century). In the 12th–15th centuries most literary writers were Anglo-Irish and probably studied overseas. (Lack of a university made Ireland an intellectual backwater.) Authors often remained abroad (e.g., Peter of Ireland who *c.*1240 taught philosopher Thomas Aquinas in Italy). The most notable was Richard FITZRALPH (d. 1360), churchman and theologian. The only known Gaelic Irish Latinist was Maurice O'Fihely (Muiris Ó Fithcheallaigh, *c.*1460–1513), editor of writings by philosopher Duns Scotus.

Latin writing by Irishmen flourished again from the later 16th to early 18th centuries, partly because advanced education became available at Continental Catholic colleges and seminaries (part of the Counter-Reformation). Theology predominated, alongside philosophy and history. Many authors lived abroad, such as Luke Wadding (1588–1657), historian of the Franciscans, and Augustine Gibbon Burke (1613–76), who refuted LUTHERANISM and CALVINISM. The less numerous Protestants included Richard Stanihurst (1547–1618) and James USSHER (d. 1656). From the 18th century, Latin continued in Ireland in GRAMMAR SCHOOL education and in the Catholic Church. *See also* EDUCATION, IRELAND.

LATIN, USE IN BRITAIN Latin was spoken and written in ROMAN BRITAIN (1st–early 5th centuries AD), especially in government, the army and towns. Though it largely disappeared, it survived where the Christian Church continued, particularly in western regions (as exemplified by GILDAS), and was strengthened in the 5th–6th centuries by MONASTICISM. Latin learning spread to Ireland, and from there to N Britain (*see* IONA).

Latin was widely revived in southern Britain with the adoption of Christianity by Germanic kingdoms (*see* CONVERSION OF ANGLO-SAXONS). It was used by clergy in liturgy, in learning and writing at MINSTERS, and for documents (*see* EDUCATION AND LEARNING, ENGLAND BEFORE 1066), though from the late 9th century alongside Old English.

After the NORMAN CONQUEST of England (1066–70s) Latin remained the language of clergy, and some Latin was acquired by kings, BARONS, KNIGHTS and merchants though FRENCH was used extensively. Latin became the standard written language of central government (e.g., in DOMESDAY BOOK), and was also used for Church records, some legal records, local record-keeping (e.g., manorial records, property charters) and some literary genres (e.g., chronicles, saints' lives, legal treatises such as *BRACTON*).

Similar developments occurred in Scotland. Latin was central to GRAMMAR SCHOOL education and UNIVERSITY learning (from the 12th and 15th centuries respectively in England and Scotland). Latin of the 12th–15th centuries tended to be plain. Its use in record-keeping declined in the 16th century, and English and Scots were preferred to Latin in Church services from the REFORMATION.

From the later 15th century, Latin in schools and universities became based on 'classical' Roman Latin, under the influence of HUMANISM; literary works (e.g., by George BUCHANAN) imitated classical Latin. Latin continued as a main language of religious, scholarly and scientific publications until the 18th century, and remained important in post-elementary education into the 20th century.

LATIN AMERICA, BRITISH INVOLVEMENT In the 19th century, Great Britain developed commercial interests in Latin America of far greater significance than its territorial holdings (BRITISH GUIANA, BRITISH HONDURAS). Expeditions to capture the Spanish imperial city of Buenos Aires failed in 1806–7, but internal revolutions after 1810 destroyed the Spanish trade monopoly. In the 1820s the foreign secretary George CANNING used British naval supremacy to deter foreign intervention, and the new republics reciprocated with favourable commercial treaties. Latin America traded foodstuffs and raw materials for manufactures, notably COTTON and machinery. The British invested in agriculture, mining and railways, especially in Brazil and Argentina.

By 1913 Latin America accounted for about 10% of British trade and 20% of British overseas investment. British business communities flourished in Buenos Aires (Argentina), Rio de Janeiro (Brazil) and Valparaiso (Chile). Britain tried not to intervene in internal politics, but launched some 30 small-scale military operations to protect lives and property. Between 1914 and 1945, the USA took over as the main commercial power in Latin America. *See also* FALKLAND ISLANDS.

LATITUDINARIANISM A theological attitude ascribed to some Church of ENGLAND clergy of the late 17th century (e.g., John TILLOTSON). 'Latitude-men' were deemed to have broadened theology to include reason, and to stress morality in preference to doctrine. They were sympathetic to WHIGS, and preferred to win support from DISSENTERS rather than coerce them. Historians have also linked latitudinarianism to an interest in science and support for toleration. Latitudinarianism is also held to characterize much 18th-century Protestant Christianity.

LAUD, WILLIAM (b. 7 Oct. 1573 at Reading, Berkshire, England; d. 10 Jan. 1645 at London, England, aged 71). A clergyman and opponent of PURITANISM and CALVINISM within the Church of ENGLAND, Laud was appointed bishop of ST DAVIDS in 1621. Supported by the duke of BUCKINGHAM initially (d. 1628) and King CHARLES I, he became bishop of Bath and Wells (1626), a privy councillor (1627), bishop of London (1628), archbishop of CANTERBURY (1633).

During Charles's 'personal rule' without Parliament (1629–40), Laud was associated with the approach to government called 'THOROUGH'. His attempt to ensure uniformity and decency in worship irritated many, not just Puritans (*see* COMMUNION TABLES). He was deeply involved in Church reforms in Scotland which resulted in the REVOLT OF 1637, Wars of the COVENANT (1639–40), and recall of the English Parliament (1640; *see* SHORT PARLIAMENT).

The LONG PARLIAMENT began IMPEACHMENT proceedings against Laud in Dec. 1640, though he was not tried until 1644. It proved impossible to convict him of TREASON. Instead he was attainted and executed (*see* ATTAINDER).

Laud's anti-Puritanism was seen as motivated by ARMINIANISM, but he is unlikely to have espoused the doctrine. 'Laudianism' came to describe an emphasis on ceremony which became an aspect of the later HIGH CHURCH movement.

LAUDABILITER (Latin, meaning 'Laudably'). Name of a bull, of uncertain authenticity, allegedly issued by Pope ADRIAN IV in 1155. It allowed King HENRY II of England to enter Ireland and reform religious and moral behaviour. If genuine, it shows that Henry was interested in conquering Ireland soon after his accession (1154) but failed to act. *Laudabiliter* was not invoked when Henry eventually visited Ireland (1171–2). *See also* HENRY II AND IRELAND; CHURCH REFORM, MEDIEVAL IRELAND.

LAUDERDALE, 2ND EARL OF (b. 24 May 1616 at Lethington, SE Scotland; d. 20 Aug. 1682 at Tunbridge Wells, Kent, England, aged 66). John Maitland (great-nephew of William MAITLAND) succeeded as earl in 1645. Wanting presbyterianism to be extended to England, he collaborated with English Parliamentarians in 1643–4 (e.g., signing the SOLEMN LEAGUE AND COVENANT). After Parliament reneged on the League's religious provisions, he negotiated the ENGAGEMENT with King CHARLES I (26 Dec. 1647). In 1651 he was captured, fighting for King CHARLES II at WORCESTER (W England), and imprisoned (until March 1660).

After the RESTORATION (1660), Lauderdale was Charles's SECRETARY OF STATE for Scotland until 1680 and KING'S COMMISSIONER from 1669. Although based at court, he effectively ruled Scotland for 20 years. He complied with the restoration of episcopacy and combated COVENANTERS, at first with indulgences (1669–73), then with persecution (1673–9). He was created duke of Lauderdale in 1672. *See also* CIVIL WARS, SCOTTISH PARTICIPATION; RISING OF

1679; CABAL; COUNCIL FOR SCOTTISH AFFAIRS; MIDDLETON, JOHN; ROTHES, 7TH EARL OF.

LAUDIANISM *see* LAUD, WILLIAM

LAUDIANISM, IMPACT ON IRELAND The promotion of Church authority and dignified worship associated in England and Wales with Archbishop William LAUD (1630s) was extended to the Church of IRELAND mainly by Thomas Wentworth (lord deputy 1632–40) and John Bramhall (bishop of Derry 1634–61). In 1634 the Church's Convocation (assembly) adopted new canons (laws), required clergy to subscribe to the English Thirty-nine Articles, and ordered COMMUNION TABLES to be placed at the east end of churches. Sympathetic clergy were appointed from England, and Bramhall implemented schemes to improve clergy incomes. Developments generated opposition to Wentworth. *See also* WENTWORTH, THOMAS, AND IRELAND; ARTICLES OF RELIGION; USSHER, JAMES.

LAURIER, WILFRID (b. 20 Nov. 1841 at St Lin, Quebec, Canada; d. 17 Feb. 1919 at Ottawa, Ontario, Canada, aged 77). Laurier, a lawyer, became a Liberal member of the Canadian Parliament in 1874, Party leader in 1887, and prime minister in 1896 (the first French-Canadian). He was knighted in 1897. Laurier awarded the UK a preferential tariff in 1897, and supported involvement in the (Second) BOER WAR (1899–1902). But he opposed proposals to centralize government of the BRITISH EMPIRE. In 1910 he created a Royal Canadian Navy.

Laurier's Party lost the 1911 election because of opposition to a trade agreement with the USA. In Opposition, Laurier supported Canada's voluntary involvement in WORLD WAR I but opposed conscription (1917). *See also* CANADA.

LAW, BONAR (b. 16 Sept. 1858 at New Brunswick, Canada; d. 30 Oct. 1923 at London, England, aged 65). Leader of the British CONSERVATIVE PARTY 1911–21, 1922–3; prime minister 1922–3.

The son of a presbyterian minister, Law left Canada aged 12 and attended school in GLASGOW (Scotland) before entering the iron trade. A Conservative MP from 1900, he emerged as Party leader in 1911. TARIFF REFORM and Ulster were his priorities, and he co-operated with the Unionist leader E.H. CARSON (*see* UNIONISM, IRELAND).

Law became colonial secretary in the first wartime coalition government (1915–16). Dissatisfied with the leadership of H.H. ASQUITH, Law helped to oust him (Dec. 1916). He was then central to the coalition under the Liberal David LLOYD GEORGE, as chancellor of the Exchequer and leader of the House of Commons 1916–19, lord PRIVY SEAL 1919–21.

Law retired on health grounds in March 1921 (succeeded by Austen CHAMBERLAIN) but returned to intervene decisively at the CARLTON CLUB MEETING (Oct. 1922). Resuming the Conservative leadership and succeeding Lloyd George as prime minister, he won a general election (Nov.). Cancer forced his resignation (May 1923; succeeded by Stanley BALDWIN). Dour in character, Law was dubbed 'the unknown Prime Minister' by Asquith.

LAW, ENGLAND BEFORE 1066 After the adoption of Christianity in Anglo-Saxon kingdoms, laws were written down and preserved by clergy. The first law code is that of King ÆTHELBERT of KENT (d. 616). Important later codes include those of INE (d. 726), ALFRED (d. 899), ATHELSTAN (d. 939) and CNUT (d. 1035). It is unclear whether early codes were responses to particular problems or assertions of royal authority. Tenth-century codes were especially concerned with public order, curbing blood feud, and supporting the Church.

In the late 10th century lawsuits were brought before public assemblies or COURTS (at the levels of SHIRE, hundred or wapentake, and BURH). The defendant swore an oath and was supported by compurgators (men who attested his innocence). The number required varied with the charge. If the accused failed to obtain the full number of oath-helpers he had to pay penalties or suffer trial by ordeal (immersion in water or carrying a hot iron). After a conviction the majority of offences could be compounded for (settled) by making compensation to injured parties. In the case of homicide, WERGELD was paid to kindred. Laws offered protection to widows and absolved wives from complicity in their husbands' crimes. *See also* WULFSTAN.

LAW, ENGLAND FROM 1066 The NORMAN CONQUEST (1066–70s) supplemented sources of law through the introduction of new private courts (*see* HONOUR) and 'feudal' landholding (or TENURE); by the early 12th century Church courts were being established. Overriding justice could sometimes be obtained from kings, until the ANARCHY (1139–54).

The reassertion of royal authority by King HENRY II included (from 1166) measures that cumulatively created a distinctive type of law: known as COMMON LAW, it featured procedures for disputes about landholding (*see* POSSESSORY ASSIZES), tours by royal justices (*see* EYRE), and COURTS at WESTMINSTER. Existing legal institutions continued (notably SHIRE, MANOR and TOWN courts), while the Church acquired jurisdiction over marriage and bequests of movable goods (retained to mid 19th century).

Common law was strengthened in the 13th century by formation of a legal PROFESSION, emergence of STATUTES (written laws) authorized by the COUNCIL or PARLIAMENT, and restraint of Church jurisdiction (*see* PECHAM, JOHN).

After 1215, juries replaced ordeals in criminal trials. From the later 14th century common law was implemented locally through assize courts and JUSTICES OF THE PEACE. Between the mid 14th and mid 16th centuries new royal courts operating on different principles (particularly 'equity') were established, notably CHANCERY and PREROGATIVE COURTS.

Most prerogative courts were abolished by Parliament in 1641, leaving common law pre-eminent. Judges gained greater independence from 1714 (*see* SETTLEMENT, ACT OF). From the 1690s Parliament greatly increased capital offences to protect property (to 160 by 1765), and law developed to meet new requirements of commerce.

During the 19th century fundamental reforms occurred, such as revision of criminal law (1820s) and creation of a Supreme Court of Judicature with fusion of common law and equity (1875). Important subsequent changes included replacement of assizes with Crown Courts (1972), subordination to law of the EUROPEAN ECONOMIC COMMUNITY (1973–2020), and the HUMAN RIGHTS ACT (1998). *See also* PRAEMUNIRE, STATUTES OF; EQUITY COURTS; BLACKSTONE, WILLIAM; LEGAL REFORMS, ENGLAND AND WALES, 1820s; DIVORCE, LAW RELATING TO.

LAW, IRELAND BEFORE LATE 12TH CENTURY *see* BREHON LAW

LAW, IRELAND FROM LATE 12TH CENTURY After the Anglo-Norman invasion (1169–70), English-type COURTS with English law and customs – most notably COMMON LAW – were introduced in English-controlled areas. Irish-ruled areas retained BREHON LAW, and Irish in English-controlled areas were excluded from English law. England remained a source of law; WRITS were replicated in Ireland, and relevant legislation was adopted. England's Parliament sometimes legislated for Ireland. Legislation for Irish conditions was issued by the Irish COUNCIL and PARLIAMENT (e.g., Statute of KILKENNY). Parliament's legislative capacity was reduced by POYNINGS' LAW (1495). From the 12th century the Church promoted canon law for its governance and regulation of lay behaviour.

During the 14th–15th centuries, areas under English law shrank as Gaelic Irish lordships expanded. In the 15th–early 16th centuries, Anglo-Irish magnates used English and brehon law (e.g., English land law, brehon law affecting personal matters).

The reassertion of English authority in the 16th–17th centuries sought to establish English law throughout Ireland and involved new PREROGATIVE COURTS (*see* PRESIDENCIES, IRELAND; CASTLE CHAMBER, COURT OF). As SHIRES were re-instituted, so too were assizes and quarter sessions (*see* JUSTICES OF THE PEACE, IRELAND). (Brehon law was declared incompatible with common law in 1607.) Law was also used for religious and social ends. The attempt in the 16th–17th centuries to impose Protestant Christianity partly through legal requirements largely failed (*see* RECUSANCY, IRELAND). Law was used more successfully after the WILLIAMITE WAR (1688–91) to exclude Catholics from civil authority, and suppress the Catholic Church and education (*see* ANTI-CATHOLIC LEGISLATION, IRELAND, 1691 TO 1740s). (Restrictions were removed from the late 18th century.)

During the 18th century Parliament had greater freedom to legislate, but from 1801 to 1922, during the UNION OF IRELAND AND GREAT BRITAIN, legislation was passed by the UK Parliament. It responded to Irish requirements and extended British practices to Ireland. *See also* NORMANS, IMPACT ON IRELAND; IRELAND, ENGLISH CONQUEST, 16TH CENTURY; SURRENDER AND REGRANT.

LAW, NORTHERN IRELAND *see* COURTS AND LAW, NORTHERN IRELAND

LAW, SCOTLAND Before the mid 9th century, peoples in N Britain had varied legal customs, though kin groups controlled land and took action for victims (*see* LEGES INTER BRETTOS ET SCOTTOS). After the formation of the Scottish kingdom (from 840s) Irish practices spread, with judges (like Irish BREHONS) serving as arbitrators.

In the 12th–13th centuries kings sought to centralize law making and justice using institutions and concepts from England and France, although customary practices survived (in the HIGHLANDS until the 18th century). DAVID I (ruled 1124–53) introduced JUSTICIARS and sheriffs (*see* SHERIFFDOM) who applied a COMMON LAW. Development of the COUNCIL, COUNCIL-GENERAL and PARLIAMENT reinforced central law making. Land law was elaborated (*see* TENURES, SCOTLAND) and the Church and BURGHS developed courts and bodies of law. English influence remained strong until *c*.1300 (*see* REGIAM MAJESTATEM), then declined.

During the 16th century the development of the Court of SESSION, staffed by professional judges, encouraged the emergence of a legal profession. In the 17th century links with Roman-based European law were strengthened by students' attendance at Dutch universities. New areas of law were developed (e.g., company law, trusts). Treatises were written (notably the *Institutions* by Viscount STAIR, 1681), which gave coherence by integrating sources (custom, common law, legislation, etc.).

After the UNION OF ENGLAND AND SCOTLAND (1707) English influence revived, partly through involvement by the House of Lords (*see* GREENSHIELDS' CASE), though Scottish legal writing flourished during the ENLIGHTENMENT. The survival of a distinctive legal system contributed to preserving Scottish identity. In the 19th century law was adapted to industrial society.

During the 20th century Scottish law's distinctiveness was eroded by the scale of legislation applied throughout Great Britain and assimilation to European law after entry to the EUROPEAN ECONOMIC COMMUNITY (1973). However, a new Scottish Parliament (from 1999) began to reverse the trend, and withdrawal from the European Union implied reduction of European influence (*see* BREXIT). *See also* COURTS, SCOTLAND; JUSTICIARY, HIGH COURT OF.

LAW, SOUTHERN IRELAND The 'Dáil courts' of 1919–22 were authorized to cite various sources of law (e.g., BREHON LAW, Roman law), but not English law.

From Dec. 1922 there were four major sources of law in the IRISH FREE STATE (IFS): (a) its constitution and amendments; (b) pre-1922 law, derived from English COMMON LAW, and Irish and UK legislation; (c) legislation of the IFS Parliament; (d) judicial development. A new hierarchy of courts was created in 1924. The replacement constitution of 1937 provided for the continuity of previous law and established a broader range of rights (e.g., private ownership of property). They were extended from 1965 through judicial development of 'unenumerated rights'. The Republic of Ireland's entry into the EUROPEAN ECONOMIC COMMUNITY (1973) subordinated Irish law to Community law, and the European Convention on Human Rights Act (2003) required Irish law to be interpreted with reference to the Convention (1950). *See also* COURTS, SOUTHERN IRELAND.

LAW, WALES FROM 1536 *see* UNION OF WALES WITH ENGLAND; LAW, ENGLAND FROM 1066

LAW, WELSH Medieval laws survive in about 40 Welsh and five Latin texts from the 12th century or later, though they include earlier material. Legal collections exhibit considerable unity, partly because they were copied and taught by quasi-professional jurists. Welsh law adapted to new circumstances, and in the 12th and 13th centuries rulers were involved in making law and dispensing justice. The laws cover a wide variety of topics: status and SOCIAL STRUCTURE; FAMILY AND KINSHIP; marriage, homicide, suretyship; land TENURE and inheritance; and elements of KINGSHIP.

Laws were resorted to, and order maintained, at local level: witnesses were expected to guarantee contracts; kin were responsible in cases of murder and theft; neighbours ensured that obligations were fulfilled and debts paid. In S Wales judgments were made by local notables, meeting in assemblies.

Some Welsh customs were retained by Norman lords in the MARCH OF WALES (from late 11th century) and the English also incorporated elements of Welsh custom in the legal framework imposed after the English Conquest (1282–3; *see* RHUDDLAN OR WALES, STATUTE OF). By *c*.1500 these vestiges were in decline. They were formally abolished by the Act of Union (1536–43; *see* UNION OF WALES WITH ENGLAND), though partible inheritance continued into the 17th century. *See also* HYWEL DDA, LAWS OF; LAW, ENGLAND FROM 1066.

LAW COMMISSIONS Independent statutory authorities which advise on the modernization and improvement of law. In 1965, as part of legal reforms instigated by Lord Gardiner (lord CHANCELLOR 1964–70), the UK Parliament established the Scottish Law Commission and Law Commission of England and Wales. Recommendations from both bodies produced extensive revisions of law. From 1999 the Scottish commission was sponsored by the Scottish Executive, and became largely concerned with areas of law devolved to the Scottish Parliament (*see* DEVOLUTION, SCOTLAND). In 2014 the commission for England and Wales was authorized to advise ministers of the devolved Welsh government.

The Republic of Ireland's parliament established a Law Reform Commission in 1975. Charged with keeping the State's laws under review, it undertook fixed-term programmes of law reform. Following the BELFAST AGREEMENT (1998), the UK Parliament created a Northern Ireland Law Commission (2002, effective from 2007), though it became non-operational in 2015 because of budgetary constraints.

LAW LORDS Popular term for the 'lords of appeal in ordinary', who were added to the UK House of Lords by the 1876 Appellate Jurisdiction Act, as salaried life peers, to undertake its work as the highest appeal court (except for Scottish criminal appeals). They were also allowed to speak on legal matters in debates. When the House's judicial role was terminated in 2009 the law lords became justices of a new UK Supreme Court. *See also* LEGAL REFORMS, ENGLAND AND WALES, 1870s.

LAWRENCE, D.H. (b. 11 Sept. 1885 at Eastwood, Nottinghamshire, England; d. 2 March 1930 at Vence, Alpes Maritimes, France, aged 44). A coalminer's son, David Herbert Lawrence became a teacher (1908–11) and prolific writer. In 1912 he eloped to Germany with a professor's German wife, Frieda Weekley (they married in 1914). Lawrence's novels *Sons and Lovers* (1913), *The Rainbow* (1915) and *Women in Love* (1920) made him well-known, and were influential for their portrayal of industrialization, and of relations between men and women. The Lawrences travelled abroad in the 1920s, living mainly in Italy from 1926. In 1960 Lawrence's final novel, *Lady Chatterley's Lover* (published privately 1928), was the subject of a famous trial (*see* LANE, ALLEN). *See also* ENGLISH LITERATURE, ENGLAND.

LAWRENCE MURDER A death which had far-reaching consequences for British society. On 22 April 1993 the black 18-year-old student Stephen Lawrence was killed at a bus stop in SE LONDON by white youths. Although two suspects were soon charged, a prosecution was dropped because identification evidence was considered unreliable. An attempted private prosecution of three suspects by Lawrence's parents also failed (1994–6). A review of the Metropolitan Police Service's investigation by another police force (1997) revealed incompetence but denied racist attitudes.

The extensive publicity for the case caused the government to commission a public inquiry, headed by retired judge Sir William Macpherson. The 'Macpherson Report' (1999) concluded that the original police investigation had failed because of institutionalized racism (a concept which gained popular currency). Recommendations were made for tackling racism in police forces.

Pressure continued to obtain convictions for Lawrence's murder, but legal action was prevented by the 'double jeopardy' rule, whereby a person could not be tried twice for the same offence. Parliament abolished the rule (from 2005), and a 'cold case' review (2006–7) found new evidence relating to the murder. Two suspects were eventually convicted (2012). Stephen Lawrence's mother Doreen, who had campaigned relentlessly for justice, was created a baroness (2013).

LAWRENCE OF ARABIA (b. 16 Aug. 1888 at Tremadoc, Caernarfonshire, Wales; d. 19 May 1935 at Bovington, Dorset, England, aged 46). T.E. (Thomas Edward) Lawrence was an archaeologist in Syria before joining British Military Intelligence (1915). His exploits during WORLD WAR I as a liaison officer with the Arab Revolt (Oct. 1916–Oct. 1918), organizing sabotage against the Turks, made him a national hero in Britain. He promoted Arab self-government in 1919, and advised on Middle Eastern affairs at the Colonial Office (1921–2). Disappointed by rejection of his ideas, Lawrence then joined the Royal Air Force, adopting the name T.E. Shaw. He died in a motorcycle accident. He recounted his exploits in *Seven Pillars of Wisdom* (1926). *See also* OTTOMAN EMPIRE, BRITISH RELATIONS WITH.

LAWSON, NIGEL (b. 11 March 1932 at London, England). Lawson worked in journalism from 1956 and was a Conservative MP 1974–92. He served in the British government under Margaret THATCHER as financial secretary to the Treasury (alongside Geoffrey HOWE) 1979–81, and as energy secretary from 1981. As chancellor of the Exchequer from 1983, he reduced income tax and reformed company taxation. But rapid economic growth created INFLATION. His policy from 1988 of 'shadowing' the

German Deutschmark, in anticipation of joining the EXCHANGE RATE MECHANISM, angered Thatcher. Lawson resigned (26 Oct. 1989) over exchange rate policy and Thatcher's use of an outside economic adviser. He was created Lord Lawson (1992).

LEAD INDUSTRY, WALES Lead mining was significant in Flintshire (NE Wales) by the 14th century and in Cardiganshire (W Wales) from the early 17th century. The industry was most prosperous in the 1860s when it employed 6000 people in mid Wales. Output in 1870 was 27,000 tons, but only 11,000 in 1890. Most mines had closed by 1914, leaving ghost villages and poisonous spoil-heaps. *See also* INDUSTRY, WALES BEFORE/FROM 18TH CENTURY.

LEAGUE OF NATIONS, BRITISH INVOLVEMENT Established by the treaty of VERSAILLES (1919), this international organization was promoted by President Woodrow Wilson of the USA, though British diplomats shaped its structure. The League aimed to maintain peace through collective security.

The refusal of the US Senate to join the League, and absence of the USSR, left Great Britain as the strongest member, but British governments felt they had nothing to gain by limiting their freedom of action through League commitments. Popular support in Britain compelled lip service to the League and its procedures from British leaders, but most treated it as just a talking shop. Britain rejected the Draft Treaty of Mutual Assistance (1923) and Geneva Protocol (1924), which proposed wide-ranging security obligations. France envisaged the League as an anti-German alliance, but Austen CHAMBERLAIN secured membership for Germany (1926).

Between 1931 and 1936, uncontained Japanese and Italian aggression discredited the League; Germany and Japan left in 1933, Italy in 1937. The League's principles obstructed APPEASEMENT, so Britain effectively abandoned it. (The League was replaced by the United Nations in 1945.)

LEAGUE OF NATIONS, IRISH INVOLVEMENT *see* FOREIGN RELATIONS, SOUTHERN IRELAND

LEARNED CLASSES, IRELAND An order within Gaelic society, collectively termed *áes dána* (OIr., meaning 'men of art'). Recorded from the 7th century AD, it possibly originated in the 1st millennium BC (*see* PREHISTORIC IRELAND, SOCIAL STRUCTURE). Roles were inherited within kindreds.

The *áes dána* included *fili* (poet and seer, perhaps originally with a priestly function); *brithem* (jurist), responsible for BREHON LAW; *lia* (physician). There were also historians, musicians and skilled craftsmen (workers of ferrous metals were excluded). Christian clergy were included

from the 5th century, enabling Christianity to be integrated into Gaelic culture. The *áes dána* were closely associated with nobility. They enjoyed considerable mobility, and could travel freely between kingdoms. They gave cultural unity to Gaelic Ireland and preserved traditions.

By the 14th century Anglo-Irish families also employed members of the learned classes (e.g., musicians, jurists). They flourished into the 17th century, with some of their activities (e.g., bardic schools) continuing thereafter. *See also* SOCIAL STRUCTURE, GAELIC IRELAND.

LEE, ROWLAND (fl. from *c.*1510; d. 28 Jan. 1543 at Shrewsbury, Shropshire, England). Bishop of Coventry and Lichfield (England) and president of the COUNCIL OF THE MARCHES IN WALES 1534–43 who led a harsh attempt to pacify the Anglo-Welsh border country. Contemptuous of the Welsh, Lee opposed Thomas CROMWELL's policy of entrusting judicial administration to native JUSTICES OF THE PEACE; *see* UNION OF WALES WITH ENGLAND.

LEEDS A city and unitary authority in N England, by the R. Aire; formerly in Yorkshire (W Riding).

A small town was created alongside a village in 1207 which became a centre of the CLOTH INDUSTRY, flourishing strongly from the late 15th century. A new cloth hall was built in 1755.

Industry (e.g., engineering, flax spinning) expanded rapidly from the later 18th century, due to convenient coal and iron ore. With a CANAL to LIVERPOOL (from 1816) and RAILWAYS to major centres (from 1830s–40s), Leeds became an important communications centre and diversified industrial town (including locomotive manufacture). It gained parliamentary representation (1832), city status (1893) and a university (1904).

In the 20th century electronics and service industries (e.g., finance) offset a decline of textiles, while motorways helped to sustain commerce. Two additional universities were created (by upgrading): Leeds Metropolitan (1992; renamed Leeds Beckett, 2014), Leeds Trinity (2012).

Est. popn: 1300, 1500; 1600, 4500; 1800, 53,000; 1900, 429,000; 2000, 715,000.

LEFT WING, RIGHT WING Terms referring (as adjectives or nouns) to individuals, groups or parties who hold, respectively, progressive or conservative opinions, particularly in politics (also implying polarization). They originated during the French Revolution, after the NOBILITY and clergy joined the National Assembly formed by commoners (27 June 1789); those who were loyal to the monarchy and Church sat to the right of the king's chair (because being at the right hand implied trust). Radical members, by default, sat to the left. In time, *la droite* ('right') and *la gauche* ('left') became terms for political tendencies.

The concepts spread to Great Britain, where 'right wing' similarly implied loyalty to monarchy, aristocracy, Church, Union and Empire, and 'left wing' denoted radicalism.

British politics were notably polarized along such divisions in the 1920s–40s and 1960s–70s when the LABOUR PARTY favoured – and the CONSERVATIVE PARTY resisted – extensive social reform and NATIONALIZATION. *See also* BUTSKELLISM; THATCHERISM.

LEGAL REFORM, ENGLAND AND WALES, 1650s
In the late 1640s, radicals (e.g., LEVELLERS) sought reforms, particularly to reduce the expense and slowness of litigation. The RUMP PARLIAMENT abolished Latin and Law French in legal proceedings in 1650, and in 1652 established a commission. Its proposals included county courts (to avoid the expense of going to WESTMINSTER) and county land registers. But lawyers managed to prevent implementation. Oliver CROMWELL, as lord protector, implemented reforms of the Court of CHANCERY in 1654. In general, popular pressure for reform was frustrated by conservatism. *See also* COMMONWEALTH AND PROTECTORATE; LAW, ENGLAND FROM 1066.

LEGAL REFORMS, ENGLAND, REIGN OF EDWARD I
Reforms made 1275–90 which sought to improve and extend legal procedures, reduce disorder, and increase royal power. They were implemented by STATUTES, which usually dealt with various matters, including improvements to the POSSESSORY ASSIZES.

Statutes included Statutes of Westminster (I, 1275, II, 1285), the latter providing for land to be entailed (i.e., inherited only within a family); Statute of Gloucester (1278), improving novel disseisin; Statute of Acton Burnell (confirmed 1285) for recovery of mercantile debts; Statute of Winchester (1285) which reformed criminal law. *See also* EDWARD I; *QUIA EMPTORES*; OYER AND TERMINER, COMMISSIONS OF; LAW, ENGLAND FROM 1066.

LEGAL REFORMS, ENGLAND AND WALES, 1820s
Legislation passed by the UK Parliament which updated criminal law and reorganized prisons. From the 1770s reforming groups (EVANGELICAL Christians, QUAKERS, UTILITARIANS) had pressed for reforms, though little was achieved because of the FRENCH REVOLUTIONARY AND NAPOLEONIC WARS. In 1819 a parliamentary select committee made recommendations which were implemented by Robert PEEL, home secretary 1822–7.

The 1823 Gaols Act consolidated legislation relating to gaols and regulated conditions. Eight STATUTES reformed criminal law, replacing 278 earlier Acts. The number of capital offences was reduced. The reforms sought to clarify criminal law and improve enforcement. *See also* BLACK ACT; ROMILLY, SAMUEL; MACKINTOSH, JAMES.

LEGAL REFORMS, ENGLAND AND WALES, 1870s
Reform of central courts was undertaken partly under pressure from business interests because commercial litigation had become complex and time-consuming. A Judicature Commission (1867–9) made recommendations; reforms were enacted mainly under Lord Selborne (lord CHANCELLOR 1872–4).

The Judicature Act of 1873 (modified 1875) abolished jurisdictions and created a Supreme Court of Judicature comprising a High Court of Justice and Court of Appeal (effective from 1 Nov. 1875). The former incorporated the COMMON LAW courts, and courts of CHANCERY, Admiralty, probate and divorce. All courts and judges were to administer common law and EQUITY. (The Common Pleas and Exchequer courts remained separate until 1880.)

Before the Act took effect, it was decided to retain the House of Lords as the superior court (thereby also retaining its jurisdiction in Ireland and Scotland). It was provided with salaried judges from 1876 (*see* LAW LORDS). *See also* COURTS, ENGLAND FROM 1660.

LEGES INTER BRETTOS ET SCOTTOS
(Latin, meaning 'Laws between Britons and Scots'). A Latin legal document, also including Gaelic terms, from Scotland; possibly of the early 11th century. It classifies people in British society (non-Gaelic inhabitants of Scotland) against those in Scottish (i.e., Gaelic) society according to the compensation due to a murdered man's kindred. It is the only legal code from Scotland which predates the arrival of English and French influences in the reign of King DAVID I (1124–53). *See also* LAW, SCOTLAND; WERGELD.

LEICESTER, ROBERT EARL OF
(b. 24 June 1532 in England; d. 4 Sept. 1588 at Cornbury House, Oxfordshire, England, aged 56). Fifth son of John Dudley (*see* NORTHUMBERLAND, JOHN DUKE OF), Robert Dudley married in 1550. After the accession of Queen ELIZABETH I, he was nominated master of the horse (Nov. 1558). By April 1559 he was Elizabeth's favourite, but any ambition he held to marry her was ruined by the manner of his wife's death (Sept. 1560; *see* ROBSART, AMY). Dudley remained influential, becoming a privy councillor (1562) and earl of Leicester (1564).

Elizabeth's partiality for Leicester survived his remarriage (1578). She appointed him commander of military forces in the Netherlands, against Spanish forces, but he was largely unsuccessful (campaigned 1585–6, 1587), and his health deteriorated. Leicester organized Elizabeth's triumphant visit to Tilbury (Essex) after the defeat of the SPANISH ARMADA (8–9 Aug. 1588). *See also* ANGLO-SPANISH WAR.

LEICESTER HOUSE
In England, a large house in Leicester Square, London, 1630s–1790s. From 1717 to 1720

George, prince of Wales, who was estranged from his father King GEORGE I, made Leicester House a centre for opponents of the government. When Prince George was king (as GEORGE II), his heir FREDERICK, PRINCE OF WALES, established a rival court at Norfolk House (from 1737) and then at Leicester House (1743–51). In both instances opposition politicians took advantage of the prince's 'reversionary interest', i.e. his prospective succession to the throne and powers of PATRONAGE.

LEINSTER A provincial kingdom (later lordship and province) in E Ireland, formed by the 5th century when it probably extended from the Boyne Valley southwards to the Celtic Sea. The northern part, MEATH, was taken by the Southern UÍ NÉILL in the 6th century. Leinster's name, meaning 'Territory of the Laigin', referred to an early dynastic confederation.

From the early 8th century Leinster was dominated by the Uí Dúnlainge and Uí Chennselaig dynasties (in N and S Leinster respectively); from the mid 8th century to c.1046 the former near monopolized the province's high-kingship. In the mid 9th and early 10th centuries Leinster suffered raids by VIKINGS, who established coastal settlements (notably DUBLIN).

By c.1046 an Uí Chennselaig king, Diarmait mac Máel na mBó (d. 1072), had taken Leinster's high-kingship. It was retained by his successors, who adopted the surname Mac Murchada (English, MacMurrough). But in 1166 Diarmait MAC MURCHADA was expelled; he regained the high-kingship with the help of Anglo-Normans (1169), thereby starting the Anglo-Norman invasion (see NORMANS, IMPACT ON IRELAND).

In 1171 Diarmait's successor, the Anglo-Norman STRONGBOW (d. 1176), surrendered Leinster to King Henry II of England, who regranted it as a lordship. It passed in 1189 from temporary Crown control to Strongbow's son-in-law William MARSHAL (d. 1219), then successively to Marshal's five sons, and in 1245 was divided between their five sisters.

Leinster's identity nonetheless survived. From 1328 heads of the MacMurrough dynasty claimed to be kings of Leinster (until the execution of Murchad MacMurrough by the English in 1557). In the 16th–17th centuries Leinster's boundaries were fixed by the definition of CONNACHT, MUNSTER and ULSTER for administrative purposes, though Leinster was not used as a governmental unit. See also MEATH; OSRAIGE; MACMURROUGH, ART; PROVINCES, IRELAND.

LEITH, CONCORDAT OF An agreement made in Jan. 1572 (at Leith, SE Scotland), during the regency of John Erskine, earl of Mar (for King JAMES VI), between royal councillors and Church ministers. It provided for the reintroduction of bishops and archbishops, with authority over

historical dioceses, in the reformed Church of SCOTLAND. They would be nominated by the Crown and entitled to sit in Parliament. Appointees had to be reformed ministers and would be answerable to the Church's General Assembly in spiritual matters. See also CHURCH ORGANIZATION, SCOTLAND FROM 16TH CENTURY; TULCHAN BISHOPS; BLACK ACTS.

LEIX-OFFALY PLANTATION The first English colonial plantation in Ireland in the 16th–17th centuries (in LEINSTER, E Ireland). It was intended to replace military control (based on forts), defend the PALE and demonstrate civility to the Gaelic Irish. Planned from 1550, the Plantation was developed from 1557 by the earl of SUSSEX (with 'shiring' of Leix and Offaly as Queen's and King's Counties, and land confiscations); 500 English newcomers gradually settled. See also PLANTATIONS, IRELAND; IRELAND, ENGLISH CONQUEST, 16TH CENTURY.

LEMASS, SEÁN (b. 15 July 1899 at Ballybrack, Co. Dublin, Ireland; d. 11 May 1971 at Dublin, Republic of Ireland, aged 71). A participant in the EASTER RISING (1916), Lemass opposed the ANGLO-IRISH TREATY (1921), which created the IRISH FREE STATE. He fought briefly for the IRISH REPUBLICAN ARMY during the IRISH CIVIL WAR (interned Dec. 1922–Oct. 1923). He helped Éamon DE VALERA to found FIANNA FÁIL (1926), and served in his governments (1932–48, 1951–4, 1957–9), mainly as minister for industry and commerce. During the 1930s he encouraged house and road building, and industrial development.

In June 1959 Lemass succeeded as taoiseach (premier). He pressed ahead with the economic development programme originally proposed by T.K. WHITAKER (see ECONOMIC EXPANSION, PROGRAMMES FOR), and applied for entry to the European Economic Community (1962). He also sought better relations with NORTHERN IRELAND (e.g., met Terence O'NEILL, Belfast, 14 Jan. 1965), and recognized the need to conciliate Unionists. He resigned in Nov. 1966 (succeeded by Jack LYNCH). See also SOUTHERN IRELAND FROM 1922.

LEND-LEASE SCHEME The arrangement during WORLD WAR II whereby the USA provided military goods to the UK (and later China and the USSR) without receiving cash payments. It ran from 11 March 1941 to 2 Sept. 1945. In return the British pledged to fight the Axis powers (Germany and Italy) and to liberalize post-war trade. The USA provided aid worth $27 billion.

LENNOX, 4TH EARL OF (b. 21 Sept. 1516 at Dumbarton Castle, W Scotland; d. 4 Sept. 1571 at Stirling, C Scotland, aged 54). Matthew Stewart, earl from 1526 (in France 1532–42), was captured by the English at the battle of Solway Moss in 1542 (*see* JAMES V). He returned in 1543, but in Jan. 1544 went back to England, lured by King HENRY VIII, and accompanied the 1545 English invasion of Scotland. In Oct. his lands were forfeited.

Lennox lived in N England until restored to his lands and honours in autumn 1564 (probably for his Catholicism) by MARY, QUEEN OF SCOTS, who married his son Lord DARNLEY (1565). In Sept. 1565 Lennox suppressed the earl of MORAY's revolt, but complicity in David RIZZIO's murder (1566) lost him Mary's support. Following Darnley's murder Lennox fled briefly (April–July 1567) and fought Mary at LANGSIDE (1568). He succeeded Moray as regent for King JAMES VI in Jan. 1570, but was killed in 1571 during an attempted coup by Mary's supporters. *See also* SCOTTISH–ENGLISH RELATIONS 1357 TO 1603; MARIAN CIVIL WAR.

LENNOX, 7TH EARL OF *see* STEWART, ESMÉ

LEOBA (fl. from 740s in Wessex; d. 28 Sept. 782 at Schornsheim, Francia). The noblewoman Leoba, originally called Leofgyth, became a nun. Exceptionally learned, she was invited by her kinsman BONIFACE to participate in Christian missionary work in eastern Francia (possibly 748). She advised rulers and bishops, and eventually became abbess of Tauberbischofsheim monastery (resigned *c.*770). She was buried near Boniface (at Fulda). *See also* MISSIONS TO CONTINENTAL EUROPE, ANGLO-SAXON.

LESLIE, ALEXANDER (b. *c.*1580 in Coupar Angus, E Scotland; d. 4 April 1661 at Balgonie, Fife, E Scotland, aged about 81). After continental service as a mercenary (becoming a field marshal in Sweden), Leslie returned to Scotland in late 1638 and commanded Scottish forces during the Wars of the COVENANT against King CHARLES I (1639–40). Charles, seeking Leslie's support, made him earl of Leven (Oct. 1641). The move failed: in 1644–5 Leven commanded Scottish forces that aided the English Parliamentarians against Charles under the SOLEMN LEAGUE AND COVENANT. Leven received Charles's surrender (5 May 1646), later handing him over to the English (30 Jan. 1647).

Leven returned to Scotland, where he remained involved in affairs though not active militarily. He opposed the ENGAGEMENT but supported CHARLES II. In Aug. 1651 Leven was captured by English invaders and held until 1654, when he retired to his estate. *See also* COVENANTING REVOLUTION; CIVIL WARS, SCOTTISH PARTICIPATION.

LEVELLERS In England, in the late 1640s, a radical movement which advocated political and social reform and religious liberty; named after anti-enclosure rioters who levelled hedges. It emerged particularly from within the NEW MODEL ARMY, and was associated with John LILBURNE,

Richard Overton and William Walwyn. The last was largely responsible for *An Agreement of the People* (Oct. 1647), a constitutional scheme discussed at the PUTNEY DEBATES.

In 1649 (after the execution of King CHARLES I), Levellers incited a soldiers' mutiny: three regiments congregated at Burford (Oxfordshire) on 13 May. They were dispersed or imprisoned by Oliver CROMWELL and Lord FAIRFAX (14–15 May). Three mutineers were shot (17 May). Levellers remained active until 1653. *See also* ENGLISH REVOLUTION SECTS.

LEVELLERS' REVOLT In SW Scotland (Dumfriesshire, Kirkcudbrightshire, Wigtownshire), protests in 1723–5 by rural people against CLEARANCES by landlords. (Tenants were being evicted and open fields enclosed to facilitate large-scale sheep and cattle farming.) Gangs of protesters killed cattle and destroyed dykes (field walls). The Revolt was quelled by troops, who captured several leaders in a confrontation on 2 June 1724. *See also* AGRICULTURE, SCOTLAND FROM 18TH CENTURY.

LEVEN, EARL OF *see* LESLIE, ALEXANDER

LEVERHULME, LORD (b. 19 Sept. 1851 at Bolton, Lancashire, England; d. 7 May 1925 at Hampstead, London, aged 73). Involved in his family's grocery business from 1867, William Lever studied American marketing techniques and in 1874 launched a brand of soap. In 1884 he and a brother founded 'Lever Brothers' which manufactured soap from vegetable oils instead of tallow, marketed other brands of cleaning products, and acquired overseas supplies of materials. Lever also created a model 'factory village' for employees at Port Sunlight, Cheshire (1888). A Liberal MP 1906–9, Lever was created a baronet (1911), lord (1917) and viscount (1922). He was a notable philanthropist, establishing a trust which funded academic research. *See also* ADVERTISING.

LEWES, BATTLE OF *see* BARONIAL CONFLICT AND WARS

LEWIS, SAUNDERS (b. 15 Oct. 1893 at Wallasey, Cheshire, England; d. 1 Sept. 1985 at Cardiff, S Glamorgan, Wales, aged 91). Chief founder of PLAID CYMRU in 1925, and its president and leading theorist 1926–39, Lewis was imprisoned for (token) arson at a ROYAL AIR FORCE bombing school (1936). In 1962 his radio lecture *Tynged yr Iaith* ('The Fate of the Language') stimulated foundation of the WELSH LANGUAGE SOCIETY. The author of plays, novels, poetry and literary studies, Lewis was the outstanding figure in 20th-century Welsh literature. In 1932 he became a CATHOLIC and undertook his political and literary work self-consciously in the context of European Catholic Christendom. *See also* WELSH LANGUAGE AND LITERATURE.

LEWIS, WILLIAM THOMAS (b. 5 Aug. 1837 at Merthyr Tydfil, Glamorgan, Wales; d. 27 Aug. 1914 at Hean Castle, Pembrokeshire, Wales, aged 87). Welsh industrialist; created Lord Merthyr (1911). Lewis's coalmines included the Universal Colliery at Senghenydd (Glamorgan), the scene of Great Britain's worst mining disaster (14 Oct. 1913) when 439 men were killed. *See also* COAL INDUSTRY, WALES.

LIBELLE OF ENGLYSHE POLYCYE An anonymous English poem, written *c*.1437 during the HUNDRED YEARS WAR. It criticized the concentration of the war effort in Normandy, urging the government to recognize the importance of trade and to protect the sea crossing to CALAIS, the location of the English STAPLE.

LIBERAL DEMOCRATS A British political party created on 3 March 1988 by merger of the allied LIBERAL PARTY and SOCIAL DEMOCRATIC PARTY (as Social and Liberal Democratic Party until Oct. 1989). Initially with 19 MPs, and Paddy Ashdown as leader, the Party advocated constitutional reform, European integration and higher education spending. The 20 'Lib Dem' MPs elected at the 1992 UK general election increased to 46 in 1997, reflecting unpopularity of the Conservatives, and to 52 in 2001, 62 in 2005. Ashdown was succeeded by Charles Kennedy (leader 1999–2006), Sir Menzies Campbell (2006–7), Vince Cable (acting leader, Oct.–Dec. 2007) and Nick Clegg (2007–2015).

The 57 MPs elected in 2010, when no party won a majority, enabled the Liberal Democrats to determine the composition of the UK government. Declining an offer from Labour, the Party accepted coalition with the Conservatives, based on an agreed policy programme. It received five Cabinet posts, including Clegg as deputy prime minister. Implemented Liberal Democrat policies included the 'Pupil Premium' of additional school funding for pupils from disadvantaged backgrounds (2011). At the 2015 election, Liberal Democrat MPs fell to eight. The party won 12 seats in 2017 and 11 in 2019. Clegg was succeeded as leader by Tim Farron (2015–17), Sir Vince Cable (2017–19) and Jo Swinson (2019).

LIBERALISM A tradition of social and political thought which emphasizes freedom and rights of the individual. It favours limited government and free markets. Liberalism has influenced all major British political parties, but especially the LIBERAL PARTY in the 19th century. *See also* NEW LIBERALISM.

LIBERAL PARTY A mainly British political party which emerged from the union of WHIGS, Radicals, and PEELITES in the 1860s. It was identified with LIBERALISM, FREE TRADE, PARLIAMENTARY REFORM, and peace. A centralized organization, the National Liberal Federation, was created in 1877.

Dominated by W.E. GLADSTONE until 1894, Liberals formed a notable reforming government (1868–74). They divided over Irish HOME RULE in 1886, when the duke of DEVONSHIRE and Joseph CHAMBERLAIN seceded as LIBERAL UNIONISTS. The weakened Party rallied to oppose TARIFF REFORM and won a landslide victory in the 1906 general election. Henry CAMPBELL-BANNERMAN and H.H. ASQUITH introduced innovative social legislation inspired by NEW LIBERALISM, which moderated the previous emphasis on individualism.

WORLD WAR I had a disastrous impact. After David LLOYD GEORGE took power (Dec. 1916), the Liberals split into 'Coalition Liberals' and 'Asquithian Liberals' (1916–23). Divided, they failed to cope with the expanded franchise (1918) and shrank to a small third party. They never formed a government again.

In the 1930s, the Liberal Nationals (or National Liberals) led by John SIMON effectively joined the Conservatives. The rump Liberal Party was down to six MPs by the 1950s. Revival appeared possible from Jo GRIMOND's time, but no breakthrough occurred. The Liberals allied with the SOCIAL DEMOCRATIC PARTY in 1981, and then merged as LIBERAL DEMOCRATS (1988).

LIBERAL PARTY, SCOTLAND, AND LIBERAL DEMOCRATS With its predecessors, the LIBERAL PARTY was the dominant Party in Scotland 1832–1918, winning the majority of parliamentary seats (except in the 'KHAKI ELECTION' of 1900). It won most BURGH seats and usually a majority of shire seats. (Liberals achieved a record 59 seats, of 72, in Jan. 1910.) They were supported by WHIG aristocrats, urban middle classes, and (from 1868) working-class radicals.

Liberals promoted causes popular in Scotland (e.g., FREE TRADE, TEMPERANCE, land reform, Disestablishment of the Church of Scotland, Home Rule), although a section separated in 1886 over Irish Home Rule (*see* UNIONISM, SCOTLAND). The East, and West, of Scotland Liberal Associations were founded in 1876 and 1877 respectively; they combined as the Scottish Liberal Association in 1881 ('Federation' from 1918). The Party remained independent of the English and Welsh Liberal Party.

Parliamentary seats fell to 28 in 1922, to nine in 1924. In 1931, after the Party split, independent and National Liberals won eight seats each. The Nationals (allies of the Conservatives) retained 5–8 seats until 1964. The continuing Liberal Party fell to three seats in 1935, to none in 1945. It won 1–5 in the 1950s–70s, eight in 1983, nine in 1987.

In 1988 the Party merged into the LIBERAL DEMOCRATS. The new Party won 9–11 seats in general elections from 1992 to 2010. But following the period in coalition under David CAMERON, the Party collapsed, winning one seat in 2015 and four in 2017 and 2019. In elections for the new

Scottish Parliament, the Liberal Democrats won 16–17 seats in the elections of 1999–2007, but only four seats in 2011 and 2016. Its results in 1999 and 2003 (coming third) enabled it to participate in devolved coalition administrations with the LABOUR PARTY. *See also* GRIMOND, JO; PARLIAMENTARY REPRESENTATION, SCOTLAND; DEVOLUTION, SCOTLAND.

LIBERAL PARTY, WALES, AND LIBERAL DEMOCRATS A majority of members of the UK Parliament from Wales were Liberals from 1865 (when they supplanted CONSERVATIVES) until 1922 (replaced by LABOUR), giving Welsh causes prominence in British politics (*see* TEMPERANCE MOVEMENT, WALES; DISESTABLISHMENT, CHURCH OF ENGLAND IN WALES). The Party was supported by NONCONFORMITY, tenant farmers, industrial workers and most industrialists. In 1906 it won 34 of the 35 Welsh seats (the other was Labour).

The Party dominated County Councils 1889–1920s, and remained influential in rural Wales until the 1950s. Local Party organization developed in association with organization in England until 1966, when the Welsh Liberal Party became autonomous within the British Liberal Party. The most prominent Welsh Liberal was David LLOYD GEORGE.

The Party merged with the Social Democratic Party in 1988 as the LIBERAL DEMOCRATS. Following DEVOLUTION (1999), the 'Lib Dems' participated in Welsh coalition governments (2000–3, from 2016). *See also* RICHARD, HENRY; ELLIS, TOM; PARLIAMENTARY REPRESENTATION, WALES.

LIBERAL TORIES A loose grouping of British TORY politicians in the 1820s, led by George CANNING, William HUSKISSON and Viscount GODERICH. Their readiness to countenance CATHOLIC EMANCIPATION, freer trade, penal reform and TRADE UNIONISM, and their general openness to new ideas, distinguished them from ULTRA TORIES. The core group of Liberal Tories, the CANNINGITES, left the Tory ministry in 1828 and joined the WHIGS in 1830.

LIBERAL UNIONISTS A political party formed in Great Britain by Liberal opponents of Irish HOME RULE who broke with W.E. GLADSTONE in 1886 and secured the re-election of 78 MPs. Led by Joseph CHAMBERLAIN and the 8th duke of DEVONSHIRE, the Liberal Unionists cooperated with the Conservatives. Closely allied from 1895, the two parties formally merged in 1912.

LIBERATION SOCIETY An organization founded in 1844 by NONCONFORMIST Edward Miall (1809–81) as the British Anti-State Church Association to campaign for disestablishment of the Church of England; renamed 1853. It championed other nonconformist issues (e.g., abolition of CHURCH RATES), enjoying support in England and Wales until

the 1870s. In Wales its branches organized the registration of eligible nonconformists as voters. Disbanded 1971. *See also* DISESTABLISHMENT, CHURCH OF ENGLAND IN WALES.

LIBERTY Term sometimes used for an area situated within a larger territorial unit (e.g., a town or county) which was exempt from the jurisdiction over the surrounding area. For example, in YORK (N England), before the DISSOLUTION OF RELIGIOUS HOUSES, various religious houses and churches with associated lands were areas or liberties independent of the city's governing corporation. The term is also used (in the plural) for rights or privileges granted by kings or lords to GUILDS or townsmen (*see* BOROUGH).

LIB-LAB PACT In Great Britain, a parliamentary alliance made on 23 March 1977 by James CALLAGHAN, the Labour prime minister, and David Steel, leader of the LIBERAL PARTY, to enable the Labour government to command a parliamentary majority and remain in office. It bound Liberal MPs to provide support in crucial votes in return for consultation about policy. Steel ended the pact on 25 May 1978. Callaghan's government survived until 28 March 1979.

LICENSING OF DRINKING PREMISES, ENGLAND AND WALES Concerned from 1495 about disorder in alehouses (Vagabonds Act), PARLIAMENT in 1552 required keepers to be licensed by JUSTICES OF THE PEACE (JPs) (Alehouses Act). In 1553 wine selling was confined to towns, also under licensing. Developments included annual licensing (from 1618).

Except in 1617–21, inns did not ordinarily require licences until the late 17th century (brought under alehouse licensing by JPs). From 1729 retailing of spirits required a licence (Gin Acts), and JPs also controlled wine licensing from 1792. Legislation was consolidated in 1828 (Alehouse Act), when closure during Sunday church services was ordered.

In 1830, to promote free trade, beer licensing was liberalized; the Beerhouse Act allowed sale of beer, ale and porter under an annual excise (tax) licence, although opening hours were restricted. 'Beerhouses' proliferated. (Separate licences for consumption on and off premises were introduced in 1834.) Defined opening hours were extended to all public houses ('pubs') in 1839–40, and excise licences introduced for wine outside alehouses or beerhouses in 1860.

TEMPERANCE campaigning increased restrictions; new beerhouse licences required a JPs' certificate from 1869, and licensing by JPs was fully reinstated in 1872. Sunday closing was enacted for Wales (1881; until 1961–96). Termination of licences by pro-temperance JPs was facilitated with compensation (1904), but a Bill to allow compulsory reductions of houses provoked protests and was rejected by the House of Lords (1908).

During WORLD WAR I (1914–18) restrictions were tightened to assist the war effort, including: authorization for local reductions of opening times (1914); establishment of a Central Control Board (1915) to regulate premises near munitions production and military activity (e.g., introducing afternoon closed period). The last change was retained (1921 Licensing Act).

Licensing remained largely unaltered until the 2003 Licensing Act transferred licensing to local authorities, and ended prescribed opening hours (implemented 2005). *See also* ALEHOUSES, TAVERNS, INNS.

LICENSING OF DRINKING PREMISES, IRELAND

In 1635 Ireland's PARLIAMENT required alehouse keepers and retailers of ale or beer to be licensed annually by commissioners, including JUSTICES OF THE PEACE (JPs). Legislation was repeated in 1662, and in 1665 licensing for wines and spirits became obligatory. Closure of premises during Sunday church services was required from 1695. In 1737 licensing was transferred to EXCISE commissioners and collectors, though from 1759 a licence required a JPs' certificate.

In 1833 the UK Parliament consolidated legislation, authorizing revenue commissioners to renew licences and JPs to consider new applications, and specifying maximum opening hours (Licensing (Ireland) Act). Arrangements were later modified to encourage alternatives to spirits: wine refreshment houses and retail sales were permitted under excise licences (1860), also 'beerhouses' (1864).

As elsewhere, the TEMPERANCE MOVEMENT influenced legislation; the 1872 English Licensing Act reduced opening hours in Ireland, and the 1878 Sale of Liquors on Sunday (Ireland) Act prohibited Sunday opening of public houses except in five urban areas (included 1906). The Licensing (Ireland) Act of 1902 began reduction of public houses by largely prohibiting new licences. During WORLD WAR I, local reductions of opening times were authorized (1914).

Following Ireland's partition (1921), the 1902 Act was largely re-enacted in NORTHERN IRELAND in 1923. Sunday closing was maintained, although afternoon opening otherwise allowed. Licence reduction was accelerated. Some Sunday opening began under a 1987 order in Council. SOUTHERN IRELAND in 1924 retained Sunday closing and introduced afternoon closing on other days (except in large centres). Sunday closing was ended, against Church opposition, in 1960. Subsequent decades saw further liberalization. *See also* ALEHOUSES, TAVERNS, INNS.

LICENSING OF DRINKING PREMISES, SCOTLAND

In 1756 the British PARLIAMENT legislated for a system similar to the English one, whereby an annual licence was required from JUSTICES OF THE PEACE (JPs) for keeping an alehouse or inn (Alehouses Act). From 1808, under legislation by the UK Parliament, JPs and town magistrates instead issued certificates permitting acquisition of an excise (tax) licence.

The 'Home Drummond Act' of 1828 entrusted licensing power to JPs and town magistrates, and compelled closure of public houses ('pubs') during church services. In 1853, influenced by the TEMPERANCE MOVEMENT, the 'Forbes Mackenzie Act' distinguished between pubs and 'off licences', closed pubs on Sundays and otherwise specified maximum opening times. Legislation was consolidated in 1903. Temperance reformers persisted; in 1913 the Temperance (Scotland) Act authorized prohibition in localities by popular vote, including closure of licensed premises.

Regulations made during WORLD WAR I (1914–18) mostly included Scotland (*see* LICENSING OF DRINKING PREMISES, ENGLAND AND WALES). The 1921 Licensing Act (for Great Britain) continued many wartime restrictions, notably afternoon closure.

In 1962 standard 'permitted hours' were prescribed; in 1976 Sunday opening was allowed and licensing transferred to local authorities. In 2005 the Licensing (Scotland) Act of the Scottish Parliament included replacement of permitted hours with individual operating plans, and personal licences for managers (implemented 2009). *See also* ALEHOUSES, TAVERNS, INNS.

LICHFIELD HOUSE COMPACT A political alliance brokered by Lord John RUSSELL, at the London home of Lord Lichfield on 18 Feb. 1835, between WHIGS and RADICALS and the influential Irish MP Daniel O'CONNELL. They agreed to co-operate in voting down Sir Robert PEEL's minority government in the UK Parliament. Peel resigned as prime minister in April. His successor, Viscount MELBOURNE, promoted reforms in Ireland. *See also* DRUMMOND, THOMAS.

LIDDELL HART, BASIL (b. 31 Oct. 1895 at Paris, France; d. 29 Jan. 1970 at Medmenham, Buckinghamshire, England, aged 74). A British soldier 1914–23 (with surname Hart until 1921), Liddell Hart wrote on military subjects from 1918. Military correspondent of the *Daily Telegraph* 1925–35, and advocate of mechanized warfare (use of TANKS, motorized infantry, air support), he became influential with the War Office and Army. He was defence correspondent of *The Times* 1935–9. Liddell Hart's influence in Great Britain waned in the late 1930s because he advocated a defensive response to German threats, though he opposed APPEASEMENT. Germans later claimed that Liddell Hart influenced their *Blitzkrieg* strategy in WORLD WAR II. He was knighted in 1966.

LIMERICK A city in the Republic of Ireland, by the R. Shannon; centre of Co. Limerick; from Irish, Luimneach, meaning 'Bare spot'.

Situated at the lowest fording point of the R. Shannon, Limerick was founded as a trading centre by VIKINGS (922) and developed into a town. After capture by Brian BÓRUMA (977), it was a centre of O'BRIEN control of MUNSTER (S Ireland) until captured by Anglo-Normans (1175). Limerick subsequently traded with SW England and S Wales.

Limerick expanded in the 17th century; the siege of Limerick ended the WILLIAMITE WAR of 1688–91. During the 18th century Limerick flourished from trans-Atlantic trade. Its area was extended and fine houses were built. But Limerick declined in the 19th and 20th centuries, until industrial development in the 1970s (e.g., alumina extraction, electronics) generated revival. In 1989 an institute was upgraded as the University of Limerick. *See also* TOWNS, IRELAND.

Est. popn: 1300, 2000; 1600, 2000; 1800, 60,000; 1900, 40,000; 2000, 50,000.

LIMERICK, TREATY OF Signed on 3 Oct. 1691 (at LIMERICK, W Ireland) between Baron van Ginkel (for King WILLIAM III) and Patrick Sarsfield, commander of forces supporting (the former king) JAMES VII/II ('Jacobites'). The treaty ended the WILLIAMITE WAR (1688–91). Afterwards, Jacobites surrendered Limerick and other areas.

The treaty contained 'military' and 'civil' articles. The former permitted Jacobite soldiers to go to France. (12,000 left by 22 Dec.) The latter allowed Catholics to exercise their religion, and provided for restoration of estates confiscated during the war. Catholic gentlemen could retain arms, and others could practise trades and professions.

The treaty was confirmed by the Irish Parliament in 1697, but in a narrower version (e.g., with a time-limit for claims on estates). Its terms were subsequently breached by ANTI-CATHOLIC LEGISLATION.

LIMITED LIABILITY The restriction under law of an owner's loss in a business to the capital he or she has subscribed (rather than extending to all personal assets). This developed in England and Scotland from the late 17th century for joint-stock companies established under royal charter or Act of Parliament (e.g., with specified limits to calls on capital). From 1856 most firms in the UK could become limited-liability companies by displaying 'Ltd' after their name. *See also* BUSINESS ORGANIZATION.

LINCOLN A city in E England, by the R. Witham; centre of Lincolnshire.

Around 60 the Romans founded a legionary fortress (called Lindum, Latin from Brittonic, Lindon, meaning 'Lake'), followed *c*.90–6 by a *colonia* (called (Domitiana) Lindensium). From *c*.300 Lindensium was probably capital of the province Flavia Caesariensis (*see* ROMAN BRITAIN, GOVERNMENT).

Abandoned in the 5th century, Lincoln (from 'Lindon colonia') was revived possibly in the late 8th century; it became a cathedral city in 1072. An important centre of the CLOTH INDUSTRY in the 12th and 13th centuries, it then declined. Lincoln manufactured agricultural machinery from the late 19th century, when it was also famous for horse-race meetings. An existing university (renamed University of Lincoln in 2001) was centred at Lincoln from 2002, and in 2012 a college was upgraded as Bishop Grosseteste University. *See also* ROMAN BRITAIN, TOWNS.

Est. popn: 200, 5000; 1086, 4000; 1300, 7000; 1600, 2500; 1800, 7000; 1900, 49,000; 2000, 86,000.

LINCOLN JUDGMENT *see* RITUALISM

LINDSAY OR LYNDSAY, SIR DAVID (b. *c*.1487, probably near Cupar, Fife, Scotland; d. 1555, aged about 68). Scots poet, satirist and herald; a courtier of King JAMES V. Lindsay's responsibility for organizing royal entertainments encouraged his literary flair. His greatest work, the morality play *Ane Satyre of the Thrie Estaitis*, was first performed before James in 1540.

LINDSEY, KINGDOM OF A small kingdom roughly equivalent to modern N Lincolnshire (E England), which originated as a British (Brittonic-speaking) kingdom (probably in the 5th century). Its name is derived from the Roman name for LINCOLN. It was under Germanic rule by the 7th century, when MERCIA and BERNICIA competed for dominance. EGFRITH of Bernicia and Deira became ruler by 675, but Mercia was supreme from 679 (Mercian victory in battle of the Trent). *See also* POST-ROMAN BRITAIN; KINGSHIP, ANGLO-SAXON.

LINEN INDUSTRY, IRELAND Linen cloth, made in homes and workshops, was exported in the 15th and 16th centuries. Yarn and cloth production, derived from locally grown flax, expanded significantly in NE Ireland (within ULSTER) from the later 17th century, and cloth exports (mostly to Britain) increased by over 60 times 1700–80. Many workers also cultivated small pieces of land. They tended to be presbyterians.

From 1825 mechanical wet spinning of yarn was developed and factories were built (or cotton factories adapted). Weaving was mechanized from the 1850s. The industry became concentrated in BELFAST and the Lagan Valley. Expansion continued until the 1870s, and was further stimulated by demand during WORLD WAR I (1914–18), when 90,000 people were employed (mainly women). The industry then declined, and despite revival during WORLD WAR II (1939–45) effectively closed in the 1960s. *See also* INDUSTRY, IRELAND 18TH CENTURY TO 1921; NORTHERN IRELAND.

LINEN INDUSTRY, SCOTLAND *see* TEXTILE INDUSTRIES, SCOTLAND

LIPTON, THOMAS (b. 10 May 1850 at Glasgow, Scotland; d. 2 Oct. 1931 at East Barnet, Hertfordshire, England, aged 81). A grocer's son, Lipton spent 1865–70 in the USA. From 1871 he opened grocers' shops in Scotland which he promoted with American-style ADVERTISING; during the 1880s he expanded his business through England and Wales. Lipton acquired meat-packing plants in the USA and a tea plantation in CEYLON as sources of supply. A millionaire by age 30, he was knighted in 1898 (created baronet 1902), and after 1899 devoted himself to yacht racing.

LISTER, JOSEPH (b. 5 April 1827 at Upton, Essex, England; d. 10 Feb. 1912 at Walmer, Kent, England, aged 84). After studying in London, Lister moved to Scotland (1853), becoming a surgeon in EDINBURGH and professor of surgery at GLASGOW University (1860). His experience stimulated interest in the management of injuries and wounds. When he learnt of the Frenchman Louis Pasteur's discovery (1865) that putrefaction in cuts was caused by minute organisms in the atmosphere, Lister sought a means to protect wounds with a chemical barrier. In 1867 he announced a system of 'antiseptic surgery', using carbolic acid. As professor of clinical surgery at Edinburgh from 1869, Lister improved conditions for operations. He served as professor of surgery at King's College, London (1877–92) and president of the ROYAL SOCIETY (1895–1900). He was created a baronet (1883) and Lord Lister (1897), the first medical man to receive a peerage. *See also* MEDICINE AND PUBLIC HEALTH.

LITERACY, ENGLAND In the 7th–11th centuries, literacy was confined mainly to clergy, who primarily used LATIN, though also Old English, for reading and writing religious works and documents (e.g., property conveyances). Some nuns (e.g., LEOBA) and a few laymen (e.g., King ALFRED) were also literate.

Following the NORMAN CONQUEST (1066–70s) nobles, townsmen and some rural people became increasingly able to read and often write – variously in Latin, FRENCH and ENGLISH – due to expansion of EDUCATION and production of documents. During the 15th century senior churchmen feared that increasing literacy would promote circulation of heretical writings (*see* LOLLARDY, ENGLAND). Literacy rates in the mid 16th century are estimated at 20% for men, 5% for women.

New factors further expanded literacy. Lay reading of the BIBLE was encouraged, and PRINTING made books and pamphlets cheaper and widely available. By 1640, probably 30% of men and 10% of women were literate (more in S England), with greater capability in reading than writing. Literacy varied strongly according to status: most GENTRY and PROFESSIONALS were literate, as were 60% of yeomen (substantial farmers) and 10–30% of husbandmen (small farmers). New forms of schooling sustained the increase (*see* EDUCATION, ENGLAND). By the mid 18th century estimated literacy was 60% for men, 40% for women.

Literacy continued to increase except in some urban industrial areas (e.g., in Lancashire), where rates declined to 42% for men, 19% for women, before rising again (from *c.*1815). Regional statistics for 1839, recording capacity to write a signature, show rates of 55–88% for men, 36–76% for women. They were highest in LONDON and some northern areas. By 1900, after elementary schooling had become compulsory (1880), literacy exceeded 95%.

LITERACY, IRELAND OGHAM writing of the 4th–6th centuries, used for Irish inscriptions, implies some literacy. Literacy in Latin developed in the 5th–6th centuries with the CONVERSION OF IRELAND to Christianity. Laws were written in Irish from the 7th century. Literacy was confined to the Gaelic LEARNED CLASSES (e.g., clergy, jurists, physicians), who flourished into the 17th century. From the 12th century there were professional lay scribes.

Administration of the English colony from the later 12th century depended on literacy (*see* GOVERNMENT, IRELAND 12TH–17TH CENTURIES). The main literate groups were clergy, lay administrators, and some merchants. The government attempted to expand literacy in English from the 16th century to spread reformed Christianity (*see* REFORMATION, IRELAND).

Literacy spread more widely in the 18th century with educational expansion, including elementary HEDGE SCHOOLS for Catholics. It was particularly valued within PRESBYTERIAN SOCIETY in N Ireland. In 1841, 47% of the population over 5 could read or write (over 70% in Cos. Down and Antrim, NE Ireland). NATIONAL EDUCATION (from 1831) produced a largely literate society: by 1891 only 18% of the population was completely illiterate. *See also* EDUCATION, IRELAND.

LITERACY, SCOTLAND By the 15th century clergy and merchants were usually literate, as were lords (peers) and LAIRDS by the 17th century. At the REFORMATION (1560), reformers called for universal literacy so that all people could read the Bible; but school provision only expanded in the 17th century (*see* EDUCATION, SCOTLAND). By *c.*1650 male literacy in the rural Lowlands was around 25% (now including wealthier tenants, craftsmen, traders), making parts of Scotland the most literate areas in Europe; female literacy was under 10%. Between the later 17th century and *c.*1750 literacy rose to 65% for men and 20–30% for women (making Lowland Scotland more literate than England, except N England where rates were similar). The (Gaelic) HIGHLAND population remained largely illiterate until the 18th century, when the provision of parish schools and work of the SOCIETY IN SCOTLAND FOR PROPAGATING CHRISTIAN KNOWLEDGE raised literacy to around 50% by c.1800.

From c.1780 to c.1830 overall rates declined as people migrated to industrial centres where school provision was poor. Rates then improved as new schools were founded (reaching slightly higher levels than in England). In 1861–71 rates were: Lowlands, 83–99% for men, 69–97% women; Highlands, 65% for men, 49% for women. Illiteracy was virtually eliminated after the 1872 Education (Scotland) Act made school attendance compulsory (by c.1900).

LITERACY, WALES Before the 15th century only clergy and lawyers were usually literate, variously in Welsh, English and Latin (*see* LAW, WELSH). Merchants, GENTRY and farmers increasingly became literate in English and Welsh in the 15th and 16th centuries, as did craftsmen and artisans during the late 17th and early 18th centuries. In the 1730s–80s literacy in Welsh was extended by the 'circulating schools' of Griffith JONES to perhaps 40 per cent of the population, but then declined.

Literacy increased again in the 19th century with the growth of Sunday schools and church schools. The majority of the population was literate from the late 19th century, following the arrival of compulsory elementary education in 1880. *See also* EDUCATION, WALES; PRINTING, WALES; NEWSPAPERS, WALES.

LITERARY REVIEWS Term referring to high-class periodicals which have functioned as forums for literary, intellectual and political debate. Though the earliest date from the late 17th century, such publications were most influential in the 19th century. The *Edinburgh Review* (1802–1929) supported the WHIGS, the *Quarterly Review* (1809–1967) was TORY, and PHILOSOPHIC RADICALS founded the *Westminster Review* (1824–1914). Important later reviews included the *Times Literary Supplement* (from 1902, separate publication from 1914).

LITERARY REVIVAL, WELSH A movement from the mid 18th century which revived poetry, and literature and culture more generally. It was a response to the decline of the bardic tradition (professional poets) from the late 17th century, which withered for want of GENTRY patronage. A leading figure was Goronwy Owen (1723–69), who reused medieval metres to treat classical subjects. He and others were encouraged by middle-class patrons, many in London and associated with WELSH NATIONAL SOCIETIES. A further revival began in the 1890s, influenced by Owen Morgan EDWARDS and the creation of the federal University of Wales (1893). *See also* WELSH LANGUAGE AND LITERATURE; EISTEDDFOD.

LIVERPOOL A city, port and metropolitan borough in NW England, by the R. Mersey; formerly in Lancashire.

Liverpool was founded by King JOHN in 1207 to facilitate communication with Ireland. Its name means 'Pool with muddy water'. Trade with the Americas in the 18th century transformed it into a cosmopolitan seaport involved in the SLAVE TRADE (abolished 1807). It was linked to MANCHESTER by waterways (river and CANAL) from 1776.

From c.1800 Liverpool was the main import centre for raw cotton for the rapidly expanding Lancashire COTTON INDUSTRY, a role enhanced by its RAILWAY to Manchester (opened 1830). For much of the 19th century it was England's second-largest urban centre. There was large-scale Irish immigration. Between 1840 and 1900 Liverpool's docks increased from 16 to 40. City status was awarded in 1880, and two cathedrals were built (Church of England, 1904–8; Catholic, consecrated 1967).

Shipping declined in the late 20th century, resulting in population decline, but electrical engineering and food-processing remained significant. Determined regeneration from the 1980s brought media and leisure activities to the City (e.g., museums and galleries). Liverpool gained three universities (by upgrading): Liverpool (1903), Liverpool John Moores (1992), Liverpool Hope (2005). *See also* BEATLES, THE; HIGHER EDUCATION, EXPANSION OF.

Est. popn: 1300, 1000; 1600, 2000; 1800, 77,000; 1900, 685,000; 2000, 442,000.

LIVERPOOL, 2ND EARL OF (b. 7 June 1770 at London, England; d. 4 Dec 1828 at Kingston-upon-Thames, Surrey, England, aged 58). Robert Jenkinson was elected an MP in 1790 and known as Lord Hawkesbury from 1796. He held junior office 1793–6, 1799–1801, under William PITT the Younger. While foreign secretary, 1801–4, under Henry ADDINGTON, he negotiated the Peace of AMIENS (1802). In 1803 he moved to the House of Lords. He served as home secretary 1804–6, 1807–9, under Pitt and the duke of PORTLAND, and succeeded his father in 1808 (*see* JENKINSON, CHARLES). As secretary for war 1809–12 he supported the Peninsular campaign.

In May 1812 Liverpool, a TORY, succeeded Spencer PERCEVAL as prime minister. His incumbency saw victory in the NAPOLEONIC WARS (1815), renewal of the CORN LAWS (1815), repeal of INCOME TAX (1816), and PETERLOO and the SIX ACTS (1819).

From 1822, as economic conditions improved, Liverpool encouraged LIBERAL TORYISM (e.g., promotion of international trade by lowering customs). He maintained neutrality on CATHOLIC EMANCIPATION. Though many regarded him as mediocre, he skilfully held ULTRA TORIES and Liberals in alliance. Illness forced his resignation (March 1827), after which the Tory Party fragmented. *See also* CANNING, GEORGE.

LIVERY AND MAINTENANCE *see* BASTARD FEUDALISM

LIVINGSTONE, DAVID (b. 19 March 1813 at Blantyre, Lanarkshire, Scotland; d. 1 May 1873 at Chief Chitambo's Village, southern Africa, aged 60). From a poor background, Livingstone studied to become a Christian missionary. From 1841, working for the London Missionary Society, he made journeys from southern Africa northwards, discovering Lake Ngami (in modern Botswana) in 1849. In 1853–5 he found a route northwest to the Atlantic (at Luanda in modern Angola). After travelling to the E coast, he returned to England (arrived Dec. 1856) and published *Missionary Travels* (1857). Livingstone then headed a government-sponsored expedition in Africa (1858–63), which explored inland from Quelimane (in modern Mozambique), assessing prospects for colonization.

Back in Africa from 1866, Livingstone explored the Lake Tanganyika region for sources of the R. NILE. In 1871 he was tracked down by the journalist Henry Stanley, who reputedly said: 'Dr Livingstone, I presume?' Livingstone was buried in WESTMINSTER Abbey, England. *See also* MOFFAT, ROBERT; MISSIONARY SOCIETIES, ENGLAND AND GREAT BRITAIN.

LIVINGSTONE, KEN (b. 17 June 1945 at Lambeth, London, England). A laboratory technician (1962–70), Livingstone was a Labour member of Lambeth and Camden Councils in LONDON (respectively 1971–8, 1978–82), and from 1973 of the Greater London Council (GLC).

In 1981, following his victory in GLC elections, Labour's moderate GLC leader was ousted in favour of the more extreme Livingstone. His reduction of fares on London's public transport ('Fares Fair' policy) was thwarted by a legal judgment (Dec. 1981). Provocative behaviour by Livingstone (e.g., public support for Republicans in NORTHERN IRELAND) encouraged the Conservative prime minister, Margaret THATCHER, to abolish the GLC and other metropolitan councils (1986). Livingstone became an MP (1987–2001).

When Tony BLAIR (Labour prime minister) instituted an elected mayor for London, Livingstone was prevented from becoming Labour's candidate (2000). He won as an independent (becoming Britain's first directly elected executive government officer), and implemented a traffic 'congestion charge' in C London (2003). In 2004 he was re-elected, as Labour's candidate, but lost elections in 2008 and 2012 to the Conservative Boris JOHNSON. In 2016 he was suspended from the Labour Party for making an offensive remark about Adolf Hitler and Zionism. He resigned from the Party in 2018. *See also* LONDON, GOVERNMENT OF.

LLANDAFF A district of CARDIFF city, SE WALES; Welsh, meaning 'Church on R. Taff'. Llandaff became the site of a cathedral church by the early 11th century, though its diocese (SE Wales) was not defined until 1129–34 (*see* URBAN OF LLANDAFF; LLANDAFF, BOOK OF). Much of the 12th- and 13th-century cathedral (dedicated to St TEILO) was rebuilt 1843–57 and again after bombing (1941) in WORLD WAR II. Llandaff was added to Cardiff in 1922. *See also* CHURCH ORGANIZATION, WALES.

LLANDAFF, BOOK OF A Latin manuscript (in National Library of Wales, Aberystwyth), compiled under Bishop URBAN OF LLANDAFF in the early 12th century to demonstrate the antiquity of Llandaff church (SE Wales), and to show (falsely) that it had an equally old extensive diocese. It contains saints' lives and charters (*see* GLYWYSING). *See also* CHURCH ORGANIZATION, WALES.

LLOYD, SELWYN (b. 28 July 1904 at West Kirby, Cheshire, England; d. 17 May 1978 at Preston Crowmarsh, Oxfordshire, England, aged 73). A barrister and British Army officer, Lloyd became a Conservative MP in 1945. As foreign secretary 1955–60, he unhappily followed Anthony EDEN's policy during the SUEZ CRISIS (1956). As chancellor of the Exchequer he implemented the expansionist policy of Harold MACMILLAN, but was forced to introduce a 'pay pause' to combat inflation (July 1961; *see* INCOMES POLICIES). He was replaced by Reginald MAUDLING in Macmillan's drastic Cabinet reshuffle (July 1962). Lloyd was speaker of the House of Commons 1971–6. Created Lord Selwyn-Lloyd in 1976. *See also* NATIONAL ECONOMIC DEVELOPMENT COUNCIL.

LLOYD GEORGE, DAVID (b. 17 Jan. 1863 at Manchester, Lancashire, England; d. 26 March 1945 at Llanystumdwy, Caernarfonshire, Wales, aged 82). British prime minister 1916–22; leader of the LIBERAL PARTY 1926–31.

David George added the name Lloyd to acknowledge a shoemaker uncle who supported his family at Llanystumdwy. He became a solicitor (1884) and Liberal MP (1890). Opposition to the (Second) BOER WAR made him famous. As president of the Board of Trade (1905–8) and chancellor of the Exchequer (1908–15) he advanced reforms (*see* PEOPLE'S BUDGET; NATIONAL INSURANCE), and survived the MARCONI SCANDAL.

During WORLD WAR I, Lloyd George achieved success as munitions minister in the coalition government (May 1915–July 1916), then became war secretary. Dissatisfied with strategy, he ousted and replaced H.H. ASQUITH as prime minister (7 Dec. 1916) but split the Liberals. After the Allied victory (Nov. 1918) he was celebrated as 'The Man who Won the War'.

The post-war COUPON ELECTION re-elected Lloyd George's coalition. He attended the PARIS PEACE CONFERENCE and negotiated an Irish treaty (1921), but the GEDDES AXE curtailed reforms. The CARLTON CLUB MEETING forced his resignation. Liberal reunion (1923) failed to restore Party fortunes. Lloyd George sat as an Independent Liberal from 1931. Created Earl Lloyd-George 1945. *See also* NEW LIBERALISM.

LLOYD GEORGE, DAVID, AND IRELAND Lloyd George became closely involved while minister for munitions; after the EASTER RISING (April 1916) he was appointed (24 May) by the British prime minister, H.H. ASQUITH, to negotiate a workable HOME RULE scheme. He persuaded the Unionist E.H. CARSON to accept Home Rule with exclusion of six counties in ULSTER, but nationalist leader John REDMOND rejected the proposal (24 July). As prime minister (from Dec. 1916), Lloyd George delegated the problem, unsuccessfully, to an IRISH CONVENTION (1917–18).

From Jan. 1919 Britain's authority in Ireland was challenged by the self-proclaimed Dáil Éireann ('Assembly of Ireland'), formed by SINN FÉIN MPs, and by violence incited by the IRISH REPUBLICAN ARMY; both groups sought an independent, all-Ireland republic. Lloyd George attempted both to suppress republicans and enact Home Rule. The GOVERNMENT OF IRELAND ACT (Dec. 1920) partitioned Ireland, providing separate Parliaments and governments in N and S. Northern Unionists accepted the scheme, but republicans rejected it. By now violence was extensive.

Eventually Lloyd George arranged a truce with Éamon DE VALERA (9 July 1921), and negotiated the ANGLO-IRISH TREATY (Dec.) which created the IRISH FREE STATE (26 counties). The 'dual solution' permitted British withdrawal, but resulted in the IRISH CIVIL WAR and longer-term problems. *See also* IRISH INDEPENDENCE, WAR OF; NORTHERN IRELAND.

LLOYD-JONES, MARTYN (b. 20 Dec. 1899 at Cardiff, Glamorgan, Wales; d. 1 March 1981 at London, England, aged 81). In 1927 a religious conversion led Lloyd-Jones to abandon a medical career to serve the Presbyterian Church of Wales (*see* CALVINISTIC METHODISTS). As minister of Westminster Chapel, London, 1938–68 he won a wide reputation as an uncompromising exponent of EVANGELICALISM. He wrote numerous books on scripture and theology.

LLYWELYN AP GRUFFUDD OR LLYWELYN THE LAST (b. *c*.1225; d. 11 Dec. 1282, near Builth, C Wales, aged about 57). Last independent ruler of GWYNEDD (NW WALES), 1246–82; PRINCE OF WALES, 1258–82.

Llywelyn ruled jointly with his brother Owain from the death of their uncle DAFYDD AP LLYWELYN (1246), and with DAFYDD AP GRUFFUDD, another brother, from 1247. Llywelyn was party to the treaty of WOODSTOCK (1247). As sole ruler from 1255, Llywelyn began expansion at the expense of the English (*see* BERFEDDWLAD, Y) and of native Welsh rulers – of Meirionydd (W Wales), DEHEUBARTH (SW Wales), and Powys (C Wales). By 1258 Llywelyn was overlord of most of native Wales and adopted the title 'prince of Wales', recognized by King HENRY III of England in 1267 (treaty of MONTGOMERY).

Relations with England deteriorated in the early 1270s because of Llywelyn's repeated failure to do homage to King EDWARD I and Edward's harbouring of Llywelyn's brother and rival Dafydd and of Gruffudd ap Gwenwynwyn of S Powys. Edward declared war on 12 Nov. 1276. His first campaign (1277) led to the treaty of ABERCONWY. In 1278 Llywelyn married Eleanor, daughter of Simon de MONTFORT, with Edward's approval.

In March 1282 Llywelyn assumed leadership of a revolt against the MARCH OF WALES, provoking Edward's second campaign, 1282–3, during which Llywelyn was slain; *see* WALES, ENGLISH CONQUEST OF. *See also* ANGLO-WELSH RELATIONS, 6TH–13TH CENTURIES.

LLYWELYN AP IORWERTH OR LLYWELYN FAWR, 'THE GREAT' (b. *c*.1175, possibly at Dolwyddelan, Gwynedd; d. 11 April 1240 at Aberconwy Abbey, Gwynedd, aged about 65). Prince of GWYNEDD (NW WALES) 1199–1240.

A grandson of OWAIN GWYNEDD, Llywelyn established his position in the 1190s mainly by evicting his uncles; by 1199 he controlled most of Gwynedd. During 1201–10 good relations with King JOHN of England (*see* SIWAN) enabled him to extend his influence over neighbouring polities such as POWYS (C Wales) and CEREDIGION (W Wales) – advances only partly set back by John's campaigns in Wales in 1211. Llywelyn made further advances in 1212–18, exploiting the weakness of English kings (*see* WORCESTER, TREATY OF) and good relations with Marcher lords (*see* MARCH OF WALES).

By 1220 Llywelyn was undisputed overlord of Welsh rulers. During the 1220s and 1230s he sought recognition from King HENRY III of England of himself as PRINCE OF WALES and of his son DAFYDD AP LLYWELYN as his sole heir. Henry refused. *See also* ANGLO-WELSH RELATIONS, 6TH–13TH CENTURIES.

LOCAL GOVERNMENT, NORTHERN IRELAND When the province was created in May 1921 it comprised six counties (Antrim, Armagh, Down, Fermanagh, Londonderry, Tyrone) with lower-tier rural and urban districts and boroughs, and two county boroughs (BELFAST, LONDONDERRY). Many local councils with nationalist majorities (elected 1920 under proportional representation) had adhered to the DUBLIN-based 'Dáil government' (*see* GOVERNMENT, SOUTHERN IRELAND). Northern Ireland's Unionist government legislated to dissolve councils that refused to recognize its authority (21 dissolved by April 1922).

In 1922 legislation replaced proportional representation with election by simple majority votes, and authorized the redrawing of ward boundaries. Ward revision enabled 'gerrymandering' – use of boundaries to produce Unionist-dominated councils in some areas with nationalist majorities. These measures, together with retention of property qualifications and business votes, and new residence requirements (1928, 1934), gave Unionists disproportionate control of local government, including patronage over jobs and HOUSING.

From 1966 Northern Ireland's Unionist government, facing criticism, considered reform. It was implemented after the outbreak of the TROUBLES (1968). Universal suffrage was introduced (under legislation in 1969 and 1971), and from Oct. 1971 a central authority took over local-authority housing. In 1973, following the 'Macrory Report' (1970), authorities were replaced by 26 single-tier districts with limited responsibilities, elected by proportional representation. Some functions (education, libraries, health) were transferred to area boards with nominated and elected members. Counties were retained for some ceremonial purposes. On 1 April 2015, the districts were reduced to 11 authorities (eight districts, two boroughs and Belfast city). *See also* GOVERNMENT, NORTHERN IRELAND.

LOCAL GOVERNMENT, SOUTHERN IRELAND

The IRISH FREE STATE (created 1922) retained the structure of 1899, comprising four county boroughs (CORK, DUBLIN, LIMERICK, WATERFORD) and 26 counties with lower-tier rural or urban districts, all with elected councils. (Co. Tipperary consisted of two separate 'ridings'.) About 30 towns, belonging to rural districts, retained elected town commissions. Rural districts were abolished in 1925 and their functions transferred to counties. The historical PROVINCES (Connacht, Leinster, Munster, Ulster) remained nominal entities.

Later modifications included the granting of borough status to some urban districts (1920s–60s), separation of Galway as a county borough (1986), and division of Co. Dublin into three (1994).

In the 1920s–30s some rebellious councils were temporarily replaced with government-appointed commissioners. Consequent improvements in administration, and US experience, encouraged adoption of the city or county manager system whereby control of administration was delegated to a professional manager. First introduced in Cork in 1929, it was made obligatory in 1940 (implemented 1942). Central control was increased by the abolition of domestic rates (1978) and rates on agricultural land (1982), which were replaced by central funding. A local property tax was re-instituted in 2013.

In 2014 major reforms were made to reduce costs. Authorities were reduced to 31 (26 counties, two county-and-city authorities, cities of Cork, Dublin, Galway). Local responsibilities included housing, planning, roads, water supply and sewerage, and recreational facilities. Managers were renamed chief executives. Twenty-five authority areas were also subdivided into municipal districts with their respective councillors empowered to take certain decisions.

LOCAL GOVERNMENTAL STRUCTURES, ENGLAND

Anglo-Saxon kingdoms (5th–10th centuries) contained small districts (or SHIRES), from which renders (e.g., food) were obtained and through which services were possibly mobilized (*see* THREE PUBLIC SERVICES). In WESSEX, in the 8th–9th centuries, larger shires were created, each administered by an EALDORMAN. By the 9th century small 'private' jurisdictions were developing (*see* MANOR).

After creation of a single kingdom, large shires were formed outside Wessex (mid 10th–11th centuries). Groups of shires (called 'provincial earldoms' by historians) were sometimes administered by an ealdorman (or EARL), assisted by shire-reeves (*see* SHERIFF). Shires were usually subdivided into 'hundreds' ('wapentakes' in northern England); some became private jurisdictions (*see* FRANCHISE).

After the NORMAN CONQUEST (1066–70s) provincial earldoms were discontinued, leaving shires (or 'counties') as primary units administered by sheriffs. Private jurisdiction expanded (*see* HONOUR), and some towns obtained autonomy (*see* TOWN GOVERNMENT, ENGLAND).

In the 14th–19th centuries JUSTICES OF THE PEACE were leading judicial and administrative officers in each county, headed from the later 16th century by a LORD LIEUTENANT. From the 16th century the PARISH (or township) extensively superseded the manor for civil purposes.

After 1834 parishes were grouped into unions for POOR RELIEF; sanitary districts were also created (1848–72; *see* PUBLIC HEALTH ACTS). In 1889 administrative powers of JPs were transferred to elected county councils (and also 'county boroughs'), and in 1894–5 most sanitary districts became 'rural districts' or 'urban districts' with councils; 'civil parishes' were created, some with councils.

In 1974 reorganization constituted six conurbations (outside London) as 'metropolitan counties', with lower-tier 'metropolitan districts' (36), and formed 39 other counties with districts (296). Metropolitan county councils were abolished in 1986, with districts becoming unitary (all-purpose) administrative authorities. Some unitary authorities were later created elsewhere. In 2015 there were 36 metropolitan district authorities; 55 other unitary authorities; 27 counties with 201 districts. *See also* LONDON, GOVERNMENT OF; PREROGATIVE COURTS.

LOCAL GOVERNMENTAL STRUCTURES, IRELAND

Administrative territories were instituted by Anglo-Normans from the later 12th century, based on arrangements in England and Wales. SHIRES (or counties) were created in areas under royal control for revenue collection and exercise of justice, administered by SHERIFFS (later assisted by keepers of the peace; *see* JUSTICES OF THE PEACE, IRELAND). They were subdivided into cantreds (called BARONIES from the 16th century). Extensive areas were also granted to Anglo-Irish lords as liberties (or PALATINATES), and administered by their officers. English-controlled territory contracted in the 14th–15th centuries (*see* PALE, IRELAND).

The reassertion of English authority from the mid 16th century included the suppression of Gaelic Irish lordships (by early 17th century) and Anglo-Irish liberties (by early 18th century), and the spread of local structures – regional PRESIDENCIES (to 1672), shires and baronies. Shire-based government (including JPs' quarter sessions') became fundamental. County grand juries (panels of landowners, chosen by sheriffs, who confirmed indictments) were involved in civil administration, initially (1634) through authorizing bridge building and taxation ('county cess'). During the 18th century their powers were extended (e.g., 1708, given responsibility for gaols and court houses). Catholics were generally excluded 1691–1793, making local administration part of the PROTESTANT ASCENDANCY.

From 1838 poor law unions were important local units, administered by elected boards and supervised by a central government board (in England until 1847). Local boards were given additional responsibilities in 1866 (see PUBLIC HEALTH ACTS), and supervised from 1872 by the Local Government Board. Sanitary districts (subdivisions of unions) were created in 1874.

The 1898 Local Government (Ireland) Act implemented (from 1899) the new English two-tier pattern of administrative counties and subordinate rural or urban districts, all with councils. (There were also six unitary county boroughs.) County councils received the administrative and fiscal powers of grand juries. See also TOWNLAND; TOWN GOVERNMENT, IRELAND; POOR RELIEF, IRELAND; LOCAL GOVERNMENT, NORTHERN IRELAND/SOUTHERN IRELAND.

LOCAL GOVERNMENTAL STRUCTURES, SCOTLAND

Before the mid 12th century the main unit within kingdoms in N Britain was the THANAGE, used by kings and nobles for gathering tribute and administering justice. From c.1120 David (heir to Alexander I) introduced SHERIFFDOMS (or shires), areas modelled on English (large) SHIRES in which sheriffs administered royal interests (holding courts and collecting revenues). Within a century sheriffdoms covered most of mainland Scotland, although their main day-to-day function was running areas outside the old earldoms, great lordships and (from the 14th century) REGALITIES, and supervising lords of local BARONIES. After the REFORMATION (1560), KIRK SESSIONS and presbyteries organized poor relief and education. (For towns, see TOWN GOVERNMENT, SCOTLAND.)

After union with England (1707), shire-based government was developed. JUSTICES OF THE PEACE (introduced, ineffectively, in 1609) received new powers (1708, 1718), as did COMMISSIONERS OF SUPPLY (formed 1667). The two groups, for example, dealt with law and order, and road and bridge maintenance. After abolition of HERITABLE JURISDICTIONS (1747), sheriffs' courts were strengthened (see COURTS, SCOTLAND).

In 1845 poor relief was transferred from kirk sessions to partly elected parochial boards (they also administered water supply and public health from 1867). Elected parochial school boards managed education from 1872. The 1889 Local Government (Scotland) Act instituted elected county councils, though commissioners of supply remained partly responsible for POLICE forces. In 1894 parochial boards were replaced by elected parish councils, and in 1918 school boards by county boards.

The Local Government (Scotland) Act of 1929 abolished most authorities other than county and burgh councils. Most county councils became all-purpose authorities, with responsibilities in some burghs. In 1975 counties and burghs were replaced by nine 'regions' and 53 subordinate 'districts'. Three island unitary authorities and local 'community councils' were also created. In 1996 regions and districts were replaced by 29 unitary authorities.

LOCAL GOVERNMENTAL STRUCTURES, WALES

In the 11th–13th centuries (and probably earlier) Welsh kings exercised authority through the COMMOTE, which may have superseded the CANTREF (see KINGSHIP, WALES 5TH–13TH CENTURIES; ROYAL REVENUES, WALES). In the 12th and 13th centuries, officers' importance increased, especially in GWYNEDD (NW Wales). In lands seized by NORMANS and taken into the MARCH OF WALES (from late 11th century) the primary unit was the lordship. In SW Wales, Norman invaders created the English-style shire of PEMBROKESHIRE.

Lands in W and SW Wales captured for King EDWARD I of England in 1277 were governed by a JUSTICIAR (from 1280) and developed as the shires of Cardiganshire and Carmarthenshire. After the conquests of 1282–3, Edward treated NW Wales as a province, giving it a justiciar with a Chancery and a chamberlain with an Exchequer. Flintshire was formed in NE Wales, under the justiciar of Chester (NW England), and the shires of Anglesey, Caernarfonshire, and Merionethshire in NW Wales, each under a sheriff and court. Commotes were retained as English-style 'hundreds', for collection of dues and administration of justice. Each justiciar held Courts of Great Sessions.

In 1536 Marcher lordships were abolished. GLAMORGAN became a shire, and some lordships were attached to Welsh and English shires, while five new shires were created, with hundreds (subdivisions): Breconshire, Denbighshire, MONMOUTHSHIRE, Montgomeryshire, Radnorshire. From 1543 a Court of Great Sessions operated in all counties except Monmouthshire and JUSTICES OF THE PEACE were introduced, who remained the main judicial and administrative officers of shires until 1889 when they lost powers to newly elected county councils and county boroughs. From the late 16th century the PARISH also served civil purposes (replaced by community councils in 1974).

In 1974 shires were replaced by eight 'regions' (under county councils) and 37 subordinate 'districts' (under district councils).

In 1996 both tiers were replaced by 22 unitary authorities (with various titles). *See also* TOWN GOVERNMENT, WALES.

LOCARNO, TREATY OF The main international agreement negotiated at Locarno in Switzerland in 1925 (5–16 Oct.) by the British foreign secretary Austen CHAMBERLAIN, signed on 1 Dec. Britain and Italy guaranteed the borders of GERMANY with BELGIUM and FRANCE against aggression from either side. This promoted Franco-German reconciliation, but critics point to British refusal to guarantee the borders of CZECHOSLOVAKIA and POLAND with Germany.

LOCKE, JOHN (b. 29 Aug. 1632 at Wrington, Somerset, England; d. 28 Oct. 1704 at Oates, Essex, England, aged 72). A scholar and teacher at OXFORD University, Locke was an adviser from 1666 of Anthony Ashley Cooper (*see* SHAFTESBURY, EARL OF). He lived in France 1675–9, and for safety in the Dutch Republic from 1683, following the EXCLUSION CRISIS and attacks on WHIGS. He returned in 1689, after the fall of King JAMES VII/II.

During the 1660s–80s Locke developed arguments for popular sovereignty and the right to resist tyrannical rulers, and also for religious toleration. He saw national churches as voluntary associations, and preferred rationalism in religion to dogma. His publications include *Two Treatises of Government*, *An Essay Concerning Human Understanding* (both 1689), and *The Reasonableness of Christianity* (published anonymously, 1695). Locke's philosophy greatly influenced 18th-century politics and religion. *See also* ENLIGHTENMENT.

LOFTUS, ADAM (b. *c.*1533 at Swineside, Yorkshire, England; d. 5 April 1605 at Dublin, Ireland, aged about 71). Educated at CAMBRIDGE University, Loftus went to Ireland in 1560 as chaplain to chief governor SUSSEX. Archbishop of Armagh (1563–7) and of Dublin (1567–1605), he was a leading promoter of the Reformation. From 1565 he served on the new Court of Ecclesiastical Causes, which sought (unavailingly) to enforce Protestantism. Loftus also served as keeper of the great seal (intermittently 1573–81) and chancellor (1581–1605). Instrumental in the foundation of Trinity College, Dublin, Loftus was first provost (1593–4). *See also* REFORMATION, IRELAND; UNIVERSITIES, IRELAND; PERROT, JOHN.

LOLLARDY, ENGLAND A Christian heresy which emerged in the 1380s and survived until the 1530s. Its core teachings, derived mainly from writings of John WYCLIF (d. 1384), were that the Pope's claims to authority over the Church were false; that TRANSUBSTANTIATION did not occur during the Eucharist (Mass); and that penance, devotion to images, and pilgrimages lacked scriptural basis and were irreligious. It promoted study of the BIBLE in English – the earliest English Bible was a lollard translation instigated by

Wyclif but completed and widely transmitted by lollards. The term 'lollard', meaning 'a mumbler of prayers', began as a term of contempt (probably derived from Middle Dutch *lollaerd*, meaning 'mumbler' or 'mutterer').

Early lollards, supported by artisans and even noblemen, sought to advance their cause through action against the government. A protest at WESTMINSTER (1395) was followed by OLDCASTLE'S RISING (1414), and another revolt (1431). The response was persecution, beginning with the statute *DE HERETICO COMBURENDO* (1401).

After 1414 lollardy was driven underground but survived in London, SE England, Coventry and parts of N England. *See also* ARUNDEL, THOMAS; CHICHELE, HENRY; PECOCK, REGINALD; CHURCH, MEDIEVAL ENGLAND; CENSORSHIP, ENGLAND AND WALES.

LOLLARDY, SCOTLAND Lollardy reached Scotland by the end of the 14th century and concerned the authorities. (ST ANDREWS University was founded in 1412 partly to defend the orthodox faith.) Lollardy proved unimportant. The only lollards burnt in Scotland were John Resby, an English priest (1406 or 1407), and Paul Crawar, a Bohemian scholar (1433). Later in the 15th century members of the Campbell family of Kingencleuch (SW Scotland) were accused of heresy, as were the 'Lollards of Kyle', a group of 29 lay people and a priest (tried in GLASGOW, 1494). None was executed. There are no proven links between lollards and early Protestants.

LOLLARDY, WALES Lollardy had little effect on Wales. Only a few relevant incidents are known. In 1386, two Welsh students at OXFORD University, England, were excommunicated, having probably espoused the heresy at Oxford. In 1391 the lollard William Swinderby was active in the Welsh border country, and had Welsh followers; they included Gwallter Brut, who declared that God had chosen the Welsh to overthrow the Pope.

The lollard rebel Sir John OLDCASTLE was captured in Powys (C Wales) in 1417. He was suspected of contact with supporters of Welsh rebel OWAIN GLYN DŴR. But they probably did not share Oldcastle's lollardy. *See also* CHURCH, MEDIEVAL WALES.

LONDON Capital of the UK, in SE England alongside R. Thames. The meaning of its (Brittonic) name is unknown.

London (Latin, Londinium) was founded by the Romans by AD 60 on the N bank by a river crossing (bridged *c.*85–90). The main focus of Roman Britain's road network, it was conveniently close to northern Europe. London was abandoned in the 5th century (*see* POST-ROMAN BRITAIN).

During the 7th century St Paul's Cathedral was founded within the Roman walls (604) and a WIC (trading centre) outside to the W. London was thereafter Britain's pre-eminent city. Situated in ESSEX, it was appropriated by MERCIA

(8th century), and by ALFRED of Wessex (886) who restarted intramural development (replacing the wic). By 1200 London was an internationally important trading and manufacturing centre, with nearby WESTMINSTER serving as the royal CAPITAL.

In the late 14th–15th centuries London's population was much reduced (*see* PLAGUE, ENGLAND). FOREIGN TRADE became overwhelmingly centred on London, especially CLOTH exporting. Population re-expanded from the later 15th century. During the CIVIL WARS (1642–8) London adhered to Parliament. It recovered swiftly from a GREAT PLAGUE (1665–6) and GREAT FIRE (1666), and by 1700 was Europe's largest city (575,000 people).

From the 18th century finance and professional services were important (*see* FINANCIAL REVOLUTION); cultural activity flourished (*see* LONDON SEASON). During the 19th century RAILWAYS facilitated expansion (*see* SUBURBS AND SUBURBIA), and the original city became mainly a business centre (21,000 inhabitants by 1921). By 1900 London was the focus of the world's trade and finance, and its largest city (to 1930s).

During the 1920s–30s London's built-up area doubled. The BLITZ (1940–1), during WORLD WAR II, necessitated reconstruction. The decline of docks (1960s–80s) and manufacturing was offset by growth in finance. IMMIGRATION (from 1990s) created a 'majority-minority population'. London remained an outstanding centre for arts and tourism. *See also* LONDON, GOVERNMENT OF; BOUDICCA; BIG BANG; MULTICULTURAL SOCIETY.

Est. popn: 200, 30,000; 1086, 20,000; 1300, 60,000; 1600, 200,000; 1800, 900,000; 1900, 6,500,000; 2000, 7,200,000.

LONDON, GOVERNMENT OF In the 7th–12th centuries London was under (differing) royal authority, administered by REEVES (called SHERIFFS in the 11th century). Inhabitants participated through folkmoots (assemblies, in St Paul's churchyard). A smaller husting court was created (possibly late 9th century). By the 11th century 24 wards existed, each with a wardmote (court) under an alderman. Following London's surrender to WILLIAM I (1066), its customs were confirmed, though William overawed London with three CASTLES.

From the 12th century Londoners obtained self-government. Possibly from 1129 they elected sheriffs; by 1194 a mayor was head of the citizens or freemen (later elected). By 1220 a court of mayor and aldermen was displacing the husting as the main court. Guilds became important, and from 1319 controlled admission to citizenship. Soon afterwards freemen were elected as ward representatives to an assembly (successor of the folkmoot) which became the Court of Common Council. Election of the mayor was restricted from 1465 to guild liverymen (senior members). In the 21st century London's financial district remained under the City Corporation – mayor, Court of Common Council (primary body from 18th century), Court of Aldermen.

In the 16th–19th centuries, population increased outside the City's jurisdiction; in these areas MANORS and especially PARISHES were the main units. By 1850 London had 300 administrative bodies.

Comprehensive government outside the City began with policing (from 1748; *see* POLICE, ENGLAND). From 1855 an elected Metropolitan Board of Works undertook sewerage and other schemes. It was succeeded in 1889 by the London County Council; subordinate metropolitan boroughs were added in 1899 (including WESTMINSTER). In 1965 the Greater London Council (GLC) and 32 boroughs were instituted covering a larger area. The former was abolished in 1986 (*see* LIVINGSTONE, KEN). Provision for strategic government was restored in 2000 with an elected Greater London Authority and directly elected mayor. *See also* TOWN GOVERNMENT, ENGLAND; COMMUNES, ENGLAND; POPLARISM; LAMBETH.

LONDON, (1518) TREATY OF Signed on 5 Oct. in England by representatives of 20 European states, including England, France, Venice and the Holy Roman Empire. Signatories agreed to maintain peace. The treaty was negotiated by Cardinal Thomas WOLSEY, chief minister of King HENRY VIII, and was intended to reconcile European countries so they could challenge the Ottoman Turks. The treaty had little effect.

LONDONDERRY A city in Northern Ireland, by the R. Foyle; centre of Co. Londonderry; originally called Derry, from Irish Doire, meaning 'Place of the oaks'.

Derry was an ecclesiastical centre (monastic and lay settlement) 6th–16th centuries, and diocesan centre from 1254. A fort founded at Derry by the English in 1600 helped them to win the NINE YEARS WAR.

In 1613 Derry was granted by King JAMES VI/I to LONDON livery companies and renamed. A new town was laid out and fortified with walls and gates. It became a marketing centre and Protestant stronghold (*see* WILLIAMITE WAR), and later an important shirt-making centre (1850s–1960s). By 1921 a majority of the population were Catholics.

In 1968 rioting in Londonderry contributed to the outbreak of sectarian conflict in Northern Ireland (*see* TROUBLES). Londonderry became divided along sectarian lines, and an exodus of Protestants left behind a predominantly Catholic population. From the 1990s new activities were attracted (e.g., telephone 'call centres', electronics factories). *See also* O'DOHERTY'S REBELLION; BLOODY SUNDAY (1972).

Est. popn: 1800, 11,000; 1900, 39,000; 2000, 90,000.

LONDONDERRY, SIEGE OF An attempt in 1689 by (mainly Catholic) forces supporting James VII/II ('Jacobites') to capture LONDONDERRY (in N Ireland), the main initial centre of Protestant resistance during the WILLIAMITE WAR (1688–91). The siege began on 18 April 1689, in James's presence. A boom placed across the R. Foyle by Jacobites was broken by relief vessels on 28 July. Jacobites withdrew on 31 July, after 105 days. Their failure was a major setback for James. *See also* JAMES VII/II AND IRELAND.

LONDON SEASON The period each year when English NOBILITY and wealthy GENTRY lived in LONDON instead of the countryside to pursue social activities and arrange marriages. It developed from the later 16th century, and flourished vigorously after the GLORIOUS REVOLUTION (1688–9) when Parliament met annually. In the 18th century, when it extended from October to May, visitors frequented pleasure gardens and assembly rooms. In the early 19th century the Season's height was April to July, and it included the presentation of débutantes (young women entering society) to the monarch.

In the 1830s–50s influential women developed greater formality (e.g., use of 'calling cards'), and from the 1880s wealthy families from commerce and manufacturing participated. The Season declined in the 1920s–50s (presentation of débutantes ended in 1958), although some events (e.g., 'Royal Ascot' race meeting, Henley Royal Regatta) continued to flourish.

LONG BARROWS, BRITAIN Elongated mounds often raised over deposits of disarticulated human remains dating from the Early and Middle NEOLITHIC (*c.*4300– *c.*2800 BC). They are contemporaneous with cairns, chambered tombs and early PASSAGE TOMBS. Used for ancestral and funerary rites by dispersed communities of kin, they are regionally varied. Some long barrows saw use over many generations.

LONGCHAMP, WILLIAM (b. near Argenton, Normandy; d. Jan. 1197 at Poitiers, Poitou). RICHARD I of England appointed Longchamp as CHANCELLOR (Aug. 1189), bishop of Ely (Dec.), and (with Hugh du Puiset, bishop of Durham) as co-justiciar (Dec.) during his absence. Longchamp excluded Hugh in March 1190, becoming head of the royal COUNCIL. But after Longchamp's men imprisoned the archbishop of York, Longchamp's enemies forced him from office (5 Oct. 1191) and he left England (29 Oct.). Despite retaining Richard's support (e.g., continuing as chancellor), he was unable to regain authority.

LONG PARLIAMENT In England, the second Parliament summoned in 1640 by King CHARLES I, following his defeat in the Wars of the COVENANT; so called because of its duration (to 1660, with break; *see also* SHORT PARLIAMENT). It met from 3 Nov. 1640.

In 1641 Parliament forced Charles to concede the TRIENNIAL ACT (Feb.); execution of Thomas WENTWORTH, earl of Strafford (May); outlawing of IMPOSITIONS without Parliament's consent (June); abolition of STAR CHAMBER, Court of High Commission, COUNCIL OF THE NORTH and COUNCIL IN THE MARCHES OF WALES (July). In Dec. the Commons narrowly passed the GRAND REMONSTRANCE, criticizing Charles's policies of 1625–40. By now many members (e.g., Edward Hyde, later earl of CLARENDON) were alarmed by Parliament's radicalism. After Charles attempted to arrest several opponents (Jan. 1642; *see* FIVE MEMBERS INCIDENT), Parliament sought to control the militia (*see* MILITIA ORDINANCE). Charles's rejection of the Parliament's NINETEEN PROPOSITIONS (June) led to CIVIL WAR (Aug.). Royalists had already withdrawn.

After Parliament's victory (June 1646), Charles's refusal to make serious concessions in negotiations (July–Oct.) deepened divisions within Parliament between (political) 'Presbyterian' and 'Independent' groups. The Army's support for Independents led to the exclusion of Presbyterian MPs in PRIDE'S PURGE (Dec. 1648). The continuing, so-called RUMP PARLIAMENT (to 1653) secured Charles's execution (Jan. 1649), and abolished the House of Lords and monarchy (March).

The Rump was revived in 1659, and members excluded in 1648 were readmitted in Feb. 1660. The Parliament dissolved itself on 16 March. Succeeded by the CONVENTION PARLIAMENT. *See also* PYM, JOHN; LAUD, WILLIAM; BISHOPS' EXCLUSION BILL; CIVIL WARS, POLITICAL ASPECTS; COMMONWEALTH AND PROTECTORATE.

LORD ADVOCATE The Crown's chief prosecutor in Scotland and a government minister; styled thus since 1598. The post, originally 'king's advocate' (for the king of Scotland), dates from the 15th century. Between 1746 and 1885 the lord advocate was a pre-eminent British government officer in Scotland. Notable office-holders include Thomas HAMILTON, George MACKENZIE and Henry DUNDAS. *See also* SECRETARY OF STATE, SCOTLAND; SECRETARY FOR SCOTLAND.

LORD LIEUTENANT In England and Wales from the later 16th century, the senior representative of the Crown in each county. The post originated in England with the appointment of three noblemen as king's lieutenants during the PILGRIMAGE OF GRACE (1536), each commanding military forces from a group of counties. Similar arrangements were then made sporadically in all counties, especially during crises.

From 1585 (in the reign of Queen ELIZABETH I) rulers usually appointed a lord lieutenant for each county, usually a leading local nobleman, to supervise the MILITIA (in place of the SHERIFF), a responsibility that continued until

1871; they also levied men for overseas service. Each lieutenant was assisted by several deputy lieutenants. Lieutenants were given other responsibilities such as supervising JUSTICES OF THE PEACE. They were regarded as the heads of county government until county councils were created after 1888.

In Ireland, lieutenants were appointed from 1715 (the head of government was known as the lord lieutenant). They were abolished in the IRISH FREE STATE in 1922 but continued in NORTHERN IRELAND. In Scotland, lieutenants were appointed to some areas from 1715 and throughout the country from 1794. *See also* GOVERNMENT, ENGLAND WITH WALES 1509 TO 1642; NOBILITY.

LORDSHIP *see* FEUDALISM

LORDS OF PARLIAMENT Important lords, ranking below dukes and earls, who received a personal summons to the Scottish PARLIAMENT under an Act of 1428, which sought to increase lords' attendance. Summonses developed into a hereditary right, and 'lord of Parliament' became the lowest rank of the Scottish PEERAGE.

After the UNION OF ENGLAND AND SCOTLAND (1707) lords (with other Scottish peers) participated in the election of 16 'representative peers' to the House of Lords in the new British Parliament (UK Parliament from 1801), and sat by right from 1963 to 1999. (In 1999 there were 11 lords and three ladies without British or UK peerages.) Thereafter they could be elected as 'excepted' peers. *See also* SOCIAL STRUCTURE, NORTH BRITAIN AND SCOTLAND.

LORDS OF THE ARTICLES A committee (20–40 members), elected by the estates in the Scottish PARLIAMENT, which received petitions and prepared legislation during parliamentary sessions; it originated in the 1450s, having developed from earlier committees. Often accused of being a royal board of control, it was not until 1612 that manipulation by the Crown was achieved. For most of its history it was a pragmatic solution to drafting legislation in short parliamentary sessions. The lords were abolished in 1640, restored in 1661, and abolished again in 1689 (*see* REVOLUTION SETTLEMENT, SCOTLAND).

LORDS OF THE COMMITTEE In England during the reign of ANNE (1702–14), a small subgroup of members of the Cabinet-council (usually five or six leading ministers) which met regularly without the queen. It discussed problems and policies, often consulting other parties, before making recommendations to the Cabinet-council. *See also* CABINET.

LORDS OF THE CONGREGATION Nobles who championed the Scottish REFORMATION. Their movement grew from five men, who signed the 'First Bond' to promote

Protestantism on 3 Dec. 1557, to include a large proportion of the nobility. They spread Church Reform in 1559–60, deposed MARY OF GUISE (1559), and took over government until 1561. *See also* COVENANTS, SCOTLAND; MORTON, 4TH EARL OF; MAITLAND, WILLIAM, OF LETHINGTON.

LOTHIAN Originally the area in N Britain between the Rivers Tweed and Forth (modern SE Scotland), including EDINBURGH. (Lothian's Brittonic name is unexplained.) The eastern part was occupied by the British Votadini tribe (recorded 2nd–5th centuries) and continued as the kingdom of GODODDIN (6th–early 7th centuries). Lothian became part of the Anglian (English) kingdom of BERNICIA by 638, which continued from 679 as the kingdom of NORTHUMBRIA, and from 927 as the earldom of Northumbria (associated with WESSEX/England).

Indulf, king of Scots (reigned 952–62), appears to have seized Edinburgh, but the earliest unambiguous record of Lothian as a territory of Scottish kings (with English endorsement) dates from 1095. The time of its transfer is unclear. It may have been ceded by EDGAR of England to KENNETH II in 973 (and part of Lothian returned in 1006); or by Earl Eadulf Cudel to MALCOLM II following the battle of CARHAM (1018); or (more likely) by King CNUT to Malcolm II by 1026.

Lothian remained considerably English in culture (e.g., settlement names). By the 12th century the name was often restricted to the northern part, the southern part being called the Merse (Scots, meaning 'Marsh'). *See also* BORDER, ANGLO-SCOTTISH.

LOVELL'S CONSPIRACY In England, an insurrection against King HENRY VII in 1486 planned by the YORKISTS Francis, Viscount Lovell, and Humphrey Stafford, both former supporters of RICHARD III. They intended to capture Henry during his progress from LONDON to YORK, March–June. Their support collapsed (April). Lovell fled to Flanders; Stafford was executed. *See also* SIMNEL, LAMBERT.

LOWE, ROBERT (b. 4 Dec. 1811 at Bingham, Nottinghamshire, England; d. 27 July 1892 at Warlingham, Surrey, England, aged 80). A WHIG MP from 1852, Lowe led the ADULLAMITES in bringing down the government of Lord John RUSSELL in 1866. Declaring himself betrayed when the Conservatives passed the Reform Act of 1867, he served W.E. GLADSTONE as chancellor of the Exchequer (1868–73) and home secretary (1873–4).

LOYALIST Term used to denote supporters of the UNION OF IRELAND AND GREAT BRITAIN (1801) and, from 1921, of the retention of NORTHERN IRELAND within the UK. It was generally interchangeable with 'Unionist'. In the early 1970s, during the TROUBLES, the term was adopted by

Unionist PARAMILITARY ORGANIZATIONS in Northern Ireland to refer to people who were determined to preserve their way of life (e.g., in phrase 'loyalist paramilitaries'). *See also* UNIONISM, IRELAND.

LOYAL NATIONAL REPEAL ASSOCIATION *see* REPEAL ASSOCIATION

LOYAL REMONSTRANCE In Ireland following the RESTORATION (1660), a statement drafted by Catholic laymen in Dec. 1661 to demonstrate their loyalty to the (Protestant) King CHARLES II in the hope of winning toleration of Catholicism. Because it denied the Pope's claimed power to release Catholics from temporal loyalty to a king, it was eventually rejected by a meeting of clergy (June 1666). Their modified version, which implicitly recognized some papal power, was rejected by Ireland's chief governor, the duke of ORMOND, leaving Catholic–government relations unstable. *See also* WALSH, PETER; CATHOLICS AND CATHOLIC CHURCH, IRELAND FROM 16TH CENTURY.

LUCAS, CHARLES (b. 16 Sept. 1713 at Ballingaddy, Co. Clare, Ireland; d. 4 Nov. 1771 at Dublin, Ireland, aged 58). In 1741 Lucas, a (Protestant) apothecary, joined the Common Council of Dublin Corporation and alleged that the aldermen had usurped powers belonging to the entire corporation. With others he took legal action, but their suit was obstructed. In 1748 and 1749 he campaigned for election to the Irish House of Commons, attacking British influence in Ireland. When his election seemed likely (Oct. 1749), he was declared an enemy in Parliament and fled abroad. He returned in 1761 and, despite strong opposition, was elected to the Commons. He served until his death, supporting the Patriot leader Henry FLOOD. *See also* PROTESTANT ASCENDANCY; PATRIOTS, IRELAND.

LUDDITES Impoverished craftsmen, mainly textile workers, who riotously attacked FACTORIES in England in the early 19th century to destroy machinery that made their skills redundant. The name was derived from 'Ned Ludd', a probably mythical leader. Trouble began in Nottinghamshire (1811) and spread into Yorkshire and Lancashire (1812). Several thousand soldiers were stationed near disaffected areas. Further trouble occurred in Nottinghamshire in 1814–16. *See also* INDUSTRY, ENGLAND FROM LATE 18TH CENTURY.

LUDLOW A small town with a castle in Shropshire (W England), by the R. Teme. The castle was established as a stronghold near the Welsh border by Roger de Lacy by 1085 and enlarged by Roger MORTIMER in the early 14th century. It was the seat of the COUNCIL IN THE MARCHES OF WALES 1473–83, 1493–1689 (except for 1640s–50s).

The town was developed in the late 11th–12th centuries and was an important centre of the WOOL TRADE in the 13th–16th centuries. It remained an important market and social centre.

Est. popn: 1300, 2500; 1600, 2000; 1800, 4000; 1900, 4500; 2000, 8500.

LUGARD, FREDERICK (b. 22 Jan. 1858 at Madras, India; d. 11 April 1945 near Abinger, Surrey, England, aged 87). Imperialist. Lugard, a former soldier, worked for the Imperial British East Africa Company 1888-92 (*see* MACKINNON, WILLIAM). In 1894 he led a military force for the Royal Niger Company (RNC) to Borgu (in modern Nigeria and Benin) to prevent a French or German presence by making an agreement with the local ruler.

In 1897 Lugard was appointed commissioner to the Nigerian hinterland by colonial secretary Joseph CHAMBERLAIN. When the British government assumed authority in NIGERIA from the RNC (1900), Lugard became high commissioner of the Northern Nigeria PROTECTORATE. He expanded British rule by developing 'indirect rule' (government involving tribal chiefs), a practice adopted elsewhere, and conquering territory (1903). He resigned in 1906 and served as governor of HONG KONG 1907-12. Lugard returned to Nigeria (1912–18) as governor of both Northern and Southern Nigeria (amalgamated 1914). He was knighted (1901) and created Lord Lugard (1928). He married Flora SHAW (1902).

LUNAR SOCIETY OF BIRMINGHAM An outstanding regional club, focused on BIRMINGHAM (Warwickshire, C England), which was interested in natural philosophy (science) and technology. It originated informally in the 1760s in friendships between the doctor Erasmus Darwin (1731-1802), manufacturer Matthew BOULTON and instrument-maker John Whitehurst (1713-88).

More formal organization began in 1775 with monthly meetings on Sundays nearest the full moon, to obtain light for homeward journeys (hence the Society's name). Members (maximum 14) were leading manufacturers, doctors and natural philosophers, including the inventor James WATT, pottery manufacturer Josiah WEDGWOOD and (from 1780) scientist and minister Joseph PRIESTLEY. Many were DISSENTERS and some had connections with scientists in Scotland. Discussions included such subjects as chemicals, electricity, magnetism, GEOLOGY and minerals. Experiments were undertaken.

After Priestley's arrival, meetings were moved to Mondays to avoid interference with his religious duties. The Society was disrupted in 1791 by the 'Priestley Riots' in Birmingham, though continued until 1813. Some members' descendants became distinguished scientists (e.g., Charles DARWIN). *See also* EVOLUTION.

LUSIGNANS Historians' term for four French half-brothers of King HENRY III of England: Aymer, Geoffrey and Guy de Lusignan and William de Valence. They were the sons of Henry's mother, Isabella of Angoulême, by her second marriage (1220) to Hugh de Lusignan, a noble of Poitou (W France). Henry invited the Lusignans to England in 1247. His favouritism for them in the 1250s (e.g., gifts of land and offices), and their rapaciousness and arrogance, enraged leading nobles. (Aymer de Lusignan was elected bishop of WINCHESTER in 1250.)

On 1 April 1258 followers of Aymer de Lusignan attacked men of the baron John fitz Geoffrey in a dispute about a church. When Henry favoured Aymer, seven leading barons formed a sworn confederation and demanded the expulsion of aliens and reform of the realm, launching the baronial reform movement (*see* BARONIAL CONFLICT AND WARS). In June 1258 the Lusignans opposed the Provisions of OXFORD and fled to Winchester. Parliament decreed their expulsion, and they returned to France (July).

LUSITANIA, SINKING OF Incident on 7 May 1915, during WORLD WAR I, when a German submarine sank the British liner *Lusitania* off S Ireland, killing 1198 people (including 124 Americans). It sparked anti-German riots in several British cities and raised hopes of US intervention in the war. Though the German Navy did not target the *Lusitania*, it claimed that the sinking was justified because the cargo included war materiel.

LUTHERANISM A Protestant Christian theology based on writings of German reformer Martin Luther (1483–1546). Lutheranism taught that salvation was achieved by faith alone, rather than by good works undertaken under the Church's authority, and that doctrine was derived from scripture.

Luther's writings reached England from 1519 and were debated in London and in UNIVERSITIES in the 1520s. They were influential in the 1530s through the prominent positions of Thomas CRANMER, Thomas CROMWELL, Hugh LATIMER and others. From the late 1540s Swiss ideas prevailed. Luther's works were influential in Scotland from the 1520s to 1560s when they were supplanted by CALVINISM. *See also* FISHER, JOHN; MORE, THOMAS; CENSORSHIP, ENGLAND AND WALES/SCOTLAND.

LYELL, CHARLES (b. 14 Nov. 1797 at Kinnordy, Forfarshire, Scotland; d. 22 Feb. 1875 at Marylebone, Middlesex, England, aged 77). Raised in England, Lyell was attracted to GEOLOGY by William Buckland's lectures while studying at OXFORD University (1816–19). Though he became a barrister (practised 1825–7), he preferred geology. He studied rock formations in France (1823), Scotland (1824), Continental Europe (1828–9) and Germany (1831), and was elected to the ROYAL SOCIETY (1826).

In 1830–3 Lyell published *Principles of Geology* (three volumes), which used natural processes (rather than divine design) to explain geological formations, and showed from fossil evidence that species appeared and disappeared. His *Elements of Geology* (1838) dealt with stratigraphy and palaeontology. Lyell's presentation of geological time influenced Charles DARWIN, and in *The Antiquity of Man* (1863) Lyell supported Darwin's theories of natural selection of species and human evolution. Lyell was knighted in 1848 and made a baronet in 1864.

LYNCH, JACK (b. 15 Aug. 1917 at Cork, Co. Cork, Ireland; d. 20 Oct. 1999 at Dublin, Republic of Ireland, aged 82). A lawyer and sportsman, Lynch was elected a FIANNA FÁIL TD for Cork in 1948. From 1951 he held ministerial posts under Éamon DE VALERA and Seán LEMASS.

In Nov. 1966 Lynch succeeded Lemass as taoiseach (premier). His government launched a third Programme for ECONOMIC EXPANSION (1969) and joined the EUROPEAN ECONOMIC COMMUNITY (Jan. 1973). After the TROUBLES erupted in Northern Ireland (late 1968), Lynch condemned violence by the IRISH REPUBLICAN ARMY, and stipulated that a united Ireland could be created only by consent. He lost the Feb. 1973 election, but headed a second government from June 1977. He retired in Dec. 1979 (succeeded by Charles HAUGHEY). *See also* SOUTHERN IRELAND FROM 1922.

M

MAASTRICHT, TREATY OF Agreed on 10 Dec. 1991 at Maastricht, Netherlands, by the European Council of Heads of State or Government (signed 7 Feb. 1992). The treaty combined the European Economic Community, renamed as the 'European Community' (EC), with new common foreign and security policies, and police and judicial co-operation, as the European Union (EU). The powers of EEC institutions were enhanced, and the EU gained additional authority in some policy areas (e.g., employment). Provision was made for a central bank and common currency. John MAJOR (prime minister) negotiated 'opt-outs' for the UK from the currency and employment 'social chapter' (regulations). The treaty was soon approved in the Republic of Ireland by a referendum (18 June 1992), but opposition in several countries delayed implementation (until 1 Nov. 1993).

In the UK, despite the 'opt-outs', strong opposition developed within the parliamentary Conservative Party, especially after the Party's return to government at the April 1992 general election. The treaty was ratified by the House of Commons by only three votes (4 Nov.). Continuing division among Conservatives over the EU (especially its currency) undermined Major's premiership, leading to election victory for Labour (1997). *See also* EUROPEAN ECONOMIC COMMUNITY/EUROPEAN UNION, IMPACT ON BRITISH POLITICS.

MABINOGI, Y (Welsh, meaning 'The Tale of Youth'). Middle Welsh prose tales, composed *c*.1050–1120, which survive in the RED BOOK OF HERGEST and WHITE BOOK OF RHYDDERCH. The 'Four Branches of the Mabinogi' concern legendary kings of DYFED (SW Wales) and GWYNEDD (NW Wales). Associated texts include romances about ARTHUR. *See also* WELSH LANGUAGE AND LITERATURE.

MABON (b. 14 June 1842 at Cwmafan, Glamorgan, Wales; d. 14 May 1922 at Pentre, Glamorgan, aged 79). Popular name of William Abraham, a nonconformist preacher and first Welsh miners' leader to become an MP (for RHONDDA 1885–1918, Rhondda West 1918–20).

As a leading trade unionist, Mabon helped to create the 'sliding scale' for relating miners' wages to prices and profits (operated 1875–1902). He was the first president of the S Wales Miners' Federation (1898–1912). Believing that owners and employees had common interests, he was unsympathetic to militants (e.g., Noah ABLETT). In the UK Parliament he was a 'Lib-Lab' (workers' representative supporting radical LIBERALS); he joined the LABOUR PARTY in 1909. *See also* COAL INDUSTRY, WALES; MINERS' UNIONS.

McADAM, JOHN LOUDON (b. 21 Sept. 1756 at Ayr, Ayrshire, Scotland; d. 26 Nov. 1836 at Moffat, Dumfriesshire, Scotland, aged 80). Using money made in America (1770–83), McAdam purchased an Ayrshire estate, became a turnpike road trustee and experimented with road surfaces. He moved to S England in 1798 and in 1815 was appointed surveyor of BRISTOL roads where he built well-drained

A Dictionary of British and Irish History, First Edition. Edited by Robert Peberdy and Philip Waller.
© 2021 John Wiley & Sons Ltd; © editorial matter and organisation Robert Peberdy and Phillip Waller.
Published 2021 by John Wiley & Sons Ltd.

roads with surfaces of small stones which were compacted by traffic. His design, which was cheap to maintain, was widely adopted by TURNPIKE TRUSTS.

MAC ALPIN KINGS Historians' name for the (Gaelic-speaking) kings of Alba/Britain (modern Scotland, N of the FORTH–CLYDE ISTHMUS) from KENNETH I MAC ALPIN (king of SCOTS 840-58, also of PICTS c.842-58) to MALCOLM II (ruled 1005-34). They are so named from Kenneth I's father, Alpin.

From c.889 (accession of DONALD II) to 1005 (death of Kenneth III) the kingship alternated between the lineages (descendants) of Constantine I (ruled 862-76) and Aed (876-8), the two sons of Kenneth I, a pattern similar to that of the kingship of Tara in Ireland (claimed high-kingship). The practice possibly enabled the ruling family to maintain power bases in both northern and southern Pictish areas (Constantine's lineage in the S, Aed's in the N, probably MORAY).

After the death of Malcolm II (1034), the kingship passed through female descent (by daughter Bethóc) to Malcolm's grandson (see DUNCAN I). After Duncan, disruption followed: the kingship was seized by a member of a related kindred, MACBETH (succeeded by stepson Lulach). The previous line was restored by MALCOLM III, but his sons were excluded by DONALD III (brother of Malcolm III). The ousting of Donald by EDGAR (1097) resulted in establishment of the MAC MALCOLM RULERS. *See also* KINGSHIP, SCOTTISH; SCOTLAND.

MACAULAY, LORD (b. 25 Oct. 1800 at Rothley, Leicestershire, England; d. 28 Dec. 1858 at London, England, aged 58). British historian and WHIG MP (1830-4, 1838-47, 1852-6). Thomas Babington Macaulay eloquently advocated PARLIAMENTARY REFORM in 1831-2. He devised the Indian Penal Code while serving on the governor-general's Council (1834-8). His popular *History of England* (published from 1849) proclaimed the Whig interpretation of the GLORIOUS REVOLUTION. He was created Lord Macaulay in 1857.

MACBETH (Gaelic, Mac Bethad mac Findlaich; d. 15 Aug. 1057 at Lumphanan, Moray). King of Scots (Scotland) 1040-57.

Macbeth of MORAY (king or MORMAER from 1032), killed and replaced King DUNCAN I (14 Aug. 1040). He defeated attacks by Crinán (Duncan's father; killed by Macbeth in 1045) and by Siward, earl of NORTHUMBRIA, NE England (1046). In 1050 Macbeth visited Rome (the only reigning king of Scots to do so). In 1054 Siward invaded again, with Duncan's son Malcolm. Macbeth fled and was killed by Malcolm in 1057, though his supporters recognized his stepson Lulach (Lulach mac Gille Comgáin) as king (killed 1058). *See* MALCOLM III.

MacBRIDE, SEÁN (b. 26 Jan. 1904 at Les Mouettes, Coleville, France; d. 15 Jan. 1988 at Dublin, Republic of Ireland, aged 83). MacBride opposed the ANGLO-IRISH TREATY (1921), which created the IRISH FREE STATE, and fought with the IRISH REPUBLICAN ARMY (IRA) during the IRISH CIVIL WAR (1922-3). He helped to organize SAOR ÉIRE (1931). He was IRA chief of staff 1936-8, but considered that Ireland's 1937 quasi-republican constitution made the IRA unnecessary. He therefore left (1939).

In 1946 MacBride founded CLANN NA POBLACHTA, to press for social improvement (e.g., action against tuberculosis), and served as a Dáil member 1947-57. He was minister for external affairs in the 1948-51 inter-party government, when he helped to obtain US loans (*see* MARSHALL AID). He worked abroad in the 1960s-70s, and was co-founder of Amnesty International (1961). He was awarded the 1974 Nobel Peace Prize. *See also* SOUTHERN IRELAND FROM 1922; MOTHER AND CHILD SCHEME.

MacDIARMID, HUGH (b. 11 Aug. 1892 at Langholm, Dumfriesshire, Scotland; d. 9 Sept. 1978 at Edinburgh, Scotland, aged 86). Poet; pseudonym of C.M. Grieve. After training as a teacher (1908-11), Grieve worked in journalism, politics and various jobs. He was awarded a Civil List pension in 1950 and from 1951 lived at Biggar (Lanarkshire). He helped to found the National Party of Scotland in 1928 and was later a Communist (1934-8, 1957-78). From the 1920s Grieve wrote in Scots. His best-known work is the modernist monologue *A Drunk Man Looks at the Thistle* (1926). *See also* SCOTS LANGUAGE AND LITERATURE.

MacDONALD, LORDS OF THE ISLES A powerful Gaelic CLAN in the WESTERN ISLES and Highland Scotland; descendants of SOMERLED (d. 1164) and his second son, Ranald (d. c.1207), kings of the Isles; named from Ranald's son Donald of Islay (fl. early 13th century). Donald's grandson Angus Og (d. 1328) supported King ROBERT I. Angus's son John of Islay (d. 1387) styled himself 'lord'. King JAMES IV annexed the lordship in 1493 (from John's great-grandson John, d. 1503) to suppress turmoil. *See also* MacDOUGAL, LORDS OF LORNE; ISLES, LORDSHIP OF THE.

MacDONALD, RAMSAY (b. 12 Oct. 1866 at Lossiemouth, Morayshire, Scotland; d. 9 Nov. 1937 at sea, aged 71). Leader of the British LABOUR PARTY 1911-14, 1922-31; prime minister 1924, 1929-35.

Born in poverty, MacDonald went to London in 1886 and worked intermittently in journalism. Marriage in 1896 provided financial security. Having joined the FABIAN SOCIETY and INDEPENDENT LABOUR PARTY, he became secretary of the Labour Representation Committee in 1900 (Labour Party from 1906), and was an MP 1906-18, 1922-35, 1936-7.

Opposition to WORLD WAR I cost MacDonald the Labour leadership in 1914 (resigned Aug.), but he was re-elected in 1922 and became Opposition leader. In Jan. 1924, he formed the first (minority) Labour government. An enthusiast for the LEAGUE OF NATIONS, MacDonald was his own foreign secretary. The WORKERS' WEEKLY INCIDENT and ZINOVIEV LETTER contributed to electoral defeat in Nov.

MacDonald's second minority government (1929–31) was overwhelmed by the GREAT DEPRESSION. His Party refused to join a NATIONAL GOVERNMENT: from 1931 until 1935 MacDonald headed a Conservative-dominated coalition (with just 13 'National Labour' MPs). The Labour Party expelled MacDonald and accused him of betraying the working class. He remained lord president of the Council 1935–7. *See also* CLYNES, J.R.; SHINWELL, EMANUEL; BALDWIN, STANLEY.

MacDOUGAL, LORDS OF LORNE A CLAN in the WESTERN ISLES and W Scotland (including Lorne); descendants of SOMERLED (d. 1164) and his eldest son, Dougal. Ewen MacDougal supported the acquisition of the Isles from Norway by King ALEXANDER III (1266). In 1309 John MacDougal forfeited his lands after being defeated at the Pass of Brander by ROBERT I. (MacDougals had supported the COMYN FAMILY.) The mainland estates were restored, but the lordship of Lorne passed from the family through the daughter of Ewen MacDougal (d. 1375) on his death. *See also* MACDONALD, LORDS OF THE ISLES.

McGUINNESS, MARTIN (b. 23 May 1950 at Londonderry, Co. Londonderry, Northern Ireland; d. 21 March 2017 at Londonderry, aged 66). A supposed commander in the PROVISIONAL IRISH REPUBLICAN ARMY in NORTHERN IRELAND 1970–90s, McGuinness also pursued the republican policy of cultivating electoral support. He represented PROVISIONAL SINN FÉIN (PSF) in the provincial ASSEMBLY (1982–6) and stood for the UK Parliament (was an abstentionist MP 1997–2013).

By 1990 McGuinness, like others, sought a more effective pursuit of republican aims. When a PEACE PROCESS was established, McGuinness participated (1997–8) in negotiations that produced the BELFAST AGREEMENT. He joined a new Assembly (from 1998) and the short-lived devolved Executive of David TRIMBLE (as minister of education 1999–2002). In 2003, PSF became the Assembly's largest nationalist party.

The DEMOCRATIC UNIONIST PARTY (DUP) resisted resumption of devolved government until 2006 (*see* ST ANDREWS AGREEMENT). McGuinness then served as deputy first minister to DUP first ministers (from 2007). His seemingly friendly collaboration with Ian PAISLEY (2007–8) earned them the nickname the 'Chuckle Brothers'.

(McGuinness withdrew briefly in 2011 to stand for president in the Republic of Ireland.) His resignation in Jan. 2017 terminated the Executive. In 2012 McGuiness famously shook hands with ELIZABETH II during a royal visit to Northern Ireland. *See also* ADAMS, GERRY; EXECUTIVES, NORTHERN IRELAND.

MacHALE, JOHN (b. 6 March 1791 at Tubbernavine, Co. Mayo, Ireland; d. 7 Nov. 1881 at Tuam, Co. Galway, Ireland, aged 90). Educated at MAYNOOTH SEMINARY, MacHale was ordained a Catholic priest (1814) and as coadjutor-bishop (1825; succeeded as bishop of Killala 1834). He was the first Irish Catholic bishop since the 16th century who had studied for the priesthood in Ireland. A polemicist, in the 1820s he attacked the KILDARE PLACE SOCIETY in newspaper letters, and as archbishop of Tuam (from 1834) denounced the NATIONAL EDUCATION scheme (1838) for undermining Catholicism. He supported the UNION REPEAL MOVEMENT (1840s), and opposed the non-denominational Queen's Colleges (1845–50).

By 1860 MacHale was marginalized within the Catholic episcopate by Archbishop Paul CULLEN. In the 1860s–70s MacHale supported the IRISH REPUBLICAN BROTHERHOOD tacitly and the HOME RULE MOVEMENT openly. He was esteemed as a 'patriot bishop'. *See also* CATHOLICS AND CATHOLIC CHURCH, IRELAND FROM 16TH CENTURY.

MacHETH, MALCOLM (Gaelic, Máel Coluim mac Áeda; fl. from 1130; d. 1168). Possibly son of a deprived earl of Ross (N Scotland), MacHeth rebelled against DAVID I (1130–4) and was imprisoned. His sons later rebelled (with their uncle SOMERLED) against MALCOLM IV (1154). MacHeth was released in 1157 and made earl of Ross but after his death the earldom did not pass to his heirs.

MACHINE TOOLS INDUSTRY, GREAT BRITAIN Advanced equipment for making industrial machinery, usually for metal working, was developed from the later 18th century. It facilitated the mass production characteristic of the INDUSTRIAL REVOLUTION. Production of machine tools became a significant British industry.

Henry Maudslay (1771–1831), the 'father of machine tools' based near London, notably designed a slide-rest lathe (1794), which directed cutting of metal mechanically rather than by hand, and a micrometer (1805). He helped French immigrant Marc Brunel (1769–1849) to make machines for manufacturing pulley-blocks for the NAVY (by 1808). Other important advances were made by two of Maudslay's pupils. Joseph WHITWORTH (d. 1887) devised standardized screw threads, which gave the British machine tools industry world leadership. James Nasmyth (1808–90), a Scotsman, established a business in MANCHESTER (1834) and invented the steam hammer (1839) and hydraulic punch. Machine tools companies developed in manufacturing districts, and engineering companies also developed machine tools.

In the late 19th century, the USA and Germany overtook Britain. The industry was stimulated by requirements of the BICYCLE, MOTORCYCLE, MOTOR and AIRCRAFT industries. ELECTRICITY replaced steam as the main power source, and in the late 20th century computer-controlled systems were introduced. From the 1960s, the British industry declined due to competition from Japan. In 2014 it ranked 11th in the world. There remained notable concentrations of businesses in England in the W Midlands and W Yorkshire. *See also* ENGINEERING, GREAT BRITAIN.

MACKENZIE, GEORGE, OF ROSEHAUGH (b. 1636 at Dundee, E Scotland; d. 8 May 1691 at Westminster, Middlesex, England, aged about 55). An advocate from 1659, knighted by 1668, Mackenzie became LORD ADVOCATE in 1677 and prosecuted COVENANTERS for the government (until the mid 1680s), gaining the nickname 'Bluidy Mackenzie' He also prosecuted the 9th earl of ARGYLL (convicted of treason Dec. 1681). In 1689, following the flight of King JAMES VII/II, Mackenzie opposed the opinion of Scotland's CONVENTION PARLIAMENT that James had forfeited the Crown. But rather than rebel, he moved to England.

As dean of Scotland's Faculty of Advocates (from 1682) Mackenzie established the Advocates' Library (opened 1689), the forerunner of the National Library of Scotland (founded 1925). *See also* GLORIOUS REVOLUTION, SCOTLAND.

MACKINNON, WILLIAM (b. 31 March 1823 at Campbeltown, Argyllshire, Scotland; d. 22 June 1893 at London, England, aged 70). In the 1850s–60s Mackinnon developed a major shipping company. In 1878 he agreed the lease of a large area of E Africa with Sultan Seyyid Barghash but the British government rejected involvement. In 1888 Mackinnon was permitted to form the Imperial British East Africa Company which acquired a coastal area in E Africa (in modern KENYA) and sought to abolish the SLAVE TRADE. The British government took over the territory in 1895. Mackinnon was created a baronet in 1882. *See also* EAST AFRICA, BRITISH INVOLVEMENT.

MACKINTOSH, JAMES (b. 24 Oct. 1765 at Aldourie, Inverness-shire, Scotland; d. 30 May 1832 at London, England, aged 66). British lawyer, politician, lecturer and philosopher (knighted 1803). A judge in India (1804–11), Mackintosh became a WHIG MP in 1813. In 1819 he opposed the SIX ACTS and obtained the establishment of a parliamentary select committee on capital punishment. Its report, advocating fewer capital offences, influenced the reforms subsequently implemented by Robert PEEL. *See also* LEGAL REFORMS, ENGLAND AND WALES, 1820S.

MACLEAN, JOHN (b. 14 Aug. 1879 at Pollokshaws, Lanarkshire, Scotland; d. 29 Nov. 1923 at Glasgow, Scotland, aged 44). Born into poverty, Maclean studied at GLASGOW University and became a schoolmaster. In 1903 he joined the SOCIAL DEMOCRATIC FEDERATION and lectured in Glasgow and Lanarkshire on Marxism (influencing James MAXTON). He opposed WORLD WAR I, organized a rent strike, and was imprisoned (1916). After release he advocated the formation of soviets (councils of soldiers and workers) and in late 1917 was named consul of Great Britain by Bolshevik (Russian) revolutionaries. He was imprisoned again in 1918. In 1920 he tried, unsuccessfully, to create a Scottish Communist Party. *See also* RED CLYDESIDE.

MACLEOD, IAIN (b. 11 Nov. 1913 at Skipton, Yorkshire, England; d. 20 July 1970 at London, England, aged 57). A Scottish doctor's son, Macleod became a Conservative MP in 1950. He achieved prominence on the Party's 'liberal' wing as an advocate of the State's capacity to improve social conditions. He was British minister of health (1952–5) and of labour (1955–9). His advocacy, as colonial secretary (1959–61) under Harold MACMILLAN, of rapid British withdrawal from Africa antagonized right-wingers and he faced difficulties as Party chairman (1961–3). Having supported 'Rab' BUTLER as Macmillan's successor, Macleod refused office under Alec DOUGLAS-HOME. In 1965 he supported the election of Edward HEATH as Party leader. He became chancellor of the Exchequer a month before his death from a heart attack. *See also* DECOLONIZATION.

MAC LOCHLAINN, MUIRCHERTACH (fl. from 1136 in Ireland; d. 1166 in NE Ireland). High-king of the Cenél nEógain branch of the Northern Uí NÉILL from 1145, and dominant in N Ireland by 1147, Muirchertach challenged the high-king of Ireland, Toirrdelbach UA CONCHOBAIR (from CONNACHT, W Ireland).

After Toirrdelbach's death (1156) Muirchertach became high-king, but was beset by enemies, especially Toirrdelbach's son Ruaidrí UA CONCHOBAIR. He died in a skirmish following the invasion of the Cenél nEógain kingdom by the high-king of AIRGIALLA.

MAC MALCOLM RULERS Historians' name for a Scottish royal dynasty, descended from King MALCOLM III (ruled 1058–93). Following disruption by Malcolm's brother (*see* DONALD III), it was established by Malcolm's son (by his second marriage) EDGAR (ruled 1097–1107). From Edgar, the kingship was transmitted by male primogeniture (succession of eldest son, or of a younger brother if there was no son), rather than by the earlier descent system of the MAC ALPIN KINGS (alternation between two lineages). The system sometimes produced MINORITIES. The main line of descent ended with MARGARET, 'THE MAID OF NORWAY' (d. 1290). *See also* KINGSHIP, SCOTTISH; GREAT CAUSE.

MACMILLAN, HAROLD (b. 10 Feb. 1894 at London, England; d. 29 Dec. 1986 at Birch Grove, East Sussex, England, aged 92). British prime minister and leader of the CONSERVATIVE PARTY 1957–63.

After serving in WORLD WAR I, Macmillan joined his family's publishing business. He was an MP 1924–9, 1931–45, 1945–64. He advocated economic planning and social reform in *The Middle Way* (1938), and criticized APPEASEMENT. During WORLD WAR II he served as colonial undersecretary (1942) and minister of state in N Africa (1942–5). As minister of housing 1951–4, his priority was COUNCIL HOUSING. Macmillan then became minister of defence (1954–5), foreign secretary (1955), and chancellor of the Exchequer (1955–7).

Appointed prime minister after the SUEZ CRISIS, Macmillan worked to improve Anglo-American relations and Conservative morale. He favoured expansionary economic policies and won the 1959 election, claiming that people had 'never had it so good'. Inflation prompted an INCOMES POLICY (1961). Macmillan accelerated DECOLONIZATION and attempted to enter the EUROPEAN ECONOMIC COMMUNITY and mediate in the COLD WAR. A drastic Cabinet reshuffle (July 1962) failed to revitalize his government. Harold WILSON depicted him as complacent, though illness attended his resignation (Oct. 1963). He was created earl of Stockton (1984), and deprecated THATCHERISM. *See also* CHURCHILL, WINSTON; EDEN, ANTHONY; LLOYD, SELWYN; MACLEOD, IAIN.

MAC MURCHADA, DIARMAIT (MACMURROUGH, DIARMUID) (b. *c*.1110 in Ireland; d. *c*. 1 May 1171 at Ferns, Leinster, E Ireland, aged about 61). High-king of LEINSTER by 1132, from 1149 Diarmait supported Muirchertach MAC LOCHLAINN (from N Ireland) against the high-king of Ireland Toirrdelbach UA CONCHOBAIR of Connacht (W Ireland; d. 1156). In 1152, while Toirrdelbach and Muirchertach were co-operating against Tigernán Ua Ruairc, high-king of BRÉIFNE and Diarmait's rival in MEATH, Diarmait abducted Tigernán's wife Derbforgaill (to 1153).

After Muirchertach's death in 1166, Tigernán took revenge by helping to oust Diarmait. Diarmait sought help abroad; he swore loyalty to King HENRY II (in SW France, late 1166), recruited military supporters in Wales (including STRONGBOW), and returned in Aug. 1167, immediately regaining his core lands. In 1169 foreign troops arrived, effectively beginning the Anglo-Norman invasion of Ireland. Ruaidrí UA CONCHOBAIR (high-king of Ireland) conceded the high-kingship of Leinster to Diarmait. He was succeeded by his son-in-law Strongbow. *See also* NORMANS, IMPACT ON IRELAND.

MacMURROUGH, ART (Irish, Art Mac Murchada; b. 1357 in Ireland; d. Dec. 1416 or Jan. 1417 in Leinster, E Ireland, aged about 59). A descendant of Diarmait MAC MURCHADA, high-king of LEINSTER, MacMurrough became king of Leinster in 1375. From S Leinster he harassed the English colony's government (based at nearby Carlow). The English sought his co-operation by appointing him keeper of roads (Carlow to Kilkenny) and awarding an annuity (1379). But disputes continued.

In 1394 MacMurrough submitted to King RICHARD II, during his visit to Ireland, but later resumed attacks on the English colony. When Richard revisited Ireland briefly in 1399, MacMurrough retreated into mountainous areas. MacMurrough continued to attack Anglo-Irish inhabitants and exact 'black rent' (protection money). *See also* GAELIC REVIVAL, IRELAND 13TH–15TH CENTURIES; RICHARD II AND IRELAND.

MacMURROUGH, DIARMUID *see* MAC MURCHADA, DIARMAIT

MacNEILL, EOIN (b. 15 May 1867 at Glenarm, Co. Antrim, Ireland; d. 15 Oct. 1945 at Dublin, southern Ireland, aged 78). A (Catholic) Gaelic scholar, MacNeill co-founded the GAELIC LEAGUE (1893) and was professor of early Irish history at University College, Dublin (from 1908). In 1913 he became, by invitation, leader of the IRISH VOLUNTEERS.

On 22 April 1916 MacNeill learnt of plans for a rebellion the following day, Easter Sunday. He therefore cancelled planned Irish Volunteer 'exercises' (a 'front' for the rebellion), enabling British forces to crush the EASTER RISING. (He was nonetheless convicted of complicity.) MacNeill supported the 1921 ANGLO-IRISH TREATY, which confirmed partition of Ireland; was minister of education in the Irish Free State (1922–5); and served on the BOUNDARY COMMISSION (resigned Nov. 1925). *See also* IRISH FREE STATE, FOUNDING OF.

McQUAID, J.C. (b. 28 July 1895 at Cootehill, Co. Cavan, Ireland; d. 7 April 1973 at Loughlinstown, Co. Dublin, Ireland, aged 77). John Charles McQuaid was professed in the Catholic Holy Ghost religious order (1914) and ordained priest (1924). From 1925 he taught at the order's school Blackrock College (president 1931–9). In 1936–7 McQuaid advised his friend Éamon DE VALERA, premier of the IRISH FREE STATE, on the country's new CONSTITUTION.

As archbishop of Dublin (1940–72), McQuaid promoted welfare work related to the EMERGENCY (to 1945), but in the 1950s attacked increased State welfare and other social policies in the Republic of Ireland, notably helping to defeat the MOTHER AND CHILD SCHEME (1951). He supervised the provision of additional parishes, churches and schools for

Dublin's increasing population, but was lukewarm about 1960s reforms in the Catholic Church. *See also* CATHOLICS AND CATHOLIC CHURCH, IRELAND FROM 16TH CENTURY; CHURCH–STATE RELATIONS, IRELAND FROM 1922.

MADOG AP LLYWELYN (b. *c*.1250; d. after 1312 at London, England, aged over 62). A leader of the 1294–5 Welsh revolt, who claimed the title PRINCE OF WALES.

A minor member of the dynasty of GWYNEDD (NW Wales), Madog was provoked into rebellion by heavy taxes and oppressive English administration in Wales. Welshmen attacked English castles in Wales from late Sept. 1294; King EDWARD I invaded N Wales, but was effectively besieged in Conwy until March or April 1295. English fortunes elsewhere improved: Madog was defeated near Welshpool (C Wales) on 5 March. (The revolt was crushed by July.) Madog was imprisoned for life in the Tower of London.

MADOG AP MAREDUDD (b. *c*.1100; d. Feb. 1160, perhaps at Winchester, Hampshire, England, aged about 60). King of POWYS (C Wales), 1132–60. Madog took advantage of the ANARCHY in England to capture Oswestry (Shropshire, England) in 1149, but sought help from England in the 1150s against OWAIN GWYNEDD, king of Gwynedd (NW Wales), and supported King HENRY II's 1157 invasion of Wales. Madog maintained the unity of Powys, but it failed to survive his death. *See also* ANGLO-WELSH RELATIONS, 6TH–13TH CENTURIES.

MAEATAE One of two main groupings of British (or Pictish) tribes N of ROMAN BRITAIN in the late 2nd and 3rd centuries (the CALEDONIANS were the other). In 197 they broke a treaty with Rome, threatening the province and eventually prompting direct intervention (208–11) from the emperor, Septimius Severus. The Maeatae are thought to have lived immediately N of the FORTH–CLYDE ISTHMUS.

MAELGWN GWYNEDD OR MAELGWN HIR, 'THE TALL' (fl. from *c*.500; d. 547, perhaps in Rhos, N Wales). King of GWYNEDD (NW Wales); the most powerful British king chastised by GILDAS; ancestor of rulers of Gwynedd. He allegedly killed several relatives. His own death was possibly caused by plague.

MÁEL SECHNAILL MAC DOMNAILL (b. 948 in Ireland; d. 2 Sept. 1022 in Meath, E Ireland). From 980 Máel Sechnaill was high-king of the Southern Uí NÉILL (in E Ireland) and high-king of Ireland ('king of Tara'). Though he demonstrated authority by subjugating Viking DUBLIN (980), he was challenged from 984 by BRIAN BÓRUMA, high-king of MUNSTER (S Ireland). In 997 they agreed to share the high-kingship of Ireland (the N to Máel Sechnaill, S to Brian).

In 1002 Brian forced Máel Sechnaill to submit, ending the Uí Néill monopoly of Ireland's high-kingship (supposedly claimed since the 5th century). Máel Sechnaill remained loyal, but possibly deserted Brian on the eve of the battle of CLONTARF (1014). Afterwards Brian was killed, enabling Máel Sechnaill to resume the high-kingship. *See also* KINGSHIP, IRELAND.

MAFEKING, SIEGE OF An episode during the (Second) BOER WAR, when the small town of Mafeking in CAPE COLONY (a British colony) was besieged by an army from the Boer republics, 12 Oct. 1899–17 May 1900. The defenders, commanded by Robert BADEN-POWELL, were celebrated for heroism by British newspapers. When news of the 'relief of Mafeking', led by Lord ROBERTS, reached Britain (18 May 1900), it was celebrated wildly.

MAGNA CARTA Schedule of terms conceded by JOHN, king of England, to rebel BARONS; agreed at Runnymede (Surrey) on 15 June 1215 (finalized 19 June). Negotiations had started in Jan., with Archbishop Stephen LANGTON as conciliator. Intermediate documents include the 'Articles of the Barons' (10 June).

Drawing on antecedents (e.g., 'Coronation Charter' of HENRY I, 1100), Magna Carta sought to protect barons by restricting royal power (e.g., fixing payments to the king for inheritance of land). It also protected KNIGHTS, towns, merchants and 'every free man', emphasizing that concessions must be allowed to barons' free tenants. Magna Carta thereby purportedly protected rights of 'the whole community'. Most radically it created a Council of 25 to enforce the terms by punishing the king for infractions. It also required consent by counsel for the levying of a general aid (tax).

Magna Carta was initially unsuccessful: it was annulled by Pope Innocent III (24 Aug.) and fighting recommenced. Following John's death (Oct. 1216) it was revised and reissued, in 1216, 1217 (with forest-related clauses separated into a 'Charter of the Forest'), and 1225. The name 'Magna Carta' (Latin, meaning 'Great Charter') was first used in 1217. The 1225 version was confirmed in later PARLIAMENTS, considered the first statute in COMMON LAW, and cited in CHARLES I's reign. In 2019 four clauses and part of a clause remained in force.

The 1216 and 1217 versions were adapted for Irish conditions, and the former became part of Irish statute law. In 2007 it was designated a 'Retained Statute' in the Republic of Ireland under the Statute Law Revision Act, titled 'Magna Carta Hiberniae'. *See also* FOREST LAW; FEUDAL INCIDENTS.

MAGNATE Historians' term for a leading nobleman who had frequent dealings with the king and was supported by followers or a retinue, particularly in the 10th–16th centuries;

derived from Latin *magnates* (meaning 'great lords' or 'noblemen') Examples of magnates include: (England) ATHELSTAN 'HALF-KING', Simon de MONTFORT, the APPELLANTS, leaders of the BEAUFORT and de la POLE families; (Ireland), 7th, 8th and 9th earls of Kildare (*see* KILDARE ASCENDANCY); (Scotland) Alexander STEWART, William DOUGLAS. *See also* FEUDALISM; BASTARD FEUDALISM.

MAGNUS MAXIMUS (fl. from *c*.367; d. July 388 at Aquileia, NE Italy). Of Spanish extraction, Maximus (Macsen Wledig in later Welsh literature) was a successful commander in ROMAN BRITAIN under Count THEODOSIUS (*c*.367–9) and Emperor Theodosius I (382). Hailed as emperor (i.e., a pretender) in 383, he ruled Britain, Gaul and Spain after killing the legitimate ruler Gratian, then invaded Italy (387), expelling Valentinian II, before being beaten by Theodosius I in NE Italy and executed.

MAGONSÆTE A Germanic group which in the 7th–8th centuries inhabited a kingdom equivalent to modern Herefordshire and southern Shropshire (W England). They were a 'buffer' between MERCIA and W Britain (Wales). The kingdom's origin is obscure. Its first documented king, Merewalh, lived *c*.625–85. A bishopric was founded at HEREFORD by 680. The last king, Mildfrith, ceased to rule by 740. The Magonsætan kingdom became an ealdomanry of Mercia (*see* ÆTHELBALD). *See also* KINGSHIP, ANGLO-SAXON.

MAGUIRE, CONNOR (b. *c*.1612 in Co. Fermanagh, Ireland; d. 20 Feb. 1645 at Tyburn, Middlesex, England, aged 32 or 33). Maguire succeeded his pro-English, Gaelic Irish father as Lord Enniskillen in 1633. In Feb. 1641 he joined anti-English conspirators, hoping to regain former family lands. On 23 Oct. Maguire was captured (*see* DUBLIN CASTLE PLOT). He was taken to England (June 1642) and eventually hanged. *See also* ULSTER RISING.

MAHDI REBELLION A revolt against Egyptian rule in SUDAN from 1881 by an Islamic reformist movement led by the so-called Mahdi. Rebels captured the capital Khartoum in Jan. 1885, killing the British commander Charles George GORDON. Though the Mahdi died in June, British and Egyptian forces did not suppress the rebellion until 1898 (*see* KITCHENER, LORD). Sudan then became an Anglo-Egyptian condominium (jointly ruled country). *See also* BARING, EVELYN.

MAIDEN CASTLE A massive multivallate HILLFORT near Dorchester, Dorset, SW England, founded *c*.500 BC (in the IRON AGE), overlying a CAUSEWAYED ENCLOSURE of the NEOLITHIC. About 400 BC it was extended to 47 acres (19 ha), with increasingly complex ditches and ramparts. It was abandoned after the CLAUDIAN INVASION, *c*. AD 70.

MAITLAND, JOHN *see* LAUDERDALE, 2ND EARL OF

MAITLAND, WILLIAM, OF LETHINGTON (b. between 1520 and 1530 in Scotland; d. 9 June 1573 at Leith, SE Scotland). SECRETARY OF STATE to the pro-French regent MARY OF GUISE from 1558, Maitland was pro-English. In Oct. 1559 he joined the pro-Protestant LORDS OF THE CONGREGATION and negotiated the treaties of BERWICK and EDINBURGH (1560), for the removal of French troops.

As secretary during the personal rule of the Catholic MARY, QUEEN OF SCOTS, Maitland negotiated (1561–4) for recognition of Mary as heir to ELIZABETH I of England. He probably encouraged the murders of David RIZZIO (1566) and Lord DARNLEY (1567), to preserve his pro-English policy. After Mary's deposition (1567) Maitland appeared to support King JAMES VI, but switched to Mary's side in 1569 and held Edinburgh Castle. He died after its capture, possibly by suicide. *See also* MARIAN CIVIL WAR; LAUDERDALE, 2ND EARL OF.

MAJOR, JOHN (b. 29 March 1943 at London, England). Leader of the CONSERVATIVE PARTY and British prime minister 1990–7.

A retired circus performer's son, Major left school at 16, tried various jobs, and became a banker (1965). He served on Lambeth Borough Council 1968–71, and was a Conservative MP 1979–2001. He was a Party whip (1983–5) and junior minister at the Health Department before becoming chief secretary to the Treasury (1987). A surprise choice as foreign secretary in July 1989, he was appointed chancellor of the Exchequer in Oct. (succeeding Nigel LAWSON).

After Margaret THATCHER was ousted as prime minister, she favoured Major as her successor. He won the Party leadership (27 Nov. 1990) and succeeded her. He offered a conciliatory style, abolished the COMMUNITY CHARGE, and negotiated the MAASTRICHT TREATY.

The unexpected Conservative election victory in 1992 was a triumph for Major, but a sterling crisis damaged his credibility (*see* BLACK WEDNESDAY). Efforts to bring reconciliation to NORTHERN IRELAND began a successful PEACE PROCESS. Major struggled against Party divisions over the EUROPEAN UNION and voluntarily fought a leadership election in July 1995 to restore his authority (*see* HESELTINE, MICHAEL). He resigned after losing the 1997 general election. He was knighted in 2005. *See also* EXCHANGE RATE MECHANISM; PERSIAN GULF WAR, BRITISH INVOLVEMENT; YUGOSLAV WARS, BRITISH INVOLVEMENT.

MAJOR-GENERALS, RULE OF A system of local military authorities imposed on England and Wales from 9 Aug. 1655 by the lord protector, Oliver CROMWELL, following PENRUDDOCK'S RISING. In each of ten (later 11) districts a major-general (an experienced soldier) acted as governor, with a militia financed by a tax on Royalists' property. The major-generals sought to promote Puritan social values (e.g., enforcing laws against sabbath breaking and drunkenness). The system ended in Jan. 1657. *See also* COMMONWEALTH AND PROTECTORATE.

MAKARIS (Scots, meaning 'Poets'). 15th- and 16th-century Scots poets; the term is derived from the title of the poem *Lament for the Makaris* by William DUNBAR (*c*.1460–*c*.1520). The Makaris included Dunbar, Gavin Douglas (*c*.1475–1522), Robert Henryson (*c*.1450–1506) and Alexander Montgomerie (*c*.1545–97). Their vigorous language influenced later poets, especially Hugh MACDIARMID (1892–1978). *See also* SCOTS LANGUAGE AND LITERATURE.

MALACHY (MÁEL MÁEDOC UA MORGAIR) (b. 1094 or 1095 at Armagh, N Ireland; d. 1 or 2 Nov. 1148 at Clairvaux, France, aged 53). Promoter of CHURCH REFORM. As abbot of BANGOR (N Ireland) 1123–7, Malachy revived strict living but suffered expulsion. (He was also bishop for Connor from 1124.) As archbishop of ARMAGH from 1132, he was denied the church's possessions by its hereditary controlling families. In 1136 he became bishop of Down.

In 1139, while in France (travelling to Rome), Malachy met Bernard of Clairvaux, a leading figure among the Cistercians, and also visited Arrouaise (a house of canons). Pope Innocent II appointed him a PAPAL LEGATE in Ireland and instructed him to hold a council. Back in Ireland, he persuaded cathedral clergy to adopt the Arrouaisian rule and encouraged the foundation of Cistercian houses (both starting in 1142). Malachy was canonized in 1190. *See also* MONASTICISM, MEDIEVAL IRELAND.

MALAWI *see* NYASALAND

MALAYA A peninsula in SE Asia, the S part of which was formerly under British control. The EAST INDIA COMPANY bought the islands of Penang (1786) and SINGAPORE (1819). Great Britain occupied the Dutch colony of Malacca on the mainland 1795–1818 and acquired it in 1824 by ceding part of Sumatra in exchange. Britain also gained Singapore in 1824.

From 1826 Penang, Malacca and Singapore were administered together from INDIA as the Straits Settlements (alongside the Malacca Strait). They became a CROWN COLONY in 1867.

British influence thereafter spread inland, resulting in first the FEDERATED and then the UNFEDERATED MALAY STATES. Chinese and Indian immigrants laboured to produce rubber, pepper, tobacco and tin. JAPAN occupied the peninsula 1941–5, after which the British united their possessions (except Singapore), initially as the Malayan Union,

a crown colony (1946–8), then as the Federation of Malaya. The Federation was granted independence as a constitutional monarchy (1957), despite the MALAYAN EMERGENCY, and in 1963 incorporated Singapore and parts of BORNEO to form Malaysia.

MALAYAN EMERGENCY Term used for a communist-led rebellion in MALAYA from June 1948. It was provoked by Great Britain's creation of the Federation of Malaya (Jan. 1948), replacing the Malayan Union, which alienated some of the Chinese minority population by empowering Malay rulers. The British fought the guerrillas and relocated rural Chinese. Several thousand civilians were killed. Serious violence was over by 1955, though the end was not declared officially until 1960.

MALCOLM I (Gaelic, Mael Coluim mac Domnaill; d. 954 in Mearns, E Scotland). King of Scots (Scotland) from between 940 and 945 to 954.

A son of DONALD II, Malcolm succeeded his second cousin CONSTANTINE II. After his accession he raided MORAY (NE Scotland), killing Cellach, possibly a king. In 945 he gained recognition from EDMUND, king of England, of Scottish control over STRATHCLYDE, and in 950 raided NORTHUMBRIA (SE of Scotland). He also defeated a VIKING force (952), but was eventually killed by men of Moray.

Malcolm was succeeded by his cousin Indulf, son of CONSTANTINE II (Gaelic, Illulb mac Causantín; ruled 954–62); by Dubh, son of Malcolm I (Dub mac Mael Coluim; 962–6); by Culen son of Indulf (Cuilén mac Illuilb; 966–71); and by KENNETH II, younger son of Malcolm I. *See also* MAC ALPIN KINGS.

MALCOLM II (Gaelic, Mael Coluim mac Cinaeda; d. 25 Nov. 1034 at Glamis, Angus, E Scotland). King of Scots (Scotland) 1005–34.

The son of KENNETH II (ruled 971–95), Malcolm killed his cousin Kenneth III (25 March 1005) to become king. In 1018 he defeated Northumbrians (English) at CARHAM, and soon afterwards his grandson Duncan was ruling STRATHCLYDE. By 1026 he probably acquired LOTHIAN from King CNUT of England. Cnut invaded in 1031 and possibly compelled Malcolm's submission for harbouring his enemies. Malcolm was the last successor by male descent of KENNETH I, the king who began the UNION OF SCOTS AND PICTS, and is considered the last of the MAC ALPIN KINGS. He was succeeded by DUNCAN I, son of his daughter Bethóc.

MALCOLM III (Gaelic, Mael Coluim Ceann Mór; b. *c*.1031; d. 13 Nov. 1093 at Alnwick, Northumberland, England, aged about 62). King of Scots (Scotland) 1058–93.

A son of DUNCAN I (d. 1040), Malcolm was exiled in England after Macbeth usurped the Scottish kingship (1040). He returned to Scotland in 1054 (with Siward, earl of Northumbria, NE England), and killed Macbeth (15 Aug. 1057) and Macbeth's stepson and successor Lulach (17 March 1058). Malcolm married Ingibiorg, daughter of Earl Thorfinn of Orkney (by 1065; she d. probably by 1069).

In 1070, following the NORMAN CONQUEST OF ENGLAND, Malcolm gave refuge to Edgar ætheling, Anglo-Saxon claimant to the kingship of England (see ÆTHELING), and married his sister MARGARET (also 1070). His actions provoked invasion by King WILLIAM I who compelled Malcolm's submission (at ABERNETHY). Scottish retaliatory raids in 1079 and 1091 provoked invasions by ROBERT CURTHOSE (1080) and WILLIAM II and Robert (1091). In 1092 William II seized Carlisle from Scotland, strengthening the BORDER. Malcom died while attacking NE England. He was called 'Canmore' (from Gaelic, Ceann mór, meaning 'Chief'); succeeded by DONALD III. See also MAC ALPIN KINGS; MAC MALCOLM RULERS.

MALCOLM IV (b. 1141; d. 9 Dec. 1165 at Jedburgh, SE Scotland, aged 24). King of Scots (Scotland) 1153–65. Malcolm succeeded his grandfather David I when aged 12 (24 May 1153). His accession was resented; rebellions broke out (early Nov. 1153, 1154). In May 1157 King HENRY II of England compelled Malcolm to return lands formerly in N England (held since 1136, 1139 and 1141; see DAVID I). Malcolm did homage to Henry and in summer 1159 joined him on campaign in SW France, which provoked new opposition; in 1160 six earls revolted and besieged Malcolm at Perth (C Scotland). The revolt was subdued with difficulty. Malcolm died unmarried; succeeded by WILLIAM I. His nickname, 'the Maiden', dates from the 15th century. See also MAC MALCOLM RULERS; SOMERLED.

MALDON, BATTLE OF Fought by the coast near Maldon, Essex (SE England), on 10 or 11 Aug. 991. VIKINGS defeated an English army. Later that year King ÆTHELRED II bought peace by paying tribute (OE *gafol*). The battle is commemorated by the Old English poem *The Battle of Maldon. See also* GELD.

MALORY, THOMAS (b. between 1415 and 1418 in Warwickshire, England; d. 14 March 1471 at London, England). A minor landowner, Malory was knighted in 1441 and fought in GASCONY (SW France) in 1442–3. In the 1450s he was imprisoned for violence. As a YORKIST, he supported the usurpation of King EDWARD IV (1460). In the late 1460s he turned against the king.

Imprisoned in the Tower of London 1468–70, Malory wrote the *Morte Darthur* ('Death of Arthur'), the longest

and most influential English version of the Arthurian legends. It was printed by William CAXTON in 1485. *See also* ARTHUR.

MALTA A former British territory in the C Mediterranean comprising the island of Malta and two smaller islands. From 1799 the British helped Maltese combat French occupiers (during the NAPOLEONIC WARS). After the French surrendered (1802), islanders appointed the British king as sovereign, with guaranteed rights for the Catholic population. Malta became a CROWN COLONY in 1813, and British possession was confirmed in 1814 (treaty of Paris). Malta served as headquarters of Britain's Mediterranean fleet 1814–1937. The island was bombed by Germans and Italians in 1940–3, during WORLD WAR II (awarded George Cross 1942).

During the 19th and 20th centuries internal dissension frustrated attempts to establish a constitution, and in 1955–8 integration with the UK was proposed. Thereafter independence was sought. An interim constitution of 1961 led to independence under the British monarch in 1964. Malta became a republic in 1974, and the last British forces left in 1979. Approx. population in 1921, 224,000; in 1963, 318,000.

MALTHUS, T.R. (b. 13 Feb. 1766 at Wotton, Surrey, England; d. 29 Dec. 1834 at Bath, Somerset, England, aged 68). (Thomas) Robert Malthus, a clergyman, challenged the belief of Radicals that social conditions could be improved. His influential *An Essay on the Principle of Population* (1798) argued that population normally increases faster than food supply. This inevitably created poverty, and population growth had to be discouraged by subsistence wages and abolition of poor relief. Malthus became a history professor in 1805 and published tracts on economics. *See also* NATIONAL AND IMPERIAL CENSUSES.

MALTOLT (French, meaning 'evil tax'). Nickname given to an emergency additional 'aid' or 'subsidy' (tax) paid on English wool exports, granted by an assembly of merchants to King EDWARD I in 1294 to fund the GASCON WAR. It was condemned in the REMONSTRANCES (22 Aug. 1297). Following further protest it was cancelled (23 Nov.).

EDWARD III levied *maltolts* in 1333, for his Scottish campaign, and from 1336 to fund war against France (see HUNDRED YEARS WAR). The subsidies of 1333–8 were granted by merchants, though PARLIAMENT asserted a right to grant the tax in 1340. Edward conceded in 1362 that taxes on overseas trade required Parliament's consent. Renewal of the wool subsidy in the 1360s, in peacetime, made it a regular part of the CUSTOMS. *See also* WOOL TRADE, ENGLAND.

MAN, ISLE OF An island (with islet 'Calf of Man') within the BRITISH ISLES, about 33 mi (12 km) in length, in the

Irish Sea between BRITAIN and IRELAND; a self-governing 'dependency' of the British Crown, associated with, but outside, the UNITED KINGDOM. Douglas is the capital. Est. popn in 2015: 88,000. Man's central area is mountainous.

Man became physically separate probably in the 8th millennium BC, and was inhabited by 8000 BC. By the 6th century AD Irish people were settling among Brittonic-speaking inhabitants. Their language developed into Manx Gaelic, which became dominant (superseded by English in 19th century). The island's Manx name, Ellan Vannin, means 'Manannan's island', referring to a god. Early Irish inhabitants also built Christian chapels.

From the 9th century Man also belonged to the VIKING world, and was taken under Norwegian sovereignty probably by King Harald Fairhair (reigned 872–930). From c.1079 it was ruled, under Norwegian rulers, with the WESTERN ISLES by Godred Crovan and his descendants (with interruptions). Magnus IV of Norway sold suzerainty in 1266 to ALEXANDER III of Scotland, who also bought out the heir to the local kingship.

Man was annexed by EDWARD I of England in 1290, though repossessed by the Scots 1313–15, 1317–33. It was ruled under the English Crown (British from 1707) by noble families (styled kings or lords). STANLEY FAMILY members were lords 1406–1736 (with breaks). In 1765, concerned about smuggling, the British Parliament bought the effective sovereignty from the duke and duchess of Atholl and vested it in the Crown (sovereigns have since been styled 'lord of Man').

Man's legislature, the Tynwald, dates to the Scandinavian period. It received considerable self-government in 1866. The economy was mainly agricultural (with fishing) until the late 19th century when tourism developed. From the 1960s the island became a leading 'offshore' financial centre (so-called 'tax haven').

MANCHESTER A city and metropolitan borough in NW England; formerly in Lancashire.

Originally a Roman fort and town called Mamucium (1st–4th centuries), a new town existed by the 13th century. (The name element 'chester', meaning 'Walled town', refers to Roman origins.) Under lordly rule, Manchester became a centre of the (woollen) CLOTH INDUSTRY. From the later 16th century fustian (linen and cotton) began to replace wool.

Increasing mechanization of cotton spinning and weaving caused rapid growth from the 1790s (see COTTON INDUSTRY, ENGLAND). Raw cotton was imported via LIVERPOOL, to which Manchester became linked by waterways (1776, river and CANAL) and a RAILWAY (1830). Machine-building and CHEMICALS developed as subsidiaries. In the 19th century Manchester was England's third-largest urban centre.

Manchester gave rise to the MANCHESTER SCHOOL and its citizens led campaigns for FREE TRADE and PARLIAMENTARY REFORM. Electing its first MPs in 1832, Manchester gained a town council (1838), bishopric (1847), city status (1853), and a university (1880, when Owens College inaugurated a federal Victoria University; independent from 1904 as Victoria University of Manchester).

With the decline of textiles in the 20th century, Manchester faced major readjustments. A polytechnic was upgraded as Manchester Metropolitan University in 1992 and the University of Manchester Institute of Science and Technology became an autonomous university in 1994 (merged 2004 with Victoria University as University of Manchester). In the 21st century Manchester remained the metropolis of NW England with a diversified economy.

Est. popn: 1300, 1000; 1600, 4000; 1800, 95,000; 1900, 540,000; 2000, 440,000.

MANCHESTER 'MARTYRS' The name conferred on three 'Fenians' ('physical force' Irish nationalists, William Allen, Michael Larkin, Michael O'Brien) who were hanged on 23 Nov. 1867 at Salford (NW England), for murdering a policeman. (The crime occurred on 18 Sept. during the rescue of two Fenians from a police van in Manchester.) The executions increased support in Ireland for the IRISH REPUBLICAN BROTHERHOOD. *See also* HOME RULE MOVEMENT, IRELAND.

MANCHESTER SCHOOL In Great Britain, a school of liberal thought which was propagated at meetings of the Manchester Chamber of Commerce (founded 1820). It emphasized CLASSICAL ECONOMICS, FREE TRADE, LAISSEZ-FAIRE, and a peaceful foreign policy. Its spokesmen were Radicals such as Richard COBDEN (d. 1865) and John BRIGHT (d. 1889). *See also* MANCHESTER.

MANDATE OR MANDATED TERRITORY An arrangement adopted after WORLD WAR I (ended Nov. 1918) for the government of former non-Turkish provinces of the OTTOMAN EMPIRE and former German colonies. Mandated territories were classified according to their intended future status (independent, colonial possession, or integrated territory). Great Britain and other powers were given mandated responsibility for territories under the supervision of the LEAGUE OF NATIONS. In 1946 the supervisory role was transferred to the United Nations. Britain's 'mandates' included IRAQ and PALESTINE (to become independent) and TANGANYIKA (as a colony).

MANDELSON, PETER (b. 21 Oct. 1953 at Hampstead Garden Suburb, London, England). A grandson of Herbert MORRISON and television producer (1982–5), Mandelson was director of campaigns and communications for the

LABOUR PARTY (1985–90) and MP (1992–2004). His transfer of support from Gordon BROWN to rival Tony BLAIR during the 1994 Party leadership election provoked lasting animosity from Brown. As strategist and SPIN DOCTOR, Mandelson worked closely with Blair and Alastair CAMPBELL to achieve victory at the 1997 general election, attacking the Conservatives for 'sleaze'.

After serving Blair as Cabinet minister without portfolio (1997–8), Mandelson became trade and industry secretary only to resign for concealing a loan (1998). Recalled as NORTHERN IRELAND secretary (1999–2001), he resigned again for helping a rich Indian to obtain British citizenship. After serving as a European Commissioner (2004–8), he was recalled by Brown (prime minister) to bolster his government, created Lord Mandelson, and appointed business secretary (2008–10) and also first secretary of state (effectively deputy prime minister, 2009–10).

MANNERS, SOCIETIES FOR THE REFORMATION OF Societies founded from the 1690s in England and Wales, mainly in towns, to promote moral reform by bringing prosecutions for vice (e.g., swearing, drunkenness) before JUSTICES OF THE PEACE. Supported by DISSENTERS, Low-Church members of the Church of ENGLAND and 'country' WHIGS, they were a response to the decline of Church courts and the perceived immorality of society. They had limited success, and declined by c.1740.

MANNING, HENRY (b. 15 July 1808 at Totteridge, Hertfordshire, England; d. 14 Jan. 1892 at Westminster, London, England, aged 83). After studying at OXFORD University, Manning became a Church of England clergyman (1832) and held posts in S England. Influenced by the OXFORD MOVEMENT, he was concerned to guard the Church against State interference. After a government committee ruled on a doctrinal matter in the GORHAM JUDGMENT (1850), Manning became a Roman Catholic (1851) and was ordained as priest. From 1865, as archbishop of WESTMINSTER, he led the Catholic Church in England and Wales. He developed schools and other children's institutions, and mediated in the 1889 DOCK STRIKE. As an ULTRAMONTANIST, Manning supported the definition of papal infallibility (1870), and was created a cardinal in 1875. *See also* CATHOLICS AND CATHOLIC CHURCH, ENGLAND.

MANOR A territorial unit, belonging to a lord, and associated rights over physical resources (e.g., arable land, meadow, woodland) and inhabitants. Manors were being formed in Anglo-Saxon kingdoms (southern Britain) by the 9th century through fragmentation of large estates (sometimes equivalent to a (small) SHIRE). Before the NORMAN CONQUEST of England (1066–70s) small estates were sometimes termed *land* (OE).

After the Conquest the invaders coined the Latin term *manerium* for estates, from OFr. *maneir*, meaning 'dwelling' or 'residence' (from which 'manor' is derived). The Latin term may connote a preoccupation with estate centres (principal dwelling and other buildings) as bases for exploitation. Other terms (e.g., English, 'hall') were also used into the 13th century. Manors varied considerably in size; for example, a village and its land could be divided between several manors; or a manor could equate to a village and its land; or a manor could cover several villages, townships or farmsteads.

As detailed in the 13th century, a manor typically comprised land reserved for the lord's use ('demesne', from OFr. *demeine*, meaning 'belonging to a lord') and tenant land (held by peasants and cultivated for themselves). Tenants varied in status. Unfree tenants had to undertake LABOUR SERVICES on the demesne and pay exactions or 'incidents' to their lord (e.g., head tax called 'chevage'). Free tenants paid money rents. A manor was administered through a court.

Manorial authority declined after the BLACK DEATH (1348–9), when lords abandoned incidents and replaced services with money rents (*see* COPYHOLD), and leased demesnes. From the 16th century, the parish eclipsed the manor as a unit of local administration, though manorial tenures continued until abolition in 1922. Lords sometimes retained residual rights in the 21st century.

Manors were created in Wales from the late 11th century (*see* MARCH OF WALES), and in Ireland from the late 12th century (*see* NORMANS, IMPACT ON IRELAND). *See also* FEUDALISM; SERFDOM; TENURES, ENGLAND FROM 1066.

MANRENT In Scotland, mid 15th–early 17th centuries, the bond given by an inferior (the 'man', generally a LAIRD or lesser lord) to a superior (generally a lord), promising life-long support. In return the lord generally gave a bond of maintenance promising protection to the 'man'. Manrent extended relationships found between kin to men unrelated by blood. The principle was adopted and extended by the COVENANTERS. *See also* COVENANTS, SCOTLAND.

MANUMISSION The process whereby people of unfree social status (e.g., slaves, villeins) were given legal freedom by their lords (e.g., by declaration or charter). In medieval Britain and Ireland slaves were sometimes manumitted as acts of charity (5th–12th centuries). In England in the 12th–14th centuries villeins sometimes bought manumission, and the abolition of villeinage (villein status and conditions) was demanded during the PEASANTS' REVOLT (1381). Unfree social conditions largely disappeared throughout the British Isles in the 14th–15th centuries as a result of changing economic and demographic conditions. *See also* SOCIAL STRUCTURE, ENGLAND 1066 TO 16TH CENTURY; SERFDOM.

MAORIS AND BRITISH, MID 19TH CENTURY
Colonization of NEW ZEALAND in the 1830s prompted the British government into acquisition. It annexed South Island in 1839, but sovereignty over North Island was acquired in 1840 through the treaty of Waitangi agreed with Maoris (indigenous inhabitants). In return the British would safeguard Maori rights.

The seizure of Maori land by British settlers, and imprecise drafting of the treaty, generated resentment. Conflict broke out in 1845–6, 1847, 1860–1, and intermittently until 1872. Maori resistance was eventually suppressed using troops from Australia. Maoris retreated to peripheral areas. Their numbers also fell because of European diseases.

MAR, 6TH EARL OF (b. Feb. 1675 at Alloa, E Scotland; d. May 1732 at Aix-la-Chapelle, aged 57). John Erskine succeeded as 6th earl in the Erskine line in 1689. A leading proponent of union with England, he was appointed a SECRETARY OF STATE for Scotland in 1705, and in 1706 was a commissioner for negotiating the treaty of Union (effective 1707). He was dismissed as secretary in 1709, reinstated (as third secretary) in 1713, and dismissed again in Sept. 1714, following the accession of King GEORGE I. Now embittered, he instigated the JACOBITE REBELLION of 1715, which failed. Mar fled to France (Feb. 1716). He was nicknamed 'Bobbing John' for his side-changing.

MARCH, EARLS OF *see* MORTIMER FAMILY

MARCH OF WALES The parts of WALES conquered by NORMANS and Anglo-Normans *c*.1070– *c*.1170 which were controlled by lords, holding from the English Crown, until the early 16th century. The March (from OFr. *marche*, meaning 'frontier') was distinct from Welsh-ruled lands, most of which were administered by the English Crown from 1283 (*see* WALES, ENGLISH CONQUEST OF).

The March extended along the S coast and ran W of the BORDER with England. It comprised about 40 lordships in four regions: (a) SW Wales from the Teifi river E to the Gower Peninsula; (b) SE Wales from SWANSEA E to Chepstow (including GLAMORGAN) and then N along the border; (c) E Wales from Brecon N to Montgomery, including the lordship of Brecon and periodically BUILTH; (d) from Montgomery N to Chester (NW England), including Oswestry and periodically 'The Four Cantrefs' (*see* BERFEDDWLAD, Y).

A lordship was centred on a castle, usually with an adjacent town. Rural population comprised areas of English settlers, imported by the lord, and native Welsh. In the more fertile parts, RURAL SETTLEMENT AND SOCIETY were based on the imported manorial system (*see* MANOR), though Welsh land-holders often lived under Welsh TENURES and customs.

Lordships descended by inheritance and sometimes passed through heiresses to new families. Important Marcher families included those of BRAOSE, CLARE, FITZALAN and MORTIMER, and later BOHUN and DESPENSER. Lords had considerable independence, including the right to wage war. The March was dangerous for English kings, because disaffected English lords with Marcher estates could withdraw to the March and organize opposition.

By 1509 the English Crown held the majority of lordships, enabling the March to be abolished and converted into shires in 1536; *see* UNION OF WALES WITH ENGLAND.

MARCONI, GUGLIELMO (b. 25 April 1874 at Bologna, Italy; d. 20 July 1937 at Rome, Italy, aged 63). Of Italian and Irish parentage, Marconi studied physics in Italy, becoming interested in the electro-magnetic theory of light formulated by James Clerk MAXWELL. He perceived the potential for using electrical waves for wireless telegraphy and developed transmitters and receivers for conveying electrical signals (1894–5).

In Feb. 1896 Marconi moved to Great Britain, sensing opportunities for his work. He demonstrated signal transmissions, and in July was granted the first patent for wireless telegraphy. By July 1897 Marconi could transmit signals over 11 mi, 18 km (in Italy, from land to a warship), and he formed his first British company. Soon he transmitted Morse code signals across the English Channel (27 March 1899) and the Atlantic (12 Dec. 1901). He experimented from 1916 with stronger short waves, which became the basis for long-distance radio communication. Marconi was awarded the 1909 Nobel Prize in Physics (shared with K.F. Braun). *See also* ELECTRONIC COMMUNICATIONS, GREAT BRITAIN; RADIO BROADCASTING, GREAT BRITAIN AND NORTHERN IRELAND.

MARCONI SCANDAL The revelation in Aug. 1912 that two British government ministers, David LLOYD GEORGE and Rufus Isaacs, had planned to profit personally from a government contract with the English Marconi Wireless Telegraphy Company. They had acquired shares in the separate American Marconi Company, which had depreciated. A parliamentary inquiry cleared them of corruption but criticized their imprudence (1913).

MARE, PETER DE LA (fl. from mid 1360s in Herefordshire, England; d. in or after 1387 in England). A member of PARLIAMENT for Herefordshire, de la Mare was chosen by the House of Commons during the GOOD PARLIAMENT (April–July 1376) to present their accusations to the House of Lords, making him the Commons' first named speaker. When JOHN OF GAUNT recovered control of the Council in Nov. 1376, de la Mare was imprisoned. He was released after King EDWARD III's death (21 June 1377), pardoned, and re-elected as speaker (Oct.). He attended several more Parliaments (1380–3).

MARGARET (b. *c*.1046 in Hungary; d. 16 Nov. 1093 at Edinburgh, SE Scotland, aged about 47). Queen of Scots (Scotland) 1070–93.

Margaret was born (in exile) into the English royal family (she was grand-daughter of EDMUND IRONSIDE and brother of Edgar ætheling). She returned with her family to England in 1057. In 1070, following the Norman invasion of England (*see* WILLIAM I), she fled with her brother to Scotland. There she married (also 1070) King MALCOLM III, thereby introducing English influences to the Scottish court. Deeply religious, she probably founded DUNFERMLINE Priory (E Scotland), introducing monks from CANTERBURY (SE England), and encouraged devotion to Scottish saints (e.g., through restoring monks to IONA). She died of grief after the deaths of her husband and son Edward. She was canonized in 1249. *See also* DONALD III.

MARGARET, 'THE MAID OF NORWAY' (b. *c.* April 1283 in Norway; d. 26 Sept. 1290 in Orkney Islands, aged 7). Grand-daughter of ALEXANDER III, king of Scots (Scotland), by his daughter Margaret (d. 1283) and King Eric II of Norway. Margaret succeeded Alexander on 19 March 1286, aged 2 or 3. Her death en route probably to England sparked a succession crisis: *see* BIRGHAM, TREATY OF; GREAT CAUSE. *See also* MAC MALCOLM RULERS.

MARGARET OF ANJOU (b. 23 March 1430 at Pont-à-Mousson or Nancy, Lorraine, France; d. 25 Aug. 1482 at Dampierre, Anjou, France, aged 52). Margaret married King HENRY VI of England (22 April 1445) to secure a truce (*see* HUNDRED YEARS WAR). She allied in England with the dukes of SUFFOLK and SOMERSET, increasingly against Richard, duke of YORK, her hostility deepening after she bore an heir, Edward (13 Oct. 1453). After Somerset's death (1455), she led opposition to York.

Conflict recommenced in 1459. Henry was captured at the battle of Northampton (July 1460), and Margaret fled to Wales and Scotland. After York was killed (30 Dec.), Lancastrians led by Margaret defeated Yorkists at St Albans and recovered Henry (17 Feb. 1461). But York's heir Edward seized the throne (4 March; *see* EDWARD IV), Lancastrians were defeated at Towton, Yorkshire (29 March), and Margaret fled to Scotland and France.

In July 1470 Margaret was reconciled with the Yorkist rebel Richard, earl of WARWICK, who reinstated Henry as king (Oct.). She returned with Prince Edward (14 April 1471) but Edward IV had regained the throne. Lancastrians were defeated (4 May) at Tewkesbury (Gloucestershire); Prince Edward was killed. Henry was murdered, and Margaret imprisoned until ransomed by the French king. *See also* YORKIST–LANCASTRIAN CONFLICT.

MARIAN CIVIL WAR Conflict in Scotland between factions supporting the restoration of MARY, QUEEN OF SCOTS ('Marians' or 'Queen's Party'), and the infant King JAMES VI ('King's Party'). Conflict broke out after Mary's escape from prison on 2 May 1568. Violence was widespread. (Mary fled to England on 16 May, after the battle of LANGSIDE.) Each side included Protestants and Catholics. By 1572 the King's Party was prevailing. The war ended after the Pacification of PERTH (1573).

MARKETS AND FAIRS Markets (frequent gatherings for trade) probably took place in SE Britain in the 1st century BC. In Roman Britain (1st–4th centuries AD), large towns included market places (*see* ROMAN BRITAIN, TOWNS), but markets were also held elsewhere. Official approval was required. Markets ceased when commercial activity declined in the 5th century.

From the 7th century, in Germanic-ruled southern Britain, informal markets were held at meeting-places (e.g., MINSTERS, WICS). In 10th-century England, larger BURHS (fortified centres), usually founded by rulers, became important market centres; DOMESDAY BOOK (1086) recorded 112 boroughs (urban centres) and another 39 markets (an under-recording). Markets probably also occurred alongside churches elsewhere in Britain and in Ireland, and in VIKING towns in Ireland. Fairs (seasonal gatherings) were probably also held. In Ireland, fairs have been more important than markets.

From *c*.1100 to *c*.1300, commercial facilities expanded (*see* COMMERCIALIZATION). Markets were central to new TOWNS in Britain and Ireland. In England and Scotland, markets and fairs required royal licences. In England, there were 700 markets by 1200; in the 13th century, another 1140 markets and 1280 fairs were 'chartered', many in rural locations (not all became established). Traded commodities included basic foodstuffs (grain, meat). Most rural markets and fairs ceased in the late 14th–15th centuries because of depopulation and economic decline. In Scotland and Ireland, more towns and markets were founded in the 17th–18th centuries, extending marketing networks.

From the late 17th century, in England, foodstuffs were increasingly traded outside markets, and in Britain in the 18th–19th centuries fairs became confined largely to livestock trading, hiring and entertainment. In the 19th century, 'respectable' market halls were built (starting with St John's Market, LIVERPOOL, 1822). More were constructed in the 1950s–60s. In the 21st century, recreational fairs remained widespread, and many towns retained a weekly market despite competition from other retailers. *See also* SHOPS AND RETAILING.

MARKIEVICZ, COUNTESS (b. 4 Feb. 1868 at London, England; d. 15 July 1927 at Dublin, Irish Free State, aged 59). From c.1909 Markievicz, an Irishwoman (Constance Gore-Booth) who had married a Polish count, was involved in Irish radical movements (e.g., member of IRISH CITIZEN ARMY). She participated in the republican EASTER RISING (1916) and was court-martialled. Her death sentence was commuted (released from prison, June 1917).

In Dec. 1918 Markievicz was the first woman to be elected to the UK Parliament, but she abstained. She joined Sinn Féin's self-proclaimed republican Dáil Éireann ('Assembly of Ireland'; formed Jan. 1919), and the Dáil government (April 1919–Aug. 1921). She opposed the 1921 ANGLO-IRISH TREATY, which created the Irish Free State (IFS), and supported 'Anti-treatyites' in the IRISH CIVIL WAR. Elected to the IFS Dáil for Sinn Féin in 1923, she again abstained. In 1926 Markievicz helped to found FIANNA FÁIL, was re-elected (1927), but died without taking her seat. *See also* IRISH FREE STATE, FOUNDING OF.

MARLBOROUGH, DUKE OF *see* CHURCHILL, JOHN

MARLBOROUGH, STATUTE OF In England, legal provisions issued on 18 Nov. 1267 by King HENRY III in a Great Council at Marlborough (Wiltshire), following the BARONIAL CONFLICT AND WARS. It confirmed legal regulations made in the Provisions of WESTMINSTER (1259) and Dictum of KENILWORTH (1266), and required MAGNA CARTA (1225 version) to be observed. The Statute sought to pacify the country and demonstrated Henry's acceptance of parts of his opponents' reform programme. Some sections remained in force in the early 21st century.

MARLOWE, CHRISTOPHER (b. Feb. 1564 at Canterbury, Kent, England; d. 30 May 1593 at Deptford, Kent, England, aged 29). A shoemaker's son, educated at Cambridge University, Marlowe translated Latin poetry and became famous as a playwright in London with *Tamburlaine the Great* (1587). His other plays include *Dido, Queen of Carthage*, and *Dr Faustus*. He was probably also a government spy. In May 1593, following accusations of atheism and blasphemy, Marlowe was arrested and bailed. He died in a fight over a bill. *See also* ENGLISH LITERATURE, ENGLAND.

MARPRELATE TRACTS Seven pamphlets, aimed at a popular readership, which ridiculed archbishops and bishops of the Church of ENGLAND. Ostensibly funded by 'Martin Marprelate, gentleman', they were printed clandestinely between autumn 1588 and summer 1589. The authors, Job Throckmorton and others, were Puritans and presbyterians. In response, Archbishop John WHITGIFT ordered a search for the printing press (seized Aug. 1589)

and imprisoned leading Puritans, including Thomas CARTWRIGHT. *See also* PURITANISM, ENGLAND.

MARRIED WOMEN'S PROPERTY ACTS Legislation that provided separate ownership of property in England, Ireland and Wales. The 1870 Married Women's Property Act conferred ownership of wages and savings; the 1882 Act enabled women to own and control property; the 1893 Act placed wives and unmarried women on the same footing regarding new property. Campaigning for such legislation started in the 1850s (*see* LANGHAM PLACE CIRCLE). In England from the 13th century married women could not own property, though from the 16th century it could be held separately in trust for women. *See also* WOMEN'S MOVEMENT 1850S TO 1918, GREAT BRITAIN.

'MARROW' CONTROVERSY A doctrinal dispute in the Church of SCOTLAND, sparked by the republication in 1718 of *The Marrow of Modern Divinity* (1645) by the English PURITAN Edward Fisher, which minimized Calvinistic belief in predestination. The book was condemned by the Church's General Assembly in 1720 and 12 ministers sympathetic to its theology (the 'Marrowmen', including Ebenezer ERSKINE) were rebuked.

MARSHAL, ENGLAND A senior officer in the ROYAL HOUSEHOLD. The earliest 'master marshal', in the late 11th century, was responsible for horses. By 1130 he also supervised payment of servants and soldiers. The post descended by hereditary right from the early 12th century, and became important through the prominence of William MARSHAL (d. 1219). From the 14th century the holder was styled 'earl marshal' and supervised the officers of arms (heralds). He later became responsible for organizing CORONATIONS. Since 1672 the post has been held continuously by the HOWARD FAMILY (earls of Norfolk).

MARSHAL, WILLIAM (b. 1146 or 1147 in England; d. 14 May 1219 at Caversham, Oxfordshire, England, aged 72). A son of the master marshal to King HENRY I, William became a renowned knight through service to ELEANOR OF AQUITAINE (served 1168–70), HENRY THE YOUNG KING (1170–83), HENRY II (1186–9) and RICHARD I (1189–90). In Oct. 1191 Marshal helped to oust William LONGCHAMP as regent. He succeeded a brother as master marshal (1194), and was made earl of Pembroke (1199).

In May 1213 Marshal was recalled to court by JOHN, whom he supported during the crisis that ended in MAGNA CARTA (1215). After John's death, during the minority of HENRY III, Marshal served as 'guardian of the king and kingdom' (Nov. 1216–April 1219) and persuaded French forces to withdraw (*see* ENGLAND, FRENCH INVASION (1216–17)). *See also* STRONGBOW.

MARSHALL, ALFRED (b. 26 July 1842 at Bermondsey, Surrey, England; d. 13 July 1924 at Cambridge, Cambridgeshire, England, aged 81). Marshall taught at CAMBRIDGE University and University College, BRISTOL, before serving as professor of POLITICAL ECONOMY at Cambridge (1885–1908). He developed economics as an academic subject in England, and was highly influential – his *Principles of Economics* (1890) remained a standard text until the mid 20th century. An exponent of neoclassical economics, Marshall represented ordinary behaviour through mathematics, developing such concepts as demand elasticity, and increasing and diminishing returns. *See also* CLASSICAL AND NEOCLASSICAL ECONOMICS.

MARSHALL AID Name given to the financial assistance provided by the USA to Western Europe 1948–50, following WORLD WAR II and early in the COLD WAR. A 'European Recovery Programme' was proposed in June 1947 by the US secretary of state, George Marshall, to promote economic revival and thus discourage COMMUNISM. The USA provided $12.7 billion in loans and grants, of which $3.3 billion went to the UK and $133 million to southern Ireland.

MARTINEAU, HARRIET (b. 12 June 1802 at Norwich, Norfolk, England; d. 27 June 1876 at Ambleside, Westmorland, England, aged 74). Despite poor health and deafness, Martineau made a living from journalism and fiction writing from the 1820s. She achieved recognition from popularizing the theories of T.R. MALTHUS and David RICARDO (in *Illustrations of Political Economy* and other works, 1832–4). Travel in the USA (1834–6) converted her to abolition of slavery, while a tour of the Middle East (1846–7) stimulated an interest in comparative religion. She was also an early advocate of women's legal rights, work and education (from late 1830s). *See also* UNITARIANS.

MARTINEAU, JAMES *see* UNITARIANS

MARX, KARL (b. 5 May 1818 at Trier, Rhenish Prussia; d. 14 March 1883 at London, England, aged 64). A German political philosopher and economist; the originator of MARXISM.

Marx lived in exile in London from Aug. 1849, supported latterly by his collaborator Friedrich Engels (1820–95), a MANCHESTER cotton manufacturer. While promoting the international LABOUR MOVEMENT, Marx did not engage directly in British politics. His writings, notably *Das Kapital* (*Capital*, 1867–94), inspired Communist movements in the 20th century (*see* COMMUNISM).

MARXISM A historical and social theory formulated primarily by the German political philosopher and econo-

mist Karl MARX (1818–83). He argued that society consisted of classes with antagonistic interests. The resultant class conflict generated fundamental historical change. Thus a 'feudal mode of production', in which agriculture was predominant and the nobility pre-eminent, was succeeded, after a period of 'transition', by a 'capitalist' mode dominated by trade and later industry, created by a 'bourgeoisie' (an entrepreneurial class). A revolutionary working class would eventually overthrow CAPITALISM, leading to SOCIALISM and COMMUNISM, in which society would be collective and classless. Marx relegated such aspects of society as religion, law and art to a secondary 'superstructure'. *See also* FEUDALISM; COMMUNIST PARTY.

MARY, QUEEN OF SCOTS (b. 8 Dec. 1542 at Linlithgow Palace, SE Scotland; d. 18 Feb. 1587 at Fotheringhay Castle, Northamptonshire, England, aged 44). Queen of Scots 1542–67 (personal rule, 1561–7).

The daughter of King JAMES V and MARY OF GUISE, Mary became queen aged six days, with the earl of ARRAN as regent. Sent to France in 1548, she married the dauphin (heir), Francis (1558), and became queen consort (1559). Francis died (1560); Mary returned to Scotland (arrived 19 Aug. 1561). She also claimed the Crown of England, as heiress of MARY I (d. 1558), although Scottish nobles had recognized ELIZABETH (*see* EDINBURGH, (1560) TREATY OF).

Mary acknowledged the REFORMATION (1560) but remained a Catholic. On 29 July 1565 she married her cousin Lord DARNLEY, strengthening her claim to England. MORAY, her pro-English, Protestant adviser, rebelled and was driven into exile. Mary's marriage soon deteriorated (*see* RIZZIO, DAVID), though a son was born (*see* JAMES VI). She acquiesced in Darnley's murder (10 Feb. 1567) and married the Protestant BOTHWELL (15 May). Nobles, led by MORTON, revolted: on 15 June they imprisoned Mary; on 24 July they forced her abdication (*see* CONFEDERATE LORDS). She escaped (2 May 1568), but was defeated at LANGSIDE and fled to England; civil war followed (*see* MARIAN CIVIL WAR). Mary remained a prisoner until executed for allegedly plotting Elizabeth's assassination. *See also* MAITLAND, WILLIAM, OF LETHINGTON; CATHOLIC PLOTS, ENGLAND.

MARY I (b. 18 Feb. 1516 at Greenwich, Kent, England; d. 17 Nov. 1558 at Westminster, Middlesex, England, aged 42). Eldest daughter of King HENRY VIII, Mary suffered the annulment of her parents' marriage (1533) and bastardization (1536), and was compelled to accept Henry's supremacy in the Church (1536) though she remained loyal to Catholicism. Henry's successor as king of England and Ireland, the Protestant EDWARD VI (d. 6 July 1553), nominated Lady Jane GREY as his successor. Mary rejected this.

On 19 July Jane was imprisoned and Mary proclaimed queen. Aged 37, she decided to marry and chose (Oct.) Philip of Spain as husband (without regal power), provoking WYATT'S REBELLION (Jan. 1554). The marriage was celebrated at WINCHESTER Cathedral on 25 July 1554.

Mary's priority was to restore Catholicism and papal jurisdiction. She immediately allowed Mass, and in Oct. 1553 Parliament repealed Edward's religious legislation. On 30 Nov. 1554 England was reconciled to the papacy by Cardinal Reginald POLE. Anti-papal laws were repealed and anti-heresy laws reinstated (from Jan. 1555). During 1555–8 almost 300 Protestants were burnt.

On 7 June 1557, under pressure from Philip, England declared war against France. CALAIS was lost (Jan. 1558). Mary died childless; succeeded by ELIZABETH I (half-sister). *See also* SUCCESSION ACTS; REFORMATION, ENGLAND/IRELAND; PAULET, WILLIAM.

MARY I AND IRELAND After accession as queen (July 1553) Mary acted quickly on religious practices. In Sept. Anthony ST LEGER was appointed lord deputy and instructed to restore Catholic rites; in 1554 George Dowdall, archbishop of ARMAGH, was ordered to deprive married clergy of livings. The restoration of papal authority took longer: Paul IV asserted authority in 1555 by raising Ireland to kingdom status, and in 1557 Ireland's Parliament readopted papal jurisdiction by repealing anti-papal statutes.

Only one monastery was restored. As Protestantism was weak, there were no burnings, though Bishop John BALE fled. Mary (d. 1558) continued the assertion of English power by implementing the planned LEIX-OFFALY PLANTATION (authorized by Parliament 1557). *See also* SUSSEX, THOMAS EARL OF, AND IRELAND; REFORMATION, IRELAND; IRELAND, ENGLISH CONQUEST, 16TH CENTURY.

MARY II (b. 30 April 1662 at Westminster, Middlesex, England; d. 28 Dec. 1694 at Kensington Palace, Middlesex, aged 32). The elder daughter of James, duke of York, Mary was brought up as a Protestant despite her father's conversion to Catholicism (1669). In 1677 she was married to William of Orange, stadholder (lieutenant) of the Dutch Republic, and then lived in the Republic. Her father became king of England, Ireland and Scotland in 1685 (*see* JAMES VII/II).

In 1688 Mary supported her husband's invasion of England to assist her father's enemies. She went to England in Feb. 1689, following her father's flight. She rejected proposals that she should become sole monarch or regent. She and William were crowned joint sovereigns on 11 April, though William exercised monarchical powers. (Mary reluctantly exercised authority during William's absences abroad.) She promoted piety, though her last years were embittered by estrangement from her sister (*see* ANNE). *See also* WILLIAM III; GLORIOUS REVOLUTION.

MARYLAND A former English colony in N America (British from 1707), around Chesapeake Bay, NE of VIRGINIA. It was authorized in 1632 when King CHARLES I granted a charter to the 2nd Lord Baltimore (Cecil Calvert), a Catholic and son of the deceased original petitioner. Maryland was named after Queen HENRIETTA MARIA. It was the first 'proprietary colony' (colony granted to an owner).

Settlers arrived from March 1634, both Protestants and Catholics. An assembly first met in 1638. Liberty of religion for Christians was granted by the assembly's Maryland Toleration Act of 1649, partly to protect Catholics. Like Virginia, Maryland prospered from tobacco cultivation. Puritans replaced Baltimore's government 1654–7, and WILLIAM III suspended proprietorial rights from the 3rd Lord Baltimore (1692; restored to 5th Lord in 1715). Est. population 1770: 200,000.

Many colonists opposed the STAMP ACT (1765) and fought for AMERICAN INDEPENDENCE (declared July 1776). Maryland became a State of the USA, confiscated the proprietor's rights, and in Nov. 1776 replaced its charter with a constitution. *See also* NORTH AMERICAN COLONIES.

MARY OF GUISE (b. 22 Nov. 1515 at Bar, duchy of Bar; d. 11 June 1560 at Edinburgh, SE Scotland, aged 44). A widow, Mary married King JAMES V of Scotland (14 June 1538). Their surviving third child, MARY, QUEEN OF SCOTS, succeeded as queen soon after birth (1542); the latter's heir, the (2nd) earl of ARRAN, became regent and allied with England (Aug. 1543). Preferring a French alliance, Mary of Guise joined his opponents, who forced him to renege (Sept.); English invasions followed (1544, 1545, 1547) during which Mary organized resistance.

In April 1554 Mary of Guise replaced Arran as regent. Though a Catholic, she co-operated with pro-Protestant nobles. But her authority was undermined by heavy taxation (1556–7), her daughter's marriage to the French heir (1558), and repression of Protestants (1559). Anti-Church riots in PERTH (May 1559) provoked the pro-Protestant LORDS OF THE CONGREGATION to drive Mary from Edinburgh (29 June) and depose her (21 Oct.). She recaptured EDINBURGH (late March 1560) but died soon afterwards. *See also* BEATON, DAVID; BERWICK, (1560) TREATY OF; SCOTTISH–ENGLISH RELATIONS 1357 TO 1603.

MASHAM, ABIGAIL (b. in 1670 at London, England; d. 6 Dec. 1734 at Otes, Essex, England, aged 64). Abigail Hill entered the service of Princess ANNE by 1700 through her cousin Sarah CHURCHILL (later duchess of Marlborough). Anne became queen in 1702, and Hill married a courtier, Samuel Masham, in 1707 (created Lord Masham, 1711).

By 1707 Mrs Masham, a TORY and also cousin of the politician Robert HARLEY, was giving political advice to the queen, causing the queen's relations with the duchess of

Marlborough to deteriorate. In early 1710 the duke of Marlborough tried to remove Mrs Masham. Anne defended her, eventually dismissing the duchess of Marlborough from her household and replacing the earl of GODOLPHIN with Harley as chief minister. After Anne's death (1714), Lady Masham lived in obscurity.

MASQUE A type of entertainment involving singing, dancing and dressing up (including mask wearing). Masques were staged at the English royal court from 1512 (reign of HENRY VIII), but were developed into highly sophisticated productions, sometimes containing political messages, from 1605 (reign of JAMES VI/I) by Ben JONSON and Inigo JONES. They continued in the reign of CHARLES I, until the CIVIL WAR (1642).

MASSACHUSETTS A former English colony in N America, in NEW ENGLAND (British from 1707). It was developed from 1628 by Puritan 'separatists' (separated from the Church of England), who obtained a charter from King CHARLES I in 1629 constituting the joint-stock Massachusetts Bay Company, under a governor and court elected by stockholders (freemen).

Small groups went to Massachusetts in 1628–9, followed by 11 ships in March 1630. The latter party took the royal charter (to remove control from England) and founded Boston. From 1634 each settlement elected two deputies for the colony's court (1632). Harvard College was founded for training clergy in 1636. In 1641 the court effectively authorized a congregational form of Church government.

In 1684 CHARLES II, dissatisfied with lack of influence, annulled the 1629 charter. WILLIAM III provided a replacement (1691, including PLYMOUTH and Maine), making Massachusetts a CROWN COLONY with an appointed governor. Est. population 1770: 299,000.

From 1765 Massachusetts forcefully resisted British impositions (*see* AMERICAN INDEPENDENCE, ORIGINS OF). It became a State of the USA in 1776. *See also* NONCONFORMITY AND DISSENT, ENGLAND; NORTH AMERICAN COLONIES; NEW ENGLAND, DOMINION OF.

MASS OBSERVATION A social research organization founded in 1937 by anthropologist Tom Harrisson (1911–76) and poet Charles Madge (1912–96) to record the everyday life of ordinary people of Great Britain, through observation, questionnaires and diary keeping. Employed by the government during WORLD WAR II to monitor civilian morale, Mass Observation continued work into the early 1950s. Its archive is kept at Sussex University (Brighton).

MATILDA (b. 7 Feb. 1102 at Sutton Courtenay, Berkshire, England; d. 10 Sept. 1167 near Rouen, Normandy, aged 65). The daughter of HENRY I, king of England and duke of Normandy, Matilda married (1114) Emperor Henry V (d. 1125) and Geoffrey of Anjou (1128). From 1117 (coronation), she was called 'Empress' (Latin *Imperatrix*).

After the WHITE SHIP DISASTER (1120) Matilda was Henry I's direct heir. He sought to ensure her succession by obtaining oaths from the nobility (1127, 1131). But after his death (Dec. 1135) STEPHEN was accepted as ruler.

From Sept. 1139 Matilda and her (illegitimate) half-brother ROBERT OF GLOUCESTER campaigned in England. After Stephen was captured at LINCOLN (Feb. 1141), a legatine council under HENRY OF BLOIS declared her 'Lady of the English' (7 April). But her attempts to capture London (June) and WINCHESTER (Sept.) failed. She retreated to OXFORD, from which she escaped in Dec. 1142. She lived mainly at Devizes (Wiltshire) until early 1148 (returned to Normandy), leaving others to challenge Stephen (*see* HENRY II). After her husband's death (1151) Matilda lived a life of religious retirement, intervening occasionally in politics (e.g., rebuking Henry for his treatment of Thomas BECKET).

MAUDLING, REGINALD (b. 7 March 1917 at London, England; d. 14 Feb. 1979 at London, aged 61). A protégé of 'Rab' BUTLER and, from 1950, a Conservative MP, Maudling encouraged his Party to accept greater State involvement in providing health services and education, and in creating full employment. He held various offices in British governments, including the posts of economic secretary (1952–5) and colonial secretary (1961–2). As chancellor of the Exchequer under Harold MACMILLAN and Alec DOUGLAS-HOME (1962–4), he sought to increase economic growth. Edward HEATH defeated him in the 1965 Conservative leadership contest. Appointed home secretary in 1970, Maudling sanctioned internment without trial in Northern Ireland (*see* TROUBLES). He was forced to resign by the POULSON AFFAIR (1972). He served Margaret THATCHER briefly as shadow foreign minister (1975–6).

MAU MAU REVOLT A rebellion in KENYA by a Kikuyu African movement against British settlers and their African employees. It began in Oct. 1952, when a state of emergency was declared by the colonial government. The Mau Mau sought return of lands and expulsion of non-Africans. The revolt was suppressed by Nov. 1956 but the emergency continued until Feb. 1960. About 1800 Africans and 70 Europeans and Asians were murdered. Possibly 20,000 Mau Mau were killed, and about 150,000 sympathizers were detained in camps. About 200 British and African security personnel were killed.

MAURICE, F.D. (b. 29 Aug. 1805 at Normanston, Suffolk, England; d. 1 April 1872 at London, England, aged 66). A Church of England clergyman, Frederick Denison Maurice was a professor at King's College, London, from 1841, becoming professor of theology in 1846. As co-founder of Queen's College, London (1848), he influenced the women's movement, and through involvement with working-class organizations he became a leader of CHRISTIAN SOCIALISM. In 1853 his *Theological Essays* provoked controversy for scepticism about eternal punishment after death. King's forced him to resign. Maurice became principal of the new Working Men's College (1854), and professor of moral theology and philosophy at CAMBRIDGE University (1866). *See also* GIRLS' AND WOMEN'S EDUCATION, BRITAIN.

MAXTON, JAMES (b. 22 June 1885 at Pollokshaws, Lanarkshire, Scotland; d. 23 July 1946 at Largs, Ayrshire, Scotland, aged 61). Graduating from GLASGOW University, Maxton entered teaching (1905). In 1904 he had joined the INDEPENDENT LABOUR PARTY (ILP). He opposed involvement in WORLD WAR I and was imprisoned for sedition (1916–17).

From 1922 until his death Maxton was ILP MP for Bridgeton (Glasgow). An eloquent maverick, he was often suspended from the House of Commons. He took a pacifist stance at the outbreak of WORLD WAR II. Chairman of the ILP 1926–31, 1934–9. *See also* RED CLYDESIDE.

MAXWELL, JAMES CLERK (b. 13 June 1831 at Edinburgh, Scotland; d. 5 Nov. 1879 at Cambridge, Cambridgeshire, England, aged 48). Interested in science as a child, Maxwell studied at EDINBURGH and CAMBRIDGE Universities (elected fellow of Trinity College 1855). He was professor of natural philosophy (science) at Marischal College, ABERDEEN (1856–60), and at King's College, London (1860–5), and professor of experimental physics at Cambridge (1871–9). He was elected to the ROYAL SOCIETY in 1861.

Maxwell's early work included experiments concerning colour and optics, and a paper about the rings of Saturn (1859). As a student, Maxwell had studied *Experimental Researches in Electricity* (1839) by Michael FARADAY. This led him to formulate theorems for the relationship between electric currents and magnetic forces. Experiments showing that the velocities of electric current and light are similar led Maxwell to the fundamental observation (1861) that they are related phenomena (electro-magnetic theory of light). Maxwell synthesized this work in his *Treatise on Electricity and Magnetism* (1873).

MAY, ERSKINE (b. 8 Feb. 1815 at Kentish Town, Middlesex, England; d. 17 April 1886 at Westminster, Middlesex, aged 71). An assistant to the librarian of the UK House of Commons from 1831, May devised procedural changes to help the Commons cope with increased business.

His *Parliamentary Practice* (1844) became the authoritative guide to parliamentary procedure, and influential overseas. May was a clerk assistant of the Commons from 1856 and clerk from 1871 (knighted 1866, created Lord Farnborough after retiring in 1886). *See also* PARLIAMENT, UNITED KINGDOM 1801 TO 1921.

MAY, THERESA (b. 1 Oct. 1956 at Eastbourne, East Sussex, England). Leader of the CONSERVATIVE PARTY and British prime minister 2016–19.

The daughter of a Church of ENGLAND clergyman, Theresa Brasier became interested in politics while at school (in Oxfordshire). After attending OXFORD University (1974–7), she married another Oxonian (Philip May, 1980). She worked for the BANK OF ENGLAND (1977–83), held banking-related posts (1983–97), and participated in local politics in LONDON (1986–94).

Elected an MP in 1997, when only 165 Conservatives were returned (of 659), May progressed quickly, becoming an Opposition spokesman (1998–9) and Shadow Cabinet member (1999–2010). As her Party's first woman chairman (2002–3), she sought to 'modernize' the Conservatives, but blundered by claiming they were considered the 'nasty party'.

As home secretary from 2010, under Prime Minister David CAMERON, May failed to reduce IMMIGRATION as promised. After the UK voted to leave the EUROPEAN UNION (2016), she succeeded Cameron despite having supported EU membership. She initiated withdrawal (March 2017), then held a general election (June) to increase her Commons majority. But seats were lost, creating conditions that nullified her withdrawal strategy. Conservatives eventually pressurized her into resigning (*see* BREXIT). Succeeded by Boris JOHNSON.

MAYNOOTH GRANT CONTROVERSY The dispute over a proposed increase in the UK Parliament's annual grant to the Roman Catholic MAYNOOTH SEMINARY in Ireland (from £9000 to £26,000). It was advocated in 1844 by the Conservative prime minister Sir Robert PEEL to conciliate Ireland's Catholic Church and clergy and discourage rural unrest. Though a grant had been paid since 1795 (originally by Ireland's Parliament), the increase was opposed within CABINET by W.E. GLADSTONE, who resigned as a minister (Jan. 1845). In early 1845 there was widespread popular Protestant opposition. The measure divided the CONSERVATIVE PARTY but received strong support in the House of Commons from WHIGS. It was passed in April 1845, supported by Gladstone. *See also* CATHOLICS AND CATHOLIC CHURCH, IRELAND FROM 16TH CENTURY.

MAYNOOTH SEMINARY Popular name for the Royal College of St Patrick at Maynooth (Co. Kildare, Ireland), founded in 1795 by Ireland's Parliament to provide a home seminary for Catholic ordinands after the FRENCH REVOLUTIONARY WARS impeded overseas training. Parliament also sought to exclude Continental revolutionary ideas. Lay students were admitted until 1817. Maynooth became Ireland's national seminary.

From 1909 Maynooth was also a recognized college of the National University of Ireland. Following the readmission of lay students (1966), four faculties became a university within the National University of Ireland (1977). *See also* MAYNOOTH GRANT CONTROVERSY; CATHOLICS AND CATHOLIC CHURCH, IRELAND FROM 16TH CENTURY; UNIVERSITIES, IRELAND.

MEATH A region of Ireland, from Lough Ree eastwards to the Irish Sea, including the Boyne Valley. Its Irish name, Mide, means 'Middle'. In the 5th century it probably belonged to LEINSTER (to the S) but it was dominated from the 6th to the late 11th century by the Southern Uí Néill from CONNACHT (W Ireland; *see* Uí NÉILL, SOUTHERN).

After the death in 1073 of Conchobar Ua Máel Sechlainn, high-king of the Southern Uí Néill, Meath lacked an effective high-king. High-kings of Ireland, or their challengers, frequently intervened. In the 1070s–mid 1080s Toirrdelbach Ua Briain (d. 1086) of MUNSTER (S Ireland) dominated Meath. In 1094 his son Muirchertach UA BRIAIN (d. 1119) expelled Meath's high-king and partitioned it. Toirrdelbach UA CONCHOBAIR (d. 1156) of Connacht again partitioned Meath in 1125, imposed his son as king in 1143 (he was killed), and repartitioned Meath in 1143 and 1144. Toirrdelbach's challenger Muirchertach MAC LOCHLAINN (d. 1166), from N Ireland, partitioned Meath in 1150 and 1152.

In 1172 Henry II of England, self-appointed lord of Ireland, granted Meath as a lordship to the Anglo-Norman Hugh de LACY (d. 1186), who granted lands to his followers. He was succeeded (1194) by his son Walter, after whose death (1241) Meath was divided between two granddaughters. *See also* HENRY II AND IRELAND; PROVINCES, IRELAND.

MECHANICS' INSTITUTES Educational centres which provided part-time evening lectures for working men, often on scientific topics, together with libraries and reading rooms. The first was the School of Arts at EDINBURGH (Scotland), founded in 1821. It was quickly imitated: in Great Britain at LIVERPOOL, GLASGOW and LONDON (1823), and in Ireland at BELFAST (1825). By 1850 there were about 700 institutes in Britain (610 in England). They declined in the late 19th century as State education developed.

MEDICINE AND PUBLIC HEALTH Until the 19th century treatments were often provided by family members, wise-women or other empirics (unqualified persons). Remedies included herbs, potions and spells. Childbirth

was managed by midwives. In Ireland and Gaelic N Britain there were also hereditary (male) physicians (*see* LEARNED CLASSES, IRELAND).

Clerical and lay surgeon-physicians (OE *læces*, meaning 'leeches') are recorded in Anglo-Saxon (southern) Britain from the 7th century. They practised 'humoral medicine' as expounded by the Greek Galen (129–*c*.210): health depended on maintaining an internal balance of four 'humours' (fluids), blood, black bile, yellow bile, phlegm. The most common treatment for imbalance was bloodletting. Surgery dealt with external matters; techniques included cauterization (searing tissue) and amputation.

From the 12th century UNIVERSITIES trained physicians, while in TOWNS surgeons and apothecaries belonged to GUILDS. Leprosy (11th–15th centuries) and PLAGUE (14th–17th centuries) were major medical problems, countered mainly by quarantine (e.g., lepers isolated in HOSPITALS).

From the mid 17th century new approaches superseded 'Galenic medicine', including understanding based on anatomy; treatments (e.g., mercury) partly reflecting the 'chemical' ideas of the Swiss Paracelsus (*c*.1493–1541); pioneer training that combined lectures and clinical instruction (in Leiden, Dutch Republic, from 1714; in EDINBURGH, Scotland, from 1726). Medicine flourished during the 18th century, with new hospitals and emergence of provincial 'general practitioners'.

Industrialization and urbanization (from 1780s) created insanitary living conditions which fostered infectious diseases. Outbreaks (e.g., CHOLERA from 1831) stimulated State responses, notably PUBLIC HEALTH ACTS, compulsory smallpox vaccination (England and Wales 1853, Scotland and Ireland 1863), and registration of medical practitioners (1858 Medical Act). Advances in anaesthesia (from 1850s) and antisepsis (1860s) facilitated surgical progress.

In the 20th century State-supported health services were developed, notably the UK NATIONAL HEALTH SERVICE (1948). From the 1920s mortality from infectious diseases declined, accelerated by chemotherapy and antibiotics. 'Life-style' diseases (e.g., cancer, diabetes) then became prevalent. *See also* PROFESSIONS; HARVEY, WILLIAM; CONSUMER REVOLUTION; CULLEN, WILLIAM; JENNER, EDWARD; LISTER, JOSEPH; SPANISH FLU.

MEDINA DEL CAMPO, TREATY OF Agreed on 27 March 1489 at Medina del Campo, Castile, Spain, by representatives of King HENRY VII of England and of Spanish rulers Ferdinand and Isabella. The treaty created a political alliance, aimed primarily against France, and provided for KATHERINE OF ARAGON, daughter of Ferdinand and Isabella, to marry Henry's heir ARTHUR. Each side was not to aid rebels against the other. The marriage took place in 1501. *See also* FOREIGN RELATIONS, ENGLAND 16TH CENTURY TO 1707; SPAIN, ENGLISH AND BRITISH RELATIONS WITH.

MEGALITHIC MONUMENTS, BRITAIN Chambered tombs and passage tombs of the NEOLITHIC (*c.*4300–*c.*2300 BC) in which construction involved the use of large stone uprights and lintels (megalith means 'large stone'). Examples most commonly occur in W and N Britain, with parallels in Ireland and Atlantic Europe. The term is occasionally used more loosely to refer to all Neolithic and BRONZE AGE monuments in which large stones are structural elements.

MEGALITHIC MONUMENTS, IRELAND Monuments incorporating large stones (megaliths) which were a distinctive feature of the NEOLITHIC, CHALCOLITHIC PERIOD and BRONZE AGE. In the Neolithic (*c.*3800– *c.*2500 BC) the main monuments were tombs: structures covered by a mound or cairn and with an external revetment. Types of megalithic tombs are distinguished by architectural variation, as court, portal, passage and wedge tombs. Tomb construction (wedge tombs) continued through the Chalcolithic (*c.*2500– *c.*2000 BC) and into the overlapping Bronze Age (*c.*2300– *c.*700 BC) but the focus shifted to the construction and use of open-air megalithic monuments: standing stones, stone rows, STONE CIRCLES and four posters.

MEILYR BRYDYDD, FAMILY OF Poets of the Middle Welsh period. Meilyr (fl. *c.*1100–37) was *pencerdd* ('chief poet') under GRUFFUDD AP CYNAN of Gwynedd (NW Wales). His son Gwalchmai (fl. *c.*1130–80) praised OWAIN GWYNEDD of Gwynedd and MADOG AP MAREDUDD of Powys (C Wales). Two or three of Gwalchmai's sons were poets. *See also* WELSH LANGUAGE AND LITERATURE.

MELBOURNE, 2ND VISCOUNT (b. 15 March 1779 at London, England; d. 24 Nov. 1848 at Brocket, Hertfordshire, England, aged 69). Originally a FOXITE Whig, William Lamb sat as an MP 1806–12, 1816–26, 1827–8, but long attracted attention chiefly as husband (from 1805) of the eccentric Lady Caroline Ponsonby (1785–1828). He served alongside LIBERAL TORIES as chief secretary for Ireland (1827–8) before inheriting a viscountcy in 1828.

As home secretary 1830–4 under Earl GREY, Melbourne suppressed social unrest. He succeeded as prime minister in July 1834, but King WILLIAM IV dismissed him (Nov.) because of his readiness to make concessions to Irish nationalists (followed by duke of WELLINGTON and Robert PEEL). The LICHFIELD HOUSE COMPACT (Feb. 1835), which provided Irish support, secured Melbourne's return in April 1835.

Melbourne seemed a passive leader, yet his detachment enabled him to referee a disputatious CABINET and preserve a fragmented majority in Parliament. Though Melbourne disliked reform, his ministry introduced the MUNICIPAL CORPORATIONS ACT (1835) and converted

TITHES to cash payments (1836). He enjoyed being a mentor to Queen VICTORIA, who obstructed his replacement in 1839 (*see* BEDCHAMBER CRISIS). He ceased to be prime minister when the Whigs lost the election of 1841. Succeeded by Peel. *See also* TOLPUDDLE MARTYRS.

MELLIFONT, TREATY OF An agreement between Lord MOUNTJOY, chief governor (lord deputy) of Ireland, and the 2nd earl of Tyrone (Hugh O'NEILL), which ended the NINE YEARS WAR. Tyrone submitted at Mellifont Abbey (Co. Louth) on 30 and 31 March 1603 (respectively in person, in writing). He renounced the title of O'Neill (i.e., chieftainship); authority over subordinate chiefs; allegiance to the king of Spain. He agreed to support English sheriffs and garrisons; was granted ownership of his lordship (Tyrone); and was promised a pardon and restoration of his earldom. *See also* FLIGHT OF THE EARLS.

MELVILLE, ANDREW (b. 1 Aug. 1545 at Baldovie, Angus, E Scotland; d. 1622 at Sedan, France, aged about 77). Educated in Scotland and France, Melville became a professor at the Geneva Academy, Switzerland (1569), and befriended the Calvinist theologian Theodor Beza. He returned to Scotland in 1574. As principal of GLASGOW University and then (from 1580) St Mary's College, ST ANDREWS, he introduced new subjects and teaching methods.

Melville became prominent in Church politics, serving as moderator of the General Assembly on several occasions and being involved in drafting the 'Second Book of Discipline' (completed 1578). He clashed with King JAMES VI over the Church's independence on numerous occasions. In 1606 James (now also king of England) summoned Melville to London for demanding the Church's liberty from State influence: Melville was imprisoned (1607–11) and then released into exile. *See also* CALVINISM; DISCIPLINE, BOOKS OF; CHURCH ORGANIZATION, SCOTLAND FROM 16TH CENTURY.

MELVILLE, VISCOUNT *see* DUNDAS, HENRY

MENZIES, ROBERT (b. 20 Dec. 1894 at Jeparit, Victoria; d. 15 May 1978 at Malvern, Victoria, Australia, aged 83). Member of the Victoria Parliament 1928–34, of the Australian Parliament 1934–66. As leader of the United Australia Party and prime minister from April 1939, Menzies led Australia into WORLD WAR II (Sept.), before discovering (late 1940) that Great Britain was too weak to provide military assistance. In 1941, after Labor refused to enter a coalition government, he resigned his positions (re-elected UAP leader 1943).

In 1945 Menzies replaced the UAP with the Australian Liberal Party, and served as prime minister 1949–66. Fundamentally conservative, he admired the British

Empire and monarchy, while also working with the USA to oppose communism. He supported British intervention in Egypt (*see* SUEZ CRISIS), and began Australia's involvement in the Vietnam War (from 1962). He received two knighthoods (Scottish 1963, Australian 1976).

MERCANTILISM Term used from the mid 18th century to characterize the economic policies of governments in Europe in the 16th–19th centuries. They sought to increase national wealth by encouraging the inflow of bullion through promotion of exports. Practices also included restrictions affecting importing and shipping. The English government strongly promoted mercantilist policies from the 1620s (e.g., NAVIGATION ACTS; CORN LAWS). Mercantilism was criticized by Adam SMITH (1723–90). *See also* ECONOMY, STATE INVOLVEMENT, BRITAIN; FREE TRADE.

MERCHANT ADVENTURERS *see* OVERSEAS TRADING COMPANIES

MERCIA A Germanic-ruled kingdom (6th–10th centuries), which expanded across Midland England from the N Midlands (modern Staffordshire, around Tamworth). 'Mercians' means 'border people', i.e., people living near the W Britons (Welsh).

During the 7th century Mercian kings exercised authority over adjacent smaller kingdoms and peoples (e.g., MAGONSÆTE, HWICCE, MIDDLE ANGLES), and sought dominance beyond (*see* TRIBAL HIDAGE). They clashed with DEIRA and BERNICIA (*see* PENDA, WULFHERE). During Wulfhere's reign (658–75) Christianity became widespread (669, see established at Lichfield).

During the 8th century Mercia absorbed subordinate kingdoms and expanded beyond them, making it the dominant Anglo-Saxon kingdom. King ÆTHELBALD (ruled 716–57) probably integrated the Magonsæte and Middle Angles, and annexed LONDON and adjoining lands. OFFA (757–96) added KENT, SUSSEX and part of WESSEX (land in Thames Valley). CENWULF sustained their gains (796–821).

In 826 Wessex seized Mercian territories in S and SE England (*see* EGBERT), and in 874 VIKINGS conquered eastern Mercia. Æthelred ruled western Mercia 883–911, but in subordination to ALFRED, king of Wessex. (Wessex sources described Æthelred as an EALDORMAN rather than king.) Æthelred's marriage to Alfred's daughter ÆTHELFLÆD (886 or 887) strengthened the alliance. After Æthelred's death, Æthelflæd ruled as 'Lady of the Mercians' (d. June 918). Her successor, Ælfwynn (daughter), was deposed by King EDWARD THE ELDER (Dec.) who annexed Mercia to Wessex. *See also* KINGSHIP, ANGLO-SAXON.

MERCILESS PARLIAMENT Name given to the English PARLIAMENT of Feb. 1388, held at WESTMINSTER, which asserted judicial authority against King RICHARD II. Influenced by the APPELLANTS, it convicted five of Richard's 'friends' of TREASON (two were executed); impeached other royal supporters; and banished judges who had recently affirmed Richard's powers to Ireland. Richard was placed under the guidance of a new Council. *See also* IMPEACHMENT.

MERFYN FRYCH, 'THE FRECKLED' (fl. from *c.*800; d. 844). King of GWYNEDD (NW Wales) 825–44. Although possibly from the Isle of Man, Merfyn acquired the kingship of Gwynedd and was the ancestor of later kings through his son RHODRI MAWR. Merfyn apparently encouraged Latin learning at his court; *see* NENNIUS.

MERTHYR RISING An insurrection from 2 June 1831, when armed ironworkers and supporters took control of MERTHYR TYDFIL, S Wales. It was caused by wage cuts at the Cyfarthfa ironworks, the behaviour of the local debtors' court, and fear that PARLIAMENTARY REFORM would fail. About 20 protesters were shot dead by soldiers (3 June). The movement collapsed on 6 June. One leader, miner Richard Lewis (known as Dic Penderyn), was afterwards hanged.

MERTHYR TYDFIL A town in S Wales; centre of Merthyr Tydfil unitary authority (Welsh, Merthyr Tudful, meaning 'Shrine of Tudful').

Until the late 18th century, Merthyr parish was thinly populated. Its area was rich in ironstone and coal. Between 1759 and 1782 four ironworks were established, which smelted iron with coke (derived from local coal), a process pioneered by Abraham DARBY. By the 1830s Merthyr, under its 'iron kings' (*see* BACON, ANTHONY; CRAWSHAY FAMILY; GUEST FAMILY), had become the world's chief iron-making centre (famous for railway rails). Population reached almost 81,000 in 1911. Merthyr was radical in politics, electing such MPs such as Henry RICHARD and Keir HARDIE (*see also* MERTHYR RISING).

Iron and steel making declined from 1918 (most had gone by the 1930s); coal mining declined from the 1920s. The resulting hardship encouraged emigration (strong in the 1930s). By 1990 population had fallen to 39,000. Light manufacturing (electrical industries, washing machines) developed from 1945 onwards. By 2016 the population had increased to 59,800.

Merthyr was successively in Glamorgan (until 1974) and the county of Mid Glamorgan (to 1996); it then became the centre of Merthyr Tydfil unitary authority (*see* LOCAL GOVERNMENTAL STRUCTURES, WALES).

MESOLITHIC PERIOD, BRITAIN Literally the 'Middle Stone Age', the period *c.*8500– *c.*4300 BC (following the PALAEOLITHIC PERIOD). Dispersed populations of gatherers and hunters practised cycles of movement and settlement as part of a seasonal round. Human activity in the period is commonly recognized by the presence of microliths (small stone tools), harpoons of bone and antler, or features such as shell middens, hearths and stake holes. Pollen evidence suggests that the scale of woodland management increased after *c*.6000 BC. *See also* GATHERING AND HUNTING.

MESOLITHIC PERIOD, IRELAND The 'Middle Stone Age', from *c*.8000 to *c*.3800 BC, the earliest period of Irish PREHISTORY. Flint and chert implements provide the main evidence. In the early Mesolithic (to *c*.5500 BC) there was a microlithic industry (producing, e.g., arrowheads, small knives). In the later Mesolithic the focus was the production of large flakes with hard hammers. Settlement and subsistence centred on the use of low-lying wetland areas for gathering and fishing. The Mesolithic was followed by the NEOLITHIC. *See also* GATHERING AND HUNTING.

METAL WORKING, PREHISTORIC BRITAIN Gold and copper working started in Britain in the late 3rd millennium BC with beaten sheet ornaments, and axes cast in open moulds. In the Early BRONZE AGE (*c*.2300–*c*.1600 BC) bivalve moulds appeared, and copper was regularly alloyed with tin to make bronze; core casting to make hollow implements started *c*.1500 BC. Copper mines occur at Great Orme (Clwyd, NW Wales). In the IRON AGE (*c*.700 BC–AD 43) *cire perdue* (lost wax) casting was used for horse trappings, and beaten metalwork culminated in La Tène-style masterpieces such as the Battersea Shield (British Museum, London, England). Iron working was introduced *c*.700 BC, initially for weapons and tools.

METAL WORKING, PREHISTORIC IRELAND Copper mining occurs at Ross Island, Co. Kerry in the period *c*.2400–*c*.2200 BC and slightly later at Mount Gabriel, Co. Cork (both in SW Ireland), i.e., during the CHALCOLITHIC PERIOD (*c*.2500–*c*.2000 BC). Metal axes were used on a wooden trackway in Corlea bog, Co. Longford (C Ireland), dated to *c*.2260 BC. From *c*.2000 BC (i.e., in the Early BRONZE AGE), increasing numbers of copper and bronze objects were being cast in stone open moulds (later in bivalve moulds). Sheet gold working also begins at this time. Major developments in bronze and gold working took place after 1000 BC with clay moulds now the norm for casting bronze. The beginnings of iron working probably date to *c*.700 BC.

METHODISM The most important 18th-century British EVANGELICAL MOVEMENT. Following evangelical conversions in the 1730s, the Church of ENGLAND clergymen

John WESLEY and George WHITEFIELD began itinerant preaching, urging conversion and holy living, and seeking to reinvigorate the Church. (Their 'Holy Club' at OXFORD had been nicknamed 'Methodists'. Wesley was ARMINIAN in outlook, Whitefield a CALVINIST.) Despite hostility from other clergymen and JUSTICES OF THE PEACE, Methodism flourished in rural areas where the Church of England's hold was shaky, in mining districts, among industrial outworkers, and later among factory workers in industrial towns. Many women were converted. John Wesley and later leaders (e.g., Jabez Bunting, 1779–1858) were hostile to political radicalism and aspects of popular culture: Methodism encouraged self-discipline, hard work and sobriety. It became strong in Wales (*see* METHODIST REVIVAL, WALES), and Methodists evangelized in Ireland (*c*.1800, 23% of Wesleyans in the British Isles were Irish).

After John Wesley's death (1791), English Wesleyan Methodists drifted from the Church of England. They had an efficient, hierarchical organization (Conference at the head, districts and circuits, societies), though fragmentation occurred, notably with the New Connexion (1797), Primitive Methodists (1807) and Wesleyan Reformers (1849). Yet Methodism continued to expand. Methodists sought converts in poor districts of 19th-century cities, endeavouring to improve their characters and circumstances, and in the BRITISH EMPIRE. About 22,000 Wesleyan members existed in England in 1767, 135,000 in 1811, and 273,000 in 1836. Total membership of English Methodist churches in 1836 was 364,000 (with 'hearers' probably three times more numerous), and in 1914 about 778,000. A broad union was created in Great Britain in 1932.

During the 20th century membership and attendances declined, to 500,000 members in Britain in 1990, 200,000 in 2013 (and 14,000 members in the autonomous Methodist Church in Ireland). A proposed union with the Church of England failed in 1972. *See also* SOPER, DONALD.

METHODIST REVIVAL, WALES An EVANGELICAL MOVEMENT within Welsh areas of the Church of England. It developed from the spiritual awakenings of Howel HARRIS, Daniel ROWLAND and William WILLIAMS in 1735–8, who made preaching tours exhorting Christians to feel and display an awareness of Christ's sacrifice. From 1737 Harris and Rowland formed local societies (Welsh *seiadau*), led by lay 'exhorters', which from 1742 were supervised by a Welsh Association (*Sasiwn*). After a meeting of Welsh and English leaders in 1743 Welsh Methodist theology was Calvinistic (*see* CALVINISM).

Methodism expanded from its base in S Wales through the N from the 1780s (*see* CHARLES, THOMAS). In 1811 Thomas ordained Methodist ministers, inaugurating a separate Church of CALVINISTIC METHODISTS. *See also* ELIAS, JOHN; NONCONFORMITY AND DISSENT, WALES.

MIDDLE ANGLES About 20 Germanic groups, each probably with its own ruler, who lived (alongside Brittonic-speaking people) in the E and S Midlands in the 7th and 8th centuries (possibly extending S to the R. Thames). The adjacent stronger kingdoms of MERCIA and EAST ANGLIA competed for dominance over the Middle Angles. King PENDA of Mercia possibly tried to unify them by imposing his son Peada as king (c.653). (Peada accepted Christianity and encouraged missionary activity.) The Middle Angles were probably absorbed into Mercia by King OFFA (ruled 757–96). *See also* KINGSHIP, ANGLO-SAXON.

MIDDLETON, JOHN (b. c.1608, probably at Caldhame, E Scotland; d. June 1674 at Tangier, aged about 66). A mercenary soldier, Middleton returned to Scotland from overseas service in 1639 to fight for the COVENANTERS; in 1645 he contributed to the defeat of the marquis of MONTROSE at Philiphaugh.

In 1648 Middleton became a Royalist and supporter of the ENGAGEMENT; he fought (in England) at Preston for King CHARLES I (1648) and at WORCESTER (1651) for CHARLES II, where he was captured. He escaped to France. In 1653 he returned to Scotland and helped to lead the unsuccessful GLENCAIRN RISING (1653–4), returning afterwards to France (created earl of Middleton 1656).

After the RESTORATION (1660) Middleton was KING'S COMMISSIONER to Scotland (1660–3). He restored episcopacy and private patronage to the Church of SCOTLAND, resulting in the removal of 270 dissenting parish ministers and the growth of CONVENTICLES. He lost his position because of enmity with LAUDERDALE (based in England) and was appointed governor of TANGIER (English colony in NW Africa). *See also* CIVIL WARS, SCOTTISH PARTICIPATION.

MIDLOTHIAN CAMPAIGN A speaking tour undertaken by British Liberal politician W.E. GLADSTONE in Nov.–Dec. 1879. He travelled from LIVERPOOL (NW England) to Midlothian (SE Scotland), his prospective constituency, denouncing the foreign policies of the prime minister, Benjamin DISRAELI.

The campaign was the first major example of public political campaigning. Gladstone made a similar tour before the 1880 general election. Thereafter public campaigning became common practice.

MILITARY SERVICE, ENGLAND BEFORE 1066 The central fighting force in early Anglo-Saxon kingdoms (5th–8th centuries) was the king's hearthtroop (or warband, or retinue; Latin *comitatus*), which included royal kin and other nobles. Other freemen were sometimes expected to serve. Kings rewarded successful combatants with land and gifts. Powerful kings also used armies from subordinate kingdoms.

As kingdoms grew (8th–9th centuries) arrangements became formalized. Estates were assessed (in HIDES) and provided men accordingly (typically one freeman for five hides). The OE term for an army or other military force was *fyrd*.

In WESSEX (from 8th century) and Wessex-conquered England (late 10th–11th centuries) armies were raised from each SHIRE and commanded by EALDORMEN and thegns. Combatants sometimes included bishops and abbots. Armies travelled on horseback but usually fought on foot. *See also* THREE PUBLIC SERVICES; HOUSECARL; NAVAL FORCES, ENGLAND BEFORE LATE 11TH CENTURY; MILITIAS, ENGLAND AND WALES.

MILITARY SERVICE, ENGLAND 1066 TO MID 17TH CENTURY After the NORMAN CONQUEST (1066–70s) kings used four types of forces: (a) household troops (KNIGHTS and other men based in the ROYAL HOUSEHOLD); (b) 'feudal' forces, i.e., EARLS, BARONS and knights who owed service for landholdings; (c) other freemen (successors to the Anglo-Saxon *fyrd*), summoned within each SHIRE; (d) hired forces (mercenaries), often from overseas.

In 1166 about 5000 landed knights each owed 40 days' service (or were charged SCUTAGE, payment for avoidance of service). Their number declined from the late 12th century. The last 'feudal summons' was made in 1327. From the late 13th century kings had also contracted with magnates to provide forces drawn from followers and tenants (called 'quasi-feudal' forces by historians; *see* BASTARD FEUDALISM). Serving for wages, such forces remained important into the 17th century.

Meanwhile the obligation of service by ordinary freemen was maintained. The Assize of Arms (1181) altered its basis from land to wealth, specifying the arms men should keep (redefined 1285 by Statute of Winchester). Kings drew on these forces when they assembled large armies (e.g., for the wars of King EDWARD I). Men were paid by the Crown from the point of muster onwards.

In the 16th century the government increased the role of shire forces (now called the 'militia'); in 1558 it repealed the provisions of 1181 and 1285 and required most men (aged 16–60) to attend musters, keep arms and serve. From 1573 small units met more regularly and used firearms (called 'trained bands' from the 1590s). The effectiveness of shire forces declined in the early 17th century. When Civil War broke out in 1642 new forces had to be created. *See also* SOCIAL STRUCTURE, ENGLAND 1066 TO 16TH CENTURY; MILITIAS, ENGLAND; NEW MODEL ARMY; ARMY, ENGLISH AND BRITISH.

MILITARY SERVICE, IRELAND BEFORE 17TH CENTURY In the 5th–10th centuries a Gaelic king's only permanent military force was a small, hired bodyguard. If he needed to repel invaders, display his strength, or invade another territory, he could by custom summon a mounted warband of free clients or larger forces consisting of men of varying social status.

VIKINGS in the 9th–10th centuries had to be countered with larger armies. Payment was introduced, often as plunder. In the 10th–12th centuries leading kings who operated over large areas raised forces by contracting with their important followers to provide men. Soldiers received wages and might be billeted on local populations. During the 13th century this system was replaced by hiring of GAL-LOGLASSES – Scottish mercenaries who were retained on a permanent basis and billeted upon native populations (so-called 'coyne').

After the Anglo-Norman invasion (1169–70), the CHIEF GOVERNOR was protected by hired soldiers and could summon extra troops based on 'knight service', the practice whereby lay magnates were required to provide KNIGHTS. Lords settled followers on lands ('knights' fees') to meet obligations and also provide retinues for their own use. They also hired Gaelic infantry known as KERNS.

By the late 13th century, the division of fees between heiresses weakened knight service. Governors relied more on hired forces or troops from England. In the 13th–16th centuries, as the strength of central government declined and warfare with Gaelic chiefs increased, Anglo-Irish lords retained troops by indenture (*see* BASTARD FEUDALISM) and imitated Gaelic chiefs by imposing coyne on rural populations to support kerns. *See also* KINGSHIP, IRELAND.

MILITARY SERVICE, SCOTLAND BEFORE 18TH CENTURY In the 12th–17th centuries Scotland relied for defence on a 'common army' raised from dependants and tenants by noblemen and sheriffs. All able-bodied men between 16 and 60 were liable for 40 days of unpaid service per year.

Between 1638 and 1651 the Covenanting regime organized an efficient national conscript army with quotas of men raised from each parish. After 1660 (*see* RESTORATION, SCOTLAND) the Crown maintained a small standing army, mainly for garrison and police duties against western COVENANTERS. Some regiments established then (e.g., Cameronians, Royal Scots, Scots Guards) were later incorporated in the British ARMY.

MILITARY SERVICE, WALES 5TH–13TH CENTURIES From possibly the 5th to the 13th centuries the primary institution was the ruler's retinue or *teulu* (Welsh, meaning 'family'), composed of selected young warriors, maintained and given horses by the ruler. Its commander was the *penteulu* ('head of the *teulu*'), a close kinsman of the ruler. All freemen (over 14) also owed service as foot-soldiers, for six weeks annually outside the kingdom and indefinitely within.

The system served well for raids into neighbouring kingdoms. But by the mid 13th century rulers, needing to mount large-scale campaigns, introduced armoured knights and longer service. After the English Conquest of 1282–3, some freemen raised contingents of soldiers for English kings. *See also* KINGSHIP, WALES 5TH–13TH CENTURIES.

MILITIA ACT, 1852 Legislation which re-established part-time military forces within England and Wales, provoked by fear of French power. It provided for 80,000 troops to be raised by voluntary enlistment, to serve for five years. Forces were commanded by lord lieutenants until 1881 when they were associated with regular forces. The militia continued until 1908. *See also* ARMY, ENGLISH AND BRITISH.

MILITIA ISSUE, SCOTLAND The new provisions for compulsory militia service introduced only in England and Wales from 1757 caused offence in Scotland, which lacked a militia. Scots presumed they were tainted by the JACOBITE REBELLION of 1745 and considered unreliable. Campaigning followed (until the 1780s), but was unsuccessful. (Landed gentlemen saw militia service as a way of restoring their social position in an increasingly commercialized world.)

A militia, conscripted by ballot, was founded by the Militia Act of 1797, to provide defence during the NAPOLEONIC WARS. Its provision for overseas service and exemptions for wealthy people provoked widespread rioting. *See also* MILITIAS, ENGLAND AND WALES.

MILITIA ORDINANCE In England, legislation passed by the LONG PARLIAMENT on 5 March 1642, despite its rejection by King CHARLES I. It provided for Parliament to nominate LORD LIEUTENANTS and thereby control county MILITIAS. John PYM had sought the measure since autumn 1641 to prevent CHARLES I mobilizing armed force against parliamentary opponents. Though not considered an Act, Parliament insisted that it had the force of law. It provided a precedent for future parliamentary ordinances. *See also* CIVIL WARS; NINETEEN PROPOSITIONS.

MILITIAS, ENGLAND AND WALES 'Militias' are forces of temporary, non-professional soldiers, either 'official' or voluntary. From possibly the 5th century, freemen sometimes reinforced mounted warbands in Anglo-Saxon kingdoms; from the 8th century, starting in WESSEX, contingents were organized by (large) SHIRE. Participation in shire- (or county-) based musters remained an important type of obligatory MILITARY SERVICE, managed by SHERIFFS; required arms were specified by legislation (1181, 1285), though in the 13th–17th centuries rulers often used retinues raised by noblemen (*see* BASTARD FEUDALISM).

County forces were revived for home defence in the 16th century (e.g., musters in 1522, from 1539). Legislation in 1558 obliged men to hold up-to-date weapons, and from 1573 county authorities were instructed to employ professional soldiers as muster-captains to teach modern techniques to small groups (called 'trained bands' from 1590s). Thereafter musters were restricted to trained men. Bands were re-equipped with muskets and pikes in 1625–9.

From 1539 musters were sometimes raised by temporary 'lieutenants'; from 1585 LORD LIEUTENANTS were consistently appointed in counties to maintain their militias. Musters also now took place in Wales. In March 1642 Parliament seized control of militias from Charles I (*see* MILITIA ORDINANCE), though during the CIVIL WARS (1642–6, 1648) and 1650s militia forces were less important than paid armies (except in London).

The militia was re-established following the RESTORATION (by statutes, 1660–3), and bands were abolished except in London. Now overshadowed by a standing ARMY, militia activity declined in the 18th century. It was revived in 1757–9 (during the SEVEN YEARS WAR) with able-bodied men aged 18–50 being selected by ballot for 20 days of annual service for three years.

The militia declined after 1815; from 1852, service was voluntary. It was treated as a manpower reservoir for recruitment to regular forces from the 1880s, and abolished in 1908 (*see* HALDANE, R.B.).

MILITIAS, IRELAND Voluntary and official militias were formed from the early 17th century for defence and political purposes. Unofficial militias operated in ULSTER (N Ireland) in the early 17th century. The government authorized official militias 1666–85 and 1690s–1760s (the latter exclusively Protestant). Organized under county governors, arrays were infrequent (usually in times of danger) and hampered by shortage of arms. A voluntary militia founded in 1778 agitated for removal of restrictions on trade and the Irish Parliament (*see* VOLUNTEERS). Suppressed in 1793, it was immediately replaced with an official militia which helped to suppress the RISING OF 1798 and continued to 1834.

During the 19th century the government developed POLICE to maintain order. Unofficial militias were created in 1913 to oppose and advance HOME RULE, respectively the ULSTER VOLUNTEER FORCE (UVF) and IRISH VOLUNTEERS. Many UVF men joined the ULSTER SPECIAL CONSTABULARY (founded 1920). The Irish Volunteers split in 1914 with a minority retaining the name, participating in the EASTER RISING (1916), and later joining the IRISH REPUBLICAN ARMY. The DEFENCE FORCES of southern Ireland claim descent from the Irish Volunteers. *See also* ARMY, ENGLISH AND BRITISH, IN IRELAND, LATE 17TH–18TH CENTURIES.

MILL, J.S. (b. 20 May 1806 at London, England; d. 8 May 1873 at Avignon, France, aged 66). John Stuart Mill was educated intensively by his father James Mill (1773–1836), a follower of Jeremy BENTHAM and PHILOSOPHIC RADICAL. J.S. Mill worked for the East India Company 1823–58, becoming its administrative head, and served as an MP 1865–8. An essayist from the 1820s, he established a formidable reputation as a philosopher with his *System of Logic* (1843) and *Principles of Political Economy* (1848), which was consolidated by his classic defence of LIBERALISM, *On Liberty* (1859). Mill's relationship with Mrs Harriet Taylor, whom he married in 1851, influenced him towards women's concerns and SOCIALISM (she died in 1858). In 1867 Mill was co-founder of the first WOMEN'S SUFFRAGE society. He also published *The Subjection of Women* (1869). *See also* UTILITARIANISM.

MILLENARY PETITION *see* HAMPTON COURT CONFERENCE

MILLER, HUGH (b. 10 Oct. 1802 at Cromarty, Cromartyshire, Scotland; d. 23 Dec. 1856 at Edinburgh, Scotland, aged 54). A journeyman mason from 1822 and published poet from 1829, Miller combined a religious temperament with interest in science, especially geology. From 1840 (until 1854) he edited the periodical *Witness*, building up opposition to private patronage in the Church of SCOTLAND which led to the DISRUPTION of 1843. In his scientific writings Miller attempted to reconcile fossil evidence with the Bible's Creation story. He died from suicide, caused by depression.

MILNER, ALFRED (b. 23 March 1854 at Giessen, Duchy of Hesse, Germany; d. 13 May 1925 at Sturry Court, Kent, England, aged 71). British imperialist. A public servant (knighted 1895), Milner served as governor of CAPE COLONY (1897–1901) and British high commissioner in S Africa (1897–1905). His assertion of British supremacy, supported by Joseph CHAMBERLAIN, resulted in the (Second) BOER WAR against the Boer-dominated Transvaal (or South African Republic) and Orange Free State (1899–1902). Milner was created Lord Milner (1901) and Viscount Milner (1902).

After the war, as governor of the defeated countries, Milner promoted economic expansion, though his importation of Chinese workers for gold mines aroused opposition in Britain. His attempt to promote British cultural domination through immigration and education largely failed. He resigned in 1905. Milner later served in the WAR CABINET of David LLOYD GEORGE (1916–18) and as colonial secretary (1918–21). *See also* SOUTH AFRICA; AMERY, LEOPOLD.

MILTON, JOHN (b. 9 Dec. 1608 at London, England; d. 9 or 10 Nov. 1674 at London, aged 65). A scrivener's son, educated at CAMBRIDGE University (1625–32), Milton became a poet. During the political troubles of the 1640s he supported Parliament (*see* CIVIL WARS, POLITICAL ASPECTS), publishing tracts against episcopacy (1641–2) and censorship (*Areopagitica*, 1644). A difficult marriage led him to write pamphlets advocating divorce (1643–5). His poetry was published from 1646.

Following the execution of King CHARLES I, Milton served the Council of State as Latin secretary (1649–60), supporting the COMMONWEALTH with polemical works (e.g., *A Defence of the People of England*, in Latin, 1649). By 1652 he was blind. After the RESTORATION (1660) he published the epic Christian poem *Paradise Lost* (1667) and other works. *See also* ENGLISH LITERATURE, ENGLAND.

MILTON, LORD (b. probably in 1692 in Scotland; d. 15 Dec. 1766 at Brunstane, Haddingtonshire, Scotland, aged 74). A nephew of Andrew FLETCHER of Saltoun, Andrew Fletcher became an advocate (1717). In 1724, aged 32, he was made a lord of SESSION (titled Lord Milton). He also served as lord justice clerk (1735–48) and presided at the trial of Captain Porteous (*see* PORTEOUS AFFAIR). As agent to the earl of ISLAY, Milton advised on the dispensation of government patronage in Scotland, making him a powerful figure (1735 until Islay's death). After the JACOBITE REBELLION of 1745 Milton was lenient to Jacobites, and worked to promote trade and agriculture.

MINERS' STRIKE, 1984–5 In Great Britain, a bitter year-long strike over the future of the COAL INDUSTRY. In March 1984 the National Union of Mineworkers called strikes in protest at the proposed closure of 'uneconomic' coalmines. By 12 March miners at 100 pits had responded. The NUM leader, Arthur SCARGILL, refused to hold a national strike ballot and organized picketing of some 20 pits still working (mainly in Nottinghamshire).

Violent clashes occurred between miners and police, notably at the Orgreave coking works in Yorkshire (May–June, so-called 'battle of Orgreave'). But stockpiles of coal allowed power stations to continue operating. Miners drifted back to work, and the strike ended without settlement on 4 March 1985, after the loss of 26.1 million working days. The government of Margaret THATCHER was perceived as having defeated militant trade unionism. The miners' action facilitated a faster contraction of the coal industry. *See also* MINERS' UNIONS.

MINERS' STRIKE AND ENERGY CRISIS, 1973–4 From late 1973 international and domestic problems caused disruption in Great Britain. After Egypt and Syria attacked Israel (6 Oct.), Arab states reduced oil production (from 17 Oct.); prices quadrupled. In Britain the National Union of Mineworkers demanded a pay rise outside the Conservative government's INCOMES POLICY. It began an over-time ban (12 Nov.) and rejected any settlement within government policy (21 Nov.).

On 13 Dec. the prime minister, Edward HEATH, ordered industry to work a three-day week to counter energy shortages (ran 1 Jan.–9 March 1974), and on 7 Feb. he called an election, asking 'Who Governs Britain?' Miners went on strike from 10 Feb. Heath lost the election (28 Feb.); the coalminers won their dispute (11 March). *See also* MINERS' UNIONS.

MINERS' UNIONS Few workers' organizations were formed in the scattered COAL INDUSTRIES of Britain and Ireland before the 1800s–30s when combinations were briefly created (e.g., 'Hepburn Union' in Northumberland and Co. Durham, 1836). As mining expanded in N England in the 1840s, county unions and (in 1842) the Miners' Federation of Great Britain and Ireland were started. But a four-month strike in Northumberland and Co. Durham (1844) failed and the Federation collapsed (1848).

The institution of elected, paid checkweighmen at collieries (by 1860 Mines Act) facilitated union growth. Alexander Macdonald formed the National Miners' Association (1863), while militant critics founded two short-lived breakaways, notably the Amalgamated Association of Miners (1869), based mainly on Lancashire, W Midlands and S Wales. The latter collapsed after a strike (1875), having stimulated unionization in S Wales (*see* MABON). The NMA ceased in 1889.

Activism in the 1880s produced the powerful Miners' Federation of Great Britain (1888). Based initially on Yorkshire, Lancashire and the Midlands, it contributed to 'Lib-Lab' politics and affiliated to the LABOUR PARTY (1909). Its national strike for minimum wages in 1912 (Feb.–April) won concessions and demonstrated disruptive capacity. Worse was threatened by the TRIPLE ALLIANCE of 1914. But owners' lockouts (1921, 1926, the latter precipitating a GENERAL STRIKE) imposed reduced terms, and a moderate union was formed in Nottinghamshire ('Spencer Union', 1926–37).

The Federation was renamed the National Union of Mineworkers in 1945 (industry nationalized 1947). National strikes in 1972 and 1974 won concessions, but a strike against pit closures (1984–5) was weakened by formation of the Union of Democratic Mineworkers (Nottinghamshire) in response to lack of a pre-strike ballot. The industry and union membership shrank drastically in the 1980s–90s. *See also* MINERS' STRIKE AND ENERGY CRISIS, 1973–4; MINERS' STRIKE, 1984–5.

MINORCA One of the Balearic Islands in the W Mediterranean, which was British territory in the 18th century. Captured from Spain in 1708, during the War of the SPANISH SUCCESSION, it was awarded to Great Britain in 1713. As a naval base it proved hard to defend. It was lost to France 1756–63, and to Spain 1782–98. Minorca reverted to SPAIN under the treaty of AMIENS (1802). *See also* BYNG, JOHN.

MINORITIES, ROYAL In England, minors could become king effectively from the 10th century when kings were chosen from sons or grandsons rather than a larger kindred (*see* ÆTHELING). Minorities occurred occasionally from the accession of EDWARD THE MARTYR (975) to that of EDWARD VI (1547).

There was no customary arrangement for a minority or a definite age of majority, though a council often exercised authority and the king was entrusted to a guardian. Guardians (e.g., Hubert de BURGH; Edward, duke of SOMERSET) could exploit their position. Richard, duke of Gloucester, deposed EDWARD V. The longest minorities were those of HENRY III and HENRY VI.

In Scotland, kings tried to restrict succession to a single line of descendants from the mid 11th century. Minorities were frequent from the mid 13th century (*see* ALEXANDER III). In 1290 the succession was disputed (*see* GREAT CAUSE). From JAMES I (king from 1406), each new ruler was a minor. As in England there was no fixed arrangement for a minority, but groups of guardians were often appointed. Factions headed by magnates often fought for power, which usually involved taking possession of the ruler. *See also* KINGSHIP AND MONARCHY, ENGLAND 1066 TO 1680s; KINGSHIP, SCOTTISH.

MINSTER Term used for any church in Anglo-Saxon England (from the late 6th century) with a community of priests, monks or nuns (OE *mynster* is derived from Latin *monasterium*, meaning 'monastery'). Minster communities might serve large 'minster parishes' containing several settlements. The authority of minsters declined in the 11th century as lords established churches on estates within minster territories. *See also* CONVERSION OF ANGLO-SAXONS; PARISH SYSTEM, ENGLAND, FORMATION OF; TOWNS, ENGLAND.

MISSIONARY SOCIETIES, ENGLAND AND GREAT BRITAIN The SOCIETY FOR PROMOTING CHRISTIAN KNOWLEDGE (founded 1699) and SOCIETY FOR THE PROPAGATION OF THE GOSPEL (1701), started by Church of ENGLAND clergy and laity, undertook overseas missionary work in the 18th century, the former in S India, the latter in N America.

Overseas exploration, imperial expansion and EVANGELICALISM stimulated the foundation of more societies in Great Britain from the later 18th century, starting (1792) with what became the Baptist Missionary Society. Others included London Missionary Society (Congregationalist, 1795), Scottish Society and Glasgow Society for Foreign Missions (both Church of Scotland and Secession Church, 1796), Society for Missions to Africa and the East (Church of England, evangelical, 1799), Wesleyan Methodist Missionary Society (1818). They organized a limited amount of overseas work, mainly by lay people rather than ordained clergy.

More societies were started in the mid 19th century, including the Mission to Central Africa (Church of England, 1857) and China Inland Mission (interdenominational, 1865). By 1916 there were 7500 British Protestant missionaries abroad. The societies established Protestant Christianity in Asia and Africa, although problems arose over the extent to which missionaries should retain control over new churches. Missionary activity declined markedly from the 1940s. *See also* ANGLICAN COMMUNION.

MISSIONS TO CONTINENTAL EUROPE, ANGLO-SAXON In the late 7th and 8th centuries English monks and nuns worked as missionaries in Continental Europe, especially in Frisia (modern Netherlands) and eastern Francia (modern Germany and Austria). Sustained work in Frisia was started by Wihtberht (late 680s). The most important figures were WILLIBRORD (d. 739) from NORTHUMBRIA and BONIFACE (d. 754) from WESSEX, who both founded monasteries and churches under the patronage of Frankish kings. They also created or reorganized dioceses under papal authority. Nuns (e.g., LEOBA) made a major contribution to evangelization. Later missionaries included Willibald (d. 787) and Willehad (d. 789). Boniface's letters reveal strong English interest in missionary work.

MISSIONS TO CONTINENTAL EUROPE, IRISH *see* SELF-EXILE FROM IRELAND, 6TH–8TH CENTURIES

MITCHEL, JOHN (b. 3 Nov. 1815 near Dungiven, Co. Londonderry, Ireland; d. 20 March 1875 near Newry, Co. Down, Ireland, aged 59). A (presbyterian) lawyer, Mitchel worked for *The Nation* newspaper from 1845 (*see* YOUNG IRELAND MOVEMENT). Radicalized by the GREAT FAMINE, he resigned (Dec. 1847) and published *The United Irishman* (from 12 Feb. 1848), advocating revolution and a republic. He was arrested, convicted and transported (May), eventually to VAN DIEMAN'S LAND (1850). In 1853 Mitchel escaped to the USA. In Feb. 1875 he was elected MP for Co. Tipperary and returned to Ireland. He died soon afterwards, while contesting disqualification.

MOFFAT, ROBERT (b. 21 Dec. 1795 at Ormiston, Haddingtonshire, Scotland; d. 8 Aug. 1883 at Leigh, Kent, England, aged 87). Scottish missionary. Moffat was sent to

S Africa in 1816 by the London Missionary Society. In 1824 he established a pioneering inland mission station at Kuruman (modern South Africa), from which David LIVINGSTONE advanced northwards in 1841. Moffat returned to England in 1870, having translated the Bible into the local Tswana language. *See also* MISSIONARY SOCIETIES, ENGLAND AND GREAT BRITAIN.

MONASTICISM, MEDIEVAL ENGLAND Germanic kingdoms were converted to Christianity by monks with Continental or Irish backgrounds (*see* CONVERSION OF ANGLO-SAXONS). Monastic communities became widespread in the 7th–8th centuries, following rules compiled by their founders, though St Benedict's rule (*c*.540) was influential (*see* MINSTER). They included 'double houses', i.e., associated communities of men and women (*see* HILD). Outstanding intellectual and artistic activity occurred (*see* BENEDICT BISCOP; BEDE).

Monasticism declined from the late 8th century. Communities were often replaced by secular clergy, and VIKINGS destroyed some monasteries (late 8th–9th centuries). It was revived in the 10th century, based on St Benedict's rule (*see* TENTH-CENTURY REFORMATION). In 1066 there were 35 houses for men and nine for women, mostly in southern counties. After the Norman invasion (1066), Normans replaced English abbots and Norman lords founded more Benedictine houses. Many were subordinate to overseas houses, including 35 'Cluniac' Benedictine houses founded from 1077 (*see* ALIEN PRIORIES). From 1072–3 monasticism was reintroduced in NE England.

In the 12th century, kings and lords founded numerous new houses, mostly belonging to Continental orders. They included communities of Augustinian canons from *c*.1100 (eventually about 200); 'Savigniac' Benedictines from 1124 (11 houses); Cistercians from 1128 (about 64 houses, including Savigniacs from 1147); Premonstratensian canons from 1143 (45 houses); a Carthusian house (or 'Charterhouse') in 1178. New nunneries included about 70 Benedictine houses and from the 1130s Cistercian houses (about 25). The Englishman Gilbert of Sempringham founded women's communities from 1139 and also 'double houses'. In 1300 there were over 800 houses containing about 14,000 religious men and 3000 women.

The only major later developments were the foundation of seven Charterhouses (1340–1414) and Syon Abbey for Birgittine (or Bridgettine) nuns (1415). Alien priories were suppressed by 1414 and over 30 houses dissolved in the early 16th century to fund educational colleges. Otherwise monastic life continued to flourish. *See also* RELIGIOUS ORDERS; CHURCH, MEDIEVAL ENGLAND; APPROPRIATION OF CHURCHES, ENGLAND; DISSOLUTION OF RELIGIOUS HOUSES, ENGLAND.

MONASTICISM, MEDIEVAL IRELAND Monasticism was prominent in the 5th–12th centuries. PATRICK (5th century) promoted asceticism, and many young women became nuns. From the late 5th century individuals withdrew to deserted places. Some lived as hermits while others founded communities (e.g., Íte of Kileedy, d. *c*.570; Ciarán of CLONMACNOIS; possibly BRIGIT of Kildare). Communities followed simple rules (e.g., rule of COLUMBANUS). Despite a revival promoted by CULDEES (8th–12th centuries), communities were dominated from the 8th century by lay abbots and hereditary control.

In the 12th century, as part of the broader CHURCH REFORM movement, Continental orders were introduced. Most older communities either were replaced or disappeared in the 12th–13th centuries. (Two communities of culdees allegedly survived until the 16th century.) Houses of Augustinian canons and Cistercians monks, founded from 1142, proved the most popular orders. Very few Benedictine houses were started. Monastic endowments often included revenues appropriated from secular clergy (*see* APPROPRIATION OF CHURCHES, IRELAND). In the early 16th century there were about 200 religious houses, including over 100 houses of Augustinian canons, 35 of Cistercians, and 36 nunneries. *See also* RELIGIOUS ORDERS; CHURCH, MEDIEVAL IRELAND; APPROPRIATION OF CHURCHES, IRELAND; DISSOLUTION OF RELIGIOUS HOUSES, IRELAND; MALACHY.

MONASTICISM, MEDIEVAL NORTH BRITAIN AND SCOTLAND Irish-type monasteries were founded in N Britain from the 6th century by SCOTS from Ireland, notably those connected with IONA (founded 563). From the 8th or 9th century, there were also CULDEE communities. Many monasteries were destroyed by VIKINGS in the 790s and 9th century, though some culdees survived.

From the late 11th century Irish-type foundations were superseded by European orders (with foundations continuing until 1273). Only two Benedictine houses were founded (DUNFERMLINE, probably by 1093; Coldingham, *c*.1139) compared with ten Augustinian houses (including SCONE, *c*.1115). New French orders were popular: 11 Cistercian houses were founded (including Melrose, 1136, and Sweetheart, 1273); five Tironensian; six Premonstratensian (including Whithorn); two Cluniac; and three Valliscaulian houses (13th century; only foundations outside France). The sole important later house was the Charterhouse at PERTH (1429). Cistercian houses contributed considerably to the development of Lowland sheep farming. Nunneries were few (11 by 1273) – the lowest number in Europe in relation to men's houses.

In the mid 16th century there were 55 houses of monks and regular canons and ten houses of nuns. Monks and nuns were fewer than in the 13th century, but regular life continued, until houses were attacked in 1559–60. *See also* RELIGIOUS ORDERS; CHURCH, MEDIEVAL NORTH BRITAIN AND SCOTLAND; APPROPRIATION OF CHURCHES, SCOTLAND; COMMENDATION OF ABBEYS, SCOTLAND; DISSOLUTION OF RELIGIOUS HOUSES, SCOTLAND; MARGARET; DAVID I; BALLIOL, DERVORGUILLA.

MONASTICISM, MEDIEVAL WALES Monastic organization was a basic feature of the Church in W Britain (later Wales) from the 5th century. Important churches were monastic 'mother churches' (Welsh *clasau*; singular, *clas*). Each comprised an abbot (sometimes doubling as bishop) and clergy. Communities became increasingly secular, with clergy holding property and marrying.

From the late 11th century, *clasau* were replaced as Continental religious orders were introduced into the Norman-controlled MARCH OF WALES and native Wales. Between 1070 and 1121 Normans founded 12 Benedictine priories, 11 as dependents of abbeys in England or France. (The exception, Carmarthen Priory, was dissolved *c.*1125.) Two Cluniac houses were founded in the 12th century, and three houses of Augustinian canons. Three *clasau* in GWYNEDD (NW Wales) were later reformed as houses of Augustinian canons (Bardsey, Beddgelert, Penmon). A Benedictine nunnery was founded at Usk by 1236.

Between 1130 and 1226, 13 Cistercian houses were established (e.g., STRATA FLORIDA, Tintern); six were daughters of foreign abbeys. A Cistercian nunnery was founded at Llanllyr (W Wales) *c.*1170–80. Until *c.*1300 Cistercian houses were important in transmitting Welsh literature and history. (Tironians also founded three houses and Premonstratensians two houses – all in the 12th century.)

In the 15th century, Benedictine priories linked to French abbeys became independent or were attached to English abbeys. By *c.*1500 houses were impoverished. Most were dissolved in 1536. *See also* RELIGIOUS ORDERS; CHURCH, MEDIEVAL WALES; APPROPRIATION OF CHURCHES, WALES; DISSOLUTION OF RELIGIOUS HOUSES, WALES.

MONCK, GEORGE (b. 6 Dec. 1608 at Great Potheridge, Devon, England; d. 3 Jan. 1670 at Westminster, Middlesex, England, aged 61). An English seaman and soldier (1620s–30s), Monck fought for King CHARLES I in the Wars of the COVENANT (1639–40), in Ireland (1642), and in the (First) Civil War in England (1643–4). He was imprisoned by Parliamentarians (1644–6) but then recruited by them; he served in Ireland.

In 1650 Oliver CROMWELL took Monck to Scotland and in Aug. 1651 left him to complete the country's conquest. After fighting the Dutch at sea in 1652–3, Monck returned to Scotland (early 1654) to suppress the GLENCAIRN RISING; he remained as head of government.

On 1 Jan. 1660, following the establishment of military government in England, Monck marched into England, where he oversaw the dissolution of the LONG PARLIAMENT, the election of the CONVENTION PARLIAMENT, and welcomed back King CHARLES II (25 May), who created him duke of Albemarle. Monck fought against Dutch attacks in 1666 and 1667. *See also* UNION OF ENGLAND AND SCOTLAND, 1650S; RESTORATION, ENGLAND; ANGLO-DUTCH WARS.

MONCKTON, WALTER (b. 17 Jan. 1891 at Plaxtol, Kent, England; d. 9 Jan. 1965 at Folkington, East Sussex, England, aged 73). A lawyer, Monckton advised King EDWARD VIII during the ABDICATION CRISIS (1936). As a British Conservative MP 1951–7, he was a conciliatory minister of labour (1951–5), under Winston CHURCHILL, then defence minister under Anthony EDEN. In Oct. 1956 he was transferred to the post of paymaster-general because he opposed military action in the SUEZ CRISIS. He left politics in Jan. 1957 and was created Viscount Monckton.

MOND, LUDWIG (b. 7 March 1839 at Kassel, Hesse, Germany; d. 11 Dec. 1909 at St Marylebone, London, England, aged 70). A German-Jewish chemist, Mond settled in England in 1867. After buying rights to the 'Solvay process' for making soda (1872), he and business partner John Brunner built a soda-manufacturing plant at Widnes (Cheshire). By the 1890s 'Brunner Mond' was the world's largest soda producer. Mond also improved the nickel manufacturing process and built a refinery at Clydach, S Wales (opened 1902). Mond's wealth enabled him to become a philanthropist and art collector. *See also* CHEMICALS INDUSTRY, GREAT BRITAIN; IMPERIAL CHEMICAL INDUSTRIES.

MONDAY CLUB A pressure group of right-wing British Conservatives founded on 1 Jan. 1961 in response to Harold MACMILLAN's support for African nationalism. It sought the application of TORY principles to Conservative government policy instead of expediency. Associated groups were created, attracting several thousand members. In the 1970s the club was notorious for supporting white supremacy in RHODESIA and opposing black IMMIGRATION. Its influence declined in the 1990s, and the CONSERVATIVE PARTY ended formal links in 2001 though the club remained active.

MONETARISM A school of economic thought, associated notably with US economist Milton Friedman (1912–2006), which argues that tight control of money supply should be central to public policy, particularly to combat INFLATION and stimulate economic activity. (The term was invented in 1968 by Swiss economist Karl Brunner.) Superseding INCOMES POLICIES, monetarism was influential in Great Britain from 1976 (introduction of broad money targets), and especially during the 1980s, although difficult to implement in practice. *See also* HEALEY, DENIS; THATCHER, MARGARET; ECONOMY, STATE INVOLVEMENT, BRITAIN.

MONEY BILL DISPUTE Controversy in Ireland 1753–6. Archbishop George STONE and allies sought to diminish the power of the House of Commons speaker Henry BOYLE. Boyle allowed the defeat of a government (financial) Supply Bill (17 Dec. 1753), to demonstrate his authority. Boyle and some allies were dismissed from government posts (1754), but in April 1756 Boyle made an advantageous 'peace agreement' with Ireland's new chief governor (the marquess of Hartington). During the controversy Boyle's supporters expressed PATRIOT attitudes. The incident is viewed as a weakening of British influence. *See also* PONSONBY, JOHN; PROTESTANT ASCENDANCY.

MONK, GEORGE *see* MONCK, GEORGE

MONMOUTH, DUKE OF *see* MONMOUTH'S REBELLION

MONMOUTHSHIRE A shire (or county) in SE Wales (abutting England) 1536–1974; from 1996, a unitary authority occupying the eastern part of the former county.

Formed from several lordships in the MARCH OF WALES, Monmouthshire, unlike the rest of Wales, was not subject to the COURT OF GREAT SESSIONS from 1543 but was attached to an English ASSIZE circuit. Consequently it was considered detached from Wales and was often included with England for taxation and other purposes (e.g., NATIONAL CENSUSES). It was fully recognized as part of Wales by local government reorganization in 1974, when it became the regional authority of Gwent (replaced by four unitary authorities in 1996).

Monmouthshire contained the eastern part of the S Wales coalfield and became heavily industrialized with ironworks from the mid 18th century (to mid 19th) and coalmines in the 19th century (to late 20th). *See also* GWENT; NEWPORT; CATHOLICS AND CATHOLIC CHURCH, WALES; COAL INDUSTRY, WALES.

MONMOUTH'S REBELLION In England, an attempt in 1685 to depose the new king, JAMES VII/II (formerly duke of York), led by his nephew James, duke of Monmouth (b. 1649), an illegitimate son of James's predecessor, CHARLES II. During the earlier EXCLUSION CRISIS, Monmouth had been seen as a Protestant alternative to the Catholic York (the legitimate heir), and had been involved in plots against York.

Monmouth's rebellion began on 11 June when he landed in Dorset (S England). He gathered about 3000 people, but they were routed when they attacked a royal army at Sedgemoor (Somerset) in the night of 5–6 July. Many rebels

were afterwards tried at the BLOODY ASSIZES. Monmouth was executed in London under an Act of ATTAINDER on 15 July. *See also* ARGYLL RISING.

MONS GRAUPIUS, BATTLE OF A decisive set-piece battle (according to TACITUS) between Romans and Britons (CALEDONIANS) in 83. Fought somewhere in N Britain (modern NE Scotland), it marked the successful completion of AGRICOLA's campaigns and the northern limit of Roman advance in Britain. *See also* ROMAN BRITAIN.

MONTAGU, RICHARD (b. Nov. 1575 at Dorney, Buckinghamshire, England; d. 13 April 1641 at Norwich, Norfolk, England, aged 65). A clergyman and from *c*.1615 a chaplain to King JAMES VI/I, Montagu caused an outcry in 1624 with his tract *A New Gagg for an Old Goose*. He claimed that the Church of ENGLAND (except for Puritans) did not accept Calvinist doctrines. He was alleged to be an Arminian, and complaints were made about him in Parliament in 1625–6. His appointment as bishop of Chichester by King CHARLES I in 1628 was seen as representing the advancement of popery and ARMINIANISM. Montagu later became bishop of Norwich (1638). *See also* CALVINISM.

MONTFORT, SIMON DE (b. *c*.1208 in France; d. 4 Aug. 1265 at Evesham, Worcestershire, England, aged about 57). A Frenchman, Montfort went to England (1229) where King HENRY III granted him former family lands (1231) and recognized him as earl of Leicester (1236). In 1238 he married Henry's sister Eleanor. He joined RICHARD OF CORNWALL on CRUSADE (1240–2) and fought with Henry in Poitou, France (1242). As lieutenant in unstable GASCONY from 1248, his use of force further aggravated the region and exhausted funds. Tried in England but acquitted (1252), he briefly returned to Gascony and was sent again to quell rebellion (1253–4). But relations with Henry deteriorated.

From 1258 Montfort was a leader of BARONS seeking reform of royal government. He supported the Provisions of OXFORD (1258), which restricted Henry's authority (1258–61), and negotiated with France (May 1259; *see* PARIS, TREATY OF). In 1263 Montfort briefly dominated the government (July–Nov.). In 1264 fighting broke out between reformers and royalists. On 14 May Montfort captured Henry at Lewes (Sussex), becoming effectively head of government. He rallied support with meetings of PARLIAMENT, but the barons' divisions weakened his position. From May 1265 Henry's son Edward led a royalist resurgence. His army killed Montfort in battle. *See also* BARONIAL CONFLICT AND WARS; KENILWORTH.

MONTGOMERY, BERNARD (b. 17 Nov. 1887 at London, England; d. 23 March 1976 at Isington, Hampshire,

England, aged 88). A soldier, Montgomery was appointed commander of the British Eighth Army in NE Africa in Aug. 1942, during WORLD WAR II. He defended EGYPT against German and Italian forces, then repulsed them in the first successful offensive against German forces (*see* EL ALAMEIN, (SECOND) BATTLE OF). In 1944 Montgomery commanded ground forces in the Allied invasion of France (*see* OVERLORD). He later accepted the German surrender in NW Europe (4 May 1945). Montgomery's clarity of purpose won admiration; his egoism caused difficulties. He was deputy supreme commander of NATO 1951–8. 'Monty' was knighted (1942) and created Viscount Montgomery (1946).

MONTGOMERY, TREATY OF Agreed on 29 Sept. 1267 (at Montgomery, in MARCH OF WALES); the high point of relations between LLYWELYN AP GRUFFUDD, prince of GWYNEDD (NW Wales), and HENRY III, king of England, following the BARONIAL CONFLICT AND WARS. It acknowledged Llywelyn as PRINCE OF WALES and ruler of the PRINCIPALITY OF WALES (including the overlordship of Welsh rulers and territorial gains such as Y BERFEDDWLAD); and required Llywelyn to pay tribute and to provide for his brother DAFYDD AP GRUFFUDD. *See also* ANGLO-WELSH RELATIONS, 6TH–13TH CENTURIES.

MONTGOMERY FAMILY A family from NORMANDY (N France), who were involved in Wales 1073–1102. Roger of Montgomery (earl of Shrewsbury by 1071; d. 1094), based in Shropshire (W England), founded Montgomery (Powys, C Wales) in 1073 and attacked W and SW Wales (1073–4). In 1093–4, with his son Arnulf of Montgomery, he overran CEREDIGION (W Wales) and founded Pembroke (SW Wales).

Roger was succeeded as earl by his sons Hugh (d. 1098) and Robert de Bellême (d. 1113). In 1102 Arnulf and Robert revolted against King HENRY I of England and forfeited their lands. *See also* NORMANS, IMPACT ON WALES.

MONTROSE, 5TH EARL OF (b. 1612 at Montrose, E Scotland; d. 21 May 1650 at Edinburgh, SE Scotland, aged 37 or 38). James Graham, earl from 1626, was a leading supporter of the NATIONAL COVENANT (1638) and fought against King CHARLES I in the Wars of the COVENANT (1639–40). But he was disturbed by the loss of royal authority in Scotland (*see* COVENANTING REVOLUTION) and opposed the 1643 alliance with English Parliamentarians (*see* SOLEMN LEAGUE AND COVENANT).

In 1644 Charles commissioned Montrose as his lieutenant-general in Scotland (Feb.) and promoted him to marquis (May). Following the Parliamentarian victory at Marston Moor (July), Montrose inflicted defeats on Covenanters, mainly in the Scottish HIGHLANDS (from Sept. 1644), until defeated at Philiphaugh, SE Scotland (13

Sept. 1645). Montrose went abroad (Sept. 1646), returning in March 1650, with the private support of King CHARLES II, to mount another attack. He was defeated, captured, and hanged by authority of the Scottish Parliament (without trial). *See also* CIVIL WARS, SCOTTISH PARTICIPATION.

MORANT, ROBERT (b. 7 April 1863 at Hampstead, Middlesex, England; d. 13 March 1920 at London, aged 56). A teacher, Morant spent 1886–94 in Siam (Thailand) tutoring the crown prince and reorganizing educational provision. As a British civil servant from 1895, he proved influential. He implemented the BALFOUR EDUCATION ACT (1902) for England and Wales (e.g., issuing important regulations), and legislation providing free school meals for poor children (1906) and medical inspections (1907). As chairman of the National Insurance Commission for England from 1911, he instigated NATIONAL INSURANCE, and was permanent secretary of the new Ministry of Health from 1919. He was knighted in 1907. *See also* CIVIL SERVICE, ENGLAND AND GREAT BRITAIN.

MORAY Name recorded from the mid 10th century (as Gaelic, Moréb) for a territory N of the MOUNTH (in modern NE Scotland), related to the area of FORTRIU. From 876 Moray may have been the power base of Aed, king of Scots and Picts, and of those of his descendants who also held the kingship (to Constantine III, d. 997; *see* MAC ALPIN KINGS).

Another kindred (possibly related and originally MORMAERS) may have taken advantage of the end of Aed's lineage to take control of Moray. In 1040 MACBETH, ruler of Moray, killed King DUNCAN I and seized the kingship of Scotland. Though he and his stepson were killed, Moray remained semi-independent under its own rulers until 1130, when Angus was killed. King DAVID I of Scotland then introduced Flemish settlers. *See also* MALCOLM I; ALEXANDER II; MURRAY FAMILY; MORAY, EARLS OF.

MORAY, EARL OF *see* RANDOLPH, THOMAS

MORAY, EARLS OF In 1312 King ROBERT I of Scotland created an EARLDOM and REGALITY in NE Scotland for Thomas RANDOLPH, based on a former territory (*see* MORAY). After the death of Randolph's grandson John Randolph (1346) it passed by marriage or grant to other families until MARY, QUEEN OF SCOTS, created her half-brother James Stewart earl in 1563 (*see* MORAY, JAMES EARL OF). His descendant John Douglas Stuart succeeded as 21st earl in 2011. *See also* MORAY, THE 'BONNY' EARL OF.

MORAY, JAMES EARL OF (b. 1531 or 1532 in Scotland; d. 21 Jan. 1570 at Linlithgow, SE Scotland, aged about 38). An illegitimate son of King JAMES V, Protestant from the mid 1550s, James Stewart joined the rebellion of the LORDS OF

THE CONGREGATION against the French Catholic MARY OF GUISE (1559) and secured their alliance with England (*see* BERWICK, (1560) TREATY OF). After her death (1560), Stewart accompanied his Catholic half-sister MARY, QUEEN OF SCOTS, from France (1561) and secured her acknowledgement of the REFORMATION. He received the earldom of Moray (1562) and status of earl (1563; *see* HUNTLY, 4TH EARL OF).

After Mary's anti-English marriage to Lord DARNLEY (1565), Moray rebelled (Aug.–Sept., the 'Chaseabout Raid'). Defeated by the earl of LENNOX, he fled to England (Oct.), but was pardoned after David RIZZIO's murder (March 1566). Dismayed by Mary's affair with the earl of BOTHWELL, Moray withdrew to France. When Mary abdicated (1567) she selected Moray as regent (for King JAMES VI); he returned. In 1568 Moray defeated Mary at LANGSIDE, but was later assassinated by one of her supporters. *See also* MARIAN CIVIL WAR.

MORAY, THE 'BONNY' EARL OF (b. 1565 or 1566 in Scotland; d. 7 Feb. 1592 at Donibristle, Fife, E Scotland, aged 26 or 27). James Stewart received his title in 1580 by marriage to the previous earl's daughter (*see* MORAY, JAMES EARL OF). He was involved in government action against Jesuits which, along with a long-standing feud, led to conflict with the Catholic (6th) earl of HUNTLY in NE Scotland. In 1591 King JAMES VI, perhaps jealous of his wife's affection for Moray, granted Huntly a warrant for Moray's arrest. Huntly took advantage: his men besieged Moray at Donibristle and he was murdered as he fled.

MORE, THOMAS (b. 7 Feb. 1478 at London, England; d. 6 July 1535 at London, aged 57). A lawyer and MP (1504, 1510, 1523), More entered the service of King HENRY VIII through the PATRONAGE of Thomas WOLSEY (appointed councillor 1517). He served as a diplomat and was knighted (1521). In 1523 he was elected speaker of the House of Commons. More succeeded Wolsey as CHANCELLOR (1529). He also wrote works of political philosophy (e.g., *Utopia*, 1516) and anti-Lutheran polemic (from 1523; *see* LUTHERANISM).

More opposed the anti-papal policy pursued by Henry to obtain a divorce from KATHERINE OF ARAGON (*see* GREAT MATTER). After the clergy were forced to submit collectively to Henry (15 May 1532), More resigned as chancellor (16 May). In 1534 he refused to swear to the Act of Succession because it implicitly denied papal authority. He was imprisoned (17 April), convicted of treason for denying Henry's supremacy in the English Church (1 July 1535), and executed. Canonized 1935. *See also* REFORMATION, ENGLAND; SUPPLICATION AGAINST THE ORDINARIES.

MORGAN, WILLIAM (b. *c.*1541 at Penmachno, Caernarfonshire, Wales; d. 10 Sept. 1604 at St Asaph,

Flintshire, Wales, aged about 63). Translator. Educated at CAMBRIDGE University, Morgan produced a Welsh version of the Bible, translating the Old Testament from Hebrew and revising William SALESBURY's New Testament translation. Morgan's profound knowledge of Hebrew and Greek and feel for Welsh resulted in a masterpiece (published 1588), making Welsh, as a poet put it, 'one of the dialects of the revelation of God'. Morgan was vicar of Llanrhaeadr ym Mochnant, Denbighshire (1578–95), and bishop of LLANDAFF (1595–1601) and of ST ASAPH (1601–4). *See also* REFORMATION, WALES; BIBLE, WELSH; HUMANISM.

MORGANNWG *see* GLYWYSING

MORLEY, JOHN (b. 24 Dec. 1838 at Blackburn, Lancashire, England; d. 23 Sept. 1923 at London, England, aged 84). Morley edited the *Fortnightly Review* (1866–82) and expounded individualist LIBERALISM, agnosticism and anti-imperialism.

In 1883 Morley became an MP. W.E. GLADSTONE made him chief secretary for Ireland (1886, 1892–5), but he clashed with William HARCOURT and the earl of ROSEBERY. Morley introduced reforms as Indian secretary (1905–10; *see* INDIAN INDEPENDENCE) and oversaw the Parliament Act (1911) as lord president of the Council (*see* PEOPLE'S BUDGET). Created Viscount Morley in 1908, he resigned (2 Aug. 1914) in opposition to British participation in WORLD WAR I. His writings include biographies of Gladstone and Richard COBDEN.

MORMAER Gaelic term for a provincial governor in the kingdom of Alba (i.e., modern Scotland, N of the FORTH–CLYDE ISTHMUS), first recorded in 918. It probably means 'great steward', but 'sea steward' has also been suggested (possibly originating in maritime DÁL RIATA). There were probably around 12 mormaers, each of whom provided military leadership and enforced royal justice in a large territory. Mormaers were called 'earls' (English) from the 12th century. *See also* EARLDOMS, SCOTLAND.

MORRIS, WILLIAM (b. 24 March 1834 at Walthamstow, Essex, England; d. 3 Oct. 1896 at London, England, aged 62). Designer, poet and SOCIALIST. A believer in craftsmanship, Morris joined the SOCIAL DEMOCRATIC FEDERATION (1883) to oppose industrial capitalism. Forming a rival Socialist League in 1884, he described his ideal society in *A Dream of John Ball* (1887) and *News from Nowhere* (1890). His writings and ideas remained influential.

MORRIS, WILLIAM (d. 1963) *see* NUFFIELD, LORD

MORRISON, HERBERT (b. 3 Jan. 1888 at Brixton, London, England; d. 6 March 1965 at Sidcup, Kent, England, aged 77). Prominent in LABOUR PARTY politics in London from 1920, Morrison was also an MP 1923–4, 1929–31, 1935–59. He was minister of transport in the second government of Ramsay MACDONALD (1929–31), and leader of the London County Council 1934–40.

During WORLD WAR II, Morrison was minister of supply (1940) and home secretary (1940–5) in the coalition government of Winston CHURCHILL. Afterwards, as deputy prime minister to Clement ATTLEE (1945–51), he co-ordinated policy implementation, especially NATIONALIZATION, and was briefly foreign secretary (1951). Morrison contested the Labour Party leadership in 1935 and 1955. Created Lord Morrison in 1959. *See also* MANDELSON, PETER.

MORTIMER, ROGER (b. *c.*1287 in March of Wales; d. 29 Nov. 1330 at London, England, aged about 43). A landowner in the MARCH OF WALES and soldier, Mortimer was alienated by the DESPENSERS (counsellors of King EDWARD II) and attacked their lands in the March (May 1321). After surrendering to Edward (Jan. 1322), he was sentenced to death (July) but reprieved. In Aug. 1322 he escaped to Paris (France) where he became the lover of Edward's queen, ISABELLA (by March 1326). They returned to England (Sept.) and deposed the Despensers and Edward.

From Jan. 1327 Mortimer dominated government under EDWARD III, receiving lands and lordships. He was created earl of March (1328). But his high-handed behaviour offended other nobles. On 19 Oct. 1330 he was arrested in Nottingham (C England). He was declared guilty of various offences by Parliament (26 Nov.) and executed. *See also* DESPENSER FAMILY AND WALES.

MORTIMER FAMILY A noble family with estates in Herefordshire (W England), the MARCH OF WALES and ULSTER (N Ireland) who were powerful in English politics in the 14th–15th centuries. Roger MORTIMER (*c.*1287–1330), lord of Wigmore, deposed King EDWARD II (1327–8) and took the title earl of March (1328). He effectively ruled England until ousted.

Roger's great-grandson Edmund Mortimer (1352–81), the 3rd earl, married Philippa, granddaughter of EDWARD III. Their son Roger (1374–98), and his infant son Edmund (1391–1425) were recognized as heirs to the childless King RICHARD II (ruled 1377–99). When Richard was deposed, Henry Bolingbroke seized the throne, ignoring Edmund's claim (*see* HENRY IV). Edmund was loyal to Henry and his successors.

Edmund died childless. His titles and claim passed via his sister, Anne Mortimer (d. 1411), to her son Richard Plantagenet (1411–60), the 6th earl. He was recognized as duke of York from 1425 and asserted his claim in 1460 (*see* YORK, RICHARD DUKE OF). His son became king in 1461 (*see* EDWARD IV). *See also* SOUTHAMPTON PLOT; YORKISTS.

MORTMAIN, STATUTE OF Enacted by the English Parliament in 1279 in response to land acquisitions by some major monasteries, this legislation prohibited further grants of property to religious corporations because as perpetual bodies their possession was permanent, consigning valuable assets to their 'dead hand' (French *morte main*). The Statute allowed for exemptions under royal licence, but although licences were granted from 1280 it deterred landowners from monastic patronage, compelling monasteries to diversify their income. Enforced in Ireland by 1301, the Statute was retained in English law until the 19th century. The concept was abolished in 1960. *See also* CHANTRIES, ENGLAND AND WALES.

MORTON, 4TH EARL OF (b. *c.*1516 in Scotland; d. 2 June 1581 at Edinburgh, SE Scotland, aged about 65). James Douglas became earl in 1553 (through marriage). Though he signed the 'First Bond' of the pro-Protestant LORDS OF THE CONGREGATION (1557), he only committed himself to implementing Protestant Church reform at a late stage (May 1560; *see* REFORMATION, SCOTLAND).

During the personal rule of MARY, QUEEN OF SCOTS (from 1561), Morton served as CHANCELLOR (from 1563). He helped to suppress MORAY's rebellion (1565), but was involved in David RIZZIO's murder (1566) and was dismissed. He knew of plans to murder Lord DARNLEY (1567), and led the CONFEDERATE LORDS who deposed Mary (1567).

During the ensuing MARIAN CIVIL WAR (1568–73), Morton was a leading supporter of King JAMES VI (a minor), and in Oct. 1572 was appointed regent (the fourth). He concluded the war (*see* PERTH, PACIFICATION OF), imposed doctrinal uniformity on the Church (Act of Uniformity, 1573), and attempted to pacify the country. In early 1578 Morton's enemies obtained his deposition. He recovered control (26 April 1578), but was arrested (31 Dec. 1580), tried for complicity in Darnley's murder, and executed. *See also* STEWART, ESMÉ; STEWART, JAMES.

MORTON, JOHN (b. *c.*1420 in Dorset, England; d. 15 Sept. 1500 at Knole, Kent, England, aged about 80). A LANCASTRIAN clergyman and lawyer, Morton fled abroad in 1461, following the deposition of King HENRY VI by Edward, duke of York (EDWARD IV). He joined the court of MARGARET OF ANJOU, returning to England in 1470 with Richard, earl of WARWICK. After Warwick's revolt failed, Morton was pardoned by King Edward (1471) and served as a minister and ambassador. He was appointed bishop of Ely (1478).

In Oct. 1483 Morton was involved in Buckingham's abortive rebellion against RICHARD III. He escaped to Flanders (1484) and organized opposition. After Henry Tudor (HENRY VII) deposed Richard (1485), Morton was appointed archbishop of CANTERBURY (1486) and CHAN-CELLOR (1487), making him Henry's chief minister. He was created a cardinal in 1493. *See also* FOXE, RICHARD.

MOSLEY, OSWALD (b. 16 Nov. 1896 at London, England; d. 3 Dec. 1980 at Orsay, France, aged 84). A Conservative MP from 1918, Mosley became an Independent (1920), then joined the Labour Party (1924). He inherited a baronetcy in 1928. In 1930 he resigned from the British government of Ramsay MACDONALD in frustration at its unwillingness to combat unemployment by stimulating economic activity.

In March 1931 Mosley launched the New Party but failed to win seats at the next general election (Oct.). Renamed the British Union of Fascists (BUF) in Oct. 1932, it held rallies and marches, in imitation of Continental European fascist organizations, until constrained by the Public Order Act (1936). Mosley was interned 1940–3 (during WORLD WAR II), then remained intermittently active in fringe politics. *See also* FASCISM, GREAT BRITAIN.

MOTHER AND CHILD SCHEME In the Republic of Ireland, a controversial plan to provide free health care and education for mothers and children. Proposed by health minister Noel Browne in 1950, it was opposed by the Catholic bishops (letter to taoiseach, John COSTELLO, 4 April 1951). Browne resigned, at Seán MACBRIDE's request, on 10 April; the government fell soon afterwards. The crisis confirmed the fears of Protestants in NORTHERN IRELAND about the influence of the Catholic Church in the Republic, but also strengthened anti-clericalism. *See also* CHURCH–STATE RELATIONS, SOUTHERN IRELAND FROM 1922.

MOTORCYCLES AND MOTORCYCLE INDUSTRY Two-wheeled motorcycles powered by petrol engines were developed in the 1890s and quickly became popular for transport, leisure and sport. Early organizations for motorcyclists included the Motor Cycle Union of Ireland (founded 1902). Sports included time-trial 'TT' (tourist trophy) races on public roads on the Isle of MAN (from 1907), which became a prestigious annual event. Motorcycling thrived; in 1929 there were 790,000 registered motorcycles in Great Britain. In the 1950s motorcycles became identified with YOUTH CULTURE. In 2010 there were about 1.1 million registered motorcycles in Britain, 26,000 in Northern Ireland, and 40,000 in the Republic of Ireland.

Motorcycles were manufactured in Britain from 1896. By the mid 1920s there were about 120 manufacturers, falling to 32 by 1939. BSA was the largest in the 1950s, but lost ground to Japanese competition in the 1960s. Its motorcycle production was merged in 1973 into 'Norton Villiers Triumph', which soon failed (1975). A government-supported co-operative, 'Triumph Meriden',

continued production 1975–83. A new company restarted manufacturing of Triumph motorcycles (1984), and by 2014 produced about 50,000 motorcycles per year using advanced production methods.

MOTOR INDUSTRY, GREAT BRITAIN Serial manufacturing of cars was started in 1897 at Coventry, Warwickshire, by Daimler, using German Daimler patents. Almost 400 firms entered the market, with 113 surviving in 1914. Wolseley, founded 1901 in BIRMINGHAM, was the largest manufacturer until the 1920s. Luxury vehicles made by ROLLS-ROYCE also became renowned. The US company Ford produced its cheap 'Model T' at Trafford Park (MANCHESTER, NW England) 1911–27. Production was protected by import tariffs 1915–56 (except 1924–5). Specialist companies also made trucks and buses.

In the 1920s Morris Motors (at OXFORD) and the Austin Motor Company (Birmingham) developed as mass car manufacturers, using Ford-type assembly lines. In 1929 they held 65% of the market. General Motors of the USA bought Vauxhall in 1922, and in 1931 Ford inaugurated a plant at Dagenham (Essex). Although British manufacturers declined from 88 (1922) to about 20 (late 1930s), Britain's industry was the second largest in the world (after USA) 1922–55. Morris and Austin merged in 1952 as the British Motor Corporation (BMC).

The industry flourished into the 1960s, with BMC taking 37% of the domestic market in 1964, Ford 28%. BMC lost sales and profitability, and in 1968 made a government-encouraged merger with Leyland Motors, primarily a truck maker, as British Leyland (BL). Unsuccessful, it was nationalized in 1974. Attempts to regain profitability failed, thwarted by overseas competition and poor labour relations. BL was broken up and privatized 1984–8, enabling some sections to flourish under foreign ownership. The last British-owned part closed in 2005.

Vehicle production peaked in 1972 (1.9 million cars, 408,000 commercial vehicles), then declined until the mid 1980s, when new Japanese-owned plants brought about a revival. In 2015, 1.58 million cars and 94,000 commercial vehicles were produced, though the major car factories belonged to Japanese, German and Indian companies. *See also* NUFFIELD, LORD.

MOTOR INDUSTRY, IRELAND *see* MOTOR VEHICLES, MOTORING AND MOTOR INDUSTRY, IRELAND

MOTORING ORGANIZATIONS The Self-Propelled Traffic Association was founded in 1895 by Sir David Salomons to remove restrictions on road 'locomotives' (achieved 1896). In 1897 F.R. Simms organized the Automobile Club of Great Britain and Ireland as an independent riposte to a manufacturer's Motor Car Club (1895);

it operated as a social club, campaigning organization, and (from 1901) service provider (e.g., roadside repairs). The prefix 'Royal' was granted in 1907. (Salomons' Association joined the Automobile Club in 1898.) The Irish Automobile Club was inaugurated in 1901. Its activities during WORLD WAR I (e.g., provision of ambulances) won the prefix 'Royal' (1918). It remained largely a social club.

The Motor Union of Great Britain and Ireland (1901) provided legal support and information, and the Automobile Association (1905) helped drivers to avoid police speed traps under the 1903 Motor Car Act. It was active in Ireland from 1910. (The Motor Union merged with the AA in 1910.)

The major organizations (RAC, AA) became primarily service providers. The RAC's service organization was separated in 1978, extended to the Republic of Ireland in 1991, and demutualized in 1998. The AA was demutualized in 1999. In 2015 they had, respectively, 8 million and 14.5 million members in Britain and Ireland. *See also* MOTOR VEHICLES AND MOTORING, GREAT BRITAIN.

MOTOR VEHICLES, MOTORING AND MOTOR INDUSTRY, IRELAND Steam-powered vehicles were used from the mid 19th century, and the first petrol-powered car was demonstrated in 1895. By 1909 there were 3790 cars. From 1865 to 1921 Ireland was usually included under vehicle legislation enacted by the UK Parliament (*see* MOTOR VEHICLES AND MOTORING, GREAT BRITAIN). In 1903 Ireland was famously the venue for the international Gordon Bennett trophy race, held on roads in Co. Kildare under special legislation.

After PARTITION (1921), cars became common in SOUTHERN IRELAND though were only affordable by wealthier people until the 1960s. In 1948 there were 60,000 cars. Petrol pumps spread widely from 1923. Legislation included the 1933 Road Transport Act, which set 25 mi/hr (40 km/hr) as the main speed limit and required insurance or an indemnity. The upper limit was raised to 50 mi/hr (80 km/hr) in 1963, and in 1964 a driving test was introduced. Later changes included metrication of speed limits (2005). Licensed vehicles increased to 390,000 by 1970, 1 million by 1990, and 1.7 million by 2007.

In NORTHERN IRELAND, car ownership spread among the middle classes in the 1920s–30s. In 1931 there were 35,000 licensed vehicles, and by 1939 one family in seven had a car. Insurance became compulsory in 1930, but driving tests began only in 1955. Cars increased to 501,000 in 1988, 840,000 in 2007.

The first manufacturer was Chambers Motors of BELFAST (1904–29). A plant at CORK, founded by US manufacturer Henry Ford, produced vehicles (initially tractors) from 1919 to 1984. In 1934 southern Ireland's government severely limited car imports and encouraged overseas manufacturers to assemble cars from kits (to 1980s). Occasional attempts were made to manufacture distinctive cars: in southern Ireland, the large Shamrock (1959–60) and TMC Costin sports car (1983–7); in Northern Ireland, the futuristic DeLorean (1981–3). *See also* MOTORING ORGANIZATIONS.

MOTOR VEHICLES AND MOTORING, GREAT BRITAIN The earliest engine-driven vehicles were steam-powered coaches (1830s). Their damage to roads, and engine explosions, curtailed their use. Steam traction engines (from 1850s) were more successful, prompting the 1861 Locomotive Act (for Britain) which set speed limits. The 1865 Locomotives Act (for UK) reduced limits to 2 mi/hr (3.2 km/hr) in built-up areas and 4 mi/hr (6.4 km/hr) elsewhere, and required a man with a red flag to precede a vehicle. The requirements later applied to petrol-powered motor cars (imported from 1889).

Following a campaign, the 1896 Locomotives on Highways Act (for UK) abolished the warning requirement and made 14 mi/hr (22 km/hr) the speed limit for 'light locomotives'. Expense initially limited motoring to wealthy people. Concern about casualties resulted in the 1903 Motor Car Act (for UK), which from 1904 introduced vehicle registration, number plates, driving licences, driving offences, and a 20 mi/hr (32 km/hr) speed limit. By 1914 there were 132,000 private cars; 51,000 taxis, buses and coaches; 82,000 goods vehicles. Vehicles carried petrol supplies.

During the 1920s–30s cheaper cars extended motoring to the middle classes (2 million cars by 1939). Petrol stations were introduced (1919), and roadside garages and cafés. Roads were classified (completed 1922), and bypasses and arterial roads built. The 1930 Road Traffic Act (for Britain) introduced compulsory third-party insurance and standardized signs, and abolished the speed limit. The 1934 Road Traffic Act (for Britain) introduced a driving test and a 30 mi/hr (48 km/hr) speed limit in built-up areas (a maximum speed of 70 mi/hr, 112 km/hr, was imposed in 1965, reduced in 1977 to 60 mi/hr, 96 km/hr, for single-carriageway roads).

Mass motoring developed from 1945. By the 1990s traffic congestion and pollution were major political concerns. At end 2015 there were 30.25 million cars and 5 million other vehicles (excluding MOTORCYCLES). *See also* TRANSPORT COMMUNICATIONS, ENGLAND/SCOTLAND/WALES; MOTORING ORGANIZATIONS; MOTORWAYS, GREAT BRITAIN; HORE-BELISHA, LESLIE.

MOTORWAYS, GREAT BRITAIN High-speed arterial roads restricted to motor traffic were constructed mainly in the 1950s–80s, later than in other major European countries, and designated by 'M' numbers. A short section of the M6, the so-called 'Preston Bypass' (NW England), was opened in 1958, followed in 1959 by a long section of the

LONDON–Yorkshire motorway (M1, completed 1966). An 'orbital motorway' around London, the M25, was completed in 1986. In 2014 there were 2300 mi (3,700 km) of motorways, mostly in England. *See also* TRANSPORT COMMUNICATIONS, ENGLAND/SCOTLAND/WALES.

MOTORWAYS, IRELAND *see* TRANSPORT COMMUNICATIONS, IRELAND

MOUNT BADON, BATTLE OF Fought at an unidentified location in POST-ROMAN BRITAIN, in the mid or late 5th century; recorded by GILDAS. After a long period of inconclusive warfare, Britons decisively defeated 'Saxons'. The battle allegedly helped to stem Germanic expansion for a half-century. *See also* AMBROSIUS AURELIANUS; GERMANIC IMMIGRATION, SOUTHERN BRITAIN.

MOUNTBATTEN, LORD (b. 25 June 1900 at Windsor, Berkshire, England; d. 27 Aug. 1979 at Mullaghmore, Co. Sligo, Republic of Ireland, aged 79). A great-grandson of Queen VICTORIA, known as Prince Louis of Battenberg until 1917, Lord Louis Mountbatten became a British naval officer. During WORLD WAR II he was supreme allied commander SE Asia (1943–6). He oversaw the British withdrawal from INDIA as viceroy (1947) and governor-general (1947–8). He was created Earl Mountbatten in 1947. After serving as first sea lord (1955–9), Mountbatten was chief of the defence staff until 1965. He was assassinated by the PROVISIONAL IRISH REPUBLICAN ARMY. *See also* INDIAN INDEPENDENCE.

MOUNTH A ridge of hills in NE Britain (modern Scotland) extending eastwards from the Grampian Mountains to the North Sea coast (N of Stonehaven, Aberdeenshire). The name is derived from *monadh*, a Scots Gaelic term meaning 'mountain range', which itself is derived from Brittonic. As a barrier between the far NE of Britain and lowlands to the S, the Mounth has been an important physical border in British and Scottish history (*see* PICTS; MORAY).

MOUNTJOY, LORD (b. 1563 in England; d. 3 April 1606 at London, England, aged 42 or 43). A soldier (and constant smoker), Charles Blount (knighted 1586) succeeded his brother as Lord Mountjoy in 1594. In early 1600 Queen ELIZABETH I sent him to Ireland as chief governor (lord deputy), to suppress the extensive rebellion led by Hugh O'NEILL, 2nd earl of Tyrone (from N Ireland). Mountjoy organized the pacification of MUNSTER (S Ireland) and LEINSTER (E); constructed forts around ULSTER (N); and wasted Tyrone's lordship. In Dec. 1601 he defeated Tyrone at KINSALE.

In 1603 Mountjoy received Tyrone's submission (March); was raised to king's lieutenant (April); suppressed the REVOLT OF THE TOWNS (April–May); and left Ireland (May). He was created earl of Devonshire in 1603. *See also* NINE YEARS WAR; IRELAND, ENGLISH CONQUEST, 16TH CENTURY.

MUIR, THOMAS (b. 24 Aug. 1765 at Glasgow, Scotland; d. 27 Sept. 1799 at Chantilly, Oise, France, aged 34). A merchant's son, Muir became an advocate (1787). In Dec. 1792, at the first convention of the Scottish Association of the Friends of the People, he read a message from the UNITED IRISHMEN, for which he was arrested (2 Jan. 1793). Released on bail, he went briefly to France and Ireland. On return to Scotland he was found guilty of sedition in a notoriously partial trial (Aug. 1793) and sentenced to 14 years' transportation in Australia. With American help he escaped in 1796 and settled in France (1798) where he wrote anti-British propaganda. *See also* FRENCH REVOLUTION, IMPACT ON SCOTLAND.

MULTICULTURAL SOCIETY Term for a society which contains minority populations with distinctive ethnic, religious or other cultural identities, usually constituting a minority collectively within the total population. Commonly used in CANADA from the early 1970s, it became current in Great Britain in the 1970s–80s, although a multicultural society was developing from the late 1940s through IMMIGRATION. The term implies that minorities are accommodated rather than absorbed by the indigenous population.

Official British attitudes towards minorities ('multiculturalism') have varied. In the 1950s–70s minorities were left to adjust to British society, assisted by anti-discrimination legislation (e.g., Race Relations Acts 1965, 1968, 1976), a stance called 'liberal multiculturalism'. From the 1980s, the increasing separatism of some groups (e.g., MUSLIMS) was accepted and even facilitated (e.g., with translations of official documents). After the emergence of Islamic radicalism *c.*2001, awareness of British culture was promoted (e.g., citizenship ceremonies from 2004, citizenship test from 2005). By 2011 some urban centres (e.g., LONDON, Luton, Leicester) exhibited a different type of multicultural society, namely 'majority-minority populations' in which no group predominated. The Republic of Ireland and Northern Ireland also became multicultural societies from the 1990s, marking a fundamental change from their previous cultural identities. The Republic introduced citizenship ceremonies in 2011. *See also* ETHNIC AND NATIONAL MINORITIES, ENGLAND/IRELAND/SCOTLAND/WALES.

MUNGO *see* KENTIGERN OR MUNGO

MUNICH CRISIS An international crisis in Europe in 1938, when Germany threatened war unless CZECHOSLOVAKIA ceded the Sudetenland, a German-speaking region. Neville

CHAMBERLAIN, the British prime minister, pressed the Czech government to yield. He brokered an agreement at a conference in Germany, at Munich (29–30 Sept.), whereby Great Britain, France and Italy accepted and condoned German annexation of the territory. It was the apogee of APPEASEMENT.

MUNICIPAL CORPORATIONS ACT Legislation concerning town and city government in England and Wales, 1835, passed for the WHIG government following the 1832 Reform Act (*see* PARLIAMENTARY REFORM). The Act reformed 178 borough corporations (often self-perpetuating oligarchies), instituting councils with two-thirds of members elected by permanent male ratepayers (the other members were aldermen co-opted by elected councillors). The Act also provided for unincorporated places to become boroughs. *See also* BURGH REFORM ACTS; TOWN GOVERNMENT, ENGLAND/IRELAND/WALES.

MUNICIPAL CORPORATIONS (IRELAND) ACT Legislation to reform town government which was passed by the UK Parliament in Aug. 1840. It originated as a measure to end Protestant domination, demanded by Daniel O'CONNELL under the LICHFIELD HOUSE COMPACT (1835). The Act dissolved 58 town corporations and reorganized the remaining ten, creating elective councils. Although the franchise was limited to male householders with property worth at least £10 per year, most surviving corporations came under Catholic control. O'Connell was elected mayor of DUBLIN (1841). *See also* TOWN GOVERNMENT, IRELAND.

MUNICIPAL REFORM, SCOTLAND *see* BURGH REFORM ACTS

MUNSTER A former provincial kingdom covering SW and S Ireland, formed by the 5th century; it was bounded by CONNACHT and MEATH (to N) and LEINSTER (E). Munster was dominated from the late 5th to mid 10th century by the Eóganachta federation of dynasties (possibly from W Munster). Various branches held the Munster high-kingship (based at CASHEL, E Munster). In the 9th and early 10th centuries Munster was raided by VIKINGS, who also founded WATERFORD, LIMERICK and CORK within Munster.

By the early 8th century the Déisi federation had also established itself (called Dál Cais from early 9th century), with groups in SE and NW Munster (modern Cos. Waterford and Clare). In 964 Mathgamain mac Cennétig, king of the Dál Cais, seized Munster's vacant high-kingship. The Dál Cais retained it until 1118; high-kings included BRIAN BÓRUMA (king 976–1014); Toirrdelbach Ua Briain (1063–86), who dominated S Ireland; and Muirchertach UA BRIAIN (1086–1116, retirement).

From 1114 the high-king of Connacht (W Ireland), Toirrdelbach UA CONCHOBAIR, supported the Eóganacht dynasty of Mac Carthaig (English, MacCarthy) against Muirchertach Ua Briain. In 1118 Toirrdelbach partitioned Munster: Tuadmumu ('N Munster'; English, Thomond) went to two of Muirchertach's nephews (Ua Briain dynasty; English, O'BRIEN); Desmumu ('S Munster'; English, Desmond), to Mac Carthaig. Munster remained divided, though Cormac Mac Carthaig was briefly its high-king (1127–38).

In 1177 King HENRY II of England granted Desmond and Thomond to Anglo-Normans. By 1250 Munster was mostly divided between English lords, and in the 14th–16th centuries was dominated by the earls of DESMOND and Ormond. The MacCarthys and O'Briens nevertheless survived in small 'rump' kingdoms and accepted English earldoms in the 16th century (*see* SURRENDER AND REGRANT). Munster's identity was later revived and defined geographically by the English provincial presidency of Munster (1570–1651, 1660–72). *See also* IRELAND, ENGLISH CONQUEST, 12TH–13TH CENTURIES; BUTLER FAMILY, IRELAND; PROVINCES, IRELAND.

MUNSTER PLANTATION An English colonial plantation in Ireland, which occupied lands in MUNSTER (S Ireland) forfeited after the Second DESMOND REBELLION; planned from 1584. By 1588, 35 UNDERTAKERS were in possession, who settled 3700 English people within five years. The Plantation was destroyed in 1598 (during the NINE YEARS WAR), but refounded in 1601. It established a large, Protestant, NEW ENGLISH minority in S Ireland (22,000 by 1641). *See also* PLANTATIONS, IRELAND.

MURDOCH, RUPERT (b. 11 March 1931 at Melbourne, Victoria, Australia). Media tycoon. After study and work in England, Murdoch in 1954 returned to Australia where he developed an inherited newspaper company. He expanded his business into Great Britain from 1968, and into the USA from 1973. He became a US citizen in 1985.

In Britain, Murdoch's acquisitions included the *News of the World* (1968), *Sun* (1969), *Times* and *Sunday Times* (1981). The overnight transfer of their production to new facilities (24–25 Jan. 1986) helped to reduce trade union power within the newspaper industry. In 1989 Murdoch founded the subscription satellite television broadcaster 'Sky' (merged into 'BSkyB' in 1990). From the 1980s he was influential with politicians (e.g., Margaret THATCHER, Tony BLAIR), but the PHONE-HACKING SCANDAL (2010–11) damaged his standing. *See also* NEWSPAPERS, ENGLAND.

MURRAY, GEORGE (b. 4 Oct. 1694 at Huntingtower, near Perth, C Scotland; d. 2 Oct. 1760 at Medemblik, Dutch Republic, aged 65). A son of John, duke of Atholl, Lord

George Murray was involved in the JACOBITE REBELLIONS of 1715 and 1719. He then went into exile. He returned in Aug. 1724 and was pardoned (1725).

Murray joined the JACOBITE REBELLION of 1745, led by Prince Charles Edward. As a senior commander, he was largely responsible for victory at Prestonpans (21 Sept. 1745). He opposed the planned invasion of England, but was overruled. He then resigned his commission, but was reinstated. During the later Jacobite retreat, Murray secured victory at Falkirk (Jan. 1746). He opposed fighting at CULLODEN. After surviving defeat there, he escaped abroad. *See also* MURRAY FAMILY.

MURRAY FAMILY A Scottish noble family; descendants of Freskin, of Flemish stock, who was given land (after 1130) in MORAY (NE Scotland) and elsewhere by King DAVID I. They used the name 'de Moray' from the early 13th century, and from 1252 had a second power base at Bothwell (S Scotland).

In 1296 Andrew Murray from Moray, together with his father and uncle (lords respectively in N and S Scotland), was captured while fighting for King John BALLIOL against the forces of King EDWARD I of England. Andrew Murray escaped in 1297 from England, returned to Moray, and took leadership of the rebellion against English rule in N Scotland, harassing English garrisons. He and supporters fought with the forces of William WALLACE at STIRLING BRIDGE (11 Sept. 1297). Murray died from wounds.

Andrew Murray's posthumous son Sir Andrew Murray (1297–1338) became 'guardian' of Scotland after the battle of DUPPLIN (1332) but was captured by supporters of Edward BALLIOL and imprisoned (1332–4). His victory at CULBLEAN (1335), against Edward's lieutenant in N Scotland, led to reappointment as guardian (spring 1336). In 1336–7 Murray attacked English strongholds in Scotland, leading to a truce in 1338. He died soon afterwards.

Later family members included the earls of Atholl (title created 1629) and the Jacobite George MURRAY (d. 1760). *See also* SCOTTISH–ENGLISH RELATIONS 1290 TO 1357.

MUSCOVY COMPANY A company of merchants, formed in London in 1555 initially as a JOINT-STOCK COMPANY, with a monopoly of English trade with RUSSIA. It sent ships to Archangel, and hoped to find a North-east Passage to China. England sold woollen and metal goods to the Russians, and bought hemp, fur, timber and fish oil. Though it lost its monopoly in 1698, it remained in business until 1917. *See also* OVERSEAS TRADING COMPANIES.

MUSIC HALL A form of entertainment (also called 'Variety'), consisting of short varied performances (singing, dancing, comedy, melodrama, etc.), which became organized *c.*1850 in the London area. It spread rapidly to towns and cities throughout Great Britain and Ireland, becoming a popular form of entertainment. Early performances took place in extensions to public houses, but dedicated theatres were also built (e.g., 'Dan Lowrey's Star of Erin Music Hall', DUBLIN, 1879). Performers, usually professionals, were introduced by a chairman. Food and drink were often provided. Music halls declined in the 1920s–30s, displaced by RADIO and CINEMA.

MUSLIMS IN GREAT BRITAIN Although a purpose-built mosque opened in 1889 (at Woking, Surrey, S England, for students), there were few Muslims until the 1950s–60s when immigrants from Pakistan-ruled Kashmir settled mainly in towns in northern and Midland England. They were followed by Indian Muslims (Gujuratis) from Africa, who became concentrated in Leicester (C England), and Bangladeshis (Sylhetis), who lived mainly in E London. Kashmiris and Bangladeshis were mostly from rural backgrounds. Muslims mainly formed self-contained communities. During the 1970s–80s they built mosques and madrasas, and from 1982 Sharia councils were formed (about 30 in UK by 2012). Continuing immigration by spouses and imams reinforced homeland culture. By the late 1980s there were about 500,000 Muslims.

Muslims asserted themselves publicly in 1988–9 with protests against Salman Rushdie's novel *The Satanic Verses* (*see* RUSHDIE AFFAIR). Their actions led to creation of a National Interim Committee (1994) and Muslim Council of Britain (1997). From 1997 hostile attitudes by non-Muslims were branded as 'Islamophobia'.

The government of Tony BLAIR (elected 1997) was initially supportive (e.g., allowing State-funded Muslim schools), but after Al-Qaeda terrorist attacks in New York, USA (2001), Muslim 'extremism' became a problem in Britain. Often involving British-born Muslims, it was abetted by propaganda and information obtainable from the Internet and overseas television channels. Britain's controversial military presence in the Muslim countries of AFGHANISTAN (2001–14) and IRAQ (2003–10) provided a pretext for terrorism. The worst incident, four co-ordinated suicide bombings in London on 7 July 2005, killed 52 civilians plus the bombers. Responses included anti-terrorism legislation and, from 2005, 'Prevent' – initiatives against extremism within Muslim communities.

By 2011 the Muslim population rose to 2.7 million, mostly in England and predominantly Sunni, with two-thirds ethnically Asian, though also including Somalis. There were about 1700 mosques. In 2016 London elected a Muslim, Sadiq Khan, as mayor. *See also* SOUTH ASIANS IN GREAT BRITAIN; AFRICANS IN GREAT BRITAIN; ETHNIC AND NATIONAL MINORITIES, ENGLAND/SCOTLAND/WALES.

MYANMAR *see* BURMA

MYLN, WALTER, EXECUTION OF Myln, an elderly priest, was burnt in ST ANDREWS (E Scotland) on 28 April 1558 for heresy (Protestantism) by Archbishop John HAMILTON. The first such execution for 12 years, it aroused fear of an anti-heresy campaign and arguably boosted support for Protestant reformers. Thirteen months later, riots in PERTH marked the beginning of the REFORMATION crisis.

MYNYDD CARN, BATTLE OF Fought N of ST DAVIDS (SW Wales) in 1081. GRUFFUDD AP CYNAN, challenger for GWYNEDD (NW Wales), and RHYS AP TEWDWR, king of DEHEUBARTH (SW Wales), defeated rivals Trahaearn ap Caradog (of Gwynedd), Caradog ap Gruffudd and Meilyr ap Rhiwallon.

MYSTERY PLAYS Christian dramas, usually performed by town GUILDS, which flourished in Europe in the late Middle Ages (14th–16th centuries). Typically performed at Whitsun (Sunday after Easter) or around Corpus Christi (after 1311), they were suppressed in England and Wales in the 16th century, a consequence of the REFORMATION. Four English cycles of plays survive (from Chester, YORK, Wakefield, and another northern town) and four Welsh plays.

N

NAITON SON OF DER-ILEI (fl. from 707; d. 732, probably in N Britain). Naiton succeeded his brother BRIDEI SON OF DER-ILEI as king of FORTRIU and the other Pictish areas in 707. His early years as king were troubled, partly because of opposition to IONA's new supremacy. That was addressed in (probably) 715, when, following advice from NORTHUMBRIA, he instituted reforms similar to those of the synod of WHITBY (660), relating particularly to the dating of Easter and the tonsure – thus aligning the far N of Britain with the Roman Church. Subsequently, new Easter tables were distributed, and Northumbrian stonemasons built a stone-and-mortar church dedicated to St Peter. Then, in 717, Naiton expelled clergy associated with Iona – probably conservative opponents of the reforms – from Pictland, which in effect ended Iona's ecclesiastical supremacy. Thereafter his reign seems to have been uneventful, and when he abdicated and entered a monastery in 724 that was probably due to his age (55–60?), not coercion. But internal warfare broke out, and in 729 the eventual victor, ONUIST SON OF VURGUIST, restored him as king. He ruled until his death in 732, whereupon Onuist succeeded. *See also* PICTS; EASTER CONTROVERSY.

NAPOLEONIC WARS *see* FRENCH REVOLUTIONARY AND NAPOLEONIC WARS, BRITISH INVOLVEMENT

NATAL A former British colony in southern Africa. Great Britain annexed Natal, a territory recently occupied by Boers (Calvinist farmers), to CAPE COLONY in 1843 and made it a separate CROWN COLONY in 1856 (self-governing from 1893). Zululand was added in 1897, and parts of the Transvaal after the (Second) BOER WAR. Approx. population in 1907: 1,164,000 (including 92,000 whites, about 8%). Natal became a province of the dominion of SOUTH AFRICA in 1910.

NATIONAL AND IMPERIAL CENSUSES An official census of Great Britain's population was first held in 1801 (during the NAPOLEONIC WARS), influenced by magazine editor John Rickman (1771–1840) who believed it would benefit military planning and other matters (e.g., food supply). It was also influenced by the pessimistic attitude to population growth of T.R. MALTHUS. Based on parishes, the census enumerated three matters: houses, male and female inhabitants, employment. Information was collected in England and Wales by overseers of the poor, and in Scotland by schoolmasters. The exercise was repeated in 1811, and in 1813–15 an abortive attempt was made to cover Ireland (grand juries proved incompetent or unco-operative).

From 1821 to 1911 (inclusive) a census of the United Kingdom occurred every ten years; likewise thereafter in Britain (except for 1941, during WORLD WAR II, and with an experimental census in 1966). More diverse information was collected.

A census was avoided in Ireland in 1921 because of the War of IRISH INDEPENDENCE. In NORTHERN IRELAND

A Dictionary of British and Irish History, First Edition. Edited by Robert Peberdy and Philip Waller.
© 2021 John Wiley & Sons Ltd; © editorial matter and organisation Robert Peberdy and Phillip Waller.
Published 2021 by John Wiley & Sons Ltd.

censuses were held in 1926, 1937, 1951 and then as in Britain at ten-yearly intervals (with an additional census in 1966). In SOUTHERN IRELAND censuses were held in 1926, 1936, 1946, then usually at five-yearly intervals (the 1976 census was delayed to 1979 to save expenditure).

From the 18th century population enumerations were made in some imperial territories (e.g., N American colonies); in the 19th century census taking became more widespread and regular (e.g., in NEW SOUTH WALES from 1828, WEST INDIES colonies from 1844, INDIA from 1867–72). From the 1840s administrators in Britain desired to organize an imperial census coinciding with the UK census; this proved impractical. From the 1860s to 1930s digests of population figures and estimates were published alongside UK figures, and in 1906 as a separate volume, *Census of the British Empire, 1901*.

NATIONAL ASSOCIATION FOR THE PROMOTION OF SOCIAL SCIENCE An influential organization founded in Great Britain in 1857 on the initiative of G.W. Hastings (1825–1917) to discuss social policy, including legal and penal reform, education, public health and welfare. It held annual congresses and published proceedings. Members included politicians, administrators, lawyers, doctors and women (notably from the LANGHAM PLACE CIRCLE). It influenced reforming legislation such as PUBLIC HEALTH ACTS and the 1870 MARRIED WOMEN'S PROPERTY ACT. Disbanded 1886.

NATIONAL ASSOCIATION OF IRELAND A political organization established on 29 Dec. 1864 to combine nationalism and Catholicism. Its aims included the establishment of 'tenant right' (*see* 'THREE FS') and DISESTABLISHMENT of the Church of Ireland. Supporters included Archbishop Paul CULLEN who hoped it would deflect support from Fenianism (*see* IRISH REPUBLICAN BROTHERHOOD). It declined after disestablishment was granted (1869). *See also* DILLON, J.B.

NATIONAL COVENANT A religious and political statement, protesting at the arbitrary government of King CHARLES I (e.g., Book of CANONS, 1637 PRAYER BOOK), which was subscribed to in 1638 by Scots after Charles ignored the REVOLT OF 1637. Drafted by Alexander HENDERSON and Archibald JOHNSTON (23–27 Feb.), the Covenant was endorsed in EDINBURGH and distributed throughout the country; 300,000 people signed. It included the anti-Catholic NEGATIVE CONFESSION (1581) and rejected episcopacy. Charles revoked the innovations (Sept.) and allowed a General Assembly to meet, which implemented the Covenant's demands (*see* GLASGOW ASSEMBLY). *See also* COVENANTS, SCOTLAND; COVENANTING REVOLUTION; COVENANTERS.

NATIONAL CURRICULUM Originally a detailed curriculum for children aged 5–16 in State-funded schools in England and Wales, authorized and outlined by the 1988 Education Reform Act. Initially comprising three 'core' subjects (English, maths, science) and seven other 'foundation' subjects, it required assessment of children at 'key stages' against 'attainment targets'. The curriculum was subsequently modified, with separate changes in Wales from 2004. A Northern Ireland Curriculum, based on the English and Welsh approach, was introduced in 2009.

NATIONAL DEBT The debt owed by a State to individuals and corporate organizations, usually referring to long-term debt requiring regular interest payments. Originating in 14th-century Italy, such public debt was first raised in England with the 'tontine loan' of 1693 (under which the shares of deceased holders were reallocated to survivors). Subsequent schemes included foundation of the BANK OF ENGLAND (1694). The Bank administered the debt from 1715.

Long-term debt was incurred initially to help fund the War of the GRAND ALLIANCE (1689–97), which left the debt at £16.7 million. Acceptance of long-term borrowing enabled Great Britain to act as a major power. With subsequent wars, the debt rose to £37.4 million (1715), £78 million (1750), £232 million (1783), £840 million (1820). Attempted reductions, through SINKING FUNDS and consolidation at 3% interest (1749–55), had little effect.

Britain's national debt was accepted as an institution by the 1720s–30s, and considered a sound form of investment because of Parliament's authorization. But it was regressive in that wealthy individuals generally held capital while ordinary people funded interest payments through taxation (*see* EXCISE). Between the early 18th and mid 19th centuries, debt servicing absorbed roughly 30–50% of central government expenditure, thereafter declining. UK debt included Ireland from 1817 to 1922 (*see* NATIONAL DEBT, IRELAND).

UK debt was increased by WORLD WAR I (1914–18) to £7800 million, by WORLD WAR II (1939–45) to £21,000 million. As a percentage of gross domestic product (GDP), it reached almost 238% in 1948, declining below 48% in 1974, and below 26% in 1991, before rising to almost 39% in 2008. Following the 2008 financial crisis, declining tax receipts and increased welfare spending rapidly increased the debt to over 80% (2016), despite cuts in government expenditure. *See also* FINANCIAL REVOLUTION; FISCAL–MILITARY STATE; SOUTH SEA BUBBLE.

NATIONAL DEBT, IRELAND The Irish government initiated long-term borrowing in 1716. By 1760 its debt was relatively low, at (Irish) £5300. It increased substantially in the 1780s, following the War of AMERICAN INDEPENDENCE, though servicing cost only 10 per cent of total expenditure. It then rocketed during the FRENCH REVOLUTIONARY AND NAPOLEONIC WARS (1793–1815), reaching £38 million by 1804 and £107 million in 1816. The Irish and British debts were amalgamated in 1817 (*see* EXCHEQUER, IRELAND, ABOLITION OF).

After foundation of the IRISH FREE STATE (1922), southern Ireland sustained a national debt. It remained relatively low until the 1970s, when international oil crises and wage inflation increased it to (Irish) £313 million (1977). Attempted stimulation of economic growth then raised the debt to £7000 million (1981), and £23,000 million (1986; 116% of gross domestic product or GDP). Through retrenchment and economic expansion the debt was reduced to 23% of GDP (2006), but it increased rapidly after the 2008 financial crisis, reaching 119% (2012), largely due to bank failures. By 2016 the debt was reduced to 73%.

NATIONAL DETERIORATION Term used from *c.*1902 for a widely held belief that the health of Great Britain's urban working class was progressively declining, threatening the country's future. It arose from social surveys (e.g., by Charles BOOTH, Seebohm ROWNTREE) and the high proportion of would-be Army recruits rejected for unfitness during the (Second) BOER WAR (1899–1902). A government report in 1904 excluded hereditary decline, but resulted in medical inspection of elementary school-children in England and Wales from 1907.

NATIONAL ECONOMIC DEVELOPMENT COUNCIL An organization created by Harold MACMILLAN (prime minister) and Selwyn LLOYD (chancellor of the Exchequer) as a forum for discussion between the British government, employers and trade unions; it was inaugurated in 1962. Though purely consultative, the NEDC (popularly known as 'Neddy') helped to set growth targets and formulate INCOMES POLICIES. Under Margaret THATCHER (prime minister 1979–90) its importance diminished. It was abolished by Thatcher's successor, John MAJOR, in 1992. *See also* ECONOMY, STATE INVOLVEMENT, BRITAIN.

NATIONAL EDUCATION, IRELAND State-funded elementary education introduced in 1831 and intended as non-denominational (*see* STANLEY LETTER). The government paid for buildings and teachers' salaries, and appointed a central supervisory board. Individual schools were supervised by local managers (often clergy). Teaching posts were closed to clergy, and denominational religious material was forbidden, but schools naturally reflected local religious allegiances. The creation of 'non-vested' status for schools in 1840 to placate presbyterians (allowing the building of schools with voluntary funds), included acceptance of denominational religious education. By 1870

elementary education became effectively denominational. *See also* EDUCATION, IRELAND.

NATIONAL FRONT *see* FASCISM, GREAT BRITAIN

NATIONAL GOVERNMENT Name of the Conservative-dominated British coalition government of 1931–40, led by Ramsay MACDONALD, Stanley BALDWIN and Neville CHAMBERLAIN.

In 1931, when the Labour government split over spending cuts required to obtain loans during a currency crisis, King GEORGE V urged party leaders to co-operate in a National Government. Despite opposition from most Labour MPs, MacDonald, the Labour leader, formed a coalition (25 Aug.). Though half the Liberals left in Oct. 1932, the Conservatives collaborated with 'Liberal Nationals' (led by John SIMON) and a handful of 'National Labour' MPs until 10 May 1940 (formation of wartime coalition). The National Government is associated with the GREAT DEPRESSION and APPEASEMENT. *See also* HENDERSON, ARTHUR.

NATIONAL HEALTH SERVICE Term applied to State-funded medical services established in the UK in the late 1940s, as recommended by the 1942 'Beveridge Report' (*see* BEVERIDGE, WILLIAM). The UK Labour government created services in England and Wales (National Health Service Act, 1946) and Scotland (1947). Both were launched in 1948. Northern Ireland's Unionist government created a similar service (legislation in 1946, 1948).

The English and Welsh service was initially supervised by a British government minister. The Welsh section was transferred to the secretary of state for Wales in 1969, and to the Welsh Assembly and government in 1999. The Scottish service was supervised by the secretary of state for Scotland, then transferred to the Scottish Parliament and Executive in 1999. Northern Ireland's service was transferred to British ministers during periods of 'direct rule' from 1972 (*see* EXECUTIVES, NORTHERN IRELAND).

Free primary, hospital, dental and optical treatment were funded from NATIONAL INSURANCE and general taxation. Hospitals were nationalized but general practitioners ('GPs') and dentists remained independent and could accept private patients (as could hospital surgeons). Some prescription charges were introduced from 1951 (e.g., for dentures and spectacles). Services in England and Northern Ireland were periodically restructured to restrain costs and relocate power (e.g., as between managers and GPs). 'NHS Trusts', with considerable self-government, were established within the English NHS from 1990. By the late 20th century the UK's health services were collectively the country's largest providers of employment.

NATIONAL INSURANCE A compulsory State-organized welfare scheme created by the 1911 National Insurance Act, funded by employees, employers and government. Implemented in Great Britain and Ireland, and administered through friendly societies, it insured most employed persons against sickness, disablement and maternity costs, and provided unemployment benefits to 2.25 million workers in certain trades.

Major reorganization under the 1946 National Insurance Act (for Great Britain) made a Ministry of Pensions and National Insurance responsible for administration, extended benefits, subsidized costs from taxation, and allocated funds towards the NATIONAL HEALTH SERVICE. The arrangements were replicated by the government of NORTHERN IRELAND. *See also* SOCIAL SERVICES AND WELFARE, SOUTHERN IRELAND.

NATIONALIST PARTY The main nationalist political party in NORTHERN IRELAND following the province's creation (1921); a continuation of the IRISH PARLIAMENTARY PARTY. It represented the province's minority Catholic population, and sought reunion with southern Ireland.

Initially led by Joe DEVLIN (d. 1934), the Party held about ten seats in the Northern Ireland Parliament, though it abstained until 1925 and refused to be the 'official' Opposition until 1965. It lacked a central organization before the 1960s. Although it supported the CIVIL RIGHTS MOVEMENT (1960s), it declined (1969–73) and was effectively replaced by the SOCIAL DEMOCRATIC AND LABOUR PARTY. *See also* PARLIAMENTARY REPRESENTATION, NORTHERN IRELAND.

NATIONALIZATION State acquisition of land, other property, industry or business, advocated from the 19th century by SOCIALISM, COMMUNISM and some TRADE UNIONS. Extensive nationalization of industries was implemented in Great Britain by the Labour government of 1945–50, including COAL MINING (1946), electricity (1947), TRANSPORT (1947), GAS (1948), IRON AND STEEL (1949). Further instances occurred in the 1960s–70s. Some nationalized industries proved inefficient and required subsidies. Many were returned to private ownership in the 1980s–90s (*see* PRIVATIZATION). In southern Ireland the State developed some industries from the 1920s through State-owned holding entities (*see*, e.g., ELECTRIFICATION, IRELAND). *See also* ECONOMY, STATE INVOLVEMENT, BRITAIN; NEW LABOUR.

NATIONAL LEAGUE In Ireland, a political organization founded on 17 Oct. 1882 to replace the proscribed LAND LEAGUE. It advocated land reform, HOME RULE, franchise extension and other causes. It also absorbed the HOME RULE LEAGUE and acted as the local organization of the IRISH PARLIAMENTARY PARTY, which dominated its central council. It split during 1890–1 (with anti-Parnellites forming the Irish National Federation) and was replaced in 1900 by the UNITED IRISH LEAGUE. *See also* PLAN OF CAMPAIGN.

NATIONAL PATRON SAINTS Patron saints became established in differing circumstances, usually based on important cults. In Wales, the cult of DAVID, an ascetic monk (*c*.530–89), was disseminated by the Norman BERNARD OF ST DAVIDS, bishop of ST DAVIDS 1115–48. Drawing on native ambitions (exemplified by Rhigyfarch's recent *Life of St David*), he obtained papal approval of David's cult (1120), and later sought archiepiscopal status for his see.

In Ireland the cult of PATRICK, a British missionary (5th century), was promoted in the later 12th century by the Anglo-Norman John de COURCY, an invader in NE Ireland. He commissioned a *Life of St Patrick* (by Jocelin of Furness), and in 1185 claimed to have discovered Patrick's body. St Patrick was promoted in association with ARMAGH as Ireland's primary see. Patrick was accepted by Anglo-Normans as well as Gaelic Irish.

In Scotland a cult of the apostle Andrew (d. *c*.60) existed by the late 8th century (*see* ST ANDREWS). His protection was first invoked nationally in 1286 by the guardians appointed for the minority of MARGARET, 'THE MAID OF NORWAY'. He was invoked again, alongside COLUMBA, during the Wars of Independence (*see* SCOTTISH–ENGLISH RELATIONS 1290–1357), and afterwards considered the patron of the Scottish kingdom and Church.

In England, Edmund (d. 869), the last king of EAST ANGLIA, and King EDWARD THE CONFESSOR (ruled 1042–66), became important saints. From the 1260s the royal family displayed interest in the martyr St George (d. possibly *c*.303 in Palestine), who was associated with KNIGHTS, and in 1349 King Edward III named him patron of the Order of the GARTER. He was invoked as England's patron from 1415, during the HUNDRED YEARS WAR.

NATIONAL PENSIONERS' CONVENTION An organization formed in Great Britain in 1979 on the initiative of Jack Jones, former general secretary of the TRANSPORT AND GENERAL WORKERS' UNION, to defend pensioners' interests. Supported initially by the TRADES UNION CONGRESS, it organized an annual Pensioners' Action Day and encouraged local organizations. It became independent in 1992.

NATIONAL SERVICE *see* CONSCRIPTION

NATIONAL SOCIETY FOR THE PREVENTION OF CRUELTY TO CHILDREN An organization founded in England in 1889 to campaign for State action against the abuse of children, concerting the efforts of local societies (started from 1883). It helped to obtain the 1889 Prevention of Cruelty to Children Act, most of which applied throughout the UK. A Scottish Society was founded in 1889.

The societies employed inspectors, with the NSPCC operating in England, Wales and Ireland. A separate Irish Society assumed responsibility in the Republic of Ireland from 1956. *See also* CHILD WELFARE; CHILD WELFARE, SOUTHERN IRELAND.

NATIONAL TRUST Short name for the National Trust for Places of Historic Interest or Natural Beauty, a conservation organization founded in 1895 by Octavia HILL and constituted under legislation from 1907. From 1937 it could accept properties (e.g., country houses) as donations in lieu of estate duty. The Trust has operated in England, Wales and Northern Ireland. Its membership reached 4 million in 2011, when the Trust held over 600,000 acres (243,000 ha) of land and 300 historic houses. A National Trust for Scotland, incorporated in 1931, had 310,000 members and held 190,000 acres (77,000 ha) of land and other properties. *See also* HERITAGE INDUSTRY.

NATIONAL UNEMPLOYED WORKERS MOVEMENT An organization founded in Great Britain in 1921 (as the National Unemployed Workers' Committee Movement, renamed 1929). It organized 'hunger marches', advised unemployed people, and opposed 'means testing' for benefits. Led by Wal Hannington and (in Scotland) Henry McShane, it presented itself as a 'trade union of the unemployed', though the TRADES UNION CONGRESS and LABOUR PARTY shunned it as a COMMUNIST front organization. The NUWM was most active in Lancashire (NW England), Scotland and S Wales. Though claiming 50,000 members at its peak (1932), it failed to channel many into the COMMUNIST PARTY. Inactive from 1939; dissolved 1946.

NATIONAL UNION OF WOMEN'S SUFFRAGE SOCIETIES An organization founded in 1897 to co-ordinate the work of British suffrage societies, led by Millicent Garrett FAWCETT. Unlike the militant Women's Social and Political Union (1903–17) its methods remained constitutional and law abiding. It sought cross-party support for enfranchising women on the same terms as men, but from 1912 allied with the LABOUR PARTY which supported universal adult suffrage. Branches rose from 200 in 1910 to 600 in 1914. WORLD WAR I brought divisions between patriots and pacifists, but limited enfranchisement for women over 30 was enacted in 1918. In 1919 the Union became the National Union of Societies for Equal Citizenship, led by Eleanor Rathbone. *See also* WOMEN'S SUFFRAGE MOVEMENT, GREAT BRITAIN.

NATIONAL VOLUNTEERS *see* IRISH VOLUNTEERS

NAVAL FORCES, ENGLAND BEFORE LATE 11TH CENTURY Powerful 7th-century Anglo-Saxon kings utilized ships, though the method of procurement is unknown.

Occupations of ANGLESEY and the Isle of MAN by EDWIN of Deira (ruled 616 or 617–33) required shipping, as did the raid on Ireland (684) by EGFRITH of Bernicia.

In the 9th–10th centuries kings of WESSEX fought at sea mainly against VIKINGS, initially with small fleets. Athelstan, son of ÆTHELWULF and subking of Kent, attacked a VIKING fleet in 851 – the first recorded Anglo-Saxon naval battle. ALFRED intermittently attacked Vikings (875–82, 885) and in 896 commissioned a fleet employing a new ship design. EDWARD THE ELDER mobilized a large fleet – allegedly 100 ships – against Vikings (910); ATHELSTAN, king of England, used ships in an expedition against Scotland (934).

A system for funding and manning ships was introduced, possibly during the reign of EDGAR (959–75). It was based on 'ship-sokes': groups of three 'hundreds' (small administrative territories), beginning with sokes of bishops and abbots. Landowners provided ships (possibly 30–60) and areas provided crews, although skilled seamen must have been employed. The arrangements enabled ÆTHELRED II to counter renewed Viking activity (992, 999, 1009). The Danish ruler of England CNUT (1016–35) also maintained ships from *heregeld* ('army geld'). They were paid off by EDWARD THE CONFESSOR (by 1051), who obtained supplementary services from ports in SE England (*see* CINQUE PORTS). The ship-soke system appears to have dwindled after the NORMAN CONQUEST (1066–70s). *See also* MILITARY SERVICE, ENGLAND BEFORE 1066.

NAVAL RACE, GREAT BRITAIN AND GERMANY Rivalry in sea power in the early 20th century, which was a major cause of Anglo-German antagonism before WORLD WAR I (1914–18). In 1900 Germany proposed a fleet of 60 capital ships. Perceiving a threat to its maritime supremacy, Great Britain constructed a naval base at Scapa Flow (in ORKNEY ISLANDS, off NE Scotland), concentrated the Royal NAVY in home waters, and pursued a policy of German containment.

Britain's introduction of the *Dreadnought*-class of heavily armed battleships in 1906 intensified competition by making older vessels semi-obsolete. When Germany accelerated its naval programme (1908), the Liberal government of H.H. ASQUITH became bitterly divided about how many 'Dreadnoughts' to build. David LLOYD GEORGE and Winston CHURCHILL tried to curb defence spending until 1911. By 1914, Britain was winning the Naval Race (with 22 'Dreadnoughts' to Germany's 13). *See also* GERMANY, BRITISH RELATIONS WITH; FISHER, LORD; PEOPLE'S BUDGET.

NAVAN FORT *see* EMAIN MACHA

NAVIES, NORTH BRITAIN AND SCOTTISH The Scots of DÁL RIATA levied men and resources to maintain ships (6th–9th centuries). Until the 16th century Scottish merchant skippers acted as privateers (e.g., Andrew Wood of Largo, c.1455–1515; Robert, John, and Andrew Barton of Leith, fl. early 16th century).

In 1505 King JAMES IV instituted a ship-building pro-gramme, under which four large and several small ships were constructed. The *Margaret* (launched 1506) displaced about 700 tons, anticipating England's *Mary Rose* (1509); the *Michael* (1511) displaced 1000 tons and had 12 cannons a side. Thereafter efforts dwindled; in 1707 the Navy com-prised two frigates, operating mainly against French privateers.

NAVIGATION ACTS Legislation that restricted the transport of goods in overseas trade to a country's own ships, to encourage SHIP BUILDING and SHIPPING business, and sometimes to exclude other countries. England's first Act in 1381 required Englishmen to ship goods in English ships. Acts of 1463, 1485 and 1489 required wine and woad from SW France to be imported in English ships.

The 1651 Navigation Act passed by the RUMP PARLIAMENT began the creation of a 'navigation system'. Aimed against the Dutch, it required imports to come directly from countries of origin and be carried in ships from the originating countries or English ships. Imports from Asia, Africa and America had to be carried in English ships (*see* ANGLO-DUTCH WARS). After the RESTORATION (1660), the replacement 1660 Navigation Act made similar rules for the import of specified commodities and required English-owned foreign-built ships to be registered. The Staple Act of 1663 required most imports of European goods to English colonies to be purchased in England and carried in English-owned ships. Restrictions were strength-ened in 1673 and 1696.

Scottish shipping was included under the 1651 Act (*see* UNION OF ENGLAND AND SCOTLAND, 1650s) but excluded at the Restoration. Scotland passed a retaliatory Navigation Act (1661). English legislation applied again to Scotland from 1707 (*see* UNION OF ENGLAND AND SCOTLAND). The Navigation Acts were repealed, except for coastal trade, in 1849 (for coastal trade in 1854).

Navigation Acts also controlled Irish trade. England excluded Ireland from most colonial trade in 1663, and direct imports of sugar and tobacco to Ireland were banned in 1671. Ireland was allowed access to trans-Atlantic trade in 1731. Commercial legislation against Irish trade was repealed in 1779. *See also* MERCANTILISM; FREE TRADE; FOREIGN TRADE, IRELAND, ENGLISH AND BRITISH REGULA-TION; ECONOMY, STATE INVOLVEMENT, BRITAIN.

NAVY, ENGLISH, BEFORE 1660 Before the 16th century kings used sailing ships from the CINQUE PORTS and contracted others from merchants. HENRY V (ruled

1413–22) exceptionally acquired 39 ships. HENRY VII (1485–1509) developed facilities (e.g., dry dock) at Portsmouth (Hampshire).

HENRY VIII (1509–47), influenced by the Scottish Navy, established a permanent Navy by developing a fleet (including 46 commissioned warships and 38 others) and an administration (notably instituting a naval council, 1546, later the Navy Board). From the mid 1530s some warships included gun decks. ELIZABETH I (1558–1603) maintained about 30 warships. Ships continued to be hired as neces-sary. The ANGLO-SPANISH WAR (1585–1604) included defeat of the SPANISH ARMADA (1588).

Under King JAMES VI/I (1603–25) maintenance stag-nated (a strong fleet was considered unnecessary for for-eign policy), although ten ships were built. When CHARLES I renewed war against Spain, a naval assault on Cádiz, SW Spain, failed (1625), as did expeditions to La Rochelle, SW France (1627, 1628). In the 1630s Charles sought a stronger navy, and built ten additional ships (1634–40); squadrons cruised in the English Channel to demonstrate power. But funding was stymied (*see* SHIP MONEY).

As CIVIL WAR approached in 1642, the Navy sided with PARLIAMENT. It was used to deter foreign intervention, protect overseas trade (to sustain CUSTOMS revenues), and provide tactical support for land forces. In 1648 nine crews defected, providing Royalists (in Dutch Republic) with a small fleet (*see* RUPERT, PRINCE). After the abolition of monarchy (March 1649), the Navy aided the conquest of Ireland (1649–50) and Scotland (1650–1).

From 1649 Parliament funded expansion, for defence against Royalists and protection of expanding overseas trade: by 1655 there were 133 ships (compared with 40 in 1640). The Navy fought the Dutch (1652–4; *see* ANGLO-DUTCH WARS), and challenged Spanish power in the Caribbean (*see* WESTERN DESIGN). *See also* NAVIES, NORTH BRITAIN AND SCOTTISH; HAWKINS, JOHN; SHIP-BUILDING INDUSTRY, ENGLAND.

NAVY, ENGLISH AND BRITISH, FROM 1660 After the RESTORATION the 'Royal Navy' was improved (e.g., bet-ter training), although further ANGLO-DUTCH WARS (1665–7, 1672–4) produced stalemates. From 1674 operations included protection for trade in the Mediterranean. During the Wars of the GRAND ALLIANCE (1689–97) and SPANISH SUCCESSION (1702–13) the Navy was increased from 109 to 180 major ships. It notably defeated the French at La Hogue (1692), and captured MINORCA from Spain (1708).

After 1713 Great Britain maintained a strong Navy (usually 150–300 ships), including fleets in distant waters, to sustain trade and empire, and assert power. During the SEVEN YEARS WAR (1756–63) the Navy operated worldwide. During the FRENCH REVOLUTIONARY AND NAPOLEONIC WARS (1793–1815), with expansion to almost

400 ships, it blockaded French ports and inflicted a major strategic defeat at TRAFALGAR (1805).

Although subsequently reduced, the Navy remained overwhelmingly the world's largest until the 1860s. Technological developments were adopted, for example steam engines (1845), iron warships (1860). Larger and faster vessels culminated in *Dreadnought*-class battleships (1906); submarines were introduced (1901). From 1900 Germany challenged British naval power (*see* NAVAL RACE, GREAT BRITAIN AND GERMANY).

During WORLD WAR I (1914–18) the Navy blockaded Germany and (from 1917) escorted convoys. Air power was developed, including the first aircraft carrier, *Argus* (1918). At end 1918 the Navy had 780 ships (including 147 submarines), but was smaller than the US Navy. It was again reduced, and air power atrophied. During WORLD WAR II (1939–45) the re-expanded Navy notably protected convoys (*see* ATLANTIC, BATTLE OF THE) and facilitated invasion of Normandy (*see* OVERLORD).

From the 1950s new technology (e.g., missiles) required drastic change. The Navy prioritized anti-submarine warfare against Soviet power (*see* COLD WAR), and from 1968 provided submarine-based nuclear deterrence. After the FALKLANDS WAR (1982), it developed expeditionary capabilities. In 2016 the Navy had 67 ships (including ten submarines). *See also* PEPYS, SAMUEL; FISCAL–MILITARY STATE; SHIP-BUILDING INDUSTRY, ENGLAND; ANGLO-GERMAN NAVAL AGREEMENT; ATOMIC AND NUCLEAR WEAPONS.

NAVY, SOUTHERN IRELAND *see* DEFENCE FORCES, SOUTHERN IRELAND

NECHTANSMERE, BATTLE OF *see* DÚN NECHTAIN, BATTLE OF

NEGATIVE CONFESSION A confession of faith rejecting Catholicism, drawn up by the Church of SCOTLAND and voluntarily subscribed by King JAMES VI of Scotland (28 Jan. 1581), his cousin and favourite Esmé STEWART, earl of Lennox (a former Catholic), and members of the royal household. James's purpose was to counter fears of renascent Catholicism in government. *See also* COVENANTS, SCOTLAND; RUTHVEN RAID; NATIONAL COVENANT.

NEHRU, JAWAHARLAL (b. 14 Nov. 1889 at Allahabad, Agra and Oudh Provinces, India; d. 27 May 1964 at Delhi, Punjab, India, aged 74). Educated partly in England (1905–12), Nehru became involved with the Indian National Congress after returning to India and in Dec. 1916 met Mohandas GANDHI. He became a strong opponent of the British in India after the AMRITSAR MASSACRE (1919). He campaigned with Gandhi against British rule but lacked his appeal to the masses. From 1921 he was often imprisoned.

From 1945 Nehru was the chief negotiator for the Congress over INDIAN INDEPENDENCE and became interim prime minister in 1946. Independence was implemented in Aug. 1947, and Nehru remained prime minister until his death, promoting industrialization through State planning.

NELSON, LORD (b. 29 Sept. 1758 at Burnham Thorpe, Norfolk, England; d. 21 Oct. 1805 off Cape Trafalgar, Spain, aged 47). A naval officer's nephew, Horatio Nelson joined the British NAVY in 1770, aged 12. After war with France began (1793) he held commands in the Mediterranean. He lost sight in his right eye while on Corsica, leading an artillery assault (July 1794), and his right arm after assaulting Santa Cruz de Tenerife (22–25 July 1797). Following recuperation, he defeated a French fleet near Alexandria (battle of the Nile, 1–3 Aug. 1798), halting an invasion of Egypt. Made Lord Nelson, during 1798–1800 he lived mostly in Naples, helped to save its royal family from an insurrection, and began a lasting affair with Lady Emma Hamilton, wife of the British envoy.

In 1801 Nelson destroyed the Danish fleet (battle of Copenhagen, 2 April), ultimately ending the anti-British 'Armed Neutrality' of Baltic States. Now Viscount Nelson, he also commanded raids on Boulogne (N France) to deter a French invasion of Britain (Aug.).

In service again from 1803, Nelson rejoined the Mediterranean fleet in Sept. 1805, but was killed while defeating a Franco-Spanish fleet at TRAFALGAR. He was an outstanding leader and naval strategist. *See also* FRENCH REVOLUTIONARY AND NAPOLEONIC WARS, BRITISH INVOLVEMENT.

NENNIUS The name traditionally but incorrectly given to the author of the *Historia Brittonum* ('History of the Britons'), composed (in Latin) by an unknown author within the kingdom of MERFYN FRYCH of GWYNEDD (NW Wales) in 829 or 830. The *Historia* is the earliest surviving historical work from Wales.

NEOLITHIC PERIOD, BRITAIN Literally the 'New Stone Age', the period *c*.4300–*c*.2300 BC (following the MESOLITHIC PERIOD), often divided into Early (to *c*.3200 BC), Middle (to *c*.2800 BC), and Late phases. It is associated with the first widespread use of domesticated plants (cereals) and animals, pottery, polished stone tools, tombs and ceremonial monuments. Regionally varied, these reflect an increased concern with ancestral rites, exchange and public ceremonies as central to the reproduction of relations between dispersed communities. Changes in the Neolithic were traditionally regarded as products of colonization from Continental Europe, though they may also reflect changes in social and economic practice adopted by communities in Britain. The Neolithic was succeeded by the BRONZE AGE.

NEOLITHIC PERIOD, IRELAND The 'New Stone Age'; in Ireland dating from *c*.3800 to *c*.2500 BC. Material culture was diverse, with stone items and pottery being the main surviving artefacts. Rectangular and circular houses were built (rectangular houses appear to be earlier). Both open and enclosed settlements occur. The period has left a range of ceremonial sites, including four main types of MEGALITHIC MONUMENTS: court, portal, passage and wedge tombs. The Neolithic was followed by the CHALCOLITHIC PERIOD.

NEST (b. *c*.1080; d. after 1136, aged at least 56). A famously beautiful daughter of RHYS AP TEWDWR, king of DEHEUBARTH (SW Wales). Nest married Gerald of Windsor, Norman constable of Pembroke (SW Wales), *c*.1100; their daughter Angharad was mother of GERALD OF WALES. Abducted in 1109 by Owain ap Cadwgan of CEREDIGION (W Wales), Nest later married two more Normans in Wales and was a mistress of King HENRY I of England, perhaps *c*.1114.

NETHERLANDS, ENGLISH AND BRITISH RELATIONS WITH England (Great Britain from 1707) has taken a close strategic interest in the northern Netherlands, to prevent its use as a base for invasion. Following the declaration of independence against Spanish rule by the United Provinces (or Dutch Republic) in 1581, English forces supported the (Protestant) rebels against (Catholic) SPAIN 1585–1604 (*see* ANGLO-SPANISH WAR). (Dutch independence was widely recognized from 1609.)

In the 17th century, commercial rivalry resulted in two naval wars (1652–4, 1665–7), while English subordination to FRANCE caused a third (1672–4; *see* ANGLO-DUTCH WARS). England seized Dutch territory in N America in 1664, thereby connecting its two regions of colonization (*see* NORTH AMERICAN COLONIES).

The acquisition of the English Crown in 1689 by the stadholder (lieutenant) of the Dutch Republic, William of Orange, created a firm alliance (*see* WILLIAM III). It lasted throughout the Wars of the GRAND ALLIANCE (1689–97), SPANISH SUCCESSION (1702–13) and AUSTRIAN SUCCESSION (1740–8). After conflict over Dutch trade with rebels in British N America (1780–4, 'Fourth Anglo-Dutch War'), the alliance was resumed in 1788.

Following French dominance and rule of the Netherlands (1795–1813), the British foreign secretary, Viscount CASTLEREAGH, promoted a 'United Kingdom of the Netherlands', including the southern Netherlands (1815); subsequently, however, Lord PALMERSTON helped to force the Dutch to withdraw from the southern section (1839; *see* BELGIUM). Later relations were generally amicable, though Dutch opinion resented the (Second) BOER WAR (1899–1902). Britain and the Netherlands were founder members of the NORTH ATLANTIC TREATY ORGANIZATION (1949).

NEVILLE FAMILY A noble family whose members were influential in N England in the 15th century, acting as a counter-balance to the PERCY FAMILY, and also of national importance. They originated as barons of Raby (Co. Durham). Ralph Neville (*c*.1354–1425), 4th baron, was created earl of Westmorland in 1397 for supporting King RICHARD II against the APPELLANTS. His children married into leading noble families and supported the LANCASTRIAN kings. Ralph's eldest son from his second marriage, Richard Neville (1400–60), was created earl of Salisbury (1429). Richard's son, also Richard (1428–71), was created earl of WARWICK (1449).

In the 1450s the Nevilles feuded with the Percys. They also became leading supporters of Richard, duke of YORK, and were England's most influential family in the 1460s under EDWARD IV. Warwick's rebellion against Edward effectively ended their power. *See also* YORKIST–LANCASTRIAN CONFLICT.

NEVILLE'S CROSS, BATTLE OF Fought W of DURHAM (NE England) on 17 Oct. 1346. A Scottish army under King DAVID II, which had invaded England to support France (invaded by England), was heavily defeated. David was captured and Edward BALLIOL was able to make another invasion of Scotland. *See also* SCOTTISH–ENGLISH RELATIONS 1290 TO 1357.

NEW BRUNSWICK A former British colony in N America. The area, NE of NEW ENGLAND, was settled sparsely in the 17th century by French, English and Scots. Control was disputed. From 1713 it was part of the British colony of NOVA SCOTIA. Following an influx of loyalists from the USA (independent from 1776), the area was separated in 1784 as the CROWN COLONY of New Brunswick, named for King GEORGE III, a descendant of the house of Brunswick. It was granted RESPONSIBLE GOVERNMENT, including an assembly, in 1848, and joined the dominion of CANADA in 1867. *See also* CANADIAN CONFEDERATION.

NEWCASTLE, DUKE OF (b. 21 July 1693 in Sussex, England; d. 17 Nov. 1768 at London, England, aged 75). Thomas Pelham took the surname Pelham-Holles on inheriting extensive estates in 1711. Lord Pelham from 1712, he was created earl of Clare (1714) and duke of Newcastle (1715) by King GEORGE I. Through land ownership and co-ordination of noble and royal PATRONAGE he became the leading manager of WHIG politicians and elections for Robert WALPOLE (prime minister 1721–42) and his own younger brother Henry PELHAM (1743–54).

As SECRETARY OF STATE (southern 1724–48, northern 1748–54) Newcastle supervised foreign policy. Unlike Walpole, he favoured involvement in the War of JENKINS'

EAR (from 1739) and alliance with Austria in the War of the AUSTRIAN SUCCESSION (1740–8).

In 1754 Newcastle succeeded his brother as first lord of the Treasury (i.e., PRIME MINISTER), but seemed unsuitable. After unintentionally provoking the DIPLOMATIC REVOLUTION and mishandling the start of the SEVEN YEARS WAR, he resigned (1756; replaced by duke of DEVONSHIRE).

Newcastle served again 1757–62, in coalition with William PITT the Elder (until Oct. 1761). He was succeeded by the earl of BUTE. A period as lord PRIVY SEAL (1765–6) under Lord ROCKINGHAM concluded Newcastle's career. *See also* PELHAMS; GEORGE II; BYNG, JOHN; ROBINSON, THOMAS.

NEWCASTLE PROGRAMME The radical election manifesto adopted by the Conference of the LIBERAL PARTY at NEWCASTLE UPON TYNE (NE England) on 1–2 Oct. 1891 and accepted by its leader, W.E. GLADSTONE. Its pledges included HOME RULE for Ireland, district and parish councils, DISESTABLISHMENT of Churches in Wales and Scotland, employers' liability for accidents, triennial Parliaments, and a local veto on alcohol sales.

NEWCASTLE PROPOSITIONS Terms presented on 30 July 1646 to King CHARLES I by commissioners of the English Parliament, for settling their conflict, at NEWCASTLE UPON TYNE (Northumberland), where Charles was a prisoner of the Scots. They required Charles to enforce the SOLEMN LEAGUE AND COVENANT in England, Ireland and Scotland; to accept abolition of episcopacy; and to implement anti-Catholic measures. Parliament would control military forces for 20 years, and nominate officers of State and judges. Various penalties would be imposed on Royalists. Charles requested time for consideration, and permission to negotiate at WESTMINSTER. No further terms were considered until July 1647. *See also* CIVIL WARS, POLITICAL ASPECTS.

NEWCASTLE UPON TYNE A city in NE England, by the R. Tyne; formerly centre of Northumberland (to 1974).

Founded by ROBERT CURTHOSE in 1080, together with a royal castle, Newcastle expanded in the 13th century, exporting COAL, lead and WOOL. In 1334 it was the fourth wealthiest place in England and the leading town N of YORK. Like most towns it contracted in the 15th century.

From the late 16th century coal exports from the Tyne Valley increased dramatically, with LONDON as the major market. In the 19th century Newcastle also became a large financial and industrial centre (heavy engineering, brewing, etc.). In 1882 a diocese was founded and Newcastle was designated a city. It suffered from industrial decline in the 1920s–30s, and from contraction of coal mining in the 1980s. Two universities were created by upgrading existing institutions: Newcastle University (1963) and Northumbria University (1992).

Est. popn: 1300, 3800; 1600, 10,000; 1800, 33,000; 1900, 214,000; 2000, 265,000.

NEWCOMEN, THOMAS (b. Feb. 1664 at Dartmouth, Devon, England; d. 5 Aug. 1729 at London, England, aged 65). Originally an ironmonger, Newcomen designed the first reliable steam engine, for industrial use. Constructed at Dudley (Worcestershire) and exhibited at London in 1712, it improved Thomas Savery's 'atmospheric engine' (a steam-powered device for pumping water from mines, patented 1699).

Newcomen's engine condensed steam in a cylinder to create a vacuum, which drove a piston. The piston rocked a beam, which moved rods connected to a pump. The engine was quickly adopted for draining mines, and remained important until the late 18th century. Over 100 were built by 1733. *See also* COAL INDUSTRY, ENGLAND; WATT, JAMES.

NEW ENGLAND The name applied in 1614 to a region in N America (now the NE part of the USA) by the English explorer Captain John Smith (1580–1631) after he mapped its coastal area. Smith argued that the region's soils and climate provided a favourable place for recreating English society in America (better than the difficult conditions in VIRGINIA). Continuous English settlement began in 1620 (*see* PLYMOUTH PLANTATION OR COLONY). At AMERICAN INDEPENDENCE (1776), New England comprised CONNECTICUT, MASSACHUSETTS, NEW HAMPSHIRE, and RHODE ISLAND. The US States of Vermont and Maine were formed subsequently (1791, 1820). *See also* NORTH AMERICA, ENGLISH EXPLORATION.

NEW ENGLAND, COUNCIL FOR An English company, led by Sir Fernando Gorges (1568–1647), to which King JAMES VI/I granted land in N America in 1620. It was effectively a revival of the Plymouth group of the earlier VIRGINIA COMPANY. Rather than finance colonization, the Council made sub-grants of lands and settlement rights to companies wishing to fund settlements. Its awards included two grants to the company supporting the PLYMOUTH PLANTATION (1621, 1630), and a land grant (1629) to the Massachusetts Bay Company (*see* MASSACHUSETTS). The Council was dissolved in 1635. *See also* NORTH AMERICAN COLONIES.

NEW ENGLAND, DOMINION OF A combination of English colonies in N America ordered by JAMES VII/II (king of England 1685–8). His scheme developed policies of CHARLES II, who sought greater control of American colonies from the mid 1670s and nullified the charter of MASSACHUSETTS by legal action (1684). He and James envisaged the amalgamation of England's colonies into several larger territories, akin to Spanish viceroyalties, which would be under strong royal control.

The dominion was implemented from May 1686 (arrival of president), and consisted initially of Massachusetts with Maine Province, NEW HAMPSHIRE, PLYMOUTH PLANTATION and part of RHODE ISLAND. A governor, Sir Edmund Andros, arrived in Dec. 1686. He added the remainder of Rhode Island and CONNECTICUT (1687), and (1688) NEW YORK and the Jerseys (*see* NEW JERSEY). In 1689, following King James's flight, a popular uprising in Boston (Massachusetts) overthrew Andros. The dominion collapsed (April–May), and individual colonies were allowed to resume autonomy. *See also* NORTH AMERICAN COLONIES, GOVERNMENTS OF.

NEW ENGLISH Term used from the later 16th century to describe English settlers who arrived in Ireland from the late 1530s onwards as the English government exerted authority across Ireland. They usually became, or were, Protestants. From the later 16th century they gradually excluded the OLD ENGLISH (Catholic English of earlier origin) from power. Many New English were involved in PLANTATIONS. From the later 17th century they tended to be called 'Protestants'. *See also* IRELAND, ENGLISH CONQUEST, 16TH CENTURY; IMMIGRATION TO IRELAND; CROMWELLIAN LAND SETTLEMENT.

NEWFOUNDLAND A former English CROWN COLONY in N America (British from 1707). Newfoundland island was visited in 1497 by the English-sponsored explorer John CABOT, who annexed territory, and then reclaimed for England in 1583 by Humphrey GILBERT. England valued its cod fisheries but settlement was discouraged until the 18th century. Governors were appointed from 1729, initially residing seasonally. France maintained a claim until 1713, and retained fishing rights until 1904. From 1763 Newfoundland was awarded an increasing area of Labrador to the N (final establishment of boundaries, 1927).

The first permanently resident governor was appointed in 1817. Immigration accompanied the development of sealing and mining. A legislature was finally established in 1855. Newfoundland rejected confederation with Canada in 1869 and 1895, and was granted DOMINION status in 1917.

Newfoundland returned to British colonial rule in 1934 when nearly bankrupted by the Great Depression. It became the tenth province of CANADA in 1949, following a referendum, and was officially called Newfoundland and Labrador from 2001. Approx. population (Newfoundland and Labrador) in 1921, 263,000; in 1948, 339,000. *See also* UTRECHT, PEACE OF.

NEWGRANGE The central NEOLITHIC passage tomb at the BEND OF THE BOYNE (Co. Meath, E Ireland). Dating from *c*.3000 BC, the mound is 280 ft (85 m) in diameter and 50 ft (15 m) high. It covers a cruciform tomb. The mound is surrounded by a kerb of 97 stones, including a highly decorated entrance stone. A concentration of quartz has been reconstructed as a facade. The mound is aligned on the sunrise at the mid-winter solstice, when the sun shines into the central chamber via a 'roof-box'. After the tomb went into disuse, there was settlement in front of it in the BEAKER period (*c*.2500– *c*.1700 BC), followed by the construction of a large timber and pit circle. Then a STONE CIRCLE was placed around the mound. In late prehistory Roman material was deposited close to the entrance. Newgrange is probably Ireland's most famous prehistoric monument. *See also* PASSAGE TOMBS.

NEW HAMPSHIRE A former English colony in N America, in NEW ENGLAND (British from 1707). The name 'New Hampshire' was originally given to land N of MASSACHUSETTS which was granted to John Mason in 1629 by the Council for NEW ENGLAND. English settlements had been founded there since 1623. By 1643 they acknowledged the authority of the Massachusetts colony.

From 1659 Mason's grandson and heir Robert Tufton Mason sought to exclude Massachusetts' jurisdiction. His claim was resolved when King CHARLES II issued a charter creating a separate province and CROWN COLONY (1679). WILLIAM III and MARY II issued a replacement charter (1691). New Hampshire was governed by a governor and council, appointed by the English Crown, and an elected assembly. Its boundaries were disputed. Est. population 1770: 60,000.

Following conflict with Great Britain, the governor fled in Sept. 1775 (*see* AMERICAN INDEPENDENCE, ORIGINS OF). In 1776 New Hampshire adopted a new constitution and became a State of the USA. *See also* NORTH AMERICAN COLONIES; NEW ENGLAND, DOMINION OF.

NEW IMPERIALISM Term used for the sudden and striking change in Europe's political relations with the rest of the world 1870–1900. The British, French, German and Russian Empires were greatly enlarged. Italy also participated in competition for territories, and Belgium and Portugal added to their possessions. *See also* SCRAMBLE FOR AFRICA; IMPERIALISM OF FREE TRADE; BRITISH EMPIRE.

NEW IRELAND FORUM A conference of three major political parties in the Republic of Ireland and the SOCIAL DEMOCRATIC AND LABOUR PARTY of Northern Ireland to review attitudes to Ireland's future, especially the status of Northern Ireland. Promoted by Garret FITZGERALD, it met intermittently May 1983–May 1984. Though the British government rejected the Forum's proposals, it conceded greater co-operation with Ireland in the HILLSBOROUGH AGREEMENT. *See also* NORTHERN IRELAND; TROUBLES.

NEW JERSEY A former English colony in N America (British from 1707). It was part of a larger area organized from 1624 as New Netherland by the Dutch East India Company (incorporating 'New Sweden' from 1655). In March 1664 King CHARLES II granted New Netherland, though not in English possession, to his brother James, duke of York (see JAMES VII/II); in July, York granted part of the territory, SW of the Hudson River, to Lord Berkeley and Sir George Carteret. It was named New Jersey in honour of Carteret, who had been Royalist lieutenant-governor of Jersey (in the CHANNEL ISLANDS) during the CIVIL WARS. York's forces seized the New Jersey area in Sept. (see NEW YORK).

In 1674 Carteret and Berkeley's successors divided New Jersey into East and West Jersey. Each was developed (including provision of government) by groups of proprietors (Carteret's heirs sold his rights in 1681). But conflict occurred between inhabitants and owners. In 1702 the proprietors surrendered their governmental rights to the English Crown, making New Jersey a CROWN COLONY. It was then ruled by a Crown-appointed governor (until 1738 the governor of New York) and elected assembly. Est. population 1770: 110,000.

New Jersey joined resistance to British policies in the 1760s–70s (see AMERICAN INDEPENDENCE, ORIGINS OF). In 1776 the governor was arrested (June), a constitution was adopted (2 July), and New Jersey became a State of the USA. See also NORTH AMERICAN COLONIES; NEW ENGLAND, DOMINION OF.

NEW LABOUR Name used from autumn 1994 as a 'rebranding' of the British LABOUR PARTY to broaden its electoral appeal following four general election defeats. Proposed in early 1994 by political consultant Philip Gould, it was deployed by Alastair CAMPBELL after the election of Tony BLAIR as leader.

'New Labour' referred to incipient 'modernization' of Party organization (e.g., reduction of union influence in leadership elections) and policies (e.g., being 'tough on crime' and, in April 1995, replacement of Labour's commitment to NATIONALIZATION), and to the Party's intent to pursue modernizing centrist rather than partisan policies in government. It is also used to characterize aspects of Blair's government (1997–2007), such as retention of the Conservatives' trade union reforms and some reforms of public services (e.g., 'Trust' hospitals). Blair's rival and successor Gordon BROWN demonstrated limited co-operation (see SPENCE AFFAIR); Brown's successor (from 2010), Ed Miliband, abandoned the term.

NEW LIBERALISM Term used from the 1880s for the development of British LIBERALISM in response to social problems (e.g., UNEMPLOYMENT, poverty, malnutrition). New liberalism advocated greater State intervention in

society to provide individuals with greater economic and social freedom. It advocated graduated direct TAXATION (e.g., death duties, income tax) to generate funds for redistribution, thereby increasing consumption and employment, together with social welfare (e.g., health insurance, pensions). New liberalism underlay the reforms of the 1905–15 Liberal government. See also GREEN, T.H.; PEOPLE'S BUDGET; SOCIAL SERVICES.

NEWMAN, JOHN HENRY (b. 21 Feb. 1801 at London, England; d. 11 Aug. 1890 at Birmingham, Warwickshire, England, aged 89). Of evangelical outlook (from 1816), Newman became a fellow of Oriel College, OXFORD (1822), and a Church of England clergyman (1824). He served as vicar of the University Church in Oxford (St Mary's) from 1828. When the OXFORD MOVEMENT was launched (1833), Newman organized and published the Tracts for the Times to spread its views. He challenged liberal theology (see HAMPDEN, RENN), and promoted the Church of England as a via media ('middle way') between Protestantism and Roman Catholicism.

Newman eventually doubted the Church's integrity. He resigned from St Mary's (1843), and in Oct. 1845 left Oriel and became a Roman Catholic. He was ordained priest in Rome in 1847 and joined the Oratorians. He founded an oratory (community of secular priests) in England (1848), and attempted to found a Catholic university at DUBLIN, Ireland (1851–7). He was created a cardinal in 1879. Newman's writings included hymns, the autobiographical work Apologia pro vita sua (1864), and influential works of theology (e.g., An Essay in Aid of a Grammar of Assent, 1870). Newman was beatified in 2010 and canonized in 2019. See also KINGSLEY, CHARLES; ELGAR, EDWARD.

NEW MODEL ARMY In England, the Army established by the LONG PARLIAMENT on 4 April 1645, during the First CIVIL WAR, which replaced existing armies as part of a new strategy to achieve victory (see SELF-DENYING ORDINANCE). Weaknesses in Parliament's military effort had resulted in demands for 'new modelling' of its armies. Though based on existing forces, it valued efficiency rather than social standing (as seen in the choice of officers).

The Army initially consisted of 22,000 officers and men, commanded by Sir Thomas FAIRFAX (succeeded, June 1650, by Oliver CROMWELL). Political radicals within the Army strongly influenced politics (see CIVIL WARS, POLITICAL ASPECTS; COMMONWEALTH AND PROTECTORATE), and units invaded Ireland (1649) and Scotland (1650). The Army reached a peak of 70,000 in 1652, and was still 42,000 strong in 1660. Divisions among the Army's leaders sapped its political strength before the RESTORATION (1660), after which it was mostly disbanded, with a few regiments being retained by King CHARLES II. See also ARMY, ENGLISH AND BRITISH.

NEW MONARCHY, ENGLAND A concept proposed by the English historian J.R. Green in 1874. He claimed that King EDWARD IV (ruled 1461–70, 1471–83) and King HENRY VII (1485–1509) asserted authority over the NOBILITY, quelling the YORKIST–LANCASTRIAN CONFLICT. Green viewed this as despotism, but others saw it as strong government producing peaceful conditions. Both rulers demonstrably strengthened the Crown by increasing revenues, and Henry VII employed officers of modest background (so-called 'new men', such as Edmund DUDLEY, Richard EMPSON).

Critics accepted that Edward and Henry were assertive, but argued that their methods were unoriginal: 'new men' had precedents, and government was little changed. Nobles remained powerful, although kings harnessed their authority in localities. The 1530s probably saw more important changes. *See also* GOVERNMENT, ENGLAND 1066 TO 1509; TUDOR REVOLUTION IN GOVERNMENT; RESUMPTION ACTS.

NEW MONARCHY, SCOTLAND A concept derived from English history (*see* NEW MONARCHY, ENGLAND), proposed as a characterization of the government of King JAMES IV (ruled 1488–1513). James raised ROYAL REVENUES to a new height, built a substantial NAVY and created a judicial COUNCIL which developed into the Court of SESSION. But other kings (e.g., DAVID II, JAMES I) had increased revenues and improved government, and during James IV's reign there was no fundamental change in the basis of royal authority in the country: he depended on achieving good relations with hereditary territorial MAGNATES (rather than using officials extensively or 'new nobles' created by the king).

NEW PARTY A pro-government group in the Scottish PARLIAMENT 1704–5, including former opposition members (*see* COUNTRY PARTY). Formed by the (2nd) marquis of TWEEDDALE, it aimed to secure the HANOVERIAN SUCCESSION (already adopted by England), by diluting the Act of SECURITY, and to raise taxation. It secured the latter only by conceding the Act. England responded with the anti-Scottish ALIEN ACT (1705) and the Party was broken by the *WORCESTER AFFAIR*. Some members later formed the *SQUADRONE VOLANTE*.

NEWPORT A city in SE Wales by the R. Usk; centre of Newport unitary authority (Welsh, Casnewydd, meaning 'New castle'.)

Newport was founded probably in the early 12th century, alongside a castle (centre of the lordship of Newport). It remained a market town until the mid 19th century, when the building of docks made it the chief port of the eastern S Wales coalfield. Coal exporting and population increased rapidly: by 1900 Newport was the fourth largest

town in Wales. Coal exporting declined from 1913. Industrial development after 1945 brought renewed growth (engineering, chemicals and steel making and working at nearby Llanwern from 1959). In the late 20th century, Newport was the third largest town in Wales. It was formerly in MONMOUTHSHIRE (1536–1974) and Gwent (1974–96). Newport was granted city status in 2002. *See also* NEWPORT RISING; CANALS, WALES; CATHOLICS AND CATHOLIC CHURCH, WALES.

Est. popn: 1300, 1000; 1600, 800; 1800, 1100; 1900, 67,000; 2000, 137,000.

NEWPORT RISING An incident on 4 Nov. 1839 when 5000 Chartists (including many miners and ironworkers) marched into NEWPORT, SE Wales, probably attempting to start a general insurrection. It was suppressed by soldiers, at the Westgate Hotel, who shot dead 20 rioters and wounded over 50. Three leaders were condemned to death, but the sentences were commuted to TRANSPORTATION for life. *See also* CHARTISM, WALES.

NEW SOUTH WALES A former British colony in Australia. The name was applied by James COOK to Australia's E coast after he annexed it in 1770. A CROWN COLONY, initially for transported convicts, was founded in 1788 (*see* TRANSPORTATION). Some convicts chose to stay and were given land; free settlers arrived from the early 19th century.

The developing colony was deemed to comprise eastern and C Australia. From 1825 new colonies were formed by subdivision (*see* AUSTRALIA). Alongside agriculture and sheep grazing, mining was developed (gold was discovered in 1851). Transportation ended in 1850.

In 1855 the British Parliament granted New South Wales a new constitution and RESPONSIBLE GOVERNMENT. It joined the Commonwealth of Australia in 1901 (*see* AUSTRALIAN FEDERATION). Approx. population in 1901: 1,366,000. *See also* BOTANY BAY; BLIGH, WILLIAM; NEW ZEALAND.

NEWSPAPERS, ENGLAND Of various short-lived news-sheets published in LONDON in the early 17th century, the *Weekly Newes* (1622) may be considered the first regular newspaper. The First CIVIL WAR (1642–6) stimulated journalism, and lighter regulation after 1695 encouraged a proliferation of weekly and tri-weekly titles, although stamp duty (1712–1855) impeded the growth of a cheap popular press. The first London daily was the single-sheet *Daily Courant* (1702–35). Notable early provincial publications include the *Worcester Post-Man* (from 1709) and the *Leeds Intelligencer* (1754; renamed *Yorkshire Post* 1866).

The Times (started 1785 as *The Daily Universal Register*; renamed 1788) won national pre-eminence in the 19th century. The steam press, distribution by RAILWAYS, creation of news agencies, and linotype permitted all-round expansion and the rise of mass-circulation dailies serving the entire UK (including Ireland), such as the *Daily Telegraph* (1855). Sunday newspapers date from 1791 (with the *Observer and Courier*). The sensationalistic *News of the World* proved best-selling (1843–2011).

A more populist approach was developed from the later 19th century, by such papers as the *Daily Mail* (1896), *Daily Express* (1900) and *Daily Mirror* (1903). As advertising revenue became increasingly important, editors boosted circulation by adding more entertainment (e.g., crossword puzzles, comic strips), though political partisanship remained common. The chief centre for national newspaper publishing was Fleet Street, London, until 1986 when the proprietor Rupert MURDOCH began a move to other locations to reduce trade union power. In the late 20th century there were over 1200 local newspapers. But competition from electronic media caused considerable reorganization from the 1990s, and in the early 21st century circulations suffered marked declines. In mid 2016 there were ten national daily papers, divided between 'quality' and 'popular tabloid', with the *Sun* (started 1964) as the best-seller. *See also* ROTHERMERE, LORD; BEAVERBROOK, LORD; PHONE-HACKING SCANDAL.

NEWSPAPERS, IRELAND The *Irish Monthly Mercury* (1649–51) was the first newspaper, published at CORK by the English Parliamentary army (*see* CROMWELL, OLIVER, AND IRELAND). Papers appeared intermittently in the 1660s–90s, then became longer lasting (e.g., *Pue's Impartial Occurrences*, 1703–73). Though attacks on the government provoked taxes (1774) and a Libel Act (1784), papers devoted to causes were not deterred (e.g., over Catholic Emancipation in 1820s).

Repeal of tax on advertisements (1853) and stamp duty on newspapers (1855) stimulated expansion. Titles increased from about 100 to almost 300 by 1910. Many promoted outlooks or causes (e.g., Unionism by the *Irish Times* from 1859). The most influential nationalist paper was the *Freeman's Journal* (1763–1924); others such as *Sinn Féin* and *Irish Freedom* were outlawed in 1914. English 'new journalism' and popular presentation (e.g., pictures) were influential from 1904 (relaunch of the *Irish Independent* modelled on Britain's *Daily Mail*). Notable in the IRISH FREE STATE was Éamon DE VALERA's *Irish Press* (1931–95). The *Sunday Press* (from 1949) was the most popular. In the early 21st century national and local newspapers faced growing competition from other media. British newspapers have also always been influential.

NEWSPAPERS, SCOTLAND The first news publication was a reprint of English parliamentary proceedings from

Dec. 1641 to Jan. 1642. In 1651 the irregular *Mercurius Scoticus* lasted for 21 editions; other short-lived titles appeared after the RESTORATION (1660). Durable papers were established in Edinburgh in 1699–1720 (including the revived *Edinburgh Gazette*, from 1699), though they were hampered by stamp duty (1712–1855). The twice-weekly *Caledonian Mercury* (1720) appeared five times a week from 1726. Papers generally supported the HANOVERIAN SUCCESSION. Lasting provincial papers began with *Aberdeen's Journal* (from 1747). The *Glasgow Advertiser* (1783; retitled *Glasgow Herald*, 1805) was Glasgow's first long-lived paper.

Publications steadily increased in the 19th century, including the *Edinburgh Review* (1802), *Blackwood's Magazine* (1817), and *The Scotsman* (1817). The *North British Daily Mail*, founded in Glasgow (1847), was Scotland's first daily newspaper. The *Sunday Post*, founded by D.C. Thomson of DUNDEE in 1920, became exceptionally popular. (The company also produced famous children's comic papers.) In the 1920s there were about 20 national papers, which fell to 12 after closures in the 1960s–70s. In the mid 1990s about 190 local newspapers were also published, including 'free sheets' supported by advertising.

By 2017 the advent of the Internet was causing serious losses of readership and advertising, and closures. There remained four daily national newspapers (*Daily Record*, with largest circulation, *The Herald*, *The Scotsman*, and *The National*, the last launched in 2014 to support Scottish independence), four Sunday nationals (*Sunday Mail*, associated with *Daily Record*, *Sunday Herald*, *Scotland on Sunday*, and *Sunday Post*) and about 120 local newspapers. UK national newspapers also continued to publish Scottish editions.

NEWSPAPERS, WALES Apart from a one-issue publication of 1735, Welsh-language periodicals appeared in the later 18th century, some spreading ideas from the FRENCH REVOLUTION. Most were short-lived. *Seren Gomer* ('Star of Gomer'), launched in SWANSEA (S Wales) in 1814, lasted as a weekly for 85 issues (and was later revived). By 1850, 139 periodicals had been launched, many having campaigned for radical causes such as CHARTISM and repeal of the CORN LAWS. Most failed.

Durable publications, some allied to nonconformist denominations, were established in the second half of the 19th century, with Thomas GEE's (Liberal) *Baner ac Amserau Cymru* ('Banner and Times of Wales') winning a substantial circulation (1857–1989). Welsh-language periodicals were also published in England (Liverpool and London) and the USA.

Wales's first English-language weekly was *The Cambrian*, launched in Swansea in 1804 (continuing until 1930). The first daily, also published in Swansea, was the (Liberal) *Cambria Daily Leader* (1861–1930). Another morning daily, the (Conservative) *Western Mail*, was published in CARDIFF (SE Wales) from 1869, followed by the (Liberal) *South Wales Daily News* from 1872. (From 1928 the *Western Mail* incorporated the *Daily News*.) The N was served from the late 19th century by the Wales edition of the *Liverpool Daily Post*. In 2003 this became a separate regional newspaper, the *Daily Post*.

In 2017 the *Western Mail* (the only Wales-based British national newspaper) and *Daily Post* remained the main newspapers, both containing Welsh-language content. Other news publications included about 60 regular Welsh-language newsletters produced by volunteers (called *papurau bro*, 'local papers').

NEWTON, ISAAC (b. 25 Dec. 1642 at Woolsthorpe, Lincolnshire, England; d. 20 March 1727 at Kensington, Middlesex, England, aged 84). A farmer's posthumous son, Newton studied at Trinity College, CAMBRIDGE, from 1661. While in Lincolnshire 1665–7 (avoiding PLAGUE), he made fundamental advances in mathematics, analysis of light, and awareness of gravitation (the last allegedly inspired by seeing an apple fall from a tree). He became a fellow of Trinity (1667) and Lucasian professor of mathematics (1669). Newton's submission of a telescope to the ROYAL SOCIETY won him election as a fellow (1672).

In 1687 Newton published *Philosophiae Naturalis Principia Mathematica* ('Mathematical Principles of Natural Philosophy', known as the *Principia*), which explained cosmology mathematically. His other publications included *Opticks* (1704). He secretly explored ALCHEMY and was anti-Trinitarian (*see* UNITARIANS).

In mid life, Newton entered public affairs, becoming an MP (1689–90, 1701–2), and warden of the Royal Mint (1696; master from 1699); he resigned his Cambridge positions in 1701. From 1703 he served as president of the Royal Society, and was knighted in 1705. One of the greatest natural philosophers (scientists), Newton was famously celebrated by Alexander Pope (1730): 'Nature and Nature's laws lay hid in night; / God said, *Let Newton be!* and all was light.' *See also* HOOKE, ROBERT; SCIENTIFIC REVOLUTION.

NEW YORK A former English colony in N America (British from 1707). It was part of an earlier, larger area, called 'New Netherland' from 1614, in which the Dutch West India Company organized settlements from 1624 (*see also* NEW JERSEY). In 1626 it purchased Manhattan Island from local Indians, on which New Amsterdam had already been started (later the principal settlement).

In March 1664 King CHARLES II of England granted the New Netherland territory, though not in English possession, to his brother James, duke of York, who sent a fleet. The Dutch colony's director-general surrendered on 27 Aug. The colony and New Amsterdam were renamed New

York after the duke. (The Dutch briefly repossessed their former territory in 1673–4.) The colony's first elected assembly met in 1683 and drafted a frame of government. New York became a CROWN COLONY in 1685 when York became king (*see* JAMES VII/II). It was ruled from 1689 to 1691 by a popular assembly led by Jacob Leisler (*see* NEW ENGLAND, DOMINION OF). Est. population 1770: 185,000.

New York resisted British impositions from 1765 but reluctantly became a State of the USA in 1776 (*see* AMERICAN INDEPENDENCE, ORIGINS OF). Many battles took place in New York State during the AMERICAN WAR OF INDEPENDENCE. *See also* NORTH AMERICAN COLONIES.

NEW ZEALAND A former British DOMINION in the SW Pacific, comprising two large and several smaller islands. Charted by James COOK in 1769–70, New Zealand was then frequented by British whalers. Missionaries followed from 1814. Edward Gibbon Wakefield (1796–1862) organized colonization in the 1830s, and Great Britain annexed South Island in 1839. Maori chiefs ceded sovereignty over North Island by the treaty of Waitangi (1840), but land disputes led to intermittent conflict with the Maoris (1845–7, 1860–72; *see* MAORIS AND BRITISH, MID 19TH CENTURY). New Zealand was considered part of NEW SOUTH WALES until made a CROWN COLONY in 1841.

New Zealand was granted a constitution in 1853, and RESPONSIBLE GOVERNMENT in 1856. Central government took over public works and immigration policy from the provinces in the 1870s. Pastoral farming flourished in the late 19th century, boosted from 1879 by the development of refrigerated ships. The Liberal Party predominated 1891–1912, introducing old age pensions (1898) and female suffrage (1893). New Zealand adopted dominion status in 1907. The Reform Party, in power 1912–28, supported farming interests and imperial unity.

During WORLD WAR I (1914–18), 130,000 New Zealanders fought in France and at GALLIPOLI. Between 1935 and 1949, Labour governments introduced social reforms. WORLD WAR II (1939–45) saw New Zealand send troops to Europe and N Africa while relying on the USA for defence from 1942. Formal independence (under the British Crown) was established in 1947, and British membership of the EUROPEAN ECONOMIC COMMUNITY (1973) led New Zealand to seek closer relations with AUSTRALIA and E Asia. Approx. population in 1921, 1,320,000; in 1946, 1,759,000.

NIALL GLÚNDUB (NIALL 'BLACK-KNEE') (fl. from 896 in Ireland; d. 15 Sept. 919 at Islandbridge, near Dublin, Leinster, E Ireland). The dominant king in N Ireland from 896 (high-king of both the Cenél nEógain dynasty and the Northern UÍ NÉILL), Niall became king of TARA (claimed high-king of Ireland) in 916. He faced renewed VIKING incursions. After an indecisive encounter at CASHEL (S Ireland), he was killed by Sitric Gale, (Viking) king of DUBLIN. In the 11th century Niall's descendants adopted his name as their surname; *see* O'NEILL FAMILIES.

NIALL NOÍGIALLACH (NIALL 'OF THE NINE HOSTAGES') (fl. in early 5th century in Ireland). A king in CONNACHT (W Ireland), Niall was the principal ancestor from whom the Northern and Southern Uí NÉILL dynastic federations claimed descent. (The federations dominated N Ireland and MEATH from respectively the 5th and 6th centuries.) The 'Nine Hostages' were possibly hostages given by nine subordinate dynasties in AIRGIALLA. Later sources claimed Niall as king of TARA (supposed high-king of Ireland). *See also* ULSTER; KINGSHIP, IRELAND.

NIGERIA A former British territory in W Africa. The English acquired slaves from the Niger Delta and other riverine areas from the mid 17th century (*see* ROYAL AFRICAN COMPANY), but from 1808 the British sought to suppress the SLAVE TRADE. Great Britain annexed Lagos as a base in 1861 and declared a PROTECTORATE over coastal areas in 1885 (the Niger Districts Protectorate; renamed Oil Rivers Protectorate 1891, Niger Coast Protectorate 1893). From 1886 the Royal Niger Company, formed by George GOLDIE, also administered extensive areas.

In 1900 the British territories became the protectorates of Northern and Southern Nigeria. Frederick LUGARD conquered the northern emirates (1903) and later united the territories as a single colony (1914). Cotton and cocoa were staples.

Nigeria was federated in 1954, and became independent under the British Crown (1960) and a republic (1963). Approx. population in 1921, 18,365,000; in 1959, 41,611,000. *See also* WEST AFRICA, ENGLISH AND BRITISH INVOLVEMENT; SHAW, FLORA; SCRAMBLE FOR AFRICA.

NIGHTINGALE, FLORENCE (b. 12 May 1820 at Florence, Italy; d. 13 Aug. 1910 at London, England, aged 90). From a privileged background, Nightingale became concerned about hospital administration after visiting a German women's religious community at Kaiserwerth which served the sick and deprived (1850). In 1854 she took a party of nurses to Turkey and ministered to British troops in the CRIMEAN WAR. *The Times* newspaper called her 'The Lady of the Lamp'. After returning to England (1856), she used her fame to improve military medicine, nurse training, and public health in India. *See also* MEDICINE AND PUBLIC HEALTH.

NILE, BRITISH INTERESTS Although the British explorers Richard BURTON and John Speke sought the source of the R. Nile in the 1850s (in eastern Africa), British strategic interest began when Great Britain became involved in EGYPT (1882). Egyptian agriculture relied on land irrigation from the Nile, which would be threatened by hostile control of the headwaters.

Britain's position was challenged by the MAHDI REBELLION in SUDAN (from 1881), which Britain initially failed to suppress (*see* GORDON, CHARLES GEORGE). Britain secured its position by taking over UGANDA and KENYA, pacifying Sudan (1898), and seeing off a French challenge at FASHODA (Sept.–Nov. 1898). *See also* SCRAMBLE FOR AFRICA.

NINETEEN PROPOSITIONS In England, the manifesto published by the LONG PARLIAMENT on 1 June 1642, demanding that King CHARLES I should accept parliamentary approval in the appointment of councillors, ministers and judges. It was rejected in the 'King's Answer' of 18 June. A few weeks later, CIVIL WAR began. *See also* PYM, JOHN.

NINE YEARS WAR In Ireland, conflict between Gaelic Irish and English, May 1593–March 1603. From May 1593 Irish chieftains in ULSTER (N Ireland) routinely attacked English officials and garrisons who ventured into their province. They were openly joined from May 1595 by the 2nd earl of Tyrone (Hugh O'NEILL), who defeated an English force at Clontibret (Co. Monaghan, 13 June 1595). A truce followed (to May 1596).

With Spanish encouragement the Irish renewed the war. After inconsequential warfare, and another truce (Dec. 1597–June 1598), Tyrone heavily defeated an English force at the Yellow Ford (Co. Armagh, 14 Aug. 1598). English strength in Ireland collapsed: CONNACHT and MUNSTER (W and S Ireland) were lost. A new English governor, the 2nd earl of ESSEX (in Ireland April–Sept. 1599), agreed another truce (7 Sept.–Jan. 1600), after which Tyrone campaigned in Munster (Feb.–March 1600).

After Lord MOUNTJOY arrived as chief governor (Feb. 1600), the English regained Munster and established forts in Ulster. When a Spanish army arrived (Sept. 1601), it was besieged in Kinsale (S Ireland), and Mountjoy defeated Tyrone nearby (24 Dec.; *see* KINSALE, BATTLE OF). During 1602 Mountjoy wasted Ulster, causing Tyrone to submit in March 1603 (*see* MELLIFONT, TREATY OF). Mountjoy's victory completed the English conquest of Ireland (*see* IRELAND, ENGLISH CONQUEST, 16TH CENTURY).

NINIAN OR NYNIA (fl. possibly in 6th century; d. in N Britain). According to BEDE, writing in 731, the British bishop 'Nynia' built a stone church, called the 'White House' (Latin, Candida Casa), at WHITHORN in N Britain (in modern Dumfries and Galloway, SW Scotland), and also preached to the southern PICTS.

Some have doubted aspects of Bede's account and even Ninian's existence. Others have suggested that he should be identified with Uinniau (*c*.495–589), a British monk with whom the young COLUMBA studied in Ireland, and who founded a monastery at Moville (in modern Co. Down, Northern Ireland). A connection between Uinniau and GALLOWAY is suggested by church dedications (to St Finnian), but the religious site excavated at Whithorn is of a later date. *See also* POST-ROMAN BRITAIN; CONVERSION OF NORTH BRITONS, PICTS AND SCOTS.

NKRUMAH, KWAME (b. probably 18 Sept. 1909 at Nkroful, Gold Coast; d. 27 April 1972 at Bucharest, Romania, aged 62). A headmaster, Nkrumah studied in the USA from 1935, where he participated in radical African-American circles, and in Great Britain from 1945. Returning to the GOLD COAST (a British colony) in 1947, he worked for the United Gold Coast Convention, then founded the Convention People's Party but was imprisoned (both 1949). After his Party won the 1951 election, Nkrumah was released (1952) and immediately became prime minister. The country became independent as Ghana (1957), and then a republic with Nkrumah as president (1964). His authoritarianism created enemies. He was ousted by Ghana's army while abroad (1966), and remained in exile.

NOBILITY Term for the élite stratum of historical SOCIAL STRUCTURES. Noble status usually reflected wealth, social authority and lifestyle. It was often conferred by kings and hereditary.

The earliest recorded nobilities (5th–8th centuries) were military élites who accompanied kings. In Ireland and Brittonic/Pictish N Britain they possibly originated from IRON AGE TRIBES. In southern Britain they emerged from Brittonic societies (5th century) and Anglo-Saxon peoples (6th–7th centuries). Senior noblemen (EALDORMEN or EARLS), and others (usually 'thegns') were important in England's GOVERNMENT (10th–11th centuries).

The NORMAN CONQUEST (1066–70s) replaced the English nobility with a Continental élite (170 BARONS, several thousand lesser noblemen, including KNIGHTS). Its members expanded into Wales (11th–12th centuries), Scotland and Ireland (12th–13th centuries). In Wales, indigenous nobles were displaced or descendants eventually became gentry. In Ireland, some Gaelic noble kindreds survived until the 17th century. In Scotland, indigenous and immigrant noble families coexisted.

Some noblemen became principal members of PARLIAMENTS in England, Ireland and Scotland (from 13th century). In the 14th–15th centuries they evolved into PEERAGES (bodies of established hereditary members, with various ranks); nobilities became equated with peers, and other noblemen lost noble status (16th–17th centuries). New peers were created by rulers.

From the RESTORATION (1660) noblemen became less involved in military activity. Peers lost political importance in Scotland and Ireland with termination of the countries' Parliaments (respectively 1707, 1800). Nobles (or aristocrats), including Scottish and Irish 'representative peers', remained influential in the UK Parliament until 1911 (abolition of Lords' veto). The decline of LANDED SOCIETY eroded other roles.

From 1922 CONSTITUTIONS for SOUTHERN IRELAND prohibited new noble titles. In the UK non-judicial life peers were appointed from 1958, and few hereditary peers were created from 1964. Most hereditary peers were removed from Parliament in 1999. In 1995 hereditary peers had totalled: 746 English/British/UK, 43 Scottish, 70 Irish. *See also* POST-ROMAN BRITAIN; NORMANS, IMPACT ON IRELAND/SCOTLAND/WALES; MAGNATE; GENTRY; LAIRD; LORD LIEUTENANT; HONOURS SYSTEM.

NONCONFORMIST CONSCIENCE Term used originally for the moral rectitude and dismay expressed by some British nonconformists and LIBERAL PARTY supporters when faced with the revelation that C.S. PARNELL, leader of the IRISH PARLIAMENTARY PARTY, had been cited as a corespondent in a divorce case (Nov. 1890). Parnell was forced to resign. The phrase was afterwards applied to a supposedly distinct nonconformist concern for standards of decency in public life and social legislation. *See also* NONCONFORMITY AND DISSENT, ENGLAND/WALES.

NONCONFORMISTS, DISSENTERS 'Nonconformist' was used from the early 17th century for someone who accepted the doctrines of the Church of ENGLAND, and remained within the Church, but refused to conform to practices required by the PRAYER BOOK (e.g., kneeling to receive Holy Communion). Puritans tended to be nonconformists and sought to change practices and Church government (*see* PURITANISM, ENGLAND/WALES). From the 1660s the term usually denoted someone who accepted the idea of an established Church but rejected conformity to the Church settlement imposed after the RESTORATION (episcopal government, 1662 Prayer Book), and often worshipped outside the Church (e.g., Richard BAXTER). The term 'dissenter' was used from the 1640s for people who disagreed with the idea of an established Church, or desired tolerance for Protestant 'gathered churches' outside the established Church.

Both nonconformists and dissenters were usually called dissenters in the later 17th and 18th centuries, and nonconformists from the 19th century. Catholics were sometimes called nonconformists, but more usually 'recusants' (late 16th–early 19th centuries). *See also* CHURCH, ENGLAND AND WALES, 1640s–50s; NONCONFORMITY AND DISSENT, ENGLAND/IRELAND/WALES; DISSENT, SCOTLAND.

NONCONFORMITY, SCOTLAND *see* DISSENT, SCOTLAND

NONCONFORMITY AND DISSENT, ENGLAND

Between the 1550s and 1640s, 'nonconformist' is applied primarily to adherents of the (Protestant) Church of ENGLAND who criticized ceremonies and episcopal Church government (effectively an alternative term to 'Puritan' or sometimes 'presbyterian'; *see* PURITANISM, ENGLAND). There were also radical Protestants who rejected a corporate Church and founded independent 'gathered congregations' (including ones in the Dutch Republic and NEW ENGLAND). They were sometimes called 'nonconformists' but also variously 'separatists', 'BROWNISTS', 'BAPTISTS' or 'Anabaptists' (rejecters of infant baptism), and (from 1640s) 'Independents', 'dissenters'. Separatism flourished during the 1640s–50s when religious uniformity collapsed (*see* ENGLISH REVOLUTION; QUAKERS).

After the RESTORATION, many Church of England nonconformists rejected the terms of reimposed religious uniformity and became separatists, notably 1760 clergy who left parish livings (1660–3; *see* CLARENDON CODE). Separatists were usually called 'dissenters'. Though granted freedom of worship in 1689 (*see* TOLERATION ACT), they endured disabilities until the 19th century (*see* TEST AND CORPORATION ACTS). Dissenting congregations worshipped in houses or chapels, and founded schools and DISSENTING ACADEMIES. There were 300,000 dissenters by 1700, mostly Independents, presbyterians and Baptists, declining to 50,000 by 1740. A few ministers abandoned orthodox theology (*see* UNITARIANS).

Dissent re-expanded from the late 18th century, influenced by EVANGELICALISM and augmented by Methodist denominations (*see* METHODISM). Dissenters founded MISSIONARY SOCIETIES from the 1790s, and denominations created associations (e.g., General Union of Particular Baptists, 1813). By 1851, a quarter of the population attended dissenting (or nonconformist) worship, mostly Methodist, CONGREGATIONALIST (i.e., Independent) or Baptist. Nonconformists became prominent in politics, especially through the LIBERAL PARTY. Congregations built grander chapels. Membership of the main denominations peaked in 1906–8 (in 1905, Methodist, Baptist and Congregationalist membership totalled about 1.3 million; attendance was larger). Decline through the 20th century, especially from the 1960s, greatly reduced adherence (to about 400,000 members in 2010 for Methodists, Baptists, United Reformed Church). *See also* NONCONFORMISTS, DISSENTERS; SACHEVERELL AFFAIR; PLYMOUTH BRETHREN; TEMPERANCE MOVEMENT, ENGLAND; UNIVERSITY REFORM, ENGLAND; NONCONFORMIST CONSCIENCE; SOPER, DONALD.

NONCONFORMITY AND DISSENT, IRELAND

In the later 16th and early 17th centuries, CHIEF GOVERNORS and Church of IRELAND bishops were uninterested in outward conformity by clergy and laity (e.g., in dress, ceremonies). It was inconsequential for the Church's theology (*see* CALVINISM); the primary concern was combating Catholicism. The Church accommodated Puritans (e.g., John CLOTWORTHY) and nonconformists, so unlike in England and Wales there was no coherent nonconformist or Puritan movement. Even presbyterian settlers from Scotland, concentrated in ULSTER (N Ireland), were initially accepted (e.g., with ministers holding Church livings). In the 1630s a campaign for greater discipline provoked opposition (*see* LAUDIANISM, IMPACT ON IRELAND). Separate presbyterian organization began in the 1640s (*see* PRESBYTERIANISM, IRELAND).

Apart from presbyterians, there were few dissenters until Independents (i.e., CONGREGATIONALISTS) and BAPTISTS arrived with the Parliamentary NEW MODEL ARMY in 1649. QUAKERS established a presence from 1654. Non-presbyterian dissenters remained fairly strong in the 1650s–60s, especially in DUBLIN, then declined.

The imposition of uniformity in the Church of Ireland (1666), following the RESTORATION, caused presbyterianism to develop separately (*see* PRESBYTERIAN SOCIETY, IRELAND). Otherwise, by the early 18th century there were only 2000 Baptists, 6500 Quakers and a few Independent congregations. Like presbyterians, they were excluded from civil offices by an addition to the 1704 Popery Act, though worship was permitted from 1719 (*see* TOLERATION ACT, IRELAND).

From 1747 revivalist METHODISM developed alongside the Church of Ireland, becoming a denomination in the 19th century. After the legalization of Unitarianism (1813) a few congregations emerged. Except for presbyterianism, Protestant dissent was slight (e.g., 4% of population in 1871).

Following the PARTITION OF IRELAND (1921), presbyterianism remained strong in NORTHERN IRELAND (19% of population in 2011; other dissenters below 9%). In southern Ireland, dissenters (including presbyterians) were few (below 1.5% in 2011).

NONCONFORMITY AND DISSENT, WALES

Protestant dissenting congregations, independent of the Church of England (which included Wales), were started from 1639 (developing from PURITANISM) and increased in number during the COMMONWEALTH AND PROTECTORATE (1649–60). More were founded after 118 clergy were ejected in 1660–2 (*see* CLARENDON CODE). In the 1670s there were 4000 dissenters, most in S Wales.

After the 1689 TOLERATION ACT dissenters built chapels and became organized. Principal denominations were

CONGREGATIONALISTS (Independents), BAPTISTS, QUAKERS, and the newer PRESBYTERIANS (followed later by UNITARIANS). Numbers remained small until the 1780s, but many were prosperous (as farmers, craftsmen) and important locally. From the 1730s some growth was generated by copying Methodist evangelical methods (see METHODIST REVIVAL, WALES). In the 1790s radicals were usually nonconformists (e.g., Richard PRICE).

Expansion into new industrial areas (see INDUSTRY, WALES FROM 18TH CENTURY) and the Methodists' separation from the Church of England in 1811 (see CALVINISTIC METHODISTS) enhanced nonconformity's position. Rapid expansion followed: by 1850, 80% of churchgoers attended chapels, with Methodists and Congregationalists being the largest denominations. Late 19th-century Welsh society, culture and politics were imbued with nonconformist values (see TEMPERANCE MOVEMENT, WALES; DISESTABLISHMENT, CHURCH OF ENGLAND IN WALES; LIBERAL PARTY, WALES).

Nonconformist church membership peaked at 550,000 in 1905 and then fell, hit by emigration in the 1920s and 1930s and later by increasing SECULARIZATION. By the 1990s nonconformity had lost its pre-eminence. See also DISSENTING ACADEMIES, WALES; EDUCATION, WALES; CATHOLICS AND CATHOLIC CHURCH, WALES; WALES, CHURCH IN.

NON-IMPORTATION MOVEMENT In Ireland, a campaign in 1778–9 which called for the avoidance of goods imported from Great Britain. It developed partly in response to a trade depression, and contributed to widespread unrest about Britain's treatment of Ireland. Because the British government was concerned for Ireland's loyalty during the AMERICAN WAR OF INDEPENDENCE, it removed restrictions on Irish trade in early 1780. See also PATRIOTS, IRELAND; HELY-HUTCHINSON, JOHN; FOREIGN TRADE, IRELAND, ENGLISH AND BRITISH REGULATION.

NON-JURORS In England and Wales, a small episcopal Church which originated in 1689 when some Church of ENGLAND clergy refused to swear oaths of allegiance and supremacy to King WILLIAM III and Queen MARY II, following the GLORIOUS REVOLUTION. They were unwilling to supersede their earlier oaths to King JAMES VII/II. Six bishops, including Archbishop William SANCROFT, and about 400 other clergy were deprived of livings by Act of Parliament. More deprivations followed the refusal of some clergy to swear allegiance to GEORGE I (king from 1714). The Church continued until 1805.

NORFOLK, 3RD DUKE OF (b. 1473, possibly in Norfolk, England; d. 25 Aug. 1554 at Kenninghall, Norfolk, aged about 81). Thomas Howard, a courtier and soldier (prominent at FLODDEN, 1513), was created earl of Surrey in 1514 and succeeded as duke in 1524. He was TREASURER

under King HENRY VIII 1522–46. Hostile in the 1520s to Cardinal Thomas WOLSEY, Norfolk was briefly a leading councillor after Wolsey's fall (1529), but was eclipsed by Thomas CROMWELL (by 1533). He quelled the PILGRIMAGE OF GRACE (1536).

In the late 1530s Norfolk supported a conservative reaction in religion (see SIX ARTICLES) and helped to discredit Cromwell (deposed 1540). Henry appointed him to command military forces in Scotland (1542) and France (1544), but he was sidelined by the Seymour family. In 1546, following involvement by his son in a plot, Norfolk was arrested (12 Dec.). He was attainted (27 Jan. 1547) but escaped execution because of Henry's death the next day.

Norfolk remained in prison during the reign of EDWARD VI (1547–53). He was released by MARY I (Aug. 1553) and the attainder was nullified. See also HOWARD FAMILY; SURREY EXPEDITION.

NORMAN, MONTAGU (b. 6 Sept. 1871 at Kensington, Middlesex, England; d. 4 Feb. 1950 at Kensington, London, England, aged 78). A banker's son, Norman joined the BANK OF ENGLAND in 1915. As governor from 1920, he helped to reschedule WORLD WAR I debt payments to the USA (1923), and influenced the decision to restore sterling to the GOLD STANDARD at its pre-war level (1925), a move criticized by J.M. KEYNES and later blamed for contributing to high unemployment. He also extended the Bank's influence in the City of London and promoted rationalization of struggling staple industries (e.g., COTTON). Following suspension of the gold standard (1931), Norman encouraged the creation of an informal STERLING AREA. He retired in 1944 and was created Lord Norman.

NORMAN CONQUEST OF ENGLAND From early 1066 William II, duke of NORMANDY, prepared to seize the English kingship after his claim was disregarded (see WILLIAM I). He obtained expressions of support from the Pope and Holy Roman Emperor, built ships and recruited followers (by Aug.). His force sailed to England on 27–28 Sept., landing at Pevensey (Sussex). King HAROLD was in N England (see STAMFORD BRIDGE, BATTLE OF). He marched S, and was defeated and killed (14 Oct.) near HASTINGS (Sussex).

The Normans initially failed to capture LONDON (repulsed at London bridge). After marching W and N, they crossed the R. Thames at Wallingford (Berkshire). Leading Englishmen submitted at Berkhamsted (Hertfordshire), including Londoners and Edgar ætheling, the English claimant (see ÆTHELING). William was crowned on Christmas Day in WESTMINSTER Abbey.

The Normans had to suppress rebellions: in 1068 by the city of Exeter (Devon) and in the W Midlands; in 1069–70 in the W Midlands and N England (see HARRYING OF THE

NORTH); in 1070 in NE England (*see* SWEIN ESTRITHSON); in 1070–1 in the FENS (E England). In 1072 William invaded Scotland (*see* ABERNETHY, TREATY OF). The last major revolt occurred in 1075 (*see* REVOLT OF THE EARLS). Rebels usually forfeited their lands.

By William's death (1087) England was profoundly changed. Most English nobles were replaced by Continental lords (about 170). Society became more rigidly hierarchical (or 'feudal'), with major lords holding land from the king, and 'subtenants' holding land from lords (*see* HONOUR). Both king and lords built CASTLES at important centres. English bishops and major abbots were replaced with Continental clergy, and merchants from Continental Europe settled in many towns. French became widely used. English forms of GOVERNMENT continued largely unchanged. *See also* NORMAN EMPIRE; NORMANS, IMPACT ON IRELAND/SCOTLAND/WALES; TENURES, ENGLAND FROM 1066.

NORMANDY A territory in N France, adjacent to the English Channel; it was created in the 10th century and powerful in the 11th and 12th centuries. It originated in 911 when the Frankish king Charles the Simple allegedly conceded the city of Rouen and surrounding land to Rollo (d. *c*.928), a VIKING and pagan, possibly to stem attacks by other Vikings. It was extended westwards by grants to Rollo and his successor William Longsword (924, 933). Longsword, a Christian (ruled *c*.928–42), called himself 'count of Rouen'. He and his successors remained theoretically subordinate to the kings of France.

Vikings settled around Rouen in the early 10th century. By the time of Richard I (ruled 942–96) their descendants had become Christians and Frankish in culture. Important social changes occurred *c*.1000, following developments elsewhere. Powerful families adopted primogeniture (succession to property by eldest son, rather than control by a kindred). Nobles asserted status by building castles, founding towns and monasteries, and recruiting bands of horse-mounted knights (*see* FEUDALISM).

Richard II (ruled 996–1026) was titled 'duke', and the territory was now called Normandy (Latin, *Normannia*), meaning 'Land of the north men', possibly to stress separateness from France. Richard was succeeded by Richard III (1026–7) and Robert I (1027–35). William II (1035–87) attacked neighbouring territories and conquered England (1066–70s), creating a NORMAN EMPIRE and spreading Norman culture. Other Normans settled in southern Italy and Sicily from *c*.1060.

From 1144 Normandy was part of the ANGEVIN EMPIRE. It was conquered by King Philip II of France in 1202–4. *See also* NORMAN CONQUEST OF ENGLAND; NORMAN KINGS.

NORMAN EMPIRE Historians' term for lands amassed by William II, duke of NORMANDY (N France) 1035–87, namely Maine (held 1063–92) and England (invaded 1066; *see* WILLIAM I). Normandy and England became connected by a common ruler (who in England was king), and by landholders with estates in both territories. They retained their own governments.

Normandy and England had separate and rival rulers 1087–96, 1100–6, 1144–54, which created problems of loyalty for cross-Channel landholders (*see* ROBERT CURTHOSE; WILLIAM II; HENRY I; STEPHEN). Normandy became part of the ANGEVIN EMPIRE in 1144, England in 1154. *See also* NORMAN CONQUEST OF ENGLAND; NORMAN KINGS.

NORMAN IRISH FAMILIES OR OLD ENGLISH Terms used for descendants in Ireland of the 12th-century Anglo-Norman invaders and associated settlers (*see* NORMANS, IMPACT ON IRELAND). Until the later 16th century they were described as English, then called 'Old English' to distinguish them from a recent new stream of English immigrants, the so-called 'NEW ENGLISH'.

During the REFORMATION (16th century) the Old English remained predominantly Catholic and were gradually excluded from power by the New English. This led to alliances between Old English and Gaelic Irish families, culminating in collaboration during the IRISH WARS of 1641–52. English, Old English, and New English were also styled 'Anglo-Irish'. *See also* IRELAND, ENGLISH COLONY IN, 13TH–15TH CENTURIES.

NORMAN KINGS Historians' term for the kings of England whose dynasty originated in the duchy of NORMANDY (theoretically within the French kingdom); namely WILLIAM I (ruled 1066–87), WILLIAM II (1087–1100), and HENRY I (1100–35). STEPHEN (1135–54) is usually included though he came from Blois (S of Normandy). Succeeded by the PLANTAGENETS. *See also* NORMAN EMPIRE.

NORMANS, IMPACT ON ENGLAND *see* NORMAN CONQUEST OF ENGLAND

NORMANS, IMPACT ON IRELAND In 1169–70, over a century after the Norman invasion of England, LEINSTER (E Ireland) was invaded from Wales by mercenaries. They are conventionally called 'Anglo-Normans', but sometimes 'Cambro-Normans' (Welsh Normans) because many had Norman and Welsh parents (*see* GERALDINES). Irish chroniclers usually called them 'English'.

The invaders were brought to Ireland by Diarmait MAC MURCHADA who offered land in return for helping him regain the high-kingship of Leinster. In 1171, during an expedition to Ireland, King HENRY II of England assumed the lordship of Ireland; he later granted away land outside Leinster. By *c*.1250 lordships held under the English Crown covered two-thirds of Ireland (*see* IRELAND, ENGLISH CONQUEST, 12TH–13TH CENTURIES).

The Anglo-Normans (or English) introduced military, social, economic and governmental institutions from England (themselves a combination of Norman and pre-Norman institutions). Holders of lordships (e.g., STRONGBOW in Leinster) created 'knights' fees' on which they settled followers (*see* MILITARY SERVICE, IRELAND BEFORE 17TH CENTURY). Major lords and knights built castles and organized their lands as MANORS containing villages with open fields. They settled English immigrants who practised arable-based mixed farming. Anglo-Normans also founded small towns and encouraged CHURCH REFORM, the formation of PARISHES, and reformed MONASTICISM. From the late 12th century a central government and legal institutions were developed. *See also* GOVERNMENT, IRELAND 12TH–MID 17TH CENTURIES.

NORMANS, IMPACT ON SCOTLAND Norman involvement comprised immigration and the import of features of Norman England, not conquest. King DAVID I (ruled 1124–53), a landholder in England, provided lordships particularly for landless younger sons of Norman (and other) families recently settled in England (*see*, e.g., STEWART FAMILY; BRUCE FAMILY). Settlement occurred initially in S Scotland except GALLOWAY (spreading the use of English) and in lowland MORAY (NE Scotland). It continued elsewhere into the 13th century. Immigrants founded many families which have been prominent throughout Scottish history.

David reorganized the court to resemble the Anglo-Norman court and built royal castles. (He also introduced BURGHS, coinage and sheriffdoms, features of pre-Norman England.)

NORMANS, IMPACT ON WALES Norman adventurers (such as ROBERT OF RHUDDLAN, William fitz Osbern and Roger of MONTGOMERY) moved from W and NW England into N WALES from the early 1070s, soon after the Norman invasion of England (1066). But only after the death of RHYS AP TEWDWR, king of DEHEUBARTH (SW Wales), in 1093 did Normans seize extensive territories further S (encouraged by Kings WILLIAM II and HENRY I of England), eventually creating the MARCH OF WALES. The Welsh regained territories during the reign of STEPHEN of England (1135–54) and in the early years of HENRY II's reign (to 1171).

The creation of Norman lordships (eventually about 40) meant the loss of native political control in the areas concerned. The March became partly non-Welsh with the founding of towns, English immigration, and the introduction of English laws, customs and land tenures. The Normans' control of churches influenced the native Welsh Church, opening it to mainstream European movements

such as Continental MONASTICISM, FRIARS, and the development of territorial structures (*see* CHURCH ORGANIZATION, WALES).

NORTH, LORD (b. 13 April 1732 at Piccadilly, Middlesex, England; d. 5 Aug. 1792 at London, England, aged 60). The son of a WHIG nobleman, Frederick North was known as Lord North from 1752 and became an MP in 1754. From 1759 to 1765 he was paymaster-general in the ministries of the duke of NEWCASTLE, earl of BUTE, and George GRENVILLE. He took a leading role against John WILKES. In 1767 North replaced Charles TOWNSHEND as chancellor of the Exchequer under the duke of GRAFTON.

In 1770 North succeeded Grafton as PRIME MINISTER (first lord of the Treasury). Supported by King GEORGE III, he enacted legislation he disliked for the king (e.g., ROYAL MARRIAGES ACT, 1772). His reaction to the crisis and war (from 1775) with the American colonies was a confused mixture of coercion and conciliation. Depressed by defeats, and from 1777 desperate to resign, he continued at the king's insistence. He resigned in March 1782 following the defeat of British forces.

North returned to government in 1783 (April–Dec.) in a coalition with Charles James Fox nominally led by the duke of PORTLAND, angering the king. North remained in opposition during the ensuing administration of William PITT the Younger. He succeeded as earl of Guilford in 1790. *See also* AMERICAN WAR OF INDEPENDENCE; ROBINSON, JOHN.

NORTH AMERICA, ENGLISH EXPLORATION Sailors from BRISTOL possibly reached N America during Atlantic voyages from 1480. The first known English-sponsored crossing took place in 1497 (*see* CABOT, JOHN). Probably seeking Asia, it reached NEWFOUNDLAND.

In 1524 the Italian Giovanni Verrazzano discovered that the coastline between Florida and the Newfoundland area was continuous. This prompted Englishmen to seek a route to Asia farther N, the NORTH-WEST PASSAGE. But after John Rut's voyage (1527), activity largely ceased, though the Frenchman Jacques Cartier discovered the St Lawrence gulf and river (in modern Canada) in the 1530s–40s.

English exploration for the passage was resumed in the 1570s by Martin FROBISHER, who discovered Baffin Island, Frobisher Bay and the Hudson Strait (later names). Francis DRAKE sought the passage from the Pacific (1579). Voyages by John Davis (1585–7) worked out the relationship of Greenland to NE America, and explored the Davis Strait and Baffin Bay.

From the 1560s English curiosity was also motivated by colonization ambitions. In 1584 the area off modern N Carolina was surveyed for Walter RALEGH to facilitate colonization (*see* ROANOKE SETTLEMENTS). War with Spain then deterred activity, and *c.*1600 the French became active in the St Lawrence Gulf area. Renewed English interest concentrated on an area S of the French (named NEW ENGLAND in 1614) and on Chesapeake Bay (modern Virginia). Voyages to New England in 1602–5, and to Chesapeake Bay in 1602–3, encouraged merchants to found the VIRGINIA COMPANY (1606). It started the first successful colony in 1607 (see VIRGINIA). Chesapeake Bay was further explored by John Smith (1607) who also mapped New England (1614).

NORTH AMERICAN COLONIES After ventures in the 1580s (see GILBERT, HUMPHREY; ROANOKE SETTLEMENTS), English colonization concentrated on two regions. One was around and S of Chesapeake Bay: VIRGINIA was founded in 1607, and later MARYLAND (1632) and NORTH and SOUTH CAROLINA (1663). The other, farther N, was 'NEW ENGLAND', where 'separatist' PURITANS were influential. Colonies included PLYMOUTH PLANTATION (1620), MASSACHUSETTS (1629), and later CONNECTICUT, RHODE ISLAND, and NEW HAMPSHIRE.

Dutch and Swedes were active in the intervening 'middle' region until the English seized 'New Netherland' in 1664, thereby linking New England and the Chesapeake. It was reorganized as NEW YORK, NEW JERSEY, PENNSYLVANIA and DELAWARE. GEORGIA, below South Carolina, was added in 1732.

Relations with indigenous 'Indians' ranged from cooperation to warfare. The largest conflict was King Philip's War (1675–6) in New England. From the mid 17th century England developed a 'colonial economic system', requiring its American and West Indies colonies to trade within the Empire and use English or colonial ships (see NAVIGATION ACTS; MERCANTILISM). Most Americans were farmers, with tobacco being an important staple in Virginia and Maryland. Slaves were imported from Africa, in large numbers from the 1680s.

In the 18th century, population increased from 275,000 to over 2 million by the 1760s (including 350,000 slaves). Immigrants included Europeans of various origins (e.g., Germans and so-called Scotch-Irish from N Ireland). Although there were established churches in nine colonies, no denomination predominated. A religious revival, the 'Great Awakening', began in the 1720s (encouraged by George WHITEFIELD), albeit dividing churches. European ENLIGHTENMENT ideas also became popular. Several colonies wanted to expand westwards but were impeded by French territory E of the Mississippi River. It was acquired by Great Britain after the SEVEN YEARS WAR (1754–63). But defence costs generated friction, leading eventually to the AMERICAN WAR OF INDEPENDENCE (1775–81) and creation of the USA (1776). See also NORTH AMERICA, ENGLISH EXPLORATION; NORTH AMERICAN COLONIES, GOVERNMENTS OF; NEW ENGLAND, DOMINION OF; CANADA.

NORTH AMERICAN COLONIES, GOVERNMENTS OF Starting from the early 17th century, governments were mostly established by the corporations or personal proprietors who founded or administered colonies under authority from the English monarch. (For exceptions, see PLYMOUTH PLANTATION, CONNECTICUT.) They usually appointed a governor and council, and allowed an elected assembly.

Governors commanded militias, appointed some officials, summoned assemblies, and could initiate and veto legislation. Councils usually acted as advisers to governors, as judges, and as the 'upper' part of the legislature. Elected assemblies voted taxes and could initiate legislation. Tripartite colonial legislatures therefore partly resembled the English Parliament. But assemblies became more representative than England's House of Commons, with 50–80% of adult white males being entitled to vote, though voting qualifications varied. Legislation required approval from the English or British PRIVY COUNCIL (normally granted).

For varying reasons, seven colonies eventually became CROWN COLONIES, with the monarch appointing the governor, and usually the governor appointing the council (see THIRTEEN COLONIES). The English or British Parliament provided a framework for trade through the NAVIGATION ACTS, but was otherwise little involved before the 1760s. Colonies dealt with the Privy Council, lords of trade and plantations (from 1675), or Board of TRADE (from 1696).

Arrangements for local government varied. In NEW ENGLAND, township meetings were important (e.g., to elect officers). In southern colonies, with scattered settlement, counties were primary territories and many officers were appointed. See also NEW ENGLAND, DOMINION OF; AMERICAN INDEPENDENCE.

NORTHAMPTON, ASSIZE OF In England, instructions to itinerant justices issued by King HENRY II and his COUNCIL (1176). They revised the Assize of CLARENDON (1166), providing for harsher penalties and increased powers for justices-in-eyre at the expense of SHERIFFS. The Assize includes the first surviving appearance of novel disseisin and *mort d'ancestor* (see POSSESSORY ASSIZES). See also EYRE; COMMON LAW.

NORTHAMPTON, TREATY OF see EDINBURGH, (1328) TREATY OF

NORTH ATLANTIC TREATY ORGANIZATION, BRITISH INVOLVEMENT This alliance for common defence, often called 'NATO', was established by the North Atlantic Treaty of 4 April 1949. It allied the USA and Canada with ten W European countries, including the UK, primarily against the USSR.

Following WORLD WAR II, and with the development of the COLD WAR (from 1947), the British had strongly encouraged continuing US commitment to the defence of Western Europe. The USA had based strategic bombers in Britain from 1948, and Ernest BEVIN, the British foreign secretary, had arranged the Brussels Pact (17 March 1948) to facilitate the North Atlantic Treaty.

NATO had an integrated defence force under US command from Dec. 1950. Britain kept four Army divisions (55,000 men) in West Germany, and the Royal NAVY guarded Atlantic sea-lanes. Britain supported nuclear deterrence and resisted any loosening of the alliance – as was evident in the support for intermediate-range nuclear weapons in the 1980s by Margaret THATCHER (*see* ATOMIC AND NUCLEAR WEAPONS).

The alliance expanded after its foundation, and following the dissolution of the USSR (1991) it was joined by countries in E Europe. By 2009 NATO had 29 members.

NORTH BORNEO *see* BORNEO

NORTH BORNEO COMPANY *see* BRITISH NORTH BORNEO COMPANY

NORTH CAROLINA A former English colony in N America (British from 1707). The earliest English settlements in America were made on an island in later North Carolina (*see* ROANOKE SETTLEMENTS). The term 'Carolana', referring to King CHARLES I, was applied to land S of VIRGINIA in 1629 when Charles granted a patent for colonization to Sir Robert Heath, a lawyer. Little happened. Some Virginians settled in the territory in the 1650s.

In 1663 King CHARLES II made a substitute grant to eight proprietors, who created two counties. The northern one was named Albemarle after the duke of Albemarle (George MONCK), a proprietor. It was given a governor and council (appointed by the proprietors) and elected assembly. By 1689 Albemarle was called North Carolina. It was ruled 1691–1712 by a deputy of the SOUTH CAROLINA governor, then by its own governor. In 1729 GEORGE II bought out seven owners, making North Carolina a CROWN COLONY. It grew slowly until the 1740s–50s when immigration accelerated. Est. population 1770: 230,000.

North Carolina protested against the Stamp Act (1765) and 'Townshend duties' (1767). The governor's flight in 1775 ended royal rule. In 1776 North Carolina's assembly advocated AMERICAN INDEPENDENCE (April; declared July) and became a State of the USA. *See also* NORTH AMERICAN COLONIES.

NORTHCOTE, STAFFORD (b. 27 Oct. 1818 at London, England; d. 12 Jan. 1887 at London, aged 68). Northcote succeeded as a BARONET in 1851. As a member of commissions for CIVIL SERVICE reform, he was co-author of the 'NORTHCOTE–TREVELYAN REPORT' (1853). A Conservative

politician and MP (1855–7, 1858–85), Northcote was chancellor of the Exchequer (1874–80) under Benjamin DISRAELI and Party leader in the UK House of Commons (1876–85). The FOURTH PARTY scorned his deference to the Liberal W.E. GLADSTONE (whose private secretary he had once been), and Lord SALISBURY beat him to the premiership (1885). Created earl of Iddesleigh in 1885, he served as foreign secretary under Salisbury (1886–7). *See also* SINKING FUND.

'NORTHCOTE–TREVELYAN REPORT' Recommendations for reform of the British CIVIL SERVICE, finalised in Nov. 1853 and published in 1854 (as *Report on the Organisation of the Permanent Civil Service*). The report was prepared by Sir Stafford NORTHCOTE, a member of commissions investigating Civil Service costs, and Charles TREVELYAN, assistant secretary (administrative head) of the British Treasury. It had been requested by the chancellor of the Exchequer, W.E. GLADSTONE.

Recommendations included abolition of PATRONAGE as a basis for appointments; entry to the service (rather than recruitment to a specific department); entrance by examination; promotion by merit; division of work into 'mechanical' and 'intellectual'. Although implementation took 20 years, the recommendations fundamentally changed the character of the Civil Service, notably through promoting coherence, impartiality and professionalism.

NORTH-EAST PASSAGE *see* ARCTIC, ENGLISH AND BRITISH EXPLORATION; MUSCOVY COMPANY

NORTHERN IRELAND A province of six counties in the island of IRELAND which are part of the UK; it was constituted on 3 May 1921 (population 1.2 million). Northern Ireland was created for 'Unionists' within ULSTER who opposed inclusion in a self-governing all-Ireland jurisdiction (*see* GOVERNMENT OF IRELAND ACT, 1920). It comprised, deliberately, a Protestant Unionist majority and 'nationalist' minority (mainly Catholic). The latter suffered discrimination, and many desired reunification with southern Ireland. Principal economic activities were AGRICULTURE, LINEN manufacturing and SHIP BUILDING.

Northern Ireland was self-governing from 7 June 1921, and dominated until 1972 by the ULSTER UNIONIST PARTY. Its first government, led by James CRAIG, suppressed resistance by the IRISH REPUBLICAN ARMY (IRA), and during the 1920s strengthened Unionist control (e.g., abolition of proportional representation in local government, 1922). Industry, depressed during the 1930s, was reinvigorated by war-time demand (1939–45). From 1946 the British WELFARE STATE was replicated, though the government of Basil BROOKE largely ignored nationalists' concerns.

From the mid 1960s the government of Terence O'NEILL was challenged by the CIVIL RIGHTS MOVEMENT. Protests in 1968–9 escalated into sectarian violence, the so-called TROUBLES, which required long-term deployment of British troops. An attempt to suppress disorder with 'internment' (detention of suspected troublemakers, 1971–5) failed. After 'BLOODY SUNDAY' (30 Jan. 1972) the British government replaced the province's government and Parliament with 'direct rule' (24 March), during which legislation consisted of orders in Council (issued by the UK Privy Council under enabling Acts).

Great Britain sought a new inclusive governmental arrangement, but a power-sharing Executive (1974) was destroyed by the ULSTER WORKERS' STRIKE (see FAULKNER, BRIAN). The Republic of Ireland was granted involvement under the HILLSBOROUGH AGREEMENT (1985). In the 1990s a PEACE PROCESS resulted in ceasefires by PARAMILITARY ORGANIZATIONS and the BELFAST AGREEMENT (1998). A new Assembly was established, and an Executive of Unionists and nationalists (including republicans) operated 1999–2002, 2007–17, and from Jan. 2020. Peaceful conditions encouraged economic expansion. See also ORANGE ORDER, IRELAND.

NORTHERN IRELAND CIVIL RIGHTS ASSOCIATION A political organization, including Catholics, republicans and liberal Protestants, which sought an end to sectarian discrimination in NORTHERN IRELAND. It was inaugurated on 9 April 1967; active 1967–8. Its principal aims were fair allocation of public housing; 'one man, one vote' in council elections; replacement of 'gerrymandered' electoral boundaries.

The Association's march in LONDONDERRY on 5 Oct. 1968, held despite a ban, ended in confrontation with police. Violent scenes were televised worldwide, and are considered the beginning of the TROUBLES. See also O'NEILL, TERENCE; PEOPLE'S DEMOCRACY.

NORTHERN ISLES see ORKNEY ISLANDS; SHETLAND ISLANDS

NORTHERN REBELLION Initially an attempt by some English noblemen to settle the uncertain succession to the English throne, 1569, given the unwillingness of Queen ELIZABETH I to marry or agree a successor. The plotters planned to marry MARY, QUEEN OF SCOTS, the principal claimant, to the (4th) duke of Norfolk (Thomas Howard, d. 1572).

When the plot was discovered, Norfolk was imprisoned (Nov. 1569). His main accomplices, the Catholic earls of Westmorland and Cumberland, were called to court. Panicking, they rebelled, raised support in northern England, and occupied DURHAM (14 Nov.) and other places. The rebellion collapsed when the rebels were challenged by a royal army (Dec.). Over 500 rebels were executed. Westmorland escaped abroad, Northumberland was executed. See also CATHOLIC PLOTS, ENGLAND; HOWARD FAMILY.

NORTHERN RHODESIA A former British territory in S-C Africa. The BRITISH SOUTH AFRICA COMPANY of Cecil RHODES negotiated treaties with local chiefs from 1890 and created two PROTECTORATES, North-Western Rhodesia (1899), North-Eastern Rhodesia (1900), which it administered. They were amalgamated as Northern Rhodesia in 1911, which became a Crown protectorate in 1924.

Copper extraction dominated the economy from the 1920s. Racial tension mounted in new mining towns, and the North Rhodesian African Congress (founded 1948) unsuccessfully opposed the inclusion of Northern Rhodesia in the FEDERATION OF RHODESIA AND NYASALAND (1953–63). In Jan. 1964 the United National Independence Party won a general election, and Northern Rhodesia became independent as the Republic of Zambia (Oct.). Approx. population in 1921, 983,000 (of whom 3600 were white); in 1963, 3,490,000. See also SOUTHERN RHODESIA.

NORTHERN TERRITORY A former British territory in AUSTRALIA. The British attempted to establish settlements in N-C Australia from 1824 to forestall Dutch or French interest. The area was administered from NEW SOUTH WALES until 1863, from SOUTH AUSTRALIA until 1911, and by Australian federal authorities until 1978. It then became a self-governing state (population, 104,000). The economy was based on sheep farming and mineral extraction.

NORTH SEA GAS AND OIL INDUSTRIES In the early 1960s surveying indicated plentiful energy resources below the North Sea. The British government placed exploration under State regulation with the 1964 Continental Shelf Act. Gas was discovered from 1965 and brought ashore from 1967; oil followed in 1969 and 1975. Great Britain became a net exporter of oil by the early 1980s, of gas by the mid 1990s. The Yarmouth–Lowestoft area (England) and ABERDEEN (Scotland) became leading centres of the industry. Production was marred by the Piper Alpha disaster (1988), a gas-rig explosion that killed 167 men. Gas and oil output peaked in 1999, declining by 2013 to 62% of UK oil consumption, 50% of gas. Gas output began to rise in 2014, oil in 2015.

North Sea energy improved the UK's trade balance, increased government revenues and generated employment, but inflated sterling's value. It also became a political issue, in that campaigners for Scottish independence demanded appropriation of tax revenues for Scotland (e.g., in referendum campaign, 2014). See also GAS INDUSTRY, GREAT BRITAIN; OIL INDUSTRY; GAS AND OIL INDUSTRIES, REPUBLIC OF IRELAND.

NORTHUMBERLAND, EARLS OF see PERCY FAMILY

NORTHUMBERLAND, HENRY EARL OF see PERCY, HENRY

NORTHUMBERLAND, JOHN DUKE OF (b. 1504 at London, England; d. 22 Aug. 1553 at London, aged about 49). A courtier, soldier and naval commander under King HENRY VIII, John Dudley (knighted 1523) was created Viscount Lisle in 1542. After the accession of the EDWARD VI, a minor (Jan. 1547), Lisle supported the protector, Edward, duke of SOMERSET. He was created earl of Warwick (Feb.). In Sept. he helped to defeat the Scots at Pinkie. In Aug. 1549 he suppressed KETT'S REBELLION.

In Oct. 1549 Warwick conspired to oust Somerset and became effectively England's ruler. In 1550 he made peace with France and withdrew forces from Scotland. He was created duke of Northumberland (Oct. 1551) and became president of the PRIVY COUNCIL (Feb. 1552). He supported continuing reform in the Church.

In 1553 Northumberland's position was threatened by the prospect of Edward's death. In June he allegedly forced Edward to nominate his own Protestant daughter-in-law as successor (*see* GREY, JANE). But after Edward's death (July), the Catholic claimant, MARY, rallied support. Lady Jane was deposed, and Northumberland's supporters deserted him. He was arrested (23 July) and executed for TREASON. *See also* DUDLEY, EDMUND; PAULET, WILLIAM; REFORMATION, ENGLAND.

NORTHUMBRIA A Germanic-ruled kingdom (7th–10th centuries) which was formed when King EGFRITH of BERNICIA annexed DEIRA (679). It extended from the R. Humber N to the R. Forth (modern N England and SE Scotland). Egfrith (king 670–85) probably also absorbed ELMET and RHEGED to the W. Northumbria competed mainly with MERCIA for influence over other kingdoms.

Following defeat by the PICTS in 685, Northumbria was weakened internally by violent rivalry between branches of the royal kindred. Several kings were killed after short reigns. (Eadbert exceptionally ruled 737–58.) In the 9th century Northumbria was raided by VIKINGS, who in 867 conquered the southern part (*see* YORK, VIKING KINGDOM OF).

The northern part (essentially the former Bernicia) remained under English rule. In 927 its king, Ealdred, submitted to ATHELSTAN, king of the Anglo-Saxons. Ealdred died possibly in 933. His successors were known as ealdormen of Bamburgh. *See also* KINGSHIP, ANGLO-SAXON; ENGLAND, FORMATION OF.

NORTH-WEST PASSAGE A hypothetical sea route westwards from Europe to China and the East Indies, going N of America. It engaged Englishmen (especially merchants) from the 16th century because it would avoid Spanish and Portuguese routes and territories.

Sebastian Cabot (son of John CABOT), based in BRISTOL, possibly searched for the passage in 1508–9; John Rut sought it in 1527. In the 1560s Humphrey GILBERT urged investigation. Voyages were led by Martin FROBISHER (1576–8), Francis DRAKE (1579, from Pacific), John Davis (1585–7) and others. Henry HUDSON discovered Hudson Bay (1610). The North-west Passage Company sponsored voyages from 1612. In 1616 William Baffin explored Baffin Bay, but concluded (incorrectly) that there was no outlet. Further voyages, until 1632 and from the early 18th century, mainly explored the Hudson Bay area. In 1778 James COOK, commissioned by the British Admiralty, investigated the passage's western end: his navigation through the Bering Strait showed that N America was separated from Asia.

In 1817 a report of melting Arctic ice stimulated John Barrow of the Admiralty, an advocate for British seapower, to organize expeditions (1818): one commanded by David Buchan sailed northwards past Spitsbergen until blocked by ice; a second, commanded by John Ross, rediscovered Baffin Bay and affirmed Baffin's conclusion. In 1819–20, however, Edward Parry sailed from Baffin Bay through Lancaster Sound to Melville Island. (Parry also commanded official voyages in 1821–3, 1824–5; Ross led a private expedition in 1829–33.) Another Admiralty expedition in 1845, commanded by Sir John Franklin, disappeared.

The passage was discovered in 1850 by Robert McClure while searching for Franklin: he sailed round Alaska to Banks Island from which he observed Melville Island; he then completed a transit (1854), partly by land. Franklin was later credited with the discovery (in 1848). Sailings through the passage were achieved from 1905 by other countries. *See also* NORTH AMERICA, ENGLISH EXPLORATION.

NORWAY, 'MATTER OF' Term for a diplomatic problem arising from treaty of PERTH (1266). Scotland gained the WESTERN ISLES from the king of Norway for an agreed annual payment of 100 marks, but it was hardly ever paid. The matter was finally resolved in 1468 when arrangements for the marriage of Margaret of Denmark-Norway to King JAMES III included cancellation of the payment.

NORWICH A city in E England, by the R. Wensum; centre of Norfolk.

Norwich probably originated *c.*700 as an international trading centre. (Its name means 'North wic'; *see* WIC.) It was an important centre of pottery production in the 10th–11th centuries.

Following the Norman invasion (1066) a castle was built, and the episcopal see for East Anglia was moved to Norwich from Thetford (1095). In the 12th–19th centuries Norwich was a cloth-manufacturing centre, and by *c.*1500 the wealthiest city after London, retaining its position until the 18th century (replaced by BRISTOL). Numerous Protestant refugees settled in the 1560s–70s, creating England's second largest immigrant community (a third of Norwich's population), and again after 1685 (*see* HUGUENOTS).

Although Norwich's population increased in the 19th and 20th centuries, the rate was far exceeded in other cities. The University of East Anglia was founded at Norwich in 1963; in 2013 a college was upgraded as Norwich University of the Arts. *See also* ETHNIC AND NATIONAL MINORITIES, ENGLAND.

Est. popn: 1086, 6500; 1300, 12,000; 1600, 15,000; 1800, 36,000; 1900, 110,000; 2000, 120,000.

NOTTINGHAM, 2ND EARL OF (b. 2 July 1647 at London, England; d. 1 Jan. 1730 at Burley, Rutland, England, aged 82). Daniel Finch, an MP from 1673, opposed the exclusion of James, duke of York, from the succession (*see* EXCLUSION CRISIS). He succeeded as earl in 1682. After York became king (1685), Nottingham opposed his pro-Catholic policies (*see* JAMES VII/II).

Though a TORY, Nottingham accepted replacement of James by WILLIAM III and MARY II (1688–9). As a SECRETARY OF STATE from March 1689, he promoted Bills for inclusion of moderate NONCONFORMISTS within the Church of England and toleration for some other Protestants. The former failed, but the latter became the 1689 TOLERATION ACT. He was dismissed in Nov. 1693 when William appointed more WHIG ministers.

Under Queen ANNE, Nottingham served as secretary of state from 1702, resigning in 1704 when Lord GODOLPHIN and the duke of MARLBOROUGH refused to dismiss WHIG ministers, and then supported attempted outlawing of OCCASIONAL CONFORMITY. In 1711 his opposition to Tory terms for ending the War of the SPANISH SUCCESSION won Whig support for action against Occasional Conformity. Nottingham supported the accession of GEORGE I (1714) and served as president of the Council 1714–16. He succeeded as earl of Winchilsea in 1729.

NOTTING HILL RIOTS In Great Britain, a major racial episode when each evening from Saturday 30 Aug. to Wednesday 5 Sept. 1958, 300–400 white people invaded the poor, overcrowded Notting Hill area of W LONDON, attacking the homes of West Indian immigrants and shops. (The events were allegedly sparked by a public argument on 29 Aug. between a white Swedish woman and her black Jamaican husband. They did not strictly constitute riots.) Afterwards, 72 white and 36 black people were charged with offences.

Policing was deemed inadequate, and the experience encouraged West Indian protests against prejudicial treatment. The 'riots' also strengthened anxieties about large-scale immigration, encouraging the eventual introduction of controls. From 1965 a Caribbean street festival (Notting Hill Carnival) sought to promote a more positive view of the area. *See also* AFRICAN CARIBBEANS IN GREAT BRITAIN; IMMIGRATION AND ASYLUM LEGISLATION, UNITED KINGDOM BEFORE 1973.

NOVA SCOTIA A former Scottish colony in N America (British from 1707). The area was visited by John CABOT in 1497. French settlers (1604–7) called it 'Acadia'. Sir William ALEXANDER, who was granted the area by King JAMES VI/I in 1621, named it Nova Scotia (Latin, meaning 'New Scotland'). Possession of Nova Scotia peninsula was contested with the French until the Peace of UTRECHT (1713). Nearby Cape Breton Island was added in 1758 (separate again 1784–1820). Nova Scotia had a House of Assembly from 1758 and RESPONSIBLE GOVERNMENT from 1848 (the first instance in the British Empire). It joined the dominion of CANADA in 1869. *See also* HALIFAX, 2ND EARL OF.

NOVEL A form of literature in prose consisting of a sustained fictional narrative with the appearance of reality. The term is derived from Italian *novella*, meaning 'short story', which itself comes from Latin *novus*, meaning 'new'. Novels were originally distinguished by featuring new rather than traditional stories.

The form developed in Continental Europe in the 16th and 17th centuries, and became established in England in the early 18th century. Leading novelists have included: (England) Daniel DEFOE, Jane AUSTEN, Charles DICKENS, George ELIOT, D.H. LAWRENCE; (Ireland) Jonathan SWIFT; (Scotland) Sir Walter SCOTT; (Wales) Daniel Owen, T. Rowland Hughes.

NUFFIELD, LORD (b. 10 Oct. 1877 at Worcester, Worcestershire, England; d. 22 Aug. 1963 at Nuffield, Oxfordshire, England, aged 85). A farm bailiff's son, William Morris made motor cars in OXFORD from 1912. During the 1920s–30s his business was one of Great Britain's largest manufacturers of low-priced cars. It merged in 1952 into the British Motor Corporation. Morris was created a baronet (1929), Lord Nuffield (1934) and Viscount Nuffield (1938), and retired in 1954. Childless, he was also a philanthropist. He founded Nuffield College, Oxford (1937), funded the Nuffield Foundation (for social and scientific research, 1943), and supported medical research. *See also* MOTOR INDUSTRY, GREAT BRITAIN.

NYASALAND A former British territory in SE Africa. Explored by David LIVINGSTONE in the 1860s, and declared a PROTECTORATE in 1891 (as the British Central African Protectorate), Nyasaland became an exporter of tobacco and tea. It was called Nyasaland Protectorate 1907–53. Its inclusion in the FEDERATION OF RHODESIA AND NYASALAND (1953–63) angered Africans. Nyasaland was granted self-government under the British Crown in 1963 and became independent as the republic of Malawi in 1964. Approx. population in 1921, 1,202,000; in 1963, 3,702,000.

O

O'BRIEN, WILLIAM (b. 2 Oct. 1852 at Mallow, Co. Cork, Ireland; d. 25 Feb. 1928 at London, England, aged 75). From 1881 O'Brien, a (Catholic) journalist, was an agitator for Irish land reform and HOME RULE, and supporter of C.S. PARNELL. He sat in the UK Parliament 1883–95, 1900–9, 1910–18.

In 1886, after the House of Commons rejected Home Rule, O'Brien developed the PLAN OF CAMPAIGN. When the IRISH PARLIAMENTARY PARTY (IPP) split in 1890 O'Brien joined the anti-Parnellite side. His UNITED IRISH LEAGUE (founded 1898) helped to reunite the Party (1900). From *c.*1900 O'Brien sought a final transfer of landownership in Ireland to tenants. This provoked other parties to take action (*see* LAND CONFERENCE). In 1903 O'Brien broke with John REDMOND, leader of the IPP, because Redmond failed to restrain strongly nationalist MPs. He later founded the small, inclusive 'All for Ireland League' of MPs (1909). O'Brien strongly opposed partition of Ireland. He retired in 1918. *See also* LAND AGITATION AND REFORM, IRELAND.

O'BRIEN, WILLIAM SMITH (b. 17 Oct. 1803 at Dromoland Castle, Co. Clare, Ireland; d. 18 June 1864 at Bangor, Caernarfonshire, Wales, aged 60). A (Protestant) Irish landowner, O'Brien sat in the UK Parliament from 1828. He initially opposed repeal of the UNION OF IRELAND AND GREAT BRITAIN. In 1843, disillusioned by anti-reform attitudes in Parliament, he joined the REPEAL ASSOCIATION, but seceded with other members of the YOUNG IRELAND MOVEMENT in July 1846.

In July 1848, partly in response to the GREAT FAMINE, O'Brien led a rebellion (*see* REBELLION OF 1848). He was convicted of treason and transported. He was pardoned in 1854 and returned to Ireland in 1856.

O'BRIEN FAMILY An Irish family (Irish, Ua/Ó Briain) whose members were kings in S Ireland. They were descendants of BRIAN BÓRUMA (d. 1014), who was high-king of the Dál Cais dynastic federation and of Munster and Ireland (*see* MUNSTER). They adopted Brian's name as a surname in the late 11th century and were high-kings of Munster until it was partitioned in 1118. They then ruled Thomond (N Munster).

Parts of Thomond were seized after 1185 by Anglo-Normans and later by members of the English CLARE FAMILY (1277–1318). The O'Brien kings survived with a 'rump' kingdom (modern Co. Clare). In 1543 it was surrendered by Murrough O'Brien (king 1539–51) to HENRY VIII, king of England and Ireland, and granted back with the titles earl of Thomond and Baron Inchiquin (*see* SURRENDER AND REGRANT). Murrough also accepted the REFORMATION. The titles descended in separate lines (the earldom until 1741). Unlike most Irish noble families, the titled O'Briens were usually Protestants.

O'CASEY, SEAN (b. 30 March 1880 at Dublin, Ireland; d. 18 Sept. 1964 at Torquay, Devon, England, aged 84). John Casey, a poor Protestant, became involved in Irish cultural

A Dictionary of British and Irish History, First Edition. Edited by Robert Peberdy and Philip Waller.
© 2021 John Wiley & Sons Ltd; © editorial matter and organisation Robert Peberdy and Phillip Waller.
Published 2021 by John Wiley & Sons Ltd.

and political activities, joining the GAELIC LEAGUE and Gaelicizing his name (1906), and participating in the IRISH CITIZEN ARMY (1913–14). A playwright from *c*.1916, he achieved success (under a modified name) with explorations of the impact of political conflicts on ordinary people (e.g., *Juno and the Paycock*, 1924). In England from 1926, O'Casey in the 1950s wrote anti-clerical dramas which were condemned in the Republic of Ireland.

OCCASIONAL CONFORMITY The practice from the 1670s whereby Protestant dissenters circumvented a prohibition on holding government offices in England and Wales by taking Holy Communion in the Church of ENGLAND once a year (*see* TEST AND CORPORATION ACTS). From the later 17th century TORIES campaigned against occasional conformity.

Three Bills to prevent office-holding by occasional conformity were passed by the House of Commons in 1702–4 but rejected by the Lords. An Occasional Conformity Act was passed in 1711 through a deal between Tories and WHIGS. It provided for civil and military officers found in dissenting CONVENTICLES to lose their positions. The Act was repealed by Whigs in 1719 to conciliate dissenters. *See also* NOTTINGHAM, 2ND EARL OF; NONCONFORMITY AND DISSENT, ENGLAND.

OCKHAM, WILLIAM (b. *c*.1287 at Ockham, Surrey, England; d. 10 April 1347 at Munich, Bavaria, aged about 60). A Franciscan friar, Ockham studied at OXFORD University from *c*.1308 and later taught there and in London. In 1323 an enemy reported him to the Pope for errors. Summoned to the papal court at Avignon, Ockham defended his ideas but was drawn into the Franciscans' conflict with the Pope over their rule. He fled Avignon, passing from Pisa (Italy) to Munich (Germany), there securing protection from the Holy Roman Emperor. As a philosopher, Ockham's influence was immediate, particularly his 'nominalism', the view that only individuals and individual phenomena exist rather than universal entities. *See also* FRIARS, ENGLAND.

O'CONNELL, DANIEL (b. 6 Aug. 1775 near Cahirciveen, Co. Kerry, Ireland; d. 15 May 1847 at Genoa, Kingdom of Sardinia, aged 71). A (Catholic) lawyer, O'Connell opposed the UNION OF IRELAND AND GREAT BRITAIN (1801). From 1803 he nevertheless participated in campaigns for Catholic Emancipation (principally admission of Catholics to the UK Parliament). Following the death of Henry GRATTAN (1820), he founded the CATHOLIC ASSOCIATION OF IRELAND to campaign for Emancipation (1823), developing it as a mass organization. When O'Connell was elected an MP in 1828, despite his ineligibility, the British government was forced to concede Emancipation (*see* COUNTY CLARE BY-ELECTION).

As an MP, O'Connell in Feb. 1835 joined the LICHFIELD HOUSE COMPACT (to defeat Robert PEEL's Conservative government) in return for reforms in Ireland (implemented by the WHIGS). But by 1838 he feared loss of popular support and revived opposition to the union, founding the REPEAL ASSOCIATION (1840). When Robert Peel again became prime minister (1841), O'Connell anticipated an end to reforms. He campaigned in Ireland, demanding repeal (1843), until compelled to cancel the CLONTARF MEETING (Oct.). He was arrested, convicted of conspiracy, and imprisoned (May–Sept. 1844). Afterwards he disputed strategies with younger nationalists (*see* YOUNG IRELAND MOVEMENT). *See also* CATHOLIC RELIEF AND EMANCIPATION, IRELAND; UNION REPEAL MOVEMENT, IRELAND.

O'CONNOR, FEARGUS (b. 18 July 1796 at Connorville, Co. Cork, Ireland; d. 30 Aug. 1855 at Notting Hill, Middlesex, England, aged 59). Chartist leader. Of Irish nationalist antecedents, O'Connor was a Radical MP (1832–5, 1847–52). Unseated for lacking the property qualification in 1835, he denounced FACTORIES and the new poor law at mass meetings throughout N England (*see* POOR LAW AMENDMENT ACT, 1834).

From 1838 O'Connor campaigned for the People's Charter with passionate oratory and his popular journal the *Northern Star*. Identified with 'physical force' and imprisoned for seditious libel (1840–1), O'Connor became Chartism's figurehead, but the National Land Company (1846), his scheme to acquire smallholdings for ex-factory workers, collapsed. Erratic and egocentric, O'Connor was certified insane in 1852. *See also* CHARTISM, ENGLAND.

O'CONNOR, RORY *see* UA CONCHOBAIR, RUAIDRÍ

O'CONNOR, TURLOUGH *see* UA CONCHOBAIR, TOIRRDELBACH

O'CONNOR FAMILY An Irish family (Irish, Ua/Ó Conchobair) whose members were kings in CONNACHT (W Ireland). They were descendants of Conchobar mac Taidg, who was high-king of both the Uí Briúin Aí dynasty and Connacht (967–73). Ua Conchobair kings monopolized the high-kingships from Conchobar's reign onwards and adopted his name as their surname by the 11th century. Toirrdelbach (d. 1156) and Ruaidrí UA CONCHOBAIR (king 1156–83) were also high-kings of Ireland. Ruaidrí allowed Anglo-Normans to establish themselves in E Ireland, though he retained his high-kingships (*see* NORMANS, IMPACT ON IRELAND).

In 1226 the English confiscated Connacht from Áed Ua Conchobair. O'Connor kings endured but could not re-establish extensive authority, even as English authority declined (14th century). They were weakened by rapid succession of kings (13 kings, 1274–1315) and disputes between two branches (1384–1461). Thereafter the kingship was not claimed though the family continued.

OCTAVIANS A commission of eight men appointed in 1596 by King JAMES VI of Scotland to tackle his desperate financial circumstances. They reduced household expenses, sought to improve collection of rents from Crown lands, raised import duties and introduced the first tariff on imports (1597), and probably promoted a heavy tax. Their enemies alleged that some were Catholics, which stirred criticism in the Church. James dismissed them in late 1597. *See also* ROYAL REVENUES, SCOTLAND; HAMILTON, THOMAS.

OCTENNIAL ACT Legislation passed by the Irish Parliament in Feb. 1768 which limited a Parliament's life to eight years (instead of a monarch's reign). It had been demanded by PATRIOT MPs, and was conceded by the chief governor, Viscount TOWNSHEND, to encourage the grant of extra funding for the Army. *See also* FLOOD, HENRY; PARLIAMENT, IRELAND.

OCTOBER CLUB In England, a group of TORY MPs (1710–14) who pressed Robert HARLEY, chief minister of Queen ANNE, to pursue more forthright Tory policies: peace, lower taxation, and strong support for the Church of ENGLAND. The Club met at the Bell tavern, Westminster (Middlesex), and took its name from October ale, a drink of country gentlemen.

O'DOHERTY'S REBELLION In Ireland, an anti-English insurrection in 1608 by Sir Cahir O'Doherty, Gaelic Irish lord of Inishowen, ULSTER (N Ireland). Previously loyal, O'Doherty was alienated by the contemptuous attitude of Sir George Paulet, governor of DERRY (arrived 1607). O'Doherty seized Culmore fort and burned Derry (18, 19 April 1608). He was killed at Kilmacrenan, Co. Donegal (5 July). Occurring soon after the FLIGHT OF THE EARLS, O'Doherty's Rebellion persuaded the English to modify plans for the ULSTER PLANTATION to include large-scale immigration.

O'DONNELL FAMILY Irish family (Irish, Ó Domhnaill) whose members were kings of Tyrconnell, NW Ireland (Irish, Tír Conaill; modern Co. Donegal and adjacent lands), from the early 13th century. They were a branch of the Cenél Conaill (*see* UÍ NÉILL, NORTHERN), named (from the early 11th century) after a 10th-century ancestor.

The last inaugurated king (1592) was Hugh O'Donnell ('Red Hugh', 1572–1602), who was defeated by the English at KINSALE (1601) and fled to Spain. His brother and nominated successor, Rory O'Donnell (1575–1608), submitted and was created earl of Tyrconnell (1603), but fled in the FLIGHT OF THE EARLS (1607). Tyrconnell was then seized for plantation. *See also* ULSTER; ULSTER PLANTATION.

ODO OF BAYEUX (b. *c.*1030 in Normandy; d. 6 Jan. 1097 at Palermo, Sicily, Italy, aged about 66). A half-brother of William II, duke of Normandy, Odo became bishop of Bayeux in 1049 or 1050. In 1066 he participated in his half-brother's invasion of England (*see* NORMAN CONQUEST OF ENGLAND). His rewards included the earldom of Kent. He helped to suppress revolts and often acted as William's deputy. But in 1082 or 1083 Odo was imprisoned in Normandy, possibly because he was scheming to become Pope (released Sept. 1087).

In 1088 Odo unsuccessfully led a revolt in England against King WILLIAM II, in favour of ROBERT CURTHOSE. He was exiled to Normandy. Odo died on CRUSADE. *See also* BAYEUX TAPESTRY.

O'DUFFY, EOIN (b. 28 Oct. 1890 at Cargaghdoo, Co. Monaghan, Ireland; d. 30 Nov. 1944 at Dublin, southern Ireland, aged 54). A member of the IRISH REPUBLICAN ARMY (IRA), O'Duffy supported the 1921 ANGLO-IRISH TREATY, which created the Irish Free State. During the ensuing IRISH CIVIL WAR he was initially a commander in the National Army, fighting the IRA.

In Aug. 1922 O'Duffy was appointed commissioner (head) of the recently founded police force, Gárda Síochána. He vigorously repressed anti-treaty republicans. But in Feb. 1933 the new prime minister, Éamon DE VALERA, dismissed him. O'Duffy then (July) became leader of the ARMY COMRADES' ASSOCIATION (so-called 'Blueshirts'), and first leader of FINE GAEL (Sept.; resigned Aug. 1934). He later fought for the Nationalists in the Spanish Civil War. *See also* IRISH FREE STATE, FOUNDING OF; POLICE, SOUTHERN IRELAND.

ÓENACH TAILTEN (OIr., meaning 'Assembly at Tailten'). In Ireland, a public festival held at Teltown in MEATH (E Ireland), dating from the IRON AGE (700 BC–AD 400) and associated with Lughnasa (festival of the god Lug). Convened from the 6th century under the patronage of the Uí NÉILL province-kings, the event included proclamations, games and contests, and commerce. It declined from the early 10th century and was last held in 1168, by the high-king Ruaidrí Ua CONCHOBAIR (of CONNACHT). *See also* KINGSHIP, IRELAND.

OFFA (fl. from 757 in Mercia; d. 29 July 796 in Mercia). In 757 Offa became king of MERCIA (C England) by driving out Beornred, successor of ÆTHELBALD (Offa's remote cousin). He greatly extended Mercian territory. By 764 he had authority in KENT (lost 776–mid 780s). He invaded SUSSEX in 771 and subordinated its king. Around 780 he terminated the ruling dynasty of the HWICCE. By 789 his son-in-law Beorhtric was king in WESSEX. In the 790s Offa was exercising some authority in EAST ANGLIA.

Offa also strengthened authority within Mercia. He issued high-quality silver coins, and possibly founded towns. He commanded the labour that built OFFA'S DYKE. Offa undermined the archbishopric of CANTERBURY by obtaining the elevation of Lichfield into an archbishopric (787). He corresponded with the Frankish emperor Charlemagne.

In 787 Offa arranged the unprecedented consecration of his son and intended successor Egfrith as king. But Egfrith died soon after his father. *See also* KINGSHIP, ANGLO-SAXON; CENWULF.

OFFALY, LORD (b. 1513 in London, England; d. 3 Feb. 1537 at London, aged 23 or 24). Thomas Fitzgerald, known as Offaly, was heir to the 9th earl of KILDARE. He was appointed acting governor (vice-deputy) of Ireland by his father before Kildare left for England in Feb. 1534. After Offaly was himself summoned (May), he denounced Henry VIII's policies to the Irish COUNCIL and resigned (11 June). When Henry imprisoned Kildare (29 June), Offaly initiated a rising (*see* KILDARE REBELLION). He surrendered in Aug. 1535 and was executed with five uncles in 1537.

It remains unclear whether Offaly caused trouble in May 1534 to challenge Henry or intended rebellion. He succeeded briefly as 10th earl (Sept. 1534 until forfeiture on 1 May 1536). He was called 'Silken Thomas' from the silk helmet fringes worn by supporters. *See also* KILDARE ASCENDANCY; HENRY VIII AND IRELAND.

OFFA'S DYKE An earthwork frontier (earthen bank with ditch) which was constructed between the Germanic-ruled kingdom of MERCIA (C England) and POWYS in W Britain (Wales), to deter raids into Mercia. It is attributed to OFFA, king of Mercia 757–96. It ran 64 mi (103 km) N–S from Llanfynydd (Flintshire) to Rushock Hill (Herefordshire). Much of the bank survives.

OGHAM An alphabet used in southern Ireland and W Britain (Wales), consisting of incised lines and notches. It was developed for the Irish language in the 4th century, influenced by contact with the Roman world. The earliest texts are mainly funerary inscriptions on stone pillars. Ogham was superseded for inscriptions by Latin writing *c.*600. The term possibly derives from Ogmios, god of learning. *See also* IRISH COLONIZATION IN BRITAIN, 4TH–6TH CENTURIES; IRISH LANGUAGE AND LITERATURE.

OGILVIE, JOHN (b. 1580 at Drum-na-Keith, NE Scotland; d. 10 March 1615 at Edinburgh, SE Scotland, aged about 35). Raised as a Protestant, Ogilvie studied in France and became a Catholic (1596), Jesuit (1601) and

priest (1610). He returned to Scotland (1613) to minister and preach. In 1615 he was arrested, tortured and hanged for treason, for refusing to acknowledge the supremacy of King JAMES VI over the Pope in matters spiritual. He was canonized in 1976. *See also* CATHOLICS AND CATHOLIC CHURCH, SCOTLAND.

O'HIGGINS, KEVIN (b. 7 June 1892 at Stradbally, Queen's County, Ireland; d. 10 July 1927 at Booterstown, Co. Dublin, Irish Free State, aged 35). A member of SINN FÉIN, and of the self-proclaimed republican Dáil Éireann ('Assembly of Ireland'; formed Jan. 1919), O'Higgins became minister for local government in the Dáil government (Aug. 1921). He supported the ANGLO-IRISH TREATY (Dec. 1921) which created the Irish Free State (IFS). He was minister for economic affairs (from Jan. 1922) in both the Dáil government and IFS provisional government. From Aug. 1922 O'Higgins served as minister for home affairs, retaining office after inauguration of the IFS (6 Dec. 1922; post redesignated minister for justice 1924). He was a leading member of CUMANN NA NGAEDHEAL.

After the IRISH CIVIL WAR, O'Higgins suppressed the ARMY MUTINY (1924) and implemented Public Safety Acts against unrest and crime. At the Imperial Conference of 1926 he helped to formulate the principle of equality between the UK and DOMINIONS (including the IFS). O'Higgins was murdered by republican gunmen. *See also* IRISH FREE STATE, FOUNDING OF; POLICE, SOUTHERN IRELAND.

OIL INDUSTRY Oil was produced in Scotland from cannel coal (1851–1880s) and oilshale (1860s–1962), initially for lighting and lubricants. Two major international businesses were also developed from Great Britain, which mainly supplied petrol and diesel.

In 1892 Marcus Samuel (1853–1927) began shipping oil from Russian C Asia to Europe via the SUEZ CANAL. Renamed Shell Transport and Trading in 1897, his company explored new sources from 1903 in collaboration with a Dutch company. In 1907 they formed Royal Dutch Shell Group, with Dutch and British holding companies. By 1930 it was a world leader, involved in production, shipping, refining and distribution. Its later new oil sources included the Gulf of Mexico (1949), Nigeria (1958), Oman (1960s), and the North Sea (1970s). From 2005 Shell had a single holding company, incorporated in Britain with headquarters in the Netherlands.

In 1901 financier William Knox D'Arcy (1849–1917) obtained a 60-year oil concession covering much of Persia (modern Iran). After discovering oil (1908), he created the Anglo-Persian Oil Company (1909), thereby starting the Middle East oil business. Britain's government bought a majority stake in 1914 to safeguard supplies for the NAVY. In 1917 Anglo-Persian acquired distribution facilities in

Britain formerly owned by 'British Petroleum'. (Anglo-Persian was renamed 'Anglo-Iranian' in 1935.) Following nationalization of Iranian oil assets in 1951, the company resumed operations under a new arrangement (1954), and was renamed 'British Petroleum' (1954). BP's other Middle East oil assets were extensively nationalized in the 1970s, forcing reliance on oil mainly from Alaska and the North Sea. The company was damaged in 2010 by the explosion of its 'Deepwater Horizon' oil rig in the Gulf of Mexico, which caused the largest ever oil spill.

The development of North Sea oil in the 1970s enabled the UK to be self-sufficient in oil from 1981 to c.2010. *See also* KUWAIT; NORTH SEA GAS AND OIL INDUSTRIES.

OLDCASTLE, JOHN (b. mid 1370s, probably in Herefordshire, England; d. 14 Dec. 1417 at London, England). Oldcastle, a knight, served as MP (1404) and sheriff (1406–7) for Herefordshire. In 1408 he inherited the estates and title of his father-in-law, Lord Cobham, giving him magnate status. In 1413 he was tried for heresy (adherence to LOLLARDY). Sent to the Tower of London to recant, he escaped (19 Oct.). Soon afterwards (Jan. 1414) he led an unsuccessful rebellion (*see* OLDCASTLE'S RISING). He remained in hiding until captured in Nov. 1417, and was executed for TREASON.

OLDCASTLE'S RISING The attempted overthrow of the English government on 9 Jan. 1414 by several hundred lollards led by Sir John OLDCASTLE. They planned to seize LONDON and assassinate King HENRY V. But Henry was forewarned. When rebels tried to enter the city they were killed, arrested or dispersed by royal forces. Oldcastle escaped. *See also* LOLLARDY, ENGLAND.

OLD COLONIAL SYSTEM Name given to the MERCANTILIST regulation of trade within the English or BRITISH EMPIRE from the NAVIGATION ACTS of the mid 17th century until the adoption of FREE TRADE (1840s–50s). England tried to monopolize trade with its colonies through preferential tariffs and a ban on colonial exports to other countries. *See also* NORTH AMERICAN COLONIES.

OLD ENGLISH *see* NORMAN IRISH FAMILIES OR OLD ENGLISH

OLYMPIC GAMES After the revival of the ancient Olympic Games in 1896, LONDON was the only city in the world to host the games three times (on behalf of the UK). The 1908 games were relocated from Rome (Italy) when allocated funds were diverted (for reconstruction after the 1906 eruption of Mt Vesuvius). The 1948 games were awarded to London following cancellation of planned games there in 1944 (because of WORLD WAR II). Valued

for raising national morale, they were organized at minimal cost using existing facilities due to austere post-war conditions. Games held in 2012 were used to regenerate part of E London and improve transport facilities.

The separate jurisdictions within the UK and Irish nationalism complicated involvement in the Olympic Games from the British Isles. Before 1922 some Irish participants resented designation as British. In 1908, as a concession, the UK team was called 'Great Britain/Ireland', and Irish teams were permitted in hockey and polo. After the foundation of the IRISH FREE STATE (1922), the varying organization of sports within Ireland created difficulties (*see* SPORT, IRELAND), and even the name used for southern Ireland was contentious. Athletes from NORTHERN IRELAND joined British or southern Irish teams. Between 1896 and 2016, Great Britain won the third largest numbers of medals and gold medals (summer and winter games combined).

O'MAHONY, JOHN (b. 1816 in Kilbeheny, Co. Limerick, Ireland; d. 7 Feb. 1877 at New York, USA, aged about 60). A supporter of YOUNG IRELAND, O'Mahony joined the REBELLION OF 1848 and escaped afterwards to France (with James STEPHENS). By 1853 he was in New York (USA), where he founded the FENIAN BROTHERHOOD (1858), advocated independence for Ireland, and worked for nationalist causes. In 1865 he sent men and money to Ireland for a rising planned by Stephens, but was discredited by Stephens' failure. After the further failure of the INSURRECTION OF 1867 O'Mahony lost influence.

O'NEILL, HUGH (b. *c.*1550 in Tyrone lordship, N Ireland; d. 20 July 1616 at Rome, Italy, aged about 66). Irish chieftain. In 1559 O'Neill was prevented from succeeding his grandfather (Conn Bacach O'Neill) as lord of Tyrone by his uncle Shane O'NEILL (d. 1567). He grew up in Anglo-Irish and English households. In 1585 the English styled him (2nd) earl of Tyrone (confirmed 1587) and supported him against Shane's successor, Turlough Luineach O'Neill. By 1593 he effectively controlled Tyrone.

The English expected Tyrone to assist their extension of government into ULSTER (N Ireland). But he feared loss of local support or English confiscation of Tyrone. In 1595 he joined resistance to English advances (May), and on Turlough Luineach's death (Sept.) was elected chieftain ('The O'Neill'). Tyrone's rebellion, which expanded across Ireland, was defeated at KINSALE (Dec. 1601). He submitted in 1603 (*see* MELLIFONT, TREATY OF) and quit Ireland in 1607 (*see* FLIGHT OF THE EARLS). *See also* O'NEILL FAMILIES; NINE YEARS WAR; IRELAND, ENGLISH CONQUEST, 16TH CENTURY.

O'NEILL, OWEN ROE (b. 1583 at Loughall, NE Ireland; d. 6 Nov. 1649 at Cloughoughter Castle, Co. Cavan, Ireland, aged about 66). O'Neill returned to Ireland from

Spanish service (July 1642) to join Catholic rebels (*see* IRISH WARS, 1641–52). He was appointed commander of the CATHOLIC CONFEDERATION's Ulster army (Aug. 1642).

In 1645–8 O'Neill backed the uncompromising stance of Archbishop RINUCCINI, defeated Robert Monro's Scottish army (at Benburb, 5 June 1646) and threatened Governor ORMOND (1647). In 1648 he supported Rinuccini's excommunication of Catholics who favoured the truce with Lord INCHIQUIN (a Protestant). The Confederation declared O'Neill a traitor (30 Sept.).

After Rinuccini departed (Feb. 1649), Ormond sought O'Neill's participation in a Royalist coalition against Parliamentary forces. O'Neill resisted until Parliament's armies had conquered much of Ireland. Terms were agreed (20 Oct.) but O'Neill died.

O'NEILL, PHELIM (b. 1603 in Ireland; d. 10 March 1653 at Dublin, Ireland, aged about 50). A leading member of the O'NEILL FAMILY, Phelim (knighted 1639) joined (Catholic) anti-English conspirators in 1641 and led the ULSTER RISING. He captured Charlemont fort, Co. Armagh (22 Oct.), and commanded rebel forces until May 1642 when he retreated to Charlemont. (He was replaced in Aug. by Owen Roe O'NEILL.) On 14 Aug. 1650 English Parliamentarian forces retook Charlemont. O'Neill escaped and was not captured until 4 Feb. 1653; he was later executed. *See also* IRISH WARS, 1641–52.

O'NEILL, SHANE (b. *c*.1530 in Ireland; d. 2 June 1567 at Cushendun, Antrim, N Ireland, aged about 37). Irish chieftain. In 1559, on the death of his father Conn Bacach O'Neill, earl of Tyrone, Shane O'Neill obtained the chieftainship of the O'Neills, and the lordship of Tyrone (N Ireland), by Irish succession custom. He thereby ignored his father's intended successor by primogeniture (Hugh O'NEILL). Shane sought dominance in ULSTER, and English acknowledgement as earl of Tyrone. His alleged usurpation and intrigues with Scots and French threatened English authority.

In 1561 O'Neill survived a military campaign led by the English chief governor SUSSEX, and in 1562 (Jan.–May) attended the English court when Queen ELIZABETH I recognized him as 'captain' of Tyrone. He survived further campaigns (1563), before submitting to Sussex (11 Sept. 1563).

From Sept. 1566 the new chief governor, Henry SIDNEY, sought to suppress O'Neill. On 8 May 1567 O'Neill attacked an Irish rival, Hugh O'Donnell of Tyrconnell, at Farsetmore, only to be defeated. He fled to the Scottish settlements of the MacDonnells in Antrim, where he was killed. *See also* O'NEILL FAMILIES; IRELAND, ENGLISH CONQUEST, 16TH CENTURY.

O'NEILL, TERENCE (b. 10 Sept. 1914 at London, England; d. 12 June 1990 at Lymington, Hampshire, England, aged 75). An ULSTER UNIONIST PARTY member of Northern Ireland's Parliament from 1946, and minister from 1956, O'Neill succeeded Basil BROOKE as prime minister on 25 March 1963. He sought better relations with the Republic of Ireland and welcomed its taoiseach (premier), Seán LEMASS, to Northern Ireland (14 Jan. 1965). He also encouraged public spending on infrastructure development, but was unable to halt the decline of staple industries (textiles, ship building).

After the CIVIL RIGHTS MOVEMENT led to violent clashes from Oct. 1968, followed by resurgent IRISH REPUBLICAN ARMY activity, O'Neill offered reforms ('five-point programme', 22 Nov.), but failed to quell discontent. Though he won an election (24 Feb. 1969), Unionist criticism compelled him to resign (28 April; succeeded by James Chichester-Clark). He was created Lord O'Neill (1970). *See also* NORTHERN IRELAND.

O'NEILL FAMILIES Irish families (Irish, Ua/Ó Néill) whose members were kings in N Ireland. The first family were descendants of NIALL GLÚNDUB (d. 919), who were high-kings of the Cenél nEógain and of the broader Northern Uí Néill federation. Their territory was called Tír Eógain (English, Tyrone). They adopted Niall's name as a surname in the early 11th century. Around 1033 they were replaced as high-kings by their Mac Lochlainn kinsmen.

Ua Néill rule was apparently restored in 1167 when Tír Eógain was partitioned by the high-king of Ireland, Toirrdelbach UA CONCHOBAIR, and half was granted to Áed Ua Néill (d. 1177). In 1241 his descendant Brian Ó Néill (king 1238–60) killed Domnall Mac Lochlainn and took the remainder of Tír Eógain; in 1258 he claimed the high-kingship of Ireland. Domnall O'Neill (king 1283–1325, with interruptions) supported the BRUCE INVASION. Henry O'Neill (king 1455–83; d. 1484) achieved overlordship over most of N Ireland.

In 1542 the O'Neill lands were surrendered by Conn Bacach O'Neill (king 1519–59) to HENRY VIII, king of England and Ireland, and were regranted with the title earl of Tyrone (*see* SURRENDER AND REGRANT). The last inaugurated ruler (1593) was Hugh O'NEILL, who left Ireland in the FLIGHT OF THE EARLS (1607). Tyrone was confiscated and used for plantation. *See also* ULSTER; O'NEILL, SHANE; ULSTER PLANTATION.

ONUIST SON OF VURGUIST (fl. from 728; d. 761, probably in N Britain). Onuist's base was probably Dunnottar, in the northernmost part of southern Pictland (in modern NE Scotland). In 728–9 he removed the kings who had replaced NAITON SON OF DER-ILEI (Elphin in the S, Drest in the N), and restored Naiton's kingship. After Naiton died (732), Onuist became king of all Pictland (the title 'king of FORTRIU' lapsed).

Onuist was soon challenged by Naiton's half-brother, with support from DÁL RIATA; but a Dál Riatan lord delivered the half-brother to Onuist, who had him drowned. Then, between 736 and 741, Onuist conquered Dál Riata, and in 744 fought Britons of Clyde Rock (later STRATHCLYDE). Also, from 740 he was allied with King ÆTHELBALD of Mercia (d. 757) which enabled dual campaigns against NORTHUMBRIA and even WESSEX; together they dominated Britain. In 750, however, Onuist's brother was defeated and killed by Clyde Rock Britons, and Wessex successfully rebelled. But Onuist's power was only partly diminished, and in 756 (now in alliance with Eadbert of Northumbria), he forced the Clyde Rock Britons to submit. Onuist is also the most likely founder of the abbey at Cennrígmonaid (later ST ANDREWS; first recorded 747). His long reign was the most successful in Pictish history. *See also* KINGSHIP, NORTH BRITAIN.

ONUIST SON OF VURGUIST (d. 836) *see* CONSTANTÍN SON OF VURGUIST

OPINION POLLS Investigations of public attitudes and voting intentions by analysis of data drawn from small representative samples. Polling began in Great Britain in 1937 and proliferated in the 1960s. Polls have guided politicians in the selection of policies and election dates, but their influence is hard to measure.

Harold WILSON (Labour Party leader 1963–76) paid assiduous attention to polls; Margaret THATCHER (Conservative leader 1975–90) professed to ignore them. If poll findings encouraged ABORTION law reform (1967), public support for capital punishment did not prevent its abolition (1969). Frequent opinion polls can affect party morale during general election campaigns, but failure to predict the correct outcomes in 1970, 1992, 2015 and 2017 cast recurrent doubt on their reliability. The development of the Internet from the 1990s enabled larger groups of people to be polled frequently.

OPIUM WARS *see* CHINA, ENGLISH AND BRITISH RELATIONS WITH

OPPIDUM In Britain oppidum (Latin, meaning 'town') indicates large lowland sites of 740 acres (300 ha) to 7.7 sq mi (20 sq km) defined by linear dykes, which date to the first centuries BC and AD. Some represent élite estates, others had urban characteristics, such as COLCHESTER, capital of CUNOBELIN.

ORANGE ORDER, IRELAND A Protestant men's social, religious and political organization (with associated women's order), based in NORTHERN IRELAND. It was started for self-defence and preservation of the PROTESTANT ASCENDANCY, and named in honour of King WILLIAM III

(William of Orange), whose victory over the Catholic JAMES VII/II in 1688–91 was the basis of the Ascendancy (*see* WILLIAMITE WAR).

The Order was founded at Loughgall (Co. Armagh) on 21 September 1795 by ex-VOLUNTEERS after they had defeated (Catholic) DEFENDERS in the 'battle of the Diamond'. A central Grand Lodge was founded in DUBLIN in 1798 which established rules (e.g., regarding ritual) and created a hierarchy of local lodges. It adopted 12 July as its day of celebration, the anniversary (after a calendar change) of the battle of the BOYNE (1690). The Order included men from all Protestant denominations and social classes. Lodges celebrated 'The Twelfth' with 'walks' (marches).

The Order was viewed suspiciously by British governments in the 19th century and was twice dissolved (1825–8, 1836–45). It expanded considerably in the N from the 1880s in response to agitation by the LAND LEAGUE, IRISH NATIONAL LEAGUE, and HOME RULE MOVEMENT, and mounted protests against Home Rule (1880s–*c*.1920). In 1905 the Order was allocated 50 seats on the ULSTER UNIONIST COUNCIL.

Following the PARTITION OF IRELAND (1921), the Grand Lodge moved to Belfast (1922). About one-third of Northern Ireland's male Protestant population were members (about 100,000), including most Unionist politicians. In southern Ireland the Order declined and many Orange halls were destroyed in 1920–3. Lodges were founded in Great Britain and elsewhere. *See also* ORANGE ORDER, SCOTLAND; KNIGHTS OF COLUMBANUS; ANCIENT ORDER OF HIBERNIANS.

ORANGE ORDER, SCOTLAND The first lodge was established at Maybole (Ayrshire) *c*.1800; by the 1830s there were many lodges among Protestant Irish immigrants (often unskilled textile workers) in the SW (Ayrshire) and Glasgow region (W-C Scotland), which remained the heartland. New skilled immigrants (metalworkers, shipbuilders) joined from the 1850s. By 1900 the Order was a large working-class movement, often involved in sectarian conflict with CATHOLICS. In 1900–14 it developed links with the CONSERVATIVE PARTY to resist Irish HOME RULE.

By the late 20th century lodges were primarily sectarian social clubs (total membership in 2000, about 50,000). In 2012, concerned about the possibility of Scottish independence, the Order established the organization 'British Together' which campaigned against independence in the referendum of 2014. *See also* ORANGE ORDER, IRELAND.

ORDAINERS *see* ORDINANCES

ORDINANCES In England, constitutions for reform of royal government compiled by BARONS and bishops, so-called 'Ordainers', following demands for reform made to King EDWARD II in the 1310 PARLIAMENT. Published and adopted in Aug. 1311, they stipulated parliamentary supervision of government (e.g., appointment of officers) and banishment of Edward's favourite Piers GAVESTON. The Ordinances remained in force until after the execution of Edward's opponent THOMAS OF LANCASTER (March 1322). Revoked by Parliament May 1322.

OREGON Former disputed territory in N America, between the Rocky Mountains and Pacific Ocean (now Oregon, Washington and Idaho in USA, and part of British Columbia in CANADA). After fur traders arrived, Great Britain and the USA both claimed the area (1792). They occupied it jointly from 1818 to 1846 when US diplomacy secured its partition.

O'REILLY, EDMUND (b. 2 or 3 Jan. 1598 in Co. Dublin, Ireland; d. March 1669 at Saumur, France, aged 71). A Catholic priest, O'Reilly became vicar-general of the archbishop of DUBLIN by 1641 (effectively diocesan leader). During the IRISH WARS (from 1641), he supported the papal nuncio Archbishop RINUCCINI against other Catholics (1645–9; *see* CATHOLIC CONFEDERATION), and in 1649 negotiated with the Parliamentarian Michael JONES on behalf of Owen Roe O'NEILL. During the English conquest (1649–52) he participated in resistance in the Wicklow Mountains (*see* CROMWELL, OLIVER, AND IRELAND). O'Reilly was arrested in 1652, convicted of supporting murders (1653), and deported (1655).

Created archbishop of ARMAGH in 1657, O'Reilly lived again in Ireland 1658–61, and returned to oppose the LOYAL REMONSTRANCE (1666). *See also* CATHOLICS AND CATHOLIC CHURCH, IRELAND FROM 16TH CENTURY.

ORFORD, EARL OF (b. 1652 at Chiswick, Middlesex, England; d. 26 Nov. 1727 at Chippenham, Cambridgeshire, England, aged about 75). A naval officer from 1666 (in the reign of King CHARLES II), Edward Russell resigned his command after the RYE HOUSE PLOT (1683) when a cousin was executed. Opposed to the pro-Catholic policies of King JAMES VII/II, in June 1688 he signed the letter inviting William of Orange to England (*see* GLORIOUS REVOLUTION).

Russell was treasurer of the NAVY 1689–99. In 1692, as admiral of the fleet, he defeated the French at La Hogue, preventing an invasion (*see* GRAND ALLIANCE, WAR OF THE). A member of the WHIG JUNTO, he became first lord of the Admiralty in 1694 and commanded a Mediterranean fleet in 1694–5. He left active service in 1695 and was created earl of Orford in 1697. Although forced to resign as treasurer and first lord in 1699, he served again as first lord 1709–17. From 1705 his protégés included Robert WALPOLE.

ORIEL *see* AIRGIALLA

ORIENTALISM Term used for the depiction of Middle Eastern and E Asian cultures in Western culture. It was also employed by the Palestinian-American scholar Edward Said (1935–2003) for his controversial thesis claiming that European study of Africa and Asia was partly motivated and shaped by an ambition to dominate the non-European world. European identity, Said argued, depended upon its self-created sense of superiority over non-Europeans.

ORKNEY ISLANDS An archipelago within the BRITISH ISLES, about 10 mi (16 km) off NE BRITAIN; part of SCOTLAND within the UNITED KINGDOM. There are about 70 islands and skerries (small, rocky islands), of which 20 are permanently inhabited. 'Mainland' is the principal island, Kirkwall the capital. Est. popn in 2015: 21,000 (75% on Mainland). (The Orkney Islands and SHETLAND ISLANDS are called the Northern Isles.)

The Orkney Islands retain considerable remains from PREHISTORY (e.g., SKARA BRAE village). The 'Ork' element, recorded in the 1st century AD (in Latin, Orcades), may have referred to a young pig. Possibly from the 3rd century the islands' inhabitants were among the so-called PICTS. They became Christian by the 8th century, just before the islands were taken into the VIKING world: after suffering raids, they were settled by Norse (9th century), and ruled by Norse *jarls* (earls) under kings of Norway and Denmark. A variant of Norse, Norn, became the principal language. Although replacement by Scots began in the 14th century, Norn was spoken until the 17th century. The Norse called the islands Orkneyjar, meaning 'Seal islands'. From the 1360s the Scottish Sinclair family became associated with the islands (through marriage); Henry Sinclair was created earl of Orkney with lands and rights (1379).

In 1468 Christian I, king of Denmark-Norway, pledged the islands towards the dowry for the marriage of his daughter Margaret to King JAMES III of Scotland. James compelled Earl William (Sinclair) to surrender his earldom (1470), and annexed the islands (1472, with the SHETLAND ISLANDS).

The islands' economy has mainly consisted of agriculture and fishing. Population peaked in 1861 at 32,200 before declining to 17,000 in 1971. Scapa Flow anchorage was used as a naval base 1914–57, and a major oil terminal was opened in 1977 (*see* NORTH SEA GAS AND OIL INDUSTRIES).

ORLÉANS, SIEGE OF The English siege of a French town SW of Paris, 7 Oct. 1428 to 8 May 1429, during the HUNDRED YEARS WAR. English forces commanded by William de la POLE, seeking to establish a base for attacking the Loire Valley, were eventually routed by a French army led by JOAN OF ARC. The French success led to further English losses.

ORMOND, 2ND DUKE OF (b. 29 April 1665 at Dublin, Ireland; d. 5 Nov. 1745 at Avignon, France, aged 80). James

Butler was a grandson of the 1st duke of Ormond, whom he succeeded in July 1688 (*see* ORMOND, 12TH EARL OF). He supported King JAMES VII/II in England (e.g., in suppressing MONMOUTH'S REBELLION), until Nov. 1688 when he defected to William of Orange (*see* WILLIAM III). Though a TORY, he fought in William's armies in Ireland and Continental Europe (*see* WILLIAMITE WAR; GRAND ALLIANCE, WAR OF THE). Under Queen ANNE (from 1702), Ormond fought in Spain (1702) and was lord lieutenant of Ireland (1703–7, 1710–13). He succeeded the duke of MARLBOROUGH as captain-general in 1711 (*see* SPANISH SUCCESSION, WAR OF THE).

In 1714 Ormond seemingly supported the new Hanoverian king GEORGE I, but was suspected of Jacobite sympathies. In Aug. 1715 he fled to France. He tried to land in SW England in Sept. (to support the JACOBITE REBELLION) and was nominal commander of the 1719 rebellion. Thereafter he lived in Continental Europe. *See also* JACOBITISM, IMPACT ON BRITISH POLITICS.

ORMOND, 12TH EARL OF (b. 19 Oct. 1610 at Clerkenwell, Middlesex, England; d. 21 July 1688 at Kingston Lacy, Dorset, England, aged 77). James Butler, of the Irish Catholic BUTLER FAMILY, was raised as a Protestant and succeeded as earl in 1633. As commander of government troops in the IRISH WARS (appointed Nov. 1641) he defeated Catholics at Kilrush, Co. Clare (15 April 1642). He was raised to marquess of Ormond (Aug.).

In April 1643 King CHARLES I ordered Ormond to negotiate with the CATHOLIC CONFEDERATION. Ormond achieved a 'CESSATION' (15 Sept.), and was appointed chief governor (king's lieutenant, 13 Nov.). But his treaty (March 1646) was blocked by RINUCCINI (Aug.). With Charles now captive, Ormond surrendered DUBLIN to England's Parliament (June 1647) and left Ireland (28 July).

Ormond returned in Oct. 1648 to win Ireland for Charles through a Protestant–Catholic coalition. The Confederation supported him (Jan. 1649), but Owen Roe O'NEILL resisted (until Oct.). Ormond failed to halt Oliver CROMWELL's conquest and withdrew (11 Dec. 1650).

After the RESTORATION (1660) Ormond was created duke of Ormond. He served as governor (lord lieutenant) 1662–9, 1677–85, favouring reconciliation of Catholics. He supported the Act of Explanation (1665), which recovered land for Catholics, but rejected the revised LOYAL REMONSTRANCE (1666). *See also* GLAMORGAN TREATIES; ORMOND TREATIES; JONES, MICHAEL; WALSH, PETER; PLUNKETT AFFAIR.

ORMOND, EARLS AND DUKES OF *see* BUTLER FAMILY, IRELAND

ORMOND TREATIES Two treaties made between the marquess of ORMOND, chief governor of Ireland (for King CHARLES I), and leaders of the CATHOLIC CONFEDERATION.

The first, agreed 28 March 1646 and proclaimed in DUBLIN on 30 July, granted Catholics an unspecific place in public life. The papal nuncio Archbishop RINUCCINI contrived its rejection (at Synod of Waterford, 12 Aug.).

A second treaty, agreed 17 Jan. 1649, recognized the Catholic Church and Catholic worship pending consideration of the issue by a free Parliament. Rinuccini's opposition was ignored. The treaty created a Protestant–Catholic Royalist coalition; but it proved unable to defeat the Parliamentarian invasion of Aug. 1649. *See also* IRISH WARS, 1641–52.

ORSINI AFFAIR A diplomatic incident which brought down the government of Lord PALMERSTON in Great Britain in 1858. Italian exiles in Britain conspired to assassinate Napoleon III, the emperor of France. The plot was implemented in France, unsuccessfully, by Pietro Orsini on 14 Jan. Palmerston proposed to make conspiracy to murder a capital offence. Accused of bowing to French pressure, he resigned when his Bill was defeated (19 Feb.).

ORWELL, GEORGE (b. 25 June 1903 at Motihari, Bengal, India; d. 21 Jan. 1950 at London, England, aged 46). Pseudonym of Eric Blair. Resident in England from *c.*1906, Blair returned to India to serve in the Burma Police (1921–7). He then concentrated on writing while intermittently taking employment. Alongside journalism, he published reportage (e.g., *The Road to Wigan Pier*, 1937), and novels (e.g., *Burmese Days*, 1934, a critical portrayal of British colonialism). Experiences in the SPANISH CIVIL WAR were recounted in *Homage to Catalonia* (1938).

During WORLD WAR II Blair was a producer for the BRITISH BROADCASTING COMPANY (1941–3) and literary editor for the left-wing newspaper *Tribune* (1943–4). His novel *Animal Farm* (1944), a parody of Stalinism, won international acclaim, and his attack on totalitarianism in the novel *Nineteen Eighty-four* (1949) was enduringly influential. *See also* ENGLISH LITERATURE, ENGLAND.

OSRAIGE (OSSORY) A kingdom in SE Ireland, between LEINSTER (E Ireland) and MUNSTER (S Ireland), based around the Nore Valley. It existed by the 7th century when it was ruled by the Corcu Loígde dynasty, who were superseded by the Dál mBirn. In the late 10th and early 11th centuries its ruling dynasty, now called Mac Gilla Pátraic (English, MacGillapatrick), sometimes seized part of Leinster (e.g., Donnchad Mac Gilla Pátraic, 1033–9). Osraige was constituted a diocese in 1111.

In 1171 Domnall Mac Gilla Pátraic (d. 1185) gave allegiance to King HENRY II of England and afterwards aided the Anglo-Normans. His descendants were allowed to survive, but Osraige was absorbed into Leinster. In 1541 Barnaby MacGillapatrick was created Lord Fitzpatrick of Upper Ossory (*see* SURRENDER AND REGRANT).

OSTMEN Term used in Ireland in the 10th–12th centuries, derived from Old Norse, Austmenn ('East men'), for the Hiberno-Scandinavian populations of towns founded by the Norse (i.e., Norwegians), namely CORK, DUBLIN, LIMERICK, WATERFORD and WEXFORD. Gaelic Irish were sometimes called Vestmen (i.e., 'West men'). *See also* VIKINGS, IMPACT ON IRELAND.

OSWALD (b. 603 or 604; d. 5 Aug. 642 at 'Maserfelth', Mercia, aged 38). In 616 Oswald (from Bernicia) escaped into exile when his father, Æthelfrith, king of Bernicia and Deira (NE England), was killed by EDWIN (from Deira). He lived in (Scottish) DÁL RIATA (modern W Scotland), where he accepted Christianity.

In 634 Oswald killed CADWALLON AP CADFAN (of Gwynedd), who had seized Bernicia and Deira (633), and became king. He requested a bishop from the monastery of IONA (in Dál Riata): they sent AIDAN (635). Oswald claimed to be overking of the Anglo-Saxons, Britons, PICTS, and SCOTS. By 638 he conquered GODODDIN, extending Bernicia N to the R. Forth. He was killed by PENDA of MERCIA at 'Maserfelth' (probably Oswestry in W Mercia), and was afterwards venerated as a saint. Succeeded by Oswiu. *See also* CONVERSION OF ANGLO-SAXONS; KINGSHIP, ANGLO-SAXON.

OSWALD (fl. from 940s in England; d. 29 Feb. 992 at Worcester, Worcestershire, England). From an Anglo-Danish family, the monk Oswald lived in the 950s at the reformed Benedictine monastery at Fleury in Francia (returned to England 958 or 959). In 961 King EDGAR appointed him bishop of WORCESTER. Oswald founded monasteries at Westbury-on-Trym (Gloucestershire, 963 or 964) and Ramsey (Huntingdonshire, 966), reformed Worcestershire monasteries, and began to replace secular clergy with monks at Worcester. From 971 or 972 Oswald was also archbishop of YORK. *See also* TENTH-CENTURY REFORMATION.

OSWIU (b. 611 or 612; d. 15 Feb. 670, aged 58). In Aug. 642 Oswiu (a Bernician) succeeded his brother OSWALD as king of BERNICIA and DEIRA (NE England/SE modern Scotland). Deira resisted his rule. Oswiu attempted to rule through subkings, but probably removed them for defiance: Oswine of Deira (ruled from 644; murdered 651); Oswald's son Œthelwald (651–5); his own son Alhfrith (655–64). Oswiu also married a Deiran (c.643, Eanflæd, daughter of King EDWIN).

At his accession Oswiu was subordinate to PENDA, king of MERCIA. He killed Penda in 655, ruled Mercia until 658 (*see* WULFHERE), and spread Christianity there. He was acknowledged as overking of southern Anglo-Saxons. In 664 Oswiu held a synod to resolve religious differences (*see* WHITBY, SYNOD OF). He died, unusually for a 7th-century king, from illness. Succeeded by EGFRITH. *See also* KINGSHIP, ANGLO-SAXON.

O'TOOLE, LAURENCE (UA TUATHAIL, LORCÁN) (b. *c*.1128 in Ireland; d. 14 Nov. 1180 at Eu, Normandy, aged about 52). Abbot of GLENDALOUGH from 1153, O'Toole became archbishop of DUBLIN in 1162. In 1169 he negotiated on behalf of Dublin before it was captured by Anglo-Norman invaders (*see* NORMANS, IMPACT ON IRELAND). He visited King HENRY II in England in 1172–3, and witnessed the treaty of WINDSOR (1175) which defined the extent of Anglo-Norman rule in Ireland. In Rome in 1179 for the Third Vatican Council, O'Toole was appointed resident PAPAL LEGATE in Ireland. He then held a synod at Clonfert to proclaim the Council's decrees. He was canonized in 1225. *See also* CHURCH REFORM, MEDIEVAL IRELAND.

OTTAWA AGREEMENTS Measures of TARIFF REFORM adopted by the UK and DOMINIONS at the Imperial Economic Conference held in Canada (21 July–20 Aug. 1932) in response to the GREAT DEPRESSION. Twelve trade agreements established limited 'imperial preference'. They were extended to include CROWN COLONIES in 1933. Though the scheme's economic impact was less than expected, it lasted until the UK joined the EUROPEAN ECONOMIC COMMUNITY (1973).

OTTERBURN, BATTLE OF Fought NW of Otterburn, C Northumberland (NE England) during the night of 5 Aug. 1388. Scots under the earls of Douglas, March and Moray defeated an English force led by Henry PERCY. The Scottish raid and a parallel one in NW England were an attempt to pressurize England following the coup against favourites of King RICHARD II by the APPELLANTS. *See also* SCOTTISH–ENGLISH RELATIONS 1357 TO 1603.

OTTOMAN EMPIRE, ENGLISH AND BRITISH RELATIONS WITH Starting with the foundation of the Turkey Company in 1581, English relations with the Ottoman Empire (areas of C and SE Europe, the Middle East and N Africa under the rule of Muslim Ottoman emperors from Istanbul) were tangential. In the 17th and 18th centuries, England (Great Britain from 1707) regretted that the HABSBURG EMPIRE was distracted by Turkish wars from opposing FRANCE.

The emergence in the 1780s of the EASTERN QUESTION led Britain to take a close interest in the Ottoman Empire in the BALKANS, Levant (eastern Mediterranean) and PERSIAN GULF. It generally supported the contraction of Ottoman rule in the Balkans (e.g., GREECE in the 1820s, ROMANIA in 1878). Support for the Empire in the CRIMEAN WAR (1854–6) was followed by a conditional guarantee of its Asiatic possessions at the Congress of BERLIN (1878). Estrangement followed, especially after the ARMENIAN MASSACRES (1896), and EGYPT became the focus of British regional strategy. The Ottoman Empire allied itself to GERMANY in WORLD WAR I (1914–18). Military campaigns in PALESTINE and Mesopotamia resulted in a major role for Britain in the post-war partition of the Empire (1918–23).

Britain was initially hostile to the new nationalist-ruled Turkey (*see* CHANAK CRISIS), but developed wary co-operation against the USSR (Turkey joined the NORTH ATLANTIC TREATY ORGANIZATION in 1952). From the 1950s, Britain's handling of CYPRUS was a sensitive issue, as was Turkey's desire from the 1980s to join the EUROPEAN ECONOMIC COMMUNITY. *See also* SYKES–PICOT AGREEMENT; IRAQ, BRITISH MANDATE; SAUDI ARABIA, BRITISH RELATIONS WITH.

OVERLORD Code-name for the Allied invasion of Normandy (N France) in 1944, during WORLD WAR II. It began on D-Day (6 June 1944), when 4000 assault craft landed 156,000 troops, primarily US, British and Canadian, commanded by Dwight Eisenhower and Bernard MONTGOMERY, on five beaches. ('D-Day' is a standard military term for the day on which an operation commences.) The forces created a front for further operations by 12 June.

OVERSEAS EXPLORATION, ENGLISH AND BRITISH Exploration from Europe was pioneered in the 14th–15th centuries by Portugal and Spain (Castile): Spanish ships reached the Americas in 1492; Portuguese reached India in 1498. Englishmen sought lands in the Atlantic Ocean possibly from 1480 (from BRISTOL), with John CABOT finding NEWFOUNDLAND (1497).

Until the 1630s the English invested mostly in searches for a northern trade route to E Asia, avoiding Portuguese and Spanish routes (*see* ARCTIC, ENGLISH AND BRITISH EXPLORATION). From the 1570s the Atlantic coastal area of N America was also explored for colonization (*see* NORTH AMERICA, ENGLISH EXPLORATION). CIRCUMNAVIGATIONS were also made (1570s–80s), and voyages to India (from 1591–4). The Dutch started exploration of the Australian and New Zealand coasts and looked for a southern continent (17th century).

Between the mid 17th and early 18th centuries, English exploration was less assertive. The buccaneer William Dampier visited Australia (1686) and commanded an Admiralty expedition (1699–1701) which discovered New Britain (now in Papua New Guinea). The Hudson Bay area (N America) was explored (partly for the NORTH-WEST PASSAGE).

New British activity from the 1760s, motivated partly by scientific curiosity, often concerned new areas. James COOK explored the Pacific region (1760s–70s), including parts of NEW ZEALAND and AUSTRALIA. Renewed interest in the North-west Passage produced Cook's discovery (1778) that Asia was separated from America. The NW

coast of N America was surveyed (1792–4) by George Vancouver. Investigation of Africa's interior was developed by James Bruce (1768–73) and by expeditions sponsored by the African Association (1788–1831).

In the 19th century searches for the North-west Passage succeeded. Research was undertaken in ARCTIC and ANTARCTIC areas, including Antarctica (from 1890s). Africa and Asia were further explored (e.g., Africa by David LIVINGSTONE, 1840s–70s; Asia by Francis YOUNGHUSBAND, from 1880s). By 1914, European awareness of the world was extensive. *See also* BRITISH EMPIRE.

OVERSEAS TERRITORY *see* DEPENDENT TERRITORY

OVERSEAS TRADING COMPANIES Mercantile companies were prominent in English FOREIGN TRADE in the 14th–19th centuries. They obtained privileges from the Crown to regulate trade, reduce competition and benefit profitability. Most companies were 'regulated' associations of individual traders; a few were joint-stock companies (*see* BUSINESS ORGANIZATION).

The earliest company was the Fellowship of the Staple, an association of wool and hide exporters created in 1363 when the wool STAPLE (compulsory export market) was established at CALAIS (English-held town in NE France). 'Staplers' controlled four-fifths of wool exports until wool exporting was prohibited in 1614. After the loss of Calais (1558) staplers were increasingly involved in the domestic wool trade. The company survived until 1928 (*see* WOOL TRADE, ENGLAND).

A company of merchants who exported cloth to the Low Countries developed during the 15th century. Known as 'merchant adventurers', they were granted privileges by King HENRY IV in 1407, and were recognized as a fellowship by the corporation of London in 1486. They included merchants from various English towns but Londoners predominated. The Crown suspended their monopoly 1624–34; their privileges were terminated in 1689. Exports went mainly to Antwerp until 1564, and from 1611 also through Hamburg where the company survived until 1806.

As merchants started trade with new places in the 16th century, the Crown authorized new monopolistic companies: the Andalusia Company, 1531, trading to Spain; the Muscovy Company, 1555, trading to Russia; the Eastland Company, 1579, trading to the Baltic and Poland; the Turkey Company, 1581, and the Venice Company, 1583 (merged 1592 as the Levant Company); the Barbary Company, 1585, trading to Morocco; the Africa Company, 1588. Merchants traded on their own account but operated collectively. Most companies declined in the late 17th century and often lost their privileges (e.g., Eastland Company, 1673; ROYAL AFRICAN COMPANY, 1697). The important survivor was the EAST INDIA COMPANY, founded 1600 (a joint-stock company).

OWAIN GLYN DŴR (b. *c*.1354; d. between 5 July 1415 and 24 Feb. 1416, aged about 61). Descendant of former rulers of Powys (C Wales) and Deheubarth (SW Wales); leader of the 1400–10 Welsh revolt, which recovered most of Wales from English control by 1404.

The revolt arose probably from a dispute between Owain (lord of Glyndyfrdwy and Cynllaith, both NE Wales) and Reginald, Lord Grey of Ruthin (NE Wales), but was fuelled by Welsh leaders' resentment of English rule (*see* Wales, English Conquest of). Owain received support partly because of his distinguished ancestry.

On 16 Sept. 1400 Owain was proclaimed Prince of Wales at Glyndyfrdwy; Ruthin castle was besieged; and an uprising occurred on Anglesey (NW Wales). Despite initial setbacks, the rebels gained ground, helped by the independent revolt of Henry Percy against Henry IV in England. The Welsh revolt culminated in 1404 with a Welsh Parliament at Machynlleth (Powys), an alliance with Charles VI of France (14 July 1404), and an agreement with leaders of the English revolt.

The tide then turned. Owain suffered defeats and loss of French and some Welsh support (1405–6). His family was captured in 1408, and many Welsh leaders were killed or imprisoned during fighting in 1410. Owain then disappeared; he is last recorded as alive in 1415. The revolt provoked Penal Laws and caused economic decline.

OWAIN GWYNEDD (b. *c*.1110; d. 23 Nov. 1170, aged about 60). King of Gwynedd (NW Wales) 1137–70; dominant Welsh ruler in the 1160s. Owain succeeded his father Gruffudd ap Cynan, but struggled against his brother Cadwaladr (exiled 1152).

From the late 1140s Owain advanced into NE Wales and Powys (C Wales), especially after the death of Madog ap Maredudd in 1160 (expansion only halted briefly by Henry II of England's invasion in 1157). Owain assumed the title 'prince of the Welsh' and leadership (with Rhys ap Gruffudd) of the Welsh revolt against Henry in 1164–5. More gains followed in 1166–7, though Owain was excommunicated by the archbishop of Canterbury mainly for an illegal marriage. *See also* Anglo-Welsh relations, 6th–13th centuries.

OWAIN LAWGOCH, 'RED HAND' (b. *c*.1330 at Tatsfield, Surrey, England; d. July 1378 at Mortagne-sur-Gironde, Poitou, W France, aged about 48). Welsh soldier in French forces during the Hundred Years War. As a great-nephew of Llywelyn ap Gruffudd he claimed Gwynedd (NW Wales) and organized expeditions in 1369, 1372 (with French aid) and 1377 (with Castilian aid); none reached Wales. Rumour of the last led to his assassination by an English agent.

OWEN, HUGH (b. 14 Jan. 1804 at Llangeinwen, Anglesey, Wales; d. 20 Nov. 1881 at Mentone, France, aged 77). A London-based civil servant who campaigned for non-denominational education in Wales. Owen championed expansion of (elementary) National Schools (from 1843); a University of Wales (from 1854), resulting in University College, Aberystwyth (1872); Normal College (teachers' college), Bangor (from 1856; opened 1858); a teachers' college for women, Swansea (opened 1871); and secondary education (Welsh Intermediate Education Act, 1889; *see* County Schools). He supported the Eisteddfod and Welsh National Societies. He was knighted in 1881. *See also* Universities, Wales.

OWEN, ROBERT (b. 14 May 1771 at Newton, Montgomeryshire, Wales; d. 17 Nov. 1858 at Newton, aged 87). In 1799 Owen, a successful cotton-mill manager in Manchester (NW England), helped to purchase cotton mills at New Lanark (S Scotland). There he provided housing and education in order to improve his employees' behaviour and efficiency, and also developed proposals for communes. Owen withdrew from New Lanark in 1829 and involved himself in trade unionism, unsuccessfully leading the Grand National Consolidated Trades Union (1833–4). Thereafter he concentrated on spreading socialist ideas and co-operativism. *See also* Socialism.

OWEN GLENDOWER *see* Owain Glyn Dŵr

OXFORD A city in C England, at the confluence of the Rivers Thames and Cherwell; centre of Oxfordshire.

Oxford originated by the early 8th century as a double monastery (governed by the Mercian royal abbess Frideswide) and settlement. They stood near routeways from the south-west and north, the former including the ford across a channel of the R. Thames from which the city's name is derived (Oxford means 'Ford used by oxen'). In the late 9th century a burh (fortified centre) was added (the central part of the modern city). A cloth-making industry operated in the 11th–16th centuries.

A university (England's first) was started by the late 12th century. Most students lived in halls (lodging houses run by university masters): by 1310 there were over 120. From the 1260s there were also endowed colleges. Town and university populations declined from the late 14th century, though more colleges were founded. By 1513 only 18 halls survived. From the 16th century colleges dominated the university. Both university and town expanded from the late 16th century. In 2019 there were 39 colleges. Oxford became a Church of England see in 1542.

From 1912 William Morris developed car manufacturing (*see* Nuffield, Lord). Book-publishing and science-based companies also expanded from the late 20th century.

A polytechnic received university status in 1992 as Oxford Brookes University. *See also* UNIVERSITIES, ENGLAND.

Est. popn: 1086, 3200; 1300, 6000; 1600, 7000; 1800, 12,000; 1900, 52,000; 2000, 130,000.

OXFORD, EARL OF *see* HARLEY, ROBERT

OXFORD, PROVISIONS OF A scheme for reform of English royal GOVERNMENT, 1258. It was formulated by a committee of 24, which consisted of magnates critical of King HENRY III and royal councillors, and was influenced by Simon de MONTFORT and Hugh BIGOD. The Provisions were adopted during a PARLIAMENT at OXFORD (June), and included the creation of an elected Council of 15 to supervise royal government, revival of the justiciarship (*see* CHIEF JUSTICIAR) and provision for Parliament to meet three times a year. They were declared invalid in 1261 by Pope Alexander IV because they undermined royal authority. *See also* BARONIAL CONFLICT AND WARS.

OXFORD MOVEMENT A movement in the 19th and 20th centuries which promoted a view of the Church of ENGLAND as a divinely instituted body which should resist State control partly by following the example of the early Church (1st–4th centuries). It was inspired by the 'assize sermon' preached at OXFORD University in 1833 by John KEBLE. Its leaders, notably J.H. NEWMAN and E.B. PUSEY, spread their ideas through *Tracts for the Times*, causing supporters to be nicknamed 'Tractarians'. They claimed that the Church of England stood between Protestantism and Catholicism. The Tracts ended in 1841 when Oxford University and bishops condemned Newman's Tract 90 for claiming that the Church's Thirty-nine Articles could be interpreted in a Catholic sense (*see* ARTICLES OF RELIGION). Newman converted to Roman Catholicism in 1845.

The movement influenced theology, liturgy, Church architecture and music until the late 20th century (*see* ECCLESIOLOGISTS). From the 1840s the revival of pre-REFORMATION practices (e.g., incense, eucharistic vestments) and adoption of Roman Catholic usages generated controversy and was called RITUALISM.

OYER AND TERMINER, COMMISSIONS OF In England, special groups of justices appointed by the Crown. Started in 1275 to relieve pressure on justices conducting general eyres, commissions were authorized to indict people suspected of criminality (e.g., trespass) and impose punishments. They could be appointed at a person's request on payment of a fee. The use of commissions dwindled in the late 14th century as JUSTICES OF THE PEACE became prominent. 'Oyer and terminer', from French, means 'to hear and stop'. *See also* EYRE; LEGAL REFORMS, ENGLAND, REIGN OF EDWARD I.

P

PACIFICO INCIDENT A dispute resulting from an attack by a mob on the home of Don Pacifico, a Portuguese Jew, in Athens (Greece) in 1847. When the Greek government refused Pacifico's request for compensation, he appealed to Lord PALMERSTON, the British foreign secretary. (David Pacifico, born at GIBRALTAR, was a British citizen.) Palmerston ordered a naval blockade of the Piraeus (15 Jan.–27 April 1850), and justified his action in a celebrated speech (25 June). *See also* GUNBOAT DIPLOMACY.

PACIFISM Term applied from the 1900s to the principles that international disputes should be settled by arbitration, not force, and that waging and participating in war are wrong. During WORLD WAR I, the introduction of CONSCRIPTION in Great Britain (Jan. 1916) included accommodation of pacifism by tribunals; 7000 conscientious objectors accepted non-combatant service, 3000 were sent to labour camps, 1500 'absolutists' refused all service. Pacifism flourished in the 1920s–30s (e.g., Peace Pledge Union, founded 1934). Tribunals were re-employed during WORLD WAR II (1939–45). More sympathetic than the earlier ones, they registered 47,000 men as conscientious objectors. Later movements influenced by pacifism included the CAMPAIGN FOR NUCLEAR DISARMAMENT (founded 1958).

PAGANISM, ANGLO-SAXON ENGLAND The areas of former ROMAN BRITAIN settled by Anglo-Saxons (from 5th century) contained sites used for pagan worship since the IRON AGE (e.g., distinctive natural places such as wells and springs). The Anglo-Saxons instituted their own shrines, possibly small enclosures surrounded by ditches or fences, which were served by priests (e.g., Coifi, mentioned by BEDE).

Anglo-Saxons honoured deities venerated in northern Europe, such as Tiw, Woden, Thor and Frig whose names were perpetuated in day-names (Tuesday, Wednesday, Thursday, Friday). Festivals were held. Many native British people accepted Anglo-Saxon paganism. Paganism declined in the 7th and 8th centuries. *See also* GERMANIC IMMIGRATION, SOUTHERN BRITAIN; CEMETERIES, EARLY GERMANIC.

PAGET, WILLIAM (b. 1505 or 1506, probably at London, England; d. 9 or 10 June 1563, probably at West Drayton, Middlesex, England, aged about 57). Paget worked for King HENRY VIII from 1528 (secretary 1543–8, knighted 1544). After Henry's death (Jan. 1547) he helped to change Henry's arrangements for the minority of EDWARD VI. He was appointed comptroller of the ROYAL HOUSEHOLD and was a principal adviser to the protector (*see* SOMERSET, EDWARD DUKE OF). When the protector was deposed (Oct. 1549), Paget lost office. Though he was created Lord Paget, his influence declined and he was briefly imprisoned in Oct. 1551 (*see* NORTHUMBERLAND, JOHN DUKE OF).

After Edward's death (1553), Paget led the councillors who declared for MARY I (instead of Lady Jane GREY). She appointed him keeper of the PRIVY SEAL (1555). He was not favoured by ELIZABETH I.

A Dictionary of British and Irish History, First Edition. Edited by Robert Peberdy and Philip Waller.
© 2021 John Wiley & Sons Ltd; © editorial matter and organisation Robert Peberdy and Phillip Waller.
Published 2021 by John Wiley & Sons Ltd.

PAINE, THOMAS (b. 29 Jan. 1737 at Thetford, Norfolk, England; d. 8 June 1809 at New York, USA, aged 72). Propagandist. Following failure in careers and marriage, Paine emigrated to Pennsylvania, N America, in 1774. There he published a hugely influential pamphlet, *Common Sense* (1776), which argued for AMERICAN INDEPENDENCE. He returned to England in 1787. A fervent admirer of the FRENCH REVOLUTION, he published *Rights of Man* (1791–2) in response to the *Reflections* by Edmund BURKE, attacking aristocratic government and advocating republicanism.

Paine fled to France (1792) and in his absence was convicted of seditious libel (publishing words stirring disaffection). But he was imprisoned during the Terror (1793–4). His book *The Age of Reason* (1794–6), an attack on orthodox religion, was widely condemned. He returned to America in 1802. *See also* ENLIGHTENMENT.

PAISLEY, IAN (b. 6 April 1926 at Armagh, Co. Armagh, Northern Ireland; d. 12 Sept. 2014 at Belfast, Northern Ireland, aged 88). An anti-Catholic pastor, Paisley in 1951 co-founded the Free Presbyterian Church (moderator to 2008). When the TROUBLES erupted in NORTHERN IRELAND (late 1960s), he encouraged opposition to Terence O'NEILL and the CIVIL RIGHTS MOVEMENT. He was elected (1970) to the Northern Ireland and UK Parliaments for the ULSTER UNIONIST PARTY, but in 1971 co-founded the DEMOCRATIC UNIONIST PARTY (DUP).

As DUP leader, Paisley opposed developments that threatened Northern Ireland's position within the UK, including British imposition of 'direct rule' (1972), the HILLSBOROUGH AGREEMENT (1985), BELFAST AGREEMENT (1998), and involvement of PROVISIONAL SINN FÉIN in government by Unionist David TRIMBLE (1999) without formal arms 'decommissioning' by the PROVISIONAL IRISH REPUBLICAN ARMY (PIRA). (Devolved government was suspended in 2002.)

At Assembly elections in 2003 the DUP became the largest Party, but Paisley refused to form a government without decommissioning. Following a PIRA statement (2005) and the ST ANDREWS AGREEMENT (2006), Paisley entered power sharing with Sinn Féin; as first minister he led a government (alongside Martin McGUINNESS) from May 2007 to June 2008, when he also retired as DUP leader. In 2010 Paisley was created Lord Bannside. *See also* PEACE PROCESS, NORTHERN IRELAND.

PAKISTAN *see* INDIAN INDEPENDENCE

PAKISTAN, BRITISH RELATIONS WITH A DOMINION and COMMONWEALTH member from 1947, and republic from 1956, Pakistan initially supported the West in the COLD WAR. It allied with Great Britain in the Baghdad Pact (1955) and Central Treaty Organisation (1958), but British arms sales to INDIA caused a breach (1962). Sceptical of British impartiality, the Pakistanis preferred mediation by the USSR to settle the Indo-Pakistani War (1965). They cultivated links with Communist powers and left the Commonwealth (1972–89) in protest at the recognition of Bangladesh (former East Pakistan).

Pakistan resumed co-operation with the USA and (secondarily) Britain after the USSR's invasion of Afghanistan (1979). Its Commonwealth membership was suspended in 1999 following a military coup, but Britain supported reinstatement in 2004 in return for Pakistan's support for the US-led 'War on Terror'. (Membership was suspended again Nov. 2007–May 2008, for prolonged maintenance of emergency rule.) In the 21st century Britain funded development projects in Pakistan. Relations were affected by the presence in Britain of the world's largest Pakistan-derived community (1.2 million people in 2011). Cricket has been a strong common interest. *See also* SOUTH ASIANS IN GREAT BRITAIN; MUSLIMS IN GREAT BRITAIN.

PALAEOLITHIC PERIOD, BRITAIN Literally, the 'Old Stone' Age', the period 450,000–10,500 BP, which is divided into three phases: Early (450,000–200,000 BP), Middle (200,000–35,000 BP), and Upper (35,000–10,500 BP). The Palaeolithic spans the arrival of hominids in Europe (c.70,000 BP, but perhaps earlier) and the emergence of modern *Homo sapiens sapiens* (in Europe, c.40,000 BP).

Some of the earliest Palaeolithic remains in Britain have been recovered at sites such as Pontnewydd cave (Clwyd, NE Wales) and Boxgrove (Sussex, S England). Typical stone tools include handaxes and flint blades which are occasionally found in caves and in gravel deposits along river valleys. Extensive use was also made of bone, antler and ivory, and artefacts made from these materials have been recovered at a number of sites, including Creswell Crags (Derbyshire, N England). The Upper Palaeolithic saw dispersed populations of gatherers and hunters practising cycles of movement and settlement as part of a seasonal round in the tundra and harsh climate of the last Ice Age. Succeeded by the MESOLITHIC PERIOD (the earliest period of Irish prehistory). *See also* GLACIATIONS; GATHERING AND HUNTING.

PALATINATE An area in which a lord exercises quasi-royal powers (e.g., holding courts equivalent to royal courts). Several palatinates (e.g., Chester) appeared in England after the NORMAN CONQUEST (1066–70s), though the term (derived from Latin *palatium*, meaning 'palace') was used only from the 14th century. The main ecclesiastical palatinate belonged to the bishop of DURHAM (abolished 1836). *See also* LANCASTER, DUCHY OF.

PALE, IRELAND The area within the English lordship of Ireland which remained directly controlled by the Dublin-based government 1420s–1540s, following the loss of authority elsewhere (leaving Anglo-Irish lords and towns to defend themselves). It comprised Co. Dublin and parts of Cos. Louth, Meath and Kildare (E Ireland).

In 1428 the area was divided into an inner 'maghery' (from Irish *machaire*, meaning 'plain') and outer marches where residents were encouraged to build defences (e.g., towerhouses, dykes). The term 'English Pale' (from Latin *palus*, meaning 'stake') was first used in 1495, when the Parliament held by Sir Edward POYNINGS ordered the construction (never completed) of a rampart and ditch between the maghery and the marches. The Pale lost its distinctiveness when English rule expanded in the mid 16th century (*see* IRELAND, ENGLISH CONQUEST, 16TH CENTURY). *See also* IRELAND, ENGLISH COLONY IN, 13TH–15TH CENTURIES.

PALESTINE, BRITISH MANDATE One of two MANDATES in the Middle East established in 1920 under British rule and the nominal supervision of the LEAGUE OF NATIONS. (Great Britain had captured the region from the OTTOMAN EMPIRE in 1917–18.) The eastern part was separated in 1921 as the emirate of TRANSJORDAN.

From 1920 the British applied the BALFOUR DECLARATION, which provided for Jewish settlement in Palestine (incorporated in official mandate 1922). Immigrants sought to build a 'national home'. Approx. population in 1922, 757,000 (of whom 78% were Muslims).

Arab opposition to increasing Jewish settlement led to guerrilla war (1936–9), while British controls on Jewish immigration provoked Jewish terrorism. Subsequent partition plans failed. Britain referred Palestine to the United Nations and withdrew (1948). Jews then proclaimed the State of ISRAEL within the mandated territory.

PALEY, WILLIAM (b. July 1743 at Peterborough, Northamptonshire, England; d. 25 May 1805 at Bishopwearmouth, Co. Durham, England, aged 61). A CAMBRIDGE University don and LATITUDINARIAN Church of England clergyman, who was appointed to numerous Church posts from 1769, Paley was the author of *The Principles of Moral and Political Philosophy* (1785), *Evidences of Christianity* (1794) and *Natural Theology* (1802). He defended Christianity through reason, arguing that the natural world was rationally ordered by divine design. His works were highly influential until challenged by the evolutionary theory of Charles DARWIN (published 1859). *See also* ENLIGHTENMENT.

PALLADIUS (fl. 429–31). In 431 Palladius, a deacon, was consecrated bishop by Pope Celestine I and sent to 'the Irish believing in Christ'. His mission to Ireland seems to have been intended to reinforce the earlier mission of GERMANUS to Britain (429). Its results are unknown, though later tradition associated Palladius with LEINSTER

(E Ireland). He may have originated from Auxerre, NE Gaul (modern France). *See also* CONVERSION OF IRELAND.

PALMERSTON, 3RD VISCOUNT (b. 20 Oct. 1784 at Broadlands, Hampshire, England; d. 18 Oct. 1865 at Brocket Hall, Hertfordshire, England, aged 80). British Whig prime minister 1855–8, 1859–65, and long-serving foreign secretary; he is generally known as Lord Palmerston.

Henry Temple inherited his Irish peerage in 1802 and became a TORY MP in 1806. A junior lord of the Admiralty (1807–9) and secretary at war (1809–28), he was a CANNINGITE over CATHOLIC EMANCIPATION and supported the WHIGS from 1829.

As foreign secretary (1830–4, 1835–41) Palmerston handled the independence of BELGIUM, the QUADRUPLE ALLIANCE, EASTERN QUESTION and OPIUM WAR. His sympathy for liberal causes abroad and assertion of the national interest won him popularity. Critics called him a blustering bully, pointing to the PACIFICO INCIDENT (1850) during his third term as foreign secretary (1846–51).

After serving as home secretary (1852–5), Palmerston became prime minister during the CRIMEAN WAR, succeeding the earl of ABERDEEN. His ministry suppressed the INDIAN MUTINY, though the ORSINI AFFAIR ousted him briefly (1858–9). His misjudgement of the SCHLESWIG-HOLSTEIN QUESTION suggested failing powers.

'Pam' exhibited the hearty style of an old-fashioned aristocrat, and while his opposition to further PARLIAMENTARY REFORM angered Radicals, he dominated foreign policy in the mid 19th century.

PANKHURST FAMILY Militant campaigners for WOMEN'S SUFFRAGE in Great Britain. Emmeline Pankhurst (1858–1928), widow of radical lawyer Richard Pankhurst (d. 1898), founded the Women's Social and Political Union in 1903. As leader of the 'suffragettes', she damaged property, went to prison (1908–9, 1911), and led hunger strikes before suspending direct action after the outbreak of WORLD WAR I (1914). Her three daughters assisted her, especially Christabel (1880–1958), who organized an arson campaign from 1912. Sylvia (1882–1960), an artist and sometime Communist, worked for Abyssinian (Ethiopian) independence (1935–41). Adela (1885–1961) emigrated and co-founded the Australian Communist Party.

PAPACY, ENGLISH AND BRITISH RELATIONS WITH *see* HOLY SEE, ENGLISH AND BRITISH RELATIONS WITH

PAPAL LEGATES Senior clergy who hold authority delegated by the Pope. Until the 16th century, some archbishops (including those of CANTERBURY, YORK, ST ANDREWS, GLASGOW) held powers as perpetual legates (in Latin *legatus natus*, meaning literally 'born legate'). Other legates, usually cardinals, were sent to Churches or governments for particular purposes, such as resolving disputes, holding councils for Church reform, or collecting papal taxation. Such a legate was a *legatus a latere* ('legate from the side [of the Pope]'). They were frequently Italians, though occasionally a clergyman was appointed *legatus a latere* in his own country.

Two legates held a council in England in 786. Legates *a latere* were then frequently sent to the British Isles between the late 11th and 16th centuries. In England, Archbishop STIGAND was deposed by a legatine council (1070), and another 20 councils were held by the early 14th century. Thomas WOLSEY was appointed a legate in 1518, and exceptionally legate for life in 1524. Reginald POLE was a legate 1553-7. Legates in Scotland included David BEATON (1544-6), and in Ireland MALACHY (1140-8).

From the 16th century legates were generally superseded by representatives called nuncios (from Latin *nuncio*, meaning 'I announce'). Nuncios sent to Ireland included Giovanni Battista RINUCCINI. *See also* GREAT MATTER; HOLY SEE, ENGLISH AND BRITISH RELATIONS WITH.

PAPAL VISITS, GREAT BRITAIN Pope John Paul II made the first visit in 1982 (28 May–2 June), during war against the mainly Catholic Argentina (*see* FALKLANDS WAR). Primarily a pastoral visit to CATHOLICS, he celebrated Mass at WESTMINSTER Cathedral, LIVERPOOL, GLASGOW and CARDIFF, visited Queen ELIZABETH II (as supreme governor of the Church of ENGLAND), and attended an ecumenical service in CANTERBURY Cathedral (*see* RUNCIE, ROBERT).

Benedict XVI made a State visit to the UK in 2010 (16–19 Sept.), instigated by Gordon BROWN. Engagements included: an 'Address to Civil Society' in WESTMINSTER HALL; a meeting with Prime Minister David CAMERON; beatification of John Henry NEWMAN in BIRMINGHAM.

PAPAL VISITS, IRELAND The first visit, a pastoral journey to the Republic of Ireland by John Paul II, took place in 1979 (29 Sept.-1 Oct.), 42 years after Ireland's CONSTITUTION recognized the 'special position' of the Catholic Church. The Pope appealed for an end to violence in NORTHERN IRELAND, and attracted 1.2 million people to an open-air Mass in Dublin's Phoenix Park. Benedict XVI (Pope 2005-13) was discouraged from visiting by Church-related scandals.

In 2018 Pope Francis visited the Republic (25–26 Aug.) to attend a Festival of Families. During a meeting with political leaders and others in Dublin Castle, the taoiseach (premier), Leo VARADKAR, expounded the 'shared mistakes' of Church and State (e.g., child abuse by clergy, mistreatment of girls in 'Magdalene laundries'), outlined profound changes in Irish society since 1979, and declared that religion would no longer be central to society. The

Pope condemned abuse and acknowledged the Church's failures, and met victims. His concluding open-air Mass in Phoenix Park was attended by 150,000 people. *See also* CATHOLICS AND CATHOLIC CHURCH, IRELAND FROM 16TH CENTURY; CHURCH–STATE RELATIONS, SOUTHERN IRELAND FROM 1922.

PAPINEAU, LOUIS-JOSEPH (b. 7 Oct. 1786 at Montreal, Lower Canada; d. 25 Sept. 1871 at Montebello, Quebec, Canada, aged 84). Elected to the House of Assembly of Lower Canada (modern Quebec) in 1809, Papineau, a French-Canadian, led the *Parti canadien* from 1815 and the more radical *Patriotes* from 1826. In 1834 he helped to draft the 'Ninety-two Resolutions' that demanded changes to the colony's government (e.g., an elected rather than appointed legislative council). After their rejection by the British government (March 1837), Papineau led a protest movement. When his arrest was ordered (Nov.), he fled abroad. (The 'Lower Canada Rebellion' continued into 1838. Afterwards the British government united Lower and Upper Canada.) Back in Canada from 1845, Papineau was elected to the Legislative Assembly (1848), and became an advocate of union with the USA. He retired in 1854. *See also* CANADA.

PARAMILITARY ORGANIZATIONS, NORTHERN IRELAND Paramilitary organizations were prominent in the TROUBLES and perpetrated most killings from 1969 to 1994. They were usually associated with 'front' political organizations.

The main nationalist organizations were the PROVISIONAL IRISH REPUBLICAN ARMY (PIRA), started in 1969, and smaller Irish National Liberation Army (INLA), started in 1974. The main pro-Unionist or 'loyalist' groups were the ULSTER VOLUNTEER FORCE, founded in 1966 to oppose conciliatory unionism; the Ulster Defence Association (1971); and Ulster Freedom Fighters (1973).

Organizations claimed to be advancing a principal cause (an all-Ireland republic for nationalists, defence of the union with Great Britain for loyalists), and protecting their community. Loyalists were influential in the ULSTER WORKERS' STRIKE (1974); republicans organized the 1981 HUNGER STRIKES. All were involved in criminal activity. Organizations tended to split. For example, from the mid 1980s the 'Continuity IRA' opposed relaxation of 'abstentionism' (refusal to join Parliaments) by PROVISIONAL SINN FÉIN (PSF, associated with the PIRA).

From the mid 1990s paramilitary organizations co-operated with the PEACE PROCESS, though opposition to arms 'decommissioning' hindered progress. The PIRA announced a ceasefire in Aug. 1994, loyalists in Oct. The PIRA ceasefire was broken in Feb. 1996, but reinstated in July 1997, enabling PSF to participate in talks. The INLA declared a ceasefire in Aug. 1998, after the BELFAST

AGREEMENT. The PIRA put weapons 'beyond use' in 2005, and the INLA and main loyalist paramilitaries decommissioned arms in 2009–10.

Paramilitary violence continued after the ceasefires. Republicans opposed to a claimed 'sell-out' by PIRA/PSF formed 'dissident' organizations, notably the 'Real IRA'. It sought to destroy the Belfast Agreement with its bomb at Omagh (Co. Tyrone) on 15 Aug. 1998, the worst ever atrocity which killed 29 people. After the reform of policing (2001) it often attacked Catholic police officers. Loyalist paramilitaries pursued criminal activities within Protestant areas rather than anti-nationalist violence.

PARIS, MATTHEW (b. *c*.1200 in England; d. May or June 1259 at St Albans, Hertfordshire, England, aged about 59). A Benedictine monk at St Albans Abbey from 1217, Paris wrote (in Latin) and illustrated numerous histories. They included the *Chronica majora* ('Greater Chronicle', 1240–59), an important account of contemporary politics. He became the intimate of kings and nobles, and led a diplomatic mission to Norway for Pope Innocent IV and King Louis IX of France (1248–9).

PARIS, PEACE OF A comprehensive peace agreement signed on 10 Feb. 1763 in Paris between representatives of Great Britain, France, Spain and Portugal, ending the SEVEN YEARS WAR. Territorial concessions greatly expanded the BRITISH EMPIRE and made Britain the world's leading power.

In N America, France ceded to Britain land E of the Mississippi River, CANADA, and Cape Breton Isle, near NOVA SCOTIA (it received some fishing rights and bases). In the WEST INDIES, France ceded Dominica, GRENADA, the Grenadines, St Vincent and Tobago (it recovered several islands). In WEST AFRICA, France ceded the Senegal River and forts (it recovered Gorée). In INDIA, conquests (except for French forts) were in theory restored to the 1749 situation, but French power was not reconstituted. In Europe, France returned MINORCA to Britain (and recovered Belle Île).

Spain ceded Florida (N America) to Britain and allowed log cutters in Honduras (C America). (Britain restored Havana in Cuba and Manila in the Philippines to Spain.) Other provisions dealt with the Netherlands and N Europe. The treaty of Hubertusburg (15 Feb. 1763) made peace arrangements between Prussia, Saxony and the Habsburg Empire. *See also* BEDFORD, 3RD DUKE OF; BUTE, 3RD EARL OF; FOX, HENRY; QUEBEC ACT; AMERICAN INDEPENDENCE, ORIGINS OF.

PARIS, TREATY OF Concluded on 4 Dec. 1259 in Paris, France, between HENRY III, king of England, and Louis IX, king of France. It ended over 50 years of Anglo-French territorial disputes. Henry renounced claims to Normandy, Anjou, Maine and Touraine (all lost to France

1202–4), and to Poitou (lost 1224), but retained GASCONY as a fief (lordship under feudal law) and the Channel Islands, held from the king of France. *See also* ANGEVIN EMPIRE; FRANCE, CLAIMS BY RULERS OF ENGLAND.

PARISH, CIVIL FUNCTIONS, ENGLAND From the 16th century, following the decline of manorial authority (*see* MANOR), central government utilized ecclesiastical parishes (or subsidiary 'townships' in large parishes) as units for civil purposes, alongside Church activities.

From 1536 churchwardens were required to make weekly collections for the poor, and from 1555 each parish had to elect annually a surveyor of highways to supervise maintenance. In 1572 parishes were instructed to elect 'overseers of the poor' (normally two) and collect a 'poor rate'. Elections and rate setting took place at meetings of ratepayers (substantial householders) called 'vestries', named after the church vestry (storage room for vestments etc., used for meetings). Vestries also elected constables where they were not appointed by a manor court. Vestries sometimes delegated responsibilities to wealthier inhabitants (so-called 'select vestry'). Parish officers were also responsible to JUSTICES OF THE PEACE (JPs). (From 1691 JPs appointed highway surveyors.)

In the 18th–19th centuries parish autonomy was eroded by compulsion and preference. Legislation in 1722 and 1782 enabled parishes to form poor-relief unions. TURNPIKE TRUSTS could impinge on highway responsibilities. From the 1780s JPs sometimes specified relief rates for an area. The MP William Sturges Bourne, who distrusted parish organization, instituted reforms (e.g., 1819 Vestries Act, to encourage select vestries).

The POOR LAW AMENDMENT ACT of 1834 had a major impact by transferring organization of relief to new units and reducing overseers to rate collectors (to 1929). Some constables became redundant from 1839 when county police forces were permitted (remainder in 1856; office abolished 1872). Elected school boards existed in some parishes 1870–1902 (*see* FORSTER'S EDUCATION ACT).

In 1894 civil and Church functions were separated by the Local Government Act which instituted councils for some civil parishes (elected by qualified ratepayers, men and women). Highway surveyors were also abolished, although earlier legislation (1835, 1862) had permitted highway unions. *See also* POLICE, ENGLAND; TOWN GOVERNMENT, ENGLAND.

PARISH, CIVIL FUNCTIONS, IRELAND Church of IRELAND parishes (about 2200) were used for civil purposes from the early 17th century. In 1615 the Irish Parliament made parishes responsible for road maintenance, requiring labourers to work for six days per year (abolished 1760). In the 18th century parishes could levy funds for road repairs and care of foundlings (abandoned infants), and appoint a constable. Business was conducted by vestries (meetings of parishioners), which were dominated by Protestants in the 17th–18th centuries. (Vestries were abolished in 1864.) The State also used parishes as census units in the 19th century. Although civil parishes were replaced in 1898 by poor law districts as a basic local administrative unit, they were not abolished. *See also* LOCAL GOVERNMENTAL STRUCTURES, IRELAND.

PARISH, CIVIL FUNCTIONS, SCOTLAND The parish was used for civil purposes mainly between 1845 and 1930, after the Church of SCOTLAND had become unable to provide national poor relief, because of the DISRUPTION (1843), growth of separate churches and population movements.

The POOR LAW (SCOTLAND) ACT of 1845 established parochial boards to administer POOR RELIEF, their jurisdiction including any BURGHS within their parish. Boards comprised elected members and representatives of KIRK SESSIONS, HERITORS and sometimes burgh magistrates. From 1855 boards provided CIVIL REGISTRATION (births, marriages, deaths), and from 1867 received duties relating to water supply and public health (transferred to county councils from 1890). Boards were replaced by elected parish councils in 1894, which were abolished with effect from 1930 (powers transferred to county and burgh councils).

From 1872 elected parochial school boards held responsibility for school provision (transferred to county boards in 1918). From 1974 elected community councils were created (over 1000) to represent local opinion and undertake voluntary projects. *See also* LOCAL GOVERNMENTAL STRUCTURES, SCOTLAND.

PARISH, CIVIL FUNCTIONS, WALES Civil functions were imposed on Welsh ecclesiastical parishes (or on 'hamlets' within large parishes) after the UNION OF WALES WITH ENGLAND (1536–43), when the English PARLIAMENT included Wales in legislation affecting parishes. Functions included way (road) maintenance under highway surveyors (1555) and POOR RELIEF organized by parish overseers (1572), which continued until 1835 and 1834 respectively. Parish officials were appointed and supervised by JUSTICES OF THE PEACE. In large unincorporated centres, e.g., MERTHYR TYDFIL, the vestry (parishioners' meeting) provided the main local government until the later 19th century.

Civil functions were separated from Church ones by the Local Government Act of 1894 which instituted councils for civil parishes (elected by all qualified ratepayers, men and women). Councils might provide local facilities such as allotments. They were replaced by Community Councils in 1974.

PARISH REGISTRATION In 1538, Thomas CROMWELL, as vicegerent (deputy) in spiritual affairs for King HENRY VIII in England and Wales, ordered that baptisms, marriages and burials should be recorded for each parish, as part of his broader regulation of parish life (e.g., ordering instruction of parishioners in scripture). Bound registers were compulsory from 1597. The comprehensiveness of registration declined from the 18th century as NONCONFORMIST churches kept separate registers.

In Scotland the (Catholic) Church ordered the keeping of registers of baptisms and marriage banns in 1552. In 1565, after the REFORMATION, the Church of SCOTLAND additionally required registration of burials. Few records were kept. More effective record keeping began following an order from the Privy COUNCIL in 1614.

Registration was ordered in the Church of IRELAND in 1617 but had little effect. It improved after another order (1634). Presbyterian churches kept registers from the late 17th century, and Catholics mainly from the 18th century.

Parish registration was effectively superseded by CIVIL REGISTRATION in the 19th century though church registers were maintained. *See also* HARDWICKE MARRIAGE ACT.

PARISH SYSTEM, ENGLAND, FORMATION OF In the mid and late Anglo-Saxon period (7th–10th centuries) religious and pastoral care was provided mainly from MINSTER churches, whose clerical communities served large areas containing several hamlets or villages (so-called 'minster parishes'). From *c*.950 lords – especially thegns (lesser nobles) – built churches on estates, usually near a lord's hall, thereby fragmenting minster territories. Estate churches were often served by a clergyman, who was supported by TITHES (levy of a tenth of produce). After the Norman Conquest (1066–70s) lords also increasingly diverted tithes from minsters to estate churches. By the 13th century, except in N England, the small 'parish', often containing a single village, was considered the principal local ecclesiastical territorial unit. Over 9200 parishes were formed.

PARISH SYSTEM, IRELAND, FORMATION OF Small parishes were established mainly in the 13th century, following the creation of a diocesan structure in the early 12th century (*see* CHURCH REFORM, MEDIEVAL IRELAND). The definition of parishes was encouraged by a decree of the synod of CASHEL (1172) requiring every man to pay a tithe (a tenth of produce) to his parish.

Parishes largely reflected patterns of settlement and landholding. In Gaelic Irish areas, parishes coincided with the lands of kindred groups. In English areas, parishes tended to be smaller and equate with lands held by feudal tenure (e.g., MANORS). Parishes existed throughout Ireland by the early 14th century. The system continued after the REFORMATION as the territorial organization of the Church of IRELAND. *See also* CHURCH ORGANIZATION, IRELAND; IRELAND, ENGLISH COLONY IN, 13TH–15TH CENTURIES.

PARISH SYSTEM, SCOTLAND, FORMATION OF

Parishes were the outcome of a two-stage process. Churches were no doubt founded at the centres of 'multiple estates' in N Britain from the 8th century, creating a pattern similar to that of 'MINSTER parishes' in England. From the early 12th century immigrant NORMANS and other lords built and endowed churches for their newly acquired estates (*see* BARONY). DAVID I (ruled 1124–53) and later kings promoted the imposition of TEINDS (tithes), which required the definition of teind-paying areas and thereby parish boundaries. By the late 13th century most of Scotland was divided into parishes (about 1100 in all), though sizes varied. In sparsely populated areas, especially the W, ancient shrines also attracted devotions. *See also* CHURCH ORGANIZATION, NORTH BRITAIN AND SCOTLAND BEFORE THE REFORMATION; APPROPRIATION OF CHURCHES, SCOTLAND.

PARISH SYSTEM, WALES, FORMATION OF

The definition of local parishes probably started by the 11th century, but accelerated with the Norman invasions from the 1070s (*see* NORMANS, IMPACT ON WALES). In S Wales (especially the lowlands), parishes were quickly formed: they were usually small and often co-terminous with knights' fees. By the late 13th century, parishes existed throughout ST DAVIDS and LLANDAFF dioceses (S and C Wales). In N Wales (BANGOR and ST ASAPH dioceses), development was slower and continued into the 14th century. Parishes here were generally larger, especially in upland districts. About 850 parishes were created. Their clergy were appointed mainly by bishops (though *see* APPROPRIATION OF CHURCHES, WALES). *See also* CHURCH, MEDIEVAL WALES; CHURCH ORGANIZATION, WALES.

PARIS PEACE CONFERENCE

The congress of victors in WORLD WAR I held in the French capital from 18 Jan. 1919 to 20 Jan. 1920 to arrange a post-war settlement. During its proceedings, treaties were signed with Germany, Austria and Bulgaria, respectively the treaties of VERSAILLES (28 June 1919), St Germain (10 Sept.) and Neuilly (27 Oct.). The chief British negotiators were David LLOYD GEORGE and A.J. BALFOUR, though the DOMINIONS sent envoys and signed treaties separately for the first time. Demands for recognition from representatives of the self-proclaimed Irish Republic were rebuffed (*see* FOREIGN RELATIONS, SOUTHERN IRELAND).

Great Britain's role was pivotal. The USA favoured a liberal peace based on national self-determination, whereas France sought a punitive peace to weaken Germany permanently. Desiring a BALANCE OF POWER in Europe, the British opposed an independent Rhineland (to shield France from Germany) and tried to moderate French demands for REPARATIONS, a large POLAND, and demilitarization of Germany. Britain itself wanted to deprive Germany of colonies and to destroy the German fleet.

The resulting compromise both humiliated Germany and left France feeling insecure when promised Anglo-American guarantees lapsed after the treaty of Versailles was rejected by the US Senate (March 1920).

PARKER, MATTHEW

(b. 6 Aug. 1504 at Norwich, Norfolk, England; d. 17 May 1575 at Lambeth, Surrey, England, aged 70). A scholar and clergyman, Parker was attracted by evangelical theology from the late 1520s. He served as chaplain to Anne BOLEYN (1535) and King HENRY VIII (1537), and as master of Corpus Christi College, CAMBRIDGE 1544–53. In 1552, under EDWARD VI, he was appointed dean of Lincoln Cathedral; but was deprived of office under MARY I (1554) and withdrew into private life.

After the accession of ELIZABETH I (1558), Parker was the first archbishop of CANTERBURY to be appointed after the (1559) ELIZABETHAN SETTLEMENT of the Church (consecrated 17 Dec. 1559). Under pressure from Elizabeth, he upheld the Settlement, particularly against PURITANS, by publishing the 'Advertisements' (instructions concerning vestments and services, 1566), superintending a standard Bible translation (Bishops' Bible, 1568), and requiring clergy to accept the Thirty-nine Articles (from 1571). *See also* REFORMATION, ENGLAND.

PARLIAMENT, ENGLAND 1230s TO 1520s

Parliament emerged under HENRY III as an assembly summoned by the king for taking counsel on important matters (e.g., taxation, laws, foreign affairs). It expanded the use of COUNCILS in GOVERNMENT, particularly for obtaining consent to general aids (taxation) as required by MAGNA CARTA (1215). The term Parliament (first used officially 1236) is derived from OFr. *parlement*, meaning 'deliberative council or assembly'.

Between 1235 and 1257 there were 46–54 Parliaments, usually at WESTMINSTER, attended by royal ministers, senior clergy (archbishops, bishops, heads of some religious houses), earls and BARONS (varying numbers), and occasionally KNIGHTS and townsmen (BURGESSES). (In 1254 each county elected two knights.) Lesser clergy often attended from 1295.

Parliament became more institutionalized, with consistent participation, from the reign of EDWARD II (1307–27). County and town (BOROUGH) representatives were usually summoned from 1312 (normally from 1325), and with lesser clergy were seen as 'Commons' (commoners) representing the COMMUNITY OF THE REALM. Consistency in summoning lords (from late 1320s) produced a hereditary PEERAGE by *c*.1350. From the 1330s (under EDWARD III) attendance by lesser clergy decreased (ended late 14th century), and 'Commons' and 'Lords' (councillors, spiritual and temporal lords) met separately, creating a bicameral (two-house) structure.

It became accepted in the 1340s–70s (during the HUNDRED YEARS WAR) that Parliament (rather than other assemblies) agreed taxation; from the 1390s the Commons primarily made grants. By mid century Parliament's Acts (or STATUTES) could override COMMON LAW custom. In 1376 a 'speaker' (Commons' representative) emerged, and Parliament tried ministers (*see* GOOD PARLIAMENT; IMPEACHMENT).

Around 1400 the 'Upper House' comprised two archbishops, 19 bishops (from England and Wales), 27 heads of religious houses and 50 lay peers; the 'Common House' included 74 county and 180 borough representatives. From the late 14th century Parliament regulated itself (e.g., shire franchise, 1429). Many towns elected gentlemen instead of merchants, creating a Commons dominated by GENTRY. *See also* OXFORD, PROVISIONS OF; MONTFORT, SIMON DE; ORDINANCES.

PARLIAMENT, ENGLAND AND WALES 1530s TO 1660
Taxation and legislation remained central purposes. Starting with the REFORMATION PARLIAMENT (1529–36), the implementation of religious changes by STATUTE raised Parliament's importance (*see* REFORMATION, ENGLAND). Parliament was also used to annex Wales (1536); other legislation was voluminous. Parliament became characterized as a governing corporation (of king/queen, Lords, Commons), rather than consultative body.

Alterations to Parliament's composition occurred. Removal of heads of religious houses made the House of Lords predominantly secular (from 1540); additions to the Commons included members for Welsh counties and towns, and for additional English towns (MPs increased 1529–1603 from 310 to 462). In the 1620s the Lords' role as an appeal court became settled.

Rulers generally obtained co-operation, through management, and permitted limited criticism. But for a century from the late 1590s MPs frequently attacked royal policies (e.g., those of ELIZABETH I in 1597–8, 1601; those of JAMES VI/I in 1610, 1621). Criticism impelled CHARLES I to rule without Parliament (1629–40). Its extraction of concessions in 1640–2 (including removal of spiritual lords, Feb. 1642) resulted in CIVIL WARS (1642–8).

Following Parliament's victory, the Commons was 'purged' of conciliatory MPs (Dec. 1648; *see* PRIDE'S PURGE). The resulting RUMP PARLIAMENT executed Charles, abolished monarchy and the Lords, and declared a Commonwealth under Commons sovereignty (1649). It was suppressed (1653) by MP and Army commander Oliver CROMWELL, and replaced with a nominated assembly, which also represented Ireland and Scotland (*see* BAREBONE'S PARLIAMENT). Parliamentary rule was replaced by a Protectorate (1653–9), including a (single-chamber) Parliament with Irish and Scottish members. From 1658 an 'Other House' of nominated lords provided balance.

In 1659 the Army reinstated the Rump Commons; excluded members were readmitted (Feb. 1660). The Parliament dissolved itself (March) in favour of a newly elected CONVENTION PARLIAMENT, to which Lords returned. It recalled CHARLES II. *See also* UNION OF WALES WITH ENGLAND; PEERAGE, ENGLISH; SHORT PARLIAMENT; LONG PARLIAMENT; COMMONWEALTH AND PROTECTORATE.

PARLIAMENT, ENGLAND AND WALES 1660 TO 1707
Following RESTORATION of the monarchy (May 1660), CHARLES II restored lawful parliamentary authority (under royal authority) by authorizing the CONVENTION PARLIAMENT (June). The subsequent, strongly Royalist, CAVALIER PARLIAMENT (from 1661), declared ordinances of 1642–60 invalid and restored spiritual lords to the House of Lords (May 1661). Crown powers affecting Parliament were revived (summoning, proroguing, dissolving Parliament; vetoing legislation; dispensing individuals from statutes; suspending statutes), and even the 1641 Triennial Act was weakened (1664; *see* TRIENNIAL ACTS, ENGLAND AND WALES). The House of Commons gained power through larger responsibility for funding royal GOVERNMENT.

Yet disputes reoccurred (e.g., over toleration for DISSENTERS and CATHOLICS), although Charles retained the Parliament until 1679 fearing election of a more hostile Commons. The earl of DANBY (treasurer 1673–9) cultivated support by awarding pensions and government posts, creating a 'court party' within Parliament. Tensions culminated in the EXCLUSION CRISIS (1678–81), when some members sought to exclude the Catholic James, duke of York, from the succession or limit his powers as king. (Catholics were excluded from Parliament in 1678.) Supporters and opponents of exclusion formed WHIG and TORY parties. Improved finances then enabled Charles to dispense with Parliament.

JAMES VII/II, after provoking opposition in Parliament (1685), purged BOROUGH corporations to produce a compliant Commons. Before elections were held, William of Orange invaded (Nov. 1688), advocating a free Parliament. Another CONVENTION PARLIAMENT effectively created a limited monarchy (*see* GLORIOUS REVOLUTION).

From 1689, Parliament was a permanent institution, mainly because of recurrent involvement in warfare. Continuous need for taxation, and (from 1693) creation of long-term debt under Parliament's authority, required annual sessions. Another Triennial Act (1694) resulted in elections every two or three years. Because party rivalries persisted (so-called 'rage of parties'), general elections became more important, and party strengths influenced rulers' choices of ministers from among members. *See also* COURT AND COUNTRY; POLITICAL PARTIES; RIGHTS, DECLARATION AND BILL OF; NATIONAL DEBT; MILITARY-FISCAL STATE; SETTLEMENT, ACT OF; PLACEMAN.

PARLIAMENT, GREAT BRITAIN Following the UNION OF ENGLAND AND SCOTLAND (1707), England's Parliament at WESTMINSTER became the Parliament of GREAT BRITAIN. The House of Commons was augmented with 45 MPs from Scotland, the Lords with 16 'representative peers' (*see* PEERAGE, SCOTTISH). Legislation sometimes involved separate provision for Scotland. The Lords exercised partial appellate jurisdiction over Scotland from 1711 (*see* GREENSHIELDS' CASE), and jurisdiction over Ireland 1720–82 (*see* SIXTH OF GEORGE I).

From 1715, when King GEORGE I created an all-WHIG government (following a JACOBITE REBELLION), Whigs secured dominance in government and Parliament (until 1760s). Already having a Commons majority, they enacted the SEPTENNIAL ACT (1716), which extended the maximum length of Parliaments to seven years, dampening party rivalry at general elections. Robert WAPOLE (effectively first PRIME MINISTER, 1721–42), the PELHAMS and successors used Crown patronage (pensions, posts) to obtain support in Parliament, though Commons majorities could not be guaranteed (*see* EXCISE CRISIS). Ministers were usually appointed from within Parliament.

Whig noblemen increased influence by obtaining control over many BOROUGH constituencies and election of sons. In a less partisan way, Parliament was used by local élites for authorizing initiatives (e.g., IMPROVEMENT ACTS), and lobbied by commercial interests (e.g., WEST INDIES merchants).

The fading of JACOBITISM (after 1745), collapse of the TORIES as a party (early 1760s), fracturing of WHIGS into factions, and interventionist approach of GEORGE III created a complex situation in Parliament. From the 1760s critics argued that it required reform because Crown influence was growing and electors' influence declining. The PETITIONING MOVEMENT (1779–85) sought reforms to improve representation, and the ECONOMICAL REFORM movement, supported by ROCKINGHAM WHIGS, achieved reductions in Crown patronage from 1782 (though George's appointment of William PITT the Younger as premier in 1783 required patronage to build parliamentary support). Substantial reform was inhibited by the FRENCH REVOLUTION (1789). Landed families remained dominant. *See also* KING'S FRIENDS; DUNNING'S RESOLUTION; PARLIAMENT, UNITED KINGDOM, 1801 TO 1921.

PARLIAMENT, IRELAND Meetings are recorded from 1264. In the late 14th century, three 'houses' emerged: Lords (temporal and spiritual), Commons (representatives of SHIRES, liberties and towns), and Clerical Proctors (from 1371, representing lower clergy). Most members were Anglo-Irish or English. Commons approval became required for taxation. In the 14th–15th centuries membership shrank as English-controlled territory contracted. In

1460, to protect the exiled Richard, duke of YORK, Parliament asserted Ireland's autonomy (*see* PARLIAMENTARY INDEPENDENCE, DECLARATION OF). HENRY VII later increased control through POYNINGS' LAW (1494), requiring royal approval for meetings and legislation.

In the 16th century Parliament was used to implement religious change (*see* REFORMATION, IRELAND; the Clerical Proctors were removed in 1537). By 1569 bishops provided a Protestant majority in the Lords, but Catholic OLD ENGLISH dominated the Commons until 1585–6. When Parliament next met, in 1613, a Protestant Commons majority had been created with new boroughs (*see* TOWNS, IRELAND). In the 1650s English Parliaments included Irish members (*see* COMMONWEALTH AND PROTECTORATE, IRELAND). Following the RESTORATION, revenue grants enabled CHARLES II to dispense with Parliament from 1666, and 'Catholicization' under JAMES VII/II briefly produced a Catholic Parliament (1689; *see* PATRIOT PARLIAMENT). Afterwards Catholics were excluded from the Commons by England's Parliament (1691).

From 1692 Parliament was more assertive, and from 1695 imposed legislation (e.g., ANTI-CATHOLIC LEGISLATION) on the government in return for funding. From 1703 it met every two years, managed through the UNDERTAKER system until 1769. Catholic peers were excluded in 1716, making Parliament part of the PROTESTANT ASCENDANCY (housed in a new building from 1732).

From the 1760s, Anglo-Irish 'Patriot' MPs sought to reduce English influence. They achieved a maximum length for Parliaments in 1768 (*see* OCTENNIAL ACT), and considerable independence in 1782 (*see* CONSTITUTION OF 1782; GRATTAN'S PARLIAMENT), only for Parliament to be dissolved in 1800 (*see* UNION OF IRELAND AND GREAT BRITAIN). *See also* PEERAGE, IRISH; PATRIOT PARLIAMENT; SIXTH OF GEORGE I; FRANCHISE, IRELAND BEFORE 1801.

PARLIAMENT, NORTHERN IRELAND Following the PARTITION OF IRELAND, a legislature with delegated legislative powers, within the UK, convened on 7 June 1921 (formally opened 22 June by GEORGE V). Located in BELFAST, it comprised the sovereign, House of Commons elected largely by proportional representation (replaced 1929 by a plurality system), and Senate mostly elected by the Commons.

From 1932 the Parliament was based in a grandiose building on the Stormont Estate. Continuously dominated by the ULSTER UNIONIST PARTY, it was suspended on 24 March 1972 during the TROUBLES (abolished 1973). Northern Ireland also continued to send representatives to the UK Parliament. *See also* NATIONALIST PARTY; ASSEMBLIES, NORTHERN IRELAND.

PARLIAMENT, SCOTLAND From *c*.1230, an assembly for legislating, legal judgments, administration and tax-raising, operating alongside the COUNCIL and COUNCIL-GENERAL (later Convention of Estates). Parliament developed from meetings of the king with officers, senior clergy (bishops, abbots) and major lords. ROBERT I (ruled 1306–29) added lesser lords and BURGH commissioners. From 1357 Parliament formally represented 'three estates' of clergy, nobility (lords) and royal BURGESSES, meeting in one chamber. A hereditary PEERAGE was formed from 1428. In 1469 attendance comprised 25 clergy, 54 nobles and 22 burgh commissioners. Meetings became irregular from *c*.1496.

From the mid 16th century Parliament regained status, implementing the REFORMATION (1560) and endorsing removal of MARY, QUEEN OF SCOTS (1567). After 1560 titular bishops and lay 'abbots' continued to sit (latter secularized from 1587; *see* COMMENDATION OF ABBEYS, SCOTLAND). From 1587 shire commissioners were included. After the UNION OF CROWNS (1603), meetings became less frequent and royal control strengthened through the LORDS OF THE ARTICLES (drafting committee).

In 1640, following the REVOLT OF 1637 and abolition of bishops (1638), Parliament abolished the lords of the articles, passed a Triennial Act, established an executive Committee of Estates superseding the Privy Council, and took control of appointment of Crown officers. For supporting monarchy after the execution of CHARLES I, Scotland was invaded by an English Army and its Parliament abolished (1651).

In 1661 Parliament was restored and the 1640s reforms were swept aside (*see* RESTORATION, SCOTLAND). Parliament reasserted itself at the GLORIOUS REVOLUTION (1689) when annual meetings were introduced and bishops and lords of the articles were again abolished.

Before Scotland's union with England (1707), Parliament comprised 154 peers, 92 shire commissioners and 68 burgh commissioners. It was then superseded by a British Parliament with Scottish representation. A new Parliament, with delegated authority and elected by proportional representation, was inaugurated by Queen Elizabeth on 1 July 1999 (*see* DEVOLUTION, SCOTLAND). *See also* LORDS OF PARLIAMENT; COVENANTING REVOLUTION; PARLIAMENT, GREAT BRITAIN.

PARLIAMENT, SOUTHERN IRELAND A Dáil Éireann ('Assembly of Ireland'), later called the 'First Dáil', was formed in Dublin on 21 Jan. 1919 by 27 SINN FÉIN MPs who had been elected in the UK general election of Dec. 1918 but had then abstained from the UK Parliament. It adopted a CONSTITUTION, proclaimed Ireland's independence, later appointed a government (1 April), and held meetings into 1921.

A two-chamber Parliament was prescribed for 'Southern Ireland' by the UK's GOVERNMENT OF IRELAND ACT (Dec. 1920), but after an election in May 1921 it was boycotted by Sinn Féin members. They formed their own

'Second Dáil' (16 Aug.). On 7 Jan. 1922 the Dáil approved the ANGLO-IRISH TREATY, and continued to meet until June. The House of Commons of Southern Ireland met on 14 Jan. to elect a provisional government for the IRISH FREE STATE under the treaty.

A 'Third Dáil' was elected on 16 June 1922 under the treaty and approved a constitution (25 Oct.). It provided for a Parliament (Irish, Oireachtas) comprising monarch, Dáil and Senate (Irish, Seanad). Under the 1937 constitution the king was replaced by an elected president.

PARLIAMENT, UNITED KINGDOM 1801 TO 1921 At the UNION OF IRELAND AND GREAT BRITAIN (1801) the Parliament of Great Britain became the UNITED KINGDOM Parliament, with 100 MPs from Ireland in the House of Commons, and 28 'representative peers' and four Church of IRELAND bishops in the Lords. Readmission of Catholics, to conciliate Irish Catholics, was rejected (conceded 1829; *see* CATHOLIC EMANCIPATION, IMPACT ON BRITISH POLITICS). The expanded Commons comprised 658 MPs; the Lords, 30 spiritual and about 300 temporal lords. The Lords reacquired appellate jurisdiction over Ireland. In 1834 fire destroyed the Palace of Westminster, requiring a new Parliament building (Lords' chamber opened 1847, Commons' 1852).

Industrialization and urbanization invigorated demands for reform (*see* INDUSTRIAL REVOLUTION). Agitation and threatened creation of supportive peers helped to bring about the Great Reform Act (1832), enfranchising prosperous middle-class men. Further democratization followed for men (*see* PARLIAMENTARY REFORM), and WOMEN'S SUFFRAGE was sought. Secret ballots were introduced (1872), and more equal single-member constituencies (1885).

From the early 19th century clearer party identities redeveloped (notably TORY/CONSERVATIVE identification). From 1830 general elections usually determined choice of PRIME MINISTER and governing party, though coherent government and Opposition sides only dominated the Commons from 1868.

In 1886 a LIBERAL split over Irish HOME RULE produced Conservative and Unionist domination of the Lords. Following a dispute, the Lords' veto of public Bills was replaced in 1911 with a two-year delaying power, establishing Commons supremacy (*see* PEOPLE'S BUDGET). The maximum length of Parliaments was reduced to five years, and payment of MPs began, enabling broader social representation. Women's franchise was partially granted in 1918.

The first woman MP, Countess MARKIEVICZ, was elected in Dec. 1918. Like other Irish SINN FÉIN MPs, she joined a breakaway Dáil Éireann ('Assembly of Ireland'). The first woman to sit at Westminster was Nancy ASTOR (1919). In 1919 devolution started (of powers to a Church Assembly). *See also* PEERAGE, IRISH; POLITICAL PARTIES; CHARTISM, ENGLAND; LAW LORDS; IRISH FREE STATE, FOUNDING OF.

PARLIAMENT, UNITED KINGDOM FROM 1921 In 1921–2 Parliament's jurisdiction was reduced by Irish developments: from June 1921 a NORTHERN IRELAND Parliament exercised devolved powers; in Dec. 1922 southern Ireland became the independent IRISH FREE STATE (constituencies abolished Oct. 1922). Parliament retained members for Northern Ireland and existing Irish 'representative peers' (until death). In 1941 bombing destroyed the Commons' chamber (during WORLD WAR II; reopened 1950).

Franchise alterations were made in 1928, 1948 and 1969 (*see* PARLIAMENTARY REFORM). From 1973 Parliament's sovereignty was diminished by membership of the EUROPEAN ECONOMIC COMMUNITY (European Union from 1993). Jurisdiction was further reduced by devolution of powers to a Scottish Parliament (1999) and Welsh Assembly (2007, 2012). From 2000 legislation had to be compatible with the European Convention on Human Rights (*see* HUMAN RIGHTS ACT). The referendum decision to leave the European Union (2016) implied regaining of sovereignty (*see* BREXIT).

Many changes within Parliament concerned the House of Lords, which was criticized as unrepresentative. After the LABOUR PARTY election victory of 1945, the 'Salisbury Convention' accepted that the Lords should enact proposals in a governing party's election manifesto (named for Lord Cecil, prospective marquess of Salisbury). In 1949 the Lords' delaying power was reduced to one year. Non-judicial (nominated) life peerages were instituted in 1958, introducing women to the House. Viscount Stansgate's campaign to renounce his peerage resulted in the 1963 Peerage Act, which permitted disclaiming; it also admitted hereditary peeresses and all Scottish peers. Constitutional reforms by Labour from 1997 included removal of most hereditary peers (1999) and ending of the Lords' judicial role (2009). Numerous life peerages were created.

Proceedings were broadcast by radio from 1978, by television from 1985 (Lords) and 1989 (Commons). In 2020 the Commons contained 650 members (including 220 women); the Lords, 26 spiritual lords, 90 hereditary peers and 679 life peers (total 795, including 217 women). *See also* PEERAGE, BRITISH AND UNITED KINGDOM/IRISH; ASSEMBLIES, NORTHERN IRELAND; DEVOLUTION, SCOTLAND/WALES; PARLIAMENTARY EXPENSES SCANDAL.

PARLIAMENT, WALES OWAIN GLYN DŴR allegedly held a parliament at Machynlleth (lordship of Powys) in 1404. He summoned four men from each COMMOTE in July 1405 to a parliament at Harlech (Merionethshire).

On 26 May 1999 Queen ELIZABETH II inaugurated an elected National Assembly for Wales in CARDIFF, empowered by the UK Parliament to exercise powers previously vested in the secretary of state for Wales (administered through the WELSH OFFICE). It marked the culmination of a century of campaigning. Additional powers were devolved to the Assembly from 2007 onwards (*see* DEVOLUTION, WALES). In 2020 it was renamed the Welsh Parliament.

PARLIAMENTARY CONSTITUENCIES AND ELECTIONS From the mid 13th century, representatives were elected for England's PARLIAMENT from SHIRES (or counties) and BOROUGHS (selected towns). Additional boroughs were enfranchised, notably in the 16th century, and OXFORD and CAMBRIDGE Universities (1604).

Constituencies in WALES were added from 1544, in SCOTLAND from 1708, and in IRELAND from 1801. In 1801 the UK House of Commons represented 39 shire and 202 borough constituencies in England (with two universities), 13 and 13 in Wales (including MONMOUTHSHIRE), 30 and 15 (mostly burgh-groups) in Scotland, and 32 and 33 in Ireland (with a representative for DUBLIN University). Most English constituencies elected two representatives; others elected one or two.

General elections for England's Parliament were initiated with WRITS from the monarch to county SHERIFFS. In theory, shire representatives were elected at a SHIRE COURT session held by the sheriff. Until the 17th century, courts normally confirmed candidates already agreed informally by leading landowners. From 1429 a voting FRANCHISE required possession of freehold land worth 40s.

Sheriffs also instructed boroughs to elect members. Electorates varied in size and qualifications, from members of small corporations to all freemen (enfranchised townsmen), rate-payers or self-sufficient residents. Voters usually assented to representatives chosen by civic leaders.

Contested elections increased during the 17th century; in autumn 1640, 86 contests occurred (*see* LONG PARLIAMENT). The EXCLUSION CRISIS generated party conflict (WHIGS against TORIES) and contests (a record 101 in March 1679). Following the 1694 TRIENNIAL ACT, contests were similarly numerous. Electors were often bribed or intimidated, though national and local concerns mattered. Contests diminished after the SEPTENNIAL ACT (1715), to 46 in England (1761). During the 18th century, many small electorates became subject to 'control' by individual noblemen.

During the 19th century franchises were reformed, seats redistributed and corruption reduced (*see* PARLIAMENTARY REFORM). Although contests increased, general elections with near-total contests became normal only from 1906. *See also* POLITICAL PARTIES; ROTTEN BOROUGH; FRANCHISE, SCOTLAND; REFORM ACTS, SCOTLAND; FRANCHISE, IRELAND 1801–1921.

PARLIAMENTARY EXPENSES SCANDAL The revelation from 8 May 2009 that numerous members of the UK House of Commons (389 of 752 sitting or recent MPs) had exploited its expenses and allowances system (funded by taxpayers) with extravagant or wrongful claims. They were exposed by the *Daily Telegraph* using leaked information. The scandal was symbolized for many by a claim for an ornamental duck house (disallowed).

MPs (including Prime Minister Gordon BROWN) were required to make repayments, and some decided not to stand for re-election. The Commons' speaker was pressured into resigning for his inept handling of the matter (19 May). Five MPs and two peers were later imprisoned, and an MP was placed under a supervisory order. Reforms included creation of an Independent Parliamentary Standards Authority. The scandal badly damaged the public reputation of politicians.

PARLIAMENTARY INDEPENDENCE, DECLARATION OF The declaration by Ireland's PARLIAMENT in Feb. 1460 that Ireland was a separate land and that English laws applied only if affirmed by Ireland's Great COUNCIL or Parliament. Its immediate purpose was to justify Parliament's confirmation of Richard, duke of YORK, as chief governor (lieutenant), following his deprivation by England's Parliament (Nov. 1459). The Declaration has also been interpreted as a claim to 'home rule' by Anglo-Irish magnates. *See also* YORKIST–LANCASTRIAN CONFLICT, ROLE OF IRELAND.

PARLIAMENTARY PETITIONS Written petitions were submitted to the English PARLIAMENT from the 1270s, possibly following procedure introduced by King EDWARD I. Composed by individuals or groups (e.g., COUNTY COMMUNITIES), and addressed to the king, they usually requested remedy of grievances. Because such 'private' petitions quickly became numerous, 'receivers' and 'auditors' (examiners) were appointed. The latter redirected petitions to an appropriate person or body (e.g., king's COUNCIL). From the 1330s, petitioners tended to bypass Parliament.

By the 1320s the Commons in Parliament also presented 'common petitions' to the king and Council, so called because they dealt with matters of common concern to the community. Some petitions (or Bills) resulted in STATUTES (laws), thereby developing the Commons' involvement in legislating. By the mid 15th century it was usual for Bills to be read three times in the Common and Upper Houses. From the later 14th century, some private petitions were submitted to the Commons to seek support from an MP, from which developed the presentation of 'private' Bills (measures concerning localities or individuals, for enactment).

Large-scale, vigorous petitioning of Parliament occurred during the 1640s–50s, such that in 1661 the Tumultuous Petitioning Act limited the presentation of a petition to ten people. Petitioning remained a means whereby all people, including the unenfranchised, could address Parliament and the monarch. The record number of petitions presented in a parliamentary session occurred in 1843 at 33,898. Notable petitions included the Chartist petitions to the UK Parliament (1839, 1842, 1848; *see* CHARTISM, ENGLAND). From 2006 the public could propose and support petitions to the UK Parliament using electronic technology. Petitioning systems were also introduced for the Scottish Parliament (1999), Welsh Assembly (2007) and parliament of the Republic of Ireland (2012).

PARLIAMENTARY PRIVILEGE Rights enjoyed by a legislature and its members to enable them to perform their functions. In England PARLIAMENT sporadically acquired rights mainly between the late 14th and late 17th centuries.

The first rights were acquired by speakers (i.e., representatives) of the House of Commons (elected from 1376); by 1485 each new speaker customarily requested the privileges and liberties enjoyed by his predecessors. The main rights (as recorded in the 16th century) were right of access, as Commons' representative, to the monarch and House of Lords; freedom to speak candidly; freedom to correct errors made while undertaking duties. From 1523, starting with Thomas MORE, speakers also obtained a royal grant of freedom of speech for MPs during debates. By the 1540s MPs claimed freedom from arrest for civil matters (e.g., debt) for themselves and their servants, so they could attend the Commons. In 1542, in a test case, the Commons first obtained an MP's release on its own authority.

In the late 16th and 17th centuries the extent of liberties, especially freedom of speech, was often limited or contested. For example, ELIZABETH I (ruled 1558–1603) sought to prohibit discussion of State affairs by the Commons. Under JAMES VI/I and CHARLES I, MPs' use of freedom of speech to criticize royal policies was sometimes opposed or thwarted. James, for example, in 1621 removed a 'Protestation' of privileges from the Commons' Journal (record), while Charles responded to the Commons' assertion of rights by ruling without Parliament (1629–40; *see* CHARLES I, PERSONAL RULE).

Politicians exploited the flight of JAMES VII/II to strengthen Parliament's rights: his proposed successors, William of Orange and Mary, were required to accept (1689) freedom of speech in Parliament (including immunity from civil legal action) and freedom for MPs and Lords to control their affairs. They were enshrined in legislation (*see* RIGHTS, DECLARATION AND BILL OF). *See also* GLORIOUS REVOLUTION.

PARLIAMENTARY REFORM Term referring primarily to changes in the electoral basis of the UK House of Commons. At the UNION OF IRELAND AND GREAT BRITAIN (1801), voting depended on ownership, rental or lease of property. There was a distinction between COUNTIES (main qualification, freehold property worth 40s. a year) and BOROUGHS (varied franchises).

The Great Reform Act (1832) for England and Wales addressed anomalies. Passed by the Whig EARL GREY amid political crisis and popular unrest, it standardized the borough franchise and introduced additional county franchises. By enfranchising prosperous middle-class men, the electorate was expanded from 516,000 to 809,000. Constituency redistribution added numerous growing towns and abolished many ROTTEN BOROUGHS. There were separate Acts for Ireland and Scotland, and another for Ireland in 1850.

After a Bill promoted by the Whig Lord John RUSSELL was defeated in 1866 (see ADULLAMITES), the Conservative Benjamin DISRAELI devised the Second Reform Act (1867) for England and Wales, responding again to Radical agitation. It extended the borough franchise to all householders and lodgers paying over £10 rent a year. Better-off urban workers gained votes. In counties, men occupying land worth over £12 a year were enfranchised. In England and Wales, one in three men now voted. Similar measures applied to Ireland and Scotland. The Liberals' Ballot Act (1872) introduced secret ballots.

The Liberal W.E. GLADSTONE obtained a Third Reform Act (1884) to enfranchise better-paid rural workers. It set a uniform household franchise throughout the UK and lowered the land qualification. Two-thirds of Englishmen and half of Irishmen could subsequently vote. A Redistribution of Seats Act (1885) created more equal constituencies, often by merging boroughs into counties.

The Representation of the People Act (1918) enfranchised all men over 21. WOMEN'S SUFFRAGE was granted in 1918 and 1928. 'One person, one vote' was enacted in 1948 when plural voting based on university seats and business property was abolished. The voting age was lowered to 18 in 1969 (from 1970). See also FRANCHISE, IRELAND 1801 TO 1921; FRANCHISE, SCOTLAND; REFORMS ACTS, SCOTLAND; CORRUPT PRACTICES ACT.

PARLIAMENTARY REPRESENTATION, ENGLAND
In 1679, when party identifications were adopted, 95% of MPs in the WESTMINSTER Parliament represented English constituencies (490, with 27 for WALES). England's representation remained overwhelming despite changes in Parliament's national composition: 87% after formation (1707) of GREAT BRITAIN (486 of 558 seats); 74% after formation (1801) of the UNITED KINGDOM or UK (486 of 658); 80% from 1922 after southern Ireland's independence (492 of 615).

Before 1832 electorates varied greatly in size. At 16 general elections 1679–1715, overall majorities swung between WHIGS and TORIES, because of competition in larger electorates. From 1715 to 1760 Whigs dominated representation because Tories were excluded from government and

Whigs gained extensive control of small borough electorates. From 1760, when GEORGE III began appointing ministers irrespective of party, Tories lost coherence as a party and representation became factional (e.g., KING'S FRIENDS; ROCKINGHAM WHIGS). The description 'Tory' was revived from c.1807 for the government and its main supporters.

From 1830 to 1846 majority representation swung between Whigs and CONSERVATIVES, with winners also achieving a UK majority except for 1837–41 when a Whig government had a minority of MPs in England (supported by Irish Repealers). (From 1846 to 1868 Conservative division produced coalitions or minority governments; see PEELITES.)

Between 1868 and 1915 majorities usually changed at elections. Most governments held an English majority (LIBERAL PARTY governments held minorities 1892–5, 1910–15). English majorities of Conservatives and LIBERAL UNIONISTS (1886–92, 1895–1906) were also UK majorities. (A broad coalition functioned 1915–22.)

Between 1922 and 2019 Conservatives won majorities in England at 20 of 27 general elections (amounting to UK majorities on eight occasions). These usually supported a Conservative or Conservative-dominated government; the LABOUR PARTY formed four governments with an English minority (1924, 1929–31, 1950–1, 1964–6). Labour achieved a UK majority in England only in 1945. At the 2019 general election Conservatives won 345 seats, Labour 180, Liberal Democrats 7, Green Party 1. (Other parties were unsuccessful.) See also POLITICAL PARTIES; PARLIAMENTARY CONSTITUENCIES AND ELECTIONS; PARLIAMENTARY REFORM.

PARLIAMENTARY REPRESENTATION, IRELAND
From 1801 Ireland was represented in the UK PARLIAMENT by 100 MPs (105 from 1832, 103 from 1874, 105 from 1918). Catholics were barred until 1829.

Until 1832 only 20–30 MPs committed themselves to a British political identification (WHIGS or TORIES). Two-thirds were generally persuaded, sometimes by PATRONAGE, to support the government irrespective of its party allegiances.

From 1832 MPs usually identified loosely with British party identities or represented Irish causes. Until 1874, normally 30–45 MPs were CONSERVATIVES. Following the Party's division in 1846, 11 PEELITES were elected in 1847, but only two in 1852. In 1859 Conservatives exceptionally achieved a small majority (55 MPs).

From 1832 to 1852 there were two other main groups: (a) Repealers (or Liberal Repealers, or O'Connellites), i.e., supporters of the UNION REPEAL MOVEMENT led by Daniel O'CONNELL; (b) Liberals. Each group won roughly 30–40 seats. After the 1835 election, O'Connell persuaded most non-Conservatives to support the Whigs (to 1841; see LICHFIELD HOUSE COMPACT). In 1852 the IRISH TENANT LEAGUE secured the election of 48 MPs committed to land reform, who formed the Independent Irish Party; 15 Liberals were also elected. The Irish Party soon fractured and declined. From 1859 non-Conservatives were Liberals.

The HOME RULE MOVEMENT altered representation from 1874, when 60 home rule supporters, ten Liberals and 33 Conservatives were elected. Home-rulers constituted the IRISH PARLIAMENTARY PARTY, which remained the largest bloc until 1918 (divided 1890–1900 between major-ity anti- and pro-PARNELL factions). On gaining a balance of power in 1885, 1892 and 1910, it supported British Liberals. Conservatives fell below 20 MPs from 1885, and were called Irish Unionists from 1886. There were 2–4 LIBERAL UNIONISTS 1886–1912.

In 1918 pro-independence SINN FÉIN won 73 seats, starting new developments that resulted in the establish-ment of NORTHERN IRELAND and the IRISH FREE STATE. See also FRANCHISE, IRELAND 1801–1921.

PARLIAMENTARY REPRESENTATION, NORTHERN IRELAND From Nov. 1922 there were 13 seats in the UK PARLIAMENT (12 from 1950, 17 from 1983, 18 from 1997). Representation has broadly reflected the division of the population between the majority (mainly Protestant) Unionists and minority (mainly Catholic) nationalists, but parties and party strengths on each side have changed.

Unionists predominated, with the ULSTER UNIONIST PARTY (UUP) until 1970 occupying at least nine seats. It then lost seats to disaffected groups, notably the DEMOCRATIC UNIONIST PARTY (DUP) from 1974. In 1997, for example, the UUP won ten seats, the DUP two seats, UK Unionist one seat. The DUP's resistance to nationalists dur-ing the PEACE PROCESS enabled it to become the primary unionist party from 2005, when it won nine seats. In 2017 the DUP won ten seats, an Independent Unionist one seat.

The NATIONALIST PARTY was the main minority party until 1955, usually winning one or two seats. The short-lived Republican Labour Party won a seat in 1966 and 1970, and the SOCIAL DEMOCRATIC AND LABOUR PARTY (SDLP) from Feb. 1974 to 2015 won 1–4 seats. The repub-lican nationalist party PROVISIONAL SINN FÉIN (PSF) regu-larly won representation from 1983, and from 2001 (four seats) was the main nationalist party. In 2017 it won seven seats. Its MPs on principle abstained from attending Parliament. At the 2019 general election the DUP won 8 seats, PSF 7, SDLP 2, and the Alliance Party (liberal) 1 seat. See also PARLIAMENT, NORTHERN IRELAND; ASSEMBLIES, NORTHERN IRELAND.

PARLIAMENTARY REPRESENTATION, SCOTLAND Most of the 45 MPs elected in 1708 (first election after the UNION OF ENGLAND AND SCOTLAND) were Whig support-ers (nine *Squadrone Volante* MPs, 27 others); nine were Tories. In 1710 (national Tory landslide) Tories won 23–25,

Whigs 19–22 (some allegiances are uncertain). In 1713 (Tory landslide) Tories won 15, Whigs 24. In 1715 (Whig landslide), Whigs won 38, Tories seven.

From the 1720s until his death (1761) the earl of ISLAY acted as government manager for Scotland, using patron-age to control elections (so-called 'management') and provide prime ministers with reliable support (e.g., in 1727, 42 Whigs were elected). (The system failed in 1741 when Islay's brother, the disaffected 2nd duke of ARGYLL, secured the election of 21 opposition Whigs. See PORTEOUS AFFAIR.) Management became weaker in the 1760s, when ministries were short-lived (and party identities faded), though many MPs supported the king's ministry. It was revived from the mid 1770s by Henry DUNDAS (in 1796, for example, he secured 43 pro-government MPs), and contin-ued from 1811 to 1827, though less effectively, under his son Robert Dundas (2nd Viscount Melville). From c.1800 government supporters were often called Tories.

From 1832 to 1918 the LIBERAL PARTY won the majority of seats, except in 1900 (Conservative victory; see KHAKI ELECTION), then declined. The LABOUR PARTY became the largest single party in 1922 (29 of 74 seats), thereafter until the 1950s vying with the CONSERVATIVE PARTY for majorities.

From 1959 Labour consistently won majorities (e.g., 41 of 59 seats in 2010). Conservatives collapsed from the late 1980s, winning no seats in 1997 and only one from 2001 to 2015. The SCOTTISH NATIONAL PARTY (SNP) was relatively successful in the 1970s and from the late 1990s. In 2015 it dramatically displaced Labour, winning 56 seats. At the 2017 general election the SNP won 35 seats, Conservatives 13, Labour 7, Liberal Democrats 4. (Other parties were unsuccessful.) At the 2019 election the SNP won 48 seats, Conservatives 6, Labour 1, Liberal Democrats 4. See also REFORM ACTS, SCOTLAND; FRANCHISE, SCOTLAND.

PARLIAMENTARY REPRESENTATION, WALES In the later 17th century, after the declaration of party sympa-thies, about three-quarters of Wales's 27 elected members of the British Parliament were TORIES (the remainder were WHIGS). From 1715 parties were balanced, and Whigs achieved a majority in the 1727 election; the Tory minority contracted after the failure of the JACOBITE REBELLION of 1745. Thereafter identification with party declined, as did the number of contested elections. Until 1832 at the earliest the parliamentary representation of both county and bor-ough constituencies was dominated by a small number of landed families who, on the whole amicably, negotiated among themselves the distribution of their respective parliamentary seats.

From the 1830s, following the revival of POLITICAL PAR-TIES, most Welsh members of the UK Parliament were CONSERVATIVES. From 1865 the LIBERAL PARTY held the majority of seats, until 1922 when the LABOUR PARTY won 18 of 36, which rose to 25 in 1929 and 32 in 1966. There was a Conservative upsurge in the late 1970s; the Party won 14 seats in 1983, but only six in 1992 and none in 1997 and 2001. A revival then followed.

In the late 1990s and early 21st century there were three political zones: the borderlands and lowland SE where Conservatives polled well; the former S Wales coalfield, which was overwhelmingly Labour; and the W, where PLAID CYMRU held over half the seats. At the 2017 general election Labour won 28 seats, Conservatives 8, Plaid Cymru 4. (Other parties were unsuccessful.) At the 2019 election Labour won 22 seats, Conservatives 14, Plaid Cymru 4. *See also* PARLIAMENT, WALES.

PARNELL, ANNA (b. 13 May 1852 at Avondale, Co. Wicklow, Ireland; d. 20 Sept. 1910 near Ilfracombe, Devon, England, aged 58). A sister of C.S. PARNELL, Anna Parnell returned from the USA to Ireland (summer 1880) at the behest of Michael DAVITT to organize the Ladies' Land League (launched 31 Jan. 1881). When the (male) LAND LEAGUE was proscribed (30 Oct.), the LLL continued land agitation. It was dissolved by Parnell in Aug. 1882. Miss Parnell, appalled by her brother's compromise with W.E. GLADSTONE (*see* KILMAINHAM TREATY), never spoke to him again. She retired to England, later showing sympathy with SINN FÉIN politics. She died from drowning. *See also* LAND AGITATION AND REFORM, IRELAND.

PARNELL, C.S. (b. 27 June 1846 at Avondale, Co. Wicklow, Ireland; d. 6 Oct. 1891 at Brighton, Sussex, England, aged 45). An Irish (Protestant) landowner, Charles Stewart Parnell was elected to the UK Parliament in 1875 as a Home Ruler. He promoted the cause from 1877 by disrupting parliamentary business, and from 1879 by encouraging land agitation, serving as president of the LAND LEAGUE. The government imprisoned him (13 Oct. 1881). He was released (2 May 1882) after agreeing to quell disorder (*see* KILMAINHAM TREATY).

In 1886 Parnell's support enabled W.E. Gladstone to form a Liberal government. Gladstone introduced a Home Rule Bill, but it was defeated (June). Parnell concentrated on parliamentary affairs rather than supporting land agitation. But in early 1887 he was accused by *The Times* newspaper of inciting crime in Ireland and condoning the PHOENIX PARK MURDERS. A commission largely acquitted him (Sept. 1888–Feb. 1890).

On 16 Nov. 1890, in a divorce case, Parnell effectively admitted involvement in adultery. Irish MPs defiantly re-elected him as their leader (25 Nov.). Gladstone, however, threatened withdrawal of support for Home Rule, causing 45 Irish MPs to repudiate Parnell (6 Dec.). In 1891 Parnell campaigned publicly for his views, and married his mistress Katharine O'Shea (25 June). But his health collapsed. *See also* HOME RULE MOVEMENT, IRELAND; LAND AGITATION AND REFORM, IRELAND; IRISH PARLIAMENTARY PARTY; DEVOY, JOHN; NONCONFORMIST CONSCIENCE.

PARR, KATHERINE (b. 1512 in England; d. 5 Sept. 1548 at Sudeley Castle, Gloucestershire, England, aged 36). Katherine married King HENRY VIII on 12 July 1543, as his sixth wife. (He was her third husband.) In 1544 she presided over a regency council while Henry campaigned in France. In 1546 religious conservatives threatened her position because of her association with leading evangelicals, but she dissimulated to avoid Henry's wrath. After his death (Jan. 1547) Katherine married Thomas Seymour, brother of Edward, duke of SOMERSET, but was excluded from Somerset's council. She died in childbirth. *See also* HENRY VIII, WIVES OF.

PARTITION OF IRELAND Division into two jurisdictions was an unintended outcome of the HOME RULE movement (launched 1870). Home Rule was promoted from 1874 by MPs of the IRISH PARLIAMENTARY PARTY, and supported from 1885–6 by many British Liberals, but opposed by Unionists throughout Ireland and by British Conservatives.

In March 1905, after Unionists in southern Ireland seemingly made concessions over Home Rule, northern Unionists founded the ULSTER UNIONIST COUNCIL (UUC). Ulster then emerged as the main centre of opposition. Its Protestants feared inclusion in a Catholic-dominated self-governing Ireland. From 1910, when the British Liberal government seemed likely to enact Home Rule, Ulster Unionists prepared for armed resistance, and considered exclusion of six Ulster counties from Home Rule (*see* ULSTER VOLUNTEER FORCE; BUCKINGHAM PALACE CONFERENCE). Only mobilization for WORLD WAR I (began Aug. 1914) prevented conflict when Home Rule was enacted (Sept.). (Implementation was suspended.)

Wartime attempts to negotiate a settlement acceptable to Ulster Unionists failed. Afterwards David LLOYD GEORGE appointed a Cabinet committee, chaired by the Unionist Walter Long (Oct. 1919), which produced a Bill (Feb. 1920) prescribing two self-governing provinces: Northern Ireland (six counties), Southern Ireland (26 counties). A Council of Ireland was envisaged as a forum for later reunion.

By now republicans were fighting for Irish independence. The UUC accepted Long's scheme (May) despite Unionist opposition in three Ulster counties assigned to Southern Ireland. (The six-county arrangement produced an overall Protestant majority.) Under the GOVERNMENT OF IRELAND ACT (Dec. 1920), Northern Ireland and the Council existed from 3 May 1921. Republicans rejected Home Rule, and Ireland eventually received DOMINION status (6 Dec. 1922). The new Irish Free State included Northern Ireland, but it opted out on 7 Dec., rejoining the UK. The Council was abolished in 1925. *See also* ULSTER; IRISH FREE STATE, FOUND-ING OF; NORTHERN IRELAND; BOUNDARY COMMISSION.

PASSAGE TOMBS Collective funerary monuments found in N and W Britain and Ireland, dating from the NEOLITHIC (*c.*4300– *c.*2500 BC in Ireland; to *c.*2300 BC in Britain). Considerable variation occurs in scale and charac-ter of sites, from small examples such as Bryn Celli Ddu (Anglesey, NW Wales) to Maes Howe (Orkney) or NEWGRANGE (Co. Meath, E Ireland). Common features include an extended passage leading to a central chamber and alignments on solstice sunrises and sunsets. They are also closely associated with abstract rock carvings: incised spirals, chevrons and zig-zags on stones which are often referred to as 'passage grave art'.

PASTON LETTERS Term generally used for about 1050 letters and related documents written between 1422 and 1520 by three generations of the Paston family and other correspondents. The Pastons were a GENTRY family based in Norfolk (E England). The letters are the earliest substan-tial collection of letters in English. They provide detailed evidence for late-medieval social, economic and legal his-tory. Most of the letters, together with later correspond-ence, belong to the British Library (London).

PATENTS AND MONOPOLIES Terms used for licences to produce or distribute certain goods (e.g., soap), or provide services, which were regularly conferred or sold by the Crown in England and Wales from the 1560s as a prerogative right, for income or favours. The practice was frequently attacked in PARLIAMENT. The Monopolies Act of 1624 restricted the recipients of monopolies. King CHARLES I evaded it during his 'personal rule' by making grants to companies (1632–5). These were revoked in 1639, and monopolies were largely abolished in 1641 by the LONG PARLIAMENT. *See also* OVERSEAS TRADING COMPANIES.

PATRICK (fl. in 5th century). A British Christian mis-sionary in Ireland. A deacon's son, born in Britain in the early 5th century, Patrick was captured (aged 16) by Irish raiders and sold into slavery. After six years in Ireland, he escaped to Britain but decided to return, undertaking mis-sionary activity in NE Ireland. British clergy accused him of self-promotion and exceeding his authority. Relationships deteriorated further when he excommunicated Coroticus, a Christian British magnate who enslaved converts to Christianity. A subsequent trial caused Patrick to write his self-justificatory *Confession*.

Later traditions portrayed Patrick as bishop of ARMAGH, ascribed his death to 461 or 493, and placed his burial at Downpatrick (NE Ireland). He was considered a saint and

apostle of the Irish by the 7th century. *See also* POST-ROMAN BRITAIN; CONVERSION OF IRELAND; ARMAGH, BOOK OF; STRATHCLYDE (CLYDE ROCK), KINGDOM OF; NATIONAL PATRON SAINTS .

PATRIMONY Legal term referring to land inherited from an ancestor (especially a father). After the NORMAN CONQUEST (1066–70s) it became customary in England for a landowner's patrimony to descend to his eldest son and for lifetime acquisitions to be bequeathed to other children. This happened at the highest level in 1089 when ROBERT CURTHOSE succeeded WILLIAM I in NORMANDY while England went to WILLIAM II.

PATRIOT PARLIAMENT A meeting of the Irish Parliament held by James VII/II, former king of England, 7 May–18 July 1689 (*see* JAMES VII/II AND IRELAND). James sought funds for military campaigns, and to retain remain-ing Protestant support, whereas attendees were mostly Catholics (predominantly OLD ENGLISH) who pursued partisan ends.

James reluctantly allowed a Declaratory Act denying the right of England's Parliament to legislate for Ireland, and conceded restoration of landholding to the 1641 situation (i.e., overturning the CROMWELLIAN LAND SETTLEMENT). An Act of ATTAINDER made 2400 exiled Protestants liable for treason (with possible loss of land). Religious liberty was declared, and congregations could pay TITHES to their own ministers. A Navigation Act extended direct involvement in trade with English colonies. But James thwarted repeal of POYNINGS' LAW (to retain control over Parliament). The Parliament's Acts were annulled by the Irish Parliament in 1695. Its name was devised by C.G. DUFFY in 1893. *See also* TYRCONNELL, EARL OF; WILLIAMITE WAR.

PATRIOTS, IRELAND Term used generally for people who claimed greater self-government for Ireland in the late 17th and 18th centuries (e.g., Jonathan SWIFT; Charles LUCAS), and specifically for members of the Irish Parliament in the 1760s–80s who campaigned against British influence and restrictions (e.g., POYNINGS' LAW; SIXTH OF GEORGE I). In the House of Commons, Patriots were led by Henry FLOOD (1760s–70s) and Henry GRATTAN (late 1770s–80s).

Patriots' campaigns partly brought about the OCTENNIAL ACT (1768), limiting the length of Parliaments; removal of British restrictions on Irish trade (1780); and the CONSTITUTION OF 1782 (legislative and judicial independ-ence). Patriots also advocated economic development, but as members of the PROTESTANT ASCENDANCY many were unsympathetic to CATHOLIC RELIEF. Many gains were nul-lified by the UNION OF IRELAND AND GREAT BRITAIN (1801). *See also* AMERICAN WAR OF INDEPENDENCE, IMPACT ON IRELAND.

PATRONAGE The practice whereby a powerful or influential person assists another to advance (e.g., by granting office, status or other rewards, or protection), either for the patron's own purpose or to enable the recipient to progress. The exercise of patronage often involves the expectation or obligation that the recipient or client will continue to support or give service to the patron.

Patronage has been important in political life and social relations in Britain and Ireland since at least the 12th century. Kings used patronage to empower non-noble supporters as counterweights to hereditary nobles (e.g., GEOFFREY FITZ PETER). But patronage had to be distributed carefully to avoid challenge, especially when favourites were indulged (e.g., Piers GAVESTON, the DESPENSERS). Patronage was intrinsic to the social relations system known as BASTARD FEUDALISM (14th–15th centuries).

From the 18th century the British PRIME MINISTER exercised much of the monarch's patronage, in both Britain and Ireland, including choice of senior ministers, ambassadors and senior clergy. Leading politicians (e.g., earl of ISLAY, duke of NEWCASTLE) used patronage to sustain support in PARLIAMENT.

Political patronage was criticized from the later 17th century. Certain PLACEMEN were excluded from the English Parliament from 1699, and more from 1782 (*see* ECONOMICAL REFORM). Patronage was further checked in the 19th century (e.g., by reform of CIVIL SERVICES), yet it remains extensive in the 21st century (e.g., rewarding MPs for loyalty to the British government with knighthoods).

Other areas in which patronage has been important (for personal advancement) include EDUCATION, award of apprenticeships, appointments in Churches, and artistic activity.

PATRONAGE ACT, 1712 An Act of the British Parliament, following GREENSHIELDS' CASE, which restored the right of private patrons to present ministers to parish livings in the Church of SCOTLAND. (Patronage had been transferred to HERITORS and elders by the Scottish Parliament in 1690; *see* REVOLUTION SETTLEMENT, SCOTLAND.) The Act arguably broke the terms of the UNION OF ENGLAND AND SCOTLAND by infringing the Church's guaranteed rights. Although a congregational veto was vaguely permitted, patronage became a contentious issue. *See also* SECESSION CHURCH; RELIEF CHURCH; DISRUPTION.

PATRON SAINTS *see* NATIONAL PATRON SAINTS

PAULET, WILLIAM (b. 1480s at Fisherton de la Mere, Wiltshire, England; d. 10 March 1572 at Basing, Hampshire, England). Paulet held posts in the household of King HENRY VIII from the 1520s. He was knighted (by 1525) and created Lord St John (1539). Under EDWARD VI he was president of the Council (1547–50). In 1549 St John helped to depose the protector, Edward, duke of SOMERSET. He was created earl of Wiltshire and appointed TREASURER (1550), and promoted to marquess of Winchester (1551).

In 1553, when the duke of NORTHUMBERLAND sought to make Lady Jane GREY queen, Winchester proclaimed MARY I. He remained treasurer during her reign (1553–8), continuing under ELIZABETH I. He had an accommodating attitude to religious change. *See also* REFORMATION, ENGLAND.

PAX BRITANNICA Late 19th-century term, meaning 'British Peace', which denoted peace and stability conferred by British rule and likened it to the 'Pax Romana' created in Europe and elsewhere by the Roman Empire. Joseph CHAMBERLAIN so described the condition of INDIA in 1893. Historians sometimes use Pax Britannica to signify the whole period of comparative peace and British naval supremacy from 1815 to 1914.

PEABODY, GEORGE (b. 18 Feb. 1795 at Danvers, Massachusetts, USA; d. 4 Nov. 1869 at London, England, aged 74). A poor farmer's son, Peabody became a merchant. Settled in England from 1837, he developed his business into the leading American trading and banking company in London, involved in financing railway development in the USA. He also became one of the first American large-scale philanthropists, his gifts including a donation to build model housing for respectable working people in London (1862). In the early 21st century his London charity, the Peabody Trust, housed over 55,000 people. *See also* SLUMS.

PEACE AND WAR, ACT ANENT A companion to the Act of SECURITY, passed by Scotland's Parliament in 1703. It stipulated that after the death of Queen ANNE the ruler should consult Parliament about ('anent') war declarations and peace treaties if Scottish funds and soldiers were involved. It thereby limited the scope for Scotland to become involved in England's wars. *See also* UNION OF ENGLAND AND SCOTLAND.

PEACE PRESERVATION ACT Legislation initiated by Robert Peel and enacted by the UK Parliament in 1814 which created the Peace Preservation Force, a body of paramilitary policemen at the disposal of the lord lieutenant of Ireland for use in disturbed districts. These original 'Peelers' were merged into the Constabulary of Ireland in 1838. *See also* PEEL, ROBERT, AND IRELAND; POLICE, IRELAND.

PEACE PROCESS, NORTHERN IRELAND Political initiatives and negotiations, from the 1990s, which diminished the violent TROUBLES and created a new governmental structure (to replace British 'direct rule').

A political 'settlement' needed a policy change by 'republican nationalists' after failing to coerce Unionists into an all-Ireland republic through violence against British authorities. Between 1988 and 1993, the 'constitutional nationalist' John HUME persuaded Gerry ADAMS, president of PROVISIONAL SINN FÉIN (PSF), that advancement of nationalist ambitions required co-operation with Unionists. The PROVISIONAL IRISH REPUBLICAN ARMY (PIRA) also indicated, through secret contacts with the British government, a readiness to allow talks (early 1990s). In Dec. 1993 the governments of Great Britain and the Republic of Ireland made the DOWNING STREET DECLARATION. PARAMILITARY ORGANIZATIONS declared ceasefires (PIRA, 31 Aug. 1994; loyalists, 13 Oct.), and the governments issued the 'Frameworks' document as a basis for negotiations (22 Feb. 1995).

The IRA broke its ceasefire (London bombing, 9 Feb. 1996). When multi-party talks began (10 June), PSF was excluded. Reinstatement of the ceasefire (19 July 1997) enabled it to participate (from 15 Sept.). The talks resulted in the BELFAST AGREEMENT (10 April 1998), which was endorsed by referendums in Northern and southern Ireland (22 May).

An ASSEMBLY was elected (25 June 1998) and in 1999 Britain devolved power to an EXECUTIVE led by the 'mainstream' ULSTER UNIONIST PARTY and the constitutional nationalist SOCIAL AND DEMOCRATIC LABOUR PARTY (Executive suspended in 2002). They were overtaken at elections in 2003 by the anti-Agreement DEMOCRATIC UNIONIST PARTY (DUP) and the republican PSF, but the DUP refused to form an Executive without thorough 'decommissioning' of PIRA arms. After the PIRA put arms 'beyond use' (2005), the ST ANDREWS AGREEMENT (2006) enabled formation of an Executive (2007). It collapsed in Jan. 2017 because of a financial scandal about a government renewable heating scheme. A new Executive was established in Jan. 2020. See also TRIMBLE, DAVID; PAISLEY, IAN; MCGUINNESS, MARTIN; POLICE, NORTHERN IRELAND.

PEARSE, PATRICK (b. 10 Nov. 1879 at Dublin, Ireland; d. 3 May 1916 at Kilmainham, Co. Dublin, Ireland, aged 36). Active in the GAELIC LEAGUE (from 1896) and a school headmaster in Dublin (from 1908), Pearse concluded that Irish independence could be obtained only by force and was motivated in large measure by ideals of martyrdom and blood sacrifice. He joined the IRISH VOLUNTEERS and IRISH REPUBLICAN BROTHERHOOD in 1913.

From May 1915 Pearse helped to prepare the IRB's intended anti-British rebellion. On Monday 24 April 1916, Pearse proclaimed a republic and provisional government of which he was president. He surrendered on behalf of the rebels on 29 April, and was court-martialled and shot. See also EASTER RISING.

PEASANTS' REVOLT An uprising in 1381 in London and SE England; one of the most serious rebellions in English history. Disturbances began in late spring, and a combined force from Essex and Kent massed outside London in early June led by Walter (or Wat) Tyler. Entering London on 13 June, they ransacked the Savoy Palace of JOHN OF GAUNT. King RICHARD II met Tyler on 14 June; simultaneously the mob captured and beheaded the CHANCELLOR and TREASURER. Next day Richard again met Tyler, who demanded an end to lordship, VILLEINAGE and Church endowment. A scuffle ensued, Tyler was killed, and Richard convinced the rebels to withdraw. Despite isolated risings elsewhere, the government recovered control.

The revolt's immediate cause was the POLL TAX of 1381. It can also be connected with economic and social tensions arising from the BLACK DEATH (1348–9), restrictions imposed under the Statute of LABOURERS (1351), failures in the HUNDRED YEARS WAR, and religious tensions associated with LOLLARDY. See also SOCIAL STRUCTURE, ENGLAND 1066 TO 16TH CENTURY.

PECHAM, JOHN (b. c.1230, probably at Patcham, Sussex, England; d. 8 Dec. 1292 at Mortlake, Surrey, England, aged 62). A distinguished scholar and Franciscan friar, Pecham was appointed archbishop of CANTERBURY by Pope Nicholas III in Jan. 1279. He quickly held a council at Reading, Berkshire (29 July), which reissued canons defending the Church's rights. Further measures announced in 1281 caused King EDWARD I to warn bishops against infringing his rights, though he recognized some concerns with the WRIT Circumspecte agatis (Latin, 'Act circumspectly'), which sought to define the jurisdiction of Church courts (1285). After Edward's conquest of Wales (1282–3), Pecham toured Wales (1284), urging the Church to help reconcile Welsh and English. See also CANTILUPE, THOMAS DE; FRIARS, ENGLAND.

PECOCK, REGINALD (b. c.1392, probably in Pembrokeshire, Wales; d. in or after 1459 at Thorney, Cambridgeshire, England). Bishop of St Asaph from 1444 and of Chichester from 1450, Pecock challenged LOLLARDY by writing expositions of Christianity in English (from 1440s). But his sympathy for opponents' arguments caused his books to be examined for heresy. In late 1457 he was forced to admit and abjure heresy, and to resign his bishopric. He was sent into retirement at Thorney Abbey. His books were publicly burned at OXFORD.

PEEL, ROBERT (b. 5 Feb. 1788 at Bury, Lancashire, England; d. 2 July 1850 at London, England, aged 62). A cotton manufacturer's son, Peel became an MP in 1809. He was British under-secretary for colonies 1810–12 (under Spencer PERCEVAL) and chief secretary for Ireland 1812–18 (under the earl of LIVERPOOL). As home secretary 1822–7, 1828–30 (under Liverpool and the duke of WELLINGTON), he undertook penal reforms and founded the Metropolitan POLICE. He succeeded to a baronetcy in 1830.

From 1828 Peel led TORIES in the House of Commons, though his acceptance of CATHOLIC EMANCIPATION (1829) alienated ULTRA TORIES. From Dec. 1834 he was prime minister of a minority government. He issued the TAMWORTH MANIFESTO (18 Dec.), seeking broader support at the forthcoming election (Jan.–Feb. 1835). He lost, and his government was defeated (see LICHFIELD HOUSE COMPACT). Peel resigned in April.

After refusing office in 1839 (see BEDCHAMBER CRISIS), Peel again became prime minister after the 1841 election (succeeding Viscount MELBOURNE). His ministry reintroduced INCOME TAX and passed the Mines Act (1842), BANK CHARTER ACT and a Factory Act (both 1844). Movement towards FREE TRADE culminated in repeal of the CORN LAWS, which Peel had pledged to maintain. Tory MPs became divided, and 'Protectionists' voted down the government. Peel resigned (June 1846). *See also* PEEL, ROBERT, AND IRELAND; CONSERVATIVE PARTY; PEELITES.

PEEL, ROBERT, AND IRELAND As CHIEF SECRETARY FOR IRELAND (1812–18), Peel recognized the rural population's precarious conditions. He combated lawlessness (1814, establishment of Peace Preservation Force), promoted education (1815, grant), and provided emergency seed supplies (early 1817). As home secretary (1822–7, 1828–30) he opposed political Emancipation of Catholics, and was attacked (and nicknamed 'Orange Peel') by Daniel O'CONNELL, but was finally compelled to accept Emancipation in 1829 (see CATHOLIC RELIEF AND EMANCIPATION, IRELAND).

As prime minister (1841–6), Peel broke O'Connell's UNION REPEAL MOVEMENT (1843–4; see CLONTARF MEETING). He attempted to conciliate Catholic clergy and wealthier laymen to the State: e.g., commission into land tenure (1844), foundation of non-denominational Queen's Colleges (1845), increased grant to the Maynooth Seminary (1845; see MAYNOOTH GRANT CONTROVERSY). He reacted to the GREAT FAMINE by initiating relief (1846) and using it to justify repeal of the CORN LAWS.

PEELITES A faction in the UK Parliament formed from the 112 Conservative MPs who supported the abolition of the CORN LAWS (1846) promoted by the prime minister Sir Robert PEEL. Led by Lord ABERDEEN from 1850 (following Peel's death), they co-operated with the WHIGS and formed a coalition government with them (1852–5). By 1860, remaining Peelites had merged into the LIBERAL PARTY. *See also* CONSERVATIVE PARTY.

PEEP O'DAY BOYS Nickname of rural Protestants in Ulster (N Ireland) who from 1784 to the mid 1790s raided the homes of Catholics, often at dawn (hence their name), to seize weapons and break linen-weaving equipment. They also fought DEFENDERS. Organized as a secret society, the Boys claimed to be enforcing anti-Catholic Penal Laws. Many Boys joined the ORANGE ORDER.

PEERAGE, BRITISH AND UNITED KINGDOM After the formation of GREAT BRITAIN (1707), new peerages, or promotions, constituted a British peerage. (Creations of English and Scottish peerages ceased.) English ranks were retained. English peers continued in the British House of Lords; Scottish peers elected 16 'representative peers' for each Parliament. Scottish peers with British titles were prevented from sitting as British peers until 1782.

After the formation of the UNITED KINGDOM (1801), creation of British peerages ceased and a UK peerage was commenced, although creation of Irish peerages continued. Irish peers elected 28 'representative peers' to the UK Lords, each serving for life.

The parliamentary peerage became subject to partisan political influences (e.g., reflecting party policies). In 1711 Queen ANNE agreed to create 12 peers to provide a Lords majority for peace preliminaries (see HARLEY, ROBERT). In 1719 Earl STANHOPE attempted to limit the creation of peerages (Peerage Bill) to preserve a favourable House against possible future IMPEACHMENT. From 1784 numerous peerages were created to provide support for William PITT the Younger (the peerage increased from about 180 parliamentary peers to almost 270 by the early 19th century). Large creations were threatened to force through the Great Reform Act (1832) and 1911 Parliament Act (see PARLIAMENTARY REFORM; PEOPLE'S BUDGET).

Until the later 19th century new peers were usually members of landed families; recipients of peerages then included industrialists and businessmen (e.g., Lord ARMSTRONG). Judicial life peerages were created from 1876 (to 2009; see LAW LORDS), and non-judicial life peerages from 1958 (barons and baronesses).

During the 20th century hereditary peers' economic power and political influence declined; the creation of non-royal hereditary peers mostly ceased in 1964. In 1999 most hereditary peers were removed from the House of Lords (two royal officers and 90 other peers were retained). Numerous life peers were created as replacements. *See also* NOBILITY; PEERAGE, ENGLISH/IRISH/SCOTTISH; PARLIAMENT, UNITED KINGDOM FROM 1921; HONOURS SYSTEM.

PEERAGE, DISCLAIMING OF The renunciation of noble status to avoid membership of the House of Lords in the UK PARLIAMENT. Previously impossible, it was brought about by A.N. Wedgwood BENN after he succeeded in 1960 as (2nd) Viscount Stansgate and unwillingly forfeited membership of the House of Commons. His campaign to renounce his peerage, including an invalid re-election to the Commons (1961), resulted in the Peerage Act (1963) to facilitate renunciation. It enabled Lord Home to become prime minister based in the Commons (*see* DOUGLAS-HOME ALEC). *See also* PEERAGE, BRITISH AND UNITED KINGDOM.

PEERAGE, ENGLISH By the mid 15th century 'peerage' was the collective term for noblemen who were summoned individually to PARLIAMENT (Upper House) by hereditary right (derived from OFr. *per*, meaning 'equal' or 'nobleman').

The peerage developed during the 14th century from the wealthier section of the NOBILITY (so-called 'baronage'). In the early 14th century, 80–100 lay lords or 'peers' (EARLS and BARONS) were sometimes summoned to Parliament, but from the late 1320s only around 60. Thereafter summons were sent to mostly the same men and their successors. Peers (with spiritual lords) met separately within Parliament from the 1330s. By *c.*1350 a settled peerage largely existed (including a 'duke', a more senior title first bestowed in 1337). By the 16th century the peerage largely constituted the nobility. Spiritual lords were deemed 'lords of Parliament' rather than peers (affirmed 1692).

New 'peerages' (title with place in Parliament) were granted individually by rulers from 1387. The introduction of 'marquess' (above earls) in 1397 and 'viscount' (below earls) in 1440 produced five ranks (duke, marquess, earl, viscount, baron).

In the 15th–16th centuries rulers created few peerages (there were 55 peers in 1603). Thereafter numbers were increased sporadically. JAMES VI/I and CHARLES I created peers to ennoble favourites or raise money: by 1628 there were 126. CHARLES II and JAMES VII/II created 40 peers, and WILLIAM III 20 peers, mainly to reward important supporters. By 1707 there were about 190 peers. Most new peers were from landed backgrounds. Women normally acquired noble rank by marriage, but sometimes in their own right by inheritance; a few were created peeresses from 1397 (without eligibility for Parliament).

At the UNION OF ENGLAND AND SCOTLAND (1707) a British peerage was inaugurated. Creations of English and Scottish peers ceased, though English peers remained members of the House of Lords (*see* PEERAGE, BRITISH AND UNITED KINGDOM). *See also* HONOURS SYSTEM.

PEERAGE, IRISH Ireland's PARLIAMENT (from 1264) included individually summoned Anglo-Irish lords. Called 'peers' from the 1340s, they met (with spiritual lords) as a separate house from the late 14th century. Many were of lower status than English peers. (In 1375, 42 laymen were summoned: three earls, 20 knights, 19 others.) The title of 'earl' was granted from the early 14th century, 'baron' (officially) from 1462,

'viscount' from 1478. Falling numbers gave spiritual lords a House of Lords majority by the 1530s–40s, although temporal lords were augmented with a few Gaelic Irish chieftains (*see* SURRENDER AND REGRANT). During the REFORMATION, few peers became Protestants. In 1615 there were 17 Catholic peers, five Protestants, three minors.

King JAMES VI/I (from 1616) and CHARLES I expanded the peerage (to 99 by 1632), partly to create a Protestant majority. New peers included NEW ENGLISH settlers and men unconnected with Ireland, who provided proxy votes to the government. The first 'marquess' was created in 1642 (*see* ORMOND, 12TH EARL OF). Catholic peers were formally excluded from the Lords in 1716.

In 1700 there were 108 peers. More peerages were awarded mainly for political purposes (e.g., 11 WHIG peers created in 1715 to overcome TORY bishops in the Lords). A great increase from 1750 raised the total to about 230 by 1800. Many peerages were awarded to government supporters with influence over Commons constituencies, and also as honours to men unconnected with Ireland (about 60). Some Irish peers were relatively poor.

After the UNION OF IRELAND AND GREAT BRITAIN (1801) Irish peers elected 28 'representative peers' to the UK House of Lords. Each sat for life and was then replaced. (Elections ceased with foundation of the IRISH FREE STATE in 1922, although existing representatives were retained; the last died in 1961.) Limited creations of Irish peerages continued until 1898. Irish peers were eligible for the Commons. *See also* NOBILITY; HONOURS SYSTEM.

PEERAGE, SCOTTISH A parliamentary peerage (noblemen with right of individual summons to PARLIAMENT) developed from 1428 when Parliament enacted that the king should summon the spiritual and temporal lords he wished to attend. Senior MAGNATES (dukes and earls) received summons. ('Earl' as primarily a personal title dated from 1358; more senior 'dukes' were created from 1398.) By 1445 the status of hereditary LORD OF PARLIAMENT was granted as a third rank. In 1460 there were 44 peers. Formation of the peerage encouraged perception of the Scottish NOBILITY as divided into lords and LAIRDS (by late 16th century).

Few peerages were created during the 16th century. ('Marquis', above earl, was adopted effectively from 1599, 'viscount' below earl in 1606.) From 1603 King JAMES VI and CHARLES I doubled the peerage (from 57 in 1603 to 119 in 1649). Generally from landed backgrounds, new peers included courtiers, lawyers or other professionals, and especially lay lords of former ecclesiastical properties (so-called 'lords of erection'; *see* COMMENDATION OF ABBEYS, SCOTLAND). Some were Englishmen without property in Scotland: their presence in Parliament was condemned in 1640, and they were barred in 1703. By 1707 there were 153 peers. Two women were created as peeresses (ineligible for Parliament).

At the UNION OF ENGLAND AND SCOTLAND (1707) the creation of Scottish peers ceased and a British peerage was inaugurated in which some Scottish peers were awarded titles (see PEERAGE, BRITISH AND UNITED KINGDOM). Scottish peers elected 16 'representative peers' to the House of Lords for each British (later UK) Parliament until 1963, when all Scottish peers were admitted. Their entitlement to sit ceased in 1999 (became eligible for election as 'excepted' peers). See also EARLDOMS, SCOTLAND; ISLAY, EARL OF.

PELAGIUS (fl. from c.400; d. 418 or later). Probably British-born, Pelagius moved to Rome (c.400) and then Palestine (c.412), espousing a doctrine of free will that attracted considerable support but also the opposition of prominent Christians, including Jerome, Augustine and Orosius. His excommunication (417) failed to eradicate his ideas, and 'Pelagianism' survived into the later 6th century. See also GERMANUS.

PELHAM, HENRY (b. 26 Sept. 1694 at London, England; d. 6 March 1754 at London, aged 59). The younger brother of the duke of NEWCASTLE, Henry Pelham, a WHIG, became an MP in 1717. A minister under Robert WALPOLE, Pelham continued to defend him after his fall (1742).

In 1743 Pelham succeeded the earl of WILMINGTON as first lord of the Treasury (during the War of the AUSTRIAN SUCCESSION), but Lord CARTERET remained influential with King GEORGE II. In Nov. 1744 Pelham and Newcastle compelled George to remove Carteret (now Earl Granville). They reorganized the ministry, against George's wishes, creating the so-called 'Broad Bottom ministry' of 'Old Corps Whigs' (former supporters of Walpole), 'New Allies' (former opposition Whigs) and a few TORIES. During Pelham's ministry the JACOBITE REBELLION of 1745 was defeated. The ministry resigned (1746) when George refused to appoint William PITT and the earl of Chesterfield. He was forced to reappoint Pelham and his colleagues when Lord CARTERET and the earl of BATH were unable to form a ministry.

After war ended in 1748, Pelham's ministry maintained a pacific foreign policy and economical home administration, consolidating the NATIONAL DEBT and reducing the Army and Navy. The ministry survived Pelham's sudden death. He was succeeded by Newcastle. See also PELHAMS; HALIFAX, 2ND EARL OF; HARDWICKE, LORD; FREDERICK, PRINCE OF WALES.

PELHAMS Term used to refer to the brothers Henry PELHAM (1696–1754) and Thomas Pelham-Holles, duke of NEWCASTLE (1693–1768), both WHIGS. They served under Robert WALPOLE (British PRIME MINISTER 1721–42) and broadly preserved his legacy; both became prime minister.

The Pelhams achieved extraordinary political dominance in Great Britain in the 1740s–50s, the younger in the House of Commons, the elder in the House of Lords. Their parliamentary support enabled them to compel King GEORGE II: in 1744 they forced him to dismiss Lord CARTERET, and in 1746 their ministry (led by Henry Pelham) resigned in order to obtain new ministerial appointments.

PEMBROKE, EARLS OF see HERBERT FAMILY; MARSHAL, WILLIAM

PEMBROKESHIRE The earliest shire in WALES, created by NORMANS who conquered the area (SW Wales) in the late 11th century from DEHEUBARTH. It was heavily settled by Flemish and English and remained English-speaking thereafter. Earls of Pembroke included Arnulf of MONTGOMERY (deposed 1102) and members of the CLARE and Marshal families (12th and 13th century respectively). Extended in 1536, the shire continued until 1974; it was reconstituted as a unitary authority in 1996. See also LOCAL GOVERNMENTAL STRUCTURES, WALES.

PENAL LAWS, IRELAND see ANTI-CATHOLIC LEGISLATION, IRELAND, 1691 TO 1740s

PENAL LAWS, WALES Legal restrictions imposed by English on the Welsh: by King EDWARD I (as ordinances) after the revolt of MADOG AP LLYWELYN (1294–5); by Parliament (ordinances and STATUTES, especially in 1401–2) in response to OWAIN GLYN DŴR's revolt.

Welshmen were banned from public offices, and from becoming burgesses in the towns of N Wales. In 1401–2 Welshmen were banned from buying land in towns; Englishmen married to Welsh women could not become burgesses. The laws were reconfirmed to c.1450, then became ineffective; repealed 1624.

PENDA (b. early 7th century; d. 15 Nov. 655 at the R. 'Winwæd', Deira). The first notable king of MERCIA (C England); ruled from 626 or 633 (possibly after killing EDWIN of Deira and BERNICIA).

Penda extended the area under Mercian influence, becoming the first Mercian king with extensive authority over Anglo-Saxon kingdoms. He regularly attacked Deira and Bernicia (Mercia's main rivals), and killed King OSWALD (642). He also ravaged EAST ANGLIA, the Welsh, and the Gewisse, ousting King Cenwealh (645; see WESSEX). He remained a pagan, but permitted Christianity and the conversion of his son Peada (653). He was killed by Oswald's brother Oswiu. See also KINGSHIP, ANGLO-SAXON.

PENICILLIN An 'antibiotic' drug (used against bacteria), created in Great Britain, which enormously reduced infectious diseases from the 1940s. Although it was long known that moulds (minute fungi) could destroy bacteria, a phenomenon named 'antibiosis' in 1889, penicillin originated in 1928. On 3 Sept. Alexander Fleming (1881–1955), a bacteriologist at St Mary's Hospital, Paddington (London), noticed that mould on a dish was emitting juice that dissolved bacteria. He concluded (in a paper, 1929) that the juice, which he named penicillin, was of limited medical use.

In 1938 Howard Florey (1898–1968) and Ernst Chain (1906–79) at OXFORD University began studying microorganisms that produced anti-microbial substances, including penicillin. Chain cultivated mould obtained from Fleming in 1929 and discovered his paper. Tests on mice (1940) and humans (1941) produced remarkable cures, which suggested that the drug could help in WORLD WAR II. As limited manufacturing assistance was available in Britain, Florey obtained support from pharmaceutical companies in the USA (June 1941). Large-scale production was developed, and penicillin was administered to troops from summer 1943. Fleming, Florey and Chain received the 1945 Nobel Prize in Physiology or Medicine.

The success of penicillin (deemed a 'wonder drug') encouraged preparation of other antibiotics in the USA and Britain. But by the early 21st century, bacteria were becoming resistant, threatening serious decline in human health. *See also* MEDICINE AND PUBLIC HEALTH; HODGKIN, DOROTHY.

PENN, WILLIAM (b. 14 Oct. 1644 at London, England; d. 30 July 1718 at Ruscombe, Berkshire, England, aged 73). An admiral's son, Penn in 1666 joined the QUAKERS (in Ireland). Thereafter (in England) he preached, wrote tracts, advocated religious toleration, and was intermittently imprisoned. In the late 1670s he also articulated WHIG ideas.

From 1676 Penn was involved with other Quakers, as a trustee and owner, in NEW JERSEY in N America. Finding the complicated situation unsatisfactory, in 1681 he acquired rights in land W of the Delaware River. His colony was named PENNSYLVANIA, and developed as a refuge for Quakers and others. Penn visited the colony in 1682–4. During the reign of King JAMES VII/II (1685–8) Penn obtained the release of Quaker prisoners, but afterwards he was viewed suspiciously by WILLIAM III and MARY II. He revisited Pennsylvania 1699–1701. *See also* DELAWARE.

PENNSYLVANIA A former English colony in N America, N of MARYLAND (British from 1707). From the early 1640s the area was settled by Swedes and Finns as part of 'New Sweden' (*see also* DELAWARE). It was seized by Dutch Americans in 1655, then by the English in 1664 (acting for James, duke of York; *see* JAMES VII/II).

In 1681 William PENN obtained a grant of land W of the Delaware River from King CHARLES II, partly to create a refuge for fellow QUAKERS. Charles named it in honour of Penn's father, Admiral William Penn. (The Latin 'Pennsylvania' means 'Penn's woodland'.) In 1682–3, 50 ships took settlers from England to Pennsylvania. Penn also founded the capital Philadelphia, which was laid out in rectangular blocks. The colony was governed mainly by deputy lieutenants acting for Penn and his heirs. There was a legislative assembly from 1682. Laws were influenced by Quaker principles, and an Act of Dec. 1682 enshrined religious tolerance. Religious liberty attracted immigrants from varied origins, including Dutch, Germans, and Scotch-Irish.

In the 18th century Philadelphia became a vigorous commercial and intellectual centre. Est. population of Pennsylvania 1770: 235,000. Like other colonies, it opposed British taxes in the 1760s–70s and became a State of the USA in 1776. The Penn family were deprived of proprietary lands in 1779. *See also* NORTH AMERICAN COLONIES.

PENRHYN, LORD (b. 30 Sept. 1836 at Luton Springs, Yorkshire, England; d. 10 March 1907 at London, England, aged 70). The autocratic owner of the world's largest slate quarry, at Penrhyn (NW Wales), which he inherited with his title in 1886. Hostile to unions, Penrhyn (formerly George Douglas-Pennant) twice responded to demands by locking out the workforce (1896–7, 1900–3), radicalizing the quarrymen. *See also* SLATE INDUSTRY, WALES; TRADE UNIONISM, WALES.

PENRUDDOCK'S RISING In England, 1655, the only significant rising against the Protectorate, intended as part of a national rebellion. The Royalists Colonel John Penruddock and Sir Joseph Wagstaff seized Salisbury (Wiltshire, S England) and marched through SW England with 400 men (11–14 March). Few others joined them, and the rising was suppressed by an Army troop. Penruddock was executed. *See also* COMMONWEALTH AND PROTECTORATE.

PENSIONS Before the 20th century, poor older people and widows were sometimes supported by statutory or charitable POOR RELIEF. State-funded, non-contributory pensions were introduced in Great Britain and Ireland from Jan. 1909 for persons aged over 70 (with means and 'character' tests, and excluding those on poor relief).

In 1925, in the UK, State pensions became contributory for workers included in NATIONAL INSURANCE, payable at 65 (implemented 1928). The 1946 National Insurance Act brought State pensions within National Insurance; provision became near universal based on compulsory contributions. An additional 'State Earnings Related Pensions Scheme' introduced in 1975 was replaced with a less generous 'Second State Pension' in 2002. Increases in pension ages were announced in 2010.

In the Republic of Ireland, contributory pensions payable at 70 were introduced in 1960 (except for the self-employed, public servants and high-earners). The pension age was reduced to 66 in the 1970s, and excluded groups were later included. In 2013 the State pension system consisted of six mutually exclusive payments.

Occupational pension schemes were also developed during the 20th century, with payments related to earnings. In the 21st century, higher costs necessitated increased contributions and reduced benefits. *See also* SOCIAL SERVICES.

PENTLAND RISING A rising of COVENANTERS in GALLOWAY (SW Scotland) in Nov. 1666; provoked by the government's policy of seeking religious uniformity and using soldiers to harass CONVENTICLES. 1000 men marched on Edinburgh, demanding concessions, but were defeated at Rullion Green in the Pentland Hills (28 Nov.). 50 were killed and others executed. *See also* ROTHES, 7TH EARL OF.

PEOPLE'S BUDGET Name applied by newspapers to the British government Budget of 1909. Introduced on 29 April by David LLOYD GEORGE, the Liberal chancellor of the Exchequer, it proposed a tax on land values and a super-tax on high incomes to pay for PENSIONS and the NAVAL RACE. A constitutional crisis ensued after its rejection by the Conservative-dominated House of Lords (30 Nov.).

The prime minister, H.H. ASQUITH, determined to abolish the Lords' power of veto. The Lords accepted the Budget (29 April 1910), following a general election (Jan. 1910). After a second election (Dec. 1910), the threatened creation of hundreds of Liberal peers induced the Lords to accept the Parliament Act (10 Aug. 1911), which removed the House's power to reject money Bills and reduced its power to delay legislation.

PEOPLE'S DEMOCRACY In NORTHERN IRELAND, a group founded by students at Queen's University, Belfast, on 9 Oct. 1968; a radical, confrontational offshoot of the NORTHERN IRELAND CIVIL RIGHTS ASSOCIATION which sought equal civil rights, irrespective of religious affiliation. It was active 1968–9. Its 'Long March' from BELFAST to LONDONDERRY, 1–4 Jan. 1969, ended with a violent police ambush at Burntollet bridge which inflamed the TROUBLES.

PEPYS, SAMUEL (b. 23 Feb. 1633 at London, England; d. 26 May 1703 at Clapham, Surrey, England, aged 70). Pepys was an administrator in the English NAVY from 1660, effectively becoming head of administration in 1673. He obtained Parliament's approval for building 30 new ships. Dismissed and imprisoned in 1679 for alleged TREASON (at the time of the POPISH PLOT), he cleared his name and was restored by King CHARLES II in 1684. Pepys retired in 1689, after the flight of JAMES VII/II, having made the

Navy an effective force. He is now best known for his intimate diary of 1660–9 which vividly portrays London life after the RESTORATION.

PERCEVAL, SPENCER (b. 1 Nov. 1762 at London, England; d. 11 May 1812 at Westminster, Middlesex, England, aged 49). A barrister from 1786 and evangelically pious, Perceval became an MP in 1796 and supported the ministry of William PITT the Younger. He served as solicitor-general (1801–2) under Henry ADDINGTON, attorney-general (1802–6) under Addington and Pitt, and as chancellor of the Exchequer (1807–9) under the duke of PORTLAND. His opposition to CATHOLIC EMANCIPATION made him acceptable to King GEORGE III.

Perceval succeeded Portland as PRIME MINISTER in Oct. 1809. A TORY, he was the dominant force in a weak ministry, and proved himself a shrewd leader. During negotiations to create a regency in 1810–11, he persuaded the prince of Wales (later GEORGE IV) to retain his ministry, outmanoeuvring the opposition under Earl GREY and Lord GRENVILLE. Perceval's administration was marked by success in the NAPOLEONIC WARS, especially in Spain under Viscount WELLINGTON, but troubled by domestic problems (e.g., machine breaking by LUDDITES).

Perceval was shot dead in the lobby of the House of Commons by John Bellingham, a bankrupt merchant. He is the only British prime minister to have been assassinated. He was succeeded by the 2nd earl of LIVERPOOL.

PERCY, HENRY (b. 10 Nov. 1341 in N England; d. 19 Feb. 1408 at Bramham Moor, Yorkshire, England, aged 66). Henry Percy became Lord Percy by inheritance in 1368. After the accession of King RICHARD II he was created earl of Northumberland (1377). By the mid 1390s he was dissatisfied with Richard. He and his son Henry supported Henry Bolingbroke's seizure of the throne in 1399 (*see* HENRY IV). Percy was rewarded with appointment as warden of the West March (western sector of Anglo-Scottish BORDER). In 1402 the Percys defeated the Scots (*see* HUMBLETON, BATTLE OF).

Charged by King Henry with subduing the Welsh rebellion led by OWAIN GLYN DŴR, Northumberland and his son were blamed when the conflict persisted. In 1403 they rebelled. Northumberland was briefly reconciled (Aug. 1403; pardoned Feb. 1404) but joined the Scrope-Mortimer rebellion in 1405, fleeing to Scotland when it failed. He was attainted (forfeited life, titles and estates), and was killed while invading England. *See also* PERCY FAMILY; SCROPE, RICHARD.

PERCY, HENRY (b. 20 May 1364 at Alnwick, Northumberland, England; d. 21 July 1403 at Shrewsbury, Shropshire, England, aged 39). The eldest son of Henry PERCY, earl of Northumberland, Percy fought in Prussia,

Ireland and Scotland. He was warden of the East March (eastern sector of Anglo-Scottish BORDER) 1385–6, 1388–94, from 1396. The Scots nicknamed him 'Hotspur' for his readiness to attack, though he was captured at OTTERBURN (Northumberland) in 1388.

Like his father, Percy supported Henry Bolingbroke's seizure of the throne in 1399 (*see* HENRY IV). As lieutenant in N Wales in 1402 he led the response to the Welsh revolt of OWAIN GLYN DŴR, supported by his father; together they quashed an opportunistic Scottish invasion at HUMBLETON. But tension with King Henry caused Percy to rebel, with his father, in July 1403. His forces were defeated before Northumberland could reinforce them and he was killed. *See also* PERCY FAMILY.

PERCY FAMILY A noble family, based in Northumberland, whose members were influential in N England in the 14th–16th centuries. Their importance originated with Henry de Percy (1273–1314) who acquired Alnwick and estates in Northumberland. Henry PERCY (1341–1408) was created earl of Northumberland in 1377 by King RICHARD II. He and his son, also Henry PERCY (1364–1403), supported Henry Bolingbroke's seizure of the throne but rebelled (*see* HENRY IV). Henry Percy (1394–55), 2nd earl and a supporter of HENRY VI, died at the battle of St Albans. In the 1450s the Percys engaged in local warfare against the NEVILLE FAMILY. Henry Percy (1421–61), 3rd earl and also a LANCASTRIAN, died at the battle of Towton. EDWARD IV confiscated the earldom. He restored it to Henry Percy (*c*.1449–89) in 1470.

Percys held the earldom until 1670 (except for 1537–57; *see* NORTHUMBERLAND, DUKE OF). The male line failed in 1670. Algernon Seymour (1684–1750), grandson of a Percy, was created earl (1749). His son-in-law Sir Hugh Smithson (1715–86) took the surname Percy in 1750. His line continued into the 21st century. *See also* YORKIST–LANCASTRIAN CONFLICT.

PERMISSIVE SOCIETY Term for a society exhibiting liberal and tolerant attitudes. In the USA and Great Britain from the 1950s it acknowledged acceptance of affluence, consumerism and new outlooks (e.g., psychiatric understanding), and also tolerance for YOUTH CULTURE. From the 1960s the term became associated in Britain, often critically, with the decriminalization of certain behaviours (e.g., 1961 Suicide Act, for England and Wales; 1967 Sexual Offences Act permitting private adult male homosexual acts in England and Wales; 1967 Abortion Act, for Britain), and also with hedonism (e.g., use of recreational drugs such as cannabis) and rejection of moral constraints (e.g., extramarital sexual activity). The Republic of Ireland moved in the same direction from the 1990s partly under the influence of the WOMEN'S MOVEMENT. *See also* ABORTION, GREAT BRITAIN/IRELAND; HOMOSEXUALITY, LAW RELATING TO.

PERRERS, ALICE (b. in Hertfordshire, England; d. between 20 Aug. 1400 and 3 Feb. 1401 at Upminster, Essex, England). The mistress of King EDWARD III from *c*.1364, Perrers dominated Edward after the death of Queen Philippa (1369) despite marrying a knight (1373 or 1374). Having interfered in the Council, Crown finance and PATRONAGE, she was convicted of corruption during the GOOD PARLIAMENT (1376) and banished from court. Edward pardoned her (22 Oct.); she remained with him until his death (June 1377). Afterwards she was convicted of interfering with legal processes and sent abroad (1377–9).

PERROT, JOHN (b. *c*.1527, probably at Harroldston, Pembrokeshire, Wales; d. Sept. 1592 at London, England, aged about 65). A courtier and alleged illegitimate son of King HENRY VIII, Perrot (knighted 1547) was the first president of MUNSTER (S Ireland; served Feb. 1571–July 1573), where he brutally suppressed the First DESMOND REBELLION.

As chief governor of Ireland (lord deputy), 1584–8 (under Queen ELIZABETH I), Perrot campaigned in ULSTER (N Ireland), where he created three lieutenancies (1584; replaced by nominal shires 1585). He encouraged the MUNSTER PLANTATION. His major achievement was a new COMPOSITION in CONNACHT (W Ireland), which made the Connacht presidency self-financing (1585). Disagreements with Archbishop Adam LOFTUS led to his recall to London and conviction for treason in 1592. *See also* IRELAND, ENGLISH CONQUEST, 16TH CENTURY; PRESIDENCIES, IRELAND.

PERSIA (IRAN), BRITISH RELATIONS WITH British diplomats were active in Persia from the early 19th century, concerned to counter Russian expansionism to safeguard British interests in India. After a brief Anglo-Persian War (1856–7), to protect Herat, Britain delineated Persia's border with India. In the later 19th century Russia and Britain were rivals for concessions (e.g., oil concession granted in 1901 to a British financier). The ANGLO-RUSSIAN CONVENTION of 1907 divided Persia into spheres of influence.

From 1918 British interests predominated, partly because of Persia's importance as a primary oil source (*see* OIL INDUSTRY). The Anglo-Persian Oil Company (founded 1909) supported Reza Khan, the army officer who seized power in 1921 and became shah (king) in 1925. (The country was renamed Iran in 1935.)

From 1941 to 1946, British and USSR forces occupied Iran to exclude German influence. Resentment of British economic dominance culminated in NATIONALIZATION of Anglo-Iranian's assets (March 1951). Although an agreement enabled the company to resume operations, US influence became predominant.

Following the establishment of an Islamic Republic (1979), Britain suspended diplomatic relations. Resumed in

1988, they were cut in 1989 by Iran after Ayatollah Khomeini demanded execution of a British author (*see* RUSHDIE AFFAIR). Relations were normalized in 1998, though embassies were closed 2011–15 after the British embassy in Tehran was attacked. In 2015 the UK was a signatory, with Iran and five other countries, to the Joint Comprehensive Plan of Action (popularly known as the 'Iran nuclear deal'), which sought to limit Iran's ability to develop nuclear weapons.

PERSIAN GULF, BRITISH INVOLVEMENT The EAST INDIA COMPANY ran a trading post at Bandar Abbas (in modern Iran, by Strait of Hormuz) from 1619, and British influence extended to the Arabian coast in the 18th century. Starting with Muscat in 1798, Great Britain made a variety of treaty relations with 40–50 sultanates and sheikdoms, designed to protect the route to INDIA, control their foreign relations, suppress piracy, and in the 20th century to secure oil rights. Policy was directed from India until 1947. The British gradually withdrew from commitments in the Gulf, ending in 1971. *See also* KUWAIT.

PERSIAN GULF WAR, BRITISH INVOLVEMENT Iraq's invasion of oil-rich KUWAIT on 2 Aug. 1990 was immediately condemned by Great Britain. It joined the USA in mounting a naval blockade, defending SAUDI ARABIA, and obtaining economic sanctions through the United Nations. Britain's prime minister, Margaret THATCHER, encouraged the resolve of the US president, George H.W. Bush, telling him it was 'no time to go wobbly'. The situation was complicated by Iraq's capture of British and other foreign citizens in Kuwait. Following visits to Iraq by Edward HEATH (21–23 Oct.) and others, foreign hostages were released (by late Dec.). British policy was sustained despite a crisis within the governing Conservative Party (Thatcher was replaced by John MAJOR on 28 Nov.).

British forces participated in a US-led (and UN-authorized) aerial bombing campaign in Kuwait and Iraq (from 16 Jan. 1991) and in an invasion of Kuwait which expelled the Iraqis (24–27 Feb.). During the crisis Britain provided 45,000 service personnel; 24 were killed. *See also* UNITED STATES OF AMERICA, BRITISH RELATIONS WITH; WAR CABINET.

PERSIAN GULF WAR, SECOND, BRITISH INVOLVEMENT *see* IRAQ WAR, BRITISH INVOLVEMENT

PERTH A city in C Scotland; on the W bank of the R. Tay. Centre of Perth SHERIFFDOM (*c*.1165–1975); centre of Perthshire and Kinross (from 1996).

Perth (possibly Brittonic, meaning 'Copse') was founded as a BURGH by King DAVID I (ruled 1124–53). Three friaries were established (13th century) and a Carthusian monastery (1429). Parliament sometimes met in Perth in the 14th and 15th centuries. In 1559 John KNOX's sermon in St

John's Church, attacking idolatry, provoked riots and the destruction of religious houses, leading to the REFORMATION. Linen and cotton manufacturing flourished from, respectively, the late 17th and late 18th centuries to the 20th century. Perth was also a major market for agriculture and livestock. It historical city status was discontinued in 1975 but reinstated in 2012.

Est. popn: 1300, 2000; 1600, 3000; 1800, 14,800; 1900, 33,500; 2000, 43,000.

PERTH, PACIFICATION OF An agreement made on 23 Feb. 1573 at Perth (C Scotland). Leading supporters of the deposed MARY, QUEEN OF SCOTS (notably the Hamilton faction) renounced their allegiance and acknowledged JAMES VI as king, effectively ending the MARIAN CIVIL WAR (started 1568). *See also* MORTON, 4TH EARL OF.

PERTH, TREATY OF Agreed 2 July 1266 (at PERTH, C Scotland). King Magnus IV of Norway sold the WESTERN ISLES and Isle of MAN to King ALEXANDER III of Scotland for 4000 marks and an annuity of 100 marks. It was the culmination of a diplomatic and military campaign (1261–6). *See also* LARGS, BATTLE OF; NORWAY, 'MATTER OF'.

PETERLOO The ironic name (echoing WATERLOO) given to a mass political demonstration at St Peter's Field, MANCHESTER (NW England), on Monday 16 Aug. 1819 which was violently dispersed. Over 60,000 people assembled to protest against hardship and hear Henry HUNT call for PARLIAMENTARY REFORM. Eleven were killed and over 400 wounded when mounted yeomanry charged at the crowd (so-called 'Peterloo Massacre'). *See also* CASTLEREAGH, VISCOUNT.

PETITIONING MOVEMENT A political movement, 1779–85, which sought reform of the British House of Commons to reduce government influence on MPs and increase their accountability to electors.

Launched in Yorkshire in 1779 by Christopher WYVILL, the movement demanded triennial Parliaments (i.e., more frequent elections), abolition of ROTTEN BOROUGHS, and more MPs representing counties. Counties and boroughs presented petitions to the Commons in 1780, 1782 and 1785. Leading politicians with similar concerns liaised with the movement in 1780 (*see* ECONOMICAL REFORM), and Wyvill persuaded William PITT the Younger to press for reform in 1782. *See also* SEPTENNIAL ACT.

PETITION OF RIGHT In England, a petition to King CHARLES I agreed by Parliament in 1628 in response to the FORCED LOAN of 1626 and FIVE KNIGHTS' CASE of 1627. It requested that imprisonment without demonstrated reason, non-parliamentary taxation, billeting of troops and martial law should be declared illegal. Charles, faced with Parliament's refusal to grant taxation, gave assent (7 June). *See also* COKE, EDWARD.

PETTY, WILLIAM (b. 26 May 1623 at Romsey, Hampshire, England; d. 16 Dec. 1687 at Piccadilly, Middlesex, England, aged 64). Educated at Leiden, Paris and OXFORD Universities, Petty was appointed professor of anatomy at Oxford (1651). In 1652 he went to Ireland as physician-general of the Parliamentary Army. He surveyed lands forfeited by Catholics (1654–9, the 'Down Survey') and became a landowner.

After the RESTORATION, Petty was a founder of the ROYAL SOCIETY (1660) and was knighted (1662). He advocated scientific analysis of social and economic conditions (*see* POLITICAL ECONOMY). His publications included *A Treatise of Taxes and Contributions* (1662) and *Hiberniae Delineatio* (1685), the first atlas of Ireland. *See also* CROMWELLIAN LAND SETTLEMENT.

PHARMACEUTICALS INDUSTRY *see* INDUSTRY, ENGLAND FROM LATE 18TH CENTURY; INDUSTRY, SOUTHERN IRELAND

PHILOSOPHIC RADICALS A group of Radical MPs and intellectuals (e.g., J.S. MILL) which flourished in Great Britain from 1817 to the 1840s. They preached the moral philosophy of Jeremy BENTHAM and James Mill (*see* UTILITARIANISM). Their zeal for remodelling public institutions according to rational principles influenced WHIG reforms of the 1830s (*see* GREY, 2ND EARL; MELBOURNE, 2ND VISCOUNT).

PHOENIX PARK MURDERS In Ireland, the assassination (by knives) of the new CHIEF SECRETARY FOR IRELAND, Lord Frederick Cavendish, and under-secretary Thomas Henry Burke in Phoenix Park, Dublin, on 6 May 1882. They were killed by members of the 'Invincibles', a FENIAN splinter group. The murders encouraged the Irish leader C.S. PARNELL to maintain support for the British government (*see* KILMAINHAM TREATY), and caused the British prime minister, W.E. GLADSTONE, to continue coercion. Five men were eventually hanged for the murders (May–June 1883). *See also* LAND AGITATION AND REFORM, IRELAND.

PHONE-HACKING SCANDAL A controversy affecting British politics caused by allegations from 2009 of extensive illegal 'phone-hacking' (listening to private messages recorded on telephones) by reporters working for the *News of the World* newspaper, controlled by Rupert MURDOCH.

From May 2010 the allegations threatened the new prime minister, David CAMERON, because a former editor of the newspaper (2003–7), Andy Coulson, had worked for him since 2007 (latterly as government communications director), and because Coulson's predecessor (2000–3),

Rebekah Brooks, was a friend. From summer 2010 Cameron publicly defended Coulson against calls for his sacking from Ed Miliband, the Labour Party leader. (Coulson resigned in Jan. 2011.)

On 6 July 2011, after a newspaper claimed that the mobile telephone of a murdered teenage girl had been hacked, Cameron sought to defuse the crisis by announcing a public inquiry into press ethics and behaviour ('Leveson Inquiry', chaired by Sir Brian Leveson, a senior judge). On 7 July, closure of the *News of the World* was announced; Coulson and Brookes were arrested (respectively 8 and 17 July) and charged. After Coulson was convicted of conspiracy to hack 'phones, Cameron apologized for having employed him (June 2014).

Leveson recommended a new system of press regulation (Nov. 2012), but it was only partly implemented because of disagreement between political parties and resistance from publishers who argued that reporters' misdemeanours might be exploited to curb press freedom. The Inquiry had also ignored the Internet.

PHONEY WAR Term applied from autumn 1939 to the seeming military inactivity in western Europe at the start of WORLD WAR II (from Sept. 1939, when Germany invaded Poland). France maintained defensive readiness and the UK imposed a blockade against Germany. The period was ended by the German invasions of Norway (April 1940) and France (May).

PICQUIGNY, TREATY OF Concluded on 29 Aug. 1475 at Picquigny (a town under Burgundian rule, now in N France) between King EDWARD IV of England and King Louis XI of France, terminating Edward's brief military expedition to the Continent (from 4 July 1475). A seven-year truce was established, and Edward agreed to withdraw his troops in return for 75,000 crowns in cash (about £18,000), an annual pension of 25,000 crowns, and consideration of his claim to the French Crown by arbitrators. The pension continued, with increases in 1519 and 1525, until surrendered in 1550. *See also* MARGARET OF ANJOU.

PICTS Term for British (Brittonic-speaking) inhabitants of N Britain, N of the FORTH–CLYDE ISTHMUS (within modern Scotland), 3rd–9th centuries (successors of prehistoric inhabitants). They were first so called in 297 by Eumenius in Roman Gaul (modern France). His Latin name 'Picti', meaning 'Painted people', denoted barbarians outside 'civilized' Roman rule and culture. During the Roman period (2nd–5th centuries) many Picts belonged to tribes (*see* CALEDONIANS; MAEATAE). In 367, when Picts attacked ROMAN BRITAIN, they reportedly comprised Di-Calidones ('Double Calidones') and Verturiones. Attacks in the 5th century are mentioned by GILDAS.

Kings are reliably reported from the mid 6th century, when BRIDEI SON OF MAILCON ruled near the Moray Firth (in modern NE Scotland), north of the MOUNTH, near the area later called FORTRIU (its name derived from the Verturiones). Christianity reached the Picts by the 5th century, and they produced distinctive carvings from the 6th century.

In the 7th century sources refer to two main Pictish areas, divided by the MOUNTH, the southern area extending to the Forth estuary. King EGFRITH of Bernicia/Northumbria (S of the Picts) probably installed BRIDEI SON OF BELI as king of Fortriu (671); Egfrith also evidently dominated southern Pictland until 679. In 685, when Egfrith attempted to re-exert authority, he was defeated by Bridei (see DÚN NECHTAIN, BATTLE OF), enabling Bridei and his successors to dominate both northern and southern Pictland. Cohesion may have been encouraged by adoption of the name 'Picts' and of Roman Christian observances (early 8th century; see NAITON SON OF DER-ILEI).

From the 8th century some Pictish kings were also high-kings of (Scottish) DÁL RIATA (see ONUIST SON OF VURGUIST; CONSTANTÍN SON OF VURGUIST), but permanent UNION OF SCOTS AND PICTS was realized from c.842 by Scottish kings. From c.900 they forged a new identity of 'Alba' (Gaelic, meaning 'Britain') and Pictish culture disappeared (with Pictish Brittonic replaced by Gaelic). See also POST-ROMAN BRITAIN; OSWALD; KINGSHIP, NORTH BRITAIN; CONVERSION OF NORTH BRITONS, PICTS AND SCOTS.

PILGRIMAGE OF GRACE A rebellion in N England, 1536, by nobles and ordinary people against the religious policies of King HENRY VIII. It began in Lincolnshire (1 Oct.), and spread to Yorkshire (by 8 Oct.). Robert Aske, a Yorkshire lawyer, emerged as leader. The rebels swore to defend the Church and wore pilgrims' badges showing Christ's five wounds.

By Nov. the 'pilgrims' numbered 30,000 and controlled England N of the R. Don. Their grievances (compiled 2–4 Dec.) included the DISSOLUTION OF RELIGIOUS HOUSES. Henry promised redress, and the pilgrims accepted a royal pardon from the (3rd) duke of NORFOLK (6 Dec.). But Henry used a later revolt (Jan. 1537) to revoke the pardon and exact vengeance: over 220 rebels were executed, including Aske. See also REFORMATION, ENGLAND.

PILGRIMS OR PILGRIM FATHERS see PLYMOUTH PLANTATION OR COLONY

PIPE ROLLS In England, nickname for the 'great rolls of the Exchequer' or 'annual rolls', parchment records which, when rolled up and stacked, looked like pipes. They were considered to symbolize the flow of revenues to the Exchequer. Each roll itself consisted of 'pipes' – pairs of membranes, sewn end to end, which were stitched together

at the head. Starting c.1110, a roll was compiled after each Michaelmas (29 Sept.) to record the annual audit of sheriffs' accounts. Rolls survive for 1129–30 and 1156–1834 (with gaps). See also EXCHEQUER; ROYAL REVENUES, ENGLAND.

PIRACY AND PRIVATEERING Piracy (robbery at sea or committed by sea-borne raiders) has occurred around the British Isles throughout most of history. VIKINGS raided extensively in the 8th–11th centuries, and African Muslims raided English and Irish ports in the early 17th century. As English trade expanded beyond Europe (16th–17th centuries), piracy became a common hazard, and British people became involved. It was rife in the Caribbean in the late 17th and early 18th centuries, the so-called 'classic age' of piracy, generated by increasing commercial traffic. Action by British authorities from 1718 helped to suppress it.

Privateering was a variant of piracy, used as a covert form of warfare, whereby private seamen were authorized to attack or capture shipping, or raid settlements. It was England's main form of maritime activity during conflict with SPAIN (1570s–1604, 1650s). In the late 16th century wealthy individuals invested in operations (to gain a share of booty), and Queen ELIZABETH I gave tacit support. Privateers included Martin FROBISHER and Francis DRAKE. See also ANGLO-SPANISH WAR.

PITT, WILLIAM, THE ELDER (b. 15 Nov. 1708 at Westminster, Middlesex, England; d. 11 May 1778 at Hayes, Kent, England, aged 69). Pitt, a WHIG, became an MP in 1735, joining the COBHAM'S CUBS who opposed Robert WALPOLE and later Lord CARTERET. He was disliked by King GEORGE II for attacking the government's concern with HANOVER. Henry PELHAM (prime minister) compelled his appointment as paymaster-general in 1746, but Pitt later attacked the duke of NEWCASTLE (Pelham's successor) and Henry FOX, and was dismissed (1755).

On Newcastle's resignation in Nov. 1756, Pitt formed a ministry with the duke of DEVONSHIRE, serving as SECRETARY OF STATE (southern). He was dismissed in April 1757 because the king disliked his strategy in the SEVEN YEARS WAR. Reappointed in June, with Newcastle, he effectively directed the war, achieving success (e.g., in CANADA, INDIA). He portrayed himself as a patriotic office-holder, the 'Great Commoner'. He resigned in Oct. 1761 over disagreements with GEORGE III and the earl of BUTE about continuing the war.

Pitt returned as prime minister in 1766, sitting in the House of Lords as earl of Chatham and holding office as lord PRIVY SEAL. Incapacitated by March 1767, he resigned in 1768. In 1770–1 he opposed the American policies of Lord NORTH. See also PITT, WILLIAM, THE YOUNGER.

PITT, WILLIAM, THE YOUNGER (b. 28 May 1759 at Hayes, Kent, England; d. 23 Jan. 1806 at Putney, Surrey,

England, aged 46). A son of William PITT the Elder, Pitt, an independent WHIG, became an MP in 1781 and served as chancellor of the Exchequer under the earl of SHELBURNE (1782–3).

In Dec. 1783, aged 24, Pitt was appointed PRIME MINISTER of Great Britain by King GEORGE III. His main achievements were financial and commercial. He tackled indebtedness from the AMERICAN WAR OF INDEPENDENCE (e.g., with a SINKING FUND, 1786). Free trade for Ireland was rejected (1785), but trade with France was liberalized (1786; see EDEN TREATY). A reformer, Pitt reorganized government of the EAST INDIA COMPANY and British India (1784, 1786), and of Canada (1791).

Britain was confronted by the FRENCH REVOLUTION from 1789, and by war from 1793. Pitt introduced repressive domestic measures (e.g., against seditious meetings), personal income tax (1799; see TAXATION), and implemented a UNION OF IRELAND AND GREAT BRITAIN (1801). But his military leadership was often inadequate. He resigned in Feb. 1801 because the king opposed CATHOLIC EMANCIPATION.

Pitt was reappointed in May 1804, during the NAPOLEONIC WARS. A threatened French invasion was prevented by victory at TRAFALGAR (Oct. 1805). Pitt's health collapsed in Jan. 1806. See also ADDINGTON, HENRY; GRENVILLE, LORD.

PLACEMAN In England, term used after the RESTORATION (1660) for an MP who held a position (or 'place') of profit under the Crown (e.g., office in the royal household, government administrative office, or pension) in expectation that he would support the government. Independent MPs feared that placemen corrupted the liberty of Parliament. 'Place Bills' to exclude placemen from Parliament were frequently introduced from the 1690s. Excise officers were excluded in 1699, customs officers in 1701, and the 1701 Act of SETTLEMENT banned placemen (inoperative). The Regency Act of 1706 prohibited the appointment of MPs to some 'old' offices and any 'new' offices; appointment to other 'old' offices required an MP to vacate his seat and seek re-election (continued until 1926). In 1739 about 200 of 558 MPs were placemen.

Many placemen were excluded from 1782 (see ECONOMICAL REFORM). By 1809, 76 MPs held posts, most of them responsible government positions. The retention of placemen meant that ministers of the British government remained members of the legislature. See also CONSTITUTION, UNITED KINGDOM.

PLAGUE, ENGLAND Between the 7th and 17th centuries England suffered outbreaks of plague (bubonic and pneumonic varieties), a deadly bacterial disease which originated in Asia. It was transmitted by fleas carried on black rats.

The earliest outbreak occurred c.664 (recorded by BEDE in his *Ecclesiastical History*). There was no further occurrence until the BLACK DEATH of 1348–9, which killed possibly 40% of the population. It was the only outbreak similar in intensity to ones in Europe and Asia. It caused profound social and economic dislocation. Further outbreaks occurred in 1361–2, 1369, and 1390, and in the 15th century (1407, 1464, 1479), contributing to demographic and economic decline.

In the 16th and early 17th centuries there were regional outbreaks in central and southern England, though mortality reached high levels only in 1550 and 1597. A more severe outbreak happened in 1665–6. Known as the GREAT PLAGUE, it killed over 70,000 in London and affected provincial towns. The period also saw a new understanding of how the disease spread. Successful precautions (e.g., watches at ports), together with a decline in the virulence of the bacillus, meant that no further major outbreaks occurred though cases are recorded until 1679. See also POPULATION, ENGLAND; MEDICINE AND PUBLIC HEALTH.

PLAGUE, IRELAND Plague is recorded c.549 (possibly introduced from Gaul) and in the 7th century (664–5, 667–8, 683–4) when the psychological impact may have encouraged the recording of cultural traditions in writing (genealogies, poetry, law). A 'great plague' occurred in 1095. The devastating plague of 1348 had far-reaching consequences (see BLACK DEATH, IMPACT ON IRELAND). There were further general outbreaks in the 14th century (1361, 1383, 1398), localized outbreaks in the 15th century (e.g., in DUBLIN 1435, 1447), and later recurrences (1520, 1575, 1602–4). The final large-scale plague, in 1649–51 (coinciding with conquest by Oliver CROMWELL), possibly originated from Spain. Its effects included a considerable fall in Dublin's population. See also POPULATION, IRELAND; MEDICINE AND PUBLIC HEALTH.

PLAGUE, SCOTLAND The first recorded outbreak was the BLACK DEATH of 1349–50, when possibly a third of the population were killed. Ten further outbreaks occurred between 1362 and 1500, which were most virulent in the S and in BURGHS. They prevented population growth and contributed to the decline of burghs. There were five outbreaks between 1500 and 1600, and others in 1600–9 and 1644–9. From the late 16th century plague was increasingly confined to Burghs. In 1644–9, 20% of burgh inhabitants were probably killed on average, though in EDINBURGH possibly one-third died in 1645 and in Brechin (Forfarshire) two-thirds. See also POPULATION, SCOTLAND; MEDICINE AND PUBLIC HEALTH.

PLAGUE, WALES Plagues occurred during the 5th–7th centuries; victims possibly included MAELGWN GWYNEDD (547). Plague returned in 1349 and recurred periodically in the late 14th and 15th centuries (see BLACK DEATH, IMPACT ON WALES). In the 16th and early 17th centuries it tended to break out in individual towns; Presteigne (Radnorshire), for example, was devastated in 1593. The last recorded occurrence was at Haverfordwest (Pembrokeshire) in 1652. *See also* POPULATION, WALES; MEDICINE AND PUBLIC HEALTH.

PLAID CYMRU (Welsh, meaning 'The Party of Wales'). A political party founded in 1925 to defend Welsh culture and seek DOMINION status for Wales; dominated initially by Saunders LEWIS. Its leaders won publicity by a token act of arson at a ROYAL AIR FORCE bombing school in Wales in 1936. Greater credibility was gained with the election of Gwynfor EVANS to the UK Parliament in 1966. The Party won four parliamentary constituencies in 1992, 1997, 2001; three in 2005, 2010, 2015; four in 2017 and 2019. In the 1990s its fundamental aim was self-government for Wales within the EUROPEAN UNION.

In 1999 Plaid Cymru became the second largest party in the new Welsh Assembly (17 of 60 seats) and won seats on most local authorities. From 2007 to 2011 it was the junior partner in the Welsh government (with Labour), with its leader, Ieuan Wyn Jones, serving as deputy first minister. *See also* DEVOLUTION, WALES.

PLAN OF CAMPAIGN In Ireland, a scheme to revive rural agitation and reduce tenant farmers' rents, which was developed by T.M. HEALY, John DILLON and William O'BRIEN for the NATIONAL LEAGUE. It was publicized anonymously in the newspaper *United Ireland* on 23 Oct. 1886. Tenants were urged to determine 'fair' rents and propose them to their landlords. (Rejected rents would be paid to trustees.) Some 20,000 tenants on over 200 estates participated. Landlords' reactions ranged from submission to making evictions. The Campaign ceased in 1891. *See also* LAND AGITATION AND REFORM, IRELAND.

PLANTAGENETS Historians' term for kings of England descended from Geoffrey, count of Anjou in France (d. 1151). They ruled from 1154 to 1485 (HENRY II to RICHARD III). The succeeding Tudors (1485–1603) were a branch of the family through the Beaufort descendants of John of Gaunt (*see* BEAUFORT FAMILY). The Plantagenets were named after Count Geoffrey's badge, a broom sprig – in Latin, *planta genista*. *See also* LANCASTRIANS; YORKISTS; TUDOR FAMILY.

PLANTATION Term for societies of mainly English migrants (with Welsh and Scots) which were established in Ireland and the Americas in the 16th–17th centuries, usually under royal authority (e.g., MUNSTER PLANTATION; VIRGINIA). The term essentially denoted the 'planting' of settlers on land, with connotations of horticulture and fruitfulness. Landholders were often called 'planters'. Plantations in Ireland were partly intended to 'civilize' the native Irish by attracting the settlement of exemplary immigrants from Britain, whereas American plantations to some extent represented emigration by individuals for their own economic or religious reasons (*see* NONCONFORMITY AND DISSENT, ENGLAND).

By the early 18th century 'plantation' tended to mean a large farm or estate, on which cash crops such as tobacco, sugar or cotton were produced, often by slaves or indentured labourers. Larger immigrant societies were instead termed 'colonies'. *See also* PLANTATIONS, IRELAND; WEST INDIES; NORTH AMERICAN COLONIES; PLANTATION INDUSTRY.

PLANTATION INDUSTRY A mode of cultivation in which a large area of land is devoted to a single crop. Settlers in many parts of the BRITISH EMPIRE produced foodstuffs and raw materials for export in this way from the 17th century, sometimes using slaves. Examples include sugar in the WEST INDIES, cotton in N America, and rubber in MALAYA. *See also* PLANTATION; SLAVE TRADE, ENGLISH AND BRITISH INVOLVEMENT.

PLANTATIONS, IRELAND Colonization projects, and the societies established by them, which were authorized or organized by the English government 1550s–1630s. They involved the 'planting' or settling of people (usually of English or Scottish culture) on land to form hierarchical societies based on arable farming. Governments deployed plantations to establish new societies in areas deemed to need pacification, designing to extend English rule and to 'civilize' the Gaelic Irish by example. In the 17th century, ambitions also included the spreading of Protestantism and commercial activity.

Major schemes were: (a) LEIX-OFFALY PLANTATION (1550s), which buttressed the PALE; (b) attempted plantation of the Ards (NE Ireland) by Sir Thomas Smith (1572–3); (c) attempted plantation of NE Ulster by the earl of Essex (1573–4); (d) MUNSTER PLANTATION in S Ireland (1580s–90s); (e) ULSTER PLANTATION in N Ireland (1610s–20s); (f) planned plantation in CONNACHT (W Ireland) by Viscount WENTWORTH (1630s). *See also* IRELAND, ENGLISH CONQUEST, 16TH CENTURY.

PLASSEY, BATTLE OF Fought on 23 June 1757 at Palashi (or Plassey) in Bengal, NE India. British and Indian troops commanded by Robert CLIVE of the EAST INDIA COMPANY defeated and ousted the nawab (ruler) of Bengal, Siraj-ud-Daulah. His successor, Mir Ja'far, a company 'client ruler', rewarded the company and Clive with land and money. Clive's victory greatly strengthened the company's presence in Bengal.

PLUNKETT, HORACE (b. 24 Oct. 1854 at Sherborne House, Gloucestershire, England; d. 26 March 1932 at Weybridge, Surrey, England, aged 77). The son of a Protestant

Irish landowner, Plunkett from 1889 managed his family's estate in Ireland. Concerned to improve conditions, he founded the non-sectarian Irish Agricultural Organisation Society (1894) to advance agricultural co-operatives. He also sat on the Congested Districts Board (1891–1918), and was a Unionist MP (1892–1900) and vice-president of the Irish Department of Agriculture (1899–1907). Knighted in 1903, Plunkett chaired the Irish Convention (1917–18) and served briefly as a senator of the Irish Free State (1922–3). He left Ireland after his house was burnt during the Irish Civil War.

PLUNKETT, OLIVER (b. 1 Nov. 1625 at Loughcrew, Co. Meath, Ireland; d. 1 July 1681 at Tyburn, Middlesex, England, aged 55). Ordained a Catholic priest at Rome (1654), Plunkett returned to Ireland in 1670 as archbishop of Armagh, determined to improve discipline in the Irish Church. Forced into hiding by renewed anti-Catholic persecution (1673), he was arrested in 1679. Though acquitted in Ireland of seeking to overthrow Protestantism, he was convicted and executed in England (*see* Plunkett affair). He was canonized in 1975. *See also* Catholics and Catholic Church, Ireland from 16th century.

PLUNKETT AFFAIR Episode during the anti-Catholic Popish Plot agitation in England (1679–81). Agitators in England claimed that Irish Catholics were involved and that Oliver Plunkett, archbishop of Armagh, was plotting to overthrow Protestantism in Ireland with French assistance. Plunkett was arrested (6 Dec. 1679), but acquitted at Dundalk by an Irish Protestant jury (24 July 1680). He was nonetheless taken to England (Oct.), convicted of treason (adhering to a superstitious religion) and executed (1 July 1681). *See also* Restoration, Ireland.

PLYMOUTH BRETHREN An evangelical Protestant Christian sect which originated in Ireland in 1829 when a group disillusioned with the Church of Ireland sought to recreate early Christian simplicity. It became named from the first English congregation, which was started at Plymouth (SW England) in 1831. The preaching of J.N. Darby (1800–82) led to the founding of congregations throughout the British Isles. Worship is focused on Holy Communion but there are no professional clergy. Brethren avoided occupations considered incompatible with the New Testament (e.g., keeping alehouses). In 1845 differences over the extent of involvement with the world resulted in division into Open and Exclusive Brethren. The Brethren have included many professional men. In 2010 there were about 70,000 Brethren in the UK.

PLYMOUTH PLANTATION OR COLONY An English settlement in N America; the first successful one in New

England, founded in 1620 by a congregation of Puritan 'separatists' (separated from the Church of England). They emigrated from England to Leiden in the Dutch Republic in 1609, and in Sept. 1620, funded by a mercantile company, they sailed for America on the *Mayflower* (founded Plymouth in Dec.).

During the trans-Atlantic voyage leading men agreed the 'Mayflower Compact' – provisions for civil society to make and obey laws. Plymouth adopted a constitution in 1636 under authority granted in 1630 by the Council for New England. No formal recognition was obtained from the English Crown. Though new settlements were started, the colony was hampered by lack of a good harbour and staple crop. On 17 Oct. 1691 Plymouth Plantation (est. population: 7400) was annexed to Massachusetts. The original settlers were called 'Pilgrims' from 1793, or 'Pilgrim Fathers' from 1820. *See also* Nonconformity and dissent, England; North American colonies; New England, dominion of.

POITIERS, BATTLE OF *see* Hundred Years War

POITOU *see* Angevin Empire

POLAND, BRITISH RELATIONS WITH Great Britain regretted the partition of Poland (1772–95), but the powers that absorbed it – Russia, Prussia, Austria – were allies against France. In 1815 the foreign secretary Viscount Castlereagh, unable to restore genuine independence, opposed re-unification under Russian auspices. Polish insurgents in 1830 and 1863 cherished misplaced hopes of diplomatic support from Lord Palmerston.

While committed to Polish independence from 1917, Britain viewed with misgiving the frontiers of a restored Poland (established 1918–21). Britain entered World War II pursuant to the Anglo-Polish Guarantee (March 1939), although realistically Poland could not be defended. After the German conquest (Sept.), a Polish government continued in exile.

At the Yalta Conference in 1945, the British prime minister Winston Churchill conceded that Poland's government-in-exile be merged with the communist puppet régime installed by the USSR. Anglo-Polish relations then became subsumed by the Cold War (from 1947). In 1988, during a visit, Prime Minister Margaret Thatcher encouraged progress towards democracy (implemented 1989). Following the end of the USSR-led Warsaw Pact (1991), Britain maintained close relations and supported Poland's entry into the North Atlantic Treaty Organization (1999) and European Union (2004). The latter produced substantial migration: 790,000 Polish-born immigrants resided in the UK by 2015.

POLE, MICHAEL DE LA (b. *c*.1330 at Hull, Yorkshire, England; d. 5 Sept. 1389 at Paris, France, aged about 59).

A merchant's son, de la Pole undertook military service under EDWARD THE BLACK PRINCE and JOHN OF GAUNT (from 1369). From 1377 he was a favoured adviser of the new king, RICHARD II. He was appointed governor of the king's person in 1381, CHANCELLOR in 1383, and was created earl of Suffolk in 1385. In 1384 he arranged a truce with France (*see* HUNDRED YEARS WAR).

In Oct. 1386, compelled by the House of Commons, Richard dismissed de la Pole as chancellor. He was impeached by the House of Commons for corruption and negligence, and imprisoned. Released in late 1387, he was convicted of TREASON by the MERCILESS PARLIAMENT (1388). He fled abroad and died in exile. *See also* POLE (DE LA POLE) FAMILY.

POLE, REGINALD (b. March 1500 at Stourton, Staffordshire, England; d. 17 Nov. 1558 at Lambeth, Surrey, England, aged 58). In 1530 Pole, a scholar and clergyman, obtained support from the University of Paris for the proposed divorce of King HENRY VIII (*see* GREAT MATTER). He moved to Italy in 1532 where he joined reform-minded Catholics. In 1536, in response to Henry's request for opinions on two theological matters, Pole wrote *De unitate*. He affirmed papal authority and condemned Henry's divorce. Pole was created a cardinal (1536) and was a papal legate to the Council of Trent (1542, 1545–6).

In Aug. 1553, following the accession of MARY I, Pope Julius III appointed Pole as PAPAL LEGATE for England. He landed on 20 Nov. 1554. On 30 Nov. he reconciled England to the papacy, though he was forced to allow lay holders to retain former Church property (24 Dec.). He held a synod (Dec. 1555–Feb. 1556) which sought effective preaching of Catholic doctrine by clergy. In March 1556 Pole became archbishop of CANTERBURY. He supported, but did not instigate, the repression of heresy.

In 1557 Pope Paul IV deprived Pole of his legatine authority and summoned him to Rome. Mary prevented his departure. He died 12 hours after the queen. *See also* REFORMATION, ENGLAND.

POLE, WILLIAM DE LA (b. 16 Oct. 1396 at Cotton, Suffolk, England; d. 2 May 1450 in Strait of Dover, aged 53). A soldier in France 1415–30, de la Pole succeeded a brother as earl of Suffolk in 1415. In 1430 he married Alice Chaucer (granddaughter of Geoffrey CHAUCER) and joined the royal Council. He was appointed steward of King HENRY VI's household (1433) and came to dominate the king. Suffolk favoured making peace with France (*see* HUNDRED YEARS WAR). He negotiated the king's French marriage in 1444 (*see* MARGARET OF ANJOU) and the surrender of Maine in 1445. He was suspicious of the duke of GLOUCESTER and arranged his arrest in 1447. (Gloucester died soon afterwards.) Suffolk was raised to duke in 1448.

In late 1449 Suffolk was blamed for losses of land in Normandy (N France) and was impeached in PARLIAMENT (March 1450). Henry, fearing Suffolk would be executed, banished him. Suffolk fled abroad, but his ship was intercepted by a privateer. Its crew lynched Suffolk. *See also* POLE (DE LA POLE) FAMILY.

POLE (DE LA POLE) FAMILY A mercantile and noble family, important in England in the 14th–16th centuries. William de la Pole (d. 1366) of Hull (Yorkshire), a leading merchant, made major loans to the government of King EDWARD III. His eldest son Michael de la POLE (d. 1389) acquired estates in East Anglia, and was appointed CHANCELLOR and created earl of Suffolk by RICHARD II. His son and successor Michael opposed Richard and supported Henry Bolingbroke's seizure of the throne (1399; *see* HENRY IV). Michael and his eldest son, also Michael, died while campaigning with HENRY V (1415). The earldom passed to the latter's brother, William de la POLE (d. 1450), counsellor to HENRY VI, who was created duke of Suffolk (1448). William's grandson Edmund de la Pole rebelled against HENRY VII (1501, executed 1513; *see* SUFFOLK REBELLION). The male line of de la Poles ended in 1539.

POLICE, ENGLAND The Statute of Winchester (1285) affirmed that all persons were responsible for law enforcement and made men liable for (unpaid) service as constables. In practice, policing was exiguous, although some parishes employed constables and part-time watchmen on low wages, chiefly to bring accused persons to court. Regular provision was usually made in towns, sometimes with annual elections of constables.

Growing concern about crime in the 18th century prompted innovations in LONDON. The magistrate (and novelist) Henry Fielding founded a force of paid 'thief-takers' (1748), later known as Bow Street Runners. A force of City Day Police was started for the City of London in 1784, and the Thames River Police in 1798. Robert PEEL, home secretary, created the Metropolitan Police (1829), a professional uniformed constabulary, answerable to his office, which regularly patrolled London's streets (excepting the City) on foot, armed with truncheons. Plain-clothes detectives were added in 1842. The 'Met.' provided a model for emulation: boroughs were required (1835), and counties permitted (1839), to provide formal policing. London's City Day Police was re-established as the City of London Police (1839).

The development of county forces was uneven until 1856, when they became compulsory and subject to Home Office inspection, with central government paying half the cost. Each borough ran its police through a Watch Committee; JUSTICES OF THE PEACE directed the county forces, in conjunction with county councillors from 1888. The first policewomen were recruited in 1915, and the first woman chief constable, Pauline Clare, appointed in 1995 (in Lancashire).

Borough and county forces gradually merged until the Police Act 1964 introduced a standardized system of local police areas and authorities (outside London), the latter comprising councillors and magistrates. They were replaced in 2012 by elected police and crime commissioners (one per force). In 2015, there were 39 police forces in England, each headed by a chief constable.

POLICE, IRELAND From 1715 the Irish Parliament authorized the appointment of high constables for BARONIES (subdivisions of SHIRES); and watches were sometimes organized in PARISHES. The first uniformed, armed police force in the British Isles operated in DUBLIN, to suppress disorder, 1786–95 and (under government control) from 1799. It was replaced in 1836 by the unarmed Dublin Metropolitan Police (DMP).

In 1814 Robert PEEL founded the paramilitary Peace Preservation Force (armed chief constable and sub-constables, nicknamed 'Peelers', under a magistrate) for temporary deployment in disturbed areas. Considered inadequate, it was supplemented by nationwide county and baronial forces from 1822, grouped into four provinces. Thomas DRUMMOND amalgamated most forces under central authority in 1838 as the Constabulary of Ireland (renamed Royal Irish Constabulary, RIC, 1867). Separate forces operated in BELFAST (1816–65), Dublin, and LONDONDERRY (1832–70). In 1870 the RIC numbered about 12,000, the DMP 1000.

During the War of IRISH INDEPENDENCE (1919–21) the RIC was reinforced by auxiliary forces such as the so-called BLACK AND TANS and the ULSTER SPECIAL CONSTABULARY, and following the PARTITION OF IRELAND (1921) was replaced. *See also* POLICE, NORTHERN IRELAND/SOUTHERN IRELAND.

POLICE, NORTHERN IRELAND The province (formed May 1921) took over part of the Royal Irish Constabulary and the ULSTER SPECIAL CONSTABULARY (USC), both armed. The former was replaced from 1 June 1922 by the armed Royal Ulster Constabulary (RUC), which became largely Protestant. Part of the USC was disbanded in 1926, leaving the part-time 'B Specials' who were almost entirely Protestant. In the late 1920s there were 3000 RUC officers and 12,000 Specials.

In the late 1960s heavy-handed policing of the CIVIL RIGHTS MOVEMENT (e.g., baton charges) inflamed sectarian conflict, resulting in the TROUBLES (1968–1990s). From Aug. 1969 British troops were also required to keep order. Following the 'Hunt Report' (Oct. 1969), the Specials were disbanded (31 March 1970) and replaced by police reserves and the Army-controlled Ulster Defence Regiment, and

the RUC was reorganized. Police primacy in peacekeeping was promoted from 1975.

As part of the 1990s PEACE PROCESS, republicans sought disbandment of the RUC. Following recommendations by the 'Patten Report' (1999), it was replaced on 4 Nov. 2001 by the (armed) 'Police Service of Northern Ireland' which sought to represent all sections of society. The new policing arrangements were endorsed by the republican PROVISIONAL SINN FÉIN at a special conference in Jan. 2007. *See also* PARAMILITARY ORGANIZATIONS, NORTHERN IRELAND.

POLICE, SCOTLAND Until the mid 19th century policing was rudimentary. Local constables are mentioned in 1456 and some BURGHS maintained town guards. From 1718 constables were appointed by JUSTICES OF THE PEACE, while burghs began establishing police forces from 1800.

In 1833 royal and barony burghs were permitted to introduce police forces, as were shires from 1839 (under COMMISSIONERS OF SUPPLY) and parliamentary burghs from 1847. From 1850 other populous places could be designated 'police burghs' and establish forces. By the 1850s most urban areas had a force. In 1857 forces were made compulsory in shires. Police authorities (commissioners or town councillors) were responsible to the home secretary until 1885, then to the SECRETARY FOR SCOTLAND. From 1890 county forces were supervised jointly by county councillors and commissioners.

Around 1900 there were 64 forces, merged into 32 by 1920, some being joint-county forces. Under the 1956 Police (Scotland) Act they were reduced to 22, and in 1975 to eight (corresponding to regions). The regional forces were amalgamated as the Police Service of Scotland in 2013. It covered the largest geographical area within the UK, and had the second largest number of staff (after London's Metropolitan Police). *See also* LOCAL GOVERNMENTAL STRUCTURES, SCOTLAND; TOWN GOVERNMENT, SCOTLAND.

POLICE, SOUTHERN IRELAND The IRISH FREE STATE recruited men for a new, armed 'Civic Guard' from Feb. 1922, to replace the Irish Republican Police (founded 1920) and Royal Irish Constabulary (disbanded Aug.). It was disarmed following a mutiny (May 1922), and established by law in 1923 as An Garda Síochána (Irish, meaning 'Guardian of the Peace'). Many early recruits were former IRISH VOLUNTEERS. The Dublin Metropolitan Police was amalgamated with the Garda in 1925. Women were recruited from 1958. In the early 21st century the force had about 12,000 officers.

POLICE, WALES From the 16th century or earlier policing was undertaken by unpaid PARISH or BOROUGH constables who were chosen annually. In 1835 boroughs were obliged to establish full-time police forces; half had done so by 1839, when JUSTICES OF THE PEACE were permitted to found county (or shire) forces. Four counties established forces by 1845; the other nine followed when county forces were made compulsory (1856).

From the late 19th century borough forces were integrated into county forces, and county forces were amalgamated from 1948 onwards. From 1964 each force was supervised by a police authority. Amalgamations of county and borough forces in 1967–9 produced four forces. Police authorities were replaced in 2012 by elected police and crime commissioners (one per force). The first woman chief constable, Barbara Wilding, was appointed in 2003 (in South Wales).

POLITICAL CARICATURE Apart from isolated early examples, satirical illustration of British politicians began with caricatures of Robert WALPOLE (prime minister 1721–42). It flourished c.1780–1820 when James Gillray (1756–1815) and Thomas Rowlandson (1757–1827) sold popular prints which savagely lampooned Charles James FOX, King GEORGE IV and others. George Cruikshank (1792–1878) and Sir John Tenniel (1820–1914) developed a less brutal style which was favoured by later 19th-century periodicals (e.g., *Punch*, *Vanity Fair*). In the 20th century newspapers published political cartoons. Sir David Low (1891–1963) dominated the form c.1920–50. From the 1960s, Gerald Scarfe (b. 1936) led a revival of grotesquerie.

POLITICAL ECONOMY An area of study similar to economics but emphasizing public policy, national wealth and moral considerations. The term was first used in French (*économie politique*) in 1615, and adopted in English in 1767 by Scotsman Sir James Steuart. Exponents included Adam SMITH, David RICARDO and J.S. MILL (18th–19th centuries). 'Economics' was preferred from the later 19th century by writers such as Alfred MARSHALL who reformulated the subject as abstract relationships (e.g., 'demand curves'). *See also* CLASSICAL AND NEOCLASSICAL ECONOMICS.

POLITICAL PARTIES Organized parties as major participants in political activity originated in England in the late 17th century during the EXCLUSION CRISIS (1678–81), when opposing sides became labelled TORY and WHIG (1679). Early parties were loose, informal organizations even when, as in the reign of Queen ANNE (1702–14), they fiercely contested elections. Allegiances spread through Great Britain and Ireland.

Whig dominance from 1715 reduced the value of party labels as indications of political allegiance: the Whigs fragmented into aristocratic factions (e.g., COBHAM'S CUBS). Party identities were revived in the early 19th century. After the GREAT REFORM ACT (1832) politics were seen as mainly a struggle between Whigs and CONSERVATIVES. Both found

that election management required more complex national and local organization (party-sponsored clubs).

Parties remained susceptible to division. The Conservatives split over the CORN LAWS (1846), creating an unstable situation until the LIBERAL PARTY emerged in the 1860s (*see* PEELITES). Between the 1860s and early 20th century, Liberals and Conservatives were the main parties, with the IRISH PARLIAMENTARY PARTY also influential. Liberals became divided over Irish HOME RULE in 1886 (*see* LIBERAL UNIONISTS).

From the 1920s the LABOUR PARTY effectively replaced the Liberals as a major party, though it split in 1931 (*see* NATIONAL GOVERNMENT). Conservatives and Labour remained the main parties until the 21st century when they were challenged by LIBERAL DEMOCRATS (formed 1988) and the SCOTTISH NATIONAL PARTY.

After the PARTITION OF IRELAND (1921), NORTHERN IRELAND was dominated by Unionist Parties (*see* ULSTER UNIONIST PARTY; DEMOCRATIC UNIONIST PARTY). Nationalists were represented by the NATIONALIST PARTY, SOCIAL DEMOCRATIC AND LABOUR PARTY, and PROVISIONAL SINN FÉIN. *See also* POLITICAL PARTIES, SOUTHERN IRELAND FROM 1922.

POLITICAL PARTIES, SOUTHERN IRELAND FROM 1922 When the IRISH FREE STATE was inaugurated (Dec. 1922), the largest party in the Dáil (Parliament) comprised members of (divided) SINN FÉIN who supported the ANGLO-IRISH TREATY (1921). In April 1923 they founded CUMANN NA NGAEDHEAL, which remained the governing party until 1932. Anti-treaty Sinn Féin members, the second largest party, abstained from the Dáil. The small LABOUR PARTY (founded 1912) acted as the Opposition. Elections to the Dáil were based on multi-member constituencies and proportional representation, a system that enabled smaller parties and independents to gain representation.

In 1926 Éamon DE VALERA founded FIANNA FÁIL, which effectively displaced Sinn Féin. It held power 1932–73 (except for 1948–51, 1954–7). Its long-term rival was FINE GAEL, formed in 1933 as successor to Cumann na nGaedhael. Labour was usually third. Other left-wing parties were usually short-lived (*see* SAOR ÉIRE; CLANN NA POBLACHTA).

From 1973 there were frequent changes of government. Fine Gael could achieve power only by making coalitions, usually involving Labour. From 1989 Fianna Fáil also made coalitions, usually with the PROGRESSIVE DEMOCRATS, a breakaway party from Fianna Fáil (1985–2009).

In the 1980s–90s other new parties were formed. They included PROVISIONAL SINN FÉIN, which entered electoral politics after the 1981 HUNGER STRIKES in Northern Ireland. It won its first Dáil seat in 1997 and in 2016 became the third largest party (23 seats). The Green Party contested parliamentary elections from 1982 (initially as the

Ecology Party). It won its first seat in 1998, six seats in 2002 and 2007, and participated in the 2007–11 governments of Bertie AHERN and Brian COWEN (Fianna Fáil). In 2016, eight parties plus independents won Dáil seats. At the 2020 general election, Provisional Sinn Féin and Fianna Fáil won the largest numbers of seats with 37 each. *See also* SOUTHERN IRELAND FROM 1922.

POLL TAXES, ENGLAND Charges imposed on adults, rather than on fixed property, possessions or income, at standard rates (from ME *polle*, meaning 'head'). They were levied intermittently from 1222 (tax to aid the defence of Jerusalem). Poll taxes were charged in 1377, 1379 and 1381 to fund war with France (*see* HUNDRED YEARS WAR); the last provoked the PEASANTS' REVOLT. They were also imposed in 1512, 1514, 1641, 1660, 1667, 1678 and 1698. A similar tax was introduced in Great Britain in 1989–90 (*see* COMMUNITY CHARGE). *See also* TAXATION, ENGLAND AND WALES BEFORE 1660; TAXATION, ENGLAND, WALES AND GREAT BRITAIN FROM 1660.

PONSONBY, JOHN (b. 29 March 1713 at Bessborough, Co. Kilkenny, Ireland; d. 12 Dec. 1789, probably in Ireland, aged 76). Ponsonby entered the Irish House of Commons in 1739 and was appointed first commissioner of revenue in 1744 (giving him some control of government patronage). In 1753–4 he and others (including Archbishop George STONE) brought about the dismissal of Commons speaker Henry BOYLE from government posts (*see* MONEY BILL DISPUTE). When Boyle retired as speaker, Ponsonby replaced him (26 April 1756), thereby enhancing his role as an 'undertaker' (power-broker).

In 1768–9 Ponsonby allowed two defeats of the government in Commons votes, allegedly because he had received insufficient reward. The chief governor, Viscount TOWNSHEND, dismissed him from the revenue commission (1770), took control of government patronage, and forced Ponsonby's resignation from the speakership (Feb. 1771). *See also* PROTESTANT ASCENDANCY.

POOR LAW AMENDMENT ACT, 1834 Legislation which reorganized POOR RELIEF in England and Wales to reduce expenditure. From *c.*1800 costs rose by over 60%, partly because underemployed men in rural areas were supported.

The Act created 'poor law unions' (15,000 parishes or townships grouped into 600 unions), requiring each to provide a workhouse for relief of the impotent (elderly, sick) and the destitute able-bodied. Outdoor relief (maintenance outside the workhouse) was generally forbidden. Unions were administered by elected guardians under government supervision. *See also* CHADWICK, EDWIN; POOR LAW GUARDIANS, BOARDS OF.

POOR LAW GUARDIANS, BOARDS OF Elected local bodies which operated the poor law (within unions or districts): in England and Wales under the 1834 POOR LAW AMENDMENT ACT, in Ireland under the 1838 POOR RELIEF (IRELAND) ACT. They were abolished in the IRISH FREE STATE in 1925, in England and Wales in 1929, and in Northern Ireland in 1946. *See also* POOR RELIEF, ENGLAND AND WALES/IRELAND.

POOR LAW (SCOTLAND) ACT Passed by the UK Parliament in 1845, following the report by a royal commission in 1844, the Act transferred poor relief from kirk sessions of the Church of SCOTLAND to the State. It established parochial boards (partly elected) and a Board of Supervision in Edinburgh. Applicants for relief were given entitlement to immediate help. Boards could combine to provide workhouses, and were required to lodge the insane poor in asylums. Arrangements continued until reformed in 1894. The Act was repealed in 1948. *See also* POOR RELIEF, SCOTLAND; PARISH, CIVIL FUNCTIONS OF, SCOTLAND.

POOR RELIEF, ENGLAND AND WALES Until the 16th century charity was the main support, from kindred, wealthy individuals and institutions (monasteries, hospitals from 11th century, almshouses from late 14th century). From the mid 14th century, poor people were categorized as respectable or undeserving. Money was collected in 'poor boxes' from the 15th century. The DISSOLUTION of monasteries, hospitals, CHANTRIES and GUILDS (1530s–40s) reduced institutional provision.

From 1495 (Vagabonds Act) the State acted over concerns about vagrants, beggars and the poor. The 1536 Vagabonds Act, requiring weekly alms collections, used the parish as the primary unit. The 1552 Poor Act imposed regular poor relief. The 1572 Vagabonds and Poor Act introduced parish overseers, assessment of needs, and taxation ('poor rate'). The Poor Relief Act of 1598 consolidated arrangements (replaced 1601), although application spread slowly. Relief consisted mostly of pensions and short-term relief. In 1662 the Act of Settlement allowed potentially needy newcomers to a parish to be returned home.

From the 1690s authorities experimented with workhouses – places providing relief and work. The 1722 Workhouse Test Act (or 'Knatchbull's Act') allowed parishes to confine relief to a workhouse and permitted unions of parishes to provide workhouses. 'Gilbert's Act', 1782, permitted unions to use both 'outdoor relief' (for able-bodied persons) and poorhouses (for others). Low rural wages were sometimes supplemented (e.g., by 1795 Speenhamland Scheme for Berkshire).

The 1834 POOR LAW AMENDMENT ACT radically reorganized relief to reduce costs. Unions became compulsory; relief was mainly confined to workhouses. But outdoor relief re-expanded because it was cheaper during economic depressions. From 1869 the CHARITY ORGANISATION SOCIETY and similar societies provided assistance.

Arrangements were replaced in the 20th century: by old age PENSIONS (1909); NATIONAL INSURANCE (1911); Public Assistance Committees providing means-tested benefits, with workhouses converted into hospitals (1929). From the 1940s a WELFARE STATE sought to prevent poverty.

POOR RELIEF, IRELAND Before the 18th century relief depended mostly on kindred, communities and religious bodies. A few charities were founded in the 17th and 18th centuries (e.g., almshouses). The Irish Parliament's Poor Relief Act (or Mendicity Act) of 1772 required counties and boroughs to establish subscription funds for relief, license beggars, and build workhouses (only six established). Landowners feared that a rate-based system, as in England, would encourage population increase.

Rural unrest in the 1810s–20s, and fear of increased Irish immigration, persuaded the British government to establish a commission on the poor (1833), but its recommendations for improving rural conditions were rejected (1836). The English system was introduced (under the English Poor Law Commission), with workhouses funded by unions of TOWNLANDS (see POOR RELIEF (IRELAND) ACT, 1838).

In 1847 the GREAT FAMINE forced the introduction of 'outdoor relief' (for the aged, poor widows, etc.) and provision of food for some able-bodied; an Irish commission was also created. Although a million people were relieved in 1848–9, the system was inadequate. In 1849 stronger unions were forced to support impoverished ones.

Subsequent developments included provision of hospitals and dispensaries (from 1851), and extension of outdoor relief (1862). In 1872 the Local Government Board assumed the commission's work. The system continued until 1925 in the IRISH FREE STATE (unions replaced by county boards), and until 1945 in NORTHERN IRELAND.

POOR RELIEF, SCOTLAND Before the mid 16th century, poor relief was a Christian duty for individuals or religious houses. Begging was allowed, though the 1424 Beggars Act distinguished 'impotent' (deserving) from undeserving poor, and banned able-bodied beggars.

At the REFORMATION (1560), reformers designated relief as a duty for local churches. KIRK SESSIONS assumed responsibility and applied general funds (from collections and fines). In 1574 an Act modelled on the 1572 English Poor Law Act required parishes to relieve their poor, by levying a stent (rate), and instituted overseers (Act reaffirmed 1579). In practice sessions retained control (recognized by Act 1592), and generally reserved rates for crises (e.g., harvest failure). Acts of 1663 and 1672 specified ratepayers as HERITORS, tenants and occupiers, while legal

judgments of 1751–2 permitted heritors to supervise administration, enabling them to resist assessments.

Industrial and town growth from the 1780s caused increased use of rating and workhouses. In the 1830s the system's inadequacy during recessions and its arbitrariness were criticized, while the DISRUPTION (1843) ended the Church's comprehensiveness. In 1845 responsibility was transferred to the State: parochial boards were instituted under a Board of Supervision (see POOR LAW (SCOTLAND) ACT). Parishes levying regular rates rose from 239 in 1839 to 644 in 1849 (27–73%).

Local administration was transferred to parish councils in 1894, to county and burgh councils in 1930. Separate rating ended in 1926. During the 20th century poor relief was replaced by Britain-wide tax-funded provisions: PENSIONS (1909), NATIONAL INSURANCE (1911), Assistance schemes (from 1930s), and the WELFARE STATE (from late 1940s).

POOR RELIEF, WALES *see* POOR RELIEF, ENGLAND AND WALES

POOR RELIEF (IRELAND) ACT, 1838 Legislation passed by the UK Parliament which instituted State-organized relief by replicating the reorganized system of England and Wales (*see* POOR LAW AMENDMENT ACT, 1834). It provided for relief in workhouses, at managers' discretion, funded by unions of TOWNLANDS. Unions (total 130) were administered by elected POOR LAW GUARDIANS who were accountable to the English Poor Law Commission. *See also* POOR RELIEF, IRELAND.

POPE, ALEXANDER (b. 21 May 1688 at London, England; d. 30 May 1744 at Twickenham, Middlesex, England, aged 56). A Roman Catholic who suffered ill health, Pope became a poet, critic and satirist (resident at Twickenham from 1719). His works include the *Essay on Criticism* (1711) and mock epic poem *The Rape of the Lock* (1712). His translations of Homer's *Iliad* (1715–20) and *Odyssey* (1725–6) made him financially independent. His satire *The Dunciad* (1729) criticized WHIG politicians. He attacked them again in *Moral Essays*, for allowing the moneyed interest to corrupt politics. *See also* ENGLISH LITERATURE, ENGLAND.

POPISH PLOT In England, 1678–81, a supposed Catholic plot, allegedly ordered by the Pope, to assassinate King CHARLES II, make his Catholic brother James, duke of York, king, and to organize uprisings in England and Ireland. It was reported to the government in Sept. 1678 by Titus Oates, a confidence trickster, and Israel Tonge.

Charles ordered enforcement of anti-Catholic laws and accepted another TEST ACT excluding Catholics from Parliament (except York). Many Catholic priests, peers and gentry were arrested (mainly Nov.–Dec. 1678), and about

35 were executed including York's former secretary. The earl of SHAFTESBURY and others exploited the plot to seek exclusion of James from the succession (*see* EXCLUSION CRISIS). Belief in the plot declined after 1681. In 1685, after James's accession, Oates was convicted of perjury. *See also* PLUNKETT AFFAIR; JAMES VII/II; RECUSANCY, ENGLAND AND WALES.

POPLARISM Term used in Great Britain in the 1920s–30s for defiance of central government by local authorities or poor law boards with LABOUR PARTY majorities, usually referring to their practice of paying wages or relief at above approved levels. It derived from the LONDON borough of Poplar where in 1921 the council, led George LANSBURY, refused to pay for central London bodies (e.g., fire brigade) in protest at the unequal burden of rates between London boroughs. This resulted in imprisonment of 30 councillors. *See also* LONDON, GOVERNMENT OF.

POPULATION, ENGLAND Using DOMESDAY BOOK, population is estimated in the late 11th century at between 1.1 and 2.25 million. During the 12th–13th centuries it doubled or even trebled, to possibly 6 million *c.*1300. It was reduced by about 15% by FAMINES in 1315–17, and by around 40% by the BLACK DEATH of 1348–9. In the late 14th century population is estimated at 2.2–3 million (using taxation records). It declined further as a result of PLAGUE and difficult economic conditions. In the 1520s population stood at 1.8–2.3 million.

Population then grew again, to 3.6 million in 1581 and 5.23 million in 1651. It declined to 5.06 million in 1701 because of disease and emigration.

Since the early 18th century growth has been continuous, due to such factors as lower ages of marriage and improved conditions. Population increased modestly to 5.63 million in 1740. From the 1740s a consistent excess of births over deaths (even in towns) caused a faster increase, and in the late 18th and early 19th centuries expansion was unprecedented, with population reaching 8.65 million in 1801 (corrected census total). For a century it rose at 10–16% per decade, reaching 21.64 million in 1871, 30.51 million 1901, and 33.65 million in 1911. Growth then fell to 5–7% per decade. Population reached 41.15 million in 1951 and 46.41 million in 1971. After stagnation in the 1970s, population growth resumed, with population reaching 50 million in 2000 and 55.9 million in 2020 (estimate). *See also* NATIONAL AND IMPERIAL CENSUSES; MALTHUS, T.R.

POPULATION, IRELAND Lack of records prevents accurate estimation before the 18th century. The population of early medieval Ireland (before 12th century) is commonly estimated at half a million. As elsewhere in Europe, population increased during the 12th and 13th centuries,

reaching roughly 1 million by 1300. The 14th century was a period of decline. The population of the English colony possibly fell by 40–50%, mainly because of the BLACK DEATH (1348), though the GAELIC REVIVAL was also a factor. Further plagues, famine and war took their toll. Mortality among Gaelic Irish was possibly lower.

By 1500 the total population had recovered to 1 million. It grew to about 1.4 million by 1600, then increased rapidly to 2.1 million by the 1640s. There was renewed decline in the late 17th century, but by the early 18th century the population numbered over 2 million. It rose slightly until 1740–1, when 10–20% were killed by famine.

From the 1750s, with economic expansion, population increased rapidly, reaching 4.4 million by 1791, 7 million by 1821, and 7.8 million by 1831. It peaked at about 8.5 million in 1845 when it was hit by the GREAT FAMINE (1845–51). With deaths and emigration, population fell to 6.5 million by 1851, and continued to decline reaching 4.4 million in 1911.

Following the partition of Ireland, the IRISH FREE STATE contained 2.97 million people and NORTHERN IRELAND 1.25 million (1926). Population declined in southern Ireland until the 1960s (1961, 2.8 million) but rose slightly in Northern Ireland (1961, 1.4 million). Populations reached 3.8 and 1.7 million by 2000, 4.9 and 1.8 million by 2020. *See also* PREHISTORIC IRELAND, POPULATION; FAMINES, IRELAND; NATIONAL AND IMPERIAL CENSUSES.

POPULATION, SCOTLAND There are no sources for making accurate estimates until 1691, although directions of change are evident. Between the 11th century and *c.*1300 population probably doubled, from possibly 500,000 to 1,000,000. It was savagely cut by the BLACK DEATH (1349–50), perhaps by a third, and further reduced by PLAGUE in the late 14th and 15th centuries, to perhaps 400,000.

Growth had resumed by *c.*1500 and population reached possibly 1.1 or 1.2 million in the 1630s. It then remained steady – the 1691 HEARTH TAX suggests 1,234,000 inhabitants. After losses from FAMINE in the later 1690s, population increased slowly until 1755, when Alexander Webster's ecclesiastical census gives 1,265,380. Growth was stronger in the later 18th century, but at a slower rate than in England. By 1801 population had risen to 1.6 million (census total), an increase of 27% on 1755.

Growth accelerated in the 19th century: population reached 2.9 million by 1851 and 4.47 million by 1901. Expansion then slowed, with population reaching 5.1 million by 1961. It then fluctuated slightly: in 2001 it was 5 million. A more vigorous increase then ensued, mainly because of IMMIGRATION. Population reached 5.5 million in 2011, 5.5 million, in 2020. Scotland's population also became markedly older, with more people aged 65 or over than 15 or younger by 2011. *See also* NATIONAL AND IMPERIAL CENSUSES.

POPULATION, WALES Because sources are poor, figures before 1801 are approximate. Around 1300 Wales contained possibly 200,000–300,000 people. Probably a third died in the BLACK DEATH (1349), and more in later plagues and in the revolt of OWAIN GLYN DŴR (1400–10). Slow recovery began in the later 15th century: by 1540, Wales contained perhaps 215,000–240,000 people.

A surge followed until *c*.1640, when population reached 370,000–390,000. Expansion was strong in N Wales, stimulating renewed inhabitation of uplands and urban growth (*see* TOWNS, WALES). Stagnation followed until the early 18th century when renewed growth raised population to 490,000 in 1750. The first NATIONAL CENSUS in 1801 recorded about 587,000 inhabitants. (Figures include MONMOUTHSHIRE.)

Industrial expansion in the 19th century caused dramatic increase: by 1901, population reached 2.02 million (*see* INDUSTRY, WALES FROM 18TH CENTURY). The SE and NE (to a lesser extent) were especially affected. Glamorgan increased from 250,000 in 1851 to 1.25 million in 1901. Rural areas, however, declined.

Between 1900 and *c*.1945 natural increase was nullified by emigration from industrial areas into England. Renewed growth thereafter generated a population of 2.9 million by 2000 (two-thirds in the SE and NE) and 3.2 million by 2020 (estimate). *See also* PLAGUE, WALES.

PORTEOUS AFFAIR An episode in Edinburgh, Scotland, 1736. After a smuggler's execution, a mob threw stones at the town guard (14 April) which opened fire, killing six and wounding about 12. Their captain, James Porteous, was found guilty of homicide. After his execution was postponed, he was seized and hanged by a mob (7 Sept.). When the British government, under Robert WALPOLE, threatened to punish Edinburgh Council for complicity, the (2nd) duke of ARGYLL was offended. The ensuing rift contributed to Walpole's fall in 1742.

PORTLAND, 3RD DUKE OF (b. 14 April 1738 at Bulstrode, Buckinghamshire, England; d. 30 Oct. 1809 at Bulstrode, aged 71). William Bentinck succeeded as duke in 1762 and entered the House of Lords where he supported WHIGS concerned about an alleged exertion of power by King GEORGE III.

In 1782 Portland was lord lieutenant of Ireland in the brief ministry of the marquess of ROCKINGHAM. Following Rockingham's death (July), he became a Whig leader. From April 1783 he was nominally PRIME MINISTER of the coalition ministry formed by Charles James FOX and Lord NORTH. He resigned in Dec. when the Lords threw out Fox's India Bill (reforming the EAST INDIA COMPANY) at the instigation of George III.

In 1794, when opposition Whigs split over dangers arising from the FRENCH REVOLUTION, conservative 'Portland

Whigs', influenced by Edmund BURKE, joined the ministry of William PITT the Younger. Portland served as home secretary (until 1801). In 1807 Portland again became prime minister but, debilitated by illness, he proved unable to manage a Cabinet containing the rivals George CANNING and Viscount CASTLEREAGH. He resigned in Sept. 1809. Succeeded by Spencer PERCEVAL. *See also* ROCKINGHAM WHIGS.

PORTSMOUTH, DUCHESS OF (b. Sept. 1649 at Kéroualle, Brittany, France; d. 14 Nov. 1734 at Paris, France, aged 85). Louise de Kéroualle joined the English royal court in 1670 and from Oct. 1671 was the main mistress of King CHARLES II. Created duchess of Portsmouth in Aug. 1673, she was given a suite of rooms at WHITEHALL PALACE in Westminster. Influential in politics and diplomacy, she supported the earl of DANBY (1670s) and enabled the earl of SUNDERLAND to regain favour (1682). She lost influence after Charles's death (Feb. 1685) and then lived mainly in France.

PORTUGAL, ENGLISH AND BRITISH RELATIONS WITH Portugal is regarded as 'England's oldest ally', based on alliances of 1373 and 1386 to assist the attempt by JOHN OF GAUNT to rule the Spanish kingdom of Castile. Mercantile rivalry caused tensions in the 16th century, and England initially failed to oppose Spanish annexation of Portugal in 1580 – a belated naval expedition by Francis DRAKE proved abortive (1589). After Portugal regained independence (1640), it bargained commercial advantages for renewed English guarantees (1642, 1654, 1661). The 1661 treaty of alliance and marriage (Catherine of Braganza to King CHARLES II of England) included the cession of Bombay (in INDIA) and TANGIER (in NW Africa) to England.

Great Britain (from 1707) generally upheld Portugal's independence by defending its neutrality. It liberated the country from the French in 1808–11. Lord PALMERSTON (foreign secretary 1830–4, 1835–41) made repeated diplomatic efforts to stabilize the Portuguese monarchy. A British and Spanish force briefly intervened in 1847.

In the late 19th century relations were dominated by the competitive SCRAMBLE FOR AFRICA. In WORLD WAR I, Portugal fought with the Allies (1916–18); in WORLD WAR II, it permitted Britain to use the Azores as a military base (1943–5). Like Britain, Portugal was a founding member of the NORTH ATLANTIC TREATY ORGANIZATION (1949); it joined the EUROPEAN ECONOMIC COMMUNITY in 1986.

POSSESSORY ASSIZES In England, legal procedures provided by King HENRY II (1160s–70s) as replacements for trial by battle in disputes over 'seisin' or justifiable possession (*see* TENURES, ENGLAND FROM 1066). Each was quick and began with the plaintiff obtaining (for a fee) a WRIT from the royal Chancery ordering a 'recognition', whereby 12 neighbours would testify to the facts on oath before royal justices (or later commissioners).

In the earliest, 'novel disseisin' ('new dispossession', c.1166), the plaintiff complained that the defendant had 'unjustly and without a judgment' deprived him of seisin. *Mort d'ancestor* ('death of an ancestor', first found in the Assize of NORTHAMPTON, 1176) settled disputes between a dead man's heirs and his lord. Darrein presentment ('last presentation', probably introduced 1179) gave advowson (right of presentation to an ecclesiastical benefice) to the last presenter or his heir. Novel disseisin became the principal land action of the 13th century. The assizes' popularity contributed to Commissioners of Assize supplanting general eyres from the late 13th century. *See also* COMMON LAW; EYRE.

POST-CHRISTIAN SOCIETY A society in which Christianity was once widely accepted and influential but which has become largely secular, leaving Christianity residual and marginal. For individuals, being unreligious is considered normal and espousing Christianity abnormal.

British society became increasingly 'post-Christian' from the 1960s, as evidenced by low rates of church or chapel attendance; abandonment of baptism, Church marriage and funerals; State promotion of moral positions antagonistic to many Christians (e.g., civil marriage for same-sex couples, instituted in Great Britain in 2014). A similar situation later became evident in the Republic of Ireland, but less so in NORTHERN IRELAND, where the polarization of Catholic and Protestant Christianity continued. While Christianity declined, IMMIGRATION established other religions. *See also* SECULARIZATION; CHURCH–STATE RELATIONS, SOUTHERN IRELAND FROM 1922.

POST OFFICE The UK's postal service, initiated in 1635 by proclamation of a Letter Office for England and Scotland by King CHARLES I. Effectively a government department, it encompassed six post roads from LONDON (developed during the 16th century, served by 'deputy postmasters' and riders) and a foreign-post monopoly (granted 1591). A near-monopoly for official and private mail, the office made standard charges for the latter (paid by recipients). During the PROTECTORATE it was re-established (1657) as the 'Post Office' (confirmed at RESTORATION, 1660). A private 'penny post' in London (started 1680) was added in 1682.

Local postmasters developed the system with 'by-posts' (branch routes) and 'cross-posts' (between roads). From 1720 such routes in SW England were 'farmed' (subcontracted) to Ralph Allen of BATH (1693–1764), who developed cross-services throughout England and Wales. Other improvements included services to colonies, more 'penny posts' (from 1770s), mail coaches (1784–1850s) and use of RAILWAYS (1830s).

In 1840 radical reforms advocated by Rowland HILL were implemented, notably the 'penny post' (cheap uniform rate) and prepayment validated by postage stamps. Other innovations included: the pillar box (1852, introduced in the CHANNEL ISLANDS by official and novelist Anthony Trollope), Savings Bank (1861), telegraph service (following nationalization, 1869), and telephone service (by 1912). Letters handled annually rose 1840–1914 from 169 million to 3.5 billion. In 1914 there were over 225,000 staff.

Overseas air services were developed in the 1920s–30s, and motor vehicles were used widely from the 1930s. Although mechanical sorting began in 1935, it was not fully adopted until the 1970s–80s. The organization was reconstituted as a public corporation (1969) and split (1981) into posts and telecommunications (latter privatized 1984 as British Telecom). After periods of varying performance, the postal service was privatized in 2013 (with 168,000 employees), although it now faced competitors and declining letter volumes caused by new ELECTRONIC COMMUNICATIONS. *See also* SECRET SERVICES, UNITED KINGDOM; POST OFFICE, IRELAND.

POST OFFICE, IRELAND Communications organized by England's government began in 1562 when it contracted a boat service from Holyhead to DUBLIN, improved riding services to Holyhead, and appointed a postmaster in Dublin. Effects were limited. More developments followed the proclamation of a postal monopoly in England (1635; *see* POST OFFICE): a new postmaster in Dublin, Evan Vaughan, began arranging distribution. By 1656, after the IRISH WARS (1641–52), there were three post roads (to N, W, S). Ireland was included in the 1657 re-establishment of the Post Office. Further expansion included new post roads and 'by-posts' (branch routes). The Dublin office was subordinated by legislation to England's postmaster-general in 1711. A cheap 'penny post' was started in Dublin in 1765.

In 1784 Ireland's newly independent PARLIAMENT made Ireland's Post Office independent. Services were improved by mail coaches (1789), road improvements resulting from UK legislation (1805), and regular steamships across the Irish Sea (1821).

The Irish and British offices were reamalgamated in 1831. Further improvements included use of Charles Bianconi's 'cars' (horse-drawn carts, from 1833), 'penny post' (1840) and railway transport (1853). The official and novelist Anthony Trollope was influential in raising efficiency (1841–51, 1853–9). The Post Office took over telephone services by 1912. In 1916 Dublin's General Post Office was briefly used by nationalist rebels as headquarters for a self-proclaimed republic (*see* EASTER RISING).

Following the PARTITION OF IRELAND, staff and services in southern Ireland were transferred to the IRISH FREE STATE (1922) and operated 1924–84 as part of the CIVIL

SERVICE; they were then reconstituted as the State-sponsored agencies An Post and Telecom Éireann (latter privatized in 1999 as eircom plc). In Northern Ireland the UK Post Office sustained a religiously balanced workforce during the TROUBLES (1968–90s). *See also* ELECTRONIC COMMUNICATIONS, IRELAND.

POST-ROMAN BRITAIN In AD 400 southern Britain belonged to the Roman Empire, though most inhabitants were Britons. Roman Britain's northern border was HADRIAN'S WALL, across the Tyne–Solway isthmus. Between the wall and the FORTH–CLYDE ISTHMUS were descendants of British IRON AGE TRIBES (Damnonii, Novantae, Selgovae, Votadini). N of the Forth–Clyde isthmus were Britons known as PICTS. Brittonic was spoken probably throughout Britain.

In the early 5th century Britain became separated from the Roman Empire: a usurper emperor, CONSTANTINE III, departed with troops (407); officials were allegedly expelled (409). Bulk imports of coinage had ended (by 402). The economy deteriorated: pottery production dwindled; coinage use ceased (by 420s); towns and VILLAS were abandoned (by 440s). Romano-British élites probably assumed authority and became warlords. Kingdoms were established in W Britain (*see* WALES), and elsewhere in former Roman Britain (e.g., DUMNONIA in SW; ELMET, DEIRA, BERNICIA, RHEGED in N). Christianity survived in western areas, and was strengthened by monasticism; it also affected Ireland (*see* CONVERSION OF IRELAND). LATIN continued to be studied (*see* GILDAS).

From the 430s, Continental Germanic people arrived in southern Britain, some probably as hired troops, others as immigrant kindreds. By 500, settlers lived in much of the E and SE; by 600, Germanic (or Anglo-Saxon) kingdoms extensively covered southern Britain (*see* KINGSHIP, ANGLO-SAXON). (British kingdoms survived in W Britain.) Britons assimilated to Germanic culture (e.g., language). Christianity was widely adopted in the 7th century, and a single English kingdom was formed in the 10th century.

N of former Roman Britain, the kingdoms of GODODDIN and Clyde Rock (STRATHCYLDE) emerged, and Irish ('Scots') immigrated into western parts, forming 'Scottish DÁL RIATA' and spreading Christianity (6th century). (Rheged and Gododdin were conquered by Germanic rulers in the 7th century.) A UNION OF SCOTS AND PICTS, from *c.*842, created a kingdom (Alba) which eventually encompassed N Britain and became Gaelic-speaking (*see* SCOTLAND). *See also* ROMAN BRITAIN; GERMANUS; VORTIGERN; AMBROSIUS AURELIANUS; GERMANIC IMMIGRATION, SOUTHERN BRITAIN; ENGLAND, FORMATION OF; ENGLISH LANGUAGE.

POTTERY, PREHISTORIC BRITAIN Pottery marks the beginning of the NEOLITHIC PERIOD (*c.*4300 BC); before long, fine bowls were produced and traded over 125 mi

(200 km). Plain, round-based vessels gradually evolved into coarser decorated wares culminating in the Collared Urns of the Early BRONZE AGE (*c.*2000 BC). Flat-based decorated BEAKERS appeared in the early 3rd millennium, interacting with the local traditions to produce the so-called Food Vessels.

In the Middle Bronze Age (*c.*1600– *c.*1200 BC) pottery-using declined, some areas giving it up until medieval times (5th century AD or later). In southern Britain new Continental fashions were adopted in the Late Bronze and early IRON AGES (*c.*1200– *c.*600 BC); the middle Iron Age (*c.*400) saw distinctive localized styles in southern Britain. In the 1st century BC the potter's wheel was introduced, and mass production started in the S and SE.

POTTERY, PREHISTORIC IRELAND Production of pottery began in the NEOLITHIC (*c.*4800– *c.*2500 BC). The basic form was the carinated bowl (a bowl with an angular shoulder). This was modified, increasingly decorated and became regionally varied through the Neolithic. A development used principally in funerary monuments was the decorated bipartite bowl. A range of uncarinated, decorated bowls occurs from 3600 BC. Grooved Ware and BEAKER pottery were in use in the CHALCOLITHIC–Early BRONZE AGE. A range of funerary pottery was used in the Early and Middle Bronze Age (*c.*2200– *c.*1200 BC), including Food Vessels (Bowl and Vase) and Cinerary Urns (Vase, Encrusted, Cordoned and Collared). In later prehistory coarse, flat-bottomed, bucket-shaped pottery was used in domestic and ceremonial activity. Analysis suggests that Irish prehistoric pottery was made and used locally.

POULSON AFFAIR In Great Britain, a corruption scandal in 1972. The bankruptcy hearing of architect John Poulson (1910–93) revealed that he had won contracts by bribing politicians and officials. The home secretary, Reginald MAUDLING, who was responsible for the (London) Metropolitan Police, resigned (18 July) because of an indirect association with Poulson. (Poulson had supported a charity of which Maudling's wife, Beryl Maudling, was a patron.)

POWELL, ENOCH (b. 16 June 1912 at Birmingham, Warwickshire, England; d. 8 Feb. 1998 at London, England, aged 85). A classical scholar, Powell became a Conservative MP in 1950. Appointed financial secretary to the Treasury in 1957, he resigned with Peter THORNEYCROFT when the British prime minister, Harold MACMILLAN, rejected spending cuts to combat INFLATION (Jan. 1958). He nevertheless served Macmillan as minister of health 1960–3.

On 20 April 1968, at the Midland Hotel, BIRMINGHAM, Powell denounced social tensions caused by coloured IMMIGRATION in his so-called 'rivers of blood' speech. Though the Conservative leader Edward HEATH dismissed him from the Shadow Cabinet, he received much public support. A fierce critic of Heath, Powell left the Conservative Party in 1974 to oppose the UK's membership of the EUROPEAN ECONOMIC COMMUNITY. He sat as an ULSTER UNIONIST MP 1974–87, and condemned the HILLS-BOROUGH AGREEMENT (1985).

POWELL, VAVASOR (b. 1617 at Heyop, Radnorshire, Wales; d. 27 Oct. 1670 at London, England, aged 52 or 53). A supporter of PURITANISM and preacher along the Anglo-Welsh BORDER, Powell fought for Parliament (1648) in the Second CIVIL WAR. As a Fifth Monarchist he was appalled by Oliver CROMWELL's assumption of power (Dec. 1653) and organized opposition, but in 1655 quelled a Royalist rising. After the RESTORATION (1660) he was frequently imprisoned. *See also* ENGLISH REVOLUTION SECTS.

POWYS A kingdom in medieval WALES, in C Wales; it originally included NE Wales and parts of modern Cheshire and Shropshire (NW and W England). Tradition claimed foundation in the 5th century by Cadell Deyrnllug, with the aid of GERMANUS. Its name is derived from Latin *pagenses*, meaning 'people of a district [*pagus*]'.

Early Powys was perhaps ruled by ancestors of the two dynasties recorded from the early 7th century, when they opposed expansion by MERCIA (C England) from the E. The southern boundary with Mercia apparently collapsed *c.*640 though the northern one survived until the mid 9th century. Powys then passed – in or after 855 – under RHODRI MAWR of GWYNEDD (NW Wales). It re-emerged as independent in the 11th century, under the dynasty of Bleddyn ap Cynfyn (d. 1097), and expanded briefly under MADOG AP MAREDUDD. On his death (1160) it was divided between his sons and his nephew Owain Cyfeiliog (d. 1197). Division proved permanent.

The separate parts of Powys were now northern Powys, or Powys Fadog ('of Madog'), with its centre at Dinas Bran, ruled by the 'lords of Bromfield'; southern Powys or Powys Wenwynwyn, named after Gwenwynwyn ab Owain Cyfeiliog (ruled 1197–1216). The dynasties were invariably dominated by Gwynedd or England.

After the English Conquest of 1282–3 northern Powys was divided into the English-held lordships of Bromfield and Chirkland (*see* MARCH OF WALES). Lands in southern Powys were restored to Gruffudd ap Gwenwynwyn (d. 1286), to reward loyalty to King EDWARD I of England (later passing to an English family by marriage).

In 1536 southern Powys formed the basis for the new Montgomeryshire (*see* UNION OF WALES WITH ENGLAND). The name Powys was later reused for a regional authority incorporating Montgomeryshire, Radnorshire and Breconshire (1974–96; a unitary authority and county from 1996).

POYNINGS, EDWARD (b. 1459, probably at South-wark, Surrey, England; d. Oct. 1521 at Westenhanger, Kent, England, aged about 62). An experienced soldier (knighted 1485), Poynings was sent to Ireland as lord deputy by King Henry VII of England. He landed with a large retinue on 13 Oct. 1494. He aimed to secure the country against the rebel Perkin WARBECK, reduce control over the government by the Kildare GERALDINES, and revive revenues. Poynings had the (8th) earl of KILDARE arrested (27 Feb. 1495) and sent to England; he also suppressed a Yorkist, pro-Warbeck rebellion in S Ireland (Aug. 1495), and was responsible for POYNINGS' LAW. He returned to England in Dec. 1495. *See also* HENRY VII AND IRELAND.

POYNINGS' LAW In Ireland, a law enacted in the 1494–5 session of Parliament by order of Sir Edward POYNINGS. Future meetings of the Parliament would require the king of England's consent, and intended legislation must first be approved by the English royal COUNCIL. Poynings' Law sought to restrict the use of Parliament by governors of Ireland for their own interests. Most controls were removed by an amendment in 1782. *See also* HENRY VII AND IRELAND; PARLIAMENT, IRELAND; YELVERTON'S ACT.

PRAEMUNIRE, STATUTES OF In England, statutes enacted in 1353, 1365 and 1393 which asserted rights of the Crown against Church courts. The first Statute effectively prevented appeals to the papal court, and the 1393 Statute enabled lawyers to remove cases from Church courts to secular courts. The Statutes were repealed in 1967. *See also* PROVISORS, STATUTES OF; HUNNE AFFAIR; CHURCH, MEDI-EVAL ENGLAND.

PRAYER BOOK, SCOTLAND In 1634–7, by order of King CHARLES I, a Prayer Book was compiled for the Church of SCOTLAND, based on the (1552) English Book of Common Prayer. Though it respected some presbyterian sensitivities, other aspects were condemned as 'popish' (e.g., provision for festivals and saints' days). Its introduction at St Giles Cathedral, Edinburgh, sparked the REVOLT OF 1637 which led to the COVENANTING REVOLUTION. *See also* GLASGOW ASSEMBLY.

PRAYER-BOOK REBELLION A rebellion in SW England, 1549, against the Protestant religious Reformation of King EDWARD VI, especially the new PRAYER BOOK. Revolts broke out in Cornwall (6 June) and Devon (11 June), and rebels besieged Exeter (Devon) unsuccessfully (2 July–6 Aug.). They demanded restoration of the Catholic religious policies of HENRY VIII (d. 1547). The rebels were defeated at Sampford Courtenay (Devon) by a royal army (16–17 Aug.). *See also* REFORMATION, ENGLAND.

PRAYER BOOKS, ENGLAND In the 16th century the government used service books to impose reformed Christianity. The first Book of Common Prayer (1549) was issued for the Church of ENGLAND by the government of Edward, duke of SOMERSET, under an Act of Uniformity. Composed in English by Archbishop Thomas CRANMER, it replaced Catholic manuals (mostly in Latin). It made morning and evening prayer the main services, and prioritized Bible lessons. Yet leading Protestant theologians regarded it as too Catholic. It was replaced in 1552 by a more radical book which viewed Holy Communion as a commemoration rather than sacrifice. When Protestantism was re-established in 1559, the 1552 Prayer Book was reissued with amendments from 1549 to conciliate conservatives (see ELIZABETHAN SETTLEMENT). The 1559 book was attacked for retaining ceremonies, and its use was banned by Parliament in 1645 (see PURITANISM, ENGLAND). A revised book was issued in 1662, after the RESTORATION, including a more dignified communion service. It remained the standard version.

A proposed replacement book was rejected by Parliament in 1928 as too Catholic. From 1965 the Church was permitted to authorize services. An Alternative Service Book was introduced in 1980 and itself replaced by Common Worship in 2000. See also REFORMATION, ENGLAND/WALES.

PRAYER BOOKS, IRELAND In 1549 a government proclamation ordered use of the new English Book of Common Prayer, to disseminate reform. Adopted mostly in English-speaking areas (e.g., the PALE), it was the first book to be printed in Ireland (1551). The more radical 1552 Prayer Book was not introduced officially, though John BALE tried to impose it (in Ossory diocese).

The 1559 version was adopted in 1560, providing standard worship for the Church of IRELAND (modified edition introduced 1604, Irish translation 1608). In 1666 a variant of the English 1662 version was imposed (Irish translation published 1712).

After DISESTABLISHMENT (1871), the Church adopted revised versions (1878, 1926, latter published in Irish 1931). A new Book of Common Prayer became the authorized service book in 2004, in English and Irish versions. See also PRAYER BOOKS, ENGLAND; REFORMATION, IRELAND; ELIZABETHAN SETTLEMENT, IRELAND.

PRAYER BOOKS, WALES see SERVICE BOOKS, WALES

PREHISTORIC BRITAIN Early PALAEOLITHIC settlement by *Homo heidelbergensis*, typified by handaxes, dates from 450,000 BP. From 80,000 Mousterian industries associated with Neanderthal man in Continental Europe appear, and from 30,000 Upper Palaeolithic blade industries used by modern man (*Homo sapiens sapiens*). Occupation ebbed with glacial expansions (see GLACIATIONS); since *c*.11,000

BC it has been continuous. Caves and open settlements on the glacial fringes were occupied. Post-glacial forestation in the MESOLITHIC (*c*.8500–*c*.4300 BC) encouraged coastal and riverine settlement, and seasonal exploitation of open highlands, where hunters, using bows and hunting dogs, followed seasonal movements of deer.

From *c*.4300 BC NEOLITHIC economic activity and technology were adopted (domestic cattle, sheep, pigs; wheat, barley; pottery and polished axes). Burial was collective under LONG BARROWS and MEGALITHIC tombs, or on ceremonial sites (CAUSEWAYED ENCLOSURES); substantial timber trackways were constructed in marshland. From the Late Neolithic (*c*.2800 BC) HENGES were built (e.g., STONEHENGE), and individual burial with grave goods suggests an increasingly hierarchical society, accentuated by copper objects (with BEAKERS) *c*.2700 BC, and, from *c*.1800 BC, bronze metallurgy. (A BRONZE AGE is demarcated from *c*.2300 BC.) Around 1300 BC, in the Middle Bronze Age, there was a decrease in burial and ceremonial monuments, but increasing deposition in hoards and rivers. The landscape was organized with linear earthworks and 'Celtic fields' (e.g., Dartmoor, Devon, SW England).

From the Late BRONZE AGE (*c*.1200 BC onwards) weapon hoards and HILLFORTS indicate institutionalized warfare, a pattern unaltered by the introduction of iron working (*c*.700 BC). In the late IRON AGE from *c*.100 BC Continental contacts increased, with Mediterranean imports known at Hengistbury Head (Dorset, SW England) and COLCHESTER. Society became markedly hierarchical with tribal states such as that ruled by CUNOBELIN. Prehistoric Britain ends with the Roman invasion of AD 43 (see ROMAN BRITAIN).

PREHISTORIC BRITAIN, AGRICULTURE The characteristic features of agriculture – use of domesticated plants (cereals) and animals (cattle, sheep, pigs) – arose piecemeal across the MESOLITHIC–Neolithic transition in the centuries around 4000 BC, eventually supplanting GATHERING AND HUNTING. Operating at subsistence level, NEOLITHIC agriculture was regionally varied and practised in parallel with the use of wild resources. It often involved limited cultivation in shifting woodland clearings and extensive animal husbandry. Some plant and animal species were introduced through contacts across the English Channel. Patchworks of woodland and grassland were reworked over time; by the Early BRONZE AGE (*c*.2300–*c*.1600 BC) there were extensive tracts of open country.

The Middle and Later Bronze Age (*c*.1600–*c*.700 BC) saw the first widespread field systems and land divisions, such as the Reaves on Dartmoor (Devon, SW England). Some systems were used for separating and containing sheep or cattle. However, lynchets within some fields indicate erosion due to cultivation by plough. (Lynchets are formed when soil eroding downslope accumulates along a boundary.)

These later patterns reflect a concern with the production of surpluses for feasting and exchange amongst kin networks. They also suggest the considered use of boundaries, and farming practice itself, to define territories held by people over generations. Animals and crops were sources of wealth and standing – to be held, exchanged or given in feasts.

PREHISTORIC BRITAIN, BURIAL PRACTICES Early NEOLITHIC burial (*c*.4300– *c*.3200 BC) is typified by excarnated (exposed) inhumations under LONG BARROWS and on CAUSEWAYED ENCLOSURES. In the Late NEOLITHIC (*c*.2800– *c*.2300 BC) single inhumation under ROUND BARROWS dominated, which was replaced by cremation in the Early BRONZE AGE (*c*.2300– *c*.1600 BC). Cremation cemeteries are known in the Middle Bronze Age (*c*.1600– *c*.1200 BC), but formal burials are rare throughout the 1st millennium BC. IRON AGE burials are only common in the Arras group of E Yorkshire (5th–1st centuries BC) and in the Aylesford cremation cemeteries of SE England (1st centuries BC and AD).

PREHISTORIC BRITAIN, COINAGE Gold coins imitating Macedonian staters were imported in the late 2nd century BC, followed by silver and potin (high-tin bronze) in the early 1st, and struck bronze coins in the late 1st century BC, perhaps indicating a market economy. Home-produced coins of the late 1st century BC bear names of rulers indicating kings and dynasties among the Catuvellauni (Tasciovanus, CUNOBELIN) and the Atrebates (Commius, Tincommius, Verica). *See also* IRON AGE TRIBES, BRITAIN.

PREHISTORIC BRITAIN, DIET AND LIVING STANDARDS Research on isotopes and trace elements in human bones suggests that there were regionally and socially varied diets for much of PREHISTORY (i.e., 450,000 BP–AD 43), involving combinations of meat, cereals and wild resources. Common ailments included arthritis although dental health was generally good. Mortality curves indicate high rates of infant mortality with another peak in the 40–50 year range. Lack of survival of soft tissues makes it impossible to establish the impact of many diseases, but life was not as short and brutish as was once supposed.

PREHISTORIC BRITAIN, FOREIGN TRADE In the NEOLITHIC (*c*.4300– *c*.2300 BC) jadeite AXES were imported from Brittany and the Alps. The advent of metallurgy from 2000 BC increased foreign trade. The use of Continental fashions in metal artefacts, and finds from wrecks, indicate that imports were common throughout the BRONZE and IRON AGES (*c*.2300–700 BC; *c*.700–AD 43) though objects are rarely found. From the 1st century BC amphorae (large

storage jars) containing wine, garum (fish paste) and figs were imported from the W Mediterranean, with bronze and silver vessels and fine pottery. Pottery from Gaul occurs commonly at the ports of Hengistbury Head (Dorset, S England) and COLCHESTER.

PREHISTORIC BRITAIN, HOUSING Though substantial rectangular timber houses are known from the NEOLITHIC (*c*.4300– *c*.2300 BC), measuring up to 82 × 13 ft (25 × 4 m), as at Balbridie (Grampian, NE Scotland), and large circular houses 50–65 ft (15–20 m) in diameter from the Late BRONZE AGE (*c*.1200–700 BC), as at Little Woodbury (Wiltshire, S England), the norm throughout PREHISTORY was the round house 33–40 ft (10–12 m) in diameter, built of stone, planks, or wattle and daub, with a thatch or turf roof. Larger buildings dating to the Late Neolithic (*c*.2800– *c*.2300 BC), as at Durrington Walls (Wiltshire, S England), or the Late Bronze Age, as at Thwing (Yorkshire, NE England), are considered to be for ceremonial use; individual social status was rarely displayed in houses.

PREHISTORIC BRITAIN, INTERNAL TRADE Stone AXES and fine pottery were traded extensively in the NEOLITHIC (*c*.4300– *c*.2300 BC). Some axes and bracelets may have doubled as ingots, and from *c*.500 BC iron 'currency bars' were produced. From the Late BRONZE AGE salt was produced on the coast (*c*.1000 BC) and at inland brine springs such as those at Droitwich (Worcestershire, England); distinctive containers document the trade. Centrally produced coins, pottery and ornaments were widely distributed in the late IRON AGE.

PREHISTORIC BRITAIN, POPULATION It is exceptionally difficult to estimate population figures, because there are few samples upon which to base estimates and no evidence from which to infer the impact of major diseases. Current estimates for population levels in Britain between the NEOLITHIC and the IRON AGE (*c*.4300 BC–AD 43) range from about 500,000 to 1.5 million. How these numbers may have fluctuated over time is unknown.

PREHISTORIC BRITAIN, RELIGIOUS PRACTICES Evidence of ritual activity occurs on CAUSEWAYED ENCLOSURES of the NEOLITHIC (*c*.4300– *c*.3300 BC) and HILLFORTS of the IRON AGE (*c*.600– *c*.300 BC) as special deposits of animal and human bones, and of artefacts such as stone axes. MEGALITHIC MONUMENTS, HENGES and STONE CIRCLES of the Neolithic (*c*.4300– *c*.2300 BC) and Early BRONZE AGE (*c*.2300– *c*.1600 BC), such as STONEHENGE and AVEBURY, show orientation on celestial bodies.

Throughout the 1st millennium BC prestige artefacts (e.g., shields, swords) were sacrificed in rivers. Temples of the late Iron Age (from *c*.100 BC), which often continued into the Roman period (*see* ROMAN BRITAIN), produce offerings of coins, weapons, and personal ornaments. There is no archaeological evidence for druids (priests).

PREHISTORIC BRITAIN, SOCIAL STRUCTURE

From the NEOLITHIC (*c*.4300– *c*.2300 BC) onwards society was hierarchical, though this is often masked in burial ritual. In the Early and Middle Neolithic only a minority were accorded formal burial, in MEGALITHIC tombs; the bodies of others were excarnated (exposed) and bones mixed to emphasize community. Single burial from the Late Neolithic (from *c*.2800 BC) emphasized individual status (wealth, sex, age, etc.), indicated by weapons, precious ornaments, and elaborate funerary structures and barrows; such burials were sometimes clustered around HENGE MONUMENTS such as STONEHENGE. In the Late BRONZE AGE (*c*.1200– *c*.700 BC) prestige objects were destroyed in ritual rather than funerary contexts, and large houses indicate high-status individuals.

In the IRON AGE (*c*.700 BC–AD 43) social differentiation was suppressed, with many individuals, male and female, owning chariots, but gold is rare, and large houses disappear. This changes in the late IRON AGE (from *c*.100 BC) when wealthy burials, rich votive offerings, inscribed coinage and documentary sources all indicate the rise of dynasties of kings and queens based in settlements with increasingly urban characteristics (OPPIDA). The best-known of these rulers include Commius and Verica of the Atrebates, Tasciovanus, CUNOBELIN and CARATACUS of the Catuvellauni, and CARTIMANDUA of the Brigantes. Cunobelin's power was partly based on control of foreign trade through the port of COLCHESTER. *See also* GATHERING AND HUNTING.

PREHISTORIC IRELAND

The earliest definite evidence for human settlement occurs soon after the last retreat of glaciers, during the MESOLITHIC (from *c*.8000 BC). For over 4000 years small bands of foragers occupied a forested landscape relying on a range of resources with limited use of hunting (*see* GATHERING AND HUNTING). Farming was established in the NEOLITHIC (from *c*.3800 BC), with long-term settlement in focal areas. The most visible aspect of the Neolithic is the use of MEGALITHIC tombs, which normally contain communal burial deposits, either cremated or inhumed. They had a number of roles. A feature particularly of PASSAGE TOMBS is their clustering in cemeteries, notably the BEND OF THE BOYNE. In southern areas there is more evidence for formal single burials from 3600 BC onwards. After a distinct tradition of rectangular houses early in the Neolithic, the use of round houses continued from the later part of the Neolithic into the later prehistoric period. Exploitation of metal (copper) began in the CHALCOLITHIC PERIOD (from *c*.2500 BC).

In the BRONZE AGE (*c*.2200– *c*.700 BC) funerary customs focused on the burial of individuals, normally in cemeteries.

Cremation became dominant. Ceremonial sites include HENGES, standing stones, stone rows and STONE CIRCLES. The deposition of metalwork in rivers and bogs became increasingly important. From *c*.1000 BC, in the Late Bronze Age, a range of metal types were used, both functional and ceremonial (bronze and gold); hoard deposition occurs; and settlements occur in a variety of environments. The construction of HILLFORTS also started in this period. Many features of the IRON AGE (*c*.700 BC– *c*. AD 400) show continuity from the Late Bronze Age, including continued activity at what in the early historic period would come to be called 'royal sites' (*see*, e.g., TARA; EMAIN MACHA).

PREHISTORIC IRELAND, AGRICULTURE

The use of domesticated plants and animals, i.e., agriculture, was established by *c*.3800 BC. All prehistoric domesticated animal species (cattle, pig – apparently not the indigenous wild pig – sheep, goat, horse, dog) and cereals (wheat, barley, rye) were introduced by man. The evidence suggests a broad, mixed farming strategy varying regionally and over time. Agriculture involved clearing forest. Thereafter some areas were maintained as open ground; in other cases there was a complex and repeated sequence of clearance, agriculture and forest regeneration. Use of woodland was an important aspect of the agricultural system.

Field systems were established during the NEOLITHIC (*c*.3800– *c*.2500 BC), the most important and largest being the co-axial (regularly patterned) field system at Céide, Co. Mayo (W Ireland). Social, technological and environmental factors resulted in a shift in the focus of farming to heavier soils and more low-lying areas during the course of prehistory. A significant expansion in settlement and farming activity took place *c*.1400– *c*.700 BC, in the Middle and Late BRONZE AGE.

PREHISTORIC IRELAND, BURIAL PRACTICES

The earliest evidence for formal burial occurs in the NEOLITHIC period (*c*.3800– *c*.2500 BC), when different practices involving inhumation (burial) and cremation were employed. Often there was a temporary burial followed by cremation of bones (frequently communal). The remains (or sometimes uncremated disarticulated bones) were then placed in a funerary structure (*see* MEGALITHIC MONUMENTS). Human bone was seen as having an important ceremonial role.

From the Early BRONZE AGE onwards (i.e., from *c*.2300 BC) there was increased emphasis on individual treatment of the dead and use of cremation. Burial deposits may contain only a token amount of cremated bone. Inhumed burials are found late in the IRON AGE (*c*. AD 100– *c*.400).

PREHISTORIC IRELAND, DIET AND LIVING STANDARDS

Life in the MESOLITHIC (*c*.8000– *c*.3800 BC) relied on the collection of a wide range of wild foods (*see*

GATHERING AND HUNTING). Thereafter the balance shifted towards agricultural resources, but wild foods were exploited throughout PREHISTORY (providing important seasonal variation and nutritional supplements). Domesticated animals and plants, particularly cereals, would have been the most important food sources (*see* PREHISTORIC IRELAND, AGRICULTURE). High infant mortality rates, short lifespans and a range of diseases, such as osteoarthritis, indicate that living conditions were difficult. It appears that men lived longer than women, perhaps reflecting differences in nutrition and health, and problems associated with multiple childbirth.

PREHISTORIC IRELAND, FOREIGN TRADE Such trade is indicated by imported artefacts in Ireland and Irish artefacts in Britain and adjacent Continental Europe. NEOLITHIC examples (i.e., from *c*.3800– *c*.2500 BC) include the export of porcellanite stone axeheads from N Ireland and the import of tuff axeheads from NW England. Copper axes were exported during the CHALCOLITHIC PERIOD (*c*.2500–*c*.2000 BC). Irish BRONZE AGE objects (i.e., from *c*.2300– *c*.700 BC), or objects of Irish inspiration such as gold lunulae, are found abroad. An import of the IRON AGE (*c*.700 BC–*c*. AD 400) is the torc from the Middle Rhine found at Knock (Co. Roscommon, W Ireland). Much of the technological change seen during the Bronze Age and Iron Age seems to be related to the inspiration of foreign objects.

PREHISTORIC IRELAND, HOUSING The earliest known house is the circular one at Mt Sandal (Co. Londonderry, N Ireland), dating to the early MESOLITHIC (*c*.8000 BC). Otherwise there is little evidence for housing in the Mesolithic. In the NEOLITHIC (*c*.3800– *c*.2500 BC) both rectangular and circular houses were in use (the most important site is Lough Gur, Co. Limerick, SW Ireland). Circular houses became the dominant form after 3000 BC, a pattern that continued for the rest of PREHISTORY. Most houses used timber for their basic structures. Dispersed and clustered, open and enclosed settlements are known.

PREHISTORIC IRELAND, INTERNAL TRADE Evidence for internal trade or exchange is present from the later MESOLITHIC period (from *c*.5500 BC onwards). It consists mainly of objects made from non-local materials, such as FLINT and chert artefacts in the Mesolithic, stone axes in the NEOLITHIC (*c*.3800–*c*.2500 BC), and metal artefacts found at a distance from the stone moulds in which they were made during the CHALCOLITHIC PERIOD (*c*.2500–*c*.2000 BC) and overlapping Early BRONZE AGE (*c*.2300– *c*.1700 BC).

PREHISTORIC IRELAND, POPULATION In the MESOLITHIC (*c*.8000– *c*.3800 BC) population may have been only a few thousand but during the NEOLITHIC

(*c*.3800– *c*.2500 BC) substantial increase can be suggested. By 2500 BC there may have been 150,000–200,000 people, though population levels would have varied through time. An estimate of 500,000 would be appropriate for the Late BRONZE AGE (*c*.1200– *c*.700 BC) and IRON AGE (*c*.700 BC–*c*. AD 400).

PREHISTORIC IRELAND, RELIGIOUS PRACTICES Religious practice can be identified in the ritual and ceremonies that surrounded the use of funerary monuments and in formal deposition of remains. In the case of MEGALITHIC tombs, especially in the NEOLITHIC (*c*.3800–*c*.2500 BC), this could involve the choice of a deliberate location, the use of fire in and around the tomb structure, the deposition of material apart from human remains, ceremonies outside the tomb and the formal blocking up of the site. In later PREHISTORY (especially from *c*.1200 BC) deposition of material in sacred places, such as rivers and lakes, appears to have become an important aspect, separate from burial practice. Deliberately made pools can occasionally be recognized, as in the case of the 'King's Stables' in the Navan (EMAIN MACHA) complex (Co. Armagh, NE Ireland).

PREHISTORIC IRELAND, SOCIAL STRUCTURE In the MESOLITHIC (*c*.8000–*c*.3800 BC) people lived in small groups, which may have continued during the Early NEOLITHIC (*c*.3800–*c*.3000 BC) but with more permanent territories. Interaction between polities is indicated by the exchange of objects and stylistic parallels in material culture. Monumental constructions of *c*.3000 BC, such as the large PASSAGE TOMBS in the BEND OF THE BOYNE, suggest greater social cohesion and perhaps regional identity. Social status may have been based on lineage and kinship, although particular individuals (males) were celebrated in death. In the BRONZE AGE (*c*.2300–*c*.700 BC) social structure appears to have been dominated by locally organized entities, with leading individuals (male and female) and related family members being buried in cemeteries.

Later prehistory sees the emergence of concern with weaponry, ornamentation and craft specialization (seen in indications of sex differentiation in hoards). This along with the use of large hill-top enclosures (*see* HILLFORTS, IRELAND) and the emergence of marked regional differences suggests the development of 'chiefdom-type' societies which can be seen as reflecting the social structure that persisted into the early historic period (*see* SOCIAL STRUCTURE, GAELIC IRELAND 5TH–12TH CENTURIES).

PREHISTORY The period of human existence known from non-written sources, especially archaeology. It begins *c*.450,000 BP in Britain, *c*.8000 BC in Ireland, and ends conventionally in Britain *c*. AD 43 (*see* ROMAN BRITAIN) and in

Ireland at the 5th century AD. The English term 'prehistoric' was introduced by the Scotsman Daniel Wilson in 1851 (in *The Archaeology and Prehistoric Annals of Scotland*). From the 1840s British prehistory was divided into Stone, BRONZE and IRON AGES, and in 1865 John Lubbock divided the Stone Age into PALAEOLITHIC and NEOLITHIC. In 1866 Hodder Westropp distinguished the MESOLITHIC before the Neolithic. *See also* PREHISTORIC BRITAIN; PREHISTORIC IRELAND.

PRE-RAPHAELITE BROTHERHOOD A group formed in 1848 by Dante Gabriel Rossetti (1828–82), William Holman Hunt (1827–1910), John Everett Millais (1829–96) and four associates to revitalize English art by taking inspiration from 14th- and 15th-century Italian art (i.e., before Raphael, 1483–1520). They depicted moral and religious subjects, sometimes from medieval literature, in brilliant colours and minute detail. The Brotherhood's members became the leading artists of mid-19th-century England, championed by John RUSKIN. Their influence is seen in the work of William MORRIS.

PREROGATIVE *see* ROYAL PREROGATIVE

PREROGATIVE COURTS Historians' term for several royal administrative and judicial bodies in England and Wales, namely the COUNCIL IN THE MARCHES OF WALES, COUNCIL OF THE NORTH, Court of REQUESTS, STAR CHAMBER, Council of the West (1539–40) and Court of High Commission. Most developed from the late 15th or early 16th century (High Commission, a Church court, from the mid 16th century). They operated under royal prerogative, drawing on civil law and EQUITY.

Some courts became intensely disliked in the 1630s because they were used by kings and royal officers against opponents. The Council of the North, Star Chamber and High Commission were abolished in 1641 by the LONG PARLIAMENT. Requests and the Council in the Marches of Wales ceased judicial work in 1642. The latter body was revived 1660–89.

Similar courts also operated in Ireland (1560s–1640s): *see* CASTLE CHAMBER, COURT OF; PRESIDENCIES, IRELAND. *See also* COURTS, ENGLAND BEFORE 1660; LAW, ENGLAND FROM 1066.

PRESBYTERIAN CHURCH OF WALES *see* CALVINISTIC METHODISTS

PRESBYTERIANISM, ENGLAND *see* NONCONFORMITY AND DISSENT, ENGLAND; CHURCH, ENGLAND AND WALES, 1640s–50s

PRESBYTERIANISM, IRELAND Presbyterian Scots migrated to NE Ireland from the early 17th century, notably for the ULSTER PLANTATION (in all, 20,000–30,000 people, including ministers). Some ministers held Church of Ireland livings. In 1642 chaplains with Robert Monro's Scottish army (sent to combat the Catholic ULSTER RISING) formed the first presbytery (court of minsters and elders). Congregationalism effectively existed during the 1650s (*see* COMMONWEALTH AND PROTECTORATE, IRELAND). A separate Church developed from 1666 when ministers were ejected from livings for rejecting the post-Restoration Church settlement (*see* IRELAND, CHURCH OF). In 1690, five presbyteries formed the Synod of Ulster (regional assembly). Earlier (1672), the government had sought presbyterians' loyalty by instituting the *REGIUM DONUM*.

Large-scale immigration in the later 17th century (60,000–100,000) generated fear of presbyterians. They were excluded from public offices by a sacramental test (added to the 1704 Popery Act; suspended from 1719, repealed 1780). In the later 18th century some presbyterians participated in the radical wing of the VOLUNTEERS and UNITED IRISHMEN.

Presbyterianism tended to splinter. In 1725 liberal opponents to subscription by ministers (to the 'Westminster Confession') separated, and a conservative 'Secession Presbyterian Church', influenced from Scotland, developed from 1746. In 1829 liberal presbyterians left the Synod of Ulster and formed the Remonstrant Synod (1830).

In the 19th century mainstream presbyterians accepted the UNION OF IRELAND AND GREAT BRITAIN and became more conservative, also accepting the Church of Ireland as a fellow Protestant body. In 1840 the Synod of Ulster (292 congregations) and Secession Synod (141 congregations) united as the Presbyterian Church in Ireland, governed by a General Assembly.

From the late 19th century presbyterians opposed HOME RULE, fearing inclusion in a Catholic-dominated State. Resistance resulted in the creation (1921) of Protestant-dominated NORTHERN IRELAND. Presbyterianism remained strong though tensions continued (e.g., with the fundamentalist Free Presbyterian Church, founded 1951 and led by Ian PAISLEY). *See also* CHURCH ORGANIZATION, SCOTLAND FROM 16TH CENTURY; PRESBYTERIAN SOCIETY, IRELAND; COOKE, HENRY.

PRESBYTERIANISM, SCOTLAND *see* SCOTLAND, CHURCH OF; DISSENT, SCOTLAND

PRESBYTERIAN SOCIETY, IRELAND During the 17th century many Scottish presbyterians migrated to Ireland, mostly to ULSTER (N Ireland). By the 1660s they formed about 20% of Ulster's population, and over 40% by the 1730s (over 200,000 persons). The largest concentrations were in Cos. Antrim and Down. Many householders were tenant farmers, some were merchants. From the later 17th century presbyterians developed an ecclesiastical structure (*see* PRESBYTERIANISM, IRELAND).

Excluded in the 18th century from many civil posts by the (Church of Ireland) PROTESTANT ASCENDANCY, presbyterians formed a separate, close-knit society, with KIRK SESSIONS (church courts) supervising moral behaviour. They used cues of identification (e.g., names) to differentiate themselves from Catholic inhabitants. Many presbyterians flourished from involvement in the LINEN INDUSTRY.

In the later 18th century a well-educated section was influenced by the ENLIGHTENMENT and FRENCH REVOLUTION; as a result, presbyterian radicals were prominent in the VOLUNTEERS, UNITED IRISHMEN and RISING OF 1798. But fear of Catholics led others to co-operate with Church of IRELAND adherents (e.g., in founding the ORANGE ORDER, 1795). In the 19th century a common 'Protestant' identity grew, which defended the UNION OF IRELAND AND GREAT BRITAIN (1801) and later resisted HOME RULE, though presbyterians retained a distrust of the British political establishment.

PRESIDENCIES, INDIA *see* INDIA

PRESIDENCIES, IRELAND Regional administrative courts through which English authority was reasserted in the 16th century. Provincial councils were proposed in the early 1550s by Thomas Cusack from the PALE, and presidencies for CONNACHT, MUNSTER and ULSTER (provinces) were advocated in 1562 by the earl of SUSSEX, modelled on English councils for the Welsh March and the North. Presidents were appointed for Connacht (W Ireland) in 1569 and for Munster (S) in 1570 (*see* SIDNEY, HENRY; PERROT, JOHN).

Presidents served under Ireland's CHIEF GOVERNOR, assisted by a council, military retinue and administrators, and funded by tax (*see* COMPOSITION). Their work included arbitration of lords' disputes. Within presidencies, SHIRES were the main local units. Presidencies were disrupted in the 1640s–50s (*see* IRISH WARS), reinstated in 1660, and abolished by King CHARLES II in 1672 to prevent their use against RECUSANTS and thereby offending the king of FRANCE. *See also* IRELAND, ENGLISH CONQUEST, 16TH CENTURY; COURTS, IRELAND; EQUITY COURTS.

PRICE, JOHN (b. *c.*1503 in lordship of Brecon, Wales; d. 15 Oct. 1555 at Hereford, Herefordshire, England, aged about 52). A Welsh lawyer, active in the REFORMATION. By *c.*1530 Price was employed by Thomas CROMWELL (and in 1534 he married Cromwell's niece Joan Williams); he then worked for King HENRY VIII, organizing the DISSOLUTION OF RELIGIOUS HOUSES and assisting at the trials of John FISHER and Thomas MORE. From 1540 he was secretary of the COUNCIL IN THE MARCHES OF WALES and was knighted in 1547 by EDWARD VI.

Price was interested in Welsh history and literature, and salvaged manuscripts from religious houses. He financed the first printed book in Welsh, *Yn y Lhyvyr hwnn* ('In this Book...'), containing the Lord's Prayer, Creed and Ten Commandments (1546).

PRICE, RICHARD (b. 6 Feb. 1723 at Llangeinor, Glamorgan, Wales; d. 19 April 1791 at London, England, aged 68). Welsh presbyterian minister, resident in London from 1740; author of advanced philosophical, mathematical and actuarial studies. During the AMERICAN WAR OF INDEPENDENCE (1775–81) Price wrote pamphlets supporting the colonists, raising the level of debate to philosophical principle. His sermon *The Love of Our Country* (1789), welcoming the FRENCH REVOLUTION and advocating the extension of civil rights and PARLIAMENTARY REFORM at home, provoked Edmund BURKE to write his *Reflections on the Revolution in France* (1790). *See also* ENLIGHTENMENT; SINKING FUNDS.

PRICE RISE, 16TH–MID 17TH CENTURIES The most sustained and powerful price inflation in Europe between the 12th and 20th centuries. The phenomenon was named the 'Price Revolution' in 1895 by the German historian Georg Wiebe. It included steep increases in the long-term prices of foodstuffs and industrial products. The main cause was probably an increase of population which exceeded increases in agricultural and industrial production. Wage labourers and landlords living on fixed rents suffered. Tenants who paid customary fixed rents benefited.

The chronology and incidence of rising prices varied. Prices began to rise in England and Wales from *c.*1515, and rapid increases were experienced in the 1540s–50s and 1590s, influenced by debasement of currency in the first period and war expenditure in both. Overall the cost of basic consumables quadrupled between 1510 and 1600. The price rise in Ireland was influenced by the import of debased coinage in the 1540s–50s. In Scotland prices rose mainly from *c.*1560, and were affected by currency debasement in the 1580s–90s. Between 1560 and 1600, commodity prices rose between three and six times. *See also* INFLATION AND DEFLATION.

PRICHARD, RHYS (b. *c.*1579, probably at Llandovery, Carmarthenshire, Wales; d. *c.* Dec. 1644 at Llawhaden, Pembrokeshire, Wales, aged about 65). Vicar of Llandovery 1597–1614, sympathetic to PURITANISM, Prichard later became a canon of ST DAVIDS (chancellor from 1626). His posthumously published didactic verses (1659–60), called *Canwyll y Cymry* ('Candle of the Welsh') from 1681, enjoyed long-lasting popularity.

PRIDE'S PURGE In England, in 1648, after the Second CIVIL WAR, the exclusion of numerous Presbyterian MPs from the House of Commons in the LONG PARLIAMENT because they supported further negotiations with King CHARLES I. Starting on 6 Dec., the expulsions were instigated by radical 'Independents' and the NEW MODEL ARMY. The remaining MPs and peers were known as the RUMP PARLIAMENT. The purge facilitated the king's trial and execution. It was named after Colonel Thomas Pride who supervised the action. *See also* CIVIL WARS, POLITICAL ASPECTS; CHARLES I, TRIAL AND EXECUTION.

PRIESTLEY, J.B. (b. 13 Sept. 1894 at Bradford, Yorkshire, England; d. 14 Aug. 1984 at Alveston, Warwickshire, England, aged 89). John Boynton Priestley was a prolific writer from the 1920s. Early in WORLD WAR II he was commissioned by the BRITISH BROADCASTING CORPORATION to give regular radio talks. He expressed a patriotic brand of left-wing radicalism which proved popular and influential, and benefited the LABOUR PARTY (5 June–20 Oct. 1940). His involvement ended when the BBC refused to meet his fee. An article written by Priestley in 1957 inspired the formation of the CAMPAIGN FOR NUCLEAR DISARMAMENT.

PRIESTLEY, JOSEPH (b. 13 March 1733 at Birstall, Yorkshire, England; d. 6 Feb. 1804 at Northumberland, Pennsylvania, USA, aged 70). A dissenter with a vocation to religious ministry, Priestley studied (1752–5) at Daventry Academy (Northamptonshire), where the curriculum included natural philosophy (science). His adoption of Arianism (denial of Christ's divinity) alienated him from his family. He pursued a life of ministry, teaching and writing on religion and science.

Priestley was a tutor at Warrington Academy (Lancashire) 1761–7, where he was ordained (1762), and a minister at LEEDS (Yorkshire) 1767–73. A spokesman for rational theology, he also investigated electricity and gases. Supported 1773–80 by the earl of SHELBURNE, and resident at Calne (Wiltshire), Priestley discovered various gases, including oxygen (1775), his most influential achievement. (The French chemist Antoine Lavoisier coined the name.) Priestley then moved to Birmingham (Warwickshire), where he joined the LUNAR SOCIETY. His involvement in organizing a dinner to celebrate the FRENCH REVOLUTION provoked the 'Priestley Riots' (14–16 July 1791). Priestley fled, settling at Hackney (Middlesex). In 1794 he emigrated to the USA, where he was fêted. *See also* DISSENTING ACADEMIES, ENGLAND; ENLIGHTENMENT.

PRIMACY DISPUTE, CANTERBURY AND YORK In England, the dispute between the Church's two archbishops over Canterbury's claim to jurisdiction throughout the British Isles (later England). It began in 1070 when LANFRANC of Canterbury demanded a profession of obedience from York

(Thomas of Bayeux). A council ruled in Canterbury's favour (1072), but confrontations reoccurred (notably Thurstan of York's resistance from 1114). The dispute was settled in 1353 when Pope Innocent VI made York 'primate of England' and Canterbury 'primate of all England'.

PRIMACY DISPUTE, DUBLIN AND ARMAGH In Ireland, the periodic assertion of status by archbishops of DUBLIN against archbishops of ARMAGH. Although Armagh (associated with St PATRICK) was formally recognized as Ireland's primatial see by the synod of Kells (1152), John Comyn, archbishop of Dublin, obtained papal recognition of extensive autonomy for his diocese (1182). Henry of London (archbishop 1213–28) acquired stronger grants (1216, 1221), covering his archdiocese. According to a seal matrix, he claimed to be 'primate of Ireland'.

Alexander Bicknor (archbishop of Dublin 1317–49) and Thomas Minot (1363–75) also claimed to be primates, despite opposition from Armagh. (In 1349 Bicknor had Archbishop Richard FITZRALPH ejected from Dublin city.) It was apparently decided, possibly by Innocent VI (Pope 1352–62), that the archbishop of Dublin should be 'primate of Ireland' and the archbishop of Armagh 'primate of all Ireland', though an award does not survive. Tensions recurred intermittently. *See also* CHURCH REFORM, MEDIEVAL IRELAND.

PRIME MINISTER The head of GOVERNMENT of Great Britain (UK from 1801), who chairs the CABINET and coordinates the government's work for the monarch. Robert WALPOLE is regarded as the first prime minister (served 1721–42). William PITT the Younger (1783–1801, 1804–6) consolidated the role after a reassertion of royal influence by King GEORGE III. The post was not officially recognized until 1905; its holder was customarily paid a salary as first lord of the Treasury. The term was considered abusive for much of the 18th century. Since 1735, 10 Downing Street in WESTMINSTER (formerly in Middlesex, now in LONDON) has been the official residence of the first lord of the Treasury.

During the 18th century monarchs were generally compelled to appoint men who could win support for the government in Parliament. They were variously peers in the House of Lords or MPs in the Commons. The convention developed that the monarch exercised powers on ministerial advice. The prime minister thereby gained extensive PATRONAGE: he effectively appointed ministers, peers, bishops, ambassadors and senior civil servants.

From 1868, following increases in the electorate, the prime minister was usually the recognized leader of the largest political party in the Commons. Lord SALISBURY was the last peer to serve as prime minister (left office 1901), and Margaret THATCHER the first woman (1979–90). *See also* TREASURER, ENGLAND.

PRIMROSE LEAGUE A Conservative organization founded in Great Britain in Nov. 1883 to rally mass support for queen, country, Church and Empire. It was named after Benjamin DISRAELI's favourite flower. Although its activities were mainly social, the League provided thousands of volunteer workers for the CONSERVATIVE PARTY at elections. By 1891 it had over 1 million members. It continued until 2004.

PRINCE OF WALES Title (Welsh *tywysog Cymru*; Latin *princeps Wallie*) accorded in March 1258 to LLYWELYN AP GRUFFUDD of GWYNEDD (NW Wales). Some 12th-century rulers (OWAIN GWYNEDD; RHYS AP GRUFFUDD) styled themselves 'prince of the Welsh' or 'prince of Wales' as principal rulers. LLYWELYN AP IORWERTH and Llywelyn ap Gruffudd claimed the latter title to denote overlordship, and sought recognition from King HENRY III of England (*see* MONTGOMERY, TREATY OF).

Prince Edward of England was styled 'prince of Wales' from May 1301, after receiving royal lands in Wales from his father King EDWARD I. Thereafter the English ruler's eldest son usually received the title. Welsh rebels also claimed it (*see* MADOG AP LLYWELYN; OWAIN GLYN DŴR). *See also* PRINCIPALITY OF WALES; KINGSHIP, WALES 5TH–13TH CENTURIES.

PRINCIPALITY OF WALES (Welsh *tywysogaeth Cymru*; Latin *principatus Wallie*). Originally territory, in NW, NE and C Wales, which was ruled directly or indirectly (as overlord) by LLYWELYN AP GRUFFUDD as PRINCE OF WALES. The term was first used in the treaty of MONTGOMERY (1267), when King HENRY III of England 'granted' the territory to Llywelyn.

From 1301 the term referred to lands held by (or reserved for) the English prince of Wales (most of Llywelyn's principality plus lands in W and S Wales, sometimes called respectively the principality of North Wales and principality of South Wales). From 1543, following the UNION OF WALES WITH ENGLAND, the 'principality' referred to all Wales (sometimes excepting MONMOUTHSHIRE).

PRINTING, ENGLAND Hand printing with movable type was introduced from Continental Europe in 1475 or 1476 by William CAXTON, based in WESTMINSTER, near London. From *c.*1500 London was the main printing centre; presses elsewhere failed for commercial reasons. Printers initially sold books; by the 1520s they were also distributed by booksellers, some of whom acted as publishers by commissioning printers. The book trade was subject to controls (*see* CENSORSHIP, ENGLAND AND WALES).

Until the 1520s the main types of printed works, predominantly in English, were religious books (e.g., by ENGLISH MYSTICS), educational books (e.g., grammars),

legal items (e.g., manuals), and popular literature (e.g., romances). The Bible was published in English from 1536 (*see* BIBLE, ENGLISH). Evangelical religious works were printed under King EDWARD VI (1547–53), defensive Catholic works under Queen MARY I (1553–8). FOXE's 'BOOK OF MARTYRS' (1563) declared printing an instrument of God's providence (for Protestants).

Supervisory powers granted to the Stationers' Company of London (1557, confirmed by ELIZABETH I in 1558) perpetuated London's dominance, although OXFORD and CAMBRIDGE Universities were each later allowed a press (1586). In the early 17th century there were about 20 printers. Output steadily increased (from 260 to 570 titles per year, 1600–40). During the CIVIL WARS (1642–8), Parliament's control of London included most printing works, forcing Royalists to install presses elsewhere. The printing of pamphlets and news-sheets boomed during the 1640s–50s. Following the RESTORATION (1660), about 1100 titles were published annually.

After controls diminished in 1695 (lapse of Licensing Act), printing businesses, publication types, and output expanded rapidly; by the 1750s most towns had a printing firm, some producing NEWSPAPERS.

Steam-powered printing, and specialist printing machinery, were developed from 1814. By the mid 19th century printing, publishing and bookselling were mostly separate businesses, although some newspaper publishers retained printing works into the 21st century. *See also* MARPRELATE TRACTS; BALLADS.

PRINTING, IRELAND The first press was established in DUBLIN by the king's printer Humfrey Powell who published the English Book of Common Prayer in 1551. The first printed book in Irish was a Protestant catechism of 1571. Although more royal printers were appointed, few works were printed until the 1640s when publications included political pamphlets and the first NEWSPAPER (1649). Printed works were also imported.

Printing expanded rapidly in the later 17th and 18th centuries, mainly in Dublin but also notably in BELFAST. The great variety of publications, mostly in English, included religious and political tracts, almanacs, legal texts, dictionaries and fiction; many works were by Irish writers (e.g., Jonathan SWIFT). In the 1790s around 4000 items were published. As copyright legislation did not apply to Ireland until 1801, Irish printers could print cheap editions for export to England. Output declined in the 19th century to 3000–4000 items per decade, mostly in English, and publishing often became separated from printing. Printing in Irish flourished from the 1890s thanks to the GAELIC REVIVAL and new scholarly emphasis on Irish history and literature.

In the 20th century publishing and printing were discouraged in the IRISH FREE STATE by the Censorship of

Publications Act 1929 (reformed 1967). Many prominent Irish writers were published abroad, though small publishing houses continued to publish new writing. *See also* CENSORSHIP, IRELAND.

PRINTING, SCOTLAND The first press, imported from France, operated in EDINBURGH from 1508 to 1510 under a patent granted by King JAMES IV to Walter Chepman and Andrew Myllar (1507). Their publications included the *Aberdeen Breviary* of William ELPHINSTONE. Other presses operated briefly in Edinburgh and ST ANDREWS between *c*.1520 and the 1550s, but little work survives. Printing expanded after the REFORMATION (1560), using mainly English type. Religious works, Acts of Parliament and royal proclamations predominated.

In the 17th century printing spread to ABERDEEN (1622), GLASGOW (1638) and Leith, near Edinburgh (1651). The COVENANTING REVOLUTION produced a boom in polemical tracts. After the RESTORATION (1660) treatises on science, medicine and law appeared, and French and Dutch types became common. English technical influence reappeared in the 18th century, but after 1750 native types were produced. Among new printing centres were PERTH, Kilmarnock (publications including *Poems* by Robert BURNS, 1786) and Kelso (including poems by Walter SCOTT, 1799). Other notable publications included *Encyclopaedia Britannica* (Edinburgh, 1768–71). In the 19th century technological advances allowed mass production. Book publishers progressively ceased printing, although Collins of Glasgow (founded 1819, HarperCollins from 1989) retained a printing plant until the 1990s. *See also* NEWSPAPERS, SCOTLAND.

PRINTING, WALES In the 16th and 17th centuries the government confined printing in England and Wales to London, Oxford, and Cambridge (England), though secret CATHOLIC presses operated in Wales in the 1580s. The first Welsh-language book, containing religious translations, appeared in 1546 (*see* PRICE, JOHN). By 1660 about 100 Welsh books had been published, mainly religious texts including the BIBLE and Prayer Book (*see* SERVICE BOOKS, WALES).

From 1695, when the 1662 Printing Act finally lapsed, Thomas Jones (1648–1713) printed books (including almanacs) at Shrewsbury (W England) which were sold throughout Wales. Shrewsbury developed as the main centre of Welsh printing outside London. The first presses in Wales were established in 1717 at Atpar (or Trerhedyn, Cardiganshire), and in 1721 at CARMARTHEN, which eclipsed Shrewsbury from the 1760s. By the 19th century most Welsh towns had printers. In the late 19th century, the 'golden age' of Welsh publishing, several hundred books were printed a year. In the 20th century printing and publishing were generally separate businesses. *See also* NEWSPAPERS, WALES; GEE, THOMAS; CENSORSHIP, ENGLAND AND WALES.

PRIVATEERING *see* PIRACY AND PRIVATEERING

PRIVATIZATION The transfer of a State-owned business or industry to private ownership. Privatization, usually through share sales, was pursued in Great Britain in the 1980s by the Conservative government of Margaret THATCHER to reduce the PUBLIC SECTOR BORROWING REQUIREMENT, improve efficiency, and spread share ownership. Businesses sold included British Telecom (1984) and other utilities. The policy was also later adopted by the LABOUR PARTY. *See also* NATIONALIZATION; ECONOMY, STATE INVOLVEMENT, BRITAIN.

PRIVY COUNCIL, ENGLAND AND GREAT BRITAIN A council which advises the monarch and was a central institution of English government 1530s–1640s. It originated as a small 'private' group of royal officers, clergy and nobles which advised King HENRY VIII about his first divorce (*see* GREAT MATTER), superseding the larger king's COUNCIL. Its existence was formalized in 1540, after the fall of Thomas CROMWELL, when a clerk was appointed and a minute book kept. Membership was normally 12–20 people (over 40 in reign of MARY I). The ruler rarely attended. It supervised royal government until spring 1646 (*see* CIVIL WARS).

The Privy Council was restored at the RESTORATION (1660) but was relatively unimportant and its membership became larger. It was superseded by CABINET government. It regained some importance in the 19th century through the creation of special committees (e.g., Judicial Committee, 1833). *See also* GOVERNMENT, ENGLAND WITH WALES 1509 TO 1642.

PRIVY COUNCIL, IRELAND A small advisory council instituted in 1520 by the earl of Surrey as chief governor (*see* SURREY EXPEDITION). Comprising mainly senior officers (e.g., chancellor), magnates were added after 1556. In 1578 there were 24 members. The Council undertook administrative and judicial business (e.g., hearing disputes over land and commerce), and prepared legislation for PARLIAMENT under POYNINGS' LAW. Some judicial business was delegated to a Court of CASTLE CHAMBER (1563–6, 1571–1640s).

The Council continued after the UNION OF IRELAND AND GREAT BRITAIN (1801) mainly as a judicial body, becoming dormant in 1922. A Privy Council of NORTHERN IRELAND, created in 1922, also became dormant (1972). *See also* COUNCILS, IRELAND, LATE 12TH–16TH CENTURIES.

PRIVY COUNCIL, SCOTLAND *see* COUNCIL, SCOTLAND

PRIVY SEAL In England, a small royal seal, ranking below the great seal, recorded from the reign of King JOHN (1199–1216). Initially kept within the royal household, it authorized use of the great seal (*see* CHANCELLOR), and authenticated other instructions (e.g., to the EXCHEQUER). From the early 14th century the seal had its own 'keeper of the privy seal', who by the late 14th century was a senior officer with a department. He mainly served the COUNCIL, issuing royal and diplomatic correspondence.

The keeper's department was abolished in 1884, but the position was retained as a CABINET post without portfolio. *See also* SIGNET.

PROCLAMATIONS ACT In England and Wales, legislation in 1539 (in reign of King HENRY VIII), which gave the force of Acts of Parliament to proclamations issued by the king with the advice of his COUNCIL. Offenders against proclamations could be punished. It was repealed after Henry's death (1547), though proclamations continued to be issued.

PROFESSIONS Occupations which usually require specialist education and qualifications, and sometimes validation by a supervisory authority. The term, commonly used from the 16th century, is derived from the profession (vows) made on full admission to a RELIGIOUS ORDER. The status of professions is unclear before the 19th century. 'Profession' could mean 'occupation' and include skilled, GUILD-regulated, manual occupations (e.g., goldsmith).

The main earliest 'learned professions' for laymen (initially alongside clergy) were in COMMON LAW in England and Ireland: by the early 14th century advocates and judges were laymen. In Scotland, law became dominated by lay professionals in the 16th century. From the 16th–17th centuries other occupations gained professional identity, notably physicians, lay administrators in central governments (*see* CIVIL SERVICE, ENGLAND AND GREAT BRITAIN), and (following the REFORMATION) Protestant clergy who increasingly were university-educated preachers. The later 17th and 18th centuries saw greater diversity, including senior ARMY and NAVY officers, civil engineers and architects. Practitioners also increased (*see* CONSUMER REVOLUTION).

In the 19th century urbanization and industrialization required more professionals (e.g., in law, engineering), and they became identified as middle class (*see* SOCIAL CLASS TERMINOLOGY). Status was asserted against unqualified people through regulatory organizations (e.g., Society of Attorneys, etc., 1825) and State action (e.g., statutory registration of medical practitioners, 1858).

From the 1890s women entered professions (e.g., Civil Service), and in 1919 prohibitions were largely removed (Sex Disqualification (Removal) Act, for UK). Both professions

and professional people (e.g., accountants, teachers) continued to increase. In the 1960s women became the majority in school teaching and social welfare work in the UK; from the 1970s numbers expanded rapidly in accountancy, banking and law. By 2018 women were a majority of solicitors in England and Wales, and substantial proportions in other professions in the UK and Ireland. In 2011, 17% of UK workers (5.2 million people) were categorized as professionals. *See also* LEARNED CLASSES, IRELAND; WOMEN, ORDINATION OF.

PROFUMO AFFAIR A sensational political scandal in Great Britain in 1963 involving sex and security issues. John Profumo, secretary of state for war, lied to Parliament (22 March) when he denied 'any impropriety' with Christine Keeler, whose lovers included a naval attaché from the USSR. Profumo eventually resigned (5 June). Despite government assurances that no breach in security had occurred, the affair damaged the reputation of the prime minister, Harold MACMILLAN. *See also* DENNING, LORD.

PROGRESSIVE DEMOCRATS In the Republic of Ireland, a political party launched on 21 Dec. 1985 by FIANNA FÁIL TDs discontented with their leader (and Opposition leader) Charles HAUGHEY, partly because of his inflexible approach over NORTHERN IRELAND. The Democrats' leaders were Desmond O'Malley (1985–1993), who had been expelled from Fianna Fáil for abstaining in a vote on prescription of contraception (opposed by his party); Mary Harney (1993–2006, 2007–8), Michael McDowell (2006–7), Senator Ciarán Cannon (2008–9). At the 1987 general election the Democrats won 14 seats, their highest total.

Progressive Democrats participated in six governments. When the 1989 election left them holding the balance of power, they joined a coalition government with Fianna Fáil, under Haughey, but forced his resignation over alleged criminal behaviour (Jan. 1992). Following an election, they continued in government with Fianna Fáil, under Albert REYNOLDS. This government collapsed (Nov. 1992) after Reynolds, at a tribunal, accused O'Malley of dishonesty.

The Democrats were again coalition partner with Fianna Fáil under Bertie AHERN 1997–2002, 2002–7, and partner with Fianna Fáil and the Green Party 2007–8, under Ahern, and 2008–9, under Brian Cowen. Progressive Democrats supported economic deregulation, a liberal approach to social issues, and conciliation of Unionists in Northern Ireland. The party was disbanded in 2009, after which its two TDs continued as independents. *See also* POLITICAL PARTIES, SOUTHERN IRELAND FROM 1922.

PROTECTIONISM The use of duties, quotas and other restrictions affecting imports in order to protect or boost domestic production and employment. Derived from MER-CANTILISM, protectionism was common practice before the 19th century (notably from the later 17th century by England and Great Britain), but did not warrant the name until it came into conflict with FREE TRADE. *See also* CORN LAWS; TARIFF REFORM.

PROTECTORATE Term used for situations in which either a ruler places his people or territory under the protection of another ruler while retaining sovereignty, or a ruler imposes a limited protective authority over another people or territory. Its main object is to prevent a third power from interfering in areas where it will threaten the trading or strategic interest of the 'protected' or 'protecting' power. Great Britain used the system extensively in the 19th century, and also often converted protectorates into CROWN COLONIES (*see*, for example, NIGERIA).

PROTECTORATE *see* COMMONWEALTH AND PROTECTORATE

PROTESTANT ASCENDANCY Term used (from 1780s) to characterize the domination of Ireland by an elite of Protestant landed and professional families (adherents of the Church of Ireland). It is considered especially appropriate for the period 1690s–1800.

Protestants owned over half the land from the 1650s (*see* CROMWELLIAN LAND SETTLEMENT), but faced Catholic challenges in the 1660s–80s (*see* RESTORATION, IRELAND; JAMES VII/II AND IRELAND). After Protestants won the WILLIAMITE WAR (1688–91), legislation excluded Catholics from the Irish Parliament, reduced landholding, and repressed the Catholic Church (*see* ANTI-CATHOLIC LEGISLATION, IRELAND, 1691 TO 1740s). Ireland's Parliament also excluded Protestant dissenters (1704–80).

England's involvement (Great Britain's from 1707) limited the power of native Protestants. Britain's Parliament asserted jurisdiction over Ireland; Britain's government appointed Ireland's chief governor and other officers, and controlled legislation through POYNINGS' LAW. The governor 'bought' support for business in Parliament (e.g., revenue grants) with patronage, recruiting so-called 'undertakers' (e.g., William CONOLLY, Henry BOYLE, John PONSONBY). British influence was resisted only when deemed excessive (*see* WOOD'S HALFPENCE AFFAIR).

In the 1760s–70s Protestant 'PATRIOTS' increasingly opposed British power, especially after Viscount TOWNSHEND increased the governor's influence (1770–2). But Protestants were challenged by the demands of Irish Catholics for 'relief'. British weakness during the AMERICAN WAR OF INDEPENDENCE enabled Catholics to obtain land rights (1778; *see* GARDINER'S ACT) but Protestants (includ-

ing the 'VOLUNTEERS'), achieved legislative and judicial independence (*see* CONSTITUTION OF 1782).

Protestant domination was curtailed following the FRENCH REVOLUTION (1789). The British government, concerned for Catholic loyalty, forced concessions to Catholics (*see* CATHOLIC RELIEF AND EMANCIPATION, IRELAND), and radicals attempted violently to establish an Irish republic (*see* RISING OF 1798). Now fearful for Britain's security, the British government created a UNION OF IRELAND AND GREAT BRITAIN (1801). It ended autonomous Protestant control, but the 'Ascendancy class' remained extensive landowners until the early 20th century. *See also* SOCIAL STRUCTURE, IRELAND FROM 17TH CENTURY; LANDED SOCIETY, DECLINE OF, IRELAND.

PROTESTORS *see* REMONSTRANTS

PROVINCES, IRELAND Historical regional subdivisions of the island of Ireland: ULSTER (N Ireland), CONNACHT (W), LEINSTER (E), MUNSTER (S and SW). Excepting Ulster, they are based on long-lasting regional kingdoms which existed by the 5th century and of which awareness continued after the Anglo-Norman invasion (1169–70). (In the N, Ulster was one of several kingdoms.) The Irish term for province, *cúige*, meaning 'fifth', acknowledges the former importance of MEATH (6th–11th centuries).

Regional units were revived for new purposes by an initiative of the (3rd) earl of SUSSEX: in 1562 he advocated administrative presidencies for Munster, Connacht and Ulster. They were instituted for Munster and Connacht (*see* PRESIDENCIES, IRELAND). The English conquest of Ulster (completed 1603) and subsequent minor adjustments established four provinces as defined groups of SHIRES (or counties). They were utilized by the Confederation of Kilkenny (1642–9) for its rebellion; each had an army, and an administrative and judicial council which raised funds and men (*see* CATHOLIC CONFEDERATION).

After the abolition of presidencies (1672), provinces were frequently used for organizing administrative activities and information, but not as governmental units (shires were the main local unit). When Ireland was partitioned in 1921, Ulster was divided: three counties remained within SOUTHERN IRELAND while six formed NORTHERN IRELAND. The latter was considered a province of the UNITED KINGDOM.

PROVISIONAL IRISH REPUBLICAN ARMY In NORTHERN IRELAND, a paramilitary organization founded on 18 Dec. 1969 by a breakaway group of the IRISH REPUBLICAN ARMY (IRA). They had become dismayed by the IRA's preoccupation with left-wing politics (rather than 'traditional' nationalist objectives), and its ineffective response to anti-Catholic violence (*see* TROUBLES). The schism's immediate cause was a dispute about whether to end 'abstentionism' from Irish and British politics. 'Provisional' referred to a claimed identity of purpose with the self-proclaimed 'Provisional Government' of 1916 (*see* EASTER RISING). Members were often called 'Provos'. The 'PIRA' soon effectively replaced the 'Official IRA'.

The PIRA's main aims were to expel British authorities from Northern Ireland and create an all-Ireland republic. Activists mainly targeted the police and British Army, but in 1979 they murdered Lord MOUNTBATTEN, a cousin of Queen ELIZABETH II, and on 12 Oct. 1984 they targeted the British prime minister Margaret THATCHER and her Cabinet with a bomb at the Grand Hotel, Brighton (S England).

From 1981, exploiting HUNGER STRIKES, the PIRA also sought 'legitimation' by parallel involvement in politics (*see* PROVISIONAL SINN FÉIN), and in the 1990s co-operated with a PEACE PROCESS. It declared a ceasefire on 31 Aug. 1994 (broken 9 Feb. 1996 with bomb at London Docklands, in protest at lack of progress; reinstated 19 July 1997). But the PIRA rejected demands for 'decommissioning' of arms.

Following the BELFAST AGREEMENT (1998), devolved government was restored to Northern Ireland (Dec. 1999) without decommissioning but it collapsed in Oct. 2002. Although the PIRA was in contact with an Independent International Commission on Decommissioning (established 1997), little happened until July 2005 when, following pressure from the USA, it announced the end of its campaign. In Sept. the Commission confirmed that arms were 'beyond use', eventually enabling formation of a new government (2007). *See also* PARAMILITARY ORGANIZATIONS, NORTHERN IRELAND.

PROVISIONAL SINN FÉIN A political organization which seeks an all-Ireland republic. It originated in Jan. 1970, during the TROUBLES in NORTHERN IRELAND, when militant members of SINN FÉIN broke away in protest at a decision to end abstention from the Irish Parliament. The split mirrored the recent one in the IRISH REPUBLICAN ARMY, and PSF served as a 'front' for the PROVISIONAL IRISH REPUBLICAN ARMY (PIRA). PSF relaxed its abstentionism in 1981 to exploit the increased support for republican nationalism created by HUNGER STRIKES in Northern Ireland.

During the 1980s PSF challenged the SOCIAL DEMOCRATIC AND LABOUR PARTY (SDLP) for nationalists' votes in Northern Ireland elections and UK general elections, and from 1982 also contested elections in the Republic of Ireland, winning Dáil seats from 1997. It was generally known as 'Sinn Féin'. Gerry ADAMS became president in 1983.

Talks between SDLP leader John HUME and Adams from 1988 helped to persuade PSF and the PIRA to co-operate with a PEACE PROCESS for Northern Ireland. Following a

PIRA ceasefire (Aug. 1994), PSF was involved in discussions with the British government (1994–5; ceasefire broken Feb. 1996). Following reinstatement of the ceasefire (July 1997), PSF participated in talks that led to the BELFAST AGREEMENT (1998). PSF won 18 (of 108) seats in a new ASSEMBLY (compared with 24 SDLP seats) and nominated two ministers in a new multi-party EXECUTIVE (1999–2002).

The cessation of PIRA violence permitted more nationalists to support PSF; at the 2003 Assembly elections it became the largest nationalist party (24 seats). But formation of a new Executive was prevented mainly by lack of substantial weapons 'decommissioning' by the PIRA. Solution of that and other problems (2005–6) resulted in a new Executive (2007) in which PSF was the principal partner with the DEMOCRATIC UNIONIST PARTY. It collapsed in Jan. 2017. Adams was succeeded as president in 2018 by Mary Lou McDonald. From Jan. 2020 PSF participated in a new Executive, and in Feb. 2020 it came equal first (with Fianna Fáil) in the general election in the Republic, winning 37 seats in the Dáil. *See also* McGUINNESS, MARTIN; PARLIAMENTARY REPRESENTATION, NORTHERN IRELAND.

PROVISORS, STATUTES OF In England, statutes enacted by Parliament to suppress the appointment of clergy, usually foreigners, by the Pope to bishoprics and collegiate churches (e.g., cathedrals) in preference to the rights of other patrons. The first Statute, in 1351, was supplemented by the Statute of PRAEMUNIRE (1353), confirmed in 1365, and modified in 1389. Papal provision nonetheless continued until the REFORMATION (1530s) and was revived in the reign of MARY I (1553–8). *See also* CHURCH, MEDIEVAL ENGLAND.

PRUSSIA, BRITISH RELATIONS WITH This state in NE Germany became a European Great Power in the early 18th century. It was allied with Great Britain in the SEVEN YEARS WAR (1756–63), but the reduction of British subsidies (1761) caused bitterness. The two countries were again allies against FRANCE (1793–5, 1813–15; *see* FRENCH REVOLUTIONARY AND NAPOLEONIC WARS, BRITISH INVOLVEMENT). Prussia then aligned itself with RUSSIA and the HABSBURG EMPIRE in the 'Holy Alliance' (*see* QUADRUPLE ALLIANCE). After vainly intervening in the SCHLESWIG-HOLSTEIN QUESTION (1863–4), the British government recognized its lack of influence over the unification of GERMANY under Prussian leadership (1870–1). *See also* DIPLOMATIC REVOLUTION; GERMANY, BRITISH RELATIONS WITH.

PRYNNE, WILLIAM (b. 1600 at Swainswick, Somerset, England; d. 24 Dec. 1669 at London, England, aged 69). A Puritan and pamphleteer, Prynne was convicted of sedition in 1633 for appearing to attack HENRIETTA MARIA, wife of King CHARLES I, in his book *Histriomastix*. He also attacked LAUDIANISM. He was convicted again in 1637 and exiled.

Prynne supported Parliament in the CIVIL WARS (1642–8) but opposed Charles's execution (1649). He was imprisoned 1649–52 for criticizing the COMMONWEALTH. As a member of the CONVENTION PARLIAMENT (1660) he supported the RESTORATION. He was appointed keeper of records in the Tower of London by King CHARLES II.

PSBR *see* PUBLIC SECTOR BORROWING REQUIREMENT

PUBLIC ACCOUNTS, COMMISSIONS OF Commissions of MPs which were originally elected annually by the English House of Commons from 1690 to supervise government expenditure (in reign of King WILLIAM III). Robert HARLEY became an influential commissioner. Commissioners influenced debates over funding. Commissions were terminated in 1697 when the WHIG JUNTO packed the Commission with WHIGS. More Commissions were elected 1702–3, 1711–13 (reign of Queen ANNE), but were used by TORIES to attack WHIG ministers. *See also* GLORIOUS REVOLUTION.

PUBLIC HEALTH ACTS Legislation which sought to improve urban sanitary conditions. A campaign for legislation was started in 1838 by Edwin CHADWICK. His report of 1842 was followed by a royal commission (reported 1844, 1845) and the 1848 Public Health Act, the first national legislation. It authorized the creation of Local Boards of Health in England and Wales where mortality was high or at the request of ratepayers (London was excluded). They were to improve sanitation, SEWERAGE and water supplies. Town councils could become Health Boards. A General Board of Health provided central supervision (replaced 1854).

The 1848 Act was replaced, and provisions modified, by the Local Government Act of 1858, which renamed Boards as 'Local Boards'. The Public Health Act of 1872 established sanitary districts where Boards did not exist, with POOR LAW GUARDIANS becoming sanitary authorities in rural areas. The legislation was consolidated by the 1875 Public Health Act. County boroughs took over urban sanitary authorities in 1888, and other authorities became urban or rural district councils in 1894.

The 1848 and other relevant Acts were extended to Ireland in 1866, and the country was divided into sanitary districts in 1874. Provisions were supplemented by the Public Health (Ireland) Act of 1878. In Scotland the Public Health (Scotland) Act of 1867 awarded responsibility for water supply and public health to parochial boards (mostly transferred to county councils in 1889). *See also* MEDICINE AND PUBLIC HEALTH; CHOLERA.

PUBLIC LIBRARIES Libraries were founded for some parishes in Britain from the 17th century. In 1699 the Church of SCOTLAND supported a scheme for parish libraries in the Highlands (80 established). The first public library in Ireland was Marsh's Library in Dublin (opened 1707). Subscription libraries were started in many towns in the British Isles in the 18th century. In the 19th century clubs and MECHANICS' INSTITUTES often had libraries.

Publicly funded provision began with the 1850 Public Libraries Act, which permitted local authorities in England and Wales to establish rate-funded libraries (extended to Scotland and Ireland in 1854 and 1855 respectively). The spread of libraries in the UK was encouraged from 1883 by the donation of buildings with funds provided by Andrew CARNEGIE (660 before 1929). The 1919 Library Act enabled county councils in Great Britain to provide library services in less populated areas. Similar arrangements were made by Northern Ireland and the Irish Free State in 1924 and 1925.

PUBLIC SCHOOL *see* GRAMMAR SCHOOL

PUBLIC SECTOR BORROWING REQUIREMENT (PSBR) Term used in the UK from the late 1960s (in preference to 'budget deficit') for the total borrowing required by central government, local authorities and public corporations to cover deficits between their aggregate annual expenditures and revenues (thereby increasing NATIONAL DEBT). Reduction of PSBR (by expenditure cuts) was a central concern of governments in the late 1970s–80s, to help reduce money supply and INFLATION. PSBR was retitled 'Public Sector Net Cash Requirement' in 1998. *See also* PRIVATIZATION.

PUBLIC WORSHIP REGULATION ACT *see* RITUALISM

PUGIN, A.W.N. (b. 1 March 1812 at London, England; d. 14 Sept. 1852 at Ramsgate, Kent, England, aged 40). Augustus Welby Northmore Pugin worked from 1827 as a designer (e.g., of stage sets). From 1836 he collaborated with architect Charles Barry (1795–1860) on the decoration of the new Houses of Parliament at WESTMINSTER. In 1835 Pugin had converted from the Church of England to Roman Catholicism. An architect from 1837, he became the leading designer of Catholic churches in England, though limited funds often compromised his work. His identification of Catholicism with Gothic architecture reinforced the Gothic revival. Pugin regarded St Giles' Church, Cheadle (Staffordshire), as his most successful work. *See also* CATHOLICS AND CATHOLIC CHURCH, ENGLAND; ECCLESIOLOGISTS.

PULTENEY, WILLIAM (b. 22 March 1684, probably in Middlesex, England; d. 7 July 1764 at Piccadilly, Middlesex, aged 80). An MP from 1705, Pulteney held posts in the WHIG ministry from 1714 (in reign of King GEORGE I), resigning with Robert WALPOLE in 1717. When Walpole returned to office in 1720, he denied Pulteney a major position. (He served as cofferer of the royal household from 1723 until dismissed in 1725.)

Pulteney went into opposition and a group of 'patriot country Whigs' formed around him. He was a leading opponent of Walpole's excise scheme (1733; see EXCISE CRISIS) and in 1738 urged action against Spain (see JENKINS' EAR, WAR OF). After Walpole's fall (Jan. 1742) Pulteney joined the CABINET and was created earl of Bath (July). In 1746, when the PELHAMS resigned, GEORGE II appointed Bath as first lord of the Treasury, but he and the earl of GRANVILLE failed to form a ministry and resigned (11–14 Feb.).

PURA WALLIA (Latin, meaning 'pure Wales'). Term used by Norman and English officials from c.1100 until the English Conquest (1282–3) for parts of WALES under native Welsh political control (as distinct from the MARCH OF WALES and areas under the English Crown).

PURCELL, HENRY (b. possibly 10 Sept. 1659 at London, or Westminster, Middlesex, England; d. 21 Nov. 1695 at Westminster, aged 36). A talented musician, Purcell was a composer for the string orchestra of King CHARLES II from 1677, organist of Westminster Abbey from 1679, and an organist of the Chapel Royal from 1682. He forged a distinctive compositional style influenced by fashionable Italian and French music. His numerous varied works, produced during a short life, include music for the stage (e.g., the pioneering opera *Dido and Aeneas*, 1689) and secular and sacred vocal music.

PURITANISM, ENGLAND A movement which sought further reformation (or purification) of the Church of ENGLAND following the ELIZABETHAN SETTLEMENT (1559). Demands included the abolition of ceremonies required by the PRAYER BOOK (e.g., kneeling at Holy Communion) and clerical dress. Some radicals sought replacement of episcopacy (government by bishops) with presbyterianism (government by presbyteries and synods). Puritans also advocated 'godly' personal life and a moral society. 'Puritan' originated as a term of abuse (1560s). ('Separatists' who rejected a corporate Church were sometimes deemed Puritans.)

The insistence by Queen ELIZABETH I, against Puritans, on conformity proved disruptive. The enforcement of clerical dress by Archbishop Matthew PARKER ('Vestiarian Controversy', 1566) caused some clergy to form independent Protestant churches. An attack on episcopacy by Thomas CARTWRIGHT (1570), and the 'Admonition Controversy' (dispute in print about Church government, 1572–7), led clergy in some counties to

establish presbyterian-type organizations (1580s). They were suppressed by Archbishop John WHITGIFT.

JAMES VI/I (king from 1603) also largely rebuffed Puritan demands (see HAMPTON COURT CONFERENCE). From c.1618 he acted against Puritans (e.g., 1622, preachers ordered to avoid controversial matters). Puritan dislike of the religious policies of Archbishop William LAUD and CHARLES I in the 1630s contributed to EMIGRATION and to the outbreak of CIVIL WAR in 1642 (see SHORT PARLIAMENT; LONG PARLIAMENT).

Parliamentary power made Puritanism influential in the 1640s–50s (see COMMONWEALTH AND PROTECTORATE). Parliament introduced simpler services (in Directory of Public Worship, 1645) and social changes (e.g., 1647, religious feasts replaced by secular holidays). But church reform, though intended, was prevented by disagreements between Presbyterians, Independents (Congregationalists) and other sects (see SOLEMN LEAGUE AND COVENANT; WESTMINSTER ASSEMBLY).

After the RESTORATION (1660), the Church of England largely rejected changes intended to accommodate Puritans (see SAVOY CONFERENCE). Numerous Puritan clergy were expelled in 1662, leaving Puritanism mostly outside the Church. It remained influential in Protestant dissenting churches and culture, and in NEW ENGLAND. *See also* REFORMATION, ENGLAND; CALVINISM; BROWNISTS; NONCONFORMITY AND DISSENT, ENGLAND; CHURCH, ENGLAND AND WALES, 1640s–50s; BAXTER, RICHARD; BUNYAN, JOHN.

PURITANISM, IRELAND *see* NONCONFORMITY AND DISSENT, IRELAND

PURITANISM, WALES From the 1580s a few Welshmen (in the Church of ENGLAND) advocated strict Puritan living (e.g., Lewis BAYLY, Rhys PRICHARD). Only John Penry advocated the radical replacement of government by bishops (episcopacy) with government by presbyteries and synods (presbyterianism); he was hanged for treason in 1593. Radical Puritans emerged from the 1630s (e.g., Vavasor POWELL), and in 1639 an independent congregation was founded at Llanfaches (Monmouthshire).

Parliament's victory in the CIVIL WARS (1642–8) strengthened Puritanism: in 1650 it passed the Act for the Better Propagation of the Gospel in Wales, under which a commission ejected clergy considered unsatisfactory and recruited preachers (lapsed 1653). After the RESTORATION of the monarchy 118 Puritan clergy were evicted from their livings (1660–2); many organized dissenting congregations outside the established Church. *See also* CLARENDON CODE; NONCONFORMITY AND DISSENT, WALES.

PURITY MOVEMENT Campaigns, 1860s–1910s, in England and Ireland which began with opposition to the

CONTAGIOUS DISEASES ACTS (1860s). Involving vigilante groups and chastity leagues, it sought to prevent the sexual exploitation of women, eliminate the double standard (the focus on women's behaviour), and promote ideals of sexual purity. It achieved the 1885 Criminal Law Amendment Act (applicable in UK), which sought to suppress brothels, raised the age of consent to 16, and prohibited male homosexual acts (styled 'gross indecency'). Campaigners also closed brothels in London. *See also* BUTLER, JOSEPHINE; STEAD, W.T.

PUSEY, E.B. (b. 22 Aug. 1800 at Pusey, Berkshire, England; d. 16 Sept. 1882 at Ascot, Berkshire, aged 82). In 1823 Edward Bouverie Pusey became a fellow of Oriel College, OXFORD, where he became friendly with John KEBLE and John Henry NEWMAN. From 1828 he was a Church of England clergyman and regius professor of Hebrew at Oxford University. In the 1830s–40s Pusey promoted the OXFORD MOVEMENT with Keble and Newman, and was regarded as its leader after Newman became a Roman Catholic (1845). He sought to combat rationalism and secularism, and to revive Catholic practices within the Church of England (e.g., encouraging personal confession).

PUTNEY DEBATES In England, 1647, following the First CIVIL WAR, discussions held near London by the General Council of the NEW MODEL ARMY, including LEVELLERS, to formulate proposals for settling the conflict between King CHARLES I and Parliament. Meeting in and around St Mary's Church, Putney (Surrey), 28 Oct.–9 Nov., with Oliver CROMWELL as chairman, the Council was presented with a radical political and religious constitutional programme (*see* AGREEMENT OF THE PEOPLE). The Debates were inconclusive. *See also* CIVIL WARS, POLITICAL ASPECTS.

PYM, JOHN (b. 20 May 1584 in England; d. 8 Dec. 1643 at London, England, aged 59). An MP from 1621, Pym, a Puritan, attacked popery and alleged Arminian clergy (e.g., Richard MONTAGU). In 1628 he supported the PETITION OF RIGHT.

In the SHORT PARLIAMENT (from April 1640), Pym was a leading critic of King CHARLES I. He liaised with the king's Scottish enemies. In the LONG PARLIAMENT (from Nov.) he co-ordinated impeachment of the earl of Strafford (Thomas WENTWORTH). After the ULSTER RISING (Oct. 1641), he sought to prevent Charles from controlling armed forces that could be used against his English enemies (*see* MILITIA ORDINANCE). In Jan. 1642 Pym was among the MPs whom CHARLES I tried to arrest (*see* FIVE MEMBERS INCIDENT).

After war began (Aug. 1642) Pym was influential in Parliament's war effort, organizing county committees and the EXCISE. He helped to negotiate the SOLEMN LEAGUE AND COVENANT with the Scots (Aug. 1643). *See also* CIVIL WARS; CIVIL WARS, POLITICAL ASPECTS.

Q

QUADRUPLE ALLIANCE An agreement between Great Britain, France, Spain and Portugal, signed 22 April 1834. Designed by Lord PALMERSTON as a liberal counterbalance to the Holy Alliance (principally Austria, Russia and Prussia), it sought to defeat absolutist pretenders to the Spanish and Portuguese thrones. It succeeded in PORTUGAL.

QUAKERS Popular name for the Religious Society of Friends, a Christian denomination that eschews clergy, liturgy and formulated creeds. It originated in England in the 1640s with preaching tours by George Fox. His followers, sometimes drawn from ENGLISH REVOLUTION SECTS, were derisively called 'Quakers' because they allegedly trembled. In 1652 Fox organized a structure of local meetings (usually monthly), district meetings (quarterly), and national meeting (annual). Women were allowed prominence. Because Quakers refused to acknowledge social superiors, they were seen as subverting social order. They also espoused pacifism.

'Quakerism' spread quickly through Britain, and to Ireland (organized by Fox, 1669), Continental Europe and the Americas. Quakers were persecuted until Toleration Acts were passed (England and Wales, 1689; Ireland, 1719). Many Quakers excelled in business. They also campaigned for abolition of the SLAVE TRADE and of SLAVERY in the British Empire (achieved in early 19th century), and in Ireland provided relief (1846–9) during the GREAT FAMINE. In the 1930s Quakers assisted Jewish refugees from Germany. In 2015 there were about 23,000 'Friends' (members and 'attenders') in Britain and about 1000 in Ireland. *See also* PENNSYLVANIA.

QUANGO Acronym used in the UK from the 1970s for 'quasi-autonomous non-governmental organization'. A quango (e.g., Audit Commission, founded 1983) is involved in government while enjoying some independence, although its senior members are usually appointed by a government minister. British CIVIL SERVICE reforms in the 1980s produced more quangos, but the coalition government elected in 2010 pledged to reduce them.

QUARTER SESSIONS *see* JUSTICES OF THE PEACE

QUEBEC ACT Legislation passed by the British Parliament, April 1774, to provide administrative and other arrangements for the former French province of Quebec (N America), captured in the SEVEN YEARS WAR. It provided an executive government, and guaranteed freedom of worship for Catholics and French legal procedures. The Act angered Protestant opinion in the British colony of MASSACHUSETTS, which associated it with the INTOLERABLE ACTS. *See also* CANADA.

QUEENSBERRY, 2ND DUKE OF (b. 18 Dec. 1662 at Sanquhar Castle, SW Scotland; d. 6 July 1711 at London, England, aged 48). In 1688–9 James Douglas supported

A Dictionary of British and Irish History, First Edition. Edited by Robert Peberdy and Philip Waller.
© 2021 John Wiley & Sons Ltd; © editorial matter and organisation Robert Peberdy and Phillip Waller.
Published 2021 by John Wiley & Sons Ltd.

the accession of William of Orange (*see* WILLIAM III) in place of King JAMES VII/II. Douglas succeeded as duke in 1695 and became a lord of SESSION and keeper of the privy seal, and was KING'S COMMISSIONER (1700), a position he retained under Queen ANNE. He was also a SECRETARY OF STATE from 1702. In 1703–4 Queensberry was implicated in Jacobite plotting and lost his offices, regaining favour in 1705. As commissioner (from 1706) he was pre-eminent in securing passage of the treaty of Union (1707) and was rewarded with English titles and offices (1708–9). He was nicknamed the 'Union Duke'. *See also* JACOBITISM, IMPACT ON BRITISH POLITICS; UNION OF ENGLAND AND SCOTLAND.

QUEEN'S COMMISSIONER, SCOTLAND *see* KING'S (OR QUEEN'S) COMMISSIONER, SCOTLAND

QUEENSLAND A former British colony in AUSTRALIA. Its area, in NE Australia, was claimed for Great Britain by James COOK in 1770 as part of NEW SOUTH WALES. Used for penal settlement 1825–40 (*see* TRANSPORTATION), Queensland was opened to free colonists in 1842. It became a separate colony, with RESPONSIBLE GOVERNMENT, in 1859. After a gold rush attracted immigrants (1858–73), the population reached 498,000 in 1901, when Queensland joined the Commonwealth of Australia (*see* AUSTRALIAN FEDERATION).

QUIA EMPTORES (Latin, meaning 'Because the buyers'). Name of a statute issued by the English PARLIAMENT in 1290 which permitted freemen to sell or alienate land or tenements freely, with the buyer replacing the seller in relation to a superior lord. It modified feudal land-holding by ending the practice of 'subinfeudation' whereby a buyer became the tenant of the seller. *See also* LEGAL REFORMS, ENGLAND, REIGN OF EDWARD I; TENURES, ENGLAND FROM 1066.

***QUO WARRANTO* INQUIRIES** Investigations by the English government 1274–5 into franchises which individuals exercised in England and Wales (e.g., manorial rights) and into the right by which they were claimed. They are so called from the Latin phrase *quo warranto* ('by what warrant [or authority]') which appears in related documents. The investigations were part of efforts by King Edward I to reform justice and increase royal authority in the provinces. *See also* LEGAL REFORMS, ENGLAND, REIGN OF EDWARD I.

R

RADAR *see* WATSON-WATT, ROBERT; DOWDING, HUGH

RADCOT BRIDGE, BATTLE OF *see* RICHARD II; APPELLANTS

RADICALS Term first used in the 1820s to describe campaigners for fundamental political reform from the late 18th century, some organized in extraparliamentary associations such as the Corresponding Societies of the 1790s. Radicals' demands from the 1760s onwards included a broader suffrage (eligibility to vote), frequent general elections, measures to prevent parliamentary corruption, and lower taxation. The term remained in general use for proponents of fundamental political and social reforms until the early 20th century.

RADICAL WAR Anti-government activity in early April 1820; the most serious challenge to authority in Scotland during the 1819–20 depression. On 1 April, 60,000 workers in and around GLASGOW (W-C Scotland) went on strike, expecting an uprising in England. A group marching on the Carron ironworks at Falkirk (Stirlingshire) was scattered ('battle of Bonnymuir'); three men were later executed. *See also* PETERLOO.

RADIO BROADCASTING, GREAT BRITAIN AND NORTHERN IRELAND In 1920 the Marconi Company made experimental broadcasts, then operated two local stations, '2MT' (1922–3) and '2LO' (from May 1922). The POST OFFICE (licensing authority) persuaded intending broadcasters to form a national British Broadcasting Company (BBC), funded partly by licences. It used 2LO's equipment, in LONDON, from 14 Nov. 1922, with John REITH becoming general manager (Dec.).

The BBC established nine linked stations which broadcast national and local material (music, drama, talks, news). By 1926 there were 1.8 million licence-holders. The company was replaced (1927) by a public corporation (*see* BRITISH BROADCASTING CORPORATION), which introduced outside broadcasts (1927), a regional structure (1930), and overseas services (1930s; *see* BBC WORLD SERVICE). From the late 1920s the BBC was challenged by livelier commercial broadcasting from Continental Europe. TELEVISION also started (1932–9).

During WORLD WAR II (1939–45) a Home Service included public information. It was supplemented by an entertainment-based Forces Service (1941–4; replaced by General Forces Service), which became the Light Programme (July 1945). A cultural Third Programme was added (1946). Licences peaked in 1950 at 11.8 million.

Revived commercial radio (from 1944) and television presented competition, as did ship-based 'pop stations' (so-called 'pirates') from 1964, which the government attempted to suppress (1967). The BBC responded with the 'pop' service Radio 1 (1967), and refashioned its other services (as Radios 2, 3, 4). New frequencies enabled development of 'local radio' (from 1967).

A Dictionary of British and Irish History, First Edition. Edited by Robert Peberdy and Philip Waller.
© 2021 John Wiley & Sons Ltd; © editorial matter and organisation Robert Peberdy and Phillip Waller.
Published 2021 by John Wiley & Sons Ltd.

Licensed independent stations started from 1973, but restricted localities caused many to fail. New legislation, implemented from 1992, allowed national commercial stations and grouped local stations. 'Digital' technology, from 1995, facilitated more stations. In 2017, the BBC operated 11 national, six regional and 38 local stations; there were about 30 national commercial stations and over 300 local services. About 90% of the population listened weekly.

RADIO BROADCASTING, SOUTHERN IRELAND
see BROADCASTING, SOUTHERN IRELAND

RÆDWALD (fl. from *c*.604; d. between 616 and 627). The first extensively documented king of EAST ANGLIA (E England), though his reign is undated. Possibly *c*.604 Rædwald was baptized a Christian in KENT (ruled by ÆTHELBERT, overking of the southern Anglo-Saxons), but he also continued to worship pagan deities.

After Æthelbert's death (616), Rædwald became overking. He defeated (616 or 617) Æthelfrith, king of BERNICIA and DEIRA (NE England), enabling the accession of EDWIN (under his protection). Rædwald possibly encouraged the expulsion of bishops from ESSEX and Kent. He is associated with the SUTTON HOO ship burial. *See also* KINGSHIP, ANGLO-SAXON.

RAFFLES, STAMFORD (b. 6 July 1781 at sea off Port Morant, Jamaica; d. 5 July 1826 at Hendon, Middlesex, England, aged 44). A proponent of British expansion in SE Asia. Employed by the EAST INDIA COMPANY from 1795, Raffles spent 1805–10 at Penang (Malaya), and in 1808 persuaded the company to retain Malacca (settlement seized from Dutch). From 1811 to 1816 he governed Java (seized from French; *see* JAVA, BRITISH INTERREGNUM IN). In 1817 Raffles published *The History of Java* and was knighted.

From 1818 Raffles was governor-general of Bengkulu, a British possession in Dutch Sumatra. Wanting to extend British influence, he was authorized to establish a settlement by the southern entrance to the Malacca Strait. In 1819 he founded SINGAPORE. He returned to England in 1824.

RAIDING, CROSS-BORDER A principal method by which Scots attacked England (until 1603; *see* UNION OF CROWNS, ENGLAND (WITH IRELAND) AND SCOTLAND). Unable to reach the government in southern England, Scots raided northern England, seeking to force local leaders to influence the government. Scots used raids intensively in 1314–23 and 1337–42 when they sought recognition of their independence. Border nobles – on both sides – also organized local raids for plunder. *See also* SCOTTISH–ENGLISH RELATIONS 1290 TO 1357/1357 TO 1603.

RAILWAYS, ENGLAND Railways developed from waggonways, which used wooden rails to ease the passage of horse-drawn coal trucks from mines to river ports. The first was built in 1603–4 in Nottinghamshire (Strelley–Lenton); others were mainly in NE England. Iron bars were added to rails at Coalbrookdale (Shropshire) in 1767. Steam locomotives (pioneered by Richard TREVITHICK) entered commercial service at Middleton (Yorkshire) in 1812 (*see* BLENKINSOP, JOHN). The Stockton and Darlington Railway (1825) first conveyed passengers by steam power.

The profitability of the LIVERPOOL and MANCHESTER Railway (1830) encouraged investment, with 'railway mania' peaks in 1835–7 and 1845–8 as over 300 JOINT-STOCK COMPANIES built lines without central planning, albeit offering a national timetable (1839) and through-ticketing (1842). Parliament authorized a standard gauge in 1846. The Crewe–BIRMINGHAM–LONDON route connected industrial NW England to the capital (1838). Isambard Kingdom BRUNEL engineered the London–BRISTOL track (1841), and George HUDSON dominated operations in NE England. By 1860 the essential network was complete, though branch construction continued for another 50 years. London underground services started in 1863. Railways largely displaced CANALS and coastal shipping. Lower transport costs stimulated industry, mass consumerism, suburban development, and seaside resorts, and made poorer people unprecedentedly mobile.

During the 20th century, competition from road transport damaged railways. Companies amalgamated into four groups in 1922–3: London, Midland and Scottish; London and North-Eastern; Great Western; and Southern. These were nationalized from 1948 as the monopoly 'British Railways' (renamed 'British Rail' 1965). Diesel and electric trains replaced steam (1947–68) except on small independent tourist railways. With the closure of uncommercial lines, especially after the 'BEECHING REPORT' (1963), route length nearly halved from its 1920s maximum. The CHANNEL TUNNEL (1994) provided a link to Continental Europe. Passenger numbers increased after reorganization into separate companies (1994) and PRIVATIZATION (1996–7). Infrastructure was returned to State control in 2002. *See also* STEPHENSON, GEORGE; TRANSPORT COMMUNICATIONS, ENGLAND.

RAILWAYS, IRELAND *see* TRANSPORT COMMUNICATIONS, IRELAND

RAILWAYS, SCOTLAND From 1722 waggonways were built for transporting coal to ports in horse-hauled trains. The Kilmarnock and Troon Railway (Ayrshire), opened 1812, also carried passengers and tested a steam locomotive (1817). Locomotives were used regularly from 1831 on the Monkland and Kirkintilloch Railway

(Dunbartonshire, opened 1826), and on the Garnkirk and Glasgow Railway (opened 1831).

The EDINBURGH and GLASGOW Railway, opened 1842, was the first passenger railway between major centres. Lines were then built southwards to England: Edinburgh to BERWICK-UPON-TWEED (1846), Edinburgh and Glasgow to CARLISLE (1848; second route from Glasgow, 1850). Routes northwards reached STIRLING and PERTH (1848, linking with the Perth and DUNDEE Railway, opened 1847), and ABERDEEN (1850). From 1850 trains also travelled between Edinburgh and Dundee using train-ferries (the world's first) across the Rivers Forth and Tay. (The Tay Bridge, opened in 1878, collapsed in 1879; replaced 1887. The Forth Bridge was opened in 1890.)

In the N, lines joined Inverness southwards to Perth (1863), westwards to Stromeferry (1870), and northwards to Wick and Thurso (1874). The western HIGHLANDS were reached last (Glasgow to Fort William, 1894; extension to Mallaig, 1901, subsidized by government to help CROFTING areas). By 1910 there were 3800 mi (6,080 km) of railways, including suburban and branch lines. They had enabled expansion of coal exporting, export of fattened livestock to London, and TOURISM.

In 1923 companies were 'grouped' into two Anglo-Scottish companies. After nationalization in 1948 a Scottish Region of British Railways was formed. Traffic fell in the 1920s–30s, recovered in the 1950s, and fell substantially in the 1970s–80s with competition from road transport and INDUSTRIAL DECLINE. From the late 1940s many lines were closed (*see* 'BEECHING REPORT'). Diesel locomotives replaced steam from the late 1950s. Railways were privatized in 1996–7. *See also* TRANSPORT COMMUNICATIONS, SCOTLAND.

RAILWAYS, WALES Waggonways were built in S Wales from the 1690s for transporting minerals in horse-hauled waggon trains, and in 1804 the world's first haulage by steam locomotive (of iron) occurred on a plateway at Penydaran, near MERTHYR TYDFIL (*see* TREVITHICK, RICHARD). From 1807 the horse-drawn Oystermouth Railway, operating along Swansea Bay, provided the world's first regular service for fare-paying passengers.

Wales's first steam railway was the Llanelli–Pontarddulais line (Carmarthenshire), which opened in 1839. Other local lines followed, mainly in S Wales. Sponsored by industrialists, they facilitated expansion of the COAL INDUSTRY. Routes across the N and S (for Ireland) were completed in 1851 and 1856 respectively, and across C Wales in 1864. By 1870 there were 1430 mi (2300 km). Railways transformed industry, stimulated agriculture, created tourist trades (along the N Wales coast and Cardigan Bay), undermined localism and enriched cultural life. They prospered until 1914.

In 1922–3 most companies were absorbed in the Great Western Railway or the London, Midland and Scottish

(nationalized 1948 within British Railways). As coal and steel declined from the 1920s, lines were closed. Another 360 mi (580 km) were closed after the 'BEECHING REPORT' (1963), leaving 270 mi (430 km). In the 1960s diesels replaced steam locomotives. The industry was privatized 1996–7. Several narrow-gauge steam railways survived as tourist attractions. *See also* TRANSPORT COMMUNICATIONS, WALES.

RALEGH, WALTER (b. 1554 at Hayes, Devon, England; d. 29 Oct. 1618 at Westminster, Middlesex, England, aged about 64). Courtier and seaman. After suppressing rebellion in Ireland (1580–1), Ralegh became a favourite of Queen ELIZABETH I (1581; knighted 1584). From 1583 he developed colonization plans made by his half-brother Humphrey GILBERT, organizing a trans-Atlantic expedition (1584) and the ROANOKE SETTLEMENTS (1585–90). A secret marriage, revealed to Elizabeth in May 1592, resulted in banishment from court.

Now preoccupied with the legendary golden city of Eldorado, Ralegh made an expedition in 1595 to 'Guiana' (N coast of S America). His participation in expeditions against Spain (1596, to Cádiz, SW Spain; 1597, to the Azores) restored him to Elizabeth's favour (1597).

JAMES VI/I, king from 1603 and influenced by Ralegh's enemies, proved hostile. Ralegh was convicted of treason on weak evidence (1603), but his death sentence was suspended and he remained in prison. He was released (1616) to make another expedition to Guiana (1617–18). He incurred James's wrath for violently infringing peace with Spain, and the death sentence was implemented. Ralegh was also a prolific author. His writings include the *History of the World* (1614). *See also* BRITISH GUIANA.

RAMSEY, MICHAEL (b. 14 Nov. 1904 at Cambridge, Cambridgeshire, England; d. 23 April 1988 at Oxford, Oxfordshire, England, aged 83). A Church of ENGLAND clergyman and theologian, with a nonconformist father, Ramsey became bishop of DURHAM (1952) and archbishop of YORK (1956). Proposed by (Conservative) Prime Minister Harold MACMILLAN, he was archbishop of CANTERBURY 1961–74.

In 1963 Ramsey attempted to calm the controversy stirred by *Honest to God* (*see* ROBINSON, JOHN). His speech on 26 Oct. 1965 supporting possible military action against white rebels in Rhodesia attracted criticism (*see* RHODESIA PROBLEM), as did his backing for liberal social legislation (e.g., decriminalization of consenting homosexual activity, though believing it remained sinful). Ramsey sought more freedom from Parliament for the Church of England and better relations with other Churches (e.g., visited Pope Paul VI, 1966). He was disappointed by defeat of proposed union of the Church of England with METHODISTS (1972).

RANDOLPH, THOMAS (b. *c.*1280; d. 20 July 1332 at Musselburgh, Lothian, SE Scotland, aged about 52). A Scottish knight who supported the English in Scotland against King ROBERT I (his mother's half-brother) 1306–8; he then fought for Robert, becoming his main commander. He was created earl of MORAY (1312) and also received Annandale and the Isle of MAN; all of these territories were held in REGALITY. As guardian (1329–32) for DAVID II, Randolph organized the king's CORONATION (1331) in response to the challenge from Edward BALLIOL.

RANULF FLAMBARD (b. *c.*1060 near Bayeux, Normandy; d. 5 Sept. 1128 at Durham, England, aged about 68). A priest's son from NORMANDY who joined the court of King WILLIAM I (1080s), Ranulf became chief officer (without official title) to WILLIAM II (ruled England 1087–1100). Nicknamed 'Torch', Ranulf enforced controversial policies (e.g., drawing revenues from vacant bishoprics and abbacies). He was appointed bishop of DURHAM (NE England) in 1099.

After the accession of HENRY I (Aug. 1100) Ranulf was imprisoned in the Tower of LONDON. He escaped (Feb. 1101) and joined ROBERT CURTHOSE in Normandy. Although later reconciled to Henry (1102), he returned to Durham only after Robert was defeated at TINCHEBRAI (1106). In Durham he was remembered as a builder and benefactor.

RAPPAREES In Ireland, name used during the WILLIAMITE WAR (1688–91) for independent forces supporting JAMES VII/II who operated against King William III's supporters in Williamite-held areas. They were prominent in the months before the battle of AUGHRIM (July 1691), when they destroyed buildings and livestock. Their name is derived from the use of half-pikes (Irish *ropairí*). It was later applied generally to bandits.

RATIONING, WORLD WAR I Great Britain depended heavily on imported food, and from Aug. 1914 the government sought to maintain supplies and encouraged self-restraint. German submarines caused food shortages by 1917: sugar rationing was introduced on 31 Dec., and rationing of meat, bacon, ham and butter started in London and SE England in Feb. 1918. Rationing was extended throughout Britain by July. Householders registered with retailers, and received coupons and ration books. Controls continued beyond the armistice (Nov.) to Oct. 1919. *See also* WORLD WAR I, IMPACT ON BRITISH SOCIETY.

RATIONING, WORLD WAR II Rationing was introduced in Great Britain and Northern Ireland at an early stage and became wide-ranging. It operated mainly through coupons. Petrol was rationed from Sept. 1939; butter, sugar and some meats from Jan. 1940; other meats from March; tea from July; clothes from 1941–2; sweets from July 1942. Other 'scarce goods' were distributed using a 'points system', and liquid milk was allocated from Nov. 1941 (remaining uncontrolled in Northern Ireland). Petrol rationing was suspended 1943–5, when supplies were low. Bread, potatoes, fruit, vegetables and fish were not rationed. Rationing was considered egalitarian, and children's diets improved. It continued beyond the war's end (1945), being withdrawn in phases in 1949–54. *See also* WORLD WAR II, IMPACT ON BRITISH SOCIETY.

RAY, JOHN (b. 29 Nov. 1627 at Black Notley, Essex, England; d. 17 Jan. 1705 at Black Notley, aged 76). A student at CAMBRIDGE University from 1644, Wray (his surname until 1670) became a fellow of Trinity College in 1649. Ordained in 1660, he forfeited his fellowship (1662) for refusing an oath (*see* CLARENDON CODE). From 1672 he was supported by an annuity bequeathed by his collaborator and patron Francis Willughby, and in 1679 returned to his birthplace.

Interested in natural philosophy (science) from the 1650s, Wray studied plants around Cambridge, and with collaborators undertook tours in Britain from 1658 and in Continental Europe in the 1660s. He published (in Latin) a *Cambridge Catalogue* (plants from Cambridge's vicinity, 1660) and *English Catalogue* (1670). His *History of Plants* (two volumes 1688, third volume 1704), describing over 16,000 species, established the species as a concept and basic unit of classification. He also brought Willughby's researches on zoology to publication, and wrote religious works. Ray was among the first to recognize fossils as remains of living things, and to question Bible-based history of the Earth (*see* USSHER, JAMES). He influenced the Swedish taxonomist Carl Linnaeus (1707–78). *See also* SCIENTIFIC REVOLUTION.

REBECCA RIOTS Attacks in SW Wales, 1839–44; initially on toll-gates, later on workhouses, JUSTICES OF THE PEACE, tithe-owners and landlords. Rioters were led by a 'Rebecca', a man often disguised as a woman, named after Rebecca in the Bible, where the wishes for her include: 'let thy seed possess the gate of those which hate them' (Genesis 24:60). *See also* TURNPIKE TRUSTS AND ROADS, WALES.

REBELLION OF 1848 An anti-British rising by members of the YOUNG IRELAND movement, inspired by revolution in France (Feb.). Rebels, led by William Smith O'BRIEN, recruited supporters in Cos. Kilkenny and Tipperary. A group clashed with police on 29 July near Ballingarry, Co. Tipperary (so-called 'battle of Widow McCormack's cabbage-patch'). The Rebellion was easily suppressed. Some participants continued 'physical force' nationalism by founding the IRISH REPUBLICAN BROTHERHOOD and FENIAN BROTHERHOOD.

RECUSANCY, ENGLAND AND WALES Recusancy was the practice of refusing to attend services of the Church of ENGLAND (from Latin *recusare*, meaning 'to refuse'). Non-attendance was punishable under the 1552 and 1559 Acts of Uniformity, the latter imposing a 12*d*. fine per absence. The term 'recusant' was used from 1568 and in practice applied to Catholics (also called 'Popish recusants'). Catholics ceased to attend parish churches from the 1570s, following the Pope's excommunication of Queen ELIZABETH I (1570). Recusancy was most common in N England, and in NE and SE Wales. The recusancy fine was raised to £20 per month in 1581. Fines were levied regularly until the 1680s.

Additional disabilities were imposed until 1605. For example, in 1581 it became treasonable to convert someone to Catholicism, from 1587 property could be seized, and in 1605 recusants were barred from public offices and professions. More disabilities were imposed in the late 17th century: recusants were barred from Parliament (1678), were subject to double land tax (1692), and were prohibited from buying or inheriting land (1700).

Disabilities were removed by the 1778 Relief Act (Catholics allowed to serve in the Army and own land), the 1791 Relief Act (Catholic worship permitted), and CATHOLIC EMANCIPATION (1829). *See also* REFORMATION, ENGLAND/ WALES; CATHOLICS AND CATHOLIC CHURCH, ENGLAND/WALES.

RECUSANCY, IRELAND From the 1570s many people openly refused to attend the Protestant Church of IRELAND as required by the religious settlement of 1560 (*see* ELIZABETHAN SETTLEMENT, IRELAND). They adhered instead to the unofficial Catholic Church, thus identifying themselves as 'recusants' (refusers). The Irish government intermittently attempted to prosecute and fine recusants, mainly in English-speaking areas; this happened notably from 1605 for several years, in 1611–12, 1615, and 1632. Proceedings usually met resistance, especially from OLD ENGLISH. *See also* CATHOLICS AND CATHOLIC CHURCH, IRELAND.

RED BOOK OF HERGEST An important Welsh manuscript (belonging to Jesus College, OXFORD, England, kept in the Bodleian Library, Oxford), which was copied by three scribes, including Hywel Fychan of BUILTH, for Hopcyn ap Thomas of Ynysforgan near Swansea 1375–1400. It includes *Y MABINOGI*; works of *cynfeirdd* ('early poets' of 6th–12th centuries) and poets of the 12th–13th centuries; *BRUT Y TYWYSOGION*; and Middle Welsh translations of GEOFFREY OF MONMOUTH's *History* and French romances. *See also* WELSH LANGUAGE AND LITERATURE.

RED CLYDESIDE Name given from 1915 to the GLASGOW area of Scotland (an important area of munitions production in WORLD WAR I), characterizing conflict (1915–16, 1922) and left-wing attitudes. The Clyde Workers' Committee (formed Feb. 1915) opposed the war and encouraged local grievances (e.g., rent strike Oct.–Nov. 1915; dispute over DILUTION Jan.–April 1916). A Soviet (workers' assembly) existed briefly in Aug. 1917.

In 1922 a strike for a 40-hour working week (27 Jan.–2 Feb.) resulted in violence. In Nov. Glasgow elected 10 MPs of the INDEPENDENT LABOUR PARTY, who were collectively known as the CLYDESIDERS. Though their impact in Parliament was limited, their home area long remained under Labour domination. *See also* MACLEAN, JOHN; MAXTON, JAMES; HOUSING LEGISLATION, SCOTLAND.

REDMOND, JOHN (b. 1 Sept. 1856 at Ballytrent, Co. Wexford, Ireland; d. 6 March 1918 at London, England, aged 61). A (Catholic) lawyer, admirer of Irish leader C.S. PARNELL, and supporter of Irish HOME RULE, Redmond was elected to the UK Parliament in 1881. After the IRISH PARLIAMENTARY PARTY split (1890), Redmond supported Parnell's minority group and became its leader after Parnell's death (1891), continuing after the Party's reunion (1900).

From 1912, when enactment of Home Rule seemed likely (in 1914), Redmond sought to ensure implementation, despite Unionists' opposition. In June 1914 he imposed control on the recently founded IRISH VOLUNTEERS, and after the UK entered WORLD WAR I (Aug.) he expressed support (to demonstrate Ireland's worthiness for self-government). When Great Britain's government tried, after the EASTER RISING (1916), to devise a Home Rule scheme acceptable to Unionists, Redmond rejected proposals involving Ulster's exclusion (July 1916, May 1917). He then participated in the IRISH CONVENTION (from July), but was increasingly marginalized by the rise of Irish republicanism. *See also* UNIONISM, IRELAND.

REEVE An officer in medieval England; the term is derived from OE *gerefa* meaning 'prefect' or 'steward', denoting a man with administrative responsibility. From the 5th or 6th century reeves collected renders (food, drink) due to kings and noblemen. Royal reeves became important in the 10th and 11th centuries, when they assumed some duties from EALDORMEN (e.g., organizing MILITARY SERVICE). Eventually a reeve in each SHIRE became recognized as principal reeve (*see* SHERIFF). In towns royal interests were administered by a portreeve.

In late Anglo-Saxon England (9th–11th centuries) villages and parishes appointed reeves as their representatives in courts and in dealings with lords. From the 12th century reeves increasingly acted as lords' officers, organizing agriculture on MANORS. *See also* KINGSHIP, ANGLO-SAXON.

REFORM ACT (SCOTLAND), 1832 *see* REFORM ACTS, SCOTLAND; FRANCHISE, SCOTLAND

REFORM ACTS, SCOTLAND Between 1707 and 1832 Scotland was represented in the British House of Commons by 30 shire and 15 BURGH members, 14 of the latter representing burgh-groups (only Edinburgh had its own MP). The 1832 Scottish Reform Act increased burgh representatives to 23. (Glasgow received two MPs, Edinburgh an extra MP, and Aberdeen, Dundee, Greenock, Paisley and Perth one each.) The Second Scottish Reform Act (1868) increased MPs to 60 (including two university MPs). The widening of the franchise by both Acts combined with the Ballot Act (1872), which introduced secret ballots, encouraged the development of organized parties. The Third (British) Reform Act (1884) enfranchised about two-thirds of adult males, while the Redistribution of Seats Act (1885) increased seats to 72, introduced roughly comparable constituencies, and abolished two burgh-groups.

In the 20th century the franchise was further widened (*see* FRANCHISE, SCOTLAND), and constituencies were increased to 74 (1918, adding a university seat). University constituencies were abolished in 1948 and burgh-groups in 1949. The number of parliamentary constituencies remained similar until reduced to 59 from 2005. *See also* PARLIAMENTARY REPRESENTATION, SCOTLAND.

REFORMATION, ENGLAND Events and movements 1531–59 which eventually established a State Church under royal and parliamentary authority, professing Protestant doctrine (*see* ENGLAND, CHURCH OF).

Although Catholic doctrine was challenged from the 1520s (*see* LUTHERANISM), the first decisive change was the repudiation of papal authority over the English Church (1530s). It happened because Pope Clement VII refused to annul the marriage of King HENRY VIII, who lacked a male heir (*see* GREAT MATTER). In 1531 Henry forced clergy to acknowledge him as 'head of the Church'; in 1532, the clergy formally submitted; in 1533, appeals to Rome were prohibited; in 1534, Parliament confirmed Henry's supremacy (*see* REFORMATION PARLIAMENT). Henry was persuaded to back further changes by reform-minded supporters, notably Archbishop Thomas CRANMER and Thomas CROMWELL. Cromwell organized the DISSOLUTION OF RELIGIOUS HOUSES (1536–40), authorized use of the English BIBLE (1536), and discouraged some Catholic practices (e.g., pilgrimages, 1536). Official doctrine was largely unchanged (*see* TEN ARTICLES; BISHOPS' BOOK; SIX ARTICLES; KING'S BOOK).

Under EDWARD VI, king from 1547 and a minor, anti-heresy legislation was repealed and counsellors implemented radical changes. Injunctions (1547) forbad many Catholic practices (e.g., images to be destroyed); CHANTRIES were dissolved (1548). In 1549 Cranmer's PRAYER BOOK imposed a reformed liturgy in English. A revised Prayer Book (1552) introduced a clearly Protestant communion service. In 1553 a statement of reformed doctrines was published (*see* ARTICLES OF RELIGION).

Edward's half-sister MARY I (ruler from 1553) sought to restore Catholicism. Mass was permitted, papal jurisdiction was readopted (1554), Edward's legislation was repealed and anti-heresy laws reinstated (1555). Numerous Protestants were burnt, including Cranmer.

Mary died before Catholicism could be entrenched. Her half-sister ELIZABETH I (ruler from 1558) restored royal supremacy and Protestant doctrine (*see* ELIZABETHAN SETTLEMENT). Most clergy and people acquiesced. But significant minorities demanded further reform or remained loyal to Catholicism (*see* PURITANISM, ENGLAND; RECUSANCY, ENGLAND AND WALES). *See also* CHURCH, MEDIEVAL ENGLAND.

REFORMATION, IRELAND As in England, HENRY VIII obtained authority over the Church through parliamentary legislation (passed by the 'Irish Reformation Parliament', 1536–7). In May 1536 Parliament declared Henry 'supreme head on earth', replacing the Pope. Other legislation vested royal succession in the children of Ann BOLEYN, replaced the Roman Curia with the Irish Court of Chancery for ecclesiastical appeals, and appropriated annates (a clerical tax). In Oct.–Dec. 1537 Parliament denied papal authority, required office-holders to acknowledge royal supremacy, transferred succession to Jane Seymour's children, and began the DISSOLUTION OF RELIGIOUS HOUSES. Religious observances were largely unaffected, though some shrines were suppressed (*see* BROWNE, GEORGE). There was no popular reform movement. But when bishoprics became vacant, both ruler and Pope made appointments, starting the development of two churches. (Henry's status was raised from lord to king in 1541.)

Under EDWARD VI (1547–53), thorough Protestant reform was envisaged by the English government, and implementation was attempted by prerogative power rather than parliamentary consent. A proclamation ordered use of the new English PRAYER BOOK, and clerical marriage was also permitted (both 1549). Catholic ceremonies were prohibited (1550), and John BALE, bishop of Ossory, promoted the 1552 Prayer Book. But few changes occurred.

MARY I (ruler 1553–8) ordered the reinstatement of Catholic rites (1553), and in 1555 Pope Paul IV bestowed kingdom status and appointed Cardinal Reginald POLE as legate. Parliament repealed anti-papal legislation, restoring papal jurisdiction (1557). Reformed bishops were deposed.

After ELIZABETH I succeeded as ruler (1558), Parliament in 1560 restored royal supremacy over the Church and prescribed the Protestant (1559) English Prayer Book (*see* ELIZABETHAN SETTLEMENT, IRELAND). As Protestant bishops and clergy were appointed, an official Church of IRELAND developed. But most people remained loyal to the continuing Catholic Church which grew separately from the 1570s. *See also* RECUSANCY, IRELAND; CATHOLICS AND CATHOLIC CHURCH, IRELAND; NEW ENGLISH.

REFORMATION, SCOTLAND Although the Reformation occurred late (1559–60) compared with other European countries, evangelical ideas were present from the 1520s: in 1525 the Scottish Parliament banned Lutheran writings (*see* LUTHERANISM), and in 1528 Patrick Hamilton was burnt for heresy. Further persecutions followed in the 1530s.

In 1542 Scotland moved closer to England, which had already left papal jurisdiction (1534): the (2nd) earl of ARRAN, regent for MARY, QUEEN OF SCOTS, allied with England and legalized a vernacular Bible. But a pro-French backlash led to repudiation of the alliance (*see* BEATON, DAVID), although consequent English invasions (1544, 1545, 1547) involved the promotion of Protestantism in SE and S Scotland. The government remained pro-Catholic and from 1554, under the regent MARY OF GUISE, was dominated by Frenchmen.

During the 1550s some nobles adopted Protestantism; in 1557 five (the LORDS OF THE CONGREGATION) signed a bond for the promotion of Protestantism. In 1558 Mary, Queen of Scots, married the French heir (24 April), fuelling fear of subordination to France. The combination of increasing support for Protestantism and anti-French feeling led to a crisis (*see* MYLN, WALTER, EXECUTION OF).

In 1559, after John KNOX provoked anti-Catholic riots in PERTH (11 May), the Lords helped to establish Protestant preaching in Perth (May), ST ANDREWS and EDINBURGH (June). Mary of Guise imported extra French troops, but on 21 Oct. was deposed by the Lords. In March 1560 English forces, acting under the treaty of BERWICK (22 Feb.), intervened. In July the French agreed to leave (*see* EDINBURGH, TREATY OF), and in Aug. Parliament met: it adopted the Calvinist SCOTS CONFESSION (17 Aug.), and (24 Aug.) repudiated papal authority and outlawed the Mass (thereby making religious houses and COLLEGIATE CHURCHES redundant.) Reformers then began the construction of a new Church, though CHURCH ORGANIZATION was to be contested for 130 years. *See also* SCOTLAND, CHURCH OF; DISSOLUTION OF RELIGIOUS HOUSES, SCOTLAND.

REFORMATION, WALES Welsh dioceses were removed from papal jurisdiction by England's Parliament in 1534 and continued within the independent Church of ENGLAND with which they were reformed during the 16th century (*see* REFORMATION, ENGLAND).

Initial alterations of status (convocation's recognition of King HENRY VIII as 'supreme head' of the Church, 1531; Parliament's anti-papal legislation, 1532–4; the break of 1534) were acquiesced in despite originating in England, as was the DISSOLUTION OF RELIGIOUS HOUSES (1536–9). Popular demand for reforms was negligible. English reformers made little impact (*see* BARLOW, WILLIAM).

Under EDWARD VI (1547–53) the prohibition of traditional observances such as holy days (1548), the dissolution of CHANTRIES (1548), and replacement of the Latin Mass by English services (in the PRAYER BOOKS of 1549, 1552) generated resentment but not rebellion (*see* CORNISH RISING). Welsh people welcomed MARY's restoration of traditional worship. During her reign (1553–8), when Wales was again under papal jurisdiction, only three Protestants were burnt and about 12 fled abroad.

ELIZABETH's accession (1558) brought renewed separation and a revised Prayer Book (both 1559). Welsh Protestants desired popular acceptance for the ELIZABETHAN SETTLEMENT (1559) and obtained an Act requiring translation of the Bible and Prayer Book (1563). The latter and the New Testament appeared in 1567 (*see* SALESBURY, WILLIAM), the complete Bible in 1588 (*see* MORGAN, WILLIAM), winning popularity. By 1600 most Welsh people accepted the Church of England. *See also* CATHOLICS AND CATHOLIC CHURCH, WALES.

REFORMATION PARLIAMENT Term used from the early 20th century for the English PARLIAMENT of 1529–36, which removed the English Church from papal jurisdiction. The southern Convocation (Church assembly) met concurrently. Thomas CROMWELL managed parliamentary business from 1532.

King HENRY VIII and Parliament initially pressurized the Church to influence the Pope into annulling Henry's marriage (*see* GREAT MATTER). In 1529 it regulated clerical abuses (e.g., setting probate charges). In 1531 Henry obtained a subsidy of £100,000 from Convocation and recognition as head of the Church (with qualification). In 1532 the Commons presented the SUPPLICATION AGAINST THE ORDINARIES (grievances) which resulted in the 'Submission of the Clergy'. The Act in Restraint of APPEALS of 1533 banned appeals to the papal courts, enabling Henry's marriage to be annulled in England. In 1534 the payment of 'first fruits' (a tax) to the Pope was terminated, the 'Submission of the Clergy' was confirmed, and succession to the throne was altered (*see* SUCCESSION ACTS).

In April 1534 news reached England of the Pope's confirmation of Henry's first marriage. In late 1534 Parliament acknowledged Henry's position as head of the English Church (Act of Supremacy) and annexed first fruits and tenths (clerical taxes) to the Crown (*see* VALOR ECCLESIASTICUS). In 1536 an Act began the dissolution of monasteries (*see* DISSOLUTION OF RELIGIOUS HOUSES, ENGLAND).

The Parliament enacted numerous other statutes, including an Act annexing Wales (*see* UNION OF WALES WITH ENGLAND). *See also* REFORMATION, ENGLAND.

REFORMATION PARLIAMENT, IRELAND *see* REFORMATION, IRELAND

REFORMED PRESBYTERIAN CHURCH A Scottish dissenting presbyterian Church, formed by CAMERONIANS (strict COVENANTERS who remained outside the Church of SCOTLAND in the late 17th century). It developed from 1743, when the Cameronians' only minister was joined by a colleague and a presbytery was organized. The Church rejected the structures and agencies of the State, because they were not based on the 1638 NATIONAL COVENANT. (Voting, for example, was forbidden to members in 1833.) Frequent schisms resulted. In 1863 there were 46 congregations with nearly 7000 members. Most congregations joined the FREE CHURCH OF SCOTLAND in 1876. In 2018 there remained five congregations with about 250 attendees and overseas congregations. *See also* DISSENT, SCOTLAND.

REFORM LEAGUE *see* REFORM UNION, REFORM LEAGUE

REFORM UNION, REFORM LEAGUE Pressure groups which campaigned in Great Britain for PARLIAMENTARY REFORM in the 1860s. The Reform Union, founded in MANCHESTER in March 1864, included Radicals of all classes. The Reform League, formed in LONDON in Feb. 1865, was dominated by ex-CHARTISTS and trade unionists. John BRIGHT persuaded the two organizations to co-operate.

REGALITY In Scotland, a lordship and territory mostly outside the royal judicial system; usually the lands of a MAGNATE in which he (rather than JUSTICIARS or SHERIFFS) exercised royal jurisdiction (Latin *regalitas*).

The first major regalities were created in the early 14th century by King ROBERT I. By the late 16th century there may have been around 200, covering perhaps a half of the country. Regalities were abolished in 1652, restored in 1661, and abolished again in 1747 following the JACOBITE REBELLION of 1745. *See also* HERITABLE JURISDICTIONS, SCOTLAND, ABOLITION OF; COURTS, SCOTLAND.

REGIAM MAJESTATEM (Latin, meaning 'Royal Majesty'). A collection of Scottish laws, called by its opening words, which was probably compiled in the early 14th century and was heavily influenced by GLANVILL and by Roman law. It remained the main compendium of Scots law for over 350 years, though it was revised by later commentators. *See also* LAW, SCOTLAND.

REGIUM DONUM (Latin, meaning 'royal gift'). An annual royal contribution to the stipends of presbyterian ministers in Ireland, initiated in 1672 by Sir Arthur Forbes, a prominent Irish supporter of King CHARLES II. Initially (Irish) £600, it sought to prevent unrest among presbyterians in Scotland spreading into ULSTER (N Ireland). Except for 1714–15, payment continued until 1869 (replaced by capital sum). *See also* PRESBYTERIANISM, IRELAND; DISESTABLISHMENT, CHURCH OF IRELAND.

REITH, JOHN (b. 20 July 1889 at Stonehaven, Kincardineshire, Scotland; d. 16 June 1971 at Edinburgh, Scotland, aged 81). A presbyterian minister's son, Reith trained as an engineer. In 1922 he was appointed general manager of the (commercial) British Broadcasting Company, Great Britain's first RADIO broadcaster. Partly on his advice it became a public corporation (1927), authorized by royal charter and funded by annual radio licences. Reith as director-general imbued it with a high-minded ethos (e.g., predominantly religious programmes on Sundays). He inaugurated an Empire Service and TELEVISION broadcasts (both 1932), and high-definition television (1936). Resigning in 1938, Reith subsequently held various government and public offices (e.g., chairman of Colonial Development Corporation 1950–9). He was knighted in 1927 and created Lord Reith in 1940. *See also* BRITISH BROADCASTING CORPORATION.

RELIEF CHURCH A Scottish dissenting presbyterian Church, founded in 1761 in Fife; so called because it offered 'relief' for congregations who objected to ministers imposed by patrons. (Congregations sometimes joined temporarily during a dispute.) The Church spread widely through the Lowlands and established a few Highland congregations. With its relatively liberal theology and relaxed discipline it appealed particularly to townspeople. In 1847 it united with the SECESSION CHURCH to form the UNITED PRESBYTERIAN CHURCH. *See also* DISSENT, SCOTLAND.

RELIGIOUS ORDERS During the first phase of MONASTICISM in Britain and Ireland (5th–11th centuries), monasteries (or MINSTERS) were not generally organized into associations, although some belonged to groups created by individuals (e.g., COLUMBA; WILFRID). The rule of St Benedict influenced religious life from the 7th century, but from the 8th century many houses became secular (e.g., with married clergy). Exceptionally, strict CULDEE communities flourished in Ireland and N Britain.

In England from the 10th century there were independent Benedictine monasteries and nunneries (*see* TENTH-CENTURY REFORMATION). A few became wealthy (e.g., WESTMINSTER Abbey), with endowments that included MANORS and peasant tenants. From 1218, following a general Church order, 'chapters' of abbots and priors met triennially.

From the late 11th century, expansion included many houses belonging to new international orders. Among the main orders, 'Cluniacs' were Benedictines associated with Cluny Abbey in Burgundy (France) or a daughter house, which emphasized worship. 'Savigniacs' were Benedictines associated with Savigny Abbey in Normandy (France). 'Cistercians' were Benedictines associated with Cîteaux Abbey in Burgundy (France), which promoted simplicity (e.g., in church decoration) and isolated locations. Opposed to manorial endowments, Cistercians organized 'granges' worked by lay brethren and pursued sheep farming. (Savigniac houses became associated with the Cistercians in 1147.) Houses of 'Augustinian canons' (from early 12th century) were not strictly monasteries but communities of priests following a rule ascribed to St Augustine of Hippo. They often served former minsters. 'Premonstratensian canons' were similar but stricter. 'Carthusians' were associated with La Grande Chartreuse in the kingdom of Burgundy, with monks living austere individual lives and meeting for services. There were similar orders or communities of nuns.

From the 13th century there were also mendicant preaching orders (or FRIARS), notably the Franciscans (started 1209 by the Italian Giovanni Francesco Bernardone) and Dominicans (started 1215 by the Spaniard Domingo de Guzmán). Both initially espoused individual and corporate poverty, and teaching. *See also* ALIEN PRIORIES; DISSOLUTION OF RELIGIOUS HOUSES, ENGLAND/IRELAND/SCOTLAND/WALES; RELIGIOUS ORDERS AND REGULAR CLERGY, IRELAND FROM 16TH CENTURY.

RELIGIOUS ORDERS AND REGULAR CLERGY, IRELAND FROM 16TH CENTURY Despite the DISSOLUTION OF RELIGIOUS HOUSES from the 1530s, some communities survived. From the later 16th century, regular clergy (particularly friars and Jesuits) helped to sustain the Catholic Church against pressures from the government and Protestant Church of Ireland (*see* REFORMATION, IRELAND). Houses of study for Irish novices were established in Continental Europe from 1606. Cistercian monks returned to Ireland in 1613. Setbacks occurred: the government attempted to close houses in 1629–30, and many

clergy fled abroad during the 1650s (*see* COMMONWEALTH AND PROTECTORATE, IRELAND).

After the RESTORATION (1660), exiled regular clergy returned but clergy were periodically threatened; e.g., ordered to leave in 1677 (during the POPISH PLOT), and in 1697 (*see* BANISHMENT ACT). The government feared regular clergy because their orders were international organizations. In 1750 there were about 800 regular clergy in Ireland. The numbers of clergy and religious houses declined in the later 18th century because of restrictions imposed in 1751 by Pope Benedict XIV, which allowed bishops and secular clergy to predominate.

Regular clergy increased during the 19th century, partly because newer orders established houses (e.g., Passionists in 1856). Some orders provided education (e.g., the Congregation of the Holy Ghost founded Blackrock College in 1860) and undertook missions. In 1904 there were about 650 regular clergy. Nuns especially increased (from about 120 in 1800 to over 8000 by 1900) and became important in teaching and nursing. Numerous Irish brothers and nuns also worked overseas. Religious orders remained strong until vocations collapsed in the 1970s (e.g., ordinations of brothers as priests fell from about 300 in 1970 to 25 in 1987). *See also* CATHOLICS AND CATHOLIC CHURCH, IRELAND.

REMONSTRANCES In England, grievances (in French) sent to King EDWARD I on 22 Aug. 1297 by BARONS dissatisfied by his handling of war against France (*see* GASCON WAR). Claiming to act for the COMMUNITY OF THE REALM, they complained about threatened overseas MILITARY SERVICE, taxation, the *MALTOLT* on wool, FOREST LAW, etc. Edward ignored the document.

REMONSTRANTS In Scotland in the 1650s, the minority radical party within the Church of SCOTLAND, strong in the W and SW; usually known as 'Protestors' from 1651. It grew from the signing of the 'Western Remonstrance' in Dumfries (SW Scotland) on 17 Oct. 1650 by leaders of the Western Association (a newly formed army), which denounced support for King CHARLES II as ungodly, rejected Oliver CROMWELL's occupation, and demanded stricter enforcement of the Act of CLASSES. Protestors sought the removal of pro-Charles clergy, and some established separate ecclesiastical courts. After the RESTORATION (1660), many Protestors became radicals outside the Church (*see* COVENANTERS). *See also* RESOLUTIONERS.

RENUNCIATION ACT Legislation by the British Parliament, passed in April 1783, which confirmed the exclusive right of the Irish Parliament to legislate for Ireland and the judicial supremacy of the Irish House of Lords. It therefore ended the British Parliament's involvement, until superseded by the UNION OF IRELAND AND GREAT BRITAIN (1801). *See also* CONSTITUTION OF 1782.

REPARATIONS Term associated with the war indemnity imposed by Article 232 of the treaty of VERSAILLES (June 1919), requiring Germany to pay compensation for damage suffered by Allied nations during WORLD WAR I. The sum was set at £6600 million in April 1921. Despite 'Make Germany Pay' rhetoric during the COUPON ELECTION (Dec. 1918), the British prime minister David LLOYD GEORGE tried to moderate excessive French demands at the PARIS PEACE CONFERENCE.

On 26 Dec. 1922 Germany was deemed to have defaulted; soon afterwards (11 Jan. 1923) French and Belgian troops occupied the Ruhr (industrial area of Germany), provoking British condemnation. Great Britain supported the Dawes Plan (1924) and Young Plan (1929) to lighten Germany's reparations burden. Payments were suspended in 1931 and never resumed, despite the formulation of a scheme by the Lausanne Conference (1932). *See also* KEYNES, J.M.

REPEAL ASSOCIATION In Ireland, a political organization launched by Daniel O'CONNELL on 13 July 1840 (as the Loyal National Repeal Association) to campaign for repeal of the UNION OF IRELAND AND GREAT BRITAIN. From late 1842 O'Connell developed the Association into a mass organization, and in 1843 held 'monster meetings' around Ireland until forced to cancel the CLONTARF MEETING (Oct.). The Association declined after O'Connell's death (1847). *See also* UNION REPEAL MOVEMENT, IRELAND; YOUNG IRELAND MOVEMENT.

REPUBLICAN MOVEMENT, 17TH CENTURY In England, a political movement which developed after the RUMP PARLIAMENT decided to abolish the monarchy (6 Feb. 1649). John MILTON, theorists James Harrington and Henry Neville, and politicians such as Algernon Sidney supported the republican principle and defended the Rump's achievements. The RESTORATION of the monarchy (1660) ended republicanism as a significant political movement, although republican sentiments were expressed by some WHIGS in the 1680s–90s. *See also* COMMONWEALTH AND PROTECTORATE.

REPUBLIC OF IRELAND *see* SOUTHERN IRELAND FROM 1922

REQUESTS, COURT OF In England, a court which heard cases mainly from the poor (e.g., rural tenants). Originally an informal branch of the king's COUNCIL, it was first mentioned in 1483 when a clerk was appointed. Using EQUITY, it operated mainly at WESTMINSTER from 1519, and was called the Court of Requests from 1529. It contin-

ued until the CIVIL WAR (withered away after 1642). *See also* PREROGATIVE COURTS.

RESIDENT MAGISTRATES, IRELAND Salaried local justices who operated alongside unpaid JUSTICES OF THE PEACE (or magistrates). They originated as supervisors of police forces who were given magistrates' powers, first in DUBLIN (1786–95), then for the Police Preservation Force (from 1814). From 1822, when police forces were reorganized, Ireland's CHIEF GOVERNOR was empowered to appoint resident magistrates (RMs) as necessary. They were intended to be less partial and more effective than JPs. By the 1840s there were 60 RMs throughout Ireland.

In the IRISH FREE STATE, RMs were renamed 'district justices' (1923) and then abolished (1924). In NORTHERN IRELAND, RMs received JPs' judicial powers (1935) and were renamed 'district judges' (2008). *See also* COURTS, IRELAND; POLICE, IRELAND.

RESOLUTIONERS In Scotland in the 1650s, the majority party in the Church of SCOTLAND (opposed to the radical REMONSTRANTS or Protestors). It originated with the 'Public Resolutions' issued by the Commission of the Church of Scotland on 14 Dec. 1650, which permitted enemies of the radical government to join a new army in support of King CHARLES II. The Resolutioners' cause was ruined by their defeat at the battle of WORCESTER (1651) and the UNION OF ENGLAND AND SCOTLAND in the 1650s. *See also* COVENANTING REVOLUTION.

RESPONSIBLE GOVERNMENT A democratic form of self-government introduced in the 1840s–50s in some British colonies (ones based on settlement by British people), whereby royal governors accepted ministers chosen from the majority party in an elected assembly instead of making their own appointments. Reflecting the growth of party-based government in the UK, responsible government was advocated by Lord Grey (3rd Earl Grey), British colonial secretary 1846–52. Starting with NOVA SCOTIA (1848), it was implemented in N American colonies (by 1854), some colonies in AUSTRALIA (1855–9), and in NEW ZEALAND (1856). It increased the colonies' autonomy, and led eventually to the creation of DOMINION status. *See also* BRITISH EMPIRE, GOVERNMENT OF.

RESTORATION, ENGLAND AND WALES The return of King CHARLES II to England from exile in 1660, after the collapse of the COMMONWEALTH, and the revival of royal authority and the Church of ENGLAND. Royal rule was restored too in Ireland and Scotland. The term 'Restoration' is also applied to the period 1660–89.

The breakdown of relations in England between the Army and RUMP PARLIAMENT from summer 1659, and loss of authority (e.g., widespread refusal to pay taxes), persuaded George MONCK, commander of the English Army in Scotland, to intervene (entered England 1 Jan. 1660, reached London 3 Feb.). He forced the Rump (21 Feb.) to readmit members of the LONG PARLIAMENT excluded in 1648, to outnumber republicans. On 16 March Parliament dissolved itself, calling new elections.

The CONVENTION PARLIAMENT (April–Dec. 1660), encouraged by Charles's Declaration of BREDA, voted to recall him (1 May; Charles arrived in London 29 May). It sought to restore the constitution as in 1641 and deal with immediate problems. Legislation passed since 1641 without royal authority was declared invalid. The Parliament provided a general pardon for the king's enemies, with some exceptions, and voted him an income. The NEW MODEL ARMY was mostly disbanded.

The Convention was followed by the CAVALIER PARLIAMENT (from May 1661), which confirmed some royal powers (e.g., Militia Act, 1661, endorsing command of the militia), but deliberately did not revive PREROGATIVE COURTS.

Charles desired a religious settlement that included presbyterians within a revived Church of ENGLAND. But MPs and bishops sought to exclude Puritans. Parliament imposed a revised PRAYER BOOK and placed restrictions on Protestant dissenters (see WORCESTER HOUSE DECLARATION; SAVOY CONFERENCE; CLARENDON CODE). See also CLARENDON, EARL OF; RESTORATION, SCOTLAND/IRELAND.

RESTORATION, IRELAND Ireland recovered parliamentary autonomy, and monarchy was reinstated, as consequences of the deposition of the protector, Richard CROMWELL (May 1659), departure of the conciliatory governor Henry Cromwell from Ireland (June), and re-emergence of Army radicalism in England (see COMMONWEALTH AND PROTECTORATE). Following Henry Cromwell's withdrawal, commissioners already appointed by England's RUMP PARLIAMENT took control.

On 13 Dec. 1659, middle-ranking Army officers of Protestant Irish background overthrew the government by seizing DUBLIN Castle and arresting senior figures. Associates also took control in CONNACHT (W Ireland) and MUNSTER (S). They called a Convention, which met from Feb. and asserted Ireland's legislative independence. Events encouraged George MONCK in England. On 14 May 1660, following developments in England, the Convention proclaimed CHARLES II as king. Episcopal government was quickly restored in the Church of IRELAND (appointments from June).

The major post-Restoration issues were the CROMWELLIAN LAND SETTLEMENT (recent transfer of land from Catholics to Protestants) and status of Catholicism. Charles largely accepted the Land Settlement, but his attempt to restore land to some Royalist Catholics disappointed other Catholics and alarmed Protestants (see SETTLEMENT AND EXPLANATION, ACTS OF). Lay Catholics and some clergy sought official tolerance of Catholicism by affirming their loyalty to the Crown, but failed to devise a statement acceptable to the government (see LOYAL REMONSTRANCE). In practice Catholics were allowed considerable freedom of worship (as were Protestant dissenters), helped by the abeyance of Parliament from 1666. But the failure to settle Catholic demands enabled Charles's successor, a Catholic, to reassert Catholicism: see JAMES VII/II AND IRELAND. See also COMMONWEALTH AND PROTECTORATE, IRELAND; ORMOND, 12TH EARL OF; IRELAND, CHURCH OF; PLUNKETT AFFAIR.

RESTORATION, SCOTLAND In mid 17th-century Scotland, unlike England, monarchy was not abolished: after the execution of King CHARLES I in England (30 Jan. 1649), CHARLES II was proclaimed king in Scotland (5 Feb.) and crowned (1 Jan. 1651), although he left soon afterwards (Aug. 1651). The Restoration (1660–2) restored royal government and private jurisdictions following English occupation (see UNION OF ENGLAND AND SCOTLAND, 1650s), and also royal powers removed in 1638–41 by the COVENANTING REVOLUTION.

Royal control was initially restored by decisions made in England, to which Charles returned in May 1660 and where he was visited by leading Scots. On 19 June he agreed to restore the Committee of Estates (standing committee of Parliament) of 1651; in July he began filling important offices, appointing the earl of MIDDLETON as KING'S COMMISSIONER and the (2nd) earl of LAUDERDALE as SECRETARY OF STATE. The Committee met on 23 Aug. It was superseded by a reinstated Privy COUNCIL in 1661.

Parliament met on 1 Jan. 1661; under Middleton's influence it passed the ACT RECISSORY (March), repealing legislation since 1633. In Aug. 1661 the Council announced the restoration of episcopacy (Church government by bishops). In 1661 private patronage (presentation of Church ministers by patrons) was restored. Ministers appointed since 1649 were required to be formally re-presented and instituted by a bishop, and to take an oath of allegiance. Nearly a third of the clergy (about 270 ministers) refused and were deprived, thereby creating a disruptive movement outside the Church (see COVENANTERS).

RESUMPTION ACTS In England, Acts of Parliament, mid–late 15th century, which reclaimed former Crown lands. Acts were passed in 1450 and 1451, reversing land grants by King HENRY VI, in an attempt to tackle the Crown's shortage of income. EDWARD IV obtained Resumption Acts (1465, 1467, 1473) to confirm possession of lands forfeited by enemies, strengthen his finances, and provide lands for distribution to key supporters. HENRY VII did likewise (1487). A similar Act of 1515 cancelled annuities and offices. *See also* NEW MONARCHY, ENGLAND.

REVOCATION OF 1625 A scheme announced on 14 July 1625, soon after the accession of King CHARLES I, whereby the Crown in Scotland would revoke grants of Church land made since 1540 (mainly to nobles) and restore revenues to the Church. Compensation was added (1627), but implementation commissions were stifled locally (into the 1630s). The revocation alienated nobles from the Crown. *See also* COVENANTING REVOLUTION.

REVOLT OF 1173–4 A crisis during the reign of HENRY II (ruler of the ANGEVIN EMPIRE, including England) arising from his provision of castles for his son JOHN in a marriage arrangement (Feb. 1173). HENRY THE YOUNG KING, Henry's eldest son who possessed little, demanded part of his future inheritance. Encouraged by ELEANOR OF AQUITAINE, he and brothers Geoffrey and RICHARD conspired with Louis VII of France, WILLIAM I of Scotland and discontented nobles.

Between May 1173 and Sept. 1174 the rebels attacked territories and strongpoints throughout the Angevin Empire but were defeated. Henry and his rebel sons were reconciled in Oct. 1174. *See also* FALAISE, TREATY OF.

REVOLT OF 1637 In Scotland, popular opposition to the imposition by King CHARLES I of a new PRAYER BOOK on the Church of SCOTLAND. The revolt began with rioting in EDINBURGH (SE Scotland) on 23 July 1637 when the Book was first used at St Giles Church. (Contrary to popular belief, there is no evidence of involvement by Jenny Geddes.) The Scottish Privy COUNCIL then received numerous petitions complaining about the Book's 'popish' content, and protesters gathered in Edinburgh. Further rioting occurred in Oct. Opposition to Charles's religious policies culminated in the NATIONAL COVENANT. *See also* COVENANTING REVOLUTION.

REVOLT OF THE EARLS In England, conspiracy and rebellion in 1075 against King WILLIAM I by three earls: Ralph Guader, earl of East Anglia (E England), a Breton; Roger de Breteuil, earl of Hereford (W England), a Norman; and WALTHEOF, earl of Northumbria (NE England), an Englishman. Their motives and aims are obscure.

Ralph fled to Brittany. Roger surrendered and was imprisoned for life. Waltheof submitted to William but was executed (1076). Meanwhile Cnut of Denmark, son of SWEIN ESTRITHSON, landed briefly in NE England. The revolt was the last against Norman rule in which Englishmen were extensively involved. *See also* NORMAN CONQUEST OF ENGLAND.

REVOLT OF THE TOWNS In Ireland, the restoration of Catholic worship and observances (e.g., processions) in KILKENNY, WEXFORD and towns in MUNSTER (S Ireland) in April 1603, following the end of the NINE YEARS WAR. Townsmen (predominantly OLD ENGLISH), who had remained loyal during the war, hoped to pressure the new king, JAMES VI/I, into sanctioning Catholicism. Instead Ireland's governor, Lord MOUNTJOY, suppressed the Revolt, requiring subscription to an oath of allegiance (April–May). *See also* REFORMATION, IRELAND.

REVOLUTION SETTLEMENT, SCOTLAND Changes to the Scottish constitution and Church of SCOTLAND were enacted by a CONVENTION PARLIAMENT and Parliament in 1689 and by Parliament in 1690. The Convention endorsed a 'Claim of Right' (11 April 1689): no Catholic could reign or hold office; the ROYAL PREROGATIVE was subordinate to law; the raising of military supply required Parliament's consent; Parliaments must be frequent and free; use of torture should be severely curtailed; episcopacy (Church government by bishops) was condemned. It also passed 'Articles of Grievance' (13 April) condemning the Crown-appointed LORDS OF THE ARTICLES who controlled parliamentary legislation. After the Convention became a Parliament (May), it abolished episcopacy, the lords of the articles, and the 1669 Act of Supremacy, which had declared the king head of the Church. In 1690 presbyterianism was formally restored in the Church and private patronage (presentation of ministers by individual patrons) abolished. *See also* GLORIOUS REVOLUTION, SCOTLAND.

REYNOLDS, ALBERT (b. 3 Nov. 1932 at Roosky, Co. Roscommon, Irish Free State; d. 21 Aug. 2014, at Dublin, Republic of Ireland, aged 81). A businessman, Reynolds became a FIANNA FÁIL TD (1977) and served in the governments of taoiseach (premier) Charles HAUGHEY (1979–81, 1982, from 1987). In Nov. 1991, after supporting a 'no confidence' motion in Haughey, Reynolds was sacked. When Haughey resigned (Feb. 1992), Reynolds was elected party leader and taoiseach.

Reynolds continued Haughey's coalition with the PROGRESSIVE DEMOCRATS. It struggled with difficult economic conditions (e.g., unemployment around 20%), and lost a referendum motion to modify the prohibition on ABORTION (Nov. 1992). The government collapsed in Nov. 1992 after Reynolds accused the Democrats' leader, Des O'Malley, of dishonesty. After a general election (25 Nov.), Reynolds formed a government with the LABOUR PARTY. It withdrew in Nov. 1994 over a controversial judicial appointment, prompting Reynolds' resignation.

In 1993 Reynolds supported private discussions about NORTHERN IRELAND between John HUME and Gerry ADAMS, and encouraged co-operation by the British prime minister John MAJOR. The outcome was the DOWNING STREET DECLARATION (Dec. 1993) which significantly advanced the Northern Ireland PEACE PROCESS. *See also* SOCIAL PARTNERSHIP; AHERN, BERTIE; BRUTON, JOHN.

REYNOLDS, JOSHUA (16 July 1723 at Plympton, Devon, England; d. 23 Feb. 1792 at London, England, aged 68). A schoolmaster's son, Reynolds was apprenticed to a London painter in 1740. He lived in Rome (Italy) 1750–2. By 1755 he was the leading British portraitist. In 1768 Reynolds was elected first president of the Royal Academy of Arts (knighted 1769). Between 1769 and 1790 he delivered 15 lectures on art, the *Discourses*. They provide a fundamental statement of 18th-century artistic theory, and influenced taste beyond Reynolds' lifetime. *See also* ACADEMIES OF ART; VISUAL ARTS, BRITAIN.

RHEGED A British (Brittonic-speaking) kingdom, around the Solway Firth (SW modern Scotland and NW England). Descended from the IRON AGE TRIBE the Novantae, it emerged after the end of Roman rule in the 5th century (*see* POST-ROMAN BRITAIN). Its main competitor was the Anglian (Germanic) kingdom of BERNICIA to the E and SE (King Urien of Rheged died *c*.590 while besieging the Bernician royal centre of Bamburgh). Rheged was extinguished by EGFRITH, king of Bernicia and Deira (Northumbria) 670–85. *See also* KINGSHIP, NORTH BRITAIN; GALLOWAY.

RHODE ISLAND AND PROVIDENCE PLANTATIONS A former English colony (British from 1707) in N America (in NEW ENGLAND), S of MASSACHUSETTS. Refugees from Massachusetts, and others, settled in the area from 1634. Roger Williams (*c*.1603–83), a minister, obtained a patent for self-government (as 'Providence Plantations') from the English Parliament in 1644 to prevent other colonies from claiming the settlements. A federation of towns was organized in 1647, and a charter was obtained from King CHARLES II in 1663 (for 'Rhode Island and Providence Plantations'). The colony was effectively self-governing, authorized to elect its own governor (subject to Crown approval). Est. population 1770: 55,000.

The British Sugar Act of 1764 damaged the colony's trade, generating support for AMERICAN INDEPENDENCE. Rhode Island and Providence Plantations became a State of the USA in 1776, though British troops occupied Newport 1776–9, during the AMERICAN WAR OF INDEPENDENCE. The State refused to ratify the US constitution until 1790. The royal charter remained the basis of government until 1842. *See also* NORTH AMERICAN COLONIES; NEW ENGLAND, DOMINION OF.

RHODES, CECIL (b. 5 July 1853 at Bishop's Stortford, Hertfordshire, England; d. 26 March 1902 at Muizenberg,

Cape Colony, aged 48). A clergyman's son, Rhodes went to NATAL (southern Africa) in 1870, returning to study at OXFORD University (Oriel College, 1873–4, 1876–81). During the 1880s he made a fortune from diamond mines in southern Africa, and from 1881 was a member of the CAPE COLONY Parliament. Ambitious to spread British power and values, Rhodes promoted involvement in BECHUANALAND (colony and protectorate established 1885). His BRITISH SOUTH AFRICA COMPANY (chartered 1889) established SOUTHERN RHODESIA and NORTHERN RHODESIA.

As prime minister of Cape Colony from 1890, Rhodes sought to unite British and Boer territories in southern Africa. His tacit support for the JAMESON RAID forced him to resign (1896). In the same year he quelled African rebellions in Southern Rhodesia through negotiations with chiefs. During the (Second) BOER WAR he organized the defence of Kimberley (1899–1900). Rhodes bequeathed his fortune for scholarships at Oxford.

RHODESIA *see* SOUTHERN RHODESIA

RHODESIA AND NYASALAND, FEDERATION OF *see* FEDERATION OF RHODESIA AND NYASALAND

RHODESIA PROBLEM A DECOLONIZATION crisis which affected British politics in the 1960s–70s. On 11 Nov. 1965 the all-white government of (Southern) RHODESIA, led by Ian SMITH, made a Unilateral Declaration of Independence (UDI) to avoid enfranchising the country's black majority. The British government came under international pressure to end the rebellion and instigate independence as a multiracial democracy.

The government of Harold WILSON immediately imposed economic sanctions, but initiatives to settle the problem (notably in 1966–7, 1970–1, 1976–7) failed. Rhodesia descended into civil war.

In Sept. 1979 the government of Margaret THATCHER persuaded parties to attend a constitutional conference in London. The 'Lancaster House Agreement' (signed 21 Dec.) briefly restored British direct rule and provided for majority rule. Rhodesia became legally independent as Zimbabwe on 18 April 1980.

RHODRI MAWR, 'THE GREAT' (fl. from 825; d. 878). King of GWYNEDD (NW Wales) 844–78; ancestor of most later Welsh rulers. Rhodri inherited Gwynedd in 844 from his father, MERFYN FRYCH; acquired POWYS (C Wales) in 855 through his mother; and added CEREDIGION (W Wales) in 872 through his wife. His reign saw VIKINGS active in Wales: he defeated them in 855, but was driven to Ireland in 877. Rhodri was killed in battle by English forces.

RHONDDA VALLEYS Two valleys in S Wales, the Rhondda Fawr ('Large Rhondda') and Rhondda Fach ('Small Rhondda'); they are popularly known as 'The Rhondda'.

Coalmining expanded rapidly in the Rhondda Valleys from the 1860s, causing population to rise from 1000 in 1850 to 169,000 by 1925. With close-knit communities and militant trade unionism, The Rhondda was the most renowned of Welsh coal-producing areas. Depression in the late 1920s and 1930s produced massive long-term unemployment and caused large-scale emigration. By 1991 population had fallen to 76,000 and the mines were closed. The Rhondda was in the county of Glamorgan until 1974, in the county of Mid Glamorgan (to 1996), and then in the unitary authority of Rhondda Cynon Taf. *See also* COAL INDUSTRY, WALES; MABON; ABLETT, NOAH.

RHUDDLAN OR WALES, STATUTE OF A decree issued on 19 March 1284 which organized the English government of former native-ruled lands in N Wales, following conquest by King EDWARD I of England, 1282–3 (*see* WALES, ENGLISH CONQUEST OF). It introduced (large) SHIRES on the English model (retaining COMMOTES as hundreds) and English legal institutions and procedures (*see* COURTS, WALES; LAW, WELSH).

RHYS AP GRUFFUDD (b. 1131 or 1132; d. 28 April 1197, aged 65). King of DEHEUBARTH (SW Wales) 1155–97; also called *Yr Arglwydd Rhys*, 'The Lord Rhys'.

King HENRY II of England's Welsh campaign of 1157–8 reduced Rhys's influence to Cantref Mawr (part of NE Deheubarth; reaffirmed 1163). But with OWAIN GWYNEDD, Rhys provoked the Welsh revolt of 1164–5 and gained territory, including CEREDIGION (W Wales; taken in 1164).

On Owain's death in 1170, Rhys became predominant in Wales, and in 1171–2 Henry II, preoccupied with Ireland, confirmed Rhys's territories. In 1176 Rhys convened the first bardic competition (*see* EISTEDDFOD).

With the accession of RICHARD I in England (1189), Rhys lost English support and raided the MARCH OF WALES (1189–96). His last years saw conflict between his sons; Deheubarth disintegrated after his death. *See also* ANGLO-WELSH RELATIONS, 6TH–13TH CENTURIES.

RHYS AP MAREDUDD (fl. from 1250; d. April 1292 at York, Yorkshire, England). Leader of the 1287–8 Welsh revolt.

A member of the dynasty of DEHEUBARTH (SW Wales), in 1271–83 Rhys supported King EDWARD I of England against LLYWELYN AP GRUFFUDD of GWYNEDD (NW Wales) and most Welsh rulers. After Edward's Conquest of Wales (1282–3), Rhys was rewarded with territories forfeited by kinsmen and styled himself 'Lord of Ystrad Tywi'.

But he was humiliated by Edward in public and harassed by Edward's officers. Rhys revolted on 8 June 1287, but failed to gain popular Welsh support. Some Welshmen supported the Marcher lords who captured Rhys's stronghold at Dryslwyn in Sept. and effectively crushed the revolt by Jan. 1288. Rhys remained free until he was betrayed and executed.

RHYS AP TEWDWR (b. *c.*1050; d. between 17 and 23 April 1093 near Brecon, Brycheiniog, C Wales, aged about 43). King of DEHEUBARTH (SW Wales) 1078–93.

Rhys was finally established as king in 1081 by the battle of MYNYDD CARN. In the same year King WILLIAM I of England crossed S Wales, probably forcing Rhys to pay the annual £40 'rent' for Deheubarth mentioned in DOMESDAY BOOK (1086).

Rhys was driven from Deheubarth by Bleddyn ap Cynfyn of POWYS (C Wales) in 1088, but restored with help from Vikings from DUBLIN (Ireland). In the 1090s NORMANS apparently sought to oust Rhys; in 1091 he slew his kinsman Gruffudd ap Maredudd, who had returned from exile in England to claim Deheubarth. Rhys was killed by Normans in BRYCHEINIOG, perhaps followers of BERNARD OF NEUFMARCHÉ. *See also* NEST; ANGLO-WELSH RELATIONS, 6TH–13TH CENTURIES.

RHYS AP THOMAS (b. 1449, probably in Wales; d. 1525 aged 75 or 76). Landowner in SW Wales and LANCASTRIAN. Rhys's followers helped Henry Tudor seize the English throne (1485; *see* HENRY VII). Rhys was knighted and given royal offices, making him Henry's chief agent in Wales (continuing under HENRY VIII). He was the last Welsh MAGNATE of vice-regal importance.

Rhys's grandson and heir, Rhys ap Gruffydd, was denied office (and later executed, 4 Dec. 1531); instead the English Crown elevated the COUNCIL IN THE MARCHES OF WALES as its main instrument of government.

RICARDO, DAVID (b. 18 April 1772 at London, England; d. 11 Sept. 1823 at Gatcombe Park, Gloucestershire, England, aged 51). Born into a Dutch Jewish family, but a UNITARIAN from 1793, Ricardo became a wealthy stockjobber (retired 1815) and MP (1819–23). Influenced by Adam SMITH, Jeremy BENTHAM and T.R. MALTHUS, Ricardo from 1810 published works on POLITICAL ECONOMY, seeking to determine fundamental laws. His chief work, *Principles of Political Economy and Taxation* (1817), linked profits and wages, and rent, to costs of food production. He argued that wages would remain close to subsistence levels, with high expenditure on POOR RELIEF depressing wages, unless FREE TRADE was adopted.

RICHARD I (b. 8 Sept. 1157 at Oxford, Oxfordshire, England; d. 6 April 1199 at Chalus, Aquitaine, aged 41). The third son of King HENRY II and ELEANOR OF AQUITAINE, Richard was recognized as duke of Aquitaine in 1169. His attempts to expand ducal authority gained him renown for military prowess. Richard also participated in revolts against his father (e.g., REVOLT OF 1173-4). He was involved in a rebellion at the time of Henry's death (6 July 1189).

Richard succeeded Henry as his oldest surviving son. After his coronation as king of England (13 Sept. 1189) Richard began planning to go on CRUSADE (departed 1190). He spent only six months of his reign in England, otherwise depending on deputies (*see* LONGCHAMP, WILLIAM; GEOFFREY FITZ PETER; WALTER, HUBERT; MARSHAL, WILLIAM). Richard conquered Cyprus (May 1191), captured Acre (July), defeated the Muslim leader Saladin (Sept.), but failed to take Jerusalem. He agreed a truce (Sept. 1192) and left the Holy Land (Oct.). While returning home Richard was captured by Leopold of Austria (Dec.) and forced to pay 100,000 marks in ransom. Released in Feb. 1194, Richard was in England March–May 1194, before attempting to restore his authority elsewhere in the ANGEVIN EMPIRE. He died suppressing a revolt.

RICHARD II (b. 6 Jan. 1367 at Bordeaux, France; d. Feb. 1400 at Pontefract, Yorkshire, England, aged 33). Son of EDWARD THE BLACK PRINCE (d. 1376), Richard succeeded EDWARD III (grandfather) as king of England and lord of Ireland (22 June 1377), aged 10. He depended on leading magnates (e.g., JOHN OF GAUNT), but personally helped to quell the PEASANTS' REVOLT (1381).

Richard gathered a group of favourites, such as Robert de Vere, earl of Oxford. In 1385 he invaded Scotland. Though nothing was achieved, he rewarded supporters (e.g., de Vere became marquess of Dublin). Widespread opposition developed. In 1386 Michael de la POLE was impeached and a Council imposed on Richard. In Nov. 1387 opponents (the APPELLANTS) made charges against Richard's favourites and defeated de Vere at Radcot Bridge, Oxfordshire (Dec.). Five of Richard's 'friends' were convicted of TREASON (1388; *see* MERCILESS PARLIAMENT). Stability from 1389 allowed Richard to secure peace with France (1396).

From 1397 Richard acted autocratically. He took revenge on the appellants (1397–8), extorted money, and in Feb. 1399 disinherited Henry Bolingbroke (former appellant). While he was in Ireland (June–Aug.) Bolingbroke invaded (July). Captured at Conwy (Aug.), Richard was deposed by Parliament (30 Sept.), imprisoned and murdered. Succeeded by Bolingbroke (*see* HENRY IV). *See also* ARUNDEL, THOMAS; RICHARD II AND IRELAND.

RICHARD II AND IRELAND Richard was the only king of England to visit Ireland between 1210 (JOHN) and 1689 (the exiled JAMES VII/II). His first expedition (2 Oct. 1394–15 May 1395) countered the growing power of Art MACMURROUGH. MacMurrough acknowledged Richard's overlordship (30 Oct.) as did most other Irish kings (Jan.–April). Conflicts between Irish and Anglo-Irish resumed after Richard's departure. The new chief governor (lieutenant), Roger Mortimer, was killed (20 July 1398).

Richard's second expedition in 1399 (1 June–27 July) made few gains (e.g., MacMurrough avoided him), and his absence from England provoked Henry Bolingbroke's invasion from France which led to Richard's deposition. *See also* GAELIC REVIVAL, IRELAND 13TH–15TH CENTURIES; IRELAND, ENGLISH EXPEDITIONS TO, LATE 14TH CENTURY.

RICHARD III (b. 2 Oct. 1452 at Fotheringay, Northamptonshire, England; d. 22 Aug. 1485 near Market Bosworth, Leicestershire, England, aged 32). The youngest brother of King EDWARD IV, Richard Plantagenet was created duke of Gloucester in 1461. During the rebellion of Richard, earl of WARWICK, and restoration of HENRY VI (1470-1), Gloucester supported Edward. They fled to Flanders in Oct. 1470, returning (March 1471) to defeat Warwick at Barnet, Hertfordshire (14 April). Richard supported Edward's rule in N England, where he was given extensive estates. He recaptured BERWICK-UPON-TWEED from the Scots in 1482.

At Edward's death (9 April 1483) and under his instruction Richard became 'protector' of the child EDWARD V. Hostile to the WOODVILLE FAMILY, he seized Edward (30 April), imprisoning him in the Tower of London. Parliament declared Edward and his brother illegitimate (25 June); the following day Richard agreed to become king. The 'princes in the Tower' disappeared soon afterwards. Richard also became lord of Ireland.

Richard's usurpation was opposed by the duke of Buckingham but his rebellion failed (Oct. 1483). Eighteen months later, exiled claimant Henry Tudor invaded, defeating Richard at BOSWORTH and seizing the throne as HENRY VII. Richard's remains were rediscovered at Leicester in 2012 and reburied in Leicester Cathedral (2015). *See also* CLARENCE, GEORGE DUKE OF.

RICHARD, EARL OF CORNWALL (b. 5 Jan. 1209 at Winchester, Hampshire, England; d. 2 April 1272 at Berkhamsted, Hertfordshire, England, aged 63). The second son of King JOHN and brother of HENRY III, Richard in 1225-7 nominally led an expedition which strengthened English possession of GASCONY and attempted to regain Poitou (*see* ANGEVIN EMPIRE). Afterwards he was created earl of Cornwall (30 May 1227). He received land grants from Henry that made him one of England's wealthiest men. Richard fought in Brittany (1230), ventured on CRUSADE to the Holy Land (1240-2), declined three papal offers of the Crown of Sicily (1250–4), and served as effectively regent for Henry (1253–4). In 1257 he secured election as king of Germany, that is of the seven German principalities, for which he was also designated king of the Romans (the title of the heir apparent to the Holy Roman Empire). Henry became dependent on loans from Richard.

During the BARONIAL CONFLICT AND WARS, Richard remained loyal to Henry and was captured at Lewes (14 May 1264) and imprisoned. Released on 6 Sept. 1265, following the royalist victory at Evesham, he helped to negotiate the Dictum of KENILWORTH (1266).

RICHARD, HENRY (b. 3 April 1812 at Tregaron, Cardiganshire, Wales; d. 20 Aug. 1888 at Treborth, Caernarfonshire, Wales, aged 76). As a congregational minister 1835–50, and secretary of the London Peace Society 1848–85, Richard became renowned as the 'apostle of peace' and was the chief interpreter in England of Welsh NONCONFORMITY. As MP for MERTHYR TYDFIL 1868–88, supporting the Liberals, Richard was a prominent parliamentary spokesman for Welsh and radical causes.

RIDLEY, NICHOLAS (b. c.1502 near Willimontswick, Northumberland, England; d. 16 Oct. 1555 at Oxford, Oxfordshire, England, aged about 53). A clergyman and scholar at CAMBRIDGE (c.1518–40s), Ridley became sympathetic to reformed theology. After the accession of King EDWARD VI and ascendancy of reformers, Ridley was appointed bishop of Rochester (1547) and London (1550). He helped to impose Protestantism (e.g., replacement of altars with COMMUNION TABLES).

After the Catholic MARY became queen (1553), Ridley was arrested. Moved to OXFORD (March 1554), he was condemned for heresy (30 Sept. 1555), degraded (15 Oct.) and burnt. *See also* REFORMATION, ENGLAND.

RIDOLFI PLOT A conspiracy against the Protestant Queen ELIZABETH I of England developed 1570–1 by Roberto di Ridolfi, a Catholic banker and papal agent in London. It envisaged that English Catholics would rebel, and a Spanish army would invade from the Netherlands. Elizabeth would be replaced by MARY, QUEEN OF SCOTS, who would marry the (4th) duke of Norfolk. Ridolfi went abroad in March 1571 to organize support. The plot was discovered in Sept. when his messenger was intercepted in SE England. Norfolk and others were arrested. Norfolk was convicted of TREASON (16 Jan. 1572; executed 2 June). *See also* CATHOLIC PLOTS, ENGLAND; HOWARD FAMILY.

RIGHT, CLAIM OF *see* REVOLUTION SETTLEMENT, SCOTLAND

RIGHT, PETITION OF *see* PETITION OF RIGHT

RIGHTS, DECLARATION AND BILL OF A Declaration of Rights was presented to William of Orange and his wife Mary on 13 Feb. 1689 by the CONVENTION PARLIAMENT after they had been offered the Crown of England (following the flight of JAMES VII/II). It stated that the Crown had no power to suspend or dispense with STATUTES, or to levy taxes or raise an army in peacetime without Parliament's consent. It guaranteed free speech in Parliament by making proceedings immune from legal action.

The Declaration was confirmed in a Bill (enacted 16 Dec. 1689), which also prohibited a Catholic from becoming ruler (and likewise inhibited the ruler's spouse). *See also* GLORIOUS REVOLUTION; WILLIAM III; SETTLEMENT, ACT OF; PARLIAMENTARY PRIVILEGE.

RIGHT WING *see* LEFT WING, RIGHT WING

RINGFORT Term applied to a variable form of early medieval enclosure in Ireland. Many ringforts comprised a small circular area, often around 98 ft (30 m) in diameter, ringed by one or more earth banks and ditches (Irish *ráth*). Others had a stone wall without a ditch (Irish *caisel* or *cathair*). About 60,000 are recorded. Built from the 4th century (possibly earlier) until the 12th century, ringforts were sometimes modified and occupied into the 17th century (occasionally later). A ringfort typically contained the farmstead (house and farm buildings) of probably a better-off farmer. Ringforts were also possibly the homes of the LEARNED CLASSES. *See also* RURAL SETTLEMENT AND SOCIETY, IRELAND.

RINUCCINI, GIOVANNI BATTISTA (b. 15 Sept. 1592 at Rome, Italy; d. 13 Dec. 1653 at Fermo, Italy, aged 61). Rinuccini, archbishop of Fermo, was papal nuncio to the CATHOLIC CONFEDERATION in Ireland 1645–9 (*see* IRISH WARS, 1641–52). He demanded recognition of Catholicism by King CHARLES I, thereby preventing a compromise agreement between Irish Catholics and Charles (embattled in the CIVIL WARS).

Rinuccini arrived in Ireland on 12 Oct. 1645 and renegotiated the GLAMORGAN TREATY (20 Dec.; afterwards disavowed by Charles). In 1646 he contrived denunciation of the First ORMOND TREATY (by Synod of Waterford, 6 Aug.). He then imprisoned leading Catholics and directed military operations. In 1648 Rinuccini excommunicated (27 May) supporters of the truce with the Protestant Royalist Lord INCHIQUIN. They protested to the Pope and Rinuccini's authority declined. Catholics agreed a second treaty with the marquess of ORMOND in 1649, despite Rinuccini's opposition. He left Ireland soon afterwards (23 Feb.). *See also* O'NEILL, OWEN ROE; WALSH, PETER.

RISING OF 1679 In Scotland, the rebellion of COVENANTERS sparked off by the murder of Archbishop James SHARP of St Andrews (3 May). The murderers joined armed Covenanters in W Scotland and on 1 June defeated a government attack, commanded by John GRAHAM, at Drumclog (S Scotland). The rebels captured GLASGOW but were routed at BOTHWELL BRIG (22 June). *See also* LAUDERDALE, 2ND EARL OF.

RISING OF 1798 An attempt by UNITED IRISHMEN to establish a republic in Ireland. Their initial planning was disrupted by the arrest of many leaders in DUBLIN (12 March) and then of Lord Edward FITZGERALD (19 May). The Rising nevertheless began on 23 May in counties around Dublin. Targets included military garrisons and landlords.

In most places the Rising was quickly suppressed. But rebels (mainly Catholics) controlled Co. Wexford (SE Ireland) from end May until 21 June (disruption of rebel camp at Vinegar Hill). Other rebels in NE Ireland (mainly Protestants) briefly held several important places in early June. The Rising was largely over by mid July. About 30,000 people died (including deaths from sectarian conflict). The Rising and other troubles (e.g., HUMBERT'S EXPEDITION) persuaded the British prime minister, William PITT the Younger, to create a UNION OF IRELAND AND GREAT BRITAIN. *See also* FRENCH REVOLUTION, IMPACT ON IRELAND.

RITUALISM Term used for a movement that introduced pre-REFORMATION and contemporary Roman Catholic practices into the 19th-century Church of England (e.g., incense, calling Holy Communion 'Mass'). Led by clergy, it developed out of the OXFORD MOVEMENT from the 1840s, stimulated partly by interest in Church history. It flourished particularly in newly built town churches. Ritualistic practices were nicknamed 'smells and bells'.

Opposition to ritualism, because it seemingly subverted Protestantism, led to the establishment of the 'Ritual Commission' (1867) which made recommendations. Their ineffectiveness resulted in the 1874 Public Worship Regulation Act, which provided for provincial Church courts to try alleged illegal practices. The subsequent imprisonment of four clergy (1877–82) discredited the Act. In 1890, when Edward King, bishop of Lincoln, was prosecuted for ritualism, Archbishop E.W. BENSON issued the 'Lincoln Judgment', which stipulated ways in which some practices were permissible (e.g., visible acts of consecration were valid). The 'Lambeth Opinions' of 1899–1900, issued by the archbishops of Canterbury and York, broadened acceptable practices. Ritualism peaked in popularity in the 1920s–30s, although some practices continued to be common thereafter (e.g., use of vestments).

RIVALLIS, PETER DE (b. in Poitou, France; fl. from 1204; d. 1262 in England). A nephew of Peter des ROCHES, Rivallis held offices in the English government by 1218, during the minority of King HENRY III, but lost power in 1221 with des Roches. After a period in France, he returned to England by 1232, securing offices (e.g., treasurer of the king's household) under the influence of des Roches, with whom he was identified as part of the 'Poitevin' faction. Ousted, with des Roches, in 1234, he was pardoned (1236) and finally readmitted to court in 1250, taking up financial posts (e.g., baron of the Exchequer from 1253). Henry dismissed him in 1258 under pressure from baronial reformers. *See also* BARONIAL CONFLICT AND WARS.

RIZZIO, DAVID (b. *c.*1533, at Pancalieri, duchy of Savoy; d. 9 March 1566 at Holyrood Palace, SE Scotland, aged about 33). A musician, hired for the Scottish court in 1561, Rizzio was appointed French secretary to MARY, QUEEN OF SCOTS (1564). Lord DARNLEY, Mary's (Catholic) husband from 1565, resented Rizzio's influence and conspired with Protestant nobles: Rizzio was murdered in the queen's presence. Mary was further alienated from Darnley and drawn towards BOTHWELL. *See also* MORAY, JAMES EARL OF.

ROADS *see* TRANSPORT COMMUNICATIONS, ENGLAND/IRELAND/SCOTLAND/WALES

ROANOKE SETTLEMENTS The first English settlements in the Americas, on Roanoke Island (off modern North Carolina, USA). They were initiated by Walter RALEGH, with authority from Queen ELIZABETH I, to obtain Mediterranean-type commodities and provide a base for attacking Spanish ships.

A party of 108 men landed in 1585. Many died; the others were evacuated in 1586 (by Francis DRAKE). A reinforcement party (15 men) landed soon afterwards but was killed by natives. A third party (117 men, women and children) arrived in 1587 but disappeared by 1590 (arrival of relief expedition). The project was abandoned. *See also* NORTH AMERICA, ENGLISH EXPLORATION.

ROBERT I (b. 11 July 1274, possibly at Turnberry Castle, W Scotland; d. 7 June 1329 at Cardross, W Scotland, aged 54). King of Scots (Scotland) 1306–29.

A grandson of Robert Bruce of Annandale (1210–95), a claimant to the vacant Scottish kingship in 1290 (*see* GREAT CAUSE), Robert Bruce was earl of Carrick from 1292 and a guardian of Scotland 1298–9 or 1300 (following the deposition of King John BALLIOL by King EDWARD I of England, 1296). By Feb. 1302 Bruce had made peace with Edward, who in 1303–4 conquered S and E Scotland.

On 10 Feb. 1306 Bruce killed his rival John Comyn, whereupon he pursued the Bruce claim. He was inaugurated as king at SCONE on 25 March, but defeated twice by the English. He fled abroad, returning in Feb. 1307. Using guerrilla warfare against Scottish supporters of Balliol and the COMYNS, he secured SW and then N Scotland. By late 1309 Robert controlled Scotland N of the R. Forth. On 23–24 June 1314, at BANNOCKBURN (C Scotland), he defeated an English army. Scots now generally accepted Robert as king. By 1318 the English were driven out (truce agreed with EDWARD II May 1323; independence recognized 1328 in treaty of EDINBURGH). *See also* SCOTTISH–ENGLISH RELATIONS 1290 TO 1357; CAMBUSKENNETH PARLIAMENT; DISINHERITED; ARBROATH, DECLARATION OF; DAVID II; BALLIOL, EDWARD; BRUCE INVASION OF IRELAND.

ROBERT II (b. 2 March 1316; d. 19 April 1390 at Dundonald, W Scotland, aged 74). King of Scots (Scotland) 1371–90; first STEWART RULER.

Son of Marjory, daughter of King ROBERT I, and Walter Stewart, (6th) hereditary steward of Scotland, Robert Stewart succeeded his father in 1326. During the minority of DAVID II (1329–41), Stewart served as 'guardian' of Scotland (1334, 1338–41). From 1333 to 1337, Scotland suffered invasions by Edward BALLIOL (supported by King EDWARD III of England); Stewart helped to lead resistance. During David's imprisonment in England (1346–57), Stewart served as 'regent' (*see* NEVILLE'S CROSS, BATTLE OF).

Succeeding David (22 Feb. 1371), Robert promoted his sons to earldoms: in the 1380s they held eight out of 16. He also granted important local offices to MAGNATES. Eventually his sons and leading magnates overshadowed him.

In late 1384 Robert's eldest son John STEWART, earl of Carrick, evidently organized a coup and was appointed 'lieutenant' (regent) by a COUNCIL-GENERAL with judicial and military powers. In 1388 Scots raided England, defeating English forces at OTTERBURN (NE England). But the death or capture of many of Carrick's supporters enabled Robert's second son Robert STEWART to wrest Carrick's authority (as 'guardian'), although Carrick succeeded King Robert (*see* ROBERT III). *See also* SCOTTISH–ENGLISH RELATIONS 1357 TO 1603; RICHARD II; MINORITIES, ROYAL.

ROBERT III (b. *c*.1337; d. 4 April 1406 at Rothesay, Bute, W Scotland, aged about 68). King of Scots (Scotland) 1390–1406.

A great-grandson of King ROBERT I, through Robert's daughter Marjory (wife of Walter Stewart), John Stewart was created earl of Carrick in 1368 (by DAVID II, ruled 1329–71). From 1384 he was 'lieutenant' (regent) for his father, ROBERT II (ruled 1371–90), but in 1388 was replaced (as 'guardian') by his younger brother Robert STEWART, earl of Fife.

King from 19 April 1390, Carrick changed first name to avoid comparison with John BALLIOL. His brother Fife remained guardian (to Feb. 1393), challenging the king's authority. To generate support for himself and his heir David STEWART (now earl of Carrick), Robert granted annuities to selected MAGNATES.

On 28 April 1398 Carrick was created duke of Rothesay, with Fife becoming duke of Albany; in Jan. 1399, the COUNCIL appointed Rothesay as lieutenant for three years. When the term was finished, Albany imprisoned Rothesay; he died between 25 and 27 March 1402, possibly of starvation. Albany was reappointed guardian (May). In 1406 King Robert dispatched his new heir, James, to France, but he was captured at sea by English pirates. Robert died after hearing the news. *See also* HUMBLETON, BATTLE OF; JAMES I.

ROBERT CURTHOSE (b. early 1050s in Normandy; d. 3 Feb. 1134 at Cardiff, Glamorgan, Wales, aged in 80s). The eldest son of WILLIAM I (d. 9 Sept. 1087), Robert succeeded as duke of NORMANDY (Robert II) while a brother became king of England (WILLIAM II). Each man desired to rule both territories (*see* NORMAN EMPIRE).

In 1088 a revolt in England in favour of Robert failed (*see* ODO OF BAYEUX). William landed in Normandy in Feb. 1091 and wrested some authority from Robert; each became the other's heir (treaty of Rouen). Robert later threatened renunciation of the treaty (1093), but ceded Normandy to William for money when he went on CRUSADE (1096–1100).

In 1100 another brother, HENRY, succeeded as king of England. Robert landed in England (July 1101), but was forced to abandon his claim (treaty of Alton). Henry ended the tension by defeating Robert at TINCHEBRAI (1106) and imprisoning him (in England and Wales). Robert's nickname means 'Short-leggings'. *See also* WILLIAM CLITO; NEWCASTLE UPON TYNE.

ROBERT OF GLOUCESTER (b. mid 1080s in Oxfordshire, England; d. 31 Oct. 1147 at Bristol, Gloucestershire, England, aged in 60s). A favourite bastard of HENRY I, king of England and duke of NORMANDY, Robert acquired extensive estates by marriage. He was recognized as earl of Gloucester by 1122.

Robert (in Normandy) reluctantly accepted STEPHEN as Henry's successor (1135), but in May 1138 withdrew allegiance and became the leading supporter of MATILDA (half-sister). They went to England (Sept. 1139). Robert captured Stephen at Lincoln (E England) in Feb. 1141, but was himself captured (Sept.) at Stockbridge (Hampshire) and exchanged for Stephen (Nov.). After spending June–Nov. 1142 in Normandy, Robert continued to challenge Stephen, defeating him again at Wilton (Wiltshire; 1 July 1143). He retained extensive authority in SW England.

ROBERT OF RHUDDLAN OR ROBERT OF TILLEUL (b. *c.*1040, probably in Normandy; d. 1093, aged about 53). Norman adventurer who advanced into N Wales in the mid 1070s with his cousin Hugh, 2nd earl of CHESTER; was established at Rhuddlan by 1075, when he aided GRUFFUDD AP CYNAN, and reached Degannwy *c.*1078. Helped by the imprisonment of Gruffudd in 1081, Robert possibly aspired to lordship of GWYNEDD (NW Wales). DOMESDAY BOOK (1086) states that Robert paid £40 'rent' annually for N Wales. He was probably slain by the Welsh, perhaps by Gruffudd. *See also* NORMANS, IMPACT ON WALES.

ROBERTS, LORD (b. 30 Sept. 1832 at Cawnpore, Oudh, India; d. 14 Nov. 1914 at St-Omer, Pas-de-Calais, France, aged 81). A British soldier in India, Frederick Roberts was honoured for bravery during the INDIAN MUTINY (1857–8). During the Second Afghan War (1878–80), he commanded forces that occupied Kabul (from Oct. 1879), to avenge the killing of a British envoy and his escort, and relieved a British garrison near Kandahar (Oct. 1880). His actions made him a hero in Great Britain. Roberts then served in India as an army commander (1881–5) and commander-in-chief (1885–93; created Lord Roberts 1892).

Back in England from 1893, Roberts was sent in Dec. 1899 to southern Africa to rescue the British position in the (Second) BOER WAR (left Dec. 1900). He was created an earl and viscount (1901) and made commander-in-chief of the British Army (1901–4). He died early in WORLD WAR I, while visiting Indian forces. *See also* AFGHANISTAN, BRITISH RELATIONS WITH.

ROBERTSON, WILLIAM (b. 29 Jan. 1860 at Welbourn, Lincolnshire, England; d. 12 Feb. 1933 at London, England, aged 73). Robertson, who enlisted in the British Army as a private in 1877, was chief of the imperial general staff from Dec. 1915 to Feb. 1918 (during WORLD WAR I). He firmly supported Douglas HAIG's strategy of offensives on the Western Front, but clashed over this with the prime minister, David LLOYD GEORGE, who forced his resignation.

ROBIN HOOD (possibly fl. in early 13th century in England). A heroic outlaw, possibly based on Robert Hod, a fugitive in Yorkshire in 1225. Robin Hood had become a legendary figure by the 1260s; references to him in rhymes were made from the late 14th century although the surviving tales date from after *c.*1450. Only later (16th century) was he depicted as robbing the rich to give to the poor. In the 19th century he was represented as a Saxon noble resisting NORMANS in Sherwood Forest (Nottinghamshire).

ROBINSON, JOHN (b. 15 July 1727 at Appleby, Westmorland, England; d. 23 Dec. 1802 at Isleworth, Middlesex, England, aged 75). A lawyer, Robinson made a reputation (1750s–60s) as the land agent and borough manager of Sir James Lowther, who secured his election as an MP in 1764. In the ministry of Lord NORTH (1770–82), as secretary to the Treasury, he became indispensable for the management of parliamentary business, PATRONAGE and electoral campaigns. He also sought to reform the EAST INDIA COMPANY. Robinson refused to join North's coalition ministry with Charles James FOX (1783), and began to collaborate with William PITT the Younger. He and North fell out in 1784. *See also* PARLIAMENTARY CONSTITUENCIES AND ELECTIONS.

ROBINSON, JOHN (b. 15 June 1919 at Canterbury, Kent, England; d. 5 Dec. 1983 at Arncliffe, Yorkshire, England, aged 64). A Church of ENGLAND clergyman and theologian, Robinson was bishop of Woolwich (in LONDON) from 1959. He controversially defended in court (1960) publication of the unexpurgated edition of *Lady Chatterley's Lover* by D.H. LAWRENCE (allegedly obscene). His own book *Honest to God* (1963), which sought to make Christianity credible for a modern age, proved a bestseller. Many thought he had abandoned his faith and should resign. At Trinity College, CAMBRIDGE, from 1969, Robinson courted controversy again with unusually conservative views about the dating of New Testament writings.

ROBINSON, MARY (b. 21 May 1944 at Ballina, Co. Mayo, southern Ireland). A professor of law at Trinity College, Dublin (1969–75), Robinson served as a LABOUR PARTY member of the Irish Senate (1969–89). In Nov. 1990 she was the first woman to be elected president of southern Ireland, and the first not nominated by FIANNA FÁIL.

Robinson used her position to express women's concerns, develop relations with NORTHERN IRELAND, and encourage the Northern Ireland PEACE PROCESS. After leaving office (1997) she served as a United Nations commissioner for human rights (1997–2002) and participated in other international organizations. *See also* SOUTHERN IRELAND FROM 1922.

ROBINSON, THOMAS (b. 24 April 1695 in Yorkshire, England; d. 30 Sept. 1770 at Chiswick, Middlesex, England, aged 75). A diplomat, Robinson served at Paris, France (1724–30), and Vienna, Austria (1730–48). He negotiated the treaty of AIX-LA-CHAPELLE (1748) which ended the War of the AUSTRIAN SUCCESSION. His concern for Hanover's security won approbation from King GEORGE II (also elector of Hanover).

Robinson was elected an MP in 1727. A WHIG, he held posts in the ministry of Henry PELHAM from 1748. After Pelham's death (1754), when the duke of NEWCASTLE became PRIME MINISTER, Robinson was SECRETARY OF STATE (southern). Newcastle also selected him to manage the ministry's supporters in the House of Commons but he proved ineffectual. He resigned as secretary in Oct. 1755.

Robinson was created Lord Grantham in 1761. He served as joint paymaster-general in the ministry of Lord ROCKINGHAM (1765–6).

ROB ROY (b. Feb. or March 1671 in Buchanan parish, C Scotland; d. 28 Dec. 1734 at Balquhidder, Perthshire, Scotland, aged 62). Nickname of Robert MacGregor (Campbell from 1693), a grazier and cattle thief, who was bankrupted in 1712 by James Graham, duke of Montrose, for embezzlement. Although Campbell was involved in the JACOBITE REBELLION of 1715, he was treated leniently. In 1722 he was arrested and tried in London, but pardoned (1725). Campbell was called 'Roy' for his hair (from Gaelic *ruaidh*, meaning 'red'). He was elevated to heroic status by the novel *Rob Roy* (1817) by Walter SCOTT.

ROBSART, AMY (b. 7 June 1532, probably at Stanfield Hall, Norfolk, England; d. 8 Sept. 1560 at Cumnor Place, Berkshire, England, aged 28). Amy Robsart married Robert Dudley on 4 June 1550. Ten years later she was found dead at the foot of a staircase while her husband was at court. A jury recorded a verdict of death by misadventure (accident), but rumour accused Dudley of organizing her murder so he could marry Queen ELIZABETH I. Amy Dudley's death probably prevented their marriage. *See also* LEICESTER, ROBERT EARL OF.

ROCHES, PETER DES (b. *c.*1178 in Touraine, France; d. 9 June 1238 at Farnham, Surrey, England, aged about 60). A French cleric who served King RICHARD I (1190s) and who, in England from 1203, was appointed bishop of WINCHESTER (1205) by JOHN. He was CHIEF JUSTICIAR from 1214, but in 1215 was replaced by Hubert de BURGH.

From 1216 des Roches was guardian of HENRY III, a minor. Returning from overseas in 1221, he lost his role as de Burgh's influence rose. He went overseas again, 1227–31, but from Jan. 1232 recovered influence over Henry, securing offices for his relative Peter de RIVALLIS and ousting de Burgh (July 1232). His dominance bred opposition to what was now identified as a 'Poitevin' faction, favouring magnates of the Crown's old French domains at the expense of their English counterparts. Baronial rebellion erupted in the Welsh MARCH. Henry was pressured to remove des Roches (April 1234) but tensions over 'Poitevins' were sustained by Henry's ties to the LUSIGNANS.

ROCHESTER, EARL OF (b. early 1642 in England; d. 2 May 1711 at London, England, aged 69). Laurence Hyde was second son of the 1st earl of CLARENDON. His sister

Anne married (1660) James, duke of York (she d. 1671). Hyde served King CHARLES II as first lord of the Treasury (1679–84) and president of the Council (from 1684). During the EXCLUSION CRISIS (1679–81) he opposed the exclusion of York, a Catholic, from the succession. He was created Viscount Hyde (1681) and earl of Rochester (1682).

In 1685 York, now JAMES VII/II, appointed Rochester as lord TREASURER. But his opposition to James's promotion of Catholicism resulted in dismissal (Jan. 1687).

At the GLORIOUS REVOLUTION (1688–9) Rochester, though a 'high TORY', accepted the regime of his niece MARY II and her husband WILLIAM III. He was lord lieutenant of Ireland from 1700, continuing (to 1703) under his niece ANNE (queen from 1702). Rochester opposed government policies 1703–10, returning to office as president of the Council (1710–11).

ROCKINGHAM, 2ND MARQUESS OF (b. 13 May 1730 at Wentworth Woodhouse, Yorkshire, England; d. 1 July 1782 at Wimbledon, Surrey, England, aged 52). Charles Watson-Wentworth, a WHIG, succeeded as marquess in 1750 and became a gentleman of the bedchamber to King GEORGE II in 1751. He resigned in 1762, angered by the anti-party policy of King GEORGE III.

After the fall of George GRENVILLE as prime minister (July 1765), 'necessity not choice' forced the king to appoint Rockingham. His ministry sought to settle disaffection in American colonies by repealing the Stamp Act and passing the Declaratory Act which asserted Parliament's right to legislate for the colonies (March 1766; *see* AMERICAN INDEPENDENCE, ORIGINS OF). The repeal angered the king who dismissed Rockingham (July).

In opposition, Rockingham's supporters, the so-called ROCKINGHAM WHIGS, developed a strong ideology influenced by Edmund BURKE. They blamed problems in 1765–6 on the 'secret influence' on the king of the earl of BUTE. Rockingham opposed war with the American colonies (began 1775), and by 1778 favoured granting independence.

After Lord NORTH resigned (March 1782), George III was forced to reappoint Rockingham as prime minister. His ministry instigated peace talks with the colonies, granted legislative independence to Ireland, and passed measures of ECONOMICAL REFORM, but collapsed after his death. *See also* CONSTITUTION OF 1782; SHELBURNE, EARL OF.

ROCKINGHAM WHIGS A party in the British Parliament led by the 2nd marquess of ROCKINGHAM, especially 1766–82 (including Rockingham's two brief periods as PRIME MINISTER). Based on former followers of the duke of NEWCASTLE, they considered themselves to be a principled organized political party. They sought to protect the GLORIOUS REVOLUTION settlement and to oppose attempts by King GEORGE III to enhance royal authority. They saw opposition to the king's ministers as beneficial, not factious. Their ideology was defined and publicized by Edmund BURKE. After Rockingham's death (1782) they were led by Charles James FOX and the duke of PORTLAND, and collaborated with other opposition Whigs. They split in 1794 over the FRENCH REVOLUTION. *See also* WHIGS; FOXITES; POLITICAL PARTIES.

ROGER OF SALISBURY (b. *c.*1067, perhaps in Avranchin, Normandy; d. 11 Dec. 1139 at Salisbury, Wiltshire, England, aged about 72). A chaplain of King HENRY I, Roger was appointed CHANCELLOR (1101) and bishop of Salisbury (1102). Around 1110 he reorganized the auditing of royal finances, introducing abacus-derived calculation (*see* EXCHEQUER, ENGLAND).

In 1135, despite previously supporting MATILDA, Roger aided STEPHEN's seizure of rule in England and Normandy. But in June 1139 Stephen arrested Roger and two episcopal nephews. A council confiscated most of Roger's possessions and he died soon afterwards.

ROLLS-ROYCE Originally a company formed in 1906 by car dealer C.S. Rolls (1877–1910) and engineer Henry Royce (1863–1933) to produce luxury cars (initially the 'Silver Ghost', 1906–25). From 1915, during WORLD WAR I, Rolls-Royce also made aero engines. During WORLD WAR II, it helped to produce Great Britain's first jet engine (*see* WHITTLE, FRANK).

In 1971 funding problems for Rolls-Royce's RB-211 jet engine resulted in emergency NATIONALIZATION. The car business was demerged and privatized in 1973; the aero engine business was privatized in 1987. Rolls-Royce cars and jet engines are among the most renowned products of British ENGINEERING. *See also* MOTOR INDUSTRY, GREAT BRITAIN; AIRCRAFT INDUSTRY, UNITED KINGDOM.

ROMAN ARMY IN BRITAIN The CLAUDIAN INVASION army (in 43) numbered around 40,000 men (including four legions). By the 2nd century, the heart of ROMAN BRITAIN (or Britannia) was largely demilitarized but C and W Britain (modern N England and Wales) remained heavily garrisoned. The army of occupation peaked in the late 1st and early 2nd centuries, at perhaps 60,000 men, a heavy drain on central Roman finances and a significant economic and social influence within Roman Britain: three legions (15,000 men) were based at Caerleon (SE Wales), Chester (NW England) and YORK (NE England), while auxiliary troops manned the forts of the frontier zones, including HADRIAN'S WALL.

The later army was smaller (perhaps 10,000–20,000 in the 4th century, reflecting the relatively peaceful conditions

in Britain), with defensive strongholds (such as the SAXON SHORE forts and signal stations in modern Yorkshire, NE England) and mobile rapid-deployment forces to counter external threats (the *comitatenses*, which supplemented the legions from the time of Constantine I, emperor 306–37). Most regular soldiers were withdrawn to Continental Europe probably in the late 4th and early 5th centuries. *See also* ROMAN BRITAIN, GOVERNMENT.

ROMAN BRITAIN Julius CAESAR twice invaded Britain (55, 54 BC), but it was CLAUDIUS I (AD 43) who conquered SE Britain and created a province (Britannia) with adjacent client states (*see* CARTIMANDUA; COGIDUBNUS). Expansion W and N (opposed by CARATACUS) was interrupted by BOUDICCA's rebellion (61), but continued under the Flavian emperors (from 71), reaching its greatest extent (into N Britain) under the governor AGRICOLA in 83 (*see* MONS GRAUPIUS). Events elsewhere then prompted a strategic withdrawal to the Tyne–Solway line, where HADRIAN's WALL was later constructed (after 122), although the frontier was briefly advanced to the ANTONINE WALL (*c.*142–60s).

The heartland of Britannia was rapidly pacified (*see* ROMANIZATION), but failure to incorporate the rest of Britain (and Ireland) initially necessitated a large garrison (*see* ROMAN ARMY IN BRITAIN). Unrest occasionally prompted personal intervention by the emperor: from Septimius Severus (208–11; *see* MAEATAE) who died at YORK; from Constantius I, who also died at York (306), where his son Constantine (the Great) was then declared emperor. Britain was relatively peaceful and prosperous in the 3rd and 4th centuries, in contrast to much of the western Roman Empire, but defensive systems had to be constructed in the later 3rd century (*see* SAXON SHORE), and episodes of unrest occurred in the mid 4th century (e.g., *see* THEODOSIUS).

The emperor Severus subdivided the province (and its army, which the governor Clodius Albinus had used to challenge him) *c.*197; the emperor Diocletian split it in four *c.*300 (*see* ROMAN BRITAIN, GOVERNMENT). Britain was part of the breakaway GALLIC EMPIRE (259–73), and was later ruled by the usurpers CARAUSIUS (286–93) and ALLECTUS (293–6). Another usurper, MAGNUS MAXIMUS, held Britain 383–8. It remained a Roman province until the early 5th century, but the emperor Honorius (395–423) failed to re-establish control after the rebellion of CONSTANTINE III (406). *See also* IRON AGE, BRITAIN; POST-ROMAN BRITAIN.

ROMAN BRITAIN, AGRICULTURE *see* ROMAN BRITAIN, SETTLEMENT AND AGRICULTURE

ROMAN BRITAIN, CHRISTIANITY IN Christianity was introduced to Britain in the later 2nd century. It probably remained a minority cult during the 3rd and early 4th centuries, when three martyrs are attested, including Alban (*see* ST ALBANS). Its status improved markedly after the conversion of the emperor Constantine in 312. Three British bishops (from LONDON, YORK and probably LINCOLN) attended the Council of Arles in SE Gaul (314), and congregational worship probably spread rapidly thereafter. *See also* PELAGIUS; ROMAN BRITAIN, INDIGENOUS RELIGIONS/ ROMAN RELIGIONS IN; POST-ROMAN BRITAIN.

ROMAN BRITAIN, CURRENCY After the CLAUDIAN INVASION (43), the Roman State-backed empire-wide coinage system replaced the late IRON AGE currencies in Britain (*see* PREHISTORIC BRITAIN, COINAGE). Quantities of gold and silver coins entered the province (the standard denomination being the silver *denarius*), principally as pay for the army but also through the activities of money-lenders. Once there they passed into general circulation in the newly established towns. The social impact was significant: wealth could be held and transported in a new way. A range of smaller denominations (in brass and copper) facilitated day-to-day transactions. From the 3rd century many taxes were levied in kind rather than cash. The result was a reduction in coin use on military sites. Civilian coin-use remained extensive, however, though largely confined to urban centres. *See also* ROMAN BRITAIN, TOWNS.

ROMAN BRITAIN, DIET AND LIVING STANDARDS In general, many inhabitants of ROMAN BRITAIN enjoyed a much higher standard of living than had the inhabitants of Iron Age Britain (*see* PREHISTORIC BRITAIN, DIET AND LIVING STANDARDS). The Roman conquerors established towns, introducing levels of engineering, architecture and civic amenities previously unknown in Britain: examples are the supply of piped water to private houses, public bath blocks and sewerage systems; and public buildings, including places of entertainment such as theatres and amphitheatres. Building in stone and brick became commonplace in Romanized contexts. Town houses for the well-to-do and Romanized farm dwellings (villas) enjoyed facilities such as underfloor heating, as well as decorative painting, plasterwork and mosaics. Roman officials, the army, and the more Romanized element of native society enjoyed a varied diet of meat (both hunted and domesticated); fowl; fish and shellfish (especially oysters, mussels and strong fish sauces); cheese; bread; fruit and vegetables (including many newly introduced species); herbs and spices; and locally produced beer and (mostly imported) wine. *See also* ROMAN BRITAIN, TOWNS/VILLAS; POST-ROMAN BRITAIN.

ROMAN BRITAIN, FOREIGN TRADE Even before the Roman Conquest, a wide range of commodities was exported from Britain to the Roman Empire, such as grain; cattle and hides; slaves; hunting dogs, and bears for the Roman arena; and metals, including gold, silver and iron. After the CLAUDIAN INVASION (43) there was rapid exploitation of resources for export, especially metal ores, including silver, copper and (later) tin. Imports into Britain included large quantities of wine and luxury goods, but especially Samian pottery from Gaul. From the 3rd century, local industry (e.g., Nene Valley pottery, from E Britain) competed successfully with imports. There were specialist exports, notably the *birrus Britannicus* ('British cloak'), hooded and made of goats' hair, and the *tapete Britannicum* ('British fabric'), a light woollen blanket.

ROMAN BRITAIN, GOVERNMENT The relatively simple bureaucracy of ROMAN BRITAIN (or 'Britannia', from the mid 1st century) was headed by a governor – a senior imperial legate of post-consular rank, who controlled the army and civil administration. He also exercised wide judicial powers, though from the Flavian period (70s) onwards a separate *iuridicus* (Latin, meaning 'legal expert') was appointed. Independent of the governor, and therefore able to act as a check on his activities, was a provincial procurator, a financial officer of equestrian rank who was in overall charge of tax collection and the operation of imperial monopolies.

Below this layer of imperial officials, the Romans allowed considerable autonomy in local administration, giving the native aristocracy a vested interest in the maintenance of Roman rule. Each urban centre (colony or *colonia*, *municipium*, and CIVITAS capital) was administered by a pair of magistrates (*duoviri*) and local senate (*ordo*), and controlled a territory (*territorium*) around it after the manner of an independent city state such as Rome itself.

The seat of government, originally at COLCHESTER, soon passed (perhaps by 60) to LONDON. Later political reorganizations split the province into two (*c.*197, into Britannia Superior and Britannia Inferior, governed from London and YORK respectively) and then four (*c.*300, with administrative capitals at London, York, Cirencester and LINCOLN), when the governors lost their military commands. A fifth province, Valentia, was established in 369 (perhaps governed from CARLISLE, in modern NW England).

ROMAN BRITAIN, HOUSING *see* ROMAN BRITAIN, SETTLEMENT AND AGRICULTURE; ROMAN BRITAIN, VILLAS

ROMAN BRITAIN, INDIGENOUS RELIGIONS Such religions survived largely unpersecuted in ROMAN BRITAIN (1st–5th centuries), though according to TACITUS the Romans attacked druids (priests) on Anglesey in W Britain (modern NW Wales) in the mid 1st century. (The importance of druids remains unclear.) Indigenous religions usually concerned the worship of deities associated with natural features, such as groves. Most deities are unknown, though some (such as the *deae matres* – Latin, meaning 'mother goddesses') are visible in Romanized form, i.e., they are shown in sculpture or are mentioned in inscriptions. Some religions survived independently, while others were equated with Roman cults; for example, Nodens, a wholly British deity depicted as a dog, was equated with the Roman gods Mars and Silvanus. *See also* PREHISTORIC BRITAIN, RELIGIOUS PRACTICES; ROMAN BRITAIN, ROMAN RELIGIONS IN/CHRISTIANITY IN.

ROMAN BRITAIN, INDUSTRY Large-scale industrial (and agricultural) output was geared to supplying the ROMAN ARMY and towns, the army producing many of its own products as well as absorbing local surpluses (thereby reducing the scale of overseas trade). The production of precious metals (e.g., silver) was State controlled; iron, however, was locally produced and worked. Commodities such as pottery, bricks, tiles and leather were produced in quantity. Other industries included window glass (fine vessels were mostly imported); fulling; spinning and weaving; production of salt (an essential preservative); and specialist and luxury items made from, for example, Whitby jet, Kimmeridge shale or Purbeck marble. *See also* ROMAN BRITAIN, FOREIGN TRADE; ROMAN BRITAIN, TOWNS.

ROMAN BRITAIN, PLACE IN ROMAN EMPIRE A relatively late addition to the Roman Empire (43), situated on its NW extremity, Britain was both geographically and politically peripheral. Of no particular strategic importance, it was initially relatively backward, but required a large standing army to prevent barbarian incursions and so was probably a net drain on the Empire's resources. However, the increasing social and military pressures on the Empire from the 3rd century were less keenly felt in Britain than elsewhere; it was relatively peaceful and prosperous, becoming increasingly independent from the overburdened central administration, which was finally unable to provide help against a Saxon invasion (*c.*410). Soon afterwards, however, the visit of GERMANUS to combat Pelagianism suggests that Britain was still regarded as a distant part of the Roman world (*see* PELAGIUS). *See also* CLAUDIUS I; ROMAN ARMY IN BRITAIN; CONSTANTINE III.

ROMAN BRITAIN, POPULATION Modern estimates suggest a population in the early 4th century of 3.6 million (with perhaps another million in parts of Britain outside the Roman province). There was some growth in numbers through the Roman period (1st–5th centuries). The majority of the population lived in rural sites; the army peaked in the late 1st and early 2nd centuries at some 60,000 (with

perhaps as many dependants); and towns contained perhaps 240,000 people (the population of LONDON may have reached 30,000; most towns were very much smaller).

ROMAN BRITAIN, ROADS The construction and maintenance of roads played an important part in the conquest and subsequent ROMANIZATION of Britain. Major roads were built in the 1st century by army units to facilitate their advance and deployment, and the movement of supplies. Accurately surveyed (and typically straight for long distances), Roman roads normally had substantial stone foundations under a gravel, cobble or paved surface, and were punctuated by milestones. These roads, many radiating from newly established towns, influenced the civilian settlement pattern, in particular the location of villas. Other roads were constructed by the *CIVITATES*. Local roads were less straight and often unmetalled, and sometimes reused prehistoric routeways. *See also* LONDON.

ROMAN BRITAIN, ROMAN RELIGIONS IN The Romans brought to Britain virtually the entire classical pantheon of deities, headed by the principal triad of Jupiter, Juno and Minerva and including eastern deities such as Mithras and Dolichenus. The imperial cult provided a unifying factor in the newly conquered province (e.g., a temple of the emperor Claudius was established at COLCHESTER). Several cults developed distinctive Romano-Celtic forms (e.g., those of Sulis Minerva and Mars Cocidius). *See also* ROMAN BRITAIN, INDIGENOUS RELIGIONS/CHRISTIANITY IN.

ROMAN BRITAIN, SETTLEMENT AND AGRICULTURE Even after the introduction of towns (from mid 1st century), over 90% of the population remained country-dwellers. Patterns of IRON AGE life continued: people lived in isolated farmsteads, hamlets and sometimes small villages; houses were usually round (though rectangular houses were predominant in lowland Britain from the 3rd century); fields were small. Some farming was above subsistence level as corn, hides and cattle were exported.

The Roman occupation increased agricultural output: the government levied grain for the army, while towns and markets (and roads) provided opportunities for selling agricultural produce. In the late 3rd and 4th centuries, technological developments are evident. Ploughs became larger and coulters were added, enabling deeper furrows to be cut and heavier soils worked. The two-handed scythe was introduced, enabling hay to be cut faster and greater quantities put aside for winter forage. Corn-drying kilns were built; farmers also used crop rotations. *See also* ROMAN BRITAIN, TOWNS/VILLAS.

ROMAN BRITAIN, SOCIAL STRUCTURE The highest social standing in ROMAN BRITAIN (as elsewhere in the Roman Empire) belonged to Roman citizens. The granting of citizenship (or lesser Latin rights) to provincial aristocracy (e.g., town magistrates in the newly established urban society in the late 1st century) was an important element of ROMANIZATION. The percentage of the population holding citizenship increased (e.g., auxiliary soldiers gained citizenship for themselves and their dependents on retirement), and eventually it was granted to virtually all free inhabitants of the provinces (212). By then a more valid distinction was between the *honestiores* (an upper class extending from senators to local councillors) and the *humiliores* or *plebei*, the peasant majority. Women in both native and Roman society enjoyed considerable freedom (though no voting rights). A slave population provided both skilled and unskilled labour; many were manumitted (freed), their offspring becoming citizens. *See also* ROMAN BRITAIN, TOWNS/DIET AND LIVING STANDARDS.

ROMAN BRITAIN, TOWNS Roman-style planned urban settlements were quickly established in S and E Britain in the wake of the CLAUDIAN INVASION (43), as a means for organizing, controlling and Romanizing the Roman Empire's new province (Britannia). At the peak were *coloniae* (Latin), chartered, self-governing towns partly for discharged soldiers. In Britain three were established (COLCHESTER, LINCOLN, and Gloucester), and YORK was later granted the same status (perhaps between 208 and 211). Below these ranked *municipia*, chartered towns with more limited citizenship, e.g., Verulamium (ST ALBANS). The majority of administrative centres fell into the lowest category, as *CIVITAS* capitals (i.e., capitals of tribal districts or *civitates*). In addition, many small towns (termed *vici*) developed both within the territory of the *civitates* and, in the less urbanized N and W, outside garrison forts (e.g., Vindolanda and Housesteads on HADRIAN'S WALL). London, founded by 60, rapidly became the largest town, though its status remains unknown. It was a commercial centre, and by *c*.100 succeeded Colchester as administrative capital of the province. *See also* ROMANIZATION; ROMAN BRITAIN, GOVERNMENT/DIET AND LIVING STANDARDS; POST-ROMAN BRITAIN.

ROMAN BRITAIN, VILLAS The term villa (Latin, meaning 'country house') implies a Roman-style complex of buildings set on a rural estate (normally, but not always, a working farm). Some villas were relatively modest (although significantly different from the native farmsteads which they sometimes overlie); others boasted elaborate Mediterranean-style courtyard buildings. The incidence of villas in ROMAN BRITAIN is closely related to the map of Roman towns and roads in the lowland S and E. Many

developed to supply agricultural produce (and sometimes industrial products) to a developing urban market whilst others provided rural retreats for the more Romanized local aristocracy. The remains of about 1500 villas are known (numbers peaking in the early 4th century) though they represent only a relatively small (Romanized) proportion of the rural population. *See also* ROMAN BRITAIN, SETTLEMENT AND AGRICULTURE/TOWNS/ROADS; ROMANIZATION.

ROMAN BRITAIN AND IRELAND While campaigning in N Britain in 81, the Roman governor AGRICOLA made preparations for a possible invasion of NE Ireland. (Graves on Lambay Island, off modern Fingal, suggest that there were already British fugitives in Ireland.) Thought to lie between Britain and (Roman) Spain, Ireland would theoretically have been a strategically valuable addition to the Empire. Though Agricola judged that Ireland could easily be taken and held (requiring just one legion and auxiliaries), no Roman military activity has been discovered in Ireland.

Roman Britain exerted economic, cultural and possibly political influence. Trade with Ireland flourished from the 2nd century, with the fortified Drumanagh headland (in modern Fingal) serving as a centre. Roman coins (including hoards) and other items (e.g., brooches) have been found, mainly in E Ireland. Irish exports possibly included slaves, wolfhounds and woollen garments. Activity temporarily declined in the third century.

Roman dealings with Ireland may have encouraged the formation of larger federations of peoples, notably the SCOTS who were mentioned from the 4th century and raided Britain in the mid 4th and 5th centuries, sometimes in co-ordination with PICTS (from N Britain) and Saxons (from Continental Europe).

From the 4th century, contact with W Britain through emigration expanded cultural influences in Ireland, as is evidenced by the Roman-influenced OGHAM alphabet used for Irish. Britain was probably also a source of Christianity (*see* CONVERSION OF IRELAND). In the 5th century, a Briton who was enslaved by Irish raiders became an influential bishop in Ireland (*see* PATRICK). *See also* IRISH COLONIZATION IN BRITAIN, 4TH–6TH CENTURIES.

ROMANIA, BRITISH RELATIONS WITH European Great Powers, including Great Britain, recognized the independence of Romania from the OTTOMAN EMPIRE in 1878 (at the Congress of BERLIN). Thereafter British influence in Romania was weak. Romanians countered pressure from Russia by alliances with Austria-Hungary and Germany (1882–1914), but joined WORLD WAR I on the Allied side (including Britain, 1916–18). Its royal family became Anglophile.

Having guaranteed Romanian independence (13 April 1939), Britain was unable to prevent the forced cession of territory to the USSR and Hungary in 1940. A German puppet in WORLD WAR II (1941–4), Romania then suffered domination by the USSR. Later, Britain encouraged the comparatively independent diplomacy of Nicolae Ceauşescu, the despotic ruler 1967–89 (e.g., by hosting a State visit, June 1978). Romania joined the EUROPEAN UNION in 2007, and from 2014 its citizens could freely enter the UK. By 2016, over 170,000 Romanians were working in Britain.

ROMANIZATION Historians' term for the acquisition of Roman cultural characteristics by native peoples in the Roman Empire (and sometimes outside). It encompasses the adoption of the Roman (town-based) way of life and modes of dress, and the use of the Latin language and Roman-style goods. In Britain, Romanization was a deliberate tool for the pacification of the province, involving the introduction of a hitherto alien social and economic structure based on a newly established network of Roman-style towns, roads and villas (*see* ROMAN BRITAIN). Its effects were most strongly felt in the lowland S and E. The marrying of Roman and indigenous characteristics over time produced a distinctive Romano-British culture peculiar to the province. The concept of Romanization has been criticized for viewing Roman rule as inherently benign, and as such akin to the declared 'civilizing mission' of 19th-century British imperialism. Critics have also claimed that it presumes that native inhabitants saw Romans as superior and wanted to emulate them. *See also* ROMAN BRITAIN, ROADS/TOWNS/VILLAS; POST-ROMAN BRITAIN.

ROMILLY, SAMUEL (b. 1 March 1757 at London, England; d. 2 Nov. 1818 at London, aged 61). A barrister (from 1783), Romilly campaigned against the SLAVE TRADE from 1787. In 1806 he became an MP and solicitor-general in the 'Ministry of All the Talents' (1806–7) under Lord GRENVILLE. In Parliament he attacked harsh laws and succeeded in repealing a few statutes (e.g., 1565 Act making pickpocketing a capital offence, repealed 1808). His *Observations on the Criminal Law of England as it Relates to Capital Punishments* (1810–11) influenced later LEGAL REFORMS.

ROSEBERY, 5TH EARL OF (b. 7 May 1847 at London, England; d. 21 May 1929 at Epsom, Surrey, England, aged 82). Leader of the LIBERAL PARTY 1894–6; British prime minister 1894–5. Known as Lord Dalmeny 1851–68.

Archibald Primrose cut a dashing figure at Christ Church college, OXFORD, which expelled him for keeping a racehorse. A Scottish landowner and earl from 1868, he helped W.E. GLADSTONE with the MIDLOTHIAN CAMPAIGN (1879). He was under-secretary for Scottish affairs at the Home Office (1881–3) and chaired the first London

County Council (1889), but his principal public work was as foreign secretary in Gladstone's ministries of 1886 and 1892–4. He clashed with Gladstone over policy towards UGANDA.

Rosebery's premiership (March 1894–June 1895) was an ordeal. The House of Lords blocked all legislation except the Budget. His relations with Sir William HARCOURT and John MORLEY were strained. His overt imperialism and aristocratic outlook proved divisive.

Liberal imperialists continued to admire Rosebery, but his repudiation of Irish HOME RULE in 1905 was the final breach and he became politically isolated.

ROSES, WARS OF THE *see* YORKIST–LANCASTRIAN CONFLICT

ROSICRUCIANISM A movement claiming secret wisdom which was publicized by two anonymous Latin pamphlets published in Germany in 1614–15. It allegedly originated in a secret society founded *c.*1407 by Christian Rosenkreuz which adopted the 'rosy cross' symbol (rose and cross). It promoted a mixture of LUTHERANISM, anti-Catholicism and ALCHEMY. Rosicrucian ideas influenced Robert BOYLE and other natural philosophers (scientists) in England who founded the ROYAL SOCIETY (1660).

ROTHERMERE, LORD (b. 26 April 1868 at Hampstead, Middlesex, England; d. 26 Nov. 1940 at Paget, Bermuda, aged 72). 'Press lord'. In 1888 Harold Harmsworth joined the newspaper business of his older brother Alfred (created Lord Northcliffe 1905). They created an empire which included the cheap, populist and influential *Daily Mail* (launched 1896). Harmsworth was created a baronet (1910), Lord Rothermere (1914) and, after service as air minister 1917–18, Viscount Rothermere (1919). In charge of the Harmsworth business from 1922 (following his brother's death), Rothermere sold *The Times* and bought the Hulton chain (1923). He then owned three national daily morning papers, three national Sundays, and two London evening papers, to which he added provincial papers (retired 1937). *See also* ZINOVIEV LETTER; NEWSPAPERS, ENGLAND.

ROTHES, 7TH EARL OF (b. 1630, probably in Scotland; d. 27 July 1681 at Edinburgh, SE Scotland, aged about 51). John Leslie, earl from 1642, was captured in 1651 at the battle of WORCESTER (W England), while fighting for King CHARLES II. Until Dec. 1658 he lived mostly under guard.

At the RESTORATION (1660) Rothes was appointed president of the COUNCIL in Scotland and in 1663 succeeded the earl of MIDDLETON as KING'S COMMISSIONER (also appointed treasurer). He collaborated with Archbishop James SHARP in actions against COVENANTERS. One consequence was the PENTLAND RISING (Nov. 1666), for which Rothes was deprived of his offices (16 April 1667). He was created duke of Rothes in 1680.

ROTHESAY, DAVID DUKE OF *see* STEWART, DAVID

ROTTEN BOROUGH Term used in the 18th and 19th centuries for BOROUGHS with very small populations, usually caused by depopulation, which elected representatives to the British, Irish or UK PARLIAMENTS (e.g., Old Sarum in Wiltshire, England, with seven voters in 1830). Usually controlled by a patron, such places were called 'the rotten part of the constitution' by William PITT the Elder in 1766. Fifty-five small borough constituencies, each electing two MPs, were abolished in 1832, and others in 1867 (*see* PARLIAMENTARY REFORM). *See also* PARLIAMENTARY CONSTITUENCIES AND ELECTIONS.

'ROUGH WOOING' *see* SCOTTISH–ENGLISH RELATIONS 1357 TO 1603

ROUND BARROWS, BRITAIN Round mounds covering single or multiple burials date from the Late NEOLITHIC and Early BRONZE AGE (*c*.2800–1600 BC). They can occur in isolation or grouped together in cemeteries as at Linga Fold (Orkney) or Winterbourne Stoke (Wiltshire, S England). Treatment of bodies and provision of grave goods suggest that round barrows drew attention to concepts of genealogy, status and inheritance for particular kin groups. They may also have marked connections between people and land or adjacent monuments.

ROUNDHEADS *see* CAVALIERS, ROUNDHEADS

ROWLAND, DANIEL (b. 1711 or 1713 at Nancwnlle, Cardiganshire, Wales; d. 16 Oct. 1790 at Llangeitho, Cardiganshire, aged 76–9). A leader of early Welsh Methodism. In 1735 Rowland was ordained a priest in the Church of England, which included Wales. Influenced by Griffith JONES, he experienced a spiritual awakening. From 1737 he made preaching tours and, in collaboration with Howel HARRIS, developed Methodist societies in S Wales. But Rowland's Methodism prevented advancement in the Church; he remained a curate at Llangeitho. In 1750, after a tense period, Harris retired, leaving Rowland as principal Methodist leader. Around 1762 he built a meeting-house at Llangeitho to which thousands flocked to hear his sermons. *See also* METHODIST REVIVAL, WALES.

ROWNTREE, SEEBOHM (b. 7 July 1871 at York, Yorkshire, England; d. 7 Oct. 1954 at Hughenden Manor, Buckinghamshire, England, aged 83). In 1895 Rowntree, a chocolate manufacturer, was shocked by seeing slums in NEWCASTLE UPON TYNE. Investigating his native city, he produced *Poverty: A Study of Town Life* (1901), which revealed that a third of York's population lived barely above subsistence. He argued that poverty often had structural rather than moral causes (e.g., family size), and popularized the 'poverty line' concept (adequate income). He influenced national social policy, regarding pensions, minimum wage and family allowances. *See also* NATIONAL DETERIORATION.

ROYAL AFRICAN COMPANY An English trading company founded in 1660 to exploit gold fields in GAMBIA, originally called the Company of Royal Adventurers Trading to Africa. Reorganized and renamed in 1672, with a monopoly of trade in gold, silver and slaves from W Africa, it built fortified trading posts between modern Gambia and NIGERIA and supplied slaves to the WEST INDIES. By 1689 it had transported around 100,000 slaves. Although it formally lost its monopoly in 1697, it remained involved in the SLAVE TRADE until 1731; dissolved 1752. High-quality gold coins based on gold supplied by the company were popularly called 'guineas' (referring to the W coast of Africa). *See also* WEST AFRICA, ENGLISH AND BRITISH INVOLVEMENT; OVERSEAS TRADING COMPANIES.

ROYAL AIR FORCE The UK's military air service. Military airpower was developed by the Army-controlled Royal Flying Corps (formed 1912) and Royal Naval Air Service (1914). During WORLD WAR I (1914–18) aircraft engaged in reconnaissance, artillery spotting, aerial combat and bombing. Because new independent roles for airpower seemed likely, the units were amalgamated on 1 April 1918, against Army and Navy opposition. In Nov. 1918 the 'RAF' had 22,000 aircraft and 300,000 personnel.

In the 1920s–30s a small RAF secured its existence partly with operations against overseas rebels, so-called 'colonial policing' (e.g., in IRAQ, 1923). By 1934 the RAF had contracted to 33,400 personnel. Expansion then recommenced to counter German rearmament, initially stressing offensive roles (e.g., bombing). From 1937 defence against bombing was prioritized, notably with the first wide-area interception system using radar and 'fighter' planes (*see* DOWDING, HUGH).

During WORLD WAR II (1939–45) the RAF participated in numerous theatres with such aircraft as Hurricane and Spitfire fighters and Wellington and Lancaster bombers. Its outstanding contributions included: deterrence of a German invasion (Battle of BRITAIN, 1940); (controversial) bombing in Germany (*see* WORLD WAR II, BOMBING OFFENSIVE AGAINST GERMANY); protection of maritime supplies (by a separate Coastal Command). In May 1945 the RAF had 55,000 aircraft and 1 million personnel.

From 1945 the RAF was shaped by changes in technology and strategy (e.g., obligations to the NORTH ATLANTIC

TREATY ORGANIZATION). Jet-powered aircraft became standard (e.g., Gloster Meteor fighter, 1944–61; Canberra bomber, 1951–2006). From 1957 to 1969, during the COLD WAR, the RAF provided Britain's nuclear deterrent, the 'V-Force' of bombers. It was also involved in such conflicts as the KOREAN WAR (1950–3) and PERSIAN GULF WAR (1991). After the Cold War (ended 1991) the RAF was reduced. In 2016 it had 806 aircraft (including 143 Typhoon fighters and 78 Tornado multi-role aircraft), and 31,000 personnel. *See also* AIR TRANSPORT, SOUTHERN IRELAND.

ROYAL COMMISSIONS Independent official bodies, usually of 3–15 members, appointed by ROYAL PREROGA-TIVE to undertake investigations, probe executive conduct or consider legislative policy. Originating as early as the 11th century (*see* DOMESDAY BOOK), they were much used *c*.1530–1630 (e.g., for implementing religious changes and investigating depopulation). They then incurred parliamentary disfavour until revived in the early 19th century when they became powerful instruments for reform (*see* CHADWICK, EDWIN). Modern commissions' conclusions have sometimes been predetermined by a government's selection of chairman and members; or division has resulted in majority and minority reports, enabling a government to avoid action.

ROYAL COURT *see* ROYAL HOUSEHOLD, ENGLAND/ SCOTLAND; ROYAL HOUSEHOLDS, WALES

ROYAL HOUSEHOLD, ENGLAND Anglo-Saxon kings (6th–9th centuries) itinerated with kin and servants (e.g., REEVES), living in halls and tents while collecting renders and asserting authority (households were centres of GOVERNMENT). Later kings of WESSEX and of ENGLAND (from 10th century) had larger households with designated officers (e.g., 'plate-thegn', OE *discÞegn*, providing food), clergy and (to *c*.1360) fighting men. By the 1060s clergy included a CHANCELLOR responsible for document writing; the major residences were houses (or palaces) at WINCHESTER and WESTMINSTER. Outsiders (e.g., MAGNATES, suitors) joined the itinerant household temporarily, forming a larger body usually called the 'court'.

From 1066 to 1204, when kings also ruled NORMANDY and the ANGEVIN EMPIRE, parts of the household moved between England and Continental Europe. By the 1130s it was organized as five main departments under officers (e.g., chapel under the chancellor; chamber for financial management under the master-chamberlain). Some governmental activities became detached, eventually settling at Westminster.

A new two-storey building at WINDSOR Castle (completed 1365) evidently encouraged the grouping of departments under the 'chamber' (for the king and senior courtiers, under the chamberlain) and 'hall' (for other servants, under the steward), though regular itineration continued. Household staff varied from 400 to 700 people (14th–15th centuries).

King HENRY VII created a dedicated bodyguard ('yeomen of the guard', 1485), and private 'privy chamber' staffed by grooms (by 1493); his court became centred on palaces near LONDON (e.g., Richmond Palace, 1501). Monarchs were more sedentary from ELIZABETH I (ruled 1558–1603), when WHITEHALL PALACE served as principal residence. It was succeeded by KENSINGTON PALACE (1689–1762) and BUCKINGHAM PALACE, although from 1698 St James's Palace (near Whitehall) was the official centre.

The court's political importance declined in the 18th century (*see* PRIME MINISTER). From 1805 (except 1837–61) the monarch's private secretary was influential. In the early 21st century the household employed 1200 people. *See also* KINGSHIP, ANGLO-SAXON; HAMPTON COURT; MASQUES; COURT AND COUNTRY; CIVIL LIST; SINECURE; GEORGE IV; ALBERT OF SAXE-COBURG.

ROYAL HOUSEHOLD, SCOTLAND Before DAVID I (ruled 1124–53) kings were probably attended by kin, nobles, clergy and servants. David introduced the formal household organization he had experienced in England and Normandy (*see* ROYAL HOUSEHOLD, ENGLAND).

The CHAMBERLAIN (usually a layman) became chief financial officer and head officer. The constable and marischal maintained peace, while departments under the steward provided food, drink, clothing and accommodation (*see* STEWART FAMILY). The CHANCELLOR (usually a churchman until the mid 16th century) was head of the 'chapel' or Chancery which produced documents. No separate treasury developed (*see* EXCHEQUER). In 1424 JAMES I instituted a master of the royal household, comptroller and treasurer and gave them (*c*.1426–8) most of the chamberlain's duties.

The household was itinerant. It effectively ended in 1603 when JAMES VI moved to London (*see* UNION OF CROWNS, ENGLAND (WITH IRELAND) AND SCOTLAND), although some hereditary posts continued. Office-holders resumed activities from 1856 when Queen VICTORIA and her successors made annual visits to EDINBURGH. *See also* ROYAL REVENUES, SCOTLAND.

ROYAL HOUSEHOLDS, WALES From the 5th or 6th century, kings were probably attended by their warband and kin, and by servants providing domestic requirements (food, clothes, etc.). By the 13th century the DISTAIN (steward) emerged as chief officer, and in GWYNEDD (NW Wales) the keeper of the bed-chamber became treasurer or chamberlain. Households were associated with a principal court (*llys*), which had a wooden hall as its centre, but also travelled to consume food renders. *See also* KINGSHIP, WALES 5TH–13TH CENTURIES.

ROYAL INSTITUTION In England, a centre founded in 1799 in LONDON to display mechanical inventions and explain natural philosophy (science) to the public. Proposed by the natural philosopher and inventor Count Rumford (Sir Benjamin Thompson, 1753–1814, originally from N America), it operated from 1800 under a royal charter. The Institution's premises included lecture theatres and laboratories. Lectures were popular with nobility and gentry, especially during the LONDON SEASON. Annual Christmas lectures for children were started in 1825, lectures for schools in 1954, and mathematics masterclasses for children in 1979. From 1981 the Institution organized masterclasses for schoolchildren in mathematics, engineering and computer science around the UK and provided other resources for schools.

Numerous distinguished scientists have been associated with the Institution, including Humphry DAVY, Michael FARADAY, and physicist John Tyndall (1820–93, professor from 1853, laboratory director 1867–87), and important research has been sustained.

ROYAL MARRIAGES ACT Legislation by the British Parliament, 1772, which required descendants of King GEORGE II to obtain the monarch's consent before marrying if under 25. Promoted by the prime minister, Lord NORTH, at the insistence of GEORGE III, it followed the clandestine marriages of the king's brothers the dukes of Cumberland and Gloucester. It was intended to prevent undesirable royal marriages. The Act was repealed in 2013 (by the SUCCESSION TO THE CROWN ACT).

ROYAL NAVY *see* NAVY, ENGLISH, BEFORE 1660; NAVY, ENGLISH AND BRITISH, FROM 1660

ROYAL OBSERVATORY In England, an astronomical observatory founded in 1675 at Greenwich, near LONDON, with support from King CHARLES II, to enable John Flamsteed (1646–1719), as astronomer royal, to survey stars (for maritime navigation). His catalogue, *Historia Coelestis Britannica* ('British Survey of the Skies'), was published posthumously (1725). From 1833 the Observatory provided a daily time signal by dropping a large ball down a roof-mounted pole, and in 1884 the 'Greenwich Meridian' was accepted internationally as the prime meridian (longitudinal division between west and east hemispheres).

Because of difficult viewing conditions, the Observatory was moved to Herstmonceux Castle (S England) in 1947–58, and to CAMBRIDGE (E England) in 1990. It was closed by the British government in 1998. The post of astronomer royal had become an honorary, advisory position (1972).

In 1822 an observatory at EDINBURGH (Scotland) was granted the title 'Royal Observatory' (absorbed into a larger organization 1998). An astronomer royal for Scotland was appointed from 1834. *See also* SCIENTIFIC REVOLUTION; HALLEY, EDMOND.

ROYAL PREROGATIVE Term for the collective powers, rights and privileges of a ruler, including waging war, creating COURTS, appointing ministers. 'Prerogative', derived from Latin and French, means 'privilege'.

The concept existed in England in the 13th century (as evidenced by the 1270s–80s tract *De praerogativa regis*, 'Of the King's Prerogative'), although royal powers had already been formally constrained by MAGNA CARTA (1215; reissued from 1216). Prerogative powers were further limited (e.g., by PARLIAMENT), but in the 16th–17th centuries royal authority was enhanced by PREROGATIVE COURTS, and in the 1630s Charles I exerted royal powers (*see* CHARLES I, PERSONAL RULE). In Great Britain from the 18th century, the Crown's rights were increasingly exercised by the PRIME MINISTER and other ministers (*see* PATRONAGE). In the 21st century, the government's authority still depended partly on royal prerogative, although its scope could be uncertain (e.g., as demonstrated in 2017 when the UK Supreme Court ruled on the authority required to initiate withdrawal from the European Union, deciding for Parliament; *see* BREXIT).

From the later 12th century rulers of England claimed extensive powers in Ireland. Largely exercised by the CHIEF GOVERNOR, they were subject in practice to considerable limitations (e.g., by power of Gaelic chieftains). In the IRISH FREE STATE (established 1922), 'the people of Ireland' replaced the Crown as the source of authority.

In Scotland the extent of royal powers was uncertain in the 12th–15th centuries. Royal authority was asserted by JAMES VI, who claimed power as judge over the people (1584) and enunciated divine right of monarchy (1598, in *The True Lawe of Free Monarchies*). CHARLES I's use of royal authority to impose a Prayer Book (1637) provoked the REVOLT OF 1637.

The concept of prerogative powers is inappropriate for other kingships within the British Isles because they operated within elaborate customary structures (*see*, e.g., KINGSHIP, IRELAND). *See also* KINGSHIP AND MONARCHY, ENGLAND 1066 TO 1680s; KINGSHIP AND MONARCHY, ENGLAND AND GREAT BRITAIN FROM 1680s; REVOLUTION SETTLEMENT, SCOTLAND; CONSTITUTION, UNITED KINGDOM.

ROYAL REVENUES, ENGLAND BEFORE 1066 Rulers of Anglo-Saxon kingdoms (5th–9th centuries) were supported by renders of food and drink (OE *feorm*, meaning 'food' or 'provision') produced by tenants and slaves on extensive estates (or small SHIRES). They itinerated between estate centres (e.g., YEAVERING), at which renders were collected. Some kings also exacted tribute from subordinate kingdoms (*see* TRIBAL HIDAGE). In the 7th–9th centuries kings additionally levied tolls (*see* WIC) and exploited Church estates.

After kings of WESSEX (S England) created the kingdom of ENGLAND (10th century), they continued to draw revenues from rural estates (including the smaller, more intensively worked estates later known as MANORS), and obtained income from SHIRE COURTS. They received rents, tolls and profits of jurisdiction from BURHS (fortified centres, many of them urban), and profited from the reminting of coins in burhs (*see* CURRENCY, ENGLAND BEFORE 1066). In the later 10th century they developed taxation based on land assessments (*see* GELD). England's kings in the late 10th and 11th centuries were among the wealthiest in Europe. *See also* KINGSHIP, ANGLO-SAXON.

ROYAL REVENUES, ENGLAND 1066 TO 1603 From the later 11th century kings received much income as FARMS; i.e., fixed annual payments from each SHERIFF, who collected revenues from his SHIRE (mainly from MANORS, BURHS (towns), and SHIRE COURTS). Other continuing sources included minting charges and GELD (taxation, until 1162).

Revenues increased thanks to new sources: FEUDAL INCIDENTS (payments arising from 'feudal' land tenure), income from vacant estates (e.g., bishops' estates), SCUTAGE, tallage (levies on tenants, intermittently 1168–1312), 'general eyres' (from 1174; *see* EYRE), and carucage (land tax, 1194–1224). Other charges were levied for special purposes, requiring consent after 1215 (from PARLIAMENT from the 1340s–70s); historians therefore differentiate 'ordinary income' (regular revenues, funding the ROYAL HOUSEHOLD and GOVERNMENT) from 'extraordinary income' (irregular grants, e.g. for war; *see* TAXATION). Kings also borrowed.

Lands (so-called 'royal demesne') were administered separately from 1236, decreasing sheriffs' 'farms'. From 1275 kings received CUSTOMS from foreign trade, some perpetually, others temporarily (usually for warfare). From the 1360s, routine renewals of discretionary customs made customs an important 'ordinary' source. From 1399 kings received revenues from the duchy of LANCASTER (administered separately; *see* HENRY IV).

By 1460 HENRY VI was impoverished because of excessive land grants and falling customs revenues. EDWARD IV and HENRY VII restored revenues by retaining nobles' forfeited estates and improving management. Customs income increased, and a French pension was acquired (1474–1550; *see* PICQUIGNY, TREATY OF). In 1509 annual ordinary income was £113,000, 37% from lands, 35% from customs.

Thomas CROMWELL increased revenues by annexation of papal taxes ('first fruits' and tenths, 1534) and monastic lands (1536–40), although lands were extensively sold. Income from feudal incidents was reinvigorated by creation of the Court of WARDS (1540). Warfare forced ELIZABETH I to sell lands (from 1585). Although by 1603 ordinary income was £300,000, the increase since 1509 scarcely matched inflation. *See also* ITALIAN BANKERS, MEDIEVAL ENGLAND; NEW MONARCHY, ENGLAND; DISSOLUTION OF RELIGIOUS HOUSES, ENGLAND.

ROYAL REVENUES, ENGLAND FROM 1603 Under JAMES VI/I (ruled 1603–25) increases in 'traditional' revenues (e.g., through IMPOSITIONS), and exploitation of newer sources (e.g., sales of PATENTS AND MONOPOLIES, and of HONOURS), to fund James's lavish lifestyle, were regularly attacked in PARLIAMENT. Charles I sought to strengthen the monarchy's finances without summoning Parliament (from 1629; *see* CHARLES I, PERSONAL RULE). Alongside improved income from principal sources (lands, FEUDAL INCIDENTS, customs), he expanded sales of monopolies, revived dormant sources (e.g., enforcement of FOREST LAW), and extended taxation under ROYAL PREROGATIVE (*see* SHIP MONEY). Income rose from £550,000 to £900,000 by 1639, but Charles's practices fuelled renewed conflict. In 1641 the LONG PARLIAMENT appropriated customs in LONDON and elsewhere, and in 1646 (during the CIVIL WARS) abolished the Court of WARDS and associated feudal incidents. After the abolition of monarchy (1649), most Crown estates were sold.

From the RESTORATION, revenues were provided by parliamentary authority, based mainly on TAXATION. The CONVENTION PARLIAMENT granted CHARLES II (1660–85) income from customs and EXCISE, and authorized repossession of lands. The CAVALIER PARLIAMENT added HEARTH TAX (1662) and 'one-off' grants (e.g., last SUBSIDY, 1663). Charles also secretly obtained a French subsidy (1670; *see* DOVER, TREATY OF). Provisions were largely continued for JAMES VII/II (1685–8). WILLIAM III surrendered the hearth tax (1689).

Costs of warfare in William's reign (1689–1702) encouraged separate consideration of civil and military requirements. From 1697 Parliament assigned revenues for certain civil expenditures (so-called CIVIL LIST, for ROYAL HOUSEHOLD and government). From 1702 its payment was unassociated with particular revenues.

From 1760 monarchs surrendered lands to the Treasury (managed by the Crown Estate from 1961). Under GEORGE III some government costs were funded separately, and from 1831 the civil list applied only to the royal household. The duchy of LANCASTER remained a personal revenue source. *See also* ROYAL REVENUES, SCOTLAND.

ROYAL REVENUES, IRELAND Gaelic kings (before early 17th century) received food, labour services, and penalties (e.g., forfeited goods) from social subordinates, and could quarter troops (recorded from 12th century). They also possessed land. Overkings commanded tribute (OIr. *cíos*) from subordinate kings' subjects (animals, bread, ale). During the GAELIC REVIVAL of the 13th–15th centuries, kings (or lords) also extracted 'protection' rents from Anglo-Irish populations (for withholding attacks).

After the Anglo-Irish invasion (1169–70), monetary charges were levied under royal authority in English-controlled areas to maintain government: rents from the ruler's MANORS, major towns, and estates temporarily under government administration; CUSTOMS on trade; fines from SHIRE and central courts; taxation (intermittent 'aids'); payments for royal 'feudal rights' (*see* FEUDAL INCIDENTS). In the 13th century, revenues yielded a surplus which was sent to England.

In the early 14th century income fell from about (Irish) £6300 to £4200 per year; then declined further, despite taxation grants, as the English-administered area contracted. After some recovery, income was about £2500 in the 1390s but under £2000 by 1485, derived mainly from the PALE and spent mostly at source (e.g., towns retaining fee-farm rents for defence). The shortage encouraged the appointment of Anglo-Irish magnates as chief governors (*see* KILDARE ASCENDANCY).

After 1534, as English authority was re-exerted, attempts were made to expand revenues, though government depended greatly on English subsidies. Increased levies in the Pale caused unrest (*see* CESS), but COMPOSITIONS (rents) were raised elsewhere (from 1570s). From the early 17th century more income was obtained from customs and minors' estates (*see* WARDS AND LIVERIES, COURT OF).

Following the RESTORATION, the Irish Parliament granted revenues to the Crown in perpetuity (1662), including customs, EXCISE (introduced 1643), and a hearth tax. With regular taxation grants, they were the mainstays of income until the Irish and UK Parliaments exerted extensive control (later 18th, early 19th centuries). *See also* KINGSHIP, IRELAND; GOVERNMENT, IRELAND 12TH–MID 17TH CENTURIES.

ROYAL REVENUES, SCOTLAND Kings in N Britain (Scotland from mid 10th century) were sustained mainly by cain (Gaelic *cáin*), i.e., tribute in kind (oats, cattle, etc.), which they consumed during visits to royal estates (*see* THANAGE), and by 'conveth' (Gaelic *coinmed*) or hospitality (food, accommodation). Following the introduction of CURRENCY (*c*.1136), rulers increasingly enjoyed money income (received by the CHAMBERLAIN). Cain and conveth were generally converted to money rents, and additional income came from new BURGHS and SHERIFFDOMS,

JUSTICIARS' courts and FEUDAL INCIDENTS; from the late 13th century there were also export CUSTOMS. But estates produced most revenues (probably over £7000 annually).

During the 14th century most Crown lands were alienated; instead, customs (quadrupled 1368) became the main income source, producing over £10,000 in some years. Direct taxation (on property values) was raised only in emergencies, and rarely caused conflict with PARLIAMENT. Armies were unpaid.

King JAMES I (personal rule 1424–37) transferred receipt of most revenues to a treasurer and comptroller (*c*.1426–8). By then customs income had declined sharply; conversely Crown lands were hugely expanded through forfeiture and escheat (reversion) of earldoms and lordships. Also, from the mid 1490s, kings drew large revenues from the Church (*see* JAMES IV; JAMES V). By 1512 royal income was at least £28,000, possibly £44,500 (though the value of £ Scots was much reduced).

Between *c*.1500 and *c*.1580 FEUING was applied to Crown lands, but the fixed feu-duties from feuars were soon devalued by inflation. JAMES VI was forced from 1581 to levy regular direct taxes, and in 1597 customs were increased and import duties introduced (*see* OCTAVIANS). Difficulties ended with the UNION OF CROWNS (1603), when rulers received English revenues. (TAXATION mainly funded government expenditure.)

From 1610 to 1708 the treasurer was also comptroller. Revenues were then received by various successive bodies until 1961 (transferred to the Crown Estate).

ROYAL REVENUES, WALES In the 12th century (as probably earlier) Welsh rulers received food from ancestral estates; they also collected food renders (or money in lieu) from freemen and bondmen while moving round their kingdoms (*see* COMMORTH). Other income included spoils of war and plunder, profits of justice, treasure trove, payments on the accession of a new ruler, and revenues from vacant bishoprics and abbacies. In the 13th century rulers exploited new sources such as tolls in towns and taxation of individuals.

In 1284 EDWARD I annexed royal revenues in native Wales to the English Crown (*see* RHUDDLAN OR WALES, STATUTE OF), though they were sometimes granted to the PRINCE OF WALES (periodically 1301–1460, and 1715–27). Revenues were administered (until 1554) by exchequers at CAERNARFON, CARMARTHEN and Cardigan. EDWARD II levied a subsidy in the principality in 1318–19. The joining of the duchy of LANCASTER to the English Crown in 1399 added revenues from duchy estates in the MARCH OF WALES.

Revenues declined sharply in the late 15th and 16th centuries. After the UNION OF WALES WITH ENGLAND (1536–43), English taxes were extended to Wales (including the

HEARTH TAXES of 1662–89). In 1760 GEORGE III surrendered the income from royal lands in Wales to the (English) Exchequer fund that paid for the CIVIL LIST. Revenues and Crown rights were administered from the 19th century by commissioners, known from 1956 as the Crown Estate Commissioners. *See also* KINGSHIP, WALES 5TH–13TH CENTURIES.

ROYAL SOCIETY In England, an organization founded in 1660 to advance natural philosophy (science) through experiments. It originated in earlier groups, especially the OXFORD Philosophical Club, which discussed experiments at Wadham College during the wardenship of John Wilkins (1648–59, during the COMMONWEALTH AND PROTECTORATE).

On 28 Nov. 1660, following the RESTORATION, a meeting of natural philosophers at GRESHAM COLLEGE in London formed a society to convene weekly, with Wilkins as chairman. Founders were connected with Oxford (e.g., Robert BOYLE, Christopher WREN) or the royal court. The Society was approved by King CHARLES II, and incorporated by royal charter in 1662 as the 'Royal Society of London' (renamed 1663 as the 'Royal Society of London for Improving Natural Knowledge'). Meetings focused on experiments (*see* HOOKE, ROBERT). Fellows also corresponded with overseas scholars, published reports (from 1665), sponsored books, and developed a museum and library.

In the 18th century the Society became more of a social organization, though it provided scientific advice to the government. It eventually responded to criticism by limiting elections (from 1847): the Society became a fellowship of scientists, and election a distinction. (Women were elected from 1945.) From the mid 19th century the Society advised on government grants for scientific work. It awarded bursaries from 1953, and research professorships from 1962 (with government-provided funds), and in 2010 opened a residential seminar centre. In 2015 there were about 1500 fellows and foreign members. *See also* SCIENTIFIC REVOLUTION; NEWTON, ISAAC; BANKS, JOSEPH; DAVY, HUMPHRY; ROYAL INSTITUTION.

RUMP PARLIAMENT In England, name given to members of the Long Parliament who continued to sit after PRIDE'S PURGE in Dec. 1648. They arranged the trial of King CHARLES I (Jan. 1649). After his execution (30 Jan.), the House of Commons resolved to abolish the House of Lords and monarchy (6–7 Feb.) and effectively became the country's executive authority. The monarchy and Lords were abolished in March, and a Commonwealth was declared on 19 May.

The Rump was expelled by Oliver CROMWELL on 20 April 1653, possibly because he feared its replacement by a hostile, conservative Parliament. It was recalled by the Army on 7 May 1659, after the failure of the Protectorate (in abeyance Oct.–Dec.). On 21 Feb. 1660 General George MONCK forced it to readmit MPs excluded in 1648 (*see* LONG PARLIAMENT). *See also* COMMONWEALTH AND PROTECTORATE.

RUNCIE, ROBERT (b. 2 Oct. 1921 at Great Crosby, Lancashire, England; d. 11 July 2000 at St Albans, Hertfordshire, England, aged 78). A veteran of WORLD WAR II (awarded the Military Cross), Runcie was ordained a Church of ENGLAND priest (1951). As archbishop of CANTERBURY 1980–91, he enjoyed friendship with the Catholic archbishop Basil HUME, and in May 1982 prayed with Pope John Paul II at Canterbury Cathedral (*see* PAPAL VISITS, GREAT BRITAIN). Runcie's sermon at an official service after the FALKLANDS WAR (26 July 1982), urging reconciliation with Argentinians, and his response to urban disturbances (the Church report *Faith in the City*, 1985), made him seem a critic of Prime Minister Margaret THATCHER. He strove to preserve Church unity over the divisive issue of women's ordination. The imprisonment of his envoy Terry Waite in Lebanon (1987–91) caused him anguish. *See also* WOMEN, ORDINATION OF.

RUNRIG In Scotland, the practice of periodically reallocating arable strips (or 'rigs') between tenants within open-field farming, in order to share the use of more fertile land. It is first recorded in 1437 but probably dates from the 12th century. It was rare by the late 17th century, although it survived into the early 20th century in the WESTERN ISLES. *See also* AGRICULTURE, SCOTLAND BEFORE 17TH CENTURY.

RUPERT, PRINCE (b. 8 Dec. 1619 at Prague, Bohemia; d. 29 Nov. 1682 at Westminster, Middlesex, England, aged 62). A German nephew of King CHARLES I, Rupert gained military experience in Germany in the late 1630s. From 1642 he was a leading Royalist commander in the CIVIL WARS in England. Initially successful, he fought at Edgehill (23 Oct. 1642) and captured BRISTOL (26 July 1643). He was created duke of Cumberland in Jan. 1644. Though defeated at Marston Moor (2 July), he was appointed captain-general (commander) in Nov. The king dismissed Rupert after he surrendered Bristol to Parliamentarians (10 Sept. 1645), though a court martial cleared him of treason.

After OXFORD (Royalist capital) surrendered (June 1646), Rupert fought in France and then commanded a small English Royalist fleet (1648–53). After the RESTORATION (1660), he was active in OVERSEAS TRADING COMPANIES and participated in the second and third ANGLO-DUTCH WARS (1665–7, 1672–4).

RUPERT'S LAND Territory in N America formerly controlled by the HUDSON'S BAY COMPANY (1670–1869).

Named after Prince RUPERT, the company's governor, it comprised all lands drained by rivers flowing into Hudson Bay (1.4 million sq mi, 3.6 million sq km). Settlement was very sparse. Despite opposition from inhabitants of French-Indian descent, the company surrendered control to the British Crown (with North-Western Territory) in 1869. The lands were granted to CANADA in July 1870.

RURAL DEPOPULATION, ENGLAND The population of many rural areas declined from 1851 into the 1920s. For example, in Brize Norton parish (Oxfordshire) it fell from 720 in 1851 to 421 in 1921. Depopulation represented shrinkage of the agricultural labour force, mainly through migration to towns but sometimes overseas. (In most counties overall population increased, with only four counties showing decreases 1851–1911.) Depopulation was encouraged by mechanization (e.g., mowing, reaping), and by shifts from arable to pastoral farming, which required less labour (notably during the AGRICUTLURAL DEPRESSION of the 1880s–90s). But many workers left to seek better conditions.

The building of rural RAILWAYS in the late 19th century, and development of bus routes after WORLD WAR I (ended 1918), encouraged repopulation based on commuting. The trend was further stimulated by the advent of relatively cheap motor cars in the 1920s–30s and mass motoring from 1945. By 1960 commuters had settled in most rural areas. The major exceptions were large parts of the SW and upland areas in the N.

RURAL DEPOPULATION, IRELAND Ireland's population peaked in 1845 at 8.5 million. The reduction of 2 million during the GREAT FAMINE (1845–9), through death and EMIGRATION, mostly affected rural areas. Rural population decline continued until the late 20th century, falling below 3 million by 1919. Causes included high emigration, migration to towns (principally DUBLIN, BELFAST), and an increase in the unmarried proportion of the population (25% of adults in their forties by 1911).

During the 20th century employment in agriculture fell from 52% of the economically active population in 1926 to below 14% the 1990s. By the 1940s many villages and towns were dominated by older people and services were uneconomic. In the later 20th century population increased in areas around major urban centres as car commuting grew. *See also* RURAL SETTLEMENT AND SOCIETY, IRELAND.

RURAL DEPOPULATION, SCOTLAND The 'improvement' of agriculture in the Lowlands from the 1760s, often involving reduction of tenant numbers, and CLEARANCES in the HIGHLANDS from the 1770s, caused steady migration (to industrializing towns or abroad). Natural increase maintained a rise in the rural population

until the 1840s. It then declined until the 1960s in the Lowlands, when car commuting generated repopulation of areas around towns, and until the 1980s in the Highlands, when retired people and business people began to settle. *See also* AGRICULTURE, SCOTLAND FROM 18TH CENTURY.

RURAL DEPOPULATION, WALES Rural population peaked in the mid 19th century when, in relation to resources, much of the countryside was overpopulated. Between 1851 and 1931 the population of the seven largely rural counties declined from 415,000 to 360,000, leaving ruined homesteads and abandoned fields in uplands. From the 1960s relatively cheap motor cars and disillusionment with towns generated repopulation of the countryside, though not to 1851 levels. *See also* AGRICULTURE, WALES FROM 18TH CENTURY.

RURAL SETTLEMENT AND SOCIETY, ENGLAND The majority of people lived in rural settlements until the mid 19th century. During the 5th–6th centuries, following the decay of Roman villas and possibly other settlements, new settlements appeared, beginning in eastern and southern areas. Started by Germanic settlers, many were hamlets of 5–10 buildings (e.g., WEST STOW), which were routinely replaced by ones nearby (so-called 'shifting settlement'). Settlements were more stable from the 7th–9th centuries as bounded building plots were established.

In the 9th–12th centuries populous villages emerged ('nucleated settlement'), mainly in a 'central region' (from NE England across the Midlands to the S) and associated with 'open-field' AGRICULTURE. Elsewhere farmsteads and hamlets remained characteristic ('dispersed settlement'), alongside small fields. Lords' residences and churches were also established; settlements became regulated by MANORS.

Settlements expanded in the 12th–14th centuries, villages commonly to 40–50 households. Manorial landholdings were typically 10–40 acres (4–16 ha). People participated in commercial transactions (*see* COMMERCIALIZATION). From the mid 14th century POPULATION fell, settlements contracted, HOUSING decayed and manorial authority weakened; 3000 villages became completely depopulated, their lands converted to pasture. Elsewhere, land availability enabled some tenants to expand holdings.

Population growth in the 16th and early 17th centuries re-expanded settlements, and larger farmers ('yeomen') prospered from higher prices. Smaller farmers ('husbandmen') did moderately well, while labourers suffered declining real wages.

In the 18th century farming and rural society were extensively restructured, particularly in the central region. Periods of low prices reduced numerous yeomen and husbandmen to labourers. Major landowners created larger farms, a process consolidated by ENCLOSURE.

Growing numbers of labourers (from 1740s) created underemployment except near industrial regions; the total peaked *c*.1850 (1,284,000 male workers, 199,000 females). Rural populations then diminished until repopulated by commuters (*see* RURAL DEPOPULATION, ENGLAND). In the 20th century mechanization reduced agricultural employment, leaving settlements mostly inhabited by urban workers. *See also* PARISH, CIVIL FUNCTIONS, ENGLAND; AGRICULTURAL REVOLUTION; TOWNS, ENGLAND.

RURAL SETTLEMENT AND SOCIETY, IRELAND

The country was predominantly rural until the mid 19th century. Until the late 12th century settlement was mostly 'dispersed', consisting of isolated homesteads or hamlets (clusters of homesteads). By *c*.900 BC some élite homesteads were situated on CRANNOGS (platforms by lakes), and by the 4th century AD some better-off farmers probably lived within RINGFORTS (small enclosures). Settlements for poorer people were probably impermanent. AGRICULTURE primarily involved cow keeping.

Following the Anglo-Norman invasion (1169–70) English lords and settlers added several hundred 'nucleated' villages and small towns, often alongside CASTLES and associated with arable-based farming. (N Ireland was little affected.) Such settlements declined, and were sometimes abandoned, in the 14th–17th centuries, due to the GAELIC REVIVAL and POPULATION changes. From the late 14th century Anglo-Irish and Gaelic Irish lords constructed tower-houses (possibly 7,000 by 17th century).

In the 16th and early 17th centuries PLANTATIONS (colonization projects) included new homesteads and villages, particularly in Ulster. Maps show that Gaelic Irish tenants sometimes lived in clusters of cabins (one- or two-room dwellings, often without windows). Increased pastoral farming in the 17th and 18th centuries reduced settlement in some areas. Elsewhere, villages grew around new Catholic chapels; landowners built houses and estate villages; and in Ulster, presbyterians built homesteads and villages. From the mid 18th century the swing towards tillage (arable farming), and rapid population expansion, increased cabin settlements, often on edges of farms or along roads.

Depopulation precipitated by the GREAT FAMINE (1845–9) and lasting into the 20th century had a substantial impact. Cabin clusters decayed, villages shrank and isolated farmsteads became fewer, though from 1898 county councils built thousands of labourers' cottages particularly in E and S Ireland. Economic growth from the 1960s created new settlements around urban centres for commuters, and bungalows were built along roads and elsewhere, a phenomenon nicknamed 'bungalization'. *See also* HOUSING, IRELAND; RURAL DEPOPULATION, IRELAND; TOWNS, IRELAND.

RURAL SETTLEMENT AND SOCIETY, SCOTLAND

By the 9th century (and probably earlier) people lived in dispersed hamlet clusters called FERMTOUNS (Gaelic *clachans*), which later accommodated small groups of joint tenants and dependant cottars. Groups of a dozen or so fermtouns formed larger estates, often called 'shires', and sometimes THANAGES. Bigger settlements developed around nuclei such as churches, mills and (from the 12th century) castles. In the SE, nucleated villages, some with regular layouts around greens, may have been introduced by Anglo-Norman landholders (12th and 13th centuries; *see* NORMANS, IMPACT ON SCOTLAND).

From the later 18th century agricultural improvement and amalgamation of holdings led to replacement of hamlets by larger steadings (farmsteads) with accommodation for farmworkers in bothies (huts) or adjoining cottages. Surplus population in many areas moved to new planned estate villages. In the HIGHLANDS in the late 18th and early 19th century peasant farmers were cleared out of interior glens to make way for commercial sheep farms, leaving depopulated landscapes and abandoned settlements. Many people were resettled in planned coastal crofting townships. Factory villages from the late 18th century, and suburbs and commuting settlements from the later 19th century, diversified traditional settlement patterns. *See also* AGRICULTURE, SCOTLAND BEFORE/FROM 18TH CENTURY; POPULATION, SCOTLAND; HOUSING, SCOTLAND; RURAL DEPOPULATION, SCOTLAND; TOWNS, SCOTLAND.

RURAL SETTLEMENT AND SOCIETY, WALES

In the 5th–18th centuries most people lived in rural settlements, either 'dispersed' farmsteads or hamlets (clusters of homesteads), or occasionally 'nucleated' villages. A group of farmsteads, hamlet or village was called a *tref* (Welsh, meaning 'vill'). Until the 14th century several *trefi* might form a *maenol* (or *maenor*), or 'multiple estate', and include a church (*llan*) and a king's or lord's hall (*llys*, meaning 'court'). A 'lowland dwelling' (*hendref*) often had an associated 'upland dwelling' (*hafoty*), inhabited during summer pasturing of animals. Bondmen tended to live in hamlets and villages, freemen in farmsteads (*see* SOCIAL STRUCTURE, WALES). As freemen's lands were divided between heirs (by partible inheritance or gavelkind), farmsteads were built around family lands creating 'girdle settlements'. In the late 11th and 12th centuries Normans and Anglo-Normans founded villages in the S and along the border (*see* MARCH OF WALES).

Many bond vills were abandoned during the 15th century (and sometimes replaced later by single freehold farms). With the rise of GENTRY and decline of native TENURES, social structure increasingly resembled that in England, consisting of gentry landlords, farmers (freeholders or tenants), smallholders (cottagers), and labourers, together with craftsmen. Most farms were small – under 30 acres (13 ha). From the late 17th century some settlements became partly industrialized as mineral working expanded (*see* INDUSTRY, WALES).

Rural population increased until the mid 19th century and then declined as people migrated to industrial centres. The widespread sale of estates in 1914–22 reduced gentry influence, and many tenants became owner-occupiers. But mechanization of farming from the 1950s encouraged amalgamation of farms and reduced employment. In the early 21st century remote areas remained sparsely populated, while city and town hinterlands were settled by commuters. *See also* AGRICULTURE, WALES BEFORE/FROM 18TH CENTURY; POPULATION, WALES; HOUSING, WALES; RURAL DEPOPULATION, WALES; TOWNS, WALES.

RUSHDIE AFFAIR An episode affecting British politics and culture provoked by Ayatollah Khomeini of IRAN. On 14 Feb. 1989, after Muslims in Great Britain and elsewhere had protested about Salman Rushdie's novel *The Satanic Verses* for insulting Islam, Khomeini issued a fatwa (pronouncement) demanding Rushdie's execution. A volatile situation developed: Rushdie went into hiding, bookshops were bombed, and Iran cut diplomatic relations with Britain (7 March). Opposition to Rushdie's book allegedly strengthened British Muslims' sense of identity, and increased self-censorship by non-Muslims. Iran's government withdrew support for the fatwa in 1998 to facilitate the restoration of diplomatic relationships. *See also* MUSLIMS IN GREAT BRITAIN.

RUSKIN, JOHN (b. 8 Feb. 1819 at London, England; d. 20 Jan. 1900 at Brantwood, Lancashire, England, aged 80). A wine merchant's son, Ruskin studied art and architecture in Europe from the 1840s and became an influential critic (through *Modern Painters*, 1843–60). His esteem for medieval architecture (in *The Seven Lamps of Architecture*, 1849, and *The Stones of Venice*, 1851–3) encouraged the Gothic revival. Ruskin became increasingly concerned about the social and aesthetic effects of the INDUSTRIAL REVOLUTION, and from the 1860s attacked LAISSEZ-FAIRE capitalism. His writings advocating social welfare (e.g., *Unto This Last*, 1862) influenced the LABOUR MOVEMENT. *See also* HILL, OCTAVIA.

RUSSELL, BERTRAND (b. 18 May 1872 at Trelleck, Monmouthshire, Wales; d. 2 Feb. 1970 at Penrhyndeudraeth, Merionethshire, Wales, aged 97). A grandson of Lord John RUSSELL, Bertrand Russell became influential as a philosopher (notably with *Principia mathematica*, 1911–13,

written with A.N. Whitehead). He was also a life-long campaigner for radical causes, starting with WOMEN'S SUFFRAGE. His opposition to WORLD WAR I led to six months in prison (1918). As president of the CAMPAIGN FOR NUCLEAR DISARMAMENT (1958–60), he urged anti-nuclear protesters to civil disobedience. He succeeded as Earl Russell in 1931. *See also* RUSSELL FAMILY.

RUSSELL, LORD JOHN (b. 18 Aug. 1792 at London, England; d. 28 May 1878 at Richmond, Surrey, England, aged 85). A leading WHIG politician; British prime minister 1846–52, 1865–6.

Third son of the 6th duke of Bedford, Russell was educated at EDINBURGH University. Elected as an MP in 1813, he advocated PARLIAMENTARY REFORM as early as 1819, and his work for the Great Reform Act (1832) made him a national figure. He was then serving as paymaster-general (1830–4). As home secretary (1834–9), he secured the MUNICIPAL CORPORATIONS ACT (1835). As secretary for war and the colonies (1839–40) he unified CANADA.

Russell formed a government in June 1846 after the fall of Sir Robert PEEL. The PUBLIC HEALTH Act (1848) was significant, but the ministry was troubled. Russell's relations with Lord PALMERSTON were strained. Russell resigned in Feb. 1852 after a Commons defeat. He participated in Lord ABERDEEN's coalition (Dec. 1852 to 1855), but withdrew from public life from 1855 until 1859, when he became foreign secretary (under Palmerston). He was created Earl Russell in 1861. Russell's second government fell after eight months when the ADULLAMITES thwarted his long-cherished plans for further parliamentary reform (June 1866).

In a time of party indiscipline, Russell was not an ideal leader. Though he was a proponent of LIBERALISM, it was W.E. GLADSTONE who consolidated the LIBERAL PARTY. *See also* RUSSELL FAMILY; GREAT FAMINE.

RUSSELL FAMILY A leading English noble family from the 16th century onwards. John Russell (*c*.1485–1555) was created earl of Bedford in 1550 for suppressing the PRAYER-BOOK REBELLION (1549). Lord William Russell (1639–83) suffered beheading for seeking the exclusion of James, duke of York, from succession to the English throne because of his Catholicism (*see* EXCLUSION CRISIS; RYE HOUSE PLOT).

Russells held high office in the 18th and 19th centuries, notably the 4th duke of BEDFORD (d. 1771) and Lord John RUSSELL (created Earl Russell in 1861; d. 1878). The latter's descendants include the philosopher Bertrand RUSSELL (3rd Earl Russell, d. 1970) and the historian Conrad Russell (5th Earl Russell, 1937–2004).

RUSSIA, BRITISH INTERVENTION The Bolsheviks' coup in Russia (Nov. 1917) and withdrawal from WORLD WAR I (Dec.) undermined the Allied war effort. Civil war also broke out in Russia. The Allies (Great Britain, France, USA, Australia, Canada) sent military forces to NW Russia. They landed at Murmansk (March 1918) and Archangel (Aug.), initially to defend stockpiles of supplies against German forces. The Allies also sought to revive the Eastern Front against the Central Powers. Their forces became involved in fighting against Bolsheviks. Meanwhile, in the Caucasus, a British force from PERSIA supported anti-Bolsheviks in Baku (July–Sept. 1918; displaced by Turks). In Aug. Britain contributed 1500 men to an Allied force in Siberia, which aided the 'White' (anti-Bolshevik) leader Admiral Alexander Kolchak.

After the western armistice (11 Nov. 1918) invalidated the intervention's original purposes, the government minister Winston CHURCHILL pressed for Allied forces to overthrow the Bolsheviks. The prime minister David LLOYD GEORGE and popular opinion were opposed. Forces remained in Russia while peace talks were attempted. British troops were withdrawn from Archangel in Sept. 1919, from Murmansk in Oct., and from Siberia in June 1920.

RUSSIA AND USSR, ENGLISH AND BRITISH RELATIONS WITH Regular trading began with foundation of the MUSCOVY COMPANY (1555). With the rise of Russian power in the 18th century, Great Britain and Russia played a secondary part in the shifting alliance strategies of the other. From the later 18th century Britain was concerned about Russian influence in SE Europe (part of the EASTERN QUESTION), though the countries co-operated in the FRENCH REVOLUTIONARY AND NAPOLEONIC WARS (1793–1800, 1805–7, 1812–15). The Eastern Question dominated relations in the 19th century, alongside rivalry in C Asia (*see* GREAT GAME). After the CRIMEAN WAR (1854–6) Prime Minister Benjamin DISRAELI again checked Russian policy in the BALKANS in 1878. The ANGLO-RUSSIAN CONVENTION (1907) eased tension and facilitated alliance in WORLD WAR I (1914–Dec. 1917).

After the Bolshevik (communist) seizure of power in Nov. 1917, Britain briefly intervened (*see* RUSSIA, BRITISH INTERVENTION). Bolshevik victory in the Russian Civil War led to creation of the Union of Soviet Socialist Republics or 'USSR' (1922), which Britain recognized in 1924, though relations were suspended 1927–9. The countries allied in July 1941, after Germany invaded the USSR (20-year treaty made 1942). Britain provided supplies by means of Arctic convoys (1941–5).

From the late 1940s the tensions of the COLD WAR pervaded British–USSR relations. They improved from the mid 1980s under the reformist Soviet leader Mikhail Gorbachev. Following the dissolution of the USSR (1991),

Queen ELIZABETH II made a State visit to Russia (1994). Relations deteriorated in the early 21st century. They were soured particularly by the murder in London in 2006 of the former Russian secret service officer Alexander Litvinenko, apparently with Russian State involvement, and by the attempted murder in Salisbury (Wiltshire) in 2018 of the former Russian military intelligence officer Sergei Skripal and his daughter Yulia by two Russian agents. (Another woman died four months later from poison discarded by the agents.)

RUTHERFORD, ERNEST (b. 30 Aug. 1871 near Nelson, Nelson Province, New Zealand; d. 19 Oct. 1937 at Cambridge, Cambridgeshire, England, aged 66). From 1895, supported by a scholarship, Rutherford worked at the Cavendish Laboratory of CAMBRIDGE University with J.J. THOMSON. Following the discovery of uranium radioactivity (in France, 1896), Rutherford found (1897) that decaying uranium emits two types of rays, which he named 'alpha' and 'beta'.

As a professor at McGill University (Canada) from 1898, Rutherford discovered a radioactive 'emanation' from thorium, which proved to be a gas; with Frederick Soddy, Rutherford argued that radioactive substances decayed into new substances ('transformation theory'). He was elected a fellow of the ROYAL SOCIETY (1903) and awarded the 1908 Nobel Prize in Chemistry.

Invited to MANCHESTER University (NW England) in 1907, Rutherford proposed (1911) that atoms comprise a nucleus orbited by electrons, a model considered his greatest achievement. In 1917 he broke debris from atoms using alpha rays (identified as protons, particles with positive electrical charge).

From 1919, as director of the Cavendish Laboratory, Rutherford oversaw fundamental advances (*see* CHADWICK, JAMES; COCKCROFT, JOHN). He became president of the ROYAL SOCIETY (1925–30) and Lord Rutherford (1931). He dismissed the possibility of atomic power, but privately advised the British government to monitor developments.

RUTHERFORD, SAMUEL (b. *c.*1600 at Nisbet, SE Scotland; d. March 1661 at St Andrews, E Scotland, aged about 61). A clergyman and academic, Rutherford was banished from SW Scotland to ABERDEEN (1636–8) for criticizing ARMINIANISM and royal policies (of King CHARLES I). In 1638 he supported the NATIONAL COVENANT, and from 1639 held posts at ST ANDREWS University. Rutherford's book *Lex Rex* (1644) denied the DIVINE RIGHT of kings; it argued that rulers held power in trust for the people. At the RESTORATION Rutherford's publications were banned (Sept. 1660) and he was charged with treason. He died before standing trial.

RUTHVEN RAID The seizure of King JAMES VI of Scotland on 22 Aug. 1582 at Ruthven Castle (now Huntingtower, near Perth, C Scotland) by William Ruthven, (1st) earl of Gowrie, and other Protestant, pro-English nobles. They forced James to dismiss his pro-French, ex-Catholic favourite Esmé STEWART, duke of Lennox. The 'Ruthven regime' ended after James escaped in June 1583. *See also* NEGATIVE CONFESSION; GOWRIE CONSPIRACY.

RYE HOUSE PLOT In England, a WHIG conspiracy in 1683 to assassinate King CHARLES II and his brother James, duke of York, to prevent the accession of York, a Catholic. The scheme was to have been implemented at Rye House in Hertfordshire. It was revealed to the government on 21 June. As a result the Whigs Lord William Russell and Algernon Sidney were executed, though their involvement was not clearly proved. Others were threatened with retribution. *See also* EXCLUSION CRISIS; JAMES VII/II.

S

SABBATARIANISM Opposition to secular activity on Sunday (e.g., recreation, work), which was sometimes promoted by Protestant Christianity. Sabbatarianism was strong in lowland Scotland from the REFORMATION (1560) to the 18th century. The Scottish Parliament prohibited activities in 1579 and 1661. Sabbatarianism was revived by EVANGELICALISM in the 19th century. From the 1830s, work and shopping were discouraged, and the TEMPERANCE MOVEMENT achieved Sunday closing of pubs (1853). Sabbatarianism was also supported by presbyterians in Northern Ireland. A broader coalition obtained Sunday closing of public houses in Ireland in 1878 (except in five urban areas; included 1906).

In England and Wales, Puritans and others sought legislation from the 1570s. King JAMES VI/I issued a proclamation against Sunday sports (1603) but later permitted them (*Book of Sports*, 1618). CHARLES I conceded an Act (1625), then reissued the *Book* (1633). The House of Commons condemned sports and dancing in 1641, and passed an ordinance (1644). Laws followed in the 1650s (*see* COMMONWEALTH AND PROTECTORATE). Legislation was resisted after the RESTORATION (1660) except for the 1677 Sunday Observance Act which banned work. Some Societies for the Reformation of MANNERS opposed Sunday trading and work (1690s–1730s). Sabbatarianism revived in the late 18th century: the Sunday Observance Society was founded in 1775, and the 1780 Sunday Observance Act (applicable in Great Britain) prohibited opening of shops and places of entertainment (e.g., theatres). The Lord's Day Observance Society, founded 1831, sought to enforce the 1780 Act. In Wales, public houses were closed on Sundays from 1881.

Sabbatarianism declined from the late 19th century, though shopworkers were protected (e.g., by 1950 Shops Act for England and Wales). Sunday opening of public houses was reintroduced (Republic of Ireland, 1960; Wales, 1961–96; Scotland, 1976; Northern Ireland, 1989). Other restrictions collapsed in Scotland in the 1980s, and the 1994 Sunday Trading Act permitted extensive opening of shops in England and Wales. *See also* PURITANISM, ENGLAND/WALES.

SACHEVERELL AFFAIR In England, political and social unrest 1709–10, in the reign of Queen ANNE, caused by Dr Henry Sacheverell (1674–1724), an outspoken HIGH CHURCH and TORY clergyman who prominently expressed Tory concerns.

On 5 Nov. 1709, in a sermon at St Paul's Cathedral, London, Sacheverell denounced 'false brethren' (WHIGS and LATITUDINARIANS in the Church hierarchy), DISSENTERS, and religious toleration. He also questioned the 1689 Revolution settlement, which was prized by Whigs (*see* GLORIOUS REVOLUTION).

Whig politicians wanted a show-trial. Sacheverell was impeached in WESTMINSTER HALL for attacking the Revolution and religious toleration, and for alleging there

A Dictionary of British and Irish History, First Edition. Edited by Robert Peberdy and Philip Waller.
© 2021 John Wiley & Sons Ltd; © editorial matter and organisation Robert Peberdy and Phillip Waller.
Published 2021 by John Wiley & Sons Ltd.

was sedition within the government (from 27 Feb. 1710). Though found guilty, he was merely banned from preaching for three years (23 March), an outcome regarded as a triumph by Tories. The events provoked rioting against dissenters in London (1 March) and aided Tory success in the 1710 general election. *See also* IMPEACHMENT; SUNDERLAND, 3RD EARL OF.

SAGADAHOC *see* VIRGINIA COMPANY

ST ALBANS A city in Hertfordshire, SE England. The late IRON AGE settlement of Verlamion (meaning unknown) became Roman Verulamium (by *c*.49), *civitas* capital of the CATUVELLAUNI. Sacked by BOUDICCA (61), it was rebuilt. In the 3rd or early 4th century Alban, a Christian, was killed nearby. Verulamium was largely abandoned *c*.450, but the place of Alban's death remained a shrine and from *c*.793 was the site of St Alban's Abbey (dissolved 1539). Abbot Wulsig laid out a new town *c*.948, which remained a market town thereafter. The surviving abbey church became a cathedral in 1877. *See also* ROMAN BRITAIN, TOWNS.

Est. popn: 200, 15,000; 1086, 450; 1300, 3000; 1600, 3500; 1800, 3000; 1900, 16,000: 2000, 82,000.

ST ANDREWS A city in Fife, E Scotland. It originated in the 8th century with the founding of an abbey in an area recorded in Ireland as Cennrígmonaid (meaning 'End of the king's upland'). The founder was probably the Pictish king ONUIST SON OF VURGUIST (ruled 732–61). Possibly soon afterwards the abbey received relics of St Andrew acquired in Rome by WILFRID. There was also a house of CULDEES by the 9th century, and by the early 10th century a bishop whose see superseded DUNKELD as Scotland's pre-eminent bishopric. The location is recorded in the 12th century as both Kilrimont (Scots English, meaning 'Church of the king's upland') and St Andrews.

An Augustinian priory and BURGH were founded *c*.1140 by Bishop Robert; a castle was built for the bishop *c*.1200; a new cathedral (Scotland's largest) was consecrated in 1318; and a centre of studies was recognized as a university in 1412 (Scotland's first university; *see* UNIVERSITIES, SCOTLAND). The bishop was raised to archbishop in 1472 (*see* GRAHAM, PATRICK).

As a theological centre, St Andrews experienced religious strife from the 1520s to the REFORMATION (1559–60). Its economy declined in the 17th century, but revived in the mid 19th with university expansion and growth of golf-related tourism. *See also* CONSTANTINE II; HAMILTON, PATRICK; WISHART, GEORGE.

Est. popn: 1300, 2000; 1600, 1800; 1800, 4000; 1900, 7600; 2000, 14,000.

ST ANDREWS AGREEMENT Concluded on 13 Oct. 2006 at ST ANDREWS (Scotland) between the British and Irish governments, after three days of talks with the main political parties of NORTHERN IRELAND (principally the DEMOCRATIC UNIONIST PARTY and PROVISIONAL SINN FÉIN). It modified the 1998 BELFAST AGREEMENT so that Northern Ireland's ASSEMBLY and devolved government could be reinstated. A timetable was stipulated, and parties were required to support the Police Service of Northern Ireland, courts and the law; provision was made for powers over policing to be devolved. If the parties rejected the Agreement, the governments would impose alternative arrangements. Though it took seven months to fulfil the requirements, a new Executive was formed on 8 May 2007. *See also* PEACE PROCESS, NORTHERN IRELAND.

ST ASAPH A cathedral city in Denbighshire, NE WALES (Welsh, Llanelwy, meaning 'Church on R. Elwy'). Originally the location of a monastery allegedly founded by KENTIGERN (d. 612) or his pupil Asaph (Welsh, Asa; d. 596), St Asaph became the see of a bishopric in 1143 (covering most of NE Wales). The present cathedral was built 1480–1770. The city was formally granted city status in 2012. *See also* CHURCH ORGANIZATION, WALES.

Est. popn: 1086, 300; 1300, 400; 1600, 250; 1800, 1500; 1900, 1700; 2000, 3300.

ST DAVIDS A cathedral city in Pembrokeshire, SW WALES (Welsh, Tyddewi, meaning 'House of Dewi/David'). St Davids was originally the location of a monastery and bishopric founded by DAVID (*c*.530–89), in DYFED. BERNARD OF ST DAVIDS (bishop 1115–48) sought – unsuccessfully – metropolitan (archiepiscopal) status for St Davids, but established authority over most of SW Wales. The present cathedral (the largest in Wales, dedicated to St Andrew and St David) dates from the late 12th century. The shrine of St David was an important pilgrimage centre until destroyed between 1538 and 1540. The city developed probably after 1115 and remained a market centre. *See also* CHURCH ORGANIZATION, WALES.

Est. popn: 1300, 600; 1600, 250; 1800, 1600; 1900, 1700; 2000, 1700.

ST JAMES'S PALACE *see* ROYAL HOUSEHOLD, ENGLAND

ST JOHN, HENRY *see* BOLINGBROKE, VISCOUNT

ST JOHN, OLIVER (b. *c*.1598, probably in Bedfordshire, England; d. 31 Dec. 1673 in Germany, aged about 75). A lawyer and MP, St John became well known as counsel for John HAMPDEN when he challenged the levying of SHIP MONEY by King CHARLES I (1637). From 1640 he was a leading opponent of royal policies in the SHORT

PARLIAMENT and LONG PARLIAMENT. He worked for Parliament's victory in the CIVIL WARS (1642–8), helping to negotiate the SOLEMN LEAGUE AND COVENANT (1643), but sought a limited monarchy in negotiations with Charles (1647–8).

From Oct. 1648 St John was chief justice of common pleas, and from 1649 a member of the Council of State. His support for Oliver Cromwell's PROTECTORATE (1653–8) was lukewarm. After the RESTORATION (1660) St John was barred from office and went into exile (1662).

ST LEGER, ANTHONY (b. *c.*1496, probably in Kent, England; d. 16 March 1559 at Ulcombe, Kent, aged about 62). A courtier who served as a commissioner in Ireland (1537–8; knighted 1539), St Leger was chief governor of Ireland (lord deputy) 1540–8. He attempted to extend royal government and English law to Gaelic Irish lordships by the SURRENDER AND REGRANT policy (1540–3), and arranged for Ireland's PARLIAMENT to grant Henry VIII and successors the title 'king of Ireland' (18 June 1541).

St Leger served again (1550–1) under EDWARD VI, when he ordered (but did not enforce) the end of Catholic Church ceremonies; and under MARY I (1553–6), when he ordered the restoration of Catholicism. *See also* IRELAND, ENGLISH CONQUEST, 16TH CENTURY; REFORMATION, IRELAND.

SALESBURY, WILLIAM (b. *c.*1520 at Llansannan, N Wales; d. *c.*1584, probably in Denbighshire, Wales, aged about 64). Translator and scholar. After adopting reformed Christianity, probably at OXFORD University, Salesbury strove to make scripture and learning available in Welsh. His early publications included *Kynniver Llith a Ban* ('So Many Lessons and Excerpts'), a translation of Bible readings (1551). He probably helped to obtain the 1563 Act of the English Parliament requiring translation of the Prayer Book and Bible into Welsh. He translated the former and most of the New Testament (published 1567), though his versions were marred by Latin usages. Work on the Old Testament was never completed. *See also* REFORMATION, WALES; BIBLE, WELSH; SERVICE BOOKS, WALES; MORGAN, WILLIAM; HUMANISM.

SALISBURY, 3RD MARQUESS OF (b. 3 Feb. 1830 at Hatfield, Hertfordshire, England; d. 22 Aug. 1903 at Hatfield, aged 73). Leader of the CONSERVATIVE PARTY 1885–1902; British prime minister 1885–6, 1886–92, 1895–1902. Known as Lord Cranborne 1865–8; marquess from 1868.

Young Lord Robert Cecil was prone to illness and melancholy. Though elected as an MP in 1853, it was marriage in 1857 that provided self-confidence, and he took up political journalism. The earl of DERBY made him secretary for India in 1866, but he resigned in protest at the Second Reform Act (1867).

Despite distrust of Benjamin DISRAELI, Salisbury returned to the India Office (1874–8) and co-operated effectively with Disraeli as foreign secretary (1878–80), before assuming the Conservative leadership in the House of Lords (1881). He saw off his rivals, Sir Stafford NORTHCOTE and Lord Randolph CHURCHILL, and headed a minority government (June 1885–Jan. 1886). Opposition to Irish HOME RULE secured LIBERAL UNIONIST backing for his subsequent ministries.

In these, Salisbury combined the offices of prime minister and foreign secretary (until 1900). Though determined to defend British interests in the Scramble for AFRICA, he pursued a balanced policy, which allowed Great Britain to retain freedom of action while co-operating informally with GERMANY. *See also* HOTEL CECIL; BALFOUR, A.J.

SALMOND, ALEX (b. 31 Dec. 1954 at Linlithgow, West Lothian, Scotland). An economist, Salmond was a SCOTTISH NATIONAL PARTY (SNP) MP 1987–2010 and Party leader (national convener) from 1990. After a Labour government was elected in 1997, he contributed to the implementation of DEVOLUTION for Scotland, although the SNP sought independence. Elected to the new Scottish Parliament in 1999, Salmond was briefly leader of its Opposition (resigned as Party and Opposition leader in 2000 over an internal Party dispute). He left the Scottish Parliament in 2001 and led SNP MPs in the UK Parliament.

In 2004 Salmond was re-elected SNP leader and a member of the Scottish Parliament. After leading an effective election campaign in 2007, he headed a minority SNP government as first minister. Success in the 2011 election enabled him to form a majority government and hold a referendum about Scottish independence (Sept. 2014). After its rejection, Salmond resigned as first minister and SNP leader. Re-elected as a UK MP in 2015, he was defeated in 2017. He resigned from the SNP in 2018 amid allegations of sexual misconduct: acquitted at trial, 2020.

SALVATION ARMY An international Christian organization for evangelistic and social work. It originated in England as the East London Christian Mission founded in 1865 by William Booth. In 1879 the Mission was renamed, and military-style organization was adopted to attract working-class support. Local branches were named 'corps', members were 'soldiers', and corps leaders (effectively ministers) were 'officers' and wore uniforms. Meeting places were called 'citadels'. Booth had extensive power as 'general'. Under the influence of Booth's wife Catherine, women were given parity and could hold all offices. The Army spread quickly abroad (in USA from 1880). By 1910 there were 100,000 members in the UK. The Army has used open-air meetings and brass bands as means of evangelization. It preaches Bible-based Protestantism, but rejects sacraments. In 2010 there were 50,000 members and 1500 officers in the UK. *See also* BOOTH FAMILY.

SANCROFT, WILLIAM (b. 30 Jan. 1617 at Fressingfield, Suffolk, England; d. 23 Nov. 1693 at Fressingfield, aged 76). A Church of ENGLAND clergyman, Sancroft as dean of St Paul's Cathedral, London, helped to organize the rebuilding of the Cathedral and City churches after the GREAT FIRE of 1666. In 1678 King CHARLES II appointed him as archbishop of CANTERBURY. Sancroft opposed the exclusion of the Catholic James, duke of York, from succession to the throne (*see* EXCLUSION CRISIS) yet later resisted the catholicizing policies of JAMES VII/II. In 1688 he and other bishops challenged a royal order and were briefly imprisoned (*see* SEVEN BISHOPS' CASE).

After James fled abroad, Sancroft presided over a provisional government. But he refused to attend the CONVENTION PARLIAMENT (1689) or to crown WILLIAM III and MARY II, regarding himself as bound by oath of allegiance to James. He was suspended from office (1 Aug. 1689) and deprived (1 Feb. 1690). He retired to Fressingfield (Aug. 1691). *See also* NON-JURORS.

SANDWICH, 4TH EARL OF (b. 13 Nov. 1718 at London, England; d. 30 April 1792 at London, aged 73). John Montagu succeeded as earl in 1729. He served as first lord of the Admiralty 1748–51 (in the ministry of Henry PELHAM) and in 1763 (under the earl of BUTE); and as SECRETARY OF STATE (northern) 1763–5 (under George GRENVILLE). He was briefly secretary again in 1770–1, then first lord of the Admiralty 1771–82 (under Lord NORTH) when he reformed the naval dockyards.

After France intervened in Great Britain's war against its rebellious American colonies (1778), Britain was unable to dominate American seas whilst also providing home defence. This contributed to defeat at Yorktown in Oct. 1781. Sandwich was held partly responsible. He invented the sandwich (1762). *See also* AMERICAN WAR OF INDEPENDENCE.

SAN STEFANO, TREATY OF Agreed on 3 March 1878 at San Stefano (now Yeşilköy near Istanbul), between representatives of the OTTOMAN EMPIRE and RUSSIA, ending the Russo-Turkish War (1877–8). The Ottoman Empire ceded most of its European provinces to a new principality of Bulgaria. The British prime minister, the earl of Beaconsfield (Benjamin DISRAELI), regarded 'Big Bulgaria' as an extension of Russian influence. His belligerent denunciation of this development in the EASTERN QUESTION led to the Congress of BERLIN and a revised settlement.

SAOR ÉIRE (Irish, meaning 'Free Ireland'). In the IRISH FREE STATE, a political party founded on 26 Sept. 1931 in DUBLIN by some members of the IRISH REPUBLICAN ARMY. Advocating the establishment of a socialist republic, it won support from some members of the LABOUR PARTY. The party's foundation occurred after two years of renewed IRA activity. It was banned on 17 Oct. 1931 as part of an anti-IRA 'crackdown'. *See also* POLITICAL PARTIES, SOUTHERN IRELAND FROM 1922; MacBRIDE, SEÁN.

SARAWAK *see* BORNEO

SAUCHIEBURN, BATTLE OF Fought near Bannockburn, S of STIRLING (C Scotland), on 11 June 1488. (The battle's name dates from the 17th century.) Rebels nominally under the future King JAMES IV defeated King JAMES III and supporters. James III was killed probably after the battle.

SAUDI ARABIA, BRITISH RELATIONS WITH From the late 19th century the House of Saud in the Arabian peninsula sought British assistance against the OTTOMAN EMPIRE. Starting in 1902, Abd al-Aziz Ibn Saud acquired territories, which Great Britain was first to recognize: in Dec. 1915 (treaty of Darin) they became a British PROTECTORATE (to defend other British protectorates by the Persian Gulf) and Abd al-Aziz joined the 'Arab revolt' against the Ottoman Turks. Britain encouraged further expansion. After Abd al-Aziz conquered the Hijaz (1924–5, including Mecca and Medina), Britain recognized (1927, treaty of Jeddah) his rule over the kingdom of Hijaz and Najd (proclaimed as the kingdom of Saudi Arabia in 1932).

The USA supplanted British influence after an American company secured exclusive oil rights (1933), and Saudi Arabia severed diplomatic relations with Britain (1956–63) over the SUEZ CRISIS. British involvement then redeveloped, particularly through arms supplies. The 'Al Yamamah' arms deal (1985) for aircraft and missiles was Britain's largest ever export agreement. The countries were allies in the PERSIAN GULF WAR (1990–1). In 2006 pressure from Saudi Arabia caused abandonment of an inquiry by the UK Serious Fraud Office into alleged bribery associated with the 1985 agreement.

SAUNDERSON, EDWARD (b. 1 Oct. 1837 at Castle Saunderson, Co. Cavan, Ireland; d. 21 Oct. 1906 at Castle Saunderson, aged 69). A landowner and (Church of Ireland) Protestant, Saunderson sat in the UK Parliament 1865–74 as a Liberal but he opposed disestablishment of the Church of Ireland, promoted by the Liberal leader W.E. GLADSTONE.

Distressed by LAND AGITATION in Ulster in 1882, Saunderson joined the ORANGE ORDER. After re-election to

Parliament, as a Conservative (1885), he helped to form, and led, the semi-autonomous Ulster Unionist group of MPs, and attacked Gladstone's Home Rule Bill (1886). After the defeat of a second Bill (1893) he concentrated on the defence of landowning. *See also* UNIONISM, IRELAND.

SAVINGS BANKS Provident societies started savings banks in Great Britain in the later 18th century for domestic servants, apprentices and journeymen. In Scotland parish savings banks for the poor began in 1810, and banks were started in Ireland from 1817. The banks' directors acted as trustees. The government established a Post Office Savings Bank in 1861.

Most savings banks in the UK were amalgamated into regional banks from 1975, and eventually united in 1985 as TSB Group PLC. Privatized in 1986, it sold its business in Northern Ireland in 1991 and merged with a clearing bank in 1995. Savings banks in the Republic of Ireland merged from the 1970s and formed TSB Bank in 1992 (sold 2002). *See also* BANKING, SCOTLAND.

SAVOY CONFERENCE In England, April–July 1661, a religious conference called by King CHARLES II to make the Church of ENGLAND more acceptable to Puritans, especially presbyterians (opponents of episcopal government). Held at the Savoy Palace, London, presbyterian clergy (e.g., Richard BAXTER) proposed revisions to the Book of Common Prayer to bishops (e.g., making some ceremonies optional). Most were rejected. The bishops' intransigence led to the BARTHOLOMEW'S DAY EVICTIONS and growth of religious DISSENT. *See also* PURITANISM, ENGLAND; CLARENDON CODE; PRAYER BOOKS, ENGLAND.

SAXONS Name used in the 7th–10th centuries (OE, Seaxe) for people of Germanic culture in south-eastern and southern parts of Britain (except initially in areas settled by JUTES). According to BEDE (in 731) they originated among Continental Saxons, who lived between the Rivers Weser and Elbe (modern NW Germany); the Saxons were one of three peoples who produced migrants to Britain (5th–6th centuries). Their name probably means 'knife-wielders'. Within Britain, 'Saxons' formed one of the two main groupings of Germanic peoples (alongside ANGLES).

By the late 6th century, kingdoms existed of so-called 'East Saxons' (ESSEX) and 'South Saxons' (SUSSEX), which doubtless also included Britons and others; from the 680s the so-called 'Gewisse' from the Upper Thames Valley were called 'West Saxons' (*see* WESSEX). A province of 'Middle Saxons', W of Essex, is recorded from the early 8th century. Although West Saxon kings formed a large kingdom, encompassing various peoples, in the 10th century, its inhabitants became known as ENGLISH, derived from the 'Angles' (*see* ENGLAND, FORMATION OF).

In the 5th–6th centuries most writers outside Britain used the name 'Saxons' (Latin, Saxones) for all Germanic settlers in southern BRITAIN, a practice followed within Britain by GILDAS (writing c.540) and later Welsh and Irish writers. It has continued as the modern Welsh and Irish terms for the English, respectively 'Saeson' and 'Sasanaig'. *See also* GERMANIC IMMIGRATION, SOUTHERN BRITAIN; ANGLO-SAXONS.

SAXON SHORE Name for the eastern and southern coastline of late ROMAN BRITAIN which was threatened by Saxon pirates. In the late 3rd century the Romans built ten defensive strong-points – the Saxon Shore forts – to guard against this threat. In the 4th century they became a unified system under a 'count of the Saxon Shore'. *See also* ROMAN ARMY IN BRITAIN.

SAYE AND SELE, VISCOUNT (b. 28 May 1582 at Broughton, Oxfordshire, England; d. 14 April 1662 at Broughton, aged 79). William Fiennes, a Puritan, succeeded as Lord Saye and Sele in 1613 and was created a viscount in 1624. From the mid 1620s he was a leading opponent among the peerage to policies of King CHARLES I (e.g., FORCED LOAN of 1626; SHIP MONEY).

During the SHORT PARLIAMENT (1640) and the LONG PARLIAMENT (from 1640), Saye supported opposition to Charles in the House of Commons, despite appointment as a privy councillor (Feb. 1641), and was a Parliamentarian during the CIVIL WARS (1642–8). But after PRIDE'S PURGE (Dec. 1648) he withdrew from politics because of growing popular radicalism. He welcomed the RESTORATION (1660).

SCANDINAVIAN EMPIRE, ENGLAND'S POSITION IN The conquest of England (1016) by CNUT, younger brother of the king of Denmark, thrust England into Scandinavian politics. In 1019–20 Cnut took power in Denmark. (His older brother's fate is unknown.) In 1026 he fought Norwegian and Swedish opponents in Sweden (battle of the Holy River). In 1028 Cnut arranged the expulsion of King Olaf Haraldson from Norway and was recognized as king. (Regents expelled 1034; *see* ÆLFGIFU.) Cnut probably attempted to re-establish Danish authority in Sweden.

Cnut gave estates and authority in England to Danes. Reverse influence was negligible: Cnut tried to reproduce the English coinage system in Denmark and encouraged co-operation between the English and Danish Churches.

Cnut (d. 1035) was succeeded by sons HARTHACNUT and HAROLD HAREFOOT. The English royal line was restored in 1042, distancing England from Denmark. *See also* ENGLAND, DANISH CONQUEST.

SCARGILL, ARTHUR (b. 11 Jan. 1938 at Barnsley, Yorkshire, England). A miner at 16, Scargill held posts in the National Union of Mineworkers (NUM) from 1960. He opposed legal restraints on trade unions and advocated industrial action for political ends. Elected NUM president in 1981, he and colleagues organized a year-long strike against mine closures in Great Britain and the government of Margaret THATCHER (see MINERS' STRIKE, 1984–5). Its failure resulted in rapid shrinkage of the industry and NUM. From 2002 Scargill was life-long honorary president of the NUM. From 1996 he also led the Socialist Labour Party. See also MINERS' UNIONS.

SCHLESWIG-HOLSTEIN QUESTION A complex 19th-century sovereignty dispute concerning two duchies between Denmark and the German Confederation. Lord PALMERSTON, the British prime minister, advocated Danish incorporation of Schleswig in 1863, but could not prevent its occupation by Austro-Prussian forces (1 Feb. 1864). This revelation of weakness made his successors more wary of intervention in Continental European affairs. See also PRUSSIA, BRITISH RELATIONS WITH.

SCIENTIFIC REVOLUTION Term for the new approach to understanding natural phenomena that developed in Europe in the 16th and 17th centuries. Formulated in the 1930s by the Russian-French philosopher Alexandre Koyré, it was popularized by the English historian Herbert Butterfield (in *The Origins of Modern Science*, 1948), though many contemporaries were aware of the reorientation.

The Revolution involved scepticism towards 'ancient' authorities (e.g., Aristotle, Galen, Ptolemy), and replacement of the 'deductive' methods (expanding knowledge by logic) used by ancient authors and university scholars. Instead, the study of cosmology and nature, known as 'natural philosophy' (i.e., science) became based on inquiry by observation and experiment, and creation of testable hypotheses (scientific method). Phenomena were explained by natural rather than supernatural causes.

The Scientific Revolution first appeared in Italy. Two important early works, published in Italy in 1543 (in Latin), were *On the Revolutions of Heavenly Bodies* by Nicholas Copernicus, which proposed a Sun-centred planetary system (rather than Earth-centred universe), and *On the Structure of the Human Body* by Andreas Vesalius, based on dissection. (Copernicus and Vesalius recognized that observations did not agree with traditional authorities.) The new philosophy was soon followed in England (e.g., by William GILBERT, Francis BACON, William HARVEY), and ideas were discussed in LONDON in the 1640s. In the 1650s a group associated with John Wilkins at Wadham College, OXFORD (e.g., Robert BOYLE), undertook important experiments. Institutional focus was provided by the ROYAL SOCIETY (founded 1660). The Revolution culminated in

the *Principia … of* Isaac NEWTON (1687), which provided a mathematical explanation of cosmology.

The Revolution broadened in the 18th century through rational approaches to human affairs (see ENLIGHTENMENT), and by the late 18th century 'scientific' understanding of the natural world was often considered consistent with Christianity (see PALEY, WILLIAM). See also GEOLOGY; EVOLUTION.

SCONE A site in Perthshire and Kinross, C Scotland (now the location of a palace and village). A Pictish royal centre (by the 7th century) and home of a CULDEE community, Scone became the traditional place for the INAUGURATION (mid 9th century–1306) and CORONATION (1331–1651) of kings of Scots. The Culdees were replaced c.1115 by an Augustinian priory (abbey from 1160; sacked 1559). See also KENNETH I MAC ALPIN; STONE OF DESTINY; ALEXANDER I.

SCOTLAND A jurisdiction within the UNITED KINGDOM comprising northern BRITAIN, the WESTERN ISLES, ORKNEY ISLANDS and SHETLAND ISLANDS; formerly a kingdom. Area: 30,100 sq mi (78,000 sq km). Est. popn in 2015: 5,373,000. The main languages are English and Gaelic; in 2011 almost 150 languages were spoken. Northern and western areas are mountainous (see HIGHLANDS).

Until the 1st century AD, N Britain experienced wider cultural changes (see PREHISTORIC BRITAIN). After invasion, it was excluded from Roman-ruled Britain (2nd–5th centuries), separated by HADRIAN'S WALL (except in 2nd century; see ANTONINE WALL).

Peoples N of the FORTH–CLYDE ISTHMUS were known from the 3rd century as PICTS. By 500 SCOTS (or GAELS) from NE Ireland were settling in the Western Isles and adjacent mainland, extending DÁL RIATA (kingdoms and overkingdom), the Irish language (Gaelic) and Irish-type Christianity to N Britain. There were other (British) kingdoms: Clyde Rock (later STRATHCLYDE, around R. Clyde); RHEGED (S of Clyde Rock); GODODDIN (E of Rheged). Gododdin and Rheged were conquered by Anglians from the S (7th century).

After intermittent associations (8th–9th centuries), Scots and Picts formed a kingdom from c.842 (later called Alba, Gaelic meaning 'Britain', then 'Scotland'), which became dominated by Irish culture, though Norway acquired the Western Isles, Orkney Islands and Shetland Islands. Scotland absorbed Anglian (English) LOTHIAN and Strathclyde (11th century).

In the 12th century Norman families were imported (see NORMANS, IMPACT ON SCOTLAND). The Western Isles were acquired in 1266. In 1290 a succession crisis resulted in warfare with England (see SCOTTISH–ENGLISH RELATIONS 1290 TO 1357/1357 TO 1603). The Orkney Islands and Shetland Islands were annexed in 1472.

In 1559–60 reformed (Protestant) Christianity was established, based on CALVINISM, though the form of Church government was contested until 1690 (*see* SCOTLAND, CHURCH OF). Scotland's ruler became king of England in 1603, and in 1707 the countries were united (*see* GREAT BRITAIN). Self-government was reinstated in 1999 (*see* DEVOLUTION, SCOTLAND). *See also* POST-ROMAN BRITAIN; CONVERSION OF NORTH BRITONS, PICTS AND SCOTS; UNION OF SCOTS AND PICTS; GAELIC LANGUAGE AND LITERATURE, SCOTLAND; BORDER, ANGLO-SCOTTISH; JACOBITE REBELLIONS, CONSEQUENCES IN SCOTLAND.

SCOTLAND, CHURCH OF Scotland's principal Church from the REFORMATION (1560), authorized by the State (through Parliament) until 1921; based on CALVINIST theology and plain services. Until the mid 19th century it served most communities, organized POOR RELIEF and EDUCATION, and regulated moral behaviour (*see* KIRK SESSION).

Until 1690 reformers (clergy and lay supporters) and the Crown struggled for control. The former sought a non-episcopal Church independent of royal authority, but in 1572 accepted Crown-nominated bishops (*see* LEITH, CONCORDAT OF). Presbyteries (courts of clergy and elders) were formed in the 1580s and presbyterian government (without bishops) authorized in 1592 (*see* GOLDEN ACT). But King JAMES VI revived episcopal authority and imposed forms of worship (*see* FIVE ARTICLES OF PERTH). The imposition of innovations by CHARLES I provoked the COVENANTING REVOLUTION and involvement in CIVIL WARS (*see* WESTMINSTER ASSEMBLY). Bishops were reintroduced in 1662 (*see* RESTORATION, SCOTLAND), but condemned in 1689 (*see* REVOLUTION SETTLEMENT, SCOTLAND). From 1690 the Church's structure was presbyterian.

In the 18th century opposition to private patronage of livings (abolished 1690; restored 1712 by PATRONAGE ACT) and theological controversy disrupted the Church. Secessions resulted (*see* SECESSION CHURCH; RELIEF CHURCH). By the 1750s 'Moderates' predominated, who accepted patronage and valued rationality alongside revelation (*see* ENLIGHTENMENT, SCOTLAND), but they were displaced in the 1830s by evangelicals. In 1843, after changes to patronage had been rejected, two-fifths of clergy and laity seceded, effectively ending comprehensiveness (*see* DISRUPTION). In 1851 only 32% of churchgoers attended the Church.

Morale later recovered. Private patronage was abolished (1874) and Parliamentary control removed (1904–25), permitting union with the UNITED FREE CHURCH OF SCOTLAND (1929). Adherents increased until the late 1950s, then declined (communicants fell 44% in 1965–95). Women were ordained as elders from 1966 and as ministers from 1969. Around 2014 there were 400,000 members. In 2018 the Church decided to provide same-sex weddings. *See also* CHURCH ORGANIZATION, SCOTLAND FROM 16TH CENTURY.

SCOTLAND, FORMATION OF *see* UNION OF SCOTS AND PICTS

SCOTS English version of the Latin term Scotti, which was used by 4th-century Roman authors and later writers to refer to inhabitants of Ireland, possibly the members of a federation of peoples. Later Irish authors and others adopted the term; it was also applied to Irish people in N Britain.

From the 10th century the term was increasingly restricted to descendants of the Irish Dál Riatai in N Britain. Their kingdom had united with the Picts in the 9th century, and by *c*.1000 Irish culture largely superseded Pictish culture throughout N Britain. From the 13th century the kingdom was called Scotland. *See also* ROMAN BRITAIN AND IRELAND; DÁL RIATA; GAELS; IRISH.

SCOTS CONFESSION The confession of faith adopted on 17 Aug. 1560 by Scotland's Reformation Parliament and in late 1560 by a council (General Assembly) of the Church of SCOTLAND. Comprising 25 articles, it displayed the influence of the Swiss Church reformers John Calvin and Ulrich Zwingli. It remained the doctrinal standard until superseded by the Westminster Confession (1647). *See also* REFORMATION, SCOTLAND.

SCOTS LANGUAGE AND LITERATURE The 'Scots' tongue, derived from northern English, developed from the language of N English immigrants and traders from the 12th century (*see* ENGLISH LANGUAGE). It replaced GAELIC in most of the Lowlands by the 14th century. The character of Scots is uncertain before the 14th century, when its literature commences with John Barbour's epic poem *The Brus* (1375). Literature flowered in the 15th and early 16th centuries with the MAKARIS ('Poets'). Scots may then have differed from English as much as Portuguese from Spanish and be considered a separate language, although the English poet Geoffrey CHAUCER (*c*.1340–1400) influenced the Makaris.

ANGLICIZATION increased markedly after the REFORMATION (from *c*.1560), when the English Geneva Bible and later the King James Bible (or Authorised Version) were used throughout Scotland (*see* BIBLE, ENGLISH). The UNIONS of 1603 and 1707 increased English influence, making southern English the main prose language. ENLIGHTENMENT figures such as David Hume (1711–76) purged their speech of 'Scotticisms', though poetry flourished in the 18th century in the writings of Allan Ramsay (*c*.1685–1758) and Robert BURNS (1759–96).

Scots survived in the 19th-century KAILYARD tradition. In the 20th century Hugh MacDIARMID (1892–1978) tried to revive it as a modern literary language. *See also* SCOTTISH LITERATURE IN ENGLISH.

SCOTT, C.P. (b. 26 Oct. 1846 at Bath, Somerset, England; d. 1 Jan. 1932 at Manchester, Lancashire, England, aged 85). Charles Prestwich Scott joined the *Manchester Guardian* newspaper (owned by a cousin) in 1871, and became editor in 1872, continuing for 57 years (resigned 1929). He established high standards of journalism and literary quality, and championed unpopular causes such as social improvement, WOMEN'S SUFFRAGE and (from 1886) HOME RULE for Ireland. As a Liberal MP 1895–1905, he opposed British imperialism in southern Africa, including the (Second) BOER WAR (1899–1902). *See also* NEWSPAPERS, ENGLAND.

SCOTT, WALTER (b. 15 Aug. 1771 at Edinburgh, Scotland; d. 21 Sept. 1832 at Abbotsford, Roxburghshire, Scotland). Writer. Though an advocate (from 1792), Scott was drawn to literature. He edited texts, notably the *Minstrelsy of the Scottish Border* (1802–3), and became famous with *The Lay of the Last Minstrel* (1805) and other narrative poems. In 1812 he settled at Abbotsford, where he built a mock-medieval house (completed 1824). From 1814 Scott published historical novels (at first anonymously), many presenting a Romantic view of Scotland's past. In 1822 he organized the visit of King GEORGE IV to EDINBURGH, which celebrated a Scotland identified with CLAN culture. Scott was made a BARONET in 1820. *See also* TOURISM, SCOTLAND.

SCOTTISH CONSTITUTIONAL CONVENTION
An unofficial assembly in Scotland, established in 1989 to formulate possible constitutional arrangements for Home Rule (or devolution). It involved representatives of the LABOUR PARTY, LIBERAL DEMOCRATS, most local councils, Churches and other organizations. (The CONSERVATIVES and SCOTTISH NATIONAL PARTY refused to participate.) A convention had been advocated in *A Claim of Right* (1988), issued by the Campaign for a Scottish Assembly in response to the treatment of Scotland by Margaret THATCHER. The breadth of the Convention's membership enabled it to claim strong support for its proposals, including that of Labour, Scotland's dominant political party. Leading participants included Donald DEWAR and David STEEL.

The Convention's report, presented on 30 November 1990 (St Andrew's day), proposed an assembly elected by proportional representation with assigned powers of taxation. After Labour came to power (1997) and won support for Home Rule in a referendum, the Convention's scheme was largely incorporated in the 1998 Scotland Act (*see* DEVOLUTION, SCOTLAND).

SCOTTISH-ENGLISH RELATIONS BEFORE 1290
At the UNION OF SCOTS AND PICTS (from *c.*842), Scotland's English neighbour (to SE, at R. Forth) was NORTHUMBRIA. Northumbria was tolerated as a buffer-kingdom against VIKING-held lands farther S. From 920 Scottish kings also dealt with kings of Wessex, who were conquering Viking lands towards Scotland. King CONSTANTINE II of Scotland allegedly 'submitted' to King EDWARD THE ELDER (920) and ATHELSTAN (927).

From 927, when Northumbria submitted to Wessex, Scotland met 'England' at the Forth, although royal authority in N England was weak and Vikings retook lands farther S (*see* BRUNANBURH, BATTLE OF; YORK, VIKING KINGDOM OF). In the late 10th or 11th century (probably by 1026, certainly by 1095) Scotland acquired Lothian, moving the eastern border to the R. Tweed. Thereafter Scots pressurized England by RAIDING or by harbouring exiles.

After the NORMAN CONQUEST OF ENGLAND (1066–70s), MALCOLM III gave refuge to Edgar ætheling, MARGARET and others (1070), and raided England (five times in 1070–93). Normans responded by strengthening control (*see* NEWCASTLE UPON TYNE; WILLIAM II), forcing submission (*see* ABERNETHY, TREATY OF), and supporting Malcolm's sons against DONALD III (1093).

Between 1097 and 1135, when Malcolm's sons reigned, relations were more harmonious, and EDGAR of Scotland was possibly a vassal of English kings. DAVID I (ruled Scotland 1124–53) imported NORMANS, but during the ANARCHY of Stephen's reign appropriated N England. MALCOLM IV surrendered it to HENRY II (1157). For 80 years the loss intermittently embittered relations. WILLIAM I of Scotland joined the REVOLT OF 1173–4 against Henry, but was captured and forced to submit at FALAISE. ALEXANDER II joined the rebellion against JOHN (1215–16) and led an army to Dover (SE England). In 1237 he abandoned Scottish claims. Thereafter he and ALEXANDER III (ruled 1249–86) had good relations with England. *See also* STRATHCLYDE (CLYDE ROCK), KINGDOM OF; ENGLAND, FORMATION OF.

SCOTTISH-ENGLISH RELATIONS 1290 TO 1357
In 1290 the death of MARGARET, 'THE MAID OF NORWAY', infant queen of Scots, thwarted a dynastic union planned by King EDWARD I of England (*see* BIRGHAM, TREATY OF). But the now vacant Scottish kingship provided another opportunity. Appointed as an arbitrator of claims, Edward forced claimants to acknowledge his declared overlordship (*see* GREAT CAUSE). Sixty years of conflict (the 'Wars of Independence') and civil war ensued.

John BALLIOL, the successful claimant, gave homage (1292). But Edward interfered, demanding military service from Scottish MAGNATES. They allied with France (Oct. 1295), whereupon Edward invaded, deposed John (1296), and occupied parts of Scotland. Scots resisted, seeking John's restoration (*see* WALLACE, WILLIAM; MURRAY FAMILY). But following more invasions (1297, 1298, 1300, 1301–2, 1303–4) most Scots capitulated (early 1304).

In 1306 Robert Bruce seized the kingship (*see* ROBERT I). Using guerrilla warfare, and helped by Edward's death (1307), he eventually expelled the English (by 1318), although many Scots opposed him (e.g., COMYN FAMILY). In 1314 Robert dispossessed his Scottish enemies, producing a party of pro-Balliol exiles, the DISINHERITED. England refused recognition of independence until, following the deposition of EDWARD II (1327), an invasion forced Roger MORTIMER to make peace (1328; *see* EDINBURGH, (1328) TREATY OF).

From 1332 a resentful EDWARD III exploited DAVID II's minority to revive English ambitions. He backed the 1332 invasion by Edward BALLIOL, claimant to the kingship (unsuccessful), and campaigned in Scotland for Balliol in 1333, 1334–5, 1335, and 1336 (receiving S Scotland in 1334). But after Edward decided to fight France (1337), Balliol was driven out (1338). Scots then raided England, demanding recognition of independence, until DAVID II was captured at NEVILLE'S CROSS (1346). Balliol then invaded again (1347), restoring much of S Scotland to English administration. David remained a captive until a ransom and truce were agreed in 1357. *See also* BANNOCKBURN, BATTLE OF; SCOTTISH–FRENCH ALLIANCE.

SCOTTISH–ENGLISH RELATIONS 1357 TO 1603
After DAVID II was released (1357), heavily ransomed, the Scots improved their situation. They withheld ransom payments (1360–5); obtained a reduction (1369, after England resumed war against France); and stopped payments (1377, on the accession of RICHARD II). They seized more English-held land in S Scotland (1384), defeated the English at OTTERBURN (1388), and then joined an Anglo-French truce (1389). In 1400, during an English invasion, ROBERT III rejected a demand for homage from HENRY IV. But a Scottish revenge raid was defeated at HUMBLETON (1402).

Between 1403 and 1502 peace, based on truces, generally persisted. Major disruptions occurred in 1436 when JAMES I attacked English-held Roxburgh castle, and in the late 1450s when JAMES II did likewise. (It fell in 1460; in 1461 the deposed HENRY VI ceded the last English-held territory, including BERWICK-UPON-TWEED.) In 1482 EDWARD IV of England ordered an invasion to support the disaffected Albany (*see* STEWART, ALEXANDER), which recaptured Berwick (Aug.), while in 1495–7 the harbouring of Perkin WARBECK by JAMES IV generated tension. HENRY

VII desired security: James accepted a treaty of Perpetual Peace (1502) and marriage to Henry's sister Margaret Tudor (1503).

After the accession of HENRY VIII (1509) Scots feared reduction to client status. They renewed the French alliance (1512), and invaded England (1513; *see* FLODDEN, BATTLE OF). Until 1560 Scottish governments were usually pro-French. England invaded in 1542 (after JAMES V failed to meet Henry in 1541) and defeated a counter-invasion (at Solway Moss, NW England, 24 Nov. 1542). In 1543 Henry persuaded regent ARRAN to make an alliance (treaties of Greenwich), but Scotland's Parliament rejected it: England invaded in 1544, 1545, 1547 (so-called 'rough wooing').

Alignments changed in 1560 when Scotland's Protestant government broke with Catholic France. MARY, QUEEN OF SCOTS, and JAMES VI remained favourable to England, hoping to succeed ELIZABETH I. *See also* SCOTTISH–FRENCH ALLIANCE.

SCOTTISH EPISCOPAL CHURCH *see* EPISCOPAL CHURCH IN SCOTLAND

SCOTTISH–FRENCH ALLIANCE In Oct. 1295 the 'guardians' of Scotland, who had taken control of the kingdom from King John BALLIOL, allied with France in defiance of King EDWARD I of England. The French continued to give diplomatic support to John Balliol even after his deposition as king by Edward (1296) and the seizure of the kingship by Robert Bruce (1306; *see* ROBERT I).

France supported Robert from 1309, resulting in the treaty of Corbeil (1326) which provided for mutual support against England. Instances include French refuge for DAVID II (1334–41), David's invasion of England (1346), French assistance in 1385 (*see* ROBERT II), and a Scottish force in France (1419–24; *see* HUNDRED YEARS WAR). Thereafter interest waned.

The alliance (known as the 'auld alliance' by the late 15th century) was renewed at French request in 1512 and reinforced by pro-French governors and French marriages (*see* STEWART, JOHN; JAMES V). The government of MARY OF GUISE (from 1554) was French-dominated. The alliance with Catholic France was renounced by Protestant leaders in 1560.

SCOTTISH LITERATURE IN ENGLISH Use of English (rather than SCOTS or GAELIC) by Scottish writers has reflected Scotland's relationship with England. Whereas Scots and Gaelic have been preserved in poetry, English has made an enduring impact through prose.

A shift to English began with the REFORMATION (16th century). English translations of the BIBLE, together with the Book of COMMON PRAYER, made English influential in religion. (A Scots version of the Bible was not produced until the 20th century.) The reformer John KNOX is an early example of a writer who chose to write in English.

The UNION OF ENGLAND AND SCOTLAND (1707) played a major role, in that English became the language of government throughout Great Britain. Although revivals of Gaelic and Scots occurred in the 18th century, they were confined mostly to verse. The use of English prose became integral to the Scottish Enlightenment. Economists, philosophers and historians (e.g., Adam SMITH, David Hume, William Robertson), made important Scottish contributions to English writing, their works gaining international renown (see ENLIGHTENMENT, SCOTLAND).

This adoption of English for intellectual discourse was consolidated in the 19th century by influential journals (e.g., *Edinburgh Review*, 1802–1929; *Blackwood's Magazine*, 1817–1980), and by the works of intellectuals, notably Thomas CARLYLE. Fiction also flourished, leading figures being James Hogg (1770–1835), Walter SCOTT, John Galt (1779–1839) and Robert Louis Stevenson (1850–94).

In the 20th and 21st centuries, education and mass media ensured the widespread use of English, in poetry as well as prose. Even writers who drew inspiration from everyday speech utilized a vernacular strongly influenced by English. Leading authors of this period included novelist Dame Muriel Spark (1918–2006). *See also* ANGLICIZATION, SCOTLAND.

SCOTTISH NATIONAL PARTY A political party founded in 1934 by amalgamation of the National Party of Scotland (founded 1928) and the Scottish Self-Government Party (1932). The Scottish National Party (SNP) sought a Parliament with sovereignty over Scottish affairs. It won by-elections to the UK House of Commons in 1945 and 1967.

The SNP enjoyed greater success in the 1970s, winning seven and 11 seats at the two 1974 general elections, but declined after the (lost) March 1979 devolution referendum, holding only two seats in May 1979. From 1988 the Party campaigned for 'Independence within Europe'. At elections from 1997 to 2010 it won 4–6 seats, but in 2015 spectacularly displaced the LABOUR PARTY, winning 56 (of 59) seats. It retained 35 in 2017 and won 48 in 2019.

The Party's success followed partly from its advancement within Scotland. In 1999 the SNP became the second largest party in the new Scottish Parliament (elected by proportional representation) with 35 seats (of 129). After falling to 27 in 2003, it became the largest party in 2007 (47 seats) and formed a minority administration, with its leader Alex SALMOND as first minister. An outright victory in 2011 (69 seats) enabled it to form a majority administration and hold a referendum on independence (2014). Its rejection caused Salmond to resign (replaced by Nicola

Sturgeon). On other matters the administration acted vigorously, capitalizing on widespread disenchantment with Labour. Although the Party's representation fell in 2016 to 63 seats, it continued in office as a minority government. Serious friction soon arose with the (Conservative) UK government, because of Scotland's preference for 'Remain' when the UK voted to leave the European Union (2016; *see* BREXIT). *See also* DEVOLUTION, SCOTLAND.

SCOTTISH OFFICE Formerly a major office of the British government. It was established at WESTMINSTER, England, in 1885 for the SECRETARY FOR SCOTLAND, who supervised government boards in Scotland (fisheries, lunacy, poor relief, prisons, transferred from the Home Office) and the Department for Scotch Education. New boards were also created (e.g., Scottish Board of Health, from 1919). In 1928 most boards were reorganized into three independent civil service departments which were supervised by the secretary: agriculture, health, prisons.

In 1939 much of the office moved to EDINBURGH (Scotland); reorganization created four main departments within the Office: agriculture, education, health, and home. During World War II, under Tom JOHNSTON, the Office became involved in economic and social development. Following a reorganization in 1996 the main departments were: agriculture, environment, fisheries; development; education and industry; health; home.

In 1999, when a new Parliament and Executive were established for Scotland, most of the office's staff were transferred to the Executive. The secretary of state for Scotland retained a small staff to administer matters reserved to the UK government. The secretary's office became known as the Scotland Office and was situated within various larger departments. *See also* GOVERNMENT, SCOTLAND FROM 1707; DEVOLUTION, SCOTLAND.

SCOTTISH TRADES UNION CONGRESS An independent association of trades councils and trade unions active in Scotland. It was founded in 1897 on the initiative of councils after they had been excluded from the TRADES UNION CONGRESS. In 1900 it helped to form the Scottish Workers' Parliamentary Election Committee (*see* LABOUR PARTY, SCOTLAND). A supporter of DEVOLUTION from the 1970s, the STUC remained in the 21st century a forceful advocate on Scottish labour, economic and other issues, although Scottish-based unions had declined and most members of its council were Scottish officers of UK-wide unions. *See also* TRADE UNIONISM, SCOTLAND.

SCRAMBLE FOR AFRICA Term used for the struggle for African territory in the last quarter of the 19th century between five European powers: France, Germany, Great Britain, Italy, Portugal. They appropriated 10 million sq mi

(25.9 million sq km), exacerbating tensions within Europe and provoking wars in Africa. Britain notably expanded in WEST AFRICA, SUDAN, EAST AFRICA and southern Africa (*see* BECHUANALAND; BRITISH SOUTH AFRICA COMPANY).

SCROPE, RICHARD (b. *c*.1350, probably at Masham, Yorkshire, England; d. 8 June 1405 at Clementhorpe, Yorkshire, aged about 55). On 29 Sept. 1399, as archbishop of YORK, Scrope headed the commission that received the 'abdication' of King RICHARD II. But in April 1405, supported by Thomas Mowbray, the MARSHAL, Scrope led a rebellion in Yorkshire against Richard's successor, HENRY IV, complaining of heavy-handed government. Their forces, some 8000–9000 men, surrendered to the earl of Westmorland, Ralph Neville, at Shipton Moor near York (29 May). Scrope was summarily tried and executed for TREASON, despite a plea for clemency by Archbishop Thomas ARUNDEL. He was briefly venerated as a saint. *See also* PERCY, HENRY (d. 1408).

SCUTAGE A charge levied instead of the MILITARY SERVICE due from knights' fees (estates held for military service). The term is derived from Latin *scutagium*, meaning 'shield money'. In England, scutage is first recorded under King HENRY I (1100–35). It continued until *c*.1330. Kings could levy scutage without consent, under military necessity. JOHN exploited scutage by making frequent levies at high rates. Consequently, MAGNA CARTA (1215) required consent for further levies. EDWARD I (1272–1307) sought to make scutage a regular tax on fees. Scutage was levied in Ireland in the 13th–16th centuries.

SEAFIELD, 1ST EARL OF (b. 11 July 1663 in Scotland; d. 15 Aug. 1730 at Cullen, NE Scotland, aged 67). A member of the Scottish Parliament from 1681 and advocate (from 1685), James Ogilvy opposed JAMES VII/II's forfeiture as king but accepted the accession of William of Orange (1689; *see* WILLIAM III). He was appointed William's SECRETARY OF STATE (1696–1702) and parliamentary manager, and created Viscount Seafield (1698) and earl of Seafield (1701).

Under Queen ANNE, Seafield was CHANCELLOR (1702–4, 1705–8, 1713–30) and a commissioner for negotiating the treaty of Union with England (1706). He famously described the demise of Scotland's Parliament in 1707 as 'ane end of ane old sang'. But he became dissatisfied with the union and in 1713 moved its repeal in the British Parliament, losing by four votes. *See also* UNION OF ENGLAND AND SCOTLAND.

SECESSION CHURCH The first Scottish dissenting presbyterian Church, founded in 1733 by Ebenezer ERSKINE and three other ministers after they were suspended by the Church of SCOTLAND for opposing private patronage of livings. Initially based in Stirlingshire, Perthshire and Fife, the Church also attracted CAMERONIANS in the SW. By 1742 there were 20 congregations, which formed the Associate Synod (1744). From 1743 members were required to take the NATIONAL COVENANT.

From 1746 the burgess oath (introduced in towns in 1745, implying recognition of the Church of Scotland) caused division into 'Burgher' and 'Antiburgher' groups. Both split in 1799–1806 into 'Auld Licht' ('Old Light', i.e., conservative) and 'New Licht' (liberal) wings on theological issues. Following removal of the burgess oath in 1819 the New Licht wings united as the United Secession Church (1820), which combined with the RELIEF CHURCH in 1847 as the UNITED PRESBYTERIAN CHURCH. The Auld Licht churches formed the United Original Secession Church (1822) and in 1852 aligned themselves with the FREE CHURCH OF SCOTLAND. *See also* DISSENT, SCOTLAND.

SECOND WORLD WAR *see* WORLD WAR II

SECRETARY FOR SCOTLAND A post in the British government created in 1885, following public pressure and advocacy by the earl of ROSEBERY, for the supervision of some government authorities within Scotland. In the first seven years there were five secretaries, but inclusion of the post in CABINET from 1892 resulted in longer periods of service. The post was upgraded to SECRETARY OF STATE in 1926. The secretary was based at the SCOTTISH OFFICE.

SECRETARY OF STATE From the 16th century, a senior officer in the English GOVERNMENT (British government from 1707), normally ranking below the CHANCELLOR, TREASURER (or PRIME MINISTER) and keeper of the PRIVY SEAL. The office originated as the post of king's secretary, recorded from 1377. It became important through the prestige of Thomas CROMWELL (king's secretary 1534–40, in reign of King HENRY VIII). From 1540 there were usually two 'secretaries of state', who directed the PRIVY COUNCIL and undertook other business, notably foreign affairs.

In 1689, after the accession of WILLIAM III and MARY II, the posts were reorganized, with a secretary each for the Southern and Northern Departments, dealing respectively with southern and northern Europe. Secretaries worked closely with rulers, and increasingly with PRIME MINISTERS.

In 1782 the Southern Department became the Home Office and the Northern Department the Foreign Office, headed respectively by home and foreign secretaries. From 1794 new secretaryships and departments were created. In June 2020 there were 17 secretaries of state in the UK government.

SECRETARY OF STATE, SCOTLAND A senior royal officer, recorded from the 1360s, who kept the privy seal (signet from early 15th century) and was a member of COUNCIL and PARLIAMENT. From the mid 16th century he was often the ruler's senior adviser (replacing the CHANCELLOR). From 1680 there were normally two secretaries. Notable secretaries include William MAITLAND, Thomas HAMILTON and the (2nd) earl of LAUDERDALE.

The post was abolished in 1709. Thereafter a British secretary usually supervised Scotland, though a separate secretaryship, with responsibility for Scotland, sometimes existed (*see* SECRETARY OF STATE). A secretaryship for Scotland was recreated in 1885; *see* SECRETARY FOR SCOTLAND.

SECRET SERVICES, UNITED KINGDOM Before the early 20th century espionage was often organized sporadically by ministers (e.g., 'spymaster' Francis WALSINGHAM). Surveillance was also undertaken by organizations such as the POST OFFICE (e.g., in its 'Secret Office' examining foreign correspondence, 1650s–1840s), ARMY and NAVY, Police SPECIAL IRISH BRANCH (from 1883) and War Office (from 1903).

In 1909, following a frenzied 'spy scare' (fear of German espionage), the British government created a civilian Secret Service Bureau. It became divided into Home and Foreign Sections, controlled respectively by the War Office and Admiralty. During WORLD WAR I (1914–18) the War Office also took over the Foreign Section (1915; renamed 'MI1c'); the Home Section was renamed 'MI5' (1916). ('MI' referred to 'Military Intelligence'.) Code breaking was developed by War Office department 'MI1b' and Admiralty 'Room 40'. The latter deciphered the ZIMMERMAN TELEGRAM.

In 1919 the Government Code and Cypher School (GC&CS) was formed for code breaking, and from the 1920s MI1c was called the Secret Intelligence Service (SIS). MI5 was renamed the Security Service in 1931, though 'MI5' continued in use.

During WORLD WAR II (1939–45) secret services made crucial contributions. Prime Minister Winston CHURCHILL gave a central role to an existing Joint Intelligence Committee. GC&CS, centred on Bletchley Park (Buckinghamshire), decrypted enemy communications (*see* COMPUTING). A Special Operations Executive (1940–6) facilitated resistance in enemy territories. (SIS became known informally as 'MI6'.)

In 1946 GC&CS was renamed Government Communications Headquarters (GCHQ). During the COLD WAR (1947–91) the services combated hostile activity by the USSR and its allies, despite embarrassing penetration by Soviet double agents (e.g., Kim Philby). Islamist terrorism later became a major concern.

In 1989, following bad publicity from the *SPYCATCHER* AFFAIR, MI5 was given legal status by legislation (also SIS and GCHQ in 1994). Stella Rimington was the first female head of a secret service (director general of MI5 1992–6).

SECULARIZATION Processes whereby societies or individuals become less religious and more worldly or secular. In Britain, aspects of Christianity were challenged intellectually from the 17th century by the SCIENTIFIC REVOLUTION, and in the 18th century by ENLIGHTENMENT rationality (e.g., scepticism of biblical miracles). In the 19th century the discovery of geological time and a possible mechanism for species formation questioned the Bible's account of divine creation (*see* LYELL, CHARLES; DARWIN, CHARLES). From the mid 19th century some people (e.g., poet Matthew Arnold) sensed that Christianity was losing cultural influence.

During the 20th century British society became increasingly secular. Regular church attendance dropped from about a third of the population to under 10% by the 1960s. Churches' social roles shrank as the State increased provision (*see* SOCIAL SERVICES; WELFARE STATE). Expanding leisure activities (e.g., SPORT) diverted attention. From the 1960s many people rejected a supernatural world-view and religious-based morality (e.g., by acceptance of ABORTION), and considered Christianity irrelevant. Secularization produced either accommodation by churches (e.g., ordination of WOMEN) or resistance (as largely happened in Ireland until the late 20th century). Contrarily, IMMIGRATION entrenched new minority communities with religious-based identities. *See also* POST-CHRISTIAN SOCIETY.

SECURITY, ACT OF An Act passed by the Scottish Parliament in 1703, in response to the English Act of SETTLEMENT (1701) which had ignored Scotland. It empowered Parliament to nominate Queen ANNE's successor as ruler of Scotland. If England's Parliament did not guarantee the Scottish Parliament's independence, the latter would select a different successor. The (2nd) duke of QUEENSBERRY, as QUEEN'S COMMISSIONER, withheld royal approval. It was given in 1704 by the (2nd) marquis of TWEEDDALE. *See also* UNION OF ENGLAND AND SCOTLAND.

SEDULIUS SCOTTUS (fl. 840s–60s or 870s). An outstanding Irish scholar, possibly from Clonard monastery (E Ireland), Sedulius worked at Liège (in Lotharingia; now in Belgium) where he was patronized by Hartgar and Franco (bishops of Liège, respectively 840–54, 854–901). He wrote grammatical treatises, biblical commentaries (involving knowledge of Greek), poetry and a treatise on Christian kingship. He was a contemporary of JOHN SCOTTUS ERIUGENA.

SELF-DENYING ORDINANCE In England, the order passed by the LONG PARLIAMENT on 3 April 1645 which prevented MPs and peers from holding civil or military office. Associated with the creation of the NEW MODEL ARMY (Feb.), it was intended to produce effective military leadership by excluding noblemen and ending rivalries among commanders. Parliament's captain-general, the earl of ESSEX, resigned in anticipation (2 April), but Oliver CROMWELL was exempted. *See also* CIVIL WARS.

SELF-EXILE FROM IRELAND, 6TH–8TH CENTURIES

With the growth of MONASTICISM, the notion of self-exile became influential from the late 6th century. It caused monks to go abroad, often permanently. Journeys were primarily for self-sacrifice, not to seek conversions.

An early exponent was Colum Cille (or COLUMBA, d. 597), founder of a monastery on IONA (off Mull, W of Scotland). Members of his community travelled into the N Atlantic and even reached Iceland (8th century). Other monks went to Continental Europe. COLUMBANUS (d. 615) founded Luxeuil monastery in Burgundy and Bobbio monastery in N Italy. One of his disciples, Gall (d. *c*.645), started a hermitage at Steinach (613) which developed into the monastery of St Gallen (in modern Switzerland). Fursa (d. 649) founded a hermitage (630s) in EAST ANGLIA (possibly Burgh castle in modern Suffolk, England), and a monastery in Neustria (*c*.640, at Lagny-sur-Marne, in modern N France). An oratory and hospice were founded at Breuil (in modern N France) by Fiachra (or St Fiacre, d. 670), who is probably to be identified with the hermit of Kilfiachra (or Kilfera, in modern Co. Kilkenny, Ireland). Fergal or Vergil (d. 784) became the distinguished abbot of St Peter's and archbishop of Salzburg (in modern Austria).

More Irishmen went abroad after Ireland was attacked by VIKINGS in the 9th century (e.g., SEDULIUS SCOTTUS, JOHN SCOTTUS ERIUGENA), but they migrated for scholarly purposes. *See also* EMIGRATION FROM IRELAND.

SELSDON PARK CONFERENCE

In Great Britain, a meeting of leading Conservative politicians, led by Edward HEATH (leader of the Opposition in Parliament), at the Selsdon Park Hotel (Surrey, S England), 30 Jan.–1 Feb. 1970, to prepare their manifesto for the next UK general election. The press alleged that right-wing policies had been adopted. Labour's Harold WILSON nicknamed participants 'Selsdon Man', which imputed a prehistoric mentality but in practice strengthened the Conservatives' reputation. *See also* CONSERVATIVE PARTY.

SEPARATE SPHERES

A concept advanced in England in the 1830s–40s by women writers (e.g., Sarah Lewis in *Woman's Mission*, 1839). It envisaged that women should concentrate on home and family life while men provided for their household and were active in business, politics and cultural activity. Though challenged by supporters of women's causes (e.g., members of the LANGHAM PLACE CIRCLE), it influenced British society until the late 20th century.

SEPTENNIAL ACT

Legislation by the British PARLIAMENT, passed 1716 (soon after the accession of King GEORGE I), which increased the maximum extent of a Parliament from three to seven years, starting with the current Parliament. Promoted by the WHIG ministry in the wake of the JACOBITE REBELLION of 1715, it replaced the TRIENNIAL ACT of 1694. The reduced frequency of general elections diminished inter-party rivalry, strengthening oligarchy and Whig domination. The extent was reduced to five years by the Parliament Act of 1911. *See also* PARLIAMENTARY CONSTITUENCIES AND ELECTIONS.

SERFDOM

Historians' term for the servile economic and social conditions experienced by peasant tenants on MANORS, which in England were at their most intense in the 13th–14th centuries. 'Servile' tenants typically inherited and held land in return for undertaking part-time LABOUR SERVICES on the directly managed land ('demesne') of a lord's manor, and were subject to the lord's justice, restrictions on movement and other impositions (e.g., payment of a death duty or 'heriot', payment of a fee for marriage of a daughter or 'merchet').

Labour service in return for land appears in the conditions attached to the tied tenants of smallholdings and stock provided by a lord in the legislation of King INE of Wessex (issued *c*.690). These resemble those of the *gebur* referred to in documents of the 10th and early 11th centuries and of later serfs. Pressure on comparatively independent peasants also increased in the 9th–12th centuries as lords, particularly of small manors, sought greater productivity. Weekly labour rent was demanded from manorial tenants who were increasingly regarded as unfree.

In the late 12th and early 13th centuries unfree tenants were largely excluded from the royal courts and COMMON LAW. Legal unfreedom was defined (generally called villeinage, from Anglo-Norman *villenage*), and tests were devised for differentiating unfree from free people. As the system of royal justice was developed, older identities persisted, such that some tenants were regarded as *nativi*, 'born unfree', while others were serfs or villeins by virtue of the services by which they held land.

Serfdom declined between the mid 14th and mid 15th centuries with the drastic decline of POPULATION started by the BLACK DEATH. Villeins refused labour services and other restrictions, and unfree tenures were often replaced by COPYHOLD. Unfree social conditions existed elsewhere in the British Isles, but within different SOCIAL STRUCTURES. *See also* FEUDALISM; PEASANTS' REVOLT.

SERVICE BOOKS, WALES Books were introduced during the REFORMATION, in English by the English government and in Welsh on local initiative. John PRICE financed *Yn y Lhyvyr hwnn* ('In this Book...') containing the Lord's Prayer, Creed and Ten Commandments (published 1546). The (English) Book of Common Prayer was imposed in 1549 but resented, though William SALESBURY translated some of its Bible readings (published 1551). The 1559 Prayer Book was published in Welsh in 1567, translated by Salesbury under the Translation of the Bible, etc., into Welsh Act of 1563. Revised versions appeared in 1599 (with Bible readings from William MORGAN's translation), 1621 and 1664, and a new bilingual Book of Common Prayer in 1984 (*see* WALES, CHURCH IN). DISSENTERS, who were influential from the late 17th century, advocated extempore prayer and so eschewed service books. *See also* PRAYER BOOKS, ENGLAND.

SESSION, COURT OF The highest civil court in Scotland. It evolved in the 15th and 16th centuries. From the mid 1420s members of the royal COUNCIL held special 'sessions' (sittings) to clear backlogs of judicial business, and from 1503 judicial business was handled mainly by a separate council (under the CHANCELLOR), usually in EDINBURGH. It was reconstituted by King JAMES V in 1532 as the Court of Session, staffed mainly by a president and 14 judges belonging to the king's new College of Justice (theoretically with salaries). (The president and seven judges were clergy until disqualified after the REFORMATION.) From 1579 judges were to be examined for suitability, while qualifications introduced in 1605 consolidated the court's evolution into a body of professional judges normally chosen from advocates. In 1711 GREENSHIELDS' CASE established that suitors could appeal to the British House of Lords. During the 19th century the Court absorbed some other courts. *See also* COURTS, SCOTLAND.

SET-ASIDE SCHEME A reform of the European Economic Community's COMMON AGRICULTURAL POLICY, adopted in 1988 (compulsory from 1992), which affected AGRICULTURE in the UK and Republic of Ireland. Intended to reduce surplus food production, the scheme required a proportion of arable land to be removed from production (initially 20%). Farmers received compensation payments. The scheme was suspended in 2008.

SETTLEMENT, ACT OF Legislation by the English Parliament passed in June 1701 to ensure Protestant succession to the English and Irish monarchies and prevent restoration of the Catholic Stuarts. It followed the death of the last Protestant Stuart heir, Princess Anne's son William, duke of Gloucester (30 July 1700). Electress Sophia of Hanover, Germany (granddaughter of JAMES VI/I), and her

Protestant descendants were named as heirs. After the death of Queen ANNE (1714), Sophia's son George succeeded (*see* GEORGE I).

The Act barred Catholics from the succession, required Parliament's approval for any war involving a ruler's possessions in Continental Europe, and banned PLACEMEN and CABINETS. It also established independence of the judiciary after the succession, making appointment as a judge dependent on good behaviour rather than at the Crown's pleasure.

The Act was the first STATUTE explicitly to limit the ROYAL PREROGATIVE in foreign affairs. Its implied preference for male primogeniture (preference to eldest son in succession) was altered in 2013. *See also* STEWART RULERS; SECURITY, ACT OF; HANOVERIAN SUCCESSION; SUCCESSION TO THE CROWN ACT.

SETTLEMENT AND EXPLANATION, ACTS OF Acts passed by the Irish PARLIAMENT, under English instruction, to modify the 1650s CROMWELLIAN LAND SETTLEMENT. After the Restoration (May 1660) King CHARLES II accepted the Settlement (to retain support from pro-English Protestants), but wished to recompense dispossessed Royalist Catholics and Protestants (Declaration, 30 Nov. 1660).

The Act of Settlement (passed 31 July 1662) vested extensive lands in the Crown and established a court to hear claims for return of land. Most were granted (mainly to Catholics), causing alarm among Protestants. The court was suspended (Aug. 1663), and the Act of Explanation was passed to resolve problems (23 Dec. 1665). It appropriated some land from recently settled Protestants to recompense Protestants dispossessed by the court. (Fifty-four named Catholics were also granted their former main residence with 2000 acres.)

The Acts increased Catholic landownership from 10% to 20% of profitable land, but disappointed Catholic hopes. Protestants considered the Acts too generous. Catholic claims continued through the 1670s–80s. *See also* RESTORATION, IRELAND; PATRIOT PARLIAMENT.

SEVEN BISHOPS' CASE A crisis in 1688 when seven bishops of the Church of England, including Archbishop William SANCROFT, challenged an order by the Catholic King JAMES VII/II requiring his second Declaration of INDULGENCE (issued 4 May) to be read in churches. The bishops petitioned James to withdraw the order because they deemed it illegal. They were charged with seditious libel (publishing words stirring disaffection), imprisoned (8–15 June), tried and acquitted (29–30 June).

SEVEN YEARS WAR A complex war, 1756–63, in Europe and elsewhere. It arose from Great Britain's change of protective alliance for HANOVER (ruled by Britain's king): from the HABSBURG EMPIRE (or Austria) to PRUSSIA (Jan. 1756, by treaty of Westminster). This triggered national re-alignments (so-called DIPLOMATIC REVOLUTION). France invaded British-held MINORCA on 18 April 1756, leading Britain to declare war on 17 May. Britain's conflict with France became widespread.

In 1756–8, in N-C Europe, Prussia fought against Russia, Sweden and Austria with varying outcomes. Meanwhile, in July 1757 France invaded Hanover, defeated the German 'Army of Observation', and imposed a ceasefire (Sept.). It was repudiated by the British minister William PITT the Elder (Nov.), who funded the Army of Observation; by March 1758 it had repulsed the French. From April, Britain subsidized Prussia. British forces attacked the French in CANADA (1757), outdid them in INDIA (1756–7), raided the French coast (1757–8), and captured forts in W Africa (1758).

In Aug. 1759, the Army of Observation defeated another French offensive towards Hanover at Minden; and in 1759–60, conflict continued between Prussia and its other enemies. A planned French invasion of Britain was foiled by two British naval victories (late 1759). British forces inflicted further defeats in India (1759–60), seized two islands in the WEST INDIES (1759), and made substantial gains in Canada (1759–60), including Quebec.

In 1761, Prussia was involved in further warfare, losing Silesia and Saxony. Britain started talks with France (March), but it allied with Spain (Aug.). Pitt resigned (Oct.) because his government resisted war against Spain. It was declared on 4 Jan. 1762. Britain made more conquests from France in the West Indies, and seized Spanish territory (Havana in Cuba in Aug., Manila in the Philippines in Oct.). War-weariness compelled the powers to make peace (*see* PARIS, PEACE OF). *See also* NEWCASTLE, DUKE OF; BYNG, JOHN; BUTE, 3RD EARL OF.

SEWERAGE Before the mid 19th century excrement and other waste were often emptied into streams. Sewage systems, employing earthenware pipes or brick tunnels flushed by water, were developed from the 1850s (*see* PUBLIC HEALTH ACTS). In LONDON the use of storm sewers for waste from 1847 polluted the R. Thames. The 'great stink' of 1858 provoked the building of a city-wide waste-disposal system (designed by Joseph Bazalgette, built 1859–75). Most towns provided systems by the later 19th century (e.g., BELFAST by 1894), though some were completed in the early 20th century (e.g., in SWANSEA, EDINBURGH). Systems were installed later in rural areas. *See also* IMPROVEMENT ACTS.

SHAFTESBURY, EARL OF (b. 22 July 1621 at Wimborne St Giles, Dorset, England; d. 21 Jan. 1683 at Amsterdam, Dutch Republic, aged 61). During the CIVIL WARS (1642–8), Anthony Ashley Cooper (a BARONET) changed from Royalist to Parliamentarian (1644). He supported the COMMONWEALTH AND PROTECTORATE but broke from Oliver CROMWELL (Dec. 1654). He helped to bring about the RESTORATION of King CHARLES II (1660), and was created Lord Ashley and appointed chancellor of the Exchequer in 1661.

After Charles dismissed the earl of CLARENDON (1667), Ashley was among the CABAL ministers. He was created earl of Shaftesbury (April 1672), appointed lord CHANCELLOR (Nov.), and was associated with promoting toleration for Protestant nonconformists (*see* INDULGENCE, DECLARATIONS OF). But his hostility to the Catholic heir, James, duke of York, resulted in dismissal (9 Nov. 1673). He was imprisoned 1676–8 for denouncing the earl of DANBY.

Shaftesbury exploited the POPISH PLOT (from Sept. 1678) to oppose York's succession, becoming a leading WHIG campaigner during the EXCLUSION CRISIS (1679–81). In 1681 he was imprisoned on suspicion of TREASON (2 July; released 28 Nov.). After prosecution was dropped (Feb. 1682), Shaftesbury became involved in conspiracies against Charles and James. He fled abroad in Nov. 1682.

SHAFTESBURY, 7TH EARL OF (b. 28 April 1801 at London, England; d. 1 Oct. 1885 at Folkestone, Kent, England, aged 84). Anthony Ashley-Cooper, styled Lord Ashley, was an MP 1826–46, 1847–51. He succeeded as earl in 1851. Driven by evangelical zeal, Ashley helped to obtain Acts of Parliament to improve working conditions in UK factories (1833, 1845, 1847) and mines (1842), to improve treatment for mental patients (1845), and to provide lodging-houses for the poor (1851). From 1844 he was president of the Ragged School Union, which fed and taught destitute children. He also supported missionary work. Concerned about RITUALISM in the Church of England, Shaftesbury pressed for the Public Worship Regulation Act (1874). *See also* EVANGELICALISM; FACTORY LEGISLATION.

SHAKESPEARE, WILLIAM (b. April 1564 at Stratford-upon-Avon, Warwickshire, England; d. 23 April 1616 at Stratford-upon-Avon, aged 52). A glovemaker's son, Shakespeare left Stratford in 1585 and by 1592 had emerged as an actor and playwright in London. By 1595 he was a member of the Chamberlain's company of actors (from 1603, the King's company). They performed Shakespeare's plays at the courts of Queen ELIZABETH I and King JAMES VI/I and from 1599 at the GLOBE THEATRE. Shakespeare also wrote narrative poems and sonnets. He retired to Stratford in 1610. The author of about 38 plays, including histories, tragedies and comedies, Shakespeare is the greatest English playwright. *See also* ENGLISH LITERATURE, ENGLAND.

SHANNON HYDROELECTRIC SCHEME In the IRISH FREE STATE, a project to generate electricity from the R. Shannon, constructed 1925–9. It was the first major enterprise commissioned by the Free State's government, inaugurating large-scale ELECTRIFICATION. It included dams, weirs, bridges and a generating plant at Ardnacrusha (Co. Clare).

SHARP, JAMES (b. 4 May 1613 at Banff, NE Scotland; d. 3 May 1679 near St Andrews, Fife, E Scotland, aged 65). Educated at ABERDEEN, Sharp lived in England (1638–43), taught philosophy at ST ANDREWS University (1643–8) and in 1649 became minister of Crail (Fife). He was imprisoned in London (1651) for supporting King CHARLES II (*see* RESOLUTIONERS).

At the RESTORATION (1660), Sharp attended court (in England) supposedly to represent Scottish presbyterians, but co-operated with the restoration of episcopacy and was appointed archbishop of St Andrews (1661). Apart from a rift in the mid 1660s, Sharp worked closely with the (2nd) earl of LAUDERDALE. From 1673 they persecuted COVE-NANTERS, a group of whom murdered Sharp and then joined the RISING OF 1679. *See also* SCOTLAND, CHURCH OF.

SHAW, FLORA (b. 19 Dec. 1852 at Woolwich, Kent, England; d. 25 Jan. 1929 near Abinger, Surrey, England, aged 76). A freelance journalist from 1887 and friend of Cecil RHODES, Shaw visited EGYPT (1888–9), S Africa and Australia (1892–3). She was colonial editor of *The Times* 1893–1900 (the first woman on the permanent staff). In 1897 Shaw coined the name NIGERIA. She promoted the BRITISH EMPIRE as a beneficial entity. In 1902 she married Sir Frederick LUGARD. She was created a dame in 1916.

SHAW, GEORGE BERNARD (b. 26 July 1856 at Dublin, Ireland; d. 2 Nov. 1950 at Ayot St Lawrence, Hertfordshire, England, aged 94). In England from 1876, Shaw became a novelist, critic and orator. After hearing Henry GEORGE speak in 1882, he advocated SOCIALISM and joined the FABIAN SOCIETY (1884). From 1892 he was also a playwright, achieving an international reputation by 1915. His works dealt with controversial topics (e.g., EUGENICS, in the play *Man and Superman*, 1903), and when published included polemical prefaces. His greatest commercial success was the play *Pygmalion* (1913). Awarded the 1925 Nobel Prize in Literature, Shaw was also a vegetarian and fascinated by phonetics. *See also* ANGLO-IRISH LITERATURE.

SHAWFIELD RIOTS Riots that occurred in June 1725 in Scottish towns after a tax of 3*d.* was imposed on a barrel of beer; named after Shawfield, GLASGOW, where the house of Daniel Campbell, MP for Glasgow, was burned.

(Campbell was presumed to support the tax.) The riots exposed the government's lack of control in Scotland and caused Prime Minister Robert WALPOLE to entrust Scottish affairs to the earl of ISLAY. *See also* FISHERIES AND MANUFACTURES, BOARD OF TRUSTEES FOR.

SHEEHY SKEFFINGTON, FRANCIS (b. 23 Dec. 1878 at Bailieborough, Co. Cavan, Ireland; d. 26 April 1916 at Dublin, Ireland, aged 37). A prominent socialist, Irish nationalist and supporter of women's suffrage (and husband of Hanna SHEEHY SKEFFINGTON), Sheehy Skeffington co-founded the Irish Women's Franchise League (1908). He opposed Irish conscription during WORLD WAR I. He was summarily arrested and shot during the EASTER RISING (1916), while attempting to prevent looting.

SHEEHY SKEFFINGTON, HANNA (b. 24 May 1877 at Kanturk, Co. Cork, Ireland; d. 20 April 1946 at Dublin, southern Ireland, aged 68). Sheehy Skeffington (a Catholic) co-founded the Irish Women's Franchise League (1908) and campaigned in Ireland and Great Britain for women's suffrage. During WORLD WAR I she participated in the EASTER RISING (1916).

Following the foundation of the IRISH FREE STATE she joined the executive of Éamon DE VALERA's new party FIANNA FÁIL (1926), but objected to the restricted place accorded to women in his 1937 constitution. *See also* WOMEN'S SUFFRAGE MOVEMENT, IRELAND; SHEEHY SKEFFINGTON, FRANCIS.

SHEFFIELD A city and metropolitan borough in N England; formerly in Yorkshire (W Riding).

The town of Sheffield existed by the late 13th century. Its name means 'Field by R. Sheaf'. Locksmiths and cutlers are recorded from the 14th century. By 1600 Sheffield was the principal cutlery-manufacturing centre outside London. A Cutlers' Company was granted supervision of the trade in 1624.

From the late 18th century cast (or crucible) steel, a high-quality steel invented by Benjamin HUNTSMAN, further stimulated cutlery manufacturing. Steel making and engineering continued to expand through the 19th century. Sheffield acquired parliamentary representation (1832), a town council (1843), city status (1893), a university (1905), and a bishopric (1914). A polytechnic was upgraded in 1992 as Sheffield Hallam University. Steel working remained important in the early 21st century.

Est. popn: 1300, 1000; 1600, 1500; 1800, 31,000; 1900, 450,000; 2000, 510,000.

SHELBURNE, EARL OF (b. 2 May 1737 at Dublin, Ireland; d. 7 May 1805 at Piccadilly, Middlesex, England, aged 68). William Fitzmaurice (Petty from 1751) was elected a British MP in 1760 and became one of the KING's FRIENDS. He inherited British and Irish peerages in 1761– Shelburne was his Irish title. (He entered the House of Lords as Lord Wycombe.) Shelburne served briefly as president of the Board of Trade under George GRENVILLE (1763).

As SECRETARY OF STATE (southern) in the ministry of William PITT the Elder (1766–8), Shelburne attempted to conciliate the disaffected American colonies (*see* AMERICAN INDEPENDENCE, ORIGINS OF). He served briefly as home secretary (the first) under the marquess of ROCKINGHAM (1782).

After Rockingham's death (July 1782), King GEORGE III appointed Shelburne as PRIME MINISTER (first lord of the Treasury). Charles James Fox and the ROCKINGHAM WHIGS, who viewed Shelburne as the king's agent, resigned. Shelburne negotiated a peace treaty with the Americans, but its rejection by the House of Commons in Feb. 1783 led to resignation. Shelburne initially supported his successor, William PITT the Younger, but in the 1790s he opposed war with France and repressive domestic legislation. He was created marquess of Lansdowne in 1784. *See also* PRIESTLEY, JOSEPH.

SHELDON, GILBERT (b. 19 June 1598 at Stanton, Staffordshire, England; d. 9 Nov. 1677 at Lambeth, Surrey, England, aged 79). A Church of ENGLAND clergyman at OXFORD University associated with Archbishop William LAUD in the 1630s (before the CIVIL WARS), Sheldon was influential among ejected Royalist clergy in the 1650s (*see* COMMONWEALTH AND PROTECTORATE; CHURCH, ENGLAND AND WALES, 1640s–50s).

After the RESTORATION (1660) Sheldon was appointed bishop of London (1660) and archbishop of CANTERBURY (1663), and was a leading figure in restoring the Church's authority. His supporters in Parliament passed the CLARENDON CODE (1662) which reimposed Anglican uniformity and sought to suppress dissenters. Sheldon's influence with King CHARLES II declined after the fall of the earl of CLARENDON (1667), though he campaigned successfully against Charles's 1672 Declaration of INDULGENCE (revoked 1673).

SHERIFF, ENGLAND An officer who administers royal interests in a SHIRE; derived from OE *scir gerefa*, meaning 'shire reeve'. The position emerged in late 10th-century England when REEVES took over duties from EALDORMEN and became important in royal GOVERNMENT. The sheriff managed royal estates, collected revenues, and assisted ealdormen (or EARLS) with courts and military activity (*see* SHIRE COURT). Sheriffs were probably appointed by kings.

After the NORMAN CONQUEST (1066–70s), kings dealt directly with sheriffs and shires, giving sheriffs local importance (e.g., presiding at the shire or county court). By the early 12th century, they had to account twice yearly at the EXCHEQUER for revenues and payments. Appointments lasted a year.

Sheriffs later lost authority to itinerant royal judges (from late 12th century), to JUSTICES OF THE PEACE (from 14th century), and to lord lieutenants (from mid 16th century). But they remained responsible for collecting revenues, executing WRITS, and attending royal judges and executions. They employed a small staff. From the mid 13th century sheriffs presided at parliamentary elections.

Reform in the 19th century abolished the fees required of sheriffs and removed their collection of Crown rents (1833). They retained legal responsibilities, and in the 20th and 21st centuries also supported police, prison and probation services.

SHERIFF, IRELAND *see* SHIRES, IRELAND; LOCAL GOVERNMENTAL STRUCTURES, IRELAND

SHERIFFDOM In Scotland, the basic local unit of royal government from the 12th century to 1975; an area, usually with natural geographical bounds, originally under a SHERIFF's jurisdiction.

Sheriffdoms were founded in LOTHIAN (SE Scotland) from *c*.1120 by David, heir to King Alexander I (*see* DAVID I). Modelled on English (large) SHIRES, they gradually replaced THANAGES. Sheriffs were based at an important centre after which the sheriffdom was named and where a BURGH and castle were founded. Sheriffs collected ROYAL REVENUES and ran a court (*see* COURTS, SCOTLAND). By 1165 (death of MALCOLM IV) there were 12 sheriffdoms (perhaps 17), covering the SE, S, C and E and perhaps MORAY (N and NE). By 1214 there were 19 (probably 23), now including most of the SW and NE (*see* WILLIAM I); some were small, others much larger, including one or more earldoms.

Later sheriffdoms were based on lordships. In 1404 the lordship of Renfrew (W), formerly in the sheriffdom of Lanark, became a separate sheriffdom; the lordship (or 'stewartry') of Kircudbright (SW) became a sheriffdom in 1455. Sheriffdoms were extended into lordships in the N in the 16th and 17th centuries: Caithness in 1503, ORKNEY and SHETLAND in 1540, Sutherland by 1582, Ross in 1661, and Cromarty in 1685 and 1698 (addition of land to Dingwall). The final number was 33.

The post of sheriff became hereditary from the late 12th century, and the importance of sheriffdoms was undermined by the expansion of private jurisdiction in the 14th and 15th centuries (*see* REGALITY). Their role re-expanded with the introduction of shire commissioners to PARLIAMENT (1587), the development of shire government after the UNION OF ENGLAND AND SCOTLAND (1707), the abolition of HERITABLE JURISDICTIONS (1747), and intro-duction of county councils (1890), though sheriffdoms (or shires) probably never developed the strong COUNTY COM-MUNITIES found in England. Sheriffdoms were abolished in 1975. *See also* LOCAL GOVERNMENTAL STRUCTURES, SCOTLAND.

SHETLAND ISLANDS An archipelago within the BRITISH ISLES, 125 mi (200 km) off NE BRITAIN; part of SCOTLAND within the UNITED KINGDOM. There are about 300 islands and skerries (small, rocky islands), of which 15 are permanently inhabited. 'Mainland' is the principal island, Lerwick the capital. Est. popn in 2015: 23,000 (80% on Mainland). (The Shetland Islands and Orkney Islands are called the Northern Isles.)

Rich in remains from PREHISTORY, the Shetland Islands were later inhabited by the people known (from 3rd century AD) as PICTS, and visited by Irish Christian mis-sionaries from the WESTERN ISLES (7th or 8th century). Norse people settled in the 9th century, and the islands became part of the earldom of Orkney under Norwegian rule. Their name is derived from Norse Hjaltland, meaning 'Highland'. A variant of Norse, Norn, was spoken until the 17th century, with Scots gaining ground from the 15th century. Shetland belonged to Scottish Sinclair earls 1379–1470 (*see* ORKNEY ISLANDS).

In 1469 Christian I, king of Denmark-Norway, added Shetland to the pledge for the dowry for marriage of his daughter Margaret to King JAMES III of Scotland. James annexed the islands in 1472 (with the Orkney Islands); Scots nobles and lairds acquired lands.

Agriculture has been the economic mainstay, though poor soil and a harsh climate make arable farming difficult. In the 18th–19th centuries, men engaged in sea fishing alongside CROFTING. Population peaked at 29,700 in 1881. In the later 19th century landlords made CLEARANCES for sheep-farming; small-scale fishing was considerably dis-placed by trawling (*see* FISHING INDUSTRY, SCOTLAND). Improved communications stimulated tourism and export of ponies for coal mines. Difficult conditions from the 1920s increased emigration, but also the marketing of knit-wear made from local fine wool. Population nonetheless declined to 17,000 by 1971. A major oil and gas terminal operated from 1978 (*see* NORTH SEA GAS AND OIL INDUSTRIES).

SHINWELL, EMANUEL (b. 18 Oct. 1884 at London, England; d. 8 May 1986 at London, aged 101). A Labour MP 1922–4, 1928–31, and 1935–70, Shinwell opposed the formation of the British NATIONAL GOVERNMENT by Ramsay MACDONALD (1931). In 1935 he stood against, and defeated, MacDonald in the general election. Appointed minister of fuel and power in 1945, by Clement

ATTLEE, Shinwell coped badly with the 1947 fuel crisis. He was a more successful war secretary (1947–50). Long con-troversial, he latterly became a national character. 'Manny' Shinwell was created Lord Shinwell in 1970.

SHIP-BUILDING INDUSTRY, ENGLAND By the 13th century, substantial wooden sailing ships were built near larger ports (e.g., LONDON, NEWCASTLE UPON TYNE). The replacement of 'shell' construction with 'skeleton' con-struction during the 16th century facilitated larger ships, including vessels capable of long ocean voyages. During the 16th–17th centuries the NAVY developed construction yards for warships (e.g., Deptford, in Kent). Major ship-building centres emerged in NE England (e.g., Hull, Yorkshire). Between the 1570s and 1750, English-owned shipping rose from 50,000 to 420,000 tons. The leading ship-building centres in the later 18th century were London and the Thames estuary, Hull, Sunderland and Newcastle upon Tyne. Ocean-going steam-powered ships were built from 1836, driven by paddle wheels. Propellers were devel-oped in the 1840s.

In the 1860s–80s, iron superseded wood (steel was then used), and steam power superseded sails, using steam tur-bines from 1894. By 1900 the British industry was the world's largest. In England, ship building became concen-trated in the NE (by Rivers Tyne, Wear and Tees), where in 1913 a third of the world's new shipping was built, pri-marily cargo vessels. Other significant centres were Barrow-in-Furness and Birkenhead (NW England), nota-bly for warships. Yards in London and Kent declined. Workers were organized in craft-specific unions, which caused demarcation disputes.

The industry was depressed in the 1920s–30s due to declining coal exports and (in 1930s) reduced world trade. Some yards closed in the late 1930s. Demand during WORLD WAR II and afterwards provided relief until the late 1950s, but decline resumed. Government-organized restructuring from 1966 included takeovers by Swan Hunter in NE England. After NATIONALIZATION in 1977 (within British Shipbuilders), capacity was greatly reduced. Businesses were privatized in the mid 1980s, but the indus-try continued to contract. North East Shipbuilders, formed 1986, closed in 1988, and Swan Hunter went into receiver-ship (1993). In 2019, Barrow-in-Furness was England's largest ship-building centre. *See also* INDUSTRY, ENGLAND BEFORE/FROM LATE 18TH CENTURY.

SHIP-BUILDING INDUSTRY, IRELAND Boat and ship building are long established. Around 1042 the VIKING warship known as 'Skuldelev 2' was built near DUBLIN. In the 17th century an expanding ship-building industry included yards at the new towns of BELFAST, Coleraine and LONDONDERRY (in N Ireland).

In the early 19th century yards at CORK (in S Ireland) dominated ship building, but declined from the 1860s. They were superseded by Belfast, where Harland and Wolff (founded 1861) became the city's largest employer (12,000 employees by 1914). Using progressive designs and technology (e.g., iron hulls), they specialized in passenger liners, most famously *Titanic*, built 1908–11 (*see* TITANIC, SINKING OF). A rival firm, Workman Clark, began in 1879.

The industry struggled in the late 1920s and 1930s, with Workman Clark collapsing in 1935. Harland and Wolff ceased to build liners from 1961 and increasingly became a diversified engineering company, including ship-related work. *See also* INDUSTRY, IRELAND.

SHIP-BUILDING INDUSTRY, SCOTLAND Notable shipyards were established in the 18th century at ABERDEEN (NE Scotland), Leith (SE) and Greenock (W), building wooden sailing vessels for fishing and trading. From the 1820s a powerful industry developed on the R. Clyde (W-C), following the development there of the world's second commercial steamship, the paddle-driven *Comet* (launched 1812; *see* BELL, HENRY). The industry expanded spectacularly from the 1840s, partly by adopting innovations such as iron construction, screw propulsion (1840s), and the fuel-efficient compound engine (1853). Use of steel from the 1870s permitted the construction of larger ships with more powerful boilers. The Clyde dominated British ship building until 1914, accounting for a third of tonnage (a fifth of world tonnage) in 1913.

Demand slackened in the 1920s, fell heavily in the 1930s, but revived during and after WORLD WAR II (1939–45). By the 1960s more productive foreign yards were undercutting the industry. Clyde yards were amalgamated into two companies (1967–8) which were nationalized and united (1977). Contraction nevertheless continued. Yards were privatized from 1985. Although few remained by 2000, the continuing construction of naval vessels remained important for the Scottish economy. *See also* INDUSTRY, SCOTLAND FROM LATE 18TH CENTURY.

SHIP MONEY Payments levied in England from maritime counties in emergencies as an alternative to the provision of ships. In 1634 King CHARLES I charged ship money on coastal towns and counties to improve the Navy, and in 1635 extended it throughout England and Wales. He claimed the right to impose the charge because it was an emergency measure. A legal challenge by John HAMPDEN (pursued by deliberately making incomplete payment to provoke prosecution) argued that it was a tax requiring authorization by PARLIAMENT. Judges narrowly supported Charles (12 June 1638), but payment then declined (1638–40). Levying of ship money was declared illegal by the LONG

PARLIAMENT (1641). *See also* NAVY, ENGLISH, BEFORE 1660; CHARLES I, PERSONAL RULE; ST JOHN, OLIVER.

SHIPPING INDUSTRIES In the 13th–16th centuries sea-going ships were owned by individual merchants or groups (to spread risk), occasionally by noblemen or bishops. Coastal shipping was important (to 19th century), particularly supply of coal from NE England to London (*see* COAL INDUSTRY, ENGLAND). Much OVERSEAS TRADE involved vessels belonging to Continental Europeans. English merchants sometimes chartered ships through OVERSEAS TRADING COMPANIES (15th–17th centuries).

During the 16th–17th centuries English and Scottish ships carried relatively more overseas trade. English ships included larger, ocean-going vessels (for sailing to the Mediterranean, Americas, W Africa, E Asia). By 1582, 177 English ships carried over 100 tons. The EAST INDIA COMPANY notably commissioned grand ships (17th–18th centuries). English and Scottish SHIP BUILDING and shipping were stimulated by legislation in the 1650s–60s (*see* NAVIGATION ACTS) and greatly increased trade.

During the 18th century ship owning, broking and marine insurance developed as separate businesses. Some ships were managed by a 'ship's husband' (part-owner). British shipping trebled 1700–88 (323,000 to over 1 million tons), including vessels designed for bulk imports (e.g., sugar, tobacco).

Regular steam-powered services, for passengers, mail and other cargo, were pioneered from 1818 between Britain and Ireland, and from 1838 across the Atlantic. Mail contracts, expanding trade and imperial territories, and EMIGRATION encouraged expansion of shipping. By 1880 the UK accounted for over half of the world's commercial tonnage. Cunard was the trans-Atlantic leader 1840–1960s, while Peninsular and Oriental ('P&O'), originating in 1837, became the world's largest shipping business in the 1920s (about 500 ships).

The UK declined relatively in shipping during the 20th century, although its fleet remained the world's largest until 1967 and peaked in 1975 (1680 vessels). Rapid contraction ensued as more modern vessels were acquired in other countries and ships were registered elsewhere ('flagged out'). In 2017 the registered UK fleet was the 18th largest.

SHIRE COURT In England, a public assembly within a (large) SHIRE, held under royal authority, for conducting administrative and legal business (e.g., settling land disputes). Shire courts existed in WESSEX by the late 9th century, but their development took place essentially from the mid 10th century. Court presidents were EALDORMEN and bishops (representing the king), assisted in the late 10th–11th centuries by SHERIFFS. Courts were attended by freemen, and usually met twice a year.

After the Norman Conquest (1066–70s) sheriffs generally presided. Courts met every four weeks. But business was removed to other courts (12th–13th centuries), and county courts declined (from 14th century). They were revived in 1846 as local civil courts, with magistrates replacing sheriffs. *See also* local governmental structures, England.

SHIRES, ENGLAND The shire was originally a unit of lordship and administration. The term is derived from OE *scir*, meaning 'district'. In Anglo-Saxon England (6th–11th centuries) there were two kinds.

The small shire contained settlements (about 12) which provided renders (e.g., food, drink) and services to a king or nobleman. Small shires as territories possibly predated Roman Britain. (For similar units in Wales and Scotland *see* commote, thanage.)

Large shires, sometimes combining several small shires, were formed in Wessex (from 8th century) and in Wessex-conquered England (mid 10th–11th centuries). Administered by ealdormen (later by sheriffs), they were units for organizing military service, taxation and justice. In the late 10th–11th centuries shires were often grouped. From the late 11th century the shire (or 'county', from OFr. *comté*) remained a principal unit of local government. *See also* shire court.

SHIRES, IRELAND English-type (large) shires (or 'counties') were created after the Anglo-Norman invasion (1169–70) as local administrative units within areas under direct royal control and within lords' liberties. Royal shires (12 by 1300) were administered by sheriffs accountable to the government in Dublin, and served for revenue collection and provision of justice. As English authority contracted in the 14th and 15th centuries, administration ceased in many shires. By 1460, only five royal shires remained in use (Louth, Meath, Dublin, Kildare, Wexford).

New shires were created, or former ones reinstated, mostly in the 16th century as English authority was re-expanded, starting with Westmeath (1543), and King's and Queen's Counties (1557). In Connacht (W Ireland) and Munster (S), shiring followed the creation of regional presidencies (1569, 1570). Nominal shires were created in Ulster (N) in 1585 and implemented later. The last shire (of 32), Wicklow, was created in 1606, though Tipperary remained a liberty of the Butler family until 1716. *See also* government, Ireland 12th–mid 17th centuries; local governmental structures, Ireland.

SHIRES, SCOTLAND *see* sheriffdom

SHIRES, WALES *see* local governmental structures, Wales

SHOPS AND RETAILING Recorded in towns from the 12th century (initially in England), and situated by market places or main streets, early shops were usually small rooms with an opening and shutter. Some were kept by merchants (e.g., drapers), others used by craftsmen for both making and selling goods (e.g., footwear). (Until the 19th century, basic foodstuffs were usually sold in markets.) In the 13th–14th centuries there were also 'selds': structures containing 20–50 trading pitches.

Shopping as a leisure activity started at the Royal Exchange in London (1568), which included 120 shops. By the mid 17th century some shopfronts included glass (small panes), and shops were becoming larger. Fascias with lettering, replacing signs, spread from the 1760s; from the 1830s larger panes of 'sheet glass' permitted variety in shopfront design.

In 19th-century Britain, increasing urbanization stimulated new retailing forms. Bazaars (numerous traders in a building) flourished from 1816 to the later 19th century. Arcades (covered pedestrian thoroughfares with shops) were built (e.g., Burlington Arcade, London, 1818). Co-operative societies became major retailers in working-class areas (from 1840s; *see* co-operative movement). Department stores developed from the 1850s, and 'chain stores' (businesses with branches and centralized distribution) likewise, using railways.

During the 1920s–30s chain stores became dominant (e.g., Burton for men's clothes), and department stores formed chains (e.g., Debenhams). 'Supermarkets' (large self-service stores, primarily selling foodstuffs) proliferated from the 1950s. Many independent retailers closed. Pedestrianized precincts and 'shopping centres' with car parks were created in towns in the 1950s–70s (e.g., Bull Ring, Birmingham, 1964), and town-edge centres from the 1970s, followed by separate 'retail parks' (e.g., MetroCentre, NE England, 1986).

In Ireland, small retailers predominated until the 1970s. Retailing changes happened mainly in Dublin, Belfast and Cork, including department stores (from 1850s), chain stores (mainly from 1920s), supermarkets (from 1960s), and British chains (from 1980s).

SHORT PARLIAMENT In England, name applied to the Parliament called by King Charles I for 17 April 1640 to obtain taxation for military action against the Scots (*see* Covenant, Wars of the, or Bishops' Wars). Charles's intention was thwarted when the House of Commons sought redress of grievances arising from his period of 'personal rule' (1629–40). Charles dissolved Parliament within three weeks (5 May). *See also* Charles I, personal rule; Long Parliament.

SHREWSBURY, 12TH EARL OF (b. 24 July 1660 in England; d. 1 Feb. 1718 at London, England, aged 57).

Charles Talbot, a Roman Catholic, succeeded as earl of Shrewsbury in 1668 and converted to Protestantism in 1679 (in the reign of King CHARLES II). In 1688, as a WHIG alienated by the pro-Catholic policies of King JAMES VII/II, he signed the letter that invited William of Orange to intervene in England.

After William became king (as WILLIAM III), Shrewsbury served briefly as a SECRETARY OF STATE (1689–90). He was reappointed, and created a duke, in 1694 when William reorganized his ministry (resigned 1698).

In 1710 Queen ANNE appointed Shrewsbury as lord chamberlain (part of her shift of power from the WHIG JUNTO towards Robert HARLEY and the TORIES), and he served as lord lieutenant of Ireland 1713–14. In July 1714 he became lord TREASURER, the last person to hold the post. His appointment thwarted the ambitions of Viscount BOLINGBROKE, and he presided over the accession of GEORGE I (resigned in Oct.).

SIDNEY, HENRY (b. probably 20 July 1529 at London, England; d. 5 May 1586 at Ludlow, Shropshire, England, aged 56). A courtier's son (knighted 1550), Sidney held posts in Ireland under Thomas, earl of SUSSEX (his brother-in-law) 1556–9, and was president of the COUNCIL IN THE MARCHES OF WALES (1559–86).

Sidney served three terms as chief governor (lord deputy) of Ireland, seeking to extend English authority. During the first (1565–7) he campaigned, at the insistence of Queen ELIZABETH I, against the rebel chieftain Shane O'NEILL (Sept.–Nov. 1566; O'Neill was killed June 1567). He also nominated (unsuccessfully) a president for Munster (*see* PRESIDENCIES, IRELAND). During the second term (1568–71) he appointed a president for CONNACHT (W Ireland; 1569), but was forced to campaign against the DESMOND REBELLION in MUNSTER (S Ireland; July–Sept. 1569; president appointed Dec. 1570).

During his third term (1575–8) Sidney attempted to make government self-financing by agreeing COMPOSITION payments with landholders in Munster and Connacht. He also annexed the Gaelic chieftainship of Thomond to Connacht (as Co. Clare), and divided the remainder of Connacht into shires (1576). *See also* IRELAND, ENGLISH CONQUEST, 16TH CENTURY; PERROT, JOHN.

SIERRA LEONE A former British territory in W Africa. The British settled freed slaves on the coast from 1787, and in 1808 Great Britain founded a CROWN COLONY, which gained a reputation as 'the white man's grave' (because of unhealthy coastal swamps). A PROTECTORATE over the hinterland was declared in 1896, and a rebellion was crushed in 1898–9. Sierra Leone became independent under the British Crown in 1961, and a republic in 1971. Approx. population in 1921, 1,500,000; in 1960, 2,241,000.

In summer 2000 a British military force, sent by the government of Tony BLAIR, halted the deterioration of peacekeeping by the UN (between forces of Sierra Leone's elected government and rebels). The British secured the main airport, facilitated evacuation by expatriates, and helped the government to repulse rebels from Freetown. A small detachment of British soldiers captured by rebels was rescued (Sept.). British forces left in July 2002, following establishment of a more peaceful situation. *See also* WEST AFRICA, ENGLISH AND BRITISH INVOLVEMENT.

SIKH WARS Two wars (1845–6, 1848–9) between the Sikh kingdom in the Punjab (NW India) and British forces. After Sikhs attacked a British post (Dec. 1845), the British imposed a loose PROTECTORATE over the Punjab with the treaty of Lahore (March 1846). Further rebellion led to a British invasion (Nov. 1848), fierce fighting, and annexation of the Punjab to British INDIA (March 1849). *See also* DALHOUSIE, 10TH EARL OF.

SILBURY HILL A massive chalk mound near AVEBURY, N Wiltshire, S England, constructed during the Later NEOLITHIC (*c.*2800–*c.*2000 BC), 130 ft (40 m) in height and covering an area of 5.4 acres (2.2 ha). The site is contained within a ditch and was constructed in three main phases. Speculation about the hill's purpose remains diverse, ranging from notions of Mother Goddess worship to competitive displays by eminent chiefs. The monument provides a platform upon which certain people would have stood to perform rites and to see other sites such as Avebury itself.

SILKEN THOMAS *see* OFFALY, LORD

SIMNEL, LAMBERT (b. 1476 or 1477 in England; d. after 1534 in England). A tradesman's son, Simnel was trained by a priest to act as a YORKIST claimant to the throne of King HENRY VII (ruled from 1485). From late 1486 Simnel impersonated Edward IV's nephew Edward, earl of Warwick (imprisoned son of George, duke of CLARENCE).

Simnel was crowned as 'Edward VI' in Dublin, Ireland (24 May 1487); he then invaded England (4 June). Supported by Yorkist nobles, including Francis, Viscount Lovell, Simnel was defeated by Henry VII at (East) Stoke, Nottinghamshire (16 June). Taken prisoner, he was made a servant in Henry's household. *See also* SIMNEL, LAMBERT, AND IRELAND; LOVELL'S CONSPIRACY.

SIMNEL, LAMBERT, AND IRELAND Because Yorkist sympathies were strong in Ireland, the Yorkist-organized Simnel rebellion was launched there. Lambert SIMNEL arrived in early 1487, was joined by English leaders and 2000 German mercenaries (5 May), and was crowned 'Edward VI' in Christ Church, Dublin (24 May). The Kildare GERALDINES were notable supporters (*see* KILDARE, 8TH EARL OF). Simnel's army sailed from Ireland for England on 4 June. *See also* YORKIST–LANCASTRIAN CONFLICT, ROLE OF IRELAND.

SIMON, JOHN (b. 28 Feb. 1873 at Manchester, Lancashire, England; d. 11 Jan. 1954 at London, England, aged 80). The son of a Congregational minister, Simon became a barrister and Liberal MP (1906–18, 1922–40). He served in the British government of H.H. ASQUITH from 1910 (also knighted), resigning in Jan. 1916 in opposition to CONSCRIPTION (*see* WORLD WAR I, IMPACT ON BRITISH SOCIETY).

In June 1931, frustrated with Liberal support for the Labour government, Simon and two others resigned the Party whip, though like other Liberals they supported the NATIONAL GOVERNMENT (formed Aug.). In Sept., more Liberals sided with Simon, becoming recognized as 'Liberal Nationals'. After a general election (Oct.), Simon became foreign secretary (served 1931–5). He was subsequently home secretary (1935–7), chancellor of the Exchequer (1937–40), and lord CHANCELLOR (1940–5). He was created Viscount Simon in 1940. Simon strongly supported the APPEASEMENT policy of Neville CHAMBERLAIN. *See also* LIBERAL PARTY.

SINECURE A nominal office or job whose holder receives an income without being required to perform any substantial duties. The term originally referred to a Church post without 'care of souls' (i.e., pastoral duties), derived from Latin *sine cura*. In the 18th century especially, British public administration and the ROYAL HOUSEHOLD included many sinecures, which were granted as rewards for political services. Increasingly regarded as corrupt, they were gradually eliminated from 1782 (*see* ECONOMICAL REFORM). Most had been abolished by the mid 19th century.

SINGAPORE A former British colony in E Asia, SE of MALAYA. In 1819 Stamford RAFFLES bought land for the EAST INDIA COMPANY on Singapore Island for a trading post. The island was ceded to Great Britain in 1824, and combined administratively with Britain's Penang and Malacca settlements as the Straits Settlements (1826). They were governed from INDIA until 1867 when they became a CROWN COLONY. Success as a port attracted Chinese and Indian immigrants to Singapore. Britain built a military base (1921).

During WORLD WAR II, Japanese occupied Singapore (1942–5; *see* SINGAPORE, FALL OF). Afterwards Singapore became a separate British colony (1946), self-governing from 1959. It joined the independent Federation of Malaysia in 1963 (withdrew as separate republic, 1965). British military bases were closed in 1971. Approx. population in 1921, 418,000; in 1958, 1,519,000.

SINGAPORE, FALL OF A major defeat for British power in E Asia in 1942, during WORLD WAR II. A Japanese army invaded SINGAPORE, a British colonial territory and location of a strategic naval base, overland from Malaya (8 Feb.). The fixed defences had been designed to counter principally a naval attack. The garrison of 70,000 British and Commonwealth troops surrendered (15 Feb.).

SINKING FUNDS Long-term funds, using allocated revenue, which are created to reduce debt. In Great Britain, following a plan by Robert WALPOLE, funds were assigned to the reduction of government debts in 1717, and united in 1718. The consolidated sinking fund continued until the 1770s without substantially reducing the NATIONAL DEBT, although it encouraged confidence in financial administration. In 1786 William PITT the Younger, influenced by Richard PRICE, created another fund to tackle debt from the AMERICAN WAR OF INDEPENDENCE, managed by Commissioners for the Reduction of the National Debt. It lasted until 1828.

In 1875 Sir Stafford NORTHCOTE started a sinking fund to demonstrate financial effectiveness (suspended 1922). Several funds were started after WORLD WAR I (ended 1918) for particular loans, and a new general fund was begun in 1923. This was divided into 'Old' and 'New' funds in 1928 (latter abolished in 1954). The use of sinking funds largely ceased in 1968, and a surviving fund ended in 2015, though the Debt Commissioners remained in post.

SINN FÉIN (Irish, meaning 'We Ourselves'). The name of a nationalist policy for Ireland, proposed in 1905 by Arthur GRIFFITH to the National Council (a nationalist forum, founded 1903): essentially independence under the British Crown.

The name Sinn Féin League was used from 1907 for a political-cultural organization created by merger of CUMANN NA NGAEDHEAL and the Dungannon Clubs. In 1908, when the League merged with the National Council, the name was shortened to Sinn Féin.

In 1916 Sinn Féin was blamed, incorrectly, for the EASTER RISING. Republicans exploited this 'fame' by adopting the name for parliamentary by-elections. In Oct. 1917 they formally made a republic their aim, and elected Éamon DE VALERA as leader. After Sinn Féin won most Irish seats at the Dec. 1918 UK general election, its MPs abstained from the UK Parliament and formed a Dáil Éireann ('Assembly of Ireland') in Dublin (21 Jan. 1919). It subsequently won elections for a British-sponsored Parliament of Southern Ireland (May 1921). Its tactics, together with attacks by the IRISH REPUBLICAN ARMY (IRA), forced Great Britain to concede effective independence. But the ANGLO-IRISH TREATY (Dec. 1921), which retained the monarchy and accepted PARTITION, split the party: pro- and anti-treaty candidates contested the Dáil election of June 1922.

After inauguration of the IRISH FREE STATE (Dec. 1922), pro-treaty Sinn Féin politicians formed (the second) CUMANN NA NGAEDHEAL. Anti-treaty Sinn Féin came second in the 1923 Dáil election, but representatives abstained. In 1926 de Valera and supporters seceded to form FIANNA FÁIL. Sinn Féin declined.

In 1970, after the IRA split, PROVISIONAL SINN FÉIN was founded. The continuing 'Official' Sinn Féin changed name to Sinn Féin, The Workers' Party (1977), and The Workers' Party (1982). In 1992 leading figures separated as Democratic Left, which participated in the 1994–7 coalition government (under John BRUTON) and merged with the LABOUR PARTY (1998). *See also* IRISH INDEPENDENCE, WAR OF.

SIWAN (b. *c*.1185; d. 30 March 1237, probably at Aberffro, Gwynedd, NW Wales, aged about 52). Welsh name of Joan, illegitimate daughter of King JOHN of England. She was betrothed (1204) and married (1205) to LLYWELYN AP IORWERTH of Gwynedd, to whom she bore DAFYDD AP LLYWELYN. She acted as intermediary between Llywelyn and John (d. 1216), and later King HENRY III. On 13 Oct. 1229 Siwan and Dafydd did homage to Henry as Llywelyn's representatives. *See also* ANGLO-WELSH RELATIONS, 6TH–13TH CENTURIES.

SIX ACTS A controversial package of legislation introduced by British home secretary Viscount Sidmouth (Henry ADDINGTON) in Nov.–Dec. 1819 to suppress radical agitation after PETERLOO. The Acts banned large public meetings and military-style drilling, strengthened libel laws and the search-powers of magistrates, limited the right of defendants to adjourn trials, and increased the tax on newspapers. *See also* LIVERPOOL, 2ND EARL OF.

SIX ARTICLES Anti-heresy legislation enforcing Catholic theology in the English Church, passed by Parliament on 10 June 1539 (in reign of King HENRY VIII). It made denial of TRANSUBSTANTIATION a capital offence. Clerical marriage was forbidden and vows of chastity were pronounced indissoluble. The Act was seen as a victory for religious conservatives (e.g., 3rd duke of NORFOLK). Repealed 1547, after accession of EDWARD VI. *See also* ARTICLES OF RELIGION; REFORMATION, ENGLAND.

SIXTH OF GEORGE I Popular name for the 1720 Declaratory Act whereby the British Parliament ended

appeals to the Irish House of Lords and awarded legal supremacy to the British Lords. It was caused by cases in which both Houses had claimed supremacy (particularly *Sherlock v. Annesley*) and included reassertion of Britain's right to legislate for Ireland. It was repealed on 21 June 1782. *See also* PROTESTANT ASCENDANCY; CONSTITUTION OF 1782.

SKARA BRAE A stone-built settlement of the Middle NEOLITHIC (*c*.3200 BC) on Mainland in the ORKNEY ISLANDS, comprising a cluster of ten cell-like buildings; similar to other Orcadian settlements such as Barnhouse and Rinyo. The houses are generally cruciform in plan, with a central hearth, side recesses for beds and a stone dresser in the rear. Similar spatial patterns are seen in certain ceremonial and funerary monuments on the island. The settlements are often associated with pottery known as Grooved Ware.

SLATE INDUSTRY, WALES Slate in the Snowdonia mountains (NW Wales) was first quarried extensively by Richard Pennant (*c*.1737–1808), who established a monopoly in 1782 and made large profits. The industry became centred on Bethesda, Llanberis and Nantlle (Caernarfonshire) and Blaenau Ffestiniog and Corris (Merionethshire), producing mainly roofing tiles. During the boom period of 1860–90s employment exceeded 20,000.

In the 20th century industrial disputes, increased transport costs, foreign competition and use of clay tiles caused contraction. Most quarries and mines were closed by the 1960s (*see* INDUSTRIAL DECLINE, WALES). The slate-quarrying communities, strongly Welsh-speaking, produced a disproportionately large number of Welsh-language writers in the 20th century. *See also* PENRHYN, LORD; CAERNARFON; INDUSTRY, WALES FROM 18TH CENTURY.

SLAVERY, ENGLAND *see* SOCIAL STRUCTURE, ENGLAND BEFORE 1066; MANUMISSION

SLAVERY, IRELAND *see* SOCIAL STRUCTURE, GAELIC IRELAND 5TH–12TH CENTURIES

SLAVERY, NORTH BRITAIN AND SCOTLAND *see* SOCIAL STRUCTURE, NORTH BRITAIN AND SCOTLAND; KINGSHIP, NORTH BRITAIN

SLAVERY, ROMAN BRITAIN *see* ROMAN BRITAIN, SOCIAL STRUCTURE

SLAVERY, WALES *see* SOCIAL STRUCTURE, WALES

SLAVERY IN BRITISH EMPIRE, ABOLITION OF British philanthropists were disappointed that the abolition of the SLAVE TRADE (implemented 1807) failed to induce PLANTATION owners to improve the treatment of slaves. Following campaigns led by William WILBERFORCE and Thomas Fowell Buxton, the UK Parliament legislated in 1834 to free slaves throughout the Empire, except for India and St Helena (where slavery was not banned until 1843).

Between 1834 and 1838, the British government paid out about £17,600,000 in compensation to 80,000 owners of 800,000 slaves, valuing slaves at about half their market rate. Ex-slaves were indentured to their former masters for 40 hours per week for a transitional period of 4–6 years.

SLAVE TRADE, ABOLITION OF Strong opposition to the trans-Atlantic slave trade developed from the 1750s in N America among QUAKERS in Philadelphia, PENNSYLVANIA. In the 1760s–70s they pressurized British Quakers to oppose the trade. Interest was also stirred by a separate campaign, led by Granville Sharp (1735–1813), to confirm the illegality of slavery in England and Wales (achieved by Somerset's case, 1772).

British Quakers publicized conditions in the trade from 1783, and helped to found a Society for the Abolition of the Slave Trade (1787), which organized popular campaigning (e.g., petitions to Parliament). Evangelical Anglicans also became involved, notably the MP William WILBERFORCE who adopted the cause in 1787 and proposed anti-trade measures in Parliament from 1789. Campaigning was hindered by the FRENCH REVOLUTION and slave uprisings in the WEST INDIES (1791), but in 1806 achieved prohibition of slave transportation in British ships (effective from 1807). Further campaigning from 1824 achieved the legal abolition of slavery in the British Empire (see SLAVERY IN BRITISH EMPIRE, ABOLITION OF). See also SLAVE TRADE, ENGLISH AND BRITISH INVOLVEMENT; CLAPHAM SECT; EVANGELICAL MOVEMENTS.

SLAVE TRADE, ENGLISH AND BRITISH INVOLVEMENT The trans-Atlantic slave trade, which shipped slaves from Africa to the Americas, was developed in the 16th and 17th centuries by the Portuguese, Spanish and Dutch. It became a lucrative business. English involvement began in the 1640s. By c.1670 England was the pre-eminent slave-trading country. Slaves were obtained by barter with African dealers on the W African seaboard. From 1672 to 1689 England's trade was in theory a monopoly of the London-based ROYAL AFRICAN COMPANY. By the 1730s, BRISTOL was the major organizing centre, supplanted by LIVERPOOL from the 1750s. In the late 17th–19th centuries at least 3.4 million Africans were transported. The trade peaked in the late 18th century.

Slaves crossed the Atlantic on dedicated ships, with many dying because of poor conditions. The trade supplied labourers to colonies in the WEST INDIES (e.g., BARBADOS,

JAMAICA), primarily for sugar cultivation. Survivors were purchased mainly by PLANTATION owners and employed in 'field gangs'. A typical operation might employ 200 slaves. Low fertility meant that new slaves had to be continually imported. Large numbers were also taken to N America from the 1680s (VIRGINIA, MARYLAND, NORTH and SOUTH CAROLINA) where fertility was higher.

Slavery as a legal institution was developed in Barbados from the mid 17th century and copied elsewhere (though slavery was not recognized in England and Wales, as was confirmed in 1772 by Somerset's case). Because rebellion was an ever-present threat, legislation was harsh, restricting movement and authorizing brutal punishments. The trade was strongly opposed from the 1780s, and abolished from 1807 (see SLAVE TRADE, ABOLITION OF). See also HAWKINS, JOHN.

SLUMS The term 'slum' (of unknown origin) was used from the early 19th century for a crowded street or neighbourhood with squalid living conditions. Overcrowding became a severe problem with the rapid growth of British and Irish towns from the later 18th century. Speculative builders constructed dwellings (tenements, courts, terraces) that lacked water supplies and SEWERAGE. Rooms were frequently shared by whole families. Distress was sometimes exacerbated by demolition programmes to create space for roads and RAILWAYS. Authors (e.g., Charles DICKENS) and social investigators (e.g., Seebohm ROWNTREE) exposed the scale of distress.

The problem was tackled by various initiatives, such as Peabody Trust housing in London from 1862 (see PEABODY, GEORGE); IMPROVEMENT ACTS obtained by Scottish cities in the 1860s–70s authorizing slum clearance; the Artizans' Dwellings Act of 1875 (for UK except Scotland), which permitted slum clearance by local authorities; municipally sponsored housing in BIRMINGHAM organized before 1914 by J.S. Nettlefold. A succession of Housing Acts from 1919 saw rapid expansion of COUNCIL HOUSING in Great Britain in the 1920s–30s: by providing subsidies, central government encouraged large-scale slum clearance and replacement building (until 1970s). See also HOUSING LEGISLATION, ENGLAND AND WALES/SCOTLAND; HOUSING, IRELAND, STATE INVOLVEMENT.

SLUYS, BATTLE OF see HUNDRED YEARS WAR

SMILES, SAMUEL (b. 23 Dec. 1812 at Haddington, Haddingtonshire, Scotland; d. 16 April 1904 at London, England, aged 91). Having been a surgeon and general practitioner in Scotland, Smiles became editor of the *Leeds Times* (1838–42) and involved with English railway companies (1845–66). From 1857 he published biographies of engineers and industrialists. He publicized his belief that success could be achieved through character and application in *Self-Help, with Illustrations of Character and Conduct* (1859), which sold over 250,000 copies within 50 years.

SMITH, ADAM (bap. 5 June 1723 at Kirkcaldy, Fife, Scotland; d. 17 July 1790 at Edinburgh, Scotland, aged 67). Political economist and philosopher of the Scottish ENLIGHTENMENT. Educated at GLASGOW and OXFORD Universities, Smith later held professorships at Glasgow (1751–64). While tutor to the (3rd) duke of Buccleuch in France (1764–6) he met leading French intellectuals, and from 1778 was a commissioner of customs in Scotland. In 1776 Smith published *The Wealth of Nations*, a work of POLITICAL ECONOMY analysing causes of economic growth. It advocated CAPITALISM based on free markets and minimal functions for the State. It considerably influenced political economists and governments. *See also* CLASSICAL AND NEOCLASSICAL ECONOMICS.

SMITH, F.E. (b. 12 July 1872 at Birkenhead, Cheshire, England; d. 30 Sept. 1930 at London, England, aged 58). Highly ambitious, Frederick Edwin Smith was a noted barrister before becoming a Conservative MP (1906). His combative attitude to the Liberal government raised Conservatives' morale.

Smith was solicitor-general (1915), attorney-general (1915–19) and lord CHANCELLOR (1919–22) in British wartime and post-war coalition governments, and was created Lord Birkenhead (1919) and earl of Birkenhead (1922). He helped to negotiate the ANGLO-IRISH TREATY (1921), and his Law of Property Act (1922) was a major reform. Too closely associated with a now discredited David LLOYD GEORGE, Birkenhead lost standing after 1922, though he served Stanley BALDWIN as India secretary (1924–8).

SMITH, IAN (b. 8 April 1919 at Selukwe, Southern Rhodesia; d. 20 Nov. 2007 at Cape Town, South Africa, aged 88). Smith entered the legislature of white-ruled SOUTHERN RHODESIA in 1948, and in 1953 transferred to the legislature of the FEDERATION OF RHODESIA AND NYASALAND. In 1962, concerned about plans for political representation of black Africans in Southern Rhodesia, he formed the Rhodesia Reform Party. It merged into the Rhodesian Front which won the 1962 Southern Rhodesian election.

In April 1964, following the Federation's dissolution (Dec. 1963), Smith became Party leader and prime minister of Rhodesia (former Southern Rhodesia). Spurning international demands to introduce black-majority rule, he declared independence (11 Nov. 1965) and a republic (1970). External pressure and internal warfare eventually forced him to institute a compliant black African government (1978). He remained prime minister until May 1979,

then served briefly as a minister. After Rhodesia became independent as Zimbabwe (1980), Smith remained in Parliament (until 1987). *See also* RHODESIA PROBLEM.

SMITH, JOHN (b. 13 Sept. 1938 at Dalmally, Argyll, Scotland; d. 12 May 1994 at London, England, aged 55). Educated at GLASGOW University, Smith, an advocate, became a Labour MP in 1970 and served in the British government under James CALLAGHAN as president of the Board of Trade (1978–9). During the 1980s he was an effective Opposition spokesman, and in 1992 was elected leader of the LABOUR PARTY (in succession to Neil KINNOCK). His unflamboyant competence won respect, and he advanced 'modernization' of the Party by ending the 'block vote' of trade unions (1993). His sudden death provided the opportunity for Tony BLAIR to become leader.

SMITH, W.H. (b. 24 June 1825 at London, England; d. 6 Oct. 1891 at Walmer, Kent, England, aged 66). William Henry Smith developed his father's newsagency (called W.H. Smith and Son from 1846) into one of Great Britain's most prominent businesses through providing bookstalls at railway stations (from 1848) and advertising space on buildings (from 1851), and becoming principal distributor of *The Times* newspaper. A Conservative MP from 1868, Smith held several Cabinet posts (first lord of the Admiralty 1877–80, secretary for war 1885–6, chief secretary for Ireland 1886, secretary for war 1886–7). He was leader of the House of Commons 1887–91; nicknamed 'Old Morality'.

SMUTS, JAN (b. 24 May 1870 at Riebeek West, Cape Colony; d. 11 Sept. 1950 at Irene, near Pretoria, South Africa, aged 80). Of Dutch descent, Smuts was disillusioned by the JAMESON RAID and in 1897 moved from CAPE COLONY to Transvaal (or South African Republic). During the (Second) BOER WAR (1899–1902) he was a leader of Boer guerrilla resistance to the British. He helped to negotiate the treaty of VEREENIGING, but opposed the policies of Alfred MILNER. In 1906, in Great Britain, he persuaded the Liberal government to grant self-government to Transvaal (now a British CROWN COLONY). He joined its government in 1907.

From 1910 Smuts served in the government of the new Union of SOUTH AFRICA, and sought co-operation between British and Boers. During WORLD WAR I, he led the conquest of German South West Africa (1915), fought in E Africa (1916–17), and served in the Imperial War Cabinet (1917–18). He was prime minister of South Africa 1919–24, 1939–48, the latter period including WORLD WAR II.

SNOWDEN, PHILIP (b. 18 July 1864 at Ickornshaw, Yorkshire, England; d. 15 May 1937 at Tilford, Surrey, England, aged 72). A weaver's son, Snowden worked for the

UK Inland Revenue until crippled by a spinal infection. In 1894 he joined the INDEPENDENT LABOUR PARTY. His SOCIALISM was ethical rather than revolutionary.

Elected as an MP in 1906, Snowden lost his seat in 1918 for opposing wartime policies. Re-elected in 1922, he served as chancellor of the Exchequer under Ramsay MacDonald (1924, 1929–31), operating orthodox policies. In 1931 his insistence on making cuts in welfare expenditure split the Labour Party and led to the NATIONAL GOVERNMENT (Aug.). In Oct. Snowden ceased to be chancellor and an MP (Nov., created Viscount Snowden). He served as lord PRIVY SEAL but resigned (Sept. 1932) after protective tariffs were adopted (see OTTAWA AGREEMENTS).

SOCIAL CLASS TERMINOLOGY A new understanding of society, based on the concept of 'class' (previously used in botany and zoology), emerged in Great Britain between the 1780s and 1830s. In the 17th–18th centuries, society was often understood as a linked hierarchy of (male-dominated) ranks or orders based primarily on land and agriculture (e.g., NOBILITY, GENTRY and PROFESSIONS, yeomen or large farmers, husbandmen or small farmers, labourers and servants, together with merchants and craftsmen). The growth of FACTORY-based industry during the INDUSTRIAL REVOLUTION, and of industrial towns (e.g., MANCHESTER), produced a larger visible group of wealthy manufacturers or capitalists, who were categorized as 'middle class'. Industrial working people were labelled 'working class', leaving nobility and gentry to be reclassified as 'upper class'. The result was a sense of society as tiered horizontal strata.

Political movements such as the middle-class ANTI-CORN LAW LEAGUE (1839–46) and working-class CHARTISM (1839–48) persuaded some that large classes existed as cohesive, purposive realities with 'class consciousness'. Others argued against this position, citing variety of occupations, skills, ranks and locations within broad class groupings (e.g., see ARISTOCRACY OF LABOUR), and preferring plural terminology ('working classes', 'middle classes', 'upper classes'). Class terminology was considered less relevant to Ireland (except for the NE) because of the continuing primacy of land and agriculture.

With DE-INDUSTRIALIZATION from the 1970s, the establishment of ethnic- and religious-based communities (through IMMIGRATION), emergence of new wealthy élites (e.g., the international 'super-rich', sports stars, entertainers), and developing predominance of women (e.g., in professions), existing social class terminology became insufficient for social analysis. See also LABOUR MOVEMENT.

SOCIAL CONTRACT Name adopted by Harold WILSON, leader of the British LABOUR PARTY, for an informal agreement made in 1973 between the Party and the TRADES UNION CONGRESS. The unions promised wage restraint in return for favourable legislation. The WINTER OF DISCONTENT (1979) destroyed the Contract. See also INCOMES POLICIES; ECONOMY, STATE INVOLVEMENT, BRITAIN.

SOCIAL DEMOCRATIC AND LABOUR PARTY A political party in NORTHERN IRELAND, often known as the 'SDLP'. Founded on 21 Aug. 1970, it originated in the CIVIL RIGHTS MOVEMENT, and won support from moderate nationalists (mainly Catholics). It gave priority to improving social conditions. As a 'constitutional nationalist' party it sought reunification of Ireland by consent (rather than force). It effectively superseded the NATIONALIST PARTY. It was represented in the UK Parliament from Feb. 1974 to 2017, and from Dec. 2019.

Initially led by Gerry Fitt, the Party participated in Northern Ireland's 1974 power-sharing EXECUTIVE. John HUME was leader 1979–2001. From 1981 the SDLP was challenged by the republican party PROVISIONAL SINN FÉIN (PSF). The SDLP took part in the NEW IRELAND FORUM (1983–4) and in the PEACE PROCESS which led to the BELFAST AGREEMENT (1998). It participated in the multi-party Executives of 1999–2000 and 2000–2 as principal partner to the ULSTER UNIONIST PARTY, with Seamus Mallon and Mark Durkan respectively serving as deputy first minister. In 2003 the SDLP was overtaken by PSF in ASSEMBLY elections, falling to fourth place. The Executives of 2007–11, 2011–16 and 2020– still included an SDLP minister. See also PARLIAMENTARY REPRESENTATION, NORTHERN IRELAND.

SOCIAL DEMOCRATIC FEDERATION A British political party founded by H.M. HYNDMAN in 1881 (as the Democratic Federation) to promote radical objectives. It adopted a socialist manifesto in 1883 and was renamed in 1884. Members included William MORRIS and John BURNS. The efforts of the 'SDF' to mobilize the unemployed attracted publicity in 1886 when its organization of a counter-demonstration (against the Fair Trade League) led to the 'West End riots' in London. An ideological influence on the wider British socialist movement in the 1880s, the SDF otherwise remained a fringe group. It collaborated in launching the LABOUR PARTY (1900), but promptly withdrew to continue the class war. In 1911 the SDF merged into the British Socialist Party, which became part of the COMMUNIST PARTY (1920).

SOCIAL DEMOCRATIC PARTY In Great Britain, a centrist political party launched on 26 March 1981 by four ex-Labour politicians repelled by the ascendancy of left-wingers in the LABOUR PARTY, namely Roy Jenkins, David Owen, William Rodgers and Shirley Williams. Supported initially by 15 MPs (defectors mostly from

Labour), it allied with the LIBERAL PARTY in late 1981. They fought the 1983 and 1987 general elections together, with the SDP winning six and five seats. The Parties merged in 1988 to form the LIBERAL DEMOCRATS. Owen rejected the merger (led continuing SDP until 1990).

SOCIALISM A school of political thought, revolutionary or constitutional, which stresses the desirability of equality and advocates State action to redistribute wealth. It rejects absolute property rights and favours collective ownership. Socialism, which developed in the 19th century, profoundly influenced the British LABOUR PARTY. *See also* CHRISTIAN SOCIALISM; NATIONALIZATION.

SOCIAL PARTNERSHIP In the Republic of Ireland, term for national agreements negotiated from 1987 onwards between the government and employers' organizations, trade unions and farmers. Reviving earlier 'corporatist' approaches to the economy, the earliest agreements were responses to difficult economic conditions: they sought to restrain inflation, discourage labour unrest, and promote economic growth by linking agreed wage increases with economic and social commitments from government. Most agreements covered a three-year period (e.g., the first, *Programme for National Recovery*, applied to 1988–90). They have been given some credit for the economic boom from the mid 1990s. The financial crisis of 2008 caused the seventh programme to collapse (2009). *See also* HAUGHEY, CHARLES; AHERN, BERTIE.

SOCIAL SERVICES Welfare services provided for communities and individuals, particularly by the State. In Britain and Ireland the State had little direct involvement before the 20th century. From the 16th century legislation required parishes to provide POOR RELIEF in England, Wales and Scotland (altered to parish unions from 1834 in England and Wales, and implemented likewise in Ireland). From the late 17th century voluntary societies in Britain and Ireland (e.g., FRIENDLY SOCIETIES) provided insurance against illness and unemployment. Their importance grew in the 19th century through involvement in EDUCATION, HOUSING and welfare (*see* CHARITY ORGANISATION SOCIETY), occasionally with government funding. 'Permissive legislation' authorized action by local authorities (e.g., housing improvement).

NEW LIBERALISM, developed in the 1880s–90s, advocated greater State intervention, funded by direct taxation. Substantial national services were introduced in Great Britain and Ireland in the early 20th century, starting with PENSIONS (1909) and NATIONAL INSURANCE (1911). From the 1940s, development of the WELFARE STATE in the UK provided universal benefits and services 'from cradle to grave'. *See also* SOCIAL SERVICES AND WELFARE, SOUTHERN IRELAND.

SOCIAL SERVICES AND WELFARE, SOUTHERN IRELAND The IRISH FREE STATE (from 1922) continued UK welfare arrangements (old age pensions, sickness and unemployment insurance), though pensions were reduced (1924–8). In 1933 the FIANNA FÁIL government extended insurance to agricultural labourers and smallholders, and other uninsured workers (Unemployed Assistance Act), and amalgamated insurance societies (National Health Insurance Act). Pensions for widows and orphans were provided from 1935.

British developments in the 1940s encouraged additional provision, though insurance and means-testing remained important (*see* WELFARE STATE). Limited children's allowances began in 1944 (extended 1952, 1963), and in 1947 a Department for Social Welfare was established (for insurance). The 1947 Health Act expanded County Councils' responsibility for health care. The 1952 Social Welfare Act unified and simplified schemes, and expanded benefits (e.g., for maternity, disability), and the 1953 Health Act introduced means-tested health care for the needy (extended by 1958 Health Care Act to over 80% of the population). In 1974 social insurance became compulsory. In 2014, 1.4 million people in the Republic of Ireland received a weekly social welfare payment. *See also* PENSIONS.

SOCIAL STRUCTURE, ENGLAND BEFORE 1066 Anglo-Saxon society mostly comprised kings, NOBILITY (including royal kindred) and peasants. In the 7th–10th centuries noblemen were called EALDORMAN ('elder' or 'great man') or *gesith* ('companion'). *Gesith* was replaced in the 9th–10th centuries by thegn (*þegn*, meaning 'servant' or 'follower'), denoting a retainer of a royal or noble household ideally with five HIDES of land.

Peasants varied in status. The most free were *ceorls*, who worked their own land, could own slaves, owed GELD, and undertook MILITARY SERVICE. Lesser peasants included *geburs*, who worked on nobles' estates as ploughmen and labourers, and had small landholdings. The lowest were slaves. Peasants called sokemen, owing less onerous services than *geburs*, are found in Danish-settled areas (from 9th century).

After marriage women retained considerable autonomy; e.g., they remained responsible for their own crimes. Widows often controlled property. *See also* KINGSHIP, ANGLO-SAXON; EARLS, ANGLO-SAXON ENGLAND.

SOCIAL STRUCTURE, ENGLAND 1066 TO 16TH CENTURY The NORMAN CONQUEST (1066–70s) resulted in a new élite (NOBILITY) and more rigidly hierarchical society based largely on landholding. King WILLIAM I granted about 50% of all land to about 170 incomers, most from NORMANDY (replacing Anglo-Saxons), who were known as BARONS (i.e., 'men'). A few were made EARLS.

Together with senior clergy (bishops, some abbots), they formed the upper nobility. They granted lands to followers called *chevaliers* (French) or KNIGHTS, who formed a lower nobility. Secular nobles embodied a military ethos (*see* MILITARY SERVICE, ENGLAND 1066 TO MID 17TH CENTURY). Landholders were normally succeeded by their eldest son ('primogeniture' inheritance).

Noble landholders (or lords) dominated through lordship; i.e., exercising authority through MANORS from which peasants held land. From the late 11th century slavery disappeared, but lords increased burdens (e.g., manorial exactions) generally on peasants. From the late 12th century 'unfree' peasants, called villeins or serfs (possibly 60% of peasants), were excluded from royal COURTS. The condition of 'unfreedom' was called 'villeinage'. Some peasants were less burdened; townspeople enjoyed extensive freedoms. Women normally retained their birth status.

During the 14th–15th centuries social structure became more varied. The regular summoning of certain lords to PARLIAMENT created a group within the upper nobility (about 60 men by late 1320s) who became known as the PEERAGE (by mid 15th century) and equated with the nobility. They were internally differentiated as five hereditary ranks: duke (from 1337), marquess (from 1397), earl, viscount (from 1440) and baron. Following a decline in knights (late 12th–13th centuries), smaller landowners adopted new titles: 'esquire' (by 1363) and 'gentleman' (by 1413). Collectively, they became regarded as GENTRY (6000–9000 families in 15th century); some exercised authority as JUSTICES OF THE PEACE.

Population decline from the mid 14th century enabled peasants to obtain greater freedom. Lords abandoned many restrictions; some peasants acquired larger landholdings and their successors became known as 'yeomen' (15th century). *See also* TENURES, ENGLAND FROM 1066; TOWN SOCIETY, ENGLAND; PROFESSIONS.

SOCIAL STRUCTURE, ENGLAND 16TH–LATER 18TH CENTURIES

Social stratification and authority remained primarily based on land. Society was headed by the monarch and hereditary NOBILITY, the latter equated with the PEERAGE (50–60 men, mostly large landowners) and their families. The lower, far larger stratum of GENTRY (several thousand men and families), was increasingly considered non-noble; it included lesser landowners, wealthier PROFESSIONALS (e.g., lawyers) and educated clergy. Deemed 'gentle', the nobility and gentry formed the 'political nation' (potential participants in national and county government, including PARLIAMENT).

Inferior rural society mostly comprised: (a) larger and smaller farmers (mainly tenants), now generally called 'yeomen' and 'husbandmen', and 'cottagers' with smallholdings; (b) craftsmen; (c) landless labourers and the destitute. Towns had separate structures (*see* TOWN SOCIETY, ENGLAND).

Population increase and other factors altered the relative sizes of social groups by the mid 17th century. The nobility expanded through creation of peers (to 126 by 1628). The gentry possibly trebled, through demographic increase and land acquisition (e.g., by merchants). Landless labourers increased (to possibly a third of adult males by 1600). Many yeomen flourished thanks to demand for agricultural produce. Conditions were disrupted in the 1640s–50s (*see* ENGLISH REVOLUTION).

From the late 17th social structure was modified by emergence of a 'monied interest' (e.g., bankers), which challenged the nobility's place (e.g., through political influence, from funding warfare). The gentry was reinforced by expansion of professions (e.g., ARMY and NAVY officers, royal officials).

The nobility (or aristocracy) nevertheless increased their dominance during the 18th century, a so-called 'aristocratic century' (e.g., many government ministers were noblemen). They sometimes extended estates through marriage or with lands acquired from yeomen and husbandmen (undermined by weak prices), which were reorganized as larger farms – effectively restructuring parts of rural society. They exploited minerals and invested in stock. From mid century, rural labourers increased significantly, and industrial communities expanded. *See also* RURAL SETTLEMENT AND SOCIETY, ENGLAND; PARLIAMENTARY CONSTITUENCIES AND ELECTIONS.

SOCIAL STRUCTURE, ENGLAND FROM LATER 18TH CENTURY

The hierarchy based on landownership was threatened by rapid industrialization (from 1780s) – the INDUSTRIAL REVOLUTION – and growing urbanization; they created the world's first industrial society (in Great Britain), thereby demoting agriculture and rural society. Industrializing TOWNS and areas, characterized by workshops and factories, were mainly in the NW (dominated by cotton textiles), NE (woollen textiles, engineering) and W Midlands (metal working, ceramics, etc.). Coal-mining communities also expanded, as did LONDON.

By the 1830s a 'class'-based sense of social structure developed, comprising an 'upper class' (aristocracy, gentry, and rich professionals, merchants and industrialists), 'middle class' (other industrialists, financiers, officials, etc.), and 'working class'. Industrial workers formed the largest sector: by 1851, 42% of the workforce was engaged in manufacturing, mining and building (21% in agriculture).

The aristocracy and gentry maintained dominance of national and county government while other classes sought influence. Concessions were made to the middle class (e.g., 1832 Reform Act), and it was deliberately strengthened through institutional reforms (schools, universities, civil service, 1850s–70s). The working-class CHARTIST Movement (1838–48) was rebuffed, but from 1867 increasing numbers of working men were enfranchised (*see* PARLIAMENTARY REFORM); TRADE UNIONISM became powerful. From the 1880s the authority of the aristocracy and landed gentry waned (to 1920s).

During the 20th century, middle-class and working-class politicians expanded State authority, shaping the lives of the majority; it included provision of education, social insurance, housing and (from 1940s) a WELFARE STATE; important industries and utilities were nationalized. Trade unions remained influential. Increasing numbers of professionals broadened the middle class.

During the 1980s–90s DE-INDUSTRIALIZATION changed society's economic basis to services (e.g., finance, entertainment), diminishing union influence. Class distinctions were blurred by new types (e.g., 'celebrities'). Women became more influential (e.g., Margaret THATCHER), and society more complex through the addition of minorities with different social structures (*see* MULTICULTURAL SOCIETY). *See also* SOCIAL CLASS TERMINOLOGY; LABOUR MOVEMENT; NEW LIBERALISM; LANDED SOCIETY, DECLINE OF, ENGLAND; ETHNIC AND NATIONAL MINORITIES, ENGLAND.

SOCIAL STRUCTURE, ENGLISH IN IRELAND BEFORE 17TH CENTURY *see* NORMANS, IMPACT ON IRELAND; IRELAND, ENGLISH COLONY IN, 13TH–15TH CENTURIES; NEW ENGLISH

SOCIAL STRUCTURE, GAELIC IRELAND 5TH–12TH CENTURIES Gaelic society was hierarchical and rigidly stratified, with few opportunities for mobility, especially upwards. Extremely patriarchal, it restricted women's roles, even within the higher social orders.

BREHON LAWS describe social orders, giving each a status that determined legal entitlements and responsibilities. At the top was the king of a *TÚATH* (kingdom). Next came the NOBILITY, essentially a warrior class, and the LEARNED CLASSES (e.g., poets, physicians). Below them were commoners, who were classified as free or unfree. The free were farmers of substance, the unfree were tenants-at-will. In addition there were land-bound serfs and those condemned to slavery, male and female, including prisoners from overseas raids.

The operational unit of society was the kin-group, especially the four-generation *derbfine* (three-generational *gelfine* after *c*.700). This was the normal property-owning unit; within royal circles it supplied successors to kings (*see* KINGSHIP, IRELAND). A married woman belonged to her husband's kin-group, whereas a single woman remained with her paternal kin. *See also* OSTMEN.

SOCIAL STRUCTURE, GAELIC IRELAND 12TH–17TH CENTURIES Social structure changed little after the Anglo-Norman invasion of 1169–70 (*see* NORMANS, IMPACT ON IRELAND). Despite losing territory to the invaders, Gaelic society continued to be governed by its traditional élite (*see* SOCIAL STRUCTURE, GAELIC IRELAND 5TH–12TH CENTURIES). In areas outside Anglo-Norman control (much of NW Ireland, small areas elsewhere), Gaelic law continued to be applied and agricultural practice was little altered. CHURCH REFORM, following Continental standards, had already started.

In areas under their control, the Anglo-Normans (or English) were a new ruling class who displaced Gaelic kings (*see* NORMAN IRISH FAMILIES OR OLD ENGLISH). Gaelic Irish peasants remained on many newly established MANORS and experienced little change in status. The invaders also introduced the PARISH SYSTEM. Gaelic rule was reasserted from the 13th century (*see* GAELIC REVIVAL, IRELAND 13TH–15TH CENTURIES).

Social structure began to change in the 16th–17th centuries (*see* IRELAND, ENGLISH CONQUEST, 16TH CENTURY). In the early 17th century many Gaelic chiefs left the country, depriving the Gaelic population of traditional leaders (*see* FLIGHT OF THE EARLS). The same period also saw the overshadowing of Anglo-Irish families by new arrivals from England (*see* NEW ENGLISH).

SOCIAL STRUCTURE, IRELAND FROM 17TH CENTURY During the 17th century society changed fundamentally. Catholic landowners were largely replaced by Church of Ireland Protestants (*see* PLANTATIONS, IRELAND; CROMWELLIAN LAND SETTLEMENT). By 1703 Catholics owned only 14% of land. The Catholic majority of the population (75%) became tenants or labourers on Protestant-owned lands. Catholic clergy assumed social leadership in Gaelic Irish communities. Scottish presbyterian immigrants in NE Ireland also formed a distinctive society (*see* PRESBYTERIAN SOCIETY, IRELAND).

In the 18th century Protestants (the PROTESTANT ASCENDANCY) monopolized politics, civil offices and most professions (*see* ANTI-CATHOLIC LEGISLATION, IRELAND, 1691 TO 1740s). Protestant middlemen often leased estates and sublet holdings to Catholic tenants, either substantial farmers (relatively few), small farmers living at subsistence level, or 'cottiers' (labourers with potato plots). Landless labourers were numerous. Some Catholics prospered as traders. Legal conditions were eased from the 1770s (*see* CATHOLIC RELIEF AND EMANCIPATION, IRELAND), but rapidly rising POPULATION increased poverty.

Population reduction caused by the GREAT FAMINE (1845–9) transformed social structure. Death and emigration reduced the extremely poor, and small landholdings became larger, making small farmers the mainstay of rural society.

The preservation of holdings for single heirs and livestock farming (requiring little labour) generated considerable EMIGRATION. In the N, a large urban working class developed, divided by religion and culture (*see* BELFAST; LONDONDERRY). Between 1885 and the 1920s tenants were enabled to become freeholders, thereby eliminating landlords (*see* LANDED SOCIETY, DECLINE OF, IRELAND).

After Partition, the mostly Catholic IRISH FREE STATE (founded 1922) remained dominated by small farmers until the 1960s, when industrial employment and urbanization increased. The growth of services from the 1980s provided extensive employment for women. NORTHERN IRELAND was created to preserve Protestant dominance. Catholics tended to be poorer and suffer greater unemployment. Resentments erupted in the TROUBLES (1968–90s). A subsequent PEACE PROCESS sought a fairer society. *See also* ETHNIC AND NATIONAL MINORITIES, IRELAND.

SOCIAL STRUCTURE, NORTH BRITAIN AND SCOTLAND From the Iron Age (*c*.700 BC onwards) tribes were basic units, possibly under kings (*see* IRON AGE TRIBES). Kingship emerges from the 6th century (*see* KINGSHIP, NORTH BRITAIN). Below kings were noblemen, who formed warbands, unfree clients owing food rents, and possibly slaves. After Scots and Picts were combined under a high-king (from *c*.842), governors called MORMAERS are found, and (by 11th century) royal agents called thanes (*see* THANAGES).

In the 12th–13th centuries immigrants received lordships (*see* NORMANS, IMPACT ON SCOTLAND) and intermarried with the native nobility. Ordinary people remained dependent tenants owing renders and LABOUR SERVICES. Lords dominated through BARONY courts and REGALITIES, and in the 16th century acquired Church and Crown lands (*see* FEUING; COMMENDATION OF ABBEYS, SCOTLAND). There were now about 2000 heads of noble families. (In the Lowlands, owner-occupiers similar to English yeomen-farmers were generally absent.) After the UNION OF ENGLAND AND SCOTLAND (1707) many magnates moved to England, while LAIRDS became locally more influential.

Between *c*.1760 and *c*.1815 Lowland society was transformed by concentration of land ownership and 'improvement', including replacement of small tenants by fewer tenant-farmers. (In 1872–3, 659 individuals owned 80% of Scotland.) Displaced people became labourers or migrated to industrializing TOWNS.

From the later 19th century landowners lost political power, though concentrated ownership survived; from the 1920s the LABOUR PARTY dominated urban areas. In the 1940s–60s councils moved slum populations to new towns. Declining heavy industry collapsed in the 1980s, increasing male unemployment. New 'service' businesses often preferred women.

In the HIGHLANDS, by the 15th century, society comprised CLAN chiefs and kindreds, middlemen 'gentry' (*see* TACKSMAN), ordinary clansmen and subtenants. From the early 18th chiefs removed tacksmen, and from the late 18th century cleared lands for sheep farming (*see* CLEARANCES). But CROFTING communities (part-time smallholders) were created, which survived in the 21st century. *See also* PEERAGE, SCOTTISH, TOWN SOCIETY, SCOTLAND; RURAL DEPOPULATION, SCOTLAND.

SOCIAL STRUCTURE, WALES According to laws of the 12th–14th centuries society comprised the king (Welsh *brenin*) or prince (*tywysog*); noble freemen (*uchelwyr*); bondmen (various ranks, including slaves). The hierarchy was probably long established.

Freemen originated probably as a military class serving kings (*see* MILITARY SERVICE, WALES, 5TH–13TH CENTURIES). They controlled most land, which was divided between heirs (partible inheritance; *see* TENURES, WALES). Bondmen (most males) held land from a lord and worked his estates. From the 12th century, increasing numbers of heirs made freemen poorer. Restrictions on bondmen declined, especially after 1349 (*see* BLACK DEATH, IMPACT ON WALES).

From the 15th century, freemen adopted primogeniture (succession by eldest son), creating a stable though poor GENTRY class which governed as JUSTICES OF THE PEACE (JPs) after the UNION OF WALES WITH ENGLAND (1536–43). Below them were wealthier farmers (Welsh *iwmon*), professionals (clergy, lawyers), small farmers, craftsmen, and cottagers and labourers (the majority). (Landed aristocrats were usually absentees.)

In the 18th century, shortage of male heirs reduced the number of gentry families, but average wealth increased as estates were joined through marriage, opening a gulf between gentry and other rural inhabitants. In 1872, 571 great landowners or squires owned 60% of land.

Industrial expansion in the 19th century created an enormous urban working class, mainly in the S (*see* INDUSTRY, WALES FROM 18TH CENTURY). Rural society weakened as people emigrated. In 1851 only 30% of the population depended on agriculture. Gentry lost power from 1889, when county councils assumed powers from JPs. Between 1914 and 1922 many estates were sold (*see* LANDED SOCIETY, DECLINE OF, WALES).

Society remained urban but became more complex in the late 20th century as mining in particular declined. By *c*.1985, service industries accounted for 60% of employment, including substantial numbers of women. *See also* FAMILY AND KINSHIP, WALES BEFORE/FROM 15TH CENTURY; ETHNIC AND NATIONAL MINORITIES, WALES.

SOCIETY FOR PROMOTING CHRISTIAN KNOWLEDGE An organization started in 1699 by clergy and laity of the Church of ENGLAND to encourage the spread of Christianity in England, Wales and overseas by promoting libraries, publications and foundation of schools. It also sought to combat immoral behaviour. In the 18th century the SPCK was the biggest publisher of religious literature in England, producing CATECHISMS, Bibles, PRAYER BOOKS and tracts. It encouraged the foundation of charity schools, and in Wales supported 'circulating schools' (*see* JONES, GRIFFITH). In 1811 the Society founded the National Society to continue its educational work. From the 1930s to 2006 it also ran bookshops. The Society remained an important publisher in the 21st century.

SOCIETY FOR THE PREVENTION OF CRUELTY TO ANIMALS

A society inaugurated on 16 June 1824 in London, on the initiative of Revd Arthur Broome (1779–1837), to enforce the 1822 Cruel Treatment of Cattle Act. Supporters included William WILBERFORCE. It appointed an inspector at Smithfield cattle market in London. The SPCA reflected objections to popular SPORTS (e.g., bear baiting, cock fighting) but accepted hunting. Similar societies were soon founded elsewhere in Great Britain and Ireland. Queen VICTORIA bestowed the prefix 'Royal' in 1840. The RSPCA and equivalent Scottish and Irish societies remained active in the 21st century. *See also* ANTI-VIVISECTIONISM.

SOCIETY FOR THE PROPAGATION OF THE GOSPEL IN FOREIGN PARTS

A MISSIONARY SOCIETY founded in 1701 by Thomas Bray (1656–1730) which sent Church of ENGLAND chaplains to N America, the West Indies and India. The 'SPG' concentrated primarily on the spiritual welfare of settlers until the 19th century when it sought to convert native peoples.

SOCIETY IN SCOTLAND FOR PROPAGATING CHRISTIAN KNOWLEDGE

An organization founded in 1708, with support from the Church of SCOTLAND, which initially aimed to 'Protestantize' and Anglicize the (Gaelic) HIGHLANDS and Islands through education. During the 18th century it was the main organization promoting education in the Highlands. By 1715 it had established 25 schools. Its work expanded between 1755 and 1784 with funds from the Board of Annexed Estates (*see* ANNEXING ACT). By 1795 there were 323 SSPCK schools in Scotland. The system continued until 1890, when it was wound up following the introduction of State education (1872). *See also* GAELIC LANGUAGE AND LITERATURE, NORTH BRITAIN AND SCOTLAND; EDUCATION, SCOTLAND.

SOCIETY PEOPLE *see* CAMERONIANS

SOKE Term derived from OE *socn* (meaning 'seeking'). In Anglo-Saxon England sokeland was land from which service was due. In the late Anglo-Saxon period (10th–11th centuries) and later, 'soke' tended to refer to a large and complex lordship, usually in eastern England, or to a special jurisdiction (e.g., an area within a town under different lordship).

SOLEMN LEAGUE AND COVENANT A political and religious agreement made at WESTMINSTER, England, on 17 Aug. 1643 (during the First CIVIL WAR), by the English Parliament and leaders of Scottish COVENANTERS. It provided for Scots to aid Parliamentary forces, and for Church reform in England after a Parliamentary victory. (Scots presumed that the Church of ENGLAND would become similar to the presbyterian Church of SCOTLAND.) The independence of national parliaments was also guaranteed and the authority of King CHARLES I, provided that he preserved the religious settlement. The alliance was confirmed in Scotland (at EDINBURGH) on 23 Nov. 1643.

Scots entered England on 19 Jan. 1644 and helped Oliver CROMWELL defeat Royalists at Marston Moor (Yorkshire, NE England) on 2 July 1644. But disagreement in England about Church reform disappointed Scots, many of whom broke the League in 1647 by transferring their allegiance to Charles (*see* ENGAGEMENT). *See also* WESTMINSTER ASSEMBLY; CLARENDON CODE.

SOLWAY MOSS, BATTLE OF *see* SCOTTISH–ENGLISH RELATIONS 1357 TO 1603

SOMERLED (Gaelic, Somhairle; fl. by 1130; d. 1164 at Renfrew, W Scotland). The lord of lands in NE Ireland and of Argyll (W Scotland), Somerled rebelled against King MALCOLM IV (1154) and won the central WESTERN ISLES for his sons from the king of MAN (1156). Reconciled to Malcolm in 1160, he died during a second rebellion. *See also* MACHETH, MALCOLM; MACDOUGAL, LORDS OF LORNE; MACDONALD, LORDS OF THE ISLES.

SOMERS, LORD (b. 4 March 1651 in Worcestershire, England; d. 26 April 1716 at North Mimms, Hertfordshire, England, aged 65). A WHIG barrister, John Somers acted as defence counsel for the bishops who opposed an order from King JAMES VII/II (June 1688; *see* SEVEN BISHOPS' CASE). An MP from 1689, he supported the replacement of James by WILLIAM III, helped to draft the Declaration of RIGHTS (1689), and was appointed to legal offices.

One of the WHIG JUNTO from the 1690s, Somers was appointed keeper of the great seal in 1693. In 1697 he became lord CHANCELLOR (April) and was created Lord Somers (Dec.), but was dismissed in 1700. Tories tried to impeach him, with colleagues, in 1701 for sealing the secret First Partition Treaty with foreign powers (1698). Though Queen ANNE disliked him, he was later appointed president of the Council at the request of the earl of GODOLPHIN (Nov. 1708; dismissed 1710).

SOMERSET, EDMUND DUKE OF *see* BEAUFORT, EDMUND

SOMERSET, EDWARD DUKE OF (b. *c.*1500, probably at Wolf Hall, Wiltshire, England; d. 22 Jan. 1552 at London, England, aged about 51). Edward Seymour was a brother-in-law of King HENRY VIII (brother of Henry's third wife, Jane Seymour, d. 1537). He was created Viscount Beauchamp (1536) and earl of Hertford (1537). After Henry's death, his executors set aside a planned regency council and appointed Hertford as protector of the realm and governor of his nephew EDWARD VI, a minor (31 Jan. 1547). Hertford was created duke of Somerset (17 Feb.).

Somerset sought to break the Scottish–French alliance and ally with Scotland. Having failed, he invaded Scotland (defeated Scots at Pinkie, 10 Sept. 1547). Within England he suppressed Catholic practices (e.g., Easter ceremonies, CHANTRIES) and introduced reforms, notably the 1549 PRAYER BOOK (causing the PRAYER-BOOK REBELLION). Heavy taxation provoked revolts.

Somerset was deposed by a coup. He was imprisoned and the protectorate was revoked (13 Oct. 1549). In 1550 he was released (6 Feb.) and restored to the PRIVY COUNCIL (10 April), then rearrested for treason (16 Oct. 1551). He was tried (1 Dec.), convicted of a felony, and executed. *See also* KETT'S REBELLION; SCOTTISH–ENGLISH RELATIONS 1357 TO 1603; NORTHUMBERLAND, JOHN DUKE OF.

SOMERSET, ROBERT EARL OF (b. probably 1585 or 1586 in Scotland; d. July 1645 at London, England, aged about 60). The Scotsman Robert Carr, in England from 1604, was the favourite of King JAMES VI/I from 1607 (knighted Dec.). From 1610 he was influential in government. He was created Viscount Rochester (1611), appointed a privy councillor (1612), and created earl of Somerset (Nov. 1613). In Dec. 1613 he married Frances Howard, countess of Essex, after her first marriage had been annulled.

The rise of the duke of BUCKINGHAM (from 1614) threatened Somerset's position. But he lost influence because of allegations surrounding his marriage. It was rumoured that Somerset's friend Sir Thomas Overbury had been murdered (Sept. 1613) to remove opposition to the marriage. The king ordered a trial. Somerset and his wife were convicted (25 May 1616) and imprisoned (until 1622). Both were pardoned.

SOMME, BATTLE OF THE A major offensive on the Western Front during WORLD WAR I. Between 1 July and 18 Nov. 1916, a series of British and French assaults on German defensive positions secured a maximum advance of 6 mi (9.6 km). Casualties were extremely heavy. The first day was the bloodiest in British Army history, when over 19,000 were killed and 57,000 injured. Overall about 100,000 of the British, Irish and imperial forces were killed and 300,000 injured. *See also* HAIG, DOUGLAS.

SOPER, DONALD (b. 31 Jan. 1903 at Wandsworth, London, England; d. 22 Dec. 1998 at Hampstead Garden Suburb, London, aged 95). A LABOUR PARTY member, socialist and Christian missionary from the 1920s, Soper regularly preached outdoors in LONDON from 1927. Ordained a Methodist minister (1929), he ran the West London Mission 1936–78, and in 1953 was president of the Methodist Conference. From 1957 he was prominent in the CAMPAIGN FOR NUCLEAR DISARMAMENT. Through radio and television in the 1950s–70s, Soper became one of Great Britain's best-known nonconformist clergy. He was created Lord Soper in 1965. *See also* METHODISM; NONCONFORMITY AND DISSENT, ENGLAND.

SOUND BITE A brief statement designed to make maximum impact on radio and television. Originally an American expression, it became popular in Great Britain in the late 1980s, when 'sound bite' journalism was blamed for reducing political debate to simplistic slogans.

SOUTH AFRICA A former British DOMINION in southern Africa, formed in 1910. CAPE COLONY, developed by the Dutch from 1652, came under British rule in 1795 (confirmed 1814). Boer inhabitants (Calvinist farmers) objected to English-language administration and the abolition of SLAVERY (1834), so many migrated farther N in the 1830s. But British immigration enlarged Cape Colony, and Great Britain annexed NATAL (to the NE) in 1843, and Griqualand West in 1871 after diamonds were discovered. Britain recognized the Boer republics of Transvaal (or South African Republic) and Orange Free State (1852–4), yet later annexed Transvaal (1877) and prosecuted the ZULU WAR, only to withdraw after conflict with the Boers (First Boer War, 1881).

After the discovery of gold in Transvaal (1886), British policy again became more aggressive, culminating in the JAMESON RAID (1894–5), (Second) BOER WAR (1899–1902) and conquest of the Boer republics (*see also* RHODES, CECIL; MILNER, ALFRED). In 1907 Britain granted internal self-government to Transvaal and Orange River Colony. They joined Cape Colony and Natal to form the federal Union of South Africa in 1910 (with dominion status).

Under Louis BOTHA and Jan SMUTS, South African forces fought for the British Empire in both WORLD WARS, and German South West Africa (modern Namibia) was acquired as a MANDATE (1919). Approx. population in 1921: 7,156,000 (of whom 1,539,000, about 21%, were white). The Statute of WESTMINSTER confirmed that South Africa was not subordinate to Britain (1931) but failed to satisfy Boer nationalism. As industrial development attracted black manual labourers into towns, discriminatory laws preserved white supremacy.

After the election victory of the National Party in 1948, 'apartheid' (racial segregation) became the governing ideology. The African National Congress, founded in 1912 to defend the black majority, was banned (1960). South Africa became a republic and left the Commonwealth in 1961. It rejoined the Commonwealth in 1994, following the dismantling of apartheid.

SOUTH AFRICA COMPANY see BRITISH SOUTH AFRICA COMPANY

SOUTHAMPTON A city and port in Hampshire, S England, by the Rivers Test and Itchen, with unusual daily double high-waters.

Hamwic, an international trading centre by the Itchen, flourished in the early 8th–9th centuries (see INE; WIC). It was succeeded in the 10th century by Hamtun, a fortified town by the Test (called Suthhamtun by 962), which became an important trans-shipment point in the NORMAN EMPIRE (1066–1204). Major exports until the 16th century were wool and cloth.

Southampton declined in the 14th century, revived in the 15th, and stagnated in the 16th–19th centuries. It became a resort and holiday town in the 18th–19th centuries. The port revived from the late 19th century, catering for trans-Atlantic and imperial shipping until the 1950s and for 'container' and cruise ships from the late 20th century. A college was upgraded as the University of Southampton in 1952; in 2005 Southampton Institute was granted university status (renamed as Southampton Solent University).

Est. popn: 1086, 1500; 1300, 2700; 1600, 4200; 1800, 8000; 1900, 105,000; 2000, 215,000.

SOUTHAMPTON PLOT In England, a conspiracy in late July 1415 to depose King HENRY V in favour of Edmund Mortimer, 5th earl of March and heir presumptive to the deposed RICHARD II, as Henry prepared to leave SOUTHAMPTON for France. It was led by Richard, earl of CAMBRIDGE (grandson of EDWARD III and Mortimer's former brother-in-law), and supported by Sir Thomas Grey, and Henry, Lord Scrope, nephew of Richard SCROPE, each aggrieved by the limited rewards for loyalty to the LANCASTRIANS. Mortimer revealed the plot. The conspirators were executed (Aug.). See also HUNDRED YEARS WAR; MORTIMER FAMILY.

SOUTH ASIANS IN GREAT BRITAIN Indian sailors, called 'lascars', settled from the mid 17th century. In the late 19th and early 20th centuries, Indian students and professionals lived in Britain. Following the partition of INDIA (1947), members of various communities migrated from the Indian subcontinent.

During the 1950s, Sikhs and Hindus from the Punjab (N India, E Pakistan), and mostly Hindus from Gujarat (W India) settled mainly in W London and towns in C England. Some had been displaced by partition, others were economic migrants. From the late 1950s, Kashmiri Pakistanis (Muslims) were recruited for textile mills in N England. The earliest settlers, usually young males, initiated 'chain migration' (immigration of male relatives, then other family members), which recreated Asian social structures in Britain. Some Kashmiris displaced by the Mangla Dam also moved to Britain. South Asian immigrants were usually from rural origins.

In 1967–8, several thousand South Asians fled to Britain from KENYA after being refused work permits; and in 1972, 28,000 arrived from UGANDA, expelled by President Idi Amin. Both groups originated mainly in Gujarat. After the independence of East Pakistan (as Bangladesh, 1971), considerable immigration resulted from the Sylhet region (NE Bangladesh).

South Asians became Britain's largest minority from the later 1970s, generally maintaining separate communities. Their economic fortunes diverged; e.g., Ugandan Asians in Leicester prospered whereas many Bangladeshis in London remained poor. From the 1980s communities increasingly expressed cultural identities in public, with individuals becoming prominent in political life (e.g., Conservative minister Baroness Warsi). Social tensions caused riots (e.g., in Bradford and elsewhere, 2001), and Muslim activism developed (see RUSHDIE AFFAIR). In 2011 there were about 3 million people of South Asian background (96% in England). See also ETHNIC AND NATIONAL MINORITIES, ENGLAND/SCOTLAND/WALES.

SOUTH AUSTRALIA A former British colony in Australia. The UK Parliament's South Australian Act of 1834 provided for controlled colonization of the territory (in SC Australia). It started at Adelaide in 1836. TRANSPORTATION was prohibited. South Australia became a CROWN COLONY in 1842, self-governing in 1856, and joined the Commonwealth of AUSTRALIA in 1901 (see AUSTRALIAN FEDERATION). Population then stood at 362,000. The economy relied on cattle and sheep.

SOUTH CAROLINA A former English colony in N America (British from 1707). The area was granted as part of 'Carolana' in 1629 but not developed (see NORTH CAROLINA). After King CHARLES II made a substitute grant in 1663 to eight proprietors, two counties were demarcated, with the southern one named Clarendon after the earl of CLARENDON (a proprietor). By 1689 it was called South Carolina.

Settlement began in 1670. The proprietors envisaged a hierarchical society of nobility and freeholders but were unable to implement it. South Carolina was governed by an appointed governor and council, and elected assembly. The Church of England was the State Church from 1706. Fur trading was important for early settlers.

In 1719 a rebellion drove out the governor, and in 1729 GEORGE II bought out most proprietors, creating a CROWN COLONY. A diversified PLANTATION economy developed, including rice cultivation, worked with African slave labour. Est. population 1770: 140,000. In 1775 mounting opposition to British policies caused the governor to dissolve the assembly and flee (15 Sept.). In 1776 South Carolina became a State of the USA and was heavily involved in the AMERICAN WAR OF INDEPENDENCE. See also NORTH AMERICAN COLONIES.

SOUTHERN IRELAND FROM 1922 In 1922, following conflict between republicans (SINN FÉIN, IRISH REPUBLICAN ARMY (IRA)) and the British government, the IRISH FREE STATE (IFS) was created (population 2.9 million, 90% Catholic). It comprised 26 of 32 Irish counties (for the remainder see NORTHERN IRELAND). The economy was largely agricultural. The IFS, though effectively independent, received informal DOMINION status under the British Crown. Many republicans rejected the settlement: civil war raged 1922–3 (see IRISH CIVIL WAR).

The new State was developed by the government of W.T. COSGRAVE, founder of CUMANN NA NGAEDHAEL (1923). Sinn Féin, the second largest party, abstained from the Dáil. In 1927 it was surpassed by FIANNA FÁIL, founded (1926) by republican Éamon DE VALERA, who served as head of government 1932–48, 1951–4, 1957–9. In the 1930s he pursued economic self-sufficiency and anti-British policies (see, e.g., ECONOMIC WAR). In 1937 a new CONSTITUTION renamed the State 'Ireland' (Irish, Éire), renamed the head of government 'taoiseach', recognized the 'special position' of the Catholic Church, and claimed jurisdiction over Northern Ireland. De Valera maintained neutrality during WORLD WAR II (1939–45).

On 18 April 1949, under Taoiseach John COSTELLO (of FINE GAEL), southern Ireland became a republic. During the 1950s the economy stagnated. Following a reappraisal of economy policy (see WHITAKER, T.K.), foreign investment was encouraged. By the late 1960s the majority of working people were employed outside agriculture, and in 1973 Ireland joined the EUROPEAN ECONOMIC COMMUNITY. But the 'oil crises' (price increases) of 1973 and 1979 caused economic difficulties. Irish politicians were also concerned about the TROUBLES in Northern Ireland.

From the 1990s politicians contributed to the PEACE PROCESS which considerably pacified Northern Ireland. Rapid economic expansion from the mid 1990s earned Ireland the nickname 'Celtic tiger', only for an international crisis (2008) to cause severe economic problems. Society became increasingly secularized. See also POLITICAL PARTIES, SOUTHERN IRELAND FROM 1922; CHURCH–STATE RELATIONS, SOUTHERN IRELAND FROM 1922.

SOUTHERN RHODESIA A former British territory in SE Africa. The BRITISH SOUTH AFRICA COMPANY of Cecil RHODES acquired mining rights S of the Zambezi River from local rulers in 1888, and in 1889 was authorized by a British royal charter to govern and develop the region. It sent settlers from 1890, and fought two Matabele Wars (1893–4, 1896–7). The area was named Rhodesia in 1895, and called Southern Rhodesia from 1898. White settlers, most of whom were farmers, rejected union with SOUTH AFRICA in 1922 and were granted limited RESPONSIBLE GOVERNMENT in Oct. 1923 as a CROWN COLONY. White immigration accelerated, while property qualifications prevented Africans from voting.

Between 1953 and 1963 Southern Rhodesia belonged to the FEDERATION OF RHODESIA AND NYASALAND. It renamed itself Rhodesia in 1964. The prime minister, Ian SMITH, under international pressure to increase political involvement by Africans, defied Great Britain by issuing a Unilateral Declaration of Independence (UDI) on 11 Nov. 1965. Most countries refused recognition, but the problem continued until 1979 (see RHODESIA PROBLEM). Rhodesia then briefly reverted to colony status before becoming the independent republic of Zimbabwe with majority rule (1980). Approx. population in 1921, 899,000 (of whom 33,600 were white); in 1979, 7,250,000 (including about 250,000 non-Africans). See also NORTHERN RHODESIA.

SOUTH SEA BUBBLE Financial speculation in Great Britain, in 1720, which collapsed with widespread consequences. The South Sea Company was founded in 1711 by Robert HARLEY as a financial corporation with some trading interests. It took over part of the NATIONAL DEBT by converting debt into company stock.

In 1720 the Company embarked on a scheme to convert £31 million (three-fifths) of the national debt. By driving up the value of its stock the Company could also sell stock at a profit. It further used stock to bribe politicians and courtiers, and an Act was passed to eliminate competitors. Feverish speculation ensued: £100 of stock was worth £128 in Jan., and over £1000 in July. Its value then crashed, ruining numerous wealthy men. The government was attacked. Ministers and King GEORGE I were defended by MP Robert WALPOLE, who was reappointed first lord of the Treasury (April 1721). See also SUNDERLAND, 3RD EARL OF.

SOVIET UNION, BRITISH RELATIONS WITH *see* RUSSIA AND USSR, ENGLISH AND BRITISH RELATIONS WITH

SPAIN, ENGLISH AND BRITISH RELATIONS WITH English kings had contacts with Spanish kingdoms from the 12th century. In 1489 HENRY VII allied with Spanish rulers Ferdinand and Isabella defensively against France (*see* MEDINA DEL CAMPO, TREATY OF), but from the mid 1520s to mid 1540s England favoured France, partly because Charles V (ruler of the HABSBURG EMPIRE, including Spain) opposed annulment of Henry VIII's first marriage (*see* GREAT MATTER). In 1554 MARY I married Philip (king of Spain from 1556, as Philip II, and ruler of the Netherlands), which led to war with France (1557–8) and loss of CALAIS.

Relations deteriorated from 1568, and war began in 1585 when ELIZABETH I assisted anti-Spanish rebels in the Netherlands (*see* ANGLO-SPANISH WAR). Spain attempted to invade England (*see* SPANISH ARMADA) and intervened in Ireland (*see* NINE YEARS WAR). JAMES VI/I of England made peace in 1604.

In the 17th century English rulers were mostly conciliatory, although war occurred in 1625 (*see* SPANISH MATCH) and Oliver CROMWELL took action in the Caribbean (1654–5) and captured JAMAICA (*see* WESTERN DESIGN); he also supported FRANCE against Spain (1656–8; *see* DUNKIRK). As Spain succumbed to French influence, despite the War of the SPANISH SUCCESSION, Spain and Great Britain were enemies during the 18th century, their conflicts sharpened by GIBRALTAR and MINORCA (ceded by Spain in 1713) and Spain's near monopoly in trade with LATIN AMERICA. During the NAPOLEONIC WARS, forces co-operated in the Peninsular campaign (1808–14). Content to see most of the Spanish Empire dissolved (1817–21), the British backed liberals internally and tried to limit French involvement.

Spain stayed neutral in WORLD WAR I (1914–18) and WORLD WAR II (1939–45). Britain promoted non-intervention in the SPANISH CIVIL WAR (1936–9). From the 1960s, Spain became popular with British holidaymakers. The Gibraltar dispute was eased by Spain's entry to the EUROPEAN ECONOMIC COMMUNITY (1986), though reignited by the UK's decision to leave (2016; *see* BREXIT).

SPANISH ARMADA The fleet sent by King Philip II of Spain in 1588 to facilitate conquest of England (during the reign of Queen ELIZABETH I); a major action during the ANGLO-SPANISH WAR. The Armada would establish control of the English Channel and escort Spanish troops, on barges, from Flanders to England.

The Armada of 122 ships was sighted by the English off the Scilly Isles on 19 July. It anchored near Calais (NE France) on 27 July, and in the night was attacked by English fireships. On 29 July the Spanish fleet was attacked again

near Gravelines (in Flanders). Many Spanish ships escaped northwards and circumnavigated the British Isles. About a third perished during the return journey to Spain. *See also* FOREIGN RELATIONS, ENGLAND 16TH CENTURY TO 1707.

SPANISH CIVIL WAR AND GREAT BRITAIN This conflict (July 1936–March 1939) between an elected left-wing Popular Front government with many anti-clerical supporters ('Republicans') and rebel 'Nationalists' with strong Catholic backing provoked divergent British responses. The government sought to prevent escalation of the conflict, resist communism, maintain freedom of commerce and shipping (especially in the Mediterranean), and avoid alienating Italy.

In Aug. 1936 Britain accepted a French proposal of non-intervention (with arms and military forces) and organized an international Non-Intervention Committee (operated from Sept.). In April 1937 the Committee oversaw the patrolling of ports and frontiers, but was unable to prevent military support for the Nationalists from Italy and Germany. In Sept. 1937 Britain arranged the Nyon Conference (in Switzerland) to counter Italian submarines in the Mediterranean with naval patrols. Britain made a separate treaty with Italy in April 1938, tacitly accepting Italian involvement in Spain, and later promoted withdrawal of foreign forces. Britain recognized the victorious Nationalists on 27 Feb. 1939.

Britain's LABOUR PARTY and TRADES UNION CONGRESS, fearful of communist influence in Spain, initially supported the non-intervention policy, but repudiated it in 1937. A popular 'Aid Spain' movement raised funds for humanitarian purposes (e.g., medical aid, food), and temporary refuge was provided in 1937 for 3800 Basque children. About 2500 Britons joined the volunteer International Brigades on the Republican side, mostly manual workers but including famous writers (e.g., W.H. AUDEN, George ORWELL). Afterwards about 200 adult refugees settled in Britain. *See also* SPAIN, ENGLISH AND BRITISH RELATIONS WITH.

SPANISH FLU Popular name for the deadly worldwide influenza pandemic of 1918–19, which overlapped the end of WORLD WAR I and unrest in Ireland (*see* IRISH INDEPENDENCE, WAR OF). It was so called because it was thought to have originated in (neutral) Spain, but was only first reported there because of lack of press censorship. The origin is unknown, and the flu strain may have arisen in 1915. An outbreak occurred in 1917 at the British military training camp at Étaples, N France.

Great Britain was affected in three waves of varying impact: June–Sept. 1918, Sept. 1918–Jan. 1919 (the most virulent phase), Jan.–May 1919. They resulted in respectively about 10%, 64% and 26% of total deaths. The pattern was roughly similar in Ireland. The flu affected 18 to 40-year-olds most severely. Est. deaths: England and Wales, 151,000; Scotland, 15,500; Ireland, 18,000.

SPANISH MATCH A project in the reign of King JAMES VI/I for a marriage alliance of England with Spain. Under discussion by 1611, it sought the marriage of Prince HENRY to Maria, daughter of Philip III (king of Spain 1598–1621). Negotiations were complicated for England by popular hostility to Catholic Spain. From 1612 Prince Charles was the English suitor. From 1620 James also hoped that the Spanish might persuade the Habsburg Holy Roman Emperor to restore his deposed son-in-law Frederick to rule in the Palatinate (in Germany).

Accompanied by the duke of BUCKINGHAM, Charles visited Spain in 1623, spending March–Aug. in Madrid. Their failure to achieve progress with Philip IV over the marriage or the Palatinate led to war against Spain in 1625 (*see* CHARLES I). A French marriage was agreed in Dec. 1624: *see* HENRIETTA MARIA. *See also* SPAIN, ENGLISH AND BRITISH RELATIONS WITH.

SPANISH SUCCESSION, WAR OF THE Conflict in Europe, 1702–13, between the 'Grand Alliance' (Dutch Republic, England, Habsburg Empire) and France (ruled by Louis XIV), Spain, and some German states, over the future of Spain and its empire. King Charles II of Spain died childless in 1700 bequeathing his territories to Philip of Anjou of France, grandson of Louis XIV, who became King Philip V. Louis supported Philip's accession, thereby rejecting a secret agreement (1699) with other powers for division of Spanish territories. The Dutch and English opposed French dominance in Europe, and feared loss of trade with Spanish America. Louis recognized the Stuart claimant to the English throne as king (Sept. 1701).

The Alliance was formed on 27 Aug. 1701 by William of Orange, stadholder (lieutenant) of the Dutch Republic and king of England (WILLIAM III). It declared war against France on 4 May 1702. (ANNE was now ruler of England.) From 1703 to 1711 the duke of MARLBOROUGH led allied forces to victories in Continental Europe. His victory at Blenheim (2 Aug. 1704) prevented a Franco-Bavarian drive against Vienna, while victories at Ramilles (12 May 1706), Oudenarde (30 July 1708) and Malplaquet (31 Aug. 1709) forced back the French in the Spanish Netherlands.

English forces also fought in Spain, seeking to oust King Philip. A landing was attempted at Cádiz (1702), and in 1703 Portugal joined the Alliance. In 1704 England captured GIBRALTAR and controlled part of the Spanish coast; and allied forces were involved in Spain 1705–13. In 1708 England captured the strategic island of MINORCA. English forces campaigned in Spain in 1710.

In England the war was supported by WHIGS, while TORIES argued for generally cheaper naval warfare in preference to expensive land campaigns. England's Tory-dominated ministry effectively withdrew from the war in May 1712. Most of the allies agreed peace terms at UTRECHT (1713–15). *See also* GODOLPHIN, EARL OF; BOLINGBROKE, VISCOUNT; FRANCE, ENGLISH AND BRITISH RELATIONS WITH; BALANCE OF POWER.

SPECIAL IRISH BRANCH In England, a unit of the (London) Metropolitan Police formed in 1883 in response to Fenian bombing (*see* IRISH REPUBLICAN BROTHERHOOD). Renamed 'Special Branch' in 1887, its remit was expanded to include political threats to British society and values. Other UK forces also established a Special Branch. In 2006 the Metropolitan force was merged into a new Counter Terrorism Command. *See also* POLICE, ENGLAND.

SPECIAL RELATIONSHIP Name for the close political understanding that supposedly exists between Great Britain and the USA on the basis of historical ties and a common language. Used from 1945 by the British politician Winston CHURCHILL to characterize co-operation in WORLD WAR II, it was later invoked notably by Harold Macmillan (British prime minister 1956–63), Margaret THATCHER (prime minister 1979–90) and George W. Bush (US president 2001–9, for his alliance with Tony BLAIR). The reality of the 'special relationship' is debatable because the warmth of Anglo-American relations has fluctuated considerably. *See also* UNITED STATES OF AMERICA, BRITISH RELATIONS WITH.

SPENCE AFFAIR An episode in British politics in 2000 when Chancellor of the Exchequer Gordon BROWN sought to assert himself as a champion of trade unionists against the privileged middle class (countering the inclusive approach of Tony BLAIR). On 25 May, during a lunch-time speech at the TRADES UNION CONGRESS, Brown attacked Magdalen College at OXFORD University for denying a place for medicine to Laura Spence, an applicant from a COMPREHENSIVE school in NE England. Brown claimed she had 'the best A-level qualifications' but was excluded by a prejudiced admissions system reminiscent of 'the old boy network'. It was later revealed that Spence had not yet taken 'A levels', and was one of 22 candidates for five places. The accepted candidates included two from comprehensive schools and three from ethnic minorities. Brown refused to apologize for his errors.

SPENCER, HERBERT (b. 27 April 1820 at Derby, Derbyshire, England; d. 8 Dec. 1903 at Brighton, East Sussex, England, aged 83). A self-educated philosopher, Spencer from the 1850s wrote a multi-volume synthesis about the natural world and human social development heavily influenced by evolutionary ideas (published 1860s–90s).

He adopted the mechanism of natural selection proposed by Charles DARWIN (1859), coining the phrase 'survival of the fittest' (1864). Spencer viewed society as a self-regulating organism, and envisaged a limited role for the State. He opposed SOCIALISM and IMPERIALISM. His ideas became influential in Europe and N America. *See also* EVOLUTION.

SPENSER, EDMUND (b. probably in 1552 at London, England; d. 13 Jan. 1599 at Westminster, Middlesex, England, aged about 46). Poet and colonizer. In 1580, after recklessly satirizing the English royal court, Spenser moved to Ireland as secretary to the CHIEF GOVERNOR (to 1582). As a clerk in the Court of CHANCERY (1581–8), he acquired a castle and land in MUNSTER (at Kilcolman, Co. Cork).

In 1589 Walter RALEGH encouraged Spenser to visit London and publish part of his masterwork *The Faerie Queene*, a verse epic honouring Queen ELIZABETH I. Probably after returning to Ireland (1591) he wrote *A Present View of the State of Ireland*, advocating methods for 'civilizing' the Gaelic Irish, which was circulated in manuscript (published 1633). He fled to England after his castle was burned during a rising (1598). *See also* ENGLISH LITERATURE, ENGLAND; ANGLICIZATION, IRELAND.

SPIN DOCTOR Nickname for a public relations expert employed by a political party or politician to put the most favourable construction on events. This American expression, relating to the spin which a baseball pitcher gives to a ball, became familiar in British politics in the 1990s. *See also* MANDELSON, PETER; CAMPBELL, ALASTAIR.

SPIRITUALISM The belief that spirits of the dead can communicate with the human world, particularly through mediums. Organized spiritualism originated in the USA after Kate Fox in New York State allegedly responded to a murder victim's spirit in 1848. She and her sister operated as mediums in the USA and England. In 1853 a spiritualist church was founded in England (at Keighley, Yorkshire) and the movement spread. Spiritualism was strong during and after WORLD WAR I (1914–18). Notable adherents included the author Arthur Conan Doyle (1859–1930). Spiritualist churches and associations continued in Great Britain and Ireland in the 21st century.

SPLENDID ISOLATION Term descriptive of Great Britain's international position in the late 19th century. Unexpected tensions with GERMANY and the USA led Joseph CHAMBERLAIN, the British colonial secretary, to declare on 21 Jan. 1896 that 'the great mother-Empire stood splendidly isolated' (quoting Canadian politician G.E. Foster). The expression was much used 1896–1902 both to promote imperial unity and (ironically) to advocate alliances. Historians often employ it to denote the policy of

freedom of action pursued by Lord SALISBURY which was ended by the ANGLO-JAPANESE ALLIANCE (1902).

SPORT, ENGLAND Individual, group and animal sports are recorded by the 14th century. Usually pursued at HOLIDAY times, they included wrestling, boxing, football, animal baiting (bulls, bears, badgers), cock fighting and horse racing. Football was widespread, often played in open country by large groups. Cricket developed in SE England during the 16th–17th centuries (a ground is mentioned in 1668) and was considered 'genteel'; by the 19th century some players were paid. Regular meetings for HORSE RACING were held widely from the later 17th century.

From the late 18th century, animal and other 'rough' sports were attacked by reformers (influenced by EVANGELICALISM). Bull baiting was suppressed under the 1822 Cruel Treatment of Cattle Act, and bear baiting, bull running and cock fighting under the 1835 Cruelty to Animals Act. Aristocratic support protected horse racing and some prize fighting.

From the 1830s, team sports using pitches and following rules, and athletics, were developed in PUBLIC SCHOOLS and by middle-class clubs, mainly in southern England. 'Governing bodies' were founded which standardized rules (e.g., 1863, Football Association; 1871, Rugby Union). During the 1860s–70s codified sports spread through northern England, including industrial towns, facilitated by RAILWAYS and Saturday-afternoon holidays.

Professional male team sports, funded by admission charges, were started in the 1840s–50s by touring cricket teams; a county championship, involving paid players, began in 1873. In 1888 leading football clubs in N and Midland England formed the Football League, which became completely professional. The Northern Rugby Football League (1895) built up professional rugby (with different rules from amateur 'rugby union'). Tennis and golf became popular middle-class amateur sports.

Football, rugby and cricket remained the main spectator sports, together with horse racing and boxing (rugby union stayed amateur until 1995). Hooliganism damaged football in the 1970s–80s but creation of an élite Premier League (1992), televised by satellite, turned leading footballers into wealthy celebrities. Amateur sports continued to flourish. *See also* SABBATARIANISM; BICYCLES AND BICYCLE INDUSTRIES; OLYMPIC GAMES; HILLSBOROUGH DISASTER.

SPORT, IRELAND Hurling, a ball-and-stick (hurley) game between teams, is recorded from the 7th century. Football and horse racing are mentioned from the 14th century. In 1752 the first 'steeplechase' (long-distance horse race across obstacles) in the British Isles was held in Co. Cork. Organized horse racing soon became popular (regulated from 1790 by Turf Club).

In the 19th century 'English' sports became prevalent, played by both Anglo-Irish and Gaelic Irish. Cricket clubs were formed from the 1820s, rugby clubs from 1854 (starting at Trinity College, DUBLIN), soccer clubs from the 1860s (starting in ULSTER). An Irish Football Association (for soccer) was formed in BELFAST in 1880.

In 1884, fearing that hurling was moribund, Michael Cusack founded the Gaelic Athletic Association (GAA) to revive it and promote athletics. It produced rules for hurling and Gaelic football, organized local clubs, instituted national championships (1887), and developed Croke Park, Dublin, as a national stadium (from 1913). The GAA flourished within a broader nationalist GAELIC REVIVAL. In 1902 it banned members from involvement with 'foreign games'. A hurling game for women, camogie, was created (1903) and run separately (from 1905).

After the PARTITION OF IRELAND (1921), sports organization continued mostly on an all-Ireland basis. The main exception was soccer: a separate association and league were formed in the IRISH FREE STATE (1922), and a national team (1924). Two all-Ireland teams co-existed until separate jurisdictions were formally instituted (1954). While Gaelic games flourished, Catholics also supported rugby from the 1930s, and in 2000 soccer was the largest sport by participation. The GAA removed its prohibition against 'foreign games' in 1971, and from 2000 allowed membership by security personnel in NORTHERN IRELAND. Horse breeding, training and racing became significant activities, centred on The Curragh (Co. Kildare) – in 2015 there were 26 racecourses. In the 21st century sport continued to be largely an amateur activity.

SPORT, SCOTLAND Several sports are long established. Shinty (Gaelic *camanachd*), a hockey-like game played mainly in the (Gaelic) HIGHLANDS, was imported from Ireland, possibly by the 7th century. Its rules were codified by the Camanachd Association, founded 1893. Curling, in which stones are slid along ice, developed in the Lowlands and from 1838 was organized by the Caledonian Curling Club ('Royal' from 1843). From the 20th century it was played on indoor rinks. Until the 19th century ball-carrying games were common in border towns; a few survived in the 21st century.

Scotland's most successful historical game, golf, is first recorded in 1457 (probably imported from the Low Countries). Clubs were established from the 18th century (Honorable Company of Edinburgh, 1744; St Andrews Club, 1754, renamed 'Royal and Ancient', 1834). The first Open Championship was held in 1860 (at Prestwick, Ayrshire). During the 19th century golf spread to England and then worldwide.

Other sports were adopted from England. Cricket was probably imported by English soldiers in the early 18th century. Clubs and leagues were formed in the 19th century. Rugby football was played from the late 1850s by independent schools, whose old boys later founded clubs. It also became popular in border towns. The first Scotland–England match took place in 1871. From 1873 Rugby was organized by the Scottish Football Union (renamed Scottish Rugby Union 1924). Both cricket and rugby remained amateur sports.

Association football, played from the 1860s, became the most popular sport. Clubs were formed from 1867 (Queen's Park, Glasgow), followed by the Scottish Football Association in 1873. The first match against England was played in 1872. A Scottish Football League was founded in 1890 and was professional from 1893. Some clubs became bases for sectarian rivalry, most notably (mainly Catholic) Celtic and (mainly Protestant) Rangers in Glasgow (the 'Old Firm'). *See also* HIGHLAND GATHERINGS.

SPORT, WALES Until the early 19th century Wales had several indigenous sports, including *bando*, a form of hockey, and *cnapan*, long-distance football; most were suppressed by Methodists (*see* METHODIST REVIVAL, WALES; CALVINISTIC METHODISTS). Fighting and boxing survived in industrial areas; in the early 20th century Wales produced several boxing world champions, including the flyweight Jimmy Wilde (1892–1969; champion 1916–23).

English team games spread into Wales in the 1850s–60s, including rugby football (introduced via St David's College, Lampeter), association football or soccer (introduced from NW England and popular in the N), and cricket (first played in MONMOUTHSHIRE in 1853). Rugby was taken up by industrial workers in the S, especially coalminers, and became closely associated with Wales. The Welsh Rugby Union was founded in 1881 and the game had successful eras in 1900–11 and 1970–9. Open professionalization of rugby developed from 1995.

SPOTTISWOODE, JOHN (b. 1565 at Mid Calder, SE Scotland; d. 26 Nov. 1639 at London, England, aged about 74). As a parish minister from 1583, Spottiswoode supported presbyterianism, but after becoming close to King JAMES VI he accepted appointment (1603) as archbishop of GLASGOW (translated to ST ANDREWS in 1615). He promoted James's ecclesiastical policy; e.g., securing approval of the FIVE ARTICLES OF PERTH. As CHANCELLOR (1635–8), he supported the introduction of a Scottish Prayer Book by CHARLES I. Spottiswoode fled to England after the REVOLT OF 1637 and was deposed by the GLASGOW ASSEMBLY (4 Dec. 1638).

***SPYCATCHER* AFFAIR** Attempts by the British government, led by Margaret THATCHER, in 1985–8 to ban publication in England and elsewhere of *Spycatcher*, the memoirs of former MI5 intelligence agent Peter Wright (1916–95). The government claimed that the book breached security and harmed the national interest. The affair made a mockery of the official secrecy that supposedly protected the government's intelligence services. The first editions of *Spycatcher* appeared in 1987. *See also* SECRET SERVICES, UNITED KINGDOM.

SQUADRONE VOLANTE (Italian, meaning 'Flying Squadron'). Name applied to a group of nobles in the Scottish PARLIAMENT Oct. 1706–Jan. 1707. Derived from the NEW PARTY, the *Squadrone* moved from opposing to supporting the UNION OF ENGLAND AND SCOTLAND, probably lured by a promise of involvement in disbursing the EQUIVALENT. This weakened the COUNTRY PARTY and ensured the acceptance of the treaty of Union (ratified 16 Jan. 1707). A few members sat in the British House of Commons from 1707 to 1715.

SRI LANKA *see* CEYLON

STAFFORDSHIRE HOARD The largest known collection of treasure from Anglo-Saxon England, containing around 4000 fragments of gold, silver and garnet from about 700 objects; so called because it was found buried in the countryside of Staffordshire in England's W Midlands. Discovered in 2009 by a metal detectorist, the hoard dates from the 6th and 7th centuries and was buried between 650 and 675. Its location was then within the kingdom of MERCIA.

The hoard has a martial character, numerous items being derived from swords (e.g., 86 pommels), although blades were absent. Other finds include parts of a helmet and Christian artefacts (e.g., crosses). The collection's nature is uncertain: suggestions include an assemblage of war spoils or treasure that belonged to Mercian kings. There is no obvious motive for its burial. *See also* KINGSHIP, ANGLO-SAXON.

STAIR, VISCOUNT (b. May 1619 at Drummurchie, W Scotland; d. 29 Nov. 1695 at Edinburgh, SE Scotland, aged 76). After fighting against King CHARLES I in the Wars of the COVENANT (1639–41) and teaching at GLASGOW University (1641–7), James Dalrymple became an advocate (1648). He was a commissioner of justice (judge) from 1657, during the English occupation, and a lord of SESSION (1660) and court president (1671) under CHARLES II. In 1681 he effectively resigned rather than take the Test Act (acknowledging the king as head of the Church). In 1684 he withdrew to the Dutch Republic, returning with William of Orange (*see* WILLIAM III), who restored him as court president (1689) and created him Viscount Stair (1690). His *Institutions of the Laws of Scotland* (published 1681) systematized Scottish law,

demonstrating the sources and principles from which it was derived. *See also* LAW, SCOTLAND.

STAMFORD BRIDGE, BATTLE OF Fought at Stamford Bridge, near YORK (NE England), on 25 September 1066. An English army led by King HAROLD II defeated Norwegians led by King Harald Hardrada, a claimant to the English kingship. Harald was killed. Three or four days later WILLIAM, duke of NORMANDY, landed in SE England to claim the kingship. *See also* HASTINGS, BATTLE OF.

STANDARD, BATTLE OF THE Fought N of Northallerton (NE England) on 22 August 1138. Scots under King DAVID I, invading England to support his niece MATILDA (claimant to the English throne), were defeated by English forces. The battle was so called from a mast hung with religious banners which accompanied the English. Despite the English victory, King STEPHEN ceded the earldom of Northumbria (NE England) to David's son Henry (April 1139). *See also* ANARCHY; SCOTTISH–ENGLISH RELATIONS BEFORE 1290.

STANDARD OF LIVING DEBATE, INDUSTRIAL REVOLUTION A controversy about whether the INDUSTRIAL REVOLUTION and large-scale urbanization improved or diminished living standards for working people, focusing on England 1780–1850. Contradictory and fragmentary statistical information has provided scope and support for opposing perspectives.

Optimists have conceded that restrictions on overseas trade during the FRENCH REVOLUTIONARY AND NAPOLEONIC WARS (1793–1815) caused problems, but argue that average real wages and living standards rose from 1815. However, they accept that the experience of regions and occupations varied.

Pessimists have emphasized these variables, drawing attention for example to the pauperization of domestic handloom weavers in N England created by more efficient factory-based weaving machinery. They have also invoked qualitative factors, such as the imposition of greater discipline in the organization of work and poor housing in industrial towns. *See also* FACTORY; COTTON INDUSTRY, ENGLAND/SCOTLAND; PUBLIC HEALTH ACTS.

STANDING ARMY, ENGLAND After the RESTORATION, King CHARLES II created the first royal standing Army for his security (1660–2). It initially comprised about 6000 men, who were known as 'guards and garrisons'. Its existence was not recognized by Parliament, and it caused concern for about 30 years because standing armies were equated with ABSOLUTISM. Fear increased when JAMES VII/ II (from 1685) rapidly increased the Army to about 35,000 troops and appointed numerous Catholic officers.

In 1689, after James's fall, the keeping of an army without parliamentary consent was declared illegal in the Bill of RIGHTS. Parliament recognized the Army in the Mutiny Act (also 1689), which provided statutory authority for military discipline and was renewed annually. *See also* ARMY, ENGLISH AND BRITISH; GLORIOUS REVOLUTION.

STANHOPE, EARL (b. 1673 at Paris, France; d. 5 Feb. 1721 at Westminster, Middlesex, England, aged about 48). A soldier, diplomat and MP, James Stanhope intermittently fought in Spain from 1702 (commander-in-chief from 1708). Captured at Brihuega in 1710, he returned to Great Britain in 1712 (*see* SPANISH SUCCESSION, WAR OF THE).

Stanhope quickly became a leading WHIG politician. After the accession of the Hanoverian King GEORGE I (1714) he was appointed SECRETARY OF STATE (southern). When some ministers went into opposition in 1717, Stanhope became first lord of the Treasury, effectively chief minister. He was secretary of state (northern) 1718–21, and was created Viscount Stanhope (1717) and earl (1718).

Stanhope sought peace and international acceptance of the HANOVERIAN SUCCESSION by creating alliances: the 'Triple Alliance' in 1716–17 (with France and the Dutch Republic), the 'Quadruple Alliance' in 1718 (addition of Austrian Empire). Britain aided the Empire by joining war against Spain (1718–20). Stanhope also tackled rivalries among Baltic powers (peace settlement, 1720). At home he advanced toleration for DISSENTERS by repealing the OCCASIONAL CONFORMITY and Schism Acts (1719). *See also* SUNDERLAND, 3RD EARL OF; WALPOLE, ROBERT.

STANLEY FAMILY An English noble family, prominent in Lancashire (NW England) from the late 14th century. Sir John Stanley (d. 1414) served as chief governor of Ireland (1389–91, 1399–1401), and in 1406 was granted the Isle of MAN by King HENRY IV. He and his male heirs were 'lords of Man' until 1736.

John's grandson Thomas Stanley (d. 1459) was created Lord Stanley (1456). His son, Thomas, Lord Stanley (*c*.1435–1504), allegedly placed the crown on Henry Tudor's head at BOSWORTH. He was created earl of Derby (1485).

In the 19th century Edward Stanley became prime minister, and his son Edward held senior government offices (*see* DERBY, 14TH/15TH EARLS OF). The 17th earl (Edward Stanley, 1865–1948) organized the 'Derby Scheme' of voluntary recruitment for the British Army in 1915 (*see* WORLD WAR I, BRITISH ARMY). The 'Derby' horse race, run at Epsom (Surrey), was founded in 1780 with support from the 12th earl (Edward Smith-Stanley, 1752–1834); *see* HORSE RACING, BRITAIN.

STANLEY LETTER In Oct. 1831 Edward Stanley, CHIEF SECRETARY FOR IRELAND, outlined for the duke of Leinster a scheme for non-denominational elementary education in Ireland. Subsequently implemented, and known as NATIONAL EDUCATION, it developed effectively into a denominational system. *See also* EDUCATION, IRELAND; DERBY, 14TH EARL OF.

STANSGATE, 2ND VISCOUNT *see* BENN, TONY

STAPLE A compulsory market for exports, usually at a specified place, intended to protect trade and associated tax revenues (from OFr. *estaple*, meaning 'market'). The English Crown instituted a staple mainly for wool in 1313 at St-Omer, Flanders (now in France). Staples were located at various towns in the Low Countries, or in England, Wales and Ireland, until 1363 when CALAIS (English-held town in NE France) became the normal location of the staple. After Calais was lost (1558), the staple was moved (1561) to Bruges (Flanders, in Spanish Netherlands). It remained there, except for 1569–74 (in Hamburg, N Germany), until wool exports were prohibited in 1614.

The Scottish Crown established a staple by the 1340s at Bruges (Flanders). It was moved in 1467 to Middelburg on Walcheren Island in Zeeland (modern Netherlands), then to nearby Veere in 1507 or 1508. Though of little importance by the 17th century, it continued until 1799. *See also* WOOL TRADE, ENGLAND; OVERSEAS TRADING COMPANIES.

STAR CHAMBER In England, name of a royal court which developed from *c*.1515 under Thomas WOLSEY (in reign of King HENRY VIII) as a continuation and expansion of the judicial business of the king's COUNCIL. It was so called because it met in a room in Westminster Palace which had a ceiling decorated with stars. Its business included misdemeanours by royal officers, riot and forgery. It used English and applied EQUITY. During the reign of CHARLES I (from 1625) it became identified with the enforcement of unpopular royal policies, and was abolished in July 1641 as a concession to Parliamentary opponents. *See also* PREROGATIVE COURTS; WESTMINSTER.

STATISTICAL ACCOUNTS Three compilations of local social and economic data about Scotland. The First, or Old, Statistical Account, produced by Sir John Sinclair of Ulbster (Caithness) in the 1790s, used information supplied by Church of Scotland ministers. The Second, or New, Statistical Account (published 1845) updated the First. The Third, from the 1940s–60s, was unsatisfactory for not giving a 'snapshot' view. Sinclair's work was a facet of the Scottish ENLIGHTENMENT.

STATUTE Written law produced by a legislative body. In England the term is applied to some laws issued by king and COUNCIL in the 13th century, but mainly to laws enacted by king and PARLIAMENT. Early statutes were formulated in response to petitions and complaints. The earliest significant body of statutes were the LEGAL REFORMS of King Edward I (1275–90), but collections have usually started with MAGNA CARTA (1225 version). Statutes were accepted by courts as overriding COMMON LAW custom and ROYAL PREROGATIVE by the mid 14th century. By the early 15th century Parliament was considered the sole source of statutes.

English statutes were also applied in Wales and sometimes Ireland. The separate PARLIAMENTS of Ireland and Scotland also enacted statutes. *See also* ASSIZE; PARLIAMENTARY PETITIONS; LAW, ENGLAND FROM 1066.

STEAD, W.T. (b. 5 July 1849 at Embleton, Northumberland, England; d. 15 April 1912 in N Atlantic, aged 62). A journalist in NE England from the 1860s, William Thomas Stead supported radical causes (e.g., repeal of the CONTAGIOUS DISEASES ACTS). He moved to London in 1880 to join the *Pall Mall Gazette*, and, as editor, in 1885 was briefly imprisoned after breaking the law to expose child prostitution; but this helped to bring about the Criminal Law Amendment Act (*see* PURITY MOVEMENT). In 1890 he founded the *Review of Reviews*. He drowned in the sinking of the *TITANIC* liner.

STEELBOYS A rural protest movement of presbyterians in Ulster (N Ireland) which developed *c*.1769 in protest against high fines for renewal of leases on Lord Donegall's estates (Co. Antrim). The self-styled Steelboys extended their campaign by protesting against TITHES and high rents, and demanding regulation of corn and potato prices (to 1772). *See also* AGRICULTURE, IRELAND 17TH CENTURY TO 1921.

STEPHEN (b. *c*.1096 in Blois, France; d. 25 Oct. 1154 at Dover, Kent, England, aged about 58). A grandson of WILLIAM I through William's daughter Adela, Stephen was raised by HENRY I (uncle), king of England and duke of NORMANDY. When Henry designated MATILDA as his successor, Stephen swore support (1127). But after Henry's death (1 Dec. 1135), Stephen was accepted as ruler (crowned king 22 Dec.).

Support in England ebbed from 1138: rebellions occurred in SW England, and ROBERT OF GLOUCESTER withdrew allegiance. The arrest of three bishops (June 1139) antagonized the Church. From Sept. Stephen's rule was contested by MATILDA and Robert. Stephen was captured at LINCOLN (E England) on 2 Feb. 1141 and imprisoned. His brother Bishop HENRY OF BLOIS defected, and a legatine council proclaimed Matilda 'Lady of the English' (8 April). Stephen's queen, also Matilda, obtained his release (1 Nov.) and Stephen re-established extensive authority, especially in SE England.

Neither side could win (though Geoffrey of Anjou conquered Normandy 1142–4). After Robert of Gloucester died (1147) and Matilda withdrew (1148), Matilda's son Henry challenged Stephen's rule. After the deaths of Stephen's queen (May 1152) and son Eustace (Aug. 1153), Stephen accepted Henry as successor (Nov.–Dec.). Stephen died soon afterwards. *See also* ANARCHY; DAVID I; HENRY II.

STEPHEN, LESLIE (b. 28 Nov. 1832 at Kensington, Middlesex, England; d. 22 Feb. 1904 at Kensington, London, England, aged 71). From an evangelical background (a CLAPHAM SECT family), Stephen became a Church of England clergyman but developed doubts about Christian doctrine. From 1864 he worked as a journalist (resigned his religious orders 1870). Stephen helped to make agnosticism (scepticism about religion) respectable, publishing *An Agnostic's Apology* (1869). His major work *English Thought in the Eighteenth Century* (1876–81) was a study of rationalism. From 1882 he edited the multi-volume *Dictionary of National Biography*. He was the father of the novelist Virginia Woolf (*see* BLOOMSBURY GROUP).

STEPHENS, JAMES (b. 1824 at Kilkenny, Co. Kilkenny, Ireland; d. 29 March 1901 at Blackrock, Co. Dublin, Ireland, aged 76 or 77). An engineer, Stephens participated in Young Ireland's unsuccessful REBELLION OF 1848 and afterwards escaped abroad (returned 1856).

Stephens aspired to organize a rising in Ireland using Irish-American money. In March 1858, after obtaining American funds, he founded a secret society in Ireland, later known as the IRISH REPUBLICAN BROTHERHOOD. He then helped to reorganize the American FENIAN BROTHERHOOD. In 1865 he finally planned to mount a rising, but was arrested (11 Nov.). After escaping to the USA (March 1866), he promised (Oct.) to instigate another rising but cancelled his plans (Dec.). He was deposed as IRB leader (21 Dec.). He lived mainly in France from 1867, in Ireland from 1891. *See also* O'MAHONY, JOHN.

STEPHENSON, GEORGE (b. 9 June 1781 at Wylam, Northumberland, England; d. 12 Aug. 1848 at Tapton House, Derbyshire, England, aged 67). From a poor family, Stephenson became familiar with colliery steam engines, and from 1811 maintained machinery for several collieries. He designed a safety lamp for miners (1815), though his achievement was overshadowed by the lamp invented by Humphry DAVY. In 1815–18 Stephenson improved Killingworth waggonway (Northumberland) by replacing wooden rails with cast-iron edge-rails and building an improved steam locomotive, demonstrating that locomotives could operate on smooth iron rails.

From 1821 Stephenson developed the Stockton and Darlington Railway (opened 1825), the first to convey passengers using a steam locomotive (*Locomotion No. 1*, designed by son Robert). Also engineer to the Liverpool and Manchester Railway from 1824, Stephenson won its locomotive competition (1829) with *Rocket*. (The railway opened in 1830.) Stephenson engineered railways around the English Midlands and in Continental Europe, sometimes assisted by his son Robert (1803–59) and nephew George Robert (1819–1905). The Stephensons spread the 'standard' gauge of 4 ft 8½ in (1435 mm). *See also* RAILWAYS, ENGLAND.

STERLING AREA Countries which linked the value of their currencies to the UK currency (sterling), also holding sterling reserves and gold in LONDON. It developed informally after the UK left the GOLD STANDARD in 1931. Most members belonged to the British Empire (later Commonwealth). Arrangements were formalized by UK legislation in 1940 as a wartime measure. The UK imposed exchange controls on members in 1972 when sterling became a floating currency. Their removal in 1979 effectively ended the area.

STEWARD, WALES *see DISTAIN*

STEWART, ALEXANDER (b. *c.*1345; d. *c.* 20 July 1405, aged about 60). The fourth son of Robert Stewart (King ROBERT II of Scotland, ruled 1371–90), Stewart was a major landholder in N Scotland and royal lieutenant there from 1373. (He was created earl of Buchan by King Robert in 1382.) Stewart, however, pursued his own ends, which brought him into conflict with the government. In 1390 he burned Elgin Cathedral after the bishop of Moray (Alexander Bur) sought 'protection' elsewhere. He was called the 'Wolf of Badenoch'.

STEWART, ALEXANDER (b. 1454; d. late 1485 at Paris, France, aged about 31). Brother of King JAMES III of Scotland (ruled 1460–88); created (3rd) duke of Albany in 1457 or 1458.

In the late 1470s Albany dangerously opposed James's policy of peace with England, and James imprisoned him (spring 1479). He soon escaped and fled (to France). In Aug. 1482 he returned with English help (James had been weakened by a revolt), but failed to establish authority. Albany fled again (spring 1483), made another raid on Scotland (1484), and paid a final low-key visit (summer 1485). He died in exile. *See also* STEWART, JOHN; SCOTTISH–ENGLISH RELATIONS 1357 TO 1603.

STEWART, DAVID (b. 24 Oct. 1378; d. between 25 and 27 March 1402 at Falkland, Fife, E Scotland, aged 23). Eldest son and heir of John Stewart (King ROBERT III, ruled 1390–1406); earl of Carrick from 1390 (in succession to his father). At King Robert's accession, his uncle Robert STEWART, earl of Fife, was 'guardian' of the kingdom (i.e., effectively ruler), a situation that ended by Feb. 1393.

From the mid 1390s Carrick became increasingly active in government. On 28 April 1398 King Robert made him duke of Rothesay, and Fife duke of Albany. Next Jan., the COUNCIL, dissatisfied with King Robert's governance, appointed Rothesay as 'lieutenant' (regent) for three years. He appears to have acted often in an arbitrary way. After the term expired (Jan. 1402), Albany had Rothesay arrested and he died in custody. A COUNCIL-GENERAL exonerated Albany from blame (May); he replaced Rothesay, as 'guardian'. (Rothesay was succeeded as heir to the kingship by his brother James, later JAMES I.)

STEWART, ESMÉ (b. *c.*1542 in France; d. 26 May 1583 in France, aged about 41). A Catholic French nobleman (seigneur d'Aubigny from 1567), Stewart arrived in Scotland in Sept. 1579 at the invitation of his cousin King JAMES VI (a minor), whose affection he won. In March 1580 he replaced his uncle Robert Stewart as earl of Lennox (created duke 1581); in June 1580 he joined the COUNCIL and professed Protestantism; in Dec. he helped to overthrow the regent, MORTON (31 Dec.), and effectively replaced him. But Lennox was opposed by Churchmen, who feared foreign Catholic influence. To conciliate them Lennox signed the NEGATIVE CONFESSION and permitted the first presbyteries (1581). His regime ended after former allies of Morton (firm Protestants) seized the king in 1582 (*see* RUTHVEN RAID). Lennox was banished and returned to France (Dec.).

STEWART, JAMES (b. *c.*1545 possibly at Ochiltree, SW Scotland; d. 1 Dec. 1596 near Symington, SW Scotland, aged about 51). In Oct. 1580 Stewart, formerly a soldier, became popular with King JAMES VI (a minor); in Dec. he helped Esmé STEWART overthrow the regent, MORTON. In 1581 Stewart joined the COUNCIL (Feb.) and was created earl of Arran (April), but was imprisoned during the 'Ruthven regime' (1582–3; *see* RUTHVEN RAID).

From Aug. 1583 Arran was King James's senior counsellor, serving from May 1584 as CHANCELLOR. He secured the anti-presbyterian BLACK ACTS (1584) and negotiated a league with England (July 1585). In Nov. 1585 James surrendered to former supporters of the Ruthven regime who had returned from England; Arran fled; exile followed. Arran was later murdered by a nephew of Morton.

STEWART, JOHN (b. *c.*1482 in France; d. 2 July 1536 at Mirefleur, France, aged about 54). Only son of Alexander STEWART; (4th) duke of Albany from 1505; uncle and heir (until 1540) of King JAMES V of Scotland (ruled 1513–42).

Called from France to be governor of Scotland (1515), Albany returned to arrange an alliance with France (treaty of Rouen, 1517). Back in Scotland from 1521, he failed in war with England (1522). Albany visited France (1522–3) and Scotland (1523–4), and thereafter held French posts. He surrendered the governorship in 1524. *See also* DOUGLAS, ARCHIBALD (*c.*1489–1557); MINORITIES, ROYAL.

STEWART, MURDOCH (b. *c.*1362; d. 26 May 1425 at Stirling, C Scotland, aged about 62). Stewart was the successor (from 1420) to Robert STEWART (father) as duke of Albany and also as 'governor' of Scotland (until the return of King JAMES I from England, April 1424). On 21 March 1425 Albany was arrested with his younger son Alexander. Along with Albany's older son, Walter, and his father-in-law, Duncan earl of Lennox, they were tried and executed. The killing of the so-called 'Albany Stewarts' was partly to avenge the death of King James's older brother, the duke of Rothesay (David STEWART), in which Murdoch's father had been implicated. *See also* HUMBLETON, BATTLE OF.

STEWART, ROBERT (b. *c.*1340; d. 3 Sept. 1420 at Stirling, C Scotland, aged about 80). Effective ruler of Scotland 1388–93, 1402–20.

The second surviving son of Robert Stewart (King ROBERT II, ruled 1371–90), Stewart (earl of Fife from 1372) became 'guardian' for his father in Dec. 1388, in place of his elder brother John Stewart, earl of Carrick, who had been 'lieutenant'. When Carrick succeeded as ROBERT III (1390–1406), Fife retained his office, possibly until Feb. 1393. He was created duke of Albany in 1398.

In 1402, after King Robert's heir David, duke of Rothesay, ended a three-year term as lieutenant, Albany imprisoned Rothesay and allowed him to die (March; *see* STEWART, DAVID). Albany was appointed lieutenant (May).

From 1406 (nominal accession of JAMES I) until his death Albany served as 'governor' of Scotland while the king remained captive in England (until 1424). In 1412, following the disputed succession to the earldom of Ross (*see* HARLAW, BATTLE OF), Albany forced the submission of Donald, lord of the ISLES. Albany was succeeded as governor by his son Murdoch STEWART.

STEWART FAMILY Lords who flourished in Scotland from *c.*1136 when Walter, (third) son of Alan (from Brittany, France; in England from *c.*1102), was granted the hereditary stewardship of Scotland by King DAVID I. The family's power base was in W Scotland, especially Renfrew (created a lordship and sheriffdom in 1404). Robert, 7th steward, became king in 1371 (*see* ROBERT II). Alan's second son, William, founded the FITZALANS in Wales. *See also* ROYAL HOUSEHOLD, SCOTLAND; STEWART RULERS.

STEWART RULERS A dynasty of Scottish, English and British rulers, 1371–1714, named from Robert Stewart, MAGNATE and hereditary steward of Scotland (whence 'Stewart'), who succeeded to the Scottish kingship (as

ROBERT II) through his mother (Marjory, daughter of ROBERT I). MARY, QUEEN OF SCOTS (ruled Scotland in person 1561–7), adopted the spelling 'Stuart'. In 1603 her son, JAMES VI, succeeded their cousin ELIZABETH as ruler of England and Ireland (through descent from King HENRY VII of England), where he was styled James I.

Stuarts ruled Scotland and England (united as Great Britain from 1707) and Ireland until the death of ANNE (1714), although the male line from JAMES VII/II (fled 1688) continued as exiles and claimants until the death of Henry Stuart (cardinal duke of York) in 1807. *See also* HANOVERIAN SUCCESSION; JACOBITISM, IMPACT ON BRITISH POLITICS.

STIGAND (b. *c.*990 in England; d. 21 or 22 Feb. 1072 at Winchester, Hampshire, England, aged about 82). A worldly cleric, Stigand became bishop of Elmham (1043), then of WINCHESTER (1047). In 1052 he assisted the reconciliation between King EDWARD THE CONFESSOR and the GODWINE FAMILY. He was appointed archbishop of CANTERBURY (1052), retaining Winchester.

Stigand's career involved irregularities; e.g., he received his *pallium* (archbishop's mantle) from an anti-pope. This enabled WILLIAM I to obtain papal support for his invasion of England (1066). Though Stigand did homage to William, he was deposed by a Church council held by PAPAL LEGATES (1070).

STIRLING A town in C Scotland, on the FORTH–CLYDE ISTHMUS, by the main crossing of the R. Forth on the S bank (bridged by the mid 13th century); called 'the gateway to the Highlands'. Stirling was a royal centre by 1124 (*see* ALEXANDER I). King DAVID I probably developed the castle (on a prominent rock) and the adjacent BURGH.

Stirling's strategic location caused many battles to be fought nearby (e.g., STIRLING BRIDGE; BANNOCKBURN; SAUCHIEBURN). The castle was an important royal residence until 1603 and was maintained after the UNION OF ENGLAND AND SCOTLAND (1707). The town was of local economic importance and prospered from agriculture in the 19th century. Stirling University was founded in 1967.

Est. popn: 1300, 1000; 1600, 1500; 1800, 5200; 1900, 18,000; 2000, 33,500.

STIRLING BRIDGE, BATTLE OF Fought NE of STIRLING (C Scotland), on the N side of the R. Forth, on 11 Sept. 1297. A Scottish army, led by Andrew Murray and William WALLACE, defeated an English army moving N to quash rebellion against English rule in Scotland. Murray died of wounds; Wallace emerged as the principal Scottish leader. *See also* SCOTTISH–ENGLISH RELATIONS 1290 TO 1357; FALKIRK, BATTLE OF.

STOKE, BATTLE OF *see* SIMNEL, LAMBERT

STONE, GEORGE (b. 7 Jan. 1708 at London, England; d. 19 Dec. 1764 at Westminster, Middlesex, England, aged 56). Stone went to Ireland in 1731 as chaplain to the chief governor. He rapidly acquired Church of Ireland positions, becoming archbishop of ARMAGH and primate (and a privy councillor) in 1747. He also sought political influence. Through allies in the House of Commons, he attempted to diminish the powerful speaker, Henry BOYLE, and opposed the Commons' claim (against the Crown) to control surplus revenues. Stone's provocation of Boyle resulted in the latter's dismissal (1754) from government posts (*see* MONEY BILL DISPUTE). Stone now seemed supreme, but a 'peace agreement' between Boyle and a new governor (April 1756) left him with little influence. *See also* PROTESTANT ASCENDANCY; PONSONBY, JOHN.

STONE CIRCLES, BRITAIN Dated to the later NEOLITHIC and Early BRONZE AGE (*c.*2500–1600 BC), and distributed across much of Britain, circles of upstanding or recumbent stones vary in size from 33 ft (10 m) in diameter to massive settings at sites such as Long Meg and her daughters (in Cumbria, NW England). They sometimes occur as features within henge monuments, as at AVEBURY. Astronomical alignments suggest an association with seasonal rites and gatherings.

STONE CIRCLES, IRELAND There are two main groups of stone circles: (a) in Cos. Cork and Kerry (SW Ireland), (b) in C Ulster (N Ireland). In Cork and Kerry large stones are used. Circles are open to the NE and have a recumbent slab as the back stone. In the Ulster circles much smaller stones are used, and circles sometimes occur as complexes, as at BEAGHMORE. They are usually associated with other monuments such as standing stones, stone rows, cairns and boulder burials (the last also occur in Cork and Kerry). Stone circles appear to have been constructed and used in the BRONZE AGE (*c.*2300– *c.*700 BC).

STONEHENGE The most famous monument in Britain of the Late NEOLITHIC–Early BRONZE AGE (*c.*2500– *c.*1600 BC). Stonehenge stands on Salisbury Plain, Wiltshire, S England. Nearby are contemporary ROUND BARROW cemeteries and older sites such as the Long Barrows and Cursus monuments. Stonehenge appears to have been at the centre of a ceremonial landscape that was used by many groups over two millennia.

Over time, the monument's form was reworked, from a simple causewayed enclosure to timber circles and alignments. The massive stone settings that can be seen today represent some of the latest stages in the development of the complex during the final Neolithic and Early Bronze Age. Like Durrington Walls, which lies to the NE, the scale of the complex suggests a site used for periodic social gatherings, rites of passage and important political events.

STONE OF DESTINY A large stone which was formerly at Scone (in modern Perth and Kinross, Scotland), the INAUGURATION place of medieval Scottish kings. It was first recorded in 1249 (inauguration of ALEXANDER III). In 1296 King EDWARD I of England sent the stone to WESTMINSTER Abbey, England, where it was incorporated into a new wooden throne. Nationalist students secretly removed it to Scotland in 1950–1. It was officially returned from England in 1996 and placed in EDINBURGH Castle. The surviving stone, of sandstone, was quarried near Scone.

STOPES, MARIE (b. 15 Oct. 1880 at Edinburgh, Scotland; d. 2 Oct. 1958 at Dorking, Surrey, England, aged 77). An outstanding scientist, involved in teaching and research into the 1920s, Stopes experienced an allegedly unconsummated marriage (1911–16). In 1915 she met the US birth-control pioneer Margaret Sanger. Stopes became famous in 1918 through publication of her book about human sexuality *Married Love*, which she followed with controversial writings about BIRTH CONTROL. Married again in 1918, Stopes and her new husband founded birth-control clinics from 1921.

STOP OF THE EXCHEQUER In England, term used for the suspension of repayment for a year of some loans to the government, imposed on 7 Jan. 1672 by King CHARLES II. The action was intended to provide resources for war against the Dutch. War was declared on 17 March and proved unsuccessful. The Stop damaged the Crown's credit worthiness. *See also* ANGLO-DUTCH WARS; FINANCIAL REVOLUTION.

STRAFFORD, EARL OF *see* WENTWORTH, THOMAS

STRAITS SETTLEMENTS *see* MALAYA; SINGAPORE

STRANGER CHURCHES, ENGLAND Two churches founded in LONDON for Protestant Dutch and French immigrants in 1550 (in reign of King EDWARD VI). Established under a superintendent, they were allowed to have their own buildings, ministers, consistories (courts) and rites. They were encouraged as examples of reformed churches. Closed after the accession of MARY I (1553), they were re-established after the succession of ELIZABETH I (1559) under the bishop of London's authority. Both churches continued in the early 21st century. *See also* REFORMATION, ENGLAND; HUGUENOTS.

STRATA FLORIDA ABBEY A Cistercian monastic house, founded 1164 in the kingdom of CEREDIGION (W Wales), which was moved to a new site in 1165 under the patronage of RHYS AP GRUFFUDD. Its monks produced important historical and literary texts, including the *Brut y Tywysogion* and the Hendregadredd Manuscript. *See also* monasticism, medieval Wales.

STRATFORD, JOHN (b. *c.*1275, probably at Stratford-upon-Avon, Warwickshire, England; d. 23 Aug. 1348 at Mayfield, Sussex, England, aged about 73). Bishop of Winchester from 1323, Stratford supported the ousting of King Edward II (1327) and of Roger Mortimer (1330). He served Edward III as chancellor 1330–4, 1335–7, and Dec. 1339–April 1340. He was also archbishop of Canterbury from 1333.

In Nov. 1340, after suspending war against France for financial reasons, King Edward returned to London and accused ministers, including Stratford, of maladministration. Stratford made counter accusations and invoked Magna Carta, demanding a parliamentary hearing. Convened in May 1341, it rejected Edward's charges. Stratford regained the king's favour but with limited influence. *See also* Hundred Years War.

STRATHCLYDE (CLYDE ROCK), KINGDOM OF A British (Brittonic-speaking) kingdom in N Britain around the R. Clyde, originally centred on Clyde Rock, or Dumbarton Rock, a dramatic volcanic rock by the N bank of the R. Clyde (in modern West Dunbartonshire, W-C Scotland). Descended from the Damnonii and Selgovae Iron Age tribes, the kingdom is recorded only by names used by outsiders.

In the 5th century Clyde Rock may have been the centre of Coroticus, a Christian magnate excommunicated by Patrick. Kings of 'Clyde Rock' (so called in Irish and in Welsh Brittonic) are more clearly recorded from the mid 6th century. In the later 6th century a church was possibly established as a bishop's see at Glasgow (*see* Kentigern or Mungo). In the late 6th and 7th centuries the kingdom was a rival of the Picts, Dál Riata, Rheged, the Gododdin and Bernicia. Unlike some other kingdoms, it avoided absorption into Bernicia, although in 756 Britons made submissions at Clyde Rock to King Onuist of the Picts and King Eadbert of Northumbria.

In 870 Clyde Rock was sacked by Vikings. Rulers probably adopted another (unidentified) centre, and the kingdom soon became known as Strathclyde ('strath' referring to a valley). Carved stones of the 9th–11th centuries at Govan Old Parish Church (in modern SW Glasgow) suggest that Govan was an important ecclesiastical centre.

Probably in the early 10th century Strathclyde expanded southwards (across modern Cumbria, NW England) and became known in English as 'Cumberland' (by 945). It was probably associated with the kingdom of Scotland from 1018 (*see* Malcolm II; Duncan I), although a continuing existence until 1034 or 1070 has been suggested. The king-

dom's area remained demarcated as Glasgow diocese. *See also* kingship, North Britain; border, Anglo-Scottish; Constantine II.

STRATHEARN, EARLDOM OF A territory in C Scotland, around the R. Earn; formerly an important area within southern Pictland, governed by a mormaer from probably the 10th century (styled 'earl' from *c.*1128–36). Strathearn was held by a native (rather than Norman) dynasty until 1332 or 1333 (resignation of Earl Malise to King Edward III of England), and by members of Stewart family from 1357 until 1437 (forfeited by Walter Stewart for the murder of King James I); it was thereafter in Crown hands. *See also* kingship, North Britain; earldoms, Scotland.

STREET LIGHTING Before the 18th century, some lighting was provided in towns using candle-lit lanterns. From the 1680s–90s London and leading towns (e.g., Edinburgh, Norwich) introduced oil lamps in main streets (using whale oil), partly to combat crime. Provision of lighting was sometimes included in Improvement Acts (e.g., for leading Welsh towns in the 1760s–70s).

After William Murdock invented lighting with coal gas in 1794, it was tried in towns, and spread extensively from 1812 (e.g., reaching Dublin in 1825). Many town centres were illuminated by 1840, extending the working day. Electric lighting superseded gas mainly from the early 1900s, following the invention of the tungsten filament.

STRESA FRONT Diplomatic co-operation which was agreed at a meeting of British, French and Italian leaders at Stresa, Italy, on 11–14 April 1935. The three powers condemned German re-armament and reaffirmed the Locarno treaty. The common front against Germany quickly proved illusory (*see* Italy, British relations with).

STRICT SETTLEMENT A legal device developed in the 1650s whereby land in England and Wales could be vested in trustees effectively for two and more generations (with a notional owner becoming a life tenant). Its purpose was to prevent landowners from selling large estates and ensure their transmission to future generations. In the 1870s at least half of all land was held under strict settlement. The 1882 Settled Land Act enabled life tenants to sell land, and the use of strict settlement declined in the 20th century because taxation (death duties) compelled land sales. *See also* tenures, England from 1066.

STRIKES *see* industrial disputes

STRIKES AND PICKETING, LAW RELATING TO Although trade unions and strikes were permitted in the UK from 1824 (by repeal of the Combination Acts), legislation constrained union action to varying extents. The 1825 Combinations of Workmen Act inhibited picketing by criminalizing intimidation and other tactics. This was moderated by the 1859 Combination of Workmen Act which allowed peaceable persuasion to encourage support for a strike. But in 1871, after the legal position of unions was strengthened, a Criminal Law Amendment Act effectively made picketing a criminal offence. 'Peaceful picketing' was restored in 1875 by the Conspiracy and Protection of Property Act.

In 1901 the TAFF VALE CASE deterred strikes by making unions liable for commercial losses. The liability was removed by the 1906 Trade Disputes Act which also allowed peaceful picketing. After the GENERAL STRIKE (1926), some strikes were made unlawful (e.g., to coerce government) by the 1927 Trade Disputes Act (repealed 1946). The 1980 Employment Act prohibited 'secondary picketing' (i.e., against an organization not immediately involved in a dispute).

In southern Ireland from 1922, the 1906 Act remained the basis of statutory law. Some secondary picketing was allowed by the 1990 Industrial Relations Act (where one employer assists another in a dispute). *See also* TRADE UNION LEGISLATION.

STRONGBOW (b. *c*.1130; d. April 1176 at Dublin, Leinster, E Ireland, aged about 46). Nickname of Richard fitz Gilbert, a lord in Wales, member of the CLARE FAMILY, and earl of Pembroke (from 1148; deprived 1154 by King HENRY II for supporting STEPHEN).

In 1167 Strongbow was recruited by Diarmait MAC MURCHADA, exiled high-king of Leinster, to help him regain his kingship. In return Strongbow would marry Diarmait's daughter Aífe and succeed him. Strongbow landed near WATERFORD on 23 Aug. 1170, captured the town and married Aífe (25 Aug.). He succeeded Diarmait in 1171.

Strongbow's success provoked an expedition by Henry II (Oct. 1171–April 1172), to whom Strongbow surrendered his kingdom. Most of it was granted back as a lordship. Strongbow in turn granted land in Leinster to his followers.

Strongbow supported Henry in NORMANDY during the REVOLT OF 1173. His daughter Isabella married William MARSHAL. *See also* NORMANS, IMPACT ON IRELAND; LACY, HUGH DE.

STUART RULERS *see* STEWART RULERS

SUBMISSION OF THE CLERGY *see* SUPPLICATION AGAINST THE ORDINARIES

SUBSIDY Term used for taxes granted to the English Crown, usually by PARLIAMENT, above customary revenues,

13th–17th centuries. They included: (a) the MALTOLT charged on wool; (b) subsidies levied intermittently on alien residents 1440–87; (c) taxes on goods and lands 16th–17th centuries (e.g., subsidies levied in 1520s for war against France). The term is sometimes also applied to the FIFTEENTH AND TENTH. *See also* TAXATION, ENGLAND AND WALES BEFORE 1660.

SUBURBS AND SUBURBIA Suburbs (originally, inhabited areas beyond a town's defences or jurisdiction) existed around some major English towns (e.g., LONDON) by the 11th century. They often developed along approach roads or at the far end of a bridge. In the 12th–13th centuries, POPULATION growth caused the development of suburbs around many leading towns in the British Isles, but they suffered depopulation in the 14th–16th centuries. In the late 17th and 18th centuries new suburbs (outer areas) were built around London and elsewhere (e.g., GLASGOW), sometimes on a grand scale with squares and large houses (*see* TOWN PLANNING).

From the 19th century RAILWAYS, trams and later motor transport facilitated suburbs at greater distances from city centres (e.g., 10 mi,16 km), often intended for a particular class. Home and work became separated. Extensive development occurred around London from the 1860s. Extensions of its 'underground' railway from 1907, powered by ELECTRICITY, produced further spread: large housing estates were built, often with standardized semi-detached houses for the middle classes. By 1939 one-third of Britons lived in houses built since 1918.

From the late 19th century suburbs were derisively labelled 'suburbia', alleging a monotonous, conformist mode of life.

SUCCESSION ACTS Three Acts of the English Parliament by which King HENRY VIII altered succession to the throne. The 1534 Act affirmed the invalidity of Henry's first marriage, to KATHERINE OF ARAGON, and settled the succession on heirs male of Anne BOLEYN (second wife) and subsequent wives, and in default on Anne's daughter ELIZABETH. It implicitly excluded MARY (Katherine's daughter). The 1536 Act declared Henry's first two marriages invalid. Mary and Elizabeth were bastardized and Elizabeth was excluded from the succession. It was settled on the heirs of Jane Seymour (third wife). The 1544 Act restored Mary and Elizabeth to the succession after EDWARD (VI) and his heirs, though they remained illegitimate. *See also* HENRY VIII, WIVES OF; REFORMATION PARLIAMENT.

SUCCESSION TO THE CROWN ACT Legislation by the UK Parliament enacted in 2013 which altered the succession to the British Crown and related matters. It implemented the Perth Agreement of 2011 between the governments of 16 countries for which the British monarch is head of state. Its main effect was to replace male primogeniture (succession by eldest son) by absolute primogeniture (succession by eldest child, irrespective of sex). The Act came into force in 2015 after the other countries had enacted similar legislation. *See also* KINGSHIP AND MONARCHY, ENGLAND AND GREAT BRITAIN FROM 1680S.

SUDAN A former Anglo-Egyptian condominium (jointly ruled country) in NE Africa. Sudan was ruled by EGYPT from 1821 until a revolt began in 1881 (the MAHDI REBELLION), during which the British commander Charles George GORDON was killed (1885). British interests in the R. NILE prompted reconquest by Horatio KITCHENER (1896–8).

From 1898 a governor-general was nominated by Great Britain and appointed by Egypt. In effect the British governed the territory, with Egyptian officials entirely excluded 1924–36. Cotton became the staple crop. Claims to Sudan from Egypt (1951) caused Britain to promise self-determination (1953). The condominium ended in 1955; Sudan became independent as a republic in 1956 (divided into Sudan and South Sudan in 2011). *See also* BARING, EVELYN.

SUEZ CANAL An artificial waterway, 103 mi (165 km) long, within EGYPT, which connects Port Said on the Mediterranean to the Gulf of Suez and Red Sea to the S. In 1854 Egypt (then autonomous) allowed an international company based in France to build the canal and run it for 99 years. It was constructed 1859–69 and reduced the sea distance from Britain to India by almost 5000 mi (8000 km).

The British, having opposed the project, then realized its strategic importance. Benjamin DISRAELI, the prime minister, ordered the purchase of 40% of the canal company's stock (1875), making the company Anglo-French, although the Constantinople Convention (1888) pledged free passage to all ships. A British military garrison protected the canal from 1882 to 1956. Nationalization of the canal in 1956 by Egypt's president, Gamal Abdel Nasser, resulted in the SUEZ CRISIS.

SUEZ CRISIS An international crisis, July–Dec. 1956, concerning the future of the SUEZ CANAL in EGYPT. On 26 July, Egypt's president, Gamal Abdel Nasser, nationalized the canal (owned mainly by Great Britain and French investors), after Britain and the USA had refused funding for a dam. Britain and France secretly planned a military response in collusion with ISRAEL.

On 29 Oct. Israel invaded Egypt. Anglo-French forces then intervened, ostensibly to separate the belligerents but mainly to recapture the canal. Allied bombing of Egyptian bases began on 31 Oct., and Port Said (at the N end of the canal) was invaded on 5 Nov.

The United Nations condemned the actions, and the USA strongly disapproved. There was popular opposition within Britain. Sterling collapsed in value. Britain and France accepted a ceasefire (7 Nov.) and subsequently withdrew. The crisis ended Britain's dominance in the Middle East, and revealed that it was no longer an independent world power. The prime minister, Anthony EDEN, resigned.

SUFFOLK, WILLIAM EARL OF *see* POLE, WILLIAM DE LA

SUFFOLK'S REBELLION A conspiracy in 1501–2 against King HENRY VII, king of England, by Edmund de la Pole, earl of Suffolk, nephew of EDWARD IV (d. 1483) and a YORKIST claimant to the throne. Suffolk fled from England in Aug. 1501 to the court of Maximilian, the Holy Roman Emperor. In Sept. Maximilian promised him 5000 troops but later betrayed him by making a treaty with Henry (July 1502, at Augsburg, Germany). Suffolk's plot collapsed. He was outlawed in Dec. 1502. *See also* POLE (DE LA POLE) FAMILY.

SULIEN, FAMILY OF Welsh clerical scholars (working in Latin) in the 11th and 12th centuries, from Llanbadarn Fawr in CEREDIGION (W Wales). Sulien (1010–91) became bishop of ST DAVIDS (1072 or 1073–8, 1080–5). His sons Rhigyfarch (1057–99), Ieuan (d. 1137) and Daniel (d. 1127), and grandsons Sulien (d. 1146), Henry (d. 1163) and Cydifor (also d. 1163) became renowned scholars. Rhigyfarch's works include a *Life of St David*. *See also* NATIONAL PATRON SAINTS.

SUMNER, J.B. (b. 25 Feb. 1780 at Kenilworth, Warwickshire, England; d. 6 Sept. 1862 at Addington, Surrey, England, aged 82). An evangelical Church of England clergyman, John Bird Sumner was from 1828 bishop of the Chester diocese (NW England), which included industrial areas (*see* COTTON INDUSTRY, ENGLAND). Sumner increased provision of schools and consecrated 233 new churches. As archbishop of CANTERBURY from 1848, he tactfully handled the consequences of the GORHAM JUDGMENT (1850) and presided over the revived upper house of Convocation (Church assembly). He encouraged evangelical and missionary societies, but feared that the OXFORD MOVEMENT was undermining Protestantism. Sumner was a prolific author. *See also* EVANGELICALISM.

SUMPTUARY LAWS Legislation to restrain private expenditure, especially on DRESS and food, often passed for economic or social purposes. In England, a Sumptuary Act of 1336 attempted to encourage the CLOTH INDUSTRY (by reducing demand for expensive imported cloth). An elaborate Sumptuary Ordinance of 1363, advocated by GENTRY and leading townsmen, sought to deter poorer people from dressing above their rank. More Acts were passed in 1463, 1482, and until the 17th century. Sumptuary Acts in Scotland in 1430, which aimed at reducing imports, prohibited specified dress for many orders within society (e.g., yeomen not to wear coloured clothes beyond knee-length). In Ireland, similar legislation banned Anglo-Irish from adopting Gaelic Irish dress (see KILKENNY, STATUTE OF). Sumptuary legislation was ineffective.

SUNDAY SCHOOL MOVEMENT Schools developed from the mid 1780s when a Sunday school in Gloucester (W England), started in 1780 by newspaper publisher Robert Raikes (1736–1811), received publicity. Schools were founded throughout the British Isles, sponsored by the Churches of England, Ireland and Scotland, and dissenters, particularly EVANGELICALS. The Hibernian Sunday School Society (founded 1809) was influential in Ireland. Schools taught literacy and religion. In 1851 over 1.8 million children in the UK attended Sunday schools. Involvement peaked in the early 20th century. In England and Wales the development of State education reduced the schools' role in non-religious education. Schools remained strong until the 1950s. By the 1980s, fewer than 10% of children attended.

SUNDAY SCHOOL MOVEMENT, WALES Schools were introduced by Methodists in the mid 1780s, soon after the first Sunday school in England (see METHODIST REVIVAL, WALES). Pioneer organizers included Thomas CHARLES. Other denominations also soon started schools. Attended equally by adults and children, Sunday schools provided important instruction in reading (alongside religious teaching) until elementary education became generally available in the 1870s, contributing to high LITERACY levels, especially among Welsh-speakers. In 1900 around half the population had links with the schools, whose activities included parades and trips. Schools declined from the time of WORLD WAR I (1914–18) and by the 21st century had a very small attendance. See also EDUCATION, WALES.

SUNDERLAND, 2ND EARL OF (b. 5 Sept. 1641 at Paris, France; d. 28 Sept. 1702 at Althorp, Northamptonshire, England, aged 61). Robert Spencer succeeded as earl in 1643 after his Royalist father was killed in the First CIVIL WAR. King CHARLES II appointed him a privy councillor (1674) and SECRETARY OF STATE (1679). But his support for the second Exclusion Bill resulted in dismissal (Jan. 1681; see EXCLUSION CRISIS). He regained favour in 1682 with help from the duchess of PORTSMOUTH, a royal mistress (Sunderland reappointed secretary 1683).

Sunderland remained in office under JAMES VII/II (king from 1685). As effectively chief minister from Jan. 1687, he

promoted James's catholicizing policies, and in June 1688 openly became Catholic. He was dismissed on 27 Oct. for making James grant concessions to Anglicans to save his throne. Sunderland fled to the Dutch Republic (Dec.).

In 1690 James's successor WILLIAM III allowed Sunderland to return. He declared himself a Protestant and from 1692, as a non-party man, advised the king and liaised with party leaders in Parliament. See also ROCHESTER, EARL OF.

SUNDERLAND, 3RD EARL OF (b. 23 April 1675 in England; d. 19 April 1722 at Piccadilly, Middlesex, England, aged 46). Charles Spencer, a WHIG MP from 1695, became son-in-law of the earl of MARLBOROUGH through his second marriage (1700). He succeeded as earl of Sunderland in 1702 and became a member of WHIG JUNTO. In 1706 Queen ANNE, under pressure from Lord GODOLPHIN and Marlborough, reluctantly appointed him SECRETARY OF STATE (southern). Sunderland's involvement in organizing the impeachment of Henry SACHEVERELL (Feb. 1710) resulted in his dismissal (June). He then led Whigs in opposition.

After the accession of the pro-Whig Hanoverian king GEORGE I (1714), Sunderland was appointed lord lieutenant of Ireland (1714) and lord PRIVY SEAL (1715). In 1717 his intrigues with the king contributed to the dismissal of Viscount TOWNSHEND. Sunderland replaced him as secretary of state (northern). In 1718 he swapped posts with Viscount STANHOPE, becoming first lord of the Treasury. Sunderland supported the takeover of NATIONAL DEBT by the South Sea Company, but was forced to resign (March 1721) by the ensuing scandal (see SOUTH SEA BUBBLE).

SUNNINGDALE AGREEMENT A political agreement reached on 9 Dec. 1973, during the TROUBLES, at Sunningdale, Berkshire (S England), by the prime ministers of Great Britain and the Republic of Ireland (Edward HEATH, Liam COSGRAVE) and by party leaders involved in the power-sharing Executive in NORTHERN IRELAND (led by Brian FAULKNER). It provided consensus on key issues before the Executive took office (1 Jan. 1974), notably Northern Ireland's continuance in the UK and the establishment of a Council of Ireland. The latter, involving the Republic, was unacceptable to many Unionists in Northern Ireland. See also EXECUTIVES, NORTHERN IRELAND; ULSTER WORKERS' STRIKE.

SUPPLICATION AGAINST THE ORDINARIES In England, a schedule of grievances concerning the Church presented by the House of Commons to King HENRY VIII on 18 March 1532, during the REFORMATION PARLIAMENT. ('Ordinaries' are holders of jurisdiction within the Church, especially archbishops or bishops.) It attacked the right of Convocation (Church assembly) to make laws and also the operation of Church courts. Convocation replied (about 27 April), only for Henry to make more demands (10 May).

On 15 May 1532 Convocation accepted that its laws required royal approval (so-called 'Submission of the Clergy'; confirmed by statute 1534). The submission was a major step in the establishment of royal control over the Church. *See also* REFORMATION, ENGLAND.

SUPPLICATION OF THE BEGGARS *see* FISH, SIMON

SURPLICE RIOTS Disturbances in 1844–5 in Exeter, Devon (SW England), which resulted from Bishop Henry Phillpotts' attempt to enforce the wearing of the surplice by parish clergy at public worship in his diocese. He sought uniformity to remove symbols of allegiance to parties within the Church of England, but the requirement was considered by many to indicate a HIGH CHURCH policy. In Jan. 1845, when Exeter's mayor asked a clergyman to cease wearing a surplice to preserve public order, Phillpotts reluctantly agreed. *See also* GORHAM JUDGMENT.

SURRENDER AND REGRANT Historians' term for an English policy in Ireland attempted in 1540–3 by Anthony ST LEGER (also in the later 16th century). Gaelic Irish chieftains were pressured into surrendering their territories and receiving them back as lands held from, and subject to, the English ruler (Henry VIII). Chieftains also accepted English-style noble titles, law and customs. The policy sought to extend English rule without the expense of conquest. It was largely unsuccessful. *See also* IRELAND, ENGLISH CONQUEST, 16TH CENTURY; PEERAGE, IRISH; O'NEILL FAMILIES; O'BRIEN FAMILY.

SURREY EXPEDITION An English military expedition to Ireland (May 1520–March 1522); sent by King HENRY VIII and led by Thomas Howard, earl of Surrey, as chief governor (king's lieutenant). Henry desired to extend English rule throughout Ireland. Surrey obtained formal submissions from many Irish chieftains (June–Oct. 1520), but advised Henry that conquest and colonization were required (June 1521). Henry shirked the challenge. *See also* IRELAND, ENGLISH CONQUEST, 16TH CENTURY; NORFOLK, 3RD DUKE OF.

SUSSEX, KINGDOM OF A Germanic-ruled kingdom (6th–8th centuries), occupying modern Sussex and adjacent lands (S England). 'Saxons' settled in the area in the 5th–6th centuries. The kingdom probably existed by the late 6th century, and was sometimes ruled jointly by several kings.

Sussex was vulnerable to outsiders. King Æthelwalh recognized the overlordship of WULFHERE, king of Mercia (d. 675). In 685–6 Cædwalla, king of WESSEX, became overking (succeeded by INE). A bishopric was founded at Selsey between 704 and 709.

Probably in 771, King OFFA of Mercia demoted the kings of Sussex to *duces* (Latin, meaning 'leaders'), effectively ending Sussex's autonomy. Sussex was appropriated by Wessex

in 826 (*see* EGBERT). It retained identity as a SHIRE (divided into two counties 1888). *See also* KINGSHIP, ANGLO-SAXON.

SUSSEX, THOMAS EARL OF (b. 1526 or 1527 in England; d. 9 June 1583 at Bermondsey, Surrey, England, aged about 57). Thomas Radcliffe, styled Lord Fitzwalter (from 1542), won the favour of MARY I (queen from 1553), despite previously supporting Lady Jane GREY. He succeeded his father as earl of Sussex in 1557.

From 1556 Fitzwalter served in Ireland. He restored papal jurisdiction and developed plantations. Under ELIZABETH I (queen from 1558) he imposed a new religious settlement. After returning to England (1564) he was appointed president of the COUNCIL OF THE NORTH (1568) and suppressed the Catholic NORTHERN REBELLION. Sussex's last years (from 1572) were spent at court.

SUSSEX, THOMAS EARL OF, AND IRELAND Lord Fitzwalter followed Anthony ST LEGER as chief governor (lord deputy) of Ireland under Queen MARY I in April 1556, serving until Dec. 1558. He succeeded as earl of Sussex on 17 Feb. 1557. He asserted himself with military campaigns (in Antrim, July 1556, in Offaly, July 1557); developed the LEIX-OFFALY PLANTATION; and presided over Parliament's restoration of papal jurisdiction and Catholicism (June 1557).

Following the accession of ELIZABETH I (Nov. 1558), Sussex was reappointed (July 1559; raised to queen's lieutenant May 1560). He imposed the ELIZABETHAN SETTLEMENT on the Church (Jan. 1560), and campaigned against Shane O'NEILL of Tyrone, N Ireland (June–July, Sept. 1561; April 1563). Failure to suppress O'Neill, and disaffection caused by Sussex's methods (e.g., charges on PALE inhabitants) forced him to leave (May 1564; resigned late 1565). Sussex contributed significantly to English policy in Ireland by advocating regional PRESIDENCIES (1562; instituted by Sir Henry SIDNEY). *See also* IRELAND, ENGLISH CONQUEST, 16TH CENTURY; REFORMATION, IRELAND.

SUTHERLAND CLEARANCES The reorganization in 1807–21 of estates of Elizabeth, countess of Sutherland, in Sutherland (N Scotland), for large-scale sheep-farming. It is regarded as the most notorious example of CLEARANCES because of its scale and brutality: over 8000 people were forced to resettle on coastal crofts (smallholdings). Estate managers James Loch and Patrick Sellar sometimes cleared townships by burning houses. *See also* AGRICULTURE, SCOTLAND FROM 18TH CENTURY.

SUTTON HOO The site of a cemetery, in Suffolk (E England), which yielded the richest burial from Anglo-Saxon England (found 1939). Covered by an earthen mound, it included remains of a sea-going ship and goods from around Europe (e.g., helmet, sword, spears, coins). The goods match the heroic society portrayed in *BEOWULF*.

The burial is tentatively associated with King RÆDWALD (d. *c*.624). *See also* EAST ANGLIA, KINGDOM OF.

SWANSEA A city in SW WALES; centre of Swansea unitary authority; from Old Norse, Sveinnsey, meaning 'Sweyn's island' (Welsh, Abertawe, meaning 'Mouth of R. Tawe').

Swansea may first have been a VIKING trading station (9th–10th centuries). A castle and town were founded in 1106 by the Norman Henry de Beaumont, as the centre of the lordship of Gower.

Swansea was primarily a market centre until 1716 when copper smelting began, using local coal and ore from Cornwall (SW England). Other metal industries followed (zinc processing from 1755, TINPLATE manufacturing from 1845), making Swansea 'the metallurgical capital of Wales'. Coal mining expanded, and large docks were opened in 1851 and 1881, from which metal products and anthracite were exported. Swansea was the second largest town in Wales in 1800.

Swansea's early industries declined from 1918: copper smelting ended in 1921, zinc mostly by 1930, tinplate by 1966, coal mining in 1968, and copper working in 1980. Meanwhile new industries developed, including oil refining from 1921. Swansea was created a city in 1969. *See also* TOWNS, WALES; UNIVERSITIES, WALES.

Est. popn: 1300, 800; 1600, 1200; 1800, 6000; 1900, 130,000; 2000, 170,000.

SWEIN ESTRITHSON (b. *c*.1020 in Denmark; d. 28 April 1076 in Denmark, aged about 55). King of Denmark from 1047, Swein claimed the kingship of England as a cousin of HARTHACNUT (ruled England 1040–2). In summer 1069, soon after the Norman invasion of England, Swein sent a force to England (R. Humber) which joined an attack on Normans in YORK. Anti-Norman revolts broke out elsewhere. In spring 1070 Swein himself arrived, provoking a revolt in E England. King WILLIAM persuaded him to withdraw. Swein's son Cnut landed briefly in England in 1075. *See also* NORMAN CONQUEST OF ENGLAND.

SWEIN FORKBEARD (fl. from 986; d. 3 Feb. 1014 at Gainsborough, Lincolnshire, England). King of Denmark from 986, Swein raided England to exact tribute (early 990s; 1003–5).

In 1013, probably fearing attack by Thorkell, a Dane with English support, Swein invaded England. Operating from Gainsborough, he was accepted as king in N England and eastern MERCIA (former Danish-ruled areas). He then moved SW and received submissions of OXFORD and SW England (at BATH). London also capitulated. In Dec. King ÆTHELRED II fled abroad. But Swein died, enabling Æthelred to return. Swein's nickname is recorded from the 12th century. *See also* MALDON, BATTLE OF; CNUT; VIKINGS, IMPACT ON ENGLAND.

SWIFT, JONATHAN (b. 30 Nov. 1667 at Dublin, Ireland; d. 19 Oct. 1745 at Dublin, aged 77). Of English parentage, Swift was educated and ordained priest (1695) in the Church of Ireland. He held secular posts in England (from 1689), and Church of Ireland livings, while developing into a powerful satirist. In 1710 he abandoned his WHIG affiliation and wrote propaganda for the English TORY Lord HARLEY. He was appointed dean of St Patrick's Cathedral, DUBLIN, in reward (1713).

After the proscription of Tories (1714, following the accession of King GEORGE I), Swift lived mainly in Ireland. He championed Irish interests and often contested British policy, notably in 1724 with his anonymous *Drapier's Letters* (pamphlets opposing the new copper coinage; *see* WOOD'S HALFPENCE AFFAIR). His works include *A Tale of a Tub* (1704) and *Gulliver's Travels* (1726). *See also* ANGLO-IRISH LITERATURE.

SWING RIOTS Agrarian unrest which swept across England in autumn 1830. Though attributed to a mythical instigator called 'Captain Swing', the riots were unco-ordinated protests against low wages and poor-law allowances and against labour-saving threshing machines. They added menace to the debate over PARLIAMENTARY REFORM.

SWYNFORD, KATHERINE (b. *c*.1350 in Hainault; d. 10 May 1403 in Lincoln, Lincolnshire, England, aged about 53). The daughter of a Hainaulter in the English royal household, Katherine Roelt married (*c*.1365) Sir Hugh Swynford (d. 1371) and became governess to the children of JOHN OF GAUNT (1369). She was Gaunt's mistress from possibly 1372 and bore four children (1372–7). They were named Beaufort. Katherine and Gaunt married in 1396 and their children were legitimized. Gaunt died in 1399. *See also* BEAUFORT FAMILY.

SYKES–PICOT AGREEMENT A secret Anglo-French deal, made with Russian assent, concluded on 16 May 1916 (negotiated by diplomats Sir Mark Sykes and François Georges-Picot). It provided for division of the OTTOMAN EMPIRE in the Middle East into spheres of influence after WORLD WAR I. Designed to allay French fears of British regional hegemony, it contradicted pledges made to Arabs under Ottoman rule. The eventual settlement was revised to take account of the BALFOUR DECLARATION and MANDATES. *See also* FRANCE, ENGLISH AND BRITISH RELATIONS WITH.

SYNDICALISM A revolutionary movement which sought to overthrow CAPITALISM by means of strikes, thereby to establish a workers' State based on trade union representation (term derived from French *syndicalisme*, meaning 'trade unionism'). Syndicalism developed in France *c*.1900 and had some influence on the industrial unrest that afflicted Britain 1911–14 (e.g., strikes by seamen, dockers, miners), but most union leaders were dismissive of it.

T

TACITUS (b. 56 or 57 in S France or N Italy; d. after 115, aged over 58). Publius or Gaius Cornelius Tacitus became a Roman senator and eventually consul (97), and was governor of Asia (in modern Turkey) 112–13. His principal historical works, the *Histories* (covering 69–96, though only the first portion survives) and the *Annals* (covering 14–68, of which the majority survives), include valuable passages on the initial period of ROMAN BRITAIN. In addition, one of his earliest works, the *Agricola* (published *c*.98), a biography of his father-in-law AGRICOLA, includes a detailed (if eulogistic) account of the expansion of Britannia under Agricola's governorship.

TACKSMAN In Scotland, the holder of a written lease or 'tack'. In the HIGHLANDS and Islands from the 17th century the term was applied to a CLAN chief's immediate subordinates (so-called 'clan gentry'). They individually held lands from a chief (now by formal lease) which they sublet, by township (Gaelic *baile*), to joint-tenants. (Tacksmen also mobilized clan members for fighting.) From the 1730s (accelerating from the 1770s) chiefs eliminated tacksmen in order to gain the full rent of tenant-clansmen. Some tacksmen became large tenants (often specializing in cattle ranching), others became estate agents (managers), while others emigrated. Removal of tacksmen weakened clan cohesion and enabled CLEARANCES to take place. *See also* SOCIAL STRUCTURE, NORTH BRITAIN AND SCOTLAND.

TAFF VALE CASE Legal action taken in 1901 by the Taff Vale Railway Company of S Wales against the Amalgamated Society of Railway Servants. It sued for £23,000 for damage caused by a strike. The company's success left unions in the UK liable for commercial losses arising from industrial action. They drew closer to the LABOUR PARTY to lobby for freedom from liability (gained by the Trade Disputes Act of 1906). *See also* TRADE UNION LEGISLATION.

TAIT, ARCHIBALD (b. 21 Dec. 1811 at Edinburgh, Scotland; d. 3 Dec. 1882 at Addington, Surrey, England, aged 70). From a presbyterian background, and educated at GLASGOW and OXFORD Universities, Tait was ordained in the Church of England in 1836. Of moderately liberal theological sympathies, he opposed the OXFORD MOVEMENT. As bishop of LONDON from 1856 he organized missions to poor areas. In 1868 Tait was the first Scotsman to be appointed archbishop of CANTERBURY. He accepted the DISESTABLISHMENT of the Church of Ireland (1871), and was largely responsible for the Public Worship Regulation Act of 1874 which sought to suppress RITUALISM.

TALBOT-ORMOND FEUD Conflict in Ireland, 1410s–40s, between factions of Anglo-Irish inhabitants headed by the Talbot brothers and the (4th) earl of Ormond. Dissension broke out between Sir John Talbot, Lord Furnival (*c*.1387–1453), and Ormond (*c*.1390–1452) after Talbot's arrival in Ireland as lieutenant in 1414. In 1417

A Dictionary of British and Irish History, First Edition. Edited by Robert Peberdy and Philip Waller.
© 2021 John Wiley & Sons Ltd; © editorial matter and organisation Robert Peberdy and Phillip Waller.
Published 2021 by John Wiley & Sons Ltd.

Talbot seized Ormond's estates. After Talbot left in 1419 his faction centred on his brother Richard, archbishop of Dublin from 1417 (d. 1449). The factions struggled for control of the Dublin-based government (e.g., in 1420 Ormond, now lieutenant, removed Talbot supporters). The Talbot faction also feared that Ormond desired greater independence from England. The feud weakened the English colony. It waned after marriage was arranged in 1444–5 between John Talbot's eldest son and Ormond's daughter Elizabeth. *See also* IRELAND, ENGLISH COLONY IN, 13TH–15TH CENTURIES; BUTLER FAMILY, IRELAND.

TALIESIN (fl. in late 6th century). A Welsh 'early poet'. His works concern the N British kings Urien and Owain of RHEGED and Cynan Garwyn, king of POWYS (C Wales). Originally composed in Primitive Welsh, they survive in Old Welsh (9th–11th centuries). *See also* WELSH LANGUAGE AND LITERATURE.

TALLIS, THOMAS (b. probably *c*.1505 in England; d. 23 Nov. 1585 at Greenwich, Kent, England, aged about 80). Church composer and from probably 1543 until his death a gentleman (lay singer) of the Chapel Royal. Tallis adapted his output of compositions according to the changing forms of religion, setting Catholic Latin texts under King HENRY VIII, English anthems and canticles under EDWARD VI, Latin Masses and motets under MARY I, and English and Latin texts under ELIZABETH I. In later life he had connections with many Catholics, including the composer William BYRD. *See also* REFORMATION, ENGLAND.

TAMWORTH MANIFESTO An election address issued by the newly appointed British prime minister Sir Robert PEEL to his constituents at Tamworth (Staffordshire) on 17 Dec. 1834, but also published throughout Great Britain. It accepted the 1832 franchises and approved the principle of reform where necessary. The manifesto sought to make the CONSERVATIVE PARTY attractive to new middle-class voters and is regarded as a significant step in the Party's evolution. *See also* PARLIAMENTARY REFORM.

TANGANYIKA A former British-held territory in E Africa. It was part of German East Africa from 1885. Great Britain administered the territory from 1919 (following WORLD WAR I) under a MANDATE from the LEAGUE OF NATIONS. A few thousand settlers grew coffee and cotton. Tanganyika became independent in 1961 under the British Crown, and a republic in 1962. It was united with ZANZIBAR in 1964 and the joint country was renamed Tanzania. Approx. population in 1921, 4,120,000; in 1960, 9,000,000. *See also* EAST AFRICA, BRITISH INVOLVEMENT; GROUNDNUT SCHEME.

TANGIER A fortified city and enclave in NW Africa, near the confluence of the Atlantic and Mediterranean, which were ceded by Portugal to England in 1661 in a treaty of alliance and marriage (Portugal's Catherine of Braganza to England's King CHARLES II). Tangier seemed valuable as a base for protecting trade around the Strait of Gibraltar.

England sought to secure Tangier with a garrison (initially 3000 men, from Jan. 1662) and by building forts. But these were frequently attacked by Moors, whose leader regarded Tangier as his possession. In 1684, unwilling to invest in further defence, Charles abandoned the territory. *See also* PORTUGAL, ENGLISH AND BRITISH RELATIONS WITH.

TANISTRY A former practice in Wales, Ireland and (Scottish) DÁL RIATA whereby a king's (or chief's) successor or 'tanist' (Irish *tanaise*) was designated from among his kin. Succession might alternate betvween segments (branches) of a kindred. Tanistry lasted in Wales until the 13th century, in the WESTERN ISLES of Scotland until the 16th century, and was declared illegal in Ireland in 1608. It was replaced by male primogeniture (succession by eldest son).

TANK A military armoured vehicle with 'caterpillar-type' tracks which was created in Great Britain during WORLD WAR I to overcome stalemate on the Western Front; possibly conceived in Oct. 1914 by official war correspondent Ernest Swinton (1868–1951). Because of War Office scepticism, the idea was developed by the 'Landships Committee' of the Admiralty (1915–16), encouraged by Winston CHURCHILL. The designation 'tank' was used to provide secrecy (chosen because machines resembled water tanks).

Tanks entered warfare at the SOMME (Sept. 1916), achieved a breakthrough at CAMBRAI (1917), and contributed to victory (1918). During the 1920s–30s, J.F.C. Fuller (1878–1966), Basil LIDDELL HART and others developed tank-based warfare strategies. But British tank development was surpassed by German advances.

TARA A complex of prehistoric monuments in the Republic of Ireland (in Co. Meath, E Ireland), including an IRON AGE hill-top enclosure. (Tara may mean 'Hill with a view', from OIr. *Temair*.) Tara was appropriated by the 6th century AD by the Southern UÍ NÉILL rulers, who styled themselves 'king of Tara' (Irish *rí Temro*) to denote high status and, by the 8th century, high-kingship of Ireland. Tara's importance declined in the early 11th century when the possession of VIKING towns became symbolic of high-kingship. *See also* FEIS TEMRO; KINGSHIP, IRELAND; CAPITALS.

TARIFF REFORM Name given to proposals in Great Britain in the late 19th and early 20th centuries to move away from FREE TRADE (trade largely free of duties or customs). Initially called FAIR TRADE, tariff reform was a protectionist response to foreign industrial and agricultural competition (*see* PROTECTIONISM). To this was added the patriotic appeal of 'imperial preference' – the use of tariffs to induce people to buy British Empire goods by cheapening their prices relative to other imports.

Joseph CHAMBERLAIN argued that tariffs could unify the Empire, finance social reform (e.g., pensions) and reduce unemployment. The CONSERVATIVE PARTY divided over the issue from 1903. Opponents maintained that tariffs would increase food prices. Tariff reform remained contentious until the NATIONAL GOVERNMENT imposed a 10% general tariff and negotiated the OTTAWA AGREEMENTS (1932). *See also* BEAVERBROOK, LORD.

TASMANIA *see* VAN DIEMEN'S LAND

TAX CREDITS A system for raising the incomes of poor people, derived from the USA and introduced in the UK in 2003; a 'flagship' policy of Gordon BROWN as chancellor of the Exchequer. Tax credits to encourage take-up of employment and reduce poverty were part of Brown's 'redistributionist' approach to public policy. The system provided a Child Tax Credit, generally for mothers of school-age children, and a Working Tax Credit for employees. 'Credits' were effectively means-tested supplements to wages.

The system was developed and administered under Brown's control at the Treasury (rather than by a welfare department). Its introduction was chaotic. Applicants found tax credits difficult to understand and budget for. A specially designed IT system was soon overloaded. Numerous errors were made, including extensive overpayment. Criminal gangs stole large sums. In the longer run, it was claimed that credits expanded dependence on the State and encouraged some employers to reduce wages (because they would be automatically supplemented). Tax credits were phased out from 2013.

TAXATION, ENGLAND AND WALES BEFORE 1660 The earliest significant tax (raised alongside customary ROYAL REVENUES) was GELD, levied by kings on land in England from 991 for paying off VIKINGS and funding military forces. It was retained after the NORMAN CONQUEST (until 1162), and similar 'carucage' was levied intermittently 1198–1224.

Kings of England imposed other taxes incidentally from the 12th century usually for specific purposes, notably from 1166 'fractional taxes' (a fraction of an individual's movable wealth or income, imitating TITHE). They were similar to 'general aids' (an emergency FEUDAL INCIDENT, as raised in 1193 for ransoming RICHARD I). Customs duties on overseas trade were also charged occasionally (e.g., 1202–6).

The unpopular levying of a 'thirteenth' by JOHN (1207) without a specified purpose probably influenced a stipulation in MAGNA CARTA (1215) whereby aids required consent from 'common counsel', indicating an assembly. Kings thereafter periodically requested tax grants from various bodies, including PARLIAMENT; the latter developed a monopoly during the 1340s–70s. From 1275 customs grants were obtained to supplement royal revenues and fund warfare, becoming an important component of royal income (from 1360s). Clergy were also taxed (from mid 13th century). Wales was taxed by Welsh and English rulers and by Marcher lords (from 13th century).

From 1334 fixed charges (sometimes multiples), known as FIFTEENTHS AND TENTHS, were levied from communities. Often granted for warfare, they were important until 1624. New taxes on individuals were tried in the late 14th and 15th centuries (e.g., POLL TAXES). From 1523 to 1663 SUBSIDIES were frequently levied from individuals, usually for war. Wales was taxed uniformly after 1543. Local taxation began in 1572 for POOR RELIEF.

Attempts by CHARLES I (1620s–30s) to impose taxation under ROYAL PREROGATIVE (e.g., SHIP MONEY) caused Parliament to prohibit non-parliamentary taxes (1641). During the CIVIL WARS (1642–8) Parliament introduced (1643) 'assessment' (regular charges) and EXCISE (commodity taxes), which continued through the 1650s.

TAXATION, ENGLAND, WALES AND GREAT BRITAIN FROM 1660 Following the RESTORATION (1660), the CONVENTION PARLIAMENT levied taxes to pay off the NEW MODEL ARMY (e.g., POLL TAX) and based finance for royal GOVERNMENT mainly on taxation, thereby strengthening parliamentary control and making inland taxation routine.

King CHARLES II (1660–85) was supported principally by CUSTOMS and EXCISE duties ('consumption taxes'), and HEARTH TAX (from 1662), with additional imposts (e.g., poll taxes; SUBSIDIES). From 1663 corn duties furthered MERCANTILISM (*see* CORN LAWS). Tax 'farming' (delegation to contractors) was ended: customs management was transferred to a board of commissioners in 1671, excise in 1683; both became large employers. WILLIAM III abandoned the unpopular hearth tax (1689), and was granted LAND TAX (1692), stamp duty (tax on legal documents, 1694) and window tax (1697).

Because of wars between 1689 and 1815, financed partly by NATIONAL DEBT, taxation became primarily concerned with warfare and long-term debt (*see* FISCAL–MILITARY STATE; CIVIL LIST). The main taxes remained land tax, and customs, excise and stamp duties (also in Scotland after 1707). INCOME TAX was also raised from the wealthy 1798–1816.

From the 1820s to 1850s taxation policy sought to encourage commerce and manufacturing, by lowering or abolishing customs duties; income tax was reintroduced from 1842 (*see* FREE TRADE). Taxation in Ireland was also assimilated (by 1855). Local rates increased considerably in the later 19th century as local government activities expanded.

From the 1890s taxation (mainly 'direct' taxation on wealth, incomes and profits) increasingly served social reform, e.g., funding pensions (1909) and other SOCIAL SERVICES, and the WELFARE STATE (from 1944). WORLD WARS I and II also required high taxation. From 1979 direct tax levels were reduced. In 2013–14 income tax provided 27% of UK tax revenues; national insurance (introduced 1911) 19%; value-added tax (or VAT, introduced 1973) 18%; corporation tax (introduced 1965) 6%; other taxes 30%. *See also* TAXATION, SCOTLAND; AMERICAN INDEPENDENCE, ORIGINS OF; TAXATION, IRELAND; NEW LIBERALISM; COMMUNITY CHARGE.

TAXATION, IRELAND Irish kings or chiefs (before early 17th century) levied tributes in cattle and foodstuffs, and by the 12th century quartered troops on households (*see* ROYAL REVENUES, IRELAND).

In the 13th century the English government levied CUSTOMS on overseas trade and obtained grants of taxes on English-controlled areas (e.g., fifteenth of moveable wealth agreed by assembly 1292; *see* EDWARD I AND IRELAND). SUBSIDIES were regularly granted by PARLIAMENT from the 14th century.

Governors of Ireland also levied cess (foodstuffs, services, money) for their household and military retinue. Their increasing demands from the mid 16th century produced a crisis in the 1570s (*see* CESS). Starting in 1575, the government obtained fixed payments from Gaelic Irish and Anglo-Irish lords as English authority was reasserted (*see* COMPOSITION). Local taxation began in 1634 when Parliament authorized collection of 'county cess' for bridges.

Additional taxes from the mid 17th century directly or indirectly affected many of the adult population. EXCISE (taxation on consumables, primarily alcohol) started as a wartime measure in 1643. Following the RESTORATION, Parliament in 1662 granted customs and excise as perpetual revenues to the Crown, and introduced a HEARTH TAX (property tax based on number of hearths). Poll (head) taxes were levied in 1660–1, 1695, 1697, and land tax in 1698.

In the 18th century parliamentary subsidies were granted continuously mainly to fund the ARMY, and local taxation increased (for roads, infirmaries, etc.). Poorer people were exempted from hearth tax in 1793 and 1795, and a window tax on larger properties was introduced in 1799.

After the UNION OF IRELAND AND GREAT BRITAIN (1801), the taxation regime largely continued. Hearth and window taxes were abolished in 1822, but poor rates, pay-

able by property owners, were introduced under the POOR RELIEF (IRELAND) ACT, 1838. Irish taxation was assimilated to UK taxation in 1853–5 (e.g., 1853, introduction of INCOME TAX). *See also* ROYAL REVENUES, IRELAND.

TAXATION, SCOTLAND Until the 1580s many taxes were raised for exceptional, non-military purposes, which minimized unrest. (Kings were expected to live off ROYAL REVENUES.) In the 12th–13th centuries 'aids' (compulsory payments) were sometimes taken from nobles (e.g., for 1189 'Quitclaim of Canterburgh'; *see* WILLIAM I), and from the late 13th century CUSTOMS were levied. The ransom for King DAVID II (1357) was raised by payments on incomes and goods (levied 1358–60, 1365–70). From 1468 nobles, clergy and burghs were taxed as separate 'estates' by grant of PARLIAMENT or COUNCIL-GENERAL. JAMES V obtained a perpetual tax on the clergy from the Pope in 1531. (The Pope had taxed the clergy for CRUSADES 1220s–90s.)

From 1581 JAMES VI levied regular taxes for royal expenditure, including £1,200,000 (Scots) plus a twentieth of annual rents (over four years) granted in 1621. CHARLES I obtained larger sums in the 1630s, contributing to the unpopularity which resulted in the COVENANTING REVOLUTION. The Covenanting regime (1640–51) taxed incomes, and from 1643 land values (by assessment or 'cess'). The English funded their occupation (1651–60) from heavy taxation. It continued after the RESTORATION (1660); £480,000 per year was granted in 1661. The cess was reintroduced in 1667 (*see* COMMISSIONERS OF SUPPLY). In the 1690s hearth and poll taxes were also levied to fund foreign wars (*see* WILLIAM III). Under union with England (1707) English arrangements were applied. The cess continued until 1854.

Taxation for local purposes began with rates for POOR RELIEF (1574). Major reforms were made in the 1850s. In the 1980s pressure from Scotland for reform of rating contributed to the introduction of the COMMUNITY CHARGE (1989). Deeply unpopular, it was replaced by the Council Tax (1993). From 1999 tax-varying powers were devolved to a new Scottish Parliament and Executive, which subsequently obtained greater powers over taxation (*see* DEVOLUTION, SCOTLAND). *See also* TAXATION, ENGLAND, WALES AND GREAT BRITAIN, FROM 1660.

TECHNICAL EDUCATION In the 14th–19th centuries craft skills were transmitted mainly through apprenticeship (usually seven years' training with a master craftsman). By the mid 19th century this was considered insufficient for industrial skills. In Scotland, engineering was developed at university level, with professorships being founded at GLASGOW (1840) and EDINBURGH (1868). Existing institutions were developed into technical colleges (Heriot-Watt at Edinburgh, 1885; Glasgow and West of Scotland, 1886).

In England, pressure from LONDON livery companies resulted in the founding of the City and Guilds Institute of London (1880) and Finsbury Technical College (1883). The Regent Street Polytechnic, an adult-education institute that provided technical classes, was also started in London (1882). The government's Samuelson Commission (reported 1884) resulted in the Technical Instruction Act (1889), which authorized local authorities in England, Wales and Ireland to support technical education. Many technical colleges were founded.

University-level courses were developed in technical colleges in England and Wales from the 1950s (as recommended by the 'Percy Report' of 1945), and 'colleges of advanced technology' were designated from 1956, funded from 1962 by the Ministry of Education. Industrial training boards were created in Great Britain under the Industrial Training Act of 1964.

From 1969 some English and Welsh colleges were upgraded to degree-awarding polytechnics, and became universities from 1992. Scotland's two major colleges also became universities (*see* UNIVERSITIES, SCOTLAND). In the Republic of Ireland, nine regional technical colleges were opened in the 1970s, and expanded from 1992 into 14 Institutes of Technology. Three were amalgamated in 2019 as the Technological University Dublin. *See also* HIGHER EDUCATION, EXPANSION OF.

TEILO (fl. in 6th century). A founder and abbot of the monastery of Llandeilo Fawr (SW WALES). He is the dedicatee, as saint, of churches in SW Wales (about 25, making him second to DAVID) and in Brittany. *See also* CONVERSION OF WALES; MONASTICISM, MEDIEVAL WALES.

TEIND (Scots, meaning 'tenth' or 'tithe'). The tenth of agricultural produce given annually in Scotland by parish inhabitants to their local church for support of its clergyman. Payment was widespread by the late 12th century. By the mid 16th century a majority of teinds had been diverted through APPROPRIATION. As a result of COMMENDATION, many recipients were lay lords.

From 1562 a third of teinds not paid to incumbent clergy was levied to support ministers of the Church of SCOTLAND (*see* THIRDS OF BENEFICES). Following the 1925 Church of Scotland (Property and Endowments) Act, a final valuation of teinds was made, payments in kind were converted to fixed charges, and teinds could be redeemed.

TELEVISION, GREAT BRITAIN AND NORTHERN IRELAND John Logie BAIRD gave the first demonstration of television transmission by radio in LONDON in 1926, and his company made experimental broadcasts 1929–32 through BRITISH BROADCASTING CORPORATION (BBC) transmitters. The BBC ran the world's first regular service 1932–5, using Baird's system. Authorized in 1936 to develop television, it operated 'high definition' television in the London area, with mechanical and all-electronic systems (former until 1937), until the outbreak of WORLD WAR II (1939).

When broadcasting resumed (1946), set-owners were required to pay an annual licence fee (including RADIO). Set ownership and viewing were stimulated by televising the coronation of ELIZABETH II (1953), seen by 20 million people. By 1955, 40% of the UK population received television, rising to 82% in 1960. Its popularity caused declines in CINEMA attendance and radio listening, and encouraged greater home-centredness.

In 1955 independent television, funded by advertisements, began. It was managed by an Independent Television Authority, which established transmitters and awarded franchises to regional companies (for local and national programming). Because competition encouraged popularization, the BBC was granted a second channel for more serious programmes, BBC2 (1964). It began broadcasting in colour from 1967, with other channels soon following; programmes included *Civilisation* by Kenneth Clark (1969). The public-sector, commercially funded Channel 4 was added in 1982, to serve minority interests, together with a Welsh service (*see* BROADCASTING, WALES). Channel 5, an entertainment channel, was launched in 1997.

From the 1980s a bigger multi-channel world developed, which fragmented the viewing market. Limited satellite broadcasts started in 1983, and cable television was developed from 1984. Two companies launched multi-channel satellite services in 1989–90 (merging in 1990 as British Sky Broadcasting). Services moved to 'digital' technology from 2002. In 2017, about 70 main channels were available and numerous other services.

TELEVISION, SOUTHERN IRELAND *see* BROADCASTING, SOUTHERN IRELAND

TELFORD, THOMAS (b. 9 Aug. 1757 in Westerkirk parish, Dumfriesshire, Scotland; d. 2 Sept. 1834 at Westminster, Middlesex, England, aged 77). A shepherd's son, Telford became a stonemason and from 1782 worked in England, by 1786 as an architect.

In 1793 Telford was appointed engineer for the Ellesmere Canal Company. He built numerous CANALS, roads, harbours and churches in Great Britain and elsewhere, and was responsible for outstanding civil engineering works such as the Caledonian Canal (1804–22), Pontcysyllte aqueduct (opened 1805), and the London–Holyhead road (1815–26, including the Menai Straits suspension bridge). *See also* TURNPIKE TRUSTS AND ROADS, ENGLAND/SCOTLAND/WALES.

TEMPERANCE MOVEMENT, ENGLAND Organized campaigning for temperance (abstinence from alcohol, or restraint in consumption) developed from the 1830s with Radicals seeking to encourage working-class self-improvement. Those who pledged abstinence were typically artisans, shopkeepers and clerks. The movement grew especially strong in NW England, home of the COTTON INDUSTRY. Temperance groups developed rituals and regalia, and provided alternative entertainment to public houses in temperance halls.

NONCONFORMISTS took the lead as local societies federated into the London-based National Temperance Society (1842), the provincial British Temperance League (1856), the Band of Hope (1847) for children, and the British Women's Temperance Association (1876). Nathaniel Card (1805–56), a Quaker and cotton manufacturer, formed the United Kingdom Alliance (1853) to lobby for prohibition of the liquor trade. The LIBERAL PARTY increased statutory restrictions by restoring licensing by justices of the peace (1869, 1872; *see* LICENSING OF DRINKING PREMISES, ENGLAND AND WALES). By 1900 perhaps 10% of adults were teetotal, but the movement thereafter declined.

TEMPERANCE MOVEMENT, IRELAND Europe's first known abstinence society was founded in 1817 at Skibbereen (Co. Cork) by Jeffrey Sedwards, a nailer, though Germans in Ireland possibly founded earlier societies. Catholics and Protestants started similar societies in the 1820s–30s.

Temperance became a mass movement from 1838 through campaigning by Theobald Mathew (1790–1856), a Catholic friar from CORK. Concerned about social problems caused by excessive alcohol consumption, he persuaded 3 million people to pledge abstinence. His campaign declined from *c*.1843 and was disrupted by the GREAT FAMINE. Catholics and Protestants continued nonetheless to promote temperance.

In 1898 James Cullen (1841–1921), a Jesuit, launched the Pioneer Total Abstinence Association of the Sacred Heart to combat poverty. It grew into one of Ireland's largest Catholic lay societies, with 280,000 members in 1921. Despite decline from the 1960s, it remained active in the 21st century. Ireland's temperance movement generally encouraged individual rather than State action, though from 1878 legislation restricted pub opening (*see* SABBATARIANISM).

TEMPERANCE MOVEMENT, SCOTLAND The movement spread rapidly after two temperance societies were founded in 1829 in W-C Scotland. Campaigners advocated abstinence from spirits, while some (from the 1830s) championed teetotalism. In 1844 the Scottish Temperance League was founded to unite local societies. Temperance was also promoted by radical movements (*see*

CHARTISM, SCOTLAND) and Churches (especially evangelicals). In 1853 the 'Forbes Mackenzie Act' was passed, which introduced Sunday closing of pubs and other restrictions.

From the 1880s the movement's strength increased, under Church leadership (including the Catholic Church). In 1908 the Temperance League had 147,000 members. The Liberal and Labour Parties gave support and a Scottish Prohibition Party was founded in 1901. In 1913 the Temperance (Scotland) Act was passed, allowing local votes on prohibition of alcohol, and in 1922 Edwin Scrymgeour was elected Prohibitionist MP for DUNDEE (ousting Winston CHURCHILL). But temperance soon declined: most areas voted against prohibition in the 1920s. Sunday opening was re-permitted from 1976. Temperance survived mainly in the N and W.

TEMPERANCE MOVEMENT, WALES Temperance societies were founded from 1832 and temperance was soon championed by NONCONFORMITY. From the 1860s it was also supported by sections of the LIBERAL PARTY. The movement's initial aims were to persuade individuals to moderate their drinking, although from 1835 some went further and advocated total abstention from alcohol (by 'taking the pledge'). Its chief victory was the Welsh Sunday Closing Act of 1881, the first Act dealing with a Welsh issue (*see* DEVOLUTION, WALES), which closed public houses on Sundays (except in MONMOUTHSHIRE, included in 1921).

The movement declined from the 1920s along with nonconformity. Sundays remained 'dry' until 1961, when periodic local referendums on the issue were initiated. By 1996 voters had reintroduced Sunday opening throughout Wales. *See also* LICENSING OF DRINKING PREMISES, ENGLAND AND WALES.

TEMPLE, FREDERICK (b. 30 Nov. 1820 on Levkas, United States of the Ionian Islands; d. 23 Dec. 1902 at Lambeth, London, England, aged 82). A Church of England clergyman and from 1857 headmaster of Rugby School, Temple contributed to the controversial theological collection *Essays and Reviews* (1860). Though his chapter was orthodox, his involvement caused protest when he was appointed bishop of Exeter (1869). He supported provision of schools, TEMPERANCE, and detachment of Cornwall as a separate diocese (1877). Temple became bishop of LONDON in 1885 and archbishop of CANTERBURY in 1896. In 1899–1900 he and the archbishop of YORK (William Maclagan) issued the 'Lambeth Opinions' which permitted incense in church but denied the legality of the reserved sacrament (*see* RITUALISM). *See also* TEMPLE, WILLIAM.

TEMPLE, WILLIAM (b. 15 Oct. 1881 at Exeter, Devon, England; d. 26 Oct. 1944 at Westgate-on-Sea, Kent, England, aged 63). The son of a Church of ENGLAND bishop (*see* TEMPLE, FREDERICK), and a philosopher and theologian, William Temple became bishop of MANCHESTER (1920), archbishop of YORK (1929) and archbishop of CANTERBURY (1942).

Concerned to promote educational opportunity and social reform, Temple was president of the Workers' Educational Association (1908–24), a LABOUR PARTY member (1918–21), and in 1924 convened 'COPEC' (Conference on Christian Politics, Economics and Citizenship), which articulated collective reforming ambitions. His book *Christianity and Social Order* (1942) reinforced wartime arguments for improved welfare provision (*see* WELFARE STATE). He supported the BUTLER EDUCATION ACT (1944). Temple's involvement with the ecumenical movement (from 1910) culminated in appointment as provisional chairman of the World Council of Churches (1938) and chairman of the British Council of Churches (1942).

TENANT PROTECTION SOCIETIES, IRELAND An association to compel better treatment of tenants by landlords was established in 1849 at Callan (Co. Kilkenny) by two Catholic priests. It deterred people from renting farms from which tenants had been evicted, and advocated independent setting of rents. Twenty societies were formed by 1850 (mainly in E and S Ireland) when the IRISH TENANT LEAGUE was started to organize more extensive campaigning. *See also* LAND AGITATION AND REFORM, IRELAND.

TENANT RIGHT, GREAT BRITAIN Term used in the 19th century for claims by tenant farmers, primarily for compensation from a landlord when leaving a tenancy for 'unexhausted improvements' (e.g., those characteristic of HIGH FARMING). Compensation became customary in some areas, and the 1875 Agricultural Holdings Act provided limited compensation in England and Wales. Campaigning (e.g., by the Farmers' Alliance) led to compulsory compensation from 1884 (including Scotland). Other concerns were settled by the 1896 Agricultural Rates Act, which halved rates on land in England and Wales, and the 1906 Agricultural Holdings Act (for Britain), which ended prescribed cropping.

TENANT RIGHT, IRELAND *see* 'THREE FS'

TEN ARTICLES The first doctrinal statement made by the English Church after its separation from papal authority, published July 1536. Compiled by King HENRY VIII and advisers, the Articles sought to reassure the public on disputed matters. They endorsed many Catholic beliefs and practices, such as Christ's presence in the Mass, purgatory, seeking the intercession of saints, and veneration of images. Some Continental reformed doctrines were repudiated. *See also* BISHOPS' BOOK; ARTICLES OF RELIGION; REFORMATION, ENGLAND.

TENISON, THOMAS (b. 29 Sept. 1636 at Cottenham, Cambridgeshire, England; d. 14 Dec. 1715 at Lambeth, Surrey, England, aged 79). A Church of ENGLAND clergyman in London from 1680, Tenison was involved in 1689 in attempts to accommodate Protestant dissenters in the Church (*see* NOTTINGHAM, 2ND EARL OF). He prospered under WILLIAM III and MARY II: he was appointed bishop of Lincoln in 1691, archbishop of CANTERBURY in 1694. But Queen ANNE (ruler from 1702) disliked him for his WHIG views and largely ignored him. Tenison supported the HANOVERIAN SUCCESSION and crowned King GEORGE I (1714). He encouraged the foundation of the Society for the Propagation of the Gospel (1701; *see* MISSIONARY SOCIETIES, ENGLAND AND GREAT BRITAIN).

TENNYSON, ALFRED (b. 6 Aug. 1809 at Somersby, Lincolnshire, England; d. 6 Oct. 1892 at Aldworth, Surrey, England, aged 83). Of modest independent means, Tennyson dedicated his life to poetry. Drawing on classical myths and medieval legends, he explored heroism and tragedy in such works as *The Lady of Shalott* (1833). *In Memoriam* (1850), a tribute to his friend Arthur Hallam (1811–33), won fame and Tennyson's appointment as poet laureate. He was created Lord Tennyson in 1884, the first occasion when a peerage was awarded solely for services to literature. *See also* ENGLISH LITERATURE, ENGLAND.

TENTH-CENTURY REFORMATION Historians' term for a movement in the English Church which spread Benedictine monasticism. It originated partly in the foundation of six religious houses by King ALFRED (late 9th century), but was mainly stimulated by reformed Continental European houses which attracted English interest (e.g., from Bishop Oda of Ramsbury in 930s).

The reform movement evolved after DUNSTAN became abbot of Glastonbury (Somerset) in 940 and his pupil ÆTHELWOLD re-founded Abingdon monastery (Berkshire) *c.*954 as a strictly Benedictine house. It was reinforced by Dunstan's experience of St Peter's monastery, Ghent (during exile, 956–7), and by OSWALD's experience at Fleury-sur-Loire, Francia (950s). The movement was supported by EDGAR, king of England from 959: he promoted Dunstan to archbishop of CANTERBURY (960), Oswald to bishop of Worcester (962; also archbishop of YORK from 971), and Æthelwold to bishop of WINCHESTER (963). By 975, about 30 male religious houses had been founded or re-founded, and seven or eight nunneries established. Their communities lived by the *Regularis concordia* ('Monastic agreement'), a rule compiled by Æthelwold (early 970s) based on St Benedict's rule. The reformers particularly advocated the corporate holding of endowments, free from interference by laypeople.

Leading reformers influenced Edgar's ideas about kingship, and the movement influenced the Church through the appointment of monks as bishops. *See also* ÆLFRIC; WULFSTAN.

TENURES, ENGLAND BEFORE 1066 The main category of land in Anglo-Saxon kingdoms was probably 'folkland' (OE *folcland*), which was controlled by royal and other kindreds. Kings rewarded followers and officials with life-time loans of land. In the 10th–11th centuries some estates were specifically reserved for loan to EALDORMEN or EARLS (called 'comital estates' by historians).

Christian missionaries in the 7th century introduced BOOKLAND: land alienated, and freed by written charter, which threatened the availability of services. From the 8th century kings formalized or imposed services on all land (*see* THREE PUBLIC SERVICES). Both folkland and bookland could be leased. Leased land was called 'loanland' (OE *lænland*). *See also* ROYAL REVENUES, ENGLAND BEFORE 1066.

TENURES, ENGLAND FROM 1066 The NORMAN CONQUEST changed landholding practices (tenures). WILLIAM I gave lands in return for future military service to major supporters (later called 'tenants-in-chief'), who likewise granted lands to followers (so-called 'subinfeudation'). Military-service landholdings (and some others) were termed 'fees' (Latin singular *feodum*); fee-holding was later conceptualized as FEUDALISM. By *c*.1200 military fee-holders established hereditary right: fees descended by male primogeniture (inheritance by eldest son). Superior lords received FEUDAL INCIDENTS.

Fees could not be sold, but were transferred (for payment) by subinfeudation, with acquirers technically becoming tenants. Subinfeudation was prohibited by the statute *QUIA EMPTORES* (1290) which required substitution of a fee-holder. Prohibition of bequeathing was circumvented with the USE (14th–16th centuries), which deprived superior lords of incidents. Extensive disposal of lands by will was conceded by HENRY VIII in 1540 (Statute of Wills). In 1656 Parliament abolished military-service tenures (confirmed 1660), replacing them with 'free socage' (effectively freehold ownership).

Agricultural and settlement units belonging to fee-holders (or lords) were known as MANORS. Within manors, lands were held from lords by 'unfree' or 'free' tenures, the former involving 'servile' restrictions and burdens; the latter (sometimes called 'socage') usually required attendance at a court and payment of a small rent. Landholders in TOWNS had extensive freedom. Following the BLACK DEATH (1348–9), unfree manorial tenures were usually converted to COPYHOLDS (hereditary tenure for a fixed annual rent). In the 16th–18th centuries, copyholds were often converted into 'leases for lives' (usually three lives, extendable), effectively a contract with the landowner.

During the 18th century landowners strengthened control over land by replacing leases for lives with fixed-term leases (e.g., 21 years) and buying out copyholds. In the 19th century annual tenancies were common. From 1841 copyholders could obtain 'enfranchisement' (conversion to freehold); remaining copyholds were converted in 1925. Thereafter freehold (ownership) and leasehold were the main tenures. *See also* SERFDOM; STRICT SETTLEMENT.

TENURES, IRELAND When records begin (7th century) land belonged to kin groups of four (later three) generations linked by male (agnatic) descent. Within a group, each adult possessed a share. Lands were periodically redistributed (e.g., after a member's death). Gaelic Irish customs remained widespread until the 17th century.

After HENRY II became lord of Ireland (1171), 'feudal' tenurial structures were applied in English-ruled areas. Rulers granted estates to 'tenants-in-chief', who subgranted lands to knights for MILITARY SERVICE. Estate-holders created MANORS on which tenures were free or unfree. Tenants by free tenure were usually of English or Welsh origin, while those by unfree tenure were mostly Gaelic Irish (so-called betaghs, roughly equivalent to English villeins), who performed LABOUR SERVICES. Population decline in the late 14th–15th centuries caused replacement of labour services by rents of money or crops (sharecropping). Areas under English tenures also contracted (*see* GAELIC REVIVAL, IRELAND 13TH–15TH CENTURIES).

The reassertion of English authority in the 16th–17th centuries included English tenures. Under SURRENDER AND REGRANT (1540–3), Gaelic lords became tenants-in-chief. PLANTATIONS (1550s–1630s) involved Crown grants of large estates ('seignories') in 'socage' (a free tenure); recipients granted freeholds or leaseholds to tenants. Military tenures were abolished in 1662 (converted to socage).

By the 18th century land belonged mainly to Protestant landowners (*see* PROTESTANT ASCENDANCY). They commonly leased estates for 31 years to a 'middleman', who subgranted short leases to tenants. The system encouraged subdivision of holdings as POPULATION increased, and discouraged investment by landowners. From *c*.1800 landowners replaced middlemen with managers and let directly to tenants. Tenancy law was reformed by 'Deasy's Act' (1860).

From the late 19th century LAND AGITATION obtained new statutory rights for tenants and State-sponsored purchase of freeholds by rural tenants, creating a land of small owner-occupiers (by 1920s). Land law in the Republic of Ireland was comprehensively reformed in 2009. *See also* FAMILY AND KINSHIP, IRELAND; RURAL SETTLEMENT AND SOCIETY, IRELAND; FEUDAL INCIDENTS.

TENURES, SCOTLAND Landholding customs are obscure before the 12th century. Kings in N Britain probably allocated some land through THANAGES. At a lower social level access to land was possibly controlled by kindreds (as in W Britain; *see* TENURES, WALES).

King DAVID I (ruled 1124–53) introduced feudal tenures (derived from NORMANDY and England): landholding for service, either military service (e.g., 'knight service' – providing knights) or nominal service ('blenchferme' tenure – by token money or other rent, literally 'white rent'). Lordships or 'feus' (equivalent to English 'fees' or 'fiefs'), were granted by charter to lords (known as tenants-in-chief) and considered indivisible and heritable by primogeniture (succession by eldest son). Kings also regranted native EARLDOMS on feudal terms. Religious houses usually received land in 'free alms' tenure.

Subordinate tenants held land by 'free' tenure (nominal rents, heritable possession) or, more commonly, by 'unfree' tenure requiring work on the lord's demesne land. By the mid 14th century services were replaced by leases or 'tacks'. By the 15th century many tenants (or joint-tenants) held by annual verbal leases ('tenants at will').

During the 16th century rulers and churchmen granted extensive lands by 'feu-ferme', perpetual leases (known from the 12th century) involving payment of an annual 'feu-duty' by the tenant ('feuar') to the superior (*see* FEUING MOVEMENT). It was the commonest tenure from 1747 when military tenures were converted to blenchferme, if held of the Crown, or feu-ferme, if held of another superior (*see* JACOBITE REBELLIONS, CONSEQUENCES IN SCOTLAND).

Feu-ferme was phased out from 1974 under legislation that required conversion to freehold (by redemption of feu-duty) when feu-ferme property was sold. In 2000 the new Scottish Parliament passed the Feudal Tenure etc. (Scotland) Act which abolished feudal land tenure, including annual feu-duties (from 28 Nov. 2004). *See also* KINGSHIP, NORTH BRITAIN; ROYAL REVENUES, SCOTLAND; NORMANS, IMPACT ON SCOTLAND; KIN-BASED SOCIETY; KINDLY TENURE; FEUDALISM.

TENURES, WALES In Welsh-inhabited Wales, until the 15th century, most land was held by individuals but alienation was controlled by the kindred. Tenures were free or bond.

A kindred group (Welsh *gwely*, meaning literally 'bed'; or *gafael*, meaning 'holding') established its members' proprietorship of land by occupying it for four generations. Each male member was entitled to a share but could not alienate it without consent. Land was partible among all male heirs. Where bond tenure applied, tenures included *tir cyfrif* ('reckoned land') whereby a community held land in return for payment of fixed rents and dues to their lord.

From the 13th century tenures became more flexible. For example, *tir gwelyog* ('land of a *gwely*') allowed inheritance by bond kindred groups. Individuals were granted more scope; *tir prid* ('pledged land') allowed tenants to acquire land for successive four-year periods in return for monetary payment. The depopulation and reallocation of land after the BLACK DEATH (1349) accelerated the decline of native tenures and encouraged personal estates.

In areas ruled from *c*.1070 by Normans (later English) and settled by English (*see* MARCH OF WALES) English tenures were used (*see* TENURES, ENGLAND FROM 1066).

TEST AND CORPORATION ACTS Legislation by the CAVALIER PARLIAMENT, 1660s–70s, which asserted the authority of the Church of ENGLAND in England and Wales by excluding Protestant dissenters and Catholics from offices.

The Corporation Act of 1661 (part of the CLARENDON CODE), directed against Protestant dissenters, required members and officers of town corporations to swear loyalty to the king and to have received Holy Communion in the Church of England within six months before entering office.

The Test Act of 1673 was passed because of suspicion of the religious loyalty of James, duke of York (heir to the throne), and of other government ministers. Holders of civil or military offices were required to take oaths of supremacy and of allegiance to the Crown, receive Holy Communion in the Church of England, and declare disbelief in the Catholic doctrine of TRANSUBSTANTIATION. A second Act of 1678 applied the same tests to members of Parliament except the duke of York (*see* POPISH PLOT).

Attempts to repeal the Corporation Act failed until 1828. The Test Acts were repealed in 1829. *See also* NONCONFORMITY AND DISSENT, ENGLAND/WALES; OCCASIONAL CONFORMITY.

TETTENHALL, BATTLE OF Fought near Tettenhall in W MERCIA (modern Staffordshire, W England) on 6 Aug. 910. An Anglo-Saxon army from WESSEX and western Mercia defeated a raid by VIKINGS from N England. It was the Anglo-Saxons' first major defeat of Vikings outside Wessex. *See also* ENGLAND, FORMATION OF.

TEXTILE INDUSTRIES, ENGLAND *see* CLOTH INDUSTRY, ENGLAND; COTTON INDUSTRY, ENGLAND

TEXTILE INDUSTRIES, IRELAND *see* INDUSTRY, IRELAND BEFORE 18TH CENTURY/FROM 18TH CENTURY TO 1921; LINEN INDUSTRY, IRELAND; COTTON INDUSTRY, IRELAND

TEXTILE INDUSTRIES, SCOTLAND Until *c.*1600 cloth making was widespread and essentially for household use or local sale. During the 17th century specialisms for wider markets were developed, notably woollen plaiding (NE Scotland) and linen (W-C and E). In the 18th century linen production expanded greatly, especially around GLASGOW (W-C) and DUNDEE (E). Linen 'stamped' (approved) for sale rose six-fold 1728–80; much was exported. Production was organized by town-based merchants and took place mainly in rural homes ('putting-out system'). From the 1750s water power (usually converted meal mills) was used for scutching (beating) flax. Government support was important (*see* FISHERIES AND MANUFACTURES, BOARD OF TRUSTEES FOR).

In the 1780s–90s the COTTON INDUSTRY expanded rapidly (especially in W-C Scotland), remaining the pre-eminent textile industry until *c.*1860. Steam-powered mills, staffed predominantly by women, enabled the production of huge quantities of yarn, which generated increased numbers of domestic handloom weavers until weaving was mechanized (1820s). Linen remained important in the E (flax-spinning mechanized from 1820s, weaving from 1850s–60s). Woollen production continued in the NE and developed in the S (specialization in tweeds from 1830s; power weaving used from 1850s). From the 1830s jute production, for sacking and canvas, 'took off' in Dundee (E), after Indian jute had been softened for spinning with whale oil.

World War I (1914–18) stimulated jute production for military purposes (e.g., sandbags) but damaged export markets. Many jute, linen and cotton mills closed in the 1920s–30s, and jute production effectively ended in the mid 1960s, leaving high-quality border woollens as a major product. *See also* INDUSTRY, SCOTLAND BEFORE/FROM MID 18TH CENTURY; FOREIGN TRADE, SCOTLAND BEFORE/FROM 17TH CENTURY.

TEXTILE INDUSTRY, WALES *see* INDUSTRY, WALES BEFORE/FROM 18TH CENTURY

THANAGE Term used in Scotland from the late 12th century for long-established territories (groupings of FERMTOUNS) from which payments were drawn, originally in kind (*see* ROYAL REVENUES, SCOTLAND). Although some were given to earls and the Church, they were essentially royal estates, and were fundamental bases for early government in E Scotland between the Forth and the Moray Firth; some contained significant royal residences. Thanages were managed by thanes (from OE *Þegn*), i.e., high-ranking servant-retainers.

Thanages were similar to COMMOTES in Wales and (small) SHIRES in England; all probably derive from an age-old structure of 'multiple estates'. The English term 'shire' was applied to Scottish multiple estates by the 10th century,

and subsequently royal shires came to be known as thanages. Previous Pictish and Gaelic terminology is unknown, although some managers may have been called *maer* (Gaelic, meaning 'steward').

Thanages were the Crown's main local administrative units until the 12th century, when their functions were gradually transferred to the new SHERIFFDOMS (whose centres were mostly important thanages). Some thanages were granted away (but only occasionally to immigrants); the majority remained in Crown hands until the 14th century. Then they were mostly alienated, often with baronial powers which turned them into BARONIES.

THATCHER, MARGARET (b. 13 Oct. 1925 at Grantham, Lincolnshire, England; d. 8 April 2013 at London, England, aged 87). Leader of the CONSERVATIVE PARTY 1975–90; British prime minister 1979–90.

A grocer's daughter (originally Margaret Roberts), educated at OXFORD University, Thatcher was an MP 1959–92. She served as parliamentary secretary to the Ministry of Pensions and National Insurance (1960–4) and as education secretary (1970–4). In 1975 she defeated Edward HEATH in a Party leadership election, and in 1979, following the WINTER OF DISCONTENT, became the UK's first female and first scientist prime minister.

Thatcher's government abolished exchange controls, adopted deflationary MONETARISM and promoted PRIVATIZATION. By 1983 inflation was low but unemployment exceeded 3 million (Jan. 1982–June 1987). Trade union reform was successful. Re-elected in 1983, after the FALKLANDS WAR (1982), Thatcher dominated her administration. Surviving an assassination attempt (1984; *see* TROUBLES), she withstood a MINERS' STRIKE (1984–5) and weathered the WESTLAND CRISIS (1986). In foreign affairs, she championed the SPECIAL RELATIONSHIP.

Re-elected again in 1987, Thatcher initiated reform of the NATIONAL HEALTH SERVICE and introduced GRANT MAINTAINED SCHOOLS. The COMMUNITY CHARGE proved unpopular. Resistance to European integration divided her Party. Geoffrey HOWE and Michael HESELTINE forced her resignation (Nov. 1990). She was created Baroness Thatcher (1992). *See also* THATCHERISM; WETS AND DRIES; LAWSON, NIGEL; KINNOCK, NEIL; SCARGILL, ARTHUR; EUROPEAN ECONOMIC COMMUNITY/EUROPEAN UNION, IMPACT ON BRITISH POLITICS; ECONOMY, STATE INVOLVEMENT, BRITAIN; MAJOR, JOHN.

THATCHERISM Term denoting the political beliefs and practice of Margaret THATCHER (leader of the CONSERVATIVE PARTY 1975–90, British prime minister 1979–90). They included criticism of NATIONALIZATION and extensive welfare provision for encouraging inefficiency, and promoted such elements as MONETARISM,

PRIVATIZATION, nationalism and vigorous anti-SOCIAL-ISM using an assertive and combative style of leadership. In its essentials, Thatcherism did not claim to be original, but marked a distinct departure in British politics with its fundamental emphasis on individual freedom and responsibility. The term was used by 1977. *See also* ECON-OMY, STATE INVOLVEMENT, BRITAIN; GOVERNMENT, GREAT BRITAIN FROM LATER 19TH CENTURY.

THEOBALD OF BEC (b. *c.*1090 at Thierville, Normandy; d. 18 April 1161 at Canterbury, Kent, England, aged about 71). In 1138 King STEPHEN of England arranged for Theobald, a monk, to be elected archbishop of CANTERBURY to thwart his brother (*see* HENRY OF BLOIS). In the 1140s–50s Theobald generally remained loyal (*see* ANARCHY). But during Stephen's imprisonment (1141) he attended on MATILDA (with Stephen's agreement), and twice defied Stephen (1148, broke ban on attending a Church council; 1152, refused to crown son Eustace). Theobald helped to negotiate a settlement between Stephen and Henry Plantagenet (treaty of Winchester, 1153). His household was distinguished for attracting many intellectually able young men, including Thomas BECKET.

THEODORE OF TARSUS (b. 602 at Tarsus, Byzantine Empire; d. 19 Sept. 690 at Canterbury, Kent, aged 88). Greek by birth, the monk Theodore was chosen archbishop of CANTERBURY by Pope Vitalian to replace a nominee who had died in Rome (667).

Theodore arrived in England in 669, aged 67. He appointed to vacant bishoprics and replaced CHAD with WILFRID at YORK. He held the first council of clergy in England (at Hertford, 672 or 673) which agreed to create more bishoprics. Theodore affirmed England's support for the papacy (e.g., in 679, at the request of Pope Agatho, the council of Hatfield affirmed catholic orthodoxy). Theodore was also a considerable scholar and teacher. *See also* EDU-CATION AND LEARNING, ENGLAND BEFORE 1066.

THEODOSIUS (fl. from *c.*367; d. 375 or 376). Spanish-born, Flavius Theodosius was a Roman general under Emperor Valentinian (364–75) and father of Emperor Theodosius I (379–95). As Count Theodosius he restored ROMAN BRITAIN after a major barbarian raid (*c.*367–9) and was promoted master of cavalry. He was executed, for unknown reasons, after Valentinian's death (Nov. 375).

THEOSOPHICAL SOCIETY A religious organization founded in 1875 in the USA by Madame H.P. Blavatsky and Colonel H.S. Olcott, which had its headquarters at Madras, India, from 1882. Its leader from 1907 was the Englishwoman Annie BESANT (d. 1933). Theosophy purported to derive from Indian sacred texts, taught reincarnation (but not personal immortality), and espoused universal brotherhood. The Society developed in Britain from 1878, reaching a peak in 1927 with 5000 members in 160 lodges.

THINK TANK Colloquial term for a group of experts who are brought together to develop useful ideas. In British politics the term became familiar as a short name for the Central Policy Review Staff (1970–83), an official office established by Edward HEATH to advise the prime minister. 'Think tanks' have been established by political parties and other groups seeking to promote particular directions in public policy.

THIRDS OF BENEFICES An arrangement (1562) between the reformed Church of SCOTLAND and the Crown whereby benefice-holders who were not clergy (usually laymen who had acquired Church revenues through APPROPRIATION and COMMENDATION) would gave a third of their income (mainly TEINDS) to the Crown partly to support the Church. The arrangement followed rejection of the 'First Book of Discipline' (1561). *See also* CHURCH ORGANIZATION, SCOTLAND FROM 16TH CENTURY; DISCIPLINE, BOOKS OF.

THIRTEEN COLONIES Popular term for the British territories in N America which formally declared independence from the British Crown and Parliament through their Second Continental Congress (4 July 1776) and formed the USA.

Eight were CROWN COLONIES with Crown-appointed governors (GEORGIA, MASSACHUSETTS, NEW HAMPSHIRE, NEW JERSEY, NEW YORK, NORTH CAROLINA, SOUTH CAROLINA, VIRGINIA); two were self-governing with elected governors (CONNECTICUT, RHODE ISLAND); two belonged to proprietors under the British Crown (MARYLAND, PENNSYLVANIA). The thirteenth, DELAWARE, was technically not a colony recognized by the Crown but an autonomous part of Pennsylvania. *See also* NORTH AMERICAN COLONIES.

THISTLE, ORDER OF THE Scotland's principal order of CHIVALRY, founded in 1687 for the monarch and 8 knight-companions by King JAMES VII, probably to bolster support. It was thought 'popish' and lapsed after James's deposition. Queen ANNE revived the Order in 1703, with 12 knights (expanded to 16 in 1821).

THOMAS, DAVID ALFRED (b. 26 March 1856 at Aberdare, Glamorgan, Wales; d. 3 July 1918 at Llanwern, Monmouthshire, Wales, aged 62). MP for MERTHYR TYDFIL 1888–1910, for CARDIFF 1910.

Thomas created the Cambrian Combine Company which became the leading coalmining company in the

RHONDDA VALLEYS by 1910, when an industrial dispute led to the TONYPANDY INCIDENT. During WORLD WAR I Thomas was called from retirement to be food controller (1917–18; *see* RATIONING, WORLD WAR I). He was created Lord Rhondda in 1916, Viscount Rhondda in 1918. His daughter Margaret, Viscountess Rhondda (1883–1958), was prominent in London upper-class society in the 1920s–30s. *See also* COAL INDUSTRY, WALES.

THOMAS, J.H. (b. 3 Oct. 1874 at Newport, Monmouthshire, Wales; d. 21 Jan. 1949 at London, England, aged 74). James ('Jimmy') Henry Thomas emerged from poverty to become a railwayman and union official. A Labour MP from 1910, he served in the British government under Ramsay MACDONALD as colonial secretary (1924), lord PRIVY SEAL and minister for employment (1929–30), and as secretary of state for DOMINIONS (from 1930). In 1931 he joined the NATIONAL GOVERNMENT, retaining office, but was expelled from the Labour Party and from his position with the National Union of Railwaymen. He helped to negotiate the OTTAWA AGREEMENTS (1932). In 1935 Thomas became colonial secretary. He resigned after accidentally leaking Budget information (1936).

THOMAS OF LANCASTER (b. *c*.1278 in England; d. 22 March 1322 at Pontefract, Yorkshire, England, aged about 43). A grandson of King HENRY III, Thomas was recognized as earl of Lancaster in 1298. His inheritance of three earldoms and an advantageous marriage made him a leading magnate. In 1309 Lancaster opposed the return of Piers GAVESTON, the banished favourite of EDWARD II, and in 1310–11 supported the reform movement which produced the ORDINANCES. His presence at Gaveston's execution (June 1312) alienated him from Edward (pardoned Oct. 1313). Edward's defeat at BANNOCKBURN (June 1314) enabled Lancaster's supporters to take control of government. In Feb. 1316 Lancaster was recognized as Edward's 'chief counsellor' by Parliament. But by May he had withdrawn into isolation.

From 1319 Lancaster encouraged opposition to Edward's favourites the DESPENSERS. On 16 March 1322 he intercepted a royalist force at Boroughbridge (Yorks.) only to be captured, tried and executed. Some considered him a champion against royal autocracy, and a cult of so-called 'St Thomas of Lancaster' developed.

THOMOND *see* MUNSTER

THOMSON, J.J. (b. 18 Dec. 1856 at Manchester, Lancashire, England; d. 30 Aug. 1940 at Cambridge, Cambridgeshire, England, aged 83). After attending Owens College, MANCHESTER, Joseph John Thomson studied mathematics at Trinity College, CAMBRIDGE (1876–80), of which he was became a fellow (1881) and master (1918). In 1884 he was elected a fellow of the ROYAL SOCIETY and appointed Cavendish professor of experimental physics at Cambridge (to 1919).

Thomson's work was important in the study of electricity after James Clerk MAXWELL (d. 1879). In 1897, while studying cathode rays (electricity discharged through a vacuum), he proposed that the rays were subatomic particles, negatively charged. Soon called 'electrons', they were the first known subatomic particles. The finding inaugurated the study of subatomic physics. Thomson's discoveries were expounded in *Conduction of Electricity through Gases* (1903). He later developed the use of 'positive rays' to separate different kinds of atoms and molecules. Awarded the 1906 Nobel Prize in Physics and knighted (1908), Thomson was president of the Royal Society 1915–20.

THOMSON, WILLIAM (b. 26 June 1824 at Belfast, Ireland; d. 17 Dec. 1907 at Largs, Ayrshire, Scotland, aged 83). A mathematician's son, Thomson studied at GLASGOW and CAMBRIDGE Universities (graduated from latter 1845), and in a French laboratory. In 1846 he was elected professor of natural philosophy (science) at Glasgow, a position he retained until retirement (1899).

Thomson made important contributions to mathematics, science and technology. In the 1840s he argued that there had been different conditions on Earth over 100 million years ago. In 1848 he proposed a new absolute temperature scale. A paper on heat (1851) included an exposition of heat dissipation and version of the second law of thermodynamics. In the 1850s–60s he developed long-distance telegraphy by designing high-conductivity cables and new instruments. From 1873 he advanced maritime shipping by improving compasses and inventing underwater sounding apparatus. Thomson was knighted (1866) and created Lord Kelvin (1892; first award of a peerage to a scientist). He served as president of the ROYAL SOCIETY 1890–5.

THORNEYCROFT, PETER (b. 26 July 1909 at Dunston, Staffordshire, England; d. 4 June 1994 at London, England, aged 84). Thorneycroft, a barrister, became a Conservative MP in 1938. He served in British governments as president of the Board of Trade (1951–7), then chancellor of the Exchequer, but resigned on 6 Jan. 1958, with Enoch POWELL and Nigel Birch, when the prime minister Harold MACMILLAN rejected spending cuts to protect sterling and combat INFLATION. (Macmillan trivialized the resignations as 'little local difficulties'.) Thorneycroft was minister for aviation (1960–2) and defence (1962–4). He lost his seat in 1966 and was created Lord Thorneycroft (1967). Margaret THATCHER, approving of his stand in 1958, appointed him as chairman of the Conservative Party (1975–81).

THOROUGH A term used in the 1630s by Viscount Wentworth (Thomas WENTWORTH) to describe his attempt, as the English governor in Ireland, to make royal authority stronger and more efficient. The term has also been applied by historians to the rhetoric of King Charles I's government in England and Wales during his 'personal rule' (1629–40), which stressed the need for royal authority to override private interests for supposed common good. *See also* WENTWORTH, THOMAS, AND IRELAND; CHARLES I, PERSONAL RULE.

'THREE FS' Term used by Irish land agitators from the 1850s to summarize their demands. It referred to: fair rent, fixity of tenure (freedom from contrived eviction), and free sale (tenant's right to sell a lease, also known as 'tenant right' or ULSTER CUSTOM). The 1870 Land Act gave legal recognition to Ulster Custom where it was long established. The 1881 Land Act granted the Three Fs throughout Ireland. *See also* GLADSTONE, W.E., AND IRELAND; LAND AGITATION AND REFORM, IRELAND.

THREE PUBLIC SERVICES Term used by historians for services owed by estates (land) to kings in Anglo-Saxon England: (a) provision of men for MILITARY SERVICE; (b) provision of labour to maintain fortifications; (c) repair of bridges. The services were imposed (or formalized) in MERCIA (740s) and extended to KENT by King OFFA (792). They later appeared in WESSEX (840s) and elsewhere. *See also* KINGSHIP, ANGLO-SAXON.

THROCKMORTON PLOT A scheme in 1583, devised by the French nobleman the duc de Guise, to replace the Protestant Queen ELIZABETH I as ruler of England with the Catholic MARY, QUEEN OF SCOTS, involving invasion by a French army. Papers discovered in Paris (France) in Oct. by an agent of Francis WALSINGHAM revealed that the English Catholic Francis Throckmorton was involved. He was arrested (Nov.) and executed (10 July 1584). *See also* CATHOLIC PLOTS, ENGLAND.

THURLOW, EDWARD (b. 9 Dec. 1731 at Bracon Ash, Norfolk, England; d. 12 Sept. 1806 at Brighton, Sussex, England, aged 74). Thurlow, a barrister, became an MP in 1765 as a follower of the 4th duke of BEDFORD. He held office under Lord NORTH as solicitor-general (1770–1) and attorney-general (1771–8), and supported coercion of the rebellious American colonies, impressing King GEORGE III (*see* AMERICAN INDEPENDENCE, ORIGINS OF).

In 1778, at the king's wish, Thurlow was created Lord Thurlow and appointed lord CHANCELLOR. He saw himself as a king's man rather than party man (*see* KING'S FRIENDS). He served until April 1783 in the ministries of Lords North, ROCKINGHAM and SHELBURNE, and was reappointed in

Dec. 1783 in the ministry of William PITT the Younger. Pitt forced Thurlow's dismissal in 1792 after he attacked a government policy.

TILLOTSON, JOHN (b. Oct. 1630 at Sowerby, near Halifax, Yorkshire, England; d. 22 Nov. 1694 at London, England, aged 64). From a Puritan family, Tillotson became a Church of ENGLAND clergyman in 1661 and accepted the post-Restoration Church settlement (*see* CLARENDON CODE). A popular preacher of commonsense sermons, he was appointed dean of CANTERBURY Cathedral in 1672.

Tillotson was favoured by WILLIAM III and MARY II (rulers from 1689), and appointed dean of St Paul's Cathedral, London. He supported the TOLERATION ACT and a scheme to include most Protestant dissenters within the Church (1689; *see* NOTTINGHAM, 2ND EARL OF). He reluctantly accepted appointment as archbishop of CANTERBURY (1691), following the deprivation of William SANCROFT. *See also* LATITUDINARIANISM.

TINCHEBRAI, BATTLE OF Fought at Tinchebrai, NORMANDY (N France), on 28 Sept. 1106. The English and Norman army of HENRY I, king of England, defeated the Norman army of his older brother ROBERT CURTHOSE, duke of Normandy. Henry took over Normandy; Robert was imprisoned (until his death in 1134). *See also* NORMAN EMPIRE.

TINPLATE INDUSTRY, WALES Tinplating (coating of iron sheets with tin) was developed by John Hanbury (1664–1734) at Pontypool (Monmouthshire). The industry migrated to W Glamorgan, around SWANSEA, by *c*.1800. From *c*.1840 demand from the US canning industry drove expansion. In the 1860s steel replaced iron – open-hearth steel, made by Landore-Siemens near Swansea, proved especially suitable (from 1875). By 1891 there were 86 works in S Wales.

The 'McKinley Tariff' on imports, imposed by the US government in 1890, devastated the industry, but replacement markets were found (1900–14). In the late 1940s the British government encouraged concentration: over 50 small works were replaced by two large plants. In the early 21st century most UK tinplate production occurred in Wales. *See also* IRON AND STEEL INDUSTRIES, WALES.

***TITANIC*, SINKING OF** Incident when the British steam-powered passenger liner *Titanic*, the largest ship in the world, sank in the N Atlantic early on 15 April 1912 during its maiden voyage (England via Ireland to USA). Built with supposedly watertight compartments, *Titanic* was considered unsinkable, but was fatally damaged by an iceberg. It was equipped with lifeboats for only 1178 of its 2223 passengers and crew; 706 were saved and 1517 died. *See also* SHIP-BUILDING INDUSTRY, IRELAND.

TITHE A tenth of agricultural produce paid annually by lay people to their local church to support clergy (from OE *téoða*, meaning 'tenth'). In England, payment was decreed compulsory by King ATHELSTAN between 926 and *c.*930. Tithes were initially paid mainly to MINSTERS, supplementing or replacing earlier renders (notably churchscot). From the late 11th–12th centuries they mainly funded PARISH churches. Tithes were levied elsewhere mainly from the 12th century as the PARISH SYSTEM developed. Tithes were sometimes diverted to religious houses, and later to lay owners, through APPROPRIATION OF CHURCHES. Payments in kind were occasionally commuted for monetary payments; when land was enclosed, tithes were frequently abolished by the compensatory award of land to tithe-owners (*see* ENCLOSURE).

In the early 19th century, in England and Wales, agitation against tithes, caused partly by agricultural depression, resulted in conversion of payments in kind to rent charges, and landlords became responsible for payment (Tithe Act, 1836). They usually required tenants to make payments, effectively as agents. Agitation reoccurred in the 1880s, especially in Wales (*see* TITHE WAR, WALES). Landlords then became responsible for payment (Tithe Act, 1891), and could only recover the cost by incorporation within a tenant's rent. Agitation by small owner-occupiers in the 1930s resulted in a scheme to extinguish tithes: the government compensated tithe-owners with stock redeemable in 60 years, and tithe-payers paid a small annuity for the same period.

In Ireland, tithes were extinguished in the 19th century (*see* TITHE ISSUE, IRELAND). In Scotland, different arrangements were made (*see* TEIND).

TITHE ISSUE, IRELAND From the later 16th century, following the REFORMATION, Catholics resented paying tithes (a tenth of agricultural produce) to Church of IRELAND clergy and some lay landlords. Some presbyterian immigrants (from 17th century) also resented tithes. Payment became an overt grievance from the 1760s during periods of rural unrest (*see* WHITEBOYS; STEELBOYS).

Although in 1823 the government enabled payments to be commuted to fixed charges (under the Tithe Composition Act), radicals launched a 'Tithe War' (non-payment) in late 1830. It continued until the 1838 Tithe Rentcharge (Ireland) Act converted tithes into fixed charges payable by landlords. They were eventually extinguished following the Irish Church Act of 1869. *See also* DRUMMOND, THOMAS.

TITHE WAR, WALES Protest throughout Wales (most intense in the NE) in 1886–8 by nonconformist tenant farmers who refused to pay TITHES to the established Church of ENGLAND; caused partly by the fall of livestock

prices and farmers' incomes during the AGRICULTURAL DEPRESSION. (Since the 1836 Tithe Commutation Act, tithes in many places had been paid as fixed rent charges.) Protesters were assuaged by the 1891 Tithe Act, which transferred tithe payment to landlords (though tenants paid via their rent). The 'War' intensified demands for DISESTABLISHMENT of the Church in Wales. *See also* NONCONFORMITY AND DISSENT, WALES; ELLIS, TOM.

TOGIDUBNUS *see* COGIDUBNUS

TOLERATION ACT, ENGLAND AND WALES Legislation by the CONVENTION PARLIAMENT, passed 24 May 1689, which allowed Protestant dissenters to worship in their own meeting-houses under certain conditions. Passed to secure Protestant support for King WILLIAM III against the former king JAMES VII/II, it formally ended the aspiration to include society solely within the Church of ENGLAND. Restrictions on dissenters holding public offices were not lifted. *See also* TEST AND CORPORATION ACTS; NONCONFORMITY AND DISSENT, ENGLAND/WALES.

TOLERATION ACT, IRELAND Legislation by the Irish PARLIAMENT in 1719 which exempted Protestant dissenters from penalties for non-attendance at Church of IRELAND worship and allowed registered meeting-houses. Such toleration (provided for England and Wales in 1689) was sought by presbyterians after they resisted the Catholic JAMES VII/II (1689–90). Proposed Acts in 1692 and 1695 were thwarted, mainly by opposition from Church of Ireland bishops who saw organized presbyterianism as a threat. Legislation was eventually conceded because the alleged threat had been reduced by exclusion of presbyterians from civil offices in 1704 (by imposition of a sacramental test), and because WHIGS wished to encourage Protestant unity following the HANOVERIAN SUCCESSION. The 1719 Act was largely nominal because penalties were not enforced. *See also* NONCONFORMITY AND DISSENT, IRELAND; PRESBYTERIANISM, IRELAND.

TOLERATION ACT, SCOTLAND An Act of the British Parliament passed in 1712, following GREENSHIELDS' CASE, which permitted Episcopalians in Scotland to meet and worship using the English Prayer Book, provided that they prayed for the reigning sovereign (thus excluding Jacobites). The Act arguably breached the terms of the UNION OF ENGLAND AND SCOTLAND by infringing the secured monopoly of the Church of SCOTLAND. *See also* KIRK SESSION; PATRONAGE ACT; EPISCOPAL CHURCH IN SCOTLAND.

TOLPUDDLE MARTYRS Name given to six farm labourers who were convicted in March 1834 of swearing an illegal oath when forming a trade union branch in Tolpuddle

(Dorset, S England). They were sentenced to TRANSPORTATION for seven years, provoking large-scale protests (e.g., in London). The sentences were remitted in 1836. The labourers were considered 'martyrs' for the right to form a union. *See also* TRADE UNIONISM, ENGLAND.

TONE, WOLFE (b. 20 June 1763 at Dublin, Ireland; d. 19 Nov. 1798 at Dublin, aged 35). Tone (a Protestant) trained as a lawyer but instead entered Irish politics as a campaigner and writer (from 1790). He was influenced by the French Revolution (1789) and adopted republican ideals. In Sept. 1791 he published the pamphlet *An Argument on Behalf of the Catholics of Ireland*, which urged Catholics and Protestants to unite to seek a reformed, national Parliament. Tone also co-founded the Dublin branch of the UNITED IRISHMEN (Nov.) and worked for the CATHOLIC COMMITTEE (1792).

In June 1795, after associating with an emissary from France, Tone moved to the USA. He then went to France (Aug.) and sought forces for an invasion of Ireland, to establish an Irish republic. A naval expedition was dispatched (Dec. 1796), but was dispersed by bad weather. A second expedition was cancelled (July 1797). After the Irish RISING OF 1798 (May–July) Tone tried to organize small expeditions. He landed in Ireland on 12 Oct. only to be captured and court-martialled for treason. He was sentenced to death by hanging, but cut his throat before the execution (12 Nov.). He died a few days later. *See also* FRENCH REVOLUTION, IMPACT ON IRELAND.

TONNAGE AND POUNDAGE Term used in the 15th–17th centuries for English CUSTOMS revenues, referring to their major components: tonnage was a charge on wine imports (referring to a cask, or tun, of definite capacity); poundage was a charge on general merchandise according to its value. From 1484 (in reign of King RICHARD III) a ruler's first Parliament usually made a life-time grant of customs revenues to the ruler.

In 1625 the first Parliament of CHARLES I, angered by IMPOSITIONS, refused the grant. Charles collected the customs revenues without authorization, provoking complaints in 1629 (*see* PETITION OF RIGHT). An Act of June 1641 declared their collection without parliamentary authorization illegal but made a short-term grant. They were granted for life to CHARLES II in 1660.

TONYPANDY INCIDENT A controversial event from 9 Nov. 1910 when soldiers were sent to help police maintain order at Tonypandy (Glamorgan, S Wales) during a miners' dispute. The right-wing press praised the Liberal home secretary, Winston CHURCHILL, for his action, but he long remained unpopular in Wales where critics claimed he had suppressed the right to strike. *See also* THOMAS, DAVID ALFRED.

TORIES The term 'tory' originated in mid-17th-century Ireland (Irish *toraidhe*), referring to Catholic outlaws. It was applied (with other terms) from 1679 to supporters of the hereditary right of James, duke of York (later JAMES VII/II), to become king despite his Catholicism (*see* EXCLUSION CRISIS). (York's opponents were called WHIGS.)

After the GLORIOUS REVOLUTION (1688–9) the term was attached to HIGH CHURCH politicians (defenders of the pre-eminent position of the Church of England). Under Queen ANNE (ruled 1702–14) Tories opposed foreign involvements and religious toleration (*see* SPANISH SUCCESSION, WAR OF THE; SACHEVERELL AFFAIR).

Under GEORGE I (from 1714) and GEORGE II, toryism was condemned for its alleged association with JACOBITISM. (Whigs dominated politics.) Tories tended to be country GENTRY. They lost their coherence as a party in the early 1760s.

The term Tory was revived in the early 19th century by opponents of reform. The administration of the 2nd earl of LIVERPOOL (1812–27) was the first since Anne's reign to identify itself as Tory. From 1830 Tories increasingly preferred the term 'Conservative'. *See also* POLITICAL PARTIES; CONSERVATIVE PARTY.

TORY DEMOCRACY The populist politics of Lord Randolph CHURCHILL, intended to attract British working-class voters in 1885. Often dismissed as an empty or contradictory slogan, Tory Democracy was defined by Churchill as 'a democracy which embraced the principles of the Tory Party'. *See also* CONSERVATIVE PARTY.

TOUN *see* FERMTOUN

TOURISM, SCOTLAND Although travellers toured Scotland in the 18th century, notably Samuel JOHNSON and James Boswell (1773), tourism burgeoned from the early 19th century with the romanticization of the HIGHLANDS, especially by the novels of Sir Walter SCOTT and the visits of Queen VICTORIA (from 1842). Tours using railways and coastal steamships were organized from 1846 by the English travel agent Thomas Cook (1808–92) and from the 1860s by railway companies. From the 1920s motorized transport opened up new areas.

From 1945, with the establishment of the Scottish Tourist Board funded by local authorities, tourism was officially promoted. The Board became a statutory body in 1969, and was renamed VisitScotland in 2006. By 2014, over 15 million people visited annually, accounting for 5% of gross domestic product and supporting 217,000 jobs. *See also* CLAN, SCOTLAND; TRANSPORT COMMUNICATIONS, SCOTLAND.

TOWN GOVERNMENT, ENGLAND In the 7th–11th centuries, urban places (MINSTER centres, WICS, BURHS) were administered by officers of kings and other lords (*see* REEVE). By the 11th century larger towns (mostly royal burhs) had courts administering local customs.

In the 12th century kings formally confirmed liberties to many towns by charter (e.g., recognition of merchant guild). From 1189 perpetual 'fee farms' were also granted; i.e., royal rights were delegated (revenues, choice of officers, court, etc.) for fixed annual payments. From the 13th century self-governing towns were usually headed by a mayor (assisted by a council). Participation required admission as a 'freeman' or BURGESS. Lords also granted liberties to new small towns (the majority of towns), usually retaining some rights (e.g., MANOR court). Historians term such towns 'seigniorial boroughs'.

From the mid 14th century some town governments became legally corporate entities (*see* INCORPORATION OF BOROUGHS); a few received county status. From the later 15th century 'closed corporations' were authorized, whereby burgesses were co-opted. Grants of charters largely ceased from *c.*1700 and separate improvement commissions were established (*see* IMPROVEMENT ACTS). In seigniorial boroughs, GUILDS sometimes acted as 'shadow governments' (13th–16th centuries); PARISH organization then became important.

In the 19th century PARLIAMENT effected reforms. Legislation in 1835 prescribed partly elected councils for 157 corporations and facilitated further incorporations (*see* MUNICIPAL CORPORATIONS ACT). In 1877 incorporation was made easier; in 1882 closed corporations were abolished. In 1888 'county boroughs' were created (large towns with powers equal or sometimes superior to those of counties); other town authorities were subordinated to county councils. In 1894 non-municipal urban sanitary authorities became urban district councils.

In 1974 reorganization constituted six conurbations (outside London) as 'metropolitan counties' with subordinate 'metropolitan districts'. Other towns became districts (below counties) or lost autonomy. Metropolitan county councils were abolished in 1986, with districts becoming unitary (all-purpose) authorities. Some district-level towns were also later upgraded. *See also* LONDON, GOVERNMENT OF; COMMUNES, ENGLAND; TEST AND CORPORATION ACTS; LOCAL GOVERNMENTAL STRUCTURES, ENGLAND.

TOWN GOVERNMENT, IRELAND Monastic 'proto-towns' (from 7th century) were administered under the authority of abbots, while the complexity of VIKING towns (10th–12th centuries) implies government under royal authority (*see* TOWNS, IRELAND).

Following the Anglo-Norman invasion (1169–70), English rulers granted self-government under their authority to major towns, specifying collective and individual liberties in charters (e.g., rights of privileged 'freemen' to elect officers and participate in government). DUBLIN was placed briefly under the authority of BRISTOL in England. From the early 13th century towns (or 'boroughs') also received 'fee farm' grants (retention of royal revenues for a fixed annual payment). Founders of small towns granted liberties to attract settlers, often replicating those of Breteuil in NORMANDY. As the English-governed area contracted in the 14th–15th centuries, major towns received extra liberties; nine became autonomous (effectively of county status). In some towns, governments became self-perpetuating 'closed corporations'.

When more small towns were founded in the late 16th–early 17th centuries (e.g., BELFAST, LONDONDERRY) they often received royal grants of closed corporations to elect Protestant MPs. Catholics were excluded from other town governments in the 1650s (*see* COMMONWEALTH AND PROTECTORATE, IRELAND). During the 18th century elected commissions were established in some towns by Act of Parliament to improve facilities (*see* IMPROVEMENT ACTS).

The UK Parliament's MUNICIPAL CORPORATIONS (IRELAND) ACT (1840) dissolved most corporations. Ten survivors (e.g., CORK, Dublin) were reformed, including establishment of ratepayer-elected councils and readmission of Catholics; WEXFORD was granted borough status in 1846. Another 109 towns regained limited autonomy by adopting elected commissions under the 1828 Lighting of Towns Act, the 1854 Towns Improvement (Ireland) Act, or private Acts. But the 1898 Local Government (Ireland) Act imposed new arrangements: it granted unitary 'county borough' status to six cities (Belfast, Cork, Dublin, LIMERICK, Londonderry, WATERFORD) and limited self-government to other towns as 'urban districts' below county councils. *See also* LOCAL GOVERNMENTAL STRUCTURES, IRELAND; LOCAL GOVERNMENT, NORTHERN IRELAND/SOUTHERN IRELAND.

TOWN GOVERNMENT, SCOTLAND Most early towns or BURGHS (founded mainly by kings from the 12th century) were administered by local royal officers – sheriffs assisted by provosts or bailies (bailiffs). Officers collected rents and tolls, held a court, and accounted to the royal CHAMBERLAIN. By 1200 townsmen were usually chosen as officers; in the 13th century officers were often elected annually by townsmen. From 1319 towns received grants of feu-ferme (fee farm); i.e., BURGESSES (freemen) kept most profits due to the Crown in return for an annual payment. By *c.*1350 royal burghs were headed by a provost, assisted by bailies and a council (typically 12 members) elected by burgesses. From the 13th century townsmen could form a guild (under a dean) to control trade and hold social gatherings.

An Act of 1469 ended elections. Henceforth an outgoing council chose its replacement, and both councils with craft representatives selected officers. From 1474 four retiring councillors had to be re-selected. The result was self-perpetuating 'closed corporations'. In the late 15th–17th centuries craft guilds were also widely established. Some burghs of barony or regality, founded by lords, lacked councils and were run by lord's officers.

The 1833 BURGH REFORM ACTS introduced election of councillors by qualified parliamentary voters in royal and (new) parliamentary burghs. (Closed corporations continued elsewhere.) Under 'Police Acts' of 1833–67 townsmen in royal and other burghs could also elect police commissioners to provide policing, lighting and street-cleansing.

The 1900 Town Councils (Scotland) Act abolished 'police burghs' and vested powers in elected councils in all burghs. From 1930 burghs were ranked in three categories with different powers. Courts were retained with magistrates elected by council members. In 1975 burghs were abolished; a few towns received 'district' status while most fell within larger districts. In 1996, when unitary authorities were reintroduced, self-government was restored to ABERDEEN, DUNDEE, EDINBURGH and GLASGOW. See also TOWNS, SCOTLAND; LOCAL GOVERNMENTAL STRUCTURES, SCOTLAND; POLICE, SCOTLAND.

TOWN GOVERNMENT, WALES Many towns (or BOROUGHS) were founded c.1070– c.1300, alongside castles, by invaders (see TOWNS, WALES; MARCH OF WALES). In these towns the castle constable was usually head of the adjacent town (as steward or, later, mayor), but as in other towns leading townsmen undertook government, following arrangements in their founder's charter. Many charters reproduced terms granted c.1070 by William fitz Osbern to Hereford (England), derived from his town of Breteuil in NORMANDY (N France). A town's freemen or BURGESSES elected officers (e.g., constables) annually and nominated men as bailiff (or portreeve), for selection by the constable. The bailiffs (often two) regulated trade and order through a court.

During the 15th and 16th centuries, town leaders obtained charters creating 'closed corporations'. A common council became the central institution, comprising an elected mayor; aldermen (often 12) sitting for life; and 'capital burgesses' (often 12) elected annually by freemen. Freemen were created by nomination – relatively few were admitted. Lords retained influence through their steward. Government continued to operate through courts.

The 1835 MUNICIPAL CORPORATIONS ACT abolished numerous corporations (56); 21 towns were reformed with elected councils (two-thirds elected by ratepayers; a third, aldermen chosen by elected councillors). Boroughs retained considerable autonomy after county councils were established in 1889; from 1894 (Local Government Act), non-municipal urban sanitary authorities became urban district councils.

Town councils were abolished in 1974, though many towns became districts (beneath counties). Reorganization in 1996 made CARDIFF, MERTHYR TYDFIL, NEWPORT, SWANSEA and WREXHAM the principal areas within relatively compact unitary authorities. See also LOCAL GOVERNMENTAL STRUCTURES, WALES.

TOWNLAND Modern name for the smallest territorial unit in Ireland, averaging about 320 acres (130 ha) though very variable. Totalling about 61,000, townlands are used as location identifiers in rural areas but otherwise serve no administrative function. Formerly known by various names (e.g., balliboe, ploughland), they predate the Anglo-Norman invasion (1169–70) and may be older by many centuries. Their names are mainly of Gaelic Irish origin. Townlands have been used for assessments, and were the basis for land transfers in the 17th century (see CROMWELLIAN LAND SETTLEMENT). They were mapped in the 1830s–40s, and served as the basis of 'unions' for POOR RELIEF. Groupings of townlands constitute PARISHES.

TOWN PLANNING All periods of urban development have involved planning. Early Anglo-Saxon urban settlements (7th–8th centuries) probably included planned streets, tenements and small market places (see TOWNS, ENGLAND). Royal BURHS (9th–10th centuries; e.g., OXFORD) featured rectilinear street plans and defences.

The numerous towns created by lords throughout the British Isles in the late 11th–13th centuries (e.g., KENILWORTH, WINDSOR) used flexible standard elements (termed 'plan units'). Reflecting commercial priorities and usually undefended, they were focused on a market place (or broad market street) lined with narrow tenements. Extensions consisted of streets with adjacent tenements. A few towns utilized grid plans (e.g., CAERNARFON; New Winchelsea, East Sussex).

Planning was then rare until the 1630s when Inigo JONES created a large Italian-style rectangular piazza, with adjacent houses and church, at Covent Garden, LONDON. It proved influential; from the late 17th century extensions to London included squares. (Replanning of central London after the GREAT FIRE of 1666 was rejected.) Large-scale planning – with broad roads, squares, crescents and terraces – flourished in the 18th and early 19th centuries, particularly for spas and seaside resorts. Examples occurred at BATH, EDINBURGH (New Town) and DUBLIN.

Industrial towns (from 18th century) frequently grew piecemeal, influenced by previous field layouts. Small grids were often favoured. In reaction, from the mid 19th century suburban areas for wealthy people preferred sweeping roads with detached villas.

By 1900 many towns comprised layouts from different periods. Subsequent planning was influenced by the concepts of the GARDEN CITY (e.g., functional zoning) and garden suburb (e.g., low-density housing), and controlled through legislation (e.g., 1935 British Act against 'ribbon development'). Some city centres (e.g., Exeter, SW England) were replanned in the 1940s after the BLITZ, and 'new towns' incorporated novel ideas (e.g., isolation of motor traffic). From the 1990s Poundbury (at Dorchester, S England), created by CHARLES, PRINCE OF WALES, reasserted a human-scale approach. *See also* ROMAN BRITAIN, TOWNS; SUBURBS AND SUBURBIA.

TOWNS, ENGLAND Following the decline of Roman towns (5th century; *see* POST-ROMAN BRITAIN), urban life revived from the 7th century: in former Roman towns where bishops' sees were established (e.g., CANTERBURY); as settlements alongside MINSTER churches; as river-side trading centres (*see* WIC). Some BURHS (fortified centres) created by King ALFRED in WESSEX (later 9th century) and by EDWARD THE ELDER and ÆTHELFLÆD in MERCIA (early 10th century) developed into towns. WINCHESTER was England's capital in the 10th–12th centuries; (large) SHIRES were centred on towns.

In the late 11th–13th centuries, lords founded numerous small towns. A clear hierarchy emerged, comprising *c*.1300: LONDON, (commercial capital, 80,000 inhabitants); regional centres, with up to 13,000 inhabitants (BRISTOL, NORWICH, YORK, Exeter, NEWCASTLE UPON TYNE); other major ports (e.g., SOUTHAMPTON) and county centres (up to 5000 inhabitants); over 600 small towns (500–1500 inhabitants). Populations recovered somewhat from BLACK DEATH (1348–9), but fell in the 15th century.

During urban expansion in the 16th–17th centuries, London grew spectacularly (to 575,000 inhabitants *c*.1700). Some towns developed identities as industrial centres (e.g., BIRMINGHAM, SHEFFIELD) and spas (e.g., BATH). The largest provincial town was NORWICH (30,000 inhabitants *c*.1700); it was superseded by Bristol in the 18th century, when western ports flourished from trans-Atlantic trade.

The INDUSTRIAL REVOLUTION (later 18th century) expanded towns in Lancashire and W Yorkshire (N England). In 1800, MANCHESTER (95,000 inhabitants) and LIVERPOOL (77,000) were the largest provincial towns, with Liverpool the biggest for most of the 19th century (685,000 inhabitants in 1900). Around 1911 Birmingham superseded Liverpool. By 1850 England became the world's first country with a majority urban population.

In the 1920s–30s new light industries contributed to urban expansion in the Midlands and southern England, while older industrial centres stagnated. After 1947, 22 'new towns' were founded. From the late 20th century economies experienced DE-INDUSTRIALIZATION and growth of services (e.g., finance). *See also* TOWN PLANNING; CAPITALS; COMMERCIALIZATION; CLOTH INDUSTRY, ENGLAND; SUBURBS AND SUBURBIA; TOWN GOVERNMENT, ENGLAND; TOWN SOCIETY, ENGLAND.

TOWNS, IRELAND By the 7th century some ecclesiastical centres (monastic and lay settlements) became 'proto-towns' through developing trade and craftwork (e.g., ARMAGH, CLONMACNOIS, both situated inland). In the 10th century VIKINGS added towns near coasts to facilitate involvement in international trade (*see* CORK, DUBLIN, LIMERICK, WATERFORD, WEXFORD). Dublin became pre-eminent.

After the Anglo-Norman invasion (1169–70) Dublin was the centre of English government. In English areas, lords founded ports (e.g., Drogheda, Galway) and small towns (possibly 200), the latter as centres of trade, small-scale manufacturing and sometimes lordship. Many small places lost urban status in the 14th–15th centuries due to contraction of English areas and population decline.

More towns were founded in the 16th–17th centuries, including ones on English and Scottish PLANTATIONS. Urban development occurred notably in ULSTER (e.g., BELFAST, LONDONDERRY), where few towns previously existed. Leading established towns (e.g., Dublin, Cork) expanded in the 17th–18th centuries.

In the 18th century major towns developed BANKING and INDUSTRY (e.g., sugar-refining, BREWING). Textile industries (LINEN, COTTON) grew around Belfast, with FACTORY production from the later 18th century. Outside Ulster, much industry declined in the early 19th century. Small towns remained centres of craftwork and retailing.

After the GREAT FAMINE (1845–9) towns with over 2000 inhabitants expanded slightly, sustained by thriving small farmers. The urban population in 1871 was about 20%. Industrial development made Belfast the largest centre 1890s–1920s (also capital of NORTHERN IRELAND from 1921, containing a third of its population). Dublin then resumed first place, because of boundary expansions and internal migration.

From the 1950s urban growth accelerated. In the Republic of Ireland the urban population (in towns over 1500 people) became a majority in the 1960s. Suburbs and commuting areas around major centres expanded. In the early 21st century a third of the Republic's population lived in Dublin. *See also* TOWN PLANNING; SUBURBS AND SUBURBIA; CAPITALS; COMMERCIALIZATION; TOWN GOVERNMENT, IRELAND; TOWN SOCIETY, IRELAND.

TOWNS, SCOTLAND Before the 12th century, non-agricultural economic activities (trade, craftwork) may have taken place at religious and estate centres. The first formal towns were BURGHS founded by King DAVID I (ruled 1124–53) as administrative and trading centres; many were also SHER-IFFDOM centres adjoining royal castles. Burghs were planned settlements, usually with a street widening into a market place (e.g., STIRLING) or grid-plan (e.g., PERTH). Few had defences. Around 1300 the largest towns contained around 2000 inhabitants. Leading towns were ABERDEEN, BERWICK-UPON-TWEED, DUNDEE, and Perth, with EDINBURGH emerging as CAPITAL in the 15th century.

Following contraction of populations in the 15th century, urban growth resumed in the late 16th and 17th centuries, including the foundation of 270 small burghs and GLASGOW joining the top rank. Population increase encouraged denser building (including change from timber-frame construction to stone), and growth of SUBURBS. By the early 17th century pressure on Edinburgh's cramped site had produced high-rise tenements. By the late 17th century Edinburgh, with suburbs and ports, contained about 50,000 people, making it Britain's second largest city. But Glasgow was also growing rapidly. The proportion of Scotland's population in towns with over 2000 inhabitants rose to 12% by c.1700.

By the late 18th century, growth of trade and industry focused on W-C Scotland had brought dramatic expansion to Glasgow and satellites such as Paisley and Greenock, as well as creating smaller industrial centres. By the mid 19th century Scottish society was predominantly urban; from the late 19th century, Glasgow was Scotland's most populous city. Railways allowed cities and towns to develop middle-class commuting suburbs, while working-class populations crammed into inner-city tenements. From c.1945 population declined in large conurbations, following INDUSTRIAL DECLINE, slum clearance and migration to new towns. Glasgow underwent considerable regeneration from the 1980s (e.g., Garden Festival, 1988), and in the 21st century Edinburgh benefited from DEVOLUTION. *See also* TOWN PLANNING; COMMERCIALIZATION; TOWN GOVERNMENT, SCOTLAND; TOWN SOCIETY, SCOTLAND.

TOWNS, WALES Roman towns in W Britain (Caerwent, Carmarthen) declined in the 5th century (*see* POST-ROMAN BRITAIN). Between c.1070 and 1135, invading NORMANS founded about 26 towns in E and S Wales (e.g., CARDIFF, SWANSEA). Situated alongside castles, they were populated with English immigrants (*see* MARCH OF WALES). More towns were founded by Anglo-Norman lords in the late 12th century; by Welsh rulers (mainly in GWYNEDD) in the 13th century; and by King EDWARD I of England from 1283 (e.g., CAERNARFON; *see* WALES, ENGLISH CONQUEST OF). By c.1300, Wales contained about 105 towns – about 75 founded by Normans or English. Cardiff was largest (2000 inhabitants), most others small (150–1000).

Populations were reduced by the BLACK DEATH (1349). Some towns recovered; CARMARTHEN emerged as the largest. At least 40 were devastated in the revolt of Owain Glyn Dŵr (1400–10). Many places ceased to be towns; by c.1500, about 60 remained.

Populations increased from c.1550. In 1600 Carmarthen, WREXHAM, Brecon and Haverfordwest each contained around 2000 inhabitants; Caernarfon, Cardiff, Denbigh, Kidwelly, Monmouth, Swansea, and Tenby about 1000; others a few hundred. Hitherto, towns had been market centres; inhabitants lived off small-scale manufacturing and trade.

During the 18th century, industry expanded at Swansea (copper smelting, coal mining) and MERTHYR TYDFIL (iron working). From the mid 19th century, Cardiff and Newport expanded rapidly as coal ports. In 1900, Cardiff had 160,000 inhabitants, Swansea 130,000, Merthyr 69,000, and Newport 67,000. Most other towns remained small (under 10,000). From c.1918 heavy industries declined and were replaced, mainly from 1945, by light industry (e.g., electrical goods, plastics). Tourism stimulated expansion of coastal towns in the N from the 1930s.

Wales has lacked large trading centres and a natural capital. Towns traded in England: from N Wales with Chester and (from the 18th century) LIVERPOOL; from C Wales with Shrewsbury; from S Wales with BRISTOL. Cardiff was designated the CAPITAL in 1955. *See also* TOWN PLANNING; SUBURBS AND SUBURBIA; COMMERCIALIZATION; COAL INDUSTRY, WALES; TOWN GOVERNMENT, WALES; TOWN SOCIETY, WALES.

TOWNSHEND, CHARLES (b. 27 Aug. 1725 in England; d. 4 Sept. 1767 at Sudbrook, Surrey, England, aged 42). A younger brother of George Townshend (*see* TOWNSHEND, 4TH VISCOUNT), and a WHIG MP from 1747, Townshend was a supporter of William PITT the Elder. He served in the Pitt-DEVONSHIRE and Pitt-NEWCASTLE ministries. He then transferred allegiance to the earl of BUTE, becoming secretary at war (1761–2) and briefly president of the Board of Trade (1763). Though a prominent opponent of George GRENVILLE's ministry, he accepted office as paymaster-general (May 1765 to 1766, continuing under the marquess of ROCKINGHAM).

Townshend served as chancellor of the Exchequer from Aug. 1766 in the ministry of William Pitt (now earl of Chatham). He became notorious for introducing import duties to the American colonies in 1767 (so-called 'Townshend duties'), which provoked fierce opposition. *See also* AMERICAN INDEPENDENCE, ORIGINS OF.

TOWNSHEND, 2ND VISCOUNT (b. 18 April 1674 at Raynham, Norfolk, England; d. 21 June 1738 at Raynham, aged 64). Charles Townshend succeeded as viscount in 1687 and later sat in the House of Lords. In 1713 he married a sister of Robert WALPOLE, his friend and fellow WHIG.

After the accession of the pro-Whig King GEORGE I (1714), Townshend became a leading minister as SECRE- TARY OF STATE (northern). He helped to suppress the JACOBITE REBELLION of 1715. But in Dec. 1716, following intrigue by the earl of SUNDERLAND with the king, Townshend was demoted to lord lieutenant of Ireland. He was dismissed in April 1717. Walpole and others also resigned.

Townshend returned to office in June 1720 (president of the Council) and was SECRETARY OF STATE (northern) again from Feb. 1721. His brother-in-law Walpole was first lord of the Treasury and effectively chief minister from April. But from 1725 they disagreed over foreign policy. Townshend resigned in May 1730 after Walpole refused to replace a minister at his request. In retirement Townshend was nicknamed 'Turnip Townshend' for promoting crop rotations that included turnips.

TOWNSHEND, 4TH VISCOUNT (b. 28 Feb. 1724 at London, England; d. 14 Sept. 1807 at Raynham, Norfolk, England, aged 83). George Townshend, a soldier, suc- ceeded as (4th) Viscount Townshend in 1764. In 1767 he became chief governor (lord lieutenant) of Ireland, with instructions to expand the Army. To encourage support in the Irish House of Commons he conceded the OCTENNIAL ACT (Feb. 1768). But because he allegedly offered insuffi- cient rewards to 'UNDERTAKERS' (business managers), the Commons rejected two government Bills (May 1768, Nov. 1769).

Townshend dismissed leading adversaries from govern- ment posts (1770), remained in Ireland (becoming the first fully resident 18th-century governor), and organized sup- port himself. By diminishing the 'undertaker system' he strengthened government control. He also roused PATRIOT opposition. He left Ireland in 1772, and was created mar- quess of Raynham in 1786. *See also* PONSONBY, JOHN; PROTESTANT ASCENDANCY.

TOWN SOCIETY, ENGLAND MINSTER-based urban societies (7th–9th centuries) included clergy with servants, craftsmen and traders. WICS had larger populations (with- out clergy). In the 10th–11th centuries, towns in Danish- inhabited areas (notably YORK) included Scandinavian communities (as did LONDON). Royal BURHS (e.g., WINCHESTER) contained landowners, a range of craftsmen, craft groups (e.g., tanners, butchers), and traders. Town societies were sustained by immigration until the 19th century.

Expanding towns of the 12th–13th centuries had hierar- chies of merchants, independent craftsmen, paid journey- men, apprentices, and labourers. In larger towns, merchants and craftsmen who belonged to a 'merchant guild' (or body of freemen or BURGESSES) were socially distinct from

others (called 'foreigners'); guildsmen were entitled to trade and participate in government. Craft groups (e.g., shoemakers) sometimes formed GUILDS (associations) to defend their interests.

In the 14th–15th centuries religious and social guilds, supporting CHANTRIES, proliferated (dissolved 1548). In many towns from the later 15th century leading townsmen appropriated control of government, creating 'closed corporations'.

During renewed expansion (16th–17th centuries), poor people increased in number and proportion (up to three- quarters). Fewer than 10% of inhabitants were wealthy, occupying big houses. By the late 17th century, towns included larger 'middling' groups, so-called 'urban gentry' (e.g., PROFESSIONALS such as lawyers, and rentiers). They became more numerous and influential, alongside mer- chants, during the 18th century, and urban cultural life flourished (*see* CONSUMER REVOLUTION).

From the 1780s the INDUSTRIAL REVOLUTION created societies (e.g., MANCHESTER) perceived as stratified by SOCIAL CLASS, comprising a mass 'working class', some liv- ing in squalid conditions (*see* SLUMS), and a small 'middle class' of business owners, tradesmen and professionals. During the 19th century RAILWAYS and trams facilitated suburban growth and commuting. In the 1920s–30s COUNCIL HOUSING schemes and large private suburbs entrenched class separation. More complex societies developed from the 1950s with the establishment of eth- nic communities and DE-INDUSTRIALIZATION. *See also* TOWNS, ENGLAND; TOWN GOVERNMENT, ENGLAND; COMMERCIAL REVOLUTION; ETHNIC AND NATIONAL MINORITIES, ENGLAND; MULTICULTURAL SOCIETY.

TOWN SOCIETY, IRELAND Ecclesiastical centres that functioned as 'proto-towns' (7th–13th centuries), were governed by abbots and probably contained traders, crafts- men and agricultural tenants. Coastal towns founded by VIKINGS (10th century) included traders and craftsmen of Scandinavian origin (*see* OSTMEN).

After the Anglo-Norman invasion (1169–70), English and Welsh settled in established towns and in new ports and small towns (founded 12th–13th centuries). Towns were the main centres of the English presence, dominated by traders and craftsmen. Gaelic immigrants to new towns were sometimes confined to 'Irishtown' areas.

During the 16th century town populations generally resisted reformed Christianity (*see* REFORMATION, IRELAND); but Protestant immigrants, so-called NEW ENGLISH, settled in the 16th–17th centuries. Dublin acquired a substantial Protestant population. New towns in ULSTER (e.g., LONDONDERRY, BELFAST) were dominated by Protestants. Catholics were ousted from governments dur- ing the 1650s (*see* COMMONWEALTH AND PROTECTORATE,

IRELAND), and remained excluded after the RESTORATION (1660). Legislation (1660s) sought to exclude Catholics from towns.

Regular meetings of PARLIAMENT in Dublin in the late 17th–18th centuries generated concurrent 'seasons' of social events (e.g., dinners, balls), attended by rural (Protestant) landlords. Other larger towns (Cork, Belfast) also acquired social amenities for wealthier inhabitants (theatres, coffee houses). Industrial development (late 18th–early 19th centuries) started to create a working class in larger towns, and general population increase created impoverished 'cabin suburbs'.

Following Union with Great Britain (1801), professionals (e.g., lawyers) and businessmen gradually replaced landowners as influential residents in larger towns. Industrial decline in southern Ireland left behind extensive SLUMS, whereas expansion in Belfast and Londonderry attracted Catholics, increasing sectarian tensions. From the mid 19th century trains and tramways facilitated smart suburbs for wealthier people.

In the 1960s urban populations became a majority in southern Ireland. In NORTHERN IRELAND, tensions degenerated into the TROUBLES (1968–90s). From the 1990s immigrant communities became a significant presence. *See also* TOWNS, IRELAND; TOWN GOVERNMENT, IRELAND; CONSUMER REVOLUTION; COMMERCIAL REVOLUTION; ETHNIC AND NATIONAL MINORITIES, IRELAND; MULTICULTURAL SOCIETY.

TOWN SOCIETY, SCOTLAND Most early BURGHS (from 12th century) were craft and trading colonies, including foreigners (especially from England, NORMANDY and Flanders). Until the 16th century they remained small, tight-knit communities, with relatively little internal social difference. The growth of FOREIGN TRADE in the 13th century increased the importance of merchants, who gradually emerged as ruling élites, distinct from craftsmen. Late-medieval towns (14th and 15th centuries) enjoyed growing self-government by elected officers, including provosts, baillies (bailiffs) and burgh councils. At first all BURGESSES had some say in urban affairs, but in the 15th century government became increasingly oligarchic, with the emergence of self-perpetuating 'closed corporations'.

Urban growth in the 16th and 17th centuries (*see* TOWNS, SCOTLAND) increased social differentiation, with larger non-burgess populations and rapid growth of PROFESSIONAL groups, especially in law and medicine. The suppression of food prices kept urban poverty in check until the late 16th century. Thereafter burgh courts, merchant and craft guilds, and KIRK SESSIONS worked together to regulate society. The late 17th and 18th centuries saw the rise of EDINBURGH and other major towns as social centres. With the building of Edinburgh's 'New Town' (late 18th

century), and new residential districts elsewhere, social differences were translated into clear high- and low-status areas.

Rapid urban growth in the 19th century associated with industrialization spread the use of tenement blocks as a characteristic housing form for working and middle classes. Slum clearance from the 1950s moved many working-class families to peripheral local-authority housing developments. *See also* TOWN GOVERNMENT, SCOTLAND; CONSUMER REVOLUTION; COMMERCIAL REVOLUTION; ETHNIC AND NATIONAL MINORITIES, SCOTLAND; MULTICULTURAL SOCIETY.

TOWN SOCIETY, WALES Towns in the MARCH OF WALES, founded *c*.1070– *c*.1135 by NORMANS, were populated by English, Norman and Flemish immigrants, though Welsh people gradually settled. Fewer English lived in towns in native Wales, but most towns had mixed populations by *c*.1300. Similar developments followed in towns founded in the N and NE after the English Conquest of 1282–3 (*see* WALES, ENGLISH CONQUEST OF). Towns' economic and administrative functions resulted in populations of traders, craftsmen, administrators and clerics. Traders and craftsmen usually became freeman or BURGESSES, permitted to trade and participate in TOWN GOVERNMENT and required to help with defence. The PENAL LAWS of the 15th century forbade Welshmen to buy land in towns or become burgesses, though enforcement was lax.

In the 16th and 17th centuries towns, now populated by Welsh, comprised a merchant élite, craftsmen and numerous artisans; they were often dominated by GENTRY, who maintained residences. Professionals (e.g., lawyers, clergy) were also important. Industrial and urban expansion in the 19th century produced a large working class in the S and NE (*see* INDUSTRY, WALES FROM 18TH CENTURY), including many immigrants from England and Ireland. In the 20th and 21st centuries IMMIGRATION from numerous countries mainly affected the populations of cities and larger towns. *See also* TOWNS, WALES; CONSUMER REVOLUTION; COMMERCIAL REVOLUTION; ETHNIC AND NATIONAL MINORITIES, WALES; MULTICULTURAL SOCIETY.

TOXTETH RIOTS *see* BRIXTON AND TOXTETH RIOTS

TRACTARIANS *see* OXFORD MOVEMENT

TRADE CYCLES OR BUSINESS CYCLES Significant fluctuations in economic activity (expansions and depressions), each usually lasting several years. The British economy became noticeably affected by such cycles from the later 18th century because of the increased importance of overseas trade which was inherently variable. Other factors, such as investment levels, later became contributory elements. The worst depression occurred in the 1930s (*see* GREAT DEPRESSION, IMPACT ON GREAT BRITAIN).

TRADE UNIONISM, ENGLAND Small unions (or 'combinations') emerged among urban craftsmen during the 18th century, though many were banned. All combinations were prohibited from 1799 until 1824, when they were permitted to undertake collective bargaining (*see* COMBINATION ACTS). Unions multiplied, especially among textile workers (including women), but attempts to create a Grand National Consolidated Trades Union (1833–5) proved unsuccessful (*see* OWEN, ROBERT).

From the mid 19th century, unions dominated working-class political activity. The ARISTOCRACY OF LABOUR formed 'New Model' unions, with national organizations, full-time officials and welfare benefits. Negotiation and arbitration were regularized, and activists founded trade councils and the TRADES UNION CONGRESS (1868), whose Parliamentary Committee (renamed General Council in 1921) lobbied for favourable legislation.

In the later 19th century, following the DOCK STRIKE of 1889, SOCIALISTS promoted 'New Unionism', a mass movement including unskilled workers. Anxieties over the law of STRIKES AND PICKETING prompted unions to seek political influence through the LABOUR PARTY. Union membership increased eightfold between 1890 and 1920, when unionization of women workers peaked at 25%, though men comprised 90% of unionists. The *Daily Herald* (1911–66) became the movement's chief newspaper.

Waves of industrial unrest in 1910–14 and 1919–21 were followed by the GENERAL STRIKE of 1926. From 1940, closer relations developed between government and organized labour, embodied later in tripartite consultative councils (including industry). White-collar unionism expanded in the 1960s. INCOMES POLICIES meanwhile made union leaders politically powerful and controversial. UK union membership peaked in 1980 at 12.2 million, around half the workforce.

After industrial strife in the 1970s, THATCHERISM and high unemployment reversed several trends. The failure of the MINERS' STRIKE (1984–5) discouraged militancy. By 2000, stoppages were few, plant pay-bargaining had extensively replaced national negotiations, many unions had amalgamated, and membership had almost halved. *See also* TRADE UNION LEGISLATION.

TRADE UNIONISM, IRELAND In the 18th and early 19th centuries craftsmen in larger towns formed 'combinations' to protect conditions (e.g., carpenters in Dublin, by 1764), and unions operated in the COTTON INDUSTRY (late 18th–early 19th centuries). They existed despite the Irish Parliament's anti-combination legislation (from 1729) and the extension to Ireland in 1803 of Great Britain's 1800 Combination Act.

After repeal of the COMBINATION ACTS (1824), local unions increased and British unions established branches. A United Dublin Trades Association was founded in 1863 to co-ordinate organizations (affiliated to the British Trades Union Congress 1868). In the 1870s–90s unionism increased in BELFAST, and a Belfast United Trades Council was started (1881). An Irish Trade Union Congress (ITUC) was inaugurated in 1894 as a forum. Unions remained predominantly male because female industrial employment, notably linen manufacturing, proved hard to unionize.

Between *c*.1900 and *c*.1920 unionization and militancy grew among unskilled workers. Jim LARKIN, from Britain, organized dockers' strikes (1907), founded the syndicalist Irish Transport and General Workers' Union (1908), and organized a tram strike in DUBLIN (Aug. 1913–Feb. 1914). Union membership increased 1916–20 from 100,000 to 225,000.

The PARTITION OF IRELAND (1921) generated tensions between trade unionists in southern and Northern Ireland. In 1941 the southern government sought to rationalize unions by requiring licences (Trade Union Act). Membership expanded further in the late 1940s, but the breakaway of Irish-based unions from the ITUC (1945), as the Congress of Irish Unions, weakened the union movement. (They reunited in 1959 as the Irish Congress of Trade Unions.) Union representation in southern Ireland peaked in 1980 at 55% of the workforce. Though the proportion then declined (in an expanding workforce), governments involved unions in policy-making 1987–2009 (*see* SOCIAL PARTNERSHIP). In 2010, 35% of workers were union members (approx. 500,000), 36% in Northern Ireland (225,000). *See also* IRISH CITIZEN ARMY; TRADE UNION LEGISLATION; LABOUR PARTY, IRISH.

TRADE UNIONISM, SCOTLAND From the late 17th century groups of craftsmen founded local societies for mutual support (including welfare provision), using protection afforded by an Act of Parliament of 1661 which allowed journeymen groups to present petitions (to JUSTICES OF THE PEACE) in wage arbitrations.

During industrial expansion from the late 18th century associations were organized for workers, such as the Glasgow Association of Operative Cotton Spinners (founded 1810). (The COMBINATION ACTS of 1799–1800 were deemed in 1810 to be inapplicable in Scotland.) From 1812 strikes increased as employers rejected arbitrated wages (e.g., strike of Glasgow handloom weavers, 1812). They normally failed because leaders were arrested and union funds were insufficient. In the 1820s many unions collapsed after employers reduced wages by hiring immigrants.

During the 1850s–60s new craft unions were formed (e.g., for coopers, woodcutters), which organized trades councils (of union delegates) in major centres (e.g., Edinburgh 1853, Glasgow 1858). They remained important and in 1897 helped to found the SCOTTISH TRADES UNION CONGRESS (STUC). In heavy industries (ship building, coal mining) employers' hostility kept unionization low. In 1892 union membership was 147,000. There were over 100 Scottish unions, but most were small.

In the late 1890s–1900s (the time of 'New Unionism', appealing to semi-skilled and unskilled workers) UK-wide unions recruited railwaymen, dock workers and others (including women). By 1924 union membership was 536,000. It contracted during the 1930s slump but recovered to 900,000 in 1947. It peaked at 1,090,000 in the early 1970s, then declined to 830,000 in 1991 and 640,000 in 2011 (29.7% of employees), before increasing modestly. Meanwhile Scottish unions were absorbed in UK-wide unions: 90 were affiliated to the STUC in 1924, only nine in 1974. *See also* INDUSTRY, SCOTLAND FROM LATE 18TH CENTURY.

TRADE UNIONISM, WALES Local unions were formed in industrial areas from the early 18th century but were short-lived. Between 1799 and 1824 they were suppressed as illegal under the COMBINATION ACTS, though sporadic protests continued. Stronger interest developed during industrial unrest in the 1820s–30s. In 1830–1, for example, the Friendly Associated Coal Miners' Union Society (based in Flintshire) established numerous lodges. But its strikes were defeated (usually by lockouts) or collapsed from internal disputes. Co-ordination between localities was difficult and many nonconformists were hostile to unions.

Longer-lasting unions were established from the 1850s–60s by small groups of skilled workers (e.g., boilermakers, stonemasons): by 1861 there were at least 51, and the first trades council met in CARDIFF during the 1860s. Mass unionism remained unsuccessful; the Amalgamated Association of Miners (founded 1869) recruited 30,000 members but its major strike in 1875 was defeated. From the late 1880s (the period of 'New Unionism', catering for semi-skilled and unskilled workers) UK-wide unions successfully recruited railwaymen, dock workers and others.

The combination of seven unions as the South Wales Miners' Federation in 1898 opened a new era. By 1910 S Wales miners were the most militant in Great Britain (*see* ABLETT, NOAH), from 1919 organizing actions that culminated in the 1926 GENERAL STRIKE. Thereafter their influence declined as the COAL INDUSTRY contracted severely.

Separate Welsh unions were also established by teachers (1940) and farmers (1955), and in 1974 the Wales Trades Union Council was founded as a constituent body of the TRADES UNION CONGRESS of England and Wales to represent unions in Welsh political and economic affairs. *See also* MINERS' UNIONS; PENRHYN, LORD; TAFF VALE CASE.

TRADE UNION LEGISLATION Before the early 19th century unions (or 'combinations') were restricted or prohibited in Great Britain (*see* COMBINATION ACTS). Union organization, collective bargaining and strikes were permitted in Britain and Ireland from 1824 (repeal of 1800 Combination Act). But other legislation weakened unionism. The 1823 Masters and Servants Act made breach of contract by workers a criminal offence. The 1825 Combinations of Workmen Act outlawed intimidation and other tactics. The Hornby *v.* Close case (1867) denied protection to union funds (under 1855 Friendly Societies Act). Agitation by the Glasgow Trades Council achieved modification of legislation (Master and Servant Act, 1867).

Violence by unionists in SHEFFIELD in 1866 (so-called 'Sheffield outrages') resulted in a royal commission (1867–9) and legislation (1871): a Trade Union Act strengthened unionism by allowing registration under the Friendly Societies Act, ownership of property and employment of staff; but a Criminal Law Amendment Act created offences that inhibited picketing. Pressure from unionists resulted, in 1875, in the Conspiracy and Protection of Property Act, which protected picketing, and the Employers and Workmen Act, which made breach of contract a civil offence.

In 1901 the TAFF VALE CASE left unions liable for commercial losses caused by strikes. This was reversed in 1906 (Trade Disputes Act). The Osborne judgment of 1909 prohibited unions' expenditure on political objectives. This was altered by the 1913 Trade Union Act, though members could contract out. Contracting in was required from 1927 to 1946.

There was little further legislation in Britain and Northern Ireland until the 1971 Industrial Relations Act created a National Industrial Relations Court to register unions and regulate disputes (repealed 1974). The 1980 Employment Act outlawed secondary picketing and regulated 'closed shops' (employment involving compulsory union membership). In 1984 the Trade Union Act required union members to approve strikes through secret ballots. The Trade Union and Labour Relations (Consolidation) Act of 1992 replaced existing Acts. *See also* STRIKES AND PICKETING, LAW RELATING TO; ECONOMY, STATE INVOLVEMENT, BRITAIN; TRADE UNIONISM, IRELAND.

TRADE, BOARD OF An agency of the English/British GOVERNMENT, founded in 1696. The PRIVY COUNCIL had created temporary committees from 1622 to consult merchants and inquire into trade. In 1696 a commission was founded for promoting trade and improving PLANTATIONS. It comprised ministers and unofficial members, and its chairman was styled 'president'. The Board surveyed economic conditions and collected statistics. Colonial responsibilities were removed in 1768, and the Board was abolished in 1782 after attacks by Edmund BURKE.

A new committee was founded in 1784 (reconstituted by royal order 1786). From the early 19th century its president was a CABINET minister, and its responsibilities increased with commercial and technological developments (e.g., RAILWAYS). Some functions were removed in the 20th century (e.g., transport in 1942). It merged with the Ministry of Technology in 1970 to form the Department of Trade and Industry. The Board continued to exist for legal purposes. *See also* HALIFAX, 2ND EARL OF.

TRADES UNION CONGRESS A voluntary organization of trade unions representing most of the British union movement. Founded in 1868, it has held annual conferences for delegates of affiliated unions and related organizations to discuss common concerns. From 1871 the 'TUC' elected a permanent committee to speak for organized labour in dealings with government and employers' organizations. In 2016 there were 52 affiliated unions with almost 5.8 million members. *See also* TRADE UNIONISM, ENGLAND; SCOTTISH TRADES UNION CONGRESS.

TRAFALGAR, BATTLE OF A decisive naval battle fought on 21 Oct. 1805 off Cape Trafalgar, SW Spain, during the Napoleonic Wars. A British fleet of 31 ships, commanded by Horatio NELSON, defeated a Franco-Spanish fleet, destroying 22 of 40 ships. Although Nelson was killed, the loss of French naval forces ended Emperor Napoleon I's hopes of invading Britain. *See also* FRENCH REVOLUTIONARY AND NAPOLEONIC WARS, BRITISH INVOLVEMENT; NAVY, ENGLISH AND BRITISH, FROM 1660.

TRANSJORDAN, BRITISH MANDATE A former British territory in the Middle East, consisting of land E of the R. Jordan and SE of the Dead Sea. It was created in 1921 when Great Britain divided its MANDATE of PALESTINE to form a separate emirate, ruled by Abdullah. From 1923 Transjordan had extensive independence, and from 1928 nominal independence, under the British mandate. Approx. population in 1921: 240,000. Britain subsidized the regime and provided officers for its armed services. After the mandate expired in 1946, Transjordan became an independent kingdom. It changed name to JORDAN in 1949 after incorporating land on the W bank of the R. Jordan. *See also* JORDAN, BRITISH RELATIONS WITH.

TRANSPORT AND GENERAL WORKERS' UNION A trade union formed in 1922 by amalgamation of 14 unions with 350,000 members, predominantly dock and transport workers in Great Britain and Ireland. Led by Ernest BEVIN 1922–45, it was influential within TRADE UNIONISM and the LABOUR MOVEMENT. From 1937, following further amalgamations, it was the UK's largest union (650,000 members). Membership peaked at over 2 million

in 1977. In 2007 it merged with 'Amicus' to form 'Unite' (1.42 million members in 2015).

TRANSPORTATION Term used for the removal of convicted criminals overseas as punishment. It was permitted from England from 1597. Transportation from Britain and Ireland, often to BARBADOS, developed from the 1650s with the commutation of death sentences.

Transportation became a standard penalty from 1717 under the British Parliament's Piracy Act. Convicts were first sent to Great Britain's NORTH AMERICAN COLONIES, mainly VIRGINIA and MARYLAND (30,000 by 1760). Following the outbreak of the AMERICAN WAR OF INDEPENDENCE (1775), transportation was suspended.

Transportation to AUSTRALIA was authorized by Parliament in 1784 and implemented in 1787 (to NEW SOUTH WALES). Convicts were normally assigned to private masters for seven years, but there were legal obstacles to return. Many chose to stay and were given land. The totals of convicts transported to Australian destinations were: 80,500 to New South Wales (1788–1850); 67,500 to VAN DIEMEN'S LAND (1803–53); 10,000 to WESTERN AUSTRALIA (1850–68). Transportation ended in 1868. *See also* BOTANY BAY; GAOLS AND PRISONS, ENGLAND AND WALES.

TRANSPORT COMMUNICATIONS, ENGLAND The area taken under Germanic rule (5th–7th centuries) included: long-distance routeways of prehistoric origin; constructed Roman roads and bridges (*see* ROMAN BRITAIN, ROADS); rougher local ways. Some Roman routes survived, others were replaced. People travelled mainly on foot or horseback, sometimes driving animals; they forded rivers, though some bridge building occurred from the 8th century. Rivers and coastal sea routes were also used for transport.

Widespread bridge building (10th–mid 13th centuries), extensive use of carts (from late 12th century), and foundation of TOWNS (12th–13th centuries) enhanced the importance of certain routes. Long-distance river navigation became less efficient in the 11th–13th centuries as mills were built.

National arrangements for maintaining ways began with legislation in 1555 requiring parishioners to make repairs (six days a year from 1563). From 1663, and extensively in the 1750s–60s, PARLIAMENT authorized TURNPIKE TRUSTS to maintain roads. Dutch-style, four-wheel waggons were used from the 1560s, and waggon-coaches for passengers followed. Stage-coach services developed across the country from the 1650s. Use of packhorses declined in the 18th century. From 1888, local and national authorities took responsibility for roads.

Expanding economic activity from the late 16th century encouraged investment in transport facilities. Some rivers were improved to facilitate navigation, and waggonways were built between collieries and river hythes for horse-hauled trucks (17th–18th centuries). From the 1760s CANALS were constructed, primarily for COAL and other heavy commodities. They flourished, alongside coastal navigation, until long-distance RAILWAYS with steam-powered locomotion provided competition (from 1830s). Railways were undermined by the dramatic increase of MOTOR VEHICLES (cars, lorries, buses) from the early 20th century, which required upgrading of roads (from 1920s) and construction of MOTORWAYS (late 20th century). The railway network was drastically reduced from 1963 (*see* 'BEECHING REPORT'). *See also* AIR TRANSPORT, GREAT BRITAIN AND NORTHERN IRELAND; POST OFFICE.

TRANSPORT COMMUNICATIONS, IRELAND

Before the 18th century roads and other facilities were poor. Bridges were rare except at major river crossings (built mainly in the 12th–13th centuries). By the late 17th century the road network was mostly focused on DUBLIN. Coastal and river navigation were important.

Long-distance roads were greatly improved in the 18th century by turnpike trusts (management boards empowered to levy tolls, from 1729 to mid 19th century), and the 'presentment system' (1765–1898), whereby county grand juries levied money for road improvements. Stage coaches operated from 1737, and mail coaches from 1789. Goods transport increased with purpose-built vehicles.

From the 1730s to 1830s almost 500 mi (800 km) of canals were constructed. The earliest, the Newry Canal (1731–41, to carry coal from Ulster to Dublin), predated similar canals in Britain. Dublin was connected to the R. Shannon by the Grand Canal (built 1756–1804) and Royal Canal (1790–1817). From 1831 the Board of Works oversaw road building and canal construction and maintenance.

The first railway was opened in 1834: 6 mi (10 km) between Dublin and the port of Kingstown (Co. Dublin). By 1912 there were 3400 mi (5500 km), including about 300 mi (480 km) built after 1889 mostly with government support to promote development in remote areas (nicknamed 'Balfour lines', after A.J. BALFOUR). Dublin and Belfast were the main railway centres. The railways of the Republic of Ireland and Northern Ireland were nationalized in 1950 and 1953; line closures in the 1950s–60s reduced the network to about 1400 mi (2300 km).

The advent of motor traffic in the early 20th century brought about better roads and new roads. Motorways were opened in Northern Ireland from 1962, in the Republic from 1983. *See also* POST OFFICE, IRELAND.

TRANSPORT COMMUNICATIONS, SCOTLAND

Especially in the HIGHLANDS, communications have been hampered by rugged terrain, indented rocky coasts, lack of navigable rivers, and wet climate. Some roads in S Scotland originally built by the Romans (late 1st–early 3rd centuries) were used for many centuries. Other routeways were variable in quality. Fords and ferries were important, though timber bridges were built at strategic crossings and later rebuilt in stone (e.g., STIRLING bridge, across the R. Forth, recorded *c*.1250, rebuilt *c*.1500). In the Highlands General George WADE had over 250 mi (400 km) of military roads built in 1725–36. Another 750 mi (1200 km) were added after 1745. TURNPIKE roads were constructed in the Lowlands from the 1750s.

Because most large towns were coastal, few CANALS were built (the most important were opened between 1790 and 1822). Colliery waggonways (the first at Tranent, 1722) led to the extensive spread of RAILWAYS from the 1840s. Harbour works were few before the 17th century; many were financed then by landowners and BURGHS. The deepening of the R. Clyde in the later 18th century gave sea-going vessels access to GLASGOW. With the decline of rail traffic in the later 20th century, roads (especially MOTORWAYS) became vital links. *See also* POST OFFICE.

TRANSPORT COMMUNICATIONS, WALES

From the 5th to late 18th centuries travel was difficult because of mountainous terrain. Thereafter, economic requirements stimulated improvements, affecting mainly routes along the N and S coasts and into England.

The Romans built roads in the N and S and across the C but except in the SE, these decayed in the post-Roman period (from 5th century). People then travelled along local tracks, especially ridgeways in the uplands. Few roads were maintained. River-crossings were mainly fords; bridges were rare.

Industrial expansion from the mid 18th century stimulated better communications to export markets; from the 1750s the turnpike movement was extended into Wales (*see* TURNPIKE TRUSTS AND ROADS, WALES). In the early 19th century government intervention prompted further improvements (*see* TELFORD, THOMAS). Cars and buses in the early 20th century necessitated dramatic upgrading and expansion of roads, though the M4 along the S coast was Wales's only MOTORWAY (with bridges across the R. Severn opened in 1966 and 1996).

Because roads were poor, water transport was important until the 19th century, both along major rivers and round the coast. This was supplemented by canals from 1766 until the late 19th century (*see* CANALS, WALES). The spread of railways from the 1840s greatly improved communications (*see* RAILWAYS, WALES), until drastic reduction after 1963 (*see* 'BEECHING REPORT'), which eliminated direct N–S rail travel. *See also* POST OFFICE.

TRANSPORT REVOLUTION

Term for the development of efficient transport systems in Great Britain mostly from the 18th century. It began with TURNPIKE TRUSTS AND ROADS, and continued with CANALS (from 1760s), RAILWAYS (from 1830s) and road vehicles powered by internal combustion engines (from 1890s). Improvements required considerable capital investment. They facilitated the INDUSTRIAL REVOLUTION by enabling manufacturers to reach large markets. *See also* TRANSPORT COMMUNICATIONS, ENGLAND/IRELAND/SCOTLAND/WALES.

TRANSUBSTANTIATION A doctrine of the Catholic Church whereby during Mass the substances of bread and wine are changed into Christ's body and blood though their outward appearances remain unchanged. Elaborated in the 13th century, the doctrine was denied by John WYCLIF in *De eucharistia* (1379–80) and rejected by Protestants in the 16th century. It was excluded from the English PRAYER BOOKS of 1549 and 1552 (also used in Ireland), and rejected by Scottish reformer John KNOX by 1550. *See also* SIX ARTICLES; ARTICLES OF RELIGION; REFORMATION, ENGLAND/SCOTLAND.

TREASON Disloyalty to a ruler, other person or the State (from Anglo-Norman *treysoun*, meaning 'betrayal'). In Anglo-Saxon England, offences against the king, punishable by death, were included in laws (9th–11th centuries; *see* LAW, ENGLAND BEFORE 1066). Offences of killing or betraying the king also appear in the treatise *GLANVILL* (*c*.1187–9). In 1352, at the request of the House of Commons, EDWARD III accepted legislation to supersede arbitrary definitions of treason. The Treason Act specified offences against royalty as 'high treason' (e.g., killing, or intending to kill, the king) and against lower persons as 'petty treason' (e.g., murder of a master by his servant). Legislation was adopted in Ireland, and was frequently amended in England and Ireland (e.g., addition of new offences).

In Scotland, two main types of treason are recorded from the early 14th century (in *REGIAM MAJESTATEM*): causing the death of the king, and promoting sedition (agitation) within the realm or in the king's army. Cases were usually tried in PARLIAMENT (transferred to Court of JUSTICIARY in 1690). Treason legislation was passed from the 15th century, notably two Treason Acts in 1449.

In 1708, following a JACOBITE REBELLION, the British Parliament replaced Scotland's treason law with the English 1352 Act. The last new form of treason was created in 1796. In the UK, petty treason was abolished in 1828, and capital punishment for treason in 1998.

In the IRISH FREE STATE (founded 1922), various actions (e.g., levying war against the State) were made treasonable under the Treasonable Offences Act of 1925, punishable by death. Treasonable offences were included in the 1937 CONSTITUTION and expanded by the 1939 Treason Act. The 1352 Act was repealed in 1983, and capital punishment for treason abolished in 1990.

TREASON TRIALS, 1794 The trials for high TREASON of leading English RADICALS, such as Thomas Hardy, John Horne Tooke and John Thelwall, following the spread of revolutionary ideas from France. They were arrested in May on the order of the government of William PITT the Younger, and tried in Oct. Defended by Thomas Erskine, a FOXITE barrister, they were acquitted. But the government's action dampened revolutionary activity. *See also* FRENCH REVOLUTION, IMPACT ON ENGLAND.

TREASURER, ENGLAND A principal officer in royal GOVERNMENT, 12th–18th centuries. In late Anglo-Saxon England (10th–mid 11th centuries) royal money and plate were managed by chamberlains. The post of treasurer was created by 1130 (in reign of King HENRY I). He was a senior officer of the EXCHEQUER, and from the 13th century a leading member of the royal COUNCIL. Treasurers were usually senior clergy until the late 14th century, then laymen.

During the 17th century the post was frequently placed 'in commission', i.e., the treasurer was replaced by a board of commissioners (titled 'lord'). This remained permanent from 1714. During the 18th century the 'first lord of the Treasury' was increasingly regarded as the most important minister and called 'first minister' or PRIME MINISTER. *See also* GOVERNMENT, ENGLAND WITH WALES 1642–1707; GOVERNMENT, GREAT BRITAIN 1707 TO LATER 18TH CENTURY.

TREASURER, IRELAND *see* EXCHEQUER, IRELAND

TREASURER, SCOTLAND *see* CHAMBERLAIN, SCOTLAND; ROYAL REVENUES, SCOTLAND

TREASURY AGREEMENT *see* DILUTION OF LABOUR

TREATY PORTS *see* CHINESE TREATY PORTS

TRENT **INCIDENT** A major diplomatic incident in 1861, during the AMERICAN CIVIL WAR. On 8 Nov. a US Federal warship intercepted the British mail-steamer *Trent* and forcibly removed two envoys from the breakaway American Confederacy who were travelling to Europe. British opinion was outraged at this violation of British neutrality and war seemed possible. When Lord John RUSSELL, the British foreign secretary, drafted a protest, Prince ALBERT suggested less belligerent amendments. The American government defused the crisis by releasing the envoys (reported 29 Dec.).

TREVELYAN, CHARLES (b. 2 April 1807 at Taunton, Somerset, England; d. 19 June 1886 at London, England, aged 79). Trevelyan worked in India for the EAST INDIA

COMPANY (1827–38) and was assistant secretary (administrative head) of the British Treasury (1840–59). From 1846 he oversaw the British government's response to famine relief in Ireland. His concern for free trade (e.g., ensuring grain exports) and readiness from 1847 to rely on the Irish poor law system generated criticism (*see* GREAT FAMINE). In 1853 Trevelyan and Sir Stafford NORTHCOTE produced the 'NORTHCOTE–TREVELYAN REPORT' which led to fundamental reform of the CIVIL SERVICE. Trevelyan served again in India (1859–60, 1862–5) and was created a BARONET (1874).

TREVITHICK, RICHARD (b. 13 April 1771 at Carn Brea, Cornwall, England; d. 22 April 1833 at Dartford, Kent, England, aged 62). A mining engineer, Trevithick sought to develop steam power: he produced a high-pressure engine (1800), three steam road carriages (1801–3), and the world's first steam railway locomotive (1804) which briefly hauled loads on a tramway in Wales. In 1808 his third locomotive gave rides to the public near London. He abandoned work on railway locomotives because rails proved inadequate. Trevithick was also involved in steam dredging (1803–7), tunnelling (1807), steam-powered threshing, and mining in S America (1816–27). *See also* RAILWAYS, ENGLAND/WALES.

TRIBAL HIDAGE Name given to an Anglo-Saxon administrative document which lists 35 peoples, each assessed in HIDES. It records their liability to tribute. It was probably produced for a king of MERCIA in the mid 7th century (possibly for WULFHERE in the 660s–70s). *See also* KINGSHIP, ANGLO-SAXON.

TRIENNIAL ACTS, ENGLAND AND WALES Legislation specifying a maximum gap of three years between Parliaments, enacted to limit the powers of the Crown. The first Triennial Act was passed by the LONG PARLIAMENT on 15 Feb. 1641, in response to the long 'personal rule' of King CHARLES I. The CAVALIER PARLIAMENT replaced it with a weaker Act in Nov. 1664: it specified that the maximum gap *ought* to be three years. CHARLES II failed to comply with the Act in 1684 (*see* EXCLUSION CRISIS).

WILLIAM III vetoed two Triennial Bills (March 1693, Jan. 1694) before accepting one under pressure (Dec. 1694). The consequent Act also limited the length of Parliaments to three years. It resulted in frequent elections and intense competition between POLITICAL PARTIES, and was replaced in 1716 by the SEPTENNIAL ACT. *See also* PARLIAMENTARY CONSTITUENCIES AND ELECTIONS.

TRIMBLE, DAVID (b. 15 Oct. 1944 at Belfast, Northern Ireland). A law lecturer and from 1978 member of the ULSTER UNIONIST PARTY (UUP), Trimble was elected a UK MP in 1990. In Sept. 1995 he became UUP leader. From June 1996 Trimble participated in talks about Northern Ireland's future (initially excluding republicans; *see* PEACE PROCESS, NORTHERN IRELAND). He continued involvement, controversially, when PROVISIONAL SINN FÉIN (PSF) joined the talks (15 Sept. 1997) despite lack of arms 'decommissioning' by the PROVISIONAL IRISH REPUBLICAN ARMY (PIRA).

Following the BELFAST AGREEMENT (April 1998), Trimble was elected first minister of Northern Ireland by the new ASSEMBLY (1 July) and led a multi-party EXECUTIVE (1999–2000, 2000–2). He was (jointly) awarded the 1998 Nobel Peace Prize. Trimble's willingness to work with PSF despite little decommissioning was unpopular with many UUP members and was attacked by the DEMOCRATIC UNIONIST PARTY (DUP). In Nov. 2003 the DUP surpassed the UUP in Assembly elections, dislodging Trimble as leader of unionism. After he lost his parliamentary seat (2005) he resigned as UUP leader. He was created Lord Trimble (2006) and in 2007 joined the CONSERVATIVE PARTY. *See also* UNIONISM, IRELAND; HUME, JOHN; PAISLEY, IAN.

TRIPLE ALLIANCE An informal arrangement, made in June 1914, between three large trade unions in Great Britain (representing miners, railwaymen, dockers and carters) to terminate agreements with employers simultaneously so they could threaten a major dispute. Suspended during WORLD WAR I (1914–18), the alliance collapsed on 15 April 1921 ('Black Friday') when a planned strike in support of miners was cancelled because the miners refused to negotiate. *See also* INDUSTRIAL DISPUTES.

TROTSKYITE A supporter of the revolutionary ideology of the Russian communist ideologue Leon Trotsky (1879–1940). British Trotskyites gained influence in 1960s fringe politics, and a group called Militant Tendency infiltrated sections of the LABOUR PARTY in the 1980s. 'Trotskyism', though vague, differed from the ideology of the British COMMUNIST PARTY.

TROUBLES Term used for disorder in NORTHERN IRELAND 1968–90s, involving nationalists (mostly Catholics), Unionists (or loyalists, mostly Protestants), police and the British Army. The Troubles originated in clashes between CIVIL RIGHTS protesters, police and loyalists (1968–9), which escalated into sectarian violence. From Aug. 1969, when police failed to contain rioting in LONDONDERRY, British troops helped to maintain order. PARAMILITARY ORGANIZATIONS became heavily involved, notably the PROVISIONAL IRISH REPUBLICAN ARMY (PIRA; founded Jan. 1970). Northern Ireland's government tried to restore order with 'internment' (detention without trial, from 9 Aug. 1971). But violence increased, culminating in 'BLOODY SUNDAY' (30 Jan. 1972). Great Britain imposed 'direct rule' (transfer of authority to British government, 24 March).

Britain attempted to restore peace by contriving a power-sharing Executive (devolved government) of Unionists and nationalists (from 1 Jan. 1974), and by making the SUNNINGDALE AGREEMENT, which involved the Republic of Ireland (Dec. 1973). But opposition from anti-reform Unionists crushed the Executive (resigned 28 May 1974; see ULSTER WORKERS' STRIKE). An elected Constitutional Convention then sought, unsuccessfully, to devise a new form of government (May 1975–March 1976).

Violence increased further in the 1980s following HUN-GER STRIKES by imprisoned republicans (1981). The PIRA's political 'wing', PROVISIONAL SINN FÉIN (PSF), became involved in electoral politics and successfully challenged the 'constitutional nationalist' SOCIAL DEMOCRATIC AND LABOUR PARTY (SDLP). On 12 October 1984 the PIRA bombed the Grand Hotel in Brighton, England, almost killing the British prime minister (Margaret THATCHER). Britain sought to support 'constitutional nationalism' by making the HILLSBOROUGH AGREEMENT with the Republic (Nov. 1985).

From 1988 the SDLP leader, John HUME, held discussions with PSF leader Gerry ADAMS. They developed into a sustained PEACE PROCESS which culminated in a ceasefire by the PIRA (1994). Conditions became more peaceful, though low-level violence and paramilitary organized crime continued. The Troubles resulted in 3172 deaths. See also EXECUTIVES, NORTHERN IRELAND.

TROYES, TREATY OF Sealed on 21 May 1420 at Troyes (N France), between Queen Isabella of France, acting for King Charles VI, and King HENRY V of England. Charles adopted Henry as his heir, in place of his son Charles (the dauphin or heir). Henry would marry King Charles's daughter Catherine of Valois and become regent of France. The treaty was supported by Philip the Good, duke of BURGUNDY, whose father had been murdered by the dauphin's supporters (10 Sept. 1419).

The treaty supposedly settled Henry's ambitions but bound only the ailing King Charles and the Burgundians, excluding the rival Armagnac faction and the dauphin. Their resistance and Henry's death soon nullified the agreement. See also HUNDRED YEARS WAR; BEDFORD, DUKE OF.

TÚATH (OIr., meaning 'a people'). Term used in Ireland by the 6th century to describe a population group which formed a political entity under its own king (*rí*). Between the 6th and 12th centuries there were roughly 100–150 *túatha*. The status of kings and *túatha* declined in the 8th–12th

centuries. By the 14th century *túath* had been replaced by *oireacht* ('gathering' or 'assembly'), ruled by a *tigerna* ('lord') or *toísech* ('leader of warband'). See also KINGSHIP, IRELAND.

TUDOR, JASPER (b. *c.*1431 at Hatfield, Hertfordshire, England; d. 21 or 26 Dec. 1495 in England, aged about 64). Welsh LANCASTRIAN; second son of Welshman Owen Tudor and Catherine of Valois (widow of HENRY V of England); created earl of Pembroke 1452.

After his elder brother Edmund's death (3 Nov. 1456), Jasper raised Welsh support for the Lancastrian king HENRY VI. But from 1461 to 1470 he lived in exile (Scotland and France), following Henry's deposition by EDWARD IV. Jasper returned to England during Henry's brief reinstatement (1470–1), but on 2 June 1471, following Edward's re-accession (11 April) and Henry's death (4 May), Jasper fled to Brittany (France), taking his nephew Henry, aged 14. Jasper helped to organize Henry's return and his accession as HENRY VII (1485); he was created duke of Bedford. See also TUDOR FAMILY; YORKIST–LANCASTRIAN CONFLICT, ROLE OF WALES.

TUDOR FAMILY A landowning family in NW Wales in the 14th and 15th centuries; descended from EDNYFED FYCHAN, *DISTAIN* of GWYNEDD (fl. 1200–46). The family name was probably derived from Tudur ap Goronwy (d. 1367). Tudors were leading Welsh LANCASTRIANS during the YORKIST–LANCASTRIAN CONFLICT (*c.*1450–85).

The marriage of Owen Tudor to Catherine of Valois, widow of HENRY V of England (*c.*1428), connected the Tudors to the Lancastrian line of English kings, and the marriage of Owen's son Edmund Tudor to Margaret BEAUFORT (1455) gave their son Henry a claim to the throne of England. He became king in 1485 as HENRY VII. Tudor monarchs ruled England, Wales and Ireland until 1603. See also PLANTAGENETS; STEWART RULERS.

TUDOR REVOLUTION IN GOVERNMENT A thesis proposed in 1953 by the English historian G.R. Elton. He argued that in England in the 1530s (during the reign of the TUDOR monarch King HENRY VIII) Thomas CROMWELL carried out an administrative revolution in central government, changing a medieval form based on the king's household into a more modern bureaucratic and professional form. Now managed by the PRIVY COUNCIL, it was less dependent on the ruler's involvement. The revolution also involved new financial departments and an extension of national sovereignty, through establishing control over the English Church and Wales (see REFORMATION, ENGLAND/WALES; UNION OF WALES WITH ENGLAND).

Elton's thesis was criticized for disregarding medieval bureaucracy (see EXCHEQUER, ENGLAND), and underestimating later changes. Developments in the 16th century were also more pragmatic and evolutionary than Elton envisaged. *See also* NEW MONARCHY, ENGLAND; GOVERNMENT, ENGLAND WITH WALES 1509 TO 1642.

TULCHAN BISHOPS A contemptuous name for bishops established in the reformed Church of SCOTLAND after the Concordat of LEITH (1572). Derived from Gaelic *tulachan*, meaning 'little hillock', the term referred to the stuffing of a calf's skin to deceive a cow into giving milk; it implied that bishops had been reintroduced to give nobles access to Church revenues through appointment of their relatives. *See also* CHURCH ORGANIZATION, SCOTLAND FROM 16TH CENTURY.

TURING, ALAN (b. 23 June 1912 at London, England; d. 7 June 1954 at Wilmslow, Cheshire, England, aged 41). A student (1931–4) and fellow (from 1935) at King's College, CAMBRIDGE, Turing published a groundbreaking paper on mathematical logic, 'On Computable Numbers …', which envisaged a computing machine ('Turing machine') instructed by programmes (1936). He advanced his work as a doctoral student in the USA (1936–8).

Based during WORLD WAR II at the Government Code and Cipher School (Bletchley Park, Buckinghamshire), Turing contributed to development of the code-breaking 'bombe' machine (1940), and led decryption of German naval messages. Success in summer 1941 reduced maritime losses in the Atlantic. After visiting the USA (Nov. 1941–March 1943), Turing worked on secure voice communication.

After the war, at the National Physical Laboratory (1945–8), Turing designed the world's first stored-programme digital computer (1946), but it was not constructed. Frustrated, he moved by invitation to the MANCHESTER University computing laboratory where a pioneer computer influenced by his ideas had been built. Although Turing designed a programming system, he turned to biological research. He was elected a fellow of the ROYAL SOCIETY in 1951. Turing's death, from cyanide poisoning, was judged as suicide but may have been accidental. *See also* SECRET SERVICES, UNITED KINGDOM; COMPUTING.

TURKEY, ENGLISH AND BRITISH RELATIONS WITH *see* OTTOMAN EMPIRE, ENGLISH AND BRITISH RELATIONS WITH

TURNPIKE TRUSTS AND ROADS, ENGLAND Turnpike trusts were associations created by Acts of Parliament with powers to maintain, repair and improve roads by levying tolls from traffic. The first Act was passed in 1663 (for part of the Great North Road). More followed from the 1690s. Tolls were levied at gates placed across roads.

The first turnpiked roads were mainly near London. The system was greatly extended by 'turnpike manias' of the 1750s–60s and 1790s. Until the mid 18th century trusts mostly repaired or widened roads. Thereafter roads were increasingly reconstructed or new roads were built, often using improved methods devised by John Metcalf (1717–1810), John Loudon MCADAM (1756–1836) and Thomas TELFORD (1757–1834). By 1836 there were 22,000 mi (35,000 km) of turnpiked roads.

The imposition of tolls sometimes provoked hostility or even riots. But the system improved roads. Coaches travelled faster, and waggons transported goods more efficiently. Carrying services were stimulated.

From the 1830s competition from RAILWAYS reduced long-distance road traffic and trust incomes. Many trusts were dissolved in the 1870s–80s. In 1888 new County Councils were made responsible for main roads. *See also* TRANSPORT COMMUNICATIONS, ENGLAND.

TURNPIKE TRUSTS AND ROADS, IRELAND *see* TRANSPORT COMMUNICATIONS, IRELAND

TURNPIKE TRUSTS AND ROADS, SCOTLAND Trusts for maintaining and improving roads, funded from tolls, were introduced after the UNION OF ENGLAND AND SCOTLAND (1707), modelled on English examples. The first, for roads in Edinburghshire, was authorized by an Act of Parliament in 1713. Trusts began constructing new roads from the 1750s. (Engineers included John Loudon MCADAM and Thomas TELFORD.) By 1844 almost 350 Acts had been passed, mostly for the Lowlands. (The HIGHLANDS had been provided with new roads, for military purposes, during the 18th century.)

Trusts were abolished in 1878. Their roads were then administered by shire road boards, and from 1890 by county councils. *See also* TRANSPORT COMMUNICATIONS, SCOTLAND.

TURNPIKE TRUSTS AND ROADS, WALES The use of trusts to raise money from tollgates and loans for road improvement spread into Wales in the 1750s with the authorization of five trusts in NE Wales by the British Parliament. By 1839 over 200 schemes had been permitted, including the Shrewsbury–Holyhead road (for sea passage to Ireland), constructed 1815–26 by Thomas TELFORD with government funds.

Strict enforcement of tolls provoked the REBECCA RIOTS (1839–44), as a result of which the trusts in six southern counties were merged under county road boards. Most trusts were dissolved in the 1870s–80s. The last ran the ANGLESEY section of the Holyhead road; it ceased operating on 1 Nov. 1895. *See also* TRANSPORT COMMUNICATIONS, WALES.

TUVALU *see* GILBERT AND ELLICE ISLANDS

TWEEDDALE, 2ND MARQUIS OF (b. 1645 in Scotland; d. 20 April 1713 in Haddingtonshire, Scotland, aged 67 or 68). John Hay succeeded as marquis in 1697; from 1703 he was a leading member of the opposition COUNTRY PARTY in the Scottish Parliament. In 1704, following the fall of the duke of QUEENSBERRY, he was appointed QUEEN'S COMMISSIONER (and CHANCELLOR in Oct.). His duty was to overcome opposition to government business, but he had to concede the Act of SECURITY in order to obtain tax revenues. England's response, the ALIEN ACT (Feb. 1705), discredited him and he was dismissed (9 March 1705). He then led the *SQUADRONE VOLANTE*. *See also* UNION OF ENGLAND AND SCOTLAND.

TYNDALE, WILLIAM (b. *c.*1494 near Dursley, Gloucestershire, England; d. Oct. 1536 at Vilvorde, Netherlands, aged about 42). A scholar and clergyman, Tyndale was probably inspired to translate the New Testament into English by the Greek text published by Erasmus (1516). Denied patronage in England, he went to Germany (probably 1524). In 1526 his translation was printed in Worms. It caused alarm in England.

From 1528 Tyndale also published works advocating the authority of scripture and castigating the Church. They provoked counter-attacks by Thomas MORE. In 1530 the first part of a projected translation of the Old Testament, from Hebrew, was printed in Antwerp. Tyndale translated

more books but in 1535 was imprisoned. Condemned as a heretic, he was degraded from the priesthood (Aug. 1536), and later strangled and burnt. *See also* REFORMATION, ENGLAND; BIBLE, ENGLISH.

TYRCONNELL, EARL OF (b. 1630 in Ireland; d. 14 Aug. 1691 at Limerick, Co. Limerick, Ireland, aged 60 or 61). From early 1685 Richard Talbot, a Catholic, collaborated with his Catholic friend King James VII/II on policies for reasserting Catholicism in Ireland. (He was created earl of Tyrconnell on 20 June.) As commander of the Army from June 1686 he discharged Protestants and appointed Catholics. From Feb. 1687, as chief governor of Ireland (lord deputy), he appointed Catholics as judges, magistrates, sheriffs and town councillors.

After James fled from England (Dec. 1688), Tyrconnell held Ireland for him, despite the nominal accession of William III and Mary II (Feb. 1689). During James's campaign in Ireland (March 1689–July 1690), Tyrconnell organized the PATRIOT PARLIAMENT (May–July 1689) and prepared military forces. He fought at the battle of the BOYNE (July 1690). In Sept. 1690 he withdrew to France, but returned for James on 14 Jan. 1691 and fought at AUGHRIM (July), dying soon afterwards. *See also* JAMES VII/II AND IRELAND; WILLIAMITE WAR.

TYRONE, 2ND EARL OF *see* O'NEILL, HUGH

TYRONE'S REBELLION *see* NINE YEARS WAR

U

UA BRIAIN, MUIRCHERTACH (fl. from 1075 in Ireland; d. March 1119 at Lismore, Munster, S Ireland). King of DUBLIN from 1075, Muirchertach succeeded his father Toirrdelbach Ua Briain as high-king of MUNSTER and Ireland in 1086. Influenced by Continental European ideas, he began the practice of directly controlling other kingdoms rather than forcing the submission of kings (e.g., partitioning Meath and appointing subordinate kings in 1094). By the mid 1090s he dominated S and E Ireland but failed to impose authority in the N. From 1096 he intervened in the WESTERN ISLES (off Scotland). In 1102 he made a marriage alliance with Magnus Barelegs of Norway.

Muirchertach also promoted Church reform, presiding over synods at CASHEL (1101) and Ráith Bressail (1111). From 1114 illness and intradynastic opposition weakened his position. *See also* CHURCH REFORM, MEDIEVAL IRELAND; UA CONCHOBAIR, TOIRRDELBACH; O'BRIEN FAMILY.

UA CONCHOBAIR, RUAIDRÍ (O'CONNOR, RORY) (b. *c.*1120 in Ireland; d. 2 Dec. 1198 at Cong, Connacht, W Ireland, aged about 78). Ruaidrí succeeded his father Toirrdelbach UA CONCHOBAIR as high-king of CONNACHT in 1156 and challenged Muirchertach MAC LOCHLAINN (based in N Ireland) who had seized the high-kingship of Ireland. When Muirchertach died (1166), Ruaidrí succeeded as high-king of Ireland. He also ousted and exiled Muirchertach's ally Diarmait MAC MURCHADA, high-king of LEINSTER (E Ireland).

Diarmait returned from overseas in 1167, retook his core lands, and was joined in 1169 by foreign mercenaries, effectively beginning the Anglo-Norman invasion of Ireland. Ruaidrí allowed Diarmait to regain Leinster and then lost Dublin to the invaders (1170).

In 1171 Henry II of England arrived. Ruaidrí refused to submit, but in 1175 he agreed the treaty of WINDSOR which recognized his high-kingship in Ireland. Though Henry and the invaders soon broke the treaty, Ruaidrí made little response. He resigned his kingships in 1183 and retired to Cong monastery. *See also* NORMANS, IMPACT ON IRELAND; HENRY II AND IRELAND.

UA CONCHOBAIR, TOIRRDELBACH (O'CONNOR, TURLOUGH) (b. 1087 or 1088 in Ireland; d. 20 May 1156 at Dunmore, Connacht, W Ireland, aged 68). High-king of CONNACHT from 1106, Toirrdelbach took advantage of Muirchertach UA BRIAIN's illness to seize the high-kingship of Ireland by marching on DUBLIN (1118). He constructed fortresses in Connacht (a novel military technique), placed fleets on the R. Shannon, and dominated MUNSTER (S Ireland).

From 1131 Toirrdelbach faced revolts, but by 1140 had reasserted himself, subjugating MEATH and LEINSTER (E), only to be challenged from the mid 1140s by Muirchertach MAC LOCHLAINN (based on N Ireland). They competed for supremacy until Toirrdelbach's death. *See also* O'CONNOR FAMILY.

A Dictionary of British and Irish History, First Edition. Edited by Robert Peberdy and Philip Waller.
© 2021 John Wiley & Sons Ltd; © editorial matter and organisation Robert Peberdy and Phillip Waller.
Published 2021 by John Wiley & Sons Ltd.

UGANDA A former British territory in E Africa, to the N and W of Lake Victoria. In 1890–2 Frederick LUGARD negotiated treaties with local rulers on behalf of the Imperial British East Africa Company to prevent German domination. After the company went bankrupt (1893), Great Britain safeguarded the source of the NILE by declaring a PROTECTORATE (1894, expanded 1896).

The British ruled through four native monarchies (Ankole, Buganda, Bunyoro, Toro) and helped to develop cotton and coffee growing. After difficulties in the late 1950s when Buganda sought to secede, Uganda became independent under the British Crown in 1962 and a republic in 1963. Approx. population in 1921, 3,071,000; in 1961, 7,049,000. *See also* EAST AFRICA, BRITISH INVOLVEMENT.

UÍ NÉILL, NORTHERN Historians' name for a federation of dynasties which dominated N Ireland in the 5th–12th centuries. Like the related Southern Uí NÉILL, they claimed descent from NIALL NOÍGIALLACH (early 5th century) of CONNACHT (W Ireland).

In the 5th century the Cenél Conaill dynasty established itself in NW Ireland (modern Co. Donegal), while the Cenél nEógain occupied the Inishowen peninsula (on N coast) and also pushed the Ulaid dynasty eastwards. In the 7th and 8th centuries the Cenél nEógain expanded southwards, taking land from AIRGIALLA. (Their area was called Tír Eógain; English, Tyrone.)

Until the late 8th century the Cenél Conaill and Cenél nEógain shared the high-kingship of the Northern Uí Néill (kings were styled 'king of Ailech' after a hillfort in Donegal). Thereafter it was monopolized by the Cenél nEógain. The high-kings also shared (or contested) the kingship of TARA (claimed high-kingship of Ireland) with the Southern Uí Néill (until 1002; *see* BRIAN BÓRUMA).

In the 10th and early 11th centuries descendants of NIALL GLÚNDUB monopolized the high-kingships of the Cenél nEógain and Northern Uí Néill (using the surname Ua Néill from the early 11th century). Around 1033 they were replaced as high-kings by their Mac Lochlainn kinsmen – Muirchertach MAC LOCHLAINN (d. 1166) was effectively the last high-king of the Northern Uí Néill. After his death various areas of N Ireland continued as autonomous kingdoms or lordships under Uí Néill kings until the early 17th century (fluctuating in number and extent). *See also* ULSTER; O'NEILL FAMILIES.

UÍ NÉILL, SOUTHERN Historians' name for a federation of Irish dynasties which, like the related Northern Uí NÉILL, claimed descent from NIALL NOÍGIALLACH (early 5th century). Originating in CONNACHT (W Ireland), in the 6th century they wrested control of Meath (Lough Ree to Irish Sea) from LEINSTER. Within Meath were two main (sub)kingdoms: Mide kingdom to the W, Brega to the E.

The former was ruled by Clann Cholmáin, who were also high-kings of the Southern Uí Néill and called themselves 'kings of Uisnech' (after a hillfort in modern Co. Westmeath). From the 8th century they also shared the kingship of TARA (i.e., claimed high-kingship of Ireland) with the Northern Uí Néill, until it was lost in 1002 by MÁEL SECHNAILL MAC DOMNAILL, high-king of the Southern Uí Néill, to BRIAN BÓRUMA of Munster (S Ireland).

The last effective high-king of the Southern Uí Néill was Conchobar Ua Máel Sechlainn (ruled 1030–73). After his death Meath lost cohesion, enabling outside kings to interfere: *see* MEATH. (Conchobar's descendants retained local authority into the 13th century.)

UKIP *see* UNITED KINGDOM INDEPENDENCE PARTY

ULAID *see* ULSTER

ULSTER Name used for N Ireland or sometimes smaller units. It means 'Territory of the Ulaid', referring to the dynasty whose members were high-kings of the northern third of Ireland in the 4th and early 5th centuries, based at EMAIN MACHA. (The Ulaid, Uluti in Latin, may have been descendants of the Voluntii, recorded in the 2nd century.) The high-kingship included AIRGIALLA and Irish DÁL RIATA.

During the 5th century, Northern Uí NÉILL dynasties expanded into Ulster from the SW, taking NW and C Ulster and achieving superiority over Airgialla. The Ulaid were forced eastwards and confined to modern Cos. Antrim and Down. During the 7th century the Ulaid high-kingship was contested by the Dál nAraide and Dál Fiatach dynasties, the latter becoming dominant. The N remained divided between the Northern Uí Néill, Airgialla and Ulaid until the late 12th century, surviving VIKING raids (late 8th–10th centuries).

In 1177 the Anglo-Norman John de COURCY conquered the Ulaid kingdom, forcing its ruling dynasty S of Lough Neagh. He was replaced in 1204 by Hugh de Lacy (d. 1242), who was created earl of Ulster (1205). De BURGHS held the earldom, in Ireland's NE corner, 1263–1333. Titular earls were then absentees, enabling Niall Mór Ua Néill (d. 1393) to assert authority over N Ireland. Conn Bacach O'Neill (king 1519–59) was created earl of Tyrone (1542) by HENRY VIII.

The English re-exerted pressure from the 1580s, and in 1607 Hugh O'Neill (king from 1593) fled, ending Gaelic kingship (*see* IRELAND, ENGLISH CONQUEST, 16TH CENTURY). In 1585, eight shires had nominally been created; Co. Cavan was added by 1608, defining Ulster as nine counties. Protestant English and presbyterian Scots settled in the 17th century, creating a religiously mixed society (*see* ULSTER PLANTATION). When Ireland was partitioned in 1921, six counties remained in the UK (*see* NORTHERN IRELAND). *See also* PROVINCES, IRELAND.

ULSTER CUSTOM A practice in ULSTER (N Ireland) in the 18th–19th centuries (also called 'tenant right') whereby a departing tenant of land had the right to sell his tenancy and be paid by his successor for his 'interest' (value of improvements and of the land beyond the rent paid). From the 1850s campaigners sought to establish the practice throughout Ireland. It was protected where customary under the 1870 Land Act, and extended elsewhere in 1881. *See also* 'THREE FS'; LAND AGITATION AND REFORM, IRELAND.

ULSTER PLANTATION A colonization scheme of the English government in N Ireland, occupying land confiscated from the earls of Tyrone and Tyrconnell (Cos. Armagh, Cavan, Coleraine, Donegal, Fermanagh, Tyrone) after their flight in 1607 (*see* FLIGHT OF THE EARLS). Sir Arthur CHICHESTER (chief governor) initially envisaged allotment of land mainly to Gaelic Irish. But after O'DOHERTY'S REBELLION (1608) immigration became the priority, to 'civilize' the Irish (*see* DAVIES, JOHN).

Plans were announced in Jan. 1609 for land grants to: (a) immigrant 'UNDERTAKERS', who would recruit other immigrants (English and Scots); (b) servitors (former government officers); (c) native Gaelic Irish, who would receive inferior land. Many undertakers and servitors appeared unable to recruit sufficient tenants; so in 1610 Co. Coleraine, the towns of Coleraine and DERRY, and other land were granted to the Irish Society of London (funded by Londoners).

Substantial immigration began *c.*1615, but disappointed expectations. Irish inhabitants remained more widely spread than intended. Native Irish resentment erupted in the ULSTER RISING of 1641. (Cos. Antrim and Down were outside the scheme, but were heavily settled by Scots under private arrangements.) *See also* PLANTATIONS, IRELAND.

ULSTER RISING In ULSTER (N Ireland), a rising of (Catholic) Gaelic Irish against (Protestant) English and Scottish settlers. The rebels, led by Phelim O'NEILL and Rory O'More, sought religious liberty and restoration of estates from King CHARLES I. Beginning on 23 Oct. 1641, they evicted rural settlers, killing around 2000. (Several thousand refugees also died.) Between Dec. and spring 1642 the Rising spread throughout Ireland. The number of dead was exaggerated in England, inflaming anti-Catholic passions. *See also* DUBLIN CASTLE PLOT; IRISH WARS, 1641–52.

ULSTER SPECIAL CONSTABULARY An armed police force created in Nov. 1920 in NE Ireland, at the request of Unionists during the War of IRISH INDEPENDENCE, to counter attacks by the IRISH REPUBLICAN ARMY. Recruited extensively from the revived Protestant paramilitary ULSTER VOLUNTEER FORCE, it helped the province of NORTHERN IRELAND (instituted May 1921) to become established.

The USC comprised three classes: A Specials, paid full-time police with limited duties; B Specials, paid local part-timers; C Specials, voluntary emergency reservists. By mid 1922 there were 32,000 Specials compared with 1100 officers in the Royal Ulster Constabulary. A and C Specials were disbanded in 1926 after the cancellation of the BOUNDARY COMMISSION fixed Northern Ireland's area and borders. B Specials continued as a Protestant force resented by many Catholics until disbanded in 1970, during the TROUBLES. *See also* POLICE, IRELAND/NORTHERN IRELAND.

ULSTER'S SOLEMN LEAGUE AND COVENANT A pledge, modelled on the Scottish NATIONAL COVENANT (1638), which was signed by (Protestant) Unionists in ULSTER (N Ireland) on 28 Sept. 1912 (so-called 'Ulster Day'). The 237,300 male signatories vowed to resist the imposition of Home Rule on Ireland (threatened by the third Home Rule Bill). Some 229,000 women signed a separate declaration. The Covenant signalled a strengthening of Ulster's opposition to Home Rule. *See also* HOME RULE MOVEMENT, IRELAND; UNIONISM, IRELAND.

ULSTER UNIONIST COUNCIL A political organization constituted on 3 March 1905 in BELFAST, NE Ireland, during the DEVOLUTION CRISIS. Its purpose was to bring together diverse Unionist organizations and MPs to oppose devolution and HOME RULE. Its foundation effectively initiated the ULSTER UNIONIST PARTY (UUP), of which it remained the central body and legal representation.

During the Home Rule crisis of 1912–14 the UUP planned a separatist ULSTER provisional government, organized ULSTER'S SOLEMN LEAGUE AND COVENANT (both Sept. 1912), and founded the ULSTER VOLUNTEER FORCE (Jan. 1913). Important later decisions included approval of the GOVERNMENT OF IRELAND Bill (March 1920), rejection of the proposed Council of Ireland (Jan. 1974; *see* SUNNINGDALE AGREEMENT), and approval for UUP involvement in a new devolved government (1999; *see* PEACE PROCESS, NORTHERN IRELAND).

The UUC initially comprised 200 members: 100 nominated by local organizations, 50 co-opted, and 50 representing the ORANGE ORDER. (A small standing committee was also created.) Membership was frequently increased to expand representation (e.g., women's organizations added 1918, constituency representatives 1929). In 1946 a new constitution expanded the standing committee, empowered it to appoint (or depose) the UUP leader, and created an executive committee. In 2000 the UUC had a maximum membership of 860. A new constitution in 2004 made the UUC the supreme decision-making body within a legally constituted UUP, and in 2007 the delegation system was abandoned with all UUP members joining the UUC. *See also* UNIONISM, IRELAND.

ULSTER UNIONIST PARTY A political party dedicated to retaining Northern Ireland's place within the UK. It originated in early 1886 as an informal group of Conservative MPs who represented Irish constituencies (mainly in ULSTER). Led by Edward SAUNDERSON, they sought to resist HOME RULE and preserve Ireland's union with Great Britain. The group, which became known as the Irish Unionist Party, co-operated with other Unionist organizations (*see* IRISH UNIONIST ALLIANCE).

On 3 March 1905, following a proposal by Ulster MPs, an ULSTER UNIONIST COUNCIL (UUC) was founded (including MPs and ORANGE ORDER representatives) to co-ordinate opposition to a proposed devolution scheme (*see* DEVOLUTION CRISIS). It effectively marked the creation of an Ulster, rather than all-Ireland, Unionist Party (UUP). In 1912–14 the UUC led resistance to the likely imposition of Home Rule.

After the province of NORTHERN IRELAND was created (1921), the UUP's structure was elaborated. It comprised the UUC and affiliated organizations; Unionist MPs and lords in the UK Parliament; members and senators in the Northern Ireland Parliament (including the prime minister of Northern Ireland, who served as leader). The Party governed Northern Ireland until 'direct rule' was imposed in 1972. Its representatives in the UK Parliament sat with the Conservatives until 1974. In 1986 it withdrew from the National Union of Conservative and Unionist Associations in protest at the HILLSBOROUGH AGREEMENT.

Following the BELFAST AGREEMENT (1998), the Party, led by David TRIMBLE, participated in a multi-party devolved government (1999–2002), despite little arms 'decommissioning' by the PROVISIONAL IRISH REPUBLICAN ARMY. The controversial policy divided the Party. Many members and voters changed allegiance to the DEMOCRATIC UNIONIST PARTY, which in 2003 overtook the UUP in Assembly seats. In 2005 the Orange Order ended formal involvement, and representation in the UK Parliament also collapsed, leaving the Party in a weak state. It participated in a new Northern Ireland Executive 2007–16 and from 2020. *See also* UNIONISM, IRELAND; PARLIAMENTARY REPRESENTATION, NORTHERN IRELAND.

ULSTER VOLUNTEER FORCE A military organization in Ulster (N Ireland) founded by the (Protestant) ULSTER UNIONIST COUNCIL on 31 Jan. 1913 to resist HOME RULE. It quickly recruited about 90,000 members and imported arms illegally (April 1914). After the UK entered WORLD WAR I (4 Aug.) the UVF was incorporated in the British Army (as the 36th Ulster Division). Many ex-UVF men later joined the ULSTER SPECIAL CONSTABULARY (founded 1920).

The name was revived in 1966 for a new Ulster paramilitary force, which opposed the conciliatory unionism of Terence O'NEILL. It became Northern Ireland's leading loyalist paramilitary organization and assassinated many nationalists. It was banned 1966–74 and from 1975. The UVF declared a ceasefire in 1994, the end of its campaign in 2007, and decommissioning of weapons in 2009 but it reportedly continued violent acts and gangsterism. *See also* UNIONISM, IRELAND; IRISH VOLUNTEERS; PEACE PROCESS, NORTHERN IRELAND.

ULSTER WORKERS' STRIKE A general strike in NORTHERN IRELAND during the TROUBLES, organized by the newly formed Ulster Workers' Council and called on 14 May 1974. It was promoted by Unionists opposed to the SUNNINGDALE AGREEMENT and involvement of nationalists in a power-sharing Executive (led by Brian FAULKNER). The strike halted industrial activity. The Executive resigned on 28 May. *See also* EXECUTIVES, NORTHERN IRELAND; UNIONISM, IRELAND.

ULTRAMONTANISM A tendency within the Roman Catholic Church which stresses the authority of the papacy rather than allowing a significant role for local churches. It developed in modern form in reaction to 18th-century rationalism and the French Revolution, culminating in the declaration of papal infallibility (1870). Ultramontanism (meaning 'beyond the mountains' – the Alps) was influential in Great Britain and Ireland from the mid 19th to late 20th century. *See also* MANNING, HENRY.

ULTRA TORIES An informal faction within the British TORY Party, early 1820s to mid 1830s, associated with Lord ELDON, which doggedly resisted political change, particularly CATHOLIC EMANCIPATION (conceded 1829) and PARLIAMENTARY REFORM (conceded 1832). They helped to defeat the Tory ministry of the duke of WELLINGTON in 1830, enabling the WHIGS to take office and introduce Parliamentary reform. A severe election defeat for the Tories in 1832 reduced the Ultras' influence. *See also* LIBERAL TORIES.

UNAUTHORIZED PROGRAMME The radical manifesto presented by the British Liberal politicians Joseph CHAMBERLAIN and Jesse Collings at the 1885 general election without approval from the leaders of the LIBERAL PARTY. It included calls for free education, a graduated property tax, smallholdings for agricultural labourers ('three acres and a cow'), disestablishment of Churches, elected county councils, and manhood suffrage.

UNDERTAKERS Term used for two groups in Irish history. The first consisted of English or Scottish investors in PLANTATIONS in the 16th and 17th centuries, who received titles to land on condition that they imported significant numbers of settlers. 'Undertaking' involved considerable investment in infrastructure such as living quarters, livestock and transport facilities.

The second group comprised influential members of the Irish PARLIAMENT in the 18th century who obtained the votes required to pass government legislation in return for rewards. Examples include William CONOLLY, Henry BOYLE and John PONSONBY.

UNEMPLOYMENT Before the 20th century work-less periods were experienced in AGRICULTURE because of vagaries of weather, and in trade and INDUSTRY because of fluctuating commercial conditions (*see* TRADE CYCLES OR BUSINESS CYCLES). In Britain, financial support at unoccupied times was available from statutory POOR RELIEF (from 16th century), FRIENDLY SOCIETIES (from late 17th century) and some TRADE UNIONS (19th–20th centuries). Friendly societies and unions also existed in Ireland, but not statutory relief until 1838.

From the late 18th century rural unemployment and underemployment increased due to rapid POPULATION growth, inflating statutory relief costs. When provision was reformed in the 1830s–40s, to reduce expenditure, idleness by able-bodied people was treated as moral failure. Harsh practices sought to deter claims and force people to find work. Except in Scotland, relief initially required entering a workhouse. 'Outdoor relief' was ostensibly prohibited, though persisted in England and Wales and was introduced in Ireland in 1847.

In the 1880s demonstrations and riots in UK towns by unoccupied skilled and unskilled workers, and growing concern about urban poverty, stimulated new remedies, understanding and attitudes. Unemployment was seen as resulting from economic conditions (the term 'unemployment' was first used by the economist Alfred MARSHALL in 1888). From 1886 to 1893 central government encouraged local authorities to provide public works outside the poor law, treating unemployment as a social problem. The 1905 Unemployed Workmen Act (for UK) permitted authorities to establish labour exchanges (job-finding bureaux).

Central government then assumed and exercised responsibility UK-wide, taking power to establish labour exchanges (1909 Labour Exchanges Act) and requiring insurance against unemployment in certain trades (1911 National Insurance Act). Provision was later extended. *See also* NATIONAL INSURANCE; HUNGER MARCHES; GREAT DEPRESSION, IMPACT ON GREAT BRITAIN/IRELAND; WELFARE STATE; SOCIAL SERVICES AND WELFARE, SOUTHERN IRELAND.

UNFEDERATED MALAY STATES Former British-controlled territories on the Malay Peninsula. By the Anglo-Siamese Treaty of 1902, Great Britain expanded in Malaya by gaining sovereignty over the sultanates of Kelantan, Trengganu, Perlis and Kedah, whose rulers accepted British advisers (1909). To the S, Johore also accepted a British resident (1914) without joining the neighbouring FEDERATED MALAY STATES. Approx. population in 1921, 1,123,000. In 1946 Britain united the sultanates with the Federated States, Penang and Malacca to form the Malayan Union, a crown colony. It was replaced in 1948 by the Federation of Malaya (*see* MALAYA).

UNIONISM, IRELAND A movement, 1880s–1920, which defended the UNION OF IRELAND AND GREAT BRITAIN against the HOME RULE movement. Thereafter it defended retention of NORTHERN IRELAND within the UK. Most Unionists were Protestants.

Home Rule agitation in 1885 alarmed Protestants. Southern Unionists formed the Irish Loyal and Patriotic Union (May). The 'conversion' of W.E. GLADSTONE to Home Rule (Dec.) provoked formation (Jan. 1886) of the Ulster Loyalist Anti-Repeal Union. Unionists protested against Gladstone's Home Rule Bill (defeated June 1886).

During the 1890s unionism developed in Ulster, though Gladstone's second Bill (1893) caused protests throughout Ireland. The DEVOLUTION CRISIS of 1904–5 provoked the creation (March 1905) of the ULSTER UNIONIST COUNCIL (UUC), effectively the formation of the ULSTER UNIONIST PARTY (UUP). After another Bill was introduced (April 1912), Ulster Unionists threatened violent resistance. (Home Rule was enacted in Sept. 1914 but suspended.)

On 20 March 1920 the UUC accepted a self-governing 'Northern Ireland' within the UK. It was dominated by the UUP until challenged by the CIVIL RIGHTS MOVEMENT (1960s). Concessions were opposed notably by Ian PAISLEY and William Craig, who respectively founded (1971) the DEMOCRATIC UNIONIST PARTY (DUP) and Ulster Vanguard (pressure group).

Britain's imposition of 'direct rule' (1972) ended Unionist rule. Britain advocated power sharing with nationalists. Though attempted with some Unionist support (1974), it was destroyed by Unionist opposition (*see* ULSTER WORKERS' STRIKE). The UUP and DUP opposed the HILLSBOROUGH AGREEMENT (1985) but diverged over the 1990s PEACE PROCESS. The UUP accepted the BELFAST AGREEMENT (1998) and led a power-sharing EXECUTIVE (1999–2002; *see* TRIMBLE, DAVID). However, support declined and at ASSEMBLY elections in 2003 it was overtaken by the DUP. It rejected power sharing unless the PROVISIONAL IRISH REPUBLICAN ARMY 'decommissioned' arms. After they were put 'beyond use' (2005), the ST ANDREWS AGREEMENT (2006) enabled the DUP to form an Executive alongside its former foe PROVISIONAL SINN FÉIN (2007–17, revived 2020). *See also* IRISH UNIONIST

ALLIANCE; ORANGE ORDER, IRELAND; PARAMILITARY ORGANIZATIONS, NORTHERN IRELAND; PARLIAMENTARY REPRESENTATION, NORTHERN IRELAND.

UNIONISM, SCOTLAND The belief that Scotland and England should be more fully joined; periodically advocated in the 17th century, following the UNION OF CROWNS. Proposals for union came primarily from rulers: from JAMES VI/I (in 1604–8), CHARLES II (1668, 1670), WILLIAM III (II of Scotland, 1689). During the 1650s Scotland was forcibly united with England. 'Union' could refer to various arrangements, including free trade, a federal arrangement or parliamentary incorporation. The last prevailed in 1707.

Between 1886 and 1914 'Unionism' flourished in Scotland as a defence of the integrated UNITED KINGDOM (including the 1707 English–Scottish union), in reaction to W.E. GLADSTONE's promotion of HOME RULE for Ireland and demands for Scottish Home Rule. A Unionist section broke from the Scottish LIBERAL PARTY (1886) and cooperated with the (pro-union) Conservatives. Unionists feared weakening of the British Empire and the consequences of a semi-independent Ireland, particularly the fate of Irish Protestants in a Catholic State. *See also* UNION OF ENGLAND AND SCOTLAND, 1650s; UNION OF ENGLAND AND SCOTLAND; DEVOLUTION, SCOTLAND.

UNIONIST PARTIES, IRELAND *see* UNIONISM, IRELAND

UNION OF CROWNS, ENGLAND (WITH IRELAND) AND SCOTLAND In 1603 JAMES VI, king of Scotland, was invited to succeed his distant cousin ELIZABETH I, queen of England (and also of Ireland), who had died without an English heir. James's accession inaugurated a century during which England and Scotland had a common ruler but otherwise remained distinct (1603–1707, except 1649–60).

The STEWART RULERS of Scotland had been the closest relations of the TUDOR rulers of England since the marriage in 1503 of Margaret Tudor, daughter of HENRY VII of England, to JAMES IV of Scotland, though the Stewarts were never recognized as heirs. (James VI was the great-grandson of Margaret and James IV.) The union was made possible by the Scottish REFORMATION (1560), which meant that both England and Scotland had rejected papal authority, and by a realignment of foreign policy which had produced peace between the countries (*see* SCOTTISH–ENGLISH RELATIONS 1357 TO 1603).

In 1603 Scotland lost a resident monarch and royal artistic patronage. Within Scotland the COUNCIL became the main instrument of royal authority. England experienced an influx of Scotsmen into court positions. It has been argued that the difficulties of managing a multi-State monarchy led to the CIVIL WARS and the 1707 incorporating UNION OF ENGLAND AND SCOTLAND. *See also* UNIONISM, SCOTLAND.

UNION OF ENGLAND AND SCOTLAND England pushed Scotland into union after Scotland resisted the HANOVERIAN SUCCESSION, which England had adopted (to ensure a Protestant succession) by means of the Act of SETTLEMENT (1701). Scotland succumbed partly because of economic weakness (*see* DARIEN SCHEME).

After discussions about union in 1702–3 failed, the Scottish Parliament asserted its freedom with the Act of SECURITY and Act anent PEACE AND WAR (1703–4). England responded with the ALIEN ACT (1705), demanding new discussions. At a moment of low attendance by opposition members (1 Sept. 1705), the Scottish Parliament authorized Queen ANNE to nominate commissioners for union negotiations, thereby ensuring pro-union representatives.

Between 16 April and 22 July 1706 two teams of commissioners (31 on each side) prepared an international treaty of 25 articles. It provided for an 'incorporating union' creating the kingdom of 'Great Britain' with one ruler, parliament, flag, fiscal system and coinage. Scotland would have free trade with England and its colonies, would retain its laws and legal system, and would be represented in Parliament by 45 MPs and 16 'representative peers' (English representation remained unchanged). It would be compensated for sharing England's pre-union national debt (*see* EQUIVALENT). BURGHS and HERITABLE JURISDICTIONS would be preserved. In Jan. 1707 a Scottish Act also guaranteed the Church of SCOTLAND's independence. Scotland's Parliament ratified the treaty on 16 Jan. 1707, England's in March. It came into force on 1 May 1707. *See also SQUADRONE VOLANTE*; QUEENSBERRY, 2ND DUKE OF.

UNION OF ENGLAND AND SCOTLAND, 1606 SCHEME Detailed proposals for union which were prepared by commissioners in 1604–6, including commercial union and naturalization of Scots. A union (as 'Great Britain') was proposed by JAMES VI of Scotland in 1604, after his accession as king of England, to prevent internal hostility. The proposals were rejected by England's Parliament (1607), partly because of dislike of the Scots. Some hostile English laws were repealed, and in 1608 James obtained a court judgment (in the collusive Calvin's case) whereby a child born in Scotland after the UNION OF CROWNS (1603) was considered an English subject under COMMON LAW.

UNION OF ENGLAND AND SCOTLAND, 1650s The countries were declared one Commonwealth by England's Parliament on 28 Oct. 1651, following conquest of much of Scotland in 1650–1 by the NEW MODEL ARMY (*see* DUNBAR, BATTLE OF). In Jan. 1652 Scottish burghs and sheriffdoms were instructed to elect representatives to give consent. Union was formally proclaimed in Scotland on 4 Feb. 1652; in April representatives were elected to discuss terms. Oliver CROMWELL, lord protector, issued an ordinance for union on 12 April 1654, and this was converted in an Act of Union by the second Protectorate Parliament on 26 June 1656.

The union's initial basis was military government (under eight major-generals) and military occupation (10,000–18,000 troops stationed in five large forts and subsidiary garrisons). Private REGALITIES and BARONIES were abolished. From the GLENCAIRN RISING (1653–4) onwards, General George MONCK was commander-in-chief and then the leading member of a Council of Scotland (instituted 1655).

Scotland was granted five seats in the nominated Parliament of 1653 (see BAREBONE'S PARLIAMENT) and 30 seats in the Protectorate Parliament (1654–9), but most MPs were government nominees. Union ended with the RESTORATION (1660). See also CIVIL WARS, SCOTTISH PARTICIPATION.

UNION OF IRELAND AND GREAT BRITAIN Union was promoted by the British prime minister William PITT the Younger in response to the RISING OF 1798 and HUMBERT'S EXPEDITION, though the idea had been floated for commercial reasons some time before. Pitt sought to guarantee Great Britain's security by strengthening control of Ireland and its defences (e.g., against France), and reducing sectarian rivalry. Many Irish Protestant politicians opposed union, whereas many Catholics welcomed it, attracted by Pitt's intention to enact 'Emancipation' (admission of Catholics to the union Parliament).

The terms of union were proposed by the British government, but required ratification by the Parliaments of Ireland and Britain. The Irish House of Commons initially rejected the principle of union (24 Jan. 1799). After lavish disposal of patronage (e.g., award of peerages and pensions), the Irish Parliament completed its approval on 6 June 1800. Britain's Parliament agreed on 2 July. Union took effect on 1 Jan. 1801.

The Union Acts created a United Kingdom of Great Britain and Ireland. The UK Parliament included 100 representatives of Irish constituencies in the House of Commons, and 28 'representative peers' and four bishops in the House of Lords. The Acts also created a United Church of England and Ireland, confirmed the UK Lords as the supreme court, and formed a customs union. Ireland retained its own administration (as a branch of the British government), though further integration took place (e.g., amalgamation of Exchequers, 1817; assimilation of currencies, 1826).

Because of opposition from King GEORGE III, Pitt was unable to effect Catholic Emancipation. Even when it was conceded (1829), many Irish people remained opposed to the union and British rule, though both endured until 1921–2. See also CATHOLIC RELIEF AND EMANCIPATION, IRELAND; UNION REPEAL MOVEMENT, IRELAND.

UNION OF SCOTS AND PICTS From c.500 SCOTS (Irish) from DÁL RIATA in NE Ireland settled in western N Britain, forming kingdoms under a high-king of (Scottish) Dál Riata and gradually intermingling with their neighbours the PICTS (see ATHOLL, KINGDOM OF). From the 8th century some kings of the Picts, possibly with kindred connections to Dál Riata, seized the high-kingship of Dál Riata (see ONUIST SON OF VURGUIST; CONSTANTÍN SON OF VURGUIST), creating temporary unions.

From c.842 KENNETH I MAC ALPIN, high-king of Dál Riata, created a firmer, Scots-dominated union. Based on the fertile C and E Lowlands, it was the political unit that eventually expanded to include all N Britain. See also SCOTLAND; DONALD II.

UNION OF WALES WITH ENGLAND Wales was annexed by England, brought under English law and systems of government, and represented in England's PARLIAMENT, by legislation passed in 1536 and 1543 (known since 1901 as the 'Act of Union'). Union replaced rule by English lords (including the king) in the MARCH OF WALES and by the Crown in the PRINCIPALITY OF WALES.

Union was partly the culmination of attempts since the 1470s to improve order through the COUNCIL IN THE MARCHES OF WALES. It resulted more immediately from the strengthening of Crown powers in distant areas by Thomas CROMWELL, to prevent Catholic countries (France, Spain) from inciting rebellion following the removal of England and Wales from papal jurisdiction (see REFORMATION, ENGLAND).

The Wales Act of the English Parliament in 1536 annexed Wales. It abolished the March, converted the lordship of GLAMORGAN into a SHIRE, and created five new shires in place of other lordships. JUSTICES OF THE PEACE were to be appointed in each county. English law was to apply, with legal proceedings held in English. Each shire was to elect an MP, as were each shire's BOROUGHS. (MONMOUTHSHIRE received two MPs.)

The Laws in Wales Act of 1543 tidied boundaries, regulated the Council, instituted a sheriff in each shire, and extended the COURT OF GREAT SESSIONS to all counties except Monmouthshire. See also WALES; LOCAL GOVERNMENTAL STRUCTURES, WALES.

UNION REPEAL MOVEMENT, IRELAND After Ireland was united with Great Britain in 1801 opposition to the union continued. But leading opponents (Henry GRATTAN, Daniel O'CONNELL) concentrated first on obtaining Catholic Emancipation (conceded 1829). O'Connell then advocated repeal in the UK House of Commons, but was repulsed (repeal motion defeated, April 1834). He turned briefly instead to achieving reforms (see LICHFIELD HOUSE COMPACT; DRUMMOND, THOMAS).

O'Connell revived the repeal cause *c*.1838, founding the REPEAL ASSOCIATION in 1840. After Sir Robert PEEL became British prime minister (Aug. 1841), O'Connell saw little prospect for reforms or repeal. He developed the Repeal Association into a mass movement, though at the cost of equating nationalism with Catholicism, and in 1843 organized 'monster meetings' around Ireland. O'Connell hoped that popular demonstrations would exact repeal. But the government banned the final CLONTARF MEETING (Oct.), and O'Connell was arrested and imprisoned. Momentum was lost. Revival of the movement was prevented by arguments between O'Connell and younger Irish nationalists (*see* YOUNG IRELAND MOVEMENT), and by the GREAT FAMINE. When campaigning recommenced (*c*.1870) it sought HOME RULE within the UK. *See also* PARLIAMENTARY REPRESENTATION, IRELAND.

UNITARIANS Christian dissenters who deny the divinity of Jesus Christ and the doctrine of the Trinity. Unitarian theology was developed in England from the early 18th century by a few dissenting ministers, and adopted in the late 18th century by some congregations of General Baptists and presbyterians. The first new Unitarian chapel was founded in 1774. Unitarian public worship was theoretically illegal until permitted by the Doctrine of the Trinity Act of 1813. A Scottish Unitarian Association was formed in 1813, and was superseded by a British and Foreign Unitarian Association in 1825 (disbanded 1867). A General Assembly of Unitarian and Free Christian Churches was created in 1925.

British Unitarians were few in number (e.g., 229 congregations in 1851) but from the 1830s until the early 20th century they included many provincial business and political leaders (e.g., Joseph CHAMBERLAIN). The minister, philosopher and writer James Martineau (1805–1900), brother of Harriet MARTINEAU, became prominent in English religious life. He contended that faith must not defy reason, and controversially argued against scriptural authority. The first woman to be given pastoral charge of a dissenting chapel (1904), Gertrude von Petzold (1876–1952), was a Unitarian. In 2010 there were about 5000 Unitarians in Great Britain. *See also* NONCONFORMITY AND DISSENT, ENGLAND.

UNITED FREE CHURCH OF SCOTLAND A Scottish dissenting presbyterian Church formed in 1900 by merger of a majority of the FREE CHURCH OF SCOTLAND and of the UNITED PRESBYTERIAN CHURCH. The new Church was the largest in Scotland, but failed to expand. It opposed the established position of the Church of SCOTLAND, but soon entered into negotiations for union, which took place in 1929. *See also* DISSENT, SCOTLAND.

UNITED IRISH LEAGUE An organization founded on 23 Jan. 1898 by William O'BRIEN and Michael DAVITT to campaign for land reform and other aims, including HOME RULE. Its success encouraged the divided IRISH PARLIAMENTARY PARTY to reunite in Jan 1900. The Party then united with the League (June), the latter serving as the Party's local and fund-raising organization (replacing the NATIONAL LEAGUE). The UIL contracted sharply after 1916. *See also* LAND AGITATION AND REFORM, IRELAND.

UNITED IRISHMEN, SOCIETY OF A political organization which began in 1791 with the founding of clubs in BELFAST (Oct.) and DUBLIN (Nov.) and spread throughout Ireland. Influenced by the FRENCH REVOLUTION, it sought to unite Irishmen of different religious backgrounds (Church of Ireland, Presbyterian, Catholic) to campaign for parliamentary reform. It was suppressed in May 1794.

From late 1794 members in NE Ireland revived the Society as a network of secret associations committed to establishing a republic. By 1797 it was operating throughout Ireland and mounted the unsuccessful RISING OF 1798. *See also* TONE, WOLFE; FITZGERALD, LORD EDWARD; DEFENDERS; EMMET'S RISING.

UNITED KINGDOM Short name for the United Kingdom of Great Britain and Northern Ireland, the largest sovereign jurisdiction within the BRITISH ISLES. Est. popn in 2015: 65,110,000 (97% in Britain).

The 'UK' was created in 1801 as the United Kingdom of Great Britain and Ireland by union of two separate kingdoms (*see* UNION OF IRELAND AND GREAT BRITAIN). The British PARLIAMENT at WESTMINSTER became the UK Parliament, expanded with Irish representation. The governments of Britain and Ireland were only partly unified, though continuing executive departments in Ireland were ultimately controlled from Britain (*see* GOVERNMENT, IRELAND, 19TH–20TH CENTURIES). The UK government continued to be called the 'British government' (or even the 'English government'). Likewise, territories ruled by the UK continued as the 'British Empire', despite involvement by Irish people. Est. popn in 1801: Britain, 10,500,000; Ireland, 5,200,000.

Although much of Ireland became independent under the Crown in 1922 (as the IRISH FREE STATE), the UK's name was retained. Alterations were made by legislation in 1927 (following collapse of the BOUNDARY COMMISSION and issue of the BALFOUR DEFINITION): the Westminster Parliament was styled the Parliament of the United Kingdom of Great Britain and Northern Ireland, and George V became king of 'Great Britain, Ireland ...'. Following southern Ireland's change to republic status in 1949, ELIZABETH II was styled queen of the 'United Kingdom of Great Britain and Northern Ireland ...' from

1953. The UK joined the EUROPEAN ECONOMIC COMMUNITY in 1973 ('European Union' from 1993), but in 2016 voted to leave (*see* BREXIT).

UNITED KINGDOM INDEPENDENCE PARTY A political party founded in 1993 to seek withdrawal of the UK from the European Union (EU). It originated in the cross-party Anti-Federalist League started in 1991 by the British historian Alan Sked (b. 1947) to oppose the MAASTRICHT TREATY. Sked viewed the EU as anti-democratic, corrupt and inimical to the UK's national interest. He led 'UKIP' until 1997, resigning in protest against factionalism.

UKIP proved most successful in elections to the European Parliament, when it benefited from proportional voting within large constituencies. It won three seats (of 87) in 1999, 12 in 2004, 13 in 2009. In 2014 it achieved the largest UK party representation with 24 seats (26% of the vote). Other success was minimal, though growing support in 2013–15 threatened the Conservatives, and two Conservative MPs defected to UKIP in 2014 (one survived at the 2015 UK general election). Nigel Farage (b. 1964), a plain-speaking former commodity broker, was UKIP's most effective leader (2006–9, 2010–16).

UKIP's threat to the Conservatives influenced the decision of Prime Minister David CAMERON to hold a referendum on membership of the EU in 2016 (*see* BREXIT). The public vote to leave realized UKIP's ambition. UKIP subsequently became associated with political extremism, causing Farage to leave (Dec. 2018). He founded the Brexit Party (Feb. 2019), which replaced UKIP in the European Parliament in 2019 (winning 29 seats). *See also* EUROPEAN ECONOMIC COMMUNITY/EUROPEAN UNION, IMPACT ON BRITISH POLITICS.

UNITED PRESBYTERIAN CHURCH A Scottish dissenting Church formed in 1847 by merger of the SECESSION CHURCH and RELIEF CHURCH. It was headed by a synod of ministers and elders. Although it adhered to the Westminster Confession (1647), it rejected aspects urging intolerance. It believed in free communion (i.e., taking the sacrament without examination) and voluntaryism (congregations' right to choose ministers) and later rejected CALVINISM (1879). In 1851 the Church was attended by almost 20% of Scottish churchgoers. There were over 500 congregations, mainly in cities and towns. It then declined. In the later 19th century it was drawn to the FREE CHURCH OF SCOTLAND through participation in campaigns for disestablishment of the Church of Scotland. The two united in 1900 as the UNITED FREE CHURCH OF SCOTLAND. *See also* DISSENT, SCOTLAND.

UNITED STATES OF AMERICA, BRITISH RELATIONS WITH Following six years of war (1775–81), Great Britain recognized AMERICAN INDEPENDENCE in 1783, and JAY'S TREATY settled many outstanding issues (ratified by USA 1795). Distant political relations thereafter, and sometimes disputes, were offset by continuing ties of trade, migration and culture.

Armed conflict in 1812–15 arose mainly from maritime disputes during the Napoleonic Wars (*see* WAR OF 1812), and the American Civil War (1861–5) caused diplomatic tensions (*see* AMERICAN CIVIL WAR AND GREAT BRITAIN). Frontiers with CANADA were agreed in 1818, 1846 and 1903.

By the early 20th century, the USA was outstripping Britain economically, and the reduction of British garrisons in the western hemisphere implied recognition of American regional paramountcy. The participation of US military forces in WORLD WAR I (1917–18) enabled the Allies to defeat Germany, and President Woodrow Wilson influenced the PARIS PEACE CONFERENCE (1919). But revived US isolationism (e.g., absence from LEAGUE OF NATIONS) limited co-operation.

After Britain declared war on Germany in 1939, President F.D. Roosevelt provided materiel (*see* LEND–LEASE SCHEME). The countries became allies after Japan bombed the US naval base of Pearl Harbor and Germany declared war against the USA (Dec. 1941). After the war, the UK benefited from US-provided MARSHALL AID (1948–50).

The wartime alliance persisted throughout the COLD WAR (1947–91) and beyond, with the USA retaining military bases in Britain. The countries were allies in the NORTH ATLANTIC TREATY ORGANIZATION (from 1949) and in the KOREAN WAR (1950–3). British leaders posited a SPECIAL RELATIONSHIP. Britain avoided involvement in the Vietnam War (mid 1960s), but supported the USA in the PERSIAN GULF WAR (1990–1), AFGHANISTAN WAR (2001–14), and IRAQ WAR (2003–10). *See also* ATOMIC AND NUCLEAR WEAPONS.

UNITED STATES OF AMERICA, IRISH RELATIONS WITH *see* FOREIGN RELATIONS, SOUTHERN IRELAND

UNIVERSITIES, ENGLAND A university (centre of higher studies), organized with faculties, is recorded at OXFORD (SW Midlands) *c*.1187. Closed 1209–14, following a dispute, it reopened under a chancellor and new statutes. From 1209 scholars developed a university at CAMBRIDGE (E England). For six centuries England had two universities, though additional foundations were attempted. From the 15th century, inns of court at LONDON were centres of legal education.

Starting at ages 15–17, students lived in academic lodgings run by masters (halls in Oxford, hostels in Cambridge), and mainly sought degrees as bachelors and masters of arts (studying, e.g., rhetoric, arithmetic). Many afterwards became clergy. From the late 13th century endowed colleges were founded, mainly for advanced students. There were also monastic colleges and friaries (closed in 16th century). During the 15th century many lodgings closed, leaving colleges to become primary centres of student education. Classical studies became important. After expansion in the late 16th–17th centuries, student numbers fell. In the 16th–19th centuries, adherence to the Church of ENGLAND was required. In the late 17th–18th centuries higher studies also flourished at DISSENTING ACADEMIES.

In the early 19th century new institutions were founded: London University (non-denominational, 1828), King's College London (Church of England, 1831), federal University of London (1836, with London University renamed University College); DURHAM University (Church of England, 1833). London degrees were opened to external candidates (1858).

Further foundations, sometimes to expand scientific education, raised the total to 11 universities in 1914, 17 in 1960, 37 in 1970 (including the 'Open University' for distance learning, 1969). From the late 19th century many institutions admitted women. University status was granted to an independent college at Buckingham in 1983.

Legislation in 1992 allowed older 'polytechnics' to become universities. Redesignations increased universities to 60 by 1995. With subsequent promotions, there were 106 universities in 2015. *See also* UNIVERSITY REFORM, ENGLAND; HIGHER EDUCATION, EXPANSION OF; GIRLS' AND WOMEN'S EDUCATION, BRITAIN.

UNIVERSITIES, IRELAND Trinity College was founded in 1592, as the only college of the University of DUBLIN, partly to educate clergy for the (Protestant) Church of IRELAND. Catholics were effectively excluded from 1637 (restriction removed 1793 by HOBART'S ACT). The Catholic MAYNOOTH SEMINARY educated lay students 1795–1817.

In the mid 19th century the British government, following the example of LONDON University, expanded provision with non-denominational 'Queen's Colleges' (at BELFAST, CORK, Galway, 1845), and Queen's University as their examining and degree-awarding authority (1850). The papacy condemned such 'Godless colleges' (1847), and a separate Catholic University was started (1854). Unable to award degrees, it struggled financially (*see* NEWMAN, JOHN HENRY). In 1880 the Royal University of Ireland replaced Queen's University, providing degrees for the Queen's Colleges, the Catholic University (renamed University College, Dublin, 1882), and additional colleges. Women graduated from 1884. Reorganization in 1908 produced two universities: Queen's University, Belfast, and the National University of Ireland (including reconstituted University Colleges at Cork and Galway, University College, Dublin, with Maynooth as a 'recognized college' from 1909).

There was little change until the late 20th century. NORTHERN IRELAND acquired a second university in 1968 (alongside Queen's, Belfast) with the opening of the New University of Ulster at Coleraine, Co. Londonderry (united in 1984 with Ulster Polytechnic as University of Ulster). In the Republic of Ireland, the University of Limerick and Dublin City University were founded in 1989 by upgrading existing institutions. In 1997 four colleges within the National University became largely autonomous (Cork, Dublin, Galway, and part of Maynooth). In 2019 three Institutes of Technology were amalgamated to provide an eighth university, namely the Technological University Dublin. *See also* EDUCATION, IRELAND; HIGHER EDUCATION, EXPANSION OF.

UNIVERSITIES, SCOTLAND The first university, at ST ANDREWS, was founded in 1412 when Bishop Henry Wardlaw recognized a centre of studies (Latin *studium*) as a university. In 1450 Bishop James KENNEDY founded St Salvator's College at St Andrews for the study of theology. GLASGOW University (1451) and King's College, ABERDEEN (1495), were founded as part of a rapid expansion of higher education in Renaissance Europe (*see* HUMANISM). Further colleges were also established at St Andrews (1513, 1538). After the REFORMATION, the city council at EDINBURGH founded Edinburgh University (1583), and Marischal College, Aberdeen, was founded by George Keith, (5th) Earl Marischal (1593; amalgamated with King's College 1860).

The 18th century saw a great expansion of student numbers, reform of curricula, and the intellectual achievements of the ENLIGHTENMENT. Relatively cheap to attend, Scottish universities may have catered for a slightly greater proportion of poor scholars than English universities.

In the 1960s university provision expanded as part of general expansion in Great Britain. The technical colleges of Edinburgh and Glasgow received royal charters as Heriot-Watt University (1966) and Strathclyde University (1964), and in 1967 Queen's College, Dundee, became Dundee University and Stirling University was founded. With further upgrading of colleges and polytechnics to university status from the 1990s, Scotland had 12 universities by 1995, 15 by 2012. The Open University (founded 1969), based in England, also operated in Scotland. *See also* UNIVERSITY REFORM, SCOTLAND.

UNIVERSITIES, WALES The 1406 manifesto of OWAIN GLYN DŴR proposed two universities, and similar aspirations were voiced later. In England, Jesus College at OXFORD University, founded in 1571 by the Welshman Hugh Price, had strong Welsh connections into the 19th century. From the 1670s university-level education was provided in Wales by DISSENTING ACADEMIES, and in 1822 St David's College, Lampeter (Cardiganshire), was founded (*see* BURGESS, THOMAS), chiefly to train clergy for the Church of England, which included Wales. The first teachers' training college was established at Brecon (Breconshire) in 1846.

In the 1850s Welsh patriots made the foundation of a Welsh university a principal ambition (*see* OWEN, HUGH), and in 1863 launched a fund: University College opened at Aberystwyth (Cardiganshire) in 1872. (Students studied for London University degrees.) The Aberdare Report (1881) recommended the creation of two university colleges: they were founded at CARDIFF (SE Wales) in 1883 and BANGOR (NW) in 1884. Most students were Welsh.

In 1893 the university colleges were brought into a federal, degree-granting University of Wales, which was enlarged with University College, Swansea (1920), the Welsh National School of Medicine (1931), the Institute of Science and Technology (1967), and St David's, Lampeter (1971), though by the 1970s over half the students came from England. In 1992 the Polytechnic of Wales (a polytechnic from 1970) was recognized as the University of Glamorgan.

From 1996 there were numerous reorganizations of higher education institutions, including alteration of the federal structure of the University of Wales to a federation of independent institutions (2007). By 2018 Wales had eight universities. *See also* EDUCATION, WALES; HIGHER EDUCATION, EXPANSION OF.

UNIVERSITY REFORM, ENGLAND In the late 18th century OXFORD and CAMBRIDGE Universities were often considered inferior to Scottish universities. They were criticized for poor teaching, narrow classical curricula, and religious exclusiveness (restriction to male adherents of the Church of England), though mathematics was becoming prestigious at Cambridge (with new examinations from 1780). In response, they improved teaching by emphasizing tutors' responsibilities, and Oxford reformed its examinations in 1800. From the 1830s new universities provided additional competition (*see* UNIVERSITIES, ENGLAND).

Following a royal commission (appointed 1850), Acts of Parliament were passed (for Oxford 1854, Cambridge 1856). They reformed university government, and allowed nonconformists to study and take bachelors' degrees. Colleges were required to revise their statutes, increasing access to some scholarships and fellowships. The Universities Tests Act of 1871 abolished most remaining religious tests. Women also studied at Cambridge from 1873, at Oxford from 1879. The 1877 Universities of Oxford and Cambridge Act forced colleges to release more funds for professorships and university institutions. Subject ranges were broadened in the late 19th century, while science

expanded dramatically in the 20th century. *See also* GIRLS' AND WOMEN'S EDUCATION, BRITAIN; SOCIAL STRUCTURE, ENGLAND FROM LATER 18TH CENTURY.

UNIVERSITY REFORM, SCOTLAND There were three phases. Between 1708 (Edinburgh) and 1735 universities revitalized teaching by ending 'regenting' (masters teaching all subjects). Professors lectured on specialisms and new chairs were founded. New medical faculties at Edinburgh (1726) and Glasgow achieved renown. Intellectual life flourished (*see* ENLIGHTENMENT, SCOTLAND) and students increased (e.g., at Edinburgh: 400 attending c.1700, 1300 in 1790s, 2300 in 1824).

In 1858 the Universities (Scotland) Act reformed constitutions by instituting a court as the supreme authority in each university (above professorial senates) and establishing graduate councils. The Act followed from the long-debated report (1831) of a royal commission which had been established (1826) after disputes.

Debate about curricula in the 1870s resulted in another report (1878) and the 1889 Universities (Scotland) Act which created a commission (until 1897). Its reforms included two-tier degrees (ordinary and honours), the establishment of science faculties, and the admission of women (1892). *See also* UNIVERSITIES, SCOTLAND.

UNIVERSITY SETTLEMENT MOVEMENT An arrangement whereby university undergraduates, usually from middle- or upper-class backgrounds, lived temporarily among the poor for experience of their privations and to provide education, welfare and recreation. It started in England in 1884 with the foundation of Toynbee Hall in London by Samuel BARNETT, who believed that poor relief was hampered by misunderstanding between classes. By 1913, 27 residences existed in London, 12 elsewhere in England, and five in Scotland. The movement declined from the 1930s, and residence by students largely ceased in the 1950s. Many houses became social centres. The movement influenced reformers such as William BEVERIDGE and Clement ATTLEE.

URBAN OF LLANDAFF (fl. from c.1065; d. 1133 or 1134 at Pisa, NW Italy). Bishop of LLANDAFF (SE Wales), 1107 until death. Urban claimed an extensive diocese for his church, which had been a bishop's see only since the early 11th century, provoking BERNARD OF ST DAVIDS to claim superior and extensive authority for ST DAVIDS. Against Bernard, Urban recognized the archbishopric of CANTERBURY in England as superior, but gained limited territory. *See* LLANDAFF, BOOK OF; CHURCH, MEDIEVAL WALES.

USE A form of trust employed in the 14th–17th centuries whereby the title to an estate was vested in trustees (so-called 'feoffees') for the use of a specified beneficiary. The term is derived from the legal French phrase *cestuy [a] que use* (meaning 'he to whose use'). Uses were regularly utilized in England from the late 1330s, when instances were licensed by Edward III, to protect the interests of heirs whose fathers were undertaking military service (*see* HUNDRED YEARS WAR). They became popular because they circumvented feudal rules for the descent of estates and avoided FEUDAL INCIDENTS. (Land held for military service could not be devised by will.) By 1500 much land had been assigned to uses.

Because uses were not recognized by courts of COMMON LAW, disputes were addressed to the royal COUNCIL and Court of CHANCERY – the latter's rise was impelled partly by cases concerning uses. HENRY VII (ruled 1485–1509) and HENRY VIII (1509–47) resented the loss of Crown income from feudal incidents; in 1536 the Statute of Uses made heirs of beneficiaries liable to incidents. The new situation was modified by the Statute of Wills (1540), which allowed freeholds and two-thirds of land held by military service to be devised. Employment of uses declined, although trusts and trust law continued to develop. Uses were also employed in Wales and Ireland. A Statute of Uses was enacted in Ireland in 1634. *See also* TENURES, ENGLAND FROM 1066.

USSHER, JAMES (b. 4 Jan. 1581 at Dublin, Ireland; d. 21 March 1656 at Reigate, Surrey, England, aged 75). An early student at Trinity College, Dublin (1594), Ussher became a college fellow (1600), Church of IRELAND priest (1601), professor of divinity (1607–21), bishop of Meath (1621–5), and archbishop of ARMAGH (from 1625). A Calvinist, he contributed to the Irish Articles of 1615 (*see* ARTICLES OF RELIGION).

Following the arrival in Ireland of Thomas WENTWORTH, lord deputy, in 1633, Ussher failed to prevent greater doctrinal unity between the Churches of Ireland and England, and in 1635 retired from public life (*see* LAUDIANISM, IMPACT ON IRELAND). In England from 1640, he lived at OXFORD 1642–5, during the First CIVIL WAR. A prolific scholar, Ussher argued that the Church of Ireland was an authentic descendant of the early Irish Church (*see* CHURCH, MEDIEVAL IRELAND). He also claimed, from study of the Bible, that the world was created in 4004 BC.

USSR, BRITISH RELATIONS WITH *see* RUSSIA AND USSR, ENGLISH AND BRITISH RELATIONS WITH

UTILITARIANISM A moral philosophy which maintains that an action is right if it promotes the greatest happiness of the greatest number of people. Developed by the English philosopher Jeremy BENTHAM (d. 1832) and refined by John Stuart MILL (d. 1873), it inspired the PHILOSOPHIC RADICALS (1810s–40s) and influenced WHIG reforms in the 1830s. *See also* GREY, 2ND EARL; MELBOURNE, 2ND VISCOUNT.

UTRECHT, PEACE OF Treaties made in 1713–15 at Utrecht in the Dutch Republic, ending the War of the SPANISH SUCCESSION. On 16 March 1713 Spain agreed to cede GIBRALTAR and MINORCA to Great Britain and to allow Britain to supply slaves to its American colonies (by means of a 30-year monopoly licence, known by the Spanish term *asiento*, referring to a government contract). On 31 March France accepted the HANOVERIAN SUCCESSION in Britain, agreed to end aid to the Stuarts (*see* JACOBITISM, IMPACT ON BRITISH POLITICS), and ceded territories including NEWFOUNDLAND and NOVA SCOTIA. In Britain, WHIGS attacked TORY ministers for accepting Philip V, the French claimant, as king of Spain, and later impeached four Tories. *See also* BOLINGBROKE, VISCOUNT; HARLEY, ROBERT; GEORGE I.

V

VAGRANCY In England, vagrants attracted exceptional concern from public authorities from the later 15th to mid 17th centuries. There were thought to be thousands of vagrants, many in gangs, who committed crimes. From 1495 Parliament passed numerous Acts against vagrants, to force them back home and impose work. Whipping was introduced in 1531. Most vagrants were young single people seeking work or assistance from relatives. *See also* POOR RELIEF, ENGLAND AND WALES.

VALOR ECCLESIASTICUS An assessment of the yearly value of Church incomes in England and Wales, including those of parish clergy and religious houses. It was compiled in 1535 to calculate taxes due to the Crown under the Act of First Fruits and Tenths (1534). The Act had annexed 'first fruits' (a year's income due from new office-holders, previously paid to the papacy) and had imposed a tax of a tenth of incomes. The *Valor* was published 1810–34. *See also* REFORMATION PARLIAMENT; FIFTEENTH AND TENTH.

VAN DIEMEN'S LAND A former British colony and island off the SE coast of mainland AUSTRALIA. Discovered in 1642 by Dutch explorer Abel Tasman, it was named after an official, Antony van Diemen. It served as a British penal colony 1803–53 (*see* TRANSPORTATION), initially as part of NEW SOUTH WALES, and also attracted free settlers from elsewhere in E Australia. By 1804 there were three settlements.

A separate CROWN COLONY was created in 1825, and a Parliament and RESPONSIBLE GOVERNMENT were instituted in 1856 when the colony was renamed Tasmania. Violence and disease wiped out the aboriginal inhabitants by 1876. Tasmania joined the Commonwealth of Australia in 1901 (*see* AUSTRALIAN FEDERATION). Its population was then 172,000.

VARADKAR, LEO (b. 18 Jan. 1979 at Dublin, Republic of Ireland). The son of an Irish-born Catholic mother and Indian-born Hindu father, who settled in Ireland (1973), Varadkar attended Catholic and Protestant schools before studying law and medicine at Trinity College, Dublin (1997–2003). He worked as a junior doctor, and qualified as a general practitioner (2010). Involved in politics from school days, Varadkar served on FINGAL County Council for FINE GAEL (co-opted 2003; elected member 2004–7) and in 2007 was elected to the Dáil.

After Enda KENNY became taoiseach (premier), Varadkar was minister for transport, tourism and sport (2011–14), health (2014–16) and social protection (from 2016). In Jan. 2015 he disclosed his homosexuality, and campaigned prominently for approval of same-sex marriage in a referendum (enacted Oct.; *see* HOMOSEXUALITY, LAW RELATING TO).

In 2017, after Kenny announced his intended resignation, Varadkar won his party's leadership and succeeded as taoiseach (14 June), aged 38. He quickly announced a referendum on ABORTION. Held in May 2018, it approved

A Dictionary of British and Irish History, First Edition. Edited by Robert Peberdy and Philip Waller.
© 2021 John Wiley & Sons Ltd; © editorial matter and organisation Robert Peberdy and Phillip Waller.
Published 2021 by John Wiley & Sons Ltd.

removal of the constitutional prohibition, further demonstrating the dwindling influence of the Catholic Church. Varadkar's premiership also asserted Ireland's importance in setting the European Union's terms for the UK's withdrawal from the European Union (*see* BREXIT). In Feb. 2020, following a general election in which Fine Gael came third, Varadkar was retained in office until a new government could be formed. *See also* CHURCH–STATE RELATIONS, SOUTHERN IRELAND FROM 1922; PAPAL VISITS, IRELAND; ETHNIC AND NATIONAL MINORITIES, IRELAND.

VAUGHAN WILLIAMS, RALPH (b. 12 Oct. 1872 at Down Ampney, Gloucestershire, England; d. 26 Aug. 1958 at London, England, aged 84). Drawn to musical composition from childhood, Vaughan Williams studied in CAMBRIDGE, London and Paris. He collected English folk songs (1903–10) and was influenced by 16th-century English music. Achieving recognition with *On Wenlock Edge* (song-cycle, 1909) and *Fantasia on a Theme by Thomas Tallis* (for strings, 1910), he was regarded in the 1920s–30s as England's leading composer (succeeding Edward ELGAR). His large and diverse output included nine symphonies.

VENUTIUS (fl. from 68 or 69; d. 71 or later). Consort of CARTIMANDUA, the queen of the Brigantes in C Britain (modern N England), Venutius headed an anti-Roman faction in the kingdom of Brigantia. Divorced by Cartimandua (who married his armour-bearer Vellocatus), he attacked and deposed her (68 or 69), precipitating a Roman invasion (71) in response. Venutius' defeat, perhaps at Stanwick (in modern Yorkshire, NE England), was followed by the incorporation of Brigantia into ROMAN BRITAIN.

VEREENIGING, TREATY OF The agreement that ended the (Second) BOER WAR. Final terms offered by the British government were accepted by delegates from the Boer territories of Transvaal and Orange River Colony on 31 May 1902 at Vereeniging, a village in the Transvaal. They were signed later the same day in Pretoria by Boer and British leaders.

The Boer territories accepted British sovereignty on condition of receiving self-government (implemented 1907). Boer prisoners who took an oath would be released, and the Afrikaans language would be safeguarded. Great Britain granted funds for economic recovery. *See also* SOUTH AFRICA.

VERSAILLES, TREATY OF Signed on 28 June 1919 at the Palace of Versailles, France, by representatives of the Allied Powers in WORLD WAR I (except Russia) and of Germany, during the PARIS PEACE CONFERENCE. The treaty imposed terms on Germany as a defeated party. They included acceptance of guilt for causing the war and payment of REPARATIONS; loss of various German-speaking territories; placement of the Saarland under international control; limitations on the German Army and other military restrictions; the reconstitution of Poland with a corridor through German territory to the port of Danzig (as a free city). The treaty also established the LEAGUE OF NATIONS, which received responsibility for Germany's colonies. These were entrusted to countries under MANDATES of the League. (Britain received TANGANYIKA and parts of Cameroon and Togoland; *see* WEST AFRICA, ENGLISH AND BRITISH INVOLVEMENT.) The USA failed to ratify the treaty, and German resentment contributed to the rise of Adolf Hitler (see WORLD WAR II, DEBATE OVER ORIGINS). *See also* ANGLO-GERMAN NAVAL AGREEMENT.

VESTRY *see* PARISH, CIVIL FUNCTIONS, ENGLAND/IRELAND/WALES

VICTORIA (b. 24 May 1819 at Kensington Palace, Middlesex, England; d. 22 Jan. 1901 at Osborne, Isle of Wight, England, aged 81). Queen of Great Britain and Ireland 1837–1901; empress of India 1876–1901.

Only child of Edward, duke of Kent (1767–1820), Victoria succeeded her uncle WILLIAM IV on 20 June 1837. Her political mentor was Viscount MELBOURNE, and the BEDCHAMBER CRISIS (1839) marked her as a WHIG partisan, but marriage to Prince ALBERT in 1840 brought her an able adviser. Though relations with Lord PALMERSTON and W.E. GLADSTONE proved difficult, the conventions of a modern constitutional monarchy were firmly established during her reign. Victoria insisted on her right to be consulted and informed.

Victoria idolized Albert and mourned his death (1861) to an extreme degree. Her virtual disappearance from public life provoked criticism, but Benjamin DISRAELI rekindled her interest in State affairs. By the time of her Jubilees (1887, 1897) she enjoyed great affection and respect as matriarch of the British Empire and, through the dynastic marriages of her nine children, 'Grandmother of Europe'. Succeeded by EDWARD VII. *See also* KINGSHIP AND MONARCHY, ENGLAND AND GREAT BRITAIN FROM 1680s.

VICTORIA A former British colony in AUSTRALIA. Visited by James COOK in 1770, the area (in SE Australia) was initially part of NEW SOUTH WALES. Settled by migrants from 1834, a separate colony was demarcated in 1851. The discovery of gold immediately afterwards encouraged immigration. Victoria was granted RESPONSIBLE GOVERNMENT, along with New South Wales, in 1855. In 1901 Victoria (population 1,201,000) joined the Commonwealth of Australia (*see* AUSTRALIAN FEDERATION).

VIKINGS Term widely used for Scandinavian raiders who were active across Europe and elsewhere (e.g., Iceland, Greenland, N America, Byzantium) mainly in the 9th–11th centuries. They were known by other names, including 'Danes', 'Northmen' and 'heathen'. 'Viking' was first used occasionally in England in the 9th century, and may refer to men of Viken, a district in south-east Norway. Viking activity was based on superbly designed ships. Initial raiders sought wealth (e.g., by robbing churches); later activity involved trade, settlement and sometimes conquest. *See also* ORKNEY ISLANDS; SHETLAND ISLANDS; NORMANDY.

VIKINGS, IMPACT ON ENGLAND 'Vikings' (Scandinavians, initially from Norway) raided WESSEX (S England) for booty from 789 and sacked Lindisfarne monastery (off NE England) in 793. Danes raided eastern England from the 830s. In the 850s armies occasionally over-wintered.

In 865 a 'Great Army' entered eastern England and conquered Anglo-Saxon areas: southern NORTHUMBRIA (867), EAST ANGLIA (869), eastern MERCIA (874). Danes established kingdoms and territories. Only (northern) Northumbria, (western) Mercia, and Wessex remained under Anglo-Saxon rule.

In the 870s Danes attempted to conquer Wessex. They overran much of the kingdom in 878, but were defeated at EDINGTON (Wiltshire) by King ALFRED, who recovered lost territory. Under EDWARD THE ELDER (ruled 899–924) Anglo-Saxons conquered Danish-ruled lands in the Midlands and East Anglia. ATHELSTAN seized York in 927. (Viking rule was re-established 939–44, 947–8, 949–54; *see* YORK, VIKING KINGDOM OF.)

Danes raided England again from 980 (so-called 'Second Viking age'), and in 1016 conquered the country. Danish kings ruled until 1042 (*see* ENGLAND, DANISH CONQUEST). Harald Hardrada of Norway invaded in 1066 (*see* STAMFORD BRIDGE, BATTLE OF), SWEIN ESTRITHSON of Denmark in 1080.

Danes settled in the E Midlands, East Anglia and N, though numbers are uncertain. Norwegians settled in NW England. Bishoprics (except York) and local churches disappeared. Scandinavian words entered the English language, and practices influenced social customs. Connections with Scandinavia stimulated trade and towns, notably YORK and LINCOLN. ÆTHELRED II (ruled 978–1016) sought to conciliate Danes by issuing laws for the E Midlands (so-called 'Five Boroughs'). Settlers gradually adopted Christianity, and were eventually absorbed into English society. *See also* ENGLAND, FORMATION OF.

VIKINGS, IMPACT ON IRELAND The first recorded attack occurred in 795 (on Rathlin Island off NE Ireland, or Lambay Island off E Ireland). Thereafter Norse Vikings raided ecclesiastical centres near the NE and SW coasts, seeking slaves and valuables (gold, silver, jewels). From 824 raids became more frequent and widespread (including the E coast). From 836 fleets moved inland along rivers, including the Boyne and Liffey.

Starting in 841, Vikings established *longphoirt* (Irish, meaning 'ship-camps'): enclosed bases for inland raids and over-wintering. They also settled along the N and E coasts. They failed to conquer Irish kingdoms, but established territories within them, pre-eminently around DUBLIN (a *longphort* founded in 841). Consequently Vikings were drawn into Irish affairs (e.g., allying with one king against another). Activity declined in the late 9th century, when Dublin (902) and other settlements were destroyed.

From 914 Viking fleets made new attacks, provoking resistance (*see* NIALL GLÚNDUB). Vikings also founded trading centres which became towns: WATERFORD (914), CORK (915), Dublin (re-founded 917), LIMERICK (922), WEXFORD (935). Dublin regained pre-eminence, though from 944 its kings submitted to high-kings of Ireland. Military activity generally ceased from the mid 10th century.

The towns retained their Scandinavian character into the 13th century (*see* OSTMEN). As dynamic centres from the late 10th century they contributed vigorously to trade and craftwork. Scandinavian culture also influenced Irish literature and art. *See also* CLONTARF, BATTLE OF; TOWNS, IRELAND.

VIKINGS, IMPACT ON SCOTLAND Viking attacks on N Britain (later Scotland) began on the W in the 790s and possibly earlier on the Northern Isles (ORKNEY and SHETLAND, off the NE). One immediate effect was the decline of IONA (off W Scotland) as an ecclesiastical centre (by mid 9th century). Raids continued for a century. They had a profound effect: the Vikings' major defeat of the PICTS in 839 probably helped KENNETH I MAC ALPIN to bring about the UNION OF SCOTS AND PICTS.

In N Scotland, the later Caithness, Sutherland and Ross were settled heavily; so were the WESTERN ISLES and Northern Isles, which fell under Norse rule: it lasted until, respectively, 1266 (*see* PERTH, TREATY OF) and 1472 (*see* JAMES III).

VIKINGS, IMPACT ON WALES Vikings, mainly from Ireland, attacked WALES from the late 8th to the late 11th centuries with attacks occurring most frequently in the mid 9th and late 10th centuries. They raided coastal monasteries (especially ST DAVIDS, SW Wales), and fertile Anglesey (NW Wales), mainly in search of booty.

The Welsh response varied. RHODRI MAWR of GWYNEDD defeated the Viking Gorm in 856, but was later driven out by Vikings. His descendant Maredudd ab Owain (ruled

986–99) was forced to pay tribute to Vikings in 989 yet employed Scandinavian mercenaries (992).

Some Viking settlement occurred, mainly near coasts (especially in the S and SW – *see* SWANSEA), probably reflecting interest in maritime trade routes to BRISTOL and Chester (SW and NW England). Vikings appear generally to have been uninterested in seizing Welsh kingdoms; none was taken, though Dublin Vikings attempted to conquer ANGLESEY (909).

VILLEINAGE *see* SERFDOM

VIRGINIA The name used by English people from 1584 to the early 17th century for lands along the E coast of N America, in honour of ELIZABETH I (the virgin queen). It was then applied mainly to England's first successful PLANTATION or colony in N America, W of Chesapeake Bay. Its promoters hoped to obtain gold and to profit from Mediterranean-type agriculture (e.g., cultivation of olive trees).

On 13 May 1607, 102 men sent by the VIRGINIA COMPANY (London group) founded Jamestown on the James River. The strict leadership of John Smith (1607–9) enabled it to survive initial harsh conditions and high mortality. Tobacco exporting (from 1612) provided economic strength. New settlements were started. In 1619 an annual legislative assembly was inaugurated (governor, council, with burgesses elected by adult males). After the company's charter was revoked (1624), King CHARLES I imposed a Crown-appointed governor and council (1625), making Virginia England's first CROWN COLONY. The colonial assembly was recognized by the Crown in 1639. A parliamentary commission supervised Virginia 1652–60. The colony adhered to the Church of ENGLAND in religion.

Virginians were prominent in anti-British agitation in the 1760s–70s (*see* AMERICAN INDEPENDENCE, ORIGINS OF). The most populous of the THIRTEEN COLONIES (est. population 1770: 450,000), Virginia became a State of the USA in 1776. *See also* NORTH AMERICAN COLONIES; WASHINGTON, GEORGE.

VIRGINIA COMPANY An English mercantile company authorized by King JAMES VI/I on 10 April 1606 to establish settlements (or PLANTATIONS) in Virginia (E seaboard of N America). It comprised two groups (or companies): the Plymouth group to operate in N Virginia, the London group for S Virginia. They were supervised by a Council of Virginia.

The Plymouth group attempted to found a settlement at Sagadahoc, in modern Maine, USA (Aug. 1607–Sept. 1608). The London group established Jamestown (1607), which grew into VIRGINIA colony.

In 1609 the London group was reorganized as the Virginia Company with a new charter and larger territory (but without a royal supervisory council). A third charter (1612) was revoked in 1624 because of insolvency (Virginia became a CROWN COLONY). The Plymouth group was dissolved in 1619, and revived in 1620 as the Council for NEW ENGLAND. *See also* NORTH AMERICAN COLONIES; BERMUDA.

VISUAL ARTS, BRITAIN Among the earliest artistic products were NEOLITHIC indigenous Grooved Ware (3rd–2nd millennia BC) and Beaker pottery derived from Continental Europe (late 3rd–early 2nd millennia BC). IRON AGE works in Celtic styles (4th century BC–1st century AD) included the Battersea Shield (in British Museum, London). Artistic work during the Roman period (1st–4th centuries) included mosaics and paintings.

In southern Britain activity revived following GERMANIC IMMIGRATION (5th–6th centuries), notably in jewellery and weapons. From the 7th century much artistic work was undertaken under Church patronage. Achievements included illuminated manuscripts and sculpture (e.g., on crosses). In N Britain the PICTS produced vivid carvings on large stones (6th–9th centuries). After the NORMAN CONQUEST (1066–70s), Romanesque and Gothic styles from Continental Europe were influential (e.g., in illumination, metalwork).

In the 16th century the DISSOLUTION OF RELIGIOUS HOUSES and REFORMATION drastically constricted Church patronage, and much art was destroyed by iconoclasts. Portraiture developed as a court art, inspired by the German Hans HOLBEIN the Younger, and Nicholas Hilliard perfected an English school of miniature painting.

During the 17th century, when royal patronage was again a major force, the Flemish painter Anthony VAN DYCK introduced a baroque style of portraiture. In the more affluent 18th century, when patronage widened greatly, a distinctively British school emerged. It encompassed genre painting (e.g., William Hogarth), portraiture (Joshua REYNOLDS, Thomas Gainsborough), caricature (James Gillray, George Cruickshank), visionary art (William Blake) and animal painting (George Stubbs). Landscape painting flourished in the 19th century (J.M.W. Turner, John Constable); the PRE-RAPHAELITE BROTHERHOOD and ARTS AND CRAFTS MOVEMENT (applied arts) were also significant.

During the 20th century artists responded to international styles, although figurative art remained strong (Walter Sickert, Francis Bacon, Lucian Freud). Several sculptors achieved international reputations (Jacob Epstein, Henry Moore). *See also* ARCHITECTURE, BRITAIN.

VISUAL ARTS, IRELAND The earliest art works in any number, from *c.*300 BC onwards, are jewellery, stone carvings and weapons in Celtic styles derived from Continental Europe. Christianity (especially monasteries) gave Celtic art new significance and vitality: outstanding works from the 6th–12th centuries include fine metalwork (e.g., Ardagh Chalice, *c*.700), illuminated manuscripts (e.g., Book of KELLS, *c*.800) and carved stone crosses (e.g., Cross of Muiredach, Monasterboice, Co. Louth). Later works show VIKING, or from the 11th century, Romanesque influences (e.g., in the metal Cross of Cong).

Gothic styles, from England and Continental Europe, considerably influenced sculpture, metalwork and illumination in the 12th–16th centuries. An outstanding example of illumination is a Psalter of 1397 from Christ Church, DUBLIN (at the Bodleian Library, Oxford). Native forms survived in illuminated works produced outside monasteries by members of the LEARNED CLASSES (to 19th century).

The DISSOLUTION of many religious houses and REFORMATION (16th century) reduced artistic activity, and English iconoclasts destroyed Irish art, although production of tomb sculpture continued.

A modest revival began after the RESTORATION (1660), mainly in portraiture and topographical painting. Sculpture was chiefly associated with architecture (e.g., carved chimney-pieces). In the 18th century the number and quality of works increased, mostly from noble patronage, with English styles influential. The portraitist James Latham (1696–1747) was outstanding.

After the UNION OF IRELAND AND GREAT BRITAIN (1801), noble patronage declined. Artists increasingly catered for middle-class tastes. In the early 20th century Ireland's greatest artist Jack B. Yeats (1871–1957) created a highly expressive style. During the rest of the century and beyond Irish artists responded to international styles. *See also* ARCHITECTURE, IRELAND.

VOLUNTEERS In Ireland, a voluntary militia (mainly GENTRY and middle-class Protestants), active 1778–93. Companies were formed spontaneously for peace keeping after regular troops were moved to coastal areas (following France's alliance with the USA, Feb. 1778, during the AMERICAN WAR OF INDEPENDENCE). (The government refused to fund an official militia.)

The Volunteers were also recruited by PATRIOT members of Parliament for political campaigns. Volunteer demonstrations (1779) encouraged the British government to end restrictions on Irish trade, while the campaign for 'legislative independence' was launched at the Volunteers' Dungannon Convention (Feb. 1782; *see* CONSTITUTION OF 1782). In Sept. 1783 Volunteers meeting at Dungannon began a campaign for parliamentary reform. Support declined after the American War. The Volunteers were suppressed in 1793 and replaced by an official militia. *See also* CHARLEMONT, EARL OF; PROTESTANT ASCENDANCY; MILITIAS, IRELAND.

VORTIGERN (fl. *c*.430 in Britain). The name given by BEDE (in 731) to an unnamed British leader who was mentioned (as a 'proud tyrant') by GILDAS (6th century). Perhaps *c*.430 'Vortigern' admitted 'Saxons' to Britain to repel SCOTS (Irish) and PICTS, and guard eastern Britain. But the Saxons apparently rebelled (possibly in 440s). *See* POST-ROMAN BRITAIN; AMBROSIUS AURELIANUS.

W

WADE, GEORGE (b. 1673 at Killavalley, West Meath, Ireland; d. 14 March 1748 at London, England, aged 75). A career soldier in the British ARMY, Wade became commander-in-chief of North Britain (1724–40) and built 240 mi (385 km) of roads and 40 bridges in the HIGHLANDS of Scotland (1726–38), to facilitate the rapid movement of troops in case of rebellion. He was made lieutenant general (1727), general (1739), and became a privy councillor in 1742. In 1743–4 Wade commanded British troops in the War of the AUSTRIAN SUCCESSION in Flanders. As commander-in-chief in England (from 1744) he was confronted with the JACOBITE REBELLION of 1745 but was unable to cope and was replaced by the duke of CUMBERLAND.

WALES Effectively a jurisdiction within the UNITED KINGDOM comprising the western part of southern BRITAIN and offshore islands. Area: 8000 sq mi (20,700 sq km). Est. popn in 2015: 3,099,000. Wales includes mountainous areas and coastal plains. Until the 19th century it was mostly Welsh-speaking. In 2015, around 100 languages were spoken.

Before the 8th century AD, W Britain was culturally part of southern Britain (see PREHISTORIC BRITAIN; ROMAN BRITAIN), including Christianity from the 3rd century (see CONVERSION OF WALES). After Roman rule ended (5th century), kingdoms emerged, notably: GWYNEDD, POWYS, CEREDIGION, DYFED, BRYCHEINIOG, GLYWYSING, GWENT.

The spread of Germanic rule and culture (including language) in southern Britain (5th–7th centuries) isolated W Britain as an area of British culture and language (see GERMANIC IMMIGRATION, SOUTHERN BRITAIN). Inhabitants called themselves, and Britons elsewhere, Cymry, meaning 'Compatriots'; W Britain became Cymru, meaning 'Land of the compatriots', although Britain ('Brytaniaid') was also used (until 12th century). The English name Wales is derived from OE, Wealas, meaning 'Foreigners'.

From the 1060s, areas were seized by Normans and English, and became lordships held from the king of England (see MARCH OF WALES). The remainder was conquered for King EDWARD I in 1277 and 1282–3 (see WALES, ENGLISH CONQUEST). The Church was integrated with the English Church from the 12th century, and removed from papal jurisdiction in 1534 (see REFORMATION, WALES). English legislation in 1536 abolished the March, annexed Wales, and imposed English law and government (see UNION OF WALES WITH ENGLAND). Wales was incorporated in England by statute in 1746.

In the 18th–19th centuries Wales was transformed by industrialization (see INDUSTRY, WALES FROM 18TH CENTURY), IMMIGRATION, the rise of religious NONCONFORMITY, and extensive adoption of English. Heavy industry and nonconformity declined in the 20th century. In 1967 'England' officially ceased to include Wales, and from 1999 Wales expressed a stronger identity through DEVOLUTION. *See also* POST-ROMAN BRITAIN; BORDER, ANGLO-WELSH;

A Dictionary of British and Irish History, First Edition. Edited by Robert Peberdy and Philip Waller.
© 2021 John Wiley & Sons Ltd; © editorial matter and organisation Robert Peberdy and Phillip Waller.
Published 2021 by John Wiley & Sons Ltd.

PRINCE OF WALES; PRINCIPALITY OF WALES; WELSH LANGUAGE AND LITERATURE; PARLIAMENTARY REPRESENTATION, WALES; MONMOUTHSHIRE; CARDIFF.

WALES, CHURCH IN A voluntary Anglican Church and province coterminous with Wales, formed from the four Welsh dioceses of the Church of ENGLAND on 1 April 1920, the day after DISESTABLISHMENT. It operates under a Governing Body of bishops, clergy and laity, with its assets vested in a Representative Body (both created in 1918), according to a Constitution (adopted 1922).

Until the 1950s administration and fund raising preoccupied the Church. It created separate dioceses for populous areas (Monmouth 1921, Swansea and Brecon 1923), and grouped rural parishes to save money. From the 1960s it publicly promoted bilingualism. Once considered a minority 'alien church', by the 1990s it was the largest Christian denomination (despite reduced attendance) and was integrated into Welsh culture. Women were ordained as deacons from 1980, as priests from 1997, and as bishops from 2017. *See also* EDWARDS, ALFRED GEORGE.

WALES, ENGLISH CONQUEST OF Native-ruled WALES was conquered by two English campaigns, in 1277 and 1282–3. On 12 Nov. 1276 King EDWARD I of England declared LLYWELYN AP GRUFFUDD of GWYNEDD (NW Wales) a rebel for his failure to do homage and other offences. In 1277 Edward's forces seized land in SW and W Wales, C Wales, and N Wales. Llywelyn agreed terms in the treaty of ABERCONWY. Edward retained lands in W and SW Wales and in C and NE Wales (*see* COURTS, WALES).

The conquest of native Wales was completed by Edward's second campaign (1282–3). He invaded again in response to the Welsh rebellion of late March 1282 (when the Welsh attacked towns and castles in the MARCH OF WALES and England). Edward determined to end the 'Welsh problem' (periodic resistance of Welsh rulers to English overlordship).

As in 1277, forces entered N, C and S Wales (summer 1282), while ANGLESEY was captured from the sea (Aug.). Edward's aim was to isolate the main resistance in Gwynedd. Llywelyn's death on 11 Dec. 1282 demoralized the Welsh, although resistance continued until July 1283 under his brother DAFYDD AP GRUFFUDD. Edward then disinherited Gwynedd's royal dynasty for rebellion, a feudal offence. He similarly dispossessed most of the dynasties of POWYS (C Wales) and DEHEUBARTH (SW Wales), leaving a few minor rulers who had remained loyal.

The conquest was consolidated militarily by castle building (*see* JAMES OF ST GEORGES), and administratively by the establishment of English administration (*see* LOCAL GOVERNMENTAL STRUCTURES, WALES). It ended Welsh independence, leaving most of Wales directly under the English

Crown or under lordships held from the Crown in the March. *See also* UNION OF WALES WITH ENGLAND.

WALLACE, ALFRED RUSSELL *see* EVOLUTION

WALLACE, WILLIAM (b. *c*.1270, probably in W Scotland; d. 23 Aug. 1305 at London, England, aged about 35). Wallace led resistance to the English after King EDWARD I invaded Scotland (March 1296) and deposed King John BALLIOL (July). On 11 Sept. 1297 Wallace defeated the English at STIRLING BRIDGE (C Scotland) and was made guardian. He lost to Edward in 1298 (at battle of FALKIRK, 22 July). Wallace resigned and disappeared. Captured on 3 Aug. 1305, he was executed for treason. From 1306 the anti-English cause was led by ROBERT I. *See also* MURRAY FAMILY.

WALLER, WILLIAM (b. *c*.1597 at Knole, Kent, England; d. 19 Sept. 1668 at Osterley House, Middlesex, England, aged about 71). Knighted in 1622, and an MP from 1642, Waller commanded Parliamentary forces in the CIVIL WARS, successfully in S and W England in 1642–3 (nicknamed 'William the Conqueror'), less successfully in 1643–4. He was defeated at Roundway Down (Wiltshire) on 13 July 1643, and by King CHARLES I at Cropredy Bridge (Oxfordshire) on 29 June 1644.

Waller lost his command under the SELF-DENYING ORDINANCE (1645). Sympathetic to Presbyterians, he spent 1647–8 in exile, fearful of threats from Independents. He was excluded from Parliament by PRIDE'S PURGE (Dec. 1648). Between 1648 and 1658 Waller was frequently in prison, suspected of sympathy for Royalists. In 1660 he supported the return of CHARLES II (*see* RESTORATION, ENGLAND AND WALES).

WALPOLE, ROBERT (b. 26 Aug. 1676 at Houghton, Norfolk, England; d. 18 March 1745 at London, England, aged 68). A WHIG MP from 1700, Walpole was secretary at war (1708–10) and treasurer of the NAVY (1710–11) under Queen ANNE. The TORIES expelled him briefly from Parliament (1712) for alleged corruption as war secretary.

After the accession of the pro-Whig King GEORGE I (1714), Walpole became paymaster-general of the armed forces. First lord of the Treasury from 1715, he resigned after Viscount TOWNSHEND was dismissed (1717).

Like Townshend, Walpole returned to office in 1720 (paymaster-general). In April 1721 he was reappointed first lord, effectively chief minister (*see* SOUTH SEA BUBBLE). He exploited the Atterbury Plot (1722) to defame Tories as Jacobites. Walpole was knighted in 1725 and retained by GEORGE II (1727). He used royal PATRONAGE (e.g., appointments, pensions) to increase support in the House of Commons, and developed CABINET government. He is regarded as Great Britain's first PRIME MINISTER.

Townshend resigned in 1730 and parliamentary opposition increased. In 1733 Walpole had to withdraw an excise extension (*see* EXCISE CRISIS; COBHAM'S CUBS). After maintaining peace (and low taxes), Walpole was pushed into war (1739; *see* JENKINS' EAR, WAR OF). He resigned (Feb. 1742) after losing a vote and was created earl of Orford. *See also* ORFORD, EARL OF; ISLAY, EARL OF; PORTEOUS AFFAIR; JACOBITISM, IMPACT ON BRITISH POLITICS; CARTERET, LORD.

WALSH, PETER (b. *c.*1618 at Mooretown, Co. Kildare, Ireland; d. 15 March 1688 at London, England, aged about 69). A Franciscan friar and pro-Royalist intellectual, Walsh opposed (1645–9) Archbishop RINUCCINI's intransigence during the IRISH WARS. He was excommunicated by Rinuccini (1 Sept. 1646) for supporting the First ORMOND TREATY. He fled abroad after the Cromwellian Conquest (1652).

Walsh returned to Ireland in 1662, following the RESTORATION (1660), and sought support from Catholic clergy for the LOYAL REMONSTRANCE. But at a meeting organized by Walsh (11–25 June 1666), clergy added implicit recognition of papal powers, making it unacceptable to the duke of ORMOND (chief governor). From 1669 Walsh lived in London under Ormond's patronage. *See also* CATHOLICS AND CATHOLIC CHURCH, IRELAND FROM 16TH CENTURY.

WALSH, WILLIAM (b. 30 Jan. 1841 at Dublin, Ireland; d. 9 April 1921 at Dublin, aged 80). Walsh served as (Catholic) archbishop of DUBLIN 1885–1921. As an Irish nationalist, he controversially supported the HOME RULE MOVEMENT (from 1870s) and the PLAN OF CAMPAIGN (1886–91), though he opposed C.S. PARNELL after the divorce case (Dec. 1890). Following the EASTER RISING of 1916, Walsh signalled support for SINN FÉIN (1917). He opposed the PARTITION OF IRELAND.

WALSINGHAM, FRANCIS (b. *c.*1532 at London, England, or Foot's Cray, Kent, England; d. 6 April 1590 at London, aged about 58). A lawyer and ardent Protestant, Walsingham served Queen ELIZABETH I by 1568. He was ambassador to France 1570–3, and a SECRETARY OF STATE and privy councillor from 1573 (knighted 1577). As ambassador he worked for a defensive alliance with France (concluded in treaty of Blois, 1572). As secretary he was concerned mainly with foreign affairs, advocating war to support Protestants in France and the Netherlands. He employed spies throughout England and Europe, partly to protect Elizabeth from life-threatening plots. He helped to discover the RIDOLFI PLOT (1571) and the THROCKMORTON PLOT (1583–4), and obtained evidence that enabled the chief Catholic claimant to Elizabeth's throne, MARY, QUEEN OF SCOTS, to be executed (1587).

WALTER, HUBERT (b. *c.*1140–5, probably at West Dereham, Norfolk, England; d. 13 July 1205 at Teynham, Kent, England, aged in 60s). A royal officer (from 1180s), Walter was appointed bishop of Salisbury by King RICHARD I (1189). Away on CRUSADE 1190–3, he commanded English forces at Acre Nov. 1190 to June 1191. After Richard was captured in Austria (Dec. 1192), Walter negotiated (March 1193) terms for his release.

Returning to England (April 1193), Walter was elected archbishop of CANTERBURY (May). He suppressed a revolt by JOHN (1193–4) and collected the ransom for Richard's release. He effectively ruled England (as CHIEF JUSTICIAR) Dec. 1193 to 1198 (resignation), during Richard's absence. After John's accession, Walter was appointed CHANCELLOR (May 1199). He probably began the systematic copying of royal charters (*see* CHANCERY ROLLS).

WALTHEOF (b. *c.*1050 in England; d. 31 May 1076 near Winchester, Hampshire, England, aged about 25). Created an earl in 1065 or 1066, Waltheof submitted to King WILLIAM I (1066). He rebelled in 1069–70 but was pardoned and married to the king's niece Judith; in 1072 he was made earl of Northumbria (a position once held by his father Siward). But after admitting complicity in another rebellion (1075), he was tried and beheaded. *See also* REVOLT OF THE EARLS.

WARBECK, PERKIN (b. *c.*1474 at Tournai, Flanders; d. 23 Nov. 1499 at London, England, aged about 25). From 1491 Warbeck claimed the throne of King HENRY VII of England by impersonating Richard, duke of York (younger son of EDWARD IV), who had disappeared in 1483.

In June 1495, supported by Emperor Maximilian I and Margaret, dowager duchess of Burgundy (Edward IV's sister), he sailed from Flanders. After failing to land in Kent (SE England) and at Waterford (SE Ireland), he was welcomed in Scotland by JAMES IV (20 Nov.). In Sept. 1496 he and James raided Northumberland. On 7 Sept. 1497 he landed in Cornwall (SW England), but in Somerset he abandoned his supporters (21 Sept.), fled into sanctuary and surrendered to Henry. Warbeck was executed for alleged involvement in another conspiracy to overthrow Henry. *See also* WARBECK, PERKIN, AND IRELAND; EDWARD V.

WARBECK, PERKIN, AND IRELAND Warbeck visited Ireland three times, seeking support from Yorkist sympathizers: (a) from Nov. 1491 to spring 1492, when he adopted the persona of Richard, duke of York, and was widely supported in Munster (S Ireland); (b) in July 1495, moving between England (after a failed landing) and Scotland; (c) in 1497 (26th July–Sept.), between Scotland and England, when he received meagre support. Ireland's initial support for Warbeck provoked vigorous English intervention (*see*

HENRY VII AND IRELAND). *See also* YORKIST–LANCASTRIAN CONFLICT, ROLE OF IRELAND; KILDARE, 8TH EARL OF.

WAR CABINET A small group of government ministers formed in wartime to facilitate efficient handling of war-related business. In Dec. 1916, during WORLD WAR I, Great Britain's new prime minister, David LLOYD GEORGE, formed a War Cabinet of five members, in place of the normal larger CABINET, to prosecute the war with increased vigour. Served by a new secretariat, it met almost daily. It continued after the war's end (Nov. 1918), though in 1919 met rarely because of peace negotiations (*see* PARIS PEACE CONFERENCE). The normal Cabinet was reinstated in Nov. 1919.

After Britain's entry to WORLD WAR II (3 Sept. 1939) the prime minister, Neville CHAMBERLAIN, replaced the Cabinet with a War Cabinet of nine members, four holding war-related offices. When Winston CHURCHILL succeeded Chamberlain (May. 1940), membership was reduced to five, though numerous changes were made subsequently. When Churchill's wartime coalition government ended (23 May 1945) the War Cabinet was dissolved and a normal Cabinet reinstated.

War Cabinets were formed during the FALKLANDS WAR (1982, seven members) and during the PERSIAN GULF WAR (1990–1, five members). Both operated alongside the normal Cabinet. *See also* WORLD WAR I, IMPACT ON BRITISH EMPIRE AND COMMONWEALTH.

WARD, MRS HUMPHRY (b. 11 June 1851 at Hobart Town, Van Diemen's Land; d. 24 March 1920 at London, England, aged 68). A granddaughter of Thomas ARNOLD, Mary Arnold married an OXFORD don in 1872. A writer from 1881, known by her married name, she achieved fame with her novel *Robert Elsmere* (1888), which argued that 'religion consists alone in the service of the people'. She promoted the UNIVERSITY SETTLEMENT MOVEMENT (1890s) and from 1908 headed the Women's Anti-Suffrage Association, which campaigned against female suffrage (for Parliament), though she advocated greater involvement by women in local government and provision of better childcare facilities.

WARDS AND LIVERIES, COURT OF, ENGLAND AND WALES An administrative court created in 1540 (in the reign of King HENRY VIII), as the Court of Wards, to regulate and exploit the Crown's feudal right of wardship (control over the person and estate of an under-age heir to a tenant-in-chief of the Crown). The court took over the work from a master of wards, and in 1542 added that of the master of liveries (legal delivery of real property).

Creation of the court was a response to the increase in tenants-in-chief that arose from the sale of estates confiscated in

the DISSOLUTION OF RELIGIOUS HOUSES. It survived a major administrative reorganization in 1554. The court's mastership was highly lucrative through sale of Crown rights (e.g., marriage of heirs, administration of estates). Holders included William and Robert CECIL. The court's abolition was proposed in 1610 (*see* GREAT CONTRACT).

In the 1630s wardship was exploited to sustain the Crown's financial independence (*see* CHARLES I, PERSONAL RULE). Francis COTTINGTON raised annual income from £54,000 to £84,000 (1635–40). Parliament abolished the court in 1646; this was confirmed by the CONVENTION PARLIAMENT (1660). *See also* FEUDAL INCIDENTS; EQUITY COURTS.

WARDS AND LIVERIES, COURT OF, IRELAND A court established in 1622 (replacing commissioners), based on the English Court, which oversaw the guardianship of minors who had inherited estates. It frequently compelled guardians to raise RECUSANT minors as Protestants, and increasingly required wards to take the oath of supremacy (acknowledging royal authority over the Church of IRELAND). It was discontinued in 1645 and abolished in 1662. *See also* COURTS, IRELAND; EQUITY COURTS.

WARHAM, WILLIAM (b. *c.*1450 at Church Oakley, Hampshire, England; d. 22 Aug. 1532 at Hackington, Kent, England, aged about 82). A clergyman and diplomat who served King HENRY VII from 1493, Warham was appointed bishop of London (1501), archbishop of CANTERBURY (1503) and CHANCELLOR (1504).

Under HENRY VIII (king from 1509) Warham's political role declined with the rise of Thomas WOLSEY (1512–14). Warham resigned as chancellor in 1515. From 1527 Warham supported Henry's attempt to obtain a divorce from KATHERINE OF ARAGON, and in 1531 he accepted the declaration of Henry as head of the English Church (with qualification). But in early 1532, now troubled, he protested publicly against violation of the papacy's rights, though shortly before his death he accepted the 'Submission of the Clergy' (*see* SUPPLICATION AGAINST THE ORDINARIES). *See also* REFORMATION, ENGLAND.

WAR OF 1812 Conflict in N America, 1812–15, during the Napoleonic Wars in Europe, caused by US resentment of British activities. On 1 June 1812, under pressure from nationalistic members of Congress nicknamed 'War Hawks', US President James Madison specified British offences in a 'war message' to Congress: restrictions on trade; harassment of shipping off the US coast; impressment of sailors seized from US ships; incitement of Indians against US citizens in border areas. On 18 June, Congress declared war on Great Britain. The USA mounted two invasions of CANADA. The first (1812) was repulsed. During the second (1813), Canada's capital, York (now Toronto), was captured and public buildings burned, including the Parliament building (27–30 April). Ships of the US Navy and privateers inflicted damage on British ships.

In 1814 Britain dispatched 20,000 troops to Canada and developed an effective naval blockade. It invaded MAINE, and sent an expedition through Chesapeake Bay which captured the US capital, Washington (24 Aug.), burning the White House (presidential residence) and other buildings. After attacking Baltimore, the force withdrew. Another offensive action from Canada was defeated.

Agitation against the war within the USA, and the apparent conclusion of war in Europe (ending the need for trade restrictions) enabled peace to be agreed at Ghent (in modern Belgium) on 24 Dec. 1814, though a US force defeated the British at the battle of New Orleans (8 Jan. 1815) before the news reached America. The British invasions were the only significant attacks on the US mainland between the American War of Independence (1775–81) and '9/11' (2001; see IRAQ WAR, BRITISH INVOLVEMENT).

WAR POETS Popular term for English authors who created a powerful poetical response to WORLD WAR I (1914–18), extensively based on military service, which influenced popular memory and understanding. The main war poets were: Edmund Blunden (1896–1974), Rupert Brooke (1887–1915), Robert Graves (1895–1985), Ivor Gurney (1890–1937), Wilfred Owen (1893–1918), Isaac Rosenberg (1890–1918), Siegfried Sassoon (1886–1967) and Edward Thomas (1878–1917). A memorial in Poets' Corner of Westminster Abbey, London (unveiled 1985), commemorates 16 poets.

WARRISTON, LORD see JOHNSTON, ARCHIBALD

WARWICK, RICHARD EARL OF (b. 22 Nov. 1428 in England; d. 14 April 1471 at Barnet, Hertfordshire, England, aged 42). Richard Neville claimed the Warwick earldom by marriage (1449). Amid rivalries destabilizing King HENRY VI's government, Warwick opposed Richard, duke of YORK, then supported him (1453) against the duke of SOMERSET. They defeated Somerset at St Albans (22 May 1455). Warwick became captain of CALAIS (1456), acquiring a military powerbase.

In 1459, demanding removal of royal counsellors, York and Warwick confronted royalists (Lancastrians) at Ludlow Bridge (Shropshire), but supporters deserted (12 Oct.). Warwick fled to Calais. He returned (June 1460) to support York, who was recognized as Henry's heir (Oct.), but York was killed (Dec.) and Warwick fled defeat at St Albans (17 Feb. 1461).

Warwick supported York's successor Edward (see EDWARD IV) from his deposition of Henry (4 March 1461)

to decisive victory at Towton, Yorkshire (29 March). Relations soured over Edward's marriage and foreign policy. Warwick fled to France (1 May 1470), joining Henry's queen MARGARET OF ANJOU (22 July). He returned (13 Sept.) and Edward fled (2 Oct.). Henry was restored with Warwick as 'lieutenant' (6 Oct.). But Edward returned, defeating Lancastrians at Barnet where Warwick was killed. He was called 'the kingmaker' from the 16th century. *See also* YORKIST–LANCASTRIAN CONFLICT; NEVILLE FAMILY.

WASHINGTON, GEORGE (b. 11 Feb. 1732 in Westmoreland County, Virginia, N America; d. 14 Dec. 1799 at Mt Vernon, Virginia, USA, aged 67). Military and political leader. Washington worked as a surveyor from 1749, and from 1754 occupied a family estate at Mt Vernon. He undertook military service on the Virginian frontier against French and Indians (1753–63), and was a member of Virginia's House of Burgesses (1758–74). In the 1760s–70s he strongly opposed Great Britain's colonial policies (*see* AMERICAN INDEPENDENCE, ORIGINS OF).

When the AMERICAN WAR OF INDEPENDENCE broke out in 1775, Washington was appointed commander-in-chief of the Continental Army. (THIRTEEN COLONIES declared independence and formed the USA in 1776.) He defeated the British (1781), and when their forces had been withdrawn resigned his commission (1783). Washington shared the belief that the USA required a stronger central authority (*see* AMERICAN INDEPENDENCE). He presided in 1787 over the Constitutional Convention that prepared a new constitution, and was elected first president (1789). He retired after a second term (1793–7).

WATER CLOSETS A water-flushing closet (i.e., toilet) was invented in England in the 1590s by the courtier Sir John Harington, but few were made. Interest revived in the 18th century when London watchmaker John Cumming patented a closet (1775). The first successful closet was designed by John Bramah in the 1780s, but adopted slowly because the required water supplies and SEWERAGE systems were rare until the mid 19th century.

After Thomas Crapper made improvements (1860s–80s), closets proliferated, initially in S England and seaside towns. They became a standard fitting in British and Irish town houses from the later 19th century. Closets were important in reducing deaths from CHOLERA and other infectious diseases.

WATERFORD A city in the Republic of Ireland, by the R. Suir; centre of Co. Waterford; from Norse, Vadrefjord, meaning 'Ram inlet' (Irish, Port Láirge, meaning 'Láirge's port').

Waterford was started as a trading centre in 914 by VIKINGS, who were attracted by a fine harbour near the confluence of the Rivers Suir and Barrow. A town developed which was captured in 1170 by Anglo-Normans (*see* STRONGBOW). Situated in MUNSTER (S Ireland), Waterford was probably Ireland's second largest city until the 17th century (overtaken by CORK). It traded with Wales, England, France and Flanders. Wool, hides and grain were major exports; French wine a major import. Waterford suffered some decline in the 14th–15th centuries because of competition from nearby New Ross.

Waterford grew from the 17th century. Cloth exports were important in the late 17th century. In the 18th century, streets were added, lined with elegant houses. Glass manufacturing was notable from the 1780s to 1840s. Waterford stagnated during the 19th century and only grew markedly again from the 1960s. Glass manufacturing was revived in 1947; industrial development in the later 20th century included pharmaceutical and electronics factories. *See also* TOWNS, IRELAND.

Est. popn: 1300, 2000; 1600, 2500; 1800, 20,000; 1900, 25,000; 2000, 44,000.

WATERLOO, BATTLE OF Fought on 18 June 1815 near Brussels (modern Belgium) in the Kingdom of the Netherlands. A French army commanded by Emperor Napoleon I was crushed by British and Dutch forces (commanded by the duke of WELLINGTON) and a Prussian army. The defeat ended Napoleon's second brief period of rule (from March 1815) and the NAPOLEONIC WARS.

WATER SUPPLIES *see* PUBLIC HEALTH ACTS

WATSON-WATT, ROBERT (b. 13 April 1892 at Brechin, Forfarshire, Scotland; d. 5 Dec. 1973 at Inverness, Invernessshire, Scotland, aged 81). After studying and teaching at Scottish universities, Watson Watt joined the British government's Meteorological Office (1915), where he researched into devices for locating thunderstorms (for air navigation). In 1927 he became head of a Radio Research Station.

In 1935 Watson Watt proposed the use of pulsed radio waves to detect aircraft. Feasibility was quickly demonstrated, and because another war with Germany was feared, he and a team were commissioned to develop the concept. A system was demonstrated in June 1937, and a detection network, 'Chain Home', was inaugurated in Sept. 1938, which contributed to success in the Battle of BRITAIN (1940). The detection system was named 'radar' (from 'radio detection and ranging') in 1939 in the USA. Watson Watt was elected a fellow of the ROYAL SOCIETY (1941) and knighted (1942, also hyphenating his surname). *See also* DOWDING, HUGH.

WATT, JAMES (b. 19 Jan. 1736 at Greenock, Renfrewshire, Scotland; d. 25 Aug. 1819 at Handsworth, Warwickshire,

England, aged 83). A maker of scientific instruments, Watt experimented with steam engines in GLASGOW from the early 1760s. In 1765 he improved the design of James NEWCOMEN by adding a separate steam condenser, air pump and double-acting pistons (patented 1769). In 1773 Matthew BOULTON acquired a share in Watt's patent, and from 1775 they manufactured engines near BIRMINGHAM (England).

In the 1780s Watt made further developments, including a mechanism to produce rotary motion. This enabled steam engines to power a wide range of machinery. Watt made a fundamental contribution to the INDUSTRIAL REVOLUTION. He also worked as a surveyor for canal and harbour companies. *See also* LUNAR SOCIETY OF BIRMINGHAM; ENGINEERING, GREAT BRITAIN.

WEBB, SIDNEY AND BEATRICE British SOCIALISTS who influenced the LABOUR PARTY. Sidney Webb (1859–1947) was a civil servant 1878–91. In 1892 he married the wealthy Beatrice Potter (1858–1943). Both members of the FABIAN SOCIETY, they studied trade unionism and local government, devised schemes for welfare reform, and with George Bernard SHAW founded the London School of Economics and Political Science (1895) to promote research. Sidney, an MP 1922–9, was created Lord Passfield in 1929. He served in the two inter-war Labour governments: as president of the Board of Trade (1924) and colonial secretary (1929–31).

WEDGWOOD, JOSIAH (b. 12 July 1739 at Burslem, Staffordshire, England; d. 3 Jan. 1795 at Etruria, Staffordshire, aged 55). Apprenticed to a potter in 1744, and in business from 1752, Wedgwood (a UNITARIAN) developed innovative designs, modelling and colours for pottery. From 1759, based at Burslem, he introduced new manufacturing processes and glazes, and division of labour. From 1769 Wedgwood's business operated from the new 'Etruria' works. He introduced distinctive neo-classical designs from the 1760s, and from the 1770s his high-quality earthenware, 'Queen's Ware', dominated the European market. He was also involved in CANALS and TURNPIKE TRUSTS AND ROADS. *See also* LUNAR SOCIETY OF BIRMINGHAM; CONSUMER REVOLUTION.

WEINSTOCK, ARNOLD (b. 29 July 1924 at Stoke Newington, London, England; d. 23 July 2002 at Westminster, London, aged 77). A statistician, Weinstock in 1954 joined his father-in-law's radio and television manufacturing company. In 1961 it merged with the General Electric Company (GEC), the combined business retaining the latter's name. As managing director from 1963, Weinstock led takeovers of rivals – Associated Electrical Industries (1967), English Electric (1968) – creating a world-scale manufacturer of electrical equipment and the kind of large, rationalized business which Great Britain's Labour government advocated. GEC flourished in the 1970s, but was later criticized for accumulating substantial reserves and avoiding innovation. Weinstock was knighted (1970) and created Lord Weinstock (1980), retiring in 1996.

WELFARE STATE Comprehensive social security provided by the State, as implemented in Great Britain and Northern Ireland in the 1940s. The term originated in 19th-century Germany, acquiring its social meaning in the late 1940s.

The UK Welfare State extended the limited State-organized SOCIAL SERVICES introduced in Britain and Ireland by the Liberal governments of 1906–14, such as PENSIONS (1909) and NATIONAL INSURANCE (1911). After WORLD WAR I (1914–18) the State also funded house-building.

A desire during WORLD WAR II (1939–45) for better social conditions than in the 1920s–30s was focused by the 'Beveridge Report' (1942), which recommended wide-ranging welfare provision without means-testing. The wartime coalition government sponsored the BUTLER EDUCATION ACT (1944, for England and Wales), Family Allowances Act and Disabled Persons Employment Act (both 1945, for Britain). The subsequent Labour government added (for Britain): National Insurance Act (1946), providing extensive benefits (e.g., for unemployment, sickness, retirement, death), NATIONAL HEALTH SERVICE (1946–7), and National Assistance Act (1948), supporting people outside national insurance (e.g., disabled). The system was replicated by the (Unionist) government of NORTHERN IRELAND (1946–9). Despite criticisms, comprehensive welfare provision continued with numerous modifications into the 21st century. *See also* BEVERIDGE, WILLIAM; SOCIAL SERVICES AND WELFARE, SOUTHERN IRELAND.

WELLESLEY, RICHARD (b. 20 June 1760 at Dangan Castle, Co. Meath, Ireland; d. 26 Sept. 1842 at London, England, aged 82). Wellesley succeeded as 2nd earl of Mornington (Irish peerage) in 1781, and became an MP in the British Parliament in 1784. As governor-general of INDIA 1795–1805 he decisively expanded British-controlled territory by defeating some rulers (e.g., Tipu Sultan, of Mysore, 1799), subordinating others, and annexing lands. He made the British the leading power in India. He was created Marquess Wellesley in 1799.

In 1809 Wellesley was sent as a diplomat to Spain to secure support for the Peninsular War (against Napoleonic France). He served as foreign secretary under Spencer PERCEVAL (1809–12), then avoided office until 1821 when he became lord lieutenant of Ireland. Wellesley sought to reconcile Protestants and Catholics, but resigned (1828)

when the prime minister, his younger brother the duke of WELLINGTON, opposed CATHOLIC EMANCIPATION. He served a brief second term in Ireland (1833–4).

WELLINGTON, DUKE OF (b. 29 April 1769 at Dublin, Ireland; d. 14 Sept. 1852 at Walmer, Kent, England, aged 83). Arthur Wellesley joined the British ARMY in 1787. Service in Flanders (1794–5) and India (1796–1805) provided extensive experience. He was also an MP (1806–9) and chief secretary for Ireland (1807–9) under the duke of PORTLAND. He participated in the Copenhagen expedition (1807).

In 1808 Wellesley was sent to the Iberian Peninsula where he fought the French (1809–14). His achievements were crowned by victory over Napoleon at WATERLOO (1815). He was created Viscount Wellington (1809), marquess (1812) and duke (1814).

Wellington re-entered British politics in 1818, joining the TORY Cabinet of Lord LIVERPOOL. His opposition to George CANNING's appointment as prime minister in 1827 contributed to Tory divisions. Wellington became prime minister in 1828 but was unable to reconcile Tory factions, offending both ULTRA TORIES and CANNINGITES. After the Catholic victory in the COUNTY CLARE BY-ELECTION (July 1828), Wellington implemented CATHOLIC EMANCIPATION to avoid unrest in Ireland (1829). He opposed PARLIAMENTARY REFORM, which resulted in his government's defeat and resignation (Nov. 1830).

Wellington served as foreign secretary (1834–5) and minister without office (1841–6) under Sir Robert PEEL. *See also* FRENCH REVOLUTIONARY AND NAPOLEONIC WARS, BRITISH INVOLVEMENT.

WELSH *see* WALES

WELSH ASSEMBLY *see* PARLIAMENT, WALES

WELSH LANGUAGE ACTS Legislation removing legal discrimination against Welsh and promoting use of the language. Discrimination stemmed from the UNION OF WALES WITH ENGLAND (1536–43) which made English the language of legal proceedings in Wales. Monoglot Welsh-speakers had to pay for translators.

The Welsh Courts Act of 1942, passed by the UK Parliament, removed the payment. The Welsh Language Act of 1967 gave Welsh equal validity with English in official documents. The Welsh Language Act of 1993 established the Welsh Language Board to oversee schemes for enhancing the status of Welsh (abolished 2011).

Further legislation was passed by the Welsh Assembly. The Welsh Language (Wales) Measure of 2011 gave official status to Welsh and created the post of Welsh language commissioner. From 2015 exhaustive legal regulations were imposed on public bodies, including the requirement for extensive provision of bilingual services. *See also* DEVO-LUTION, WALES.

WELSH LANGUAGE AND LITERATURE Welsh belongs to the Brittonic division of Celtic languages. Five periods are distinguished: Primitive Welsh (*c*.600– *c*.800); Old Welsh (*c*.800– *c*.1100); Middle Welsh (*c*.1100– *c*.1400); early Modern (*c*.1400– *c*.1600); late Modern (from *c*.1600). Welsh was the first language of Welsh people until the 18th century, when GENTRY adopted English. In the 19th century English IMMIGRATION reduced the Welsh-speaking population. By 1891, only 54.4% spoke Welsh; by 1990, under 20% (most in the NW and W), and 19% in 2011.

Little Primitive and Old Welsh literature survives, though later, updated texts preserve works by 'early poets' (Welsh *cynfeirdd*): *see* ANEIRIN, TALIESIN. The substantial legacy of early Middle Welsh (*c*.1100– *c*.1250) includes works by poets such as CYNDDELW BRYDYDD MAWR, HYWEL AB OWAIN GWYNEDD and MEILIR BRYDYDD (*see also* MABINOGI, Y; LAW, WELSH). During the later Middle Welsh period (*c*.1250– *c*.1400) important manuscripts were copied (*see* BLACK BOOK OF CARMARTHEN; RED BOOK OF HERGEST; WHITE BOOK OF RHYDDERCH; HENDREGADREDD MANUSCRIPT).

As Modern Welsh evolved in the 14th century, poets such as DAFYDD AP GWILYM and IOLO GOCH developed the *cywydd* metre. The bardic tradition flowered in the 15th century, under gentry patronage, with such poets as Guto'r Glyn (*c*.1435– *c*.1493), GUTUN OWAIN, and Lewys Glyn Cothi (*c*.1420–89). Bardic culture was party transmitted orally, through apprenticeship and poets' gatherings (*eisteddfodau*), but grammars, aimed at poets, survive from the early 14th century.

Late Modern Welsh emerged in the 16th century (*see* BIBLE, WELSH; MORGAN, WILLIAM), but by the late 17th century the bardic tradition had declined, though poetry was stimulated from 1789 by revival of the EISTEDDFOD. The modern novel was initiated by Daniel Owen (1836–95) and developed by T. Rowland Hughes (1903–49). The pre-eminent 20th-century writer was Saunders LEWIS. *See also* LITERARY REVIVAL, WALES; WELSH LANGUAGE ACTS.

WELSH LANGUAGE SOCIETY (Welsh *Cymdeithas yr Iaith Gymraeg*). A campaigning society constituted in 1963, following a radio lecture by Saunders LEWIS (1962), which sought official status for the Welsh language. It can claim partial responsibility for bilingual road signs and official forms, the Welsh-language television channel, the Welsh Language Board, inclusion of Welsh as a core subject in the Welsh National Curriculum, and the official status granted to Welsh. *See also* WELSH LANGUAGE ACTS.

WELSH LEAGUE OF YOUTH (Welsh *Urdd Gobaith Cymru*, meaning 'The League of the Hope of Wales'). A movement in Wales founded in 1922 by Ifan ab Owen Edwards (1895–1970; son of Owen Morgan EDWARDS) to promote Welsh culture among children. In 2017 it had several hundred branches and three residential centres (including one in Hungary). Its annual EISTEDDFOD was one of Europe's largest youth festivals, involving over 15,000 children.

WELSH-MEDIUM SCHOOLS Schools teaching in Welsh. During the 19th century schools in Wales taught in English and discouraged Welsh, sometimes with harsh punishments. Attitudes changed from 1889, when State schools began to offer Welsh lessons. By the 1930s most primary schools in solidly Welsh-speaking districts taught at least partly through Welsh but those in linguistically mixed or largely Anglicized districts continued in English. A private Welsh-medium school was established at Aberystwyth (Cardiganshire) in 1939, assisted by the WELSH LEAGUE OF YOUTH.

The first State primary school designated 'Welsh-medium' (1947) was at Llanelli (Carmarthenshire). Thereafter provision expanded greatly, especially at CARDIFF, where a school founded in 1949 engendered eight others by the 1990s. Flintshire acquired the first Welsh-medium secondary school in 1955; by the 1990s over 45 secondary schools taught some subjects in Welsh. In 1988 the UK Parliament made Welsh a core subject in the National Curriculum in Wales. In 2015 there were 435 Welsh-medium primary schools and 50 secondary schools (respectively 33% and 24% of all schools). *See also* EDUCATION, WALES.

WELSH NATIONAL SOCIETIES Cultural associations founded from the mid 18th century, partly replacing previous patronage by GENTRY. The first ambitious society, the Cymmrodorion ('Aborigines'), was founded in London in 1751 and encouraged the LITERARY REVIVAL. Defunct in 1787, it was revived 1820–43 and from 1878, when it sponsored the National EISTEDDFOD Society (founded 1880) and promoted educational ventures such as COUNTY SCHOOLS and the University of Wales (*see* UNIVERSITIES, WALES). The Gwyneddigion ('Scholars of Gwynedd'), also in London (1770–*c*.1837), included Edward WILLIAMS among its members, published manuscripts and periodicals, and sponsored Eisteddfods from 1789. The more radical Cymreigyddion ('Welsh Scholars') Society was active in London 1794–1855. Its offshoot Cymreigyddion y Fenni (Cymreigyddion of Abergavenny, Monmouthshire) was active 1833–54 and held regional eisteddfods.

WELSH OFFICE A department of the British government, under a secretary of state with CABINET rank, which was created (in London) in 1964. Its foundation was a development from the practice of designating a senior minister as 'minister for Welsh affairs' (home secretary 1951–7, minister of housing and local government 1957–64).

The Welsh Office initially administered housing and local government. Primary and secondary education were added in 1970; industry and employment in 1974; and most higher education and agriculture in 1977, making the administration of Wales autonomous. By 1992 it also supervised 55 QUANGOS. From 1971 the Welsh Office worked mainly from CARDIFF, S Wales.

In 1999, when DEVOLUTION was implemented, most powers were transferred to a Welsh Assembly. The Welsh Office was replaced by a department for the secretary of state for Wales (in the UK government), known informally as the Wales Office. *See also* GRIFFITHS, JAMES.

WELSH REVOLT *see* BALFOUR EDUCATION ACT AND WALES

WELSHRY The parts (often upland) of a lordship in the MARCH OF WALES (late 11th–16th centuries) inhabited by Welsh. They held land under native tenures (*see* TENURES, WALES), paid native dues (e.g., cattle) and maintained some native laws (*see* LAW, WELSH). Lords recognized Welshries as distinct areas in the 13th century. *See also* ENGLISHRY.

WELSH TRUST A scheme founded in 1672 by Thomas Gouge (1605–81), an ejected English clergyman (*see* CLARENDON CODE), after visiting Wales (1671–2). Funded by London Welshmen and Welsh GENTRY, supported by Anglicans and DISSENTERS, and organized by the ejected Welsh clergyman Stephen Hughes (1622–88), the Trust distributed Welsh religious literature and sponsored schools (possibly 300). The schools' use of English limited their influence while the authorities considered them subversive. The Trust was closed after Gouge's death. *See also* EDUCATION, WALES.

WENTWORTH, THOMAS (b. 13 April 1593 at London, England; d. 12 May 1641 at London, aged 48). An MP from 1614, Wentworth opposed the aggressive foreign policy of the duke of BUCKINGHAM (mid 1620s) and the 1626 FORCED LOAN (imprisoned June–Dec. 1627). In 1628 he supported the PETITION OF RIGHT. But soon afterwards, when King CHARLES I reconciled some opponents, he was created Lord Wentworth. In Dec. he was promoted to Viscount Wentworth and appointed president of the COUNCIL OF THE NORTH. A privy councillor from Nov. 1629, he became friendly with William LAUD.

From 1632 Wentworth was lord deputy of Ireland (arrived July 1633). His heavy-handed efforts to strengthen royal finances and recover Church property alienated leading Irishmen (*see* WENTWORTH, THOMAS, AND IRELAND). He dubbed his policy of strong government 'THOROUGH'.

In 1639 Wentworth was recalled by Charles to combat the Scots (*see* COVENANT, WARS OF THE, OR BISHOPS' WARS). He was created earl of Strafford in Jan. 1640. In Nov. the LONG PARLIAMENT voted to impeach Strafford for TREASON. His vigorous defence at his trial (March–April 1641) caused Parliament to attaint him instead. Charles reluctantly accepted the decision and Strafford was executed. *See also* ATTAINDER.

WENTWORTH, THOMAS, AND IRELAND As chief governor (lord deputy) from Jan. 1632 Viscount Wentworth increased government revenues. By halting RECUSANCY prosecutions, he persuaded OLD ENGLISH Catholics to extend subsidy payments. In Ireland from July 1633, he obtained subsidies from PARLIAMENT (July 1634) by suggesting that the 1628 GRACES (proposed concessions to Catholics) might be enacted. But subsequent duplicity, and the threat of new PLANTATIONS (involving land confiscation), alienated leading Old English and Gaelic Irish Catholics.

Wentworth strengthened the Church of IRELAND (e.g., by raising clerical incomes), and increased conformity with the Church of ENGLAND (*see* LAUDIANISM, IMPACT ON IRELAND). Such policies offended NEW ENGLISH Puritans. Wentworth lived in a quasi-regal manner and acquired great wealth.

During the 1638–9 crisis in Scotland, Wentworth prevented the (Catholic) 2nd earl of Antrim (supported by King CHARLES I) from raising an army to invade Scotland, fearing revival of Gaelic Irish power in ULSTER. He countered the Scottish NATIONAL COVENANT by forcing (Scottish) Ulster presbyterians to take the 'Black Oath' of allegiance (from May 1639). In March 1640 Wentworth (now earl of Strafford and lord lieutenant) revisited Ireland to obtain funds for an army mostly of Catholics. When Wentworth was impeached in England, 16 of 28 charges related to Ireland. *See also* THOROUGH; CLOTWORTHY, JOHN.

WERGELD In Anglo-Saxon England (6th–11th centuries), a payment due to a murdered person's kinsmen, payable by the murderer or his kin. (The OE term means 'man-money'.) Rates were specified by law codes (in monetary values), and varied according to the victim's status. Wergeld payment largely replaced blood-feud (violent retaliation). It declined in the 11th century and was superseded by royal assumption of responsibility for providing justice. *See also* LAW, ENGLAND BEFORE 1066.

WESLEY, CHARLES (b. 18 Dec. 1707 at Epworth, Lincolnshire, England; d. 29 March 1788 at Marylebone,

Middlesex, England, aged 80). A younger brother of John WESLEY, Charles Wesley studied at OXFORD University from 1726. In 1727–8 he formed a 'Holy Club' which attended Holy Communion several times a week. Its members were nicknamed 'Methodists'. Wesley was ordained a clergyman in the Church of England (1735) and worked briefly in GEORGIA, N America (1736).

After experiencing an EVANGELICAL conversion (21 May 1738), Wesley undertook itinerant preaching. He lived in BRISTOL from 1756 and moved to LONDON in 1771. He was outraged by his brother's decision to ordain ministers in 1784. Charles Wesley is chiefly remembered as the hymn-writer of the Methodist revival: he composed over 6000 hymns. *See also* METHODISM.

WESLEY, JOHN (b. 17 June 1703 at Epworth, Lincolnshire, England; d. 2 March 1791 at London, England, aged 87). Educated at OXFORD University, Wesley became a Church of England clergyman (1725) and a fellow of Lincoln College (1726). In 1729 he joined the informal 'Holy Club' in Oxford, which fostered regular devotion (to 1735). Its members were nicknamed 'Methodists'. He visited GEORGIA, N America, 1735–7.

On 24 May 1738 Wesley experienced an EVANGELICAL conversion. He felt called to proclaim salvation by faith. (He rejected the CALVINISM of fellow preacher George WHITEFIELD.) But his enthusiasm barred him from parish churches. He created local societies with lay preachers, in Great Britain and Ireland, forming the Methodist movement of which he was leader. In 1784 Wesley controversially ordained preachers to serve in the USA. *See also* WESLEY, CHARLES; METHODISM.

WESSEX A Germanic-ruled kingdom (6th–10th centuries), which expanded across S England and created the kingdom of 'England' (10th century).

In the late 6th century the 'Gewisse' ('reliable ones'), a Germanic group in the Upper Thames Valley, expanded NE and NW under King Ceawlin. King Cynegils in 635 accepted Christianity and founded a see at Dorchester (in modern Oxfordshire). During the 7th century the kingdom expanded S and SW: the see was moved S to WINCHESTER (early 660s), and by 680 the Gewisse controlled Exeter (SW England). Under Cædwalla (685–8) the name 'West Saxons' replaced 'Gewisse'.

INE (ruled 688–726) fought MERCIA, DUMNONIA and ESSEX. He probably established Hamwic (*see* SOUTH-AMPTON), and possibly replaced subkingdoms within Wessex with lower-status SHIRES (*see* EALDORMAN). Wessex subsequently lost its original lands to Mercia (*see* OFFA), but under EGBERT gained SE England (826).

From the 840s Wessex was attacked by VIKINGS (*see* ÆTHELWULF). In 878, after retreating into western Wessex

(Somerset), King ALFRED defeated the Vikings decisively at EDINGTON (Wiltshire), and later captured LONDON (886).

In 909 King EDWARD THE ELDER began a period of expansion in which Wessex captured Viking-held lands, annexed other Anglo-Saxon kingdoms, and created the kingdom of England. Wessex retained identity as an ealdormanry or earldom (*see* GODWINE). *See also* KINGSHIP, ANGLO-SAXON; ENGLAND, FORMATION OF.

WEST AFRICA, ENGLISH AND BRITISH INVOLVEMENT English merchants traded in W Africa from the 1530s, acquiring gold, pepper and later slaves, etc. The ROYAL AFRICAN COMPANY developed trading near the GAMBIA, Volta and Niger rivers in the later 17th century, and in the 18th century the British dominated the SLAVE TRADE. This was suppressed from 1808 by a British naval squadron based in SIERRA LEONE.

Imperial rivalry with FRANCE and GERMANY prompted expansion in the hinterland of W Africa in the late 19th century, with military campaigns against native states in the GOLD COAST and NIGERIA. Parts of Togoland and Cameroon were acquired from Germany in 1919 (following WORLD WAR I). Great Britain governed extensively through the cheap system of 'indirect rule', pioneered by Frederick LUGARD from *c*.1900.

Britain withdrew from its W African territories between 1957 and 1965, under pressure from local nationalism and the expense of maintaining its rule (*see* DECOLONIZATION). *See also* BRITISH EMPIRE.

WESTERN AUSTRALIA A former British colony in AUSTRALIA. The SW area of Australia was explored by the Dutch (17th century), and a penal colony was organized from NEW SOUTH WALES in 1826. A colony was founded in 1829 as the Swan River Colony (renamed Western Australia in 1832). It was used for TRANSPORTATION 1850–68. In the later 19th century farmers and graziers expanded the settled area. Western Australia was granted self-government in 1890 and joined the Commonwealth of Australia in 1901 (*see* AUSTRALIAN FEDERATION). Its population was then 187,000. A referendum vote in 1933 favouring secession was repudiated by Great Britain and Australia.

WESTERN DESIGN Contemporaneous name for an English scheme (or 'design') against Spain's western empire instigated in 1654–5 by Oliver CROMWELL, lord protector. After concluding peace with the Dutch Republic (*see* ANGLO-DUTCH WARS), Cromwell and his Council decided to act against (Catholic) Spain, which was considered hostile to England and Protestantism.

On 20 Dec. 1654, 30 ships and 3600 troops sailed for the West Indies to capture the island of Hispaniola, establish an English presence in the C Caribbean, seize Spanish treasure ships, and break Spain's monopoly of trade. Having failed to capture Hispaniola's capital, Santo Domingo (14–25 April 1655), the force seized JAMAICA. Cromwell interpreted the setback as a divine rebuke, and renewed efforts to enforce Puritan moral values (*see* MAJOR-GENERALS, RULE OF). Jamaica, deemed worthless, soon proved immensely valuable. *See also* SPAIN, ENGLISH AND BRITISH RELATIONS WITH; NAVY, ENGLAND BEFORE 1660.

WESTERN ISLES An archipelago (also called the Hebrides) within the BRITISH ISLES, off NW BRITAIN; part of SCOTLAND within the UNITED KINGDOM. There are about 500 islands (including small islands), forming two groups: the Inner Hebrides, close to the mainland, with 35 inhabited islands, of which the largest are Skye and Mull; the Outer Hebrides, with 15 inhabited islands, of which Lewis and Harris is the largest. Est. popn in 2015: Inner Hebrides, 22,000; Outer Hebrides, 27,000.

The islands contain numerous remains from PREHISTORY (e.g., Callanish Standing Stones on Lewis, 3rd millennium BC). By AD 500 SCOTS from NE Ireland had settled on many of the Inner Hebrides and adjacent mainland, establishing kingdoms under the Irish overkingdom of DÁL RIATA. The Irish also brought Christianity (*see* CONVERSION OF NORTH BRITONS, PICTS AND SCOTS).

From the 8th century the Isles were raided by Norwegians and became part of the VIKING world. They were taken under Norwegian sovereignty probably by King Harald Fairhair (reigned 872–930). The Norse called the Isles Suðreyjar, meaning 'Southern isles'. Various men sought to become local kings. From *c.*1079 Godred Crovan established rule over the Isle of MAN and the Isles, but *c.*1156 a descendant lost many islands to SOMERLED, whose descendants retained local lordships.

In 1266 King ALEXANDER III of Scotland bought the suzerainty (including Man) from the king of Norway, though it took several years to obtain recognition from local lords. (Man was seized by England in 1290.) The Isles remained a heartland of Gaelic (Irish) language and culture (*see* GAELIC LANGUAGE AND LITERATURE, SCOTLAND; GAELDOM, SCOTLAND). Visitors were attracted from the 18th century (e.g., Samuel JOHNSON, 1773).

In the late 18th and 19th centuries landowners cleared lands for sheep keeping, moving inhabitants to smallholdings (*see* CROFTING). In 1846–7, potato blight caused suffering (*see* FAMINES, BRITAIN). In the late 20th century church attendance remained strong. *See also* MACDONALD, LORDS OF THE ISLES; MACDOUGAL, LORDS OF LORNE; ISLES, LORDSHIP OF THE; CATHOLICS AND CATHOLIC CHURCH, SCOTLAND; FREE CHURCH OF SCOTLAND; FREE PRESBYTERIAN CHURCH.

WEST INDIES A tropical archipelago of 1200 islands in C America, which separate the Atlantic Ocean from the Caribbean Sea. Ten States were formerly British colonies: Antigua and Barbuda, The Bahamas, BARBADOS, Dominica, GRENADA, JAMAICA, St Kitts-Nevis, St Lucia, St Vincent and the Grenadines, and Trinidad and Tobago. Another five countries remained British overseas territories in the early 21st century: Anguilla, Montserrat, British Virgin Islands, Cayman Islands, and the Turks and Caicos Islands.

Named in 1492 by Christopher Columbus, who believed that he had found a western route to India, the West Indies were first colonized by Spain, concentrating on the Greater Antilles group in the NW. The English, turning to the Lesser Antilles (SE), settled St Kitts (1624) and then, after King CHARLES I granted a charter to Lord Carlisle (1627), Barbados (1627), Nevis (1628), Antigua and Montserrat (both 1632). Settlers grew tobacco until the Dutch introduced sugar cane in the 1640s. They imported slaves from WEST AFRICA for PLANTATIONS, and from *c.*1660 the slave population exceeded the white population. During intense rivalry in the 17th and 18th centuries, England captured JAMAICA from Spain (1655; *see* WESTERN DESIGN) and other islands from France. In the 18th century Great Britain's 'sugar islands' were among its most valuable overseas possessions. The Bahamas became a crown colony in 1718.

Following the abolition of slavery (1834), some colonies used INDENTURED LABOUR from India. Total population of the British colonies in 1921 was 1,676,000. Falling sugar prices in the 1920s produced riots in the 1930s which Britain countered with economic assistance. Britain gradually established internal self-government, and created a Federation of the West Indies in 1958, but it foundered on strong local loyalties (1962).

Jamaica and Trinidad and Tobago were granted independence (1962), followed by Barbados (1966). The smaller British islands then formed the West Indies Associated States (1967), and most became independent (1974–83). The Bahamas became independent in 1973. *See also* SLAVE TRADE, ENGLISH AND BRITISH INVOLVEMENT; PARIS, PEACE OF; PIRACY AND PRIVATEERING.

WESTLAND CRISIS A dispute between British government ministers over the future of the ailing Westland helicopter company (a supplier of military helicopters) in 1986. When a CABINET meeting supported an American takeover bid, the defence secretary, Michael HESELTINE, resigned and dramatically walked out (9 Jan.). (Heseltine had preferred an alternative arrangement.) Leon Brittan, the trade and industry secretary, also had to resign (24 Jan.), after he leaked a letter to discredit Heseltine. The integrity of the prime minister, Margaret THATCHER, was also questioned.

WESTMINSTER A borough within Greater LONDON with city status; seat of the UK government and Parliament.

Westminster was originally the site of a MINSTER (7th century). A new abbey was founded there *c*.959 by DUNSTAN. King EDWARD THE CONFESSOR (d. 1066) established a residence (or palace) and rebuilt the abbey church. WILLIAM II (d. 1100) added a grand hall to the palace (*see* WESTMINSTER HALL). By the late 12th century departments of English royal government and law courts were situated at the palace, and a small town developed nearby; Westminster was superseding WINCHESTER as the royal administrative CAPITAL. From the 15th century PARLIAMENT usually met at Westminster Palace. After a fire at the palace in 1512, rulers ceased to live there.

In the late 17th century extensive house building joined Westminster to the urban area around London. Another fire in 1834 destroyed most of the palace, which was afterwards rebuilt to meet Parliament's requirements (designed by Charles Barry and A.W.N. PUGIN). Westminster was made a Metropolitan borough in 1899 and a city in 1900. In 1992 a polytechnic was upgraded as the University of Westminster. *See also* EXCHEQUER, ENGLAND; WHITEHALL PALACE; LONDON, GOVERNMENT OF.

Est. popn: 1300, 2500; 1600, 4500; 1800, 150,000.

WESTMINSTER, PROVISIONS OF In England, legal reforms issued on 24 Oct. 1259 by the new royal Council formed under the Provisions of OXFORD. They extended the reform of royal government by modifying the application of COMMON LAW. They redefined the roles of bailiffs and SHERIFFS, and removed common abuses of the judicial process. *See also* BARONIAL CONFLICT AND WARS.

WESTMINSTER, STATUTE OF Legislation by the UK Parliament, enacted Dec. 1931, whereby the DOMINIONS of the British Empire were recognized as States in their own right, and Parliament renounced its right to legislate for them unless requested to do so. It finalized the new concept of dominionhood outlined in the BALFOUR DEFINITION of 1926. The dominions in 1931 were: AUSTRALIA, CANADA, IRISH FREE STATE, NEWFOUNDLAND, NEW ZEALAND, SOUTH AFRICA.

WESTMINSTER ASSEMBLY A conference of Puritan clergy and laymen held at WESTMINSTER Abbey, England, from 1 July 1643. It was convened by the LONG PARLIAMENT to reform the Church of ENGLAND, including replacement of episcopacy (government by bishops). Scottish representatives were added after Parliament agreed the SOLEMN LEAGUE AND COVENANT (Aug. 1643). It met regularly until 1649 (including Scots until Nov. 1647), and occasionally until 1653.

The Assembly produced a Directory of Public Worship (1645) and recommended a presbyterian scheme of Church government (July 1645). It also composed two CATECHISMS (1647) and the 'Westminster Confession of Faith' (1648). *See also* PURITANISM, ENGLAND; CHURCH, ENGLAND AND WALES, 1640s–50s.

WESTMINSTER HALL A hall of immense size in the Palace of Westminster, London, built in 1097–8 for King WILLIAM II. It has been used for banquets (including CORONATION banquets to 1821), and once housed the main law courts (13th–early 19th centuries). It was also the venue for State trials, including that of King CHARLES I (1649). It survived a fire that destroyed most of the palace (1834), and remained in use in the 21st century. *See also* WESTMINSTER; COMMON LAW.

WESTON, RICHARD (b. early 1577 at Chicheley, Buckinghamshire, England; d. 13 March 1635 at London, England, aged 58). An MP from 1601, Weston became chancellor of the Exchequer in 1621; in 1625–7 he raised money for King CHARLES I for war against Spain and France (*see* BUCKINGHAM, DUKE OF).

In 1628 Weston was appointed TREASURER and created Lord Weston. He strengthened the Crown's financial position by paying off war debt and increasing 'ordinary' income and CUSTOMS revenues. He was created earl of Portland in 1633. Weston's work helped Charles to rule without calling Parliament (from 1629). *See also* CHARLES I, PERSONAL RULE.

WEST STOW The site of an excavated early Germanic hamlet, in Suffolk (E England); occupied 5th–7th centuries. Its inhabitants (maximum four households) lived in hall-houses and used sunken-floor huts for storage and craftwork. They grew cereals, kept livestock (especially sheep), and made pottery. Farmsteads were enclosed with ditches and fences in the 7th century. Part of the hamlet was reconstructed from the 1970s. *See also* HOUSING, ENGLAND BEFORE 1066; RURAL SETTLEMENT AND SOCIETY, ENGLAND.

WETS AND DRIES Nicknames for informal factions in the British CONSERVATIVE PARTY in the early 1980s. The prime minister, Margaret THATCHER, decried Party critics of her policies, especially MONETARIST economics, as 'wet' (a colloquialism for 'feeble'). They adopted the term; conversely her supporters became known as 'Dries'. After 1983 CABINET members were overwhelmingly Dries. *See also* THATCHERISM.

WEXFORD A town in the Republic of Ireland, by the estuary of the R. Slaney; centre of Co. Wexford; from Norse, Waesfjord, meaning 'Inlet of the mudflats' (Irish, Loch Garmain, meaning 'Headland lough').

Founded by VIKINGS as a trading centre in 935, Wexford grew into a port which had important trade with BRISTOL

(SW England). It was the first town to be captured by Anglo-Norman invaders (1169; *see* NORMANS, IMPACT ON IRELAND). Situated in LEINSTER, Wexford flourished into the 13th century, but suffered from competition from New Ross. Some 1,500 inhabitants were killed at Wexford in 1649 (*see* CROMWELL, OLIVER, AND IRELAND), and in 1798 it was captured by rebels (*see* RISING OF 1798). During the 18th century Wexford was involved in trans-Atlantic trade. A new dockyard was opened in 1832. Factories were established by overseas companies in the later 20th century. *See also* TOWNS, IRELAND.

Est. popn: 1300, 1500; 1600, 1000; 1800, 10,000; 1900, 11,000; 2000, 17,000.

WHARTON, THOMAS (b. Aug. 1648 in England; d. 12 April 1715 at London, England, aged 66). An MP from 1673, Wharton supported attempts to exclude the Catholic James, duke of York, from succession to the throne (1679–81; *see* EXCLUSION CRISIS). By Nov. 1685 (in reign of King JAMES VII/II) he was a leader of the WHIGS.

In Nov. 1688 Wharton joined the invasion army of William of Orange, and on 29 Jan. 1689 nominated William and his wife Mary in the CONVENTION PARLIAMENT to succeed James (*see* GLORIOUS REVOLUTION). He was appointed comptroller of the royal household. In the 1690s, as one of the WHIG JUNTO, Wharton was an important link between King WILLIAM III and Whig MPs. He succeeded as Lord Wharton in 1696.

Queen ANNE dismissed Wharton in 1702, but created him earl of Wharton in 1706. He served as lord lieutenant of Ireland 1708–10. GEORGE I appointed him as lord PRIVY SEAL (1714) and marquess of Wharton (1715).

WHEATLEY, JOHN (b. 24 May 1869 at Bonmahon, Co. Waterford, Ireland; d. 12 May 1930 at Glasgow, Scotland, aged 60). Taken to Lanarkshire, Scotland, in 1878, Wheatley was later a coalminer, grocer and publisher. In 1906 he joined the INDEPENDENT LABOUR PARTY and also founded the Catholic Socialist Society which persuaded many Liberal-voting Catholics to support Labour. From 1910 he served for the ILP on Lanarkshire County Council, transferring to Glasgow Council when his area (Shettleston) was incorporated in 1912.

In 1922 Wheatley was elected ILP MP for Shettleston. As minister of health under Ramsay MACDONALD (1924), he sponsored the 'Wheatley Act' which increased council housing subsidies. *See also* RED CLYDESIDE; HOUSING LEGISLATION, ENGLAND AND WALES.

WHEELHOUSE A structure named after its plan: a circular stone house subdivided by radiating piers. Often semi-subterranean, they lack the visual impact of the BROCHS whose distribution they share (northern Hebrides, northern Scotland, Orkney and Shetland). Some may be contemporary with brochs (from *c*.700 BC), but they flourished as late as AD 300.

WHIG JUNTO In England, name applied to a close-knit group of WHIG leaders on whom King WILLIAM III came to rely as leading ministers from 1693: John Somers (Lord SOMERS from 1696), Charles Montagu (Lord HALIFAX from 1700), Thomas WHARTON (Lord Wharton from 1696), and Edward Russell (earl of ORFORD from 1697). They provided war finance through control of the House of Commons (*see* GRAND ALLIANCE, WAR OF THE). Most were dismissed in 1699–1700 after peace with France had weakened their influence. Enemies attempted to impeach Somers, Halifax and Orford in 1701. Joined by the 3rd earl of Sunderland, some held office again under Queen ANNE, 1706–10.

WHIGS The term 'whig' (or 'whiggamore') originated in Scotland in the mid 17th century, referring to cattle thieves and rebellious presbyterians. It was applied in England from 1679 (among other terms) to those who sought to exclude the Catholic James, duke of York, from succession to the English throne (*see* EXCLUSION CRISIS). Whigs were England's first organized political party (from autumn 1679). (Their opponents became known as TORIES.) Party identities were adopted elsewhere in the British Isles.

After the GLORIOUS REVOLUTION (1688–9), Whigs supported constitutional monarchy, religious toleration, and later the HANOVERIAN SUCCESSION. After the accession of King GEORGE I (1714), when toryism was tainted with JACOBITISM, Whigs were the dominant, establishment party.

Party coherence declined in the mid 18th century but revived from the late 1760s. Whigs remained important in British politics until they were absorbed into the LIBERAL PARTY in the 1860s. Notable Whigs included Robert WALPOLE, the PELHAMS, Edmund BURKE, Charles James FOX and Earl GREY. *See also* POLITICAL PARTIES; SHAFTESBURY, EARL OF; WHIG JUNTO; ROCKINGHAM WHIGS.

WHISKY INDUSTRIES First recorded in Scotland in 1494, whisky was a lower-class drink, produced domestically by the 'pot-still' method. In the 1830s commercial distilleries introduced the more economical 'patent still-grain method', patented (1830) by the Irishman Aeneas Coffey. In the late 19th century 'Scotch', usually a blend, became popular among upper-class people throughout Britain; between 1850 and 1900 production expanded from 9 to 25 million gallons (41–110 million litres). Many firms closed during the depressed 1920s–30s, but exporting generated revival from the 1950s. In the late 20th century about 100 distilleries remained, benefiting from the popularity of single malts.

In the 18th century 'whiskey' became popular in Ireland, where production was concentrated in towns after the introduction of an EXCISE in 1779–80. Coffey's method was adopted in the N, where distilleries flourished until the late 1920s. Older methods continued in the S.

WHITAKER, T.K. (b. 18 Dec. 1916 at Rostrevor, Co. Down, Ireland; d. 9 Jan. 2017 at Dublin, Republic of Ireland, aged 100). (Thomas) Kenneth Whitaker joined the Civil Service of the IRISH FREE STATE in 1934 and obtained an external economics degree from LONDON University. Appointed secretary of the Republic of Ireland's Department of Finance in 1956, aged 39, he greatly influenced the government's 'white paper' *Programme for Economic Expansion* (1958). Whitaker's advocacy of foreign investment and free trade helped to redirect Ireland's economy from stagnation to expansion. He served as governor of the Central Bank of Ireland 1969–76. *See also* LEMASS, SEÁN; ECONOMIC EXPANSION, PROGRAMMES FOR.

WHITBY, SYNOD OF A meeting in 664 of senior clergy and laymen at Whitby in DEIRA (NE England) under the presidency of OSWIU, king of Bernicia and Deira. It was convened, probably at the instigation of Alhfrith (subking of Deira) and WILFRID, to decide whether the Church in Bernicia and Deira should retain Ionan ('Irish') practices (e.g., the timing of Easter) or adopt 'Roman' ones. Opting for the latter, it increased unity within the Anglo-Saxon Church. *See also* HILD; CONVERSION OF ANGLO-SAXONS; EASTER CONTROVERSY.

WHITE BOOK OF RHYDDERCH An important Welsh manuscript (kept as several manuscripts in the National Library of Wales, Aberystwyth), which was copied *c.*1340. It includes *Y MABINOGI* and Middle Welsh religious texts. *See also* WELSH LANGUAGE AND LITERATURE.

WHITEBOYS Rural secret societies which developed in Munster (S Ireland) from *c.*1760 and appeared in Leinster (E Ireland) in the 1770s, continuing into the 19th century. Named after members' white shirts, Whiteboys protested against enclosure and TITHES by attacking landlords, crops and other property. The government legislated against 'Whiteboyism' from 1776. *See also* AGRICULTURE, IRELAND 17TH CENTURY TO 1921.

WHITEFIELD, GEORGE (b. 16 Dec. 1714 at Gloucester, Gloucestershire, England; d. 30 Sept. 1770 at Newburyport, Massachusetts, N America, aged 55). An innkeeper's son, Whitefield was educated at OXFORD University where he joined John and Charles WESLEY in the 'Holy Club' (1733), the original so-called 'Methodists'. In 1735 he experienced an EVANGELICAL conversion. Though ordained in the Church of England (deacon 1736, priest 1739), Whitefield was critical of the Church and became an itinerant preacher. Unlike the Wesleys, he adhered to CALVINISM.

A dramatic, fervent preacher, Whitefield toured Great Britain and Ireland and frequently visited N America, where he was given an estate and slaves. He died after returning to America in 1769. *See also* METHODISM.

WHITEHALL PALACE A principal English royal residence in the 16th and 17th centuries, at WESTMINSTER, Middlesex (now part of London). A house of the archbishops of YORK from the mid 13th century, 'York Place' was seized in 1529 by King HENRY VIII from Cardinal Thomas WOLSEY and renamed. Henry undertook extensive new building. During the PROTECTORATE, Whitehall Palace was the home of Oliver CROMWELL (1653–8). WILLIAM III and MARY II moved elsewhere in 1689 (*see* KENSINGTON PALACE), and in 1698 most of Whitehall Palace was destroyed by fire. Only the Banqueting House survives above ground (*see* JONES, INIGO). *See also* ROYAL HOUSEHOLD, ENGLAND.

WHITE SHIP DISASTER The accidental sinking on 25 Nov. 1120 in the English Channel (near Barfleur, Normandy) of the ship carrying William ætheling, the only direct male heir of King HENRY I, king of England and duke of NORMANDY. Henry, a widower, afterwards remarried (1121) but failed to produce another male heir. He therefore sought the succession of his daughter, MATILDA.

WHITGIFT, JOHN (b. 1530 or 1531 at Grimsby, Lincolnshire, England; d. 29 Feb. 1604 at Lambeth, Surrey, England, aged about 74). A scholar and clergyman at CAMBRIDGE University, Whitgift, as vice-chancellor, deprived Thomas CARTWRIGHT of his professorship for condemning the structure of the Church of ENGLAND (1570). He defended the ELIZABETHAN SETTLEMENT in contributions to the 'Admonition Controversy' (1572, 1574), a dispute over Church government. He was appointed bishop of Worcester (1577), archbishop of CANTERBURY (1583), and privy councillor (1586).

As archbishop, Whitgift worked with Queen ELIZABETH I to enforce uniformity of religion against Puritan and Catholic dissenters. He required clergy to support 'Three Articles' (1583–4), affirming the Church's episcopal structure, but met considerable resistance. He was attacked in the MARPRELATE TRACTS (1588–9). In 1593 Whitgift obtained an Act of Parliament against Protestant sectaries (Conventicle Act), the only one in Elizabeth's reign.

After the accession of JAMES VI/I he attended the HAMPTON COURT CONFERENCE (Jan. 1604). *See also* REFORMATION, ENGLAND; PURITANISM, ENGLAND.

WHITHORN A town in Dumfries and Galloway, SW Scotland. It was long thought to have been one of the earliest Christian sites in N Britain (possibly 5th century), and to have been the location of the church called the 'White House' which according to BEDE (in 731) was founded by NINIAN. This appeared to have been confirmed by excavations in the 1980s, until reinterpretation of the earliest finds suggested a secular rather than religious centre.

Whithorn was a bishop's see (with interruptions) from 731 or earlier until 1689 (in the expanded kingdom of BERNICIA until the 9th century). Whithorn Cathedral was governed by Premonstratensian canons *c*.1175–*c*.1560. *See also* CHURCH ORGANIZATION, NORTH BRITAIN AND SCOTLAND BEFORE THE REFORMATION; GALLOWAY.

WHITTINGTON, RICHARD (b. *c*.1350 at Pauntley, Gloucestershire, England; d. 23 or 24 March 1423 at London, England, aged about 73). A landowner's son who became a London mercer (cloth dealer), Whittington made large loans to the Crown from the 1380s. He served LONDON as alderman, sheriff and MP, and was mayor three times (1397–8, 1406–7, 1419–20). He died childless, leaving his fortune to charity.

From the early 17th century Whittington's name, as 'Dick' Whittington, was attached to a legend about a country orphan who went to London, married his master's daughter, and became mayor. It appeared frequently in children's stories, and later in pantomimes and films.

WHITTLE, FRANK (b. 1 June 1907 at Coventry, Warwickshire, England; d. 9 Aug. 1996 at Columbia, Maryland, USA, aged 89). Whittle joined the ROYAL AIR FORCE (RAF) as an apprentice (1923) and qualified as a pilot (1928). In 1929–30 he drafted a patent for a gas turbine to produce jet propulsion for aircraft, but failed to obtain official or commercial interest. He studied at the RAF engineering school from 1932 and at CAMBRIDGE University (1934–6).

In 1935 interest was shown in Whittle's engine, and he formed Power Jets to develop the idea (1936). A prototype was operated in 1937, and in July 1939 the Air Ministry commissioned a test plane and engine. The first jet-powered plane flew on 15 May 1941, during WORLD WAR II (Gloster E.28/39), and the RAF received service aircraft in May 1944 (Gloster Meteor I with successor engine). In April the government had nationalized Power Jets, and Whittle had ceased to be involved. He was knighted, and left the RAF, in 1948, emigrating to the USA in 1976. *See also* AIRCRAFT INDUSTRY, UNITED KINGDOM.

WHITWORTH, JOSEPH (b. 21 Dec. 1803 at Stockport, Cheshire, England; d. 22 Jan. 1887 at Monte Carlo, aged 83). An engineer, Whitworth in 1833 founded a tool-making company in MANCHESTER (NW England). By 1841 he developed a system of standard screw threads which became widely adopted (by 1860s), facilitating mass-production engineering. Whitworth also improved military rifles and created 'Whitworth steel'. He was created a baronet (1869). *See also* MACHINE TOOLS INDUSTRY, GREAT BRITAIN.

WIC OE term (from Latin *vicus*, meaning 'port') used to denote large, unfortified trading centres on major rivers in eastern and southern England. They were developed from the early 7th century, probably by kings, in parallel with wics in northern Europe. Some had planned streets. Examples include: YORK, NORWICH, Ipswich, LONDON (probably the largest) and SOUTHAMPTON. Wics declined in the 9th century and were replaced by fortified centres (BURHS). *See also* TOWNS, ENGLAND; TOWN PLANNING.

WILBERFORCE, WILLIAM (b. 24 Aug. 1759 at Hull, Yorkshire, England; d. 29 July 1833 at Chelsea, Middlesex, England, aged 73). A merchant's son, friend of William PITT the Younger, and independent MP (1780–1825), Wilberforce experienced an EVANGELICAL conversion in 1785. Thereafter he worked for religious and social causes, such as moral reform (e.g., lobbying for a royal proclamation against vice; issued 1787). Wilberforce was a leading member of the CLAPHAM SECT (resident at Clapham 1792–1808).

Wilberforce's greatest concerns were to end British involvement in the slave trade and slavery. He worked against the trade from 1787, achieving its abolition by Parliament in 1807. (Slavery in the British Empire was abolished after his death.) *See also* YOUNG, ARTHUR; SLAVE TRADE, ABOLITION OF.

WILFRID (b. *c*.634 in Northumbria; d. probably 24 April 710 at Oundle, Mercia, aged about 75). After visiting Rome, and studying Roman observances (e.g., calculation of Easter), Wilfrid became (*c*.658) abbot of Ripon (in DEIRA). In 664 he persuaded OSWIU, king of BERNICIA and Deira, to adopt Roman practices (*see* WHITBY, SYNOD OF). He was appointed bishop of Northumbria; but his patron Alhfrith (subking of Deira) died and he was excluded until 669 (*see* CHAD). As bishop he moved the see from Lindisfarne to YORK and founded Hexham monastery.

In 678 Wilfrid was expelled by EGFRITH. After going first to Rome he took refuge in SUSSEX (S England, from 680 or 681), and was then made bishop in WESSEX (685). He was restored to York (691), but the now reduced size of the diocese discontented him. He moved to MERCIA (C England) by 692. A council deprived Wilfrid of most possessions (703). His monasteries at Ripon and Hexham were eventually returned (706), but he refused restoration to York and died in Mercia. *See also* WILLIBRORD.

WILKES AFFAIR Episode in the 1760s–70s when British governments sought to silence the propagandist John Wilkes (1725–97).

From 1762 Wilkes, an MP, lampooned the earl of BUTE, George GRENVILLE and the royal family in his newspaper the *North Briton*. Issue 45 (23 April 1763) was seen as a treasonable attack on King GEORGE III. Wilkes was imprisoned. After his release, the House of Commons voted that issue 45 contained seditious libel (words stirring disaffection). Wilkes went abroad and the Commons expelled him (Jan. 1764).

Wilkes returned in 1768. He was elected MP for Middlesex but imprisoned, provoking riots. Parliament again expelled him. He was re-elected and expelled twice more (1769). Parliament's behaviour seemingly thwarted the will of a large constituency electorate, and Wilkes claimed to represent liberty against arbitrary government. He received widespread support (e.g., from Wilkes Clubs). In London he was elected an alderman (1769), sheriff (1771), and lord mayor (1774). He served again as an MP 1774–90. Wilkes was the first individual in British history to create a popular campaign on constitutional matters. *See also* GRENVILLE-TEMPLE, RICHARD; GRAFTON, 3RD EARL OF; NORTH, LORD.

WILLIAM, PRINCE *see* CAMBRIDGE, WILLIAM DUKE OF

WILLIAM I OR WILLIAM THE CONQUEROR (b. 1027 or 1028 at Falaise, Normandy; d. 9 Sept. 1087 at Rouen, Normandy, aged 59 or 60). Duke of NORMANDY who conquered England.

William succeeded as duke (William II) in 1035, aged 7, and was declared of age *c*.1042. His position remained precarious until he defeated Guy of Brionne (claimant to Normandy) in 1047. After the deaths (1060) of rivals Henry I of France and Geoffrey Martel, count of Anjou, William established Norman predominance in N France by conquering Maine (1063) and attacking Brittany (1064 or 1065).

On 28 Sept. 1066 Normans invaded England, killing HAROLD II at HASTINGS (14 Oct.). Norman chroniclers claimed that William removed a usurper (William had allegedly been designated heir in 1051 by his kinsman EDWARD THE CONFESSOR). English chroniclers considered William an aggressor. Many English submitted but between 1068 and 1072 revolts broke out which William suppressed ruthlessly, ending the idea of a collaborative Anglo-Norman realm. In 1070 William purged the Church, replacing STIGAND of Canterbury with LANFRANC.

From 1072 to 1080 William lived mainly in Normandy. During his final visit to England (1085–6) he commissioned a survey (see DOMESDAY BOOK). He was succeeded by ROBERT CURTHOSE in Normandy, by WILLIAM II in England. *See also* NORMAN CONQUEST OF ENGLAND.

WILLIAM I OR WILLIAM THE LION (b. *c*.1143; d. 4 Dec. 1214 at Stirling, C Scotland, aged about 71). King of Scots (Scotland) 1165–1214. William succeeded his elder brother MALCOLM IV (9 Dec. 1165). He had previously held the earldom of Northumberland in NE England (from his father's death in 1152 until dispossessed by King HENRY II of England in 1157). To regain the earldom, William joined the REVOLT OF 1173–4 against Henry II, but was captured near Alnwick, NE England (July 1174), and taken to NORMANDY (N France). To obtain release he had to do homage to Henry (Dec. 1174) and accept English garrisons in Scotland (*see* FALAISE, TREATY OF). The treaty was annulled by RICHARD I for 15,000 marks in the 'Quitclaim of Canterbury', 1189.

William's capture provoked revolt in GALLOWAY (SW Scotland), which William eventually suppressed in 1185. He then dealt with Donald Macwilliam (of MORAY, NE Scotland), claimant to the kingship, who was killed in 1187. King JOHN of England, however, sought to reimpose English authority, and in 1209 compelled William to pay 15,000 marks (treaty of Norham, confirmed 1212). William (called 'the Lion' from the 14th century) was succeeded by ALEXANDER II. *See also* MAC MALCOLM RULERS; HUNTINGDON, DAVID EARL OF.

WILLIAM II OF SCOTLAND *see* WILLIAM III

WILLIAM II OR WILLIAM RUFUS (b. *c*.1060 in Normandy; d. 2 Aug. 1100 in New Forest, Hampshire, England, aged about 40). The second surviving son of WILLIAM I, William was sent by his dying father (7 or 8 Sept. 1087) from NORMANDY to England where he became king (crowned 26 Sept.). His older brother, ROBERT CURTHOSE, became duke of Normandy. Each ruler desired to control both territories (*see* NORMAN EMPIRE).

In 1088 ODO OF BAYEUX led a revolt in England in favour of Robert. It was quickly suppressed. In Feb. 1091 William, in Normandy, forced Robert to agree that each would be the other's heir (treaty of Rouen). They collaborated on pacifying parts of Normandy, N England and Wales (*see* MALCOLM III), but then quarrelled (late 1091). Robert returned to Normandy. In March 1094 William, again in Normandy, denounced the treaty but achieved little (returned to England Jan. 1095). He received custody of Normandy in 1096 when Robert mortgaged it to pay for crusading.

William's ambitions resulted in harsh exactions (e.g., from the Church), mainly organized by RANULF FLAMBARD. William was accidentally killed by an arrow while hunting. Succeeded by HENRY I. The nickname Rufus (Latin, meaning 'Red'), referring to William's hair, was recorded from the 12th century. *See also* ANSELM; BORDER, ANGLO-SCOTTISH; DUNCAN II; WESTMINSTER HALL.

WILLIAM III (b. 4 Nov. 1650 at The Hague, Dutch Republic; d. 8 March 1702 at Kensington Palace, Middlesex, England, aged 51). William of Orange was appointed stadholder (lieutenant) of the Dutch Republic in 1672. Until 1679 he led Dutch forces in war against France. In 1677 he married Mary, elder daughter of James, duke of York, of England (King JAMES VII/II from 1685). William was a nephew of King CHARLES II.

In July 1688 William, a Protestant, was invited to intervene in England by opponents of James's pro-Catholic policies. He landed in Devon on 5 Nov. 1688. James fled. William and Mary became joint sovereigns (proclaimed 13 Feb. 1689), after accepting a Declaration of RIGHTS. William exercised monarchical powers. (Mary died in 1694; *see* MARY II.)

William soon faced renewed war. James, with French support, attempted to regain his thrones from Ireland (1689–90; *see* JAMES VII/II AND IRELAND). From 1691 to 1696 William fought France in Continental Europe (*see* GRAND ALLIANCE, WAR OF THE).

William initially ruled in England with a ministry of WHIGS and TORIES, including the earls of NOTTINGHAM and DANBY. But from 1694 he became reliant for war finance on the so-called WHIG JUNTO. After the 1698 election more Tories were appointed (e.g., earl of ROCHESTER). *See also* GLORIOUS REVOLUTION; GLORIOUS REVOLUTION, SCOTLAND; TRIENNIAL ACTS, ENGLAND AND WALES.

WILLIAM IV (b. 21 Aug. 1765 at Westminster, Middlesex, England; d. 20 June 1837 at Windsor, Berkshire, England, aged 71). The third son of King GEORGE III, William served in the British NAVY (1779–83, 1785–9) and was created duke of Clarence (1789). He lived from 1797 to 1811 with actress Dorothy Jordan (1761–1816), who bore ten children. In 1818 he married Princess Adelaide of Saxe-Meiningen (1792–1849). Their two daughters died young. In 1827 William became heir to GEORGE IV and served briefly as lord high admiral.

William succeeded as king of Great Britain, Ireland and HANOVER, on 26 June 1830. Soon afterwards, following an election, the Tories were defeated in Parliament and he appointed Earl GREY as prime minister, who supported PARLIAMENTARY REFORM. This passed in 1832 after William agreed reluctantly to threaten the creation of peers (if required) to obtain approval of the House of Lords.

In Nov. 1834 William dismissed the government of Viscount MELBOURNE because he disapproved of its policy towards Ireland. His successor, Sir Robert PEEL, was unable to win an election, resulting in Melbourne's reappointment. It was the first instance where the electorate overruled the king's choice of minister.

Lacking legitimate offspring, William was succeeded (except in Hanover) by his niece VICTORIA.

WILLIAM CLITO (b. 25 Oct. 1102 in Normandy; d. 28 July 1128 at Aalst, Flanders, aged 25). The son and heir of ROBERT CURTHOSE (ousted as duke of NORMANDY by King HENRY I of England in 1106), William went into exile (1112). From 1114 his claim to Normandy was championed by Henry's enemies. In 1127, supported by King Louis VI of France, William was elected count of Flanders (adjacent to Normandy). Henry encouraged opposition, preventing William from establishing authority. He died during a siege. 'Clito' (Latin) means 'Prince'.

WILLIAMITE WAR Struggle for control of Ireland, 1688–91, between forces loyal to James VII/II, former (Catholic) king of England, Scotland and Ireland ('Jacobites'), and forces supporting his successors, (the Protestant) WILLIAM III and MARY II ('Williamites').

After William invaded England (5 Nov. 1688), James's chief governor in Ireland, the earl of TYRCONNELL, retained control but Protestants in N Ireland seized key places. The (Catholic) earl of Antrim attempted to capture their main centre, LONDONDERRY, but was rebuffed: 13 apprentices closed the city gates (7 Dec.). James arrived in S Ireland (from France) on 12 March 1689 and advanced on Londonderry (18 April). But it refused to capitulate (*see* LONDONDERRY, SIEGE OF).

William decided to attack James in Ireland. He sent military forces to NE Ireland from Aug. 1689, and landed there himself on 14 June 1690. On 1 July he defeated James's army in E Ireland (*see* BOYNE, BATTLE OF THE). James fled soon afterwards (4 July). William moved S, then W, and unsuccessfully besieged LIMERICK (9–30 Aug.). He left Ireland on 5 Sept. The Williamites, under the earl of Marlborough, captured the southern ports of Cork (28 Sept.) and Kinsale (15 Oct.). They now held all but W Ireland.

English forces advanced westwards (from DUBLIN) in mid 1691, and captured Athlone (21–30 June). The Jacobite commander, the marquis of St-Ruth (a Frenchman), decided to fight, but his forces were decisively defeated at AUGHRIM (12 July). The Jacobites, now led by Patrick Sarsfield, retreated to Galway (surrendered 21 July), then to Limerick. It was besieged from 25 Aug. until a ceasefire was arranged (23 Sept.). The subsequent treaty (signed 3 Oct.) made generous concessions to Catholics (*see* LIMERICK, TREATY OF). *See also* GLORIOUS REVOLUTION, ENGLAND; JAMES VII/II AND IRELAND; RAPPAREES; CHURCHILL, JOHN; PROTESTANT ASCENDANCY.

WILLIAMS, EDWARD (b. 10 March 1747 at Llancarfan, Glamorgan, Wales; d. 18 Dec. 1826 at Flemingston, Glamorgan, aged 79). A stonemason learned in Welsh literature, Williams (known as Iolo Morganwg) fabricated early Welsh verse and in 1792 founded the *Gorsedd Beirdd*

Ynys Prydain ('Assembly of the Bards of the Isle of Britain'), claimed as a revival of druidism (pre-Roman British religion). The *Gorsedd* met that year at midsummer on Primrose Hill, London, and from 1819 at EISTEDDFODS in Wales, from 1858 performing druidical ceremonies devised by Williams. *See also* FRENCH REVOLUTION, IMPACT ON WALES; WELSH NATIONAL SOCIETIES.

WILLIAMS, JOHN (b. March 1582 at Conway, Caernarfonshire, Wales; d. 25 March 1650 at Gloddaeth, Caernarfonshire, aged 67 or 68). A clergyman, Williams prospered under King JAMES VI/I. He was appointed dean of Westminster Abbey (1620), keeper of the great seal and bishop of LINCOLN (1621). But CHARLES I, encouraged by William LAUD, disliked Williams. He was barred from Charles's coronation and lost the keepership (1625). From 1628 he was charged in STAR CHAMBER, and in 1637 suspended from his offices, fined and imprisoned.

In 1640, when Charles needed support (*see* LONG PARLIAMENT), Williams was released. In Nov. 1641 he was appointed archbishop of YORK (but then imprisoned with other bishops by order of the House of Lords). In the CIVIL WARS (from 1642), Williams held Conway Castle for Charles, until his Royalist rival Sir John Owen seized it (1645). Williams then helped Parliamentarians retake the castle (Nov. 1646).

WILLIAMS, WILLIAM (b. 1717 at Llanfair-ar-y-bryn, Carmarthenshire, Wales; d. 11 Jan. 1791 at Llanfair-ar-y-bryn, aged 73 or 74). Hymn-writer and Methodist leader. From a dissenting family, Williams was converted (1738) to the Church of England, which included Wales, by the preaching of Howel HARRIS. He became a deacon and curate, but was denied ordination as priest (1743) because of involvement in Methodism. He became an itinerant preacher, based at Pantycelyn (Carmarthenshire).

Williams wrote around 860 hymns, which helped to define the METHODIST REVIVAL. The best are a matchless expression of the concepts of the Redeemer's sacrifice and the love of God.

WILLIBRORD (b. 657 or 658 in Deira; d. 7 Nov. 739 at Echternach, Francia, aged 81). A pupil of WILFRID at Ripon, Willibrord lived in Ireland (678–90) before becoming one of the most important Anglo-Saxon missionaries in Continental Europe, working in Francia and Frisia (modern Netherlands) and attempting to convert the Danes. He was consecrated probably as an archbishop in Rome in 695, and established his see at Utrecht in Frisia (by 704). ALCUIN composed a Life of him. *See also* MISSIONS TO CONTINENTAL EUROPE, ANGLO-SAXON.

WILMINGTON, EARL OF (b. c.1674 in England; d. 2 July 1743 at Westminster, Middlesex, England, aged about 69). From a TORY family, Spencer Compton joined the WHIGS soon after becoming an MP in 1698. He was elected speaker of the House of Commons in 1715 (in the first Parliament of King GEORGE I), serving until 1728. He also served, in the ministry of Robert WALPOLE, as paymaster-general (1722–30), lord PRIVY SEAL (1730), and lord president of the Council (Dec. 1730–42). A favourite of GEORGE II (king from 1727), Compton was created Lord Wilmington in 1728 (to remove him from the Commons) and earl of Wilmington in 1730.

When Walpole fell in 1742, Wilmington succeeded him as first lord of the Treasury, though the ministry was effectively headed by Lord CARTERET.

WILSON, HAROLD (b. 11 March 1916 at Huddersfield, Yorkshire, England; d. 24 May 1995 at London, England, aged 79). Leader of the LABOUR PARTY 1963–76; British prime minister 1964–70, 1974–6.

An industrial chemist's son, Wilson became an academic economist before joining the Civil Service (1940). An MP from 1945, he held junior office at the ministry of works (1945–7), then entered the Cabinet as president of the Board of TRADE. He resigned in April 1951 in protest at health charges but was not a committed BEVANITE. In 1963, after the death of Hugh GAITSKELL, he won the Party leadership, defeating George BROWN and James CALLAGHAN.

Wilson won election victories in Oct. 1964 and March 1966. There were balance of payments crises, and little came of a 'National Plan' for economic growth. The government ordered COMPREHENSIVE EDUCATION, grappled with the RHODESIA PROBLEM, and tried to enter the EUROPEAN ECONOMIC COMMUNITY (EEC).

Though defeated in 1970, Wilson formed a minority government in March 1974. The SOCIAL CONTRACT helped secure a small majority in Oct. 1974. The economic situation was bad: inflation reached 26.9% (Aug. 1975). A referendum confirmed EEC membership (June 1975). Wilson unexpectedly retired in April 1976. Created Lord Wilson in 1983. *See also* KITCHEN CABINET; HEATH, EDWARD.

WINCHELSEY, ROBERT (b. c.1240, probably at Winchelsea, Sussex, England; d. 11 May 1313 at Otford, Kent, England, aged about 73). A scholar, clergyman and administrator, Winchelsey was elected archbishop of CANTERBURY in 1293. In early 1297 the clergy resisted King EDWARD I's demand for taxation, with Winchelsey invoking the bull *CLERICIS LAICOS*. Edward outlawed the clergy and charged them for pardons. In July he and Winchelsey were reconciled. The clergy granted the tax on condition that that they collected it.

Antagonism between Winchelsey and Edward continued. In 1305 Edward charged Winchelsey with plotting against him. Winchelsey was suspended from office by the

Pope (Feb. 1306) and went abroad. He was recalled (1307) by EDWARD II, though he then supported the barons against Piers GAVESTON (1308).

WINCHESTER A city in S England, by the R. Itchen; centre of Hampshire.

Winchester was originally the Roman city and CIVITAS capital Venta Belgarum, (meaning 'Market ...' or 'Place of the BELGAE'; 1st–5th centuries). Following abandonment, redevelopment began in the mid 7th century: King Cenwalh of the Gewisse (later WESSEX) built a church or MINSTER (later called Old Minster) near the former Roman forum (c.650) and appointed a bishop (between 660 and 663). There was probably already a royal residence. The town's English name (OE, Uintancaestir, meaning 'Walled place of Venta') is recorded from the 8th century.

Under ALFRED (king 871–99) a grid of streets was laid out in Winchester's central area; in the early 10th century EDWARD THE ELDER founded a New Minster, N of Old Minister. The population and economy expanded in the 10th–11th centuries, when Winchester was effectively England's CAPITAL.

After the Norman invasion (1066) a castle was built, the royal residence (or palace) was expanded, and the two minsters were replaced by a new cathedral – one of the largest in Christendom. The palace was destroyed in 1141 (see ANARCHY). From the late 12th century, WESTMINSTER superseded Winchester as the royal administrative capital. A new palace built in 1683–5 for King CHARLES II by Christopher WREN remained an empty shell until it became Army barracks in 1796 (destroyed by fire 1894 and replaced).

Cloth manufacturing was significant in the 12th–16th centuries, but the city declined considerably after the BLACK DEATH (1348). Since the late 17th century Winchester has been a shopping, services, administrative and social centre. Winchester College, founded 1382 by William of WYKEHAM, became a leading school. In 2005 a teacher-training college was upgraded as the University of Winchester.

Est. popn: 1086, 6000; 1300, 8000; 1600, 5000; 1800, 11,000; 1900, 46,000; 2000, 93,000.

WINDSOR A town in Berkshire (S England) and location of a pre-eminent royal castle.

Windsor Castle, built in the late 11th century on a cliff by the R. Thames, superseded an older nearby royal centre called Windsor (from OE, Windlesora, meaning 'Landing place with windlass'). A town was created outside the castle by 1131 (called 'New Windsor' until 1974).

Windsor Castle's original wooden buildings were rebuilt in stone in the 12th–13th centuries. King HENRY III defined the boundary of the 5000-acre (2000-ha) royal hunting ground later known as the Great Park. EDWARD III founded the Order of the GARTER at Windsor Castle (1349) and developed the castle into a palace for his court. EDWARD IV began a rebuilding of the garter chapel of St George (1475–1528). The castle was extensively rebuilt in 1824–8 for WILLIAM IV. Further rebuilding followed a fire in 1992. St George's chapel contains numerous royal tombs. Windsor town has served the castle and adjacent area. Since the arrival of a railway in 1849, Windsor was been a popular destination for tourists. *See also* ROYAL HOUSE-HOLD, ENGLAND.

Est. popn: 1300, 1500; 1600, 2000; 1800, 3000; 1900, 9000; 2000, 26,000.

WINDSOR, TREATY OF Confirmed on 6 Oct. 1175 at WINDSOR, S England, between representatives of Ruaidrí Ua CONCHOBAIR, high-king of Ireland, and King HENRY II of England. Following Henry's establishment of lordship in Ireland, it defined spheres of influence: Ruaidrí was confirmed as high-king of Ireland (under Henry's protection) while Henry and Anglo-Normans would retain areas they controlled (principally LEINSTER, MEATH, and part of MUNSTER). The treaty was soon broken by the English. *See also* HENRY II AND IRELAND; NORMANS, IMPACT ON IRELAND.

WINGATE, ORDE (b. 26 Feb. 1903 at Naini Tal, United Provinces, India; d. 24 March 1944 near Bishnupur, Assam, India, aged 41). A charismatic but independent-minded British Army soldier (from 1921), Wingate served in SUDAN (1928–33) and PALESTINE (1936–8). During WORLD WAR II, he led the 'Gideon Force' that in 1941 overthrew Italian rule of Abyssinia (Ethiopia) and reinstated the exiled Emperor Haile Selassie. Following the Japanese occupation of BURMA, Wingate commanded two expeditions of 'Chindits', small units supplied by aircraft which infiltrated Burma and harassed enemy forces (1943, 1944). Named after a mythical Burmese temple guardian, they were an early example of military 'special forces'. Wingate died in an air crash.

WINSTANLEY, GERRARD (b. Oct. 1609 at Wigan, Lancashire, England; d. 10 Sept. 1676 at London, England, aged 66). Winstanley, a failed cloth trader in London, began writing radical religious works in 1648. Seeking to implement a vision of a reformed society, he led a group which communally cultivated common land at St George's Hill, Surrey, from 1 April 1649 (soon after the establishment of the COMMONWEALTH). Known as 'Diggers', they moved to Cobham Heath in Aug. and were forcibly dispersed in spring 1650. Winstanley continued to publish works attacking landlords, lawyers, merchants and clergy, and envisaging an equal society without private property and wage labour (e.g., *The Law of Freedom*, 1652). He died a Quaker. *See also* ENGLISH REVOLUTION SECTS.

WINTER OF DISCONTENT In Great Britain, name applied to the surge of strikes in public services and transport Jan.–March 1979. They wrecked the INCOMES POLICY of the Labour government led by James CALLAGHAN, destroyed the Party's claim to have a uniquely harmonious relationship with the trade unions, and helped Margaret THATCHER to win a UK general election (May). The name was applied by the *Sun* newspaper, alluding to a phrase by William SHAKESPEARE (in *Richard III*).

WISEMAN, NICHOLAS (b. 2 Aug. 1802 at Seville, Spain; d. 15 Feb. 1865 at London, England, aged 62). Educated in Ireland, England and Rome, Wiseman became a Roman Catholic priest in 1825. He was rector (head) of the English College in Rome 1828–40 and author of theological works. Consecrated as bishop in 1840, he served as president of Oscott College (Catholic seminary and school in England) 1840–7. In 1847 Wiseman advised Pope Pius IX that a hierarchy should be reinstated in England and Wales. This was implemented in 1850, against popular Protestant protests. Wiseman became the first archbishop of WESTMINSTER and a cardinal. He encouraged provision of schools for poor children and work by religious communities among the poor. *See also* CATHOLICS AND CATHOLIC CHURCH, ENGLAND.

WISHART, GEORGE (b. *c*.1513 in Angus, E Scotland; d. 1 March 1546 at St Andrews, Fife, E Scotland, aged about 33). A clergyman, Wishart adopted reformed Christianity by 1538. After spending time in England (1538–9), he fled overseas where he translated the Swiss Church reformers' 'First Helvetic Confession' (1536) into SCOTS (published 1548). Returning to Scotland (from CAMBRIDGE, England) in 1543, he preached Protestant doctrines until arrested (Jan. 1546) and burnt for heresy. Wishart influenced John KNOX and linked Scotland with Swiss reform movements (*see* CALVINISM). *See also* BEATON, DAVID.

WISHART, ROBERT (fl. from 1271; d. 1316 in Glasgow diocese, Scotland). Bishop of GLASGOW from 1273 and a 'guardian' of Scotland 1286–92 (*see* GREAT CAUSE), Wishart did homage to King EDWARD I of England after the deposition of King John BALLIOL (1296), but then encouraged resistance to the English occupation of parts of Scotland. He was captured (June or July 1297) and imprisoned until 1300.

In 1305 Wishart apparently co-operated with Edward over Scottish government, but supported seizure of the kingship by Robert Bruce in Feb. 1306 and participated in Robert's inauguration (25 March; *see* ROBERT I). Wishart

was captured on 19 June 1306 and imprisoned in England; released 1314, after the battle of BANNOCKBURN.

WITAN OE term meaning 'wise men'; used by historians for royal councils (or their members) in Anglo-Saxon kingdoms (recorded from 7th century). They consisted of king, nobles, leading officers, senior clergy (bishops, abbots). Council meetings or assemblies helped to integrate the early kingdom of England (mid 10th–mid 11th century). *See also* KINGSHIP, ANGLO-SAXON; ENGLAND, FORMATION OF; COUNCIL, ENGLAND, FROM 1066.

WITCHCRAFT, ENGLAND AND WALES Witchcraft (malevolent use of magical power) was prosecuted in Church courts by the 13th century, but cases were few and penalties light. A STATUTE of 1542 introduced the Continental mania for persecuting suspected women (repealed 1547). A statute of 1563 was replaced in 1604. Prosecutions peaked in the 1590s, thereafter declining rapidly, until a spate of trials in 1645–7, resulting from activity by Matthew Hopkins, the so-called 'witch-finder general'. Cases were relatively fewer in Wales. Most prosecutions were of poor women.

Although belief in witchcraft was common, there were always sceptics (e.g., Reginald Scot in *Discoverie of Witchcraft*, 1584). By the late 17th century educated opinion was generally doubtful. The last hanging for witchcraft occurred in 1685 (Alice Molland, in Exeter), and the last civil trial in 1717 (in Leicester). The 1604 statute was repealed in 1736, though belief in witchcraft persisted long afterwards.

WITCHCRAFT, SCOTLAND In 1563, with the Witchcraft Act, the Scottish Parliament made witchcraft (malevolent use of magical power) a capital offence. By 1736, when the British Parliament repealed the Act, many people (mostly women) had been executed (by burning or strangulation), though it is difficult to reach an accurate estimate. It is commonly suggested that executions numbered about 1500; if correct, Scotland would have been a leading country of persecution. (For comparison, possibly about 1000 were executed in the more populous England.) Most executions occurred between 1591 and 1662 during five 'witch scares'. The accused were usually tried by the Privy COUNCIL or High Court of JUSTICIARY. Those attacked as witches were usually 'wise women'. Many communities included a wise woman, who offered remedies, involving incantations, for medical and other problems. Persecutions usually happened during economic crises, primarily in the Lowlands where State authority was stronger. The last execution was in 1727.

WOLFENDEN COMMITTEE Short name for the Committee on Homosexual Offences and Prostitution, established by David Maxwell-Fyfe, British home secretary, in 1954 in response to increasing street prostitution and convictions for (illegal) homosexual activity by prominent men. It was chaired by Jack Wolfenden, a university vice-chancellor and experienced inquiry chairman. Presenters of evidence included homosexual men and representatives of Churches.

The resulting 'Wolfenden Report' (1957) argued that law should govern public order but leave private activity to be governed by personal morality. It recommended that law concerning street prostitution should be strengthened (soon implemented), and that homosexual activity in private by consenting adult males should be decriminalized. The latter proposal was not immediately implemented for fear it would undermine social cohesion, though the report encouraged public discussion of homosexuality. *See also* HOMOSEXUALITY, LAW RELATING TO; PERMISSIVE SOCIETY.

WOLLSTONECRAFT, MARY (b. 27 April 1759 at London, England; d. 10 Sept. 1797 at London, aged 38). Wollstonecraft, a schoolkeeper, began to write for a living in 1786 and became active in dissenting and RADICAL circles (also involving Richard PRICE). Enthused by the FRENCH REVOLUTION, she published *A Vindication of the Rights of Man* (1791), a reply to the *Reflections* of Edmund BURKE. Her book *A Vindication of the Rights of Women* (1792), criticizing women for their preoccupation with marriage instead of education, made her the best-known female political writer in Europe. From 1796 she lived with, then married (1797), fellow Radical William GODWIN, and died after giving birth to their daughter Mary (later, as Mary Shelley, the author of *Frankenstein*).

WOLSEY, THOMAS (b. 1470 or 1471 at Ipswich, Suffolk, England; d. 29 Nov. 1530 at Leicester, Leicestershire, England, aged about 59). A butcher's son, Wolsey became chaplain to King HENRY VII (1507) and served as a diplomat. Under HENRY VIII he was appointed almoner (1509) and a councillor (1510). He organized military expeditions to Spain (1512) and France (1513), and was rewarded with appointment as bishop of Lincoln and then archbishop of York (both 1514), and as CHANCELLOR (Dec. 1515). From 1514 he was Henry's chief minister. In 1518 Wolsey asserted Henry's importance in Europe with the treaty of LONDON. He was also created a cardinal (Sept. 1515). As a papal legate from 1518 (sole legate from 1519) he had authority over the English Church.

Wolsey supported Henry's attempts to reconquer land in France (raid into Picardy 1522, invasion 1523). When Henry decided on rapprochement, Wolsey negotiated the treaty of The More (Aug. 1525). But Wolsey's domestic policies, especially taxation for war, made him unpopular (*see* AMICABLE GRANT).

In July 1529 Wolsey failed to obtain annulment of Henry's marriage (*see* GREAT MATTER). In Oct., pressurized by Wolsey's enemies, Henry removed Wolsey from most of his posts. He was arrested for high TREASON (4 Nov. 1530) and died while travelling to the Tower of London. *See also* HAMPTON COURT.

WOMEN, ORDINATION OF Nonconformist denominations began the acceptance of women as ministers and clergy in the British Isles in the early 20th century. In England, the Unitarian Gertrude von Petzold was the first woman to qualify as a minister and receive charge of a chapel (1904), while Constance Coltman, a Congregationalist, was the first to be ordained to Christian ministry (1917, as Constance Todd). The Baptist Union of Great Britain and Ireland ordained women from 1922. The Methodist Church (of Great Britain) voted in favour of women ministers in 1938 and 1971 though delayed implementation until 1974.

Women were ordained as ministers by the (presbyterian) Church of Scotland from 1969, and by the Presbyterian Church in Ireland from 1973.

The ordination of women to the hierarchies of national episcopal Churches proved particularly controversial. Women were ordained as deacons from the 1980s, first in the Church in Wales (1980); and as priests from the 1990s, first in the Church of Ireland (1990). Ordination as bishops was agreed by the Church of Ireland in 1990; by the Scottish Episcopal Church in 2003; by the Church in Wales in 2013; by the Church of England in 2014. The first woman bishop was consecrated in Ireland in 2013 (Pat Storey). Ordination of women bishops in the Church of England began in 2015 (with Libby Lane), in the Church in Wales in 2017 (Joanna Penberthy), and in the Scottish Episcopal Church in 2018 (Anne Dyer). The Catholic Church retained its traditional male hierarchy.

WOMEN'S EDUCATION *see* GIRLS' AND WOMEN'S EDUCATION, BRITAIN; EDUCATION, IRELAND; UNIVERSITIES, IRELAND

WOMEN'S MOVEMENT 1850s TO 1918, GREAT BRITAIN Though women's rights were advocated from the late 18th century (*see* WOLLSTONECRAFT, MARY; MARTINEAU, HARRIET), campaigning began from the 1850s. Women such as Barbara Leigh Smith (or BODICHON) and Emily Davies sought mainly property rights and post-elementary education (*see* LANGHAM PLACE CIRCLE). Groups also campaigned from 1867 for parliamentary suffrage (*see* WOMEN'S SUFFRAGE MOVEMENT, GREAT BRITAIN). Predominantly middle-class, campaigners secured significant changes: women ratepayers could vote in municipal elections from 1869; legislation from 1870 expanded property ownership (*see* MARRIED WOMEN'S PROPERTY ACTS);

the CONTAGIOUS DISEASES ACTS were repealed (1886). Women became eligible for election to school boards (from 1870 in England and Wales, 1873 in Scotland), to boards of poor law guardians in England and Wales (from 1894), and to borough and county councils (from 1907). They also developed skills of public speaking and leadership (previously discouraged by the SEPARATE SPHERES concept) through participation in charitable societies. From the 1890s, aspirations were denoted by the term FEMINISM.

In the early 20th century some campaigning for parliamentary suffrage became more militant. Alongside peaceful activity by 'suffragists', the Women's Social and Political Union ('suffragettes') mixed rallies and marches with violence, especially against property (see PANKHURST FAMILY). When adult male suffrage was granted in 1918, women aged over 30, subject to other qualifications, became eligible to vote (see WORLD WAR I, IMPACT ON BRITISH SOCIETY). See also GIRLS' AND WOMEN'S EDUCATION; WOMEN, ORDINATION OF.

WOMEN'S MOVEMENT 1860s TO 1930s, IRELAND From the later 18th century some women, mostly middle-class Protestants, showed interest in writings by women's advocates (e.g., Mary WOLLSTONECRAFT) and became involved in philanthropic activities (e.g., visiting women prisoners). Women's contributions to education and social work also expanded during the 19th century as Catholic nuns became more numerous.

Campaigning for particular causes developed from the late 1860s. Two influential figures were Isabella Tod (1836–96), a presbyterian of Scottish-Irish parentage, and Anna Haslam (1829–1922), a Quaker. They campaigned, often with associates in Great Britain, for reform of property laws, access to education, repeal of the CONTAGIOUS DISEASES ACTS (1864–9), which operated in Ireland, and formal involvement in politics. Tod helped to expand educational opportunities (e.g., foundation of Ladies' Institute of Belfast, 1867; inclusion of girls in Intermediate Education (Ireland) Act, 1878), and organized Ireland's first suffrage society (in Belfast, 1871; see WOMEN'S SUFFRAGE MOVEMENT, IRELAND). Responses included the admission of women to examinations by the Royal College of Physicians of Ireland (1877, under permissive legislation), to university colleges (from 1880s), and to franchises (from 1887).

Women also participated in political movements (e.g., Ladies' Land League, 1881–2; see PARNELL, ANNA), and women's trade unions were founded from 1880. In the early 20th century many women gave priority over suffrage to HOME RULE (promotion or resistance) or Irish independence (e.g., Maud Gonne, founder in 1900 of Inghinidhe na hÉireann, 'Daughters of Ireland').

Nationalist women were influential in obtaining Irish independence; in the IRISH FREE STATE (founded 1922)

women received an equal citizenship, based on the EASTER RISING declaration (1916) and CONSTITUTION. But conditions were eroded in the 1920s–30s, despite opposition (e.g., exemption from jury service, 1927). Few women participated in politics, and the 1937 constitution protected women's domestic roles. See also MARRIED WOMEN'S PROPERTY ACTS.

WOMEN'S MOVEMENT FROM 1960s, GREAT BRITAIN Campaigning for women's concerns was revitalized from the late 1960s by new feminist analysis of social relationships and the student protest movement (see YOUTH CULTURE 1950s TO 1970s, GREAT BRITAIN). Demands were specified in 1970 at a national conference organized by the Women's Liberation Movement (WLM): (a) equal pay; (b) equal education and job opportunities; (c) free contraception and on-demand ABORTION; (d) free 24-hour nurseries.

High-profile political and media campaigns were launched by numerous groups, with WLM conferences acting as centres for debate (to 1978). Considerable success was achieved with the Sex Discrimination Act (1975) which established the Equal Opportunities Commission. Female authors and journalists, and businesswomen, became powerful symbols (e.g., Germaine Greer, Australian-born author of *The Female Eunuch*, 1970; Anita Roddick, founder in 1976 of 'The Body Shop', a cosmetics company). In the 1980s 'radical' and 'socialist' feminist groups emerged; other campaigns sought to influence the mainstream political agenda. The LABOUR PARTY and trade unions gave commitments to increase the number of female MPs and representatives, which were followed by other political parties. The UK's first female prime minister was a Conservative, Margaret THATCHER (1979–90), though she appointed only one woman to her CABINET (Baroness Young of Farnworth, 1981–3). Nicola Sturgeon became the first female first minister of Scotland (2014), and Theresa MAY the UK's second female prime minister (2016–19). See also WOMEN, ORDINATION OF.

WOMEN'S MOVEMENT FROM 1960s, IRELAND An increase of women in higher education and the workforce stirred interest in issues affecting women. In 1968 women's organizations in the Republic of Ireland, responding to a United Nations directive, elected a committee to brief the government (e.g., concerning equal pay, girls' education), and a government-established commission subsequently made recommendations. Radical movements influenced by US feminism also made demands. They included the Irish Women's Liberation Movement (1970–2), which flagrantly imported illegal contraceptive devices from Northern Ireland on a 'contraceptive train' (1971), and Irish Women United (1975–7), which sought ABORTION (also illegal).

Entry to the EUROPEAN ECONOMIC COMMUNITY (1973) began considerable legal change. Marriage-related restrictions in the Civil Service were abolished (1973) and discriminatory pay scales outlawed (1974). The Employment Equality Act (1977) prohibited general discrimination. Legal action ended the ban on import of contraceptive devices (1973), and limited provision was permitted from 1979. But many considered feminism as anti-Catholic and anti-Irish, and feared acceptance of abortion. A 'pro-life' campaign obtained a constitutional prohibition (1983). A referendum legalizing divorce was also defeated (1986; accepted 1995). But women gained prominence in public life, notably with the presidency of Mary ROBINSON (1990–7). Liberal provision of abortion was legalized in 2018.

In NORTHERN IRELAND women, especially Catholics, were prominent in the CIVIL RIGHTS MOVEMENT (1960s), and radical groups emerged (1970s). Women benefited from UK legislation but local activity was impeded by the TROUBLES (1968–90s), although in 1976 Mairéad Corrigan and Betty Williams co-founded 'Women for Peace', organized marches and received the Nobel Peace Prize. In 2016 Arlene Foster became the first female first minister. *See also* BIRTH CONTROL, SOUTHERN IRELAND.

WOMEN'S SUFFRAGE MOVEMENT, GREAT BRITAIN The demands of women for voting rights sprang from aspirations by middle-class women in the 1850s–60s (*see* LANGHAM PLACE CIRCLE) and from the broader campaign for PARLIAMENTARY REFORM. Lydia Becker (1827–90) founded the first national campaigning group in MANCHESTER in 1867, the National Society for Women's Suffrage. Local societies founded in following years affiliated to the NATIONAL UNION OF WOMEN'S SUFFRAGE SOCIETIES (formed 1897 by merger of two societies). Campaigners were called 'suffragists'.

Women ratepayers (e.g., spinsters, widows, or independent property owners) were granted votes in corporate towns in England and Wales in 1869, and in Scotland in 1882, and in the local government franchises granted in 1888 (England and Wales), 1889 (Scotland), and 1894 (England and Wales). Neither the Liberal nor the Conservative Party backed female parliamentary suffrage, so private members' Bills (from 1872) repeatedly failed.

Militant campaigners, nicknamed 'suffragettes', formed the Women's Social and Political Union (1903). The PANKHURSTS led them in dramatic demonstrations and low-level violence. This action was suspended on the outbreak of WORLD WAR I (1914).

Following agreement at an all-Party conference chaired by the speaker of the House of Commons (1916–17), the Representation of the People Act (1918) enfranchised women over 30 who (or whose husbands) were local government electors. All adult women could vote in the UK from 1928.

WOMEN'S SUFFRAGE MOVEMENT, IRELAND A movement developed in the 1860s–70s based on local organizations (e.g., North of Ireland Women's Suffrage Committee, founded 1871 by Isabella Tod; Dublin Women's Suffrage Association, 1876, later renamed). Campaigners were mainly middle-class Protestants. Women ratepayers were enfranchised in BELFAST in 1887 (in connection with drainage improvement), and in Blackrock and Kingstown (both in Co. Dublin) in 1894. From 1896 women could become Poor Law guardians. All other local franchises (in boroughs, rural and urban districts, and counties) were granted to women, on the same qualifications as men, in 1898, and women could become council members, except for counties (restriction removed 1911).

Campaigners continued to press for the parliamentary franchise and eligibility for the UK Parliament. Hanna and Francis SHEEHY SKEFFINGTON, despairing of peaceful tactics, launched the Irish Women's Franchise League (1908) which permitted physical protests (e.g., breaking windows). The Irish Women's Suffrage Federation (1911) co-ordinated efforts by several scattered organizations. The movement was weakened by the HOME RULE problem: many supporters of women's suffrage considered it more important to obtain, or defeat, Home Rule.

In Feb. 1918, despite opposition from many Irish MPs, UK-wide legislation granted the parliamentary franchise to women aged 30 and over who (or whose husbands) were local government electors. Equal franchise (from 21) was granted in the IRISH FREE STATE by its constitution (1922). *See also* FRANCHISE, IRELAND 1801 TO 1921.

WOOD'S HALFPENCE AFFAIR Controversy in Ireland caused when a patent was sold in 1722 to William Wood (of Wolverhampton, England) for issuing bronze halfpence and farthings for Ireland. Opponents (including members of the Irish Parliament, government officers and, especially, Jonathan SWIFT) resented lack of consultation and feared the economic consequences. Robert WALPOLE, British prime minister, withdrew the patent in 1725. *See also* CARTERET, LORD, AND IRELAND; PROTESTANT ASCENDANCY.

WOODSTOCK, TREATY OF Agreed on 30 April 1247 (at Woodstock, Oxfordshire, England); between LLYWELYN AP GRUFFUDD and his brother Owain, joint rulers of GWYNEDD (NW Wales), and HENRY III, king of England; it followed English attacks on Gwynedd. Llywelyn and Owain were recognized as rulers of Gwynedd, holding by Henry's grant, but conceded territories (including Y BERFEDDWLAD). *See also* ANGLO-WELSH RELATIONS, 6TH–13TH CENTURIES.

WOODVILLE, ELIZABETH (b. *c.*1437 in England; d. 8 June 1492 at Bermondsey, Surrey, England, aged 55).

Elizabeth, a widow, secretly married King EDWARD IV on 1 May 1464 (marriage publicized Sept.). During the restoration of HENRY VI (1470–1) Elizabeth took sanctuary in WESTMINSTER Abbey.

After Edward's death (9 April 1483), the duke of Gloucester seized the new king, EDWARD V (a minor). Elizabeth returned to Westminster Abbey. Gloucester seized the throne (26 June; see RICHARD III) and Elizabeth's two sons disappeared (summer). Her marriage was formally declared invalid (Jan. 1484), and she submitted to Richard (March). After HENRY VII deposed Richard (1485), he married Elizabeth's daughter Elizabeth of York, uniting the Lancastrian and Yorkist lineages (see YORKIST–LANCASTRIAN CONFLICT). Elizabeth retired to Bermondsey nunnery (1487).

WOODVILLE FAMILY A noble family of modest origins in Northamptonshire (C England) whose wealth and status increased dramatically from the mid 15th century through fortuitous marriages. Richard Woodville married the widow of John, duke of BEDFORD (late 1430s), and was created Lord Rivers in 1448. His daughter Elizabeth WOODVILLE, one of 11 children, married King EDWARD IV in 1464.

Edward promoted Elizabeth's relatives. Lord Rivers was created Earl Rivers and appointed TREASURER in 1466, and became dominant at court. (He was executed during the attempted rebellion by Richard, earl of WARWICK, in 1469.) The Woodvilles were even more influential during the 1470s. After the accession of EDWARD V (April 1483), a minor, the Woodvilles' influence was feared by the 'protector', the duke of Gloucester. He had Anthony Woodville, 2nd Earl Rivers, arrested and executed (30 April, 25 June) before he seized the throne (see RICHARD III).

WOOLLEN TEXTILE INDUSTRY, ENGLAND see CLOTH INDUSTRY, ENGLAND

WOOLTON, LORD (b. 23 Aug. 1883 at Salford, Lancashire, England; d. 14 Dec. 1964 at Walberton, West Sussex, England, aged 81). A social scientist and successful retailer, Frederick Marquis became involved with the British government in the 1920s–30s. Knighted in 1935, he participated in planning for wartime, and in 1939 was created Lord Woolton. As minister of food (1940–3), during WORLD WAR II, he implemented an efficient RATIONING system. (A vegetable pie for which he publicized the recipe was nicknamed the 'Woolton pie'.) Woolton's independence made him an effective minister of reconstruction (1943–5). In 1946 he joined the CONSERVATIVE PARTY and served as chairman 1946–55. He was created a viscount (1953) and earl (1955). See also WORLD WAR II, IMPACT ON BRITISH SOCIETY.

WOOL TRADE, ENGLAND Exporting increased from the late 11th century mainly to supply the expanding cloth industry in Flanders (part of modern Belgium and adjacent areas). In the 12th–14th centuries wool was England's pre-eminent export commodity. Much wool left through East Coast ports, notably Boston (Lincolnshire). In the 1270s, following disputes with Flanders, Italian merchants largely replaced Flemings as the main exporters. Exports were taxed from 1275, resulting in permanent arrangements for CUSTOMS collection.

Exports peaked in 1304–11 at 39,500 sacks per year (average). From 1313 kings established STAPLES (compulsory places of sale and taxation) at varying places. From 1363 there was a single staple at CALAIS (English-held town in NE France), governed by the first English trading company (fellowship of the staple). English merchants now dominated exporting (except for wool exported by Italians from SOUTHAMPTON to the Mediterranean under special licence).

Exports declined significantly from the 1360s due to the HUNDRED YEARS WAR, taxation, and demand from English cloth-makers. 20,000 sacks were exported in 1390, 9000 in 1440. Calais was lost in 1558. By the 1580s little wool was exported. Wool exporting was prohibited in 1614. See also FOREIGN TRADE, ENGLAND, 1066 TO EARLY 17TH CENTURY.

WORCESTER A city in W England, by the R. Severn; centre of Worcestershire.

Originally a Roman small town (1st–5th centuries), Worcester was revived as a bishop's see for the HWICCE (679 or 680) and expanded by Æthelred, ruler of western MERCIA (890s). Worcestershire was created in the mid 10th century.

Worcester remained a small county and cathedral town. King JOHN and Arthur (son of King HENRY VIII) were buried in the cathedral (1216, 1502 respectively). A CLOTH INDUSTRY flourished in the late 15th–18th centuries, and new industries developed in the 18th–19th centuries (porcelain, glove making, engineering). Worcester retained a mixed economy in the 21st century. A college was upgraded as the University of Worcester in 2005.

Est. popn: 1086, 2000; 1300, 4000; 1600, 5000; 1800, 11,000; 1900, 46,000; 2000, 93,000.

WORCESTER, BATTLE OF Fought on 3 Sept. 1651 at WORCESTER (Worcestershire, W England); the final significant battle of the mid-17th-century conflict (see CIVIL WARS). The Army of the English Commonwealth, commanded by Oliver CROMWELL, defeated a Royalist Scottish army led by King CHARLES II, which had invaded England to rally Royalist support. Charles escaped to France. See also RESOLUTIONERS; COMMONWEALTH AND PROTECTORATE.

WORCESTER, TREATY OF Agreed during March 1218 (at Worcester, Worcestershire, England); the high point of relations between LLYWELYN AP IORWERTH, prince of GWYNEDD (NW Wales), and King HENRY III of England. Henry recognized Llywelyn's territorial gains, including Y BERFEDDWLAD, and gave Llywelyn two English castles in SW Wales and lands of Gwenwynwyn of POWYS (C Wales). *See also* ANGLO-WELSH RELATIONS, 6TH–13TH CENTURIES.

WORCESTER AFFAIR An anti-English episode in Scotland. On 12 Aug. 1704 the English ship *Worcester* was seized in the Firth of Forth by the Company of Scotland in retaliation for the seizure of their last ship by the EAST INDIA COMPANY. The *Worcester*'s crew was found guilty, without cause, of piracy (March 1705) and the captain and two others were hanged (11 April). The Scottish Privy Council allowed the executions to proceed to appease public anger over England's role in the DARIEN SCHEME and over the ALIEN ACT.

WORCESTER HOUSE DECLARATION Name for the 'Declaration Concerning Ecclesiastical Affairs', a proposed religious settlement for England and Wales issued by King CHARLES II on 25 Oct. 1660. It was based on discussions by Charles with Church of England clergy of conformist and presbyterian attitudes (the latter including Richard BAXTER) held at Worcester House, London (residence of Edward Hyde). It advocated inclusion of presbyterians (opponents of episcopal government) within the Church by allowing lesser clergy to assist bishops, omission of some ceremonies, and revision of the PRAYER BOOK. The proposals were rejected by the CONVENTION PARLIAMENT. *See also* PURITANISM, ENGLAND; RESTORATION, ENGLAND AND WALES; SAVOY CONFERENCE.

WORDSWORTH, WILLIAM (b. 7 April 1770 at Cockermouth, Cumberland, England; d. 23 April 1850 at Grasmere, Westmorland, England, aged 80). A poet from childhood, Wordsworth visited France 1791–2 and was enthused by the FRENCH REVOLUTION. Great Britain's subsequent war with France caused him consternation. In 1798 he and Samuel Taylor Coleridge published *Lyrical Ballads*, a celebration of nature and the ordinary. Wordsworth lived mostly in the Lake District (NW England) from 1799. In later life he became more conservative. He was appointed poet laureate in 1843. Wordsworth's emphasis on the senses rather than reason in poetic response influenced European Romanticism. *See also* ENGLISH LITERATURE, ENGLAND.

WORKERS' WEEKLY INCIDENT A political episode in Great Britain in 1924 which followed the charging of J.R. Campbell, editor of the COMMUNIST newspaper *Workers'* *Weekly*, with inciting soldiers to mutiny (5 Aug.). When the prosecution was dropped, Conservatives accused ministers in the Labour government with interference in the justice system. Defeat on the matter in Parliament brought down the government of Ramsay MACDONALD (9 Oct.).

WORKS, BOARD OF, IRELAND A government agency created in 1831 by Edward Stanley, CHIEF SECRETARY FOR IRELAND, from several public bodies with power to make loans for public works or private improvements. The Board was an important source of funds for economic development (e.g., supporting land drainage, canals, railways), and the main public provider of employment (e.g., road and bridge work) during the GREAT FAMINE (1845–9). It was transferred in 1922 to the Department of Finance of the IRISH FREE STATE. *See also* GOVERNMENT, IRELAND 19TH–20TH CENTURIES; DERBY, 14TH EARL OF.

WORLD WAR I, BRITISH ARMY When war began (Aug. 1914), the Army comprised almost 250,000 regular soldiers. All were volunteers, by contrast with conscripted Continental European armies. By end Dec., Parliament authorized recruitment of another 4 million troops. British and Irish men responded enthusiastically, some joining 'Pals battalions' recruited from places or businesses. Senior (commissioned) officers were selected from university and public school men. By end 1914 over 1 million men volunteered.

Declining recruitment during 1915 was met by harder campaigning and reduction of physical standards. Men and women were registered in Aug. 1915. The 'Derby scheme' (Oct.–Dec.) investigated whether recruitment targets could be met voluntarily: men were asked to 'attest' (declare readiness to serve). The scale of refusal resulted in CONSCRIPTION (Jan. 1916, mainly of unmarried men aged 19–40; extended to married men in May); but exclusions (e.g., for inadequate health) resulted in lower recruitment (only 820,000 in 1917). The upper age for conscription was raised to 50 in April 1918.

By 1918 the Army was shrinking. When the government decided to extend conscription to Ireland (April), this provoked resistance (*see* WORLD WAR I, IMPACT ON IRELAND). In all, 5.7 million men served. *See also* PACIFISM.

WORLD WAR I, BRITISH INVOLVEMENT Great Britain declared war against Germany on 4 Aug. 1914, after Germany invaded Belgium, whose independence Britain had guaranteed. This aligned Britain with FRANCE and RUSSIA. A British Expeditionary Force under John FRENCH helped slow the German advance across Flanders. A 'Western Front' through Belgium and France stabilized in Oct. 1914 and varied little until 1918. Allied and German trenches faced each other, separated by 'no man's land'

(British in northern sector). Offensives at Neuve Chapelle (March 1915) and Loos (Sept. 1915) secured small gains. The deadlock encouraged eastern strategies aimed at nullifying Germany's allies, Turkey and Austria-Hungary. None succeeded. The GALLIPOLI CAMPAIGN (1915) failed after eight months. An Anglo-French force landing at Salonika (Oct. 1915) was obstructed by Greek political divisions. An invasion of Mesopotamia initially ended with surrender (Kut-al-Imara, April 1916).

The Royal NAVY meanwhile drove German warships from the seas and imposed a blockade. Germany retaliated with submarine warfare in the Atlantic (Feb.–Sept. 1915). The naval battle at Jutland (31 May–1 June 1916) appeared inconclusive, but Germany's battle fleet stayed in port thereafter. Zeppelins (airships) raided Britain from June 1915. The Royal Flying Corps engaged in reconnaissance and aerial combat.

Douglas HAIG ineffectually committed British armies to the SOMME on the Western Front (1916). Attacks in 1917 at Arras (April), YPRES and CAMBRAI also produced no decisive breakthrough. German resumption of unrestricted submarine warfare (Feb. 1917) gravely affected British shipping until convoys were devised. US involvement (from April 1917) was offset by Russian departure (Dec. 1917). Minor successes occurred in Palestine, Mesopotamia and Africa.

The Allies repulsed a final German offensive in July–Aug. 1918. A rapid advance from Salonika defeated Bulgaria. Turkey and Austria-Hungary collapsed. Germany surrendered, accepting an armistice (11 Nov.). The PARIS PEACE CONFERENCE followed. British, Irish and imperial forces totalled 9,669,000; 947,000 were killed. Mobilization from the UK totalled 6,120,000; 886,000 were killed. *See also* ROYAL AIR FORCE.

WORLD WAR I, IMPACT ON BRITISH ECONOMY

After the outbreak (Aug. 1914), the government took control of RAILWAYS, much shipping, and sugar and wheat supplies. Its powers were extended according to necessity: DILUTION OF LABOUR and control of munitions factories and workshops were instituted in March 1915; in Aug., the Munitions of War Act enabled other concerns to be 'controlled'. During 1917–18 there was extensive government purchase of raw materials and price controls. Controls over COAL MINING (implemented 1915–18) amounted to virtual NATIONALIZATION. Steel-making and ship-building capacity were expanded (continuing beyond the war), and the acreage of arable agriculture (from 1917), though control of food was more important. Trade union membership was encouraged to facilitate bargaining (increased 4–8 million, 1913–19). New production techniques were promoted in industry.

A decline in exports created an adverse balance of payments (from 1915), and loss of some export markets.

About 10% of overseas assets were liquidated. Industrial overcapacity, losses of markets, and indebtedness left the post-war economy (from Nov. 1918) much weakened. *See also* ECONOMY, STATE INVOLVEMENT, BRITAIN.

WORLD WAR I, IMPACT ON BRITISH EMPIRE AND COMMONWEALTH

Military forces from DOMINIONS and colonies supported the British war effort (1914–18), fighting on the Western Front and in the Middle East (*see* GALLIPOLI CAMPAIGN). The Empire also supplied food and vital raw materials. The government of SOUTH AFRICA suppressed a pro-German internal rebellion and conquered German South West Africa. The British prime minister, David LLOYD GEORGE, created an Imperial War Cabinet to co-ordinate imperial involvement (1917–18).

The war had important repercussions for the Empire. Britain and the dominions were styled an 'Imperial Commonwealth' from 1917, a conception that led to the BALFOUR DEFINITION (1926) and Statute of WESTMINSTER (1931). An Empire delegation also attended the PARIS PEACE CONFERENCE. Nationalism was stimulated. The British had to concede reforms in Indian government (*see* INDIAN INDEPENDENCE). The war also expanded the Empire, as Britain was awarded former German colonies and Turkish provinces as MANDATES. *See also* BALFOUR DECLARATION.

WORLD WAR I, IMPACT ON BRITISH POLITICS AND GOVERNMENT

When war began in 1914 only a radical fringe opposed hostilities but the apparent wartime irrelevance of LIBERALISM weakened the governing LIBERAL PARTY, which dithered over whether to introduce CONSCRIPTION. To postpone a general election, the prime minister, H.H. ASQUITH, formed a coalition with the CONSERVATIVE and LABOUR PARTIES (25 May 1915). The IRISH PARLIAMENTARY PARTY declined to be involved.

A Ministry of Munitions (created 19 June 1915, under David LLOYD GEORGE) pioneered industrial intervention, while increased trade union power strengthened the Labour Party. The Cabinet argued over strategy: 'Westerners' against 'Easterners' (i.e., whether Germany could be defeated only on the Western Front or from eastern positions).

Lloyd George, calling for greater vigour and supported by the Conservative Bonar LAW, forced Asquith to resign (7 Dec. 1916). Lloyd George became prime minister, but the Liberal Party split. Lloyd George founded a Cabinet secretariat under Maurice HANKEY and ran a small WAR CABINET until Oct. 1919. He created Ministries of Labour, Shipping and Food (and later National Service). DOMINION ministers were included in an Imperial War Cabinet (1917–18). Efforts towards 'social reconstruction' occurred, including an Education Act and PARLIAMENTARY REFORM (1918).

WORLD WAR I, IMPACT ON BRITISH SOCIETY

The war's duration (1914–18), industrial requirements and impact on the civilian population have caused it to be deemed the first 'total war'. Almost 5 million people, mostly men and boys, joined the armed forces, devastating family life and communities. (Allowances and pensions for dependants were introduced in Oct. 1915.) The government obtained extensive powers through DEFENCE OF THE REALM ACTS, including censorship of the press, right to place workers, and controls over public houses and alcohol (*see* ALCOHOL LICENSING LAW, ENGLAND AND WALES). German airships ('Zeppelins') made about 40 bombing raids, causing little damage but creating fear.

Women extensively replaced men in paid work (e.g., transport and administration), and were recruited for war production. About 700,000 worked in factories, including munitions plants (*see* DILUTION). Their incomes often improved children's health. The doubling of income tax and its extension to more workers, together with inflation, reduced real incomes. The government sought to maintain food supplies, but shortages in late 1917 led to RATIONING. Popular demand for improved post-war conditions in return for wartime sacrifices prompted the government to create a Ministry of Reconstruction (1917). Limited parliamentary franchise was conceded to women in 1918; *see* PARLIAMENTARY REFORM. *See also* WORLD WAR I, BRITISH ARMY; DAYLIGHT SAVING; COUNCIL HOUSING.

WORLD WAR I, IMPACT ON IRELAND

The UK's entry into war (4 Aug. 1914) halted a crisis in Ireland: Home Rule was about to be enacted, but armed resistance seemed likely in ULSTER (N Ireland). Both Home Rule nationalists and Unionists joined the British Army (about 150,000, of whom 49,000 were killed; *see* ULSTER VOLUNTEER FORCE; IRISH VOLUNTEERS). Ireland's economy benefited from war, especially agriculture which enjoyed higher prices. Industry was stimulated by demand for ships, aircraft, clothing, etc.

Republican nationalists used the cover of war to mount an uprising (April 1916; *see* EASTER RISING). Though it was crushed, it prompted the British government to seek a solution to the Home Rule problem, but without success (*see* HOME RULE MOVEMENT, IRELAND). In April 1918 the government took powers to introduce conscription in Ireland; it provoked outrage and the extensive transfer of public support from the IRISH PARLIAMENTARY PARTY to the republican SINN FÉIN. At the post-war election (Dec. 1918) Sinn Féin won most constituencies and then created its own Assembly which re-proclaimed an Irish republic: *see* IRISH FREE STATE, FOUNDING OF.

WORLD WAR II, BOMBING OFFENSIVE AGAINST GERMANY

When the ROYAL AIR FORCE (RAF) first attacked industrial targets in Germany (May–June 1940), it suffered heavy losses in daylight raids, and night bombing was inaccurate. Bomber Command therefore adopted the strategy of 'area bombing' (i.e., carpet bombing of built-up areas) in early 1942. Arthur HARRIS, commander-in-chief from Feb. 1942, argued that systematic devastation of German cities would end the war by destroying production facilities and morale. From Jan. 1943 the RAF operated in co-ordination with the United States Army Air Force: the former continued night-time area bombing while the latter focused on key military targets.

British attacks included the 'Thousand Bomber Raid' on Cologne (May 1942), Operation Gomorrah against Hamburg ((July–Aug. 1943), and the Battle of Berlin (Nov. 1943–March 1944). Operation Thunderclap against Dresden (13–14 Feb. 1945) caused some 100,000 casualties.

The strategic value and moral justification of the bombing offensive have been disputed. It enabled Britain to assist the USSR in its war with Germany by pressuring German heartlands, and to retaliate against Germany, while preparations were being made for a 'second front' in western Europe (instituted June 1944). Germany was forced to divert resources to air defence, but its war industries did not collapse until late 1944, and civilian morale was never broken.

WORLD WAR II, BRITISH INVOLVEMENT

After Germany invaded Poland on 1 Sept. 1939, the UK honoured its ANGLO-POLISH GUARANTEE and, with France, declared war (3 Sept.), though conflict began only in April 1940 with unsuccessful intervention in Norway (*see* PHONEY WAR). When Germany invaded France (May), British forces had to retreat (*see* DUNKIRK, WITHDRAWAL FROM). ITALY declared war on Britain (10 June) and Germany occupied the CHANNEL ISLANDS, but the battle of BRITAIN (July–Oct.) averted invasion. Bombing of UK cities continued into 1941 and thereafter re-occurred periodically. Mercantile shipping was threatened from 1939 (*see* ATLANTIC, BATTLE OF THE).

The British occupied Iraq, Syria and Persia (*see* IRAN) and tried to defend GREECE (April–May 1941). Early successes against Italians in N Africa were reversed by German reinforcements (Feb.). German invasion of the USSR (June) prompted an Anglo-Soviet alliance (12 July 1941).

Japanese attacks on American and British Pacific bases (from 7 Dec. 1941), caused the USA to join the war. Japan humiliated Britain by capturing SINGAPORE (Feb. 1942), though India was defended.

In 1942–3, Italo-German forces were defeated at EL ALAMEIN and swept from N Africa. This, coinciding with Soviet victory at Stalingrad (Jan. 1943), proved the turning point. Despite calls for a second front in N Europe, Winston CHURCHILL promoted a Mediterranean-based strategy, while continuing a bombing offensive against Germany. In July, Anglo-American forces invaded Italy (surrendered 3 Sept.), but Germany contained the advance.

In 1944 the Allies liberated France (*see* OVERLORD). The Germans counter-attacked in the Ardennes, Belgium (Dec. 1944), but British troops crossed the Rhine on 23 March 1945. Soviet forces reached Berlin. 'Victory in Europe' Day was 8 May. Japan conceded on 14 Aug. ('VJ' Day), after being attacked with ATOMIC WEAPONS (surrendered formally, 2 Sept.).

The UK engaged 5,896,000 men, of whom 265,000 died. Bombing claimed 60,000 British civilian lives. Cost: £34.4 billion. *See also* BROOKE, ALAN; MONTGOMERY, BERNARD; WORLD WAR II, BOMBING OFFENSIVE AGAINST GERMANY.

WORLD WAR II, DEBATE OVER ORIGINS In *The Origins of the Second World War* (1961), the British historian A.J.P. Taylor (1906–90) challenged the view that the German Nazi leader Adolf Hitler intentionally caused war in western Europe in 1939. Taylor argued that Hitler sought only, by opportunistic means, the undoing of the treaty of VERSAILLES (1919). France and Great Britain allowed Hitler to break international treaties and remilitarize the Rhineland in 1936. After Germany secured Austria (1938) and the Sudetenland (from Czechoslovakia, 1939) by applying pressure, Hitler could never have expected Britain to abandon APPEASEMENT and fight a hopeless war for Danzig (a 'Free City' which proclaimed union with Germany on 1 Sept. 1939). Other historians (e.g., H.R. Trevor-Roper) retorted that Hitler's earlier statements (e.g., in his book *Mein Kampf*, 'My Struggle') and later actions prove that military conquest was always his objective. The dispute between historians has involved moral judgement as well as conventional historical research.

WORLD WAR II, IMPACT ON BRITISH ECONOMY Fear of war stimulated the economy from 1936 through rearmament (e.g., expansion of aircraft production). Other economic preparations included announcement of 'reserved occupations' (spring 1939), to retain skilled labour, and subsidized ploughing of grassland for cereal production (1939).

After the outbreak (Sept. 1939), the government controlled RAILWAYS, and regulated and reduced 'ordinary' production and consumption through RATIONING and higher taxes, pressing workers to transfer to war-related production. Aircraft remained a priority: production rose from 2800 in 1938 to 26,000 in 1943. Overall economic mobilization was sluggish until late 1941, following the appointment (May 1940) of Ernest BEVIN as minister of labour and national service, and policy development (including routine representation of unions). Unemployment was reduced, and by 1943, 3.3 million people worked in armaments

production (excluding chemicals, explosives, iron and steel). Government generally preferred indirect means, rather than direct controls, to manage industry, such as DILUTION OF LABOUR (e.g., agreements with engineering unions, summer 1940), direction of skilled workers (from March 1941), and allocations of materials. The aircraft, electrical, general engineering and chemicals industries, and AGRICULTURE, benefited from the war, though bombing caused widespread damage to industry. Shortage of labour affected coalmining, for which workers were conscripted from 1943 (so-called 'Bevin boys').

The cost of war, met by sales of overseas assets, borrowing, US 'lend-lease', and Canadian aid, reduced the UK to a major international debtor. War damage and loss of export markets impeded post-war recovery. *See also* ECONOMY, STATE INVOLVEMENT, BRITAIN.

WORLD WAR II, IMPACT ON BRITISH EMPIRE AND COMMONWEALTH As in WORLD WAR I (1914–18), imperial manpower bolstered Great Britain's capacity to wage war (1939–45). For example, the success of the Eighth Army at EL ALAMEIN (late 1942) depended upon contingents from Australia, New Zealand, South Africa and India. But nationalism within the Empire was stronger than in the 1914–18 conflict. In INDIA, the decision of the viceroy, the marquess of Linlithgow, to declare war (Sept. 1939) without consulting Indian political parties resulted (Aug. 1942) in the threat of civil disobedience if Britain withheld independence. Meanwhile defeats in SE Asia, especially the fall of SINGAPORE (Feb. 1942), led many Australians to accuse Britain of failing to safeguard it against Japanese attack. The war proved a major catalyst for DECOLONIZATION.

WORLD WAR II, IMPACT ON BRITISH POLITICS AND GOVERNMENT The pre-war NATIONAL GOVERNMENT, led by Neville CHAMBERLAIN (Conservative), remained in office during the PHONEY WAR (from Sept. 1939). But MPs' anger over the failure of British intervention against Germany in Norway caused Chamberlain to resign as prime minister (10 May 1940). Winston CHURCHILL (Conservative) formed an all-party coalition government. Heading a five-man WAR CABINET, he concentrated on strategy and diplomacy, leaving planning for the 'home front' to Clement ATTLEE (his deputy), Ernest BEVIN, and Herbert MORRISON, and also to non-party men such as John ANDERSON and Lord WOOLTON. Conservatives associated with the pre-war APPEASEMENT policy were sidelined.

The emergence of the COMMON WEALTH PARTY (founded 1942) reinforced a desire, and planning, for post-war social and economic reconstruction. The war created a new centre-left consensus in politics, exemplified by the wide support for the 'Beveridge Report' (Dec. 1942),

BUTLER EDUCATION ACT (1944), and proposals for full employment.

After Germany was defeated, the Labour Party left the coalition (25 May 1945) and Churchill headed a Conservative 'caretaker' government, pending the outcome of a general election. Labour won the election, and Attlee formed a government on 27 July. The war against Japan ended on 14 Aug.

WORLD WAR II, IMPACT ON BRITISH SOCIETY

The government openly prepared for war from early 1938, 18 months before the outbreak, primarily fearing large-scale German bombing. 'Air Raid Precautions' wardens were recruited from March; during the MUNICH CRISIS (Sept.), gas masks were issued and evacuation began. Information was distributed. On 1 Sept. 1939, two days before war was declared, mass EVACUATION started and nightly blackouts were instigated (street lights, windows). Men aged 18–41 were made liable for military CONSCRIPTION (4 Sept.). RATIONING was introduced (extensive from Jan. 1940). RADIO was an important news source. Censorship was restrained.

Little happened until April 1940 when German offensives began in western Europe (see PHONEY WAR). Invasion was feared until late 1942, and prompted formation of the Local Defence Volunteers (May 1940; Aug., renamed Home Guard). From May 1940, Prime Minister Winston CHURCHILL provided leadership. Between 7 Sept. 1940 and 21 May 1941 there was relentless aerial bombing of LONDON and other centres, followed by further attacks (see BLITZ). Bombing destroyed 475,000 houses and damaged 3.5 million.

The Emergency Powers Act (May 1940) gave government control over industrial resources and workers. Women were recruited into industry and onto the land (e.g., 87,000 in Women's Land Army, 1943). By 1944, 48% of civil servants were women. From Dec. 1941 there was limited conscription of women, for armed services, civil defence and industry. By June 1945, 4.6 million people were in the armed forces. From 1942 to 1944, Britain also experienced the presence of several million American servicemen.

Planning for post-war social improvement encouraged morale, especially following the 'Beveridge Report' (Dec. 1942; see BEVERIDGE, WILLIAM) and BUTLER EDUCATION ACT (1944). Public opinion moved leftwards, with the LABOUR PARTY winning the 1945 general election. The war entailed 60,000 civilian deaths. See also WORLD WAR II, IMPACT ON IRELAND; DAYLIGHT SAVING.

WORLD WAR II, IMPACT ON IRELAND In southern Ireland the taoiseach (premier) Éamon DE VALERA

declared neutrality on 2 Sept. 1939 and subsequently resisted pressure to join the Allies. The wartime period (1939–45) was known as 'The Emergency'. Informally the Irish government assisted the Allied war effort (e.g., tolerating active British intelligence agents, repatriating crashed pilots). About 175,000 men emigrated to Great Britain to take advantage of labour shortages. Their remittances helped to sustain the southern Irish economy. An estimated 42,000 people also joined the Allied armed forces.

NORTHERN IRELAND entered the war as part of the UK. Its heavy industries manufactured munitions (e.g., ships, planes). Unionists pressed for the extension of military conscription to Northern Ireland, but the British government refused for fear of inflaming opposition from nationalists. In April–May 1941 BELFAST was heavily bombed by the Germans, killing over 1100 people. See also SOUTHERN IRELAND FROM 1922.

WREN, CHRISTOPHER (b. 20 Oct. 1632 at East Knoyle, Wiltshire, England; d. 25 Feb. 1723 at Westminster, Middlesex, England, aged 90). Originally a mathematician and scientist, Wren practised as an architect from the early 1660s. He was responsible for the rebuilding of many London churches after the GREAT FIRE (1666), notably St Paul's Cathedral (under construction 1675–1710). As surveyor general to the king 1669–1714 he designed many other public buildings. Wren perfected a distinctive English style of baroque architecture, although shortly after his death it was replaced by a more academic, 'Palladian' style. See also ARCHITECTURE, BRITAIN; ROYAL SOCIETY; WINCHESTER.

WREXHAM A town in NE Wales; centre of Wrexham unitary authority (Welsh, Wrecsam); both names mean 'Water-meadow of Wryhtel'.

A market town from the 12th or 13th century, Wrexham expanded as a wool-trading centre in the late 14th century. The parish church was rebuilt, greatly enlarged, c.1463. By 1550 Wrexham almost matched CARMARTHEN, Wales's largest town, in population. Elihu Yale (1649–1721), after whom Yale University (Connecticut, USA) was named, was buried in Wrexham churchyard.

Wrexham was briefly Wales's largest town c.1800, thanks to late 18th-century industrial expansion (iron working, coal mining). Further expansion of coal mining around Wrexham in the 19th century stimulated continuing growth. Wrexham was granted self-government as a BOROUGH in 1857. Mining declined in the 20th century (the last mine closed in 1986), and from 1945 light industry developed (chemicals, plastics, food processing). In the 20th century Wrexham was the largest town in N Wales.

Wrexham was in the kingdom of N Powys (to 1272), the Marcher lordship of Bromfield and Yale (1282–1536), Denbighshire (1536–1974), and Clwyd county (1974–96), and then became the centre of Wrexham county borough unitary authority.

Est. popn: 1300, 800; 1600, 2000; 1800, 6900; 1900, 14,500; 2000, 42,500.

WRIT OE term meaning 'a writing'; in Anglo-Saxon England, a written instruction sent from a senior royal officer to a local officer (e.g., SHERIFF). They are known in WESSEX (S England) from the reign of ALFRED (871–99). Writs (or writ-charters) also served as property titles. Latin became their standard language in the reign of WILLIAM I (1066–86).

Writs were extensively developed from the 12th century for legal purposes (e.g., POSSESSORY ASSIZES). They were used in Scotland from c.1100, in Ireland from 1210, in the MARCH OF WALES from the mid 13th century, and in other parts of Wales from 1284.

WULFHERE (fl. c.655–75). A son of the pagan King PENDA (d. 655) of MERCIA (C England), Wulfhere, a Christian, became king in 658 when Mercians revolted against OSWIU, the king of Bernicia and Deira (NE England) who had annexed Mercia.

Wulfhere acted as overking of southern Anglo-Saxon kingdoms. In 661 he ravaged the Gewisse (see WESSEX); in the 670s his authority was acknowledged by Frithuwold, sub-king of Surrey (SE England). Around 674 Wulfhere attacked EGFRITH of Bernicia and Deira but was defeated. Wulfhere was a founder and benefactor of churches in Mercia and elsewhere. See also CHAD; KINGSHIP, ANGLO-SAXON.

WULFRED (fl. from 803; d. 24 March 832 at Canterbury, Kent, Wessex). Archbishop of CANTERBURY from 805, Wulfred was suspended from office (817 or 818) by the Pope at the request of CENWULF, king of Mercia. He had alienated Cenwulf by asserting authority over two MINSTERS in Kent (part of Mercia), infringing royal rights. He was reinstated (821) after conceding land and money to Cenwulf. Wulfred lost authority and further land after Wessex seized Kent (see EGBERT).

WULFSTAN (fl. from 996 in England; d. 28 May 1023 at York, Yorkshire, England). The monk Wulfstan was bishop of London 996–1002, bishop of Worcester 1002–16, and archbishop of YORK 1002–23. He sustained the ideals of the TENTH-CENTURY REFORMATION. He wrote and preached influential homilies on Christian life, notably the 'Sermon of the Wolf to the English' (1014) which denounced sin and crime, and treachery against kings. He composed law codes for both King ÆTHELRED II and King CNUT. See also LAW, ENGLAND BEFORE 1066.

WULFSTAN OF WORCESTER (b. c.1008 at Itchington, Warwickshire, England; d. 20 Jan. 1095 at Worcester, Worcestershire, England, aged about 86). After serving as a secular priest, Wulfstan became a monk at Worcester Cathedral priory. He was prior from c.1055, until made bishop of WORCESTER (1062). He systematically toured his diocese, and promoted clerical celibacy. After the Norman invasion (1066) he submitted to King WILLIAM I and was loyal to WILLIAM II. As the last Anglo-Saxon bishop, Wulfstan conveyed English values to the Norman-dominated Church.

WYATT, THOMAS (b. c.1503 at Allington, Kent, England; d. Oct. 1542 at Sherborne, Dorset, England, aged about 39). Wyatt held posts in the household of King HENRY VIII from 1524 and undertook diplomatic missions in Continental Europe in the 1520s–30s (knighted probably 1535). He was imprisoned in 1536, because his family was associated with Anne BOLEYN, and in 1541, after the fall of his patron Thomas CROMWELL. Wyatt translated literary works into prose and verse, and composed poetry. He was the first known English author of sonnets. His son Thomas (1521–54) rebelled against MARY I (see WYATT'S REBELLION). See also ENGLISH LITERATURE, ENGLAND.

WYATT'S REBELLION In England, a rising against the planned 'Spanish marriage' of Queen MARY I, 1554. Anti-Catholic nobles planned to advance on London in March to overthrow the government. Mary would be replaced by ELIZABETH (half-sister). When the plot was discovered, Sir Thomas Wyatt of Kent (SE England) acted prematurely. He raised support in Kent (25 Jan.) and marched to London (arrived 3 Feb.), but the capital remained loyal to Mary. Wyatt surrendered (7 Feb.) and was executed (11 April). See also GREY, JANE.

WYCLIF, JOHN (b. c.1325, probably near Richmond, Yorkshire, England; d. 31 Dec. 1384 at Lutterworth, Leicestershire, England, aged about 59). A theologian at OXFORD University from c.1350, at several colleges, Wyclif obtained a doctorate (c.1372). Awarded church livings, he undertook government service (e.g., 1374, negotiated abroad with papal officials). In 1375–6, in De civili dominio ('On civil power'), Wyclif argued that clergymen should not own property. He was summoned before a bishops' council (Feb. 1377); it was disrupted by a riot, but papal condemnation followed (May). The bishops resummoned him (March 1378), but action was delayed by his patrons, and by the Pope's death.

Wyclif developed his ideas, rejecting TRANSUBSTANTIA-TION and papal authority. He was blamed for the PEASANTS' REVOLT (1381) and withdrew to his living at Lutterworth. Comprehensive condemnation came from a council at Blackfriars (church) in London (May 1382), but Wyclif's writings remained influential. In 1428 his bones were exhumed and burnt. *See also* LOLLARDY, ENGLAND/SCOTLAN D/WALES.

WYKEHAM, WILLIAM OF (b. *c.*1324 at Wickham, Hampshire, England; d. 27 Sept. 1404 at South Waltham, Hampshire, aged about 80). A clergyman, Wykeham served King EDWARD III as clerk of works at WINDSOR Castle 1356–61 and keeper of the PRIVY SEAL 1363–7. By 1365 he was the largest pluralist (holder of multiple Church posts) in Canterbury archdiocese. He was elected bishop of WINCHESTER in 1366 and appointed CHANCELLOR in 1367 (dismissed 1371).

During the GOOD PARLIAMENT (1376) Wykeham opposed courtiers accused of corruption, but was himself impeached by supporters of JOHN OF GAUNT for malad-ministration while chancellor (pardoned 1377 by RICHARD II). He founded Winchester College school (1378) and New College, OXFORD (1379). He was chancellor again 1389–91.

WYNDHAM, GEORGE (b. 29 Aug. 1863 at London, England; d. 8 June 1913 at Paris, France, aged 49). A member of the UK Parliament 1889–1913, Wyndham served as (Conservative) CHIEF SECRETARY FOR IRELAND from Nov. 1900. He continued his Party's policy to 'kill Home Rule with kindness', notably with the far-reaching 1903 Land Act ('Wyndham Act'), which resulted from the 1902 LAND CONFERENCE. Wyndham resigned on 6 March 1905 after being accused of complicity in a proposal for administrative devolution (*see* DEVOLUTION CRISIS).

See also LAND REFORM LEGISLATION, in IRELAND 19TH AND EARLY 20TH CENTURIES.

WYNDHAM, WILLIAM (b. *c.*1688 at Trentham, Staffordshire, England; d. 17 June 1740 at Wells, Somerset, England, aged about 52). Wyndham inherited a baronetcy in 1695 and was an MP from 1710. A TORY, he served in the ministry of the earl of Oxford (Robert HARLEY) under Queen ANNE (appointed secretary at war 1712, chancellor of the Exchequer 1713). After the accession of King GEORGE I (1714) he planned a Jacobite rising in SW England. Though imprisoned (late 1715–July 1716), he escaped charges.

In the 1720s–30s Wyndham led the Tory opposition to Robert WALPOLE in the House of Commons, guided by Viscount BOLINGBROKE. An effective orator, he attempted unsuccessfully to co-operate with disaffected WHIGS to defeat Walpole. He was unable to end the prohibition against Tories holding office. *See also* JACOBITISM, IMPACT ON BRITISH POLITICS.

WYVILL, CHRISTOPHER (b. Dec. 1738 at Edinburgh, SE Scotland; d. 8 March 1822 at Constable Burton, Yorkshire, England, aged 84). A clergyman in England from 1763, Wyvill inherited estates in 1774 and became a country gentleman in Yorkshire. In 1779, dismayed by British military failure in America, he joined the move-ment for parliamentary reform. He was the driving force behind the Yorkshire Association (founded 1779), which inspired 40 similar bodies, all part of the wider PETITIONING MOVEMENT. Wyvill sought more county seats, triennial Parliaments, and abolition of ROTTEN BOROUGHS to reduce government control of Parliament. From the mid 1780s he supported Charles James Fox, and later advocated CATHOLIC EMANCIPATION. *See also* AMERICAN WAR OF INDEPENDENCE; ECONOMICAL REFORM.

Y

YEATS, W.B. (b. 13 June 1865 at Sandymount, Co. Dublin, Ireland; d. 28 Jan. 1939 at Menton, Alpes-Maritimes, France, aged 73). Of Anglo-Irish, Protestant origin, William Butler Yeats lived in Ireland and England, and as a professional writer from 1887 drew on Irish mythology in his poems and plays. Between 1899 and 1907 he also managed the Irish Literary Theatre (Abbey Theatre from 1904). Though his relationship with Ireland was ambivalent (e.g., he disliked its religious cultures), Yeats served as a senator of the IRISH FREE STATE (1922–8). Acclaimed as a 'modernist', he was the first Irish writer to win the Nobel Prize in Literature (1923). His remains were reburied in Ireland in 1948. *See also* ANGLO-IRISH LITERATURE.

YEAVERING A site in Northumberland (NE England), which was occupied in the late 6th–mid 7th centuries; possibly the royal estate centre *ad Gefrin* mentioned by BEDE (in 731). Archaeologists have identified five phases of development, each with a new wooden hall or halls, and found a unique wooden amphitheatre. The centre was probably used by Kings Æthelfrith, EDWIN, OSWALD and OSWIU. *See also* ROYAL REVENUES, ENGLAND BEFORE 1066.

YELVERTON'S ACT Popular name for the legislation passed in July 1782 by the Irish Parliament which amended POYNINGS' LAW (1494–5). It ended the involvement of the British and Irish royal Councils in formulating Irish legislation, thereby giving primacy to the Irish Parliament. It was named after the MP Barry Yelverton who sponsored the Bill. *See also* CONSTITUTION OF 1782; PARLIAMENT, IRELAND.

YORK A city in NE England, by the Rivers Ouse and Foss; formerly the centre of Yorkshire. Established in 71, Eboracum (Latin from Brittonic, meaning 'Yew grove') became a permanent legionary fortress in Roman Britain (*see* ROMAN ARMY IN BRITAIN). The adjacent town became Britain's fourth *colonia*, perhaps in 208–11 (*see* ROMAN BRITAIN, TOWNS). From *c*.197 Eboracum was capital of the second province, Britannia Inferior, and from *c*.300 capital of Britannia Secunda (*see* ROMAN BRITAIN, GOVERNMENT). Two emperors died at York (Severus in 211, Constantius I in 306); Constantine (the Great) was acclaimed there (306; *see* ROMAN BRITAIN). A bishopric was founded before 314 (*see* ROMAN BRITAIN, CHRISTIANITY IN), but the city was largely abandoned in the 5th century.

By *c*.600, Eoforwic (OE, meaning 'Boar wic' – *see* WIC) or Eoforwicceaster ('Boar wic walled town') had become a major centre of DEIRA, a kingdom ruled by Angles (*see* GERMANIC IMMIGRATION, SOUTHERN BRITAIN). King EDWIN was baptized there in 627 by PAULINUS (effectively the city's first archbishop). The city was conquered by VIKINGS in 867; for 100 years Yorvik (the Viking name, from which 'York' derives) was the centre of Scandinavian power in Britain.

York fell to the Normans in 1069; they built two castles (Clifford's Tower, rebuilt in the 13th century, survives). York

---

A Dictionary of British and Irish History, First Edition. Edited by Robert Peberdy and Philip Waller.
© 2021 John Wiley & Sons Ltd; © editorial matter and organisation Robert Peberdy and Phillip Waller.
Published 2021 by John Wiley & Sons Ltd.

Minster (erected 1220–1447) is the latest church overlying the Roman *principia* (headquarters). In the 13th and 14th centuries York was England's second city (prosperous from the wool trade and cloth manufacturing), but then declined. From 1537 to 1641 it was the seat of the COUNCIL OF THE NORTH. The late 19th century saw renewed prosperity, derived from confectionery and railway works. In 1974 York ceased to be the centre of Yorkshire and was absorbed into N Yorkshire. York University was founded in 1963, and a college was upgraded as York St John University in 2006.

Est. popn: 200, 12,000; 1086, 4000; 1300, 8000; 1600, 11,000; 1800, 17,000; 1900, 75,500; 2000, 137,000.

YORK, RICHARD DUKE OF (b. 22 Sept. 1411 in England; d. 30 Dec. 1460 at Wakefield, Yorkshire, England, aged 49). Richard Plantagenet was recognized as duke of York in 1425. He also inherited a claim to the English throne (*see* MORTIMER FAMILY). He was lieutenant of France (1436–7, 1440–5) and of Ireland (from 1447; went to Ireland 1449).

In Sept. 1450 York denounced the government of King HENRY VI, following CADE'S REBELLION and the loss of Normandy (*see* HUNDRED YEARS WAR). He was ignored, but later served as 'protector' (March 1454–Feb. 1455) while Henry was ill. On 22 May 1455 York's supporters clashed with royalists (or 'Lancastrians') at St Albans (Hertfordshire). York's rival, the duke of Somerset (Edmund BEAUFORT), was killed and York again became protector, Oct. 1455–Feb. 1456 (ousted by Queen MARGARET OF ANJOU).

In late 1459 York and the earl of WARWICK demanded removal of 'evil counsellors'. While confronting Lancastrians at Ludlow Bridge (Shropshire), they were deserted by supporters (12 Oct.). York fled to Ireland. He returned in Sept. 1460, approaching London for control of Henry and, if supported, the throne. He settled for recognition as heir and went north to face royalist resistance, dying in battle. *See also* CAMBRIDGE, EARL OF; EDWARD IV; YORKIST–LANCASTRIAN CONFLICT; YORKIST–LANCASTRIAN CONFLICT, ROLE OF IRELAND.

YORK, VIKING KINGDOM OF A kingdom in NE England ruled by Vikings, 867–927, 939–44, 947–8, 949–54; formerly the southern part of Anglo-Saxon NORTHUMBRIA (former DEIRA), between the Rivers Humber and Tees. (Northern Northumbria remained under Anglo-Saxon rule.)

The kingdom's founder, Halfdan (a Dane), was succeeded by about ten kings until (927) ATHELSTAN, king of the Anglo-Saxons, seized the kingdom (after death of King Sihtric).

After Athelstan's death (939), Olaf Guthfrithson, a Viking from DUBLIN (Ireland), re-established the king-

dom. His successor (from 941), Olaf Sihtricson (cousin), and rival Ragnall Guthfrithson were expelled by King EDMUND (944).

The kingdom was briefly re-established (947–8) by the Norwegian Eric Bloodaxe (expelled by Northumbrians). In 949 Olaf Sihtricson retook York. He was expelled (952) only for Eric Bloodaxe to return (expelled 954). York thereafter remained under English rule.

The kingdom's involvement in the Viking world (from Ireland to Scandinavia) stimulated commercial activity, especially at York. Its rulers issued coins, and were assisted by archbishops of York. *See also* VIKINGS, IMPACT ON ENGLAND/IRELAND.

YORKIST–LANCASTRIAN CONFLICT The struggle, 1450s–85, between English nobles headed by dukes of York ('YORKISTS') and by King HENRY VI and Queen MARGARET OF ANJOU ('LANCASTRIANS'); also called 'Wars of the Roses' from the white and red roses depicted on Yorkist and Lancastrian badges.

From 1450 Richard, duke of YORK, denounced royal counsellors, notably the duke of Somerset (Edmund BEAUFORT). Their factions fought at St Albans, Hertfordshire (22 May 1455). Somerset was killed. When Lancastrians threatened leading Yorkists in 1459, conflict re-erupted. After a skirmish at Blore Heath, Staffordshire (23 Sept.), the parties prepared for battle near Ludlow, Shropshire (12 Oct.). Some Yorkists deserted, causing their leaders to flee abroad. They were condemned to death (Nov.). Richard, earl of WARWICK, returned in June 1460 and defeated Lancastrians at Northampton (10 July). York returned in Sept. and claimed the throne. Parliament made him heir instead of Prince Edward (24 Oct.), but while tackling resistance in Yorkshire York was killed (battle of Wakefield, 30 Dec.). Although Yorkists were defeated again (at St Albans, 17 Feb. 1461), York's successor, Edward, duke of York, seized the throne (4 March 1461; *see* EDWARD IV). He defeated Lancastrians at Towton, Yorkshire (29 March); Henry, Margaret and Prince Edward fled to Scotland. Though resistance continued, Henry was eventually arrested (1465).

In 1469 Warwick, now disaffected, attempted rebellion. He fled to France in May 1470, returning in Sept. King Edward fled (2 Oct.) and Warwick reinstated Henry (3 Oct.). But Edward returned (14 March 1471) and killed Warwick (at Barnet, Hertfordshire, 14 April), just as Margaret and Prince Edward returned. Yorkists defeated Lancastrians at Tewkesbury, Gloucestershire (4 May), killing Prince Edward. Afterwards Henry was murdered.

King Edward's successor, EDWARD V, was deposed by his uncle, RICHARD III, who was deposed by the Lancastrian HENRY VII (1485). Although Henry married ELIZABETH OF YORK, Yorkist resistance continued until the 1520s.

YORKIST-LANCASTRIAN CONFLICT, ROLE OF IRELAND In late 1459, following the collapse of YORKIST forces at Ludford Bridge, near Ludlow in Shropshire (12 Oct.), Richard, duke of YORK, fled to Ireland. He aimed to exploit support: since 1447 (except for 1453–4) he had been chief governor (lieutenant) and had recruited a large faction. (He had lived in Ireland in 1449–50.)

On 20 Nov. 1459 England's Parliament convicted York of treason, thereby cancelling his offices. Ireland's Parliament responded (Feb. 1460) by confirming York as governor and asserting independence (*see* PARLIAMENTARY INDEPENDENCE, DECLARATION OF). York returned to England in Sept. 1460 (killed at Wakefield, 30 Dec.).

Ireland's allegiances became crucial again after the LANCASTRIAN Henry Tudor seized the English throne and lordship of Ireland (1485). Yorkist sympathies remained alive in Ireland, which encouraged both Lambert SIMNEL and Perkin WARBECK to launch anti-Tudor revolts there. In response, Henry intervened to strengthen English influence (*see* HENRY VII AND IRELAND). *See also* KILDARE ASCENDANCY.

YORKIST-LANCASTRIAN CONFLICT, ROLE OF WALES Because both LANCASTRIANS and YORKISTS held lands in WALES (including the MARCH OF WALES), Wales was drawn into the struggle of *c.*1450–85. Lancastrians controlled Chester (NW England), Flintshire, ANGLESEY, Caernarfonshire, Merionethshire (all N Wales), Cardiganshire (W Wales) and Carmarthenshire (SW Wales), and four Marcher lordships. On the Yorkist side, Richard, duke of YORK (1411–60), had inherited large lordships of the Mortimer family (N, C and SW Wales) in 1425. Each side had supporters among Marcher lords and Welsh gentry. Important Lancastrians included the TUDOR FAMILY, such as Jasper TUDOR, half-brother of HENRY VI of England. On the Yorkist side, Sir William HERBERT (*c.*1423–69), earl of Pembroke, was friend and councillor of the Yorkist king EDWARD IV.

Though the major battles occurred in England, Wales had strategic importance as a place from which parties drew support at vital moments, and to which participants retreated. Richard, duke of York, marched from Wales, with Welsh supporters, to the battle of St Albans in May 1455; Edward IV's victorious army of 29 March 1461 (battle of Towton) was largely Welsh. On the other hand, in 1460, after the battle of Northampton (10 July), Queen Margaret (wife of Henry VI) sought refuge in Harlech (NW Wales) and then Pembroke (SW Wales) before sailing to Scotland. Military conflict first occurred near the Anglo-Welsh border in 1459 (battles of Blore Heath, 23 Sept., and Ludford Bridge, 12 Oct., Shropshire, W England); while the conflict was finished by Henry Tudor's 1485 campaign, which began on 7 Aug. when he arrived from France and landed at Milford Haven, SW Wales (*see* HENRY VII).

YORKISTS Historians' term for: (a) Richard, duke of YORK (d. 1460), and his supporters as opponents of King HENRY VI and MARGARET OF ANJOU in England and elsewhere in the 1450s; (b) Richard's descendants who were kings of England, namely EDWARD IV (son), EDWARD V (grandson), RICHARD III (son), and their supporters.

Richard, duke of York, and Edward IV claimed the throne as descendants of Lionel, duke of Clarence (1338–68), the second son of EDWARD III. Their Lancastrian opponents (descendants of the third son, JOHN OF GAUNT) argued that the Yorkist claim was invalid because it involved transmission through the female line (via Lionel's daughter Philippa and Anne Mortimer). *See also* MORTIMER FAMILY; YORKIST–LANCASTRIAN CONFLICT.

YORKTOWN, BATTLE OF The siege by American and French armies (commanded by George WASHINGTON) of a British army (commanded by Charles CORNWALLIS) at Yorktown, VIRGINIA (N America), 28 Sept.–19 Oct. 1781. The British had withdrawn to the port of Yorktown on 7 Aug. to maintain naval communications with New York, but were blockaded by a French fleet. The British surrender effectively ended the AMERICAN WAR OF INDEPENDENCE. Lord NORTH, the British prime minister, later resigned.

YOUNG, ARTHUR (b. 11 Sept. 1741 at Westminster, Middlesex, England; d. 12 April 1820 at London, England, aged 78). A journalist and farmer, Young published works on AGRICULTURE from 1767 (e.g., his *Tours*, such as *The Farmer's Tour through the East of England*, 1771) and edited the periodical *Annals of Agriculture* (1784–1815). He promoted progressive practices, including cultivation of 'waste' (land such as heath). He was secretary of the Board of Agriculture for England and Wales from 1793.

Young witnessed initial stages of the French Revolution (1789–90). The experience made him more conservative, while a daughter's death (1797) and friendship with William WILBERFORCE made him more religious. He became concerned for rural poverty and the effects of ENCLOSURE.

YOUNG ENGLAND A small group of young CONSERVATIVE MPs which formed around Lord John Manners and George Smythe 1837–45. Repelled by industrial blight and the manufacturing classes, they extolled a paternalistic and chivalrous aristocracy. Their Romanticism appealed to Benjamin DISRAELI.

YOUNGHUSBAND, FRANCIS (b. 31 May 1863 at Murree, Punjab, India; d. 31 July 1942 at Lytchett Minster, Dorset, England, aged 79). A British soldier, Younghusband explored areas beyond British-ruled India. In 1887, after participating in a mission to Manchuria, he travelled from

China westwards through the Gobi desert and across the Himalayas into NW India. In 1903–4 he led a military mission from India to Tibet, to investigate any Russian presence and establish relations. Despite massacring 700 Tibetans (April 1904), he negotiated a treaty (Sept.). Younghusband was British resident in Kashmir (NW India) from 1906. After retiring to England (1910), he was involved in religious, mystical and philosophical movements. *See also* GREAT GAME.

YOUNG IRELAND MOVEMENT A nationalist political movement formed by Thomas DAVIS (Protestant), J.B. DILLON, C.G. DUFFY (Catholics), and others which promoted a cultural (rather than Catholic) Irish identity and advocated an Irish Parliament. They joined the REPEAL ASSOCIATION, founded (1840) by Daniel O'CONNELL, and supported his UNION REPEAL MOVEMENT in their weekly newspaper *The Nation* (founded Oct. 1842), around which the Young Ireland movement developed.

After failure of the repeal movement, O'Connell and the Young Irelanders quarrelled; e.g., they supported (and O'Connell denounced) the non-denominational Queen's Colleges founded (1845) by Robert PEEL. (Davis died in Sept. 1845.) In July 1846 Young Irelanders seceded from the Association after refusing to repudiate violence. As the GREAT FAMINE deepened, leading Young Irelanders became increasingly radical. The authorities arrested Duffy and John MITCHEL, but Dillon and William Smith O'BRIEN mounted a feeble rebellion (*see* REBELLION OF 1848). Though Young Ireland was ineffectual, its ideas influenced later nationalists.

YOUNG WALES (Welsh *Cymru Fydd*, meaning 'Wales of the Future'). An association for promoting Welsh culture, founded 1886 in London (influenced by YOUNG IRELAND); it also sought Home Rule. Branches were founded in Wales from 1892. From 1894 David LLOYD GEORGE, wanting to push Welsh causes in the LIBERAL PARTY, sought to amalgamate Young Wales with the Liberal Federations in Wales. A meeting in Jan. 1896 rejected his plan and the movement collapsed.

YOUTH CULTURE 1950s TO 1970s, GREAT BRITAIN A novel, predominantly working-class 'youth culture' developed with its own styles, identity and political views, resulting from demographic changes, wider education (e.g., under the BUTLER EDUCATION ACT, 1944) and increased affluence. The first manifestations were rock 'n' roll music imported from the USA and 'teddy boy' culture (Edwardian style of dress adopted by often aggressive gangs). They were regarded by the press, politicians and Churches as signs of moral decline. American influences were evident too in the expanding British fashion

industry focused on the youth market (notably, from 1957, boutiques in Carnaby Street, London), films reflecting youthful aspirations (e.g., *Billy Liar*, 1963), and 'pop' music, especially that of The BEATLES and The Rolling Stones (prominent from respectively 1963, 1964). Teddy boys were followed in the 1960s by 'mods and rockers' (respectively fashionably dressed youths with motor scooters, and leather-wearing motorcyclists).

The commercial exploitation of youth culture caused a reaction in the mid 1960s, symbolized by the 'counterculture' of 'hippies' (term derived from 'hipster', a jazz enthusiast in USA). It involved drugs and sexual liberty (using new contraceptive pills for women), and drew on the anti-materialism of Eastern religions and generalized political protest against pollution, arms expenditure, war and university administration (there were protests at many universities 1965–73). Unlike 1950s youth culture, it was essentially a middle-class phenomenon. *See also* YOUTH ORGANIZATIONS.

YOUTH CULTURE 1950s TO 1970s, IRELAND Despite low disposable incomes and prevailing religious and cultural conservatism, young people in the 1950s became aware of youth culture in the USA and elsewhere through magazines and films (e.g., 'teenpics' produced in Hollywood, USA). Some obtained radios and record players. British 'teddy boys' were imitated in DUBLIN and other urban centres, mostly without violence. Rock 'n' roll music was played at dance halls, and international stars gave concerts, usually in Dublin and BELFAST (e.g., Bill Haley and The Comets in Dublin, 1957). Skiffle music was popular in the late 1950s.

In the 1960s The BEATLES and Rolling Stones performed in Dublin (1963, 1965 respectively). Irish youth culture produced its own international stars from the 1970s, notably Van Morrison (from NORTHERN IRELAND), The Boomtown Rats (including Bob Geldof), and U2 (including Paul Hewson, alias 'Bono'). Hippie culture had little impact, though a commune lived on Dorinish Island (off Co. Mayo) 1970–2 at the invitation of its owner, John Lennon of The Beatles.

YOUTH ORGANIZATIONS Usually associated with religious activity, organizations sought to build character through discipline, physical exercise and recreation. From 1844 the Young Men's Christian Association (YMCA) offered support to newcomers to LONDON and other cities. A women's organization was also created (1853). In 1883 William Smith, influenced by the YMCA and military service, founded the Boys' Brigade in GLASGOW (Scotland) to improve lives in drab areas. Members wore uniforms and undertook drill. The 'BB' spread quickly through the UK, British Empire and USA. Companies were usually associated with churches. Girls' organizations began in

Ireland (1893), Scotland (1900) and England (1902), and amalgamated in 1964. The Girls' Friendly Society, started in England in 1875, provided accommodation in towns for working girls from the country. The Church Lads' Brigade, associated with the Church of ENGLAND, was founded in 1891, and the Jewish Lads' Brigade in 1895. Boy Scouts, developed by Robert BADEN-POWELL from 1908, were less associated with churches and emphasized outdoors activities. Girl Guides were inaugurated in 1910. In Ireland, British-derived organizations were associated with unionism. In the late 20th century organizations struggled against the desire of young people for greater independence. Boys' and Girls' Brigades declined but scouting proved more resilient. *See also* YOUTH CULTURE 1950s TO 1970s, GREAT BRITAIN.

YPRES, THIRD BATTLE OF A British-led offensive during WORLD WAR I on the Western Front in Flanders (Belgium); also known as Passchendaele. After an artillery bombardment (from 16 July 1917), infantry advanced (from 31 July) on a 15-mi (21-km) front. Assaults continued into the autumn in bleak conditions (e.g., rain and extensive mud fields). British and Canadian forces, making limited tactical gains, suffered 300,000 casualties.

YUGOSLAVIA, BRITISH RELATIONS WITH Before 1914, Austro-Russian rivalry excluded British influence from Serbia (independent from 1878). Great Britain supported the creation of the larger 'Kingdom of Serbs, Croats and Slovenes' in 1918, after WORLD WAR I, but France was its principal patron. (The kingdom, which included a large Muslim minority, was renamed Yugoslavia in 1929.) During German occupation (1941–4) in WORLD WAR II, Winston CHURCHILL, the British prime minister, controversially switched British military aid from the Serbian nationalist resistance (Chetniks) to communist-led Partisans (1943), who were considered more effective.

Yugoslavia became a republic in 1945. After its prime minister, the former Partisan leader Josip Tito, asserted independence from USSR influence in 1948, British–Yugoslav relations improved. In the 1990s Britain was among the powers that attempted to manage the disintegration of Yugoslavia (*see* YUGOSLAV WARS, BRITISH INVOLVEMENT; KOSOVO WAR, BRITISH INVOLVEMENT).

YUGOSLAV WARS, BRITISH INVOLVEMENT Through a series of conflicts, 1991–2001 (sometimes overlapping), secessionist movements dismembered Yugoslavia into independent countries. Before they started, Yugoslavia (created 1918) comprised six 'republics': Bosnia-Herzegovina, Croatia, Macedonia, Montenegro, Serbia (with two autonomous provinces), Slovenia. At first the Yugoslav People's Army tried to preserve Yugoslavia, but by 1994 it was dominated by Serbs who sought a 'Greater Serbia' comprising Serbia itself and Serb-inhabited parts of Croatia and Bosnia-Herzegovina. Great Britain was involved in attempts to control the disintegration, often through international organizations.

Britain had no involvement in the brief Slovenian War (or Ten-Day War) of 27 June–7 July 1991. Slovenia's independence was recognized, together with Croatia's, by members of the European Economic Community (including Britain) on 15 Jan. 1992. During the Croatian War of Independence (1991–5), the United Nations imposed an arms embargo (Sept. 1991) and Britain contributed military forces to 'UNPROFOR' (United Nations Protection Force), which secured Serb-inhabited havens within Croatia from Feb. 1992 to March 1993. UNPROFOR also operated during the Bosnian War of 1992–5, involving conflict between Bosniaks, Serbs and Croats. Britain participated in an informal 'Contact Group' of concerned powers (including the USA and Russia). Its foreign secretary, Douglas Hurd, controversially supported the arms embargo, which disadvantaged the Bosniaks, to minimize the war's duration. Britain contributed to three military forces that attempted to entrench peace in Bosnia and Herzegovina: IFOR (Implementation Force, Dec. 2005–Dec. 2006, which replaced UNPROFOR), SFOR (Stabilization Force, Dec. 1996–2004) and EUFOR Althea (from 2004). Britain also intervened in the KOSOVO WAR (1998–9).

YUPPIE OR YUPPY Colloquial term of US origin, originating in the 1980s, derived from 'Young Urban Professional' (also presumed to mean 'Young Upwardly Mobile Professional'). In Great Britain it was applied to young employees of financial businesses in the City of LONDON who prospered after 'BIG BANG' (deregulation, 1986) and were considered beneficiaries of THATCHERISM.

Z

ZAMBIA *see* NORTHERN RHODESIA

ZANZIBAR A former British territory in E Africa, comprising the islands of Zanzibar and Pemba and a small coastal strip. Zanzibar was an Arab sultanate from 1699 and a commercial centre. The British declared a PROTECTORATE over the sultanate (1890) and sought to suppress the local slave trade. In 1963 Zanzibar became independent under the sultan. He was overthrown in 1964 and Zanzibar combined with TANGANYIKA as Tanzania. *See also* EAST AFRICA, BRITISH INVOLVEMENT.

ZIMBABWE *see* SOUTHERN RHODESIA

ZIMMERMANN TELEGRAM The enciphered message sent on 19 Jan. 1917, during WORLD WAR I, by German foreign minister Arthur Zimmermann to his envoy in Mexico proposing an alliance (possibly also with Japan) against the USA (a neutral power). British naval intelligence intercepted the telegram and informed the USA. Published on 1 March, it stimulated US entry into the war (6 April).

ZINOVIEV LETTER In 1924, a message allegedly sent by Grigori Zinoviev, a leading politician in the USSR, to the British COMMUNIST PARTY, urging it to violent revolution. Published in the British *Daily Mail* newspaper on 25 Oct., four days before a general election, it discredited the LABOUR PARTY, which had favoured a diplomatic accommodation with the USSR. The letter was probably forged with that aim.

ZULU WAR A British offensive in southern Africa which suppressed Zulu power, 1879. When Great Britain annexed the Transvaal (Boer republic in southern Africa) in 1877, it inherited a territorial dispute with the Zulu kingdom. To impress the Boers (Calvinist farmers), the British high commissioner, Sir Bartle Frere, determined to limit Zulu military power. He demanded (Dec. 1878) disbandment of military forces and acceptance of a British resident. The ultimatum was rejected.

On 11 Jan. 1879, British troops (5000 European, 8200 natives), commanded by Lord Chelmsford, invaded Zululand. A detachment was heavily defeated at ISANDLWANA, but a simultaneous heroic stand at Rorke's Drift prevented Zulu occupation of NATAL (both 22 Jan.). Victory at Ulundi (4 July) enabled the British to disband the Zulu army and divide the kingdom into 13 weak chieftainships. *See also* SOUTH AFRICA.

A Dictionary of British and Irish History, First Edition. Edited by Robert Peberdy and Philip Waller.
© 2021 John Wiley & Sons Ltd; © editorial matter and organisation Robert Peberdy and Phillip Waller.
Published 2021 by John Wiley & Sons Ltd.

BRITISH ISLES *c.* AD 40

MAP 1

Decantae   Tribes

– – – –   Approximate limit of coin usage in south-east Britain

▨   Kingdom of Cunobelin of the Catuvellauni

•   Chief centre of Cunobelin

Shetland Islands

Orkney Islands

ATLANTIC OCEAN

Decantae

Boresti

Taexali

Caledonii

Vacomagi

Venicones

North Sea

Damnonii

Votadini

Novantae

Selgovae

Brigantes

Vennikni

Robogdii

Darini

Voluntii

Carvetii

Parisi

Nagnatai

Eblani

Cauci

Irish Sea

B R I T A I N

IRELAND

Manapii

Usdiae

Coriondi

Brigantes

Deceangli

Cornovii

Corieltauvi

Iceni

Auteini

Gangani

Vellabori

Iverni

Ordovices

Demetae

Silures

Dobunni

Catuvellauni

Atrebates

Trinovantes

Camulodunon (Colchester)

Cantii

Celtic Sea

Dumnonii

Durotriges

English Channel

0   100 miles
0   160 kilometres

A Dictionary of British and Irish History, First Edition. Edited by Robert Peberdy and Philip Waller.
© 2021 John Wiley & Sons Ltd; © editorial matter and organisation Robert Peberdy and Phillip Waller.
Published 2021 by John Wiley & Sons Ltd.

BRITISH ISLES *c.* 400   MAP 2

Picts   Major peoples
-----   Northern frontier of Britannia
-·---   Earlier frontier (140s–150s or 160s)
-----   Conjectural boundaries of
                   Roman provinces
▨   Diocese of the Roman
                   Empire (Britannia)
○   Major royal
                   ceremonial centres
●   Provincial
                   capitals

*Shetland
Islands*

*Orkney
Islands*

Verturiones
(subgroup of Picts)

Picts

*ATLANTIC
OCEAN*

*North
Sea*

ANTONINE
WALL

Damnonii   Votadini

Novantae   Selgovae   HADRIAN'S WALL

Dál Riata   ● Carlisle

Airgialla   VALENTIA
Ulaid
Emain Macha   BRITANNIA
(Navan Fort)   SECUNDA

Cruachain   ○ Tara   York ●
(Rathcroghan)
                             Lincoln ●
*Irish
Sea*   FLAVIA
Laigin   CAESARIENSIS

Dún Ailinne
(Knockaulin)   *BRITAIN*

IRELAND   BRITANNIA
                             PRIMA   MAXIMA
Érainn   ● Cirencester CAESARIENSIS
                                          ◉
*Celtic
Sea*   London
                                      (diocesan capital)

English Channel

0   100 miles
0   160 kilometres

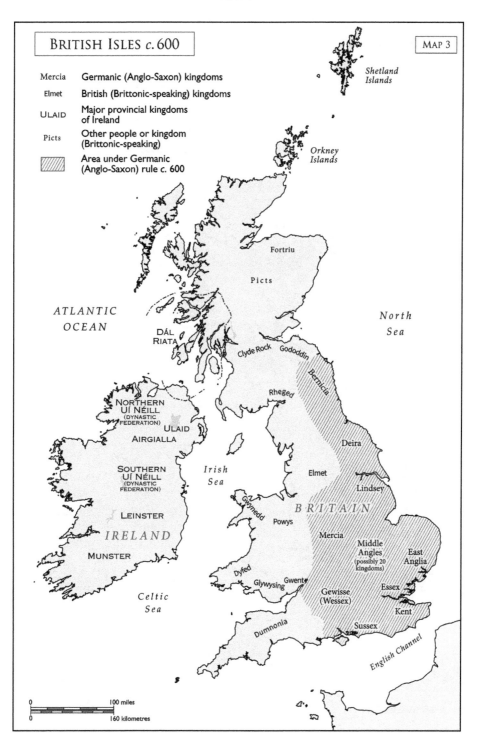

BRITISH ISLES *c.*600   MAP 3

Mercia — Germanic (Anglo-Saxon) kingdoms

Elmet — British (Brittonic-speaking) kingdoms

ULAID — Major provincial kingdoms of Ireland

Picts — Other people or kingdom (Brittonic-speaking)

— Area under Germanic (Anglo-Saxon) rule *c.* 600

Shetland Islands

Orkney Islands

Fortriu

Picts

ATLANTIC OCEAN

DÁL RIATA

North Sea

Clyde Rock

Gododdin

Bernicia

Rheged

NORTHERN UÍ NÉILL (DYNASTIC FEDERATION)

ULAID

AIRGIALLA

Deira

Elmet

SOUTHERN UÍ NÉILL (DYNASTIC FEDERATION)

Irish Sea

Lindsey

B R I T A I N

LEINSTER

IRELAND

MUNSTER

Gwynedd

Powys

Mercia

Middle Angles (possibly 20 kingdoms)

East Anglia

Dyfed

Glywysing

Gwent

Gewisse (Wessex)

Essex

Kent

Sussex

Celtic Sea

Dumnonia

English Channel

0   100 miles

0   160 kilometres

BRITISH ISLES *c.* 940   MAP 4

Territories under
Norwegian rule

Dyfed   Welsh kingdoms

ULAID   Major provincial kingdoms
            of Ireland

o   Viking trading centres
            in Ireland

*Shetland
Islands*

*Orkney
Islands*

*Western
Isles*

ATLANTIC
OCEAN

*Kingdom
of
Alba*

*North
Sea*

Dunkeld
Scone   St Andrews
Glasgow   Edinburgh
Govan   Bamburgh

*Kingdom of Strathclyde
(British)*

*Earldom of Northumbria
(associated with England)*

Chester-le-
Street

NORTHERN
UÍ NÉILL
(DYNASTIC
FEDERATION)
                ULAID
            AIRGIALLA
BRÉIFNE
                        *Isle of
                        Man*
                                 *Viking
                                 Kingdom
                                 of York*   York

CONNACHT
        SOUTHERN
        UÍ NÉILL
        (DYNASTIC
        FEDERATION)
IRELAND
        LEINSTER
                    Dublin

*Irish
Sea*

Gwynedd

Lincoln

*Kingdom
of
England*

Limerick
                                                    Norwich
Waterford   Wexford
MUNSTER   Dyfed Buellt
Cork   Glywysing Gwent   Oxford
                                                                London
*Celtic
Sea*   Kingston
                                            upon Thames   Canterbury
                            Winchester

English Channel

0   100 miles
0   160 kilometres

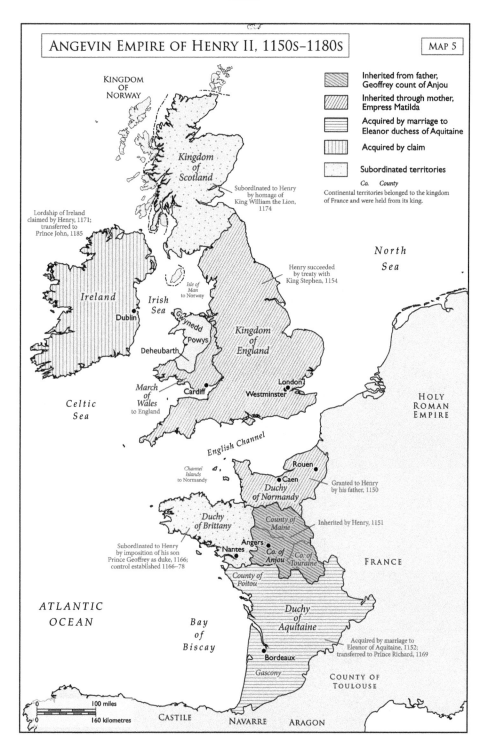

ANGEVIN EMPIRE OF HENRY II, 1150s–1180s   MAP 5

KINGDOM
OF
NORWAY

Kingdom
of
Scotland

Subordinated to Henry
by homage of
King William the Lion,
1174

Lordship of Ireland
claimed by Henry, 1171;
transferred to
Prince John, 1185

North
Sea

Inherited from father,
Geoffrey count of Anjou

Inherited through mother,
Empress Matilda

Acquired by marriage to
Eleanor duchess of Aquitaine

Acquired by claim

Subordinated territories

Co.   County

Continental territories belonged to the kingdom
of France and were held from its king.

Ireland   Irish
Sea

Isle of
Man
to Norway

Henry succeeded
by treaty with
King Stephen, 1154

Dublin

Gwynedd

Powys

Deheubarth

March
of
Wales
to England

Celtic
Sea

Cardiff

Kingdom
of
England

London
Westminster

HOLY
ROMAN
EMPIRE

English Channel

Channel
Islands
to Normandy

Rouen

Caen

Duchy
of Normandy

Granted to Henry
by his father, 1150

Duchy
of Brittany

County of
Maine

Inherited by Henry, 1151

Subordinated to Henry
by imposition of his son
Prince Geoffrey as duke, 1166;
control established 1166–78

Angers

Nantes

Co. of
Anjou

Co. of
Touraine

FRANCE

County of
Poitou

ATLANTIC
OCEAN

Bay
of
Biscay

Duchy
of
Aquitaine

Acquired by marriage to
Eleanor of Aquitaine, 1152;
transferred to Prince Richard, 1169

Bordeaux

Gascony

COUNTY OF
TOULOUSE

100 miles

160 kilometres   CASTILE   NAVARRE   ARAGON

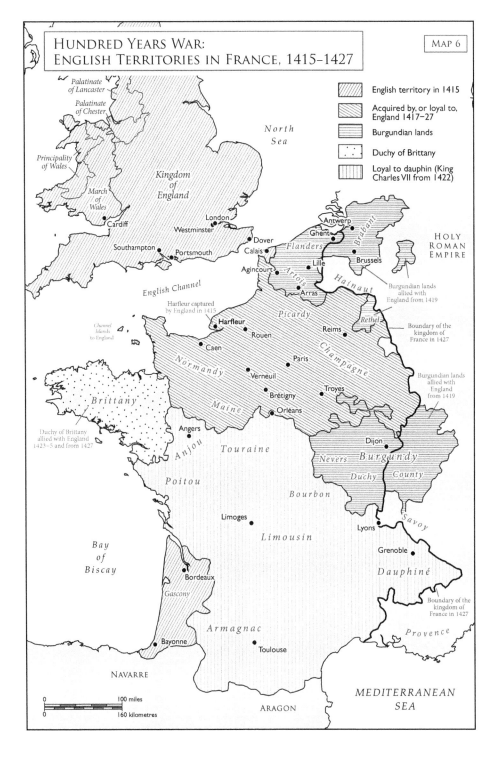

HUNDRED YEARS WAR:
ENGLISH TERRITORIES IN FRANCE, 1415–1427

MAP 6

Key:
- English territory in 1415
- Acquired by, or loyal to, England 1417–27
- Burgundian lands
- Duchy of Brittany
- Loyal to dauphin (King Charles VII from 1422)

Palatinate of Lancaster

Palatinate of Chester

North Sea

Principality of Wales

March of Wales

Kingdom of England

London

Westminster

Dover

Cardiff

Calais

Southampton
Portsmouth

Agincourt

English Channel

Flanders

Antwerp

Ghent

Brabant

Lille

Brussels

Artois

Arras

HOLY ROMAN EMPIRE

Hainaut

Burgundian lands allied with England from 1419

Channel Islands to England

Harfleur captured by England in 1415

Harfleur

Rouen

Picardy

Reims

Rethel

Boundary of the kingdom of France in 1427

Caen

Normandy

Paris

Champagne

Verneuil

Brétigny

Troyes

Maine

Orléans

Burgundian lands allied with England from 1419

Brittany

Duchy of Brittany allied with England 1423–5 and from 1427

Angers

Anjou

Touraine

Dijon

Nevers

Burgundy

Duchy

County

Poitou

Bourbon

Savoy

Limoges

Lyons

Limousin

Grenoble

Bay of Biscay

Bordeaux

Dauphiné

Gascony

Boundary of the kingdom of France in 1427

Armagnac

Bayonne

Toulouse

Provence

NAVARRE

MEDITERRANEAN SEA

0   100 miles
0   160 kilometres

ARAGON

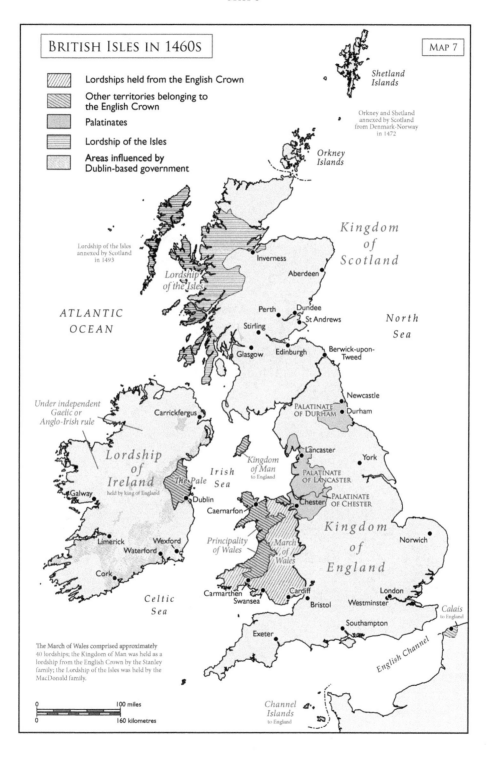

BRITISH ISLES IN 1460S | MAP 7

- Lordships held from the English Crown
- Other territories belonging to the English Crown
- Palatinates
- Lordship of the Isles
- Areas influenced by Dublin-based government

Shetland Islands

Orkney and Shetland annexed by Scotland from Denmark-Norway in 1472

Orkney Islands

Lordship of the Isles annexed by Scotland in 1493

Kingdom of Scotland

Lordship of the Isles

Inverness

Aberdeen

ATLANTIC OCEAN

Perth • Dundee
Stirling • St Andrews

North Sea

Glasgow • Edinburgh • Berwick-upon-Tweed

Under independent Gaelic or Anglo-Irish rule

Carrickfergus

Newcastle
PALATINATE OF DURHAM • Durham

Lordship of Ireland
held by king of England

Galway

Kingdom of Man
to England

Irish Sea

Lancaster
PALATINATE OF LANCASTER

York

The Pale
Dublin
Caernarfon

Chester
PALATINATE OF CHESTER

Limerick • Wexford
Waterford

Principality of Wales

March of Wales

Kingdom of England

Norwich

Cork

Carmarthen • Cardiff
Swansea

London
Westminster

Bristol

Southampton

Celtic Sea

Exeter

Calais
to England

English Channel

The March of Wales comprised approximately 40 lordships; the Kingdom of Man was held as a lordship from the English Crown by the Stanley family; the Lordship of the Isles was held by the MacDonald family.

Channel Islands
to England

0 — 100 miles
0 — 160 kilometres

DIVIDED KINGDOMS, AUGUST 1642   MAP 8

Areas mainly Parliamentarian

Areas divided, contested or would-be neutral

Areas mainly Royalist

Areas in Ireland held for royal government

°Cork   Towns in Ireland held for royal government

at the outbreak of Civil War in England and Wales

Shetland Islands

Orkney Islands

Kingdom of Scotland ruled by Charles I

Inverness

Aberdeen

ATLANTIC OCEAN

Perth • Dundee • St Andrews

Stirling

Glasgow • Edinburgh • Berwick-upon-Tweed

North Sea

Kingdom of England ruled by Charles I

Newcastle • Durham

Carlisle

Loyal to the Catholic Confederation

Coleraine • Londonderry • Carrickfergus

Ulster Belfast

Lancaster

York • Hull

Kingdom of Ireland ruled by Charles I

Connacht

Galway

Drogheda • Dublin

Irish Sea

Isle of Man

Manchester

Chester

Nottingham

Leinster

Kilkenny

Limerick • Waterford • Wexford

Munster

Cork

Loyal to the Catholic Confederation

Wales

Norwich

Pembroke • Carmarthen • Gloucester • Oxford

Cardiff • London

Swansea • Westminster

Bristol • Southampton

Exeter

English Channel

War against Parliamentary enemies was declared by Charles I at Nottingham, 22 August 1642. Scotland was formally neutral towards war in England and Wales but sympathetic to the English Parliament. Kilkenny was the centre of the Catholic Confederation.

Channel Islands

0   100 miles
0   160 kilometres

SHIRES & COUNTIES, 18TH CENTURY

MAP 9

Shire and county boundaries

Other internal boundaries

National borders

International borders

Co.   County
Sh.   Shire

Berw.   Berwickshire
Cl.   Clackmannanshire
Du.   Dunbartonshire
Eds.   Edinburghshire (or Midlothian)
Hadds.   Haddingtonshire
Kinr.   Kinross-shire
Kirkcud.   Kirkcudbrightshire
Lin.   Linlithgowshire
Nn.   Nairnshire
Pbl.   Peeblesshire
Ren.   Renfrewshire
Roxb.   Roxburghshire
Selk.   Selkirkshire
Stirl.   Stirlingshire
Wigt.   Wigtownshire

Shetland Islands

Shetland and Orkney comprised a single county of Scotland

Orkney Islands

North Sea

Caithness

Sutherland

Cromartyshire

Ross-shire

Elgin.

Nn.

Banffshire

Aberdeenshire

Kincardineshire

Kingdom of Great Britain
created in 1707

Scotland

Inverness-shire

Forfarshire

Perthshire

Cl.

Kinr.

Fife

ATLANTIC OCEAN

Argyllshire

Du.

Stirl.

Ren.

Lanarkshire

Lin.

Eds.

Hadds.

Berw.

Berwick-upon-Tweed
North Durham

Bute-shire

Pbl.

Selk.

Ayrshire

Roxb.

Kingdom of Ireland

Co. Donegal

Co. London-derry

Co. Antrim

Co. Tyrone

Ulster

Co. Down

Fermanagh

Co. Monaghan

Armagh

Dumfriesshire

Northumberland

Wigt.

Kirkcud.

Cumberland

Co. Durham

Westmor-land

Beds.   Bedfordshire
Bucks.   Buckinghamshire
Cambs.   Cambridgeshire
Herts.   Hertfordshire
Hun.   Huntingdonshire
Mdsx.   Middlesex
Oxon.   Oxfordshire
Rut.   Rutland
Worcs.   Worcestershire

Co. Sligo

Co. Mayo

Co. Leitrim

Co. Cavan

Co. Roscommon

Co. Long-ford

Co. Louth

Isle of Man

Yorkshire

Co. Galway

Westmeath

Co. Meath

Co. Dublin

Irish Sea

Lancashire

Connacht

King's County

Co. Kildare

Queen's County

Co. Wicklow

Co. Clare

Co. Tipperary

Co. Kilkenny

Co. Carlow

Co. Wexford

Leinster

Anglesey

Denbigh-shire

Cheshire

Derbyshire

Nottingham-shire

Lincoln-shire

Caernarfonshire

Fl.

Merioneth-shire

Montg.

Shrop-shire

Stafford-shire

Leicester-shire

Rut.

Norfolk

Co. Limerick

Munster

Co. Kerry

Waterford

Cardiganshire

Rad.

Hereford-shire

Worcs.

Warwick-shire

Northampton.

Hun.

Cambs.

Suffolk

England

Wales

Co. Cork

Pembrokeshire

Carm.

Brecon.

Mon.

Gloucester.

Oxon.

Beds.

Herts.

Essex

Glamorgan

Mdsx.

Celtic Sea

Wilt-shire

Berkshire

Surrey

Kent

Somerset

Hamp-shire

Sussex

Devon

Dorset

English Channel

Cornwall

Brecon.   Breconshire
Carm.   Carmarthenshire
Fl.   Flintshire
Mon.   Monmouthshire
Montg.   Montgomeryshire
Rad.   Radnorshire

Channel Islands

France

0   100 miles

0   160 kilometres

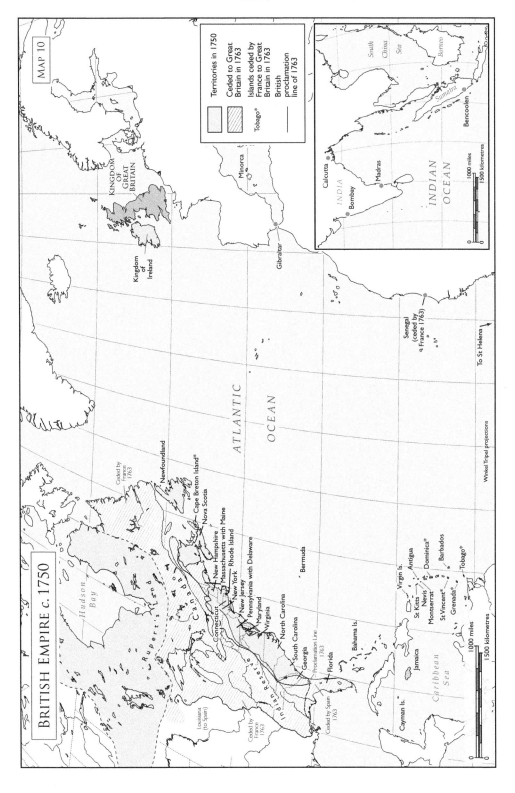

MAP 10

BRITISH EMPIRE *c.* 1750

Territories in 1750
Ceded to Great Britain in 1763
Islands ceded by France to Great Britain in 1763
British proclamation line of 1763

Tobago*

KINGDOM OF GREAT BRITAIN

Kingdom of Ireland

Minorca

Gibraltar

ATLANTIC OCEAN

Senegal (ceded by France 1763)

To St Helena

Winkel Tripel projections

Hudson Bay

Rupert's Land

Newfoundland

Cape Breton Island*

Nova Scotia

Ceded by France 1763

New Hampshire
Massachusetts with Maine
New York
Rhode Island
Connecticut
New Jersey
Pennsylvania with Delaware
Maryland
Virginia
North Carolina
South Carolina
Georgia
Proclamation Line 1763
Florida

Louisiana (to Spain)

Ceded by France 1763

Ceded by Spain 1763

Bermuda

Bahama Is.

Cayman Is.

Jamaica

Caribbean Sea

Virgin Is.
Antigua
St Kitts
Nevis
Montserrat
Dominica*
Barbados
St Vincent*
Grenada*
Tobago*

1000 miles
1500 kilometres

South China Sea

Borneo

Sumatra

Bencoolen

INDIA

Calcutta

Bombay

Madras

INDIAN OCEAN

1000 miles
1500 kilometres